Twentieth Century Authors
FIRST SUPPLEMENT

THE AUTHORS SERIES

Edited by Stanley J. Kunitz and Howard Haycraft

AMERICAN AUTHORS: 1600-1900
BRITISH AUTHORS BEFORE 1800
BRITISH AUTHORS OF THE NINETEENTH CENTURY
THE JUNIOR BOOK OF AUTHORS
TWENTIETH CENTURY AUTHORS

Edited by Stanley J. Kunitz
TWENTIETH CENTURY AUTHORS: FIRST SUPPLEMENT

THE H. W. WILSON COMPANY
950-972 University Avenue
New York 52, N. Y.

TWENTIETH CENTURY AUTHORS

FIRST SUPPLEMENT

A Biographical Dictionary of Modern Literature

Edited by
STANLEY J. KUNITZ

Assistant Editor
VINETA COLBY

NEW YORK
THE H. W. WILSON COMPANY
NINETEEN HUNDRED FIFTY-FIVE

15532

Preface

THE foundation-volume of *Twentieth Century Authors*, published in 1942, included biographies of approximately 1850 writers of this century, of all nations, whose books are familiar to readers of English. The present First Supplement brings the original biographies and bibliographies up to date and contains some 700 new biographies, 670 with portraits, mostly of authors who have come into prominence since 1942, though with the inclusion of a small number of older authors whose omission from the earlier volumes it has seemed advisable to rectify. The total listing of approximately 2550 names is to be found in this Supplement, incorporated into a single alphabet. When the main sketch of an author is located in the original volume, that circumstance is clearly indicated.

It is gratifying to note the large proportion of living authors who responded favorably to our invitation to write their own sketches, whether new or supplementary. Many who did not contribute autobiographies were extremely helpful in supplying needed biographical and bibliographical data. Only a handful of authors have had to be omitted because of insufficiency of material. Those who are present in the work, aside from their diversity of nationality, comprise almost every conceivable variety of aesthetic judgment, political belief, and religious faith; they have been granted the opportunity to express themselves freely in their first-person reports—their opinions, naturally, are their own. Our editorial policy, in offering a descriptive commentary on an author's work, has been not to attempt an independent appraisal but to give a fair summation of representative critical response.

No rigid formula has been adopted to determine the selection of authors. Some are here because of their literary reputation, others because of outstanding popularity—or, happily, since the two factors are not always mutually exclusive, for both reasons. Various writers, scholars, and librarians have been consulted in the preparation of the list, but there has been little unanimity of preference, except for the celebrated few, so that the responsibility for the final selection must rest with the editor, who is more than ready to confess his fallibility.

The work has been planned with the American reader largely in mind. Primary emphasis has been on professional men and women of letters whose vocation is the writing of fiction, poetry, drama, history, philosophy, biography, essays, and criticism, but some writers from specialized fields— for example, the natural and social sciences, psychology, psychoanalysis, theology—have been included when their work seemed to be of sufficiently wide interest or influence to justify admission. With respect to foreign authors, their inclusion has been dependent on the availability of their work in English translation rather than on their reputation in their native lands or tongues.

As was stated in the preface to the foundation-volume:

By and large, in the selection of authors the editors have been guided less by their personal critical preferences than by an effort to satisfy the general taste. *Twentieth Century Authors* is a reference work, not a judgment-seat. Its ideal realization would be to contain the lives of all modern writers in whom all readers are interested. This is manifestly impossible, and no doubt every reader who consults this volume will be disappointed by the omission of some authors and surprised at the inclusion of some others. The editors, however, are sanguine enough to hope that most readers will find herein most of the modern authors whose names they know or whose books they enjoy. Future supplementary volumes will be able to rectify the omissions and to include, as well, the names of newcomers to the literary scene. . . .

The generous praise accorded *Twentieth Century Authors* on publication and its acceptance, for more than a decade, as one of the best-thumbed of standard reference works in American and foreign libraries would seem to confirm the validity of the editorial premises on which it and the present Supplement are based.

The length of each entry has been influenced to some extent by the amount of material available on the author in question, the term and variety of his career, and the adequacy of previous treatment (if any) in the foundation-volume. Library of Congress name forms and pseudonym policy have been followed, in accordance with general library practice, except when modification has seemed advisable for ease of reference. Pronunciation of names has been indicated whenever authoritative information could be secured. The lists of principal works by each author, with original dates of publication, and of biographical and critical sources about the author, are designed to be selective and practical rather than definitive in nature. During the more than three years that the Supplement has been in progress, the master-list having been composed in 1952, these bibliographical entries have been checked many times and brought up to date at every proof-reading. Advantage has also been taken of the opportunity to correct biographical and bibliographical errors that appeared in the original edition.

Acknowledgment is gladly made of the cooperation of dozens of publishing houses and authors' agents in the task of gathering biographical data and acquiring reproducible photographs. In the course of this project it has been a pleasure to associate with an unusually gifted staff of research specialists and writers. Sketches have been contributed by Josephine Herbst, Ruth Herschberger, Eleanor Kunitz, Vivian Mercier, Irene Orgel, Jessie M. Rella, and Elizabeth Pollet Schwartz. Luella O. Beaman has been in charge of photographs. As assistant editor, Vineta Colby has been with this book from its inception, performing prodigies of labor. She has been the most resourceful, indefatigable, and imperturbable of colleagues, and has made a major contribution to the substance of the entire work.

September 1955   S.J.K.

KEY TO PRONUNCIATION

(Based on Webster's Guide to Pronunciation)

ā	āle	N	Not pronounced, but indicates the nasal tone of the preceding vowel, as in the French *bon* (bôN).	ū	cūbe	
â	câre			û	ûrn; French eu, as in *jeu* (zhû); German ö, oe, as in *schön* (shûn), *Goethe* (gû'tĕ)	
ă	ădd					
ä	ärm					
à	àsk			ŭ	tŭb	
ē	ēve	ō	ōld	ü	Pronounced approximately as ē, with rounded lips: French u, as in *menu* (mē-nü'); German ü, as in *grün*.	
ĕ	ĕnd	ô	ôrb			
ẽ	makẽr	ŏ	ŏdd			
		oi	oil			
ī	īce	oo	ōoze			
ĭ	ĭll	oŏ	foŏt			
		ou	out			
к	German ch as in *ich* (iк).	th	thin	zh	azure	
				' =	main accent	

vii

Twentieth Century Authors

First Supplement

ABBOTT, ELEANOR HALLOWELL
(September 22, 1872-). For autobiographical sketch and list of works and references, see TWENTIETH CENTURY AUTHORS, 1942.

* * *

Eleanor Hallowell Abbott lives in Wilton, N.H. Her husband, Dr. Fordyce Coburn, died several years ago. Her only recent publication is a short story, "My Love Affair with the British," which appeared in the *Canadian Home Journal.* She writes to the editors of this volume that chronic arthritis "has relegated me more or less to a correspondence from a lapboard in a wobbly rocking chair."

ABBOTT, LYMAN (December 18, 1835-October 22, 1922). For biographical sketch and list of works and references, see TWENTIETH CENTURY AUTHORS, 1942.

* * *

ABOUT: Brown, I. V. Lyman Abbott, Christian Evolutionist; Jones, E. D. Royalty of the Pulpit.

ABDULLAH, ACHMED (May 12, 1881-May 12, 1945). For autobiographical sketch and list of works and references, see TWENTIETH CENTURY AUTHORS, 1942.

* * *

Achmed Abdullah died of a heart attack at Columbia-Presbyterian Medical Center, New York, on his sixty-fourth birthday. The paid death notice in the New York *Times* the following day described him as the "beloved son of the late Grand Duke Nicholas Romanoff and Princess Nourmahal Durani." He was apparently christened Alexander Nicholayevitch Romanoff, but after his mother divorced his father—she was the second of the Grand Duke's three wives—her parents made him a Moslem, brought him up in Afghanistan, and sent him to school at Eton. Achmed Abdullah were his Moslem given names; he was also known as Prince Nadir Khan Durani. Mr. Abdullah's first wife was Jean Wick, author's agent, who died in 1939. *Deliver Us from Evil* is dedicated to her and to the Reverend Martin J. Scott, S.J. "whose example . . . showed me the road to . . . the Catholic Faith."

ADDITIONAL WORKS: *Fiction*—Bucking the Tiger, 1917; The Honourable Gentleman and Others, 1919; The Man on Horseback, 1919; The Mating of the Blades, 1920; Night Drums, 1921; The Year of the Wood-Dragon, 1926; Ruth's Rebellion (with F. Baldwin) 1927; They Were So Young, 1929; The Veiled Woman, 1931; Girl on the Make (with F. Baldwin) 1932.

ABOUT: Hoehn, M. (ed.) Catholic Authors, I; New York Times May 13, 1945; Publishers' Weekly June 2, 1945.

ABERCROMBIE, LASCELLES (January 9, 1881-October 27, 1938). For biographical sketch and list of works and references, see TWENTIETH CENTURY AUTHORS, 1942.

* * *

ABOUT: Dictionary of National Biography 1931-1940.

ADAMIC, LOUIS (March 23, 1899-September 4, 1951). For autobiographical sketch and list of earlier works and references, see TWENTIETH CENTURY AUTHORS, 1942.

* * *

Louis Adamic died at fifty-two under mysterious circumstances at his home in Riegelsville, N.J. His body was found on the couch of his second-floor bedroom-study; a bullet from the .22 rifle that lay across his knees had penetrated the brain. Both the lower floor of the house and the garage across the road had been set on fire with rags soaked in fuel oil. Although it was rumored that he might have been murdered by Communist agents because of his pro-Tito views, his widow, then convalescing in Los Angeles, attributed his death to suicide induced by overwork and anxiety about world conditions. The New Jersey authorities finally accepted this view, in spite of reports of frequent threats made to Adamic since 1949, culminating in a brutal beating earlier in 1951.

The last ten years of Adamic's life were lived under great stress, caused by the fatal disunity of his homeland, Yugoslavia, and by his own political insecurity. During World War II, he had switched from support of the Yugoslavian leader General Mikhailovitch to the position of spokesman to the American people for the Partisans, who, he felt, were putting up the more effective resistance to

Hitler and Mussollini (see *My Native Land,* October 1943). A stay in Yugoslavia from January to August 1949 made him more pro-Tito than ever, so that much of his posthumous *The Eagle and the Roots* is a biography of Tito.

Although several times consulted by President Roosevelt and other high officials during the war years and very active in rallying foreign-born Americans behind the U.S. war effort, Adamic was frequently cited as a subversive in the post-war period. After Tito broke with Stalin in 1948, the Communists joined in the attack on Adamic.

A "dinner at the White House" with the Roosevelts and Winston Churchill on January 13, 1942, led four years later to the publication of a book by that title.

In January 1947 Churchill successfully sued Adamic for libel on the basis of a footnote in the book. Both President and Mrs. Roosevelt had been impressed by the thesis of *Two-Way Passage:* "I propose that we take to Europe—in person—the American Revolution, the American Experience. . . ."

For hostile and friendly pen-portraits of the later Louis Adamic, see respectively the *American Mercury* and *Nation* articles listed below.

ADDITIONAL WORKS: Two-Way Passage, 1941; What's Your Name? 1942; My Native Land, 1943; Nation of Nations, 1945; Dinner at the White House, 1946; The Eagle and the Roots, 1952.

ABOUT: Adamic, L. Laughing in the Jungle, The Native's Return, Dinner at the White House, The Eagle and the Roots; McWilliams, C. Louis Adamic & Shadow-America; American Mercury December 1951; Current Biography 1940; Nation September 22, 1951; Newsweek September 17, 1951; New York Times March 16, 1941, January 16, 1947, August 3, 4, 1948, September 5, 6, 27, 1951.

ADAMS, FRANKLIN PIERCE ("F.P.A.") (November 15, 1881-). For biographical sketch and list of earlier works and references, see TWENTIETH CENTURY AUTHORS, 1942.

* * *

For a brief period in 1946 "F.P.A." returned to the New York *Post* with a new column, "This Little World." He has published very little of his own writings in recent years—a loss to his reading public which is perhaps explained in part by his comment to an interviewer that "the only people who like to write [are] the people who write terribly."

ADDITIONAL WORKS: Innocent Merriment: An Anthology of Light Verse (ed.) 1942; Nods and Becks, 1944; F.P.A. Book of Quotations (ed.) 1952.

ABOUT: National Cyclopedia of American Biography (1946); Atlantic Monthly January 1948; Current Biography 1941; Newsweek February 11, 1946; Scholastic March 10, 1947; Time February 11, 1946.

ADAMS, JAMES TRUSLOW (October 18, 1878-May 18, 1949). For autobiographical sketch and list of earlier works and references, see TWENTIETH CENTURY AUTHORS, 1942.

* * *

James Truslow Adams died in his seventieth year at his home in Southport, Conn., after a short illness. His wife survived him.

The last decade of Dr. Adams' life was almost as productive as the two which preceded it, though *Big Business in a Democracy* was his last original work. An associate of the publishing house of Charles Scribner's Sons, he acted as editor-in-chief of the *Atlas of American History* and the five-volume *Album of American History,* the last volume of which appeared in the year of his death. No work of his ever again won such popularity as *The Epic of America,* which headed the best-seller lists in 1932 and had sold nearly 360,000 copies in all editions (including translations into eight European languages) by his death. Academic historians were inclined to be somewhat grudging in their praise for Dr. Adams, perhaps because, as Professor Michael Kraus wrote in his *History of American History,* "for himself he . . . fulfilled the ambition of Macaulay—that his volumes should replace the latest novel on the drawing-room table." "His *Founding of New England,"* said the obituary in the *American Historical Review,* "will still stand as a rare blend of scholarship and literary skill." Professor Kraus concurred, but included the two later New England volumes also among Adams' permanent achievements. Of the more popular works, such as *The Epic of America,* Professor Kraus wrote that although these books "teach little to the members of the historical guild," they have "kept hundreds of thousands of readers awake while they read in smoothly flowing prose and quoted poetry an interpretation of our past that has made use of the latest historical research."

ADDITIONAL WORKS: The American, 1943; Atlas of American History (ed.) 1943; Frontiers of American Culture, 1944; Album of American History (ed.) 1944-49; Big Business in a Democracy, 1945.

ABOUT: Kraus, M. History of American History; American Historical Review July 1949; Current Biography 1941; New York Times May 19, 1949; Publishers' Weekly June 11, 1949.

ADAMS, JOHN CRANFORD (October 11, 1903-), American Shakespearean scholar and educator, writes: "I was born in

Boston, attended public schools in Brookline and removed upon my father's retirement to the old family farm sixteen miles west of Syracuse two years before entering Cornell University. There I began a liberal arts program with the intention of transferring in a year or two to architecture or engineering, but instead remained to graduate with a major in English, doubtless because of the spell which a great department of English scholars then wove about the subject. In particular I remember with gratitude and affection Martin Wright Sampson, Joseph Quincy Adams, and J. William Hebel—teachers and scholars who combined international renown with great human warmth and personal charm.

Fabian Bachrach

"The following two years were spent at King's College, Cambridge, England, with sufficient study almost to justify the happy hours in a number of students' clubs, in rowing in the college eight-oared shell, or in scurrying about the English countryside in a rickety old car.

"Returning from Cambridge I joined the English department of Syracuse University as instructor, and married the following summer, in Scotland, Alice deBois Murray, a member of a family well-known in Glasgow in academic, literary, musical and civic circles. Several years then followed in the English department at Cornell while earning a Ph.D. (1935), serving on committees, and developing that detestation of the handwritten word which marks all those who have corrected a million freshman themes.

"In 1936-37 a fellowship at the Folger Shakespeare Library in Washington, D.C., gave a welcome break and offered an opportunity to conclude a study of Shakespeare's stage which had been undertaken as a doctoral thesis. This research had enlarged to embrace the total structure of the Globe Playhouse and to inquire into the theory and techniques of Elizabethan dramatic production. It was published in 1942 with the title *The Globe Playhouse: Its Design and Construction*. Since that time a number of articles bearing upon related problems have appeared in various English journals. Allied to this has been the opportunity to lecture at

a dozen eastern universities and in Stratford on the staging of Shakespearean plays and to correspond with scholars interested in the topic on both sides of the Atlantic.

"In 1944 my wife, children (Murray, age 13, Joan, age 12) and I left Cornell when I became the president of Hofstra College in central Long Island, and we have had the excitement of watching it grow from an enrollment of 350 to a present figure (1953) of 4,300. In the early years of this post time was found to complete a scale model of the Globe Playhouse which at present is on loan at the Folger Shakespeare Library. Some 25,000 pieces and ten years of work went into the model with the most brilliant assistance by a talented artistic friend, Irwin Smith, who is chiefly responsible for the tapestries, carvings, figures, tile and brick work which brought the model to life.

"It is perhaps no accident that the dramatic department at Hofstra in recent years has constructed a full scale replica of Shakespeare's stage or that it produces each year a Shakespearean play staged in accordance with the principles of Elizabethan dramatic art. This distinctive festival has grown to sell-out proportion and attracts national notice as one of the significant contributions to the understanding of Shakespeare's art.

"The administrator dreams of finding time in a busy schedule to write those other books he had in mind when living the life of the scholastic teacher, but when he faces his daily round."

PRINCIPAL WORK: The Globe Playhouse, 1942.

ABOUT: Christian Science Monitor Magazine June 17, 1950; Scholastic April 5, 1950.

ADAMS, LÉONIE (December 9, 1899-), American poet, writes: "The fifth of six children of Henrietta Rozier and Charles Frederic Adams, I passed most of childhood and girlhood in my birthplace in Brooklyn, N.Y., much secluded except for school. There I sought out foreign-named companions, for a fellowship that was absolute and abstract, beyond our mute sep-

arate converse with dimly known and receding regions of source. My mother's forebears had all come from Scotland or England to Maryland and Virginia in the seventeenth century, and she was born on a Potomac plantation held since then by her father's family. Our Adams forebears were of neighboring planter stock, but my father was born in Santiago, Cuba, where his father had sugar and banking interests, had been created a Spanish don and was American consul; and my father's mother was Spanish by race and Venezuelan by birth. This fact and a New England schooling made him the more devoutly American. A lawyer, he was also a crusading lecturer for various reforms. Pure daughter of her early world, my mother without trying gave me a rustic disposition and a disposition I only begin to plumb toward faith. My father, more deliberately, made me a childhood agnostic—I am now a Roman Catholic—and political zealot—a calling from which I soon guiltily shrank—and by his fine voice and memory for *Hamlet* and *Lycidas* a lover of the poets.

"I composed in metres by seven and by eleven wished vaguely to be a writer and read with unexamined wonder the English poets. The little modern free verse I saw at about fifteen I disliked, and the first living poet who delighted me was Yeats, found in the high school library. I knew nothing of the little magazines, and at college (Barnard) we did not then study contemporaries. I first discriminated an interest in poetic techniques through rediscovery there of certain Elizabethan poets, whose auditory effects I tried to emulate.

"Friends encouraged me, and one, Marian Smith, showed poems of mine to Louis Untermeyer, who wrote that he had placed some with Max Eastman and Ridgely Torrence.

"For most of my twenties I supported myself sketchily in New York, with intervals at my widowed mother's home, then on a Ramapo mountaintop, at the edge of woods. I visited New Mexico and even Europe (as companion) and made a few literary friends, of whom Raymond Holden took my first collection to McBride's. This period ended when in 1928 I received a Guggenheim fellowship and left the Metropolitan Museum editorial office for a first taste not of Paris but of the literary life and to get together a second book.

"In the early depression years, Eda Lou Walton found me a teaching job at Washington Square College of New York University. There I met and in 1933 married the critic William Troy, and in 1935 we joined the faculty of Bennington College. We lived in the Bennington community, and I taught writing and poetry a good part of the time,

until 1944. Since then we divide our time between teaching in New York (I am now at Columbia) and an old house in Connecticut which we moved to its present site in 1934 and have lived in, when we could, ever since.

"In 1948-49 I passed an eventful year as consultant in poetry at the Library of Congress and after years of broken writing began to prepare a selected poems. In 1949 I received an award for lyric poetry from the National Institute of Arts and Letters and in 1950 a D. Litt. from New Jersey College for Women. Since 1949 I have been a Fellow in American Letters of the Library of Congress, since 1951 a member of the National Institute of Arts and Letters, and am a member of Phi Beta Kappa and P.E.N. I am a very liberal democrat."

* * *

Léonie Adams' work has been described as "metaphysical" and "mystical." Louise Bogan speaks of an "Elizabethan" coloring in her early verse, by which "Miss Adams' sensitively interpreted nature, thought, and feeling have an intensity which often seems to slip over into mystic vision." She was a co-winner (with Louise Bogan) of the 1954 Bollingen prize in poetry, for her *Poems: A Selection.*

PRINCIPAL WORKS: Those Not Elect, 1925; High Falcon, 1929; This Measure, 1933; Lyrics of François Villon (ed. and trans.) 1933; Poems: A Selection, 1954.

ABOUT: Bogan, L. Achievement in American Poetry; Gregory, H. & Zaturenska, M. A History of American Poetry, 1900-1940; Untermeyer, L. Modern American Poetry; Commonweal November 26, 1954; Poetry March 1930.

ADAMS, SAMUEL HOPKINS (January 26, 1871-). For autobiographical sketch and list of earlier works and references, see TWENTIETH CENTURY AUTHORS, 1942.

* * *

Samuel Hopkins Adams continues to divide his time between winters in his home in South Carolina and summers on the shores of Lake Owasco in New York. Badly crippled now, he gets around with "one stylish metal crutch." In 1946 Adams received the Critics' Award for his biography of his fellow alumnus from Hamilton College, Alexander Woollcott. (Adams said of him, "I had an affection for Aleck Woollcott, often admiring, sometimes complicated with shudders.") His novel *The Harvey Girls* was made into a successful musical film. Of Average Jones, his detective story hero whose "death" Adams announced some years ago, he now writes, "Maybe the death of Average Jones is exaggerated, as I have just had a television offer for him." Adams' reminiscences of his grandfathers Hopkins and Adams, *Grandfather Stories,* published when he was eighty-four, was a Book-of-the-Month Club selection. Some of these sketches had appeared earlier in the *New Yorker.*

The statement in TWENTIETH CENTURY AUTHORS, 1942, that Adams studied medicine is incorrect.

ADDITIONAL WORKS: The Harvey Girls, 1942; Tambay Gold, 1942; Canal Town, 1944; A. Woollcott, His Life and His World, 1945; Banner by the Wayside, 1947; Plunder, 1948; Sunrise to Sunset, 1950; Pony Express (juvenile) 1950; The Santa Fe Trail (juvenile) 1951; The Erie Canal (juvenile) 1953; Wagons to the Wilderness, 1954; Grandfather Stories, 1955.

ABOUT: Van Gelder, R. Writers and Writing; Saturday Evening Post January 7, May 27, 1950; Saturday Review January 15, 1955.

ADE, GEORGE (February 9, 1866-May 16, 1944). For autobiographical sketch and list of works and references, see TWENTIETH CENTURY AUTHORS, 1942.

* * *

George Ade died at seventy-eight in Brook, Ind., after a series of heart attacks, leaving an estate of more than $400,000. His big house, Hazelden Farm, was given by his trustees to Newton County for a George Ade Memorial Hospital. Purdue University and Sigma Chi filled a large part of Ade's later life. He was Grand Consul of Sigma Chi, 1909-11, put up much of the money for the Delta Chapter House at Purdue, 1912, and wrote the Sigma Chi Creed, 1929. The Ross-Ade Stadium at Purdue, dedicated in 1924, is named after Ade and David E. Ross, who together made it possible.

Critical opinion on Ade has covered a wide range since his heyday. In 1908 Mark Twain wrote to W. D. Howells of Ade's *Pink Marsh*: "Pink—oh, the shiftless, worthless, lovable black Darling! Howells, he deserves to live forever." William Allen White said, "I would rather have written *Fables in Slang* than be President," and several Presidents, including Franklin D. Roosevelt, almost agreed with him.

Recent appraisal of Ade inclines rather to the view of Bergen Evans, who, writing in the *American Mercury,* called the fable in slang, "a perfect vehicle for the country hick turned city slicker who has gotten wise to himself and learned not to take any wooden nickels. And its success was largely due to its appearance at a time when the majority of Americans were becoming urbanized and had achieved just such wisdom."

ADDITIONAL WORKS: Stories of the Streets and of the Town (ed. F. J. Meine) 1941; The Permanent Ade (ed. F. C. Kelly) 1947. *Plays*—The Sultan of Sulu, 1902; Peggy from Paris, 1903; The County Chairman, 1903; The Sho-Gun, 1904; The College Widow, 1904; The Bad Samaritan, 1905; Just Out of College, 1905; Marse Covington, 1906; Mrs. Peckham's Carouse, 1906; Father and the Boys, 1907; The Fair Co-Ed, 1908; The Old Town, 1909; Nettie, 1914.

ABOUT: Kelly, F. C. George Ade; McCutcheon, J. T. Drawn from Memory; Russo, D. R. Bibliography of George Ade; American Mercury March 1950; Magazine of Sigma Chi October-November 1944; New York Times May 17, 18, 1944; Saturday Review of Literature April 12, 1947; Time May 29, 1944.

ADLER, ALFRED (February 7, 1870-May 28, 1937). For biographical sketch and list of works and references, see TWENTIETH CENTURY AUTHORS, 1942.

* * *

ABOUT: Dreikurs, R. Fundamentals of Adlerian Psychology; Way, L. M. Adler's Place in Psychology.

ADLER, FELIX (August 13, 1851-April 24, 1933). For biographical sketch and list of works and references, see TWENTIETH CENTURY AUTHORS, 1942.

* * *

ABOUT: Cohen, J. H. They Builded Better Than They Knew; Neumann, H. Spokesmen for Ethical Religion.

ADLER, MORTIMER JEROME (December 28, 1902-), American philosopher and educator, was born in New York City, the son of Ignatz Adler, a jewelry salesman, and Clarissa (Manheim) Adler, a former school teacher. A brilliant student, he left high school at fifteen ("I had a difference of opinion with the principal as to who was running the school"), worked

Halsman

briefly on the New York *Sun* and, after discovering Plato at seventeen, resolved to become a philosopher instead of a journalist. To this end he entered Columbia University on a scholarship, finished the four-year course in three years, received a Phi Beta Kappa key, but failed to win the B.A. degree because he refused to take the required swimming test. The lack of a degree proved

5

no handicap for Adler. He was appointed instructor in psychology at Columbia and, in addition, taught the famous General Honors Course (a forerunner of the "Great Books" course) set up by John Erskine. Meanwhile he wrote a thesis on musical appreciation for which Columbia granted him a Ph.D. in psychology in 1928.

While still an undergraduate Adler launched his lively philosophical rebellion against pragmatism and its leading intellectual proponent, John Dewey, under whom Adler had studied philosophy. Adler opposed the pragmatic position ("truth is whatever is useful to a given society at a specific stage in its history") and affirmed his belief in absolute and universal truths and values. He read St. Thomas Aquinas and found in that great medieval thinker the moral and intellectual system and order which, he felt, pragmatism and allied schools of thought had thrown to the winds. The best evidence of the chaos which pragmatism produces, Adler argued, is progressive education, and here he won the enthusiastic support of a number of distinguished educators who agreed that current pragmatic trends in education were producing a half-educated or uneducated public, trained for jobs and money-making, but not for thinking and leading the "good life."

Adler's opportunity to put his educational theory to practice came in 1928 when he met Robert Maynard Hutchins, then acting dean of the Yale Law School. In 1929 Hutchins became president of the University of Chicago and invited Adler to join the faculty, first as a member of the philosophy department, but then, when Adler's views clashed too violently with those of other members of the department, Hutchins created for him the post of associate professor of the philosophy of law. The Hutchins-Adler combination very soon revolutionized the educational program of the university. Strict departmentalization and rigid but frequently meaningless academic requirements were discarded in favor of a broad training in the humanities, an education based not so much on the acquiring of a mass of factual data gathered from textbooks as on the close reading of original texts, the "Great Books," as they have come to be called. Hutchins and Adler enlarged their educational program to include non-academic students and in 1946 organized the Great Books Program. Under this program discussion groups made up of adults from all walks of life meet biweekly to discuss a book from a set list of Great Books which ranges widely, but with uniform seri-

ousness and erudition, from Homer to Hegel, and from Dante to Freud. To make these texts available to members of the group and to the general public, Hutchins and Adler conceived the idea of reprinting the books in a complete set. The cost of the undertaking was covered by the *Encyclopaedia Britannica* and the University of Chicago. In 1952 the 54-volume set (443 works by 76 authors: price, $249.50) was published.

Adler's ambitious contribution to the project was the preparation of an index of "Great Ideas" called the *Syntopticon* (a synthesis of topics). To assist him he had a staff of scholars at the University of Chicago who spent altogether seven years on the task. But the *Syntopticon* was planned as only the beginning of an elaborate scholarly project for the analysis of the basic ideas in the thought of the Western world. In June 1952 Adler resigned from the University of Chicago to found the Institute for Philosophical Research, in San Francisco, endowed with grants from the Old Dominion Foundation and the Fund for the Advancement of Education. The Institute plans to publish a series of studies on the Great Ideas, as outlined in the *Syntopticon,* and produce ultimately a *Summa Dialectica* which will encompass the ideas of twentieth century Western thought as St. Thomas' *Summa Theologica* did for medieval thought.

Although the bulk of Adler's writings is devoted to such recondite subjects as Thomism, the philosophy of law, ethics, and esthetics, he is best known for two popular "how to" books—*How to Read a Book*, in which he observes that there is more *real* illiteracy in the United States today than in the eighteenth century and advises that reading is a serious job involving the most intense mental activity; and *How to Think About War and Peace*, a hard-hitting analysis of questions on peace and post-war planning.

Adler's has not been the quiet life of the ivory-towered scholar. Few academic personalities are as controversial; few have engaged in so many bitter polemics, and probably few enjoy them as much as Adler does. "He aspires to be the great codifier and systematizer of Western culture, to write its Code Napoléon," Dwight MacDonald commented. To him, MacDonald continued, "ideas seem as objective and distinct as marbles, which can be arranged in definite, logical patterns. He has the classifying mind, which is invaluable for writing a natural history or collecting stamps."

Since he has staked out all knowledge as his province, Adler is naturally in a hurry—speaks rapidly, writes rapidly, likes fast cars, and rarely relaxes. He has been married since 1927 to Helen Leavenworth Boyton, and they have two sons.

PRINCIPAL WORKS: Dialectic, 1927; Music Appreciation: An Experimental Approach to its Measurement, 1929; Diagrammatics (with M. P. Hutchins) 1932; Crime, Law, and Social Science (with J. Michael) 1933; Art and Prudence, 1937; What Man Has Made of Man, 1937; Saint Thomas and the Gentiles, 1938; Problems for Thomists, 1940; How to Read a Book, 1940; How to Think About War and Peace, 1944; Syntopticon (ed.) *in* Great Books of the Western World (ed. R. M. Hutchins) 1952.

ABOUT: Current Biography 1952; New Yorker November 29, 1952; Saturday Review of Literature April 3, 1948; Time April 24, 1950, June 4, 1951, March 17, June 16, 1952.

"A.E." See RUSSELL, G. W.

AGAR, HERBERT (September 29, 1897-). For biographical sketch and list of earlier works and references, see TWENTIETH CENTURY AUTHORS, 1942.

* * *

Herbert Agar was the first president of Freedom House, an organization for the promotion of peace and international cooperation, which he helped to found in 1941. When the United States entered the Second World War, Agar became a lieutenant commander in the Navy, but shortly after his enlistment he was appointed special assistant to the American ambassador to Great Britain, the late John G. Winant. He served in this office until 1946, and during the last year of that period was Counsellor for Public Affairs in the United States Embassy in England. Another wartime duty was as civilian adviser to "Army Talks," training officers to be group leaders for army discussion groups.

After the war Agar remained in England to edit *Freedom and Union*, an organ of the federal world government movement. He resumed his writing and published a history of the American political system, *The Price of Union*, which Avery Craven called "a wise book, well written and highly provocative," and G. M. Stephenson described in the *American Historical Review* as "the work of a brilliant writer and seasoned historian, whose instincts are sharp, whose judgments are sound, and whose industry is adequate." In 1952 his *Declaration of Faith* appeared, an interpretation of history through the texts of

such "modern moralists" as Unamuno, Bernanos, Michael Roberts and Toynbee.

Agar now lives in England, dividing his time between London and a country home in Sussex. His third marriage took place in 1945 to Mrs. Euan Wallace.

ADDITIONAL WORKS: A Time for Greatness, 1942; Adams, H. The Formative Years (ed.) 1947; The Price of Union (in England: The United States: The Presidents, the Parties and the Constitution) 1950; A Declaration of Faith, 1952.

ABOUT: Current Biography 1944; Time November 9, 1942, December 9, 1946.

AGATE, JAMES EVERSHED (September 9, 1877-June 6, 1947). For biographical sketch and list of earlier works and references, see TWENTIETH CENTURY AUTHORS, 1942.

* * *

James Agate died of a heart attack in his London apartment at the age of sixty-nine. Just four days before, he had written the last words of his diary-autobiography *Ego 9*. He had decided that this was to be the last volume of the series, the diary portion of which had begun on June 2, 1932. His bad health, including chronic asthma, had given him premonitions of death. The last entry in the diary refers to his debts, large as always, saying, "Something has always turned up, and something will turn up now."

In amplification and correction of the sketch in TWENTIETH CENTURY AUTHORS, 1942, the following facts are important: Agate left Giggleswick School in 1893 and attended Manchester Grammar School for the next three years. On leaving school he entered his father's cotton mill in Nelson, Lancashire, and worked there for a year. For the next five years he worked on commission as a cotton manufacturer's agent in the Manchester office of his father's firm. On his twenty-fifth birthday he was taken into partnership; he made anything up to $20,000 a year until the first World War temporarily ruined the cotton business. His dramatic criticism for two Manchester papers, the *Daily Dispatch* and the *Guardian*, was therefore an avocation. In May 1915 he joined the Royal Army Service Corps and spent the remaining war years in Provence, "baling and despatching hay to the army in Salonika."

After the war was over, his French wife and he obtained a divorce on the friendliest possible terms, since neither could bear to live permanently in the other's homeland. She remarried, though he did not. The partnership in the cotton firm having "come to an end," Agate had nothing but his army gratuity. With it he bought a small candy, newspaper and tobacco store in the South Lambeth Road and proceeded to go broke. His *Saturday Review* job finally started him on his true path just after his forty-fourth birthday. In 1928 he had a nervous breakdown, allegedly because Leonard Rees of the *Sunday Times* always cut his criticisms. He reviewed books for the London *Daily Express* as well as doing his theatre and film criticism. Furthermore, he *did* write a play (in collaboration), a dramatization of his novel *Blessed Are the Rich;* he was booed when he tried to make a speech at the final curtain, and the play was taken off after a few performances.

J. B. Priestley wrote of Agate after his death that he was "a ripe character . . . one of the best dramatic critics of this century. . . . His novels are readable, but . . . not those of a novelist." Priestley characterized Agate's view of the theatre as escapist. Of the *Egos* he said, "The James Agate we meet in these diaries is not the whole man, freely and candidly expressing himself, but a character performance, brilliant and astonishingly sustained." Jacques Barzun, on the other hand, said of the *Egos* that "nine volumes of this ideal bedside reading are none too many," and again, "To me he outranks Pepys." Alan Dent summed him up as "a great character, undeniably a great dramatic critic, and possibly a diarist. . . . His style was lively and prickly, but not that of a great stylist. He knew this and admitted it honestly."

ADDITIONAL WORKS: Thursdays and Fridays, 1941; Express and Admirable, 1941; Brief Chronicles, 1943; Ego 5, 1943; Noblesse Oblige, 1944; Ego 6, 1944; Red Letter Nights, 1944; Immoment Toys, 1945; Ego 7, 1946; Around Cinemas, 1946; Contemporary Theatre, 1946; Ego 8, 1947; Thus to Revisit, 1947; Ego 9, 1948; Around Cinemas (second series) 1949; The Later Ego (8 & 9 in 1 vol.) 1951.

ABOUT: Agate, J. Ego 5, Ego 6, Ego 7, Ego 8, Ego 9, The Later Ego; Manchester Guardian June 9, 1947; New Statesman and Nation June 14, 1947; New York Times June 7, 1947; Saturday Review of Literature February 24, 1951; Time May 14, 1951.

*AGEE, JAMES (1909-), American poet, novelist, and miscellaneous writer, was born in Knoxville, Tenn. He attended school there and in the Cumberland Mountain country of Tennessee and spent some of his school vacations working as a harvest stiff

* Died May 16, 1955;   ā'jē

in the wheat fields of Kansas and Nebraska. Out of this background and experience he developed "a deep love of the land," which has been reflected in much of his later writing. He continued his education at Exeter Academy and at Harvard, where he received the coveted Poetry Prize and edited the Harvard *Advocate.* He graduated from Harvard in 1932 and two years later a collection of his verse, *Permit Me Voyage,* was published in the Yale Series of Younger Poets. In a foreword to the book, Archibald MacLeish commended especially Agee's "technical apprenticeship successfully passed, a mature and in some cases a masterly control of rhythms, a vocabulary at once personal to the poet and appropriate to the intention and, above everything else, the one poetic gift which no amount of application can purchase and which no amount of ingenuity can fake—a delicate and perceptive ear."

Walker Evans

In the same year in which his first book was published Agee joined the staff of *Fortune* magazine. As one of his assignments for *Fortune* he spent some weeks in the summer of 1936 living with an Alabama sharecropper family. He was so stirred by what he observed there that he gave up his job to devote himself to writing a report on sharecropper life. This was published as the text for a series of photographs by Walker Evans which appeared in 1941 as *Let Us Now Praise Famous Men.* Agee's text was written with bitterness and passionate sympathy in a style which one reviewer found "superior, highly original, accurately poetic writing." Another reviewer suggested, however, that from time to time the reader would curse the author as "a confused adolescent, an Ezra Pound in Wolfe's clothing, a shocking snob, or a belligerent mystic posing with a purple pencil on the Left Bank of *Fortune.*"

Agee went to work for *Time* in 1939, and in 1943 he became motion picture reviewer for the *Nation,* a post which he held until 1948 when he resigned to devote full time to writing. Most of Agee's recent work has been for motion pictures and television. He has published one short novel, *The Morning Watch,* a finely drawn study of a single day in the life of an adolescent boy, a student in an Anglo-Catholic school in the Tennessee hills. Agee's film credits include the commentary and dialogue for the widely acclaimed documentary film *The Quiet One,* and adaptations for the screen of Stephen Crane's story "The Brides Comes to Yellow Sky" (for the film *Face to Face*) and of C. S. Forester's *The African Queen.* Early in 1953 he wrote a television series on the life of Abraham Lincoln for the Ford Foundation's "Omnibus" program. He is married, has three children, and lives in New York City.

PRINCIPAL WORKS: Permit Me Voyage (poems) 1934; Let Us Now Praise Famous Men (with W. Evans) 1941; The Morning Watch, 1951.

ABOUT: MacLeish, A. *Foreword to* Permit Me Voyage; The Reporter April 14, 1953.

AIKEN, CONRAD POTTER (August 5, 1889-). For biographical sketch and list of earlier works and references, see TWENTIETH CENTURY AUTHORS, 1942.

* * *

In 1952 Conrad Aiken published his autobiography, in the form of a poetic essay told in the third person about a character named simply D. The book was called *Ushant* and, athough only two years in the writing, Aiken had begun it nearly twenty years earlier. Malcolm Cowley pronounced it "one of the great American autobiographies," and Mark Schorer found it profoundly original, "an almost stunning outpouring of prose, an incredibly subtle reconstruction of 'the soul's landscape.'" That *Ushant* is a strange and difficult book (Alfred Kazin called it "pretentiously difficult") was generally agreed by the critics. There is no regular chronological sequence. It would be impossible to piece together a factual record of Aiken's life from the book. But writing such a record was clearly not his purpose. Rather, he undertook to write, and in the main succeeded in writing, an autobiography of the creative spirit: ". . . he had kept firmly to his own slightly conservative bias, in the persistent belief that form must be form, that inventions of form must keep a basis in order and tradition, that a mere surrender to the pleasure (which was undoubtedly to be had) of charm-making in the bright colors of the colloquial and the colloquial cadence was not enough, not a substitute for the dark and difficult and, yes, painful process of cryptopoiesis, and that this, in turn, must, like a compass, have its true North in the shape of a conscious and articulated *Weltanschauung,* a consistent view. The consistent view had shaped itself slowly and intermittently out of the incredibly rich pour of new

discoveries, new ideas, the miraculously rapid expansion of man's knowledge, inward and outward, whether into the ever farther-reaching astrophysics of the heavens, or of man's mind" (*Ushant,* p. 219).

Aiken has published much poetry in recent years and has remained secure in his position as one of America's leading poets. He had the Library of Congress' Chair of Poetry in 1950-1951. His *Collected Poems* won the National Book Award as the most distinguished volume of poetry published in 1953. Delmore Schwartz observed in the *New Republic* that "the inclusive character of the volume makes possible a new experience of all of Aiken's work. Poems which at first seemed unimportant in themselves gain a new and profound meaning as phases and stages of a long progress and pilgrimage. And other poems, which seemed when they appeared separately to be only charming and delightful lyrics, exist now in a new light, possessing an underlying seriousness which was not at first apparent."

The publication of Aiken's collected *Short Stories* in 1950 reminded readers of his stature as a writer of fiction. Although his "Mr. Arcularis" and "Silent Snow, Secret Snow" are frequently anthologized, Aiken's fiction has been largely neglected. Of his quietly told stories, with their subtle, imaginative and sometimes horrifying probing of the human spirit, Mark Schorer has said: "We have, I think, no other body of contemporary fiction like this—so centrally coherent, its very coherence derived from a contemplation of the intransigence of that incoherence that lies scattered on all sides of us, and above and below."

Aiken and his artist-wife Mary Hoover live in a large rambling house in Brewster, Mass., where he likes best to write "at my own very dark and very disordered ping-pong table . . . or a table in my attic with windows on a level with trees." Part of the writing of *Ushant* was done in a small apartment on New York's East Side.

ADDITIONAL WORKS: *Poetry*—Brownstone Eclogues and Other Poems, 1942; The Soldier, 1944; The Kid, 1947; Divine Pilgrim, 1949; Skylight One, 1949; Collected Poems, 1953. *Prose*—Great Circle (novel—omitted from list of works in 1942 edition) 1933; Short Stories, 1950; Ushant, 1952.

ABOUT: Aiken, C. Ushant; Brown, C. S. Music and Literature; Gregory, H. & Zaturenska, M. History of American Poetry, 1900-1940; Hoffman, F. J. Freudianism and the Literary Mind; London Times Literary Supplement February 12, 1954. New Republic March 31, 1952, November 2, 1953; New York Herald Tribune Book Review September 24, 1950, October 12, 1952; New York Times Review October 26, 1952; Wake 11 (periodical).

AKINS, ZOË (October 30, 1886-). For biographical sketch and list of earlier works and references, see TWENTIETH CENTURY AUTHORS, 1942.

* * *

A slight but pleasant comedy by Zoë Akins, *Mrs. January and Mr. Ex,* ran for forty-three performances in New York City in 1944. The leading characters in the play were a feather-brained wealthy widow and a retired ex-President of the United States. George Jean Nathan found it a story spun "with the airy technique of knitting needles employed upon a candy spider web." The play was produced in Sweden under its original title, *Plans for Tomorrow.*

Other recent dramatic works listed by Miss Akins as having been produced are *Another Darling,* 1950, and *The Swallow's Nest,* 1951.

ADDITIONAL WORKS: *(dates of publication):* Puget, C. Happy Days (adaptation) 1942; Mrs. January and Mr. Ex, 1948.

ALAIN-FOURNIER. See FOURNIER

ALBERTI, RAFAEL (1902-), Spanish poet now living in South America, was born in Santa María, Cadíz, and educated in a

Jesuit academy. Little is known of his early life except that in 1917 he settled in Madrid. His early poetry was refined and scholarly, much of it based on folk themes. His collection of songs about the sea and sailors, *Marinero en Tierra,* won the National Prize for Literature in 1924. Succeeding volumes—*La Amante, El Alba del Alheli, Cal y Canto*—reflect Alberti's search for a poetic form. He imitated, with great virtuoso success, the elaborate verse forms of sixteenth and sevententh century Spanish poetry. His verse, at this stage, was very similar to the work of his contemporary and personal friend García Lorca, but, Sir Maurice Bowra writes, "he lacked Lorca's instinctive joy and instinctive melancholy." Alberti moved steadily toward his own modern idiom and a more intense self-analysis, finding his subjects, Bowra writes, "more and more in himself, in his own struggles and contradictions, and problems."

His masterpiece is *Sobre los Angeles* (1929), a collection of brilliantly introspec-

tive poems in which Alberti plumbs the depths of personal anguish and despair, and emerges neither triumphant nor defeated but prepared to find new reason for existence, new "angels," new powers of the spirit. The total, Pedro Salinas finds, conveys "an impression of distress, of anguish, that is the product of the fatal intimacy between the most beautiful and the most ugly . . . in that imaginary world of angels."

In 1934 Alberti announced that his poetry had ceased to serve purely "aesthetic reason and now obeys revolutionary reason." He traveled in Europe and the Soviet Union, actively interested in political movements of the Left. During the Spanish Civil War he fought on the Loyalist side as an airman, and after the defeat of the Loyalist forces, he emigrated to Buenos Aires where he now lives. From here he has continued to publish his poetry, as well as a number of dramas, essays, and collections of Spanish fables and poetry of the sixteenth and seventeenth centuries.

Very little of Alberti's work is available in English translation, a particular loss since his intellectual and highly concentrated poetry, Lloyd Mallan writes, "is not only accessible emotionally to all non-Spaniards but at the same time it offers new techniques, new forms of expression and an originality that might be incorporated to advantage in the poetic expressions of other languages." Mallan regards Alberti as "internationally . . . perhaps the most important poet of the new generation in Spanish literature." Salinas and other critics have found his work occasionally obscured with "the torments and incoherencies brought to literature by the winds of surrealism." But the result, Salinas concludes, "is never shapeless or spiritually obscure. . . . His crudest moments of expression retain an inevitable verbal charm which constitutes the essence of his poetic personality."

PRINCIPAL WORKS IN ENGLISH TRANSLATION: A Spectre Is Haunting Europe, 1936; Selected Poems, 1944.

ABOUT: Bowra, C. M. The Creative Experiment; Columbia Dictionary of Modern European Literature; Mallan, L. *Introduction to* Selected Poems of Alberti; Poetry December 1945.

"ALBRAND, MARTHA" (pseudonym of Heidi Huberta Freybe Loewengard) (1913-), German-American novelist, writes: "I was born in Rostock, Germany, but I went to school all over Europe, in Switzerland and France, Italy and England, sometimes privately tutored, sometimes going to public or private schools. This was mainly due to the conditions in Germany after the First World War and partly because my family had so many ties with other countries. There was  Polish, French, Danish and English blood all mixed up in this one Prussian officer's family. Maybe being rather lonely, always the new little girl, having to leave friends almost as soon as I had made them, was what made me start writing when still a child. My first novel, published by Ullstein in Berlin when I was seventeen, appeared under the name of 'Katrin Holland.'

"Somehow growing up in different countries, speaking different languages, adjusting or having to adjust to all sorts of mentalities only made me want to see more of the world, and so I became a journalist instead of going to college. Gradually I was sent about—to Austria, Hungary, Czechoslovakia, Yugoslavia, Poland, the Balkans, Spain, Morocco, Turkey, Palestine, Greece, Egypt, Iraq, and Persia. The northern countries I knew well. Having had a Danish great-grandfather (from whom I later borrowed my pen name), I had relatives in Denmark and spent many holidays there as well as in Norway and Sweden. But I never got to America though I longed to see it since the fairy tales of my childhood were the tales my American-born grandmother told. Her father, my great-grandfather, a Polish count, had dropped his title to become a missionary and had gone to spread the gospel among the Indians. My grandmother was the first white child to be born among the Chippewas, was stolen by a jealous medicine man for comparison with a newborn baby of another tribe and was, luckily, returned. Of all my great-grandfather's children who, later, when he was called to India, grew up as British citizens, my grandmother was the only one to finish her education in Germany where she met and married a German minister, my grandfather.

"My husband and I left Germany before Hitler's rise to power, and for a time we made our home on an island in northern Italy, San Giulio, in the Lago di Orta. There I managed to indulge in my favorite sport, swimming, to work in my garden, and to escape all kinds of speed, like cars and planes which I hate. From there too I finally managed to get to America. And the moment I came here I knew this was where I wanted to stay so I became an American citizen. In 1941 I bought a small dairy farm in New Jersey and this is where we live. I have never liked to live in cities, no matter how beautiful Paris, London, Rome and others are. I have always preferred the country which I seem to need in order to write. It took me quite a time to learn to write in English.

"From my own experiences it has always seemed of great importance that people in different countries should know about each other, and for that reason I have tried to tell of people of different nationalities and with different mentalities in my books."

PRINCIPAL WORKS: No Surrender, 1942; Without Orders, 1943; Endure No Longer, 1944; None Shall Know, 1945; Remember Anger, 1946; Whispering Hill, 1947; After Midnight, 1949; Wait for the Dawn, 1950; Desperate Moment, 1951; The Hunted Woman, 1952; Nightmare in Copenhagen, 1954; The Mask of Alexander, 1955.

ABOUT: New York Times Book Review June 22, 1947; Saturday Evening Post December 30, 1950; Wilson Library Bulletin June 1944.

ALDANOV, M. A. (1888-). For biographical sketch and list of earlier works and references, see TWENTIETH CENTURY AUTHORS, 1942.

* * *

M. A. Aldanov emigrated to the United States from Paris in 1941 and lives in New York. Since the publication of *The Fifth Seal* in 1943, his works have been read with increased interest by American readers. While pointing out the flaws in the structure of *The Fifth Seal* and deploring its "frigidity and lack of conviction about anything," Clifton Fadiman praised Aldanov as "an ingenious and practiced novelist." This has been the consensus of much of the critical writing on Aldanov, who displays a subtlety which can frequently turn into obscurity, an irony and brilliant imagination which sometimes produce an uneven, disconnected effect, and a detachment toward his characters which renders them sometimes cold and lifeless. Peter A. Pertzoff suggested that in his interest in individual characters and social movements, he is in the great tradition of the Russian novel. But, Pertzoff continues, "he interprets that tradition after his own manner, blending pessimism with irony, realism with symbolical interpretation."

ADDITIONAL WORKS IN ENGLISH TRANSLATION: The Fifth Seal, 1943; For Thee the Best, 1945; Before the Deluge, 1947; Tenth Symphony, 1948; Escape, 1950; A Night at the Airport (stories) 1949; To Live as We Wish, 1952.

ABOUT: Columbia Dictionary of Modern European Literature; Gray, J. On Second Thought; Ledré, C. Trois Romanciers Russes.

*ALDINGTON, RICHARD (1892-).

For biographical sketch and list of earlier works and references, see TWENTIETH CENTURY AUTHORS, 1942.

* * *

Richard Aldington has published little poetry and fiction since the Second World War. His most important writings in recent years have been biographies. Here his creative talents and sound scholarship have combined to produce several significant biographical studies—outstanding among them *The Duke*, a portrait of Wellington, which received the James Tait Black Memorial Prize in 1947; *The Strange Life of Charles Waterton*, a warm and witty study of the eccentric British explorer and ornithologist; and his *D. H. Lawrence*, which the London *Times* called "an admirable biography, honest in intention, affectionate in spirit, and generous in appreciation." In 1955, however, his biography of T. E. Lawrence was bitterly attacked in England for the unfavorable picture it presented of Lawrence's character and life.

Aldington has also done a considerable amount of editing, including an edition of the works of Oscar Wilde in the Viking Portable series, a collection of classic French novels, and an anthology of English verse. He lives in Montpellier, in the south of France.

ADDITIONAL WORKS: *Poetry*—Dream in the Luxembourg, 1946; Complete Poems, 1949. *Prose*—The Duke (in England: Wellington) 1943; A Wreath for San Gemignano, 1945; The Romance of Casanova, 1946; Four English Portraits, 1801-1851, 1948; The Strange Life of Charles Waterton, 1949; D. H. Lawrence: Portrait of a Genius but . . . 1950; Pinorman, 1954; Lawrence of Arabia, 1955.

ABOUT: Kershaw, A. Bibliography of the Works of Richard Aldington from 1915-1948; Revue de Littérature Comparée October-December 1951.

* A footnote in the second and third printings of TWENTIETH CENTURY AUTHORS, 1942, erroneously reported an obituary for Mr. Aldington.

ALDRICH, Mrs. BESS (STREETER) (February 17, 1881-August 3 1954).

For autobiographical sketch and list of earlier works and references, see TWENTIETH CENTURY AUTHORS, 1942.

* * *

Bess Streeter Aldrich died in Lincoln at the age of seventy-three. Several months before her death, she wrote to the editors of this volume: "My address is no longer Elmwood, Nebr., for in spite of my love for the small town where I lived for so many years, I built a home in Nebraska's state capitol, Lincoln, moving here in 1946. There was a vacant lot next door to my only daughter and, as my three sons had all left home by that time, I succumbed to the temptation to have my home near my daughter's family. Although Lincoln is a city with over one hundred thousand population, there are large cities in our country by the side of which Lincoln is still 'a small town,' so my liking for small towns as set forth in the 1942 volume has not changed.

"Since the earlier publication of TWENTIETH CENTURY AUTHORS, I worked one winter for Paramount Studios in Hollywood as a writer. Later helped supervise the filming of my book *Miss Bishop* for United Artists."

ADDITIONAL WORKS: The Lieutenant's Lady, 1942; Journey Into Christmas, 1949; The Bess Streeter Aldrich Reader, 1950.

ABOUT: National Cyclopedia of American Biography (1952); New York Times August 4, 1954; Scholastic November 13, 1944.

ALDRIDGE, JAMES (1918-), Australian novelist, was born in White Hills, Australia, where his father published a country newspaper, and spent his boyhood there and on the Isle of Man, in the Irish Sea. He began his newspaper career at sixteen as an office boy on the Melbourne *Sun*. In 1939 he went to England, studied briefly at Oxford and at the London School

Cosmo-Sileo

of Economics, and wrote feature articles for the London *Sketch*.

By the time World War II broke out, he was a seasoned reporter. When he could find no newspaper to send him to the front, he proceeded to cover the war on a freelance basis. He was in Finland at the time of the Russian attack on that country and was the only correspondent to see action on all the Finnish fronts. He was also one of the first correspondents to cover the Italian-Greek war, and was in Greece at the time of the German invasion. As a result of an injury received during the Syrian campaign, Aldridge was invalided home to Australia.

He flew to the United States while convalescing to take a temporary position in the foreign department of *Time* magazine. After six months, in February 1942, he returned to the front as war correspondent for the North American Newspaper Alliance.

Aldridge wrote his first novel, *Signed With Their Honour*, in off-hours from his *Time* job. Drawing heavily upon his war experiences, he set his story in Greece, and the most memorable scenes in the book are those concerned with the air fighting of the R.A.F. over Greece. Aldridge's skill as a reporter—his eye for detail, his terse, vivid, lucid prose—were displayed at best advantage here. The love story itself was full of Hemingway echoes, reminding one reviewer of *A Farewell to Arms,* another of *For Whom the Bell Tolls.* This was merely a surface resemblance, Robert van Gelder pointed out. "There is neither challenge nor swagger beneath the style. Instead there is curiosity and youth, the excitement of telling an important story and the pleasure of telling that story well."

In the novels which followed Aldridge continued to draw upon his war experiences, but with less happy results than in his first book. It was not until 1950, when he published *The Diplomat*, that there was, to quote Richard Lauterbach in the *New Republic,* "a tremendous forward stride in Aldridge's development from neo-Hemingway to a style and stature of his own." *The Hunter* was an even more extreme departure, concerned as it was with the life of a trapper in the Canadian North Woods. What remains of the "earlier" Aldridge is, apparently, the straightforward, authoritative style, and the faithful, detailed rendering of a "locale."

Aldridge has lived in recent years in Australia, Cambridge, Mass. (where he wrote *The Diplomat),* Canada (where he wrote *The Hunter*), and in France. His wife is Egyptian. Some years ago a newspaper reporter described him as having a diffident, "almost apologetic" manner—"quite deceptive behavior as he heads straight into anything that interests him, even if it's belched right up out of hell."

PRINCIPAL WORKS: Signed With Their Honour, 1942; The Sea Eagle, 1944; Of Many Men, 1946; The Diplomat, 1950; The Hunter, 1950; Heroes of the Empty View, 1954.

ABOUT: Current Biography 1943; New York Sun September 14, 1942; New York Times Book Review May 20, 1951.

*ALEGRÍA, CIRO (November 4, 1909-   ), Peruvian novelist, was born in Sartimbamba (province of Huamachuco), northern Peru, in the Marañon River region he describes in his *Golden Serpent*, of Spanish-Irish parents, José Alegría Lynch and Herminia Bazán Lynch. He was raised in the country and early became familiar with Indian life—an influence which was to

shape all his later writing. He received his secondary education at the Colegio Nacional de San Juan, in Trujillo. In 1926 Alegría became a reporter for the newspaper *El Norte.* He dropped out of journalism, after about a year, to work on construction and road-building projects, but in 1930 he returned to Trujillo and his job on *El Norte.* He attended classes at the University of Trujillo but did not take a degree. Meanwhile he began writing, publishing some poems and short stories in various periodicals in Peru.

Also in 1930 Alegría became a leader in the *Aprista* movement, a political group dedicated to the reformation of the Latin-American social and economic structure, with particular emphasis upon improving the lot of the poverty-stricken and down-trodden Indians. The Peruvian government quickly clamped down upon *Aprista* activity, and in 1931 Alegría was arrested and jailed for six months. He was liberated by an armed revolt of the *Apristas,* but when the uprising was suppressed, he was recaptured and condemned by court martial to ten years' imprisonment in the penitentiary in Lima.

Alegría was released from prison after a year and sent into exile in Santiago, Chile, in 1934. Here, penniless and in very poor health, he began to write again, contributing a monthly short story to a Buenos Aires newspaper. One of his stories, rejected by the newspaper because it was too long, he expanded into a novel, *La Serpiente de Oro* (published in the U.S. as *The Golden Serpent*) and submitted to a novel competition sponsored by a Santiago publisher. The book won first prize and was published in 1935. It is the story of the Indians who live in the region of the Marañon River, where Alegría grew up; "a strong and beautiful book," Carleton Beals called it, a sensi-

* ä lä grē′ä

13

tive study of the river and the men and women who live beside it, win their livelihood from it, and battle it in flood.

Three years later Alegría's second novel, *Los Perros Hambrientos* (The Hungry Dogs), was published. Once again the scene is northern Peru, but now no longer the river banks but the highlands above the river, populated by shepherds and farmers who live precariously, at the mercy of drought and a tyrannical landowner who exploits them. Before the publication of this novel Alegría deleted one episode which he later expanded into his third and most successful novel, *El Mundo Es Ancho y Ajeno (Broad and Alien Is the World)*. He submitted this book in a contest sponsored by the Pan-American Union, the publishers Farrar & Rinehart, and *Red Book* magazine. Unanimously judged the best of all the novels submitted (John Dos Passos, one of the judges, called it "one of the most impressive novels I've ever read in Spanish"), it received the $2,000 award, was published in the United States and Great Britain, and was translated into Swedish, Danish, German, Russian, and Portuguese.

In *Broad and Alien Is the World*, as in his earlier novels, Alegría considers a rural village in northern Peru and the attempts of a wealthy landowner to exploit the villagers. In spite of the power of its theme and the fact that it clearly described conditions that existed not merely in one isolated community but over a far larger section of South America (one critic called it a South American *Grapes of Wrath*), *Broad and Alien Is the World* was not primarily a propagandistic novel. What makes the book so satisfying, Milton Rugoff wrote, is its "fullness, authenticity, compassion." It thus becomes "the tragedy of the poor and helpless everywhere who . . . are despoiled of their little possessions, their dignity and their hope." For most readers, especially those outside South America, the main interest of Alegría's work lies in its rich depiction of the region, the life and the culture of the Indians of Peru. Harriet de Onís, who has translated his novels into English, finds his style "a blend of the language that has been preserved in the more remote regions of Peru, rich, sober, with a somewhat archaic flavor, the crisp direct manner that has probably come from his work as a journalist, and with a lyrical tone that reveals the poet who walks hand in hand with the novelist."

Alegría visited the United States in 1941 and was described by Robert van Gelder as

black-haired, stocky, and "healthy as a prizefighter." In recent years he has written Spanish dialogue for American-made motion pictures, articles, poems, short stories, and a number of children's stories, but he has published no novels. During World War II he worked for the Coordinator of Inter-American Affairs and for the Office of War Information. Alegría lived in the United States for eight years and is now teaching at the University of Puerto Rico.

PRINCIPAL WORKS IN ENGLISH TRANSLATION: Broad and Alien Is the World, 1941; The Golden Serpent, 1943.

ABOUT: Onís, H. de (ed.) The Golden Land; Spell, J. R. Contemporary Spanish-American Fiction; Wade, G. E. & Stiefel, W. E. *Introduction to Alegría's El Mundo Es Ancho y Ajena* (1945); Bulletin Pan-American Union June 1941; Current Biography 1941.

"ALEICHEM, SHALOM." See RABIN-OWITZ, S. J.

ALGREN, NELSON (March 28, 1909-), American novelist and short story writer, was born in Detroit, Mich., but has lived most of his life in Chicago. The Chicago of his childhood and young manhood—the slums, the cheap taverns, the looming shadow of the "El," the Polish immigrant community of the city's West Side— has been the background for most of

Robert McCullough

his brutal, hard-hitting novels and short stories. He attended the University of Illinois and took a degree in journalism, but he has worked only three weeks of his life on a newspaper. Finishing college in the middle of the great depression, he drifted about the South and Southwest for a while as a door-to-door salesman and a migratory laborer. In 1933, stranded in an abandoned filling station outside Rio Hondo, Tex., he wrote his first short story, "So Help Me," and sent it to Whit Burnett who published it in *Story*. This was sufficient encouragement to launch Algren on a writing career—a brief stint on a W.P.A. writers' project, another as co-editor with Jack Conroy of an experimental magazine, *The Anvil*.

His first novel, *Somebody in Boots*, was a stark and bitter portrayal of "depression youth"—which he dedicated to "those innumerable thousands: the homeless boys of America." The novel, as Maxwell Geismar writes, was "in the straight documentary style of the 1930's: a thesis novel of social protest in which the characters are social types." It had a spectacularly unsuccessful sales record (about 750 copies were sold) and was promptly forgotten until 1942 when *Never Come Morning* was published. With this powerful story of poverty and crime among the Poles of Chicago's West Side, Algren was recognized as a novelist of importance. Reviewers compared him to the acknowledged master of the "Chicago school of realism"—James T. Farrell, and to Richard Wright, author of *Native Son*. But Algren was no mere imitator. Philip Rahv points out that his realism "is so paced as to avoid the tedium of the naturalistic stereotype, of the literal copying of surfaces." His writing is perhaps self-conscious and stylized, but it is rich with creative detail and shrewd observation, shocking but not sensationalized.

Algren's most mature and significant work to date is the novel *The Man With the Golden Arm*, a study of Frankie Machine, dealer in a gambling club, and the cheap, sordid world of petty crime in which he operates. The scene is again Chicago's West Side, sharply and vividly realized in a host of minor characters—"a *Winesburg, Ohio* of the demented slum dwellers," Geismar calls it. It is a violent, unsparing novel, a "world of ruins," yet touched with warmth and compassion, retaining "the notion of hope and chance in a blind and very often hostile but not absolutely fatal universe." Algren wrote *The Man With the Golden Arm* on fellowships from the Newberry Library in Chicago and the American Academy of Arts and Letters. It became a best seller and received the National Book Award as the most distinguished American novel of 1949.

Algren is a shy, diffident man—"medium height, medium slim, medium sandy hair." From 1942 to 1945 he served in the Army ("I went in the Army a private, stayed three years, came out a private"). He is married and lives in Gary, Ind., within easy commuting distance of Chicago. Some years ago Malcolm Cowley called him the "poet of the Chicago slums." In his *Chicago: City on the Make*, a prose-poem that one reviewer described as "both a social document and a love poem," he writes about the city with a combination of brutal frankness and warm compassion that reminded some of his readers of Carl Sandburg's Chicago poetry. But Algren

has few pretensions—literary or otherwise. He thinks Faulkner and Hemingway are "in another league over and above Washington Irving, Henry James, or Hawthorne." Hemingway, who was born not far from Chicago, returns some of that admiration and has named Algren after Faulkner as among America's first writers.

As a novelist, Algren writes in the tradition of native American realism—the tradition of Stephen Crane's *Maggie,* Frank Norris' *McTeague,* and Dreiser's *Sister Carrie*. He has, from time to time, succumbed to some of the dangers of that tradition—the tendency toward over-simplification of character and motive, toward over-writing (one reviewer speaks of his occasional "floods of poetic rhetoric") and melodrama. But, as Maxwell Geismar points out, "he also represents a solid and enduring part of the American heritage of dissent."

PRINCIPAL WORKS: Somebody in Boots, 1935; Never Come Morning, 1942; The Neon Wilderness (short stories) 1947; The Man With the Golden Arm, 1949; Chicago: City on the Make, 1951.

ABOUT: Warfel, H. R. American Novelists of Today; English Journal March 1953; New York Herald Tribune Book Review October 7, 1951; New York Times Book Review October 2, 1949.

ALLEN, FREDERICK LEWIS (July 5, 1890-February 13, 1954). For autobiographical sketch and list of earlier works and references, see TWENTIETH CENTURY AUTHORS, 1942.

* * *

Frederick Lewis Allen died in New York City several days after being stricken by a cerebral hemorrhage. A few months before his death he wrote to the editors of this volume: "I have received in the interim [since 1942] two honorary Litt. D. degrees—one from Northeastern University and the other from Dartmouth. My term of service as a trustee of Bennington College ran only from 1937 to 1944, but I have served as an Overseer of Harvard from 1942 to 1948 and began a second term in 1950 which is still running. I also served for a time as a member of the Council of the Authors Guild; as a member of the Council of the Authors League; and as a director of the Foreign Policy Association, of which I am now an honorary director."

There is some disagreement among the readers of Mr. Allen's books as to whether he should be called a "social historian" or an "historical journalist." On one thing, however, they agree—that his books caught the unique flavor and spirit of the changing

American scene of the first half of the twentieth century. Edward Weeks of the *Atlantic Monthly* wrote: "Mr. Allen . . . has the memory of an elephant, a social conscience that smiles as it recalls, and a talent for terse and telling résumé which is the envy of any historian." Early in 1953 Frederick Lewis Allen resigned as editor-in-chief of *Harper's Magazine* to devote more time to his own writing. He continued, however, as a vice-president and director of Harper & Brothers until his death.

ADDITIONAL WORKS: I Remember Distinctly (with A. Rogers) 1947; The Great Pierpont Morgan, 1949; The Big Change, 1952.

ABOUT: Van Gelder, R. Writers and Writing; New York Herald Tribune Book Review October 12, 1952; New York Times February 14, 1954; Saturday Review of Literature April 2, 1949; Time July 12, 1948.

ALLEN, HERVEY (December 8, 1889-December 28, 1949). For biographical sketch and list of earlier works and references, see TWENTIETH CENTURY AUTHORS, 1942.

* * *

Hervey Allen died in his sixtieth year at his home, The Glades Estate, Coconut Grove, Fla., of a heart attack. He was at work on *The City in the Dawn*, the fourth of five novels about Colonial America; the complete series was to have been called *The Disinherited*. While none of his later novels matched *Anthony Adverse* in popularity, the four of them together had by his death outsold *Anthony Adverse*'s huge world-wide total of over 1,500,000 copies. In all, Allen's lifetime sales were well over three million.

Hervey Allen's Florida plantation was the successor to those he had previously owned in Bermuda and Maryland. His taste for big books and big estates matched his big (six-foot-four-inch) frame. He served his country bravely in World War I. (See *Toward the Flame* for an account of his front-line experiences.) In World War II he worked with the War Manpower Commission. He rendered further public service as a member of the board of governors of St. John's College, Annapolis, and as trustee of the University of Miami. Among his more cherished honors were Phi Beta Kappa, a fellowship in the Royal Society of Arts, and membership in the National Institute of Arts and Letters. From 1943 until his death he edited the *Rivers of America* series with Carl Carmer.

Anthony Adverse, wrote Harrison Smith, "was a revolution in a popular form of literature that had become formalized and sterile." The same writer said of his former *Saturday Review of Literature* colleague that "success had never altered his even temper or diminished his generous sympathy and his understanding for all mankind." No one who is interested in Allen either as a man or as a writer should miss his own article "The Sources of *Anthony Adverse*" in the *Saturday Review of Literature* for January 13, 1934.

ADDITIONAL WORKS: The Forest and the Fort, 1943; Bedford Village, 1944; Toward the Morning, 1948; The City in the Dawn (including the three foregoing) 1950.

ABOUT: National Cyclopedia of American Biography (1951); New York Times December 29, 1949; New York Times Book Review January 8, 1950; Saturday Review of Literature August 28, 1948, January 14, 1950.

ALLINGHAM, MARGERY (1904-). For autobiographical sketch and list of earlier works and references, see TWENTIETH CENTURY AUTHORS, 1942.

* * *

Margery Allingham's home is at Tolleshunt D'Arcy, in Essex, where she writes her "literate, highly readable" (to quote Will Cuppy) crime detection novels. She takes her work seriously and told Harvey Breit, of the New York *Times Book Review*: "If you have an intelligent mind and you like to read, and you need to escape, then you require an intelligent literature of escape. I make no distinction between the novel and the thriller, between Dorothy Sayers' *The Nine Tailors*, for instance, and Elizabeth Bowen's *The Heat of the Day*." One of the most ambitious of her recent novels, *The Tiger in the Smoke*, was described by the London *Times Literary Supplement* as a novel "in which the characters and their motives are as round and deep as those we might hope to find in a serious novel as opposed to an entertainment."

In 1949 Miss Allingham made her first visit to the United States. Breit described her as "a woman in her forties, with a warm, spontaneous manner."

ADDITIONAL WORKS: Galantrys (in England: Dance of the Years) 1943; Pearls Before Swine (in England: Coroner's Pidgin) 1945; Deadly Duo (in England: Take Two at Bedtime) 1949; More Work for the Undertaker, 1949; The Tiger in the Smoke, 1952; No Love Lost, 1954; The Estate of the Beckoning Lady, 1955.

ABOUT: New York Times Book Review March 20, 1949; Saturday Evening Post September 29, 1951.

ALTSHELER, JOSEPH ALEXANDER
(April 29, 1862-June 5, 1919). For biographical sketch and list of works and references, see TWENTIETH CENTURY AUTHORS, 1942.

*ALVÁREZ QUINTERO, SERAFÍN
(March 26, 1871-April 12, 1938) and
JOAQUÍN (January 21, 1873-June 14, 1944). For biographical sketch and list of earlier works and references, see TWENTIETH CENTURY AUTHORS, 1942.

* * *

Joaquín Alvárez Quintero died in his sixty-first year at his home in Madrid after a long illness.

The youngest of the Quintero brothers—there were three, of whom Pedro was the eldest—besides being a member of the Spanish Academy, was a founder member of the Society of Spanish Authors and a corresponding member of the Seville Academy of Belles Lettres and of the Hispanic Society of America. Since his death the *Obras Completas* of Serafín and Joaquín Alvárez Quintero have been published in six volumes (Madrid, 1947-49) containing 8,503 pages in all. The 228 dramatic works included begin with *Esgrima y Amor*, first performed on January 30, 1888, and end with *Los Burladores*, first staged on December 10, 1948. The brothers founded two weeklies in their earlier years, *Perecito* in Seville and *El Pobrecito Hablador* in Madrid.

The double issue of *Cuadernos de Literatura Contemporanea* listed below contains five items dealing with the Quintero brothers: a' brief obituary, three literary studies, and a bibliography of which the portion listing English translations bristles with misprints and seems to include a great many translations that were never published.

ADDITIONAL WORK IN ENGLISH TRANSLATION:
By the Light of the Moon, n.d. (1943-48).

ABOUT: Columbia Dictionary of Modern European Literature; Hoehn, M. (ed.) Catholic Authors, I; Cuadernos de Literatura Contemporanea (Madrid) 13/14, 1944; Hispania May 1949; New York Times June 15, 1944.

* äl'vä räth kĕn tä'rō

ALVERDES, PAUL (May 6, 1897-). For biographical sketch and list of works and references, see TWENTIETH CENTURY AUTHORS, 1942.

* * *

Paul Alverdes lives in Munich where, since 1934, he has edited the literary magazine *Das Innere Reich.* He publishes widely —stories, anthologies, non-fiction, children's books, book reviews, and articles—but his recent works are not available in English translation.

ABOUT: Columbia Dictionary of Modern European Literature.

AMBLER, ERIC (June 28, 1909-), English novelist and screenwriter, is a Londoner by birth and, apparently, by inclination. He was born there, the son of Alfred Percy and Amy Madeline Ambler, educated there, at Colfe's Grammar School and London University, and currently lives there. Ambler's early talents were scientific. He studied engineering on a scholarship  at London University and served an apprenticeship in engineering following his graduation. But a taste for literature and the stage dictated a change in plans. After a brief flurry with the theatre—during which time he wrote songs and toured England as a vaudeville comedian—he settled down to write advertising copy. He wrote technical ads for a firm of engineers, press releases for a theatrical agency, and general copy on a variety of subjects "ranging from baby foods to non-ferrous alloys." By 1937 he was the director of a large London agency, but at about the same time his "extracurricular" writings—short stories and novels—had proved profitable enough for him to resign to become a full-time professional writer.

In the period from 1937 to 1940 Ambler produced four of his most successful novels in a genre which has been variously called the "suspense novel," "the novel of intrigue," or simply, "the spy story"—*Background to Danger, Cause for Alarm, A Coffin for Dimitrios,* and *Journey Into Fear.* The prime elements of these stories, as Ben Ray Redman suggests, are "danger, mystery, and speed." But they must be strictly separated from the lurid "thriller" novel of brutal sensation and violence. Ambler's peculiar talent is for creating tension, and he is often able to accomplish this with a minimum of violence and derring-do. "Ambler's intrigue is urbane, his killings sophisticated, his double-crosses sheer artistry," Bernard Kalb writes. His heroes are well-meaning average men who, usually innocently or accidentally, become involved in a sinister maze of international spying and intrigue. The problem for Ambler has been, as he writes in a note to a 1951 edition of his *Epitaph for a Spy*, to add a touch of realism to the "familiar cloak and dagger stereotypes." But still he recognizes the deeper and more subtle psychological issues involved in his material. "In most human beings ideas of spying and being spied upon touch fantasy systems at deep and sensitive levels of the mind," he writes.

Ambler enlisted as a private in the British Army in 1940 and wrote no more novels until 1951. He was discharged from the Army in 1946 a lieutenant-colonel, after having served in Italy in a combat filming unit and as assistant director of Army kinematography in the War Office. He was in charge of all military training, morale and educational films for the British Army. After the war he continued to write and produce motion pictures. Among his recent screenplays are *The Magic Box* (1951), *Gigolo and Gigolette*, an adaptation of a Somerset Maugham story, for *Encore* (1952), and the adaptation of Nicholas Monsarrat's novel *The Cruel Sea* (1953).

With *Judgment on Deltchev* and *The Schirmer Inheritance*, his two recent novels, Ambler has demonstrated a tendency towards slower pace and more careful and detailed construction and documentation. *The Schirmer Inheritance*, indeed, does not introduce a note of violence until it is more than halfway through, and much of it is taken up with an account of some complicated litigation. What the book lacks in "physical excitement," C. Day Lewis observes, "it makes up for in expertise and verisimilitude." These qualities, Lewis continues, throw "the glamour of reality over the features of romance."

Ambler was married in 1939 to Louise Crombie, an American. For the present he is very much satisfied with his busy schedule of writing films and writing books. When asked by an interviewer whether the two interfered with each other, he replied, "No. Only that I'd like 600 days in the year. When I finish a movie I want to do a novel, and vice versa."

PRINCIPAL WORKS: Dark Frontier, 1937; Uncommon Danger (in U.S.: Background to Danger) 1937; Epitaph for a Spy, 1938; Cause for Alarm, 1938; A Coffin for Dimitrios (in England: Mask of Dimitrios) 1939; Journey Into Fear, 1940; Judgment on Deltchev, 1951; The Schirmer Inheritance, 1953. *As "Eliot Reed" (with C. Rodda)*—Skytip, 1950; Tender to Danger (in England: Tender to Moonlight) 1951; The Maras Affair, 1953.

ABOUT: Hitchcock, A. *Preface to* Intrigue: An Ambler Omnibus; New York Times Book Review July 26, 1953, August 9, 1953; St. Louis Star-Times September 15, 1944; Saturday Review July 18, 1953; Wilson Library Bulletin June 1943.

*AMMERS-KÜLLER, Mrs. JO VAN (August 13, 1884-). For autobiographical sketch and list of earlier works and references, see TWENTIETH CENTURY AUTHORS, 1942.

* * *

Mrs. van Ammers-Küller writes from Bussum, Holland: "The years of the war and after stopped my traveling abroad and also the publishing of my books in foreign countries. Many relations were lost. My books are prohibited now in the countries behind the iron screen, where I am (with many others) considered a 'bourgeois' author with capitalistic tendencies. The last book published in many languages (six) was *Elzelina*, the story of a Dutch parson's daughter who followed the armies of Napoleon as the mistress of Marshal Ney. The heroine was my great-grandmother's niece. Another historical novel deals with the witchery of Jeanne d'Arc; another tells the story of Louis XVII, the lost son of Louis XVI of France and Marie Antoinette. My next novel will, however, deal with modern times: the years after the war. In about thirty-five years I have published some twenty novels and six plays. The novels have appeared in fifteen countries."

* äm'ērs kül ēr

AMORY, CLEVELAND (September 2, 1917-), American social historian and novelist, was born in the resort town of Nahant, Mass., "Boston society's answer to Newport," a proper birthplace for a writer who was to become the chronicler of America's "society" resorts. His father, Robert Amory, is a textile manufacturer, and the Amory family has long been identified

Blackstone

with Boston society. Young Cleveland attended the Milton Academy and Harvard College, from which he was graduated in 1939. He devoted most of his time in college to the undergraduate daily, the *Harvard Crimson*. In his senior year he was president of the *Crimson*. By this time—influenced perhaps by an interview he had with the swimmer Eleanor Holm who received him at the Ritz-Carlton and served him champagne —Amory was determined to become a reporter. After a brief apprenticeship on the Nashua (N.H.) *Telegraph,* he became editor of the *Saturday Evening Post*'s "Postscripts" page—the youngest editor ever hired by that journal.

In World War II, Amory served in Washington, D.C., as second lieutenant with the Military Intelligence Division of the General Staff. He was discharged from the army for reasons of health in 1942 and went to Arizona where, he says, he quickly lost his Boston accent. Settling in Tucson he became a reporter for the *Arizona Star* and later he moved to Prescott as managing editor of the *Evening Courier.* After a year and a half in Arizona and a brief stay in Hollywood, Amory returned to the East as a free-lance writer. He became a specialist in what is called the "institutional" article—the detailed, anecdotal, and shrewdly-observed profile of almost any institution that is a representative part of American society. Amory's subjects have ranged from essays on Groton and Harvard to one on Stillman's Gymnasium (where New York's professional boxers train), and they have appeared in the *Saturday Evening Post, Life, Holiday, Harper*'s, and other magazines.

In 1947 Amory published in book-form his most ambitious institutional study up to that time—the history of Boston society and its first families from colonial times to the present—*The Proper Bostonians.* For his material Amory drew on family writings, legends, interviews, and his own store of memories and impressions, and wrote, Edward Weeks commented in the *Atlantic,* "with enough impudence, accuracy, affection, and respect to make the First Families anxious lest there be a second volume." As a scholarly history of a formidable social institution, Amory's book may have left something to be desired, but as a spirited, chatty, and at times acid-edged portrait, it was completely successful. It was, Perry Miller said, "weak on history, but rich in anecdote and written *con amore.*"

The Last Resorts, Amory's witty and informative study of the great society resorts of the last century and the early part of this one—Newport, Palm Beach, Southampton, Bar Harbor, etc.—followed in 1952 and proved equally popular.

Amory has taken time off from social history to write a novel, *Home Town,* a satire on book publishing and publicity. The inspiration for *Home Town,* he says, was his own gruelling experience as lecturer, luncheon guest, and autograph signer during the publicity campaign for *The Proper Bostonians.* Amory is described as "a tall, amiable-appearing man . . . seemingly more western than New England." He appears frequently on television panel shows.

PRINCIPAL WORKS: The Proper Bostonians, 1947; Hometown (novel) 1950; The Last Resorts, 1952.

ABOUT: New York Herald Tribune Book Review January 22, 1950.

ANDERSEN NEXØ. See NEXØ

ANDERSON, FREDERICK IRVING (November 14, 1877-December 24, 1947). For autobiographical sketch and list of works and references, see TWENTIETH CENTURY AUTHORS, 1942.

* * *

Frederick Irving Anderson died in St. Luke's Hospital, Pittsfield, Mass., at seventy after a fortnight's illness. Though he still made his home at East Jamaica, Vt., his last illness overtook him while visiting friends at Sandisfield, South Berkshire County, so that he died among the Berkshire Hills which had provided the setting for so many of his stories. It should be noted that his marriage to Emma Helen de Zouche took place on March 23, 1908, the year inadvertently given as that of her birth in TWENTIETH CENTURY AUTHORS, 1942.

ABOUT: New York Times December 25, 1947.

ANDERSON, MAXWELL (December 15, 1888-). For biographical sketch and list of earlier works and references, see TWENTIETH CENTURY AUTHORS, 1942.

* * *

In 1954, with a successful Broadway production of his dramatization of William March's novel *The Bad Seed,* Maxwell Anderson entered his thirty-first year as a playwright. He is a prolific and curiously uneven writer. None of his recent plays has had the great popularity and literary success of his earlier *Winterset* or *Elizabeth the Queen,* but he has has never written a play that has failed to entertain and to stimulate some portion of the theatre-going public. Some of his later work has been termed naïve, sentimental, and sometimes pompous.

These objections are especially valid for his wartime plays, *Candle in the Wind, The Eve of St. Mark, Storm Operation,* and *Truckline Cafe.* In historical drama, where his blank verse proves less unwieldy and his lofty sentiments less incongruous, Anderson has fared better. Both *Joan of Lorraine,* in which Ingrid Bergman starred as Joan of Arc, and *Anne of the Thousand Days,* a drama of the tempestuous romance and marriage of Anne Boleyn and Henry VIII, had successful productions. *Barefoot in Athens,* a portrait of Socrates as an early spokesman for democracy in a society ruled by totalitarian tyranny, had a mildly favorable critical reception. Anderson wrote the libretto for Kurt Weill's opera *Lost in the Stars,* based on Alan Paton's novel *Cry the Beloved Country.*

If Anderson has not yet written the great American drama which his earlier plays had promised, he has nevertheless kept alive in the theatre the tradition of serious dramatic writing. John Mason Brown thinks of him as "a playwright who believes in the beauty of great words nobly used, a philosopher who dares to ponder upon the imponderables. . ." Anderson himself has spoken of the lofty nature of the drama, as he conceives it: "The theatre is a religious institution devoted entirely to the exaltation of the spirit of man." He has referred to the theatre as "a temple of democracy." On this kind of idealism George Jean Nathan has commented shrewdly: "No man writing for our theatre has greater sincerity than Anderson, and no man a higher goal. But none, also, has a mind more critically incapable of meeting the demands it imposes upon itself."

Most of Anderson's recent plays were written in a small wooden shack in the woods back of his home in Rockland County, N.Y. He writes his first drafts in longhand and spends very little time rewriting. However, some six or seven months are spent plotting a play before he puts anything on paper. His wife, the former Gertrude Maynard, died early in 1953. His oldest son Alan has directed the television productions of some of his father's plays and also the play *Barefoot in Athens.*

ADDITIONAL WORKS: *Plays (dates of publication)*—The Eve of St. Mark, 1942; Storm Operation, 1944; Truckline Cafe, 1946; Joan of Lorraine, 1946; Anne of the Thousand Days, 1948; Lost in the Stars, 1950; Barefoot in Athens, 1952; The Bad Seed, 1955. *Essays*—Off Broadway, 1947.

ABOUT: Brown, J. M. Still Seeing Things; Morris, L. R. Postscript to Yesterday; American Literature May 1944; Current Biography 1953; South Atlantic Quarterly January 1945.

ANDERSON, SHERWOOD (September 13, 1876-March 8, 1941). For biographical sketch and list of works and references, see TWENTIETH CENTURY AUTHORS, 1942.

* * *

ADDITIONAL WORKS: Letters of Sherwood Anderson (ed. H. M. Jones) 1953.

ABOUT: Anderson, S. Letters; Gregory, H. *Introduction to* Portable Sherwood Anderson; Howe, I. Sherwood Anderson; Rosenfeld, P. *Introduction to* Sherwood Anderson Reader; Schevill, J. Sherwood Anderson; American Mercury May 1951; Atlantic Monthly June 1953; Nation May 19, 1951; New Republic August 15, 1949; New York Herald Tribune Book Review April 12, 1953; New York Times Book Review June 14, 1953; Saturday Review of Literature September 4, 1948, April 28, 1951, June 30, 1951; Time February 28, 1949.

ANDREEV. See ANDREYEV

ANDREWS, CHARLES MC LEAN (February 22, 1863-September 9, 1943). For autobiographical sketch and list of earlier works and references, see TWENTIETH CENTURY AUTHORS, 1942.

* * *

Charles McLean Andrews died at the New Haven Hospital, New Haven, Conn., at eighty, after a long illness. His wife, son, and daughter survived him. In an estimate published in 1951, A. S. Eisenstadt described Charles Andrews as "one of America's greatest historians . . . great not so much because of the answers he gave as because of the questions he asked." Some of these questions impelled him to reorient the study of the colonial period of American history. In his own words, "The years from 1607 to 1783 were colonial before they were American or national, and our Revolution is a colonial and not an American problem."

According to the obituary notice in the *American Historical Review,* "He became convinced that the most fruitful approach to a historical period was through its institutions and that the colonies could be understood only when placed against the English background. These two principles underlay nearly all his writings."

The Colonial Background of the American Revolution and the four volumes of *The Colonial Period of American History* are regarded as his most important achievements. Apparently three further volumes of the latter work were planned but never completed. His influence continues not only through his books, but also through the teaching and writing of the large number of his students upon whom he left a deep impression.

ADDITIONAL WORKS: Guide to the Manuscript Materials for the History of the United States to 1783 in the British Museum, 1908; The Colonial Period, 1912; Jonathan Dickinson's Journal, or God's Protecting Providence (ed. with E. W. Andrews) 1945.

ABOUT: Ausubel, H. (ed.) Some Modern Historians of Britain; Gipson, L. H. Charles McLean Andrews and the Re-Orientation of the Study of American Colonial History; American Historical Review January 1944; New York Times September 11, 1943.

ANDREWS, Mrs. MARY RAYMOND (SHIPMAN) (186?-August 2, 1936). For biographical sketch and list of works and references, see TWENTIETH CENTURY AUTHORS, 1942.

ANDREWS, ROY CHAPMAN (January 26, 1884-). For autobiographical sketch and list of earlier works and references, see TWENTIETH CENTURY AUTHORS, 1942.

* * *

Dr. Andrews retired as director of the American Museum of Natural History on January 1, 1942 and was appointed honorary director. In the following year he published the first volume of his autobiography, *Under a Lucky Star,* a lively and non-technical account of his explorations and scientific discoveries. A few years later, in *An Explorer Comes Home,* he continued his autobiography, describing the purchase of his farm home in Colebrook, Conn., and his life in the country. He now spends his summers there and his winters in Tucson, Ariz.

ADDITIONAL WORKS: Under a Lucky Star, 1943; Meet Your Ancestors, 1945; An Explorer Comes Home, 1947; Quest in the Desert, 1950; Heart of Asia, 1951; Nature's Ways, 1951; All About Dinosaurs (juvenile) 1953; Beyond Adventure, 1954.

ABOUT: Andrews, R. C. Under a Lucky Star, An Explorer Comes Home; Current Biography 1953; National Cyclopedia of American Biography (1946); New York Herald Tribune Book Review October 7, 1951; Science February 7, 1944.

*****ANDREYEV, LEONID NIKOLAE-VICH** (June 18?, 1871-September 12, 1919). For biographical sketch and list of works and references, see TWENTIETH CENTURY AUTHORS, 1942.

* * *

ABOUT: Columbia Dictionary of Modern European Literature; Guerney, B. G. (ed.) Portable Russian Reader; Martin, W. W. L. (ed.) New Spirit; Snow, V. Russian Writers.

* ŭn dryă′yĕf

"ANDRÉZEL, PIERRE." See BLIXEN, K. D.

"ANET, CLAUDE." See SCHOPFER, J.

ANGELL, Sir NORMAN (December 26, 1874-). For autobiographical sketch and list of earlier works and references, see TWENTIETH CENTURY AUTHORS, 1942.

* * *

From 1940 to 1951 Sir Norman Angell spent at least half of every year in the United States writing and lecturing. In 1951 he published his autobiography, *After All*— a record of a long lifetime devoted to the cause of international peace. Close to eighty and in poor health, Sir Norman wrote, near the end of the book: ". . . I find that I have not *quite* the energy I had until just recently for continent-wide lecture tours, sleeping on trains at night and lecturing or debating during the day. So, as I prepare to leave for England this spring, which I have done for nearly every year of this last decade, to return in the autumn, the feeling grows that this time I may not return; and that as I watch the skyscrapers fade into the distance, it may be my last look at the country where so much of my life has been spent."

In a review of *After All,* Alvin Johnson commented on the great influence that John Stuart Mill's essay "On Liberty" had upon Sir Norman Angell's life and work. Johnson wrote: "I have ever since [first meeting Sir Norman] associated Mill and Angell as the two most honest, bravest, wisest thinkers of the English-speaking world. In their infinite humanity, in their devotion to honest reason, Mill and Angell are father and son. But Angell became a movement. He wrapped the Great Illusion around his slender body and issued upon the world the most powerful movement for international peace and understanding of our time."

ADDITIONAL WORKS: Let the People Know, 1943; The Steep Places, 1947; After All, 1951.

ABOUT: Angell, N. After All; Christian Science Monitor Magazine July 31, 1948; Current Biography 1948; Saturday Review of Literature January 24, 1948, March 15, 1952.

ANGLE, PAUL MC CLELLAND (December 25, 1900-), American historian, writes: "I was born in Mansfield, Ohio, the first child of John Elmer and Nellie (McClelland) Angle. There I attended the public schools, graduating from the Mansfield

High School in 1918. That fall I entered Oberlin College but didn't like it and transferred to Miami University at the end of the first year. At Miami I majored in history and political science and received an A.B. degree, *magna cum laude*, in 1922. "Having no particular bent, I yielded to the blandishments of a well-meaning alumnus and started to sell life insurance in Rochester, N.Y. I quickly discovered that that was one occupation I was not cut out for, and decided to go to graduate school with the intention of preparing for college teaching. I spent the year 1923-24 at the University of Illinois and emerged with a master's degree and a sizable personal debt. To pay the debt I went to work as a textbook salesman for the American Book Company.

"In the spring of 1925, as I was about to accept a teaching position at Miami, I was offered the secretaryship of the Abraham Lincoln Association (then called the Lincoln Centennial Association) at Springfield, Ill. I held that position until 1932, when I became librarian of the Illinois State Historical Library and secretary of the affiliated organization, the Illinois State Historical Society. In 1945 I resigned to become director of the Chicago Historical Society.

"In college, and for some time afterward, I had no intention of becoming a professional writer. However, my position with the Abraham Lincoln Association called for historical research, and in that connection I discovered that I had a certain skill with words. I began to write, and have never stopped. I can count the books for which I am responsible, but I have no idea of the number of pamphlets, articles, book reviews, and sheer hack jobs that I have turned out.

"On June 17, 1926 I married Vesta Verne Magee of Piqua, Ohio. We have two children, Paula, and John Edwin, now adults. I am a member of the Sigma Chi fraternity, the Phi Beta Kappa Society, and the usual string of social clubs and professional organizations. Although a registered Republican—a distinct minority in Chicago—I go off the reservation without much provocation. I have no church affiliation."

PRINCIPAL WORKS: New Letters and Papers of Lincoln (comp.) 1930; Mary Lincoln, Wife and Widow (with C. Sandburg) 1932; Lincoln: 1854-1861, 1933; "Here I Have Lived": A History of Lincoln's Springfield, 1935; A Shelf of Lincoln Books, 1946; The Lincoln Reader (ed.) 1947; Bloody Williamson: A Chapter in American Lawlessness, 1952; By These Words (ed.) 1954.

ABOUT: Foreword in Angle, P. M. (ed.) Abraham Lincoln: His Autobiographical Writings; Book-of-the-Month Club News January 1947.

ANKER LARSEN, JOHANNES (September 18, 1874-). For autobiographical sketch and list of earlier works and references, see TWENTIETH CENTURY AUTHORS, 1942.

* * *

Johannes Anker Larsen writes: "My life since 1942 has not showed any incident worth noticing. After some traveling years (France, Italy, North Africa), I lead a calm, retired life in Copenhagen, without—as far as it is possible—being affected by all the exciting incidents of modern times.

"My latest novel, *Hansen*, appeared in 1949. None of my later novels has been translated into English. A big novel, *Olsens Dårskab* ('The Folly of Olsen'), 1942, has been published, however, in Holland 1943, in France 1949, and is going to appear in Italy."

ANNUNZIO, GABRIELE D' (March 12, 1863-March 1, 1938). For biographical sketch and list of works and references, see TWENTIETH CENTURY AUTHORS, 1942.

* * *

ABOUT: Columbia Dictionary of Modern European Literature; Harding, B. L. Age Cannot Wither; Atlantic September 1950; Saturday Review of Literature October 27, 1945.

*ANOUILH, JEAN (June 23, 1910-), French playwright, was born in Bordeaux of French-Basque parents. His mother was a violinist and his father, Anouilh writes, "was a tailor's cutter. He was a good and simple man who was a thorough master of his craft. That was his pride. When I was drawn into the wicked ways of literature, I always dreamed of becoming as skilled a craftsman as my father. Even my critics admit I have succeeded in that." At ten young Anouilh started writing plays in verse,

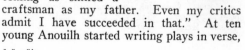

* ă nü′y

ambitious imitations of the plays of Edmond Rostand. He attended school in Paris at the Collège Chaptal and at the University of Paris where he spent a year and a half as a law student. For the next two years he wrote advertising copy for "products ranging from noodles to automobiles." This experience, he insists, was valuable training for a playwright, because it taught him more about "precision, conciseness, and agility of expression" than he would have learned in years of formal education. At nineteen, in collaboration with Jean Aurenche, he wrote his first play, a one-act farce, *Humulus le Muet*, the story of a young man who is able to speak only one word a day. He prudently saves the words up and offers them, all at one time, to a pretty young lady.

The first of Anouilh's plays to have a relatively successful production was *L'Hermine*. It was one of the several plays Anouilh was later to describe as *pièces noires*, a term which applies more accurately to the spirit and mood of the play than to its action. His "sable" plays end in death, just as his *pièces roses*, his "shell-pink" plays, end happily, in the conventional sense. But, as Paule Scott-James points out, the color is no real key to the plays. "The tragic ones, in the conventional sense of the word, are the only ones in which the heroes achieve bliss, where love is absolute, permanent and pure in death. . . ." The *pièces noires* "are in the long run the happy plays. Death saves those who have throughout the play won our sympathy from the tragedy of life."

Eric Bentley says that Anouilh is an artist "whose complex mind requires a complex vehicle." His plays fall into one large and subtle design as though, to quote Bentley again, "they are all the same play." His characters appear and reappear in different plays, and he frequently reworks the same theme from one play to another. He retells old stories—drawing upon the Bible *(Jezabel)*, Greek drama *(Eurydice, Antigone, Medée)*, Shakespeare *(Roméo et Jeannette)* or reworks some trite and time-worn device (like the "twin-comedy" in *Ring Round the Moon*) with refreshing new charm. In *The Rehearsal, or Love Punished* he quite literally incorporates Marivaux' comedy *Double Inconstancy* as a play within a play. "The astonishing thing," Edward Owen Marsh writes, "is not that he can keep on writing the same theme but that he can arrive at such a variety of solutions." His greatest dramatic virtues, Marsh finds, are "the characters and the poetry that is in them, the brilliantly sensitive manner in which he builds up our relationship to them and swings us into their tragic or fantastic predicament."

Philosophically, Anouilh's work is existentialist, although, as Bentley suggests, his closest tie is not to Jean-Paul Sartre but to the pre-existentialist Italian dramatist Luigi Pirandello. His adaptation of the *Antigone* of Sophocles, which to audiences in Paris during the German occupation in 1944 and in New York in 1946 (where Katherine Cornell played the title role) was a parable of the struggle of the Resistance (in Antigone) against the collaborationist (in Creon), was probably far less a political play than audiences took it to be. It is a *pièce noire* in which, Paule Scott-James says, "Hope is in death. Antigone and her lover Hemon have pierced through the compromise, the deadly materialism of this world; order, the reasons of state, politics, common obedience they know not of, and because they are true to themselves, to their passion, to their love, death embraces them, in their purity."

Anouilh is today regarded as the most popular living playwright in Europe. In America, however, his plays have so far had only limited success. Two of them, *Cry of the Peacock* (translation of his *Ardèle*) and *Legend of Lovers* (translation of *Eurydice*) were failures on the New York stage. *Antigone* and *Ring Round the Moon* (in Christopher Fry's translation) were somewhat more favorably received and *Mademoiselle Colombe* (1954), though it had a chilly critical reception, ran for sixty performances. *The Rehearsal (La Répétition)* was presented in French in New York late in 1952 by Jean-Louis Barrault's company. An early *pièce rose*, *Thieves' Carnival*, had a successful off-Broadway production in 1955. Anouilh has also written several films—among them the highly praised *Monsieur Vincent*.

Anouilh was married to the actress Monelle Valentin, who acted in productions of some of his plays, including the title role in *Antigone*. They have a daughter, Catherine. He is a shy, youthful-looking man, who dresses simply and wears gold-rimmed spectacles. He shuns publicity and is generally regarded as an "unsociable recluse." Marsh writes that his conversation "is unusually lucid and colorful, for he drops unhesitatingly on the exact word he requires—there is an almost legal precision in his terms and a vivid artistic compactness in image. He talks as he writes."

PRINCIPAL WORKS IN ENGLISH TRANSLATION: Antigone, 1946; Ring Round the Moon, 1950; Eurydice (with Antigone) 1951; Colombe, 1952; Legend of Lovers, 1952; Thieves' Carnival, 1952.

ABOUT: Current Biography 1954; Dictionnaire Biographique Français Contemporain; Gigoux, H. Jean Anouilh (in French); Marsh, E. O. Jean Anouilh: Poet of Pierrot and Pantaloon; Christian Science Monitor Magazine November 25, 1950, December 16, 1950; Contemporary Review May 1951; New Republic December 22, 1952; Nineteenth Century May 1948, June 1948; Theatre Arts November 1950.

"ANSTEY, F." See GUTHRIE, T. A.

ANTHONY, KATHARINE SUSAN (November 27, 1877-). For autobiographical sketch and list of earlier works and references, see TWENTIETH CENTURY AUTHORS, 1942.

* * *

To her list of biographical subjects Miss Anthony has added, since 1942, the Lambs, (Charles and Mary), Dolly Madison, and Susan B. Anthony. Her emphasis on abnormal psychology in her study of the tragic Lamb family produced a lively and controversial book. Dumas Malone called her *Dolly Madison* "the fullest and best account of Dolly Madison which has yet appeared in print."

Miss Anthony contributed an essay on "Writing Biography" to *The Writer's Handbook*, edited by Helen Hull, 1950. Here she outlined her own theory of biography as a combination of the skills of the novelist, the scholar and the historian. She wrote that "lifelikeness of the central character is the primary aim of all life histories. The human being who actually lived, thought, acted, suffered, failed, prevailed, triumphed and molded circumstances must be brought before us in his own unique and inimitable voyage and personality. To do this by the magic of language remains the principal reason for writing a biography."

ADDITIONAL WORKS: The Lambs, 1945; Dolly Madison: Her Life and Times, 1949; Susan B. Anthony: Her Personal History and Her Era, 1954.

ANTIN, MARY (1881-May 15, 1949). For autobiographical sketch and list of works and references, see TWENTIETH CENTURY AUTHORS, 1942.

* * *

Mary Antin died at the Pinehurst Nursing Home, Suffern, N.Y., after a long illness. She was sixty-seven years old. Her daughter, Mrs. Josephine E. Ross, and four sisters survived her, but her husband, Professor Grabau, had died in 1946. In her last nine years Miss Antin continued to be "still the author of *The Promised Land*," her plan for a book on her search for God never having attained fulfilment. *The Promised Land* had sold 85,000 copies in thirty-four printings by her death.

ABOUT: New York Times May 18, 1949; Publishers' Weekly June 11, 1949.

APOLLINAIRE, GUILLAUME (Wilhelm Kostrowitzki) (August 26, 1880-November 10, 1918). For biographical sketch and list of works and references, see TWENTIETH CENTURY AUTHORS, 1942.

* * *

PRINCIPAL WORKS IN ENGLISH TRANSLATION: Cubist Painters (1913) 1944; Selected Writings, 1950.

ABOUT: Adema, M. Apollinaire; Bowra, C. M. The Creative Experiment; Columbia Dictionary of Modern European Literature; Fowlie, W. Age of Surrealism; Books Abroad Spring 1947; Mercure de France April 1952; Saturday Review of Literature October 7, 1950, March 31, 1951.

APPEL, BENJAMIN (September 13, 1907-). For autobiographical sketch and list of earlier works and references, see TWENTIETH CENTURY AUTHORS, 1942.

* * *

Benjamin Appel writes: "I was still living in New York City on December 7, 1941, but by the following spring I had moved from my native town and haven't lived there since. Prior to December 7, 1941, an accident almost killed me. I was in an explosion and was severely burned—and if a writer looks for symbols, this was the symbol that came for me out of the blue. My whole life would change. I moved to Patchogue, Long Island, and once I was completely recovered I went to work as an aviation mechanic in the Republic Aviation Co., working a fifty-eight hour week. After six months here, I moved to Washington, D.C., in 1943 where I wrote speeches and articles for John B. Martin, acting director of the Office of Civilian Defense. In 1944 and 1945 I was a special writer for Paul V. McNutt, War Manpower Chairman. When Mr. McNutt was appointed U.S. High Commissioner to the Philippines, he appointed me his special assistant. In Manila I had the simulated rank of full colonel. On my return to Washington in 1946 I worked for seven months for John Steelman at the Office of War Mobilization and Reconversion, and when this agency was terminated by Congress I decided to return to fiction writing again. I moved to Roosevelt, N.J., in the fall of 1947 and have lived since then in this small town of eight hundred population. To complete the personal data, I might add that I am married to the same wife, Sophie Marshak, and have two daughters, Carla and Willa.

"My writing during the war years was, of course, a spotty affair. I hastily wrote one novel, *The Dark Stain,* in 1942, about race relations, concluding my brain guy trilogy. My novel *But Not Yet Slain,* about the last days of the New Deal and Washington bureaucracy, was published in 1947. *Fortress in the Rice,* my most ambitious novel since the brain guy trilogy, concerned itself with the Philippines of the war years.

"I did another novel about the Philippines, titled *Plunder,* published as a paper-back original. Some thirteen of my stories were also published in a paper-back collection called *Hell's Kitchen.* Otherwise, I am finishing a new novel for my "hardback" publisher. And soon I hope to begin a long novel about America over the last fifty years that will include not only what I have to say about middle-class people, but also contain everything I have to say—and by everything I mean just that."

ADDITIONAL WORKS: The Dark Stain, 1943; But Not Yet Slain, 1947; Fortress in the Rice, 1951; Plunder, 1952; Hell's Kitchen (short stories) 1952; Sweet Money Girl, 1954.

ABOUT: Van Gelder, R. Writers and Writing; Warfel, H. R. American Novelists of Today.

ARAGON, LOUIS (1897-). For biographical sketch and list of earlier works and references, see TWENTIETH CENTURY AUTHORS, 1942.

* * *

Louis Aragon and his wife, Elsa Triolet, lived in Nice during the first uneasy days of the Vichy government. In the fall of 1942, when the Italian Army entered Nice, they left and, in his words, "went under the deep and pleasant cover of illegality." Aragon joined the French Resistance. He organized intellectuals in the movement, edited a clandestine paper, *Les Etoiles,* and wrote poems which rapidly became a kind of folk-poetry of the Maquis who recited them around campfires. In all, Aragon published six books of poetry during the war—"a record of the wartime emotions of French soldiers and civilians—and all those in Allied countries who were committed to the war—such as no other poet has attempted to give," Malcolm Cowley wrote.

It was the war, Cowley points out, that made Aragon a poet again after a career in journalism. To his war poems he brought a

freshness and vigor too rare in the literature of World War II. Karl Shapiro said of Aragon's work in 1945: "The range of his pen is astonishing to a reader 'who has searched the poetry of this war for the love poem free of bitterness, cynicism, perversion or intellectualization; for the patriotic poem free of hysteria and tin; for the political poem free of fuzzy abstraction and cant; for the moral poem free of nasal rectitude."

In nearly all critical discussions of Aragon, his work is divided into three periods: a first stage when he participated in the *avant-garde* literary movements—cubism, dadaism, surrealism; a second period of Communism and "social realism"; and the third period, when he was the spokesman for the French Resistance. Since the end of World War II, Aragon has entered a new phase. What this "fourth period" will be called, or how Aragon will emerge, if he ever does, from it, no one can yet say. Aragon returned to Communism after the war and continues to serve the Communist Party. He is recognized, according to Genêt, as "French Communism's undisputed intellectual, literary and artistic leader."

As a Communist in post-war Europe, Aragon has had a strange and turbulent career. The Communist newspaper *Ce Soir,* which he edited and published, ceased publication in March 1953 because, he charged, rising costs, the Marshall Plan's support of non-Communist papers, and the French Government's opposition combined to destroy it. More telling, probably, is the fact that the circulation of *Ce Soir* dropped from some 600,000 in 1946 to only a little over 100,000 in 1952. Aragon then became editor of the Communist weekly *Les Lettres Françaises.* In the spring of 1953 this journal published the now-famous portrait of Stalin by Picasso —a picture which displeased a number of Communists and brought Aragon a sharp reprimand from the French Communist Party. In a personal statement Aragon admitted an "error in esthetics," but offered no humble apology. Instead he ended the article with a salute to Picasso. Such incidents as these have not apparently disillusioned or discouraged Aragon with Communism. More discouraging—perhaps to him and certainly to the readers who admired his wartime poetry—is the fact that he has produced no writing of serious literary merit since 1947.

Two books by Elsa Triolet (Madame Aragon) appeared in English translation in 1946 and 1947 respectively: a novel, *The White Charger,* which she wrote in 1942, a story of life in Paris between the two wars;

and a collection of three narratives of the French underground, *Fine of 200 Francs*. In 1944 she received the Prix Goncourt.

ADDITIONAL WORKS IN ENGLISH TRANSLATION: Aragon, Poet of the French Resistance (ed. H. Josephson and M. Cowley) 1945; Aurelien, 1947; Passengers of Destiny, 1947.

ABOUT: Aragon, Poet of the French Resistance (ed. H. Josephson and M. Cowley); Liebling, A. J. The Republic of Silence; Columbia Dictionary of Modern European Literature; Commonweal February 8, 1946; Nation January 15, 1944; New Republic July 5, 1943, August 13, 1945, December 17, 1945; New Yorker May 2, 1953; Saturday Review of Literature April 29, 1944, January 6, 1945, January 20, 1945, November 10, 1945.

ARCHER, WILLIAM (September 23, 1856-December 27, 1924). For biographical sketch and list of works and references, see TWENTIETH CENTURY AUTHORS, 1942.

ARDREY, ROBERT (1908-), American playwright and novelist, was born in Chicago and educated in the public schools of Chicago and at the University of Chicago. Here, in 1930, he studied writing with Thornton Wilder, and he spent the next five years as an "apprentice" writer, aiming primarily to develop his own personal style rather than to sell his writings. To support himself during his apprenticeship he had a colorful variety of jobs in which his average earnings amounted to about fifty dollars a month—statistician, piano player with dance orchestras, lecturer on the pre-Columbian Indians at the Chicago Century of Progress Fair, and bank clerk.

Sam Perkins

Ardrey wrote his first play, *Star Spangled*, in 1935. It was rejected by three producers before Arthur Hopkins finally produced it in 1936. The play, Ardrey cheerfully admits, was a flop, but it was not without its ádmirers. On the strength of it he was granted a Guggenheim fellowship. In 1938 he had two more plays, *How to Get Tough About It* (a Guthrie McClintic production) and *Casey Jones* (a Group Theatre production, directed by Elia Kazan), completed and in simultaneous rehearsals for Broadway productions. The two plays opened eleven days apart and both failed. On this Ardrey drily comments: "Business of having two failures at once so sensational, I became slightly famous and in

great demand in Hollywood. My value seemed to double and I went to work for Sam Goldwyn."

After three months in Hollywood, Ardrey went to Nantucket and began work on a new play, *Thunder Rock*, a philosophical fantasy about a young idealist who isolates himself in a lighthouse and creates a ghost world peopled with the passengers of a ship that foundered on Thunder Rock in 1839. The play opened in New York, under the direction of Elia Kazan, in 1939, and theatrical history repeated itself. "Biff, boom, worst notices I ever got. Artistic success my eye. This is what critics say these days to cover up. Three weeks closed." Thus Ardrey summed it up. He quietly departed for Hollywood to work on a screen treatment of Sidney Howard's play *They Knew What They Wanted*. A year later, however, *Thunder Rock* opened in London, and there, to the amazement of the New York theatre public and of the playwright himself, it became an "enormous, hysterical success." It played in London through the blitz, toured England, and was made into a successful English film.

During World War II, Ardrey worked for the Office of War Information in New York. In 1944 his first novel, *Worlds Beginning*, a fantasy about post-war life in America in the 1960's, was published. The reviewers were, on the whole, disappointed with it. Ardrey returned to the West Coast in the following year to settle there permanently. But he was back in New York briefly to attend the opening of another of his plays, *Jeb*, which Herman Shumlin produced in 1946—a very brief visit, since the play was a failure. Once more Ardrey went back to Hollywood, vowing to give up the Broadway theatre for good. "If and when I get at playwriting again, it will be because I've found some approach other than the usual routine of writing a new play, finding a producer and turning the script into the Broadway mill. There are just too many hazards in that. . . ." He published a second novel, *Brotherhood of Fear*, in 1952—like the first one an imaginative account of life in a mythical, totalitarian state. The British *New Statesman and Nation* found it "an exciting, readable middle-brow novel." American reviewers considered it a promising book, though lacking, as Anne Brooks wrote in the New York *Herald Tribune*, "the finer shades of characterization, the subtleties of emotion which make the distinction between an excellent thriller and a really analytical novel."

In October 1954 a new play by Ardrey, *Sing Me No Lullaby*, was produced in New

York by the Phoenix Theatre group. The story of a brilliant mathematician suffering in the 1950's for his political radicalism of the 1930's, it was a timely and forceful play, but not a popular success. *Time's* reviewer said that Ardrey's concern was not with a particular abuse but with what he saw as a national sickness. "Such a subject is not only highly complex; it is also not very dramatic."

As a script writer Ardrey has produced a new picture every twelve to eighteen months. This involves about three or four months of work for which, in 1947, he earned $6500 a week—a record salary which he does not expect to equal again. Ardrey and his wife, who was a former classmate at the University of Chicago, and their two young sons live in Los Angeles. As for Hollywood, he says: "Lovely thing Hollywood, if you handle it right. Live quiet, save your money, and always say *no*."

PRINCIPAL WORKS: *Plays*—Star Spangled, 1937; Thunder Rock, 1941. *Novels*—Worlds Beginning, 1944; Brotherhood of Fear, 1952.

ABOUT: Theatre Arts June, October 1940.

"A. RIPOSTE." See MORDAUNT, E. M. C.

ARLEN, MICHAEL (November 16, 1895-). For biographical sketch and list of works and references, see TWENTIETH CENTURY AUTHORS, 1942.

* * *

Time has stood happily still with Michael Arlen, who has published nothing since *The Flying Dutchman* in 1939. Ten years later a *New Yorker* reporter described him as "slender of waist, bushy of eyebrow, neatly sideburned, elegantly mustached, poised, urbane . . . and apparently the world's best-adjusted writer." Actually the image of the idle, dapper man-about-town, so carefully cultivated by Arlen, is not quite accurate. English by naturalization, he served as Civil Defense Public Relations officer for the West Midlands in 1940 and 1941 and was in Coventry during the terrible bombings of that city. When invalided out of service, he went to Hollywood in 1942 to write for MGM. Of his two years there he has said: "I did absolutely nothing. I was perfectly content. I'm a very indolent man. I'm a loller." In spite of his claim that "I hate writing. And I really mean it," he has been working on and off for the past several years on a play, "The Humble Peacock."

ABOUT: New York Times Book Review February 15, 1953; New Yorker April 9, 1949; Time February 11, 1946.

ARMSTRONG, HAMILTON FISH (April 7, 1893-). For biographical sketch and list of earlier works and references, see TWENTIETH CENTURY AUTHORS, 1942.

* * *

Hamilton Fish Armstrong is editor of *Foreign Affairs,* as he has been since 1928. He has served in a number of government posts in recent years. He was a member of the State Department Advisory Committee on Post-War Foreign Problems for the years 1942-44. In September 1944 he was appointed special assistant to Ambassador John G. Winant in London, with the rank of Minister, to advise the Ambassador on matters concerning the European Advisory Commission. He was also at this time a special adviser to Secretary of State Edward R. Stettinius. In 1945 he was an adviser to the United States delegation at the San Francisco conference of the United Nations and a member of the President's Advisory Committee on Political Refugees.

Armstrong's principal writings since the war have been on United States foreign policy and international affairs. In *The Calculated Risk* he urged all-out support for the Marshall Plan and changes in the veto policies of the Security Council of the United Nations. His *Tito and Goliath,* an analysis of the rift between Yugoslavia and the Soviet Union, was praised by John Gunther as "erudite, close packed, and definitive," and Vincent Sheean called it "so fully informed and coolly reasoned that one could wish it under the eyes and into the minds of all who have to deal with foreign policy."

Armstrong lives in New York City. His second wife was the novelist Carmen Barnes, whom he married in 1945; in 1951 he married Christa von Tippelskirch.

ADDITIONAL WORKS: The Calculated Risk, 1947; Tito and Goliath, 1951.

ABOUT: Current Biography 1948; New York Herald Tribune Book Review October 8, 1950, January 14, 1951; Time September 29, 1947.

ARMSTRONG, MARGARET NEILSON (September 24, 1867-July 18, 1944). For biographical sketch and list of earlier works and references, see TWENTIETH CENTURY AUTHORS, 1942.

* * *

Miss Armstrong died at her home, 58 West 10th Street, New York City, at seventy-six, after an illness of several months. Her last book, *The Blue Santo Murder Mystery,* had appeared three years before. From 1910 until her death she was a member of the board of directors of the Association for the Aid of Crippled Children; from time to time she served as chairman of important committees of this organization.

ADDITIONAL WORK: The Blue Santo Murder Mystery, 1941.

ABOUT: New York Times July 19, 1944.

ARMSTRONG, MARTIN DONIS-THORPE (October 2, 1882-). For autobiographical sketch and list of earlier works and references, see TWENTI-ETH CENTURY AUTHORS, 1942.

* * *

In 1951 Martin Armstrong's short stories, some of them "slightly Beerbohmish" and bizarre, were praised by the *Times Literary Supplement* for "neatness, orderliness, and frequent ingenuity." The same journal pronounced his book on George Borrow, in the English Novelists Series, "an interesting study of the man, a less sympathetic one of his books." Armstrong lives in Pullborough, Sussex.

ADDITIONAL WORKS: The Butterfly, 1941; Said the Cat to the Dog, 1945; Said the Dog to the Cat, 1948; George Borrow, 1950; Selected Stories, 1951.

ARMSTRONG, PAUL (April 25, 1869-August 30, 1915). For biographical sketch and list of works and references, see TWENTIETH CENTURY AUTHORS, 1942.

* * *

ABOUT: New Yorker December 30, 1950 (A. Johnston, "Profiles: Legend of a Sport").

ARNOLD, ELLIOTT (1912-), American journalist and novelist, writes: "I was born and educated in New York City. I  started working as a newspaperman there when I was eighteen, going to school in the afternoon and evening. I covered almost everything for the paper, beginning with Police Headquarters (lobster trick), covering the courts, City Hall, and the district shacks, which newspapers had in those days. I covered fires and murders and executions at Sing Sing and in the end I worked as a rewrite man and feature writer.

"I thought about writing books all the time and I wrote my first one when I was twenty

and it was published, which was a mistake. I recovered from that and wrote two more. Almost nobody read those first three. Just before the war I had an idea for a book dealing with the Commando operations out of England but I didn't know too much about that show until one day someone steered me on to a man from the Commandos who was on his way to Canada to train men. With the technical information he gave me I started in just before Pearl Harbor and the book almost wrote itself. When it was published it was read by a lot of people and I was a private in the air force.

"I was commissioned after a while and trained as an Intelligence Officer and sent to North Africa and then to Italy. Lieutenant General Ira C. Eaker, the air boss of the Mediterranean, ordered me to write the official air history of the theatre in collaboration with Richard Thruelsen, which I did. Then General George C. Kenney, who ran the air show in the South Pacific, requested that Donald Hough and I do a similar book on that theatre, which was done. In between I managed to get a novel about Italy down on paper.

"I got married during the war to an Arizona girl named Helen Emmons, and when I was discharged, as a captain, we went up to a summer house we owned in Maine and while there she happened to read to me a short magazine article dealing with the Apache Indian chief Cochise. The story fascinated me and we headed out for Tucson (which was probably in the back of her head all the time) and out of that came a book called *Blood Brother*. This was made into a fine film, *Broken Arrow*. The picture was especially good, I thought, because it started a new kind of thinking in Hollywood. From then on Indians got a break in films and it was about time.

"From my memories of what went on in Washington during the war I wrote a satire, called *Everybody Slept Here*, and then I wrote a fictional biography of the late Sigmund Romberg, and then another war book about Italy. I then plunged into another historical novel dealing with a relatively little known period in American history, the conquest of New Mexico, and it is the longest and, I hope, the best of them all—*The Time of the Gringo*.

"My books have been translated into French, Italian, Spanish, and Norwegian, and have almost all been published in London as well.

"Besides the books there have been short stories and articles in *Story Magazine, Cos-*

mopolitan, *Saturday Evening Post*, *Atlantic Monthly*, *Tomorrow*, *Liberty Magazine*, *Reader's Digest*, *Arizona Highways* and others. I'm not very good at the short stuff. I don't know why. I get cramped when I have to write to size. Maybe I'll get over that but I have so many novels running through my head I may never try hard enough.

"The Arizona business stuck, of course, which my wife also probably figured out in advance, and we now live about twelve miles out of Tucson and have two children, Tommy and Mary, an Irish setter, Jamie, and some of the most exciting country in the world and I hope I can keep on making enough money writing books to stay there."

PRINCIPAL WORKS: *Novels*—Two Loves, 1934; Personal Combat, 1936; Only the Young, 1939; The Commandos, 1942; Tomorrow Will Sing, 1945; Blood Brother, 1947; Everybody Slept Here, 1948; Walk with the Devil, 1950; The Time of the Gringo, 1953. *Biography*—Finlandia, the Story of Sibelius (juvenile) 1941; Deep in My Heart, 1949. *History*—Mediterranean Sweep (with R. Thruelsen) 1944; Big Distance (with D. Hough) 1945.

ABOUT: Warfel, H. R. American Novelists of Today.

ARNOLD, THURMAN WESLEY (June 2, 1891-   ), American lawyer and political scientist, writes:

"I was born in Laramie, Wyo. My boyhood was spent when Wyoming still had the atmosphere of the Wild West. My father owned cattle ranches while at the same time he practiced law in town. My education was at Princeton and Harvard Law School. I returned to Laramie in 1919 after service in the first World War. My ambitions were not literary but for a political career. I served in the state legislature when Harding was elected as the only Democrat to survive the landslide. I later became mayor of my home town.

"After practicing law for seven years I was unexpectedly offered the deanship of the law school at the University of West Virginia. Later I was appointed professor of law at Yale University in 1930. At that time the Yale Law School was in revolt against the narrowness of the traditional legal curriculum. In an attempt to broaden the base of legal training I became associated with a distinguished psychologist, Professor E. L. Robinson, in an attempt to study legal institutions from the point of view of public psychology. This approach to law lacked form and definition and for that reason students called our course the 'Cave of the Winds.' It was considered around the school as a frill lacking in practical moneymaking significance.

"Out of it grew my first two books—*The Symbols of Government* and *The Folklore of Capitalism*. The latter book received considerable public acceptance, which was probably the reason that President Roosevelt appointed me Assistant Attorney General in charge of the Anti-trust Division in 1938. This was after the NRA had been declared unconstitutional and the Administration had decided to reverse its field and try out the ideas of old fashioned competition for which I had considerable enthusiasm. With the Administration's support, I succeeded in enlarging the Anti-trust Division from a body capable of handling a few selected suits into an economic operation on a nationwide scale. This was the first time in the history of the Sherman Act that this had been done. Out of my efforts to promote competition as a national economic policy came two other books—*The Bottlenecks of Business* and *Democracy and Free Enterprise*. My first two books were written from the point of view of objective analysis, the second two from the point of view of an advocate—extremely different platforms from which to view society.

"My articles in popular magazines and scholarly publications are too numerous to detail. Most of them deal with economic and legal problems.

"In 1943 I was appointed a member of the United States Court of Appeals of the District of Columbia. The work of the Appellate Court, while most important, I found so different from my principal interest, the art of advocacy, that I resigned and entered the practice of law in 1946 with two close friends, Abe Fortas, who had been Under Secretary of the Interior, and Paul A. Porter, who had occupied a number of distinguished government positions. We practice in Washington, D.C."

* * *

In his witty and iconoclastic analysis of legal institutions in *The Folklore of Capitalism*, Arnold had described the effect of the anti-trust laws as actually promoting the growth of industrial monopolies "by deflecting the attack on them into purely moral and ceremonial channels." But during his tenure as United States Assistant Attorney General in charge of anti-trust cases, 1938 to 1943, he became known as the nation's "number one trust-buster," filing more than 200 suits against alleged conspiracies in restraint of trade.

Arnold has been described by Louis Cassels as "a fight-loving Westerner, who has a flamboyant sense of humor and one of the best legal minds in the country." The firm of Arnold, Fortas, and Porter has a thriving practice. Among its clients are the Coca Cola Company, Pan American Airways, Lever Brothers, and other large corporations. At the same time the firm has also handled without pay the defense for more than one hundred cases of government employees dismissed from their jobs for alleged disloyalty.

PRINCIPAL WORKS: The Symbols of Government, 1935; Cases on Trials, Judgments and Appeals (with F. James) 1936; The Folklore of Capitalism, 1937; The Bottlenecks of Business, 1940; Democracy and Free Enterprise, 1942.

ABOUT: Current Biography 1940; American Mercury June 1942; Harper's November 1951; Political Science Quarterly September 1943.

* ARTSYBASHEV, MIKHAIL PETRO-VICH (October 18, 1878-March 3, 1927). For biographical sketch and list of works and references, see TWENTI-ETH CENTURY AUTHORS, 1942.

* * *

ABOUT: Columbia Dictionary of Modern European Literature; Clark, B. H. & Freedley, G. (eds.) History of Modern Drama; Snow, V. Russian Writers.

* ŭr tsĭ bä'shĕf

ARVIN, NEWTON (August 23, 1900-). For autobiographical sketch and list of earlier works and references, see TWENTIETH CENTURY AUTHORS, 1942.

* * *

Newton Arvin has been professor of English at Smith College since 1940. His study of Herman Melville, published in the American Men of Letters Series, received the National Book Award for non-fiction in 1951. In 1952 he was elected a member of the National Institute of Arts and Letters.

ADDITIONAL WORKS: Short Stories of Nathaniel Hawthorne (ed.) 1946; Herman Melville, 1950; Selected Letters of Henry Adams (ed.) 1951.

ASBURY, HERBERT (September 1, 1891-). For biographical sketch and list of earlier works and references, see TWENTIETH CENTURY AUTHORS, 1942.

* * *

Herbert Asbury contributes articles to the New Yorker, the Saturday Review, Cosmo-politan, and other magazines. He was on the staff of Collier's Weekly from 1942 to 1948. His Great Illusion: An Informal History of Prohibition was reviewed as a solid and expert work of social history. Divided into two parts, the book covered the history of the temperance movement in America (in which his ancestor Bishop Asbury was a prominent figure) and the history of the corrupt and crime-ridden prohibition era.

Asbury was married to Edith S. Evans in 1945.

ADDITIONAL WORK: The Great Illusion: An Informal History of Prohibition, 1950.

ASCH, NATHAN (July 10, 1902-). For autobiographical sketch and list of works and references, see TWENTIETH CENTURY AUTHORS, 1942.

* * *

Nathan Asch writes: "I served three years overseas in the Air Force, flying several combat missions. At the war's end, my wife (formerly Caroline Tasker Miles of Philadelphia), who served in the WAC, and I were both in Paris. We decided we wanted to live in Northern California. We have a small home in Mill Valley, which is across the Golden Gate Bridge from San Francisco. We raise Siamese cats, and as a hobby I make furniture. I have published pieces, some of which have been reprinted in anthologies both here and in England, in the New Yorker, the Virginia Quarterly, Commentary. At the moment I am finishing a novel."

ASCH, SHOLEM (November 1, 1880-). For biographical sketch and list of earlier works and references, see TWENTIETH CENTURY AUTHORS, 1942.

* * *

The trilogy about the life of Jesus and the growth of early Christianity which Sholem Asch began with The Nazarene in 1939 was continued in 1943 with The Apostle, a study of the life of St. Paul, and completed in 1949 with Mary. Edmund Fuller described Asch's achievement as "an epic work in the grand tradition, intellectually, spiritually, and in literary stature." Asch handled his Biblical materials with dignity and restraint. His scholarship and erudition and his profound grasp of the spiritual bases of Christianity and Judaism, while not on the level of Thomas Mann's Joseph series, were regarded as far superior to the run of current popularizing novels on Biblical subjects. Asch's trilogy grew out of a belief that he has held for nearly half a century. Since visiting

Palestine in 1906, he has said, "I have never thought of Judaism or Christianity separately. For me it is one culture and one civilization, on which all our peace, our security and our freedom are dependent."

This recognition of the interdependence of the two faiths was the basis of Asch's very popular contemporary novel, *East River*. Set in New York City, the novel considers the fortunes of two Jewish families and their Jewish and Christian neighbors, and its dramatic crisis involves the marriage of a Catholic and a Jew, the conflicts and the ultimate reconciliation of the couple. Inevitably the objection has been raised that Asch has drifted away from his own faith. This he denies. "I have never done anything in my life to justify the rumor that I have left the Jewish religion. . . . I am a Jewish writer, a writer of the Jewish spirit."

Past seventy now, Asch lives in Florida. He is described as "still vigorous looking, with grey-white hair, a lined strong face, and a vibrant voice." His novels are written in Yiddish and then translated into English.

ADDITIONAL WORKS: *Fiction*—The Apostle, 1943; East River, 1946; Tales of My People, 1948; Mary 1949; Moses, 1951; A Passage in the Night, 1953. *Non-fiction*—My Personal Faith, 1942; One Destiny: An Epistle to the Christians, 1945.

ABOUT: Columbia Dictionary of Modern European Literature; English Journal November 1950; New York Herald Tribune Book Review April 15, 1951, October 7, 1951; New York Times Book Review October 9, 1949; Religion in Life Winter 1950; Saturday Review of Literature October 8, 1949.

ASHLEY-MONTAGU, MONTAGUE FRANCIS. See MONTAGU, A.

ASHTON, HELEN ROSALINE (October 18, 1891-). For biographical sketch and list of earlier works and references, see TWENTIETH CENTURY AUTHORS, 1942.

* * *

In two of her later novels Helen Ashton has again turned to the materials of English literature, as she had done in her earlier *William and Dorothy*, writing fictionized biographies of Jane Austen and the once famous but now forgotten poet Letitia Landon. With *Parson Austen's Daughter*, Miss Ashton daringly entered the hallowed and zealously guarded territory of the Janeites. Her story, based on a careful study of Jane Austen's letters and family memoirs, was a labor of love, written (the *Spectator* found) "with uncommon skill, grace and integrity." But of course the book suffered by comparison with the subject herself. Since Miss Ashton's Jane Austen was neither so clever nor so charming as Miss Austen's Elizabeth Bennett, readers were inevitably disappointed. "All the excitement, the inspiration, the interest, lies in the novels," Shirley Jackson wrote, "and the second-hand characters who creep into the biography are stale and lifeless beside their fictional counterparts."

With a lesser figure like Letty Landon, the outward events of whose life were also far more colorful and dramatic than Jane Austen's, Miss Ashton had an almost unqualified success. Michael Sadleir praised the book for its several brilliant incidental portraits of nineteenth century personalities which "show Miss Ashton at her intuitive best." And Carlos Baker felt that while, in less skillful hands, Letty Landon's story might have been a maudlin romance, Miss Ashton had elevated her "to something like the stature of a tragic heroine."

Helen Ashton's other recent novels have had contemporary settings. One of these, *Yeoman's Hospital*, like her earlier *Dr. Serocold*, covered twenty-four hours in the life of a provincial English hospital. It was made into a motion picture in England under the title *White Corridors*. Miss Ashton lives in Lechlade, Gloucestershire.

ADDITIONAL WORKS: Joanna at Littlefold (in U.S.: Joanna) 1942; Yeoman's Hospital, 1944; The Captain Comes Home (in U.S.: The Lost Captain) 1947; Parson Austen's Daughter, 1949; Letty Landon, 1951; Footman in Powder, 1954.

ASHTON, WINIFRED. See DANE, C.

ATHERTON, Mrs. GERTRUDE FRANKLIN (HORN) (October 30, 1857-June 14, 1948). For autobiographical sketch and list of earlier works and references, see TWENTIETH CENTURY AUTHORS, 1942.

* * *

Mrs. Atherton died in Stanford Hospital, San Francisco, at ninety, of "ailments connected with her advanced age." She had been in the hospital for almost a month.

In 1943, at the request of the Library of Congress, Mrs. Atherton presented a number of manuscripts and memorabilia to the Library. *My San Francisco*, subtitled *A Wayward Biography*, was her 56th and last book to be published. She wrote it on her accustomed schedule of arising at 6:30 A.M. and working about four or five hours before knocking off for the day. As usual, she made one longhand and two typewritten drafts of each chapter without assistance. When receiving a gold medal from the City of San Francisco on her ninetieth birthday, she said she "couldn't endure to have a secretary about when I'm writing."

Editorially the New York *Times* wrote at her death, "It will take some time to determine her niche in literature. . . . For the most part she succeeded in remaining contemporary, entering with gusto into the crowding debates of her time from feminism to communism. Of course a good deal of what she wrote was journalism rather than great literature. But at her best she wrote with strength, skill and surety." Also, one might add, with vividness, humor, and a keen sense that her best stock-in-trade was her own rich, courageous, unembittered personality.

ADDITIONAL WORKS: The Horn of Life, 1942; Golden Gate Country, 1945; My San Francisco, 1946.

ABOUT: Atherton, G. My San Francisco; Life November 11, 1946; National Cyclopedia of American Biography (1950); New York Times June 15, 16, 1948.

ATKINSON, BROOKS. See ATKINSON, J. B.

ATKINSON, ELEANOR (STACKHOUSE) (January 7, 1863-November 4, 1942). For autobiographical sketch and list of earlier works and references, see TWENTIETH CENTURY AUTHORS, 1942.

* * *

Mrs. Atkinson died in a hospital at Orangeburg, N.Y., at seventy-nine. She had been living with her daughter "Eleanor Blake" (d. 1952) at Nyack. Her other daughter still lives in Manhasset, Long Island. Mrs. Atkinson was the daughter of Isaac M. and Margaret (Smith) Stackhouse.

ABOUT: Banta, R. E. Indiana Authors and Their Books; New York Times November 11, 1942.

ATKINSON, JUSTIN BROOKS (November 28, 1894-   ). For biographical sketch and list of earlier works and references, see TWENTIETH CENTURY AUTHORS, 1942.

* * *

In the fall of 1942 Brooks Atkinson temporarily gave up his post as drama critic and began a new career as foreign correspondent for the New York *Times*. He was first assigned as war correspondent to Chungking, China, from 1942 to 1944, and then from

1945 to 1946 he was news correspondent in Moscow. His reporting from the Russian capital was bitterly attacked in *Pravda* but won him the Pulitzer prize for journalism in 1947. He returned in 1946 to his post as drama critic on the *Times* where his reviewing continues to be marked, John Mason Brown comments, by "felicity, wisdom, and perception."

Atkinson's life is neatly (and not at all schizophrenically) divided between Times Square and the "Walden Pond" atmosphere of his farm home in the Catskill region of New York. His latest collection of essays, *Once Around the Sun,* is a day-by-day chronicle of life in the city and in the country—summed up by John Mason Brown as: ". . . life in war-torn China or Russia, life on his farm, life on New York's streets and piers, wild life and the seasonal changes of nature, life wherever the sun shines and the human spirit is tested."

Mrs. Oriana Atkinson wrote an account of her ten-months' stay in the Soviet Union with her husband in *Over at Uncle Joe's* (1947). She has also published several historical novels.

ADDITIONAL WORKS: Broadway Scrapbook, 1947; Once Around the Sun, 1951.

ABOUT: Current Biography 1942; Nation July 20, 1946; New Yorker July 27, 1946; Saturday Review of Literature August 11, 1951; Time July 22, 1946.

* AUBRY, OCTAVE (September 1, 1881-March 28, 1946). For biographical sketch and list of earlier works and references, see TWENTIETH CENTURY AUTHORS, 1942.

* * *

Octave Aubry died of a heart attack in Paris at sixty-four. He was to have been received as a member of the French Academy next day, having been elected on February 14, 1946. The Academy suspended its sitting of March 28 immediately after convening, as a mark of respect for the deceased. Former Premier Edouard Herriot succeeded to M. Aubry's chair the following December.

The last years of Octave Aubry's life were devoted to a history of the French Revolution, planned in four volumes. Volumes I and II, subtitled *Destruction de la Royauté* (1942) and *La République* (1945) respectively, deal with the Revolution proper. The projected subtitles of Volumes III and IV were *L'Empire National* and *Grandeur et Chute de Napoléon.* The foreword to Volume I is short and obviously full of a sense

* ō brē′

of France's unhappy war-time predicament, but it reveals with the utmost clarity the author's attitude toward Napoleon ("the great man of the Revolution") and toward the writing of history. Of the whole historical period 1789-1815 Aubry writes, "It shows us forcefully how major a share individuals have in events, and how, if one wishes to seize facts and link them together, he must first brood over human beings, try to make them live again as Ulysses did the shades from the Styx, and question them about the heart of the matter." One might well expect such views from a writer who, as M. Prévost has pointed out, "evolved from the historical novel to novelized history, and thence to history *tout court.*"

ADDITIONAL WORK IN ENGLISH TRANSLATION: The Private Life of Napoleon, 1947.

ABOUT: Dictionnaire de Biographie Française; New York Times February 15, March 29, December 6, 1946; Wilson Library Bulletin May 1946.

AUDEN, WYSTAN HUGH (February 21, 1907-). For biographical sketch and list of works and references, see TWENTIETH CENTURY AUTHORS, 1942.

* * *

The stature of W. H. Auden has risen considerably in the past decade. Now no longer merely the facile, brilliant and witty young virtuoso-poet, he is widely recognized as a major figure in contemporary poetry, probably, as Louise Bogan has said, after T. S. Eliot "the strongest influence in American and British poetry." This is not to suggest that a growing seriousness and depth of feeling in his work have subdued his audacious wit. Auden is still a daring and sometimes a flamboyant poet. He ranges freely from the impressive Christmas oratorio *For the Time Being* and *The Age of Anxiety* (which Marianne Moore called "a deep and fearless piece of work matched by a mechanics of consummate virtuosity") to the lusty and grotesque Hogarthian spirit of his libretto for Igor Stravinsky's opera *The Rake's Progress* (on which he collaborated with Chester Kallman).

Such a range inevitably produces unevenness in the quality of the poetry. This is further complicated by Auden's intellectual and spiritual development over the past years. His emigration to the United States, his slow but steady shifting of viewpoint from youthful Marxism to his present-day Anglo-Catholicism, his constant experimenting in poetic forms—these may account for what Richard Hoggart, in a full-length critical study of Auden, calls "the unsatis-

factoriness of so much of Auden's recent work, for the disconcerting changes of tone, the switches, say, from subtle wit to childish cruelty . . . or from an obviously *clever* manner to a somewhat heavy seriousness." However the issues are resolved, Hoggart continues, Auden will always be "a civilizing force" and he will continue to write poetry. "Poetry is his natural way of speaking, and he is too concerned with man in society and too anxious to communicate ever to let himself be silent for long."

Auden has become a United States citizen. ("The attractiveness of America to a writer," he told an interviewer in 1940, "is its openness and lack of tradition.... You are forced to live here as everyone else will be forced to live. There is no past. No tradition. No roots—that is, in the European sense. . . . But what is happening here is happening everywhere.") He has taught and lectured at a number of American colleges and universities. In 1950 he became associate professor of English at the University of Michigan, and in January 1953 he was appointed William Allen Neilson Research Professor at Smith College. He was named a Guggenheim Fellow in 1942 and in 1945 received an award for poetry from the American Academy of Letters. In addition to his creative writing, he has edited a collection of Edgar Allan Poe's *Selected Prose and Poetry* and (with Norman Holmes Pearson) a five-volume anthology called *Poets of the English Language.* In 1955 he was compiling an anthology of modern American verse for publication in England. Part of his time he spends at his villa on the Italian island of Ischia, near Capri.

ADDITIONAL WORKS: *Poetry*—For the Time Being, 1944; Collected Poetry, 1945; The Age of Anxiety: A Baroque Eclogue, 1947; Collected Shorter Poems, 1930-1944, 1950; Nones, 1951; The Shield of Achilles, 1955. *Prose*—The Enchaféd Flood, or The Romantic Iconography of the Sea, 1950.

ABOUT: Hoggart, R. Auden; Scarfe, F. Auden and After, W. H. Auden; Southworth, J. F. Sowing the Spring; Canadian Forum September 1948; Christian Century January 16, 1946; Commonweal December 8, 1944, May 25, 1945, May 14, 1948; English Journal February 1949; Nation October 28, 1948; New Yorker April 14, 1945; Nineteenth Century January 1947; Poetry January, March, July 1945, November 1947, September 1951; Saturday Review of Literature April 28, 1945, July 19, 1947; Time July 21, 1947, April 30, 1951; Virginia Quarterly Review July 1945, October 1946.

AUMONIER, STACY (1887-December 21, 1928). For biographical sketch and list of works and references, see TWENTIETH CENTURY AUTHORS, 1942.

AUSLANDER, JOSEPH (October 11, 1897-   ). For biographical sketch and list of works and references, see TWENTIETH CENTURY AUTHORS, 1942.

* * *

Joseph Auslander is lecturer in poetry at Columbia University. He was associated with the Library of Congress from 1937 to 1944, as consultant in English poetry (1937-43) and as gift officer (1942-44).

Auslander's poems on the Second World War, collected and published under the title *The Unconquerables,* were praised in some sources as a passionate tribute to the victims of tyranny and war. Elizabeth Drew found them "full of movement and color." But S. H. Hay, in the *Saturday Review of Literature,* while commending the spirit in which the poems were written, thought that they might have been more worthy of their theme had they been written "with less haste, with more discipline, with a greater regard for the strict phrase and the inevitable word." His verse on popular themes appears frequently in *This Week,* the syndicated Sunday magazine.

With his wife Audrey Wurdemann, Auslander has collaborated on two novels—one, *My Uncle Jan,* a warm and pleasant story of a Czech-American family in Wisconsin; the other, *Islanders,* a poetically-told story of a Greek family living in Florida, praised by Elizabeth Yates for its "subtle language" and by Philip Wylie for "its beautiful display of meanings in mankind."

ADDITIONAL WORKS: *Poems*—The Unconquerables, 1943. *Novels (with A. Wurdemann)*—My Uncle Jan, 1948; Islanders, 1951.

AUSTIN, Mrs. MARY (HUNTER) (September 9, 1868-August 13, 1934). For biographical sketch and list of works and references, see TWENTIETH CENTURY AUTHORS, 1942.

* * *

ABOUT: Hunt, R. D. California's Stately Hall of Fame.

AYALA. See PÉREZ DE AYALA

* **AYMÉ, MARCEL** (March 28, 1902-   ), French novelist and playwright, was born in Joigny, the son of a blacksmith. When he was two years old his mother died and he went to live in Jura with his maternal grandparents who were tile-makers. At seven he was sent to live with his mother's sister in Dôle. His schooling was irregular. "I had a horror of school," he has said, "and even

* ā mā'

today, in my most horrible nightmares, I dream that I am in the classroom." In spite of his antipathy for formal study, he submitted to family pressure and enrolled in medical school. But after a year he dropped out. He settled in Paris and tried a variety of jobs— bank clerk, motion picture "extra," insurance agent, journalist—with no particular success.

Studio Lipnitzki

His dominant interest since the age of sixteen, when he discovered the writings of Villon and Balzac, was literature. An illness forced him to spend six months at Dôle, and during this period of enforced leisure he read widely and completed his first novel, *Brûlebois.* The manuscript came to the attention of Jacques Reboul, editor of the *Cahiers de France,* who helped Aymé to get it published. He wrote and published regularly and rapidly after that. In 1929 his fourth novel, *Table aux Crevés,* won the Théophraste Renaudot prize as the best novel of the year. Aymé's early novels drew heavily upon the peasant life he had observed at first hand around Dôle. His first novel to appear in English translation, *The Hollow Field,* was a somber picture of this life. V. S. Pritchett called it "a little masterpiece, imperturbably observant, grave, merry, cruel and delicate."

It was not until after World War II, however, that Aymé first came to the general notice of American critics, and by this time he had developed into a satirist, a suave, witty, ironic and completely detached observer. *The Transient Hour,* his quite unidealized portrait of life in Paris during the German occupation, *The Barkeep of Blémont,* with its sharp-eyed view of a small town immediately after the Liberation, and *The Miraculous Barber,* a novel of France in the throes of the 1936 political riots, were all the more remarkable for their lack of powerful political passion. Like many great satirists (Justin O'Brien classes him with Molière, Daumier, and Anatole France in this respect, and Morris Bishop believes that he writes "in the Voltairean tradition"), Aymé has a lean, spare style. He reports horrors as objectively and as cheerfully as he might report the most tender and charming incidents. He is a writer who, Nicola Chiaromonte comments, "is authentically non-committed to the questions of our time and entirely free from any anguish."

Like his novels, Aymé's plays are hard and brilliant satires. His *Clérambard*—a thoroughly amoral farce which was denounced by François Mauriac for "frivolous impiety"—was the greatest success of the 1950 season in Paris. His *La Tête des Autres*, produced in Paris in 1953, was hailed as "an uproarious satire" on the court system in France. Aymé also writes essays, literary criticism, and children's books. He is a confirmed Parisian. According to legend, which may be apocryphal, he never appears out of doors without a pair of large, dark sun glasses. The reason for this, he tells curious reporters, is, "So that I can sleep while I walk." Aymé and his wife visited the United States in 1949. At that time Harvey Breit described him as tall and lean, having "a quiet air about him, quite catlike in its stillness."

PRINCIPAL WORKS IN ENGLISH TRANSLATION: The Hollow Field, 1933; The Green Mare, 1938; The Transient Hour, 1948; The Barkeep of Blémont, 1950; The Miraculous Barber, 1951; The Wonderful Farm (juvenile) 1951; The Second Face, 1953; The Secret Stream, 1954; The Magic Pictures (juvenile) 1954.

ABOUT: Dictionnaire Biographique Français Contemporain; New York Times Book Review August 7, 1949; Partisan Review September 1950.

*AYSCOUGH, Mrs. FLORENCE (WHEELOCK) (1878-April 24, 1942). For biographical sketch and list of works and references, see TWENTIETH CENTURY AUTHORS, 1942.

* * *

Mrs. Ayscough (by her second marriage Mrs. Harley F. MacNair) died in the Chicago Osteopathic Hospital after a long illness. She had published nothing since *Chinese Women: Yesterday and Today* (1937), but after her death Professor MacNair discovered among her papers the exceedingly interesting correspondence which he edited and published in 1945 under the title *Florence Ayscough and Amy Lowell: Correspondence of a Friendship*. The published correspondence begins in December 1917, although the two women had known each other from childhood, and ends with Miss Lowell's death in 1925. Most of the letters deal with their collaboration on *Fir-Flower Tablets*. The book contains a variety of other matter of interest to students of Chinese literature or of Miss Lowell's poetry, including "Reminiscences of Amy Lowell"

* ās′kō

taken from a letter of Mrs. Ayscough's to Ada Russell, a mutual friend.

Mrs. Ayscough had been president of American Friends of China, Chicago, since 1939; she was a member of the Royal Asiatic Society of London, the Royal Central Asian Society, the Society of Women Geographers, and other learned societies. Acadia University, Wolfville, Nova Scotia, awarded her an honorary Litt.D. in 1923.

ABOUT: MacNair, H. F. (ed.) Florence Ayscough and Amy Lowell; New York Times April 25, 1942; Poetry February 1919, June 1942.

"AYSCOUGH, JOHN." See BICKER-STAFFE-DREW, F. B. D.

"AZORÍN." See MARTÍNEZ, RUIZ, J.

BABBITT, IRVING (August 2, 1865-July 15, 1933). For biographical sketch and list of works and references, see TWENTIETH CENTURY AUTHORS, 1942.

* * *

ABOUT: Hough, L. H. Great Humanists; Kazin, A. On Native Grounds.

BABEL, ISAAK EMMANUILOVICH (1894- ?). For biographical sketch and list of works and references, see TWENTIETH CENTURY AUTHORS, 1942.

* * *

Since 1936 there has been no mention of Isaak Babel's name in Soviet publications. His fate has been the subject of a number of conflicting rumors. Raymond Rosenthal writes in *Commentary* that Babel's wife, who lives in Paris, heard a report that he was jailed in 1941 for making some indiscreet remark while traveling in a remote part of Russia as a correspondent. According to this story he contracted typhus fever and died in jail. Another report has it that he is alive and well, living in the country. The only fact that emerges out of this fog of mystery and rumor is that Babel stopped writing. His works were never under official Soviet condemnation. His silence, Rosenthal suggests, "seemed to be a voluntary act." Probably, according to the late Nikander Strelsky, it stemmed from "the enforced proletarization of literature under the first Five-Year Plan and . . . Babel's unwillingness to submit his pen to a dictated tendentiousness."

Translations of Babel's stories have appeared in recent years in *Commentary* and *Partisan Review*. His work is now ignored in the country of its origin, but scholars recognize him as "a typical and brilliant representative of the 'romantic' period in Soviet literature." In Strelsky's judgment he was "uniquely gifted within limits . . . unrivalled for the concentration, impact, and brevity of his stories and for his mastery of dialect."

ABOUT: Columbia Dictionary of Modern European Literature; Guerney, B. G. (ed.) The Portable Russian Reader; Struve, G. Soviet Russian Literature, 1917-50; Commentary February 1947.

BACHELLER, IRVING (September 26, 1859-February 24, 1950). For autobiographical sketch and list of works and references, see TWENTIETH CENTURY AUTHORS, 1942.

* * *

Irving Bacheller died in the Westchester division of New York Hospital, White Plains, N.Y., at ninety, after a long illness.

The *Winds of God* (1941) was his last book; in it he told of the man he might have been—an Adirondack guide and timber cutter with frustrated scholarly leanings—if he had married at sixteen, as for a time he wanted to, instead of going to college as his mother wished.

Irving Bacheller, like many others, claimed to be the discoverer of Stephen Crane, having serialized *The Red Badge of Courage* in 1893. In 1917 he served as a war correspondent in France. His first wife died in 1924, and the following year he married Mrs. Mary Elizabeth Sollace (d.1949). In 1939 he was made an honorary LL.D. of Rollins College and given a dinner jointly by the alumni of St. Lawrence University and Rollins in honor of his eightieth birthday.

Eben Holden sold over a million copies in its author's lifetime, but his own favorites among his books were *A Man for the Ages* and *The Light in the Clearing.*

ADDITIONAL WORK: The Master of Chaos, 1932.

ABOUT: Van Gelder, R. Writers and Writing; New York Times February 25, 1950; New York Times Book Review December 21, 1941; Publishers' Weekly March 18, 1950.

BACON, Mrs. JOSEPHINE DODGE (DASKAM) (February 17, 1876-). For biographical sketch and list of works and references, see TWENTIETH CENTURY AUTHORS, 1942.

* * *

Mrs. Bacon occasionally contributes articles and stories to the Girl Scout magazine *American Girl.* She lives in New York City and spends her summers in the Catskills, where she is an active member of the Onteora Club. She is founder and curator of the club's

famous art collection, "A Hundred Years of American Art," and she has assembled during the last fifteen years a unique group of the works of artists who have lived in the colony since its founding in 1887.

Correction: In the list of Mrs. Bacon's principal works, *Down in the Closet*, 1940, should read *Door in the Closet.*

BACON, LEONARD (May 26, 1887-January 1, 1954). For biographical sketch and list of works and references, see TWENTIETH CENTURY AUTHORS, 1942.

* * *

Leonard Bacon died at his home in South Kingston, R.I., at the age of sixty-six.

Bacon received an honorary M.A. from Yale University in 1941. In 1951 he was elected to the American Academy of Arts and Letters.

Like his Pulitzer prize-winning *Sunderland Capture*, Bacon's collection of wartime lyrics, *Day of Fire*, was more meditative and reflective than much of his earlier satiric work. "He muses on the causes which have brought us to our present pass," Elizabeth Drew wrote, "[and] . . . finds a sustaining power in the undying life of natural forces." In 1950 Bacon published his translation of the sixteenth century Portuguese epic *The Lusiads* of Luis de Camões. Dudley Fitts found the translation admirable in every respect—". . . one cannot say too much in tribute to his skill as a translator and his taste as a poet." Thomas G. Bergin was equally pleased with the translator's introduction and notes to the work—"easy and urbane without condescension, witty without pretentiousness."

ADDITIONAL WORKS: Day of Fire, 1943; Camões, L. de, The Lusiads (tr.) 1950.

ABOUT: New York Times January 3, 1953.

BAGNOLD, ENID. For autobiographical sketch and list of earlier works and references, see TWENTIETH CENTURY AUTHORS, 1942.

* * *

Enid Bagnold (Lady Jones) writes from Sussex: "Her recreations (now she is older) are gardening and gardening only. Her daughter Laurian is now married to the Honorable Rowland Winn, M.C., and published a novel some four years ago, called *Prince Leopold and Anna.* Her son Timothy Jones, a barrister, has published two novels, —*The Small Hours of the Night* and *Mr. Twining and the God Pan.*"

In recent years Enid Bagnold has turned to writing for the stage. Her study of a psychotic theatre-struck young girl, *Lottie Dundass*, had a successful run in London, co-starring Ann Todd and Dame Sybil Thorndyke. Another play, *Poor Judas*, was performed in London. American audiences, however, gave a chilly reception to *Gertie* which had a four-day run in New York in 1952. Far more enthusiastic was the American reception of her novel *The Loved and the Envied*, a perceptive study of an aging beauty and the social world in which she lives. Leo Lerman described it in the New York *Times* as an "intricately designed fan of a book, folding and unfolding some fifty years of life ... one of those reports that are being written by those who realize that their worlds are dying and know exactly why."

Miss Bagnold figures as a character in H. G. Wells' novel *The Dream*.

ADDITIONAL WORKS: *Plays* (dates of publication)—Lottie Dundass, 1941; Theatre (Lottie Dundass *and* Poor Judas) 1951. *Fiction*—The Loved and the Envied, 1951; The Girl's Journey (The Happy Foreigner, pub. 1920, and The Squire, pub. 1938) 1954.

ABOUT: Atlantic October 1952; New Yorker January 19, 1952.

BAILEY, HENRY CHRISTOPHER

(February 1, 1878-). For autobiographical sketch and list of earlier works and references, see TWENTIETH CENTURY AUTHORS, 1942.

* * *

Henry Christopher Bailey retired from the staff of the London *Daily Telegraph* in 1946. He lives in Llanfairfechan, North Wales.

ADDITIONAL WORKS: Nobody's Vineyard (in England: Dead Man's Shoes) 1942; Mr. Fortune Finds a Pig, 1943; The Cat's Whisker, 1944; Queen of Spades (in England: Slippery Ann) 1944; The Wrong Man, 1945; Life Sentence, 1946; Honour Among Thieves, 1947; Save a Rope, 1948; Shrouded Death, 1950.

BAILEY, TEMPLE (188?-July 6, 1953).

For biographical sketch and list of earlier works and references, see TWENTIETH CENTURY AUTHORS, 1942.

* * *

Temple Bailey died at her home in Washington, D.C. She was probably in her seventies.

Once one of the highest paid and most popular writers in America, she wrote little in her last years. Her fiction adhered strictly to a romantic formula which a reviewer once described as "high-flown romance with a bland disregard for realities." Her writing, within its limitations, was, however, expert. "Temple Bailey always writes a good novel," a reviewer said in the *Christian Century* in 1942, "agreeable in tone, smooth in style, sound in construction, never so tense in its situations as to subject the reader's nerves to serious strain."

ADDITIONAL WORKS: Pink Camelia, 1942; Red Fruit, 1945.

ABOUT: New York Times July 8, 1953.

BAKELESS, JOHN EDWIN (December 30, 1894-). For biographical sketch and list of earlier works and references, see TWENTIETH CENTURY AUTHORS, 1942.

* * *

John Bakeless became associate professor of journalism at New York University in 1940 and was appointed to the graduate faculty of the university in 1948. He received a second Guggenheim Fellowship in 1946. A captain in the infantry reserve, Bakeless went on active duty as a major in the infantry in 1941; he became major and later lieutenant colonel in the General Staff Corps in 1942. In 1944 he was assistant military attaché to Turkey and in the following year, with the rank of colonel, a member of the American section of the Allied Control Commission for Bulgaria. His present home is in Seymour, Conn.

In 1942 Bakeless expanded and completed his earlier work on Christopher Marlowe in the two-volume *The Tragicall History of Christopher Marlowe*. The product of some twenty years of research, this was hailed as "one of the most informative books" yet written on the great English poet and dramatist. Since the end of the war Bakeless has worked mainly in the field of early American discovery and exploration. His combined biography of Lewis and Clark was praised for its exhaustive research and its lively and readable presentation of the material. Equally successful in its appeal to the general reader as well as to the scholar was *Eyes of Discovery*, a book which attempts to show America as it appeared to the first white men. *Time* found it "a fascinating view of what the land was like before the first highway went through and the first billboard went up."

ADDITIONAL WORKS: The Tragicall History of Christopher Marlowe, 1942; Lewis and Clarke, Partners in Discovery, 1947; Fighting Frontiersman (juvenile) 1948; Eyes of Discovery, 1950.

ABOUT: Altick, R. The Scholar Adventurers.

BAKER, Mrs. DOROTHY (DODDS)

(April 21, 1907-   ). For autobiographical sketch and list of earlier works and references, see TWENTIETH CENTURY AUTHORS, 1942.

* * *

Mrs. Baker writes: "My home is no longer Cambridge, Mass., but Terra Bella, Calif., where we live on the extremely variable fat of the land in the business or businesses of raising oranges, olives, and, in a small way, cattle.

"Furthermore, we now have not just one daughter but two, the second being named Joan, born in 1943.

"And on the literary side: I have written two novels since *Young Man With a Horn*. *Trio* was published in 1943; and the year following, my husband and I collaborated on a stage version of it, which was produced in New York in 1945. The play starred Lydia St. Clair, Lois Wheeler, and Richard Widmark. It ran some seventy performances and then was banned by the City Commissioner as immoral, which was, I thought, a very odd conclusion for the City Commissioner to come to, since the novel (to which the play very faithfully adhered) was not considered in the least immoral and indeed was awarded the Gold Medal for Literature of the Commonwealth Club of California in 1943. However, since the time of the New York banning, the play has been successfully presented and respectfully received in Los Angeles, San Francisco, Woodstock, N.Y., (summer circuit), and at the Arts Theatre in London.

"My latest (and I hope not my last) novel was published almost five years ago in 1948. It is entitled *Our Gifted Son*. Since that time I have lectured, or talked, rather, about writing at Stanford University and at Pomona College. I have also started three or four novels, none of which has got to chapter two, which is a good distance short of first base. However, this may be the year."

ADDITIONAL WORKS: Trio, 1943; Our Gifted Son, 1948.

ABOUT: Current Biography 1943.

BAKER, FRANK

(May 22, 1908-   ), English novelist and dramatist, writes: "I was born in London, the only child of musical parents. Music was in our blood, but I was the first to take to literature. Educated at Winchester Cathedral School, where I came under the influence of the late Dean Hutton, who encouraged my earliest writing. Went straight from school to work in the City;

clerk in the Underwriting Room of the London Assurance for five years. When I was twenty-one I resigned this job, and, because of my love of music, undertook secretarial work to a college for church musicians. Within a year I had revolted against the academic attitude to life and art and taken myself off to the Land's End, where, with twenty pounds and a small piano, I started to live sensibly. My first published article was in the *Radio Times*, a little later. I then wrote masses of stories, poems, and composed much music, as well as a first novel, sensibly rejected by publishers. My second novel, *The Twisted Tree*, was a Cornish tragedy, 'a dark and terrible tale,' said one reviewer. 'If Mr. Baker will quiet down,' said Gerald Gould in the *Observer*, 'he may go far.' A second novel, *The Birds*— which was a bitter satire on human folly in the Wellsian manner—followed a year later. 'Tediously unconvincing,' said the *Daily News*. 'A vividly imaginative tour de force,' said the *Illustrated London News*. But it did not sell.

"Moving about from place to place, earning my living by playing village organs, I did not publish again for some years. Then I wrote *Miss Hargreaves* as a joke. It was rejected by nine publishers; but I persisted, because I liked it. It was finally accepted, has since been reissued, translated into Italian and French, and published in America. Although I have written nine books since then, *Miss Hargreaves* is the only one most people remember, which maddens me as much as Sherlock Holmes must have maddened Conan Doyle. I have since adapted her for television, for sound-radio, for the theatre; and in each version Miss Hargreaves was played by Margaret Rutherford. Most people were astonished to learn that I did not write the play for her; in fact, she read the book and was so determined to play the part that my adaptations naturally followed. It was a superb performance from England's leading comedy actress.

"As well as many novels and stories, etc., I have written many plays, both for radio and the theatre. Only one of my stage plays, apart from *Miss Hargreaves*, has seen production: a modern version of *Punch and Judy* which was toured to remote service camps in Scotland and the Orkneys during the war, myself playing Punch. Six of my radio plays have been produced, and I have read my own stories over the air. Not long ago I broadcast a series of English popular songs, from the Middle Ages to the present day, from Paris radio. And for eighteen months I was accompanist at the Victorian cabaret, the Players Theatre, in Albemarle Street, London.

"In 1938 I was received into the Catholic Church, baptized in Winchester, England's ancient capital, where my education had been begun. In 1943 I married Kathleen Lloyd, an actress, on tour with Sir Lewis Casson's and Dame Sybil Thorndike's production of the *Medea* to Welsh and Durham miners, in which I also had a small part. We have three children, two boys and a girl, and have resided in Cornwall until recently.

"Although reviewers both in England and America have written very favorably of my work, I have never achieved the distinction of becoming a best-seller. Of one of my books the New York *Times* remarked: 'Of one thing you can be certain with Frank Baker—you are not going to be bored.' I hope this continues to be true."

PRINCIPAL WORKS: The Twisted Tree, 1935; The Birds, 1936; Miss Hargreaves, 1940; Allanayr (in U.S.: Full Score), 1941; Sweet Chariot, 1942; Playing with Punch (play) 1944; Mr. Allenby Loses the Way, 1945; Before I Go Hence, 1946; Embers, 1946; My Friend the Enemy, 1948; The Road Was Free, 1948; The Downs So Free, 1948.

ABOUT: Current Biography 1948.

BAKER, GEORGE PIERCE (April 4, 1866-January 6, 1935). For biographical sketch and list of works and references, see TWENTIETH CENTURY AUTHORS, 1942.

* * *

ABOUT: Kinne, W. P. George Pierce Baker and the American Theatre; Atlantic Monthly February 1948.

BAKER, RAY STANNARD (April 17, 1870-July 12, 1946). For biographical sketch and list of earlier works and references, see TWENTIETH CENTURY AUTHORS, 1942.

* * *

Ray Stannard Baker died of a heart attack at his home in Amherst, Mass., at seventy-six. He had been suffering from a heart condition for some time, but had continued to write and was working on another book to be published under the pseudonym of "David Grayson." In January 1946 he and his wife, who survived him, celebrated their fiftieth wedding anniversary. His last published work was *American Chronicle,* the second volume of his autobiography, which told his life-story from his first days as a cub reporter in Chicago down to the death of President Wilson and then summarized briefly the fourteen years he devoted to the Wilson biography and to the five tons of documents which supplied the raw material for it. *American Chronicle* revealed that Mr. Baker kept a diary continuously from 1897; it amounted to about two million words in 1945. He drew on it extensively for his two autobiographies and the David Grayson books.

In 1918 Mr. Baker acted as State Department special commissioner in Great Britain, France, and Italy. He was then given the thankless post of director of the press bureau of the American Commission to Negotiate Peace in 1919. He helped his wife to write a biography of her father, Professor William James Beal, under the title *American Pioneer in Science* (1925). In 1928 he was a Democratic presidential elector from Massachusetts. Amherst College conferred a Litt.D. on him in 1925, as did Duke University in 1938. He acted as technical adviser during the production by Twentieth Century-Fox Film Corporation of the motion picture *Wilson,* 1943-44.

The New York *Times* commented editorially on his death: "Perhaps he best summed up his own credo when he said that a man's aim should be 'to understand the wonder and truth of life—and then to make other people understand.' It is a modest aim that another generation could re-learn to its profit."

ADDITIONAL WORKS: Under My Elm (by "David Grayson") 1942; American Chronicle, 1945.

ABOUT: Baker, R. S. American Chronicle; Morris, L. R. Postscript to Yesterday; Newsweek March 12, 1945; New York Times July 13, 1946; Saturday Review of Literature April 14, 1945; Time March 12, 1945.

BALCHIN, NIGEL (MARLIN) (December 3, 1908-), British novelist, was born in Wiltshire, the son of William E. and Ada Elizabeth Balchin. He attended Dauntsey's School and Peterhouse College, Cambridge, where he was exhibitioner and prizeman in natural science. In his professional career Balchin has sought "to combine business and authorship in varying proportions," and he has balanced his time successfully between research work in science and industry and writing in private life. He says that he finds it possible to write only when doing what would be considered a full-time job in other directions. At present he no longer holds a full-time industrial job, but he still has a variety of business interests.

Balchin's earliest published writing was  a series of humorous sketches for *Punch* explaining (and delightfully distorting) various phases of business. Collected and published in book form under the pseudonym of "Mark Spade" in *How to Run a Bassoon Factory: or Business Explained,* they proved "agreeably animated nonsense," with enough sound business knowledge for a background to make them real satire. His humorous writings are not so well known on this side of the Atlantic, however, as are his serious novels. *The Small Back Room,* his closely-observed attack on wartime British Civil Service bureaucracy, is generally regarded as his finest novel. The detached view of the satirist, the technical assurance of a man who knows business, and the perception of a skillful novelist were combined in a book that Kate O'Brien described as "witty, trim, hard and beautifully made—an accomplished and exciting entertainment." Probably his most popular novel is the psychological thriller *Mine Own Executioner.* Balchin subsequently wrote the scenario for the motion picture version of this novel, which starred Burgess Meredith. His novels are literate and fast-paced. James Sandoe has said: "Balchin is a novelist worth reading now and one whose future novels are an uncommonly rich prospect because of . . . [his] accuracy of ear, because of the honesty of his subjects, because of the abounding vitality of his characters."

In 1933 Balchin married Elizabeth Evelyn Walshe, and they had three daughters. They were divorced in 1951. During World War II he acted as Deputy Scientific Adviser to the Army Council, with the rank of brigadier. He lives in the country, in an old cottage in Sussex, likes music, gardening, all sorts of sports (except polo), and says of himself, "There is practically nothing in which I am not or can not be intensely interested."

PRINCIPAL WORKS: No Sky, 1934; The Simple Life, 1935; Lightbody on Liberty, 1936; Income and Outcome, 1936; Darkness Falls from the Air, 1942; The Small Back Room, 1943; Mine Own Executioner, 1945; Lord, I Was Afraid, 1947; The Borgia Testament, 1948; A Sort of Traitors (in U.S.: Who Is My Neighbor?) 1949; The Anatomy of

Villainy, 1950; A Way Through the Wood, 1951; Private Interests, 1953. *As "Mark Spade"*—How to Run a Bassoon Factory, 1934; Business for Pleasure, 1935.

ABOUT: New York Herald Tribune Book Review October 8, 1950; Saturday Evening Post July 8, 1950.

*   *   *

BALDWIN, FAITH (October 1, 1893-). For autobiographical sketch and list of earlier works and references, see TWENTIETH CENTURY AUTHORS, 1942.

*   *   *

In July 1951 Faith Baldwin moved from Fable Farm in New Canaan, Conn., to a smaller house in Norwalk, Conn. She still publishes novels at the rate of about two a year and writes for the women's magazines. In addition, she has made several radio and television appearances and is a regular contributor to the *Christian Herald.* She writes: "A great many of the books, old and new, have been translated, now that publishing abroad has picked up somewhat since the war; they appear in Holland, Italy, South America, France, Scandinavia. They are always published in England."

Correction: Miss Baldwin's first novel was *Mavis of Green Hill,* not *Alimony.*

ADDITIONAL WORKS: Five Women in Three Novels (Star on Her Shoulder; Detour; Let's Do the Town) 1942; The Rest of My Life With You, 1942; Washington, USA, 1943; You Can't Escape, 1943; He Married a Doctor, 1944; Change of Heart, 1944; Arizona Star, 1945; A Job for Jenny, 1945; No Private Heaven, 1946; Sleeping Beauty, 1947; Give Love the Air, 1947; Marry for Money, 1948; They Who Love (four stories) 1948; The Golden Shoestring, 1949; Look Out for Liza, 1950; The Whole Armor, 1951; The Juniper Tree, 1952; Widow's Walk (poems) 1954.

ABOUT: Van Gelder, R. Writers and Writing; Christian Science Monitor Magazine January 11, 1947; Collier's May 27, 1944; New York Times Book Review May 1, 1949, May 7, 1950.

BALDWIN, HANSON WEIGHTMAN (March 22, 1903-), American journalist and writer on military affairs, was born in Baltimore, Md., the son of Oliver Perry and Caroline (Sutton) Baldwin. His father was managing editor and editorial writer for the Baltimore *Sun.* Young Baldwin attended the Boys' Latin School in Baltimore and the U.S. Naval Academy  at Annapolis, from which he was graduated, with an ensign's commission, in 1924. In the next three years he saw service aboard battleships and a destroyer on the East Coast, in the Caribbean, and in the European squadron. He resigned from the Navy in 1927 as a lieutenant, j.g., and, after another year of travel, joined the staff of the Baltimore *Sun* as a "cub" reporter. In 1929 Baldwin became a general assignment reporter on the New York *Times* and has been with the newspaper ever since—as military and naval corespondent since 1937 and as military editor from 1942 to the present time. For the *Times* Baldwin has covered naval and military maneuvers all over the world. He has written special interpretation and background articles, news stories, Sunday feature articles, book reviews, and editorials. His sound and clearly-written analyses of complicated matters of strategy have won him a wide and appreciative reading public.

In the autumn of 1942 Baldwin visited a number of American bases in the battle area of the South Pacific and reported his observations in a series of articles for which he received the Pulitzer prize for journalism. He wrote another such series on England and the battle areas of North Africa which he visited in 1943. He was present at the Normandy invasion and made a front line survey after covering the actual landings aboard the cruiser Augusta. Baldwin remained in France until after the St. Lô breakthrough. When the war ended he continued to make periodic visits to Army and Navy camps, bases and installations in the United States and abroad for first-hand material for feature and news stories. He reported the second atom bomb test at Bikini in the Pacific, and in 1947 and 1950 made a cross-country tour of military posts, including guided missile and rocket firing installations. In 1950 also he made a survey trip to Korea, Japan, Formosa, Hong Kong, and French Indo-China. His writings now deal chiefly with military-political problems and their ramifications and with the organization of our military forces for the atomic age and what he calls a "bi-polar world."

Baldwin contributes articles to a number of popular and technical journals. His books are lucid and comprehensive presentations of military information. He writes in a straightforward and sober style, making no attempt to "talk down" to his non-military readers nor to "dramatize" and sensationalize his material. He is currently doing research for a history of World War II which he expects "will take most of the rest of his lifetime."

Baldwin made a motion picture short on "Our Third Year of War" in 1944. He appears frequently on radio and television discussion programs. The School of Journalism of the University of Syracuse awarded him a medal for distinguished service in 1944, and he received an honorary degree from Drake University in 1945. Baldwin has been married since 1931 to Helen Bruce, and they have two daughters. He likes to relax at swimming and sailing but he says that he "has had little time for sports since the war. His daughters and the world situation keep him on the move."

PRINCIPAL WORKS: Men and Ships of Steel (ed. with W. F. Palmer) 1935; The Caissons Roll, 1938; We Saw It Happen (ed. with S. Stone) 1938; Admiral Death, 1939; United We Stand, 1941; What the Citizen Should Know About the Navy, 1941 (reprinted as What You Should Know About the Navy, 1943); Strategy for Victory, 1942; The Navy at War, 1943; The Price of Power, 1947; Great Mistakes of the War, 1950; Power and Politics, 1950.

ABOUT: Current Biography 1942; Time November 9, 1942.

BALFOUR, ARTHUR JAMES, 1st Earl (August 25, 1848-March 19, 1930). For biographical sketch and list of works and references, see TWENTIETH CENTURY AUTHORS, 1942.

* * *

ABOUT: Salter, J. A. Personality in Politics; Quarterly Review July 1947.

BANG, HERMAN JOACHIM (April 20, 1857-January 29, 1912). For biographical sketch and list of works and references, see TWENTIETH CENTURY AUTHORS, 1942.

* * *

ADDITIONAL WORK IN ENGLISH TRANSLATION: Brothers, a Play, 1943.

BANGS, JOHN KENDRICK (May 27, 1862-January 21, 1922). For biographical sketch and list of works and references, see TWENTIETH CENTURY AUTHORS, 1942.

* * *

Francis Hyde Bangs, author of *John Kendrick Bangs, Humorist of the Nineties* (1941), sends the following corrections and additions to his father's biographical sketch: "John Kendrick Bangs was born in Yonkers and was removed to New York City by his parents when he was four years old. He grew up in New York City, attended private school and Columbia College in New York City. After being graduated from Columbia, he attended the Columbia Law School, but retired from it in 1884 when he became associate editor of *Life*. In the middle of the Eighties he returned to Yonkers and resided there until the autumn of 1904. After 1904 he did not reside in Yonkers. He was a citizen of Ogunquit, Maine, from 1906 until his death in 1922."

F. H. Bangs adds that his father was editor of "The Drawer" of *Harper's Magazine* until 1900 and conducted *Literature* (An International Gazette of Literary Criticism) in its American edition from January 1899 to November 1899, when he became editor of *Harper's Weekly*. In 1886 he married Agnes Lawson Hyde. Bangs describes his father as "about five feet ten inches in height... and his weight was usually about 170 pounds. As a young man he was lean and lank. In his fifties he tended toward corpulency, but kept his weight in hand by an exceedingly active physical life." Of his father's literary achievement he writes: "Bangs was a storyteller with a pleasant sense of humor and had no axes to grind. He was not trying to reform society. He was writing to please certain audiences of readers through such media as existed, the leading magazines and newspapers, and he was considered extraordinarily successful at the job. You say that the House Boat books were somewhat in the vein of Mark Twain's diaries of Adam and Eve. Since Mark Twain's 'diaries' were written subsequent to the House Boat books, why not say that Mark Twain's 'diaries' were in the same vein, somewhat, as the House Boat books, but neither so good nor so popular?"

F. H. Bangs disagrees that his father's career was "the record of a typical small town American of the latter half of the nineteenth century." If true, he comments, "small town Americans must have been quite different from what they are now. Bangs was even unusual in Yonkers... in the Elegant Eighties and the Nineties probably the most beautiful suburb of the American Metropolis... the home of many distinguished people, especially distinguished in New York City."

BANNING, Mrs. MARGARET (CULKIN) (March 18, 1891-). For autobiographical sketch and list of earlier works and references, see TWENTIETH CENTURY AUTHORS, 1942.

* * *

During the second World War, Margaret Culkin Banning was a member of the advisory committee of the Writers' War Board.

In 1942, at the invitation of the British Ministry of Information, she visited England, studying industrial and home conditions there. Mrs. Banning is active in club work, a director of the National Council of Community Chests of America, a trustee of the National Health and Welfare Retirement Association. She has served as chairman of Program Coordination for the National Federation of Business and Professional Women's Clubs, and she is presently on the Women's Advisory Committee. She lectures and speaks frequently on the radio. In the summers of 1946, 1948, and 1951 she visited Europe, studying postwar conditions, and in 1952 she revisited South America.

Mrs. Banning's recent novels have been praised for their "sincere and straightforward" treatment of domestic problems. One reviewer remarked that they bring "fresh emotional focus" to familiar situations.

In 1952 an article which Mrs. Banning wrote for the *Reader's Digest*, "Filth on the Newsstands," attracted wide attention. She was called as one of the witnesses at the hearings of the House of Representatives Select Committee on Current Pornographic Materials where she testified that she was opposed to any kind of political censorship, but urged the organization of public opinion to destroy the demand for indecent publications, and the enforcement of laws against mailing material fraudulently described as educational.

In 1944 Mrs. Banning was married to LeRoy Salsich, of Duluth, then president of the Oliver Iron Mining Company of United States Steel Corporation and now retired. Her daughter by her first marriage, Dr. Mary Banning Friendlander (Mrs. Gardner Friedlander), is a research physicist; her son, a lieutenant commander in the U.S.N.R.

ADDITIONAL WORKS: Letters from England, 1943; Conduct Yourself Accordingly (with M. L. Culkin) 1944; The Clever Sister, 1947; Give Us Our Years, 1950; Fallen Away, 1951; The Dowry, 1955.

ABOUT: Current Biography 1940.

"BARBELLION, W. N. P." See CUMMINGS, B.

BARBER, MARGARET FAIRLESS ("Michael Fairless") (May 7, 1869-August 24, 1901). For biographical sketch and list of works and references, see TWENTIETH CENTURY AUTHORS, 1942.

* * *

ABOUT: Branch, W. G. By Unknown Ways.

BARBUSSE, HENRI (May 17, 1874-August 30, 1935). For biographical sketch and list of works and references, see TWENTIETH CENTURY AUTHORS, 1942.

* * *

ABOUT: Columbia Dictionary of Modern European Literature.

BARCLAY, Mrs. FLORENCE LOUISA (CHARLESWORTH) (December 2, 1862-March 10, 1921). For biographical sketch and list of works and references, see TWENTIETH CENTURY AUTHORS, 1942.

* * *

ABOUT: Harper's October 1947.

*BAREA, ARTURO (September 20, 1897-), Spanish autobiographer, short story writer, novelist, and critic, writes: "I  was born in Badajoz, Spain, but the place of my birth was sheer bad luck: my parents had gone there on my father's business, and he had fallen gravely ill in a shabby little hotel. There I was born, and there he died soon after my birth. My mother took me home to Madrid to her three older children and turned herself into a washerwoman and domestic help to keep us afloat. I was virtually adopted by an uncle and aunt who were childless and well-to-do; in return, my mother did their housework. This early experience of a world divided into comfort and miserable toil left a decisive impression on me, even while I profited from the comfort myself. I hoped to be able to become a mechanical engineer, but my uncle's death destroyed this hope and cut short my attendance at school, the 'Pious School' conducted by Escolapians where I was just working for my school certificate. At the age of thirteen I became first shop assistant, then clerk at a big bank. In various commercial jobs I learnt to know all regions and corners of Spain, till I was called up in 1920. Three years in the corrupt army in Morocco, during a disastrous colonial war, taught me to hate violence. Back in Madrid, I married; though my private life soon became unhappy, I was successful in my career as the technical manager of a big patent agent's firm.

* bä rä'ä

"During all those years I had no more than a hankering after writing. The immediate needs of existence absorbed me. The great turning point came in the Spanish Civil War, which broke out in 1936. As a democratic socialist, I put myself at the disposal of the Republican authorities and at the beginning of the siege of Madrid was made chief of the Foreign Censorship Office, a branch of the Ministry for External Affairs. There I met the Austrian who soon was to become my second wife and also my constant collaborator. And at that time, under the impact of the civil war and of a profound nervous shock, I began to write in earnest. My illness together with the dangerous disfavour of the Communist groups, which had driven me and Ilsa, my wife, out of our war work in the Foreign Censorship and the radio, forced us in 1938 to go to France. After a miserable year of refugee existence, we went to England, where we made our home, always in the country and never in towns.

"My illness was cured by the peace of the English countryside, even though the World War had broken out in the meantime. In 1940 I started to broadcast, as a free lance, commentaries on the Latin-American service of the BBC, work which I am still doing at the moment of writing this. My first book came out in Republican Spain in 1938, my first serious work—in English translation—in London in 1941. Since then I have made my living as writer, broadcaster and lecturer. I always write in Spanish and my wife translates it into English; all of my books after the first one have been launched in an English version long before a Spanish version. It was a great thing for me when my autobiographical trilogy, published in the United States in a single volume as The Forging of a Rebel, appeared in the Spanish original in Buenos Aires, ten years after its first part had been published in English.

"My quiet life, which consists of pottering about with odd jobs about the house and of writing, was only twice interrupted, when I went in 1947 on a tour through Denmark where I had turned out to be a best-seller, and when I went as visiting professor of Spanish literature to Pennsylvania State College for the spring semester and summer school of 1952. I do not know how many short stories and essays I have published, and exactly in how many languages my books have been published: I believe, apart from English and Spanish, in eight. I am working at a new novel now.

"I am, I suppose, a writer of the realist school, but I am trying to get beyond the flat surface realism and, even when I start, as I must, from my direct Spanish experiences and feelings, to reach some general human truths. But as I am not an intellectual writer, I have no particular theory about myself; I only know that I have to find my own way and express what I call my own truth if I want to make people feel and think more clearly—which is my great ambition."

PRINCIPAL WORKS IN ENGLISH TRANSLATION: The Struggle for the Spanish Soul, 1941; Lorca, the Poet and his People, 1944; The Forging of a Rebel (The Forge, The Track, The Clash) 1946; The Broken Root, 1951; Unamuno, 1952.

ABOUT: Barea, A. The Forging of a Rebel; New Republic December 23, 1946; Saturday Review of Literature December 28, 1946; Time December 30, 1946.

BARING, MAURICE (April 27, 1874-December 14, 1945). For autobiographical sketch and list of earlier works and references, see TWENTIETH CENTURY AUTHORS, 1942.

* * *

Maurice Baring died at Beaufort Castle, Beauly, Scotland, at seventy-one. He had been a victim of the steady advance of *paralysis agitans* since 1936. In August 1940 his illness forced him to leave Half-Way House, Rottingdean, Sussex, his home since 1930, and go to live with the family of Lord Lovat, with whom he remained until his death. His last book, *Russian Lyrics*, appeared in 1943.

Richard Church wrote that Dame Ethel Smyth's study of Baring "shows a person of rare charm, with a playful humor and a wayward attitude toward the conventions of life," but notes that "both in verse and prose he writes with a deliberate flatness, a drooping rhythm, as though a great weariness and desolation of spirit possess him." The Rev. C. C. Martindale, S.J., described him as "like a crystal cut into very many facets, reflecting a thousand colored lights, and shadows, and strange images, yet lit by a steady light interiorly." His old commanding officer, Lord Trenchard, quoted Marshal Foch as saying, "There never was a staff officer in any country, in any nation, in any century, like Major Maurice Baring," and added, "He was the most unselfish man I have ever met or am likely to meet." François Mauriac said to a friend, "What I most admire about Baring's work is the sense he gives you of the penetration of grace." Anne Fremantle granted him "the stature of Mauriac and of Bernanos."

ADDITIONAL WORKS: *Novels*—Passing By, 1921; Overlooked, 1922; When They Love, 1928. *Plays*—The Grey Stocking, 1912; His Majesty's Embassy, 1923. *Short Stories*—Orpheus in Mayfair, 1909; The Glass Mender, 1910. *Autobiography*—Round the World in Any Number of Days, 1919; R.F.C., H.Q., 1920. *Miscellaneous*—Landmarks in Russian Literature, 1910; Letters from the Near East, 1913; An Outline of Russian Literature, 1915; Punch and Judy (essays) 1924; What I Saw in Russia, 1927; Russian Lyrics (verse translations) 1943.

ABOUT: Church, R. British Authors; Hoehn, M. Catholic Authors, I; Lovat, L. L. F. Maurice Baring; Reilly, J. J. Of Books and Men; Atlantic Monthly October 1947; Catholic World February 1946, September 1946; Commonweal February 15, 1946; London Times December 17, 1945; New York Times December 16, 1945.

BARKER, AUDREY LILLIAN (April 13, 1918-), English novelist and short story writer, is very reticent about herself. She sums her autobiography up by stating that she has led "a well-grooved and mundane life." She was born in St. Paul's Cray, Kent, England, the daughter of Elsie (Dutton) and Henry H. Barker. She has been writing, she says, since the age of

Mary Marney

nine when she composed "a particularly sickly little verse about a violet." Since then she has wasted no time. She was educated at Beckenham and Wallington secondary schools. After leaving school at sixteen, she began to work in an office in the City in London. From there she went on to a literary agent's office, and thence to the Amalgamated Press where she describes her position as "a very-assistant, very-junior subeditress." During World War II she spent six months in the Land Army and over three years with the National Fire Service. She is currently on the staff of the B.B.C.

Meanwhile A. L. Barker wrote poetry, what she calls "bad plays," short stories, and "an unpublished and unpublishable novel." Her short stories, which began to appear in British periodicals after the war, attracted favorable notice. In 1946 she was offered—but was unable to accept—an Atlantic Award in Literature, a grant of two hundred pounds which would have enabled her to devote a year entirely to writing. A year later a collection of short stories, *Innocents*, won her the Somerset Maugham Award. These stories, dealing mainly with children and their responses to emotional crises, revealed, according to the London *Times Literary*

Supplement, "a real and specific gift." In them Charles Rolo found the qualities that have also marked Miss Barker's later work—"highly individual sensitivity, precision and control, a refreshing sense of structure and a wonderful ability to fuse character and incident."

This later work includes a novel, *Apology for a Hero,* and another collection of stories under the title *Novelette.* Her novel is a strong and perceptive study of a middle-aged English clerk who comes suddenly into a situation of violence and uncertainty. It is not a completely successful work. R. D. Charques, in the *Spectator,* found that it "strains too visibly for descriptive and psychological effect," and other critics complained that it did not show "a mastery of the larger form." But in spite of weaknesses in technique—failings which can be accounted for largely by Miss Barker's youth and relative inexperience as a writer—reviewers of her work are in agreement that she is a writer of unusual ability and promise—"detached," Hugh I'Anson Fausset says of her, "but with an intimate feeling for what is both sad and absurd in the drama. . . ." She writes memorably, William Peden comments, "about what Elizabeth Bowen has so aptly termed the problem of human unknowableness."

PRINCIPAL WORKS: The Innocents, 1947; Apology for a Hero, 1950; Novelette, and other Stories, 1951.

BARKER, Sir ERNEST (September 23, 1874-), English political scientist, was born in East Cheshire, the son of George Barker. After attending the Church elementary school in his village, he entered the Manchester Grammar School on a scholarship. In 1892 he received a classical scholarship to Balliol College, Oxford, where he studied both classics and modern history. On completion of his course, he went to Merton College on a fellowship in classics. He began teaching modern history at Wadham College in 1899. From 1909 to 1913 he was Fellow and Lecturer at St. John's College, and then transferred to New College where he taught until 1920 (one of his students was the late Harold Laski). After a year in the United States as visiting professor at Amherst College, Sir Ernest

became Principal of King's College in the University of London. He held this post until 1927 when he was invited to be the first holder of the Chair of Political Science in Cambridge and was made a Fellow of Peterhouse College. Here he remained until his retirement in 1939.

Sir Ernest Barker's writings reflect his extensive education in the classics as well as in modern history. His earliest published work was on ancient Greek political theory, and as recently as 1946 he published a translation of Aristotle's *Politics.* He is best known, however, for his sound and lucid expositions of present-day political theory. Learned, moderate in tone, and eminently readable, his books demonstrate a combination of scholarship and philosophical reflection all too rare in modern writing in the field. He admits to a "want of that sort of knowledge of politics which comes from actual experience," but, T. P. Peardon writes in the *Political Science Quarterly,* "his great historical and philosophical knowledge, his eclectic approach and complete freedom from sectarianism give a rare breadth and richness to his argument."

Essentially, Sir Ernest's approach to his material on political theory is philosophical rather than historical or governmental. His valuable *Ideas and Ideals of the British Empire* is, to quote Allan Nevins, "a study of general forms, and of those basic ideas which create forms." Similarly, in his *Reflections on Government* and his more recent *Principles of Social and Political Theory,* he is concerned not so much with the historical development of institutions as with the ideas and ideologies behind them. The latter book, which contains an inquiry into the principles behind the National Society and the National State, has been called "the author's most comprehensive statement of his own political theory." The *Manchester Guardian* described it as "a strong and learned and beautifully balanced book . . . true to a great tradition."

Sir Ernest has continued to live in Cambridge since his retirement. He is a Fellow of the British Academy, an honorary Fellow of Merton College, Oxford, and of Peterhouse. He has honorary degrees from British, continental, and American universities, and has been decorated by the governments of France, Norway, Belgium, the Netherlands, and Greece for services rendered during World War II to the Conference of Allied Ministers of Education. He was knighted in 1944. His first wife, whom he married in 1900, Emily Isabel Salkeld, died in 1924, leaving him one son and two daughters. He married Olivia Stuart Horner in 1927, and they have one son and one daughter.

PRINCIPAL WORKS: The Political Thought of Plato and Aristotle (rev. ed. titled Greek Political Theory) 1906; Political Thought in England from Herbert Spencer to Today, 1915; The Crusades, 1923; The National Character and the Factors in its Formation, 1927; Values of Life, 1939; Ideas and Ideals of the British Empire, 1941; Reflections on Government, 1942; Britain and the British People, 1942; Essays on Government, 1945; Aristotle's Politics (trans.) 1946; The Character of England (ed.) 1947; Father of the Man 1948; Traditions of Civility, 1948; Principles of Social and Political Theory, 1951; Age and Youth, 1953.

ABOUT: Barker, Sir E. Father of the Man, Age and Youth; American Political Science Review September 1952.

BARKER, GEORGE (GRANVILLE) (February 26, 1913-), British poet and novelist, was born in Loughton, Essex, of an  Irish mother, Marion Frances Taaffe Barker, and an English father, George Barker. He attended the Marlborough Road School in Chelsea and the Regent Street Polytechnic. At fourteen he dropped out of school and went to work, trying his hand at "an incredible miscellany of jobs," among them wall-paper designer and garage mechanic, and at times so poor that he was reduced to sleeping "on Putney Common with newspapers wrapped around the body for warmth."

At eighteen Barker wrote his first novel, *Alanna Autumnal.* Two years later, in 1933, both this novel and a first volume of verse, *Thirty Preliminary Poems,* were published. In the same year he married Jessica Woodward and moved to a cottage in Dorset. Here he wrote the volume *Poems,* which was published in 1935 and which received favorable critical notice. As David Daiches commented some years later, Barker was younger than the Auden-Spender-Lewis group which dominated British poetry in 1935. His work was distinct and individual; "he belonged to no school and his entrance was unaccompanied by manifestos." His early poetry was lyrical, intensely personal, and tragic— all the more striking in an era which produced so much poetry of revolution and "social passion." The main weakness of these early poems, Daiches pointed out, was

the inherent danger that the poet might lose control of his material—"Working as he does from the inside, he is not always able to impose a unity that is clearly apparent to the observer."

Barker received grants for further work from his publishers, from the Royal Society of Literature, and from the King's Bounty. William Butler Yeats selected several of his poems for inclusion in the *Oxford Book of Modern Verse* in 1936. In 1939 Barker visited Japan as professor of English literature at the Imperial Tohoku University, and in the following year he came to the United States where he stayed until 1943, when he returned to England. The poems which he published during this interval show an increasing mastery of form and technique. Harvey Breit wrote of his *Selected Poems* in 1941: "He has gotten rid of, in the last poems, the excessiveness, the over-zealousness, that diminished rather than affirmed the natural tension in the work." By 1944 when his *Eros in Dogma* was published, his poems showed him, to quote David Daiches again, "at his full stature as a lyric poet." Other critics, however, have objected to Barker's continued use of a "mannered" style, what Dudley Fitts describes as "the too surprising distortion of language, the quaintness too arch . . . the bizarre paraphernalia. . . ." And Conrad Aiken wrote of Barker's *Sacred and Secular Elegies*: "With a trifle less preciosity and affectation, they could be superb." To an editor who recently asked him to state his attitude to the craft of poetry, Barker replied, "I can tell you quite simply. It is an amorous attitude."

In 1950 Barker published another novel, *The Dead Seagull,* a brooding and highly symbolic story that had many passages of impressive, evocative writing, but on the whole was judged to be "self-conscious and without true moving power." He lives on a farm in Haslemere, Surrey, with his wife and their three sons and three daughters.

PRINCIPAL WORKS: Poetry—Thirty Preliminary Poems, 1933; Poems, 1935; Calamiterror, 1937; Lament and Triumph, 1940; Selected Poems, 1941; Sacred and Secular Elegies, 1943; Eros in Dogma, 1944; Love Poems, 1947; News of the World, 1950; A Vision of Beasts and Gods, 1954. Prose—Alanna Autumnal, 1933; Janus, 1935; The Dead Seagull, 1950.

ABOUT: Poetry December 1941, March 1947, April 1948; Wilson Library Bulletin June 1942.

BARKER, GRANVILLE-. See GRAN-VILLE-BARKER

BARKER, SHIRLEY (April 4, 1911-), American poet and novelist, was born in Farmington, N.H. Her ancestors were early  settlers in New England. Some of them, she believes, attended the Salem witch trials, and this may account for her affinity with the rugged Puritan town, reflected in her novel *Peace, My Daughters*. She received her B.A. from the University of New Hampshire in 1934, her M.A. from Radcliffe in 1938, and a degree in library science from the Pratt Institute in 1941. While she was still an undergraduate at the University of New Hampshire her first book, *The Dark Hills Under*, was published in the Yale Series of Younger Poets. The poems dealt almost exclusively with the New England scene, and their author was highly praised for her mature grasp of character and locale and for her mastery of poetic forms, particularly the narrative ballad.

Miss Barker did little writing from then until 1944 when she began work on *Peace, My Daughters*. In the interim she moved to New York City (which she loves because of the anonymity it offers a writer: "In New York you can be nothing—in smaller communities you must show a face to the world and be a social character with known attributes. Here you do not have to be anything except the book you're writing.") and established herself in the library profession. Until 1954 she worked in the American History Department of the New York Public Library —an ideal spot for a historical novelist who managed, as she did, to "eat lunch in ten minutes right here in the building and have fifty minutes left for research."

It is the combination of the librarian's painstaking research and the poet's discriminating sense of language that has raised Miss Barker's first two novels above the level of routine historical fiction. *Peace, My Daughters*, her story of the Salem witchcraft trials, was, Lloyd Morris wrote, "finely conceived and, on the whole, finely executed.' Herschel Brickell commended it as "a beautifully written novel that gives sharp reality to the Salem scene of 1692-97." Miss Barker did equally extensive historical research for *Rivers Parting*, a novel set in early colonial days in her native state of New Hampshire. This novel was originally conceived as an epic poem, and Miss Barker wrote "two books" of verse before she decided—influenced in part by the success of her first novel— to change her medium to prose. *Rivers Parting*, strangely enough, is a less "poetic" book than *Peace, My Daughters*— more crowded with incident, adventure and excitement. If not exactly notable for its literary merit, Charles J. Rolo commented in the *Atlantic*, it is notable "for its freedom from synthetic lustiness and gustiness, and for its sensible characterizations." Her later novels have been similarly praised for skillful writing and for sound scholarship.

When planning a novel Miss Barker works leisurely and methodically at her research. When the new book reaches the writing stage, however, she quickens her pace and writes furiously. She is unmarried. In 1954 she gave up her New York apartment and moved to New Hampshire.

PRINCIPAL WORKS: The Dark Hills Under (poems) 1933; Peace, My Daughters, 1949; Rivers Parting, 1950; A Land and a People (poems) 1952; Fire and the Hammer, 1953; Tomorrow the New Moon, 1955.

ABOUT: New York Herald Tribune Book Review January 7, 1951.

BARLOW, JANE (1857-April 17, 1917). For biographical sketch and list of works and references, see TWENTIETH CENTURY AUTHORS, 1942.

BARNES, DJUNA. For biographical sketch and list of works and references, see TWENTIETH CENTURY AUTHORS, 1942.

* * *

ABOUT: Sewanee Review Summer 1945.

BARNES, HARRY ELMER (June 15, 1889-). For autobiographical sketch and list of earlier works and references, see TWENTIETH CENTURY AUTHORS, 1942.

* * *

Harry Elmer Barnes writes: "While I joined with such leading historians and students of international relations as Charles Austin Beard and Edwin M. Borchard in opposing our entry into the Second World War, holding that it was a mistake, especially after June 22, 1941, once war was declared I entered into government work assisting the successful prosecution of the war.

"In 1943-1944, I served as historian and consultant to the Prison Industries Branch of the War Production Board, under the Hon. Maury Maverick. This organization was devoted to putting inmates of state prisons, then virtually idle, to work on munitions of warfare. The effort was highly successful. I wrote the standard history of this experiment, *Prisons in Wartime*, which also included an account of how more than 100,000 convicts and former convicts were inducted successfully into the armed forces of the United States.

"In 1945-1946, I served as historian and consultant to the Smaller War Plants Corporation, also under Mr. Maverick. I edited a gigantic manuscript history in some thirty volumes on the origins and work of the Corporation which was deposited in the Library of Congress and the National Archives.

"After the war, I continued my work for the government in the field of penology, supplying the text for the publication of the Federal Bureau of Prisons, entitled *Handbook of Correctional Design and Construction* (1950), the most complete work on the physical aspect of prisons, penitentiaries and correctional institutions ever published in any language. The technical material was supplied by the architects and engineers of the Federal Bureau of Prisons.

"Also following the war, I resumed my university teaching from time to time, serving as visiting professor of sociology at Temple University, 1946, University of Colorado, 1948-1949, and the University of Indiana, 1951. In the summers of 1950 and 1951, I directed tour groups of teachers and students to Europe under the auspices of 'Study Abroad.'

"At present, my main scholarly and literary efforts are devoted to work on the diplomatic and political background of the Second World War, in the effort to promote a revival of the Revisionism which flourished after the First World War and was exemplified by such books as my *Genesis for the World War* and Sidney Bradshaw Fay's *Origins of the World War*. The need for such a resumption of Revisionism, as applied to the Second World War, was set forth in my widely-read and heatedly-discussed monograph on *The Struggle Against the Historical Blackout* (nine editions, 1949-1952). I inspired and helped to guide such books as William Henry Chamberlin's *America's Second Crusade* and Charles Callin Tansill's *Back Door to War*. I edited such books as F. J. P. Veale's *Advance to Barbarism*, a searching study by an able English lawyer of the recent barbarization of war and international jurisprudence. I intend to prosecute this line of work as long as feasible.

"Following out the statement of belief in the 1942 edition of TWENTIETH CENTURY AUTHORS, I find little intellectual or spiritual contact with the Totalitarian Liberals of the mid-century. My spiritual home remains with the pre-1937 Liberals who prized peace as well as liberalism and recognized that only in peace can liberalism thrive. This vintage of Liberals is now a fast disappearing race. Only a few, such as John Haynes Holmes, Roger Baldwin, Norman Thomas, and the like, still survive—and they are getting old."

ADDITIONAL WORKS: The American Way of Life (with O. M. Ruedi) 1942; New Horizons in Criminology (with N. K. Teeters) 1943; Introduction to the History of Sociology (ed.) 1948; Historical Sociology, 1948; The Struggle Against the Historical Blackout, 1949; Perpetual War for Perpetual Peace (ed.) 1953.

BARNES, Mrs. MARGARET (AYER)
(April 8, 1886-   ). For autobiographical sketch and list of works and references, see TWENTIETH CENTURY AUTHORS, 1942.

* * *

Mrs. Barnes writes from Chicago: "I have nothing to add to the sketch . . . except that my husband, Cecil Barnes, died in July 1949, and that now, in the age of possible atomic war, I am a more puzzled pacifist than ever and not an unqualified isolationist."

*BAROJA Y NESSI, PÍO (December 28, 1872-   ). For autobiographical sketch and list of works and references, see TWENTIETH CENTURY AUTHORS, 1942.

* * *

In his eighties now, Pío Baroja lives in Madrid. He is still writing industriously—six volumes of memoirs (*Desde la Ultima del Camino*) and several novels, but none of his recent work has appeared in English translation. In Spain Baroja is respected and honored; he is a member of the Royal Spanish Academy, and his books, one critic writes, are "the glory and pride of Spain." According to a report in *Les Lettres Françaises* in May 1947, Baroja was winning a larger audience of French readers, who admire his deep understanding of his country, his keen observation of people, and the resultant variety of characters in his works. A French critic described him as "a kind of omnipresent movie camera that misses nothing."

Both in literature and in politics Baroja continues to occupy an ambiguous and inconsistent position. As José A. Balseiro

* bä ró′hä

points out, he is a recalcitrant individualist, consistent only in his uncompromising sincerity and in his absolute skepticism of all social organization. He expresses open contempt for "the modern myths of equality and fraternity," and yet it is in the lower classes that he has found his inspiration and his material. He is not, however, a "popular" writer in the sense of having a large Spanish reading public. Possibly, it has been suggested, this is because his work is "so negative, so destructive and so relentless in its pessimism."

Correction: The province in which Baroja was born is Guipuzcoa, not Guipuzcua.

ABOUT: Balseiro, J. A. Ibáñez, Unamuno, Valle-Inclán, Baroja: Cuatro Individualistas de España; Columbia Dictionary of Modern European Literature; Books Abroad Winter 1948; Hispanic Review October 1944, January 1947, April 1950.

BARON, ALEXANDER (December 4, 1917-), British novelist, writes: "I came to creative writing by way of a long and, I think, unhelpful detour by way of journalism. I was born of a working-class Jewish family whose Anglicisation (Bernstein became Baron) was reflected in my upbringing. The usual family sacrifices made it possible for me to have secondary (high) school education; but when I was seventeen, I was driven by shame at not earning my own living to forego a university scholarship I had won and to take a job as a municipal clerk.

"I became embroiled in the politics of the period (an interest which lasted only till the war) and began to work as a journalist in my spare time. The desire to write creatively was—at this time—something that I had consciously suppressed, together with my desire to go to college, because it seemed to stand in the way of becoming financially independent. In 1938 I became assistant editor of the literary-political weekly *The Tribune* and continued at this type of journalism until I joined the British Army in June 1940.

"My work as a journalist did not help me to develop technically as a writer; I learned to deal in second-hand thoughts and phrases and had to struggle later to overcome the habit. However, my travels about Britain among all conditions of people, together with my childhood experiences in the poorer quarters of London, laid the foundation for my future literary work.

"I spent six years in the army, as pioneer and infantryman, seeing active service in Sicily, Italy, France, and Belgium. It was during this time that I 'came to life' both in terms of human experience and of literature. I began to read seriously for the first time in my life; I admitted and accepted my ambition to write; and I made the first attempts, in the forms of short stories.

"I was badly knocked about towards the end of the war and came home with an invalid's pension in 1946. I got a job as assistant editor of a theatre magazine, became editor in 1947 and remained in this post till 1948.

"For the first three years after the war I lost about three months in each year through ill-health—I seem to have recovered now—but managed, besides holding down the magazine job, to complete a first novel in 1947 (*From the City, From the Plough*) which became a best seller. Since then I have published several other novels. I do occasional film work and reviewing but am able to live basically, on the royalties of my books.

"I spend as much time reading as I do writing. My masters are Balzac, Dickens and Hardy, and I find it hard to admit that any fiction of importance has been written in the English language since 1914."

* * *

From the City, From the Plough, the story of an English battalion in World War II, was well received and widely admired in England and in America. It was described by the *Manchester Guardian* as "a sober, firm narrative, devoid of all spurious sensationalism." Another war story, *Wine of Etna*, was equally restrained but effective. "This is a novel limited in scope," David Daiches wrote in the New York *Times*, "with a clean surface and a craftsmanlike prose style." In 1954 Baron made a radical departure from his simple and realistic subject matter drawn from contemporary life to write a long historical novel about the Spanish conquest of Mexico, *The Golden Princess*. The London *Times Literary Supplement* called it "an excellent historical novel," and the New York *Herald Tribune*'s reviewer found it "interesting and exciting and genuinely concerned with human relationships and the nature of man."

PRINCIPAL WORKS: From the City, From the Plough, 1948; There's No Home (in U.S.: Wine of Etna) 1950; Rosie Hogarth, 1951; With Hope, Farewell, 1952; The Human Kind, 1953; The Golden Princess, 1954.

BARR, ROBERT (September 16, 1850-October 21, 1912). For biographical sketch and list of works and references, see TWENTIETH CENTURY AUTHORS, 1942.

BARR, STRINGFELLOW (January 15, 1897-), American educator and world federationist, writes: "I was born in Suffolk, Va., son of an Episcopal clergyman. I spent my childhood in Richmond, Norfolk, Lynchburg, and New Orleans. At fifteen I entered Tulane University but stayed there only a year. I then returned to Virginia to complete my undergraduate education at the University of Virginia, where I also took a Master's degree. After two years in the army in World War I, I took up a Rhodes Scholarship I had won and spent two years at Balliol College, Oxford, where I took a B.A. in Modern History, with Honours, in 1921. In the same year, I married Gladys Baldwin, who was then studying theology at King's College, London. After a year in Paris, where I worked on the Paris edition of the old New York *Herald*, I won a fellowship in history and studied a year at the University of Ghent, Belgium.

"In 1923 I returned to this country and, after spending a year in Asheville, N.C., accepted an assistant professorship in history at the University of Virginia. After serving successively as assistant professor, associate professor and full professor in the School of History, I took a year's leave of absence to serve on a committee which President Robert M. Hutchins of the University of Chicago had set up to investigate the undergraduate curriculum of American colleges and universities. After a year's research, I accepted the presidency of St. John's College in Annapolis, Md., for the purpose of introducing a four-year, all-required curriculum based on the study of the great books of Western civilization from the Greeks to the present and including rigorous training in mathematics and laboratory science.

"I resigned from St. John's at the close of 1946 to start a similar college in Massachusetts, a venture subsequently abandoned. In 1948 I accepted the presidency of the newly established Foundation for World Government and remain in that post.

"In 1951 I returned to the University of Virginia on a two-year appointment as visiting professor of political science, while retaining my connection with the Foundation for World Government. "

PRINCIPAL WORK: Mazzini—Portrait of an Exile, 1935; Pilgrimage of Western Man, 1949; Let's Join the Human Race, 1950; Citizens of the World, 1952.

ABOUT: Current Biography 1940; Harper's June 1939; Newsweek March 1, 1943, August 26, 1946, December 23, 1946; Saturday Review of Literature April 3, 1948, July 23, 1949, December 13, 1952; School and Society March 23, 1940; Time October 24, 1938, August 19, 1946.

*BARRÈS, MAURICE (September 22, 1862-December 5, 1923). For biographical sketch and list of works and references, see TWENTIETH CENTURY AUTHORS, 1942.

* * *

ABOUT: Brogan, D. W. French Personalities and Problems; Columbia Dictionary of Modern European Literature; Lalou, R. Maurice Barrès; Mauriac, F. Men I Hold Great; Saurat, D. Modern French Literature; Slochower, H. No Voice Is Wholly Lost; Romanic Review April 1949.

* bà rěs'

BARRETTO, LARRY (May 30, 1890-). For biographical sketch and list of earlier works and references, see TWENTIETH CENTURY AUTHORS, 1942.

* * *

During World War II Larry Barretto served as enlistment officer for the American Field Service and later as war correspondent in the Caribbean area and the China-Burma-India theatre. He lives now in Carmel, Calif.

Much of Barretto's fiction has been concerned with the problem of the man-of-good-will who seeks spiritual peace in a materialistic and war-torn world. His post-World War II novel, *Great Light*, considers just such a problem. "In its metaphysical undertones," Harry R. Warfel writes, "the novel suggests that the plane of the spirit has hardly been touched in contemporary thinking." Rose Feld found that the secondary characters in the novel were successfully realized, but that Barretto's philosophy was somewhat vague. "It is undefined, mainly because Dirck [the hero] remains vague and unreal. He never reaches the stature of spiritual greatness indicated by his quest."

ADDITIONAL WORK: Great Light, 1947.

ABOUT: Warfel, H. R. American Novelists of Today.

BARRIE, Sir JAMES MATTHEW, Bart.
(May 9, 1860-June 19, 1937). For biographical sketch and list of works and references, see TWENTIETH CENTURY AUTHORS, 1942.

* * *

ADDITIONAL WORK: Letters (ed. V. Meynell) 1947.

ABOUT: Barrie, J. Letters; Blake, G. Barrie and the Kailyard School; Bowen, E. Collected Impressions; Christian Science Monitor Magazine November 1, 1947; Dictionary of National Biography 1931-1940.

"BARRINGTON, E." See BECK, L. M. A.

BARRY, PHILIP (June 18, 1896-December 3, 1949). For biographical sketch and list of earlier works and references, see TWENTIETH CENTURY AUTHORS, 1942.

* * *

Philip Barry died suddenly of a heart attack at his New York City apartment, 510 Park Avenue, at fifty-three. Mrs. Barry and their two sons were at his side when he died. *Second Threshold,* the play Philip Barry had been working on at his death, was revised by Robert Sherwood and produced at the Morosco Theatre, New York, on January 2, 1951. Thirty years before, *A Punch for Judy,* his first play to reach Broadway, was put on at the same theatre. "In *Second Threshold,* finally," wrote John Gassner, "he actually succeeded in fusing his talent for high comedy with his less manageable but very real talent for expressing human anguish." Robert Sherwood wrote of "his Irish, impish sense of comedy, and his profound, and also Irish, sense of the ultimate sadness of life on earth, the 'endless assault' of evil upon good."

Philip Barry's last three Broadway plays before his death were something less than smash hits. *Without Love,* with Katharine Hepburn, opened on November 10, 1942; *Foolish Notion,* with Tallulah Bankhead, opened on March 13, 1945; *My Name Is Aquilon,* an adaptation of Jean-Pierre Aumont's *L'Empereur de Chine,* which opened on February 9, 1949, was a failure, despite performances by M. Aumont himself and Lilli Palmer. The film versions of two earlier hits, *Holiday* and *Philadelphia Story,* have won frequent revival. In 1943 a film entitled *One More Tomorrow* was made from Barry's play *The Animal Kingdom.*

John Mason Brown summed up Philip Barry as "both a man of the theatre and a man of letters," one who "stood apart from —and above—the brassy competence and spiritual emptiness of the commercial theatre. . . . He employed the means of Congreve to preach sermons against divorce that a Cardinal would have approved of." Yet Mr. Brown sorrowfully reaches the conclusion that Barry never fulfilled himself: "The biggest things for which Phil reached may have eluded his grasp."

ADDITIONAL WORKS: Without Love, 1943; Second Threshold, 1951.

ABOUT: Barry, P. Second Threshold (Preface by R. E. Sherwood); Brown, J. M. Still Seeing Things; Flexner, E. American Playwrights 1918-1938; Gagey, E. M. Revolution in American Drama; Hamm, G. The Drama of Philip Barry; Hoehn, M. (ed.) Catholic Authors, I; Krutch, J. W. American Drama Since 1918; National Cyclopedia of American Biography (1951); New York Times December 4, 1949; Theatre Arts December 1951; Wilson Library Bulletin February 1950.

BARTH, KARL (May 10, 1886-   ), Swiss theologian, was born in Basel, the son of Friedrich Barth, a theologian of the Reformed Church, and Anna Sartorius Barth. He studied in Bern, and at the German universities of Berlin, Tübingen, and Marburg. For a brief period he worked on a newspaper, *Die Christliche Welt,* and in 1909 he entered the ministry. His first  pastorate was a small Reformed church in Geneva. He moved from there, in 1911, to the pastorate of Safenwil, a small Swiss village, where he remained for ten years.

In 1918 Barth's *Epistle to the Romans* was published. The book began, he has said, as "an essay to help me know my own mind," but upon publication it rapidly became "a burning topic of theology in all the Protestant countries of Europe." Barth saw the church in a state of intellectual contradiction and chaos, as a result largely of the flexible "liberalism" of nineteenth century Protestant theology and the "God-forgetting humanism" which it produced. With this book, and with later ones in which he has modified and enlarged upon his original thesis, Barth has established the movement of "neo-orthodoxy" within the Protestant Church. "Faith," he argues, "not reason, is the basis of Christian knowledge." It is significant that much of Barth's early theology was developed during the critical years of the First World War under the influence of Sören Kirkegaard's existentialism. Through later years it has taken on even more profound significance and has come to be known as the "Theology of Crisis." It offers no easy and pleasant solutions to the dilemmas of human existence. Instead, as the British theologian M. Chaning-Pearce has said, "to the acute and almost unbearable tensions of our life it brings a tension yet more intense—the tension of absolute faith." One can meet the tensions of human life, Barth says, only "with the greater tension of faith which Pauline theology, Pauline Christianity, with the word of resurrection at its center, shows to us."

In 1921 Barth was invited to the University of Göttingen as professor of reformed theology. Four years later he moved on to the University of Münster in Westphalia, and in 1930 he joined the faculty of the University of Bonn. Here he remained until 1934 when he defied the Hitler government in Germany by refusing to take an oath of loyalty to it. He was immediately dismissed from the post and banned from Germany. He returned to Switzerland to teach at the University of Basel and became an energetic and outspoken foe of Nazism, lecturing against Hitler, cooperating in programs of aid to refugees from Germany, and joining the Swiss Army—at the age of fifty-four—to serve sentry duty on the Swiss-German frontier.

As soon as the war ended, Barth returned to Germany on a visit. In 1946 and 1947 he was guest professor at summer sessions at Bonn and he lectured in many other German cities. In 1948 he visited Hungary and there endorsed the stand of the Reformed Church in refusing to fight the Communist government. For this action Barth was severely criticized and the charge was even made that he had been "converted" to Communism. This Barth vigorously and thoroughly denied. He stated his position in a revealing two-part article, "How My Mind Changed, 1938-1948," in the *Christian Century* (March 9 and 16, 1949): "I am of the opinion that Communism can be warded off only by a 'better justice' on the part of the Western world, not by the all too cheap denials in which the fear of the West is now expressing itself. . . . The locus of Christianity is to be sought above today's conflict between East and West." In September 1951 Barth addressed a letter to the head of the Hungarian Reformed Church sharply attacking him for making his "affirmation of Communism a part of the Christian message"

and deploring the encroachments of political propaganda upon the faith.

Barth is a modest, unassuming man who lives simply with his wife, the former Nelly Hoffmann, whom he married in 1913, in a house that is always crowded with students and visitors. They have five children and eight grandchildren. One son is a missionary in Borneo. Barth is a powerful writer and speaker, stylistically influenced by years of pulpit oratory. Although he is universally acknowledged as the founder of a major field of thought that bears his name— "Barthian theology"—he is personally opposed to any such identification. "No better method can be devised of keeping away the truth than to stamp it out with this or that name," he has said. His influence on contemporary thought has been considerable. The six large volumes of his major work, *Kirkliche Dogmatik*, one commentator says, "may turn out to be the most imposing theological work of modern times." He has many critics. Heinrich Emil Brunner, who worked closely with him some years ago, now objects that Barth denies "all contact between theology and the general consciousness of man," and Reinhold Niebuhr has charged that Barth's doctrine, by concentrating on the Kingdom of God, makes no provision for the practical and frequently tragic decisions that Christian men and nations must make on earth. But even his most severe critics would accept Hugh Ross Mackintosh's statement that his theology "is the Christian thinking of a great Christian mind . . . of incalculable import for the Church of our time." No one, Mackintosh continues, will "deny his unrivalled power to wake up the sleeping intelligence of the Christian society and to insist that theology shall be Biblical in its essence from end to end. He is compelling us to face again the problems of life and death."

PRINCIPAL WORKS IN ENGLISH TRANSLATION: Christian Life, 1920; The Word of God and the Word of Man, 1928; Credo: Chief Problems of Dogmatics, 1936; Doctrine of the Word of God, 1936; Epistle to the Romans, 1933; Resurrection of the Dead, 1933; God in Action, 1936; The Holy Ghost and the Christian Life, 1938; The Church and the Political Problems of Our Day, 1939; Church and State, 1939; The Knowledge of God and the Service of God, 1939; Reformation Old and New, 1947; Dogmatics in Outline, 1949; Prayer According to the Catechisms of the Reformation, 1952; Against the Stream, 1954.

ABOUT: Brunner, H. E. Theology of Crisis; Camfield, F. W. Revelation and the Holy Spirit; Chaning-Pearce, M. The Terrible Crystal; Chapman, J. A. The Theology of Karl Barth; Fairweather, A. The Word as Truth; Hanson, W. G. The Message of Karl Barth; Heath, C. The Challenge of Karl Barth; Hoyle, R. B. The Teaching of Karl Barth; Keller, A. Karl Barth and Christian

Unity; Kent, F. Karl Barth and His Teaching; Leitch, J. W. Theology of Transition; Lowrie, W. Our Concern with the Theology of Crisis; McConnachie, J. Significance of Karl Barth, Barthian Theology and the Man of Today; Mackintosh, H. R. Types of Modern Theology; Pauck, W. Karl Barth; Spencer, S. Shall We Follow Karl Barth?; Van Til, C. The New Modernism; Weber, O. Karl Barth's Church Dogmatics: An Introductory Report; Zerbe, A. S. Karl Barth Theology; Christian Century March 9, 16, 1949.

BARTLETT, VERNON (April 30, 1894-). For biographical sketch and list of earlier works and references, see TWENTIETH CENTURY AUTHORS, 1942.

* * *

Vernon Bartlett remained in Parliament representing the Bridgewater Division of Somerset until 1950. He was a member of the United Nations Advisory Committee of Experts in 1948 and is honorary consultant to the Department of Public Information of the United Nations. Since 1934 he has been on the staff of the London *News Chronicle*. Joseph Barnes considers Bartlett "one of the best of all living foreign correspondents." His book on his visit to the Soviet-satellite countries in 1949, *East of the Iron Curtain*, was widely praised for sound and level-headed reporting, a realistic but sanguine outlook, and a dispassionate approach to controversial issues. Albert Guérard called his earlier *Tomorrow Always Comes*—a "diary of the future," warning of the dangers of the postwar period—"a generous, an entrancing book, and a wise one."

ADDITIONAL WORKS: Tomorrow Always Comes, 1943; Go East, Old Man, 1948; East of the Iron Curtain, 1950; Report from Malaya, 1955.

BARZUN, JACQUES (November 30, 1907-). For biographical sketch and list of earlier works and references, see TWENTIETH CENTURY AUTHORS, 1942.

* * *

Jacques Barzun calls himself "a student of cultural history." This designation, rather than simply "historian," more accurately indicates the breadth of Barzun's interests. In the past decade his most important books have been in the fields of criticism, education, and musicology—all of them having in common the combination of sound scholarship and fresh, independent interpretation which is the mark of the humanist man-of-letters.

Nowhere is Barzun's wise and witty approach to the subject-at-hand seen to better advantage than in his *Teacher in America*, which the late Christian Gauss called "one of the few volumes on education by which no intelligent reader can be bored." A teacher and lecturer himself, Barzun is here concerned not with theories of education but with the essence of education—the teacher, his teaching, and the resources of the human mind. "The test and the use of a man's education," Barzun wrote in an article in *Life* in 1950, "[is] that he finds pleasure in the exercise of his mind."

His re-evaluation of the great figures of nineteenth century romanticism, *Romanticism and the Modern Ego*, was widely praised as a provocative and illuminating study, lacking the high seriousness of Irving Babbitt's *Rousseau and Romanticism* but displaying (Harry Levin felt) "all the intellectual flexibility and esthetic sympathy that are conspicuously absent from Babbitt's work." His two-volume biography of Hector Berlioz, while questioned by some reviewers on points of technical information, was praised by many more for the qualities Charles J. Rolo singled out in his review in the *Atlantic*— "monumental scholarship; elegant and eloquent writing; the pervasive imprint of a deeply civilized mind; and a wealth of insights into the life of art." In 1954 Barzun published his reflections on American life in *God's Country and Mine*, subtitled "A Declaration of Love Spiced with a Few Harsh Words." His views were fresh and stimulating. "He has no sacred cows," D. W. Brogan wrote in the New York *Times*, "and his book will startle, infuriate, enlighten and rejoice different types of readers."

Barzun became professor of history at Columbia University in 1945. He appears frequently as a guest on the radio discussion program *Invitation to Learning*. He has been married since 1936 to Mariana Lowell and has two sons and a daughter.

ADDITIONAL WORKS: Romanticism and the Modern Ego, 1943; The Teacher in America, 1945; Berlioz and the Romantic Century, 1950; The Pleasures of Music (ed.) 1951; Letters of Byron (ed.) 1953; God's Country and Mine, 1954.

ABOUT: Morgan, C. Liberties of the Mind; Life October 16, 1950; New York Herald Tribune Book Review May 21, 1950; Saturday Review of Literature May 13, 1950.

BASSETT, JOHN SPENCER (September 10, 1867-January 27, 1928). For biographical sketch and list of works and references, see TWENTIETH CENTURY AUTHORS, 1942.

BASSHE, EMJO (1900-October 28, 1939). For biographical sketch and list of works and references, see TWENTIETH CENTURY AUTHORS, 1942.

BASSO, HAMILTON (September 5, 1904-). American novelist and biographer.

NOTE: This biography, at the request of the writer, supersedes the sketch which appeared in TWENTIETH CENTURY AUTHORS, 1942.

Hamilton Basso was born in New Orleans, La., where his family has been established since before the Civil War. He was educated in the New Orleans public schools and attended Tulane University from 1922 to 1926. Leaving the university before he graduated, he went to New York with the idea of making a literary career for himself, and ended up working in a print shop and trucking freight. Returning to New Orleans, where he had previously been associated with the so-called *Double Dealer* group, he became a reporter for the now deceased *Tribune,* and later worked on the *Item* and the *Times-Picayune.*

It was about this time (1929) that he published his first novel, *Relics and Angels.* Following his marriage to the former Etolia Simmons in 1930, he moved to the mountains of North Carolina, where he lived, off and on, until 1941. He also spent considerable time in the Southwest, in South Carolina, and in Europe. He and Mrs. Basso spent the year 1937-38 in a little village in southern France and also traveled in England and Italy, returning to the United States in the early summer of 1939. Since then he has traveled throughout this country and in the Caribbean. He was an associate editor of the *New Republic* from 1935 to 1937, a contributing editor of *Time* in 1942 and 1943, and after 1943 an associate editor of the *New Yorker,* for which magazine he has been a literary critic and to which he has contributed a number of short stories and profiles. He has also written for various other magazines. The Bassos, who have one son, now live in Weston, Conn.

Hamilton Basso's novel *Days Before Lent* received the Southern Authors Award and was made into a motion picture. His *The View from Pompey's Head,* a study of a small Southern town and its rigid and complex social structure, was highly praised, and, Basso told an interviewer in October 1954, may be the basis for at least two more novels forming "a sort of social history of the South."

In the field of non-fiction he has published a biography of General Beauregard; a collection of biographical essays, *Mainstream,* intended to serve as a study of the American character; and an edition of William Lewis Herndon's *Exploration of the Valley of the Amazon,* first published in 1842. With his wife he was co-editor of *The World from Jackson Square,* a collection of writings about New Orleans.

PRINCIPAL WORKS: Relics and Angels, 1929; Beauregard: The Great Creole (biography) 1933; Cinnamon Seed, 1934; In Their Own Image, 1935; Courthouse Square, 1936; Days Before Lent, 1939; Wine of the Country, 1941; Sun in Capricorn, 1942; Mainstream (essays) 1943; The World from Jackson Square (ed. with E. S. Basso) 1948; The Greenroom, 1949; Herndon, W. H. Exploration of the Valley of the Amazon (ed.) 1952; The View from Pompey's Head, 1954.

ABOUT: Warfel, H. R. American Novelists of Today; New York Herald Tribune Book Review October 24, 1954; New York Times Book Review October 24, 1954; Publishers' Weekly February 3, 1940; Wilson Library Bulletin October 1939.

BATES, ERNEST SUTHERLAND (October 14, 1879-December 4, 1939). For biographical sketch and list of works and references, see TWENTIETH CENTURY AUTHORS, 1942.

BATES, HERBERT ERNEST (May 16, 1905-). For biographical sketch and list of earlier works and references, see TWENTIETH CENTURY AUTHORS, 1942.

* * *

During the Second World War, H. E. Bates wrote steadily and with ever-increasing popular success in England and in the United States. He was the first short story writer commissioned by the British government to write about the R.A.F. Under the pseudonym of Flying Officer X, he published a number of short pieces that, according to Meyer Berger, conveyed to "the reader a clearer conception of the combat flier's thinking, fighting, living, than anything that has come before." Under his own name Bates published one of the most popular of wartime novels, *Fair Stood the Wind for France* (a Book-of-the-Month Club selection in the United States), the story of a British bomber crew forced down in occupied France. Before the war ended, Bates was sent to Burma to write about the war in that theatre. Some of what he calls the "leftover" material from his Burma experiences he used to good effect in *The Purple Plain* and *The Jacaranda Tree.*

Essentially Bates is a reporter of action. Reviewers sometimes complain that his fiction is disjointed or artificially well-made

("One is aware that life has been arranged," the *Spectator* commented on his *Scarlet Sword*), his characterization thin, and what one reviewer calls his "thematic range" narrow. But rarely absent from Bates' work is "the spell-binding power of the good story teller." He writes with the economy and virtuosity of a master. "He has, besides," Richard Match comments, "a special quality quite his own, an antenna-like sixth-sense perception of the color of a place, an hour or an emotion that identifies his best work as surely as the title page."

In February 1953 Bates visited the United States, for the first time since 1937, en route to the Bahamas where he planned to spend several months gathering material for a history of the islands. His home is still in Little Chart, Kent. He now has four children—two sons and two daughters.

ADDITIONAL WORKS: In the Heart of the Country, 1942; The Bride Comes to Evensford, 1943; O More than Happy Countryman, 1943; Fair Stood the Wind for France, 1944; Days of Glory (play) 1945; Cruise of the Breadwinner, 1947; The Purple Plain, 1947; Thirty-One Selected Tales, 1947; The Jacaranda Tree, 1948; The Scarlet Sword, 1950; The Modern Short Story: A Critical Survey, 1950; Edward Garnett: A Portrait, 1951; Colonel Julian and Other Stories, 1951; Cut and Come Again: Fourteen Stories, 1951; Love for Lydia, 1952; The Face of England, 1953; The Nature of Love, 1954; The Feast of July, 1954. As Flying Officer X— Greatest People in the World, 1942; How Sleep the Brave, 1943; There's Something in the Air, 1943.

ABOUT: Current Biography 1944; New York Herald Tribune Book Review February 15, 1953; New York Times Book Review February 15, 1953; Saturday Review of Literature December 13, 1947.

BATES, KATHARINE LEE (August 12, 1859-March 28, 1929). For biographical sketch and list of works and references, see TWENTIETH CENTURY AUTHORS, 1942.

* * *

ABOUT: Burgess, D. The Dream and the Deed: The Story of Katharine Lee Bates.

BATES, RALPH (November 3, 1899-). For biographical sketch and list of earlier works and references, see TWENTIETH CENTURY AUTHORS, 1942.

* * *

Ralph Bates lives in New York City where, since 1948, he has been adjunct professor of literature at New York University. He was married in 1940 to Eve Salzman and has a son. His novel *The Dolphin in the Wood* came as something of a surprise to readers familiar with his forceful and incisive novels of Spain and Mexico. This latest book, the first-person narrative of a young Englishman born in a quiet English village at the beginning of the twentieth century, was full of evocative regional detail. R. D. Charques, of the *Spectator*, wrote that it "wears its liveliness and strength of imagination or memory with genuine charm."

ADDITIONAL WORK: The Dolphin in the Wood. 1949.

BAUM, LYMAN FRANK (May 15, 1856-May 6, 1919). For biographical sketch and list of works and references, see TWENTIETH CENTURY AUTHORS, 1942.

BAUM, VICKI (January 24, 1888-). For autobiographical sketch and list of earlier works and references, see TWENTIETH CENTURY AUTHORS, 1942.

* * *

Vicki Baum lives in Hollywood, Calif. Since 1938 she has been writing her novels in English instead of German. She now lists dancing and traveling as her "main vices."

In 1945 Didier, Publishers, of New York, published a novel of Miss Baum's, *Once in Vienna*. Miss Baum protested that this was an unauthorized publication of her first novel which she had written at fifteen and which had been originally published in Germany in 1919. Didier replied that the publication had been authorized under an earlier contract with Miss Baum's English publisher. There is considerable confusion as to the number of books Miss Baum has written. She is not sure herself. In 1953 she told an interviewer: "Sometimes when I'm trying to get to sleep I go over them. Did this book come after I had the baby or before? What was the name of the one following? Sometimes I get thirty-one, sometimes twenty-five. But it's an agreeable way to put yourself to sleep." *The Mustard Seed*, her novel about a faith healer in California, was submitted to the publisher (and accepted) under a pseudonym. Her reason, she says, was that "I didn't want always to be the girl who wrote *Grand Hotel*."

ADDITIONAL WORKS: The Weeping Wood, 1943; Hotel Berlin '43, 1944; Once in Vienna, 1945; Mortgage on Life, 1946; Headless Angel, 1948; Danger from Deer, 1951; The Mustard Seed, 1953.

ABOUT: Warfel, H. R. American Novelists of Today; New York Times Book Review October 11, 1953; Publishers' Weekly February 3, 1945.

BAXTER, JAMES PHINNEY, 3d (February 15, 1893-), American historian and educator, was born in Portland, Maine, the son of James Phinney Baxter, an industrialist and banker, and Nelly Furbish (Carpenter) Baxter. He is of old New England ancestry. His grandfather served five

terms as mayor of Portland and wrote books and monographs on early American history. His uncle, Percival Proctor Baxter, was twice governor of Maine. Young Baxter was educated at the Portland High School, Phillips Academy at Andover, Mass., and Williams College, where he majored in history, was active in debate and student government, and was elected to Phi Beta Kappa. After graduation, *summa cum laude,* in 1914, he worked for a year for the Industrial Finance Corporation in New York. During the course of a long illness, from 1915 to 1921, Baxter decided to make a career of the study of history. In 1921 he joined the faculty of Colorado College as instructor in history. A year later he went to Harvard to study for his M.A., which he received in 1923. He traveled on a John Harvard Fellowship in 1924 and 1925 and then returned to Harvard to teach history and to do further graduate study. In 1926 he received his Ph.D. His thesis, *The Introduction of the Ironclad Warship,* won the Toppan Prize for "exceptional merit." He remained on the faculty of Harvard, rising in academic rank to full professor, until 1937 when he became president of Williams College.

In World War II, Baxter organized the research and analysis section of the Office of the Coordinator of Information (which became the Office of Strategic Services in 1942). He resigned from this post in 1943 to become historian of the Office of Scientific Research and Development, holding the job until 1946 on a part-time basis, by permission of the trustees of Williams College. Baxter also headed the Commission on Liberal Education of the Association of American Colleges. In 1945 he was elected president of the A.A.C.

During the summer of 1945 Baxter began work on *Scientists Against Time,* an official history of the Office of Scientific Research, the first volume in a planned series, Science in World War II. *Scientists Against Time,* of which Baxter wrote all but six chapters on chemistry and military medicine, was hailed as "a monumental record of . . . the greatest scientific and engineering undertaking of all

time . . . an invaluable, as well as entertaining, source of information." It received the 1946 Pulitzer prize in history.

Baxter has also written many articles on naval affairs and diplomatic history. He has lectured at the Lowell Institute in Boston (1931), at Cambridge University (1936), and at the Army War College (1946). He has honorary degrees from a number of American universities and colleges, and is a trustee of Radcliffe College, Phillips Andover Academy, the American Military Institute, and the World Peace Foundation. Baxter lives in Williamstown, Mass. In 1919 he married Anne Holden Strang, and they have three sons.

PRINCIPAL WORKS: The Introduction of the Ironclad Warship, 1933; Scientists Against Time, 1945.

ABOUT: Current Biography 1947; New York Times May 6, 1947.

*BAZIN, RENÉ (December 26, 1853-July 21, 1932). For biographical sketch and list of works and references, see TWENTIETH CENTURY AUTHORS, 1942.

* * *

ADDITIONAL WORKS IN ENGLISH TRANSLATION: Take This Child. . . 1948; Juniper Farm, 1951.

ABOUT: Columbia Dictionary of Modern European Literature; Gilson, Sister M. A. Analysis of the Realistic Elements in the Novels of René Bazin; Hoehn, M. (ed.) Catholic Authors, I.

* bà zăN'

BEACH, JOSEPH WARREN (January 14, 1880-   ), American critic, poet, and educator, writes: "Most of my life I have spent as a college professor and critic of literature. In rare moments of leisure I have tried my hand at fiction (best forgotten), but what I have most enjoyed is writing poetry. As a critic, I do not aim so much to render final judgments and deliver

certificates of greatness, which is something manifestly impossible and a trifle ridiculous, as to analyze and interpret stories and poems as expressions of our humanity and as effective works of art.

"I was born and bred in Gloversville, N.Y., a typical bustling small manufacturing town, which my mother found lacking in 'class' in comparison with her native Stamford, Conn., but which had a high school that in those days gave a fine 'classical' education. My most distinguished ancestor was John Davenport, an English Puritan divine, who was one of the founders of the New Haven colony and made a lot of trouble in the theological world both there and in Boston. Our line represents what Matthew Arnold called 'the dissidence of dissent and the protestantism of the Protestant religion.' I had my college education (B.A. 1900) at the University of Minnesota in the smell of the lumber yards, the hum of the flour mills and the splashing of St. Anthony Falls. I took my Ph.D. at Harvard (1907) under guidance of George Lyman Kittredge, philologist, medievalist, benevolent dictator, and terror of the undergraduates in his Shakespeare course. My unpublished thesis, on Chaucer, was really a study of folk tales dealing with the transformation of humans into animals and back again. I later pitched my tent in the Romantic and Victorian 'fields,' and have even made some raids into the field of contemporary American literature.

"From 1907 to 1948 I was in the English faculty at Minnesota going through the usual grades; for some years I was department chairman. The university world was already rocking with the epic battle between the 'scholars' and the 'critics.' In this battle I did not take sides, believing that scholarship and criticism are equally indispensable in the study of literature. This was also a period notable for the attaching of creative writers to college faculties. Our luckiest stroke during my term of office was bringing Robert Penn Warren to Minnesota. I have taught summer school at several universities and at the Salzburg Seminar, and have been visiting professor at the Universities of Washington, Harvard, Illinois, Paris, Strasbourg, and Johns Hopkins.

"I have been twice married, have two grown sons and plenty of grandchildren. I early formed the habit of going abroad whenever possible, but am not a good traveler and generally get comfortably stuck in Paris. I am not good at any games, but, in summer camp on the St. Croix River, can be happy swimming, chopping wood, and making paths that follow the contours so that guests may not have heart failure getting up and down the hills. Beyond this, my biography is a list of books. I have lived longest (among writers in English) with Chaucer, Wordsworth, Meredith, Hardy, Henry James, Conrad, Faulkner, and (for American poets) with Sandburg, Frost, Eliot, Wallace Stevens. Strange bedfellows!"

PRINCIPAL WORKS: The Comic Spirit in George Meredith, 1911; The Method of Henry James, 1918; The Technique of Thomas Hardy, 1922; Meek Americans and Other Foreign Trifles, 1925; The Outlook for American Prose, 1926; The Twentieth Century Novel, 1932; The Concept of Nature in Nineteenth Century English Poetry, 1936; American Fiction 1920-1940, 1941; A Romantic View of Poetry, 1944. Novel—Glass Mountain, 1930. Poetry —Beginning with Plato, 1944; Involuntary Witness, 1950.

ABOUT: O'Connor, W. V. (ed.) Forms of Modern Fiction: Essays Collected in Honor of Joseph Warren Beach.

BEACH, REX ELLINGWOOD (September 1, 1877-December 7, 1949). For biographical sketch and list of earlier works and references, see TWENTIETH CENTURY AUTHORS, 1942.

* * *

Rex Beach committed suicide by shooting himself through the head at his lakeside home in Sebring, Fla., at seventy-two. He had been suffering from incurable cancer of the throat for two years and was going blind. He is buried beside his wife, who died in 1947, on the campus of Rollins College.

Beach wrote little in his later years compared with his earlier prolific output, but left a novel, *Woman in Ambush*, almost completed at his death. Having made a fortune from novels and motion pictures, he had gone on to make another from flower and vegetable growing and cattle raising in Florida. The sale of lily bulbs alone grossed him $200,000 in a single season. Having achieved success with flowers and vegetables, he sold out to his employees and went on to apply scientific methods to cattle raising. At one time he owned 7,000 acres near Sebring and 2,000 more at Avon Park.

Motion picture history must always find room for the name of Rex Beach, "the first author to insert a clause about movie rights in his contract" and the producer of the first six-reel film, *The Spoilers* (1912). Beach always refused to sell his stories outright to Hollywood, thus profiting every time *The Spoilers* was re-made. In all, fourteen of his novels and sixteen of his original scenarios were made into films. In 1948 he sold the film rights to *Woman in Ambush* for $100,-000, the highest price ever paid by Hollywood for an unpublished manuscript.

Beach, who had to run a laundry to earn his tuition at Rollins Preparatory (which he entered in 1891) and at Rollins College, left

$100,000 to Rollins for a student-loan fund, and $50,000 to Notre Dame College, Wilcox, Saskatchewan, for the same purpose.

ADDITIONAL WORKS: World in His Arms, 1946; Woman in Ambush, 1951.

ABOUT: Van Gelder, R. Writers and Writing; New York Times December 8, 1949; Publishers' Weekly December 24, 1949; Reader's Digest January 1951.

BEALS, CARLETON (November 13, 1893-). For autobiographical sketch and list of earlier works and references, see TWENTIETH CENTURY AUTHORS, 1942.

* * *

Carleton Beals writes: "During the ten years since the previous sketch was written, vast cataclysms have occured, changing the map of the world and every human soul. I built a house in Guilford, Conn., overlooking Long Island Sound, and moved in just after Pearl Harbor shook the United States out of isolationism. This was the first time I had ever had a permanent place for my large library, more than twenty years of clippings and files, and a quiet place to work.

"I published several more books on Latin America, including one on Chile, which represented further travels to South America. A novel, *Dawn over the Amazon,* was taken by the Literary Guild.

"Feeling the need for revitalizing local initiative in a period of overriding governmental centralization, I have turned in part to writing the local history of various Connecticut communities to be used as texts in the high schools and colleges, the first time such history has been introduced into the regular curriculum of public schools. The story of the making of New Haven was published in 1951, and that of Bristol in 1953. I have also written a biography of *Stephen Austin: Father of Texas.*

"The greater concentration of government and official controls over all phases of industry and individual activities, the greater concentration of publishing due to higher costs, the excess of biased propaganda, lowered standards of journalism, thought, and taste, make the role of the free-lance writer much more difficult than when I started writing. The disease of collective uniformity, which we are fighting abroad, creeps in upon us, limiting all independent opinions.

"Among writers who influence me, not previously mentioned, have been Ibsen, Dostoevsky, Turgenev Flaubert, and Heine. Of the contemporaries of the previous period, only Faulkner continues to interest me,

far more than before. I have since read more widely in Latin American literature. *Rebellion in the Backland (Os Sertões)* by Euclides da Cunha, for me, is one of the greatest books of all time. Numerous Chilean writers are decidedly worth reading, but not many have been translated. I keep on reading Cervantes and have read a great deal more of Lope de Vega.

"In short, I find no contemporary thinker or writer who impresses me very much, although numerous individual books have meant a great deal to me. Offhand I think of Lillian Smith's *Strange Fruit,* Rachel Carson's *The Sea Around Us,* quite a few biographies. Joyce Cary is a great delight."

ADDITIONAL WORKS: Rio Grande to Cape Horn, 1943; Dawn over the Amazon, 1943; What the South Americans Think of Us: A Symposium, 1945; Lands of the Dawning Morrow, 1948; Chile: The Long Land, 1949; Our Yankee Heritage: The Making of Greater New Haven, 1951; Our Yankee Heritage: The Making of Bristol, 1953; Stephen Austin: Father of Texas, 1953.

ABOUT: Collier's August 2, 1947; Current Biography 1941.

BEARD, CHARLES AUSTIN (November 27, 1874-September 1, 1948). For biographical sketch and list of earlier works and references, see TWENTIETH CENTURY AUTHORS, 1942.

* * *

Charles A. Beard died in the Grace-New Haven Community Hospital in Connecticut at seventy-three, a victim of aplastic anemia.

In the closing years of his life, the "grand old man of the study of American politics in historical perspective," as the *Yale Law Journal* has characterized him, emphasized his differences with the internationalist viewpoint. Although the *Basic History of the United States,* written with his wife and published in 1944, was praised for its objectivity by H. S. Commager, who termed it "the best short history of the United States yet written," *American Foreign Policy in the Making* (1946) and *President Roosevelt and the Coming of War, 1941* (1948), were called isolationist by many critics. The National Institute of Arts and Letters award of its gold medal to the historian raised controversy in the membership of that body. In 1944 Beard was made an honorary Doctor of Letters by Columbia University.

"Nothing in Beard's writing quite reveals the radiant personality of the man," his associates on the *American Historical Review* observed. "He was a great historian," Max Lerner has said, "mainly because he was more than a historian. He was a political theorist, and a dabbler in philosophy. But his real stature as historian came from his being a satirist; that is what gives strength, bite and pungency to his work."

ADDITIONAL WORKS: The American Spirit: A Study of the Idea of Civilization in the United States (vol 4 of The Rise of American Civilization, with M. Beard) 1942; The Republic, 1943; A Basic History of the United States (with M. Beard) 1944; American Foreign Policy in the Making, 1932-1940, 1946; President Roosevelt and the Coming of the War, 1941, A Study in Appearance and Realities, 1948.

ABOUT: Beale, H. K. (ed.) Charles A. Beard; Kazin, A. On Native Grounds; Reither, J. (ed.) Masterworks of History; American Political Science Review December 1948; Atlantic Monthly August 1948; Christian Century September 22, 1948; Nation September 11, 1948, September 25, 1948; New Republic October 25, 1948, November 1, 1948; New York Times September 2, 1948; Virginia Quarterly Review October 1949.

BEARD, DANIEL CARTER (June 21, 1850-June 11, 1941). For autobiographical sketch and list of works and references, see TWENTIETH CENTURY AUTHORS, 1942.

BEARD, Mrs. MARY (RITTER) (August 5, 1876-). For biographical sketch and list of earlier works and references, see TWENTIETH CENTURY AUTHORS, 1942.

* * *

Mary R. Beard lives in New Milford, Conn. An "indomitable and delightful scholar and propagandist," she has continued to work energetically in the cause of women's rights. Her *Woman as a Force in History* was a detailed and impressive history of woman's place in our society. In 1953 she completed a study of the place of women in Japanese history. Her husband and collaborator, the noted historian Charles A. Beard, died in 1948.

ADDITIONAL WORKS: Woman as a Force in History, 1946; Force of Women in Japanese History, 1953. *With C. A. Beard*—The American Spirit (vol. 4 of Rise of American Civilization) 1942; A Basic History of the United States, 1944.

ABOUT: Banta, R. E. Indiana Authors and their Books; Reither, J. (ed.) Masterworks of History.

BEAUCHAMP, KATHLEEN MANS-FIELD. See MANSFIELD, K.

BEAUCHAMP, MARY ANNETTE. See RUSSELL, M. A. B. R.

*BEAUCLERK, HELEN DE VERE (September 20, 1892-). For autobiographical sketch and list of earlier works and references, see TWENTIETH CENTURY AUTHORS, 1942.

* * *

Miss Beauclerk sends a correction for her 1942 sketch: her father was nephew, not son, of the late Sir Alan Bellingham and therefore not a baronet.

She also adds that the description of her as a "typical English blonde" is erroneous: "I am greying now but have been very dark."

ADDITIONAL WORKS: Shadows on a Wall, 1941; Where the Treasure Is, 1944; There Were Three Men, 1949.

* bō'clâr

* BEAUVOIR, SIMONE DE (January 9, 1908-), French novelist and existentialist philosopher, was born in Paris and educated in private schools and at the Sorbonne, where she took her degree in philosophy in 1929. A fellow student at the Sorbonne was Jean-Paul Sartre, with whom she became associated in the French existentialist movement.

Elliott Erwitt

In 1931 Mlle. de Beauvoir went to Marseille to teach philosophy in a *lycée*. From 1933 to 1937 she taught at Rouen, and in 1938 she returned to Paris where, for the next five years, she taught at the Lycée Molière and the Lycée Camille-Sée. In 1943 she gave up teaching to devote herself to her writing. That same year her first novel, *L'Invitée*, appeared, and in the following year she published an existentialist essay, *Pyrrhus et Cinéas*, and the novel *Le Sang des Autres* (*The Blood of Others*). In 1945 her play *Les Bouches Inutiles*—posing a characteristically existentialist moral question: Should a besieged city rid itself of those 'useless mouths' which cannot aid in its struggle for survival?—was produced in Paris.

The literary reputation of Simone de Beauvoir has something of the legendary about it. As a leading exponent of the much-publicized existentialist movement, she became, along with Jean-Paul Sartre, the center of a lively literary and philosophical cult, headquarters of which were two side-

* bō vwàr'

walk cafés of the Left Bank of Paris, the Deux Magots and the Flore. Allied with Sartre she edited the existentialist magazine *Les Temps Modernes*. A handsome woman, energetic, and profoundly learned, she wrote, traveled and lectured widely. In 1947 she visited the United States on a nation-wide tour, lecturing under the auspices of the French Cultural Service on the moral problems of the post-war writer. The first of her novels to be published in translation in America, *The Blood of Others*, though marked with what one reviewer called "sincere humanity," was in some ways a disappointment to readers who had come to expect so much of her, since it was, for the most part, a conventional novel of the French Resistance. But her vigorous and challenging essays and philosophical writings on existentialism gave substance to the de Beauvoir legend. As Bernard Kalb has pointed out, "Mlle. de Beauvoir is a major existentialist, not merely a dulcet-voiced carbon-copy of Sartre." W. E. Garrison reported, after reading her essay *The Ethics of Ambiguity*, that she is a thorough-going humanist, "whose zest for life equals Sartre's disgust for it." Here she writes her own interpretation of existentialism—one which does not differ radically from Sartre's premise that "man is condemned to be free," to strive, to seek, but not to find, but which offers a more affirmative interpretation of that view. Man's freedom, she writes, "can be achieved only through the freedom of others. He justifies his existence by a movement which, like freedom, springs from his heart but which leads outside of him."

Early in 1953 *The Second Sex*, Simone de Beauvoir's study of the status of the human female, was published in the United States. (It had been published in France in 1949.) An exhaustive and encyclopedic work, crammed with erudition and penetrating analysis, the book has provoked lively controversy. The *Saturday Review* carried six reviews of it in a single issue, ranging from Dr. Karl Menninger's judgment that it is a scholarly but at the same time "a pretentious and inflated tract on feminism," through Philip Wylie's statement that it is "one of the few great books of our era." Nearly all the reviewers of *The Second Sex* agreed, however, that it is an impressive and beautifully written book. Margaret Mead's comments on it are a good summary of the general critical reaction: "Theoretically, the book violates every canon of science and disinterested scholarship in its partisan selectivity, but as a piece of writing it provides

a rare, exasperating, but unfailingly interesting experience. It is torrential, brilliant, wonderfully angry. Read in context, it should give good insight into the psychology of one woman whose society has convinced her that it is terrible to be born a woman."

Mlle. de Beauvoir says at the beginning of *The Second Sex* that she writes from the perspective of existentialist ethics. Her thesis is that the secondary place of the female in our society derives from social forces and traditions which deprive her of human dignity as a free and independent existent. As Dr. Menninger puts it, "Whereas our society treats men as subjects, existents, transcendents, it treats women as objects, beings, and immanents." Lacking independence, woman lacks real *existence*, lacks "fulfillment as a human being." In her observations of woman's place in contemporary civilization, Mlle. de Beauvoir feels that only in the Soviet Union does woman have anything approaching real status, a point on which many of her reviewers had serious doubts.

More controversy, though of a less academic nature, was stimulated by the publication of Mlle. de Beauvoir's *America Day by Day*, a diary covering her tour of America a few years before and crowded with some shrewd observations on the American scene, but more often, in the opinion of William Phillips of *Partisan Review*, "a catalogue of the latest anti-Americanisms abroad . . . a handbook of popular distortions and stale panaceas." William Pfaff noted in *Commonweal* that her book "is of interest not for what it says about America, but for what it says about its author."

Mlle. de Beauvoir is unmarried. She lives in a hotel in Paris. William Phillips has described her as she appeared on that visit to America as "quite handsome, with a sturdy outdoor figure; her face, though full and rosy, was finely drawn. . . . She had quick luminous eyes. . . . Her manner was confident, leaving no doubt she knew what she wanted—all business and no nonsense."

In 1954 she received the Goncourt prize for her novel *Les Mandarins*.

PRINCIPAL WORKS IN ENGLISH TRANSLATION: The Blood of Others (novel) 1948; The Ethics of Ambiguity, 1948; She Came to Stay (novel) 1949; America Day by Day, 1952; Marquis de Sade: An Essay, 1953; The Second Sex, 1953; All Men Are Mortal (novel) 1954.

ABOUT: Beauvoir, S. de America Day by Day; Dictionnaire Biographique Français Contemporain; Commentary July 1953; New Yorker February 22, 1947; Saturday Review February 21, 1953.

BECK, Mrs. LILY (MORESBY) ADAMS ("E. Barrington," "Louis Moresby," pseuds.) (?-January 3, 1931). For biographical sketch and list of works and references, see TWENTIETH CENTURY AUTHORS, 1942.

* * *

ABOUT: Thomas, C. Canadian Novelists, 1920-1945.

BECKER, CARL LOTUS (September 7, 1873-April 10, 1945), American educator and historian, was born in Lincoln Township, Iowa, to Carl DeWitt and Almeda Becker. It was in the Middle West that Becker grew up, received his education, and laid the foundation for his lifework. He attended Cornell College in Iowa, and the University of Wisconsin from

Kaiden-Kazanjian

which he received a B.Litt. degree in 1896 and a Ph.D. in 1907. Awarded a fellowship in Constitutional Law, he studied at Columbia University in 1898-99. After short teaching assignments at Penn State College in 1899 and Dartmouth in 1901, Becker went to the University of Kansas, where he taught European history for fourteen years. In 1917 he was appointed professor of history at Cornell University; he was named professor emeritus and university historian in 1941.

Becker, interested in almost all historical epochs, was perhaps most at home in the eighteenth century. His popular book *The Heavenly City of the Eighteenth Century Philosophers* (1932) is evidence of this. He was a keen student of liberalism and the democratic process both here and in Europe. He was greatly concerned with the challenge that democracy is presenting to the United States; such a book as *The United States— an Experiment in Democracy* (1920) is a grave examination, not untinged with disillusionment, of this question.

Professor Becker appeared to his contemporaries as a questioner of and a Socratic gadfly to the body politic, rather than a formulator of a complete political system. His role, as he conceived it, was not to rouse men to fight for democracy, but to make them think more clearly about it, convinced as he was that little progress could be made with the prevailing understanding of political issues. Hope for the future, he thought, lay in the establishment of international agencies which would regulate currency, tariffs, foreign investments, food, raw materials, and labor. He felt that the great obstacles to international amity would be uncurbed nationalism, power politics, and imperialism.

Becker was highly esteemed by fellow historians and critics. His literary ability (as a youth Becker wanted to be a professional writer) contributed to his reputation. Writing of *Modern Democracy* (1941), Reinhold Niebuhr commented. "The value of the book lies in the clarity and economy of thought and word with which the problem of democracy is analyzed so that one feels oneself carried toward his conclusions by an irresistible logic." Becker's point of view, however, did not always go unchallenged. In the opinion of Edmund Wilson, Becker was "an old-fashioned liberal with a kind of abstract political realism but no very immediate sense of what is going on in the world in our time."

Carl Becker was a member of many professional groups, among them the American Historical Association (he was president in 1931), the Institute of Arts and Letters, the American Academy of Arts and Sciences. He was awarded honorary degrees by Yale, Rochester, and Columbia Universities. Becker died in Ithaca, N.Y., after a brief illness. He was survived by his wife, the former Maude Hepworth whom he had married in 1901, and their son, Frederick DeWitt Becker.

PRINCIPAL WORKS: Political Parties in the Province of New York from 1765 to 1776, 1908; Kansas, 1910; Beginnings of the American People, 1915; Era of the American Revolution, 1918; The United States—an Experiment in Democracy, 1920; The Declaration of Independence, a Study in the History of Political Ideas, 1922; The Spirit of '76, 1922 (with W. E. Dodd & G. M. Clark); Modern History, 1931; The Heavenly City of the Eighteenth Century Philosophers, 1932; Every Man His Own Historian, 1935; Progress and Power, 1936; Story of Civilization (with Frederick Duncalf) 1938; Modern Democracy, 1941; New Liberties for Old, 1942; How New Will the Better World Be? 1944; Freedom and Responsibility In the American Way of Life, 1945.

ABOUT: American Historical Review July 1945; Nation April 28, 1945; National Cyclopedia of Biography (1947); New York Times April 11, 1945; School and Society April 21, 1945; William and Mary Quarterly July 1952.

BECKER, Mrs. MAY (LAMBERTON) (August 26, 1873-). For autobiographical sketch and list of earlier works and references, see TWENTIETH CENTURY AUTHORS, 1942.

* * *

May Lamberton Becker writes from Epsom, Surrey: "My report in the 1942 volume of TWENTIETH CENTURY AUTHORS left off with the varied activities it recorded in full swing. So was the Second World War, during which, in the intervals of conducting in the New York *Herald Tribune* both the 'Reader's Guide' and the reviews in 'Books for Young People,' I managed to write *Introducing Charles Dickens* and otherwise occupy the hours of a somewhat extended working day. In 1948 the Women's National Book Association gave me its Constance Lindsay Skinner medal.

"The absorbing adventure of 'Books Across the Sea' began with the idea—tossed over in a cable from my daughter Beatrice Warde in London through the blitz—that a list of books published in America since war began, chosen to represent to English readers the customs, background and ideals of America, and sent over in exchange for a corresponding selection of English books, would be a practical aid to international understanding. The Guide, calling on its clients to collaborate on such a list, asked each one to suggest books true to life in his own region, with the result that the list, 'Sixty Books About America,' really represented our country, not Manhattan and large cities only. The actual books were sent over one by one; my daughter, at the height of submarine warfare, brought here from England a corresponding selection of English books. Today 'Books Across the Sea,' established under its name as a committee of the English Speaking Union in both countries, carries on the work.

"After the Dickens book there was but one other introductory biography for which I had the same sort of equipment: a book for beginners about Jane Austen. I had made her acquaintance through *Pride and Prejudice* when I was twenty; scarce a day since then has passed without my taking one of her novels from my nearest bookcase. On many English journeys afoot I have visited just about every place associated with her or her characters. So I took five years for the actual writing of *Presenting Miss Jane Austen*. The book to my surprise was welcomed not only by beginners but by seasoned Janeites as well."

* * *

The citation of the Women's National Book Association to Mrs. Becker read in part: "For her contributions to better international understanding through the very practical and inspiring program of 'Books Across the Sea' in Britain and America, For her work as author, editor. . . , anthologist, Dickens authority, with keen understanding of readers' interest, young and old, and of the books needed, For her intangible gifts to the world of books as an enthusiastic book-lover, omnivorous reader, and friend to all who write, publish or sell books."

On May 1, 1955, Mrs. Becker discontinued her "Reader's Guide" column in the New York *Herald Tribune Book Review*. The editor of the *Book Review*, Irita Van Doren, wrote of her on that occasion: "Learned, witty, human and wise, she has established an almost personal relationship with hundreds of readers, so that they have acquired the habit of putting before her their problems, confident of helpful guidance. The warmth of her sympathies, the breadth of her knowledge, the miracle of her memory have been theirs over the years."

ADDITIONAL WORKS: Youth Replies I Can: Stories of Resistance (ed.) 1945; Home Book of Laughter (ed.) 1948; Rainbow Book of Bible Stories (ed.) 1948; Presenting Miss Jane Austen, 1952.

ABOUT: Library Journal June 1, 1948; New York Herald Tribune Book Review May 1, 1955; Publishers' Weekly April 3, May 8, 1948.

BECKETT, SAMUEL (1906-), Irish poet, novelist, and playwright, who writes in French, was born in Dublin and educated at Portora Royal School at Enniskillen, County Fermanagh, and at Trinity College in Dublin, where he received his B.A. in French and Italian in 1927. From 1928 to 1930 he was in Paris as lecturer in English at the Ecole Normale Supérieure. His first  book, *Whoroscope*, a long poem, was printed in Paris in 1930. In the following year Beckett returned to Trinity College as lecturer in French and took his M.A. At this time he published his first critical work, a study of Marcel Proust. In 1932 he resigned from his teaching post and spent the next four years traveling on the Continent, with extended stays in France, Germany, and London. During this period he published a volume of short stories, *More Pricks than Kicks*, a collection of poems, *Echo's Bones*, and in 1936 an essay on James Joyce in the ponderously titled *Our Exagmination round His Factification for Incamination of Work in Progress*. Beckett was closely associated with Joyce, served as his secretary, and worked on the French translation of *Anna Livia Plurabelle*.

In 1937 Beckett settled permanently in Paris. He remained in France during World War II, spending 1942 to 1944 in the Unoccupied Zone. In 1945-46 he worked as storekeeper and interpreter with the Irish Red Cross Hospital at St. Lô and was decorated for his services. In 1945 Beckett abandoned his native language and began writing in French. Since then all his new works have appeared in his adopted language. He himself did the English translation of his play *Waiting for Godot*, and in 1954 Patrick Bowles was at work on English translations of three of his novels—*Molloy* (1951), *Malone Meurt* (1951), and *L'Innommable* (1953). *Watt*, a narrative composed in English, was published in Paris in 1953. The opening section of *Molloy* was published, in English translation, in *New World Writing, No. 5*.

Waiting for Godot (En Attendant Godot), which the author describes as a tragicomedy, was first presented at the Théâtre de Babylone in Paris in the winter of 1952, a production which the French playwright Jean Anouilh called "as important as the première of Pirandello put on in Paris by Pitoëff in 1923." It became a great success with the critics and audiences alike, and was the first of Beckett's works to be published in America. The play has only five characters—two tramps, a landowner, a slave, and a boy—and almost literally no action. The characters merely gather on a country road, where the tramps wait hopelessly for one Godot, a mysterious figure whom none of them has ever seen. Anouilh described the play's extraordinary evocation of madness, boredom, human suffering and cruelty as follows: "Nothing happens, nobody comes, nobody goes, it is *terrible.*" Edwin Kennebeck wrote of it in a review in *Commonweal*: "Neither edifying nor purgative, the play nonetheless has an effect; it is appalling and desperate, and not false or pretentious."

Some critics have hailed *Waiting for Godot* as a crystallization of Beckett's work, placing him next to Joyce and Kafka for the originality of his work and for the importance of its contribution to modern literature. There are only the slightest vestiges of his Irish background in his writings. Niall Montgomery, a fellow Dubliner, calls him "the Irish Steve Brody," who "took the big plunge, cast off race and genus," and became a Frenchman. His French novels, written since the end of the war, have reminded more than one reviewer of the work of Sartre and Camus. "There is a common sense of imprisonment, solitude, pervasive misery, the voice sobbing in the dry throat," Montgomery writes. His work is still little known and appreciated outside France, and its tortuous obscurity is not calculated to win a wide audience. His characters—abject, paralyzed in will, often sick and deformed in body—move inside a framework of highly personal symbolism. Anthony Hartley wrote in the *Spectator*: "Mr. Beckett's characters create and are created. That is their singularity. Just as the author imposes a pattern on them by means of his imagination, so they impose a pattern on the world by means of theirs.... At the last, Mr. Beckett's characters renounce all action. They busy themselves with creating myths in the darkness of their own minds. It is that that makes them tick." Hartley points out that Beckett's stream of consciousness technique is "sometimes a bit of a bore," and that the lack of rationally connected incidents in the narrative plagues the reader. Nevertheless, he concludes, "His taut, poetic style, purged of the Irishry and conceited wit of the first novels, can convey appeasement or beauty as well as abjection."

PRINCIPAL WORKS IN ENGLISH: Whoroscope (poem) 1930; Proust, 1931; More Pricks than Kicks, 1934; *in* Our Exagmination round His Factification for Incamination of Work in Progress (essays) 1936; Echo's Bones (poems) 1936; Murphy, 1938; Watt, 1953; Waiting for Godot: A Tragicomedy, 1954.

ABOUT: *Biographical note in* Beckett's Waiting for Godot; Books Abroad Summer 1949; Mercure de France August 1951; New World Writing, No. 5 (1954); New York Times Book Review April 11, 1954; Spectator October 23, 1953.

BEDEL, MAURICE (December 30, 1884-October 15, 1954). For biographical sketch and list of works and references, see TWENTIETH CENTURY AUTHORS, 1942.

* * *

Maurice Bedel died at his estate near Chatellerault in France at the age of seventy. In his last years he wrote a number of books and articles on travel. None of his later books was translated into English. Several months before his death he was a candidate for the seat of Jérome Tharaud in the French Academy, but because neither he nor any other candidate received a majority in the election, the seat remained vacant.

ABOUT: New York Times October 16, 1954.

BEDFORD-JONES, HENRY (April 29, 1887-May 6, 1949). For autobiographical sketch and list of works and references, see TWENTIETH CENTURY AUTHORS, 1942.

* * *

H. Bedford-Jones died at his home in Beverly Hills, Calif., at sixty-two. He had suffered from a heart ailment for two years before his death.

Publishing at times under the pen names "John Wycliffe" and "Gordon Keyes," he is credited with having written approximately one hundred novels and an uncounted number of short stories. His last published novel, *John Berry*, written in collaboration under the pseudonym of "Donald F. Bedford," told of the development of California from 1846 to 1850.

The historical novels that comprised the major part of his work were based on notably careful and scholarly research, including painstaking tracing of documents and other source material.

ADDITIONAL WORK: John Berry (as "Donald F. Bedford" with Donald Friede & Kenneth Fearing) 1947.

ABOUT: New York Times May 7, 1949.

* BÉDIER, JOSEPH (January 28, 1864-August 30, 1938), French medievalist and literary historian, was born in Paris, of Breton family origin.  He was educated at the Lycée de Saint-Denis and the Ecole Normale Supérieure. Graduated from the latter institution at twenty-two, he studied romance philology at the Collège de France under Gaston Paris, the great French medievalist and founder of the philological journal *Romania*. He continued his studies in Germany under Hermann Suchier and completed his work for the doctorate in letters at the Ecole Normale Supérieure in 1893.

Bédier began his long and distinguished teaching career in 1889 at the University of Fribourg in Switzerland. Two years later he returned to France to teach at the University of Caen, and in 1893 he was appointed to the faculty of his alma mater, the Ecole Normale Supérieure. In 1903 he accepted a professorship at the Collège de France where

* bā dyā'

64

he remained until his retirement in 1936. He spent his last years working on a history of the editions of the *Chanson de Roland*. This study has not been published. Bédier married in 1891 and had two sons and a daughter.

The extent of Bédier's scholarship and the importance of his contributions to our knowledge of medieval literature are vast. Urban T. Holmes has said that his investigations "have at one time or another embraced every phase of early French literature." His work was concentrated primarily on the Old French epic, but the ramifications of his subject included the fable, the folk tale, and the romance as well. He studied not only manuscripts and literary texts to establish his theory of the origin of the French epic, but medieval art, iconography, churches, monuments, tombs, the routes taken by pilgrims. It was Bédier's theory (now modified but still held in substance by many contemporary scholars), outlined in his *Les Légendes Epiques* (1908-1913), that the Old French *chansons de geste* or epics originated not spontaneously or in the mouth-to-mouth, generation-to-generation popular tradition of the folk tale, but as the work of creative individuals, primarily among the educated clergy of the Middle Ages. The epics, he argued, were extensions of the literary form known as the saint's life, sung in the churches and at shrines and other holy places. Frequently heroes, both legendary and historical, were also buried in these places. Some time around the year 1000, in the age of the crusades, Bédier claimed, the medieval poet began to develop and exploit the theme of the hero in long historical narrative poems. The first such hero was naturally Charlemagne, who saved France from the Moslems, but soon other figures whose shrines dotted the main pilgrimage routes of France became heroes of their own epic cycles. The most famous of all French epics, the *Chanson de Roland*, Bédier concluded, was not a survival of an epic contemporaneous with the events of the eighth century which it describes, but, in the words of William A. Nitze, "an original composition inspired by the enthusiasm for the First Crusade."

In the course of his studies of the origins of literary forms, Bédier also made contributions to medieval textual studies. One of his earliest published works was an edition of the Old French poem, the *Lai de l'Ombre*, in 1890, when he established a text by the then conventional method of grouping manuscripts into families and in cases of conflict accepting the reading which appeared in two manuscripts or more of different families. This method, Bédier later decided, produced an unreal, composite text, far removed from the normal version of the poem. In 1913 he published a new edition of the same poem, confining himself to one manuscript which he reproduced with the minimum number of corrections. Professor John Orr, of the University of Edinburgh, points out that this method is now generally recognized as the only truly "scientific" method. "But none the less it still leaves ample scope for scholarship and taste on the part of an editor."

Non-academic readers know Bédier best for his modern French prose translation of the *Roman de Tristan et Iseult*, first published in 1900. Professor Nitze has said: "Here—at a stroke—the modern troubadour opened up the Middle Ages to the cultivated reading public. Noteworthy is the fact that philology now becomes the handmaid of art and that factual research scores one of its greatest triumphs." An English translation of Bédier's version was made by the late Hilaire Belloc. Reviewing a recent edition of this translation (with additions by Paul Rosenfeld), Joseph Campbell wrote: "Inspired by a love for the French medieval past, and implemented with a close knowledge of the field, as well as a delicate sense for the nuances of style, Joseph Bédier made of himself, for the moment of his task, a reincarnation of the spirit of the courtly trouvères. Like them he composed at once in accordance with tradition and under the inspiration of a fresh, personal realization."

Bédier's professional activities were not confined to medieval scholarship. In 1903 he published *Etudes Critiques* with critical essays on Chateaubriand, Diderot, and others. He took an active part also in the administration of the Collège de France and, Professor Nitze says, was "an ardent revisionist in the Dreyfus case." During World War I he wrote propaganda pamphlets and in 1921 he was a founder of the journal *Revue de France*. He was tall and thin, shy in manner, but a thoroughly stimulating teacher. Among the many honors he received were election to the French Academy, the Légion d'Honneur, and the academies of Copenhagen, Oslo, Marseilles, Bucharest and Rome. He received honorary degrees from Oxford, Harvard, Louvain and other universities.

PRINCIPAL WORK IN ENGLISH TRANSLATION: Romance of Tristan and Iseult, 1907.

ABOUT: Columbia Dictionary of Modern European Literature; Holmes, U. T. History of Old French Literature; Lot, F. Joseph Bédier; Orr, J. *in* Studies in French Language, Literature, and History, Presented to R. L. Graeme Ritchie.

* **BEEBE, WILLIAM** (July 29, 1877-   ). For biographical sketch and list of earlier works and references, see TWENTIETH CENTURY AUTHORS, 1942.

* * *

Well past seventy, William Beebe still works in his laboratory at the New York Zoological Society. In 1949 he published an account of his last three expeditions to the Venezuelan Andes—*High Jungle*. The book was described happily by its reviewers as "the mixture as before"—the same combination of fascinating scientific reporting and entertaining writing that has so long delighted Beebe's readers. The naturalist Edwin Way Teale commented that his latest book "stands very high, indeed, on that ridge where literature and natural history meet."

ADDITIONAL WORKS: The Book of Naturalists: An Anthology (ed.) 1944; High Jungle, 1949; Unseen Life of New York, 1953.

ABOUT: Cooper, A. C. & Palmer, C. A. Twenty Modern Americans; Von Hagen, V. W. The Green World of the Naturalists; New York Herald Tribune Book Review June 5, 1949; New York Times Book Review June 5, 1949.

* bē'bē

BEEDING, FRANCIS (pseud. of John Leslie Palmer, 1885-August 5, 1944, and Hilary Aidan St. George Saunders, January 14, 1898-December 16, 1951). For biographical sketches and list of earlier works and references, see TWENTIETH CENTURY AUTHORS, 1942.

* * *

John L. Palmer, one of the collaborators who wrote under the name of "Francis Beeding," died at a hospital in Hampstead, England, at fifty-eight.

Although a major part of Palmer's literary output was pseudonymous, he achieved recognition in England as a novelist and particularly as a literary and dramatic critic in his own name. At the time of his death, the first volume of a projected trilogy on Shakespeare's characters, *Political Characters of Shakespeare*, was on the press. Hamilton Basso noted the imagination and contemporary meaning in the work, adding that "though a great deal of scholarship has gone into it, the seams never show." "By his death," in the opinion of the London *Times*, "the world of English letters has lost a critic of candor and a writer of distinction."

* * *

Hilary Aidan St. George Saunders, who shared with Palmer the pen-name of "Francis

65

Beeding," died in the Prospect Hospital at Nassau, the Bahamas, at fifty-three, of asthma contracted during service in World War II.

During and following the war, Saunders wrote a number of books (he preferred to be called a pamphleteer) on various aspects of Britain's armed forces; of these, *Per Ardua*, the story of British air power, has been called "a work of permanent value to the military historian," while *The Green Beret* (the official history of Britain's commandos) and *The Red Beret* (concerning a famous parachute regiment) were especially popular. After a trip to the United States at the invitation of the Office of War Information, he published a slight but amusing book of his impressions of America, *Pioneers! Oh Pioneers!*

From 1946 to 1950, Saunders served as librarian of the British House of Commons. At the time of his death he was engaged in writing a history of the Bahamas.

* * *

All in all, some forty detective and historical novels appeared over the name of Francis Beeding. Saunders once explained the collaboration by saying that "Palmer can't be troubled with description and narrative, and I'm no good at creating characters or dialogue." The composite author was characterized by a London *Times* critic as "coming into the front rank of those who succeed in making their readers sit up until the book is finished."

ADDITIONAL WORKS: *"Francis Beeding"*—There Are Thirteen, 1946; *H. Saunders and "D. Pilgrim"* (J. L. Palmer)—The Grand Design, 1943; Emperor's Servant, 1946; *J. L. Palmer*—Political Characters of Shakespeare, 1946; *H. Saunders*—Per Ardua: Rise of British Airpower, 1945; Pioneers! Oh Pioneers!, 1944; Left Handshake: The Boy Scout Movement During the War, 1948; The Green Beret, 1949; Red Cross and the White, 1949; Valiant Voyaging, 1949; Middlesex Hospital, 1950; The Red Beret, 1950; Sleeping Bacchus, 1951; Westminster Hall, 1951.

ABOUT: *"F. Beeding"*—Saturday Review of Literature October 28, 1944; *J. L. Palmer*—London Times August 7, 1944; New York Times August 8, 1944; *H. Saunders*—Hoehn, M. (ed.) Catholic Authors, I; London Times December 17, 1951; New York Times December 18, 1951.

BEER, THOMAS (November 22, 1889-April 18, 1940). For biographical sketch and list of works and references, see TWENTIETH CENTURY AUTHORS, 1942.

* * *

ABOUT: Atlantic April 1943; Saturday Review of Literature November 15, 1947.

BEERBOHM, Sir MAX (August 24, 1872-). For biographical sketch and list of earlier works and references, see TWENTIETH CENTURY AUTHORS, 1942.

* * *

It becomes increasingly difficult to separate Max Beerbohm the legend, from Max Beerbohm, the quiet little old man who lives in retirement in Rapallo, Italy. He is in the unusual and perhaps uncomfortable situation of having lived to see his works become "classics" (Edmund Wilson and Louis Kronenberger agree that Beerbohm will be read much longer than Chesterton or Belloc), of having outlived his contemporaries, and of having survived the shattering transition from the Victorian age in which he was born to the atomic age. Recent photographs show Beerbohm frail and perilously ancient but still dapper. Alan Dent, who visited him in 1952, reported that he was enchanted to find "his mental vigor, his gaiety, his lambent wit absolutely unimpaired."

Beerbohm spent the years of World War II in England where he lectured and broadcast occasionally for the B.B.C. After the war he returned to his villa in Italy. Lady Beerbohm (the former Florence Kahn) died in 1951.

ADDITIONAL WORKS: Lytton Strachey, 1943; Mainly on the Air (essays and broadcasts) 1947; Around Theatres, 1953.

ABOUT: Bottome, P. From the Life; Tinker, C. B. Essays in Retrospect; Wilson, E. Classics and Commercials; Blackwood's Magazine November 1946; Saturday Review of Literature June 21, 1947, October 18, 1947; Saturday Review August 30, 1952; Spectator December 13, 1946.

BEHRMAN, SAMUEL NATHANIEL (June 9, 1893-). For autobiographical sketch and list of earlier works and references, see TWENTIETH CENTURY AUTHORS, 1942.

* * *

Like the hero of his sparkling success of the 1939 theatrical season, *No Time for Comedy*, S. N. Behrman has apparently grappled with the dilemma of the comic dramatist in a war-torn world. And like his hero, after some wavering, Behrman has followed his bent—continuing during the 1940's to write his pleasant high comedies, full of brilliant talk, charming people, and brittle situations. The single exception was *Dunnigan's Daughter*, subtitled a comedy though actually a more ambitious and serious treatment of the conflict of ideologies. The play was a failure. The most successful of Behrman's later plays have been *The Pirate* (adapted by him from Ludwig Fulda's play), a romantic farce which served mainly as a vehicle for the acting team of Alfred Lunt and Lynn Fontanne; *Jacobowsky and the Colonel* (an adaptation of a play by Franz Werfel), a contemporary comedy ironically played against the tragic background of the Nazi invasion of France; and *Jane* (adapted from a W. S. Maugham story), a return to the polished comedy of manners at which Behrman is such a master. In 1954 he adapted Marcel Pagnol's trilogy *Fanny* for a Broadway stage musical.

Behrman's ambition to write a novel has not yet been realized, but he has made his mark in non-dramatic literature with a stylish and entertaining biography of the famous art dealer Joseph Duveen. Originally written as a "Profile" for the *New Yorker*, his study of Duveen and the world of priceless art and fabulous wealth in which he lived was later expanded and published as a book. He has also published in the *New Yorker* several reminiscent pieces on his early days as the child of a poor Jewish family in Worcester, Mass. These were collected in a volume called *The Worcester Account*.

Behrman has been married since 1936 to Elza Heifetz, sister of the violinist Jascha Heifetz. They have a son.

ADDITIONAL WORKS: (Date of publication)— The Pirate, 1943; Jacobowsky and the Colonel, 1944; Dunnigan's Daughter, 1946; I Know My Love (adapted from M. Achard's Auprès de Ma Blonde) 1951; Jane, 1952; Duveen (biography) 1952; The Worcester Account, 1954.

ABOUT: Gagey, E. M. Revolution in American Drama; Morris, L. R. Postscript to Yesterday; Current Biography 1943; New Republic February 18, 1952; New York Herald Tribune Book Review October 24, 1954; New Yorker June 29, 1946, January 18, June 28, December 6, 1947, July 17, 1948, January 26, 1952, January 16, 1954; Theatre Arts May 1952.

BEITH, Sir JOHN HAY ("Ian Hay") (April 17, 1876-September 22, 1952). For biographical sketch and list of earlier works and references, see TWENTIETH CENTURY AUTHORS, 1942.

* * *

Sir John Hay Beith died from a lung infection in a private hospital near Petersfield, Hampshire, in England, at seventy-six.

Under his pen-name of "Ian Hay," Beith remained a prolific writer of light novels, short stories, and plays "verging on farce." Many of his plays were dramatizations of his own or of others' novels; most of them were very successful in London productions. *Hattie Stowe*, based on the life of Harriet

Beecher Stowe, did not meet with success in a New York production in 1947. More serious in intent than the author's usual work were several books written on themes growing out of World War II (*The Unconquered Isle*, a story of the siege of Malta, is an example), for which Hay's light, deft style was deemed inappropriate by critics.

Noting that Hay himself would have been the last to claim profundity for his work, the London *Times* adds, "But within the limits set by his particular talents, he was a careful and conscientious draftsman who would have scorned to give to a loyal public less than the best of which he was capable."

ADDITIONAL WORKS: Little Ladyship, 1941; The Unconquered Isle, 1943; America Comes Across, 1943; Peaceful Invasion, 1946; Let My People Go, 1949.

ABOUT: London Times September 23, 1952; New York Times September 23, 1952; Theatre Arts May 1947; Time November 8, 1943.

BEKESSY, JEAN. See HABE, H.

BELASCO, DAVID (July 25, 1859-May 14, 1931). For biographical sketch and list of works and references, see TWENTIETH CENTURY AUTHORS, 1942.

* * *

ABOUT: Dickson, S. San Francisco Is Your Home; Middleton, G. These Things Are Mine; New York Times Magazine July 25, 1948.

* BELFRAGE, CEDRIC (1904-). For biographical sketch and list of earlier works and references, see TWENTIETH CENTURY AUTHORS, 1942.

* * *

Cedric Belfrage wrote to the editors of this volume in 1952: "Moved to the United States in 1936 and has since resided here, in California and now in New York. Two children. War service: British Security Co-Ordination, New York, 1941-1943; Psychological Warfare Division of SHAEF in France and Germany, 1944-1945. Guggenheim Fellow, 1946, to write history of the revival of a democratic press in Germany, in which he took part as PWD-SHAEF press officer from Aachen (January 1945) to Frankfurt (October 1945). Since 1948, editor of the *National Guardian*, progressive newsweekly, New York. Object: to keep alive the fundamentally democratic spirit with which America is endowed—now almost obliterated from public life."

* Belfrage: "rhymes with Selfridge"

Belfrage, who had lived in the United States since 1936 as a permanent alien resident, was ordered deported in June 1953 on the grounds that he "had been an active member of the Communist party, resided in Russia on official business for the party, and had been closely associated with leaders of the Communist party and with persons known to have engaged in espionage" (New York *Times*, June 10, 1953). Belfrage denied the charges and filed an appeal. His divorced wife, Mrs. Mary Beatrice Belfrage, was also ordered deported, but left voluntarily for England in 1954. Belfrage's appeal was denied in May 1955 by The Board of Immigration Appeals and he was jailed.

ADDITIONAL WORK: Abide With Me (novel) 1948.

ABOUT: New York Times June 10, 1953, May 13, 1955.

* **BELITT, BEN** (May 2, 1911-   ), American poet, writes: "My birthplace in New York City is an empty datum, since my childhood, up to my tenth year, stops at the  graveled driveways of a large public orphanage in upper Manhattan, and my memories, with the exception of an illuminated clock-dial over the main entrance, seen for the first time from the *outside* after dark, are institutional and hermetic. My birth begins in the early '20's, after the re-marriage of my mother, when I found myself in a meandering frame house on the corner of Madison and Ninth Streets in Lynchburg, Va., among grape-arbors, fruit-trees, a chicken-yard, gooseberry bushes, and a high, stilted porch from which I once flew cicadas on a thread and dropped a kitten to test the myth of the indestructible equilibrium of the cat. There, in an alcove divided sparingly between an old-fashioned wardrobe, a bedstead, and myself, I wrote my first poems and stories for Mrs. Addie T. Eure and Miss Evelina O. Wiggins of the E. C. Glass High School, behind closed doors. I took the world of the impossible for my subject: oriental shahs, dying circus-riders and ballet-dancers with names out of Maupassant, and assassins in the diabolical image of Poe—several of which found their way to the State competitions conducted annually by the

* bĕl'ĭtt

University of Virginia Extension Department and returned bemedaled.

"It was on the occasion of a public reading of a prize story in the University auditorium —a militant story about a pacifist school teacher in World War I—that I resolved to enter the University of Virginia in the following fall; and there, aided by scholarships, fellowships, and the interest of the English faculty, I remained for eight successive years. I received my Bachelor of Arts degree in 1932, my Master's in 1934, and had completed all doctoral requirements, with the customary exception of the dissertation (on Katherine Mansfield) by 1936. By that time my stories had ebbed to a trickle published principally in the old *Midland Magazine* and starred encouragingly by O'Brien, while poems, articles, and reviews began to appear in *Poetry, New Outlook, Virginia Quarterly Review,* and the books sections of the New York *Times* and *Herald Tribune,* a number of Virginia newspapers, and the *Nation.* In the winter of 1936-37 during a Christmas visit—my first—to the office of the *Nation,* I was offered the position of editorial assistant by Joseph Wood Krutch, then editing the Books and the Arts Section of the magazine. I promptly resigned from the university to begin an unforgettable apprenticeship in the practical and professional aspects of magazine journalism in the twilight of the great reporters and the heyday of the foreign correspondents. I was encouraged to attempt a little of everything by the tolerant and kindly Mr. Krutch: drama, film, book criticism, articles, and I watched with a wondering eye while the best of a vanishing age of American reportage flowed in and out of the offices of 20 Vesey Street. I cherish particularly a long poem called 'Battery Park,' toward which most of my luncheon walks were directed on fine afternoons for the next year and a half, and a shorter poem about a charwoman assigned to the Vesey Street office building—both of which found their way into my first volume of poems published by Knopf in 1938 under the title *The Five-Fold Mesh.*

"Since 1938—with the exception of the war years, two of which were spent in the U.S. Army as private, and one as civilian editor-scenarist for the Historical Films Section of the U.S. Army Signal Corps Photographic Center in Astoria—I have taught gladly enough at Bennington College in Vermont. I have published in a number of literary periodicals in this country, received the Shelley Memorial Award for

Poetry in 1936, and a Guggenheim grant in 1946. My work includes, besides *The Five-Fold Mesh,* a volume of translations from Rimbaud, a translation of Federico García Lorca's *Poet in New York,* to be published by the Grove Press of New York City, a new book of poems called *Wilderness Stair* which has long gone unpublished. A prose journal called *School of the Soldier* which I like to regard as my 'war book,' was published in its entirety by the *Quarterly Review of Literature* and awarded their Fiction Prize for 1950."

* * *

In the course of his career as a poet, Ben Belitt has developed, as the editors of *This Generation* remark, "from an unusually good craftsman and lyric poet into a poet who recognizes his relationship to the social world." In the poem "Battery Park" particularly he combines the intense personal reflection of the lyric with an objective and dramatic approach to his subject—"to talk in terms both of himself and mankind—without the confusion apparent in the poetry of those earnest revolutionary writers who wish to identify themselves with the laboring class to which they do not belong and whose thoughts and feelings they cannot evaluate."

PRINCIPAL WORKS: The Five-Fold Mesh, 1938; Four Poems by Rimbaud: The Problem of Translation, 1948; School of the Soldier, 1950; Wilderness Stair, 1955.

ABOUT: Anderson, G. K. & Walton, E. L. This Generation.

BELL, ADRIAN (October 4, 1901-). For biographical sketch and list of earlier works and references, see TWENTIETH CENTURY AUTHORS, 1942.

* * *

A reviewer wrote in the *Times Literary Supplement* in 1947: "Mr. Adrian Bell as farmer-writer . . . has become something of a present-day British institution. With him there is no sententious moralizing about 'back to the land,' but a practical conviction that agriculture is, or should be, culture." He is a part-time writer. For weeks together he works his Suffolk farm, ploughing and stocking his grain, and forgetting that he has ever written a book. Then out of his farming experiences he writes, and in his writings— most of them called novels although they are too personal and anecdotal to fit properly into the category of fiction—"experience and what transcends it are well harmonized." All of his books reveal his "sure instinct for natural beauty," and his "ringing faith in the English soil and those who live by it."

ADDITIONAL WORKS: Apple Acre, 1942; Budding Morrow, 1947; The Black Donkey, 1949; The Flower and the Wheel, 1949; The Path by the Window, 1952.

ABOUT: Fortnightly Review January 1945.

BELL, BERNARD IDDINGS (October 13, 1886-), American clergyman and educator, was born in Dayton, Ohio, son of Charles Wright and Vienna Valencia (Iddings) Bell. He received his B.A. in 1907 from the University of Chicago, majoring in social history, with a lively interest in dramatics and college publications on the side. Bell took his theological

Wide World

training at the Western Seminary in Chicago (now Seabury-Western)—Bachelor of Sacred Theology in 1912. In 1910 he was ordained deacon and priest of the Episcopal Church. He held various church offices in and around Chicago until 1913 when he went to Fond du Lac, Wisc., to become dean of St. Paul's Church and examining chaplain to the bishop. During World War I he was a chaplain at the Great Lakes Naval Training Station.

In 1919 Bell joined the staff of the small and rapidly failing St. Stephen's College at Annandale-on-the-Hudson, N.Y. Within the next fifteen years he led a group of interested patrons in reorganizing the college, its educational philosophy, and its curriculum. It became a constituent college of Columbia University in 1930. Over a million dollars was raised to support an educational program described as one "which encouraged emphasis on intellectual achievement of unusually competent students and withstood the tendency of American education to standardize its product and lower its standards." St. Stephen's died in the depression in 1933. Its physical property is now used by Bard College which has no other connection with St. Stephen's. From 1930 to 1933 Bell also was a Professor of Religion at Columbia.

After spending the years from 1933 to 1946 in Providence, R.I., as canon of St. John's Cathedral, Bell went to Chicago as consultant on education to the Bishop of Chicago and canon of the Cathedral of St. Peter and St. Paul. Here he represented the Church in its relations with the University of Chicago and was Episcopal chaplain at the

University. Early in 1955, his eyesight failing, Canon Bell retired from this post and accepted a position as consultant in Christian education to the Episcopal bishop of Chicago.

Through books like *Crisis in Education* and *Crowd Culture,* and by numerous magazine articles and lectures, Canon Bell has become known as an outspoken and formidable critic of the undisciplined and materialistic attitudes which he feels that John Dewey's ideas have produced and encouraged. He has made the charge that American educators are setting up a false and unrealistic goal for American students, a belief "that there can be reward without quest, wages without work, a master's prestige without a master's skill, marriage without fidelity, national security without sacrifice." Canon Bell has been equally sharp in his criticism of the Christian Church which, he argues, like the schools has compromised and debased its spiritual and ethical standards until "its only moral function [is] to bless whatever the multitude at the moment regards as the American way of life." As a result, the Church is responsible for a condition of "religious illiteracy" parallel to the "educational illiteracy" fostered by the schools. Canon Bell's criticism of both school and church is founded on his resistance to the popular American concept of "mass man" and to the pressures which reduce the individual to conform to the lowest common denominators in our culture.

Canon Bell, a member of Phi Beta Kappa, has honorary degrees from Western Theological Seminary, the University of the South, Columbia University, Colorado College, Coe College, Ohio Wesleyan University, and the University of the State of New York. He has been married since 1921 to Elizabeth Wood Lee (their only son is deceased) and lives in Chicago.

PRINCIPAL WORKS: Right and Wrong After the War, 1918; Postmodernism, and Other Essays, 1926; Common Sense in Education, 1928; Beyond Agnosticism, 1929; Unfashionable Convictions, 1931; Holy Week, 1933; Men Wanted, 1933; Preface to Religion, 1935; O Men of God, 1936; A Catholic Looks at His World, 1936; In the City of Confusion, 1938; Religion for Living, 1939; Understanding Religion, 1941; The Church in Disrepute, 1943; The Altar and the World, 1944; God Is Not Dead, 1945; A Man Can Live, 1947; Crisis in Education, 1949; Crowd Culture, 1952.

ABOUT: Catholic World May 1951; Current Biography 1953; New York Post Magazine July 1, 1949; Time April 25, 1949, March 27, 1950, October 20, 1952.

BELL, CLIVE (September 16, 1881-   ). For autobiographical sketch and list of works and references, see TWENTIETH CENTURY AUTHORS, 1942.

* * *

Clive Bell lives in Lewes, Sussex. He has published no full-length book since 1934, but is a frequent contributor of articles on art and art criticism to British and American periodicals.

BELL, ERIC TEMPLE ("John Taine") (February 7, 1883-   ), British-American mathematician and writer of science fiction, writes: "Born in Aberdeen, Scotland, younger son of James Bell and his wife, Helen Lyndsay Lyall. My father came of a prominent mercantile family in the City of London; my mother's people were classical scholars for several generations back. At  one time we lived on a hill overlooking the old Crystal Palace grounds in Croydon, now a landing field. That was the beginning of a life-long interest in those magnificently amoral brutes, the dinosaurs. There were a few restorations of the great reptiles grouped about a small lake in the grounds. Many years later I wrote *Before the Dawn* (1934), the one of all my science fiction novels that I like best. It was published under my own name; the other sixteen so far published are by 'John Taine.'

"My education was by tutors till I entered the Bedford Modern School, where the late E. M. Langley converted me to mathematics. To escape being shoved into Woolwich or the India Civil Service, I left England and came on my own at nineteen to California, where I matriculated at Stanford University. There (in 1902) the free elective system was still in force. I took only mathematics. Langley had done such a good job of teaching that in two years I covered all the mathematics offered. The rest of my education was one year at the University of Washington and another at Columbia University, where (1912) I took my Ph.D. in mathematics. In the meantime, I had worked as a ranch hand, a mule skinner in Nevada, a surveyor, partner in a telephone company in San Francisco and had gone broke in the great earthquake and fire of 1906. After clearing up with my partners our obligations,

I quit business for good and returned to mathematics and, as a recreation, writing. My academic experience has been at the Universities of Washington and Chicago, at Harvard University, and at the California Institute of Technology. In 1910 I married Jessie L. Brown, a widow. She died in 1940. We had one son, Taine, now an M.D. In all I have published about 250 papers on mathematical research, one of which was awarded the Bôcher prize in 1921 for mathematics in the preceding five years; nine books on the less inhuman aspects of mathematics, including mathematicians (of which *Men of Mathematics*, 1937, was awarded the Gold Medal of the Commonwealth Club); seventeen science fiction novels. The excuse for the last is that if they made money for publishers, some publisher might be interested in more serious books. It worked, and some have gone into several foreign languages."

PRINCIPAL WORKS: Algebraic Arithmetic, 1927; Queen of the Sciences, 1931; Numerology, 1933; The Search for Truth, 1934; Before the Dawn (novel) 1934; Men of Mathematics, 1937; Handmaiden of the Sciences, 1937; Man and His Lifebelts, 1938; The Development of Mathematics, 1940; The Magic of Numbers, 1946; Mathematics, Queen and Servant of Science, 1951. *Science Fiction (as "John Taine")*—The Purple Sapphire, 1924; Quayle's Invention, 1926; The Gold Tooth, 1927; Green Fire, 1928; The Greatest Adventure, 1929; The Iron Star, 1930; The White Lilly, 1930; Seeds of Life, 1931; "1287," 1935; The Time Stream, 1946; The Forbidden Garden, 1947; The Cosmic Geoids, 1949; The Crystal Horde, 1952; G.O.G. 666, 1952.

BELL, MACKENZIE (March 2, 1856-December 13, 1930). For biographical sketch and list of works and references, see TWENTIETH CENTURY AUTHORS, 1942.

"BELL, NEIL." See SOUTHWOLD, S.

BELLAH, JAMES WARNER (September 14, 1899-). For autobiographical sketch and list of earlier works and references, see TWENTIETH CENTURY AUTHORS, 1942.

* * *

James Warner Bellah was divorced in 1942 and married to Helen Hopkins. There are two children by this marriage, John Lasater and Stephen Hopkins. During the Second World War he served in the 1st and 80th Infantry Divisions and on the staff of Admiral Lord Louis Mountbatten at headquarters of the Southeast Asia Command, as an American officer. He had combat service with General Stilwell, General Wingate, and Colonel Philip Cochran in Burma, and emerged from the war with the rank of colonel, the Legion of Merit, the Bronze Star Medal, Air Medal, and Commendation Medal.

Bellah's numerous short stories and serials (which appear usually in the *Saturday Evening Post*) are now included in over twenty-five anthologies, and his works have been translated into fifteen foreign languages. One of his stories, "Command," was requested by the State Department for translation into the Thai language for the "This Is America" program. He has written technical articles on troop training for infantry, cavalry, and artillery journals. His screenplay adaptation, *She Wore a Yellow Ribbon*, was a successful motion picture. He also did the dialogue for the official Navy documentary film, *This Is Korea*.

Bellah received an M.A. in history from Georgetown University in 1945. He is president of James Warner Bellah, Inc., and vice president of the Lancaster and Chester Railroad.

ADDITIONAL WORKS: Ward Twenty, 1946; Irregular Gentleman, 1948; The Valiant Virginians, 1953.

ABOUT: Bellah, J. W. Irregular Gentleman; Van Gelder, R. Writers and Writing; Saturday Evening Post June 8, 1946.

BELLAMAN, HENRY (April 28, 1882-June 16, 1945). For biographical sketch and list of earlier works and references, see TWENTIETH CENTURY AUTHORS, 1942.

* * *

Henry Bellaman died of a heart attack, at his home in New York City, at sixty-three.

Although he had been ill for several months, he worked up to the time of his death on a sequel to his enormously popular novel *Kings Row*. His plan was to write a trilogy encompassing the development of a small mid-Western town into a modern city. *Parris Mitchell of Kings Row* was completed by his wife, Katherine Jones Bellaman. *Time* referred to it as "a mass psychoanalysis . . . in language that seems lifted from a handbook of psychiatric clichés."

A New York *Times* critic observed that Bellaman semed to have evolved a literary formula composed of "equal parts of Gothic melodrama and ideas."

ADDITIONAL WORKS: Victoria Grandolet, 1943; Parris Mitchell of Kings Row (with K. J. Bellaman) 1948.

ABOUT: Current Biography 1942; New York Times June 17, 1945.

BELLOC, HILAIRE (July 27, 1870-July 16, 1953). For biographical sketch and list of works and references, see TWENTIETH CENTURY AUTHORS, 1942.

* * *

Hilaire Belloc died in Guildford, England, eleven days before his eighty-third birthday, of burns suffered when he fell into a fire-place in his home.

With Chesterton, Shaw, and Wells, Belloc had been one of the "Big Four" of the Edwardian world of letters. He was probably the most versatile and certainly one of the most prolific of modern English writers. As Britain's "foremost Roman Catholic apologist," Belloc was a forceful and robust controversialist. He may have antagonized as many readers as he persuaded, but he had the greatest asset a controversialist can have —the power of attracting undivided attention. "What Belloc writes," a commentator said in 1939, "goes *home;* they could no more ignore him than they could ignore a tiger on the doorstep."

Belloc's last years were spent in retirement in his Sussex home. He stopped writing in 1941 after the death of his son Peter, of pneumonia, in an army camp in Scotland. Ten years later, on the occasion of the publication of an anthology of his writings, there was something of a critical re-evaluation of Belloc's work. Some of it, the critics said, was of little or no lasting value—trivial and ephemeral. But more of it, they felt, would remain memorable, for its brilliance, wit, and sheer craftsmanship. His verse too is now receiving an increased measure of critical recognition. Belloc, as Maurice B. Reckitt points out, "was not a poet in the modern vaticinatory manner, but he has written some of the loveliest lines in English verse." Here, as in his prose, are revealed his particular talents—"his uniquely individual handling of our language, springing from his immense zest for life, coupled with his deep sense of the 'tears of things,' which for fifty years had made him beloved over all to those who had once fallen under his spell." Another critic wrote of him: "What posterity will value in him as an artist is the power to give to his writing precisely the diversity of feeling that has distinguished him as a man."

ADDITIONAL WORKS: The Servile State (American ed.; originally published in England in 1912) 1946; Hilaire Belloc: An Anthology of his Prose and Verse (ed. W. N. Roughead) 1951.

ABOUT: Hamilton, R. Hilaire Belloc; Hoehn, M. (ed.) Catholic Authors, I; Sheed, F. J. Sidelights on the Catholic Revival; Slochower, H. No

Voice Is Wholly Lost; Wilhelmsen, F. Hilaire Belloc, No Alienated Man; Catholic Library World November 1950; Catholic World October 1953; Commonweal June 29, 1951; New Statesman and Nation July 25, 1953; New York Times July 17, 1953; Saturday Review August 8, 1953; Spectator March 16, 1951; Time December 24, 1951, July 27, 1953.

BELLOC LOWNDES. See LOWNDES

BELLOW, SAUL (July 10, 1915-), American novelist, writes: "My parents emigrated to Canada from Russia in 1913— my father, a businessman, has often told me that he imported Egyptian onions into St. Petersburg — and settled in the town of Lachine, Quebec. I was born there in 1915, the youngest of four children. Until I was nine years old we lived in one of the

Victoria Lidov

poorest and most ancient districts of Montreal, on the slope of St. Dominick Street between the General Hospital and Rachel Market.

"In 1924 we moved to Chicago. I grew up there and consider myself a Chicagoan, out and out. Educated after a fashion in the Chicago schools, I entered the University of Chicago in 1933. In that year the Hutchins revolution was already under way and the university was, for me, a terrifying place. The dense atmosphere of learning, of cultural effort, heavily oppressed me; I felt that wisdom and culture were immense and that I was hopelessly small. In 1935 I transferred to Northwestern University. Northwestern had less prestige, but my teachers there appreciated me more. And of course I wanted to be appreciated. My intelligence revived somewhat and I graduated with honors in anthropology and sociology in 1937.

"Graduate school didn't suit me, however. I had a scholarship at the University of Wisconsin, and I behaved very badly. During the Christmas vacation, having fallen in love, I got married and never returned to the University. In my innocence, I had decided to become a writer.

"I will say this for my choice: there are many professions that one may follow without enthusiasm, but though there may be as many unenthusiastic novelists, proportionately, as there are unenthusiastic engineers or dentists, they must consider themselves infidels and they feel their unbelief and treason keenly. Vividness is what they must desire most and so they must value human existence or be unfaithful to their calling.

"It's obvious to everyone that the stature of characters in modern novels is smaller than it once was, and this diminution powerfully concerns those who value existence. I do not believe that human capacity to feel or do can really have dwindled or that the quality of humanity has degenerated. I rather think that people appear smaller because society has become so immense. Hugest of all are the fears that surround us. These are what make it hard for us to determine our proper size and the importance of our deeds."

* * *

Since the publication of Bellow's first novel in 1944, he has been recognized by a small but devoted group of admirers as a novelist of unusual power and originality. In 1953, when *The Adventures of Augie March* appeared, that group was greatly enlarged and Bellow was hailed as one of the most promising of the younger American novelists. The novel received the National Book Award as "the most distinguished work of fiction published in 1953."

The Adventures of Augie March follows no model in form, unless it be the long, crowded, picaresque novels which Fielding and Smollett wrote in the eighteenth century. It was written in a conscious rebellion against the current critical concern with severity of style and exactness of form. Bellow has said: "Today the novelist thinks too much of immortality and he tries to create form. He tries to make his work durable through form. But you have to take your chances on mortality, on perishability. That's what I felt. I kicked over the traces, wrote catch-as-catch-can, picaresque. I took my chance." His hero, whom Robert Gorham Davis describes as "a West-Side Chicago Tom Jones, a Wilhelm Meister of the depression years," moves steadily through a series of seemingly unconnected experiences —family crises, odd jobs, love affairs, a hunting expedition, shipwreck. But they are not without their effects on Augie March. If he does not identify himself with them, if, as Davis says, "it ends without Augie's either finding or transcending himself, it leaves him with the conviction that both achievements are possible, and that they may be simply different names for the same thing."

Bellow is married to Anita Goshkin, a social worker. They have one son. Bellow

has held a Guggenheim Fellowship and a National Institute of Arts and Letters Award. He has taught at the University of Minnesota, Princeton, New York University, and Bard College.

PRINCIPAL WORKS: Dangling Man, 1944; The Victim, 1947; The Adventures of Augie March, 1953.

ABOUT: Warfel, H. R. American Novelists of Today; New York Herald Tribune Book Review October 11, 1953; New York Times Book Review September 20, 1953, January 31, 1954.

BEMELMANS, LUDWIG (April 27, 1898-). For biographical sketch and list of earlier works and references, see TWENTIETH CENTURY AUTHORS, 1942.

* * *

In the past ten to fifteen years Ludwig Bemelmans has emerged from a slyly humorous writer and a casual and delightfully unorthodox illustrator of children's books to a satirist of real stature and a "proper" painter whose canvases are exhibited in art galleries. Fortunately this course of evolution has not dampened his ebullient spirits and his extravagant, edge-of-madness charm. He remains a writer-artist whose pre-eminent characteristic is an inexhaustible capacity for enjoying life. In 1952 he told a newspaper interviewer: "My trouble is that I have always set out to write in a book a very bitter social satire. But I have a great leaning toward people who are a little larcenous. By the time I'm halfway through the book I fall in love with my characters. I just can't seem to hate the people I write about."

Book reviewers are sharply divided into pro- and con-Bemelmans camps. Those who admire him, admire him wildly. Those who fail to be amused—and some of these are critics whose senses of humor are above question—find that much of his work "falls sadly flat." Orville Prescott wrote in the *Yale Review* that Bemelmans' first novel, *Now I Lay Me Down to Sleep,* was not a novel at all. To be sure, this picaresque account of the voyage of an elderly, wealthy Ecuadorian general from Biarritz home to South America has very little of the form and structure one expects of a novel. "You say 'Preposterous!' but continue to chuckle," Charles Marriott observed of the book in the *Manchester Guardian.* James Stern, of the *Nation,* was enthusiastic. He found that it contained "many passages of superb writing." And, he continues, "Bemelmans doesn't seem to know what a literary cliché is.

73

Parts of his book have behind them the quality and the mentality of the late Ronald Firbank—but of a less precious, more prolific Firbank, whose day begins before lunch and whose evenings are spent in the *demi-* rather than the *beaumonde*." Whatever the division of opinion on Bemelmans, probably most of his readers would agree with Richard Watts, who wrote: "There can be no doubt by now that his is one of the original talents of current American letters."

Cosmopolite and gourmet, Bemelmans recently opened a small but elegant café in Paris.

ADDITIONAL WORKS: I Love You, I Love You, I Love You, 1942; Rosebud, 1942; Now I Lay Me Down to Sleep, 1943; Blue Danube, 1945; Hotel Bemelmans, 1946; Dirty Eddie, 1947; Best of Times: An Account of Europe Revisited, 1948; Eye of God, 1949; Sunshine: A Story About the City of New York, 1950; How to Travel Incognito, 1952; The Happy Place, 1952; Madeline's Rescue, 1953; Father, Dear Father, 1953; The High World, 1954; To the One I Love the Best, 1955.

ABOUT: Bemelmans, L. Father, Dear Father; Mahoney, B. E. (ed.) Illustrators of Children's Books, 1744-1945; American Artist May 1951; Collier's February 19, 1944; Horn Book August 1954; New York Herald Tribune Book Review September 15, 1952, August 23, October 11, 1953; New York Times Book Review August 30, 1953; Time July 2, 1951, March 31, 1952.

BEMIS, SAMUEL FLAGG (October 20, 1891-   ). For biographical sketch and list of earlier works and references, see TWENTIETH CENTURY AUTHORS, 1942.

* * *

Samuel Flagg Bemis received his second Pulitzer prize (the first, 1926, was in history, for *Pinckney's Treaty*) in 1950 for his biographical study *John Adams and the Foundation of American Foreign Policy*. A sound, scholarly interpretation of a vast amount of historical material, including personal and official papers of the Adams family, the book was described by one reviewer as "the work of an historian's historian."

Bemis was Carnegie visiting professor in Cuba in 1945. In that same year he was appointed Sterling professor of history and inter-American relations at Yale University, where he has taught since 1935.

ADDITIONAL WORKS: The Latin-American Policy of the United States, 1943; John Quincy Adams and the Foundation of American Foreign Policy, 1949; The United States as a World Power, 1900-1950 (previously published as pt. 3 of A Diplomatic History of the United States) 1950; A Guide to the Diplomatic History of the United States, 1775-1921, 1952.

ABOUT: Current Biography 1950; New York Herald Tribune May 2, 1950; New York Times May 2, 1950.

*BENAVENTE Y MARTINEZ, JACINTO (August 12, 1866-July 14, 1954). For biographical sketch and list of works and references, see TWENTIETH CENTURY AUTHORS, 1942.

* * *

Jacinto Benavente died in Madrid of a heart ailment at the age of eighty-seven. He had been active in Spanish literary circles until shortly before his death, contributing literary criticism to periodicals, and writing plays. In 1952 he wrote five new satirical plays which were produced in Madrid. His last play, *The Bronze Husband*, was produced in April 1954.

During the Spanish Civil War, according to Clark and Freedley in their *History of Modern Drama*, he "fled Madrid with the Republic, was captured in Valencia, taken back to Madrid by Franco forces, and kept under guard in his own house. Later he made his peace with Franco." Benavente received a number of honors from Generalissimo Franco's government. As recently as 1939 he appeared on the stage, acting the role of Crispin in his *Bonds of Interest*, for the benefit of war victims.

ABOUT: Clark, B. H. & Freedley, G. A History of Modern Drama; Columbia Dictionary of Modern European Literature; Hoehn, M. (ed.) Catholic Authors, I; Nicoll, A. World Drama; Ogrizek, D. Spain and Portugal; Oxford Companion to the Theatre; Current Biography 1953; Hispania February 1951; New York Times July 15, 1954.

* bā'nä vän'tä

BENCHLEY,   ROBERT   CHARLES (September 15, 1889-November 21, 1945). For biographical sketch and list of earlier works and references, see TWENTIETH CENTURY AUTHORS, 1942.

* * *

Robert Benchley died, at fifty-six, at the Harkness Pavilion of the Columbia-Presbyterian Medical Center in New York. The cause of death was a cerebral hemorrhage; although he had been seriously ill for a week, the death was described as "sudden."

The versatile humorist spent a large part of his last years in Hollywood, and was frequently heard on radio broadcasts. Of nine major motion pictures in which he appeared in the last year of his life, three were being shown on Broadway at his death. He was once classified as an author, a playwright, an actor, a columnist, a humorist, a critic, and a radio star. A friend has said that he led "one of the most insanely complicated private lives of our day, and did it, on the whole, with extraordinary composure."

In the opinion of Wolcott Gibbs, Benchley was "by far the most brilliant and consistent of the school, originating with Leacock, who performed such dizzy miracles with parody, *non sequitur*, garbled reference, and all the other materials of off-center wit." Stephen Leacock himself called Benchley "perhaps the most finished master of the technique of literary fun in America."

ADDITIONAL WORKS: Benchley Beside Himself, 1943; Benchley—Or Else! 1947; Chips Off the Old Benchley, 1949.

ABOUT: National Cyclopedia of American Biography (1947); Good Housekeeping November 1948; New York Times November 22, December 16, 1945; New Yorker December 1, 1945, January 5, 1946; Reader's Digest February 1946; Scholastic February 25, 1946.

---

*BENDA, JULIEN (December 28, 1867-   ). For autobiographical sketch and list of earlier works and references, see TWENTIETH CENTURY AUTHORS, 1942

* * *

Julien Benda writes from Paris: "In France he published nothing openly during the German occupation, but the (clandestine) Editions de Minuit brought out *Chroniques Interdites*, 1944, and in America there appeared *La Grande Epreuve des Démocraties*, 1943.

"Immediately after the liberation, J. Benda began to publish the work completed during the years of enforced silence: *Exercice d'un Enterré Vif*, 1944; *La France Byzantine*, 1945; *Le Rapport d'Uriel*, 1946; *Tradition de l'Existentialisme*, 1947; *Du Poétique*, 1947; *Trois Idoles Romantiques: Le Dynamisme, L'Existentialisme, La Dialectique Matérialiste*, 1948; *Deux Croisades pour La Paix*, 1948; *Du Style d'Idées*, 1948; *La Crise du Rationalisme*, 1949; *De Quelques Constants de L'Esprit Humain*, 1950; *Cahiers d'un Clerc*, 1950; *Mémoires d'Infra-Tombe*, 1951."

In the works which Julien Benda has published in recent years he has again demonstrated his independence, his intransigence, and his iconoclasm. He defies classification in any literary "school" and remains the sharp critic of emotion and sensation. Linton C. Stevens wrote of him in 1950: "Benda seems to be quite unperturbed by his isolated position as an independent thinker, denounced by philosophers like Jean Paulhan, execrated by writers whose

* băN dà′

pretensions he pierces, and tolerated by critics, who regard him as an intruder upon their sacred preserves. In spite of this equivocal position, Benda has a certain prestige among a small group of readers who admire his audacity in daring to criticize the reigning literary favorites. As Pierre Brodin says: 'Whoever has the taste for ideas will read him with pleasure.' "

ABOUT: Columbia Dictionary of Modern European Literature; Commentary January 1948; Modern Language Notes March 1948; South Atlantic Quarterly April 1950.

BENEDICT, RUTH (FULTON) (June 5, 1887-September 17, 1948), American anthropologist, was born in New York City and spent the first six years of her life on the family farm at Norwich, N.Y., to which her ancestors had come from Connecticut in 1799 on a bob-sled with a cow tied behind to give milk for the babies. Her father, Fred S. Fulton, a physician,  died when she was two years old and her mother, Beatrice J. (Shattuck) Fulton, supported her family by teaching. She and her sister followed their mother in teaching posts, keeping house for her through Missouri and Minnesota. After her graduation from Vassar in 1909 she spent the next year in Europe, settling with Swiss, German, Italian, and English families. Upon her return she taught English in a girls' school in California where she first became interested in the Japanese, Chinese, and Koreans. In 1914 she came east and married Dr. Stanley R. Benedict, a biochemist, who died in 1936.

In 1919 she began the study of anthropology with Franz Boas at Columbia University and for twenty years afterwards worked closely with him. Her first field studies were made among the Serrano Indians in California in 1922. Upon completing her doctorate in 1923 she was named lecturer at Columbia University and in 1930 became assistant professor, advancing to associate professor in 1936, acting head of the department in 1939, and full professor in 1948. As a specialist in behavior patterns she was head of the Basic Analysis Section, Bureau of Overseas Intelligence, Office of War Information, from 1943 to 1945, and during the last summer of her life she was connected with one of the most comprehensive research undertakings of her career as director of Research in Contemporary Cultures, supported by Medical Services Branch of Naval Research.

She was editor of the *Journal of American Folklore*, 1923-39; a fellow of the American Academy of Arts and Sciences, and President of the American Ethnological Society and of the American Anthropological Association. On May 2, 1946, she received an American Design award of $1000 with a citation stating that "she had endured much hardship in her chosen task in order to give the world an understanding of its different citizens through her studies of various civilizations of all races." In June 1946 the American Association of University Women gave her its Achievement Award of $2500.

In the course of many field trips Dr. Benedict made extensive studies of the Pueblo, Apache, Pima, and Blackfoot Indians of the American West. A social path-finder, she applied related technics to the materials of anthropology and then went a step further to apply the findings of her science to the fundamental problems of our day. In the thirties when psychoanalysts began to appreciate the insight to be gained through direct collaboration with anthropologists, she was among the first to give active cooperation. Her studies· were frequently cited by the opponents of Fascist theories and racial discrimination. She was a scientist who had focused her analytic gifts on the differences between people and people, not in order to forge weapons of discrimination nor even of scientific manipulation, but in order to understand the crowning purpose of being individual and different.

As director of the Naval Research project she spent the last summer of her life giving a two weeks' seminar on education for the United Nations Educational, Scientific and Cultural Organizations in Czechoslovakia, and visiting Poland, Belgium, France, and the Netherlands. Shortly after her return she died at New York Hospital of a coronary thrombosis at the age of sixty-one.

Reserved as a person, restrained in expression, sympathetic and kindly, her close associates described her as "civilized utterly and without abatement"—qualities reflected in her writings that combined scientific precision with an artist's sensitivity. As a writer of verse she contributed poems to the *Nation*

and to *Poetry* during 1928-33 under the name of Anne Singleton.

Dr. Alfred Kroeber wrote that "her most famous book, *Patterns of Culture,* became at once a milestone in the development of anthropology." And Margaret Mead writing of the same work in the *Nation* said, "Dr. Benedict's work is based upon a scholarly knowledge of the sources, combined with first hand experience of American Indian tribes, but she has taken her material and reworked it, simplifying it to the extent that she has related it to a more universal context, the philosophy of history."

PRINCIPAL WORKS: The Concept of the Guardian Spirit in North America, 1923; Tales of the Cochiti Indians, 1931; Patterns of Culture, 1934; Zuni Mythology, 1935; Race, Science and Politics, 1940; The Chrysanthemum and the Sword, 1946.

ABOUT: American Anthropologist July 1949; Current Biography 1941, 1948; Journal of American Folklore October 1949; National Cyclopedia of American Biography (1950); New York Times September 18, 1948; Wenner-Gren Foundation for Anthropological Research 1949.

BENEFIELD, BARRY (1877-   ). For autobiographical sketch and list of earlier works and references, see TWENTIETH CENTURY AUTHORS, 1942.

* * *

Barry Benefield writes from Peekskill, New York, that "having been for some thirty years a whole-time or part-time editor in publishing houses, [he] retired in 1947 to the whole-time delight of reading, instead of works still suffering editorial judgment, works already accepted, already printed and bound and in circulation."

Correction: Date of birth 1877, not 1880, as given in TWENTIETH CENTURY AUTHORS, 1942.

ADDITIONAL WORKS: Eddie and the Archangel Mike, 1943.

*BENÉT, STEPHEN VINCENT (July 22, 1898-March 13, 1943). For biographical sketch and list of earlier works and references, see TWENTIETH CENTURY AUTHORS, 1942.

* * *

Stephen Vincent Benét died as the result of a heart attack, at forty-four, at his home in New York City. Although he had been ill for some time, he had given unflagging energy to writing "designed to help mobilize the emotions of this country for war." Much of this output, including a radio series on "Your Army" and a "Prayer for the United

* bĕ nā′

Nations" which was read by President Franklin D. Roosevelt on a Flag Day broadcast in 1942, was published posthumously in *We Stand United*. At the request of the Office of War Information for "a short, interpretative history of the United States that could be translated into many languages and distributed abroad," he wrote *America*, which was published in 1945.

To devote himself to these occasional works, Benét had interrupted the writing of a long narrative poem on the period of American colonization. The "noble fragment" which he completed, published under the title *Western Star*, "continued and prolongs the American search for a home and an emblem" according to Paul Engle, who finds in the poem "the small, living, warm texture of the years of men, and over all the vast conception of the westward motive."

The 1943 gold medal award of the National Institute of Arts and Letters was to have been given to Benét a few weeks after his death. In 1953 his *John Brown's Body* was successfully presented on a wide tour of the United States as a dramatic reading by an all-star cast headed by Raymond Massey.

Despite his versatility, poetry was "his first and dearest love." The London *Times* remarked at the time of his death that he "was not, it now seems probable, a poet whom later generations will turn to for the deeper delights of poetry, but he was a real poet, and he may turn out to have been the Longfellow of his age—and that is no minor politico-poetical office to hold." H. S. Commager has noted that Benét "loved his country passionately, gave his life to singing her beauty and her glory."

ADDITIONAL WORKS: They Burned the Books (poetic drama) 1942; Western Star, 1943; America, 1944; We Stand United, 1945; Last Circle, 1946.

ABOUT: Gregory, H. & Zaturenska, M. History of American Poetry; Van Gelder, R. Writers and Writing; New York Times March 14, March 28, July 11, 1943; Scholastic September 17, 1945.

BENÉT, WILLIAM ROSE (February 2, 1886-May 4, 1950). For autobiographical sketch and list of earlier works and references, see TWENTIETH CENTURY AUTHORS, 1942.

* * *

William Rose Benét suffered a heart attack and died on a New York street as he was on his way to attend a meeting of the council of the National Institute of Arts and Letters. He was sixty-four.

In addition to his own creative work, which in the last years of his life included three volumes of poetry and a child's book in verse, Benét engaged in considerable editorial activity. Two anthologies of poetry and *The Reader's Encyclopedia* (of world literature and the arts) were published within a three-year span. As a contributing editor of the *Saturday Review of Literature*, he had just completed editorial work on that journal's annual poetry issue at the time of his death.

"To intensity he added integrity—and a pervasive kindness," Louis Untermeyer has observed. "His poetry was the man: generous, sometimes too lavish, overflowing with forthrightness and brotherly good will."

Of his last book of poems, *Spirit of the Scene*, Milton Crane remarked in the New York *Times*: "The collection ranges freely from celebrations of fellow-poets and beloved ancestors to disturbed speculations on man and his fate: from the most casual and genial of light verse to the bitterest indictments of the wrongs Benét saw and hated in the world around him. And, above all, illuminating his work, is a profound religious conviction, an affirmation of his faith in God and man."

ADDITIONAL WORKS: Day of Deliverance, 1944; (ed. with Norman Cousins) Poetry of Freedom, 1945; (ed. with Conrad Aiken) Anthology of Famous English and American Poems, 1945; Stairway of Surprise, 1947; Timothy's Angels, 1947; (ed.) The Reader's Encyclopedia, 1948; (with C. Morley) Poetry Package, 1950; Spirit of the Scene, 1951.

ABOUT: Gregory, H. & Zaturenska, M. History of American Poetry; National Cyclopedia of American Biography (1951); New York Times May 5, 1950; Saturday Review of Literature May 20, 1950, June 10, 1950, July 21, 1951.

BENNETT, ARNOLD (May 27, 1867-March 27, 1931). For biographical sketch and list of works and references, see TWENTIETH CENTURY AUTHORS, 1942.

* * *

A new biography of Bennett by Reginald Pound was published in 1952. A long and detailed study, it drew upon Bennett's *Journals* and on his unpublished correspondence with H. G. Wells, Joseph Conrad, G. B. Shaw, and others.

ABOUT: Allen, W.E. Arnold Bennett; Clarke, D. W. Modern English Writers; Dictionary of National Biography 1931-1940; Flower, Sir N. Just as It Happened; Gray, J. On Second Thought; Maugham, W. S. The Vagrant Mood; Pound, R. Arnold Bennett; Sitwell, Sir O. *in* Lehmann, J. (ed.) Orpheus; Saturday Review July 18, 1953.

*BENOÎT, PIERRE (July 6, 1886-   ). For biographical sketch and list of works and references, see TWENTIETH CENTURY AUTHORS, 1942.

* * *

Pierre Benoît lives in Paris. Since 1930 he has published an average of one novel a year. These are love-and-adventure stories, "cleverly done," and eminently readable. None of his recent works has appeared in English translation.

ABOUT: Columbia Dictionary of Modern European Literature; Dictionnaire Biographique Français Contemporain.

* bē nwȧ'

BENSON, ARTHUR CHRISTOPHER (April 24, 1862-June 17, 1925). For biographical sketch and list of works and references, see TWENTIETH CENTURY AUTHORS, 1942.

BENSON, EDWARD FREDERIC (July 24, 1867-February 29, 1940). For biographical sketch and list of works and references, see TWENTIETH CENTURY AUTHORS, 1942.

BENSON, GODFREY RATHBONE. See CHARNWOOD, G. R. B.

BENSON, ROBERT HUGH (November 18, 1871-October 19, 1914). For biographical sketch and list of works and references, see TWENTIETH CENTURY AUTHORS, 1942.

* * *

In the past decade there has been a revival of interest in the writings of Monsignor Benson, and several of his books have had posthumous publication. This revival is perhaps explained by the current interest in prophetic and visionary literature. Anne Fremantle writes: "His accounts of the end of the world anticipated our current atomic anxieties and his account of the stages by which persecution sets in are anticipatory of what is happening in Hungary and Czechoslovakia today, as well as George Orwell's *1984.*"

ADDITIONAL WORKS: (Newly published or omitted from earlier list)——The Papers of a Pariah, 1907; Lord of the World, 1908; The Dawn of All, 1911; Christ in the Church, 1942; The Upper Room: A Drama of Christ's Passion, 1943; The History of Richard Raynal, Solitary, 1945.

ABOUT: Commonweal November 11, 1949.

BENSON, SALLY (September 3, 1900-), American short story writer, was born Sara Mahala Redway Smith in St. Louis, Mo., the daughter of Alonzo Redway and Anna (Prophater) Smith. Her family moved to New York City when she was eleven, and she attended and was graduated from the Horace Mann School. At seventeen she took her first job, "singing into dictaphones," she says, at the National City Bank. Two years later she married Reynolds Benson, an administrative officer at Columbia University. A daughter, Barbara, was born the next year.

John Engstead

Mrs. Benson began her writing career as a newspaperwoman on the old *Morning Telegraph* in New York, interviewing visiting celebrities, mainly authors, actors and actresses. She continued her interviewing even after she moved to her next job, reviewing movies (some thirty-two a month was her average) for a pulp-paper house. She wrote her first short story in 1930, sent it off bravely to the *New Yorker* which, to her amazement, promptly accepted it and asked for more. More was not forthcoming for another year while Mrs. Benson enjoyed the shock and satisfaction of her first sale, but after that, getting "broker and broker," she started writing again, selling most of her material to the *New Yorker.* One of her stories, "The Overcoat," refused by the *New Yorker,* was published in the *American Mercury* and republished in the O'Brien collection of best short stories. But her steady market was the *New Yorker,* this, she explained to Robert van Gelder in an interview, "probably because I haven't tried other markets. My style fits here and it wouldn't most places. Every once in a while editors of some of the national magazines have asked for my stuff, but what they really want are healthy, clean-limbed hearty young people on a raft, and that isn't for me."

Ironically, it is for her "healthy, clean-limbed hearty young people" that Mrs. Benson is best known, especially for her memorable archetype of adolescence, the awkward, ungainly yet curiously appealing Judy Graves, heroine of the *Junior Miss* stories. At the beginning of her career, however, Mrs. Benson seemed the most unlikely author imaginable to portray the charms of adolescence. Her short stories up to that time were, in the words of a reviewer for the Boston *Transcript,* "brilliant with a knife-like cut, ruthless in their satire, and penetrating often to the point of tragedy." In 1938, with the publication of another collection of her stories, *Emily,* some reviewers observed that the acid of her satire had been neutralized a little. She was especially successful here in her stories about young girls—"compassionate in a way impossible to anyone except the very kind and the very wise," Frances Woodward wrote.

Mrs. Benson wrote her first Judy Graves story for the *New Yorker* and, after doing another, she tired of the idea and wanted to drop it. The late Harold Ross urged her to continue, and she has had no occasion to regret that advice. *Junior Miss* appeared in 1941, was a Book-of-the-Month Club choice, and a distinct critical success. In that same year a highly successful dramatization of the book by Jerome Chodorov and Joseph Fields opened on Broadway, and, with added episodes, it became a popular radio series.

Judy Graves' successor in the realm of thoroughly human and natural literary children was Tootie Smith, the six-year-old younger sister of *Meet Me in St. Louis,* Mrs. Benson's next book. For this warm, nostalgic picture of life in St. Louis in the early part of the century, she drew upon her own childhood memories and the diaries which her older sister had kept in St. Louis in 1902 and 1903 when she was sixteen. Mrs. Benson sold *Meet Me in St. Louis* to Hollywood where it was made into a very popular musical film starring Judy Garland.

From time to time Mrs. Benson has reviewed mystery stories for the *New Yorker.* In recent years most of her writing has been for motion pictures, however. Among the films she has collaborated on are *Shadow of a Doubt, Anna and the King of Siam,* and *Come to the Stable.*

PRINCIPAL WORKS: People Are Fascinating, 1936; Emily, 1938; Stories of the Gods and Heroes, 1940; Junior Miss, 1941; Meet Me in St. Louis, 1942; Women and Children First, 1943.

ABOUT: Current Biography 1941; Van Gelder, R. Writers and Writing.

BENSON, STELLA (1892-December 6, 1933). For biographical sketch and list of works and references, see TWENTIETH CENTURY AUTHORS, 1942.

* * *

ABOUT: Dictionary of National Biography 1931-1940; Nineteenth Century April 1947.

BENT, SILAS (May 9, 1882-July 30, 1945). For autobiographical sketch and list of works and references, see TWENTIETH CENTURY AUTHORS, 1942.

* * *

Silas Bent died, at sixty-three, in the Stamford, Conn., hospital after an illness of three days.

For the last twenty-three years of his life, the former newspaper man lived in Old Greenwich, Conn., engaged in free-lance writing, chiefly articles. His last book was a biography of Zachary Taylor, *Old Rough And Ready,* written with a cousin, Silas Bent McKinley, and published in 1946 (incorrectly dated 1941 in earlier sketch).

ABOUT: National Cyclopedia of American Biography (1948); New York Times July 31, 1945.

BENTLEY, EDMUND CLERIHEW (July 10, 1875-). For autobiographical sketch and list of earlier works and references, see TWENTIETH CENTURY AUTHORS, 1942.

* * *

E. C. Bentley retired from the staff of the *Daily Telegraph* in 1947. His wife died in 1949, and he lives now in a London hotel. He writes that "the fourth and by far the most successful film version of *Trent's Last Case* was produced by Herbert Wilcox in 1951."

ADDITIONAL WORKS: Elephant's Work, 1950; Clerihews Complete, 1951.

BENTLEY, ERIC RUSSELL (September 14, 1916-), Anglo-American critic and stage director, writes: "I was born at Bolton, Lancashire, England. At eleven I won a scholarship to Bolton School. My chief interest there was the annual school play. I played Lacy in *The Shoemaker's Holiday,* Macbeth, Malvolio, and Masefield's 'Pompey.' On the side I studied  piano and became Licentiate of the Guildhall School of Music. In 1935 I won a history scholarship that took me to Oxford. Here my biggest experience was to act under John Gielgud in *Richard III* and under Esme Church in *Twelfth Night* (this time I played not Malvolio but Sir Toby).

"After Oxford, Yale; where I took my doctorate in comparative literature (at that time designated 'History, the Arts, and Letters'). Although I'd contributed to a student anthology while at Oxford, my writing career proper began with the revision of my Ph.D. thesis which was about the cult of hero-worship in modern literature. In 1942 I began selling bits of it to the literary reviews (*Partisan Review* being the first). In 1944 the thesis blossomed as a book under the title *A Century of Hero Worship*. Meanwhile I was teaching history, literature, and drama in various parts of the United States. At Black Mountain College (1942-44) I took to directing plays, but at the University of Minnesota (1944-48) my academic work was limited to the lecture room. I used to emerge, however, see all the Broadway shows, and write about them—for *Harper's* and other magazines. In my study at Minneapolis I completed two books: *The Playwright as Thinker* and *Bernard Shaw*.

"In 1948 a Guggenheim Fellowship took me to Europe, and I decided to leave academic life, at least for a time, and devote myself to theatre. I stayed in Europe till 1951. The Rockefeller Foundation contributed to my upkeep; as did *Theatre Arts* and *Kenyon Review*, to both of which I was sending regular reports on the drama in Europe. But my principal job, at this point, was directing. I was guest director at the Abbey, Dublin; the Schauspielhaus, Zurich; the Teatro Universitario, Padua. I was Bertolt Brecht's assistant in his own production of *Mother Courage* (Munich, 1950). I directed seven Irish plays for a Dublin group which toured the United States in 1951 as the Young Ireland Theatre Company. Returning to the United States, I directed in summer stock and was subsequently guest director at the Brattle Theatre and the Westport Country Playhouse, Penn Valley Playhouse and elsewhere. In 1952 I accepted the post of drama critic to the *New Republic*."

* * *

Eric Bentley is widely regarded as one of the keenest and most literate of present-day drama critics and writers on the theatre. He is a critic rather than a mere reviewer of plays, bringing to his work a generous background of scholarship and fresh insight into the esthetic and practical aspects of the drama. He has been married twice—to Maja Tschernjakow (who collaborated with him in his translations of the works of Bertolt

Brecht) and in 1953 to Joanne Davis. He lives in New York City. In 1954 he became Brander Matthews Professor of English at Columbia University. He has held Rockefeller and Guggenheim fellowships and in 1953 he received a National Institute of Arts and Letters Award.

PRINCIPAL WORKS: *Criticism*—A Century of Hero-Worship (in England: The Cult of the Superman) 1944; The Playwright as Thinker (in England: The Modern Theatre) 1946; Bernard Shaw, 1947; In Search of Theatre, 1953; The Dramatic Event: An American Chronicle, 1954. *Anthologies (ed.)*—The Importance of Scrutiny, 1948; From the Modern Repertoire, I, II, 1949, 1952; The Play, 1951. *Translations and Editions*—Brecht, B. Private Life of the Master Race, 1944, Parables for the Theatre, 1948; Pirandello, L. Liola (*in* Naked Masks, Five Plays by Pirandello) 1952; Pirandello, L. Right You Are, 1954.

ABOUT: Accent Spring 1948; Kenyon Review Winter 1945; Partisan Review Fall 1944; Saturday Review of Literature September 30, 1944, June 22, 1946, February 7, 1948; Theater der Zeit (Berlin) July 1950; Theatre Arts December 1944, November 1946; (London) Times Literary Supplement August 23, 1947.

BENTLEY, PHYLLIS (November 19, 1894-). For autobiographical sketch and list of earlier works and references, see TWENTIETH CENTURY AUTHORS, 1942.

* * *

Phyllis Bentley served in the American Division of the Ministry of Information in London from 1942 to 1944. She is vice president of the English Center of PEN, a member of the North Regional Advisory Council of B.B.C. and of the Brontë Society Council, and president of the Association of Yorkshire Bookmen. In 1949 she received an honorary D.Litt. from Leeds University.

In her fiction Miss Bentley continues to write of the region she knows and loves best, the West Riding of Yorkshire. Out of this region too has grown her interest in the Brontës on whom she wrote a book in the English Novelists Series. (She has also edited the works of the Brontës in the Heather edition). Her own theory of the novel is outlined in *Some Observations on the Art of Narrative*.

Miss Bentley notes the following corrections to be made in the original sketch: "My tour in Holland took place in 1934, not 1935 as mentioned. My novel *Manhold* should be spelt thus and not with an 'e.' Also my novel *The Power and the Glory* was published in England under the title *Take Courage*."

ADDITIONAL WORKS: Here Is America, 1941; The Rise of Henry Morcar, 1946; Some Observations on the Art of Narrative, 1946; The Brontës, 1947; Life Story, 1948; Quorum, 1950; Panorama, 1952; The House of Moreys, 1953.

ABOUT: Gray, J. On Second Thought; New York Herald Tribune Book Review October 11, 1953.

*BERCOVICI, KONRAD (June 22, 1882-). For biographical sketch and list of earlier works and references, see TWENTIETH CENTURY AUTHORS, 1942.

* * *

Konrad Bercovici's two latest novels have been "fictionized biography" or "biographical fiction," both characterized by vigor and vividness of imagination. *Exodus* was an ambitious retelling of the biblical story, with Moses as its hero. Inevitably the novel invited comparison with Thomas Mann's Joseph trilogy and Sholem Asch's *Nazarene* and *Apostle*. J. H. Holmes, writing in the New York *Herald Tribune*, found that Bercovici's book "has neither the power nor the profundity of these earlier masterpieces. But it has imagination, beauty, and a certain strange timeliness which arouse interest and hold attention." *Savage Prodigal,* based on the life of the French poet Arthur Rimbaud, was described by the *New Yorker* as "very lively whether it's Rimbaud or simply Mr. Bercovici."

ADDITIONAL WORKS: Exodus, 1947; Savage Prodigal, 1948.

ABOUT: Warfel, H. R. American Novelists of Today.

* bŭr kō vē'sē

*BERDYAEV, NIKOLAI ALEKSANDROVICH (1874-March 24, 1948). For biographical sketch and list of earlier works and references, see TWENTIETH CENTURY AUTHORS, 1942.

* * *

Nikolai Berdyaev died at his home in Clamart, a suburb of Paris, at seventy-three.

Many of his books have been translated into English in recent years, including *Dream and Reality*, an autobiography written during and immediately after World War II for publication after his death, and *The Beginning and the End*, which has been called "a kind of spiritual biography." The former work was characterized (by the *New Yorker*) as "the record of a quest for the absolute which took him through Marxism, Chris-

* byĕr dyä'yĕf

tianity, and Existentialism, and ended with his discovery of faith, if not truth."

B. Evan Owen has called Berdyaev "a symbol of our time, for he embraced all the dilemmas that confront our world within the complexity of his philosophy." The London *Times* observed that he "possessed a breadth of vision on world history which few today could approach."

ADDITIONAL WORKS IN ENGLISH TRANSLATION: Solitude and Society, 1938; Spirit and Reality, 1939; The Russian Idea, 1948; Slavery and Freedom, 1948; The Divine and the Human, 1949; Towards a New Epoch, 1949; Dream and Reality, 1950; The Beginning and the End, 1952; The Realm of Spirit and the Realm of Caesar, 1953; Truth and Revelation, 1954.

ABOUT: Clarke, O. F. Introduction to Berdyaev; Attwater, D. Modern Christian Revolutionaries; Lampert, E. Nicolas Berdyaev and the New Middle Ages; Orton, W. A. Liberal Tradition; Seaver, G. Nicolas Berdyaev: an Introduction to His Thought; Sorokin, P. Social Philosophies of an Age of Crisis; Spinka, M. Nicolas Berdyaev: Captive of Freedom; Catholic World October 1951; Commonweal August 13, 1948; Contemporary Review June 1948; Fortnightly December 1950; Time April 5, 1948.

BERENSON, BERNARD (June 26, 1865-). For biographical sketch and list of earlier works and references, see TWENTIETH CENTURY AUTHORS, 1942.

* * *

After a lifetime of the most devoted study of art, Bernard Berenson has turned his eye upon himself and published two searching and revealing volumes of memoirs—*Sketch for a Self-Portrait* and *Rumor and Reflection*. The portrait of Berenson that emerges is richly delineated and reveals, John Walker wrote in the New York *Times*, "a witty, perceptive human being, the heir in a sense of all the cultures of the past, learned in his own field but with a universal knowledge rare in modern scholarship."

The greater part of these two volumes was written in Italy during the war when Berenson had left his villa, I Tatti, near Florence, and was in hiding from the Nazis. The memoirs show Berenson, to quote the *New Yorker*, as "one of the few surviving completely civilized men." Nazism and Fascism, anti-Semitism, war, the destruction of so much of the Italy that he loved—Berenson observed and recorded all this with rare objectivity and dispassion, reflecting what the London *Times Literary Supplement* called "the triumph of that disciplined mind over all circumstances."

In the Epilogue to *Sketch for a Self-Portrait,* written after the war ended, Berenson

81

said, "I have come through it spiritually un-harmed and physically undamaged, although aged and enfeebled." He returned then to his villa, with his books, his art treasures, and his photographs. Here he leads a semi-retired life, but visitors report that he is still the same brilliant conversationalist, charming personality, and shrewd critic of art as ever he was.

ADDITIONAL WORKS: Aesthetics and History in the Visual Arts, 1948; Sketch for a Self-Portrait, 1949; Rumor and Reflection, 1952; Seeing and Knowing, 1953; Caravaggio, 1953.

ABOUT: Behrman, S. N. Duveen; Berenson, B. Sketch for a Self-Portrait, Rumor and Reflection; Linklater, E. Art of Adventure; Horizon October 1949; Life April 11, 1949; New York Herald Tribune Book Review October 12, 1952; New York Times Magazine July 8, 1951; Saturday Review of Literature July 18, 1949; Time July 5, 1948.

BERESFORD, JOHN DAVYS (March 7, 1873-February 2, 1947). For auto-biographical sketch and list of earlier works and references, see TWENTIETH CENTURY AUTHORS, 1942.

* * *

J. D. Beresford died at Bath, England, at seventy-three.

He continued almost until his death to publish novels at the average rate of one a year. The London *Times* notes as admirable his "patient and practiced novelist's re-source" and observes that, although his work declined in artistic power, at its best he "produced work of genuine distinction, all of it showing fine and careful craftmanship."

ADDITIONAL WORKS: What Dreams May Come. . . , 1941; Common Enemy, 1942; Bene-factor, 1943; Long View, 1943; If This Were True. . . , 1944; Riddle of the Tower, 1944; Prisoner, 1946; Hampdenshire Wonder, 1948. *With E. Wynne-Tyson:* Men in the Same Boat, 1943; Gift, 1947.

ABOUT: London Times February 4, 1947; New York Times February 4, 1947.

BERGSON, HENRI (October 12, 1859-January 4, 1941). For biographical sketch and list of works and references, see TWENTIETH CENTURY AUTHORS, 1942.

* * *

ABOUT: Columbia Dictionary of Modern Euro-pean Literature; D'Amato, G. A. Portraits of Ideas; McElroy, H. C. Modern Philosophers; Scharfstein, B. Roots of Bergson's Philosophy; Tomlin, E. W. F. Great Philosophers; France Illustration February 17, 1951; Saturday Review of Literature August 23, 1947.

"BERKELEY, ANTHONY." See COX, A. B.

BERNANOS, GEORGES (1888-July 5, 1948). For biographical sketch and list of earlier works and references, see TWENTIETH CENTURY AUTHORS, 1942.

* * *

Georges Bernanos died in the American Hospital in Neuilly, France, at sixty, two weeks after he had been flown there from Tunisia for an emergency operation.

Following World War I, in which he served as a volunteer, he made a living for his family as an insurance inspector. In 1938, shortly before Munich, he migrated with his wife (a lineal descendant of Jeanne d'Arc, and bearing the same name) and his six children to Brazil because, he said, he felt the need for deep self-examination to find "valid reasons for living" in the world as he found it, and "the air we breathe today in my country is unhappily not very favor-able to such an examination of conscience."

In South America he explored many re-mote regions, was an honored member of the "literary, political and social élite" of Brazil, wrote as a journalist and for the radio, and issued *Plea for Liberty,* which G. N. Shuster has called "a searing profession of faith; curiously also one of the few optimistic books written during the war." Bernanos was one of the first French writers to join the de Gaullist movement, and during his last year in Brazil, according to André Rous-seaux, "Bernanos' words, printed in news-papers and books and broadcast over the radio, were given greater and greater cur-rency in the world at war," and "high emis-saries" of the embassies of the United States, Canada, England and the de Gaullist Free France movement frequented his home at Barbecena, La Croix des Ames.

In 1945 Bernanos and his family returned to France, "to find no happiness there," and settled finally in Tunisia. He was one of fifty of Europe's leading intellectuals who met at Geneva in September, 1946, in a "peace conference of thought." At the time of his death, Bernanos was engaged in writ-ing a life of Jesus which W. M. Frohack believes "might have been the keystone of his work."

According to Frohack, Bernanos was "the least literary of men," writing "because he felt that he had to. . . . He regarded writing not as a profession but as a vocation." Es-sentially independent in his political thinking, he has been called by Ernest Erich North "an honest man in the fullest sense of the word, [who] has left everywhere profound traces of his prodigious personality." The *Columbia Dictionary of Modern European Literature* has characterized him as "both a novelist of rare originality and an effective polemicist; a firm believer in the essential dignity of man and a militant Christian for whom sanctity constituted the highest form of adventure and heroism."

ADDITIONAL WORKS IN ENGLISH TRANSLATION: Plea for Liberty: Letters to the English, the Americans, the Europeans, 1944; Open Mind, 1945; Joy, 1946; Sanctity Will Out: an Essay on St. Joan, 1947; Tradition of Freedom, 1950; The Fearless Heart, 1952; Last Essays, 1955.

ABOUT: American Mercury June 1944; Books Abroad Winter 1949; Catholic World March 1945, March 1949; Commonweal December 17, 1943, June 16, 1944, July 16, 1948; Emporium March 1947; France Illustration February 17, 1951; Le Figaro Littéraire December 27, 1952; Life October 14, 1946; New York Times May 31, 1951.

BERNSTEIN, ALEC. See BARON, A.

BERNSTEIN, HENRY (1876-November 27, 1953). For biographical sketch and list of earlier works and references, see TWENTIETH CENTURY AUTHORS, 1942.

* * *

Henry Bernstein, "easily the most durable figure of the modern French theatre," came to the United States as a refugee in 1940. With his fellow French artist André Maurois, he played an active role in the Free French movement in this country. After the war he returned to France, resumed the directorship of the Théâtre des Ambassadeurs, where his new play *La Soif*, starring Jean Gabin, was produced. In 1950, photographing Bernstein for *Life* magazine, Yousuf Karsh commented that he was "very much the gentleman who has been, and still is, full of sex appeal." He was reported to have been one of Europe's richest playwrights.

Bernstein died in Paris at seventy-seven following an operation.

ABOUT: Columbia Dictionary of Modern European Literature; Commonweal April 13, 1945; Dictionnaire Biographique Français Contemporain; Life August 7, 1950; New York Times November 28, 1953.

BERRYMAN, JOHN (October 25, 1914-), American poet and critic, was born in McAlester, Okla. He went to school in South Kent, Conn., and has degrees from Columbia College and the University of Cambridge. On his return from study in England, he spent a year teaching English at Wayne University in Detroit. Since then he has taught at Harvard, where he held a Briggs-Copeland instructorship, and at Princeton.

Berryman's first published poems appeared in the late 1930's in the *Southern Review, Kenyon Review, Partisan Review, Nation,* and *New Republic.* In 1940 twenty of his poems were published by New Directions in *Five Young American Poets.* At that time he wrote in a prefatory note: "One of the reasons for writing verse is a delight in craftsmanship—rarely for its own sake, mainly as it seizes and makes visible its subject. Versification, rime, stanzaform, trope, are the tools. They provide the means by which the writer can shape from an experience in itself usually vague, a mere feeling or phrase, something that is coherent, directed, intelligible." Berryman's verse has, on the whole, admirably demonstrated his theory. He has, as one reviewer puts it, "structure and craft." In his best work David Daiches finds "grave and quiet precision." Dudley Fitts speaks of him as "a poet whose gifts . . . are salient; a poet of discriminating sensibility and a saving wit." But Fitts has found in all but the very best of his work "an aura of academic contrivance, a certain 'muzziness' that is as hard to define as it is to ignore." The Poetry Society of America named him recipient of the Shelley Memorial Award in 1948.

In addition to his poetry Berryman has written short stories (one, "The Imaginary Jew," received the *Kenyon*-Doubleday award for 1945 and has been widely reprinted), literary criticism, and a biography of Stephen Crane, published in the American Men of Letters Series. This volume was widely praised as the first scholarly and comprehensive critical and biographical study of Crane. As a creative writer himself, Berryman approached his subject with sympathy and insight. "The discrepancies that set so many biographers hopelessly apart from their main literary subjects simply do not obtain here," Morgan Blum wrote of the book in *Poetry.* Although Blum objected to certain characteristics of the book—"the sweeping statement, the dogmatic exaggeration"—he considered it generally distinguished, especially in "those areas where criticism and biography meet."

In 1953 Berryman took a leave from Princeton to travel and write in Europe. He has been at work for some time on a biographical study of Shakespeare.

PRINCIPAL WORKS: "Twenty Poems" *in* Five Young American Poets, 1940; Poems, 1942; The Dispossessed (poems) 1948; Stephen Crane, 1950.

ABOUT: Five Young American Poets, 1940; Poetry October 1948, August 1951.

BERTO, GIUSEPPE (December 27, 1914-), Italian novelist, writes in Italian: "My life is an example of how one may

Meldolesi, Rome

become a writer even without being one by vocation. I was born in Mogliano Veneto, a small town not far from Venice, where my father owned a hat shop and occasionally made a sale. Of the five children he had, I was the only one he was able to send to school. At the age of six I thought of becoming a priest. By the time I was twelve I had changed my mind and wanted to be a doctor. But when I reached eighteen my father told me that he could not afford to spend any more on my education, so I enlisted in the army and, with money saved out of my pay, enrolled in the university. I selected the Faculty of Letters because, of the several schools, it was the least expensive.

"In 1935 I was sent to fight in Ethiopia. When I returned to Italy, a new war was already in the making. I barely had time to take my degree before finding myself again in uniform, this time in North Africa. When the resistance in Tunisia ended, I was taken prisoner and transported to a concentration camp at Hereford, Texas. I was then almost twenty-nine and still had no clear notion as to what I would do with my life. For thirty months I was kept inside a barbed-wire enclosure in the middle of the Texas prairie. The most serious problem that confronts a prisoner is that of keeping his mind occupied. I myself solved it by beginning to write.

"Italian literature, during the period in which my intellectual growth had taken place, could furnish me with no models. The writers who had turned to Fascism were high-sounding and barren of thought. The remainder, in part because political conditions were not conducive to a sincere examination of social problems, and in part because of the Italian tendency to consider literature an intellectual activity sufficient unto itself, had retired more than ever into their ivory tower and into a kind of writing which, however refined, intelligent, and formally perfect it may have been, was arid and worthless. I had neither the desire nor, probably, the talent to become one of them. But slight contact with American literature—being able to read two or three books and to see how those writers boldly and without too great a concern with fine writing face up to problems —sufficed to demonstrate that I might become a writer like them.

"In 1946, no longer a prisoner, I returned to my father's house in Mogliano Veneto. I had no money whatever, but possessed almost unlimited faith in the two manuscripts I had carried from America: the stories contained in *The Works of God* and the novel *The Sky Is Red*. And one day I took them and set out for Milan, the publishing center of Italy.

"The trip was a failure. I knew no one, neither editors, critics, nor other writers, and obviously no one had heard of me. I departed, leaving the manuscripts to be read, warmly entrusting them to some secretaries, and returned home with the vague promise that sooner or later I would hear something from them. Several months passed with no word, and so, borrowing some money, I made a second trip to Milan. This time fortune led me to knock at the door of an editor who was looking for an Italian novel that was new both in conception and form. He read *The Sky Is Red* and accepted it immediately. The book was at once a popular success, and the following year a commission of leading Italian men of letters awarded it the Premio Firenze for literature. I was able finally to regard myself as a writer.

"The success of my first novel gave me courage to write a second, *The Brigand*, and assisted in finding means by which to live. At present I live in Rome, working for the film industry and occasionally writing stories for magazines. I am thinking of writing a satirical novel with my hometown as its setting."

* * *

Giuseppe Berto's *The Sky Is Red* is one of the most distinguished of a number of Italian novels that have appeared since the end of World War II—all of them capturing, or attempting to capture, the bitter tragedy of Italian Fascism. Berto's book is a poignant picture of the effects of war on four teen-aged children. "It has a reality that stands out clearly in the glow of a steady, subdued light," Harold Clurman wrote of it in the *New Republic*. Alfred Kazin has pointed out that Berto's work shows the "enormous" influence of Ernest Hemingway, especially in the bare simplicity of its style. But, Kazin feels, the Hemingway influence has not been altogether happy. "Berto lacks Hemingway's secret lyricism and above all Hemingway's insistence on the ultimate dignity of man."

PRINCIPAL WORKS IN ENGLISH TRANSLATION: The Sky Is Red, 1948; The Works of God, and Other Stories, 1949; The Brigand, 1951.

ABOUT: New York Times Book Review October 3, 1948; Time October 25, 1948, November 26, 1951.

* * *

BESANT, Mrs. ANNIE (WOOD) (October 1, 1847-September 20, 1933). For biographical sketch and list of works and references, see TWENTIETH CENTURY AUTHORS, 1942.

* * *

ABOUT: Dictionary of National Biography 1931-1940; Venkatachalam, G. Profiles.

BESIER, RUDOLF (July 1878-June 15, 1942). For biographical sketch and list of works and references, see TWENTIETH CENTURY AUTHORS, 1942.

BESSIE, ALVAH CECIL (June 4; 1904-). For autobiographical sketch and list of earlier works and references, see TWENTIETH CENTURY AUTHORS, 1942.

* * *

Alvah Bessie writes: "October 5, 1940, married Helen Clare Nelson. Eva Christine Bessie, daughter, born March 1, 1944, Los Angeles. Contract screenwriter, Warner Brothers, Burbank, Calif., January 1943 to January 1946; free-lance screenwriter, January 1946 to January 1948. In October 1947 subpoenaed together with eight other screenwriters, directors, producers, by the House Committee on Un-American Activities, engaged in investigating 'subversive activity' in the motion picture industry. As a result of refusing to surrender the Bill of Rights into the hands of this committee, was blacklisted by motion picture industry, indicted for 'contempt of Congress,' and after conviction served twelve-month sentence in Federal Correctional Institution, Texarkana, Tex. (June 1950 to April 1951). Since August 15, 1951, associate editor of *The Dispatcher*, official newspaper, International Longshore-

men's & Warehousemen's Union, San Francisco, and associate information director of that union."

ADDITIONAL WORKS: Mirbeau, O. Torture Garden (tr.) 1949; The Heart of Spain (ed.) 1952.

ABOUT: Warfel, H. R. American Novelists of Today.

BESTON, HENRY (June 1, 1888-). For autobiographical sketch and list of earlier works and references, see TWENTIETH CENTURY AUTHORS, 1942.

* * *

Henry Beston writes: "Ten years have passed since I wrote the foregoing sketch, and still the fragrance of yellow birch blows off from the chimneys of 'Chimney Farm.' The decade has seen me settling down more and more into the country way of life as we know it in coastal Maine. Not only am I a born countryman by temperament, but also I chance to hold that in order to live a really human life, 'Man' must be in a living relation to a community. Half farmer, half writer, and growing respectably old, I manage rather pleasantly, my horticultural specialty being the growing and testing of grapes hardy in the higher north.

"Of my older books, *The Outermost House*, 1928, now in its fourteenth printing, has apparently established itself as something of a 'classic' in American nature-writing, and has, moreover, been honored with an excellent translation into French, Paris 1953. The old *Fairy Tales* I wrote on emerging from service in War I are still vigorously alive after some thirty-three years of continuous publication and have just been reissued, together with various new stories, in a first collected edition, New York 1952. My 'St. Lawrence,' too, holds its significant place and was the first of the River Series to appear in a British edition, London 1951.

"Of my newer books, *Northern Farm* (1948) seems to be a living favorite with those who like an account of the country world, whilst my regional reader of the State of Maine, *White Pine and Blue Water* (1950), is on all the regional lists and has been widely read. At the moment I am working towards a new study of an aspect of Nature, together with a study of the relation of that aspect to the Spirit of Man.

"I help with the foreign agricultural students who come to Maine, and I occasionally lecture at the colleges. Two years ago Harvard made me an honorary Phi Beta Kappa, an honor for which I remain profoundly grateful.

"My beliefs, my 'philosophy of life,' all this has not changed. The malady of our age, as I see it, is a loss of power to perceive reality in terms of the poetic spirit, and this I lay to an alienation from Nature unexampled in human history. What is needed is not a change of political forms but a rebirth of wonder, reverence, and poetry. God builds on Nature.

"Midmorning, and the December rain is changing into snow, and my lovely lady whom the world knows as Elizabeth Coatsworth is calling to me to please put another stick of wood on the kitchen fire."

ADDITIONAL WORKS: Northern Farm: A Chronicle of Maine, 1948; White Pine and Blue Water: A State of Maine Reader (ed.) 1950; Henry Beston's Fairy Tales, 1952.

ABOUT: Beston, H. Northern Farm; Kunitz, S. J. & Haycraft, H. The Junior Book of Authors (rev. ed.).

* BETJEMAN, JOHN (1906-), British poet and architectural authority, was born in England, and was educated at Marlborough and at Oxford. He is a communicant of the Church of England. In 1933 he married Penelope, the daughter of Field Marshal Sir Philip Chetwode. He has a son and a daughter. During 1941-43 he was the British Press Attaché in Dublin, and in 1944 he held a post with the British Admiralty. At the end of 1944 he was appointed to the British Council, and he remained with this organization until 1946.

Cecil Beaton

He first became celebrated as a poet, occupying a place that no literary critic has yet succeeded in defining. W. H. Auden said, "His poems are slick but not streamlined." He is a satirist with a delicate lyrical gift, a lover of the past who delights to evoke the present, the author of comic verse whose sense of fun is perpetually trembling on the verge of seriousness. In advice to young writers John Betjeman has said that if he could live his life over again, he would probably take up some handicraft such as making stained glass, or weaving, or French polishing, and with this to fall back on and to satisfy the manual side of him, without disturbing his creative energies, he would write with vigor and confidence. He

* bĕt'jĕ màn

insists however, that writing would be his primary occupation.

He loves architecture next to poetry best of all human manifestations, and believes that the life of a place is as important as its appearance. When he writes of the country, he writes as a poet, when he writes about buildings he never forgets the human beings for, and by whom, they were built, so that his scholarship is never dead but invested with a warmth and a living expressive love.

Betjeman received the Heinemann Award in 1948 for his *Selected Poems*. American readers know him best for a collection of his poems and short pieces called *Slick But Not Streamlined*, selected and introduced by W. H. Auden. Much of Betjeman's work suggests Auden in its polish and wit. His architectural and topographical writings, his poetry, and his prose have in common not only wit, however, but the quality of slipping over into another dimension, as Louise Bogan says, "where sensibility is all." The net result is therefore "highly civilized entertainment," and also, Irwin Edman found, a quality "of tenderness and understanding of things English, and of wry insight into the mixture of the new and the traditional, the traditional and the sceptical, in modern English intelligence."

Betjeman lives in the town of Wantage, in Berkshire.

PRINCIPAL WORKS: *Poetry*—Mount Zion, 1933; Continual Dew, 1937; Old Bats in New Belfries, 1940; Old Lights for New Chancels, 1945; Slick But Not Streamlined, 1947; Selected Poems, 1948; A Few Late Chrysanthemums, 1954. *Prose*—Ghastly Good Taste, 1933; Cornwall Shell Guide (ed.) 1934; Devon Shell Guide (ed.) 1936; English, Scottish and Welsh Landscape (comp. with G. Taylor) 1944; (with J. Piper) Murray's Architectural Guides to Buckinghamshire, 1948; Berkshire, 1949; Shell Guide to Shropshire, 1951; First and Last Loves, 1952.

ABOUT: Auden, W. H. *Introduction to Betjeman's* Slick But Not Streamlined; Poetry December 1947.

BEVERIDGE, ALBERT JEREMIAH (October 6, 1862-April 27, 1927). For biographical sketch and list of works and references, see TWENTIETH CENTURY AUTHORS, 1942.

* * *

ABOUT: Banta, R. E. Indiana Authors and their Books; Thomas, B. P. Portrait for Posterity: Lincoln and his Biographers; Tarkington, B. *in* American Academy of Arts and Letters Commemorative Tributes (1905-1941); Journal of Southern History May 1954; Mississippi Valley Historical Review March 1949.

BIBESCO, MARTHE LUCIE (LAHO-VARY), Princesse (1887-). For biographical sketch and list of works and references, see TWENTIETH CENTURY AUTHORS, 1942.

* * *

Prince George Bibesco died in 1941. Since 1945, when Rumania went under Communist control, Princess Bibesco has discontinued her visits to her native country. She now divides her time between France and England. In 1950 she published a rambling and reminiscent book on Marcel Proust, which included some previously unpublished papers and letters of Proust to the Duc de Guiche.

ADDITIONAL WORKS IN ENGLISH TRANSLATION: Prince Imperial, 1949; Veiled Wanderer: Marcel Proust, 1950.

ABOUT: Hoehn, M. (ed.) Catholic Authors, II.

BICKERSTAFFE-DREW, FRANCIS BROWNING DREW, Count (February 11, 1858-July 3, 1928). For biographical sketch and list of works and references, see TWENTIETH CENTURY AUTHORS, 1942.

BIGGERS, EARL DERR (August 26, 1884-April 5, 1933). For biographical sketch and list of works and references, see TWENTIETH CENTURY AUTHORS, 1942.

BINDLOSS, HAROLD (1866-December 30, 1945). For biographical sketch and earlier works and references, see TWENTIETH CENTURY AUTHORS, 1942.

* * *

Harold Bindloss died at seventy-nine in Carlisle, England.

Since turning to writing in 1902, after he was thirty, because of a breakdown in health, he had written over sixty novels. His last book was published in the year of his death.

The Boston *Transcript* found that Bindloss combined "most of the qualities of the experienced teller of tales. He knows his background; he keeps his narrative relatively simple and uncomplicated of minor whirlpools of action. And more important his characterization is for the most part well imagined." Will Cuppy described his work as "leisurely, well-bred and somewhat meandering adventure, with plenty of fine, ringing sentiments."

ADDITIONAL WORKS: Caverhills, 1943; Laird o' Borrans, 1945; Richardsons of the Forge, 1946.

ABOUT: New York Times January 2, 1946.

BINGHAM, ALFRED MITCHELL (February 20, 1905-). For autobiographical sketch and list of earlier works and references, see TWENTIETH CENTURY AUTHORS, 1942.

* * *

Alfred M. Bingham writes: "I am now practicing law in Norwich [Conn.]. In the last few years, I have been active in public affairs, locally and in the state, my most recent state position being that of Workmen's Compensation Commissioner, 1950-1952. During World War II, I served two years overseas as a military government officer, terminating with the rank of major.

"Family-wise, I have added one son since your previous biography. My home is still in Salem, which is near Colchester, and uses the Colchester post office."

ADDITIONAL WORKS: The Techniques of Democracy, 1942; The Practice of Idealism, 1944.

BINNS, ARCHIE (July 30, 1899-). For biographical sketch and list of earlier works and references, see TWENTIETH CENTURY AUTHORS, 1942.

* * *

Archie Binns' home is in Menlo Park, Calif. Since 1950 he has been teaching creative writing at the University of Washington, in Seattle. He is married to the former Mollie Windish and they have two daughters.

Binns' two latest novels have again had the Pacific Northwest, a region which he describes with intimate knowledge and lively sympathy, for their backgrounds. His novels have the clean-cut outlines of motion picture scenarios. Milton Hindus said of his *Timber Beast*: "Hollywood scenario writers would be out of their jobs if every novelist composed his work with so unerring an eye for pace, characterization, dialogue, and other apparatus of the profession." His dramatic non-fiction history of the Northwest, *The Sea in the Forest*, is regarded as "the standard history of Puget Sound." Richard L. Neuberger wrote of it that Binns' "fine panoramas of sea and timber and glacial summit excel even the magnificent descriptions written by Viscount Bryce." Binns has also been successful with his books for children. *Radio Imp* was a pleasant sentimental fantasy set in New York's lower East Side, and *Sea Pup* was a lively story of a boy's adventures in the Puget Sound area.

ADDITIONAL WORKS: Timber Beast, 1944; You Rolling River, 1947; The Radio Imp (juvenile) 1950; Sea in the Forest (non-fiction) 1953; Sea Pup (juvenile) 1954.

ABOUT: Warfel, H. R. American Novelists of Today.

BINYON, LAURENCE (August 10, 1869-March 11, 1943). For autobiographical sketch and list of earlier works and references, see TWENTIETH CENTURY AUTHORS, 1942.

* * *

Laurence Binyon died in a nursing home at Reading, England, at seventy-three.

A memorial loan fund to encourage travel, established at Oxford in the poet's name, attests to Binyon's belief "that art and beauty are in the nature of a common language, uniting all nations, accessible to everyone." Ranjee G. Shanhani has declared that India remembers Binyon as "one of our true friends—one who tried to interpret our thought and feeling without prejudices and postjudices," while Basil Gray suggests that "he may in perspective appear the central figure in the period of appreciation of oriental art that has been characteristic of the last fifty years."

Binyon has been described as "at once gentle and brave. He hated cruelty and injustice; but he was always prepared to defend such things as he loved. He refused to recognize any ultimate values except truth, beauty, goodness and holiness." The *Manchester Guardian* assayed his volume of poems *North Star* as "standing well in the English tradition of Wordsworth and Arnold."

ADDITIONAL WORKS: North Star, 1941; Burning of Leaves, 1944; Madness of Merlin, 1947.

ABOUT: Ars Islamica 1946; Asiatic Review January 1947; Atlantic Monthly February 1944; London Times March 11, 1943; New York Times March 11 1943; Poetry April 1943, February 1946; Saturday Review of Literature November 24, 1945.

"BIRMINGHAM, GEORGE A." See HANNAY, J. O.

BIRRELL, AUGUSTINE (January 19, 1850-November 20, 1933). For biographical sketch and list of works and references, see TWENTIETH CENTURY AUTHORS, 1942.

* * *

ABOUT: Dictionary of National Biography 1931-1940.

BISHOP, ELIZABETH (February 8, 1911-), American poet, was born in Worcester, Mass. She attended Walnut Hill School at Natick, Mass., for three years before entering Vassar College from which she was graduated in 1934. She has lived in Nova Scotia and New England, made a walking trip in Newfoundland in 1932 and

from 1935 to 1937 traveled in France, Spain, North Africa, Ireland, and Italy. From 1938 to 1942 she made her home in Key West, Fla., and during 1943 lived in Mexico. She has spent recent summers in Yaddo, Saratoga Springs, N.Y., and her latest journeying has taken her to Brazil.

Joseph Breitenbach

The first volume of her verse, *North and South,* won the Houghton Mifflin Poetry Fellowship award of $1000 in 1945. Publication followed in 1946. She was awarded a Guggenheim Fellowship in 1947 and has served as Consultant in Poetry to the Library of Congress. In April 1951 the first Lucy Martin Donnelly Fellowship, with a grant of $2500, awarded by Bryn Mawr College went to Miss Bishop. She is represented in several anthologies. Recently she has written short stories for the *New Yorker* and elsewhere.

The poems in *North and South* fall into two classes, fantasies and straight descriptive verse, some of it based on the author's experiences in Florida. Marianne Moore wrote in the *Nation*: "At last we have a prize book that has no creditable mannerisms. At last we have someone who knows, who is not didactic." Louise Bogan wrote: "Miss Bishop's poems are not in the least showy. They strike no attitudes and have not an ounce of superfluous emotional weight, and they combine an unforced ironic humor with a naturalist's accuracy of observation."

Miss Bishop is extremely diffident about discussing herself or her work. "No matter what theories one may have," she has written, "I doubt very much that they are in one's mind at the moment of writing a poem. . . . Theories can only be based on interpretation of other poets' poems, or one's own in retrospect, or wishful thinking. The analysis of poetry is growing more and more pretentious and deadly. After a session with a few of the highbrow magazines one doesn't want to look at a poem for weeks, much less start writing one. The situation is reminiscent of those places along the coast where warnings are posted telling one not to walk too near the edge of the cliffs because they have been undermined by the sea and may collapse at any minute. This does not mean that I am opposed to all close analysis and criticism. But I am opposed to making poetry monstrous or boring and proceeding to talk the very life out of it."

The editors of *This Generation*, in a comment on Miss Bishop's poems, remark: "The fact that she has been able to devote herself wholly to her work and to live on a private income in a pleasant home in Key West has not made Miss Bishop eclectic. Instead, she has had time to mature slowly, to escape the mistakes of youth, and to observe closely the events of her own day."

PRINCIPAL WORK: North and South, 1946.

ABOUT: *in* Mid-Century Poets (ed. by John Ciardi); *in* This Generation (ed. by G. K. Anderson and E. L. Walton); Vogue April 1953.

BISHOP, JOHN PEALE (May 21, 1892-April 4, 1944), American poet and essayist, was born in Charles Town, W.Va., the son  of John Peale and Margaret Miller (Cochran) Bishop. His people were mainly Virginians though the family of his paternal grandfather had come from New London, Conn., and his mother's lineage was full of ancient Scotch names. He went to day-school at Hagerstown, Md., to boarding school at Mercersburg, Pa., and to college at Princeton, 1913-17. His father, a physician, had studied art before medicine and taught his son to paint at the age of four. Until he was seventeen he considered painting his lifework.

His first published verse, written at Mercersburg Academy, was published in *Harper's Weekly*, September 12, 1912. At Princeton he was managing editor of the *Nassau Literary Magazine* when Edmund Wilson was editor, succeeding him in the editorship the following year. Wilson reports that he was known to his classmates as one "who lived chiefly for poetry, who took no interest in politics, little in personalities, rarely read history or fiction and did not care to discuss general ideas." But he sold stories and poems to various periodicals and walked off the campus with four literary prizes.

Shortly after graduation he published a volume of verse, *Green Fruit*. During the war he served as first lieutenant of infantry and following the armistice commanded a company guarding 500 German prisoners of war. His war experience was crucial; he was to be haunted by a sense of change and

decay and "the greatness and glory that was France." Upon his return to New York he joined the staff of *Vanity Fair*, soon thereafter becoming its managing editor. While on the magazine he collaborated with Edmund Wilson on *Undertaker's Garland*, a potpourri of verse and prose celebrating death.

In 1922 he married Margaret Grosvenor Hutchins and they went abroad for two years. He lost much of his early *élan*, forgot the Swinburne and Shelley of his college days and echoed Pound and Eliot in his verse. His Italian and French improved; he studied ancient Provençal with the intent of translating the troubadours.

Returning to America in 1924, he was shy about exposing his writing, did not much care for the excitement of the twenties and returned to France in 1927. He bought the Chateau Tressancourt at Orgeval, Seine-et-Oise, forty minutes from Paris, where he lived with his family until 1933. Three sons were born there. In 1931 his first work of prose fiction was published, *Many Thousands Gone*, to be followed in 1935 by his one novel, *Act of Darkness*. His first volume of collected poems, *Now with His Love*, came out in 1933 after his return to America. Settling down with his family at South Harwich, Cape Cod, he entered a new phase in his development. In Europe he had reversed himself; now he read fiction, biography, and history. His new interests were reflected in thoughtful essays, many of them never published until after his death, when *Collected Essays* with an introduction by Edmund Wilson appeared (1948).

Although Bishop was usually associated with John Crowe Ransom, Allen Tate, and Robert Penn Warren as belonging among the poets of the Southern Renaissance, the powerful impression of his days in France kept him from becoming strictly a regional poet. In contrast with the posthumous evaluation of his work, R. P. Blackmur in 1941 judged *Selected Poems* as the work of an occasional poet, an amateur, whose works never reached "a unity of substance or theme or sensibility, as with the full poet whether major or minor." Robert Penn Warren writing of his earlier *Now with His Love* had come to somewhat the same conclusion. But Allen Tate wrote that "he is not a poet of personal moods and idle sensation" but "constantly strives for formal structure," explaining that form meant a coherent framework of moral values. The boldness of his Princeton days gave way in later years to reticence. He was inclined to hold back his work for improvement. In 1941-42 he spent almost a year in New York as director of publishing of the Bureau of Cultural Relations of the Council of National Defense. The violence of his reaction to the fall of France indicated that he had located there "the good society" which he liked to imagine and which had faded from modern Virginia. At the death of his friend and classmate at Princeton, F. Scott Fitzgerald, he wrote an elegy, "The Hours," and seemed launched on a period of creative activity initiating a new phase of his poetry. In 1943 he was offered a post in the Library of Congress by Archibald MacLeish but a leaking heart and other disorders obliged him to return to Cape Cod where he had built a home, "Sea Change," at South Chatham in 1937. There until his death at fifty-one, he continued to work on unfinished poems. He was survived by his wife and three sons.

Edmund Wilson wrote: "The verse of John Peale Bishop is probably the finest poetic instrument that we have had in the United States since Pound and Eliot left. His ear is musically perfect and he is a magician of color and light. He is perhaps the single American poet whose verse is truly sensual." In a summation of his work in *Sewanee Review* Joseph Frank concluded that "he was that rare thing in American literature, a true type of the second-rate writer who, though incapable of supreme literary achievement, keeps alive a sense for the highest values."

Edmund Wilson described him during Princeton days as "something like a Wycherley who had adapted himself to the Nineties," and F. Scott Fitzgerald parodied the young poet, his classmate, as the collegiate literary genius Thomas Parke D'Invilliers in *This Side of Paradise*. In his mature years he might have passed for a well-dressed businessman—his interest in clothes was proverbial from college days—but his eyes were quick, alert and responsive—the eyes of a poet.

Two poets paid tribute to him in verse: Allen Tate in "Seasons of the Soul" in his volume, *The Winter Sea* (1945); Nicholas Moore, in "Aquatic Stag: Poem in Memory of John Peale Bishop," *Sewanee Review* January 1946.

PRINCIPAL WORKS: Green Fruit, 1917; Undertaker's Garland (with Edmund Wilson) 1922; Many Thousands Gone, 1931; Now with His Love, 1933; Act of Darkness, 1935; Minute Particulars, 1935;

Selected Poems, 1941; Collected Essays (with introduction by Edmund Wilson) 1948; Collected Poems (with preface and memoir by Allen Tate) 1948.

ABOUT: Kenyon Review Spring 1942; Nation April 12, 1941; Princeton University Library Chronicle 1946; Sewanee Review January 1947; Wilson Library Bulletin February 1944.

BISHOP, MORRIS GILBERT (April 15, 1893-), American humorist, poet, biographer, writes: "I was born in the Main Building of the Willard (New York) State Hospital for the Insane. My father, Dr. Edwin Rubergall Bishop, was a Canadian; my mother, Bessie E. Gilbert, was the daughter of the Steward of the Willard State Hospital. My mother died when I was a year old, my father when I was eight. I was educated at the Yonkers (N.Y.) High School and Cornell University. At Cornell I was much influenced by Professor Martin Wright Sampson, who inspired the malleable young men in his Manuscript Club to control the wild fancy, to love reason, to laugh at folly. Thus the Cornell School of his time (Frank Sullivan, William Hazlett Upson, E. B. White and others) are friends of wit, lovers of the sharp, shining phrase, foes of spiritual bombast.

"On leaving Cornell in 1914 with an M.A. in Romance Languages, I went to work for Ginn and Company, textbook publishers, in Boston. I served with a Massachusetts cavalry troop on the Mexican border in 1916, attended the first Plattsburg camp in 1917, and went to France as a first lieutenant of infantry. After the armistice I was sent to Finland as a member of the American Relief Administration mission. This was the high point of my career. Reduced to civilian insignificance, I worked for a year for a New York advertising agency and did not like it at all. The work seemed to me intellectual whoredom, and I did not do it very well. In the spring of 1921 I seized an opportunity to teach French and Spanish at Cornell. This was probably the most sensible thing I ever did. Except for leaves of absence, spent abroad, two and a half years' rather bewildered service in the Office of War Information and in Psychological Warfare during the Second War, and a year as

Visiting (Fulbright) Professor of American Life and Civilization at the University of Athens, I have lived in Ithaca, N.Y., happily teaching, reading, and writing. In 1927 I married Alison Mason Kingsbury of Greenwich, Conn. One daughter, Alison.

"I began writing, and publishing in the *St. Nicholas* League, at about ten. In college and afterward I wrote a lot of poetry, some of which was published, even reaching the anthologies. But I had to recognize that I had nothing to say which had not been better said by others. The lyric urge of youth dwindled and died, leaving behind a certain amount of technique, which would serve, I discovered, for light verse. When, badly wounded, I abandoned the business battle, I found that I could sell my little witticisms in verse and prose. So for thirty years I have contributed to the old *Life*, the *Saturday Evening Post,* and the *New Yorker*. Two volumes of my light verse have appeared, and maybe there will be another.

"Though I have done the usual editing and translating and compounding of scholarly articles and bibliographies, and have published a mystery novel under an assumed name, my chief interest has been biography. I have done two full-length studies of explorers, Cabeza de Vaca and Champlain, and three biographies of great French literary men, Pascal, Ronsard, and La Rochefoucauld. There can be few happier occupations that the writing of a biography. For about three years one lives the life of another and greater man; one suffers with him, falls into his errors, gossips with his friends. One comes to know him better than one does one's self. And then he dies; one buries him and weeps him and writes his enormous epitaph. But one survives, and looks about for a new host upon whom to attach one's self."

PRINCIPAL WORKS: Gallery of Eccentrics, 1928; Paramount Poems, 1929; Love Rimes of Petrarch (trans.) 1932; The Odyssey of Cabeza de Vaca, 1933; Pascal: The Life of Genius, 1936; Ronsard, Prince of Poets, 1940; Split Milk, 1942; Champlain, the Life of Fortitude, 1948; The Life and Adventures of La Rochefoucauld, 1951; A Bowl of Bishop, 1954. *As "W. Bolingbroke Johnson"*—The Widening Stain, 1942.

ABOUT: Wilson Library Bulletin April 1943.

BJÖRKMAN, EDWIN AUGUST (October 19, 1866-November 16, 1951). For biographical sketch and list of earlier works and references, see TWENTIETH CENTURY AUTHORS, 1942.

* * *

Edwin Björkman died at eighty-five at his home in Asheville, N.C. His final publication two years before his death was a translation, in collaboration with N. Ericksen, of eight plays by Strindberg.

The novelist, poet, critic, translator and newspaperman wrote "with a refreshing freedom from either sentimentality or swagger," observed the *Dial*, which also praised his "fine perception, artistic restraint, and narrative skill." His "delightful sense of word values and his intellectual sophistication" were noted by the New York *Times.*

ABOUT: New York Times November 17, 1951.

BLACKMUR, RICHARD P. (1904-). For biographical sketch and list of earlier works and references, see TWENTIETH CENTURY AUTHORS, 1942.

* * *

R. P. Blackmur has published two volumes of poetry since 1942 and two volumes of critical essays, *Language as Gesture* and *The Lion and the Honeycomb*. An announced critical biography of Henry Adams and a study of Henry James have not yet appeared. With this relatively small output, Blackmur nevertheless stands as a leading American critic—sound, learned, imaginative. Unlike many of his fellow critics, he has little taste for polemics. For this reason, possibly, he is not so well-known as other less significant critics. On this Blackmur comments modestly: "I believe that it is due to my own defects—of style and sensibility and scope—that my audience is so limited; I have no personal justification for complaint." Students of his works, however, hold Blackmur in the highest esteem. Stanley Edgar Hyman describes him as a critic who combines "wide learning, hard labor, imaginative brilliance, and humble honesty." And R. W. B. Lewis, although objecting that he can be "the most obscure, often the most irritating and superficially one of the least engaging of contemporary critics," nevertheless continues, ". . . he seems to me pretty well assured of being one of the two or three very likely to endure."

Blackmur has been at Princeon University for the past few years, first as a staff member of the Institute for Advanced Study, then as lecturer in the Creative Arts Program under Allen Tate, and more recently as Resident Fellow in Creative Arts. He was abroad in 1952-53.

Correction: The volume "Henry James," listed among Blackmur's principal works, was not published.

ADDITIONAL WORKS: *Poetry*—Second World, 1942; The Good Europeans, and Other Poems, 1947. *Criticism*—Language as Gesture, 1952; The Lion and the Honeycomb, 1955.
ABOUT: Hyman, S. E. The Armed Vision; Kenyon Review Summer 1951.

BLACKWELL, ALICE STONE (September 14, 1857-March 15, 1950). For autobiographical sketch and list of works and references, see TWENTIETH CENTURY AUTHORS, 1942.

* * *

Alice Stone Blackwell died at her home in Cambridge, Mass., after a week's illness, at ninety-two.

In recent years her translations of the work of South American poets, particularly Amado Nervo and Gabriela Mistral (winner of the 1945 Nobel prize for literature), appeared in periodicals. As journalist, translator and lecturer, her work for rights for women, Negroes, workers and the oppressed of other countries continued "almost to the end of her long life," according to the *Nation*, which observed that "her death has ended an amazing career; it also marks the end of an amazing generation."

ABOUT: Nation March 25, 1950; New York Times March 16, 1950.

BLACKWOOD, ALGERNON (1869-December 10, 1951). For autobiographical sketch and list of works and references, see TWENTIETH CENTURY AUTHORS, 1942.

* * *

Algernon Blackwood died in London at eighty-two, after a two-months' illness.

A large selection of his short stories of the supernatural was published in 1949. Toward the end of his life he achieved "an immense reputation" in England as a teller of ghost stories on television, "a role in which he was terrifyingly effective."

The London *Times* observes that it was only now and then that Blackwood, in his supernatural tales, "slipped past the guard of incredulity which ensures a good night's rest even to the habitual reader of ghost stories," but that when he did so "he had his authentic triumphs—more, perhaps, than almost any of his contemporaries. . . . He had a genuinely poetic vein of language and an individual inventive fancy."

ADDITIONAL WORKS: The Doll, and One Other, 1946; Tales of the Uncanny and Supernatural, 1949.
ABOUT: London Times December 11, 1951; New York Times December 11, 1951.

BLAKE, GEORGE (October 28, 1893-). For biographical sketch and list of earlier works and references, see TWENTIETH CENTURY AUTHORS, 1942.

* * *

In his novels and non-fiction of past years George Blake continues to write his sturdy, minutely-observed chronicles of Scottish life. He is most at home in the region around the Clyde River, and his novels set in that area display what a reviewer for the *Times Literary Supplement* calls "an almost Arnold-Bennett-like love of material detail." It is perhaps characteristic of his work that the region is sometimes more richly and successfully portrayed than are his characters. Thus the *Times* comments on his novel *The Westering Sun*: "To the river Mr. Blake brings intuition and love; to the social scene knowledge and sympathy; to the individual man or woman, a somewhat commonplace insight."

One of Blake's recent works of non-fiction was a history of the 52d (Lowland) Division, of which he was a member, from 1940 to 1945—*Mountain and Flood*. Blake lives in Clackmannanshire.

ADDITIONAL WORKS: *Novels*—The Constant Star, 1945; The Westering Sun, 1946; The Five Arches, 1947; The Paying Guest, 1949; The Piper's Tune, 1950; The Voyage Home, 1952. *Non-Fiction*—Mountain and Flood, 1950; Barrie and the Kailyard School, 1951; The Firth of Clyde, 1952.

"BLAKE, NICHOLAS." See DAY LEWIS, C.

BLAKER, RICHARD (March 4, 1893-February 19, 1940). For biographical sketch and list of works and references, see TWENTIETH CENTURY AUTHORS, 1942.

BLAND, Mrs. EDITH (NESBIT). See NESBIT, E.

BLANSHARD, PAUL (August 27, 1892-), American sociologist and journalist, writes: "My writing career has been a series of spasms rather than a lifework. I have always dreamed of full-time writing, but I was never able to find the time and means for the venture until I was past fifty years of age and then I was as much astonished as anyone else with the success of my best-seller books on Roman Catholic policy.

"I was born in Fredericksburg, Ohio, the son of a Congregational minister, Francis  George Blanshard, who had come over from Canada and been naturalized with his wife Emily. My twin brother and I—Brand Blanshard is now professor of philosophy at Yale—grew up in considerable poverty. Our parents died when we were young. We graduated from Detroit Central High School and the University of Michigan, and then went on for graduate work, my brother to Oxford and I to Harvard and Columbia. I studied theology and was ordained a Congregational minister, but soon abandoned my profession simply because I was more interested in social work and the labor movement. Becoming a Socialist under the inspiration of Norman Thomas, I served successively as a labor union organizer and educational director for the Amalgamated Clothing Workers, and as field secretary for the League for Industrial Democracy, the American counterpart of the Fabian Society. I began writing articles for liberal magazines in those days and served for about two years in the late twenties as an associate editor of the *Nation*. Then, when reform impulses started to show themselves in New York City politics, I became executive director of the City Affairs Committee, research director for LaGuardia in his first campaign for mayor, and later New York City Commissioner of Investigations under him for four years.

"Abandoning politics in 1938 I tried desperately to realize my writing dream on a small farm in Alabama which I had inherited from an aunt, but failed in both poetry and fiction. Meanwhile, I had become a lawyer by studying at night and tried practicing for a short time in New York, later serving as director of the Society for the Prevention of Crime. I had by this time written several books on labor and reform, *An Outline of the British Labor Movement*, and (with Norman Thomas) *What's the Matter with New York*. After four years in the State Department during World War II, I wrote *Democracy and Empire in the Caribbean*, and then took the final plunge by retiring to a small farm in Thetford Center, Vt., where I wrote my two books on Catholic policy. In writing the latter of these two, I went to Rome for the Holy Year of 1950

as a representative of the *Nation*. [Blanshard's study of Irish Catholicism, undertaken at the suggestion of an Irish Jesuit scholar, was begun in Dublin, continued in London, and finished in Boston.]

"In spite of three or four careers in politics, the law, etc., my primary interest in life has always been in moral problems, and I hope to devote the rest of my life to writing in philosophical-moral territory. My interest in the Catholic Church sprang partly from a burning moral conviction that birth control was and is one of the world's greatest necessities for the poor, and that the priests are imposing on their subjects a fundamentally immoral rule on that question. Also, I have always been a believer in the public school as the basis of American democracy, and I was drawn into the struggle against Catholic policy largely because of the bishops' mandate against the attendance of Catholic children at public schools."

PRINCIPAL WORKS: An Outline of the British Labor Movement, 1923; What's the Matter with New York (with N. Thomas) 1932; Democracy and Empire in the Caribbean, 1947; American Freedom and Catholic Power, 1949; Communism, Democracy and Catholic Power, 1951; The Irish and Catholic Power, 1953.

ABOUT: O'Neill, J. Catholics and American Freedom; Atlantic Monthly May 1950, August 1951; Newsweek May 21, 1951, June 4, 1951.

* **BLASCO IBÁÑEZ, VICENTE** (January 1867-January 28, 1928). For biographical sketch and list of works and references, see TWENTIETH CENTURY AUTHORS, 1942.

* * *

ABOUT: Balseiro, J. A. Blasco Ibáñez, Unamuno, Valle-Inclán, Baroja: Cuatro Individualistas de España; Columbia Dictionary of Modern European Literature; Flower, Sir N. Just as It Happened; Peers, E. A. St. John of the Cross and Other Lectures.

* bläs'kō ē bä' nyäth

BLIVEN, BRUCE ORMSBY (July 27, 1889-). For biographical sketch and list of earlier works and references, see TWENTIETH CENTURY AUTHORS, 1942.

* * *

Bruce Bliven became editorial director of the *New Republic* (with which he has been associated since 1923) in 1946. From 1927 to 1947 he was New York correspondent of the *Manchester Guardian*. Bliven is primarily a publicist, and his works have been praised as useful, timely, informative, and eminently readable. His recent books have been collections of essays—some his own, some the work of others—on contemporary problems.

ADDITIONAL WORKS: What the Informed Citizen Needs to Know (ed. with A. G. Mezerik) 1945; Twentieth Century Unlimited (ed.) 1950; Preview for Tomorrow, 1953.

BLIXEN, KAREN (DINESEN), Baronesse (1885-). For autobiographical sketch and list of earlier works and references, see TWENTIETH CENTURY AUTHORS, 1942.

* * *

In 1944, during the Nazi occupation of Denmark, a novel by one "Pierre Andrézel" was published in Copenhagen under the title *Ways of Retribution* and became a best seller. To the German censors it was apparently a typical Gothic romance, an old-fashioned story, hair-raising but harmless. After the war the book was published in the United States as *The Angelic Avengers*, and careful readers recognized beneath the melodramatic lines of the story a subtle symbolism and an unmistakable parallel between the innocent-appearing but thoroughly corrupted villain of the novel and the Nazi conquerors of Denmark. With the war over, there was no longer any need for disguise, and "Pierre Andrézel" was revealed to be the Baroness Blixen of Rungstedlund, or "Isak Dinesen" as she is better known. Under the latter pen name she continues to write her deliciously diabolic tales. Her most recent short stories have appeared in America in the *Saturday Evening Post* and the *Ladies' Home Journal*.

ADDITIONAL WORKS: As "Pierre Andrézel"—The Angelic Avengers, 1947.

ABOUT: Claudi, J. Contemporary Danish Authors; Saturday Evening Post December 10, 1949.

BLOCH, JEAN-RICHARD (May 25, 1884-March 15, 1947). For biographical sketch and list of works and references, see TWENTIETH CENTURY AUTHORS, 1942.

* * *

Jean-Richard Bloch died in Paris at sixty-two and was buried at Père Lachaise.

At the time of his death he was a member of the Upper House of the French legislature, and a director of the Communist newspaper *Ce Soir*, which he had helped to found in 1937. After World War II he was among those who urged that the death sentence for Marshel Pétain be carried out. He held the Croix de Guerre and the rank of Officer of the Legion of Honor.

Upon the announcement of the dropping of the first atomic bomb, Bloch reaffirmed his humanism in an article in *Ce Soir* (reprinted in this country in *Poetry*) in which he said, "Let us not forget that the human spirit remains untouched by the atom bomb. . . . Man remains the supreme value, the value which is the beginning and the end of all creation."

Bloch was "not perhaps one of the most original talents of his generation," in the opinion of the *Saturday Review of Literature*, "and yet by reason of his strength and sanity of outlook [he] will be understood and welcomed beyond most of his contemporaries." The same journal has characterized him as "a writer who possesses a deep insight into human character and a rare ability to trace the sociological factors by which human destinies are swayed." René Lalou believes that "if they were arranged to retrace, step by step, his own itinerary, his collected essays would form a panorama of the spiritual life of France during a quarter of a century."

ABOUT: New York Times March 16, 1947.

BLOK, ALEXANDR ALEXANDRO-VICH (1880-August 9, 1921). For biographical sketch and list of works and references, see TWENTIETH CENTURY AUTHORS, 1942.

* * *

ADDITIONAL WORKS IN ENGLISH TRANSLATION: Song of Fate (n.d.); Spirit of Music, 1946.

ABOUT: Columbia Dictionary of Modern European Literature; Gorky, M. Reminiscences; Snow, V. Russian Writers; Yarmolinsky, A. (ed.) A Treasury of Russian Verse; Russian Review January 1953.

BLUNDEN, EDMUND CHARLES (November 1, 1896-). For biographical sketch and list of earlier works and references, see TWENTIETH CENTURY AUTHORS, 1942.

* * *

Edmund Blunden was on the staff of the Oxford University Senior Training Corps from 1940 to 1944. He was sent to Tokyo in 1948 as a member of the United Kingdom Liaison Commission and was elected an honorary member of the Japan Academy. In 1945 he married Claire Margaret Poynting.

In an evaluation of Blunden's later poetry, Hugh I'Anson Fausset admits that there is some truth to the prevailing attitude that he "has failed to come to grips with contemporary reality and is for that reason inevitably only a minor poet. . . ." His poetry lacks the fever and the dynamic force of the times, but out of that lack emerges its beauty, its tranquility, and its integrity. Fausset writes: "He does not stand between two worlds, one dead, one struggling to be born, but in a world of his own, secure and at peace, though tempests rage without or its tranquil air quivers now and then at the thud of distant explosions."

One of the most important of Blunden's recent works is his biography of Shelley which displayed, most reviewers agreed, a happy combination of poetic sympathy and sound scholarship.

ADDITIONAL WORKS: Thomas Hardy, 1942; Romantic Poetry and the Fine Arts, 1942; Cricket Country, 1944; Shells by a Stream: New Poems, 1945; Shelley, 1946; Selected Poems, 1947; After the Bombing, and Other Short Poems, 1949; Sons of Light, 1949; Selected Poetry and Prose (ed. K. Hopkins) 1951.

ABOUT: Church, R. B. Eight for Immortality; Ensor, R. C. K. *Introduction to* Selected Poems of E. Blunden; Fausset, H. I. Poets and Pundits; Nineteenth Century June 1941.

*BOAS, FRANK (July 9, 1858-December 21, 1942), German-American anthropologist, was born at Minden, Westphalia, the  son of M. and Sophie Meyer Boas. He studied at the universities of Heidelberg and Bonn from 1877 to 1881, and received his Ph.D. from Kiel University the following year. His keen interest in geography led to his joining an expedition to the Arctic in 1883. It was then he decided to take up anthropology as his lifework, and he spent a year in a small Eskimo settlement in Baffin Land. Upon his return he was appointed assistant at the Royal Ethnological Museum in Berlin and also docent of geography at the University of Berlin.

In 1886 he left Germany to conduct ethnological investigations among the Indians of British Columbia for the British Association for the Advancement of Science. His first academic position in this country was as docent of anthropology at Clark University from 1888 to 1892. He was appointed chief assistant of the Department of Anthropology at the Chicago Exposition, 1892-95, and in 1896 went to Columbia University where he became first professor of anthro-

* bō'ăs

pology in 1899 and held that position until his retirement in 1936. From 1936 to 1938 he was professor emeritus in residence at Columbia and emeritus following 1938.

A pioneer in the study of the effect of social and environmental conditions on race physique and of the results of racial crossing, his written works began with *The Growth of Children.* His special field of interest was the "race question." Even before the First World War he was debunking the "blond superman" and exposing what he called "this Nordic nonsense." When Hitler came to power in the Germany that had previously heaped academic honors upon Dr. Boas his books were among the first to be burned in 1933, but the underground continuously circulated his articles and letters.

For some time before his death he had been working on a study of the Kwakiutl Indians of Vancouver Island whose history and characteristics he had been studying for more than fifty years. His expeditions in this region resulted in many treatises, among which are *The Social Organization and Secret Societies of the Kwakiutl Indians, Contributions to the Ethnology of the Kwakiutl,* and *The Religion of the Kwakiutl.*

His retirement from academic duties accelerated his activity in the political field in behalf of intellectual freedom and democratic equality. He believed that it was not possible to keep one's scientific knowledge from influencing one's attitude and actions in the world of affairs and was outspoken against all abrogation of civil liberties and against conditions in the school system which limit intellectual freedom. For forty years he worked to further cultural understanding between the United States and the Far East, between the United States and Latin America.

Dr. Boas was honorary philologist of the Bureau of Ethnology from 1901 to 1919. He was corresponding secretary of the Germanistic Society of America and member or fellow of the following societies or associations: American Academy of Sciences; American Philosophical Society; American Antiquarian Society; American Folklore Society, of which he was editor for seventeen years and president in 1931; American Association for the Advancement of Science (vice-president in 1895 and 1897 and president in 1931); New York Academy of Sciences (president 1910); American Anthropological Society (president 1907-1908); American Academy of Arts and Sciences.

He was corresponding member of societies in Berlin, Brussels, Florence, Moscow, Paris, Rome, Stockholm, and Washington.

Besides his books and treatises Dr. Boas wrote numerous studies dealing with the fundamental problems of anthropology. Sixty-two of his most important papers are collected in the volume *Race, Language and Culture*. Many of the theses presented here were basic in the development of anthropology during a period of forty years. He was a frequent contributor to magazines and newspapers.

Dr. Boas married Marie A. E. Krackowizer in 1887. She was killed in an automobile accident in 1929. Recognized as one of the world's leading authorities on the study of man and his inheritance, he was active to the day of his death when at the age of eighty-four he died of a heart attack during luncheon at the Men's Faculty Club of Columbia University. He was survived by a son, Dr. Ernest P. Boas, assistant professor of clinical medicine at Columbia University, and two daughters, Mrs. Helene Marie Yampolsky and Mrs. Marie Franziska Michelson.

From his early training in physics and mathematics, Franz Boas brought to the social sciences a mind sensitive to the necessity of framing scientific questions so that they could be answered by investigation, and a conviction that most problems needed new, first-hand investigation, and could not be answered by mere examination of stale, existing knowledge. By pressing forward in the social sciences on the basis of these rules, he laid the foundations for modern anthropology and was himself responsible for many of its greatest achievements.

In a summation of his life and work, Dr. Ruth Benedict wrote in the *Nation*: "All his studies of other cultures reinforced his conviction that cultural differences are vital and valuable. He believed the world must be made safe for differences. . . . He had an incomparable right to the title of elder statesman in science, yet he evoked more enthusiasm from the younger generation than from those closer to him in years. At eighty-four he had not sold out, or stultified himself, or locked himself in a dogmatic cage. He had set a standard of intensive scientific work in all fields of anthropology which no student could hope to match."

PRINCIPAL WORKS: The Growth of Children, 1896; The Mind of Primitive Man, 1911; Primitive Art, 1927; Anthropology and Modern Life, 1928; General Anthropology (ed.) 1938; Race, Language and Culture, 1940.

ABOUT: Herskovits,M. J. Franz Boas; American Historical Review April 1943; American Journal of Sociology March 1943; Current Biography 1943; Encyclopedia of American History; Nation January 2, 1943; New York Times December 22, 1942; Science April 9, 1943.

BODENHEIM, MAXWELL (May 26, 1893-February 6, 1954). For biographical sketch and list of earlier works and references, see TWENTIETH CENTURY AUTHORS, 1942.

* * *

Maxwell Bodenheim and his third wife, Ruth Fagen (whom he is said to have married in 1952, two years after the death of his second wife, Grace Finan), were found murdered in the dingy fifth floor furnished room of one Harold Weinberg, on the fringes of New York City's Bowery. Weinberg, who had once been an inmate of a mental hospital, was arrested and confessed to the crime. He was declared insane.

In the last years of his life Bodenheim had been reduced to begging in the streets and peddling manuscripts of his poems in Greenwich Village bars. In 1952 he was arrested for sleeping in a New York subway and charged with vagrancy. Funeral arrangements for the penniless poet were made by his first wife, Minna, and a colleague of his early literary days, Ben Hecht. At the funeral services the poet Alfred Kreymborg eulogized Bodenheim as a modern-day Edgar Allan Poe or Heinrich Heine and said, "He was a great lover and wit. We need not worry about the future. He will be read."

ADDITIONAL WORKS: Lights in the Valley, 1942; Selected Poems, 1914-44, 1946; My Life and Loves in Greenwich Village (autobiography) 1954.

ABOUT: New York Times February 8, 1954; Poetry July 1942.

BODKIN, MAUD (1875-   ), British scholar and critic, writes, "I was born in the quiet country town, as it then was, of Chelmsford, Essex. There my father, having left his family home in Ulster, carried on his medical practice, and my mother, partly relieved of the care of her family by the help of the domestic service then obtainable, devoted herself to charitable works in connection with her congregational church.

"To the services of this church we children were taken from a tender age, though none of us, to my mother's grief, cared to join it. My father had little sympathy with my mother's outlook and spent his leisure mainly in reading contemporary and recent works of philosophy. Though I did not at the time make much response consciously to the expressed views of either of my parents, I have thought lately, turning  the much marked and many times re-read pages of my father's copy of William James' *Varieties of Religious Experience,* that my life's quest has been, perhaps, a continuation of his.

Lionel Wood.

"In my recent book *Studies of Type Images,* I have spoken of the effect on my mind of the study at college of the *Dialogues* of Plato. The other main influence felt at this time was that of William James, coming to me from both his psychological and philosophic writings. When, on leaving college, I began work as a lecturer in a training college in Cambridge, I thought of my task mainly as an attempt to bring such psychological thinking as that of James, at once empirical and speculative, within reach of young minds often without much inclination or capacity for psychological thought of any kind.

"While still holding this teaching post I was granted a year's leave to visit America to study there methods of teaching educational psychology. Though during this visit I received much kindness and encouragement, I remained troubled by the difficulty of bringing psychology, as I understood it, into helpful relation with the work of the schools and, influenced partly by declining health, decided on early retirement to devote myself to literary and philosophic studies.

"For some years I made a particular study—with medical help in relation to my own experience—of the psychology of Dr. C. G. Jung; and his hypothesis concerning the power upon the mind of archetypes present in poetry became the starting point of my first book. The center of my own interest, however, has never been so much in the distinctive theories of Jung as in the thought—more fully developed in my latest book—that there are in our whole literary and philosophic, as well as in our religious heritage, deeply rooted images and patterns of thought which we may regard as God-given, and as offering, to those of us who cannot accept as uniquely revealed the dogmas of any religion, some clues to life's meaning."

* * *

Stanley Edgar Hyman writes in *The Armed Vision*: "It is Maud Bodkin's distinction to have made what is probably the best use to date of psychoanalysis in literary criticism." He points out that her emphasis has rightly been upon the work of art itself rather than upon the pathology of the artist and that by so extending its limits, "she has furnished psychological criticism with endless vistas." Miss Bodkin has neither sought nor received widespread recognition of her work, but it remains a solid achievement in contemporary literary criticism.

PRINCIPAL WORKS: Archetypal Patterns in Poetry, 1934; The Quest for Salvation in an Ancient and a Modern Play, 1941; Studies of Type Images in Poetry, 1951.

ABOUT: Day Lewis, C. The Poetic Image; Hyman, S. E. The Armed Vision; Folk-Lore March 1935; Hibbert Journal January 1952; Life and Letters January 1935; Theology December 1951.

BOGAN, LOUISE (August 11, 1897-   ). For biographical sketch and list of earlier works and references, see TWENTIETH CENTURY AUTHORS, 1942.

* * *

Louise Bogan was Fellow in American Letters at the Library of Congress in 1944, and from 1945 to 1946 she had the Chair of Poetry there. She has been visiting lecturer in poetry at the University of Washington and at the University of Chicago. In 1948 she won the Harriet Monroe Poetry Award. She contributes verse to *Poetry,* the *Nation,* the *New Yorker,* and other periodicals. Her "bright and terse" reviews of current poetry for the *New Yorker* have been called "the only sustained criticism of modern poetry that the general reader can follow."

In 1951 Miss Bogan contributed a volume on the history of American poetry from 1900 to 1950 to the Twentieth-Century Literature in America series. Within the limits of this small volume she compressed a formidable amount of factual and critical material. Milton Crane wrote that the book was "full of acute, spirited, and authoritative judgments of writers and works, expressed with grace and wit." In 1954 a collection of her poems written over the past three decades was published. This volume, Richard Eberhart wrote in the New York *Times,* gives the reader for the first time the full dimension of her talent. "The feeling is of somber strength, of a strong nature controlling powerful emotions by highly conscious art. There is marked skill in her restraint. Her best poems read as if time would not be likely to break them down."

Miss Bogan was co-winner (with Léonie Adams) of the 1954 Bollingen prize in poetry for her *Collected Poems*.

ADDITIONAL WORKS: Achievement in American Poetry, 1900-1950, 1951; Collected Poems, 1954.

BOILEAU, ETHEL (YOUNG), Lady (1882?-January 16, 1942). For biographical sketch and list of works and references, see TWENTIETH CENTURY AUTHORS, 1942.

* * *

ADDITIONAL WORK: Challenge to Freedom (with M. Baxter-Ellis) 1947.

* BOJER, JOHAN (March 6, 1872-). For autobiographical sketch and list of works and references, see TWENTIETH CENTURY AUTHORS, 1942.

* * *

Johan Bojer lives near Oslo, Norway. He is still writing, and his latest novel, *Skyld,* was published in 1948. None of his works has been translated into English since 1940. In a fairly recent evaluation of Bojer's achievement, Einar Haugen pointed out that his work lacks great depth and power. But, he adds: "His appeal lies in his humanism, his kindliness, and that undogmatic religion which fills his best characters with an abiding faith in the glory of hard work and the mysterious power of love."

ABOUT: Columbia Dictionary of Modern European Literature.

* boi′ĕr

BOK, EDWARD WILLIAM (October 9, 1863-January 9, 1930). For biographical sketch and list of works and references, see TWENTIETH CENTURY AUTHORS, 1942.

* * *

ABOUT: Morris, L. R. Postscript to Yesterday.

* BOLITHO, HECTOR (1898-): For autobiographical sketch and list of earlier works and references, see TWENTIETH CENTURY AUTHORS, 1942.

* * *

Since the end of World War II, Hector Bolitho has given some 130 lectures in the United States. He has written a number of books on British history and the British monarchy. In the winter of 1951-52 he went

* bō li′thō

to Pakistan to write the official biography of Mohammed Ali Jinnah, creator of the young Moslem state. He gave up the plan, the New York *Times* reported, when a split of opinion developed in Pakistan over the propriety of having the book done by a foreigner.

Bolitho has not yielded to his earlier temptation to settle in California: instead, he has made his home in the The Close, Salisbury, England. He explains the change of mind by saying: "I am too old to uproot myself and settle in America. My habits are too fixed for the adventure into a new world —I realize this now. America is for the young, who are restless with ambition. At fifty a man is no longer restless or ambitious —that is, if he has learned anything on the way. But I still believe that the only hope for the world is in the close relationship and unsuspicious sympathy between the British and American peoples."

With reference to the sketch in TWENTIETH CENTURY AUTHORS, Mr. Bolitho comments to the editors: "If you knew the truth about the Abdication, and if you read my book, you would not accuse me of an 'abrupt change' from adulation to criticism of the Duke of Windsor."

ADDITIONAL WORKS: War in the Strand, 1942; Combat Report, 1943; Command Performance, 1946; The Romance of Windsor Castle, 1946; The British Empire (ed.) 1948; The Reign of Queen Victoria, 1948; A Biographer's Notebook, 1950; A Century of British Monarchy, 1951; Their Majesties, 1951.

ABOUT: Bolitho, H. Command Performance.

BOLITHO, WILLIAM (1890-June 2, 1930). For biographical sketch and list of works and references, see TWENTIETH CENTURY AUTHORS, 1942.

"BOLTON, ISABEL." See MILLER, M. B.

BONE, Sir DAVID WILLIAM (1874-). For biographical sketch and list of earlier works and references, see TWENTIETH CENTURY AUTHORS, 1942.

* * *

Sir David Bone was knighted in 1946. Three years earlier he had been named Commander of the Order of the British Empire. He is retired Master Mariner, Commodore of the Anchor Line, and lives in Glasgow.

ADDITIONAL WORKS: Merchantman Rearmed, 1949; The Queerfella, 1952.

BONSAL, STEPHEN (March 29, 1865-June 8, 1951), American historian and journalist, was born in Baltimore, Md., son of Stephen Bonsal, a wealthy coffee importer and shipowner, and Frances (Leigh) Bonsal. He attended St. Paul's School in New Hampshire and studied at the universities of Heidelberg, Bonn, and Vienna, specializing in German and Italian literature.  Edward Burks

Soon after his return to the United States a portion of the Bonsal family fortune was wiped out in a horse race. He then turned to journalism for a career and joined the staff of the New York *Herald* as a reporter.

As a newspaperman Bonsal covered virtually every news event from the Bulgarian-Serbian War of 1888 to World War I. Along with Richard Harding Davis and Arthur Brisbane he was tagged one of the "Three Musketeers of New York journalism." In 1887 he became a foreign correspondent for the *Herald* and subsequently traveled over much of Europe, Asia, South America, and Africa. He left the *Herald* briefly in 1893 after a dispute with its famous owner, James Gordon Bennett, and entered the United States diplomatic service, serving in the legations in Madrid, Peking, and Tokyo. Meanwhile, the quarrel with the *Herald* was patched up, and Bonsal reported some of the major news events of the next few years—the Sino-Japanese War in 1894-95, the Cuban insurrection of 1897, and the Spanish-American War.

In the first years of the twentieth century Bonsal continued to cover uprisings, revolutions and wars all over the world. In 1913 and 1914 he was in the Philippines, first as secretary to the Governor General, then as commissioner of public utilities. He went to Germany in 1915 to report on the progress of General von Hindenberg's army on the East Front. At the invitation of Colonel Edward House, President Wilson's aide and representative to Europe during this period, Bonsal became an interpreter, sitting in on important conferences with German political leaders. When the United States entered the war, he was commissioned a major in the A.E.F. in France. After the armistice, he was on the scene during all of the secret meetings of the "Big Four"—Wilson, Clemenceau, Lloyd George, and Orlando—acting as confidential interpreter for Wilson and House.

The notes which Bonsal took on these negotiations were the only eye-witness reports of them, since no official stenographic records were made. For many years Bonsal refused to publish them on the grounds that this "might be indiscreet on the part of a professional writer who had been given access to confidential information." It was not until 1944, under the pressure of friends who urged him to publish because "we were beginning to repeat the same mistakes that led to the tragedy of Versailles," that Bonsal released them in *Unfinished Business.* The great value of his material as source history was immediately recognized by readers of the book. Allan Nevins commented that "a more timely book than this could hardly be imagined." Bonsal wrote, the *New Yorker* said, with "a sharp reporter's eye, an excellent sense of selection, the ability to tell a story, and something of the historian's objective point of view." For this volume he received the 1944 Pulitzer prize in history.

Bonsal continued his account of post-war negotiations and of the Paris Peace Conference of 1918-1919 in another book, *Suitors and Suppliants.* He also continued, until his very last years, to take an active part in movements for world peace, attending conferences in Europe and at the United Nations in New York. Until his last years, too, he contributed many articles and short stories to magazines. He was married in 1900 to Henrietta Fairfax Morris and had four sons. The Bonsals lived in the Georgetown section of Washington, D.C., and it was there that he died at the age of eighty-six.

PRINCIPAL WORKS: The Real Condition of Cuba, 1897; The Fight for Santiago, 1899; The Golden Horseshoe (ed.) 1900; The American Mediterranean, 1912; Edward Fitzgerald Beale, 1822-1903, 1912; Heydey in a Vanished World (autobiography) 1937; Unfinished Business, 1944; When the French Were Here, 1945; Suitors and Suppliants, 1946.

ABOUT: Bonsal, S. Heyday in a Vanished World; Collier's January 4, 1947; Current Biography 1945; Saturday Review of Literature June 1, 1946.

BONSELS, WALDEMAR (February 21, 1881-August 1, 1952). For biographical sketch and list of works and references, see TWENTIETH CENTURY AUTHORS, 1942.

* * *

Waldemar Bonsels died at his home at Lake Starnberg, near Munich, Germany, at seventy-one.

No new work of his had appeared for several years, but a new edition of his widely popular *The Adventures of Maya the Bee* was published in English translation the year before his death. Victor Lange, who finds in this and in Bonsels' other entomological fantasies "an incredibly sentimental gospel of love for nature, for a vaguely conceived God, and for his fellow beings," found more value in "his earliest books ... in which the supernatural and German folk themes are happily fused."

ABOUT: Columbia Dictionary of Modern European Literature; New York Times August 2, 1952.

BOOTHE, CLARE (Mrs. HENRY ROBINSON LUCE) (April 10, 1903-).
For biographical sketch and list of earlier works and references, see TWENTIETH CENTURY AUTHORS, 1942.

* * *

In February 1953 Clare Boothe Luce was appointed Ambassador to Italy by President Dwight D. Eisenhower. She is the second woman ambassador in American history and the first assigned to a major world power. The prelude to Mrs. Luce's appointment was a long and lively political career which she began in 1940 when she worked for the election of the Republican candidate, Wendell L. Willkie. Her candidate was defeated, but Mrs. Luce's enthusiasm for politics was not dampened. She was elected to Congress in 1942 as a Representative from Connecticut. In her first speech on the floor of Congress she captured the headlines with a sharp attack on the then Vice President Henry A. Wallace's proposals for establishing freedom of the air for all nations, characterizing the plan with the epithet "globaloney." Mrs. Luce held the headlines consistently during the remainder of her two terms in Congress.

In 1946 Mrs. Luce withdrew from political life. In that same year she entered the Roman Catholic Church, and since then most of her writing—including magazine articles, a film scenario *Come to the Stable*, and a play *Child of the Morning*—has been on religious subjects. She returned to politics in 1952. After an unsuccessful attempt to win the Republican nomination for United States Senator from Connecticut, she began to campaign actively for General Eisenhower.

Mrs. Luce assumed her duties in Italy in April 1953. Her home in America is in Ridgefield, Conn. Her only daughter, Ann

Brokaw, was killed in an automobile accident in California in 1944.

ADDITIONAL WORKS: Twilight of God (essay) 1949; Saints for Now (ed.) 1952

ABOUT: Harriman, M. C. Take Them Up Tenderly; Henle, F. Au Clare de Luce; Hoehn, M. (ed.) Catholic Authors, I; American Scholar January 1948; Collier's March 27, 1943; Current Biography 1953; New Republic August 28, 1943; Saturday Evening Post July 17, 1947; Time September 1, 1942, August 26, 1946, February 16, 1953.

*BORDEAUX, HENRY (January 29, 1870-).
For biographical sketch and list of earlier works and references, see TWENTIETH CENTURY AUTHORS, 1942.

* * *

Henry Bordeaux lives in Paris. In 1950 he became dean of elections of the French Academy. After a long period of silence, during which Bordeaux was all but forgotten by many readers, a new novel appeared in 1953—*A Pathway to Heaven*. It was in all respects a typical Bordeaux novel—pleasant, warm, devout, facile. "He belongs to a bygone generation," Laurence LeSage wrote, "that produced idealistic and moralizing novels for the delectation of the high bourgeoisie and preached an arch-conservative social program based upon church, home, and fatherland."

ADDITIONAL WORK IN ENGLISH TRANSLATION: A Pathway to Heaven, 1953.

ABOUT: Columbia Dictionary of Modern European Literature; Dictionnaire Biographique Français Contemporain; Hoehn, M. (ed.) Catholic Authors, I; Saturday Review March 7, 1953.

* bôr dō'

BORDEN, MARY (1886-).
For biographical sketch and list of earlier works and references, see TWENTIETH CENTURY AUTHORS, 1942.

* * *

In World War II, Mary Borden conducted a mobile hospital unit in France, Syria, Tobruk, Cairo, and the Middle East, and her husband, Sir Edward Spears, headed the British Mission to General de Gaulle. She wrote an account of their wartime experiences in *Journey Down a Blind Alley*. As a novelist Miss Borden remains a writer of considerable depth and seriousness whose works, while perhaps not distinguished by "brilliance of imagination," have solid merit. *Catspaw*, a study of a prince of a small European state who discovers that he has been used by the Communists, was hailed by Richard Sullivan as "the best, the soundest, the most illuminating novel about Communism I've read since Koestler's classic *Darkness at Noon." You, the Jury,* the story of an idealist who tries, with tragic results, to follow literally the teachings of Christ in modern-day England, was a strange and uneven novel, interesting mainly for a skillfully handled trial scene. It sold widely in England and was a Book-of-the-Month Club selection in the United States.

Miss Borden lives in Berkshire. In the fall of 1952 she visited the United States where her nephew-by-marriage, Adlai Stevenson, was then Democratic nominee for President of the United States.

ADDITIONAL WORKS: Journey Down a Blind Alley, 1946; Number 2 Shovel Street, 1949; Catspaw (in England: For the Record) 1950; You, the Jury (in England: Martin Merriedew) 1952; Margin of Error, 1954.

ABOUT: Borden, M. Journey Down a Blind Alley; New York Herald Tribune Book Review October 8, 1950.

*BORGESE, GIUSEPPE ANTONIO (November 12, 1882-December 4, 1952). For autobiographical sketch and list of earlier works and references, see TWENTIETH CENTURY AUTHORS, 1942.

* * *

Giuseppe Borgese died suddenly, ·at the age of seventy, of a cerebral thrombosis, in Fiesole, Italy. He is survived by his wife, Elizabeth Mann Borgese, and two daughters from this marriage, Angelica and Dominica.

Shortly after his death, Mrs. Borgese wrote of her husband to the editors of this volume: "His last American years, 1946-1951, were dedicated to the purpose of world unity in the political sense. In 1946 he founded, in intimate cooperation with Chancellor Robert M. Hutchins, Professor Mortimer Adler, and Professor Robert Redfield, the Committee to Frame a World Constitution at the University of Chicago, which, after two years' labor, published, as a collective work, *A Preliminary Draft of a World Constitution* (1948). The Chancellor relieved him of all his teaching duties, and he dedicated his full time to this effort, as Secretary General of the Committee and as Director of its monthly publication, *Common Cause.* A philosophical work, *The Foundations of the World Republic,* was completed in manuscript before Mr. Borgese left the United States.

"From 1951 on Mr. Borgese worked under a Ford grant on the preparation of

* bōr jä'sä

another philosophical work, tentatively entitled *Hagia Sophia.* It was to be a reinterpretation of Christianity in the light of modern science and the philosophy of one world. Of this book there are only notes and small fragments extant.

"Mr. Borgese had been 'reintegrated' as Professor of Aesthetics at the University of Milan and resumed his classes there. His collected works, in thirty volumes, are now being published by Mondadori in Milan."

ADDITIONAL WORKS: The City of Man (with H. Agar and others) 1940; Common Cause, 1943; Foundation of the World Republic, 1953.

ABOUT: Columbia Dictionary of Modern European Literature; Current Biography 1947; Newsweek July 14, 1947; New York Times December 5, 1952; Poetry April 1953; Saturday Review of Literature July 21, 1951; Sewanee Review January 1942.

BOTKIN, BENJAMIN ALBERT (February 7, 1901-   ), American folklorist, writes: "I was born in East Boston (Noddle Island), Mass., the younger of two sons of Albert and Annie (Dechinick) Botkin. I know very little of my parents' background, except that they had come to America from Vilna (then in Lithuania) and that my father's name had originally

Viola Kantrowitz

been Rabotnik (worker). (This is my answer to the many Botkins of Irish and English extraction who have written to ask if I am related to them). My father, a barber and something of a student and teacher himself, taught me to read and write before I started to school at four-and-a-half, in Quincy. Since we moved almost every time he moved his shop I never sank my roots in any one of our four home towns (which included Everett), unless it was Dorchester, where I lived nine years, through graduation from grammar school, high school, and college. During my four years at Harvard (1916-1920), I commuted and saw little of college life outside of classes and the library, and developed little college spirit, except a profound sense of obligation to my teachers—'Copey,' 'Kitty,' John L. Lowes, and Byron S. Hurlbut, under the last of whom I wrote my first extensive work, an autobiographical 'Story of a Boy.' I earned a scholarship each year and worked summers as Railway Express sheet writer, Massachusetts General Hospital floor boy, wholesale drug house dumb-waiter operator, and restaurant cashier. I first broke into print in high school and college magazines, Boston newspaper 'columns,' and the *Stratford Journal.*

"From Boston I went to New York in 1920 to take my master's degree in English at Columbia, working under John Erskine, Brander Matthews, and Carl Van Doren. My master's essay on the Manx poet, Thomas Edward Brown, was probably my introduction to folklore. My folklore activity, like my education, really began, however, when in 1921, through a teachers' agency, I was appointed instructor in English at the University of Oklahoma. After two years of teaching and taking part in the campus and state poetry boom and a summer working and hitchhiking on the West Coast, I returned to New York. Here for two years I took (and cut) classes at Columbia, worked sporadically in a cramming school and around settlement houses, taught English to foreigners, saw as many plays as I could, hitchhiked to Battle Creek, Mich., and drifted in and out of rooming houses and my brother's art studio. In 1925, on a visit to Quincy, I met and married Gertrude Fritz, a music teacher.

"Back at the University, I began collecting folklore among students and townspeople and became identified with the Southwest 'renascence' as founder and editor of an annual, *Folk-Say* (1929-32), a monthly 'little magazine,' *Space* (1934-35), contributing editor of the *Southwest Review,* and a book reviewer for the Sunday *Oklahoman.* In 1930-31 I taught at the University of Nebraska, where I took my doctorate in English and anthropology under Louise Pound in 1931. In the summers of 1932 and 1933 I taught and took part in writers' conferences in Montana and New Mexico and toured the Northwest and Southwest in our 1932 'Chevvie.' In 1934 and 1937 our daughter and our son were born, and we made several car trips back East. During this Oklahoma period (which closed officially with my resignation from the university in 1940), I contributed articles on regionalism and folklore to regional, little, and professional magazines and attended a good many regional and national conferences.

"In 1937 I went to Washington on a Rosenwald fellowship to do research at the Library of Congress in Southern folk and regional literature. From 1938 to 1941 I was national folklore editor of the Federal Writers Project (also co-founder and chair-man of the Joint Committee on Folk Arts, WPA) and chief editor of the Writers' Unit of the Library of Congress Project. In 1941, under Archibald MacLeish, I became Library of Congress Fellow in Folklore and in 1942 head of the Library's Archive of American Folk Song. In 1945, having published *A Treasury of American Folklore* (1944) and while serving as president of the American Folklore Society, I resigned from the Library and moved to Croton-on-Hudson to devote full time to writing and editing, with occasional field trips and lectures on the side. In 1946 I became a contributing editor of the *New York Folklore Quarterly,* for which I began writing a regular column in 1950. In 1951 I began work on a study of contemporary folklore on a Guggenheim fellowship.

"My writing has been more or less incidental to my work as teacher, editor, and collector. The word *folk-say* (which I coined in 1928) sums up the two phases of my interest—collecting and compiling what people have to say about themselves, especially in their own words, and interpreting America through its basic oral culture, popular fantasy, folkways, symbols, and myths. In each period my development has been marked as much by unlearning a good deal of what I had previously learned as by breaking new ground or experimenting with new ways of reconciling my scholarly and creative interests, the local and the universal."

PRINCIPAL WORKS: *Editor*—Folk-Say, 1929, 1930, 1931, 1932; The American Play-Party Song, 1937; A Treasury of American Folklore, 1944; Lay My Burden Down, 1945; A Treasury of New England Folklore, 1947; A Treasury of Southern Folklore, 1949; A Treasury of Western Folklore, 1951; A Treasury of Railroad Folklore (with A. F. Harlan) 1953; Sidewalks of America, 1954.

ABOUT: New York Post May 4, 1944.

*BOTTOME, PHYLLIS (May 31, 1884-). For biographical sketch and list of earlier works and references, see TWENTIETH CENTURY AUTHORS, 1942.

* * *

Some of Phyllis Bottome's most interesting writings in recent years have been the two volumes of intensely revealing and detailed autobiography, *Search for a Soul* and *The Challenge.* Her novelist's talent for depicting subtle human relationships, combined with her interest in Adlerian psychology, have produced sensitive and objective auto-

* bŏ tŏm'

biography which one reviewer described as "certainly one of the most remarkable self-revelations made by a living novelist." Miss Bottome's fiction continues to show the competence and craftsmanship of an experienced practitioner. Her wartime novel *Survival*, like her earlier *Private Worlds*, has a psychoanalyst for its hero and is sprinkled with the influence of (as well as quotations from) Alfred Adler. In the five stories in *Man and Beast*, Miss Bottome made fresh use of her knowledge of psychology. The suspense of each story is supplied "by crisis or tragedy in the relationships between man and animal." Edmund Fuller called them "psychological tales equally penetrating with both the human and the animal characters."

Miss Bottome lectured for the Ministry of Information from 1940 to 1943. She lives in St. Ives, Cornwall.

ADDITIONAL WORKS: Survival (in England: Within the Cup) 1943; From the Life, 1944; The Life Line, 1946; Search for a Soul (autobiography) 1948; Under the Skin, 1950; Fortune's Finger (short stories) 1950; The Challenge, 1953; The Secret Stair, 1954; Man and Beast (short stories) 1954.

ABOUT: Bottome, P. Search for a Soul, The Challenge; Independent Woman February 1944; Saturday Review of Literature November 6, 1948.

BOTTOMLEY, GORDON (February 20, 1874-August 25, 1948). For biographical sketch and list of works and references, see TWENTIETH CENTURY AUTHORS, 1942.

* * *

Gordon Bottomley died at Oare, near Marlborough, England, at seventy-four.

The dramatist continued almost to the time of his death his crusade for the revival of poetic drama in England. Two plays of his own were published, in 1944 and 1945, and in articles contributed to *Theatre Arts* magazine and *Life and Letters Today* he carried on "his special self-imposed task... to raise the standard of verse-speaking."

Noting that Bottomley's "instinct for the stage was not particularly strong or sure," the London *Times* nevertheless observed that his "diction was very close to the 'real language of men'...the blank verse he employed seldom lacked life or dignity. Of his integrity of thought and craftsmanship as a poetic dramatist there can be no question."

ADDITIONAL WORKS: Deirdre: drama in 4 acts in Gaelic and English, 1944; Kate Kennedy: a comedy in 3 acts, 1945; Poems and Plays, 1953.

ABOUT: Abbott, C. C. Introduction to Poems and Plays of Gordon Bottomley; London Times August 27, 1948; New York Times August 27, 1948.

*"**BOUCHER, ANTHONY**" (pseudonym of William Anthony Parker White) (August 21, 1911-   ), American critic, detective story, and science fiction writer and editor, writes: "I was born in Oakland, Calif.— not only a native Californian but a second generation native, with a family background of medicine, the law, and the navy. I am told that at an early age I resolved  to be an admiral; later resolves shifted in many directions until now I have none except to do the next interesting job that turns up and hope that in the next forty years it will all seem to make some kind of pattern.

"I went through high school (Pasadena) thinking I was going to be a physicist; in junior college (also Pasadena) my main interest shifted to linguistics, and this persisted through university (B.A., University of Southern California, 1932) and postgraduate work (M.A. in German, University of California, 1934). All through my college life I spent as much time in little theatre (acting, directing, writing) as in curricular work, and finally decided that this appealed to me more than academic scholarship: I was going to be a playwright. After a few years of not selling plays, I tried a mystery novel and sold it, in 1936, which fixed my activities for the next six years.

"Then I got fascinated by science fiction and fantasy; the field is fun to write in... and even pulp rates paid better than mystery books in those days before the growth of reprints and book clubs. So the period 1941 to 1944 was mostly magazine stories, science-fantasy and detective. In 1945 a chance cocktail party meeting led me into radio, and for three years I was plotting as many as three half-hour shows a week ('Sherlock Holmes,' 'Gregory Hood,' and one that is still a dread secret). Radio and I began to collapse at about the same time.

"I had been extremely fortunate, from the beginning of my professional writing, in working with wonderfully creative and sympathetic editors (Lee Wright and Marie Rodell in mystery novels, John W. Campbell

* "Technically, my name is William Anthony Parker White; but the Boucher pseudonym, originally adopted to keep the mysteries separate from my supposed career as a dramatist, has taken over so fully that White is used chiefly for voting, income tax, and paying the mortgage. Boucher, a French-Irish family name, rhymes with *voucher*, not *touché*."

Jr. in science fiction, Ellery Queen in detective shorts, Joseph Henry Jackson in reviewing, Edna Best in radio), and editing had come to interest me strongly as a profession. In 1949 J. Francis McComas and I founded *The Magazine of Fantasy and Science Fiction,* published by Lawrence Spivak —an attempt to do for science fiction what Ellery Queen had accomplished in stressing quality and originality in the detective short story. I'm now also editing for Spivak a line of mystery reprints and (with McComas) *True Crime Detective;* and editing is just as absorbing a profession as I'd imagined . . . and far more complex than I'd dreamed.

"Meanwhile, back in 1942, I'd become a professional book reviewer for the San Francisco *Chronicle,* specializing in mysteries and science fiction. After five years on the *Chronicle* and briefer sessions on the Chicago *Sun-Times* and *Ellery Queen's Mystery Magazine,* another cocktail party (at which I wasn't even present) landed me on the New York *Times,* whose 'Criminals at Large' column I now run. As 'H. H. Holmes,' I also have a column on science-fantasy in the New York *Herald Tribune.*

"Now that I'm chiefly an editor and reviewer, I feel, of course, more itch to write than I ever did as a full-time writer; it's fairly pleasant, with a limited output, to be able to confine myself to subjects I love, such as Sherlock Holmes, theological speculation, opera, football, classic murders, cooking, party politics, and historical record collecting.

"I am a member of the Catholic Church, the Democratic Party, the Baker Street Irregulars, the Authors League of America, Mystery Writers of America, and the Elves', Gnomes', and Little Men's Science Fiction Chowder and Marching Society. I am married and have two sons, and live in Berkeley, Calif., with wife, sons, mother, and cats.

"In looking over this synopsis, I feel like a block of marble from which unlikely strokes are somehow gradually causing the inherent shape to emerge. I wonder what cocktail party will next cause what stroke."

PRINCIPAL WORKS: The Case of the Seven of Calvary, 1937; The Case of the Crumpled Knave, 1939; The Case of the Baker Street Irregulars, 1940 (rewritten as Blood on Baker Street, 1953); The Case of the Solid Key, 1941; The Case of the Seven Sneezes, 1942. *As "H. H. Holmes"*—Nine Times Nine, 1940; Rocket to the Morgue, 1942. *Anthologies*—The Pocket Book of True Crime Stories, 1943; Great American Detective Stories, 1945; Four-&-Twenty Bloodhounds, 1950; (with J. F. McComas) The Best From Fantasy and Science Fiction, 1952, Second Series, 1953.

*BOURGET, PAUL CHARLES JOSEPH (September 2, 1852-December 25, 1935). For biographical sketch and list of works and references, see TWENTIETH CENTURY AUTHORS, 1942.

* * *

ABOUT: Hoehn, M. (ed.) Catholic Authors, I; Columbia Dictionary of Modern European Literature; Secor, W. T. Paul Bourget and the Nouvelle; South Atlantic Quarterly October 1946.

* bōōr zhĕ'

BOURNE, RANDOLPH SILLIMAN (May 30, 1886-December 22, 1918). For biographical sketch and list of works and references, see TWENTIETH CENTURY AUTHORS, 1942.

* * *

ABOUT: Filler, L. Randolph Bourne; Madison, C. A. Critics and Crusaders.

BOWEN, CATHERINE (SHOBER) DRINKER (January 1, 1897-), American biographer, was born in Haverford, Pa. and spent her childhood in Bethlehem, Pa., where her father, Henry Sturgis Drinker, was president of Lehigh University. From her mother, Aimee Ernesta (Beaux) Drinker, young Catherine acquired a passionate love of music, and  her earliest ambition was to be a professional musician. She attended boarding school at St. Timothy's in Catonsville, Md., and, story has it, rebelled at going to college when a relative, looking at her high forehead, commented that it was "a forehead that will go to Bryn Mawr and write a book." "Never, never to Bryn Mawr! I swore it, kneeling against the sofa. Never to any of their stuffy colleges, to be a spinster with a forehead and her skirt hanging wrong. I would play the violin. I would work until I could play like Kreisler, like two Kreislers."

She enrolled at the Peabody Conservatory of Music in Baltimore where she studied from 1915 to 1917. From there she proceeded to New York to take a teacher's certificate from the Institute of Musical Art. In 1919 she gave up her plans for a career in music to marry Ezra Bowen. Two years later she had a son, three years later a daughter, and by this time she had learned to balance marriage and a career well enough to give music lessons to her own and the neighbors' children and to write articles for the popular magazines on yachting and on music.

Mrs. Bowen's first successful book grew out of her love for music. It was *Friends and Fiddlers*, a group of gay, anecdotal essays on the delights of music from an amateur's point of view. Two years later she made her first venture into the field in which she has achieved greatest success—popular biography—with *Beloved Friend*, the story of the stormy friendship-in-letters between Tchaikowsky and his patroness, Nadejda von Meck. For this work Mrs. Bowen had access to the letters themselves, plus the assistance of Barbara von Meck, distantly related to Nadejda von Meck. The book proved to be a happy vehicle for combining Mrs. Bowen's musical and literary interests, sold over 150,000 copies in this country, and was published in Sweden, Denmark, Germany, France and England. In 1937, as soon as *Beloved Friend* was finished, Mrs. Bowen began research for her biography of two other great musical figures—Anton and Nicholas Rubinstein, and in the course of her work she traveled to Russia, Germany, and France to interview people who had known them.

With this book behind her she planned to prepare a biography of Mendelssohn, but World War II prevented her from going abroad for research. Seeking a subject closer to home, she decided on Oliver Wendell Holmes, Jr., and the result, after four years of work, was the best-selling *Yankee from Olympus,* a lively and sympathetic portrait of the Chief Justice, which historian Henry Steele Commager hailed as "a beautiful piece of workmanship, each piece fitted perfectly into the whole, no exaggeration, no straining for effect, not too much sentiment." The major objection to Mrs. Bowen's book came from reviewers who deplored the "fictionized" form of biography. Edmund Wilson cited the "imaginary" conversation, the probings of Justice Holmes' thinking—a failing of the form, he pointed out, rather than of Mrs. Bowen's writing specifically; and Max Lerner commented that "the semi-fictional form becomes in itself a symbol of the effort, in the literature of recognition, to make things easy that will never be anything but hard." Mrs. Bowen herself acknowledged that she disapproves of this kind of biography but adds: "Without the scenes I have to create, my biographies read like children's notebooks."

Mrs. Bowen was divorced from her first husband. She has been married since 1939 to Dr. Thomas McKean Downs and lives in Bryn Mawr, Pa., near the college she once so vehemently refused to attend. She is described as "a rangy, forceful woman," with angular features and a preference for tweed clothes. She is a popular speaker and lecturer and remains an enthusiastic amateur musician.

PRINCIPAL WORKS: History of Lehigh University, 1924; Story of the Oak Tree, 1924; Rufus Starbuck's Wife (novel) 1932; Friends and Fiddlers (essays) 1935; Beloved Friend (with B. von Meck) 1937; Free Artist: The Story of Anton and Nicholas Rubinstein, 1939; Yankee from Olympus: Justice Holmes and His Family, 1944; John Adams, and the American Revolution, 1950.

ABOUT: Bowen, C. D. Friends and Fiddlers; Current Biography 1944; New York Herald Tribune Book Review July 9, 1950; New York Times Book Review July 2, 1950; Saturday Review of Literature June 17, 1950; Wilson Library Bulletin January 1940.

BOWEN, ELIZABETH (June 7, 1899-). For biographical sketch and list of earlier works and references, see TWENTIETH CENTURY AUTHORS, 1942.

* * *

With the publication of *The Heat of the Day* in 1949, Elizabeth Bowen moved "out of the ranks of interesting minor writers," the critic David Daiches wrote, "to become a major modern novelist." Long a favorite of a small group of discriminating readers, Miss Bowen is now in the rare position of being a writer of "quality" fiction whose works really sell (*The Heat of the Day* was a Literary Guild selection in the United States). Essentially she is, and has always been, a woman's novelist: a term too often used disparagingly to suggest thinness and sentimentality—charges which can never be brought against Elizabeth Bowen's work. But she is a woman's novelist in the sense that she has been concerned primarily with affairs of the heart, with "the simple love story," told not in conventional terms, but with a delicacy and sensitivity that raises some of her writings to the level of those of Virginia Woolf, Katherine Mansfield, and Henry James.

Miss Bowen spent the war years in London working days for the Ministry of Information and nights as an air-raid warden, and writing, as she has said, "continuously— the only interruption being the necessity to clean up my house from time to time when it had been blasted." Her war writings are a remarkable record of what she calls the "overcharged subconsciousness," of the reaction of the civilian under siege and bombing. In both her collection of short stories *Ivy Gripped the Steps*, and her novel *The Heat of the Day*, war is the framework and the backdrop against which her characters move. Yet her focus is never upon war, but upon war's impingement upon individuals. In these later works, as in her earlier novels, she is concerned primarily, as Daiches points out, with "the difficulty of living with one's true nature in a world whose behavior patterns are all social and public...with the terror of personality...with the divorce between public belief and behavior on the one hand and private intuition on the other. . . ."

Her permanent home is Bowen's Court in County Cork, Ireland, but she has lately spent considerable time in the United States writing and lecturing. Since 1941 she has been writing literary criticism and book reviews for *The Tatler* and other journals. She has also written scripts for the B.B.C.

ADDITIONAL WORKS: Seven Winters: Memories of a Dublin Childhood, 1942; Ivy Gripped the Steps, and Other Stories (in England: Demon Lover) 1946; Anthony Trollope: A New Judgment, 1946; The Heat of the Day, 1949; Collected Impressions, 1950; The Shelbourne Hotel, 1951; A World of Love, 1955.

ABOUT: Bowen, E. Seven Winters; Commonweal March 23, 1951; English Journal June 1949; Mercure de France September 1949; New Republic September 21, 1942; New York Herald Tribune Book Review March 26, 1950, October 8, 1950; New York Times Book Review March 6, 1949, March 26, 1950; Partisan Review November 1949; Saturday Review of Literature February 19, 1949; Time April 15, 1946.

*

"BOWEN, MARJORIE." See Long, G. M. V. C.

BOWER, B. M. (November 15, 1871-July 23, 1940). For biographical sketch and list of works and references, see TWENTIETH CENTURY AUTHORS, 1942.

BOWERS, CLAUDE GERNADE (November 20, 1879-). For biographical sketch and list of earlier works and references, see TWENTIETH CENTURY AUTHORS, 1942.

* * *

Claude G. Bowers was United States Ambassador to Chile from 1939 to 1953. Long active in inter-American cultural and diplomatic affairs, he was the chairman of the American delegation to the first United Nations Conference for Latin-America at Santiago, and chairman of the United States delegation to the fifth congress of the Inter-American Institute of History and Geography, also at Santiago, in 1950. The United States War Department awarded him the Order of Freedom for work for hemisphere solidarity during World War II, and in 1950 he was decorated by the Chilean government. He is a member of the National Institute of Arts and Letters.

In 1945 Bowers completed his Jefferson trilogy, which he wrote backward, with *Young Jefferson*, a study of Jefferson's career up to the time he became Washington's first Secretary of State. Five years later he published a biography of another Revolutionary figure—this time a Girondist, the now little-known French lawyer and orator Pierre Vergniaud. In 1954 Bowers published his long-awaited report on Spain in the period just before and during the Spanish Civil War. With the thesis that World War II began in Spain in 1936, *My Mission to Spain* was a powerful book. Lewis Gannett called it "the most significant American contribution to the history of republican Spain yet written."

ADDITIONAL WORKS: Young Jefferson, 1743-1789, 1945; Pierre Vergniaud: Voice of the French Revolution, 1950; My Mission to Spain, 1954; Making Democracy a Reality, 1954.

ABOUT: Banta, R. E. Indiana Authors and Their Books; Current Biography 1941.

BOWLES, PAUL (FREDERIC) (December 30, 1910-), American composer, novelist, and short story writer, reports: "I  was born in the Mary Immaculate Hospital at Jamaica, Long Island, N.Y. (My parents were not Catholics, nor, indeed, were they even believers of any sort. I don't recall any member of my family, including my grandparents, as ever having been affiliated with any church—save one great-uncle, who was for many years Unitarian minister at Exeter, N.H.) My childhood was a typical suburban one. I was an only child. My father was a dentist, and played golf constantly, so that a good deal of time was spent at the country-club. The era I remember best was that following the passage of the Prohibition Act, and the accent was of course on clandestine liquor, its procural and its consumption. After I was graduated from high school I went to art school for a season, having a vague idea I might like to become an artist. Then I decided to go to the University of Virginia, because Poe had gone there. During the first term I managed to secure a passport and escape to France, leaving everyone in doubt as to my whereabouts. In my last year at high school I had sent poems to the old *transition* in Paris and had them published, and considered that an enormous feather in my cap. Using the prestige of that first success, I went on writing poems and sending them to all the then extant little magazines here and abroad, and managing to get them accepted. Thus during my first stay in Paris I thought of myself as a poet.

"On returning to the United States I met Aaron Copland, who offered to give me lessons in musical composition. I accepted, broke into the routine for a few months to complete my first year at college, and then returned to Europe, where I studied in Berlin and in Paris, still writing poetry in my spare time. During the summer of 1931, when I was visiting Gertrude Stein at Bilignin, she told me that I was definitely not a poet. Then she suggested I go to Tangier, which I did, at the same time determined never to write again. However, from there I posted her a short story I had written a year earlier, and she wrote me an approving letter, saying: 'I take back all the harsh things I said about your writing. It makes a picture and that is always good. But it is alright to learn to play Bach in writing too.'

"Still, I had made my decision and I did not alter it. Thus for the next fifteen years I devoted myself entirely to music and music criticism. It was the latter which treacherously made it possible for me to get back into writing. While I was on the staff of the New York *Herald Tribune* as a music critic I decided to translate Jean-Paul Sartre's *Huis Clos* for Broadway. (I had been writing theatre music since 1936.) Then I wrote a few stories, sold them all to *Harper's Bazaar*, *Partisan Review* and *Mademoiselle*, and gained sufficient confidence to accept when Doubleday offered me an advance on a novel. I went back to Tangier and wrote the book wandering about Morocco, Spain and the Sahara, places which had already been my stamping-ground for a period of four years back in the early thirties. I sent *The Sheltering Sky* to Doubleday and they immediately refused it, saying it was not a novel. Eventually New Directions published it. I had already bought a little house in the Casbah of Tangier, so I had a headquarters from which to wander further. I went to India and Ceylon in 1949, and saw an island off the south coast of Ceylon which pleased me immensely, but which was not for sale. I began to write *Let It Come Down* out there, and finished it back in Tangier, all the while keeping a lookout for some possibility of purchasing the island. Then in 1952 I went back to Ceylon and finally managed to buy it. Now I hope to live between Ceylon and Morocco, since both are good places in which to work."

* * *

In 1941 Paul Bowles went to Mexico on a Guggenheim Fellowship where he completed his opera *The Wind Remains* (performed at the Museum of Modern Art in New York in 1943), with a libretto by García Lorca. In addition to his opera, he has composed a number of functional scores for the theatre, a ballet *Pastorela*, an orchestral work *Danza Mexicana*, and many piano pieces and songs. John W. Aldridge wrote that Bowles' first novel, *The Sheltering Sky*, "is a book-length metaphor of the modern world, particularly of the new postwar world in which all morality is relative and life is gray and destined to become grayer as more of the blacks and whites are canceled out." In this novel and the works which have followed it, Bowles has identified himself with the spokesmen for the so-called "new lost generation" —his theme the disintegration and sterility of the modern spirit. Tennessee Williams has called Bowles "probably the American writer who represents most truly the fierily and blindly explosive world that we live in so precariously from day and night to each uncertain tomorrow."

Bowles' wife, Jane, is a playwright. Her play *In the Summer House* was produced in New York in 1954, starring Judith Anderson. Bowles composed the background music for the play.

PRINCIPAL WORKS: The Sheltering Sky, 1949; The Delicate Prey, and Other Stories, 1950; Let It Come Down, 1952.

ABOUT: Aldridge, J. W. After the Lost Generation; Ewen, D. American Composers Today; Howard, J. T. Our American Music; Reis, C. Composers in America; New York Times Book Review March 9, 1952; Saturday Review of Literature February 11, 1950.

BOWRA, Sir CECIL MAURICE (April 8, 1898-), British classical scholar and literary historian, the son of Cecil A. V. Bowra, of the Chinese Customs Service, was educated at Cheltenham College and at New College, Oxford. After joining the R.F.A. and serving in France, 1917-18, he became a fellow and tutor at Wadham College, Oxford, from 1922 to 1938, when he was appointed warden. From 1946 to 1951 he  was professor of poetry and in 1951 was made vice-chancellor of Oxford University. He was knighted in 1951.

Sir Maurice says of himself: "I am a professional don and my life lacks interest. I spent many years as a classical scholar but have moved on to other studies in recent years because though I am devoted to Greek poetry I like modern poetry as well and have wanted to write about it. I am an old-fashioned European who likes most European countries and before the war I spent a good deal of time in Italy and Greece, and I have even managed to visit them since the war. I call myself not a literary critic but a literary historian, as I do not like to pass judgments but try to understand what a writer does. Though I can read several European languages, I cannot talk a single one well, though I am fairly fluent in some."

His early works, beginning with a translation of Pindar's *Pythian Odes* (in collaboration with H. T. Wade), were studies in Greek poetry, including *Tradition and Design in the Iliad.* In 1938, following publication of *Early Greek Elegists,* he moved away from ancient to modern literature and in *The Heritage of Symbolism* discussed the influence of the symbolist movement in France upon Rilke, Valéry, Stefan George, and Yeats. His conviction that the study of literature need not always be conducted by exclusive specialists on parallel lines which never meet was further demonstrated when he edited *A Book of Russian Verse* in new English translations, followed in four years by a second volume which included the forerunners of Pushkin and Russian poets since 1917.

Described by the *London Church Times* as something of a Halley's comet, he has scintillated over a vast field since 1940, turning from Pindar and Homer to Valéry, Apollinaire, Pasternak, Eliot, and Lorca. He has discussed Edith Sitwell and in *The Romantic Imagination* traced the achievements and limitations of romantic poetry. In his study of the literary epic, *From Vergil to Milton,* he applied a method of comparative technique which proved even more effective

later in his *Heroic Poetry,* concerned with that kind of oral poetry found in the *Iliad* and *Odyssey* and still surviving in Russia under conditions he considers not far different from those which shaped the epics of Homer.

His writing displays his apparent distaste for anything that savors of an emotive style. As a professor of poetry Bowra was known for his refusal to pander to any popular desire for the fireworks of rhetoric. Though his subject matter has often followed untrodden ways, displaying versatility as well as scholarship, he has been content as a lecturer and writer to rely upon his material rather than to seek to impress or to intrude his own personality.

He was the Norton lecturer at Harvard University, 1948-49. He has an honorary LL.D. from Dublin University and is an officer of the Legion of Honor. He claims to have "no recreations."

PRINCIPAL WORKS: Pindar's Pythian Odes (with H. T. Wade) 1928; (co-editor) Oxford Book of Greek Verse, 1930; Tradition and Design in the Iliad, 1935; Ancient Greek Literature (Home University Series) 1935; Pindari Carmina, 1935; Greek Lyric Poetry, 1936; Early Greek Elegists, 1938; The Heritage of Symbolism, 1943; A Book of Russian Verse, 1943; Sophoclean Tragedy, 1944; From Vergil to Milton, 1945; Edith Sitwell, 1947; Second Book of Russian Verse, 1948; The Creative Experiment, 1949; The Romantic Imagination, 1950; Heroic Poetry, 1952; Problems in Greek Poetry, 1953.

ABOUT: London Church Times October 24, 1952; Saturday Review of Literature February 12, 1949.

BOYD, ERNEST AUGUSTUS (June 28, 1887-December 30, 1946). For biographical sketch and list of works and references, see TWENTIETH CENTURY AUTHORS, 1942.

* * *

Ernest Boyd died at his home in New York City at fifty-nine.

Though bitterly attacked by some who found his satire "synthetic" and his critical attitude that of a "bad boy," he was praised (by Lewis Galantière) for "familiarity with his subject, intelligence, a civilized point of view, and a straightforward, unaffected style." In a review of *Studies From Ten Literatures,* the *Nation* characterized its author as follows: "As a reporter, he reveals a greater erudition in modern foreign literatures than is to be found in anyone else now writing in America. As a critic he has a distinct preference for the solid, realistic, intellectual and sophisticated; he is the enemy of all cults, of sciolists, and of aesthetics. As a wit he brutally knocks down what as a rule is not deserving of much tenderness."

ABOUT: London Times January 1, 1947; New York Times December 31, 1946.

BOYD, JAMES (July 2, 1888-February 25, 1944). For biographical sketch and list of earlier works and references, see TWENTIETH CENTURY AUTHORS, 1942.

*   *   *

James Boyd died at fifty-five while he was participating in a wartime course given for members of the British armed services at Princeton University. Death was the result of the serious sinus infection which had made him a semi-invalid since World War I.

During the last two years of his life Boyd had returned to an earlier interest in the writing of serious poetry. His friend Struthers Burt found the poems, many of which were published in the *Atlantic Monthly* and other periodicals, "profound and deeply moving." Ruth Lechlitner commented on the "slightness" of the verses published in *Eighteen Poems*, but considered them "the work of a sensitive draftsman and genuine character: as such they add to the stature of a creative figure in American writing." Boyd published the *Pilot*, a periodical issued at Southern Pines, N.C., where he lived. A book of short stories, selected by his widow, Katharine Boyd, published in 1952, was called (by Henry Cavendish) "another step in the gradual enlargement of our picture of Boyd as one of the leading American novelists." Richard Sullivan, in the New York *Times*, called the collection "an impressive little book . . . the general feeling here is one of firm, steady control and clear, objective vision."

Boyd will be remembered primarily for his novels based on American history, in which his writing "belongs to that school which effaces itself as writing—which has no need for poetry," observed Morris Markey. "His pages go marching on, with rarely a variation of pace, rarely a change of cadence. His words come easily against the mind, and past them grow images that are not readily forgotten."

ADDITIONAL WORKS: Eighteen Poems, 1944; Old Pines and Other Stories, 1952.

ABOUT: New York Times February 26, 1944; Saturday Review of Literature April 1, 1944.

BOYD, THOMAS (July 3, 1898-January 27, 1935). For biographical sketch and list of works and references, see TWENTIETH CENTURY AUTHORS, 1942.

BOYLE, KAY (February 19, 1903-   ), American novelist, short story writer, and poet.

NOTE: This biography at the request of the writer supersedes the sketch which appeared in TWENTIETH CENTURY AUTHORS, 1942.

Miss Boyle writes: "Kay Boyle traveled extensively in Europe while a child, and after her marriage to a French engineer [Richard Brault], who had just graduated from the University of Cincinnati, she went with him to France, and settled there. She wrote two novels, with life as she knew it in France as a background, during those years, and a novel of her girlhood in America (which was never published). She also wrote much poetry during that period of extreme loneliness among a strange people, and a long poem entitled 'Harbor Song,' written in Le Havre, was published in Harriet Monroe's magazine, *Poetry*.

"In 1931, following her divorce from Richard Brault, Kay Boyle married Laurence Vail, an American painter and writer, and they lived and worked in France, Austria, and England, until 1936, when they bought a house in the French Alps, near Mont Blanc. There they settled with their six children (Kay Boyle's four daughters, and Laurence Vail's son and daughter by a former marriage). They remained in their mountain chalet until 1941, and then made their way to Lisbon and returned by 'Clipper' to New York. Three books covering this period of the war in France were written by Kay Boyle before leaving the country, and after her return to America—*Primer for Combat, Avalanche,* and *1939*.

"She lived with her children in Nyack and in Mount Vernon from 1941 to 1943, completing her books, writing short stories and articles for the *New Yorker, Harper's Bazaar,* the *Saturday Evening Post,* and other magazines. She taught a night course in short story writing at the Nyack High School and was active in war and relief work. In 1943, having been granted a divorce from Laurence Vail, she married Baron Joseph von Franckenstein, a former Austrian, then serving in the American Army. Kay Boyle and Joseph Franckenstein have a daughter and son.

"After the war, Joseph Franckenstein returned to work in occupied Germany with the War Department, and Kay Boyle and her children joined him there. They now reside in Bad Godesberg, Germany, where Joseph Franckenstein is employed with the Public Affairs Division of the State Department.

Kay Boyle is a correspondent for the *New Yorker* in Germany, and a book of her short stories on Germany appeared in 1951."

PRINCIPAL WORKS: Wedding Day and Other Stories, 1929; Plagued by the Nightingale, 1930; Year Before Last, 1931; The First Lover and Other Stories, 1932; Gentlemen, I Address You Privately, 1933; My Next Bride, 1934; The White Horses of Vienna and Other Stories, 1935; Death of a Man, 1936; Monday Night, 1937; Glad Day (poems) 1938; The Youngest Camel (juvenile) 1939; The Crazy Hunter (novelettes) 1940; Primer for Combat, 1942; Avalanche, 1943; Frenchmen Must Die, 1946; Thirty Stories, 1946; 1939, 1948; His Human Majesty, 1949; The Smoking Mountain: Stories of Postwar Germany, 1951; The Seagull on the Step, 1955.

ABOUT: Van Gelder, R. Writers and Writing; Wilson, E. Classics and Commercials; Bookman June 1932; Current Biography 1942; New York Herald Tribune Book Review April 22, 1951, October 7, 1951; New York Times Book Review November 24, 1946, April 10, 1949; Poetry September 1939; Reader's Digest September 1940; Saturday Review of Literature November 30, 1946; Time December 26, 1938.

*BOYLESVE, RENÉ (1867-January 15, 1926). For biographical sketch and list of works and references, see TWENTIETH CENTURY AUTHORS, 1942.

* * *

ABOUT: Columbia Dictionary of Modern European Literature.

* bwà làv′

BOYNTON, PERCY HOLMES (October 30, 1875-July 8, 1946). For autobiographical sketch and list of works and references, see TWENTIETH CENTURY AUTHORS, 1942.

* * *

Percy Holmes Boynton died of cerebral hemorrhage, at seventy, in a New London, Conn., hospital, after a brief illness. He was survived by his wife, the former Florence Brinkman Rice, and two sons by a previous marriage. His first wife, Lois Damon Boynton, died in 1939.

Boynton was appointed professor emeritus after his retirement as professor of English at the University of Chicago in 1941. He had been the original member of the University staff to appear on the radio program "Chicago Roundtable of the Air." He taught at the University of Puerto Rico (1944-45) and at Rollins College, Winter Park, Florida (1945-46).

Books found his critical works written in a "lecture-like, jaunty, witty, discursive man-

ner," and Cyril Clemmons has spoken of them as "scholarly, splendidly written and stimulating."

ABOUT: New York Times July 9, 1946; School and Society July 20, 1946.

BRACE, GERALD WARNER (September 23, 1901-   ), American novelist, writes: "I was born in the village of Islip on Long Island, N.Y. My family lived at Dobbs Ferry, on the Hudson, and later moved to New York. My forebears were New Englanders, particularly from Hartford and Litchfield, Conn. One great grandfather, John Pierce Brace, was a writer,  author of two novels, and editor of the Hartford *Courant.* His son, my grandfather, was Charles Loring Brace, a sociologist and writer of books on many subjects.

"My early schools were in Connecticut and Massachusetts. I went to Amherst College, then to Harvard graduate school for a doctor's degree. Since 1924 I have taught in New England colleges—at various times at Radcliffe, Williams, Dartmouth, Mount Holyoke, and Amherst. I am now at Boston University as a regular full time faculty member. I live in Belmont, am married, have three children now of college age.

"My writing began early, and I owe a good deal to George Whicher of Amherst and Dean Briggs of Harvard for their encouragement. *The Islands,* my first novel, had its beginnings in Dean Brigg's English 5, though it took me ten more years to finish it. There are no great events in my career, either as writer or teacher. I learned about New England from long and solitary wanderings in the back country, from getting to know people and places in Vermont and Maine. I have spent a lifetime of summers at Deer Isle, Maine, and am a designer and sailor of small boats. I used to do a lot of mountain climbing (in New England) and camping and skiing. My writing is mainly done in the summer months. I work at painting also, mostly water colors."

* * *

In 1941, on the publication of Gerald Warner Brace's third novel, a reviewer for the *Christian Science Monitor* observed that his writings "voice an intuitive response to New England's natural beauty, accompanied by an almost paradoxically intellectual approach in the observation of life and nature." He is thus not simply a regionalist, but a keen and knowledgeable observer of life and manners in general. His most successful novel to date is *The Garretson Chronicle*, a study of three generations of a New England family and the conflict of ideas among them, which Rose Feld described as "a rich and thoughtful book, written with maturity of understanding that holds satire as well as sympathy."

PRINCIPAL WORKS: The Islands, 1936; The Wayward Pilgrims, 1938; Light on a Mountain, 1941; The Garretson Chronicle, 1947; A Summer's Tale, 1949; The Spire, 1952.

ABOUT: Wagenknecht, E. Cavalcade of the American Novel; Warfel, H. R. American Novelists of Today; Current Biography 1947.

BRADBURY, RAY (August 22, 1920-), American writer of science fiction, reports: "I was born in Waukegan, Ill. My father comes from a line of editors and publishers, Bradbury & Sons, who owned a Chicago firm at the turn of the century, and whose forebears came to this country in 1630. My mother was born in Stockholm, Sweden, and arrived here in 1890.

"I became interested in books and writing at the age of seven, through the attention of my aunt, Neva Bradbury, who read to me from Edgar Allan Poe, Wilkie Collins, and the Oz books. In 1928 my life was drastically changed by the advent of Buck Rogers in the comic pages of our newspaper. Through Buck Rogers and Tarzan and the magazine *Amazing Stories*, I became aware of the fabulous world of the future, and the world of fantasy. I became a boy magician, received my first rabbit from Blackstone, the illusionist, when I was eleven, and had my first typewriter, a toy, but more than adequate, when I was twelve. I lived completely in a world of fantasy and illusion, collecting Buck Rogers and Flash Gordon strips, doing magic shows, appearing in plays, reading the comics to children on Saturday nights over a radio station in Arizona, and writing my first stories on my toy machine, profusely illustrated.

"When I was fifteen I began reading on a somewhat higher level and decided that some day I must appear in the *Best American Short Stories*. I started sending stories to the *Post, Collier's*, and *Esquire* in 1935, while still in high school, taking a short story course from Jennet Johnson, my good teacher there. Otherwise I have had no formal training in the short story. When I graduated from high school I went to sell newspapers on a street corner for three years, while I wrote one or two thousand words a day, year after year. Most of this I burnt. My first story (no payment), at the age of nineteen, went to Rob Wagner's *Script*, a West Coast magazine. My first sale involving money was a collaboration with Henry Hasse which appeared in *Super Science Stories* on my twenty-first birthday.

"From 1941 until 1945 I sold continuously to *Weird Tales, Amazing Stories, Astounding Science Fiction, Thrilling Wonder Stories, Astonishing, Captain Future*, and other pulps, including many detective magazines. Simultaneously I was writing and submitting stories to the quality magazines. My first quality sale went to the *American Mercury* in 1945: 'The Big Black and White Game,' which appeared in *The Best American Short Stories of 1946* edited by Martha Foley. My dream had at last come true, after ten years. Within three months of my first quality sale, I sold stories to *Charm, Mademoiselle*, and *Collier's*, each story being listed on the Roll of Honor for their year by Martha Foley. The total so far seems to be sixty appearances in short story anthologies, both in hard- and paper covers, since 1946. My first book of stories, *Dark Carnival*, got all of my night-sweats and terrors down on paper. My second, *The Martian Chronicles*, showed my concern for the future, as did my third, *The Illustrated Man*. I seem to be addicted to the short story form, but hope some day to finish several novels I've been working on for many years.

"I think that science fiction and fantasy offer the liveliest, freshest approaches to many of our problems today, and I always hope to write in this vivid and vigorous form, saying what I think about philosophy and sociology in our immediate future. An ancestor of mine, Mary Bradbury, was tried as a witch in Salem in the seventeenth century; from her, I suppose, I get my concern and dedicated interest in freedom from fear and a detestation for thought-investigation or thought-control of any sort. Science fiction is a wonderful hammer; I intend to use it when and if necessary, to bark a few shins or knock a few heads, in order to make people leave people alone.

"I do not read and have not read (for ten years at least) the magazines I write for; believing that it is the writer's task to be fresh and new to whatever market he wishes to sell. He must, then, be himself, and only himself. Which means that an author must never slant his stories for any particular market. A good story is a good story. For example: I wrote a story, 'The Man Upstairs,' to please myself. *Weird Tales* rejected it. I turned around and sold it to *Harper's* magazine. A bad story fits only *one* magazine. A good story can go to many, if not all.

"My wife Marguerite and I (married in 1947) have two fine girls, Susan and Ramona, and now live, and hope to go on living, in Los Angeles, Calif. I have just written my first film and am starting a second. [Bradbury did a scenario of *Moby Dick* for director John Huston.] I would like to do one film a year, for the challenge it offers, and for the imaginative possibilities inherent in the form."

* * *

Christopher Isherwood considers Bradbury's "a very great and unusual talent." He objects to calling him simply a science-fiction writer. "If one must attach labels . . . he might be called a writer of fantasy, and his stories 'tales of the grotesque and arabesque' in the sense in which those words are used by Poe." Anthony Boucher says: "He has literary integrity of a high order, and an intense desire to utilize popular fiction to express the ideas that seem to him to need saying." Bradbury has been described as "a pretty big fellow, looking more like football material than like interplanetary stuff."

PRINCIPAL WORKS: Dark Carnival, 1947; The Martian Chronicles, 1950; The Illustrated Man, 1951; The Golden Apples of the Sun, 1953; Fahrenheit 451, 1953; Switch on the Night, 1955.

ABOUT: Current Biography 1953; New York Times Book Review August 5, 1951; Ray Bradbury Review (ed. William E. Nolan, San Diego, Calif., 1952); The Reporter June 26, 1951; Tomorrow October 1950.

BRADFORD, GAMALIEL (October 9, 1863-April 11, 1932). For biographical sketch and list of works and references, see TWENTIETH CENTURY AUTHORS, 1942.

* * *

ABOUT: Carver, G. Alms for Oblivion; American Academy of Arts and Sciences, Commemorative Tributes, 1905-41.

BRADFORD, ROARK (August 21, 1896-November 13, 1948). For biographical sketch and list of earlier works and references, see TWENTIETH CENTURY AUTHORS, 1942.

* * *

Roark Bradford died at fifty-two, after a two-year illness, at his home in New Orleans, of amoebiasis, contracted in French West Africa while serving there with the Navy in 1943.

In the last few years Bradford had lectured at Tulane University on various phases of writing. A posthumously published book, *The Green Roller*, a collection of short sketches built around an itinerant Negro preacher, was called by Marc Connolly, the author's friend and collaborator, "a happy last testament of a singularly rich talent and a human heart."

Critics have mentioned his gift for storytelling, his gentle humor, above all his uncannily accurate ear for the speech of those around him. "He lived a full and busy life," Harrison Smith has said. "He was a skilled fisherman and horseman, a student, a talented writer, and a fascinated listener who could catch the colorful and sad nuances in sung and storied legend of the deep South."

ADDITIONAL WORK: Green Roller, 1949.

ABOUT: New York Times November 14, 1948; Saturday Review of Literature June 24, 1944, November 27, 1948, December 4, 1948.

BRADLEY, ANDREW CECIL (March 26, 1851-September 2, 1935). For biographical sketch and list of works and references, see TWENTIETH CENTURY AUTHORS, 1942.

* * *

ABOUT: Dictionary of National Biography 1931-40; Murry, J. M. Katherine Mansfield and Other Literary Portraits; Studies in Philology April 1947.

BRADLEY, JOHN HODGDON, Jr. (September 17, 1898-   ). For autobiographical sketch and list of earlier works and references, see TWENTIETH CENTURY AUTHORS, 1942.

* * *

John Hodgdon Bradley writes from Escondido, Calif.: "Though still a runaway from the campus, I have been closer this past decade to the problems of education than ever before. In 1940 and 1941, I entered the field of secondary education when I became co-author of a series of three textbooks in general science for the junior high school (*Adventuring in Science*) and of a senior high school textbook in general science (*Our World and Science*). With the war my interest shifted to geography, specifically to the problem of combatting what one leading educator had called the geographic illiteracy of the American people. The result was *World Geography* (1945), a textbook which is now being taught in thousands of American and Canadian high schools. Though I have since been pretty busy with the never-ending job of keeping these textbooks up-to-date, I have done some writing for adult readers and I am planning a great deal more.

"In 1950, my personal and professional life was shattered when my wife and silent collaborator in all my work for twenty-eight years died. With the help of Elinor M. Downie, whom I married in 1952, I am currently attempting to close the ranks and carry on."

ADDITIONAL WORKS: Adventuring in Science (with S. R. Powers and others) 1940-41; Our World and Science (with S. R. Powers and others) 1941; World Geography, 1945.

BRAILSFORD, HENRY NOEL
(1873-). For biographical sketch and list of earlier works and references, see TWENTIETH CENTURY AUTHORS, 1942.

* * *

Henry Noel Brailsford contributes articles on political affairs to British and American periodicals. His major interests in recent years have been the problems of postwar Germany and independence for India. In 1944 he published *Our Settlement With Germany*, which argued for the ultimate inclusion of a defeated Germany in the post-war community of nations. Some reviewers questioned whether Brailsford's proposals were sufficiently "realistic," but they agreed that his approach was "sane and judicious." In *Subject India* he urged that India be granted its freedom, and in subsequent articles he has commented with clarity and sympathy on the issues involved in Indian independence. Brailsford lives in London.

ADDITIONAL WORKS: Subject India, 1943; Our Settlement With Germany, 1944; Mahatma Gandhi (with H. S. L. Polak) 1949.

BRAITHWAITE, WILLIAM STAN-LEY BEAUMONT (December 6, 1878-). For biographical sketch and list of earlier works and references, see TWENTIETH CENTURY AUTHORS, 1942.

* * *

William Stanley Braithwaite undertook the difficult task of retelling the story of the Brontës and their work in *Bewitched Parsonage*. The result, Alfred Ames wrote, was an altogether successful study—"knowledgeable but not pedantic . . . a labor of love . . . written with literary skill." A recent collection of his poems displayed versatile craftsmanship. David Daiches found echoes of the imagery and diction of Victorian poetry in his work. "His poetry is filled with individual perceptions of man and nature, speculations on history and morality, moods and introspections." His scope as a poet is limited, but, as A. M. Sullivan points out, "His gift is as quiet and consistent as the pleasure it evokes."

ADDITIONAL WORKS: Selected Poems, 1948; Bewitched Parsonage: The Story of the Brontës, 1950.

ABOUT: Barton, R. C. Witnesses for Freedom; Gregory, H. & Zaturenska, M. History of American Poetry, 1900-1940; Saturday Review of Literature February 12, 1949.

"BRAMAH, ERNEST." See SMITH, E. B.

BRANCH, ANNA HEMPSTEAD (March 18, 1875-September 8, 1937). For autobiographical sketch and list of works and references, see TWENTIETH CENTURY AUTHORS, 1942.

* * *

ADDITIONAL WORK: Last Poems, 1944.

ABOUT: Torrence, R. *Foreword to* Last Poems of A. H. Branch; Saturday Review of Literature March 31, 1945.

BRAND, MAX (May 29, 1892-May 12(?), 1944). For biographical sketch and list of earlier works and references, see TWENTIETH CENTURY AUTHORS, 1942.

* * *

Frederick Schiller Faust, whose most familiar pseudonym was "Max Brand," was killed in battle "about May 12," 1944, at fifty-one. Attached to the Fifth American Army in Italy during World War II on a reportorial assignment for *Harper's*, the writer elected to accompany infantry units leading an attack on Santa Maria Infante, then in German hands. He was killed in the first half-hour of assault, and was buried in a soldier's grave.

His amazing productivity in the pulp magazine, adventure novel and motion picture script fields continued to the time of his death, and half-a-dozen books by "Max

Brand" and "Evan Evans" (another nom de plume) have been published since that date. Other names under which Faust wrote were Frank Austin, George Owen Baxter, Walter C. Butler, George Challis, and P. H. Morland; he is credited with at least 115 published books and over 350 magazine serials and novelettes.

According to his friend Leonard Bacon, Faust (though he achieved no reputation as a poet) was "poetry incarnate. He lived, moved, and had his being in, for, and because of it. . . . Homer, Dante, Chaucer, Shakespeare were part and essence of his mind. The writing of verse was to him a sacred art." He is described as spending the fresh morning hours working "like a lapidary" at poetry, then using the flagging energy of afternoon to turn out "the three or four thousand words necessary . . . for bread and circuses." A great capacity for friendship and enormous generosity were outstanding characteristics of the writer; he financed the education of dozens of young men, and supported "an army of unemployables." *Time* has described him as "a massive man with a long, chiseled face" whose "appetites for work and living were enormous."

ADDITIONAL WORKS: Man From Mustang, 1942; Silvertip, 1942; Silvertip's Strike, 1942; Silvertip's Trap, 1943; Silvertip's Chase, 1944; Fighting Four: A Silvertip Story, 1944; Mountain Riders, 1946; Border Bandit (as Evan Evans) 1947; Hired Guns, 1948; Rescue of Broken Arrow (as Evan Evans) 1948; Smiling Desperado, 1952.

ABOUT: New York Times May 15, 1944, May 17, 1944; Saturday Review of Literature May 27, 1944; Time May 29, 1944.

BRAND, MILLEN (January 19, 1906-). For autobiographical sketch and list of earlier works and references, see TWENTIETH CENTURY AUTHORS, 1942.

* * *

Millen Brand writes: "I now belong to the Authors League and the NAACP, do not have a farm in Pennsylvania, refuse to play chess, and almost never listen to music. From this it might be suspected that my world has been narrowing. It has narrowed almost entirely to the written word and the experience that conveys itself in the written word, which will appear for good or bad as I get words published. I now not only write but edit the writing of others at Crown Publishers and teach others to write at the Seminar and Clinic for Professional Writers at New York University.

"In 1947 I published my third novel, *Albert Sears,* about Negroes opening up a new

neighborhood to Negro tenancy in my place of birth, Jersey City. The end of the same year I went to Hollywood and wrote (with Frank Partos) the screenplay of *The Snake Pit,* for which I received the Screen Guild Award and the Robert Meltzer Plaque.

"I am now (1952) halfway through a long novel on psychiatry which is under contract to Crown. Over the last ten years I've been working on a long book of poetry, 'Local Lives,' parts of which have appeared in magazines and in *Cross-Section 1945.*"

ADDITIONAL WORKS: Albert Sears, 1947; Some Love, Some Hunger, 1955.

ABOUT: Warfel, H. R. American Novelists of Today.

BRANDE, Mrs. DOROTHEA (THOMPSON) (January 12, 1893-December 17, 1948). For biographical sketch and list of works and references, see TWENTIETH CENTURY AUTHORS, 1942.

* * *

Dorothea Brande died at fifty-five, in Boston. She had made her home in Wonalancet, N.H., in her last years. She was survived by her husband, Seward B. Collins, her son by a former marriage, Justin Herbert Brande, and an adopted son, Gilbert Collins.

ABOUT: New York Times December 18, 1948.

* BRANDES, GEORG MORRIS COHEN (February 4, 1842-February 19, 1927). For biographical sketch and list of works and references, see TWENTIETH CENTURY AUTHORS, 1942.

* * *

ABOUT: Columbia Dictionary of Modern European Literature; YIVO Annual of Jewish Social Science (Yiddish Scientific Institute) 1947-48.

* brän' děs

BRANT, IRVING NEWTON (January 17, 1885-), American historian and biographer, writes: "My first book, published in 1933, was a questions - and - answers primer in economics, a subject of which I was fully as ignorant as the economists had proved themselves to be. The highest compliment it received came from a member of the Capitol Parks Police who stopped  me ten years later, asked me if I wrote *Dollars and Sense,* and said he still consulted it when confused by what was going on. He must have read it every day. In 1936 *Storm Over the Constitution* was published. When referred to today, it is always called a book written to defend President Roosevelt's 1937 court-packing plan. To be sure, it did have that effect, except for a footnote opposing the method of Supreme Court reformation chosen by FDR in the following year. I never thought footnotes were of much importance, but this one prevented the publication of a special issue of 100,000 copies.

"The writing of *Storm* led directly to the *Life of James Madison.* That was undertaken partly because I wanted to develop the significance of Madison's crossover from nationalism to state rights under the stress of politico-economic issues, partly because the head of the Bobbs-Merrill publishing house thought that oldtime biographers had not done well by his fellow alumnus of Princeton University. My scholastic training in American history was adequate. It consisted of a one-semester course in the fifth grade, which left me free of accumulated misinformation. Added to this was the knowledge, gained through twenty-five years of editorial writing, that the public utterances of statesman seldom reveal the reasons for what they do—a principle too seldom applied in distant retrospect.

"In 1937, just as the research for this biography was starting, I declined an invitation to write another book because this one-volume work would require two years to complete. Fifteen years later, with the fourth volume finished and one more to come, there still seems to be about two years' work ahead.

"During a seven-year respite from newspaper work, beginning in 1923, my time was chiefly devoted to playwriting. A modest part of the output reached little-theatre production, but the authentic response of Broadway producers seemed to be: "We would have put this on two or three years ago, but it is not immoral enough for today." Since 1938, full time has been spent on the Madison biography, except for a two-year effort to help the Chicago *Sun* rise, and a few months devoted to showing *The Road to Peace and Freedom* to a world that trod on the book instead of the path.

"My education at the University of Iowa, blended with daily work on my father's standpat Republican newspaper in Iowa City, did nothing to undermine a virginal belief that William Howard Taft was a rather dangerous radical. A few years later the writings of Henry George (though not his tax theory) subverted me to what might be called the Brandeis end of Wilsonian democracy. Educationally, the most valuable year of my life began at the age of thirteen, when another boy's well-directed throw of a croquet ball kept me out of school for a year and taught me the difference between a tufted titmouse and a piedbilled grebe. The resulting inclination toward outdoor recreation found expression, especially after marriage to likeminded Hazeldean Toof (a 1909 classmate at the University of Iowa), in hiking, canoeing, camping, mountain climbing, etc., and also led to the writing of many pamphlets on wildlife and forest conservation. Two years spent as consultant to Secretary of the Interior Ickes were chiefly devoted to working for the establishment of the Olympic and Kings Canyon National Parks."

* * *

Brant was born in Walker, Iowa. He worked as a newspaperman on the Iowa City *Republican* from 1909 to 1914; was editor of the Clinton (Iowa) *Herald* 1914 to 1915; associate editor of the Des Moines *Register and Tribune* 1915 to 1918; editorial writer of the St. Louis *Star* 1918 to 1923 and of the St. Louis *Star-Times* 1930 to 1938; and of the Chicago *Sun* 1941 to 1943.

PRINCIPAL WORKS: Dollars and Sense, 1933; Storm Over the Constitution, 1936; James Madison: I (The Virginia Revolutionist) 1941, II (The Nationalist) 1948, III (Father of the Constitution) 1950; The Road to Peace and Freedom, 1943; The New Poland, 1946; James Madison: IV (Secretary of State) 1953.

ABOUT: Saturday Review of Literature April 8, 1953.

BRAWLEY, BENJAMIN GRIFFITH
(April 22, 1882-February 1, 1939). For biographical sketch and list of works and references, see TWENTIETH CENTURY AUTHORS, 1942.

* * *

ABOUT: Phylon, vol. 10 (1949).

BREASTED, JAMES HENRY (August 27, 1865-December 2, 1935). For biographical sketch and list of works and references, see TWENTIETH CENTURY AUTHORS, 1942.

* * *

ABOUT: Breasted, C. Pioneer to the Past; The Story of James Henry Breasted.

BRECHT, BERTOLT (February 10, 1898-). For biographical sketch and list of earlier works and references, see TWENTIETH CENTURY AUTHORS, 1942.

* * *

Bertolt Brecht lived in California from 1941 to 1947, when he returned to Europe to work at the playhouse in Zürich. During his years in the United States, Brecht wrote one play, *The Caucasian Chalk Circle.* Two earlier plays, *The Private Life of the Master Race* and *Galileo,* had professional productions here (in 1945 and 1947 respectively).

In 1949 Brecht returned to Germany. He settled in East Berlin, creating his own theatrical company (the Berliner Ensemble), and produced an outstanding series of plays for the Deutsches Theater. These included his *Mother Courage* and *Puntila* and dramas from both the classical and contemporary repertories. For a while, Edouard Roditi writes in the New York *Times,* the Deutsches Theater was "the cynosure of the German literary world as well as Europe's most important subsidized *avant-garde* theatre." The production of Brecht's *The Trial of Lucullus,* first written some years earlier, as an opera with a score by Paul Dessau, however, was severely criticized by the Communist press as "formalistic." *Lucullus* was reported banned and was withdrawn from the stage. But, according to a letter in the *New Statesman and Nation,* June 9, 1951, Brecht announced at an All-German Congress at Leipzig that it had been withdrawn at his own wish until he could make certain revisions in the text. At latest reports, Brecht is still living in East Berlin.

A large measure of credit for the wider recognition of Brecht in the United States is due to the drama critic Eric Bentley, who has translated several of Brecht's plays and has written several sound critical appreciations of him. He studied Brecht's productions in post-war Germany and was his assistant in the 1950 production of *Mother Courage* in Munich. Bentley finds that "the one fresh style in German theatre today is that of Brecht." He is not only a playwright, but a producer and director too, actively concerned with the production as a whole. "In his art there is stage-illusion," Bentley writes in *The Playwright as Thinker,* "suspense, sympathy, identification. The audience is enthralled and—most important of all—the highly personal genius of Brecht finds expression."

ADDITIONAL WORKS IN ENGLISH TRANSLATION: *Poetry*—Selected Poems, 1947. *Plays*—Round Heads, Peak Heads, or Rich and Rich Make Good

Company, *in* Internationale Literatur May 1937; Señora Carrar's Rifles, *in* Theater Workshop April-June 1938; Mother Courage (early version) *in* New Directions in Prose and Poetry (ed. J. Laughlin) 1941; The Trial of Lucullus, 1943; The Private Life of the Master Race, 1944; Two Plays (He Says Yes, He Says No) *in* Accent Autumn 1946; The Horatians and the Curatians, *in* Accent Autumn 1947; Parables for the Theater (The Good Woman of Setzuan, The Caucasian Chalk Circle) 1948; The Threepenny Opera, *in* From the Modern Repertoire, Series One (ed. E. Bentley) 1949; The Baby Elephant, *in* Wake Autumn 1949; The Lesson, *in* Harvard Advocate February 1951; Galileo, *in* From the Modern Repertoire, Series Two (ed. E. Bentley) 1952; Puntila: Two Episodes, *in* Accent Spring 1954.

ABOUT: Bentley, E. The Playwright as Thinker, In Search of Theater; Cole, T. & H. K. Chinoy (eds.) Directing the Play; Gassner, J. The Theatre in Our Times; Gorelik, M. New Theatres for Old; Hewitt, B. Theatres of Yesterday and Today; Nicholson, H. A. Voyage to Wonderland and Other Essays; Richman, R. (ed.) The Arts at Mid-Century; Nation May 19, 1951; New Statesman and Nation April 21, June 9, July 7, July 21, 1951; New York Times Book Review December 7, 1952, January 4, 1953; Poetry December 1945; Theatre Arts February 1948, June 1949; Western Review Spring 1948.

BRENAN, GERALD (1894-), British journalist and historian, writes: "My father was an officer in the British Army and my mother the daughter of a Belfast manufacturer. Both were Protestants. My early childhood was spent in South Africa and India, but in 1902 my father retired and we settled in a village in the south of England. I was given the usual  Spartan education meted out to English middle class boys, which consists in their being taught nothing and made as miserable as possible. The result was that I turned against the whole of middle class life and, influenced by Thoreau and the tramp poet W. H. Davies, ran away from home and travelled with a donkey and cart from Paris to the Balkans, living on a few cents a day. These six months taught me more than the whole of my schooling had done.

"Compelled in the end to return home, I was sent to Germany to continue my education. A year later the war broke out and I joined up in the infantry. I found the war much more bearable than school and, chiefly on account of the high mortality among my fellow officers, soon reached the rank of captain. This meant that when the armistice came and I was still alive, I had saved enough money to be independent for some time. I was thus able to take a passage to the south of Spain and to settle there in a remote village with a large number of books. Here I lived for five years, reading and teaching myself to write. After this I returned to England, making friends among the literary group known as Bloomsbury. When in 1930 I inherited a little money I married Elisabeth Gamel Woolsey, of Aiken, S.C., a poet and half-sister of the famous federal judge of that name. We bought a house near Malaga and lived in it till the Civil War broke out.

"The books I wrote before 1936 came out under a pseudonym. The only ones I will mention here are *The Spanish Labyrinth,* 1943 (revised edition, 1950)—a political-sociological study of modern Spain; *The Face of Spain,* 1950—a travel book; and *The Literature of the Spanish People,* 1951 —a critical history of Spanish literature from Roman times to the present century.

"As I have written a political book on Spain, perhaps I should add that my political opinions have never been anything else but liberal. I am an individualist and value liberty above everything else."

* * *

Gerald Brenan, as the *New Yorker* points out, is "an accomplished writer and a knowledgeable traveler; he is able in a few words to convey the mood of a town or a landscape, catch the characteristic nuances of a foreign culture, or describe how people look and act." His books on Spain are not mere travelogues, but works of real literary merit in their own right. They are the products of scholarship, of years of on-the-scene experience and—equally important—a deep personal sympathy for and understanding of Spain and its people.

PRINCIPAL WORKS: The Spanish Labyrinth, 1943; The Face of Spain, 1950; The Literature of the Spanish People, 1951

ABOUT. New York Times Book Review January 27, 1952.

* **BRETON, ANDRÉ** (February 18, 1896-), French Surrealist poet and leader of the Surrealist movement, was born in Tinchebray (Orne), the son of a Norman shopkeeper. As a young student in 1913 he met and came under the influence of the French symbolist poet Paul Valéry. He began to read the poetry of the earlier sym-

* brĕ tôN'

bolist Arthur Rimbaud who, Breton wrote some years later, "opened to poetry an entirely new path by systematically defying all the habitual forms of reaction to the drama of the world. . . ." Breton's intention at this time, however, was to become a doctor. His special interest was mental disease and, although he never practiced medicine, his readings in psychiatry, especially in the works of Freud, shaped his later definition of Surrealism as "pure psychic automatism."

French Embassy

In 1916 Breton met Jacques Vaché, a Dadaist, sometimes called the founder of Surrealism, and Guillaume Apollinaire, one of its leading disciples. In 1919, with Louis Aragon and Philippe Soupault, he founded the magazine *Littérature,* where he published his first truly Surrealist work, *Les Champs Magnetiques,* a collection of so-called "unconscious writing." In 1921 he visited Freud in Vienna. A year later he took over the editorship of *Littérature* and thus became the undisputed leader of the Surrealist movement. The definition of Surrealism as "psychic automatism" was published by Breton in 1924 in his *Manifeste de Surréalisme.* The aim of the movement, as stated here, was to dispose of the "flagrant contradictions" of (to quote Breton) "being awake and sleeping (of reality and dream), of reason and madness, of objectivity and subjectivity, of perception and representation, of past and future, of collective and individual love, even of life and death." Art, he believed, should be a "real process of thought," freed from all the control exercised by reason, quite beyond rational, esthetic, or moral preoccupations. As Charles Weir, Jr., has pointed out, Surrealism, under Breton's leadership, became thus not simply an esthetic movement but a way of life, "which combined an extravagant scorn of all accepted values with a corresponding exaltation of the importance of the subconscious."

Alone, and writing in collaboration with fellow Surrealists like Aragon, Paul Eluard, and Soupault, Breton published poems, polemical tracts, and essays. His best creative work was the poetic novel *Nadja* (1928) which Weir calls "one of the most remarkable books in modern literature." It is the story of a love affair between the author and a woman "of marked psychic tendencies," who relies upon pure intuition and is, Simone de Beauvoir writes, "so wonderfully liberated from regard for appearances that she scorns reason and the laws." Of his poems Mlle. de Beauvoir remarks, "There is only one world; poetry is objectively present in things. . . ." Outside the Surrealist movement, Breton is probably better known as a personality than as a literary artist. His main importance in literature, Weir has pointed out, is as a "controlling force of a school," rather than as a creative writer.

During the 1920's the Surrealist movement became more and more involved in social and political matters. Breton, Aragon, and other leaders joined the Communist Party, but Breton always stressed in his writings that Surrealism should be free of "all external controls, even Marxism." The *Seconde Manifeste de Surréalisme,* published in 1930, tried to define better the philosophic position of the movement and pointed out the need for guarding it from all outside political pressure. A new review edited by Breton, *Surréalisme au Service de la Révolution,* defended the same position. In 1935 Breton broke with Communism, announcing his decision in a tract, *Du Temps que les Surréalistes Avaient Raison.* In the following year, on the occasion of the International Surrealist Exhibition held in London, he wrote, "We therefore reject as *erroneous* the conception of *'socialist realism'* which attempts to impose upon the artist the exclusive duty of describing proletarian misery and the struggle for liberation in which the proletariat is engaged." Breton remained a Marxist, however. In 1938 he went to Mexico where he met the exiled Leon Trotsky. Together they founded *La Fédération de l'Art Révolutionnaire Indépendant.* Breton became an exile himself during the German occupation of France. He emigrated to New York and in America found new disciples and new facets for the Surrealist movement. In 1942 he organized a Surrealist exposition at Yale University. In 1945 he visited Indian reservations in Arizona and New Mexico and studied American Indian art. He then turned to the West Indies where he organized another Surrealist exposition and studied native art and poetry in the Antilles and in Haiti.

Breton returned to France in 1946. He organized the Surrealist exhibit of 1947 and has now collected a new Surrealist group around him. Probably his best-known Surrealist associates today are Nicholas Calas and Salvador Dali. (It has been said that in America "it was by Reason of Dali, out of Breton, that Surrealism was reproduced.")

PRINCIPAL WORKS IN ENGLISH TRANSLATION: What Is Surrealism? 1936; Limits Not Frontiers of Surrealism, *in* Surrealism (ed. H. Read) 1936; Young Cherry Trees Secured Against Hares (poems) 1946; Yves Tanguy, 1946.

ABOUT: *In French*—Bédouin, J. L. André Breton; Carrouges, M. André Breton; Dictionnaire Biographique Français Contemporains; Mauriac, C. André Breton; Nadeau, M. Histoire du Surréalisme. *In English*—Beauvoir, S. de The Second Sex; Columbia Dictionary of Modern European Literature; Fowlie, W. Age of Surrealism; Lemaître, G. E. From Cubism to Surrealism in French Literature; New Directions 1940.

BRETT YOUNG. See YOUNG, F. B.

BREUER, ELIZABETH (October 18, 1892-). For autobiographical sketch and list of earlier works and references, see TWENTIETH CENTURY AUTHORS, 1942.

* * *

Bessie Breuer received second prize in the 1944 O. Henry Award for her short story, "Home Is a Place." A collection of her short stories was published in 1947. Her play, *Sundown Beach,* directed by Elia Kazan, which dealt with the rehabilitation attempts of a group of World War II fliers, opened in New York in September 1948 and closed after seven performances.

ADDITIONAL WORKS: The Bracelet of Wavia Lea and Other Short Stories, 1947.

BRIDGE, ANN (pseudonym of Lady Mary Dolling Sanders O'Malley, 1889-). For biographical sketch and list of earlier works and references, see TWENTIETH CENTURY AUTHORS, 1942.

* * *

Ann Bridge's talent for combining travelogue with romantic fiction has been employed to good effect in several of her latest novels. *The Singing Waters* did for Albania, its scene, what her earlier *Illyrian Spring* had done for Yugoslavia—introducing a country and a people to her readers in the guise of an entertaining story. *The Dark Moment,* one of her most popular recent novels, considers a much-neglected period in Turkish history, the great national revolution under Mustafa Kemal Ataturk. Once again the elements of history, romance, and exotic background are neatly blended. Miss Bridge's interest in Turkish history was stimulated in 1940 when her husband, Sir Owen O'Malley, now retired from the British Diplomatic

Service, was stationed in Turkey. Here she met and interviewed many of the men and women who had been associated with Ataturk and visited the historic scenes she later incorporated into her novel.

During World War II, Miss Bridge was active in war relief work. In the course of this work she made a round-the-world trip and spent more than a year in the United States. She now lives in the country in Ireland. "It is the perfect place to write in," she says. "A soothing climate, great tranquillity, extreme beauty out of every window and just the right number of delightful neighbors, after a life overcrowded with people." In 1948 she was received into the Roman Catholic Church.

Correction: In the 1942 volume it was stated incorrectly that she had two sons. She has one son and two daughters.

ADDITIONAL WORKS: Frontier Passage, 1942; The Singing Waters, 1946; And Then You Came, 1948; The Selective Traveller in Portugal (with S. Lowndes) 1949; The House at Kilmartin (juvenile) 1951; The Dark Moment, 1952; A Place to Stand, 1953.

ABOUT: Hoehn, M. (ed.) Catholic Authors, II.

BRIDGES, ROBERT (October 23, 1844-April 21, 1930). For biographical sketch and list of works and references, see TWENTIETH CENTURY AUTHORS, 1942.

* * *

ABOUT: Gorden, G. S. Robert Bridges; Pinto, V. de S. Crisis in English Poetry; Thompson, E. J. Robert Bridges, 1844-1930; Wright, E. C. Metaphor, Sound and Meaning in Bridges' The Testament of Beauty.

* BRIEUX, EUGÈNE (January 19, 1858-December 6, 1932). For biographical sketch and list of works and references, see TWENTIETH CENTURY AUTHORS,

* * *

ABOUT: Columbia Dictionary of Modern European Literature; Lancaster, H. C. Adventures of a Literary Historian.

* brē ŭ'

*BRIFFAULT, ROBERT STEPHEN (1876-December 11, 1948). For biographical sketch and list of earlier works and references, see TWENTIETH CENTURY AUTHORS, 1942.

* * *

Robert Briffault died of tuberculosis at seventy-two at St. Helen's Hospital in Sussex, England. He had returned to his native country a month before his death, after having lived in France for seventeen years.

* brē'fō

At the close of World War II it was revealed that he had remained in Paris throughout the German occupation. At least part of that time he spent in a Nazi prison in reprisal for publishing "two critical books of English history" through the underground Communist press.

His last book, *The New Life of Mr. Martin* (1946), is "a compound of adventure story, social satire and philosophical inquiry" dealing with world crises in the years 1926 to 1936. Nash K. Burger felt that once more Briffault's fiction was "a vehicle for his political, religious and moral views."

It has been said that Briffault considered himself one of the "lost generation of intellectuals" who believed in the coming "day of destiny" of the world's masses, but who could not "comfortably identify" themselves with the masses. The New York *Times* has said of him: "The bitter things he had to say in his novels about politics and economic systems, religion, morals and social relationships, were as controversial as his scientific theories in his non-fiction books. Curiously, there was little controversy about Briffault himself. Critics were pretty well agreed on admiring his books for their erudition, broad scope, intense emotion and stimulating thought, but they also generally disapproved his weak characterization, lack of unified dramatic story-line and a style 'unbelievably ornate' and tedious."

ADDITIONAL WORKS: The New Life of Mr. Martin (novel) 1947.

ABOUT: London Times December 15, 1948; New York Times December 14, 1948; Science January 14, 1949.

BRIGHOUSE, HAROLD (July 26, 1882-). For biographical sketch and list of earlier works and references, see TWENTIETH CENTURY AUTHORS, 1942.

* * *

Harold Brighouse lives in London. He has published no novels in recent years, but has written several plays, including *Hallowed Ground*, *The Inner Man*, and *Sporting Rights*, a one-act comedy.

ADDITIONAL WORKS: Sporting Rights, 1943; Albert Gates (one-act play, originally pub. 1937) 1946.

BRIGHT, Mrs. MARY CHAVELITA (DUNNE) ("George Egerton") (December 14, 1860-August 13, 1945). For biographical sketch and list of works and references, see TWENTIETH CENTURY AUTHORS, 1942.

* * *

Mary Dunne Bright died at her home at Ifield Park, Crawley, in Sussex, England, at eighty-four.

"George Egerton," in the opinion of L. Ruth Middlebrook, "wrote not because she wanted to write, but because she had to write down woman's world as she lived it—in all its ghastly compromise and mocking inadequacy." Thus her first book of short stories, *Keynotes*, although not praised for its literary quality, has been called by Mrs. Middlebrook the most courageous analysis of England's "new woman" of the 1890's, and undoubtedly "a compelling and significant contribution to the emancipation of woman."

ABOUT: College English December 1948; London Times August 13, 1945; New York Times August 14, 1945.

BRILL, ABRAHAM ARDEN (October 12, 1874-March 2, 1948), American psychiatrist, teacher and practitioner of psycho-

analysis, was the first to introduce the writings of Sigmund Freud to the English speaking world. Many new phrases, such as "libido" and "Oedipus complex" were first introduced into the American language by Dr. Brill.

Born in Kanczuga, Austria, he arrived in New York in 1889, a boy of fifteen, alone and almost penniless. During the day he worked at all sorts of jobs open to a youth in his teens, but by studying at night he prepared himself to enter the College of the City of New York. Compelled to interrupt his studies for lack of funds, he did not graduate from New York University until 1901 nor receive his M.D. degree from the College of Physicians and Surgeons, Columbia University, until 1903 when he was twenty-nine years old. After four years as assistant physician at Central Islip State Hospital, he went abroad in 1907, first to the neurological clinics in Paris and then to the hospital at Burghölzli in Zurich where he came in contact with Eugen Bleuler, Carl Jung, and Karl Abraham, who were applying Freud's theories to the study of psychoses. Appointed an assistant at Burghölzli, Brill remained about a year. After he had translated into English Jung's *Psychology of Dementia Praecox* he met Freud and arranged to become his translator.

Upon his return to New York in 1908 he married Dr. K. Rose Owen and began his practice of psychoanalysis at a time when Freud's theories met with indifference or violent opposition. Unconventionally blunt, Dr. Brill lost no opportunity, whether through the spoken or written word, to defend psychoanalysis. In debate he yielded ground to no one and pugnaciously returned to resume the contest.

In 1911-12 he was chief of the clinic of psychiatry at Columbia University; from 1913 to 1920 lecturer on psychoanalysis and abnormal psychology at New York University; from 1914 to 1918 assistant professor of psychiatry at New York Post Graduate Medical School; in 1927 lecturer on psychoanalysis and psychosexual sciences at Columbia University; in 1945 clinical professor of psychiatry at New York University.

The first of his many translations of the works of Sigmund Freud, *Selected Papers on Hysteria*, appeared in 1909, followed by *Three Contributions to the Theory of Sex* in 1910, and *Interpretation of Dreams* in 1912.

Besides translating the works of Freud, Dr. Brill was the author of many original works on psychoanalysis. He wrote numerous pamphlets on psychiatric subjects, edited the English edition of Eugen Bleuler's *Textbook of Psychiatry*, Breuer and Freud's *Studies in Hysteria*, and *The Basic Writings of Sigmund Freud*.

In 1911 Dr. Brill founded the New York Psychoanalytic Society and a few months later was active in the formation of the American Psychoanalytic Association. He was president of both these associations on several occasions. A member of many psychiatric associations in the state and nation, he was elected to the presidency of the New York Neurological Society, the New York Psychiatric Society, the New York Society for Clinical Psychiatry, and the Section on Neurology and Psychiatry of the New York Academy of Medicine. Shortly before his death Phi Beta Kappa conferred upon him an honorary membership.

In World War I he discontinued his practice to serve with a psychiatric unit at Plattsburg, N.Y., and again in World War II, at the age of seventy, he volunteered as consultant in psychiatry to the Selective Service System. Known here and abroad as the first American psychoanalyst, Dr. Brill was the teacher of two generations of psychiatrists and psychoanalysts. Though his first and foremost thought lay in clinical medicine he found time for many other interests, including music, the classics, languages, ornithology, sociology, and education.

After a few days' illness, he died of a heart ailment at Mount Sinai Hospital in his seventy-third year. His wife, the former Dr. K. Rose Owen; a daughter, Mrs. Philip G. Bernheim; a son, Dr. Edmund R. Brill, a research biologist; and two grandchildren, Thomas Owen and Lynn Bernheim, survived him.

PRINCIPAL WORKS: Psychoanalysis: Its Theories and Practical Application, 1912; Fundamental Conceptions of Psychoanalysis, 1922; Freud's Contribution to Psychiatry, 1944; Lectures on Psychoanalytic Psychiatry, 1946. *Principal Translations*: (C. G. Jung) Psychology of Dementia Praecox, 1909; Association Method, 1909; (Sigmund Freud) Selected Papers on Hysteria, 1909; Interpretation of Dreams, 1912; The Psychopathology of Everyday Life, 1914; Leonardo da Vinci, 1916; Wit and the Unconscious, 1916; History of the Psychoanalytic Movement, 1916; Totem and Taboo, 1917; Exploring the Hidden Mysteries of the Mind, 1924; Three Contributions to the Theory of Sex, 1930; Basic Writings of Sigmund Freud, 1938; (Eugen Bleuler) Textbook of Psychiatry, 1924; (Joseph Breuer and Sigmund Freud) Studies in Hysteria, 1936.

ABOUT: American Medical Association Journal May 29, 1948; New York Times March 3, 1948; Psychoanalytic Quarterly April 1948.

BRINIG, MYRON (December 22, 1900-). For biographical sketch and list of earlier works and references, see TWENTIETH CENTURY AUTHORS, 1942.

* * *

Myron Brinig has long been a thoroughly practiced and seasoned novelist. He writes prolifically, always with serious intention, but with varying degrees of success. None of his later works has had the sustained power of the earlier *The Sisters* and *May Flavin*, John Barkham has commented upon "Brinig's sentimental streak and his sympathetic touch with characters [which] usually lend his books a warm glow of humanity, if not of art." It is these qualities that the critics have found generally lacking in his recent novels. Brinig lives in Taos, N.M.

ADDITIONAL WORKS: The Family Way, 1942; The Gambler Takes a Wife, 1943; You and I, 1945; The Hour of Nightfall, 1947; No Marriage in Paradise, 1948; Footsteps on the Stair, 1950; The Sadness in Lexington Avenue, 1951; The Street of the Three Friends, 1953.

ABOUT: Warfel, H. R. American Novelists of Today.

BRINNIN, JOHN MALCOLM (1916-), American poet, writes: "I was born in Halifax, Nova Scotia, where my father, a native Bostonian, was scenic artist for the theatre repertory company of Sidney Toler (later Hollywood's 'Charlie Chan'). It was there he met and married my mother, Frances Malcolm, a descendant of early Scotch settlers engaged in ship-building. When I was four we moved to Detroit, returning to Nova Scotia every summer for many years afterwards.

"I was educated by Dominican nuns and Jesuit priests until the later years of high school when, having left the Catholic Church, I also left its schools. My college career began inauspiciously at Wayne University. When my first English instructor told me that my enthusiasm for the works of Marcel Proust was both specious and inappropriate, I decided I would seek an unrestricted education. For several years then I pursued, in the Detroit Public Library, an absurdly systematic program of self-education, from Anthropology to Zoology, and as a side line edited three self-consciously *avant garde* literary journals (*Prelude, New Writers, Signatures*), worked in book stores old, rare, and new, and in 1936 spent a summer wandering about northern Europe. By this time, my rebellious adolescence having simmered down, I recognized the need of a formal education and entered the University of Michigan. The death of my father two months later threatened another abrupt break in my attempts to get through college but, falling back upon my experience in the book trade, I opened a shop, The Book Room, on the Ann Arbor campus. The Book Room became a literary haven for undergraduate literati and brought me an income which, supplemented by literary prizes from the Avery Hopwood Awards committees and frequent publications of poems, supported me until graduation.

"After a summer in residence at Bennington College studying relationships between modern dance and poetry, I left Ann Arbor for New York City, in 1940. Nine months there brought me the never-relaxed conviction that I could never creatively exist as a New Yorker, and in 1941 I entered Harvard as a graduate student. After a year in Cambridge, I went to Vassar College as instructor in English and remained there for five years, teaching a wide range of subjects. In the summer of 1947, I travelled for three months over most of the United States with the

French photographer, Henri Cartier-Bresson, and with him published a number of articles.

"Moving to Westport, Conn., in 1947, I did free-lance work, served on a committee basis as associate editor for the New York publisher Dodd, Mead and Company, spent a semester as poet-in-residence at Stephens College, taught for a summer at the University of California, lectured frequently, taught courses in literature to adults in New York City, and spent parts of each summer in residence at Yaddo, in Saratoga Springs.

"I became director of the Poetry Center of the YM-YWHA in New York City in 1949 and have served in that capacity to the present time, organizing and conducting yearly series of reading appearances by poets, among whom have been T. S. Eliot, Robert Frost, Edith Sitwell, W. H. Auden, Wallace Stevens, Marianne Moore, E. E. Cummings, Stephen Spender, Dylan Thomas, William Carlos Williams, and most of the other significant poets in England and America.

"In recent years I have maintained a residence in Cambridge, Mass., while teaching at the University of Connecticut, overseeing the activities of the Poetry Center, lecturing at colleges and universities, and making annual summer trips to London and Venice.

"I did not mean to assume the role of promoter of modern poetry that my recent activities suggest, but have never been able to resist opportunities various individuals and agencies were kind enough to open to me. My happiest role is as a teacher when creative and academic drives are allowed to function in harmony."

PRINCIPAL WORKS: The Garden Is Political, 1942; The Lincoln Lyrics, 1942; No Arch, No Triumph, 1945; The Sorrows of Cold Stone, 1951; Modern Poetry: American and British (ed. with K. Friar) 1951.

ABOUT: Daiches, D. Some Notes on Contemporary American Poetry *in* Modern American Poetry (B. Rajan, ed.); Junior Bazaar December 1946; Poetry April 1945, November 1947, June 1952; Saturday Review of Literature December 29, 1951.

BRINTON, CLARENCE CRANE (February 2, 1898-). For autobiographical sketch and list of earlier works and references, see TWENTIETH CENTURY AUTHORS, 1942.

* * *

Crane Brinton has been professor of history at Harvard University since 1942. In the same year he became chairman of the Society of Fellows of Harvard, having been a Senior Fellow since 1939. During the Second World War he was special assistant in the Office of Strategic Services, European Theatre of Operations. In 1950 he was elected a Chevalier of the Legion of Honor and vice president of the *Société d'Histoire Politique et Constitutionelle*. He received the honorary degree of L.H.D. from Ripon College in 1951 and from Kenyon College in 1952. He was married to Cecelia Roberts in 1946.

Professor Brinton's *Ideas and Men*, published in 1950, was an examination of the intellectual history of Western thought from its Hebrew and Greek origins to the present time. Geoffrey Bruun called the book a "scholarly, sane, and stimulating survey," and Hans Kohn wrote in the *New Republic*, "Brinton has the great and rare gift of writing about very difficult and complex problems with an easy grace and lucid simplicity."

ADDITIONAL WORKS: The United States and Britain, 1945; From Many One (lectures) 1948; Ideas and Men, 1950; The Temper of Western Europe, 1953.

BRISBANE, ARTHUR (December 12, 1864-December 25, 1936). For biographical sketch and list of works and references, see TWENTIETH CENTURY AUTHORS, 1942.

BRISTOW, GWEN (September 16, 1903-). For autobiographical sketch and list of earlier works and references, see TWENTIETH CENTURY AUTHORS, 1942.

* * *

Gwen Bristow writes: "My novel *Tomorrow Is Forever* was published in 1943 and was made into a moving picture in 1945. In 1950 I published *Jubilee Trail*, an historical novel of the Americans who traded in California before the gold rush. This has been made into a moving picture by Republic Studio; the shooting script was prepared by my husband, Bruce Manning.

"My present home is in Northridge, a suburban village in the San Fernando Valley of California. We have a small house and a big yard, where we grow oranges, avocados, guavas, tangerines, peaches, all sorts of vegetables, and a family of cats."

ADDITIONAL WORKS: Tomorrow Is Forever, 1943; Jubilee Trail, 1950.

ABOUT: Warfel, H. R. American Novelists of Today; Current Biography, 1940; New York Herald Tribune Book Review February 12, 1950; Wings (Literary Guild) March 1950.

BRITTAIN, VERA MARY (1896?-   ). For autobiographical sketch and list of earlier works and references, see Twentieth Century Authors, 1942.

* * *

Vera Brittain (Mrs. George E. G. Catlin) writes: "I have now changed my address and live in Westminster at 4, Whitehall Court, which is the block of flats where Bernard Shaw had his London home for a number of years. The little daughter of ten whom your sketch mentions is now a young woman in her twenties, who was a Scholar of Somerville College, Oxford, and has just completed a course at Columbia University, where she studied American political institutions as a Smith-Mundt Scholar and the holder of a Fulbright grant. She expects to stand for Parliament at an early date."

Among Miss Brittain's recent published works are two novels, a biography of John Bunyan, and a travel book, *Search After Sunrise*, which described a long tour of India and Pakistan during which she attended several conferences and also lectured. "In preparation at present," she writes, "are a history of women in this century [published as *Lady into Woman*, 1954] and the sequel to *Testament of Youth*, entitled 'Testament of Experience.'"

ADDITIONAL WORKS: Humiliation with Honor, 1943; Account Rendered (novel) 1944; Seed of Chaos, 1944; On Being an Author, 1948; Born 1925 (novel) 1949; Valiant Pilgrim (in England: In the Steps of John Bunyan) 1950; Search After Sunrise, 1951; Lady into Woman: A History of Women from Victoria to Elizabeth II, 1954.

ABOUT: Brittain, V. On Being an Author; Gray, J. On Second Thought; New York Herald Tribune Book Review May 22, 1949.

BRIUSOV. See BRYUSOV

BROADHURST, GEORGE H. (1866-January 31, 1952). For biographical sketch and list of works and references, see Twentieth Century Authors, 1942.

* * *

George Broadhurst died at eighty-five, after an illness of several months, at his home in Santa Barbara, Calif., where he lived for the last ten years of his life.

The playwright had been quoted as saying, at the time of his virtual retirement in 1926, that "one characteristic absolutely necessary for playwriting is imagination, and that is an attribute of youth." Despite this dictum, he and his wife collaborated in 1950, when he was eighty-four, on his last play, *The Man in Brown*.

The New York *Times* has called Broadhurst's record of successfully produced plays "a career that has few parallels in the world of the drama."

ABOUT: New York Herald Tribune July 4, 1950; New York Times February 1, 1952; Variety September 6, 1939.

*BROCH, HERMANN (November 1, 1886-May 30, 1951). For biographical sketch and list of earlier works and references, see Twentieth Century Authors, 1942.

* * *

Hermann Broch died as the result of a heart attack, at sixty-four, at his home in New Haven, Conn.

An émigré to the United States in 1939, he became an American citizen, did philosophical and psychological research, on a Rockefeller Fellowship, at Princeton (1942-44), and lectured on German literature at Yale. Although he did little formal teaching, he "wielded a great and stimulating influence" at both institutions. He studied intensively in the fields of economics, politics, social psychology, and value research, and wrote epistemological studies, political essays and notes on the philosophy of language. In 1942 he was elected a member of the American Institute of Arts and Letters.

At the time of his death Broch was working on a novel set in his native Austrian mountains. His last finished novel was *Die Schuldlose* (*The Guiltless*). *The Death of Virgil*, published in 1945, was called "perhaps the best novel by a European since Thomas Mann's *The Magic Mountain*" (by Hamilton Basso), and "a work of great learning, remarkable psychological understanding, and startling symbolical subtlety" (by Leonard Bacon). Begun while the author was in a Nazi prison, "as a private preparation for death," completed and published in America, the "cosmological epic" deals with Virgil's recreation of "the world and the universe and man and God" in the moment before his death.

"Hermann Broch belongs in that tradition of great 20th Century novelists," says Hannah Arendt, "who have transformed, almost beyond recognition, one of the classic art forms of the 19th century. . . . The novelist's ambition to create the illusion of a higher reality . . . has yielded to the intention to involve the reader in something which is at

* brŏk

123

least as much a process of thought as of artistic invention."

The writer has been described by his translator, Jean Starr Untermeyer: "Broch, though having the keenest eye and mind, which overlooked very little, was socially shy. There was nothing shy in his intellectual make-up. His was almost a Paracelsus character, Faustian in that he wanted to encompass the whole world of knowledge in his own Ego. In appearance he was tall, with extremely short overbody and overlong legs. He stooped as do many scholars. His head was arresting: of his face, with its prominent nose, its almost femininely sensitive mouth, but his piercing eyes and noble brow, one could only say that it deserved the designation of *countenance*. His influence over people was remarkable." Henry Seidel Canby has called Broch "one of the significant minds as well as one of the most persuasive personalities of our time."

In TWENTIETH CENTURY AUTHORS, 1942, Broch was called a "German novelist." Jean Starr Untermeyer points out that this is incorrect. She writes: "Broch was a born and bred Austrian, and he was likewise born a Jew. In early manhood he became a Catholic, but it was well known among his intimate friends that in his last years he had planned to make a formal return to the faith of his fathers." She goes on to say that Jewish thinking, and especially Jewish mysticism, played a decisive role in his philosophy.

ADDITIONAL WORKS IN ENGLISH TRANSLATION: The Death of Virgil, 1945.

ABOUT: Books Abroad Winter 1952; Columbia Dictionary of Modern European Literature; Kenyon Review, No. 3, 1949; Publications of the Modern Language Association June 1947; New York Times May 31, 1951; Saturday Review of Literature June 23, 1951.

BROCK, CLUTTON-. See CLUTTON-BROCK

*BROD, MAX (May 27, 1884-). For biographical sketch and list of earlier works and references, see TWENTIETH CENTURY AUTHORS, 1942.

* * *

An ardent Zionist, Max Brod has lived in Tel Aviv since 1939. He has continued his work as composer with the Habima Theatre and, in addition, has written two novels—*The Master*, a story of Palestine in the early Christian era, and *Unambo*, a

* brōt

novel of contemporary times concerned with the Arab-Israeli conflict. Some reviewers found in *Unambo* (the title refers to a "magic" gadget which enables the protagonist to be two personalities simultaneously) a trace of the influence of Kafka's mystic imagery, though "none of the simple, fascinating prose style that makes Kafka so readable."

ADDITIONAL WORKS IN ENGLISH TRANSLATION: Franz Kafka: A Biography, 1947; The Master, 1951; Unambo, 1952.

ABOUT: Bergel, L. *in* The Kafka Problem (ed. A. Flores); Liptzin, S. Germany's Stepchildren; Saleski, G. Famous Musicians of Jewish Origin.

BROGAN, DENIS WILLIAM (August 11, 1900-), British historian and political scientist, has been described as "an Irishman born in Scotland and educated in France, England, and America." He was born in Glasgow, eldest son of Denis and Elizabeth Nixon (Toner) Brogan. He attended the University of Glasgow and Balliol College, Oxford. On a grant from the Laura

British Broadcasting Corp.

Spelman Rockefeller Foundation he spent two years, 1925 to 1927, at Harvard, where he took an M.A. in American history. Upon his return to England he lectured on American history at the University of London and on American government at the London School of Economics, and was appointed a Fellow and tutor of Corpus Christi College, Oxford. Since 1939 he has been professor of political science at Cambridge University.

Brogan's interest in American life is said to date back to his boyhood. His father had spent two years in California many years before, and subscribed to a number of American newspapers and magazines which the young boy read eagerly. With this background, supplemented by his studies and visits to this country, Brogan was ideally suited for the position of interpreter of American life to his British readers and interpreter of British life to American readers. Reinhold Niebuhr has spoken of his "extraordinary gift for understanding and illuminating the woof of constitutional principles and the warp of political tactics in the fabric of democratic history, whether in his own or in other nations." It is this quality which makes his writings on America not only useful to British readers but "instructive and entertaining" to American readers as well. His writing is crisp, urbane, and witty, soundly and shrewdly observed. "He can make any subject interesting merely by writing about it." Herbert Agar commented. "His wit, his liveliness and his range of allusion are all first class."

Brogan is also highly regarded as an authority on modern France. His *France Under the Republic*, a political history of France from 1870 to 1939, was hailed as an authoritative account of the period and a work of immense learning. André Maurois wrote: "His qualities of style implemented with a dry Scotch humor make the reading of this history as provocative as it is moving." Even on controversial French political matters covered in his *French Personalities and Problems* he writes, Justin O'Brien said, "with such admirable impartiality that anyone concerned with the growth of modern nationalism or the antecedents of Vichy cannot ignore this book."

During World War II, Brogan worked for the B.B.C.'s European Service as an intelligence officer, preparing special broadcasts aimed at the Resistance movement in France. In 1946 he received the Legion of Honor for his wartime services to that country. He also acted as adviser on current American history for the B.B.C.'s North American Service. In 1944 he participated in a trans-oceanic quiz program sponsored jointly by the B.B.C. and the Blue Network.

In 1941, while convalescing from an attack of the mumps, Brogan wrote a detective novel, *Stop on the Green Light*, and published it under the pseudonym of "Michael Barrington." A fast-paced and humorous story, it introduced one character whose mastery of American slang astonished and delighted readers who knew "Barrington's" identity. Brogan was married in 1931 to Olwen Kendall, the archeologist. They have four sons and a daughter, and live in Cambridge, England.

PRINCIPAL WORKS: The American Political System (in England: Government of the People) 1933; Proudhon, 1934; Abraham Lincoln, 1935; France Under the Republic (in England: Development of Modern France) 1940; Is Innocence Enough? Some Reflections on Foreign Affairs, 1941; Politics and Law in the United States, 1941; U.S.A.: An Outline of the Country, its People and Institutions, 1941; The English People: Impressions and Observations, 1943; The American Character (in England: The American Problem) 1944; The Free State, 1945; French Personalities and Problems, 1946; American Themes, 1948; The Era

of Franklin D. Roosevelt, 1950; The Price of Revolution, 1951; Politics in America, 1954. *As "Maurice Barrington"*—Stop on the Green Light, 1941.

ABOUT: Book-of-the-Month Club News October 1944; Current Biography 1947; New Yorker October 14, 1944.

BROMFIELD, LOUIS (December 27, 1896-   ). For biographical sketch and list of earlier works and references, see TWENTIETH CENTURY AUTHORS, 1942.

* * *

Just before the outbreak of World War II, Louis Bromfield and his family settled on his 1,000-acre farm (named Malabar after the Indian coastal region locale of *The Rains Came*), near his birthplace of Mansfield, Ohio. He has become, John Bainbridge writes, "one of America's most famous farmers and easily its most eloquent champion of the farm as a way of life." Malabar is now a showplace, worked with the latest scientific farm equipment, the house usually filled with guests from all over the world, and humming with activity. Bromfield's farming has brought him almost as wide a fame as his novels. As a practicing farmer, he became an outspoken critic of the New Deal's food administration during the war. In 1944 he left the Democratic Party (of which he had been a lifelong member) to campaign for the Republican presidential candidate Thomas E. Dewey. Since then—in lectures, magazine articles and books—he has passionately urged decentralization of government and industry. R. L. Duffus describes him (in a review of *A Few Brass Tacks*) as "an angry gentleman farmer, striding up and down his sitting room and front parlor and . . . dictating and not revising."

Bromfield's later novels are distinctly inferior to his earlier ones. One of these, *Mrs. Parkington*, was sold to Hollywood on the basis of a synopsis before the book was even written. Another, *What Became of Anna Bolton*, was devastatingly reviewed by Edmund Wilson as a novel "in which there is not a single stroke of wit, not a scene of effective drama, not a phrase of clean-minted expression, and hardly a moment of credible behavior." Only in *The Wild Country*, the story of a young boy's life on a Missouri farm, is there a reminder of the close perception and expert craftsmanship of the earlier Bromfield. His most interesting recent writings have come out of Malabar Farm itself—the two volumes of autobiographical reminiscence, *Pleasant Valley* and *Malabar Farm*, and *Out of the Earth*, a book on agriculture which the New York *Times* suggested, might be compared with Jefferson's *Notes on Virginia* and the writings of William Cobbett.

ADDITIONAL WORKS: *Fiction*—Mrs. Parkington, 1943; The World We Live In, 1944; What Became of Anna Bolton, 1944; Colorado, 1947; Kenny, 1947; The Wild Country, 1948; Mr. Smith, 1951. *Non-fiction*—Pleasant Valley, 1945; A Few Brass Tacks, 1946; Malabar Farm, 1948; Out of the Earth, 1950; A New Pattern for a Tired World, 1954.

ABOUT: Bromfield, L. Pleasant Valley, Malabar Farm; Gray, J. On Second Thought; Van Gelder, R. Writers and Writing; Wilson, E. Classics and Commercials; Current Biography 1944; Life October 11, 1948; New York Herald Tribune Book Review October 7, 1951; Saturday Review of Literature November 1, 1947.

BROOKE, CHARLES FREDERICK TUCKER (June 4, 1883-June 22, 1946), American Shakespearean scholar and critic, was born in Morgantown, W.Va., the son of St. George Tucker Brooke, dean of the Law School of West Virginia University, and Mary Harrison (Brown) Brooke. He received his B.A. and M.A. from West Virginia University in 1901 and 1902 respectively, and was awarded a fellowship in German at the University of Chicago where he studied in 1903 and 1904. In the latter year he was appointed the first Rhodes Scholar from West Virginia, and he proceeded to Oxford University, taking a B.A. with first class honors in 1906 and a B.Litt. in 1907.

Brooke served as senior demy at Magdalen College, Oxford, in 1907-1908. His first American teaching appointment was as instructor in English at Cornell University, from 1908 to 1909. In 1909 he joined the English faculty of Yale University. Except for time out in 1920 when he was an exchange professor at the University of London, during the academic year 1928-1929 when he was research associate at the Huntington Library, and other periods when he lectured at Stanford, Harvard, the Universities of Chicago, California, Southern California, and Texas, Brooke taught at Yale for the rest of his life. At the time of his death he was Sterling Professor of English and a Fellow of Calhoun College.

Both of Brooke's teaching and of his scholarship the highest praise that can be given is that he wore his vast learning lightly. Milton Crane wrote of him: "As editor, scholar, teacher, and critic, he stood consistently and steadfastly for the reasonable, the median, the predominantly sensible viewpoint, fortified by sound knowledge." Brooke's achievements in Shakespearean scholarship and in the history of Tudor and Elizabethan drama were considerable. His first published work, *The Shakespeare Apocrypha*, his B.Litt. thesis at Oxford, made accessible for the first time the texts of fourteen plays sometimes ascribed to Shakespeare but not generally accepted as his work. His Christopher Marlowe studies set the way for the lively and revealing Marlowe scholarship of modern times. His work in the history of the Elizabethan and Tudor drama contributed significantly to our knowledge of the physical stage, the production of plays, and their social and intellectual backgrounds. One of his most valuable works for present-day scholars was his editorship of the Yale Shakespeare series, with their sound annotation and careful attention to textual problems and source materials. Brooke's scholarship was also distinguished by a felicitous and witty style. Oscar James Campbell, reviewing the posthumously published *Essays on Shakespeare and Other Elizabethans*, commented that they "reveal his admirable qualities and many of the facets of his wise and whimsical personality." Each essay, Campbell continues, whether intended for the average reader or for the serious scholar "bears the indelible stamp of an acute and original mind."

Brooke was a member of a number of scholarly and honorary societies—among them, the American Philosophical Society, the Modern Language Association, the Bibliographical Society of London, and Phi Beta Kappa, and he had honorary degrees from Yale (M.A., 1921) and Lawrence College (D.Litt., 1935). He died in New Haven at the age of sixty-three, leaving a wife, the former Grace Drakeford, of Hertfordshire, England, and one son and one daughter.

PRINCIPAL WORKS: The Shakespeare Apocrypha (ed.) 1908; The Works of Christopher Marlowe (ed.) 1910; The Tudor Drama, 1911; Common Conditions (ed.) 1915; The Reputation of Christopher Marlowe, 1922; Shakespeare of Stratford, 1926; Songs of William Shakespeare (ed.) 1929; English Drama, 1580-1642 (ed. with N. B. Paradise) 1933; Shakespeare's Sonnets (ed.) 1936; Essays on Shakespeare and Other Elizabethans, 1948.

ABOUT: National Cyclopedia of American Biography (1950); New York Times June 24, 1946.

BROOKE, JOCELYN (November 30, 1908-), British novelist and naturalist, writes: "I was born at Sandgate, Kent, England, the son of a wine merchant. I was educated at a series of preparatory schools—all of which I heartily detested—and in 1922 was sent to the King's School, Canterbury, from which I promptly ran away. After this I went to Bedales, the first co-educational school to be founded in England. Subsequently I spent a year at Worcester College, Oxford, but left without taking a degree. During the next ten years I worked in the book and wine trades, and in 1940 joined the Royal Army Medical Corps, in which I remained till I was demobilized in 1945. Bored by civilian life, I re-enlisted in 1947, but bought my discharge after a year's

W. Fisk-Moore

service. For a short time I worked as a Talks Producer at the B.B.C., but since 1949 have occupied myself solely with writing. Chief hobbies: books and botany."

* * *

Jocelyn Brooke has been writing only since 1946, after a busy career as bookseller, publisher, wine merchant, and wartime medical orderly in Italy and the Middle East. His writings include autobiography, verse, a children's book, a masterly and exhaustive botanical study of the British orchid, and three neatly effective psychological novels. He has said that he finds "any purely conscious writing"—a business letter or a review—painfully difficult to write. But the things he wants to write, he finds, "write themselves, almost in a trance."

PRINCIPAL WORKS: The Military Orchid, 1948; A Mine of Serpents, 1949; The Wonderful Summer (juvenile) 1949; The Goose Cathedral, 1950; The Wild Orchids of Britain, 1950; Ronald Firbank, 1951; The Flower in Season, 1952. *Novels*—The Scapegoat, 1948; The Image of a Drawn Sword, 1950; The Passing of a Hero, 1953. *Poetry*—December Spring, 1946; The Elements of Death, 1952.

ABOUT: Brooke, J. The Military Orchid, A Mine of Serpents, The Goose Cathedral; New York Herald Tribune Book Review February 11, 1951.

BROOKE, RUPERT (August 3, 1887-April 23, 1915). For biographical sketch and list of works and references, see TWENTIETH CENTURY AUTHORS, 1942.

* * *

ADDITIONAL WORKS: Democracy and the Arts, 1946.

ABOUT: Stringer, A. J. Red Wine of Youth; Nineteenth Century April 1945; Time August 16, 1948.

BROOKS, CHARLES STEPHEN (June 25, 1878-June 29, 1934). For biographical sketch and list of works and references, see TWENTIETH CENTURY AUTHORS, 1942.

BROOKS, CLEANTH (October 16, 1906-), American scholar and critic, was born in Murray, Ky., son of the Rev. Cleanth Brooks and Bessie Lee (Witherspoon) Brooks. He studied at the McTyeire School in McKenzie, Tenn., and at Vanderbilt (B.A. 1928) and Tulane (M.A. 1929) universities. From 1929 to 1932 he was a Rhodes Scholar at Oxford University,

Fonville Winans

from which he received a B.A. with honors in 1931 and a B.Litt. in 1932. He returned to the United States and joined the English department of Louisiana State University, where he taught for the next fifteen years and, from 1935 to 1942, in collaboration with Robert Penn Warren, edited the journal *Southern Review*. During this period he published a linguistic study of the Alabama-Georgia dialect and contributed numerous critical articles and reviews to *Poetry, Kenyon Review, Virginia Quarterly Review, Yale Review,* the *New Republic,* and the *Saturday Review*. He has been visiting professor of English at the Universities of Texas, Michigan, and Chicago, and at the Kenyon School of English. Since 1947 he has been professor of English at Yale University. In addition to his teaching and his critical writing, Brooks is the general editor (with David N. Smith) of the letters of Thomas Percy, ten volumes projected since 1942, and a member of the advisory committee on the Boswell papers.

Brooks is a teacher of poetry as well as a critic of it, and his critical writings show the concern of the teacher with clarification or exegesis of difficult poetry. With his colleagues Robert Penn Warren and Robert Heilman he wrote a series of college textbooks—*Understanding Poetry, Understanding Fiction, Understanding Drama*—which have had considerable influence on the teaching of literature. The Brooks-and-Warren method is that of close reading and careful structural analysis. Though much simplified in textbook form, it is in substance the method of the "New Criticism," of which Brooks is an active practitioner. In *The Well-Wrought Urn* he states his critical position as follows: "I insist that to treat the poems discussed primarily as poems is a proper emphasis, and very much worth doing. For we have gone to school to the anthropologists and the cultural historians assiduously, and we have learned their lesson . . . so well that the danger now . . . is not that we will forget the differences between poems of different historical periods, but that we may forget those qualities which they have in common . . . those qualities that make them *poems* and which determine whether they are *good* poems or *bad* poems."

These qualities, for Brooks, are wit, irony, paradox, symbolism, ambiguity, dramatic structure. In his search for them in English poetry he has produced what George F. Whicher describes as "masterly exercises in the kind of close critical explication that enriches our appreciation of the poems examined and confers a new dignity on the work of the poet." Stanley Edgar Hyman calls him "a confessedly eclectic critic of real acuteness." Other critics of Brooks' work have objected, however, to the narrowness of his approach. Some of his readings, they point out, produce "not a poem but simply a piece of subtle dialectic." Ronald S. Crane, in an essay called "The Critical Monism of Cleanth Brooks," suggests that his fundamental error is that he starts not with the poem as a whole but with only one of "the several internal causes of poems"—their linguistic matter.

Brooks was married in 1934 to Edith Amy Blanchard. He lives in Northford, Conn.

PRINCIPAL WORKS: The Relation of the Alabama-Georgia Dialect to the Provincial Dialects of Great Britain, 1935; Approach to Literature (ed. with R. P. Warren and J. T. Purser) 1936; Understanding Poetry (ed. with R. P. Warren) 1938; Modern Poetry and the Tradition, 1939; Understanding Fiction (ed. with R. P. Warren) 1943; The Well-Wrought Urn, 1947; Understanding Drama (ed. with R. Heilman) 1947; Modern Rhetoric (ed. with R. P. Warren) 1949; Poems of Mr. John Milton (ed. with J. E. Hardy) 1951.

ABOUT: Crane, R. S. (ed.) Critics and Criticism; Hyman, S. E. The Armed Vision.

BROOKS, GWENDOLYN (June 7, 1917-), American poet and novelist, writes: "I was taken from Chicago to Topeka, Kan., my mother's home, to be born. A month after my birth my mother and I returned to Chicago, where we have lived ever since. (She is Keziah Wims Brooks, my father is David Anderson Brooks. I have one brother, Raymond.)

"I loved poetry very early and began to put rhymes together at about seven, at which time my parents expressed most earnest confidence that I would one day be a writer. At the age of thirteen my first poem, 'Eventide,' was accepted and printed by a then well-known children's magazine, *American Childhood.* I received in payment six copies of the issue in which it appeared, and a kind, encouraging note from the editor.

"In my last two years at high school, I wrote a few themes, and two or three little stories, in verse, and these attracted attention from one or two teachers. When I was seventeen I began submitting poems to the Chicago *Defender,* a Negro newspaper. Over seventy-five of these confident items appeared in a variety column of the *Defender* called 'Lights and Shadows.'

"My education ended with graduation from Wilson Junior College here in Chicago, June 1936. I was nineteen then. Subsequently I typed in various offices until shortly after my marriage to Henry Blakely on September 17, 1939. Our son Henry, Jr., was born October 10, 1940. We also have a daughter, Nora, born September 8, 1951.

"In July of 1941 a poetry writing class was formed by Inez Stark Boulton at the South Side Community Art Center here. Here I learned more about modern poetry—from one who had an excellent understanding of it. The class was maintained for almost two years.

"I won, in 1943, '44 and '45, four first prizes in the poetry division of the Midwestern Writers' Conference. In August of 1945 my first book of poetry, *A Street in Bronzeville,* was published. The following December I was chosen by *Mademoiselle* magazine as one of 'Ten Women of the Year.' The following March I was given a $1000 American Academy of Arts and Letters award, and a Guggenheim fellowship. The latter was renewed in March of 1947.

"In August of 1949 *Annie Allen,* a second book of poetry, was published. In October of that year I received the Eunice Tietjens Memorial Award given by *Poetry* magazine. In 1950 I received the Pulitzer prize for *Annie Allen.*"

* * *

The strength of Gwendolyn Brooks' poetry consists, Rolfe Humphries wrote in 1949, "of boldness, invention, a daring to experiment, a naturalness that does not scorn literature but absorbs it, exploits it, and through this absorption and exploitation comes out with the remark made in an entirely original way, not offhand so much as forthright." Another critic remarked that in her poetry she draws upon her own personal, social, and racial experiences in such a way that they become "not merely personal or racial but universal in their implications."

In 1953 Miss Brooks published her first novel, *Maud Martha,* the story of a young Negro girl growing up in Chicago. In form the book is a series of sketches which suggest sensitively and with restraint the emotional depths of a seemingly simple and uneventful life. Within this framework, Coleman Rosenberger found "the bright imprint of her identity . . . the same sharp insights, the warmth, the joy in the work that words can do, the polished simplicity of line, the perfection of word and phrase" that distinguish Miss Brooks' verse.

PRINCIPAL WORKS: A Street in Bronzeville, 1945; Annie Allen, 1949; Maud Martha (novel) 1953.

ABOUT: Dreer, H. American Literature by Negro Authors; Current Biography 1950; New York Times May 2, 1950; Phylon 11 (1950); Poetry April 1950; Saturday Review of Literature September 17, 1949, May 13, 1950, May 20, 1950.

BROOKS, VAN WYCK* (February 16, 1886-). For autobiographical sketch and list of earlier works and references, see TWENTIETH CENTURY AUTHORS, 1942.

* * *

Van Wyck Brooks writes: "His first wife, the former Eleanor Kenyon Stimson [not Eleanor Kenyon, as incorrectly given in the earlier volume], died in 1946. He then left Westport, Conn., where he had lived for twenty-six years and settled for two years in New York. Then, marrying Gladys Rice Billings, he returned to Connecticut, spending a year at Cornwall and subsequently buying a house at Bridgewater, where he has lived ever since.

"Since 1942 he has received honorary degrees from Dartmouth and Union colleges, and Northwestern, Northeastern, and Boston universities. Since 1942 he has also become a Fellow of the Royal Society of Literature (London) and the American Academy of Arts and Sciences (Boston)."

Brooks has now published the three concluding volumes of the series collectively titled "Makers and Finders: A History of the Writer in America, 1800-1915." These are *The World of Washington Irving, The Times of Melville and Whitman,* and *The Confident Years.* His *The Writer in America,* published in 1953, was undertaken, he writes, "to explain the author's reasons for writing his historical series. Beginning with

* văn wĭk'

this, he then went on to explain his philosophy of life and letters."

Edmund Wilson and other commentators on the work of Van Wyck Brooks have observed that Brooks' reputation as a critic has been radically revised in the past quarter century. He began his career as a controversial or "opposition" critic with a handful of readers. He became popular—"the darling of the women's clubs," Wilson puts it—and won a Pulitzer prize. And now, Wilson writes, "the highbrows are trying to drop him."

That may be overstating the case a little. As a critic, Brooks belongs to the so-called "biographical" school, which approaches a writer's work through studying his life, his personality, and his character. The approach has been a useful one, often making an obscure writer more attractive to wider numbers of readers or casting valuable new light upon an already popular writer. But the biographical approach lacks method; it focuses upon the critic's insight, intuition, or imagination, rather than upon the literary work that is being studied. A striking example of this kind of faulty emphasis was offered in the long and bitter controversy between Bernard De Voto and Brooks over their interpretations of the life of Mark Twain. In 1944, when De Voto published his angry indictment of the American literature of the twenties, *The Literary Fallacy,* he devoted almost half his book to an attack on Brooks. "The attack," Stanley Edgar Hyman wrote, "boiled down to the charge that Brooks hadn't begun to hate modern literature until 1940, whereas De Voto had been hating it at least since 1920."

Within the limits and limitations of his critical framework, Brooks has made significant contributions to American literary history—especially in his re-creation of the cultural life of nineteenth century New England and in his exhaustive survey of the minor as well as the major writers of the American past. Reviewing *The Confident Years* Malcolm Cowley wrote: "It isn't Mr. Brooks' definition of the American tradition that is important for the world today; it is his recovery of the tradition in volume after volume; it is his proof that in literature this country has long possessed a usable past. It is, beyond this, his love of letters as an art and his integrity as a lonely scholar."

ADDITIONAL WORKS: The World of Washington Irving, 1944; The Times of Melville and Whitman, 1947; A Chilmark Miscellany, 1948; The Confident Years: 1885-1915, 1952; The Writer in America, 1953; Scenes and Portraits, 1954; John Sloan: A Painter's Life, 1955.

ABOUT: Brooks, V. W. Scenes and Portraits; Dupee, F. W. *in* The Partisan Reader; Hyman, S. E. The Armed Vision; Kazin, A. On Native Grounds; Wilson, E. Classics and Commercials; Van Gelder, R. Writers and Writing; College English November 1946; New Republic October 9, 1944; Saturday Review of Literature November 8, 1947; Time October 2, 1944.

BROPHY, JOHN (December 6, 1899-   ). For autobiographical sketch and list of earlier works and references, see TWENTIETH CENTURY AUTHORS, 1942.

* * *

John Brophy writes from London: "In the past ten years he has published several novels, including *Sarah,* the 1803 love story, set in Dublin, of Robert Emmet and Sarah Curran; *Portrait of an Unknown Lady,* which expounds the strange ways of picture dealers; *Julian's Way,* set in Jerusalem and Haifa, a sympathetic depiction of British-Jewish personal relations during the last years of the Mandate; and *Turn the Key Softly,* the story of the first twelve hours spent by three women after their release from a London prison. Mr. Brophy has also made a substantial success with three works of non-fiction: *The Human Face,* the first comprehensive and historical study of this subject; its successor, *Body and Soul;* and a lively and unconventional journal, *The Mind's Eye.* Each of these three books is illustrated with old master and modern drawings from the author's private collection. His books are translated into most European languages west of the Iron Curtain. In the same period Mr. Brophy has played a prominent part in the British book trade, serving on the executives of the National Book League, the London PEN Club, and the Society of Authors. In addition, he has lately aroused intense controversy by advocating a new development in the method by which authors are paid—the 'Brophy penny' which those who use public and commercial circulating libraries in Great Britain are to be asked to pay for the benefit of the author on each volume borrowed.

"Three of his novels have been filmed: *Immortal Sergeant,* by 20th Century-Fox in 1943 and again in 1951 as *Fixed Bayonets,* with a Korean setting; *Waterfront,* by Rank in 1949; and *Turn the Key Softly,* by Rank in 1952-53."

ADDITIONAL WORKS: Spearhead, 1943; Target Island, 1944; The Human Face, 1945; Portrait of an Unknown Lady, 1945; City of Departures, 1946; Woman from Nowhere, 1946; Sarah, 1948; Body and Soul, 1948; Julian's Way, 1949; The Mind's Eye, 1949; Turn the Key Softly, 1951.

ABOUT: Brophy, J. The Mind's Eye.

*BROUN, HEYWOOD CAMPBELL (December 7, 1888-December 18, 1939). For biographical sketch and list of works and references, see TWENTIETH CENTURY AUTHORS, 1942.

* * *

ABOUT: Hoehn, M. (ed.) Catholic Authors, I; Kramer, D. Heywood Broun.

* brōōn

BROWN, ABBIE FARWELL (1872-March 4, 1927). For biographical sketch and list of works and references, see TWENTIETH CENTURY AUTHORS, 1942.

BROWN, ALICE (December 5, 1857-June 21, 1948). For autobiographical sketch and list of works and references, see TWENTIETH CENTURY AUTHORS, 1942.

* * *

Alice Brown died in Boston, Mass., at ninety.

A friend who saw her seven weeks before her death described her as "a white-haired lady, smooth-faced and deaf, and with a voice as clear as a little bronze bell."

Acknowledging that she was prone to sentiment and to "a gentle mysticism," F. L. Pattee said that "she worked with an artistry sonnet-like in its form and finish and with materials and motifs not merely localized, but universal." Grant Overton mentioned her "vigorousness of mind, fine perception, integrity of purpose and poetic feeling."

ABOUT: America February 19, 1949; New York Times June 22, 1948.

BROWN, HARRY PETER M' NAB (April 30, 1917-   ), American novelist, poet, and playwright, writes: "I was born in Portland, Maine, the son of Bessie Hiles and Harry McNab Brown. After a normal public school education, I entered Harvard with the Class of 1940, remaining there through my sophomore year. My leave-taking of Harvard was an amiable

G.M. Kesslere

one and due to no lack of scholarship on my part; I merely got bored.

"The fall of 1939 found me an office-boy in the morgue at *Time.* I had already started to contribute to the *New Yorker,* and the late

Harold Ross, rest him, disapproved of contributors who worked for the Luce publications. He hired me as a sub-sub-editor.

"In line with *New Yorker* policy, my duties were never made quite clear to me. Looking back, all I can say is that they required a full two-hour working day, and that most of my daylight hours were spent in the bar of the Algonquin Hotel, a place in which one can learn a great deal about people. This was a very happy period in my life.

"It came to an abrupt end in July 1941 when I, who cannot pound a nail without smashing a finger or two, found myself in the Corps of Engineers at Fort Belvoir, Va.

"When *Yank* was started I joined the magazine in New York. In December 1942 I was sent to its London office, where I remained until the winter of 1943-44. Then, for reasons which still bewilder me, I turned up in the Films Division of the Office of War Information, in London still, and on loan from the army. This organization eventually lent me back to the army—specifically to the Anglo-American Film Unit which, under Garson Kanin and Carol Reed, made *The True Glory.* I was returned to the States in August 1945 and was discharged in October of the same year.

"I am possibly the only Harvard man who, after more than four years in the army, came out a private. For a short and giddy period I was a staff sergeant, but I managed, one way or another, to make myself stripeless.

"I wrote a novel, *A Walk in the Sun,* which was published in 1944 and enjoyed a small success—but sufficient to develop in me a taste for luxury which intrigues me more each year. At one time I was the only private of any army, including the Russian, living at the Ritz in London.

"The short Broadway run of a play of mine, *A Sound of Hunting,* in November 1945, left me with two things: (a) no prospects, and (b) a certain amount of cash. I spent most of the latter on a mink coat for my former wife (it was *cold* that winter), and then began looking around for some vaguely honest work.

"A film had been made from *A Walk in the Sun,* and Lewis Milestone, the director, had come east for the première. He persuaded me to try my hand at a screen original. So I came to Hollywood in January 1946, and I have been here, working on films, ever since. The California sun is no detriment to luxury.

"I first started writing in, I believe, 1934, and my first publication was in *Poetry.* Since then, in addition to books, I have appeared in the *New Yorker, Atlantic Monthly, Vogue, Harper's Bazaar, Town and Country, Virginia Quarterly Review, Horizon,* and several others whose names escape me.

"Since coming to Hollywood I have twice been nominated for an Academy Award, and in 1952 I was given an Oscar (along with Michael Wilson) for the screenplay of *A Place in the Sun,* based on Dreiser's *An American Tragedy.* I should say I've worked on between fifteen and twenty films.

"My avocations are hunting, fishing, guns and everything to do with them, avoiding work, being dull at parties, and not answering letters."

PRINCIPAL WORKS: *Poetry*—The Poem of Bunker Hill, 1941; The End of a Decade, 1941; The Violent, 1943; Poems, 1941-1944, 1945; *Novels*—A Walk in the Sun, 1944; Artie Greengroin, 1945. *Drama*—A Sound of Hunting, 1946.

ABOUT: Warfel, H. R. American Novelists of Today; New York Herald Tribune June 24, 1944; New York Times November 30, 1941; Poetry January 1948; Saturday Review of Literature December 24, 1949.

BROWN, IVOR JOHN CARNEGIE (April 25, 1891-), English word-specialist, essayist, novelist, and journalist, was born in Penang, Malaya. He comes of a Scottish family and was educated at Cheltenham College and Balliol College, Oxford. In 1915 he entered Home Civil Service from which he resigned to take up literary work.

He is a life-long writer about the theatre, although he has never really specialized, preferring to practice journalism and authorship in many forms. He claims he has been writing ever since he could spell and has a book he wrote and illustrated at the age of five. In his youth he wanted to write like Compton Mackenzie, then like C. E. Montague of the *Manchester Guardian,* lastly, Somerset Maugham, that is, richly, then austerely.

He was dramatic critic and leader writer for the *Manchester Guardian,* 1919-35, and dramatic critic for the London *Saturday Review,* 1923-30. He was an editor of the London *Observer,* 1942-48, and at various times dramatic critic for *Punch, Weekend Review,* and other papers.

His first novel was published in 1915 and his fourth and latest in 1932. Between those dates he wrote numerous other works ranging in subject from politics to literature and the drama. With the exception of a volume titled *Shakespeare* appearing in 1949 the decade of the forties was given over to a series of essays on word lore. The third of his double-volume excursions into word lore, *No Idle Words, and, Having the Last Word,* appeared in the United States with an introduction by J. Donald Adams. Commenting on the series, the *New Yorker* wrote: "The author has a witty way with words; he likes to poke into their genealogies and is delighted when he can turn up a bar sinister. From "alien" to "yoicks" he discusses all manner of words—common, recherché and slang." The London *Statesman and Nation* accused him of "being insensible to verbal magic among his contemporaries and overlooking the most word-intoxicated of English writers, Joyce and Virginia Woolf, deserting them to look for Elizabethan glories."

During the winter of 1950 he decided to set down a record of how one Londoner made the best of the four dark months of winter. His attitude was "that a man is a fool who does not savour the place in which he lives." *Winter in London,* 1951, was the result of his strolls and explorations through London streets. The *Manchester Guardian* considered it "a glowing and original book, and that is much to say of a book on so well served a theme."

He is married to Irene Hentschel, a theatrical director, and lives in London. In 1950 the honorary LL.D. degree was conferred upon him by the University of St. Andrews and the University of Aberdeen.

He thinks he writes best when feeling rather ill physically, for it is drudgery to sit at a desk when in good health. His clubs are the Garrick and the Savile of London and the Royal and Ancient Golf Club of St. Andrews. He is an active golfer, but thinks of himself as a less active but appreciative spectator of any aspect of the human comedy.

PRINCIPAL WORKS: Years of Plenty, 1915; Security, 1916; Meaning of Democracy, 1919; English Political Theory, 1920; Lighting Up Time, 1920; H. G. Wells, 1922; Masques and Phases, 1926; First Player, 1927; Parties of the Play, 1928; Now on View, 1929; Brown Studies, 1930; Marine Parade, 1932; I Commit to the Flames, 1934; Master Sanguine, 1934; The Heart of England, 1935; The Great and the Goods, 1937; Life Within Reason, 1939; This Shakespeare Industry (with George Feron) 1939; A Word in Your Ear, 1942; Just Another Word, 1943; I Give You My Word, 1945; Say the Last Word, 1947; No Idle Words,

1949; Shakespeare, 1949; Having the Last Word, 1950; Winter in London, 1951; I Break My Word, 1951; Summer in Scotland, 1952.

ABOUT: Brown, I. Confessions, *in* Saturday Book, edited by Leonard Russell.

BROWN, JOHN MASON (July 3, 1900-). For biographical sketch and list of earlier works and references, see TWENTIETH CENTURY AUTHORS, 1942.

* * *

In a recent two-part *New Yorker* "Profile," Herbert Warren Wind described John Mason Brown as "a graying, ebullient, high-strung Kentucky thoroughbred, out of Harvard by Broadway, whose specialty is literature and the theatre." To many audiences all over the United States, he is also "the greatest lecturer of the present day." Brown generally prefers to think of himself as a man-of-letters rather than as a popular lecturer, and there is no denying his claim to literary distinction—his witty, sensitive, and often tender and moving essays, and his shrewd, sophisticated theatre criticism. If he is better known as a lecturer, this is a commentary not on the deficiencies of his writing but on the super-abundant success of his personality on the lecture platform. Urbane, poised, quick-witted, energetic and enthusiastic, he is a kind of cultural ambassador from the theatre and publishing circles of New York to the outermost reaches of the country.

Brown's busy schedule includes—in addition to some seventy-five lecture appearances a year—the writing of "Seeing Things," his column of theatre criticism (and more recently articles on politics and world affairs) for the *Saturday Review,* and books, essays, prefaces, and miscellaneous articles; appearances as master of ceremonies at any number of literary and theatrical functions, and on radio and television programs; meetings of the board of overseers of Harvard and the board of trustees of the Metropolitan Museum of Art; and keeping a paternal eye on two energetic sons (described with engaging good humor in *Morning Faces*). He has an apartment in New York and a summer home at Martha's Vineyard. During World War II he was a lieutenant in the Navy, an aide to Admiral Alan G. Kirk, and participated in the Sicily and Normandy landings.

ADDITIONAL WORKS: Insides Out: Being the Saga of a Drama Critic Who Attends His Own Opening, 1942; To All Hands: An Amphibious Adventure, 1943; Many a Watchful Night, 1944; Seeing Things, 1946; Seeing More Things, 1948; Morning Faces, 1949; Still Seeing Things, 1950; As They Appear, 1952; Daniel Boone (juvenile) 1952.

ABOUT: New Yorker October 18, October 25, 1952; Newsweek November 22, 1943; Saturday Evening Post October 2, 1943; Saturday Review of Literature September 21, 1946, December 2, 1950; Theatre Arts October 1943.

BROWN, ROLLO WALTER (March 15, 1880-). For autobiographical sketch and list of earlier works and references, see TWENTIETH CENTURY AUTHORS, 1942.

* * *

Rollo Walter Brown published his autobiography, *The Hills Are Strong*, in 1953. More than a factual record of a busy and fruitful life, the book records the author's intellectual and philosophical development. During World War II, Brown relates in his book, he wrote editorials for the Boston *Herald* and traveled over the country lecturing at many colleges on "The Creative Spirit and Durable Peace." He stressed the importance of "work that provided growth," creativeness, originality. "The more there is of growth, of reality, for individual persons," he writes, "the more there is of a transfiguring power running through the whole of life, giving to existence a sustaining miraculousness, on and on ahead."

Brown lives in Cambridge, Mass. In the early winter of 1953 he gave eight talks in the famous Lowell Lectures at the Boston Public Library.

ADDITIONAL WORKS: Harvard Yard in the Golden Age, 1948; Dr. Howe and the Forsyth Infirmary, 1952; The Hills Are Strong, 1953.

ABOUT: Brown, R. W. The Hills Are Strong.

BROWN, YEATS-. See YEATS-BROWN

BROWN, Mrs. ZENITH (JONES) ("Leslie Ford," "David Frome," pseuds.) For biographical sketch and list of earlier works and references, see TWENTIETH CENTURY AUTHORS, 1942.

* * *

Whether she writes as "Leslie Ford" or as "David Frome," Mrs.. Brown is equally successful, producing a series of sleek and entertaining detective novels, written in the best Anglo-American tradition. Messrs. Pinkerton and Bull, her British sleuths, are "amiable as ever"; and Grace Latham, who narrates her American tales, is emerging, Anthony Boucher wrote in 1953, "as an extremely lively, likeable and real person."

ADDITIONAL WORKS: *As "David Frome"*— Homicide House: Mr. Pinkerton Returns (in England: Murder on the Square) 1950. *As "Leslie Ford"*—Murder in the O.P.M. (in England: Priority Murder) 1942; Siren in the Night, 1943; All for the Love of a Lady (in England: Crack of Dawn) 1944; Philadelphia Murder Story, 1945; Honolulu Story, 1946; The Woman in Black, 1947; The Devil's Stronghold, 1948; Date with Death (in England: Shot in the Dark) 1949; Murder Is the Pay-Off, 1951; The Bahamas Murder Case, 1952; Washington Whispers Murder, 1953; Invitation to Murder, 1954.

ABOUT: Saturday Evening Post January 18, 1947.

BROWNE, LEWIS (June 24, 1897-January 3, 1949). For autobiographical sketch and list of earlier works and references, see TWENTIETH CENTURY AUTHORS, 1942.

* * *

Lewis Browne committed suicide by taking poison at his home in Santa Monica, Calif., at fifty-one. Under treatment for an eye ailment, the author left a note saying "the doctors have done their best for me" and regretting "what I am about to do."

During World War II Browne served as civilian lecturer in the orientation section of the War Department. A novel about a pre-Pearl Harbor American Fascist organization, *See What I Mean?*, was published in 1943.

It was described by Joseph Henry Jackson as "a readable, shrewdly put together pamphlet with plenty of story to carry the message the author wishes to deliver."

ADDITIONAL WORKS: See What I Mean? 1943; Wisdom of Israel (ed.) 1945; World's Great Scriptures (ed.) 1946.

ABOUT: New York Times January 4, 1949.

BROWNELL, BAKER (December 12, 1887-), American sociologist and educator, writes: "I was born in St. Charles, a small, old-fashioned town in the Fox river valley of northern Illinois. My parents were Mid-Westerners of New England colonial stock. I was the fifth of their six widely spaced children. My father, a veteran of the Civil War, was a paper manufacturer. His mill, a small one, is one of my earliest memories. In St. Charles I followed the rhythm of school and long, easy-going summers, football every fall, and many days alone in the woods and on the

water. I had a passion for the river. My home was full of books and I still possess with pride our old ninth edition of the *Britannica*. My older sister, Harriet, a person like my father of remarkable seriousness and dignity of purpose, greatly influenced my early life. In high school I discovered the arts and sciences. I began—too late—the study of the violin, took up sketching and later oil painting, but before I left high school the *Scientific American* accepted an article of mine, written in long hand and illustrated painfully by the author, on the air thermometer.

"College in general did me more harm than good until my fourth year when I arrived at Harvard. I came just at the end of the great period in philosophy and knew well Royce, Santayana, Palmer, Woods, R. B. Perry. William James was still a familiar figure in Emerson Hall. I also knew Bliss Perry, Wendell, Dean Briggs. In 1912-13 I held the James Walker Traveling Fellowship in Philosophy (the same once held by Santayana) and studied, or dreamed, at Tübingen, Germany, and Cambridge, England. I returned from England in 1913 and went on the Chicago *Tribune* as cub reporter at $12 a week. Walter Howey, the man who became the symbol of the hard-boiled newspaper man, hired me. He really was a kind person.

"Ten years in many places followed. There was newspaper work, teaching, editing an educational journal, writing poetry for Harriet Monroe's magazine *Poetry*, and other magazines, marriage to Helena Van Arsdale Maxwell, miscellaneous military service in the National Guard, the Army and finally the Navy where I was critically ill for a long time with pneumonia and its complications. Towards the end of this period I left the Chicago *Daily News* where I was editorial writer and took a similar position on the Chicago *Tribune*.

"The *Tribune* at that time retained a good deal of the Progressive character of Teddy Roosevelt days. Colonel McCormick and Captain Patterson served alternately each month as editor. Tiffany Blake was chief editorial writer. During these years on the *Tribune* and the *Daily News* I never was asked to write anything not of my own choosing. At about this time I also entered the faculty of Northwestern University and served successively as professor of journalism, professor of contemporary thought, and professor of philosophy. Thus after

twenty-five years, I was back in the field of my early choice.

"I wrote a book during this period on the average about every three years and edited twenty-six more. Some of my books reached a goodly number of printings and received high comment from a diversity of people all the way from John Dewey and Bertrand Russell to Zona Gale and Carl Sandburg. I traveled widely, including the famous trip to Galapagos Islands in 1930 as a guest on the yacht of Commander E. F. McDonald, Jr. I married Adelaide Howard in 1933 and have a son, Eugene.

"Since World War I my ideas have become more and more liberal. I never have fallen into that snare of liberals called Communism, but I believe that the social evils that have given rise to Communism must be faced, if our American freedom and democracy is to endure. During the last fifteen years I have turned to study and field work in small communities, or primary communities, for the answer to this critical problem. From 1944 to 1946 I served as director of a community service project, the Montana Study, financed initially by the Rockefeller Foundation, and continued that work in other areas until 1953 on two successive grants from the same source. At present I am entering this work towards the rehabilitation of the American small community in my own state. As Director of Area Services at Southern Illinois University and Professor of Philosophy at Northwestern University I am trying to integrate two major interests of my youth, philosophy and the small community or home town. The problem is more important than most professional and business men realize."

PRINCIPAL WORKS: The New Universe, 1926; Earth Is Enough, 1933; Architecture and Modern Life (with F. L. Wright) 1937; Art Is Action, 1939; The Philosopher in Chaos, 1941; Life in Montana (with J. K. Howard and P. Meadows) 1945; The Human Community, 1950; The College and the Community, 1952.

ABOUT: Poston, R. W. Small Town Renaissance.

BROWNELL, WILLIAM CRARY (August 30, 1851-July 22, 1928). For biographical sketch and list of works and references, see TWENTIETH CENTURY AUTHORS, 1942.

* * *

ABOUT: Perry, B. *in* American Academy of Arts and Letters Commemorative Tributes, 1905-1941; Pritchard, J. P. Return to the Fountains; Bulletin of Bibliography January-April 1953; University of Texas Studies in English 1945-1946.

BRUCE, WILLIAM CABELL (March 12, 1860-May 9, 1946). For autobiographical sketch and list of works and references, see TWENTIETH CENTURY AUTHORS, 1942.

* * *

William Cabell Bruce died at his home in Baltimore, Md., at eighty-six, after an illness of several months. His wife had died six months earlier.

Mr. Bruce has been called "a seasoned public servant, a scholar and a widely known orator and author." In connection with his Pulitzer prize-winning biography of Benjamin Franklin, the Boston *Transcript* praised its author's "keen critical insight and deep understanding of human nature . . . a fine sense of proportion, and a literary manner which renders the work eminently readable."

ABOUT: New York Times May 10, 1946.

BRULLER, JEAN (pseudonym "Vercors") (February 26, 1902-), French novelist, essayist, and graphic artist, was born in Paris on the centenary of Victor Hugo's birthday, a detail he considers significant. He  has had two distinct careers, one as a graphic artist under his own name; the other, born in the French Resistance during World War II, as a writer under the name "Vercors."

In spite of the literary auspices of his birth he felt drawn in early youth not at all to letters but to art and science. After graduating from the Ecole Alsacienne in Paris, he studied mathematics at the Paris University, then switched to a technical college which he left with a diploma of an electrical engineer. After a year's military service in Tunis, he decided he was not made for either science or industry. In Tunis he had begun to paint and little remains of his first career except a keen interest in scientific problems and a consuming admiration for Albert Einstein. Returning to Paris, he went to art school where he abandoned painting for the kindred arts of drawing, etching, aqua-fortis. In 1926 he published his first album of satirical drawings, *21 Recettes de Mort Violente,* later republished in New York under the title *21 Delightful Ways of Committing Suicide.* An immediate success, it was followed by *Hypotheses on Art Lovers,*

1927; *A Man Cut up in Slices,* 1929; *A New Key to Dreams,* 1929; *This Is Hell,* 1935; *Comforting Visions of the War,* 1936; *Silences,* 1937. From 1932 to 1938 he published a series of prints, *Quarterly Accounts,* which was eventually to appear in a volume of 160 plates under the title *The Dance of the Living.* He also illustrated a number of books including the works of Racine, Kipling, Maurois, Coleridge, and Poe.

In 1940 Lieutenant Jean Bruller was serving an Alpine regiment at the foot of a mountain plateau called Vercors when the collapse of France and the armistice came. He returned to his village, twenty-five miles from Paris, to hire out as a journeyman carpenter. Writing every night "to keep his brain in trim" he eventually came in contact with the French intellectual Resistance movement. With other members of the group, he founded the leading clandestine publishing house in France, Les Editions de Minuit. Its first publication, *Le Silence de la Mer,* was written by Vercors. Smuggled to England and America for translation and republication, *The Silence of the Sea* was attributed to all the great writers of France. His example was followed with works by the leading Resistance writers, François Mauriac, Paul Eluard, Louis Aragon, and Jean Cassou. In 1943, a second work, *La Marche à l'Etoile* by Vercors, was issued by the underground publishing house.

Since the war Vercors, retaining his pseudonym, has written a number of novels, *L'Imprimerie de Verdun, Les Armes de la Nuit* and its sequel, *La Puissance du Jour;* short stories and essays. His recent novel, *Les Animaux Dénaturés,* translated into English, *You Shall Know Them,* by his wife, Rita Barisse, merges his crisp, satirical style with Vercors' moral and philosophical preoccupations. What concerns him is the postwar world and the necessity to determine the basic notion underlying the term "human." On a visit to the United States as a lecturer in 1946 he spoke to his audiences on the danger of the atomic bomb. In an interview with a reporter of the *New Yorker* he stated that the feature of the contemporary world most frightening to him was the progressive indifference to the concept of death. While in America the spot he most wanted to see was the TVA project.

In 1952 the artist Jean Bruller caught up once more with the writer. Adding one more to his several professions, he developed a new manual technique for reproducing modern oil paintings and pastels, the work of

Van Gogh, Monet, Braque and others. The first Paris exhibition of his replicas astounded Picasso and Léger who claimed they could not distinguish, at first sight, their own work from the copies.

A slight, bright-eyed man with delicate features and hands and dark hair, Jean Bruller continues his several careers in Paris.

PRINCIPAL WORKS IN ENGLISH TRANSLATION: The Silence of the Sea, 1945; Three Short Novels, 1947; You Shall Know Them, 1953.

ABOUT: Columbia Dictionary of Modern European Literature; Mahony, B. E. Illustrators of Children's Books; New York Herald Tribune Book Review June 28, 1953; New Yorker March 9, 1946.

BRUNNER, (HEINRICH) EMIL (December 23, 1889-   ), Swiss theologian, was born in Switzerland, the son of Emil and Sophie Brunner, and educated at the *gymnasium* in Zurich. He received his doctorate in theology from the University of Zurich in 1913 and did further study in theology in Berlin and in New York. He has received honorary degrees in divinity from the universities of Münster, Edinburgh, Utrecht, Oxford, Oslo, Princeton, and St. Andrews, and holds an honorary Doctor of Laws degree from the University of Bern.

Like his contemporary Karl Barth, he began his career as a minister in the Swiss Reformed Church, taking over his first pastorate in 1912. After a brief period of high school teaching in Leeds, England, he returned to Switzerland as a pastor in the Canton of Glarus, where he remained from 1916 to 1924. In the latter year he was appointed lecturer in theology at the University of Zurich. Two years later he became professor of systematic and practical theology there.

Brunner has lectured at many universities in Europe, Great Britain, and the United States. At the invitation of the Princeton Theological Seminary he was guest professor of systematic theology for the academic year 1938-1939. When World War II became imminent, he chose to return to the University of Zurich where, from 1942 to 1944, he was rector of the university, and where he is currently professor of theology. In 1948 he delivered the Gifford Lectures at St. Andrews University in Fife, Scotland, and these were later published under the title *Christianity and Civilization*. In these lectures Brunner attempted to clarify the relationship between present-day Christianity and civiliza-

tion and the world which we hope for in the future. Late in 1952 he accepted the post of professor of Christian ethics and philosophy at the new Japan International Christian University. Brunner was married in 1917 to Margrit Lauterburg, and they have two sons living (two other sons are deceased).

Emil Brunner and Karl Barth are the cofounders of a reform movement within the Protestant Church which bears the name "Theology of Crisis," and in their writings the main trends of the movement have been fully developed. They have rejected any theology based upon human experience and observation as having significance, Brunner writes, "only for the knowledge of man, not for the knowledge of God." The knowledge of God which the theologian seeks, Brunner continues, is not to be founded in man but "beyond all human possibilities—truth which is given in the event which constitutes revelation." The point at which Barth and Brunner diverge is on the issue of the divine image in man. Barth holds that in the fall of man the image of God in man was destroyed by sin, and "the necessary point of contact" with God can be restored only by faith, in the act of revelation. Brunner believes, to quote John McCreary, that man still has "traces of the divine image, however defaced by sin they may be." For both Barth and Brunner, however, as M. Chaning-Pearce writes, "it remains the essential truth that there is no way from man to God apart from the grace of God which is His free gift and is to be found only by faith." As Brunner defines it, "Faith is neither a psychological function, nor a combination of such functions; it is the life-utterance of the total self in its unanalysable unity . . . the totality act of personality."

Brunner's theological inquiries have taken him into other fields of knowledge—cultural history, ethics, philosophy, psychology. Unlike Barth, he favors an active participation of the church in matters of "earthly justice and the earthly welfare of men," though he warns that these must always remain "secondary matters." He wrote, in the *Christian Century* (July 11, 1951): "Today . . . our eyes are opened to the terrible danger that life may lose its human quality through the constant narrowing down of the life of the soul and the scope of the personal by the abstract powers—the state, society, civilization. The totalitarian state is simply the maximum of this collectivization."

Brunner is a powerful writer; his style is lucid and his exposition aimed at a more "popular" level than are Barth's writings.

But this is not to suggest that he is a "popularizer" or that his work lacks profundity. Daniel D. Williams observed: "Brunner's writing has a deceptive smoothness and simplicity on the surface. Underneath there is a dialectical restlessness and a continuous subtle movement."

ADDITIONAL WORKS IN ENGLISH TRANSLATION: Theology of Crisis, 1929; The Word and the World, 1931; The Mediator, 1934; The Divine Imperative, 1936; God and Man: Four Essays on the Nature of Personality, 1936; Our Faith, 1936; Philosophy of Religion, From the Standpoint of Protestant Theology, 1937; The Church and the Oxford Group, 1937; Man in Revolt: A Christian Anthropology, 1939; The Divine-Human Encounter, 1943; Justice and the Social Order, 1945; Reason and Revelation, 1946; Christianity and Civilization, 1948; The Christian Doctrine of God (Dogmatics, I) 1950; The Scandal of Christianity, 1951; Misunderstanding of the Church, 1952; The Christian Doctrine of Creation and Redemption, 1952.

ABOUT: Chaning-Pearce, M. The Terrible Crystal; Moran, J. W. Catholic Faith and Modern Theologies; Rolston, H. A Conservative Looks to Barth and Brunner; Van Til, C. The New Modernism; Christendom Spring 1947; Christian Century August 4, 1948, September 15, 1948, October 15, 1952; Journal of Religion April 1940, April 1948; Time August 16, 1948, December 5, 1949.

BRUNNGRABER, RUDOLF (1900-).

For autobiographical sketch and list of works and references, see TWENTIETH CENTURY AUTHORS, 1942.

* * *

Rudolf Brunngraber remained in Germany during World War II at considerable personal risk—because his wife was part Jewish and because he was an anti-Nazi. In 1940, Ernst Waldinger reports in *Books Abroad*, Brunngraber was investigated by the Gestapo but was not arrested. In 1944 he was commissioned by the government to write a book on logistics in World War II, and shortly after he was placed under civil arrest and forced to live and work at the staff headquarters of General Nagel, just outside of Berlin. During the chaotic days of the battle for Berlin, he escaped and went into hiding until the war was over.

Brunngraber has written several essays shrewdly analyzing the German Fascist movement. He has also published two stories, *Der Tierkreis* and *Irrelohe*, and two novels, *Prozess auf Tod und Leben* (1948) and *Der Weg durch das Labyrinth* (1949). None of these has appeared in English translation. Lately he has been working as a motion picture writer and producer. He was recently elected to the Deutsche Akademie für Sprache und Dichtung.

ABOUT: Books Abroad Autumn 1952.

BRUSH, Mrs. KATHARINE (INGHAM) (August 15, 1902-June 10, 1952).

For biographical sketch and list of earlier works and references, see TWENTIETH CENTURY AUTHORS, 1942.

* * *

Katharine Brush died at St. Luke's Hospital in New York City at forty-nine, after an illness of several months.

At her death she left an unfinished novel "Lover Come Back," on which she had worked for two years. A selection of sketches from her syndicated magazine column *Out of My Mind*, published in 1943, seemed to L. S. Munn to appear "more original and amusing" then the material actually was, because of Miss Brush's "flair for phrasing and adept appreciation of the generation and era in which she lived."

Repeating the frequent comparison of her work with that of F. Scott Fitzgerald, the New York *Times* describes her fiction as "a product of the post-World War I period—entertaining, brittle, superficial and in revolt against sentimentality and other qualities of the Victorian period."

ADDITIONAL WORKS: Out of My Mind, 1943; This Man and This Woman (four short novels) 1944.

ABOUT: Van Gelder, R. Writers and Writing; American Home December 1946; American Magazine January 1944; Scholastic February 4, 1947.

*BRUUN, GEOFFREY (October 20, 1898-), Canadian-American historian,

writes: "An old village near Montreal and a new one near Vancouver framed my childhood, but in retrospect the Laurentian hills and the mountains and forests of British Columbia loom as the palpable realities. The impalpable realities were books. To my parents books and memories of England were a refuge from the emptiness of the Canadian frontier and like all children of exiles I grew up in two worlds. The other-world of literature took on a timeless peripheral intensity.

"Some chastening months in the Royal Air Force (1918), limited to fighting mumps and influenza, brought free tuition at the University of British Columbia. A mistaken enthusiasm for chemistry died of unbalanced equa-

* "The spelling of my name (Norwegian originally) troubles many people. Pronunciation: Jeffrey Broon."

tions. Gay escapades mismanaging the college weekly pointed toward journalism, yet somehow I ended up in history and went east to Cornell in 1924 on a graduate fellowship.

"From Joseph Quincy Adams I learned what made the Elizabethans great; from Preserved Smith the meaning of science for Western man; from Carl Becker insights too numerous to list. It was he who first convinced me that books are not made, they grow, and he detected that my desire to write was not so much an urge to communicate as an impulse to sort things out, as best I might, for my own satisfaction.

"Luck and the generosity of publishers have let me indulge the impulse, even within the unpromising pattern of history texts. During the 1930's, when the revival of authoritarianism dismayed all liberals, I tried to trace its roots through the enlightened despots of the eighteenth century and the rule of Napoleon. A counter-search for the strands, strong and weak, from which democracy was woven, led me to biographies of Saint-Just and Clemenceau.

"Since 1945 I have forsaken college teaching except for occasional semesters at Columbia and Cornell. A lively family and forbearing friends help to keep me human, travel keeps me leavened, and writing keeps me solvent. My favorite game of solitaire with filing cards is the search for a pattern that will make Western civilization more intelligible to me, and my publishers seem reckless enough to speculate on my speculations."

PRINCIPAL WORKS: Saint-Just: Apostle of the Terror, 1932; Europe and the French Imperium, 1938; Clemenceau, 1943.

ABOUT: Historical Outlook February 1933; New Republic August 17, 1938, December 6, 1943; Saturday Review of Literature May 7, 1938, November 20, 1943.

BRYANT, Sir ARTHUR (February 18, 1899-   ), British historian, the son of Sir Francis Bryant, Sergeant-at-Arms to King  George V, left Harrow at eighteen to become a pilot in the Royal Flying Corps and was one of the original officers of the newly formed R.A.F. He served in the first squadron to bomb the Rhineland cities in World War I and was at one time the only Britisher attached to a training unit of American pilots sent overseas in 1917.

Upon demobilization he went to Oxford —although he had won a scholarship at Cambridge—but left the university to teach in London. For a time he ran a children's library in Charles Dickens' old house in a slum that has since been bombed out of existence. At twenty-three he was appointed principal of the Cambridge School of Arts, Crafts, and Technology, becoming the youngest headmaster in England. After raising the student body from two hundred to two thousand in three years, he resigned to read for the Bar and to write history. The pursuit of his new careers did not prevent him from becoming a producer of monster pageants. Among his productions were the Cambridge, Oxford, and Hyde Park pageants and the Naval Night Pageant at Greenwich, attended by the King and Queen, the Prince of Wales, the British Cabinet and members of the World Economic Conference. He was acclaimed by the press as an "English Reinhardt."

His first published work, *King Charles II*, was an immediate popular success. Since 1931 he has published seven works on the later seventeenth century as well as a trilogy (*The Years of Endurance, Years of Victory, Age of Elegance*) on Britain's struggle during the French Revolution and the Napoleonic Wars and a three-volume *Life of Samuel Pepys*, based on diaries newly discovered by the author in 1934 and 1935.

An indefatigable lecturer, he has been heard in many of the leading cities and schools of Great Britain and has been invited to lecture in the United States and in fourteen European countries. In 1935 he delivered the Alfred Watson lectures on American history, literature, and biography for the Sulgrave Manor Trust. The lectures were subsequently published as *The American Ideal*.

In 1936 he succeeded G. K. Chesterton as writer of "Our Note Book" page in the *Illustrated London News*. Throughout his writing career he has been a frequent contributor to leading London papers and magazines. In radio he has broadcast on subjects allied to his historical preoccupations and a collection of his scripts appeared in a volume titled *The National Character*.

Bryant's dramatization of the life of Samuel Pepys in collaboration with W. P. Lipscomb had a run of one hundred and fifty performances in London. He has written several radio plays for B.B.C. During the Forties he moved away from the seventeenth century in his writings, edited Neville Chamberlain's speeches, and wrote *English*

Saga, a survey of the last hundred years of England's history culminating in the epic of Dunkirk.

His travels have taken him to Spain, Portugal, Germany, Italy, and the West Indies, and he was in France at the outbreak of World War II. Even his residence reflects his bent toward history. He lives in a house which has been described as "one of the most beautiful of the smaller seventeenth century English houses," and which once belonged to Edmund Verney, the son of the member of Parliament whose shorthand notes gave the world the story of Charles I's attempt to arrest the Five Members. He collects old furniture, pictures and books and claims that even his cat is literary and has corresponded with a cat owned by Walter de la Mare. He is married to Anne Brooke, the daughter of Bertram Brooke, the brother and heir presumptive to the Raja of Sarawak.

He is a Fellow of the Royal Historical Society and a member of the Advisory Talks Council of the British Broadcasting Corporation.

Age of Elegance, the last volume of his historical trilogy, appeared in 1950. The *Yale Review* commented, "Mr. Bryant writes in a spirit of sober though unashamed patriotism. But the great story he so splendidly tells is one that in its nature and significance belongs to the entire free world." The *New Statesman and Nation* admired his virtuosity in painting Waterloo but warned that the historians' "love of military music is liable to carry them away." But as the main subject of the book is not military but a description of the state of England toward the end of the Regency, "Mr. Bryant's gifts of exposition and analysis are fully tested for the period was one of the utmost complexity." Christopher Sykes in the *Spectator* conceded that he was "left finally with a sense of unreserved admiration for the finish, capaciousness, efficiency, and the pleasant design of Mr. Bryant's highpowered Time machine."

PRINCIPAL WORKS: King Charles II, 1931; Macaulay, 1932; Samuel Pepys, 3 vols., 1933-1939; The National Character, 1934; The England of Charles II, 1934; Letters and Speeches of Charles II, 1935; George V, 1936; The American Ideal, 1936; Postman's Horn, 1936; Stanley Baldwin, 1937; Humanity in Politics, 1938; Unfinished Victory, 1940; English Saga, 1940; The Years of Endurance, 1942; Dunkirk, 1943; Years of Victory, 1944; Historian's Holiday, 1947; The Age of Elegance, 1950; The Story of England, 1954.

ABOUT: New Statesman and Nation November 11, 1950; Yale Review Autumn 1951.

BRYHER, WINIFRED (Mrs. Kenneth Macpherson) (September 2, 1894-), English novelist, was born in Margate, Kent, England, the daughter of John Reeves Ellerman (later Sir John Ellerman, Bart.), prominent industrialist and financier, and Hannah (Glover) Ellerman. She was taken abroad for many long trips to France Italy, Switzerland and  Egypt between 1900 and 1908, and was privately educated during this period. Later, 1910-1912, she was a student at Queenwood (School), Eastbourne, spending many of her holidays in the Scilly Isles, from one of which she was to take the pen-name of Bryher. The outbreak of World War I forced her to give up the formal study of archeology which she had begun after leaving school. During 1917-1918 she worked on reviews and articles for the *Saturday Review*, then edited by A. A. Baumann, and occasionally for the *Sphere*, edited by Clement Shorter. She has always said that she owes them much for her early training as a writer. She was similarly indebted to Havelock Ellis who took a lively interest in her literary apprenticeship.

Bryher's first novel, *Development*, a study of schoolgirl adolescence, was published in 1919, and was well received by the critics. During a trip to America in 1919-20 she gathered material for her travel book, *West*; and in 1920, in New York City, she was married to Robert McAlmon, the American writer and later publisher of *avant-garde* literature at the Contact Press. They settled in Montreux, Switzerland, in 1920; and though traveling widely thereafter, she has maintained her residence in that country.

In 1927 she was divorced, and was married to Kenneth Macpherson, a Scotsman, author, and authority on the cinema. She helped him to establish *Close Up*, perhaps the finest of the magazines devoted to the art of the silent film, and assisted in its operation until its demise in 1933.

Bryher's novels have been praised by critics like Marianne Moore, for her "undeceived eye for beauty and her passion for moral beauty," and for her ability to recreate the mood of the past without the obtrusion of unassimilated historical data. As a stylist she is recognized as being in the first rank of modern writers of prose, and as the creator of a new genre of the historical novel. Short, bereted, and immensely energetic, she is likely to turn up anywhere unexpectedly, except at formal literary gatherings. A friend to many writers in England, on the continent, and in America, she prefers them individually to *en masse*.

PRINCIPAL WORKS: Amy Lowell, A Critical Appreciation, 1918; Development, 1920; Arrow Music, 1922; Two Selves [1923]; West, 1924; A Picture Geography, 1925; Civilians, 1927; Film Problems of Soviet Russia, 1929; The Lighthearted Student (with Trude Weiss) 1930; Paris 1900, 1940; Beowulf, 1948; The Fourteenth of October, 1952; The Player's Boy, 1953; Roman Wall, 1954.

BRYSON, LYMAN (July 12, 1888-), American educator and social scientist, writes: "I was born in the sandhills of

Pach

northwestern Nebraska, they tell me, where, in the middle eighties, my father and mother had gone in a covered wagon. My father was a druggist and his business changes took us, in a dozen years, up and down the Elkhorn River valley; my childhood memories are of little Nebraska towns and ranches. All my life, working on Omaha and Detroit newspapers, going to college and beginning to teach in Ann Arbor, working for five years in Geneva and Paris, after the first World War, afterward in California and for nearly twenty years in New York, I have thought of myself as a westerner and the child of pioneers.

"My serious writing began at the age of nine with an epic. This was a prophecy of the early verses which were put together, as a ten years' harvest, in *Smoky Roses*. A few short stories got into print; the inevitable novels remained in piles of typescript. A one act play, "The Grasshopper," won a prize and was produced in Detroit. But teaching and lecturing, directing an anthropology museum in San Diego, voyaging around the world on international relief missions and other things that were generally educational in purpose, distracted me from any but educational writing for a long time. In 1937, after coming to Teachers College, Columbia, where we carried on an experiment in popular writing on serious subjects, I contributed to The People's Library the political tract *Which Way America?*

"For the Kappa Delta Pi lectureship I wrote *The New Prometheus* and this small book was a bridge between professional adult educational writing and the volumes in which I have been trying to build a social philosophy for our times. *Science and Freedom* and *The Next America* have made a beginning. In the meantime, and with the same purpose, I have been an editor and frequent contributor to the thirteen volumes of proceedings of the Conference on Science, Philosophy and Religion, and to the essays published by the related Institute for Social and Religious Studies, especially the volume called *The Communication of Ideas*.

"If broadcast conversations are a literary form, the record is substantial since I have, on the Columbia Broadcasting System, discussed politics alone or with partisans, for fourteen years and have criticized some three hundred of the world's great books, with various critics and companions, on 'Invitation to Learning.' "

PRINCIPAL WORKS: Smoky Roses, 1916; Adult Education, 1936; Which Way America? 1939; The New Prometheus, 1941; Science and Freedom, 1947; Communication of Ideas (ed.) 1948; The Next America, 1952; The Drive Toward Reason, 1954.

ABOUT: Finkelstein, L. (ed.) American Spiritual Autobiographies; Current Biography 1951; Saturday Review of Literature, August 19, 1950.

*BRYUSOV, VALERY YAKOVLE-VICH (December 13, 1873-October 9, 1924). For biographical sketch and list of works and references, see TWENTIETH CENTURY AUTHORS, 1942.

* * *

ABOUT: Yarmolinsky, A. (ed.) A Treasury of Russian Verse.

* bryōō′sôf

*BUBER, MARTIN (February 8, 1878-), Jewish theologian and philosopher, now living in Jerusalem, was born in Vienna and raised in Galicia in the home of his grandfather, Solomon Buber, a noted Hebrew scholar and a leader of the Jewish *Haskalah* or Enlightenment. Here the young boy grew up in an atmosphere of solemn Hebrew tradition. Here too he was exposed for the

first time to Hasidism, the mystical movement at that time largely degenerated into superstition but later to be revived by Buber into a vital religious philosophy. At the same

* bōō′bĕr

time the boy's secular education was not neglected, and he was thoroughly trained "in the West European intellectual tradition of reason, logical criticism, and historical research." He studied philosophy and the history of art at the universities of Vienna, Berlin, and Zurich from 1896 to 1899 and was for most of this period alienated from Judaism altogether. In 1900, however, while studying at the University of Leipzig, he joined the Zionist movement and from that time forward he dedicated his life to the cause of Judaism.

Buber became primarily a cultural Zionist, rather than a political one. Through Zionism he foresaw a Jewish cultural renascence, a reawakening of the great intellectual and philosophical traditions of his people. At the outset Buber was to some extent involved in Zionist politics. In 1901 he edited the Zionist paper *Die Welt*, and a year later he became one of the founders of a Jewish publishing house, *Jüdischer Verlag*. But the essence of the Jewish national character for Buber lay in the mystical Hasidic tradition through which, he felt, there was the most direct communion with the Divine. In 1904 —the same year in which he received his Ph.D. from the University of Vienna with a thesis on German mysticism—he gave up his activities as journalist and lecturer for Zionism to study the Hasidic literature. For five years he devoted himself to this study, publishing numerous traditional Hasidic tales and parables retold in his own words. Buber did not remain too long, however, in the cloistered life of the scholar. From 1916 to 1924 he edited *Der Jude* (of which he was also a founder), the leading periodical of German-speaking Jewry, and from 1926 to 1933 he was one of the editors of the religious journal *Die Kreatur*. He began his long and distinguished teaching career in 1923 when he became professor of comparative religion at the University of Frankfort. When, in 1933, the Nazis came to power and excluded all Jewish students from German educational institutions, Buber resigned from the university to head the Central Office for Jewish Adult Education in Germany and to direct the *Frankfurter Jüdische Lehrhaus*, a free college for Jewish adult education. In 1938 he emigrated from Germany to Palestine and joined the faculty of the Hebrew University in Jerusalem, where he remained until his retirement in 1951. Since then he has continued active in educational work as director of the Institute for Adult Education which he founded in 1949 to train teachers for work in the immigration camps of Israel.

He visited the United States for the first time in 1951 when he delivered a series of lectures later published in *Eclipse of God* and *At the Turning.*

Commentators on Buber's work have pointed out that he is in the truest sense the living embodiment of the ancient *Zaddik* tradition, the rabbis or "perfect men" who were teachers, who brought the word of God to men, and who were the unifying forces and spiritual leaders of their communities. Of equal importance is the fact that Buber has served as an interpreter of modern Jewish thought to the non-Jewish world. He has had an influence on thinkers of other faiths— Catholic and Protestant alike. Reinhold Niebuhr has called him "the greatest living Jewish philosopher," and Will Herberg writes that he is "one of the great formative influences in contemporary religious thought."

Buber's theology, Herberg says, "falls in with the general movement of religious existentialism," of which "he is one of the main contemporary sources." He strives for a meeting, a "dialogue," with God, with Man as "I" and God as "Thou," as opposed to what he considers the impersonal and meaningless "I-IT" relationship that exists between most men and the universe in which they live. This theory Buber outlined in *I and Thou.* Elsewhere, in an essay called "God and the Soul," he wrote: "He is the great lover, Who has placed man in the world that He might be able to love him—but there is no perfect love without reciprocity, and He, the original God, longs thereafter that man should love Him."

The extension of Buber's all-embracing love of God is love of the world and love of one's fellow men—"for man cannot love God in truth without loving the world, in which He has put His strength." Carried into the realm of social philosophy, Buber's theory rejects any form of powerful state control and favors the small, self-governing and self-sustaining community in which men live in direct personal relationship (a kind of decentralized socialism such as one finds in the Israeli *kibbutzim*). "You cannot truly love God," he writes, "if you do not love your fellow man, and you cannot truly love your fellow man if you do not love God."

Buber lives in Talbiyeh, Jerusalem. His wife, Paula Winkler, whom he married in 1899, writes fiction under the name "George Mundt." He is a small, slight man, with a flowing white beard and penetrating, dark eyes—an appearance and bearing which strikingly recall the paintings of the prophets of ancient times. He has received many honors for his work—including honorary degrees from the University of Aberdeen in Scotland, Hebrew Union College in Cincinnati, and the Hebrew University in Jerusalem. The citation accompanying the Goethe Prize, awarded Buber by the University of Hamburg, read in part that he was receiving the prize "... to honor your great scholarly work, but, more than that, your activity in the spirit of a genuine humanity."

PRINCIPAL WORKS IN ENGLISH TRANSLATION: Jewish Mysticism and the Legends of Baalshem, 1931; I and Thou, 1937; For the Sake of Heaven, 1945; Mamre, 1946; Between Man and Man, 1947; Tales of the Hasidim (ed.) 1947-48; Hasidism, 1948; Israel and the World, 1948; Paths in Utopia, 1949; The Prophetic Faith, 1949; The Way of Man, 1951; Images of Good and Evil, 1952; Two Types of Faith, 1952; At the Turning, 1952; Eclipse of God, 1952; Israel and Palestine, 1952; Right and Wrong, 1952; For the Sake of Heaven: A Chronicle, 1953.

ABOUT: Agus, J. B. Modern Philosophers of Judaism; Kohn, H. Martin Buber: Sein Werk und Seine Zeit; Lewisohn, L. Cities and Men; Liptzin, S. Germany's Stepchildren; Schwarz, L. W. Memoirs of My People; Current Biography 1953; Menorah Journal April 1938; Yale Review Winter 1953.

*BUCHAN, JOHN, 1st Baron Tweedsmuir (August 26, 1875-February 11, 1940). For biographical sketch and list of works and references, see TWENTIETH CENTURY AUTHORS, 1942.

* * *

ADDITIONAL WORK: Clearing House: A Survey of One Man's Mind, 1946.
ABOUT: Buchan, S. John Buchan, By His Wife and Friends; Mansbridge, A. Fellow Men; Turner, A. C. Mr. Buchan, Writer; London Quarterly Review October 1947.

* bŭk'ăn

*BUCHHOLTZ, JOHANNES (1882-1940). For autobiographical sketch and list of works and references, see TWENTIETH CENTURY AUTHORS, 1942.

* * *

Johannes Buchholtz died at the age of fifty-eight of "paralysis of the heart." His widow, Olga Buchholtz writes from Struer, Denmark: "He died in the midst of his geniality and love of work, and left me in deep grief. We had lived a very happy life together from the days of our youth until the last hour. The loss was felt by his many friends and admirers too. He was a very noble and amiable man. His books are still read by many in Denmark and in other countries too, and as for *Susanne*, this novel has recently been filmed in this country and became a great success."

* bŏŏk'hŏlts

BUCK, PAUL HERMAN (August 25, 1899-). For biographical sketch and list of earlier works and references, see TWENTIETH CENTURY AUTHORS, 1942.

* * *

Paul Herman Buck became professor of history and dean of the faculty of Harvard University in 1942. He has held a number of other important educational and administrative offices—including the chairmanship from 1947 to 1948 of the Committee for Advancing Higher Education and Research of the Rockefeller Foundation and the chairmanship of the Committee on American Culture for the American Council of Learned Societies. Since 1941 he has been on the board of editors of the *Journal of Southern History*.

ADDITIONAL WORK: General Education in a Free Society (with others) 1945.

BUCK, Mrs. PEARL (SYDENSTRICKER) (June 26, 1892-). For autobiographical sketch and list of earlier works and references, see TWENTIETH CENTURY AUTHORS, 1942.

* * *

Richard J. Walsh, president of The John Day Company, publishers, and husband of Pearl Buck, writes: "In 1941 Pearl Buck founded the East and West Association, devoted to 'mutual understanding between peoples,' a purpose which she pressed vigorously throughout the war and for several years after. She still continues to devote much time and attention to making the opposite sides of the world know one another better. In 1949 she founded Welcome House, a non-profit organization for the care and adoption of American-born children who have Asian ancestry. Near her home in Pennsylvania are two houses where such children have been gathered and are being brought up under the care of permanent parents; in one house nine, in the other five, including Chinese-American, Japanese-American, Korean-American and Indo-American. An even larger number of children have been placed for adoption in American homes in various parts of the country.

"In 1951 Pearl Buck was elected a member of the American Academy of Arts and Letters, one of only two women in that body of fifty life members."

ADDITIONAL WORKS: The Promise, 1943; Portrait of a Marriage, 1943; What America Means to Me, 1943; Tell the People, 1945; Talk about Russia, 1945; Pavilion of Women, 1946; Far and Near: Stories of China, Japan and America, 1947; How It Happens: Talk about the German People,

1947; Peony, 1948; Kinfolk, 1949; American Argument, 1949; The Child Who Never Grew, 1950; God's Men, 1951; The Hidden Flower, 1952; Come, My Beloved, 1953; My Several Worlds, 1954. *Juveniles*—Chinese Children Next Door, 1942; Water Buffalo Children, 1943; Dragon Fish, 1944; Yu Lan, Flying Boy of China, 1945; The Big Wave, 1948; One Bright Day, 1950; The Man Who Changed China, 1953.

ABOUT: Buck, P. My Several Worlds; Gray, J. On Second Thought; Van Gelder, R. Writers and Writing; Yaukey, G. S. ("Cornelia Spencer") The Exile's Daughter; Christian Science Monitor Magazine February 5, 1944; New York Herald Tribune Book Review October 7, 1951.

BULEY, R. CARLYLE (July 8, 1893-), American historian, was born in Floyd County, Ind., of ancestry he describes as  "English, Scotch-Irish, German, and Irish all mixed up." His father was David Marion Buley, a doctor, and his mother, the former Nora Keithley, was the daughter of a Civil War veteran who, Buley recalls, "told tales and helped introduce me to the woods." Buley writes that his early interest in American history, "particularly the midwest pioneer period, came from tales of 'catamounts' (panthers or wildcats) and Indians from the lips of my great-grandmother Riley in Floyd County, and from tales of the Civil War told by my grandfather Keithley. The interest was further developed by my early environment at Vincennes, Ind., where we learned of the early French settlements in the Middle West, of George Rogers Clark's conquest of Vincennes for Virginia, and where we read Thompson's *Alice of Old Vincennes* and many other historical novels."

Buley was educated in the public schools of Vincennes and at the University of Indiana, where he took a B.A. in history and government in 1914 and an M.A. in 1916. Before he completed work for the latter degree, he published his first articles on the history of Indiana and the Middle West. Buley began his career as a teacher in the high schools of Delphi and Muncie, Ind. In World War I he served in the U.S. Army Signal Corps, and at the end of the war he returned to teaching. He was head of the history department and assistant principal of the Springfield, Ill., High School until 1923 when he went to the University of Wisconsin to teach and to work on his doctorate. He received that degree in 1925, with a thesis on *The Political Balance in the Old Northwest, 1820-1860.* By this time Buley's fields of scholarly interest were clearly marked: "the Middle West, particularly the period prior to the Civil War; recent United States history (since the Civil War); American biography; United States economic history."

Buley returned to his native state to join the faculty of the University of Indiana in 1925 as instructor in American history (he is now full professor). He published his thesis and a number of articles and book reviews in scholarly journals. In 1943 he edited *The Indiana Home* of the late Logan Esarey, a former colleague at the university. Two years later he collaborated with Madge E. Pickard on a history of medicine in the pioneer days of the Midwest. In 1950 his two-volume *The Old Northwest Pioneer Period,* a comprehensive social history of the region from Ohio to Wisconsin, 1815-1840, was published. The historian James G. Randall praised Buley's study for "its uncommon fullness, competence, wealth of source material, and authentic flavor," and it is generally regarded as one of the most valuable histories of the frontier period now available. For this book Buley received the 1951 Pulitzer prize in American history.

Buley has been instrumental in acquiring for the Indiana University Library a number of collections of manuscripts and papers —among them the Oakleaf Lincoln collection and the "Mitten" and "Sweet" War of 1812 collections. His chief ambition, he says, is "to write a first class historical novel— which I shall never do." For relaxation he favors landscape gardening, golf, and travel. Buley's first wife, Esther Giles, whom he married in 1919, died in 1921. In 1926 he married Evelyn Barnett.

PRINCIPAL WORKS: The Political Balance in the Old Northwest, 1820-1860, 1926; The Midwest Pioneer, His Ills, Cures, and Doctors (with M. E. Pickard) 1945; The Old Northwest: Pioneer Period, 1815-1840, 1950; The American Life Convention: A Study in the History of Life Insurance, 1953.

ABOUT: Current Biography 1951; New York Times May 8, 1951; Publishers' Weekly June 30, 1945; Saturday Review of Literature May 19,

BULLEN, FRANK THOMAS (April 5, 1857-February 26, 1915). For biographical sketch and list of works and references, see TWENTIETH CENTURY AUTHORS, 1942.

BULLETT, GERALD (December 30, 1893-), English novelist, poet, biographer and critic.

NOTE: This biography at the request of the writer supersedes the sketch which appeared in TWENTIETH CENTURY AUTHORS, 1942.

Gerald Bullett writes: "Gerald Bullett was born at Forest Hill, a south-eastern suburb of London, the third and youngest son of parents who had migrated from the midland counties. He was educated at a private school and afterwards at Jesus College, Cambridge, where he graduated with First Class Honours in 1921, his university career having been preceded by four years' service with the armed forces in France and Egypt. His first novel, written at the age of twenty, was published in 1916. After coming down from Cambridge he became a regular contributor to the *Times Literary Supplement* and other weeklies, and began writing short stories, essays, and more novels. He married at the end of 1921. Though born a Londoner, he is a country-man by ancestry and adoption. For the past quarter of a century he has lived in an Elizabethan farmhouse in Sussex. He belongs to no church and to no political party. He believes that no culture, no real civilization, is possible without freedom of thought and expression. The extremists of Right and Left would probably describe him as an old-fashioned Liberal.

"His published works fall naturally into two groups, the dividing line being the Second World War, during which he worked in an overseas section of the British Broadcasting Corporation. The best-known novels in the earlier group are *The Pandervils* (1928) and *The Jury* (1935). Since the war he has published six more novels, a biography of George Eliot, a study of *The English Mystics*, and three small volumes of verse of which the latest is *News from the Village*. In addition to writing, he has done a good deal of broadcasting, of book talks and his own short stories. His anthologies include: *The Testament of Light, The English Galaxy of Shorter Poems,* and *Readings in English Literature.* He is a member of the selection committee of the Book Society (England), founded by Alan Bott and Hugh Walpole."

PRINCIPAL WORKS: *Fiction*—The Progress of Kay, 1916; The Street of the Eye (short stories) 1923; Mr. Godley Beside Himself, 1924; The Baker's Cart (short stories) 1925; The Panther, 1926; The Spanish Caravel (juvenile) 1927; The History of Egg Pandervil, 1928; The World in Bud (short stories) 1928; Nicky Son of Egg, 1929;

Marden Fee, 1931; Remember Mrs. Munch (juvenile) 1931; I'll Tell You Everything (with J. B. Priestley) 1932; Helen's Lovers (short stories) 1932; The Quick and the Dead, 1933; Eden River, 1934; The Jury, 1935; The Happy Mariners (juvenile) 1935; The Snare of the Fowler, 1936; The Bending Sickle, 1938; Twenty-Four Tales (short stories) 1938; A Man of Forty, 1939; When the Cat's Away, 1940; The Elderbrook Brothers, 1943; Judgment in Suspense, 1946; Men at High Table, 1948; The House of Strangers, 1948; Cricket in Heaven, 1949; The Trouble at Number Seven, 1952. *Miscellaneous*—The Innocence of G. K. Chesterton, 1923; Walt Whitman, 1924; Modern English Fiction, 1926; Germany, 1930; The Testament of Light (ed.) 1932, second series, 1934; The English Galaxy (ed.) 1933; The Bubble (poems) 1934; The Story of English Literature, 1935; Poems in Pencil, 1937; Problems in Religion, 1938; The Jackdaw's Nest (ed.) 1939; The Golden Year of Fan Cheng-ta (poems) 1946; George Eliot, 1947; Poems, 1949; The English Mystics, 1950; Sydney Smith, 1951; News from the Village (poems) 1952.

*BULOSAN, CARLOS (November 24, 1914-), Filipino poet and memoirist, writes: "I was born in a small village in the Philippines. The province is Pangasinan, the town is Binalonan, and the village is Mangusmana. When I was born Mangusmana was still a wilderness; the great forest on the eastern slope of the village teemed with wild game, and the mountains to the north were untrodden by man.

F. Belandres

On the south were the wide fertile plains of Luzon, extending as far as Manila, the capital of the Philippines; while on the west were rivers, crisscrossing growing towns and expanding sugarcane plantations until they met the China Sea. I started working when I was five.

"Today the village of Mangusmana is nearly gone, eaten away by the Tagamusin River, a tributary of the Agno River which flows to Lingayen Gulf. I lived in Mangusmana with my father until I was seven years old. We lived in a small grass hut; but it was sufficient, because we were peasants. My father could not read or write, but he knew how to work his one hectare of land, which was the sole support of our big family.

"The rest of the family lived in a palm-leaf house in Binalonan. It consisted of four brothers and two sisters. Here my mother was the driving force, who sold salted fish

* bōō lō'săn

in the public market to feed and clothe her children. Being the youngest of the five brothers, I was obligated to help my mother in the house and in the marketplace. My mother could not read or write; but she was such a dynamic little peasant woman that, when her sons had all grown up and were scattered in many lands, she gathered the numerous grandchildren in fold and raised them alone as she had done to her own children. Today, at the age of eighty, she is still supporting her last five grandchildren by selling salted fish in the public market of Binalonan.

"Off and on I went to the public school of Binalonan until I was thirteen, then to the high school in Lingayen, where I stayed for three semesters. Then I quit school forever and went to work in Baguio, the summer capital of the Philippines. Later I returned to Binalonan and worked on the farm until I came to the United States in 1931.

"The next period of my life is recorded in my autobiography, *America Is in the Heart*. Between 1931 and Pearl Harbor day, I lived violent years of unemployment, prolonged illnesses and heart-rending labor union work on the farms of California. It was when I was dying of tuberculosis in the Los Angeles County Hospital that I had the opportunity to seriously read books which opened all my world of intellectual possibilities—and a grand dream of bettering society for the working man.

"I stayed in this hospital two years. But it took me another five years before I was able to put my grand dream on paper in a literate form. When it began—my relentless creative activity began. And many things followed from my typewriter for two restless years—poetry, short stories, articles on political and cultural subjects. And books— *The Laughter of My Father* (written in twelve days), *The Voice of Bataan* (three days), *America Is in the Heart* (twenty-four days), *Chorus for America*, *Letter from America*, and two books for children, as well as *The Dark People*.

"Today I have published poetry, short stories and serious articles in many magazines—enough to fill three more books.

"I am sick again. I know I will be here (Firland Sanitarium, Seattle, Wash.) for a long time. And the grass hut where I was born is gone, and the village of Mangusmana is gone, and my father and his one hectare of land are gone, too. And the palmleaf house in Binalonan is gone, and two brothers and a sister are gone forever.

"But what does it matter to me? The question is—what impelled me to write? The answer is—my grand dream of equality among men and freedom for all. To give a literate voice to the voiceless one hundred thousand Filipinos in the United States, Hawaii, and Alaska. Above all and ultimately, to translate the desires and aspirations of the whole Filipino people in the Philippines and abroad in terms relevant to contemporary history.

"Yes, I have taken unto myself this sole responsibility."

PRINCIPAL WORKS: Chorus for America (ed.) 1942; Letter from America (poems) 1942; The Voice of Bataan (poem) 1943; The Laughter of My Father, 1944; The Dark People, 1944; America Is in the Heart, 1946.

ABOUT: Bulosan, C. America Is in the Heart; Current Biography 1946; Saturday Evening Post March 6, 1943.

*BUNIN, IVAN ALEXEYEVICH (October 22, 1870-November 8, 1953). For biographical sketch and list of earlier works and references, see TWENTIETH CENTURY AUTHORS, 1942.

* * *

Ivan Bunin died at eighty-three of a heart attack in his home in Paris. During the years of the Nazi occupation of France, Bunin—a declared anti-Nazi—wrote nothing. He is said to have helped a number of refugees from Nazism and to have sheltered a Jewish journalist for the whole period of the occupation. In 1951 he published a small volume of autobiography and literary reminiscences, *Memories and Portraits*, which contained, in addition to its personal information on the author, valuable glimpses of some of his contemporary Russian authors and artists. Bunin was an honest and outspoken critic and, in his last volume, demonstrated the same candor and shrewdness that characterized his earlier work. "He writes with detachment," John Cournos observes. "His warmest admirations are tempered with the critical spirit."

Mark Aldanov had visited Bunin in Paris in 1950 and reported that he was "a man bedridden and living in semi-obscurity."

ADDITIONAL WORKS IN ENGLISH TRANSLATION: Dark Avenues, and Other Stories, 1949; Memories and Portraits, 1951.

ABOUT: Bunin, I. Memories and Portraits; Columbia Dictionary of Modern European Literature; Snow, V. Russian Writers; Yarmolinsky, A. (ed.) A Treasury of Russian Verse; New York Times November 9, 1953; New York Times Book Review November 26, 1950.

* bŏŏ'nyĭn

BURGESS, GELETT (January 30, 1866-
September 18, 1951). For biographical
sketch and list of earlier works and
references, see TWENTIETH CENTURY
AUTHORS, 1942.

* * *

Frank Gelett Burgess died of a heart
attack at eighty-five at the Peninsula Community Hospital in Carmel, Calif., where he
had lived for his last two years.

S. J. Woolf once said of Burgess that
"like most humorists he is sad, and like
many funny men he is serious." Burgess
himself has furnished the best third-person
analysis of his own work: "G. B. loves
tours-de-force. He loves machinery, and the
intricacies of technique. He adores the extravagant, the outrageous. But he used his
gift always to demonstrate the absurdities of
life. He creates his characters only to destroy them. He formulates complex theories
and blows them up with blasts of laughter.
He is amused at everything, respects nothing."

ADDITIONAL WORK: New Goops and How to
Know Them, 1951.

ABOUT: Mahony, Bertha E. (ed.) Illustrators
of Children's Books; Van Gelder, R. Writers and
Writing; Life October 1, 1951; New York Times
September 19, 1951.

BURGESS, PERRY (October 12, 1886-),
American novelist and memoirist, lecturer,
and administrator, writes: "The world I was

born in no longer
exists—the lawless
foothills of the
Ozarks with Indian
Territory only a short
distance away. Here
at sixteen I became
a 'boy preacher,' a
phenomenon that was
not uncommon at that
time. After preach-
ing my way through
college I became national field director of
the Near East Relief Campaign, an assignment which led to a wonderful year with
Dr. Wilfred Grenfell, the Labrador doctor,
raising funds to carry on the work of that
remarkable man.

"But the continuing adventure of my life
began when Governor-General Leonard
Wood of the Philippines appealed to the
American public to create a research foundation for the study of Hansen's disease (leprosy).

" 'Do people still have that?' I exclaimed,
and so I began to learn something of the
story of the most tragic people on the face of
the earth. From the outset I realized that
this work was something I had to do. From
that day to this I have been a man fired by
excitement and driven toward a goal, not
yet in sight, but never out of mind.

"With the founding of the Leonard Wood
Memorial (American Leprosy Foundation),
a research organization devoted solely to the
study of that single disease, I began the
journeys that have taken me not over the
highways but into the byways of the world;
I have poked my nose into almost every
country on earth. I am not an orthodox
traveler, for after a quarter century of
roaming I have yet to see many of the wonders of the world, but I have seen many of
its grim sights. I have met men, women and
children, exiled from the world by age-old
fear, living in jungle huts, in unspeakable
Indian villages, even in graveyards. And I
have seen their gallantry and courage in the
face of despair.

"In 1936 I married Cora [L. Turney],
who has been my companion and my fellow
worker ever since, carrying her brightness
into the dark places of the world. Certainly
hers must have been the strangest honeymoon on which a woman ever embarked for
it took us into most of the leprosaria of the
world.

"My first book, *Who Walk Alone*, a factual novel, was written in an attempt to build
a greater understanding of this baffling illness called leprosy and to paint a picture of
man's indomitable courage in the face of
disaster. An autobiography, *Born of Those
Years*, followed. It is a record of what has
been accomplished to date, and a signpost
pointing out what remains to be done in our
tireless but hopeful battle."

* * *

Perry Burgess was born in Joplin, Mo.
He graduated from Baker University in
1912, and studied at Drew and Columbia
universities. In 1925 he became national director of the Leonard Wood Memorial for
the Eradication of Leprosy, and since then
has devoted himself to that cause. His novel
Who Walk Alone went through thirty-two
printings in the decade after its publication.
It was named a "Discovery" Book by the
National Booksellers Association and received a gold medal from the Society for the
Libraries of New York University.

PRINCIPAL WORKS: Who Walk Alone (novel)
1940; Born of Those Years (autobiography) 1951.

ABOUT: Burgess, P. Born of Those Years;
Publishers' Weekly February 15, 1941, March 29,
1941, June 12, 1948.

"BURKE, FIELDING." See DARGAN, O. T.

BURKE, KENNETH (May 5, 1897-). For biographical sketch and list of earlier works and references, see TWENTIETH CENTURY AUTHORS, 1942.

* * *

In two important books, *The Grammar of Motives* and *The Rhetoric of Motives* (part of a planned trilogy to conclude with a "Symbolic of Motives"), and a number of articles and lectures, Kenneth Burke has continued to develop the thesis implicit in his early literary criticism that literature is "symbolic action." The aim of his work, Stanley Edgar Hyman writes, "is no less than the comprehensive exploration of human motives and the forms of thought and expression built around them, and its ultimate object...is to eliminate the whole world of conflict that can be eliminated through understanding."

Burke's profound and provocative thinking and his "craggy," formidable presentation of it in his writings have limited his reading audience mainly to fellow critics and teachers and graduate students in the universities. But his influence is considerable, and he is certainly no longer merely the "critic's critic," read and appreciated only in esoteric literary circles. R. P. Blackmur, Malcolm Cowley, and Francis Fergusson are only a few of many critics who have felt that influence. The ambitious critical system which he is still in the process of developing is an attempt, Stanley Edgar Hyman writes, "to do no less than to integrate all man's knowledge into one workable critical frame." Work of such tremendous scope, especially when supported with such breadth and depth of learning and imagination as Burke's, must inevitably be a shaping force in criticism. To quote Hyman again: "If it has seemingly had a lack of focus, gone after a bewildering number of quarries in no apparent sequence, it has had the compensatory virtue of endless fertility, suggestiveness, an inexhaustible throwing off of sparks."

Correction: Burke has three daughters, not two, from his first marriage.

ADDITIONAL WORKS: A Grammar of Motives, 1945; A Rhetoric of Motives, 1950.

ABOUT: Hyman, S. E. The Armed Vision; Rosenfeld, I. *in* Kenyon Critics (1951); Poetry March 1946.

BURKE, THOMAS (1886-September 22, 1945). For autobiographical sketch and list of earlier works and references, see TWENTIETH CENTURY AUTHORS, 1942.

* * *

Thomas Burke died in London at fifty-nine following an operation.

He was writing his short stories, essays, and observations about England and particularly London to the end of his life; two volumes were published posthumously. A collection of the best of his short stories was published in 1950.

Burke "enjoyed mystification" about the facts of his own life, according to John Gawsworth, who quotes the author as saying that in *The Wind and the Rain*, which has been accepted by many critics as being autobiographical, "the treatment is at five or six removes from the actual."

A drive "to tell a story as ably as Ambrose Bierce and to see and write as clearly as Stephen Crane" was Burke's own definition of his literary credo. "The London he bodied forth in his novels and miscellaneous writings," says the London *Times*, "was produced out of the alembic of a romantic imagination. At times its sentiment came near the borders of sentimentality and its drama verged on melodrama; but Burke had authentic talent of a high order and he built on a foundation of true and keen observation."

ADDITIONAL WORKS: Victorian Grotesque, 1942; Travel in England from Pilgrim and Packhorse to Light Car and Plane, 1942; English Inns (*Britain in Pictures* series) 1943; Dark Nights (short stories) 1944; Son of London, 1946; English Townsman as He Was and as He Is, 1947; Best Stories (ed. J. Gawsworth) 1950.

ABOUT: London Times September 24, 1945; New York Times September 24, 1945.

BURLINGAME, ROGER (May 7, 1889-). For biographical sketch and list of earlier works and references, see TWENTIETH CENTURY AUTHORS, 1942.

* * *

Roger Burlingame was with the Office of War Information from 1942 to 1943. In 1945 he visited the European and Mediterranean theatres as war correspondent and in the following year he visited Australia. His writings—which include magazine and reference work articles as well as books—are factual, sound, and always lively and readable. His history of the first hundred years of the publishing firm of Charles Scribner's Sons, *Of Making Many Books*, was "told so congenially and so fairly," Edward Weeks wrote, "that I could wish the book in the hands of every beginning writer and as a source in our schools of journalism." *Backgrounds of Power*, like his earlier *March of the Iron Men* and *Engines of Democracy*, was a history of technology in American society. Stuart Chase pointed out that while the book is not "the definitive work on mass production," it is "by all odds the best survey to date, philosophically as well as technically—a wise, learned and stimulating book."

Burlingame has also contributed articles to the *Dictionary of American Biography*, the *Dictionary of American History*, and many magazines.

ADDITIONAL WORKS: Victory Without Peace (with A. Stevens) 1944; Of Making Many Books, 1946; Inventors Behind the Inventor, 1947; Backgrounds of Power: The Human Story of Mass Production, 1949; General Billy Mitchell, 1952; Mosquitoes in the Big Ditch: The Story of the Panama Canal, 1952; Machines That Built America, 1953; Henry Ford, 1955.

BURMAN, BEN LUCIEN (December 12 1895-). For biographical sketch and list of earlier works and references, see TWENTIETH CENTURY AUTHORS, 1942.

* * *

Ben Lucien Burman was the first war correspondent to reach the Free French in North Africa after the collapse of the French government. His news reporting from North Africa won him the French Legion of Honor. He described his wartime experiences in *Miracle on the Congo*. Africa was also the scene of *Rooster Crows for Day*, which was awarded the Thomas Jefferson Memorial Prize in 1945; but in his later works Burman has reverted to the scenes he knows best and always describes with affection and sympathy—the Mississippi valley and the Kentucky mountains region. His writing is "simple, direct, and homespun," and reflects his attitude toward the region and the people, an attitude Joseph Henry Jackson describes as "warmly understanding, interpretive, gently humorous, and mildly philosophical." Many of Burman's books are illustrated by his wife, Alice Caddy.

ADDITIONAL WORKS: Miracle on the Congo: Report from the Free French Front, 1942; Rooster Crows for Day, 1945; Everywhere I Roam, 1949; Children of Noah, 1951; High Water at Catfish Bend (juvenile) 1952; The Four Lives of Mundy Tolliver, 1953.

ABOUT: Warfel, H. R. American Novelists of Today; Publishers' Weekly April 28, 1945; Saturday Review of Literature November 26, 1949.

BURNETT, Mrs. FRANCES ELIZA (HODGSON) (November 24, 1849-October 29, 1924). For biographical sketch and list of works and references, see TWENTIETH CENTURY AUTHORS, 1942.

* * *

ABOUT: Laski, M. Mrs. Ewing, Mrs. Molesworth and Mrs. Hodgson Burnett; Life December 5, 1949.

BURNETT, HALLIE SOUTHGATE. See BURNETT, WHIT

BURNETT, WHIT (August 14, 1899-). For autobiographical sketch and list of earlier works and references, see TWENTIETH CENTURY AUTHORS, 1942.

* * *

Whit Burnett writes: "My editorial life is still bound up with *Story*, but the magazine's part-time angel departed in 1941, its co-founder Martha Foley quit a few months later, and with Hallie Southgate Burnett, short story writer and novelist, the magazine acquired a new co-editor and its editor acquired a new wife and since 1942 a new family named John Southgate, now ten, and later Whitney Ann Beekman Burnett, aged seven [1953].

"*Story*, continuing its policy of presenting new and established short story writers from America and most other parts of the world, went through the 'forties in a bi-monthly publishing rhythm until 1948 when it became a quarterly and left the newsstands for the bookstores. Publishing costs, borne by the editors alone, and other difficulties, caused its suspension for a couple of years, but it reappeared in book form under the editorship of Whit and Hallie Burnett in 1951 and is now appearing under the imprint of the Story Press with A. A. Wyn, Inc., N.Y., at regular six-month intervals.

"Since 1942 a number of writers who first appeared in its pages have continued with widening prestige with their own books among many publishers. Norman Mailer, author of *The Naked and the Dead*, was a winner of one of the nation-wide college short story contests conducted by *Story* when he was still in his teens at Harvard; Truman Capote's first short story to be purchased appeared in *Story*; and in an anthology of fifty-odd stories chosen from several hundred printed, the editors presented in *Story: The Fiction of the 'Forties* a noteworthy culling of the short story writing of the decade as they had discovered it between 1942 and 1950.

"With the cooperation of thousands of literary persons in the United States who voted on the literary great of their time, it seemed a simple jump from editing short stories to assembling material from well-known writers already published, and with *This Is My Best*, an anthology of ninety-three of America's greatest living authors picking their own most representative work, I contributed to what for several seasons was to be a flood of anthologies. I even contributed several times later to the same stream with *The Seas of God*, great stories of the human spirit, which joined *This Is My Best* as one of the favorite books of the armed forces. Then came *Time to Be Young, Two Bottles of Relish, A Pocket Story Book, Story: The Fiction of the 'Forties* (with Hallie Burnett), and Hallie even did one of her own, with an associate editor of *Story*, Eleanor Gilchrist; the book was about parenthood, entitled *Welcome to Life* (1948). About this time *Story* inaugurated a new literary long story form to interest Hollywood in stories, but the only result was the sale to Twentieth-Century Fox of a short novel treating the love life of Robert Burns, entitled 'Immortal Bachelor,' which once bought from me has lain on the shelf, I am sorry to say, during the entire cinematic slump.

"I gave up teaching the short story at Columbia in 1943, but have never ceased editing short stories, although the editing at *Story* is not a one-man job, since for ten years past it has involved the hard-working and practical editorial point of view of a practicing writer, Hallie Burnett, who since her first appearance as a short story writer in *Story* with a story which won an O. Henry Memorial Award, has worked very closely with all the writers *Story* has published since 1942, and without her work the magazine would long since have ceased as the outlet for new writers in America.

"In 1953 the Burnetts knocked off for a couple of months and took their two children to introduce them to France, seeing authors they once 'discovered,' looking for new ones as usual—Mrs. Burnett with two novels behind her, *A Woman in Possession* (1951), *This Heart, This Hunter* (1953), and engaged on her third, and this autobiographee attempting to seek out old haunts on the Left Bank of Paris which knew him more than twenty years before as a young man with a beard and on this visit observed that unlike the beards of his era, Pirandello, John Macrae, Count Sforza, Shaw, and J. Berg Essenwein, he had not yet quit the scene entirely but had shaved."

ADDITIONAL WORKS: *As editor*—This Is My Best, 1942; Two Bottles of Relish, 1943; Seas of God, 1944; Time To Be Young, 1945; American Authors Today (with C. E. Slatkin) 1947; Story: The Fiction of the 'Forties (with H. Burnett) 1949; World's Best, 1950; Sextet: Six *Story* Discoveries in the Novella Form (with H. Burnett) 1951.

BURNETT, WILLIAM RILEY (November 25, 1899-). For autobiographical sketch and list of earlier works and references, see TWENTIETH CENTURY AUTHORS, 1942.

* * *

W. R. Burnett writes: "As of 1952 I have published eighteen novels: best known of my later books *The Asphalt Jungle*. It was made into an excellent movie by MGM, and has been translated into French, Dutch, Spanish, Italian, Portuguese and German. Also published in London. It was a best-seller in Paris, having sold over 40,000 copies.

"My favorite novel since 1942: *Little Men, Big World* (1951). It was not as successful as the *Jungle*, but a better book, I think. It has also been translated into the above languages. And it was performed as a television drama very successfully on 'Studio One.' I have done considerable movie writing in the last ten years. *The Asphalt Jungle; Little Men, Big World*; and *Vanity Row* were designed as a trilogy, showing the gradual collapse of a city administration through corruption—characters do not continue, merely the situation—and each book is a complete unit in itself. *Vanity Row* received an excessively bad press in New York; wonderful reviews in the rest of the country.

"I am married for the second time—to Whitney Forbes Johnstone—and have two young sons: William Riley B. III and James Addison B. I still live in southern California."

ADDITIONAL WORKS: Nobody Lives Forever, 1943; Tomorrow's Another Day, 1945; Romelle, 1946; The Asphalt Jungle, 1949; Little Men, Big World, 1951; Vanity Row, 1952; Adobe Walls, 1953; Captain Lightfoot, 1954.

ABOUT: Saturday Evening Post February 15, 1947.

BURNHAM, Mrs. CLARA LOUISE (ROOT) (May 26, 1854-June 20, 1927). For biographical sketch and list of works and references, see TWENTIETH CENTURY AUTHORS, 1942.

BURNHAM, JAMES (November 22, 1905-   ), American philosopher and social historian, was born in Chicago, the son of Claude George Burnham, a railroad executive, and Mary May (Gillis) Burnham. His brother David Burnham is a novelist, and another brother, Philip Burnham, is a journalist and former editor of *Commonweal* magazine. James Burnham attended Princeton, taking his B.A. in 1927, *summa cum laude*. After graduation he traveled in Europe and studied at Balliol College, Oxford, from which he received a B.A. in 1929 and an M.A. in 1932. In 1929 he returned to the United States and joined the philosophy department of the Washington Square College of New York University, where he now holds the rank of professor. In 1950 Burnham went on leave, traveling in Europe and Asia, doing research in Washington, D.C., and lecturing at the Naval War College in Newport, the Air War College in Maxwell Field, Ala., the National War College, the School for Advanced International Studies, and other similar institutions. He has also taught comparative literature and mathematics (to army groups during World War II). From 1930 to 1934 he was co-editor, with Philip Wheelwright, of the critical and philosophical quarterly *The Symposium*.

In the classroom Burnham is a serious, soft-spoken, rather characteristically academic personality. It is outside the classroom, in a series of controversial and strikingly original books that began with *The Managerial Revolution* in 1941, that Burnham has made his reputation as a social and political philosopher. His interest in politics was first aroused in the depression days of the early 1930's. In 1933 he became associated with the revolutionary anti-Stalinist Communist group known as "Trotskyists" or "Fourth Internationalists." He was an editor of the *New International,* "then generally recognized as the theoretical Marxist journal," and contributed to many labor and radical publications. By 1939, however, Burnham had become involved in a bitter quarrel with Trotsky (who was then living in Mexico), and early in 1940 he broke completely with Marxism. "The basic reason for the break," he said, "was my conclusion that Marxism is false, and

that Marxist politics in practice lead not to their alleged goal of democratic socialism but to one or another form of totalitarian despotism."

The Managerial Revolution was published only a few months before the United States entered World War II. Its thesis—that we are in the midst of a revolution in which power will be transferred from capitalist-private ownership to the hands of the "managers," the administrators of our complex technological economy—was hotly debated. Of even greater interest, at the time of the publication of the book, were Burnham's predictions about the future—his forecast that the managerial trend would be accelerated by the war, and that from this acceleration would ultimately emerge gigantic managerial super-states, their headquarters in the main industrial centers of Europe, Asia, and America. Charges of defeatism and even pro-Hitlerism were made against the book, but most reviewers agreed that essentially it was an ingenious and compelling analysis. Malcolm Cowley wrote: "Mr. Burnham is a better critic and analyst than he is a prophet. . . . The real value of his book is that it casts a clearer light on the present."

Burnham employed the same method of razor-sharp analysis of so-called "sentimental" and "idealistic" notions of government and society in his next book, *The Machiavellians,* a study of the disciples of political expediency from Machiavelli himself down through Mosca, Michels, and Pareto. By this time, though admiring Burnham's erudition and analytical powers, some of his reviewers deplored his cynicism. Benedetto Croce commented on the book: "By confining himself too narrowly to the purely political forces he makes liberty a purely political product. He thus degrades man to a *homo politicus,* by not recognizing and emphasizing another element, active and indeed superior, which may be called either his moral or his religious nature."

Since the end of World War II, Burnham has focussed his attention on the thorny problem of Communist aggression. His initial premise is that the aim of Soviet-Communism is to conquer the world. In *The Struggle for World Power* he advocated that the United States abandon its foreign policy of "benevolent neutrality" and take aggressive steps (setting up what he calls an "American empire" among the non-Communist nations) to block Soviet expansion. In *The Coming Defeat of Communism* he suggested that Communism has the seeds of its destruction within itself, and he offered a plan for defeating it without war—a plan based on a counter-offensive of resistance and propaganda. In *Containment or Liberation?* he altered his plan by attacking the policy of "containment" of Russia and urging a program of active political warfare aimed at the destruction of the Soviet government.

Probably the most thoroughgoing critique of Burnham's work up to 1945 is the late George Orwell's essay, "Thoughts on James Burnham." Orwell noted that Burnham's specific political predictions in 1940—a German victory in World War II, defeat of the Soviet by Germany, and later (in 1944) the prophecy that the Soviet would launch a program of world conquest—represent "a continuation of the thing that is happening." Orwell wrote: "Power-worship blurs political judgment because it leads, almost unavoidably, to the belief that present trends will continue. Whoever is winning at the moment will always seem to be invincible." Arthur Schlesinger, Jr., evaluating Burnham's later work, finds that he is "a stock figure of our age. . .he is the man in a permanent apocalypse. . . Burnham has said shrewd and sound things. But the general picture is of the evolution, not of an intelligence, but of a neurosis."

Burnham was married in 1934 to Marcia Lightner. They have a daughter and two sons, and live in Kent, Conn.

PRINCIPAL WORKS: Introduction to Philosophical Analysis (with P. E. Wheelwright) 1932; The Managerial Revolution, 1941; The Machiavellians: Defenders of Freedom, 1943; The Struggle for the World, 1947; The Case for DeGaulle (with A. Malraux) 1948; The Coming Defeat of Communism, 1950; Containment or Liberation?, 1953; What Europe Thinks of America (ed.) 1953; The Web of Subversion, 1954.

ABOUT: Croce, B. My Philosophy; Lerner, M. Actions and Passions; Orwell, G. Shooting an Elephant; Current Biography 1941; New Republic March 16, 1953; New York Times Book Review February 26, 1950.

BURNS, JOHN HORNE (October 7, 1916-August 10, 1953), American novelist, died of a cerebral hemorrhage at Leghorn, Italy, at the age of thirty-six. Several months before his death he wrote the following sketch for this volume:

"John Horne Burns was born in Andover, Mass., at midnight of 7 October, 1916, the feast of the Most Holy Rosary. He was a large baby, weighing eleven pounds, and the first of seven children, the other six of whom are far more extraordinary than he. He did not talk or walk until past two years old,

a fact which gave rise to a suspicion of backwardness and uselessness which has later been confirmed. At the age of four and a half he was sent to Saint Augustine's School, run by the Sisters of Nôtre Dame de Namur, where he spent eight years acquiring the discipline of the three R's—and the Sisters are hard taskmistresses. Then he attended Phillips Academy in his home town, a stern and sumptuous private school, where he distinguished himself in no visible manner. Followed four years at Harvard College, during which, since he was allowed to do exactly as he pleased, he graduated Phi Beta Kappa in English literature.

"In the fall of 1937 he was offered a post as instructor in English at the Loomis School in Windsor, Conn., where he remained until 1942, when Mr. Roosevelt's long arm plucked him into the infantry. After a year, since the Pentagon heard he knew Italian, instead of being sent to the slaughter at Salerno, along with his other little friends, he went to the Adjutant General's School in Washington, and was commissioned a second lieutenant. He sat out the war reading prisoner of war mail in Africa and Italy. Released from active duty in 1946, he went back to teaching for a while, but the war had made him nervous, or possibly the publication of his first novel, *The Gallery*, in 1947, went to his head. It was a considerable success, and he decided to come out of the cloister.

"In 1949 his second novel, *Lucifer With a Book*, met with raucous opposition. He managed to keep alive by writing eleven articles on travel for *Holiday* magazine. His third book, *A Cry of Children* (1952), was admired by practically no one. He is at present living in a chilly villa outside Florence, Italy, finishing his fourth novel, which will deal with Saint Francis of Assisi in modern life. If that novel is a fiasco, he will take up gardening and write a book about that too. He has written this account in the third person because, with all his faults, he is shy about his worth, even to the point of doubt, a sin against the Holy Ghost."

* * *

Of the three novels which John Horne Burns published in his short lifetime, *The Gallery,* a series of portraits of Americans and Italians in Naples in 1944, testified best to what John W. Aldridge called "the remarkable range and intensity of Burns' talent as a writer." His intention in the book was "to affirm the values of human dignity and love in a milieu of war." He failed to do this—to his credit—because, Aldridge says, "Burns was too scrupulous an artist. . . He had no choice but to let the real meaning of his material carry him where it would even if it meant a serious and inevitable weakening of his total achievement."

PRINCIPAL WORKS: The Gallery, 1947; Lucifer With a Book, 1949; A Cry of Children, 1952.

ABOUT: Aldridge, J. W. After the Lost Generation; New York Times August 14, 1953; New York Times Book Review April 3, 1949; Saturday Review of Literature February 14, 1948.

BURR, Mrs. ANNA ROBESON (BROWN) (May 26, 1873-September 10, 1941). For biographical sketch and list of works and references, see TWENTIETH CENTURY AUTHORS, 1942.

BURROUGHS, EDGAR RICE (September 1, 1875-March 19, 1950). For biographical sketch and list of earlier works and references, see TWENTIETH CENTURY AUTHORS, 1942.

* * *

Edgar Rice Burroughs died at his California home at seventy-four. As the result of a series of heart attacks he had been confined to a wheelchair for several years, and had been seriously ill for three months before his death.

Witnessing the attack on Pearl Harbor, Burroughs, at sixty-six, got himself accredited as war correspondent for the Los Angeles *Times* and spent four years in the Pacific Islands. Invalided home, he spent his remaining years quietly in a modest home at Encino, Calif. At his death he left fifteen unpublished novels, and had just signed contracts for fifteen Tarzan motion pictures to be made in the following ten years. Several of his earlier books have been reprinted since his death.

Burroughs "never regarded his literary work too seriously," according to his friend Cyril Clemens, who quotes the author as saying, "My writing helped me escape being broke." F. L. Mott has observed, "On the whole, the first Tarzan is a pretty good story of its kind. It is better than most of its sequels, because it is simple. . . . It has vigorous imagination, plenty of suspense, and an interesting setting."

ADDITIONAL WORKS: Deputy Sheriff of Comanche County, 1940; Land of Terror, 1944; Escape on Venus, 1946; Tarzan and the Foreign Legion, 1947; Llana of Gathol, 1948.

ABOUT: Mott, F. L. Golden Multitudes; Hobbies May 1950; New York Times March 20, 1950.

BURT, Mrs. KATHARINE (NEWLIN) (September 6, 1882-). For autobiographical sketch and list of earlier works and references, see TWENTIETH CENTURY AUTHORS, 1942.

* * *

In recent novels Mrs. Burt has widened her range of setting and subject matter—colonial Virginia, the Smoky Mountains, main-line Philadelphia, and the stately homes along the upper Hudson in New York. In reviewing *Strong Citadel* Virginia Kirkus described her work succinctly as "feminine fiction, with more animation than most, by an editor and practitioner in the field."

Correction: Mrs. Burt was fiction editor of the *Ladies' Home Journal* from 1939 to 1940, not 1928 to 1930.

ADDITIONAL WORKS: Captain Millett's Island, 1944; The Lady in the Tower, 1946; Close Pursuit, 1947; Still Water, 1948; Strong Citadel, 1949; Escape from Paradise, 1952.

ABOUT: Warfel, H. R. American Novelists of Today.

BURT, MAXWELL STRUTHERS (October 18, 1882-August 28, 1954). For autobiographical sketch and list of earlier works and references, see TWENTIETH CENTURY AUTHORS, 1942.

* * *

Struthers Burt died at his summer home in Jackson, Wyo., after a long illness. He was seventy-one. His history-biography of his native city, *Philadelphia, Holy Experiment,* was published in 1945 and described by one reviewer as "the story of a man in love—with a city." The author confessed cheerfully to the charge. "I am a Philadelphian," he wrote, "bone of the bone, and so I cherish a passion, often against my better judgment, for the city I am going to berate, compliment, despise and hold up to admiration."

ADDITIONAL WORKS: Philadelphia, Holy Experiment, 1945.

ABOUT: Gray, J. On Second Thought; Warfel, H. R. American Novelists of Today.

"BURTON, THOMAS." See LONGSTREET, S.

BURY, JOHN BAGNELL (October 16, 1861-June 1, 1927). For biographical sketch and list of works and references, see TWENTIETH CENTURY AUTHORS, 1942.

BUSCH, NIVEN (April 26, 1903-   ), American novelist and journalist, writes: "I was born in New York City. My father was

at this time a member of the New York Stock Exchange. My mother, Christine Marie Fairchild, was one of four daughters of a British wine importer. She had grown up in Bellport, Long Island, and, being fond of this area, persuaded my father to buy a house in Oyster Bay on the north shore of the island. Long Island was not then the fashionable and lavish community it has since become. A boy could grow up there with many outdoor diversions to choose from, and I spent happy years going to school, sometimes in the country and sometimes in New York; summers were filled with such activities as fishing, swimming, camping and sports, with rides in the hills where on the bridle trails we sometimes encountered the stocky, spectacled figure of ex-President Theodore Roosevelt, who never passed without a cherry 'hello' and a wave of his hand.

"When I was fourteen, I was sent to boarding school as was the fashion of the day. The school chosen for me was Hoosac, a small establishment located in the Berkeley hills not far from Williamstown, Mass. Although there were never more than fifty boys in the school, we maintained a monthly literary magazine, the *Owl*, which bore comparison to the magazines put out by far larger schools. About five minutes after I had arrived in the school I began to write a composition for the *Owl*—a poem entitled 'The Wind.' (I believe that the first poem of most embryonic writers is titled 'The Wind.') As soon as I saw my creation and my name in print the deed was done: I had chosen my trade. A couple of years later I became editor of the *Owl* and before leaving Hoosac I had sold verse and sketches to several paying magazines, including *McClure's, Leslie's,* and some of the poetry magazines. At Princeton I wrote for the *Nassau Literary Magazine, Tiger,* and *Daily Princetonian.* Looking back now, I can see how fortunate I was to attend a school and then a college where literary tradition was highly regarded. When lack of funds forced me to leave Princeton in 1924, I was able to get a job with *Time,* then two years old. The offices were then on the third floor of a warehouse located on 39th Street between 2d and 3d Avenues. Briton Hadden, a cousin of mine, was the editor. I have always advised young writers in beginning their career to make sure they have a cousin who is the editor of a national publication. Henry R. Luce was business manager; others on the board at that time were Thomas J. C. Martyn, J. S. Martin, and John Farrar, now head of the publishing firm of Farrar and Strauss. Before long, *Time* absorbed the *Saturday Review of Literature,* thus adding to our staff in the loft editorial rooms such eminent literary figures as Christopher Morley, Henry S. Canby, Bill Benét, and Miss Amy Loveman.

"The *New Yorker* magazine began publication at this time, and before long I was contributing stories, news columns, and profiles to editor Harold Ross. Ross's tuition improved my style considerably, but my work for his publication brought me an ultimatum from *Time.* I must either drop my outside work or my recently acquired *Time* position as associate editor. The following year I accepted the ultimatum, also saying farewell to Mr. Ross; I was able to leave New York (for good, as it turned out) since I had secured a job with Warner Brothers Pictures, Inc.

"For the next eight years I worked hard writing screenplays. I wrote a number of pictures and to my great good fortune several became hits. I think that my best pictures in this early period were *The Crowd Roars, In Old Chicago,* and *The Westerner.* In 1939 I wrote my first novel, *The Carrington Incident.* Since then I have spent most of my time writing novels, retaining contact with the motion picture business by doing one or at the most two screenplays a year.

"The screen still interests and challenges me, and I have tried hard to do something worthwhile in that medium. In recent years I successfully adapted James M. Cain's story *The Postman Always Rings Twice;* I also wrote and helped to produce three original screenplays with western backgrounds: *Pursued, The Captured,* and *Distant Drums.* I have just completed at this writing [February 1953] a fourth screenplay of this series, *The Moonlighter.* All of these stories are

153

really psychological dramas laid against western scenery. This is a formula which fascinates me and in which I hope to work considerably in the future.

"I have travelled, I think, quite some distance, both spiritually and actually, from my journalistic beginnings in the big damp office buildings of Manhattan. I now live with two of my sons on a combined fruit and cattle ranch in San Benito County, Calif. A third son, Peter, is in the Army; my small daughter, Mary Kelly, lives with my divorced wife, Teresa Wright, in Los Angeles."

PRINCIPAL WORKS: The Carrington Incident, 1941; Duel in the Sun, 1944; They Dream of Home (Till the End of Time) 1944; The Furies, 1948; The Hate Merchant, 1953; The Actor, 1955.

ABOUT: Warfel, H. R. American Novelists of Today; Harper's November 1946; Saturday Review of Literature February 5, 1944, June 15, 1946.

BUSH, (JOHN NASH) DOUGLAS (March 21, 1896-), Canadian-American scholar, literary historian, and educator,

writes: "I was born at Morrisburg, Ontario. My father had a veneration for writing and wrote a little verse himself; my mother read Dickens to my sister and me before we could read. Along with Dickens, my first great passion was Macaulay (whose brassy faults every freshman can catalogue); I read his every word, and was led by him to Burke and many others. I had six years of Latin and five of Greek in high school and, entering Victoria College in the University of Toronto as Prince of Wales scholar, I took the course in Classics; I still think a classical education, under good teachers, the best there is. A fellowship in English at Victoria was followed by two years at Harvard, where, in odd hours between linguistic courses, I had a few glimpses of literature; and I had the happy experience of writing my Ph.D. thesis under John Livingston Lowes. While many friends were disciples of Irving Babbitt, I—it now seems odd to remember—was too much of a romantic to enter the fold. After a year abroad on a fellowship, I spent three years as a tutor and instructor at Harvard. In 1927 I was married to Hazel Cleaver, a college classmate, and we went to the University of Minnesota for what were to be eight happy years (in 1934-35 we were in London on a Gug-

genheim fellowship). In 1936 we moved to Harvard, where any scholar is happy to go before he dies, or even after. In 1940 we became American citizens, one immediate motive being the desire to vote for Roosevelt.

"I enjoy teaching and hope I am better at it than I was at first. I like intelligent students and I have had to do with a lot of them. Possibly a literary son has helped to keep my arteries from hardening altogether. In the matter of scholarly writing I seem to have either raised or lowered my sights. When I began, 'research' was the established ideal, and I have done a fair amount; but I have come to believe that, in the present state of our civilization, at home as well as in the world at large, the chief need is to keep the humanities alive and to help to enlarge the saving remnant who find light and strength in great literature."

PRINCIPAL WORKS: Mythology and the Renaissance Tradition in English Poetry, 1932; Mythology and the Romantic Tradition in English Poetry, 1937; The Renaissance and English Humanism, 1939; Paradise Lost in our Time, 1945; English Literature in the Earlier Seventeenth Century (Oxford History of English Literature), 1945; Science and English Poetry, 1950; Classical Influences in Renaissance Literature, 1952; English Poetry: the Main Currents from Chaucer to the Present, 1952.

BUTLER, ELIZA MARIAN (December 29, 1885-), British critic and scholar, whose writings are signed E. M. Butler,

reports: "I was born in the little village of Bardsea in Lancashire as one of a large and lively family of boys and girls, whose father, Theobald Fitzwalter, was a brilliant, daring and eccentric Irishman, and his wife a shrewd, charming and lovable Yorkshirewoman. A Norwegian governess attempted to keep us in order; Irish uncles, aunts and cousins undid most of the good she tried to do; the moors were all round us; the sea lay spread out before us. It was a dramatic and enviable childhood. My father's love of languages was the reason why we were all educated abroad; and our own unruliness and embarrassing number accounted for the fact that we were packed off to school at an early age, for I was barely eleven when I was wafted off to Hanover. From there I went to Paris and finally to a school for domestic economy in Germany, where I enjoyed myself madly but could not learn to cook and did not become a practically useful member of society.

"My intimate knowledge of French and German resulted in reading Modern Languages at Cambridge; but it was my love of adventure that made me learn Russian at the beginning of the first World War in order to obtain a post with the Scottish Women's Hospitals in Russia under Dr. Elsie Inglis. I succeeded in getting out as stores-orderly, and later accompanied the unit to Macedonia and Yugoslavia. When the war was over, I returned reluctantly to academic life; and from 1921 onwards held successive posts at Newnham College and in the University of Cambridge as supervisor in Modern Languages and lecturer in German. My sabbatical year (1934-35) was spent in Egypt, Burma, and India, the latter country in particular being a revelation to me, and ranking with the time in Russia as one of the two great awakenings and enrichments of my life. Hardly had I returned and settled back into my pleasant Cambridge groove before I was invited to fill the Henry Simon Chair of German in the University of Manchester; and the nine years I spent there (though unfortunately including the period of the second World War) taught me many things for which I shall always be profoundly grateful. But the call to Cambridge, which came in 1945, was too strong to resist; and the last six years of my academic life as Schröder Professor in that lovely and beloved university passed like a happy dream.

"Yet, had I been born a man, or even a very rich woman, I should have chosen the life of an explorer. At it is, I have travelled as widely through Europe and beyond as time and money allowed. I have also pandered to my ruling passion by attempting explorations into the minds of men and women, as mirrored in literature, life, and magical tradition. And the magic of poetry has made all these voyages of discovery a source of perennial delight, although no one is more vividly aware than I am of the unfathomable nature of the human mind."

PRINCIPAL WORKS: The Saint-Simonian Religion in Germany, 1926; The Tempestuous Prince, 1929; Sheridan, a Ghost-Story, 1931; The Tyranny of Greece over Germany, 1935; Rainer Maria Rilke, 1941; Romantic *Germanentum* in the German Mind and Outlook, 1945; The Myth of the Magus, 1948; Ritual Magic, 1949; The Fortunes of Faust, 1952. *Novels*—Daylight in a Dream, 1951; Silver Wings, 1952.

BUTLER, ELLIS PARKER (December 5, 1869-September 13, 1937). For biographical sketch and list of works and references, see TWENTIETH CENTURY AUTHORS, 1942.

BUTTERFIELD, HERBERT (October 7, 1900-   ), British historian, the son of Albert and Ada Mary (Buckland) Butterfield, was educated at the Trade and Grammar School, Keighley, Yorkshire. He was a scholar at Peterhouse, Cambridge, and has been a fellow of Peterhouse since 1923. From 1924 to 1925 he was a visiting-fellow at Princeton University.  He was a lecturer in History at Peterhouse, Cambridge, from 1930 to 1944, becoming professor of Modern History at Cambridge in 1944.

His first published work was *The Historical Novel* in 1924, but he won his reputation seven years later with an adventurous work, *The Whig Interpretation of History.* Upon its republication in 1951 the *Hibbert Journal* commented: "Terse and tidy, it contains a lively, and often illuminating discussion of the underlying assumption of the historian, of the historical process itself, of judgments of value and moral judgments in history, and of the art of the historian." The decade of the Forties was productive for Butterfield, resulting in the publication of six volumes dealing with various periods and phases of European history. *George III, Lord North and the People* (1949), from original sources, was described by the *New Statesman and Nation* as "an admirable piece of research." The same journal complained of his way of writing as showing evidence of "his too long success as a lecturer." But the *Political Science Quarterly* proclaimed that the book was "brilliantly written."

Origins of Modern Science and *Christianity and History* crowded into the year of 1949 in quick succession and once more drew conflicting views as to style from commentators . The New York *Times* compared *Christianity and History* with the work of Toynbee, commenting: "He is always perceptive if not what is often called profound. Readers who fell in with Toynbee may be dissatisfied but here is more authentic feeling for history and a deeper understanding of religion." The volume had its origin in a collection of lectures given over B.B.C.

His latest work comprises a series of essays on historiography and the philosophy of history. In *History and Human Relations,* Butterfield ranges "from a candid analysis of the inevitability of conflict between two powers oriented as are the U.S. and the U.S.S.R. (regardless of the 'goodness' of their respective governments) to a consideration of the power of love—of God and of man—in human relationships."

Accused by some critics of being too diffuse and lacking bite and precision, he has been praised by others (Ordway Tead in *Survey*) for his "lucid and cogent writing at its best." Even the *New Statesman and Nation* reversed its customary criticism of his style to remark about *History and Human Relations* that it was "his most effective book. . . . He is still not a brilliant writer but this is all to the good."

Professor Butterfield married Edith Joyce Crawshaw in 1929. They have three sons. He is the editor of the *Cambridge Historical Journal* and calls himself "a confirmed Christian and a Yorkshire Methodist."

PRINCIPAL WORKS: The Historical Novel, 1924; The Peace Tactics of Napoleon, 1929; The Whig Interpretation of History, 1931, The Statecraft of Machiavelli, 1940; The Englishman and His History, 1944; George III, Lord North and the People, 1949; The Origins of Modern Science, 1949; Christianity and History, 1949; History and Human Relations, 1951; Christianity, Diplomacy, and War, 1953.

*BYNNER, WITTER (August 10, 1881-). For biographical sketch and list of works and references, see TWENTIETH CENTURY AUTHORS, 1942.

* * *

Witter Bynner's American version of *The Way of Life* of Lao Tzu, published in 1944, was widely praised for its faithful expression of the calm, serene wisdom of the Chinese philosopher. The *New Yorker* wrote: "A fresh simplicity and humane common sense prevail here . . . and the poems provide a delightful coolness for our present discordant times." A collection of Bynner's own poems, *Take Away the Darkness,* revealed similar ingratiating qualities of humanity and "warm openness." Dudley Fitts observed, however, that these qualities are inadequate for raising the book above the level of mediocrity. Bynner's verse, he felt,

* bĭn'ẽr

156

represents the tradition of "Poetry as a Decorative Art."

Probably the most interesting of Bynner's recent works is his portrait of D. H. Lawrence and his wife in *Journey With Genius.* Bynner had spent considerable time with the Lawrences in New Mexico in 1922 and 1923 and his recollections of the novelist are sharp and vivid. The critical reception of the book was strangely mixed. Paul Horgan found it "the most persuasive, penetrating, and literate" of all the many new books on Lawrence, and George F. Whicher commented on Bynner's "good humor, wit, lively anecdote, perfection of phrase, and moving eloquence." But Mark Schorer pronounced it a work "drenched in malice," and Joe Dever of *Commonweal* observed that Bynner could not apparently make up his mind whether this was to be "a grudge book or a love book." Bynner lives in Santa Fe, N.M.

ADDITIONAL WORKS: The Way of Life, According to Laotzu: An American Version, 1944; Take Away the Darkness, 1947; Journey With Genius, 1951.

BYRD, RICHARD EVELYN (October 25, 1888-). For biographical sketch and list of works and references, see TWENTIETH CENTURY AUTHORS, 1942.

* * *

In World War II, Rear Admiral Richard E. Byrd (now retired) served with Fleet Admiral King in Washington and Fleet Admiral Nimitz in the Pacific. He saw overseas duty in both the Atlantic and the Pacific, and was twice awarded the Legion of Merit Medal. In 1946 Byrd was appointed commanding officer of the United States Navy Antarctic Expedition. The announced purpose of this expedition was to study mineral deposits in the area. Admiral Byrd's permanent home is in Boston, Mass.

In March 1955 it was announced that Admiral Byrd would head an expedition to the Antarctic in the summer of 1955 to begin work on observation sites.

ABOUT: Henry, T. R. White Continent; Current Biography 1942; National Geographic October 1947; Newsweek December 16, 1946; Time April 28, 1947.

BYRNE, DONN (November 20, 1889- June 18, 1928). For biographical sketch and list of works and references, see TWENTIETH CENTURY AUTHORS, 1942.

* * *

ABOUT: Wetherbee, W. Donn Byrne: A Bibliography.

CABELL, JAMES BRANCH (April 14, 1879-   ). For biographical sketch and list of earlier works and references, see TWENTIETH CENTURY AUTHORS, 1942.

* * *

In *Quiet, Please,* a collection of autobiographical essays published in 1952, James Branch Cabell comments that "remarkably few persons" appear to read his books today. This does not surprise him, he says. "Yet do I find it perceptible—here to riot in understatement—that I, who was once a leading personage in and about those scanty playgrounds of human interest which we nickname literature, seem now to have become, for all practical results, unheard-of thereabouts."

The passage is characteristic of Cabell's idiosyncratic style, which John Peale Bishop once described as a rhetoric consisting sometimes "of vague and sonorous sentiment added merely for general impressiveness." Cabell has not, however, retired to so complete an obscurity as he would suggest in *Quiet, Please.* During the 1940's he wrote a trilogy of novels on life in Florida—the last volume of which was his fiftieth book. He now spends every winter in St. Augustine, Fla., but in spirit he remains a Virginian through and through. Probably his most important work of recent years is a collection of essays on "the remarkable commonwealth of Virginia"—*Let Me Lie.* A quick survey of reviews of his latest books will show also that he is still the subject of controversy—mellowed, perhaps, but still lively. The anti-Cabell faction balks at his mannered style, his irreverence, his iconoclasm. (D. H. Mosely wrote in *Commonweal:* "It is the tiresome Swan Song of that generation which had as a primary purpose in writing the blasting of tradition and the exhibition of its own shallow cleverness...") The pro-Cabells, on the other hand, delight in these same qualities and in what Edward Wagenknecht has called "the familiar Cabell mixture of bleak disillusion and amused persiflage, with good sense and good humor persistently breaking in."

Mrs. Priscilla Cabell died in 1948. In 1950 Cabell married Margaret Waller Freeman.

ADDITIONAL WORKS: *Novels*—The St. Johns (with A. J. Hanna) 1943; There Were Two Pirates, 1946; The Devil's Own Dear Son, 1949. *Non-Fiction*—Let Me Lie, 1947; Quiet, Please, 1952.

ABOUT: Bishop, J. P. Collected Essays; Cabell, J. B. Quiet, Please; Wagenknecht, E. Cavalcade of the American Novel; New York Herald Tribune Book Review April 10, 1949; New York Times Book Review September 1, 1946, April 17, 1949; Saturday Review of Literature April 11, 1942; Time February 25, 1952.

*CAHAN, ABRAHAM (July 7, 1860-August 31, 1951). For biographical sketch and list of works and references, see TWENTIETH CENTURY AUTHORS, 1942.

* * *

Abraham Cahan died at Beth Israel Hospital in New York at ninety-one. He had retired from the editorship of the *Jewish Daily Forward* a few years earlier. In 1947 he was honored at a celebration of the fiftieth anniversary of the newspaper held at Madison Square Garden.

"Like the *Forward* he was an institution," commented the New York *Times,* which credits his work and writings with much influence in the birth and development of the needle trades and other labor organizations, and the "vast improvement in working and living conditions of the East Side masses and their colonies." So widely copied were the features of the *Forward* that Cahan has been called the editor of all the Jewish newspapers in the United States.

"Cahan made the *Forward* a transmission belt between the old culture and the new Americanism," observed *Newsweek.* "Many an immigrant schooled himself for citizenship via *Forward's* serialized lessons in English and American history. But Cahan never neglected the Jewish tradition."

ABOUT: Villard, O. G. The Disappearing Daily; American Mercury August 1947; Commentary August 1952; Commonweal June 6, 1947; Newsweek May 26, 1947; New York Times September 1, 1951; Time September 18, 1950.

* kä'hàn

CAIN, JAMES MALLAHAN (July 1, 1892-   ). For biographical sketch and list of earlier works and references, see TWENTIETH CENTURY AUTHORS, 1942.

* * *

Although none of James M. Cain's later novels has had the tremendous popular success of *The Postman Always Rings Twice,* he has gained a new and even wider audience in recent years through motion picture versions of his works. The relatively neglected short novel *Double Indemnity,* originally published as a magazine serial, became the most successful of his films (1944), "a landmark in the art of the cinema." This was followed by film versions of *Mildred Pierce* and, after long delays over censorship, *The Postman Always Rings Twice.*

These three films, Cain estimated, earned their producers over twelve million dollars, as compared to slightly over one hundred thousand dollars which he received for them. To protect authors whose works are bought for the screen and to correct the disproportion in the financial returns, Cain proposed to establish an "American Authors' Authority" (A.A.A.) which would be controlled by representatives of the four guilds affiliated with the Authors' League of America. The plan, supported by the Screen Writers' Guild, met with strong opposition from other members of the Authors' League who objected to its compulsory features—including a limitation on publishers' profits and the required "signing away" of copyrights to the A.A.A. In 1947 a compromise was reached in which the Authors' League agreed to adopt some of the A.A.A. features but not those involving censorship and copyright.

Cain's later novels have, for the most part, followed the pattern of the earlier ones—hard-hitting, fast-paced, sordid, violent. As he points out in his preface to *Three of a Kind,* he has deliberately cultivated the technique of shocking and jolting the reader. W. M. Frohock says that he is one of the few American writers "who are really sure-handed in the manipulation of their materials." Edmund Wilson considers him merely a Hollywood writer, one of the "poets of the tabloid page." Frohock similarly points out that "nothing he has ever written has been entirely out of the trash category." But, Frohock continues, in spite of this, he has been read and imitated by "an inordinate number" of intelligent people (among them the French novelist Albert Camus in *The Stranger*).

Cain lives in Hollywood. He was divorced from his second wife and married Florence Macbeth Whitwell, a former opera singer, in 1947.

ADDITIONAL WORKS: Love's Lovely Counterfeit, 1942; Three of a Kind (Sinful Woman, Double Indemnity, The Embezzler) 1943; Past All Dishonor, 1946; The Butterfly, 1947; The Moth, 1948; Galatea, 1953.

ABOUT: Frohock, W. M. The Novel of Violence in America; Lerner, M. Public Journal; Wilson, E. Classics and Commercials; Current Biography 1947; Look January 23, 1945; Wilson Library Bulletin December 1941.

CAINE, Sir HALL (May 14, 1853-August 31, 1931). For biographical sketch and list of works and references, see TWENTIETH CENTURY AUTHORS, 1942.

* * *

ABOUT: Dictionary of National Biography 1931-1940; Atlantic Monthly August 1949.

CALDWELL, ERSKINE (December 17, 1903-). For autobiographical sketch and list of earlier works and references, see TWENTIETH CENTURY AUTHORS, 1942.

* * *

Erskine Caldwell writes: "Divorced from Margaret Bourke-White, 1942; married to June Johnson, of Phoenix, Ariz., 1942, and we have one son; have been editor of *American Folkways* since 1942, and the series to date [1952] contains twenty-three volumes; from 1942 to 1945 lived in Beverly Hills, Calif.; from 1946 to present lived in Tucson, Ariz.; during past seven years have devoted much time to travel, including several trips around the United States, one to all countries in South America, one to all countries in Europe, and several trips to England and France."

It is safe to say that in terms in sheer quantity Erskine Caldwell is the best best-selling author in the United States today. Among paper-bound reprint editions his *God's Little Acre* has led all other books, and in 1949 his publishers estimated that approximately 20,000,000 copies of his books, in all editions, had been distributed. Caldwell's phenomenal success has continued in spite of (and possibly because of) the fact that his works have been subjected to more censorship than those of any other American author. *God's Little Acre* had been taken into court in 1933 under a charge of obscenity instituted by the New York Society for the Suppression of Vice. The charge was dismissed, but that novel, the later novel *Tragic Ground,* and the stage production of *Tobacco Road* have all had their day in the courts. In the face of repeated attempts to ban his books, Caldwell is sanguine, pointing out that if people can still get excited about *God's Little Acre* after so many years, "I am encouraged to think it must take a pretty good novel to create so much interest." He is, however, seriously concerned about the threat of censorship to the freedom of the writer, the publisher and bookseller, and the public. He has said: "Censorship, in cases where obscenity or salaciousness is not clearly defined or evident, is now a basic threat to the freedom of the press, and to writing and reading in general. Sooner or later it can touch everyone."

ADDITIONAL WORKS: Moscow under Fire: A Wartime Diary (also called: All Out on the Road to Smolensk) 1941; All Night Long, 1942; Georgia Boy, 1943; A Day's Wooing, and Other Stories, 1944; Stories of Erskine Caldwell, 1944; Tragic Ground, 1944; A House in the Uplands, 1946; The Sure Hand of God, 1947; This Very Earth, 1948; Place Called Estherville, 1949; Episode in Palmetto, 1950; Call It Experience: The Years of Learning How to Write, 1951; The Courting of Susie Brown, 1952; A Lamp for Nightfall, 1952; Complete Stories of Erskine Caldwell, 1953; Love and Money, 1954.

ABOUT: Burke, K. Philosophy of Literary Form; Caldwell, E. Call It Experience; Cantwell, R. Introduction to The Humorous Side of Erskine Caldwell; Frohock, W. M. The Novel of Violence in America; Gray, J. On Second Thought; Snell, G. D. Shapers of American Fiction; Van Gelder, R. Writers and Writing; Current Biography 1940; Life October 1, 1945; New Republic November 6, 1944; Newsweek September 24, 1951; New York Herald Tribune Book Review October 8, 1950; New York Times Book Review May 30, 1948, November 22, 1953; Publishers' Weekly May 14, 1949.

CALDWELL, JANET TAYLOR (September 7, 1900-   ). For autobiographical sketch and list of earlier works and references, see TWENTIETH CENTURY AUTHORS, 1942.

* * *

Taylor Caldwell writes to the editors of this volume: "I want to thank you now for giving me an opportunity to correct flagrant errors in this biographical data. Most of it was thought up by foolish press-agents, who had told me that the 'public liked that sort of thing.' And some of it you have evidently picked up from prejudiced sources.

"The only correct matters in your data are the date of my birth, the place of my birth, the names of my parents and their Scots background, my marriages, my education, the time I began writing, the general religious background of my family.

"It is all as erroneous as the statement that I am a 'tall, nervous, blonde housewife.' I am medium height, not nervous, and am a decided brunette. I am not, and never was, a housewife. I never wrote confession stories, as your data states, and never had anything published prior to Dynasty of Death, not even a 'letter to the editor.' I was not a 'stenographer' in the Immigration Service in Buffalo. I was one of a three-member panel called the Board of Special Inquiry.

"Dynasty of Death was not written 'in nine months—typed at a kitchen table.' My husband, who is my collaborator, business manager, researcher and editor and partner, and I, began to write this book in 1934 and it was not until the spring of 1938 that it was finished. It was written in an office we established in our home. We worked on it at night, for that was the only time available to us.

"The idea of my 'writing three novels simultaneously' was another wild dream of idiot press-agents, who insisted on publishing this error against my protests. Our novels take us from three to five years each, at least, and almost all that has been published since 1938 dates back to the middle twenties, with some later minor corrections. This Side of Innocence, for instance, published in 1946, was begun in 1927 and not finished (first draft) until four years later. Until 1945 it was worked on occasionally, until its last draft, in 1946.

"Other errors in your data are not so mischievous, but could bear correcting. Our family stems from the Clan of MacGregor, of which the Taylors are a subsidiary Clan. I have one-third Irish blood.

"Another small correction: I have no hobbies except reading. I never, if I can get out of it, attend parties of any kind. I do not 'keep house.'"

ADDITIONAL WORKS: The Arm and the Darkness, 1943; The Turnbulls, 1943; The Final Hour, 1944; The Wide House, 1945; This Side of Innocence, 1946; There Was a Time, 1947; Melissa, 1948; Let Love Come Last, 1949; The Balance Wheel, 1951; The Devil's Advocate, 1952; Maggie—Her Marriage, 1953; Never Victorious, Never Defeated, 1954.

ABOUT: Warfel, H. R. American Novelists of Today; New York Times Book Review April 28, 1946, April 10, 1949; Report to Writers February 1953.

CALLAGHAN, MORLEY (1903-   ). For biographical sketch and list of earlier works and references, see TWENTIETH CENTURY AUTHORS, 1942.

* * *

Morley Callaghan lives in Toronto. He is generally recognized as one of the most distinguished of contemporary Canadian authors. He contributes articles and short stories to American periodicals. Callaghan is an active worker for his alma mater, the University of Toronto. His novel The Varsity Story, described by one reviewer as "a sort of intellectual guidebook to the University of Toronto cast into the form of fiction," was written in answer to a fundraising appeal made by the university to its alumni. Callaghan signed over the royalties on the book to the university. In quite a different vein was his sensitive and tragic study of Negro-white racial relations in *The Loved and the Lost*. The novel is set in Montreal and offers a vivid picture of "café society" life in that city. Many reviewers of the book, however, felt that it suffered from a "vagueness" and "remoteness" of theme, what Riley Hughes, in *Catholic World*, called "an uneasy alliance between an extreme radicalism and a frantic symbolism."

PRINCIPAL WORKS: Luke Baldwin's Vow (juvenile) 1948; The Varsity Story, 1948; The Loved and the Lost, 1951.

ABOUT: Hoehn, M. (ed.) Catholic Authors, I; Phelps, A. L. Canadian Writers; Thomas, C. Canadian Novelists, 1920-1945; Scholastic May 14, 1945; Time February 7, 1949.

"CALVERT, JOHN." See LEAF, M.

CALVERTON, VICTOR FRANCIS (June 25, 1900-November 20, 1940). For autobiographical sketch and list of works and references, see TWENTIETH CENTURY AUTHORS, 1942.

"CAMBRIDGE, ELIZABETH." See HODGES, B. K. W.

*CAMMAERTS, EMILE LÉON (March 16, 1878-November 2, 1953), Belgian poet and essayist, who made his home in England for more than forty years, was born in Brussels. His parents were divorced, and he was raised by his mother, a well-educated and intelligent woman who exerted a great influence on her young son. An admirer of the writings of Rousseau, she instilled in the boy a reverence toward all living things and succeeded, Cammaerts wrote, "in eliminating from my mind any idea that nature was ruthless." It was not until years later that Cammaerts underwent religious conversion and came to recognize the fundamental error in the assumption that nature was good and a thing to be worshipped in itself. "This error," he wrote in his autobiographical *The Flower of Grass*, "is caused by the confusion between the impression of comfort and beauty and the virtue of goodness."

* käm'ärts

Cammaerts was often ill during his childhood and was therefore educated at home by a tutor. When he was at last sent to school, a secular state institution, he was wretchedly unhappy until he learned to adjust himself to the harshness of everyday reality. He studied at the University of Brussels and discovered the works of Michelangelo, Rabelais, and Shakespeare. He read Shakespeare first in a bad French translation but was stirred deeply enough by his reading to study English for the purpose of translating great works of literature. When he completed his university studies, Cammaerts traveled to Italy for a time. The works of art which he saw there opened a new world to him and many of his later books reflect his passionate interest in art. One of the greatest influences upon him at this time was Ruskin, and he resolved to translate that English author's guidebook, *Mornings in Florence*, into French. Cammaerts' translation, supplemented with his own notes, grew into a four-volume translation of Ruskin's work. It was a useful task—"I had . . . begun my training as a writer, for there is no better training for a beginner than the stern discipline of translation."

Cammaerts settled in England in 1908. By that time he was already well known in Belgium as a lyric poet. Besides his verse and verse plays, he wrote art criticism, historical studies, a book on G.K. Chesterton, and a considerable amount of political commentary on Belgian affairs. In 1914 his poem "Carillon," inspired by the German invasion of his homeland, was recited in public in England by the poet's wife, the English actress Tita Brand Cammaerts. Mrs. Cammaerts translated many of her husband's books into English and was co-author with him of a children's book, *Boy of Bruges*.

Cammaerts relates, in *The Flower of Grass*, that he met his future wife when he went as a reviewer for a newspaper to a recital in which she performed. When they married it was his hope that he might write plays for her to act in, but with the coming of a family (they had six children), Cammaerts took up teaching duties at the University of London and—he wrote—"we left the aristocracy of art for the democracy of family life." Under his wife's influence Cammaerts entered the Church of England, to which he had long been drawn. The record of his spiritual development may be found in *The Flower of Grass*, a book which W. H. Auden compares with the writings of Saint Augustine and Cardinal Newman as "not so much an autobiography as a paragraph in the biography of the Divine Grace."

American readers know Cammaerts best for this autobiography and for another intense and deeply personal volume, *Upon This Rock,* a poignant expression of the author's grief over the death of his son Peter who had been a fighter pilot with the R.A.F. In England, where Cammaerts was professor of Belgian studies and institutions at the University of London, he was recognized as the foremost interpreter of Belgian culture. His histories of Belgium, his biography *King Albert of Belgium,* his vindication of King Leopold, who surrendered to Hitler, in *The Prisoner at Laeken,* and his articles on Belgian politics, which appeared regularly in the *Contemporary Review,* were all distinguished by sound scholarship and a sympathetic but unprejudiced approach to Belgian affairs.

Cammaerts was an officer of the Order of Leopold and a Commander of the British Empire. He was corresponding member of the Royal Society of Literature in England and held an honorary LL.D. from Glasgow University. He died at his home in Radlett, Hertfordshire.

PRINCIPAL WORKS IN ENGLISH TRANSLATION: Belgian Poems, 1915; New Belgian Poems, 1916; Messines and Other Poems, 1918; Boy of Bruges (with T. B. Cammaerts) 1918; Belgium from the Roman Invasion to the Present Day, 1921; The Childhood of Christ as Seen by the Primitive Masters, 1922; Treasure House of Belgium, 1924; The Poetry of Nonsense, 1925; Discoveries in England, 1930; Rubens: Painter and Diplomat, 1932; Albert of Belgium, 1935; The Laughing Prophet: G. K. Chesterton, 1937; Child of Divorce (novel) 1938; Keystone of Europe: History of the Belgian Dynasty, 1939; The Prisoner at Laeken: King Leopold, Legend and Fact, 1941; Upon This Rock, 1942; The Flower of Grass, 1944; The Peace That is Left, 1945; Flemish Painting, 1945; Principalities and Powers (with J. Lindley) 1947; The Devil Takes the Chair, 1949; For Better, For Worse, 1950.

ABOUT: Cammaerts, E. Upon This Rock, The Flower of Grass; New York Times November 3, 1953.

CAMPBELL, JOSEPH (1904-   ), American mythologist, writes: "My interest in mythology began when I was a boy. We lived next to the New Rochelle (N.Y.) public library, and after a year or two of reading American Indian lore in the children's room, I was admitted to the stacks. There I found the *Annual Reports* of the Bureau of Ethnology, Morgan's *League of the Iroquois,* and the works of Franz Boas, which I read

avidly until I went to prep-school and had to begin working toward college. My serious studies were not resumed until one year after graduation from Columbia, when I realized, while reading for my M.A. in English literature, that many motifs in the Arthurian legends resembled themes that I could recall from my American Indian studies. From that moment to the present the  problem of the mythological archetypes has been the *primum mobile* of all my research.

"Columbia awarded me a traveling fellowship for two years (1927-29) on which I went first to Paris, where I studied Old French and Provençal but discovered *Ulysses* and modern art, and then to Munich, where I studied Sanskrit and Indo-European philology, but discovered Freud, Jung, Mann, Goethe, and Hinduism. I returned to America just in time for the Wall Street crash and a long season of no jobs, but since I had much to assimilate, my forced retreat to the forest was not unfortunate. I learned to live on nothing, and for three years did little but read and take notes.

"The first employment that came to me was in my old prep-school, where I taught German, French, Ancient History, and fifth-form English for one year. Chancing to sell a short story for three hundred dollars, however, I returned to the forest when my teaching contract expired, for another fifteen months of reading. Since 1934 I have been a member of the literature department of Sarah Lawrence College where I conduct a course in comparative mythology. In 1938 I married Jean Erdman of Honolulu who was at that time a member of the Martha Graham Company and has since founded a dance company and school of her own. I have learned that the dance, like practically everything else, is a function of myth.

"My writing began at prep-school where I wrote for the school paper and the literary quarterly, becoming business manager of the former and editor of the latter. At college my interests were athletic and I ceased writing. I tried short stories for a while when I returned from Europe, but contracted an allergy to the popular press and so abandoned the pen until 1939 when my friend

Henry Morton Robinson persuaded me to collaborate with him on a key to *Finnegans Wake.* The following year another friend, Heinrich Zimmer, introduced me to the founders of the Bollingen Series and I edited their first volume, *Where the Two Came to Their Father: A Navaho War Ceremonial.* These two works opened a gusher, and I have been writing ever since."

PRINCIPAL WORKS: Where the Two Came to Their Father: A Navaho War Ceremonial (with J. King and M. Oakes) 1943; A Skeleton Key to Finnegans Wake (with H. M. Robinson) 1944; Grimm's Fairy Tales: Folkloristic Commentary, 1944; The Hero with a Thousand Faces, 1949; *Editor*—Zimmer, H. Myths and Symbols in Indian Art and Civilization, 1946, The King and the Corpse, 1948, Philosophies of India, 1951; The Portable Arabian Nights, 1952; Zimmer, H. The Art of Indian Asia, 1955.

CAMPBELL, ROY (October 2, 1901-). For autobiographical sketch and list of earlier works and references, see TWENTIETH CENTURY AUTHORS, 1942.

* * *

In the current volumes of *Who's Who* Roy Campbell lists himself as "wine-grower and cattle-breeder." Poetry is still listed as merely "recreation," although as recently as 1952 Stephen Spender referred to him as "one of the most distinguished poets writing in the English language." His talents as a poet have made him a successful translator of the poetry of others—notably St. John of the Cross, Baudelaire, and García Lorca. Of his critical study of the latter, Wallace Fowlie wrote that Campbell "demonstrates a very real understanding of Spain and the Spanish temperament, and a poet's kinship with Lorca." Others objected that he was using Lorca as a stalking-horse for his Rightist political views.

A colorful and highly controversial personality, Campbell has completed another breathless and dashing volume of autobiography covering his life up to 1935—*Light on a Dark Horse.* He makes no pose of false modesty. He is egotistic, bombastic, and, as one reviewer suggested, "self-consciously romantic." But all this is part of the Campbell pattern. Iain Hamilton wrote of the book in the *Manchester Guardian:* "Even the unrestrained sounding of his own wreathed horn is in the old epic tradition and perfectly in character. This must irritate a good many people ... but it has at least the virtue of complete naturalness—forceful, but unforced."

Campbell left Spain in 1942 to join the British Army as a private. He saw service in East and North Africa until he was disabled and discharged with the rank of sergeant in 1944. His present home is in Sintra, Portugal.

ADDITIONAL WORKS: *Poetry*—Sons of the Mistral, 1941; Talking Bronco, 1946; Collected Poems, 1949; Poems of St. John of the Cross (tr.) 1951; Selected Poems, 1955. *Prose*—Light on a Dark Horse, 1951; Federico García Lorca, 1952; The Mamba's Precipice, 1954.

ABOUT: Campbell, R. Light on a Dark Horse; Hoehn, M. (ed.) Catholic Authors, I.

CAMPBELL, WALTER STANLEY ("Stanley Vestal") (August 15, 1887-). For autobiographical sketch and list of earlier works and references, see TWENTIETH CENTURY AUTHORS, 1942.

* * *

Walter Stanley Campbell continues to balance neatly the careers of college professor and teacher of writing and (as "Stanley Vestal") author of a score of solid, colorful books on the Old West. His academic headquarters are the University of Oklahoma, where he has taught since 1915. In 1939 he became director of courses in professional writing, and out of this experience has come a number of books and articles of practical advice for beginning writers. As a chronicler of the life and times of the West, he has produced, in recent years, two biographies (*Jim Bridger* and *Joe Meek*), a study of the Missouri in the Rivers of America series, an historical study of the Plains Indians from 1851 to 1891, and a lively re-creation of Dodge City in the 1880's. Vestal, a reviewer wrote in 1952, "is an old hand at getting the best out of western frontier material." He holds fast to the record, Stewart Holbrook commented, "without even a side glance at Hollywood."

ADDITIONAL WORKS: Writing Non-Fiction, 1944; The Missouri, 1945; Jim Bridger: Mountain Man, 1947; Warpath and Council Fire: The Plains Indians' Struggle for Survival in War and in Diplomacy, 1948; Writing: Advice and Devices, 1950; Queen of Cowtowns, Dodge City, 1872-1886, 1952; Joe Meek: A Biography, 1952.

CAMPBELL, WILLIAM EDWARD MARCH ("William March") (September 18, 1893-May 15, 1954), American novelist and short story writer, died of pneumonia at his home in the French Quarter of New Orleans at the age of sixty. Several months before his death, he wrote to the editors of this volume: "I was born in Mobile, Ala., the second child in a family of eleven children. My father was John Leonard Campbell and my mother Susy March Campbell. On my mother's

side the family was of English descent; on my father's, Scotch, with perhaps an admixture of Irish. In boyhood I lived mostly in a series of small, sawmill towns in Alabama and Florida. Later I went to Valparaiso University for one year; the following year I took law at the University of Alabama; in 1916 I dropped out in order to earn enough money to complete my studies and wound up in New York as a law clerk and subpoena server for one of the large law firms there.

"In 1917 I enlisted in the Marine Corps. I participated in all action that Marines saw during the First World War. I was wounded and gassed. I was decorated with the Distinguished Service Cross, the Navy Cross, the Croix de Guerre with Palm.

"On my demobilization I returned to Mobile. Later I became one of the organizers of the Waterman Steamship Corporation, which has grown to be the largest steamship company in the world. As a vice president of that organization, I opened offices in various cities in the United States. In 1932 I went to Germany, with Hamburg as a base, to work westbound cargoes to the United States. Later I used London for the same purpose. I returned to the United States late in 1937 and lived in New York City for the next ten years. Since that time I've lived in Mobile. [He moved to New Orleans several months before his death.]

"I began to write short stories in 1928. My first novel, Company K, was published in 1933, although written several years earlier."

* * *

Early in William March's writing career a reviewer took note of his skill in handling the eccentric and the horrible "with a simple matter-of-courseness which somehow tempers their strangeness." His novels and short stories—many of them set in Alabama—treat small-town Southern life with something of Faulkner's starkness and artistry. But March was not an imitator, nor did he write within any fixed framework or tradition. Stanley Edgar Hyman said of him: "It is a pleasure to read a writer with a

knowledge of his craft and so full an awareness of the material he is manipulating." His last novel, The Bad Seed, a terrifying story of a little girl who is a mass murderess, was widely read. In the fall of 1954 it was dramatized by Maxwell Anderson and produced on Broadway with great success.

PRINCIPAL WORKS: Company K, 1933; Come in at the Door, 1934; The Little Wife and Other Stories, 1935; The Tallons, 1936 (in England: Song for Harps); Some Like Them Short (short stories) 1939; The Looking Glass, 1943; Trial Balance (short stories) 1945; October Island, 1952; The Bad Seed, 1954.

ABOUT: Warfel, H. R. American Novelists of Today; New York Times May 16, 1954; Saturday Review July 17, 1954; Wilson Library Bulletin June 1943.

*CAMUS, ALBERT (November 7, 1913-), French novelist, essayist, and playwright, was born in Mondovi, a town in northeastern Algeria, of a Spanish mother and an Alsatian father. His father died during World War I, and the family was very poor. He attended public schools in Algiers and worked his way through the University of Algiers

where, in 1936, he passed his *aggrégation* in philosophy with a thesis on Plotinus and Saint Augustine.

From 1935 to 1938 Camus took an active part in the intellectual life of the city of Algiers. His absorbing interest was the theatre. Beginning in 1935 he managed and acted with a theatrical company, L'Equipe (The Team). The first production of the group was an adaptation of Malraux's novel Le Temps du Mépris. The next play undertaken, a four-act drama based on a labor uprising in 1934, was banned by the Algerian government, but the company continued to produce successfully a distinguished list of classical and contemporary dramas—works by Gide, Synge, Ben Jonson, Dostoevsky, and a translation made by Camus of the Prometheus of Aeschylus.

Camus' first book, L'Envers et l'Endroit, a collection of personal essays, was published in Algiers in 1937. In the following year he published another volume of essays, Noces, and traveled abroad for the first time, visiting Central Europe, Italy, and

* că mü'

France. On his return to Algiers he worked as a journalist for *Alger Républicain* until 1940 when he went back to France to join the staff of *Paris-Soir*. In June 1940, when France fell to the German armies, he returned to North Africa and taught for two years in a private school in Oran. This was a period of intense literary activity for Camus, and when he went back to Paris in 1942 he had completed his novel *L'Etranger (The Stranger)*, and a philosophical essay, *Le Mythe de Sisyphe*.

In France Camus played an important role in the Resistance movement. The brilliant editorials and reviews he wrote for the underground press—*Combat, Revue Libre, Cahiers de la Libération*—won him wide attention. After the Liberation his position in French intellectual life was major and unchallenged. He continued, now in the open, as editor of *Combat*, to write a series of moving, deeply philosophical essays which reached to the heart of the moral and intellectual dilemmas of post-war France. Like his plays and novels, these editorials represented, John L. Brown commented in the New York *Times*, "a noble, courageous, but resolutely atheistic humanism."

The essence of Camus' thought is probably best captured in the allegory of the Sisyphus legend, the hopeless, meaningless, eternal up-hill labor, which, Camus suggests, is human life. But just as he rejects a facile optimism, so too does Camus reject the all-embracing negativism of existentialism. Kermit Lansner, in an article on Camus in the *Kenyon Review*, speaks of the "singleness of his own moral purpose." He asks only one question, "What does it mean to be a man?" and his answer, always tentative and subject to revision as metaphysical speculation must be, takes many forms—essays, novels, plays. The problem is stated over and over again. Man is alone, an alien in a hostile, illogical world. He is always the "stranger,"' nameless and isolated. Camus' earlier work echoed a nihilism, a sense of the absurdity of all things, which is strikingly similar to the *nausea* of Sartre's existentialism. His most recent writings, however, suggest that he is moving in the direction of what Lansner calls "a secular humanism." *L'Homme Révolté* (translated under the title *The Rebel*) is in part an historical analysis of revolution in the Western world, and in part Camus' account of his own attitudes toward the political ideologies of our time. Nicola Chiaromonte wrote of the book: "He felt intellectually

responsible for his political commitments and attempted to live up to this responsibility." As a result, Camus presents a closely-reasoned argument that we live in an era of nihilism, the logical extension of which is the justification of murder and war; that rebellion or revolt, carried to its limits, produces the very negation of the freedom which it attempts to establish. Camus' essay was generally received with acclaim in France. The most interesting dissenting opinion was in the pages of *Les Temps Modernes*, the journal edited by the existentialist Jean-Paul Sartre. Camus' criticism of Marxism and Stalinism was deplored as "objectively reactionary." The debate continues, but one conclusion is sure—Sartre and Camus, whose intellectual positions had run parallel at many periods, were now clearly, sharply, and probably irrevocably divided.

Camus resigned from *Combat* in 1945 to devote his time to his own writing. In 1946 he made a lecture tour of the United States where the publication in that year of his novel *The Stranger* created a lively stir in literary circles. *The Stranger* is a first-person narrative by a clerk living in Algiers. He moves in emotional isolation (hence a "stranger") through a series of experiences which ultimately drive him to murder and his own death. The novel is written in the form of a philosophical tale. Camus' message, Justin O'Brien commented, "will have a universal appeal to some minds, to those who like Kafka and Dostoevsky, who know why they like Gide and Malraux." Two years later *The Plague*, a parable depicting the life of a modern city during an epidemic of bubonic plague, was published in England and the United States. It was hailed by the *Spectator* as "one of those very rare combinations, an intellectual book that is also a good novel." To the critics who objected that the allegory obtruded (Orville Prescott, for example, said in the *Yale Review* that "instead of writing about particular people he has written about people who are abstract symbols of various political and moral attitudes..."), Stephen Spender answered: *"The Plague* stands or falls by its message. The message is not the highest form of creative art, but it may be of such importance for our time that to dismiss it in the name of artistic criticism would be to blaspheme against the human spirit."

The dramas of Albert Camus are less well known in America and England than is his fiction. A considerable amount of critical attention has, however, been given to some of them—particularly *Caligula,* written in 1938 and published in 1944, a prophetic drama about the Roman emperor who is driven, through a sense of the terror and meaninglessness of life, into the acts of monstrous cruelty for which history remembers him. Other plays by Camus are *L'Etat de Siège* and *Les Justes.*

Since 1947 Camus has taken an active interest in movements for world government. He was the founder of the Committee to Aid the Victims of Totalitarian States. He is, as one critic remarked, "a superb example of the artist who has not attempted to retreat from the horror of the contemporary world." He is still a young man. In the decade and a half that he has been writing, he has shown great and profound philosophical development, and there is every reason to believe that his position will be reshaped and altered in the years to come. It is for this reason that he remains a figure of such vital interest to readers on both sides of the Atlantic. Wallace Fowlie writes: "Camus has been called by some of his younger admirers their conscience, an irritable, uneasy conscience which is making a valiant effort to understand the age and to prepare a renascence from the ruins. His writings deal with the tragic aspects of our time, but they also call upon the will of man to dominate the absurd aspect of man's fate."

Camus has been married since 1940 and has a son and a daughter. He is described as tall and thin, dark-haired but blue-eyed, intense looking—and a chain smoker. He lives in Paris, where he is a director of the publishing house Librairie Gallimard.

PRINCIPAL WORKS IN ENGLISH TRANSLATION: The Stranger, 1946; The Plague, 1948; Caligula, and Cross Purpose: Two Plays, 1948; The Rebel, 1953.

ABOUT: Beaton, C. & Tynan, K. Persona Grata; Columbia Dictionary of Modern European Literature; Dictionnaire Biographique Français Contemporain; Lerner, M. Actions and Passions; Peyre, H. The Contemporary French Novel; Arizona Quarterly Winter 1953; Christian Science Monitor February 24, 1953; Commonweal May 30, 1952; France Illustration January 5, 1952, September 20, 1952; Kenyon Review Autumn 1952; Mercure de France January 1952; New Republic April 29, 1946; New York Herald Tribune Book Review April 7, 1946; New York Post June 5, 1945; New York Times Book Review April 7, 1946, January 10, 1954; New Yorker April 20, 1946, May 30, 1953; Partisan Review November-December 1952; Saturday Review of Literature July 31, 1948; Spectator March 18, 1949; Time May 20, 1946.

CANBY, HENRY SEIDEL (September 6, 1878-   ). For autobiographical sketch and list of earlier works and references, see TWENTIETH CENTURY AUTHORS, 1942.

* * *

Henry Seidel Canby taught writing and literary criticism at Yale until 1941, with many later distinguished writers among his students. He received an LL.D. from the University of Delaware in 1946 and in 1951 was elected a Fellow of the Royal Society of Literature.

During World War II Canby worked for the Writers' War Board. In 1945 he was sent by the Office of War Information to Australia and New Zealand. There, he writes, "My mission was to explain the cultural history of the United States as made articulate in its literature to nations with a democratic experience like our own."

Canby's major work in the past decade has been in the fields of biography and autobiography. He has published a life of Walt Whitman, and in *Turn West, Turn East,* a comparative biographical study of Henry James and Mark Twain—James reflecting the eastward stream of American culture toward Europe, tradition, and refinement, Twain the hearty and robust culture of the West and the frontier. In 1947 Canby completed his autobiographical trilogy which had begun with *The Age of Confidence* (1934) and *Alma Mater* (1936). Now, with a new section, "Brief Golden Age," his autobiography appeared as *American Memoir.* Here Canby sums up his more than forty years in American literary life, affirming—near the end of the book—"I am quite sure that if I could be shot back along the time line to the Concord of Thoreau and Emerson, I should be most impressed by both the change and the persistence of American values since that day. And should find much to confirm, and probably something to disprove, my own theories of the history of American literature. For literature is not only the best index of values in a given age; it can also be said to consist of values on which imagination builds, and for whose expression techniques are invented. And the best defense of a literary memoir like this one . . . was that if its theories were only deductions, its memories were the same source material as was used in the making of all good books."

ADDITIONAL WORKS: Walt Whitman, An American, 1943; Family History, 1945; American Memoir, 1947; Turn West, Turn East, 1951.

ABOUT: Canby, H. S. American Memoir: Current Biography 1942; Newsweek September 1, 1947; Saturday Review of Literature August 30, 1947; Time August 25, 1947, August 8, 1949.

CANFIELD, DOROTHY. See FISHER, D. F. C.

CANNAN, GILBERT (June 25, 1884-   ). For biographical sketch and list of works and references, see TWENTIETH CENTURY AUTHORS, 1942.

* * *

Gilbert Cannan's long silence as a writer has been unbroken since 1924. His translation of a poem by Heine appeared in the *Contemporary Jewish Record* for October 1943, but he has been otherwise unpublished.

CANNAN, JOANNA (1898-   ). For biographical sketch and list of earlier works and references, see TWENTIETH CENTURY AUTHORS, 1942

* * *

Joanna Cannan lives in Oxford. She divides her writing time between books for children (which reflect her lively interest in horses and in hunting) and urbane detective stories. She writes the latter with skill and humor. Her plots are slight, but her portraits of English life are subtle and satirical. A reviewer in the New York *Herald Tribune* commented that her work "reads like a cross between Margery Sharp and Angela Thirkell."

ADDITIONAL WORKS: Blind Messenger, 1942; Little I Understood, 1948; Poisonous Relations (in England: Murder Included) 1950. *Juveniles*—More Ponies for Jean, 1943; They Bought her a Pony, 1944; I Had Two Ponies, 1947; I Wrote a Pony Book, 1950.

CANNON, Mrs. CORNELIA (JAMES) (November 17, 1876-   ). For autobiographical sketch and list of works and references, see TWENTIETH CENTURY AUTHORS, 1942.

* * *

Mrs. Cannon writes from Cambridge, Mass.: "My husband [Dr. Walter B. Cannon] died in 1945, and since then I have taken two trips alone round the world, seeing Australia and New Zealand, the Philippines, India, and the new and interesting state of Israel, which is a great addition to the democracies of the free world. Nineteen grandchildren keep me in touch with youth and inspired with hopes for the future

in which I hope they will not have to kill and be killed."

Correction: Mrs. Cannon notes that the description of her in TWENTIETH CENTURY AUTHORS, 1942, as "tall and slender" is inaccurate.

CANNON, LE GRAND, Jr. (December 1, 1899-   ), American novelist, writes: "I was born in New Haven, Conn., the second child of LeGrand and Florence Pond Cannon, and together with two sisters grew up— so the calendar said —in the pleasant shelter of a closely-knit family. As children we were, I presume, under the influence— certainly we were regularly exposed to it!  —of the Congregational church and Sunday school and of the public school of a relatively gentle neighborhood. But most of all we were under the influence of—and are still indebted to—the devotion as well as the discipline of my mother and father. It was a privileged boyhood.

"I recall with dismal clarity the fact— equally well perceived at the time—that I was not good at anything, neither at games nor at lessons nor at anything else. I did like to read. I don't know whether I was good at reading or not; I don't know how you tell. But I know I enjoyed it.

"Vacations, we went as a family into the woods in Maine. We loved it, we children, more than anything that I can remember out of those years.

"Following grammar school and high school, I went to the Yale of those days, saw no more of the war than a distant view of its outermost fringe, and having received an unearned degree in June of 1920, I went to Labrador for the summer to work for the Grenfell Mission. So did Jeannette Peabody of Cambridge. We were married two years later. Meantime, apparently, I'd attended the Harvard Business School in Cambridge.

"For some six years I worked in the wholesale grocery business in New Haven under my father, and when he retired and the business was discontinued, I indulged in a brief and very expensive career as a promoter. The venture had something to do with patents; it included two trips to England, and the promoters as well as the stockholders lost all they put in That over with, I started to try to write.

"I wrote some short pieces, and a little verse, and I wrote a book, and I couldn't sell any of them. So then I wrote another book which was published as *A Mighty Fortress* in 1937. For a first novel, it did fairly well—something under five thousand copies—and I received a half-cent an hour for the time I'd put in on it. My next book, *The Kents*, didn't do quite so well.

"My wife continuing loyally and cheerfully to support the family—there were four children by now—I set out to write another book. It took four years, but published under the title of *Look to the Mountain*, this one really did pretty well. It has continued to do pretty well. In the first half of 1952 it sold more copies than there were copies of its successor returned. That was a pretty good record—because there were an awful lot of copies of *Come Home at Even* (1951) returned.

"Our four children are now dispersed about their various ways of life, and my own time is divided about evenly between New Haven and Chocorua, N.H.

"Mrs. Cannon died in 1948 after an illness of many years. Her beauty, her kindness, her courage, and her laughter are the lasting joy of her family and a help to everyone who knew her."

* * *

Chocorua, N.H., where Cannon spends his summers, was the scene of his best-selling and highly-praised novel of pioneering life in pre-Revolutionary days—*Look to the Mountain*. A solid and leisurely book, it was hailed at the time of its publication as one of the finest of American historical novels. The historian Allan Nevins commented: "Seldom do we find a transcript from the American past executed with so much sincerity, clarity, and delicacy."

PRINCIPAL WORKS: A Mighty Fortress, 1937; The Kents, 1938; Look to the Mountain, 1942; Come Home at Even, 1951.

ABOUT: Book-of-the-Month-Club News October 1942; Current Biography 1943.

CANTWELL, ROBERT (January 31, 1908-). For autobiographical sketch and list of earlier works and references, see TWENTIETH CENTURY AUTHORS, 1942.

* * *

Robert Cantwell left the staff of *Time* magazine in 1945 to become literary editor of *Newsweek*. His home is in Riverdale, N.Y. In 1948 he published the first volume

of a projected two-volume biography of Nathaniel Hawthorne, covering that author's early life up to 1850 and the publication of *The Scarlet Letter*. The book reflected a staggering amount of research—a fact which disturbed some reviewers, who found it overloaded with small detail. Cantwell's purpose was to dispel the mystery that has surrounded Hawthorne's early years and the popularly-held notion that until his marriage Hawthorne was a lonely recluse. He tried instead to show him as an active politician and journalist in this period.

ADDITIONAL WORKS: Nathaniel Hawthorne: The American Years, 1948; The Humorous Side of Erskine Caldwell (ed.) 1951.

ČAPEK, KAREL (1890-December 24, 1938). For biographical sketch and list of works and references, see TWENTIETH CENTURY AUTHORS, 1942.

* * *

PRINCIPAL WORKS IN ENGLISH TRANSLATION: How They Do It, 1945; Apocryphal Stories, 1949; Three Novels: Hordubal, An Ordinary Life, Meteor, 1949; In Praise of Newspapers, and Other Essays on the Margin of Literature, 1951.

ABOUT: Columbia Dictionary of Modern European Literature; Stern, A. K. C.: A Short Account of His Works, *in* Prayer for Czechoslovakia.

*CAPOTE, TRUMAN (September 30, 1924-), American novelist, playwright, and short story writer, writes: "I was born in New Orleans. My mother was from Alabama, and I spent a great lot of my childhood in that state, though I lived in several other parts of the South. Later I spent winters in schools in the East, particularly the Trinity School in New York City and

Cecil Beaton

the high school in Greenwich, Conn.—where Miss Catherine Wood, who taught English there at the time, offered me great kindness and encouragement. But I believe I was a nuisance and a bother to most all my other teachers; certainly I was never a good student, and so intense was my relief when graduation finally came that I did not consider college.

"Instead I spent a winter in an apartment of my own in New Orleans—reading, writing short stories, working on a novel. I was

* "Capote is pronounced Ca-poe-tee."

seventeen. The novel came to nothing, indeed was never finished, but one of the stories written during this period was subsequently published by the magazine *Story*.

"The following year I went to New York wanting a job, which was not easy to find, particularly because I looked too young, thirteen or fourteen at the most. One day, however, I went round to the *New Yorker* magazine—and left with a glorious-sounding job in their Art Department; in actuality I turned out to be a kind of errand boy; still I enjoyed the year I stayed there—though certain personages might have been surprised to hear it.

"I spent the following winter on a farm in Alabama, and it was then that my stories began to appear with some regularity in a number of magazines—including 'Miriam,' 'Shut a Final Door,' which won the O. Henry prize of that year, and the title story from my first collection, *A Tree of Night*. It was then also that I began work on a novel, *Other Voices, Other Rooms*, which was finished three years later on Nantucket Island.

"I prefer travel to any other form of entertainment and do not know that I should ever care to be settled in any specific place. During the last six years I've lived in the West Indies, Paris, New York, Tangiers, Venice, and for quite long stretches in Sicily. To live and work in this somewhat scattered manner is very agreeable to me— I think because I do not have much instinct for ownership, do not want in the least to be surrounded by the personal possessions that can root one's life. I wish to have only those things that are transportable. Or so it would appear at the moment.

"None of my work is autobiographical; except, in an obscure way, in a way that even I cannot define, my second novel, *The Grass Harp*. It was written to commemorate my affections for two beloved friends, long dead, who appear in the book as Miss Dolly Talbo and Catherine Creek. I wrote a play, more or less based on the book, and with the same title, which was produced in New York in March of 1952.

"The content of my work is 'literary'; as opposed, that is, to writing inspired by political or religious convictions, of which I have, in the very orthodox sense, none: so that my source, my point of view, is a matter of private imagination, personal moral beliefs. The 'message' of a story should be after all the story itself. Though I have always been conscious of style, I have not a 'fixed' style and hope that I never do, for

each story requires a new setting of tone, a language that will contain the story as a glass contains water. Just generally, however, I work toward a certain sound, the rhythms of speech, and try to make each sentence read as though it could also, in a natural voice, be said."

* * *

In 1948 when Truman Capote's *Other Voices, Other Rooms* was published, he was hailed as a boy wonder. The publication of a stylized photograph of him draped over a couch, his eyes fixed in a stare of childlike wonder behind straggling bangs, only reinforced the popular impression that he was the *enfant terrible* of contemporary American letters. Probably more attention was given to the author than to the intrinsic qualities of the novel itself, a strange and gripping little book, peopled with grotesque characters who moved in a neo-Gothic world of decadence and degeneracy. In the years and the books that have followed, Capote has at last come to the place where he can be read and evaluated apart from the hullabaloo of publicity campaigns. Traces of the precocious, slightly diabolical but charming child still exist in his works. The world in which his characters move is fundamentally a child's world—isolated, self-centered, richly and sometimes exotically imaginative. (John W. Aldridge speaks of the "purity" of Capote's world—a purity not of experience but "the sort that can be attained only in the isolation of a mind which life has never really violated, in which the image of art has developed to a flowerlike perfection because it has developed alone.") But the eerie short stories in *The Tree of Night* and the warm-hearted fantasy of *The Grass Harp* give evidence of a sound and considerable talent. There is similar evidence in Capote's non-fiction—*Local Color*, a collection of sketches about places Capote has visited from New Orleans and Brooklyn to Spain and North Africa—that he is, in Gouverneur Paulding's words "a conscientious and thoughtful artist."

In 1952 Capote turned to another form, the drama, with an adaptation of *The Grass Harp* which was favorably received by the New York critics. Richard Hayes wrote in *Commonweal*: "Mr. Capote excels as the dramatist of sensibility, of the small, the delicate and eccentric; he displays, moreover, the essential flintiness of mind from which a good scene may be struck." Capote has also done motion-picture writing, and in Italy in 1953 he wrote the script for the Humphrey Bogart-John Huston production *Beat the Devil.* In 1954 he wrote the book for the colorful and exotic musical comedy *House of Flowers,* which had a moderate Broadway run. Capote spends much time in Taormina, Sicily, where he has bought a villa once occupied by D. H. Lawrence.

PRINCIPAL WORKS: Other Voices, Other Rooms, 1948; A Tree of Night and Other Stories, 1949; Local Color (essays) 1950; The Grass Harp (novel) 1951, (play) 1952.

ABOUT: Aldridge, J. W. After the Lost Generation; Current Biography 1951; New York Times Book Review February 24, 1952; Saturday Review of Literature February 12, 1949.

CARCO, FRANCIS (July 31, 1886-)
For biographical sketch and list of works and references, see TWENTIETH CENTURY AUTHORS, 1942.

* * *

When World War II broke out, Francis Carco was living at L'Isle-Adam, near Paris. During the German occupation, he published nothing and resisted all efforts to elect suspected collaborationists to the Goncourt Academy. He finally fled from the German zone to the south of France where, cut off from funds, he supported himself by singing in nightclubs. After the Germans took over the remainder of France, he moved on to Geneva. There he began to write again. After the war he returned to France and his home at L'Isle-Adam.

Seymour S. Weiner, Carco's biographer, points out that during all the political upheavals of recent years, Carco has remained aloof and apolitical. He has friends on both the Right and the Left. His later writings—novels and poetry (none translated into English as yet)—reflect a growing morbidity and horror, "the miasma of mind and sentiment and environment." Weiner speaks of the "hallucinatory quality of some of Carco's work . . . an irrational feeling that all is occurring under incomprehensible circumstances." Weiner considers that Carco does not belong in the first rank of contemporary French literature—his range and specialization are too narrow. "Carco is not among the giants," he writes, "but within the scope which he has set himself he is an artist of high importance. His finesse, his ability to follow without didacticism the serpentine convolutions of the heart's and the mind's complexities, is extensive."

ABOUT: Columbia Dictionary of Modern European Literature; Weiner, S. S. Francis Carco: The Career of a Literary Bohemian.

"CARLSON, JOHN ROY." See DE-ROUNIAN, A. A.

CARMAN, BLISS (April 15, 1861-June 8, 1929). For biographical sketch and list of works and references, see TWENTIETH CENTURY AUTHORS, 1942.

* * *

ADDITIONAL WORKS: Pipes of Pan (definitive edition) 1942.

ABOUT: Edgar, P. Bliss Carman, *in* Leading Canadian Poets (ed. W. P. Percival); Morse, W. I. Bliss Carman, Bibliography.

CARMER, CARL LAMSON (October 16, 1893-). For autobiographical sketch and list of earlier works and references, see TWENTIETH CENTURY AUTHORS, 1942.

* * *

Carl Carmer is one of the best known of American regional writers. The region is upper New York State, where he was born and raised, and where he now lives (in an old octagonal-shaped house at Irvington-on-Hudson). He has long been a collector of American folk songs, legends, and ballads. In 1949 he published a long and lively "cycle of York State years" called *Dark Trees to the Wind*—the effect of which, a fellow New Yorker, Samuel Hopkins Adams, wrote, "is that of an old-time panorama accompanied and explained with the charm and persuasiveness of a master narrator."

Carmer has also written a number of books for young readers—all of them full of local color and charm. Some of these books were illustrated by his wife, Elizabeth Black Carmer.

ADDITIONAL WORKS: America Sings (ed.) 1942; Songs of the Rivers of America (ed.) 1942; The Jesse James of the Java Sea, 1945; Taps Is Not Enough (dialogue in verse) 1945; American Scriptures (ed. with C. Van Doren) 1946; Dark Trees to the Wind, 1949; The Susquehanna, 1954. *Juveniles*—Wildcat Furs to China, 1949; Hurricane Luck, 1949; Too Many Cherries, 1949; Windfall Fiddle, 1950; A Flag for the Fort, 1952.

ABOUT: Holiday September 1949; New York Herald Tribune Book Review November 20, 1949, October 11, 1953; New York Times Book Review November 13, 1949; Saturday Review January 29, 1955.

CAROSSA, HANS (December 15, 1878-). For biographical sketch and list of earlier works and references, see TWENTIETH CENTURY AUTHORS, 1942.

* * *

Hans Carossa lives in Passau, Germany, where he had first settled half a century ago to practice medicine. He managed, in the years of the Nazi domination of his country, to remain aloof from political matters. During World War II he published only one book, the autobiographical *Das Jahr der Schönen Täuschungen* (translated into English a decade later as *The Year of Sweet Illusions*)—an account of a year of his student life in Munich in 1897-98. Since the end of the war he has published a volume of poems (*Stern über der Lichtung*) and, in 1951, a personal account of his life under Nazism—*Ungleiche Welt*. In this book (according to a sketch in Hoehn's *Catholic Authors*) he described the Nazi era as one "when German fate fulfilled itself" and when the life of the spirit "was condemned to a catacomb existence."

In all of his writings Carossa has shown a spiritual, even mystical, detachment from the world of action. "He shrinks from uncompromising clarity. . . ," Ruth J. Hofrichter wrote, "preferring a floating and luminous haze to any merciless light or focus." With himself, however, he is candid. Hugh W. Puckett wrote of his autobiographical volume: "His confessions are the product of modesty and of that clairvoyance which honesty of intellectual dealing can achieve." The strongest literary influence upon his work was not Rilke, whom he knew well, but Goethe (appropriately, he received the Goethe prize in 1938). It is as a poet, Professor Hofrichter says, that "he seeks to resolve the problems set up by the impact of the total world on the individual. In the ideas of metamorphosis, of sublimation, of sacrifice and responsibility, his poems combine the demands of life on earth with the selfish instincts of man, and assimilate to a certain degree the great spiritual forces from whose immediate experience Carossa shrinks."

ADDITIONAL WORKS IN ENGLISH TRANSLATION: The Year of Sweet Illusions, 1951.

ABOUT: Carossa, H. The Year of Sweet Illusions; Columbia Dictionary of Modern European Literature; Hoehn, M. (ed.) Catholic Authors, I; Hofrichter, R. J. Three Poets and Reality.

CARR, EDWARD HALLETT (June 28, 1892-), British political scientist, received his early education at the Merchant Taylors' School in London. He attended Trinity College, Cambridge, and in 1916 joined the British Foreign Office. He was attached to the British delegation to the Peace Conference of 1919 and in recognition of his work was made, in 1920, a Commander of the Order of the British Empire.

In the same year, he was sent to the British Embassy in Paris for work with the Conference of Ambassadors. In 1925 he was Second Secretary in the British Legation in Riga, Latvia. From 1930 to 1933 he was an assistant adviser on League of Nations affairs. In the latter year he became a First Secretary.

After twenty years in the diplomatic service—during which he acquired an impressive background in foreign affairs—Carr resigned in 1936 to enter academic life. For the next decade he was Wilson Professor of International Politics at the University College of Wales. When World War II broke out, he returned to government service for a time as director of foreign publicity for the Ministry of Information. From 1941 to 1946 he was an editor of the London *Times*, writing editorials and critical and historical articles for the *Literary Supplement*. Since 1946 he has devoted himself to the study of Soviet history in preparation for his comprehensive *History of Soviet Russia*.

In a sense all of Carr's earlier writings have been preparation for his history of the Soviet Union. His first books were biographical studies, and his subjects were nineteenth century figures who played important roles in Russian revolutionary history. Especially valuable were his *Romantic Exiles*, a study of a group of nineteenth century Russian and German political revolutionaries, and his biography *Michael Bakunin*, which A. J. P. Taylor called "a masterpiece of scholarship and wit," and Avrahm Yarmolinsky praised for "candor, vivacity, amused understanding, and strict adherence to the record." In 1937 Carr published the first of several books on international relations. In this field his Foreign Office experience, C. D. Burns wrote in the *Spectator*, "has given him what is best in the tradition of diplomacy, a capacity for calm in the midst of crises and alarms." His analyses are cautious, balanced, and, said the London *Times*, "trustworthy." Of his *Conditions of Peace*, "a positive and unflinching" book on peace policies after World War II, Harold Butler wrote in the *Spectator*: "It is full of an independence and breadth of vision, a loftiness of aim and a sobriety of judgment which are rare in themselves and still rarer in combination. No more penetrating study has been made of the revolutionary epoch through which we are passing or of the conditions required for the building up of a new and stable society."

Carr published a series of lectures he had given at Oxford in 1946 as *The Soviet Impact on the Western World*. This study of the wide influence of Soviet concepts on the institutions and the thinking of the Western democracies attracted wide and favorable attention in Britain and in the United States. It was the subject of an editorial in the New York *Herald Tribune* for January 30, 1947, which said that the book "is likely to have a very considerable impact in Western democratic thought." The long-awaited *History of Soviet Russia: 1917-1923* was published from 1951 to 1953. Carr announced in his preface to the first volume that his purpose was not to write a history of the events of the revolution, "but of the political, social and economic order which emerged from it." The first volume concentrated primarily on political institutions, the second on economics, and the third on foreign policy. The entire study is merely a preliminary work to the narrative proper which, according to Carr's original plans, begins with the death of Lenin.

The critical reception of these volumes has been, on the whole, excellent. Even those critics who objected to Carr's reliance on Soviet sources and to what Hajo Holborn, in the *Yale Review,* called "his inclination to measure events almost exclusively in terms of success," agreed that the work was the soundest, most carefully documented and most comprehensive in its field.

PRINCIPAL WORKS: Dostoevsky: A Biography, 1931; The Romantic Exiles, 1933; Karl Marx, 1934; International Relations Since the Peace Treaties, 1937; Michael Bakunin, 1937; The Twenty Years' Crisis, 1919-1939, 1939; Britain: A Study of Foreign Policy, 1939; The Conditions of Peace, 1942; Nationalism and After, 1945; The Soviet Impact on the Western World, 1946; Studies in Revolution, 1950; History of Soviet Russia, 3 vols., 1950-53; German-Soviet Relations Between the Two World Wars, 1919-1939, 1951; The New Society, 1951; The Interregnum: 1923-1924, 1954.

ABOUT: Rowse, A. L. End of an Epoch; Wilson, E. Shores of Light; Hibbert Journal July 1940; Twentieth Century February 1953.

CARR, JOHN DICKSON (1905-). For biographical sketch and list of earlier works and references, see TWENTIETH CENTURY AUTHORS, 1942.

* * *

John Dickson Carr writes under only two names now—his own and "Carter Dickson."

The dropping of the third name, "Carr Dickson," in no way reflects a diminishing in the number of his books, however. He still produces four, and sometimes as many as six, books a year and innumerable short stories. In addition, he has tried his hand, with considerable success, at two other genres—the historical novel, in *The Bride of Newgate*—and biography, in his authorized study, *The Life of Sir Arthur Conan Doyle*. Finally in collaboration with Adrian Conan Doyle (Sir Arthur's youngest son), he wrote a series of stories concerning the further adventures of the immortal Sherlock Holmes, entitled *The Exploits of Sherlock Holmes.* The first of these, "The Adventure of the Seven Clocks," was published in *Life* magazine for December 29, 1952.

Carr, his wife, and their three children returned to the United States from England in 1948. They now have a home in Mamaroneck, N.Y. There Carr writes in an attic room, the walls of which are lined with book shelves holding one of the finest crime reference libraries in the world. In 1949 he was elected for a term as president of the Mystery Writers of America. He was the subject of a two-part *New Yorker* profile by Robert Lewis Taylor in 1951 (see reference below).

ADDITIONAL WORKS: *As John Dickson Carr—* The Emperor's Snuff-Box, 1942; Till Death Do Us Part, 1944; He Who Whispers, 1946; Sleeping Sphinx, 1947; Below Suspicion, 1949; The Life of Sir Arthur Conan Doyle, 1949; The Bride of Newgate, 1950; The Devil in Velvet, 1951; The Nine Wrong Anaswers, 1952; Great Escapes in Life and Story, 1952; (with A. Conan Doyle) Exploits of Sherlock Holmes, 1954; The Third Bullet, and Other Stories, 1954; Captain Cut-Throat, 1955. *As Carter Dickson—*She Died a Lady, 1943; He Wouldn't Kill Patience, 1944; Curse of the Bronze Lamp, 1945; My Late Wives, 1946; Skeleton in the Clock, 1948; Graveyard to Let, 1949; Night at the Mocking Widow, 1950; Behind the Crimson Blind, 1952; The Cavalier's Cup, 1953.

ABOUT: Life December 29, 1953; New Yorker September 8, 15, 1951.

*CARREL, ALEXIS (June 28, 1873-November 4, 1944). For biographical sketch and list of earlier works and references, see TWENTIETH CENTURY AUTHORS, 1942.

* * *

Alexis Carrel (sometimes spelled Carrell) died of a heart ailment at seventy-one at his home in Paris. His widow has said that his heart condition was aggravated by the "superhuman task" on which he was work-

* kăr′ĕl

ing, by accusations of collaborating with the Germans, and by the physical rigors endured during the German occupation of France.

Under the Vichy regime in occupied France Carrel had established the Foundation for the Study of Human Relations, dedicated to the study of "the reconstruction of man from the physical as well as the mental viewpoint." On August 29, 1944, following the liberation, he was dismissed from his post and a few days later was arrested on charges that he had attempted to supplant French universities with his foundation by forcing university laboratories to close when their staff members were reluctant to join the faculty of his institute. Carrel denied collaborating with the Germans, and stated, "I am convinced I did not do anything against France." A committee of three French scientists was appointed to investigate the charges against him. A week before his death, the French government officially denied that proceedings had been started against him.

One of Carrel's last projects was a study of blood circulation, fatigue, and sleep. A book on the influence of prayer was his last work to be published in France before his death. *Reflections on Life*, published here in 1953, is an unfinished account, on which he was working to the time of his death, of the theories on which his "Foundation" was projected. Anne Carrel has described her husband's plan as a study of man "as a whole, in the totality of his physiological, mental and spiritual makeup," by a "small group of men of the highest calibre" living in "an atmosphere of calm which would allow them to concentrate themselves into a genuine 'collective brain.'" Here they would, in Carrel's own words, "work for the development of beings superior to any who have hitherto inhabited the earth" by helping the strong rather than the unfit and the defective ("only the *élite* makes the progress of the masses possible"), and confining their work to "individuals belonging to the races who produced the Western civilization to which they belong."

Of Carrel's literary style, a "feeling for word and phrase quite unusual in the writings of most scientists" was noted by Hans Zinsser, who added that "the style is simple without dryness—picturesque without affectation. At times the form rises to the level of distinguished prose." The scientist's friend and collaborator Charles A. Lindbergh has said: "To me, his true greatness lay in the unlimited penetration, curiosity, and scope of his mind, in his fearlessness of opinion, in his deep concern about the trends of modern civilization and their effect upon his fellow man."

ADDITIONAL WORKS: Prayer, 1947; Voyage to Lourdes, 1950; Reflections on Life, 1953.

ABOUT: Hoehn, M. Catholic Authors, I; Leonardo, R. A. Lives of Master Surgeons (Supplement I); Lerner, M. Public Journal; Kaempffert, W. B. Science Today and Tomorrow (2nd Series); Catholic World December 1944; Scientific American January 1942; New York Times November 6, 1944.

*CARRERA ANDRADE, JORGE (September 28, 1903-   ), Ecuadorian poet, was born in Quito, son of Abelardo Carrera Andrade, a minister of the Supreme Court of Justice, and Carmen Vaca Andrade, descendant of a colonel in the Ecuadorian army. One of eleven children, the poet grew up on a country estate where he developed an intense love for his natural surroundings and for the rich native Ecuadorian traditions. In later life Carrera Andrade has traveled much and his writing has taken on what H. R. Hays called a "cosmopolitan elegance." But, Hays pointed out, his work "retains the impress of his native land: his particular kind of sensitivity, his exquisite sensuality, is truly Latin-American."

Carrera Andrade was educated in preparatory schools in Ecuador and studied law at the University of Quito. At fifteen he was editing a literary review, and his first two volumes of poetry—*Estanque Inefable* and *La Guirnalda del Silencio*—were published when he was in his early twenties and still a university student. He continued his studies in philosophy and literature in France, Germany, and Spain, and for the next two decades of his life traveled all over the world in the Ecuadorian foreign service. He served in the Ecuadorian consul in Marseilles from 1929 to 1930; in Barcelona for the next three years (where his third book, *Boletines de Mar y Tierra* was published), then returned to Ecuador briefly as secretary of the National Senate in 1933 and to teach at the Instituto Nacional Mejía. In the following year he was sent to the consulate in Paita, Peru; from there to Le Havre, and then to Yokohama. From 1940 to 1944

* kär rĕ'rä än drä'thä

he was in the United States with the Ecuadorian consulate in San Francisco. He returned to South America to spend three years in Caracas, Venezuela, then abroad again in 1947 for a year in London. In 1948-49 he was director of protocol in the Ministry of Foreign Affairs in Ecuador. Since 1950 he has been vice-president of the Casa de la Cultura. He lives in Quito. His wife is the former Paulette Collin.

Carrera Andrade is generally regarded as the leading poet of Ecuador and one of the most important of contemporary Latin-American poets. His poems are usually brief, terse, strongly imagistic, full of immediacy and objectivity. "All his poetry has its own accent," Muna Lee wrote, "its own freshness: and most of its images . . . are set down with the shrewdness and the sagacity of a peasant or a child." The Spanish critic Trincado said, "He feels the life in things," and the late John Peale Bishop called him "a natural poet . . . a poet who has never doubted his own nature." His poetry has been shaped by three major streams of influence—his travel abroad, his reading, and his innate sympathy for life around him. The first influence has produced sensitive poetic sketches of foreign cities. Of his reading—particularly the work of the French poet Francis Jammes—Carrera Andrade has said: "The bare simplicity, the fervid love of humble lives, the fresh and fragrant peace that characterize the poetry of that solitary of the French Pyrenees, left a profound impression on me, since they harmonized with my turn for country life and my sympathy for the country folk and the Indians of Ecuador." Finally, his poetry shows the impress of his discovery of his own environment and his identification with the traditions and problems of his fellow Ecuadorians. He has written many poems dealing with the labor movement and social problems. In Spain he took an active part in the proclamation of the Republic. His poetry, however, is itself part of no political movement. It is born, H. R. Hays has commented, "of a sensitive individualism and he is an aesthetic aristocrat." In Carrera Andrade's own words: "Poetry is *creation* rather than construction. I do not believe it should be facility or craftsmanship. The poet does not deliberately sit down at a table to manufacture poetry; the latter comes unexpectedly from the heights, like a tremendous wind, like a militant angel who shakes and tortures the man, and the victim argues with himself in his agony and stammers some broken fragments which constitute the poem. For true poetry is only that which has fallen from the combat with the angel."

PRINCIPAL WORK IN ENGLISH TRANSLATION: Secret Country, 1946.

ABOUT: Bishop, J. P. *Introduction to* Secret Country; Books Abroad Autumn 1941, April 1943; Poetry February 1942.

CARROLL, Mrs. GLADYS (HASTY)
(June 26, 1904-). For autobiographical sketch and list of earlier works and references, see TWENTIETH CENTURY AUTHORS, 1942.

* * *

Mrs. Carroll writes from South Berwick, Maine: "World War II, by calling up all our young men and taking the older men into defense plants, brought an end to the annual production of the neighborhood folk-play and to rural life as we had known it. Since then more and more of our young people have gone on to college and to occupations which require that they spend the greater part of the year away from us, but they come home for winter and summer holidays. Community projects are now supported by public suppers, fairs, auctions, and so on.

"During the war my husband joined the faculty of the University of New Hampshire and became chairman of the department of psychology. Our daughter, Sarah Frances Linden Carroll, was born in 1941. My mother passed on in May 1952, and my father now makes his home with us.

"The University of Maine conferred an Litt.D. degree on me in 1939, and Bates College in 1945. I am now serving a five-year term as alumni representative on the Bates Board of Overseers. Our son Warren was a member of the Bates Class of '53; history major, Phi Beta Kappa, and varsity debater. At present I am county chairman for the Pine Tree Society for Crippled Children and Adults."

ADDITIONAL WORKS: Dunnybrook, 1943; While the Angels Sing, 1947; West of the Hill, 1949; Christmas Without Johnny, 1950; One White Star, 1954.

ABOUT: Publishers' Weekly October 6, 1951.

CARROLL, PAUL VINCENT (July 10, 1900-). For autobiographical sketch and list of earlier works and references, see TWENTIETH CENTURY AUTHORS, 1942.

* * *

Paul Vincent Carroll writes: "In 1943 I assisted the late James Bridie, the famous Scottish playwright, to found the Glasgow

Citizens' Theatre, and became a director of this theatre and productions adviser. The Citizens' is now admitted to be the second finest repertory theatre in Great Britain and is flourishing in Glasgow.

"In 1945 I moved to London to be in closer touch with the British film industry. In 1948 I wrote for Sir Alexander Korda the film entitled *Saints and Sinners*, which was a big success in the United States.

"As I am more interested in the repertory movement than in the metropolitan theatre, I spend a lot of my time visiting many of the little theatres that are scattered all over Britain and are keeping the living theatre strong and healthy. Since the war I have visited Italy and Sweden, two countries in which my various plays receive much serious attention.

"I have just finished my latest play, a satirical extravaganza entitled 'The Devil Came from Dublin.' I hope that this play will bring me back to Broadway where I had my first big successes in the theatre. At the moment I am doing short Irish films for Douglas Fairbanks [Jr.] for exhibition on television screens in the U.S.A. I try to keep the quality of these short films on a high plane, as I believe in the future importance of TV.

"I live quietly in a small garden flat in Bromley, Kent, which is the garden of England."

* * *

Paul Vincent Carroll's satire on the devil's efforts to trap a gentle Irish priest came to Broadway early in 1955 as *The Wayward Saint*. He described it as "a romp, but with deep dramatic overtones." The critics found it a warm and charming play, but it had only a brief run.

ADDITIONAL WORKS: The Old Foolishness, 1944; Three Plays: The White Steed; The Things That Are Caesar's; The Strings, My Lord, Are False, 1944; The Green Cars Go East, 1947; The Wise Have Not Spoken, 1947.

ABOUT: Hoehn, M. (ed.) Catholic Authors, I; Kavanagh, P. The Story of the Abbey Theatre; Theatre Arts May 1945.

CARSON, RACHEL LOUISE (May 27, 1907-), American marine biologist, writes: "The question I am most often asked is when and how I acquired my interest in the sea. Neither heredity nor early environment influenced me in this direction —none of my ancestors had been seafaring people and I grew up inland, without a glimpse of the sea until I had graduated

from college. Among my earliest conscious memories, however, are two things: a feeling of absolute fascination for everything relating to the ocean, and a determination that I would some day be a writer. At the age of ten I began contributing to the prose department of the *St. Nicholas* League, and at twelve or thirteen turned professional by selling to *St. Nicholas* a

Brooks

little piece I had written about that magazine. The pay, I believe, was a cent a word.

"As a child I spent long days out of doors, in fields and woods, happiest with wild birds and creatures as companions. I read a great deal. I attended the public schools of Springdale, Pa., where I was born, and of the neighboring town of Parnassus, and then entered Pennsylvania College for Women. There my childhood interest in natural history found a new and clearer focus in the biological sciences. This interest became so strong that I felt I had to make a choice between science and writing, for in my youthful zeal it never occurred to me that I could combine the two. The 'choice' presumably made, I graduated with a degree in zoology and enrolled as a graduate student in the Zoology Department of Johns Hopkins University, where I received the Master's degree in 1932.

"After a brief period of teaching in the University of Maryland, the old desire to write began to reassert itself. I joined the U.S. Bureau of Fisheries (now the Fish and Wildlife Service) as an aquatic biologist, but in a position involving some writing and editing. About this time I began to write for the *Sunday Magazine* of the Baltimore *Sun*, and in 1937 the *Atlantic Monthly* accepted and published a little essay on the ocean called "Undersea." Out of this grew the idea for my first book, *Under the Sea-Wind*, published in November 1941, on the eve of Pearl Harbor.

"Engrossed in war work, I did little personal writing for several years thereafter, serving as information officer in the Coordinator of Fisheries' Office, returning to Fish and Wildlife after the war, and becoming its chief editor in 1949. Meanwhile, the science of the sea was undergoing revolutionary changes. Because of war conditions governments were pouring funds into oceanographic research, and with new techniques and intensified study we were gaining an entirely new conception of the ocean. I decided to write a book that would summarize what modern man knows of the sea. The result was *The Sea Around Us*, published in July 1951 in the United States, and since then in England, Sweden, France, Norway, Holland, Mexico, Denmark, Japan, Germany, and Italy. Because of interest in this book, *Under the Sea-Wind*, which had been out-of-print, was republished in 1952.

"In the meantime I had received a Guggenheim fellowship for special studies of the sea shore as a basis for a book interpreting the lives of shore creatures for vacationists and general readers. In July 1952 I resigned from the Government to devote my entire time to writing. Besides the shore book, I have definite plans for several others. I write slowly, often in longhand, with frequent revision. Being sensitive to interruption, I write most freely at night.

"As a writer, my interest is divided between the presentation of facts and the interpretation of their underlying significance, with emphasis, I think, toward the latter. Much of my scientific work in marine biology has been done in the laboratories at Woods Hole, Mass., and Beaufort, N.C. It was at Woods Hole, as a student, that I first knew the ocean as a reality, beyond my dreams of it. My favorite 'laboratory,' of course, is the sea and its shores, and I cannot remain long away from them. I am deeply interested in the preservation of the few remaining areas of undeveloped sea shore, where plants and animals are preserved in their original relations, in the delicate balance of nature. In such places we may answer some of the eternal 'whys' of the riddle of life."

* * *

Chapters of *The Sea Around Us* were published first in the *New Yorker* in June of 1951, and the haunting loveliness of Miss Carson's style, as well as the sheer weight of the information she presented, caught the attention of a reading public which had largely ignored her earlier, and equally valuable, *Under the Sea-Wind. The Sea Around Us*, published in book form in July 1951, topped the non-fiction best-seller lists for months and by October of the same year went into its ninth printing. It was the winner of the National Book Award for non-fiction for that year. In February 1953 Miss Carson was elected to the National Institute of Arts and Letters. She was the first science writer elected to the group in thirteen years.

PRINCIPAL WORKS: Under the Sea-Wind, 1941; The Sea Around Us, 1951.

ABOUT: Current Biography 1951; New York Herald Tribune Book Review July 29, 1951, October 7, 1951; New York Times Book Review July 8, 1951; Newsweek July 7, 1951; Saturday Review of Literature July 7, 1951.

CARSWELL, Mrs. CATHERINE (MAC FARLANE) (March 27, 1879-February 18, 1946). For biographical sketch and list of earlier works and references, see TWENTIETH CENTURY AUTHORS, 1942.

* * *

Catherine Carswell died at Camden Town, England, where she had lived alone throughout World War II, at sixty-six.

She left a desk full of notes toward an autobiography, which was edited and published after her death by her son, John Carswell, also a writer. There is little in the book about her own literary life or that of her friends; it consists chiefly of childhood reminiscences and, in the words of the London *Times Literary Supplement,* of "random reflections of varying interest and value, on youth and age, men and women, work and leisure, and so on."

As a biographer she did her best work, writing "a firm, flexible, and excellent prose, never wordy, never ornate." Edgar Johnson has said of her biographical achievement: "She goes in for no narrative tinsel or hypothecated dialogues. Her scholarship is sound and often revealing; her judgments scrupulous. She has intellectual courage and does not hesitate to make a choice among possible interpretations and state it without temporizing."

ADDITIONAL WORKS: Lying Awake (autobiography) 1950.

ABOUT: Carswell, C. Lying Awake.

CARTER, HODDING (February 3, 1907-), American journalist, novelist, and regionalist, was born William Hodding Carter, Jr., in Hammond, La., son of William Hodding and Irma (Dutartre) Carter, whose ancestors were early settlers in the Louisiana territory. A firm believer in the importance of "having roots" in a region, Carter has spent most of his life in the Mississippi Delta country of the South and has written about it "with intimate, instinctive feeling and knowledge." He attended college in the North, however, receiving a B.A.

from Bowdoin in 1927 and a B.Litt. in journalism from Columbia University in the following year. In the academic year 1928-29 he taught freshman English at Tulane University in New Orleans, a brief but illuminating experience in~which he discovered, he writes, "the sad state of secondary-school education."

In 1929 Carter joined the staff of the New Orleans *Item-Tribune* as a reporter. From there he moved to a night bureau managership with the United Press in New Orleans and then to an Associated Press bureau managership in Jackson, Miss. He was dismissed from this post for "insubordination," and finding himself with a newly acquired wife (Betty Brunhilde Werlein whom he married in 1931), drastically limited funds, and a burning urge to be a newspaperman, he returned to Hammond, bought a broken-down press, and started his own paper, the *Daily Courier*. With ingenuity, luck, and the financial and moral support of Carter's parents and his wife, the paper managed to survive the lean years of the depression and the threats of the Huey Long machine, which the *Courier* bitterly opposed.

In 1936, a year after Long's death, Carter sold the paper at a profit and, on the invitation of David Cohn and the late William Alexander Percy, moved to Greenville, Miss., to publish a new paper, the *Delta Star*, in a region that offered an even greater challenge to an editor with liberal and crusading views. Two years later he bought out his competitor and merged the two papers into the *Delta Democrat-Times*. In 1939 Carter received a Nieman fellowship which enabled him to spend a year studying at Harvard University. While at Harvard he met Ralph Ingersoll, who invited him to come to New York on the staff of the newly-established tabloid *PM*. Carter was *PM*'s press editor during its first months in 1940 but he left in the fall of that year, convinced, he writes, that "I wasn't made for big cities or big newspapers or for working for somebody else if I could help it. I probably knew this all along, but it was good to make sure."

For the next five years Carter was in the army, serving first with the National Guard, then in Washington with the Army Bureau of Public Relations (during this stint he was co-author of a book on civilian defense). In 1943 he was sent to Cairo to launch and edit Middle East editions of *Stars and Stripes* and *Yank*. At the time of his discharge in 1945 he was a major in the Intelligence Division. He returned to Greenville and the *Democrat-Times* and began to write the series of editorials on racial, religious, and economic intolerance which won him the 1945 Pulitzer prize for distinguished editorial writing. The chief targets of Carter's editorial scrutiny were the Mississippi congressmen Theodore Bilbo and John Rankin who campaigned on a "white supremacy" platform. The *Democrat-Times*, and a new daily which Carter started publishing in 1946, the *Morning Star*, won national attention for their editorial policy and their unbiased presentation of the news. Carter's own position on southern problems, as stated in his autobiographical *Where Main Street Meets the River*, is that "persuasion is a more effective and democratic weapon than compulsion. . . ." He favors abolition of the poll tax by constitutional amendment and an "advisory" but not "coercive" Fair Employments Practices Commission. He points proudly to the record of steadily improving racial relations in the South and to the sharp decline in the number of lynchings and urges the use of "reason, spiritual appeal and local censure" to abolish these evils altogether.

In both his fiction and his non-fiction, Carter maintains a reputation for what Nash K. Burger has called "intelligent, honest, constructive writing on important southern themes." His novels, the reviewers find, tend to be more polemical than dramatic, but they have been praised for their conviction and objectivity. His regional writings—for the Rivers of America and the American Folkway series—are sound and thoroughly documented; and his discussion of southern attitudes and traditions—in *Southern Legacy* and *Where Main Street Meets the River*, are considered just and representative expressions of liberal southern opinion. Ralph McGill, editor of the Atlantic *Constitution*, said of him: "More than any other person who has written on the 'why' of the South, I believe he has come closest to an answer which can be understood and accepted as true and reasonable by all save the unreasonable."

Carter, his wife, and their three sons make their home in Greenville and spend their summers in Maine. There he has roots almost as deep and tenacious as his southern ones. "Maine is still the closest to Heaven that I've yet come," he writes, "and the place I'd be willing to settle on for a celestial abode."

PRINCIPAL WORKS: Lower Mississippi, 1942; Southern Legacy, 1950; Gulf Coast Country (with A. Ragusin) 1951; Where Main Street Meets the River, 1953. *Fiction*—Winds of Fear, 1944; Flood Crest, 1947.

ABOUT: Carter, H. Where Main Street Meets the River; Current Biography 1946; New Republic September 9, 1946; New York Times Book Review February 28, 1948; Saturday Evening Post June 14, 1947; Saturday Review of Literature February 4, 1950.

CARTER, JOHN FRANKLIN ("Jay Franklin") (April 27, 1897-). For biographical sketch and list of earlier works and references, see TWENTIETH CENTURY AUTHORS, 1942.

* * *

"Jay Franklin" still conducts a syndicated newspaper column from his headquarters in Washington, D.C. During the war years he did special intelligence work for the White House. Since 1950 he has also served as an economic research consultant for New York State. Once a New Dealer, Carter now lists his political affiliation as Republican. His *Republicans on the Potomac* (1953), which gave a series of sketches of the prominent new figures in the Eisenhower government—was not well received. W. S. White wrote in the New York *Times* that it was below his usual standards—"with something of the tired, contrived ecstasy of advertising copy."

ADDITIONAL WORKS: Catoctin Conversation, 1947; Champagne Charlie, 1950; Rat Race, 1950; Republicans on the Potomac, 1953.

ABOUT: Current Biography 1941.

*CARUS, PAUL (July 18, 1852-February 11, 1919). For biographical sketch and list of works and references, see TWENTIETH CENTURY AUTHORS, 1942.

* kä′rōōs

CARY, (ARTHUR) JOYCE (LUNEL) (December 7, 1888-), British novelist, was born in Londonderry, Ireland, of a Devonshire family settled in Ireland since the seventeenth century. He was given for first name, according to a common Anglo-Irish practice, his mother's surname of Joyce. The boy's mother died when he was eight, and although he was educated in England, he spent much time in Ireland, "shuttling from house to house and living in a tumble

of relatives." His first schools were Tunbridge Wells and Clifton College. At sixteen, with an independent income and an even more independent spirit, he went to Edinburgh to study art and later moved on to Paris. He soon realized that he could not express himself in art (although he became a very good painter), and entered Trinity College, Oxford, taking his degree with an apparent minimum of labor in 1912. A college friend, John Middleton Murry, claimed that he "never saw him do a spot of work."

Soon after leaving Oxford, Cary volunteered for duty with a Montenegrin battalion in the Balkan war of 1912-1913. "I didn't think there were going to be any more wars," he explains, "and I didn't want to miss it. And of course I did have some idea about this sort of freedom stuff." He went to the front with a British Red Cross party, and was later decorated by the King of Montenegro. Upon his return to England, Cary studied Irish Cooperation under Sir Horace Plunkett, and in 1913 joined the Nigerian Political Service. He fought in the Nigerian regiment during World War I, and was wounded at Mora Mountain. On returning to political duty as magistrate and executive officer, he was sent to Borgu, a remote and isolated district, where he was the only white administrator in a primitive and rebellious native community.

His war injuries and ill health forced him to retire from African service in 1920. He returned to England, settled in Oxford, and with characteristic determination and enthusiasm set out to become a writer. Cary was much dissatisfied with his early writing. "I couldn't control it. I had immense invention, but I hadn't decided what I meant." What he needed, he decided, was not so much literary technique as a new education in philosophy, history, and politics. His apprenticeship was therefore long and painful. His first book, many times rewritten, did not appear until 1932. It was *Aissa Saved*— the story of a primitive African girl converted to Christianity. The book took a long time to finish, Cary has explained, because it kept on raising questions which he had not properly considered before, and he felt that as a professional writer he ought not to deal

177

in problems to which he had no answer. This first book sold badly; the second did no better. It was not until 1936, when *The African Witch* became a Book Society choice that Cary had any real financial compensation for his work. But success was still slow in coming. *Mister Johnson,* a rich and exuberant study of a native African clerk (which *Time*'s book reviewer considers "the best novel ever written about Africa"), sold only some 5,000 copies when it was first published. American readers were not introduced to Cary's work until after World War II with the publication of his trilogy—*Herself Surprised,* the story of a cook who marries her master and rises in the world; *To Be a Pilgrim,* concerning this woman's employer, an old conservative who hates change and yet knows that it must come; and *The Horse's Mouth,* about an artist who seduces this same woman and abandons her.

With the publication of *Prisoner of Grace,* Cary was recognized on both sides of the Atlantic as one of the most distinguished of contemporary novelists and probably the only living English novelist writing in the great tradition of Dickens and Hardy. His penetrating and absorbing study of Chester Nimmo, the self-made politician who rises to a cabinet office, and his straying and thoroughly human wife, fully demonstrated his remarkable ability to project warm, breathing life into his varied and colorful characters. Whether he writes of the rich or poor, the English, the Irish, or the Africans, V. S. Pritchett remarked, "the assimilation is quick, delectable, sometimes profound. Many novelists have a wide range of characters, but it is often merely a range of conscientious guesses: Mr. Cary goes further and becomes the person." He is no "historian of fine consciences," and his prose is more vigorous than refined. The novelist Elizabeth Janeway has pointed out that there is no one like Cary writing today —"no one who is at once so unsentimental, so rational and so perceptive; no one who can combine, as he does, the toughest-minded realism with mood and insight and character-drawing that is like a lightning flash."

Since the death of his wife (the former Gertrude Ogilvie) in 1949, Cary has lived alone in Oxford. He has four grown sons. In spite of a lifetime of poor health, he is spry and wiry, takes long daily walks, and in every way reflects the heartiness and lively spirits of the characters he has created. According to *Time*: "He writes his books in bits and pieces, may drop one sec-

tion to tackle another, and some times drops the whole thing to work on something else. . . . He has schemes for at least eight more novels."

PRINCIPAL WORKS: Aissa Saved, 1932; The American Visitor, 1933; The African Witch, 1936; Castle Corner, 1938; Mister Johnson, 1939; Charley Is My Darling, 1940; Herself Surprised, 1941; House of Children, 1941; To Be a Pilgrim, 1942; The Horse's Mouth, 1944; A Fearful Joy, 1945; The Moonlight, 1946; A Prisoner of Grace, 1952; Except the Lord, 1953. *Non-Fiction*—Power in Men, 1939; The Case for African Freedom, 1941; The Process of Real Freedom, 1943; Marching Soldier (narrative poem) 1945; Drunken Sailor (ballad epic) 1947.

ABOUT: Current Biography 1949; Holiday March 1950; New York Herald Tribune Book Review January 29, 1950, October 8, 1950; New York Times Book Review February 18, 1951; Time October 20, 1952.

*CASPARY, VERA (1904-   ), American novelist, writes: "I come from a family of bridge-players whose lives, when I was young, seemed of such extraordinary dullness that I decided that I must become a writer, a woman of the world, and independent. My father was a millinery buyer in a Chicago department store, my mother a mother and also an excellent housekeeper.  When I was four or five years old I discovered that stories were in storybooks because people, not necessarily dead, had written them. I vowed to write stories as soon as I learned to write; this is what I have been trying to do ever since.

"It was a struggle, sometimes hopeless, but never without the driving passion. At the end of high school in Chicago I counted the cost and years of college and knew I could not afford it. No Chicago paper would give me a job, so I learned stenography and after eighteen months of answering advertisements, got into an advertising agency where they allowed me to write booklets, pamphlets and advertisements promoting the sale of milking machines, washing tablets, and correspondence courses in finger-printing and voice culture. I organized a mail order school of ballet, wrote a complete course ($5 down and $5 a month) in photoplay writing and ran a weekly magazine for

* "In Europe, where I have been living this year [1952] they call me Cahs-*pahr*-y, which is the original pronunciation of my name. In America we call it Caspary to rhyme with Raspberry.

a public ballroom. When I was twenty-four I went to New York to become editor of the *Dance Magazine* for Bernarr Mac-Fadden.

"In 1929 *The White Girl* was published. This was about a Negro girl in Chicago and a number of newspapers said it was my autobiography. The real story of my family and background is in *Thicker than Water* which is about a middle class Jewish family in the Middle West during the early part of this century. While I was writing this book in 1931 and 1932, after the failure of my first play, I needed some money quickly and wrote what Hollywood calls "an original." Since then I have written a number of stories for pictures, some of which have been good ones and popular, but I never work for more than four months a year for studios, although I live in Beverly Hills and am married to I. G. Goldsmith, a movie producer.

"After I wrote *Laura* and *Bedelia*, I became known as a mystery writer and many people, mostly publishers, wanted me to do nothing else. But since I was more interested in telling stories about people and the forces that make them what they are, I could not keep to crime. In spite of two murders, *Stranger than Truth* is actually the story of the theft of an idea, and in *The Weeping and the Laughter* I make use of the suspense-story technique to investigate the causes of suicide. With *Thelma* I threw out the technical tricks entirely and told a straight story of character. This is the way I like to write and shall go on, although I still enjoy suspense enough to try my hand at it now and then."

PRINCIPAL WORKS: The White Girl, 1929; Ladies and Gents, 1929; Music in the Street, 1930; Thicker than Water, 1932; Laura, 1943; Bedelia, 1945; Stranger than Truth, 1946; The Weeping and the Laughter, 1950; Thelma, 1952.

ABOUT: Collier's September 14, 1946; Current Biography 1947.

CASSERES. See DE CASSERES

*CASSIRER, ERNST (July 28, 1874-April 13, 1945), German-born philosopher and historian, was born in Breslau, the son of a wealthy Jewish tradesman. At the *gymnasium* in Breslau he was at first only an average student, but when he was twelve, under the influence of his grandfather who was a scholarly man and had a fine library, Cassirer acquired a

* kä sē'rēr

passion for learning which shaped the entire course of his life. He graduated from the *gymnasium* with the highest honors and entered the University of Berlin at eighteen to study jurisprudence. He soon switched to studies in German philosophy (with a course in Kant given by Georg Simmel) and literature. He took additional courses at the universities of Leipzig and Heidelberg. In

1896 he went to Marburg to study philosophy under the neo-Kantian Hermann Cohen. Cohen later said that from Cassirer's first brilliant answers to his classroom questions he realized "that this man had nothing to learn from me." But Cassirer remained in Marburg as one of Cohen's disciples, continuing his studies in philosophy, languages, literature, mathematics, and science.

Cassirer's doctoral thesis was on the philosophy of Leibniz. It won an award from the Berlin Academy and he received his doctorate *summa cum laude*. His formal education completed, Cassirer returned to Berlin, married in 1901, and began work on his history of epistemology, the first volume of which was published in 1906 under the title *Das Erkenntnisproblem in der Philosophie und Wissenschaft der Neuen Zeit* ("The Problem of Knowledge in Philosophy and Science in Modern Times"). This study has become a standard work in the history of human thought. The second volume appeared in 1908, the third in 1920, and the fourth and final volume, carrying the history up to 1932, was published posthumously in English in 1950.

Cassirer hesitated for some time before he entered the academic world to teach philosophy. Although he became an eminently successful teacher (a former student, Dimitry Gawronsky, writes; "He was a true *paidagogos* in the Platonic sense, deeply convinced that the teacher is largely to blame for the insufficiencies of his pupils"), he preferred the more secluded life of the scholar. Furthermore, as a Jew in Germany he was sensitive to the anti-Semitic pressures he would meet in many universities. He at last applied for and received an appointment at the University of Berlin where he remained until the outbreak of World War I. During the war he was drafted for civil service, and his work consisted of the reading and analysis of foreign newspapers. After the war

179

he accepted a full professorship at the University of Hamburg, and in 1930 he was elected rector and represented the university at all manner of academic functions. Immediately after Hitler became chancellor of Germany, however, Cassirer resigned from his post and emigrated to England. From 1933 to 1935 he lectured at Oxford, and in September 1935 he accepted an offer from the University of Göteborg in Sweden. When he came to the United States in 1941 to teach at Yale, he planned to stay only two years (he had already become a Swedish citizen). The outbreak of World War II prevented his return to Sweden, and he remained at Yale until 1944 when he was invited to teach at Columbia University. There he died, very suddenly on his way to class, in April 1945, survived by his wife, two sons and a daughter.

Ernest Cassirer has been called "the last true scion of the classic tradition of German idealism." Beginning as a neo-Kantian, studying and analyzing the forms and methods of human knowledge and human thought, Cassirer proceeded to an epistemology which, Hajo Holborn has said, "included the methodology of history and moreover of all forms of creative civilization, finally encompassing even the expressions of pre-scientific human thought and imagination as revealed in language and mythology." His theory of knowledge is thus a "theory of mental activity" (to use Suzanne Langer's phrase), which begins not with logic and the development of "orderly thought about facts," but with myth and with language, the symbolization of thought, what Cassirer called "symbolic forms"—language, myth, art, religion, history, science.

The scope of his work was enormous and his scholarship was painstaking and exhaustive. Gawronsky writes that he had "an incredibly fine mind for the slightest nuances of thought, for the minutest differences or similarities, for all that was fundamental or of secondary importance." He was the first, Gawronsky continues, to introduce the work of scientists like Kepler, Galileo, and Newton into the history of philosophy. Mathematics and physics were as fundamental to his philosophy as were history, religion, and art.

The four years which Cassirer spent in the United States before his death won him as important a place in American philosophy as he had made for himself in Germany in the pre-Hitler years. Since the middle 1940's a number of his books have been published

in English. Cassirer himself wrote some of his later books and articles in English ("clearly, fluently, and with a nice sense of the meanings of the language," Charles W. Hendel commented)—including his *Essay on Man*, which he intended as a kind of revision and abridgement of his major *Philosophie der Symbolischen Formen*, published in Germany 1923-29. His *Myth of the State*, an interpretation of the contemporary world in the light of his philosophy of history, first appeared in abridged form in *Fortune* magazine for June 1944.

With Cassirer's death, Hajo Holborn wrote, "one of the great philosophical interpreters of human civilization has been taken from us." He was a humanist in the richest sense of the term—keeping always in sight the ideals of human dignity and intellectual achievement. His own academic life he described, only a year before his death, as an Odyssey, a pilgrimage "that led me from one university to the other, from one country to the other, and, at the end, from one hemisphere to the other. This Odyssey was rich in experiences—in human and intellectual adventures."

PRINCIPAL WORKS IN ENGLISH TRANSLATION: Substance and Function, and Einstein's Theory of Relativity, 1923; An Essay on Man, 1944; Rousseau, Kant, Goethe, 1945; Language and Myth, 1946; Myth of the State, 1946; The Problem of Knowledge, 1950; The Philosophy of the Enlightenment, 1951; The Platonic Renaissance in Italy, 1953; The Philosophy of Symbolic Forms, I, 1953, II, 1955; Substance and Function, and Einstein's Theory of Relativity, 1953; The Question of Jean-Jacques Rousseau, 1954.

ABOUT: Klibansky, R. & Paton, H. J. (eds.) Philosophy and History; Schilpp, P. A. (ed.) The Philosophy of Ernst Cassirer (Library of Living Philosophers, vol. VI).

CASTLE, EGERTON (March 12, 1858-September 16, 1920). For biographical sketch and list of works and references, see TWENTIETH CENTURY AUTHORS, 1942.

*CATHER, WILLA SIBERT (December 7, 1873-April 24, 1947). For biographical sketch and list of earlier works and references, see TWENTIETH CENTURY, AUTHORS, 1942.

* * * *

Willa Cather died of cerebral hemorrhage, at seventy-three, at her home in New York City. She had never wholly recovered from the effects of an operation performed in

* The date of Miss Cather's birth was definitely established as 1873 by the late E. K. Brown in his biography of her. The name is pronounced căth'ẽr.

1942, and had spent much of the intervening period in virtual retirement at Northeast Harbor, Maine.

The National Institute of Arts and Letters honored Miss Cather in 1944 with the presentation of the society's gold medal. Her last work consisted of three long short stories published as *The Old Beauty* a year after her death. A collection of her critical writings issued the following year was called by H. N. Doughty, "the record of an artistic sensibility that knew perfectly its own direction and believed in it thoroughly."

The quality in Willa Cather's work which prompted Henry Steele Commager to call her "a traditionalist and a conformer" caused Morton Dauwen Zabel, who believes that a few of her novels are American classics, to say that when she died "she had already come to appear as the survivor of some distant generation, remote from the talents and the problems of the past two anxious decades." This anachronistic aspect of her nature and work is described by Maxwell Geismar as "that of an inherent aristocrat in an equalitarian order, of an agrarian writer in an industrial order, of a defender of the spiritual graces in the midst of an increasingly materialistic culture."

In a personal reminiscence of the novelist, Henry Seidel Canby observes that her mind had "the precision of a scholar's, the penetration of a critic's, and the warm intellectuality of a creative artist's." Although the place she made for herself was "a subtle and interesting world of her own," says Alfred Kazin, her influence on American writing was positive. "As an indigenous and finished craftsman, she seemed so native, and in her own way so complete, that she restored confidence to the novel in America."

ADDITIONAL WORKS: The Old Beauty, 1948; On Writing, 1949; Writings from Willa Cather's Campus Years (ed. J. R. Shively) 1950.

ABOUT: Brown, E. K. (& Edel, L.) Willa Cather; Bennett, M. R. World of Willa Cather; Daiches, D. Willa Cather; Geismar, M. D. Last of the Provincials; Gray, J. On Second Thought; Jessup, J. L. Faith of Our Feminists; Kazin, A. On Native Grounds; Lewis, J. Willa Cather Living; Moorhead, E. These Two Were Here; Louise Homer and Willa Cather; Morris, L. R. Postscript to Yesterday; Nation June 14, 1947; New York Times April 25, 1947; Nineteenth Century November 1949; Publishers' Weekly February 5, 1944; Saturday Review of Literature May 10, 1947.

CATTON, (CHARLES) BRUCE

CATTON, (CHARLES) BRUCE (October 9, 1899-), American journalist and historian, was born in Petoskey, Mich., the son of George Robert Catton and Adella Maude (Patten) Catton. His family moved

to nearby Benzonia when his father, a Congregational minister, became principal of Benzonia Academy, a small preparatory school. Benzonia, he recalls with nostalgia, was "about as small a small town as there ever was, and I think about as pleasant a place, in the last of the pre-automobile age, for a child to grow up."

Catton attended Benzonia Academy and entered Oberlin College in 1916. He left college during World War I, spent two years in the Navy as an enlisted man, and then returned to Oberlin, where his extracurricular activities included waiting on table in the village hotel for his board and helping to get out the college paper. But at the end of his junior year he left to become a professional newspaper man, choosing his career "more or less automatically." From 1920 to 1926 he reported for the Cleveland *News,* the Boston *American,* and the Cleveland *Plain Dealer;* from 1926 to 1941 he was with the Newspaper Enterprise Association service—writing editorials and book reviews, running a Sunday section, or acting as a Washington correspondent. His more creative attempts of the 1930's, a couple of novels, he now dismisses as "quite worthless."

In 1942 Catton became a government man, serving as director of information for the War Production Board and holding similar posts after the war with the Department of Commerce and the Department of the Interior. It was his W.P.B. experience which provided background for his 1948 book, *The War Lords of Washington.*

Since 1952 he has devoted all his time to literary work, and although his Washington columns and book reviews have appeared in the *Nation* for several years, his chief occupation has been Civil War history. Gathering material from diaries, letters, and soldiers' reports, he wrote *Mr. Lincoln's Army,* the story of the early years. A New York *Times* review by A. F. Harlow lauded Catton's "rare gift of doing enormous research and then presenting it in what is almost a motion picture in color of march, camp and field, with brief vivid closeups of generals." When Catton continued with the chronicle of the bloody 1862-1863 campaigns in *Glory Road,* Avery Craven, in the Chicago *Sunday Tribune,* called the work "military history . . . at its best. . . . [He] has come remarkably close to catching the feelings and reactions of citizen soldiers. . . . He imparts an air of reality to camp and battle."

A Stillness at Appomattox was the third volume in Catton's trilogy on the Union Army of the Potomac. It won the Pulitzer prize for history in 1954. Earlier in the same year Catton had received the National Book Award for the volume. The N.B.A.'s citation read: "Mr. Catton has combined historical accuracy with poetic insight to present the story of the Army of the Potomac in the final years of the Civil War. Writing from the point of view of the citizens who found themselves soldiers, he has reaffirmed the great American tradition of a peace-loving people who, faced with necessity, can also produce greatness in war."

Catton and his wife, the former Hazel Cherry, live in Bethesda, Md. They have one son. A journalist turned historian, Catton retains something of the spirit of the newspaper reporter. Lewis Nichols writes in the New York *Times Book Review* that he "resembles not in the slightest the storied historian who pursues through a lifetime the substance of a footnote." Catton himself has said: "Writing history is the same thing as being a reporter. You try to get the real facts, not the made-up stories. It has the advantage that you don't get talked back to."

PRINCIPAL WORKS: The War Lords of Washington, 1948; Mr. Lincoln's Army, 1951; Glory Road, 1953; A Stillness at Appomattox, 1953; U.S. Grant and the American Military Tradition, 1954.

ABOUT: Current Biography 1954; New York Times May 5, 1954; New York Times Book Review November 29, 1953.

"CAUDWELL, CHRISTOPHER." See SPRIGG, C. ST. J.

*CAVAFY, CONSTANTINE P. (April 17, 1863-April 29, 1933), Greek poet, was born and spent most of his life in Alexandria, Egypt. The correct form of his name is Kavafis—Cavafy being the genitive case in Greek used on all his books. Except for the publication of a few of his poems by E. M. Forster in *Pharos and Pharillon*, his works were little known by the English-reading public until 1952 when a collection of his poems, translated by John Mavrogordato, appeared.

Cavafy is considered by many the greatest poet of modern Greece, although he made only two brief visits to Greece in his life-

* kä vä' fē

time. But Greek was his mother-tongue; and Greece, its history and its mythology, provided the subject matter of much of his poetry. It must be emphasized, however, that he followed no Greek national tradition. As a man and as a poet he cut himself off from all traditions and connections —European and Eastern alike. "His manner was his own invention," C. M. Bowra

writes, "the reflection of his temper and his circumstances, guided by a natural instinct for words." His poems are peopled with figures from the Hellenistic past—Homeric characters and historical persons. But these are not abstract symbols; rather, as Bowra says, they are "human beings who through something universal in their characters or their situations have the clarity of individual symbols and the reality of living persons." The fall of Troy, in his poem "Trojans," for example, evokes the somber knowledge of our own imminent disaster:

And yet our fall is certain. Up above,
Up on the walls the wailing has begun.
Memories weeping and sensations of the past,
Bitterly for us weep Priam and Hecuba.

Cavafy spent his childhood in Alexandria where his father was in the export-import trade. When the boy was thirteen, his father died and he was taken to England where he lived for three years. He returned to Alexandria briefly, then spent three and a half years in Constantinople, his mother's native city. Except for short trips later to London, Paris, and Athens, he remained in Alexandria until his death from cancer of the throat in 1933. He began to write early but published little in his lifetime and destroyed many of his own poems. His first book, containing fourteen poems, was privately printed when he was forty-one. Five years later he reissued the volume, adding seven poems. He never published another book, but distributed his poems on broadsheets to his friends. Kimon Friar writes in the *New Republic* that he lived most of his adult life in one house in Alexandria, "amid dimly-lit rooms filled with Arabian furniture, ornate petrol lamps and candles. He would honor an especially beautiful guest by lighting another candle, taking care to remain in the shadows himself."

His work falls roughly into two groups—the contemplative and historical poems, and his personal and erotic poems, many of them frankly homosexual. The latter poems, Friar points out, "are integrally important because they are ... the only poems which depict the lusts, guilts, anxieties, and nostalgic satisfactions of an illicit love without sentimentality." Cavafy's use of the "Greek Past"—not the Classical past but the Hellenistic, Greco-Roman, and Byzantine—is perfectly controlled and sustained. These poems, Friar writes, "are neither emotional nor lyrical, but dramatic, narrative, objective, realistic, a recounting of facts and episodes with subtlety and irony in a tone of voice which is dry, precise, deliberately prosaic, and, above all, ironic." In the past, as Bowra shows, Cavafy was free from his immediate cares and could extend himself and enlarge his vision in the richest, most concrete terms. "By his dramatic handling of his material he was able to enter into many strange corners of the human soul, and so firm was his grasp on the essentials of reality that he seems always to deal with something of fundamental importance."

The world of Cavafy's poetry is neither heroic nor epic. It is a world that some might describe as decadent. But, Rex Warner writes in his introduction to Cavafy's poems, "it is a world that existed and exists. It can be examined minutely and dispassionately. And to this examination Cavafy brings a peculiar point of view together with a singular integrity."

PRINCIPAL WORK IN ENGLISH TRANSLATION: The Poems of C. P. Cavafy, 1952.

ABOUT: Bowra, C. M. The Creative Experiment; Dalven, R. Modern Greek Poetry; Forster, E. M. Pharos and Pharillon; Warner, R. *Introduction to* Poems of C. P. Cavafy; Horizon September 1948; New Republic January 26, 1953.

*CAZAMIAN, LOUIS FRANÇOIS (April 2, 1877-   ). For autobiographical sketch and list of earlier works and references, see TWENTIETH CENTURY AUTHORS, 1942.

* * *

Louis Cazamian writes from Paris that he retired from the Sorbonne in 1945. From 1948 to 1949 he was in the United States as visiting professor at Grinnell College in Iowa. In 1950 he was elected a Fellow of the Royal Society of Literature. His recent publications in French are *L'Humour de*

* "The name," Cazamian writes, "is pronounced with no perceptible stress, and the normal values of the sounds in French."

Shakespeare, 1945, *Anthologie de la Poésie Anglaise,* 1946, *Symbolisme et Poésie,* 1947, and a French translation of Wordsworth's *Prelude.* In 1952 Cazamian's *The Development of English Humor,* Parts I and II, was published in the United States. This volume incorporates his history of English humor from earliest times to the Renaissance, which had appeared in 1930, and his *L'Humour de Shakespeare,* and brings the study forward to the Restoration.

ADDITIONAL WORKS IN ENGLISH: The Development of English Humor, Parts I and II, 1952.

CECIL, Lord EDWARD CHRISTIAN DAVID (April 9, 1902-   ). For biographical sketch and list of earlier works and references, see TWENTIETH CENTURY AUTHORS, 1942.

* * *

Lord David Cecil has been Goldsmiths' Professor of English Literature at Oxford since 1948. His university lectures, his radio talks, and his written essays are all distinguished by impeccable scholarship and a felicitous style. He does not pretend to be a literary critic of any of the present-day "schools" of criticism. (A reviewer in *Poetry* points out that he has "no special critical apparatus, no fulfilled scholarly aptitude.") Rather, he takes the broad view of the cultivated "man of letters." He possesses, Professor George F. Whicher has said, "the wide knowledge of the past, the nice judgment of men, and the esthetic appreciation that ideally equip him for the work."

ADDITIONAL WORKS: Hardy, the Novelist: An Essay in Criticism, 1946; Two Quiet Lives: Dorothy Osborne, Thomas Gray, 1948; Poets and Story-Tellers; A Book of Critical Essays, 1949; Melbourne, 1954.

ABOUT: New York Herald Tribune Book Review October 24, 1954.

"CELINE, LOUIS FERDINAND." See DESTOUCHES, L. F.

*CENDRARS, BLAISE ("Frederic Sauser") (September 1, 1887-   ). For biographical sketch and list of earlier works and references, see TWENTIETH CENTURY AUTHORS, 1942.

* * *

Blaise Cendrars writes: "In September 1939, with the outbreak of the World War, I could not make the world tour on board a Finnish three-master as I had hoped to; at

säN drär'

183

CESTRE

the very start I went up to the front as a war correspondent. Accredited to headquarters of the British Expeditionary Corps, where I represented some ten Parisian, French, Algerian, and Moroccan newspapers, I followed the fortune, or rather the misfortune, of the armies up to the fatal armistice of June 1940.

"The day of their entry into Paris, the Germans came to search my house in the Avenue Montaigne (the same as they were to do later in my houses in the country and in Biarritz), but they drew a blank. I was already in the free zone, and I hadn't left a scrap of paper behind me.

"During the four years of the occupation I did not write or publish a line, not because the Germans had put me on the index in designating me on their 'Otto' list as a Jewish writer of French 'expression' (that's the limit!), but because I did not have the heart to work in the face of the calamities of the country and my own unhappiness. My two sons were prisoners, and after his escape, my younger son, a pursuit pilot, was killed in an accident while escorting American planes in Morocco.

"Since the Liberation I have been working overtime and have published about ten works up to now and still have a good ten or so on the fire.

"I did not return to Paris until 1950. Meanwhile I was remarried, to Madame Raymone, the comedian, the greatest comic actress in France. By the way, I am a grandfather."

ADDITIONAL WORKS IN ENGLISH TRANSLATION: Antarctic Fugue, 1948.

ABOUT: Levesque, J. H. Blaise Cendrars; McMillan, D. & G. An Anthology of the Contemporary French Novel; Miller, H. The Books in My Life; Parrot, L. Blaise Cendrars.

CESTRE, CHARLES (May 9, 1871-). For biographical sketch and list of works and references, see TWENTIETH CENTURY AUTHORS, 1942.

* * *

Since the end of World War II, Charles Cestre has published several books on American literature and civilization (Les Américains, 1945; Histoire de la Littérature Américaine, 1946; Les Poètes Américains, 1948) and an English grammar (Grammaire Complète de la Langue Anglaise, 1949). To date, none of these volumes has appeared in English translation. He lives in Paris.

184

CHAMBERLAIN, JOHN RENSSELAER (October 28, 1903-). For biographical sketch and list of earlier works and references, see TWENTIETH CENTURY AUTHORS, 1942.

* * *

John R. Chamberlain was book editor of Harper's Magazine from 1939 to 1947. During part of this period (1942-44) he was also a book columnist for the New York Times. From 1945 to 1950 Chamberlain was an editor of Life, writing editorials and occasional articles on contemporary literature for that journal. He resigned from Life in 1950 to take over the editorship (with Henry Hazlitt) of The Freeman, a far-right-wing political magazine. In 1953 Chamberlain resigned from this post following a split among the editors and directors over questions of editorial policy (Chamberlain favoring the continuation of a "militant" policy "appealing to strong emotion").

ADDITIONAL WORK: Living, Reading and Thinking: Essays in Exposition (ed. with others) 1948; (with C. A. Willoughby) MacArthur, 1941-1951, 1954.

ABOUT: Newsweek October 16, 1950; Time January 26, 1953.

CHAMBERLIN, WILLIAM HENRY (February 17, 1897-). For biographical sketch and list of earlier works and references, see TWENTIETH CENTURY AUTHORS, 1942.

* * *

Since 1940 William Henry Chamberlin has been lecturing and writing on political affairs, with special emphasis on the United States' foreign policy and relations with the Soviet Union. He is bitterly critical of the administration of the late President Franklin D. Roosevelt for the so-called "soft" policy toward Communism. His America's Second Crusade (1950) argues that in World War II (our involvement in which he blames largely on Roosevelt and his advisors) the United States "gained nothing and lost a great deal." Because Chamberlin's book was so highly controversial, reviews ranged from praise of it as a "lucid, profound, and extremely interesting book" (Chicago Tribune) to the charge (in the Saturday Review of Literature) that the author was "ladling out" the same type of propaganda as did Gayda and Goebbels.

Chamberlin has been a contributing editor of New Leader and an editorial contributor to the *Wall Street Journal*. He lives in Cambridge, Mass.

ADDITIONAL WORKS: Canada Today and To-morrow, 1942; The Russian Enigma, 1943; America: Partner in World Rule, 1945; European Conflict, 1947; America's Second Crusade, 1950.

CHAMBERS, CHARLES HADDON (April 22, 1860-March 27, 1921). For biographical sketch and list of works and references, see TWENTIETH CENTURY AUTHORS, 1942.

* * *

ABOUT: Dictionary of Australian Biography.

CHAMBERS, Sir EDMUND KERCH-EVER (March 16, 1866-January 21, 1954). For biographical sketch and list of earlier works and references, see TWENTIETH CENTURY AUTHORS, 1942.

* * *

E. K. Chambers died at eighty-seven, at his home in Devon. His works, according to Hugh I'Anson Fausset, "combined attractively the precision of the scholar with the breadth of sensitiveness of the humanist." In 1945 he contributed to the monumental *Oxford History of English Literature* a volume on English literature at the close of the Middle Ages, especially valuable for a lively chapter on Sir Thomas Malory.

ADDITIONAL WORKS: A Sheaf of Studies, 1942; Shakespearean Gleanings, 1944; English Literature at the Close of the Middle Ages (Oxford History of English Literature, vol. II, pt. 2) 1945; Sources for a Biography of Shakespeare, 1946; Matthew Arnold: A Study, 1947.

ABOUT: London Times January 22, 1954.

CHAMBERS, ROBERT WILLIAM (May 26, 1865-December 16, 1933). For biographical sketch and list of works and references, see TWENTIETH CENTURY AUTHORS, 1942.

*CHAMSON, ANDRÉ (June 6, 1900-). For autobiographical sketch and list of earlier works and references, see TWENTIETH CENTURY AUTHORS, 1942.

* * *

André Chamson writes from Paris: "André Chamson served in the campaign of 1939-40 as liaison officer under General de Lattre de Tassigny, then a young division general. After the defeat of the French Army, he stayed in the Southern zone, in

* shäN sôN'

isolation, and was assigned, by the national museums, to the protection of the master-pieces of the Louvre from German greed.

"During the Occupation he published nothing, except, in the clandestine Editions de Minuit, under the pseudonym of 'Lauter,' an extract from *Puits des Miracles*. He took an active part in the organization of the *Maquis* in Lot. When the First French Army of General de Lattre de Tassigny disembarked in Provence, in August 1944, he found himself at the borders of Lot and Corrèze with the Alsatian Maquis; he rejoined his old chief at Aix-en-Provence. Along with André Malraux—'Colonel Berger' in the Resistance he organized the Alsace-Lorraine brigade which was incorporated into the First Army. With it he took part in the liberating battles of Alsace, defended Strasbourg, and fought in the campaign in Germany. After the armistice, he became curator of the Petit Palais (Musée des Beaux-Arts de la Ville de Paris). In this capacity he organized four very important exhibitions: Masterpieces of French Painting (paintings from the Louvre which had been exhibited provisionally at the Petit Palais since 1946); Treasures of the Vienna Museums (winter 1947-48); Masterpieces from the Pinacothèque in Munich (winter 1948-49); and The Virgin in French Art (1950).

"The last work published by André Chamson before the invasion of France was called *Quatre Mois: Carnet d'un Officier de Liaison*, which appeared shortly before the armistice.

"During the five years of silence which he observed, André Chamson wrote: *Ecrit en 40, Le Puits des Miracles, Le Dernier Village*, and *Les Fragments d'un Liber Veritatis*. None of these books appeared until after the liberation of France.

"In 1948 Chamson published a philosophical tale, *L'Homme Qui Marchait devant Moi*. This man, who is perhaps only our shadow, a double which will not detach itself from us, leads Chamson to reflect that men today have surely lost the eternal part of themselves and that most of them are no more than living dead men. With *La Neige et La Fleur*, published in 1951, Chamson seems to have found the road of hope again. The contemporary generation, he says, is in the process of rediscovering the sense of great vocations.

"In 1952 Chamson had his first play produced in Paris. *On ne Voit pas les Coeurs*, dealing with the problem of fidelity in separation. Several of his novels have been made into films: *L'Auberge de l'Abîme, Tabusse, Le Crime des Justes.*"

ADDITIONAL WORKS IN ENGLISH TRANSLATION: The Times of Calamity, and Poems, *in* New Writing, 1946; A Mountain Boyhood, 1947.

ABOUT: Columbia Dictionary of Modern European Literature; Lehner, F. *Foreword to* Chamson, A. L'Auberge de l'Abîme (Harper, 1949); Mercure de France July 1950; Nouvelle Revue Française March 1936.

CHANDLER, RAYMOND (July 23, 1888-), American detective story writer, writes: "I was conceived in Laramie, Wyo.,

and if they had asked me, I should have preferred to be born there. I always like high altitudes and Chicago is not a place where an Anglophile would choose to be born. My mother was of an Anglo-Irish Quaker family in Waterford, Ireland, one of a family of ten. All the girls but one were beauties and all but one (the same one) made poor marriages to get away from home. My father was also of Quaker stock, Pennsylvania. My mother divorced him when I was young and we went to England where I grew up and went to school. By British law she became a British national again, but I did not. I wanted to be a barrister (and still do, for that matter) but there wasn't enough money and I was no Patrick Hastings who could do it on the cuff. So I drifted into that vague kind of journalism on the fringe which is called free-lancing. At school I displayed no marked literary ability. My first poem was composed at the age of nineteen, on a Sunday, in the bathroom, and was published in *Chambers' Journal*. I am fortunate in not possessing a copy, but I can remember some of it and I think it would go over well if recited by Margaret O'Brien. I had, to be frank, the qualifications to become a pretty good second-rate poet, but that means nothing because I have the type of mind that can become a pretty good second-rate anything, and without much effort. I used to do mostly paragraphs (which I lifted from foreign language papers) for the *Westminster Gazette* and verses and sketches. For the *Academy*, lately edited by Lord Alfred Douglas but not in my time, I did essays and book reviews.

"I entered the United States with some difficulty (I feel sure, although I don't remember anything about it) because I had an English accent you could cut with a baseball bat and yet insisted I was an American. I got a job in St. Louis where the canaille referred to me as Lord Stoopentakit, which didn't bother me in the least but the climate did, and there seemed a great deal of spitting going on, which we didn't do in England. A crusty old boy informed me with an immense fraudulent dignity that 'the American gentleman did not spit.' I said, 'Good, perhaps I'll meet him some day.' This didn't go over good either. I moved to the Pacific coast and went to work. I was offered a job as a bookkeeper. As I knew nothing whatever about bookkeeping, I went to a night school and in six weeks the instructor asked me to leave; he said I had done the three years' course and that was all there was. This incident convinced me that a classical education, unless one had a sharp bent for science or mathematics, was by all odds the most practical there was. I have never wavered in that belief.

"After the war (World War I) in which I served with the Canadian forces and the R.A.F.—it was still natural to me to prefer a British uniform—I had another feeble fling at writing and almost sold the *Atlantic* a Henry James pastiche which was not much more ludicrous than Elizabeth Bowen's current unconscious parody of the Henry James' third manner, but I didn't get anywhere, so I went to work in an English bank in San Francisco and I think I then, for the first time, began to dislike the kind of English who don't live in England, don't want to live in England, but bloody well want to wave their Chinese affectations of manner and accent in front of your nose as if it was some kind of rare incense instead of a distillation of cheap suburban snobbery which is just as ludicrous in England as it is here. Then I went into the oil business and became a corporation executive and soon after the year of wrath came in 1929 I went out of the oil business, or what was left of it.

"Often, I suppose, I've been asked why, with my sort of background, I wrote the kind of lowlife fiction I did. The question comes, I should guess, from a middle-class or slick magazine point of view, the kind of mind that sees life through a full page ad in *Collier's* or the *Post*. You might as well ask me why I don't play golf with the country club set. The answer is I'll be dead long enough and I don't need to practice for it now. A better reason might be that I had no talent for fiction, just had to learn it like anything else, and it seemed easier to learn it in the pulps which went in for this sort of writing. A third, and possibly the best reason of all, is that this elaborate over-tooled civilization of ours just strikes me that way. The story of our time to me is not war nor atomic energy but the marriage of an idealist to a gangster and how their home life and children turned out."

* * *

Raymond Chandler has been called "one of the most aware, articulate, and literarily gifted of American detective novelists." He is a leading exponent of the so-called "tough" school of crime fiction and his hero Philip Marlowe (along with Dashiell Hammett's memorable Sam Spade) is the archetype of the hard-boiled, hard-hitting "private eye." Chandler has a sober, workmanlike approach to his type of fiction. He holds no high-flown ideas about its esthetics, but he recognizes its importance as a literary form, which he names appropriately "The Simple Art of Murder." In an essay with that title, Chandler acknowledges his debt to Dashiell Hammett, and his comments on him are equally appropriate to his own work: "Hammett gave murder back to the kind of people that commit it for reasons, not just to provide a corpse. . . . He put these people down on paper as they are, and he made them talk and think in the language they customarily used for these purposes. He had style, but his audience didn't know it, because it was in a language not supposed to be capable of such refinements." He is keenly aware of the abuses to which such a style is subject: "The realistic style is easy to abuse: from haste, from lack of awareness, from inability to bridge the chasm that lies between what a writer would like to be able to say and what he actually knows how to say. It is easy to fake; brutality is not strength, flipness is not wit, edge-of-the-chair writing can be as boring as flat writing. . . ."

Chandler himself has successfuly avoided these pitfalls. His incidents are lurid; he writes in the idiom of "hard-boiled" American speech; but what distinguishes his work from its imitators is primarily his sense of timing and his recognition of the salient fact that "the crime . . . is not half so important as its effect on the characters. . . . The reactions of the people to the crime are what makes the story."

Chandler's books have been published in England, France, Denmark, Spain, Portugal, and Latin America. They have been dramatized on the radio and made into motion pictures. He also writes for motion pictures, and one of his most successful "scripting" jobs was on James M. Cain's *Double Indemnity*. Chandler lives in California with his wife, the former Pearl Eugenia Hurlburt, whom he married in 1924. He leads a quiet life, dislikes crowds and social games, and for recreation and relaxation favors travel, music, reading, walking, tea, and pipe-smoking.

PRINCIPAL WORKS: The Big Sleep, 1939; Farewell, My Lovely, 1940; The High Window, 1942; The Lady in the Lake, 1943; Five Murderers, 1944; Five Sinister Characters, 1945; Red Wind, 1946; The Little Sister, 1949; The Simple Art of Murder, 1950; The Long Goodbye, 1954.

ABOUT: Current Biography 1946; Atlantic March 1945; Newsweek May 14, 1945; Town and Country October 1945.

CHANNING, EDWARD (June 15, 1856-January 7, 1931). For biographical sketch and list of works and references, see TWENTIETH CENTURY AUTHORS, 1942.

* * *

ABOUT: Saveth, E. N. American Historians and European Immigrants, 1875-1925.

CHAPMAN, FRANK MICHLER (June 12, 1864-November 15, 1945). For biographical sketch and list of works and references, see TWENTIETH CENTURY AUTHORS, 1942.

* * *

Frank Michler Chapman died at eighty-one, at New York's St. Luke's Hospital, after a long illness. He was survived by his son, Frank M. Chapman, Jr., a concert and opera singer and the husband of Gladys Swarthout.

In 1935 Chapman, who had been the founder of the publication *Bird Lore*, and its publisher and editor for thirty-six years, presented the magazine to the Audubon Society. He retired as Curator of the Department of Ornithology of the American Museum of Natural History in New York on July 1, 1942, and was appointed Curator Emeritus of Birds.

Author of sixteen books and numerous articles on ornithology, and the originator of the habitat idea of museum exhibition, he has been called "the most influential man since Audubon in getting people interested in birds." In 1950 the Chapman Memorial Fund for ornithological research was established in his memory.

ABOUT: Von Hagen, V. W. Green World of the Naturalists; National Academy of Sciences Biographical Memoirs (vol. 25); Audubon Magazine January 1949, January 1950; New York Times November 17, 1945.

CHAPMAN, JOHN JAY (March 2, 1862-November 4, 1933). For biographical sketch and list of works and references, see TWENTIETH CENTURY AUTHORS, 1942.

* * *

ABOUT: Atlantic Monthly February 1947.

CHAPMAN, JOHN STANTON HIGHAM. See Chapman, M.

CHAPMAN, MARISTAN (John Stanton Higham Chapman, May 21, 1891- , and Mary Hamilton Ilsley Chapman, September 10, 1895-). For biographical sketch and list of earlier works and references, see TWENTIETH CENTURY AUTHORS, 1942.

* * *

In 1948 the Chapmans announced their plans to publish six historical novels covering the Tennessee region from 1540 to 1918. To date, two novels in the series have appeared —*Rogue's March*, dealing with the period of the American Revolution, and *Tennessee Hazard*, covering the early days of the Republic. Both novels have been praised as "rousing, good old-fashioned" romances. In the juvenile field, writing as "Maristan Chapman" and as "Jane Selkirk," they continue to produce pleasant and lively mystery-adventure stories.

ADDITIONAL WORKS: *As Maristan Chapman*—Mystery on the Mississippi, 1942; Trail Beyond the Rockies, 1943; Secret of Wild Cat Cave, 1944; Treasure Hunters, 1945; Rogue's March, 1949; Tennessee Hazard, 1953. *As Jane Selkirk*—Mystery of the Hectic Holidays, 1944; Blue Smoke Mystery, 1946; Mystery of Horseshoe Caves, 1948; Treasure Box Mystery, 1951.

ABOUT: Warfel, H. R. American Novelists of Today.

CHARDONNE, JACQUES (1884-). For biographical sketch and list of works and references, see TWENTIETH CENTURY AUTHORS, 1942.

* * *

Jacques Chardonne has written several books of fiction and personal reminiscences in the past decade. In the post-war period

he was out of favor as one of the few outstanding writers accused of collaborating with the Germans during the Occupation. None of his recent works has appeared in English translation. An edition of his complete works was published in Paris in 1951.

ABOUT: Columbia Dictionary of Modern European Literature.

CHARNWOOD, GODFREY RATHBONE BENSON, 1st Baron (November 6, 1864-February 3, 1945). For biographical sketch and list of works and references, see TWENTIETH CENTURY AUTHORS, 1942.

* * *

Lord Charnwood died at Cadogan Court in London at eighty. His wife had predeceased him by three years. One daughter, Theodora Benson, is a novelist and writer of books of travel.

The popularity of Lord Charnwood's biography of Abraham Lincoln led to an invitation to visit this country to attend the unveiling of a statute of Lincoln at Springfield in 1918. At the end of World War II he gave a series of lectures in the United States on behalf of the British government.

"Few modern biographies have shown stronger qualities of sympathy and understanding," the London *Times* has said of *Abraham Lincoln*, and of its author: "Under a manner superficially reticent, and even a little austere, he kept a simple, candid disposition, and a singularly kind heart."

ABOUT: London Times February 5, 1945; New York Times February 6, 1945.

*CHARTERIS, LESLIE (May 12, 1907-). For autobiographical sketch and list of earlier works and references, see TWENTIETH CENTURY AUTHORS, 1942.

* * *

Leslie Charteris writes from Beverly Hills, Calif.: "First, in your 1942 edition, you perpetuated a rather common error which probably originated with a misprint somewhere. My original name was Leslie Charles Bowyer Yin, not 'Lin.' The Yins are a much more distinguished family, having been emperors of China from about 1760 to 1120 B.C. (otherwise known as the Shang dynasty): my father happens to be their direct lineal descendant. I legally took the name of

---

* "The name *Charteris* seems to need a note on pronunciation, judging by the labored versions with which I am often addressed—usually *Shartris* or *Char-terrace*. It should be pronounced quite simply like the word *charter* (ch as in *church*) plus a sibilant *is*, thus: *tchar' ter-iss.*"

Leslie Charteris in England in 1928. I re-affirmed this change of name when I was naturalized a U.S. citizen in July 1946. (Note that your original biography starts off by calling me 'English.' The nearest to the truth you can get now would be to call me 'British born.') I have, of course, as a good American, renounced all claim to the throne of China.

"You will notice that my output indicates a considerable spell of most enjoyable lazi-ness—not due, however, to the vegetative existence which I indicated at the end of my last autobiographical notes. That didn't last too long.

"In 1943 I was divorced again, and about that time I firmly discarded the monocle, which I decided was a pretty outworn prop, and stopped brushing my hair and dressing to please tailors. I took a brief flurry in a publishing venture, in which I lost my shirt. This left me a complete sartorial zero. I married again—Betty Bryant Borst, a singer.

"I realized from my unhappy experience that being a solid business man was not for me, and that it was much more fun to be a high-class bum. As soon as the war would let me, I started crashing around the world again, sailing about the West Indies, and going back to Europe. My trailer became obsolete and was replaced by a boat. I decided that commercial airlines were more comfortable than flying myself, and turned to skin-diving and spear-fishing for my favorite sport.

"I didn't write much about the Saint, but amused myself with articles on travel and cooking. I produced a series of radio shows on the Saint, and also launched him in a comic strip, which is still running. [*The Saint Detective Magazine* was launched in 1953.]

"This year [1952] my third divorce be-came final, and I remarried for the fourth time—Audrey Long, a movie actress who decided that she'd prefer to play with me. We are just setting off for at least a year's wandering around the world, during which I seriously intend to write some more and also plan to produce a series of Saint pic-tures for television; but mostly we shall have all kinds of fun and slaughter fish.

"Basically, I guess, I haven't changed much."

ADDITIONAL WORKS: The Saint at Large, 1943; The Saint Steps In, 1943; The Saint on Guard, 1944; The Saint Sees It Through, 1946; Call for the Saint, 1948; Saint Errant, 1948; The Second Saint Omnibus, 1951; The Saint in Europe, 1953; The Saint on the Spanish Main, 1955.

ABOUT: Editor and Publisher October 2, 1948.

CHASE, MARY (COYLE) (February 25, 1907-), American playwright, was born in Denver, Colo., the daughter of Frank Bernard and Mary (McDonough) Coyle. Her parents were from Ireland, having come in their early youth to the Ameri-can West. From them Mary inherited a taste for Celtic poo-kas and banshees, and probably a liter-ary frame of mind.
By the age of eight she had read *A Tale of Two Cities;* and three years later she saw her first Denver matinee. In 1922 she was graduated from the West Denver High School, after which she went to the Univer-sity of Denver where she stayed for two and a half years. At Boulder, she attended the University of Colorado but at the end of the year accepted a job as reporter for the *Rocky Mountain News.* On June 7, 1928, she married Robert Lamont Chase, also a reporter, who later became managing editor of the *News.*

Quitting her job after marriage, Mary Chase went into several occupations, at one time fighting for the rights of Spanish-Americans in Denver, and at another run-ning a "quiet effective lobby" for an oleo-margarine concern. She wrote a weekly radio program for the Teamsters' Union, meanwhile working on her own short stories and plays. Also active as a free-lance cor-respondent, Mrs. Chase was employed by the International News Service and United Press (1932-36).

Her first play, *Me Three* (1937), was produced in the Federal Theater. Having attracted the interest of Brock Pemberton, this political satire was brought to New York with the new title, *Now I've Done It.* The play was a failure but Pemberton en-couraged its author to continue her writing. *The Banshee* and others, fantasies, comedies and tragedies, were completed but experi-enced little theatrical success. During this time (1941-44) Mrs. Chase was publicity director for the National Youth Administra-tion in Denver, along with being a housewife and raising three children.

Looking for an "escapist plot" during World War II, she came upon the idea of her Pulitzer prize-winning comedy, *Harvey.* The title was the name of a six-foot invisi-ble rabbit which represented a spirit similar to that of Gaelic faery folk. The hero of the play, an imaginative alcoholic, may have been prompted by the early advice of Mrs. Chase's mother to her children: "Never be unkind or indifferent to a person others say is crazy. Often they have deep wisdom." With Brock Pemberton producing, Antoinette Perry directing, and Frank Fay cast in the leading role, the première was a tremendous Broadway success. There were, however, divided reactions among critics. While Pemberton spoke of Mary Chase's being "an adroit playwright who knew her material upside down and inside out," Louis Kronenberger contended that the play's "fresh and imaginative side" was marred by much routine farce writing." Nevertheless, it made box-office records and was later published by the Oxford University Press, since then having been translated into almost every foreign language including Japanese.

Her next two plays, *Mrs. McThing* and *Bernadine*, both enjoyed highly successful New York runs. But Mrs. Chase has said that she does not write her comedy for money, and only desires to make unhappy people laugh. With her husband and children she lives in Denver, maintaining a full domestic and social life. She is a member of the Dramatists' Guild; and among other honors she was recipient (1944) of the William MacLeod Raine award from the Colorado Authors League. In 1947 she was given a Litt.D. by the University of Denver.

Mary Chase has been described as a beautiful woman with wide gray eyes and a white imperious face. It is said that she seldom smiles and there is often melancholy in her expression. But "nicely contrasted with her Madonna appearance, she has a sharp flip tongue" and a whimsical imagination.

PRINCIPAL WORKS: Harvey, 1950; Mrs. McThing, 1952; Bernadine, 1953.

ABOUT: Current Biography 1945; Ladies' Home Journal February 1951; Saturday Evening Post September 1, 1945.

CHASE, MARY ELLEN (February 24, 1887-). For biographical sketch and list of earlier works and references, see TWENTIETH CENTURY AUTHORS, 1942.

* * *

After nearly thirty years of teaching at Smith College, Mary Ellen Chase retired in June 1955. Her recent writings reflect her characteristically wide range of interests— fiction, biography, scholarship. The subject matter is varied, but all her books have in common felicity of style and what C. M.

Brown has described as an "almost unbearable awareness of the human heart." One of the most successful of her recent books is her simple but sound and scholarly interpretation of the Scriptures as literature and as history—*The Bible and the Common Reader,* which the late Sigrid Undset called "her fine labor of love."

ADDITIONAL WORKS: The Bible and the Common Reader, 1944; Jonathan Fisher, Maine Parson, 1768-1847, 1948; The Plum Tree (novel) 1949; Abby Aldrich Rockefeller, 1950; Recipe for a Magic Childhood, 1951; Readings from the Bible (ed.) 1952; The White Gate, 1954.

ABOUT: Chase, M. E. Recipe for a Magic Childhood, The White Gate; Current Biography 1940; Taves, I. Successful Women; Warfel, H. R. American Novelists of Today; New York Herald Tribune Book Review October 24, 1954.

CHASE, RICHARD VOLNEY (October 12, 1914-), American critic, scholar and biographer, writes: "I was born in Lakeport, N.H. My family has lived in New Hampshire and Massachusetts since the 1630's, and I am, in fact, the first in my direct line to marry or live outside of New England. My wife, who writes on child psychology, was born Frances Walker, in Youngstown, Ohio.  I was educated at Dartmouth College and Columbia, taking my Ph.D. at this latter institution in 1946. After teaching English for three years at Connecticut College, I joined the faculty of Columbia College in 1949, where I am an associate professor of English.

"The fact that I have taken up an academic career but that my writing extends beyond strictly academic limits I attribute to the temper of the times. The times have been very favorable, during the last fifteen years, to that combination of an academic career with non-academic writing which has distinguished the work of nearly all contemporary American literary critics and many contemporary poets and novelists as well. I got my start as a critic and reviewer in 1943 by writing for the *Partisan Review,* and since then I have been contributing not only to this magazine but also to the *Kenyon Review, Sewanee Review, Nation, Commentary,* and so on.

"My book called *Herman Melville: A Critical Study* showed rather strongly the intellectual imprint of the 1940's, being concerned with literary and moral values as seen in Melville's use of myth and symbols. The study of mythology as a literary phenomenon had been the subject of my doctor's dissertation, *Quest for Myth*. My book on Emily Dickinson was published as one of the volumes in the American Men of Letters Series. This book was rather more eclectic and conventional than the *Melville*, and was received with more equanimity by the reviewers.

"Although I have been associated in various ways with the so-called New Critics (partly as a Fellow of the Kenyon School of English and of the School of Letters at the University of Indiana) and have learned a good deal from them, I do not consider myself to be of their number. By temperament I lean rather to the historical, moral, or naturalistic approach of such contemporary critics as Lionel Trilling and Edmund Wilson. In politics I am a liberal conservative or a conservative liberal—a statement which may make more sense if I add that Edmund Burke is my idea of the political thinker *par excellence*.

"I am currently at work on a study of Walt Whitman, also for the American Men of Letters Series, which, I believe, will be the last of my books on American authors and my final contribution to that critical movement within the study of American literature which is gradually replacing the academic 'history of ideas' approach with a method which may variously be called 'cultural,' 'historical,' or 'naturalistic.' "

PRINCIPAL WORKS: Quest for Myth, 1949; Herman Melville: A Critical Study, 1949; (ed.) Selected Tales and Poems of Melville, 1950; Emily Dickinson, 1951; Walt Whitman Reconsidered, 1955.

CHASE, STUART (March 8, 1888-).
For autobiographical sketch and list of earlier works and references, see TWENTIETH CENTURY AUTHORS, 1942.

* * *

Stuart Chase writes from Georgetown, Conn.: "My interests, changing with time and history, veer farther than ever away from ideologies. These always seemed less important to me than practical measures to abolish poverty. Economics now seems less important than the broader field of social science, where I have undertaken an assignment as a sort of integrator—a non-specialist who tries to fit the specialties together and interpret their achievements. My latest two books are in this field—*The Proper Study of Mankind*, a survey of the broad area of social science, and *Roads to Agreement,* an inventory of techniques, in labor-management and elsewhere, for resolving conflict. I am now at work on a third, which began as a revision of *The Tyranny of Words,* but is rapidly assuming the proportions of a whole new opus [published in 1954 as *The Power of Words*]."

ADDITIONAL WORKS: Men at Work (with M. Tyler) 1945; The Proper Study of Mankind, 1948; Roads to Agreement (with M. Tyler) 1951; The Power of Words, 1954. *"Twentieth Century Fund Series"*—Goals for America, 1942; Where's The Money Coming From? 1943; Democracy Under Pressure, 1945; Tomorrow's Trade, 1945; For This We Fought, 1946.

ABOUT: Parks, G. Camera Portraits; Current Biography 1940; Saturday Review March 6, 1954.

CHENEY, SHELDON (June 29, 1886-).
For autobiographical sketch and list of earlier works and references, see TWENTIETH CENTURY AUTHORS, 1942.

* * *

Sheldon Cheney writes: "Between 1942 and 1952 Sheldon Cheney published only one major new book, *Men Who Have Walked With God* (1945). A history of mysticism through the ages, told through biographical sketches of outstanding seers and saints, this met with a divided critical reception, with adjectives ranging all the way from 'superb' to 'foggy.' The public response was generous, however, and the volume was reprinted four times within three months of publication. It elicited, the author reports, more letters from grateful readers than had all his earlier books together.

"For the rest, the author gave this decade to three activities: to lecturing, first under contract with W. Colston Leigh, then independently at colleges, universities and museums over the country; to revision of earlier books, and to extended work on a monumental history of sculpture, as yet unpublished.

"Revisions have included *A Primer of Modern Art* (in its seventeenth printing and still widely circulating twenty-eight years after publication), *Expressionism in Art,* and *The Theatre: 3000 Years of Drama, Acting and Stagecraft.* The last-named reappeared in 1952 with a carefully revised text, additional chapters, new bibliographies and many added illustrations. (Cheney has pointed out that nothing could be more indicative of the surprises, uncertainties and vagaries of the publishing game than the history of this book. Published first in 1929 at $10, a second edition soon followed at $5.

Too successful ever to be remaindered, the book yet was sold during the Great Depression into the hard-back reprints and was merchandised in drugstores, stationery shops and the like at $1.69, then $1.89 and finally $1.98. During the 'forties it steadied down at $3.50; and in 1952 the enlarged edition appeared at $8.)

"Now looking back over his writing career to date, Sheldon Cheney, with six major 'surveys' in the field of the arts to his credit, regards *A World History of Art* (1937) as his most widely useful contribution to the field of education.

"Recently he has been working upon projects for translations of the *World History* and of *A Primer of Modern Art*—always a special problem where hundreds of illustrations are involved. A translation of *Men Who Have Walked With God* appeared in German in 1949 under the title *Vom Mystischen Leben*. As to illustrations, as if a few hundred did not pose problems enough, he has assembled a set of one thousand photographs for 'The Art of Sculpture.' Present address, New Hope, Pa."

ADDITIONAL WORK: Men Who Have Walked With God, 1945.

CHESNUTT, CHARLES WADDELL (June 20, 1858-November 15, 1932). For biographical sketch and list of works and references, see TWENTIETH CENTURY AUTHORS, 1942.

* * *

ABOUT: Chesnutt, H. M. Charles Waddell Chesnutt: Pioneer of the Color Line; Gloster, H. M. Negro Voices in American Fiction; Phylon, vol. 14 (1953).

CHESTER, GEORGE RANDOLPH (1869-February 26, 1924). For biographical sketch and list of works and references, see TWENTIETH CENTURY AUTHORS, 1942.

CHESTERTON, GILBERT KEITH (May 29, 1874-June 14, 1936). For biographical sketch and list of works and references, see TWENTIETH CENTURY AUTHORS, 1942.

* * *

ABOUT: Dictionary of National Biography 1931-1940; Hoehn, M. (ed.) Catholic Authors, I; Kenner, H. Paradox in Chesterton; Ward, M. Gilbert Keith Chesterton, Return to Chesterton; Commonweal March 21, 1947, October 27, 1950; Fortnightly October 1950; London Quarterly Review October 1943; Time March 10, 1952; Virginia Quarterly Review April 1947.

*CHEVIGNY, HECTOR (June 28, 1904-   ), American novelist, radio and television dramatist, writes: "Our name is actually Chevigny de La Chevrotière and the family seems to have had a great tendency to wander from its bases in French Canada. Great-grandfather Pierre Menard is one name cropping up in the annals of exploration and the fur-trade; he was the

Pete Martin

Missouri Company's factor at St. Louis around 1815. My parents, born in French Canada, settled in western Montana in its rawer territorial days, my one sister and I being born late in their lives. Father was a carpenter and contractor. Missoula was our home town but we also lived in Butte and much of my childhood I passed near Frenchtown, in a rugged mountain valley homesteaded by relatives in the 1870's. That now I write television plays, having known in my own life a period when even rural electrification seemed a wild dream, appears to me less cause for wonder, however, than the fact it seems to give no cause for wonder at all. I am constrained to wonder how I became a writer only because others have done so. Perhaps the family propensity for wandering had something to do with it. Wandering can take place over the cultural map too. More probably it was the influence of the Carnegie library system, the effect of which on communities like Missoula social historians overlook. I was often ill, was forever immersed in a sea of print. They call what I had nowadays allergic. My people called it *le riffe* and some tried dog-grease on it. My conscious wish was to study medicine and I still think a good pediatrician was lost in me. Working as a butcher's helper, lumbercamp cook's assistant, hotel clerk and, for three years, as a hospital orderly, I put myself through Gonzaga University (1927) and a year's graduate work in languages at the University of Washington. But in 1928 I found myself at a typewriter as a scriptwriter in a Seattle radio station. Now it is twenty-four years, five books, one motion picture and several short stories later. I suppose I am a pioneer in the medium. Certainly when I came to work on it the broadcast play was wholly derived from the stage and nobody trusted it really to tell an orig-

* shĕv'nē

inal story entirely in dialogue. I worked in Hollywood from 1935 to 1943, quitting staff-writing in 1937 after serving as script-chief for CBS at KNX, to become a free-lance fiction writer.

"Shortly after arriving in New York in 1943 I lost sight, suddenly, through bilateral detachment of the retinas. I was, and still am, annoyed to find that gave me more notoriety than my work. I live in a rambling old apartment on Manhattan's Gramercy Park with a wife, two almost-grown children and a Seeing Eye dog. Television dismays me mostly because it represents another technological change I must face and another pioneer period to be undergone."

* * *

Hector Chevigny's broadcast plays are in a number of anthologies, notably *Best TV Plays of 1951-52*. His two first books are among the few serious works in English on the history of the early Russians in Alaska and California. One is a literary prizewinner. The impact of his experiences after loss of sight on his social concepts he told in *My Eyes Have a Cold Nose*. He has for ten years been a councilman of the Authors' League; he is a founder of the Radio Writers' Guild. Since his loss of sight he has engaged in research into the influence of handicap on personality, work recognized by several professional societies and publications. Although a layman, he is a member of the psychology section of the New York Academy of Sciences. With clinical psychologist Sydell Braverman he is co-inventor (under grant from the American Foundation for the Blind) of the Braverman-Chevigny Auditory Projective Test, a method for evaluating emotional factors without visual cues.

PRINCIPAL WORKS: *Non-Fiction*—Lost Empire, 1937; Lord of Alaska, 1942; My Eyes Have a Cold Nose, 1946; The Adjustment of the Blind (with S. Braverman) 1950; *Novel*—Woman of the Rock, 1949.

ABOUT: Chevigny, H. My Eyes Have a Cold Nose; Hoehn, M. (ed.) Catholic Authors, I; American Magazine October 1945; Collier's October 6, 1945; Time October 12, 1942, June 30, 1947; Variety October 25, 1945, April 1, 1949.

CHIANG, YEE (May 19, 1903-), Chinese artist and travel writer, was born in Kiukiang, China, one of a large family, son of Chiang Ho-an, an artist who specialized in flower and bird paintings, and Tsai Hsiang-Lin. His mother died when he was five, and he was raised by his grandmother, "who ruled the household by strict Confucian principles." He was educated at the Kiukiang provincial school and at the National South-Eastern University in Nanking, from which he was graduated, in 1925, with a B.Sc. degree. After a year of military service and a brief stint as a journalist, Chiang Yee taught school for two terms and for one year lectured in chemistry at the National Chi-Nan University.

Chiang Yee became a "silent traveller" (his Chinese pen-name, *Yahsin-che* means "dumb walking man") after holding down what he describes as the "tiresome talking job" of governor and director of four districts, Yushan, Wuhu, Tangtu, and Kiukiang, for five years. In 1933 he went to England. He now lives in Oxford when not traveling—silent but busy with pen-and-ink, paint brush, eyes, and ears. "I live very simply, with a roomful of books and the necessary desk and bed; a quiet surrounding is essential while writing, though I can paint amidst noise." At home he relaxes, going to the cinema and the theatre, reading his favorite authors (including Wordsworth, Keats, Shelley, Stevenson, Yeats, Longfellow, Whitman, and Thoreau), arranging flowers and occasionally preparing a Chinese meal. He is married and has two sons and two daughters.

In 1935 Chiang Yee became lecturer in Chinese at the School of Oriental Studies of London University. In 1938 he was placed in charge of the Chinese section of the Wellcome Historical Medical Museum. Meanwhile he had held a number of successful one-man shows of his paintings and drawings in London, and his works were exhibited on the continent. In 1942 he designed the decor and costumes for the Sadler's Wells ballet "The Birds."

Chiang Yee began writing in his college days in 1924 when he edited a periodical, *New Kiukiang*, for his native city and contributed articles to various Chinese magazines. A volume of his poems was published in Shanghai in 1934. His first book published in England was *The Chinese Eye*, a study of the history, philosophy, and principles of Chinese painting. In 1937 the first of his "Silent Traveller" books appeared— this an account of a tour of the Lake Country of England, charmingly illustrated with the author's pen-and-ink sketches. With this and succeeding volumes, which have taken him to London, Dublin, Edinburgh, and New York, readers found Chiang Yee a "gentle, understanding, and diverting visitor." He illustrates his books with precise and charming black-and-white drawings and delicate oriental water colors. His observations are casual, but they are also shrewd. Roger Pippet wrote of his *Silent Traveller in Edinburgh*: "This book is a boon to a driven world, for it is pictorial art at its happiest, work done in tranquility by a man for whom 'wisdom is a butterfly and not a gloomy bird of prey.'"

PRINCIPAL WORKS: The Chinese Eye, 1935; The Silent Traveller in Lakeland, 1937; Chinese Calligraphy, 1938; The Silent Traveller in London, 1938; Birds and Beasts, 1939; Chin-Pao and the Giant Panda, 1939; The Silent Traveller in Wartime, 1939; A Chinese Childhood, 1940; The Silent Traveller in the Yorkshire Dales, 1941; Chin-Pao at the Zoo, 1941; Men of the Burma Road, 1942; The Silent Traveller in Oxford, 1944; The Silent Traveller in New York, 1950; The Silent Traveller in Edinburgh, 1951; The Silent Traveller in Dublin, 1953.

ABOUT: Chiang, Y. A Chinese Childhood; Mahony, B. (ed.) Illustrators of Children's Books; New York Herald Tribune Book Review October 7, 1951; Newsweek December 25, 1950.

CHIDESTER, ANN (1919-), American novelist, writes: "I was born in Stillwater, Minn., where my grandparents were early

Lotte Jacobi

settlers. This is a New England town, almost the oldest in the state, settled by lumber men, the Irish and Scandinavians, on a winding river, the St. Croix, where the logs could be shipped. My mother's people are of Irish descent; my father's came from Wales and fought in the American Revolution. I am the eldest of three daughters and was educated in Stillwater and later at St. Catherine's College in St. Paul. I began writing very young, and I was a serious writer in my late teens, more interested at that time in the novel than in the short story. Very fortunately, I met Maxwell Perkins of Scribner's who published my first books, and more recently I have been lucky in having as a friend and agent Elizabeth Otis of McIntosh and Otis. I have published short stories in almost all the well known magazines, and at the moment [1952] I am living and writing in Mexico."

* * *

Mary Ross commented in 1947 that Ann Chidester's writing "has originality, sensitiveness, and punch." Although her books have been, from time to time, uneven and occasionally over-wrought, she has shown promise of a developing and maturing talent. Hers is "a genuine literary talent," M. S. Ulrich said in the *Saturday Review of Literature* in 1943. "She writes always with zest and often with unusual sensitiveness and beauty; she has a sincere feeling for her characters . . . , and she has the born storyteller's sense of drama."

PRINCIPAL WORKS: Young Pandora, 1942; No Longer Fugitive, 1943: The Long Year, 1946; Mama Maria's, 1947; Moon Gap, 1950.

ABOUT: Warfel, H. R. American Novelists of Today.

CHIDSEY, DONALD BARR (May 14, 1902-), American biographer and novelist, writes: "Born, Elizabeth, N.J. High school graduate, no college. Newsboy, soda jerker, golf caddy, bellhop, etc., etc. Newspaper reporter or rewrite man in Elizabeth; New York City; Newark, N.J.; Union City, N.J.; Denver; Jacksonville, Fla.; New Orleans; Honolulu; Paris, etc.,  for ten years more or less. Always a wanderer. Have knocked around Europe, Near East, Far East, South America, West Indies, etc., but especially in the south Pacific, and most especially in eastern Polynesia—the Societies, Gambiers, Cooks, Australs, Tuamotus. Ran a copra plantation for five years at Punaauia, Tahiti. Once ran a tea room in Bermuda, a bridge club in Greenwich Village, a poker game-speakeasy in Honolulu. Drove an ambulance for American Field Service in World War II, with British Eighth Army in Libya, Syria, Tunisia. After the war married and settled down in Lyme, Conn. Proud possessor of a private pilot's license. Pillar of local P.T.A., C.A.P., volunteer fire company, Cub Scout organization, etc. Democrat. Crazy about modern music. Sports used to be chiefly boxing, fencing, mountain climbing; now, with waistline, chiefly sailing and stunt flying. Sometimes lecture. Stories or travel articles published in *Saturday Evening Post, Esquire, Adventure, Cosmopolitan, Redbook, Collier's* and many, many other magazines."

* * *

Donald Barr Chidsey's biographies are written in a rapid, popular style—at times flippant but more often full of gusto and the color and spirit of the period involved. Donald Douglas wrote that "in every line one recognizes the man who understands men and women as they exist in their own nature." Chidsey's novels have not been distinguished for depth and penetration, but he can write what Victor Hass calls "a tale of thumping adventure," an expert blend of romance, action, and suspense.

PRINCIPAL WORKS: *Biographies*—Bonnie Prince Charlie, 1928; Marlborough: the Portrait of a Conqueror, 1929; Sir Walter Raleigh, 1931; Sir Humphrey Gilbert, 1923; The Gentleman from New York: a Life of Roscoe Conkling, 1935; John the Great: the Times and Life of John L. Sullivan, 1942. *Novels*—Pistols in the Morning, 1930; Weeping Is for Women, 1936; Each One Was Alone, 1938; Panama Passage, 1946; Stronghold, 1948; Captain Adam, 1953; Lord of the Isles, 1954; Captain Bashful, 1955. *Juvenile*—Rod Rides High, 1950.

ABOUT: Warfel, H. R. American Novelists of Today.

CHILDE, VERE GORDON (April 14, 1892-), British anthropologist and archeologist, was born in Sydney, New South Wales, Australia, son of the Reverend S. H. Childe, Rector of St. Thomas' Church in North Sydney. He was educated at the Church of England Grammar School and the University of Sydney, and in 1914 left Australia with a graduate scholarship in classics to study at Oxford. Childe received his B.Litt. from Oxford in 1916 with a thesis on "Indo-European Elements in Prehistoric Greece." In 1917 he took first class honors in Literae Humaniores (Classics) at Oxford. He returned to Australia and from 1919 to 1921 served as private secretary to the Premier of New South Wales. After a period of travel and study in Greece, the Balkans and Central Europe, Childe settled in London. From 1925 to 1927 he was librarian of the Royal Anthropological Institute. Meanwhile he had published his *Dawn of European Civilization*, a comprehensive study of the neolithic age, which impressed scholars and archeologists as "a contribution to prehistoric archeology of first-rate importance," and a book which would have a profound effect on future lines of study and research.

Childe was appointed Abercromby professor of Prehistoric Archeology at the University of Edinburgh in 1927, a post which he held until 1946. During this period he took several leaves from the university to work with archeological expeditions in the Orkney Islands (excavating the neolithic village of Skara Brae) in 1928-30, and to travel to Mesopotamia and India in 1933-34. He was a founding member of the International Congress of Prehistoric and Protohistoric Sciences in Berne in 1931 and served as British secretary to the Congress from that time until 1947 when he became British representative on its Permanent Council. Professor Childe has made a number of visits to the United States. He was visiting professor at the University of California in 1939 and has honorary degrees from Harvard and the University of Pennsylvania. Since 1946 he has been professor of Prehistoric Archeology and director of the Institute of Archeology of the University of London.

Although Professor Childe's books are intended primarily for scholars and specialists in the fields of anthropology and archeology, they are so lucid, timely and comprehensive that they have appealed to the nonspecialist reader as well. His work is distinguished by the integration as well as the thoroughness of his scholarship. A reviewer in the *New Statesman* wrote of his *Most Ancient East*, a study of the "prehistory" of the Nile Valley and Mesopotamia: "Not only has he summarized the facts, he has also related them with each other and with the stages in human development which preceded and followed them. . . . And he has done all this in a book that the layman can understand and the expert respect and enjoy." The anthropologist Ashley Montagu regards him as "the most widely informed and the ablest of archeologists."

Professor Childe was elected a Fellow of the British Academy in 1940. He is a member of a large number of British and international honorary societies. In 1948 he delivered the Mason lectures in anthropology at the University of Birmingham on "Social Evolution" (these lectures were published in 1951) and the Hobhouse Memorial Lecture at the University of London on "Social Worlds of Knowledge" (published in 1949). He delivered the Frazer Lecture at the University of Liverpool in 1949 on "Magic, Craftsmanship and Science." In 1950 he lectured in Oslo for the Instittutet f. Samlignende Kulturfoskning on "Prehistoric Migrations in Europe" (published that same year). He lists his recreations as bridge, walking, and motoring.

PRINCIPAL WORKS: Dawn of European Civilization, 1925; The Aryans, 1926; The Danube in Prehistory, 1929; Most Ancient East, 1929; The Bronze Age, 1930; Skara Brae, 1931; New Light on the Most Ancient East, 1934; The Prehistory of Scotland, 1935; Man Makes Himself, 1936; Prehistoric Communities of the British Isles, 1940; Progress and Archaeology, 1944; Social Worlds of Knowledge, 1949; Prehistoric Migrations in Europe, 1950; Social Evolution, 1951.

ABOUT: Nature March 9, 1946.

CHILDERS, ERSKINE (June 25, 1870-November 24, 1922). For biographical sketch and list of works and references, see TWENTIETH CENTURY AUTHORS, 1942.

CHILDS, MARQUIS WILLIAM (March 17, 1903-   ), American journalist and novelist, was born in the Mississippi river town of

James R. Dunlop

Clinton, Iowa, where his father was a lawyer and all his forebears, from his grandfather back, had been farmers.

Childs was graduated from the University of Wisconsin in 1923 with a B.A. degree. Shortly thereafter he went to work for the United Press in Chicago and the Midwestern area. He interrupted his newspaper career to return to the University of Iowa to teach English composition, to meet his future wife and take his M.A. degree in 1925. He then joined the United Press again but this time in New York City.

In 1926 Childs joined the staff of the St. Louis *Post-Dispatch* as a feature writer. He traveled widely, laying down a solid base of 'observation knowledge' of the relationship of politics to the social and economic status of people. In 1930 Childs took a leave of absence from the *Post-Dispatch* to attend a housing exposition in Sweden. Two years later he returned to Europe, visiting most European countries, including Nazi Germany. In 1934 he joined the Washington bureau of the *Post-Dispatch*. In 1936 he wrote *Sweden: The Middle Way*, a study of the cooperative movement in Sweden and its effect on production, distribution, and consumption. This book received such wide acclaim that it prompted the government to send a special commission abroad to study cooperative systems in Europe. The book was revised in 1947 and has gone through several editions since that time. In 1937 Childs again returned to Europe on another fact-finding tour and collected material for

his book *This Is Democracy: Collective Bargaining in Scandinavia*, a detailed study of the operation of capital-labor collaboration in Scandinavia. After finishing his study of the Scandinavian political scene he traveled to Spain and wrote a series of articles on the Spanish Civil War for the *Post-Dispatch*, spending some time in Madrid during the siege.

The next country in line for Childs' critical appraisal was Mexico. His series of articles on the oil expropriation was so hot that a senatorial investigation followed. Childs was denounced on the Senate floor by Senator Joseph Guffey of Pennsylvania. He subsequently sued and won a full apology on the floor of the Senate from Guffey.

Childs began writing his column, "Washington Calling," in February of 1944. His sources range from the small towns of America, where he knows and understands the feelings and beliefs that eventually take form in political decisions in Washington, to the chancelleries of Europe and the top offices in every world capital. In 1945 he was given the Sigma Delta Chi award 'for sustained insight in national affairs, firsthand reporting and effective writing'; and in 1951, the University of Missouri's annual award for distinguished service in journalism.

Speaking frequently on the radio, Childs is now also taking an active interest in television. He has appeared frequently on such programs as *Meet the Press* and *Who Said That?* More recently he has inaugurated a discussion program called *Washington Spotlight* which appears on television screens in most American cities. He has lectured in the School of Journalism at Columbia University and at the University of Oregon.

Childs lives in Chevy Chase, Md., with his wife, the former Lue Prentiss, of Iowa City, Iowa. They recently observed their twenty-fifth wedding anniversary. Their son, Henry Prentiss, is a graduate of Yale University and their daughter, Malissa, now Mrs. H. J. Redfield III, was graduated from Leland Stanford in California.

PRINCIPAL WORKS: Sweden—the Middle Way, 1936; Washington Calling, 1937; This Is Democracy, 1938; Toward a Dynamic America (with W. T. Stone) 1942; This Is Your War, 1942; I Write from Washington, 1942; The Farmer Takes a Hand: the Electric Power Revolution in Rural America, 1952; Ethics in a Business Society (with D. Cater) 1954. Novel—The Cabin, 1944.

ABOUT: Current Biography 1943; New York Herald Tribune October 15, 1942; New York Times October 14, 1942; Saturday Evening Post April 19, 1941.

CHILTON, ELEANOR CARROLL
(September 11, 1898-February 8, 1949). For autobiographical sketch and list of works and references, see TWENTIETH CENTURY AUTHORS, 1942.

* * *

Eleanor Carroll Chilton died at Doctors Hospital in New York City, at fifty, after a long illness.

Of her poetry, William Rose Benét said, "She is accomplished in the sonnet. She writes good lyrics. Her poems have sincerity, movement, grace. But they do not 'startle and waylay.'" He admired the "intense individuality" of her prose.

Gladys Grabom found in her novels a "delicate distinction of style, almost mystical interpretation of nature, and scalpel-like analysis of personality," and Elizabeth Bowen declared that Miss Chilton's last novel, *Follow the Furies*, has "the solidity of a Mrs. Wharton novel, an equally sober and unobtrusive excellence of style."

ABOUT: New York Times February 9, 1949.

*CHOLMONDELEY, MARY (June 8, 1859-July 15, 1925). For biographical sketch and list of works and references, see TWENTIETH CENTURY AUTHORS, 1942.

* chǔm'lǐ

CHRISTIANSEN, SIGURD WESLEY
(November 17, 1891-October 23, 1947). For autobiographical sketch and list of works and references, see TWENTIETH CENTURY AUTHORS, 1942.

* * *

Sigurd Christiansen died in Norway at fifty-five. In 1941 his novel *Mannen fra Bensinstasjonen* ("The Man from the Gas Station") was published. In 1942 he wrote a short biography of the Norwegian painter Henrik Soerensen celebrating his sixtieth birthday. Christiansen's trilogy, which began with *Dream and Life* and continued with *The Lonely Heart*, was completed in 1945 with *Menneskenes Lodd* ("The Lot of Humans"). In the same year his play *Alexander Paulovitsj* was given at the National Theatre in Oslo. Just before his death he rewrote *Doeperen* ("The Baptist") which was published in 1947.

Christiansen's collected works appeared in nine volumes published in 1949-50. These later works of Christiansen have not been translated into English.

CHRISTIE, Mrs. AGATHA (MILLER)
(1891-). For autobiographical sketch and list of earlier works and references, see TWENTIETH CENTURY AUTHORS, 1942.

* * *

In 1950 the publication of Agatha Christie's fiftieth mystery novel, *A Murder Is Announced*, was celebrated in both England and the United States. At that time the total world sales of her books was estimated at between 75,000,000 and 100,000,000. (They have been translated into almost every modern language, including Japanese.) Her success is not hard to explain. The appeal, as Margery Allingham has pointed out, "is made directly to the honest human curiosity in all of us." An admirer, former British Prime Minister Clement Attlee, wrote: "I . . . delight in the ingenuity of Agatha Christie's mind and in her capacity to keep a secret until she is ready to divulge it." Her major achievement, Margery Allingham said, is the fact that she has entertained "more people for more hours at a time than almost any other writer of her generation."

In addition to producing a steady stream of smooth mystery stories, Miss Christie has adopted a pseudonym, "Mary Westmacott," under which she has written two "straight" novels. Under her own name she has also published *Come, Tell Me How You Live*, a good-humored personal account of the various expeditions to Syria that she made with her archeologist husband Max Mallowan.

On the successful London opening of her mystery play, *Witness for the Prosecution*, in the fall of 1953, W. A. Darlington wrote to the New York *Times*: [Agatha Christie] "has a miraculous faculty for constructing puzzles which seem to have one solution and turn out to have another equally plausible. With this she combines an ability to draw characters which actors can play with effect." The play proved equally successful on Broadway in the 1954-55 season and won the New York Drama Critics Circle Award as the best foreign play of the year.

ADDITIONAL WORKS: The Moving Finger, 1942; Murder in Retrospect, 1942; Towards Zero, 1944; Death Comes as the End, 1944; Remembered Death (in England: Sparkling Cyanide) 1945; Come, Tell Me How You Live, 1946; The Hollow, 1946; Labors of Hercules, 1947; There Is a Tide (in England: Taken at the Flood), 1948; Witness for the Prosecution, and Other Stories, 1948; Crooked House, 1949; A Murder Is Announced, 1950; Three Blind Mice, and Other Stories, 1950; They Came to Baghdad, 1951; Under Dog, and Other Stories, 1951; Mrs. McGinty's Dead, 1952; Murder with

Mirrors, 1952; Funerals Are Fatal, 1953; A Pocket Full of Rye, 1954; So Many Steps to Death, 1954. *As "Mary Westmacott"*—Absent in the Spring, 1944; The Rose and the Yew Tree, 1948.

ABOUT: Christie, A. Come, Tell Me How You Live; Current Biography 1940; New York Times November 15, 1953; New York Times Book Review June 4, 1950; Newsweek June 12, 1950; Publishers' Weekly July 1, 1950.

CHURCH, RICHARD (March 26, 1893-). For biographical sketch and list of earlier works and references, see TWENTIETH CENTURY AUTHORS, 1942.

* * *

Richard Church has long been known as an accomplished poet, novelist, and essayist. In recent years he has entered other literary fields—editing anthologies, writing travel books and children's books. Of the latter, his *A Squirrel Called Rufus* has been the most successful, in England and the United States. The story of a war between the native English red squirrels and the invading grey squirrels, its allegorical implications were unmistakable, and its appeal was not limited to juvenile readers. Some reviewers were reminded by it of Kenneth Grahame's classic, *The Wind in the Willows*.

ADDITIONAL WORKS: *Poetry*—The Solitary Man, 1941; Twentieth Century Psalter, 1943; The Lamp, 1946; Collected Poems, 1948; The Prodigal, 1953. *Prose*—The Sampler, 1942; British Authors, a Twentieth Century Gallery, 1943; Rufus (in U.S.: A Squirrel Called Rufus) 1941; Green Tide, 1945; Kent, 1948; The Cave (in U.S.: Five Boys in a Cave) 1950; A Window on a Hill, 1951; Portrait of Canterbury, 1952.

CHURCHILL, WINSTON (November 10, 1871-March 12, 1947). For biographical sketch and list of earlier works and references, see TWENTIETH CENTURY AUTHORS, 1942.

* * *

Winston Churchill died of a heart attack at seventy-five, shortly after his arrival at Winter Park, Fla., where he had spent several winters. His wife had died two years earlier. He left a daughter and two sons, with one of whom he was collaborating on a book at the time of his death.

At the age of forty-six Churchill virtually retired to his estate at Cornish, N.H., where he painted, read, carpentered, and occasionally wrote work seen only by a small circle of friends. He reluctantly authorized the writing of a biography of himself in 1941, but later withdrew permission, saying he had spent twenty-seven years of his life "in an attempt to eliminate publicity."

Churchill once said of his own work, "I have always concerned myself with American history and with current social problems." On another occasion he said, "I never was really literary. I wrote the novel for pleasure or adventure." Frederick Taber Cooper speaks of his novels as "born of an inexhaustible patience, a dogged determination to be true to his own stern exactions both in style and substance . . . carefully fashioned upon the great mid-Victorian models."

ABOUT: Walcutt, C. C. Romantic Compromise in the Novels of Winston Churchill; Hobbies May 1947; New York Times March 13, 1947; Saturday Review of Literature June 9, 1951, August 25, 1951; Scholastic November 9, 1949.

CHURCHILL, Sir WINSTON LEONARD SPENCER (November 30, 1874-). For biographical sketch and list of earlier works and references, see TWENTIETH CENTURY AUTHORS, 1942.

* * *

Probably no figure in twentieth century public life has had so rich, so varied, and so distinguished a career as Sir Winston Churchill. In 1953, at seventy-nine, he received two of the highest honors which his country and the world could offer him— knighthood (on April 24, 1953, Queen Elizabeth II knighted him and presented him with the insignia of the Most Noble Order of the Garter) and the Nobel prize for literature (awarded him October 15, 1953, for his six volumes of memoirs, *The Second World War*). On November 30, 1954, his eightieth birthday, he was acclaimed by the Queen, by Parliament, and by his whole country as "the greatest living Briton."

It is not, however, for the honors he has received that Sir Winston is known and respected throughout the world. It is for his gallant and indomitable leadership of Britain in the terrible days of World War II. As prime minister during these years he was more than a statesman. He was a symbol of the dignity and courage of the whole impassioned defense of democracy against tyranny. His wartime speeches were singled out by the Swedish Academy in the citation accompanying the Nobel award— "For his historical and biographical presentations and for the scintillating oratory in which he has stood forth as a defender of eternal human value."

After the surrender of Germany in May 1945 Churchill, as prime minister and leader of the Conservative government, tendered his resignation to King George VI. In the general election of July 1945 he and his party were overwhelmingly defeated by the Labour Party. For Churchill this was a bitter but not a crushing blow. He declined an offer of knighthood at that time, feeling that his leadership had been repudiated. For the next six years he sat in Parliament as leader of His Majesty's Loyal Opposition. At the invitation of President Harry S. Truman he visited the United States in 1946 and, at Fulton, Mo., made his challenging "Iron Curtain" speech in which he warned the Western democracies to stand firm behind the United Nations and to build up their military strength. In the general election of 1950 the Labour Party was continued in office, but this time with a very slim majority. In 1951 the Conservative Party was re-elected to power by a small margin and Churchill once again became prime minister.

During the six-year period in which he was opposition leader, Churchill did the greater part of the compilation and writing of his magnificent wartime memoirs. The first volume, *The Gathering Storm*, appeared in 1948, and the final volume, *Triumph and Tragedy*, which carries the account through D-Day and his defeat at the polls in 1945, appeared in 1953. It was an open secret that Churchill would have preferred the Nobel Peace Prize to the literature award, and there were some objections raised to the award that his work was political rather than literary. But in Churchill's rhetoric, in his "grand style," as in Cicero's, it would be difficult and pointless to try to draw a line between what is politics and what is literature. The elements of literary distinction are there—intelligence, a sense of history, and a gift for language such as few writers in the twentieth century possess.

In June 1953 Churchill retired to his country home, Chartwell Manor, to recuperate from what the New York *Times* described as "strain from overwork." (Not until March 1955 did he reveal that he had suffered a paralytic stroke.) He returned to London in the fall, noticeably feeble but still active in state and international affairs. In speeches in Parliament during the latter part of 1953 he urged "informal talks at the highest level" between representatives of the Western democracies and the Soviet Union. In April 1955 he retired from the prime ministership and was succeeded by Sir Anthony Eden. In his retirement, he announced, he would continue his active interest in politics and would complete his history of England as his crowning literary achievement.

ADDITIONAL WORKS: *War Speeches*—The Unrelenting Struggle, 1942; The End of the Beginning, 1943; Onward to Victory, 1944; The Dawn of Liberation, 1945; Secret Session Speeches, 1946; Victory, 1946. *Post-War Speeches*—Sinews of Peace, 1949; Europe Unite, 1950; In the Balance, 1951; Stemming the Tide, 1953. *The Second World War*—The Gathering Storm, 1948; Their Finest Hour, 1949; The Grand Alliance, 1950; The Hinge of Fate, 1951; Closing the Ring, 1951; Triumph and Tragedy, 1953.

ABOUT: Ausubel, H. (and others) Some Modern Historians of Britain; Broad, C. L. Winston Churchill; Coulter, J. Churchill; Cowles, V. Winston Churchill; Davenport, J. and Murphy, C. J. V. The Lives of Winston Churchill; Eade, C. (ed.) Churchill by his Contemporaries; Eden, G. Portrait of Churchill; Hawthorne, H. The Long Adventure; Hilditch, N. (comp.) In Praise of Churchill; Hughes, E. Winston Churchill in War and Peace; Kiernan, R. H. Churchill; Lockhart, J. G. Winston Churchill; MacNalty, A. S. The Three Churchills; Morton, H. C. V. Atlantic Meeting; Nicolson, H. Winston Churchill; Taylor, R. L. Winston Churchill; Thomson, M. Life and Times of Winston Churchill; Wingfield-Stratford, E. C. Churchill: the Making of a Hero; Current Biography 1953; New York Times April 10, 1955; New York Times Magazine November 27, 1949.

*CHUTE, MARCHETTE GAYLORD (August 16, 1909-), American biographer and literary historian, writes: "My grand-

Morrice A. Baer

father came to Minnesota in the days of the fur traders and built a house by the falls of St. Anthony. My father was born there, in the town that later became Minneapolis, and both men were influential in the growth of the city. My father married an Englishwoman and they lived in a country home near Minnehaha Creek. My two sisters and I grew up there, and before we left Hazelwood we had all become professional writers.

"I was tutored through the grades. Then I spent four years at Central High School in Minneapolis, one year at the Minneapolis School of Art, and three at the University of Minnesota. I was given two literary awards when I graduated, but this made no difference to my intention of becoming a writer. No other possibility had occurred to me.

"My first book was a set of verses for children, which I illustrated with silhouettes and called *Rhymes About Ourselves*. It was

* "The name is pronounced Marshette Choot."

accepted immediately by a publisher, but my experience with my next book was more normal. It was a study of the Bible called *The Search for God* and was turned down steadily for years. Once published, it has remained in print, and there have been English and German editions (the latter was published in Switzerland). The book was an attempt to interpret the Bible directly instead of by the light of later commentaries. It ended with the Gospel of John, but a sequel, *The End of the Search*, carried the discussion through the remaining books of the Bible.

"I did another book for children, *Rhymes About the Country*, and then moved to New York. The result was another juvenile, *Rhymes About the City*, which I was now able to dedicate to a small niece.

"The first summer in New York I did a fourteenth-century story called *The Innocent Wayfaring* and discovered the wonderful resources of the New York Public Library. I enjoyed living in the fourteenth century, so I next wrote *Geoffrey Chaucer of England*. No full-length biography of Chaucer had previously been written, since comparatively little is known about his life; but I found that if the background was handled vividly enough, the figure of the poet could be made to emerge clearly against it.

"For my next book I tried the same method in a more difficult and controversial field. *Shakespeare of London* was an attempt to look at a great man through the eyes of his contemporaries. As in the case of *Geoffrey Chaucer of England*, I tried to place the man clearly against his background, and as in the case of *The Search for God* I tried to avoid being influenced by later commentaries. The Shakespeare biography was a selection of the Book-of-the-Month Club, and I used the extra income on my first trip to England. London looked very familiar to me, although I had encountered it only in the New York Public Library.

"I like writing because of the freedom it gives. It is one of the few professions in which you can be left entirely alone, free to do the best you can privately and in your own way.

* * *

Not the least remarkable feature of Marchette Chute's biographies of Chaucer, Shakespeare, and Ben Jonson is the fact that these sound and pleasantly written books were based almost entirely upon research done in the New York Public Library. Her *Ben Jonson of Westminster* is dedicated,

"with affection and respect," to the reading room staff of the library. Miss Chute is one-third of a literary family—consisting of herself, her sister B. J. (Beatrice Joy) Chute, a novelist and magazine writer and author of books for boys, and another sister, M. G. (Mary Grace), also a novelist and short story writer.

PRINCIPAL WORKS: Rhymes About Ourselves, 1932; The Search for God, 1941; Rhymes About the Country, 1941; The Innocent Wayfaring, 1943; Geoffrey Chaucer of England, 1946; Rhymes about the City, 1946; The End of the Search, 1947; Shakespeare of London, 1949; An Introduction to Shakespeare, 1951; Ben Jonson of Westminster, 1953; The Wonderful Winter, 1954.

ABOUT: Book-of-the-Month Club News March 1950; Current Biography 1950; Minneapolis Sunday Tribune May 28, 1950; New York Herald Tribune Book Review April 2, 1950, October 11, 1953; New York Times Book Review October 18, 1953; Saturday Review of Literature April 1, 1950.

*CIARDI, JOHN (June 24, 1916-), American poet, writes: "Born Boston, Mass. Father Carminantonio Ciardi, mother Concetta DeBenedictus.  In 1921, two years after father was killed in an automobile accident, the family (mother, three sisters and I) moved to Medford, Mass., where I went through the public schools.

"In 1933 I entered Bates College, Lewiston, Maine, transferred to Tufts College in the middle of my sophomore year. Took a B.A. (*magna cum laude*) at Tufts, 1938. Entered graduate school at Michigan and took M.A. in 1939. While at Michigan won Major Award in Poetry in the Hopwood Awards Contests.

"In 1940 went to Kansas City University as instructor in English. Stayed there until 1942. Enlisted in the Air Corps. Combat service 1944-45 as aerial gunner on B-29. Based on Saipan. Discharged October 1945 as Technical Sergeant.

"Returned Kansas City one semester and married Judith Hostetter of Frankford, Mo., then went to Harvard as Briggs-Copeland Instructor in English, 1946-47. Was appointed Briggs-Copeland Assistant Professor, 1948.

"On leave 1950-51 lectured at Salzburg Seminar in American Studies, then settled in Rome and completed a translation of the

* chē är'dē

200

Inferno I had been working on for some time.

"Currently [1952] on a grant from the Fund for the Advancement of Education to study methods of teaching poetry in connection with other arts.

"In 1949 entered into association with Mr. Jacob Steinberg and became editor, later executive editor, of Twayne Publishers. Have lectured at Bread Loaf Writers Conference since 1947."

* * *

David Daiches wrote in 1949 that John Ciardi "is a poet of genuine if unequal gifts, whose best poetry has wit, perception, and humanity." As teacher, editor, translator, and critic—as well as practicing poet—he has worked energetically in the cause of modern poetry. He seeks a middle ground, in his poetry and in his theory of poetry, between what he calls "baroque poetry" ("that sort of writing that addresses itself inward to other writing, rather than outward to the lives of men") and mere "poesy"—the trite, the sentimental, the commonplace. He argues that a poem should be understandable, though—he hastens to add—not "paraphrasable," and he reminds the impatient reader that he "is as liable to error as the poet, and that when the poem fails to communicate, the failure may as reasonably be charged against the one as the other." The poets of the past whom he most admires are Dante, Chaucer, Shakespeare, and Donne. Among modern poets, he names Yeats, "the early Eliot," Spender, and MacLeish.

Ciardi regularly contributes poetry reviews to the *Nation*. In 1953 he joined the faculty of Rutgers University as lecturer in creative writing. In 1954 his long-awaited translation of Dante's *Inferno* was published. Dudley Fitts (in the New York *Times*) hailed the translation as "Dante for the first time translated into virile, tense American verse; a work of enormous erudition which (like its original) never forgets to be poetry; a shining event in a bad age." His translation was rhymed, but did not follow Dante's *terza rima* scheme. Rather, Ciardi aimed to reproduce "the common speech of the original." Ciardi has recorded on LP records his reading of some cantos from his translation.

PRINCIPAL WORKS: Homeward to America, 1940; Other Skies, 1947; Live Another Day, 1949; (ed.) Mid-Century American Poets, 1950; From Time to Time, 1951; (tr.) Dante's Inferno, 1954.

ABOUT: Peragallo, O. Italian-American Authors and Their Contributions to American Literature; Poetry June 1947, May 1948.

CLAPP, MARGARET ANTOINETTE (April 11, 1910-), American educator and biographer, was born in East Orange, N.J., the daughter of Alfred Chapin and Anna (Roth) Clapp. On her father's side she was descended of English and Scottish Puritans, who came to Massachusetts in the first half of the seventeenth century. Her mother's family dated to the nineteenth century in America, German Lutherans who had settled in New York at that time. Margaret Clapp herself was reared in the town of her birth, with a sister and two brothers. She attended public schools and was graduated in 1926 from the East Orange High School. After that, she entered Wellesley College and majored in economics. Here she was drawn to the career of educator. Later, when asked what had influenced this choice, she said, "Offhand, I'd recall Henry Mussey at Wellesley, whose constant query, when students talked of injustices in large terms, was: 'What are you going to do about it?' "

Underwood & Underwood

After graduating from Wellesley in 1930, she attended Columbia University, receiving her M.A. in 1937. At Todhunter School she taught English and history until 1939; she then taught at the Dalton School, the New Jersey College for Women, and Columbia where she gave extension courses for veterans. During World War II she did research for the British Broadcasting Corporation (1942-43) and worked for the Red Cross. In 1946 she received her Ph.D. from Columbia.

Her Pulitzer prize-winning biography *Forgotten First Citizen: John Bigelow* (1947) began as a dissertation on a relatively obscure nineteenth century New Yorker at the suggestion of Professor Allan Nevins, the historian. "Writing with clarity and detachment," observed the San Francisco *Chronicle*, "she has shown how man reaches full development and fruition. She has done a worthy deed in recalling John Bigelow to the American people."

In 1949, Miss Clapp was appointed president of Wellesley College, the school from which she was graduated when she was twenty. Aside from administrative duties, she has continued to write. In 1948 she contributed a chapter, "The Social and Cultural Scene" to *The Greater City*, edited by Allan Nevins, John A. Krout, and herself. *The Modern University* (1950), edited by Miss Clapp, appeared both in England and America. She is a trustee of the Walnut Hill School in Natick, Mass., and a director of Filene's, the Boston department store.

She calls herself an independent voter. Her religious affiliation is Protestant. Research is one of her greatest pleasures, and she loves to spend time in the libraries. Her favorite writers, she reports, are Scott, Henry James, Emerson, Whitman, and Emily Dickinson. She is fond of swimming, walking, music, and the theatre. At the time she assumed the presidency of Wellesley, she was described as slim and pretty, with a calm, gracious countenance.

PRINCIPAL WORKS: Forgotten First Citizen: John Bigelow, 1947; The Modern University (ed.) 1950.

ABOUT: Current Biography 1948; National Cyclopedia of American Biography (1952); Time October 10, 1949.

CLARK, BARRETT HARPER (August 26, 1890-August 5, 1953). For autobiographical sketch and list of earlier works and references, see TWENTIETH CENTURY AUTHORS, 1942.

* * *

Barrett H. Clark died in his home at Briarcliff Manor, N.Y., at sixty-two. Several months before his death, he wrote to the editors of this volume: "I have continued, as director of Dramatists Play Service and otherwise, to broaden the scope of the living theatre by enabling playwrights to extend their audiences throughout the country—into the schools and colleges and community theatres: in a word, into the nonprofessional theatre. As publisher, agent, lecturer, instructor, and writer, I have tried to help bring what was best in the professional theatre to the far wider audience that now exists practically everywhere outside the narrow limits of New York.

"At Columbia University I have at more or less regular intervals (in the English Department and the School of General Studies) continued the sort of instruction undertaken years ago; also at Queens College and the College of the City of New York.

"My interest in American history and drama resulted in the completion of a project to discover and publish several early American plays. A twenty-volume set of *America's Lost Plays* was published, 1940-42. This was supplemented later by a volume *Favorite American Plays of the Nineteenth Century*. In 1947 I edited, with George Freedley, *A History of Modern Drama*, contributing the section on 'Drama in the United States.' *European Theories of the Drama* was supplemented and reissued in 1947. My book *Eugene O'Neill* (originally published in 1925) was rewritten and published in 1947, and brought up to date subsequently for translations into the Spanish and Greek, which were published in Buenos Aires and Athens; and into German, which will be published soon. My latest published book (on Gorky, Galsworthy, Sidney Howard, Edward Sheldon, and George Moore) appeared in 1951, as *Intimate Portraits*.

"During the late 'thirties and in the 'forties I have been active as editor, advisor and radio commentator and moderator, on various NBC and Mutual programs (Great Plays Series, Broadway Talks Back, etc.).

"Continuing concern over providing texts of basic standard works is evidenced by the compilation of children's classics (in collaboration with M. Jagendorf), *A World of Stories for Children* in 1943. (Similar to my three volumes of *Great Short Stories of the World*, *Great Short Novels of the World*, and *Great Short Biographies of the World*.)"

ADDITIONAL WORKS: Favorite American Plays of the Nineteenth Century (ed.) 1943; A World of Stories for Children (ed. with M. Jagendorf) 1943; A History of Modern Drama (ed. with G. Freedley) 1947; Intimate Portraits, 1951.

ABOUT: New York Times August 7, 1953; Theatre Arts July 1942.

CLARK, ELEANOR (1913-   ), American novelist, short story writer, and essayist, writes: "Born in California, my mother's family having been natives of that state, but remember nothing before Roxbury, Conn., which has always been my home —although combined with family and other affiliations with New York. Father, Frederick Huntington Clark, mining engineer. Grandfathers, economist John Bates Clark, and Charles Henry Phelps, a lawyer but of literary inclination and exercise, as poet and editor.

Lotte Jacobi

"Attended what now seem innumerable schools, a one-room country one in Roxbury, a French convent on the Riviera and another in Paris, among others mainly Rosemary Hall in Greenwich, Conn. After a year in Italy (Rome), went to Vassar and graduated from there. Was doing the usual writing and puppy-editing all the time, although for some years was more inclined toward music, professionally speaking (for myself) a bad fallacy. Also inclined, always, to waste a lot of time on various sports and hope not to outlive the possibility of doing so. Began publishing reviews, short stories and essays early, along with having all sorts of jobs, publishing, translating, ghosting, etc., etc. 1943-45 in O.S.S. in Washington. *The Bitter Box*, a novel, was published in 1946. Received an award that year in creative writing from American Academy of Arts and Letters, and a Guggenheim fellowship. Began a series of long stays in Italy, mostly in and near Rome, from which resulted *Rome and a Villa*, published 1952. Then resumed writing fiction, never having meant to depart from it. Am married to Robert Penn Warren."

* * *

Eleanor Clark's first novel, *The Bitter Box*, was a clever and carefully wrought study of a mild-mannered little bank clerk who becomes involved in a radical political movement. It was recognized by the critics as a novel of unusual distinction, tasteful, sensitive, and sophisticated. "Her writing," Rose Feld commented, "has an almost polished beauty, a poetic absorption with the inner meaning of the outward symbol." Nowhere was the subtlety of her prose better demonstrated than in the series of impressionistic essays of *Rome and a Villa*, an intricate re-creation of the spirit and the charm of the Eternal City. Katherine Anne Porter called the book "the distillation of a deep personal experience; it is autobiography in the truest sense, in terms of what outward impact set the inner life in motion toward its true relation to the world."

Eleanor Clark and her husband Robert Penn Warren, the novelist and poet, whom she married in 1952, live in Connecticut. They have one daughter.

PRINCIPAL WORKS: The Bitter Box, 1946; Rome and a Villa, 1952.

ABOUT: Commonweal June 13, 1952; New York Times Book Review April 20, 1952; Newsweek April 14, 1952; Time April 14, 1952.

CLARK, Sir KENNETH (July 13, 1903-), English art critic, was the only son of Kenneth McKenzie and Margaret Alice (McArthur) Clark. His father, who was founder of the thread-manufacturing firm Clark and Co., and the possessor of a large fortune in England, retired at the age of forty to travel about the continent, taking his family with him. Young Kenneth spent winters in Scotland, summers in Cape Martin near Monte Carlo and autumns in Suffolk. Although the Clarks had no particular interest in art, the boy developed by the age of nine a passion for the subject; and six years later he determined to make art writing his profession.

Fayer

After attending Winchester and Trinity College, he became a student at Oxford, and there began his first book, on the revival of Gothic architecture. At this time he made the acquaintance of Bernard Berenson who invited Clark to help him with the revision of his *Florentine Drawings*. Two years later, with Berenson, the young man went to Florence where he continued his researches into the Italian Renaissance. Upon his return to England he finished *The Gothic Revival* (1929), which was well received by both critics and artists. From 1931 to 1933 he served as keeper of the Department of Fine Arts at the Ashmolean Museum at Oxford. Then in 1934, at the age of thirty, Kenneth Clark was invited to occupy the position of Director at the National Gallery, becoming the youngest man ever to have been granted that office. Concurrently he was given the post of Surveyor of the King's Pictures, a task which involved looking after the world's largest private collection, in Hampton Court, Buckingham Palace, Windsor Palace, and various other places. "I've dealt," he once said, "with three kings, George V, Edward VIII, and George VI."

Meanwhile, Clark's monumental catalogue of *Leonardo da Vinci's Drawings at Windsor*, which places Da Vinci's drawings for the first time in chronological order, was published (1935) and recognized as a work of foremost scholarship. In 1936 Clark visited America as Ryerson Lecturer at Yale University. There he gave a series of talks on Da Vinci which later formed the basis of a book, *Leonardo Da Vinci*, "the best short account of that master." In addition to writing and lecturing, Clark continued to act in positions of public responsibility; he became Director of Film Divisions in England, and later Controller of Home Publicity and Minister of Information (1939-41). Resigning from the National Gallery in 1946, he then became Slade Professor of Fine Arts at Oxford. Here he remained for five years, during which period he wrote three more books. At the same time, Sir Kenneth was gaining reputation as a writer and lecturer on a wide range of subjects: baroque architecture, Chinese painting, the poetry of Wordsworth, and nineteenth century English landscape painting. Clive Bell has remarked on his particular talent "for historical generalization, the scholar's gift of drawing inferences from apparently disconnected facts—and above all, a love of painting."

In England Kenneth Clark is especially known for his encouragement of modern art, of which he has formed a large collection. But, in keeping with his catholicity of viewpoint, this same collection includes art objects from several different centuries, some dating back to predynastic Egypt. He is a member of various organizations, the Advisory Council of the Victoria and Albert Museum, the National Art Collection Fund, the Contemporary Art Society, and the Covent Garden Opera Trust. Sir Kenneth is also the only Englishman ever to have been elected to the French *Conseil Artistique de la Réunion des Musées Nationaux*.

He lives with his wife, the former Elizabeth Martin, at Hampstead Heath with their three children. During a recent visit to America, Kenneth Clark was described by the *New Yorker* as being a busy, "modest but confident man." When his wife was asked by a reporter if they had seen much of the city, she answered, "We never seem to have time for a walk, except of course, walks in museums."

PRINCIPAL WORKS: The Gothic Revival, 1929; Commemorative Catalogue of Exhibition of Italian Art (part author and editor) 1930; Catalogue of Drawings of Leonardo da Vinci in the Collection of His Majesty the King at Windsor Castle, 1935; One Hundred Details in the National Gallery, 1938; Leonardo da Vinci, 1939; Last Lectures of Roger Fry (ed.) 1939: L. B. Alberti on Painting, 1944; Constable's Hay Wain, 1944; Florentine Painting: Fifteenth Century, 1945; Ruskin, J. Praeterita (Introduction) 1949; Landscape into Art, 1949; Piero della Francesca, 1951.

ABOUT: New Yorker March 10, 1951.

CLARK, WALTER VAN TILBURG

(August 3, 1909-   ), American novelist and short story writer, was born in East Orland, Maine, spent his early childhood in West Nyack, N.Y., and in 1917 moved with his family to Reno, Nev., where his father, Dr. Walter Ernest Clark, was president of the University of Nevada. He was educated in

the public schools of Reno and at the University of Nevada (B.A. 1931, M.A. 1932). Clark then returned to his native New England, where he studied for two years at the University of Vermont (M.A. 1934). He spent the next ten years in the small upstate New York town of Cazenovia, teaching English, dramatics, and sports in the public schools. In 1945, by then the author of two published novels and a number of short stories (one of these, "The Wind and the Snow of Winter," won the O. Henry prize in 1945), he gave up teaching to devote full time to writing. With his wife, the former Barbara Morse whom he married in 1933, and their two children, he returned to the West. For a while he lived in Taos, N.M., and now he is settled (feeling, he says, "as permanent as anybody can these days") in an old frame house on top of a mountain in Virginia City, Nev. He occasionally attends and lectures at writers' conferences, but he despises formal lecturing and "popular music, slanted journalism, advertising English, radio serials, big cities, hurry, political speeches, cover girls in the flesh or on paper, and all theories, political, historical, scientific, religious or literary, which pretend to authority and finality."

Walter Clark is a regionalist in the sense that he writes about and identifies himself completely with a region—the American West. But Clark's West is not the West of conventional cowboy fiction, although superficially the materials are the same—the frontier town, the hard-bitten, tough-minded characters, the rigors of the climate, and the loneliness and magnificence of the scene. To these materials, however, Clark has brought the inquiring mind of the artist. The excellence of his fiction, as Frederic I. Carpenter pointed out in an article in the *English Journal*, "lies in the originality and richness of his re-creation of the life of the American West—past and present, real and ideal, savage and civilized. Within this complex life he has sought to describe the motives, or 'gods,' which actually determine men's actions." In his first novel, the remarkable *Ox-Bow Incident* (made into an equally remarkable motion picture), Clark dealt with a situation fairly common in Western fiction—a reported murder, the forming of a posse, the arrest and lynching of three suspicious-looking strangers who, it is discovered later, were innocent of the crime. What was unique in his treatment was the total "re-interpretation" of traditional Western stock-type characters and the subdued but penetrating insight into their motives, their human and universal passions. Carpenter wrote: "The novel is the story of the tragic failure of an ideal in action—the 'western' ideal of law and justice. It can also be taken, if you will, as a parable of the tragedy of Western civilization."

Of its genre *The Ox-Bow Incident*, the critics agreed, was a minor classic, "so perfect," Clifton Fadiman wrote, "that it seems to deny the possibility of growth on the author's part." But even if Clark has not produced another novel so perfectly realized and self-contained as his first one, the novels which followed have given positive evidence of continuing growth. *The City of Trembling Leaves* was a Western novel only in its Nevada setting. Its subject—the adolescence of a sensitive young boy growing up in Reno —was sufficiently universal to inspire a number of critics to a comparison of the book with Thomas Wolfe's autobiographical novels. They noted the same "sprawling" exuberance, rich but uneven, the same intensity, passion, and evocativeness of the prose. But perhaps because *The City of Trembling Leaves* lacked the taut economy of his first novel, its fine and precise objectivity, it was considered a less successful book. "It seems too easy-going and good-natured, too lacking in organization, always dissolving into an even sunshine, always circumventing by ample detours what one expects to be sharp or direct," Edmund Wilson commented.

The Track of the Cat is Clark's most ambitious novel to date. Like *The Ox-Bow Incident* it finds its tragic subject in the sheer physical and emotional force of the West, only this time it is not an issue of a community rising, of man against man, but of man in isolation, against something far more sinister and formidable—literally a panther, symbolically a force of absolute evil. Once again, Carpenter reminds us, as in *The Ox-Bow Incident*, Clark offers "a parable of the tragedy of Western man." Some critics felt that as a parable the novel was unsuccessful. They found some of the symbolism obtrusive (inevitably, Clarke's "cat" was compared to Melville's whale in *Moby Dick*), the whole conception too patly and self-consciously arranged. But on the question of the novel's general effectiveness, its sheer force and impact, there was agreement. Mark Schorer

wrote of it: ". . . this is the real beauty of Walter Clark's masterful prose—its wonderful capacity to evoke from the homeliest circumstances the quality of grief and loneliness that exists deep in or under every human effort."

An adopted rather than a native westerner, Clark enjoys the advantage of belonging to a region and yet of having a degree of detachment from it. He describes his work as a "constant effort to personalize the land and put the human tragedy back into its natural setting." The richness and promise of his work lies in his use of the West for this purpose, and, as Carpenter remarks, "He has steadily pursued his fictional quest . . . with single-mindedness and a considerable measure of success."

PRINCIPAL WORKS: Ten Women in Gale's House, and Shorter Poems, 1932; The Ox-Bow Incident, 1940; The City of Trembling Leaves, 1945; The Track of the Cat, 1949; The Watchful Gods, and Other Stories, 1950.

ABOUT: Warfel, H. R. American Novelists of Today; English Journal February 1952; Holiday October 1949; New York Herald Tribune Book Review June 19, 1949, October 8, 1950; New York Times Book Review June 5, 1949; Saturday Review of Literature June 4, 1949.

CLARKE, ARTHUR CHARLES (December 16, 1917-), British novelist and science-writer, reports: "I was born at the coast town of Mine-head, England, the eldest of four children. My youth was spent alternating between the seaside and my parents' small farm, and I became interested in science at an early age, constructing my first telescope at thirteen.  My first literary connections were with the school magazine, and after I had entered the civil service as an auditor in 1936 I was concerned with various amateur 'science-fiction' publications. As treasurer, I was also closely connected with the early development of the British Interplanetary Society, of which I have been chairman since 1949.

"Joining the Royal Air Force in 1941, I specialised in radar and was eventually in charge of the first Ground Controlled Approach (G.C.A.) unit during its experimental trials, taking it over for the R.A.F. from its American inventors. During this period I published a number of papers on electronics and also sold my first science-fiction stories. After demobilization, I resigned from the civil service to become a student at King's College, London, where I obtained my B.Sc. (First Class Honours) in mathematics and physics in 1948. From 1949 to 1951 I was assistant editor of *Science Abstracts* and continued writing sparetime until it became obvious that my job, interesting though it was, was less profitable than authorship. Since 1952 I have been a full-time writer and have also given numerous radio and TV programmes on spaceflight, as well as many lectures.

"I am a Fellow of the Royal Astronomical Society, and was a council member of the British Astronomical Association 1949-52. My main relaxations are 35mm photography (particularly color), and I hope soon to take my camera underwater as I have become fascinated by 'frogman' techniques.

"My literary interests are divided equally between fiction and non-fiction: I have also had a short play performed on TV. A Book-of-the-Month Club selection enabled me to spend three months in the United States in 1952, and I hope to be a regular visitor there in future."

* * *

Like the poet's poet, Arthur C. Clarke is something of the science-fiction writer's science-fiction writer. He has supplied a sound non-fiction base for his work, and for the writings of many of his contemporaries, in two volumes on space travel ("astronautics") which are widely regarded as lucid, comprehensive, and definitive works. What gives these books their charm, Roy Gibbons wrote, "is Clarke's ability to reduce complex subjects to simple language and his steadfast avoidance of fantasy as a substitute for factual narration."

His fiction is thoughtful, imaginative, and written with real style. Basil Davenport wrote in 1953 that with *Childhood's End* Clarke "joins Olaf Stapledon, C. S. Lewis, and probably one should add H. G. Wells, in the very small group of writers who have used science-fiction as the vehicle of philosophical ideas—not merely ideas about the nature of future society, but ideas about the End of Man."

PRINCIPAL WORKS: *Non-Fiction*—Interplanetary Flight, 1950; The Exploration of Space, 1951; *Fiction*—Prelude to Space, 1950; The Sands of Mars, 1951; Islands in the Sky, 1952; Against the Fall of Night, 1953; Childhood's End, 1953; Expedition to Earth, 1953; Going into Space, 1954; Earthlight, 1955.

ABOUT: Book-of-the-Month Club News June 1952; New York Herald Tribune August 10, 1952; New York Times Book Review March 14, 1954.

CLARKE, AUSTIN (1896-   ), Irish poet, dramatist, and novelist, was born in Dublin, son of Augustine and Eileen Patten (Browne) Clarke.

His family had long been settled in Dublin and were staunch Irish nationalists. Clarke studied at the Jesuit Belvedere College (where James Joyce had also been a student) and received his B.A. from University College, Dublin. There he studied the Irish language under Douglas Hyde and literature under Thomas MacDonagh, the poet, who was executed by the British in 1916 for his part in the Easter Week uprising. Clarke succeeded MacDonagh as lecturer in English in 1917, the year in which his first volume of poetry, *The Vengeance of Fionn*, was published.

Although he was only about twenty when this poem was composed, Clarke was promptly recognized as a poet of rich promise. His earliest poems were lyrics, full of the haunting loveliness of Irish legend and the Irish country side. Succeeding volumes were long narrative poems—two dealing with the Gaelic legendary period, and one, *The Fires of Baal*, with the heroic age of Israel. Whatever the period or scene Clarke wrote about, he identified himself with it completely. In *The Cattledrive in Connaught* he captured the boisterous, extravagant spirit of the old epic. Padraic Colum said of it: "And as Austin Clarke does not lose sight of the actual Irish landscape, so he does not lose sight of the actual Irish character." In the poems in *Pilgrimage* (which won the national Tailteann award), written in the assonantal patterns of Gaelic poetry, Colum finds that Clarke identifies himself with the Gaelic poets of the seventeenth and early eighteenth century: "He writes in the temper of these dispossessed men, as if he were actually trudging the roads they trudged, crossing the waters they crossed, and, like them, separating themselves from the people they sing to by dealing only with the most tragic figures in their tradition."

Clarke lived in England for a number of years, doing free-lance writing for newspapers and periodicals. His writings were much admired by English critics—especially his two "medieval" novels (both of which were banned by the Irish censorship board). Richard Church said of one of these, *The*

Singing Men of Cashel, that "it leaves the reader with a feeling of having read in one of those ancient illuminated manuscripts such as the *Book of Kells.*" In 1937 he returned to Ireland and settled permanently in Templeogue, a village near Dublin. His reputation in his native country at this time was slight. Only one of his plays had been produced in Ireland (by the Gate Theatre), and the Abbey Theatre had shown little interest in his verse drama. He therefore decided to establish his own company and began by recruiting a choir which he trained and led in verse-reading. Clarke himself is an effective reader. Vivian Mercier says that "he happens to possess a very beautiful speaking voice as well as the ability to read poetry rhythmically and intelligently." His group became the Dublin Verse Speaking Society, giving weekly radio recitals and producing full length verse plays under the title of the Lyric Theatre Company.

Clarke's plays reveal an intimate knowledge of theatrical technique. Their subject matter is generally taken from medieval Catholic tradition. Padraic Colum called them "more inwardly medieval than any modern version of medieval life written in English that I know of." *The Flame,* for example, concerns the reactions of a community of Irish nuns toward a supposed miracle. In this play, as in most of his serious dramas, Mercier writes, "Clarke dramatizes the persecution by the group of the individual who will not conform." Although the scene is the dead past, the analogy to the political situation of his own time in Ireland is always evident. His dramas are usually written in a wide-ranging blank verse—a line "less supple, more liturgical, than Shakespeare's," Mercier comments— which produces powerful theatrical effects.

Clarke has described Irish poetry as "a medium in which could be expressed the drama of conscience and of inner conflict." He has himself used the medium daringly (as in his experiments in assonance) and inventively. Colum wrote of him: ". . . in a period of literary innovation he is one of the very few poets whose innovations have gone beyond the blurred and the experimental and he has made poetry which comes fresh, clear, and lovely through the use of newly moulded verse-structure." In 1950 Clarke became president of the Irish Academy of Letters. He is married and has three sons.

PRINCIPAL WORKS: *Poetry*—The Vengeance of Fionn, 1917; The Fires of Baal, 1930; The Sword of the West, 1921; The Cattledrive in Connaught, 1925; Pilgrimage, 1929; Collected Poems, 1936; Night and Morning, 1938; *Verse-Plays*—The Flame, 1930; Black Fast, 1941; As the Crow Flies, 1943; Viscount of Blarney, and Other Plays, 1944; Second Kiss, 1946. *Novels*—Bright Temptation, 1932; The Singing Men at Cashel, 1936; The Sun Dances at Easter, 1952. *Essays*—First Visit to England, 1946.

ABOUT: Colum, P. *Introduction to* Collected Poems of Austin Clarke; Griffin, G. The Wild Geese; Mercier, V. and Greene, D. 1000 Years of Irish Prose; Life and Letters April 1947.

*CLAUDEL, PAUL (August 6, 1868-February 23, 1955). For biographical sketch and list of earlier works and references, see TWENTIETH CENTURY AUTHORS, 1942.

* * *

Paul Claudel died of a heart attack in Paris at eighty-six. He spent his last years in retirement, dividing his time between his Paris home in the Boulevard Lannes and his chateau on the banks of the Rhône, in the province of Dauphiné. He devoted himself to the study of the Bible and the writing of Biblical commentaries in which he rejected modern textual criticism and exegesis in favor of medieval symbolic interpretation. "What do I care for the critical sense?" he told an interviewer in 1949. "The proof of a book is in the effect it produces, just as the proof of life is that it gives life. I hate those people who walk through life with a magnifying glass in one hand and a scalpel in the other."

Claudel was intensely and passionately Catholic. "Doubt," he said, "is something I have never known." His religion informed and shaped his thought and his work. No more vivid illustration of this fact is available than the remarkable correspondence between Claudel and the free-thinking André Gide, published in 1952. Over a period of more than twenty-five years these two brilliant men carried on a relentless struggle—Claudel, the proselytizer, writing and speaking at times so powerfully that Gide confesses in his journal: "In the presence of Claudel I am aware only of what I lack; he dominates me; he overhangs me; he has more base and surface . . . than I. I think only of obeying without a word." In the end, however, Claudel failed in his purpose to convert Gide, and the friendship was dissolved.

One of Claudel's major dramas, *The Satin Slipper,* written just after the first World War, received its first stage production by the Comédie Française in Paris in 1943. It had long been thought an "unplayable" play because of its great length and variety of scenes, and for the Comédie Française pro-

* klō dĕl'

duction it was cut radically. But even in the abridged version the performance lasted four hours. A decade later the theatrical company of Madeleine Renaud and Jean-Louis Barrault produced his *Le Livre de Christophe Colomb* in Paris. This "spectacle" had originally been written for Max Reinhardt in 1927 but was not produced at that time. Claudel's plays, as Paul D'Estournelle has pointed out in an article in *Theatre Arts,* were slow to gain public acceptance. Their length and their lofty symbolism, their religious significance in an age of universally secular drama, have kept them from becoming "popular" successes. But there is a continued and a growing interest in these plays. This D'Estournelle explains as follows: "Whatever objection one may validly have to the poet's conception of drama and to his dramatic style, it is difficult to remain unmoved by the conflicts within the human person which his work brings to life."

Claudel was elected to the French Academy in 1946.

ADDITIONAL WORKS IN ENGLISH TRANSLATION: Coronal (hymns) 1943: Three Plays: The Hostage, Crusts, The Humiliation of the Father, 1945; Lord, Teach Us to Pray, 1948; Poetic Art, 1948; The Eye Listens, 1950; Correspondence, 1899-1926, between Paul Claudel and André Gide, 1952.

ABOUT: Bondy, L. J. Claudel and the Catholic Revival *in* The Thomist, V (1943); Chiari, J. The Poetic Drama of Paul Claudel; Claudel, P. Correspondence with André Gide; Columbia Dictionary of Modern European Literature; Fowlie, W. Clowns and Angels; Hoehn, M. (ed.) Catholic Authors, I; O'Flaherty, K.M.J. Paul Claudel and The Tidings Brought to Mary; Ryan, M. Introduction to Paul Claudel; Slochower, H. No Voice Is Wholly Lost; Accent Winter 1954; America April 2, 1949; New York Times February 23, 1955; New Yorker March 12, 1955; Theatre Arts May 1946.

CLEGHORN, SARAH NORCLIFFE

(February 4, 1876-). For biographical sketch and list of earlier works and references, see TWENTIETH CENTURY AUTHORS, 1942.

* * *

In 1945 Sarah Cleghorn published a small volume of essays on lovingkindness and the part it can play in life today. It was, like her poems, a simple and quiet work. F. E. Johnson wrote, in *Survey Graphic:* "In these pages a rare person has revealed her insight, and it is that of a gentle but courageous spirit."

ADDITIONAL WORKS: Poems of Peace and Freedom, 1945; The Seamless Robe, 1945.

CLENDENING, LOGAN (May 25, 1884-

January 31, 1945). For biographical sketch and list of earlier works and references, see TWENTIETH CENTURY AUTHORS, 1942.

* * *

Logan Clendening ended his own life at sixty-one. He was found in bed in his home in Kansas City with his jugular vein pierced. He had been in ill health for some time.

Clendening's reputation as a writer was based principally on what the New York *Times* called "his notable faculty for the clear, simple and readable statement for lay reading of medical developments and findings."

ADDITIONAL WORKS: Source Book of Medical History (ed.) 1942; Methods of Diagnosis (with E. H. Hashinger) 1947.

ABOUT: National Cyclopedia of American Biography (1948); New York Times February 1, 1945.

CLEUGH, Mrs. SOPHIA (1887?-). For

biographical sketch and list of works and references, see TWENTIETH CENTURY AUTHORS, 1942.

*CLEWES, WINSTON (DAVID ARMSTRONG) (March 20, 1906-), British

novelist, writes: "I was born in Leeds, Yorkshire, the eldest son of James L. Clewes and Clara Sharpe Clewes. My father was a railwayman and consequently my earliest years were spent in a great many places as he moved around.

"I went to school in the city of York and from there we moved to Derry in Northern Ireland. This was in 1914, about a month before the outbreak of the first World War. I went to the preparatory school of Foyle College until 1917 when we moved back to London, a good deal of my novel *Troy and the Maypole* being based on childish recollections of Derry.

"We arrived in London in time for the Zeppelin raids which served as an early training or preparation for the London blitz of the last war. In London I went to Merchant Taylors' School, leaving in 1923 to join the Crosse & Blackwell Co., with whom I have been ever since; traveling abroad during vacations during one of which I met

* "Pronunciation of name: Klooz."

my wife in Tangier, North Africa. I was married in 1932 to Dorothy (Parkin) Clewes, also a writer of novels, teen-age novels, and books for small children.

"I have always, as long as I can remember, been interested in writing and have somewhere about the house a trunk full of juvenilia which were never even submitted for publication. Apart from a few poems in the school magazine and a short story in the old *Saturday Review*, my first literary earnings were for a number of short stories for radio, starting in 1941, although I had been writing seriously for publication since 1937. I withdrew my first novel because no publishers by whom I wished to be published would accept it. My second was thrown away half finished on the outbreak of war. It was to have been called 'Peace for Free Men,' and after September 3, 1939, struck me as a little untopical. Consequently my first published novel was *The Violent Friends*, a story based on the life of Jonathan Swift; and almost at the same time a play on the same theme was produced in this country, did very well in the provinces, and was due to open in London the week the first flying bombs began to arrive. It did not open.

"More novels followed. In 1949 *The Violent Friends* play was revived, this time reaching London for a run of exactly ten performances. I have not yet been lucky with the stage although I have had a radio play and a television play done and am still hoping.

"I write in spare time, my daily work being Organisation and Methods Manager for Crosse & Blackwell, Ltd.

* * *

Critics in America and in England found *The Violent Friends* a searching, delicate, and powerful treatment in fiction of the Swift-Stella-Vanessa triangle. When Clewes' second novel appeared, the (London) *Times Literary Supplement* hailed him as "among the most promising of our young novelists." His more recent novels have been characterized by what the *Christian Science Monitor* calls "inspired commonplaceness" and "refreshing, quietly exact craftsmanship."

Winston Clewes' younger brother, Howard Clewes, is also a novelist, author of *The Long Memory* and *Epitaph for Love*.

PRINCIPAL WORKS: The Violent Friends, 1944; Sweet River in the Morning, 1946; Journey into Spring, 1948; Troy and the Maypole, 1949; Men at Work, 1951; Peacocks on the Lawn, 1954.

CLIFFORD, Mrs. LUCY (LANE) (?-April 21, 1929). For biographical sketch and list of works and references, see TWENTIETH CENTURY AUTHORS, 1942.

CLOETE, STUART (July 23, 1897-). For autobiographical sketch and list of earlier works and references, see TWENTIETH CENTURY AUTHORS, 1942.

* * *

Stuart Cloete has lived in Paris, London, New York, and the British West Indies, but he returned to South Africa after World War II and has settled there again. Africa is the scene of the two novels he has published since 1942—*Congo Song* and, more recently, *The Curve and the Tusk*. He has also written, in *Against These Three*, a biographical study of the three most dramatic figures in the turbulent history of South Africa—Paul Kruger, Cecil Rhodes, and Lobengula, king of the Matabeles. From time to time reviewers have found his rhetoric "over-charged" and "undisciplined," but in general Cloete's style, in both fiction and non-fiction, is noted for its vividness and clarity.

Cloete's *The Third Way* is an expression of his personal faith and his search for moral values in the atomic age. His 'third way' is a plea for a higher private and public morality. He has said of himself: "The war showed me death and caused me to wonder about it. Farming showed me life and also caused me to wonder about it. This strange tie between noise and silence, between the city and the hills, between the man and the woman, between life and death, is what makes men write. Out of these two wonderings and a great love of the wilds and the cities has come my work."

TWENTIETH CENTURY AUTHORS, 1942, incorrectly stated that Cloete was unmarried. He was married at twenty-one, divorced, and in 1940 he married Mildred Ellison.

ADDITIONAL WORKS: Congo Song, 1943; Against These Three, 1945; The Third Way, 1947; The Curve and the Tusk, 1952.

ABOUT: Cloete, S. Preface to The Third Way; Van Gelder, R. Writers and Writing; Collier's April 12, 1947; Life May 4, 1953; Scholastic April 21, 1947.

"CLOSE, UPTON." See HALL, J. W.

CLUTTON-BROCK, ARTHUR (March 23, 1868-January 8, 1924). For biographical sketch and list of works and references, see TWENTIETH CENTURY AUTHORS, 1942.

COATES, ROBERT MYRON (April 6, 1897-). For autobiographical sketch and list of earlier works and references, see TWENTIETH CENTURY AUTHORS, 1942.

* * *

Robert M. Coates writes: "I was divorced in 1946 and am now married to Astrid Peters, writer. I live in Old Chatham, N.Y. and have one son, Anthony."

Coates is still art critic for the *New Yorker*. His three published books since 1942 are two novels and a collection of short stories. All these have in common the economy, restraint, and understatement so characteristic of *New Yorker* fiction. But beneath the smooth spare surface there are, as Weldon Kees puts it, "violent patterns of action." William Soskin has written of Coates' work: "Few writers are able to sustain psychological atmosphere and at the same time achieve the strength, the tragic statement and the compassion Robert Coates has."

ADDITIONAL WORKS: All the Year Round (short stories) 1943; The Bitter Season, 1946; The Wisteria Cottage, 1948.

COATSWORTH, ELIZABETH (May 31, 1893-). For autobiographical sketch and list of earlier works and references, see TWENTIETH CENTURY AUTHORS, 1942.

* * *

Elizabeth Coatsworth writes: "Miss Coatsworth's work has been divided into three periods. The first came when she was known primarily as a poet and a writer of short stories which appeared in the *Dial* and the *Atlantic*. In 1927 she published the first of many books for children and in 1930 (with the Oriental tale of *The Cat Who Went to Heaven*) won the Newbery award for the best book for children of the year. Eight years later, her first novel, *Here I Stay*, appeared, and since then she has written four others and three books of sketches of New England people and places.

"Her husband and she now live entirely in Maine. One daughter goes to Bennington College and one is in California, and both are interested in writing and drawing."

Corrections: Miss Coatsworth studied at Radcliffe, not the University of California. Her first book of poetry was *Fox Footprints* (1923), not *Fox Footsprings*; there was no co-author for *Runaway Home* (1942).

ADDITIONAL WORKS: *Poetry*—Country Poems, 1942; Summer Green, 1948; The Creaking Stair, 1949; Night and the Cat, 1950. *Juveniles*—Thief Island, 1943; Twelve Months Make a Year, 1943; Trudy and the Tree House, 1944; Wonderful Day, 1946; Plum Daffy Adventure, 1947; Up Hill and Down (stories) 1947; The House of the Swan, 1948; Little Haymakers, 1949; First Adventure, 1950; Door to the North, 1950; The Captain's Daughter, 1950; Dollar for Luck, 1951; The Wishing Pear, 1951; The Last Fort, 1952; Old Whirlwind, 1953. *Novels and Non-Fiction*—Country Neighborhood, 1944; Maine Ways, 1947; South Shore Town, 1948; The Enchanted, 1951; Silky, 1953; Mountain Bride, 1954; The Sod House, 1954.

ABOUT: Kunitz, S. J. & Haycraft, H. (eds.) The Junior Book of Authors (rev. ed.); Warfel, H. R. American Novelists of Today; New York Herald Tribune Book Review October 7, 1951.

COBB, HUMPHREY (1899-April 25, 1944). For biographical sketch and list of works and references, see TWENTIETH CENTURY AUTHORS, 1942.

* * *

Humphrey Cobb died at forty-four of coronary thrombosis, resulting from his service in the Canadian Army in World War I, at his home in Port Washington, Long Island, N.Y.

He has been described as "a doughty, flushfaced, amusingly irascible little man with his clipped speech, tart judgments and inevitable rightness about issues and persons."

At death, Cobb left an unpublished manuscript of a book titled "Nov. 11, 1918, the Story of the Armistice." His reputation will rest chiefly on *Paths of Glory*, which, in the opinion of Carey McWilliams, "described war as few Americans have ever described it. It will unquestionably rank with *The Red Badge of Courage* and the best of Bierce and will never be forgotten by those who have read it."

ABOUT: New Republic May 22, 1944; New York Times April 26, 1944.

COBB, IRVIN SHREWSBURY (June 23, 1876-March 10, 1944). For autobiographical sketch and list of works and references, see TWENTIETH CENTURY AUTHORS, 1942.

* * *

Irvin S. Cobb died of dropsy, after a two-years' illness, in New York City, at sixty-seven.

Anticipating his death, he sent some verses entitled "Schedule for Plan for Going Elsewhere" to a friend with the message, "To kill time, before Time kills me, I write doggerel like this." Three months before his death he wrote his burial instructions, suggesting for an epitaph "Anyhow he left here."

The humorist had campaigned for Wendell Willkie for president in 1940. He joined the America First Committee in the early days of World War II, but resigned after the attack on Pearl Harbor. His autobiography *Exit Laughing* was his last major literary work. A collection of his "gay stories, grim stories, and Judge Priest stories" was published posthumously.

Cobb once stated as his philosophy of humor, "You have to be able to poke fun at yourself before you can poke fun at anyone else without hurting his feelings." The New York *Times* has said that "he was endowed with a robust, genial talent for humor that was characteristically American, in the best tradition of Bill Nye, Artemus Ward, Mark Twain, and Will Rogers."

ABOUT: Cobb, E. My Wayward Parent; Van Gelder, R. Writers and Writing; Christian Science Monthly May 13, 1944; New York Times March 10, 1944.

*COCTEAU, JEAN (July 5, 1891-). For biographical sketch and list of earlier works and references, see TWENTIETH CENTURY AUTHORS, 1942.

* * *

Now in his middle sixties, Jean Cocteau shows no signs of tempering the reputation of "erratic genius" which he acquired so many years ago. Through his plays and motion pictures—*The Eagle Has Two Heads, Beauty and the Beast, Orpheus, The Strange Ones*—he has won a wide and appreciative audience in America as well as in Europe. In the motion picture his daring imagination has had full play, and he has ranged from grim psychological studies of decadence and perversion like *The Strange Ones* to an enchanting fairytale like *Beauty and the Beast.* His documentary account of the filming of the latter, published as *Diary of a Film*, graphically demonstrates the qualities of the man—mercurial, vastly energetic, hypochondriachal, perverse, utterly dedicated to his work. Eva Putnam wrote in a review of the book in the San Francisco *Chronicle*: "The mind rejects Cocteau the man for an outrageous egotism that reduces the universe to the measure of his personal activities; but the emotions yield, spellbound, to Cocteau the artist, battling titanically for the realization of a dream."

In 1941 Cocteau's play *Le Machine à Ecrire* was banned by the German occupa-

* kŏk tō'

tion authorities after they had seen it in rehearsal. He had considerable difficulties with the authorities after that. In 1943, however, another play, a fairytale, *Renaud et Armide*, was produced by the Comédie Française, and he returned to motion picture making with *Le Baron Fantôme* and, in 1944, *L'Eternel Retour.* Since the end of the war, in addition to the writing of plays and scenarios and the composition of two ballets, he has published in France two volumes of poems, *Léone* and *La Crucifixion*, a collection of essays on poetry, *Poésie Critique*, and one on painting, *Le Greco*, and also philosophical works, essays on the theatre, and a personal account of a trip he made to Egypt, *Maalesh.* He illustrates many of his own books. On March 10, 1955, Cocteau was elected a member of the Académie Française.

Late in 1951 Cocteau became involved in a lively controversy with François Mauriac, the conservative Catholic novelist and editor of *Figaro*. As Genêt reported it in the *New Yorker*, the quarrel centered on Cocteau's play *Bacchus*, produced by Jean-Louis Barrault. Mauriac found the play, which dealt with the issue of freedom of the mind during the Reformation in Germany, sacrilegious and reprimanded Cocteau, also a Catholic, for its sentiments. Cocteau's answer was written in the form of Zola's famous *"J'Accuse"* letter in the Dreyfus case. He accused Mauriac of being a bad Christian, if a good Catholic, and of "seeing only the ignoble in the world, and of limiting nobility to another world, which escapes us as incomprehensible. . . ."

ADDITIONAL WORKS IN ENGLISH TRANSLATION: The Eagle Has Two Heads (play) 1948; The Typewriter (play) 1948; Blood of a Poet (film) 1949; Diary of a Film, 1950; The Human Voice, 1951; Cocteau on the Film, 1954.

ABOUT: Columbia Dictionary of Modern European Literature; Dictionnaire Biographique Français Contemporain; Maritain, J. Art and Faith: Letters between Jean Cocteau and Jacques Maritain; New York Times Magazine January 11, 1948; New Yorker January 8, 1949, January 12, 1952; Poetry May 1954; Theatre Arts April 1947.

COFFIN, ROBERT PETER TRISTRAM (March 18, 1892-January 20, 1955). For autobiographical sketch and list of earlier works and references, see TWENTIETH CENTURY AUTHORS, 1942.

* * *

Robert P. Tristram Coffin died suddenly in Portland, Maine. He was sixty-two. In 1952 he wrote to the editors of this volume from his home in Brunswick: "Since its inauguration in 1938 I have taught at the Writers' Conference at the University of New Hampshire every summer; and for the past five years have taught poetry and the short story at the Fine Arts Colony, Corpus Christi, Tex.

"I gave the Patten Lectures at Indiana University in 1940-41 and was special lecturer in 1942. In 1945 I gave the Samuel Harris Lectures at Bangor Theological Seminary. I inaugurated the George Elliston Chair of Poetry at the University of Cincinnati in 1951. I have just been named as Class of 1898 Lecturer in Poetry at Haverford College for 1953. And I have this year [1952] been nominated by the University of Athens, in Greece, to the Chair of American Literature and Civilization there; and under a State Department and Fulbright set-up will be in Athens for the year 1953-54.

"In the past ten years, I have given upwards of a thousand lectures or readings across our country, carrying on my life-work of making poetry a center of the lives of the American people; and the response to my lectures has been most gratifying. Three of my poems are available to schools, in my reading of them, on the recording of the National Council of Teachers of English, of which I am an honorary member for life; twenty or so more of my readings of my poems are available on the recordings in the Modern Poets Series of the Harvard University Vocarium; and fifty-odd, not for sale, are recorded, in my reading of them, in the Library of Congress.

"As for literary honors, I was elected in 1945 a member of the National Institute of Arts and Letters, and made a Fellow of the American Academy of Arts and Sciences in 1949. My own college, Bowdoin, honored me with a Robert Coffin Day, on July 9, 1948, at which I read from my poems, and there was an exhibition of my water-colors and pen-and-inks and the unveiling of my murals of the Maine Coast in the Moulton Union.

"For family happenings, these: my older son, Robert Jr., won many decorations as a Naval aviator in the Pacific in the Second World War and now teaches Latin and English at St. Paul's School, Concord, N.H. My second daughter, Peggy, won the Durham Chapbook Award at the Writers' Conference, University of New Hampshire, and her first book, *Two Against Time* was published in 1950. My wife died in April 1947.

"I am just finishing my longest and most ambitious work, an epic of modern times, "Vip," which, in view of its great length, complexity, and daring may well be a long time in getting published; but if so, I can work the rest of my life upon it."

ADDITIONAL WORKS: *Poetry*—Primer for America, 1943; Poems for a Son with Wings, 1945; People Behave Like Ballads, 1946; Collected Poems (new ed.) 1948; One-Horse Farm, 1949; Apples by Ocean, 1950. *Prose*—Book of Uncles, 1942; The Substance That Is Poetry, 1942; Mainstays of Maine, 1944; Seventeenth Century Prose and Poetry (ed. with A. M. Witherspoon) 1946; Yankee Coast, 1947; Coast Calendar, 1949; The Third Hunger, and The Poem Aloud, 1949; Maine Doings, 1950; On the Green Carpet, 1951.

ABOUT: Christian Science Monitor Magazine July 21, 1945; New York Times January 21, 1955; Scholastic November 18, 1946.

COHEN, MORRIS RAPHAEL (July 25, 1880-January 28, 1947). For biographical sketch and list of earlier works and references, see TWENTIETH CENTURY AUTHORS, 1942.

* * *

Morris Raphael Cohen died at sixty-six, after an illness of several weeks, at his home in Washington, D.C. He had retired from teaching five years earlier, following a heart attack, and had concentrated on writing. During these last years he worked on several books simultaneously, often dictating to two secretaries and one of his sons.

His autobiography, *Dreamer's Journey*, published posthumously, was called by Felix Frankfurter "an effort, and a triumphant one, as was Morris Cohen's whole life, after things that are of 'perennial value.'" In the opinion of Perry Miller, "It will demand a permanent place among the classics of immigrant narrative, and one not too far behind the greater classics of intellectual biography."

The New York *Times* has noted that through his former College of the City of New York students, many of whom later filled positions of major importance in law, industry, education and government, Cohen exerted "a deep and wide influence on American life." "He was a whole man," Milton R. Konvitz said. "He sought the truth, and was willing to open many doors in his search." S. I. Hayakawa attributed to him "that combination of learning and ethical earnestness and sweetness of temper that Matthew Arnold called 'urbanity,'" and Sidney Hook has spoken of "the qualities of intellectual penetration and practical wisdom which made him a unique figure in contemporary American philosophy."

ADDITIONAL WORKS: Preface to Logic, 1945; Faith of a Liberal (essays) 1946; Meaning of Human History, 1947; Source Book in Greek Science (with I. E. Drabkin) 1948; Dreamer's Journey, 1949; Studies in Philosophy and Science, 1949; Reason and Law, 1950; Reflections of a Wondering Jew, 1950.

ABOUT: Cohen, M. R. Dreamer's Journey; American Mercury May 1946; Antioch Review December 1947; New York Times January 30, 1950; Saturday Review of Liberature August 13, 1949.

COHEN, OCTAVUS ROY (June 26, 1891-   ). For biographical sketch and list of earlier works and references, see TWENTIETH CENTURY AUTHORS, 1942.

* * *

Octavus Roy Cohen lives in Los Angeles, Calif. In addition to his slick and suave mystery novels, published on an average of about one a year, he continues to contribute short stories and serials to popular magazines and has written a number of motion picture scenarios and radio scripts. In 1953 he departed rather radically from his usual style with an historical novel, *Borrasca*, which takes place in Virginia City, Nev., during the Comstock Lode days.

ADDITIONAL WORKS: Sound of Revelry, 1943; Romance in the First Degree, 1944; Danger in Paradise, 1945; Dangerous Lady, 1946; Love Has No Alibi, 1946; Don't Ever Love Me, 1947; More Beautiful than Murder, 1948; My Love Wears Black, 1948; A Bullet for My Love, 1950; Borrasca, 1950; Love Can Be Dangerous, 1955.

ABOUT: American Magazine July 1954.

*COIT, MARGARET LOUISE (May 30, 1919-   ), American biographer, writes:

"I was born in Norwich, Conn., and, like O. Henry, 'raised' in Greensboro, N.C. I can never remember any vague 'wanting to write,' but always knew that I would be a writer, for I always had something I wanted to say. My first literary effort (6th grade) was a story of the private life and home-habits of the caveman, written from the point of view of the caveman's wife.

"At fifteen I was writing a little news column for a country weekly in Little River, Fla., and literally obsessed by politics and history. The family history intensified my love of American history; my father's family fought, cousin against cousin, in the Civil War.

* koit

"The personality of John C. Calhoun overwhelmed me while I was still in high school, and I knew then that I was going to write his life. The book that touched off the initial spark was Christopher Hollis' *The American Heresy*. At the Woman's College of the University of North Carolina where I was graduated in 1941, the note-taking got under way. I had good teachers, in both English and history, the former doing much to polish off my rough edges in composition, the latter to tone down my dogmatisms (but never my enthusiasms). I wrote for the college newspaper and edited the magazine. My early 'influences' were biographers and historians like Gerald Johnson, Marquis James, Bernard Mayo, Carl Sandburg, Claude Bowers, and Esther Forbes. In fiction I liked Thomas Wolfe, Ellen Glasgow, and Edna Ferber, with equal relish, and still consume the sea yarns of C. S. Forester with the avidity with which Presidents and presidential candidates eat up mystery stories. Charles Dickens was my first reading 'excitement,' my latest, Thomas Hardy.

"One of the ideas I stress at the University of New Hampshire Writers' Conference where I teach biography is: 'Write the kind of stuff you like to read.' You cannot rise above—or sink below—your own level. You cannot write like Eudora Welty if you really prefer Sophie Kerr, or vice versa.

"In 1941 I came North with my family and a year later started writing *John C. Calhoun*. Nothing could have been more fortunate for the book. Before that I had seen Calhoun in two dimensions, only, as a great personality and a great Southerner; it took the northward move for me to see him in perspective as a great American and as one of America's two or three greatest contributions to the mainstream of political philosophy in the nineteenth century.

"The book took seven years to write, while I earned my living 'covering' fires, funerals, and town meetings for small Massachusetts newspapers. In 1948 I staggered up to Breadloaf, Vt., as a Fellow, weighted down with sixteen pounds of Calhoun manuscript. Bernard De Voto helped me cut out a lot of nonsense and a lot of words, as did my Houghton Mifflin editors whose faith and help sustained me through the entire incubation period.

"The book was published in March 1950. It was one hundred years after the death of Calhoun. I was dazed and rather shaken by the publicity. Everything began to happen at once: lectures, a 'return trip' to Calhoun's South Carolina, a debate with Jonathan

Daniels, a Phi Beta Kappa key from the Woman's College in Greensboro, papers before the American Historical Association— and romance. (I have been engaged, but am currently free from 'entangling alliances.') The climax came with a congratulatory telephone call from elder statesman Bernard M. Baruch, which resulted in my next project— the first biography of Baruch to be written from his private papers. It was all so much, and when *Calhoun* received the Pulitzer prize in 1951, I just broke down and cried.

"Although there is still another big political biography I want to write some day, I don't want to get typed. I want to try fiction. Right now I have four ideas in mind: a nineteenth century sea yarn, a Civil War story (of course), a modern 'political novel' of small town New England, and 'something Irish,' and modern too. What has been most overwhelming is getting used to the idea of 'being an author.' "

PRINCIPAL WORKS: John C. Calhoun, American Portrait, 1950.

ABOUT: Current Biography 1951; Shoreliner Magazine June 1952.

COLBY, FRANK MOORE (February 10, 1865-March 3, 1925). For biographical sketch and list of works and references, see TWENTIETH CENTURY AUTHORS, 1942.

* * *

ABOUT: South Atlantic Quarterly October 1952.

COLE, GEORGE DOUGLAS HOWARD (September 25, 1889-). For autobiographical sketch and list of earlier works and references, see TWENTIETH CENTURY AUTHORS, 1942.

* * *

G. D. H. Cole was a Fellow of University College, Oxford, from 1925 to 1944. Since 1944 he has been Chichele Professor of Social and Political Theory at Oxford, and Fellow of All Souls College. He is also a Fellow of Nuffield College, Oxford, of which he was formerly Sub-Warden. He is now president of the Fabian Society. During World War II he was director of the Nuffield College Social Reconstruction Survey and worked with Lord Beveridge on the Man-Power Survey.

Mrs. Cole has been chairman of the Further Education Committee of the London County Council since 1950, and an alderman of the Council since 1952. Since 1942 the Coles have written extensively on politics, as well as on economics and sociology.

The Coles' elder daughter is married to an American and settled in New York.

ADDITIONAL WORKS: Europe, Russia, and the Future, 1941; Chartist Portraits, 1941; Great Britain in the Post-War World, 1942; Fabian Socialism, 1943; Money, Present and Future, 1944; A Century of Cooperation, 1945; Local and Regional Government, 1947; The Meaning of Marxism, 1948; Samuel Butler (English Novelists Series) 1948; A History of the Labour Party, 1948; World in Transition, 1949; Socialist Economics, 1950; Essays in Social Theory, 1950; Introduction to Economic History, 1952; Socialist Thought: the Forerunners, 1789-1850, 1953; Marxism and Anarchism, 1954. *Economics and Sociology by M. I. Cole*—Books and the People, 1938; Democratic Sweden (ed.) 1938; Evacuation Survey (with R. Padley) 1940; Our Soviet Ally (ed.) 1943; Beatrice Webb, 1945; Makers of the Labour Movement, 1948; Our Partnership (ed. with B. Drake) 1948; Growing Up into Revolution, 1949; The Webbs and their Work (ed.) 1949; Beatrice Webb's Diaries (ed.) 1952; Robert Owen, 1953. *Detective Stories by G. D. H. & M. I. Cole*—Toper's End, 1942; Death of a Bride, 1945; Birthday Gifts, 1946; Fatal Beauty, 1948; In Peril of His Life, 1948; Toys of Death, 1948.

COLE, Mrs. MARGARET ISABEL (POSTGATE). See COLE, G. D. H.

COLES, CYRIL HENRY. See "COLES, M."

"COLES, MANNING," English author of detective stories and thrillers, writes: " 'Manning Coles' is a partnership of Adelaide Frances Oke Manning and Cyril Henry Coles, who live in adjacent houses at the village of East Meon in Hampshire, England. Both were born in London and were taken by their families to live in the country at an early age. C. H. Coles was  educated at Churchers College, Petersfield, Hants., and Adelaide Manning at the High School for Girls, Tunbridge Wells, Kent.

"Both served in the first World War. A. F. O. Manning in munition factories and later as a clerk at the War Office. C. H. Coles was apprenticed to the famous ship building firm of John I. Thornycroft at Southampton from which he fled to join the Hampshire Regiment under an assumed name and an optimistic estimate of his age. He served in France for some time with the Twenty-Ninth Division until his gift for languages and an uncanny knack of emerging unscathed from incursions into German lines

came to the notice of the authorities and he was transferred to British Intelligence. He lived in Germany for the remainder of the war and for some time after, when he returned to Thornycroft's at Southampton.

"During the slump life became too unbearably dull and he began to travel, visiting most of the countries of the world except the Far East. His longest stay in any one country was in Australia, where at different times he worked on the railway, managed a garage, and later wrote a column a day for a Melbourne paper.

"He returned to England in 1928 and in 1929 the Mannings moved from Buckinghamshire into the house next door as tenants of Mr. Coles senior. In due course A. F. O. Manning, driven by want of money, took to writing, but her first novel, though receiving an excellent press, did not sell and C. H. Coles suggested that he had a book in mind which was begging to be written and perhaps they could write it together. The book was *Drink to Yesterday,* a factual account of intelligence work in the first World War; it started a vein of such stories upon which the partners are still working."

* * *

Drink to Yesterday and *A Toast to Tomorrow,* "the two first, inseparable, and incomparable Tommy Hambledon adventures," have already found their places in the lists of classic spy stories. Succeeding Hambledon adventures have been uniformly full of action, humor, and thrills. "Coles" is not always expert in construction, but, as Anthony Boucher points out, he can be relied upon to produce "a nice exercise in good-humored implausibility."

PRINCIPAL WORKS: Drink to Yesterday, 1940; Pray Silence, 1940 (In U.S.: Toast to Tomorrow); They Tell No Tales, 1941; This Fortress, 1942; Without Lawful Authority, 1943; Great Caesar's Ghost (juvenile) 1943 (in England: The Emperor's Bracelet); Green Hazard, 1945; The Fifth Man, 1946; A Brother for Hugh (in U.S.: With Intent to Deceive) 1947; Let the Tiger Die, 1947; Among Those Absent, 1948; Diamonds in Amsterdam, 1949; Not Negotiable, 1949; Dangerous by Nature, 1950; Now or Never, 1951; Alias Uncle Hugo, 1952; Night Train to Paris, 1952; All that Glitters, 1953; Brief Candles, 1954; The Man in the Green Hat, 1954.

COLETTE, SIDONIE GABRIELLE CLAUDINE (January 28, 1873-August 3, 1954). For biographical sketch and list of earlier works and references, see TWENTIETH CENTURY AUTHORS, 1942.

* * *

Colette died at eighty-one in her Paris apartment at the Palais-Royal. She was given a state funeral—"the only honor of [its] kind to be given a French woman writer in the history of all the four republics," and the highest posthumous honor a citizen can receive—and her death was regarded in France as the greatest literary loss since the death of André Gide. Thousands of Parisians attended her funeral in the courtyard of the Palais-Royal. She lay in state, Genêt wrote in the *New Yorker,* "on a great catafalque loosely covered with tricolor silk, which the wind billowed, and her glittering cross of a Grand Officer of the Legion of Honor and its scarlet ribbon were attached to a black velvet pillow that leaned against her coffin." Colette was survived by her daughter, Mme. Colette Jouvenel, and by her third husband, Maurice Goudeket. (Her second marriage, to Henri de Jouvenel, ended in divorce.) A request by members of her family that she be given a Catholic burial was refused by the Archbishop of Paris on the grounds that she had married twice outside the Church and was a noncommunicant of the Church at the time of her death. A bitter controversy followed upon the Archbishop's decision, and a dramatic protest against it was written by the Catholic novelist Graham Greene, and published in *Le Figaro Littéraire.* Greene addressed himself respectfully to the Archbishop but objected strongly that the decision "has given the impression that the Church pursues an error even beyond the deathbed."

Colette spent the last years of her life as an invalid, crippled by arthritis, confined to her apartment. Her bed was placed near a window in the apartment so that she might overlook the Palais-Royal Garden, and in that spot, surrounded by her books, photographs, and her adored cats, she wrote and received visitors. A plaque, to be placed on the garden wall of the house, will read: "Here lived, here died Colette, whose work is a window wide-open on life." Few writers have looked more sympathetically into the human heart. Probably no other writer has better summed up "certain French essences, as in her love for excellent foods and wines, her perfect feeling for the written or spoken French phrase, and her literary sense *de l'époque*, whether the epoch was that of aging cocottes or of nubile provincial schoolgirls" (Genêt, in the *New Yorker*). In an address at her funeral, the French Minister of National Education, Jean Berthoin, described her as a writer who was "pagan, sensuous, Dionysiac." Her style, Glenway Wescott pointed out in 1951, was a wonderful combination of sensuousness, elegance, brevity, clarity—"and those turns of phrase, speedy and forceful and neat, and with a sense of fun, for which the French have the word *esprit*." For American readers who are only now discovering her work (a number of translations have appeared since 1950, and a dramatization of her *Gigi* was a Broadway success in 1951), Colette's appeal may be harder to define. Beyond her candor and her worldly charm, there was her depth of characterization, her instinctive knowledge of human weaknesses, her wise and sympathetic grasp of feminine psychology. In the words of another speaker at her funeral services, Germaine Beaumont: "She had . . . more aptitude than others for observing, seizing, holding."

In 1945 Colette was elected to the Goncourt Academy (the only woman to be so honored) to sit among the ten "living literary immortals" who annually award the coveted Prix Goncourt for fiction. For that occasion she left her invalid's bed and hobbled to the Academy's meeting. Her hopes for the future, she told reporters at that time, were simple—"to love . . . to live a little . . . to have flowers . . . strawberries . . . to live in a more tranquil universe."

ADDITIONAL WORKS IN ENGLISH TRANSLATION: Short Novels, 1951; Three Novels (Gigi, Chance Acquaintance, Julie de Carneilhan) 1952; My Mother's House, and Sido, 1953; The Vagabond, 1955.

ABOUT: Colette, G. My Mother's House, and Sido; Columbia Dictionary of Modern European Literature; Crossland, M. Madame Colette, a Provincial in Paris; Wescott, G. *Introduction to Short Novels of Colette*; Atlantic Monthly July 1946; France Illustration September 1954; Life May 28, 1945, August 16, 1954; Mercure de France December 1953; New Republic September 6, 1954; New York Times August 4, 1954; New York Times Magazine January 22, 1950; New Yorker November 12, 1949, August 21, 1954; Time May 14, 1945, August 23, 1954.

COLLIER, JOHN (May 3, 1901-). For biographical sketch and list of earlier works and references, see TWENTIETH CENTURY AUTHORS, 1942.

* * *

Two collections of John Collier's short stories have appeared in the past decade and have been the occasion for rejoicing among the ever-widening circle of his admirers. A favorite activity in this circle is attempting to define the peculiar talent which is Collier's. As Clifton Fadiman has pointed out, his stories "are not profound or beautiful or even memorable." But, Fadiman continued, "they are refreshingly odd, aromatic and spicy. . . . His mind is limited and subtle, working only with the unexpected, the wild, and the lightly diabolic. He has the genuine *soufflé* touch." Probably the writer he most closely resembles is Saki—casual, whimsical, diabolical, and witty. He remains, Basil Davenport said, "the master of an irony so perfectly balanced that his horror is hardly ever quite free of humor, nor his humor of horror."

In recent years Collier has been living in Los Angeles, Calif., where he had "a little matter of business" in Hollywood. The business, Collier wrote in 1951, "I sweetened by the occasional nostalgic planting of a rose bush or two, playing some weak chess, and a good deal of erratic tennis." He was divorced from his first wife in 1943 and in 1945 married Margaret Elizabeth Eke.

ADDITIONAL WORKS: A Touch of Nutmeg, 1943; Fancies and Good Nights, 1951.

ABOUT: Fadiman, C. *Foreword to* A Touch of Nutmeg; New York Herald Tribune Book Review October 7, 1951.

COLLINGWOOD, ROBIN GEORGE (1889-January 9, 1943), British philosopher and archeologist, was the son of William Gershom Collingwood, friend and biographer of John Ruskin. The boy was educated at home until he reached thirteen. He began Latin at four, Greek at six, and not much later started reading everything in the natural sciences that he could lay his hands on. He entered Rugby on a scholarship in 1902 where, he recalled years later in his *Autobiography*, he learned a considerable amount of modern history, "dis-

Lafayette

covered Bach, learned to play the violin, studied harmony and counterpoint and orchestration, and composed a good deal of trash." At Rugby he also acquired a serious and incurable knee injury while playing football.

Collingwood went up to University College, Oxford. In 1910 he took first class Honours Moderations and in 1912 he took first class in Classics. In the latter year he received a philosophical fellowship to Pembroke College. His interests were divided about equally among philosophy, history, and archeology. He spent most of his life teaching philosophy at Oxford—variously a fellow, tutor, lecturer, and from 1935 to 1941 Waynflete Professor of Metaphysical Philosophy. During the years of World War I he worked with the British Admiralty Intelligence Division. He spent many summers on excavations, pursuing his historical and archeological studies. Archeology, he wrote, impressed on him "the importance of the questioning activity in life." His field of specialization was Roman Britain and his writings on this period were widely regarded as lucid, well-arranged, and trustworthy presentations of exhaustive scholarship.

At the root of Collingwood's varied and ambitious researches was a single aim—the search for a rapprochement between philosophy and history. He took a firm and independent philosophical position and, in 1917, announced himself "an opponent of the realists," describing philosophical realism as "the undischarged bankrupt of modern philosophy." He developed his own system of logic, declaring, "In logic I am a revolutionary," and rejected so-called "propositional logic" in favor of a logic of question-and-answer. He describes the origin of this new system very amusingly in his *Autobiography,* explaining that he developed it during the war years when his duties at the ministry in London forced him to pass the Albert Memorial every day. Struck by the ugliness of the structure, he began to wonder why it was so bad, why an artist would deliberately and conscientiously create such a monstrosity. Why was something that appeared ugly to Collingwood apparently beautiful to others? One could not answer this question, he reasoned, with a single proposition. A proposition is not true or false, he wrote, "until you know what question it is intended to answer." As a teacher Collingwood insisted that his students must seek in the philosophical text under study the questions that the philosopher intended his philosophy to answer. Truth was not the property of any single proposition but the product "of a complex consisting of questions and answers."

Collingwood's work on esthetics (where he followed Croce very closely) was described by John Cournos as "factual and precise . . . the product of an ordered mind which puts everything in its place." His last book, written during the war years while he was in ill health, was a study of "man, society, civilization and barbarism" based on the famous *Leviathan* of Thomas Hobbes. R. M. MacIver wrote of it: "Amid the niceties of its logic it has some wise and witty things to say, but . . . the social thinking of the author remains peculiarly private, remote from the tangled affairs of political life." Less "remote," however, was the personal statement Collingwood made in 1939 at the conclusion of his autobiography: "I know that Fascism means the end of clear thinking and the triumph of irrationalism. I know that all my life I have been engaged unawares in a political struggle, fighting against these things in the dark. Henceforth I shall fight in the daylight." Collingwood was a Fellow of the British Academy. He had married Ethel Winifred Graham in 1918, and they had a son and a daughter.

PRINCIPAL WORKS: Religion and Philosophy, 1916; Ruskin's Philosophy, 1920; Roman Britain, 1921; Speculum Mentis, or the Map of Knowledge, 1924; Outlines of a Philosophy of Art, 1925; Archaeology of Roman Britain, 1930; Essay on Philosophical Method, 1933; Roman Britain and the English Settlements (Oxford History of England, Volume I, with J. N. L. Myres) 1936; Human Nature and Human History, 1936; Britain, 1937; Principles of Art, 1938; Autobiography, 1939; Essay on Metaphysics 1940; The First Mate's Log, 1940; The New Leviathan, 1942; The Idea of Nature, 1945; The Idea of History, 1946.

ABOUT: Collingwood, R. G. Autobiography; McCallum, R. B. & others, Robin George Collingwood; Richmond, I. A. Robin George Collingwood; Nature February 6, 1943; New York Times January 12, 1943.

COLLINS, DALE (April 7, 1897-   ). For biographical sketch and list of earlier works and references, see TWENTIETH CENTURY AUTHORS, 1942.

* * *

Dale Collins worked as a press censor during World War II and did no creative writing. Since the end of the war, however, he has published a considerable amount of fiction and non-fiction and several books for children. He publishes some of his books under the pseudonym "Stephen Fennimore." Collins lives in Australia.

ADDITIONAL WORKS: Utility Baby, 1944; Ah, Promised Land, 1946; Bright Vista (autobiography) 1946; The Far-Off Strands (short stories) 1946; A Sister for Susan, 1947; Voyage of the Landship, 1947; Winds of Chance, 1947; The Happy Emigrants, 1948. As Stephen Fennimore—Simple Simon Smith, 1949, Vanishing Boy, 1949; Robinson Carew—Castaway, 1949; Bush Holiday, 1949; Bush Voyage, 1950; Shipmates Down Under, 1950.

ABOUT: Collins, D. Bright Vista; Roderick, C. A. Twenty Australian Novelists.

COLLINS, NORMAN RICHARD (October 3, 1907-), British novelist and radio, television, and motion picture producer, is

the son of the late Oliver Norman Collins. He has lived most of his life in London and was educated at the William Ellis School in Hampstead. Before he was well beyond his teens, Collins had gained a foothold in the publishing business. He was with the Ox-

Howard Coster

ford University Press from 1926 to 1929. From 1929 to 1933 he was assistant literary editor of the (London) News-Chronicle. By this time too he was an established literary critic, having published a lively and very well-received history of the English novel, The Facts of Fiction. At twenty-four he became deputy chairman of the publishing house of Victor Gollancz, Ltd. During his seven years of active association with Gollancz, he managed to write and publish six novels—all of them popular successes in England and in the United States.

The novelists to whom Collins is most often compared are Arnold Bennett and J. B. Priestley. Although he has written several adventure and suspense stories, he is most expert in the "local" novel, the warm, comfortable and homey novel of English middle-class life. The best and the most typical of these in his Dulcimer Street (published in England as London Belongs to Me). A long and leisurely story of a group of tenants living at 10 Dulcimer Street from 1938 to 1940, it pleasantly and nostalgically echoes the late Victorian and Edwardian novels—"a sound, old-fashioned novel," the New Yorker called it, ". . . like those that were popular family reading three or four decades ago. . . ." The ground he covers is

usually familiar, but, as Clifton Fadiman pointed out in a review of another of his novels, "He arranges his narrative so artfully that you follow him with pleasure even as you feel you have been through all this before."

Collins joined the staff of the British Broadcasting Company in 1946. He served as controller of the Light Programme, as general overseas director, and from 1947 to 1950 he was in charge of B.B.C. television. In the latter year he resigned from the B.B.C. to work with the British Film Institute, of which he had been elected governor in 1949, and the Radio Industries Club, of which he was president. He is currently head of the Associated Broadcasting Developing Company, producing films for television. His aim, according to an interview in the British magazine Courier, is to make possible "the first marriage of films and television through assisting in the development of television in the world at large, eventually producing alternative independent services in Britain."

"Compact, alert, and dapper," Collins carries on his many activities in radio, television, and literature with fierce energy—"He has the incapacity to sit still which goes with the incapacity to stay mentally at rest." He lives in London and has a country cottage "in the very heart of John Bunyan's Bedfordshire." He has been married since 1931 to Sarah Helen Martin, who had been an actress before their marriage, and they have two daughters and a son, ranging in ages from sixteen to four. "Through my children," Collins writes, "I am thus kept forcibly in touch with something better than half a generation of contemporary thought and rising opinion."

PRINCIPAL WORKS: The Facts of Fiction, 1932; Penang Appointment, 1934; The Three Friends, 1935; Trinity Town, 1936; Flames Coming Out of the Top, 1937; Love in Our Time, 1939; "I Shall Not Want" (In U.S.: Gold for My Bride) 1940; Anna (in U.S.: The Quiet Lady) 1942; London Belongs to Me (in U.S.: Dulcimer Street) 1945; Black Ivory, 1948; Children of the Archbishop, 1951; The Bat that Flits, 1952.

ABOUT: Courier (magazine) December 1953; New York Herald Tribune Book Review October 7, 1951.

COLLIS, MAURICE (January 10, 1889-), British writer on oriental subjects and art critic, writes: "I was born in Dublin. My family belonged to the Protestant gentry, a class descended from English settlers from the time of the Tudors onwards, and who, though Irish in many ways, had little sym-

pathy with the national aspirations of the Catholic Irish. In accordance with the ideas of such a family I was educated in England from

Baron

my ninth year, going at fourteen to Rugby School and at eighteen to Corpus Christi College, Oxford. After getting first class honours at Oxford in history, I decided on an active career and entered the Indian Civil Service which then offered brilliant prospects to those who could pass the difficult examination. I was posted to Burma (then a province of the Indian empire) and arrived there in 1912. But I became aware that I was not an Imperial civil servant of the normal type. The movement for liberation which was gathering force in my native country had my sympathy and suggested to me at an early date that the Burmese deserved a similar emancipation. In addition to this view on politics, I also found that I had strong literary inclinations.

"In spite of the first World War I continued in my official capacity until in 1917 I was permitted to join the armed forces and became an officer in a Burmese regiment on the Palestine front in 1918 where I took part in Allenby's victory over the Turks.

"My inclination was now to leave the Indian Civil Service and devote myself to writing, but having a family to support I found it impossible to do this and returned to Burma after the war. Between 1920 and 1934 when I finally left Burma, I wrote without much success a good deal of poetry, some of which was published. It was in this period that the movement for Burmese emancipation gained force. Being a civil officer in Imperial employ, it was of course impossible for me to do more than sympathize privately with Burmese aspirations. A crisis, however, arose in 1930, which is fully described in my book *Trials in Burma*. As district magistrate of Rangoon I was obliged in a series of criminal cases to give judgment in favour of the Burmese point of view. The government was deeply offended by my attitude, which however was correct at law and could not be interfered with.

"These events had an adverse effect upon my prospects as a civil servant, but were of great advantage to me in that they determined my literary future. When I left Burma in 1934 I had the material for several of the books that I afterwards wrote. My first book, *Siamese White,* published in January 1936, was a great success and brought me into prominence, though by that time I was forty-seven years of age. I then entered with vigour upon a life of letters. The books listed below show that since then I have published twenty-five volumes and most of them concerned with oriental subjects. They have been translated into the principal European languages and nine have been published in America.

"In addition to writing on oriental subjects, I interested myself in the modern movement in painting and sculpture and was for two and a half years the art critic of the London *Observer* and for ten years the art critic of *Time and Tide.*

"The first volume of my autobiography appeared in September 1952 and when it is completed in three volumes will give in detail the story I have sketched here."

* * *

A curious, inquiring mind, a background of both scholarship and on-the-scene experience, and a lively imagination combine, in the best of Maurice Collis' work, "to make the exotic past live and breathe for us," as Eudora Welty has said. His most successful oriental studies include a volume on Confucius and Confucianism, *The First Holy One* ("intended to give pleasure rather than to instruct," the Sinologist Arthur Waley pointed out, but, a reviewer in the *Saturday Review of Literature* said, "written in a style that is so learned, so lucid, so graceful and yet instructive, that Confucius himself would surely have approved of it"); a biography of the Portuguese explorer of the Far East, Fernão Mendes Pinto, *The Grand Peregrination;* a reconstruction of life in seventeenth century Burma and India under Portuguese domination, based on the *Travels* of the Augustinian Friar Manrique, *The Land of the Great Image;* and an account of the opium wars of the 1830's in China, *Foreign Mud.*

PRINCIPAL WORKS: Siamese White, 1936; She Was a Queen, 1937; Trials in Burma, 1938; Lords of the Sunset, 1938; Sanda Mala, 1939; The Dark Door, 1940; The Great Within, 1941; British Merchant Adventurers, 1942; The Land of the Great Image, 1943; The Motherly and Auspicious, 1943; The Burmese Scene, 1944; White of Mergen (play) 1945; Quest for Sita, 1946; Foreign Mud, 1946; The First Holy One, 1948; The Descent of the God, 1948; The Grand Peregrination, 1949; Marco Polo, 1950; The Mystery of Dead Lovers, 1951; The Journey Outward (autobiography) 1952.

ABOUT: Collis, M. The Journey Outward; Leasor, J. Author by Profession.

COLUM, Mrs. MARY GUNNING (MAGUIRE) (188?-). For biographical sketch and list of earlier works and references, see TWENTIETH CENTURY AUTHORS, 1942.

* * *

From time to time Mrs. Colum contributes book reviews and critical articles to the *Saturday Review, New Republic*, and other journals. In 1947 she published a volume of her literary memories, *Life and the Dream*, which Carl Van Doren described as "the best chronicle I know of an individual Irish contribution to the intellectual life of America." It is a spirited book, not without its prejudices, but giving a rich picture of the literary circles—especially in Dublin before the First World War—in which Mrs. Colum has moved. Edmund Wilson said that she got into the book "the nobility and the fire of the movement, and her pictures of its personalities have . . . humanity and . . . dignity."

In 1953 Mrs. Colum was elected to the National Institute of Arts and Letters.

ADDITIONAL WORKS: Life and the Dream, 1947.

ABOUT: Colum, M. Life and the Dream; Hoehn, M. (ed.) Catholic Authors, I.

COLUM, PADRAIC (December 8, 1881-). For autobiographical sketch and list of earlier works and references, see TWENTIETH CENTURY AUTHORS, 1942.

* * *

Padraic Colum has received two signal honors in recent years—the award of the American Academy of Poets in 1952 and, in 1953, the Gregory Medal of the Irish Academy of Letters for distinguished work in Irish literature. "It is as an ever new singer in a very old tradition that Padraic Colum will always be remembered," John L. Sweeney wrote. His immortality, as Yeats long ago noted, is assured by the fact that at least one of his poems ("She Moves Through the Fair") has been set to music and has already acquired the status of a folksong.

ADDITIONAL WORKS: The Frenzied Prince, Being Heroic Stories of Ancient Ireland, 1943; An Anthology of Irish Verse (ed.) 1948; Collected Poems, 1953; The Vegetable Kingdom, 1954; A Treasury of Irish Folklore (ed.) 1955.

ABOUT: Hoehn, M. (ed.) Catholic Authors, I; Kunitz, S. J. & Haycraft, H. Junior Book of Authors (rev. ed.); New York Herald Tribune Book Review October 11, 1953.

COLVIN, Sir SIDNEY (June 18, 1845- May 11, 1927). For biographical sketch and list of works and references, see TWENTIETH CENTURY AUTHORS, 1942.

COMFORT, ALEXANDER (February 10, 1920-), British novelist, poet, and sociologist, who writes as Alex Comfort, was

born in North London and educated at Highgate School and Trinity College, Cambridge, where he was Styring Scholar in Classics and Senior Scholar in Natural Sciences. At the London Hospital he was qualified in medicine in 1944. In addition to varied writing pursuits, Dr. Comfort is engaged in biological and medical research.

His publications include literary and critical work, studies in zoology, chemistry and social psychology, and a long series of articles and pamphlets. His literary reputation rests chiefly on his novels *The Power House* (1944) and *On This Side Nothing* (1949). Both these and his other works express a philosophy based on humanism, pacifism, and a form of anarchism which he bases upon his interpretation of social anthropology and psychiatry. As a pacifist he refused military service in World War II, and was for a time blacklisted as a broadcaster as a result of his bitter attacks upon the policies of the Western Powers, particularly the adoption of indiscriminate bombing. He received amends in the post-war years when he was invited to broadcast a series of talks on the philosophy of humanism, and has continued since then to broadcast regularly. As a sociologist and anarchist, Dr. Comfort has remained intensely critical of both Soviet Communism and of Western social democracy; as a pacifist he has worked consistently in recent years, both through his literary work and his political activities, to prevent war between them. As a member of the Executive of the pacifist Peace Pledge Union and of the Authors' World Peace Appeal he has devoted much time to campaigning against militarism and in favor of a sociological and scientific assessment of world tensions. In his book *Authority and Delinquency in the Modern State* he put forward a theory of the relation between delinquency and the impulse to govern.

Of his work he writes: "My first book appeared in 1936, when I was still at school. If the mixture of books and pamphlets which I have produced since then seems confused, I can only say that it represents a unified effort as far as I am concerned. While the suspicion of propagandist art is sound, it obscures the fact that all writing has content. The content of mine is what I think and believe about human responsibility, and accordingly everything I write is didactic, since I have tried to express my preoccupations both in action and in print."

The (London) *Times Literary Supplement* writes that Alex Comfort is the only young English novelist of the post-World War II era "who appears in his work thoroughly committed to any particular view of life." The viewpoint he adopts, the *Times* says, is anarchism. His first novel, *The Power House*, was described as a "formidable Zolaesque story about French workers after the fall of France." It was an ambitious and talented work, "densely woven, tough-fibered, intense." His writings are controversial, his style thorny, and the reviews are necessarily mixed. But there would probably be general critical agreement with the *Times'* evaluation of his work in 1952—"There must always be a feeling about a writer as talented as Mr. Comfort that he has an exceedingly bulky something up his sleeve." His poetry, Louise Bogan commented, "illustrates something with which we are all so familiar, the border line between emotion and dream. His emotions, as well as his language, keep slipping into a haze. He can use ordinary language with good effect . . . but usually he is merely murmuring about eerie, obsessive pictures." Other critics have praised his verse for its force, deep human appeal, and "sensuous awareness of the tragic undertone of his age." He has, Kenneth Rexroth writes, "a maturity and grasp, a sense of mastery of his material, which is rare in so young a man."

PRINCIPAL WORKS: *Fiction*—The Almond Tree, 1942; The Power House, 1944; Letters from an Outpost, 1947; On This Side Nothing, 1949; A Giant's Strength, 1952. *Verse*—A Wreath for the Living, 1942; Elegies, 1944; The Song of Lazarus, 1945; The Signal to Engage, 1946; All But He Departed, 1951; A Giant's Strength, 1952. *Non-Fiction*—Art and Social Responsibility, 1946; First-Year Physiological Technique, 1948; The Novel and Our Time, 1948; The Pattern of the Future, 1949; Authority and Delinquency in the Modern State, 1950; Sexual Behaviour in Society, 1950.

ABOUT: Jarrell, R. Poetry and the Age; Rexroth, K. New British Poets; Stanford, D. The Freedom of Poetry; Arizona Quarterly 1952; Humanist (6) 1951.

COMFORT, WILL LEVINGTON (January 17, 1878-November 2, 1932). For biographical sketch and list of works and references, see TWENTIETH CENTURY AUTHORS, 1942.

COMMAGER, HENRY STEELE (October 25, 1902-), American historian, was born in Pittsburgh, Pa., the son of James Williams and Anna Elizabeth (Dan) Commager. He received his early education in the cities of Toledo and Chicago, and enrolled at the University of Chicago to obtain his Ph.B. and M.A. in philosophy, 1923 and 1924 respectively. After a year

Manny Warman

of study at the University of Copenhagen in Denmark (where he wrote a Ph.D. thesis on Danish history) he returned to Chicago for his doctorate. At New York University (1926-1938) he became instructor of history, ascending the academic ladder from the position of assistant professor to that of full professor. Meanwhile, Commager served as visiting professor at such universities as Duke, Harvard, the University of Chicago and the University of California.

In 1930 he made his first book-length contribution to the literature of American history with *The Growth of the American Republic*, written in collaboration with Samuel Eliot Morison. This work was said by Allan Nevins to be "the most entertaining, stimulating and instructive single-volume history of the United States as yet written on the plane that meets a demand for all principal facts." Three years later Commager's second book was published; done in collaboration with William Edward Dodd and Eugene Campbell Barker, it was one of the volumes of the Our Nation historical series, entitled *Our Nation's Development.* Also in that year (1934) Commager edited *Documents of American History,* "a monumental source book" which he later suggested might be regarded as his most valuable work.

After this he continued yearly to bring out books of contemporary and historical import, some of which were published in England and then translated into French, German and Italian. In 1939 Commager left New York University, transferring to Columbia to take a post as professor of American history. Around this time he completed *The Heritage of America,* in collaboration again with Allan Nevins. Shortly after, Commager's approach to his subject could be said to have taken another turn; in 1943 he had left the path of straight history for discussion and special pleading in the publication of *Majority Rule and Minority Rights.* Also, with the coming of World War II, he moved out into a more diversified activity. Articles for periodicals, *Current History, Scholastic,* the *American Mercury,* the *Nation,* etc., although not taking precedence over his former interests, began to occupy a major part of his time. From 1942 to 1943 he lectured in American history at Cambridge University in England, returning there a year later to speak on wartime living in the United States. At this period, he was also consultant of the Office of War Information, writing numerous articles, booklets and broadcasts. In Paris (1945) he served in the Information and Education Division of the Army, holding the assimilated rank of colonel.

Coming back to the United States, Commager resumed his teaching at Columbia, never ceasing a remarkable output of material and ideas in the form of university courses and publications. Indeed, as it has sometimes been noted, in the case of Commager it is difficult to locate the man behind the works. This is perhaps due (as the *Saturday Review* put it) to his intentional and "locked up disdain for any homely autobiography." That he is a Jeffersonian Democrat is generally recognized and referred to more than often in reviews about his work. Commager himself has stated that the American historian he most admires is Vernon Parrington, who was also a Jeffersonian with a liberal slant of mind.

In 1928 Commager received the Herbert B. Adams award of the American History Association. He is a Fellow of the American Scandinavian Society, a member of the American History Association, of the Massachusetts Historical Society, the American Antiquarian Society, and the Century Association. Along with the duties of his career, he follows local affairs closely (in the American press), subscribes to a dozen English periodicals, and for relaxation reads three or four novels a week. Married to the former Evan Carroll, Commager has three children and lives in Rye, N.Y. In appearance he is of medium height and stocky and has been described (in the *Saturday Review of Literature*) as "the very model of a tweedy professor of constitutional and intellectual history." It may be said of Commager that his viewpoint is the mirror that reflects the man. Reporting and observing on recent and modern times, he arrives at this conclusion in one of his later books: "The great danger that threatens us is neither heterodox thought nor orthodox thought, but the absence of thought."

PRINCIPAL WORKS: The Growth of the American Republic (with S. E. Morison), 1931; Our Nation's Development (with W. E. Dodd & E. C. Barker), 1934; (ed.) Documents of American History 1934 (1940,1950); Theodore Parker, 1936; The Heritage of America (with A. Nevins) 1939; Our Nation (with E. C. Barker) 1941; America: the Story of a Free People (with A. Nevins) 1942; Majority Rule and Minority Rights, 1943; (ed.) Tocqueville's Democracy in America, 1946; America in Perspective, 1947; (ed.) Blue and Gray, 1950; American Mind, 1950; (ed.) Living Ideas in America, 1951; America's Robert E. Lee, 1951; Chestnut Squirrel, 1952; Freedom, Loyalty, Dissent, 1954.

ABOUT: New York Herald Tribune May 19, 1950; New York Times Book Review May 12, 1950; Saturday Review of Literature March 11, 1950.

COMPTON-BURNETT, IVY (1892-   ), British novelist, was born in London, daughter of James and Katharine (Rees) Compton-Burnett. She was educated first at home, then at the Royal Holloway College of London University, taking a degree in classics. She has traveled extensively on the continent and made a number of visits to the Alps where she

Walter Bird

has pursued one of her chief interests—the study and collection of Alpine wild flowers. She is extremely reticent about the details of her life. "Autobiography," she writes, "is not in my line and my life has to the outside eye been uneventful. I have had my own flat in London for many years, and for over thirty of them I lived with Margaret Jourdain, the authority on old furniture, who died in April of this year [1951]. I am interested in all kinds of literature."

About her work, however, Miss Compton-Burnett is a little less reticent. This she discusses with the dry precision and subtle depth of the novels themselves. Her art has been described as "oblique," but it seems so only because readers are conditioned to expect the fullest exposition, narrative, and description from the novels they read. On this score Miss Compton-Burnett shocks the convention-bound reader—and at times may even irritate and exasperate him. He never knows what her characters look like. (Elizabeth Bowen once commented: "Costume and accessories play so little part that her characters sometimes give the effect of being physically, as well as psychologically, in the nude, and of not only standing and moving about in but actually sitting on thin air.") He has only a hazy notion of the time and place of the action. He may, for that matter, have only a hazy notion of the action itself. What the novel offers him, as a rule, is a series of brilliant conversations: witty, ironic, but sometimes, beneath the polished surface, filled with bitter, brooding intensity and horror. Although she disclaims any conscious plan behind her technique ("I cannot tell you why I write as I do, as I do not know. I have even tried not to do it, but find myself falling back into my own way"), she has characteristically terse and satisfying explanations for it. She cannot see why exposition and description are necessary parts of a novel. "They are not of a play, and both deal with imaginary human beings and their lives." She relies on the reader to imagine her characters: "However detailed such description is, I am sure that everyone forms his own conceptions that are different from every one else's, including the author's." As for the stylized "unnatural" talk of her characters (unnatural in the sense that it is too clever for ordinary human talk), Miss Compton-Burnett explains that it is not her intention to use either characters or dialogue from real life: "I think that actual life supplies a writer with characters much less than is thought. . . . People in life hardly seem to be definite enough to appear in print. They are not good enough or bad enough, or clever enough or stupid enough, or comic or pitiful enough. As regards plots I find real life no help at all. Real life seems to have no plots."

The world of Miss Compton-Burnett's novels is narrow. Her characters are wealthy, live in spacious but damp and drafty country houses and are attended by impeccable and inscrutable servants. The most remarkable of her characters are the children—precocious, miniature adults behind whose innocence always lurks something of the malice and the malevolence of the grown-up world. The time is the past—vaguely the Edwardian era: "I do not feel that I have any real or organic knowledge of life later than about 1910. I should not write of later times with enough grasp or confidence. I think this is why so many writers tend to write of the past. When an age is ended, you can see it as it is."

Superficially the novelist Ivy Compton-Burnett comes closest to resembling is Jane Austen. Actually, as the English novelist Elizabeth Taylor pointed out: "As soon as that is said, disparities come to mind. There is nothing lyrical in Miss Compton-Burnett and her wit is more excoriating." Miss Compton-Burnett herself says of the resemblance: "I have read Jane Austen so much, and with such enjoyment and admiration, that I may have absorbed things unconsciously. I do not think myself that my books have any real likeness to hers. I think that there is possibly some likeness between our minds."

PRINCIPAL WORKS: Pastors and Masters, 1925; Brothers and Sisters, 1929; Men and Wives, 1931; More Women than Men, 1933; A House and Its Head, 1935; Daughters and Sons, 1937; A Family and a Fortune, 1939; Parents and Children, 1941; Elders and Betters, 1944; Bullivant and the Lambs (in England: Manservant and Maidservant) 1948; Two Worlds and their Ways, 1949; Darkness and Day, 1951; Mother and Son, 1955.

ABOUT: Bowen, E. Collected Impressions; Johnson, P. H. I. Compton-Burnett; Liddell, R. A. Treatise on the Novel; New York Herald Tribune Book Review April 8, 1951; Vogue (London) July 1951.

CONAN DOYLE. See DOYLE

CONKLING, Mrs. GRACE WALCOTT (HAZARD) (1878-). For biographical sketch and list of works and references, see TWENTIETH CENTURY AUTHORS, 1942.

* * *

Mrs. Conkling lives in Northampton, Mass., where she is professor of English at Smith College. Her poems appear from time to time in *Poetry*, the *New Yorker*, and other magazines.

CONKLING, HILDA. See CONKLING, G. W. H.

"CONNELL, NORREYS." See O'RIORDAN, C. O'C.

CONNELL, RICHARD EDWARD (October 17, 1893-November 22, 1949). For autobiographical sketch and list of works and references, see TWENTIETH CENTURY AUTHORS, 1942.

* * *

Richard Connell died at his home in Beverly Hills, Calif., as the result of a heart attack, at fifty-six. He had been working on a play up to the time of his death.

Of the short stories which comprised the bulk of his writing, the New York *Times* has observed that "the very tricks which have given him a large and remunerative public have continued to rob him of the critical rewards which come to a man of his talents if he devote them to a shrewder and more critical study of the contemporary scene."

ABOUT: New York Times November 24, 1949.

CONNELLY, MARCUS COOK (December 13, 1890-). For biographical sketch and list of works and references, see TWENTIETH CENTURY AUTHORS, 1942.

* * *

In 1947 Marc Connelly joined the faculty of Yale University to teach playwriting. Teaching and helping young playwrights get their start has been his major interest ever since. He has also produced a few plays (which *Time* magazine describes as "a couple of minor successes and a couple of major turkeys"), acted a bit, and written dialogue for motion pictures. Only one new play by Connelly has had a recent Broadway production—a fable called *Story for Strangers,* about a talking horse who caused a whole town to reform. The play opened in October 1948 and ran for fifteen performances. John Chapman summed up critical opinion with the comment, "It had charm, but not enough charm." *The Green Pastures* was revived in 1951, but did not repeat its earlier Broadway success.

ABOUT: Time May 19, 1947.

"CONNINGTON, J. J." See STEWART, A. W.

CONNOLLY, CYRIL (VERNON) (September 10, 1903-), British essayist and critic, was born in Coventry, the only son of Major Matthew Connolly, an Army officer, and Muriel (Vernon) Connolly. From his Irish mother he acquired, he says, "just enough Irish blood to be afraid of the Irish temperament . . . an addiction to melancholy and to an exaggerated use of words." When he was five he was taken to South Africa where his father's regiment was stationed. His parents remained in Africa, but

Larry Burrows

the boy was sent back to England for his education and spent many of his holidays with his mother's family in Ireland.

In the autobiographical sections of *Enemies of Promise,* Connolly confesses that he was a spoiled child—"a vicious little golden-haired Caligula." His career in boarding school was relatively successful. He was popular, he says, because "I had embarked on the career which was to occupy me for the next ten years of 'trying to be funny,' " a process which he later identified as "my defence mechanism." Among other schools he attended St. Wulfric's, where two of his classmates were George Orwell and Cecil Beaton. From St. Wulfric's Connolly went up to Eton College on a scholarship. There he suffered all the miseries of the English public school caste system but also managed to acquire an excellent education. ("By the time I had left Eton I knew by heart something of the literature of five civilisations.") He won a history prize at Eton and a history scholarship to Balliol College, Oxford. (He says characteristically: "In history I was on the side of the underdog; I liked the past, the personal element, the Ages of Faith, the policies with no future. Most stimulating were the Dark Ages, there was 'no damned merit' about them, they were obscure, their futility a standing criticism of humanity.")

In the opening lines of *The Unquiet Grave* Connolly writes: "The more books we read, the sooner we perceive that the true function of a writer is to produce a masterpiece and that no other task is of any consequence." His own writing career has developed apparently out of his early and candid recognition of the fact that he could not write an epic poem or a great novel. Consequently, in 1927, he turned to literary journalism—writing articles and reviews for the *New Statesman* and other periodicals. The critical essays that he wrote over the next fifteen years and more were sharp, bold, and incisive. He believes, as R. G. Lienhardt pointed out in *Scrutiny,* that "the distinction between true criticism and creation is nonexistent," and that his merits as a critic are "somewhat practical and earthy." He is not, and does not pretend to be, a systematic critic Rather, his criticism is based on a series of personal judgments—shrewd, witty, and erratic.

In January 1940, in association with Stephen Spender and Peter Watson, Connolly published the first issue of a critical review, *Horizon.* The strength of *Horizon,* Spender has said, "lay in the vitality and idiosyncrasy of the editor"—Connolly. He published what he liked, and his taste was eclectic—new poets like Laurie Lee, W. R. Rodgers, Francis Scarfe, short novels like Evelyn Waugh's *The Loved One* and Mary McCarthy's *The Oasis,* the memoirs of Augustus John, war reporting, scholarly articles on eighteenth century French literature, his own sparkling and iconoclastic editorials. Spender left the staff in 1941 after a series of friendly disagreements with Connolly—mainly over the fact that *Horizon* lacked a clearly thought-out editorial policy on the war and the post-war world. (Probably the closest thing to a statement of *Horizon's* principles on the war appeared in June 1945: "*Horizon* has always hated war; but it is not pacifist, for it has hated fascism more and therefore recognized the value of that patriotism which derives from the healthy human desire to protect our liberties and to fight for our country against an invader.")

By 1949, Spender writes, *Horizon* "showed obvious signs of editorial tiredness." Regretfully but resignedly, Connolly ceased publication of the magazine on its tenth anniversary, announcing in his closing editorial that the move was a result of a variety of causes—a drop in subscription, the lack of sufficient excellent material, but principally, as Connolly saw it, the failure of the public to support it. This factor, he felt, was symptomatic of a general cultural decline: ". . . it is the closing time in the gardens of the West and from now on an artist will be judged only by the resonance of his solitude or the quality of his despair." When he wrote this Connolly had hoped to start publication again in a year, but this has not been done. As an editor, Spender remarks, Connolly was "like a cook, producing with each number a new dish with a new flavor. Sometimes the readers objected, finding it too light, too sweet, too lumpy, or too stodgy, but he had somehow created in them a need to taste more." *Horizon* died a natural death, but in its short lifetime it made a major contribution to contemporary literature.

Connolly's published books include one novel, *The Rock Pool*—a story of the rapid ruin of a smug young Englishman who spends a summer in an art colony on the Riviera, written in the "off-hand and brittle manner" of Norman Douglas' *South Wind* —and several volumes of essays. Perhaps the most remarkable of these is *The Unquiet Grave,* a slender volume of little essays, epigrams, and aphorisms which Anne Fremantle called "the haphazard autobiography

of [his] beleaguered ego." Edmund Wilson found it one of the best written books that came out of wartime England. *The Unquiet Grave* was written under the pseudonym of "Palinurus," the Trojan helmsman of Aeneas, who fell (or jumped) into the sea, and after drifting for three days, landed on a shore where he was murdered by the inhabitants. In Connolly's interpretation, Palinurus stands for "a certain will-to-failure or repugnance-to-success, a desire to give up at the last moment, an urge towards loneliness, isolation and obscurity."

In his life as in his work Connolly is consistently inconsistent and iconoclastic. Spender describes how he would call on him at noon "to find him lying in bed, a picture of the man of letters who writes unwillingly (though at the age of a little over forty he had written four books better than most of those of any of our generation), reading Catullus or eager to discuss the metric of Tennyson's poem 'The Daisy.' " He has, inevitably, as many critics as he has admirers. His sharpest critic is himself: "I have always disliked myself at any given moment; the total of such moments is my life." Edmund Wilson says that he has described his faults "more brilliantly than anyone else is likely to do," and concludes that "he is one of those fortunate Irishmen, like Goldsmith and Sterne and Wilde, who are born with a gift of style, a natural grace and wit, so that their jobs have the freshness of *jeux d'esprit,* and sometimes their *jeux d'esprit* turn out to stick as classics."

Connolly describes himself as a passionate reader, sight-seer, house-hunter, motorist, food and wine sampler. He has traveled extensively in Europe and he visited the United States in 1947.

PRINCIPAL WORKS: The Rock Pool (novel) 1935; Enemies of Promise, 1938; The Unquiet Grave, 1944; The Condemned Playground, 1945; Ideas and Places, 1953; (ed.) The Golden Horizon, 1953.

ABOUT: Connolly, C. Enemies of Promise, The Condemned Playground; Lienhardt, R. G. *in* The Importance of Scrutiny (ed. E. Bentley); Wilson, E. Classics and Commercials; Atlantic April 1946, December 1950; Commonweal August 2, 1946; Current Biography 1947. New Yorker December 14, 1946; Time March 25, 1946.

CONNOLLY, JAMES BRENDAN

(1868-   ). For biographical sketch and list of earlier works and references, see TWENTIETH CENTURY AUTHORS, 1942.

* * *

James Brendan Connolly's stories of Gloucester fisherman have become "near classics" in the literature of the sea. In 1944 he published his autobiography, *Sea-Borne*, a lively record of his adventures on land and sea. He lives in Boston, Mass.

ADDITIONAL WORKS: Master Mariner: Life and Voyages of Amasa Delano, 1943; Sea-Borne: Thirty Years Avoyaging, 1944.

ABOUT: Connolly, J. B. Sea-Borne; Hoehn, M. (ed.) Catholic Authors, I; Marriner, E. C. Jim Connolly and the Fishermen of Gloucester; Commonweal July 14, 1944; New York Herald Tribune Book Review June 12, 1949.

"CONNOR, RALPH." See GORDON, C. W.

CONRAD, JOSEPH (December 3, 1857-August 3, 1924). For biographical sketch and list of works and references, see TWENTIETH CENTURY AUTHORS, 1942.

* * *

ABOUT: Bowen, E. Collected Impressions; Guérard, A. J. Joseph Conrad; Leavis, F. R. The Great Tradition; Retinger, J. H. Conrad and his Contemporaries; Warner, O. Joseph Conrad; Woolf, V. The Captain's Death Bed and Other Essays; Wright, W. F. Romance and Tragedy in Joseph Conrad; Zabel, M. D. *Introduction to Viking Portable Conrad.*

*CONSTANTIN-WEYER, MAURICE (April 24, 1881-). For autobiographical sketch and list of works and references, see TWENTIETH CENTURY AUTHORS, 1942.

* * *

Since the end of World War II, Constantin-Weyer has published a number of books of fiction and non-fiction. Among the latter are historical studies (including a history of Vichy, France) and a volume on natural history with special attention to John James Audubon. None of these has appeared in English translation.

* kôns tän tăn' vä yâr'

COOK, GEORGE CRAM (October 7, 1873-January 14, 1924). For biographical sketch and list of works and references, see TWENTIETH CENTURY AUTHORS, 1942.

COOKE, (ALFRED) ALISTAIR (November 20, 1908-), British-born essayist and journalist, was born in Manchester, England, the son of a Wesleyan preacher, Samuel Cooke, and the former Mary Elizabeth Byrne. He grew up in his native Lancashire, and entered Jesus College, Cambridge, as a candi-

date for an honors degree in 1927. He received his B.A., having passed the English tripos, in 1930, and spent another year at Cambridge studying for the Diploma in Education. In his college days Cooke intended to become an actor, and he was a founder of the Cambridge University Mummers, a dramatic society. In 1931 he published the first of a number of articles in the American *Theatre Arts Monthly*—this one on the Cambridge Festival Theatre.

Cooke's first visit to the United States was in 1932 when he came to Yale on a Commonwealth Fund fellowship and specialized in the study of the American language. The fellowship was renewed, and he spent the following year studying at Harvard. He then returned to England and joined the British Broadcasting Company as a cinema critic. His duties were soon extended to general radio reporting. In 1936 he became London correspondent of the National Broadcasting Company. He covered a number of news events for American radio audiences—among them the abdication of King Edward VIII, the Munich Conference, and the Wimbledon tennis matches.

In 1938 Cooke returned to the United States as commentator on American affairs for the B.B.C. and as special correspondent for the London *Times*. He began to contribute articles regularly to American and British periodicals—his subjects ranging widely from pieces on American films (his first book published in America was on the actor Douglas Fairbanks) to observations on the American scene based on a 20,000-mile, six-month auto trip all over the country. In 1941 he became an American citizen. Four years later Cooke became American correspondent for the internationally-known *Manchester Guardian*. His most distinguished reporting for this paper was the series of articles he wrote on the two perjury trials of Alger Hiss in 1949 and 1950. In the Hiss case Cooke found a theme of real tragic stature, but he never forgot that his own job was that of a reporter. "A reporter's job is to see and record, however inconclusive or contradictory his impressions may be," he told Harvey Breit in an interview. "You don't line up the heroes and the villains, and a man can be both at the same time."

It was Cooke's willingness to suspend judgment on an issue as controversial and heated as the Hiss case which made his book-length report on it, *A Generation on Trial*, so valuable a document. *Time* called it "a model of balance and lucidity," and Richard Rovere, in the *New Yorker*, hailed it as "one of the most vivid and literate descriptions of an American political event that has ever been written." The book was prefaced by a long essay which recalled the shifts in political thinking in the era between the two world wars. In the historical light in which Cooke saw it, his report was a study of "the trials of a man who was judged in one decade for what he was said to have done in another."

Since 1947 Cooke has been giving a series of broadcasts for the B.B.C. interpreting American life to British audiences. Cooke calls these talks "radio essays." They are leisurely, carefully constructed, and charmingly written pieces. Published as *One Man's America*, they proved to be no solemn attempt to study American social institutions, but a collection of shrewd and witty observations which many a more serious scholar might have overlooked in his researches. In 1952 Cooke made his debut as host on the Ford Foundation's television program *Omnibus*. He has an eminently successful television personality—poised, friendly, casual, urbane but never supercilious. Harvey Breit has described him as "tall, slim, nattily dressed, and all in all [he] has a kind of King George look—but he hardly ever sounds it." Cooke lives in New York City with his wife, the former Jane (White) Hawkes, whom he married in 1946. He has a daughter from this marriage and a son from an earlier marriage, in 1934, to Ruth Emerson.

PRINCIPAL WORKS: Garbo and the Night Watchmen (ed.) 1937; Douglas Fairbanks, 1940; Generation on Trial: U.S.A. vs. Alger Hiss, 1950; One Man's America (in England: Letters from America) 1952; Christmas Eve, 1952.

ABOUT: Current Biography 1952; Life August 25, 1952; Look September 11, 1951; New York Herald Tribune Book Review October 1, 1950; New York Times Book Review October 8, 1950; Time March 19, 1951.

COOKE, CROFT-. See CROFT-COOKE

COOPER, COURTNEY RYLEY (October 31, 1886-September 29, 1940).
For biographical sketch and list of works and references, see TWENTIETH CENTURY AUTHORS, 1942.

* * *

ADDITIONAL WORK: Action in Diamonds, 1942.

COOPER, LOUISE FIELD (March 8, 1905-), American novelist and short story writer, reports: "I was born in Hartford, Conn., and enjoyed a most conventional uneventful childhood and upbringing. School began when I was eight. Fresh air had just become fashionable and the neighborhood children sat for four years in a bleak, porch-like structure, our legs stuffed into felt bags and our heads bowed in grey hoods.  Ink froze in the inkwells from, as I recall it, November to May, and the canvas sheeting that was supposed to protect us from the winds of winter soon resembled sails that had battled around the Horn. Four more years in another day school, mercifully indoors, and three years at boarding school in Farmington completed such formal education as came my way. Then I did very minor jobs on a newspaper for one winter and the next, in company with another girl, managed to run into the ground a small library and branch of the best book shop in town; this was not intentional, but perhaps it was inevitable. Soon after this I married a lawyer and we moved to New Haven.

"We live in a long white house against a hill in the country to the west of town, and over the past twenty-odd years have been bringing up a variety of children and many generations of large birds. The children are three of our own, two English girls who spent the war years here, and now a Chinese boy who came for a visit to the United States when he was eleven and stayed on.

"Mornings I write and afternoons I often garden. Even in the cold New England winters I am concerned with more flats of seedlings than there is room for; I always believe every single seedling will eventually burst into wonderful bloom, and often they do. I find that what one is writing can be kept quietly under control and private, in a few notebooks and a neat pile of papers, but that carnations and lavender and wallflower seedlings spread all over the place. This is as it should be, because I never talk about my writing, but I am willing to go on endlessly, to anyone who will listen, about the facts of horticulture, new to me but doubtless known for hundreds of years to all gardeners' boys.

"Now that the children are all married or away at school or college, one might suppose one would have more time, but it doesn't seem to work out that way, and it is probably all for the best. More time spent on them would not improve my books, and there are not enough gardens on the place to accommodate the wallflowers as it is. I live now by the same routine I always have, and continue to enjoy it. In recent years we have gone several times to Europe, taking an old station wagon which can carry many children and a moderate amount of luggage. England is the country we most often visit, probably because there they produce the world's best of the two things I most admire—short story, poetry and novel writing, and gardens."

* * *

Louise Field Cooper's first short stories appeared in the *New Yorker* and her writing has, in common with many stories published in that magazine, the qualities of restraint, subtle humor, and personal detachment. Her most successful novel to date is *The Boys from Sharon*, which was a Book-of-the-Month Club selection. This story of the visit of two little boys to the home of a stuffy and overbearing elderly lady was praised for its "appealing human quality."

PRINCIPAL WORKS: The Lighted Box, 1942; The Deer on the Stairs, 1943; Love and Admiration (short stories) 1944; Summer Stranger, 1947; The Boys from Sharon, 1950; The Cheerful Captive, 1954.

ABOUT: Warfel, H. R. American Novelists of Today; Current Biography 1950.

COPPARD, ALFRED EDGAR (January 4, 1878-). For biographical sketch and list of earlier works and references, see TWENTIETH CENTURY AUTHORS, 1942.

* * *

A. E. Coppard lives in a country home in Essex. Several volumes of his short stories have appeared in recent years, some of them new, many of them reprints of earlier stories. He has published no poetry lately, but, if such a thing is possible, his poetry is in his prose. William Peden wrote of him: "If he is first of all a teller of tales, Coppard is next a poet and an artist. Passages of real lyric beauty appear and reappear in his stories; the final effect of much of his work is closer to that evoked by poetry than by prose."

ADDITIONAL WORKS: Ugly Anna, and Other Tales, 1944; Fearful Pleasures (short stories) 1946; The Dark-Eyed Lady: Fourteen Tales, 1947; Collected Tales, 1948; Lucy in Her Pink Jacket, 1954.

CORBETT, ELIZABETH FRANCES (September 30, 1887-). For biographical sketch and list of earlier works and references, see TWENTIETH CENTURY AUTHORS, 1942.

* * *

Elizabeth Corbett continues to write her pleasant and unpretentious novels with the ease and authority that come of long years of experience. She publishes a new novel nearly every year and contributes stories to the popular magazines. Isabelle Mallet once pointed out that Miss Corbett has made a fair bargain with her readers: "In exchange for a little interest and a little more credulity, she offers conscientious entertainment, pleasantly written and easy on the nerve centers."

ADDITIONAL WORKS: Early Summer, 1942; Excuse Me, Mrs. Meigs, 1943; Golden Grain, 1943; Red-Haired Lady, 1945; Lady With a Parasol, 1946; Immortal Helen, 1948; Eve and Christopher, 1949; Duke's Daughter, 1950; Portrait of Isabelle, 1951; Richer Harvest, 1952; In Miss Armstrong's Room, 1953.

ABOUT: Warfel, H. R. American Novelists of Today.

CORBUSIER. See LE CORBUSIER

CORELLI, MARIE (1855-April 21, 1924). For biographical sketch and list of works and references, see TWENTIETH CENTURY AUTHORS, 1942.

* * *

ABOUT: Mott, F. L. Golden Multitudes; Life and Letters Today June 1944; New Statesman and Nation August 2, 1947.

COREY, LEWIS (October 13, 1894-September 16, 1953). For biographical sketch and list of earlier works and references, see TWENTIETH CENTURY AUTHORS, 1942.

* * *

Lewis Corey, who had been born Louis C. Fraina in Italy and brought to the United States as a child, died in New York City of a cerebral hemorrhage. He was survived by his wife, Esther, and a daughter, Olga. After playing an important part in the organization of the Communist Party in the United States, Corey left the party and became an active anti-Communist. He served for a time as educational director of the International Ladies' Garment Workers' Union, as research director of the Union for Democratic Action, and as educational director of the A.F. of L.'s Amalgamated Meat Cutters and Butcher Workmen. For the latter group he wrote *Meat and Man: A Study of Monopoly, Unionism, and Food Policy*, the aim of which, he said in the preface, was "to study the meat industry, within the complex of general economic organization and its relation to other food industries." It was praised as a well-organized and valuable collection of useful information on the food problems of the world. From 1942 to 1951 Corey was professor of political economy at Antioch College.

In 1949 Corey filed application for United States citizenship, but just nine months before his death, the Department of Justice began deportation proceedings against him under the McCarran Act. On his attorney's advice, Corey applied for an Italian visa, planning to leave the United States and then to apply for re-entry. He died before the government could act on his application.

ADDITIONAL WORK: Meat and Man, 1950.

ABOUT: Antioch Review Winter 1953-54; New York Post October 20, 1953; New York Times September 17, 1953.

COREY, PAUL (July 8, 1903-). For biographical sketch and list of earlier works and references, see TWENTIETH CENTURY AUTHORS, 1942.

* * *

Paul Corey began his own private "back-to-the-soil" movement some years ago. With the end of World War II and the increased de-urbanization which the housing shortage brought, he has found an ever-widening and more enthusiastic audience for his forthright and practical books on country living and self-help. In *Buy an Acre* Corey suggests that in this movement America will find a "Second Frontier"—"a crusade," as one reviewer put it, "against mass production and living up to the Joneses." John T. Frederick called *Buy an Acre* "one of the most truly far-seeing and most deeply significant books about our times that I've read."

The Coreys now live in Sonoma, Calif., in a home which they built themselves. Since 1950 he has been writing a series of articles on building and carpentry for *Popular Science* magazine. He has also written several books on farm life for children and teen agers.

ADDITIONAL WORKS: Buy an Acre, 1944; Build a Home, 1946; Acres of Antaeus (novel) 1946; Homemade Homes, 1950. *Juveniles*—Red Tractor, 1944; Five Acre Hill, 1946; Little Jeep, 1946; Shad Haul, 1947; Corn Gold Farm, 1948.

ABOUT: Warfel, H. R. American Novelists of Today.

CORKERY, DANIEL (1878-), Irish critic, dramatist, poet, and writer of fiction, writes: "My family name though rare still survives in southwest  Ireland. I was born in Cork City, the son of many generations of craftsmen who had lived and died there. Schooled by the Presentation Brothers I became a teacher and worked as such till 1922. Literature and art were my private studies. In 1901 I became an enthusiast in the struggle to make the Irish language once more the vernacular of the country. I am still an enthusiast. In that language I found unbroken literary tradition of 1500 years, its poetry uniquely distinctive since its moulds and spirit had easily resisted the impact of the Classical Renaissance, a strange thing considering that its writers were learned in the classics and spoke Latin 'like a vulgar tongue.' Many of them were churchmen living under the protection of the native Irish princes.

"In 1908 Terence MacSwiney, who later was as Lord Mayor of Cork to die in London on hunger-strike, myself and a few others founded in Cork a dramatic movement something like Yeats' movement in Dublin. We held that Dublin should never have been chosen: Bergen, not Christiania, the capital of Norway, had been chosen by Ibsen for his somewhat similar venture. Capitals incline to be cosmopolitan. Of our little theatre I was producer; I also wrote plays. So did MacSwiney and others. It lived until actors, writers, and all went into the movement to free Ireland. In 1922 I gave up school-teaching and became a teacher (itinerant) of art in the county of Cork.

"Some years later I became an organizer of adult classes for the study of Irish in the same county. Always I had been writing in journals and papers. I had my first book of short stories published in 1916. I took out my M.A. degree and in 1931 was appointed professor of English in the Cork College of the National University of Ireland. When I retired in 1947 the University conferred the D. Litt. degree on me. In 1951 Mr. de Valera nominated me Senator of the Republic of Ireland."

* * *

Corkery considers *The Hidden Ireland*, published in 1925, his most important work. "It is," he writes, "a study of the voluminous poetry produced in Munster under the most dire conditions by the penalised, enslaved Irish people. Although that poetry gives a moving and beautifully wrought picture of the life of the people as a people apart from, and perhaps six or eight times as numerous as the alien English-minded Ascendancy that ruled the country, the professional historians, men like Lecky, had never looked at it when writing the history of Ireland in that self-same century! Hence the name of the book."

Corkery's only novel, *The Threshold of Quiet*, "may well be his masterpiece," Vivian Mercier and David H. Greene comment in their *1000 Years of Irish Prose*. Probably his most controversial book was his *Synge and Anglo-Irish Literature*. No biography of Corkery would be complete, Mercier and Greene write, without reference to his influence, "both directly and through his writings, on such younger Corkmen as Sean O'Faoláin, Frank O'Connor, and the gifted sculptor Seamus Murphy, author of *Stone Mad*."

PRINCIPAL WORKS: *Drama*—The Labour Leader, 1920; The Yellow Bittern and Other Plays, 1920. *Short Stories*—A Munster Twilight, 1916; The Hounds of Banba, 1920; The Stormy Hills, 1926; Earth out of Earth, 1939; The Wager (collected stories) 1950. *Criticism*—The Hidden Ireland, 1925; Synge and Anglo-Irish Literature, 1931. *Novel*—The Threshold of Quiet, 1917. *Poetry*—A Book of Lyrics, 1926.

ABOUT: Boyd, E. A. Ireland's Literary Renaissance; Colum, P. Cross Roads in Ireland; De Blacam, A. S. Gentle Ireland; De Blacam, A. S. Irish Literature; Gwynn, S. L. Irish Literature and Drama; Mercier, V. and Greene, D. H. 1000 Years of Irish Prose; Shuster, G. N. The Catholic Spirit in Modern English Literature.

*CORLE, EDWIN (May 7, 1906-), American novelist, biographer, and writer on the Southwest, writes: "I was born in Wild-

wood, N.J. I attended public schools in both Wildwood and Philadelphia. When I was seventeen my parents moved to California (we had traveled widely in California several years before) and I completed high school at Hollywood. The next four years I spent at the University of California at Los Angeles, majoring in English and taking a number of courses in history and philosophy and science. I received a degree of Bachelor of Arts in 1928. I spent

* "Corle is pronounced korl."

the next two years at Yale University as a graduate student in the College of Fine Arts, in particular in the Department of Drama, where I studied playwriting under the late George Pierce Baker.

"Leaving Yale in the spring of 1930 I returned to California and wrote mostly for radio, with a few brief stints in MGM and RKO. In 1932 I left radio to devote all my time to creative writing. In November of that year Ellery Sedgwick, editor of the *Atlantic Monthly*, accepted a short story which I called 'Amethyst' and which had a Mojave Desert setting. This was my first professional appearance in print. The story has since been reprinted a number of times and was chosen by Edward J. O'Brien for his *Best Short Stories of 1934*. While I rarely write short stories any more, in those early years I contributed to the *New Yorker, Harper's, Forum, Liberty, Scribner's, Esquire, Yale Review, Virginia Quarterly, Prairie Schooner, American Mercury*, and a number of others. My short stories have appeared in about a dozen anthologies of which *The New Yorker Book of Stories* is probably the best known.

"In 1938 I traveled over most of Europe and wrote articles for newspaper publication on those troubled times. Some of my European experiences were used for background material for the novel *Three Ways to Mecca*.

"The novel *People on the Earth* was awarded a silver medal by the Commonwealth Club of San Francisco. In 1941 I received a Guggenheim Fellowship for creative writing and traveled throughout Mexico for six months.

"My desire to write began early. My parents bought me all the books I wanted, and I read day and night. At fifteen I was devouring such contrasting authors as Mark Twain, William Shakespeare, Jack London, Henry Fielding, Sinclair Lewis, Daniel Defoe, Harry Leon Wilson, Booth Tarkington, and William Wordsworth. If anyone ever 'learned' to write at all, I certainly learned a great deal, at an impressionable age, from those authors. Without my knowing it, I was receiving a course in authorship.

"It was inevitable that the time would come when I would want to write a story myself. This happened at sixteen—a schoolboy novel that has yet to see the light of day —and I have been writing ever since.

"At present I am at work on a series of novels about California, to be interspersed with occasional non-fiction books about the American Southwest.

"In 1944 I married Jean Armstrong of Winnetka, Ill. We have one daughter, Jean Corle, born June 27, 1945. I am a member of the Players Club of New York, and our home is in Santa Barbara, Calif."

PRINCIPAL WORKS: *Fiction*—Mojave (short stories) 1934; Fig Tree John, 1935; People on the Earth, 1937; Burro Alley, 1938; Solitaire, 1940; Coarse Gold, 1942; Three Ways to Mecca, 1947; In Winter Light, 1949; Billy the Kid, 1953. *Non-Fiction*—Desert Country, 1941; Listen, Bright Angel, 1946 (republished as The Story of the Grand Canyon, 1951); John Studebaker: An American Dream, 1948; The Royal Highway, 1949; The Gila: River of the Southwest, 1951.

ABOUT: Wilson Library Bulletin March 1943.

CORNFORD, FRANCIS MACDONALD

(February 27, 1874-January 3, 1943), British classical scholar, was the son of the Reverend James Cornford and Mary (Macdonald) Cornford. He attended St. Paul's School and entered Trinity College, Cambridge, on a classical scholarship. In 1904 he became lecturer in classics at Trinity; and—except for interruptions in 1914-18 when he served as sergeant major and musketry instructor in the Home Force, and in 1928 when he visited the United States to give a lecture series at Harvard University—Cornford spent the rest of his life at Cambridge. In 1931 he was made the first holder of the newly-created chair of Ancient Philosophy. He was married in 1909 to the poet Frances Darwin (daughter of the botanist Sir Francis Darwin) whom he had met when they were both studying under Jane Harrison, the distinguished classical scholar. They had three sons and two daughters.

The influence upon Cornford of Jane Harrison's teaching was very strong. Her studies in primitive Greek religion and ritual and in comparative mythology—along with the anthropological work of another Cambridge scholar, Sir James Frazer—showed him the need "to realize the atmosphere of thought and feeling" in which the ancient Greeks lived. His particular merit as a scholar, W. K. C. Guthrie has pointed out, was "his constant awareness that all systems of religious and philosophical thought have two sides, the conscious and the unconscious or . . . the intellectual and the instinctive."

His quest was an understanding of the Greek mind. His first book, *Thucydides Mythistoricus*, a study of the mind and art of the ancient historian, was considered by conservative scholars a daring and unorthodox work of scholarship. By 1912, however, with the publication of his *From Religion to Philosophy*, the soundness and validity of his scholarship were widely recognized. By this time Cornford had formulated the major problem of his life's work. "The origin of philosophy," he wrote, "cannot be understood without a study of the representations which philosophy inherits from religion." And these representations, he adds, religion inherits in turn from "the social order of the primitive tribe." To understand Heraclitus, or even Plato, one must understand the atmosphere of thought and feeling in which they lived and the habits of thought they inherited from the past. His valuable study *The Origin of Attic Comedy* was an illustration of this thesis, tracing various fixed elements in comedy back to the fertility rituals of Dionysus.

In 1927 Cornford agreed to complete the translation, with notes and commentary, of Aristotle's *Physics* which had been started by Dr. Joseph Wicksteed but abandoned because of the latter's ill health. Two years later volume I of this translation was published in the Loeb Classical Library. Cornford's interest in the broad social and intellectual bases of Greek culture and his clear and forthright English prose style, combined with a sound linguistic background, suited him ideally for the role of translator and annotator of ancient Greek texts. He adapted to his translations his classroom method of presenting a paragraph of the text, then following it with his explanation and comments. As a result he was able to present in lucid terms one of the most difficult of Plato's dialogues, the *Timaeus*, to give a complete exposition of Plato's theory of knowledge in his translations of the *Theatetus* and *Sophist*, and to offer a new translation of the *Republic* which, Jacques Barzun wrote, "will rank with the best Elizabethan and Victorian work, with Florio and Scott-Moncrieff." Sir Maurice Bowra, reviewing the *Timaeus* translation, was especially impressed with Cornford's commentary —"Concise and clear, it shirks no difficulty and is never irrelevant. One is torn between amazement at Mr. Cornford's easy mastery of a vast literature and admiration for the self-effacing way in which he keeps his knowledge in strict control."

Cornford was a stimulating classroom teacher. His lectures, W. K. C. Guthrie recalls, "gave one the peculiar sensation of mental well-being which comes from following a skilfully and closely woven pattern of argument, of necessity intricate but never obscure." He took an active part in the organization and administration of the Working Men's College. His friends remembered him as a witty and charming personality, with a talent for writing parodies and composing Latin valentines. One of his earliest books, *Microcosmographia Academica*, was a lively university satire, still in print and still timely academic reading. Gilbert Murray writes of him: "He combined great personal charm and courtesy with a certain aloofness and apparent indifference to worldly values and received opinions. A rather lonely thinker, he pursued a particular path of research which at first was not fully defined even to himself, but from tentative beginnings became gradually clearer and gave a unity to his intellectual life."

PRINCIPAL WORKS: Thucydides Mythistoricus, 1907; Microcosmographia Academica, 1908; From Religion to Philosophy, 1913; The Origin of Attic Comedy, 1914; Greek Religious Thought, 1923; (tr. & ed. with P. H. Wicksteed) Aristotle's Physics, 2 vols., 1929, 1930; Laws of Motion in Ancient Thought, 1932; Before and After Socrates, 1932; (tr. & ed.) Plato's Theory of Knowledge (Theatetus & Sophist) 1935; (tr. & ed.) Plato's Cosmology (Timaeus) 1937; (tr. & ed.) Plato and Parmenides (Parmenides' Way of Truth & Plato's Parmenides) 1939; (tr. & ed.) Plato's Republic, 1941; The Unwritten Philosophy, and Other Essays, 1950; Principium Sapientiae, 1952.

ABOUT: Guthrie, W. K. C. Introduction to Cornford's The Unwritten Philosophy; Murray, G. F. M. Cornford, 1874-1943 (Proceedings of British Academy, vol. 29) 1944; London Times Literary Supplement January 9, 1943; Nature January 30, 1943.

*CORTISSOZ, ROYAL (1869-October 17, 1948). For biographical sketch and list of works and references, see TWENTIETH CENTURY AUTHORS, 1942.

* * *

Royal Cortissoz died at his home in New York City at seventy-nine. He had suffered for three years from the heart ailment which caused his death. From the onset of his illness he had been on leave from the New York *Herald Tribune*, after fifty-three years as that journal's art critic.

A self-avowed traditionalist, Cortissoz stated his own creed of art criticism: "that a work of art should embody an idea, that it

* kôr tĕ′sŭz

should be beautiful, and that it should show sound craftsmanship." *Art Digest*, referring to him as the "staunch and revered dean of art critics," says that "a scholarly turn of mind, vast reading, cultivated as well as instinctive taste and a warm heart contributed to his success that came early and the veneration that followed." His interests spread far beyond the field of art," according to the New York *Times*, "and he was as catholic and sound in his knowledge of books, music and architecture as in the sphere distinctively his own."

ABOUT: Art Digest November 1, 1946; Art News November 1948; New York Times October 18, 1948.

"CORVO, BARON." See ROLFE, F.

CORWIN, NORMAN LEWIS (May 3, 1910-), American radio dramatist and novelist, writes: "I was born into the age of fission and psychiatry in Boston at a time when the great tradition of that city still hung comfortably on her. The interests of my boyhood vacillated between the Boston Symphony, the Boston Braves, and the Boston Public Library. I was an in-different student, doing well only in subjects which appealed to me, and either flunking or barely passing those which didn't. I cannot reconcile my early scholastic *ennui* with the areas of later interest, for the very studies which bored me most in my schooling (mathematics, languages, history) fascinated me in adult life.

"Having gladly rid myself of formal schooling, I went fresh from high school to newspaper work, and for ten years, through and beyond the Depression, I covered everything from politics through crime to music, and was at various times a sports writer, movie critic and radio editor. In 1936 I first let myself into the mixmaster of New York City, and after some skidding and churning I landed, more or less upright, in the program department of the Columbia Broadcasting System. I became a director of dramatic programs, and, after acquiring the techniques of production, I began to write plays.

"Fortunately for myself, radio was then in a period of relative freedom—freedom to experiment, freedom to speak, freedom from the vulgarity, venality and even cowardice that, in later years, was to blight the medium. In 1941 I was presented by CBS with the Columbia Workshop to do with what I wished, and I did. The series '26 by Corwin' came out of this, as did two later series called 'Columbia Presents Corwin.' Besides these, productions too numerous to cite here were scattered across the years 1938-1948—probably one hundred and fifty original broadcasts. At the beginning of 1949 I left CBS over a matter of principle involving, of all things, the self-ownership of subsidiary rights to my radio writing.

"In 1946, as recipient of the Wendell Willkie One World Flight Award, I flew around the world, recording interviews and impressions toward the production of a series of broadcasts called 'One World Flight.' The material that went into the series—comprising interviews with leaders of state, workers, farmers, housewives, unemployed, the Pope, Nehru, Attlee, MacArthur (in his Tokyo days), Beneš, Chou En Lai, Roxas, Katchaturian, Prince Bertil, Viscount Wavell, etc., etc., was addressed to the objective of defining and reporting on the areas of agreement in the world, where the late Willkie's concept of global unity had taken hold, or had the best chance of surviving. Alas, no more ephemeral or forlorn enterprise could have been undertaken, for the cold war, with all its ugly consequences, placed the One World idea in a glacial deep-freeze, from which it may not emerge in our time.

"In 1949 I joined the United Nations as Chief of Special Projects in Radio, and under its aegis produced several documentaries for worldwide distribution. In between radio broadcasts I wrote two motion pictures and several books.

"Politically I am a liberal, which does not add years to one's life in a period conspicuous for its lack of liberalism. As for my radio, which was my first love, my emotion is that of sadness for an old friend, now bedridden, who has been kind and generous to many writers, including me. This disease is probably incurable: radio may die, as a cultural force, of the after-effects of the birth of television; and, worst of all, it will be succeeded by this half-breed that is neither pictures nor radio but both, an omniphage devouring everything around it, chomping steadily into the economy of books, sports, movies, and the theatre itself.

"I have a number of projects before me —books, plays, raising a family and keeping gophers at bay on my California hillside. I believe these will give me plenty to cope with in the immediate future."

PRINCIPAL WORKS: *Plays*—They Fly Through the Air with the Greatest of Ease, 1939; Thirteen by Corwin, 1942; More by Corwin, 1944; On a Note of Triumph, 1945; Untitled and Other Radio Dramas, 1947; The Plot to Overthrow Christmas, 1952. *Novel*—Dog in the Sky, 1953.

ABOUT: Brown, J. M. Seeing Things; Hamburger, P. The Oblong Blur; Coronet Magazine December 1945; Current Biography 1940; Newsweek September 26, 1949; New York Times Magazine August 2, 1942; Theatre Arts September 1942; Time March 4, 1946, January 27, 1947.

*COSTAIN, THOMAS BERTRAM (May 8, 1885-   ), Canadian-American novelist, historian, and editor, was born in Brantford, Ontario, the son of John Herbert Costain and Mary (Schultz) Costain. His father came from the Isle of Man. He was educated in the public schools of Brantford and in 1952 the honorary degree of D.Litt. was conferred upon him by the University of Western Ontario.

Karsh, Ottawa

While still in high school, Thomas Costain wrote three unpublished novels. The acceptance and publication of a mystery story by the Brantford *Courier* led to his being offered a job as reporter for that paper. In 1908 he progressed to the editorship of the Guelph (Ontario) *Daily Mercury*. Two years later he joined the staff of the Maclean Publishing Company (now The Maclean-Hunter Publishing Corporation) in Toronto, first as editor of three of their trade journals, later becoming editor of *Maclean's Magazine*, which position he held until he came to this country in 1920 to become chief associate editor for George Horace Lorimer on the *Saturday Evening Post*. He stayed with the *Post* for fourteen years during which time he discovered and developed the talents of a number of writers who later attained considerable renown. In 1934 he became eastern story editor for 20th Century-Fox Film Corporation, and in 1937, took on the editorship of *American Cavalcade*. From 1939 to 1946 Costain was advisory editor of Doubleday and Company, Inc. His first three novels and a collaboration on a biography were written and published during these years while he was still handing out plots and ideas, still encouraging other writers. Since 1946 he has devoted himself exclusively to his own writing.

* kŏs'tăn

233

In the ten years from 1942, when his first
novel appeared, to 1952, he wrote seven full-
length novels, each of which was made a
selection of one of the major book clubs;
two volumes of English history; and a biography (in collaboration). The work and the
plans for work continue unabated. Early
in 1953, he had a volume of Canadian history well on the way toward completion, an
outline for the next historical novel ready,
and reservations in hand for sailing to England on a research trip in connection with
the third volume of The Pageant of England
series.

It was while he was running the Guelph
Mercury that young Costain met Ida Randolph Spragge of that city, having first seen
her when she sang the part of Ruth in an
amateur production of *The Pirates of Pen-
zance.* They were married in 1910. Theirs
is a charming close-knit family consisting of
two daughters, Molly (Mrs. Howard Haycraft) and Dora (Mrs. Henry D. Steinmetz),
and one grandson, Thomas Costain Steinmetz.

Tall, broad-shouldered and erect in his
late sixties, he has snow-white hair, a pink
and white complexion, and clear blue eyes.
Everything about him is quick, alert, nervous,
underneath a calm and poised exterior, that
is, calm except for his eager buoyancy and,
on occasion, his righteous indignation.

An evaluation of Mr. Costain as author of
histories and historical romances is attempted
in the citation by the University of Western
Ontario granting him the honorary degree
of Doctor of Letters. His "inherent gifts"
are designated as "the fundamental interest
in people, the power as a story-teller, the
facility as a writer, the capacity as an
historian, the skillfulness as a craftsman."
The citation concludes: "Democracy is a
philosophy of life; Mr. Costain is the historian of that philosophy."

PRINCIPAL WORKS: For My Great Folly, 1942;
Ride With Me, 1943; Joshua (in collaboration
with Rogers MacVeagh), 1943; The Black Rose,
1945; The Moneyman, 1947; High Towers, 1949;
The Conquerors, 1949; Son of a Hundred Kings,
1950; The Magnificent Century, 1951; The Silver
Chalice, 1952; The White and the Gold, 1954.

ABOUT: Chicago Sunday Tribune Magazine of
Books September 16, 1951; Cosmopolitan Maga-
zine October 1947; Current Biography 1953; Mac-
lean's Magazine January 15, 1946; Mayfair February
1952; New York Herald Tribune Book Review
December 11, 1949, August 10, 1952; New York
Times Book Review, August 17, 1952; New York
World Telegram June 2, 1949; Saturday Review
February 23, 1952; Wilson Library Bulletin No-
vember 1945; Writers' Digest June, 1949.

COUCH. See QUILLER-COUCH

*COULTER, ELLIS MERTON (July
20, 1890-), American historian, writes: "I
was born in Catawba County, N.C., five miles
from a railway, of
German ancestry,
which came to Amer-
ica from the Palatin-
ate Rhine in colonial
times. My forebears
first settled in Penn-
sylvania, but before
the Revolution they
migrated to North
Carolina in a party
with Daniel Boone,

locating in the Catawba River valley and refusing to follow Boone farther—the grant of
land on which they settled still remains in
the ownership of my family. When I was
two years old my father moved to a little
railway station, first called Icard, then Happy
Home, and finally Connelly Springs in the
adjoining county of Burke, where he engaged
extensively in the lumber business and where
some members of the family have continued
to live. Longevity is a family trait, both
grandmothers living to be more than ninety,
and my father and mother eighty-seven and
eighty-nine respectively. Both grandfathers
were Confederate soldiers, one not returning
from the war.

"I received my first education in a one-
room schoolhouse and my high schooling in
a small Methodist institution called Ruther-
ford College. I was half way through it
before I found out that it was not really a
college (it had one time been so) and that
there was further knowledge to be had. As
my father wanted me to be a minister in the
Lutheran Church, the faith of the family,
he sent me to a Lutheran school, Concordia
College in Conover, N.C. Not wanting to
be a minister, I remained there one year
and then entered the University of North
Carolina where I received the A.B. degree in
1913. The next year I was principal of a
high school in Glen Alpine, N.C. Being interested in history as far back as I can
remember, I decided to temper my Southern,
Confederate heritage with what a Middle
Western institution had to offer; and so I
attended the University of Wisconsin for the
next three years and in 1917 I received the
Ph.D. degree, having in 1915 been made a
Master of Arts. Later I received the honorary degree of Litt.D. from Marietta Col-

* kōl'tēr

lege and the LL.D. from the University of North Carolina.

"I began my career as a college teacher in Marietta College, Marietta, Ohio. Desiring to be connected with a larger institution, but with no preference for the South, I began two years later to teach in the University of Georgia, where I have remained—except for short periods at the Louisiana State University and the University of Texas, and in summers at a dozen other universities in the United States and one in Mexico City.

"My moving around for short spells to other institutions is somewhat an expression of my yen for travel. When not teaching in summers I have generally traveled to most of the countries of Europe, to Canada, Alaska, Mexico, Central America, and the West Indies. I like the outdoors, hiking, and easy mountain-climbing—much of which I have done in the Appalachians, the Rockies, and in Alaska.

"I have a love for books, especially old and rare ones, for old newspapers and other old historical documents and manuscripts; and I have always had an urge to write history and nothing else. Truth being stranger than fiction, I have stuck to the former, never having had the slightest desire to attempt the latter or even to read much of it. As the historian must be governed by what he writes, by the material at hand (less so now than formerly), I have largely confined myself to regional history. I also find it stimulating and worth while to pioneer into small fields and bring out an article of only a dozen or more pages for some historical magazine. I have written more than three dozen such articles."

* * *

In 1953 E. M. Coulter spent six months in Israel as visiting professor of American history at the University of Jerusalem. He joined the history faculty of the University of Georgia, in Athens, in 1919 and since 1923 has been professor of history there.

PRINCIPAL WORKS: History of Kentucky (with W. E. Connelley) 1922; The Cincinnati Southern Railroad and the Struggle for Southern Commerce, 1865-1872, 1922; The Civil War and Readjustment in Kentucky, 1926; College Life in the Old South, 1928; A Short History of Georgia, 1933; (ed.) Georgia's Disputed Ruins, 1937; William G. Bronlow, Fighting Parson of the Southern Highlands, 1937; (ed.) The Other Half of Old New Orleans, 1939; (ed.) The Course of the South to Secession, 1939; Thomas Spalding of Sapelo, 1940; John Jacobus Flournoy, Champion of the Common Man in the Antebellum South, 1942; The South During Reconstruction, 1947; (comp.) Travels in the Confederate States, A Bibliography, 1948; (with A. B. Saye, eds.) A List of Early Settlers of Georgia, 1949; The Confederate States of America, 1950.

*COULTON, GEORGE GORDON (October 15, 1858-March 4, 1947), British historian, was born in King's Lynn, West Norfolk, England, son of John James and Sarah (Radley) Coulton. His father, like his father before him, was a solicitor, and both parents were of sturdy yeoman stock. Young George was raised in a large, happy family. He attended grammar school briefly in King's Lynn, but when he was only seven his father sent him to France with an older brother to study at the Lycée Impérial in St. Omer. He completed his preparatory schooling at Felsted School in Essex, and entered St. Catharine's College, Cambridge in 1877 with a classical scholarship. In 1882 Coulton resolved to take Holy Orders and began to read for his examination. He was ordained deacon in 1883 and took up parish work at Offley, a little village not too far from London where he went in every spare moment to do research in the British Museum Reading Room. He soon found himself with feelings of doubt about his religious faith. As Coulton wrote many years later in his autobiography, Fourscore Years: "It seemed more and more obvious that I must either spend my life in misleading conformity, or proclaim nonconformity, perhaps with increasing emphasis, and take the consequences." He resolved at last in 1885 to leave the ministry—"until I could recover certainty in my own mind."

Coulton thereupon began a teaching career which lasted more than half a century. He taught in a grammar school in Wales, at an English school in Heidelberg (where he had an opportunity to attend lectures at the university), at Sherborne Grammar School, Sedbergh Grammar School (where one of his colleagues was H. W. Fowler, author of Modern English Usage), and at Dulwich College. In 1895, under the influence of what he described as "an over-mastering and decisive impulse," he began to devote himself to the study of medieval history. He had by now met the great Oxford medievalist Hastings Rashdall and read sufficiently to resolve that "our modern problems can often be studied best in the Middle Ages." After a period of study and travel in France and Italy, Coulton returned to England to teach at the Eastbourne School in South Lynn

* kōl't'n

235

where he remained for the next thirteen years.

Coulton did not embark seriously on what was to be his life's work until well into his forties. Up to 1905 when his first historical writings were published, his research had been voluminous but scattered. A friend once said to him, "You have the biggest collection of perfectly useless knowledge I ever came across." Slowly but surely Coulton organized that collection into one of the most useful and exhaustive collections of medieval scholarship ever assembled. Coulton's publication record was prodigious. With meticulous care he reconstructed from the records of the Middle Ages the panorama of medieval life. His style was vivid and vigorous, his learning massive in depth and scope, and his conclusions, though frequently challenged, were strongly supported by evidence from medieval records. "He was inquisitive, original and encyclopedic, just as Roger Bacon was in his day," Sir Maurice Powicke wrote. His lectures were "learned and fascinating and discursive," and his books "made medieval life real and delightful to thousands of readers." As a teacher he trained and influenced other historians—Eileen Power, Margaret Deansley, H. S. Bennett—and under his editorship the Cambridge Studies in Medieval Life and Thought (which Powicke has called "the finest memorial of his work in Cambridge") published many valuable historical studies.

Coulton throve on controversy. H. S. Bennett wrote of him: "The idea that 'the historian's business is not to judge but to understand' was meaningless to him." He did judge, and strongly. Even his admirers admit that he had "magnificent prejudices." Kingsley Martin remembers him as "a very doughty and lovable fighter." The main target of Coulton's scholarly wrath was the Roman Catholic scholar Cardinal Gasquet whose interpretation of the English Reformation included a defense of the moral conditions of the monasteries. Coulton challenged this, and a number of acrimonious disputes followed. In time Coulton himself became the target of a considerable amount of criticism from Catholic sources. G. K. Chesterton and Hilaire Belloc, among others, entered the lists against him. Coulton threw himself with equal fervor into another, non-academic controversy, when he took an active stand, during World War I, in favor of universal military conscription, in support of which he wrote books and pamphlets.

Although soon after the publication of his first writings Coulton became recognized as a scholar who had much to contribute to his field, he did not have a permanent and secure university connection until he was sixty-one years old. After years of teaching in preparatory schools and lecturing in university extension courses, he was appointed Birkbeck Lecturer at Trinity College, Cambridge, in 1911. But interest in medieval studies was lagging during this period. By 1919, however, he was in great demand as a lecturer in both the History and the English Tripos, and in that year he was appointed to the lectureship in English left vacant by the death of G. C. Macaulay and also received a fellowship at St. John's College. He retired from his lectureship in 1934 but continued active in his work. When World War II broke out he went to Canada as a guest lecturer at the University of Toronto. He returned to England in 1944 and spent his last years in Cambridge, going to the university for research regularly until just a short time before his death. Coulton was survived by his wife, the former Rose Ilbert, whom he had married in 1904, and two daughters. In 1948 his daughter Sarah published a memoir of her father. She remembers him as a great man, but opinionated, obstinate, and hard to live with. "His life seems to me to have been deliciously balanced between an uninhibited pleasure in things and the growlings of a Victorian conscience which reminded him one must pay for one's pleasures."

PRINCIPAL WORKS: From St. Francis to Dante (Chronicle of Fr. Salimbene) 1906; Chaucer and His England, 1908; A Medieval Garner, 1910 (2d ed. published as Life in the Middle Ages, 1928-30); Medieval Studies, 1907, 1915; (comp.) Social Life in Britain from the Conquest to the Reformation, 1918; Five Centuries of Religion (3 vols.) 1923-36; The Medieval Village, 1925; Art and the Reformation, 1928; The Inquisition, 1929; The Medieval Scene, 1930; The Black Death, 1930; Ten Medieval Studies, 1930; Froissart: Chronicler of European Chivalry, 1930; In Defence of the Reformation, 1931; Papal Infallibility, 1932; Two Saints, 1932; Scottish Abbeys and Social Life, 1933; Medieval Panorama, 1938; Inquisition and Liberty, 1938; Fourscore Years, 1944.

ABOUT: Bennett, H. S. George Gordon Coulton (in Proceedings of British Academy, vol. 33); Campion, S. Father: A Portrait of G. G. Coulton at Home; Coulton, G. G. Fourscore Years; Cambridge Historical Journal, vol. 9 (1947); New York Times March 5, 1947.

COUNTS, GEORGE SYLVESTER (December 9, 1889-), American educator, writes: "According to the record in the family Bible and the testimony of my parents, I was born on a farm near Baldwin, Kan., the year before the official announcement of

the closing of the geographical frontier. I was the third of six children, three brothers and two sisters, with whom I played and quarreled and worked during childhood and adolescence. My people came almost altogether from colonial and pioneer stock— English, Scotch, Welsh, Dutch, German, and perhaps French.

"As boy and youth, both during vacations and before and after school, I worked long hours, usually from before sun-up to after sun-down on my father's farm. I helped to clear and plow the land, to plant, cultivate, and harvest the crops, to take care of the farm animals, to do the chores morning and evening. Except for Sunday, which was always rigorously observed in the spirit of uncorrupted Methodism, my holidays were few and far between.

"By way of recreation I went swimming and skating, played Indian, indulged in snipe-hunting, participated in spelling bees, broke and rode horses, went to neighborhood picnics, read stories of adventure, and dreamed of going down the Mississippi on a houseboat. I made collections of stamps, birds' eggs, and arrowheads. John James Audubon and Daniel Boone were my favorite heroes.

"In my teens I developed a passion for hunting and trapping the game and fur-bearing animals of the region. During autumn, winter, and early spring I would rise daily long before dawn, visit my line of traps by lantern-light, perform my assigned tasks around house and barn, and then go to school. From the sale of furs I made practically all the money I could call my own. What a thrill it was to catch a mink, a raccoon, or even a 'possum! I am still of the conviction that no one has really lived who has never wandered through the October woods, with the crisp brown leaves of autumn under his feet, a rifle over his shoulder, a hatchet in his belt, and a dozen or more traps dangling by chain from his hand.

"When seventeen years of age I 'shipped' as a laborer from Kansas City to a lumber camp in the Big Horn Mountains of Wyoming. Here I acquired some of the skills of the lumberjack. Also I met three French-Canadian trappers who promised to take me with them in the coming autumn to their na-tive haunts to the North. Unfortunately the foreman fired me for riding logs down the flume in violation of his expressed orders. With a sad heart I returned to farm and college in Kansas.

"As I look back from the vantage point of years I can see that the process of en-slaving a free spirit began early. My parents decided to send me to a one-room rural school built of sandstone, but by no means 'red.' Here I remained two years, completing four grades and learning to read and write and cipher. I then went to the public school in Baldwin and on finishing the twelfth grade entered Baker University. At college I specialized in Latin, Greek, mathematics, and philosophy, football, basketball, and student activities generally. I even passed the Rhodes Scholarship examination. In my senior year I met a girl, Lois H. Bailey, the daughter of a distinguished Methodist minister, and abandoned forever the thought of becoming a trapper.

"On graduation from college in 1911 I proceeded to do something that I had always contended I would never do. I turned to teaching, and for two years I taught science and mathematics and coached athletics in the high schools of Kansas. By this time I myself was completely trapped. We were married in 1913. From this union there came in the course of time two children, Esther and Martha, who began life quite as free and untrammeled as I had been in my childhood. But they too are now thoroughly 'civilized.'

"In the year of my marriage I entered the graduate school of the University of Chicago, specializing in sociology, psychology, and education. Here I studied three years, making my own way by working at various jobs and winning scholarships and fellowships.

"In 1916 I was awarded the degree of doctor of philosophy with honors. Thus the final seal was placed on my fate. From that time on I was destined to work in the colleges and universities of the nation and 'contribute to the advancement of knowledge and learning.'

"My first post after leaving Chicago was at Delaware College. From there I moved successively to Harris Teachers College, the University of Washington, Yale University, and the University of Chicago. In 1927 I came to Teachers College, Columbia University, where I have remained ever since and often brought embarrassment to the constituted authorities.

"I have traveled over a good part of Europe and Asia. In 1925 I served as a member of an educational commission to the Philippines. In 1927, 1929, and 1936 I visited the Soviet Union for extended periods. On the second trip I took a Ford car with me and traveled six thousand miles through the forests, across the steppes, and over the mountains of European Russia. In 1946 I went to Japan on an educational mission for the State Department.

"Politics has always interested me since William Jennings Bryan ran for the presidency in 1896. I was New York State Chairman of the American Labor Party from 1942 to 1944, when in the 'era of good feeling' towards 'our great democratic ally' the Communists captured control. In 1952 I ran for the United States Senate on the Liberal Party ticket and polled almost half a million votes. For many years I was a Bull Mooser. Today I am an unreconstructed New Dealer.

"In the spring of 1953 I received the Educators Award of B'nai B'rith as the 'educator in the metropolitan area who has contributed to democratic human relations among students, teachers and in the community generally.' Thus was my career brought to its unknown but probably preordained destination.

"As a way of escape from the many frustrations of 'civilization' I devote an occasional holiday to the care of ornamental shrubs and trees on a small farm near New Hope, Pa. Apparently this interest is about all that remains of my 'original nature.'"

PRINCIPAL WORKS: The Selective Character of American Secondary Education, 1922; Principles of Education (with J. C. Chapman) 1924; The Senior High School Curriculum, 1926; The Social Composition of Boards of Education, 1927; School and Society in Chicago, 1928; The American Road to Culture, 1930; A Ford Crosses Soviet Russia, 1930; The Soviet Challenge to America, 1931; Dare the School Build a New Social Order? (pamphlet) 1932; The Social Foundations of Education (with others) 1934; The Prospects of American Democracy, 1938; The Education of Free Men, 1941; Education and the Promise of America, 1945; The Country of the Blind—The Soviet System of Mind Control (with N. Lodge) 1949; American Education through the Soviet Looking Glass, 1951; Education and American Civilization, 1952.

ABOUT: American Mercury April 1937; Book-of-the-Month Club News May 1931, November 1949; Current Biography 1941; Fortune July 1936; Literary Digest March 7, 1936; New York Times August 23, 1940, September 15, 1941; New Yorker September 24, 1938; Newsweek April 2, 1951; School and Society October 25, 1941; Time July 20, 1936.

COUPERUS, LOUIS MARIE ANNE (June 10, 1863-July 16, 1923). For biographical sketch and list of works and references, see TWENTIETH CENTURY AUTHORS, 1942.

* * *

ABOUT: Columbia Dictionary of Modern European Literature.

COURNOS, JOHN (March 6, 1881-). For autobiographical sketch and list of earlier works and references, see TWENTIETH CENTURY AUTHOR, 1942.

* * *

John Cournos writes from New York City: "I have little that is personal to add to my record. I still have the same wife, and a half dozen grandchildren. As for the rest, it's books, books, books."

ADDITIONAL WORKS: A Treasury of Russian Life and Humor (ed.) 1943; A World of Great Stories (ed. with H. Haydn) 1947; Best World Short Stories (ed. with S. Norton) 1949. Juveniles (all with S. Norton)—Famous Modern American Novelists, 1952; Famous British Novelists, 1952; Famous British Poets, 1952; Pilgrimage to Freedom: The Story of Roger Williams, 1953; Candidate for Truth: The Story of Daniel Webster, 1953; John Adams: Independence Forever, 1954.

COURTHOPE, WILLIAM JOHN (July 17, 1842-April 10, 1917). For biographical sketch and list of works and references, see TWENTIETH CENTURY AUTHORS, 1942.

* * *

ABOUT: Thompson, F. Literary Criticisms Newly Discovered (ed. T. L. Connolly).

COUSINS, NORMAN (June 24, 1912-), American editor and essayist, was born in Union, N.J., the son of Samuel and Sara Barry (Miller) Cousins. Young Cousins' earliest interests were reading, writing, and baseball. Throughout his school years he participated in all three with equal zest. In 1933 he was graduated from Teachers College at Columbia University. But instead of going into teaching, he became education editor of the New York *Evening Post*, where he remained until 1935.

In 1935 Cousins took a job as book critic for the magazine *Current History*, where he was elevated to the literary and managing editorship, a position which he occupied until 1940. Then he became executive editor of the *Saturday Review of Literature*, a publication which had emerged out of the literary pages of the New York *Evening Post* some twenty years before. According to *Newsweek*, Mr. Cousins transformed the character of the *Review* in the sense that he "began tying the *Review's* other-worldliness down to the world of today." Circulation increased 50 per cent; writers who were specialists on their subjects were brought in to contribute articles about literature and culture. At the same time, Cousins continued to write editorials and book reviews, never hesitating to speak frankly his own opinions. In 1943 he criticized the American Congress for what he thought was its prejudice, greed, and lack of unity. "Can it be," he said, "that a nation born in the blood of freedom's battle has so far wandered from its heritage as to be ignorant of the bold requirements of continued freedom and self-preservation?" But as ready to give room to affirmative sentiments, Cousins had written in 1942 *The Good Inheritance: The Democratic Chance*, and previous to that he had produced a collection of the aphorisms of freedom, *A Treasury of Democracy*. This was followed by *The Poetry of Liberty*, edited in collaboration with William Rose Benét.

During World War II Norman Cousins worked with the Office of War Information and other governmental agencies. When the atomic bomb was dropped on Hiroshima, he wrote an editorial for the *Review* with the striking title *Modern Man Is Obsolete*. This piece was enlarged into a book and became his best known work, being translated into several different languages. His interest in ideas, people, and current events took Cousins into a variety of subjects and into many parts of the world. After the war he was made honorary citizen of Hiroshima, and since then has visited that city twice. At the Bikini experiments he was an observer; and in 1948 during the blockade on Berlin he flew the airlift while doing work on a democratization survey set up by General Clay. Early in 1951 he was sent by the American government to India, Pakistan, and Ceylon. When he returned from his travels, he wrote *Who Speaks for Man?*, a series of observations about his tours and a plea for World Federation. Adlai Stevenson, in reviewing this book, spoke of the

"penetrating and often moving account of man's present dilemma . . . which, according to Mr. Cousins, results from the fact that MAN has no spokesman, no collective voice, no effective representation of his own most vital interests." And Stevenson adds, "With his passionate concern for mankind . . . Cousins has filed a formidable brief in the case for enforceable world laws."

In 1948 Cousins received the Thomas Jefferson Award for the Advancement of Democracy in Journalism. He is a trustee of Briarcliff College in New York, and is active in several educational groups, being Chairman of the Connecticut Fact-Finding Commission of Education, and serving on the Board of Directors of the Conference on Science, Philosophy, and Religion of Columbia University. He is also a member of the Library Development Committee of Columbia University, and a member of the Council of Foreign Relations.

Cousins is married to the former Ellen Kopf, and they live in Norwalk, Conn., with their four daughters. In appearance he is brown-eyed with an alert sharp face and a manner of great energy and awareness. His hobby is music; his recreations are many, not the least of them being the literary hoax and the practical joke. Walt Whitman is his favorite figure in literature, and in history he leans toward the era of ancient Greece and the period of the Reformation.

PRINCIPAL WORKS: A Treasury of Democracy (ed.) 1941; The Good Inheritance: The Democratic Chance, 1942; An Anthology of Poetry of Liberty (ed.) 1942; Modern Man Is Obsolete, 1945; Writing for Love or Money (ed.) 1949; Who Speaks for Man? 1953.

ABOUT: Current Biography 1943; Life April 4, 1949; Newsweek April 4, 1949.

COWARD, NOEL PIERCE (December 16, 1899-). For biographical sketch and list of earlier works and references, see TWENTIETH CENTURY AUTHORS, 1942.

* * *

Noel Coward has emerged from World War II, the post-war crises, and the natural ravages of time and age temporarily battered but little the worse for wear. He is still the dapper, impeccable man-about-town, given to sudden bursts of serious sentiments —but happiest and most successful, as actor or playwright, in brittle, epigrammatic society comedies like *Design for Living, Private Lives*, and *Blithe Spirit*. He has written only one such new comedy since the end of the war—*Present Laughter*—and the critics found it below par. A revival of *Private Lives* in 1947, starring Tallulah Bankhead, had a triumphant run, however, and proved that though Coward's comedies are dated, in a good production they retain a surprising amount of their original flavor, what George Jean Nathan calls their trick "of successfully passing off foam for champagne." His recent musical plays—*Pacific 1860* (1946) and *Ace of Clubs* (1950) had moderately successful runs in London. In 1952 his comedy *Quadrille* proved a pleasant vehicle-play for the acting talents of Alfred Lunt and Lynn Fontanne in a London production and in 1954 in New York.

Coward suffered some unfavorable publicity during the first years of World War II. He traveled widely and made many public appearances at fund-raising benefits and to entertain the Allied troops. In 1943 he toured North Africa and the Middle East and, in the next year, published a record of the trip, *Middle East Diary*. The traditional Coward flippancy and sparkle, so successful in his plays, struck many readers as in poor taste. Margaret Marshall referred, in her review in the *Nation*, to his "imperial provincialism," and John Mason Brown objected that the book would create bad feeling between Britain and America. Some hard feelings were indeed created—especially by a slurring reference Coward made to soldiers from Brooklyn. Brown felt that in his pose of wartime sophisticate Coward failed to do justice not only to the troops on whom he was reporting, but to himself. "The wonder is that Mr. Coward, having traveled such distances to entertain the troops, should go to such lengths as a diarist to detract from one of his best performances."

Coward has devoted much of his time in recent years to motion picture making. His first independent production, which he wrote, directed and starred in, was the moving story of a British destroyer and its crew, *In Which We Serve* (1943). Equally successful were *This Happy Breed* (1944), a saga of English family life, the sensitive and quietly-told *Brief Encounter* (1945), and the sparkling film version of his play *Blithe Spirit* (1945). He has residences in London, at St. Margaret's Bay on the English Channel, and has recently built a home in Jamaica, in the British West Indies, with a view of the Caribbean. The dominant influences on his life, he wrote in 1951, have been "the theatre and books, but while, apart from human relationships, they have been the most important things in my life, their dominion is

not quite unchallenged and their challenger is the sea."

ADDITIONAL WORKS: Middle East Diary, 1944; Star Quality: Six Stories, 1951; The Noel Coward Song Book, 1953; Future Indefinite, 1954. *Plays (dates of publication)*—Present Laughter, 1947; This Happy Breed, 1947; Peace in Our Time, 1948.

ABOUT: Brown, J. M. Seeing Things; Coward, N. Middle East Diary, Future Indefinite; Greacen, R. The Art of Noel Coward; American Mercury January 1949; Collier's January 2, 1943; Current Biography 1941; Life December 8, 1947; New York Herald Tribune Book Review October 7, 1951; New York Times Magazine February 14, 1943, December 11, 1949; New Yorker February 3, 1951; Theatre Arts January 1944, August 1949; Time July 7, 1947.

COWLEY, MALCOLM (August 24, 1898-). For autobiographical sketch and list of earlier works and references, see TWENTIETH CENTURY AUTHORS, 1942.

* * *

Malcolm Cowley writes: "Since 1942 I have continued to live in Sherman, Conn., with a few commotions and catastrophes, but only minor ones. I note in your earlier volume references to wife, son and FHA mortgage; they are respectively (1) still charmingly here, (2) at Harvard, (3) paid off. I have been making a series of studies of American literature, represented by various edited volumes, with more to come; also I have been doing some lecturing at various universities, from Puget Sound to Casco Bay. Since 1948 I have been a literary adviser to the Viking Press."

In 1951 Malcolm Cowley published a revised edition of *Exile's Return*, originally published in 1934, adding new material on Ezra Pound, F. Scott Fitzgerald, Hart Crane, and other writers, and a new introduction and epilogue. Of the new volume Lloyd Morris wrote: "Present-day readers will find it an unusual and important book. The most vivacious of all accounts of literary life during the fabulous 1920's, *Exile's Return* offers an intimate, realistic portrait of the era that produced a renaissance in American fiction and poetry." In 1954 appeared another collection of critical essays, *The Literary Situation*, concerned primarily with the problems of the American writer.

Correction: *The Lost Generation*, 1931, listed among Cowley's Principal Works was never published, but was an "announced" title for *Exile's Return*, 1934.

ADDITIONAL WORKS: The Literary Situation, 1954. *Editions*—The Portable Hemingway, 1944; The Portable Faulkner, 1946; The Complete Walt Whitman, 1948; The Portable Hawthorne, 1948; The Stories of F. Scott Fitzgerald, 1951.

ABOUT: Burke, K. The Philosophy of Literary Form; Cowley, M. in Rahv, P. Discovery of Europe; New York Herald Tribune Book Review October 7, 1951

COX, ANTHONY BERKELEY (1893-).
For autobiographical sketch and list of works and references, see TWENTIETH CENTURY AUTHORS, 1942.

* * *

A. B. Cox writes from London: "There is nothing to add to my biography and certainly no further publications. I don't know if it is worth mentioning that I was on the *Daily Telegraph* literary staff, reviewing ordinary novels, for about five years before the war; and am now doing the crime fiction for the Sunday *Times.* I shouldn't think so. There is no secret now about my being 'Francis Iles.' To regain a decent anonymity I shall have to think about a new pseudonym."

COYLE, KATHLEEN (1886-March 25, 1952).
For autobiographical sketch and list of earlier works and references, see TWENTIETH CENTURY AUTHORS, 1942.

* * *

Kathleen Coyle died at sixty-six at the Hahnemann Hospital in Philadelphia. At the time of her death she was engaged in writing the story of her life and a play about Philadelphia, where she had lived since the previous June. Her husband, Charles O'Maher, predeceased her; she was survived by a daughter, Michele O'Maher, an artist, and a son, Kirstal O'Maher.

Margaret Wallace called Miss Coyle "one of the most moving and individual of English writers"; Mary Ross spoke of the "scrupulous perceptiveness of her work," and found her books "sensitive and luminous with intelligence." According to the New York *Times,* "Beauty and sorrow crowded the life of Miss Coyle, whose power to evoke emotion was her chief writing glory."

ADDITIONAL WORKS: Major, 1942; Magical Realm (autobiography) 1943.
ABOUT: Coyle, K. Magical Realm; Wagenknecht, E. (ed.) When I Was a Child; New York Times March 29, 1952.

COZZENS, JAMES GOULD (August 19, 1903-).
For biographical sketch and list of earlier works and references, see TWENTIETH CENTURY AUTHORS, 1942.

* * *

James Gould Cozzens' *Guard of Honor* won the Pulitzer prize for the best novel of 1948. It was generally agreed that such recognition of his distinguished writing was long overdue. Three months before Cozzens received the award, Bernard De Voto, in his "Easy Chair" column in *Harper's Magazine,* had belabored those "formulators of literary judgment" who failed to recognize Cozzens' abilities—his sheer "professionalism" as a writer, his sureness of technique and purpose. But Cozzens has not been so neglected as De Voto's charge might suggest. Each of his novels, in its turn, as Mark Schorer pointed out, "has been better than its predecessor." Recognition has been slow but, like the progress of the novels themselves, sure and steady. In 1942 Herbert Gorman hailed *The Just and the Unjust* as a novel of "major dimensions," and Harry Sylvester spoke of its author as "a great American novelist come of age."

In that same year Cozzens enlisted in the United States Army Air Force where he served, rising to the rank of major, until 1945. A few days after his discharge, he began work on *Guard of Honor,* a rich and compelling story of three days in 1943 in an air-training camp in Florida. The novel is the most complex of his works to date. Granville Hicks commented that "the skill with which he sustains its multiple themes can scarcely be overestimated." Perhaps its most striking feature—and one which is characteristic of Cozzens—is its objectivity, what Hicks calls his "passionate detachment" from his material. If this is the source of the strength of Cozzens' work, it is perhaps also the source of the weakness of it. The artistic discipline which he imposes upon himself, Hicks writes, "frequently strains out some part of the vitality that is the essence of imaginative literature." Brendan Gill similarly speaks of "the sense one gets of an absence of deep feeling in Cozzens' novels, of a fastidious shying-off on the part of the novelist, of an inconspicuous but nagging failure to commit himself beyond irony."

ADDITIONAL WORK: Guard of Honor, 1948.
ABOUT: College English January 1950; Current Biography 1949; Harper's February 1949; Pacific Spectator Winter 1951.

CRAIG, GORDON (January 16, 1872-).
For biographical sketch and list of works and references, see TWENTIETH CENTURY AUTHORS, 1942.

* * *

Gordon Craig has lived in France for the past twenty years. During the German occupation he was briefly held in a detention camp and then returned to Paris. After the war he retired to the small village of Corbeil, some fifty kilometers from Paris, where he is now engaged in the massive project of re-editing his works and writing his memoirs. John Savacool, who visited Craig in 1950, reported in *Theatre Arts* magazine that he has mellowed and "is no longer the rebellious artist who preached destruction of all we know about stagecraft in order to start anew and remake the craft into an art." He is now resigned to the role of prophet, Savacool says, a precursor of the "real theatre." In Craig's words: "The *real* theatre, the theatre which is an art in its own right like music and architecture, is yet to be discovered and may not come for several generations."

ABOUT: Theatre Arts June 1950.

CRAIG, HARDIN (June 29, 1875-), American Shakespearean scholar writes: "I was born on a farm in Daviess County, Ky.,  six miles east of Owensboro. My father, Robert Craig, was born in New Cumnock, Scotland, in 1830 and immigrated to Kentucky in 1850. My mother was Mary Jane McHenry, daughter of John Hardin McHenry of Hartford, Ky., lawyer and member of Congress. Hardin and McHenry are pioneer names in the settlement of the West. I was educated in the district schools of my community and still think of them as excellent institutions. One of my later teachers was Malcolm McIntyre, a Bowdoin graduate, and from him I was enabled to learn the Latin, Greek, and mathematics required for entrance into the Centre College of Kentucky. From that institution I was graduated as Ormond Beatty Senior Prizeman in 1897. The prize was sixty very welcome and potent dollars. The next year I taught Latin, Greek, and mathematics in an academy at Stanford, Ky., and in September 1898 I entered Princeton University as a post-graduate student. I was in that institution as student and teacher over a period of twelve years except for somewhat less than two years that I spent at Jena in Germany and at Exeter College, Oxford. My training was mainly philological, and my Ph.D. dissertation, *Two Coventry Corpus Christi Plays*, was published by the Early English Text

Society (1902). My Princeton period covered the progressive and stimulating years when Woodrow Wilson was president of the University. I was instructor in English and, on the establishment of the Preceptorial System in 1905, I was appointed Edgerstoune Preceptor of English. I owe much to the five years spent in that position, not only to the ideals and intellectual efforts of the time, but to the fact that a preceptor carried the same groups of students through their entire course and was obliged to rise to a high level of scholarly proficiency in the whole range of English and American literature.

"In 1906 I married Gertrude Carr of Ashby, Mass. She lived until 1941, and we had one son, Hardin Craig Jr., now professor of history in the Rice Institute, Houston, Tex.

"I went as professor of English in 1910 to the University of Minnesota and remained there until the spring of 1917 when I entered the United States Army. I was graduated from an officers' training school at Fort Snelling as second lieutenant, Q.M.C. I served during the first World War at Camp Dodge, Camp Johnston, and in Washington and was discharged as captain, Q.M.C., about the first of the year 1919. I had little chance to go abroad because of the need in the service of persons who could teach and who knew educational organization. I worked very hard and did what I was told to do.

"In 1919 I became professor of English and head of department at the State University of Iowa, then prospering under the presidency of Walter A. Jessup. I succeeded in building up a strong department, and during the nine years I was there I improved my ability as a Shakespeare scholar. The work of those years is embodied in numerous articles and in a widely used textbook, *Shakespeare: A Historical and Critical Study with Annotated Texts of Twenty-One Plays* (1931). In 1928 I accepted a call to Stanford University as professor of English. I had about that time some deanships and headships offered me, which I refused in favor of teaching, research, and writing. Stanford was going forward under the presidency of Dr. Ray Lyman Wilbur, and my years there were both happy and productive. I spent a good deal of time at the Huntington Library, and for a period of about two years I was research associate of that institution. I published, besides the *Shakespeare, The Enchanted Glass* (1936) and a good many editions and articles.

"After the death of my dear wife in 1941 I left Stanford for a temporary position at the University of North Carolina and remained at Chapel Hill for more than seven years. During that time I did a good deal of careful and laborious work on my *The Complete Works of Shakespeare* (1951), edited a hitherto unpublished Elizabethan translation of Machiavelli's *The Prince* (1944), published *Literary Study and the Scholarly Profession* (Walker Ames Lectures, 1944), *An Interpretation of Shakespeare* (1948), and *Freedom and Renaissance* (1949). The last-mentioned book gives a pretty good idea of my life and work at the University of North Carolina. One thing I should like to mention, if only as an example of patient and useful work—from 1925 until 1950 I compiled annually, for a long time single-handed, for the April numbers of *Studies in Philology*, an extensive bibliography, 'Recent Literature of the Renaissance.'

"About three years ago I came to the University of Missouri on a temporary appointment to teach Shakespeare and Renaissance literature and have been here since. In 1951 I published *The Complete Works of Shakespeare*, and last spring *An Introduction to Shakespeare*. After this very considerable publication in Shakespeare I have turned back to my original field of specialization and am now engaged on a history of the English religious drama of the Middle Ages.

"It will be noticed that I have lived, taught, and worked in most of the principal sections of our country and for considerable periods of time. I am more impressed with the unity of the United States than with its diversity."

PRINCIPAL WORKS: Two Coventry Corpus Christi Plays (ed.) 1902; Shakespeare: a Historical and Critical Study, 1931; The Enchanted Glass, 1936; Literary Study and the Scholarly Profession, 1944; An Interpretation of Shakespeare, 1948; Freedom and Renaissance, 1949; The Complete Works of Shakespeare (ed.) 1951; An Introduction to Shakespeare (ed.) 1952.

ABOUT: Kirk, R. *in* Renaissance Studies in Honor of Hardin Craig.

CRANE, HART (July 21, 1899-April 27, 1932). For biographical sketch and list of works and references, see TWENTIETH CENTURY AUTHORS, 1942.

* * *

ADDITIONAL WORK: Letters (ed. B. Weber) 1952.

ABOUT: Crane, H. Letters; Southworth, J. G. Some Modern American Poets; Tate, A. On the Limits of Poetry; Waggoner, H. H. The Heel of Elohim; Weber, B. Hart Crane; American Literature March 1949; Partisan Review July 1949; Publications of the Modern Language Association March 1951; Sewanee Review January 1950, July 1950; Time March 22, 1948.

CRANKSHAW, EDWARD (1909-   ),

English critic, novelist, and expert on Russia, was born at Woodford, Essex. He was educated at Bishop's Stortford College, but left school early to travel on the continent. Between 1931 and 1935 Crankshaw wrote regularly for numerous British publications on a variety of topics, ranging from studies of the twelve-tonalists to reviews of  books, art, and the theatre. After 1935 he gave up journalism and devoted himself to translations from the German and to critical writing. *Joseph Conrad: Some Aspects of the Art of the Novel* appeared in 1936. This was both an original study of Conrad's method and an analysis of the novelist's art in general, with special reference to Flaubert and Henry James.

Although Edward Crankshaw became an authority on Russia by an accident of war, his Russian orientation follows in logical progress from his first interest in Conrad. It can also be traced indirectly to the prevailing emotional climate of the '30's, which was fatalistically obsessed with Europe's "decline and fall." In 1938, after Hitler's uncontested *Anschluss* of Austria and Germany, Crankshaw wrote *Vienna: The Image of a Culture in Decline*. In it the author attempted to evoke "the dead or dying culture before it lies too far behind. . . ." This nostalgic evocation of the doomed city through its art and music and its historical monuments elicited mixed reactions from the critics, who found the book at once passionate and sensitive, but lacking in balance.

Crankshaw had been commissioned in the British Territorial Army in 1937. In 1941 he went to Russia with the British Military Mission, remaining there for two years. At that time, he also had the opportunity of traveling in a number of Eastern European countries. In 1947 he revisited Moscow for the foreign ministers' conference. Out of his travels and contacts within and on the fringes of the Soviet empire came a series of books, all of which attempt to decipher the riddle of Russian behavior through an understanding of national history and national character.

After his first return from that country in 1943, Edward Crankshaw wrote a small book, *Russia and Britain,* which the author described as a mild antidote to the prevailing atmosphere of hero-worship. *Russia and the Russians* (1947) attempted to present a more detailed picture of the Soviet reality. Beginning with an analysis of the Russian "heritage of the plain" (which has left Russia historically open to invasion) and taking into account the mutually troublesome pre-war relations with the West, Crankshaw interpreted the Iron Curtain as basically a Russian defense against a hostile outer world. We must come to understand Russia, he concludes, or we must destroy her—and in so doing, destroy ourselves, too.

Russia by Daylight (in U.S., *Cracks in the Kremlin Wall*) appeared in 1951. Written before the death of Stalin, it predicted the probable future course of Soviet foreign policy. Here the author pointed to the inherent weaknesses in the Soviet system—the absence of civil liberties, slave labor, technical backwardness, discontent—and concluded that the Russians were unlikely therefore to resort to further expansion or to initiate a major war in this generation. Rather than being shrewd or far-sighted, Russian foreign policy he saw as essentially blundering and inept. The Soviet character, which he interpreted "psychoanalytically," Crankshaw saw as remaining the same under both Czarist and Soviet regimes; and Soviet expansion has merely furthered the classical Russian patterns of expansion under the Romanoffs.

In 1952 Crankshaw published *The Forsaken Idea: A Study of Viscount Milner* ("the man who made the Boer war"). This book was a reassessment of British imperialist policy in the light of the post-war world and Britain's declining world position. According to the liberal *Manchester Guardian,* "Milner is the peg on which hangs a spirited defense of British imperialism."

Crankshaw's writing has drawn, all along, a wide range of critical opinion. His major work on Russia has been praised as an example of "genius . . . extraordinary in its penetration" (New York *Times Book Review*) and simultaneously decried as "an interesting and aromatic fiction" (by Harvey Breit, the *Atlantic*). Altogether, the author seems to prefer an impressionistic approach to his subject, relying on his personal insights and observations, rather than subjecting himself to any specific disciplines.

Edward Crankshaw is also the author of two novels, *Nina Lessing* (1938) and *What Glory* (1940), and he is currently at work on a third. Crankshaw makes his home in Kent. He has been the London *Observer's* Russian expert since 1947, and also broadcasts on Russian matters for the B.B.C. He holds the commission of lieutenant-colonel in the Territorial Army.

PRINCIPAL WORKS: Joseph Conrad: Some Aspects of the Art of the Novel, 1936; Nina Lessing (novel) 1938; Vienna: The Image of a Culture in Decline, 1938; What Glory (novel) 1940; Russia and Britain, 1944; Russia and the Russians, 1947; Russia by Daylight (in U.S.: Cracks in the Kremlin Wall) 1951; The Forsaken Idea: a Study of Viscount Milner, 1952.

ABOUT: Atlantic Monthly September 1951; New Statesman and Nation July 19, 1947; New York Times Book Review February 15, 1948; Saturday Review of Literature April 3, 1948.

CRAPSEY, ADELAIDE (September 9, 1878-October 8, 1914). For biographical sketch and list of works and references, see TWENTIETH CENTURY AUTHORS, 1942.

CRAVEN, THOMAS (January 6, 1889-). For biographical sketch and list of earlier works and references, see TWENTIETH CENTURY AUTHORS, 1942.

* * *

ADDITIONAL WORKS: Story of Painting from Cave Pictures to Modern Art, 1943; Cartoon Cavalcade (ed.) 1943.

ABOUT: Current Biography 1944.

CREEKMORE, HUBERT (1907-), American poet and novelist, writes: "Born in Water Valley, Miss., I was the third (and last) son of my parents' four children. Maternal and paternal grandfathers were planters, owning moderately large farm lands first in Tennessee and then in northeastern Mississippi, and descended from Virginia settlers of the late eighteenth century, though my mother's family, the Hortons,  were in this country earlier. My father was a lawyer, as are both my brothers, and most of the uncles and cousins on both sides of the family are doctors. During high school I wrote poems and stories, fantastic, romantic, melodramatic and finally somewhat realistic, and continued to do so at the University of Mississippi with considerable improvement in fiction.

"While there, the publication of the first books of William Faulkner, in his famous 'post-office period' during my freshman year, served as an encouragement to me to abandon the idea of law as a career and try the unheard-of in Mississippi—be a writer; and I managed to complete a feverish novel which found no publisher. After college, where my main interests were literature, languages, music (I had played the piano since childhood), and theatre, I studied drama at the University of Colorado and playwriting at Yale under Professor George P. Baker. The following winter by lucky chance I appeared in a Broadway play (spear-carrier in Belasco's *Mima*) and shortly after that, by unlucky chance, in the Depression. I worked briefly in the draughting rooms of the Mississippi Highway Department (my parents had moved to Jackson in 1928), later for the Veterans' Administration and the Social Security Board in Washington and, after an interim of graduate study at Columbia University, for the Mississippi Writers Project. Another year at Columbia completed my work for an M.A. degree in American literature. Then followed a year with New Directions (during its infancy), a brief return to the Writers Project and service in the Navy (yeoman and lieutenant), including a sojourn in New Caledonia where most of the poems in *The Long Reprieve* were written.

"After the war, I worked some months for *Tomorrow* and Creative Age Press and a second time for New Directions, at last located in New York, where I remained until 1948 when I became 'Visiting Lecturer, Fiction' in the University of Iowa Graduate Writers' Workshop. Since 1949, I have devoted all my time to writing, either in Mississippi, New Orleans, California, or New York.

"My first real publication came in 1934 with poems in *Poetry* and 'Operation' in *Story;* and in that year I issued one number of an undistinguished little magazine, *The Southern Review,* and began *The Chain in the Heart.* After this there was little comparable success and, when World War II involved the USA, I had almost given up hope or even thought of being able to see a book accepted. My first novel, though it appeared after the war, was written several years before its outbreak. Since then I have tried to make up for production lost during the previous years of discouragement. However, I write poetry very slowly and not very

often; fiction I write usually rather fast, but cannot work long at a sitting and ponder it a great deal. Revisions, reconsiderations . . . such eat up the rest of the time. While working on a book, I sometimes interrupt to do book reviews for the New York *Times, Nation,* and *Poetry.*

"Having just finished my third novel, I am now continuing my translations of Rimbaud's letters, Mallarmé's complete poems and a group of Provençal lyrics, before beginning another book."

* * *

Hubert Creekmore's novels of the South are written with passionate sincerity and reflect a wide and sound knowledge of the region and its people. His recent novel *The Chain in the Heart* is a chronicle of three generations of a Southern Negro family, from the post-Civil War period to the late 1930's. Harrison Smith, in the *Saturday Review,* called it "a persuasive and powerful book."

Ralph Gustafson wrote of Creekmore's verse in 1944 that "it is sincere and technically well stated, but it seems imaginatively undramatic." *The Long Reprieve* was a promising collection. Ruth Lechlitner found some of these poems "among the most remarkable to come from a war experience," and the *New Yorker's* reviewer commented that "his seriousness and powers of observation are apparent, in spite of his often baffling form and over-wrought language."

PRINCIPAL WORKS: *Poetry*—Personal Sun, 1940; The Stone Ants, 1943; The Long Reprieve, 1946; Formula, 1947; No Harm to Lovers, 1950; A Little Treasury of World Poetry (ed.) 1952. *Novels*—The Fingers of Night, 1946; The Welcome, 1948; The Chain in the Heart, 1953.

ABOUT: Warfel, H. R. American Novelists of Today.

*CRICHTON, KYLE SAMUEL (November 6, 1896-). For biographical sketch and list of works and references, see TWENTIETH CENTURY AUTHORS, 1942.

* * *

Kyle Crichton resigned from *Collier's* in 1949 after sixteen years on the editorial staff. He now lives in Newtown, Conn., and is a free-lance writer. He has published two novels in the past decade—one, *Proud People,* a story of a Spanish family in New Mexico, and the other, *The History of the Adventures of George Whigham and His Friend Mr. Claney Hobson,* a farce

* kri't'n

about New York society which Joseph Henry Jackson called "fun even if it is completely mad." Crichton's most popular book of recent years is his biography of the Marx brothers—"as winningly daft a family as ever got on paper," Robert Bendiner wrote.

ADDITIONAL WORKS: Proud People, 1944; The Marx Brothers, 1950; The History of the Adventures of George Whigham and His Friend Mr. Claney Hobson, 1951.

*CROCE, BENEDETTO (February 25, 1866-November 20, 1952). For biographical sketch and list of earlier works and references, see TWENTIETH CENTURY AUTHORS, 1942.

* * *

Benedetto Croce died at eighty-six in Naples as the result of chronic bronchitis aggravated by influenza and kidney trouble. His family refused a state funeral, but 50,000 people watched his funeral cortege of 2,000 mourners.

Throughout the Mussolini regime, Croce's was the strongest anti-Fascist voice in Italy. He published an anti-Fascist magazine, *La Critica*, was responsible for the publication of many liberal books, and worked with youth groups through the country "to keep the flame of moral and intellectual resistance alive." Enzo Tagliacozzo has said that "thanks to his work, thousands of young Italians who had been influenced by Fascist propaganda in their teens switched to liberalism in their university years." Although he was granted extraordinary freedom of person and publication, a nocturnal attack by "Fascist roughs" once threatened his library and his life.

In September 1943, following the German occupation of Italy, Croce was rescued by a British naval detachment and taken to safety on Capri. He became president of the reconstituted Liberal Party, and was a Minister without Portfolio in Italy's two first postwar cabinets and a member of the Constituent Assembly in 1946-47.

He retired from active politics in 1947 and founded the Italian Institute for Historical Study at Naples, "devised to provide and foster post-graduate research in the field of the humanities, of law, and economics." This was the philosopher's first formal teaching experience; he presided over the institute until his death.

In his late years Croce considered himself "a Christian outside the Church." In a measure responsible, by virtue of his early

* krō′chĕ

interest and support, for the fact that "Communism in Italy has retained a much more authentic cultural status than in countries relatively unschooled in idealist dialectics," according to Cecil Sprigge, Croce "for decades belabored the Communists and derided the Soviet paradise" but "regarded the Communists as allies of the Liberals in the opposition against Fascism, and always maintained courteous relations with them."

Bernard Wall noted that Croce's lifework gives an unparalleled "impression of unruffled continuity and organic growth." E. K. Bramstedt pointed out that "the red thread which runs through most of his work, both historical and philosophical, is the idea of liberty." Sprigge has called him "the spokesman of an anti-mystical and anti-Utopian Humanism." Croce's outstanding characteristics, in the opinion of the London *Times*, were "an immense erudition, a wide and almost unceasing production, the highest possible quality of scholarship and a peculiar felicity in bringing learning into contact with life."

ADDITIONAL WORKS: Germany and Europe, 1944; Politics and Morals, 1945; My Philosophy, 1949; Croce, the King and the Allies: Extracts from a Diary, July 1943-June 1944, 1950.

ABOUT: Romanelli, P. Croce versus Gentile; Sprigge, C. J. Benedetto Croce, Man and Thinker; Atlantic Monthly March 1944; Comparative Literature Winter 1953; Contemporary Review November 1945, April 1951; Current Biography 1944; Life November 22, 1943; Nation January 3, 1953; New Statesman and Nation November 29, 1952; New York Times July 8, 1951, November 21, 1952; Saturday Review of Literature August 19, 1944, September 2, 1944, October 14, 1944; Time October 16, 1944, February 27, 1950; Twentieth Century January 1953.

CROCKETT, SAMUEL RUTHER-FORD (September 24, 1860-April 21, 1914). For biographical sketch and list of works and references, see TWENTIETH CENTURY AUTHORS, 1942.

* * *

ABOUT: Saturday Review of Literature April 7, 1945, September 8, 1945.

CROFT-COOKE, RUPERT (1903-). For biographical sketch and list of earlier works and references, see TWENTIETH CENTURY AUTHORS, 1942.

* * *

Rupert Croft-Cooke joined the British Army in 1940, saw service in Africa and India, and until 1946 when he was discharged, he wrote nothing. He has subsequently made up for this lost time with a prodigious number of books—novels, short stories, travelogues, books on his pet interests, the circus and gypsies. In 1950, after four years of life in a flat in London, he bought a two-hundred-year-old Georgian house in Sussex, which he remodeled with infinite and loving care and made the subject of a book, *The Life for Me.*

As a novelist Croft-Cooke specializes in the smart, well-made novel—neither deep nor entirely superficial. James Hilton wrote that his *Another Sun, Another Home* is "excellently written, its characters live, and there is a passionate sincerity." The only serious objection raised to the book was that the author's antipathy to the British Labor government was so evident that it sometimes produced distortions and exaggerations.

ADDITIONAL WORKS: Darts, 1938; Escape to the Andes, 1938; The Circus Has No Home (memoirs) 1941; Ladies Gay, 1946, Miss Allick (in England: Octopus) 1947; Moon in My Pocket: Life with the Romanies, 1948; Rudyard Kipling (English Novelists Series) 1948; How to Enjoy Travel Abroad, 1948; The Circus Book (ed.) 1948; Another Sun, Another Home (in England: Wilkie) 1949; White Mountain, 1949; Brass Farthing, 1950; Football for the Brigadier, and Other Stories, 1950; Three Names for Nicholas, 1951; Sawdust Ring (with W. F. Meadmore) 1951; Cities (with N. Barber) 1951; Nine Days with Edward, 1952; Buffalo Bill (with W. F. Meadmore) 1952; The Life for Me, 1953; The Blood-Red Island, 1953; Harvest Moon, 1953.

ABOUT: Croft-Cooke, R. The Circus Has No Home, The Life for Me.

CROFTS, FREEMAN WILLS (June, 1879-   ). For autobiographical sketch and list of earlier works and references, see TWENTIETH CENTURY AUTHORS, 1942.

*　*　*

Freeman Wills Crofts writes from Guildford, Surrey, England: "Since the previous notice I have written nine books, including a detective story for boys and a religious book on the Gospels. I have had translations into Norwegian, Spanish, Japanese, and Esperanto in addition to the languages mentioned. In all I have done over fifty short stories and some thirty short radio plays for the B.B.C."

ADDITIONAL WORKS: Fear Comes to Chalfont, 1942; The Affair at Little Wokeham (in U.S.: Double Tragedy) 1943; Enemy Unseen, 1945; Death of a Train, 1946; Young Robin Brand, Detective (juvenile) 1947; Murderers Make Mistakes (short stories) 1947; Silence for the Murderer, 1948; The Four Gospels in One Story, 1949; French Strikes Oil (in U.S.: Dark Journey) 1951.

CROLY, HERBERT DAVID (January 23, 1869-May 16, 1930). For biographical sketch and list of works and references, see TWENTIETH CENTURY AUTHORS, 1942.

*　*　*

ABOUT: Time April 22, 1946.

CRONIN, ARCHIBALD JOSEPH (July 19, 1896-   ). For biographical sketch and list of earlier works and references, see TWENTIETH CENTURY AUTHORS, 1942.

*　*　*

A. J. Cronin was in the United States, working for the British Ministry of Information, from 1941 to 1945. During this period he lived in Blue Hills, Maine, and in Greenwich, Conn. In recent years he has made his permanent home here, in New Canaan, Conn.

Cronin's later novels have sold well and received generally favorable notices, but they have not matched the popularity of *The Citadel* or *The Keys of the Kingdom*. *The Green Years* and its sequel, *Shannon's Way,* comprise a gently told, pleasant and sincere account of the childhood and manhood of an Irish boy who is raised in Scotland. Edwin Seaver commented on the novels: "Dr. Cronin remains the pale but legitimate inheritor of the Victorian storytellers. . . . If his story line and characterization go back to the horse-and-buggy days, it must be admitted that Old Dobbin and the one-horse shay still get there in their own good time." It is in the role of storyteller that Cronin wrote his autobiography, *Adventures in Two Worlds,* a collection of anecdotes drawn from his early life as a physician. There, as in his fiction, the essential appeal of Cronin to the reader is demonstrated. As Edward Weeks wrote: "He carries you forward in his recital not by any compulsion of style, wit, or originality, but by his genuine interest in men and women whom he doctored as best he could and whose problems and heartaches will appeal to many." Of his novel *Beyond This Place,* the *New Yorker* wrote: "The writing is stiff and earnest, and owing to the author's sincerity, the occasional descents into melodrama are touching."

ADDITIONAL WORKS: The Green Years, 1944; Shannon's Way, 1948; The Spanish Gardener, 1950; Adventures in Two Worlds, 1952; Beyond This Place, 1953.

ABOUT: Hoehn, M. (ed.) Catholic Authors, I; Cronin, A. J. Adventures in Two Worlds; Current Biography 1942; New York Herald Tribune Book Review September 17, 1950.

CROSS, WILBUR LUCIUS (April 10, 1862-October 5, 1948). For autobiographical sketch and list of earlier works and references, see TWENTIETH CENTURY AUTHORS, 1942.

* * *

Wilbur Lucius Cross died at his home in New Haven, Conn., at eighty-six, of pneumonia and a weakened heart.

In 1942 Cross edited the *Yale Review Anthology*, and the following year published his autobiography, *Connecticut Yankee*, which K. T. Willis called "the straightforward story of a good American." The work was characterized by the *New Yorker* as "free-flowing and witty, with a good, pithy turn of phrase, and one of the pleasantest autobiographies of the season."

Cross was "a man who maintained peace with himself and the world," in the words of H. M. Ayres, "while he kept everlastingly busy doing what he wanted to do." Of his political service the New York *Times* remarked that "in addition to bringing a keen, analytical mind to the head of the state government of Connecticut, he brought to it also a kindliness of spirit, a sprightliness of outlook and a literary flavor which found enthusiastic response." James Truslow Adams said: "He was a politician when a scholar and remained a scholar when a politician. In a word, he has always been in the best Platonic and Greek sense a 'whole man.'"

ADDITIONAL WORK: Connecticut Yankee, 1943.

ABOUT: Cross, W. L. Connecticut Yankee; Current History January 1944; Life December 13, 1948; New Republic November 8, 1943; New York Times October 5, 1948; Saturday Review of Literature October 16, 1943; Yale Review Winter 1943, Winter 1949.

*CROTHERS, RACHEL (1878-). For biographical sketch and list of works and references, see TWENTIETH CENTURY AUTHORS, 1942.

* * *

Rachel Crothers lives in retirement in her home in Redding, Conn. Her last Broadway success was *Susan and God* (1937). The question of whether her brittle and charming plays will survive is as yet unsettled. In the grim years of World War II and after, they were not revived in the professional theatre. To many readers they now seem dated. But if their situations are too slight for serious consideration, they remain admirable plays, written, as Joseph Mersand has said, "with skill, good taste, and humor."

* krŭth'ẽrz

ABOUT: Mersand, J. The Play's the Thing; Sapieha, V. P. R. Eminent Women; Independent Woman January 1946.

CROTHERS, SAMUEL MC CHORD (June 7, 1857-November 9, 1927). For biographical sketch and list of works and references, see TWENTIETH CENTURY AUTHORS, 1942.

* * *

ABOUT: Eliot, S. A. (ed.) Heralds of a Liberal Faith.

*CROUSE, RUSSEL (February 20, 1893-), American playwright and journalist, was born in Findlay, Ohio, the son of Hiram Powers Crouse, a newspaper editor, and Sarah (Schumacher) Crouse. He was educated in the public schools and high schools of Toledo, and began his writing career at seventeen as a reporter on the Cincinnati *Commercial-Tribune*. From 1911

Kesslere

to 1916 he was a news and sports reporter on the Kansas City (Mo.) *Star,* and in 1917 he returned to Cincinnati as political reporter for the *Post*. Crouse joined the Navy during World War I, serving as yeoman 2d class from 1917 to 1919. When his enlistment was up, he broke into the New York newsrooms and for the next ten years he worked as a reporter and columnist for the New York *Globe, Evening Mail,* and *Evening Post*.

In 1928 Crouse made his theatrical debut with an eight-line role in Ward Morehouse's *Gentlemen of the Press*. Although it was a not particularly auspicious beginning in the theatre, it was an important first step. He continued to write his column for the *Evening Post*, but he also began writing scenarios for short films on newspaper life. In 1931 he did the libretto for a musical comedy, *The Gang's All Here*, with results described as "not memorable" (the show ran for three weeks). But the lure of the theatre was irresistible. By 1933 he was the co-author (with Corey Ford) of a successful musical comedy book—*Hold Your Horses*—and a press agent for the Theatre Guild. He was also, by this time, an author in his own right, with two pleasantly nostalgic books on nineteenth century American life to his credit: *Mr. Currier and Mr. Ives* and *It*

* krous

Seems Like Yesterday, and a collection of essays on some classic unsolved New York murders, *Murder Won't Out.*

One of the happiest of theatrical collaborations was launched in September 1934 when Crouse met Howard Lindsay and they went to work on the book for the musical *Anything Goes.* Since then their partnership has produced some of the most successful comedies and musical comedies in American theatrical history—*Life With Father,* based on the late Clarence Day's charming family reminiscences; *Arsenic and Old Lace,* a zany comedy which completely upset all murder and horror story conventions; the Pulitzer prize-winning *State of the Union,* a satire on American politics so timely that dialogue had to be rewritten from day to day; and *Call Me Madam* (with music by Irving Berlin), which produced a campaign slogan for the 1952 presidential elections ("I Like Ike").

Lincoln Barnett has called Lindsay and Crouse "the most successful team of dramaturgists since Gilbert and Sullivan." Unlike Gilbert and Sullivan, however, there is not the slightest conflict between them. They are good personal friends as well as working associates, and they work together so smoothly that it is almost impossible to know which one has contributed what to the play. "We don't complement each other," Lindsay has said. "We supplement each other. If any two people can be said to think alike, we do." According to Crouse, Lindsay has the greater knowledge of the theatre. According to Lindsay, Crouse has the sharper sense of comedy. Theatre-goers find that the distinctions between them are unimportant. What matters is their smooth and efficient collaboration—warm, humorous, always good-natured, and thoroughly knowledgeable about all the tricks of the theatre. Several of their plays have had successful productions abroad as well as at home. *Arsenic and Old Lace* had almost as long a run in London as it had in New York. Nearly all of their plays have been made into motion pictures.

Crouse was married in 1923 to Alison Smith, who died in 1943. In 1945 he married Anna Erskine, daughter of the late John Erskine, and they have two children. He lives with his family in a town house in New York City.

PRINCIPAL WORKS: Mr. Currier and Mr. Ives, 1930; It Seems Like Yesterday, 1931; Murder Won't Out, 1932. *Plays (with H. Lindsay)—year of production*—Anything Goes, 1934; Red Hot and Blue, 1936; Hooray for What, 1937; Life With Father,

1939; Arsenic and Old Lace, 1940; Strip for Action, 1942; State of the Union, 1945; Life With Mother, 1948; Call Me Madam, 1950; Remains to Be Seen, 1951; The Prescott Proposals, 1953.

ABOUT: Barnett, L. K. Writing on Life; Current Biography 1941; National Cyclopedia of American Biography (1946); New York Times Magazine January 13, 1946; Saturday Evening Post May 27, 1944; Theatre Arts February 1944, October 1951; Time November 26, 1945.

CROW, CARL (1883-June 8, 1945). For biographical sketch and list of earlier works and references, see TWENTIETH CENTURY AUTHORS, 1942.

* * *

Carl Crow died at the Lenox Hill Hospital in New York City, after a long illness, at sixty-one.

His last book, *The City of Flint Grows Up,* published posthumously, was written "with the financial help" of the Buick Division of General Motors, and has, according to one reviewer, "the character of a glorified advertisement."

In reviewing Crow's more familiar books about China, Leo Kennedy called him "an old and skilled hand at a kind of innocent oversimplicity." Pearl Buck has praised his "balanced understanding and humor" and Lin Yutang spoke of his "keen, observant mind coupled with a very lively, humorous imagination."

ADDITIONAL WORKS: The Great American Customer, 1943; China Takes Her Place, 1944; The City of Flint Grows Up, 1945.

ABOUT: Current Biography 1941; National Cyclopedia of American Biography (1950); New York Times June 10, 1945.

CROY, HOMER (March 11, 1883-). For autobiographical sketch and list of earlier works and references, see TWENTIETH CENTURY AUTHORS, 1942.

* * *

Homer Croy writes from New York City: "Six or eight of my things have been made into motion pictures. Now and then somebody comes along and buys the movie rights to one and makes me happy. Once I danced in the street.

"*Jesse James Was My Neighbor* was sold last semaine to Republic as a movie. They have to keep my title.

"*He Hanged Them High,* my latest opus, deals with a Hangin' Judge in Fort Smith, Ark., who hanged everybody he could get his hands on.

"And at this moment [November 1952] I am working on the life of Will Rogers. I have until December first to turn it in;

if I don't, hell will pop. No title as yet. I wrote more of his motion pictures than did any other hombre; that was the reason I was picked to write the so-called 'definitive' life. I'm not sure what 'definitive' means, but I'm writin' something, anyway. [Signed] Croy, Enemy of Sin and the Dutch Elm Disease."

Correction: Croy's birthplace was Maryville, Mo., not Marysville.

ADDITIONAL WORKS: Country Cured, 1943; Wonderful Neighbor, 1945; Corn Country, 1947; What Grandpa Laughed At, 1948; Jesse James Was My Neighbor, 1949; He Hanged Them High, 1952; Our Will Rogers, 1953; Wheels West, 1955.

ABOUT: Harper's October 1946; New York World-Telegram and Sun April 26, 1952.

CROZIER, JOHN BEATTIE (April 23, 1849-January 8, 1921). For biographical sketch and list of works and references, see TWENTIETH CENTURY AUTHORS, 1942.

CULLEN, COUNTEE (May 30, 1903-January 9, 1946). For biographical sketch and list of earlier works and references, see TWENTIETH CENTURY AUTHORS, 1942.

*   *   *

Countee Cullen died at New York City's Sydenham Hospital at forty-two.

For the last eleven years of his life he taught French at the Frederick Douglass High School and lived in Tuckahoe, N.Y. His last work was a play, *St. Louis Woman*, written with Arna Bontemps.

Cullen's poetry has been described by W. Tasker Witham as "sophisticated in language and emotion, conventional in form, and precise in meter." Alfred Kreymborg called him "an authentic poet some of whose lyrics vie with the finest in America," and James Weldon Johnson remarked, "The old forms come from his hands filled with fresh beauty." Bontemps has observed that although Cullen did not live to experience a resurgence of his own creative powers "comparable with the impulse that produced his first three books of poetry," he did live to see "a second generation of the Harlem renaissance, owing much to him, on the way."

ADDITIONAL WORKS: On These I Stand (anthology) 1947.

ABOUT: Drier, H. American Literature by Negro Authors; Gregory, H. & Zaturenska, M. History of American Poetry; New York Times January 10, 1946; Saturday Review of Literature February 23, 1946, March 22, 1947.

CULLUM, RIDGWELL (August 13, 1867-November 3, 1943). For biographical sketch and list of works and references, see TWENTIETH CENTURY AUTHORS, 1942.

*   *   *

Ridgwell Cullum died at seventy-six. His ingenious adventure and mystery novels showed "no great mastery of his human material," as the Springfield *Republican* has said, but he "used a large canvas, composed a sweeping background and filled in with effective scenic descriptions."

CUMMINGS, BRUCE FREDERICK ("W. N. P. Barbellion") (September 7, 1889-October 22, 1919). For biographical sketch and list of works and references, see TWENTIETH CENTURY AUTHORS, 1942.

*   *   *

ABOUT: New Statesman and Nation July 21, 1945, July 28, 1945.

CUMMINGS, EDWARD ESTLIN (October 14, 1894-   ). For biographical sketch and list of earlier works and references, see TWENTIETH CENTURY AUTHORS, 1942.

*   *   *

In 1952 E. E. Cummings was invited to give the annual Charles Eliot Norton lectures in poetry at Harvard University. In characteristic Cummings fashion he announced to his audience that he hadn't "the remotest intention of posing as a lecturer" and proceeded to give a series of informal, witty talks and readings which he called "nonlectures." Published late in 1953 as *i: six nonlectures*, they proved a charming and valuable memoir, "an aesthetic self-portrait," an "autobiographical self-discovery," a fresh and lively exploration of Cummings' quest to discover, "Who, as a writer, am I?"

Alfred Kazin wrote in 1954 that "Cummings' poetry has ripened amazingly in recent years, but it has not grown." In his later work Cummings retains his eccentricities of language, punctuation, typography. J. G. Southworth says that his claim to a place in modern poetry must rest "not on what he says—but upon his way of saying it—his technical achievements in extending the capabilities of poetry." But fundamentally, as the late Theodore Spencer pointed out, his poetic technique is a direct consequence of his point of view. To isolate Cummings' technique and to discuss it apart from the poems themselves is therefore profitless. He writes the way he does because he is what he is—an iconoclast, an individualist, an enemy of systems and restriction and regimentation. In one of the "nonlectures" Cummings asserted: "So far as I am concerned, poetry and every other art was and is and forever will be strictly and distinctly a question of individuality. . . . If poetry is your goal, you've got to forget all about punishments and all about rewards and all about selfstyled obligations and duties and responsibilities etcetera ad infinitum and remember one thing only: that it's you—nobody else—who determine your destiny and decide your fate."

In Cummings' poetry, Horace Gregory wrote, "one is refreshed by the revival of courtly music and compliment, of poetic wit, and the art of burlesque that Italian players brought into being with the commedia dell' arte." Spencer considered him "the most truly delightful lyric poet in America," and Lloyd Frankenberg, in a review of χαιρε (the Greek word for "rejoice") called him "one of the major lyric poets of our time."

Cummings exhibited his paintings in one-man shows at the American-British Art Centre in 1944 and 1949 and at the Rochester Memorial Gallery in 1945. He is a member of the National Institute of Arts and Letters. In 1955 he received a special citation from the National Book Awards Committee for his *Poems, 1923-1954*.

ADDITIONAL WORKS: 1 x 1, 1944; Anthropos: The Future of Art, 1945; Santa Claus: A Morality, 1946; χαιρε : Seventy-One Poems, 1950; i: six nonlectures, 1953; Poems, 1923-1954, 1954.

ABOUT: Bishop, J. P. Collected Essays; Cummings, E. E. i: six nonlectures; Frankenberg, L. Pleasure Dome; Southworth, J. G. Some Modern American Poets; Spencer, T. in Modern American Poetry (ed. B. Rajan); American Literature January 1943; New Republic September 18, 1950; New Yorker January 2, 1954; Poetry November 1944, July 1947.

CUNLIFFE, JOHN WILLIAM (January 20, 1865-March 18, 1946). For autobiographical sketch and list of earlier works and references, see TWENTIETH CENTURY AUTHORS, 1942.

* * *

John William Cunliffe died at eighty-one, in Ogunquit, Maine.

Of his style (specifically in *Leaders of the Victorian Revolution*) S. A. Coblentz said: "The author's method is such as to enlist the reader's sympathy and confidence and to

allure by a steady glow that does not grow dim or cold until the last page has been reached."

ABOUT: Carnegie Foundation for the Advancement of Teaching: Annual Report 1945-46; New York Times March 19, 1946.

CUNNINGHAME GRAHAM, ROBERT BONTINE (May 24, 1852-March 20, 1936). For biographical sketch and list of works and references, see TWENTIETH CENTURY AUTHORS, 1942.

* * *

ADDITIONAL WORK: The Essential R. B. Cunninghame Graham, 1953.

ABOUT: Bloomfield, P. Preface to The Essential R. B. Cunninghame Graham; Child, W. S. The Contribution of Cunninghame Graham to the Literature of Travel; Dictionary of National Biography 1931-1940; Grieve, C. M. (Hugh MacDiarmid) Cunninghame Graham: A Centenary Study; Niles, B. R. (ed.) Journeys in Time.

CUPPY, WILLIAM JACOB (August 23, 1884-September 19, 1949). For autobiographical sketch and list of earlier works and references, see TWENTIETH CENTURY AUTHORS, 1942.

* * *

Will Cuppy died at New York's St. Vincent's Hospital at sixty-five after a long period of failing health.

The humorist's prodigious research methods had filled many boxes of 3x5 cards with notes, from which his literary executor, Fred Feldkamp, compiled two volumes which were published posthumously.

The late William Rose Benét, who once described Cuppy as having "the haunted look of the true humorist," declared that "he had something that poets have, the harassment of 'wonder,' though in him it took fantastic prose form." C. B. Palmer has spoken of the writer's "wryness, skepticism, personal delight and excellent taste." Will Davidson says: "Mr. Cuppy was one of those rare writers who can make nonsense, delightful, warming nonsense, out of the most unlikely subjects. His serious approach, his enchanting use of footnotes to add *non sequiturs* to clichés and his gentle but rather deadly spoofing of the human race give him a literary stature that is not often achieved in the field of humor."

ADDITIONAL WORKS: World's Great Detective Stories (ed.) 1943; World's Great Mystery Stories (ed.) 1943; Great Bustard and Other People, 1944; Murder Without Tears (ed.) 1946; How to Attract the Wombat, 1949; Decline and Fall of Practically Everybody, 1950; How To Get from January to December, 1951.

251

ABOUT: Banta, R. Indiana Authors and Their Books; New York Times September 20, 1949, October 8, 1950; Saturday Review of Literature October 15, 1949.

*CURTI, MERLE (September 15, 1897-), American historian and university professor, writes: "Both the frontier and immigration  helped to shape my early interest in American history. I was born in Papillion, Neb., where as a boy I knew first settlers from the older parts of the country, like the Vermont family of my mother, Alice Hunt, and the Swiss-American family of my father, John Eugene Curti. Moving with my family to Omaha I became aware of many more immigrant groups and of the importance of cities in the national life. After graduating from South High School, I entered Harvard in 1916, served briefly during World War I in the Student Army Training Corps, and took my degree, *summa cum laude* in history, in 1920. Such distinguished historians as Edward Channing, Samuel Eliot Morison, and especially Frederick Jackson Turner guided my studies; and a Sheldon Traveling Fellowship enabled me, during study at the Sorbonne, to make the acquaintance of Charles Cestre, one of the pioneer European scholars to cultivate seriously an interest in American culture. I took my Ph.D. from Harvard in 1927.

"My teaching included brief sojourns at Beloit College, Simmons College, and, through summer teaching, the University of Chicago, the University of California at Los Angeles, the University of Vermont, and other institutions. Thus I became better acquainted with various parts of the country. Research interests took me to the South. My chief academic home was Smith College, where I began as an assistant professor in 1925 and became the Dwight Morrow Professor of History in 1936. From 1937 to 1942 I was a member of the Teachers College (Columbia) faculty, and of the faculty of political science of Columbia. In 1942 I went to the University of Wisconsin and became Frederick Jackson Turner Professor of History in 1947.

"My researches in the social and intellectual history of the United States have emphasized the integral relations of our his-

* kûr′tē

torical experience with that of Europe and, indeed, of the world. A Guggenheim fellowship, a visiting professorship to the Indian universities under the auspices of the Watumull Foundation, and participation in the first historical Congress of United States and Mexico and in the first Fulbright Conference on American Studies in England have given me a deeper understanding of America and a larger perspective. My writings include histories of the peace movement, of American patriotism, and of the social ideas of American educators. *The Growth of American Thought* (1943) was the first synthesis of our intellectual history. My interest in education has been reflected in the textbooks I have written in collaboration with others, for the high schools and for colleges, as well as in a history of the University of Wisconsin, in collaboration with Vernon Carstensen. As chairman of the committee on historiography of the Social Science Research Council I learned a good deal about the theory of history. The committee's report, *Theory and Practice of History*, has had warm admirers and severe critics. This is the place to acknowledge my indebtedness to one of the members of the S.S.R.C. committee on historiography, the late Charles A. Beard.

"I have been a Curator of the Wisconsin Historical Society and am a Fellow of it; a member of the Board of Advisors of the American Council of Learned Societies; of the Social Science Research Council; of the American Philosophical Society; of the American Academy of Arts and Sciences; of the American Historical Association; and of the Mississippi Historical Association, of which I was president in 1951-52. Northwestern University conferred the L.H.D. on me in 1950, and in 1952 I gave at Northwestern the Norman Waite Harris lectures on the history of American technical and advisory missions overseas under the title 'Prelude to Point Four.' In 1952 I completed my term as a Senator of Phi Beta Kappa.

"In 1925 I married in Paris Dr. Margaret Wooster. We have two daughters, Nancy Alice Gardner, and Martha. Mountain climbing and folksongs have been my favorite recreations. We spend the academic year in Madison, Wis., and summers at Lyme Center, N.H."

* * *

In May 1944 Professor Curti received the Pulitzer prize in history for *The Growth of American Thought.*

PRINCIPAL WORKS: Austria and the United States, 1848-1852, 1927; The American Peace Crusade, 1815-1861, 1929; The Social Ideas of American Educators, 1935; Peace or War: the American Struggle, 1636-1936, 1936; The Learned Blacksmith: Letters and Journals of Elihu Burritt (ed.) 1937; The Growth of American Thought, 1943; The Roots of American Loyalty, 1946; The University of Wisconsin: a History, 1848-1925 (with V. L. Carstensen) 1949; American Scholarship in the Twentieth Century (with others) 1953; Prelude to Point Four (with K. Birr) 1954; Probing Our Past, 1955.

ABOUT: Saturday Review of Literature May 6, 1944.

CURWOOD, JAMES OLIVER (June 12, 1878-August 13, 1927). For biographical sketch and list of works and references, see TWENTIETH CENTURY AUTHORS, 1942.

* * *

ABOUT: Flower, Sir N. Just as It Happened. wood.

CURZON OF KEDLESTON, GEORGE NATHANIEL CURZON, 1st Marquis (January 11, 1859-March 20, 1925). For biographical sketch and list of works and references, see TWENTIETH CENTURY AUTHORS, 1942.

* * *

ABOUT: Flower, Sir N. Just As It Happened.

CUTLIFFE HYNE. See HYNE

DABNEY, VIRGINIUS (February 8, 1901-), American historian, biographer and journalist, writes: "I was born at the University of Virginia, where my father, Richard Heath Dabney, a Heidelberg Ph.D., served on the faculty for forty-nine years. He and my aunt taught me at home until I was thirteen, when I entered Episcopal High School, near Alexandria, Va. After my graduation there three years later, I took B.A. and M.A. degrees from the University of Virginia (1920 and 1921). It was not until 1922, when I was teaching school, that my father asked me if I had ever thought of entering newspaper work. I had been floundering around trying to decide what career appealed to me, when this suggestion struck a responsive chord. I went to Richmond and

Foster Studio

obtained a job as a cub reporter on the *News Leader,* effective at the end of the school year.

"After I had been on the paper six years, and had written for various newspapers and magazines, I joined the staff of the rival paper, the Richmond *Times-Dispatch.* In 1930 I accepted an invitation from the University of North Carolina Press to write a book on liberal movements in the South from Jefferson's time to the present. Two and a half years of hard work, done at night and on week-ends, resulted in *Liberalism in the South.* It appeared in the fall of 1932, when the great depression was virtually at its worst, so that sales were small, but the book can be said to have been a critical success.

"Six months in Central Europe on a fellowship in 1934 were followed by my appointment as chief editorial writer of the *Times-Dispatch,* and in 1936 as editor. An engagement at Princeton University as lecturer on the New South for the second semester, session of 1939-40, led Appleton-Century to invite me to write a book on developments in the South since the appearance of my first book. The result was *Below the Potomac.* This had the bad luck to be published in the spring of 1942, some four months after Pearl Harbor when the eyes of the nation were focused on the Second World War. While the reception the book had from the reviewers was as good as I had hoped for, most citizens were too absorbed in the war to give much thought to an analysis of regional domestic problems.

"Throughout the war, I was so loaded down with editorial duties because of the shortage of help, that I found it impossible to do any outside writing, except occasional articles for the magazines and book reviews. When the war was over, I decided to complete a project on which I had done a great deal of spadework in the 1930's—a biography of Bishop James Cannon, Jr., key figure in the prohibition movement since the turn of the century, and an amazingly devious and slippery figure. This appeared in 1949.

"I have always been primarily a newspaperman, and have written books only when I could find time from my journalistic duties. My economic and social philosophy has undergone a shift in the conservative direction since my first book was published, but in that book I stressed the importance of states' rights."

* * *

The Pulitzer prize in journalism was awarded to Virginius Dabney in 1948 for his editorials in the Richmond *Times-Dispatch.*

He was married in 1923 to Douglas Harrison Chelf and they have three children. Their home is in Richmond, Va.

PRINCIPAL WORKS: Liberalism in the South, 1932; Below the Potomac, 1942; Dry Messiah: the Life of Bishop James Cannon, Jr., 1949.

ABOUT: Current Biography 1948; Richmond News Leader May 5, 1948; Saturday Review of Literature April 16, 1949; Time December 4, 1944.

DAGLISH, ERIC FITCH (August 29, 1892-). For autobiographical sketch and list of earlier works and references, see TWENTIETH CENTURY AUTHORS, 1942.

* * *

Eric Daglish writes from Speen, Aylesbury, England: "From 1940 to 1948 I served with the R.A.F. in staff appointments with the rank of Squadron Leader."

Since his release from the service, Daglish has written several books on nature study and dog breeding. He has also illustrated a number of books—among them editions of Walton's *Compleat Angler*, Thoreau's *Walden* and Gilbert White's *Selborne*. He is editor and illustrator of the Open Air Library.

ADDITIONAL WORKS: Birds of the British Isles, 1948; The Dog Breeder's Manual, 1951; Name This Insect, 1952; Enjoying the Country, 1952; The Popular Dachshund, 1952.

ABOUT: Mahony, B. E. Illustrators of Children's Books, 1744-1945.

DAHLBERG, EDWARD (July 22, 1900-), American novelist, poet, and critic, writes: "I was born in Boston, but up until  I was past six, my mother, Elizabeth Dahlberg, an itinerant hairdresser, took me from one city to another to get bread. We lived in Louisville, Memphis, New Orleans, Dallas and Denver before settling in Kansas City, Mo., where my mother opened up a ladies' barber shop underneath the 8th Street viaduct which shambled down toward the old railroad depot in the factory West Bottoms. The shop, about half an alley block from the Grand Opera House, which seemed to me so immense, and where I played behind the stage, is one of the early memories of Harry S. Truman. How wizened it was, but then everything to a child is very big and to a man so small, and

close to dust and nothing. The ladies' barber shop was a popular hangout for out-of-town cattle ranchers, local Democratic aldermen, railroad hands from the roundhouse, and wealthy commission house men from lower Walnut Street. The shop, the cowboys and politicians and big horse and mule traders that came to it, are the basis of my first novel, *Bottom Dogs*, which appeared in London in 1929 and in New York in 1930, with a long introduction by D. H. Lawrence.

"I still think there was more health in the wild, ruttish Kansas City streets than in my later experiences in Paris, London, Florence and Brussels. My greatest teachers were not Lao Tze, Heraclitus, Pliny or Sir Thomas Browne, whom I read with bacchic avidity, but my mother, Kansas City, the Cleveland orphanage, where I was an inmate until my seventeenth year, and the roving boxcars in which I hutted and slept as a hobo in 1919. Later, the minds that seeded my life and books were Alfred Stieglitz, the Socratic camera seer, and Theodore Dreiser who taught me how to read Shakespeare and who turned my attention to neglected writers like Henry B. Fuller, Hamlin Garland, Kirkland, Harris Merton Lyon, Edgar Howe. The most significant intellect for me after these men was Randolph Bourne, the hunchback gnome and son of a Bloomfield, N.J., minister, and the author of *Untimely Papers* and *The History of a Literary Radical*.

"After some years abroad as a deracinated K. C. urchin of the Muses, I decided that the only land I could understand was the United States. I saw that I read the wise Europeans to comprehend American locality and the genius of Thoreau, Whitman, Melville, Dickinson, and Sherwood Anderson. The land that so drew Cortez, La Salle, De Soto, and Thoreau was my mare's nest and fate.

"Besides *Bottom Dogs* I published *From Flushing to Calvary*, another novel dealing with my mother, in part apocryphal, and the Cleveland orphanage memories. There was also the small prose-poem titled *Kentucky Blue Grass Henry Smith*, brought out by the White Horse Press, Cleveland, and *Those Who Perish*, also fiction. The little magazine, *This Quarter*, of Paris, Milan, and Roquebrune, had printed short stories, verses and essays of mine, and *Pagany* of Gramercy Square had also printed me. In 1941 *Do These Bones Live* came out. Ford Madox Ford took the manuscript with him to Deauville where he died. He was going to do a preface to it. In 1947 it was republished in London with a foreword by Herbert Read, who also did an introduction to my last book,

The Flea of Sodom, published in London and by New Directions in New York. In 1950 I married R'lene L. Howell, and since then have contributed poetry to the *New Directions Annual* and to *Poetry*, Chicago, as well as a piece on Garcilaso de la Vega's marvelous history of Florida and De Soto."

PRINCIPAL WORKS: Bottom Dogs, 1929; From Flushing to Calvary, 1932; Those Who Perish, 1934; Do These Bones Live, 1941; Sing, O Barren, 1947; The Flea of Sodom, 1950.

ABOUT: American Mercury June 1941; Poetry January, April 1951.

*DAICHES, DAVID (September 2, 1912-), English critic, writes: "I was born in the north of England, but, my parents moving to Edinburgh  shortly afterwards, I grew up in Scotland. I was educated at George Watson's College, Edinburgh, and at Edinburgh University, taking my degree in 1934 with first class honours in English literature and language. I had been interested in literature and in writing since I was a small boy, and from the age of nine had produced reams of poetry, stories, and plays. I think I was eighteen when I wrote and helped produce a musical comedy.

"My university studies turned my literary ambitions into more academic channels for a time, and when I won a scholarship at Edinburgh that sent me on to Balliol College, Oxford, to do research, I embarked on an ambitious study of English Bible translation which eventually won me the Oxford D.Phil. (Part of it was published as *The King James Bible: A Study of its Sources and Development*, by the University of Chicago Press in 1941.) But even while I was engaged in this research I had also less academic literary interests and wrote a fair amount of poetry, including some light verse, and some miscellaneous prose. I also took time off from my research to write critical essays on modern writers, in whom I was beginning to be much interested. This resulted in my book *New Literary Values*, published in 1936. A year later, under the influence of new ideas about the social background of literature, I wrote my *Literature and Society*, a breezy sketch of the social background of English literature which I dashed off in two months as a pleasant change from working on my

* dä'tchĕz

thesis. In 1936 I was appointed Bradley Fellow of Balliol College, Oxford, and the following year I married Isobel Janet Mackay of Aberdeen and Edinburgh.

"After my marriage I became rather restless in the conventional academic world and we decided to go to France for a year when I would try to earn my living by my pen. But we had only been in France for a few months when I received an offer from the University of Chicago to go over and teach there, and as we were quite broke at the time and the prospect seemed interesting, we went to America at the end of 1937, intending to stay a few years before returning to Britain or France.

"The war, of course, changed our plans as it changed so many people's. I stayed at Chicago until the spring of 1943, when I left to go into British Government service. I worked at British Information Services in New York for a while, and was then appointed Second Secretary at the British Embassy in Washington. I was back in London for some brief spells, working first at the Ministry of Information and then at the Foreign Office. Then in June, 1946, I resigned my position at the British Embassy and we all returned —we had three children by now—to Scotland. While I was wondering what I was going to do next I received an offer from Cornell University, so back to America we went late in 1946, and I remained at Cornell as professor of English and, from 1948, chairman of the Division of Literature, until 1951, when I resigned to take up a position as university lecturer in English at Cambridge, England.

"In my fourteen years in America I did a great deal of writing, largely critical, but also including some poetry and short stories, and I contributed regularly to a number of periodicals and reviews.

PRINCIPAL WORKS: The Place of Meaning in Poetry, 1935; New Literary Values, 1936; Literature and Society, 1938; The Novel and the Modern World, 1939; Poetry and the Modern World, 1940; The King James Version of the Bible, 1941; Virginia Woolf, 1942; Robert Louis Stevenson, 1947; A Study of Literature, 1948; Robert Burns, 1950; Willa Cather, 1951.

DALLIN, DAVID JULIEVICH (May 24, 1889-), Russian-born political economist, was born David Julievich Levin, son of Jule and Sara Levin, in Rogachev. In 1909 he was arrested for participation in an anti-Czarist underground organization and imprisoned for two years. He escaped to Germany where he lived from 1911 to 1917 and completed his studies, taking a Ph.D. from the University of Heidelberg in 1913. In that

same year he published his first book, a study of wages and social movements, in Germany. Ten days after the Russian Revolution in 1917 he returned to Russia. He was elected a member of the Moscow Soviet and served in it as an opposition (Menshevik) deputy from 1918 to 1921. He was arrested by the Soviet authorities in 1920 but released. In 1922, on the verge of arrest again, he fled to Germany. During the next two decades Dallin lived in Berlin, Warsaw, Paris, Stockholm, London, and Copenhagen. He supported himself by lecturing and writing for magazines and newspapers on political and economic questions. He published a second book, on political affairs, in Berlin in 1923. In 1940, with his wife and son, he came to the United States.

Since Dallin has been in the United States he has published a number of books on Soviet affairs which are widely recognized as authoritative in that field. Although he is, and has long been, anti-Soviet, his books are scholarly and well-documented political analyses rather than emotion-charged personal indictments. When judged from the perspective of the middle 1950's, Dallin's sober warnings of potential Soviet aggression and expansion in the middle 1940's take on added significance. At the time of the publication of his *The Real Soviet Russia* and *The Big Three,* many reviewers and political commentators had a more sanguine view of relations between the Soviet Union and the Western democracies. Even then, however, the soundness of his work was recognized. Hans Kohn wrote of *The Real Soviet Russia*: "Probably his picture is as one-sided as all presentations of Soviet Russia tend to be. But it is one that no serious student of Russia, whatever his point of view may be, should overlook." Of *The Big Three,* in which (in 1945) Dallin warned of Soviet expansion in the Far East and the Middle East as well as in Europe, the *United States Quarterly Book Review* commented: "Dallin is an historian of some skill, not an irresponsible alarmist. If one accepts his premises and employs the evidence he sup-

plies, the conclusions he reaches are not illogical." In 1945 some reviewers questioned his premises (though his evidence was not seriously challenged), but within the next few years they found widespread approval and acceptance. Hans Kohn hailed his *Soviet Russia and the Far East* as "a cool and factual book which marshals the facts . . . into an intelligent and intelligible pattern," and R. J. Kerner (in the *Yale Review*) called the book "superior to any work heretofore published" on the subject.

Dallin lives in New York City. Articles by him appear frequently in the *Yale Review* and other periodicals. He is a contributing editor of the *New Leader* magazine.

PRINCIPAL WORKS IN ENGLISH TRANSLATION: Soviet Russia's Foreign Policy, 1942; Russia and Postwar Europe, 1943; The Big Three, 1945; The Real Soviet Russia, 1947; Forced Labor in Soviet Russia (with B. I. Nicolaevsky) 1947; Soviet Russia and the Far East, 1948; The Rise of Russia in Asia, 1949; The New Soviet Empire, 1951; (ed.) What Happened in Salem? 1952.

ABOUT: Steinberg, J. (ed.) Verdict of Three Decades; Saturday Review of Literature July 2, 1949.

DALY, ELIZABETH (October 15, 1878-), American writer of mystery stories, was born in New York City, the daughter of Joseph Francis Daly, a justice of the Supreme Court of the County of New York, and Emma Barker Daly. She was the niece of Augustin Daly, the famous playwright and theatrical producer of the '90's, whose personal library con-

tained a first folio of Shakespeare. Miss Daly grew up immersed in the world of literature and the theatre, reading intensively both in her father's library and in that of her uncle Augustin.

After attending Miss Baldwin's School, Elizabeth Daly went to Bryn Mawr College, receiving her B.A. there in 1901, and taking her M.A. at Columbia the following year. In 1904 she returned to Bryn Mawr as a reader in English. She remained there in that capacity for two years, coaching and producing amateur plays, and thereafter directing pageants.

Miss Daly started boldly on her literary career at the age of sixteen, when she began publishing light verse and prose in the old

Life, Puck, and *Scribner's.* But it was not until 1940, when she was past sixty, that *Unexpected Night,* the first of her mystery novels featuring Henry Gamadge, the suave bibliophile-detective, appeared. Since that date she has published no fewer than seventeen books, praised for their literary quality, credibility, and intellectual excitement.

For many readers Henry Gamadge has become an actual person; mail addressed to him has been sent to her door. Miss Daly has described her amateur detective-hero as "the semi-bookish type, but not pretentious. . . . He represents everything in a man eager to battle the forces of evil. . . . He is basically kind but at times can be ruthless."

Unexpected Night, which dealt with a conspiracy to obtain a legacy, was followed by *Deadly Nightshade,* the story of a case of poisoning. The success of her third book, *Murders in Volume 2* (1941), a problem in the fourth dimension, led to British editions of her works. In the year 1941 Miss Daly brought out, as a change of diet, *The Street Has Changed,* a novel of manners mirroring forty years of the theatre, as seen through the life of a retired actress—in which she put to good use her background in theatrical history. *The Book of the Dead* (1944) made use of murder clues provided by a copy of Shakespeare's plays.

Miss Daly traces her own interest in detective fiction to a taste for games and puzzles of all kinds and back to an early admiration for the novels of Wilkie Collins. A careful worker, who "takes as much pains as Proust," she usually makes four drafts of each book. She considers the detective novel, at its best, a high form of literary art and says she has no further desire to write any other kind of fiction.

Described as a shy retiring person, Miss Daly makes her home and creates her Henry Gamadge stories in a modest New York apartment. She is unmarried.

PRINCIPAL WORKS: Unexpected Night, 1940; Deadly Nightshade, 1940; Murders in Volume 2, 1941; The Street Has Changed, 1941; The House Without the Door, 1942; Nothing Can Rescue Me, 1943; Evidence of Things Seen, 1943; Arrow Pointing Nowhere, 1944; The Book of the Dead, 1944; Any Shape or Form, 1945; Somewhere in the House, 1946; Wrong Way Down, 1946; Night Walk, 1947; The Book of the Lion, 1948; And Dangerous to Know, 1949; Death and Letters, 1950; The Book of the Crime, 1951.

ABOUT: New York World-Telegram June 1, 1949; Wilson Library Bulletin December 1944.

DALY, THOMAS AUGUSTINE (May 28, 1871-October 4, 1948). For autobiographical sketch and list of works and references, see TWENTIETH CENTURY AUTHORS, 1942.

* * *

T. A. Daly died at seventy-seven at the Philadelphia General Hospital. He had continued writing his newspaper column throughout a long illness until he suffered a paralytic stroke two months before his death.

Although many critics regarded his poems as "journalistic verse but definitely not poetry" and "chipper doggerel," William Lyon Phelps said of Daly's Italian dialect verses, "they are revelations of individual men and women. They are exactly what they ought to be." William Rose Benét described him as "a genial humanist, no propagandist, a clever technician, a boon companion."

ABOUT: New York Times October 5, 1948.

DAMON, SAMUEL FOSTER (February 22, 1893-). For biographical sketch and list of works and references, see TWENTIETH CENTURY AUTHORS, 1942.

* * *

S. Foster Damon lives in Providence, R.I., where he is professor of English and curator of the Harris Collection of American Poetry at Brown University. Although more recent studies of the poet William Blake have amplified our knowledge of him and cast new light on his work, Damon's *William Blake: His Philosophy and Symbols* (1924) remains one of the most important and most comprehensive volumes on him. Damon's recent scholarship has been in the field of American folklore and culture, with special emphasis on folk songs and folk dancing.

*DAMPIER, Sir WILLIAM CECIL (December 27, 1867-December 11, 1952), British historian of science, was born William Cecil Dampier Whetham, in London, son of Charles Langley Whetham and Mary Ann Dampier, both of West Country families. "My ancestors," he wrote in his autobiography (*Cambridge and Elsewhere*), "belonged to the class of yeomen or small landowners who made little fortunes in the industrial revolution of the early nineteenth century, the Whethams and Tuckers as manufacturers of canvas, twine, and nets, the historic products of Bridport, and the Dampiers, with their

* dăm′pĭ ĕr

257

relatives the Bides, as owners of glove factories, carrying the staple industry of Yeovil. . . . As a boy, I had bad health, and could not

go to a public school—a deprivation I felt keenly in later years. . . . I was diffident, shy, somewhat halting in my speech, and distrustful of my own power. . . . The problem of a future profession was a recurrent nightmare. . . . I went up to Cambridge with the idea of studying chemistry . . . became more and more interested in physics . . . was placed in the first class in the two parts of the Natural Science Tripos in 1888 and 1889. . . . In 1889 I was awarded the Coutts Trotter Studentship for research, which provided me with an income at a time which, owing to the death of my father, was financially difficult for my family. . . . The studentship kept me going until my election to a fellowship (at Trinity College) in October 1891 on the results of my research. In 1895 I was made a lecturer of Trinity College, and in 1907 a tutor." His highly-prized connection with Trinity College lasted through life, including several years as Senior Fellow. His early research was on the mechanics of moving liquids, and on problems of electrolysis, leading to the writing of *Solution and Electrolysis* for the Natural Science Manuals of the Cambridge University Press, later enlarged and improved as *The Theory of Solution*, and followed by *The Theory of Experimental Electricity*. In 1901 he was elected a Fellow of the Royal Society on the strength of his electrolytic experiments. *The Recent Development of Physical Science* was the first of his books to deal with the historical and philosophical aspects of science. Though fully occupied with lecturing and with college and university administration, he continued to write, his next books being the product of studies in family history, pursued in conjunction with his wife (Catherine Durning, daughter of Robert Durning Holt of Liverpool, whom he married in 1897; they had six children). A life of *Colonel Nathaniel Whetham, a Forgotten Soldier of the Civil Wars*—a far-off cousin—was succeeded by books on heredity and eugenics, expounding the recently rediscovered work of Mendel and its bearings on sociology and politics.

The inheritance from an uncle of land in Dorset led to the change of name to Dampier, to experiments in dairy farming and cheese-making, and to work that resulted in the establishment of an industry for making lactose and pig-food from whey. His consideration of the economic and financial aspects of agriculture bore fruit in papers on the economic lag of farming, and on the effects of monetary instability on agriculture, and in a book on *Politics and the Land*. Becoming known for his application of scientific knowledge to agricultural problems, he was drawn into administrative work of various kinds—on the Councils of the Royal Agricultural Society of England, the Lawes Agricultural Trust, and the National Institute of Agricultural Botany, on committees on agricultural machinery, agricultural policy, and land settlement, and on the Agricultural Wages Board. His services to the public were recognized in 1931 by a knighthood. A four years' appointment as secretary of the newly-formed Agricultural Research Council followed, and appointment as a Development Commissioner in 1933 was renewed for many years. Other long spells of service were devoted to local committees and councils in Cambridge and Dorset.

"My beginnings as a physicist and my somewhat amateurish studies in theoretical biology and practical agriculture gave me a wide if superficial interest in science as a whole, and my inquiries into family history taught me something about the methods of historical research. It was natural that I should be drawn to weave all these threads into a history of science. . . . About 1925 I started to write in the intervals of other employment, and in 1929 the book was . . . published by the Cambridge University Press as *A History of Science and its Relations with Philosophy and Religion*." The book was successful in both Britain and the United States, and was issued in numerous editions and several languages, and also in simpler form as *A Shorter History of Science*. Sir William Dampier continued to contribute conscientious services on many committees until almost the end of his life, in spite of poor general health, and recurring spells of illness. He was slight in build, taller than his "scholarly stoop" allowed him to appear; he wore a pointed beard which early became white. His combination of the intellectual interests of a Cambridge don with administrative and business experience, and with attachment to country life and the country sports of shooting and hunting, brought him an exceptionally wide range of friends, and his varied activities were reflected in the careers taken up by his daughters, in biochemistry, nursing, agricultural science (in two cases), and economics. He had ten grandchildren and a great-grandson at the time of his death.

PRINCIPAL WORKS: Solution and Electrolysis, 1895; The Theory of Solution, 1902; The Recent Development of Physical Science, 1904; The Theory of Experimental Electricity, 1905; The Foundations of Science, 1913; The War and the Nation, 1917; Matter and Change, 1924; Politics and the Land, 1927; A History of Science, and its Relations with Philosophy and Religion, 1929; A Shorter History of Science, 1944; Cambridge and Elsewhere, 1950. *With C. D. Dampier*—Studies in Nature and Country Life, 1903; Colonel Nathaniel Whetham, a Forgotten Soldier of the Civil Wars, 1907; The Family and the Nation 1909; Back to the Land, 1910; Science and the Human Mind, 1912; An Introduction to Eugenics, 1912; Heredity and Society, 1912. *With M. Dampier Whetham*—Cambridge Readings in the Literature of Science.

ABOUT: Dampier, W. C. Cambridge and Elsewhere; Illustrated London News December 27, 1952; Nature January 31, 1953.

DANE, CLEMENCE (pseudonym of Winifred Ashton). For biographical sketch and list of earlier works and references, see TWENTIETH CENTURY AUTHORS, 1942.

* * *

Clemence Dane's *Come of Age* (with incidental music by Richard Addinsell) was revived in New York City in February 1952, with Judith Anderson starring in the leading role as she had done in the first American production in 1934. Although the earlier production had been a failure, it had attracted many admirers, mainly because of its unusual use of a jazz background for a play that was essentially poetic fantasy. The revival, however, was also unfavorably received. More successful with American critics was Miss Dane's historical novel *He Brings Great News*, a story of English life in the Napoleonic era, which the *New Yorker* praised as "a beautifully told, exciting narrative pulsing with the breath of life."

ADDITIONAL WORKS: *Novels*—He Brings Great News, 1944. *Plays*—Call Home the Heart, 1947; The Saviours *(with R. Addinsell)* 1942; The Lion and the Unicorn, 1943.

DANIELS, JONATHAN (April 26, 1902-). For biographical sketch and list of earlier works and references, see TWENTIETH CENTURY AUTHORS, 1942.

* * *

Jonathan Daniels was administrative assistant to President Franklin D. Roosevelt from 1943 to 1945. In the latter year he became the President's press secretary. He has described the Washington of this period in a series of lively profiles in *Frontier on the Potomac*. Since 1947 Daniels has represented the United States on the United Nations subcommittee on the Prevention of Discrimination and Protection of Minorities. He became a member of the public administrative board of the Economic Cooperation Administration in 1948, and in the following year was elected Democratic National Committeeman from North Carolina. Daniels' father, Josephus Daniels, died in 1948, and his son then became officially the editor of the Raleigh (N.C.) *News and Observer*. Later that same year Daniels accompanied President Truman on his pre-election campaign tour. In 1950 he published his biography of the President, *Man of Independence*, a sympathetic and admiring but—most of the reviewers concluded—also a fair and objective portrait. Probably the most interesting of his recent books is *The End of Innocence*, a study based on the voluminous diaries of his father, Josephus Daniels, of the political chessboard of Washington during the years of Woodrow Wilson's presidency. Claude G. Bowers found the book "rich in revealing historical data, in wit, humor, whimsey, and a charm that sometimes reminds the reader of *The Education of Henry Adams*."

ADDITIONAL WORKS: Frontier on the Potomac, 1946; Man of Independence, 1950; The End of Innocence, 1954.

ABOUT: Saturday Review of Literature September 30, 1950, June 19, 1954.

DANNAY, FREDERIC. See QUEEN, E.

D'ANNUNZIO. See ANNUNZIO

DARGAN, Mrs. OLIVE (TILFORD) ("Fielding Burke"). For biographical sketch and list of earlier works and references, see TWENTIETH CENTURY AUTHORS, 1942.

* * *

Under the name "Fielding Burke," Mrs. Dargan has published one novel in the past decade—*Sons of the Stranger*, a story of the struggle for social justice in a Western mining community at the turn of the century. A long and turbulent novel, its "tough, authentic background of labor war" was in strange and sometimes confusing contrast to Mrs. Dargan's "romantic view" of her characters. D. L. Adams wrote in the *Atlantic*: "The author's sympathies are warm and always on the right side, but they have led her into exploring far too many aspects of a period that was complicated enough."

ADDITIONAL WORK: Sons of the Stranger, 1947.

ABOUT: North Carolina Authors (1952); Warfel, H. R. American Novelists of Today.

*DARÍO, RUBÉN (January 18, 1867-February 6, 1916). For biographical sketch and list of works and references, see TWENTIETH CENTURY AUTHORS, 1942.

* * *

ABOUT: Davis, H. E. Latin American Leaders; Stewart, W. & Peterson, H. F. Builders of Latin America; United Nations World September 1951.

* dä rē′ō

DARK, ELEANOR (O'REILLY) (August 26, 1901-   ), Australian novelist, was born and educated in Sydney. She married

Dr. Eric Dark in 1922, has one son, and lives with her family in New South Wales. Her recreations are reading, bush-walking, and gardening.

Mrs. Dark's first novel was published in 1932. Her second novel, *Prelude to Christopher*, won the Australian Literature Society's Gold Medal for the best novel by an Australian published in 1934, and two years later she won the award again with *Return to Coolami*. Her novels have been well received in both England and the United States. Especially successful was *The Timeless Land*, an historical novel about the early English settlers in Australia, which became a Book-of-the-Month Club selection in the United States.

All of Mrs. Dark's novels have been set in Australia. For the most part, however, they have not been regional novels. Australia is the scene, the background—frequently described with striking sensitivity—but the primary interest of the author is her drama on the human level: the emotional problems of mature, intelligent, and well-meaning people. Her first three books were love stories—"romantic in the conventional sense," as Barnard Eldershaw wrote, and

"conventional in the romantic sense." What distinguished them from the run-of-the-mill brand of novels, however, was her technique —what Eldershaw calls her "technical subtlety"—shifting points of view and her manipulation of time sequences. Alfred Kazin wrote that the characters in her *Return to Coolami* "rise to their full stature only as they think deep enough into the past." As a result, Kazin found, the novel is built in fragments which come together only from time to time. But, he continued, "it is a significant indication of Mrs. Dark's talent that her novel should possess the constant interest that it does "

Each succeeding book by Mrs. Dark, Eldershaw remarks, "shows a definite gain on its predecessor in maturity and skill of treatment." *The Timeless Land* was praised by Klaus Lambrecht in the *Saturday Review of Literature*, as "a novel of stern beauty and profound reality," and the New York *Times'* reviewer found it "a novel of towering stature, beautifully molded, soundly and broadly based." A more recent historical novel, *Storm of Time*, was equally sound and thorough. R. D. Charques of the *Spectator* admired the breadth, sympathy and justice of Mrs. Dark's picture of nineteenth century Australian life. "It is competence of this order, after all," he wrote, "not the fashionably pretentious or febrile, that helps to keep the novel alive." The critical consensus is that Mrs. Dark is an intelligent and conscientious novelist. Her experiments in technique have at times produced uneven results, but it is always work that is worthy of the reader's serious attention.

PRINCIPAL WORKS: Slow Dawning, 1932; Prelude to Christopher, 1934; Return to Coolami, 1936; Sun Across the Sky, 1937; Waterway, 1938; The Timeless Land, 1941; The Little Company, 1945; Storm of Time, 1948.

ABOUT: Eldershaw, B. Essays in Australian Fiction; Scholastic November 5, 1945.

DARROW, CLARENCE SEWARD (April 18, 1857-March 13, 1938). For biographical sketch and list of works and references, see TWENTIETH CENTURY AUTHORS, 1942.

* * *

ABOUT: Stone, I. & Kennedy, R. (eds.) We Speak for Ourselves; Antioch Review March 1953.

DAVENPORT, MARCIA (June 9, 1903-   ), American novelist, was born in New York City. Her mother was the famous lyric soprano Alma Gluck, and the little girl was raised in the glamorous but frequently trying atmosphere of the concert halls and opera stages of Europe and America.  "My life," she says, "was not what most people would consider a normal life for a child; that is, my mother had no room in her world for a child. I was fitted into my mother's existence along with the other exigencies. If I wanted companionship I had to come up to adult standards. . . . I had a very lonely childhood except for books. I read fairy stories, and the people in them were my first companions." She was educated in the United States and attended the Friends School in Philadelphia and the Shipley School at Bryn Mawr. She studied at Wellesley for two years, then went to Europe where she received her bachelor's degree from the University of Grenoble in France. In 1923 she married Frank D. Clarke. A year later a daughter, Patricia, was born, and shortly after that she was divorced.

Resuming her maiden name of Gluck, Mrs. Davenport became a writer of advertising copy. From 1928 to 1931 she was a member of the editorial staff of the *New Yorker*. She married Russell Davenport, managing editor of *Fortune*, in 1929 (they were divorced in 1946; he died in 1954) and they had one daughter, born in 1934. From 1934 to 1939 Mrs. Davenport was music critic of *Stage* magazine. In 1936 she was commentator on the Metropolitan Opera Saturday afternoon broadcasts. Her first book was a biography of Mozart which she described as "neither a romance nor a textbook." Her second book, and first novel, was *Of Lena Geyer,* a warm and vivid portrait of a great opera singer. With her second novel, a lengthy and heavily detailed saga of life in the steel mills of Pittsburgh, *The Valley of Decision,* Mrs. Davenport made the top ranks of the best-seller lists and remained there for a comfortable stay. The novel was made into a motion picture.

Mrs. Davenport writes: "In 1947 I published the novel *East Side, West Side.* This was promptly pounced upon by the quidnuncs as autobiographical, which it definitely is not, but such denials only accuse one of protesting too loudly. The book is a cross-section portrait of the human hodgepodge which is New York. It was suggested to me by my beloved editor, Maxwell Evarts Perkins, who died on June 17, 1947, while he and I were in the midst of revising that novel. It was the last book that he edited. Somehow it got finished and published, but thereafter the loss of Max and then of the other major interest and incentives of my existence suspended me in a long retreat, both geographical and from all activity. *East Side, West Side* was made into a film by M.G.M.

"All during the late war I was deeply absorbed in work for the Czechoslovak people and their cause. This grew out of my long-standing attachment to their country and my innumerable visits to it in the days of the Republic. As the war drew to a close I began to shape up a long novel, most of which I intended to place in Bohemia, the rest in the American Middle West. At the same time I was active on the Executive Board of American Relief for Czechoslovakia which, I am thankful to say, was never infiltrated here or in Prague by Communists. This organization was promptly disbanded upon the Communist *coup d'état* in 1948.

"The late President Beneš had assured me that I should go to Prague to work at all my jobs as soon as it should be possible, and I did arrive there in the early summer of 1945. I remained there, with intermittent trips to New York, digging myself in and settling down to a life that I had planned for many years, until the Communist *putsch.* I left Prague on March 7, 1948, leaving my beautiful home and everything around which I had made my life. I have never been back. My agony of mind over the temper and fate of the Czechoslovaks, and my bitter disillusionment have torpedoed the novel I had so long been planning.

"I wandered by way of England and other stopping-places down to the Lake of Como, which I have known since infancy when I used to go there with my mother. Its atmosphere of gentleness was so welcome that I took a small house there, which four years ago I bought. Having resisted furiously all previous attempts to trap me into living in the country, I have now become at least two-thirds a rustic. I am passionately interested in my garden, where I raise quite extraordinary roses, and on a tiny bit of land an enormous variety of fruits and vegetables. I have about two hundred olive trees which produce very nice oil. My Italian house is perched directly on the shore of the Lago di Como. I hear (and work over) a lot of music. I dare brag that I am a magnificent cook. I do needlepoint embroidery and nearly burst with pride when the Metropolitan Museum borrowed a wing chair of mine for an exhibition of contemporary needlework some years ago. I now spend about half the year in Italy and the other half in my apartment on the East River in New York, where I have lived for nearly twenty-five years. I fly back and forth to Italy accompanied by a wonderful English peke who is a far better traveler than most of the human passengers.

"I am now finishing a novel still untitled. I must stick to my phobic refusal ever to say what an unpublished book is about. I hope it wins the same international favor as my previous novels, which have been translated into a collective total of twelve different languages. I have also in hand chunks and fragments of two non-fiction books at which I have been chipping away for many years. One or other of them is likely to follow the current novel." [The "current novel" was *My Brother's Keeper,* an immediate best seller, the story of two recluse brothers which was suggested in part by the real-life case of the recluse Collyer brothers in New York City.]

PRINCIPAL WORKS: Mozart, 1932; Of Lena Geyer, 1936; Valley of Decision, 1942; East Side, West Side, 1947; My Brother's Keeper, 1954.

ABOUT: Van Gelder, R. Writers and Writing; Warfel, H. R. American Novelists of Today; Current Biography 1944; New York Herald Tribune Book Review October 24, 1954; Wilson Library Bulletin September 1937.

DAVIDSON, DAVID (ALBERT) (May 11, 1908-), American novelist, writes: "I was born in New York, a city mysteriously

Vandamm

elusive to the novelist, that refuses to let itself be captured as Paris was captured by Balzac and Proust, Chicago by Dreiser. A traveling scholarship from Columbia University in 1931 turned my own lenses toward Europe. Each of my three novels to date is set in a foreign land, and each shows Americans in inter-action with other cultures. For the future, however, I hope to show Americans among Americans.

"My boyhood was spent in the jungles of lower Harlem, where my contemporaries ran to future hoodlums, boxing champions

of the world, and killers. Willing but balked at finding a place for myself in the hierarchy of violence, I had to look elsewhere for success. From the age of thirteen on, I habitually thought of myself as a novelist-to-be, though without doing much to bring this about. When at thirty-eight I wrote and published my first novel it was with a sense of both inevitability and surprise.

"Education, previously, consisted of the public elementary schools; Townsend Harris High School, in New York, where the four-year curriculum was compressed into three, for no discernible reason; the College of the City of New York (B.A. 1928) and the Columbia University School of Journalism (B. Lit. 1930). This appallingly lengthy process leaves me with resentment that I should have been taught so little and learned less. What I know has been acquired since then, and on the fly, so that I emerge one of the best half-informed men in America.

"Ten years of newspaper work followed schooling—on the now-defunct New York *World*, the Baltimore *News-Post* and the New York *Post* among others, as reporter, feature writer, rewrite man and foreign correspondent. It took me some time to get over the hollow city-room legend that masterpieces are written on deadlines.

"I published some short stories and attempted a play meanwhile. In 1938 I stumbled into commercial radio and ran up a score of almost 2,000 produced scripts. This, at least, developed a facility for writing fluently and massively, if not classically. In 1942 while winding up one of these scripts, my phone rang and I was asked if I would go to South America for the Office of Inter-American Affairs. 'Anything,' I replied, 'rather than write another.'

"It led to a three-year association with Latin-American matters in Ecuador, Washington, and New York. Early in 1945 there was another phone call, asking me to go to Germany with SHAEF and Military Government to help build a German anti-Nazi press. (Everything pivotal in my life has happened by phone.) Besides being feverishly interested in 'saving the peace,' I had an absolute hunch that this was the setting for which I had long been waiting. Violence, from my childhood, had been a haunting subject with me, and I had seen enough of Germany in 1931 to know even then that this country was the very cockpit of violence.

"In the next year, 1945-6, I traveled 25,000 miles by jeep throughout Bavaria searching for anti-Nazi editors and publishers, setting up six newspapers, and meeting with a torrent of self-revelation from 2,500 interviewees that almost engulfed me. Every moment was like being a character in a drama on a stage.

"On returning from Germany I set to at once to write *The Steeper Cliff*, the first novel I had ever tackled, more with the feeling that I knew things which must be told, than with any notion that the book could have commercial success. It was taken by Random House on the basis of the first two chapters, the first publisher who saw it.

"There followed *The Hour of Truth*, based on impressions of South America in 1942; and *In Another Country*, harking back to my residence in England in 1931. There have been reprints of these, variously, by the Book-of-the-Month Club, the Fiction Book Club, Bantam Books, Popular Books, and *Omnibook*, and publication in England, France, Denmark, Italy, and Australia. Further, 20th Century-Fox bought *The Steeper Cliff* in 1950, and is still wondering how to make it.

"Other recent activities have included an enjoyable six months in Hollywood, a year of participating in an *ad lib* roundtable program on a world-wide network of Voice of America, and a summer of teaching creative writing at Montana State University to agreeably talented students with a down-to-earth background and ability to use same that I envy. At present, while planning a fourth novel, I make my living from writing for television.

"I am married to Hilde Abel, herself the author of three novels. We have one child, Carla, born in 1940, and already a confirmed painter and future writer."

* * *

David Davidson's first novel, *The Steeper Cliff*, received wide acclaim for its illuminating picture of life in American-occupied Germany. With his second novel, *The Hour of Truth*, he was assured (Harrison Smith wrote in the *Saturday Review of Literature*) "of an established and firm place among that small group of young novelists to whom the public can now look, confident of their destiny." Davidson's television play *P.O.W.*, a story of a group of repatriated G.I.'s who had been prisoners in Korea, produced in the fall of 1953, was hailed as "one of the finest, most stirring, most honest, and most disturbing plays ever projected onto television screens" (Philip Hamburger in the *New Yorker*).

PRINCIPAL WORKS: The Steeper Cliff, 1947; The Hour of Truth, 1949; In Another Country, 1950.

ABOUT: Warfel, H. R. American Novelists of Today; Life September 1, 1947, August 16, 1948; Saturday Review of Literature February 14, 1948; Time August 4, 1947, December 15, 1947.

DAVIDSON, DONALD (August 18, 1893-). For autobiographical sketch and list of earlier works and references, see TWENTIETH CENTURY AUTHORS, 1942.

* * *

Donald Davidson writes: "I have recently collaborated with the composer Charles Faulkner Bryan in an opera, *Singin' Billy*, for which Mr. Bryan wrote the music and I wrote the drama and lyrics. First production was at Vanderbilt University Theatre, April 23, 1952; now being produced elsewhere at university theatres. In 1948 Washington and Lee University honored me with the degree of Litt.D."

Donald Davidson contributed a two-volume study of the Tennessee to the Rivers of America Series. In the first volume he dealt with the recorded history of the river from 1541 to the start of the Civil War; in the second he brought the history up through the installation of TVA. His work was considered one of the most distinguished studies in the series. G. W. Johnson wrote: "His prose is not merely correct, it is lucid, smooth, supple; few Americans have a more carefully chiseled style, agreeable to the eye and ear without trumpery ornamentation, clear to the understanding without falling into puerility. In addition to that, his training as a scholar carries over from his own field into that of history."

Davidson lives in Nashville, Tenn., and teaches at Vanderbilt University.

ADDITIONAL WORK: The Tennessee, 2 vols., 1946, 1948.

ABOUT: Rubin, L. D. & Jacobs, R. D. (eds.) Southern Renascence; Georgia Review Spring 1952; Nashville Tennessean Magazine September 4, 1949.

DAVIES, RHYS (November 9, 1903-), Anglo-Welsh novelist and short story writer, writes: "A pure-blood native of Wales who writes his books in English could, I suppose, be thought of as a dog of indeterminate breed. The Welsh, in my opinion, have remained even more distinct from their English conquerors than the Irish and the Scotch; they possess their own ancient and still flourishing language (my grandparents, living in a rural and remark-  ably pristine district of Wales, knew only a few words of English), and there is an output of literature which is read widely in Wales and seldom translated into English. In addition, we have the fervent Nationalist guardians of Wales, warriors who, among more political ideals, fight for the preservation of the native language. By these the writer who gabbles in English is sometimes referred to as a disgrace if not a traitor.

"During the last thirty years or so, however, several Welsh-born writers have appeared who wish to bathe in the blessedly non-local stream of literature. Viewers and critics have alleged that, like the earlier Irish school, they have brought a fresh current into English writing. Until the 1939-45 war intervened we were able to run two literary magazines, *Wales* and *The Welsh Review*, and nowadays there is never an English publishing season without several books of Welsh origin.

"My own load of novels, short stories and miscellaneous writing began in 1927, with my first novel *The Withered Root*. It dealt with a religious revival in a Welsh coal-mining valley. I was born in such a district, the Rhondda Valley, in 1903, and spent my first eighteen years there. It was a turbulent place of high-minded religious disputes, industrial warfare—its riotous strikes were famous—and singing festivals known as Eisteddfods. From the Rhondda I went to London where, until my first novel was published, I worked at various jobs in offices and stores. Then I left for France, whose writers had been my main influence. There, in Paris and the Riviera, I mixed with writers and painters in the 'expatriate' manner of the period; it was a civilizing if sometimes rank and headlong time. In Bandol and Paris I stayed with D. H. Lawrence whose work, for the young writers of that day, seemed to crystallize, more than any other, their own problems and searchings. This was an educative period of my life in strong contrast to my stern upbringing in the grim Welsh mining valley with its fundamental economic and social struggles.

"I have lived since in London, with frequent visits to Wales, France, Italy and Germany. Most of my writing takes Wales for its background, but I have always tried to avoid a strictly 'regional' bias and quality. I try to create my characters first as human beings—tears and smiles, rage, greed, love and malice seem to me universal!—but Wales certainly is a country with its own internal non-English flavour. (My feeling is that the Welsh have more natural affinities with the Spanish and the Italians than with the English to whom, in an economic way, they are bound inextricably now.) That Wales, a tiny nation, has succeeded in retaining this individual flavour I regard as a sweet miracle. I hope it is to be found in my books.

"During the war I worked in the London War Office. An interest in the theatre keeps me hankering after this mess of pottage. In 1945 a musical play, *Jenny Jones,* based on one of my Welsh stories, was produced at the London Hippodrome. I have had another play produced, rather ruthlessly, in the West End.

"At present I am engaged on a novel with a London background. I think it is necessary for a writer to graze in fresh pastures every few years."

PRINCIPAL WORKS: *Novels*—The Withered Root, 1927; Count Your Blessings, 1932; The Red Hills, 1932; A Time to Laugh, 1937; Jubilee Blues, 1938; Under the Rose, 1940; Tomorrow to Fresh Woods, 1941; The Black Venus, 1944; The Dark Daughters, 1947; Marianne, 1951; The Painted King, 1954. *Short Stories*—A Pig in a Poke, 1931; Love Provoked, 1933; The Things Men Do, 1936; A Finger in Every Pie, 1942; The Trip to London, 1946; Boy With a Trumpet, 1949. *Miscellaneous*—My Wales, 1936; Sea Urchin, Life and Adventures of Jorgen Jorgensen, 1940; The Story of Wales (Britain in Pictures) 1943.

ABOUT: Adam, G. F. Three Contemporary Anglo-Welsh Novelists; Bates, H. E. The Modern Short Story; Griffith, W. The Welsh; Megroz, F. L. Rhys Davies, A Critical Sketch; International Observer (Paris) March 27, 1947; John O' London's October 1952; Literary Digest (London) Summer 1947; (London) Times Literary Supplement October 15, 1938; Voices Autumn 1946; Wales December 1946; Welsh Review November 5, 1946.

DAVIES, WILLIAM HENRY (April 20, 1871-September 26, 1940). For biographical sketch and list of works and references, see TWENTIETH CENTURY AUTHORS, 1942.

* * *

ADDITIONAL WORK: Collected Poems, 1942.

ABOUT: Sitwell, O. Noble Essences; Dictionary of National Biography 1931-1940; (London) Times Literary Supplement August 10, 1951.

"DAVIOT, GORDON." See MACKINTOSH, E.

DAVIS, CLYDE BRION (May 22, 1894-). For autobiographical sketch and list of earlier works and references, see TWENTIETH CENTURY AUTHORS, 1942

* * *

Clyde Brion Davis writes: "Hobbies: No longer cultivating weeds. They now cultivate me. Occupations: I never said I was a steamfitter's helper; a friend said that about me. Since this sketch was written I put in ten months in Hollywood for the usual reason; went to Europe in 1941 for a newspaper syndicate; worked two years as an associate editor of Rinehart & Company in New York. For last six years have been living in Salisbury, Conn., trying to make a living from books. Family: My wife died January 14, 1952; I acquired a grandchild February 12, 1952. Appearance: My hair is still thick but is now quite gray. Favorite authors: I don't know how I overlooked Melville because I regard *Moby Dick* as the greatest novel written in America. Prospects: At 58 [1952] I feel I now have learned my trade and expect to do better work in the future. Inasmuch as my people all live approximately one hundred years, I should have twenty-five or thirty good working years left."

In the half-dozen novels published by Clyde Brion Davis during the past ten years, he has ranged widely over the American scene. Probably the most ambitious of his works is *Thudbury*, subtitled *An American Comedy*, a novel depicting the life of one Otis Paul Thudbury, a small-town businessman.

Davis has published one work of non-fiction in recent years—*The Age of Indiscretion*. This volume is partly a personal memoir of his life in Missouri in the early years of the century, and partly a polemic against T. S. Eliot who, in *Notes Towards a Definition of Culture*, had suggested that the modern age was one of cultural disintegration and decline.

ADDITIONAL WORKS: The Rebellion of Leo McGuire, 1944; The Stars Incline, 1946; Jeremy Bell, 1947; Temper the Wind, 1948; Playtime Is Over, 1949; The Age of Indiscretion (non-fiction) 1950; North Woods Whammy (juvenile) 1951; Thudbury, 1952; Eyes of Boyhood (ed.) 1953; The Newcomer, 1954.

ABOUT: Davis, C. B. The Age of Indiscretion; Warfel, H. R. American Novelists of Today; New York Herald Tribune Book Review October 12, 1952; Saturday Review of Literature June 18, 1949.

DAVIS, ELMER HOLMES (January 13, 1890-). For biographical sketch and list of works and references, see TWENTIETH CENTURY AUTHORS, 1942.

* * *

Elmer Davis headed the Office of War Information from 1942 to 1945. Under his administration the O.W.I. organized and carried out a vast program of war information, establishing branch offices in several of the larger American cities and in the capitals of most of the allied and neutral nations abroad. It recruited outstanding authors and political and economic experts for its education and propaganda programs. Although the agency was disbanded after the war, many of its activities were taken up and continued by existing government agencies; and the importance of large-scale information programs, especially in those countries where Communist pressures are heavy, has been recognized, mainly through the successful precedents set up during the war years by O.W.I. Davis' administration of the agency was a stormy one; *Newsweek* described it as "one of the most harried in the wartime administration." Bluntly honest, belligerently liberal in politics, he tangled with Congress, with the Army and Navy, and with the press on numerous occasions. His enemies called him the "Goebbels" of the American propaganda machine, but his friends (and they included President Roosevelt) pointed out that he had to his credit the establishment and maintenance of one of the most powerful agencies of the United States government in the struggle for democracy.

At the end of the war Davis resumed his broadcasting work as a news commentator for the American Broadcasting Company. His shrewd, independent, acidly humorous analyses of the news have three times won him the Peabody Award for distinguished radio broadcasting. In 1953 he received the Lauterbach Award for his contribution to the cause of civil liberties. In the fall of 1953 Davis discontinued his broadcasts temporarily for reasons of health. Early in 1954 he returned to radio and began a weekly television series. He lives in Washington, D.C. His *But We Were Born Free* was hailed as one of the most thoughtful and stimulating books of recent years on the American political scene.

ADDITIONAL WORK: But We Were Born Free, 1954; Two Minutes Till Midnight, 1955.

ABOUT: Banta, R. Indiana Authors; National Cyclopedia of American Biography (1946); Harper's February 1943; Life May 3, 1943; New Republic June 28, 1943; Newsweek June 28, 1943, February 7, 1944; Time September 13, 1943.

DAVIS, HAROLD LENOIR (October 18, 1896-). For autobiographical sketch and list of earlier works and references, see TWENTIETH CENTURY AUTHORS, 1942.

* * *

Like his contemporaries A. B. Guthrie, Jr., and Walter Van Tilburg Clark, H. L. Davis is a "literary pioneer" of the American West, rediscovering and reinterpreting its rich past with the eyes of an artist, "reclaiming the realities of Western experience," as Dayton Kohler writes, "from the writers of two-gun epics and the clichés of Hollywood." As early as 1935, with his first novel, *Honey in the Horn*, Davis established himself as a distinguished novelist of the West. His next novel, *Harp of a Thousand Strings*, which appeared twelve years later, was also a Western—but in a far different pattern. The story of the naming of a western town, its scene was Tripoli during the Napoleonic wars, and its main characters important figures in the French Revolution.

With the two novels and one collection of short stories which have followed, Davis has continued to explore the materials of the West with humor, insight, and sensitivity. The poet Thomas Hornsby Ferril wrote that Davis' *Beulah Land* was "a passionate apprehension of American experience told plainly, lyrically, tragically, sometimes comically and, above all, by a man deeply sensible of the energies that make history." Davis' novels are loosely plotted, at times almost picaresque; his style is quiet, and his characters are not sharply realized. What sets his work above the run of Western fiction is his mood—what Charles Lee has called "the magic qualities of place and emotion that are peculiarly Mr. Davis'."

ADDITIONAL WORKS: Harp of a Thousand Strings, 1947; Beulah Land, 1949; Winds of Morning, 1952; Team Bells Woke Me (short stories) 1953.

ABOUT: College English December 1952; New York Herald Tribune Book Review January 27, 1952.

DAVIS, OWEN (January 29, 1874-). For biographical sketch and list of earlier works and references, see TWENTIETH CENTURY AUTHORS, 1942.

* * *

Owen Davis lives in a midtown Manhattan hotel where, he told an interviewer in 1949, "I'm still at work. It's a silly habit, but at seventy-five it's hard to break." In his more than fifty years in the theatre he has written close to three hundred plays;

practically every one of them, he has said, was a money-maker. George Jean Nathan called Davis "in percentage by volume the Lope de Vega of the American theatre." His most recent Broadway production, a farce comedy *The Snark Was A Boojum* (a dramatization of a novel by Richard Shattuck), proved an exception to Davis' glittering record of hits. It opened and closed in September 1943 after five performances.

ADDITIONAL WORKS: No Way Out (play) 1945; My First Fifty Years in the Theatre, 1950.

ABOUT: Davis, O. My First Fifty Years in the Theatre; New Yorker February 5, 1949.

DAVIS, RICHARD HARDING (April 18, 1864-April 11, 1916). For biographical sketch and list of works and references, see TWENTIETH CENTURY AUTHORS, 1942.

* * *

ABOUT: Time July 1, 1946.

DAVIS, WILLIAM STEARNS (April 30, 1877-February 15, 1930). For biographical sketch and list of works and references, see TWENTIETH CENTURY AUTHORS, 1942.

DAWSON, CHRISTOPHER HENRY (October 12, 1889-), British social historian and philosopher of history, was born at Hay Castle, Wales, the son of Lt.-Col. H. P. Dawson and Mary (Bevan) Dawson, whose father was Archdeacon of Brecon. He was educated at Winchester and at Trinity College, Oxford. In 1911 he went to Sweden to study economics  under Gustav Cassel, and a year later he returned to Oxford for graduate studies in history and sociology. About that time Dawson became deeply interested in the writings of Ernest Troeltsch on the problem of the relation of religion and culture. His life's work has been the study of the history of culture, showing "how changes of culture are accompanied and conditioned by changes in man's religious beliefs and spiritual attitude to life."

In 1914 Dawson entered the Roman Catholic Church. The Church, he believes, is "the representative in a changing world of an unchanging spiritual order." In the light of historical knowledge, Dawson wrote in 1950, we can appreciate the "vital function of religion both as a principle of continuity and conservation and as a source of new spiritual life." To illustrate this thesis Dawson has undertaken to demonstrate, in his *Religion and the Rise of Western Culture* and in other writings, that it was the medieval Catholic Church, with its continuous tradition, which shaped and gave meaning to the moral and intellectual development of Western Europe, and which sustains it today in the face of totalitarian pressures.

As a Catholic historian Dawson has made distinct and valuable contributions to present-day knowledge of the past. One of the most important of these is his interpretation of the so-called Dark Ages—in *The Making of Europe*—during which, he shows, "the elements which are the basis of European unity were painfully fused into synthesis." Aldous Huxley wrote of this volume: "The Dark Ages lose their darkness, take on form and significance. Thanks to Mr. Dawson's erudition and his gift of marshalling facts, we begin to have a notion of what it is all about. . . ." Dawson writes a fresh and pleasantly direct prose. Philip Burnham said of his style: "There is no parade of learning and laboring of points, but rather discipline and modesty—and also a kind of confidence in the reader, not assuming unusual knowledge but trusting his reasonableness and imagination."

Dawson was lecturer in the history of culture at University College, Exeter, from 1930 to 1936. In 1934 he was Forwood Lecturer in the philosophy of religion at the University of Liverpool (these lectures were published as *Medieval Religion*). He delivered the Gifford Lectures at the University of Edinburgh in 1947 and in 1948 (published as *Religion and Culture* and *Religion and the Rise of Western Culture*). He has contributed many articles to British periodicals—among them *Criterion*, the *Dublin Review*, and the *Hibbert Journal*—and in America his articles appear frequently in *Commonweal*. In 1940 he became editor of the *Dublin Review*. Dawson married Valery Mills in 1916. They have one son and two daughters and live in Oxford.

PRINCIPAL WORKS: The Age of the Gods, 1928; Progress and Religion, 1929; Essays in Order (ed. with T. F. Burns) 1931; The Making of Europe, 1932; Enquiries into Religion and Culture, 1933; The Spirit of the Oxford Movement, 1933; The Modern Dilemma, 1933; Medieval Religion, 1934; Religion and the Modern State, 1935; Beyond Politics, 1939; Christianity and the New Age, 1940; Judgment of the Nations, 1942; Religion and Culture, 1948; Religion and the Rise of Western Culture, 1950; Understanding Europe, 1952; Medieval Essays, 1954.

ABOUT: Alexander, C. The Catholic Literary Revival; Hoehn, M. (ed.) Catholic Authors, I; Schlesinger, B. P. Christopher Dawson and the Modern Political Crisis; Sheed, F. J. Sidelights on the Catholic Revival; Catholic World May 1949.

DAWSON, CONINGSBY WILLIAM (February 26, 1883-). For biographical sketch and list of works and references, see TWENTIETH CENTURY AUTHORS, 1942.

* * *

Coningsby Dawson lives in Santa Monica, Calif. His last published book appeared in 1941.

DAY, CLARENCE SHEPARD (1874-December 28, 1935). For biographical sketch and list of works and references, see TWENTIETH CENTURY AUTHORS, 1942.

* * *

The prodigiously successful dramatization of Clarence Day's sketches of his irascible but irresistibly charming father—Howard Lindsay's and Russel Crouse's *Life With Father* (1939)—assured Day of a permanent place in American letters. The play had one of the longest runs in Broadway theatrical history, toured triumphantly, was made into a motion picture, and in the winter of 1953 became the nucleus for a television series. Lindsay and Crouse also dramatized *Life With Mother* (1948), which was well received but was generally eclipsed by the memory of *Father*.

DAY, HOLMAN FRANCIS (November 6, 1865-February 19, 1935). For biographical sketch and list of works and references, see TWENTIETH CENTURY AUTHORS, 1942.

DAY LEWIS, CECIL (April 27, 1904-). For biographical sketch and list of earlier works and references, see TWENTIETH CENTURY AUTHORS, 1942.

* * *

C. Day Lewis served from 1941 to 1946 as editor of books and pamphlets for the Ministry of Information. In the latter year he returned to academic life, after a ten-year absence, as Clark lecturer at Trinity College, Cambridge. (These lectures were published as *The Poetic Image*.) In 1951 he was appointed professor of poetry at Oxford University. He was divorced from his first wife in 1951 and married Jill Balcon.

As a practicing poet, Day Lewis has mellowed and quite abandoned the revolutionary fervor of his earlier work. His poems written from 1936 to 1943 and published in *Short Is the Time* were described by F. W. Dupee as "exceedingly well written, and even though the effectiveness of the poems is more in the part than in the whole, they testify to an observant and cultivated mind." He appears at his best in simple shorter lyrics. Robert B. Heilman commented: "When Lewis can stay away from the rhetorical flourish, keep to the proper materials of which he has no lack, submit to the discipline of his form, and let the hot metal of enthusiasm be poured into firm molds instead of splashing all over the shop, he can write first-rate poetry." A later collection, published in 1948, proved disappointing to the critics—lacking the excitement, "the ignition" as a British reviewer put it, of his early poems. But with *An Italian Visit* (1954), Lewis was praised for having matured his art, as "a good grammarian of movement and of love" (V. S. Pritchett).

In 1952 Day Lewis published his translation of Virgil's *Aeneid* which had been commissioned for broadcasting (and actually broadcast) by the B.B.C. for its Third Programme. A rapid, conversational translation in a loose six-stress meter, it was admirably suited for the purposes for which it was made, although less satisfactory as a literary translation. "The poem on the page," Dudley Fitts wrote, "by no means measures up to the poem spoken." As "Nicholas Blake," Cecil Day Lewis has continued to write his expert and literate detective stories. He has also done some writing for children and teen agers—a pleasant and useful introduction to the study of poetry, *Poetry for You,* and a mystery thriller, *The Otterbury Incident.*

ADDITIONAL WORKS: Poetry for You: A Book for Boys and Girls on the Enjoyment of Poetry, 1944; Short Is the Time (poems) 1945; The Poetic Image, 1947; Poems, 1943-1947, 1948; The Otterbury Incident 1948; The Aeneid of Virgil (trans.) 1952; An Italian Visit (poems) 1954. As "Nicholas Blake"—Minute for Murder, 1948; Head of a Traveller, 1949; The Dreadful Hollow, 1953; The Whisper in the Gloom, 1954.

ABOUT: Daiches, D. Poetry and the Modern World; Grierson, H. J. C. & Smith, J. C. Critical History of English Poetry; Southworth, J. G. Sowing the Spring; Weygandt, C. The Time of Yeats; Nation October 13, 1945; New Republic August 6, 1945; Poetry September 1948; Saturday Review of Literature August 25, 1945.

DEAN, VERA *MICHELES (March 29, 1903-   ), American editor and writer on international affairs, was born in St. Petersburg, Russia, daughter of Alexander and Nadine Micheles. She was educated privately until she came to the United States in 1919 and entered Radcliffe College. She received her B.A. from Radcliffe in 1925. In 1926 she received an M.A. from  Yale University. In 1928 she completed her graduate studies with a Ph.D. from Radcliffe. In that same year she became a naturalized American citizen. A year later she married William Johnson Dean (who died in 1936). She has a son and a daughter from that marriage.

Mrs. Dean joined the Foreign Policy Association as a research associate in 1928. In 1933 she became an editor, and since 1938 she has been research director of the organization. In addition to her books in the field of foreign relations, she is the author of a number of pamphlets and reports for the Foreign Policy Association. She has also published many articles in magazines, among them the *Nation, New Republic, Christian Science Monitor, Christian Century, Yale Review,* and *Reporter.* Mrs. Dean is an expert on Russian affairs and has written extensively on the economy and foreign policy of that country. Since the early 1930's she has been an active proponent of collective security and a firm believer in international collaboration in the interests of world peace. She has traveled widely in Europe, Asia, and South America, and has attended and participated in a number of international conferences and meetings.

Mrs. Dean's writings for the Foreign Policy Association and for other sources are uniformly sound, clear and thought-provoking. Her audience is the average intelligent reader who seeks to be well-informed but not pressured on major issues of foreign policy. Her style is restrained and succinct. Walter Millis said of one of her earlier books: "She has a really remarkable ability to pack a maximum of complicated historical detail into a minimum of wordage; the flavor, as is likely to be the case with concentrated foods, may be a trifle dry, but the nutritive value is considerable." In 1953

* mĭ shĕ'lĕs

Geoffrey Bruun wrote of her *Foreign Policy Without Fear:* "Everything she writes in her lucid and persuasive style bears the stamp of a liberal and courageous mind."

A stately and handsome woman with a vigorous and direct platform manner, Mrs. Dean is a popular lecturer. She has organized and taught a course on "Contemporary India and Its Role in World Affairs" at Smith College. She has honorary degrees from Wilson College and the University of Rochester and is an alumnae trustee of Radcliffe College. She lives in New York City.

PRINCIPAL WORKS: New Governments in Europe (ed. R. L. Buell) 1934; Europe in Retreat, 1939; Four Cornerstones of Peace, 1946; Russia: Menace or Promise, 1947; The United States and Russia, 1947; Europe and the United States, 1950; Foreign Policy Without Fear, 1953.

ABOUT: Current Biography 1943.

DE AYALA. See PEREZ DE AYALA

*DE CASSERES, BENJAMIN (1873-December 6, 1945). For autobiographical sketch and list of works and references, see TWENTIETH CENTURY AUTHORS, 1942.

* * *

Benjamin De Casseres died at seventy-two at his home in New York. He had continued his work as an editorial writer for the New York *Mirror*, a Hearst tabloid, throughout a year of illness.

Critics have spoken of his "flashy, bombastic rhetoric" (New York *World*) and his "staccato, ejaculatory, striking, brilliant style" (Boston *Transcript*). G. S. Hellman noted "the richness of Mr. De Casseres' cultural background, with art and literature as intimately his domains as the realm of metaphysics."

De Casseres perhaps best described his own quality when he called himself a "gustatorian," that is, "a critic whose judgments are founded on spontaneous, intuitional taste and who does not analyze or weigh, but apotheosizes or slays."

ABOUT: New York Times December 7, 1945.

* dĕ kăs'ĕr ĕs

DEEPING, WARWICK (1877-April 20, 1950). For autobiographical sketch and list of earlier works and references, see TWENTIETH CENTURY AUTHORS, 1942.

* * *

Warwick Deeping died at Weybridge, England. To the end of his life he continued to produce, at least once a year, "a nice story about interesting people topped off with proper sentiments and a happy ending," in the words of one reviewer.

"Deeping was by no means without talent," the London *Times* commented, "and was certainly serious enough in all he wrote, but his gift was very much for the sentimental and all too human narrative." The New York *Times*, also noting the sentimentality of his some sixty novels, commended them for "British solidity, a gentlemanly goodness and fun, and well-woven plots."

ADDITIONAL WORKS: I Live Again, 1942; Slade, 1943; Cleric's Secret, 1944; Reprieve, 1945; Impudence of Youth, 1946; Fox Farm, 1946; Laughing House, 1947; Playboy, 1948; Old Mischief, 1950.

ABOUT: New York Times April 21, 1950.

DE FORD, MIRIAM ALLEN (August 21, 1888-). For autobiographical sketch and list of earlier works and references, see TWENTIETH CENTURY AUTHORS, 1942.

* * *

Miriam Allen de Ford writes from San Francisco: "About all I have to add biographically is that I have won for the third time one of the prizes in the annual contest of *Ellery Queen's Mystery Magazine*, and that most of my current work for magazines is in true crime, fantasy, and science fiction. The most reprinted thing I ever had published was a story in *Harper's* in 1946 ["Last Generation"] which, besides three magazine reprints (one in England) and an anthology for college students, has been spread in French, Italian, and Dutch all over the world by the British Bureau of Information.

"I might add that the Order of Bookfellows no longer exists and that I am no longer honorary local secretary of the Rationalist Press Association, though I still belong to it and the American Newspaper Guild, and that at present I am on the steering committee of our branch of the Authors Guild."

Revised editions of Miss de Ford's *They Were San Franciscans* and *Who Was When?* appeared in 1947 and 1950 respectively. She was a contributor to *British Authors Before 1800*, published in 1952.

ADDITIONAL WORKS: Psychologist Unretired: The Life-Pattern of Lillian J. Martin, 1948.

DE GOURMONT. See GOURMONT

DE HARTOG. See HARTOG

*DE JONG, DAVID CORNEL (June 9, 1905-). For autobiographical sketch and list of earlier works and references, see TWENTIETH CENTURY AUTHORS, 1942.

* * *

David S. DeJong writes: "Please amend the final paragraph of my autobiographical sketch: Weight, rather constant 175 (height, the same as in sketch). Since 1949 have been married to the former Helen Elizabeth Moffitt. Permanent address, West Barrington, R.I. Also I object a bit to the next paragraph. I am not a pronounced reddish blond, am in fact as pale blond as you can make them, nor have a small mustache, sorry. However, the little description doesn't bother me too much."

DeJong has entered two new fields of the arts since 1942—poetry (he has published three volumes of poems) and painting (his water colors appear on the dust jacket of *With a Dutch Accent*). But his most successful work continues to be his simple and warm characterization of Dutch-American family life. Of his autobiography, *With a Dutch Accent*, R. A. Cordell wrote in the *Saturday Review of Literature*: "This skilfully told story . . . deserves an honorable position alongside the autobiographies or thinly disguised autobiographical fiction of such adopted sons of America as Rölvaag, Lewisohn, Adamic, and McFee.

ADDITIONAL WORKS: *Fiction*—Benefit Street, 1942; Somewhat Angels, 1945; Snow-on-the-Mountain (short stories) 1946; The Desperate Children, 1949; Two Sofas in the Parlor, 1952. *Poetry*—Across the Board, 1943; Domination of June, 1944. *Autobiography*—With a Dutch Accent, 1944.

ABOUT: DeJong, D. C. With a Dutch Accent; Current Biography 1944; Poetry June 1943.

* "How to pronounce my name? Make the *Jong* sound as if it were *Young*. That's close enough, unless you're a Dutchman yourself."

DE JOUVENEL. See COLETTE

DE KRUIF, PAUL (March 2, 1890-). For biographical sketch and list of earlier works and references, see TWENTIETH CENTURY AUTHORS, 1942.

* * *

Paul De Kruif lives in Holland, Mich. In recent years he has contributed numerous articles on medical research to the *Reader's Digest*. He remains the best known and most successful American "popularizer" of scientific and medical subjects. His work has not always been sympathetically received by doctors and specialized writers on these subjects. They object to the sensationalism, the tendency toward oversimplification which can produce a demand "for quick, unsubstantiated cures." But few critics would challenge De Kruif's effectiveness as a writer. Waldemar Kaempffert of the New York *Times* writes: "There is no question about the skill with which he draws his characters. He is verbose, slangy, sometimes ungrammatical, but never dull."

ADDITIONAL WORKS: Kaiser Wakes the Doctors, 1943; The Male Hormone, 1945; Life Among the Doctors (with R. B. De Kruif) 1949.

ABOUT: Reader's Digest December 1946, January 1947.

DE LACRETELLE. See LACRETELLE

"DELAFIELD, E. M." (1890-December 2, 1943). For biographical sketch and list of earlier works and references, see TWENTIETH CENTURY AUTHORS, 1942.

* * *

Mrs. Arthur Paul Dashwood ("E. M. Delafield") collapsed while lecturing at Oxford and died a few weeks later at her home at Cullompton, Devon, Engand, at fifty-three.

Her last novel, *Late and Soon*, published shortly before her death, was characterized by L. S. Munn as "a successful amalgamation of 'drawing room drama' with the crass realities of an era in which artificial barriers are being destroyed by war." The story of "a middle-aged romance," a plot one reviewer described as "incredibly Edwardian," it was nevertheless a delicately-handled and credible novel.

The author of the "Provincial Lady" series was described (by *Time*) as "a nice mixture of Jane Austen, *Punch*, and her own 'provincial lady.'" The London *Times* said: "She had an almost uncanny gift for converting the small and familiar dullnesses of everyday life into laughter. But though all her work was, superficially at least, lightly and gaily written, her more serious novels showed not only a preoccupation with the amusing or deplorable foibles of her own sex but a deep interest in the social conditions of their lives."

ADDITIONAL WORK: Late and Soon, 1943.

ABOUT: London Times December 3, 1943; New York Times December 3, 1943.

*DE LA MARE, WALTER JOHN (April 25, 1873-). For biographical sketch and list of earlier works and references, see TWENTIETH CENTURY AUTHORS, 1942.

* * *

Walter de la Mare is one of the most highly respected and widely admired of living English writers. In 1948 he was named Companion of Honour by the late King George VI, and he holds honorary degrees from many universities—Oxford, Cambridge, Saint Andrews, Bristol, and London. Now past eighty, his "late harvest" (as one reviewer described his recent poetry) is rich. Horace Gregory has pointed out that no contemporary poet "has relied so completely upon the resources of his imagination as de la Mare has done; the view is singular and minute in detail, an independent view that remains unconcerned with fashions in writing verse. . . ." The note of the "old and familiar" in his work is neatly balanced with new freshness and insight. "His lyrics," Wallace Fowlie wrote in 1951, "are the debris of an adventure from which he is always returning, heartened and terrified. He looks at our world as if from some planet, and sees it chaotic and dazzling." In a poem honoring de la Mare on his seventy-fifth birthday, T. S. Eliot speaks of his peculiar talent for rendering the familiar scene "suddenly strange"—

> . . . by those deceptive cadences
> Wherewith the common measure is refined;
> By conscious art practised with natural ease;
>
> By the delicate, invisible web you wove—
> The inexplicable mystery of sound.

His prose tales, like his poems, are filled with an air of wonder, with childlike innocence penetrating sharply and deeply into a less innocent and often distinctly evil reality. "There is no comfort in the best writings of de la Mare for soft-hearted children and their parents," Gregory writes. "If and when he is whimsical, whatever exists between his lines, or on the other side of a green tinted mirror of the world, has in it somewhere the chill of ice, or the rational touch of snow."

ADDITIONAL WORKS: *Poetry*—The Listeners, 1942; Collected Rhymes and Verses, 1944; Motley, 1944; The Burning Glass, 1945; Rhymes and Verses, 1947; The Winged Chariot, 1951. *Prose*—The Old Lion, and Other Stories, 1942; Magic Jacket, and Other Stories, 1943; The Scarecrow and Other Stories, 1945; Dutch Cheese, and Other Stories, 1946; Collected Stories for Children, 1947; Collected Tales, 1950.

* dē lä mâr′

ABOUT: Atkins, J. A. Walter de la Mare: An Exploration; Duffin, H. C. Walter de la Mare: A Study of His Poetry; Kunitz, S. J. & Haycraft, H. (eds.) Junior Book of Authors (rev. ed.); Wagenknecht, E. *Introduction to* Collected Tales of Walter de la Mare; Tribute to Walter de la Mare on his Seventy-Fifth Birthday (London, 1948); Library Journal April 15, 1948; New York Herald Tribune Book Review October 7, 1951; Poetry May 1946, July 1952.

DELAND, Mrs. MARGARET WADE (CAMPBELL) (February 28, 1857-January 13, 1945). For biographical sketch and list of works and references, see TWENTIETH CENTURY AUTHORS, 1942.

* * *

Margaret Deland died at the Hotel Sheraton in Boston, where she had lived for several years, at eighty-seven.

She has been called (by the New York *Times*) "the mildest and most serene of gentlewomen." Her last two books, which were autobiographical, were written with "the light and shade, the sensitive humor, the delicate insight into varied and dramatic human values, that mark the author's fiction," according to V. D. Scudder in the *Atlantic*.

ABOUT: Boynton, P. H. America in Contemporary Fiction; National Cyclopedia of American Biography (1947); New York Times January 14, 1945.

DE LA PASTURE. See DELAFIELD

*DE LA ROCHE, MAZO (1885-). For biographical sketch and list of earlier works and references, see TWENTIETH CENTURY AUTHORS, 1942.

* * *

Few institutions in twentieth century life are more solid and permanent than the Whiteoak family. Since 1927 Mazo de la Roche has been raveling and unraveling her history of the members of the family. Her narrative moves forward and backward in time. Three of the later Jalna novels actually pre-date the first one, the *Atlantic* prize winner *Jalna*, in their action. *The Building of Jalna* (1944), first in point of time, describes the founding of the family when Philip and Adeline Whiteoak migrated to Canada in the 1850's. Others carry the action through the growing-up and marriage of "Young Renny's" daughter. To Miss de la Roche's numerous readers in Canada, the United States, and in Europe (in 1949

* dē lä rōsh′

her sales were estimated at about 2,000,000 and her books had been translated into fifteen languages), Jalna is a symbol of a way of life—a sanctuary of peace and the sturdy domestic virtues. Edward Weeks commented in the *Atlantic* that Miss de la Roche's achievement "makes me think of Trollope and Galsworthy: I am too close to her work to attempt a comparison in quality, but I do know that neither of them ever created more living people."

Miss de la Roche lives very quietly in Toronto with her life-long friend Caroline Clement, and two adopted children.

ADDITIONAL WORKS: *Fiction*—Two Saplings, 1942; The Building of Jalna, 1944; Return to Jalna, 1946; Mary Wakefield, 1949; Renny's Daughter, 1951; A Boy in the House, and Other Stories, 1952; The Whiteoak Brothers: Jalna—1923, 1953; Variable Winds at Jalna, 1953. *Non-Fiction*—Quebec: Historic Seaport, 1944.

ABOUT: Thomas, C. Canadian Novelists, 1920-1945; Time January 17, 1949.

DE LA SERNA. See GÓMEZ DE LA SERNA

*DE LA TORRE, LILLIAN (March 15, 1902-), American crime writer, writes: "Racially I call myself a typical American—

a blend, that is, of pioneers of many stocks. My father, José Rollin de la Torre Bueno, was born in Lima, and traced his ancestry in a direct line from one of the famous Thirteen Conquistadors of Peru, Pizarro's *maestre de campo,* Don Juan de la Torre. My mother, Lillian Sarah Reinhardt, was born in Montreal of German-Yankee parentage. Her paternal grandfather, Gottlieb Reinhardt, was an *Auswanderer* of the revolution year of 1848. Her mother, Myra James, traced her forebears back to men who in 1776 took up arms with the Minute Men and the Green Mountain boys, as well as to a baffled emigrant of 1620 who planned to sail on the Mayflower, missed the boat, and had to follow ingloriously on the Ann.

"These diverse pioneer stocks combined in me when I was born in New York in 1902. There I grew up, and there I met and married George Sutherland McCue, a Staten Islander of Irish-Scotch antecedents. He brought me west. We make our home in Colorado Springs, where he is a professor of English at Colorado College.

"I had always intended to write. As a student at Columbia and Radcliffe, as a teacher in New York, as a wife, I stocked my mind and kept my pen busy until the day when, at forty, I found the thing I wanted to say. I have been saying it ever since.

"As a scholar I had specialized in the history and literature of eighteenth century England. As a reader, I had rejoiced in the literature of crime ever since at eight years of age I started raiding my father's library, which included a fine collection of early crime stories. The day the lines crossed was the day my writing career opened.

"The spark that kindled me was the sudden perception that in Dr. Johnson, the great philosopher of the Age of Reason, with James Boswell, his famous biographer, there was a new Holmes-Watson combination, in a setting that was fresh and fascinating, full of crime and chicanery of an entirely new flavor. The result was a series of short stories, still running in *Ellery Queen's Mystery Magazine,* in which the Great Cham solves (fictitiously) the most challenging unsolved mysteries of his day, and his Boswell (*The* Boswell) narrates the story.

"My study of unsolved mysteries soon led me to solving them. My most serious work is in this vein. In *Elizabeth Is Missing* I solved, by reinterpreting the evidence, a hitherto unsolved disappearance of 1753. *The Heir of Douglas* brings to light the hidden truth about the mysterious boy who in 1762 inherited the Douglas fortune. These books (and others in preparation), based on research, illuminate the social scene which they depict at the same time that they cast light on mysteries hitherto dark.

"As an enthusiastic amateur actress, I soon turned to writing crime plays. *Women Don't Hang* is a series of four thrillers for casts of women, based on the careers of four famous women, Katharine Nairn, Constance Kent, Madeline Smith, and Lizzie Borden. *Goodbye, Miss Lizzie Borden* has been twice anthologized, televised, and played by amateurs in many places—including Fall River, Mass., the scene of the crime.

"Today I have several books and no children. Acting for fun, cooking for fun, traveling for research and for fun, fill my time and compete with a full writing schedule.

---

* Miss de la Torre writes that her name is pronounced "in the Spanish manner, with two syllables in Tor-re—dĕ lă Tŏr rĕ."

'My purpose in writing about crime is neither sociological nor sensational, but humanistic. I believe that the intense light generated when human relationships burst into flame in some great crime leads to the illumination of the soul of man, which is man's proper study. That is why I took the motto for *The Heir of Douglas* from the mouth of Dr. Johnson, when he said of an earlier book on the same subject: 'Sir, I think such a publication does good, as it does good to show us the possibilities of human life.' "

PRINCIPAL WORKS: Elizabeth Is Missing, 1945; Dr. Sam: Johnson, Detector, 1946; Villainy Detected, 1947; The 60 Minute Chef (with C. Truax) 1947; Goodbye, Miss Lizzie Borden, 1948; The Heir of Douglas, 1952; The White Rose of Stuart, 1954.

ABOUT: Current Biography 1949; Rocky Mountain Life September 1948; Colorado Springs Gazette Telegraph June 11, 1949; Denver Post August 3, 1952.

*DELEDDA, GRAZIA (September 27, 1872-August 16, 1936). For biographical sketch and list of works and references, see TWENTIETH CENTURY AUTHORS, 1942.

* * *

ABOUT: Columbia Dictionary of Modern European Literature.

* dä lĕd'dä

DELL, FLOYD (June 28, 1887-). For biographical sketch and list of works and references, see TWENTIETH CENTURY AUTHORS, 1942.

* * *

Floyd Dell did editorial work for various federal government agencies from 1935 to 1947. He is now a free-lance writer. He lives in Washington, D.C.

DELMAR, Mrs. VIÑA (CROTER) (January 29, 1905-). For biographical sketch and list of earlier works and references, see TWENTIETH CENTURY AUTHORS, 1942.

* * *

The generation that grew up during the years of World War II knew little or nothing of Viña Delmar. Although by no means in retirement (she was raising a son, writing magazine serials, short stories, and Hollywood scenarios), Mrs. Delmar was identified primarily with *Bad Girl*, a thoroughly dated and hence forgotten novel. Since 1950, however, she has produced three popular novels—*About Mrs. Leslie* (a *Grand Hotel* type of novel set in a Beverly Hills rooming house), *The Marcaboth Women* (a smoothly-told story of a wealthy and snobbish family), and *The Laughing Stranger* (a romantic melodrama in the *Rebecca* style). In 1945 Mrs. Delmar's domestic comedy *The Rich Full Life* had a brief Broadway run. In the spring of 1953 her play *Midsummer* opened in New York to generally favorable notices. It was a warm and at times moving portrait of a stage-struck young man, his sympathetic wife (played very effectively by Geraldine Page) and his alarmingly precocious little daughter (played by Jenny Hecht, daughter of the author Ben Hecht).

Shortly before the opening of the play, Mrs. Delmar told an interviewer that all of her work—from *Bad Girl* to date—has been done in collaboration with her husband Eugene Delmar. Once the epitome of the "flapper" age—Dutch bob and all—Mrs. Delmar is now a trim, slim grey-haired matron. Her home is in Beverly Hills, Calif.

ADDITIONAL WORKS: The Rich Full Life (play) 1946; About Mrs. Leslie, 1950; The Marcaboth Women, 1951; The Laughing Stranger, 1953.

ABOUT: New York Post January 14, 1953.

DEL VALLE-INCLÁN. See VALLE-INCLÁN

DE MADARIAGA. See MADARIAGA

DE MONTHERLANT. See MONTHERLANT

DE MORGAN, WILLIAM FREND (November 16, 1839-January 15, 1917). For biographical sketch and list of works and references, see TWENTIETH CENTURY AUTHORS, 1942.

DENNETT, TYLER (June 13, 1883-December 29, 1949). For biographical sketch and list of works and references, see TWENTIETH CENTURY AUTHORS, 1942.

* * *

Tyler Dennett died at sixty-six, at Geneva, N.Y., of a heart attack.

His last published works were articles dealing with aspects of the war in the Pacific area, printed in 1944 and 1945 in *Pacific Affairs* and *Far East Survey*.

Of his most distinguished book, the biography of John Hay, the historian Henry

Steele Commager has said: "Professor Dennett's volume is a triumph of condensation, balance, scholarly accuracy, discriminating criticism, philosophical interpretation, and pleasing presentation."

ABOUT: American Historical Review April 1950; New York Times December 30, 1949.

DENNIS, GEOFFREY POMEROY
(January 20, 1892-). For biographical sketch and list of earlier works and references, see TWENTIETH CENTURY AUTHORS, 1942.

* * *

Geoffrey Dennis was a major in the Intelligence Corps of the British Army during World War II. In 1945 he joined the British Broadcasting Company as head of the Italian section. In 1949 he represented the B.B.C. in the former Italian colonies. He is currently associated with UNESCO in Paris. Dennis has contributed many articles to British periodicals. He was the general editor of a four-volume history of World War II.

ADDITIONAL WORK: (ed.) The World at War: A History of World War II, 4 vols., 1951.

DE POLNAY, PETER (March 8, 1906-),
British novelist and miscellaneous writer, is the son of a Hungarian diplomat. Truly a

cosmopolite, he was privately educated in England, Switzerland, and Hungary. "It is one of the boasts of my life," he writes, "that I belong nowhere." In 1932 he went to Africa to farm in Kenya. There de Polnay began to write. His first novel, An Angry Man's Tale, a slight but clever story with a Majorca setting, was published in 1938. Wilfrid Gibson found the book "an extremely accomplished ironic comedy, related with a witty assurance that betrays nowhere the crude touch of the beginner."

De Polnay returned to Europe before the outbreak of World War II and was living in Paris when the Germans entered the city. He enlisted in the French Army but was not called up. Meanwhile his Hungarian national status afforded him some measure of safety, but his open hatred of the Nazis and his work with the French Resistance led to his arrest and imprisonment. After several months in prison, during which he suffered great hardship, he escaped to England. In The Germans Came to Paris he describes these experiences vividly—but not without humor.

The most widely admired of de Polnay's novels is The Umbrella Thorn, a story of the life of an English farmer living in Kenya. His own residence in the British colony gave him the material for an interesting and authentic background to his story. In her review of the book, Elizabeth Bowen hailed the author as a striking arrival on the English literary scene. And a reviewer in the London Times Literary Supplement wrote: "Mr. de Polnay has made a real advance as novelist, adding substance to his gifts of irony and satire, and gives promise of still better work to come." His later novels reflect his versatility and the variety of his interests, but some of them suffer from what the London Times calls their "lack of focus" —"He has any number of excellent ideas and a lively, economical way of expressing them; but this good measure is at times almost an embarrassment, in so much that it involves him in dealing with diversified and often incongruous elements." His study of the English poet and translator Edward Fitzgerald, Into an Old Room, written more in the form of a familiar essay than a scholarly biography, was a smooth and lively memoir, though hardly a definitive work. "De Polnay's Fitzgerald," a reviewer in the New York Times observed, "is interesting and human. Whether he is the real Fitzgerald, readers and scholars can decide for themselves."

Although his permanent home is in England, de Polnay confesses a "split allegiance" in his love for France which he visits whenever possible. His first wife, whom he married in 1942, was Margaret Mitchell-Banks. They had one son. She died in 1950, and in 1952 he married Daphne Taylor. De Polnay's recreations are collecting French furniture and shooting. He is a confirmed dog-lover.

PRINCIPAL WORKS: An Angry Man's Tale, 1938; Children, My Children, 1939; Boo (in U.S.: The Magnificent Idiot) 1941; Death and Tomorrow (in U.S.: The Germans Came to Paris) 1942; Water on the Steps, 1943; Two Mirrors, 1944; The Umbrella Thorn, 1946; A Pin's Fee, 1947; The Moot Point, 1948; Fat of the Land, 1948; Somebody Must, 1949; Into an Old Room: Memoir of Edward Fitzgerald, 1949; The Next Two Years, 1951; An Unfinished Journey to Southwestern France and the Auvergne, 1952; Death of a Legend: The True Story of Bonny Prince Charlie, 1952; The Beast in View, 1953; When Time Is Dead, 1954.

ABOUT: De Polnay, P. Death and Tomorrow.

*DERLETH, AUGUST WILLIAM

(February 24, 1909-). For autobiographical sketch and list of earlier works and references, see TWENTIETH CENTURY AUTHORS, 1942.

* * *

August Derleth writes from Sauk City, Wisc.: "Since publication of TWENTIETH CENTURY AUTHORS, I have left my office on the local Board of Education, and I am no longer lecturing regularly at the University of Wisconsin, though I occasionally go to other colleges and universities as guest lecturer for limited periods. I have also abandoned the contributing editorship of *Outdoors Magazine*. Since 1941, however, I have been literary editor of *The Capital Times* of Madison, Wisc.

"Through 1953, so far only, counting only books definitely scheduled, I will have had published 70 books; 22 others are ready, awaiting publication."

August Derleth's claim in 1942 that he was probably "the most versatile and voluminous writer in quality writing fields" remains unchallenged. Writing methodically and industriously, he has acquired a bibliography that is almost book-length itself. His ambitious Sac Prairie Saga now consists of eight novels, three collections of short stories, three books of miscellaneous prose, and eight collections of poems. His "Judge Peck" mystery series still flourishes, and his reincarnation of Sherlock Holmes in the person of his detective Solar Pons has supplied the material for three collections of short stories. In addition he has written many books for young people, and he has edited some dozen anthologies of stories of the supernatural and science fiction.

Derleth was married in April 1953 to Sandra Evelyn Winters.

ADDITIONAL WORKS: *Poetry*—And You, Thoreau! 1944; Selected Poems, 1944; The Edge of Night, 1945; Habitant of Dusk, 1946; Rendezvous in a Landscape, 1952; Psyche, 1953. *Novels and Short Stories*—Shadow of Night, 1943; The Shield of the Valiant, 1945; Sac Prairie People, 1948; The House of Moonlight, 1953. *Mystery Stories*—Mischief in the Lane, 1944; "In Re: Sherlock Holmes": Adventures of Solar Pons, 1945; No Future for Luana, 1947; The Memoirs of Solar Pons, 1951; Three Problems for Solar Pons, 1952; Fell Purpose, 1953; Death by Design, 1953. *Miscellaneous*—The Wisconsin: River of a Thousand Isles, 1942;

* "The name *Derleth* is pronounced with the accent on the first syllable, though just as many people pronounce it with the accent on the second. It was originally d'Erlette, accent on second syllable; Germanized, it became Derleth, and the accent shifted, carrying the accent over from the German pronunciation to the English."

H. P. L.: A Memoir, 1945; Writing Fiction, 1946; Village Daybook, 1947; The Milwaukee Road: Its First 100 Years, 1948; Empire of Fur (juvenile) 1953; Land of Gray Gold, 1954.

ABOUT: Bishop, Z. The Curse of Yig; Warfel, H. R. American Novelists of Today; Hobbies June 1945; Poetry July 1945, December 1945; Report to Writers (magazine) September 1952; Scholastic September 20, 1943.

DEROUNIAN, AVODIS ARTHUR

("John Roy Carlson") (April 9, 1909-), American journalist, writes: "My story is quite the ordinary story of an immigrant who dreamed long and hard, and realized some measure of success in a land of opportunity. My parentage is Armenian, my birthplace Alexandropolis, Greece. In the next twelve years my parents, two  brothers, and I witnessed two wars, and wandered from country to country seeking refuge. Fortunately we escaped the horrible Turkish massacres in which countless Armenians died. In 1921 we left the Old World, sick and exhausted by its eternal feuds and tyrannies, and dreamed of our new stake in America. At the time I spoke six languages, but knew only two words of English.

"My new life began in Mineola, L.I., in April 1921, at the age of twelve, when I was enrolled in the third grade. Away from the 'nationality islands' of teeming New York City, our Americanization was rapid. Mother already knew English, but father learned it by reading the New York *Times*. In a peaceful environment, among kindly neighbors, I grew in the new climate, participating in numerous school and communal activities. A deep sense of gratitude toward my adopted country began to develop during these formative years. To my rather serious European-trained mind, Americans of my age seemed flippant and too comfortably ignorant of Old World evils to take their country or its problems seriously. It puzzled me then; worries me now! I've been an American citizen since 1926.

"I worked my way through New York University School of Journalism as reporter for small-town newspapers, and as literary editor of the centennial yearbook. Aspirations toward a singing career and following father in his importing business gradually faded as I found myself turning more and more to writing for self-expression, finding in the mastery of the new language a new challenge. Elbert Hubbard and Emerson inspired me to pour out my philosophical thoughts. Influenced by Lincoln Steffens and Jacob Riis, I 'investigated' the Bowery, a few blocks from my *alma mater*, went with the Bonus Marchers to Washington, probed into conditions in slum areas, gradually became aware of a world outside the idyllic Mineola. Dreiser and Sinclair Lewis, too. helped in the process of my social awakening.

"I graduated in 1932 with a B.S. degree in journalism. The depression was on. My first job was that of gardener. Borrowing $100 from the banker who employed me, I hitch-hiked across the country, discovering other unexpected facets of America. On my return I was editor of a conservative Anglo-Armenian publication, the *Spectator*. A shocking experience on Christmas Sunday, 1933, was to set the course of my future thinking and writing: the murder of my beloved Archbishop in the Armenian Holy Cross Church (Eastern Orthodox Rites) by a terrorist group belonging to the Armenian Revolutionary Federation. All nine assassins were convicted. I gave up the *Spectator* and worked editorially with several national magazines. About this time Louis Adamic introduced me to the idea of the integration of Old and New World cultures, and I did research for the U.S. Office of Education for their nation-wide program, 'Americans All—Immigrants All.' I did some post-graduate study at Columbia University.

"That my adopted America could fall prey to the age-old hatreds from which we had fled was further dinned into me in 1938 when *Fortune* engaged me on a part-time basis to report on subversive meetings. The Hitler-worship and mass hatred I witnessed convinced me that a sizable portion of our people were being victimized by ideologies which, while foreign to the American spirit, were capable of seeping into the fabric of our nation. When *Fortune* discontinued the project, I gave up editorial work and joined the staff of Friends of Democracy, engaged in research on the enemies of democracy from the Left and Right. Four years' investigation resulted in the publication of *Under Cover* in 1943. During this period I found it necessary to assume a pen name to safeguard my identity.

"Prior to its acceptance on the twenty-eighth round, *Under Cover* had been rejected twenty-seven times by eighteen different publishers—some of whom had received it for consideration over a period of three years. It sold in excess of 700,000 copies. *Under Cover* revealed the kinship in the thinking of respectable Americans with these not so respectable.

"In 1946 I wrote *The Plotters*, disclosing efforts of Communists and Fascists to capture the veterans' mind. For exposing some of our bigots I received the Thomas Jefferson Award in 1947 from the Council Against Intolerance. In 1951 I wrote *Cairo to Damascus*, based on eyewitness observation of the Arab-Israel War and life in the Middle East. It was also published in Israel, Germany, Canada. I am now at work on 'Germany Speaks,' based on two trips there, and closing a political cycle begun in the U.S.A. in 1938.

"I usually write slowly, from a rough outline based on extensive notes made throughout my travels, with frequent revisions of pages. I start early in the day, often working past midnight—with catnaps in between. I eat voraciously during my 'pregnancy,' do not drink or smoke. I've written for the old *Forum and Century, Liberty, American Mercury, Christian Herald, Pageant*, and helped in the preparation of 'Voices of Defeat' for *Life*. I lecture widely, and have spoken frequently on the radio and television. I have also done an adventure comic strip, 'The Underground,' for the New York *Herald Tribune* Syndicate.

"I have a deep and abiding faith in God, and detest all forms of hypocrisy, ostentation, and bigotry. Politically, I'm a registered Wendell Willkie-type Republican, and have no sympathy with the die-hard school. I'm essentially a 'missionary' hoping to usher in the good by exposing the evil. I look forward to living long enough to see a world which has learned that war, hate, imperialism, dictatorship, Communism, and Fascism do not pay."

PRINCIPAL WORKS: Under Cover, 1943; The Plotters, 1946; Cairo to Damascus, 1951.

ABOUT: Carlson, J. R. Under Cover, Cairo to Damascus; Current Biography 1943; Forum November 1939; Life January 17, 1944; New York Post October 7, 1943; Saturday Review of Literature August 28, 1943.

DE SÉLINCOURT, ERNEST (September 24, 1870-May 22, 1943). For biographical sketch and list of earlier works and references, see TWENTIETH CENTURY AUTHORS, 1942.

* * *

Ernest De Sélincourt died after a brief illness, at seventy-two, at Kendal, Westmoreland, England.

"De Sélincourt was a devoted servant of the English muses," the London *Times* commented, "and the benefactor of all who would study their utterances seriously. He was both a careful textual critic and a discerning interpreter. Upon himself and others he imposed a rigorous and relentless standard of exact scholarship. There lay in him also a warmth of feeling and a steady if sometimes hidden enthusiasm."

ADDITIONAL WORK: Wordsworthian and Other Studies, 1947.

ABOUT: London Times May 25, 1943; New York Times May 25, 1943.

DE SERNA, ESPINA. See ESPINA

*DESTOUCHES, LOUIS FERDINAND ("Louis Ferdinand *Céline") (1894-). For biographical sketch and list of works and references, see TWENTIETH CENTURY AUTHORS, 1942.

* * *

Céline lives in exile in Denmark with his Danish wife, Lucette. He is sick, poor, and embittered—"a crippled giant," as Milton Hindus described him in the intense and intimate little book of that title.

Openly Fascistic, and author of a number of scurrilous anti-Semitic tracts, Céline had little difficulty in getting along with the German conquerors of France. He kept aloof from political life and practiced medicine in two dispensaries near Paris. When the collapse of the Nazi power became imminent, he recognized his own personal danger as a known collaborationist, and he followed the members of the Vichy government into flight. For a while he was one of the attending physicians to the aged and ailing Marshal Petain. With the complete military defeat of Germany, he fled to Denmark. Here he lived safely—his identity disguised under his real name—as Dr. Destouches. French authorities learned of his whereabouts, however, when letters which he wrote to friends in Paris were discovered. France moved to have him extradited. He was arrested in Denmark, imprisoned (in prison he contracted pellagra), but subsequently freed, and extradition proceedings were never carried through. Tried in absentia in Paris, he was given a suspended sentence of one year and subsequently permitted to return to France.

Since the end of the war, Céline has lived a marginal existence in a seaside cabin, a pariah, under the strict surveillance of the local police. Hindus, who visited him in the summer of 1948, reported that he was partially paralyzed, tormented by insomnia, and close to madness ("still on the same side of the boundary line as we are, although closer to it perhaps and full of impulses, threats, intentions and fears of crossing over momentarily to the other side"). What remains of Céline is a pitiful wreck of a brilliant, imaginative, and thoroughly perverse artist. Hindus writes of him: "He hid the good in himself assiduously and successfully and he exploited, exhibited, flaunted the evil. But it did not become his character—or he would have perished at the war's end either by the hands of others or his own. He lives and wants to return to health but does not know how. . . ."

ADDITIONAL WORK IN ENGLISH TRANSLATION: Guignol's Band, 1954.

ABOUT: Columbia Dictionary of Modern European Literature; Dictionnaire Biographique Français Contemporain; Hindus, M. The Crippled Giant.

DE UNAMUNO. See UNAMUNO

DEUTSCH, BABETTE (September 22, 1895-). For autobiographical sketch and list of earlier works and references, see TWENTIETH CENTURY AUTHORS, 1942.

* * *

Babette Deutsch writes from New York City: "Since 1942 Babette Deutsch has continued to write poetry and criticism, as well as other prose, to give poetry readings, and to lecture on poetry. She was visiting lecturer on poetry at Queens College in 1942, and was appointed to the faculty of Columbia University in 1944, where, as guest professor of English, she gives a course on modern poetry. Columbia University accorded her an honorary degree of Litt.D. in 1946. Her *Walt Whitman — Builder for America* won the Julia Ellsworth Ford Award for 1941, and a Spanish translation of it was sponsored by the American Council of Learned Societies. Several of her books have been published in England as well as here, and one was translated into Dutch. She is the author of a few juveniles and a number of translations, some of which have also been published in England."

Among Miss Deutsch's publications in recent years are a fictionized biography of the French poet François Villon—*Rogue's Legacy*; a reworking of fifteen of Shakespeare's plays into narrative form, *The Reader's Shakespeare,* of which Lionel Trilling wrote that the author had "succeeded won-

* dā tōōsh'; sā lĕn'

derfully" in combining "sensitivity of perception" with the "directness and simplicity that the intention of the book required"; and a critical survey of twentieth century American and British poetry, *Poetry in Our Time*, which W. H. Auden called "an excellent job in judgment, insight and presentation."

Take Them, Stranger, a collection of her own poems, appeared in 1944. Irwin Edman wrote of the volume: "Miss Deutsch has a poetic conscience not simply toward her craft but toward her world. It makes her book a rich experience in love and understanding."

ADDITIONAL WORKS: Rogue's Legacy, 1942; Take Them, Stranger (poems) 1944; The Reader's Shakespeare, 1946; Poetry in Our Time, 1952; Animal, Vegetable, Mineral (poems) 1954.

ABOUT: Bishop, J. P. Collected Essays.

DEVAL, JACQUES (June 27, 1893-). For biographical sketch and list of works and references, see TWENTIETH CENTURY AUTHORS, 1942.

* * *

Jacques Deval returned to France after World War II and now lives in Paris. Two new plays by him have been produced in America in recent years. One was *Bathsheba* (1947), a Biblical drama. A dispute arose between the playwright and James Mason, who was starring in the play, over whether it should be played as tragedy or comedy. Deval insisted that it was tragedy, but Mason, influenced by audience laughter during an out-of-town tryout, wanted to do it as comedy. What New York finally saw— for a brief twenty-nine performances—was, in the words of one critic, "a rather weak compromise." The other play, *Tonight in Samarkand* (written with Lorenzo Semple, Jr.), had a brief run in 1955. *Tovarich* was revived for fifteen performances by the New York City Center Company in 1952. The critics found it a pleasant but dated comedy.

DEVLAN, EUGENE. See FOWLER, G.

DE VOTO, BERNARD AUGUSTINE (January 11, 1897-). For biographical sketch and list of earlier works and references, see TWENTIETH CENTURY AUTHORS, 1942.

* * *

One of the liveliest literary battles of the 1940's was set off by Bernard De Voto with the publication in 1944 of his *The Literary Fallacy*. The object of De Voto's attack in the volume was the literature of the 1920's and '30's—tried and found guilty on the grounds that the writers (among them Lewis, Hemingway, Dos Passos, and Faulkner) were "completely separated from the experiences that alone give life and validity to literature." The "literary fallacy," De Voto said, "is the belief that a culture may be understood and judged solely by means of its literature, that literature embodies truly and completely both the values and the content of a culture, that literature is the highest expression of a culture, that literature is the measure of life, and finally that life is subordinate to literature." This controversial thesis in itself was enough to provoke a loud cry of critical protest, including a bitter denunciation of it by Sinclair Lewis in the *Saturday Review of Literature* called "Fools, Liars and Mr. De Voto." But fuel (and some ironic humor) was added to the fire by the fact that De Voto found the personification of the literary fallacy in a fellow critic, Van Wyck Brooks, who, he argued, neglected and ignored the great native American tradition for the "decadent" and "alien" culture of Europe. Since Brooks has developed into one of the most conservative critics of the day and an ardent spokesman for the American tradition himself, De Voto's charges had the effect, as Henry Seidel Canby pointed out, of throwing off "more heat than light." Essentially something of the same pugnaciousness, the same blunt, stubborn and rough-shod approach to literature characterizes all of De Voto's literary criticism. But his work—however limited and opinionated—is invariably stimulating and challenging.

In 1952 De Voto resigned from the staff of *Harper's Magazine* (where he had conducted the "Easy Chair" department since 1935) to give full time to his major interest —the study of primitive America and the frontier. Probably the most successful of his works in this field to date was *The Year of Decision: 1846*—"a monumental narrative," based on contemporary diaries and other records, of a single but vastly significant year in the history of the American West. His scholarship is sound and thorough, his style vigorous and dramatic, but most important—as Struthers Burt said of De Voto's *Across the Wide Missouri*—he has "a passion as strong as a Chinook wind —as just and as lucid as the mountain-clearness of the original America idea." De Voto's research has been extensive. It has taken him from his Cambridge, Mass., home on numerous trips to the West, where he crossed the Missouri River and followed the trail of Lewis and Clark, whose journals he has edited. His *Course of Empire,* a survey of the history of the exploration of the American continent up to 1805, was hailed by historian Henry Steele Commager as "the best book that has been written about the West since Webb's *Great Plains,* and it is the best written book about the West since Parkman."

ADDITIONAL WORKS: *Fiction*—Mountain Time, 1947; (as "John August") The Woman in the Picture, 1944. *Non-Fiction*—Mark Twain at Work, 1942; The Year of Decision: 1846, 1943; The Literary Fallacy, 1944; Across the Wide Missouri, 1947; The World of Fiction, 1950; The Hour, 1951; The Course of Empire, 1952; The Journals of Lewis and Clark (ed.) 1953.

ABOUT: Hyman, S. E. The Armed Vision; Rahv, P. Image and Idea; Van Gelder, R. Writers and Writing; Current Biography 1943; Harper's Magazine June 1952; Saturday Evening Post July 22, 1950.

DEWEY, JOHN (October 20, 1859-June 1, 1952). For biographical sketch and list of earlier works and references, see TWENTIETH CENTURY AUTHORS, 1942.

* * *

John Dewey died of pneumonia at his home in New York City, at ninety-two. Active to the end of his long life, he left several outlined projects uncompleted. In 1946 he had been married a second time, to the former Mrs. Roberta Lowit Grant; they had adopted two children, who were twelve and nine at the time of Dewey's death.

Activities of his last years included involvement in the organization (1944) of a Council for a Democratic Germany, conferences (1946) with labor leaders on a third-party movement, and the founding of a University-in-Exile for scholars who were refugees from their European homes during World War II. He was an active member of the New York Teachers Guild, the International League for Academic Freedom, the Committee for Cultural Freedom, and a month before his death was elected honorary chairman of the Liberal Party of New York State. His ninetieth birthday was widely celebrated.

Max Eastman has called Dewey "not only American, but you might almost say average American." Irwin Edman described him, at ninety, as "a homespun, almost regional, character . . . a modest, gray-haired, stoop-shouldered man with a Green Mountain drawl and a chuckle and a grin." "He was free of all formalities and complacency," the London *Times* has observed, "and showed little of the academic temper, for he

remained a son of the soil, a rebel against traditionalism." Dewey's impact on his time has been stated by Jan Christian Smuts: "He, more than any other American thinker, has wedded philosophy to life and striven to make it a real force, not only in the thought, but also in the practice of his day."

ADDITIONAL WORKS: Problems of Men, 1946; Wit and Wisdom (ed. A. H. Johnson) 1949; Knowing and the Known (with A. F. Bentley) 1949.

ABOUT: Buswell, J. O. Philosophies of F. R. Tennant and John Dewey; Fisher, D. F. American Portraits; Hagedorn, H. Americans; Hook, S. (ed.) John Dewey, Philosopher of Science and Freedom; Mack, R. D. Appeal to Immediate Experience; Morris, L. Postscript to Yesterday; Nathanson, J. John Dewey: the Reconstruction of the Democratic Life; White, M. G. Origin of Dewey's Instrumentalism; American Scholar Winter 1947; Nation's Schools November 1946; New Republic October 17, 1949, October 31, 1949; Newsweek October 24, 1949; New York Times October 16, 1949, June 2, 1952; Pacific Spectator Spring 1953; Saturday Review January 17, 1953; Saturday Review of Literature October 22, 1949; Time June 24, 1946.

DICKINSON, GOLDSWORTHY LOWES (August 6, 1862-August 3, 1932). For biographical sketch and list of works and references, see TWENTIETH CENTURY AUTHORS, 1942.

* * *

ABOUT: Dictionary of National Biography 1931-1940.

DICKINSON, THOMAS HERBERT (November 9, 1877-). For autobiographical sketch and list of works and references, see TWENTIETH CENTURY AUTHORS, 1942.

* * *

Thomas H. Dickinson writes: "During recent years he has been active in both state and national affairs, having been a member of the Connecticut House of Representatives, and during and after the Second World War engaged in various official enterprises for the promotion of international understanding and peace. He maintains homes in Washington, D.C., and Wilton, Conn."

From 1943 to 1945 Dickinson was a member of the Connecticut General Assembly. He worked with the United Nations Relief and Rehabilitation Administration from 1945 to 1946. Since 1941 he has been director of the Fairfield County Planning Association. Mrs. Dickinson died in 1943.

"DICKSON, CARTER (or CARR)." See CARR, J. D.

DI DONATO, PIETRO (1911-). For biographical sketch and list of works and references, see TWENTIETH CENTURY AUTHORS, 1942.

* * *

Short stories by Pietro Di Donato have appeared in recent years in *Esquire,* the *American Mercury,* and *Best American Short Stories.* His story "The Widow of Whadda-You-Want" appeared in *Discovery No. 2.* He is currently at work on a novel to be called "The Purificat."

ABOUT: Discovery No. 2 (Pocket Books, 1953); Peragallo, O. Italian-American Authors and Their Contribution to American Literature.

DILLON, GEORGE (November 12, 1906-). For autobiographical sketch and list of works and references, see TWENTIETH CENTURY AUTHORS, 1942.

* * *

From 1942 to 1945 George Dillon served with the United States Army Signal Corps in Africa and Europe. In 1949 he resigned from the staff of *Poetry* magazine. At that time he wrote: "My name has appeared continuously on the masthead of *Poetry* for twenty-four years, during most of which time my relationship to the magazine has been functional rather than honorary. I now look forward to reading each new issue with no knowledge of what will be in it, for this, I believe, is the proper reward of ex-editors." Dillon, who has written little in recent years, lives in Richmond, Va.

*DIMNET, ERNEST (July 9, 1866-December 8, 1954). For autobiographical sketch and list of works and references, see TWENTIETH CENTURY AUTHORS, 1942.

* * *

Abbé Dimnet died in Paris at the age of eighty-eight. In an editorial on his death, *Commonweal* remarked: "He was an almost classic type of the *salon abbé*—cultivated, witty, sophisticated, tolerant, charitable, a Christian humanist in the best sense of the term."

In 1940 the Abbé Dimnet joined the many refugees who were crowding the roads of France seeking escape from the invading German armies. He had planned to come to America and was engaged for a lecture series here, but he decided at last to remain in France. In an essay called "Living With

* dĕm nĕ'

the Boche," published in the *Atlantic Monthly* in November 1945, he explained his decision. "I did not feel like running away from home in a crisis like this. America would be too comfortable from the material standpoint, too uncomfortable at a time when France must be regarded as a quitter. No, Paris should be my choice." Although his name was on the German blacklist, he was able to report at the end of the war that nothing had happened to him during the four years of occupation: "I was only one of the millions who were hungry and cold, irritated and ironical, hopeful and disappointed, ever expectant optimists." The Abbé visited the United States in 1945 and again in 1947.

ABOUT: Hoehn, M. (ed.) Catholic Authors, I; Atlantic Monthly November 1945; Catholic World May 1955; Commonweal December 31, 1954; New York Times December 16, 1954.

"DINE, S. S. VAN." See WRIGHT, W. H.

"DINESEN, ISAK." See BLIXEN, K. D.

"DIPLOMAT." See CARTER, J. F.

DITMARS, RAYMOND LEE (June 20, 1876-May 12, 1942). For autobiographical sketch and list of earlier works and references, see TWENTIETH CENTURY AUTHORS, 1942.

* * *

ADDITIONAL WORKS: Animal Kingdom: The Way of Life in a Zoo, 1941; Twenty Little Pets from Everywhere, 1943.

ABOUT: Kunitz, S. J. & Haycraft, H. Junior Book of Authors (rev. ed.); Wood, L. N. Raymond L. Ditmars, 1944.

DITZEN, RUDOLPH ("Hans Fallada") (July 21, 1893-February 6, 1947). For autobiographical sketch and list of earlier works and references, see TWENTIETH CENTURY AUTHORS, 1942.

* * *

Rudolph Ditzen died at fifty-three at a hospital in the suburbs of Berlin, where he had been reading the final proofs of his last book, *Every Man Dies Alone.*

The writer remained in Germany throughout World War II. In 1943 his books were pronounced "undesirable" by the Nazis, although the London *Times* has observed that his work during these years suffered from his compulsion to write "books that could in no way be interpreted as hinting at any criticism of the Nazi régime." In 1944 Ditzen was imprisoned for attempted murder, a charge of which he was later acquitted. While in prison he wrote *The Drinker,* described by Edwin Kennebeck as "a bare, harsh story of a man's retreat from reality." Following the defeat of Germany in 1945 the Berlin City Government banned Ditzen's novel *Iron Gustav* as Nazi propaganda, an action which the American military occupation called "illicit."

Lionel Trilling has spoken of Ditzen's "sound, minor talent," while Alfred Kazin says "Fallada's power is never a deep thrust, a forward glance, but the slow, meticulous, affectionate envelopment of suffering." The London *Times* comments: "Fallada was not, in the sense of inspiration, an artist, which is doubtless the clue to his comparative failure and decline, certainly as a 'social' writer, after 1934. He had not the inner certainty of purpose that might have enabled him to take a line of his own either inside or outside Germany, in the Nazi era; he retreated into the whimsical, sentimental and trivially charming. But there is much evidence that he was far from happy in his own conscience."

ADDITIONAL WORK IN ENGLISH TRANSLATION: The Drinker, 1952.

ABOUT: London Times February 11, 1947, March 14, 1953; New York Times February 7, 1947.

DIVER, Mrs. MAUD (MARSHALL) (1867?-October 4, 1945). For autobiographical sketch and list of earlier works and references, see TWENTIETH CENTURY AUTHORS, 1942.

* * *

Maud Diver died, at seventy-eight, in Hindhead, Surrey, England, where she had lived for several years with her daughter-in-law.

She had been at work, up to the time of her final illness, on one more book about British civil servants working in India, and had planned to write a study of Warren Hastings.

Her books about India are described by Orville Prescott as "popular, superficial description"; the London *Times,* noting that she avoided the subject of politics "so far as is possible," added that she wrote in "an amiable, colloquial style that should attract many readers who have neither time nor taste for the more weighty books about the States."

ADDITIONAL WORKS: Royal India, 1942; The Unsung, 1945.

ABOUT: London Times November 11, 1945; New York Times November 11, 1945.

DIXELIUS-BRETTNER, HILDUR (1879-). For autobiographical sketch and list of works and references, see TWENTIETH CENTURY AUTHORS, 1942.

* * *

Hildur Dixelius lives in Bredbyn, Sweden. Her only published book in recent years is *Stormansfru och Helgon,* published in Upsala in 1951, a novel about Saint Brigitta of Sweden.

DIXON, THOMAS (January 11, 1864-April 3, 1946). For biographical sketch and list of works and references, see TWENTIETH CENTURY AUTHORS, 1942.

* * *

Thomas Dixon died at Raleigh, N.C., at eighty-two, after several years of ill health. Dixon, who described himself as a "reactionary individualist," devoted a large part of his voluminous writing to what the New York *Times* has called "upholding the 'purity' of the white race against what he described as the dangers of Negro encroachment through social equality and miscegenation."

ABOUT: Gloster, H. M. Negro Voices in American Fiction; New York Times April 4, 1946.

DOBELL, BERTRAM (January 9, 1842-December 14, 1914). For biographical sketch and list of works and references, see TWENTIETH CENTURY AUTHORS, 1942.

DOBIE, CHARLES CALDWELL (March 15, 1881-January 11, 1943). For biographical sketch and list of earlier works and references, see TWENTIETH CENTURY AUTHORS, 1942.

* * *

Charles Caldwell Dobie died at his home in San Francisco at sixty-one. His death resulted from injuries suffered in a fall caused by a heart attack.

At the time of his death he was working on a book about California's Russian River. The San Francisco *Chronicle* calls his "a pen which for a quarter of a century chronicled the life-pulse of the city of San Francisco." Of his short stories, Katherine Fullerton Gerould wrote: "He never, as far as I know, smeared the 'stream of consciousness' down his page, permitted mood to supplant character, or loose associational revery to pinch-hit for plot."

ADDITIONAL WORK: Three Times a Day (play, with M. Meiklejohn) 1932.

ABOUT: New York Times January 13, 1943; San Francisco Chronicle January 12, 1943.

DOBIE, JAMES FRANK (September 26, 1888-   ), American regionalist, writes: "I was born, the oldest of six children, on a  ranch owned by my parents in Live Oak County, Tex.—in the brush country towards the Mexican border. That land, my stalwart parents, and the English literature on which they nurtured me have been the chief influences of my life. My father and a few neighbors built a one-teacher school on our ranch. When I was sixteen I was sent to the town of Alice to attend high school. Two years later I went to Southwestern University at Georgetown, Tex., where I took the B.A. degree (1910). What I got out of college was friendship, a passion for poetry, especially Wordsworth, Shelley, Keats, Chaucer, and Shakespeare, and the sweetheart, Bertha McKee, who became my wife in 1916.

"I was writing in college and took to teaching English because I loved poetry so much. I have never tried to write poetry however. After receiving a Master's degree from Columbia University (1914), which hardly gave me as much as the New York theatres, I became instructor in English at the University of Texas. World War I took me away for two years as first lieutenant in Field Artillery. I got to France but not into battle. Back at the University of Texas, I found that I could not make a living on my salary and resigned to manage a quarter-million-acre ranch for my uncle Jim Dobie.

"On this ranch, where I lived mostly with Mexican *vaqueros*, I came to a consciousness of the folklore of the Southwest and of range traditions. In 1922 I was back at the University of Texas and began editing the publications of the Texas Folklore Society, for which I was secretary and editor for twenty-one years. Two of these years (1923-25) I went, for more money, to Oklahoma A. and M. College as head of the English department. Here I began writing for the

Country Gentleman, which just about paid for our home in Austin, Tex.

"Back at the University of Texas I began making books, while continuing with articles and tales for magazines. The Guggenheim and Rockefeller foundations gave me grants for leaves of absence in which to write. One year we lived in Mexico. Spanish and Mexican elements are strong in several of my books. I have tried to give significance to the natural things of the Southwest and to emphasize its cultural inheritance. Yet I combat provincial-mindedness. After teaching 'Life and Literature of the Southwest' for years, I came to the conclusion that teaching 'The Trial and Death of Socrates' might be of more value to the students.

"In 1943 I was invited to lecture for a year on American history in Cambridge University, from which experience *A Texan in England* was written. I learned and grew more that year than during any other one year of my life. I went back to England with the U.S. Army in 1945, and again, for *Holiday* magazine in 1949. The University of Texas had meantime been taken over by reactionary politicians. We parted company.

"Now I am free-lance. For years I have done considerable lecturing. Intellectual integrity seems to me as rare in American writing as in American politics. I am called a folklorist, but I care little about scientific folklore. I have done hard research on range history, but I care more for the beautiful than for facts. I am a liberal in religion—a free thinker, I suppose—as in politics."

* * *

A fellow Texan and author, George Sessions Perry, describes Frank Dobie as "a gentle, modest, violent, generous man who says no when he means no, and who, I suspect, would not take one backward step before the devil carrying a bowie knife." As unmistakably Texan "as a Longhorn steer," Dobie is said to know more about Texas folklore than any other man alive. When Cambridge University awarded him an honorary M.A., the Latin citation read in part: *De bobus longicornibus quod ille non cognovit, inutile est alliis cognoscere*—"what he doesn't know about longhorn cattle isn't worth knowing."

PRINCIPAL WORKS: A Vaquero of the Brush Country, 1929; Coronado's Children, 1931; On the Open Range, 1931; Tongues of the Monte, 1935; The Flavor of Texas, 1936; Apache Gold and Yaqui Silver, 1939; John C. Duval: First Texas Man of Letters, 1939; The Longhorns, 1941; Guide to Life and Literature of the Southwest, 1943; A

Texan in England, 1945; The Voice of the Coyote, 1949; The Ben Lilly Legend, 1950; The Mustangs, 1952.

ABOUT: Day, D. Big Country Texas; Perry, G. S. Texas a World in Itself; Peyton, G. America's Heartland—the Southwest; Current Biography 1945; Esquire March 1946; New York Herald Tribune Book Review June 11, 1950, October 12, 1952; Saturday Evening Post September 11, 1943; Southwest Review Spring 1953; Time October 13, 1947.

*DÖBLIN, ALFRED (August 10, 1878-). For biographical sketch and list of earlier works and references, see TWENTIETH CENTURY AUTHORS, 1942.

* * *

After more than ten years of exile from his native land (during which time he lived in Palestine and the United States), Alfred Döblin returned to Germany in 1945. He settled in Baden-Baden where he interested himself in the publishing of a literary magazine. In 1949 he worked for the French Military Government in Baden-Baden. The latest address given for him is Mainz, Germany.

ABOUT: Columbia Dictionary of Modern European Literature; Books Abroad Spring 1954.

* dü′blēn ˎ

DOLE, NATHAN HASKELL (August 31, 1852-May 9, 1935). For biographical sketch and list of works and references, see TWENTIETH CENTURY AUTHORS, 1942.

DONATO. See DI DONATO

DONN-BYRNE. See BYRNE

"DOOLEY, MR." See DUNNE, F. P.

DOOLITTLE, HILDA (September 10, 1886-). For biographical sketch and list of earlier works and references, see TWENTIETH CENTURY AUTHORS, 1942.

* * *

The poetry of "H.D." written during and since the end of World War II has shown continuing growth in emotional depth, intellectual content, and technique. Horace Gregory commented in 1950 that her recent work has proved "the hardiness of lyric poetry in what has so often been regarded as an age of prose." Her major work during the war years was a trilogy of classical simplicity, written in short unrhymed lines—

The Walls Do Not Fall, Tribute to the Angels, and Flowering of the Rod. The first of these volumes, Louise Bogan said, "based on Egyptian symbolism and concerned with bombed London, shows tenser feeling, writing of more energy, and thought of a larger sweep than has been usual in her poetry for many years." In Tribute to the Angels, Miss Doolittle conceives the war as "an alchemist's crucible, served by an apocalyptic flame," searching through smoke and ruin for the jewel of a new life. The final volume recounts the dream of one of the three kings who brought gifts to Christ at His birth—"a legend of resurrection and regeneration, which takes the fragrant, flowering rod as its symbol of hope and survival."

Miss Doolittle's more recent By Avon River, poems and a prose essay commemorating Shakespeare Day, 1945, had (David Daiches wrote) "a charm and delicacy not often found among the tougher ironies of our modern poets and critics." Restrained, delicate and muted, these later poems demonstrate (according to Horace Gregory) "that the imagination and sensibility of a highly-gifted poet have survived a tempest in which whole groups of fashionable writers have lost their bearings."

ADDITIONAL WORKS: The Walls Do Not Fall, 1944; Tribute to the Angels, 1945; Flowering of the Rod, 1946; By Avon River, 1949.

ABOUT: Poetry April 1947, January 1950; Sewanee Review April 1948.

DOREN. See VAN DOREN

DOS PASSOS, JOHN RODERIGO (January 14, 1896-). For autobiographical sketch and list of earlier works and references, see TWENTIETH CENTURY AUTHORS, 1942.

* * *

John Dos Passos writes: "My first wife, Katharine Smith Dos Passos, lost her life in an automobile accident, September 12, 1947. In August 1949 I married Elizabeth Holdridge. Since then we have lived on a fragment of my father's old farm in Westmoreland County, Va. We have a daughter, Lucy Hamlin Dos Passos."

The most ambitious and the most controversial of Dos Passos' works in recent years is the trilogy District of Columbia, the unifying element of which is the Spotswood family—Glenn, who suffers disillusionment and finally martyrdom in the cause of labor and, later, Communism (Adventures of a Young Man); his brother Tyler, who becomes the tool of a political demagogue (*Number One*); and their father, Herbert Spotswood, who sees the ideals of the New Deal corrupted by political intrigue and bureaucracy (*The Grand Design*). Inevitably, evaluations of Dos Passos' writing have become confused with evaluations of his politics—his anti-Communism, his steady drift from the political Left to the Right, his bitterness and his pessimism. Malcolm Cowley puts the blame for this critical confusion at least in part on Dos Passos himself, writing of his novels, "Dos Passos kept obtruding his opinions as if he thought they were more important than the characters, and finally it was the opinions we had to review." But even the most politically neutral critics found weaknesses in *District of Columbia*; they found it superficial and narrow; they found the documentary style, which had been so effective in *U.S.A.*, trite and fragmentary. Few critics, however, deny the tremendous significance of Dos Passos' work in American literature—his influence upon a whole generation of younger novelists, both in the United States and abroad, his daring "kaleidoscopic" style, and (in the words of Arthur Mizener) "the passionate sincerity of his hatred of our failure, of humanity's failure, to be what it professes—and what it ought to be."

ADDITIONAL WORKS: Number One, 1943; State of the Nation (essays) 1944; First Encounter (reissue of One Man's Initiation) 1945; Tour of Duty (essays) 1946; The Grand Design, 1949; The Prospect Before Us (essays) 1950; Chosen Country, 1951; District of Columbia, 1952; The Head and Heart of Thomas Jefferson, 1954; Most Likely to Succeed, 1954.

ABOUT: Aldridge, J. W. After the Lost Generation; Frohock, W. M. Novel of Violence in America; Kazin, A. On Native Grounds; Potter, J. Bibliography of John Dos Passos; Snell, G. D. Shapers of American Fiction, 1798-1947; Antioch Review Spring 1950; Kenyon Review Winter 1950; New Republic February 28, 1949; New York Herald Tribune Book Review October 8, 1950; New York Times Book Review September 22, 1946, November 12, 1950; New Yorker July 29, 1944; Saturday Review of Literature January 8, 1949, June 30, 1951; Sewanee Review July 1947; Time October 30, 1950.

DOUGLAS, LLOYD CASSEL (August 27, 1877-February 13, 1951). For autobiographical sketch and list of earlier works and references, see TWENTIETH CENTURY AUTHORS, 1942.

* * *

Lloyd Douglas died of a heart ailment, at seventy-three, in Los Angeles.

Over two million copies of *The Robe*, published in 1942, were sold during the next few years; in 1943 an estimated $750,000 was spent on preparations for making a motion picture based on the novel; then the plans were abandoned. This experience led Mr. Douglas to stipulate that his later novel, *The Big Fisherman*, should never be made into a movie, a radio script, or condensed or serialized. Ironically, after the author's death *The Robe* was produced as the first large-screen CinemaScope film, costing over $3,500,000, with prospective earnings estimated at $20,000,000.

Douglas wrote what he intended to be a first volume of memoirs, described by Charles Lee as "a rockingchair gossip on a sunny afternoon. Optimistic, affectionate, easy-going and disjointed, it makes up in heart for what it lacks in artistic refinements and intellectual rub."

The "ill repute of Douglas' writing among the critics" has been attributed by Carl Bode to two sources—one, the writer's technical crudeness and relatively simple ideas, the other his didactic use of the novel form. "His writing is too often gaudy in its emotional effect, superficial in its characterization, and marked by lapses in literary taste," in the opinion of Bode. "However, for anyone who is a student of the relationship between contemporary American religion and contemporary American literature, Douglas' importance is great."

ADDITIONAL WORKS: Doctor Hudson's Secret Journal, 1939; The Robe, 1942; The Big Fisherman, 1948; Home for Christmas, 1949; A Time to Remember, 1951; The Living Faith (sermons) 1955.

ABOUT: Douglas, L. C. Time to Remember; Dawson, V. D. and Wilson, B. D. The Shape of Sunday: An Intimate Biography of Lloyd C. Douglas; Mott, F. L. Golden Multitudes; Van Gelder, R. Writers and Writing; Wilson, E. Classics and Commercials; Christian Century July 5, 1950; Life May 27, 1946; New York Times February 14, 1951; New Yorker August 26, 1944; Newsweek July 19, 1943; Religion in Life Summer 1950; Saturday Review of Literature November 13, 1948.

DOUGLAS, NORMAN (December 8, 1868-February 9, 1952). For biographical sketch and list of earlier works and references, see TWENTIETH CENTURY AUTHORS, 1942.

* * *

Norman Douglas died on Capri at eighty-three. His last published work was a brief sketch of the island with which he had become so closely identified.

His friend Graham Greene said of him, "One knew Douglas as a man more loved by more people than is usually the lot of any of us; a man of great personal dignity and of great charity." He has been called an uninhibited hedonist, a scientific humanist, a wit, a scholar, a prose writer of exquisite conscience. V. S. Pritchett, who considered him "a recalcitrant rather than a rebel," added that "Douglas stood in his own light on purpose. The large, committing, confusing issues rose up everywhere he turned; he put his derisive back to them and became a critic, a scholar, a worker in small things, a discreet writer of indiscreet footnotes."

ADDITIONAL WORKS: Almanac, 1945; Late Harvest, 1946; Footnote on Capri, 1952.

ABOUT: Aldington, R. Pinorman; Woolf, C. A Bibliography of Norman Douglas; Fortnightly August 1952; Kenyon Review Autumn 1952; Life and Letters December 1943, January 1944, August 1948; New Statesman and Nation February 6, 1943, May 4, 1946, March 15, 1952; New York Times February 9, 1952; New York Times Book Review February 20, 1949; South Atlantic Quarterly April 1950; Spectator February 22, 1952, March 14, 1952; Time April 15, 1946; Twentieth Century April 1952.

DOUGLAS, WILLIAM ORVILLE (October 16, 1898-), American jurist and travel writer, was born in Maine, Minn. His

father, William Douglas, was a home missionary of the Presbyterian Church, and his mother was the former Julia Bickford Fiske. Young Douglas spent his early years in a number of towns in California and Washington where his father's

Harris & Ewing

work took him. In 1904 the elder Douglas died, and Mrs. Douglas settled with her three children in Yakima, Wash. Here William O. Douglas grew up and attended high school, earning his expenses with part-time work in the town and as an itinerant farm laborer. He entered Whitman College, in Walla Walla, on a scholarship and received the B.A., with a Phi Beta Kappa key, in 1920. His college career was interrupted for several months in 1918 while he served as a private in the U.S. Army.

After two years of high school teaching in Yakima, Douglas came to New York to study for a law degree at Columbia University. He supported himself with a variety of jobs, among them tutoring and supplying cases to illustrate law textbooks. In law school, where he ranked second highest in his class and was an editor of *Law Review*, Douglas became interested in the study of the relation between the law and business. After being admitted to the bar he worked for a time with a Wall Street firm, but he gave up this association to accept an assistant professorship at Columbia Law School. A year later, as the result of a meeting with Robert Maynard Hutchins, then dean of the law school of Yale University, he joined the law faculty of Yale. In 1931 Douglas was made a full professor, and in 1932 he was named Sterling Professor of Law.

While at Yale Douglas published a number of studies in his field of specialization, bankruptcy law. In 1934 he directed a study of protective committees which was sponsored by the Securities and Exchange Commission. In 1936 he was appointed a member of the commission and a year later he became its chairman. He was nominated to the Supreme Court by President Franklin Roosevelt in 1939 to fill the vacancy created by the retirement of Justice Louis D. Brandeis. In his long tenure as a Supreme Court justice, Douglas has won the reputation of being one of the most liberal judges who has ever sat in that court. In 1948 his name was prominent in discussions of possible Democratic presidential candidates, but he announced that he had no intention of running and he refused President Truman's invitation to run for vice president.

It is not as a jurist but as an author that Douglas is probably most widely-known today. Those qualities which distinguished his legal decisions and his public speeches—what *Commonweal* has called his "eloquent and optimistic devotion to civil rights and the well-being of the common man"—have been carried over into his literary writings. Orville Prescott has spoken of the disarming simplicity of his style—"Its quality lies in the character of its author, the warmth, friendliness, humanity, and bedrock idealism." In his informal autobiography, *Of Men and Mountains*, Douglas hardly mentions the courtroom and his legal work. The important part of his life, as reflected in the book, is his deep kinship with nature, his love for the out-of-doors, for the mountains. "I learned early," he writes, "that the richness of life is found in adventure. Adventure calls on all the faculties of mind and spirit. It develops self-reliance and independence. . . . But man is not ready for adventure unless he is rid of fear. For fear

confines him and limits his scope. He stays
tethered by strings of doubt and indecision
and has only a small and narrow world to
explore." Such adventure has not been without its perils for Douglas. In 1949 he was
seriously injured in a climbing accident. But
he recovered sufficiently to make a long and
difficult journey, much of it on horseback,
through the Middle East, a trip which he
reported with warm sympathy and sensitivity
in *Strange Lands and Friendly People*. A
year later he reported on a similar journey
through Central Asia in *Beyond the High
Himalayas*, and in 1953 he published an account of his observations of the struggle
between Communists and non-Communists
in the Far East, in *North from Malaya*.

Tall, sandy-haired and blue-eyed, Douglas
appears far more at home in his casual riding and mountain-climbing clothes than in
the somber robes of a Supreme Court justice.
His first wife, whom he married in 1923, was
Mildred Riddle, and they had a son and a
daughter. In 1953 they were divorced. A
year later Douglas married his research assistant, Mrs. Mercedes Hester Davidson.

PRINCIPAL WORKS: Democracy and Finance,
1940; Being an American, 1948; Of Men and
Mountains, 1950; Strange Lands and Friendly
People, 1951; Beyond the High Himalayas, 1952;
North from Malaya, 1953; An Almanac of Liberty,
1954.

ABOUT: Douglas, W. O. Of Men and Mountains; Lerner, M. Ideas Are Weapons; McCune,
W. Nine Young Men; Nizer, L. Between You
and Me; Current Biography 1950; Life August 15,
1949; New York Herald Tribune Book Review
April 23, 1950.

DOWDEY, CLIFFORD (1904-). For
autobiographical sketch and list of earlier works and references, see TWEN-
TIETH CENTURY AUTHORS, 1942.

* * *

Clifford Dowdey writes: "During the Second World War I did propaganda for the
War Department, Treasury Department, Department of Justice, and worked in the
Pentagon on a confidential assignment to the
Secretary of War. Since Tucson, I've spent
considerable time on the Mexican border,
Hollywood and New York and am now
permanently located in Richmond. I am no
longer married to the former Helen Irwin
(divorced 1944). I have been married for
the past eight years to the former Frances
Gordon Wilson of Richmond, with whom I
returned to Henrico County, Virginia. We
live in the house which was formerly my
mother's, and I work in the room which was

my bedroom as a youth. We have one
daughter, Frances Blunt Dowdey. I am
now engaged on a non-fiction work for
Doubleday's 24-volume history project, Main
Stream of America. I'm doing the South
from 1832 to 1870: it will be called 'The
Land They Fought For.' On the novels
published since the sketch, *Jasmine Street*
and *Weep for My Brother* are laid in modern settings with contemporary themes. The
novel *The Proud Retreat* returns to history
—a story based on the flight of President
Davis' Cabinet and the Confederate treasure
train.

"I see less football, much less horse-racing,
and very few fights; I walk less and read
more, now mainly research."

ADDITIONAL WORKS: Tidewater, 1943; Where
My Love Sleeps, 1945; Experiment in Rebellion
(essays) 1946; Weep for My Brother, 1950; Jasmine Street, 1952; The Proud Retreat, 1953; The
Land They Fought For, 1955.

ABOUT: Warfel, H. R. American Novelists
of Today.

DOWNES. See PANTER-DOWNES

DOYLE, ARTHUR CONAN (May 22,
1859-July 7, 1930). For biographical
sketch and list of works and references
see TWENTIETH CENTURY AUTHORS,
1942.

* * *

ABOUT: Carr, J. D. Life of Sir Arthur Conan
Doyle; Christ, J. F. Irregular Guide to Sherlock
Holmes of Baker Street; Doyle, A. C. The True
Conan Doyle; Pearson, H. Conan Doyle: His Life
and Art; Smith, E. Profile by Gaslight; Atlantic
November 1945; Collier's September 1, 1945; Satur-
day Review of Literature September 20, 1947, May
1, 1948.

DRABKIN, YAKOV DAVIDOVICH.
See ORENBURGSKY •

"DRAGONET, EDWARD." See WIL-
LIAMSON, T. R.

DREISER, THEODORE (August 27,
1871-December 28, 1945). For biographical sketch and list of earlier works
and references, see TWENTIETH CEN-
TURY AUTHORS, 1942.

* * *

Theodore Dreiser died of a heart attack
at his home in southern California at
seventy-four.

In 1944 the American Academy of Arts
and Letters had awarded its Merit Medal

for Fiction to the novelist. Several months before his death, Dreiser joined the Communist Party; at the same time there were signs of an increasingly religious philosophy in his last novels, *The Bulwark* and *The Stoic*. The latter received little critical praise. Horace Gregory declared that although *The Bulwark* lacked "the energy and force" of the earlier books, he found in it "a lyrical overtone and unexpected charm."

"Dreiser's faults are the sad, lovable, honorable faults of 'reality' itself," wrote Lionel Trilling, "or of America itself—huge, inchoate, struggling toward expression, caught between the dream of power and the dream of morality." Identifying himself with the average man of the turn of the century, bewildered by changing concepts, he wrote with painful honesty of the dilemmas of his generation. The late F. O. Matthiessen observed: "From first to last he was driven to try to understand man's place in nature, to a far more profound degree than any of his American contemporaries in fiction. . . . This is what gave Dreiser's books their peculiar breadth."

ADDITIONAL WORKS: The Bulwark, 1946; The Stoic, 1947.

ABOUT: Dreiser, H. P. R. My Life With Dreiser; Dudley, D. Dreiser and the Land of the Free; Elias, R. H. Theodore Drieser; Matthiessen, F. O. Theodore Dreiser; Morris, L. R. Postscript to Yesterday; Snell, G. D. Shapers of American Fiction; Trilling, L. Liberal Imagination; Van Gelder, R. Writers and Writing; American Literature November 1946; American Mercury June 1946; New York Times December 29, 1945; New York Times Book Review January 13, 1946; Nation April 20, 1946, April 28, 1951; New Republic January 14, 1946, June 23, 1947, April 16, 1951; New Yorker April 17, 1948; Saturday Review of Literature January 5, 1946, January 12, 1947; Theatre Arts August 1951; Time January 24, 1949.

DREW. See BICKERSTAFFE-DREW

*DRINKWATER, JOHN (June 1, 1882-March 25, 1937). For biographical sketch and list of works and references, see TWENTIETH CENTURY AUTHORS, 1942.

* * *

ABOUT: Dictionary of National Biography 1931-1940.

* drĭnk′wôter

DRUMMOND, WILLIAM HENRY (April 13, 1854-April 6, 1907). For biographical sketch and list of works and references, see TWENTIETH CENTURY AUTHORS, 1942.

DRUTEN. See VAN DRUTEN

*DU BOIS, WILLIAM EDWARD BURGHARDT (February 23, 1868-). For autobiographical sketch and list of earlier works and references, see TWENTIETH CENTURY AUTHORS, 1942.

* * *

W. E. B. DuBois was retired for age from Atlanta University in 1944 and returned to the National Association for the Advancement of Colored People as director of special research. In 1948 he was dismissed from this job. He accepted an honorary and unpaid position as vice-chairman of the Council on African Affairs which had been listed as a "subversive" organization by the United States Attorney-General. In 1948 DuBois actively supported the Progressive Party in the national elections, and in 1950 he was a candidate for United States Senator from New York on the American Labor Party ticket. Along with four other officers of the Peace Information Center, DuBois was indicted in 1951 by the Grand Jury in Washington, D.C., for "failure to register as an agent of a foreign principal." The case was brought to trial and the defendants were acquitted.

Mrs. Nina DuBois died in 1950, and in 1951 DuBois was married to the author Shirley Graham (see sketch in this volume).

ADDITIONAL WORKS: Color and Democracy, 1945; Encyclopedia of the Negro (ed. with G. B. Johnson) 1945; The World and Africa, 1947; In Battle for Peace, My 83rd Birthday, 1952.

ABOUT: Barton, R. C. Witnesses for Freedom; Drier, H. American Literature by Negro Authors; DuBois, W. E. B. In Battle for Peace; Embree, E. Thirteen Against the Odds; Gloster, H. M. Negro Voices in American Fiction; Rogers, J. A. World's Great Men of Color; American Scholar Winter 1948-49; Phylon (Tenth Anniversary Number) 1949; Survey Graphic January 1947.

* dü bwä′

"DUDLEY, FRANK." See GREENE, W.

DUFFUS, ROBERT LUTHER (1888-). For biographical sketch and list of earlier works and references, see TWENTIETH CENTURY AUTHORS, 1942.

* * *

R. L. Duffus contributes articles on political and economic affairs to the New York *Times Magazine*, the *Nation's Business*, and other periodicals. In 1944 he published an informative and charming fragment of autobiography called *The Innocents at Cedro*. The book was intended to be a memoir of the economist Thorstein Veblen, with whom Duffus lived for a year while he was a student at Stanford. It was this, but it was also something else; for it was Veblen seen through the eyes of a sensitive and intelligent nineteen-year-old boy. Duffus wrote in his foreword to the book: "I long ago resolved that I would never write anything in the autobiographical line if I could help it. I haven't been able to help it."

Duffus has also written the text for an illustrated history of the TVA and a "sane, articulate, suspenseful" novel—*Non-Scheduled Flight*. He lives in Westport, Conn.

ADDITIONAL WORKS: The Innocents at Cedro, 1944; The Valley and its People: A Portrait of TVA, 1944; Non-Scheduled Flight (novel) 1950.

ADDITIONAL WORKS: The Innocents at Cedro,

DU GARD. See MARTIN DU GARD

DUGGAN, ALFRED LEO (1903-), English novelist, was born in Buenos Aires, Argentina. He is partly of American descent,  for his mother's father, Joseph Monro Hinds, was born in Illinois in 1843, and met the author's grandmother (born in Argentina of English parents) when appointed Consul General in Rio de Janeiro, Brazil. Duggan himself, though born in South America, was taken to England at the age of two, and England has been his home ever since. After his education at Eton College and Balliol College, Oxford, he worked for the British Natural History Museum, collecting specimens. At the age of twenty-one he sailed in the 600-ton barquentine, St. George, from England via Madeira, Trinidad, and Panama to the Galapagos Islands, pursuing his job for the Museum. Duggan is one of the few people in recent years to have crossed the Atlantic under sail. In later years he traveled extensively in Greece and Turkey, studying Byzantine monuments, and in 1935 helped to excavate Constantine's Palace, Istanbul, under the auspices of the University of St. Andrews (Scotland). From 1938 to 1941, when he was discharged as medically unfit, he served in the London Irish Rifles (T.A.), seeing active service in Norway. For the rest of World War II he worked in an airplane factory.

A prolific writer of historical fiction, Duggan has turned out more than one book a year recently. His first was *Knight With Armour*, written in 1946 and published in 1950. He had visited all the places mentioned in this work except Antioch, where neither the French nor, later, the Turks encouraged foreign visitors. Next came his novels *The Conscience of the King* and *The Little Emperors*, the latter dealing in lively fashion with the decline and fall of the western Roman Empire as it impinged upon the life of a British civil servant. "As one novel follows another in pleasant succession," wrote Thomas Caldecot Chubb in the New York *Times*, "it dawns upon this constant reader of historical fiction that in Alfred Duggan he has found an extremely gifted writer who can move into an unknown period and give it life and immediacy." "A specialist in decline and fall," in *Lady for Ransom* he dealt with one of the preliminary crises of Byzantine politics. "Mr. Duggan's characters are sharply drawn," writes Chubb, "and, as always, he keeps his eye on the flow of history." His "cheerful cynicism" and satirical view of men and politics "have introduced a refreshing new element into current historical fiction," Orville Prescott wrote in the New York *Times*, "Mr. Duggan looks upon the past with a connoisseur's relish of villainy and violence." His recent novel *Leopards and Lilies* was found by some critics deficient in characterization and human interest. But Geoffrey Bruun wrote: "If the milieu and the actors are not quite up to the high mark Duggan set in his previous novels, his terse realistic style, which has been compared to that of Defoe, retains all its wizardry."

PRINCIPAL WORKS: Knight With Armour, 1950; The Conscience of the King, 1951; The Little Emperors, 1951; Thomas Becket of Canterbury, 1952; The Lady for Ransom, 1953; Leopards and Lilies, 1954.

ABOUT: New York Herald Tribune Book Review October 24, 1954.

*DUGUID, JULIAN (May 24, 1902-). For autobiographical sketch and list of earlier works and references, see TWENTIETH CENTURY AUTHORS, 1942.

* * *

Julian Duguid is a special correspondent for the British Broadcasting Company, covering assignments in the East, Israel, and South Africa. He reported on a trip he made through the Khyber Pass in *Harper's* for January 1952.

ABOUT: Harper's January 1952.

* dü gēd'

*DUHAMEL, GEORGES (June 30, 1884-). For biographical sketch and list of earlier works and references, see TWENTIETH CENTURY AUTHORS, 1942.

* * *

Georges Duhamel remained in Paris throughout the German occupation, at considerable personal risk, since he had declared his opposition to Hitler. His books were banned, three members of his family were arrested, but Duhamel himself managed to escape arrest. During this period he worked busily, mainly on his memoirs. He was acting secretary of the French Academy and belonged to the National Committee of Authors, a group which published the clandestine *Les Lettres Françaises*, to which Paul Eluard, Louis Aragon, and François Mauriac, among others, contributed. Duhamel himself contributed an anonymous account of the German destruction of Oradour-sur-Glane.

Within a few hours after the liberation of France in 1944, the National Committee of Authors issued a statement pledging itself to strive for full victory, the "new France" and world security. The first signature on the statement was Duhamel's—followed by those of Paul Valéry and Mauriac. Henry C. Wolfe, who visited Duhamel soon after the liberation, described him as follows: "A tall, gray, bespectacled man, his worn face bespoke the physical privations and spiritual strain of the occupation years." Duhamel was proud of the spirit of the French underground resistance. Before he could begin to write again, he announced, he wanted to go forth and mingle with the people of France, "which I have seen mute and frozen in the grip of men who thought themselves conquerors, not knowing that victory is a thing of the spirit."

Duhamel is now engaged in publishing his memoirs, one volume of which (covering his early years) has appeared in English. He has also published two additional novels in the *Pasquier Chronicles* series, these said to be the concluding works. In these later novels critics found the same "sureness of touch" that had distinguished the earlier novels, but, Robert Gorham Davis wrote in the New York *Times*, as a conclusion they are "a most abrupt and melancholy close, without a coda, or resolution of themes." Taken as a whole, however, the *Pasquier Chronicles* represent Duhamel's greatest literary achievement and a positive and affirmative expression of "the enduring

* dü á měl'

stuff" of French life. The series has often been compared to John Galsworthy's *Forsyte Saga* and there are superficial resemblances. But, as A. E. Ballard has pointed out in an article in the *National Review*, Galsworthy's series was essentially a nostalgic record of a dying class. The Pasquiers, however, "bowed but not beaten, survived the recent temporary eclipse of France and will rebuild her greatness."

Duhamel visited Canada and the United States in 1945. He lives in Paris.

ADDITIONAL WORKS IN ENGLISH TRANSLATION: Light on My Days: Autobiography, 1948; Suzanne [and] Joseph: Two Novels from the Pasquier Chronicles, 1949; Cry Out of the Depths, 1953.

ABOUT: Columbia Dictionary of Modern European Literature; Dictionnaire Biographique Français Contemporain; Duhamel, G. Light on My Days; Books Abroad Winter 1946; Contemporary Review April 1948; National Review July 1948; New York Times Magazine September 17, 1944; Saturday Review of Literature October 14, 1944, March 17, 1945.

DULLES, FOSTER RHEA (January 24, 1900-), American historian and sociologist, writes: "I was born in Englewood, N.J., and started at a fairly early age to peck at a typewriter with two fingers—a method of getting something on paper which I have followed more or less consistently ever since. Editorship of the *Daily Princetonian* led me into journalism, and a desire to see the world suggested China. Taught at school known as Princeton-in-Peking, worked with English-language news service, and for a time served as correspondent for the *Christian Science Monitor*. Back in this country after two years, I was a reporter for the old New York *Herald*, briefly with the magazine *Foreign Affairs*, and then two years abroad in the Paris office of the New York *Herald Tribune*. There I met my future wife (Marion Richardson) and after a honeymoon trip around the world, returned once more to New York. Several years as editorial writer on the New York *Evening Post* and spare time in taking courses at Columbia University where I eventually obtained (1940) a Ph.D. in American history. Also began writing a number of books on historical topics which interested me.

"A Guggenheim Fellowship in 1938-39 finally served as a transition from the journalistic to the teaching world. After temporary appointments at Bennington, Smith, and Swarthmore, joined the history faculty at Ohio State University in 1941 and have been teaching there ever since. If I entered the profession in part to have more time and opportunity to write, have come to enjoy the teaching more and more and find the two activities a stimulating and satisfying combination.

"Other phases of life during these years would include helping my wife to bring up a family of four daughters, occasional travel, and recreational activities embracing canoe trips in the Canadian woods, gardening, water coloring and domestic chess."

* * *

Foster Rhea Dulles has been called "one of the abler craftsmen in the historical profession." He writes, as Floyd Taylor has pointed out in the *Christian Science Monitor*, "with the knowledge of a scholar and with a journalist's talent for telling a story." For his books on China and the Near East he drew upon a rich background of personal experiences as well as careful scholarship. A. Whitney Griswold described his *Road to Teheran* as "a book which combines the timeliness of good journalism with the objectivity and perspective of good history."

PRINCIPAL WORKS: The Old China Trade, 1930; Eastward Ho, 1931; America in the Pacific, 1932; Lowered Boats, 1933; Harpoon (juvenile) 1935; Forty Years of American-Japanese Relations, 1937; America Learns to Play, 1940; The Road to Teheran, 1944; Twentieth Century America, 1945; China and America, 1946; Labor in America, 1949; The American Red Cross, 1950; America's Rise to World Power, 1955.

DUMARCHAIS (or DUMARCHEY), PIERRE. See MAC ORLAN, P.

*DU MAURIER, DAPHNE (May 13, 1907-). For autobiographical sketch and list of earlier works and references, see TWENTIETH CENTURY AUTHORS, 1942.

* * *

Daphne du Maurier now lives in an old manor house on the Cornish seacoast, "Menabilly," where she spends part of her day writing and the rest of it with her family—two daughters, Flavia and Tessa, and a son, Christian. Miss du Maurier's husband, Lt. Gen. Sir Frederick Browning, was chancellor of the exchequer in the household of Princess Elizabeth before her accession to the

* dū mō′rĭ ā

throne of England and is now treasurer to the Duke of Edinburgh.

Rebecca proceeds rapidly on its way toward becoming a minor classic among popular novels (some critics have called it "a twentieth century *Jane Eyre*"). That it is part of a large and ever-popular tradition of romantic novels was demonstrated dramatically in 1941 and again in 1948 when charges of plagiarism were brought against Miss du Maurier. The first case was based on claims of similarity to a Portuguese novel, *A Sucesora*, by Carolina Nabuco, and was never brought to court. The second was a suit by J. Clifford MacDonald, son of the late Edwina MacDonald whose short story "I Planned to Murder My Husband" and novel *Blind Windows* were alleged to have been sources of *Rebecca*. Miss du Maurier came to New York to testify, and the suit was dismissed largely on the grounds that the resemblances between the themes of the two books were coincidental and that, as Harrison Smith of the *Saturday Review of Literature* pointed out in his testimony, the "second wife" plot is well-worn in literature today. Smith wrote of the case that if *Rebecca* could be attacked on grounds of plagiarism, "then any author who writes a successful book on any subject that has been used before places his reputation and his fortune in hazard."

With *Hungry Hill, The King's General,* and *The Parasites*, Miss du Maurier received less favorable critical response, but the novels sold well. In *My Cousin Rachel*, published in the United States in 1952 and promptly made into a motion picture, she returned to the formula which had made *Rebecca* so successful—the enigmatic heroine, the brooding tortured hero, and the Gothic atmosphere of the rugged Cornish coast. Both in *Rachel* and again in a collection of short stories, *Kiss Me Again, Stranger*, Miss du Maurier displays a predilection for horror and suspense.

She has written two plays, *The Years Between* and *September Tide* (in which the late Gertrude Lawrence starred on the London stage), published an edition of the letters of her grandfather, George du Maurier, and a biographical novel about her great-great-grandmother Mary Anne Clarke.

ADDITIONAL WORKS: Hungry Hill, 1943; The Years Between (play) 1945; The King's General, 1946; The Parasites, 1949; September Tide (play) 1949; My Cousin Rachel, 1951; The Young George du Maurier: Letters, 1860-1867, 1951; Kiss Me Again, Stranger, 1952; Mary Anne, 1954.

ABOUT: Church, R. British Authors; Current Biography 1940; Life September 11, 1944; New York Herald Tribune Book Review January 1, 1950; New York Times Book Review March 16, 1952; Publishers' Weekly January 31, 1948; Saturday Review of Literature February 7, 1948, February 9, 1952.

DUNKERLEY, WILLIAM ARTHUR.
See OXENHAM, J.

DUNNE, FINLEY PETER ("Mr. Dooley") (July 10, 1867-April 24, 1936).
For biographical sketch and list of works and references, see TWENTIETH CENTURY AUTHORS, 1942.

* * *

ABOUT: Brogan, D. W. American Themes; Hoehn, M. (ed.) Catholic Authors, I; Morris, L. R. Postscript to Yesterday; Atlantic Monthly June 1946; New Republic March 22, 1948.

*DUNSANY, EDWARD JOHN MORETON DRAX PLUNKETT, 18th Baron (July 24, 1878-).
For biographical sketch and list of earlier works and references, see TWENTIETH CENTURY AUTHORS, 1942.

* * *

Lord Dunsany made a twelve-week visit to the United States—his first since 1928—in the spring of 1953, spending more than half his time in California. His home is Dunsany Castle in County Meath, Ireland, but he now lives most of the year in England on his estate, Dunstall Priory, in Kent. He was in England during World War II—a volunteer in the Home Guard. In the war years he wrote more poems "than in all the rest of my life put together"—sometimes as many as one a day, for the *Evening Standard*, the *Evening News*, and the *Sunday Express*. He is still a rapid and fertile writer ("I never rewrite and I never correct"). He wrote five stories on his American visit and the total of his published books is over fifty. A handsome man in his middle seventies, Lord Dunsany was described in 1953 as "slightly stooped but still an inch or two over six feet, flowing white hair and white goatee." His opinions—whether on literature, travel, or the cutting off of dogs' tails ("foolish cruelty")—are clear-cut and delivered "staccato-fashion." He regards Walter de la Mare as "the greatest living poet in English." On prose writers he says crisply: "I can't think of any great prose writers who have come up to the standards I

* dŭn săʹ nĭ

have set for prose." Returning to the United States for a lecture tour early in 1955, Lord Dunsany inveighed against the "obscurity" of modern poetry.

ADDITIONAL WORKS: *Poetry*—Journey, 1943; Wandering Songs, 1943; While the Sirens Slept, 1944; The Sirens Wake, 1945; The Year, 1946; To Awaken Pegasus, 1949. *Prose*—Guerilla, 1944; Donellan Lectures, 1945; Glimpse from a Watch Tower, 1946; Fourth Book of Jorkens, 1948; The Man Who Ate the Phoenix, 1949; The Last Revolution, 1951; The Sword of Welleran, 1954.

ABOUT: New York Herald Tribune Book Review June 21, 1953; New Yorker June 27, 1953.

DUPEE, FREDERICK WILCOX (June 25, 1904-), American editor, biographer, and critic, writes: "I was born on the South Side of Chicago. My father was Leroy Church Dupee, a graduate of Yale and resident of Chicago. My mother was Fannie Wilcox, of Joliet, Ill. My family moved about a good deal because my father was always looking for better business con-

Erich Hartmann

nections. During my childhood I lived variously, and went to public school, in Chicago, Joliet, and Rockford. But if I have a home town, it is mainly Joliet and to a lesser extent Grand Haven, Mich., where we spent our summers. I was graduated from the University High School of Chicago, attended the University of Illinois for one semester, the University of Chicago for a couple of years, and finally received a Ph.B. degree from Yale in 1927. At Yale I was very proud to be a member of the Elizabethan Club. At the latter, in conversation with Dwight MacDonald, Wilder Hobson and others, I became a convinced literary man. We read and worshipped Spengler, Proust, Joyce, Sherwood Anderson, Henry James, and Irving Babbitt—it then seemed possible to admire them all equally. The interest in Babbitt signified that the '20's were coming to an end and that we were in search, very vaguely, of order and orthodoxy. Scott Fitzgerald, whom I had loved in high school, seemed as dated as Byron.

"This tendency had consequences some years later, when, with Dwight MacDonald and others, I edited a dismal little-magazine called *The Miscellany*, which in its two years of existence printed few good things but managed to attack, in its reviews, some of the best poems and novels of the late '20's. Then, a few years later, I read *The Coming Struggle for Power* and the *Marxist Handbook* and was for a couple of years caught up, with so many others, in the 'orthodoxy' of Communism. For a few months I was literary editor of the *New Masses*, until its policies and developments in Spain and Moscow sickened me with Communism. In 1937, with several others, I began to edit the revived *Partisan Review*, which for some years devoted its main energies to the battle with Stalinism. This ended the fascination with orthodoxies.

"Meanwhile I had taught English for two years (1927-29) at Bowdoin, spent a couple of years in Mexico, and lived for the remainder of the time in New York, writing book reviews. In 1940 I became an instructor in English at Columbia. From 1944 to 1948 I taught at Bard College. I then returned to Columbia where I am now associate professor of English. In 1952 I received a Guggenheim fellowship to spend the year 1952-53 in Europe preparing to write a book on modern literature."

PRINCIPAL WORKS: The Question of Henry James (ed.) 1945; Henry James (American Men of Letters Series) 1951; Great French Short Novels (ed.) 1952.

DURANT, WILLIAM JAMES (November 5, 1885-). For biographical sketch and list of earlier works and references, see TWENTIETH CENTURY AUTHORS, 1942.

* * *

Will Durant's monumental "Story of Civilization" has now been carried through the Renaissance. He plans to complete the entire series in 1963. His work does not rival that of the great creative historians, but it is widely admired as both informative and delightful reading. The historian Geoffrey Bruun said of volume IV: "Rarely has a historian writing for the general public combined such a readable style with such assiduous documentation, encyclopedic interest, and indefatigable zest." The outstanding merits of his books, another reviewer has said, are vividness, intelligibility, and honesty.

In 1935 Durant and his wife moved to Los Angeles where he taught philosophy at U.C.L.A. His home is still in Los Angeles. He told an interviewer in 1953 that he is neither a philosopher nor an intellectual. "I am a lover of the lovers of wisdom. I am an historian who loves philosophy."

ADDITIONAL WORKS: *Story of Civilization*—III. Caesar and Christ, 1944; IV. The Age of Faith, 1950; V. The Renaissance, 1953.

ABOUT: New York Post November 22, 1953; This Week Magazine January 17, 1954.

DURANTY, WALTER (May 25, 1884-). For biographical sketch and list of earlier works and references, see TWENTIETH CENTURY AUTHORS, 1942.

* * *

Walter Duranty's long experience in the Soviet Union has given his recent work on Soviet affairs special interest and authenticity. Hans Kohn found his *U.S.S.R.* a "sober and well-informed book," remarkable not only for the author's first-hand knowledge of his subject but also for "a sincere effort at objectivity and dispassionate analysis." His more recent *Stalin & Co.* was praised by Edgar Snow as "an impartial book, sympathetic with humanity on both sides of the world and one which refrains from passing any moral judgment upon the men whose lives it chronicles."

Duranty's two ventures into fiction in the past decade have been less favorably received. *Search for a Key* was a fictional autobiography, vividly written but, F. H. Bullock wrote, "a little self-indulgent, a little lacking in the discipline that a stricter form would have imposed on it." His novel of peasant life in post-war Europe, written with Mary Loos, *Return to the Vineyard*, was found, by a reviewer in the New York *Times*, "crude and sentimental in style and . . . lacking in probability."

In 1951 *Time* reported that Duranty, then living in Hollywood and in poor health, had launched an unusual literary service. For one dollar a month he offered to send subscribers a "personal" (but multigraphed) letter each week on any subject of their choice, ranging from travel and world politics to love letters —"imaginary of course." Aside from the income which the service would bring him, he announced, he wanted to share with others his experience and knowledge.

ADDITIONAL WORKS: Search for a Key, 1943; U.S.S.R., 1944; Return to the Vineyard (with M. Loos) 1945; Stalin & Co.: The Politburo—the Men Who Run Russia, 1949.

ABOUT: Collier's January 19, 1946; Time March 25, 1946; New York Herald Tribune Book Review April 3, 1949.

DURRELL, LAWRENCE ("Charles Norden") (1912-), British poet and novelist, writes: "I was born in India, educated in England, St. Edwards College, Canter-

bury. Have been a Foreign Service press officer in Athens, Cairo, Rhodes, and Belgrade; a British Council lecturer in Argentina and Greece. I have also worked at other things—once as a pianist in a night club.

"I am Irish, have been twice married and have two daughters, Penelope and Sappho-Jane. About my work: I deplore much of it, but have been continuously growing so it gets better and better, I hope. I haven't yet produced the mature work of my middle life and only hope it will be coming along soon. I regard writing as a fascinating bore: and wish it were better paid. I intended to die young and have the following words on my tomb: 'Lawrence Durrell wishes you great passions and short lives.' If I die old it will only need altering by one word.

"I am now living like a hermit on the island of Cyprus with my two-year-old daughter Sappho. My poems constitute the only honest sketch of myself I have ever made. I suggest you reprint them all and let your readers judge."

* * *

Like his friend Henry Miller, Lawrence Durrell has made no attempt to cater to the reading tastes of a wide popular audience. Like Miller he lives quietly and simply, in rugged isolation from 'literary' society. His readers, though few in number, are wildly enthusiastic about his work. "His genius," Lawrence Clark Powell has pointed out, "is versatile and abundant." His Joycean novel *The Black Book*, which has been compared to Miller's 'Tropics' novels, is a rich and sophisticated "study of moral exhaustion." Kenneth Rexroth has said of the book: "It is as though Pascal had turned his scientific and passionate eye on the behavior of some trivial diabolist of the gutter." His poetry is distinguished by a rare purity of style, what Rexroth describes as his "uniquely self-sufficient tranquillity," and by an ability to convey "the excitement of the senses," as the *Times Literary Supplement* puts it, to "recreate in sharp, intellectually conceived yet sensuously executed images the classical civilization" of the Aegean scene which is the background for most of his writings.

In 1950 Durrell lectured in Argentina, under the auspices of the British Council, to an audience of graduate teachers of English. These lectures were subsequently published as *A Key to Modern Poetry*. Reviewers generally agreed that although Durrell offered some fresh and challenging opinions on some English poets, his thesis (that

modern poetry is an expression of the disruption of materialist thought and mechanical psychology) was not well supported. "He shows himself here," the *New Statesman and Nation* commented, "not so much a critic by vocation as an imaginative writer doing his best off his main beat."

PRINCIPAL WORKS: Ten Poems, 1933; Transition, 1934; The Pied Piper of Lovers, 1935; The Black Book (novel) 1938; A Private Country (poems) 1943; Prospero's Cell: Guide to the Landscape and Manners of the Island of Corcyra, 1945; Cities, Plains and People (poems) 1946; Cefalu (novel) 1947; On Seeming to Presume (poems) 1948; Sappho: A Play in Verse, 1950; A Key to Modern (British) Poetry, 1952. *As "Charles Norden"*—Panic Spring (novel) 1937.

ABOUT: Powell, L. C. *Preface to* Durrell's A Landmark Gone (pamphlet, privately printed); Rexroth, K. (ed.) New British Poets.

*DUTOURD, JEAN (January 14, 1920-   ), French novelist and satirist, was born in Paris. He studied at the Sorbonne, where he took a degree in philosophy. Drafted into the French Army in June 1940, he was captured in July by the Germans and in August escaped from his captors by jumping off a train that was taking him to Germany. In 1943 he was recaptured by the

British Broadcasting Corp.

Gestapo and sentenced to death but again escaped. For the remainder of the war he was a fugitive from the Gestapo and an active worker in the French Resistance movement. In May 1942 Dutourd married Camille Lemercier in Paris. They have two children and live in Paris. He speaks English well and lived in London for several years. He paints and fences for recreation and was at one time fencing champion of Paris.

Dutourd's first novels were slight but humorous satires—*Le Complexe de César, Le Déjeuner de Lundi*. He first won fame with the publication in 1950 of his fantasy *Une Tête de Chien (A Dog's Head)*, a character study of an ordinary middle class Frenchman who was born with a dog's head. This extraordinary tale—told, as Henri Peyre observed, "with an incisive humor reminiscent of a Voltairean *conte*"—was hailed in France as a satire of the first rank. American reviewers, while shocked at the ferocity of the satire, were deeply impressed by the book. The New York *Herald Tribune* called it "a

* dü tōor'

293

tiny masterpiece in the French classical tradition . . . stylish, elegant, and witty." The New York *Times* found that the book "has the classic virtues of brevity, lucidity, and concentration."

As a satirist Dutourd has inevitably invited comparison with satirists from Voltaire and Swift through Evelyn Waugh. With his second novel to appear in English translation—and to date his most successful book—*The Best Butter,* subtitled An Extravagant Novel, Dutourd established himself securely as a social satirist in the tradition of Balzac. *The Best Butter (Au Bon Beurre)* is a savage but comic portrait of middle class French society in post-war France. It is a realistic picture of black-marketeering and profiteering, of the rise to wealth and social success of a family who keep a dairy shop. Anthony West, in the *New Yorker,* described the novel as "a laconic comedy about the behavior of the common man." Like most powerful social satires, *The Best Butter* reveals beneath its surface of ribald comedy a brooding sense of the tragedy of human society. John K. Hutchens wrote in the New York *Herald Tribune:* "Its expression is the comedy of despair, the weapon against corruption so grim that, approached in any other fashion, it would invite something like madness." The novel received the Prix Interallié in France and was a selection of the French book club Choix.

Dutourd describes his writing as his "homework." He holds a full-time job on the staff of the *Nouvelle Revue Française* and does his writing after office hours, productive on an average of five double-spaced typewritten pages in an evening. In spite of his claim that writing is only an avocation, he is a writer of real promise. Henri Peyre writes in evaluation of his work: "The author promises to be one of the good minor talents of his generation and one of the rare entertaining writers of an age that prefers to wallow in its anguish rather than to laugh at it."

PRINCIPAL WORKS IN ENGLISH TRANSLATION: A Dog's Head, 1951; The Best Butter, 1955.

ABOUT: Peyre, H. The Contemporary French Novel.

*DUUN, OLAV** (November 21, 1876-September 13, 1939). For biographical sketch and list of works and references, see TWENTIETH CENTURY AUTHORS, 1942.

* * *

ABOUT: Columbia Dictionary of Modern European Literature.

* dōōn

DYKE. See VAN DYKE

EARLY, ELEANOR, American travel writer, reports: "I was born in Massachusetts, attended school in Wellesley and was graduated (a kindergartner) from Miss Wheelock's School in Boston, after which I went to work on the Boston *American* where I became a reporter and did a column called 'Girls in Sports.' The column landed my picture on the cover of the *Police Gazette,* but made no impression elsewhere.

"On my first vacation, I visited Cuba where I had such a good time that I determined to free lance, in order to travel. In one year I wrote three novels, *Daughter of Magdalene, Whirlwind,* and *Orchid. Daughter of Magdalene,* which was mostly autobiographical, was lost in the mails. Fortunately, there was no carbon. The Newspaper Enterprise Association took *Whirlwind* and *Orchid.* Whereupon I went to Paris and wrote *The Shining Talent,* also for N.E.A. Following newspaper syndication, the three were published by Grosset & Dunlap.

"Then I did a Washington column for International News Service, wrote a book about Washington, and had a Washington radio program (Mutual Network). Also did Washington date-line stuff for King Features. Traveled in the British Isles, Europe, West Indies, South America, and North Africa.

"While covering the Braves at training camp in Florida, I began a book on Boston (*And This Is Boston*). Since then I have written eleven travel books and a little number called *She Knew What He Wanted,* reprinted as *She Knows How,* allegedly a guide for girls who wanted a man or who had a man and wanted to keep him. Also edited *The Constance Letters of Charles Chapin.*

"My best selling books are about Boston, Cape Cod, and New York. The ones I like best are about the West Indies where I have spent some of the happiest months of my life.

"I love seeing new places and the digging business that goes into a travel book, but find it extremely difficult to get started writing. I should like to visit Japan, fly around the world, and drive across the U.S.A. Some day I shall return to a little island where the sun always shines and the palms forever sway. There I hope to write something *much* better than I have ever written before.

"Meantime, I live in Manhattan, in an apartment that overlooks Central Park. The two cities in the world which I really love are New York and Paris. And New York, I think, is even more wonderful than Paris."

* * *

Eleanor Early's travel books are animated, full of lively gossip and little-known facts about the places she has visited. Virginia Kirkus calls her "my favorite travel guide," and a New York *Times* reviewer once wrote: "Nobody writes better guide books than Eleanor Early—better, more interesting, more charming."

PRINCIPAL WORKS: *Travel*—And This Is Boston! 1930; And This Is Washington! 1934; Behold the White Mountains, 1935; Ports of the Sun, 1937; Adirondack Tales, 1939; Lands of Delight, 1939; A New England Summer, 1940; An Island Patchwork, 1941; New Orleans Holiday 1947; Cape Cod Summer, 1949; New York Holiday, 1950; New England Cookbook, 1954; Washington Holiday, 1955. *Fiction and Miscellaneous*—Orchid, 1929; Whirlwind, 1930; Love's Denial (pub. serially as The Shining Talent) 1932; Detour to Happiness, 1935; She Knew What He Wanted, 1941.

ABOUT: Hoehn, M. (ed.) Catholic Authors, II; Boston Sunday Herald July 10, 1949.

EASTMAN, MAX (January 4, 1883-). For autobiographical sketch and list of earlier works and references, see TWENTIETH CENTURY AUTHORS, 1942.

* * *

Max Eastman completed and published his autobiography, *Enjoyment of Living*, in 1948. The volume covers only the first thirty-three years of his life—to 1917—but it covers this period with amazing, at times alarming, candor and detail. Eastman wrote in a foreword to the book: "It is the story of how a pagan and unbelieving and unregenerate, and carnal and seditious and not a little idolatrous, epicurean revolutionist emerged out of the very thick and dark of religious America's deep, awful, pious, and theological zeal for saving souls from the flesh and the devil." Granville Hicks found it "an ardently honest attempt at self-revelation," though he, and many other readers of the book, confessed to being puzzled about

the turbulent self that was revealed. Edmund Wilson has commented on Eastman's "anomalous role of preacher-teacher-critic-poet." He has never been an easy personality to categorize. In recent years, however, he has followed a more regular and consistent pattern than in the past. A long-time bitter foe of Communism, he has found a large and sympathetic reading public for his articles on that subject in such periodicals as *American Mercury, Reader's Digest,* and *Saturday Evening Post*. In 1951 he published a new and expanded edition of his very popular *Enjoyment of Poetry*. Eastman lives in Chilmark, Mass.

ADDITIONAL WORKS: Lot's Wife (poem) 1942; Enjoyment of Living, 1948; Poems of Five Decades, 1954; Reflection on the Failure of Socialism, 1955.

ABOUT: Eastman, M. Enjoyment of Living; Wilson, E. Classics and Commercials; Reader's Digest March 1948.

EATON, EVELYN SYBIL MARY (December 22, 1902-), Canadian-American novelist and memoirist, was born in Montreux, Switzerland, of Canadian parents— Col. Vernon Eaton, director of military training in Canada, who was killed in 1917 at the battle of Vimy Ridge, and Myra Fitz Randolph Eaton. Miss Eaton was educated in Canada, at the Sorbonne,

Yolla Niclas

and at the fashionable Heathfield School in England (her four years there, she writes, "armed me to meet frustrations with indifference, and loneliness with relief") and she was duly presented at Court in 1920. Rebellion set in, however, at an early age. She borrowed money from an indulgent aunt to attend secretarial school and worked in a variety of jobs. In 1925, after a tour through Belgium, Switzerland, and Corsica, she settled in Paris, where she did translations and wrote movie scenarios for the Paramount Studios at Joinville (the movie studio background figures prominently in her first novel—*Desire, Spanish Version*). In the middle thirties she returned to England for a while where she became secretary to the Bodleian Appeal Committee at Oxford. In 1938 and 1939 she worked in New York City with the literary agent Ann Watkin. Since 1944 Miss Eaton has been an American citizen. She was a war correspondent in the Far East during World War

II and covered over 33,000 miles by plane and jeep.

Since the end of the war Miss Eaton has lived in New York and in Virginia. She recently acquired a farm in New Hampshire. Her short stories appear frequently in the *New Yorker* and she contributes book reviews to the New York *Times* and the *Saturday Review*. She has taught English at Columbia University and is currently on the faculty of Sweet Briar College in Virginia. From 1948 to 1951 she was president of Pen and Brush. She was married in 1928 to Ernest Richard Viedt. They had one daughter, Teresa Neyana (known as "Terry" in her mother's autobiographical writings), and were divorced in 1934.

In her writing, as in her life, Evelyn Eaton has never allowed herself to fall into an easy pattern of routine. She has written on a variety of subjects and in a variety of forms—poetry, prose poems, children's books, historical romances, travel and personal essays. Her most successful book has been *Quietly My Captain Waits*, which was sold to Hollywood and became a Literary Guild selection. A colorful historical novel, set in French Canada of the early eighteenth century, it was swiftly and vigorously told— "high romantic drama," Clifton Fadiman called it. Her two books of personal reminiscences—*Every Month Was May* and *The North Star Is Nearer*, parts of which appeared in the *New Yorker*—are a series of light-hearted sketches with sharply-drawn portraits of French peasant life, English and continental nobility, and the rigors of the life of a wartime correspondent. They reveal, in Miss Eaton herself, a sturdy, vivacious, intelligent woman with a rich sense of humor and a warm sympathy for her fellow human beings. Her novel *Flight* was described by John Metcalf in the *Spectator* as "a remarkably sensitive and civilized attempt to communicate a mystical experience in modern metaphor and simple language."

PRINCIPAL WORKS: Stolen Hours (poems) 1923; Desire, Spanish Version, 1933; John—Film Star, 1937; Summer Dust, 1937; Pray to the Earth, 1938; Quietly My Captain Waits, 1940; Restless Are the Sails, 1941; The Sea Is So Wide, 1943; Birds Before Dawn (poems) 1943; In What Torn Ship, 1944; Every Month Was May, 1947; Heart in Pilgrimage (with E. R. Moore) 1948; The North Star Is Nearer, 1949; Give Me Your Golden Hand, 1951; Flight, 1954.

ABOUT: Eaton, E. Every Month Was May, The North Star Is Nearer; Thomas C. Canadian Novelists; Warfel, H. R. American Novelists of Today; Wilson Library Bulletin November 1944.

EATON, WALTER PRICHARD (August 24, 1878-). For autobiographical sketch and list of earlier works and references, see TWENTIETH CENTURY AUTHORS, 1942.

* * *

Walter Prichard Eaton lives in Sheffield, in the heart of the Berkshires of Massachusetts—a region on which he has written considerably. In recent years he has also contributed articles on the theatre, playwriting, and other subjects to the *Virginia Quarterly Review, Theatre Arts, The Writer,* and the *American Mercury.*

ADDITIONAL WORK: Palme, A. Berkshire through the Camera (including sketch by Eaton) 1951; essays *in* R. Peattie (ed.) The Berkshires, 1948.

EBERHART, Mrs. MIGNON (GOOD) (July 6, 1899-). For autobiographical sketch and list of earlier works and references, see TWENTIETH CENTURY AUTHORS, 1942.

* * *

Mrs. Eberhart gave up her country home in Connecticut when her husband joined the navy in World War II. After he was demobilized, his engineering work took them to Chicago where they now live. She works industriously and methodically at her writing, and hardly a year has passed since 1929 (when her first book was published) that has not seen the publication of at least one of her lively detective stories. The mixture is about the same in these, but, as the *New Yorker* remarked, "the ingredients are tested and the cook's hand is remarkably sure."

ADDITIONAL WORKS: Wolf in Man's Clothing, 1942; Hasty Wedding, 1942; The Man Next Door, 1943; The Unidentified Woman, 1943; Escape the Night, 1944; Wings of Fear, 1945; The White Dress, 1946; Another Woman's House, 1947; House of Storm, 1949; Hunt With the Hounds, 1950; Never Look Back, 1951; Dead Men's Plans, 1952; The Unknown Quantity, 1953; Man Missing, 1954.

EBERHART, RICHARD (April 5, 1904-), American poet, writes: "In the fall of 1952 (man is always falling) I am looking westward toward the Olympic mountains from our back windows in Seattle. This year I am visiting professor of English (poet in residence) at the University of Washington. I have a wife, a son six and a daughter one and a half.

"Perhaps the reader may discover me in my poetry, for that is where I have tried to discover myself. Poems are mileposts along the way.

One becomes what they are. They become what one was at the moment of composition.

"I tend to philosophize about everything, to conclude nothing, to sit on the fence, to espouse seer-states if I can, or whirlpools of violent contemplation, the fiery centers of creative consciousness. "The Olympics have an ethereal quality as I presume Japanese volcanic mountains to have. There is more pleasure in contemplating them than in climbing them. I used to travel around the world, figuratively climbing all the mountains. Poetry is the ascent of the imagination.

Henri Cartier-Bresson

"I probably derived an Olympian attitude from a certain nobility in my parents. I must have been natively susceptible to it. If it was challenged by reality, Cambridge fortified it. Thus, I have never been interested in politics. I can always see two sides, if not many, to every question. Multiple ramifications appear. I suppose this is comic, to think to live in a noble, imaginative world beyond present action, beyond time, in creative moments of vision, when one can cope with the world as it is and does not believe in the withdrawal of the poet from the concerns of everyman. I am contemplative by nature. I am also active. I suppose I am a modern dualist.

"A poet has to be two persons, at least two. He has to have superior energies, enough for the world as it is, in which he does not believe, and an abundance for the world of becoming, which he makes real. It is here that he exercises his real self. The sitting on the fence attitude allows him to escape whole decades of intellectual error, while it provides radical use of the deepest subjective states of mind toward vision felt as absolute when experienced.

"I am not a dogmatist. I am a relativist. If I am dogmatic about relativism and tend to become didactic, I consider that as part of the comic. Neither mind nor heart should dominate the being. Harmony and wholeness are goals of the good.

"What probably made me a poet was the death of my mother, at forty-eight, of cancer of the lung, when I was eighteen. I witnessed intimately her nine-month birth of death through utmost pain. I lived the allegory of life in that time.

"My father was the son of a Methodist minister. He became the vice president of George A. Hormel and Company. He was betrayed by the notorious Cy Thompson, who embezzled over a million dollars from the company. My father lost his fortune, but not his spirit, his vast recuperative powers, his sense of humor, or his powerful love of life. He was formidable, large, epical, inviolable, a masterful man.

"The violent changes in my early world subsequently drove me around the world and to Cambridge University in search of truth. The spirit of poetry is the nearest I have ever come to its profound but subtle evanescences. One should not reveal too much. Poems are masks of revelations.

"I have not sailed my kites for some time. The inventor of the Navy Mark II Target Kite introduced me to this sport. He gave me a seven footer which I still have. Most are five feet tall. They have two linen cords attached to a rudder and can be maneuvered in beautiful ways from a heavy double-reeled rig strapped over the shoulders. From Spectacle Island off the coast of Maine, seeing water all around the compass, what pleasure to sail a kite in a twenty-knot southwester out over the sea. I have dive-bombed them from two hundred feet up and five hundred feet out down almost to water and adroitly reversed them up for a fast climb to high center. Or made them go in figure eights, vertical or horizontal. Sometimes they can be dived into water and if quickly enough turned, and you reel in hard, I have drawn them up to sail again, dripping and flashing off salt water, like an osprey after a catch. Failing, a friend goes out in an outboard to pull up the submerged kite, itself a delicate operation.

"Like poetry, these elaborate kites take patience and skill. Poetry is a maneuvering of ideas, a spectacular pleasure, achievement and mastery of intractable material, not less than an attempt to move the world, to order the chaos of man, insofar as one is able. Love, harmony, order; poise, precision, new worlds.

"An artist is in a sense inscrutable, Sphinx-like. He knows all. The exaltation of such a statement should be pared down to he knows what he knows. His paradox is that he acts under compulsion, confessing truth not as something given, for that may be a blinding light, but through pain and labor communicating what is human. It is the truth of the world that hurt him into revelation. Poetry is his spiritual reality."

* * *

Richard Eberhart was born in Austin, Minn. He studied at the University of Minnesota from 1922 to 1923. He received an A.B. from Dartmouth College in 1926, a B.A. from Cambridge University (St. John's College), in 1929 and an M.A. from Cambridge in 1933. He studied at Harvard Graduate School in 1932-33. In 1930 he spent a year as tutor to the son of King Prajadhipok of Siam. From 1933 to 1941 Eberhart taught English at St. Mark's School in Southborough, Mass. In 1941 he married Elizabeth Butcher, and they have a son and a daughter. He served in the Navy during World War II and was a lieutenant commander at the time of his discharge in 1946. Since the end of the war he has managed to combine two strikingly disparate careers—poet (and lecturer at a number of American universities) and business man (vice president and member of the board of directors of a firm that manufactures floor polish).

Eberhart appeared as a poet in *New Signatures,* published in London in 1932. He was the only American poet in this collection—which also included the work of Auden, Spender, and C. Day Lewis. Then as now Eberhart's work was and is strongly individual. It is characterized by a simplicity and directness that can at times— as Arthur Mizener once pointed out—become "a weakness for moral commonplaces." More often, however, the honesty of the poetry is its strength. In his fondness for the "moral answer" and his use of "the homely image in which to clothe it," Selden Rodman suggests, Eberhart resembles Robert Frost. Rodman calls him "a natural poet" and finds in his work "an even temper, a healthy optimism, a muscular goodwill . . . that stamps his writing as peculiarly American." Louise Bogan writes that Eberhart continues to be original "because his vision is constantly self-refreshing, and he needs no masks to enhance either his meaning or his impact."

In 1950 Eberhart was a founder and first president of the Poet's Theatre, Cambridge, Mass.

In 1953 Eberhart returned from Washington to New England to teach at the University of Connecticut. His permanent home is in Cambridge, Mass. *Poetry* magazine awarded him the Guarantors' Prize in 1946 and the Harriet Monroe Memorial Prize in

1950. In 1951 he received the Shelley Memorial Award of the Poetry Society of America. He won the Harriet Monroe Poetry Award for 1955 given by the University of Chicago and also in 1955 was awarded a grant of $1000 by the National Institute of Arts and Letters. In 1954 Dartmouth College awarded him an honorary LL.D., and in the same year he accepted the post of poet-in-residence and professor of English at Wheaton College in Norton, Mass. In 1955 he was appointed a lecturer at Princeton University.

PRINCIPAL WORKS: A Bravery of Earth, 1930; Reading the Spirit, 1936; Song and Idea, 1940; Poems New and Selected, 1944; War and the Poet, an Anthology (ed. with S. Rodman) 1945; Burr Oaks, 1947; Brotherhood of Men, 1949; An Herb Basket, 1950; Selected Poems, 1951; Undercliff: Poems 1946-1953, 1953.

ABOUT: Furioso Summer 1939; Irish Statesman April 12, 1930; New York Herald Tribune Book Review October 11, 1953; New Republic December 10, 1951; New Yorker February 16, 1952; Perspectives USA #10, January 1955; Poetry June 1937, December 1942, May 1945, January 1949; Saturday Review of Literature April 11, 1942; Western Review Summer 1954.

ECKSTEIN, GUSTAV (October 26, 1890-), American physiologist and nature writer, asked at the time of his first book for a biographical sketch, submitted the following: "Born, practised dentistry, studied medicine, taught physiology, learned not much, read two or three men, learned a little, came to know two or three women, learned a good deal, made  friends with two rats, learned prodigiously, wrote about the rats, continued to write."

This, he says, still is his biography. But he adds the following explanation of his nature writing. "Oddly, even to me, I had little to do with animals when I was a child. We lived in a densely populated part of the city, brick or stone all around, and my mother was very clean, so that having a pet would have been difficult, and there weren't even too many in the neighborhood. I never had a dog, nor a cat, and I think that there was some feeling of fright about the wings of birds. It is true that Hato, the pigeon, came, or was thrust into my laboratory, before there was any canary. She was not long with me, about two years, when she flew away. Then came the 'persons', one after another, that were to make my book *Lives*. It seems unlikely, and yet it is entirely true, that each one entered by chance, and that, except for an occasional bird, I have never sought an animal. There has been a sick one, and I have tried to cure it. There has been a lost one, and someone has brought it, and I have let it stay. Always something like that, but that can bring you a good deal."

A subject that also has been suited to Dr. Eckstein's insight and literary style has been the Japanese. "I went to Japan the first time on an impulse," he writes. 'I was talking to a Japanese scientist who had worked in this country many years and was my friend, when he had the sudden idea that I ought to go, and proved that he could make it possible in spite of my small purse, provided I went on a Japanese freighter, and provided I was willing to live like a poor but respectable Japanese. I set off. . . . It was the year of the American Exclusion Act. In fact, the freighter put in on the very day the Act went into effect. . . . When the opportunity came to return to Japan I snatched at it. I returned again and again. I was more interested in Japan, I suppose, than in any country but my own.

"When Hideyo Noguchi, the bacteriologist of the Rockefeller Institute, died of yellow fever in West Africa where he was investigating it, I saw in that a subject that included both Japanese and medicine, so undertook to write his biography, and lived, as one does, for the next two years somewhere at the back of my subject's head."

The biography of Noguchi was followed by a play, *Hokusai*, and a study of the Japanese people, *In Peace Japan Breeds War*. Dr. Eckstein has published a novel and two additional plays, but his writing of his laboratory birds and animals is undoubtedly the most widely read. Joseph Wood Krutch, in his *Great Nature Writing*, says of Dr. Eckstein's stories of creatures other-than-human: "Being endowed as few men have been with the gift of empathy, he can also feel his way into the existence of any living creature until that creature lives in his imagination an intense and poignant life. But that is not all. His way of writing, like his way of feeling, is like that of no one else. . . . Sometimes colloquial, sometimes tangential, sometimes perhaps not quite in accord with the laws of English syntax, it is at once informal and mannered; or rather, it would be mannered if it were not so obviously natural to Eckstein, if to him alone."

Dr. Eckstein was born and raised in Cincinnati, Ohio. He has both the D.D.S. and M.D. degrees (the latter from the University of Cincinnati), and has also studied at Harvard. In 1922 he joined the faculty of the University of Cincinnati as instructor in physiology and since 1950 he has been a full professor. He married Francesca Bendeke in 1919.

PRINCIPAL WORKS: Noguchi, 1931; Lives, 1932; Kettle (novel) 1933; Hokusai (chronicle play) 1935; Canary: the History of a Family, 1936; Christmas Eve (play) 1940; In Peace Japan Breeds War, 1943; The Pet Shop (play) 1944; Everyday Miracle, 1948.

ABOUT: Krutch, J. W. Great American Nature Writing; Woollcott, A. Foreword *in* Eckstein, G. Friends of Mine (Lives, and Canary); American Magazine September 1937; Current Biography 1942; Science Illustrated March 1949; Time July 26, 1948.

EDDINGTON, Sir ARTHUR STAN-LEY (December 28, 1882-November 22, 1944). For biographical sketch and list of earlier works and references, see TWENTIETH CENTURY AUTHORS, 1942.

* * *

Arthur Stanley Eddington died at a nursing home in Cambridge, England, at sixty-one. At the time of his death he had nearly completed a book intended to be a definitive statement of what he called The Fundamental Theory, having to do with the unity of the forces of nature, which H. C. Plummer has called "a doctrine original in its deepest foundations, a new isomorphism between thought and nature."

An Arthur Stanley Eddington Memorial Lectureship, instituted at Trinity College, Cambridge, in 1947, honors a central aspect of Eddington's work by dealing with "some aspect of contemporary scientific thought considered in its bearing on the philosophy of religion or on ethics." Plummer, writing on Eddington's theory of "the unity of Nature working on the cosmic and the atomic scale," has said: "To launch out into unknown seas, to be venturesome even at the risk of error, Eddington felt himself called, and the reward of the pioneer came to him." The New York *Times* has noted that he was "one of the most human of scientists and the most unpretentious of men" with a "rare ability to write for popular understanding on the most abstruse scientific subjects."

ADDITIONAL WORK: Fundamental Theory, 1946.

ABOUT: Church, R. British Authors; Jacks, L. P. Sir Arthur Eddington; Low, A. M. They Made Your World; Ritchie, A. D. Reflections on the Philosophy of Sir Arthur Eddington; New Statesman and Nation June 8, 1946; New York Times November 23, November 25, December 3, 1944; Spectator May 31, 1946.

EDDY, GEORGE SHERWOOD (January 19, 1871-). For autobiographical sketch and list of earlier works and references, see TWENTIETH CENTURY AUTHORS, 1942.

* * *

Dr. Eddy writes that his European tours for American educators are still conducted annually. Mrs. Maud Eddy died in 1945, and in 1947 he married Louise Gates. His home is in Jacksonville, Ill. His autobiography was published in 1955.

ADDITIONAL WORKS: Portrait of Jesus, 1943; A Century with Youth: A History of the Y.M.C.A., 1944; I Have Seen God Work in China, 1945; Pathfinders of the World Missionary Crusade, 1945; God in History, 1947; You Will Survive After Death, 1950; Eighty Adventurous Years (autobiography) 1955.

EDMAN, IRWIN (November 28, 1896- September 4, 1954). For biographical sketch and list of earlier works and references, see TWENTIETH CENTURY AUTHORS, 1942.

* * *

Irwin Edman died in his New York City apartment, of a heart attack, at fifty-seven. He was survived by a sister. In 1950 Edman had been appointed Johnsonian Professor of Philosophy and chairman of the department of philosophy at Columbia University. He was visiting professor in recent years at Harvard and at Wesleyan; in 1945 he gave a series of lectures at the University of Brazil, under the joint sponsorship of the United States Department of State and the Brazilian government; in 1951 Edman went to France as a Fulbright lecturer, and in 1953 he lectured at Oxford. Goucher College awarded Edman an honorary degree in 1949. He became vice-president of the National Institute of Arts and Letters in 1953 and in the same year became a member of the board of directors of the American Council of Learned Societies.

Edman was one of the foremost American practitioners of the increasingly rare familiar essay. An essayist of intelligence and charm, he took the position of the "questing philosopher" whose major concerns are men and ideas. His pace was leisurely. His

attitude was serene but never smug. Gerald W. Johnson described his *Philosopher's Quest* (a companion volume to the earlier *Philosopher's Holiday*) as a "mellow, urbane and charming apology for his own life by one of our most celebrated teachers of philosophy." From 1944 until his death, Edman's essays appeared regularly in the *American Scholar.*

ADDITIONAL WORKS: Philosopher's Quest, 1947; Under Whatever Sky, 1951.

ABOUT: Edman, I. Philosopher's Quest; Current Biography 1953; New York Times September 5, 1954.

EDMONDS, WALTER DUMAUX (July 15, 1903-). For autobiographical sketch and list of earlier works and references, see TWENTIETH CENTURY AUTHORS, 1942.

* * *

Walter D. Edmonds writes in comment on the 1942 sketch: "The photograph seems very youthful, and I think 'Mr. Edmonds is a good-looking young man with crisp brown hair, a long alert face, and an invariable pipe,' is no longer appplicable on a single point. The weight has increased from 130 to 165; the hair is rapidly vanishing; the long face has broadened together with various other portions of the frame it surmounts, and I also am dubious about the alertness; smoking had to be abandoned some years ago."

In addition to three historical novels for adults and some half-dozen books for children, Walter D. Edmonds has written the first volume of an informal history of the United States Air Force (done at the request of the Air Force) in the opening year of the war in the Southwest Pacific, published in 1952 as *They Fought With What They Had.* The second volume is now in preparation. He holds the honorary degree of Litt.D. from Rutgers (1940), Colgate (1946), and Harvard (1952). He was elected an honorary member of Phi Beta Kappa in 1951. From 1944 to 1950 he was a member of the Board of Overseers of Harvard College.

ADDITIONAL WORKS: *Novels*—In the Hands of the Senecas, 1947; The Wedding Journey, 1947; The Boyds of Black River, 1953. *History*—They Fought With What They Had, 1952. *Juveniles*—Tom Whipple, 1942; Two Logs Crossing, 1943; Wilderness Clearing, 1944; Cadmus Henry, 1949; Mr. Benedict's Lion, 1950; Corporal Bess, 1952.

ABOUT: National Cyclopedia of American Biography (1946); Atlantic Monthly July 1943; Current Biography 1942; Philadelphia Record February 17, 1947; Scholastic January 20, 1947.

EDWARDS, Sir OWEN MORGAN (December 25, 1858-May 15, 1920). For biographical sketch and list of works and references, see TWENTIETH CENTURY AUTHORS, 1942.

* * *

ABOUT: Davies, A. T. (ed.) O. M.: A Memoir.

"EGERTON, GEORGE." See BRIGHT, M. C. D.

*EGGE, PETER (April 1, 1869-). For autobiographical sketch and list of works and references, see TWENTIETH CENTURY AUTHORS, 1942.

* * *

Peter Egge lives in Norway, near his birthplace in Trondheim. He published nothing during the German occupation of Norway, but he resumed work when the war ended. Since then he has published several novels and an autobiographical work —none of these as yet translated into English.

ABOUT: Columbia Dictionary of Modern European Literature.

* ăg'gĕ

*EHRENBOURG, ILYA (January 27, 1891-). For biographical sketch and list of earlier works and references, see TWENTIETH CENTURY AUTHORS, 1942.

* * *

Ilya Ehrenbourg spent all of the World War II years at the front as a correspondent, turning out some 3,000 articles during that period. Some of these eye-witness dispatches were published in America under the title *The Tempering of Russia*. In the spring of 1946 Ehrenbourg flew to the United States, along with two other Soviet journalists (one of them the novelist Konstantin Simonov), to be interviewed by the American Society of Newspaper Editors. He spent several weeks traveling through this country, and after his return to Russia he wrote a series of articles for *Izvestia* giving his impressions of this country. (Translations of these were published in *Harper's* for December 1946.) He admired some things American (the superhighways, for instance), but mainly he warned against the menace of a third world war which, he claimed, American "industrialists" were fomenting. Another post-war journey made by Ehrenbourg was a tour through the Bal-

* ă'rĕn bŏŏrg

kans, on which he reported in a travel diary published as *European Crossroad*. This volume, Joseph Barnes wrote in the New York *Herald Tribune,* "has meaning for those who can read it with politically bifocal glasses. Its style is neither more taxing nor more compelling than the soundtrack of a motion-picture travelogue."

Ehrenbourg's novel *Storm,* which won the Stalin prize in 1947, had a chilly reception in the United States and Great Britain. Reviewers found this lengthy story of Russia and France during World War II heavy-handed and mechanical. Ehrenbourg is reported to be living in a luxurious apartment in Moscow. From time to time quotations from his speeches and articles—all of them bitterly anti-American—appear in the press, but generally little is heard of him on this side of the Iron Curtain.

ADDITIONAL WORKS IN ENGLISH TRANSLATION: The Fall of Paris (novel) 1943; The Tempering of Russia, 1944; European Crossroad: A Soviet Journalist in the Balkans, 1947; The Storm (novel) 1949

ABOUT: Columbia Dictionary of Modern European Literature; Guerney, B. G. Portable Russian Reader; Yarmolinsky, A. Treasury of Russian Verse; Commentary August 1947; Deutsche Rundschau November 1952; Nation July 6, 1946; New Republic July 1, 1946; Saturday Evening Post January 6, 1951; Time, April 29, 1946, June 10, 1946, July 8, 1946, July 14, 1952.

EHRLICH, LEONARD (1905-). For biographical sketch and list of earlier works and references, see TWENTIETH CENTURY AUTHORS, 1942.

EIKER, MATHILDE (January 5, 1893-). For autobiographical sketch and list of earlier works and references, see TWENTIETH CENTURY AUTHORS, 1942.

* * *

Under the pseudonym of "March Evermay," Miss Eiker has written several literate and smoothly plotted detective stories. The late Will Cuppy described one of these as "a joy for its admirable prose and all-around narrative interest." Miss Eiker lives in Washington, D.C.

ADDITIONAL WORKS: As "March Evermay"— They Talked of Poison, 1938; This Death Was Murder, 1940; Red Light for Murder, 1951.

EINSTEIN, ALFRED (December 30, 1880-February 13, 1952), musicologist, was born in Munich, Bavaria, the son of Ludwig and Johanna (Guttenstein) Einstein. He was a distant cousin of the physicist Albert Einstein. He received his Ph.D. from the University of Munich in 1903 with a dissertation on German literature for the viola da gamba.

As a private music scholar he explored the museums and libraries of Europe, discovering and copying priceless old music manuscripts. Among his most ambitious undertakings in music scholarship were the preparation of three editions of Riemann's *Musik-Lexikon* (1919, 1922, 1929) and a complete revision of the nineteenth century Köchel catalogue of Mozart's compositions (1937, American edition 1947). In the course of his Mozart researches, Einstein discovered some twenty new Mozart works and proved another dozen works spurious.

Einstein was one of the most distinguished and influential of music critics in pre-Hitler Germany. From 1918 to 1933 he was editor of the *Zeitschrift für Musikwissenschaft* and in 1927 he became music critic of the *Berliner Tageblatt*. With the rise of the Nazis to power in Germany, Einstein decided to leave his native land. He shipped ahead to England his large collection of music manuscript copies and went himself to Italy to study Italian music of the sixteenth and seventeenth centuries. In 1939 Einstein came to the United States and was appointed William Allan Neilson Professor of Music at Smith College. He also held visiting lectureships at Columbia, the University of Michigan, Yale, Princeton, and the Julius Hartt School of Music at Hartford, Conn. He retired from Smith in 1950 after being honored in a three-day celebration at the college during which students and faculty played and sang the music he admired most—Italian madrigals, works of Mozart and Schubert and, from the contemporary scene, works of Roger Sessions and Benjamin Britten. He died in 1952 in El Cerrito, Calif. He had married, in 1906, Hertha Heumann, and they had one daughter.

Einstein wrote all his books in German. He was never a "popularizer." Although he wrote from time to time for "lay" readers, not specialists, his works demand a greater degree of musical sophistication and experience than the average beginner may possess.

His enthusiasm for his subject, however, tempered the profundity and abstruseness of his scholarship. As Roger Sessions has pointed out, Einstein was "outstanding among musical scholars as one who, by virtue of a warm and vivid love for music and a genuine and even racy human wisdom, understands the limits and the limitations, the illusions and the pitfalls of mere scholarship." American readers know best his sound and detailed *Mozart: His Character, His Work*. Equally impressive among his later works, however, are *Music in the Romantic Era*, his three-volume history *The Italian Madrigal*—the latter being regarded as the definitive work on the subject—and his book on Franz Schubert.

PRINCIPAL WORKS IN ENGLISH TRANSLATION: Gluck, 1936; A Short History of Music, 1936; Greatness in Music, 1941; Mozart: His Character, His Work, 1945; Music in the Romantic Era, 1947; The Italian Madrigal, 1949; Schubert: A Musical Portrait, 1951.

ABOUT: Haggin, B. H. Music in The Nation; Deutsche Rundschau January 1951; Music Library Association Notes December 1950; Musical Quarterly January 1951; New York Times February 17, 1952; Time April 24, 1950.

ELIOT, GEORGE FIELDING (June 22, 1894-   ). For autobiographical sketch and list of earlier works and references, see TWENTIETH CENTURY AUTHORS, 1942.

* * *

Major Eliot was news analyst of the Columbia Broadcasting Systen from 1939 to 1947 and, during the same period, he was military and naval correspondent for the New York *Herald Tribune*. He wrote a column for the New York *Post* from 1947 to 1949. Since 1950 his newspaper writing has been carried by the General Features Syndicate. Also in 1950 he joined the staff of the Mutual Broadcasting System as military analyst. Major Eliot made a tour of the Middle East early in 1948, recording his impressions in the book *Hate, Hope, and High Explosives*. In other recent books he has proposed and analyzed military plans for the post-war world. He served for two terms as president of the Association of Radio News Analysts, in 1943 and 1951. From 1942 to 1945 he was president of the Committee for National Morale. Major Eliot and the former Sara Hodges were divorced in 1942. He married June Cawley on January 1, 1943.

ADDITIONAL WORKS: Hour of Triumph, 1944; The Strength We Need, 1946; Hate, Hope, and High Explosives, 1948; If Russia Strikes, 1949.

ABOUT: Fisher, C. Columnists; Atlantic Monthly July 1945; Current Biography 1940.

ELIOT, THOMAS STEARNS (September 26, 1888-   ). For biographical sketch and list of earlier works and references, see TWENTIETH CENTURY AUTHORS, 1942.

* * *

Probably the most extraordinary phenomenon in T. S. Eliot's long and distinguished career is his having become, in recent years, something of a "popular" figure. This is not to suggest that Eliot's work is generally more widely or popularly read today than it was twenty years ago (although no contemporary poet is more thoroughly studied in the colleges and graduate schools). But he has moved slowly and steadily forward in the public's consciousness until today he is almost universally recognized as "the world's most distinguished living poet" (so he was designated in an article in *Life* magazine in 1954). In 1948 he received the highest honor a writer can win—the Nobel prize in literature. With characteristic spareness he remarked, shortly after hearing the news: "The process of advancement is interesting. One seems to become a myth, a fabulous creature that doesn't exist. One doesn't feel any different, though. It isn't that you get bigger to fit the world; the world gets smaller to fit you. You remain exactly the same." In that same year Eliot was honored with the Order of Merit, awarded by King George VI of England; and also in 1948 he visited the United States, where he made his headquarters at the Institute for Advanced Study at Princeton University. He returned to the United States in 1950, when he gave the first Theodore Spencer Memorial Lecture at Harvard on "Poetry and Drama" and spent several months teaching and lecturing at the University of Chicago.

The source of Eliot's current popularity is his drama. Since 1950 he has written two verse dramas that won general attention—*The Cocktail Party* and *The Confidential Clerk*—the first of which was the greater theatrical success both in England and in the United States. Eliot's two earlier plays, *Murder in the Cathedral* and *The Family Reunion*, had been basically poetic, rather than dramatic, achievements. In *The Cocktail Party* Eliot succeeded where, in his own opinion at least

(see *Poetry and Drama*), he had failed before: he created a poetry of "strict dramatic utility," a poetry which on the printed page is unmistakably poetry but which—as spoken by skillful actors—has the subtlety and variety of prose rhythms. He created, moreover, a situation that had complete relevance for contemporary audiences, and within the framework of modern-day society—smart, well-dressed people, the cocktail party itself, the psychiatrist—he nevertheless managed to suggest the most profound and universal of themes—heavenly grace and human salvation. Less profound, perhaps, though likewise allegorical, was his *Confidential Clerk*—a comedy of manners and errors, of misplaced illegitimate children and their parents, and of man's search for a father and a belonging-place. Finally, no discussion of Eliot's attempt to bridge the gap between poetry and popular entertainment is complete without mention of the fine, somber, and meticulously faithful screen adaptation of *Murder in the Cathedral* in which Eliot himself appeared (though only on the sound track) reading the role of the Fourth Tempter.

Eliot's major poetic work of recent years has been his *Four Quartets*, which some commentators now regard as his finest poetic achievement to date. The four long poems which comprise the volume are "Burnt Norton," "East Coker," "The Dry Salvages," and "Little Gidding," and they echo in their combined effect the melancholy but also the serenity of the poet's deep religious faith. "His unique distinction among English poets," Helen Gardner writes, "is the balance he has maintained between the claims of his vision and the claims of his art. . . . When we read *Four Quartets* we are left finally not with the thought of 'the transitory Being who beheld this vision,' nor with the thought of the vision itself, but with the poem, beautiful, satisfying, self-contained, self-organized, complete."

ADDITIONAL WORKS: Complete Poems and Plays, 1952. *Essays*—Notes Towards the Definition of Culture, 1949; Selected Essays (new ed.) 1950; Poetry and Drama, 1951; The Three Voices of Poetry, 1954; Religious Drama: Mediaeval and Modern, 1954. *Plays*—The Cocktail Party, 1950; The Film of Murder in the Cathedral (with G. Hoellering) 1951; The Confidential Clerk, 1954. *Poetry*—Later Poems, 1925-1935, 1941; Four Quartets, 1943.

ABOUT: Drew, E. T. S. Eliot: The Design of His Poetry; Gallup, D. C. T. S. Eliot (bibliography); Gardner, H. The Art of T. S. Eliot; March, R. & Tambimutta, M. J. (eds.) T. S. Eliot: A Symposium; Maxwell, D. E. S. The Poetry of T. S. Eliot; Rajan, B. (ed.) T. S. Eliot: A Study of His Writings by Several Hands; Unger, L. (ed.) T. S. Eliot: A Selected Critique; Williamson, G. A Reader's Guide to T. S. Eliot; Wilson, F. A. C. Six Essays on the Development of T. S. Eliot; American Scholar Autumn 1947; Life February 1, 1954; New York Times Book Review November 21, 1948, July 19, 1953; New York Times Magazine February 7, 1954; New Yorker August 1, 1953; University of Toronto Quarterly Autumn 1954; Yale Review March 1949.

"ELIZABETH." See RUSSELL, M. A. B. R.

ELLIS, HAVELOCK (February 2, 1859-July 8, 1939). For biographical sketch and list of works and references, see TWENTIETH CENTURY AUTHORS, 1942.

* * *

ADDITIONAL WORKS: From Marlowe to Shaw: Studies, 1876-1936, 1950; The Genius of Europe, 1950; Sex and Marriage: Eros in Contemporary Life, 1952.

ABOUT: Delisle, F. R. Friendship's Odyssey, 1946; Dictionary of Australian Biography, I; Dictionary of National Biography 1931-40.

ELLSBERG, EDWARD (November 21, 1891-). For autobiographical sketch and list of earlier works and references, see TWENTIETH CENTURY AUTHORS, 1942.

* * *

Rear Admiral Ellsberg writes: "Upon the outbreak of World War II, I volunteered for active duty, was recommissioned in the Navy, and was sent to the Red Sea as commanding officer to rehabilitate the sabotaged Italian naval base at Massawa, Eritrea, and to salvage some dozens of wrecks there, including two invaluable sunken drydocks. For the speedy accomplishment of this task under terrible climatic conditions where white men were not supposed to be able to work, I was shortly promoted to Captain, USNR, and awarded the newly created Legion of Merit.

"When the Allied Forces invaded North Africa, I was immediately detached from the Red Sea and ordered to join General Eisenhower as his Principal Salvage Officer for that Mediterranean campaign, which task involved opening the vital harbor of Oran and the salvage from Morocco to Tunisia of numerous torpedoed and bombed vessels both at sea and in port. A second Legion of Merit was awarded for this task.

"In the Normandy invasion I took part in the establishment at the Omaha Beach of the vital Artificial Harbors and in other salvage work along the invasion coast.

"For this last, and for the work in the Red Sea and in the Mediterranean in support of the Royal Navy, the British decoration of the Order of Commander of the British Empire was bestowed on me.

"Upon conclusion of World War II, I returned to Southwest Harbor on the Maine coast, which is now my permanent home. Since then I was promoted to Rear Admiral, USNR, in recognition of my services in actual combat during the war, and placed on the retired list."

ADDITIONAL WORKS: Under the Red Sea Sun, 1946; Cruise of the Jeannette (juvenile: based on Hell on Ice, 1938) 1949; No Banners, No Bugles, 1949; Passport for Jennifer, 1952; Mid Watch 1954.

ABOUT: Ellsberg, E. Under the Red Sea Sun, No Banners, No Bugles; Kunitz, S. J. & Haycraft, H. (eds.) Junior Book of Authors (rev. ed); New York Herald Tribune Book Review October 16, 1949, October 12, 1952.

ELTON, OLIVER (1861-June 4, 1945). For biographical sketch and list of works and references, see TWENTIETH CENTURY AUTHORS, 1942.

* * *

Oliver Elton died, at Oxford, England, at eighty-four.

His principal contribution to literary criticism, the *Survey of English Literature*, has been described (by the London *Times*) as "large in scale, humane, balanced and judicious in tone, founded on first-hand acquaintance with the works not only of major but of minor writers."

Samuel S. Chew attributes the value of Elton's critical work to "an exact knowledge of every aspect of the subject, a sound scholarship, and especially the ability of the teacher to put it into a form that is both informative and interesting." Edwin Clark places Elton "among the minority of literary historians who are men of letters as well."

ABOUT: Martin, L. C. Oliver Elton; London Times June 7, 1945.

*ELUARD, PAUL (December 14, 1895-November 18, 1952), French poet, was born Eugène Grindel in the Parisian suburb of Saint-Denis. His father was an accountant and his mother a seamstress. From his early years he lived near the factories of the proletariat, first at Saint-Denis and later at Aulnay-sous-Bois. He attended the Ecole Communale, where he was a very good student. The family moved to Paris, and Eluard was registered at the Ecole Primaire Supérieure Colbert, where, by his own admission, he was a very poor stu-

* ā′lü är

dent. His studies were interrupted by illness, and, at the age of sixteen, he left Paris for Davos, Switzerland, to spend a year and a half in a sanatorium.

French Embassy

Shortly after his return to Paris, he entered the army and did service in the trenches, where he had further contact with suffering —his own and that of others; he was gassed and stricken with gangrene of the bronchi. While at the sanatorium he read a great deal of poetry, including the works of Rimbaud, Lautréamont, and Vildrac. Although his experience of suffering impressed him deeply and pervades his writings, his outlook remained a hopeful one. He was moved by a strong desire to change the world and to alleviate misery. Eluard felt an affinity with Walt Whitman, whose *Leaves of Grass* he read many times over. He extended his reading to the English and German novelists, and to Shelley, Novalis, and Heraclitus.

His own poetic career started early. *Le Devoir et l'Inquiétude* was published in 1917, and in 1918 *Poèmes pour la Paix* appeared. These were the first of over 70 volumes published in his lifetime. In Paris Eluard met other young writers, notably André Breton, Louis Aragon, Philippe Soupault, and Tristan Tzara, who were then active in the Dadaist movement. From the anarchy of Dada they moved to Surrealism, with its elaborate discipline. Eluard was a signer of the original Surrealist manifestoes, and his poetry acquired a new character resulting from these researches. In 1921 *La Nécessité de la Vie et la Conséquence des Rêves* was published. Though Eluard adhered to Surrealist tenets throughout his life, his talent is of a somewhat different nature, and he is acknowledged to be the truest poet of the group. Surrealism, "a state of mind" rather than a "school," according to its adherents, attracted many artists, and Eluard included among his close friends Picasso, Ernst, Chirico, Arp, Miró, Tanguy, and Dali.

He took a very active part in the group's work and controversies, which were often carried on until dawn in a café. Eluard was married—he had met his wife, Gala, in Switzerland in 1912—and had a daughter, Cécile. This marriage was doomed to failure, and in March 1924 Eluard disappeared from the Paris scene. Word of his death

spread in Paris; no one knew that he had taken the first boat sailing from Marseilles to lose himself in a trip around the world. Among the places he visited during this seven-month voyage were Panama, New Zealand, Australia, Java and Sumatra, India, Indo-China, and Ceylon.

On his return to Paris, he resumed his role in Surrealist endeavors; among his responsibilities was the editing and directing of the group's reviews, *Révolution Surréaliste* and *Surréalisme au Service de la Révolution*.

In 1926, with the publication of *Capitale de la Douleur*, his reputation was established. Here, as in so much of his work, he writes of love, of the woman loved, and of the unity of lovers.

With André Breton, he produced, in 1931, an unusual volume, called *L'Imaculée Conception*. In this work they tried to reproduce the actual manifestations of different forms of mental disorders; Surrealism is fused with "surrationalism," involuntary poetry with intentional poetry.

It was about this time that a new love appeared in Eluard's life: Nusch, to whom he was devoted and who inspired much of his poetry. Their marriage was a very happy one, lasting until her death in 1946.

The Spanish Civil War aroused Eluard's passions and fired his poems with a new tone. In 1936 he wrote, in *L'Evidence Poétique*, that "the time has come when poets have a right and a duty to maintain that they are profoundly involved in the lives of other men, in communal life." In this essay, too, he submitted that bread is more useful than poetry, but that love is not; man, who puts himself at the top of the scale of living things, cannot deny the value of his feelings, non-productive though they may be. The poet, he states, is he who inspires rather than he who is inspired. Eluard was alarmed at the world's deafness to cries for help and in *Cours Naturel* (1938) he expressed his alarm.

In 1939 Eluard, for the second time in his life, was called to do military service. During the German occupation of France, he engaged in underground activity, living in constant danger of arrest. He delivered secret papers and editions and assisted in the publication of clandestine literature. His *Poésie et Vérité 1942* was denounced by the Germans, and Eluard and his wife were forced to move to a different residence every month. At one point, in flight from the Gestapo, he took refuge in an insane asylum at Saint-Alban, where the misery of the inmates touched him deeply; during his months there he worked on a manuscript which was published after the war under the title, *Souvenirs de la Maison des Fous.* His poems of the Resistance years were poems of circumstance, of the events of the day, which were multigraphed and circulated among the *maquis,* with a powerful effect on French morale. Among the best-known poems of this time are *Liberté* and *Rendezvous Allemand.* During this period Eluard used the pseudonyms Jean du Hault and Maurice Hervent. In 1942 he joined the underground Communist Party.

Poésie Ininterrompue, a volume of five poems, appeared in 1946. Louis Parrot has written of the title poem as the most revealing testimony of "a life which is an incessant effort toward that moral and intellectual perfection which a poet always seeks to attain."

In November of the same year *Le Dur Désir de Durer,* illustrated by Marc Chagall, was published. That month was tragically marked by the unexpected death of Nusch, whose memory survives in so many poems of Eluard and in numerous portraits by Picasso.

In accordance with his belief that "poetry must have as its aim practical truth," Eluard continued to write poems of circumstance, and in 1948 *Poèmes Politiques,* a collection of such poems, was published. Eluard was very active in Communist affairs, mainly from the aspect of cultural relations. He was an ambassador of the new poetry and traveled extensively, visiting England, Belgium, Switzerland, Czechoslovakia, Italy, Greece, Yugoslavia, Bulgaria, Albania, Poland, Hungary, Rumania, Mexico, and Soviet Russia. He attended many Communist-inspired cultural congresses.

With him at his death, at the age of fifty-six, was his wife of his last years, Dominique, to whom he had written the poem, *Dominique Aujourd'hui Présente.*

Claude Roy has described Eluard as "large with lightness, much too attentive to be called large as a cloud, . . . infinitely too *present,* a man of flesh, hair, hands, looks, to be called as large as a cloud of smoke. . . . A handsome face, well covered with flesh, with years, with thoughts and *good* sentiments."

PRINCIPAL WORKS IN ENGLISH TRANSLATION: Selected Writings of Paul Eluard, 1951.

ABOUT: Alexander, L., Aragon, L., Parrot, L. & Roy, C. *Essays in* Selected Writings of Paul Eluard; Carrouges, M. Eluard et Claudel (in French); Cassou, J. Pour la Poésie (in French); Parrot, L. & Marcenac, J. *in* Paul Eluard (Poètes d'Aujourd'hui, I, 1953); Partisan Review Fall 1939.

ELWIN, MALCOLM (June 6, 1903-), English biographer and critic, writes: "My Elwin ancestors farmed the same acres at Stalisfield, near Charing, in Kent, for more than three centuries before my great-grandfather, an artist, migrated northward at the time of the Industrial Revolution. My grandfather, a friend of Holyoake and Bradlaugh, was eminent  among early trade-unionists; my father was a factory owner in Nottingham. I was born and bred near Nottingham—about as far from the city on its eastern side as was D. H. Lawrence on its westward side. As my mother came of stock long settled in Nottinghamshire and Yorkshire, I am probably as purely Anglo-Saxon as anybody can be, and owe to my ancestry, besides impatience with insincerity and shams, the saving grace of humour and the belief that 'what is worth doing is worth doing well.'

"As a child I wanted to write, and to equip myself I read everything within reach. I discovered decided preferences, but how did one learn to recognise good writing from bad? I discovered the answer in Arnold Bennett's *Literary Taste: How to Form It;* Bennett led me to Charles Lamb and thence to Hazlitt, who opened windows upon a new world and offered a new scale of values.

"My discovery of Hazlitt coincided with my leaving school at fifteen. From school, which thwarted specialized study by teaching a smattering of everything, I long desired to escape, and my end was achieved by leading rebellion against the rights of prefects to administer corporal punishment. Successively to both Nottingham newspapers I applied for the post of junior reporter; kindly considerate, both editors informed me that I was too young, and one of them gave me an introduction to the principal of the local University College with a view to my studying political economy as a preparation for journalism. When I complained that political economy seemed a scientific fiction based on false premises, my tutor surprisingly agreed, and directed me to read English literature and the classics.

"When I went up to University College in 1920, I was probably the youngest undergraduate at Oxford. After leaving Oxford, where I enjoyed life and went on reading, I edited a provincial weekly newspaper till the effort of combining editorial responsibilities with the functions of leader writer, dramatic critic, sports correspondent, and racing tipster resulted in a nervous breakdown. I retired to an Oxfordshire cottage to read and write, and have been reading and writing ever since. After writing three novels (one appeared as a newspaper serial), I published my first book in 1928.

"My inclination to biography was instinctive: if a book interested me, I wanted to know more of its writer—to know how and why he had come to write that book and to assume that particular habit of thought. As Lytton Strachey remarked, biography properly treated is 'the most delicate and humane of all branches of the art of writing.' It requires greater powers of sympathy and imaginative projection than fiction, because the novelist can always make his creations act according to character, whereas, as Somerset Maugham has pointed out, in life people do not act according to character—they are never 'all of a piece.' But biography is also the best training for the writing of fiction, and perhaps because passing years inspire inclination to the easier task, in my fiftieth year I feel that I am likely to write more fiction than biography in the future.

"During the nineteen-thirties I sought bread-and-butter by reviewing—in the *London Mercury, Saturday Review, Observer, John o'London's Weekly*. Since the paper shortage extinguished reviewing in England and there is no butter, I earn bread by a more rewarding exercise of the critical faculty as a publisher's adviser. When I moved to North Devon in 1938, I wondered why I had lived so long away from the sea. My second wife is an American-born novelist, Mary Turner, elder daughter of David Bryant Turner, of Colorado Springs."

PRINCIPAL WORKS: Charles Reade, 1931; Thackeray, a Personality, 1932; Victorian Wallflowers, 1934; De Quincey, 1935; Old Gods Falling, 1939; Savage Landor, 1941; Life of Llewelyn Powys, 1946; The First Romantics, 1947; Pleasure Ground, a Miscellany of English Writing (ed.) 1947; The Essential Richard Jefferies (ed.) 1948; The Strange Case of Robert Louis Stevenson, 1950; Autobiography and Journals of Benjamin Robert Haydon (ed.) 1950; Essays of Robert Louis Stevenson (ed.) 1950; Charles Lamb's Elia (ed.) 1952; The Little Hangman (novel) 1953.

EMPSON, WILLIAM (September 27, 1906-   ), British poet and critic, writes: "I was born in Yorkshire, was educated at Winchester and Magdalene College, Cambridge, graduated in mathematics, and got a First in English Literature in a fourth year, leaving in 1929. My first book of literary criticism, *Seven Types of Ambiguity,* came out in 1930. For the three years 1931-  34 I was in Tokyo as Professor of English Literature, then came back to England; *Poems* and the book of literary criticism, *Some Versions of Pastoral,* came out in 1935 (many of the poems had been written at college).

"In autumn 1937 I went to Peking to teach English Literature at its National University, arriving on a Japanese troop train as a war had just started; I caught up with the refugee university at Changsha and spent two years with it, ending at Kunming on the Burma Road. In autumn 1939 I was granted indefinite wartime leave because the European war was clearly impending; I returned to England through the United States. In 1940 I joined the B.B.C. Monitoring Department, editing summaries of foreign broadcasts, and next year was transferred to the then developing Far Eastern Section, where I became Chinese Editor, organizing news broadcasts and talks in Chinese. A second book of poems, *The Gathering Storm,* was printed in 1940.

"In 1941 I married Hester Henrietta Crouse, a South African who was broadcasting in Afrikaans; we have two sons, called William Hendrick Mogador and Jacobus Arthur Calais, since each had to have an English name, an Afrikaans name, and the name of a town captured by the Allies on the day he was born. In 1947 I went back to the Peking National University with the family; I now received extra pay from the British Council as one of its 'subsidized poets,' which does not involve other than university work. In 1948 and 1950 I flew to America for the Kenyon Summer School, returning to Peking for next term by boat; in the second case the Korean war was just beginning, and the boat was carrying troops to Japan.

"I came home with the family in 1952; the British Council had decided to close its activities in China, and we had already decided that the children needed education at home. I have now (1953) been appointed professor of English Literature at Sheffield University. A third prose book, *The Structure of Complex Words,* came out in 1951; it was greatly expanded and rewritten in Peking, but the main material had been written before the Second World War, though left in confusion and almost forgotten. American editions of the three prose books came out concurrently with the English ones, except that the American *Pastoral* was given an absurd name, but the first American edition of my verse was a combined one of 1949.

"My verse was much connected with the revival of interest in seventeenth century metaphysical poetry, which it probably imitated more directly than anyone else, though this doesn't mean it wasn't felt directly too. I have almost stopped writing verse; at least, I have tried to do some in recent years but haven't thought the results good. Of the prose books, *Ambiguity* examines the complexity of meaning in poetry; *Pastoral* examines the way a form for reflecting a social background without obvious reference to it is used in a historical series of literary works, and *Complex Words* is on both those topics; it offers a general theory about the interaction of a word's meanings and takes examples which cover rather the same historical ground as *Pastoral.* Roughly, the moral is that a developing society decides practical questions more by the way it interprets words it thinks obvious and traditional than by its official statements of current dogma."

* * *

Since its publication more than twenty years ago, *The Seven Types of Ambiguity* has become one of the classic documents of the "New Criticism." The work shows strikingly the influence of I. A. Richards, under whom Empson studied at Cambridge, in its emphases on language and the meanings of words. With Empson, however, the reading of poetry becomes not a matter of explicating the text by precisely defining the words, but a study of the complexity, the multiplicity of meanings which the language of the poem holds. Stanley Edgar Hyman writes that the book contains "certainly the most elaborate and probably the finest close reading of poetry ever put down, the fantastic, wonderful, and almost endless spinning out of implications and linguistic possibilities." Critics of Empson's method (and

even those who are generally sympathetic to it) have complained that such readings can become mere displays of virtuosity, more dazzling than illuminating. But there is no doubt that Empson has stimulated the modern critical tendency toward the close, lively, imaginative and analytical reading of poetry. Cleanth Brooks speaks of him as "one of our ablest critics and one of our soundest," and finds that his work "is fraught with revolutionary consequences for the teaching of all literature and for the future of literary history."

Empson's poetry has received far less attention than his prose. Richards admires the poetry greatly, rating him as among the finest of contemporary poets. The poet Robert Lowell has, similarly, called him one of the five best (then) living English poets (along with Auden, MacNeice, Thomas, and Graves). His poetry, like his criticism, is highly intellectualized (Richards calls it "metaphysical in the root sense")—subtle, sophisticated, and complex.

PRINCIPAL WORKS: *Criticism*—Seven Types of Ambiguity, 1930 (revised in 1947); Some Versions of Pastoral (in U.S. English Pastoral Poetry) 1935; The Structure of Complex Words, 1951. *Poetry*—Poems, 1935; The Gathering Storm, 1940; The Collected Poems of William Empson, 1949.

ABOUT: Hyman, S. E. The Armed Vision; Ransom, J. C. The New Criticism; Accent Summer 1944; Furioso Spring 1940; Modern Philology May 1950; Partisan Review December 1937; Poetry July 1949, June 1950; Saturday Review of Literature March 19, 1949; Sewanee Review April 1944; Time April 18, 1949.

ENGSTRAND, STUART DAVID

(March 13, 1904-   ), American novelist, writes: "I was one of the youngest of seven children of Swedish immigrant parents. I was born in Chicago, but shortly after my birth my family moved to what was then the country town of Wheaton, Ill. There were fields to roam and creeks to swim. There were chickens  and a cow to tend, which in some small way supplemented my father's earnings as a small merchant. These early years developed in me a love for the earth and the things that grew on it. In spite of living my mature life in very urban places, I always felt this kinship with my rural boyhood unbroken.

"After finishing Wheaton High School I entered Wheaton College, an extremely fundamentalist school. But sectarianism did not make me happy, and after one year I enrolled at the Illinois State Teachers College at DeKalb. There I 'finished' my education. I made my living during these high school and college years with all manner of jobs—driving a truck, trimming trees, selling.

"Having felt early that I was to be a writer, I did not take a teaching job. I felt that if I got into the teaching profession my writing ambition and endeavors would be drowned out. At a loss as to how I could sustain myself, and write, I took the easy way out. I went 'adventuring.' After hiking out to the West Coast, I hired out on a freighter bound for China. I stayed on this ship, the *Islip*, about a year, visiting all the Oriental ports. There was a strong temptation to stay at sea and work toward a captaincy. But I knew that this type of life would interfere with the unexplainable ambition to be a writer.

"I rented a room in Los Angeles, and with money I had saved I set out on my career. My savings lasted only a short time, and then I had to supplement them doing odd jobs. Writing was much harder than I had ever dreamed. I sent stories off to the magazines and invariably they were returned. I was in that tiresome, oft-repeated experience of the novice. And a year went by. There had been no payoff, not even any feeling that I had improved, or learned more about writing. In disgust, I returned to Chicago, and there hired out again as a truck driver. I saved my money for another try at writing.

"When I felt I had a minimum stake, I moved to Ashland County, Wis. I built a cedar shack in the woods. There I sat for three years, turning out poems, short stories, and novels. A few of the smaller pieces sold. But in this big piece of dedicated time I learned how to write. Not knowing what to do with the manuscripts, I went to the University of Chicago and visited James Weber Linn. He invited me to join his class in writing, but advised against registering, as that would require tuition payment. His criticism and enthusiasm greatly fired me, and I shall always remain in his debt.

"In 1935 I married Sophia Belzer, who, like myself, was devoted to writing. We moved to Phoenix, Ariz., where I set to writing *The Invaders*, my first published novel. This was the beginning of my professional life as a writer. After the birth of our daughter, Stephanie, I settled down to earnestly earning a living with my typewriter. After several more novels were published, our son Steven came along. In 1942 we moved to Beverly Hills, Calif. and this is now our home.

"Although critics and publishers have labeled me as a 'psychological' writer, my feeling is that I am not. I have always, with few exceptions, written about the Middle West. That is my milieu. The roots are there."

PRINCIPAL WORKS: The Invaders (in England: The Tomato Field) 1937 They Sought for Paradise, 1939; Spring, 1940, 1941; The Sling and the Arrow, 1947; Beyond the Forest, 1948; Son of the Giant, 1950; A Husband in the House, 1952; The Scattered Seed, 1953.

ABOUT: Warfel, H. R. American Novelists of Today.

ERENBURG. See EHRENBOURG

"ERICSON, WALTER." See FAST, H.

ERNLE, ROWLAND EDMUND PROTHERO, 1st Baron (September 6, 1851-July 2, 1937). For biographical sketch and list of works and references, see TWENTIETH CENTURY AUTHORS, 1942.

* * *

ABOUT: Dictionary of National Biography 1931-1940.

ERSKINE, JOHN (October 5, 1879-June 2, 1951). For biographical sketch and list of earlier works and references, see TWENTIETH CENTURY AUTHORS, 1942.

* * *

John Erskine died at seventy-one at his home in New York City, as the result of a heart ailment from which he had suffered for eighteen months. He left his widow, Helen Worden Erskine; his marriage to Pauline Ives Erskine had been terminated by divorce in 1945. He was also survived by two children from his first marriage.

In his last years John Erskine completed and published three autobiographies, each dealing with a different aspect of his many-faceted career. Two projected works, a fourth autobiographical volume to be titled "My Life As a Writer," and a version of Chaucer's *Canterbury Tales*, were cancelled by his death.

His later satiric novels declined in popularity. Probably Erskine's greatest contribution will prove to have been in the field of education. The New York *Times* has said that "his tenure at Columbia University [1909-37] came at the time when the University was a focal point of an American cultural development in which music, literature and teaching, itself, were important and exciting. Mr. Erskine helped to generate much of this excitement."

ADDITIONAL WORKS: Complete Life, 1943; Philharmonic-Symphony Society of New York, 1943; Voyage of Captain Bort, 1943; What is Music? 1944; Musical Companion (ed.) 1944; Human Life of Jesus, 1945; Memory of Certain Persons, 1947; My Life as a Teacher, 1948; Venus, the Lovely Goddess, 1949; My Life in Music, 1950.

ABOUT: Erskine, J. Memory of Certain Persons, My Life as a Teacher, My Life in Music; Newsweek October 30, 1950; New York Herald Tribune October 8, 1950; New York Times April 27, 1947, June 3, 1951; Saturday Review of Literature May 17, 1947, June 19, 1948, November 25, 1950; Time October 29, 1945, April 17, 1950.

ERTZ, SUSAN (1894?-   ). For biographical sketch and list of earlier works and references, see TWENTIETH CENTURY AUTHORS, 1942.

* * *

The recent novels of Susan Ertz, like her earlier ones, have clearly demonstrated her competence and good taste as a writer. Hamilton Basso pointed out in 1947 that while she is not "one of the really fine novelists of our time ... she is a better writer on almost every count than several of her contemporaries who have managed to acquire larger and noisier reputations." Miss Ertz, who is the wife of Major J. Ronald McCrindle (not McCrinkle, as erroneously given in TWENTIETH CENTURY AUTHORS, 1942), divides her time between London and her country home, Pooks Farm, in Sussex.

ADDITIONAL WORKS: Anger in the Sky, 1943; Mary Hallam (in England: Two Names Upon the Shore) 1947; Prodigal Heart, 1950; Invitation to Folly (in England: The Undefended Gate) 1953.

*ERVINE, ST. JOHN GREER (December 28, 1883-   ). For biographical sketch and list of earlier works and references, see TWENTIETH CENTURY AUTHORS, 1942.

* * *

Frank Swinnerton has observed that although St. John Ervine is best known as a playwright, it is actually in his novels (Swinnerton cites *Mrs. Martin's Man* and *The Wayward Man*) that his talent "reaches

* ûr′vĭn, sĭn jŭn

310

its most natural expression." Among his plays *The First Mrs. Fraser* has proved the heartiest. Revived in New York in 1947, it had a short run and was pronounced "dated" by some of the critics. But, Wolcott Gibbs pointed out, many of Mr. Ervine's remarks on divorce "are entertaining and sensible, and he is eloquent about the endless, bitter war between age and youth."

Ervine lives in Devon, preferring the country to the city because, he writes, "the country renovates itself every year, and never has that worn and battered look every city has."

ADDITIONAL WORKS: Sophia, 1941; Oscar Wilde, 1951. Plays—Friends and Relations, 1947; Private Enterprise, 1948; Christies, 1949.

ABOUT: Swinnerton, F. The Georgian Literary Scene 1910-1935; New York Herald Tribune Book Review October 12, 1952.

*ESPINA, CONCHA (April 15, 1869- May 19, 1955). For autobiographical sketch and list of earlier works and references, see TWENTIETH CENTURY AUTHORS, 1942.

* * *

Concha Espina died in Madrid after a long illness. Although her age was reported in the press as seventy-six, the editors of TWENTIETH CENTURY AUTHORS learned through the Spanish Royal Academy that she had been born in 1869. She was survived by four sons, fourteen grandchildren, and fifteen great-grandchildren. Blind since 1937, she had continued to write industriously. Her novel *Un Valle en el Mar* received the National Prize in Literature in 1952. Other recent works include a study of the writings of Antonio Machado and a novel, *Una Novela de Amor*, published in 1954. Her first novel, *La Niña de Luzmela*, was so popular that in 1949 the Spanish government changed the name of the town Mazcuerras to Luzmela, and a bust of Concha Espina was erected in the town.

ABOUT: New York Times May 20, 1955.

* ās pē′nä

ETSU. See SUGIMOTO

EVANS, CARADOC (1883-January 11, 1945). For autobiographical sketch and list of earlier works and references, see TWENTIETH CENTURY AUTHORS, 1942.

* * *

Caradoc Evans died of pneumonia in Aberystwyth, Wales, at sixty-one.

Toward the end of his life he not only returned to his native Wales to live, but wrote short stories "full of love for Wales," according to the London *Times,* "with none of the bitternesss for his fellow countrymen which had made him unpopular among Welsh people."

Gwyn Jones, who called Evans "the most important single figure of the Anglo-Welsh group," and described him as a "gifted, perverse, and in all ways fascinating man," observed that "Caradoc's style at its best is remarkable for its purity, strength and precision. His writing, with all its fine qualities, was irremediably stylized; it was designed for one set of effects, and with those he was content. What he saw and chose to write about he saw with extraordinary, and at times furious, intensity; but he was blinkered."

ADDITIONAL WORKS: Pilgrims in a Foreign Land, 1942; Morgan Bible, 1943; Earth Gives All and Takes All, 1947; Mother's Marvel, 1949.

ABOUT: Sandys, O. Caradoc Evans; London Times January 13, 1945; New York Times January 13, 1945.

EVARTS, HAL GEORGE (August 24, 1887-October 18, 1934). For biographical sketch and list of works and references, see TWENTIETH CENTURY AUTHORS, 1942.

"EVERMAY, MARCH." See EIKER, M.

"EVOE." See KNOX, E. G. V.

***FABRICIUS, JOHAN WIGMORE** (August 24, 1899-). For biographical sketch and list of earlier works and references, see TWENTIETH CENTURY AUTHORS, 1942.

* * *

W'⁸en World War II broke out Johan Fabricius was in Italy. From there he escaped to England where he remained until 1945. Fabricius' works had been on the German blacklist since 1933 when, at a PEN conference in Yugoslavia, he protested against the Nazi book burnings. From England Fabricius made a number of broadcasts to the occupied countries on the continent, especially to his native land, Holland. After the fall of Japan the Dutch government invited him to visit Indonesia. His permanent home is The Hague. Many of his books—

* få brē'sē ûs

both for adults and for young people—are illustrated by his own pen-and-ink sketches.

ADDITIONAL WORKS: No Return from Bali, 1941; Malayan Tragedy, 1942; Night Over Java, 1944; Flip Wonders Why (in U.S.: World at Six) 1947; Hotel Vesuvius, 1947; Java Revisited, 1947; Beggar's Banquet, 1951; Great Ordeal, 1951; Pike Beelzebub, and Heartbreak in Flanders, 1953; Dutchman at Large: Memoirs, 1952.

ABOUT: Fabricius, J. Dutchman at Large; Mahony, B. E. (comp.) Illustrators of Children's Books.

FADIMAN, CLIFTON (May 15, 1904-). For biographical sketch and list of earlier works and references, see TWENTIETH CENTURY AUTHORS, 1942.

* * *

Clifton Fadiman resigned as book editor of the *New Yorker* in 1943. Since then his literary activities have been mainly of an administrative nature—as member of the War Writers Board and the Book-of-the-Month Club Board. He has edited the short stories of Henry James (1945) and Dickens' *Pickwick Papers* (1949), written several highly readable and informative prefaces, and he regularly contributes articles to the popular journals—among them *Holiday,* the *Saturday Review,* and the *Atlantic.* In *Party of One* (1955), a collection of essays, reviews, comments, and prefaces, Fadiman assembled in a volume for the first time a quarter-century of his writing.

Fadiman is better known today in the entertainment world than in the world of letters. Until 1948 when the series ended, he was the affable and urbane master of ceremonies of "Information Please." Since that time he has moved over to television where he performs similar duties on various television "panel" programs.

PRINCIPAL WORK: Party of One: Selected Writings, 1955.

ABOUT: New York Times Book Review April 24, 1955; Time September 27, 1943.

"FAIR, A. A." See GARDNER, E. S.

FAIRBANK, Mrs. JANET (AYER) (1878?-December 28, 1951). For biographical sketch and list of works and references, see TWENTIETH CENTURY AUTHORS, 1942.

* * *

Janet Ayer Fairbank died in Milwaukee, at the reported age of seventy-three, after a long illness. Her husband had died in 1939.

Of her writing, which was only one element of her busy life, Isabel Paterson said that while Mrs. Fairbank had "no pretensions to style" her novels had "a homely pleasantness, a feeling for the time spirit and its incessant mutations, and a genuine historical perspective."

ABOUT: New York Times December 29, 1951; Wilson Library Bulletin February 1952.

FAIRCHILD, HENRY PRATT (August 18, 1880-), American sociologist, writes: "Circumstances decreed that I should first

see the light of day in Dundee, Ill., though for the whole of their long life together, both before and after that event, my parents made their home in Crete, Neb., where my father was a professor, and most of the time treasurer in Doane College. I got my preparatory education in the public schools of Crete and the academy attached to Doane College, and graduated from the college, with the degree of A.B., in 1900. I was awarded the degree of LL.D. by Doane in 1930. Immediately after graduation I went to Smyrna (now Izmir), Turkey, where for three years I taught in the American International College. My classes included such heterogeneous and ill-assorted subjects—all the way from botany (which I had never studied) to commercial correspondence—as the older American teachers did not care to concern themselves with. Returning to Crete in the summer of 1903 I accepted the position of state secretary for Doane College, and spent the next three years traveling about the state, enlisting the interest of potential students, publicizing the college, and raising the major part of the money for a new combined chapel and conservatory.

"Continuing the three-year pattern I then went to Yale and enrolled as a graduate student. Having been interested in immigration and population from my early boyhood I wanted to get a thorough grounding in those subjects. I discovered that to do so it was essential that I study sociology, and that is how I became a sociologist. I took my minor in economics, and my Ph.D. in 1909. In the same year I married Mary Eleanor Townsend, of an old New Haven family. (She died in 1928.)

"After a year as professor of economics and sociology at Bowdoin College, I returned to Yale as assistant professor of economics, and later of the 'science of society.' I resigned from Yale in 1918 to become associate director of the personnel department of War Camp Community Service, and in the fall of 1919 I joined the faculty of New York University, where I have remained ever since, becoming emeritus in 1945.

"All my life I have been interested in social and civic affairs, and have served as officer or board member of many organizations, including the American Sociological Society, the American Eugenics Society, the Town Hall Club of New York, the Teachers Insurance and Annuity Association, the American Association of University Professors, and the Authors Guild. I was the organizer and first president of the Population Association of America. I initiated and was the general editor of the Wiley Social Science Series. I have done a considerable amount of public lecturing on various subjects, particularly population and migration. In the summer of 1952 I did some special editorial work for the United Nations."

PRINCIPAL WORKS: Greek Immigration to the United States, 1911; Immigration: A World Movement and its American Significance, 1913; Outline of Applied Sociology, 1916; Elements of Social Science, 1924; The Melting Pot Mistake, 1926; The Foundations of Social Life, 1927; (ed.) Immigrant Backgrounds, 1927; Profits or Prosperity? 1932; (ed.) Survey of Contemporary Sociology, 1934; General Sociology, 1934; This Way Out, 1936; People: the Quantity and Quality of Population, 1939; Economics for the Millions, 1940; (ed.) Dictionary of Sociology, 1944; Race and Nationality, as Factors in American Life, 1947; The Prodigal Century, 1950; Versus: Reflections of a Sociologist, 1950.

ABOUT: Current Biography 1942.

"FAIRLESS, MICHAEL." See BARBER, M. F.

"FALLADA, HANS." See DITZEN, R.

FANTE, JOHN (April 8, 1911-). For autobiographical sketch and list of earlier works and references, see TWENTIETH CENTURY AUTHORS, 1942.

* * *

John Fante lives in Los Angeles and writes for motion pictures. During World War II he worked for the Office of War Information. Fante's own life—and especially the pregnancy of his wife and the birth of their son—was the subject of his latest book, *Full of Life*.

ADDITIONAL WORK: Full of Life, 1952.

ABOUT: Pergallo, O. Italian-American Authors and their Contribution to American Literature.

FARGE. See LA FARGE

*FARJEON, ELEANOR (1881-). For autobiographical sketch and list of earlier works and references, see TWENTIETH CENTURY AUTHORS, 1942.

* * *

Eleanor Farjeon lived in a cottage in Sussex until June 1940 when she returned to London to be near her brothers during the Battle of Britain. Her brother Herbert, with whom she frequently collaborated, died in 1944, shortly after the very successful production of their play with music, *The Glass Slipper*. Her elder brother, the composer Harry Farjeon, died in 1948.

When World War II ended, Miss Farjeon sold her Sussex cottage and moved to Hampstead where she now lives. She continues to write her charming and airy verses and plays for children. She also occasionally writes adult fiction, and her novel *Love Affair*, though slight and unpretentious, was praised for its "adroit composition." In 1951 she was received into the Catholic Church.

ADDITIONAL WORKS: New Book of Days, 1941; Cherrystones, 1942; The Fair Venetian, 1943; The Golden Coney, 1943; Ariadne and the Bull, 1945; The Mulberry Bush, 1945; Prayer for Little Things, 1945; The Glass Slipper (with H. Farjeon) 1946; Love Affair (novel) 1947; First and Second Love. Sonnets, 1947; Two Bouquets (with H. Farjeon) 1948; Old Nurse's Stockingbasket, 1949; Starry Floor, 1949; Silver-Sand and Snow, 1951; The Silver Curlew, 1953.

ABOUT: Hoehn, M. (ed.) Catholic Authors, II; Kunitz, S. J. & Haycraft, H. Junior Book of Authors (rev. ed.).

* fär'jŭn

*FARJEON, JOSEPH JEFFERSON ("Anthony Swift") (June 4, 1883-). For biographical sketch and list of earlier works and references, see TWENTIETH CENTURY AUTHORS, 1942.

* * *

Although Joseph Jefferson Farjeon publishes on an average of well over one suspense novel a year in England, all of them regarded as expert, his work is little known in the United States. He contributes articles to *Punch* and to several British newspapers. Farjeon has been married since 1910 to

* Died June 6, 1955.

Frances Antoinette Wood and they have one daughter. He lives in Ditchling, Sussex.

ADDITIONAL WORKS: The Judge Sums It Up, 1942; House of Shadows, 1943; Greenmask, 1944; Rona Runs Away, 1945; Peril in the Pyrenees, 1946; Back to Victoria, 1947; Smith Minor, 1947; Death of a World, 1948; Shadow of Thirteen, 1949; Cause Unknown, 1950; House over the Tunnel, 1951; Adventure for Nine, 1951; Ben on the Job, 1952; Number 19, 1952; Money Walks, 1953; Mystery of the Map, 1953. As "Anthony Swift"—Murder at a Police Station, 1943; November 9 at Kersea, 1944; Interrupted Honeymoon, 1946.

FARNOL, JEFFERY (February 10, 1878- August 9, 1952). For biographical sketch and list of earlier works and references, see TWENTIETH CENTURY AUTHORS, 1942.

* * *

Jeffery Farnol died at seventy-four, after a two-year illness, at Eastbourne, Sussex, England.

Up to the year before his death he continued to write the swashbuckling novels that were published at the rate of about one a year. The London *Times* has called him "a full-flavoured romantic novelist who entertained and endeared himself to a happily more innocent younger generation than the present."

ADDITIONAL WORKS: Valley of Night (ed.) 1942; The King Liveth, 1944; Piping Times, 1945; Heritage Perilous, 1947; Most Sacred of All, 1948; A Fool Remembered, 1949; The Ninth Earl, 1950; Glad Summer, 1951.

ABOUT: London Times August 11, 1952; New York Times August 11, 1952; Time May 8, 1944.

FARRELL, JAMES THOMAS (February 27, 1904-). For autobiographical sketch and list of earlier works and references, see TWENTIETH CENTURY AUTHORS, 1942.

* * *

A mellowed and sanguine James T. Farrell took stock of his work in 1952 and commented: "I have been writing now for something like twenty-five years. I feel as enthusiastic about writing now as I did when I first began. I hope that I may be able to go on writing for many more years. Despite the crisis in the world, I feel confident that both freedom and literature will survive. I look ahead and think of the future." Many of the plans which Farrell ambitiously drew up at the beginning of his career have now been completed, but he has new plans and new projects under way. The Lonigan trilogy has given way to the Bernard

Clare (or Carr) trilogy and the (to date) five volumes of the Danny O'Neill series.

For some time Farrell has had relatively rough treatment from the critics, and his stature as an American novelist appeared considerably diminished. Along with Dreiser and Dos Passos, he has suffered from the critical disfavor into which literary naturalism has fallen. His work has been the target of more specific and biting criticism, however, than the objections of formlessness and over-lavish detail generally raised against Dreiser and Dos Passos. W. M. Frohock concludes regretfully that "Farrell is a highly derivative writer and very much the inferior of the men in whose steps he resolutely plods along." But judged as a documentary novelist, Frohock points out, Farrell has distinct merits—"a deep moral seriousness . . . an ability to create living people." Granville Hicks found the latest volume in the Danny O'Neill saga, *The Face of Time,* "one of the best novels Farrell has ever written. It has the solidity and the absolute honesty that have always marked his work, but his characteristic effects are achieved without the usual hammering, repetitive assault upon the reader's sensibilities."

Farrell's work, despite his critics, continues to be read, and in 1955 he sold the movie rights of the *Studs Lonigan* novels. In a favorable re-appraisal of his career (*New World Writing* #5), Horace Gregory attempts to answer the question, "Why has James T. Farrell survived while so many of his contemporaries of the 1930's are scarcely more than half-remembered names and their books forgotten?" Gregory's explanation runs: "One can say that the *Studs Lonigan* trilogy and the Danny O'Neill cycle are monumental. . . . One can also say no novelist in America of Farrell's day has been so successful in extending the power of a realistic tradition in fiction to the mid-years of the present century. . . . Granting all this, the basic question of Farrell's singular position today remains unanswered. . . . The answer has something to do with Farrell's view of life, or rather a view that he conveys to the printed page: the view is elemental, humane, direct, and moral; it is far deeper than its seemingly political and economic associations, and carries with it the perspective of a Chicago writer whose second home is Paris, where so many pages of *Studs Lonigan* were rewritten."

Farrell continues to publish his volumes of essays, written, according to the *New Yorker,* with "the same slow-burning intensity, the buffalolike stubbornness, and the uncompromising honesty that made *Studs Lonigan* the book it is." James Burnham said of his *Literature and Morality*: "He never analyzes technique or form, but always content and social correlations. . . . As with almost all creative artists, Mr. Farrell's critical system is a projection and justification of his own creative work."

ADDITIONAL WORKS: *Fiction*—My Days of Anger, 1943; To Whom It May Concern, and Other Stories, 1944; Bernard Clare, 1946; When Boyhood Dreams Come True, 1946; Life Adventurous, and Other Stories, 1947; The Road Between, 1949; American Dream Girl, and Other Stories, 1950; This Man and This Woman, 1951; Yet Other Waters, 1952; The Face of Time, 1953. *Non-Fiction*—The League of Frightened Philistines, 1945; Literature and Morality, 1947; Reflections at Fifty, 1954.

ABOUT: Frohock, W. M. The Novel of Violence in America, 1920-1950; Morris, L. R. Postscript to Yesterday; Snell, G. D. Shapers of American Fiction; Van Gelder, R. Writers and Writing; America June 8, 1946; Canadian Forum August 1942; Current Biography 1942; Harper's October 1954; New World Writing #5; New York Herald Tribune Book Review October 12, 1952; Time May 20, 1946.

FARSON, NEGLEY (May 14, 1890-   ). For biographical sketch and list of earlier works and references, see TWENTIETH CENTURY AUTHORS, 1942.

* * *

A confirmed Anglo-American, Negley Farson makes his permanent home in Devon; but the scene of his latest novel, *Sons of Noah,* is his birthplace, New Jersey. In 1949 he published *Last Chance in Africa,* a report on a four months' tour through Kenya, during which he explored the territory thoroughly and interviewed a host of people, ranging from government officials to tribal chiefs. The book was lively and informative. Farson, commented Keith Hutchison in the *Nation,* "has a bountiful curiosity, a gusto for life, a love of nature, and a genuine interest in all kinds and conditions of men." His point of view is essentially that of the tourist, but, Arch Steele wrote in the New York *Herald Tribune,* his "evaluation of the people who cross his path, be they black or white, lofty or lowly, is penetrating and colorful and gives you a valuable insight into the human side of the African problem."

ADDITIONAL WORKS: Going Fishing, 1943; Last Chance in Africa, 1949; Sons of Noah (novel) 1949; Caucasian Journey, 1951.

ABOUT: Farson, N. Going Fishing.

FAST, HOWARD MELVIN ("Walter Ericson") (November 11, 1914-   ), American novelist and biographer, was born in New York City to  Barney and Ida (Miller) Fast. His father was a factory worker. Fast was educated in the public schools of New York. He left high school to join the navy. Rejected because of his youth, he began traveling around the United States as a hobo, working at odd jobs—as a laborer in a lumber camp, a shipping clerk in a New York factory, a page boy in the New York Public Library. He studied art for a while at the National Academy of Design. Fast finished his first novel at seventeen and sold his first story in 1932. His first published novel, *Two Valleys*, appeared in 1933, but it was not until 1937, when his novella "The Children" was published in *Story* magazine, that Fast was able to give up his other jobs and devote full time to writing.

Pinchot

Fast's most successful work, both in terms of sales and in the judgment of the reviewers, has been in the field of historical fiction. He has drawn much of his subject matter from American history. *Conceived in Liberty* had its setting in Valley Forge and offers a grim and vivid picture of the hardships endured there by the American army. *The Last Frontier* was the story of the flight from a reservation of a group of Cheyennes back to their home in Wyoming. With *The Unvanquished* Fast returned to the American Revolution for his scene, and the action of the novel centers around George Washington and his emerging leadership of the new nation. Fast worked in the same field with his fictional biography of Thomas Paine, *Citizen Tom Paine*.

Long associated with left-wing American political groups, Fast's position in American letters has inevitably been affected by his political position. In 1950 he served a prison sentence for contempt of Congress for withholding from the Committee on Un-American Activities of the House of Representatives records concerning the Joint Anti-Fascist Refugee Committee, listed as subversive by the Attorney General of the United States. In February 1953 his name was brought up in a congressional investigation of the Voice of America, which had used selections from Fast's works in its overseas broadcasts because (according to a State Department memo reported in the New York *Times*) "he is known as a Soviet-endorsed author . . . [and] materials favorable to the United States in some of his works may thereby be given a special creditability among selected key audiences." At this hearing Fast, invoking the Fifth Amendment, declined to say whether he was a member of the Communist Party. In December 1953 the Soviet Union awarded him the Stalin Peace Prize.

It has become increasingly difficult to arrive at a dispassionate judgment of Fast's work as a writer. His later novels, particularly *Spartacus* (which he published privately after the manuscript had been rejected by several commercial publishers), a story of the slave revolts under the Roman Empire, have suffered—as the *Saturday Review* points out—"from the fact that attention to Mr. Fast has shifted from the book page to the front page." Many of his novels had a wide popular appeal in the late 1930's and early 1940's. They were lively, and sometimes moving, interpretations of history, distinguished by what more than one critic has called Fast's "sure narrative skill." *The American* was a Literary Guild selection and *Freedom Road*, which went through eight printings within five years of its publication, was translated into twenty-one languages. Fast's major weakness as a novelist appears to be a lack of restraint. The late Stephen Vincent Benét found "hectic overwriting" in *Conceived in Liberty*, although he admired the book. Allan Nevins remarked of *Citizen Tom Paine* that "until Mr. Fast learns to combine power with more restraint, more careful accuracy, and more studied art, his books will not last."

Fast was a member of the overseas staff of the Office of War Information from 1942 to 1943. He worked on a special film project for the army in 1944, and in 1945 he went to Europe as a correspondent for *Esquire* and *Coronet* magazines. In the New York elections of 1952 he was the American Labor Party candidate for the twenty-third congressional district. He lives in New York City with his wife, Betty Cohen, whom he married in 1937, and their two children.

PRINCIPAL WORKS: Two Valleys, 1932; Strange Yesterday, 1933; A Place in the City, 1937; Conceived in Liberty, 1939; Haym Salomon, 1941; The Last Frontier, 1941; Lord Baden-Powell of the Boy Scouts, 1941; The Unvanquished, 1942; Citizen Tom Paine, 1943; Freedom Road, 1944; The American, 1946; My Glorious Brothers, 1948; Departure, and Other Stories, 1949; Literature and Reality, 1949; The Proud and the Free, 1950; Spartacus, 1952; Silas Timberman, 1954; Thirty Pieces of Silver (play) 1954. As "Walter Ericson"—Fallen Angel, 1952.

ABOUT: Current Biography 1943; Warfel, H. R. American Novelists of Today.

*FAUCONNIER, HENRI. For autobiographical sketch and list of works and references, see TWENTIETH CENTURY AUTHORS, 1942.

* * *

Henri Fauconnier lives in Nice, France. He is married and has four children. He has written novels as well as travel books, but the only one of his works available in English is The Soul of Malaya (1931). His Visions, published originally in 1938, is a collection of stories and poetic essays, and includes the autobiographical "Triptyque du Pays Natal," with Fauconnier's recollections of his childhood, and the essay "Vision," an anti-war dream allegory.

* fō kô nyā'

FAULKNER, WILLIAM (September 25, 1897-). For biographical sketch and list of earlier works and references, see TWENTIETH CENTURY AUTHORS, 1942.

* * *

William Faulkner lives, as he has lived for most of his life, in the small southern town of Oxford, Miss. Outwardly his life has shown little change in recent years. His hair is all grey now, his daughter is grown up; but he continues his routines, spending some part of the day writing, and as much time as he can hunting, fishing, visiting with old friends. The placid course of Faulkner's existence has been interrupted from time to time by trips to Hollywood for motion picture writing and by visits to his publisher in New York. His most newsworthy trip away from home was to Stockholm in 1950 to receive the Nobel prize in literature.

Since 1945 (in which year, incidentally, his books were almost entirely out of print), Faulkner has moved from relative obscurity (i.e., the admiration of coterie readers, especially in academic circles) into national and international prominence. What is most remarkable about this emergence is that it has happened not so much on the basis of Faulkner's current literary work but on the re-evaluation and rediscovery of his earlier work, which is now the subject of exhaustive study in the graduate schools and in the critical journals. The Faulkner "revival"

began with Malcolm Cowley's edition of The Portable Faulkner in 1945. In his illuminating and appreciative preface, Cowley wrote that in Oxford "Faulkner performed a labor of imagination that has not been equalled in our time, and a double labor: first, to invent a Mississippi county that was like a mythical kingdom, but was complete and living in all its details; second, to make his story of Yoknapatawpha County stand as a parable or legend of all the Deep South." Other sympathetic studies in this country and abroad (especially in France where Faulkner is much admired) have tended to confirm Robert Penn Warren's pronouncement, made in 1946: "The study of Faulkner is the most challenging single task in contemporary American literature for criticism to undertake. Here is a novelist who, in mass of work, in scope of material, in range of effect, in reportorial accuracy and symbolic subtlety, in philosophical weight can be put beside the masters of our own past literature."

Through all this attention and adulation, Faulkner moves quietly and with studied indifference. His recent works, like his early works, make little concession to popular taste. But, as always, they have a somber and haunting "staying" power. Sometimes, for example with Intruder in the Dust, the sheer force of the narrative captures wide numbers of readers. At other times, as with Requiem for a Nun (part of which is written as a play, part as a novel), the tortured sequel to Sanctuary, they miss fire. He considers his novel A Fable (1954) the most important work of his life. It is a religious allegory based on the false Armistice which took place on the battlefields of France just before the end of World War I. Faulkner himself described the work as a re-telling of the Christ story in modern terms, and the action of the novel closely parallels the structure of Christ's Passion. Reviewers were divided in their reception of the book, some finding it pretentious and obscure, others hailing it as a masterpiece. It received the National Book Award for fiction and the Pulitzer prize in 1955.

Probably the most eloquent expression of Faulkner as an artist and as an individual was the short acceptance speech which he made at the presentation ceremonies of the Nobel awards. "I feel that this award was not made to me as a man but to my work— a life's work in the agony and sweat of the human spirit, not for glory and least of all for profit, but to create out of the materials of the human spirit something which did not exist there before." Man will endure, Faulkner continued, "because he has a soul, a spirit capable of compassion and sacrifice and endurance. The poet's, the writer's, duty is to write about these things. It is his privilege to help man endure by lifting his heart, by reminding him of the courage and honor and hope and pride and compassion and pity and sacrifice which have been the glory of his past."

Two other literary figures in the Faulkner family should be mentioned here. One is Faulkner's brother John, author of the novels *Men Working* (1941), *Dollar Cotton* (1942), and *Chooky* (1950). The other, Col. William Falkner, was Faulkner's great grandfather and author of a melodramatic novel, *The White Rose of Memphis*, which was a great popular success of the 1880's. It was reprinted, with an introduction by Robert Cantwell, in 1953.

ADDITIONAL WORKS: Intruder in the Dust, 1948; Knight's Gambit, 1949; Collected Stories, 1950; Requiem for a Nun, 1951; Mirrors of Chartres Street, 1953; The Faulkner Reader, 1954; A Fable, 1954.

ABOUT: Campbell, H. M. & Foster, R. E. William Faulkner; Coughlin, R. The Private World of William Faulkner; Daniel, R. W. Catalogue of the Writings of William Faulkner; Frohock, W. M. The Novel of Violence in America, 1920-1950; Hoffman, F. J. & Vickery, O. W. William Faulkner: Two Decades of Criticism; Howe, I. William Faulkner; Kazin, A. On Native Grounds; Miner, W. L. The World of William Faulkner; O'Connor, W. V. The Tangled Fire of William Faulkner; Snell, G. D. Shapers of American Fiction; Atlantic October 1951; Commentary August 1951; Current Biography 1951; Life September 28, October 5, 1953; New York Times November 11, December 8, December 11, 1950; Partisan Review January 1951; Saturday Review of Literature September 25, 1948, November 25, 1950, July 12, 1952; Time November 20, 1950.

*FAURE, ÉLIE (April 4, 1873-October 31, 1937). For biographical sketch and list of works and references, see TWENTIETH CENTURY AUTHORS, 1942.

* * *

ABOUT: Columbia Dictionary of Modern European Literature.

* fôr

FAURE, RAOUL COHEN (September 10, 1909-), Egyptian-born novelist now living in America, was born in Cairo. He was educated in Paris: "Doctor in Law of the Faculté de Droit de Paris. Diplome de l'Ecole Libre des Sciences Politiques et Economiques, Section Diplomatique, Paris. Diplome des Hautes Etudes Commerciales de Paris."

With this distinguished background for a career in business, government, and law, he went to London to train for stock broking. Then he returned to Egypt where he worked in an import-export firm and did stock broking and cotton plantation supervising for six years. At this point Faure decided to give up business and to become a writer. He traveled in the United States, Mexico and Central America, and was in the United States, on his way to Tahiti, when World War II broke out. He settled in California, where he now lives, in a suburb of San Francisco.

Emmett E. Smith

Faure's novels have been described as brilliant exercises in prose and in imagination. He creates a strange and exotic world in his fiction. "It is a peculiar and limited world," Robert Gorham Davis wrote, "and yet one that so extends and illuminates some aspects of ordinary experience that it becomes an enlargement of life itself." He wrote his first novel, *The Spear in the Sand*, the story of a young man hopelessly marooned on a Pacific island, "maybe," he says, "as an unconscious reaction to rush and din. I used many impressions of desert shores on Mediterranean and Red Sea and some from my trip in Mexico and Central America. Have often been myself in the desert near Alexandria and on the plantation and the theme of the effects of solitude has always interested me. Perhaps, too, it's a reaction against the numerous books replete with action as consequence of the war and the unstable political and social situation." The book was highly praised for its richness and originality. Joseph Henry Jackson remarked of it: "Mr. Faure writes this unusual story in a warm, richly textured, poetic prose. His understanding of nature in its various aspects is uncanny; his ability to express this understanding and to relate it to his character, Sausal, is extraordinary."

With *Mister St. John* Faure moved over into the realm of time fantasy, introducing the Devil as a leading character, and a dream sequence for the major plot development. It was not a "popular" book—some reviewers found it turgid and contrived— but it convinced at least one reviewer, the late Thomas Sugrue, that "its author is one

of the recent writers of genuine tales."
Lady Godiva and Master Tom was a re-
telling of the famous medieval Godiva legend, heavily seasoned with modern psychoanalytic lore. And in *The Cave and the
Rock* Faure turned complete allegorist with
a story of a lizard community which, none
too flatteringly for mankind, mirrors the
foibles and practices of human community
life.

Faure's work in general has been perhaps
too esoteric and exotic to win him an important place in contemporary fiction. But
it is these very qualities of originality and
imaginativeness that distinguish his work
and give promise of important developments
to come.

PRINCIPAL WORKS: The Spear in the Sand,
1946; Mister St. John, 1947; Lady Godiva and Master Tom, 1948; The Cave and the Rock, 1953.

*FAUSET, JESSIE REDMON (1884?-).
For biographical sketch and list of
works and references, see TWENTIETH
CENTURY AUTHORS, 1942.

* * *

Jessie Fauset (Mrs. Herbert Harris) lives
in Montclair, N.J. In 1949-50 she was visiting professor of English at Hampton Institute. Although she has published no full-
length work of fiction since 1933, Miss Fauset is well remembered for her sharp and
sensitive studies of "middle-class colored
people whose lives are twisted and distorted
because of race prejudice." Hugh M. Gloster, in his *Negro Voices in American Fiction*, considers her *Comedy: American Style*
"the most penetrating study of color mania
in American fiction," and he finds that her
studies of the colored élite of Northern cities
constitute "one of the major achievements
of American Negro fiction."

ABOUT: Gloster, H. M. Negro Voices in American Fiction.

* fô' sĕt

*FAUSSET, HUGH I'ANSON (June 16,
1895-). For biographical sketch and
list of earlier works and references, see
TWENTIETH CENTURY AUTHORS, 1942.

* * *

Hugh I. Fausset contributes reviews and
critical articles regularly to the *Times Literary Supplement, Manchester Guardian,* and
other periodicals. A collection of his essays,
Poets and Pundits, was warmly received in
the United States as in Britain and praised

* fô'sĕt

especially for its "deep, spiritual insights."
His more personal philosophical work, *Towards Fidelity,* was a record of his attempt
to arrive at a satisfying outlook on life. The
reviewer for the *Times Literary Supplement*
found that it reflected "an attitude of mind
whose good faith is beyond question." Fausset lives in Saffron Walden, Essex.

ADDITIONAL WORKS: Between the Tides (novel)
1942; The Last Days (novel) 1945; Poets and
Pundits, 1947; Towards Fidelity, 1952.

"FAUST, FREDERICK." See BRAND,
MAX

*FAÿ, BERNARD (April 3, 1893-).
For biographical sketch and list of
works and references, see TWENTIETH
CENTURY AUTHORS, 1942.

* * *

Bernard Faÿ on last reports was serving
a life sentence in France for collaborating
with the enemy in World War II. In 1941
Pierre Laval had appointed him director of
the French National Library. In this capacity—according to charges brought against
him in 1946 after the liberation of France—
Faÿ "directed during the Pétain regime a
special service to combat Free Masonry."
He was accused of opening secret archives
in the French National Library which contained information on Masonry, of organizing propaganda against Masons, including
publishing pamphlets, making films and releasing lists of names of Free Masons. The
latter act, according to the prosecution, resulted in the deportation and death of thousands of them. In December 1946 Faÿ was
found guilty and sentenced to life imprisonment at hard labor.

ABOUT: New York Times August 28, 1944,
November 26, December 6, 1946.

* fä'y'

FAY, SIDNEY BRADSHAW (April 13,
1876-). For autobiographical sketch
and list of earlier works and references,
see TWENTIETH CENTURY AUTHORS,
1942.

* * *

Sidney Bradshaw Fay regularly contributes articles on international affairs to *Current History* magazine. In the academic year
1945-46 he was professor of history at Yale,
and in 1946 he served as president of the
American Historical Association. His home
is in Cambridge, Mass., and he summers in

Nantucket. His only published work in recent years is a translation of *Die Deutsche Katastrophe* by the "dean of German historians," Friedrich Meinecke.

ADDITIONAL WORK: (tr.) Meinecke, F. The German Catastrophe, 1950.

FEARING, KENNETH (1902-   ). For autobiographical sketch and list of earlier works and references, see TWENTIETH CENTURY AUTHORS, 1942.

* * *

Since 1939 Kenneth Fearing has won a wider audience with his fiction than with his poetry. His novels are in the genre of the "psycho-thriller," a notch or more above the average, thanks to his lively imagination, shrewd and original observation, and a prose which one reviewer described as "lean, vernacular and effective." The most successful of Fearing's novels to date has been *The Big Clock* (which was made into a motion picture), a chilling and sharply satiric story of murder and mayhem in the offices of a New York magazine publisher.

Fearing's poetry appears from time to time in *Poetry*, the *New Yorker* and other journals, and he has published two volumes of verse in recent years. His later work retains the sharpness and the wit which distinguished his early work, but a number of critics have observed that it lacks the passion and excitement.

Fearing's first marriage ended in divorce. In 1945 he married Nan Lurie, a painter. His home is in New York City.

ADDITIONAL WORKS: *Poems*—Afternoon of a Pawnbroker, 1943; Stranger at Coney Island, 1948. *Novels*—The Big Clock, 1946; The Loneliest Girl in the World, 1951; The Generous Heart, 1954. *As "Donald F. Bedford"* (with D. Friede & H. Bedford-Jones) John Barry, 1947.

ABOUT: Bishop, J. P. Collected Essays; Burke, K. Philosophy of Literary Form; Gregory, H. & Zaturenska, M. History of American Poetry; Poetry December 1943, July 1944.

*FEIBLEMAN, JAMES KERN (July 13, 1904-   ), American philosopher, writes: "I was born in New Orleans, La. My mother, Nora (Kern) Feibleman, was born in New Orleans of German parents, and my father, Leopold Feibleman, had come over from Germany where he had been a farmer in the Rhineland. Here in New Orleans he became the owner of a large department store, L. Feibleman and Company, Inc.

"I attended Henry W. Allen and I. Newman Training Schools in New Orleans;

* fē′bĕl màn

Horace Mann School in New York; for a short while, I attended the University of Virginia, and later I studied privately in Europe.

"From 1925 until 1929, I was assistant manager of L. Feibleman and Company, Inc., and from 1930 on I have been, and am, vice president and general manager of James K. Feibleman Realty Company, Inc.

"In 1928 I married Dorothy Steinam of New York. There was one son of this marriage, Peter S. Feibleman, born August 1, 1930. We were divorced in 1946.

"I have been teaching continuously at Tulane University in the College of Arts and Sciences since 1943. I became acting assistant professor of English in 1943; acting assistant professor of philosophy in 1945; graduate professor of philosophy in 1946, and since 1951 have been graduate professor and head of the department of philosophy.

"I have had thirteen books published; have contributed chapters to four philosophical volumes, and have had more than sixty technical essays published in professional journals both here and abroad. I have also written a number of book reviews.

"I have lectured at Yale University, Harvard University, Princeton University, Columbia University, John Hopkins University, University of Virginia, University of Connecticut, Western Reserve University School of Medicine, Vassar College, the Worcester Foundation for Experimental Biology, and others, and am on the staff of the Tulane University School of Medicine, Department of Psychiatry and Neurology, where I have lectured several times each year for the past few years. I have appeared on a number of radio programs, including several for CBS's national broadcast, 'Invitation to Learning.'

"In early 1952 I was made an honorary member of Phi Beta Kappa, and am a member of a number of professional organizations, including the Eastern and Western Divisions of the American Philosophical Association, the American Mathematical Society, the Association for Symbolic Logic, the American Society for Aesthetics, the American Association of University Professors, the Modern Language Association of America, the Southwestern Philosophical Conference, the Southern Society for Philosophy and Psychology, and am past president of the Peirce Society.

"I am engaged at the present in writing a book on technical metaphysics and one on the method of experimental research."

PRINCIPAL WORKS: What Science Really Means (with J. W. Friend) 1937; In Praise of Comedy: a Study in Its Theory and Practice, 1939; Positive Democracy, 1940; Introduction to Peirce's Philosophy, 1946; The Revival of Realism, 1946; The Theory of Human Culture, 1946; The Long Habit (novel) 1948; Aesthetics, 1949; Ontology, 1951; Philosophers Lead Sheltered Lives (memoirs) 1952; Trembling Prairie (poems) 1953.

ABOUT: Feibleman, J. Philosophers Lead Sheltered Lives.

"FEIKEMA, FEIKE." See MANFRED, F. F.

FERBER, EDNA (August 15, 1887-   ). For biographical sketch and list of earlier works and references, see TWENTIETH CENTURY AUTHORS, 1942.

* * *

"A natural born storyteller," Edna Ferber continues to write with assurance, poise, and an unrivaled ability to attract large numbers of readers. The results are facile but unfailingly interesting. Although none of her later writings has been so well received as the earlier *Show Boat, Cimarron,* and *So Big,* they have had a respectable success. The only exception was the play *Bravo!* (written with George S. Kaufman), about a Hungarian playwright and his mistress who are trying to make a place for themselves in the United States. The play was a failure and closed after forty-four performances on Broadway in 1948.

The novel *Great Son,* a saga of four generations of a Seattle family, was characteristic of her slick and entertaining fiction. The reviewers disagreed on its merits as a novel, but they were in complete agreement that it was "surefire" best-seller material. Her collection of short stories *One Basket* found her (said James MacBride in the New York *Times*) "at the top of her form—a virtuoso lightness of phrasing, a shrewd ear for dialogue, plus real understanding of the standard problems Americans have faced in the past and must go on facing."

Miss Ferber's "understanding" of the American scene was challenged by some reviewers, however, on the publication of her novel *Giant.* This large and sprawling tale of life in present-day Texas (which she describes as "that enormous and somewhat incredible commonwealth") was none too

well received by Texans, who found her picture of their state a grossly unflattering one. Miss Ferber, who had traveled through the state extensively in preparation for the book, had a forthright answer to such criticism. "Texas history is as varied, tempestuous, and vast as the state itself. Texas yesterday is unbelievable, but no more incredible than Texas today. Today's Texas is exhilarating, exasperating, violent, charming, horrible, delightful, alive."

As if to prove that she could level equally stinging charges at other parts of the country (including the city where she lived herself for many years), Miss Ferber created something of a similar furor when she announced to reporters, on her return from a European visit in April 1953, that the streets of New York City were "disgustingly filthy" and dirtier than any she had seen on her travels.

ADDITIONAL WORKS: Great Son, 1945; One Basket (short stories) 1949; Bravo! (with G. S. Kaufman) 1949; Giant, 1952.

ABOUT: Ernst, M. L. The Best Is Yet. . . ; Gray, J. On Second Thought; Van Gelder, R. Writers and Writing; New York Herald Tribune Book Review October 12, 1952; New York Times Book Review October 5, 1952.

FERGUSSON, FRANCIS (February 21, 1904-   ), American critic, writes: "I was born in Albuquerque, N.M., and spent most of my childhood there. My father, H. B. Fergusson, a lawyer, had moved to New Mexico from Alabama in the late 1870's. My mother was born in Albuquerque of German parents. Her father, Franz Huning, went there in 1849. I remember the Albuquerque of my childhood as a New Town on the railroad, and an Old Town on the Rio Grande, which still preserved the look of an eighteenth-century Mexican village.

"My father was a congressman, and in 1912 we moved to Washington for three years. My father died in 1915, and four years later my mother moved from Albuquerque to New York to secure better schooling for my sister and me. I graduated from the Ethical Culture School in 1921; went to Harvard for two years, where I studied biology, and then to Queen's College, Oxford, on a Rhodes Scholarship. There I studied philosophy and took my undergraduate degree in 1926 in the Honour School of Modern Greats.

"Back in this country after three years abroad, I entered the American Laboratory Theatre in New York. That theatre included a permanent repertory company directed by Richard Boleslavsky and a school where Maria Ouspenskaya taught acting. They were both from the Moscow Art Theatre, and the conception of the dramatic art which I learned from them has been an important influence on my work ever since. I worked there four years, as actor, stage-manager, and associate director. I also translated plays from French and Spanish for that theatre and began to write poems and critical essays.

"In 1930 our theatre succumbed to the depression, and I spent the next three and a half years in New York in a succession of jobs: dramatic critic for *The Bookman*, lecturer and executive secretary for the New School for Social Research, and reviewer for various periodicals. In 1931 I married Marion Crowne, who had been Maria Ouspenskaya's assistant at the Laboratory Theatre.

"In 1934 I was appointed to the literature faculty of Bennington College, which was then a year and a half old. My wife and I were put in charge of the college theatre in 1936 and continued in that position until 1947, experimenting with plays of many styles and periods, and participating in the building of the college. We have two children, Harvey, born in New York, and Honora, born in Bennington.

"I had written some poems, plays and essays at Bennington, but in 1948 I was made a member of the Institute for Advanced Study at Princeton for a year and a half, and that enabled me to complete a longer work, *The Idea of a Theatre*. From 1949 to 1952 I directed the seminars in literary criticism at Princeton University. I was made a Fellow of the School of Letters (now at Indiana University) in 1950; a member of the editorial board of *Comparative Literature* in 1951, and of the advisory board to the Special Program in the Humanities, at Princeton University, in 1952. I have just finished a book on Dante's *Purgatorio*. In 1952-53 I was 'visiting critic' at Indiana University." [Currently, since writing the above, Fergusson is teaching at Rutgers University.]

* * *

Francis Fergusson, brother of the novelist Harvey Fergusson and the regional writer Erna Fergusson, has come to the field of literary criticism through the theatre and is, as Stanley Edgar Hyman has pointed out, "a drama critic in the proper sense, a critic of both dramatic literature and performance." For many years a contributor to the critical journals, he published his first book on criticism, *The Idea of a Theatre*, in 1949. The book consists of studies of ten plays, ranging from the *Oedipus Rex* to Cocteau's *Infernal Machine*, which reflect in dramatic terms "the natural history of the human soul . . . its characteristic journey toward the triumphant or desperate realization of its own essence." From the roots of the drama in ancient religious ritual, from Aristotle's definition of tragedy as an imitation of an action, and from Kenneth Burke's conception of "symbolic action," Fergusson has drawn together a theory of the drama as the moving of the human soul from "purpose" to "passion" to "perception." This movement is analogous to the journey of the soul in Dante's *Purgatorio*, and Fergusson most effectively illustrates his thesis with a discussion of that great poem. In 1953 he published a full-length study of the *Purgatorio*. His *The King and the Duke* had a brief off-Broadway showing in June 1955.

PRINCIPAL WORKS: Sophocles' Electra, A Version for the Modern Stage, 1938; Poems, *in* New Directions Yearbook, 1937, 1938; The Idea of a Theatre, 1949; The King and the Duke, a Melodramatic Farce from Huckleberry Finn *in* From the Modern Repertoire, Series Two (ed. E. Bentley) 1952; Dante's Drama of the Mind: A Modern Reading of the Purgatorio, 1953.

ABOUT: Hyman, S. E. The Armed Vision.

FERGUSSON, HARVEY (January 28, 1890-). For autobiographical sketch and list of earlier works and references, see TWENTIETH CENTURY AUTHORS, 1942.

* * *

Harvey Fergusson's autobiography *Home in the West*, which was published in 1945, covers the formative years of his life and ends with his joining the staff of the Washington *Herald*. J. A. Brandt wrote of it in *Book Week*: "Harvey Fergusson's chapters on his boyhood are as fine and as understanding of the problems of sensitive youth as one will encounter in many a day." His recent novels, *Grant of Kingdom* and *The Conquest of Don Pedro*, are set in the Southwest and are full of authentic detail and local color. Fergusson lives in Berkeley, Calif.

ADDITIONAL WORKS: Home in the West, 1945; People and Power: A Study of Political Behavior in America, 1947; Grant of Kingdom, 1950; The Conquest of Don Pedro, 1954.

ABOUT: Fergusson, H. Home in the West.

*FERRERO, GUGLIELMO (July 31, 1871-August 4?, 1942). For biographical sketch and list of earlier works and references, see TWENTIETH CENTURY AUTHORS, 1942.

* * *

Guglielmo Ferrero died in Geneva, Switzerland, at seventy-one.

An exile from Italy, he had been characterized by Mussolini as "anti-Italian, anti-Roman, anti-Fascist, anti-everything alive and strong in this Italy." In Geneva, the historian and his wife (sometimes called "Italy's leading woman intellectual") established "a sort of asylum for Italian, Jewish and other refugees from Axis oppression." Mrs. Ferrero died in 1944.

Ferrero was, as F. A. Hermens has said, "a master of the art of making the past yield its real lessons for the present." John Chamberlain called *The Reconstruction of Europe* "probably the greatest single contribution to clarity in political thinking that our generation has seen." *The Principles of Power*, published here in 1942, is written, says Walter Millis, "with mature historical knowledge, with a considerable literary grace and at moments an almost poetic touch," although Millis questions the profundity of the theories expounded in this third volume of the author's historical trilogy.

The Boston *Globe* characterized Ferrero as "one of those rare composites—an erudite scholar of major proportions yet a man of letters who has both imagination and a positive flair for what in journalese is called 'the human interest touch.'"

ADDITIONAL WORK: Principles of Power, 1942.

ABOUT: Christian Century August 19, 1942; Commonweal October 22, 1943; New Republic March 15, 1943; New York Times August 5, August 6, August 7, 1942.

* fär rā′rō

FERRIL, THOMAS HORNSBY (February 25, 1896-), American poet and essayist, writes: "Thomas Hornsby Ferril was born in Denver, Colo., son of Will C. and Alice M. Ferril. His father was a newspaper editor, naturalist and historian with deep roots in the West, his people having reached

the Missouri River in 1809 and branched out on the Santa Fe and California trails. His mother was born in Rome, N.Y., and came to Colorado in 1886. Her people came from early colonial stock. The Ferrils and Hornsbys, strong abolitionists, were in the thick of the 'border-ruffian' struggles, involved in many episodes of frontier conflict between pro-slavery and anti-slavery forces and guerilla activities. As a child, Thomas Hornsby Ferril became well acquainted with the stories of such people as John Brown, Quantrell, Jesse James, Kit Carson, Jim Bridger, etc., through hearing his father telling the family lore—tales such as the James gang giving protection to the Ferrils preaching at Missouri camp meetings, or John Brown dropping in for dinner, or Jim Bridger, the West's greatest frontiersman, riding at the head of the column with Parson T. J. Ferril, grandfather of Thomas Hornsby Ferril, in the Indian campaigns in Wyoming in the 1860's. Will C. Ferril as a young lawyer and school teacher, came to Colorado in 1878 where he started a newspaper at Silver Cliff. Eugene Field, the poet, urged him to come to Denver, where Ferril subsequently edited various newspapers, wrote history books and became the first curator of the Colorado State Historical Society, building up outstanding collections of material and lecturing to thousands of school children. In 1912 Will C. Ferril acquired the *Rocky Mountain Herald*, Denver's oldest weekly paper, which he published until his death in 1939. The paper was then taken over by Helen Ray Ferril, wife of Thomas Hornsby Ferril, who continues to publish it with her husband's assistance.

"Thomas Hornsby Ferril was graduated from East Denver High School and Colorado College, B.A., with the class of 1918, he being in the army at the time. After serving as a second lieutenant in the Air Service he entered newspaper work in Denver. In 1921 he married Helen Drury Ray of Granville, Ohio. They have one daughter, Anne Folsom (Mrs. MacGregor Folsom), of Berkeley, Calif. Anne is an artist, writer and designer of jewelry. Helen R. Ferril and Anne Folsom collaborate on humorous books: *The Indoor Bird Watcher's Manual, The Second Indoor Bird Watcher's Manual,* and

Anne has written *The Care and Training of Husbands.*

"As a child Thomas Hornsby Ferril had written verses and when he went to work as a reporter on the Denver *Times* he was encouraged by Arthur Chapman, the editor, to write occasional pieces for the editorial page. These were not to his liking but by trial and error he worked toward the serious poetry which subsequently incorporated his attitudes. These early rhymes are listed in the bibliography of 'A Critical Analysis of Thomas Hornsby Ferril' written as a Master's thesis 1950, by Marian Eloise Hollister, Colorado College, Colorado Springs. The newspaper rhymes, however, brought favorable comment from such writers as Spingarn, Woodbridge, and Le Gallienne and a good many of them appeared in *High Passage* which won the competition in the Yale Series of Younger Poets, 1926.

"By 1926 it was clear to Ferril that poetry was his central interest and that he would have to work out some way of life enabling him to pay the bills and keep it going. He declined invitations to go into newspaper work in Chicago and New York and decided against teaching. In 1926 he went to work for the Great Western Sugar Company in Denver where he has since been employed, putting in a full day mostly in agricultural extension work. He writes books, makes motion pictures, radio talks, advertisements, etc., concerned with agronomy, animal husbandry, handling of farm equipment, weed controls, fertilizers, etc. He works with hundreds of farmers, 4-H and FFA boys and girls, veterans groups, etc., with emphasis on new mechanical techniques reducing or eliminating operations previously done largely by hand in the sugar beet fields.

"About the time Ferril went into the agricultural work, the pattern of the poetry writing changed. Fewer poems were written. From 1926 to today the average is around six to eight a year.

"Awards won by Ferril include the Yale Competition for Younger Poets, the *Nation's* prize, the Oscar Blumenthal prize of *Poetry*, a Doubleday-Doran prize, a *Forum* award, an award by the Academy of American Poets, the Fine Arts Medal of the City Club of Denver, the Ridgely Torrence prize of the Poetry Society of America, and two Top-Hand awards by the Colorado Authors League. Honorary degrees have been conferred on Ferril by Colorado College, Colorado University, and Denver University.

"In 1952 the poem 'Words for Time' was given symphonic interpretation by Cecil Effinger, composer. This 'Symphony for Chorus and Orchestra' was performed by the Denver Symphony Orchestra and one hundred voices from the University of Colorado. Ferril has been associated with the Writers Conference at the University of Colorado since its beginning and has taken part in many others.

"The popularity of the *Rocky Mountain Herald* has been a real problem for the Ferrils. Praise of the paper by Bernard De Voto, Bennett Cerf and various radio commentators brought a deluge of subscriptions in the spring of 1953. The Ferrils printed rejection slips and mailed back as many as 600 subscriptions in one week.

"The considerable amount of quick prose writing that has to be done to keep these various activities going might give a misleading idea as to how the poems come into being. They are very carefully done. Sometimes a single poem will go into fifty or more work sheets before it is ready for publication. Fundamental is the theme of the continuity of the human spirit outwearing its own butcheries and betrayals."

* * *

Out of his busy, and in no sense cloistered, poet-editor's life, Ferril has written of the West with intimate knowledge and affection. "His knowledge of Western history," the Western novelist H. L. Davis wrote, "gives his use of it the feeling not of some remote event with period costumes, but of something come from the past to happen over again, with none of its original meaning lost and a new and deeper one added." His poetry reflects a "trans-American" spirit, as Davis calls it. He is a regional poet in that his poetry graphically projects the Rocky Mountain country he knows and loves. But, Sara Henderson Hay says, "above the regionalism and the celebration of a particular geographical locality is that wider quality of universality, 'the long dimension' of man's spirit." Robert Frost has written of Ferril:

> A man as tall as his height
> Plus the height of his home town.
> I know a Denverite
> Who, measured from sea to crown,
> Is one mile five-foot-ten,
> And he swings a commensurate pen.

PRINCIPAL WORKS: *Poems*—High Passage, 1926; Westering, 1934; Trial by Time, 1944; New and Selected Poems, 1952. *Essays*—I Hate Thursday, 1946.

ABOUT: Davis, H. L. *Foreword to* Ferril's New and Selected Poems.

*FEUCHTWANGER, LION (July 7, 1884-   ). For autobiographical sketch and list of earlier works and references, see TWENTIETH CENTURY AUTHORS, 1942.

* * *

Lion Feuchtwanger lives in Pacific Palisades, Calif. After publishing two "topical" wartime novels—*Double, Double, Toil, and Trouble* (dealing with Nazi Germany) and *Simone* (set in occupied France), he turned to writing historical novels again, and here he has enjoyed considerable popular success. For his subjects in these recent novels he has taken three colorful historical figures—Benjamin Franklin, as the diplomat negotiator with Louis XVI and the French court, in *Proud Destiny*; the Spanish painter Goya and his tempestuous love affair with the Duchess of Alba, in *This Is the Hour*; and, in *'Tis Folly to Be Wise*, the French philosopher Jean-Jacques Rousseau, murdered (in Feuchtwanger's version) by his common-law wife's lover, and in general the victim of the covetousness of the members of his household.

Whatever the defects of Feuchtwanger's later work—its excessive length, the frequent distortions of historical fact, the occasional ponderousness of style—many critics would agree with the late Herschel Brickell who called him "the greatest living master of the historical romance." His scholarship is wide and sound, and, thanks to a lively imagination, he has been able to achieve his wish to "take over from the past . . . the fire, not the ashes."

Feuchtwanger's Ph.D. from the University of Munich, revoked by the Nazis, has now been restored. On the personal side, he supplies the following vital statistics (as reported in the New York *Times*): "I have spent fourteen years at school, seventeen days as a war prisoner, five and one-half months in military service, eleven years in Munich, and the remaining years in comparative freedom. I have written eleven dramas, including three good ones, which were never produced, one very mediocre one which has been played 2,346 times and one very bad one which has been wildly acclaimed on 167 German and foreign stages within the last two years. . . . I can write up to seven pages on the typewriter within one hour and write poetry up to four pages during the same time."

* foikt'väng ěr

ADDITIONAL WORKS: Paris Gazette, 1942; Double, Double, Toil, and Trouble, 1943; Simone, 1944; Proud Destiny, 1947; This Is the Hour, 1951; 'Tis Folly to Be Wise, 1953.

ABOUT: Van Gelder, R. Writers and Writing; Saturday Review April 25, 1953; New York Times Book Review May 17, 1953; Saturday Review of Literature May 19, 1951.

*FÉVAL, PAUL, fils (1860-March 15, 1933). For biographical sketch and list of works and references, see TWENTIETH CENTURY AUTHORS, 1942.

* * *

Paul Féval died in Paris at the age of seventy-three. Talvart and Place wrote in their *Bibliographie des Auteurs Modernes de Langue Française* (vol. 5) that all of his work was essentially of a secondary nature, repeating or continuing the themes of his father's more famous novels.

* fā vàl'

FICKE, ARTHUR DAVISON (November 10, 1883-November 30, 1945). For autobiographical sketch and list of works and references, see TWENTIETH CENTURY AUTHORS, 1942.

* * *

Arthur Davison Ficke died at the Hudson (N.Y.) Hospital, after a long illness, at sixty-two. Shortly before his death he wrote letters of farewell to his friends. He was buried on the Ficke estate, "Hardback," at Hillsdale, N.Y.

The late William Rose Benét, who asserted that Ficke wrote "some of the best sonnets in our time, and some fine lyrics," said of his last book of poems, *Tumultuous Shore*: "I do not always agree with Mr. Ficke's conclusions, nor do I always think his phraseology as fresh as it might be. But his poetry is instinct with beauty."

ABOUT: Millay, E. St. V. Letters; New York Times December 4, 1945; Poetry April 1946; Saturday Review of Literature December 22, 1945, January 12, 1946.

FIELD, RACHEL LYMAN (September 19, 1894-March 15, 1942). For biographical sketch and list of works and references, see TWENTIETH CENTURY AUTHORS, 1942.

* * *

ADDITIONAL WORK: Prayer for a Child, 1944.

ABOUT: Kunitz, S. J. & Haycraft, H. Junior Book of Authors (rev. ed.); National Cyclopedia of American Biography (1947).

FIELD, SARA BARD (1882-   ). For
autobiographical sketch and list of
earlier works and references, see TWEN-
TIETH CENTURY AUTHORS, 1942.

* * *

Miss Field writes from Los Gatos, Calif.:
"My husband, Charles Erskine Scott Wood,
died on January 22, 1944. The Huntington
Library desired all papers of every kind
written by or relating to him and to his work,
also to this writer's. I have spent the years
since his death on this project. I prepared
Collected Poems by Charles Erskine Scott
Wood for publication. It contained an extended foreword by me and an introduction
by William Rose Benét, and was published
in 1949 in a beautiful memorial edition.
Aside from a few poems appearing in magazines, I have published little else, but have
a volume of new poems in preparation."

WORKS: The Vintage Festival, 1920; To a Poet
Born on the Edge of Spring, 1925; The Pale Wom-
an, 1927; Vineyard Voices, 1930; Barabbas, 1932;
Darkling Plain, 1936; Selected Poems (with C. E. S.
Wood) 1937; Collected Poems of Charles Erskine
Scott Wood (ed.) 1949.

FIELDING, A. E. For biographical
sketch and list of works and references
see TWENTIETH CENTURY AUTHORS,
1942.

FINEMAN, IRVING (April 9, 1893-   ).
For autobiographical sketch and list of
earlier works and references, see TWEN-
TIETH CENTURY AUTHORS, 1942.

* * *

Irving Fineman writes from Shaftsbury,
Vt.: "In 1941 I went with my family to California to spend the winter writing at a
motion picture studio. Pearl Harbor and the
war kept us out there for several years; and
I wrote for a number of the studios but only
two of my efforts got to the screen, in both
cases after being subjected to devitalizing
revision. I found that while motion picture
producers were intrigued by the idea of getting something fresh from a serious writer,
they almost invariably got cold feet when it
came to putting something unusual or controversial before the cameras. The result is
that a number of my screen stories are still
awaiting liberation by some courageous independent producer, which appears to be increasingly possible as Hollywood is respond-
ing to the success of fine European films.

"I returned to novel writing with the publication of *Ruth* (1949) which, like *Jacob*
and *Hear, Ye Sons*, was another expression
of my profound attachment to that Hebraic
heritage which I still believe is basic to western civilization.

"Working with motion pictures had, however, developed my interest in the dramatic
form, and in 1950 I wrote and had performed
in Los Angeles "Akiba: A Child's Play" in
one act of a novel form, and then finished
my first full length play, "The Fig Tree
Madonna" which won the Stevens Award of
the Dramatists' Alliance at Stanford University in 1951. I am also dramatizing my
Ruth novel for production.

"In 1949 I returned with my family to
our residence in Vermont; but I am now
(December 1952) going to California for
six months on a resident fellowship at the
Huntington Hartford Foundation, where I
shall work on a novel and a play.

"I am more than ever convinced that the
most important function of the artist (like
that of the scientist, which was my first
occupation) is revelation, the essential difference being that whereas the scientist appeals
only to the intelligence, the artist first stirs
the senses and emotions."

ADDITIONAL WORK: Ruth, 1949.

FINGER, CHARLES JOSEPH (December 25, 1869-January 7, 1941). For autobiographical sketch and list of works and
references, see TWENTIETH CENTURY
AUTHORS, 1942.

FINNEY, CHARLES GRANDISON
(December 1, 1905-   ). For autobiographical sketch and list of works and
references, see TWENTIETH CENTURY
AUTHORS, 1942.

* * *

Charles Finney is a newspaperman in Tucson, Ariz. His *Circus of Dr. Lao* remains
his most memorable book. In 1951 the
theatre group ANTA announced that it
would produce a dramatization of the book,
but the plans for the production were cancelled. The editors of the *Saturday Review*
selected it as one of a group of "Books
Worth Re-Reading" in 1953. Joseph Wood
Krutch, reviewing the book at that time, commented that it is one of those rare books
which succeed in creating two worlds—one
of fantasy and one of grim reality—and in
moving back and forth successfully between
them.

ABOUT: Saturday Review July 4, 1953.

FIRBANK, ARTHUR ANNESLEY RONALD (1886-May 21, 1926). For biographical sketch and list of works and references, see TWENTIETH CENTURY AUTHORS, 1942.

* * *

A revival of interest in the works of Ronald Firbank has been marked by the publication of two collections of his eccentric but diverting novels. There has been a considerable amount of critical writing on Firbank in recent years, and Sir Osbert Sitwell has drawn a memorable portrait of him in *Noble Essences*. V. S. Pritchett points out that Firbank's contribution to English literature was an important one: ". . . technically Firbank cleared dead wood out of the English novel, in one or two convulsive laughs; laid down the pattern for contemporary dialogue twenty or thirty years ago and discovered the fact of hysterical private humour —the jokes the mind makes and does not communicate."

ABOUT: Brooke, J. Ronald Firbank; Jones, E. *Introduction to* Three Novels, by R. Firbank; Pritchett, V. S. Books in General; Sitwell, O. Noble Essences; New Yorker December 10, 1949; Time November 21, 1949; University of Toronto Quarterly January 1955.

FIRKINS, OSCAR W. (1864-March 7, 1932). For biographical sketch and list of works and references, see TWENTIETH CENTURY AUTHORS, 1942.

FISCHER, LOUIS (February 29, 1896-), American journalist and political commentator, was born in Philadelphia, son  of David and Shifrah (Kantzapolsky) Fischer. On graduating from the Philadelphia School of Pedagogy in 1916, he taught for a while in the public schools. In 1917 he volunteered for service in the British - sponsored Jewish legion which had been established to help reconquer the Holy Land. After training in Canada, England, France, Italy, and Egypt, Fischer arrived in Palestine and spent fifteen months there. In 1921 he returned to Europe as a correspondent for the New York *Evening Post*. He remained in Europe for the next eighteen years. In his autobiography, *Men and Politics*, Fischer writes: "I did not know that I would stay to see the outbreak of a second world war. My eighteen years in Europe were not years of peace; they were an armistice between two wars."

In 1922 Fischer went to the Soviet Union as a free-lance correspondent. From 1923 to 1945 he was correspondent for the *Nation*. He spent in all some fourteen years in Russia, long enough to observe at first hand many of the most important developments in the Communist government and to become one of the best informed American correspondents on Soviet affairs. Fischer entered the country with a certain amount of sympathy for the Communist experiment. "My vague sympathy for Soviet Russia was," he writes, "first of all a reaction against the chaos, disunity, dishonesty, and despair of the rest of Europe. . . . In Lenin's Russia of 1922, I looked not for a better present but for a brighter future. I also expected clean politics and a foreign policy that rejected conquest, colonies, imperialism, and the lying that is often synonymous with diplomacy." His first books on Russia, particularly his two-volume *Soviets in World Affairs*, were considered "partisan" by some reviewers (Leonard Woolf and the late Simeon Strunsky, among others), but the same reviewers found the book "of great interest and real value" and "essentially an honest piece of work." Generally Fischer's books have been rated honest and informative, written in a sound and straightforward style.

Although Fischer's headquarters were in Moscow, he found with the rise of Hitler and Mussolini that "Europe now interested me more and Russia less." He made frequent visits to Germany, Austria, Czechoslovakia, and Italy. In 1937 he went to Spain to cover the Civil War. He became the first American to join the International Brigade to fight for the Loyalist cause. "I am as proud of that as I am of anything I have done in my life. A nation was bleeding. Machine guns were being mounted on the ivory tower. It was not enough to write."

For a long time, Fischer relates in his autobiography, he had been struggling with his growing disillusionment about Soviet Russia. The Moscow trials had been a crushing blow to him, but his final break with Communism was made in 1939, with the Soviet invasion of Finland and the Russo-German pact. With his family (his Russian-born wife, an author herself, Bertha Mark, and his two sons) he returned to the United States, which has been his home ever since. Fischer has continued to travel widely, however. In recent years he has become especially interested in India and in the cause of Indian independence. He is a great admirer of the late Mahatma Gandhi, whose biography he has written. When not traveling on overseas assignments, Fischer is in great demand in the United States as a lecturer. He is a rugged-looking, square-jawed man with a deep and resonant voice, "a pleasing presence and a strong personality."

PRINCIPAL WORKS: The Soviets in World Affairs, 1930; Why Recognize Russia? 1931; Machines and Men in Russia, 1932; Soviet Journey, 1935; Men and Politics, 1941; Dawn of Victory, 1942; A Week with Gandhi, 1942; Empire, 1943; The Great Challenge, 1946; Gandhi and Stalin, 1947; Life of Mahatma Gandhi, 1952; The Life and Death of Stalin, 1952.

ABOUT: Fischer, L. Men and Politics; Current Biography 1940; Newsweek June 11, 1945; Saturday Review of Literature October 4, 1947, September 16, 1950, August 23, 1952.

FISHER, Mrs. DOROTHEA FRANCES (CANFIELD) (February 17, 1879-). For biographical sketch and list of earlier works and references, see TWENTIETH CENTURY AUTHORS, 1942.

* * *

In 1951 Dorothy Canfield Fisher retired from the editorial board of the Book-of-the-Month Club after having served with it since it was founded twenty-five years before. Except for eliminating a once-a-month trip to New York for Book-of-the-Month meetings and the reading of about 150 books a year for the Club's selections, Mrs. Fisher's retirement has involved no slackening in her many activities. From her farm home at Arlington, Vt., she has continued to write her pleasant, forthright, and indigenously American books. Her later fiction reveals, the *Christian Century*'s reviewer commented in 1949, "a storyteller of consummate skill," a quiet mastery of form and feeling, redeemed from mere slickness by what another reviewer describes as "warm tenderness that doesn't grow mawkish and sentiment that never sugars off into sentimentality." Her most ambitious book in recent years is *Vermont Tradition*, which she subtitled "The Biography of an Outlook on Life." Although she was Kansas-born, Mrs. Fisher is Vermont through-and-through, and her book begins with the statement, "I have lived in Vermont ever since 1763." Out of so strong a family tradition, she has written what Bradford Smith describes as an "informal but richly reflective statement of what Vermont is and what it means." The basic concern of Vermont tradition, Mrs. Fischer writes, "is with the conduct of human life."

Although the book contains few autobiographical details, it is an intensely personal document. The title of the book, she warns her readers, should read: "What Vermont Tradition Means to Me."

ADDITIONAL WORKS: Our Young Folks, 1943; American Portraits, 1946; Four-Square (short stories) 1949; Vermont Tradition, 1953. *Juveniles*—Something Old, Something New, 1949; Our Independence and the Constitution, 1950; Paul Revere and the Minute Men, 1950; A Fair World for All, 1952.

ABOUT: Fisher, D. C. American Portraits, Vermont Tradition; Educational Forum November 1950; Good Housekeeping November 1943; Holiday November 1949; New York Herald Tribune Book Review October 11, 1953; Publishers' Weekly January 13, 1951.

FISHER, HERBERT ALBERT LAURENS (March 21, 1865-April 17, 1940). For biographical sketch and list of works and references, see TWENTIETH CENTURY AUTHORS, 1942.

* * *

ABOUT: Dictionary of National Biography, 1931-40; George, R. E. G. Heirs of Tradition; Ogg, D. Herbert Fisher, 1865-1940.

FISHER, VARDIS (March 31, 1895-). For autobiographical sketch and list of earlier works and references, see TWENTIETH CENTURY AUTHORS, 1942.

* * *

Vardis Fisher writes from Hagerman, Idaho: "Since 1940 my third wife [Opal Laurel Holmes] and I have lived in the beautiful Thousand Springs Valley of Idaho, where without assistance we built our own house and several other structures; planted several thousand trees on a piece of abandoned wasteland; and where in preparation for my historical Testament of Man series of novels have read many additional hundreds of learned books about the past, and written most assiduously, if not always well. Since early 1941 I have published a weekly column in various Idaho newspapers, and its record will show that from the first I said the Nazi and Communist tyrannies were indistinguishable; vigorously opposed most of Roosevelt's foreign policies, which have got us where we are today; and spoke out repeatedly against the Communist conspiracy in this country, much to my loss in both fame and fortune. I mean that I was one of those whom Stalin did not deceive."

In 1952 Fisher published the seventh novel in his Testament of Man series, *The Island of the Innocent*. The series, in which twelve volumes are planned, is a vastly ambitious attempt to trace the history of man's mental and spiritual development from its earliest sources to the modern age. The first five novels are prehistoric. They begin with *Darkness and the Deep* (1943) in which Fisher describes the "dawning of the human intellect" among sub-human, ape-like creatures. He continues his anthropological survey moving from Neanderthal and Cro-Magnon man into the era of pagan worship, then to Hebrew, Greek, Roman, and early Christian history. The eleventh volume, according to Fisher's plan, will consider the struggles of the human mind for liberation in the Middle Ages and early Renaissance, and the final volume will be "the story of one man's life in our time." For this tremendous project Fisher has done extensive research. A frequently voiced criticism of his work, indeed, has been the complaint that the scholarship has tended to overweigh the narrative itself. It is, of course, too early to expect any comprehensive critical evaluation of the Testament of Man. Fisher has written of his work: "I do not imagine that my efforts will be more than an attempt to pioneer in a most exciting and very difficult field. Novelists some day will do better by those rich stores of scholarship which so many men and women, laboring obscurely in devotion to truth, have put before us."

In his original sketch Fisher referred to himself as an atheist; he now feels that "agnostic" is a more accurate term.

ADDITIONAL WORKS: The Mothers, 1943. *Non-Fiction*—God or Caesar, 1953. *Testament of Man*—Darkness and the Deep, 1943; Golden Rooms, 1944; Intimations of Eve, 1946; Adam and the Serpent, 1947; Divine Passion, 1948; The Valley of Vision, 1951; The Island of the Innocent, 1952.

ABOUT: Snell, G. D. Shapers of American Fiction, 1798-1947; Time August 12, 1946.

FITTS, DUDLEY (April 28, 1903-).

For biographical sketch and list of earlier works and references, see TWENTIETH CENTURY AUTHORS, 1942.

* * *

Dudley Fitts has been instructor in English at Phillips Academy, in Andover, Mass., since 1941. In 1948 he was awarded a grant from the American Academy of Arts and Letters and in the same year he was appointed to the Emilie Belden Cochran Foundation. Fitts married Cornelia Butler Hewitt in 1939 and they have a son and a daughter.

Fitts's most important literary work in recent years has been his translation (with Robert Fitzgerald) of the *Oedipus Rex* of Sophocles—a translation which, according to Gilbert Highet, "deserves both emulation and praise." He has also translated a number of poems from the Spanish.

ADDITIONAL WORKS: (ed.) Greek Plays in Modern Translation, 1947; (tr., with R. Fitzgerald) Sophocles' Oedipus Rex, 1949; (tr.) Aristophanes' Lysistrata 1953.

ABOUT: Gregory, H. & Zaturenska, M. History of American Poetry, 1900-1940.

FITZGERALD, FRANCIS SCOTT KEY

(September 24, 1896-December 21, 1940). For biographical sketch and list of works and references, see TWENTIETH CENTURY AUTHORS, 1942.

* * *

The F. Scott Fitzgerald legend, freely circulated even before his death, has taken on new dimension with the publication, in the past decade, of a number of serious, sympathetic, and illuminating studies of the man and his work. The legend—its tinsel-glittering hero and its pathetic conclusion with his death in Hollywood as a literary hack, his genius burnt out—is being replaced by a sober, sharply-drawn picture of a novelist of real stature, author of at least one novel, *The Great Gatsby*, which is everywhere recognized as a masterpiece of twentieth century American fiction.

In 1945 Edmund Wilson edited a collection of Fitzgerald's autobiographical papers and notebooks under the title *The Crack-Up*. The book was a candid examination of "the failure of a life's illusion." Mark Schorer wrote: "This cool analysis of a nervous breakdown and the emotional exhaustion which followed it is already a classic of literary self-revelation." In 1950 Budd Schulberg made Fitzgerald the hero of his novel *The Disenchanted*, drawing a vivid portrait of his last years in Hollywood, where Schulberg had known him. In 1951 Arthur Mizener's *The Far Side of Paradise*, the first full-length biography of Fitzgerald, appeared. It was a detailed and scholarly book, thoroughly documented with Fitzgerald's own records of his life, the recollections of his friends, and the papers and recollections of his daughter, now grown up and married.

Fitzgerald's wife Zelda died, in 1948, in a fire that swept a hospital for mental and nervous diseases in Asheville, N.C., where she had been a patient for a number of years.

ADDITIONAL WORK: The Crack-Up, 1945.

ABOUT: Aldridge, J. W. After the Lost Generation; Fitzgerald, F. S. The Crack-Up; Kazin, A. (ed.) F. Scott Fitzgerald: The Man and His Work; Mizener, A. The Far Side of Paradise; O'Hara, J. Preface to The Portable F. Scott Fitzgerald.

FITZGERALD, ROBERT (STUART)

(October 12, 1910-   ), American poet and translator, writes: "Though I was born in

Geneva, N.Y., my parents moved while I was still an infant to Springfield, Ill., where I spent my childhood and went through school. My mother died before I was three, of puerperal fever after the birth of my brother Bernard Montague. My brother died in the influenza epidemic of 1918. We were then living in the home of my grandmother while my father practiced law. In 1919, in consequence of an injury that had crippled him before, my father became an invalid with tuberculosis of the hip bone. He was nearly bed-ridden for about eight years; in 1927, under violet ray treatment, he began a recovery that was cut short by his death from pneumonia in 1929. I went to St. Agnes parochial school and to Springfield High School, usually passing through the State capitol building on my way. The old Edwards place (the house of Ninian Edwards) where Lincoln was married stood half a block from our house when I was a child. We had also, and used in the kitchen, a table that my grandfather had acquired at an auction of Lincoln's and Herndon's office furnishings; the initials A.L. were deeply carved in it.

"In high school I began writing, with the encouragement of Susan Wilcox, who had been Vachel Lindsay's teacher and friend, and of Elizabeth Graham. I played tennis and football for the school and in the summers went to Culver Naval School, where I rowed on the crew and boxed. In 1928, when Vachel Lindsay returned to Springfield to live, he spoke kindly of my verses and was afterwards kind and hospitable to me. The year 1928-29 I spent at the Choate School in Connecticut, entering Harvard in the fall. In 1931, at Vachel's suggestion, I sent a group of poems to Poetry and they were awarded the Midland Authors Prize for that year. By that time I was at Trinity College, Cambridge, studying philosophy and the classical languages. The winter vacation I spent in Switzerland and called on Ezra Pound at Rapallo; the spring vacation I spent in Paris reading Flaubert. I returned to Harvard to take my degree with my class in 1933. T. S. Eliot, who was giving the Norton lectures at Harvard that year, accepted two of my poems for the Criterion. I gave up my intention to enter the Law School and thought of going to Paris to study philosophy under Gilson at the Sorbonne. I found myself without the means to do this, and in the fall, through the good offices of my uncle, John Stuart, I was fortunate enough to get a job as a reporter on the New York Herald Tribune.

"My year and a half of work on the newspaper were intensely interesting to me and intensely frustrating at the same time, for the momentum I had gathered in the five or six years preceding would have carried me further in poetry, I felt, had it not been deflected. I worked hard and learned much from the big-city savvy of Stanley Walker, then city editor; but I never learned to write at high speed. In the spring of 1935 I quit. That summer the MacDowell Colony at Peterborough, N.H., offered me a refuge, and there I put together my first book of poems and worked on a translation of Euripides' Alcestis with my friend Dudley Fitts, who had been my teacher at Choate. Both were published late in the fall. Early in 1936 Time gave me a job as a writer, first of book notes and then of business and financial news until, late in 1937, the art department became vacant. I wrote that section of Time for the next two years, and edited the book section in 1939-40. These three years of journalism were made possible for me largely by the friendship and literary sympathy of T. S. Matthews, who was then editor in charge of the critical sections of the magazine.

"In the summer of 1940, seeing that the German army was in Paris, and having saved enough money to live on for a year, I resigned from Time and repaired to Santa Fe, N.M., to live quietly and collect myself in the face of the world's difficulties and my own. I wrote a translation of Sophocles' Oedipus at Colonus and nearly completed a second book of poems I returned to Time late in 1941 and stayed as a writer and for a time as an editor until the spring of 1943, when I received a commission in the Navy. After training at Fort Schuyler (Harold A. Stassen was commander of my battalion) I was assigned to a shore station in New York and, late in 1944, to the staff of the Commander-in-Chief, Pacific Ocean Areas, first at Pearl Harbor and then at Guam. I did no writing during these years except for a journal, later lost.

"Baptized and brought up a Roman Catholic, I had lapsed from all Catholic practice before I was twenty-five. I had married, in a civil ceremony in December 1935 Eleanor Green, a writer of fiction. In 1946 this marriage was ended by divorce. At the same time I returned to the faith and practice of the Catholic Church, under whose law it had not been a valid marriage. I began writing book reviews for *Time* and continued this until 1949, at the same time teaching literature at Sarah Lawrence College. In 1947 I married Sarah Morgan, of New York, and we have had six children. For two years, 1948 and 1949, I served as poetry reviewer for the *New Republic*. In 1949 I moved with my family to Connecticut. In the same year a translation of Sophocles' *Oedipus Rex*, done in collaboration with Dudley Fitts, was published. In 1950-51 I served as resident fellow in creative writing at Princeton, in the summers of 1951 and 1952 as a fellow of the School of Letters, Indiana University. At the present writing I have in hand a verse translation of the *Odyssey* and a long poem of my own, both of which will take several years to complete. I received a Guggenheim Fellowship, with the help of which in 1953 I moved with my family to Italy, where we remain."

* * *

As a translator from the Greek and as a poet in his own right, Robert Fitzgerald has won praise for the swiftness, delicacy, and precision of his work. Louise Bogan wrote, in her review of his *Wreath for the Sea*: "Fitzgerald's grasp of classic resonance and balance brings him out always on the side of simplicity; he is incapable of either rhetoric or bombast. His effects are sometimes rather muffled, but soon the expected translucence returns, and we are back in that humane region where the gravity of learning and the seriousness of art function, never out of sight of life." His translations of the *Antigone* (with Dudley Fitts) and the *Oedipus at Colonus* are considered worthy successors in the Sophoclean trilogy to Yeats' translation of *Oedipus the King*—producing, George F. Whicher wrote, "an idiom uncolored by colloquialisms and yet like the colloquial in its cadence and fluidity and its power to respond to the demands of any conceivable occasion."

PRINCIPAL WORKS: Poems, 1935; Euripides' Alcestis: An English Version (with D. Fitts) 1936; Sophocles' Antigone: An English Version (with D. Fitts) 1939; Sophocles' Oedipus at Colonus: An English Version, 1941; A Wreath for the Sea (poems) 1944; Sophocles' Oedipus Rex: An English Version (with D. Fitts) 1949.

ABOUT: Hoehn, M. Catholic Authors, II; Nation April 29, 1944; Poetry May 1944.

FITZMAURICE-KELLY, JAMES (June 20, 1858-November 30, 1923). For biographical sketch and list of works and references, see TWENTIETH CENTURY AUTHORS, 1942.

FLANDRAU, CHARLES MACOMB (December 9, 1871-March 28, 1938). For biographical sketch and list of works and references, see TWENTIETH CENTURY AUTHORS, 1942.

* * *

ABOUT: Newsweek December 17, 1951.

FLAVIN, MARTIN (November 2, 1883-   ). For autobiographical sketch and list of earlier works and references, see TWENTIETH CENTURY AUTHORS, 1942.

* * *

Martin Flavin writes: "In 1938 I turned away from the medium of the theatre to the novel; and to date I have written four: *Mr. Littlejohn, Corporal Cat, Journey in the Dark*, which won both the Harper and Pulitzer prizes, and *The Enchanted*. And lastly, a travel book on Africa, *Black and White*. In this field I have been a contributor to *Harper's Magazine*. I am currently engaged in the preparation of some autobiographical material.

"In 1946 I disposed of my home 'Spindrift' on the coast near Carmel, since when I have been resident at Pebble Beach, Calif., which is my present address."

The prize-winning novel *Journey in the Dark* is the life-story of a small-town, Middle Western American who acquires a fortune in business at the price of his integrity, and who finds himself then "a lonely man going nowhere in the dark." Horace Reynolds wrote of the book in the New York *Times*: "Setting aside some echoes of Dos Passos' 'newsreels,' which clot the even flow of the novel's action, Mr. Flavin is himself; he isn't trying to write like somebody else. He has taken a superficially uninteresting man and made him interesting. That alone is no mean achievement. He has also made a plain Middle Western business man a symbol of all these United States."

ADDITIONAL WORKS: Journey in the Dark, 1943; The Enchanted, 1947; Black and White, 1950.

ABOUT: Current Biography 1943; Publishers' Weekly October 2, 1943; Saturday Review of Literature May 6, 1944.

FLECKER, JAMES ELROY (November 5, 1884-January 3, 1915). For biographical sketch and list of works and references, see TWENTIETH CENTURY AUTHORS, 1942.

* * *

ABOUT: Mercer, T. S. James Elroy Flecker, from School to Samarkand; Commentary May 1951; Fortnightly June 1946.

FLEMING, PETER (May 31, 1907-). For biographical sketch and list of earlier works and references, see TWENTIETH CENTURY AUTHORS, 1942.

* * *

Peter Fleming writes the theatre reviews for the *Spectator* and contributes articles to a variety of British and American periodicals. His novel *The Sixth Column*, subtitled "A Singular Tale of Our Times," was a light-hearted satire on life in present-day Britain, described by a reviewer in the *New Statesman and Nation* as "skilfully blending *Punch* and John Buchan."

ADDITIONAL WORK: The Sixth Column, 1951.

"FLEMING, WALDO." See WILLIAMSON, T. R.

FLETCHER, JOHN GOULD (January 3, 1886-May 10, 1950). For autobiographical sketch and list of earlier works and references, see TWENTIETH CENTURY AUTHORS, 1942.

* * *

John Gould Fletcher was found drowned in a pool near his home near Little Rock, Ark., an apparent suicide.

Before his death at sixty-four he had been at work on an anthology of Southern poetry, and had planned to collaborate on an historical work with his wife. In *Johnswood*, written after his death, his widow explained his final illness and death as the results of the rage and despair of a sensitive man confronted with "the Machine Age and its machine wars."

"At heart he was more of a traditionalist than he intended to be or would have been willing to acknowledge during the rebellious early stage of his career," says Donald David-son. "In his devotion to his art there was a certain fierceness that, while it isolated him, also must have sustained him. Independent to the last degree, outspoken and frank, uncompromising where his principles were involved, yet wholly without guile, he won all that he won by the test of merit alone."

In his later work Fletcher grew away from the Imagist experiments of his youth. *Burning Mountain* (1946) expressed, in the opinion of John Holmes, "a powerful sense of the old space and quiet of the Southwest, which is his home place, and a mature realization of the vastness of time."

ADDITIONAL WORKS: Burning Mountain, 1946; Arkansas, 1947.

ABOUT: Gregory, H. & Zaturenska, M. A History of American Poetry; Simon, C. M. Johnswood; Books Abroad Autumn 1950; New York Times May 11, 1950; Poetry March 1947, December 1950; South Atlantic Quarterly January 1953; Southwest Review Summer 1953.

FLETCHER, JOSEPH SMITH (February 7, 1863-January 31, 1935). For biographical sketch and list of works and references, see TWENTIETH CENTURY AUTHORS, 1942.

FLEXNER, ABRAHAM (November 13, 1866-). For biographical sketch and list of works and references, see TWENTIETH CENTURY AUTHORS, 1942.

* * *

Abraham Flexner, who earlier in his life had administered the $600,000,000 Rockefeller General Education Board and headed the Institute for Advanced Studies at Princeton, celebrated his eighty-fifth birthday by attending classes at Columbia University, where he studied European history and Soviet public administration. In his very active retirement he has also written two sound biographies of prominent American educators, Henry S. Pritchett and Daniel Coit Gilman, and a brief but comprehensive review of the work of educational foundations in the United States.

ADDITIONAL WORKS: Henry S. Pritchett, 1944; Daniel Coit Gilman, 1946; Funds and Foundations, 1952.

ABOUT: Newsweek November 26, 1951.

FLINT, FRANK STEWART (December 19, 1885-). For biographical sketch and list of works and references, see TWENTIETH CENTURY AUTHORS, 1942.

FLYNN, JOHN THOMAS (October 25, 1882-). For biographical sketch and list of earlier works and references, see TWENTIETH CENTURY AUTHORS, 1942.

* * *

John T. Flynn was an associate editor of *Collier's* magazine from 1937 to 1942. He served on the New York City Board of Higher Education from 1935 to 1944. Since 1940 when he published his bitter attack on Franklin D. Roosevelt in *Country Squire in the White House,* he has been one of the most vociferous critics of New and Fair Deal policies, internationalism, and all political organizations and programs which are generally termed "liberal." His books have been reviewed favorably by newspapers and magazines which support the same political line and unfavorably by those which do not.

In his recent books *While You Slept* and *The Lattimore Story,* Flynn has been especially critical of United States foreign policy in the Far East. Of *While You Slept,* the New York *Times* wrote: "John T. Flynn has shed much heat but little light on one of the great issues of our time."

ADDITIONAL WORKS: As We Go Marching, 1944; Meet Your Congress, 1944; Epic of Freedom, 1947; The Roosevelt Myth, 1948; The Road Ahead, 1949; While You Slept: Our Tragedy in Asia and Who Made It, 1951; The Lattimore Story, 1953.

"FLYNT, JOSIAH." See WILLARD, J. F.

FOERSTER, NORMAN (April 14, 1887-). For biographical sketch and list of earlier works and references, see TWENTIETH CENTURY AUTHORS, 1942.

* * *

In 1944 Norman Foerster resigned from the University of Iowa, where he had been director of the School of Letters and professor of English since 1930. Two years later he published, for the University of North Carolina, a study of the place of the humanities in higher education, *Humanities and the Common Man.* Stringfellow Barr said of the book: "Norman Foerster has again struck a blow for a kind of liberal education in our country that would be worthy of a civilized society. His book is brief, cogent, spacious-minded, and eloquent." Foerster was visiting professor of English at Duke University from 1948 to 1951. His home is in Santa Barbara, Calif.

ADDITIONAL WORKS: Humanities and the Common Man: The Democratic Role of the State Universities, 1946; (ed. with H. H. Clark) Lowell, J. R. Representative Selections, 1947.

*FOGAZZARO, ANTONIO (March 25, 1842-March 7, 1911). For biographical sketch and list of works and references, see TWENTIETH CENTURY AUTHORS, 1942.

* * *

ABOUT: Columbia Dictionary of Modern European Literature.

* fō gät tsä′rō

*FÖLDES, JOLÁN (1903-). For autobiographical sketch and list of earlier works and references, see TWENTIETH CENTURY AUTHORS, 1942.

* * *

Jolán Földes lives in London. She frequently contributes short stories and articles to British periodicals, and her novels are popular in England. In the United States, however, only one of her recent works has had any particular attention. This was *Golden Earrings*—a light novel, "with continental flavor," as one reviewer described it, about a British officer who, while escaping from the Nazis, meets and becomes romantically involved with a glamorous gypsy. The novel was made into a motion picture starring Marlene Dietrich.

ADDITIONAL WORKS: Moving Freely, 1944; Women and Love (short stories) 1945; Golden Earrings, 1946; Make You a Fine Wife, 1947; Mind Your Own Murder, 1948; The Fairest Apple, 1950; Imperial Tokay, 1950; Fain Would I Change, 1951.

* fûl′děsh

FOOTE, SHELBY (1916-), American novelist, was born and raised in Greenville, Miss., and attended the University of North Carolina. He spent five years in the army and Marine Corps, plus one year in the Mississippi National Guard. In the army, Foote rose from sergeant to captain, but was courtmartialed and "kicked completely out of the army" during service  in Northern Ireland, because he went to see his girl in Belfast. He later married the girl. Returning to the United States, he worked as an Associated Press reporter for six months before joining the Marine Corps (which knew all about his army experience).

Advancing rapidly as a writer, Foote published his first book in 1949 and his fifth in 1954. *Tournament*, the story of a delta planter and his family, was received as a promising first novel. When *Follow Me Down* appeared in 1950, there was again praise of his gifts, and of his "stabbing use of language," together with criticism of a youthful virtuosity and verbal extravagance.

On the occasion of the publication of *Shiloh* (1952), Harvey Breit interviewed the author, describing him as "an attractive, tough-minded fellow of thirty-five." Foote's grandfather had fought at Shiloh. The new book was his first historical novel. No character in *Shiloh*, said Foote, "says or does anything except what I have accurate evidence of his having said or done." "A superb story of war," wrote the *Saturday Review of Literature*. "Here's one 'promising' novelist who may be said to have arrived. All of Shelby Foote's three earlier novels have worn elements of distinction. Now in *Shiloh*, he has written a *tour de force* of genuine stature." "Mr. Foote writes a clear, unaffected, and telling prose," added the New York *Times*. Most recent is *Jordan County* (1954), four short stories and three short novels, ranging in time but all with a background of Bristol, county seat of Jordan in the Mississippi delta.

Of his working habits, Foote says, "I work straight through the day, every day. I get up to New York maybe about twice a year. The rest of the time I'm working straight through, eight hours, twelve hours, it doesn't matter. And I don't have any hobbies or any other interests. Writing is a religion with me." And of influences: "Stephen Crane, Stendhal, Tolstoy all helped me. I'm not afraid of what writers did before me. Writing is a progressive thing."

PRINCIPAL WORKS: Tournament, 1949; Follow Me Down, 1950; Love in a Dry Season, 1951; Shiloh, 1952; Jordan County: a Landscape in Narrative, 1954.

ABOUT: New York Times Book Review April 27, 1952.

FORBES, ESTHER (1894?-). For biographical sketch and list of earlier works and references, see TWENTIETH CENTURY AUTHORS, 1942.

* * *

Esther Forbes' biography of Paul Revere, published in 1942, was a best seller and in 1943 received the Pulitzer prize for history. Since that time critics and the reading public have come to expect books of prizewinning calibre from her, and she has not disappointed them. Her juvenile story

Johnny Tremain won the Newbery award, and one reviewer suggested that her young eighteenth-century American hero could join those immortals of boys' fiction—Jim Hawkins and Huck Finn. *The Running of the Tide*, an historical novel set in Salem in the period between the Revolution and the War of 1812, won the M.G.M. novel award. And *Rainbow on the Road*, a fresh and unpretentious story of life in the New England of the 1830's, was a Literary Guild selection. Edmund Fuller considered it "a masterpiece of its kind, a high water mark in Miss Forbes' distinguished career," and Henry Commager praised it heartily for "the good humor, the high spirits, the sense of the richness of life and the beauty of the land."

Miss Forbes lives with a sister and a brother in Worcester, Mass. Her main interests—"listed in ascending order of importance"—are gardening, travel, and people.

ADDITIONAL WORKS: Johnny Tremain (juvenile) 1943; America's Paul Revere (juvenile) 1946; The Boston Book, 1947; The Running of the Tide, 1948; Rainbow on the Road, 1954.

ABOUT: Van Gelder, R. Writers and Writing; New York Times Book Review January 31, 1954; Newsweek December 29, 1947.

FORBES, Mrs. ROSITA (TORR) (1893-). For biographical sketch and list of works and references, see TWENTIETH CENTURY AUTHORS, 1942.

* * *

Miss Forbes, true to her plans announced before World War II, has settled down to live in the home she built in the Bahamas, at Eleuthera. During the war she traveled widely as a lecturer for the War Office and the Air Ministry. Since then she has written three volumes of autobiography, crammed with the details of her busy and exciting life, and several studies of the West Indies.

ADDITIONAL WORKS: Prodigious Caribbean, 1940; Gypsy in the Sun, 1944; Appointment with Destiny, 1946; Henry Morgan, Pirate, 1946; Appointment in the Sun, 1947; Islands in the Sun, 1950.

ABOUT: Forbes, R. Gypsy in the Sun, Appointment with Destiny, Appointment in the Sun.

FORD, FORD MADOX (Ford Madox Hueffer) (1873-June 26, 1939). For biographical sketch and list of works and references, see TWENTIETH CENTURY AUTHORS, 1942.

* * *

In 1950 and 1951 the republication of Ford's massive Tietjens tetralogy (under the title *Parade's End*) and his *Good Soldier* signaled the beginning of a Ford Madox Ford revival, after more than two decades during which his work had been largely ignored. Actually the renewal of interest in Ford began with the publication of *New Directions 1942*, which was dedicated to Ford's memory and contained a symposium, by a number of distinguished literary figures, on his life and work. There it was pointed out repeatedly that Ford was a major novelist, a "novelist's novelist," and that his work marked an important step forward in the history of the English novel. Caroline Gordon has said: "Ford brought to perfection at least one major process: the time shift. . . . He was labelled a stylist, but I think that his novels are chiefly remarkable for their form. He succeeded in doing the thing that Poe said could not be done. He produced the long work whose tensions are as nicely adjusted, whose tone is as sustained as that of the short tale or lyric poem."

ABOUT: Goldring, D. South Lodge, Trained for Genius (in England: The Last Pre-Raphaelite); Macaulay, R. *Introduction to* Ford's Parade's End; Schorer, M. *Introduction to* Ford's The Good Soldier (1951); America October 21, 1950; Dictionary of National Biography 1931-1940; Nation July 30, 1949; National Review August 1948: New Directions 1942; New Republic April 4, 1955; New Statesman and Nation April 20, 1946.

"FORD, LESLIE." See BROWN, Z. J.

FORD, WORTHINGTON CHAUNCEY (February 16, 1858-March 7, 1941). For biographical sketch and list of works and references, see TWENTIETH CENTURY AUTHORS, 1942.

* * *

ABOUT: National Cyclopedia of American Biography (1948).

FORESTER, CECIL SCOTT (August 27, 1899-). For biographical sketch and list of earlier works and references, see TWENTIETH CENTURY AUTHORS, 1942.

* * *

C. S. Forester's permanent home is in Berkeley, Calif., but, in spite of an attack of arterio-sclerosis that has left him a semi-invalid, he divides the year pleasantly by spending June in England, October in New York, and the rest in California. He was divorced from his first wife in 1944 and in 1947 married Dorothy Foster. With

the motion picture successes of the redoubtable and perennial Captain Horatio Hornblower and *The African Queen*, a grand spoof on adventure stories, which was directed by John Huston and starred Humphrey Bogart and Katharine Hepburn, Forester has made a secure place for himself in Hollywood. The demand for his Hornblower books is unceasing. Forester planned to stop writing them in 1946, but, he observed six years and several books later: "The odd thing was and is that the Hornblower plots keep coming, without any labor. You can't just look a gift horse in the mouth."

The Good Shepherd, the story of fortyeight desperate hours in the life of a North Atlantic convoy during World War II, was highly praised on its publication in 1955 as a dual Book-of-the-Month Club selection.

In a talk with Lewis Nichols of the New York *Times Book Review*, Forester (selfdescribed as "gray suit, nondescript, with glasses") revealed that "Hornblower's final adventure has been written and is in my agent's safe, against some day when I can't pay the rent or am dead." Forester planned to follow *The Good Shepherd* with a naval history of the War of 1812.

ADDITIONAL WORKS: Poo-Poo and the Dragons (juvenile) 1942; Rifleman Dodd, and The Gun (two novels) 1942; The Ship, 1943; Commodore Hornblower, 1945; Lord Hornblower, 1946; The Sky and the Forest, 1948; Mr. Midshipman Hornblower, 1950; Randall and the River of Time, 1950; Lieutenant Hornblower, 1952; Hornblower and the Atropos, 1953; The Barbary Pirates (juvenile) 1953; The Good Shepherd, 1955.

ABOUT: Fortnightly June 1945; New York Herald Tribune Book Review March 30, 1952; New York Times Book Review April 6, 1952, April 3, 1955; Saturday Evening Post April 27, 1946, March 6, 1948.

FORSTER, EDWARD MORGAN (1879-). For biographical sketch and list of earlier works and references, see TWENTIETH CENTURY AUTHORS, 1942.

* * *

The revival, or more properly the discovery, of E. M. Forster's splendid novels, was slow in coming to America. Although his *Passage to India* was known and highly admired here, it was not until 1943, when two American publishers began issuing his early novels and a number of critical studies of his work began to appear, that Forster's true stature as a novelist was recognized. Although he has published no novel since 1924, his position as one of the major novelists of the first half of the twentieth century is unchallenged.

In 1946 Forster gave up his Surrey home in the village of Abinger. He now lives in Cambridge. He writes busily, but at his own pace, in a variety of forms. His lectures (he visited the United States on a lecture tour in 1947) are restrained and disarming little essays written and delivered in his characteristically easy, graceful style. During World War II and after, he broadcast many of them over the B.B.C. Irving Howe sums up their excellences: "an utter freedom from stuffiness, an enviable assurance in dealing with the English literary tradition, a readiness to converse with the reader on terms of intellectual equality, and a shy humility—that famous minor tone—which is immensely pleasing and, in this assertive age, frequently moving." Forster has also written a pageant-play (*England's Pleasant Land*), a script for the film *Diary for Timothy,* and (with Eric Crozier) the libretto for Benjamin Britten's opera *Billy Budd.*

Forster revisited India in 1945 to attend a PEN Club conference at Jaipur. In 1953 he published, in *The Hill of Devi,* a record of his own Indian experiences of an earlier day, when in 1921 he had served briefly as secretary to the Maharajah of Dewas Senior. Since this was the period in which he was preparing to write *A Passage to India,* his recollections have heightened interest. But in their own right they stand as a brief but sharp and dramatically effective portrait of an Indian prince and his court.

In January 1953 Forster was awarded membership in the Order of Companions of Honour by Queen Elizabeth II.

ADDITIONAL WORKS: Virginia Woolf, 1942; Two Cheers for Democracy, 1951; The Hill of Devi, 1953.

ABOUT: Bowen, E. Collected Impressions; Brown, E. K. Forms of Modern Fiction, The Rhythm of the Novel; Connolly, C. The Condemned Playground; Forster, E. M. The Hill of Devi; Johnstone, J. K. The Bloomsbury Group; Trilling, L. E. M. Forster; Warren, A. A Rage for Order; Atlantic Monthly January 1949; Dublin Review October 1946; Nation August 7, 1943; New Republic September 6, 1943; New York Times Book Review June 29, 1947, June 19, 1949; New Yorker May 3, 1947; Saturday Review of Literature August 28, 1943; Time November 19, 1951.

"FORSYTHE, ROBERT." See CRICH-TON, K.

FORT, CHARLES HOY (August 9, 1874-May 3, 1932). For biographical sketch and list of works and references, see TWENTIETH CENTURY AUTHORS, 1942.

FOSDICK, HARRY EMERSON (May 24, 1878-), American clergyman, writes: "I was born in Buffalo, N.Y. My grandfather had been Superintendent of Education there, and my father also was a teacher—the combined span of their service in Buffalo's public schools extending over eighty years. At first I intended to follow this family tradition, but in my young manhood religion became of dominant concern to me in working out my philosophy of life. I was a rebel against conventional religion and had a tough struggle out of post-adolescent atheism into Christian faith. In the end, after graduating from Colgate University and Union Theological Seminary, I entered the ministry.

Pach

"After eleven years in the First Baptist Church of Montclair, N.J., I was called to a professorship in the Union Theological Seminary, and combined with it the position of stated preacher at the First Presbyterian Church in New York City. Then the Fundamentalists got after me and, attacking my liberalism which I refused to compromise, made that preaching position untenable. Resigning with regret from the service of a congregation which had unanimously supported me against the attacks of William Jennings Bryan and his fundamentalist cohorts, I accepted the call of the Park Avenue Baptist congregation to lead them in building an interdenominational church on Riverside Drive. Beginning in 1926, for twenty years I continued my professorship at the seminary and my ministry at the Riverside Church.

"Intending first to be a teacher and then deciding to be a preacher, I had the privilege of being both, but I do not recall that I had ever intended to be an author. I began writing, not with any expectation of a cordial welcome from readers, but rather to discover, by putting it down in black and white, what I honestly thought myself. So, for example, early in my ministry I wrote *The Meaning of Prayer* and sent it to my publishers saying that I was sure two thousand copies would be all they would need to print. They tell me now that the book has appeared in American, British, Indian, and Australian editions and has been translated into seventeen foreign languages. With such encouragement I have kept on writing and, somewhat shamefacedly, I acknowledge the authorship of twenty-five books.

"Four major influences, I suspect, have most affected the content of my writing. First, my own personal struggle for a reasonable Christian faith, both against the reactionary dogmatism of the orthodox and against the skepticism of the atheists. Second, my experience in radio preaching, which brought me letters from all over the world—about 125,000 annually—and aroused a natural desire to write about the problems they presented. Third, intimate personal counseling, which I called 'the Protestant confessional,' on which I spent a large portion of my time, and from which came endless stimulus to tackle in a book individual problems of faith and life. Fourth, contact with students at the seminary, presenting in personal form the critical needs of the churches and their ministers.

"Now in my seventy-fifth year, I have retired from active responsibility as a teacher and preacher, but I find that I cannot retire from writing. Sometimes I think it is a bad habit, but I am unable to break it."

* * *

On the occasion of Dr. Fosdick's seventy-fifth birthday, the Union Theological Seminary created a Harry Emerson Fosdick Visiting Professorship "to strengthen the training of the present and oncoming leaders of the Christian Church so as to enable them in their generation, as Dr. Fosdick has in this generation, to interpret the abiding truths and experiences of Christian faith in terms relevant and compelling to contemporary life." A liberal "fighting" minister, he is one of the best-known and most highly honored of American clergymen. Now in retirement, there is no slackening in his activity. He writes rapidly. In addition to sermons and lectures, he has been known to turn out as many as three books in one year. He is active in civic and social groups. Robust and ruddy-faced, he walks five miles every day near his home in Bronxville, N.Y., where he lives with his wife, the former Florence Whitney, their widowed daughter, and their two grandchildren. He spends his summers in Boothbay Harbor, Maine.

PRINCIPAL WORKS: The Second Mile, 1908; The Assurance of Immortality, 1913; The Manhood of the Master, 1913; The Meaning of Prayer, 1915; The Meaning of Faith, 1917; The Meaning of Service, 1920; Christianity and Progress, 1922; Twelve Tests of Character, 1923; The Modern Use of the Bible, 1924; Adventurous Religion, 1926; A Pilgrimage to Palestine, 1927; As I See Religion, 1932; The Hope of the World, 1933; The Secret of Victorious Living, 1934; The Power to See It Through, 1935; Successful Christian Living, 1937; A Guide to Understanding the Bible, 1938; Living Under Tension, 1941; On Being a Real Person, 1943; A Great Time to Be Alive, 1944; On Being Fit to Live With, 1946; The Man from Nazareth, 1949; Rufus Jones Speaks to Our Times (ed.) 1951; Great Voices of the Reformation (ed.) 1952; A Faith for Tough Times, 1952.

ABOUT: Finkelstein, L. (ed.) American Spiritual Biographies; Jones, E. D. American Preachers of Today; Jones, E. D. Royalty of the Pulpit; Lotz, P. (ed.) Creative Personalities; Rusterholtz, W. P. American Heretics and Saints; Shepherd, W. C. Great Preachers as Seen by a Journalist; Strong, S. (ed.) What I Owe to My Father; American Magazine March 1923, May 1926; Christian Century June 20, 1945; Churchman October 11, 1930; Congregationalist April 26, 1923; Coronet December 1947; Current Biography 1940; Epworth Herald January 19, 1929; Homiletic Review February 1931; Literary Digest November 1, 1930; Newsweek April 8, 1946; New York Times Magazine October 5, 1930, May 24, 1953; Radio Digest April 1931; Review of Reviews March 1925; Time October 6, 1930, June 18, 1945, April 8, 1946, May 25, 1953; World's Work October 1925.

*FOURNIER, ALAIN (Alain-Fournier) (October 3, 1886-September 22, 1914). For biographical sketch and list of works and references, see TWENTIETH CENTURY AUTHORS, 1942.

* * *

ABOUT: Gibson, R. The Quest of Alain-Fournier; Columbia Dictionary of Modern European Literature; Commonweal March 12, 1954; Cornhill Autumn 1947; New Statesman and Nation April 12, 1944.

* à làn' fŏor nyā'

FOWLER, FRANCIS GEORGE. See FOWLER, H. W.

FOWLER, GENE (1890-). For biographical sketch and list of earlier works and references, see TWENTIETH CENTURY AUTHORS, 1942.

* * *

Gene Fowler is the acknowledged master of "show business" biography. His biography of John Barrymore, Good Night, Sweet Prince, was hailed as "one of the best biographies ever written of an actor." The author's simple style, his scrupulous care for the truth, his affection for Barrymore, and his intimate knowledge of Broadway and Hollywood life all helped to make the book both a critical and a popular success. He has used the same method, with similar results, in biographies of Jimmy Durante and the late Jimmy Walker, and in his own autobiography (which covers his life up to 1920), *Solo in Tom-Toms*. Fowler lives in Los Angeles. In 1950 he became a Catholic.

ADDITIONAL WORKS: Good Night, Sweet Prince, 1944; Solo in Tom-Toms, 1946; Beau James: The Life and Times of Jimmy Walker, 1949; Schnozzola: The Story of Jimmy Durante, 1951; Minutes of the Last Meeting, 1954.

ABOUT: Fowler, G. Solo in Tom-Toms; Hoehn, M. (ed.) Catholic Authors, II; Van Gelder, R. Writers and Writing; Current Biography 1944; New York Times Book Review February 10, 1946; Saturday Review of Literature April 27, 1946; Time May 13, 1946.

FOWLER, HENRY WATSON (1858-December 26, 1933). For biographical sketch and list of works and references, see TWENTIETH CENTURY AUTHORS, 1942.

* * *

ABOUT: Dictionary of National Biography 1931-1940.

FOWLIE, WALLACE (November 8, 1908-   ), American poet and critic, writes: "I was born in Brookline, Mass. My mother

was born in Brookline and my father in Boston. My maternal grandparents were Irish and my paternal grandparents Scotch. I remember my Scottish grandmother telling me when I was a child that her ancestors came from France to Scotland after the Revocation of the Edict of Nantes. In Brookline I attended the Edward Devotion School and the high school. Then I went to Harvard where I received three degrees: A.B. in 1930, A.M. in 1933, Ph.D. in 1936.

"I interrupted my Harvard studies for a year's teaching at the Taft School in Connecticut. Then I returned as graduate student and instructor in French. French literature had become my central interest. I wrote my doctoral dissertation on Ernest Psichari and met in Paris the family and friends of Psichari. Two winters I lived at

the home of his mother, Mme. Noémi Renan, at 16, rue Chaptal.

"My first full-time teaching post was at Bennington College in Vermont where I taught between 1936 and 1941. Then I spent five years at Yale during which I began to publish quite regularly articles and books of literary criticism. My first book was a collection of poems I had written in French. I like to think that poetry, which was the first kind of writing I did, will be the ultimate form I shall return to. Ever since I can remember, I have been engaged in some kind of writing. The habit is daily. Although I have published mainly criticism, I have written more in the form of novels and memoirs.

"At the close of the war, I went to the University of Chicago for four years, although one of these years, 1948-49, I spent in Paris on a Guggenheim Fellowship. There I worked on a study of the poetry of Mallarmé. Rimbaud and Mallarmé are, I believe, the two principal literary influences on my life. They are the poets I return to the most willingly and the most frequently.

"In 1950 I returned to Bennington College where I am at the writing of this article (September 1952). I teach also, on Fridays, at the New School in New York and serve as advisory editor of *Poetry* magazine in Chicago. I feel the book on Mallarmé in many ways to be the fullest testimonial of what I understand about poetry. To it I would add the new study of *Les Illuminations* of Rimbaud. These two books represent what I have derived from twenty years of study and teaching of French poetry, and from twelve visits to France where I tried to learn something of the French mind, temperament, and art."

* * *

Wallace Fowlie's work has been called "the best criticism of contemporary French literature now being written in America." His feeling for the language and literature of France is more than an academic interest. In his autobiography *Pantomime*, he writes of his introduction to French, at the age of twelve, at the Edward Devotion School: "During those first two years, when I didn't know the language, and to some degree ever since, everything about French seemed enchanted to me and quite distinct from all I had learned about life." As he mastered the language, he responded to it with complete dedication and it became an esthetic, a way of life: "My being seemed merged with all others," he wrote, recalling a conversation with Jacques Maritain in Paris, "and participating at once more freely and more securely with the movement of the universe, with the past of France, whose meaning, like that of a palimpsest, I was trying to decipher, and with the unwritten pages of the future."

PRINCIPAL WORKS: *Poetry*—Matines et Vers (in French) 1936; From Chartered Land, 1938; Intervalles (in French) 1939. *Criticism*—Ernest Psichari, 1939; La Pureté dans l'Art (in French) 1941; Clowns and Angels, 1943; De Villon à Péguy (in French) 1944; Spirit of France: Studies in Modern French Literature, 1944; Rimbaud, 1946; Jacob's Night, 1947; The Clown's Grail, 1948; Age of Surrealism, 1950; Mallarmé, 1953; Rimbaud's Illuminations: A Study in Angelism, 1953. *Novel*— Sleep of the Pigeon, 1948. *Autobiography*—Pantomime, 1951. *Edited*—Mid-Century French Poets, 1955.

ABOUT: Fowlie, W. Pantomime; Chimera Autumn 1944; Poetry January 1952; Renascence Autumn 1951.

FOX, JOHN, JR. (1862-July 8, 1919). For biographical sketch and list of works and references, see TWENTIETH CENTURY AUTHORS, 1942.

* * *

ABOUT: Green, H. E. Towering Pines.

FOX, RALPH WINSTON (1900-January 3, 1937). For biographical sketch and list of works and references, see TWENTIETH CENTURY AUTHORS, 1942.

"F.P.A." See ADAMS, F. P.

"FRA ELBERTUS." See HUBBARD, E.

FRANCE, ANATOLE (April 16, 1844-October 12, 1924). For biographical sketch and list of works and references, see TWENTIETH CENTURY AUTHORS, 1942.

* * *

ABOUT: Axelrad, J. Anatole France; Columbia Dictionary of Modern European Literature; Pritchett, V. S. The Living Novel; Walton, L. B. Anatole France and the Greek World; Books Abroad January 1945; Contemporary Review April 1949; Nation April 22, 1944.

FRANCK, HARRY ALVERSON (June 29, 1881-). For autobiographical sketch and list of works and references, see TWENTIETH CENTURY AUTHORS, 1942.

* * *

Harry A. Franck writes from New Hope, Pa.: "We got back [from a South American

trip] in June 1941. I was halfway through *Rediscovering South America* when Pearl Harbor happened; applied to the Nelson Rockefeller Committee with an offer of my services, but before they got around to answering, Uncle Sam astounded me by offering me a majority in the Air Force and called me to active duty the day after my sixty-first birthday! Several U.S. assignments, with six and one half months in Europe with the Ninth Air Force in between—wrote a book on the Ninth, which the War Department has never gotten around to publish—terminal leave ended January 1947.

"Wife and I drove roundabout to California, visiting relatives and old friends; decided to retire, but found it a great bore, so became cruise lecturer on Holland-American Line's 'Nieuw Amsterdam' around South America, through Straits of Magellan, spring 1950. Pottered at what might perhaps best be miscalled an autobiography. Made two Mediterranean cruises as lecturer, spring of 1951; wife and I took party of fourteen around the world on American President Line, with lot of flying sidetrips, spring of 1952; sailed to Casablanca on a Danish freighter October 1952; took the monthly (winter only) diesel bus across the Sahara and kept on down the center of Africa, always on the ground (or river or lake steamers) to Cape of Good Hope; sailed from Capetown to England March 31, 1953; eleven days watching London get het up over the Coronation; S.S. 'United States' Southampton to New York in less than five days.

"Wife and I taking a party around the Pacific early in 1954. Oh, yes, there's life in the old dog yet."

FRANK, BRUNO (June 13, 1887-June 20, 1945). For autobiographical sketch and list of earlier works and references, see TWENTIETH CENTURY AUTHORS, 1942.

* * *

Bruno Frank died of a heart attack, at fifty-eight, at his home in Beverly Hills, Calif. His will directed that all his papers except letters to his wife and Thomas Mann should be burned "so no third person could learn anything of my personal life from my estate."

Frank's last work in Hollywood was with Ernst Lubitsch on the motion picture *A Royal Scandal*; he was working on a novel about the French moralist Chamfort at his death. A book of short stories, *The Magician*, published posthumously, had, according to *Time*, "qualities that make for engaging reading rather than great writing; a sure professional touch, quiet sophistication, an easy way with the ways of the world."

Frank belonged, says Harold von Hofe, to the rapidly disappearing "European bourgeoisie, the liberal faction of the nineteenth century middle class, which felt that wrongs were to be righted slowly by considered and painless means. Frank would have been far more in tune with the world had he lived fifty years earlier. . . . Immediacy of problematic issues only diverted his energy into channels yielding relatively small return."

ADDITIONAL WORKS IN ENGLISH TRANSLATION: One Fair Daughter, 1943; The Magician (short stories) 1946.

ABOUT: Books Abroad Winter 1946; Columbia Dictionary of Modern European Literature; New York Times June 21, 1945.

FRANK, LEONHARD (September 4, 1882-). For biographical sketch and list of earlier works and references, see TWENTIETH CENTURY AUTHORS, 1942.

* * *

Leonhard Frank lived in England until 1951 when he returned to Germany to make his home in Munich. He is married and has one son. His recent works have not attracted much attention in the United States. *Dream Mates*, a translation of a novel Frank had published in Germany in 1936, was a study of the love lives of two neurotic young women. The critics found the heavy symbolism of the book "foggy" and "murky," and they objected generally that the book was overwritten and slight in substance. *Mathilde*, the story of the adolescence and young womanhood of a Swiss girl, was a more effective novel. "His attitude to his characters is slightly obscure," the *Times Literary Supplement* commented, "giving the impression that he regards them as symbolic figures in some nebulous cosmic drama; but he writes with his usual genuine human warmth." The English novelist L. A. G. Strong wrote in the *Spectator* that *Mathilde* "is remarkable for the range of its understanding, for the poetic accuracy of the writing . . . its indomitable truth of feeling."

ADDITIONAL WORKS IN ENGLISH TRANSLATION: Dream Mates, 1946; Mathilde, 1948; The Baroness, 1950; Heart on the Left, 1954.

ABOUT: Columbia Dictionary of Modern European Literature.

FRANK, WALDO DAVID (August 25, 1889-). For autobiographical sketch and list of earlier works and references, see TWENTIETH CENTURY AUTHORS, 1942.

* * *

Waldo Frank writes from Truro, Mass.: "In 1942, just after Pearl Harbor, he was invited by a group of South American universities and other cultural institutions, Argentina's in particular, to speak on inter-American relations during the world crisis. Public enthusiasm was such that he drew great crowds, whether before university, metropolitan or provincial audiences. In Buenos Aires, he was attacked by a delegation of Fascists, disguised as police, who tried to terminate his campaign by killing him. The attempt on his life, although abortive, resulted in serious injuries and a protracted hospital convalescence, at the end of which he completed his speaking tour.

"At present, two book-size studies of his work are in preparation in the U.S.: by William Bittner, professor of English Literature at Rutgers University, and by Jerome Kloucek, of Northwestern University."

South American Journey, which Lewis Mumford called "a surpassingly good book," was a personal history of Frank's experiences in South America. In 1948 he was commissioned by the government of Venezuela to prepare a biography of Simon Bolivar; this was published three years later under the title *Birth of a World: Bolivar in Terms of His Peoples*. In 1943 Frank was married to Jean Klempner. It was his third marriage.

ADDITIONAL WORKS: South American Journey, 1943; The Jew In Our Day, 1944; Island in the Atlantic (novel) 1946; The Invaders (novel) 1948; Birth of a World: Bolivar in Terms of His Peoples, 1951; Not Heaven (novel) 1953.

ABOUT: Cargill, O. Intellectual America; Hoffman, F. J. Freudianism and the Literary Mind; Current Biography 1940; Current History October 1942.

FRANKAU, GILBERT (April 21, 1884- November 4, 1952). For biographical sketch and list of earlier works and references, see TWENTIETH CENTURY AUTHORS, 1942.

* * *

Gilbert Frankau died at his home in Hove, Sussex, England, after a long illness, at sixty-eight.

He continued his prolific writing to the end of his life, completing a novel a week before his death. A few months earlier he had announced his conversion to Catholicism.

Frankau's technique was said to be "as clearcut as a steel engraving" by the London *Times Literary Supplement.* "Every line tells us something, though it may be on occasion something we do not particularly want to know."

ADDITIONAL WORKS: World Without End, 1943; Michael's Wife, 1948; Son of the Morning, 1949; Oliver Trenton, K. D., 1951.

ABOUT: Illustrated London News November 15, 1952; New York Times, November 5, 1952.

FRANKAU, PAMELA ("Eliot Naylor") (1908-). For biographical sketch and list of earlier works and references, see TWENTIETH CENTURY AUTHORS, 1942.

* * *

Pamela Frankau began her literary career as a writer of breezy, pleasant, but insubstantial fiction. Michael Arlen's influence was everywhere, and, she comments, "I would never put anyone into my novels that did not use a foot-long cigarette holder, drive a Hispano Suiza and have peaches for breakfast." Her later novels, however, have shown a pronounced shift toward the more serious and solid. *The Willow Cabin*, probably the best-known of her works, is a smooth and sensitive love story. It shows in every line the "professional" touch. As a reviewer in the New York *Times* summed it up: "It has precision of phrase, unobtrusive economy of style and genuine passion." Her *A Wreath for the Enemy* was a serious and sensitive study of a young girl growing up on the French Riviera and was highly praised by the critics for its mature craftsmanship.

In World War II Miss Frankau served in the A.T.S. (the British W.A.C.), rising from the rank of private to major. She is married to Marshall Dill, Jr., and has lived in the United States since 1945. She visits Europe regularly, contributes articles and stories to British and American periodicals, and when in England she frequently broadcasts for the B.B.C. In 1942 Miss Frankau entered the Catholic Church.

ADDITIONAL WORKS: Shaken in the Wind, 1948; The Willow Cabin, 1949; To the Moment of Triumph (in England: The Winged Horse) 1953; A Wreath for the Enemy, 1954. As "Eliot Naylor" —The Offshore Light, 1952.

ABOUT: Hoehn, M. (ed.) Catholic Authors, I.

FRANKEN, ROSE (Rose Franken Meloney) (1898-).

* * *

The first two printings of TWENTIETH CENTURY AUTHORS (1942 and 1944)

incorrectly reported that Rose Franken's marriage to Dr. Sigmund Walter Anthony Franken ended in divorce. Actually, the marriage ended with his death in 1933. This error was corrected in the third printing of TWENTIETH CENTURY AUTHORS (1950).

ADDITIONAL WORKS: *Novels*—Another Claudia, 1943; Young Claudia, 1946; The Marriage of Claudia, 1948; From Claudia to David, 1950; The Fragile Years, 1952; Rendezvous, 1954. *Plays* (dates of publication)—Outrageous Fortune, 1944; Soldier's Wife, 1945; The Hallams, 1948.

ABOUT: Current Biography 1947.

FRANKENBERG, LLOYD (September 3, 1907-), American poet and critic, writes: "I was born in Mount Vernon, N.Y. There were pears in the backyard, a swing under the peartrees, and lilies-of-the-valley along one side of the house. When I was seven I moved to Manhattan, where I went to grammar school, George Washington High School, and Columbia. An

M. Morehouse

early disinclination for poetry was overcome under Raymond Weaver, who professed to dislike it, and John Erskine, who was beginning to write novels.

"In 1927 college was interrupted for a spell of the sea. Through the Panama Canal to San Pedro we chipped paint. On the way back we redleaded the scraped areas. The ship was a tanker taken over from a Canadian company and was changing colors in midstream.

"In 1929 or '30 I worked briefly, and for a time simultaneously, on the New York *Post* and the Brooklyn *Daily Eagle.* Occasional editorial jobs have since intervened. 1932 was a bumper year for driftwood on the ocean side of Cape Cod, then unnavigated by low-pressure tires. For $25 I put up a ten-by-twelve shack where my wife, the painter Loren MacIver, and I spent many summers and one winter. A skunk named Delilah used to dig up the tin cans we buried in the dunes.

"Poems of mine began appearing in magazines around 1937. In 1938 I was the first and last recipient of the Spenser Award. In 1939 a book of poems, *The Red Kite*, was published. The following winter, while we were in Key West, I received a Guggenheim Fellowship.

"In 1942 a Carnegie grant saved me from outside-reading jobs with Paramount and

Twentieth-Century Fox. Synopses for the first had to be in the present tense, 'vivid'; for the latter in the past, 'smooth like a story.' Mine were sometimes both.

"During the war, as a conscientious objector, I spent one year in a C.P.S. camp in Maryland, dynamiting tree-stumps, and another as attendant in a psychiatric hospital.

"In 1947 a grant from the Academy of Arts and Letters helped me finish *Pleasure Dome: On Reading Modern Poetry*. One thesis is that sound forms part of the meaning of poetry. Feeling hampered by the silence of quotations, I edited *Pleasure Dome: An Audible Anthology*, which Columbia Records brought out at the same time. In this collection, the first to be commercially produced, T. S. Eliot, Marianne Moore, E. E. Cummings, W. H. Auden, William Carlos Williams, Ogden Nash, Dylan Thomas, and Elizabeth Bishop read from their poems.

"Recently I have been working on projects to increase the already growing audience for poetry. For several seasons I arranged the series of poetry evenings at the Museum of Modern Art.

"My favorite avocation is visiting Europe. So far we've managed to indulge in it once."

PRINCIPAL WORKS: The Red Kite, 1939; Pleasure Dome, 1949.

"FRANKLIN, JAY." See CARTER, J. F.

FRAZER, Sir JAMES GEORGE (January 1, 1854-May 7, 1941). For biographical sketch and list of works and references, see TWENTIETH CENTURY AUTHORS, 1942.

* * *

ABOUT: Marett, R. R. James George Frazer, 1854-1941.

FREEMAN, AUSTIN. See FREEMAN, R. A.

FREEMAN, DOUGLAS SOUTHALL (May 16, 1886-June 13, 1953). For biographical sketch and list of earlier works and references, see TWENTIETH CENTURY AUTHORS, 1942.

* * *

Douglas Southall Freeman died of a heart attack at his home in Richmond, Va. At the time of his death he was preparing the sixth and concluding volume to his biography of George Washington. This work was undertaken after Freeman had completed *Lee's Lieutenants*, his three-volume study of the commanding officers who served under General Robert E. Lee. Both as military history and simply as interesting and rewarding reading, *Lee's Lieutenants* set a high standard and proved a worthy successor to his Pulitzer prize-winning biography of General Lee. Henry Steele Commager found in this, as in nearly all of Freeman's work, that he achieved "his purpose of recapturing the sense of things and recreating figures all but forgotten." The Washington biography, with its massive research and faithful delineation of the character of Washington himself, was recognized as the long-awaited definitive biography. Although at times the piling up of details was regarded by the critics as "excessive," the work as a whole was considered a monumental achievement. Another project which Freeman was planning at the time of his death was a history of the military operations in World War II.

In 1949 Freeman retired from the staff of the Richmond *News-Leader* which he had edited since 1915. In his retirement, however, he kept up his busy schedule of research, writing, and radio broadcasting, rising at 2:30 A.M. seven days a week and at his desk, ready to work, by 3. In addition to the tremendous research demanded by his George Washington biography, and the preparation of two daily broadcasts of news analysis, Freeman made frequent and extensive lecture tours, delivering as many as one hundred addresses a year. In 1945 he traveled 45,000 miles, mostly by air, to meet lecture engagements. At the age of sixty-three, Freeman began to take piano lessons, having had no musical instruction ever before, on the principle, he wrote, of giving himself "what should be part of every man's needful daily discipline—the attempted performance of something new, difficult, and awkward to him."

ADDITIONAL WORKS: Lee's Lieutenants (3 vols.) 1942-44; George Washington: A Biography (6 vols.) 1948-54.

ABOUT: Malone, D. *Preface to* Freeman's George Washington, VI; New York Herald Tribune Book Review October 7, 1951; New York Times June 14, 1954; New York Times Book Review October 17, 1948; Saturday Review of Literature October 16, 1948.

FREEMAN, HAROLD WEBBER (1899-). For biographical sketch and list of earlier works and references, see TWENTIETH CENTURY AUTHORS, 1942.

* * *

H. W. Freeman published no books during the war years. His recent books have been little noticed in the United States, but are admired in England. One of these is a quiet story with an agrarian setting, *Blenheim Orange.* A "solid, slow-moving, well-written book" (*Times Literary Supplement*), its unusual plot centers around a young girl who is obsessed with her grandfather's market garden, even to the extent of sacrificing career and romance for it. An odd situation around which to build a novel, the *Times* comments, "but Mr. Freeman makes it convincing and, in a mild, unhurried way, moving."

Freeman is married to Elizabeth Boedecker.

ADDITIONAL WORKS: Blenheim Orange, 1949; The Poor Scholar's Tale, 1954.

FREEMAN, JOHN (January 29, 1880-September 23, 1929). For biographical sketch and list of works and references, see TWENTIETH CENTURY AUTHORS, 1942.

FREEMAN, JOSEPH (October 7, 1897-). For autobiographical sketch and list of earlier works and references, see TWENTIETH CENTURY AUTHORS, 1942.

* * *

Joseph Freeman writes from New York City: "In 1937 I left New York, retired to the country and gave all my time to study and writing. I attempted to get back to my roots, to retrace my steps and to cover new ground in an effort to reorient myself in our rapidly changing world.

"In the spring of 1939 I completed a short book on radical literary criticism in the United States from 1900 to 1930; it was set up in type but withdrawn before publication. That spring I also spoke at Harvard University as a guest of the Nieman Fellows. That fall all my connections with Left publications and groups of every kind were completely severed.

"I was now a free lance, doing pieces for *Reader's Digest*, the *Nation*, *Fortune*, and other magazines, and some fiction for *Harper's*. I also went back to my old post as publicity director of the American Civil Liberties Union (1940-1942).

"In the spring of 1940 I began to do another short story for *Harper's* which kept writing itself till it became a 360,000 word novel, *Never Call Retreat*, published in the spring of 1943.

"In the summer of 1943 I joined the editorial staff of Information Please, where I remained till the fall of 1945. There I helped draft the radio programs and the basic plan for the *Information Please Almanac*. In the summer of 1945 I went with the show under USO and Special Services auspices to France, Germany, and Austria. Back in New York in the fall of that year I began writing *The Long Pursuit*, a novel published in the summer of 1947.

"Amidst these various activities, I continued to write poetry, completing a book of sonnets in 1944 and another in 1947. In the latter year I co-authored the script of *Dreams That Money Can Buy*, a film directed and produced by Hans Richter in cooperation with Marcel Duchamp, Ferdinand Léger, Max Ernst, John Latouche, John Cage, and other modern writers, painters, and musicians. The following spring I did publicity for The Poets' Theatre, directed by Mrs. Erwin Piscator. In the summer of 1948 I joined the staff of a leading public relations firm with which I remained till the spring of 1952. In the fall of 1952 I flew to Mexico on a writing assignment and spent a month in Chicago as a Fellow of the Newberry Library.

"All this time I continued to write poetry and to work on my third novel, begun in the early 1940's. I published a good deal of poetry in the 1920's and 1930's. Though little of my verse has appeared in print in the past decade and a half, I have kept on writing it. I like to read poetry because it tells me more about the world than any other form of communication, and I like to write it because it is the medium in which I speak most freely. I now feel that my experience in rhetoric, sociology, politics and journalism was something through which I passed on the way to my present view of the world. This is primarily ethical, occasionally mystical with a complete acceptance of science; one of my favorite modern philosophers is Alfred North Whitehead.

"I am a member of the Public Relations Committee of the American Civil Liberties Union, the Authors' League, PEN, Phi Beta Kappa and Delta Sigma Rho."

* * *

Correction: *An American Testament*, listed among Freeman's principal works, was first published in 1936, not 1938.

ADDITIONAL WORKS: Never Call Retreat, 1943; The Long Pursuit, 1947.

FREEMAN, Mrs. MARY ELEANOR (WILKINS) (October 31, 1852-March 13, 1930). For biographical sketch and list of works and references, see TWENTIETH CENTURY AUTHORS, 1942.

FREEMAN, RICHARD AUSTIN (1862-September 30, 1943). For biographical sketch and list of earlier works and references, see TWENTIETH CENTURY AUTHORS, 1942.

* * *

R. Austin Freeman died at Gravesend, England, at eighty-one, after an illness of several months.

"It would be difficult," Isaac Anderson has observed, "to find anywhere more nearly perfect stories of scientific deduction than the Dr. Thorndyke tales." The process by which Freeman constructed his absorbing chronicles in deduction has been described by P. M. Stone: "the creation of a dominant, living character, intricate yet convincing plot structure, and a background of engrossing charm against which the stirring sequence of events is skillfully presented."

ABOUT: London Times October 1, 1943; New York Times October 1, 1943; Saturday Review of Literature October 16, 1943.

FREMANTLE, ANNE (JACKSON) (June 1910-   ), Anglo-American poet, novelist, biographer, and miscellaneous writer, writes: "I was born in Savoy, France, in an old house, locally thought to have been built by the Saracens in the ninth century and therefore called La Maison du Diable. My mother was Scottish, the daughter of Sir Mounstuart Grant-Duff, sometime Under-Secretary of State for India, Governor of Madras, Rector of Aberdeen University, and for fifty years Member of Parliament for the Elgin Boroughs. My father was English, the Right Hon. Frederick Huth Jackson, president of the Institute of Bankers, Director of the Bank of England, Sheriff of London, and a Privy Councillor to the King. My parents had houses in Sussex, England, in Scotland, and in London, and until my father's death in 1921 my childhood was passed between these places.

Bertrand de Geofroy

"I began to write at seven. My earliest poem was about the Massacre of Glencoe; my second on the death of Sir Roger Casement. I took School Certificate from Cheltenham Ladies College and went on as a Scholar to Lady Margaret Hall, Oxford, where I graduated B.A. in 1930, M.A. in 1932. In 1927 I became engaged, and in 1930 was married, to the Hon. Christopher Fremantle, son of Lord Cotteslow. We have three sons, called after the Victorines, Adam, Richard, and Hugh.

"My first published work was a reply in the London *Evening News* to the query 'Should a Woman Marry or Have a Career?' Both, wrote I, and was paid five guineas (about $20). I was seventeen. At twenty-one, the Swan Press published the usual slim volume of my poems; and in the same year, Duckworth's published a life of George Eliot in their Great Lives series. I reviewed novels for the *New Statesman*, books for the (London) *Times Literary Supplement*, and wrote for dozens of different magazines—the *Blue Peter, Time and Tide, Nineteenth Century, Sunday Times, News Chronicle*, etc. I ran for Parliament against the Right Hon. Alfred Duff Cooper, as a Labor Candidate, in 1936—he got 20,000 votes, I only 5,000. We contested Charles James Fox's old constituency, St. George's Westminster. In 1936 I was the first correspondent of the London *Times* to enter Russia: I covered the Moscow Theatre Festival, and in 1937 the WPA theatre in the United States. I also did a speaking tour for the English Speaking Union, on the British Social Services, covering 423,000 miles, forty states, and going from coast to coast and Quebec to Mexico City. In 1939 I became, on the outbreak of war, ambulance driver for the London County Council; later I worked for the B.B.C., broadcasting in French and German. In 1942 I got a job as research assistant to the Agent General for India in Washington, D.C. and remained there three years. From 1945 on I have been an associate editor of *Commonweal*, and from 1948 I have been on the staff of Fordham University, and from 1950 an editor of the Catholic Book Club. I worked as an editor at the United Nations during 1949-50. My husband and I both became United States citizens, I in 1947, he in 1950."

PRINCIPAL WORKS: *Biographies*—George Eliot, 1931; Loyal Enemy (biography of Marmaduke Pickthall) 1938; Desert Calling (biography of Charles de Foucauld) 1949. *Novels*—Come to Dust, 1941; James and Joan, 1948. *Miscellaneous*—Poems, 1931; The Wynne Diaries (ed.) 1935-37; A Guidebook to Sicily, 1936; The Face of the Saints (tr.) 1947; Greatest Bible Stories (anthology) 1950; Mothers (anthology) 1951; Lives of the Saints (tr.) 1951; Christian Conversation (ed.) 1953; The Age of Belief (ed.) 1955.

ABOUT: Hoehn, M. (ed.) Catholic Authors, II; O'Brien, J. A. (ed.) Roads to Rome; Commonweal March 26, 1954; New York Herald Tribune Book Review February 27, 1955.

FRENSSEN, GUSTAV (October 19, 1863-April ?, 1945). For biographical sketch and list of works and references, see TWENTIETH CENTURY AUTHORS, 1942.

* * *

Gustav Frenssen died at his birthplace, Barin in Holstein, at eighty-one.

The nature of his novels, widely read in Germany during and after World War I, is perhaps best conveyed in his own words: "I wanted to show to the people of my home community, and to all others who would see it, the whole deep, sad truth and burden of life."

Although Frenssen was generally said to be "mediocre as a literary artist, but estimable as a preacher," Katharine G. Potts found that "the freshness and energy which attracted attention to him as a preacher are to be found in his novels also, and give them a peculiar charm, which compensates for his apparent carelessness of form." L. M. Hollander, acknowledging "glaring defects in composition, the intolerable repetitions, the undistinguished style," says that "few Germans have so well caught, and so poignantly expressed, the cry of despair, the spirit of gloomy introspection which is symptomatic of that land of misery."

ABOUT: New York Times April 20, 1945.

*FREUCHEN, PETER (1886-   ). For autobiographical sketch and list of earlier works and references, see TWENTIETH CENTURY AUTHORS, 1942.

* * *

An outspoken anti-Nazi since the early 1930's, Peter Freuchen set up a private rescue organization for German refugees on his island farm in Denmark. In the years before the German occupation of Denmark he took an active part in the underground movement. When his country was invaded, he continued his resistance work until he was arrested by the Gestapo. He escaped from a German concentration camp and fled to Sweden where he was joined by his wife and his daughter Pipaluk. Freuchen visited the United States and lectured widely on Denmark's contribution to the war. He was divorced from his second wife in 1945 and is now married to Dagmar Mueller, a New York fashion illustrator. They live in New York City and have a country home in Noank, Conn. Freuchen's recent writings include two vivid and entertaining historical novels and the hearty autobiography *Vagrant Viking*. His

* froi'kĕn

daughter Pipaluk, now married and living in Sweden, is the author of a highly-praised book for children, *Eskimo Boy* (1951).

ADDITIONAL WORKS: White Man (novel) 1946; The Law of Larion (novel) 1952; Vagrant Viking (autobiography) 1953; Ice Floes and Flaming Water, 1954.

ABOUT: Freuchen, P. Vagrant Viking.

FREUD, SIGMUND (May 16, 1856-September 23, 1939). For biographical sketch and list of works and references, see TWENTIETH CENTURY AUTHORS, 1942.

* * *

ADDITIONAL WORKS IN ENGLISH TRANSLATION: The Origins of Psychoanalysis: Letters and Notes 1887-1902, 1954.

ABOUT: Brill, A. A. Freud's Contribution to Psychiatry; Fodor, N. & Gaynor, F. (eds.) Freud: Dictionary of Psychoanalysis; Freud, S. Origins of Psychoanalysis; Hollitscher, W. Sigmund Freud; Jastrow, J. Freud: His Dream and Sex Theories; Jones, E. Life and Work of Sigmund Freud; Ludwig, E. Dr. Freud; Puner, H. W. Freud: His Life and His Mind; Sachs, H. Freud: Master and Friend; Trilling, L. The Liberal Imagination; Zilboorg, G. Sigmund Freud: His Exploration of the Mind of Man; American Scholar October 1950; Contemporary Review February 1946; New Republic December 4, 1944; New York Times Magazine November 23, 1947; Time October 30, 1944.

"FROME, DAVID." See BROWN, Z. J.

FROMM, ERICH (March 23, 1900-   ), German-born psychoanalyst, social philosopher, and author, was born in Frankfort and studied sociology and psychology at the universities of Heidelberg, Frankfort, and Munich. He received his Ph.D. from the University of Heidelberg in 1922. He was trained in psychoanalysis in Munich and later at the Psychoanalytic Institute in Berlin.

Since 1925 he has devoted his time partly to his psychoanalytical practice and partly to theoretical work. His special field is the application of psychoanalytic theory to problems of culture and society.

In an early book, *The Development of the Dogma of Christ*, published in Vienna in 1931, he attemped to demonstrate that religious doctrines and symbols have to be understood on the basis of the socio-economic situation of those groups to whom they appeal. Early in his career, he criticized the orthodox concept of Freudian theory which tended to ignore the weight of economic factors. He has been among the psychoanalytical writers who have emphasized the need for a social and cultural orientation in psychoanalysis, in contrast to orthodox Freudianism which emphasizes the biological factor.

In 1933 he visited the United States when he was invited to lecture at the Chicago Psychoanalytical Institute. In 1934 he settled in this country and later became an American citizen. He has taught at Columbia and at Yale universities, at Bennington College and at various institutes of psychiatry. Before coming to America, Dr. Fromm had published many works on various psychological subjects in German. He is best known in this country, however, for his most recent books, written in English: *Escape from Freedom*, *Man for Himself*, and *The Forgotten Language*.

In *Escape from Freedom* Dr. Fromm made a searching inquiry into the meaning of freedom for modern man. He stressed the role of psychological factors in the social process, and interpreted the historical development of freedom in terms of man's awareness of himself as a significant separate being. The book contained a diagnosis of the psychological aberration of Nazism as an extreme example of man's "Escape from Freedom." He criticized tendencies in contemporary culture which suppress spontaneity and result in a sense of isolation and powerlessness on the part of the individual which make him seek relief in authoritarianism.

Margaret Mead said of this book, "It bridges the gap between economics and psychology and shows how no theory which invokes only man's way of earning a living or man's human nature alone, is sufficient. It presents, with vivid concise statement, the dilemma of too much freedom from, too little freedom to, which is crushing man today and threatening to force him back into the authoritarianism of Nazism."

Man for Himself continued this inquiry into the interrelation of psychology and ethics, "leading to the realization of man's self and his potentialities." He stated even more clearly his humanistic philosophy that man is "for himself," that he must determine his own standards rather than follow authoritarian standards.

The Forgotten Language was a study of dreams, fairy tales and myths, which reiterated his faith in the spontaneous human mind unfettered by authoritarianism. Rollo May wrote in the New York *Times* that

readers would profit by the "broad, synthesizing compass of this book" with "its many stimulating insights."

Dr. Fromm has recently been in Mexico. He has been married twice—to Frieda Reichmann, from whom he was divorced, and, in 1944, to Henny Gurland.

PRINCIPAL WORKS: Escape from Freedom, 1941; Man for Himself, 1947; The Forgotten Language, 1951.

FROST, ROBERT (March 26, 1874-). For biographical sketch and list of earlier works and references, see TWENTIETH CENTURY AUTHORS, 1942.

* * *

On March 24, 1950, the United States Senate unanimously adopted a resolution honoring Robert Frost on his seventy-fifth birthday. His poems, the citation read in part, "have helped to guide American thought with humor, and wisdom, setting forth to our minds a reliable representation of ourselves and of all men. . . ." This honor came as a fitting climax to a series of honors, and within his own lifetime Frost has had the unique experience of seeing his work become a "classic" in American literature. He has won the Pulitzer prize for poetry four times —the latest in 1943 for *A Witness Tree*. In an age which generally ignores poetry, his work is widely known and loved. He speaks to every reader so intimately and so unaffectedly that, in Dorothy Canfield Fisher's words, "to find it on a printed page is not like reading something, but like living through a flash of the revelation which comes . . . even to poor human beings, moments in which we can see what we are, what we know— what we can only guess."

Frost lives in a modest brick house in Cambridge, Mass., and spends his summers on his Vermont farm. He visits a number of colleges every year to give lectures and readings. In 1954 Joseph Warren Beach described him (in the *Yale Review*) as "tall and well built, white-haired—very blue eyes —large, well-shaped head, rather handsome in the English manner. . . . His carriage is somewhat slouching or loose-hung, like that of a Yankee farmer stopping to talk with you over the fence. His expression has something of patriarchal benignity, but with a touch of whimsy in the eyes and round the corners of the mouth."

In recent years Frost has published two verse plays, or masques, with Biblical settings: *The Masque of Reason* (in which Job and God are the major characters) and *The*

Masque of Mercy. These poems—though fresh, witty, and graceful—lacked, according to most critical opinion, the immediacy of appeal of Frost's earlier work. His *Steeple Bush,* on the other hand, a collection of forty-three poems, was a masterful work, demonstrating in every line the sharpness and subtlety of Frost's genius—what Leonard Bacon described as "the barbed image, the penetrating wisdom, the inconspicuous grace that half conceals its own elegance, and the lancinating wit."

Frost is no longer simply the common reader's poet. In recent years, after long years of general critical neglect, he has become the subject of intensive critical study. His best poetry, Randall Jarrell commented in 1952, "deserves the attention, submission, and astonished awe that real art always requires of us." And Frost himself, Jarrell continues, "is that rare thing, a complete or representative poet, and not one of the brilliant partial poets who do justice, far more than justice, to a portion of reality, and leave the rest of things forlorn. When you know Frost's poems, you know surprisingly well how the world seemed to one man, and what it was to seem that way."

Correction: Frost was born in 1874, not 1875. This information did not come to light until 1954 when Frost announced it.

ADDITIONAL WORKS: Come In, and Other Poems (enlarged as The Road Not Taken, 1951) 1943; Masque of Reason, 1945; Masque of Mercy, 1947; Steeple Bush, 1947; Complete Poems, 1949; Hard Not to be King, 1951; Aforesaid, 1954.

ABOUT: Fisher, D. C. Vermont Tradition; Jarrell, R. Poetry and the Age; Thompson, L. R. Fire and Ice: The Art and Thought of Robert Frost; Untermeyer, L. *Preface to* Frost's Road Not Taken; American Literature January 1948; American Scholar October 1945; College English February 1947; Current Biography 1942; New York Herald Tribune Book Review May 29, 1949; New York Times Book Review November 7, 1949; New York Times Magazine March 26, 1950; Publishers' Weekly May 20, 1950; Sewanee Review October 1948; Time October 9, 1950; Yale Review Summer 1948, Winter 1954.

FRY, CHRISTOPHER (December 18, 1907-), English playwright, was born in Bristol, England, the son of Charles Harris Hammond, architect, and Emma (Fry) Hammond. His father, deeply religious, had been a lay missionary in the Bristol slums. Christopher Fry began writing early, producing a farce at eleven, a poem at twelve, and a verse drama at fourteen; at formal English studies he earned no distinction. He attended the prominent public school Bedford, leaving it at eighteen and adopting at this time his mother's

Pix

maiden name, Fry ("It was a matter of euphony") and her religious faith, that of Society of Friends, or Quakers. After a brief period of teaching, he joined the Bath Repertory Company as an actor. In this capacity, as Harold Hobson put it, "he acquired just about as much fame at the job as Shakespeare did, which is, to all intents and purposes, none at all."

There followed a period of teaching again, then eight years in repertory troupes, acting in Shakespeare, Shaw, Wilde, Barrie, Coward; whereupon he moved to London, edited a magazine, tried his hand at cartooning, worked as secretary to a novelist and wrote children's plays for the radio. For some time early in 1934 he directed the Wells Repertory Players at Tunbridge Wells, until that enterprise failed. His next effort was to write words and music for an André Charlot revue, *She Shall Have Music,* presented in London in 1935. His first play, *Siege,* has never been published or acted.

"He says he didn't write a line from the age of eighteen to twenty-eight," reports the New York *Times,* "though the desire to write plays in verse, and the inner assurance that he would, never faltered." The turning-point was John Gielgud's acting in *Richard II.* "The performance inspired me so much that I went home and was able to write easily and fluently."

Dr. Barnardo's Homes, a charitable organization caring for orphaned and abandoned children, asked him to write a play on the life of its founder, John Barnardo. This he did, and toured England with it for two years.

In 1936 Fry married Phyllis Hart, a journalist, and by 1938 "there was no money at all," but fortunately he was left a small legacy by a cousin. Fry now began work on *The Boy with a Cart* (1938), a pageant marking the fiftieth anniversary of a village church. Two other pageants were written and produced: *The Tower* and *Thursday's Child.* In 1939 he became director of the Oxford Playhouse. During the war Fry, a conscientious objector, took part in clearing away bomb damage in various parts of England, and helped fight blitz fires at Liverpool docks in 1941. After the war he returned to writing and chose verse as his medium. "It seems to have been just the proper moment. I lay the acceptance of poetry in the theatre nowadays to two things. One is the reaction to the long hold of 'surface realism'. . . . The other is that the world seems rather cut down a bit . . . and poetry provides something people lack and wish for; a richness and a reaffirmation." For a year he became one of two resident dramatists at London's private Arts Theatre Club. *A Phoenix Too Frequent*, a one-act play, was first put on at this theatre, in 1946, and was followed by sixty-four performances in the West End. This play opened in New York in April 1950, but was withdrawn after only five performances.

In 1948 *The Firstborn*, with a religous theme, was performed at the Edinburgh Festival. *Thor, with Angels* was put on during the festival week of the Friends of Canterbury Cathedral in the same year. But the most important event for Fry in 1948 was the first production of *The Lady's Not for Burning* at the Arts Theatre Club. Here it took the Shaw Prize Fund for the best play of the year. *The Lady* toured the provinces for eight weeks, then ran for eight months at London's Globe Theatre. It came to New York, with John Gielgud in the leading role, and the critics were enthusiastic.

Subsequent plays have been *Venus Observed*, a verse play; *Ring Round the Moon*, a translation of Jean Anouilh's *L'Invitation au Chateau; A Sleep of Prisoners*, a verse play on a religious theme; *The Dark Is Light Enough;* and *Tiger at the Gates*, an English version of Giraudoux' "The Trojan War Will Not Take Place." It is for his sheer virtuosity as a poet, rather than for the profundity of his ideas, that Fry is so much admired in both England and America. Reviewers and audiences alike have been dazzled by the richness of his verse, the sheer tumble of words and images, his "cartwheeling leaps of language."

Fry does most of his writing in a small cottage in an Oxfordshire village, where he lives with his wife and his son, Tam. He usually writes directly on the typewriter, beginning at ten at night and continuing until four in the morning. He is of average height, and light in weight, with a straight, clean-cut profile.

PRINCIPAL WORKS: The Boy with a Cart, 1939; The Firstborn, 1946; A Phoenix Too Frequent, 1946; The Lady's Not for Burning, 1949; Thor, with Angels, 1949; Venus Observed, 1950; Ring Round the Moon (translation) 1950; A Sleep of Prisoners, 1951; An Experience of Critics (essay) 1952; The Dark Is Light Enough, 1954.

ABOUT: Stanford, D. Christopher Fry; Current Biography 1951; Life January 14, 1952; New York Times Magazine March 12, 1950; Saturday Review of Literature March 21, 1953; Time November 20, 1950.

FRY, ROGER ELLIOT (1866-September 9, 1934). For biographical sketch and list of works and references, see TWENTIETH CENTURY AUTHORS, 1942.

* * *

ADDITIONAL WORKS: (new editions and posthumous): Chinese Art, 1947; French, Flemish and British Art, 1951; (tr.) Mallarmé's Poems, 1951.

ABOUT: Dictionary of National Biography 1931-40; Gaunt, W. Aesthetic Adventure; Johnstone, J. K. The Bloomsbury Group; Woolf, V. The Moment, and Other Essays; Spectator April 11, 1952.

*FUESS, CLAUDE MOORE (January 12, 1885-). For biographical sketch and list of earlier works and references, see TWENTIETH CENTURY AUTHORS, 1942.

* * *

Claude Fuess is active in a wide variety of educational activities. As a teacher and a school administrator he has witnessed and helped to shape vast and fundamental changes in American education over a period of four decades and more. In 1952 he published his memoirs, appropriately titled *Independent Schoolmaster*, a volume which reflects, he says, "the growth . . . of a schoolmaster who started in the conservative tradition and is ending with a passion for experimentation in the light of new knowledge."

In 1948, after completing forty years of service with Phillips Andover, Fuess retired. He now lives near Boston, in Chestnut Hill, Mass., and in his retirement, busy with lectures, research and writing, he comments: "I have since been so much occupied that I have had no idle hours in which to indulge in laments." Fuess' first wife died in 1943. In 1945 he married Lulie Blackfan.

ADDITIONAL WORKS: Unseen Harvest: A Treasury of Teaching (ed. with E. S. Basford) 1947; The College Board: Its First Fifty Years, 1950; Joseph B. Eastman (biography) 1952; Independent Schoolmaster, 1952; Stanley King of Amherst, 1955.

ABOUT: Fuess, C. Independent Schoolmaster; Journal of Education October 1948; Newsweek May 5, 1947; Time May 5, 1947.

* fēz

FULLER, HENRY BLAKE (January 9, 1857-July 28, 1929). For biographical sketch and list of works and references, see TWENTIETH CENTURY AUTHORS, 1942.

* * *

ABOUT: Theatre Arts July 1951.

FULLER, ROY (February 11, 1912-), British poet, writes from London: "I have lived in the north of England until my middle twenties and then, after my marriage, for a short time in Kent and afterwards in London. I left school at sixteen, was articled to a solicitor, and qualified at twenty-one. Since then I have always practiced as a lawyer, writing in my spare time. When I was nineteen or twenty, I came across the work of W. H. Auden and Stephen Spender and other writers of the new literary movement of the thirties and gradually weaned myself from such previous provincial influences as Rupert Brooke and Humbert Wolfe. During the thirties I contributed poetry to *New Writing, New Verse,* and other *avant-garde* periodicals, and published a first collection in 1939. I lived in south-east London during the air raids of 1940-41 and wrote several poems about them. I was called up for military service in 1941 in the Royal Navy. Like the air raids, communal life and service discipline made my verse more precise, concrete and copious, and when I published *The Middle of a War* in 1942 I found, rather to my surprise, that it achieved prominent reviews and went quickly into a second impression. My poetry was still 'highbrow' but it attempted to give a true picture of service life and to delineate universal emotions about the war and therefore found a comparatively large readership. The chances of the Navy put me in training as a radar mechanic and in 1942 I went to East Africa and worked there for a year on various naval airfields. My African poems were collected in a volume called *A Lost Season,* and during the last year of the war, when I was an officer at the Admiralty in London, I wrote a novel with an African background— a novel for boys—called *Savage Gold.*

"I was released from the Navy early in 1946 and went back to my old civilian occupation. My poetry suffered from these changed circumstances and I did not publish another collection until 1949. This book, *Epitaphs and Occasions,* was often light in form and bitter in tone, and ran counter to the romanticism which had gained a thorough hold of English *avant-garde* poetry after the war. At the moment of writing (1953) I have another book of verse in preparation, and this, I fear, is no more romantic than *Epitaphs and Occasions.* I feel, however, that the lessons I learnt in the thirties are still valid—that verse in our time must try to comprise the experience of the majority, despite working in minority terms —although the poet and his public may only be able to find each other in times of common crisis or suffering."

PRINCIPAL WORKS: Poems, 1939; The Middle of a War, 1942; A Lost Season, 1944; Epitaphs and Occasions, 1949; Second Curtain, 1953; Counterparts, 1954. *Juveniles*—Savage Gold, 1946; With My Little Eye, 1948.

ABOUT: Poetry January 1946.

*FÜLÖP-MILLER, RENÉ (March 17, 1891-). For autobiographical sketch and list of earlier works and references, see TWENTIETH CENTURY AUTHORS, 1942.

* * *

René Fülöp-Miller (also spelt Fülöp-Müller and Fueloep-Miller) lives in Westport, Conn. He is a naturalized American citizen. His wife is the poet and translator Erika Renon, and they have three children. Fülöp-Miller lectures widely on Russian civilization and sociology and contributes articles to American and British periodicals. His books are written in German and cover a variety of subjects—biography, critical studies, and fiction. The stories, or novellas, in *The Web* are based on the author's own childhood memories of legends of his native land, and are written, the *New Yorker* commented, "in a forthright, unaffected style that accords very well with the simple, folktale mood of his stories." *The Night of Time* tells the macabre story of Adam Ember ("Ember" means "man" in Hungarian), a soldier in an unknown army in a strange archetypal war. "In its nightmarish, surrealistic fashion and in its blend of the worlds of Kafka and Remarque," wrote Orville Prescott in the New York *Times,* "The Night of Time* casts a cold and sinister spell upon one's imagination."

ADDITIONAL WORKS IN ENGLISH TRANSLATION: Saints that Moved the World, 1945; Sing, Brat, Sing, 1947; Fyodor Dostoevsky: Insight, Faith and Prophecy, 1950; The Web, 1950; The Night of Time, 1955.
* fü lûp'

*FUTRELLE, JACQUES (April 9, 1875-April 15, 1912). For biographical sketch and list of works and references, see TWENTIETH CENTURY AUTHORS, 1942.
* fü trĕl'

*FYLEMAN, ROSE (1877-   ). For autobiographical sketch and list of earlier works and references, see TWENTIETH CENTURY AUTHORS, 1942.

* * *

Rose Fyleman lived for a while on a farm in Surrey, but she writes the editors of this volume that she is now living permanently in London. Her *Nursery Stories* was televised in 1949.

ADDITIONAL WORKS: Timothy's Conjurer, 1942; Hob and Bob, 1943; The Timothy Toy Trust, 1944; Adventures with Benghazi, 1946; Over the Tree Tops, 1949; Nursery Stories, 1949; Rhyme Book for Adam, 1949; Daphne and Dick, 1951.

ABOUT: Kunitz, S. J. & Haycraft, H. (eds.) The Junior Book of Authors (rev. ed.).

* file′màn

GÁG, WANDA (March 11, 1893-June 27, 1946). For autobiographical sketch and list of earlier works and references, see TWENTIETH CENTURY AUTHORS, 1942.

* * *

Wanda Gág died at fifty-three, at Doctors' Hospital in New York City. She had been seriously ill since the spring of 1945. Her last years were spent with her husband Earle Humphreys, her sister Flavia, and her brother Howard, at her home, "All Creation," in the Muscanetcong Mountains of New Jersey. Up to the time of her death, Miss Gág was working on further translations and illustrations of *Grimm's Fairy Tales* and on the writing of her childhood reminiscences.

Fellow writers have paid tribute to Miss Gág's sense of dedication to her lifework, her seriousness of purpose, and the "life, laughter and joyfulness [which] were an integral part" of her art, her writing, and her relationships with people. "With as sure an instinct for the right word for the ear as for the right line for the eye," Anne Carroll Moore has said, "Wanda Gág became quite unconsciously a regenerative force in the field of children's books."

ABOUT: Mahony, B. D. (& others) Illustrators of Children's Books; Scott, A. O. S. Wanda Gág; Zigrosser, C. Artist in America; American Artist February 1947; Horn Book September 1946, May 1947; New York Times June 28, 1946.

GAITHER, FRANCES ORMOND (JONES) (May 21, 1889-   ), American novelist, was born in Somerville, Tenn., the daughter of Annie Matilda (Smith) and Paul Tudor Jones. Her father was a doctor with manufacturing interests in Corinth, Miss.

The family moved to Corinth in Frances' early childhood, and it was there that she graduated from high school. She received her B.A. degree from the Mississippi State College for Women in Columbus, Miss., in 1909. Three years later she married Rice Gaither, newspaper writer and editor.

Mrs. Gaither sold her first story in 1918 to *All Story* and within the next ten years

Lotte Jacobi

her stories appeared in *McCall's, North American Review, Ainslee's,* and other magazines. She also wrote masques and pageants, one of which—an after-war pageant called *Shores of Happiness*—was produced at the University of Virginia in 1919. Her novel writing began with juveniles, all of them dealing with Southern history and reflecting Mrs. Gaither's lively interest in the past.

She has said that she does not believe that she is writing historical novels. "I don't base characters on actual personages. What I try to do in dealing with the past is to create an illusion of the present. I work terribly hard to get my characters to think and feel and speak as if they were living now, in this moment. My books, I like to think, are bare of costume, and trappings, of set stage and stock actions. The important thing for me in research is to absorb the period so completely that I am able to give out what I believe are its realities." *Double Muscadine*, Mrs. Gaither's most successful novel, is the product of just this kind of painstaking research. For this historical "whodunit," set in pre-Civil War days in Mississippi, Mrs. Gaither had to familiarize herself with the laws governing slavery and with the infinitely complex procedures of courtroom law. To do this, she hired a young law student as tutor, and the result was that the reviews of her novel, almost without exception, praised the "taut, expert" courtroom scenes.

The Gaithers now live in New York City where, before his retirement due to illness, Rice Gaither worked on the New York *Times.* Mrs. Gaither regards writing as a hard job. Some days a whole chapter will be produced with ease; at other times she labors long over a single passage. When the writing bogs down, there are always research, editing, and cutting to afford mental relaxation and outlets for creative energies. Usually she works out a general outline for a new novel in her mind and then begins amassing a large collection of notes before the actual writing starts. Changes do occur, however, as the story develops. No one sees the novel or hears a word about it until it is entirely finished; then her husband is the first critic.

PRINCIPAL WORKS: *Juveniles*—The Painted Arrow, 1931; The Scarlet Coat, 1934; Little Miss Cappo, 1937. *Biography*—The Fatal River: the Life and Death of La Salle, 1931. *Novels*—Follow the Drinking Gourd, 1940; The Red Cock Crows, 1944; Double Muscadine, 1949.

ABOUT: Current Biography 1950; New York Times Book Review April 3, 1949.

GALDOS. See PEREZ GALDOS

GALE, ZONA (August 26, 1874-December 27, 1938). For biographical sketch and list of works and references, see TWENTIETH CENTURY AUTHORS, 1942.

* * *

ABOUT: Library Journal December 15, 1945; Wilson Library Bulletin November 1946.

GALLICO, PAUL WILLIAM (July 26, 1897-   ), American sportswriter, short story writer, screenwriter, was born in a

Arn Glantz

New York City boarding house, the son of Paolo and Hortense (Ehrlich) Gallico. Paolo Gallico, a native of Trieste, had been to America at the age of fourteen, when he made his first appearance as a concert pianist in New York City. Ten years later he returned as solo pianist with leading American symphony orchestras, finally settling in New York as a teacher of the piano and composition. As a child Paul Gallico traveled to Europe with his parents, and recalls "a luscious, rich, enchanting Europe, friendly and trusting." He attended New York public schools, worked his way through Columbia College of Columbia University, and, after service in the navy in World War I, returned to Columbia and received his B.S. in 1921. While in college he joined in several sports, rowing on the Columbia crew for four years, as its captain in his senior year. He always

sought to study sports from the inside— "how it feels," and has tried some three dozen sports, often persuading star players to let him play against them—boxing with Jack Dempsey ("I knew all that there was to know about being hit"), golf with Bob Jones, swimming against Johnny Weissmuller, and so on through baseball, skiing, football, speedboat racing, and others.

As a student he had written fiction for pulp magazines and newspapers; in 1922 he joined the New York *Daily News* as motion picture reviewer. Not long afterwards he was transferred to the sports department, and in 1924 he was promoted to sports editor and columnist, a position he held for twelve years. "Some sportswriters build up a following by the accuracy of their forecasts," says Gallico. "I built mine up by being wrong much more often than right. I didn't have to fake it. I just was. And then admitted it, worried over it, and marveled that I should not have seen what was apparently obvious to many thousands of readers." By 1936 he was reportedly the highest-paid sports writer in New York, in a field that included Damon Runyon and Grantland Rice. In 1936 Gallico left the *News* to become a free-lance fiction writer. In 1944 he was European editor and war correspondent for *Cosmopolitan.*

His first book was *Farewell to Sport,* a collection of twenty-six chapters of reminiscences which had been serialized; it was published in 1938, was called "racy, thoroughly readable," and went into six printings. Most of his books have been collections of articles or stories printed in periodicals. *Golf Is a Friendly Game* (1942) included eight of his humorous golf tales. *The Adventures of Hiram Holliday* (1939) has been termed "pure escape fiction." In *The Secret Front* Hiram Holliday continued as a foreign correspondent. Gallico is said to have received as much as five thousand dollars for one story.

A different type of book was *The Snow Goose,* which proved to be the most popular of Gallico's works. Published in 1941, it was the story of a hunchback, the girl he loved, and the white goose which flew over his rescue craft at Dunkerque. William Lyon Phelps called it "a little masterpiece . . . a work of calm beauty." It sold over three hundred thousand copies in the United States. Gallico's anthology of his own stories and novelettes, *Confessions of a Story Writer* (1946) includes explanatory comments and a short autobiography. In 1952

Gallico said, "I like best a novel I wrote about two cats, called 'Jennie'"—published in the United States under the title *The Abandoned* (1950). The Robert Vogeler case helped spark *Trial by Terror,* his novel of 1952. More recent are *Foolish Immortals,* part-parable, part-realistic, and a shorter book, *Snowflake,* the fable of a snowflake. The first novel was termed "synthetic" and "overwritten" by one critic; but the second book was generally praised. Joseph Henry Jackson has found the secret of Gallico's great popular success in his ability "to wrap up a sermon in a story which, though it may sound fantastic (and is) somehow keeps you reading. The trick . . . is that the writer must communicate his own enthusiasm to the reader."

His screen plays include *Joe Smith, American* (1942) and *The Pride of the Yankees* (1942), and *Lili* (1953), this last an adaptation of his novel *Love of Seven Dolls.*

Gallico's first wife was Alva Taylor, daughter of Bert Leston Taylor, the Chicago *Tribune's* columnist. There were two children by this marriage. His second marriage was to Elaine St. Johns, daughter of the writer Adela Rogers St. Johns. In 1939 he married his present wife, Baroness Pauline Gariboldi, with whom he wrote the screenplay *The Clock.*

He is six-foot-three-inches tall, big and "bull-necked," and wears horn-rimmed glasses. In 1952 he said, "I used to write between ten at night and three or four in the morning. Old morning-paper habits. Now I do it more sensibly. A morning and afternoon session. Five hours a day total is the most I can write. Often when I get stuck I talk to myself on the typewriter. The mechanical effort of doing this usually by-passes the mental block· and ideas flow again."

PRINCIPAL WORKS: Farewell to Sport, 1938; The Adventures of Hiram Holliday, 1939; The Secret Front, 1940; The Snow Goose, 1941; Lou Gehrig, 1942; Golf Is a Friendly Game, 1942; Confessions of a Story Writer, 1946; The Lonely, 1947; The Abandoned (in England: Jennie) 1950; Small Miracle, 1952; Trial by Terror, 1952; Foolish Immortals, 1953; Snowflake, 1953; Love of Seven Dolls, 1954.

ABOUT: Peragallo, O. Italian-American Authors and Their Contribution to American Literature; Warfel, H. R. American Novelists of Today; Current Biography 1946; Esquire May 1943; New York Herald Tribune Book Review April 27, Post May 26, 1951; Scholastic March 8-13, 1943; 1952; New York Post Magazine November 16, Time December 13, 1937.

GALLIENNE. See LE GALLIENNE

GALSWORTHY, JOHN (August 14, 1867-January 31, 1933). For biographical sketch and list of works and references, see TWENTIETH CENTURY AUTHORS, 1942.

* * *

ABOUT: Clark, B. H. Intimate Portraits; Dictionary of National Biography 1931-40; Dupont, V. John Galsworthy: The Dramatic Artist; Gray, J. On Second Thought; McCullough, B. W. Representative English Novelists.

*GAMOW, GEORGE (March 4, 1904-), Russian-born American physicist and science writer was educated at the University of Leningrad and afterwards did research on nuclear physics in universities in Germany, Denmark and England. In 1934 he became a citizen of the United States. Since 1934 he has been professor of theoretical physics at the George Washington University in Washington, D.C. He has published about one hundred articles on nuclear physics and its application to astrophysics and cosmology, as well as a dozen books.

His special contribution to the non-scientific world lies in those of his books in which he has made the subjects of cosmology and nuclear physics intelligible and absorbing to the layman. A trilogy of books, *Birth and Death of the Sun, Biography of the Earth,* and *Creation of the Universe,* bring to the reader in rich prose and exciting narrative the knowledge which twentieth century physicists have discovered of the nature and origin of the universe. The first volume deals with the place of our sun among the stars, the second with the place of our earth among the planets, and the last one discusses the universe as a whole.

Waldemar Kaempffert reviewing the last of the books in the New York *Times* wrote: "Mr. Gamow is a skilful and ingenious popularizer of science. His book is not the kind that can be skimmed through, but one that must be absorbed. For all his rigorous reasoning, he must be regarded as a scientific poet. To create a universe in an hour and to do it in such a way as to make scientific sense is an intellectual achievement of the first order."

* gà'mov

Mr. Tompkins in Wonderland is a charming book dedicated to both Lewis Carroll and the physicist Niels Bohr, Gamow's teacher. This is a whimsical and amusing exposition of such mysteries of modern physics as the quantum theory, relativity, and curved space. It is a mixture of classical nonsense and unclassical physics. Three scientific lectures set the fictional Mr. Tomkins dreaming of various scientific wonderlands, and these three lectures have been described by the London *Times* as the best popular statements written on the subject of relativity and the quantum theory.

Gamow's books have been translated into fifteen languages. He is a member of the following learned societies: the American Physical Society, the American Astronomical Society, the American Geophysical Society, the Washington Philosophical Society, the International Astronomical Union, the Royal Danish Academy of Sciences, the National Academy of Sciences and the New York Academy of Sciences. He lists his hobbies as poetry, model electric railroads, and traveling. He is married, has one son, born in 1935, and lives in Bethesda, Md.

PRINCIPAL WORKS: Constitution of Atomic Nuclei and Radioactivity, 1931; Mr. Tompkins in Wonderland, 1939; The Birth and Death of the Sun, 1940; Biography of the Earth, 1941; Mr. Tompkins Explores the Atom, 1943; Atomic Energy in Cosmic and Human Life, 1946; One, Two, Three . . . Infinity, 1947; Creation of The Universe, 1952; The Moon, 1953.

ABOUT: Current Biography 1951; Newsweek May 5, 1952.

GANNETT, LEWIS (October 3 1891-). For autobiographical sketch and list of earlier works and references, see TWENTIETH CENTURY AUTHORS, 1942.

* * *

Since 1930 Lewis Gannett has contributed his daily "Books and Things" column to the New York *Herald Tribune*. His work keeps him in New York City for most of the year, but vacations and weekends are still given to his country home in Connecticut. This home, Cream Hill—its history and its personal memories for Gannett and his family—was the subject of a book by Gannett. The substance of *Cream Hill*, Hal Borland wrote in the New York *Times*, "is about one man's living with one piece of ground which gives him satisfaction and a sense of continuity. The warmth of his feeling is contagious, for Mr. Gannett en-joys the country with all the pores of all his senses open."

ADDITIONAL WORK: Cream Hill, 1949.

ABOUT: Gannett, L. Cream Hill; Current Biography 1941; Saturday Review of Literature May 21, 1949.

*GARCÍA LORCA, FEDERICO (June 5, 1899-August 1936). For biographical sketch and list of works and references, see TWENTIETH CENTURY AUTHORS, 1942.

* * *

ADDITIONAL WORKS IN ENGLISH TRANSLATION: III Tragedies (Blood Wedding, Yerma, Bernarda Alba) 1947; The Gypsy Ballads, 1953; Selected Poems, 1955; The Comedies, 1955.

ABOUT: Barea, A. Lorca: The Poet and His People; Campbell, R. Federico García Lorca; Columbia Dictionary of Modern European Literature; Crow, J. A. Federico García Lorca; García Lorca, Francisco, *Introduction to* García Lorca's III Tragedies; Honig, E. García Lorca; Hispania February 1950; Hispanic Review January 1946; New Republic April 24, 1944; New Yorker August 19, 1950; Poetry November 1949, April 1950; South Atlantic Quarterly October 1948; Theatre Arts October 1950; Time December 22, 1947; Virginia Quarterly Review July 1945.

* gär thē'ä lôr'kä

GARD. See MARTIN DU GARD

GARDNER, ERLE STANLEY ("A. A. Fair") (July 17, 1889-). For autobiographical sketch and list of earlier works and references, see TWENTIETH CENTURY AUTHORS, 1942.

* * *

In 1948 Erle Stanley Gardner set out to explore the rugged peninsula of Baja Calif., and, using vehicles with power winches and four-wheel drives, went from Tijuana, Mexico, to the southernmost tip of the peninsula, a distance of almost 1200 miles. His adventures on this trip were the foundation for his first non-fiction book, *The Land of Shorter Shadows*.

Shortly thereafter, Gardner associated himself with Harry Steeger, owner of *Argosy* magazine, and a staff of investigators, Dr. LeMoyne Snyder, an outstanding figure in the field of legal medicine, Raymond Schindler, internationally known private detective, and Alex Gregory, past president of the Society for the Detection of Deception, in organizing *Argosy* magazine's "Court of Last Resort." These individuals, all of whom donated their services, investigated the cases of penniless men who had been wrongfully convicted of murder and had exhausted all their legal rights. While the investigators donated their services, the magazine hired two full-time investigators, Tom Smith, penologist, former warden of the Washington State Penitentiary at Walla Walla, and Bob Rhay, penologist and psychologist, to assist in investigations. The results of these activities have been assembled by Gardner in his second non-fiction book, *The Court of Last Resort.*

Gardner covered the Willie Sutton case for *Look* magazine in 1952, reported the DeMarigny trial in the Bahamas for the New York *Journal-American* and affiliated newspapers in 1943, and, in company with Dr. LeMoyne Snyder, covered a murder case for the Denver *Post* in 1948.

In addition to volumes previously mentioned, Gardner has continued his production of mystery novels. Sales figures available in the fall of 1952 showed sales in excess of sixty-five million copies in the United States and Canada. Since 1939 Gardner has also been publishing mystery novels under the name "A. A. Fair," but it was not until 1946, in a series of articles on Gardner by Alva Johnston in the *Saturday Evening Post,* that "Fair's" identity was revealed.

ADDITIONAL WORKS: The Case of the Haunted Husband, 1941; The Case of the Careless Kitten, 1942; The Case of the Buried Clock, 1943; The Case of the Drowsy Mosquito, 1943; The Case of the Smoking Chimney, 1943; The D.A. Calls a Turn, 1944; The Case of the Crooked Candle, 1944; The Case of the Black-Eyed Blonde, 1944; The Case of the Golddigger's Purse, 1945; The Case of the Half-Wakened Wife, 1945; The Case of the Borrowed Brunette, 1946; The Case of the Backward Mule, 1946; The D.A. Breaks a Seal, 1946; The Case of the Fan-Dancer's Horse, 1947; The Case of the Lazy Lover, 1947; The Case of the Lonely Heiress, 1948; The Case of the Vagabond Virgin, 1948; The D.A. Takes a Chance, 1948; The Case of the Dubious Bridegroom, 1949; The Case of the Cautious Coquette, 1949; The Case of the Negligent Nymph, 1949; The D.A. Breaks an Egg, 1949; The Case of the One-Eyed Witness, 1950; The Case of the Musical Cow, 1950; The Case of the Fiery Fingers, 1951; The Case of the Angry Mourner, 1952; The Case of the Moth-Eaten Mink, 1952; The Case of the Grinning Gorilla, 1952; The Case of the Hesitant Hostess, 1953; The Case of the Green-Eyed Sister, 1953; Case of the Fugitive Nurse, 1954; The Case of the Runaway Corpse, 1954; The Case of the Restless Redhead, 1954; The Case of the Glamorous Ghost, 1955; The Case of the Sun Bather's Diary, 1955. *As "A.A. Fair"*— The Bigger They Come, 1939; Turn on the Heat, 1939; Gold Comes in Bricks, 1940; Spill the Jackpot, 1941; Double or Quits, 1941; Owls Don't Blink, 1942; Bats Fly at Dusk, 1942; Cats Prowl at Night, 1943; Give 'Em the Ax, 1944; Crows Can't Count, 1946; Fools Die on Friday, 1947;

Bedrooms Have Windows, 1949; The Top of the Heap, 1952; Some Women Won't Wait, 1953. *Non-Fiction*—The Land of Shorter Shadows, 1949; The Court of Last Resort, 1952; Neighborhood Frontiers, 1954.

ABOUT: Mott, F. L. Golden Multitudes; Current Biography 1944; Look November 14, 1944; New Yorker November 11, 1950; Newsweek October 25, 1943; Saturday Evening Post October 5, 12, 19, 1946; Time May 9, 1949.

GARLAND, HAMLIN (September 14, 1860-March 4, 1940). For biographical sketch and list of works and references, see TWENTIETH CENTURY AUTHORS, 1942.

* * *

ABOUT: Ahnebrink, L. Beginnings of Naturalism in American Fiction; Mencken, H. L. A Mencken Chrestomathy; Nuhn, F. The Wind Blew from the East; Taylor, W. F. The Economic Novel in America.

GARNETT, DAVID (1892-). For biographical sketch and list of earlier works and references, see TWENTIETH CENTURY AUTHORS, 1942.

* * *

David Garnett lists himself in the current volume of *Who's Who* as author, publisher, and farmer. As publisher he is a director of the firm of Rupert Hart-Davis, Ltd. As farmer he lives and farms at his home, Hilton Hall, in Huntingdon. As author and man-of-letters, Garnett has edited works on Henry James and T. E. Lawrence and written a lively first volume of autobiography, *The Golden Echo.* This book ends in 1914, when Garnett was only twenty-two, but it is crowded with literary reminiscences—Garnett's childhood memories of his parents' friends and guests— Conrad, Galsworthy, Belloc, and others. His mother, Constance Garnett, Dostoevsky's translator, died in December 1946. In 1942 Garnett married Angelica Bell, daughter of the critic Clive Bell.

ADDITIONAL WORKS: (ed.) James, H. Fourteen Stories, 1946; (ed.) The Essential T. E. Lawrence, 1951; (ed.) Selected Letters of T. E. Lawrence, 1952; The Golden Echo, 1953.

ABOUT: Garnett, D. The Golden Echo; Swinnerton, F. The Georgian Literary Scene, 1910-1935.

GARNETT, EDWARD (1868-February 21, 1937). For biographical sketch and list of works and references, see TWENTIETH CENTURY AUTHORS, 1942.

* * *

ABOUT: Bates, H. E. Edward Garnett; New Statesman and Nation December 30, 1950.

GARRETT, GARET (February 19, 1878-November 6, 1954). For biographical sketch and list of earlier works and references, see TWENTIETH CENTURY AUTHORS, 1942.

* * *

Garet Garrett, died in Atlantic City, N.J., at seventy-six, from the effects of a stroke. From 1940 to 1942 he was chief editorial writer of the *Saturday Evening Post*. In 1944 he became editor of the magazine *American Affairs*, a post he held until 1950. He was married in 1947 to Dorothy Williams Goulet; his home was in Tuckahoe, N.J. Garrett's last publications included articles in the *American Mercury* and other periodicals, several pamphlets and a book on political subjects (he was an extreme conservative politically), and a study of the business career of Henry Ford, *The Wild Wheel*.

ADDITIONAL WORKS: The Revolution Was, 1944; Ex America, 1951; The Wild Wheel, 1952; The People's Pottage, 1953; The American Story, 1955.

ABOUT: New York Times November 7, 1954.

*GARRIGUE, JEAN (December 8, 1914-), American poet and writer of fiction, reports: "I was born in Evansville, Ind., the daughter of Allan Colfax and Gertrude Heath Garrigus. It was my grandfather who in a burst of stars and stripes changed the name from Garrigues to Garrigus, rendering vaguely Irish what had been French, and it was my older sister and afterwards myself who restored the name to one at least of its proper vowels thereby causing some confusion. For with a name so French ought we not to be French? Dim Hugenot ancestors on one side—English mixed with Scotch on the other—both families have been, alas, in this country since the Revolution. My father was a postal inspector who in his early years wrote and published short stories. My mother was musical. Music, in fact, was the culture in which I grew up, for my sister, Marjorie, later to become a concert pianist, made by her playing a very paradise of sound. My older brother, Ross H. Garrigus, is a newspaper editor.

"Most of my childhood was spent in various small and large towns in Indiana,

* gà rĕg'

including Indianapolis, but I never felt the flat land to be my own very home and am happy only in mountains or cities with ports that lead to the sea.

"I 'discovered' Shelley, then Keats, then the Imagists in about the same year—when I was fourteen—but it was the Imagists who made daring to write poetry seem possible and of the Imagists, especially H.D. A teacher of English in the high school in Indianapolis I attended, Elizabeth N. Brayton, was after my sister mentor and rare guide, reading what I wrote with that sympathy so necessary for first tender-minded exertion.

"Followed a period in New York with my sister and a year in Europe with her and her husband before entering college. After graduating from the University of Chicago in 1937, some graduate work and some serious employment—editing a weekly newspaper—I came to New York in 1940. And it was only then that I felt myself delivered and as it were in possession of a tongue. All dates from that, despite a lost trunkful of the proverbial journals, notes, poems and prose—that trail of attempts and explorations the writer must blaze. . . . *Kenyon Review* introduced my work in 1941 in a group of Nine Young Poets and I appeared in New Directions' 1944 collection of *Five Young American Poets* with a group of 36 poems. Since then I have published two collections of verse, *The Ego and the Centaur* (1947) and *The Monument Rose* (1953). I have also published a number of short stories, winning a *Kenyon Review* first prize for one of them in 1944 and was at work like many others on a novel, ambitious in theme and most probably audacious.

"As for living—where are the servants to do it for us? And as for earning a living? Alas, like some writers I have been broke much of the time since I was ever determined not to sacrifice *living*, which above all includes writing, to the *earning* of living. Odd journalistic jobs sometimes sustained me in which I re-wrote technical articles for an aviation magazine or made phrases about toy trains. I have reviewed fiction for the *New Republic* and other reviews have appeared in the *Saturday Review of Literature, Kenyon Review, Tomorrow,* etc. During World War II I edited a publication sheet for the U.S.O. Receiving a scholarship to the University of Iowa, I taught as a graduate assistant while obtaining a Master's degree (1943) and later I taught at Bard College and at Queens College. Right now I am in Europe—it is the summer of 1954—and have just received a

Rockefeller grant. I plan to work on a new volume of poems and on prose.

"About poetry—I suppose one is always searching for an absolute language, that language which takes its rhythms from heartbeat and blood, wind, water, light. Interior and exterior married in a diagram, a paradigm, by metaphor and rhythm to equate perception with experience. And experience? One takes a complex of experience, trying to deal with as many of its contingents and tangents as the poem will bear. The real is incorrigible, untamable. And what is it? I think of elements that once 'made' a poem for me. Rain. A river. A graveyard. Under umbrellas you stand with friends, the brilliant living. The rust-colored lichen on chipped angel wings. The dash of rain on stone. The slip and shadowed darkness of the river. This moment in the real trembles. History and death. The long coil of the past—all bearing upon the immediacy of the moment. Thus is one compelled to write—a vision of powers interlocking at one given, endowed instant. Rain, sovereign elms, the exuberance of nature, this ambrosial wildness, within form. And love. And the nearness to death, the nearness to deaths of the great—innovators, intransigents, their death, that odd prospect of one's own, of one's world, and surrounding all this with invisible pressure, valorous force, the sense of the mystery of waters, earth, man. Elements, out of which one tries to make some whole. This is one kind of poem. Not that such lyric universals always stand so close to hand. For it is always up to the next moment, the next poem, to stumble as it can into the unexpected area of consciousness where, a butterfly caught in the hands, metaphor frees it.

"The English poets I most admire and re-read are Wyatt, Marvell, Donne, Coleridge, Blake, Hopkins, Yeats. As for the poetry of my age, especially in America, it is a medium I explore with as much delight and necessity as the world around me. Elsewise I like comets, lightning, fireworks, and feel close to nearly all furred things, especially the cat, 'mystic companion,' and the lion and the fox, because he will never submit to his captivity. This is not to forget the great heraldic beasts."

* * *

Miss Garrigue has been termed an exciting "poet of celebration" by William Arrowsmith in the *Hudson Review*, "a rare prosodist" who writes with "the mastery of dynamics and resolution that comes only with a poet's perfected style, the poem moving with the habitual movement of the mind. . . . What was once a clear case of promise in her *Ego and the Centaur* has now blossomed superbly; . . . the appearance now of *The Monument Rose* puts her easily among the best younger poets of America. To the festive air *sans* feast of her earlier book, this volume brings a banquet out of Sappho and Khayyam; to her old knack for sweetness, the creation of felt love, and for those earlier O's of incoherent ebullience, the exact exhilaration of language. In consequence, this small, sumptuous 50-page book is a fine, magnificently sustained performance; anthologists will disregard at their peril nearly half the poems in the book."

In the *Sewanee Review* Howard Nemerov refers to Miss Garrigue's speech as "ornate, elaborate of tongue and somewhat lightly, ironically impassioned. . . . The world of *The Monument Rose* is romantic in its richness and strangeness and curious elaboration of detail. . . . The character of this poetry is just where it belongs, in the play between rhythm and syntax, the wave-motion so to say, which makes the identity of passage after passage and makes all one and most fine. This thing, the weaving and stitching, is the most neglected part of poetry at present, but attention to it is a mark of mastery, and the gift for it, the melodiousness which is, as Coleridge claimed, the final and distinguishing sign of a poet, is something Miss Garrigue wonderfully has."

Miss Garrigue is five feet two, blue-eyed, with a wiry mop of tawny hair, brown flecked with gold. Her permanent residence is in Greenwich Village, New York City.

PRINCIPAL WORKS: in Five Young American Poets, 1944; The Ego and the Centaur, 1947; The Monument Rose, 1953.

ABOUT: Deutsch, B. Poetry in Our Time; Five Young American Poets; Hudson Review Winter 1953; Partisan Review February 1948; Poetry December 1953; Saturday Review of Literature June 19, 1948, January 16, 1954; Sewanee Review, Spring 1954.

GASSET. See ORTEGA Y GASSET

GAUNT, WILLIAM (July 5, 1900-), English art critic and literary historian, writes: "I was born at Hull, Yorkshire, only son of William Gaunt and Harriet (Spence) Gaunt, both of that city. Was educated at Hull Grammar School, 1910 to 1918. As a boy most wanted to be a painter (my father was graphic artist and designer) and used to draw ships on the Humber and in the docks, the grain mills on river Hull, and the beautiful churches of the East Riding.

Roye, London

"Equally interested in books, gulped down poems, novels, plays, history, biography, essays, criticism, read also as many French works as I could. First thought of a literary career came of winning a prize offered by a magazine for essay on Shakespeare's The Tempest.

"The 'Great War' had then just begun, was nearly over when I joined the army at age of eighteen. In 1919 went up to Worcester College, Oxford, read modern history, spoke now and then at the Union, tried some rowing, joined the Art Society. With honours degree in 1922 faced problem of earning a living: began to write articles on art exhibitions, wrote introduction for the Connoisseur to an album of prints illustrating 'English Rural Life in the Eighteenth Century' in 1924, settled in London as staff contributor on The Studio art magazine. 1924 to 1930 was interested spectator of the 'gay twenties'; a result being a book of sketches (words and drawings) of people and places, London Promenade. Traveled to France, Germany, Holland, Italy, Spain, and Eastern Mediterranean, influenced by modernism in art and architecture, for a while edited magazine Drawing and Design in contemporary spirit.

"1930 to 1939 wrote many occasional pieces on art but only one book (or what I thought of as a real book), Bandits in a Landscape, a study of the romantic spirit in art. During these years more and more taken up by responsibilities of editing and publishing: but with growing urge to write. Have since concentrated on authorship, producing a series of books of art, and social history, telling the story of a movement or period in terms of 'collective biography' (the phrase is that of a critic who regarded it as something of a new form). First was The Pre-Raphaelite Tragedy; followed by an account of the Aesthetic movement, The Aesthetic Adventure (written in the intervals of a wartime appointment); The March of the Moderns, an account of the modern movement; latest book, Victorian Olympus, returning to consider the classic revivals and academic figures of the last century.

"Writing books of this kind has become main occupation, apart from criticism (as art critic for London Evening Standard, subsequently for Punch). Have lectured and broadcast occasionally but feel most at home pen in hand, still use it for drawing as well as writing. Married to Mary Catherine Reilly (née Connolly), to whom The Aesthetic Adventure was dedicated: live in country cottage on Surrey-Hampshire borders. Find almost unlimited scope in the social history of the arts but have plans also for an historical novel."

PRINCIPAL WORKS: London Promenade, 1930; Bandits in a Landscape, 1937; The Pre-Raphaelite Tragedy, 1942; British Painting from Hogarth's Day to Ours, 1945; The Aesthetic Adventure, 1945; The March of the Moderns, 1949; Victorian Olympus, 1952.

ABOUT: American Magazine of Art June 1937; Connoisseur September 1942; New York Times August 1, 1937; New Yorker May 5, 1945; Time September 21, 1942, May 14, 1945.

*GEDDES, Sir PATRICK (1854-April 16, 1932). For biographical sketch and list of works and references, see TWENTIETH CENTURY AUTHORS, 1942.

* * *

ABOUT: Boardman, P. L. Patrick Geddes: Maker of the Future; Dictionary of National Biography 1931-40; Mumford, L. in Barnes, H. E. (ed.) Introduction to the History of Sociology; Tyrwhitt, J. (ed.) Patrick Geddes in India; Commonweal October 6, 1944; Magazine of Art January 1951; New Republic December 11, 1944; Saturday Review of Literature October 14, 1944; Social Forces March 1944.

* gĕd'ĭs

GEDDES, VIRGIL (May 14, 1897-   ). For autobiographical sketch and list of earlier works and references, see TWENTIETH CENTURY AUTHORS, 1942.

* * *

Virgil Geddes writes: "In 1941 I was appointed postmaster at Brookfield, Conn., where I live and where in 1932 I founded 'The Brookfield Players,' one of the first of the summer theatres. It was this group which first produced my play 'In the Tradition,' a play involving a small town undertaker who couldn't make a living because people didn't die fast enough. A petition was circulated at the time asking that the play be withdrawn and no further performances given in the community. A record of my experiences as postmaster is covered in my latest book, Country Postmaster, published in 1952.

"In 1943 I received an award from the American Academy of Arts and Letters and the National Institute of Arts and Letters for outstanding achievement in the field of literature.

"It might seem from the above that I have somewhat abandoned THE theatre, which is perhaps so. But 'The Virgil Geddes Theatre' still goes on and is as much alive as ever.

ADDITIONAL WORK: Country Postmaster, 1952.

ABOUT: Deutsch, H. & Hanau, S. The Provincetown: A Story of the Theatre; Geddes, V. Country Postmaster; Sper, F. From Native Roots.

*GEDYE, GEORGE ERIC ROWE (May 27, 1890-). For autobiographical sketch and list of earlier works and references, see TWENTIETH CENTURY AUTHORS, 1942.

* * *

G. E. R. Gedye writes: "In June 1940, after repeated applications, I induced the [New York] *Times* to transfer me from Moscow, where the existence of the Hitler-Stalin pact and the severe censorship imposed in December 1939 made real journalistic work impossible, to Istanbul. From there, the backdoor to the Balkans, I covered events in German-occupied central and southeastern Europe for a year, when I was asked to undertake special war duties connected with political warfare, and commissioned in the British 'Force 133' in the Middle East. For my war services I was awarded the British M.B.E. (Member of the Order of the British Empire). At the end of war I returned to Vienna as correspondent, first of the London *Daily Herald* for five years, and subsequently for two years as London *Observer* correspondent. At the present time I am 'Iron Curtain Correspondent' in Vienna for the Overseas News Agency, New York, and contributing regular articles on Iron Curtain and Austrian affairs to a number of American and British magazines. I am at present completing a new book dealing with my journalistic experiences of Russia at the beginning of the war, and describing how Communism was established and is being maintained in Russia's European satellites. I am also completely re-writing my *Wayfarer in Austria.*"

* * *

Gedye was divorced in 1949, and married Alice Mehler of Vienna; they have one son.

* gĕd'ē

ADDITIONAL WORKS: Marboe, E. The Book of Austria (trans.) 1948; (with others) Austria in 1953 (Fodor's Modern Guides) 1953.

ABOUT: Time September 10, 1945.

*GEIJERSTAM, GÖSTA af (1888-). For biographical sketch and list of works and references, see TWENTIETH CENTURY AUTHORS, 1942.

* * *

Gösta af Geijerstam lives in western Norway. He has published nothing in recent years.

* yĕ'ĭ ĕr shtäm

GEISEL, THEODOR SEUSS (March 4, 1904-). For biographical sketch and list of earlier works and references, see TWENTIETH CENTURY AUTHORS, 1942.

* * *

Dr. Seuss, as Geisel signs his cartoons and fantasies, lives in La Jolla, Calif., "high on a mountain overlooking the Pacific." Here he plants trees and builds rock gardens by day, and by night writes stories and draws his extraordinary animals. In addition to his books, which are ostensibly for children but have a large and devoted adult audience, he has written several screen plays for Hollywood—in 1953 a full-length motion picture, *The 5,000 Fingers of Dr. T.*; a classic animated cartoon, *Gerald McBoing-Boing*, which won an Academy Award in 1951; and another Academy Award winner, the documentary film *Design for Death* (on which his wife collaborated), in 1947.

ADDITIONAL WORKS: McElligot's Pool, 1947; Thidwick, the Big-Hearted Moose, 1948; Bartholomew and the Oobleck, 1949; If I Ran the Zoo, 1950; Scrambled Eggs Super, 1953; Horton Hears a Who!, 1954.

ABOUT: Mahony, B. E. (ed.) Illustrators of Children's Books, 1744-1945; Newsweek February 9, 1942; Publishers' Weekly April 24, 1943; Saturday Review of Literature November 11, 1950.

GEISMAR, MAXWELL DAVID (August 1, 1909-), American critic and essayist, writes: "I was born in New York City; grew up in Westchester County, where I am now living. After graduation from the Scarsdale High School, I worked for the Brooklyn *Eagle* and, that winter, in the advertising department of a music firm. I was taking writing courses at Columbia University Extension. I quit my job, in order apparently to save my mind for better things, worked at a garage in the evenings, and set out to get a regular college education.

"These decisions were all youthful, more or less instinctive, and made with a happy insouciance that I now envy. Upon gradu-

ation from Columbia College in 1931, I received a Proudfit fellowship for graduate work, but spent most of the year writing somber and tragic short stories. That was perhaps the real moment of my determination not to pursue the higher reaches of the academic life. When, having moved on to Harvard I had a choice of continuing graduate work or taking a teaching job with what seemed to me then a munificent salary, it was also a simple decision.

"The Boston relatives of my newly-acquired wife warned me against this reckless and short-sighted hedonism. Yet, my experience at Sarah Lawrence College for the next ten years was probably the most valuable part of my early training. I am firmly committed to this kind of education for both teacher and student. My first book of literary criticism appeared in 1942, and I should pay my debt here to the editor Maxwell Perkins, the critic Edmund Wilson, and the historian Van Wyck Brooks, for their help and encouragement on this work. The idea for a series of books which would contain studies of the leading American novelists as individual artists, primarily, but as writers working within a common cultural framework, had already taken hold of my mind. A Guggenheim fellowship in 1943 made the project official, as it were; a later grant from the National Institute of Arts and Letters, in 1951, was in recognition of the first two books in the series.

"For the rest, I am still married, have three children, enjoy the vicissitudes of domesticity, believe in the value of sustained human relationships of every kind for writers, and even for literary critics. This is the enduring matrix of great literature to my mind; the superstructure of 'ideas,' to which contemporary criticism is perhaps unduly addicted, has to have this base. At least, I see my own books as studies in temperament, character and craft. The cultural environment, the ruling intellectual concepts in any epoch of American life, are of importance for the historical record; but what continues to fascinate me is the nature of an artist's primary experiences, his talent, his achievement."

* * *

The three volumes which Maxwell Geismar has published on the American novel are part of a projected five-volume history of the leading American novelists from 1840 to 1940, under the general title "The Novel in America." Charles Rolo, of the *Atlantic*, describes Geismar as "an open-minded critic. . . . He is alert to the play of social forces; he is well versed in the concepts of modern psychiatry; and he knows that a critic's paramount duty is close scrutiny of the written word."

PRINCIPAL WORKS: Writers in Crisis: The American Novel 1925-1940, 1942; The Last of the Provincials: The American Novel 1915-1925, 1947; Rebels and Ancestors: The American Novel 1890-

ABOUT: Atlantic October 1953; New Republic October 19, 1953.

GELLHORN, MARTHA ELLIS (1908-). For biographical sketch and list of earlier works and references, see TWENTIETH CENTURY AUTHORS, 1942.

* * *

Martha Gellhorn was a war correspondent for *Collier's* in China in 1941 and in England, Italy, France, and Germany from 1943 to 1945. Since then she has contributed short stories and articles on foreign affairs to a variety of periodicals—among them the *Atlantic, Good Housekeeping*, the *New Republic*, and the *Saturday Evening Post*. Her fiction is "thoroughly professional." The San Francisco *Chronicle* commented, in a review of her war novel *The Wine of Astonishment*: "Among America's women authors at the moment she is perhaps the most impressive in terms of ability, though there are others who may have a greater measure of talent." She writes with the skill and facility of a practiced journalist. Her stories in *The Honeyed Peace*, Patricia Blake wrote in the New York *Times*, show "her journalistic gift of isolating the pertinent and pathetic detail that illuminates the virtually indescribable totality of a wartime situation." Miss Gellhorn's one try at dramatic writing, a comedy on which she collaborated with Virginia Cowles, *Love Goes to Press*, ran for only five performances in 1947.

In 1945 Martha Gellhorn and Ernest Hemingway were divorced. She now lives in Cuernavaca, Mexico.

ADDITIONAL WORKS: Liana, 1944; The Wine of Astonishment, 1948; The Honeyed Peace (short stories) 1953.

*GEORGE, STEFAN ANTON (July 12, 1868-December 4, 1933). For biographical sketch and list of works and references, see TWENTIETH CENTURY AUTHORS, 1942.

* * *

ADDITIONAL WORKS IN ENGLISH TRANSLATION: Poems, 1943; Works, 1949.

ABOUT: Bennett, E. K. Stefan George; Capetanakis, D. Shores of Darkness; Columbia Dictionary of Modern European Literature; Antioch Review March 1949; Commonweal September 17, 1943; Contemporary Review September 1945; Nation May 22, 1943; New Statesman and Nation April 22, 1944; New Yorker April 17, 1943; Poetry September 1943; Saturday Review of Literature July 24, 1943; Sewanee Review July 1944.

* gā ōr'gĕ

GEORGE, WALTER LIONEL (March 20, 1882-January 30, 1926). For biographical sketch and list of works and references, see TWENTIETH CENTURY AUTHORS, 1942.

GERHARDI, WILLIAM ALEXANDER (November 21, 1895-). For biographical sketch and list of works and references, see TWENTIETH CENTURY AUTHORS, 1942.

* * *

William Gerhardi lives in London. He has published no new books in recent years, but he has written many essays, articles, and broadcasts. In 1947 he wrote an introduction called "My Literary Credo" to the collected revised edition of his works. During World War II he was with the European division of the B.B.C.

*GEROULD, Mrs. KATHARINE (FULLERTON) (February 6, 1879-July 27, 1944). For biographical sketch and list of earlier work and references, see TWENTIETH CENTURY AUTHORS, 1942

* * *

Katharine Gerould died at sixty-five in Princeton, N.J., after a long illness.

Ellery Sedgwick, editor of *Atlantic Monthly*, where many of Mrs. Gerould's short stories and essays were published, has spoken of their "long acquaintance, delightful to me, and of fame to the magazine," and of her "individual distinction and her intolerance of things which were not distinguished."

ABOUT: Sedgwick, E. (comp.) Atlantic Harvest: Time August 7, 1944.

* jĕr'ŭld

GIBBINGS, ROBERT (March 23, 1889-), Irish artist and travel writer, writes: "You couldn't find a nicer place to be born than the city of Cork in the South of Ireland, and I have always been glad of my choice. I was the second son of my father, a Protestant curate in the city who later became a canon of the diocese. He could have been a dean but the deanery was a small house and my father was a tall man: he said he couldn't bear the idea of sleeping with his feet through a window. My mother was the daughter of Robert Day, a citizen of the town, whose name is well known among archeologists. From my earliest years I wanted to be an artist, but considerable opposition had to be overcome before I was allowed to follow my bent, and I was still an art student in 1914 when war broke out. In August of that year I joined the Royal Munster Fusiliers; in the following May I went with a draft of them to the Dardanelles, and on the 28th June I had a bullet through my neck that nearly sent me to Glory.

"After the war I settled in London and began my career as an artist, specializing in wood-carving. In 1924 an opportunity arose to acquire the Golden Cockerel Press, a small publishing firm devoting itself to limited editions-de-luxe. There as controller I continued that policy, but added to fine typography wood-engravings by myself and other artists. *The Four Gospels*, decorated by Eric Gill, was acclaimed by one critic as 'the greatest piece of work yet produced by the revival of printing.' In 1933 I disposed of the Press and became a free lance again until 1936 when I was offered a position at Reading University as lecturer in typography and book production; soon after my acceptance of the post the National University of Ireland conferred on me an honorary Master of Arts degree.

"From time to time then I had written a few books which, though well reviewed, had comparatively small sales. It wasn't till the publication in 1940 of my *Sweet Thames Run Softly* that a gratifying change in my royalty account made its appearance. *Sweet Thames* was followed two years later by *Coming Down the Wye*, and after another two years my first Irish book, *Lovely Is the*

Lee, knocked the wind out of me with its reception. A Book-of-the-Month selection in America, it brought my work to a very wide audience, an audience that I am happy to say still remains faithful. There came a time when a mere five months' vacation each year did not seem enough for a hard working artist, so I resigned from the university and made my way to the South Seas. As a result of this voyage I wrote *Over the Reefs.* Then came another visit to Ireland and *Sweet Cork of Thee,* a book that has a far wider range of subject than its title suggests.

"Recently I have spent a great deal of my time in France, and *Coming Down the Seine* is now with the printers and due for publication in the fall [1953]. All the books that I have written have been illustrated with my own wood-engravings, generally as many as sixty or seventy to a volume. The double role of author and artist enables me to combine text and illustrations in a happier alliance than might otherwise be possible. Now as I write these notes I am about to pack my bags for another visit to France. This time I am travelling with a paint-box and, Muses permitting, my next book (1955 *D.V.*) will have not only woodcut illustrations again, but also some plates in colour.

"In all I have written and illustrated nine full-length books, and illustrated about fifty more for other authors. In the course of my life I have been married twice and have acquired seven children. As to bulk, I am a little over six feet in height and a little over 300 pounds in weight. Though not of the ballet-dancer build, there is still, I like to think, sufficient activity in the bones to carry me through a few more travel books."

PRINCIPAL WORKS: Iorana! A Tahitian Journal, 1932; Coconut Island, 1936; John Graham, Convict, 1937; Blue Angels and Whales, 1938; Sweet Thames Run Softly, 1940; Coming Down the Wye, 1942; Lovely Is the Lee, 1945; Over the Reefs and Far Away, 1948; Sweet Cork of Thee, 1951; Coming Down the Seine, 1953.

ABOUT: Mahony, B. E. Illustrators of Children's Books, 1744-1945; Current Biography 1948; New York Times November 9, 1946.

"GIBBON, LEWIS GRASSIC." See MITCHELL, J. L.

GIBBONS, FLOYD PHILLIPS (July 16, 1886-September 24, 1939). For biographical sketch and list of works and references, see TWENTIETH CENTURY AUTHORS, 1942.

* * *

ABOUT: Hoehn, M. (ed.) Catholic Authors, I.

GIBBONS, STELLA (January 5, 1902-). For autobiographical sketch and list of earlier works and references, see TWENTIETH CENTURY AUTHORS, 1942.

* * *

Stella Gibbons and her husband, A. B. Webb, live in Highgate, London. None of her quiet, witty, and sensitive novels has matched the success of *Cold Comfort Farm,* but, as Rosemary Carr Benét wrote in the *Saturday Review of Literature* in 1946, "Miss Gibbons must suffer from this constant deprecating comparison, like a mother with one unusually precocious offspring who continually overshadows the quiet, worthy members of her brood." She was elected a fellow of the Royal Society of Literature in 1950.

ADDITIONAL WORKS: The Rich House, 1941; Ticky, 1943; The Bachelor, 1944; The Gentle Powers (in England: Westwood) 1946; The Matchmaker, 1949; Conference at Cold Comfort Farm, 1949; The Swiss Summer, 1951; Fort of the Bear, 1953. Poetry—Collected Poems, 1950.

ABOUT: Books of Today May 1949; The Leader April 28, 1945.

GIBBS, ARTHUR HAMILTON (March 9, 1888-). For biographical sketch and list of earlier works and references, see TWENTIETH CENTURY AUTHORS, 1942.

* * *

A. Hamilton Gibbs lives in Middleboro, Mass. He has been a naturalized American citizen since 1926. His ties to Europe are strong, as his most recent writings show. In his novel *A Way of Life* he considered with sympathy the problems of a love affair between a young American paratrooper and an English country girl. His long poem *One Touch of France* is a nostalgic memoir of his experiences in France as a student and as a soldier in the World War I. The poem, 188 pages of free verse, gave the author scope for a variety of asides, anecdotes, historical allusions—"all of it," Morris Gilbert wrote in the New York *Times,* "devoted, the tribute of a servant and eternal lover to a refulgent and famous beauty."

ADDITIONAL WORKS: A Way of Life, 1947; One Touch of France, 1953.

ABOUT: Gibbs, A. H. One Touch of France.

GIBBS, Sir PHILIP HAMILTON (May 1, 1877-). For biographical sketch and list of works and references, see TWENTIETH CENTURY AUTHORS, 1942.

* * *

From his country home in Shamley Green, Essex, and from London itself, Sir Philip

Gibbs was an active witness of the bombings of England during World War II. His recent writings— novels and autobiography—reflect the impact of the war on England, its social and its moral structure. In 1950 he made a tour of Germany to get first-hand material for his novel of life in post-war Berlin, *Thine Enemy,* and this, like all his novels, was marked by earnestness and by wide and sympathetic observation of his material. But however contemporary his scene may be, his work remains essentially something of the past. The novelist L. A. G. Strong wrote in 1949: "Sir Philip does not so much interpret life as project a picture, nostalgic, gentle, dignified, of a lost world. He can record the gestures of the present, but his understanding and his love are with the past."

ADDITIONAL WORKS: (ed.) Bridging the Atlantic: Anglo-American Fellowship, 1943; Interpreter, 1943; Battle Within, 1944; Through the Storm, 1945; Pageant of the Years (autobiography) 1946; Hopeful Heart, 1947; Behind the Curtain, 1948; Crowded Company (autobiography) 1949; Both Your Houses, 1949; Thine Enemy, 1950; Spoils of Time, 1951; Cloud Above the Green, 1952; The Journalist's London, 1952; Called Back, 1953; The New Elizabethans, 1953; Lady of the River, 1954.

ABOUT: Gibbs, P. Pageant of the Years, Crowded Company; Hoehn, M. (ed.) Catholic Authors, I.

*GIBRAN, KAHLIL (1883-April 10, 1931). For biographical sketch and list of works and references, see TWENTIETH CENTURY AUTHORS, 1942.

* * *

Gibran's works are widely read and studied today. As a result, a problem has arisen over the disposition of his royalties. His will had authorized that all royalties should go to his birthplace, Bechari, Lebanon. In 1952, however, when the renewal of the copyrights of several of his books came up, Gibran's sister made a claim to the royalties. Pending a final settlement of this matter, Gibran's American publishers, Alfred Knopf, have set aside all royalties. Meanwhile, the New York *Times* wrote, "the profits just keep piling up." In a recent evaluation of Gibran, Gerald Heard said that he was not a great poet. "But he helps many people if not to translate and construe at least to transpose their experience."

ADDITIONAL WORKS: Secrets of the Heart (selected works) 1947; Tears and Laughter, 1947; Nymphs of the Valley, 1948; Spirits Rebellious, 1948; Tears and a Smile, 1950.

ABOUT: Hillyer, R. *Preface to* Gibran's Tears and a Smile; Naimy, M. Kahlil Gibran; New York Times Book Review November 23, 1952; Time January 22, 1945.

* jōōb rän'

GIBSON, WILFRID WILSON (October 2, 1878-). For biographical sketch and list of earlier works and references, see TWENTIETH CENTURY AUTHORS, 1942.

* * *

Wilfrid Gibson continues his long career as "poetic interpreter of the life of the ordinary man." Reviewers found his wartime verse too plodding, too lacking in imaginative inclination. But even in this group of poems, as the reviewer for the London *Times Literary Supplement* pointed out, "the reflective element . . . is sustained by a lyrical impulse without any loss of that fidelity to homely detail which is one of his chief virtues." In 1913 Gibson published a collection of five short plays of the Border country, *Within Four Walls,* family dramas about country people. The *Times'* reviewer found the plays dramatically deficient, although he felt that "each play tells its tale with balance and compassion." Gibson lives in West Byfleet, Surrey.

ADDITIONAL WORKS: The Challenge, 1942; Searchlights, 1943; The Outpost, 1944; Solway Ford, and Other Poems, 1945; Coldknuckles, 1947; Within Four Walls (plays) 1950.

*GIDE, ANDRÉ PAUL GUILLAUME (November 22, 1869-February 19, 1951). For biographical sketch and list of earlier works and references, see TWENTIETH CENTURY AUTHORS, 1942.

* * *

André Gide died of pneumonia at his home in the Rue Vaneau in Paris at eighty-one.

In 1947 he was awarded the Nobel prize for his "extensive and artistically important authorship in which he exposed the problems and conditions of mankind." The same year saw the publication in English translation of the first volume of his *Journals,* which have been called "among the books of our time which posterity may well call great." Kenneth Scholes has said of this work: "Always honest, incisive and stimulating, they are nevertheless organically uncomposed variations upon multiple themes: Christianity, literature, Communism, travel, music, sex. . . . Measured against their time, they partially document the major intellectual interests of Europe throughout half a century." In 1950 the American Academy of Arts and Letters elected Gide an honorary corresponding member. His books have been placed on the Vatican Index of forbidden literature, and have also incurred a Communist ban.

* zhēd

When in his eightieth year he was asked what he had most enjoyed in his life, he replied: "The *Arabian Nights,* the Bible, the pleasures of the flesh, and the Kingdom of God."

After Gide's death, Nicola Chiaromonte remarked that the writer "had doubtless outlived his fame and influence"; but Jean-Paul Sartre exclaimed, "What weight this old man of eighty, who had almost given up writing, still carried in the literature of today!" He has been called the writer who "led French literature out of the romantic and symbolist movement of the late nineteenth century . . . the prophet of individualism and the castigator of social injustice."

Sartre has summed up Gide's art as seeking "to establish a compromise between the risk and the rule; in him are balanced the law of the Protestant and the non-conformity of the homosexual, the proud individualism of the grand bourgeois and the puritan's taste for social restraint, a certain dryness, a difficulty in communicating with others and a humanism of Christian origin; a lively sensuality (which would like to be innocent); the observance of the rule is united in him with the quest for spontaneity."

ADDITIONAL WORKS AVAILABLE IN ENGLISH TRANSLATION: Recollections of the Assize Court, 1941; Imaginary Interviews, 1944; Journals (4 vols.) 1947-49; Fruits of the Earth, 1949; Notes on Chopin, 1949; Persephone, 1949; Corydon, 1950; Two Legends: Oedipus and Theseus, 1950; Correspondence, 1899-1926, between Paul Claudel and André Gide, 1952; My Theater, 1952; The Secret Drama of My Life, 1952; Madeleine (Et Nunc Manet in Te) 1952; Marshlands, and Prometheus Misbound, 1953.

ABOUT: Ames, V. M. André Gide; Fayer, M. H. Gide. Freedom and Dostoevsky; Guérard, A. André Gide; Mann, K. André Gide and the Crisis of Modern Thought; March, H. Gide and the Hound of Heaven; Martin du Gard, R. Recollections of André Gide; O'Brien, J. Portrait of André Gide; Painter, G. D. André Gide: A Critical and Biographical Study; Starkie, E. André Gide; Thomas, L. André Gide: The Ethic of the Artist; Atlantic Monthly February 1947; Commonweal May 4, 1951; France Illustration March 3, 1951; Nation July 14, 1951; New Republic May 7, 1951; Nouvelle Revue Française November 1951; Saturday Review of Literature November 29, 1947, March 3, 1951, March 22, 1952; Sewanee Review October 1952.

*GIEDION, SIEGFRIED (April 14, 1893-), Swiss art and social historian, was born in Langnau, Switzerland, son of John Giedion, a manufacturer. He studied engineering; and later art history under Heinrich Woelfflin (author of *Principles of Art History*). His writing career began with a

* ge'dyŭn

play and poems, and he believes historians who are not also poets never surpass the limits of specialization. In 1938 he was a professor at Harvard, and since 1928 he has been General Secretary of the CIAM (International Congresses for Modern Architecture). He began to teach in his present position at ETH (Eidgenössische Technische Hochschule, the Federal Institute of Technology) at Zurich in 1946, and is now professor of art history there.

Giedion's first published book in English was *Space, Time and Architecture: The Growth of a New Tradition,* which came out in 1941, and has now appeared in its ninth edition. These were the Charles Eliot Norton lectures of 1938-39. 'Despite its high-kiting title," said the *Nation,* "this book contains a graphic, direct, well-illustrated, and absorbing narrative." Its reputation grew through the years, and on the publication in 1954 of a revised and enlarged edition, Ben Ray Redman wrote in the *Saturday Review of Literature*: it is "packed with interesting facts and fine photographs." Giedion, said Redman, "believes that we are suffering from a schism between thought and feeling. . . . But he thinks, or would like to think, that 'in spite of the seeming confusion there is nevertheless a true, if hidden unity, a secret synthesis, in our present civilization.' He seeks to discover this hidden unity, which has not yet become 'a conscious and active reality,' through the study of our architecture; he looks to architecture for a reflection 'of the progress our own period has made toward consciousness of itself.' " This reviewer found him "more successful as historian than as philosopher." His survey of our architectural inheritance, beginning with the "organization of space" in the early Renaissance is "masterly, selective, and instructive."

In 1948 *Mechanization Takes Command* was published, a study of the evolution of mechanization in the last century and a half, its effects on modern civilization, and its historical and philosophical implications. The *American Journal of Sociology* said, "Dr. Giedion's discussion is invariably informing, entertaining and intelligent."

Giedion is an honorary member of the Royal Institute of British Architects, a member of the Flemish Academy, Belgium, and has a diploma as engineer and a Ph.D. degree. His wife, Carola Giedion-Welcker, is well-known as the author of books and articles on modern poetry, painting and plastic art. They live in Zurich.

PRINCIPAL WORKS: Space, Time and Architecture, 1941; Mechanization Takes Command, 1948; (ed.) Decade of New Architecture, 1951; Walter Gropius, Work and Teamwork, 1954.

ABOUT: Saturday Review of Literature April 10, 1954.

GILL, BRENDAN (October 4, 1914-), American novelist and short story writer, writes: "I was born in Hartford, Conn. My

Lotte Jacobi

father was Michael Henry Richard Gill, a physician in Hartford; my mother was Elizabeth Pauline Duffy Gill. I graduated from Yale College in 1936 and have been a contributor to the *New Yorker* since that time. A novel by me, *The Trouble of One House*, was published by Doubleday in 1950. I am married and live in Bronxville, N. Y., and Norfolk, Conn."

Some years ago Brendan Gill reported the following personal data to the *Saturday Evening Post*: that he is six feet tall, known to his friends as "the black Irishman," married to Anne Barnard, and the father of a son and a daughter. He wrote then that he and his wife "like long-distance driving, movies, tennis, and being invited places for the weekend. My hobby is architecture." In recent years he has become more reticent about himself. To an interviewer for the *Saturday Review of Literature* (which had selected him as one of the more promising novelists of 1951) he protested: "Interview me? Do you have to? I'm appalled, even though I realize that comes with a very poor grace from one who earns his living as a reporter."

Gill is a serious and rigorously disciplined writer. Although he has contributed many short stories to the *New Yorker* (of which he is a staff member) and other magazines, he has published only one novel so far—*The Trouble of One House*, a taut, restrained, and sensitive study of a dying woman and the effects of her death upon those in the household around her. Gill served as a

judge of fiction on the National Book Awards committee of 1952.

PRINCIPAL WORK: The Trouble of One House, 1950.

ABOUT: Saturday Evening Post August 9, 1941; Saturday Review of Literature February 17, 1951.

GILL, ERIC ROWLAND (1882-November 17, 1940), English carver, engraver, draughtsman and writer, was born in Brighton where his father was curate of the church of "The Countess of Huntingdon's Connexion." In 1897, the family moved to Chichester and the boy was sent to art school there. His father decided to make him an architect and in 1899 he

was apprenticed in a London office. Gill did not, however, adopt this profession. His whole life was to be a protest against the artificial distinction between the artist and the ordinary man, and for this reason he chose the humbler craft of lettering in place of the more impressive profession of architecture. He made his living for some time by doing the stone carving and lettering for tombstones.

In 1910 he produced his first piece of sculpture, *Madonna and Child*, which received favorable criticism. Through the influence of Augustus John he gave an exhibition at the Chenil Gallery in London in 1911, and this brought him recognition and the independence to devote himself to his art. About this time he went through a profound spiritual struggle. Although as an exceptionally talented craftsman he was in a favored position in society and could live more or less as he pleased, he did not retreat from contemporary problems. On the contrary, his aim, as he expressed it, was "to make a cell of good living in the chaos of our world."

Through the Fabian Society, he entered the Socialist movement. His revolt against the injustice of the possessing classes was unequivocal. ("Incomparably more horrible that men of business should rule us and impose their foul point of view on the world, than it should be if the whole race of men and women should rot their bodies with lechery and drunkenness.") But he soon discovered that the Socialist movement was "not moved, still less inspired, by any ideas of man or of man's work, other than those of the capitalist world against whose injustices and cruelty it was in revolt."

He left London and helped to found an ideal community in Ditchling. When life at Ditchling was spoiled by too much publicity, he went to live alone in the wilds of Wales. When solitary life in Wales became too difficult, he came to Buckinghamshire where he found "a quadrangle of decent English brick buildings, the only decent way to live," and he lived there until he died. His experience had made him abandon all hope of reform by political means, and he felt that the essential evil—and its final remedy—lay somewhere in the sphere of religion. His spiritual pilgrimage led him, in 1913, to enter the Roman Catholic church. Once within the Church he became a fierce critic of the timidity of his fellow churchmen in dealing with social problems.

Gill's search for the good life was reflected in his work in stone and in his books. In 1913 he was commissioned to carve the Stations of the Cross in Westminster Cathedral. These sculptures are marked by stark sincerity and conviction; many critics objected to their so-called archaism. His statue *Mother and Child* is in the Tate Gallery, London, and other works are to be found in museums and churches throughout England. He expounded his religious, social, and aesthetic views in *Christianity and Art* (1927), *An Essay on Stone Cutting with a Preface about God* (1917), and finally in his autobiography, which Herbert Read found to be a noble book with "the sincerity and significance of a Pilgrim's Progress."

Gill has been described as an eccentric in appearance. He usually wore a long monk-like robe and a beard. A man of passionate convictions, he was nevertheless distinguished for his great personal humility and kindness. He was married, in 1904, to Ethel Moore, and they had four children.

PRINCIPAL WORKS: An Essay on Stone-Cutting with a Preface about God, 1917; Christianity and Art, 1927; Beauty Looks after Herself, 1934; Clothes; An Essay upon the Nature and Significance of the Garments Worn by Men and Women, 1934; Engravings, 1934; Essay on Typography, 1936; Money and Morals, 1936; Trousers and the Most Precious Ornaments, 1937; Work and Leisure, 1935; Work and Property, 1937; Autobiography, 1941; Last Essays, 1943; Letters of Eric Gill, 1948.

ABOUT: Attwater, D. Eric Gill: Workman, Modern Christian Revolutionaries; Gill, E. Autobiography; Hoehn, M. (ed.) Catholic Authors, I; Read, H. A Coat of Many Colours; Thorp, J., Eric Gill; Eric Gill (Contemporary British Artists, 1925).

GILLIGAN, EDMUND (June 7, 1899-), American novelist and newspaperman, was born in Waltham, Mass., the son of John and Ellen (Dillon) Gilligan, who had immigrated from Ireland. A good part of his boyhood was spent in West Newton, where he attended Newton High School, and near Gloucester, the background which he recreates with force and energy in many of his later novels of adventure at sea.

Gilligan's first literary venture, while still a schoolboy, was an entry in a story contest run by the Boston *Post*. The prize was the munificent sum of $5, which Daniel (Gilligan) Boone and his chum, Kit (Tedesco) Carson (or Anthony Tedesco, now well-known as a book designer) desperately wanted for the purchase of a .22 calibre rifle with which to track their imaginary wild-West, and, nearer home, a fox. As the contest was open only to women, Edmund submitted his story under the pen-name of 'Lily Lyman'; and he won. Five years later, still in his teens, he got his first newspaper job on the same paper, the Boston *Post*.

In World War I, Gilligan enlisted in the U. S. Navy—he first tried to enlist in the Royal Canadian Flying Corps—and fought as a quartermaster on a submarine chaser in the North Atlantic. His ship, working with Canadian destroyers and minesweepers, hunted the German U-boats which infested Newfoundland waters; and the patriotism, courage, and anger of the men, both Canadian and American, some of them fishermen now hunting the enemy in waters where in peacetime they earned a hard and precarious living, later provided Gilligan with the living images of good and evil, the atmosphere of danger and habitual courage which, as an author, he uses so effectively. If Gilligan has a romantic or melodramatic eye—as some of his critics have remarked— it reflects a romance and melodrama based on a profound admiration for the qualities he observed then and which he had known before in the fishermen of Gloucester.

Before the end of the war, Gilligan was transferred to the naval aviation school at Massachusetts Institute of Technology. Discharged after the Armistice, he returned to work in Boston, alternating periods of work on various papers with attendance at Harvard College where he studied English under Professors Copeland and Briggs. He graduated from Harvard College, B.S. 1926. From 1926 to 1930 he was a reporter on the Boston *Post*. Following the death of his first wife, Gilligan moved to New York City. He worked on the New York *Sun* from 1930 to 1939, and then for the Luce publications, where he was an associate editor of *Fortune* from 1939 to 1942.

Since 1937, when his first book appeared, Gilligan has been a successful and prolific writer. In his most characteristic novels, his sagas of the sea, Gilligan combines carefully plotted and dramatic narratives with a wealth of visual detail and poetic description. Typical are *White Sails Crowding*, an epic of halibut fishing off the Grand Banks in winter, "a battle of ice and sea"; and *The Gaunt Woman*, the war-time odyssey of a Gloucester schooner with a Bannon skipper who, fishing on the Grand Banks, sights a mysterious "black-hulled square-rigger," the mother-ship for a pack of German submarines.

In reviewing *The Ringed Horizon*, the *Saturday Review of Literature* said that Gilligan writes "nautical yarns as gripping, as brave, and as salty as those of Marryatt or Stevenson"; and the New York *Herald Tribune*, reviewing *Storm at Sable Island*, said that his novels "possess serious purpose, depth and a sure knowledge of evil and good in human beings." Of his dramatic novel *I Name Thee Mara*, Walter Havighurst wrote: "Too much symbolism, too many correspondences of twentieth century fishermen to too many ancient myths. The result is murky and magnificent."

Gilligan's first wife was Marjorie Work, who died in 1929. They had one daughter. In 1933 he married Nancy Rittenhouse and they have three children. He works at home in a large house on a rural slope near Woodstock, N. Y.; he is a ruddy, powerful man, somewhat moody, a genial host, and an accomplished sportsman. He often returns to the New England coast, and to Newfoundland waters. At present he is the "Rod and Gun" columnist for the New York *Herald Tribune*.

PRINCIPAL WORKS: One Lives to Tell the Tale, 1937; Boundary Against Night, 1938; White Sails Crowding, 1939; Strangers in the Vly, 1941; The Gaunt Woman, 1943; The Ringed Horizon, 1943; Voyage of the Golden Hind, 1945; I Name Thee Mara, 1946; Storm at Sable Island, 1948; Sea Dog (juvenile) 1954.

ABOUT: Wilson Library Bulletin March 1945.

GILMAN, LAWRENCE (July 5, 1878-September 9, 1939). For biographical sketch and list of works and references, see TWENTIETH CENTURY AUTHORS, 1942.

* * *

ADDITIONAL WORK: Orchestral Music: An Armchair Guide (ed. E. Cushing) 1951.

ABOUT: Haggin, B. H. Music in The Nation; National Cyclopedia of American Biography (1949); Taylor, D. Music to My Ears; House Beautiful January 1952.

GILPATRIC, GUY (January 21, 1896-July 7, 1950). For biographical sketch and list of earlier works and references, see TWENTIETH CENTURY AUTHORS, 1942.

* * *

Guy Gilpatric and his wife were found shot to death in their home in Santa Barbara, Calif. The writer, who was fifty-four, apparently had taken his wife's life and his own in a suicide agreement when they learned that Mrs. Gilpatric had cancer.

The best known of the writer's last books, *Action in the North Atlantic*, was written (according to the *Christian Science Monitor*) "with both eyes on the movies," where it subsequently appeared. Of his series of stories centered around the character of Mr. Glencannon, the *Library Journal* commented "Gilpatric's storytelling has Hollywood flexibility and makes summer entertainment for casual readers."

Gilpatric's last work was a collaboration with Norman Reilly Raine, author of the "Tugboat Annie" stories, on a novel bringing together Annie and Mr. Glencannon. *Glencannon Meets Tugboat Annie* was published posthumously as a serial in the *Saturday Evening Post*.

ADDITIONAL WOKS: Action in the North Atlantic, 1943; Mr. Glencannon Ignores the War, 1944; First Glencannon Omnibus, 1945; Flying Stories, 1946; (with N. R. Raine) Glencannon Meets Tugboat Annie, 1950; The Last Glencannon Omnibus, 1953.

ABOUT: Conrad, B. *Introduction to* The Last Glencannon Omnibus; New York Times July 8, 1950; Saturday Evening Post August 26, 1950; Time July 17, 1950.

*GILSON, ÉTIENNE HENRY (1884-). For biographical sketch and list of earlier works and references, see TWENTIETH CENTURY AUTHORS, 1942.

* * *

In 1951 Genêt, in the *New Yorker's* "Letter from Paris," described Étienne Gilson

* zhēl sôN'

as "the Collège de France's most erudite, most venerable exponent of medieval Catholic philosophy, France's greatest authority on Thomas Aquinas, and possibly the greatest living Thomist." Most remarkable about Gilson's career is the degree to which he has successfully combined the recondite aspects of his scholarship with practical contemporary political action. He attended the San Francisco Conference in 1945 as a technical adviser to the French delegation, and he was a member of the French delegation to UNESCO. In 1946 he was elected to the French Academy. A regular contributor of articles on international politics to *Le Monde,* Gilson became involved in a heated political controversy in 1950 and 1951. In an article in *Le Monde* he used the word *neutralisme* to describe a political policy he favored of keeping Europe out of any future war which, he argued, would devastate her. He urged French neutrality and criticized French cooperation with the United States in taking a firm stand against Soviet aggression. In a dramatic gesture he resigned his Collège de France chair and stated that he would live in North America rather than remain in France to see another war. Gilson thereupon moved to Toronto, Canada, where he taught at the Institute of Medieval Studies. He visited the United States in 1950 and gave a series of lectures on the medieval philosopher Duns Scotus at Notre Dame University.

ADDITIONAL WORKS IN TRANSLATION: Being and Some Philosophers, 1949; Dante the Philosopher, 1949; Heloise and Abelard, 1951; Choir of Muses, 1953; A History of Christian Philosophy in the Middle Ages, 1955.

ABOUT: Hoehn, M. (ed.) Catholic Authors, I; Nation May 12, 1951; New Yorker March 3, 1951.

*GIONO, JEAN (March 30, 1895-). For biographical sketch and list of earlier works and references, see TWENTIETH CENTURY AUTHORS, 1942.

* * *

Because Jean Giono tolerated and, according to some sources (see the *Dictionnaire Biographique Français Contemporain*), took a "rather favorable attitude toward" the Vichy government, he was blacklisted by the National Writers' Committee and from 1944 to 1947 published nothing. During this period, however, he was not idle, and his recently published works have given evidence of a revived and in some ways even more powerful talent. He has begun a pro-

* jô nō′

jected series of twenty books, of which two, *Un Roi Sans Divertissement* and *Noé,* have been published. He has translated Melville's *Moby Dick* into French and written a book on Melville, *Pour Saluer Melville.*

Two novels by Giono have appeared in English translation since the end of the war. One of these, *The Blue Boy,* was semi-autobiographical, a series of interrelated stories set in his native region of Provence, full of the color, the passion, and the simple humanity of the land and its people, saturated (as Justin O'Brien wrote) "with a rich poetry compounded of protracted, often charming images, a childlike naïveté and an intoxication with words." The other novel, *The Horseman on the Roof,* was an extraordinary study of a cholera epidemic in 1838 which ironically, in spite of its grim subject matter, revealed such *élan* and zest for life that Henri Peyre called it "one of the most cheerful novels written by a Frenchman in the last ten or fifteen years." Giono lives a simple, rather solitary life in the Provence town of Manosque where he was born. Here, Henry Miller points out, like Faulkner in Mississippi, "Giono has created his own terrestrial domain, a mythical domain far closer to reality than books of history and geography."

ADDITIONAL WORK IN ENGLISH TRANSLATION: Joy of Man's Desiring, 1940; The Blue Boy, 1946; The Horseman on the Roof (in England: The Hussar on the Roof) 1953.

ABOUT: Columbia Dictionary of Modern European Literature; Dictionnaire Biographique Français Contemporain; Miller, H. The Books in My Life; Publications of the Modern Language Association December 1948; Vogue March 1954.

GIOVANNITTI, ARTURO (January 7, 1884-). For biographical sketch and list of works and references, see TWENTIETH CENTURY AUTHORS, 1942.

*GIRAUDOUX, JEAN (October 29, 1882-January 31, 1944). For biographical sketch and list of earlier works and references, see TWENTIETH CENTURY AUTHORS, 1942.

* * *

Jean Giraudoux died in Paris at sixty-one. Although at his death he was still serving as minister of propaganda in the Vichy regime, he had forbidden the production of any of his plays during the occupation. *The Madwoman of Chaillot,* completed in 1943, he left with the actor-producer Louis Jouvet bearing the optimistic notation: "To be

* zhē rō dōō′

produced October 17, 1945." It was in fact produced on December 19, 1945.

The Madwoman of Chaillot, The Enchanted, and *Ondine* were produced and published in this country after their author's death. Their translator and adaptor, Maurice Valency, has said that Giraudoux "writes something that is neither comedy nor tragedy, in a manner that is neither realistic nor unrealistic. Paradox is the essence of his form; in these plays the equivocal is made to serve as a means of precise communication." *Tiger at the Gates,* adapted by Christopher Fry, had a 1955 London production.

Giraudoux has been called (by Allardyce Nicoll) "perhaps . . . the greatest French dramatic writer of the thirties." His successful integration into the theatre of Jouvet prompted the actor to characterize him as "one who possesses that especial eloquence, that sacred gift of speech, which differentiates the writer for the theatre and sets him alone and apart from the journeyman dramatist, as elect and predestined." Wallace Fowlie, who finds in Giraudoux "the fecund imagination of a poet who writes in prose," adds that "it may seem at first a work ridiculously clear and simple, but one has to look for a long time into clear waters in order to see their depth."

ADDITIONAL WORK IN ENGLISH TRANSLATION: The Madwoman of Chaillot, 1947; The Enchanted, 1950; Ondine, 1954.

ABOUT: Fowlie, W. Clowns and Angels; Le Sage, L. Jean Giraudoux, Surrealism, and the German Romantic Ideal; Nicoll, A. World Drama; Theatre Arts August 1949, November 1949.

*GIRONELLA, JOSÉ MARIA** (December 31, 1917-   ), Spanish novelist, was born José Maria Gironella Pous in the province

Basabe

of Gerona, in Catalonia, and educated in primary school and in an ecclesiastical seminary. He left the seminary at the age of thirteen to become an apprentice in a liquor factory and had no further formal education. In 1933 he became an apprentice in a grocery store, in 1934 a page boy in the Banco Arnus where he rose to the position of clerk. From 1936 to 1939 Gironella served at the front in the Spanish Civil War. After the war he worked for a while in the wholesale clothing business and as a second-hand

* hē rô nä′lyä

book seller. He left Spain in 1948 for Paris. "In Paris," he writes, "I drove a sand truck and gave chess lessons to tourists from the United States. Since 1949 I have lived entirely by my pen." Gironella remained in Paris until 1952 and during this period visited England and Switzerland. He had meanwhile, in 1944, published a long poem in *Entregas de Poesia* (Barcelona) with the title "Winter Has Come and You Are Not Here." His first novel, *Un Hombre* ("A Man"), appeared in 1946 and won the Nadal prize (equivalent in Spain to the Prix Goncourt in France). Two years later he published another novel, *La Marea* ("The Tide"), which was translated into French.

In 1955 an English translation of *The Cypresses Believe in God* brought Gironella immediate international fame. This long and powerful novel is planned as the first volume of a trilogy based on the turbulent history of Spain just before, during, and after the Spanish Civil War. Gironella describes his project as follows: "The book will have sequels, though it can be read independently. *The Cypresses Believe in God* [a story of a provincial middle class family and the effects of political events upon them] covers the pre-war period and the opening days of the Civil War. The second volume will cover the three years of the Civil War, 1936-39— on both sides, in one region and another, telling what I saw, what I lived through, and what I know. It will be called 'One Million Dead,' that being approximately the number who died in Spain including those killed at the front, by bombardment, and behind the lines in both zones. The third volume will be in two parts. In one I shall describe the life of Spain during the period since the war; the other will give the life of the Spanish exiles abroad. The third volume has no title as yet."

Gironella's principal ambition in this massive undertaking is to analyze impartially and objectively the problems of modern Spain. He writes: "An infinity of books has been written on the Spanish Civil War, but none impartially. Some are red, others white. . . . I have thought of my book as a reply to those books on Spain written by Hemingway, Koestler, Malraux, and Bernanos. But to say so would perhaps give the impression that it is a specifically political book, and the truth is that my book is a novel, though the characters and situations move against a background of actual facts and within a real geography. They also follow a rigorous chronological order. The books of the four authors mentioned above do not convince me—not for political reasons, but because they give a small view, a folkloric view of the Spanish drama and do not confront the theme in its totality."

The novel had extraordinary success in Spain. Gironella explains this success as follows: "My chief occupation has been objectivity, conceding to all those involved both their best and their worst motives. In Spain this objectivity (better, my desire to be just) has been what has surprised my readers and has led to the exhaustion of the first edition in one month. I can say that in Spain the appearance of the book has produced an authentic searching of consciences. People devour the book; the critics are unanimous in considering it the loftiest literary achievement of Spanish letters since the Civil War."

On its publication in the United States, *The Cypresses Believe in God* was hailed as the best novel to come out of Spain in many years. *Commonweal* called it a major literary event, announcing that "the search for a Great Catholic Novel of contemporary life can end." Thomas G. Bergin, in the *Saturday Review,* found it a richly revealing portrait of Spanish life. Some of the political details, he pointed out, may seem remote and foreign to American readers. "Yet it must be added that the political attitudes are so dramatically incarnate in the characters of the tale that at no time does the historical element become arid or detached from the humanity of the story."

Since completing his book Gironella has spent most of his time traveling in Spain, in preparation for his second volume, and writing articles for Spanish literary periodicals. His articles, which appear regularly in the periodical *ABC* (Madrid), he describes as having national importance because "for the first time since the Civil War a writer has publicly denounced things in this country that are not going as they ought to." He is married to Magda Castañer and lives in Gerona. He lists his special interests as "the 'Spanish problem' especially from the social and political point of view, Christianity, Communism, Masonry. At the present [1953] I am ardently studying universal history and everything referring to these fields. I also study chess." He belongs to no clubs, political parties, or other organizations and says: "I should like my books to be read by many Spanish exiles, who will perhaps appreciate my objective impartiality."

PRINCIPAL WORK IN ENGLISH TRANSLATION: The Cypresses Believe in God, 2 vols., 1955.

ABOUT: Commonweal April 15, 1955; Saturday Review April 16, 1955.

*GLADKOV, FEDOR VASILIEVICH (1883-). For biographical sketch and list of works and references, see TWENTIETH CENTURY AUTHORS, 1942.

* * *

Feodor Gladkov, according to recent issues of the *International Who's Who*, lives in Moscow and is one of the most highly honored of Soviet writers. He is a member of the Presidium Union of Soviet Writers and has been awarded the Order of the Red Banner and the Order of Lenin.

ABOUT: Columbia Dictionary of Modern European Literature.

* glŭt kôf'

GLAESER, ERNST (1902-). For biographical sketch and list of works and references, see TWENTIETH CENTURY AUTHORS, 1942.

* * *

Ernst Glaeser's recent works have been published only in Germany and are not available in English translation. These include a collection of tales, which appeared in 1946, and a book on the problems of German political reconstruction, in 1947. In 1951 he edited a German travel book.

GLASGOW, ELLEN ANDERSON GHOLSON (April 22, 1874-November 21, 1945). For biographical sketch and list of earlier works and references, see TWENTIETH CENTURY AUTHORS, 1942.

* * *

Ellen Glasgow died at seventy-one, following a heart attack at her home in Richmond, Va.

Miss Glasgow's last published work during her lifetime, *A Certain Measure* (1943), subtitled "An Interpretation of Prose Fiction," a collection of her prefaces to the Virginia Edition of her novels, was called by H. M. Jones "a notable contribution both to the art of fiction and to the ways by which fiction, maturely conceived, can illuminate American life." Nine years after her death, her autobiography, *The Woman Within*, was published. A personal and revealing document, reviewers found it "more engrossing, more rich, more deeply moving than her most successful novels" (Hudson Strode in the New York *Times*).

"My major theme," Miss Glasgow wrote of her own work, "is the conflict of human beings with human nature, of civilization with biology. In this constant warfare tragedy lies not in defeat but in surrender."

Her steady, coherent "endeavor to get the true values of the life she knew best into literature" has been praised by Henry Seidel Canby, who characterized her as "a major social historian of our times, who had almost single-handed rescued Southern fiction from the glamorous sentimentality of the Lost Cause, and almost alone had viewed Southern culture with sympathetic but unclouded eyes."

ADDITIONAL WORK: A Certain Measure, 1943; The Woman Within (autobiography) 1954.
ABOUT: Glasgow, E. A Certain Measure, The Woman Within; Adams, J. D. Shape of Books to Come; Cabell, J. B. Let Me Lie; Canby, H. S. American Memoir; Commager, H. S. American Mind; Geismar, M. Rebels and Ancestors; Kazin, A. On Native Grounds; Van Gelder, R. Writers and Writing; Nation October 16, 1943; 19th Century November 1949; New Republic October 25, 1943, December 10, 1945; New York Times November 22, 1945; Saturday Review of Literature October 16, 1943, December 1, 1945, December 22, 1945.

GLASPELL, SUSAN (July 1, 1882-July 27, 1948). For autobiographical sketch and list of earlier works and references, see TWENTIETH CENTURY AUTHORS, 1942.

* * *

Susan Glaspell died, at sixty-six, in Provincetown, Mass.

Miss Glaspell wrote no more plays after her Pulitzer prize-winning *Alison's House.* Her last two novels showed the same qualities of sensitive perception, sympathy, and quiet excellence that characterized her earlier work. Rose Feld called *Norma Ashe* "a searching and compassionate book that makes the reader one with its lost heroine." *Judd Rankin's Daughter* was a study of American family life, "a prevailingly hopeful picture of friendliness and honesty and grass-roots wisdom among ordinary, unassuming people."

Her maturity and her sure artistic competence did not win Susan Glaspell a wide and enthusiastic reading public, but readers who know her work will probably agree with the late Thomas Sugrue who said: "Susan Glaspell writes a story with delicacy and skill, blending the thoughts, ideas, emotions, and personalities of characters so that they intertwine, yet stand out for themselves like the pieces in a New England rag carpet. . . . The wild songs of the new prophets are all well, but the normal ear can catch but a few notes

of them. Here is a melody that can be heard entire."

ADDITIONAL WORKS: Norma Ashe, 1942; Judd Rankin's Daughter, 1945.
ABOUT: Independent Woman January 1946; New York Times July 28, 1948.

GLASS, MONTAGUE MARSDEN (July 23, 1877-February 3, 1934). For biographical sketch and list of works and references, see TWENTIETH CENTURY AUTHORS, 1942.

GLENN, ISA (1888-). For biographical sketch and list of works and references, see TWENTIETH CENTURY AUTHORS, 1942.

GLYN, Mrs. ELINOR (SUTHERLAND) (October 17, 1864-September 23, 1943). For biographical sketch and list of works and references, see TWENTIETH CENTURY AUTHORS, 1942.

* * *

Elinor Glyn died in a London nursing home at seventy-eight. She was survived by two daughters, Lady Davson and Lady Williams.

The novelist who shocked and amused a wide public during the Edwardian period has been called an "incurable romantic" beneath her "pretensions to sophistication and dalliance with 'naughtiness.' " "She was by nature intense," the London *Times* said of Mrs. Glyn, "and lived every moment of a long and adventurous life. Despite some foibles and petty vanities, she was a vital and courageous woman."

ABOUT: London Times September 24, 1943; New York Times September 24, 1943.

GODDEN, RUMER (December 10, 1907-). For autobiographical sketch and list of earlier works and references, see TWENTIETH CENTURY AUTHORS, 1942.

* * *

Rumer Godden is now settled in Buckinghamshire, England, the wife of James Haynes Dixon (whom she married in 1949). Her ties to India are still strong. In 1950 she wrote that she had been going back and forth between England and India all her life, "perpetually homesick for one or the other, but especially for Kashmir, where I lived until lately." Her present home is a seventeenth century English cottage. Here she lives with her husband, her two daughters (by a former marriage) and here, she writes, "I grow roses, breed Pekingese and listen to gossip as heard over the hedge." Her life is far more active than that statement would suggest, however, and her recent writings have established her as one of the most consistently successful of contemporary English women novelists.

India remains the background of much of Miss Godden's fiction—a background richly observed and strikingly delineated. In *The River*—a short but quietly impressive study of an adolescent girl's coming of age in India—Miss Godden produced what W. Y. Tindall called "one of the most delicate and certainly the most exotic of the novels of adolescence which have abounded since Butler's *Way of All Flesh,* Maugham's *Of Human Bondage,* and Joyce's *Portrait of the Artist.*" A work of delicacy and sensitivity, it portrays the wonder and innocence of childhood against the ancient wisdom of nature and of India. In 1951 it was made into a motion picture under the direction of Jean Renoir. But whether Miss Godden's scene is India, a remote Pacific Island (scene of *A Breath of Air*), a ballet school in London (*A Candle for St. Jude*), or an old house in London through which a small panorama of English life is projected (*Take Three Tenses*), she writes with expert craftsmanship and, in Tindall's phrase, "considerable art."

Rumer Godden's sister, Jon Godden (born in 1908), has in recent years published several well-received novels, among them *The Peacock* and *The City and the Wave.*

Correction: Rumer Godden's birthdate is 1907, not 1909, as given in TWENTIETH CENTURY AUTHORS, 1942.

ADDITIONAL WORKS: Thus Far and No Further (*in England*: Rungli-Rungliot) 1944; Bengal Journey, 1945; Take Three Tenses (*in England*: Fugue in Time) 1945; The River, 1946; Dolls' House (juvenile) 1947; In Noah's Ark (verse) 1949; A Breath of Air, 1950; The Mousewife (juvenile) 1951; Kingfishers Catch Fire, 1953; Hans Christian Andersen, 1955.

ABOUT: English Journal March 1952; New York Herald Tribune Book Review December 18, 1949, October 8, 1950.

*GOETEL, FERDYNAND (1890-).

For biographical sketch and list of works and references, see TWENTIETH CENTURY AUTHORS, 1942.

* * *

Ferdynand Goetel remained in Poland during World War II. There have been no

* gĕ'tĕl

recent reports on his whereabouts or on his works.

ABOUT: Columbia Dictionary of Modern European Literature.

GOETZ, GEORGE. See CALVERTON, V. F.

*GOGARTY, OLIVER ST. JOHN (August 17, 1878-). For biographical sketch and list of earlier works and references, see TWENTIETH CENTURY AUTHORS, 1942.

* * *

Since 1939 Oliver St. John Gogarty has lived in the United States. His official residence is the family home, Renvyle, in County Galway, but he has long maintained an apartment in New York City. A great talker and a lively wit, he has written with most success about himself, about his friends, and about the Dublin of his early days. Here—with his buoyant spirits, sharp eye, and, more often than not, his even sharper tongue—he "shines as a literary entertainer who can excite the imagination and enlarge the spirit" (wrote Horace Reynolds in the New York *Times* in 1950).

Probably the most neglected part of Gogarty's work is his poetry, overshadowed as it is by the gossipy exuberance of his prose. In the collection of his poems entitled *Perennial,* Ruth Lechlitner found "poems continuously distinguished for their classic form, their romantic manner with a touch both delicate and modern, their lively and urbane wit." Robert Hillyer hailed the publication of his *Collected Poems* in 1951 as "a literary event of the first magnitude."

ADDITIONAL WORKS: Perennial (poems) 1944; Mr. Petunia (novel) 1945; Mourning Becomes Mrs. Spendlove, and Other Portraits, Grave and Gay, 1948; Rolling Down the Lea, 1950; Intimations, 1950; It Isn't This Time of Year at All, 1954; Collected Poems, 1954; Unselected Poems, 1954.

ABOUT: Gogarty, O. St. J. It Isn't This Time of Year at All; Hoehn, M. (ed.) Catholic Authors, I; Mercier, V. & Greene, D. H. 1000 Years of Irish Prose; Weygandt, C. The Time of Yeats; Yeats, W. B. and others, *Prefaces to* Collected Poems of Oliver St. John Gogarty.

* gō'gĕr tĭ

GOLD, MICHAEL (April 12, 1894-).

For biographical sketch and list of works and references, see TWENTIETH CENTURY AUTHORS, 1942.

* * *

Mike Gold has been called "the dean of proletarian writers in the U.S.A." He is a contributing editor of the magazine *Masses & Mainstream*. In 1954 a collection of his writings over the past forty years was published as *The Mike Gold Reader*.

ADDITIONAL WORK: The Mike Gold Reader, 1954.

ABOUT: Sillen, S. *Introduction to* The Mike Gold Reader.

GOLDBERG, ISAAC (November 1, 1887-July 14, 1938). For biographical sketch and list of works and references, see TWENTIETH CENTURY AUTHORS, 1942.

GOLDING, LOUIS (November 1895-). For autobiographical sketch and list of earlier works and references, see TWENTIETH CENTURY AUTHORS, 1942.

* * *

Louis Golding writes from London that since 1941 "he has continued simultaneously the adventures of Elsie Silver and the contemporary history of Europe in a series of interlinked but independent novels: *Mr. Emmanuel, The Glory of Elsie Silver, The Dangerous Places;* and now, the culmination of the whole enormous project, 'To the Quayside,' the novel he is at present [1952] completing." He says that he would now add *Mr. Emmanuel* to *The Miracle Boy* and *Five Silver Daughters* on his list of his best work.

ADDITIONAL WORKS: Who's There Within? 1942; No News from Helen, 1943; The Pale Blue Nightgown (short stories) 1944; The Vicar of Dunkerly Briggs (short stories) 1944; The Glory of Elsie Silver, 1945; Three Jolly Gentlemen, 1946; Honey for the Ghost, 1949; The Dangerous Places, 1951; The Loving Brothers, 1952. *Non-Fiction*—The Bare-knuckle Breed, 1952.

GOLDRING, DOUGLAS (January 7, 1887-). For autobiographical sketch and list of earlier works and references, see TWENTIETH CENTURY AUTHORS, 1942.

* * *

Douglas Goldring writes: "During the war, his sons having joined the forces, he lived in a cottage in Hampshire, near Bordon Camp. On July 9, 1942, his elder son was killed in action in North Africa. In the autumn of 1945 he moved to a small Georgian house in Deal, Kent, which is his present home."

Goldring has published no fiction in recent years, but has worked mainly in the fields of biography, history, and travel writing. He has written his own personal reminiscences in *Life Interests* and his reminiscences of the *English Review* circle in *South Lodge* and in his biography of Ford Madox Ford, published in the United States under the title *Trained for Genius*.

ADDITIONAL WORKS: South Lodge, 1943; The Nineteen Twenties, 1945; Journeys in the Sun, 1946; Marching with the Times, 1947; Trained for Genius: The Life and Writings of Ford Madox Ford (in England: The Last Pre-Raphaelite) 1948; Life Interests, 1948; Home Ground, 1949; Foreign Parts, 1950; Regency Portrait Painter: The Life of Sir Thomas Lawrence, 1951; Three Romantic Countries, 1951.

ABOUT: Goldring, D. Life Interests; New Statesman and Nation January 19, 1946.

"GOLDSMITH, PETER." See PRIESTLEY, J. B.

GOLLOMB, JOSEPH (November 15, 1881-May 23, 1950). For autobiographical sketch and list of earlier works and references see TWENTIETH CENTURY AUTHORS, 1942.

* * *

Joseph Gollomb died of a heart attack at sixty-eight in his New York City home.

His last work was a biography of Albert Schweitzer written for teen-age readers. The book was generally praised, the New York *Times* saying of it, "The pace is brisk, the sequence of events rich and colorful, and the style pleasant." The series of books for boys of high-school age which formed a major portion of his work is characterized by the Chicago *Sun* as "tense, realistic, and swept by a revolving beam of idealism."

ADDITIONAL WORKS: Young Heroes of the War (with A. Taylor) 1943; Up at City High, 1945; Tiger At City High, 1946; Window on the World, 1947; Albert Schweitzer: Genius in the Jungle, 1949.

ABOUT: New York Times May 24, 1950.

GOLSSENAU. See VIETH VON GOLSSENAU

GOMBERG. See LIDIN

*GÓMEZ DE LA SERNA, RAMÓN (July 5, 1888-). For biographical sketch and list of works and references, see TWENTIETH CENTURY AUTHORS, 1942.

* * *

Long a resident of Buenos Aires, Gómez de la Serna has written a variety of books

* gō'mäth thâ lä sĕr'nä

in recent years—novels, critical studies of artists and literary figures, and an enlarged collection of his famous *greguerías*, 1940-45.

Correction: Gómez de la Serna's birth-date is 1888, not 1891, as given in TWEN-TIETH CENTURY AUTHORS, 1942.

ADDITIONAL WORKS IN ENGLISH TRANSLATION: Some Greguerías, 1944.

ABOUT: Columbia Dictionary of Modern European Literature.

GOOCH, GEORGE PEABODY

(1873-), English historian, writes: "I was born in London. My father was a junior partner in the firm of J. S. Morgan. My mother was the daughter of a Norfolk clergyman. I was educated at Eton, King's College, London, Trinity College, Cambridge, Berlin, and Paris. Though I was reared on Greek and Latin and spent most of my time at Cambridge in the study of the Middle Ages, all my writings have dealt with the history and ideologies of modern Europe.

"Though dedicated to an academic career, I devoted much time to popular lecturing at the London University Settlements, the Working Men's College, etc. As a Gladstonian Liberal I disapproved the prevailing imperialism represented by Joseph Chamberlain and Kipling, Milner, and Curzon. Like most Liberals I was critical of the policy which led to the South African War. I was elected Liberal Member for Bath in 1906. During my four years in Parliament I specialised in foreign affairs. I was defeated at Bath in 1910 and again at a by-election in Reading in 1913, which closed my brief political career. The First World War was a great grief. Though my wife is German and I had many friends among German scholars, I disliked Prussian militarism as heartily as I admired German music, literature, and philosophy.

"In addition to writing historical books, I have edited the *Contemporary Review*, the oldest of the English monthlies, since 1911. In 1924 I accepted an invitation from Prime Minister Ramsay Macdonald to select and edit documents from the Foreign Office archives illustrating British policy 1898-1914. My colleague was Harold Temperley."

* * *

Dr. Gooch contributed several chapters to the *Cambridge Modern History*, among them a study of Europe and the French Revolution (vol. VIII) and a major essay on historiography, 'The Growth of Historical Science' (vol. XII). He has received the honorary D.Litt. from both Oxford and Durham Universities and is a Fellow of the British Academy.

PRINCIPAL WORKS: English Democratic Ideas in the Seventeenth Century, 1898; Annals of Politics and Culture, 1901; History of Our Time, 1911; History and Historians in the Nineteenth Century, 1913; Life of Charles, Third Earl Stanhope, 1914; English Political Thought from Bacon to Halifax, 1915; Life of Lord Courtney, 1920; Germany and the French Revolution, 1920; Nationalism, 1920; History of Europe, 1878-1919, 1923; Franco-German Relations, 1870-1914, 1923; (ed. with A. W. Ward) Cambridge History of British Foreign Policy, 1923; (ed.) The Later Correspondence of Lord John Russell, 1925; Germany, 1925; (ed. with H. Temperley) British Documents on the Origins of the War, 1898-1914, 1926-38; Recent Revelations of European Diplomacy, 1927; Studies in Modern History, 1931; Before the War: Studies in Diplomacy, 1936-38; Studies in Diplomacy and Statecraft, 1942; Courts and Cabinets, 1944; Frederick the Great: the Ruler, the Writer, the Man, 1946; Studies in German History, 1949; Maria Theresa and Other Studies, 1951; Catherine the Great, and Other Sketches, 1954.

ABOUT: Journal of Modern History September 1954.

GOODMAN, PAUL

(September 9, 1911-), American poet, novelist, and essayist, says of himself: "Born 1911 and went thru all the New York school system. Consider myself academically trained. Fatherless, was free on the streets of the Empire City and the wild rocks along the Hudson River. . . . Have written books of drama, criticism, and social study. . . . My attempt is to reinforce the continuity between personal and public concern by drawing on the nature prior to individuality. I accept most of the propositions of Aristotle, Kant, Marx, and Freud."

Paul Goodman, whose father died before he was born, was the youngest of three children. Raised in New York, he graduated from City College (B.A., 1931); and from the University of Chicago (Ph.D., 1940). He has taught at the University of Chicago (1939-40), at the Manumit School of Progressive Education, at Black Mountain College, N.C., and at New York University. At present, he is a practicing psychotherapist affiliated with the New York Institute for Gestalt Therapy.

Paul Goodman is a prolific and versatile experimental writer. His first books appeared in 1942 when he published *Stop Light*, a group of five dance poems, and *The Grand Piano*, a novel. The poems, based on the *noh* play—a traditional form of Japanese drama in which the leading figure is a ghost —were reviewed in the *New Republic* by Lloyd Frankenburg, who wrote, "The style —a loose blank-verse interspersed with short lines and with prose—is fluid; the thought is always interesting . . ."; another reviewer observed that "the occasions . . . are ordinary enough, usually occurring in New Jersey: a visit to a cousin, a birthday, a morning awakening, a cycling trip, a stoplight on a lonely road." *The Grand Piano*, subtitled *Or, The Almanac of Alienation*, disturbed most reviewers by its lack of a clear story and the ambiguity of its meanings.

In 1945 Goodman was included in *Five Young American Poets* (a New Directions series); and in 1946 he published *Facts of Life* (stories), *State of Nature* (a novel), and *Art and Social Nature* (essays). *Facts of Life*, the *New Yorker* called "a volume of mocking, literate, and often witty short pieces by a non-realist of extreme virtuosity." Of *State of Nature*, the *Weekly Book Review* said, "Mr. Goodman is, if nothing else, a man of startling individuality. His book is always provocative—the sort of writing that seems acute even when you're not quite sure what it means."

Politically, Goodman states, he is an anarchist, and a frequent contributor to *Resistance*. In his essays he has often discussed such topics as the relations of parents and children, the social and cultural effects of the institution of marriage, etc. In collaboration with his brother Percival, an architect (who also illustrated several of his books), he wrote *Communitas* (1947), a study of modern ideas in city and regional planning.

Of his recent work *The Structure of Literature* (1954), Goodman has written, "The book is an attempt to teach reading by making the reader aware of his actual experience in reading a variety of great works"; and his publisher adds, "[here] . . . there is a sustained attempt to integrate the new textual criticism of poetry into the more classical criticism of the whole plot."

In 1940 Goodman received a fellowship from the American Council of Learned Societies; and in 1953, an award from the National Institute of Arts and Letters.

Goodman is witty, talkative, and lively, and has always been the center of a circle of friends. Twice married, he has one daughter, Susan, by his first marriage, and a son, Matthew Ready, by his second. He has recently started a new magazine, *Complex*, and he lives in New York City.

PRINCIPAL WORKS: *Poems*—Stop Light, 1942; *in* Five Young American Poets, 1945; *Fiction*—The Grand Piano, 1942; Facts of Life, 1946; State of Nature, 1946; Break-up of Our Camp, and other stories, 1950; Parents' Day, 1952; *Other Prose*— Art and Social Nature, 1946; Kafka's Prayer, 1947; The Structure of Literature, 1954; *Co-author*— Communitas, 1947; Gestalt Therapy, 1951.

GOODSPEED, EDGAR JOHNSON

(October 23, 1871-   ), American Biblical scholar, was born in Quincy, Ill., the son of Thomas Wakefield and Mary Ellen (Ten Broeke) Goodspeed. His father, a Baptist minister, was one of the founders of the present University of Chicago. After some private tutoring, young Edgar attended preparatory classes at the Old University of  Chicago and entered Denison University at fourteen to specialize in classics. He took his B.A. in 1890, spent a year doing graduate study in Semitics at Yale, and returned to Chicago for a year of teaching at Morgan Park Academy. In 1892 he entered the newly constituted University of Chicago from which he received a B.D. in 1897 and a Ph.D., having specialized in New Testament Greek, in 1898. In 1901 he married Elfleda Bond.

Dr. Goodspeed continued his studies in Europe—at the Universities of Berlin, Oxford, Cambridge, at the British Museum, and in Egypt where he joined a party excavating manuscripts from an archeological site. With the Oxford scholars Bernard Pyne Grenfell and Arthur Surridge Hunt, he edited part of these manuscript discoveries, published as *The Tebtunis Papyri*, Part II. His studies of Greek papyrus documents led to the discovery that the Greek in which the New Testament was written was the vernacular Greek of the period and not a specialized, 'literary' idiom. Some years later when he published his transcription of the New Testament in the American Translation version he tried to retain this original vernacular flavor, employing "the simple, straightforward English of everyday expression," in contrast to the lofty Elizabethan English of the King James version.

Meanwhile Dr. Goodspeed had joined the faculty of the University of Chicago in Biblical and patristic Greek. He became assistant professor in 1905, associate professor in 1910, full professor in 1915, and chairman of the New Testament Department in 1923, the year in which his *The New Testament: An American Translation*, was published. This translation was reprinted many times. (By 1946 a total of 830,000 copies, in its various forms, had been sold.) In 1930 he became a member of the committee for the revision of the American Standard Version of the Bible and shared in the production of the New Testament section of the Revised Standard Version.

With Donald W. Riddle and Harold R. Willoughby, Dr. Goodspeed edited the famous *Rockefeller McCormick New Testament*, an edition of the richly miniatured Codex 2400 of the Greek New Testament which he had discovered in Paris in 1928. To demonstrate that paleography and other forms of scholarly research are not necessarily stuffy and dull, he wrote a mystery story suggested by the manuscript adventures of himself and his colleagues, *The Curse in the Colophon*, an erudite and amusing book with, of course, a special appeal for bibliophiles.

In 1933 Dr. Goodspeed was appointed Ernest D. Burton Distinguished Service Professor at the University of Chicago. Four years later he retired, but in 1938 he returned to teaching as lecturer at the University of California at Los Angeles. He has continued his Biblical studies, concentrating on apocryphal literature, and has published a translation of the Apocrypha. Altogether his works number about seventy books and nearly two hundred articles. He lives now in Bel-Air where his home, "Vega Vista," overlooks the Los Angeles campus of the University of California.

PRINCIPAL WORKS: Greek Papyri from the Cairo Museum, 1902; The Newberry Gospels, 1902; Index Patristicus, 1907; (with B. P. Grenfell and A. S. Hunt) The Tebtunis Papyri, Part II, 1907; Chicago Literary Papyri, 1908; Index Apologeticus, 1912; The Story of the New Testament, 1916; (with E. D. Burton) A Harmony of the Synoptic Gospels for Historical and Critical Study, 1917; The New Testament: An American Translation, 1923; The Making of the English New Testament,

1925; Things Seen and Heard, 1925; (with T. W. Goodspeed and C. T. B. Goodspeed) William Rainey Harper, First President of the University of Chicago, 1928; (with J. M. Powis Smith) The Bible: An American Translation, 1931; Buying Happiness, 1932; The Meaning of Ephesians, 1933; The Story of the Old Testament, 1934; The Curse in the Colophon (mystery story) 1935; The Story of the Bible, 1936; An Introduction to the New Testament, 1937; The Apocrypha: An American Translation, 1938; (with J. M. Powis Smith) The Complete Bible: An American Translation, 1939; The Story of the Apocrypha, 1939; Christianity Goes to Press, 1940; The Four Pillars of Democracy, 1940; A History of Early Christian Literature, 1942; The Goodspeed Parallel New Testament, 1943; Problems of New Testament Translation, 1945; How to Read the Bible, 1946; Life of Jesus, 1950; As I Remember, 1953.

ABOUT: Cobb, J. H. and L. B. Jennings. A Biography and Bibliography of Edgar Johnson Goodspeed; Current Biography 1946; Goodspeed, E. J. As I Remember.

GORDON, CAROLINE (October 6, 1895-). For autobiographical sketch and list of earlier works and references, see TWENTIETH CENTURY AUTHORS, 1942.

* * *

Caroline Gordon writes: "At present my husband [Allen Tate] and I divide our time between Princeton, N.J., where we have an ancient little house on the outskirts of the town, and Minneapolis, where my husband is a member of the English faculty of the University of Minnesota. Until we moved to Minnesota I was a lecturer in English in the Department of General Studies at Columbia, teaching a course in the novel and the short story. I have also taught courses in fiction at the Woman's College of the University of North Carolina and at the College of St. Catherine in St. Paul, Minn., and at Hamline University in Minneapolis, and a course in creative writing at the University of Washington, in Seattle. I have lectured on the techniques of fiction at the University of Virginia, the University of Kansas, the University of Utah, the College of St. Thomas, and other institutions.

"I wrote my first novel on my husband's Guggenheim fellowship in 1928. In those days one was required to go abroad in order to receive the award. In France, where living was cheaper than in the United States, I was able to hire a nurse for my child. Otherwise I would not have been able to write the novel. I have never received any honors except an honorary degree from my college, Bethany, in 1946, a Guggenheim fellowship in 1932, and the second O. Henry prize in 1934. My novels do not sell well and hence have received no serious critical consideration, except for an article by Andrew Lytle in the *Sewanee Review* and an article by Vivienne Koch in the same quarterly.

"I have lived in so many different towns that I cannot even remember their names but have never felt at home in any of them, for life hardly seems worth living to me unless lived in the country."

* * *

Andrew Lytle sums up his evaluation of Miss Gordon's work as follows: "I know of no writer of fiction that other writers can study with greater profit. Her tension at times seems too severe, as if her image as mask penetrates the passion and, instead of objectifying, freezes it. It causes her characters at times to appear immobile or cold. . . . But certainly she is one of the few distinguished writers of fiction, in the shorter pieces as well as the novels." The Tates were living abroad, in Rome, in 1954.

ADDITIONAL WORKS: The Women on the Porch, 1944; The Forest of the South (short stories) 1945; The House of Fiction: An Anthology of the Short Story (ed. with A. Tate) 1950; The Strange Children, 1951.

ABOUT: Hoehn, M. (ed.) Catholic Authors, II; New York Herald Tribune Book Review October 7, 1951; Sewanee Review Summer 1946, Autumn 1949.

GORDON, CHARLES WILLIAM ("Ralph Connor") (September 13, 1860-October 31, 1937). For biographical sketch and list of works and references, see TWENTIETH CENTURY AUTHORS, 1942.

* * *

ABOUT: Dictionary of National Biography 1931-40; Thomas, C. Canadian Novelists, 1920-45.

GORDON, JANET. See WOODHAM-SMITH, C. B.

"GORDON, NEIL." See MACDONELL, A. G.

GORER, GEOFFREY (EDGAR) (March 26, 1905-), British anthropologist, was born in London, and educated at Charterhouse and Cambridge, where he took a B.A. and M.A. in classics and modern languages. He also studied abroad at the Sorbonne, and at the universities of Berlin and Florence. It had been Gorer's early intention to be a playwright and he wrote six plays, none of which was ever produced commercially. In 1933, he recalls, "with the rise of the

Nazis to power and the frequent references to 'sadism' consequent thereon," he decided to analyze the full meaning of the term by making a study of the Marquis de Sade. This study became his first published book, *The Revolutionary Ideas of the Marquis de Sade,* in 1934.

In that same year Gorer made a three months' journey through French West Africa, studying tribal customs and particularly the dances of the region. These he described in his well-received *Africa Dances.* As a result of his travels, Gorer's interests turned definitely toward social anthropology. He traveled to the Dutch East Indies and to French Indo-China for further studies. In 1936 he came to the United States and received academic training in social anthropology from Dr. Margaret Mead of the American Museum of Natural History and from Ruth Benedict of Columbia University. To put this training into practice he made an expedition in 1937, in the company of Major C. J. Morris, to study the Lepchas, a Himalayan mountain tribe living in Sikkim, on the Tibetan border on the slopes of Mount Kinchenjunga. The rigors of this journey and a bad fall from the rocks seriously impaired Gorer's health and made further field trips impossible. He accepted an invitation from the Humanities Division of the Rockefeller Foundation to study—"from an anthropological point of view"—the impact of films and radio on American audiences. This work took Gorer over a major part of the United States (he has, as a matter of fact, traveled more extensively in the United States than in England). When this survey was completed he joined the staff of the Institute of Human Relations at Yale University.

When war between the allied powers and Japan seemed imminent, Gorer turned his attention to the study of Japanese society and produced several monographs on Japanese culture. During World War II he was attached to the British Embassy in Washington, D.C., and at the end of the war he acted as a consultant to the British Control Commission in Germany. In 1948 and 1949 he was consultant and convener in research in contemporary cultures at Columbia University and studies in Soviet culture at the Museum of Natural History. In 1950 Gorer returned to England and bought a farm in Sussex where he now spends his time farming and gardening, studying and writing. His publications since the war have continued the exploration of the connections linking social anthropology, psychology, and political behavior. His best-known work is *The American People*, an informed, informative, and perceptive book of observations. He is currently at work on a volume on the English character.

PRINCIPAL WORKS: The Revolutionary Ideas of the Marquis de Sade, 1934; Africa Dances, 1935; Bali and Angkor; or Looking at Life and Death, 1936; Hot Strip Tease, and Other Notes on American Culture, 1937; Himalayan Village: Account of the Lepchas of Sikkim, 1938; The American People: A Study in National Character, 1948; The People of Great Russia, 1949.

GORKY, MAXIM (March 14, 1868-June 14, 1936). For biographical sketch and list of works and references, see TWENTIETH CENTURY AUTHORS, 1942.

* * *

ADDITIONAL WORKS IN ENGLISH TRANSLATION: Orphan Paul, 1946; The Artamonov Business, 1948.

ABOUT: Bowen, E. Collected Impressions; Clark, B. H. Intimate Portraits; Columbia Dictionary of Modern European Literature; Guerney, B. G. (ed.) The Portable Russian Reader; Holtzman, F. Young Maxim Gorky; Roskin, A. I. From the Banks of the Volga; Snow, V. Russian Writers; New Republic February 27, 1950; New Yorker April 30, 1949.

GORMAN, HERBERT SHERMAN (January 1, 1893-October 28, 1954). For autobiographical sketch and list of earlier works and references, see TWENTIETH CENTURY AUTHORS, 1942.

* * *

Herbert Gorman died, at the age of sixty-one, at his home in Hughsonville, N.Y., after a long illness. He was survived by his second wife, Claire Crawford Gorman, and a daughter, Patricia.

Gorman spent considerable time in travel and lived for extended periods in France, England, and Mexico. In the past decade he wrote three historical novels, all of them set in Mexico in the nineteenth century. The critics have found all three highly readable fusions of "historical fact and romantic fancy," remarkably free from the more glaring abuses of the historical-romance formula.

ADDITIONAL WORKS: The Wine of San Lorenzo, 1945; Cry of Dolores, 1947; The Breast of the Dove, 1950.

ABOUT: Warfel, H. R. American Novelists of Today; New York Times October 29, 1954.

GOSSE, Sir EDMUND WILLIAM (September 21, 1849-May 16, 1928). For biographical sketch and list of works and references, see TWENTIETH CENTURY AUTHORS, 1942.

* * *

ABOUT: Flower, N. Just as It Happened; Pritchett, V. S. The Living Novel; Sitwell, O. Noble Essences; Woolf, V. The Moment, and Other Essays.

GOTTSCHALK, LOUIS REICHENTHAL (February 21, 1899-), American historian, writes: "My parents were among the myriads who left the ghetto of Russian Poland around 1890 to come to the United States. They settled in Brooklyn, N.Y., and there I was born, the sixth of eight children who survived beyond infancy. When I was too young to remember, my family  moved to Albany, and my earliest childhood recollections are of the hills, the horse chestnut trees, and the snowbanks of that city. When I was eight, we were back in Brooklyn, and I was attending the public schools there. My father earned the family living by operating various kinds of small stores, but he was not very successful and between stores would return to his trade as a barber. My mother's heroic frugality kept us from poverty until the better days when my older brothers and sisters began to contribute sizeable sums to the family budget. By the time I graduated from Boys' High School in Brooklyn, my mother was able to spare from the family income a monthly allowance which, together with my summer earnings at various jobs, was sufficient to supplement the scholarships awarded me by the State of New York at Cornell University. I entered Cornell at sixteen (1915), received my B.A. in 1919, my M.A. the next year, and my Ph.D. the next, being pushed by economic necessity. In the meantime, I had served a few months in the U.S.N.R. at Cornell (1918) and had married (1920). (Five years later the marriage ended in sheer incompatibility and divorce.)

"From 1919 to 1921 I was a teaching assistant at Cornell. Primarily because of my great devotion to Carl Becker, I had done my graduate work with him in the history of the French Revolution. In 1921 I took my first teaching post at the University of Illinois, where my colleagues were invariably considerate, though I now recall with embarrassment that my favorite topic of conversation was how much better things were done at Cornell. I stayed at Illinois two years and then went to the University of Louisville, where I stayed nearly four, until my protests against presidential policies brought my dismissal. I could afford to protest because I already had reason to expect a year's appointment at the University of Chicago, which fortunately did eventuate and then developed into a longer appointment, and I have been there ever since except for visiting sessions in several other universities at home and abroad. In 1930 I married Fruma Kasdan. We have a pleasant home in Chicago and two sons, Alexander and Paul.

"Most of my writing since 1929 has centered around the career of Lafayette, who interests me not only as a gradually developing liberal but also as a witness of several revolutions. In addition, I have written about the structure of revolutions and the nature of historical knowledge. In recent years the growth of world interdependence has also become a major theme of my work, and I have been designated one of the authors of the proposed UNESCO Scientific and Cultural History of Mankind. Since association with an enlightened university administration has made it easier for me than is usual to get research funds regularly, I have been able to do a fairly large amount of what is called 'research'. So I have published about a dozen books and several dozen articles, and have won honors, fellowships, prizes, and high posts in professional societies. I often wonder what would have happened to me if my parents had remained in Poland."

PRINCIPAL WORKS: Jean Paul Marat: Study in Radicalism, 1927; Era of the French Revolution, 1929; Lafayette Comes to America, 1935; Lafayette Joins the American Army, 1937; Lady-in-Waiting: the Romance of Lafayette and Aglaé de Hunolstein, 1939; Lafayette and the Close of the American Revolution, 1942; Letters of Lafayette to Washington, 1777-1799 (ed.) 1944; The Place of the American Revolution in the Causal Pattern of the French Revolution, 1948; Lafayette between the American and the French Revolution, 1950; Understanding History, 1950; Europe and the Modern World, vol. I (with D. Lach) 1951.

GOUDGE, ELIZABETH (April 24, 1900-). For autobiographical sketch and list of earlier works and references, see TWENTIETH CENTURY AUTHORS, 1942.

* * *

Elizabeth Goudge lives in the Devon which she loves so deeply and evokes so lovingly in many of her novels. She has a wide and devoted audience in America as well as in England. Her *Green Dolphin Street,* a long historical romance (which *Time's* reviewer described as "tasty as a marshmallow and practically written in technicolor") won the $125,000 M.G.M. Literary Award, and several of her later books have appeared on bestseller lists in this country. The critical reception of her work has been friendly, although there has been strong objection to what one reviewer called her "paraphernalia of sentimentality." Horace Reynolds suggested that her chief faults are those of over-emphasis; her chief talents as a writer are a sympathetic knowledge of human nature, and a marvellous skill in portraying "the world of childhood" and the English countryside. She is a novelist, Mary Ross points out, "who recreates life, rather than dissects it, with a special feeling for the continuity of living that has flowed through countless generations down to our own."

A number of Miss Goudge's recent writings have been on religious subjects, and in 1951 she published a fictionized life of Jesus, *God So Loved the World.* She has also, in recent years, written several highly praised books for children—among them *The Little White Horse,* which received the Carnegie Medal in 1947. "I enjoy all forms of writing," she has said, "but especially for children."

ADDITIONAL WORKS: Green Dolphin Street, 1944; The Elizabeth Goudge Reader, 1946; Pilgrim's Inn (in England: Herb of Grace) 1947; Gentian Hill, 1949; Make Believe (short stories) 1949; Reward of Faith, and Other Stories, 1950; God So Loved the World, 1951; The Heart of the Family, 1933. Juveniles—The Blue Hills (in England: Henrietta's House) 1942; The Little White Horse, 1947; The Valley of Song, 1951.

ABOUT: Dobbs, R. Introduction to The Elizabeth Goudge Reader; New York Herald Tribune Book Review October 7, 1951; Time September 4, 1944.

GOULD, JOHN (THOMAS) (October 22, 1908- .), American essayist and regionalist, writes: "John Thomas Gould, born Boston, Mass. Removed to Maine and grew up in Freeport, coastal town with shipyard history. Freeport High School, 1926. Began newspaper work a stown correspondent for several papers as early as 1922, and worked on daily staffs summers during college. Bowdoin, A.B., 1931. Joined staff of weekly Brunswick, Maine, *Record* after graduation. Bought family farm at Lisbon Falls, Maine, in 1930, moved there after marriage to Dorothy Florence Wells of Arlington, Mass., in 1932. Now operates farm, including

greenhouse and local florist business. Owner-editor of weekly Lisbon *Enterprise*, 1945 to 1951. Public relations for Goddard College,

Plainfield, Vt., 1940 to 1941, Maine Development Commission, 1942. Lecturer, including journalism consultant. Two children, John, Jr., 1938, Kathryn MacLeod, 1943. Editorial contributor to the *Christian Science Monitor* (weekly 'Dispatch from the Farm') since 1942. The Gould Farm at Lisbon Falls is said to be the oldest farm in Maine always in the same family name; it was cleared in the 1700's by Jacob Gould and has always been owned by descendants."

* * *

The spare "Down East" quality of the foregoing sketch captures some of the flavor of John Gould's character and personality. Humorous in the hard-bitten, commonsensical tradition of his New England ancestry, his books are his autobiography and tell the story of how he and his wife settled in Lisbon Falls, rebuilt the family farmhouse, and raised their children.

PRINCIPAL WORKS: New England Town Meeting, 1940; Pre-Natal Care for Fathers, 1941; The Farmer Takes a Wife, 1945; The House that Jacob Built, 1947; And One to Grow On, 1949; Neither Hay Nor Grass, 1951; The Fastest Hound Dog in the State of Maine, 1953.

ABOUT: Gould, J. The Farmer Takes a Wife, The House that Jacob Built, And One to Grow On; Newsweek April 18, 1949; New York Herald Tribune Book Review May 8, 1949; Saturday Review of Literature July 3, 1948.

*GOURMONT, RÉMY DE (April 4, 1858-September 28, 1915). For biographical sketch and list of works and references, see TWENTIETH CENTURY AUTHORS, 1942.

* * *

ABOUT: Columbia Dictionary of Modern European Literature; Saurat, D. Modern French Literature, 1870-1940.

* goor môN'

*"GRACQ, JULIEN" (pseudonym of Louis Poirier, 1910-   ), French novelist, playwright, and poet, writes: "I was born at Saint Florent le Vieil (Maine et Loire) of a family of merchants. I had my secondary

* gräk

education at the *lycée* in Nantes from 1921 to 1928, then at the Lycée Henry IV in Paris where I prepared for the entrance examinations for the

Ecole Normale Supérieure. Here I studied under the philosopher Alain and was a fellow student of the sociologist Jules Monnerot, of the critic Armand Hoog, and of Maurice Schumann, who has since made a name for himself in politics. From 1930 to 1934 I was a student at the Ecole Normale Supérieure where I passed the examination for the degree of fellow in history. I also received a diploma from the Ecole des Sciences Politiques. From 1935 on I held different posts in public education, in the *lycées* of Nantes, Quimper, Amiens, Angers, as assistant of the faculty of Caen, and finally at the Lycée Claude Bernard in Paris, where I still teach. I took part in the 1939 war as lieutenant in the infantry. Taken prisoner at the time of the defense of the port of Dunkerque, I was repatriated in 1941 to France following an illness.

"After Stendhal, Wagner, and Edgar Poe, the reading of surrealist writing was, without a doubt, a determining event in the taste that I developed rather late—at twenty-eight—for writing. Although I do not accept all the ideas of surrealism, I continue to consider this movement as the great poetic event of this first half of the century—for France at least. Considered rather as a novelist, I am far from being attached exclusively to this form of expression, and I have written essays, poems in prose, and a play. I live in Paris, where my teaching keeps me, and I spend my vacations at Saint Florent le Vieil, where I have written most of my books. I consider myself a man of the West, and long stays in Britain account for the privileged place which its scenes have in my books. I have travelled a little in the Argentine, in Central Europe, in Italy, in Scandinavia. I write relatively little, slowly, and sometimes with rather long intervals of idleness."

* * *

The Prix Goncourt, the highest literary honor offered in France, was awarded to Gracq in 1951 for *Le Rivage des Syrtes*. A declared opponent of literary prizes, Gracq turned down the award ($14.28 at the prevailing currency rates) which was then used to aid needy writers. It was through the attendant publicity, rather than through his mannered and esoteric writings, that Gracq became well known even outside France. The London *Times Literary Supplement* said of him in 1952: "His novels, or rather his stories, are always interesting even to those who find his affectation somewhat exaggerated, because they represent an emphatic protest against the overwhelming majority of fictional works published today and devoted, in one way or another, to the portrayal of contemporary events." Gracq's work is a positive rejection of "Today-ism," of the Sartrian slogan, "We must write for our times." He is convinced, the *Times* points out, "that the business of novelists is to give new meanings to old myths and not to describe and judge the world which surrounds them."

PRINCIPAL WORKS IN ENGLISH TRANSLATION: The Dark Stranger, 1950; The Castle of Argol, 1951.

ABOUT: France Illustration December 15, 1951; New Yorker December 15, 1951: (London) Times Literary Supplement August 29, 1952.

GRAEFE. See MEIER-GRAEFE

GRAF, OSKAR MARIA (July 22, 1894-). For autobiographical sketch and list of works and references, see TWENTIETH CENTURY AUTHORS, 1942.

* * *

Oskar Maria Graf writes from New York City: "Since the 'German Writers' Association' was discontinued on its own accord in 1940, Oskar Maria Graf wrote two novels and many short stories, mainly, however, cultural-philosophical and literary essays. At the present time, he is working on a selection and compilation of poems he wrote over a period of forty years.

"Since 1946, the following titles appeared in Spanish: *La Vida de Mi Madre, Somos Frisoneros,* and the political and social novel, *El Abismo.*

"In Germany the following books were published: *Unruhe um einen Friedfertigen* (a novel), *Mitmenschen* (short stories), *Anton Sittinger* (satirical novel), *Einer gegen Alle* (postwar novel, English title: The Wolf), *Bayrisches Dekameron* (short stories), and *Die Eroberung der Welt* (Utopian novel).

"Since the end of the Second World War, O. M. Graf has again regularly contributed to all major German newspapers and magazines."

GRAHAM, CUNNINGHAME. See CUNNINGHAME GRAHAM

GRAHAM, DOROTHY (December 13, 1893-). For autobiographical sketch and list of earlier works and references, see TWENTIETH CENTURY AUTHORS, 1942.

* * *

Dorothy Graham writes: "I divorced my husband, James W. Bennett, in 1942. I live in New York, when not traveling in Europe to write on post-war conditions. *Wind Across the World,* my latest novel, was published in 1947, depicting life in Shanghai from the Victorian days to the Communist upheaval. The *New Yorker* commented: 'a very interesting novel, of which China is not only the setting but the principal character.'

"I am a corporate member of the MacDowell Association, founded for the encouragement of composers, writers and painters. Although a non-Catholic, I was signally honored in 1951 on the occasion of Monsignor James M. Gillis' Golden Jubilee, when he expressed appreciation for the contributions I had made for twenty-five years to the *Catholic World,* the magazine he edited. I was the only writer so honored.

"I have given many lectures to museums and clubs on my book *Chinese Gardens* and on Chinese architecture. The book has become important as a record because many of these gardens were destroyed in the Japanese war."

Correction: Dorothy Graham's mother was Emma Welton (not Weltech) Graham.

ADDITIONAL WORK: Wind Across the World, 1947.

GRAHAM, SHIRLEY (November 11, 1907-), American biographer and dramatist, writes: "I was born in Indianapolis, Ind., 'City of the Indians'. My grandfather's tribe had been pushed westward from that fertile Wabash valley about 1800. His forebears were presumably Potawatomies, though after crossing the Mississippi his people mingled and merged with the Cheyennes.  This maternal grandfather, though born in Missouri, made his way back to the shores of Lake Michigan where he settled and made fine saddles which he sold in nearby

Chicago. My mother spent her happy childhood in the lakeside suburb called Glencoe. Her maternal grandfather was a French Louisiana trader who traveled up and down the Mississippi. My paternal grandfather was a native Hoosier. His father had escaped from slavery, found work and land in Indiana and raised his family there. His farm was one of the 'under-ground railway stations' for runaway slaves. A town in Indiana is named after my paternal grandmother's family. Like Sinclair Lewis' hero I can boast that I am one hundred per cent All-American: Indian-Negro-French-Scotch.

"This is the rich heritage my father cultivated in his children. We were taught history in very personal terms. We grew up with a sense of belonging to the past and present, with a sense of responsibility for the future of our country. Father was a devout Methodist minister, the kind of pastor who was sent from place to place to 'mend broken fences,' 'to establish better race relations' in a community, to rebuild churches. Our large family, five sons and one daughter, grew up in a series of parsonages scattered all over the country. My early schooling, therefore, was uneven. Sometimes I was in a segregated school for Negro children only; sometimes I was the lone Negro child in a room filled with white children. I liked school, however, and never considered myself at any particular disadvantage. My father had endowed me with a deep and vivid kinship with every manifestation of life and he had poured into me his own love for books.

"I wonder now how my father found time to read as he did. Before I was six years old he began reading his books aloud to me. Evenings were our time—until I had to go to bed: *Ben-Hur, Quo Vadis, A Tale of Two Cities, Uncle Tom's Cabin*—modern parents would no doubt shudder at the list of books he read aloud to me. The result was that as I learned to read myself I read every book that came my way. Books crowded dolls and toys out of my life. There was, however, always time for music. How my parents managed it I do not know—but somehow there was always money for my music lessons —piano, voice, pipe-organ.

"By the time I reached high school I realized that my white schoolmates knew very little about colored people, whether they were Negroes or Indians. That's when I began to write for school papers and magazine. I acquired a reputation for reciting Paul Lawrence Dunbar's poetry and I began arranging Negro spirituals to be sung by groups selected by myself. The only thing that saved me

from being an obnoxious little busybody was that I so genuinely loved what I was doing that I managed to arouse enthusiasm for my projects. Also I have been most fortunate in the people who came my way. I recall the Japanese youth in my high school in Spokane, Wash., who coached me for an oratorical contest. Our essays had been chosen among the top submitted in a city-wide competition. When the names for the final renditions were announced this boy came to me with his offer: "My English is not good enough for me to win any farther. But I'll help you. You must win the prize." When I did, the Japanese boy was completely happy. I recall professors at Oberlin College, from which I graduated in 1934 and took an M.A. in 1935. My teachers always gave me personal help and encouragement. I recall African and Egyptian students from whom I learned so much while I was studying at the Sorbonne, in Paris in 1930. I was given two Rosenwald fellowships, 1938-40, and a Guggenheim fellowship, 1947.

"My first serious creative work was in music—a music-drama performed by the Cleveland Opera Company in 1932. I wrote a number of plays which have been performed by various Little Theatre Groups and college dramatic departments throughout the country; I've written a few books. I've just finished a book on the French Negro, Jean Baptiste Pointe De Sable, who was the first man to settle where the great city of Chicago now spreads out.

"De Sable came to New France (Louisiana-Canada) about 1761. He joined the Potawatomi tribe of Indians. There were times in writing this book that I had the feeling of writing autobiography. I'm planning a children's book on Pocahontas. If I live to be a hundred I may get half the books and songs and plays written I'd like to do about the amazing people who have had the courage, the strength and the faith to make America."

* * *

In 1951 Shirley Graham was married to the author W. E. B. Du Bois (see sketch in this volume). They live in Brooklyn, N.Y. She had two sons by an earlier marriage—one died and the other, Robert Graham McCanns, is now grown up and a veteran of World War II. Miss Graham's biography of Frederick Douglass, *There Was Once a Slave*, received the Julian Messner Award in 1946 for "the best book combating intolerance in America." In 1950 her biography of Benjamin Banneker, *Your Most Humble Servant*, won the *Saturday Review of Literature*'s Anisfield-Wolf award. In the same year she received a grant from the National Institute of Arts and Letters for "contributions to American literature."

In recent years Miss Graham's name has appeared in the press from time to time in reports of congressional investigations of allegedly left-wing and subversive organizations. Her biography of the Negro singer Paul Robeson was removed from the shelves of the United States overseas libraries by the State Department in 1953. Of this book George Streator wrote in the New York *Times* in 1946: "The author has given too little attention to chronology if the book is intended to portray to youth the details of a great struggle upward, and the rhapsodic style fails to make the hero lovable or understandable." Other critics objected that Miss Graham was "too fulsome" in her praise of Robeson and that her portrait of him lacked dimension.

PRINCIPAL WORKS: There Was Once a Slave, 1947; Your Most Humble Servant, 1949; Jean Baptiste Pointe de Sale, 1953. *Juveniles*—Dr. George Washington Carver, Scientist (with G. Lipcombe) 1944; Paul Robeson, Citizen of the World, 1946; The Story of Phillis Wheatley, 1949.

ABOUT: Christian Science Monitor April 8, 1946, April 27, 1950; Current Biography 1946; New York Post January 2, 1947; New York Times July 16, 1953.

GRAHAM, STEPHEN (1884-). For biographical sketch and list of earlier works and references, see TWENTIETH CENTURY AUTHORS, 1942.

* * *

Stephen Graham was with the B.B.C. Foreign Service from 1941 to 1949. He became a Councillor of the Poetry Society in the latter year. In 1950 he was elected a Fellow of the Royal Society of Literature. He lives in London.

ADDITIONAL WORKS: Thinking of Living? 1949; Summing Up on Russia, 1951.

GRAHAME, KENNETH (March 3, 1859-July 6, 1932). For biographical sketch and list of works and references, see TWENTIETH CENTURY AUTHORS, 1942.

* * *

ADDITIONAL WORKS: First Whisper of The Wind in the Willows (ed. E. Grahame) 1944.
ABOUT: Life November 21, 1949.

GRANBERRY, EDWIN (April 18, 1897-). For biographical sketch and list of works and references, see TWENTIETH CENTURY AUTHORS, 1942.

* * *

Edwin Granberry is Irving Bacheller Professor of Creative Writing at Rollins College in Winter Park, Fla. His novel *Strangers and Lovers*, originally published in 1928, was reprinted as a pocket book by the New American Library in 1951.

GRAND, SARAH (pseudonym of Frances Elizabeth Clark McFall) (1862?-May 12, 1943). For biographical sketch and list of works and references, see TWENTIETH CENTURY AUTHORS, 1942.

* * *

Sarah Grand died at Calne, England, at eighty-eight, according to the press, although her listed birth-date would make her eighty-one at most.

Of her twelve novels, *The Heavenly Twins* is the one for which she is best remembered. "Ill-constructed, crammed with ideas and opinions and prejudices, and often overwritten," as F. L. Mott describes it, it nevertheless was a tremendous success in both the United States and England, and has been called "the chief woman's rights novel of the period."

The London *Times* commented that she had "widened the field of English fiction by freeing it from some of its former limitations as to subject and treatment."

ABOUT: Mott, F. L. Golden Multitudes; London Times May 13, 1943; New York Times May 13, 1943.

GRANT, ROBERT (January 24, 1852-May 19, 1940). For biographical sketch and list of works and references, see TWENTIETH CENTURY AUTHORS, 1942.

* * *

ABOUT: Howe, M. A. DeW. *in* American Academy of Arts and Letters Commenorative Tributes, 1905-41.

GRANVILLE-BARKER, HARLEY GRANVILLE (1877-August 31, 1946). For biographical sketch and list of earlier works and references, see TWENTIETH CENTURY AUTHORS, 1942.

* * *

Harley Granville-Barker died in Paris, France, at sixty-nine. He had come to the United States in 1940 and until 1943 was a visiting professor at Yale and Harvard universities.

Commenting on Granville-Barker's contribution to the theatre and the *Prefaces to Shakespeare* in particular, Alan S. Downer says of these works, "What Barker has done, all great actors should do. He has left behind him ten nearly perfect productions of Shakespeare, realizations of the play, nearly perfect because of his intimate knowledge of the conditions permanently true of the arts of acting, of playwriting, and of stagecraft."

The author's reputation rests largely on the *Prefaces* and on his actual participation in the theatre as actor and director rather than on his own plays, of which Hesketh Pearson says "His plays were interesting but rather lifeless; the themes were vital, but the treatment lacked zest."

ADDITIONAL WORKS: Use of the Drama, 1945; Prefaces to Shakespeare, 1946-47.

ABOUT: Pearson, H. Last of the Actor-Managers; Harper's January 1947; New York Times September 1, 1946; Sewanee Review October 1947; Theatre Arts October 1947.

GRATTAN, CLINTON HARTLEY (October 19, 1902-). For autobiographical sketch and list of earlier works and references, see TWENTIETH CENTURY AUTHORS, 1942.

* * *

From 1942 to 1952 C. Hartley Grattan was associated with *Harper's Magazine* and contributed more articles to the magazine than any other person not a member of the editorial staff. His articles were mainly on economics, domestic and international, although he also contributed portraits of prominent people and occasional pieces on literary subjects.

Grattan continues his lively interest in Australian affairs. His *Introducing Australia* and his edition of a group of essays on Australia for the United Nations Series were described in the *Manchester Guardian Weekly* as the books which, beyond all others, have determined the image of Australia in the minds of people overseas. With Sylvan Hoffman, Grattan has worked on two popularizations of history—*News of the Nation*, a history of the United States in the form of little four-page newspapers, and, more recently, *News of the World*. He is currently engaged in a research and writing project under the sponsorship of the Fund for Adult Education. His home is in Katonah, N.Y. In 1953 he received an honorary degree from his alma mater, Clark University.

Grattan has said of his work: "I am a general writer who has operated largely within the fields of the social sciences and literature.

My special distinction is that I am one of the very few of my species who ever became an expert on a foreign country."

ADDITIONAL WORKS: News of the Nation (with S. Hoffman, eds.) 1944; Australia (ed., United Nations Series) 1947; News of the World (with S. Hoffman, eds.) 1953.

ABOUT: Newsweek April 13, 1942.

GRAVES, ROBERT (July 26, 1895-). For biographical sketch and list of earlier works and references, see TWENTIETH CENTURY AUTHORS, 1942.

* * *

Robert Graves is known in America mainly for his brilliant, if eccentric, historical novels—*I, Claudius*, and in more recent years, *Hercules, My Shipmate*—a retelling of the story of Jason and the Golden Fleece; *Wife to Mr. Milton*—a highly imaginative reconstruction of Milton's first marriage, to Mary Powell; and *King Jesus*—a bold but erudite interpretation of the life of Jesus. In 1949 the *Times Literary Supplement* hailed him, along with George Orwell, as "one of our two living masters in the plain prose style." The reviewer added, "His prose is everywhere a model of clear, forcible and unpretentious writing." His remarkable study of poetic myth, *The White Goddess*, impressed critics for the dazzling range of its scholarship, although it was not widely read. A voyage into the ancient pagan world of Celtic folklore and poetry, *The White Goddess*, the *Times Literary Supplement* said, had "the glamour of old romance and the excitement of a well-knit detective story," but many readers got lost in "the tangled brushwood and the haunted glens of Welsh mythology."

Of Graves' later poems—vigorous, rough-textured, paradoxical—Horace Gregory wrote in *Partisan Review*: "These poems are distinctly unlike any written by other poets in England or, for that matter, in the United States today; they are independent of any heritage except the peculiar Anglo-Irish tradition of Graves' childhood and his choices of later readings both of which are at a great distance from the common reading lists of the majority of contemporary poets." Having long lived apart from the literary fashions of his time, he has suffered critical neglect, but because he is apparently indifferent to praise or blame, he has emerged as a writer of "a hard-won, hard-bitten, roughly accomplished independence." He restores to the figure of the poet, Gregory says, "the image of a man who does not choose to lose himself in crowds, one whose particular genius is impatient of mediocrity."

Graves lives in Majorca, Spain.

ADDITIONAL WORKS: *Poetry*—Poems, 1938-45, 1946; Collected Poems, 1914-47, 1948; Poems and Satires, 1951; Poems, 1953. *Novels*—Wife to Mr. Milton, 1943; Hercules, My Shipmate (in England: The Golden Fleece) 1944; King Jesus, 1946; Islands of Unwisdom, 1949; Watch the North Wind Rise (in England: Seven Days in New Crete) 1949; Homer's Daughter, 1955. *Miscellaneous*—The White Goddess, 1948; Common Asphodel, 1949; Occupation: Writer, 1950; (tr.) Apuleius' The Golden Ass, 1951; (with J. Podro) The Nazarene Gospel Restored, 1953.

ABOUT: Essays in Criticism January 1955; New York Times Book Review September 18, 1949; Partisan Review January-February 1953; Saturday Review of Literature March 26, 1949.

GRAY, JAMES (June 30, 1899-   ). For biographical sketch and list of earlier works and references, see TWENTIETH CENTURY AUTHORS, 1942.

* * *

James Gray was on the staff of the St. Paul *Pioneer Press & Dispatch* as drama critic and literary editor from 1920 until 1946, when he resigned to serve for two years as literary editor of the Chicago *Daily News*. Since 1948 he has been professor of English at the University of Minnesota. His first wife died, and in 1952 he married Elizabeth B. Reeves. They live in St. Paul.

ADDITIONAL WORKS: Pine, Stream and Prairie: Wisconsin and Minnesota in Profile, 1945; On Second Thought, 1946; The University of Minnesota, 1851-1951; American Non-Fiction, 1900-1950 (with M. Brodbeck & W. Metzger) 1952.

"GRAYSON, DAVID." See BAKER, R. S.

GREEN, ANNA KATHARINE (November 11, 1846-April 11, 1935). For biographical sketch and list of works and references, see TWENTIETH CENTURY AUTHORS, 1942.

GREEN, ANNE (November 11, 1899-   ). For biographical sketch and list of earlier works and references, see TWENTIETH CENTURY AUTHORS, 1942.

* * *

Anne Green spent five years during the World War II in the United States but after the war returned to France where she now lives. In recent years she has published novels, translations from the French of some of

the writings of George Bernanos and Charles Péguy (collaborating on the latter with her brother Julian Green), and a volume of autobiography, *With Much Love*, which charmingly portrays her and her family's early years in France before the outbreak of World War I. In 1947 Miss Green became a Catholic.

ADDITIONAL WORKS: Just Before Dawn, 1943; The Old Lady, 1947; With Much Love, 1948.

ABOUT: Green, A. With Much Love; Hoehn, M. (ed.) Catholic Authors, II; Time April 26, 1948.

GREEN, FREDERICK LAWRENCE (1902-April 14, 1953), British novelist, was born in Portsmouth, England, the second son of George Edward and Elizabeth (Jermy) Green. His family was of Irish and Huguenot descent. He was educated at Salesian College in Farnborough. In 1929 he married Margaret Edwards. In 1932 he settled in northern Ireland and spent most of his life in Belfast, where he became something of an expert on Irish contributions to modern literature. He died at fifty-one in Bristol, England. Shortly before his death he wrote a terse autobiographical statement for his publishers: "Began writing at the age of four, and have since made a profession of it, eschewing such professions as the law, accountancy, provincial journalism, lecturing, commercial traveling, etc., but still indulging a frustrated talent as a painter. It is now twenty-five years since I spent some years of my youth in wandering about the south of England and writing short stories."

Green published in all fourteen novels, most of them very successful in England and translated into a dozen foreign languages. Americans were introduced to his work through the fine motion picture version of his novel *Odd Man Out*. The film, for which Green also wrote the script, was directed by Carol Reed and starred James Mason, and it is regarded as a motion picture classic. The story of an Irish revolutionist who, wounded and a fugitive from the police, spends his last eight hours of life wandering through the streets of Belfast, *Odd Man Out* was a grim psychological study, pitting a small, helpless man against the corruption and complexity of the modern world. Green's most famous novel, it is also his most characteristic, for he was always concerned with the theme of the outlaw, the man who is spiritually as well as physically a fugitive from society. In this respect he can be compared with Graham Greene. Both novelists have used the form of the "thriller" novel for deep psychological probing of man's place in the universe: the hero is a hunted man, pursued by sinister forces which he (and often the reader too) can scarcely identify; the action of the novel frequently moves in "the border-line area of human experience where a straw separates sanity and madness." Where Graham Greene, however, transformed the "thriller" into a novel of profound allegorical significance, F. L. Green was rarely able to integrate the two elements. The result was what Robert Gorham Davis described, in the New York *Times*, as "a disparity . . . between the patness of the plot and the psychological richness of the human relationships," and what another reviewer referred to as the "philosophic clutter" of some of his novels.

The New York *Times* observed in its obituary article on him: "Mr. Green's narrative skill in telling a melodramatic tale of flight and pursuit, murder and guilt, was impressive. But the pretentious moralizing with which he spoiled many of his best effects, his mystical broodings on the immortality of the soul, and his frequent passages of theological speculation were serious drawbacks."

PRINCIPAL WORKS: Julius Penton, 1934; On the Night of the Fire, 1939; The Sound of Winter, 1940; Give Us the World, 1941; Music in the Park, 1942; A Song for the Angels, 1943; On the Edge of the Sea, 1944; Odd Man Out, 1945; A Flask for the Journey, 1946; A Fragment of Glass, 1947; Mist on the Waters, 1948; Clouds in the Wind, 1950; The Magician, 1951; Ambush for the Hunter, 1952.

ABOUT: New York Times April 16, 1954.

GREEN, HENRY (1905-), English novelist, writes under a pseudonym. His real name is Henry Vincent Yorke. In an article for the New York *Herald Tribune*, he wrote: "I was born in 1905 in a large house by the banks of the river Severn, in England, and within the sound of the bells from the Abbey Church at Tewkesbury. Children in my circumstances are sent away to boarding school. I went at six and three-quarters and did not stop till I was twenty-two, by which time I was at Oxford, but the holidays were all fishing. And then there was billiards.

"I was sent at twelve and a half to Eton and almost at once became what was then called an 'aesthete,' that is a boy who consciously dressed to shock. I stayed that way at Oxford. . . . From Oxford I went into the family business, a medium-sized engineering works in the Midlands, with its own iron and brass foundries and machine shops. After working through from the bottom I eventually came to the top where for the time being

I remained, married, living in London, with one son."

Henry Green's first novel, *Blindness*, was written while he was still a schoolboy at Eton. *Living*, his second, was published in England in 1929. Ten years elapsed and then, between 1939 and 1948, *Party Going, Caught, Loving, Back*, and *Concluding* appeared. Though he was not published in America until 1949 (*Loving*), by 1952 seven of his novels were in print here, including his two latest, *Nothing* (1950) and *Doting* (1952).

Henry Green has puzzled many critics: his novels are more impressive than they have any right to be, for he writes in a mannered prose that is sometimes hard to read, while his characters are not at all heroic nor his plots particularly important. Yet Elizabeth Bowen could write, "Mr. Green's novels reproduce, as few English novels do, the actual sensations of living. At the same time, they cover ground: by the end the story has been told with an effectiveness, a power to hold the memory, that many straight, conventional novelists might envy."

American reviewers called *Party Going*, "a divertissement . . . a frivolity full of serious perceptions" (*Atlantic Monthly*); *Nothing*, "a novel like a dry and sparkling wine" (*Saturday Review*); *Loving*, a novel that "mirrors the world with a richness and a fullness that dazzle the beholder" (*New Yorker*); *Doting*, "a novel of English upperclass life in which sharp dialogue and a strange semi-poetic narrative combine" (*New Republic*). And in the New York *Times*, Diana Trilling wrote, "Beneath the pleasant surface of Mr. Green's 'light' fiction there is, in fact, a strikingly bold intelligence"; and Mark Schorer commented, "*Loving* is a fine example of Green's presentational art, the directly dramatized feel and texture of experience concretized in style."

The secret of Henry Green's identity was divulged to the American public by *Time* (1949): "In 1929 a young nobody of 24, named Henry Green, wrote *Living*, a proletarian novel about the lives of Birmingham (England) factory workers. In the same year another 24-year-old unknown named Henry Vincent Yorke, nephew of a peer named Lord Leconfield, became engaged to the Hon. Adelaide Biddulph." Since those years Henry Yorke "has graduated into big business; he is now managing director in London of his old Birmingham firm, H. Pontifex & Sons. In World War II, he worked full time as a fire-fighting 'ranker,' *i.e.*, enlisted man in the hazardous National Fire Service."

In 1950, when Henry Green visited America, *Newsweek* reported: *Novelist X* "turned out to be a tall, stoop-shouldered individual who said that he was a 45-year-old British engineer."

PRINCIPAL WORKS: Blindness, 1926; Living, 1929; Party Going, 1939; Pack My Bag, 1940; Caught, 1943; Loving, 1945; Back, 1946; Concluding, 1948; Nothing, 1950; Doting, 1952.

ABOUT: Allen, W. *in* Modern British Writing (ed. D. V. Baker); New York Herald Tribune Book Review November 8, 1950; Newsweek March 27, 1950; Partisan Review May 1949; Time October 10, 1949.

GREEN, JULIAN (September 6, 1900-).
For biographical sketch and list of earlier works and references, see TWENTIETH CENTURY AUTHORS, 1942.

* * *

Julian Green came to the United States after the fall of France and lectured at Goucher, Mills, and several Jesuit colleges. Here he completed his autobiographical *Memories of Happy Days* (the only one of his books he has written in English), winner of the Harper Book Prize in 1942—a richly nostalgic book which Katherine Woods hailed in the New York *Times* as "one of the most innately beautiful and subtly communicative books to be written by an American about France." In 1942 Green entered the United States Army and he later worked with the Office of War Information. After the Liberation in 1945 he returned to Paris where he now lives.

A French critic has spoken of Green as a "pure" writer, explaining that he has never written a line except under a kind of absolute artistic compulsion. He lives and works under a rigid self-discipline which rules out all petty distractions. In 1939, after nearly twenty years of apostasy, he returned to the Catholic faith. This "new" conversion has not had too apparent an influence upon his fiction, but it has shown itself strikingly in the several volumes of the *Journal* which Green published for 1946-50 and for which he received in 1951 the Grand Prix Littéraire of the Principality of Monaco. Here Green constantly reiterates the two-fold obligation of the artist—to himself and to God. "What is it God wants of the artist," he asks, "and how may it be known?"

Green remains better known and far more widely read in France than in America and England. The only one of his recent books to attract particular attention outside France was the novel *Moira*, a study of the grim psychological conflicts faced by a country boy, steeped in the puritanism of his American backwoods upbringing, who attends an American university in the 1920's (the scene is obviously the University of Virginia where Green had studied in the early '20's). In America the book was generally received as a better-than-average psychological novel. The London *Times Literary Supplement's* reviewer, however, more enthusiastically announced that *Moira* "takes first rank beside the best of M. Mauriac and Bernanos and Gide." In Paris the book received high praise and became a best seller. In March 1953 Green's first play, *Sud* (South) was produced in Paris. Based on his unfinished novel *Les Pays Lointains* (Distant Lands), it was a stark tragedy of a man's struggle to overcome an unnatural love, set in South Carolina just before the outbreak of the Civil War.

ADDITIONAL WORKS IN ENGLISH TRANSLATION: Memories of Happy Days, 1942; If I Were You, 1949; Moira, 1951. *Translations*—Péguy, C. Basic Verities, 1943, Men and Saints, 1944, The Mystery of the Charity of Joan of Arc (play) 1950.

ABOUT: Columbia Dictionary of Modern European Literature; Green, J. Memories of Happy Days; Hoehn, M. (ed.) Catholic Authors, II; Megroz, R. L. Thirty-One Bedside Essays; Commonweal October 15, 1954; France Illustration May 5, 1951; French Review March 1950; Georgia Review Spring 1953, Fall 1954; Journal of Abnormal and Social Psychology April 1946; New Yorker September 1, 1951.

GREEN, PAUL (March 17, 1894-). For autobiographical sketch and list of earlier works and references, see TWENTIETH CENTURY AUTHORS, 1942.

* * *

Mrs. Paul Green writes: "Since the opening of the first annual presentation of *The Lost Colony* in 1937, Paul Green has seen a great development throughout the country in this form of outdoor theatre. He has written three more plays himself and has encouraged others to write and stage similar plays. Green's own outdoor plays include *Roll, Sweet Chariot*, the story of a Negro village and a great highway that splits cruelly through it; *The Highland Call*, the story of Flora MacDonald and the Scotch Highlanders in North Carolina; *The Common Glory*, staged annually at Williamsburg, Va., and concerned with Thomas Jefferson and the beginning of government in the United States; and *Faith of Our Fathers*, written for the Sesquicentennial of the city of Washington, D.C., in 1950.

"The staging of these symphonic plays has required the evolvement of different techniques to meet the particular problems of spoken drama on large outdoor stages. Work on the production, and supervision of their annual summer performances has necessitated Green's abandonment of active teaching at the University of North Carolina. At the same time his interest in the wider aspects of history draws him into national and international organizations formed for the exchange of cultural ideas and the efforts for international peace. He has recorded talks and forum appearances for the Voice of America. He is a member of the United States National Commission for UNESCO and a member of the organization's executive board 1951-1952, also was a delegate to its Paris General Conference in 1951. He has been president of the National Theatre Conference, 1940-1942, member of the executive board of the American National Theatre and Academy, and is a member of ASCAP and of the National Institute of Arts and Letters. In 1951 he made a trip around the world with his wife under the sponsorship of the Rockefeller Foundation studying and lecturing on the theatre and its importance in a democratic way of life.

"The four Green children are now grown and there are five grandchildren. The youngest daughter attends the University of North Carolina.

"During the winter Green continues to live in Chapel Hill and frequently talks to university students and to study groups in North Carolina and neighboring states. Some of his stories have been written especially for the radio and television. Since 1941 he has published two books of essays, two volumes of short stories, two musical collections, and a new version of *Peer Gynt*. His present work-in-progress consists of a novel of the Negro, 'Stormy Banks,' a musical folk-opera, 'Hoedown,' and historical research for projected outdoor plays to be written about the dramatic events centered in Plymouth, Mass.; Santa Barbara, Calif.; Columbus, O.; and the Sea Islands of Georgia."

* * *

In 1941 Green collaborated with Richard Wright in a dramatization of the latter's powerful novel *Native Son*, produced on the New York stage by the Mercury Theatre.

ADDITIONAL WORKS: *Plays*—Native Son (with R. Wright) 1941; The Common Glory, 1948; Faith of Our Fathers, 1950; Peer Gynt: American Version, 1951; *Fiction*—Salvation on a String (short stories) 1946; Dog on the Sun (short stories) 1949. *Miscellaneous*—The Hawthorn Tree (essays) 1943;

Forever Growing (essay) 1945; Song of the Wilderness, A Cantata, 1947; The Common Glory Song Book, 1951; Dramatic Heritage (essays) 1953.

ABOUT: Adams, A. B. Paul Green of Chapel Hill; Gagey, E. M. Revolution in American Drama; Henderson, A. North Carolina; Isaacs, E. J. R. The Negro in the American Theatre; Morehouse, W. Matinee Tomorrow; Theatre Arts Anthology (1950); English Journal April 1949; New York Times Magazine April 11, 1943.

GREENBERG, CLEMENT (January 16, 1909-   ), American art critic, writes: "I was born in the Bronx, in New York City, the oldest of three sons. My father and my mother had come, in their separate ways, from the Lithuanian Jewish cultural enclave in northeastern Poland, and I spoke Yiddish as soon as I did English. When I was five we moved to Norfolk, Va., but moved back to New York—Brooklyn this time—when I was eleven, and we have more or less stayed there since. My father had by that time made enough money to change over from storekeeper (clothing) to manufacturer (metal goods). However, I can't remember there ever having been any worrying about money in our family, or any one in it lacking for anything. Which is not to say that we were rich.

Jerry Cooke

"I attended public school in Norfolk and Brooklyn, took the last year of high school at the Marquand School, and went to Syracuse University for an A.B. (1930). For two and a half years after college I sat home in what looked like idleness, but did during that time learn German and Italian in addition to French and Latin. The following two years I worked in St. Louis, Cleveland, San Francisco, and Los Angeles in an abortive, left-handed venture of my father's into the wholesale drygoods business; but I discovered that my appetite for business did not amount to the same thing as an inclination. During the next year I supported myself by translating. In 1934 I married and had a son, Daniel, a year later—and another year later I was divorced. At the beginning of 1936 I went to work for the federal government, first in the New York office of the Civil Service Commission, then in the Veterans Administration, and finally (in 1937) in the Appraiser's Division of the Customs Service in the Port of New York. Until then

I had been making desultory efforts to write, but now I began in earnest, in my office-time leisure—of which I had plenty—and fairly soon I began to get printed.

"As a child I had been a precocious draughtsman, and I had drawn and sketched obsessively until college; but gradually I became much more interested in literature than in art (which I still find it hard to read *about*), and so when I began to write it was mainly on literature. *Partisan Review* was the first place to publish my criticism, in 1938, and in 1940 I became one of its editors. Late in 1942 I resigned from both the magazine and the Customs Service, and most of 1943 I spent in the Army Air Force. After a spell of free-lancing and translating I took a job, in August 1944, as managing editor of the *Contemporary Jewish Record*, a bimonthly put out by the American Jewish Committee; when the *Record* was replaced by *Commentary* I stayed on as an associate editor of the latter, which I still am.

"In the meantime my interest in art had reawakened and become a good deal more self-conscious than before; that is, I no longer took my opinions in the matter of painting and sculpture as much for granted, and began to feel *responsible* for them. By the end of 1941 I was writing an occasional piece on art for the *Nation*, for which I had already been doing book reviews, and in 1944 I became its regular art critic. At the same time I wrote art criticism now and then for other periodicals, and enough book reviews—not all of them on art books—to give me a belly-full of reviewing in general. So in 1949 I gave up the *Nation* column, though I continued for another two years writing more or less regularly for *Partisan Review*, which, being a bimonthly, gave me more breathing space between deadlines. But in 1951 I gave that up too, and have been trying ever since then to work on things, inside and outside art, that have less to do with the current scene. The only book I have to my credit so far is a short one, *Joan Miró*. I am now preparing an even shorter book on Matisse.

"No one has written about me at any length, though some of my failings were discussed in the reviews of my Miró book—and I do get referred to, rather unfavorably on the whole, in an occasional article or book. But I was pleased when Alfred Barr, in his book on Matisse, mentioned me as a painter as well as critic; and I have been painting more and more seriously in the last ten years or so. Art criticism, I would say, is about the most ungrateful form of 'elevated' writing I

know of. It may also be one of the most challenging—if only because so few people have done it well enough to be remembered—but I'm not sure the challenge is worth it."

PRINCIPAL WORK: Joan Miró, 1948.
ABOUT: Time April 2, 1951.

GREENE, Mrs. ANNE (BOSWORTH) (1878-). For biographical sketch and list of works and references, see TWENTIETH CENTURY AUTHORS, 1942.

GREENE, GRAHAM (October 2, 1904-). For biographical sketch and list of earlier works and references, see TWENTIETH CENTURY AUTHORS, 1942.

* * *

It was Graham Greene himself who first called attention to the split character of his work—the "entertainments" (those sinister spy-chase psychological thrillers, ranging from his earliest novels through the post-World War II setting of *The Third Man*) and the works of serious, somber, moral and religious reflection, beginning with *England Made Me*, *Brighton Rock*, and *The Power and the Glory*. But, as Louise Bogan observed in a review of his more recent *The End of the Affair*, the pattern of the "entertainments," with their elements of mystery, fear, pursuit and flight, has "a close parallel in the religious drama of salvation and redemption." It is significant that Greene names as two great influences on his writing the late John Buchan, a master of the spy-thriller, and the Catholic novelist François Mauriac—an extraordinary but, on sober reflection, not impossible combination.

Greene himself has been a Catholic for many years, but it is only within recent years that he has been concerned in his novels with specific doctrinal issues. Even in his *The Power and the Glory*—whose hero, a priest, becomes a martyr, pursued by the relentless forces of a totalitarian police-state—Greene skirted an outright declaration of religious principles and told his story in the familiar hunted-versus-hunter pattern. But with *The Heart of the Matter* and *The End of the Affair* Greene has grappled fairly with the dilemmas of a Catholic in the modern world. Because he has focussed his attention on the profoundly moral problems of man in relation to God, his work has had a sharp and striking significance for non-Catholics as well. Major Scobie, the British colonial officer hero of *The Heart of the Matter*, is a well-meaning, ineffectual and essentially commonplace man who happens, seemingly only incidentally, to be a Catholic. He destroys himself and in that act appears to reject God, but out of the very violence and meaninglessness of the act arises a profound spiritual truth—a sense of what François Mauriac, in a discussion of another of Greene's novels, calls "the utilization of sin by Grace." Similarly, out of a sordid adulterous love affair in shabby post-war London there arises a saint, in *The End of the Affair*, and, in the hero-narrator of the book, a character whose personal rejection of God initiates the most powerful dramatic struggle of the book. There was serious critical objection to the introduction, in *The End of the Affair*, of supernatural incidents, specifically miracles. Here Louise Bogan wrote: "Greene's intuitions concerning the ancient and unchanging secrets of the human heart continue to be remarkable, but he is not always capable of fusing his religious faith with this psychological insight. Moments of such fusion happen, but usually on the level of shock rather than of spiritual grandeur. . . ."

Whether Greene has fulfilled completely the promise of his earlier work remains a debatable critical matter. But nothing that he has written in recent years would invalidate Morton Dauwen Zabel's critical estimate of him which appeared originally in the *Nation* in 1943: "He stands at the threshold of major fiction, a searching, irresistible talent, and a true magician in the words and spells of authentic drama. He has found an instrument for probing the temper and tragedy of his age, the perversions and fears that have betrayed it, and the stricken weathers of its soul."

A number of Greene's novels and one of his short stories ("The Basement Room" which was filmed as *The Fallen Idol*) have had successful motion picture adaptations. In 1953 his first play, *The Living Room*, was produced and generally well received in London. In 1954 it was produced in New York and Paris.

During World War II Greene served with the Foreign Office and was on special duty in West Africa in 1942-43. In 1952 he came to the United States to receive the 1952 Catholic Literary Award. His application for a visa had been delayed by the United States Department of State under the Internal Security (the McCarran) Act on the grounds that many years earlier Greene had been, for a brief time, a member of the Communist Party. Later that same year Greene applied for another visa for a longer visit. After

some delay, it was granted, but this time Greene rejected it.

In 1954 he was in Indo-China reporting on the war there for the *New Republic*. Some pages from his Indo-Chinese journal, relating his experiences as an opium-smoker, have appeared in the *London Magazine*.

ADDITIONAL WORKS: The Ministry of Fear, 1943; The Heart of the Matter, 1948; Nineteen Stories, 1949; The Third Man, 1950; The Little Fire Engine (juvenile) 1950; The Lost Childhood, and Other Essays, 1951; The End of the Affair, 1951; The Little Horse Bus (juvenile) 1952; Shipwrecked (originally published as England Made Me, 1935) 1953; The Living Room (play) 1954.

ABOUT: Allott, K. & Farris, M. The Art of Graham Greene; Greene, G. The Lost Childhood; Hoehn, M. (ed.) Catholic Authors, I; Mauriac, F. Men I Hold Great; O'Donnell, D. Maria Cross; Zabel, M. D. *in* O'Connor, W. V. (ed.) Forms of Modern Fiction; Catholic World February, April 1950; Harper's August 1952; London Magazine December 1954; New Republic December 10, 1951; New Yorker November 10, 1951; South Atlantic Quarterly July 1951; Twentieth Century March, April, October 1951.

GREENE, WARD (December 23, 1892-). For biographical sketch and list of earlier works and references, see TWENTIETH CENTURY AUTHORS, 1942.

* * *

A veteran newspaper reporter, Ward Greene continues as editor and general manager of the King Features Syndicate. He contributes fiction to magazines from time to time, sometimes using the pseudonyms "Frank Dudley" or "Jean Greene." In 1944 he published a warm and amusing novel about a typical suburban American family in wartime—*What They Don't Know*. Greene was married in 1942 to Edith Pfeil. They have one son and live in Rockleigh, N.J.

ADDITIONAL WORKS: What They Don't Know, 1944; (ed.) Star Reporters, and Thirty-Four of Their Stories, 1948.

GREENWOOD, WALTER (December 17, 1903-). For biographical sketch and list of works and references, see TWENTIETH CENTURY AUTHORS, 1942.

* * *

Walter Greenwood's recent writings have been mainly for the stage and for the screen. The motion picture version of his *Love on the Dole* was a popular success in England and in the United States in 1941. During the war he wrote a film for the merchant navy. Greenwood's play *A Cure for Love*, a pleasant comedy of Lancashire life, was produced in London in 1945, with Robert Donat in the starring role. Greenwood has also written a travel book on Lancashire.

ADDITIONAL WORKS: Something in My Heart, 1944; A Cure for Love (play) 1947; So Brief the Spring, 1952.

GREGORY, HORACE (April 10, 1898-). For autobiographical sketch and list of earlier works and references, see TWENTIETH CENTURY AUTHORS, 1942.

* * *

Horace Gregory writes: "In 1942 I received the Russell Loines award for poetry from the American Institute of Arts and Letters. In 1943 I edited *The Triumph of Life*, an anthology of devotional and elegaic verse. In 1944 I published a book of essays, *The Shield of Achilles*; in 1946 (in collaboration with my wife, Marya Zaturenska) I published *A History of American Poetry* 1900-1940; in 1949 I edited *The Portable Sherwood Anderson*; in 1951 I received a Guggenheim fellowship and published *Selected Poems of Horace Gregory*. I am a member of the English faculty of Sarah Lawrence College where I lecture on classical literature in translation and modern poetry and conduct a class in advanced writing.

"As recent photographs of the past ten years testify, I am no longer spectacled; I am still thin."

ADDITIONAL WORKS: The Triumph of Life: Poems of Consolation for the English-Speaking World (ed.) 1943; The Shield of Achilles, 1944; A History of American Poetry 1900-1940 (with M. Zaturenska) 1946; The Portable Sherwood Anderson (ed.) 1949; James Whitcomb Riley: A Victorian American, 1951; Selected Poems, 1951.

ABOUT: New Republic December 10, 1951; Poetry March 1948, November 1952; Publishers' Weekly May 16, 1942; Saturday Review of Literature April 28, 1951.

GREGORY, ISABELLA AUGUSTA (PERSSE), Lady (March 5, 1852-May 22, 1932). For biographical sketch and list of works and references, see TWENTIETH CENTURY AUTHORS, 1942.

* * *

Correction: *Cuchulain of Muirthemne* (1902) and *Gods and Fighting Men* (1904), heading the list of Lady Gregory's Principal Works, are not plays but traditional stories of Ireland's epic heroes, Cuchulain and Finn, retold by her in Kiltartan dialect.

ADDITIONAL WORK: Journals, 1916-1930 (ed. L. Robinson) 1946.

ABOUT: Colum, M. Life and the Dream; Dictionary of National Biography 1931-40; Gregory, I. Journals; Wade, A. (ed.) The Letters of W. B. Yeats; Christian Science Monitor Magazine June 7, 1947; New Yorker April 19, 1947; Review of English Studies October 1947.

GREGORY, JACKSON (March 12, 1882-June 12, 1943). For biographical sketch and list of earlier works and references, see TWENTIETH CENTURY AUTHORS, 1942.

* * *

Jackson Gregory died at sixty-one at the home of his brother, E. M. Gregory, in Auburn, Calif., shortly after completing his last novel, *The Hermit of Thunder King*.

ADDITIONAL WORKS: Man from Texas, 1942; Man from Painted Rock, 1943; Aces Wild at Golden Eagle, 1944; Hermit of Thunder King, 1945.

ABOUT: New York Times June 15, 1943.

GRENFELL, JULIAN (1888-May 26, 1915). For biographical sketch and list of works and references, see TWENTIETH CENTURY AUTHORS, 1942.

GRENFELL, Sir WILFRED THOMASON (February 28, 1865-October 9, 1940). For biographical sketch and list of works and references, see TWENTIETH CENTURY AUTHORS, 1942.

* * *

ABOUT: Comber, W. M. Wilfred Grenfell, Labrador Doctor; Miller, B. W. Wilfred Grenfell; Northcott, C. Venturers of Faith; Porrit, A. More and More of Memories.

GRESHAM, WILLIAM LINDSAY (August 20, 1909-), American novelist, sends this sketch written by his wife, the poet and novelist Joy Davidman: "William Lind-  say Gresham was born in Baltimore, Md., of a family which settled in Kent County, Md., in 1641. He was the elder of two children, both boys. His childhood was spent in Baltimore, Fall River, Mass., and finally New York City. He was educated at Erasmus Hall High School in New York City and partially completed a college course at Brooklyn College and at Upsala College, N.J.

"His early ambitions were to become a writer and/or a Unitarian minister. After graduating from high school at sixteen, however, he went to work immediately as file clerk in an insurance agency, and with the exception of brief periods in college worked steadily through the depression at a variety of trades—including kitchen equipment salesman, newspaper office boy, advertising copywriter, and once even dishwasher. He also put in three months in the C.C.C.

"During this period Gresham spent his spare time writing, mainly pulp fiction and articles, some of which was published. He also pioneered in singing American folksongs with guitar accompaniment—an art which only became popular much later—and occasionally appeared on the radio and elsewhere as a cowboy singer.

"In October, 1937, Gresham went to Spain as a volunteer soldier to aid in the unsuccessful defense of the Spanish republic against General Franco and his Italian and German allies. Gresham at first served as a private in the field artillery and was later with an anti-tank battery of 37-mm. guns with the 129th Infantry. When the foreign volunteers were repatriated shortly before the fall of the republic, Gresham returned to the United States—this was in February 1939—and spent the next year or two recovering from tuberculosis and other ailments contracted as the result of privations in Spain, and doing occasional writing.

"In 1942 Gresham, now working as the editor of a true-detective magazine, married the poet and novelist Joy Davidman. They have two sons—David, born 1944, and Douglas, born 1945. In the following years Gresham held a variety of editorial jobs, until the publication of his novel *Nightmare Alley* in 1946 established him as a free-lance writer. *Nightmare Alley* was later made into a movie starring Tyrone Power. It concerns the unscrupulous career of a carnival magician who develops into a fake spirit medium and swindler.

"After living for some time in Westchester County, N.Y., the Greshams moved in 1947 to their present residence in Staatsburg, Duchess County, N.Y. They inhabit a large and untidy house full of children, dogs, cats, goldfish, and transient snakes, frogs, and turtles. Gresham's second novel, *Limbo Tower*, appeared in 1949; Mrs. Gresham's *Weeping Bay*, in 1950. Both Greshams were also contributors to a religious symposium, *These Found the Way*, published in 1951. During recent years Gresham has written articles and fiction for many magazines, chiefly *Redbook*,

True, the *Saturday Evening Post, Collier's, Esquire,* and *Blue Book*.

"Gresham's hobbies, in addition to folksongs, include stage magic and mind-reading —he has given many public performances— and visiting friends on carnival midways.

"Gresham is six feet tall and weighs 185 pounds, with dark hair and eyes and a small mustache; he looks like a rather battered cross between King Charles II and Abraham Lincoln. Although he seldom writes humor, he is famous in private life as a humorous raconteur, and has a large repertoire of jokes and dialect stories. He has been called many things, but never dull ."

To his wife's account Gresham adds: "I have no illusions about myself as an 'author' —I am a hack writer who approaches writing as a trade like cabinet making. I have taught many classes in short story writing; the students probably learned very little but I always learned a lot, listening to myself sound off on how short fiction should be put together.

"In politics I have been everything from a Marxist (I managed to recover from this contagious paranoid psychosis just in time) to a Peter Viereck-type conservative. In religion I have been a deist, then a Unitarian, then an atheist, then a Presbyterian, and am now an Emersonian free-lance, still trying to find out God's will for me.

"I am not attached to any particular locality in spirit but find myself most at home on a carnival midway, especially if I have friends there. I am much more comfortable in a hotel room than in a palace (if anybody ever invited me to a palace, which they never have)."

PRINCIPAL WORKS: Nightmare Alley, 1946; Limbo Tower, 1949; Monster Midway, 1953.

ABOUT: Newsweek February 20, 1950; New York Times Book Review October 20, 1946.

GREY, Sir EDWARD. See GREY OF FALLODON, E. G.

GREY, ZANE (January 31, 1872-October 23, 1939). For biographical sketch and list of earlier works and references, see TWENTIETH CENTURY AUTHORS, 1942.

* * *

At the time of his death Zane Grey was reported to have left numerous unpublished manuscripts, and these are now being published posthumously, to the delight of his fans. In 1952 Edward Zern collected some of Grey's stories of his adventures in search ot big game fish and published these under the title *Adventures in Fishing*. The Zane Grey that emerges, a reviewer commented in the New York *Times*, "is an avid sportsman deeply in love with the outdoors who confessed his thrills and fears . . . with the candor of a small boy."

ADDITIONAL WORKS: Stairs of Sand, 1943; Wilderness Trek, 1944; Shadow on the Trail, 1946; Valley of Wild Horses, 1947; Rogue River Feud, 1948; Maverick Queen, 1950; Dude Ranger, 1951; Captives of the Desert, 1952; Adventures in Fishing, 1952; Wyoming, 1953; Lost Pueblo, 1954.

ABOUT: Karr, J. Zane Grey, Man of the West; Mott, F. L. Golden Multitudes; New Yorker July 19, 1952.

GREY OF FALLODON, EDWARD GREY, 1st Viscount (April 25, 1862-September 7, 1933). For biographical sketch and list of works and references, see TWENTIETH CENTURY AUTHORS, 1942.

* * *

ABOUT: Wallace, A. In Spite of All; Foreign Affairs January 1952; Spectator January 26, 1945.

GRIERSON, FRANCIS (September 18, 1848-May 29, 1927). For biographical sketch and list of works and references, see TWENTIETH CENTURY AUTHORS, 1942.

* * *

ABOUT: New Yorker September 18, 1948.

GRIERSON, Sir HERBERT JOHN CLIFFORD (1866-). For biographical sketch and list of earlier works and references, see TWENTIETH CENTURY AUTHORS, 1942.

* * *

Sir Herbert Grierson retired as Rector of Edinburgh University in 1939. He has continued to live in Edinburgh and in recent years has written and edited a number of volumes of special interest to students of literature. In 1948 he published an unusual anthology which assembled the records of man's belief in a hereafter, *And the Third Day*, ranging from Scripture, poems, and sermons to historical records, and beautifully illustrated with color plates of great works of religious art. Two years later he entered his eighty-fifth year with a collection of his essays, *Criticism and Creation*, which the London *Times Literary Supplement* described as "a book of essays full of happy, youthful quality, full of learning and the praise of learning, but vindicating everywhere the primacy of the imagination in literature and criticism."

ADDITIONAL WORKS: Rhetoric and English Composition, 1944; A Critical History of English Poetry (with J. C. Smith) 1944; (comp.) Personal Note: First and Last Words from Prefaces (with S. Wason) 1946; (ed.) And the Third Day; 1948; Criticism and Creation, 1949.

GRIEVE, CHRISTOPHER MURRAY ("Hugh McDiarmid") (August 11, 1892-). For biographical sketch and list of earlier works and references, see TWENTIETH CENTURY AUTHORS, 1942.

* * *

In 1943 Hugh McDiarmid published the first volume in a projected trilogy of autobiography—*Lucky Poet: A Self-Study in Literature and Political Ideas*. In many ways the volume was characteristic of McDiarmid's life and work—rich, sprawling, turbulent, learned, stimulating, and opinionated. His evaluation of his achievement as a poet is conceded, by critics of his work, to be entirely just: "I have been hailed in many quarters as the greatest Scottish poet since Burns . . . or—the way I prefer to put it—as one of a trinity with Burns and Dunbar." David Daiches agrees that he is "the greatest Scottish poet since Burns," and adds that he has effected, "almost single-handed, a literary revolution in Scotland." He has restored an indigenous Scottish literature and created—as Dunbar and Burns had done before him—a poetic language of wide variety, a "synthetic Scots," combining the richness of native speech with the subtle idiom of English poetry.

ADDITIONAL WORKS: Kist of Whistles, 1943; Lucky Poet (autobiography) 1943; Selected Poems, 1945; Speaking for Scotland, 1946.

ABOUT: McDiarmid, H. Lucky Poet; Poetry July 1948; Times (London) Literary Supplement August 29, 1952.

GRIFFIN, VIÉLÉ-. See VIÉLÉ

GRIGSON, GEOFFREY (1905-), British critic, poet, and editor, was born in Pelynt, Cornwall, the seventh son of Canon W. S. Grigson and Mary Beatrice Boldero Grigson. He was educated at St. John's Leatherhead, and St. Edmund Hall, Oxford. His father was sixty years old when he was born, and his grandfather had been a scholar in the reign of George III. In his autobiography, *The Crest on the Silver*, Grigson describes how his parents belonged to

another century and how, after much irresolution and suffering, he made his own way into the *avant-garde* literary life of the troubled twentieth century.

Three sons of his father's first marriage were killed in World War I. Grigson had nursery memories of these brothers, "firm foundation rocks of what should have been an affection for life." At Oxford, the modern poets Auden, Louis MacNiece, and Clere Parsons were his contemporaries, but Grigson did not know them, nor did he then appreciate modern poetry. Each vacation he returned to Cornwall where he pursued antiquarian research in barrows and prehistoric implements unearthed in the countryside, and in studying local history in the Public Records Office. He tried to like T. S. Eliot's "urbanity and alienness" but confesses that he should have preferred the then unfashionable Thomas Hardy. "Hardy's poems would have helped me not to be a traitor to the garden and the valley in which I had lived." It was in Auden's poetry that he first found what he was looking for—a blending of the tradition with an awareness of the modern world. "His mineshafts and mineral railways, his deserted waterwheels, buzzards, his windy headlands were properties not alien at all."

Upon leaving college, he first thought of working in Coleman's mustard factory, only to decide upon journalism as a more congenial way of earning his living. He joined the London staff of the Yorkshire *Post* in Fleet Street, "which has long had the tradition of taking young men from the universities and handing them on after training to the metropolitan papers."

In 1929 he married Frances Galt of St. Louis, Mo. He went to work on the *Morning Post*, a London paper, and started the *avant-garde* poetry magazine *New Verse* which he planned as a reply to the "public assault to which younger poets were treated." His wife died and he was left with a baby daughter. He wrote many unhappy poems at this time, while working for a publisher and harassed with the problems of finding nurses for his child. The poems were published in his first volume in 1939. In 1938 he married Bertshy Kunert, the daughter of an Austrian major. He has one son and one daughter by this marriage.

Upon the outbreak of World War II he was invited by the B.B.C. to join its monitoring department in Evesham. He was a member of the Literary Advisory Committee of the British Broadcasting Company, and from 1946 to 1948 was editor of *The Mint*, a literary magazine. He is a member of the Advisory Council of the Institute of Contemporary Arts. In addition to several volumes of his own poetry, Grigson has edited anthologies. He has written books of art criticism (*The Drawings of Henry Moore*) and literary criticism (*The Romantics, Before the Romantics, The Victorians*) and has edited the poems of the little known Romantic poets, John Clare and Samuel Palmer. He lives on a farm at Swindon.

PRINCIPAL WORKS: Several Observations, 1939; The Romantics, 1942; Under the Cliff and Other Poems, 1943; The Drawings of Henry Moore, 1943; The Poet's Eye, 1944; The Isles of Scilly and Other Poems, 1946; Samuel Palmer, 1947; Before the Romantics, 1947; The Harp of Aeolus, 1947; An English Farmhouse, 1948; John Caxton, Printings and Drawings, 1948; The Crest on the Silver, 1950; The Victorians, 1950; Essays from the Air, 1952; Gardenage, 1952.

Editor—The Arts Now, 1935; New Verse, an Anthology, 1939; Poems of John Clare's Madness, 1949; Poetry of the Present, 1949; Selected Poems of William Barnes, 1950; Selected Poems of John Clare, 1950.

ABOUT: Grigson, G. The Crest on the Silver.

GRISWOLD, FRANCIS (1902-). For biographical sketch and list of works and references, see TWENTIETH CENTURY AUTHORS, 1942.

* * *

Francis Griswold lives in Santa Barbara, Calif. He has published no book since *A Sea Island Lady*, but he is reported to be working on a new novel.

*GRUENING, ERNEST HENRY (February 6, 1887-). For biographical sketch and list of works and references, see TWENTIETH CENTURY AUTHORS, 1942.

* * *

Ernest Gruening was governor of Alaska from 1939 until April 1953. In that period he was a member of the commission that supervised the building of the Alcan Highway; he was chairman of the Alaska War Council, and commander-in-chief of the Alaskan Territorial Guard. During his ten-

* gre̅'nĭng

ure of office, Gruening administered the government of a wartime and post-war Alaska—a strategic military outpost during the war and a booming territory of new settlers, inflation, and housing shortages after the war. Gruening has long been active in the movement for Alaskan statehood.

ADDITIONAL WORK: The State of Alaska, 1954.

ABOUT: Current Biography 1946; Scholastic September 30, 1946; Survey Graphic October 1947; Time June 16, 1947; United States News April 22, 1949.

*GUARESCHI, GIOVANNI (1908-   ), Italian novelist, was born in Fontanelle di Parma near the Po River in Italy, where  he says, "people have heads as hard as pig iron and thus I succeeded in becoming editor-in-chief of *Bertoldo*," a humor magazine. He was born in the building that housed the Socialist party headquarters, and Fontanelle itself, he says, was at that time, "an island of Socialism in a sea of Communism." Guareschi's father was a local landowner and dealer in mechanical gadgets, and his mother was a schoolteacher. During the Italian financial crisis of 1926-27, his parents lost all their money, being even forced to sell the beds on which the family slept. He was taken out of school where he had been rather good at classical studies, got a job as doorman at a sugar refinery in Parma, and then drifted into journalism. He rose rapidly, starting as proofreader, then local news editor, sports editor, "finally I became editor-in-chief and proofreader." On the side he ran a humorous magazine for which he did his first cartoons.

In 1936 he decided to try his luck in a bigger city and went to Milan, where he got a job on a humorous weekly. At this time he married a girl he had known in Parma, now Margherita Guareschi. One night in 1942 (on "a monumental drunk," says *Life*) he went staggering about the streets of Milan roaring insults at the government. He was jailed for a week. Then, to avoid trial, he joined the Italian army as a lieutenant; but a year later Italy signed an armistice with the Allies and Guareschi, in German hands, was sent to a concentration camp in Poland. When he was released he had lost much weight: "I was

* gwä rĕs′kē

reduced to a sack of bones of which the total weight was one hundred pounds and this included lice, bedbugs, fleas, hunger, and melancholy."

In 1945 he founded *Candido*, the magazine that was to make him famous, and he is now "Italy's leading humorist as well as a devout and passionate monarchist," says Winthrop Sargeant in *Life*. The collection of stories which formed the book, *The Little World of Don Camillo* (1950), never aroused much interest in Italy until it was chosen by the Book-of-the-Month Club in America. "An utterly delightful and diverting collection of incidents," said Virginia Kirkus; and the *Library Journal* added, "told with infinite wit, whimsy, humor . . . in a mildly satirical vein." Of the movie, *The Little World of Don Camillo*—a hit in Europe—which Julien Duvivier filmed with Fernandel, the comedian, the only objection to it, said *Life*, was that "its anti-Communist punch got lost by the wayside." "The worst of it is," says Guareschi, "the Communists *like* it." *Don Camillo and His Flock*, published in 1952, was a best seller; and in 1953 *The House that Nino Built* appeared, including stories of his own life with his family. His work is warm, broadly humorous, and full of love—along with its satire—for people in general and for the people of Italy in particular. Into the bitter ideological struggles of contemporary life, Guareschi has brought sympathy, tolerance, and understanding.

Guareschi, who is barrel-chested and wears an enormous black mustache, lives in Milan with his wife and two children, but he says, "I know that I could be really happy only in Fontanelle." His name informally is "Nino."

In April 1954 he was the center of a highly publicized trial involving charges that his magazine *Candido* had published two allegedly forged political documents which libeled former Italian premier Alcide De Gasperi. Guareschi, who was already under a suspended sentence of eight months for having libeled Italian President Einaudi, was found guilty, fined, and sentenced to a year in jail. He refused to appeal his sentence and entered prison in the summer of 1954.

PRINCIPAL WORKS: The Little World of Don Camillo, 1950; Don Camillo and His Flock, 1952; The House that Nino Built, 1953.

ABOUT: Hoehn, M. Catholic Authors, I; Life November 10, 1952; New York Herald Tribune Book Review October 19, 1952; New York Times Book Review December 17, 1950; Publishers' Weekly May 8, 1954; Saturday Review of Literature August 19, 1950, February 17, 1951.

*GUEDALLA, PHILIP (March 12, 1889-December 16, 1944). For biographical sketch and list of earlier works and references, see TWENTIETH CENTURY AUTHORS, 1942.

* * *

Philip Guedalla died in a London hospital at fifty-five after an illness of five weeks. In the last years of his life Guedalla was active in the British war effort. He served as head of the Latin-American section of the British Ministry of Information for four months, after which he returned to his former position with the British Council. An R.A.F. squadron leader, in 1943 he made a 20,000 mile trip by air through the Middle East gathering information on the influence of air power. The author also made a goodwill tour of America in the early part of the war.

Guedalla's work, often termed over-brilliant, caused Richard Church to comment that in summing up his writing one might tend to think that "his anxiety to give the utmost, to present it with a maximum of explanation and humorous connecting asides, tends to overlay the structure of his works, and to make it suspect because of the exuberance with which it is draped in ornament." The same authority then goes on to state, "That would be unfair to the sound historical scholarship, and the conscientious marshalling of it, upon which Mr. Guedalla's historical studies and biographies are founded."

ADDITIONAL WORKS: Liberators, 1942; Two Marshalls, Bazaine, Petain, 1943; Middle East, 1940-1942, A Study in Air Power, 1944.

ABOUT: Church, R. British Authors; New York Times December 17, 1944.

* gwĕ dăl'å

*GUÉRARD, ALBERT JOSEPH (November 2, 1914-   ), American novelist and critic, writes: "I come to realize, as I look

Walter R. Fleischer

back, how divided a being I am. My father [Albert Léon Guérard, see sketch below] was born in France, grew up in the enthusiasms of the Dreyfus controversy, and (naturalized American) became an historian, political theorist, critic, amateur city-planner, and professor. But my mother, who has published a few short stories under the name of 'Graham Munro,'

* gä rärd'

was brought up in a household of Covenanter ministers. To this day I combine an incorrigible moralistic bias (perhaps disguised as psychiatric curiosity) and a resentment of all complacent moralisms and easy conformities. But I am not sure how much of this is French, how much Scottish-American.

"So too for place. I spent my first ten years in Houston, Tex. (and long intended to go into cotton); most of the next ten in California, and more than the last ten in Massachusetts as a teacher of literature at Harvard. But I know Paris (where I have lived some five years in all) better than San Francisco or Boston. Hence I am at home nowhere, and have no local feeling and folklore to write from. And hence I am drawn to what I do know: to the old subject of the American in Europe, for instance—the collision of a dangerous 'innocence' or uncritical idealism with an often puzzling 'experience.' I have written one college novel (*The Hunted*) as fruit of a curious year at Amherst, but I do not expect to write another.

"I am European at least in this—that I divide my energies between novels, critical books, and teaching. I do most of my novel-writing during the long vacations. Thus my great problem as a writer is to try to recover, each June and by an act of will, the necessary naiveté together with the necessary awareness of extra-curricular disorder. I think I have been saved from too restricted a life by a sufficient native leaning toward this disorder, and by two and a half years as an enlisted man in the army. In that time, working in 'psychological warfare' and for various intelligence agencies in France, I stocked up enough appalling experience and enough guilt-feeling to last out a reasonable lifetime and a good many books. *Maquisard* (written in one month in a barracks in Verdun) is my act of piety to the enthusiasms of those days and to my brief experience with French partisans. *Night Journey*—an unwitting but detailed prediction of the Korean war—is my somber act of contrition. I wrote it before I read *1984*, but it tries to say the same things.

"I won national prizes in high school and college for stories clearly sponsored by Hemingway. My first novel, *The Past Must Alter*, has the irrecoverable simplicity of books written at twenty and twenty-one, while my first critical book (*Robert Bridges*) was overly influenced by Yvor Winters, the best of my teachers. Thereafter the contradictions are less extreme between my two kinds of writing. In my books on Hardy,

Conrad, and Gide I have tried to bring to bear my knowledge of how novels are written, and of how the novelist's creative impulses may conflict (and valuably) with his rational intentions. And this is what now interests me most as a novelist: the conflict betwen conscious longings and preconscious drives. Only my most recent novel (*Night Journey*) still satisfies me as a story of normal human impulses exposed to abnormally severe pressures. I cannot pretend to see my own work clearly. I could say my subject is ambiguity, both personal and political. But that's pretty general! If one thing—any single personal note or tone—binds my first adolescent novel with what I am now writing, it is a simultaneous awareness and uncomfortable interplay of tenderness and violence. This is not what I deliberately planned to turn out, but it seems to be there in the books."

PRINCIPAL WORKS: The Past Must Alter, 1937; Robert Bridges, 1942; The Hunted, 1944; Maquisard, 1945; Joseph Conrad, 1947; Thomas Hardy, 1949; Night Journey, 1950; André Gide, 1951.

ABOUT: Hoffmann, F. The Modern Novel in America; Current Biography 1946.

GUÉRARD, ALBERT LÉON (November 3, 1880-). For autobiographical sketch and list of earlier works and references, see TWENTIETH CENTURY AUTHORS, 1942.

* * *

Albert Guérard served with the Office of War Information from 1942 to 1945. He became professor emeritus at Stanford in 1946 and since then has taught comparative literature and French civilization at San Diego State College, the University of Hawaii, the New School for Social Research, and Radcliffe. From 1950 to 1953 he was professor of comparative literature at Brandeis University.

In his autobiography, *Personal Equation,* Professor Guérard reviewed not only the major accomplishments of his life but, even more interesting and significant, the evolution of his thought. "Thinking," he wrote, "has been my pleasure, my business and my dignity." Here he outlines his humanistic faith: ". . . my work has been and is directed against all the supercilious élites, the exclusive aristocracies, the embattled professionals, the exquisite connoisseurs, the esoteric cliques, the special interests, the Pharisees in every domain. . . . Any privilege that refuses to stand the test of reason and justice is a superstition and must be challenged. . . . This

constant protest against *assumed* superiority is probably the chief factor in my personal equation."

ADDITIONAL WORKS: Napoleon III, 1943; Europe Free and United, 1945; France, A Short History, 1946; Personal Equation, 1948; Education of a Humanist, 1949; A Bottle in the Sea, 1954; Napoleon III, 1955.

ABOUT: Guérard, A. Personal Equation, Education of a Humanist, A Bottle in the Sea; Books Abroad Autumn 1950; Saturday Review of Literature April 3, 1948; Time August 8, 1949.

*GUILLOUX, LOUIS (1899-). For biographical sketch and list of works and references, see TWENTIETH CENTURY AUTHORS, 1942.

* * *

When the German armies occupied France, Louis Guilloux went to Brittany and tried unsuccessfully to escape to England. Throughout the remainder of the occupation, a fugitive from the Gestapo, he was in hiding in Toulouse. Upon the liberation of France, Guilloux was able to come out of hiding, and he served as an interpreter for the American Army. In 1949 he published his 800-page novel, *Le Jeu de Patience,* winner of the Prix Théophraste-Renaudot, a profound and sensitive summing-up of the experiences of a man of fifty, who has lived through two world wars, the Spanish Civil War, and the rise of Hitlerism. None of his later books has appeared in English translation.

ABOUT: Columbia Dictionary of Modern European Literature; Dictionnaire Biographique Français Contemporain.

* gē yoo′

*GUINEY, LOUISE IMOGEN (January 7, 1861-November 2, 1920). For biographical sketch and list of works and references, see TWENTIETH CENTURY AUTHORS, 1942.

* * *

ABOUT: Gregory, H. & Zaturenska, M. History of American Poetry, 1900-1940; Reilly, J. J. Of Books and Men; Rollins, H. E. & Parrish, S. M Keats and the Bostonians; America February 19 1949.

* gī′nĭ

*GUITERMAN, ARTHUR (November 20, 1871-January 11, 1943). For biographical sketch and list of earlier works and references, see TWENTIETH CENTURY AUTHORS, 1942.

* * *

Arthur Guiterman died in the Presbyterian Hospital of Pittsburgh, Pa.. at seventy-one

* gĭt′ĕr măn

of a heart attack. His death came late in the evening after a sudden collapse that morning in nearby Oakland where he was scheduled to make a lecture appearance. He was survived by his wife.

In a review of Guiterman's last work, *Brave Laughter*, Leo Kennedy says, "In it his rhymed journalese is as amusing, as good and as bad, as careless and as American in flavor as the nine volumes that went before it."

ADDITIONAL WORKS: Brave Laughter, 1943.
ABOUT: New York Times January 12, 1943.

*GUITRY, SACHA (February 21, 1885-   ). For biographical sketch and list of earlier works and references, see TWENTIETH CENTURY AUTHORS, 1942.

* * *

A sober and chastened Sacha Guitry, reported looking "more like seventy than sixty," served sixty days in prison in 1945 for collaboration with the Nazis and was deprived of his membership in the French Academy. Upon his release from prison for lack of evidence, Guitry returned to his museum-like Paris home, which houses his valuable art collection, and proceeded to write two books of memoirs of the period 1940-44 —*Quatre Ans d'Occupation* and *Soixante Jours de Prison*. His defense was a simple one—he was an actor, not a politician; he loved Paris and he loved the theatre; and if he had it to do again, he would not conduct himself in any other way.

Although there has been considerable bitterness toward Guitry, especially from former members of the French Resistance, his alleged collaboration has been forgotten, if not forgiven. His collected works are currently being published in France, and he continues to write plays (many on historical subjects), films (celebrating the days of France's glory), and novels. Only one of his plays has had a recent production in America. This was a comedy, *Don't Listen, Ladies*, which opened in New York in December 1948, ran fifteen performances, and was dismissed by the critics as an "extremely old-style French sex-comedy."

In 1949 Guitry was married to an actress, Lana Marconi. It was his fifth marriage.

ADDITIONAL WORK IN ENGLISH TRANSLATION: Villa for Sale (one-act play) 1943.
ABOUT: Middleton, G. These Things Are Mine; Columbia Dictionary of Modern European Literature; Dictionnaire Biographique Français Contemporain; France Illustration February 16, 1952; Time March 18, 1946.

* gē trē′

GULBRANSSEN, TRYGVE (1894-   ). For biographical sketch and list of works and references, see TWENTIETH CENTURY AUTHORS, 1942.

* * *

Trygve Gulbranssen has published nothing since the war. He owns a farm in eastern Norway and devotes his time to farming.

*GUMMERE, FRANCIS BARTON (March 6, 1855-May 30, 1919). For biographical sketch and list of works and references, see TWENTIETH CENTURY AUTHORS, 1942.

* gŭm′ĕr ê

GUNN, NEIL MILLER (November 8, 1891-   ). For autobiographical sketch and list of earlier works and references, see TWENTIETH CENTURY AUTHORS, 1942.

* * *

Neil Gunn lives in Inverness-shire where he relaxes by fishing, but spends most of his time writing novels, short stories, and travel books about Scotland. He writes of Scotland as a native, lovingly but with restraint. "The method is Wordsworthian," the *Times Literary Supplement* wrote of his *Highland Pack*, a travel memoir of the region which Gunn knows and loves so well. Of his novel *Man Goes Alone* Kate O'Brien wrote in the *Spectator*: "This author has the great merit of knowing passionately and imaginatively the beautiful remote region that he writes of, and many will find a legitimate and helpful escape from our present weary, ugly time in his evocation of natural beauty. . . ."

ADDITIONAL WORKS: *Fiction*—Young Art and Old Hector, 1942; Man Goes Alone (in England: The Serpent) 1943; The Green Isle of the Great Deep, 1944; The Key of the Chest, 1945; The Drinking Well, 1947; The Shadow, 1948; The Lost Chart, 1949; The White Hour, and Other Stories, 1950; The Well at the World's End, 1951; The Bloodhunt, 1952. *Travel*—Highland Pack, 1950.
ABOUT: Christian Science Monitor Magazine September 30, 1950.

GUNNARSSON, GUNNAR (May 18, 1889-   ). For biographical sketch and list of works and references, see TWENTIETH CENTURY AUTHORS, 1942.

* * *

Gunnar Gunnarsson lives in Reykjavik, Iceland. Since his return to his native land from Denmark, shortly before the outbreak of World War II, he has written a number of novels, several of them taking their subject matter from Icelandic history and legend. None of these later works has been translated into English. Stefan Einarsson has commented: "At his best Gunnar Gunnarsson merges land and people in a single vision of humanity's burning bush in the wilderness. With Hamsun and Duun in Norway and Johannes V. Jensen in Denmark, Gunnarsson is one of the great interpreters of the common people of the North."

ABOUT: Columbia Dictionary of Modern European Literature.

GUNTHER, JOHN (August 30, 1901-). For autobiographical sketch and list of earlier works and references, see TWENTIETH CENTURY AUTHORS, 1942.

* * *

John Gunther writes: "At present [February 1953] I am working on the fifth of my books about continents, to be entitled 'Inside Africa.' I have not returned to daily journalism since 1941 and have terminated all work on radio in order to devote myself entirely to writing books. In preparing my various books, I visited all the countries of Eastern Europe in 1948, went around the world in 1950, paying particular attention to the development of NATO.

"Your brief sketch omits all my activities as a war correspondent. I was accredited to London in 1941, visited all the Mediterranean Fronts in 1943, took part in the invasion of Sicily and Italy in 1943, and thereafter covered the Middle East in Egypt and Turkey.

"I was divorced in 1944 and in 1948 married Jane Vandercook."

That John Gunther still keeps pace with the headlines—and is, in fact, a day or two ahead of them as a rule—may be seen in the list of his works and their publication dates below. Both *Inside U.S.A.* and *Behind the Curtain* were Book-of-the-Month Club choices. *Inside U.S.A.* has been translated into fifteen or sixteen foreign languages. *Roosevelt in Retrospect* appeared in Japanese, Siamese, and Hebrew, as well as in most of the western languages.

In 1949 Gunther published a deeply moving account of the death of his young son John, two years earlier, of a brain tumor, *Death Be Not Proud.* The book appeared first serially in both the *Ladies' Home Journal* and the *Reader's Digest* and in 1953 was published in the Modern Library series.

ADDITIONAL WORKS: D-Day, 1944; The Troubled Midnight (novel) 1945; Inside U.S.A., 1947; Behind the Curtain, 1949; Death Be Not Proud, 1949; Roosevelt in Retrospect, 1950; The Riddle of MacArthur, 1951; Eisenhower: The Man and the Symbol, 1952; Alexander the Great (juvenile) 1953.

ABOUT: Gunther, J. Death Be Not Proud; Van Gelder, R. Writers and Writing; Current Biography 1941; New Yorker August 23, 1947; Saturday Review of Literature May 31, 1947, February 3, 1951; Time February 7, 1949.

GUSEV (or GUSSIEV). See ORENBURGSKY

GUSTAFSON, RALPH BARKER (August 16, 1909-), Canadian poet, writes: "Of Scandinavian-English stock, Ralph Gustafson was born in Lime Ridge, near Sherbrooke, Quebec, Canada, the son of Carl Otto and Ella Gertrude (Barker) Gustafson. He attended the Sherbrooke High School, then Bishop's University where he obtained the degrees of B.A.

Karsh, Ottawa

(1929) with first class honours in History and English, winning the Governor-General's Medal for the highest standing in the University, the Chancellor's Prize, the Ven. Archdeacon Scott's Prize for English Literature, the Mackie English Essay Prize, and a first class aggregate prize. The degree of M.A. (thesis on 'The Sensuous Imagery in Shelley and Keats') was conferred in 1930 when he again won the Ven. Archdeacon Scott's prize for an English poem.

"The following three years were spent at Oxford University on an I.O.D.E. Scholarship, where he obtained the degree of B.A. in English Language and Literature. He was a Master at St. Alban's School for Boys in Brockville, Ontario, in 1934, and thereafter lived in London, England, as tutor and journalist, until his return to Canada in 1938. In 1935, his first book of poems, *The Golden Chalice,* was published in England, and was awarded the Prix David by the Quebec Government in the same year. *Alfred the Great,* a verse drama, was published in 1937. He was with the British Information Services for four years during the war and has since lived in New York City as a free-lance writer. His poems and short stories have appeared in the foremost literary periodicals in Canada, the United States and in England.

"In 1941 a poem, *Epithalamium in Time of War,* was published in New York, and in the following year, *Lyrics Unromantic,* both in limited editions. In 1944 *Flight into Dark-*

ness, a collection of poems, was published. During these years he also edited a series of anthologies presenting contemporary Canadian prose and poetry to a wide audience, and a series of musical monographs."

* * *

Gustafson's short stories have appeared in the *Atlantic Monthly, Argosy* (London), *Cross Section* 1948, *Story, Virginia Quarterly Review,* and other magazines, as well as in *The Best American Short Stories* 1948 and 1950. His poetry, E. K. Brown wrote, shows the influence of Anglo-Saxon verse and the "passionate, contorted work" of Gerard Manley Hopkins. "Fascinating as the Hopkins techniques are in his use of them, one doubts, at times whether the substance inevitably required so intense and so elaborate a treatment. Whatever question his poetry inspires, Mr. Gustafson is always notable as a curious and striking craftsman."

PRINCIPAL WORKS: The Golden Chalice, 1935; Alfred the Great, 1937; Epithalamium in Time of War, 1941; Lyrics Unromantic, 1942; Anthology of Canadian Poetry (ed.) 1942; A Little Anthology of Canadian Poets (ed.) 1943; Canadian Accent (ed.) 1944; Flight into Darkness, 1944; Poetry and Canada, 1945.

ABOUT: Brown, E. K. On Canadian Poetry.

GUTHRIE, ALFRED BERTRAM, Jr.
(January 13, 1901-   ), American novelist, writes: "I was born in Bedford, Ind., but

have never felt like a Hoosier for the very good reason that after six months in Indiana I was taken to Choteau, Mont., a raw, small ranch town south of the Blackfoot reservation, where I grew up. My father, a teacher, went there to become the first principal of the newly-established Teton County Free High School.

"The West is in me, and I suppose always will be, not alone because of early residence, but because of an interest that found origin and encouragement from my father. He quickly developed a love for the West and for its history. Longer ago than I can very well recall we were reading pioneer journals and visiting the sites of old buffalo runs and Indian encampments.

"From teaching Dad went to newspaper publishing. In it he got the idea that perhaps my brother and I should take up journalism. We readily agreed. When we were old enough, both of us served as apprentices in the country shop, though Dad had sold it meantime. After high school I went to the University of Washington for a year and then to the University of Montana, where I was granted a degree in 1923. My brother joined me there and was graduated later.

"After a couple of rather aimless if enjoyable years in Old Mexico, California, western New York, I came to Lexington, Ky., and found a reporter's job on the Lexington *Leader.* I stayed there more than twenty years, working up from a cub's position to that of executive editor.

"Meantime, though, I had come to realize —if, indeed, I hadn't realized it all along— that I wanted to write fiction, though what attempts I made at it were clumsy and deservedly unsuccessful. I didn't think then, however, that I would ever give full time to magazine or book writing. That was to be an avocation to be indulged as newspaper work permitted.

"Then, in 1944, I won a Nieman Fellowship at Harvard and there stumbled into Theodore Morrison, the author and teacher, then head of English A at Harvard. Out of that accident grew one of my closest and most rewarding friendships. A great deal of whatever I know about writing owes itself to him. I wrote part of *The Big Sky* at Harvard while carrying on the course of studies proposed in my application for a fellowship. I finished it a year or more later after returning to Kentucky and the *Leader.*

"Early in 1947, encouraged by the reception the book got, I quit newspaper-making and went to free-lancing. *The Way West* came out in 1949. The two books and a number of short stories and magazine articles constitute my total, if you ignore an earlier novel that I hate to claim. All right, then. It's *Murders at Moon Dance.* Proceed at your own risk.

"In recent years I've taught one two-hour course in creative writing at the University of Kentucky, with pleasure to myself if with no discernible benefit to the students.

"My wife, Harriet Larson, is a Montanan, daughter of old-timers there. We grew up together in Choteau and can't recall when we didn't know each other. We have two children, Bert, who wants to be a cattle rancher, and Helen, who wants to be a thousand things.

"We spend our summers in Montana, where we have a little mountain ranch, and our winters in Lexington. It's a good arrangement. The values of each are accented by contrast with the other's.

"I enjoy horseback riding, woodworking, outdoor experiences. I used to like to hunt and fish. Now I don't want to shoot things and go fishing more for the companionship than the catch.

"After twenty years and more in a news room, I'm not bothered by noises and interruptions while at work. It's just the writing that bothers me, always, under any circumstances. Writing is a desperate business. I think I would quit it but for the high if unassayable rewards. Maybe I would anyhow if I didn't have to earn a living."

* * *

A. B. Guthrie, Jr., received the Pulitzer prize for fiction in 1949 for his novel *The Way West*. His earlier novel *The Big Sky* was a vigorous study of frontier life in the years 1830-43. The historian Allan Nevins called it a "skillfully planned and beautifully finished novel," a sensitive evocation of the land and the people who settled on it. *The Way West* continues the story of the opening of the West with an account of an emigrant trek from Missouri to Oregon in the 1840's.

PRINCIPAL WORKS: The Big Sky, 1947; The Way West, 1949.

ABOUT: Current Biography 1950; Editor and Publisher October 22, 1949; New York Herald Tribune Book Review October 23, 1949; New York Times Book Review June 1, 1947, October 23, 1949; Saturday Evening Post August 16, 1947; Saturday Review of Literature May 3, 1947, February 14, 1948, October 8, 1949.

GUTHRIE, THOMAS ANSTEY ("F. Anstey") (August 8, 1856-March 10, 1934). For biographical sketch and list of works and references, see TWENTIETH CENTURY AUTHORS, 1942.

* * *

ABOUT: Dictionary of National Biography 1931-1940.

GWYNN, STEPHEN LUCIUS (February 13, 1864-June 11, 1950). For autobiographical sketch and list of earlier works and references, see TWENTIETH CENTURY AUTHORS, 1942.

* * *

Stephen Gwynn died at the age of eighty-six in Dublin, Ireland.

A writer in many fields (the *Spectator* has said "though dissipation of talent always involves some sacrifice, the very extent of the ground Gwynn covered meant that he appealed to many different circles of readers"),

Gwynn was primarily a specialist in Irish subjects. J. M. Hone has described him as "distinguished in his country's scholarship and literature . . . a sportsman and a politician as well as a lover of scenery, a student of Irish history, antiquities and social character." The London *Times* has observed that the "chief secret of his attraction" when he wrote of Ireland was the fact that "whatever form he chose, he was at heart a poet, conscious always of the shimmering background against which the tragedies of Ireland have been played."

ADDITIONAL WORKS: Aftermath, 1946; Memories of Enjoyment, 1946.

ABOUT: London Times June 12, 1950; New York Times June 12, 1950.

*HABE, HANS (pseudonym of Jean Bekessy) (February 12, 1911-), German-American novelist and journalist writes: "I was born in Budapest, Hungary. My father was a newspaperman, my mother a school teacher. Although my heritage is entirely Hungarian, I considered myself until 1940 a German writer, for I grew up in Vienna and was raised on German culture.

"I studied in Vienna and Heidelberg, devoting myself to wine, women and duels rather than to science. In 1930 I escaped the university and entered journalism. Two years later I was faced with sudden fame by discovering that Hitler's real name was Schicklgruber. At twenty-one years of age I became Europe's youngest chief-editor, at the Viennese *Der Morgen*. Later, I spent four years as a foreign correspondent, covering the League of Nations in Geneva and traveling throughout Europe and Africa.

"I wrote my first novel *Three Over the Frontier* in 1936. I had the misfortune that this book, like most of my initial efforts, became an instant success. It was translated into eighteen languages and gave me the feeling of being a great novelist. This was, as I found out, a big mistake. Before World War II I wrote two more novels. The second of my books, *Eine Welt Bricht Zusammen* (A World Crumbles), was not translated into any languages, and several reviewers advised me to choose another profession. I did not. My third book, *Sixteen Days*, dealing with

* hä′bĕ

the Munich Conference, was published on the day war broke out in Europe.

"All my life I preferred to live than to write. Although I was the citizen of a neutral country, I immediately enlisted in the French Army. As a sergeant with the foreign volunteers I was captured by the Germans. Fortunately, they did not find out my real name and I escaped to freedom in August 1940. I received a special presidential visa and arrived in the United States in December of the same year.

"Here again my initial successes were greater than the later ones. My book *A Thousand Shall Fall*, published in 1941, became an instant best-seller. It described my experiences in the French Army and revealed the story of my escape. Hollywood turned it into the movie *Cross of Lorraine*. A year later appeared *Kathrine*, which I considered my best novel.

"I became an American citizen by enlisting in the American Army. I started as a private in America, became a second lieutenant in Africa, a first lieutenant in Italy, a captain in Luxembourg and a major in Germany. It was my privilege to participate in three invasions. After the hostilities ended I became editor-in-chief of America's eighteen newspapers in Germany. Running the *Neue Zeitung* on the presses which printed Hitler's *Völkische Beobachter* belongs to the greatest satisfactions of my life.

"I lived in Hollywood between 1946 and 1949. Here I wrote my two novels *Aftermath* and *Walk in Darkness*. *Aftermath*, a vicious attack on American womanhood, received the unfavorable reception it deserved. *Walk in Darkness*, describing a Negro soldier's experiences in occupied Germany, endeared me again to the American public.

"Having always been torn between writing and editing, I returned to Germany in 1949 to take charge of two important weeklies, the *Münchner Illustrierte* and the *Echo der Woche*. Both were violently anti-Nazi and anti-Communist and thus quite unpopular. To heal the wounds received in political battles, I wrote my novel *Black Earth*, published in America at the end of 1952. In the meantime I collected material for my newest book, *Our Love Affair With Germany*. In the summer of 1952 I came back to America, feeling even more than twelve years before that it is the only country where a free man can do and write as he pleases.

"Being an *homme à lettres*, I should add a few words about my literary preferences. As I mentioned before, I was brought up on German culture. Heinrich Heine is still my preferred poet, Friedrich Schiller my favored dramatist. I consider the Russians and the Americans the world's greatest novelists. Generally speaking, poetry is my greatest love, psychoanalysis my pet hatred.

"At present [December 1952] I am working on a most difficult book—my autobiography. It is the second book I am writing in English. Unable to live without seeing my name in print every day, I am also writing a syndicated column 'Outside USA.' "

PRINCIPAL WORKS: Three Over the Frontier, 1939; Sixteen Days, 1939; A Thousand Shall Fall, 1941; Kathrine, 1943; Aftermath, 1947; Walk In Darkness, 1948; Black Earth, 1952; Our Love Affair With Germany, 1953.

ABOUT: Van Gelder, R. Writers and Writing; Christian Century June 2, 1943; Current Biography 1943; New York Herald Tribune May 29, 1943.

HACKER, LOUIS MORTON (March 17, 1899-). For autobiographical sketch and list of earlier works and references, see TWENTIETH CENTURY AUTHORS, 1942.

* * *

Louis M. Hacker writes: "It would be strange indeed if I did not note certain changes from positions taken ten years ago. I am not so certain about Charles A. Beard; perhaps his influence—notably in helping shape an anti-capitalist bias among American historians—has not been the happy one I was, earlier, prepared to assume. I am equally dubious about Parrington and Veblen. As I contemplate the unfolding of the American story now I am prepared to give greater weight to the achievement of Hamilton than to that of Jefferson: for it was Hamilton who understood the great difficulties of a new country threatened by internal dissension and at the mercy of powerful neighbors; it was Hamilton who got the United States off to its real start. Yet, I continue to recognize my intellectual debt to the Enlightenment; but do not find my growing preoccupation with Burke, Tocqueville, and Acton necessarily a rejection of what I have learned from Locke, Adam Smith and John Stuart Mill.

"My teaching experiences in the past ten years have taken me into new worlds. I have been the Harmsworth Professor of American History at Oxford University; I have lectured at Cambridge University and in American universities all over the country. I have become the Dean of one of Columbia University's great schools—the School of General Studies.

"My writing has continued despite administrative duties. I think the following articles and lectures best represent what contributions I have sought to make to American historical writing: 'The First American Revolution' in *Columbia University Quarterly*, XXVII (1935); 'England and America: the Ties that Bind, an Inaugural Lecture' (Oxford, 1948); 'Politics and Economics in History' in the *Pennsylvania Magazine of History and Biography*, LXXII (1948); 'The Limits of Intervention' in the *American Scholar*, XIX (1950). The book of mine I like best is *The Triumph of American Capitalism*; I think it is misunderstood in America but nowhere else: for there are Spanish and Japanese translations of it, and it is well known in Britain, France, Italy and Germany."

ADDITIONAL WORKS: The United States and Its Place in World Affairs (with others) 1943; The Shaping of the American Tradition, 1947; The New Industrial Relations (with others) 1948; Government Assistance to Universities in Great Britain (with H. W. Dodds and L. Rogers) 1952; The United States in the Twentieth Century (with H. Zahler) 1952.

ABOUT: Fortune April 1952; The Historian XII (1950); Revue Internationale du Monde du Travail September-October 1952; Saturday Review of Literature July 5, 1947; Time February 4, 1952.

HACKETT, FRANCIS (January 21, 1883-). For biographical sketch and list of earlier works and references, see TWENTIETH CENTURY AUTHORS, 1942.

* * *

Francis Hackett divides his time between his American home in Bethel, Conn., and his Danish home in Holte. In 1944-45 he was a book critic for the New York *Times* and in 1947 he published a collection of his book reviews, originally written for the *Times*, the *Saturday Review of Literature*, and other journals. Hackett is a member of the National Institute of Arts and Letters in America and was honored in Denmark with the Liberty Medal, presented by King Christian X.

ADDITIONAL WORKS: The Senator's Last Night (novel) 1943; On Judging Books in General and in Particular, 1947.

"HADDON, CHRISTOPHER." See "BEEDING, F."

*HAGEDORN, HERMANN (July 18, 1882-). For biographical sketch and list of earlier works and references, see TWENTIETH CENTURY AUTHORS, 1942.

* * *

* hăg'ĕ dôrn

Hermann Hagedorn continues active in the Theodore Roosevelt Memorial Association, of which he is trustee and secretary. He has edited some of Roosevelt's letters and has made numerous biographical studies of him, including the highly praised *Roosevelt Family of Sagamore Hill*, which was a Book-of-the-Month selection. His biography of Dr. Albert Schweitzer, *Prophet in the Wilderness*, was judged by the *Christian Century* the easiest to read, the shortest and the most dramatic of all books on Schweitzer.

ADDITIONAL WORKS: Sunward I've Climbed: The Story of John Magee, Poet and Soldier, 1922-41, 1942; Americans: A Book of Lives, 1946; The Bomb that Fell on America (poetry) 1946; Prophet in the Wilderness: The Story of Albert Schweitzer, 1947; The Roosevelt Family of Sagamore Hill, 1954.

HAGGARD, Sir HENRY RIDER (June 22, 1856-May 14, 1925). For biographical sketch and list of works and references, see TWENTIETH CENTURY AUTHORS, 1942.

* * *

ABOUT: Haggard, L. R. The Cloak That I Left; Mott, F. L. Golden Multitudes; Scott, J. E. A Bibliography of the Works of Sir Henry Rider Haggard; Fortnightly December 1945.

"HAGGARD, PAUL." See LONGSTREET, S.

HAHN, EMILY (January 14, 1905-), American biographer, memoirist, and novelist, writes: "If there was anything out of the ordinary in my early life, it was the complete absence on my part of any intention to be a writer. I was born in St. Louis, a member of a large family. We were all readers; we read absolutely everything that came our way, and sooner or

later, I suppose, it was inevitable that some of us should begin to produce copy of a sort. But I meant to be the exception. I would not be an intellectual. I would breed dogs or go on a farm or do something equally vigorous. (I wasn't good at games: as a baby my legs had gone wrong for a while.)

"A sudden enthusiasm for geology came on in high school. (I wasn't good at history or languages.) At the University of Wisconsin I specialized in geology and then in mining engineering—I *was* fairly good at mathematics—and took a degree in mining. Everyone said a girl couldn't get a job as a mining engineer: with the greatest of ease I got a job, and hated it. Research was what I liked, not applied science, but it seemed too late to do anything about it. I was not good at my job, and at the end of a year I quit. Then followed several years of drifting, or as near drifting as a middle-class, well-brought-up young woman can achieve. I was in New Mexico, California, and New York. I needed money, and began to write in order to earn some.

"I taught geology at Hunter College for a while; then went to Europe, and while I was in England my first book was published at home. It was 1930, the Depression year, but I made enough to go away on. I went to the Belgian Congo and stayed there nearly two years, by which time I had long given up the struggle against being a writer. There is really nothing else to be, if you like traveling. Passing through England I decided to come back and stay there for a while and work at the British Museum in the library. I did that, and then went to China.

"I stayed in China. I would be there now, I suppose, if it hadn't been for the war. I was repatriated from Hongkong in 1943. At the end of the war I married and came to England, my husband's home, where I live in the country, but not all the time. A year ago I went to Borneo and visited Hongkong again. Nowadays, however, life is regulated by school holidays; there will be no more nine-year sojourns in the East. At least not for a long time."

* * *

Emily Hahn first came to literary prominence with her lively and intimate biography *The Soong Sisters*, the three remarkable Chinese sisters who married probably the three most influential men of recent Chinese history. Shortly after the publication of the book, Miss Hahn was interned when Hongkong, where she lived, fell to the Japanese. After her repatriation she married Major Charles Ralph Boxer, whom she had met in China, and they now live in England with their two daughters. Miss Hahn's books on China were light and disarming, their humor often coating a shrewd and discerning portrait of life there. Her later works have often exploited her gift for light humor, but a series of articles she wrote for the *New Yorker* in 1954 on her recent travels in the Orient was solid, informative reporting, and

her friendly biography of Chiang Kai-shek (1955) is at the same time an informal history of modern China.

PRINCIPAL WORKS: *Fiction*—With Naked Foot, 1934; Mr. Pan, 1942; Miss Jill, 1947. *Biography*—The Soong Sisters, 1941; Raffles of Singapore, 1946; A Degree of Prudery, 1950; Love Conquers Nothing, 1952; Chiang Kai-shek, 1955. *Memoirs*—Congo Solo, 1935; China to Me, 1944; Hong Kong Holiday, 1946; England to Me, 1949. *Juveniles*—Francie, 1951; Mary, Queen of Scots, 1953; Francie Again, 1953.

ABOUT: Hahn, E. England to Me, Hong Kong Holiday; Current Biography 1942; New York Times Book Review March 27, 1955; Saturday Review March 26, 1955; Scholastic November 6, 1937; Time December 11, 1944.

HAINES, WILLIAM WISTER (September 17, 1908-   ), American novelist and playwright, writes: "I was born in Des Moines, Iowa, the second son of Diedrich Jansen and Ella (Wister) Haines. I grew up in Des Moines attending public and private grade schools, the Culver Military Academy, and the Roosevelt Public High School in Des Moines from which I was graduated. In 1931 I was graduated from the University of Pennsylvania with the degree of Bachelor of Science in Economics.

"After college I continued for some time to work at the trade of lineman which I had followed during summer vacations, working at high voltage transmission tower construction and wire stringing for several construction companies and finally upon the electrification of the Pennsylvania Railroad.

"My first novel, *Slim*, was written about the life and work of linemen. It was published in August 1934. Since then I have published short stories in several of the popular magazines, some being reprinted in anthologies. Another novel of linemen, *High Tension*, was published in 1938. I have written motion picture scripts for several of the Hollywood studios, including the script of *Slim* which the Warner Brothers produced in 1937, starring Henry Fonda, Pat O'Brien, and Margaret Lindsay.

"In March 1942 I was commissioned in the Army Air Forces in which I served forty-one months, thirty-three of them being spent overseas. Worked variously in the Headquarters Army Air Forces, the 8th Composite

Command, 8th Fighter Command, 8th Air Force, and United States Strategic Air Forces, serving the last eighteen months of the European war for the latter Command in the office of the Assistant Chief of the Air Staff for Intelligence, Royal Air Force.

"On VJ day I applied for separation from the service which was granted two weeks later. I began immediately writing the play *Command Decision*. I sent the play script to the *Atlantic Monthly* whose editor, Edward Weeks, requested me to write it in the form of a novel. This I did and the novel *Command Decision* ran in four serial installments in the *Atlantic Monthly* before it was published January 1947. It was republished in England and has subsequently been reprinted in Dutch and Spanish.

"The play *Command Decision* was first presented for three weeks at the Cleveland Playhouse in 1946. It was presented at the Fulton Theatre in New York by Kermit Bloomgarden in October 1947 and ran there for fifty weeks before taking to the road where it played in various cities for another sixteen or seventeen weeks. It was later made into a moving picture by Metro Goldwyn Mayer."

PRINCIPAL WORKS: Slim, 1934; High Tension, 1938; Command Decision, 1947 (as play, 1948).

ABOUT: New Yorker October 18, 1947.

HALDANE, JOHN BURDON SANDERSON (November 5, 1892-).

For autobiographical sketch and list of earlier works and references, see TWENTIETH CENTURY AUTHORS, 1942.

* * *

J. B. S. Haldane writes from London: "During the Second World War I worked on the physiology of diving and was partly responsible for the methods used in clearing liberated ports. During this work I made the curious discovery that oxygen, at the pressure of about six atmospheres, has a taste. This fact may or may not have got into elementary chemistry texts by A.D. 2000. Since then I have worked on genetics and evolution, for which work I was awarded the Darwin medal of the Royal Society in 1952. In 1945 I married Helen Spurway, my colleague in underwater work. At the age of sixty I have more or less retired from politics. However, I would certainly be rated as a Red in the U.S.A., though in fact my opinions as to world politics are probably as near to those of Nehru as of any other well-known politician."

The first Mrs. Haldane, the writer Charlotte Franken Haldane, was divorced from J. B. S. Haldane in 1945. In her autobiography, *Truth Will Out*, published in 1950, she records the somewhat parallel histories of her membership in the Communist Party, which she had joined in 1937 and left in 1941, and of her marriage to Haldane.

Correction: Professor Haldane wishes it noted that he was never professor of physiology at London University and that his experiments described in the original sketch were with ammonium chloride and other salts (*not* "ether salts"). At present he is in the department of biometry of University College, London.

ADDITIONAL WORKS: Adventures of a Biologist (in England: Keeping Cool, and Other Essays) 1940; A Banned Broadcast, and Other Essays, 1946; Science Advances, 1947; What Is Life? 1947; Everything Has a History, 1951; The Biochemistry of Genetics, 1954.

ABOUT: Haldane, C. F. Truth Will Out; Current Biography 1940; Newsweek January 13, 1947; Time July 30, 1945, June 30, 1947, September 27, 1948, August 15, 1949.

HALE, NANCY (May 16, 1908-),

American novelist and short story writer, writes: "I was born in Boston, Mass., the only child of Philip L. Hale and Lilian Westcott Hale, both painters. I was brought up in Dedham, Mass., and went to the Winsor School in Boston and later, after 'coming out' in Boston, to the School of the Boston Museum of Fine Arts. I  also studied in my father's studio in the old Fenway Studios.

"I placed my first short story at the age of eleven, in the Boston *Herald*. My mother has kept a letter to an editor I wrote (I don't know why it wasn't sent) at that time: it ends, after saying I was enclosing a poem, 'My object is remuneration.' However the remuneration didn't start coming until after I married, at twenty, and went to New York, where I became an assistant editor of *Vogue*; an assistant editor of the old *Vanity Fair*; and the first woman reporter on the New York *Times*, over the period of 1928-36. During this time I sold stories to such magazines as the *New Yorker*, *Harper's*, the now defunct *Scribner's Magazine*, and Mr. Mencken's *Mercury*, besides publishing my first two novels, *The Young Die Good* and *Never Any More* and a collection of my short stories, *The Earliest Dreams*. A good number of my stories were in the O. Henry and O'Brien collections of these years, and in one year I won an O. Henry prize.

"In 1937 I came to Charlottesville where I have lived off and on ever since, my husband, Fredson Bowers, being professor of English literature at the University of Virginia. The 'off' periods include the war years when we went to Washington, and the summers which I spend on Cape Ann, Mass. In 1942 I published *The Prodigal Women*, which sold 1,250,000 copies in all editions, and the following year a collection of short stories, *Between the Dark and the Daylight*. In 1950 I published a novel, *The Sign of Jonah*. Both these latter two novels have been extremely successful in Europe; in fact I don't know what I should have lived on last year if the Germans had not unexpectedly liked *Jonah* so much.

"I have an amazing collection of ancestors—Edward Everett Hale, Harriet Beecher Stowe, Nathan Hale, Edward Everett, Lyman Beecher, etc. etc.—but the most they really ever did for me is that, as a child, knowing that Nathan Hale was hanged by the British for some reason gave me courage to go down to the cellar after dark.

"I have been anthologized a great many times, more than thirty but I don't know how many more, having lost track.

"I have lately become very much interested in writing for the theatre. I am fortunate in having been able to avail myself of the facilities of the Virginia Players at the University, who produced in the past two years my comedies *The Best of Everything* and *Somewhere She Dances*. It seems clear that small university or community drama groups such as this provide the best possible laboratories for would-be playwrights in an age where the cost of mounting a production in New York precludes experimentation.

"I am a member of the Board of Directors of the local League of Women Voters. I have two sons by former marriages: Mark Hardin, who is married, and William Wertenbaker, who is at boarding-school. At present I am engaged in writing a number of short stories, and plan another novel and another play."

PRINCIPAL WORKS: The Young Die Good, 1932; Never Any More, 1934; The Earliest Dreams (short stories) 1936; The Prodigal Women, 1942; Between the Dark and the Daylight (short stories) 1943; The Sign of Jonah, 1950.

ABOUT: Gray, J. On Second Thought; Van Gelder, R. Writers and Writing; New York Herald Tribune Book Review November 19, 1950; Wilson Library Bulletin January 1943.

HALL, GRANVILLE STANLEY (February 1, 1844-April 24, 1924). For biographical sketch and list of works and references, see TWENTIETH CENTURY AUTHORS, 1942.

* * *

ADDITIONAL WORKS: Hall, G. S. Letters to Jonas Gilman Clark (ed. N. O. Rush) 1948.
ABOUT: Journal of Applied Psychology February 1943; School and Society July 8, 1944, December 23, 1944, April 13, 1946, May 11, 1946.

HALL, HAROLD FIELDING-. See FIELDING-HALL

"HALL, HOLWORTHY." See PORTER, H. E.

HALL, JAMES NORMAN (April 22, 1887-July 5, 1951). For autobiographical sketch and list of earlier works and references, see TWENTIETH CENTURY AUTHORS, 1942.

* * *

Having returned to Tahiti from the United States in May 1941, James Norman Hall died in his Papeete home at sixty-four. In accordance with his wishes he was buried on a hill overlooking Matavai Bay, where Captain Bligh, immortalized by Hall in *Mutiny on the Bounty*, had anchored his ship.

Most of Hall's work was done with Charles Nordhoff, and Ellery Sedgwick has attempted to analyze the collaboration and each author's share in it. "With Nordhoff and Hall," he writes, "complete success was due not to the similarity but to the diversity of the component halves. Neither half lost anything of his personality, but the sum of both was ampler and richer than either alone. Nordhoff gave energy and passion, Hall meditation and understanding. Nordhoff gave action, Hall beauty. Nordhoff's humor was in a higher key. Hall gave a quieter satisfaction." Murray Welch regrets that Hall did not produce more works independently and writes of the few books done without collaboration, "Hall's poetry and philosophy of life are built with emotion, whim, color, texture, glamor, and are the products of reverie." His posthumously published autobiography, *My Island Home*, was a simple and unpretentious self-portrait. William McFee said that it was "a revelation of a writer whose books deal with the world outside, a writer whose success was largely due to brilliant editorship and an unusually hard-headed collaborator. But the character of the man himself shines serenely, a gentle spirit of flawless integrity."

ADDITIONAL WORKS: Under a Thatched Roof, 1942; Lost Island, 1944; High Barbaree (with C. B. Nordhoff) 1945; Word for his Sponsor, a Narrative Poem, 1949; Far Lands, 1950; Forgotten One, and Other True Tales of the South Seas, 1952; My Island Home, 1952.

ABOUT: Hall, J. N. Forgotten One, My Island Home; Sedgwick, E. Atlantic Harvest; Van Gelder, R. Writers and Writing; Atlantic Monthly September, October 1951; New York Herald Tribune Book Review October 8, 1950; New York Times July 7, 1951; New York Times Book Review January 14, 1951; Saturday Review of Literature July 21, 1951; South Atlantic Quarterly April 1940; Time January 19, 1942.

HALL, JOSEF WASHINGTON ("Upton Close") (February 27, 1894-). For biographical sketch and list of earlier works and references, see TWENTIETH CENTURY AUTHORS, 1942.

* * *

Upton Close continued his radio broadcasts in the first years of World War II as an expert on Far Eastern affairs. In this capacity he had a weekly broadcast for N.B.C. from April 1941 to September 1942 and continued broadcasting off and on, until 1944. He also broadcast for the Mutual Network. In 1944 N.B.C. did not renew his contract, and Close charged that various outside pressures had influenced the network's decision to drop him. This was strongly denied by N.B.C. In point of fact, there had been much objection to Close's broadcasts. An isolationist, violently anti-liberal, anti-labor, and anti-Franklin Roosevelt, Close was accused of slanting the news along the lines of his own opinions. The late Dixon Wecter made a study of Close's broadcasts (along with those of Fulton Lewis, Jr.) for the *Atlantic Monthly* in 1945. Here he wrote: "The passage of news through a commentator's personality achieves its sharpest refraction with Upton Close." At about the same time the *Saturday Evening Post* denied editorially a rumor which Close had broadcast concerning pressures brought upon the magazine to discontinue the publication of certain articles. The editorial reported that when Close had gone off the air, a short time before, *Variety*—the magazine of show business—had commented that Close's loss was America's gain. To this the editorial added:

"The *Post* emphatically agrees with that verdict."

Close married Julia Robinson in 1942. They have one son and live in Los Angeles, Calif.

ADDITIONAL WORKS: Ladder of History (with M. Burke) 1945.

ABOUT: Atlantic Monthly August 1945; Current Biography 1944; Saturday Evening Post August 11, 1945.

HALL, LELAND (July 20, 1883-). For biographical sketch and list of works and references, see TWENTIETH CENTURY AUTHORS, 1942.

HALL, RADCLYFFE (188?-October 7, 1943). For biographical sketch and list of works and references, see TWENTIETH CENTURY AUTHORS, 1942.

* * *

Radclyffe Hall died in London at the reported age of fifty-seven, after a six-months' illness. An untitled novel on which she had been working was destroyed, at her own request, after her death.

The London *Times* has said: "Radclyffe Hall had abundant sympathy and pity, and views on her controversial book [*The Well of Loneliness*] should not be allowed to rob her of credit for her sterling literary qualities, her well-controlled emotional pitch, her admirable prose style."

ABOUT: London Times October 11, 1943; New York Times October 12, 1943.

HALLGREN, MAURITZ ALFRED (June 18, 1899-). For biographical sketch and list of works and references, see TWENTIETH CENTURY AUTHORS, 1942.

HALLIBURTON, RICHARD (January 9, 1900-March 23/24, 1939). For biographical sketch and list of works and references, see TWENTIETH CENTURY AUTHORS, 1942.

* * *

ABOUT: National Cyclopedia of American Biography (1949); Newsweek March 12, 1945.

HALPER, ALBERT (August 3, 1904-). For autobiographical sketch and list of earlier works and references, see TWENTIETH CENTURY AUTHORS, 1942.

* * *

Although Albert Halper has adopted New York for his home and lives in Brooklyn, his literary roots are firmly planted in Chicago. Only one of his recent works, *Only an Inch from Glory*, has a New York setting. *The Little People* chronicles in faithful and pathetic detail the lives of a group of employees of a Chicago department store. Even closer to home for Halper is the semi-autobiographical novel *The Golden Watch* with its warm and tender reminiscences of a West Side Chicago Jewish family. Sam Ross wrote in the New York *Times*: "There is a soft folk quality in the book. It is rich in humor and the plain speech of common people, with lilts of irony and pathos." Halper's humor, Nelson Algren observed, "resembles that of Saroyan except that it is less contrived. . . . The art that conceals art is in this, for the reader's interest is thereby the more closely held."

Halper married Pauline Friedman in 1942. They have a son, Thomas. The sketch in TWENTIETH CENTURY AUTHORS, 1942, described Halper as dark, with a small mustache. He writes to the editors: "I am far from dark, and I have always been clean shaven."

ADDITIONAL WORKS: The Little People, 1942; Only an Inch from Glory, 1943; This Is Chicago: An Anthology (ed.) 1952; The Golden Watch. 1953.

ABOUT: Antioch Review December 1942.

HAMILTON, CLAYTON (November 14, 1881-September 17, 1946). For autobiographical sketch and list of works and references, see TWENTIETH CENTURY AUTHORS, 1942.

* * *

Clayton Hamilton died of coronary thrombosis at his home in New York City at sixty-four. He had been in good health up to the time of his death, his activities including lecturing on the radio and writing poetry.

Hamilton was widely popular in theatrical and literary circles. In 1932 he received Columbia's University Medal, and Union College at Schenectady, N.Y., had conferred an honorary fellowship in drama upon him.

Richard Lockridge called him "an astute and reasonable critic of the theatre, at once alert to present methods and well-grounded in those of the past, erudite and contemporary."

ABOUT: Current Biography 1946; New York Times September 18, 1946; Publishers' Weekly November 9, 1946; Time September 30, 1946; Wilson Library Bulletin November 1946.

"HAMILTON, CLIVE." See LEWIS, C. S.

HAMILTON, COSMO (187?-October 14, 1942). For biographical sketch and list of earlier works and references, see TWENTIETH CENTURY AUTHORS, 1942.

* * *

Cosmo Hamilton died of pneumonia in a nursing home in Guilford, Surrey, England, at the reported age of seventy. He had been engaged in censorship work for the British Ministry of Information up to the time of his death. Hamilton was divorced from his second wife in 1929.

Author of over forty plays and some thirty novels, he was "not only an industrious and technically expert workman," in the words of the New York *Times*, "but he had a keen sense of the saleability of his products and knew how to keep his name constantly before the public."

His brother Sir Philip Gibbs recalls that "he was a born storyteller, and the devising of plots and dramatic situations was the breath of life to him."

ADDITIONAL WORKS: Aunt of England, 1942; Brief Flower, 1943.

ABOUT: Gibbs, P. Crowded Company; London Times October 16, 1942; New York Times October 15, 1942.

HAMILTON, EDITH (1867-). For biographical sketch and list of earlier works and references, see TWENTIETH CENTURY AUTHORS, 1942.

* * *

In an essay of tribute to her, John Mason Brown wrote that Edith Hamilton is a citizen of two worlds, the ancient and the modern—"and is equally at home with the best of both." He continues: "In any period Edith Hamilton would be exceptional; in ours she is unique. At all times those people are few and far between who can—indeed, who must —be described as having nobility of mind and spirit. It is to this slim fellowship that Miss Hamilton belongs. She is as uncorrupted by the vulgarities of the present as she is undowned by its pressures." Her most recent book, *Witness to the Truth*, published in her eighty-first year, had for its subject the teachings of Jesus and the early Christians, thus—after her work on ancient Greek, Roman, and Hebrew thought—rounding out her study of the moral and intellectual sources of our modern society. The late Thomas Sugrue described *Witness to the Truth* as "brief, intense, quietly brilliant . . . luminous with understanding and perception."

In 1952 Miss Hamilton wrote a long and challenging essay in the *Saturday Review* condemning William Faulkner and all those "who detest nature and escape from reality" for creating, in their work, a world of ugliness, corruption and doom. The substance of Miss Hamilton's essay was open to debate, but it was widely admired for its forthright and lucid statement of her position.

Correction: Edith Hamilton was born in 1867, not 1869, as given in TWENTIETH CENTURY AUTHORS, 1942.

ADDITIONAL WORKS: Mythology, 1942; Witness to the Truth, 1948.

ABOUT: Brown, J. M. Seeing More Things.

HAMILTON, Mrs. MARY AGNES (ADAMSON) (1883-). For biographical sketch and list of earlier works and references, see TWENTIETH CENTURY AUTHORS, 1942.

* * *

Mrs. Hamilton has been a temporary civil servant since 1940 and has written numerous pamphlets and articles on the problems of British labor and trade unions. In 1949 she was honored with the Commander Order of the British Empire. She lives in the Chelsea district of London.

ADDITIONAL WORK: Remembering My Good Friends, 1944.

HAMILTON, PATRICK (1904-), British novelist and playwright, was born in Sussex, and attended school in Hove. At seven-teen he went on the stage, playing small parts and acting as assistant stage manager for Andrew Melville, on tour and in repertory. Melville's repertory consisted of Old Lyceum melodramas; and, while prompting, ringing curtain up and down, and performing his various other duties, Hamilton became fascinated by the techniques of melodrama which he later used more subtly in his plays *Angel Street* and *Rope*. Aware of the precarious livelihood afforded by the stage, Hamilton learned typing and shorthand by correspondence, and moved from the London suburb Chiswick to the city in order to find a job. While living at Chiswick, however, he had absorbed the mid-dle-class atmosphere later reproduced in his novel *Craven House* (1926).

Hamilton's first novel was *Monday Morning* (1925); but it was the publication of his second novel, *Craven House*, which drew enthusiastic praise from critics in America as well as in England. Hamilton's style was called "reminiscent of Dickens," in its gusto of detail, imagination, and irony.

Twopence Coloured (1928), the story of a romance within the theatre world, was less favorabiy received. Several reviewers noted that Hamilton's gift was for "light irony and kindly ridicule," rather than for anything of a graver nature. *The Midnight Bell, The Siege of Pleasure*, and *The Plains of Cement*, three novels of the trilogy *Twenty Thousand Streets Under the Sky*, followed, and showed further development of his gift for "Dickensian" characterization, his excellent ear for dialogue and for the Cockney dialect, his "warm-hearted" insight into characters, and his talent for creating suspense.

Much of Hamilton's fame, however, derives from his authorship of the play *Angel Street* (1939), which received high praise in American newspapers and periodicals and was selected for Burns Mantle's *Best Plays of 1941-42*. A "good Victorian thriller," obviously the fruit of Mr. Hamilton's early experiences with melodrama, *Angel Street* was commended by *Time* for creating suspense "not by keeping the audience in ignorance, but by making it doubt what it knows. . . . [It] builds up tension not by hurrying its pace, but by slowing it down to a nerve-racking creep." It was made into a motion picture under the title *Gaslight*. Other plays by Hamilton are *Rope* (1929), also made into a motion picture, and *The Duke in Darkness* (1943), as well as two radio plays, *Money With Menaces*, and *To the Public Danger* (both 1939).

PRINCIPAL WORKS: *Fiction*—Monday Morning, 1925; Craven House, 1926; Twopence Coloured, 1928; The Midnight Bell, 1929; The Siege of Pleasure, 1932; The Plains of Cement, 1934; Twenty Thousand Streets Under the Sky, 1935; Impromptu in Moribundia, 1939; Hangover Square, 1941, The Slaves of Solitude, 1947; The West Pier, 1951. *Plays*—Rope, 1929; Angel Street, 1939; The Duke in Darkness, 1943.

ABOUT: (London) Times Literary Supplement September 7, 1951.

HAMMETT, DASHIELL (May 27, 1894-). For biographical sketch and list of works and references, see TWENTIETH CENTURY AUTHORS, 1942.

* * *

Dashiell Hammett's Sam Spade has won

assured immortality in the ranks of "who-dunit" fiction. Probably the most sincere tribute to his stature is the number, enormous and still growing, of his imitators. These hardboiled, hard-drinking, and hard-hitting "private eyes" range from the relatively decent detective heroes who hate crime, are to some extent brutalized by their contacts with it but manage nevertheless to emerge with some shreds of decency remaining, to the out-and-out sadists who take the law into their own hands and administer, at best, a kind of cave-man justice to the criminals they track down. Spade remains the classic of the type—"not yet . . . surpassed," John Paterson wrote in the *Saturday Review* in 1953, "in the hardboiled tradition of detective fiction."

Hammett himself, Paterson commented, "abdicated the literary scene, perhaps because he had exhausted the possibilities of his subject matter." In World War II he enlisted in the Army as a private and served overseas. Long active in left-wing political groups, he has, since the end of the war, devoted himself to political work. In 1951 Hammett, as trustee of the Civil Rights Congress which had supplied bail to a group of Communists on trial for conspiracy against the United States government, was subpoenaed for questioning when four of the then convicted Communists jumped bail and disappeared. Hammett refused to name the sources of the bail fund and to produce the books of the organization. He was convicted of contempt of court and, his appeals to the higher courts failing, he served a six-months' jail sentence from July to December 1951. In April 1953 Hammett testified before a Senate subcommittee investigating charges that pro-Communist books were on the shelves of overseas libraries run by the Department of State. Three hundred copies of Hammett's books had been found in these libraries. He refused to say whether he was a Communist and said that he thought it was "impossible to write anything without taking some sort of stand on social issues."

ABOUT: Commentary May 1949: Newsweek October 31, 1949; Saturday Review May 31, 1952, August 22, 1953; Time April 6, 1953.

HAMMOND, PERCY (March 7, 1873-April 25, 1936). For biographical sketch and list of works and references, see TWENTIETH CENTURY AUTHORS, 1942.

* * *

ABOUT: Lewis, L. It Takes All Kinds.

HAMSUN, KNUT (August 4, 1859-February 19, 1952). For biographical sketch and list of works and references, see TWENTIETH CENTURY AUTHORS, 1942.

* * *

Knut Hamsun died at his home in Grimstad, Norway, in his ninety-second year. His death passed without comment in the Oslo press because this once highly honored writer had been an outright sympathizer with the Nazi conquerors of his native land during World War II and had visited Hitler in 1943. When Germany invaded Norway, Hamsun told his countrymen: "Norwegians! Throw away your rifles and return home. The Germans are fighting for us and all neutrals." His countrymen had their revenge on him in some measure during these years by sending back to him thousands of copies of his books —all of them well-worn with reading but now rejected. When Norway was liberated in 1945, Hamsun and his wife were arrested for collaboration with the enemy. Charges against him were later dropped because of his age and mental condition.

Hamsun was the only important Norwegian author to welcome the Nazis; and his stand, though completely irrational and unjustified, was consistent with his admiration for Prussian militarism in World War I. And it was not entirely inconsistent with his work—his passionate individualism, his rejection of modern industrial civilization, his obsession with rugged heroic themes. Alrik Gustafson suggests that "the primitivism which lies at the base of all his social criticism is not without direct points of contact with central tenets in the Nazi philosophy."

It may be, as W. Gore Allen has pointed out, that Hamsun revolted consciously and deliberately against the liberal society which, when he was a young man, had been content to see him starve but, when he wrote his magnificent *Hunger*, lionized him. It may be, on the other hand, that he was simply a stubborn and feeble old man. In any case, his novels remain rich and powerful works of art. "It is perhaps the task of those who read his books," Allen writes, "to measure how far the teaching they contain is against all human progress, and how far it merely recognizes limitations, takes warning from mistakes, so rendering a real advance more easy that it would otherwise have been."

ABOUT: Allen, W. G. Renaissance in the North; Columbia Dictionary of Modern European Literature; New York Times February 20, 1952; Time September 7, 1942, December 29, 1947, March 3, 1952.

HANDLIN, OSCAR (September 29, 1915-), American social historian, writes:

"I was born in Brooklyn, N.Y. My parents

were Russian immigrants, my mother having come to America as a girl in 1905, my father some nine years later. In the early years of their married life they were engaged in the trying struggle for security and independence, moving through a succession of small businesses in Brooklyn, New Haven, and Kingston. They finally settled in 1922 in Mapleton, a suburban district of Brooklyn where they operated a grocery for the next twenty years.

"Through that whole period they were above all concerned with the education of their children, both out of the love of learning itself and because they hoped education might be the instrument of advancing status. Although my formal schooling was, at first, frequently interrupted by the family movings, I was always imbued with the sense of its importance. I passed through the public elementary schools and graduated from New Utrecht High School in 1931.

"As a matter of course, with almost all my contemporaries of the neighborhood, I moved on to Brooklyn College. I had by then discovered my interest in history and was fortunate to find in college Jesse D. Clarkson, a stimulating teacher whose restlessly critical mind opened to me the first glimpses of the potentialities of the subject. Apart from that, my education was largely independent, arrived at through undisciplined but voracious reading.

"I came to Harvard to work toward the doctorate in medieval history, but within a year, found the focus of my interests had shifted toward American history, under the influence of Arthur M. Schlesinger and Frederick Merk. My dissertation, written under the direction of Professor Schlesinger, took me into the realm of social history and exposed me to the problems of the role of immigration in American culture. Published in 1941 as *Boston's Immigrants*, this work earned the Dunning Prize of the American Historical Association.

"In 1937, I married Mary Flug, whom I had met as a student in Brooklyn College. Our children (Joanna, David, and Ruth) were born between 1942 and 1947. We have

also collaborated in scholarship. Jointly we undertook a study of the role of government in the American economy for the Committee on Research in Economic History, the results of which were published in *Commonwealth* as well as in a series of articles.

"Between 1936 and 1939, I taught occasionally at Brooklyn College. In 1939 I joined the Department of History at Harvard University. I have remained there since, teaching for some years also in the Department of Social Relations. My interests are still in the sources of American culture."

* * *

In May 1952 Dr. Handlin received the Pulitzer prize in history for *The Uprooted*, a study of the great immigration movements to America after 1820. Since 1951 he has been editor of Little, Brown's "Library of American Biography" series.

PRINCIPAL WORKS: Boston's Immigrants, 1941; Commonwealth: a Study of the Role of Government in American Economy (with M. F. Handlin) 1947; This Was America (ed.) 1949; The Uprooted, 1951; The American People in the Twentieth Century, 1954; Adventure in Freedom, 1954; Chance or Destiny, 1955.

ABOUT: Current Biography 1952; New York Herald Tribune May 6, 1952; New York Times May 6, 1952; Perspectives I; Saturday Review July 3, 1954.

HANLEY, GERALD (1916-) was born in Ireland, and at the age of sixteen went to Kenya, East Africa, to take up farming. At

the outbreak of World

War II he joined the Royal Irish Fusiliers, serving in Africa with the occupying forces of the United Kingdom, then went to Burma as a war correspondent with the 11th East African Division. *Monsoon Victory* (1946), his
first book, tells the story of the 14th Army in Burma, in 1944, and its struggle against three months' bombardment by the monsoon. In August of that year, when the Japanese thrust at India had at last overreached itself, Captain Hanley marched with his division down the Khaban Valley, until, in December, when the rain had stopped, a bridgehead was established at Kalewa, which opened the way to Mandalay.

After the war, Hanley became a member of the J. Arthur Rank film organization, working in India and Pakistan. Later, he worked in England with the foreign service of the British Broadcasting Corporation. In the autumn of 1950 Hanley returned to India. He has been living near Palumpur, N.E. Punjab, which he describes as a remote spot at the foot of the Himalayas, and where his life in a thatched hut is simple, among people whose daily existence has not changed much in the last few centuries.

In Hanley's first novel, *The Consul at Sunset* (1951), the action occurs in an outpost near Ethiopia, where warrior tribal chiefs oppose both Italian and British armed forces. Hanley is particularly interested in the Indian people, and their efforts to develop an individual and unified nation. "From India," he says, "will certainly come some new kind of civilization in which the best of the past and the present will be mingled." In *The Consul at Sunset,* a reviewer noted, "the author does anything but idealize his natives. . . . He is less interested in over-all solutions of the British Colonial problems than he is in its effects on the individual conscience of those thrust into authority." His second novel, *The Year of the Lion* (1954), shows the same kind of dramatic style, full of suspense, and permeated with moral feeling, as the earlier books. The London *Times Literary Supplement* has called Hanley's style "highly sensuous . . . strongly charged with muscular effort, tactile impressions, gleams of intense vision."

PRINCIPAL WORKS: Monsoon Victory, 1946; The Consul at Sunset, 1951; The Year of the Lion, 1954.

HANLEY, JAMES (1901-). For biographical sketch and list of earlier works and references, see TWENTIETH CENTURY AUTHORS, 1942.

* * *

Until the American publication of *The Closed Harbor* in 1953, James Hanley had attracted little critical attention outside England, where he is a highly respected but not a popular novelist. At his best, the (London) *Times Literary Supplement* had observed of him, he is "a novelist of the sea of commanding realistic power. But he has always been an uneven and incalculable writer . . . apt to be capricious and uncertain." *The Closed Harbor,* however, brought him wider and more enthusiastic notice than any of his earlier works. A grim study of the moral disintegration of a French captain who has lost his ship and his honor, the novel was hailed by the *Times* as one of Hanley's greatest achievements—"and of

their kind there are none superior." Here, as in his other novels, his style is lean, "roughhewn," and unadorned, his action essentially simple and naturalistic. The scene of *The Closed Harbor* is Marseilles and the novel, as several reviewers noted, shows French as well as English influences. The book ends in abysmal despair—"a veritable Canaan of wretchedness," as Brendan Gill described it in the *New Yorker,* and, Gill continued, it "reads a little as if it were translated from the French of one of those young Existentialist authors of a few years back who seemed to teeter forever this side suicide and to be ready, should they slip, to pull the whole human race out of the window after them."

Hanley lives in a small Welsh village near the sea. The sea, as one reviewer suggested, is "the central experience of his novels." It forms his style, his plots, his characters, and, in a sense, it forms him as well.

ADDITIONAL WORKS: *Novels*—No Directions, 1943; Sailor's Song, 1943; What Farrar Saw, 1945; Winter Song, 1950; The Closed Harbor, 1952. *Short Stories*—At Bay, 1943; Crilley, 1945; Selected Stories, 1947; A Walk in the Wilderness, 1950. *Essays*—Don Quixote Drowned, 1953.

ABOUT: New Yorker November 21, 1953; Time November 16, 1953; (London) Times Literary Supplement February 27, 1953.

HANNAY, JAMES OWEN ("George A. Birmingham") (July 16, 1865-February 2, 1950). For biographical sketch and list of earlier works and references, see TWENTIETH CENTURY AUTHORS, 1942.

* * *

Rev. James Owen Hannay died in his sleep at eighty-four. His final years as the distinguished vicar of a small, well-to-do London parish "rounded off his life with a serene and happy last chapter."

His prodigious output of popular novels (written under the pseudonym of "George A. Birmingham") continued until a few weeks before his death. In describing this major portion of his work the *Saturday Review of Literature* observed that "he has a tremendous appetite for life and is amused by his own appetite; the idiosyncrasies of human nature delight him; and the ridiculous in close attendance upon the serious is the cream of his jest." When in 1946 Hannay received a degree of Doctor of Literature from Trinity College, Dublin, the London *Times* said that "he was greatly pleased to find in the Public Orator's address recognition of his work on Church history and theology, which he valued in spite of the great success of his novels."

Personally he was "a man of great charm. . . . He could tell a good story as well as he could write one."

ADDITIONAL WORKS: Potter's Wheel (non-fiction) 1940; Miss Maitland's Spy, 1941; Over the Border, 1942; Poor Sir Edward, 1943; Lieutenant Commander, 1944; Good Intentions, 1945; Piccadilly Lady, 1946; Golden Apple, 1947; Sea Battle, 1948; Laura's Bishop, 1949; Two Scamps, 1950.

ABOUT: New York Times February 3, 1950; (London) Times February 3, 1950.

HANSEN, HARRY (December 26, 1884-). For autobiographical sketch and list of earlier works and references, see TWENTIETH CENTURY AUTHORS, 1942.

* * *

In November 1948 Harry Hansen gave up his regular book reviewing assignments (although he continued for a while as reviewer for *Redbook* and *Survey*) to become editor of the *World Almanac*. His keen interest in details and stray bits of information has stood him in good stead not only in his new editorial duties, but in his own writing as well. His book on the Chicago for the Rivers of America Series was a chatty and informative history of the city. More recently, in *North of Manhattan*, a kind of informal guide to some of the historic points of New York's Westchester, Hansen produced what John K. Hutchens described as "a little book charming for its air of leisurely poking around in odd corners, and informative for the nuggets it finds there."

ADDITIONAL WORKS: The Chicago, 1942; (tr.) Habe, H. Kathrine, 1943; (ed.) The World Almanac and Book of Facts, 1949—; North of Manhattan: Persons and Places of Old Westchester, 1950; Scarsdale, 1954.

ABOUT: Current Biography 1942; Editor and Publisher November 6, 1948; Publishers' Weekly November 6, 1948; Scholastic November 3, 1948.

HANSEN, MARCUS LEE (December 8, 1892-May 11, 1938). For biographical sketch and list of works and references, see TWENTIETH CENTURY AUTHORS, 1942.

* * *

ABOUT: Common Ground, vol. II, no. 2 (1942).

HAPGOOD, HUTCHINS (May 21, 1869-November 18, 1944). For autobiographical sketch and list of works and references, see TWENTIETH CENTURY AUTHORS, 1942.

* * *

Hutchins Hapgood died at his home in Provincetown, Mass., at seventy-five, after a brief illness.

The New York *Times* noted that Hapgood had been "a leader in liberal literary circles a quarter of a century ago and in the movement which gave birth to the Greenwich Village traditions and the artists' Provincetown."

The *Christian Century* called him "an unrepentent libertine who, having great abilities and opportunities, might have accomplished much more than he ever did if he had not been so obsessed with the idea of having a good time." R. L. Duffus has pointed out, however, that although Hapgood was a bystander rather than an actor, he was "a deeply concerned bystander," and adds: "He loved life. He speaks of 'this marvelous gift of existence,' of waking every morning for years with a sense of eager expectancy."

ABOUT: National Cyclopedia of American Biography (1949); New York Times November 19, 1944.

HAPGOOD, NORMAN (March 28, 1868-April 29, 1937). For biographical sketch and list of works and references, see TWENTIETH CENTURY AUTHORS, 1942.

HARBAGE, ALFRED (July 18, 1901-), American scholar, writes: "To supply this sketch with a properly refulgent opening, I must point out that in 1557-58 when Queen Elizabeth ascended the throne of England and the father of William Shakespeare first became active in the government of Stratford-upon-Avon, the mayor of that star-marked town was Frances Harbage.  Since my father was born only twenty-five miles from Stratford-upon-Avon, I exercise my faith and claim Frances as the founder of our line. My grandfather was a Wesleyan circuit-rider before his migration to America, a highly unsuccessful pioneer in the chain-store movement afterwards. My maternal grandfather also mixed the spiritual with the temporal, as an ordained clergyman and photographer of Bucks County, Pa.

"I was born in the Kensington district of Philadelphia, the youngest of five. Financial necessity and vague aspirations to become an author after gaining a knowledge of life led me into about twenty different jobs before my graduation from the University of Pennsylvania. I was a farm-hand, a factory-hand, a labor-pusher in a water-power construction camp, an ordinary seaman (twice), an apprentice structural-steelworker (twice), etc. I look back on the structural-steelwork with particular wonder since I was physically not the type and was then as I am now afraid of heights. I began teaching at Pennsylvania in the year of my graduation, and in 1926 married my classmate, Eliza Price Finnesey. Of our four children two daughters are married, one son is an ensign in the navy, another son still happily with us.

"I became finally a professor at Pennsylvania, then at Columbia, and recently at Harvard. My teaching has centered about Shakespeare, who excites me as much now as when my father used to thunder out the soliloquies in a style no doubt inherited from the Wesleyan circuit-rider. I have never felt confident about my effectiveness as a teacher, yet have persistently declined invitations to trade the classroom for richer interiors.

"A number of essays and articles, and the books listed below, are the by-product of my teaching. Although the last of the books was awarded a prize (of an academic sort) and I should like to think that this work qualifies me as a Twentieth Century Author, I cannot believe that I have much reference interest as a result of it. In case I was invited to submit a sketch for other reasons, I must explain that my fiction can lay claim to no kind of literary distinction. When the creative impulse reasserted itself, I produced a series of humorous detective novels under a pen-name. The crime novel seems to me to have lost its harmlessness and I have shifted to short story writing, accepting the hospitality of Ellery Queen in his editorial role. I have published other forms of brief fiction under various pen-names. I am reticent about this activity only because I do not wish to be mistaken for a qualified counsellor by the college English majors (about 95 per cent of the total number) who plan to become authors."

* * *

In 1951 Professor Harbage received the Modern Language Association-Macmillan Award for his study of the Elizabethan theatre and its audience in *Shakespeare and the Rival Traditions.*

PRINCIPAL WORKS: Thomas Killigrew, Cavalier Dramatist, 1930; Sir William Davenant, Poet-Venturer, 1935; Cavalier Drama: An Historical and Critical Supplement to the Study of the Elizabethan and Restoration Stage, 1936; Annals of English Drama, 975-1700: An Analytical Record of All Plays, 1940; Shakespeare's Audience, 1941; As They Liked It: Shakespeare and Morality, 1947; Shakespeare and the Rival Traditions, 1952.

HARDING, Mrs. BERTITA (LEONARZ) (November 1, 1907-   ). For biographical sketch and list of earlier works and references, see TWENTIETH CENTURY AUTHORS, 1942.

* * *

In addition to her informative travel books on Latin-American countries, Bertita Harding has—in recent books—written of the Hapsburg family *(Lost Waltz)* with her characteristic "reverence for royal rococo" (to quote Virginia Kirkus), and—with considerable romantic dash—of the love affair of Duse and D'Annunzio *(Age Cannot Wither)*, and of the stormy life of Richard Wagner *(Magic Fire)*. Her most successful book, however, was about herself and the Mexico in which she grew up, *Mosaic in the Fountain*. As autobiography the book is a detailed and sensitive picture of her girlhood. It is equally valuable as a picture of the turbulent history of Mexico in the first quarter of this century, and her account of the siege of Monterrey, Robert Pick wrote in the *Saturday Review,* "ranks with the very best of stories about Mexican revolts."

ADDITIONAL WORKS: Lost Waltz, 1944; Age Cannot Wither, 1947; Southern Empire: Brazil, 1948; The Land Columbus Loved: The Dominican Republic, 1949; Mosaic in the Fountain, 1949; Magic Fire, 1953.

ABOUT: Harding, B. Mosaic in the Fountain.

HARDY, ARTHUR SHERBURNE (August 13, 1847-March 13, 1930). For biographical sketch and list of works and references, see TWENTIETH CENTURY AUTHORS, 1942.

HARGROVE, MARION (LAWTON, Jr.) (October 3, 1919-   ), American author, was born in Mount Olive, N.C., the son of Marion Lawton Hargrove and Emma (Jernigan) Hargrove, his family having come to that section from Virginia "a couple of hundred years ago." He attended Central High School in Charlotte, N.C., where he edited the school paper and was student director of the dramatic society. Marion Hargrove left this high school in 1938 and spent four months as a student at Belmont Abbey in North Carolina, then going to Washington where he worked for a while as a soda-jerker. Returning to Charlotte (1939), he ushered at a movie theatre, was a printer's devil, and a

publicity man, then worked as proofreader for the Charlotte *News,* becoming feature editor and the city editor's assistant. In 1941 he was drafted, and while stationed at Fort Bragg, N.C., he met Maxwell Anderson who had come down to look for local color for *The Eve of St. Mark.* Hargrove showed him a column called "In the Army Now," that he had been writing for the Charlotte *News;* Anderson recommended publication in book form. A New York publisher took his advice, and *See Here, Private Hargrove,* a collection of these articles, appeared in 1942—four months later. The critics found it delightful, but differed on how great was Hargrove's writing ability and how much was a reportorial knack. With the public the book immediately became a best seller. Hargrove reportedly made two hundred thousand dollars from it, besides selling it for $12,000 to Metro-Goldwyn-Mayer. The movie sequel rights brought him $50,000. "Light and humorous in style, this small book provides an excellent insight through a trainee's eyes into life in the army training camps today," wrote S. T. Williamson in the New York *Times.* "The selection of material is good in that it has variety and deals with most of the experiences common to all of us in the army." A "glossary of Army slang," added the *Library Journal.*

In 1942 Hargrove was transferred to New York to work as a staff writer on *Yank.* In 1943, then a sergeant, he was sent to China as *Yank* correspondent, then to India, and in 1944 returned to New York as *Yank's* feature editor. After an assignment to the Philippines in 1945, Hargrove was in the same year discharged from the Army. He then went on a lecture tour, speaking not only about his Army experiences but about the need for democratizing the Army, for providing housing for veterans, and other subjects.

In 1948 the author's first novel, appeared, *Something's Got to Give.* It was called "inconsequential fare," but the Hargrove geniality was there. "His wry sanity, his freedom from pretentiousness are pleasantly bracing," said Charles J. Rolo. "Hargrove has an easy touch," wrote the *New Republic;* "his dialogue, which comprises 99 per cent of the book, is airy and usually convincing."

In 1942 Hargrove was married to Alison Pfeiffer of Vermont, then on the staff of *Mademoiselle.* They have two children. The author dislikes parties and exercise—sleeping is said to be his favorite pastime. He has described himself as a reticent type but has a quick wit and a fine sense of humor and is rarely at a loss for a subject to talk about. In recent years Hargrove has been feature editor of *Argosy* magazine in New York.

PRINCIPAL WORKS: See Here, Private Hargrove, 1942; Something's Got to Give, 1948.

ABOUT: Current Biography 1946; New York Post March 30, 1944; Newsweek September 7, 1953.

HARKER, Mrs. LIZZIE ALLEN (WATSON) (1863-April 14, 1933). For biographical sketch and list of works and references, see TWENTIETH CENTURY AUTHORS, 1942.

HARPER, GEORGE MCLEAN (December 31, 1863-July 14, 1947). For autobiographical sketch and list of earlier works and references, see TWENTIETH CENTURY AUTHORS, 1942.

* * *.

George McLean Harper died of a heart attack at eighty-three at Princeton. *Time* described the scholar as "an erect and kindly man who loved all that was good in men and books." Of his writing, T. S. Matthews said: "This author has the rare gift of conveying the sincerity of his enthusiasm to his readers."

ADDITIONAL WORKS: Woodrow Wilson (ed. by W. S. Myers) 1946.

ABOUT: Carnegie Foundation for Advancement of Teaching, 43rd Annual Report; New York Times July 15, 1947; Time July 28, 1947.

HARRADEN, BEATRICE (January 24, 1864-May 5, 1936). For biographical sketch and list of works and references, see TWENTIETH CENTURY AUTHORS, 1942.

* * *

ABOUT: Dictionary of National Biography 1931-1940.

HARRIMAN, JOHN (1904-   ). For autobiographical sketch and list of earlier works and references, see TWENTIETH CENTURY AUTHORS, 1942.

* * *

John Harriman writes: "Since the publication of TWENTIETH CENTURY AUTHORS, I have published another novel, *The Magnate* (1946), the story of the growth and decline of a great utility empire.

"I now live in Cambridge, Mass., and do a column on economics and politics for the Boston *Globe.* This and the birth of a second daughter are the only biographical developments."

ADDITIONAL WORK: The Magnate, 1946.

HARRIS, FRANK (February 14, 1856-
August 26, 1931). For biographical
sketch and list of works and references,
see TWENTIETH CENTURY AUTHORS,
1942.

* * *

ABOUT: Dictionary of National Biography 1931-
40; Root, E. M. Frank Harris; Scully, F. Rogues'
Gallery; Saturday Review of Literature October
2, October 30, 1943, June 21, 1947.

HARRIS, SEYMOUR EDWIN (September 8, 1897-   ), American economist, writes:
"I was born in New York City and lived in

John Brook

or around New York
City in my youth. I
received an A.B. de-
gree from Harvard in
1920 and Ph.D. in
1926. Except for two
years of teaching at
Princeton, 1920-1922,
when I had Governor
Adlai Stevenson in
my first class and
taught him orthodox
economics, my teaching career has been concentrated at Harvard (except for one semester at Cornell and one summer at Stanford).
"Brought up in the classical tradition, I
gradually weakened under the impact of the
late Lord Keynes and the Great Depression.
It became increasingly clear that the discipline of the market was not enough; that
every seller did not automatically find a buyer; that depression could be treated only by
artificial creation of buying power, with the
government's province to fill the gap created
by deficiency of buying in the private economy in depression, and to channel off excess
purchasing power in inflation. The result may
be cumulative rises in the national debt, but
so long as the underlying economy is strong
and growing, the rise of the debt is of little
concern. In twenty years the annual cost of
the debt has risen by $5 billion; but the
national income which supports it by $250
billion.
"My major energies have gone into teaching, writing, and advising. I am responsible
for the only course of economics in General
Education at Harvard, 'Economics for the
Citizen,' and I am a member of the Committee on General Education.
"In presenting a photograph of my books
in the Widener Library at Harvard, the Harvard Alumni Bulletin suggested that I had
written more than any economist in history.
I am responsible for about twenty-five volumes, exclusive of articles. The writings cov-

er education, social security, mobilization and
war, monetary policy, international economics, New England, medicine, economic history, capitalism, ideology, planning. My plans
call for additional studies, of sports, a biography of Keynes, economics of medicine,
money (with Professor Hansen), America's
economic history, and social security. I am
also editor of the *Review of Economics and
Statistics* and associate editor of the *Quarterly Journal of Economics*.
"In government work, I have advised several Latin American countries, served with
several agencies during World War II, inclusive of serving as director of the Export-
Import Price Control Office of the OPA;
and in the post-war, I have advised the National Security Resources Board, the President's Council of Economic Advisers, the
Secretary of Agriculture (as a member of
the Commodity Credit Corporation and the
Agricultural Mobilization Board, by Presidential appointment), the President's Commission on the Health Needs of the Nation.
I have also been a member of the Committee
on the New England Economy reporting to
the President, and Chairman of the New
England Governors' Committee on the Textile Industry."

PRINCIPAL WORKS: Twenty Years of Federal
Reserve Policy, 1933; The Economics of Social
Security, 1941; Post War Economic Problems,
The New Economics (ed.) 1947; The National
Debt and the New Economics, 1947; How Shall
We Pay for Education?, 1948; The European Re-
covery Program, 1948; Saving American Capital-
ism (ed.) 1948; The Market for College Graduates,
1949; The Economics of New England, 1952; John
Maynard Keynes, 1955.

HARRISON, GEORGE BAGSHAWE
(July 14, 1894-   ), English author and
scholar, writes: "Dr. Harrison was born at
Hove, Sussex, Eng-
land. He was edu-
cated at Brighton Col-
lege and Queens'
College, Cambridge,
where his studies were
interrupted by the
first World War in
which he served in
the infantry and on
the staff in India and
Mesopotamia from
1914 to 1919. After taking his degree at
Cambridge in 1919, he taught at Felsted
School (Essex) and St. Paul's Training
College at Cheltenham. In 1924 he joined
the faculty of King's College, University of
London, where he remained until the second

World War in which he served in the Royal Army Service Corps and the Intelligence Corps. In 1943 he became professor and head of the English department at Queen's University Kingston, Canada, until 1949 when he joined the faculty of the University of Michigan."

* * *

G. B. Harrison, one of the most eminent of contemporary Shakespearean critics, has published a number of sound, lucid and scholarly studies of Shakespeare's plays and the background in which he wrote them. Probably his major achievement in scholarship has been his recreation, in the form of contemporary journals, of the life of Elizabethan and Jacobean England. Every important event of English political, social and cultural history in this period is chronicled. Harrison's sixteenth-seventeenth century imaginary diarist who keeps this record was described by Rose Macaulay in the *New Statesman and Nation* as "learned, inquisitive and remarkably well-informed," of versatile interests and "urbane, anecdotal pen." Harrison married Dorothy Agnes Barker in 1919, and they had five children, of whom two survived. With his wife he entered the Catholic Church in 1947.

PRINCIPAL WORKS: The Bodley Head Quartos (ed.) 1922-1926; The Church Book of Bunyan Meeting, 1928; The Elizabethan Journals, 1928-1933; John Bunyan: A Study in Personality, 1928; Shakespeare at Work, 1933; A Companion to Shakespeare Studies (ed. with H. Granville-Barker) 1934; The Life and Death of Robert Devereux, Earl of Essex, 1937; Elizabethan Plays and Players, 1940; A Jacobean Journal, 1941; Shakespeare's Tragedies, 1951; Shakespeare: The Complete Works (ed.) 1952.

ABOUT: Anthony, J. A. (ed.) The Road to Damascus; Hoehn, M. (ed.) Catholic Authors, II.

HARRISON, HENRY SYDNOR (February 12, 1880-July 14, 1930). For biographical sketch and list of works and references, see TWENTIETH CENTURY AUTHORS, 1942.

HARRISON, Mrs. MARY ST. LEGER (KINGSLEY) ("Lucas Malet") (1852-October 27, 1931). For biographical sketch and list of works and references, see TWENTIETH CENTURY AUTHORS, 1942.

* * *

ABOUT: Dictionary of National Biography 1931-1940; Hoehn, M. (ed.) Catholic Authors, I.

HART, ALBERT BUSHNELL (July 1, 1854-June 16, 1943). For biographical sketch and list of earlier works and references, see TWENTIETH CENTURY AUTHORS, 1942.

* * *

Albert Bushnell Hart died a few weeks before his eighty-ninth birthday.

The historian's later years were given largely to "promoting the study of George Washington and Theodore Roosevelt." He served as historian of the U. S. Commission for the Celebration of the 200th Anniversary of the Birth of George Washington.

The *American Historical Review* characterized Professor Hart as "the most useful historical worker of his generation," and the *American Political Science Review* described him as "more closely articulated with the stream of American life than any other academic historian of our time."

A. Chester Hanford termed Hart "a sturdy, vigorous American who exerted a wide influence upon the development of the social studies, upon public affairs, and most of all upon those who had the privilege of studying and working with him."

ADDITIONAL WORK: (ed.) American Year Book, 1942.

ABOUT: American Historical Review October 1943; American Political Science Review October 1943; New York Times June 17, 1943.

HART, Mrs. FRANCES NEWBOLD (NOYES) (August 10, 1890-October 25, 1943). For biographical sketch and list of works and references, see TWENTIETH CENTURY AUTHORS, 1942.

* * *

Frances Noyes Hart died at New Canaan, Conn., at fifty-three. She left her husband and two daughters.

None of her later work ever achieved the popularity of *The Bellamy Trial*, which was praised as "an ingenious and spirited" mystery book containing "clever characterizations, strong suspense and real comic relief."

ABOUT: New York Times October 26, 1943.

HART, LIDDELL. See LIDDELL HART, B. H.

HART, MOSS (October 24, 1904-   ). For biographical sketch and list of earlier works and references, see TWENTIETH CENTURY AUTHORS, 1942.

* * *

Of Moss Hart's dazzling career in the American theatre, Margaret Case Harriman once wrote, it "has always ignored the ups and downs of the average man and has leapt instead along empyrean summits at a sort of courteous, perplexed gallop." There have been some "downs," to be sure, in recent years—specifically his plays *Christopher Blake* (1946) and *The Climate of Eden* (1952)—(Hart's adaptation of Edgar Mittelholzer's novel, *Shadows Move Among Them*). But even these were at least minor critical successes, and are measured as failures only by the tremendous scale of his successes. The most outstanding of the latter in recent years was *Winged Victory* (1943), a wartime propaganda play in which Hart performed the "remarkable achievement" of dramatizing the United States Army Air Corps. To gather material and inspiration for the play he toured air force bases here and abroad in an army bomber. When it was finished—a simple and dramatically effective story of the training and combat experiences of a group of fliers—Hart staged and directed the play in an elaborate production, with some 350 air force men taking part in it. Proceeds from the production went to Army Emergency Relief. Rosamond Gilder wrote of it in *Theatre Arts*: "He has woven into the texture of his play the very spirit of the Air Corps—its language, its songs, its ritual; he has made palpable that profound emotion . . . the comradeship of men in war." Less exalted in theme but also effective theatrically was *Light Up the Sky* (1948), a sparkling farce about theatre people.

Hart has also directed a number of successful Broadway comedies not of his own authorship—among them *Dear Ruth* (1944) and *Miss Liberty* (1949). He is the author of the scenario of the motion picture *A Star Is Born*, one of the most popular films of 1954. He married the actress Kitty Carlisle in 1946, and they have one son, Christopher. In 1954 Hart directed Jerome Chodorov's and Joseph Field's comedy *Anniversary Waltz*, in which his wife had a starring role. The Harts divide their time between a New York apartment and his farm in Bucks County, Pa.

ADDITIONAL WORKS: *Dates of publication*—Winged Victory, 1943; Christopher Blake, 1947; Light Up the Sky, 1949; The Climate of Eden, 1953.

ABOUT: Current Biography 1940; Harriman, M. C. Take Them Up Tenderly; National Cyclopedia of American Biography (1946); Nizer, L. Between You and Me; New York Times Magazine October 31, 1943; Saturday Evening Post November 18, 25, 1944; Theatre Arts February 1944, October 1949, May 1954.

HARTLEY, LESLIE POLES (December 30, 1895-   ), English novelist, short story writer, and literary critic, was born in Whittlesea, England, the son of H. B. Hartley, Justice of the Peace for Fletton Town, Peterborough. He was educated at Harrow and at Balliol College, Oxford, graduating in 1922. L. P. Hartley is a man whose private life, at least as far as

Pearl Freeman

the public knows, is almost entirely absorbed by his literary life. Unmarried, he lives in Somerset, travels occasionally in France and Italy, and lists his recreations as rowing, swimming, and going for walks. His career has followed a line of steady, if unspectacular achievement, arriving finally at a reputation among the brightest in contemporary British fiction. Since 1922 he has reviewed novels and short stories for such papers as the *Spectator*, the *Saturday Review*, the *Weekend Review*, *Weekly Sketch*, *Observer*, and *Time and Tide*, meanwhile publishing novels and short stories of his own at respectable intervals.

After some twenty years of writing, Mr. Hartley published a novel, his second, entitled *The Shrimp and the Anemone*, a mature and, in all respects, distinguished story about two children, which brought him considerable critical acclaim. The London *Times* called it "perceptive, witty, touching: a work of art of great delicacy and hidden strength." This was followed by two novels about the same children now grown into their twenties, *The Sixth Heaven* and *Eustace and Hilda*, the latter winning him the James Tait Black Memorial Prize in 1947. As a trilogy these three works were described by the *Times* as "unique in modern writing . . . diverting and disturbing." Beneath a surface "almost overcivilized" the reviewer found "a hollow of horror."

Less successful perhaps are the two later novels, *The Boat* and *My Fellow Devils*. *The Go-Between* (1953), however, seems to fulfill all the earlier promise. Both technically and in the depth of its social perception, this is an extraordinary work in the firm and exacting tradition of the English novel.

At his best, L. P. Hartley can be compared to Henry James more than to any other writer. For all the wit and delicacy of his method, he is concerned with such depths of experience as guilt and loneliness and evil. His devotion to the craft of fiction, his respect for form, as well as his fundamentally serious approach to moral problems, are Jamesian.

PRINCIPAL WORKS: Night Fears, 1924; Simonetta Perkins, 1925; The Killing Bottle, 1932; The Shrimp and the Anemone, 1944; The Sixth Heaven, 1946; Eustace and Hilda, 1947; The Boat, 1950; The Travelling Grave, 1951; My Fellow Devils, 1951; The Go-Between, 1953.

ABOUT: Harper's Bazaar October 1953.

*HARTOG, JAN DE (April 22, 1914-), Dutch-English author, was born in Haarlem, Holland, the son of a Dutch theologian. Hav-ing run away to sea at the age of ten, he sailed with a fishing smack on the Zuyder Sea. After finishing grammar school he became a cabin boy on a two-masted schooner, and from there went on to the Amsterdam Naval college; three months later, however, he was dismissed with the notation: "This school is not for pirates." Packed off to sea again, this time as a messboy, he eventually joined the ocean-going tugboats with which he remained until he was eighteen. Thereupon he became a sub-inspector with the Amsterdam Harbor Police.

At this time, and during night watches, he began to write his first stories, submitting them to one of the big Amsterdam newspapers under a pseudonym. The stories came to the attention of the directors of the Municipal Theatre, with the result that the theatre invited de Hartog to give technical advice on a sea play then in production. This, in turn, led to playwriting on his own. The End of the 'Liberty' was the product, and it received a prize before being closed down by the censor. He was successful with a first novel, Holland's Glory, in 1940. During World War II he was one of the earliest underground resistance fighters, eventually escaping to England. He was wounded while escaping and sentenced to death in absentia by the Germans.

While Hartog's native language is Dutch, he now writes better in English than many Englishmen do. His plays Skipper Next to God and The Fourposter were produced on Broadway, the latter given an Antoinette

* här'tŏk

Perry Award. Both were made into movies. "In printed form it makes good reading," said W. P. Eaton of The Fourposter, a play about marriage. "An extremely clever job which never obtrudes its cleverness."

Of his novels, The Lost Sea is based on his childhood seagoing experiences. The Distant Shore, a Literary Guild Selection, is a war novel in two parts, the first of which appeared in England under the title Stella (1951). "It is a gripping story, uneven in the telling, but exciting reading, another tale of man against the sea," said Virginia Kirkus.

Hartog and his wife, Angela Priestley de Hartog, the oldest daughter of J. B. Priestley, and their two children live on the "Rival," the last of the Dutch seagoing tjalks, which they converted into a houseboat. During the 1952 flood in Holland, he turned the boat into a hospital ship and sailed to the devastated area. The Little Ark, published in 1953, describes the adventures of a small orphan boy and his adopted sister during the disaster. "The children—boastful, callous and loving—are most convincing; and humor as well as goodness shine unobtrusively through the horrors," wrote the (London) Times Literary Supplement. "It is surprising that such a rounded and complete work of art, not mere reportage, should be produced so soon after the tragic event."

At last reports Hartog was living in his houseboat on the Seine.

PRINCIPAL WORKS: Plays—The Fourposter, 1948; Skipper Next to God, 1949. Fiction—The Lost Sea, 1951; Stella 1951; Captain Jan: A Story of Ocean Tugboats; 1952; The Distant Shore, 1952; The Little Ark, 1953.

ABOUT: France Illustration May 26, 1951; Harper's November 1952; New York Herald Tribune Book Review August 31, 1952; New York Times Book Review August 24, 1952.

HAŠEK, JAROSLAV (April 30, 1883-1923). For biographical sketch and list of works and references, see TWENTIETH CENTURY AUTHORS, 1942.

* * *

ABOUT: Columbia Dictionary of Modern European Literature.

HATCH, ERIC (October 31, 1901-). For biographical sketch and list of works and references, see TWENTIETH CENTURY AUTHORS, 1942.

* * *

Nothing that Eric Hatch has written in recent years has rivaled the success of My Man Godfrey, but his later novels have the same pleasant lightness of touch, the froth and fluff, that characterizes all his work. Hatch lives in Hollywood.

ADDITIONAL WORKS: Little Darling: A Comedy, 1943; Words and Music, 1943; Unexpected Warrior, 1947; The Beautiful Bequest, 1950.

ABOUT: Warfel, H. R. American Novelists of Today; American Magazine May 1949; Collier's January 10, 1948.

HATCHER, HARLAN HENTHORNE
(September 9, 1898-   ). For autobiographical sketch and list of works and references, see TWENTIETH CENTURY AUTHORS, 1942.

* * *

After more than thirty years at Ohio State University, during which he rose in academic rank from instructor to professor, dean of the College of Arts and Sciences (1944-48), and vice president of the university (1948-51), Harlan Hatcher was appointed president of the University of Michigan in 1951. He now lives in Ann Arbor with his second wife, Anne Gregory Vance (his first wife died), and their two children.

Hatcher's recent writings have focused on the Great Lakes region with studies of the lakes and the history of the area. They have been highly praised for their "harmonious mingling of learning, observation and reflection" (Walter Havighurst) and for a literary style which is "happily readable" (Stewart Holbrook).

ADDITIONAL WORKS: The Great Lakes, 1945; Lake Erie, 1945; Western Reserve: The Story of New Connecticut in Ohio, 1949; A Century of Iron and Men, 1950.

ABOUT: Newsweek May 28, 1951.

HAUPTMANN, GERHART JOHANN ROBERT
(November 15, 1862-June 8, 1946). For biographical sketch and list of works and references, see TWENTIETH CENTURY AUTHORS, 1942.

* * *

Gerhart Hauptman died at his home at Agnetendorf, Silesia, of pneumonia, at eighty-three. As the major German writer remaining in Germany during the Hitler period he had been celebrated, if not entirely favored, by the régime. After the close of World War II he was asked by the Cultural Association for the Democratic Reconstruction of Germany to "help restore Germany's culture." Walter A. Reichart has defended Hauptmann against charges of collaboration with the Nazis by referring to his "aversion to politics," and declaring that "early in life he discovered that art and politics are not com-

patible." On the other hand he has been called an "opportunist and perpetual conformist" by Hermann Kesten, who says "he became the echo of all the changing political régimes of his time." Fritz Gross, explaining Hauptmann's acceptance of Hitler as "partly on account of the force of circumstances and partly by reason of his own easy-going accord," characterizes him as one who "had written so much and thought so little, had felt so much sympathy and so little loving kindness, and who, for upwards of half a century, had been *the* representative German."

Hauptmann's one basic theme, in the opinion of Oskar Seidlin, was "the failure of the poor and naked human creature faced with an inexorable, superior power." He adds that "compassion is the message of Hauptmann's work, and for the sake of this message we love him." In the words of Frederick W. J. Heuser, "Hauptmann's work will perhaps go down in history as the most complete artistic expression of the so-called historicism and the relativistic skepticism of the last fifty years."

ABOUT: Clark, B. H. and Freedley, G. (eds.) History of Modern Drama; Garten, H. F. Gerhardt Hauptmann; Nicoll, A. World Drama; Slochower, H. No Voice Is Wholly Lost; Books Abroad 1946; Commonweal January 1, 1943; Contemporary Review August 1946; Emporium October 1946; London Times June 12, 1946; Nation December 8, 1945; New York Times June 12, 1946; Saturday Review of Literature November 28, 1942; South Atlantic Quarterly July 1947.

HAUSER, ARNOLD
(1892-   ), Hungarian born art historian, writes: "I was born in Hungary. I started studying history of art and literature in the universities of Budapest, Vienna, Berlin and Paris. Of my university teachers it was the art historian Max Dvořák in Vienna, the philosopher and sociologist Georg Simmel in Berlin, Henri Bergson and Gustave Lanson in Paris by whom I was most deeply influenced.

"After the first World War I spent two years in Italy doing research work on the history of classical and Italian art. In 1921 I moved to Berlin. By that time I had come to the conclusion that the problems of art and literature, in the solution of which our time is most eagerly engaged, are fundamentally sociological problems. I felt that I had to revise the philosophical idealism of my earlier years, and from that time on I devoted myself above all to the study of sociology and economics under the guidance of Max Weber, Werner Sombart and Ernst Troeltsch. In the following years I studied, besides the works of these scholars, the writings of the great American sociologists: Thorstein Veblen, Charles H. Cooley, William G. Sumner, John Dewey, and I found a new source of inspiration in their sound rationalism and realism.

"In 1924 I settled down in Vienna. From that time on my interest was mainly focused on the problems of the film. I felt that there was a test case for most of the vital problems of art in general—a case which offered an opportunity to study the birth and the first developments of a new art and to observe the motive forces behind the evolution of art forms, as it were, in a laboratory.

"In 1938 I left Vienna and came to London. I was working on a book on the dramaturgy and sociology of the film, which I had started in Vienna, and I wrote, as a by-product, a number of essays on sociological problems connected with the film for the English periodicals *Life and Letters Today* and *Sight and Sound*. One of the essays written in that period was published in America by *Partisan Review* in January 1948.

"Since my coming to England I have widely expanded, however, the basis of my studies which resulted, after ten years of research work and writing, in my *Social History of Art*, published in two volumes in 1951 simultaneously in New York and in London. The first edition was out of print after a few months. A German, an Italian and a Portuguese edition of the book are partly in the course of publication, partly in preparation.

"In 1948 I became a naturalised British subject. Since 1951 I have been lecturer in the history of art in the University of Leeds. In 1952 I was invited by Washington University in St. Louis to participate in a symposium which was to be given in celebration of the centennial year of this university and of the cinquecentennial anniversary of the birth of Leonardo da Vinci. I lectured on 'The Conceptions of Time in Modern Art and Science,' and I was invited to repeat this lecture in the Metropolitan Museum of Art and at New York University and in the School of the Museum of Fine Arts in Boston.

"At present I am working on a kind of philosophical introduction to the history of art, concerned exclusively with methodological problems such as the scope and limitations of the sociology of art, historical materialism and the history of art, psychoanalysis and the history of art, etc."

PRINCIPAL WORK IN ENGLISH TRANSLATION: The Social History of Art, 1951.

HAUSER, HEINRICH (1901-). For biographical sketch and list of earlier works and references, see TWENTIETH CENTURY AUTHORS, 1942.

* * *

Heinrich Hauser left Germany in 1939. For the next six years he lived with his family on a farm in upstate New York and here he wrote one of the most controversial books to come out of World War II, *The German Talks Back*. Published only a few months after the Allied defeat of Germany, the book was a daring, shocking, and impassioned defense of the Prussian spirit and tradition and a bitter attack upon America and the American concept of democracy. The publishers of the book announced that they had hesitated to publish it ("We read it with anger [and] revulsion, [but] we recognized that these emotions . . . did not answer the question whether the book should or should not be published"), but it was generally agreed, as *Time* magazine put it, that "the very freedom for which the U.S. has been fighting demands that such books be given a hearing." Many reviewers perceived the real value of the book in showing that Nazism was only one aspect of a long and formidable German tradition. The importance of the book, Virginia Kirkus wrote, is "in the revelation of the persistence of the very factors that made possible Hitler's Germany, that will make its re-education virtually impossible, that—if not recognized and guarded against—will make World War III inevitable."

Hauser returned to Germany soon after the publication of the book. In 1947 he translated from the German Max Picard's highly praised analysis of Hitlerism, *Hitler in Our Selves,* and in the following year he published his translation of Leonard von Muralt's *From Versailles to Potsdam.* Hauser's later writings —all of them in German—include a novel, several travel books, and studies on German political affairs.

ADDITIONAL WORK IN ENGLISH TRANSLATION: The German Talks Back, 1945.

ABOUT: Time September 24, 1945.

HAVIGHURST, WALTER (November 28, 1901-), American novelist and regionalist, writes: "I was born on Thanksgiving Day, 1901, in Appleton, Wis., where my father was professor of history at Lawrence College. Just below my birthplace ran the Fox River, which is a part of my earliest memory. I soon learned how the French explorers, fur traders and missionaries had passed those shores on their way to the fabled Mississippi. I learned also the mood of the Wisconsin

woods, the dread of forest fires and some of the lore of the dwindling pineries.

"My later boyhood was spent in central Illinois; I attended high school in the county seat towns of Bloomington and Decatur. Before going to college I worked as a deckhand on Great Lakes freighters. At that time a few white-sailed schooners still sailed over Lake Superior, calling at the lonely ports. They roused in me a lasting desire to know about early trade routes on the Lakes—which led, twenty years later, to the writing of *The Long Ships Passing*.

"I attended Ohio Wesleyan University for two years and took an A.B. degree from the University of Denver. Later I took an M.A. at Columbia University. My college and graduate study was interrupted by service in the Merchant Marine. In 1921-22 I shipped on various vessels, from a lumber schooner to an Oriental liner, in the Pacific. In the winter of 1926 I left a Leyland Line ship in Liverpool, went down to London and enrolled at King's College to study literature. I lived in Chelsea, within sound of tugboats on the Thames, and besides unsystematic reading I tramped over all quarters of London. During vacations I bicycled through Ireland, Scotland, and France.

"In 1928 I became a member of the department of English at Miami University, where I have remained. I was married to Marion Boyd, poet and story-writer, in 1930; we have collaborated on several junior historical novels. When we are away from home and speak of Miami there is sure to be some remark about the enviable climate. Our climate includes snow, sleet and slush, for this is the old original Miami University, in Oxford, Ohio. Though the climate is nothing special, it has a fine tradition, a beautiful setting, and an enviable spirit.

"My first published novel, *Pier 17*, was based on my memories of a waterfront strike on the Pacific coast. One of its readers (there weren't many) was the late Constance Lindsay Skinner, who had just begun planning the Rivers of America series. She persuaded me to write *Upper Mississippi*, and that assignment helped to focus my interest on the American Midwest, the region for which I have most feeling and kinship. Since then my writing has attempted to show the traditions

and development of the land between the Ohio River and the Great Lakes.

"In the past century this region has grown populous, productive, vastly prosperous. Sometimes its life seems thin; it has no lost causes and few deeply cherished traditions. Yet its memories of toil and opportunity have a certain richness, accessible to all, and sometimes its sense of future illuminates the country like sunrise. In the way of literary material it seems to me quite inexhaustible."

PRINCIPAL WORKS: Pier 17, 1935; Upper Mississippi, 1937; The Quiet Shore, 1937; The Winds of Spring, 1940; The Long Ships Passing, 1942; Land of Promise, 1946; Signature of Time, 1949; George Rogers Clark: Soldier in the West, 1952; Annie Oakley of the Wild West, 1954.

ABOUT: Collier's February 28, 1948; Scholastic January 17, 1944; Wilson Library Bulletin June 1943.

HAWES, CHARLES BOARDMAN
(January 24, 1889-July 15, 1923). For biographical sketch and list of works and references, see TWENTIETH CENTURY AUTHORS, 1942.

HAWKES, JACQUETTA (HOPKINS)
(1910-   ), English archeologist and writer, was born in Cambridge, England, the younger daughter of Sir Frederick Gowland Hopkins and Jessie Anne Stephens Hopkins. Her father, a first cousin of the poet Gerard Manley Hopkins, was "a pioneer biochemist and the principal discoverer of vitamins," his daughter has said.

Jacquetta Hawkes grew up in Cambridge, reading archeology and anthropology at Newnham College, Cambridge, and taking first class honors with her B.A. Between 1931 and 1940 she pursued research and excavation in Great Britain, Eire, France and Palestine. An assistant principal in the Post-War Reconstruction Secretariat from 1941 to 1943, Mrs. Hawkes became, through the Ministry of Education, principal and secretary of the United Kingdom National Commission for UNESCO. This assignment lasted from 1943 to 1948. "In theory I greatly approved of international organizations, but in practice I found UNESCO unbearably gaseous, so in 1948 I resigned from it and from the civil service and reverted to archeology and writing." She was archeological adviser for the Festival of Britain from 1949 to 1951. Since 1950 she has been a governor of the British Film Institute, and she assists in the editing of *UNESCO History of Mankind.*

After publishing papers in specialized journals and a monograph on the archeology of the isle of Jersey, of the Channel Islands, Jacquetta Hawkes wrote *Prehistoric Britain* with her first husband, Christopher Hawkes. A history of Britain from the time of earliest man to the closing years of Roman rule, based on recent excavations, the book first appeared in a Penguin edition in 1944, and again—rewritten and expanded—in 1947. Of her book *History in Earth and Stone,* the New York *Times* wrote, "Nothing escapes her, her resonance is subtle and complete. She leaves a powerful impression of the majesty and sadness of the human process. At the same time she manages to locate more than four hundred monuments, as revealed by acount of sites mentioned in the appended gazetteer. The maps and photographs are excellent." In *Fables* (U. S. title: *A Woman as Great as the World*) the author moved into the field of prose fiction; most of the personages of these eighteen fables are animals and gods, seldom even quasi-men. "The discerning reader will find much enjoyment in these delicately and poetically told tales, whose biting moral will be appreciated by sophisticates," wrote H. R. Forbes in the *Library Journal.*

She is a regular contributor to the London Sunday *Times* and the *Spectator,* to learned journals and national periodicals. She has published a book of poems, *Symbols and Speculations* and, in collaboration with J. B. Priestley, written a play, *Dragon's Mouth,* produced in England in 1952.

She married Christopher Hawkes in 1933. They had one son, and were divorced in 1953. In that year she married J. B. Priestley. She has two homes, one in London a short distance from Piccadilly, and one "built recklessly on a hilltop" in the Isle of Wight. "I have always disliked games," she writes, "indoor or outdoor, but am fond of taking long walks, which I enjoy the more because I am interested in natural history, and can claim once to have been really knowledgeable about birds."

PRINCIPAL WORKS: The Bailiwick of Jersey, Archaeology of the Channel Islands, II 1939; Early Britain, 1945; Prehistoric Britain (with C.F.C. Hawkes) 1944; Symbols and Speculations (poetry) 1949; Guide to the Prehistoric and Roman Monuments in England and Wales (in U.S.: History in Earth and Stone) 1951; A Land, 1951; (with

J. B. Priestley) Dragon's Mouth (play) 1952; Fables (in U.S.: A Woman as Great as the World, and Other Fables) 1953; Man on Earth, 1955.
ABOUT: New York Herald Tribune Book Review October 11, 1953.

HAWKINS, Sir ANTHONY HOPE ("Anthony Hope") (February 9, 1863-July 8, 1933). For biographical sketch and list of works and references, see TWENTIETH CENTURY AUTHORS, 1942.

* * *

ABOUT: Dictionary of National Biography 1931-1940.

HAWTHORNE, JULIAN (June 22, 1846-July 21, 1934). For biographical sketch and list of works and references, see TWENTIETH CENTURY AUTHORS, 1942.

"HAY, IAN." See BEITH, J. H.

*HAYAKAWA, SAMUEL ICHIYÉ (July 18, 1906-), American educator and semanticist, was born in Vancouver, B.C., the son of Ichiro and Tora (Isono) Hayakawa. He was educated in the public schools of Calgary, Alberta, and Winnipeg, Manitoba, took a B.A. at the University of Manitoba in 1927, an M.A. at McGill University in 1928, and a Ph.D. at the University of  Wisconsin in 1935.

Leroy Sylverst

Coming to the United States in 1929 as a Fellow in English at the University of Wisconsin, he studied and taught there until 1939, the last three years with the extension division. In 1939 he joined the Armour Institute of Chicago, which became Illinois Institute of Technology. Here he remained until 1947. Since 1950 he has been a lecturer at University College of the University of Chicago.

A columnist for the Chicago *Defender* between 1942 and 1947, Hayakawa has been the editor of *ETC, a Review of General Semantics* since 1943. His interest in semantics developed through study of Middle English and American linguistics; he contributed to the *Middle English Dictionary* (University of Michigan Press, 1952). While occupied with extension teaching he felt the necessity of speeding up the educative process if democracy is to have fuller development, and he began to study general semantics with Alfred

* hä yä kä'wä

421

Korzybski in 1938. His *Language in Action* (1939) was a Book-of-the-Month Club selection and a great popular success both in the original and in the revised version, retitled *Language in Thought and Action.* "It is precisely what a popularization should be. It is very smoothly and lucidly written; it is compact; it is lively; it is logical and informative, and it reveals unusual intellectual acuteness. It makes no claim to basic originality," wrote Henry Hazlitt in the New York *Times.* Alvin Adey in *Current History* said, *"Language in Action* is a masterpiece of exposition, so simply and incisively written as to be nothing less than brilliant, and it's moreover enlivened by a constantly flashing humor and pithy common sense."

Also the author of articles, reviews, and poems, many of which have appeared in the little literary magazines, Hayakawa makes his home in Chicago. He married in 1937 Margedant Peters, a poet, and they have three children, two boys and a girl. A member of the Cooperative League of the United States, Hayakawa is on the board of Consumers Union. In spite of his Japanese surname, he speaks Japanese only with difficulty, and cannot read or write it.

PRINCIPAL WORKS: Language in Action, 1939; Language in Thought and Action (revised; with B. H. Pillard) 1949; (ed.) Language, Meaning and Maturity, 1954.

ABOUT: Consumer Reports February 1953.

HAYCOX, ERNEST (October 1, 1899-October 13, 1950), American writer of western fiction, was born in Portland, Ore., the

son of William James Haycox and Bertha (Burghardt) Haycox. His boyhood was spent in logging camps, shingle mills, ranches, and small towns. He served with his National Guard regiment on the Mexican border in 1916, and later in France with the American Expeditionary Forces for fourteen months during World War I. In 1919 and 1920 he attended Reed College, moving on to the University of Oregon, from which he graduated in 1923. Haycox first started writing while at the university, living in an abandoned chicken house where he papered three walls with rejection slips before his stories began to sell. Having majored in journalism, he worked after graduation as police court reporter for the Portland

Oregonian, writing on the side. When he felt that the time had come to "go all-out on writing," he moved to New York, "nearly starved out" for a year, married Jill Chord, an Oregon girl doing art work, then moved back west where he lived until his death in Portland.

Haycox was the author of over twenty novels, and hundreds of short stories. Four films were made from his work: *Union Pacific, Stagecoach, Apache Trail,* and *Canyon Passage.* His novel *The Adventurers,* posthumously published, was a Literary Guild selection. "I know the West, having been born in it and having been raised from shingle mill to logging camp to ranch to coal mine," Haycox wrote. "I feel this West distinctly. To me, some little faded town sitting out on the Nebraska sand hills, or tucked away in a fold of the Cascades, nourishing the memory of a more robust career, is more valid than any great city." When his first book, *Free Grass,* appeared in 1929, it was pronounced a very good tale, an exceptionally good yarn. In 1939 when *The Border Trumpet* was published, G. W. Harris in the New York *Times* called it "among the most noteworthy half-dozen historical Westerns of the last decade," adding: "In this novel Ernest Haycox has found himself at last. Never before has he written so carefully or so well." However, by 1941, with the publication of *Trail Town,* the same reviewer found it "perhaps the best Ernest Haycox has yet written." His novel, *The Earthbreakers,* published in 1952, was over four hundred pages long. "The best Western novel of the year," in the opinion of Harrison Smith, the story covered one year in the lives of a group that came to Oregon to settle in the middle 1840's. "Before his death last year," wrote V. P. Hass in the Chicago Sunday *Tribune,* "Ernest Haycox completed this, his most ambitious novel. It is a solid achievement in storytelling. With his *Bugles in the Afternoon,* that excellent fictional presentation of the Custer story, it serves to point up once again that Mr. Haycox was among the most seriously underrated of contemporary novelists."

In recent years Haycox served as chairman of Selective Service Board No. 1 in Multnomah County, Ore., was a member of the Oregon State Library Board, a president of the University of Oregon Alumni Association, a member of the American Legion, and a Methodist, Rotarian, and Republican. Married in 1925, he had a son and a daughter. At the age of fifty-one he died at his home in Portland after a long illness. He had been ill with cancer for several months and underwent surgery in August; he had been convalescing at his home but suffered a relapse in October. Surviving were his widow and two children.

PRINCIPAL WORKS: Free Grass, 1929; Chaffee of Roaring Horse, 1930; All Trails Cross, 1931; Whispering Range, 1931; Starlight Rider, 1933; Rough Air, 1934; Smoky Pass, 1934; Riders West, 1934; Silver Desert, 1935; Trail Smoke, 1936; Deep West, 1937; Trouble Shooter, 1937; Man in the Saddle, 1938; Sundown Jim, 1938; Border Trumpet, 1939; Saddle and Ride, 1940; Rim of the Desert, 1941; Trail Town, 1941; Alder Gulch (in England: No Law and Order) 1942; Action by Night, 1943; Wild Bunch, 1943; Bugles in the Afternoon, 1944; Canyon Passage, 1945; Long Storm, 1947; Rough Justice, 1950; By Rope and Lead, 1951; The Earthbreakers, 1952; The Adventurers, 1954. *Short Stories*—Pioneer Loves, 1952; Murder on the Frontier, 1953; Outlaw, 1953; Prairie Guns, 1954.

ABOUT: New York Times October 14, 1950.

*HAYDN, HIRAM COLLINS (November 3, 1907-), American novelist, critic, and editor, writes: "I was born in Cleveland, Ohio, of a family of educators and Presbyterian ministers. After being graduated from Amherst College in 1928, my means of livelihood for sixteen years was teaching. At one time or another, I have taught English at every level from third grade through graduate school. I finally left regular academic

Glidden

work in 1944, going toward publishing by the transitional route of a combination job of executive secretary of Phi Beta Kappa and editor of the *American Scholar*. The latter position, a most congenial one, I still hold, but in 1945 I resigned the secretaryship to become an associate editor with Crown Publishers. I came to Bobbs-Merrill as New York editor in July 1950. [In 1955 Haydn resigned from Bobbs-Merrill and became senior editor at Random House.]

"I suppose that what is most interesting about my being a practicing editor is that it is rare to come upon one who is also a writer. Despite the frequent conviction that one cannot continue successfully with his own writing if he is dealing every day with that of others, I have found the combination a stimulating one. My first love was the novel and in my work at Bobbs-Merrill with novelists, especially young and new ones, the Novel Workshop that I conduct in the New School for Social Research, and my own work as a

* hä'dĕn

novelist, it has turned out—at least from my point of view—a highly successful love affair.

"On the other hand, both through my own work in such books as *The Counter-Renaissance* and that as editor of *The American Scholar*, I have had a steadily growing interest in other fields than fiction and have found the working with all sorts of non-fiction at Bobbs-Merrill and elsewhere a happy complement to my work with the novel.

"Of my own creative work, I should say only that it has been marked by a constant preoccupation with the central concern of the novelist as I see it: to realize the successful combination and integration of theme, story and characterization. I have particularly been concerned, in terms of my own work and that of others, with the consistent failure of most contemporary American novelists to attain full three-dimensional characterization, and to be able to maintain in a novel at one time a true richness of texture and a representative widely meaningful context. I think that there are many and complex reasons for this being true of our time and place—social, cultural and psychological reasons—but I am thoroughly convinced that until we begin more nearly to achieve this combination, the American novel is not going to regain the pre-eminent position it once held in American life. On the one hand, we have the many talented young novelists who are rich, even thick, in allusion, style and ideas, but quite alienated from the main body of the life of their own time; on the other, we have a large number of 'reportorial' novelists who grapple with important particular problems, institutions or aspects of our time and system but focus almost sociologically upon the problem as a local or provincial matter and are very thin indeed in what I mean by texture—which involves the novelist's primary concern with the creation of fully realized human individuals and with those human relationships and values that remain permanent no matter how much their particular forms and idioms change.

"This is what most excites me of all the general problems involved in the work which I do with other writers and in my own work."

PRINCIPAL WORKS: Explorations in Living (ed. with W. H. Rogers and R. V. Redinger) 1941; By Nature Free (novel) 1943; Manhattan Furlough (novel) 1945; The Portable Elizabethan Reader (ed.) 1946; The Time Is Noon (novel) 1948; The Counter-Renaissance, 1950; A Renaissance Treasury (ed. with J. C. Nelson) 1953.

ABOUT: Warfel, H. R. American Novelists of Today; New York Times Book Review April 11, 1948; Newsweek October 14, 1946; Publishers' Weekly December 1, 1945.

*HAYEK, FRIEDRICH AUGUST VON

(May 8, 1899-   ), Austro-English economist and philosopher, writes: "I was born in

Vienna as the eldest of the three sons of August von Hayek, physician and botanist. The atmosphere of the home early directed my interest to the natural sciences, but even during my school days my moved progressively towards the problems of man and human society. The experience of war service in the polyglot Austro-Hungarian army definitely confirmed my interest in the problems of society and on my return from the war I started on the study of law— then still the recognized approach to the study of economics.

"What time I could spare from the study of law was, however, divided about equally between economics and psychology, and the first scientific paper I wrote (1920, unpublished), the germ of a book published more than thirty years later, was on physiological psychology. But soon pure economic theory was to absorb all my energy, largely as the result of the influence of two of my teachers, Friedrich von Wieser and later Ludwig von Mises. The latter soon became my immediate superior in my first job in a (temporary) government office concerned with the execution of some of the financial provisions of the peace treaty of 1919. While holding this position (1921-1926) I successively obtained doctoral degrees in law and political science at the University of Vienna; and immediately after obtaining the latter went on leave to spend some fifteen months (1923-24) on graduate work in New York.

"Largely as a result of interests acquired there, my work during the next ten years was mainly in the field of the theory of money and business cycles. It led to my appointment first as director of a newly created institute for business cycles research in Vienna (1927), later held jointly with a lectureship at the University of Vienna, and in 1931 to a professorship in the University of London (London School of Economics). Much of my further theoretical work (on the theory of capital and the problems of economic calculation under socialism) was determined by the necessity of making more explicit, and of elaborating for an audience which did not take them for granted, presuppositions on

* hi'yĕk

which my earlier work had been based. But the most important effect of the transplantation into a new environment was that it made me recognize as general intellectual trends of Western civilization certain features, of which the disputes about socialism, which had occupied so much of the mental energy of my early years in Vienna, now appeared merely as a special instance.

"A strong interest in the history of ideas, which first had expressed itself in studies in the history of economics, combined with an acute awareness of the difference in character between the natural and the social sciences, led me more and more towards the general problems of the role of reason in the conduct of human affairs, which in a way had been my starting point. It was entirely unexpected when an incidental by-product of this long-range plan, the book called *The Road to Serfdom*, became a best seller, both in the English-speaking world and nearly a dozen other countries into whose languages it was translated. But though I gladly took the opportunity which offered itself as a result, to renew after twenty-one years on a lecture tour my acquaintance with the United States, I refused to be drawn by the unintended success from the task I had set myself and for which I felt best suited; to trace the sources of the intellectual and moral confusion which threatens to destroy our civilization and whose most respectable and dangerous manifestation I still see in socialism. As this seemed to me to be due more and more to certain mistaken conclusions derived from our present scientific approach to all problems, it drew me more and more into philosophical and psychological problems. The offer of a position where I could devote myself entirely to what seemed to me most important led me in 1950 to accept the position of professor of social and moral science in the Committee on Social Thought in the University of Chicago.

"Lest this account of a development sound all too appallingly purely intellectual, I will merely add that the one other activity in which I feel thoroughly at home is mountaineering, for which, however, alas, neither London nor Chicago offers all the opportunities I could wish. But I still spend my summers as far as possible in the Tyrol."

PRINCIPAL WORKS: Prices and Production, 1931; Monetary Theory and the Trade Cycle (ed.) 1933; Collectivist Economic Planning, 1935; Monetary Nationalism and International Stability, 1937; Profits, Interest, and Investment, 1939; The Pure Theory of Capital, 1941; The Road to Serfdom, 1944; Individualism and Economic Order, 1948; John Stuart Mill and Harriet Taylor, 1951; The

Counter-Revolution of Science, 1952; The Sensory Order, 1952; Capitalism and the Historians (ed.) 1954.

ABOUT: Cole, G. D. H. Studies in World Economics; Lerner, M. Actions and Passions; American Political Science Review June 1945; Current Biography 1945; Economic Journal June 1941; Harper's July 1945; Nation April 28, 1945; Saturday Review of Literature May 12, 1945; Spectator July 7, 1944.

HAYES, ALFRED (1911-), American novelist, playwright, and poet, was born in London, England, but grew up and attended school in New York City. He has worked as a newspaperman, magazine writer, and "radio hack," all in New York. *The Big Time*, his first book of poems, deals in a realistic manner with the drab inner hells of the big city—its movie houses, dance halls, and bars.

Rose Wolfe

In 1943 Hayes went into the Army, serving in Italy. While in Rome he became acquainted with Roberto Rossellini, and worked with him on the script of the successful postwar movie, *Paisan*. Out of his war experiences he drew material for a play and novel that deal with the relations of American soldiers and Roman civilians during the trying days of the occupation. The play was *The Girl on the Via Flaminia*. The novel *All Thy Conquests* (1946) was based on an actual case of the rise and fall of a Fascist hoodlum. The book contrasts the mutual attitudes of the Americans—homesick, childishly irresponsible, but historically alert to the possible rebirth of Fascism—and the cynical-hopeful, despairing Italians. It was praised especially for its expert construction, evocation of mood, and the sensitive rendering of the Italian characters.

With *Shadow of Heaven* (1947), Hayes chose for his subject a labor organizer, Harry Oberon, who has begun to doubt the validity of his calling, of life in general, and of love. This inner drama is presented in a prose that carries the shadings and nuances of a Jamesian manner. The book was praised, as was Hayes' earlier novel, for its vivid dialogue and characterization. However, J. D. Ross, writing in the New York *Times Book Review*, claimed that in "depicting Harry Oberon, sick of himself and of people, a burned-out crusader, dead in a sense before the story opens, Mr. Hayes creates an atmos-phere of fatigue which weighs the reader down."

Meanwhile Hayes gave up hope of seeing *The Girl on the Via Flaminia* produced as a play. In 1949 he rewrote it as a short novel. In the novel, as in the play, the relations between conqueror and conquered are symbolized by the portrayal of an affair between an American soldier and a respectable girl who consents to live with him, out of need, during the desperate winter of 1944. A number of reviewers commented on the impression of tautness and control, similar to that of a play. This impression was justified when the Circle in the Square in New York City put on a successful dramatic version of *The Girl on the Via Flaminia* in February 1954; the play was adapted by the author himself. When this off-Broadway theatre was closed, the play moved up to Broadway for a successful run. Almost simultaneously with the opening of *The Girl on the Via Flaminia*, a screen version appeared, entitled *Act of Love*. In this United Artists film, the situation revolves about an American soldier and a French girl, and the scene has been transferred to Paris.

In his later non-dramatic works, Hayes has returned to exploring an inner world of increasing complexity and subjectiveness. This pattern was laid down in his second book of poems, *Welcome to the Castle* (1950), which sadly welcomes the reader to "this grim and comic castle of my middle age." His more recent novel *In Love* (1953) again makes use of the Jamesian idiom in a triangular love story, told from the point of view of a middle-aged artist. In the New York *Times*, Malcolm Cowley had this to say of Hayes: "What sets him apart from most of our younger novelists is his feeling for words and his sense of how to make them count."

Hayes went to Hollywood for Warner Brothers in 1945, and now lives permanently in California. He is married, and has a daughter. In addition to his other works, he has written two earlier Broadway plays: *Journeyman* (1938) and *'Tis of Thee*, a musical (1940).

PRINCIPAL WORKS: *Fiction*—All Thy Conquests, 1946; Shadow of Heaven, 1947; The Girl on the Via Flaminia, 1949; In Love, 1953. *Poems*—The Big Time, 1944; Welcome to the Castle, 1950. *Plays*—Journeyman (adapted from a novel by Erskine Caldwell) 1938; 'Tis of Thee, 1940; The Girl on the Via Flaminia, 1954.

ABOUT: Aldridge, John W. After the Lost Generation; Warfel, Harry R. American Novelists of Today; New York Herald Tribune Book Review October 26, 1947, March 20, 1949, April 16, 1950; New York Times Book Review October 26, 1947, March 20, 1949; Saturday Review of Literature April 2, 1949.

HAYES, CARLTON JOSEPH HUNT-LEY (May 16, 1882-), American historian, was born in Afton, N.Y., the son of

Blackstone

Dr. Philetus A. Hayes, physician and surgeon, and Permelia M. Huntley Hayes. He went to Columbia University to study law, but in his junior year his interest in history led him into that field. The year of his graduation, 1904, he was received into the Catholic Church; his parents had been Baptists. Graduate work in medieval and modern history won him his M.A. in 1905 and his Ph.D., under James Harvey Robinson, in 1909. He began teaching at Columbia in 1907 and remained there, with a few absences, until he became emeritus in 1950. From 1934 on, he was Seth Low Professor of History.

Hayes served in World War I, and during World War II was Ambassador to Spain (1942-45). He is credited with having helped keep Spain out of the war, and with having induced the Spanish government "not only to withhold the aid it had previously been giving to Nazi Germany but also to grant to the allies such facilities as releasing all aviators and refugees."

He has written a great number of books, more than twenty titles; some were written for colleges and others for high schools. Two of his most widely known and most scholarly books are *Political and Social History of Modern Europe* (1916) and *Political and Cultural History of Modern Europe* (1932 and 1939). Since World War I a subject for special study with him was nationalism, clearly distinguishing modern nationalism, or undue exaltation of the state, from patriotism. He treats of this in *Essays on Nationalism* (1926), *France, A Nation of Patriots* (1930), and *The Historical Evolution of Nationalism* (1931).

In 1930 *Modern History* (1923), a textbook written with Dr. Parker T. Moon, was removed from the approved list of textbooks for New York City schools where it had been used for seven years, "after protests had been made that it was un-American and pro-Catholic." Both Hayes and Moon denied the charges.

A Generation of Materialism 1870-1900 was published in 1941. As Lewis Gannett said, "Mr Hayes writes as a son of the established Church and a believer in traditional religion. (He writes also with easy learning and with a grace granted to few historians)." His literary style has been called "flowing," "fresh and stimulating," characterized by "fluency and elasticity."

An extremely popular teacher during his years at Columbia, Professor Hayes is recalled by one student: "It always surprised some of us that, in the midst of the lectures—first-rate theatrical performances, words shot out for emphasis, silences . . . gestures and movement deployed like those of a good actor—when we looked down at our notes they were as ordered and clear as if we had listened to a scholastic metronome. . . . Some of the barbs delivered in a dry voice by this baldish, sharp-featured man in his thirties were directed at us, at our very smugness, at our laziness, or at our fathers'."

Hayes has received many honors and citations from colleges and universities. In 1946 he was given the Laetare Medal by Notre Dame University for outstanding services by a Catholic layman. From 1925 to 1945 he was Catholic co-chairman of the National Conference of Christians and Jews.

His marriage to Mary Evelyn Carroll took place in 1920. They have two children and live at Jericho Farms, Afton, N.Y. He enjoys music, especially Mozart and Beethoven.

PRINCIPAL WORKS: Political and Social History of Modern Europe, 1916; A Brief History of the Great War, 1920; Essays on Nationalism, 1926; France, A Nation of Patriots, 1930; The Historical Evolution of Modern Nationalism, 1931; Political and Cultural History of Modern Europe, vol. 1, 1932, vol. 2, 1939; A Generation of Materialism, 1941; Wartime Mission in Spain, 1945; the United States and Spain, 1951; Christianity and Western Civilization, 1954.

ABOUT: Hintz, H. W. & Grebanier, B. D. N. Modern American Vistas 1940; Hoehn, M. Catholic Authors, I; Current Biography 1942; National Cyclopedia of American Biography (1946); New York Times April 4, 1942; Newsweek June 22, 1942; PM April 8, 1942; Time September 14, 1942, January 30, 1950.

HAYS, HOFFMAN REYNOLDS (March 25, 1904-), American novelist, critic, and playwright, writes: "I come of old New York stock. My great, great grandfather was the last high constable of the city and the first modern detective. His son, Aaron Burr Hays, was cashier of the North River Bank for forty years. His son, William J. Hays, was an artist of the frontier, notable for his painting of bison and deer. His son, William J. Hays, Jr., was also an animal painter, specializing in horses. Since my mother was a singer, my grandmother a novelist, two uncles painters, and a third a sculptor, I suppose I should have reacted away from the

arts, but somehow this didn't happen. After obtaining a B.A. in Cornell in 1925, an M.A. (in medieval literature) in Columbia, I spent  a year and a half teaching English in City College and the University of Minnesota. I almost completed work for a Ph.D. in comparative literature, studying Flemish for a year in the University of Liége, Belgium, but finally decided to chuck the academic life. I then spent some bohemian years writing for little magazines, mostly poetry and literary criticism.

Shelburne

"By the early Thirties I found I cared most about the theatre and began to try my hand at plays. My first, the *Ballad of Davy Crockett*, I wrote while working on the Federal Theatre. It was tried out by the Federal Theatre and by the Columbia University players. I still believe *Crockett* had some good writing in it though it was not a well-constructed play. A year or two later I encountered Kurt Weill and rewrote the play with lyrics to which Weill contributed a score. In those days he was not well known; consequently the play never reached Broadway. In 1940, in collaboration with Oscar Saul, I wrote a Living Newspaper, *Medicine Show*, dealing with the national medical situation, which was produced by Wharton and Gabel in 1940 with some critical success but had the bad luck to open on the day Hitler invaded Norway. The public proved to be more interested in Hitler than in medical reform. I went on writing unproduced plays which were sometimes optioned until in 1943, in disgust, I turned one of them into a novel, *Stranger on the Highway*. It was bought by the second publisher who read it, published that year, and sold to Twentieth-Century Fox, on whose shelves it has reposed ever since. *Lie Down in Darkness* was published in 1944.

"In 1939 I spent a summer in Mexico at which time I became interested in Spanish American literature. I taught myself Spanish and began translating Spanish American poetry. The result of this interest was *12 Spanish American Poets*, an anthology, translated and edited by me, and published in 1943. In 1946 I returned to Mexico to get background material for my historical novel *The Takers of the City*, dealing with the great Spanish liberal, Bishop las Casas. This was published in 1946. The following year the same firm published my translation of a Mex-

ican novel, *El Luto Humano*, by José Revueltas, as *The Stone Knife*. It got an indifferent and obtuse critical reception like most Latin American novels. *Selected Poems of Bertolt Brecht*, which I translated and edited, was published in 1948. In recent years, since the decline of publishing, I have found that television allows me to see produced themes for which there is apparently no room on Broadway. I have written a score of hour dramas chiefly for N.B.C.'s Television Playhouse. My work has also appeared on the Pulitzer Prize Theatre and Studio One. I think I was the first to bring Henry James to television with my adaptation of *The Marriages*. My biography of Vincent Van Gogh has been published in *The Best Television Plays of 1950-51*.

"As I look back my writing career seems rather chaotic but actually a certain preoccupation with social themes has run through all my novels and plays. My poetry owes a debt to William Carlos Williams and Bertolt Brecht. I still go on writing plays dealing with American history which, I believe, offers material for serious fiction and I hope to find time to write a novel which will trace the development of American spiritual and intellectual life in the great period of revolt and affirmation from 1840 to 1850. I have also not given up the struggle to promote cultural interchange between the two halves of the hemisphere."

PRINCIPAL WORKS: *Novels*—Stranger on the Highway, 1943; Lie Down in Darkness, 1944; The Takers of the City, 1946; The Envoys, 1953. *Translations*—12 Spanish American Poets, 1943; Brecht, B. Selected Poems; Revueltas, J. The Stone Knife.

"H.D." See DOOLITTLE, H.

HEADLAM, WALTER GEORGE (February 15, 1866-June 20, 1908). For biographical sketch and list of works and references, see TWENTIETH CENTURY AUTHORS, 1942.

HEARD, GERALD (October 6, 1889-). For autobiographical sketch and list of earlier works and references, see TWENTIETH CENTURY AUTHORS, 1942.

* * *

Although Gerald Heard writes under two names (using H. F. Heard for his mysteries and weird stories), he is really three writers —a writer on scientific subjects, a writer of scientific thrillers, and a writer on religion and mysticism. "Objective, subjective, and both simultaneously," writes Anne Fremantle,

"Gerald Heard plays his three parts to their capacity."

As H. F. Heard he received the Ellery Queen Award in 1946 for the best mystery story of the year, "President of U.S.A., Detective." As Gerald Heard he lectured in 1951 and 1952 at Washington University in St. Louis on the question "Can Human Nature Be Changed?" He writes that he has issued "the only continuous account of the phenomena known vulgarly as 'flying saucers' under the title *Is Another World Watching?*" In recent years he has published several studies in theology, a history of morals since 1920, and a collection of symbolic fairy tales describing evolution, *Gabriel and the Creatures.*

Heard lives in Santa Monica, Calif. Here he has continued his association with Aldous Huxley and Christopher Isherwood in the study of Vedanta. At Tzabuco, near Laguna Beach, he led a group participating in monastic community life. The group spent hours in silence and meditation, shared the work on a communal basis, and lived according to strict ascetic principles. Heard figures in Huxley's novel *After Many a Summer Dies the Swan* as the mystic, William Propter. It has also been suggested that he was the model for Bruno Rontini in Huxley's *Time Must Have a Stop.*

ADDITIONAL WORKS: Man the Master, 1941; Preface to Prayer, 1944; Recollection, 1944; The Gospel According to Gamaliel, 1945; The Eternal Gospel, 1946; The Doppelgangers: An Episode of the Fourth, the Psychological Revolution, 1997, 1947; Is God Evident? 1948; The Black Fox (novel) 1950; Is God in History? 1950; Morals Since 1920, 1950; Is Another World Watching? 1951; Gabriel and the Creatures, 1952; *As H. F. Heard*—Murder by Reflection, 1942; The Great Fog, 1944; The Lost Cavern, 1948; The Notched Hairpin, 1949.

ABOUT: Forster, E. M. Two Cheers for Democracy; Savage, D. S. Mysticism and Aldous Huxley; Commonweal January 25, 1946; Wilson Library Bulletin April 1943.

HEARD, H. F. See HEARD, G.

HEATH-STUBBS, JOHN FRANCIS ALEXANDER (July 9, 1918-   ), English poet and critic, writes: "I was born in London and am of mixed English and Welsh blood on my father's side, part Scottish on my mother's. My father, Francis Heath Stubbs, came of an old Staffordshire family, and according to family tradition, we are descended from the John Stubbs who, having written a pamphlet opposing Queen Elizabeth I's proposed French marriage, was sentenced to have his right hand cut off: he showed his

loyalty by waving his hat with the other, crying, 'God Save the Queen!' Another ancestor is said to have assisted in the escape of Charles II after the battle of Worcester and to have refused a knighthood at the Restoration. My mother, under the name of Edie Marr, was a pianist of distinction. I received a good musical education and was taught to play the cello. From my father

I learned an early interest in philosophy, science, and literature.

"When I was about six, we moved to New Milton, Hampshire, a small residential town between the New Forest and the sea. My early surroundings gave me a keen interest in natural history, especially ornithology, which I still retain. I was educated at schools in Sussex and the Isle of Wight, but at the age of sixteen was put under private tutors. My eyesight had been poor from birth, and after an operation at the age of eighteen, I was sent for a year to Worcester College for the Blind. In 1939 I entered the Queen's College, Oxford, where I stayed for four years, taking a First Class in English Language and Literature in 1942 and remaining for an additional year of research. At Oxford I became friendly with the poet Sidney Keyes, and my first printed poems (apart from schoolboy productions) appeared in *Eight Oxford Poets,* edited by him. After leaving Oxford I taught for a short time in a private preparatory school in London and later did literary hack-work as an editorial assistant on the compilation of a popular encyclopedia. Since 1947 I have devoted my time entirely to writing and lecturing. In 1952 I was appointed Gregory Fellow in Poetry (Poet-in-Residence) at the University of Leeds.

"In literature, as in politics, I am a traditionalist, who believes that traditional values can only be maintained at the price of continual change and flexibility. In religion, I subscribe to the Catholic faith, as taught by the Church of England."

PRINCIPAL WORKS: Wounded Thammuz, 1942; Beauty and the Beast, 1943; The Divided Ways, 1946; Poetry from Giacomo (tr.) 1946; The Charity of the Stars, 1949; The Swarming of the Bees, 1950; The Forsaken Garden (ed. with D. Wright) 1950; Hafiz of Shiraz: Thirty Poems (tr. with P. Avery) 1952. *Criticism*—The Darkling Plain, 1950.

ABOUT: British Weekly January 1953; Poetry June 1949; Poetry Quarterly Spring 1948.

HECHT, BEN (February 28, 1893-). For biographical sketch and list of earlier works and references, see TWENTIETH CENTURY AUTHORS, 1942.

* * *

The quiet, reflective life of the traditional man-of-letters has never been for Ben Hecht. The years have not apparently mellowed him nor his "volcanic" style. He remains a stormy figure, quick to plunge into quarrels and controversy, but endowed in all his ventures with an uncanny flair for success.

Hecht divides his time between his Nyack, N.Y., home (where his collaborator Charles MacArthur is a neighbor) and his home in Oceanside, Calif. For a number of years he has been writing, directing, and producing motion pictures. Recent ones include two done in collaboration with Alfred Hitchcock, *Notorious* and *Spellbound;* an ambitious if somewhat eccentric ballet study, *Specter of the Rose;* and a dramatization of two of his stories in a single film, *Actors and Sin.* His recent ventures into the Broadway theatre have been less successful. *Lily of the Valley* (1942) and *Swan Song* (written with MacArthur, 1946) were not well received. His stirring pageant about the struggle of the Jews for Palestine, *A Flag Is Born* (1946), was highly praised as a propaganda piece but not, in its own right, as a play. In 1953 Hecht ventured into television to write a drama series, *Tales of the City.* No survey of Hecht's contribution to the entertainment world is complete without mention of his precocious daughter Jenny, who made her acting debut, at the age of eight, in her father's *Actors and Sin* and followed this with a triumphant Broadway appearance in a major role in Viña Delmar's play *Midsummer* (1953).

Hecht's varied theatrical activities have almost—but not entirely—overshadowed his literary work. In 1944, however, he published a book that stirred up almost as much lively discussion as his earlier writings had done. This was *A Guide for the Bedevilled,* described as "a handbook of Hechtian philosophy," in which Hecht attempted to analyze anti-Semites and anti-Semitism. His approach was described (by a reviewer in the *Atlantic*) as "vitriolic and violent," and it was suggested that Hecht's belligerent tone may have done as much harm as good to his cause. But of its sincerity there was no doubt. Hal Borland, in the New York *Times,* called it "timely, fiery, full of tart truth." Hecht's passionate concern for an independent Jewish state led him into work with the American League for a Free Palestine, of which he became co-chair-

man, and the Hebrew Committee of National Liberation, an anti-Zionist group which urged prompt and violent action for their cause.

In 1945 Hecht published an edition of his collected short stories, a revealing volume which showed Hecht at his best, at his worst, and with the varying degrees in between. Ben Ray Redman wrote of the book in the *Saturday Review of Literature:* "Mr. Hecht's style is a medley of styles, all serviceable in their various ways, some more admirable than others. He loves to write with a flourish, he loves to write with a swagger, but he can also write with sobriety and restraint when he chooses." Of his autobiography *Child of the Century,* published in 1954, Saul Bellow wrote: "His manners are not always nice, but then nice manners do not always make interesting autobiographies, and this autobiography has the merit of being intensely interesting. If he is occasionally slick, he is also independent, forthright and original. Among the pussy-cats who write of social issues today he roars like an old-fashioned lion."

ADDITIONAL WORKS: Miracle in the Rain, 1943; A Guide for the Bedevilled, 1944; I Hate Actors! 1944; Collected Stories, 1945; The Cat that Jumped Out of the Window, 1947; Child of the Century, 1954.

ABOUT: Hecht, B. Child of the Century; Nizer, L. Between You and Me; Current Biography 1942; Good Housekeeping November 1945; Saturday Review of Literature June 23, 1945; Newsweek June 16, 1947, July 6, 1953; Time June 16, 1947; July 20, 1953.

*HEDIN, SVEN ANDERS (February 19, 1865-November 26, 1952). For biographical sketch and list of works and references, see TWENTIETH CENTURY AUTHORS, 1942.

* * *

Sven Hedin died at his home in Stockholm, at eighty-seven, as the result of a virus disease from which he had suffered for more than a year. His remarkable physical vitality remained almost unimpaired throughout his last years. At eighty-two he recovered, through an operation, sight in one eye which had been blinded in the early 1890's.

From 1937 to 1949 Hedin was chiefly occupied with work on the thirty-five volumes which detailed results of his expedition to Northern China sponsored by the Swedish government in 1927-35. His sympathy with the Nazi cause was often expressed during and after World War II. The London *Times,* acknowledging him to be "one of the world's most distinguished and most adventurous explorers of Central Asia," added that his books

* hĕ dēn′

are "massive, learned, fascinating, though they underrate the merits of brevity and are at times needlessly assertive in temper."

ABOUT: Hedin, S. & Bergman, F. History of the Expedition in Asia, 1927-1935; Ambolt, N. P. Karavan; London Times November 27, 1952; New York Times November 27, 1952.

HEGGEN, THOMAS (ORLO) (December 23, 1919-May 19, 1949), American writer and author of the best-selling novel  *Mister Roberts,* was born at Fort Dodge, Iowa, and grew up in Iowa, Oklahoma, and Minnesota. The son of Thomas O. and Mina (Paulson) Heggen, he came from a solid line of Norwegians, was educated in the public schools and at the University of Minnesota (B.A., 1941).

In college, Heggen was a columnist for the campus newspaper, the *Minnesota Daily,* and wrote for *Ski-U-Mah,* the campus humor magazine. He was one of the "bright, young University of Minnesota boys" whom, said *Life,* "the Eastern publishers quickly spotted."

He came East in 1941 and got a job on the *Reader's Digest.* Then in December, immediately after Pearl Harbor and America's entry into World War II, he enlisted in the U.S. Navy. He served for four years from December 1941 to October 1945, the first year in the Atlantic, the next three in the Pacific, and was on a variety of ships—a tanker, a cargo ship, an assault transport, and a battleship. Aboard an assault transport, he took part in the Guam, Peleliu, Iwo Jima, and Okinawa campaigns. At the end of the war he held the rank of lieutenant.

Released from active duty, Heggen returned to the staff of the *Reader's Digest,* and it was during the following year that he wrote his famous novel *Mister Roberts* (1946), which *Book Week* characterized as "an honest, behind-the-scenes portrayal of the Navy as it usually is—in dungarees rather than dress blues." Some of the original material for this book was first published in the *Atlantic Monthly.* When the book appeared in May 1946, it was an immediate and overwhelming success; and by the time of Heggen's death three years later, the original edition had sold more than 100,000 copies, while a Pocket Book edition with an initial printing of 750,000 was still selling at the rate of 30,000 copies a month.

Mister Roberts is a series of anecdotes and tales about life on board a Navy cargo ship operating in the back areas of the Pacific where front-line zones seem incredibly far away. The enemy, for most of the men, is tedium, boredom, and the petty persecutions of the Captain; the hero of the ship is Lieutenant Roberts, of whom Heggen once said, "he is too good to be true, he is a pure invention." For thousands of readers, however, Mister Roberts is too human to be merely or purely good, and he is certainly very real.

In February 1948 a dramatic version of the novel (co-author Joshua Logan) opened at the Alvin Theatre in New York City. Produced by Leland Hayward, and starring Henry Fonda as Mister Roberts, the play was a smash Broadway hit. *Theatre Arts* (March 1950) printed the entire play, and in a preliminary note, said: "The jokes may be Logan and Heggen, but the attitude is pure Heggen. It is an attitude that belongs to his generation: a tendency to laugh at what is inescapable, to accept no authority without reservation and to avoid illusion."

Heggen was described by the New York *Times* as "a shy, nervous, slightly built young man, full of ironic little humors." Several people who met him casually at parties have said that they were struck by his "terrific intensity." He married Carol Lynn Gilmer of Okmulgee, Okla., to whom his book was dedicated, but the marriage did not last and at the time of his death in May 1949 they had already been divorced.

Heggen's sudden death at twenty-nine by drowning in his bathtub came as a great shock to his many friends and admirers. Alan Campbell, a screen writer who shared a duplex apartment with him in New York but was then in Hollywood, said that he had spoken to Heggen on the telephone only the day before and that he had been in wonderful spirits and working well. He died at the height of his success and with a new play well under way.

PRINCIPAL WORK: Mister Roberts, 1946.

ABOUT: Life October 7, 1946, March 8, 1948; New York Times May 20, 1949; Saturday Review of Literature June 11, 1949; Theatre Arts March 1950; Vogue August 15, 1948.

*HEIDEGGER, MARTIN (September 26, 1889-   ), German philosopher, was born in Messkirch, Baden. He was a Catholic and became acquainted with Thomistic thought in his early youth. Heidegger was educated at the *gymnasium* in Freiburg and at the University of Freiburg, where he became *Privatdozent* in 1915. His first lecture at the uni-

* hi'dĕg'er

versity was on the concept of time in historical studies. From 1923 to 1928 he was professor of philosophy at the University of Marburg, and in 1928 he returned to Freiburg as professor of philosophy, succeeding the great founder of phenomenology, Edmund Husserl. In 1933, after the Nazis had come to power, Heidegger was elected rector of the university, but he soon became disillusioned with Nazism and resigned the post in 1934. He married Elfride Petri in 1917; they have two sons and one daughter.

Retired from teaching since 1945, Heidegger lives near Freiburg. He has never left this region in which he was born. Hitler invited him to Berlin in 1935, but he refused to come. He spends much of his time high up in the Black Forest mountains in a small skiing hut. Stefan Schimanski, who visited him there in 1947, described him as short and slight in appearance, his thick black hair streaked with white. "His living conditions," Schimanski wrote, "were primitive; his books were few, and his only relationship to the world was a stack of writing paper. His whole life revolved within those white sheets and it seemed to me that he wanted nothing else but to be left in peace to cover those white sheets with his writing."

Heidegger's first book, his dissertation on the medieval philosopher Duns Scotus, was published in German in 1916. Six other books in German followed. In 1949 the first volume of an English translation of his work was published. This book, *Existence and Being*, contains four essays by Heidegger and a long introduction and review by Werner Brock of Heidegger's main work, "Being and Time," which has not yet been published in its entirety. Although only a relatively small amount of his work is available in English, he is nevertheless recognized by philosophers in both Europe and America as one of the most important and original of contemporary thinkers. Heidegger himself insists that he has had nothing to do with the rise of the Existentialist movement, but Werner Brock points out that his "Being and Time," along with the writings of another German philosopher, Karl Jaspers (see sketch below), "both being stimulated by Kierkegaard . . . gave rise to the movement in our age."

Like Kierkegaard, Heidegger believes that the conditions of human experience are care, the void, dread, and death. His entire work has been devoted to the ageless philosophical question: What is meant by *being?* In the pursuit of this question Heidegger first immersed himself in the history of philosophy, finding in the works of the ancient Greeks the fullest and the purest philosophizing about this question. The Greek view of being, however, was limited, Heidegger found, to "the individual existent thing in its visibility and perceptibility." What Heidegger sought was to go beyond the individual visible thing, and this he did by attempting to analyze the problem of the structure of human existence. As Brock points out, his analysis is directed toward that aspect of human existence which was relatively neglected by the Greeks and by the later philosophers—"its temporal and historical character," of special importance to him "because it forms the horizon of all human questioning about Being, that is, of all philosophical thought." Hence his major work is called "Being and Time," and his study ranges from the relation of man to the perceptible world, to man's grasping of the existential significance of death.

In his later work Heidegger has been increasingly concerned with the function of artists, and especially poets, in the rediscovery of Being. Both the poet and the philosopher are explorers of the great question of Being and seekers of truth. His writings have been of special interest to students of German literature who find in his analysis of human existence the "existential" roots of modern German literature—"with regard to both the pessimistic pictures of human life and the attempts to give a deeper and fuller meaning to human existence" (Hans Jaeger in *PMLA*, September 1952). The resemblances to the writings of Jean-Paul Sartre, which have reflected a similar trend in modern French literature, have been frequently pointed out and sometimes overstated. Heidegger himself has refused to be classified with the current Existentialist movement. As James Collins explains the differences between the thought of the two: "The basic contrast arises from Sartre's anthropocentric view of human consciousness and freedom. For Sartre, man is all in all, with respect to both meaning and practical projects. For Heidegger, being is what counts most and provides a measure for human comprehension and freedom."

The extent of Heidegger's contribution to modern German philosophy is only now being measured. But as early as the 1930's he was recognized, along with Karl Jaspers, as one of the two living German philosophers who have, more than any others, tried to understand the essence of philosophy and its future tasks. Both Jaspers and Heidegger, Brock wrote in 1935, "succeeded further than other academic philosophers in finding a way back to that inner attitude and to those tasks which, through the rise of the autonomous sciences, had been lost to German philosophy since the era of Hegel; and . . . at the same time, they endeavoured to maintain the critical strictness and the reflection on fundamental principles, which Kant had left as a model to the epistemologists of the later nineteenth century."

PRINCIPAL WORK IN ENGLISH TRANSLATION: Existence and Being, 1949.

ABOUT: Brock, W. *Introduction to* Existence and Being, Contemporary German Philosophers; Collins, J. The Existentialists: A Critical Study; Grene, M. Dreadful Freedom: A Critique of Existentialism; Journal of Philosophy June 5, 1952; Publications of the Modern Language Association September 1952.

HEIDENSTAM, VERNER VON (July 6, 1859-May 20, 1940). For biographical sketch and list of works and references, see TWENTIETH CENTURY AUTHORS, 1942.

* * *

ABOUT: Columbia Dictionary of Modern European Literature; Allen, W. G. Renaissance in the North.

HEINLEIN, ROBERT (July 7, 1907-), American science fiction writer, writes: "I was born in Butler, Mo., one of seven children, son of Rex Ivar Heinlein and Bam Lyle Heinlein; I attended public schools in Kansas City, Mo., and graduated from Central High School there in 1924. I graduated from the U.S. Naval Academy at Annapolis in 1929, served in aircraft carriers and destroyers, and was retired for physical disability in 1934. I went back to school on retirement, to the graduate school of U.C.L.A. in order to study mathematics and physics, but again became ill and left school without completing my studies. For the next four years I dabbled in real estate, politics, mining, architecture, while regaining my health.

"I wrote my first story in 1939 and continued writing until Pearl Harbor. I spent the war as a mechanical engineer at the Naval Aircraft Factory at Philadelphia; when the war was over I resumed writing.

"I am married (Virginia Gerstenfeld) and we are now living in Colorado Springs.

"Much of my writing has been for magazines, radio, television, and motion pictures; so far, I have had thirteen trade books published. My books are usually published in French, German, and Italian as well as in English and occasionally in other languages. I occasionally write non-fiction, verse, and technical papers, as well as fiction, but fiction is my principal occupation."

* * *

Science fiction enthusiasts regard Robert Heinlein's lucid and vigorous novels of outer space as among the best being written in that field. His work combines literate style and an expert sense of construction with what one critic calls "most delightful and provocative imaginative writing (and thinking)." In 1954 the New York *Herald Tribune* wrote of his *The Star Beast*: "Regularly every year Robert Heinlein produces the best juvenile science fiction novel—and in so doing creates a work more satisfying than ninety per cent of 'adult' science fiction."

PRINCIPAL WORKS: Rocket Ship Galileo, 1947; Beyond this Horizon, 1948; Space Cadet, 1948; Red Planet, 1949; Sixth Column, 1949; Farmer in the Sky, 1950; The Man Who Sold the Moon, 1950; Waldo; and, Magic, Inc., 1950; The Green Hills of Earth, 1951; Between Planets, 1951; The Puppet Masters, 1951; Tomorrow, the Stars (ed.), 1952; The Rolling Stones, 1952; Revolt in 2100, 1953; Assignment in Eternity, 1953; Starman Jones 1953; The Star Beast, 1954.

ABOUT: Reinsberg, M. *in* Heinlein, R. The Green Hills of Earth.

HELLMAN, LILLIAN (June 20, 1905-). For autobiographical sketch and list of earlier works and references, see TWENTIETH CENTURY AUTHORS, 1942.

* * *

In 1951, when Lillian Hellman's play *The Autumn Garden* had its Broadway première, John Mason Brown observed that it was "in many ways the most mature and probing [play] to have come from her gifted pen." Although in the years immediately preceding she had written no play that, in critical or popular reception, had matched *The Children's Hour, The Little Foxes,* or *Watch on the Rhine,* every play she wrote during that period was distinguished by what Brown called "the same muscularity of mind, the same command of authentic dialogue, the same willingness to face unpleasant people as they are, and the same instinctive awareness of the theatre's needs which have always animated her writing."

During the war years Miss Hellman spent considerable time in Hollywood, adapting *Watch on the Rhine* for the screen and writing the screenplay for *The North Star*, a wartime propaganda film depicting the heroism of the Russian people in the face of the German invasion. Her only stage play in this period was *The Searching Wind* (1944), a thoughtful drama about the appeasers and the politicians who played their fateful roles behind the scenes in World War II. After the war she wrote a sequel to her memorable *The Little Foxes*. This was *Another Part of the Forest* (1946), which dealt with the earlier financial and psychological conflicts of the grasping Hubbard family, before the action of *The Little Foxes* began.

In 1949 Miss Hellman directed her own adaptation of Emmanuel Robles' play about rebellion in nineteenth-century Venezuela, *Monserrat*—"an exquisitely grim melodrama," one critic described it—in which Emlyn Williams starred. Two years later, in *The Autumn Garden*, she returned to the contemporary scene with a poignant, reflective comedy-drama about a group of people at a summer resort near New Orleans. The later development of Miss Hellman's career demonstrates clearly the fact that, successes or failures, her works are of sure theatrical effectiveness. A revival of *The Children's Hour* in 1953 showed the play a trifle dated but still exciting drama. And, in 1949, her hardy and enduring *The Little Foxes* was transformed into an American opera, *Regina*, by Marc Blitzstein.

Lillian Hellman visited the Soviet Union twice, in 1945 as an honored guest, and was active in many organizations described as "left-wing" and "Communist-front." In 1952 she was called to testify before the House Un-American Activities Committee and, while denying that she was a Communist at that time, refused to say whether she had ever been a member of the Communist Party. Subsequently Miss Hellman sent a letter to the Committee chairman in which she stated that for ethical reasons she would not testify about the political activities of her friends and associates. The Committee took no further action.

ADDITIONAL WORKS: *Date of publication*—The North Star, 1943; The Searching Wind, 1944; Another Part of the Forest, 1947; Robles, E. Monserrat (adaptation) 1950; The Autumn Garden, 1951.

ABOUT: Harriman, M. C. Take Them Up Tenderly; National Cyclopedia of American Biography (1946); Collier's March 31, 1945; Independent Woman January 1946; Saturday Review of Literature March 31, 1951; Theatre Arts January 1944; Time June 2, 1952.

HEMINGWAY, ERNEST (July 21, 1899-). For biographical sketch and list of earlier works and references, see TWENTIETH CENTURY AUTHORS, 1942.

* * *

Ernest Hemingway saw active service in World War II. In 1942-44 he volunteered himself and his launch, the *Pilar*, for anti-submarine patrol duty in the waters around Cuba. In the spring of 1944 he went to Europe as a war correspondent for *Collier's*, flew a number of missions with the American air force and the R.A.F., and was with the American army when it broke through into France and Germany. Through all this Hemingway took an active part, so active that he was the subject of a formal investigation by the Army to see if he was not violating the Geneva Convention on war correspondents. The investigation cleared him, but the award of a Bronze Star some time later suggested that Hemingway was not a passive spectator.

The role that Hemingway shaped for himself during the war is one that he has cheerfully played ever since. This was "Mr. Papa" —a jovial, generous, rough-talking but kind-hearted "regular guy." (See Lillian Ross' famous profile of him in the *New Yorker*, May 13, 1950.) As Malcolm Cowley described him in *Life* in 1949, ". . . he keeps trying to protect and lay plans for others. Younger men and women come to him for advice about their literary problems and their love affairs, while he talks to them as if he were ninety years wise instead of only forty-nine." He still wanders all over the world with the restless energy of an Odysseus. In the winter of 1954, on a hunting trip in Africa with his fourth wife, Mary Welsh (they were married in 1946 after his divorce from Martha Gellhorn), his plane crashed in the jungle and for several hours he was believed dead (some news sources issued prompt but fortunately premature obituaries). But Hemingway survived the crash, though considerably battered by it, and continued his trip. Home for Hemingway is a fifteen-acre estate in Cuba. Here he entertains, lavishly but informally, a huge and widely assorted circle of friends—sportsmen, royalty, jockeys, matadors, politicians, movie actors and actresses. He is muscular, "built like a boxer," with grey hair and a bristling beard. Cowley said of him: "When he puts on his steel-rimmed army-issue spectacles, Mr. Papa looks like a scholar poring over a Greek manuscript. When he grins, he looks like a schoolboy masquerading in an iron-gray wig."

No living American author has so captured the imagination of the American people as Hemingway has. Millions who have never read his novels know him as a personality, as they know baseball players and movie actors. In the movies and in radio and television adaptations his novels have reached an enormous audience. But it is Hemingway himself (rather than what he has written)—the burly and bearded war correspondent, fisherman, hunter, African explorer—who has brought to life the myth of the American hero. Edmund Wilson once remarked that this Hemingway "is certainly the worst-invented character to be found in the author's work." This character is adolescent, self-dramatizing, belligerent, flamboyant, and completely lacking in substance. He is the hero of one of Hemingway's later novels, *Across the River and into the Trees*, his first novel in more than ten years and, in the critical consensus, an outright disappointment, "an occasion for little but exasperated depression," Morton Dauwen Zabel commented. The hero of the book is an aging American army officer, dying of heart disease and trying desperately to crowd his last days with excitement. The scene is Venice in the chaotic days of post-World War II. "It is hard to say," Alfred Kazin wrote of the novel, "what one feels most in reading this book—pity, embarrassment that so fine and honest a writer can make such a travesty of himself, or amazement that a man can render so marvelously the beauty of the natural world and yet be so vulgar. . . . The Colonel is like all the Hemingway prize-fighters, hunters, drinkers, and soldiers in one. Yet this book is different, for it is held together by blind anger rather than the lyric emotion that gives Hemingway's best work its unforgettable poignance." Maxwell Geismar even more regretfully announced that "it is a synthesis of everything that is bad in his previous work and it throws a doubtful light on the future."

Two years later, however, with a dramatic resurgence of vitality, Hemingway published *The Old Man and the Sea*, a short, simple and compelling story of an old fisherman's struggle to bring into port a giant marlin which he has caught out in the Gulf of Mexico. Some critics interpreted the novel as an allegory of man's struggle against defeat—by nature, by old age, by his own instincts; but most readers were happy to accept it on its face value as a story of the sea and the men who eke out their living on it. The widest possible interest in the novel was assured by its publication (before its release in book form) in an issue of *Life* magazine. In 1953 the book received the Pulitzer prize in fiction—a fitting and, in the opinion of many readers, long-overdue recognition of Hemingway's contribution to American literature. The climax to the success of the book, and to Hemingway's career, was the Nobel prize for literature, which was awarded to Hemingway on October 28, 1954 with a citation reading: "For his powerful, style-forming mastery of the art of modern narration, as most recently evinced in *The Old Man and the Sea*." Because he was still recuperating from the injuries he had received in Africa some months before, Hemingway was unable to go to Stockholm to receive the award in person.

Correction: Hemingway was born in 1899, not 1898, as given in TWENTIETH CENTURY AUTHORS, 1942.

ADDITIONAL WORKS: (ed.) Men at War: The Best War Stories of All Time, 1942; Across the River and into the Trees, 1950; The Old Man and the Sea, 1952.

ABOUT: Aldridge, J. W. After the Lost Generation; Atkins, J. A. The Art of Ernest Hemingway; Baker, C. Hemingway: The Writer as Artist; Cowley, M. *Preface to* The Portable Ernest Hemingway; Fenton, C. The Apprenticeship of Ernest Hemingway; McCaffery, J. K. M. (ed.) Ernest Hemingway: The Man and his Work; Young, P. Ernest Hemingway; Life January 10, 1949, September 1, 1952, November 8, 1954; New Republic October 23, 1944; New York Times October 29, 1954; New York Times Book Review July 31, 1949; New Yorker January 4, 1947, May 13, 1950; Time December 13, 1954.

*HÉMON, LOUIS (October 12, 1880-July 8, 1913). For biographical sketch and list of works and references, see TWENTIETH CENTURY AUTHORS, 1942.

* * *

ABOUT: Columbia Dictionary of Modern European Literature; Scholastic May 14, 1945.

* ā môN′

HENDERSON, ARCHIBALD (June 17, 1877-). For autobiographical sketch and list of earlier works and references, see TWENTIETH CENTURY AUTHORS, 1942.

* * *

Now retired from the University of North Carolina, where he was a member of the faculty for more than half a century, Archibald Henderson lives in Chapel Hill. In 1945 he revived the defunct Historical Society of North Carolina, and four years later published a history of the founding and expansion of the University of North Carolina, a volume which together with his 5-volume history of the state and his *Conquest of the Old Southwest* constitute "a closely integrated original historical project." Among his many interests, Henderson writes, has been his "lifelong campaign to stimulate Southern authorship and to appraise critically the literature of that region."

A group of Henderson's colleagues and friends—among them the author Betty Smith, Frank Graham, former president of the University of North Carolina, and the late Charles A. Beard—contributed to a volume of essays on him, entitled *Archibald Henderson: The New Crichton*, in 1949.

ADDITIONAL WORKS: Pioneering a People's Theatre (ed.) 1945; The Campus of the First State University, 1949.

ABOUT: Hood, S. S. (ed.) Archibald Henderson: The New Crichton; Newsweek June 9, 1947; Time June 6, 1949.

HENDERSON, WILLIAM JAMES (December 4, 1855-June 5, 1937). For biographical sketch and list of works and references, see TWENTIETH CENTURY AUTHORS, 1942.

HENDRICK, BURTON JESSE (December 8, 1870-March 24, 1949). For biographical sketch and list of earlier works and references, see TWENTIETH CENTURY AUTHORS, 1942.

* * *

Burton Jesse Hendrick died of heart failure at the Roosevelt Hospital in New York City at seventy-eight after a short illness. He had lived at the Yale Club of New York in his final years.

His last book, *Lincoln's War Cabinet* (1946), met with general critical acclaim; G. F. Milton said that its author "writes with the perspective of the reflective historian weighing the knowns, hunching the unknowns, and shrewdly characterizing the actors' personalities and motives in the struggle for control. His scholarship is unobtrusive, his style deceptively leisurely."

The New York *Times* observed that the historian's "freshness and penetrating analysis bore the mark of his early journalistic training. This, coupled with his own scholarliness, made his writings outstanding. Each of his books was the result of several years' research."

ADDITIONAL WORK: Lincoln's War Cabinet, 1946.

ABOUT: New York Times March 24, 1949.

*HENRIQUES, ROBERT DAVID QUIXANO (December 11, 1905-   ), British novelist, writes: "Though born in London on a foggy day at the end of 1905, I do not admit to being a Londoner. I go there as rarely as possible, and much prefer to stay on my farm in the Cotswolds, rearing beef and pigs, market-gardening, and writing articles and books. As often as possible I go to France, Spain, or Italy.

"My family came over from Spain at the time when the Jewish Sefardic families fled to England in the seventeenth century. My great, great grandfather was the first Jew ever to hold the King's Commission in the British Army, and in each generation some of us have been 'career soldiers' ever since. I was educated at Rugby School and at New College, Oxford (Honours Degree in Modern History), and in 1926 entered the Regular Army and served in Egypt and the Sudan. It was a wonderful period of my life, and it served as the background for my first novel, *No Arms, No Armour*, which won the All Nations Prize Novel competition and was a Literary Guild choice in 1939.

"After seven years in the Royal Artillery, they took away our horses and gave us mechanical transport. At that time horses were the most important factor in my life; and so I resigned my Regular Commission, bought this farm in the Cotswolds, became an officer in the Territorial Army and tried unsuccessfully to write. An equally unsuccessful venture was a printing and publishing business, which I folded up in 1936 when I returned to the Sudan for a trip on the borders of Darfur and French Equatorial Africa. This was my second aggression against the big game of Africa, and it served as the basis of a book called *Death by Moonlight*.

"Although a Territorial Army officer, I was recalled to the Regular Army in July 1939. After attending a course at the Staff College, I became a brigade major, Royal Artillery, to a division which was mobilised on the outbreak of war. A year later, after the fall of France, my wife took our children to America and I went into the Commandos, which were just forming. I served as a troop commander for a year before I was appointed brigade major (chief staff officer) of the

* "The name should be pronounced in the Spanish way— *hen ri'quez* and not in the French manner."

First Special Services Brigade, which then comprised all eight Commandos stationed in Britain. In this capacity I was employed planning the various commando raids, in some of which I took part. The most exciting venture was the Vaasgo raid on the 26th December 1941. During this period I was writing *The Voice of the Trumpet*. This book was first published in America with the help of Stephen Vincent Benét who took the manuscript while I was in Washington in the autumn of 1941, edited it and wrote a preface, and saw it through the press during my absence in Africa with the American Army.

"In the meanwhile, I was officially posted to the staff of Combined Operations Headquarters, which Admiral Lord Louis Mountbatten was then commanding. Again I was employed on planning many commando raids such as that at St. Nazaire in the spring of 1942. I was then lent to General Patton, with whom I spent much of the next eighteen months as a planning staff officer. As such, I was privileged to land with the American assault forces of the renowned Third Infantry Division both at Casablanca and in Sicily. During the latter campaign, I was used as a travelling liaison officer between Generals Patton and Montgomery. In addition to the fun and friendship which I had with the American Army in Africa and Sicily, they gave me the Silver Star and Bronze Star. During this period I wrote the greater part of my third novel, *Home Fires Burning*.

"Towards the end of the war I worked on the plans for the Normandy assaults and was appointed colonel-in-charge of the planning section at Combined Operations Headquarters. I was sent to Normandy as chairman of an inter-service commission to revise the organising of beach groups (or shore regiments, in American parlance) in preparation for assaults against Japan. When that job was finished, I flew to America to serve as a representative British novelist, still in Army uniform as a colonel, on four of the 'Books and Author War Bond Rallies.' On these I had the great fun of meeting many American authors, and of going with them on various whirlwind tours, during which people came to hear us talk and bought their admission to the theatre or hall in American War Bonds. On my return from America, I was sent on various jobs to Holland and Germany, and was demobilised in the autumn of 1945.

"After demobilisation I started farming seriously and intensively, and also formed and commanded a territorial light anti-aircraft regiment. In 1950, when I resigned my command, I was appointed a full colonel on the active list of the Territorial Army, which is my present army status. During this period I wrote first an official planning monograph for the War Office, then a book on the Cotswolds in which I live, and also a long novel called *Too Little Love*. In England this book, under the title *Through the Valley*, won the James Tait Black Memorial Prize given by Edinburgh University for the best novel of 1950. Considerable confusion is sometimes caused by giving novels different titles in different countries. The *Voice of the Trumpet* was called *Captain Smith and Company* in England, and *Home Fires Burning* was called *The Journey Home* at home. So far as I am concerned, this practice must now cease! My 1953 novel, *A Stranger Here*, has the same title in both countries.

"In addition to writing novels and farming, I write a great many articles on agriculture and other subjects, and plays for television. I also do a lot of broadcasting on quiz programmes and the like. It is perhaps true to say that writers nowadays spend too much energy on the subsidiary activities of talking, either through a microphone or to live audiences, which leaves them too little time for their hobbies. Mine are shooting, fishing, and oil painting. My wife's hobbies are fox-hunting and sculpture. We have four children. Our elder son has taken over a derelict farm of 350 acres in West Wales; our elder daughter is a reporter on a newspaper; our younger son and daughter are still at school."

PRINCIPAL WORKS: Death by Moonlight (non-fiction) 1938; No Arms, No Armour, 1939; Captain Smith and Company (in U.S.: Voice of the Trumpet) 1943; The Journey Home (in U.S.: Home Fires Burning) 1944; Through the Valley (in U.S.: Too Little Love) 1950; The Cotswolds (non-fiction) 1950; A Stranger Here, 1953.

ABOUT: Publishers' Weekly November 11, 1939, May 12, 1945; Time March 8, 1943; Wilson Library Bulletin December 1945.

HENRY, O. (pseudonym of William Sydney Porter) (September 11, 1862-June 5, 1910). For biographical sketch and list of works and references, see TWENTIETH CENTURY AUTHORS, 1942.

* * *

ABOUT: Kramer, D. The Heart of O. Henry; Long, E. H. O. Henry, The Man and His Work; Morris, L. R. Postscript to Yesterday; Nolan, J. C. O. Henry; Reader's Digest August 1947; Saturday Review of Literature July 31, 1948.

HERBERT, Sir ALAN PATRICK (September 24, 1890-). For biographical sketch and list of earlier works and references, see TWENTIETH CENTURY AUTHORS, 1942.

* * *

In his autobiography, *Independent Member*, A. P. Herbert describes his service in World War II as "a queer, modest, but exciting, and, I hope, useful part in the war, divided . . . between the House of Commons and the tidal Thames." In Commons he continued to represent Oxford University as an independent member, and he remained in that office until 1949 when university seats were abolished by the Labor government. On the Thames he commanded his own cruiser, the *Water Gipsy*, as petty officer of the Royal Navy in the River Emergency Service. Mobilized one day before war broke out, Herbert served with distinction, doing mine-spotting duty, fire work, and on one occasion engaging in actual combat with a German plane. After the war, in 1945, he was knighted.

Since then, in addition to Parliamentary duties, Herbert has written busily—books, musical plays, articles for *Punch*, letters to the London *Times*. He has also studied navigation and devised a system of new names for the stars (described in his book *A Better Sky*).

ADDITIONAL WORKS: Well, Anyhow. . . ; or, Little Talks, 1942; Bring Back the Bells (poems) 1943; A.T.I.: There Is No Need for Alarm (poems) 1944; A Better Sky, 1944; Less Nonsense (poems) 1944; House by the River, 1945; Light the Lights (poems) 1945; Big Ben (light opera) 1946; Topsy Turvy, 1947; Mr. Gay's London, 1948; Topsy Omnibus, 1949; Bless the Bride (play) 1950; Independent Member, 1950; Number Nine: or, The Mind-Sweepers, 1951; Coad's Last Case, and Other Misleading Cases, 1952; Why Waterloo? 1953.

ABOUT: Herbert, A. P. Independent Member; Life April 17, 1944; New York Herald Tribune Book Review January 25, 1953; Time June 25, 1951.

HERBERT, FREDERICK HUGH (1897-), playwright, novelist, and scenario writer, who writes as F. Hugh Herbert, was born in Vienna, Austria, the son of Lionel Frederick Herbert and Paula (Knepler) Herbert. His father was a stock broker. Raised in London, he attended Gresham School (Norfolk), and the University of London, receiving from the latter a B.S. degree. During World War I he was a lieutenant in the Royal Garrison Artillery. He started his writing career in this country in 1920, at Paramount's Long Island Studios; and alone or in collaboration has been writing movies

ever since. His first play for Broadway was "Quiet, Please"; but—as he tells it—an earlier play was written: "When I was about nineteen and living in London during World War I, I wrote my first play. Fortunately I had sense enough not to try to sell it. It was dreadful. It had every possible melodramatic situation you could think of." Years later, he found this "yellowed script that had my name on it." All he salvaged from it was the title—"The Moon Is Blue," a play which by 1953 had earned him a million dollars.

Kiss and Tell was a smash hit, and featured Corliss Archer, a sub-deb known to readers of his short stories as well. *Meet Corliss Archer*, a collection of these stories, came out in 1944, after first appearing in *Good Housekeeping*. "All the stories have freshness and appeal," wrote the New York *Times*, adding that sometimes "manipulation and plotting rob the stories of their naturally convincing qualities. But the writing is always bright and easy, the characterization deft and shatteringly of this world." *The Moon Is Blue* was published in 1951 with an introduction by Ben Hecht. "Mr. Herbert's newest play, *The Moon Is Blue,* is the perfect example of successful mental comedy," wrote Hecht. "It is a play whose sole quality is wit. Its plot, characters and problems are almost as naïve as those in a musical show. Its humor, however, is as sharp and literate as the best of Shaw, Coward, and Behrman." This play ran into interesting censorship problems when it became a movie. Herbert, as president of the Screen Writers Guild, has expressed to the Production Code Administration the interest of the Guild in helping them rewrite the code.

As the author of both plays and scenarios, Herbert claims "writing a play is easy . . . it's the easiest literary medium there is, for me anyway." In a movie "you may have 150 sets to worry about," and "the bulk of a novel alone is enough to make you sweat." *The Moon Is Blue* was written in twelve days, and *Kiss and Tell* in nine. But there may be weeks and possibly months of thinking it out beforehand. "I write about the things I know best—the emotional and romantic crises that might come to my own daughters," he told Ward Morehouse. "I've dictated every word of every play I've written. I pace the room and slam things. . . . It's always been my policy to dictate my plays to young and attractive secretaries. The best I've ever had was Mary. I married her. . . . The time will come when I will do a serious play. The one I want to write will be about the American occupation in Germany and I already have the title, 'We Come as Conquerors.'" Morehouse described Herbert, in 1953, as "gay and hospitable, friendly and folksy." Wambly Bald in the New York *Post* said he is "so suave he can chuckle inaudibly," and described "a plump, baldish little man in herringbone tweed; he had a manner of remote good fellowship and superlative confidence." He reads every play that's written, sees every play on Broadway when he comes to New York. "I'm stagestruck," he says. He hates golf and outdoor sports, classifies himself as an "indoor" man, with a liking for bridge, poker, good food and good friends, and light amusing conversation.

He married his second wife, Mary Alice Herbert, in 1927; they live in Bel Air, Calif., and have two daughters. He has been often confused with the late Hugh Herbert, the actor.

PRINCIPAL WORKS: There You Are! 1925; Vengeance, a drama of the Congo, based on the motion picture story, 1930; A Lover Would Be Nice, 1935; The Revolt of Henry, 1939; Kiss and Tell, 1943; Meet Corliss Archer (short stories) 1944; For Keeps, 1944; For Love or Money, 1948; The Moon Is Blue, 1951; I'd Rather Be Kissed (novel) 1954.

ABOUT: Hecht, B. *Preface,* The Moon Is Blue; Cue April 14, 1951; New York Herald Tribune November 9, 1947, March 4, 1951; New York Post April 15, 1951; New York Times April 4, 1943, July 2, 1944; New York World Telegram-Sun April 27, 1953, November 5, 1953; New Yorker November 15, 1947; Saturday Review of Literature November 14, 1953; Screen Writer November 1946; Time November 17, 1947.

HERBST, JOSEPHINE (March 5, 1897-). For autobiographical sketch and list of earlier works and references, see TWENTIETH CENTURY AUTHORS, 1942.

* * *

Josephine Herbst writes: *"New Green World* (1954) really began a long time back, perhaps at the age of sixteen when I read Boswell and Fanny Burney and became fascinated by the eighteenth century. The fact of my own residence in Pennsylvania, where my family had lived early in the eighteenth century, added interest to Bartram, the botanist, whose experiments were made in that same soil. But my interest in the contemporary world spurred me to the actual writing and gathering together of many felt and thought attitudes; I was not interested in nostalgic recapitulation but in writing something to challenge some of our notions of today and to bring to light our most basic concepts. I like to deal with the complicated and in that sense the writing of this book ties in with my interest in fiction.

"I am finishing a new novel, 'The Watcher with the Horn'; it is about the 1920's in complicity with the 1940's as revealed in the experience of a woman. I have another work in progress, a series of stories, connected by theme and the device of the same character in the role of confidant repeated in each. These stories will be about writers in our time and their predicament. The first story, 'Hunter of Doves,' was published in *Botteghe Oscure,* Spring 1954. The stories will be published in one volume and form a different kind of novel; time and circumstance are factors as well as personalities."

* * *

Josephine Herbst's biography of the American naturalist John Bartram, *New Green World,* was her first published book in seven years. Her earlier *Somewhere the Tempest Fell,* set in Chicago during the last months of World War II, was described by Richard Sullivan in the New York *Times* as "a sound and deliberate, scrupulous and valid novel." *New Green World,* however, was "resolutely non-fiction," Alan Devoe commented in the *Saturday Review,* a straight factual biography. But, he adds, "It is written . . . with an accomplished novelist's imaginative insight, sympathetic intimacy and suave felicity in the telling."

ADDITIONAL WORKS: Somewhere the Tempest Fell, 1947; New Green World, 1954.

ABOUT: Warfel, H. R. American Novelists of Today; New York Herald Tribune Book Review May 9, 1954; New York Times Book Review May 2, 1954.

HERFORD, CHARLES HAROLD (1853- April 25, 1931). For biographical sketch and list of works and references, see TWENTIETH CENTURY AUTHORS, 1942.

* * *

ABOUT: Dictionary of National Biography 1931- 1940.

HERFORD, OLIVER (December 1863- July 5, 1935). For biographical sketch and list of works and references, see TWENTIETH CENTURY AUTHORS, 1942.

* * *

ABOUT: Reader's Digest August 1943.

*HERGESHEIMER, JOSEPH (February 15, 1880-April 25, 1954). For autobiographical sketch and list of works and references, see TWENTIETH CENTURY AUTHORS, 1942.

* * *

In 1940 Joseph Hergesheimer announced to Robert Van Gelder that he had retired as "a serious novelist." He had written ten good books which, he told Van Gelder, "represented the greatest effort of which he was capable," and he saw no reason to write more. So complete was Hergesheimer's retirement that long before his death critics wrote of him only in the past tense. Partly this was because the world of many of his novels—the elegant, refined, and decadent world of "an international leisure class"—seemed so remote to the modern reader. Like the work of his contemporary James Branch Cabell, Hergesheimer's writing had a note of the precious and the baroque. "His novels," Albert Kazin says, "were like a museum devoted to the households of the past."

Hergesheimer spent his last years at his home in Stone Harbor, N.J. He died after a brief illness, survived by his widow, Dorothy Hemphill Hergesheimer. At the time of his death the New York *Times* commented: "Without having skirted the small inner circle of the nation's greatest writers, he has left profuse evidence of the fact that he was a hard worker, a diligent scholar and a competent stylist, a teller of tales of dead days who made them live, and an inquisitive historian who brightened his facts with the art of the novelist and the disposition of a minor philosopher."

ABOUT: Kazin, A. On Native Grounds; Van Gelder, R. Writers and Writing; New York Times April 26, 1954; Saturday Review of Literature December 1, 1945.

* hûr′gĕs hī mĕr

HERRICK, ROBERT (April 26, 1868-December 24, 1938). For autobiographical sketch and list of works and references, see TWENTIETH CENTURY AUTHORS, 1942.

* * *

ABOUT: Cargill, O. Intellectual America; American Literature March 1949.

HERSCHBERGER, RUTH (MARGARET) (January 30, 1917-), American author, was born in Philipse Manor, N.Y., just outside of New York City. Her parents, Clarence B. and Grace (Eberhart) Herschberger, came from Chicago, and she returned with them to that city after two years in the

East. She grew up in Chicago and attended public schools there, the University of Chicago for three years, and Black Mountain College, in North Carolina, for one year. She also spent a summer at the University of Michigan, where she received an Avery Hopwood award in poetry in 1941, and she studied playwriting at the Dramatic Workshop of the New School for Social Research from 1942 to 1943. A radio play by her, "Edgar Allan Poe" was produced in New York City by station WNYC. More recently (1953) two verse plays, "A Ferocious Incident" and a scene from "Andrew Jackson" were produced by the Poets Company in the Playwrights Theatre Club of Chicago.

G. Herschberger

In 1948 Miss Herschberger published a book of poems, *A Way of Happening*, which won considerable critical acclaim. Dudley Fitts, writing in the *Saturday Review of Literature*, singled out for praise "the fresh, scoured diction; the sympathetic clarity of observation, particularly of animal and vegetable shapes and textures, which clothes itself in imagery at once homely, strange, and just; the urgent rhythms, controlled, yet always on the point of bursting." Selden Rodman commented on the volume, in the New York *Times*: "Miss Herschberger . . . is one of those rare poets who never write an off-key or dull poem; the shock of recognition is on every page." In the same year she also published a prose work, *Adam's Rib*, an analysis of the position of women in modern society, which the *New Yorker* described as "a clever, literate, and coldly logical analysis." Her poems and criticism frequently appear in "little magazines" and anthologies. One short story, "A Sound in the Night," was reprinted in *Best American Short Stories of 1949*. In 1953 Miss Herschberger received the Harriet Monroe Memorial Prize. She lives in Chicago.

PRINCIPAL WORKS: A Way of Happening (poems) 1948; Adam's Rib, 1948.

HERSEY, JOHN RICHARD (June 17, 1914-), American novelist and journalist, was born in Tientsin, China, the son of Grace Baird Hersey and Roscoe Monroe Hersey, for twenty-five years a Y.M.C.A. secretary in China. John Hersey spoke Chinese fluently before he knew a word of English, and lived in China until 1924. However, at the age of three he was taken by his mother on a two-year trip around the world. When he was ten, his family returned to the United States to live, and he attended Hotchkiss School and Yale, graduating from the latter in 1936. He studied for one year at Clare College, Cambridge, England. Returning to America, he became a secretary and assistant to Sinclair Lewis, then became affiliated with *Time* and *Life* magazines, serving as a war correspondent for them on both fronts during World War II.

E. M. M. Warburg

Hersey's first book was *Men on Bataan*, published in 1942. As Milton Rugoff writes, it is, "in effect, a correspondent's report," although Hersey had not reached Bataan itself; "it uncovers his characteristic freshness and restraint, and his sure, spare style." The next year Hersey wrote *Into the Valley* (1943), a brief account of a skirmish on Guadalcanal. He had gone along with a Marine company in an attack, and when they found they had by bad luck walked straight into a Japanese trap in the middle of the jungle, Hersey had an opportunity to study their reactions, as well as his own. Afterwards he remained in Guadalcanal, and was commended in 1942 by Secretary of the Navy Frank Knox for heroism in assisting the wounded under fire. Hersey very nearly lost all his notes for *Into the Valley* when his plane hit a wave in the South Pacific and capsized and sank. Extricating himself when the plane was about nine feet below the surface, he found his notebooks floating within reach. The lines on the paper notebooks were smeared but the jottings were clear.

The third book, *A Bell for Adano* (1944), dealing with Italy, had as its substance a report Hersey had written for *Life*. With this novel Hersey leaped into national fame, winning the Pulitzer prize in 1945. The novel was successfully adapted for stage production and for the motion pictures. His next book, *Hiroshima*, a journalistic tour de force and a model of objective and accurate reporting, appeared in 1946; the *New Yorker*, for which Hersey was then a correspondent, devoted an entire issue to it. Not a single scene, fact, or character was invented. The account of what happened when the first atom bomb was dropped on a city is told through the intimate record of six survivors. Dr. Fujii, one of the central characters of *Hiroshima*, told Norman

Cousins in 1950, "You know, when he was here speaking to me, and when I looked at him, I said to myself, 'This young man is the type of American the great President Lincoln must have been. He even looks like the pictures of Lincoln I have seen in the history books. He is slender and tall—one of the tallest men I have ever seen anywhere. And he is so understanding and sympathetic.'"

The Wall, a novelistic study of Poland under the Nazis, appeared in 1950, and *The Marmot Drive*, concerning a community drive to rid a New England town of a colony of woodchucks, was published in 1953. The latter, generally treated as an allegory, seemed to baffle many of Hersey's admirers and received mixed reviews. Hersey's critics are in doubt whether his novels are not actually journalism, presented in a dramatized form. In *The Marmot Drive*, wrote Irving Howe, "Mr. Hersey has made an intense effort to shake off those journalistic mannerisms. . . . But he has replaced them with a large repertoire of literary mannerisms." Others found the book bizarre but fascinating.

In 1940 Hersey married Frances Ann Cannon; they have four children and live in Connecticut. There was a time when he used to "saw the violin," but he gave it up, he says, "because I am an ardent lover of good music."

PRINCIPAL WORKS: Men on Bataan, 1942; Into the Valley, 1943; A Bell for Adano, 1944; Hiroshima, 1946; The Wall, 1950; The Marmot Drive, 1953.

ABOUT: Warfel, H. R. American Novelists of Today; Witham, W. T. Panorama of American Literature; American Mercury May 1950; Current Biography 1944; English Journal September 1950; National Cyclopaedia of American Biography (1946); New York Herald Tribune Book Review March 5, 1950, August 20, 1950; Newsweek September 9, 1946; Saturday Review of Literature March 4, 1950.

HERSKOVITS, MELVILLE JEAN

(September 10, 1895-   ), American anthropologist, writes: "I was born in Bellefontaine, Ohio, spent a part of my boyhood in El Paso, Tex., and was able to see something of Mexican modes of life when I was assigned a newspaper route in Juarez. I was an observer of sorts of the 1910 uprising led by Madero, and during the siege of Juarez had  some first-hand contact with him and with Pancho Villa. My college career was interrupted by enlistment during World War I and service in France, the post-armistice part of which was spent at the University of Poitiers, where I remember, as an outstanding impression, studying the history of the French Revolution under a Royalist professor!

"My interest in anthropology came late as these things go, since I took my first course in the subject when I was twenty-six years old. I had tried a number of things, but none of them held my interest, and I early resolved not to commit myself to a career until I found a field that would excite me and keep me excited. The breadth and freshness of the questions with which anthropology was concerned, and its relevance for such pressing problems of our times as the meaning of racial differences and the attainment of cross-cultural adjustment appealed to me. This appeal has increased with the years.

"I took my degree with Franz Boas, and, after my marriage to Frances Shapiro in 1924, continued at Columbia in association with him as Fellow of the National Research Council until 1927, when I came to Northwestern, where I initiated work in anthropology. While at Columbia, I completed my study of Negro-White crossing, which indicated that the American Negro, despite the degree of mixture he represents, is forming a homogeneous sub-type of the general population. These results seem to have been accepted, but I wish that, after the manner of science, the study could be repeated independently and thus have its findings checked, as my later work has so thoroughly been.

"Because it was important to discover where the African component in this population had been derived, I started to look for it, found it, and have been exploring the implications ever since. In 1928 and 1929 my wife, who has participated in all my field research, and I went to Surinam, Dutch Guiana, and studied the Bush Negroes, who have the purest African culture in the New World. This led us in 1931 to West Africa—Nigeria, Dahomey, the Gold Coast—then back to Haiti in 1934, to Trinidad in 1939 and Brazil in 1941. Out of all this has come the field known as Afro-American studies, which aims at discovering what happens to civilizations in contact as a general thing, by finding out in particular what happened to the African civilizations brought to the New World when they met the cultures of Europe and the American Indian.

"This research program has directed most of my writing. My first papers and books were essentially descriptive, though they ranged in form from *Rebel Destiny*, where Mrs. Herskovits and I used a literary technique to make of our Bush Negro friends more than the lay figures of the conventional monograph, to *Dahomey*, which falls under the customary rubric of the enthnographic report. With time, however, the broader implications of my studies began to point sharper theoretical formulations, as I had always been confident they would, and practical implications as well. A good example of both is *The Myth of the Negro Past*, which I did for the Carnegie-Myrdal study, and which revealed some unsuspected historical and psychological bases of American problems of race relations.

"In *Man and His Works* I tried to bring the materials of my discipline together to answer a question that is increasingly asked these days, 'What *is* anthropology?', and at the same time give my own theoretical approach to its problems. I also have compounded another interest of long standing by writing on comparative economics, a task toward which I was early directed through my contacts, first as student and then less formally with Thorstein Veblen. I felt that a cross-cultural point of view, in economics as in other disciplines that draw their materials from our own society, can throw valuable light on basic hypotheses. So I did a book on this in 1939, which I have almost completely rewritten, bringing it out in 1952 under a new title, *Economic Anthropology*.

"As graduate work in anthropology at Northwestern developed, and we began increasingly to send students into the field, the importance of integrating an emergent Africa into a nascent world scene became more and more apparent. This led to the broadening of my anthropological concerns with Africa, and I now direct our University's African Area Program, in which all the social science disciplines cooperate.

"Aside from area and theoretical concerns, I am deeply interested in the problem of the relation between the humanistic disciplines and the social sciences. In my own field research I have recorded music, collected tales, analyzed art, and have encouraged my students to do the same and to study these and other manifestations of the creative drive in man on a cross-cultural basis. For because of its breadth of approach and its special techniques of lifting the cultural horizon, I believe that anthropology must be the discipline to bridge the gap and form the basis of the new humanism we see developing on a worldwide, multi-cultural basis. In providing the empirical findings for a philosophy known as cultural relativism, which is among its most important contributions to the thought of our time, I feel that anthropology best exemplifies the breadth and freshness of outlook on long-standing problems that attracted me to it in the first place."

PRINCIPAL WORKS: The American Negro: A Study in Racial Crossing, 1928; Anthropometry of the American Negro, 1930; Rebel Destiny, Among the Bush Negroes of Dutch Guiana (with F. S. Herskovits) 1934; Surinam Folklore (with F. S. Herskovits) 1936; Life in a Haitian Valley, 1937; Dahomey, 1938; Acculturation, 1938; The Economic Life of Primitive Peoples, 1940; The Myth of the Negro Past, 1941; Trinidad Village (with F. S. Herskovits) 1947; Man and His Works, 1948; Franz Boas, 1953; Cultural Anthropology (abridged revision of Man and His Works) 1955.

ABOUT: Current Biography 1948; Saturday Review of Literature September 18, 1948.

HERZOG, ÉMILE. See MAUROIS, A.

*HESSE, HERMANN (July 2, 1877-   ). For autobiographical sketch and list of earlier works and references, see TWENTIETH CENTURY AUTHORS, 1942.

* * *

Hermann Hesse received the Nobel Prize for Literature in 1946. The prize-winning novel was *Das Glasperlenspiel* (translated under the title *Magister Ludi*), a powerful and profound fantasy about a community of men who devote their lives to a formidable but utterly sterile scholarly project. Although Hesse has been ranked with Thomas Mann as "the greatest contemporary German author," his writings are little known outside of German-speaking countries. At least two of his most important novels were not even available in English until after 1948.

Hesse has lived in Switzerland since 1912. Long a critic of German politics, he was of course bitterly opposed to Nazism. When in 1946 he was offered the Goethe Prize of the town of Frankfurt, he accepted the honor with some hesitancy, expressing the fear that his acceptance might mean that he recognized "the official Germany." He commented: "My relationship to that enigmatic people has always been thorny and intricate, two-edged and difficult."

He was divorced from his first wife, from whom he had three sons, in 1923, and in 1931 married Ninon Auslaender. Thomas Mann, long an admirer of Hesse's work, wrote of him in 1948: "I also love Hesse the man, his cheerfully thoughtful, roguishly kind ways, the beautiful deep look of his,

alas, ailing eyes, whose blue illuminates the sharp-cut face of an old Swabian peasant."

ADDITIONAL WORKS AVAILABLE IN ENGLISH TRANSLATION: Demian, 1948; Magister Ludi, 1949; Siddhartha, 1951.

ABOUT: Columbia Dictionary of Modern European Literature; Books Abroad Spring 1947, Summer 1947, Summer 1951; Contemporary Review January 1947; Modern Language Forum March 1947; New Directions 14; New York Times Book Review December 8, 1946; Poet Lore Winter 1947; Poetry July 1947; Queen's Quarterly Summer 1948; Saturday Review of Literature January 3, 1948.

HEWLETT, MAURICE HENRY (January 22, 1861-June 16, 1923). For biographical sketch and list of works and references, see TWENTIETH CENTURY AUTHORS, 1942.

* * *

ABOUT: Thompson, F. Literary Criticisms; Wagenknecht, E. Cavalcade of the English Novel.

"HEXT, HARRINGTON." See PHILLPOTTS, E.

HEYER, GEORGETTE (August 16, 1902-   ). For biographical sketch and list of earlier works and references, see TWENTIETH CENTURY AUTHORS, 1942.

* * *

Georgette Heyer has a large and devoted audience on both sides of the Atlantic. Her specialty is the historical romance, a skillful blend of the ingredients Harvey Curtis Webster lists (in the *Saturday Review*) as "not-to-be-taken-too-seriously shivers, period descriptions of clothing, hunting, castles, and love of the most unimpugnable kind." The results are invariably frothy but engrossing, and she has been highly praised by the reviewers for her recreation of Regency days in London in *The Grand Sophie* and *Cotillion.* Miss Heyer (Mrs. George Ronald Rougier) lives in London.

ADDITIONAL WORKS: Penhallow, 1943; Death in the Stocks, 1945; Friday's Child, 1946; The Reluctant Widow, 1947; The Foundling, 1948; Arabella, 1949; The Grand Sophie, 1950; Duplicate Death, 1951; The Quiet Gentleman, 1951; Cotillion, 1953; Detection Unlimited, 1953; The Toll Gate, 1954.

*HEYERDAHL, THOR (October 6, 1914-   ), Norwegian author, was born in Larvik, Norway, the son of Thor Heyerdahl, the president of a brewery and mineral water plant, and of Alison (Lyng) Heyerdahl, who was chairman of the Larvik Museum. His

* hĕs'ĕ

* hi'ĕr-däl, tŏŏr

father's enthusiasm for outdoor life and his mother's scientific studies in folk art, zoology, and the history of primitive races, were to be important factors in  Thor Heyerdahl's choice of a career. He has written this summary account of his activities: "Since early childhood interested in Natural Sciences, and opened one room zoological museum at age of 7. After Senior Matriculation in 1933 he specialized in Zoology and Geography at the University of Oslo, but changed entirely to Anthropology during his first field research among the Polynesians in the Marquesas Islands 1937-38. More field research in Northwest Indian territory of British Columbia 1939-40 to collect material for the theory of two separate American Indian movements into the Pacific. At the German invasion of Norway in 1940 he volunteered on active services with free Norwegian Military Forces in Canada and Great Britain, ending as officer in Parachute Unit serving in Finnmark on Northern Norway until armistice 1945. Continued research in Europe and U.S.A. until 1947, when he organized and lead a Kon-Tiki expedition by balsa raft from Callao, Peru, to Raroia, Polynesia. The raft, which was a replica of the prehistoric vessels used by South-American Indians, followed the Humboldt Current, and covered 4300 miles of the open Pacific in 101 days, thus proving that Peruvian Indians could have settled in Polynesia. Continued researches and lectures in U.S.A. and Europe 1948-52. In 1953 organised and led the Norwegian Archeological Expedition to the Galapagos which uncovered for the first time in this group archeological evidence of pre-European visits by South American Indians."

During his university days, Heyerdahl contributed articles on outdoor life to Norwegian newspapers; he spent his summer vacations fishing and mountaineering, his winter vacations on husky-and-sled trips into the mountains. His first book was *Paa Jagt efter Paradiset* ("On the Hunt for Paradise"), published in Oslo in 1938. His second work, *Kon-Tiki*, which tells the story of his raft expedition, was first published in Norway in 1948. Most of the leading American publishers rejected the book, but on its publication here and in England two years later, it proved an overwhelming success, and has

since been translated into twenty-four languages in all. "While this is not the first time that a log has been turned into literature," wrote the *Christian Science Monitor*, "it has seldom been done so superbly. The book is cast in terms of men-against-the-sea, which gives it a general . . . appeal." *The Saturday Review of Literature* complained that the first ninety-two pages are dull, "but Heyerdahl's limitations as a writer are forgotten once the nine balsa logs, held together only by ropes, finally reach the timeless Humboldt Current." Although the majority of anthropologists reject Heyerdahl's hypothesis (that the origins of the Polynesian people are not Asiatic), Waldemar Kaempffert has said, he "certainly proved by his epic voyage that it is possible to reach Polynesia from Peru on a balsa raft." This point, Heyerdahl reiterated later, was all he had set out to prove. In 1952 his *American Indians in the Pacific, the Theory behind the Kon-Tiki Expedition*, was published.

He has received many honors from many different countries. The movie which was made during the expedition received an Academy Award for the best documentary feature of 1951.

Heyerdahl is fair, blue-eyed, five feet eleven inches in height, and weighs about 160 pounds. His first wife was Liv Heyerdahl, who accompanied him to the Marquesas Islands in 1937. They had two sons, Thor and Bjorn. His second marriage took place in 1949, to Yvonne Dedekam-Simonsen; they have one daughter.

Among his favorite recreations are cartooning and wood carving.

PRINCIPAL WORKS IN ENGLISH TRANSLATION: Kon-Tiki, 1950; American Indians in the Pacific, 1952.

ABOUT: Current Biography 1947; Herald Tribune Book Review September 10, 1950, October 8, 1950.

*HEYM, STEFAN (April 10, 1913-), German-American novelist, was born in Chemnitz, Germany, and after attending schools there and in Berlin, entered the University of Berlin. When Hitler became Reichschancellor in 1933, Heym was still at the university. Even in his teens he had been under official scrutiny for his anti-Nazi views and when he wrote and published an anti-militaristic poem (at the age of eighteen) he was beaten up. He fled to Czechoslovakia, skiing part of the way across the mountains, and from 1933 to 1935 lived in Prague where he made a living of sorts through odd jobs

* him

and a little writing. In 1935 he won one of the graduate scholarships offered by the University of Chicago to two students of standing promise whose education had been interrupted by Hitler's coming to power. After receiving his M.A. from Chicago, Heym accepted the editorship of a small anti-Nazi German newspaper published in New York. The publication failed after two years,—but not before Heym had a chance to aid in an exposé of the activities of the Nazi Bund in America. His findings were brought together in a pamphlet *Nazis in the U.S.A.*, published in 1938. The year before, his dramatized version of Mark Twain's *Tom Sawyer* (in collaboration with Hans Burger) had been produced in Vienna and Prague.

From 1939 to 1942 Heym worked as a printing salesman and spent his leisure hours on his first novel, published in 1942. This was *Hostages*, a story of the Nazi occupation of Prague in terms of the experiences of a group of hostages who are to be shot. They are accused of causing the death of a Nazi who had been publicized as murdered, but whom the Nazis know to have been a suicide. The reviewers agreed on the whole that the book was hair-raising and a "terrifyingly effective narrative." A few of them felt that the characters did not emerge clearly; that the writing was uneven; and that it did not measure up to the standard of Koestler's *Darkness at Noon*, which handled a similar situation. *Hostages* was found by them to have "the suspense and narrowing sense of pursuit of a top-notch detective story" and to be strongest on atmosphere. Although Diana Trilling, writing in the *Nation*, found the book for the most part "only a grand scale thriller," Orville Prescott in the New York *Times* called it the best novel he had seen of life under the Nazis, "tense, tautly constructed, swift, and terrible." The book sold widely and was made into a film. Copies were distributed to soldiers overseas.

This book was followed by *Of Smiling Peace* in 1944, a year after Heym's entrance into the U.S. Army as a private. He was promoted to a lieutenancy in the psychological warfare branch and *The Crusaders*, published in 1948, was begun during his war service. *Of Smiling Peace* is a novel based on the war in Africa, a psychological study of two men. *The Crusaders* deals with the invasion of Normandy, through the liberation of Paris, to the occupation of Germany. The second book is much longer than the first, and, in the opinion of several reviewers, too long. Both books were generally commended for their pace and interest, but Malcolm Cowley in the *New Republic* states the opinion of several reviewers, "The novel [*The Crusaders*] has everything . . . combat, pursuit, cruelty, sex, a host of characters . . . and a story that plunges ahead like an armored division. . . . It also has a thesis and a sound one, namely, that the war was fought against evils some of which exist in our own army and nation. There is only one thing the novel lacks: the respect for his characters and for truth as opposed to bombast that one has a right to expect from a writer of Heym's talent."

In 1951 his novel *The Eyes of Reason* was published, a book about Czechoslovakia falling under the Communist régime. To some reviewers it appeared that Heym had weighted his narrative in favor of the upholders of the new revolutionary state.

In 1954 Heym was reported to be living in Soviet East Germany.

PRINCIPAL WORKS: Hostages, 1942; Of Smiling Peace, 1944; The Crusaders, 1948; The Eyes of Reason, 1951.

ABOUT: Warfel, H. R. American Novelists of Today 1951; Current Biography 1943; New York Times October 16, 1942; Saturday Review of Literature October 24, 1942.

HEYWARD, DU BOSE (August 31, 1885-June 16, 1940). For biographical sketch and list of works and references, see TWENTIETH CENTURY AUTHORS, 1942.

* * *

ABOUT: Durham, F. DuBose Heyward: The Man Who Wrote Porgy.

*HICHENS, ROBERT SMYTHE (November 14, 1864-July 20, 1950). For autobiographical sketch and list of earlier works and references, see TWENTIETH CENTURY AUTHORS, 1942.

* * *

Robert S. Hichens died in a Zurich hospital at eighty-five. He had lived in Switzerland for the last few years of his life.

Hichens' prolific novel-writing continued to the time of his death, and although his work declined in interest and popularity, his "singularly assured craftsmanship" made the

* hïch'ĕnz

decline a slow one. "For over a half a century," the London *Times* observed, "he entertained, shocked, fascinated, and only rarely bored his public. . . . Few have exhibited so versatile and fecund an imagination." Lisle Bell called him "a master hand at blending the exotic and emotional."

ADDITIONAL WORKS: Young Mrs. Brand (in England: Veils) 1943; Woman in the House (alternate title: Harps in the Wind) 1945; Incognito, 1947; Too Much Love of Living, 1947; Yesterday (autobiography) 1947; Man in the Mirror (short stories) 1950; Strange Lady (in England: Beneath the Magic) 1950; Mask, 1951; Nightbound, 1951.

ABOUT: Hichens, R. S. Yesterday; New York Times July 22, 1950.

HICKS, GRANVILLE (September 9, 1901-). For autobiographical sketch and list of earlier works and references, see TWENTIETH CENTURY AUTHORS, 1942.

* * *

Granville Hicks writes: "Have continued to live in Grafton, N.Y. Still reading for Macmillan and writing for various magazines. Literary consultant, *The New Leader*, since 1951.

"Though I still think I learned a lot from Marx, I do not now consider myself a Marxist, nor am I a socialist. See *Small Town*, chap. 2."

Small Town is a semi-autobiographical, semi-sociological account of a New England country town, "Roxborough," a none too thinly-veiled disguise for the upper New York State community in which Hicks has lived since 1935. Essentially the book is concerned with the problem of the intellectual adjusting and adapting himself to the standards of a rural community and making a valid and secure place for himself and his family within that community. Chapter 2, to which Hicks refers above, is called "The Natural History of an Intellectual," and is the autobiographical portion of the book.

In February 1953 Hicks testified as a "cooperative" witness before the House Committee on Un-American Activities on the question of a Communist group at Harvard during the late 1930's. He warned of a peril in the inquiries of Congressional committees, saying: "The fear in this country is in part a real and understandable fear of the Soviet Union and its agents. Above it, I think there is . . . an irrational apprehension that is not real. I feel that this has been encouraged by Congressional committees."

ADDITIONAL WORKS: Behold Trouble (novel) 1944; Small Town, 1946; There Was a Man in Our Town (novel) 1952; Where We Came Out, 1954.

ABOUT: Hicks, G. Small Town, Where We Came Out; Current Biography 1942; New Republic December 9, 1946; Newsweek December 2, 1946; New York Times February 27, 1953.

*HIGHET, GILBERT (1906-), Scottish-born author, critic and Anthon Professor of Latin at Columbia University, was born in Glasgow, son of Gilbert and Elizabeth (Boyle) Highet; and graduated from the University of Glasgow in 1928. After receiving an M.A. from Glasgow, he attended Oxford University, taking a double first in classics, an honorary scholarship

Elliott Erwitt

at Balliol College and several university distinctions. He was appointed Fellow and Lecturer in Classics at St. John's College, Oxford, where he taught for five years. During this period, he was co-founder of the Oxford University Experimental Theatre Society and editor of the *New Oxford Outlook*, a literary and political review. He began reviewing contemporary American books, in which he found an essential vitality and a sense of liberty which he appreciated.

Highet's first view of the North American continent (Canada) was as a student playing in the band of a cruise-ship. His second transatlantic visit was more ceremonial. In 1937 he was invited to Columbia University for one year and in 1938 he joined the permanent staff of Columbia as professor of Greek and Latin.

He was on leave for war service from 1941 through 1946, mainly doing U.S.-Canadian-British liaison work in Washington and New York. He was promoted to the rank of lieutenant-colonel in the British army and was one of the officers responsible for taking Nazi Party property into control to prevent its misuse, and for finding loot taken by German agencies from occupied countries in Europe.

He returned to Columbia in 1946 and was appointed Anthon Professor of Latin in 1950. In 1951 he was awarded a Guggenheim fellowship for a study of the Roman satiric poet Juvenal, and was awarded the D.Litt. of the University of Glasgow. In 1951 he became a U.S. citizen. A year later he was appointed chief book reviewer for *Harper's Magazine*. In 1954 he resigned

* hī′ĕt

from this post to become an editor of the Book-of-the-Month Club.

Highet has published books of criticism, essays and translations. *The Classical Tradition: Greek and Roman Influence on Western Literature* is a study of the various ways in which Greek and Roman authors have stimulated and educated the writers of Europe and America from the Dark Ages to the present day. *The Art of Teaching* is a description of the character and methods of the ideal teacher, illustrated by the work of great teachers from Socrates and Jesus to those of the last generation.

He has translated a massive three-volume work, *Paideia, The Ideals Of Greek Culture,* from the German of Werner Jaeger, on the educational aspects of Greek civilization. Many of his translations of Greek poems appear in the *Oxford Book of Greek Verse in Translation.* In a lighter vein, he has written parodies of Pound, Hemingway, and other contemporary writers.

In recent years, Highet has given a weekly series of radio talks over radio station WQXR in New York. Of these talks, John Crosby, radio and television critic of the New York *Herald Tribune,* said: "Since the late Alexander Woollcott, no one has managed to grapple successfully on the air with the subject of books. . . . An astonishingly literate and successful exception is the series of fifteen-minute talks by Gilbert Highet, the overwhelmingly erudite Professor of Latin Language and Literature at Columbia University. . . . They are flavorsome, scholarly, charming talks."

Highet is married to the novelist Helen MacInnes. They live in New York City and have one son, now attending Harvard.

PRINCIPAL WORKS: The Classical Tradition: Greek and Roman Influences on Western Literature, 1949; The Art of Teaching, 1951; People, Places and Books, 1953; Man's Unconquerable Mind, 1954; The Migration of Ideas, 1954; A Clerk of Oxenford, 1954; Juvenal the Satirist, 1954.

ABOUT: Harper's Magazine August 1952; New York Herald Tribune Book Review December 25, 1949.

HILL, FRANK ERNEST (August 29, 1888-). For biographical sketch and list of earlier works and references, see TWENTIETH CENTURY AUTHORS, 1942.

* * *

Frank Ernest Hill has continued his work in popular education through writing and radio. In 1946 he published a modern English verse translation of the *Canterbury Tales,*

and three years later his biography of Shakespeare (part fact and part fiction) appeared. This book was well received as a modest but useful and entertaining study. The Shakespeare scholar Alfred Harbage pronounced it "a sincere, respectful, indeed affectionate book." Hill drew upon his knowledge of the Elizabethan period again in his historical romance (for teen-age readers) *The King's Company,* a story which, Charles Lee commented in the New York *Times,* he handled "with skill and spirit." He lives in New York City.

ADDITIONAL WORKS: Tune In for Education, 1942; Chaucer's Canterbury Tales: Done into Modern English Verse, 1946; To Meet Will Shakespeare, 1949; The King's Company, 1950; The Kid Who Batted 1.000 (with R. Allison) 1951.

HILL, Mrs. GRACE (LIVINGSTON) (April 16, 1865-February 23, 1947). For biographical sketch and list of earlier works and references, see TWENTIETH CENTURY AUTHORS, 1942.

* * *

Grace Livingston Hill died at her home in Swarthmore, Pa., after a long illness, at eighty-one.

A novel on which she was working at the time of her death was completed by her daughter, Mrs. Ruth Munce. Shortly before she died Mrs. Hill had signed a contract with her publishers calling for two novels a year. Almost 4,000,000 copies of her books had been sold in the United States during her lifetime.

"Although she said she had no formula," according to the New York *Times,* "Mrs. Hill used the same ingredients over and over again, mixing romance, adventure, conflict and religion." Her biographer, Jean Karr, characterized the novels as "more than a pleasant pastime for thousands of people; they were object lessons in clean living and thinking."

ADDITIONAL WORKS: Crimson Mountain, 1942; Street of the City, 1942; Sound of the Trumpet, 1943; Spice Box, 1943; Through These Fires, 1943; Time of the Singing of Birds, 1944; More Than Conqueror, 1944; All Through the Night, 1945; Girl to Come Home To, 1945; Bright Arrows, 1946; Where Two Ways Meet, 1947; Mary Arden (with R. L. Hill) 1948; Miss Lavinia's Call (short stories) 1949.

ABOUT: Karr, J. Grace Livingston Hill; New York Times February 24, 1947.

HILLARY, RICHARD HOPE (1919-January 8, 1943), English writer and R.A.F. pilot, was killed at the age of twenty-four. He was the author of one book published in 1942 (English title, *The Last Enemy;* American title, *Falling Through Space*). This book and the nature and meaning of

his death as a war casualty in World War II have made of his life and death a legend and a symbol.

Hillary was the son of a wealthy upper-class English family. In 1939, when the war broke out, he was a student at Trinity College, Oxford, which he described as "a typical incubator of the English ruling classes before the war." Trinity College had many Blues (athletes) and Hillary, an experienced oarsman, trained for the Oxford crew. He was also on the staff of the University magazine, and a member of the University Air Squadron. Before he decided to be a writer, he had intended to go into the government of the Sudan which he describes as "that country of blacks ruled by Blues in which my father had spent many years."

The summer before the war, Hillary traveled in Germany, Hungary, and France. He had always liked to travel, and most of his school vacations had been spent on the continent.

On September 3, 1939, Hillary, with many of his closest friends, reported to the Volunteer Reserve Center at Oxford. After a lengthy training period, he was assigned to a squadron stationed in Scotland, and at the height of the Battle of Britain, his squadron was moved south to Hornchurch, an airdrome near London. In Hillary's words: "Twenty-four of us flew south that 10th day of August 1941: of those twenty-four eight were to fly back."

Hillary was not one of the eight. On September 3, 1941, he was shot down in flames over the North Sea. Spotters on the beach saw him fall and after several hours' search, he was picked up by the Margate lifeboat. He was severely burned and for the next two years was in and out of hospitals undergoing many operations and skin grafts on his face and hands. Hillary himself seemed to feel that he was living on borrowed time—almost none of his friends were still alive—and it was in this interim that he wrote and published his book.

Arthur Koestler, in an essay on Hillary, says, "Of all the writing airmen, Hillary, with St. Exupéry, form a category apart." That Hillary had a genuine literary talent is

evident from his only book as well as from his letters, many excerpts from which are quoted by Koestler. His book is not only a dramatic account of his training and battle flights, but also an attempt to analyze and describe the attitudes and outlook of young men of his class in pre-war England, and the impact that the war had on these attitudes. J. M. Murry wrote: "The late Richard Hillary's book, *The Last Enemy,* is the work of a writer born: it depicts with remarkable vividness and objectivity the experiences of an Oxford undergraduate turned airman, who crashed, was terribly burned, was patched up into the semblance of a human being by plastic surgery, and could not rest till he was flying again to a death which he knew to be certain, and which he desired."

Although a plane had to be specially fitted out so that Hillary could handle it, he managed to pass a medical board, and was returned to active duty. On January 8, 1943, Hillary was killed in an unexplained accident on a night training flight.

PRINCIPAL WORK: Falling Through Space (in England: The Last Enemy) 1942.

ABOUT: Dickson, L. Richard Hillary; Koestler, A. *in* The Yogi and The Commissar; Linklater, E. *in* Art of Adventure; Murry, J. M. *in* Katherine Mansfield and Other Literary Portraits; Time February 23, 1942.

HILLYER, ROBERT SILLIMAN (June 3, 1895-). For autobiographical sketch and list of earlier works and references, see TWENTIETH CENTURY AUTHORS, 1942.

* * *

Robert Hillyer became chancellor of the Academy of American Poets in 1942. He resigned from the faculty of Harvard University in 1944 to devote his time to writing and has been visiting professor at Kenyon College and the University of Delaware. Hillyer was divorced in 1943. Since 1945 he has lived in Greenwich, Conn. He is a sailing enthusiast and in 1946 built a small sloop-yacht "Gloriana" (named for Queen Elizabeth I) for summer cruising.

In 1949 Hillyer, then president of the Poetry Society of America, fired the first shot in a modern-day "Battle of the Books" by writing two articles in the *Saturday Review of Literature* hotly and indignantly protesting the award of the Bollingen-Library of Congress prize to Ezra Pound for his *Pisan Cantos* as "the highest achievement in American poetry" in 1948. Pound, who had been indicted for treason and declared in-

sane in 1945, was not the sole object of Hillyer's attack which included the whole school
of what he called the "new estheticism"—
"alien" and "expatriate" intellectuals. Specifically, his target was T. S. Eliot. The fury
of Hillyer's argument naturally evoked a
lively response. More than the literary co-
teries were involved in this controversy.
Congressmen challenged the award since it
was in part under Library of Congress sponsorship, and shortly after, the Bollingen prize
was transferred to the auspices of Yale University. Other readers and critics extended
Hillyer's attack to James Joyce, Marcel
Proust, and Gertrude Stein. The issue basically was that these were "coterie" writers—
alien, decadent, pretentious, obscure, and generally unwholesome. Hillyer extended the
charges himself in 1950 in an article in the
American Mercury to the so-called "New
Critics," Allen Tate, I. A. Richards, William
Empson and others, and to the teachers,
scholars, and poets associated with their theories.

Since 1942 Hillyer has published a novel,
My Heart for Hostage; a collection of his
poems; a long episodic poem in blank verse,
The Death of Captain Nemo; and a collec-
tion of satirical lyrics, *The Suburb by the
Sea*.

ADDITIONAL WORKS: My Heart for Hostage
(novel) 1942; Poems for Music, 1917-1947, 1947;
The Death of Captain Nemo, 1949; The Suburb by
the Sea, 1952.

ABOUT: Gregory, H. and Zaturenska, M. History of American Poetry, 1900-1940; Current Biography 1940; New York Times Book Review August
28, 1949.

HILTON, JAMES (September 9, 1900-De-
cember 20, 1954). For biographical
sketch and list of earlier works and
references, see TWENTIETH CENTURY
AUTHORS, 1942.

* * *

James Hilton died in Long Beach, Calif.,
after a long illness, at the age of fifty-four.
Hilton had lived in the United States since
1935. He became a familiar figure to American audiences, not only through his books
(and these continued to be popular successes,
though none matched *Goodbye Mr. Chips* and
Lost Horizon), but through magazine articles,
book reviews, motion picture dramatizations
of his stories, and radio appearances. Hilton
was a gifted raconteur. Isabelle Mallet remarked in the New York *Times* that "he
could if necessary tell an absorbing and expert story about almost nothing." She continued: "He has evolved a smooth blend of

worldly wisdom, charming simplicity and delightful ease with words which could con-
ceivably carry the multiplication table to
dramatic heights."

Hilton wrote rapidly, without preliminary
notes or synopses, sometimes, "when the
mood is on me," as much as 3,000 words a
day. "I am happy writing," he said, "though
not always happy about what I write." In
1951 Hilton reported on himself as follows
in the New York *Herald Tribune Book Review*: "I dislike organized games, swimming
pools, fashionable resorts, night clubs, music
in restaurants, and political manifestoes; I
enjoy driving from coast to coast, good food
and drink, a few friends, dogs, the theatre,
long walks, music (except grand opera), and
free conversation. I read a dozen or so books
a week (if I can find that many I want to
read); I spend three or four hours a week,
averagely, in radio listening, and an hour or
so with television."

ADDITIONAL WORKS: The Story of Dr. Wassell,
1943; So Well Remembered, 1945; Nothing So
Strange, 1947; Morning Journey, 1951; Time and
Time Again, 1953.

ABOUT: Mott, F. L. Golden Multitudes; New
York Herald Tribune Book Review October 7,
1951; New York Times December 21, 1954.

HINDUS, MAURICE GERSCHON (February 27, 1891-). For biographical
sketch and list of earlier works and references, see TWENTIETH CENTURY AU-
THORS, 1942.

* * *

Maurice Hindus traveled in the Soviet
Union from 1942 until a few months before
the end of the war in Europe as war correspondent for the New York *Herald Tribune*.
An expert on Russian affairs, he reported on
wartime conditions (in *Mother Russia*) with
sympathy and insight. Since the end of
World War II, and particularly since the
Communist *coup* in Czechoslovakia in 1948,
Hindus has become increasingly outspoken
in his criticism of the government of the
U.S.S.R. At the same time, however, he continues to affirm his faith in the people of the
U.S.S.R. In 1953 he wrote in the foreword
to *Crisis in the Kremlin*: "True enough, as
in the days of the czars, the people have had
no voice in the making of policy, internal and
external, though were war to come they, as
always, would be the chief sufferers. But
anyone who has broken bread with them, or
has slept in their homes, whether in the one
bed in the house or in the straw on the floor,
or has heard them talk and laugh and weep,

must attest that they are crusaders neither for world revolution nor world conquest."

Hindus has also traveled in recent years through the Near East—Iran, Egypt, Iraq, and Palestine. He reported on his observations in *In Search of a Future,* "a fine job of analytic reporting," according to the San Francisco *Chronicle.* In this book Hindus urged land reform as the only hope for solution to the complex social and economic problems of the region. His novel, *Magda,* the story of a Polish immigrant who comes to America and rises from farm laborer to land owner, was praised for its warm portrayal of American rural life.

ADDITIONAL WORKS: Mother Russia, 1943; The Cossacks: Story of a Warrior People, 1945; Bright Passage, 1947; In Search of a Future, 1949; Magda (novel) 1951; Crisis in the Kremlin, 1953.

ABOUT: Hindus, M. Crisis in the Kremlin.

HINKSON, Mrs. KATHERINE. See TYNAN, K.

HOBART, Mrs. ALICE TISDALE (NOURSE) (January 28, 1882-). For biographical sketch and list of earlier works and references, see TWENTIETH CENTURY AUTHORS, 1942.

* * *

Mrs. Hobart lives in Oakland, Calif. A "gentle and soft-spoken woman," forced by a spinal condition to spend long periods in bed, she nevertheless writes industriously. Her novels are sharp, vigorous and compelling. At times, however, her critics object, their "high seriousness of purpose" becomes obtrusive (the *New Yorker* describes her writing as "serene, industrious, and commonplace"). Although Mrs. Hobart is best known for her novel about Chinese life, *Oil for the Lamps of China,* she has grappled successfully with the problems of other peoples and other societies in recent works—a wine-growing dynasty in California in *The Cup and the Sword,* a California farm family in *The Cleft Rock,* the social changes in twentieth century Mexico in *The Peacock Sheds His Tail,* the ethics of the American medical profession in *The Serpent-Wreathed Staff.* "I'm enormously interested in democracy, in the breaking-up of tradition, wherever it is," she told Harvey Breit in an interview in 1951.

ADDITIONAL WORKS: The Cup and the Sword, 1942; The Peacock Sheds His Tail, 1945; The Cleft Rock, 1948; The Serpent-Wreathed Staff, 1951; Venture into Darkness, 1955.

ABOUT: New York Herald Tribune Book Review October 7, 1951; New York Times Book Review November 11, 1951 (Part I).

HOBSON, LAURA KEANE (ZAMETKIN) (June 18, 1900-), American novelist, writes: "I was born in New York City, of parents who, some twenty years earlier and separately, had emigrated from Russia in their late teens. My father, Michael Zametkin, had been a student at the University of Odessa; my mother, born Adella Kean, had had less formal education than  he. They were both intellectuals and idealists, 'old-fashioned Socialists,' dedicated to the concepts of equality and freedom, detesting everything that smacked of terrorism and despotism, economic or political, overt or slyly concealed. My father was an editor, and for a time, the editor of *The Jewish Daily Forward;* he also taught English to foreigners, and lectured widely to labor groups, chiefly in 'the needle trades' of New York, and the coal industry in Pennsylvania. My mother gave English lessons too, and in middle age began to write a newspaper column for women in *The Day,* largely about modern dietetics and child training, continuing her column for more than a decade.

"When I was about seven, my parents moved out to what was then a rather small town, Jamaica, Long Island, their motive being the passionate desire to have their two youngest children grow up in a completely American community, away from foreign accents and foreign ways. Even there, they kept on with their Socialist talk to neighbors and tradesmen and friends, and in her sixties my mother ran for Assemblywoman on the Socialist ticket in Queens, polling the largest Socialist vote ever returned from that district up to that time.

"Thus I grew up in an environment of ardent liberalism, pro-labor, agnostic, internationalist, non-sectarian. Like my twin sister and my much older brother and half-brother, I went to public schools and knew that both my parents fervently hoped I would become a teacher. My twin and my brother did become teachers, but my half-brother became a dentist and oral surgeon, and I always said vaguely that I wanted to be a writer. At high school I was the assistant editor of the school paper, and also wrote school items for the New York *Daily Mail,* averaging sixty cents a week at this exciting professionalism. I began college at Hunter, but halfway through, in profound disappointment that it seemed only like a harder high school, I transferred to Cornell University, and there took my B.A. in 1921, after two full years and a summer session.

"Apart from a small state scholarship and smaller funds from my family, I helped support myself through Cornell by summer jobs, and by writing college news for the New York *Globe* and campus fashion notes for *Women's Wear*. I also borrowed from the Student Loan Fund and from family friends. Upon my graduation, it was these debts that turned me from my hope of 'writing' to the more specific field of writing advertising. Until 1929 I worked as a copywriter, either in large agencies or as a free lance, except during 1926-7 when I became a cub reporter on the New York *Evening Post*.

"In 1929 I wrote a play, which had an offer of production from the Theatre Arts Club in London, but which never was actually produced, and sold my first magazine articles, four of them. In 1930, after my marriage to the book publisher, Thayer Hobson, I began to think of writing fiction, but the depression year of 1932 saw me back in advertising, this time doing 'high fashion' copy for a department store. However, in 1934, collaborating under the joint pseudonym of 'Peter Field,' we ground out two 'Westerns,' published by his own firm and y-clept *Outlaws Three*, and *Dry Gulch Adams*. That same year I began what was to turn into my largest business experience: writing promotion for *Time*, the March of Time, *Fortune*, and, later, *Life*. By 1940, when I resigned, I was director of promotion for *Time*.

"In 1935 my marriage had ended in divorce, and during that year I turned many of my evening hours and weekends to my first real attempt to write short stories. I sold the first two to *Collier's*, and during my remaining five years in business offices, writing fiction only in my spare time, I published half a dozen more stories in national magazines, and saw my first 'book' appear, a juvenile called *A Dog of His Own*.

"In 1937 I adopted an infant son, Michael, and in 1942, another infant, Christopher, both of whom, like me, have the middle initial Z. Despite the added responsibilities as 'Head of Family,' I left promotion in 1941, meaning only to try myself, for a limited time, as a fulltime writer of short stories. It went badly; suddenly, nothing sold. But Richard L. Simon, of Simon & Schuster, began to argue that I ought to attempt a novel; he backed up his faith, or hunch, by a startling advance and a contract. In Octo-ber, 1941, I began my first novel, *The Tres-passers*.

"The next five years were a scramble of short stories, free-lance promotion for magazines and book publishers, two summers of hack work in Hollywood—and writing books. In 1943 *The Trespassers* appeared; in 1947 *Gentleman's Agreement*. This second novel, which was made into a motion picture and translated into some thirteen foreign languages, was that turning point which all novelists dream of: since 1947 I have been able to devote my entire time to writing. *The Other Father* appeared in 1950, and in the next year, *The Celebrity*, my first attempt at social satire. I began my fifth novel in 1953, but it is long and difficult, and may remain 'work in progress' for a long while.

"Since 1953 I have had some new writing experiences—one as a five-times-a-week daily columnist that I soon found too destructive of my fiction writing, and the other as a once-a-month writer of a magazine column about books and authors, 'Thumbing Through,' in *Good Housekeeping*. This I increasingly enjoy doing, and hope to continue for a very long while. The newspaper columns I abandoned after a fourteen-month stretch, ending January 1, 1955.

"For the past fifteen years, I have been active with several political and professional organizations, which fight against racial or religious bigotry, and for civil liberties. I belong to Americans for Democratic Action, the PEN Club, United World Federalists; I serve on the National Council of the Authors' League of America, and on the Board of Directors of the New York branch of the American Civil Liberties Union."

* * *

Gentleman's Agreement, Mrs. Hobson's most celebrated novel, was the story of a journalist who posed as a Jew in order to gather material for a series of articles on anti-Semitism. It became one of the most popular novels of the post-war era and was widely praised as an honest and forceful attack on anti-Semitism. In this, as in all her novels, Mrs. Hobson writes a sharp and incisive prose, distinguished (the New York *Times* observed) for her ability "to share with the reader her rage at human idiocy without permitting him to take his eye or his mind from a vitally exciting story."

PRINCIPAL WORKS: The Trespassers, 1943; Gentleman's Agreement, 1947; The Other Father, 1950; The Celebrity, 1951.

ABOUT: Current Biography 1947; New York Herald Tribune Book Review May 28, 1950, October 7, 1951; New York Times Book Review November 4, 1951.

HOCKING, JOSEPH (1860-March 4, 1937). For biographical sketch and list of works and references, see TWEN-TIETH CENTURY AUTHORS, 1942.

* * *

HOCKING, WILLIAM ERNEST (August 10, 1873-), American philosopher and educator, writes:  "My life is not a time-string with events strung on it like beads. There are plenty of events, but to tell them would not be 'my life.' For I have lived several lives abreast, or rather braided; and the events often belong at once to two or three strands. For instance, my wife and I went to the Near East in 1928; that was 'an event.' My job was a study of mandates—philosophy, political theory—Egypt, Palestine, Syria, Turkey, ending in Geneva. At the same time, it belongs on the education strand; for a mandate was supposed to be educating backward peoples toward independence. It was also on the strand of art: I made various drawings for the hypothetical illustration of a book that appeared in 1932, without illustrations. And it was also on the strand of one's loves—the most important of all—for I fell in love with the Arabs and out of love with the Zionists (for whom I had been prepossessed), except for the cultural Zionism of such as my dear friend Judah Magnes.

"This is by way of saying that the education-strand, which is a long one—for one begins by being educated and goes on to educate others while continuing being educated—is only one of several. The other main strands are (1) the practical handwork strand, passing papers, being promoted to devil—printer's devil, surveying, engineering apprenticeship, building, architecture, farming and (2) the kindred strand of art; (3) the religious and philosophical anguish and discovery of a lifetime, whose literary side is my ostensible self as a small segment of the reading public; (4) my participation in the public catastrophes of the century, in the world wars and their problems; (5) the strand of love and friendship on the strength of which I could sum up my life in four words—I have enjoyed living: I have found it a wonderful and holy thing. And surely I ought to put in somewhere the strand of fighting; for what is life without its inner angers, wills-to-eliminate this and that blemish from a fair world? And what is love without the hatred of all that destroys or degrades it? There is a lot to hate, *ergo* a lot to fight."

* * *

William Ernest Hocking was born in Cleveland, Ohio. His father, William Francis Hocking, a Canadian by birth, was a doctor. His mother, Julia Carpenter Pratt Hocking, came from an old New England family. Hocking was raised in a religious home. His parents were Methodists, and their religion, he recalls, "was much thought-about, so that the atmosphere of our home life was at once devout and, in a wholly untechnical way, metaphysical." The boy's earliest education was at home—"an early and firm discipline in reading, spelling, and grammar," he writes. The family moved to Joliet, Ill., where he attended high school and, after his graduation, worked for four years as a civil engineering apprentice for the Elgin, Joliet, and Eastern Railroad, trying to accumulate enough money for college. He had hoped to enter the newly-founded University of Chicago, but lacking the necessary funds he enrolled in Iowa State College, in Ames.

Hocking's introduction to philosophy came very early in life. He has described the religious atmosphere of his home as "concrete, vivid, and regulatory." As a child he had several "semi-mystical" religious experiences. His first readings in philosophy, quite in contrast, were in the nineteenth century naturalists, and he found himself absorbed by mathematics and science. At fifteen he discovered Herbert Spencer's *First Principles*: "I was fascinated by Spencer, and entirely persuaded. My religion was undermined: my world, though pervaded by Spencer's Unknowable, had become clarified and desolate." The next great intellectual influence on Hocking was William James, whose *Principles of Psychology* he read in 1895. Determined to go to Harvard so that he might study under James, he devoted four years to full-time teaching in the public schools of Iowa. At the end of that time he came east to begin his studies at Harvard. He received his B.A. in 1901, his M.A. in 1902, and his Ph.D. in 1904. He spent the years 1902-03 in Germany as a traveling fellow. By this time Hocking had already begun to develop his own philosophical system. Although this system was deeply influenced by his two Harvard teachers—the Pragmatist William James and the Idealist Josiah Royce, Hocking proceeded independently His work shows, according to

James A. Martin, "modifications of absolutism as a result of empirical emphases." This has been variously described as "critical intuitive idealism," "individualistic idealism," "objective idealism." Actually it does not lend itself to easy classification. Hocking himself refers to it as "realism . . . mysticism . . . idealism also, its identity not broken"; and elsewhere as "a realism of social experience . . . or more truly a realism of the Absolute, not far removed from Absolute idealism." His most significant work has been in the field of religion: "The heart of religion for him lies in man's immediate awareness of the Infinite Whole of Reality as an Individual Mind" (Edwin A. Burtt writes). Religion, he has said, is the only agency capable of uniting the "wider prophetic purposes of man."

Hocking taught at the Andover Theological Seminary from 1904 to 1906, and at the University of California, from 1906 to 1908. In the latter year he joined the philosophy department at Yale, where he remained until 1914 when he went to Harvard as professor of philosophy. He remained at Harvard until his retirement in 1943 and is now emeritus professor. He lives in Madison, N.H. He has lectured in many universities in the United States and abroad. In 1937 and 1939 he was Gifford lecturer at Glasgow University and in 1938 he was Hibbert lecturer at Oxford and Cambridge.

With his wife, the former Agnes Boyle O'Reilly, whom he married in 1905, Hocking began a school at home to supplement the education his children were receiving in the public schools. The venture, begun in New Haven and moved to Cambridge in 1914, was extended into a large-scale cooperative school and is now the Shady Hill School. During World War I he was an instructor in military engineering and visited the American and British fronts as an observer. He has been active in religious and social organizations. He was a member of the Commission on the Freedom of the Press and author of its report, published in 1947, in which he pointed out that freedom of the press brings with it a moral responsibility and does not mean the right to publish indiscriminately and irresponsibly. "The right to be in error in the pursuit of truth," he wrote, "does not include a moral right to be deliberately in error."

PRINCIPAL WORKS: The Meaning of God in Human Experience, 1912; Human Nature and Its Remaking, 1918; Morale and Its Enemies, 1918; Man and the State, 1926; Present Status of the Philosophy of Law and of Rights, 1926; The Self: Its Body and Freedom, 1928; Types of Philosophy, 1929; Spirit of World Politics, 1932; Lasting Elements of Individualism, 1937; Thoughts on Death and Life, 1937; Living Religions and a World Faith, 1940; What Man Can Make of Man, 1942; Science and the Idea of God, 1944; Freedom of the Press, 1947; Experiment in Education: What We Can Learn from Teaching Germany, 1954.

ABOUT: Burtt, E. A. Types of Religious Philosophy; Martin, J. A. Empirical Philosophies of Religion; Wach, J. Types of Religious Experience, Christian and Non-Christian; Werkmeister, W. H. A History of Philosophical Ideas in America; Time August 11, 1947, August 17, 1953.

HODGES, Mrs. BARBARA K. (WEBBER) ("Elizabeth Cambridge") (October 7, 1893-March 3, 1949). For biographical sketch and list of works and references, see TWENTIETH CENTURY AUTHORS, 1942.

* * *

Mrs. Barbara Hodges died at Westfield, near Battle, Sussex, England, at fifty-five. Her "sensitively observed novels of English village life" often reminded critics of Jane Austen. Forrest Reid called her "a realist of Jane Austen's school. She writes with restraint and good taste . . . of people whom in actual life one would like to know."

ABOUT: London Times ·March 4, 1949; New York Times March 4, 1949.

HODGSON, RALPH (1871-   ). For biographical sketch and list of earlier works and references, see TWENTIETH CENTURY AUTHORS, 1942.

* * *

Ralph Hodgson has lived for the past several years in Minerva, Ohio. He published two volumes of verse in the early 1940's (privately printed) and some of his poems appeared in the Saturday Review of Literature for March 22, 1947. In 1946 Hodgson received from the National Institute of Arts and Letters its second annual award of $1,000 for distinguished achievement. In 1954 he was awarded the Queen's Gold Medal for Poetry.

ADDITIONAL WORKS: Silver Wedding, and Other Poems, 1941; The Muse and the Mastiff (dramatic poem) 1942.

ABOUT: Publishers' Weekly May 11, 1946.

HOFFENSTEIN, SAMUEL (October 8, 1890-October 6, 1947). For biographical sketch and list of earlier works and references, see TWENTIETH CENTURY AUTHORS, 1942.

* * *

Samuel Hoffenstein died of a heart attack at his home in Los Angeles, Calif., two days before his fifty-seventh birthday.

Among the screenplays he wrote during his Hollywood career was that for Dreiser's *An American Tragedy*.

His style in the humorous verse for which he was best known was described by the *New Yorker* as "the surprise attack, the epigrammatic grimace, the seemingly inadvertent poetic doubletake." Eda Lou Walton spoke of his "versatile, accomplished and amusing wit in verse." The late William Rose Benét declared that "at his best he can be gorgeously biting, despite his leaning toward brittle wisecrackery."

ADDITIONAL WORKS: Treasury of Humorous Verse (includes works previously listed) 1946; Pencil in the Air (poems) 1947.

ABOUT: New York Times January 2, 1947.

*HOFMANNSTHAL, HUGO HOFMANN, Edler von (February 1, 1874-July 15, 1929).

For biographical sketch and list of works and references, see TWENTIETH CENTURY AUTHORS, 1942.

* * *

ADDITIONAL WORK IN ENGLISH TRANSLATION: Selected Prose, 1952.

ABOUT: Broch, H. *Introduction to* Selected Prose of Hugo von Hofmannsthal; Lange, V. Modern German Literature; Peacock, R. The Poet in the Theatre; Columbia Dictionary of Modern European Literature; Contemporary Review February 1949; Deutsche Rundschau July 1949.

* höf'mäns täl

HOGBEN, LANCELOT THOMAS (December 9, 1895-).

For autobiographical sketch and list of earlier works and references, see TWENTIETH CENTURY AUTHORS, 1942.

* * *

Lancelot Hogben has taught at the University of Birmingham since 1941, first as Mason Professor of Zoology and—since 1947—as professor of medical statistics. Hogben visited the United States in 1940 and again in 1950. A scholar and a scientist, he has nevertheless retained the light and popular touch in his writings. The most successful of his later books has been an illustrated history of 30,000 years of human visual communication, *From Cave Painting to Comic Strip*. Hogben provided the text for the book—"witty comments and personal crotchets which add immeasurably to the effectiveness of his presentation" (New York *Times*).

Like many scientists, however, Hogben does occasionally lose himself in abstruse scientific speculation. In one such moment, in 1952, he was arrested and accused of driving while drunk (his car had backed twice into another car). Hogben testified in his defense that he was so absent-minded that he forgot his own birthday and was confused by the gears on his car. His defense was amply supported, and he was acquitted, on the testimony of a university colleague, a professor of neurology, who said: "I've known Professor Hogben for many years. I know of no other man who is more likely to be mistaken for a drunken man when he is quite sober."

ADDITIONAL WORKS: Introduction to Mathematical Genetics, 1946; From Cave Painting to Comic Strip, 1949; Chance and Choice by the Cardpack and Chessboard: An Introduction to Probability, 1950.

ABOUT: Current Biography 1941; Newsweek March 17, 1952; New York Times Book Review July 9, 1950.

HOLBROOK, STEWART HALL (August 22, 1893-), American journalist and regionalist, writes: "I was born in Newport, Vt., of old-line Yan-

kee stock, attended public school there, rural school in Lemington, Vt., and Colebrook Academy in New Hampshire. Going to Winnipeg, Man., in 1911, I worked on a newspaper, played a little semi-pro baseball, and toured the Western provinces in one of the worst repertoire companies ever seen in places like Moose Jaw, Sask., and Medicine Hat, Alba. Returning to New England in 1914, I worked in a logging camp store and scaled timber at First Connecticut Lake, from where, in 1917, I went into an American field artillery regiment and so to France, where we were engaged in minor actions and in the Meuse-Argonne defensive. Within a week after my discharge in 1919, I was coming down the Connecticut River on the log-drive; and later that year returned to the woods in a camp bossed by the remarkable Jigger Jones, who appears in my first book. In January 1920 I went to Boston, bought a fine derby hat and a round-trip ticket to Vancouver, B.C. I sold the return half and went to logging in a camp up the Fraser River; and later in another camp far up the British Columbia coast. I began writing in camp, and several American editors gave me encouragement by buying my essays and articles. Then, in 1923, I quit the woods and went to Portland, Ore., which has been my home for most of the past thirty years. From Portland I ranged the entire Pacific Northwest as a reporter for the *Lumber News*, a trade magazine and newspaper. (I later became editor.) It was a lovely assignment, and while on it I covered many forest fires, logging camp and sawmill strikes, and several I.W.W. riots. In 1934 I resigned with the intention of writing for a living. I have done nothing else since, save for three summers during World War II when I was with the Division of Forestry of the State of Washington in forest fire work.

"For two years I lived in Cambridge, Mass., where I wrote a book and lectured on American historical subjects both at Harvard and at Boston Universities. I lived in New York City for a year, doing research for a book. Still another year was spent in Seattle. For the rest, Portland, where I continue to contribute to the *Oregonian*, has been my home. My wife, who was Sibyl Walker, of Walker, Ore., is a great-granddaughter of Oregon pioneers. We have no children. We live on one of Portland's West Side hills from where we can see a great deal of handsome country. My wife is a fine handweaver, and also does metal work. My only hobby, other than for reading American history, is painting pictures which friends have described as pretty bad. I find the art most relaxing. My wife and I visit New England and New York every other year.

"Hewitt H. Howland and Henry L. Mencken gave me early encouragement in magazine writing, but it was the late Harold Ross who sent me my first magazine check. It was for $5, but later, when he had the *New Yorker*, my checks were a little larger. Harold Latham, longtime chief editor for The Macmillan Company, urged me to write my first book. His firm published it and most of my other books. My only ambition as a writer is to put into books the figures and portions of American history that I think have been largely ignored, or badly treated. My sole distinction, of which I am very proud, was my election to the American Antiquarian Society."

PRINCIPAL WORKS: Holy Old Mackinaw, 1938; Iron Brew, 1939; Ethan Allen, 1940; Murder Out Yonder, 1941; Burning an Empire, America's Great Forest Fires, 1943; (ed.) Promised Land, Anthology of Northwest Writing, 1945; Lost Men of American History, 1946; The Story of American Railroads, 1947; The Yankee Exodus, 1950; Far Corner, A Personal View of the Pacific Northwest, 1952; The Age of the Moguls, 1953; James J. Hill, 1955.

ABOUT: Boston Herald May 26, 1940; Denver Post August 12, 1947; New York Herald Tribune Book Review June 25, 1950.

HOLDEN, RAYMOND PECKHAM (April 7, 1894-). For autobiographical sketch and list of earlier works and references, see TWENTIETH CENTURY AUTHORS, 1942.

* * *

Raymond Holden writes: "After twelve years with the Book-of-the-Month Club, first as editorial consultant and later as personnel director, I gave up all direct connection with the Club and moved to North Newport, N.H., where I now make my permanent home. My *Selected Poems* was published in 1946. I have just completed a new novel entitled 'Things Too Wonderful,' and am working on a project in poetry which should keep me busy for the rest of my life. It is an attempt to do, in somewhat different form, for the modern world and its central figure, man, what Lucretius did for the ancient world. I am also keeping a journal and, at present, am writing a new mystery novel.

"In 1949 I was married to Barbara Badmington, of North Newport. In November 1952 I was elected to the New Hampshire House of Representatives."

ADDITIONAL WORK: Selected Poems, 1946.

ABOUT: Saturday Review of Literature March 22, 1947.

"HOLLAND, KATRIN." See "ALBRAND, M."

HOLLIDAY, ROBERT CORTES (July 18, 1880-December 1, 1946). For autobiographical sketch and list of works and references, see TWENTIETH CENTURY AUTHORS, 1942.

* * *

Robert Cortes Holliday died at sixty-six, in a New York City hospital, of heart disease. He had lived at The Players Club until his death. His last piece of writing was a sketch of Booth Tarkington which appeared in the *Players' Bulletin*.

A. B. Douglas expressed a rather general critical reaction when he called Holliday's work "neither unique nor profound" but added that it gave him "quiet pleasure." The Boston *Transcript* observed that "he has captured the art of saying the forever unexpected. He rambles as freely through his pages as one might see him wandering about a city, with his stick upon his arm."

ABOUT: New York Times January 2, 1947.

HOLLOWAY, EMORY (March 16, 1885-). For autobiographical sketch and list of works and references, see TWENTIETH CENTURY AUTHORS, 1942.

* * *

Emory Holloway was chairman of the English department at Queens College in New York from 1937 to 1941 and is now professor emeritus. From 1943 to 1944 he was director of the Army Special Training Program unit in the college.

Beginning in 1940 Professor Holloway was an associate editor of *American Literature* for several years, and later a member of the advisory board. In 1952 he was elected honorary member of Phi Beta Kappa. In 1950 he received the first medal for distinguished service to Brooklyn presented by the Library Associates of Brooklyn College.

ADDITIONAL WORKS: (omitted in the 1942 edition) : The Uncollected Poetry and Prose of Walt Whitman (ed.) 1921; Whitman, W. Leaves of Grass, Inclusive Edition (ed.) 1924; Walt Whitman, Nonesuch Edition (ed.) 1938.

HOLME, CONSTANCE. For biographical sketch and list of works and references, see TWENTIETH CENTURY AUTHORS, 1942.

* * *

Constance Holme lives in the house where she was born and raised, Owlet Ash, in Minthorpe, Westmoreland. She has published nothing in recent years.

HOLMES, JOHN HAYNES (November 29, 1879-), American clergyman, writes: "I was born in the city of Philadelphia, Pa.

My parents were Boston people, and it was more or less of an accident that they were living in Philadelphia at the time when I chose to arrive in the world. In my third or fourth year the little family returned to Massachusetts, where all my life was spent up to the year 1907, when I came to New York.

Editta Sherman

"I was educated in the public schools of Malden, a suburb of Boston. I graduated from Harvard College, A.B. degree, *summa cum laude*, in 1902, and from the Harvard Divinity School, S.T.B. degree, in 1904. I was elected to Phi Beta Kappa in my junior year in college.

"I have had the pleasure through the years of receiving the following honorary degrees —from the Jewish Institute of Religion, N.Y., in May 1930, D.D.; from St. Lawrence University, Canton, N.Y., in June 1931, D.D.; from the Meadville Theological School, Chicago, in June 1945, D.D.; from Benares Hindu University, India, in December 1947, the degree of Doctor of Letters; and from Rollins College, Fla., in February 1951, the degree of Doctor of Humanities.

"I began my ministry in the Third Religious Society in Dorchester (Unitarian) in 1904, and remained in this church for three years. In November 1906 I was called into the ministry of the Church of the Messiah in New York, in succession to Minot J. Savage, and began my work in the following February, 1907. Twelve years later, in 1919, I withdrew from the Unitarian ministry, deciding to work henceforth as an independent, and reorganizing my church as a free society in contrast to a sectarian church, and at that time the name of the church was changed to The Community Church of New York. On my seventieth birthday, in 1949, I retired from the ministry of the church, and am now its minister emeritus.

"I married my wife, Madeleine H. Baker, on June 27, 1904. I have two children, Roger Wellington and Frances Adria, and four grandchildren.

"Thirty-five years ago I was one of a little group of men and women who founded the American Civil Liberties Union, which began its work in the midst of the first World War as the Anti-Preparedness Committee. I have served regularly as director of this organization down to my present period of service, and for ten years was chairman of the Board of Directors. In the same way, I was a member of a little group of men and women who, in 1909, founded the National Association for the Advancement of Colored People, and through all the years since this date, have served this organization as vice chairman.

"I was chairman of the City Affairs Committee of New York from 1929 to 1938, and in association with the co-chairman, Rabbi Stephen S. Wise, led the Committee's fight for the retirement of Mayor Walker, which was achieved in due course.

"I have lectured widely here at home, and traveled extensively abroad. I went to Palestine in 1929 on a special mission for the Zionists, and in recognition of this service was given the Annual Gottheil Medal in

1933. In the fall and early winter of 1947-48, under the auspices of the Watumull Foundation, of Los Angeles, I went to India as the Rabindranath Tagore Memorial Professor to Benares University, and traveled and lectured widely in India in a three months' visit to that country. On this occasion I renewed my long-standing friendship with Mahatma Gandhi, and met and talked with Prime Minister Nehru and other prominent Indian leaders."

* * *

In addition to his theological writings, Dr. Holmes collaborated on an anti-war play with Reginald Lawrence, *If This Be Treason*. The play, produced in New York by the Theatre Guild in 1935, concerned the activities of a president of the United States who averted war with Japan by making a direct personal appeal to the leaders of that country. Dr. Holmes has also written "warmly human and reverent" fictionized versions of some of the gospel tales, published in *The Second Christmas*.

PRINCIPAL WORKS: The Revolutionary Function of the Modern Church, 1912; Is Death the End? 1915; New Wars for Old, 1916; The Life and Letters of Robert Collyer, 1917; New Churches for Old, 1922; Patriotism Is Not Enough, 1925; Palestine Today and Tomorrow, 1929; If This Be Treason (with R. Lawrence) 1935; Rethinking Religion, 1938; Out of Darkness, 1942; The Second Christmas, and Other Stories, 1943; The Affirmation of Immortality, 1947; My Gandhi, 1953.

ABOUT: Jones, E. D. American Preachers of Today; Rusterholtz, W. P. American Heretics and Saints; Current Biography 1941; Newsweek February 24, 1947.

HOLTBY, WINIFRED (1898-September 25, 1935). For biographical sketch and list of works and references, see TWENTIETH CENTURY AUTHORS, 1942.

* * *

ABOUT: Gray, J. On Second Thought; Handley-Taylor, G. Winifred Holtby: Concise and Selected Bibliography; White, E. E. M. J. Winifred Holtby as I Knew Her.

HOOK, SIDNEY (December 20, 1902-   ), American philosopher and educator, was born in New York City, the son of Isaac and Jennie (Halpern) Hook. After graduating from the public schools in Brooklyn, he went to the City College of New York, studying under Morris R. Cohen. A brilliant student, he won the Ward Medal for Logic (1922), and at his graduation (B.S., 1923) the Certificate of Merit in philosophy. While teaching in the public schools (1923-28) he pursued his graduate studies at Columbia University,

from which he received an M.A. (1926) and a Ph.D. (1927). He was the winner (1926-27) of one of the coveted University fellowships, and the following year he went abroad on a Guggenheim research fellowship, studying at the Universities of Berlin and Munich, and also at the Marx-Engels Institute in Moscow.

Hook is now chairman of the philosophy department at Washington Square College, New York University, where he was first appointed as an instructor (1927), an assistant professor (1932), an associate professor and chairman of the department (1934), and a full professor (1939). In 1948 he was named head of the department of philosophy of the New York University Graduate School, and in 1949 chairman of the division of philosophy and psychology. He also lectures at the New School for Social Research (since 1931).

John Dewey was Hook's most esteemed teacher and mentor, and he has often been spoken of as his disciple. In his many books and articles, he uses the concepts of pragmatism and rigorous logical analysis to clarify and evaluate contemporary social, cultural, and political problems, and his subjects range from what makes a good teacher to what the philosophy of a militant democracy should be. Irwin Edman once spoke of his work as revealing "the consistent (though flexible) point of view of one of the most incisive and provocative minds in contemporary social philosophy."

His first book, *The Metaphysics of Pragmatism* (1927), written as a doctoral thesis while he was still studying under Dewey, is a brilliant analysis of the philosophical principles and world outlook of pragmatism. *Towards an Understanding of Karl Marx* appeared in 1933, and in 1936 *From Hegel to Marx*. About the former, Hook declared: "The challenge of Marx's ideas to our contemporary social order is so fundamental and pervasive that every intelligent person must now define his attitude towards them"; and the *Nation* called this book, "the most significant contribution to Marxism which has yet appeared in America." *From Hegel to Marx* presents the intellectual environment of the young Marx, traces the development of Marxism out of the philosophy of Hegel, and includes detailed accounts of other German thinkers also influenced by Hegel. *Reason, Social Myths and Democracy* (1940) is a collection of essays discussing various contemporary theories and problems, and again quoting Irwin Edman, "is a salutary contribution toward the turning of democracy into a vital rather than merely verbal ideal." *The Hero in History* (1943), which won for Hook Columbia's Butler Silver Medal, was reviewed by G. K. Morrow who wrote: "With the touting of the role of the leader by contemporary fascists, and the corresponding extravagant claims made for impersonal social forces by Marxist dogma . . . it is refreshing indeed to read such a sober and sensible appraisal of the hero's role as Professor Hook gives us in this book."

Several generations of students have testified to Hook's effectiveness as a teacher: he uses his own version of the Socratic method and is a past master of the classroom techniques of argument and discussion. As he puts it in *Education For Modern Man* (1946), "The secret of intellectual vitality in the classroom . . . consists in getting the students to reach the familiar conclusion with a sense of having made their own discovery."

Believing as he does that a philosopher should be an active participant in contemporary movements, Hook is not only an educator and author, but also an organizer and leader of such groups as the Committee for Cultural Freedom; Conference on Methods in Philosophy and Science; Conference on Scientific Spirit and Democratic Faith; as well as an active member of the American Philosophical Society, the American Association of University Professors, the International Committee for Academic Freedom, and the John Dewey Society.

Hook has three children, the eldest, John Bertrand, by a first marriage to Carrie Katz (1924), and the two younger, Ernest Benjamin, and Susan Ann, by a second marriage to Ann Zinken (1935). The Hooks, who live in Brooklyn, have a summer home in New England and when they can, they "disappear," as the *Saturday Evening Post* has put it, "into a wild part of Vermont."

PRINCIPAL WORKS: The Metaphysics of Pragmatism, 1927; Towards the Understanding of Karl Marx, 1933; American Philosophy Today and Tomorrow (ed. with H. Kallen) 1935; From Hegel to Marx, 1936; Planned Society—Yesterday, Today, Tomorrow, 1937; John Dewey: An Intellectual Portrait, 1939; Reason, Social Myths and Democracy, 1940; The Hero in History, 1943; Education for Modern Man, 1946; Heresy, Yes—Conspiracy, No!, 1953.

ABOUT: Current Biography 1952.

HOOTON, EARNEST ALBERT (November 20, 1887-May 3, 1954). For biographical sketch and list of earlier works and references, see TWENTIETH CENTURY AUTHORS, 1942.

* * *

Earnest Hooton died in Cambridge, Mass., of a heart attack, at the age of sixty-six, just after returning home from two classroom lectures. He had spent his last years studying and making comparisons of Harvard generations for the purpose of determining whether changes in the physique were the result of better nutrition or simply of cyclical trends, independent of environment. During World War II Hooton was a consultant to the Quartermaster and Medical Corps of the U.S. Army and he was subsequently consulted from time to time on problems involving the human physique.

Hooton's writings never failed to stir up lively controversy. He was called "Harvard's scientific *enfant terrible.*" His gloomy predictions about the future of the human race ("Gadgets and machines are getting better and better while man is getting worse and worse"), his advocacy of human sterilization and state-supervised breeding, made headlines and made him the best-known of American anthropologists. But the value of his research in anthropology was solid and enduring, and it was to his credit as an educational administrator that Harvard's department of anthropology became "one of the best in the world."

At the time of his death Hooton's "Physical Anthropology of the Irish," a report on Harvard's expedition to Ireland in the 1930's, was in process of publication.

ADDITIONAL WORKS: Man's Poor Relations, 1942; Young Man, You Are Normal, 1945.

ABOUT: Life February 11, 1946; New York Times May 4, 1954.

"HOPE, ANTHONY." See HAWKINS, A. H.

HOPE, LAURENCE (April 9, 1865-October 4, 1904). For biographical sketch and list of works and references, see TWENTIETH CENTURY AUTHORS, 1942.

* * *

ABOUT: Coronet September 1951; Saturday Review of Literature November 15, 1941.

"HOPLEY, GEORGE." See WOOLRICH, C.

457

HORGAN, PAUL (August 1, 1903-   ).
For autobiographical sketch and list of
earlier works and references, see TWEN-
TIETH CENTURY AUTHORS, 1942.

* * *

Paul Horgan served in the Army as officer of the Army Information Branch in the
War Department, rising to the rank of lieutenant colonel, from 1942 to 1946. He was
awarded the Legion of Merit.

In 1946 he lectured at the University of
Iowa in the Graduate School of Letters. He
was a Guggenheim Fellow in literature from
1947 to 1948. Also during this period and
until 1950, when he resigned to devote full
time to writing, he was assistant to the president of the New Mexico Military Institute.

Horgan has contributed stories to *Collier's,
Saturday Evening Post, Cosmopolitan, Good
Housekeeping*, and other journals, and his
work has appeared in several anthologies including the O'Brien and the Foley "Best
Short Story" collections. *The Devil in the
Desert*, a long short story about a priest in
the Rio Grande country, was a simple and
moving tale, "beautifully told and innocent
of sentimentalizing" (to quote Virginia
Kirkus).

In 1954 he published his two-volume history of the Rio Grande, on which he had
worked for some thirteen years. The book,
Great River, was praised for its literary excellence as well as for its extensive scholarship. It received both the Pulitzer and the
Bancroft prizes for history in 1955. A "labor
of love," the book, as one reviewer put it,
"fuses the imagination of a good novelist
with a remarkable sense of a region's character." Horgan lives in Roswell, N.M.

ADDITIONAL WORKS: The Common Heart, 1942;
The Devil in the Desert, 1952; One Red Rose for
Christmas, 1952; Great River: The Rio Grande (2
vols.) 1954.

ABOUT: Hoehn, M. (ed.) Catholic Authors, I;
Mahony, B. Illustrators of Children's Books; New
York Herald Tribune Book Review October 24,
1954; Publishers' Weekly July 3, 1954; Saturday
Review October 16, 1954; Scholastic March 29,
1943.

HORN, ALFRED ALOYSIUS ("Trader"
Horn) (1861?-June 26, 1931). For biographical sketch and list of works and
references, see TWENTIETH CENTURY
AUTHORS, 1942.

* * *

ABOUT: Scully, F. Rogues' Gallery

HORN, "TRADER." See HORN, A. A.

HORNADAY, WILLIAM TEMPLE
(December 1, 1854-March 6, 1937). For
autobiographical sketch and list of works
and references, see TWENTIETH CEN-
TURY AUTHORS, 1942.

* * *

ABOUT: Hobbies December 1943, July 1944;
Nature November 1943.

HORNEY, KAREN (DANIELSEN)
(September 16, 1885-December 4, 1952),
German-American psychoanalyst and author,
was born in Ham-
burg, Germany, the
daughter of Berndt
Danielsen, a Nor-
wegian captain, and
Clothilde von Ronze-
len, of Dutch-German
origin. After studying
medicine in Freiburg,
Goettingen, and Ber-
lin, she obtained her
medical license in

1913. Between 1913 and 1915 she studied
with Dr. Karl Abraham, well-known pupil of
Freud. After serving her psychiatric intern-
ship in Berlin, she taught at the Institute for
Psychoanalysis, Berlin, and also practiced
psychoanalysis in that city. Dr. Horney was
active in international psychoanalytic conferences and was one of the participants in the
discussion on lay analysis conducted by Dr.
Freud. In 1932 she came to the United
States, where she was naturalized in 1938.
At first associate director at the Institute for
Psychoanalysis in Chicago, she became an
instructor at the Institute for Psychoanalysis
in New York (1934 to 1941), and from 1935
until her death also taught at the New School
for Social Research.

In 1941 the Association for the Advancement of Psychoanalysis was formed, after a
meeting of the New York Psychoanalytic Institute had disqualified Dr. Horney as training analyst and instructor. No special reason
was given, and it was estimated that almost
fifty per cent of the members present re-
frained from voting. One of the first steps
taken by the newly formed group was to
establish a training center, the American Institute for Psychoanalysis, of which Dr. Horney was elected dean. The Association was
designed so that no one individual's or
group's theories could control it.

A colleague, Dr. Frederik Weiss, has given
a short evaluation of her work which Dr.
Horney found accurate and pertinent. "Starting from a critical evaluation of Freud,"

wrote Weiss, "Karen Horney developed the psychoanalytical theory and therapy in a more constructive spirit. In contrast to Freud's emphasis on instinct and genesis, Dr. Horney stresses the intra-psychic and intra-human elements. She includes biological, social and cultural factors into the total picture of an autonomous and harmonious personality, with the emphasis not on negative and dangerous aggression toward self and others, but on the positive constructive drive towards self-realization." Her first book, *The Neurotic Personality of Our Time* (1937), was highly influential, and achieved considerable popularity, though reviewers were chary if not unenthusiastic. The book departed from Freud in stressing that human beings are essentially constructive, that they want happiness, want to develop, to unfold. *Self-Analysis*, published in 1942, was similarly influential. This book, while emphasizing that "severe neuroses belong in the hands of experts," offered some suggestions on self-analysis and the diagnosis of neurotic patterns. Heartily welcomed by the general reader, the volume received the usual severe strictures from professional critics, such as Lionel Trilling, who felt the author made "a weak case for her belief," or J. F. Brown, who suggested in the *New Republic* that Dr. Horney return to her "excellent technical psychoanalytic studies of feminine sexuality," and leave these "semi-popular books" of propagandizing. Her criticisms of Freud awakened strong opposition. Her last book was *Neurosis and Human Growth* which appeared in 1950. Called "an important and constructive document" by Martin Gumpert in the New York *Times,* it further developed her theory that cultural conditions were, in the last analysis, what determined the particular form of neuroses.

Of medium height, she had light brown eyes set wide apart, prominent cheekbones and a high forehead. On the lecture platform she was completely informal. Evelyn Seeley described her in 1940: "Dr. Horney is white-haired, vital, strong and direct in appearance and manner. There is a trace of German in her speech." A resident since 1934 of New York City, Karen Horney died there at the age of sixty-seven, in 1952, after an illness of two and one-half weeks. She was survived by her husband, Dr. Oscar Horney, whom she married in 1909, by three daughters, and by five grandchildren. Her daughters are Dr. Marianne von Eckardt, a psychoanalyst in Washington, D.C., Mrs. Renate Crevanna of Mexico, and Mrs.

Brigitte Tschetwerikoff, once a German actress.

PRINCIPAL WORKS: The Neurotic Personality of Our Time, 1937; New Ways in Psychoanalysis, 1939; Self-Analysis, 1942; Our Inner Conflicts, 1945; (ed.) Are You Considering Psychoanalysis? 1946; Neurosis and Human Growth, 1950.

ABOUT: American Medical Association Journal February 14, 1953; Current Biography 1941, 1953; Lancet December 20, 1952; New York Times December 5, 1952.

HORNUNG, ERNEST WILLIAM (1866-March 22, 1921). For biographical sketch and list of works and references, see TWENTIETH CENTURY AUTHORS, 1942.

* * *

ABOUT: Dictionary of Australian Biography; Orwell, G. Dickens, Dali and Others.

*HORVÁTH, ODÖN VON (1901-June 1938). For biographical sketch and list of works and references, see TWENTIETH CENTURY AUTHORS, 1942.

* hör′vät

HOTSON, JOHN LESLIE (August 16, 1897-   ), Elizabethan scholar, was born in Delhi, Ont., Canada, the son of John H. Hotson and Lillie S. Hotson. He attended Harvard, and took his B.A. in 1921, his M.A. in 1922, and his Ph.D. in 1923. During the summers of 1922 and 1925 he was a Dexter Traveling Scholar, and in 1923-24 a Sheldon Traveling Fellow. He began  his teaching career at Harvard as instructor in 1924-25; was an assistant in English (1925-26) and Sterling senior research fellow (1926-27) at Yale; and from 1927 to 1929 an associate professor of English at New York University. In 1929 he won a Guggenheim fellowship which continued until 1931. He then began teaching, as professor of English, at Haverford College, Pa. (1931-42). Hotson was the Folger Shakespeare Memorial lecturer in 1940 and 1944-46. Between 1943 and 1946 he served as 1st lieutenant and captain in the Signal Corps of the U.S. Army. A Fulbright exchange scholar at Bedford College, London, 1949-50, he was in 1953 a research associate at Yale. In 1954 he was elected a regular Fellow of King's College, Cambridge.

Hotson's first book, *The Death of Christopher Marlowe* (1925), presented new facts on the subject and brought him quickly to the attention of readers and scholars. Of his second, *The Commonwealth and Restoration Stage* (1928), the New York *Herald Tribune Book Review* said, "From his months of research in the London archives, Dr. Hotson has brought back, if nothing of such sensational interest as the discovery of the circumstances of Marlowe's death, which won him his first wide reputation, at any rate a rich harvest of new facts, not only patiently assembled but well digested. In the light of this evidence all the general histories of the 'Restoration Stage' must to a greater or less degree be rewritten." *Theatre Arts* spoke of "that amazing figure, the modern scholar. Let it be said at once that Mr. Hotson exemplifies the outstanding virtues of his class . . . [he is] able to string together a perfect maze of documentary evidence into clear, eminently readable chapters." "He is lively without jauntiness or any sort of affectation," stated the (London) *Times Literary Supplement*.

Other favorably reviewed books have followed. In *Shakespeare's Motley* Hotson discussed Shakespeare's use of the fool as a character, beginning by uncovering the exact meaning of "motley," usually misunderstood, and ending with a sketch of the life of Robert Armin, the actor who played the motley's parts. "Leslie Hotson is a scholar-detective," wrote the *Saturday Review of Literature*, "with a rare gift of writing with clarity, suspense, and informality." Hotson received the 1954 Modern Language Association-Macmillan Award for the manuscript of his book, *The First Night of Twelfth Night*.

Besides his original books, Hotson has edited Shelley's *Lost Letters to Harriet* (1930) and *Queen Elizabeth's Entertainment at Mitcham* (1953), which is attributed to John Lyly. Hotson's name is sometimes listed simply as Leslie Hotson. He married Mary May Peabody in 1919, and they live in Connecticut. His recreation is boating.

PRINCIPAL WORKS: The Death of Christopher Marlowe, 1925; The Commonwealth and Restoration Stage, 1928; Shakespeare Versus Shallow, 1931; I, William Shakespeare, 1937; Shakespeare's Sonnets Dated, and Other Essays, 1949; Shakespeare's Motley, 1952; The First Night of *Twelfth Night*, 1954.

ABOUT: Altick, R. The Scholar Adventurers.

*HOUGH, EMERSON (June 28, 1857-April 30, 1923). For biographical sketch and list of works and references, see TWENTIETH CENTURY AUTHORS, 1942.

* hŭf

460

HOUGH, HENRY BEETLE (November 8, 1896-), American author and editor, writes: "In New Bedford, Mass., when I was born there, there were still many whaleships fitting at the wharves, and the sight of them and the tiers of oil casks runs back among my earliest memories. New Bedford was then a city of some 60,000 inhabitants and at the turn of the century swept  into a period of great prosperity as the leading center of manufacture for fine cotton goods.

"When I entered the public school, the population was 90,000, and by the time I left high school it was 125,000. But by then the mills had already begun to go south; the great expansion was over, with stalemate and decline taking its place. The last whaleship had also sailed and been lost.

"Such a yeasting, turbulent period was the background of my youth. My maternal grandfather, Captain Henry W. Beetle, for whom I was named, had been a whaling captain on long Pacific voyages. My father was a newspaperman, destined to be for many decades editor of the New Bedford *Standard*.

"In 1914 I entered the School of Journalism at Columbia University, then a four year course, and was graduated in 1918 while serving as a yeoman in the Naval Reserve Force, assigned to the Office of Naval Intelligence at Washington. My first job after the war was doing publicity for the Institute of American Meat Packers in Chicago where I stayed a year.

"In 1920 I married Elizabeth Wilson Bowie; we had met at the School of Journalism. That June we became owners, editors and publishers of the *Vineyard Gazette*, a weekly newspaper published since 1846 at Edgartown on the island of Martha's Vineyard. Thirty-two years later we are still at it. During one interlude of absenteeism, I was in charge of newspaper publicity for the Western Electric Company in New York City.

"A medal for excellence was awarded to me by Columbia University in 1942; half or more of it should have gone to my wife.

"In Edgartown I served for eighteen years as a member of the school committee, for some years as president of the Dukes County Historical Society, and in various community activities. My wife and I like to grow roses

—they flourish on Martha's Vineyard—and I am a member of the American Rose Society."

PRINCIPAL WORKS: Martha's Vineyard, Summer Resort, 1936; Country Editor, 1940; That Lofty Sky, 1941; All Things Are Yours, 1942; Roosters Crow in Town, 1945; Long Anchorage, 1947; Once More the Thunderer, 1950; Singing in the Morning (essays) 1951; Whaling Wives (with E. M. Whiting) 1953; An Alcoholic to his Sons (as told to H. B. Hough) 1954.

ABOUT: Hough, H. B. Country Editor; Hough, H. B. Once More the Thunderer; Christian Science Monitor Magazine June 28, 1941; New York Herald Tribune Book Review December 3, 1950.

"HOUGHTON, CLAUDE." See OLD-FIELD, C. H.

HOUGHTON, WILLIAM STANLEY (February 22, 1881-December 11, 1913). For biographical sketch and list of works and references, see TWENTIETH CENTURY AUTHORS, 1942.

HOULT, NORAH (September 20, 1898-). For autobiographical sketch and list of earlier works and references, see TWENTIETH CENTURY AUTHORS, 1942.

* * *

Norah Hoult sends the following corrections to her 1942 sketch: "The date of my birth is September 20, 1898, not 1901. I have been married, but my marriage was dissolved. I am certainly *not* strikingly handsome, and my hair is not smooth and dark, but brown and curly, if of any interest.

"I am anti-feminist rather than feminist in my views, since I believe that feminism has done, on the whole, more harm than good to the true welfare of women. Nor as an artist am I 'against superstition and fanaticism' which exaggerations are grist to the mill! Only two books of mine are concerned with Dublin life, *Holy Ireland* and *Coming From the Fair*."

Only one of Miss Hoult's novels has been published in the United States since 1942, *There Were No Windows*, a skillful character study of an old woman in the terrible days of the London blitz. More than one reviewer described the book as a tour de force, suspenseful, almost terrifying, and brilliantly sustained.

ADDITIONAL WORKS: Augusta Steps Out, 1942; Scene for Death, 1943; House Under Mars, 1946; There Were No Windows, 1947; Farewell Happy Fields, 1948; Cocktail Bar (short stories) 1950; Frozen Ground, 1952; Sister Mavis, 1953.

ABOUT: Wilson Library Bulletin December 1941.

HOUSE, JAY ELMER (April 3, 1872-January 5, 1936). For biographical sketch and list of works and references, see TWENTIETH CENTURY AUTHORS, 1942.

HOUSEHOLD, GEOFFREY (November 30, 1900-). For biographical sketch and list of works and references, see TWENTIETH CENTURY AUTHORS, 1942.

* * *

During World War II Geoffrey Household was a British intelligence officer in the Levant. He now lives in London but lists "the Mediterranean" as his hobby in *Who's Who*. In 1942 he married Ilona M. J. Zsoldos-Gutman (his second marriage) and they have two children. Household continues to write his romantic novels about spying and international intrigue. None of his later volumes has had the popular acclaim of *Rogue Male*, but they have all been suave, professionally-written, and diverting fiction.

Correction: Household's birthdate of 1903, given in TWENTIETH CENTURY AUTHORS, 1942, was incorrect.

ADDITIONAL WORKS: Arabesque, 1948; The High Place, 1950; A Rough Shoot, 1951; A Time to Kill, 1951; Fellow Passenger, 1955.

ABOUT: Saturday Evening Post August 28, 1948.

HOUSMAN, ALFRED EDWARD (March 26, 1859-May 1, 1936). For biographical sketch and list of works and references, see TWENTIETH CENTURY AUTHORS, 1942.

* * *

ADDITIONAL WORK: Manuscript Poems (ed. T. B. Haber) 1955.

ABOUT: Brooks, C. in Kenyon Critics (1951); Connolly, C. The Condemned Playground; Dictionary of National Biography 1931-40; Robb, N. A. Four in Exile; Robinson, A. Angry Dust: The Poetry of A. E. Housman; Tinker, C. B. Essays in Retrospect; Wilson, E. The Triple Thinkers; Withers, P. The Buried Life; America August 31, 1946; Atlantic Monthly July 1946; Saturday Review of Literature February 2, February 23, 1946; Time April 1, 1946; Times Literary Supplement April 29, 1955.

HOUSMAN, LAURENCE (July 18, 1865-). For autobiographical sketch and list of earlier works and references, see TWENTIETH CENTURY AUTHORS, 1942.

* * *

With irrepressible good spirits and what the London *Times Literary Supplement* calls "his engaging and enviable innocence," Laurence Housman continues to write his plays, poems, and romantic tales and fantasies. At eighty he wrote, in the preface to *Back Words and Fore Words,* a selection of his works: "In my fifty years of authorship, I have written more books than I should have done had I given more time to second thoughts; or, at any rate, they would have contained less matter, better expressed." But at eighty-five and more he was still busily at work, with no sign of a lessening enthusiasm. Housman lives in the town of Street, in Somerset, England.

ADDITIONAL WORKS: The Preparation of Peace (essays) 1941; Palestine Plays, 1943; (with C. H. K. Marten) The Long Journey (bks. II-IV) 1943; Samuel, the King-Maker (play) 1944; Happy and Glorious, 1945; Back Words and Fore Words, 1945; Cynthia: An English Pastoral in Verse, 1947; Strange Ends and Discoveries (stories) 1948; Family Honour (play) 1950; The Kind and the Foolish (stories) 1952.

ABOUT: Mahony, B. (ed.) Illustrators of Children's Books; Publishers' Weekly October 4, 1947.

HOWARD, JOHN TASKER (November 30, 1890-), American biographer and specialist in American music, writes: "I was

born in Brooklyn, N.Y., and at the age of twelve moved with my family to New Jersey, where I have lived ever since. I started my musical education with private teachers at an early age, with no thought of making music my profession. I had my academic education at Williams College and then entered business. My interest in music continued and in my spare time I studied composition. After several of my compositions had been accepted by publishers I decided to give all of my time to music and joined the staff of a music magazine, the *Musician,* of which I later became managing editor. From this position I went to the Ampico Corporation, of which I was educational director for five years. In 1928 I became a free lance and devoted several years to writing my first book, *Our American Music.* This was published in 1931, and has been revised and brought up-to-date three times. In connection with the research for this book I became interested in the life of Stephen Foster and with the help of the Foster Hall Collection established in Indianapolis by the late Josiah K. Lilly I wrote a full-length biography called *Stephen Foster, America's Troubadour.*

"The following years were devoted to writing further books, composing music, lecturing, acting as commentator on radio music programs, and as a consultant on musical matters for book publishers, copyright lawyers, etc. In 1940 I was invited to join the staff of the New York Public Library, where I spend part of my time as Curator of the Americana Music Collection. As a specialist in American music I attempt to answer specialized questions on our native music, and to help those who are conducting research into our nation's music history. I also conduct a course in American music at the School of General Studies, Columbia University.

"One of my greatest interests is the American Society of Composers, Authors and Publishers (ASCAP) of which I have been a member since 1926 and a director since 1945. It is a privilege to have a part in protecting the rights of fellow composers and to help them gain a just financial return from the public performance of their works.

"I have been married to the same wife for nearly thirty-seven years and hope we shall both see our diamond anniversary. We have two married daughters and two grandchildren. For the past twelve years I have cultivated the hobby of oil painting, and have had a number of my pictures in exhibits and a couple of one-man shows. Recently my amateur standing has been threatened by the sale of several paintings."

PRINCIPAL WORKS: Our American Music, 1931; Stephen Foster, America's Troubadour, 1934; Ethelbert Nevin, 1935; Our Contemporary Composers (with A. Mendel) 1941; This Modern Music, 1942, A Treasury of Stephen Foster, 1946; The World's Great Operas, 1948.

ABOUT: Howard, J. T. Our American Music 3d ed., rev.) ; New York World-Telegram November 4-6, 1946.

HOWARD, JOSEPH KINSEY (1906-August 25, 1951), American regionalist, was born in Iowa and moved with his family to Montana when he was a boy. Later the family lived in Saskatchewan for several years. After his parents brought him back to Montana, Howard entered Great Falls High School. He became, first, society editor of the Great Falls *Leader,* then reporter, and in time news editor, in which capacity he led a long struggle with the wealthy interests which he considered to be despoiling Montana's natural resources.

Montana—High, Wide and Handsome, published in 1943, drew favorable reviews from many leading critics. The book was a well-documented attack on the copper, railroad, and cattle interests. He was not easy on the Montanans themselves in dealing out blame for soil erosion, "the fenced deserts in which trapped tumbleweed spun and raced nowhere all day." "Superior history . . . by an indigenous editor who understands ecology, as well as gun-play, and who is tearing mad about what a mistaken land policy, monopoly practices, dust storms, and two wars have done to his native earth," commented the *New Yorker.*

Howard was greatly interested in rural community conditions in Montana, and when the Rockefeller Foundation financed what was called "the Montana study," he was named assistant and later became director of the survey. Editor of an anthology of Montana writing called *Montana Margins,* he was at work on a story of the rebellion of the Red River Indians in Canada at the time of his death. *Strange Empire,* published posthumously in 1952, was "vivid and absorbing," according to a typical critical remark. The book describes one of the crucial struggles in the long war for the West, a significant history, written with ardor and skill.

Howard presided at the Writers Conference sponsored by the University of Montana, and was director of a Montana University project "The Round-Up of the Arts," an annual musical, artistic and literary festival.

On August 25, 1951, Joseph Kinsey Howard died after a heart attack, at the age of forty-five. He was survived by his mother, Mrs. Josephine K. Howard, with whom he had made his home. He was unmarried.

PRINCIPAL WORKS: Montana—High, Wide and Handsome, 1943; (ed.) Montana Margins, 1946; Strange Empire, 1952.

ABOUT: New York Times August 27, 1951; Time September 3, 1951.

HOWARD, SIDNEY COE (June 26, 1891-August 23, 1939). For biographical sketch and list of works and references, see TWENTIETH CENTURY AUTHORS, 1942.

* * *

Sidney Howard's last play, *Madam, Will You Walk,* scheduled for a Broadway production in 1939 which never came off, was produced in New York in December 1953 by a newly-formed repertory company, at the Phoenix Theatre. The story of a visit by the devil to the modern world, described as "a light philosophic fantasy," it was praised by the critics, although they were generally agreed that it was not destined for commercial success in the theatre.

ABOUT: Clark, B. H. Intimate Portraits; Krutch, J. W. *in* Zabel, M. D. (ed.) Literary Criticism in America (1951); Morris, L. Postscript to Yesterday.

HOWE, EDGAR WATSON (May 3, 1853-October 3, 1937). For biographical sketch and list of works and references, see TWENTIETH CENTURY AUTHORS, 1942.

* * *

ABOUT: Banta, R. E. Indiana Authors and Their Books; Saturday Evening Post October 25, 1941.

HOWE, HELEN HUNTINGTON (January 11, 1905-), American novelist and monologist, writes: "I was born in Boston. I attended private schools in and near Boston, went one year to Radcliffe College, spent a winter studying in Paris (where I studied under one of the actors of the Vieux Colombier theatre), taught for a winter in a small private school in Bos-  ton before I became convinced that I wanted to act. I went to New York, to study at the Theatre Guild School. It was there that the idea germinated which led me into writing, as well as performing my own character sketches. Beginning, without benefit of manager, at private parties for a modest fee, a career began to snowball which led me for the next fifteen years all over the United States. I appeared in my one-woman show before countless clubs, colleges, town halls, and civic organizations. I was twice invited to appear at the White House, gave recitals in several New York theatres, appeared for two seasons at the Blue Angel nightclub, and in 1936 gave recitals in London at the Arts Theatre and the Mercury Theatre. It was not until 1943 that my first novel, *The Whole Heart,* was published. I was so doubtful about trying my hand at all at this new medium that this first book is actually no more than four glorified character sketches—telling the story of a man's life in the words of four women who loved him.

John Erwin

"In 1946 my next novel, *We Happy Few*, was published, and in 1950 *The Circle of the Day*.

"In 1946 I married Reginald Allen who is assistant manager of the Metropolitan Opera Association. I cannot go so far as to say that I have given up my monologue recitals forever, but I do know that until my next novel is published I cannot think of any other profession than writing!"

* * *

Helen Howe comes of a distinguished literary family. She is the daughter of Mark A. De Wolfe Howe, author and editor of more than forty books, and Fanny Huntington (Quincy) Howe, an essayist. Her brothers are Quincy Howe, author and radio commentator, and Mark De Wolfe Howe, professor at Harvard Law School and editor of the *Holmes-Laski Letters*. In her own right Miss Howe is regarded as one of the more brightly promising of contemporary women novelists. She writes with humor and penetration of the Eastern society which she knows so well, with a "gift of satire and mimicry" which she developed and cultivated in her career as a monologist.

PRINCIPAL WORKS: The Whole Heart, 1943; We Happy Few, 1946; The Circle of the Day, 1950.

ABOUT: Riesman, D. Individualism Reconsidered; Current Biography 1954; New York Herald Tribune Book Review June 4, 1950; New York Times Book Review June 4, 1950; Saturday Review of Literature October 16, 1943.

HOWE, IRVING (1920-   ), American critic and biographer, writes: "I was born in New York City in 1920. My parents were

Jewish immigrants and now, in retrospect, I can see how important this was to my life. It meant, on the one hand, a home atmosphere of warm and binding love, and it meant, on the other hand, an atmosphere of striving, of struggle to appropriate those goods of American life which to others come almost automatically. On the whole, I suppose, the advantage was mine, since it was more important to inherit a valuable tradition and style of life, no matter how much I was later to deviate from it, than to receive a well-stocked but unread library.

"The great event of my childhood came when, during the depression years, my father lost his little grocery business and we were plunged into severe poverty. It was this which turned me to the world of books and ideas, which pulled me out of the unreflective routine of ordinary childhood. From the cast of seriousness that was then thrown over me I have been unable to escape, nor do I wish to. During the years of my early adolescence, I read an immense amount of poetry, certainly more than I ever have since; and at the same time, like so many other youngsters of my generation, I became interested in politics, developing a sympathy for socialism. Since then I have been a socialist, though in the course of years my conception of socialism has gradually been modulated and complicated. For a good part of my teens I was active in the various socialist youth groups, and unlike a good many of my contemporaries I feel no regret; never having succumbed to the falsities of Stalinism I have not had to fall into another extreme as a gesture of extenuation.

"From 1936 to 1940 I attended the City College of New York where the atmosphere was intense and stimulating; my formal education was ragged but I learned many things there which few college students ever do. I then took a half year of graduate work in English at Brooklyn College, but found the routine of graduate study appalling and quit. Though the lack of graduate work and degrees has perhaps been a professional handicap, I cannot regret this decision.

"During the war I served three and a half years in the army, one and a half of them in Alaska. There, in frozen isolation, I did an immense amount of serious reading in fields I never expect to touch again, unless some unhappy shift of events thrusts me once more into such a situation; it was graduate school, modern style.

"I began writing seriously after my discharge from the army. The editors of *Partisan Review* and *Commentary* were the first to print and encourage me.

"My work has fallen into two fields: social history and literary criticism. I have tried to strike a balance between the social and the literary; to fructify one with the other; yet not to confuse one with the other. Though I believe in the social approach to literature, it seems to me peculiarly open to misuse; it requires particular delicacy and care.

"I am married, have one child a year old [1952], and another due in early 1953. My wife is a classicist and archeologist. We try to reinforce each other in our intellectual interests, even though we start pretty much at the opposite poles of history.

"I have taught, not as a regular staff member but as a guest, at the University of Vermont and the University of Washington. I have been appointed a Fellow at the School of Letters, a graduate school in English at the University of Indiana." [In 1954 Howe became associate professor of English at Brandeis University, in Waltham, Mass.]

PRINCIPAL WORKS: The UAW and Walter Reuther (with B. J. Widick) 1949; Sherwood Anderson (American Men of Letters series) 1951; William Faulkner, 1952; A Treasury of Yiddish Stories (ed. with E. Greenberg) 1954.

ABOUT: New York Times Book Review July 20, 1952.

HOWE, MARK ANTONY DE WOLFE
(August 28, 1864-). For biographical sketch and list of earlier works and references, see TWENTIETH CENTURY AUTHORS, 1942.

* * *

The senior member of the distinguished Howe family (which includes the editor-lawyer Mark De Wolfe Howe, the radio commentator and historian Quincy Howe, and novelist Helen Howe) continues to record New England history in his scholarly and thoroughly entertaining books. Howe has been called "New England's best-known biographer." Arthur Stanwood Pier wrote of him in the *Atlantic*: "For his success as a writer of biography he laid the foundation by what he terms his steam-shovel qualities, his persistence and thoroughness in excavating significant facts from masses of documents and letters. But to the grubbing industry of the antiquarian were added the poet's imaginative insight and the artist's skill in rounding out and lighting the portrait." One of the most popular of Howe's later books is *Who Lived Here?*, a collection of photographs of famous old New England houses (by Samuel Chamberlain) with a richly informative text by Howe.

Howe lives in Boston. In recent years he has received honorary degrees from Northeastern University (1947) and Brown University (1951).

ADDITIONAL WORKS: A Tale of Tanglewood: Scene of the Berkshire Music Festivals, 1946; Boston Landmarks (with S. Chamberlain) 1946; (ed.) The Articulate Sisters: Passages from the Journals and Letters of the Daughters of President Quincy of Harvard, 1946; Who Lived Here? (with S. Chamberlain) 1952; (ed. with G. W. Cottrell, Jr.) The Scholar-Friends: Letters of Francis James Child and James Russell Lowell, 1952.

ABOUT: Atlantic Monthly April 1950.

HUBBARD, ELBERT ("Fra Elbertus") (June 19, 1856-May 7, 1915). For biographical sketch and list of works and references, see TWENTIETH CENTURY AUTHORS, 1942.

* * *

ABOUT: Rotarian April 1948; South Atlantic Quarterly July 1951.

HUBBARD, FRANK McKINNEY ("Kin Hubbard," "Abe Martin") (1868-December 26, 1930). For biographical sketch and list of works and references, see TWENTIETH CENTURY AUTHORS, 1942.

* * *

ABOUT: Kelly, Fred C. The Life and Times of Kin Hubbard; Reader's Digest September 1951; Saturday Review of Literature June 24, 1944.

*HUCH, Frau RICARDA OCTAVIA (July 18, 1864-November 17, 1947). For biographical sketch and list of works and references, see TWENTIETH CENTURY AUTHORS, 1942.

* * *

Ricarda Huch died, at eighty-three, while on a visit to relatives at Frankfort-on-the-Main. Her home was at Jena.

Remaining in Germany throughout World War II, she secretly collected material for a book on the anti-Nazi underground movement while pretending to carry on historical research. She was able to complete only the first part of this work, dealing with the revolt of the Munich students, before her death.

Frau Huch has been called Germany's "undisputed leading woman writer" of her time by Herman Boeschenstein, who describes her work as "the combining of a true epic style with the ability to discern, in a welter of conflicts and opposites, the lasting values of beauty and love." C. M. Richman placed her "among the small band of supremely gifted women writers in Europe," adding: "Drama, poetry, fiction, history, biography—in all these she has done notable, in some remarkable work." A more negative point of view has been expressed by Clifton Fadiman, who declared that "Ricarda Huch's great historical knowledge and her grave and marmoreal prose cannot atone for lack of humor and insight."

ABOUT: Columbia Dictionary of Modern European Literature; Nation May 1, 1948; New York Times November 20, 1947.

* hōōk

HUDSON, JAY WILLIAM (March 12, 1874-). For biographical sketch and list of earlier works and references, see TWENTIETH CENTURY AUTHORS, 1942.

* * *

Jay William Hudson has been emeritus professor of philosophy at the University of Missouri since 1944. Since his retirement he has lectured for the Institute of International Understanding, the Rotary International, and other groups, and he has been visiting professor of philosophy at the University of Kansas City (1945-46) and Stephens College (1945-51). Hudson lives in Columbia, Mo.

ADDITIONAL WORK: Prayers of Aspiration: For Use in Public Services and in Private Devotions, 1950.

HUDSON, STEPHEN (1869?-October 29, 1944). For biographical sketch and list of works and references, see TWENTIETH CENTURY AUTHORS, 1942.

* * *

Stephen Hudson (the pseudonym of Sydney Schiff) died of heart failure at Brighton, England; the London *Times* reported his age as seventy-five. Although little of his private life was known, he was a friend of James Joyce and Marcel Proust, and figures prominently in Proust's published correspondence. A friend has described him as "the kindest and most generous of colleagues. Of independent and fastidious taste, Stephen Hudson preferred to remain detached from social life. His increasing deafness contributed to his desire for seclusion."

Charles G. Poore has called Hudson "one of the most accomplished novelists of our time," and believes that "he has probably done as much as any living writer to perfect the form of the novel by achieving a technique that presents with extraordinary lucidity and precision the flowing series of causes and effects that is at the heart of the novelists' eternal major problem—character development."

ABOUT: London Times November 13, 1944.

HUDSON, WILLIAM HENRY (August 4, 1841-August 18, 1922). For biographical sketch and list of works and references, see TWENTIETH CENTURY AUTHORS, 1942.

* * *

ADDITIONAL WORKS: Letters to R. B. Cunninghame Graham (ed. R. Curle) 1941; Tales of the Gauchos (comp. & ed. E. Coatsworth) 1946; Letters on the Ornithology of Buenos Aires (ed. D. R. Dewar) 1951.

ABOUT: Hamilton, R. W. H. Hudson: The Vision of Earth; Looker, S. J. (ed.) William Henry Hudson; West, H. F. W. H. Hudson's Reading; Audubon Magazine September 1943; Hispania February 1946; Saturday Review of Literature April 12, 1947.

HUDSON, WILLIAM HENRY (May 2, 1862-August 12, 1918). For biographical sketch and list of works and references, see TWENTIETH CENTURY AUTHORS, 1942.

HUEFFER. See FORD, F. M.

HUGHES, DOROTHY BELLE (FLANAGAN) (1904-), American writer of mystery novels, was born in Kansas City, Mo., and educated at the University of Missouri, Columbia University, and the University of New Mexico. Her career has included newspaper work in Missouri, New York, and New Mexico, and she won an award in the Yale Series of Younger Poets for her book *Dark Certainty* (1931).  Now best known for her mysteries, she wrote several unsuccessful and unpublished mystery novels before her first, *The So Blue Marble*, was published and acclaimed (1940). "No editor ever returned a manuscript to me without receiving another one in the next mail," she said; and of the writing of mysteries: "It took twelve years to write one because it took twelve years to *learn* to write one."

Among the most popular of her works are *The So Blue Marble*, *The Fallen Sparrow*, and *The Delicate Ape*. Of the first Will Cuppy wrote in *Books*: "We're telling you that a thriller so impressive in wallop and so irresistible in manner and other merits hasn't appeared in a long time." The *New Yorker* recommended *The Fallen Sparrow* as a "beautifully told story of terror," while *Books* noted: "Chilling, eloquent and enigmatic by turns, it is right in there with a claim to top 1942 honors." *The Delicate Ape*, set in a future time, is a tale of international intrigue that won high approval among critics. "The author's passionate conviction that it must not happen again gives the story a meaning," wrote the New York *Times*, "and makes it a portent of the direction history may take in the future—if the aggressor nations of today are not carefully watched and controlled. The hero's adventures, thrilling as they are in themselves, are but the outward embellishments of a tale that is intended to make us think."

The author is married to Levi Allen Hughes, Jr., of Santa Fe, N.M. She has three children: Holly, Antony, and Suzy. Her home is in Westwood Village, Calif. In 1950 she received the Edgar from the Mystery Writers of America for mystery criticism, in her capacity as mystery critic for the Albuquerque *Tribune* and the Los Angeles *Daily News*.

PRINCIPAL WORKS: Dark Certainty (verse: by Dorothy Belle Flanagan) 1931; Pueblo on the Mesa, the First Fifty Years at the University of New Mexico, 1939; The So Blue Marble, 1940; The Cross-Eyed Bear, 1940; The Fallen Sparrow, 1942; The Bamboo Blonde, 1941; The Black-Birder, 1943; Johnnie, 1944; The Delicate Ape, 1944; Dread Journey, 1945; Ride the Pink Horse, 1946; In a Lonely Place, 1947; The Big Barbecue, 1949; The Candy Kid, 1950; The Davidian Report, 1952.

ABOUT: The Writer May 1947.

HUGHES, HATCHER (1886?-October 18, 1945). For biographical sketch and list of works and references, see TWENTIETH CENTURY AUTHORS, 1942.

* * *

Hatcher Hughes died of coronary thrombosis at his home in New York City. During the last few years of his life he divided his time between vacations at his farm in West Cornwall, Conn., and teaching playwriting and modern drama at Columbia University. He was a director of student dramatic productions of the Columbia Theatre Associates.

Hughes completed a satirical comedy shortly before his death, thirteen years after his last previous play was produced. The play for which he was best known, *Hell-Bent Fer Heaven*, was called "a particularly fine example of the native folk drama" by Burns Mantle.

ABOUT: New York Herald Tribune October 20, 1945; New York Times October 20, 1945; Saturday Review July 17, 1954; School and Society November 3, 1945.

HUGHES, LANGSTON (February 1, 1902-). For autobiographical sketch and list of earlier works and references, see TWENTIETH CENTURY AUTHORS, 1942.

* * *

During the Second World War Langston Hughes was a member of the Music War Board, the Theatre Wing of the New York Stage Door Canteen, and the Writers War Board. He wrote radio scripts and other wartime morale programs and gave poetry programs in USO centers from coast to coast. He was in residence at Yaddo for two summers as creative writer. In 1947 Hughes was visiting professor in creative writing at Atlanta University, and in the same year he received a grant from the American Academy of Arts and Letters. He was poet-in-residence at the University of Chicago Laboratory School in 1949. Since 1945 Hughes has been a columnist for the Chicago *Defender* where his short stories about the Negro Simple first appeared. These were published in 1950 as *Simple Speaks His Mind*. He is also a contributing editor to *Phylon*, the Atlanta University quarterly. He has lectured widely at colleges and universities all over the country and has made many radio and television appearances.

Among Hughes' works for the stage in recent years are the play *The Sun Do Move*, produced in Chicago in 1942; lyrics for Kurt Weill's musical version of Elmer Rice's *Street Scene* in 1947; the librettos for two operas—*Troubled Island* by William Grant Still, produced in New York in 1949, and *The Barrier* by Jan Meyerowitz, produced in New York in 1950; and the lyrics for a musical, *Just Around the Corner*.

In 1952 Hughes published a collection of twenty-four short stories, *Laughing to Keep From Crying*. Arna Bontemps wrote of this volume in the *Saturday Review*: "Langston Hughes has practiced the craft of the short story no more than he has practiced the forms of poetry. His is a spontaneous art which stands or falls by the sureness of his intuition, his mother wit. His stories, like his poems, are for readers who will judge them with their hearts as well as their heads. By that standard he has always measured well. He still does."

ADDITIONAL WORKS: *Poetry*—Freedom's Plow, 1943; Fields of Wonder, 1947; One-Way Ticket, 1949; Montage of a Dream Deferred, 1951. *Translations*—Roumain, J. Masters of the Dew (with M. Cook) 1947; Guillen, N. Cuba Libre (with B. F. Carruthers) 1948; Lorca, G. Gypsy Ballads, 1951. *Fiction*—Simple Speaks His Mind, 1950; Laughing to Keep From Crying, 1952; Simple Takes a Wife, 1953. *Miscellaneous*—The Poetry of the Negro (ed. with A. Bontemps) 1949; The First Book of Negroes 1952; Famous American Negroes, 1954; The First Book of Rhythms, 1954.

ABOUT: Barton, R. C. Witnesses for Freedom; Embree, E. R. 13 Against the Odds; Gregory, H. and Zaturenska, M. A History of American Poetry,

1900-1940; Richardson, B. A. Great American Negroes; Current Biography 1940; Opportunity September 1946; Phylon (4th quarter) 1952; Poetry February 1950; Saturday Review of Literature March 22, 1947; Scholastic February 12, 1945.

HUGHES, RICHARD ARTHUR WARREN (1900-   ). For biographical sketch and list of works and references, see TWENTIETH CENTURY AUTHORS, 1942.

* * *

Richard Hughes served in the British Admiralty from 1940 to 1945 and in recognition of his services received the Order of the British Empire. He has published little in recent years, only an occasional short story (in the *Virginia Quarterly Review* in January 1947 and in the *New Yorker* for September 29, 1951). In 1943 Paul Osborn's dramatization of Hughes' *The Innocent Voyage* was produced on Broadway. Done as "a comedy of considerable charm and imagination, but a bit too fine for the crowd" (so Burns Mantle wrote), it closed after forty performances. Mantle selected it as one of *The Best Plays of 1943-44*. Another play which Hughes had written some years before, *Minnie and Mr. Williams*, a Welsh comedy-fantasy, was produced on Broadway in 1948, starring Eddie Dowling and Josephine Hull. It closed after only five performances.

ABOUT: Virginia Quarterly Review January 1947.

HUGHES, RUPERT (January 31, 1872-   ). For biographical sketch and list of earlier works and references, see TWENTIETH CENTURY AUTHORS, 1942.

* * *

Rupert Hughes' third wife, Elizabeth Patterson Dial, died in 1945. He lives in Los Angeles. He was active in the formation of the California State Guard in 1940 and from 1941 to 1943 he was a colonel in the Guard. Hughes' later writings have been of only slight literary value. In 1950 the *New Yorker* described his prose style as "rather primitive," adding that "there is probably no author with a greater weakness for exclamation points and for capitalizing common nouns."

ADDITIONAL WORKS: His Fabulous Fortune, 1943; In a Blaze of Glory, 1945; Gyges' Ring, and Other Verse, 1949; Complete Detective: Life and Cases of Raymond Schindler (biography) 1950; The Giant Wakes: A Novel About Samuel Gompers, 1950; Triumphant Clay, 1951; The War of the Mayan King, 1952.

*HUIDOBRO, VICENTE (January 10, 1893-January 2, 1948). For biographical sketch and list of works and references, see TWENTIETH CENTURY AUTHORS, 1942.

* * *

Vicente Huidobro died in Santiago, Chile, at fifty-four.

Guillaume Apollinaire said, early in the Chilean poet's career, "His work is foreordained to be experimental and progressive. In his very progress, therefore, are the tokens of large success." Huidobro's ultimate importance, however, lay rather in his influence on other writers than in his own work. Cansinos-Assens wrote that "the youngest poets flocked to him. They had a flair for the new day that was dawning in his poems. He jarred more than one writer wide awake."

ABOUT: Holmes, H. A. Contemporary Spanish Americans; New York Times January 4, 1948; Pan American Union Bulletin May 1948.

* wē dŏ′brŏ

*HUIE, WILLIAM BRADFORD (November 13, 1910-   ), American novelist and journalist, was born in Hartselle, Ala., the son of John Bradford Huie and Margaret Lois (Brindley) Huie. He received his B.A. from the University of Alabama in 1930, was reporter for the Birmingham *Post* from 1932 to 1936, and associate editor of the *American Mercury* from 1941 to 1943. Serving as a lieutenant in the U.S. Navy from 1943 to 1945, he was—either as officer or correspondent—on every war front except the Russian.

Fabian Bachrach

In 1942 he published two books—*Mud on the Stars*, a novel, and *The Fight for Air Power*. "His central figure, Peter Lafavor," wrote N. L. Rothman of *Mud on the Stars*, "is probably autobiographical to a considerable degree. Lafavor, about to leave on a troopship, looks backward upon his remembered America, chiefly Tennessee and Alabama, from 1929 to 1942. It isn't a pretty picture, nor is it a reformer's picture pointed up with criticism."

In *The Fight for Air Power*, said the *New Yorker*, "the author charges that our long-range offensive air power has been and is being slowed up by Army and Navy ground hogs." This was the first of his controversial

* hū′ē

non-fiction books. After two books on the Seabees, Huie wrote *The Case Against the Admirals; Why We Must Have a Unified Command,* in which he tried to show that the Army and Navy had crippled the Air Corps in such a way that we had "no air power at all when Hitler began his try for world supremacy" (*Library Journal*). "His book, even before publication, roused the Navy Department into distributing to the reviewers a letter that answered a number of Mr. Huie's charges but not, it must be said, his major indictments" (*New Yorker*). One of the most hotly-debated of his books was *The Execution of Private Slovik,* the previously little-publicized story of an American soldier who was shot for desertion in 1945.

Huie was editor and publisher of the *American Mercury* until late in 1952. Since 1941 he has been a lecturer, and has throughout his career been a prolific author of magazine articles. In 1934 he married Ruth Puckett.

In October 1954, while collecting material for a book on a 1952 murder case in Florida (involving a Negro woman accused of shooting a white doctor), Huie was convicted of contempt of court and sentenced to jail for allegedly trying to influence a psychiatrist who was a witness in the case. Huie appealed the conviction, but in May 1955 the Florida State Supreme Court upheld it.

PRINCIPAL WORKS: Mud on the Stars (novel) 1942; The Fight for Air Power, 1942; Can Do! the Story of the Seabees, 1944; From Omaha to Okinawa, 1945; The Case against the Admirals, 1946; The Revolt of Mamie Stover (novel) 1951; The Execution of Private Slovik, 1954.

ABOUT: Newsweek August 25, 1952; Saturday Review of Literature September 19, 1942; Time May 30, 1949, December 8, 1952.

*HUIZINGA, JOHAN (December 7, 1872-February 1, 1945), Netherlands historian, son of a professor of medicine at the University of Groningen, The

Netherlands, was educated at the University of Groningen and graduated in philology and history. He spent a semester at the University of Leipzig in Germany, where he studied Indo-Germanic linguistics. He took his Ph.D. in Groningen in 1897, was teacher of history at a high school in Haarlem (Netherlands), *Privaatdocent* of Indian literature at the University

* hoi'zĭng à

of Amsterdam, professor of history at the University of Groningen (1905-1915), and after 1915 professor of general history at the University of Leiden.

Huizinga's first publications were in the field of Indian literature and cultural history, but his interest soon shifted toward Dutch and European history. He never became a specialist of one period or country, though his main historiographical work deals with the later Middle Ages and the Renaissance. His best book undoubtedly is *The Waning of the Middle Ages,* A Study in the Forms of Life, Thought and Art in France and the Netherlands in the Fourteenth and Fifteenth centuries, first (Dutch) edition 1919. It is the northern and medieval counterpart of Jacob Burckhardt's famous *Culture of the Renaissance in Italy.* It differs from the latter in that it includes the forms of art and literature, and that it develops a central idea, *viz.* that the civilization of declining chivalry in its bright autumn colors was the reflection of the spirit of an age fleeing from reality into a beautiful dream. The book was an international success, and was translated into eight foreign languages.

The period of the Renaissance is dealt with in numerous essays which have not been translated into English, and above all by his biography of Erasmus (1924), written for the series "Great Hollanders," edited by Edward W. Bok. In later years Huizinga's research was mostly devoted to general themes of cultural history. His most important work in this respect, though not so creative and evocative as *The Waning of the Middle Ages,* was *Homo Ludens,* A Study of the Play-element in Culture, first (Dutch) edition 1938.

Meanwhile the rise of National Socialism had drawn Huizinga's attention to the threatening symptoms of cultural decline in our own time. *In the Shadow of Tomorrow,* A Diagnosis of the Spiritual Distemper of Our Time, 1935, gave expression to his alarm at the morally disquieting decay of norms and values. He was not basically pessimistic, though, as appears also from his short essay *Conditions for a Recovery of Civilisation,* 1940. During World War II he returned to the subject in his last and posthumously published book *Outraged World,* 1945 (not translated into English). Here he calls for simplification and a sort of asceticism, and he appeals to all men of good will. Huizinga wrote two studies on American civilization "Man and Mass in America," 1918, and "Life and Thought in America," 1927. These have not been translated into English.

In addition to his professorship Huizinga held several important offices. He was a member of the Royal Netherlands Academy of Sciences, and, from 1929 to 1942, he was president of its section for Humanities. He was a member, and, in 1938 became vice-president of, the International Committee of Intellectual Cooperation of the League of Nations. He was granted honorary doctorates by the universities of Oxford and Tübingen. As one of the leaders of the resistance movement at the University of Leiden during the war he was, for some time, imprisoned as a hostage. He was not allowed to return to Leiden afterward, and he had to live near Arnhem, where in the last winter of the war the military front was quite close. Here he died after a short illness.

PRINCIPAL WORKS IN ENGLISH TRANSLATION: The Waning of the Middle Ages, 1924; Erasmus, 1924; In the Shadow of Tomorrow, 1936; Homo Ludens, 1949.

ABOUT: Inge, W. R. Rustic Moralist; College Art Journal Autumn 1946.

HULL, EDITH MAUDE. For biographical sketch and list of works, see TWENTIETH CENTURY AUTHORS, 1942.

HULL, HELEN ROSE. For autobiographical sketch and list of earlier works and references, see TWENTIETH CENTURY AUTHORS, 1942.

* * *

Helen Hull has been associate professor of English at Columbia University since 1939. From 1949 to 1952 she was president of the Authors' Guild. During this period she edited a collection of essays by prominent authors on the craft of writing—The Writer's Book. In 1943 Miss Hull wrote a brief biography of Madame Chiang Kai-shek, who had been her student at Wellesley. Her other works since 1942 have been fiction—three novels, which are dispassionate and perceptive studies of the conflicts in modern marriage, and a volume of short stories. Her recent novel Landfall, a story of a self-centered career woman, was described in one review as "ultra-sophisticated in setting and crisp in style."

ADDITIONAL WORKS: Mayling Soong Chiang, 1943; Circle in the Water (in England: Darkening Hill) 1943; The Hawk's Flight, 1946; Octave (short stories) 1947; (ed.) The Writer's Book 1950; Landfall, 1953.

"HULL, RICHARD." SEE SAMPSON, R. H.

HULME, THOMAS ERNEST (September 16, 1883-September 28, 1917). For biographical sketch and list of works and references, see TWENTIETH CENTURY AUTHORS, 1942.

* * *

ABOUT: Mason, E. A. in The Importance of Scrutiny (ed. E. Bentley); Church Quarterly October 1947.

HUME, CYRIL (March 16, 1900-). For biographical sketch and list of works and references, see TWENTIETH CENTURY AUTHORS, 1942.

* * *

Stories by Cyril Hume appear occasionally in the Saturday Evening Post and Collier's. He has published no books in recent years.

HUME, FERGUS (July 8, 1859-July 13, 1932). For biographical sketch and list of works and references, see TWENTIETH CENTURY AUTHORS, 1942.

* * *

ABOUT: Dictionary of Australian Biography.

HUMMEL, GEORGE FREDERICK (September 3, 1882-). For biographical sketch and list of earlier works and references, see TWENTIETH CENTURY AUTHORS, 1942.

* * *

George Frederick Hummel lives in his birthplace of Southold, Long Island. His only book of recent years is the novel Joshua Moore, American, a family chronicle, actually five vignettes of American life from the seventeenth century to the present. If, in the opinion of the critics, Hummel did not fully succeed in his goal of depicting America's growth in a single novel, he nevertheless managed to write a novel which was happily "neither portentous nor tiresome" (Margaret Wallace in the New York Times).

ADDITIONAL WORK: Joshua Moore, American, 1943.

HUMPHRIES, ROLFE (November 20, 1894-). For autobiographical sketch and list of earlier works and references, see TWENTIETH CENTURY AUTHORS, 1942.

* * *

Rolfe Humphries has published four volumes of his verse since 1942 and a verse translation of Virgil's Aeneid, the latter described by Anne Fremantle in Commonweal as "magnificently successful" in communicating the swiftness, vigor, and spirit of the original text. He is currently preparing translations of Ovid's *Metamorphoses* and Lorca's *Gypsy Ballads*. His *Poems: Collected and New,* Roberta Teale Swartz wrote in the New York *Times,* "demonstrate what it is to write from a richness of learning, as well as of experience."

He has taught summers at the Writers' Conference in the Rocky Mountains, held at the University of Colorado in Boulder, and at Colorado State College of Education in Greeley. In 1947 Humphries received the Shelley Memorial Award, and in 1950 he shared the Poetry Award (of Pasadena) with Hyam Plutzik. He was elected to the National Institute of Arts and Letters in February 1953.

ADDITIONAL WORKS: The Summer Landscape, 1944; Forbid Thy Ravens, 1947; The Wind of Time, 1949; The Aeneid of Virgil (tr.) 1951; Poems: Collected and New, 1954; New Poems of American Poets (ed.) 1954; The Metamorphoses of Ovid (tr.) 1955.

ABOUT: Christian Century December 6, 1944; Nation April 11, 1942; Poetry October 1942, July 1948.

HUNEKER, JAMES GIBBONS (January 31, 1860-February 9, 1921). For biographical sketch and list of works and references, see TWENTIETH CENTURY AUTHORS, 1942.

* * *

ABOUT: Mencken, H. L. A Mencken Chrestomathy; American Literature November 1951.

HUNT, VIOLET (1866-January 16, 1942). For biographical sketch and list of works and references, see TWENTIETH CENTURY AUTHORS, 1942.

* * *

Violet Hunt died at her home, South Lodge, at Campden Hill, England, at seventy-five.

Although her judgment and taste have been questioned by critics, she was generally admired for her courage, her skill in depicting certain types—"especially of disagreeable worldly women"—and the fervor and vigor of her style.

Douglas Goldring, speculating on whether future students of social life and manners will be interested in the epoch she represents, added: "If they are, it is difficult to see how Violet's personality—a catfish in that decorous aquarium if ever there was one—can fail to attract their attention to herself and her books." The latter, in his opinion, "were

brilliant in their period . . . are certainly 'dated'. . . but seem, on various grounds, to have the qualities which should make for survival."

ABOUT: Goldring, D. South Lodge; London Times January 19, 1942; The Windmill 1947.

HURLBUT, JESSE LYMAN (February 15, 1843-August 2, 1930). For biographical sketch and list of works and references, see TWENTIETH CENTURY AUTHORS, 1942.

HURST, FANNIE (October 18, 1889-   ). For biographical sketch and list of earlier works and references, see TWENTIETH CENTURY AUTHORS, 1942.

* * *

Fannie Hurst's books, said *Time* magazine in 1944, "are as numerous as Egyptian dynasties." By 1950 she had published some twenty-five in all, and there was no evidence of a slackening of her enthusiasm or her energy. Her writing, in her later works, remains vigorous and florid. Sterling North observed that it "flows a little like the Mississippi—wide, deep, and rather muddy." At her best her work is enriched by her sympathy and her sharp eye for human detail—"the pulse of life is always there," Wilbur Watson remarked in the New York *Times.* At her worst, her fiction is cheapened by sentimentality and over-writing until it is reduced to what K. S. Rosin describes in the *Saturday Review of Literature* as "a glorified *True Confessions* story."

Miss Hurst has long been active in civic and social work. In recent years she has served on the board of trustees of the Heckscher Foundation and the Russell Sage Foundation. From 1945 to 1947 she was a member of the Mayor's Committee on Unity in New York, and she has also been a member of the board of directors of the New York Urban League and the United Neighborhood Houses. She has been an officer of the Authors' Guild of America for a number of years. In addition, she lectures widely and appears frequently on radio and television programs. She lives, as she has for many years, in a fourteen-room apartment on Central Park West in Manhattan. Her husband, Jacques Danielson, died in 1952.

ADDITIONAL WORKS: Hallelujah, 1944; The Hands of Veronica, 1947; Anywoman, 1950.

ABOUT: Lotz, P. H. (ed.) Distinguished American Jews; New Yorker January 22, 1944; Time January 31, 1944.

HURSTON, ZORA NEALE (January 7, 1903-). For autobiographical sketch and list of earlier works and references, see TWENTIETH CENTURY AUTHORS, 1942.

* * *

Zora Neale Hurston is on the faculty of North Carolina College for Negroes in Durham. Her permanent home is in her native state of Florida, at Eau Gallie. In 1942 she published her autobiography, *Dust Tracks on a Road,* which won the Anisfield award for better race relations. In this simple, forthright, but dramatically told narrative, Miss Hurston described her family, her childhood, and her struggle for an education. In recent years she has contributed articles and stories to the *Saturday Evening Post* and other journals.

ADDITIONAL WORKS: Dust Tracks on a Road, 1942; Search on the Sewanee (novel) 1948.

ABOUT: Barton, R. C. Witnesses for Freedom; Dreer, H. American Literature by Negro Authors; Hurston, Z. N. Dust Tracks on a Road; Current Biography 1942.

HUTCHINSON, ARTHUR STUART-MENTETH (June 2, 1879-). For autobiographical sketch and list of earlier works and references, see TWENTIETH CENTURY AUTHORS, 1942.

* * *

A. S. M. Hutchinson lives very quietly in his Eastbourne home. His latest published work, the novel *It Happened Like This,* appeared in 1942. A subtle and carefully understated horror story, his novel was an experiment in technique, an attempt to tell three stories in one, and "to fuse the disassociated acquaintances of a man's life into a common fiction background."

Correction: Hutchinson's date of birth was incorrectly given as 1880 in TWENTIETH CENTURY AUTHORS, 1942.

ADDITIONAL WORK: It Happened Like This, 1942.

HUTCHINSON, RAY CORYTON (January 23, 1907-). For autobiographical sketch and list of earlier works and references, see TWENTIETH CENTURY AUTHORS, 1942.

* * *

R. C. Hutchinson writes from Surrey, England: "I was commissioned in the British Army in March 1940 and shortly put in command of a company in a newly-formed battalion of The Buffs. In 1943 I passed through the Staff College and then for one year served as a staff officer with rank of Major in the War Office, London. Early in 1945 I was sent on a journey through Egypt, Palestine, Persia, and Iraq in order to write a 'popular' history, for the War Office, of the Persia and Iraq Command (which in co-operation with the U.S. Persian Gulf Command established and maintained the overland aid to Russia route).

"My elder daughter now works in the foreign department of a London literary agency. My next two children—boy and girl —are both at Oxford.

"I visited—and adored—New York in 1948."

Of R. C. Hutchinson's novels published since the end of the World War II, the longest and most ambitious is *Elephant and Castle,* a crowded, panoramic study of life in the London slums that was eight years in the writing. His later novel, *Journey With Strangers,* tells the tragic story of a family of Polish aristocrats living first under Nazi, then under Communist occupation.

In an article called "If One Must Write . . . ," published in the *Saturday Review of Literature* in 1949, Hutchinson describes the desire to write novels as "a kind of disease" and calls the writing profession "the hardest, the loneliest, the most continuously exasperating" of occupations. But, he writes, "I believe that in so far as he succeeds in the artistic purpose of illuminating an area of truth—the actualities of human nature— the novelist performs a unique function which cannot be without moral value."

ADDITIONAL WORKS: Interim, 1945; Elephant and Castle, 1949; Journey With Strangers, 1952.

ABOUT: Book-of-the-Month Club News January 1949; Current Biography 1940; Saturday Review of Literature September 3, 1949.

HUXLEY, ALDOUS LEONARD (July 26, 1894-). For autobiographical sketch and list of earlier works and references, see TWENTIETH CENTURY AUTHORS, 1942.

* * *

Aldous Huxley lives in a suburb of Los Angeles where he writes his books and from time to time a movie scenario (one of these was *A Woman's Vengeance,* based on his short story "The Gioconda Smile"), and studies Vedanta and other mystic religions. Mysticism has played an ever larger role in Huxley's work. According to many reviewers, its effects upon his fiction have not been altogether salutary, leading him toward the didactic, instead of the dramatic; the fantastic, instead of the satiric. Both *Time Must*

Have a Stop, a novel with a more or less contemporary setting (part of it takes place in Limbo), and *Ape and Essence,* whose scene is a ruined and devastated Los Angeles in 2108 A.D. after a third world war, had chilly critical receptions. Huxley's most successful book of the past decade is *The Devils of Loudon* which, like *Grey Eminence,* has its source in seventeenth century French ecclesiastical history. Of this account of the mass hysteria which swept an Ursuline convent and provoked the martyrdom of the priest Urbain Grandier, Chad Walsh wrote: "This peak achievement of Mr. Huxley's career reveals his sharp skill at characterization, his ability to re-create the smell and flavor of vanished eras, his preoccupation with roads to salvation and roads to damnation."

In 1945 Huxley published an anthology of religious and mystical writings called *The Perennial Philosophy* with his commentary on the texts. Out of these writings Huxley culls "the Highest Common Factor" in all philosophies and religions, and this he summarizes as "the metaphysic that recognizes a divine Reality substantial to the world of things and lives and minds; the psychology that finds in the soul something similar to, or even identical with, divine Reality; the ethic that places man's final end in the knowledge of the immanent and transcendent Ground of all being."

ADDITIONAL WORKS: The Art of Seeing, 1942; Time Must Have a Stop, 1944; The Perennial Philosophy, 1945; Ape and Essence, 1948; Themes and Variations (essays) 1950; The Devils of Loudon, 1952; The Doors of Perception, 1954.

ABOUT: Lebowitz, M. *in* The Kenyon Critics (ed. J. C. Ransom); Savage, D. S. Mysticism and Aldous Huxley; Wilson E. Classics and Commercials; Atlantic August 1947; Collier's April 17, 1943; Commonweal September 15, 1944; Coronet February 1950; Fortnightly February 1947; Life March 24, 1947, September 20, 1948; New York Times Book Review May 21, 1950; New Yorker October 25, 1947; Saturday Review of Literature August 21, 1948; South Atlantic Quarterly July 1946; Theatre Arts May 1951; Time August 28, 1944.

HUXLEY, JULIAN SORRELL (June 22, 1887-). For biographical sketch and list of earlier works and references, see TWENTIETH CENTURY AUTHORS, 1942.

* * *

Julian Huxley was appointed Director-General of UNESCO in 1946 and served a two-year term in that office. His appointment stirred up a heated controversy. His qualifications for the job were not questioned, but his outspoken views on a number of subjects, particularly his overt atheism, caused much objection and criticism. On his appointment Huxley announced that his aim in UNESCO would be to encourage the development "of a single world culture, with its own philosophy and background of ideas, and with its own broad purpose." Huxley's tenure of office in UNESCO was stormy but constructive, in that the organization was built up and strengthened under his administration. Since the end of his term he has traveled and lectured all over the world, and he has continued to write books and articles that are distinguished for their lucidity and persuasiveness. His *Evolution in Action,* a popular history of evolution, is a collection of lectures he delivered at Indiana University and later over the B.B.C. *Heredity, East and West* was a scholarly and carefully documented attack on the Soviet-sponsored Lysenko theory of genetics. In this, as in his other works, Huxley argues vigorously and persuasively for the importance of free and independent intellectual inquiry.

In 1947 a writer in *Life* described Huxley as "a tall, bespectacled, bony-faced scholar who looks placid but erupts in fits of temper or kinetic conversation."

ADDITIONAL WORKS: Evolution, the Modern Synthesis, 1942; TVA: Adventure in Planning, 1943; On Living in a Revolution, 1944; The Future of the Colonies (with P. Deane) 1945; Man in the Modern World, 1947; UNESCO: Its Purpose and Its Philosophy, 1947; Heredity, East and West (in England: Soviet Genetics and World Science) 1949; Evolution in Action, 1953; From an Antique Land, 1954.

ABOUT: Coates, J. B. Leaders of Modern Thought; Coronet February 1950; Current Biography 1942; Life March 24, 1947; Saturday Evening Post October 2, 1948; Time December 16, 1946; United Nations Weekly Bulletin December 31, 1946.

HYDE, DOUGLAS (1860-July 12, 1949). For biographical sketch and list of works and references, see TWENTIETH CENTURY AUTHORS, 1942.

* * *

Douglas Hyde died in Dublin at eighty-nine.

Although he completely recovered from a serious illness in 1940, he then announced that he would not run again for the presidency of Eire when his term expired in 1945. The New York *Times* observed: "Ireland admired him as scholar and poet. She acclaimed him as a patriot and respected him as an elder statesman. To him was given credit for the revival of Erse, ancient Gaelic language of Erin."

ABOUT: Contemporary Review August 1945; London Times July 14, 1949; New York Times July 13, 1949.

HYNE, CHARLES JOHN CUTCLIFFE WRIGHT (Cutcliffe Hyne) (May 11, 1865-March 10, 1944).

For biographical sketch and list of works and references, see TWENTIETH CENTURY AUTHORS, 1942.

* * *

Cutcliffe Hyne died at his home in Kettlewell, by Skipton-in-Craven, Yorkshire, England, at seventy-eight.

It has been pointed out that in Captain Kettle, hero of most of his short stories, he created a character who at one time was second only to Sherlock Holmes in the affections of British readers. The London *Times* has called the creation of this series of stories "the achievement not only of a lively imagination supported by a breezy and vigorous style, but of a conscientious craftsman who went to infinite trouble and sometimes to no little risk in an almost worldwide search for his material."

ABOUT: London Times March 11, 1944; Publishers' Weekly May 6, 1944.

HYNE, CUTCLIFFE. See HYNE, C. J. C. W.

IBÁÑEZ. See BLASCO IBÁÑEZ

"ICONOCLAST." See HAMILTON, M. A. A.

IDELL, ALBERT EDWARD (June 21, 1901-),

American novelist, writes: "I was born in Philadelphia.

My mother, Melissa Barr Idell, came of a Pennsylvania Dutch family that arrived in the United States back in 1690. My father, Albert Magilton Idell, was of Irish and German descent. I started working early. In fact, looking back, I find there has been hardly a time in my life when I haven't been doing two jobs at once. While I was a student at the Germantown High School I worked evenings on a produce truck, heaving boxes of apples and cases of oranges from midnight till eight in the morning. Although I really preferred fishing and wrestling to work and school, I managed to get myself graduated from high school in 1919. For the next two years I worked my way through courses in modeling, wrought iron, and wood carving in the School of Industrial Art in Philadelphia by acting as secretary to its director. At the same time I was attending evening classes in accounting and related commercial subjects.

"Formal studies soon palled on me, however, and I left school and set out to see the world. For the next few years I was variously a pin boy in a bowling alley, a cloakroom attendant, a bar boy, a bus boy, a waiter, and a dishwasher. I did many of the fool things any adventurous kid does—riding the freights across the country, harvesting wheat in Kansas, slinging hash in California. As a seaman, or a guide to a group of artists, or a buyer of illuminated manuscripts for an American museum, I did what I had set out to do: I saw the world.

"After my marriage in 1926 to the artist Marguerite Borgiano Cadwalader, I settled down, more or less, to specialize in building and loan bank accounting, and in 1929 I acquired a partnership in a firm that manufactured fiber specialties. Taking advantage of the slack seasons, we toured Europe, Mexico, Venezuela, and the West Indies. At times, when our travels were prolonged beyond the accounting season, I turned salesman. I have successfully sold accounting systems, real estate, vacuum cleaners, and can openers.

"An incurable interest in life and people propelled me into still more diverse activities. After a period as a prize-fight promoter in Asheville, N.C., I began to study the restaurant business. In 1930 I organized a lending library in which I still own an interest. Two years later I was engaged as a consultant in school lunchrooms of the Philadelphia school system, and the following year I became supervisor. At the same time I conducted courses in restaurant management for the Philadelphia Restaurant Association.

"I began my writing career by reviewing books for newspapers. That my hand turned to creative writing was no fault of mine. My interest was forced in that direction by Harry Emerson Wildes, the literary editor of the Philadelphia *Public Ledger*. Wildes, for whom I wrote book reviews, insisted that I begin to write fiction. He is an obstinate man, and I finally gave in.

"In 1941 my first novel, *Pug*, won the $1,000 Bookman prize. In the same year, my second novel, *Cross in the Caribbean*, was published. Both novels, however, had been written simultaneously, as antidotes to each other. Since then I have been writing almost continuously. *Centennial Summer* was a Literary Guild selection and was made into a very successful motion picture, which contains the last music of Jerome Kern. Two further books about the same family were also successful and the trilogy was widely translated.

"Six years ago, I came to Guatemala, Central America, to finish a book. We fell in love with its ancient capital, Antigua Guatemala, bought a house there, and consider it our home, although we usually spend part of each year in Palm Beach, Fla., and Philadelphia, Pa., where we have houses."

PRINCIPAL WORKS: Pug, 1941; Cross in the Caribbean, 1941; Centennial Summer, 1943; Bridge to Brooklyn, 1944; (under pseudonym Phillips Rogers) Stag Night, 1946; The Sea Is Woman, 1947; The Great Blizzard, 1948; Doorway in Antigua: A Sojourn in Guatemala, 1949; Stephen Hayne, 1951; The Corner Store, 1953.

ABOUT: Boston Herald March 21, 1948; Current Biography 1943; New York Herald Tribune Book Review June 21, 1953; New York Times Book Review May 4, 1947; Publishers' Weekly January 18, 1941; Retail Bookseller May 1941.

"ILES, FRANCIS." See COX, A. B.

ILF, ILYA ARNOLDOVICH (October 16, 1897-April 14, 1937). For biographical sketch and list of works and references, see TWENTIETH CENTURY AUTHORS, 1942.

* * *

ABOUT: Columbia Dictionary of Modern European Literature; Guerney, B. G. (ed.) The Portable Russian Reader.

IMBS, BRAVIG (October 8, 1904-1946). For autobiographical sketch and list of earlier works and references, see TWENTIETH CENTURY AUTHORS, 1942.

* * *

Bravig Imbs was killed in an automobile accident in France. He was forty-two.

His last book, *Confessions of Another Young Man*, was characterized as "gay and trivial, sometimes clever and always impermanent." In June 1944 he established the first "free" radio station in Cherbourg, France, following the German occupation, as part of the American Office of War Information program. Broadcasting five shows a week up to the time of his death, Imbs became "the darling of the French airways." *Time* pointed out that he was "an American more loved in France than known in the U.S."

ADDITIONAL WORK: (trans.) Breton, A. Yves Tanguy, 1946.

ABOUT: Time June 10, 1946.

INCLÁN. See VALLE INCLÁN

*INGE, WILLIAM MOTTER (May 3, 1913-), American playwright, writes: "I was born in Independence, Kans., my parents being Luther Clayton Inge and Maude Sarah Gibson. My father was a small town merchant and traveling salesman; my mother, so it was told me, a descendant of the acting Booths. I was the youngest in a family of five children, none of whom shared my interest in the theatre. The only

Talbot

relative who did share it was an uncle, John W. Gibson, my mother's elder brother, who began his professional life with a Shakespearean troup but was recalled by his father to come home and take care of the family harness business. My uncle became one of Wichita's leading citizens but remained at heart, I believe, an unsatisfied actor.

"At the age of seven, I began to recite— poems, monologues, dialect pieces, etc. I gave my recitations at club meetings, church and school programs, and home talent shows. During my early teens, I began to act in school plays. I graduated from high school in Independence in 1930 and entered the University of Kansas the next September. There I continued acting, taking an A.B. in Speech and Drama in 1935. I lost a year of schooling when I stayed out with a tent show, what is called a 'Toby Show,' in which I was cast as the juvenile. Another summer I acted with the Maxinkuckee Mummers, a summer stock company at Culver Military Academy, Culver, Ind. That was the summer of 1934. The following summer I returned there to teach, to replace the head of the speech and drama department, Major C. C. Mather, while he was on leave. I had expected during that summer to save enough of my salary to take me into New York and finance the start of my acting career. But I saved nothing, so I accepted a scholarship at George Peabody Teachers College, Nashville, Tenn., where I went to begin work on a master's degree in English. During the year in Nashville, I despaired of ever becoming an actor and tried to accept teaching as my profession. At the end of my year there, I developed a sickness of mood and temper which caused me to leave, to return home two weeks before I was to get my degree.

* "My name is pronounced to rhyme with *hinge*."

"The following year, I floundered. During that summer (1936), I worked on a highway gang, then went to Wichita and worked as announcer and writer for a radio station. The fall of 1937, I began work as a teacher in the high school at Columbus, Kans., teaching English, speech, and dramatics. The summer of 1938, I returned to Nashville, finished my master's, and began teaching at Stephens College for Women in Columbia, Missouri, in the fall of '38. I remained at Stephens for five years, the last three of them being spent in the drama department which was headed then by Miss Maude Adams. I was restless teaching, so left in 1943 to become drama, music, movie critic for the St. Louis *Star-Times*. This job I found stimulating and enjoyable. I hated to give it up. But I was replacing a friend who returned from overseas in 1946, so there was nothing to do but vamoose. I took another teaching job, in the English department of Washington University in St. Louis, where I remained until 1949, when I came to New York to witness the production of my play, *Come Back, Little Sheba*, which the Theatre Guild was planning for its summer season in Westport, Conn.

"During my formative years, it had never occurred to me that I would ever write. While teaching at Stephens, I kept a journal, wrote a few stories (none published) and some poetry. But I never considered myself 'a writer.' I took the newspaper job because it appealed to me and I felt I could do it. I became surer of myself, writing, and developed confidence. Seeing all the plays that came to St. Louis during those years (1943-1946), I couldn't help but begin to wonder if I could not write better ones. I still needed a final motivation. In December of 1944, I traveled to Chicago to see Tennessee Williams' *The Glass Menagerie*, which I found so beautiful and so deeply moving that I felt a little ashamed for having led what I felt was an unproductive life. I returned to St. Louis and, while still working on the paper, wrote my first play, *Farther Off From Heaven*, which Margo Jones produced and directed in her Dallas theatre in June 1947. The production came off well, or well enough to encourage me to write more plays. I made two separate tries, both failures, before writing *Come Back, Little Sheba*. *Picnic* grew out of some of the writing I was awkwardly doing before *Sheba*. I began earnest work on *Picnic* the summer after *Sheba's* New York opening, February 15, 1950. *Picnic* opened in New York, February 19, 1953.

"As for my work, about all I can say at this time is that I seem to find myself looking for the surprising depths of feeling that lie far below the public surface of human personality. The only drama I can find to write about comes from the relations between people."

* * *

William Inge received the 1953 Pulitzer prize for drama for his play *Picnic*. *Picnic* also received the Outer Circle award and was named the best new American play of the 1952-1953 season by the New York Drama Critics' Circle. *Come Back, Little Sheba* won the George Jean Nathan and the Theatre Time awards. Inge's third play, *Bus Stop*, opened in New York to enthusiastic notices in February 1955 and gave every sign of matching the success of its two predecessors.

PRINCIPAL WORKS: *Dates of publication*—Come Back, Little Sheba, 1950; Picnic, 1953.

ABOUT: Current Biography 1953; New York Herald Tribune June 25, 1950; New York Times July 23, 1950, February 15, 1953, March 22, 1953; New Yorker April 4, 1953; Theatre Arts May 1950.

INGE, WILLIAM RALPH (June 6, 1860-February 26, 1954). For biographical sketch and list of earlier works and references, see TWENTIETH CENTURY AUTHORS, 1942.

* * *

Dean Inge died at his home at Wallingford, Berkshire, England, at ninety-three; he had been ill with bronchitis for several weeks. His wife died in 1949. One of his sons was killed in World War II.

During the twenty years after his retirement, Inge had continued to write lively and often controversial weekly articles for the London *Evening Standard*. When he was eighty-four a visitor described him as a pleasant old gentleman with a delightful smile, a deep, sly chuckle and rakish eyebrows, hard at work "undisturbed behind a stone wall of deafness." George Bernard Shaw called him "an extraordinarily handsome intellectual, with an enchanting smile," and "an original mind and a first-rate literary craftsman."

A few months before his death Inge told an interviewer: "All my life I have struggled to find the purpose of living. . . . I know no more now than when I started. I have done my best, and I hope I haven't entirely wasted my life. . . . But don't call me the Gloomy Dean. I never deserved that. I have tried only to face reality, to be honest and to refuse to be foolishly optimistic."

ADDITIONAL WORKS: Talks in a Free Country, 1942; Five Essays, 1944; God, King and Empire (with others) 1947; End of an Age (essays) 1948; Mysticism in Religion, 1948; Diary of a Dean; St. Paul's, 1911-1934, 1949; Rādhākrishnan: Comparative Studies in Philosophy (ed. with others) 1951.

ABOUT: Inge, W. Diary of a Dean; Jones, E. D. Royalty of the Pulpit; Atlantic Monthly May 1950; New York Herald Tribune February 27, 1954; New York Times February 18, 1945, February 26, 1954; Newsweek August 28, 1950; Time December 18, 1944, January 8, 1945, August 28, 1950, July 27, 1953.

*   *   *

INGERSOLL, RALPH (December 8, 1900-   ), American author and editor, was born in New Haven, Conn., the son of a consulting engineer, Colin Macrae Ingersoll, and Theresa (McAllister) Ingersoll. He attended the Hotchkiss School, graduated from Yale University's Sheffield Scientific School in 1921, and studied engineering at Columbia University. His first job was as a mining engineer with a California gold mine, working underground as a miner. After several months he got another job with a copper mining company in Arizona. In 1923 he became a division engineer for a mining company in Mexico.

His first book, *In and Under Mexico* (1924), won him a job as a reporter on the New York *American.* He stayed with the *American* until the end of 1924, then did free-lance writing. This led to reporting for the *New Yorker.* In 1925, when he was twenty-five, he became managing editor of the *New Yorker* and remained in that position for five years.

He next became associate editor of *Fortune,* published by Henry R. Luce, then managing editor of *Fortune,* and finally in 1935 he became vice-president and general manager of Time Incorported. In 1937 he was appointed publisher of *Time,* and remained there until 1940 when he resigned to start publishing *PM,* a New York metropolitan daily which he had planned.

PM, which was published for eight years, differed from other metropolitan newspapers, in that it did not contain a line of advertising. It kept its readers informed of bargains and sales by presenting a digest of retail advertising as news. Ingersoll formulated the liberal editorial policy as follows: "We are against people who push other people around, just for the fun of pushing; whether they flourish in this country or abroad. We are against fraud and deceit and greed and cruelty and we will seek to expose their practitioners. We are for people who are kindly and courageous and honest. We respect intelligence, solid achievement, open-mindedness, religious tolerance. We do not believe all mankind's problems are now being solved successfully by any existing social order, certainly not our own, and we propose to crusade for those who seek constructively to improve the way men live together. We are Americans and we prefer democracy to any other principle of government." *PM's* financial backers included Mrs. Marian Rosenwald Stern, daughter of the founder of Sears, Roebuck Company, and Marshall Field III. Ingersoll retained the "complete, absolute, and exclusive power" to formulate the newspaper's policies. After World War II, however, there was a serious split among the editors over the paper's allegedly pro-Communist leanings. There were also changes in policy—principally the inclusion of paid advertising. In opposition to these changes, Ingersoll resigned from *PM* in 1946.

Ralph Ingersoll's first book was *Report on England,* based on his reporting and editorials for *PM.* In 1943 he described in *The Battle Is the Pay-Off* the battle of El Guattar in Tunisia, which he had observed when he was serving as a captain in the Army Engineers. This book was highly praised for the vividness and concreteness of its reporting. Equally lively as reporting but far more controversial was his story of the Allied invasion of Europe in *Top Secret,* which was very critical of the military strategy of the British commanders. Ingersoll's novels include *The Great Ones,* a story of a love affair between a magazine publisher and an actress-novelist, which was described as being "the work of a reporter, not a novelist" by Merle Miller in *Saturday Review of Literature;* and *Wine of Violence,* a love story set against the background of World War II in Europe, which the New York *Times* judged "a lively, at times mildly moving and always readable book."

Tall, bald, and shambling, Ingersoll is a member of the Yale, Union, Racquet, Tennis, and Cloud Clubs. He was married in 1926 to Elizabeth Garden of New York. She died in 1948, and he married Mary Hill Doolittle.

PRINCIPAL WORKS: Report on England, 1940; Action on All Fronts, 1942; The Battle Is the Pay-Off, 1943; Top Secret, 1946; The Great Ones (novel) 1948; Wine of Violence (novel) 1951.

ABOUT: Current Biography 1940; Business Week March 23, 1940; Nation June 8, 1940; New Yorker November 28, 1936, May 18, 1940; Scholastic November 19, 1938; Time January 22, 1940.

"INNES, MICHAEL." See STEWART, J. I. M.

"IRISH, WILLIAM." See WOOLRICH, C.

IRVINE, WILLIAM (June 9, 1906-   ), American literary historian, was born in Carson Hill, Calif., the son of Louis A. and  Katharine (Thomas) Irvine. He was educated in California, at Stanford University (B.A. 1928), and spent a year (1928-29) studying classics in Germany at the University of Heidelberg and the University of Munich. He returned to the United States to complete his graduate studies, receiving an M.A. from Harvard in 1931 and a Ph.D. in 1934. His first teaching post was at Mills College in Oakland, Calif., from 1934 to 1935. Since 1935 he has been a member of the faculty of Stanford University, becoming professor of English in 1948. He has been visiting professor of English at the University of North Carolina (summer 1948), at Northwestern University (summer 1949), and at Harvard (summer 1951, and winter 1954). He married Charlotte Stearns in 1935 and their home is in Stanford, Calif. He is a member of World Federalists, Phi Beta Kappa, and the Modern Language Association.

Irvine's writings, which include articles in literary and historical journals as well as books, have been concerned primarily with late nineteenth century personalities who wielded a strong influence in the development of social thought—Carlyle, T. H. Huxley, Darwin, George Bernard Shaw. His first book, published in England, was a study of the nineteenth century economist and journalist Walter Bagehot. His second book, and the one with which he gained wide recognition in the United States, was *The Universe of G.B.S.*, a sound and knowledgeable study of Shaw and the world of ideas in which he lived. Hesketh Pearson, another biographer of Shaw, called Irvine's book "the most intelligent guide to Shaw's philosophy that I have read." Pearson found the book both sympathetic and critical in its approach to Shaw—"partial to the theme, impartial in treatment; it displays a general admiration and a detailed detachment, virtues and faults equally and carefully noted." John Mason Brown observed in the *Saturday Review of Literature* that Irvine's study "is a good book and a needed one. It lives up to the challenge of its title."

In *Apes, Angels, and Victorians: The Story of Darwin, Huxley, and Evolution*, Irvine tried to capture the era and the drama of the great nineteenth century controversy over evolution. He writes: "I have attempted to show how the lives of these two men were variously and dramatically interwoven through Darwin's ideas of evolution and the impact of those ideas on the world. Availing myself of a large amount of unpublished material, I have tried to give a fresh and detailed account of the personal and family lives of Darwin and Huxley." Irvine's delineation of these two powerful personalities was described by one reviewer as "masterful . . . in full dimensions of life and blood." He was also praised for his skillful evocation of the Victorian intellectual atmosphere which was the background for the controversy. "Only in certain scientific aspects," wrote I. Bernard Cohen in the New York *Times Book Review*, "will the book be found wanting." Nevertheless, Cohen concludes, "Mr. Irvine has not written a history of science so much as a history of men and the effects of scientific ideas. He has done so with remarkable effectiveness."

PRINCIPAL WORKS: Walter Bagehot, 1939; The Universe of G.B.S., 1949; Apes, Angels, and Victorians, 1955.

IRWIN, Mrs. INEZ (HAYNES) (March 2, 1873-   ). For biographical sketch and list of earlier works and references, see TWENTIETH CENTURY AUTHORS, 1942.

* * *

Inez Haynes Irwin was president of the New York chapter of PEN from 1941 to 1944. She has published one mystery story in recent years, *The Women Swore Revenge*—which the late Will Cuppy judged "meatier than most puzzle tales, easy on the ear, complex but lucid"—and more than half a dozen more of her popular "Maida" tales for young readers. Her husband, Will Irwin, died in 1948. She lives in Scituate, Mass.

ADDITIONAL WORKS: Maida's Little Village, 1942; Maida's Little Houseboat, 1943; Maida's Little Theatre, 1946; The Women Swore Revenge, 1946;

Maida's Little Cabins, 1947; Maida's Little Zoo, 1949; Maida's Little Lighthouse, 1951; Maida's Little Farm, 1953; Maida's Little House Party, 1954.

ABOUT: Saturday Review of Literature September 26, 1942.

IRWIN, MARGARET, English historical novelist, was born, the youngest of a large family, in a rambling old house on top of  Highgate Hill, where it is supposed that Charles II once spent a night. Her grandfather, Colonel Irwin, was commander of the troops in Western Australia, and the Irwin River and district were named after him. He was the last Englishman to bear the title Knight of Hanover, a now obsolete honor which had been imported by the Georges. Her maternal grandfather, General Baker, was sent out as one of the representatives to determine the boundary of Greece after the War of Liberation in which Byron lost his life. Her family has a far back connection with the publisher Jacob Tonson, who bought *Paradise Lost* from Milton for a "fiver," and who published works by Dryden, Pope and Addison.

Her parents died when she was still a child, and she went to live with her uncle, S. T. Irwin, who was well known as classical master at Clifton for over thirty-five years, and as the author of classical essays, chiefly on the literature of the seventeenth and eighteenth centuries, and of translations from Greek and Latin. Under his encouragement and scholarly influence, her natural taste for reading developed. Intimate history of a somewhat unusual nature always appealed to her; Saint-Simon's *Memoirs* and Agnes Strickland's *Lives of the Queens of England* were favorites. She was ten years old when she started reading Sir Walter Scott, and continued throughout twenty of his novels, *Quentin Durward* and *The Fair Maid of Perth* being read and re-read. Her first literary effort was written at the age of five, when, in large capitals, she printed out a ghost story. She did no more writing until she was just grown up, and then the first stories she wrote were fairy tales.

On leaving school at Clifton, Margaret Irwin went to Oxford, where she read English literature. In 1924, she published a "ghost story" that combined the eighteenth century with the present day, under the title *Still She Wished for Company.* During the next few years, there followed *These Mortals, Knock Four Times* and *Fire Down Below,* and in 1930 *None So Pretty,* which won first prize in the Historical Novel Competition organized by Chatto and Windus. The news that she had won the prize reached her on her honeymoon; she had just married J. R. Monsell, the author-artist of many children's picture, song and story books, from *The Pink Knight* to *Polichinelle,* a collection of French nursery rhymes. He also designed the jackets for Margaret Irwin's books.

Miss Irwin's "brightly tapestried" historical novels have won her great popularity in Great Britain and in the United States. She has been especially successful in her books on the Elizabethan period. These began with *The Gay Galliard,* a story of Mary Queen of Scots and her lover Bothwell, a subject which had fascinated Miss Irwin for many years. From Mary her reading led naturally to Elizabeth, on whom she has written a trilogy beginning with the highly successful *Young Bess,* a vivid and gracefully-written novel which was made into an American motion picture in 1952. Miss Irwin lives in London.

PRINCIPAL WORKS: Still She Wished for Company, 1924; These Mortals, 1925; Knock Four Times, 1927; None So Pretty, 1930; Royal Flush, 1932; Proud Servant: the Story of Montrose, 1934; The Stranger Prince, 1937; The Bride: the Story of Louise and Montrose, 1939; The Gay Galliard, 1941; Mrs. Oliver Cromwell and Other Stories, 1942; Young Bess, 1945; Elizabeth, Captive Princess, 1948; Elizabeth and the Prince of Spain, 1953; Bloodstock (short stories) 1954.

ABOUT: Current Biography 1946; New York Herald Tribune Book Review October 24, 1954.

IRWIN, WALLACE ADMAH (March 15, 1875-). For autobiographical sketch and list of works and references, see TWENTIETH CENTURY AUTHORS, 1942.

* * *

Wallace Irwin sends the following corrections to his sketch in TWENTIETH CENTURY AUTHORS, 1942: he was born in 1875, not 1876; his wife, Laetitia McDonald, was the author of three, not two novels—the third being *Golden Hammock.* Irwin adds that his "Hashimura Togo" series was "one of Mark Twain's pets."

Irwin's only literary work of recent years years was a collaboration, with Dr. Sylvester Lambert, on the latter's book about his experiences as a doctor in the South Seas, *Yankee Doctor in Paradise* (1941). Irwin lives part of the year in East Setauket, Long

Island, N.Y., and part of the year at his home in Southern Pines, N.C.

IRWIN, WILLIAM HENRY (September 14, 1873-February 24, 1948). For biographical sketch and list of earlier works and references, see TWENTIETH CENTURY AUTHORS, 1942.

* * *

Will Irwin died of cerebral occlusion, at seventy-four, at New York's St. Vincent's Hospital.

Although he wrote novels, plays, and articles, it is as a reporter that he is best remembered. Oswald Garrison Villard called him "one of the most valued and distinguished of our popular journalists." The New York *Times* observed: "Wide-ranging, versatile, personally genial, a story-teller who delighted his cronies, he searched and wrote in just about every field available to an extraordinary curiosity."

ADDITIONAL WORKS: Making of a Reporter (autobiography) 1942; (ed.) Letters to Kermit from Theodore Roosevelt, 1946; History of the Union League Club of New York City (completed after author's death by E. C. May and J. Hotchkiss) 1952.

ABOUT: Irwin, W. H. Making of a Reporter; National Cyclopedia of American Biography (1949); New York Times February 25, 1948; Saturday Review of Literature April 14, 1945, March 16, 1946, June 12, 1948.

"I.S." See SCHNEIDER, I.

ISHERWOOD, CHRISTOPHER (August 26, 1904-   ). For autobiographical sketch and list of earlier works and references, see TWENTIETH CENTURY AUTHORS, 1942.

* * *

Christopher Isherwood writes: "1941-42 I worked for the American Friends Service Committee at a hostel for refugees from Central Europe, near Philadelphia. 1943-45 I became a resident student of the Vedanta Society of Southern California in Hollywood and helped its minister, Swami Prabhavananda, edit the society's magazine, *Vedanta and the West*. I have edited two anthologies of articles taken from this magazine: *Vedanta for the Western World* and *Vedanta for Modern Man*. With Swami Prabhavananda, I have made the following translations: *The Bhagavad-Gita*, 1944; *The Crest-Jewel of Discrimination*, 1947; *How to Know God* (Patanjali's *Yoga Aphorisms*), 1953. (These translations are from the Sanskrit.)

"In 1945 I published a novelette, *Prater Violet*. In 1949, I published *The Condor and the Cows*, a South American travel-diary, illustrated with photographs by William Caskey, who accompanied me. In 1951 *I Am a Camera*, adapted by John Van Druten from two of my stories in *Goodbye to Berlin*, opened on Broadway as a stage-play with Julie Harris and William Prince. It won the New York Drama Critics' Award.

"In 1946 I became a U.S. citizen. Since then I have visited England three times and made the above-mentioned trip to South America. In 1949 I was elected a member of the National Institute of Arts and Letters. I still live in the Los Angeles area, not far from Santa Monica."

* * *

In 1954 Isherwood published his first novel with an American setting, *The World in the Evening*, a study of the loves and the two marriages of a young writer. Many reviewers found the book disappointing, "featureless and commonplace," awkward in structure. But they were nevertheless impressed with the brilliance of Isherwood's style. The London *Times Literary Supplement* commented: "At moments Mr. Isherwood writes with surprising sentimentality and at others he is unnecessarily and embarrassingly frank, but at all times he is impressive as a writer who with complete sincerity and to the best of his ability puts his considerable talent to the service of his experience."

ADDITIONAL WORKS: Prater Violet, 1945; The Berlin Stories, 1946; Vedanta for the Western World (ed.) 1946; The Condor and the Cows, 1949; Vedanta for Modern Man (ed.) 1951; The World in the Evening (novel) 1954.

ABOUT: American Mercury April 1952; New York Times Book Review December 16, 1951; Saturday Review of Literature December 14, 1946, December 27, 1947, April 12, 1952; Theatre Arts May 1946.

*ISTRATI, PANAÏT (August 11, 1884-April 16, 1935). For biographical sketch and list of works and references, see TWENTIETH CENTURY AUTHORS, 1942.

* * *

ABOUT: French Review February 1947.

* ē strä′tē

JACKS, LAWRENCE PEARSALL (1860-   ). For biographical sketch and list of earlier works and references, see TWENTIETH CENTURY AUTHORS, 1942.

* * *

L. P. Jacks retired from the editorship of the *Hibbert Journal*, which he had founded, in 1947. He continues active in literary work, publishing articles, translations of the religious writings of Alfred Loisy, and two volumes of memoirs. In 1948 he delivered the Eddington Memorial Lecture at Cambridge. Jacks' wife died in 1945. He lives in Headington, Oxford. On the occasion of his ninetieth birthday, in 1950, the trustees of the *Hibbert Journal* offered their tribute to him as one "who has devoted a long life to facing the growing challenge of religious unrest with a reverence for all in the past that was worthy and a fearless understanding of the problems of his own time."

ADDITIONAL WORKS: Confessions of an Octogenarian, 1942; Observations of a Nonagenarian, 1952.

ABOUT: Jacks, L. P. Confessions of an Octogenarian, Observations of a Nonagenarian; Hibbert Journal January 1948, October 1950.

JACKSON, CHARLES REGINALD
(April 6, 1903-), American novelist and short story writer, reports: "I was born in

Summit, N.J., the fourth child of Sarah Williams and Frederick George Jackson. My father was English, my mother's parents English too. When I was three, we moved to Newark, N.Y., a small village in Wayne County, and there I was brought up. Graduated from Newark High School in 1921, and that was the end of my formal education. Worked in a bookstore in Chicago in 1925-26, and in late 1926 went to New York City. Serious tuberculosis from 1927 to 1930. Went to Davos, Switzerland, in October 1929 for my health, stayed there till July 1931. During these years of illness I read a great deal—largely Shakespeare, Proust, the great Russians, and the Bible—and also wrote. After submitting many stories to the magazines over many years, and writing three novels (all unpublished), my first published story, 'Palm Sunday' (1939), appeared in *Partisan Review*, then a quarterly; my second, 'Rachel's Summer,' in the next issue of *Partisan Review*. Meanwhile I had worked as a staff writer for Columbia Broadcasting System for two years, and free lanced in radio generally, from 1939 to 1944. Also taught radio writing at New York University. My first published novel was *The Lost Weekend* (January 1944), my second *The Fall of Valor* (October 1946), my third

The Outer Edges (April 1948). Two years later, April 1950, a collection of short stories appeared under the name of *The Sunnier Side* (which was the name of the first story in the collection). My stories have appeared also in *Cosmopolitan, Collier's, Mademoiselle, Esquire, Good Housekeeping, Park-East,* the *New Yorker, Harper's Bazaar, Today's Woman,* and *Woman's Home Companion.*

"In 1938 I married Rhoda Booth, then an associate editor of *Fortune* magazine; we have two daughters, Sarah and Kate. Three times I have gone to Hollywood for short periods to do movie work. In 1944 we moved to Orford, N.H., and have been living here ever since. I have written a number of published articles, not very important, and a considerable number of book reviews for the New York *Times*, the Chicago *Sun*, and the *Saturday Review of Literature*. I have spoken at New York University to the writing classes, at Columbia University, often at Dartmouth College, and lectured for a year at Marlboro College, in Vermont, on the American Novel. I have appeared a number of times on radio programs such as 'The Author Meets the Critics' and 'Information Please' (ten times on the former, eight times on the latter). My chief interests outside of writing are reading, music (especially Beethoven and Mozart), and my children. There has been a great deal written about my work, both praise and blame; but, as it should, it mostly goes in one ear and out the other. The above contains the bare facts. I wish I could write you something more interesting about myself, but somehow I am unable to do this—unless it be in the form of fiction, i.e., the short stories in *The Sunnier Side.*"

* * *

Charles Jackson's study of an alcoholic in *The Lost Weekend* was called by Philip Wylie "the most compelling gift to the literature of addiction since DeQuincey." It was a best seller and was made into a successful motion picture. In the two novels which followed it, Jackson dealt penetratingly and sensitively with the problems of homosexuality (*The Fall of Valor*) and the mentally deficient (*The Outer Edges*). His short stories in *The Sunnier Side* were a curious mixture of tragedy and comedy, set in a country village in upstate New York from 1912 to 1918. "In his best stories," Frederic Morton writes of Jackson, "he catches the tune of all our existence and hums it for us with the casual, colloquially relaxed precision characteristic of his style."

PRINCIPAL WORKS: The Lost Weekend, 1944; The Fall of Valor, 1946; The Outer Edges, 1948; The Sunnier Side (short stories) 1950; Earthly Creatures (short stories) 1953.

ABOUT: Barnett, L. The Lost Novelist (pamphlet); Warfel, H. R. American Novelists of Today; Current Biography 1944; New York Herald Tribune Book Review November 3, 1946, October 11, 1953; New York Times Book Review April 30, 1950.

JACKSON, HOLBROOK (December 31, 1874-June 16, 1948). For autobiographical sketch and list of earlier works and references, see TWENTIETH CENTURY AUTHORS, 1942.

* * *

Holbrook Jackson died at seventy-three, at Bournemouth, Hampshire, England, of asthma, from which he had suffered for years.

He remained extremely active to the end of his life; his last book, a series of studies of a group of nineteenth century idealists, was published two months before his death. "His peculiar strength," according to the London *Times*, "lay in the constriction under one hat of an enormous reader, a discriminating judge of literature, and a lover of books as a material object."

ADDITIONAL WORKS: Reading of Books, 1946; (comp.) Bookman's Pleasure; A Recreation for Booklovers, 1947 (in England: Bookman's Holiday, 1945); Dreamers of Dreams, 1948.

ABOUT: London Times June 18, 1948; New York Times June 18, 1948.

*JACKSON, JOSEPH HENRY (July 21, 1894-). For biographical sketch and list of earlier works and references, see TWENTIETH CENTURY AUTHORS, 1942.

* * *

After more than thirty years of living in San Francisco, Joseph Henry Jackson's roots there are deep and strong, and he is a kind of unofficial chronicler-historian of the city. He has reached the quarter-century mark as literary editor of the San Francisco *Chronicle*. He is also a member of the editorial board of the magazine *Pacific Spectator*. On the national literary scene, Jackson served as a member of the Pulitzer prize fiction jury from 1949 to 1951, as a judge of the Harper prize novel contest in 1947 and 1949, and of the O. Henry Memorial Award in 1942 and 1951. His recent books—with one exception —reflect his chief side-interests. "California's early days and true crime: I've done books in both fields and shall probably go right on doing them." The exception was his account of a Mexican Christmas legend,

* Died July 15, 1955.

The Christmas Flower, which Richard Sullivan described in the Chicago *Sunday Tribune* as "a short story written with sensitive restraint, warm feeling, and genuine validity."

ADDITIONAL WORKS: Bad Company: The Story of California's Stage-Robbers, 1949; The Christmas Flower, 1951; My San Francisco: An Appreciation, 1953. *Edited*—Bierce, A. Tales of Soldiers and Civilians, 1943; Continent's End: A Collection of California Writing, 1944; The Portable Murder Book, 1945; San Francisco Murders, 1947; The Gold Rush Album, 1949.

ABOUT: New York Herald Tribune Book Review October 11, 1953; Time December 11, 1944.

JACKSON, LAURA (RIDING) (January 16, 1901-). For autobiographical sketch and list of works and references, see RIDING, LAURA, TWENTIETH CENTURY AUTHORS, 1942.

* * *

Laura Jackson (as the author asks to be styled) writes: "The previous record I wrote just after I had ceased to live as a poet, when I was just beginning to live again on the common plane, after twenty years of absence from it. I became a poet because I was filled with hope of human good, but could see no room for my hope except in the isolation of poetry. The life around me I found a disorder of personal patterns unrelieved by any common loyalty of hope. Especially was I unhappy in the language I heard spoken everywhere—sordidly chaotic to my ears; I felt my tongue tied, from a sense of the impossibility of speaking mere truth in the manner in which people habitually spoke. Poetry was for me a form of living, a state of being in which the redemption of human life from its deadly disorder by truth could be looked forward to. Although I had no company in that state, I sustained myself in it in the happy certainty that there was a destined fulfillment of common humanity in truth.

"I foretold in my poems the coming of a time of truth; the necessity and imminence of this was with increasing force their inspiration. In following that single vision, not distracted by literary or ideological preoccupations, I circumvented the inveterate unveraciousness of poetry as an art of creating simulacra of truth. My whole art was an anticipating of the intonations of truth; thus my word-style had a peculiar rectitude of accent. My words were still, however, the words of a careless tradition of speech, and their intractability as such drew me ever closer to the crux of the human problem: the question of the validity of words. The same while, I was gradually approaching the end of my ability to endure in a position of hope alone, with living truth a continuously suspended activity. At last the time came for the proving. This was the road by which I traveled to the making of a dictionary: the meanings of words, I had come to feel, had to be known with perfect distinctness before they could be used with perfect truthfulness. My husband reached the same decision by a road of his own.

"We knew that in the task we set ourselves (we are speaking of it jointly) we would have to break with lexicographical tradition— to what extent was not at first clear to us. Existing dictionaries and word-books define words by suggestive generalizations that correspond with the indefinite ideas of words' meanings entertained at large: we would have to define them with orderliness and exactness, holding them to the internal consistency of the language. For long, however, we found words resistant to such treatment. We did not fully understand the character of the mental operation required for definitions of the kind we wished to make until we perceived that we must liberate our minds entirely from the confused associations of usage in which the meanings of words are entangled —and that, for us, the act of definition must involve a total reconstituting of words' meanings. Much of our work has been done upon our minds, rather than upon words directly: and we have proceeded very slowly, in consequence. We know now that slowness is inevitable; also inevitable, probably, was our inability to foresee this—but we regret, nevertheless, the expectations of early completion of our work we excited during its first stages. It is still far from completion, but we must leave the matter of time to nature. Perhaps, under the pressure of a sense of the public need for such an unfolding of linguistic realities as we are making, we shall be moved some time to publish a separate portion of the work, preliminarily. Personally, we are resigned to continuing slowness and difficulty, as our portion of the mental punishment all must in one manner or another suffer for the common sin of tolerating confusion in language.

"The previous record is out-of-date in these respects: my husband [Schuyler Jackson] resigned from *Time* many years ago; we live in Wabasso, Fla., where we have sustained ourselves by shipping and growing citrus fruits."

ABOUT: Gregory, H. & Zaturenska, M. A History of American Poetry, 1900-1940.

JACKSON, SHIRLEY (1919-), American novelist and short story writer, reports: "I very much dislike writing about myself or my work, and when pressed for autobiographical material can give only a bare chronological outline which contains, naturally, no pertinent facts. I was born in San Francisco in 1919 and spent most of my early life in California. I was married in  1940 to Stanley Edgar Hyman, critic and numismatist, and we live in Vermont, in a quiet rural community with fine scenery and comfortably far away from city life. Our major exports are books and children, both of which we produce in abundance. The children are Laurence, Joanne, Sarah, and Carry; my books include three novels, *The Road Through the Wall, Hangsaman, The Bird's Nest,* and a collection of short stories, *The Lottery. Life Among the Savages* is a disrespectful memoir of my children.

"My books have almost all been published in England, and I have published short stories and miscellaneous prose in many magazines in this country and abroad. A number of the stories have been included in anthologies and performed on television and radio."

* * *

Shirley Jackson's short story "The Lottery," which first appeared in the *New Yorker* in 1948, has become a classic in its form, many times anthologized, and even dramatized for television. This precise and adroitly-written horror story reflects only one aspect of Miss Jackson's work—her concern with the darker regions of human consciousness and personality, also brilliantly reflected in her novels *Hangsaman* and *The Bird's Nest.* On the other side are a group of informal and completely engaging personal essays which have appeared in many popular magazines and are collected in *Life Among the Savages.* Chronicled here are the adventures of her large and singularly happy family, about which she writes—the *New Yorker* observes—"with a sort of nervous and observant detachment that is sometimes quite funny."

PRINCIPAL WORKS: The Road Through the Wall, 1948; The Lottery; or the Adventures of James Harris (short stories) 1949; Hangsaman, 1951; Life Among the Savages, 1953; The Bird's Nest 1954.

ABOUT: Jackson, S. Life Among the Savages; Warfel, H. R. American Novelists of Today; New York Herald Tribune Weekly Book Review May 8, 1949, July 5, 1953; New York Times Book Review June 29, 1949.

JACOB, NAOMI ELLINGTON (July 1, 1889-). For autobiographical sketch and list of earlier works and references, see TWENTIETH CENTURY AUTHORS, 1942.

* * *

Naomi Jacob's home, "Casa Micki," is in Gardone Riviera, Italy. She travels to England every spring for a visit. In 1942 she returned to the London stage briefly to act in *The Nutmeg Tree* by Margery Sharp. She produces her light and breezy novels at the rate of about two books a year. Her series of chatty autobiographical "Me" books still flourishes; she has written some half-dozen since the end of World War II.

ADDITIONAL WORKS: Me—in War Time, 1940; Leopards and Spots, 1942; Private Gollantz, 1943; White Wool, 1944; Me and the Mediterranean, 1945; Susan Crowther, 1945; Honour's a Mistress, 1947; Me—Over There, 1947; Passage Perilous, 1948; Mary of Delight, 1949; Me and Mine, 1949; Every Other Gift, 1950; Heart of the House, 1950; Me—Looking Back, 1950; Robert, Nana and—Me, 1952; Just About Us, 1953; The Gollantz Saga (2 vols.) 1952-53; Morning Will Come, 1953; Second Harvest, 1954; Me—Likes and Dislikes, 1954; Antonia, 1954.

ABOUT: Hoehn, M. (ed.) Catholic Authors, I; *see* "Me" books listed above.

JACOBS, WILLIAM WYMARK (September 8, 1863-September 1, 1943). For autobiographical sketch and list of works and references, see TWENTIETH CENTURY AUTHORS, 1942.

* * *

W. W. Jacobs died in a London nursing home a few days before his eightieth birthday.

The enormous popularity of his short stories, most of which deal with "the misadventures—financial, marital, alcoholic and what-not—of the salt in port," is evidenced by frequent comparisons of his work with O. Henry's. Christopher Morley called him "one of the most permanently delightful short story writers who ever lived." He was a conscientious craftsman, writing carefully and critically, and, in common with many humorous writers, took life so seriously as to be disposed to pessimism.

J. B. Priestley found him "a most finished, conscientious and delicate artist" whose humor is "limited, neat, finished . . . the humor of a witty dramatist, out to exploit a situation rather than a character, and achieving its end by verbal dexterity."

ABOUT: Pritchett, V. S. Books in General; National Review November 1943; London Times September 2, 1943; Publishers' Weekly September 11, 1943; Saturday Review of Literature September 18, 1943.

JAMES, HENRY (1879-December 13, 1947). For biographical sketch and list of works and references, see TWENTIETH CENTURY AUTHORS, 1942.

* * *

Henry James died at his home in New York City as the result of a heart ailment, after an illness of several weeks. He was sixty-eight years old.

Among his activities were trusteeships of the Carnegie Corporation of New York and the Rockefeller Institute for Medical Research.

James' most distinguished piece of writing was the Pulitzer prize-winning biography of Charles W. Eliot, of which H. L. Mencken said: "Mr. James pretends very little to that omniscience which has been the conceit of biographers. Mr. James has made an interesting book about Eliot and deals with him honestly and sensibly."

ABOUT: American Historical Review April 1948; New York Times December 15, 1947.

JAMES, MARQUIS (August 29, 1891-). For autobiographical sketch and list of earlier works and references, see TWENTIETH CENTURY AUTHORS, 1942.

* * *

Marquis James writes: "One of the things that a writer has to think about is making a living. When I first started writing books I kept up my magazine work simply to finance the writing of the books. About 1940 a rather novel proposal was made to me. It was to write, for an acceptable sum of money, a history of the Insurance Company of North America. Before answering the proposal I looked into the matter of corporation histories. All that I read were laudatory sagas, unworthy of belief. It may well be that objective and credible histories of businesses existed at that time. All I say is that I didn't run onto one in my cursory search.

"I told the North America people that I would write their history (which began in 1792) if I could write it the way I saw it, and not the way some officer of the company might see it. This was agreed to. I found that in the course of its long career the company had made some serious mistakes, and a time or two almost went under. The book was published in 1942 and presently I received several offers from other corporations. I picked the Metropolitan Life Insurance Company to do. After that I did a short sketch of the Texas Company and, with my former wife, did a full-scale job on the history of the world's largest bank, the Bank of America, National Trust and Savings Institution, of San Francisco.

"The only other book I have written in the meantime is *The Cherokee Strip, A Tale of an Oklahoma Boyhood*—and that about describes it.

"For ten years, however, I have been interested in the history of race relations in the United States, and in particular in the life of Booker T. Washington. Since the beginning of 1952 I have devoted my full time to the research for a biography of Washington. It is quite the largest undertaking I have tackled to date. I have no idea when the book will appear.

"On the personal side, I have been divorced and live alone in a converted barn overlooking a cove of Long Island Sound in Rye, N.Y. About a half mile down the road live my daughter and her four children."

* * *

Marquis James was elected to the National Institute of Arts and Letters in February 1953.

ADDITIONAL WORKS: Biography of a Business, 1792-1942: The Insurance Company of North America, 1942; The Cherokee Strip, 1945; The Metropolitan Life: A Study in Business Growth, 1947; Biography of a Bank (with B. R. James) 1954.

ABOUT: James, M. The Cherokee Strip; Saturday Review of Literature October 20, 1945; Time September 24, 1945.

JAMES, MONTAGUE RHODES (August 1, 1862-June 12, 1936). For biographical sketch and list of works and references, see TWENTIETH CENTURY AUTHORS, 1942.

* * *

ABOUT: Dictionary of National Biography 1931-1940.

JAMES, NORAH CORDNER (1900-). For autobiographical sketch and list of earlier works and references, see TWENTIETH CENTURY AUTHORS, 1942.

* * *

Norah C. James writes from London: "I became a recruit in the Auxiliary Territorial Service in May 1940 as a convoy driver. This lasted for six months when I got a commission. I had a training company of some 250 women and girls in the North of England. Later I was posted to the War Office to the Public Relations Department. Amongst other interesting jobs there I was a film supervisor of A.T.S. training films. I was medically boarded out of the Army after four and a half years with the rank of Captain.

"After the war I stood as a Labour candidate for the borough of Finsbury Council, was elected, and remained a Councilor until I went to live in Jersey, C.I., for health reasons. However, I was able to return to England after three years.

"I have written some B.B.C. scripts for the North American Service. I have also had a number of stories published in women's magazines. I write a novel a year and have done so ever since the last one you mention."

ADDITIONAL WORKS: Hunted Heart, 1942; Two Selfish People, 1942; Enduring Adventure, 1944; One Bright Day, 1945; Father, 1946; There Is Always Tomorrow, 1946; Penny Trumpet, 1947; Brittle Glory, 1948; Swift to Sever, 1949; Greenfingers and the Gourmet (with B. Beauchamp) 1949; Pay the Piper, 1950; Pedigree of Honey, 1951; So Runs the River, 1952; Cooking in Cider, 1952; Summer-storm, 1953; Silent Corridors, 1953; Over the Windmill, 1954.

JAMES, WILL (June 6, 1892-September 3, 1942). For autobiographical sketch and list of earlier works and references, see TWENTIETH CENTURY AUTHORS, 1942.

* * *

Will James died at the Presbyterian Hospital in Hollywood at fifty. Although he had been living in Hollywood for a year, he was not connected with the film industry.

May Lamberton Becker has observed that in telling a story in a straightforward fashion James "achieves a method the most deliberate of stylists might envy. Its tone, pace and cadence belong to the range. Its soft drawl, faintly tinged with the melancholy, the unhurried tempo of unlimited space, provide the precisely proper medium for a story." The cowboy artist and writer was looked upon as "a charming exotic" when he first appeared in print, Struthers Burt has noted, but "as we get to know our country better, he has a good chance of being regarded as a classic."

ABOUT: Scully, F. Rogues' Gallery; New York Times September 4, 1942.

JAMESON, STORM (1897-). For biographical sketch and list of earlier works and references, see TWENTIETH CENTURY AUTHORS, 1942.

* * *

As president of the English branch of PEN from 1938 to 1945, Storm Jameson had a close view of the sufferings of European intellectuals during the war. She worked actively in behalf of refugee writers and, after the war, continued her efforts in the governing body of International PEN. In 1952 she was a delegate to the UNESCO Congress on the Arts, held in Venice. A vigorous, sensitive, and intelligent woman, she has shown in both her PEN work and in her writing a passionate concern for the fundamental ethical and moral issues of modern life. In 1947 she wrote in an essay on "The Writer's Situation": "I propose a way to test the value of the writers of our day. Not a test to find out whether a writer is clever or stupid, not even whether he is honest or dishonest, brave or cowardly. No —what we should ask the writer is only this. Is he able to tell us about the destiny of man, our destiny, in such a way that we have the courage to live it, and gaily? If not, then he may be a very clever writer, he may even be honest, but he is not a great writer—not for us."

Her later novels have been for the most part sober, thoughtful explorations of such questions. "Her subject is important, her labor impressive and there is much that is sensitive and deft in her presentation," Dorsha Hayes wrote of her war novel *Cloudless May*, and it is a comment that has been echoed by reviewers of all her recent books. At times her "moral earnestness" becomes obtrusive; the action bogs down; her characters seem wooden. But her craftsmanship rarely fails. (A reviewer referred to one of her recent novels as "a first-rate second-rate novel.") Among her later books *The Green Man* has had the best reception. A study of an English family over the critical years 1930 to 1947, it was a crowded, panoramic historical novel—"in the tradition of Galsworthy and Bennett," wrote Harvey Curtis Webster in the *Saturday Review*.

In 1948 Miss Jameson and her husband, Guy Patterson Chapman, professor of modern history at the University of Leeds, visited the United States to lecture at the University of Pittsburgh.

ADDITIONAL WORKS: (ed.) London Calling, 1942; Then We Shall Hear Singing: A Fantasy in C Major, 1942; Cloudless May, 1944; The Journal of Mary Hervey Russell, 1945; The Other Side, 1946; Before the Crossing, 1947; Black Laurel, 1948; The Moment of Truth, 1949; The Writer's Situation, and Other Essays, 1950; The Green Man, 1952; The Hidden River, 1955.

ABOUT: Gray, J. On Second Thought.

*JAMMES, FRANCIS (December 2, 1868-November 1, 1938). For biographical sketch and list of works and references, see TWENTIETH CENTURY AUTHORS, 1942.

* * *

ADDITIONAL WORK IN ENGLISH TRANSLATION: Homer Had a Dog: Selections from His Poetry, 1946.

ABOUT: Columbia Dictionary of Modern European Literature; Hoehn, M. (ed.) Catholic Authors, I; Mercure de France March 1952.

* zhám

JANEWAY, ELIZABETH (October 7, 1913-), American novelist, was born in Brooklyn to Charles and Jeanette (Searle) Hall. She attended Shore Road Academy and Swarthmore College, later transferring to Barnard, from which she graduated in 1935 with a B.A. degree. Her college career was interrupted for one year during the depression when she wrote advertising copy for a Brooklyn department store. While a senior at Barnard, Mrs. Janeway won *Story* magazine's intercollegiate short story contest. It was not until 1943, however, that she published her first novel, *The Walsh Girls*, a study of the adjustment of two New England sisters, one of whom returns to the other in America after the death of her husband at Dachau.

Leonard

The press greeted *The Walsh Girls* with considerable enthusiasm, remarking on the author's talented entrance into the field of the novel with this "lucid and subtle" psychological book.

Mrs. Janeway's second novel, *Daisy Kenyon*, a study of the life and loves of a successful career woman, was generally considered to be fast-moving but "slick." *The Question of Gregory*, another psychological portrait, with Washington, D.C., and World War II as its background, was labeled as "synthetic" by some reviewers, though others regarded it more highly. With *Leaving Home* (1953), the story of a Brooklyn family in the Thirties, Mrs. Janeway won back a more united praise from the critics. "The construction of this quiet novel is expert. . . . The writing is sustained, the dialogue good," James Michener wrote in the *New York Herald Tribune,* and the *New York Times'* reviewer called it "a novel of new detachment and keen objectivity."

Mrs. Janeway is described by Harvey Breit as "a trim, slight, sleek slip of a girl," dark-haired and attractive. She expresses admiration for authors Robert Graves and William Faulkner, and, in an interview with Mr. Breit for the New York *Times,* has said, "I am trying to write the truest thing I can say about this country, about the people in it."

Married to Eliot Janeway, one of the editors of *Life* and *Fortune,* shortly after her graduation from college, Elizabeth Janeway has two sons, Michael and William. Mrs. Janeway shares with her husband, "a wide-ranging social and intellectual life, including a pragmatic fascination with politics." She thoroughly enjoys, also, she says, "such usual feminine activities as running a house, cookery, and wearing pretty clothes." The Janeways have a duplex apartment overlooking New York's East River.

PRINCIPAL WORKS: The Walsh Girls, 1943; Daisy Kenyon, 1945; The Question of Gregory, 1949; Leaving Home, 1953.

ABOUT: Current Biography, 1944, New York Times Book Review, September 11, 1949; New York Herald Tribune Book Review, October 11, 1953.

JARRELL, RANDALL (May 16, 1914-),
American poet and critic, was born in Nashville, Tenn. After his early schooling, he

R. Thorne McKenna

attended Vanderbilt University where he took two degrees, a B.A. and M.A. He studied both psychology and English, and after two years of graduate work, was already dedicated to his twin professions of writing and teaching.

In 1942, the year his first book of poems, *Blood For A Stranger,* was published, Jarrell enlisted in the Army Air Corps. By then he had already been teaching for five years, first on the English staff at Kenyon College (1937-39), and then at the University of Texas (1939-42). Of his first book *Time* said: "Some of the lyrics in *Blood for a Stranger* register the pain of human guilt as it has seldom been registered before in American poetry."

World War II and his army experiences as a CNT (control tower) operator at an airfield training B-29 crews deepened and extended Jarrell's dominant themes. And *Little Friend, Little Friend,* his second book of poems, published in 1945 while he was still in the army, is full of the pathos and horror of war; the courage of the soldiers and the tragedy of death in youth.

The war over, Jarrell was, for 1946, the acting literary editor of the *Nation* and a teacher at Sarah Lawrence College. That year too he won a Guggenheim fellowship. In 1947 he accepted a permanent position as an associate professor at the Woman's College of the University of North Carolina, and in 1948 his third book of poems, *Losses,* was published. *Poetry* magazine said of *Losses:* "The book contains war poems quite as good as any written in this century"; and Louis Untermeyer said: "The poems vibrate with an emotion which is tender and tragic, full of unsentimental pity which can smoulder with bitter outrage. An unusual intelligence is always in command."

Jarrell has said that he always loves to teach, just as he always loves to read books. Besides his permanent position, he has lectured at the Salzburg Seminar (1948); taught as a Visiting Fellow in Creative Writing at Princeton University (1951-52) and also lectured there in the Seminars in Literary Criticism; he was a visiting professor at the University of Illinois (1953); and is one of the Fellows of the School of Letters at Indiana University.

Most of Jarrell's work first appears in the literary reviews: in the *Sewanee Review, Kenyon Review, Partisan Review, Poetry,* and others; he also contributes to the *Nation, New Republic,* and the New York *Times* Sunday book section. He has received several magazine prizes for his poems, as well as a $1,000 award from the National Institute of Arts and Letters. His fourth book of poems, *The Seven-League Crutches,* was published in 1951, and a collection of his critical essays in 1953. Of the latter, titled *Poetry and the Age,* the New York *Times'* reviewer said: "Jarrell moves forward to what may very well be the beginning of a new evaluation of poetry, what it is and what it can be."

Randall Jarrell, despite his erudition, is a surprisingly unpretentious young man. He looks quite collegiate and speaks with a Western twang. He is impatient with those critics who "worry and weary their readers to death, in the most impressive way possible," and insists that books are written to be enjoyed.

In 1952 Jarrell married Mary von Schrader. His first novel, *Pictures from an Institution,* "a caricature in epigrams of a progressive college and of its faculty" (as Lewis Gannett described it) was highly praised for its sharp satire.

PRINCIPAL WORKS: *Poetry*—Blood for a Stranger, 1942; Little Friend, Little Friend, 1945; Losses, 1948; The Seven-League Crutches, 1951; Selected Poems, 1955. *Criticism*—Poetry and the Age, 1953. *Novel*—Pictures from an Institution, 1954.

ABOUT: New York Times Book Review August 16, 1953, May 2, 1954; Vogue April 15, 1953.

JARRETT, Mrs. CORA (HARDY) (February 21, 1877-). For biographical sketch and list of earlier works and references, see TWENTIETH CENTURY AUTHORS, 1942.

* * *

After nearly fifteen years of silence, Cora Jarrett published a new novel, *Return to December,* in 1951. A psychological mystery with a touch of the supernatural, it was found worthy, but not quite up to her earlier novels. August Derleth commented: "It stands ably by itself on its own merits, but there is a little too much contrived obscurity, a little less straightforward simplicity, something more of deliberate complexity instead of the easy naturalness of the earlier novels."

ADDITIONAL WORK: Return to December, 1951.
ABOUT: The Writer August 1951.

*JASPERS, KARL (February 23, 1883-), German philosopher, writes: "My course through life was not complicated and it is  almost a miracle that I escaped misfortune in this era of catastrophes. I was born in Oldenburg, close to the shores of the North Sea. My father was a lawyer and president of a bank, whose favorite hobbies were painting and hunting. My mother was a descendant of one of the oldest peasant families. After graduating from the humanistic *gymnasium,* I studied jurisprudence for three semesters, then medicine, graduated in 1908 and acquired the M.D. degree in 1909.

"In 1910 I married Gertrude Mayer, who came from a devout Jewish family. A bond of mutual trust and sympathy was soon established with my parents-in-law, after they had

* yäs'pĕrs

conquered their feelings of distress and disappointment over their beloved daughter's marriage to a non-Jew. Our marriage became the unshakable foundation of the realization of life with both beautiful as well as depressing experiences which we endeavored to master together in philosophy.

"It was also in 1910 that I became assistant to the Psychiatric Clinic in Heidelberg. In 1913 I qualified as an unsalaried lecturer on psychology in the philosophical faculty, where I became full professor of philosophy in 1921 after having declined calls to Greifswald and Kiel. In 1937 I was removed from the professorship by the National Socialist regime, for political reasons. Later, in 1945, I was reinstated with the approval of the American Occupation Army. In 1949 I accepted a call to the University of Basel.

"Since 1910 I have written articles on psychiatric research. In my publication *Allgemeine Psychopathologie* (1913), I attempted a new methodical approach and an objective recapitulation of our psychiatric understanding. This book is still available in its fifth revised edition (1948). In 1919 I published *Psychologie der Weltanschauungen* ('Psychology of World Conceptions'); *Philosophie* was published in three volumes in 1931, my book *Von der Wahrheit* ('On Truth') in 1947. In between these larger works I wrote many shorter ones, of which the following found much recognition: 1931 *Die Geistige Situation der Zeit* ('The Spiritual Outlook on Time'); 1935 *Nietzsche;* 1937 *Descartes und die Philosophie;* 1947 *Der Philosophische Glaube* ('Philosophical Faith'); 1949 *Vom Ursprung und Ziel der Geschichte* ('The Origin and Goal of History'); 1950 *Einführung in die Philosophie* ('Introduction to Philosophy'); 1951 a series of addresses and articles under the title *Rechenschaft und Ausblick* ('Accounts and Outlook').

"Among the motives of my philosophizing, two were always outstanding from the very beginning: I wanted to be sure, and science was foremost. I still distrusted philosophy while I constantly read the works of our great philosophers. But the limits of science and the possibilities of knowledge, on the other hand, disclosed to me the necessity and the great importance of philosophy in our life.

"Philosophizing as thinking opens realms which may not be objective proof to everybody, nor may it lend itself subjectively to opinions and desires, but it clarifies in methodically conscious forms transcendental thinking, as we find ourselves in this world, and the significance of being. In this sphere we realize from another origin than the knowledge of our mere mind that which man can feel and absorb only with all his powers of perception and being. And it can manifest itself only through absolute honesty, to attain which is the never-ending true urge of philosophizing. Man becomes conscious of his inner self only in border situations. Therefore, from early youth to this day, I have always tried to scrutinize even the smallest detail. Because of this desire, I chose medicine and psychiatry. Man can realize himself only through his relationship with others, never through knowledge alone. We become ourselves only to the extent our fellowmen do; we are free only as far as our fellowmen are. Since my schooldays, therefore, I considered the question of communication from man to man, first the practical, then the philosophical principle of life. I never reached finality in any of the three directions: (1) in experience in true science and philosophizing as a form of transcendent thinking, (2) experience in border situations, and (3) enlightenment in communication. The thought of being still on the path and not having reached the goal is not less intense in advanced age than it was in youth, but it has deepened through the events of our age, of which our generations are a part. It was only in 1914 that I began to grasp this condition in its intensity. Time travels with terrific speed. I tried to understand this stirring fate of mankind not as an obvious necessity of a dark, planned process of history, but as a whole which, on the basis of genuine perceptibilities that are always particular, will be determined through the elements of human freedom. Deciding this is up to the individual, and in turn, as a result of his way of life and living, his many, often unimportant daily actions, his important decisions, the individual becomes the reflection of what is possible. Through actual presence, he works unrecognizably on the pattern of the future and in this role he should consider himself not less important than in his role of casting his vote among millions of other votes.

"In this respect philosophy is ever fathomless and yet it is an ever ready foundation for concrete action for the historical purpose of our life, our faithfulness and our trustworthiness and our love."

* * *

Karl Jaspers is one of the leading existentialist philosophers of modern times. Trained as both a scientist and a philosopher, he cuts across conventional lines between modern "schools of thought." For him, James Collins writes, "philosophy of existence is but a particular, contemporary determination of perennial philosophy. . . . Jaspers stresses the need for striking a balance between tradition and original advance in the development of a truly perennial philosophy. It is mainly in Jaspers' books that the attachment of existentialism to the mainstream of philosophy is made evident." His system is a rigorously logical one, but unlike some of his fellow-existentialists (especially Sartre), he acknowledges a transcendental power toward which man strives and with whom he seeks communication. He is less iconoclastic than other existentialists and does not counsel flight from or rejection of society. In general, as William Barrett observed of him in the New York *Times*: "Jaspers shows himself . . . to be one of the most diligent and sensitive students of contemporary history. He has good eyes for the present because he knows what to fear in it—particularly, the threatened loss of individual freedom." Barrett singles out as the combination of qualities which has made Jaspers outstanding among contemporary philosophers "a lucid and flexible intelligence in the service of a genuine and passionate concern for human life."

PRINCIPAL WORKS IN ENGLISH TRANSLATION: Man in the Modern Age, 1933; The Question of German Guilt, 1947; The European Spirit, 1948; The Perennial Scope of Philosophy, 1949; The Way to Wisdom, 1951; Existentialism and Humanism, 1952; Reason and Anti-Reason in our Time, 1952; The Origin and Goal of History, 1953; Tragedy Is Not Enough, 1953.

ABOUT: Brock, W. An Introduction to Contemporary German Philosophy; Collins, J. The Existentialists; Grene, M. Dreadful Freedom.

JASTROW, JOSEPH (January 30, 1863-January 9, 1944). For biographical sketch and list of earlier works and references, see TWENTIETH CENTURY AUTHORS, 1942.

* * *

Joseph Jastrow died of a heart attack at Stockbridge, Mass., at eighty. His adopted son had been killed in World War II.

The psychologist, who had been known as "a valiant tilter at man's absurdities" rather than an originator, had in his later years begun to outline "a naturalistic conception of psychology based on the known or reasonably conjectured facts of neurology, which he hoped would bring cosmos out of the present persisting chaos," according to V. A. C. Henmon, who adds that Professor Jastrow "possessed a keen, incisive mind and an extraordinarily facile pen."

ADDITIONAL WORK: Freud, His Dream and Sex Theories, 1948.

ABOUT: New York Times January 9, 1944; Science March 10, 1944.

JEANNERET-GRIS, C.-E. See LE COR-BUSIER

JEANS, Sir JAMES HOPWOOD (September 11, 1877-September 16, 1946). For biographical sketch and list of earlier works and references, see TWENTIETH CENTURY AUTHORS, 1942.

* * *

Sir James Jeans died at his home in Dorking, Surrey, England, at sixty-nine. He had suffered from a heart malady for some time.

Jeans has been described by S. C. Roberts as a man of few friends, partly because of a temperamental shyness and partly because of "his intolerance of what he deemed to be second-rate." The extraordinary aspect of his career was the combination in one man of a major scientist (S. Chandrasekhar called him the "last remaining link with the great masters in Newtonian tradition of the 19th century") with a writer capable of communicating the complexities of his science to a wide audience.

The London *Times* called him "a man whose mathematical investigations of problems in cosmogony, radiation and molecular dynamics were penetrating and original, while his lucid exposition of the newer physics and astronomy charmed hundreds of thousands of readers in many lands."

ADDITIONAL WORKS: Physics and Philosophy, 1942; Growth of Physical Science, 1947.

ABOUT: Low, A. M. They Made Your World; Milne, E. A. Sir James Jeans; London Times September 17, 1946; New York Times September 17, 1946; Science February 28, 1947; Time September 30, 1946.

JEFFERS, ROBINSON (January 10, 1887-). For biographical sketch and list of earlier works and references, see TWENTIETH CENTURY AUTHORS, 1942.

* * *

Although Robinson Jeffers continues to live in relative seclusion at his home in Carmel, Calif., his work has been discovered by a wider audience than he has ever had before. This has been the result of the production of his *Medea*, a "free adaptation" of Euripides' tragedy, which had a flamboyantly successful production in the 1947 New York theatre season and toured many American cities. No small part of the sensation which the play caused was the overwhelming power of Judith Anderson's Medea, as savage and forceful a performance as has been seen in the American theatre in recent years. The performance, the critics agreed, quite overshadowed the play. Jeffers' adaptation was powerful and full of horror. But—as in his earlier treatment of a classic Greek theme in *The Tower Beyond Tragedy* (revived in New York in 1950 with Judith Anderson as Clytemnestra) and, more recently, his adaptation of Euripides' *Hippolytus* under the title *The Cretan Woman*—his play was melodramatic rather than tragic, violent, shocking, nerve-shattering but quite lacking the calm serene fatalism of the Greek tragedies. "He is concerned with violence rather than with genuine tragedy" (J. G. Southworth). *The Cretan Woman* "lacks every quality of tragedy as the Greeks understood it" (Dudley Fitts).

Jeffers' two latest collections of verse have had an uneven critical reception. In *The Double Axe* he announced his intention "to present a certain philosophical attitude which might be called Inhumanism, a shifting of emphasis and significance from man to notman." The poems were written in "the grand manner" that has always characterized his work, but in this volume nearly all the critics detected an ebbing of his creative powers, a "narrowness of vision," a "lack of self-renewal." In *Hungerfield*, however—especially in the shorter, lyrical poems in the volume—Dudley Fitts found traces of the best of his work: "In all of his better work there is evidence that he is sensitive, and not only to suffering; that he has clear insight into the springs of human action and dereliction; that he truly is the seer poet."

Jeffers' contribution to American poetry has been considerable. It is very likely, as Horace Gregory and Marya Zaturenska point out, that his simpler, more direct, lyrical and descriptive poems will outlast his elaborate philosophic-dramatic poems. His "philosophy," they write, may have less endurance "than those gifts which enabled him to create parables of human blindness and suffering, to see, as if for the first and last time, the austerities of a Pacific or Irish coast line."

In June 1955 *Medea*, with Judith Anderson, was presented in Paris as part of the cultural exchange program of the American National Theatre and Academy.

ADDITIONAL WORKS: Medea, 1946; The Double Axe, 1948; Hungerfield, 1954.

ABOUT: Commager, H. S. The American Mind; Gilbert, R. Four Living Poets; Gregory, H. & Zaturenska, M. History of American Poetry, 1900-1940; Southworth, J. G. Some Modern American Poets; Waggoner, H. H. The Heel of Elohim; Poetry March 1949; Saturday Review of Literature July 31, 1948, September 11, 1948; Theatre Arts June 1949.

JENNINGS, JOHN EDWARD (December 30, 1906-), American historian and historical novelist, writes: "I was born in

Brooklyn, N.Y., the son of John E. Jennings, M.D., a well remembered surgeon of that city, and Florence (Thistle) Jennings; almost equally well known as a social worker both there and in Manhattan. Seventeen and a half years later I managed, through the titanic efforts of my teachers and my parents, to graduate from preparatory school, and in September 1924 I entered Colorado School of Mines under the romantic impression that the life of a mining engineer consisted mainly of Adventure in the Andes, Romance in Rio de Janeiro, etc., etc. I think it likely that I enjoy at least one unique distinction; probably I am the only historical novelist ever to attend the School of Mines.

"My education at Mines was swift and thorough. I learned two things; first, that I was not nearly as good a football player as I thought I was, and, second, that mining engineers' knowledge of the effect of the moon on the Latin temperament was entirely extracurricular! In addition it was necessary for them to know a little geology, a touch of metallurgy, and an awesome amount of mathematics and chemical formulae. I knew my limitations! Later I attended New York University; still later Columbia, where I concentrated on courses more congenial to my temper.

"Meantime I began my travels. I went first as a deckhand in a freighter to the Mediterranean, where we delivered everything from coal to Malta to high-octane gasoline to Syria and picked up figs at Smyrna, ocher at Cyprus, cotton at Alexandria and essence of roses at Algiers. That was in 1926, when the Riff war was just ending, and I think the glimpses I had then of the mountainous coast of North Africa were the last tempting straw that lured me into the life of a writer. During the next four years I was back again

in Algeria and Tunisia, Morocco and Spain and the Balearics. In the intervals, while I was back in the United States, I wrote articles and one travel book, several short stories, and gave lectures. Only the lectures sold, thank God, and they did not do very well. But it was all good practice.

"In 1931 I married Virginia Storey, of Uniontown, Pa. In 1933 our son, John E. Jennings, III, was born. Until this time I had been 'practicing' writing between bouts of other activities which were grist to the mill eventually but which offered little recompense at the moment. Now, with these new responsibilities, it was clear that the time had come to stop practicing and be practical. Perhaps it is mildly significant that in the year my son was born I made my last grab at the romantic by taking—and passing—the examinations for the U.S. Consular and Diplomatic Service. In the same year I also sold my first story to Street & Smith.

"In that year of depression even those who passed their examinations found that appointments to the service were few and far between. In the meantime apparently the fiction market was doing well in the lower brackets. By the time I could have had an appointment I was so well established as a writer of action-adventure stories for the pulp magazines that I could not afford to accept it.

"For several years I worked in this field—again gaining what I feel was valuable experience. In 1934 I began work, against my then agent's advice, upon my first historical novel—a type of work that I had long wanted to try. Since I was without any research experience whatever, I had to feel my way, and the book—*Next to Valour*—was not finished until the end of 1937, almost four years later.

"At that time, however, I was asked by Thomas Y. Crowell and Son to do a travel book to be entitled *Our American Tropics*. This was done, completed and published in 1938. So that this was actually my first book. The novel on which I had worked so long was not sold until the end of that year, and not published until 1939.

"Since then, with the exception of time out for service with the Navy in World War II (I entered as lieutenant, junior grade, in 1942, was released in 1945, and now am a lieutenant commander, inactive), I have devoted myself mainly to writing historical stories. Besides my books my work has appeared periodically in the *Saturday Evening Post*, *Liberty*, *Omnibook*, the Toronto *Star*, Philadelphia *Inquirer*, etc., etc."

PRINCIPAL WORKS: Our American Tropics, 1938; Next to Valour, 1939; Call the New World (reprint title Land of Vengeance) 1941; Coasts of Folly (under pseudonym 'Joel Williams') 1942; Gentleman Ranker, 1942; The Shadow and the Glory, 1943; The Salem Frigate, 1946; Boston, Cradle of Liberty, 1947; River to the West, 1948; The Sea Eagles, 1950; The Pepper Tree, 1950; The Sultan's Warrior (under pseudonym 'Bates Baldwin') 1951; The Strange Brigade, 1952; Clipper Ship Days (juvenile) 1952; Rogue's Yarn, 1953; Banners Against the Wind, 1954; Shadows in the Dusk, 1955.

ABOUT: Leisy, E. E. The American Historical Novel; Current Biography 1949.

JENSEN, JOHANNES VILHELM (January 20, 1873-November 25, 1950). For biographical sketch and list of earlier works and references, see TWENTIETH CENTURY AUTHORS, 1942.

* * *

Johannes Jensen died in Copenhagen at the age of seventy-seven.

Author of more than sixty volumes of poetry, plays, short stories, and novels, and one of the most influential literary men in Denmark, Jensen was so little known in the United States that general surprise was expressed when he was awarded the Nobel prize in 1944. The award was given for his six-volume epic *The Long Journey*, published in this country in three volumes in 1923 and 1924, and in an omnibus edition in 1933. The citation read: ". . . because of the exceptional vigor and fertility of his poetic imagination, combined with an all-embracing intellectuality and bold, creative expression."

Francis Hackett has called Jensen a "full, wise, ripe human being" and "a great critic of human history, using his language creatively, a poet and a seer." The Dane's deep interest in science, and especially in evolution, infused most of his work; for the last ten years of his life he wrote only newspaper articles, chiefly on this theme. Seen in retrospect, Jens Nyholm has said, "Johannes Vilhelm Jensen's authorship may be described in terms of orientation on various levels, or a series of self-identifications—first with his own ego, then, successively, with his forebears, his race, and finally with man."

ADDITIONAL WORK: Garden Colonies in Denmark (translation) 1949.

ABOUT: Hackett, F. On Judging Books; Heepe, E. and Heltberg, N. (eds.) Modern Danish Authors; American Scandinavian Review December 1943, December 1944; London Times November 27, 1950; New Republic May 7, 1945; New York Times November 26, 1950; New Yorker April 28, 1945; Newsweek May 7, 1945; Publishers' Weekly November 18, 1944; Saturday Review of Literature December 2, 1944.

JEROME, JEROME KLAPKA (May 2, 1859-June 14, 1927). For biographical sketch and list of works and references, see TWENTIETH CENTURY AUTHORS, 1942.

JESSE, FRINIWYD TENNYSON. For autobiographical sketch and list of earlier works and references, see TWENTIETH CENTURY AUTHORS, 1942.

* * *

F. Tennyson Jesse writes from her home in St. John's Wood, London: "Since publishing *While London Burns*, I have published (for the Ministry of Information) *The Saga of San Demetrio*, and a novel, *The Alabaster Cup*. I have also, with my husband, H. M. Harwood, converted the novel *A Pin to See the Peepshow* into a play, which the Lord Chamberlain refuses to pass, and which consequently was performed at a Club Theatre."

A Pin to See the Peepshow was produced in New York in 1953 but was poorly received and closed after a very brief run. The play was based upon the sensational Thompson-Bywaters murder trial which took place in London in 1922.

ADDITIONAL WORKS: The Saga of San Demetrio, 1943; The Story of Burma, 1946; Comments on Cain, 1948; The Alabaster Cup, 1950.

JEWELL, EDWARD ALDEN (March 10, 1888-October 11, 1947). For autobiographical sketch and list of earlier works and references, see TWENTIETH CENTURY AUTHORS, 1942.

* * *

Edward Alden Jewell died in an ambulance between his New York City home and a hospital; he had been working at his job as art critic of the New York *Times* until two days before his death. He was fifty-nine years old.

The journalist was described by a friend as "a sensitive, rather lonely man with a friendly smile and a judicial gallery air," who disliked equally the dull academic in art and the school of fashionable expressionism. Stark Young has spoken of his "poetic and lucid insight" by which he perceived inner values of art without resort to schools or classification. Peyton Boswell, Jr., wrote of his friend and fellow-critic as a man who was "warm of heart and looked upon his task as art critic as a means of communication between the masses of the people and those gifted few who call themselves artists."

ADDITIONAL WORKS: *Preface to* French Impressionists and Their Contemporaries Represented in American Collections, 1944; Paul Cezanne, 1944; Georges Rouault, 1945; Vincent Van Gogh, 1947.

ABOUT: Art Digest October 15, 1947; New York Times October 13, 1947.

JOAD, CYRIL EDWIN MITCHINSON
(August 12, 1891-April 9, 1953). For biographical sketch and list of earlier works and references, see TWENTIETH CENTURY AUTHORS, 1942.

* * *

C.E.M. Joad died at his home in London at sixty-one. Bed-ridden for several months, he had continued to teach groups of students from his bed, and had finished correcting proofs on his book *Shaw and Society* the day before his death.

Participation in a B.B.C. panel-show called "Brains Trust" (1939-45) had made the philosopher a widely-known and popular figure in England. World War II caused him to reverse his position on pacifism and on religion. Long an agnostic, he announced shortly after the end of the war that he now believed that the all-pervading nature of evil was explicable only by the doctrine of original sin, and that he found the Christian belief "less implausible" than any other theory of the universe.

The London *Times*, noting the "zest, gaiety, wit, agility, combativeness and an unfailing lucidity and an equally unfailing glibness" that Joad brought to his role as a popular educator, added that "as a writer, Joad drew on the same qualities which always ensured him an audience when he talked. There was a lucidity and a springiness in his writing which gave interest to his expositions of other people's ideas. He had no original contribution to make as a philosopher."

ADDITIONAL WORKS: God and Evil, 1943; Adventures of the Young Soldier in Search of a Better World, 1944; About Education, 1945; Bookmark (essays) 1945; How Our Minds Work, 1946; More Opinions, 1946; Untutored Townsman's Invasion of the Country, 1946; Guide to Philosophy, 1947; Decadence: A Philosophical Inquiry, 1948; A Year More or Less, 1948: Shaw, 1949; Critique of Logical Positivism, 1950; Introduction to Contemporary Knowledge, 1951; The Pleasure of Being Oneself, 1951; Counter-Attack from the East: the Philosophy of Radhakrishnan, 1951; First Encounter with Christianity, 1952; The Recovery of Belief, 1952; (ed.) Shaw and Society, 1953; Folly Farm, 1954.

ABOUT: Coates, J. B. Leaders of Modern Thought; Fortnightly February 1951; London Times April 10, 1953; New York Times April 10, 1953; Time September 7, 1942, March 15, 1948, June 12, 1950.

JOHNS, ORRICK (June 2, 1887-July 8, 1946). For autobiographical sketch and list of works and references, see TWENTIETH CENTURY AUTHORS, 1942.

* * *

Orrick Johns ended his own life by taking poison at his home in Danbury, Conn., at the age of fifty-nine.

His best known work, *Time of Our Lives*, was called "intensely readable, and filled with charm and good story telling" by Floyd Dell, who added that its author had "been almost everywhere and seen almost everybody." Of his early poetry the late Genevieve Taggard declared: "It is possible to delight in him to the full, as one does in the minor Elizabethans, or in Housman."

ABOUT: New York Times July 9, 1946; Publishers' Weekly July 20, 1946.

JOHNSON, ALVIN (December 18, 1874-), American educator, author, social scientist, was born near Homer in northeastern Nebraska, the son of Danish parents, John and Edel Marie (Bille) Johnson. Raised on a farm, he left home at the age of eighteen to attend the University of Nebraska where he specialized in the classics, graduating in 1897.  Apparently the Spanish-American war was responsible for turning his interest to the contemporary political scene. After four months of army service he went to Columbia to study political science, earned his Ph.D. in 1902, and began a teaching career.

Until 1917 he devoted the major part of his time to teaching as a professor of economics at the Universities of Nebraska, Texas and Chicago, Stanford, and Cornell, at the same time writing many scholarly articles, a textbook on economics, and one forgotten novel, *The Professor and the Petticoat*. In 1917 he became editor of the *New Republic*, a magazine which he had helped to launch and with which he was associated for six years. His second book of fiction was a collection of stories first printed in that periodical, *John Stuyvesant, Ancestor*.

As an educator, his greatest challenge and most brilliant achievement came with the founding of The New School for Social Research in New York City in 1919. Working with such remarkable men as Thorstein Veblen, James Harvey Robinson, and Charles A. Beard, friends from Columbia and the *New Republic,* Johnson became director of The New School in 1923, and continued to guide the destinies of this lively new venture in adult education until his resignation in 1945.

As a writer, he has close to a thousand articles to his credit, the subject matter a catalogue of major liberal causes in the field of political thinking and education. He is the founder and editor-in-chief of *Social Research,* and chief working editor of the *Encyclopedia of the Social Sciences.* He has also written a creditable novel, *Spring Storm,* which turns to his Nebraska boyhood for its material, and an extremely readable autobiography, *Pioneer's Progress,* "the story of a long and brilliant career in American education told by the man who lived it."

Dr. Johnson lives in Nyack, N.Y., with his wife, Edith Henry Johnson, whom he married in 1904. They have seven children, all educated at home by Mrs. Johnson, whose success can be measured by their excellent college records. Retired from his more active duties, Johnson still likes to farm, reads in eight languages, and is known to friends and associates as a gifted raconteur. In spite of a long list of honorary degrees and awards, he remains an unassuming person, capable of regarding both himself and his fellows with humor.

PRINCIPAL WORKS: Rent in Modern Economic Theory, 1903; Introduction to Economics, 1909; The Professor and the Petticoat, 1914; John Stuyvesant, Ancestor, 1919; Deliver Us from Dogma, 1934; Spring Storm, 1936; The Public Library; A People's University, 1938; The Clock of History, 1946; Pioneer's Progress, 1952.

ABOUT: Johnson, A. Pioneer's Progress (autobiography); American Scholar Winter 1954-55; Current Biography 1942.

JOHNSON, EDGAR (December 1, 1901-), American biographer and novelist, was born in New York City, the son of Wal-

ter Conover Johnson and Emily Mathilde (Haas) Johnson. He took his B.A. at Columbia in 1922, then taught English there and at Hunter, Washington University, Vassar, and The New School, arriving at the City College of New York in 1927, where he is now chairman of the English Department.

His first book, a novel, was published in 1931: *Unweave a Rainbow,* a sentimental fantasy. "The author's achievement," wrote the *Nation,* "is a perfect artificiality of plot, of scene, of character . . . so well substantiated by selection of details that it is capable of arousing a very real emotion." An historical-critical book appeared in 1937, *One Mighty Torrent,* on the drama of biography. This book was later a challenge to him, he said, "to see if I could do what I told other people to do." But first came another novel, *The Praying Mantis,* followed by two surveys which he edited, one of biography and one of satire. Around this time he read *Bleak House* and was greatly impressed by what he considers Dickens' work of greatest stature. When he studied Dickens' life, what struck him was "the parodox and dramatic form his life took—the spectacular success and disillusion. I was astonished that no other biographer had done anything about this."

For seven years, from 1945 to 1952, he worked on *Charles Dickens,* a biography based on much unpublished material. Johnson's analysis of the novels relates them to the social conditions of Dickens' times. The book was published in two volumes in 1952 and met with critical acclaim. "Edgar Johnson has written the completest and most objective life of Dickens which has yet appeared. John Forster's official biography, published seventy-five years ago, is at long last superseded," commented the *Saturday Review of Literature.*

The next book planned is to be called "The Laughing Philosophers," partly biographical, partly critical, about the great comic writers, with an analysis of the comic spirit. Then another biography—perhaps (he says) "Johnson's Life of Boswell."

In 1933 he married Eleanor Kraus, and they live with their two children in New York City.

PRINCIPAL WORKS: Unweave a Rainbow (novel) 1931; One Mighty Torrent, 1937; Praying Mantis (novel) 1937; Charles Dickens, 1952.

ABOUT: New York Herald Tribune Book Review January 18, 1953; New York Times Book Review January 18, 1953; Saturday Review of Literature January 10, 1953.

JOHNSON, GERALD WHITE (August 6, 1890-), American biographer, historian, journalist, and novelist, was born in Riverton, N.C. ("pop. six kin"), the son of Archibald Johnson, a country newspaper editor, and Flora Caroline (McNeill) Johnson. At the age of twenty he established the

Thomasville (N.C.) *Davidsonian,* and a year later graduated from Wake Forest College. Two years later he became music critic—

Stanislav Rembski

he is, among other things, an amateur musician—for the Greensboro (N.C.) *Daily News* where, except for World War I service, he remained until 1924. The next year, when he was professor of journalism at the University of North Carolina, his first book was published, *The Story of Man's Work* (with W. R. Hayward). When H. L. Mencken spotted him, the "Sunpapers" in Baltimore gained a new star. He had then written three books, but it was his next, *Andrew Jackson* (1927), that made his reputation.

A prolific writer, Johnson is noted for his modesty. He will not admit he is a critic—or a historian. "Anyone who writes about the past without falling into grotesque errors of fact is called a historian. It is a rank injustice to scholars who do the real work, but there isn't much I can do about it." "The second ranking Sage of Baltimore" (the first is indubitably Mencken), as a writer in the New York *Herald Tribune Book Review* called him, writes with a graceful, tart style. His two novels are not much heard of, but his non-fiction is well known. All are in the historical vein except *A Little Night-Music,* "discoveries in the exploitation of an art." Among his best known works are *Andrew Jackson, America's Silver Age, Roosevelt: Dictator or Democrat?, Woodrow Wilson, This American People.*

Around the "Sunpapers" a favorite phrase used to be "Ask Gerald," so great was his background of information. His speed and capacity for work were also famous among his fellow workers, and a number of his most brilliant editorials were written in eight to ten minutes. Of a recent volume, *Incredible Tale, the Odyssey of the Average American in the Last Half Century,* Lloyd Morris wrote in the *Saturday Review of Literature,* "It is an eloquent and powerful book, wise, often witty, but above all a work of penetrating insight. No higher praise could be given it than to say that it explains us to ourselves."

In 1922 Johnson married Kathryn Dulsinea Hayward. They have two daughters

and make their home in Baltimore, where he has been a free-lance writer since 1943. Also a commentator on WAAM-TV, Baltimore, Johnson received a Peabody award in 1954 for his "scholarly commentary on the news."

PRINCIPAL WORKS: The Story of Man's Work (with W. R. Hayward) 1925; What Is News? 1926; The Undefeated, 1927; Andrew Jackson, 1927; Randolph of Roanoke, 1929; By Reason of Strength (novel) 1930; Number Thirty-Six (novel) 1933; The Secession of the Southern States, 1933; The Wasted Land, 1937; A Little Night-Music, 1937; America's Silver Age, 1939; Roosevelt: Dictator or Democrat? 1941; American Heroes and Hero-Worship, 1943; Woodrow Wilson, 1944; Honorable Titan, 1946; First Captain, the Story of John Paul Jones, 1947; Liberal's Progress, 1948; Our English Heritage, 1949; Incredible Tale, 1950; This American People, 1951; Pattern for Liberty, 1952; The Making of a Southern Industrialist, 1952; Mount Vernon, 1953.

ABOUT: New York Herald Tribune Book Review September 4, 1949, October 7, 1951; Saturday Review of Literature June 3, 1950.

JOHNSON, JAMES WELDON (June 17, 1871-June 26, 1938). For biographical sketch and list of works and references, see TWENTIETH CENTURY AUTHORS, 1942.

* * *

ABOUT: Barton, R. C. Witnesses for Freedom; Gloster, H. M. Negro Voices in American Fiction; Mims, E. Christ of the Poets.

JOHNSON, JOSEPHINE WINSLOW (June 20, 1910-). For autobiographical sketch and list of earlier works and references, see TWENTIETH CENTURY AUTHORS, 1942.

* * *

Josephine W. Johnson writes: "In the past few years I have published several short stories—many included in Martha Foley's collections. I am a member of the Authors' Guild, but no longer active or a member of any of the organizations mentioned in the previous biography. I have married again and have two children. My husband is Grant Cannon, managing editor of the *Farm Quarterly,* and we live in Newton, Ohio, near Cincinnati."

Miss Johnson's latest novel is *Wildwood,* published in 1946, a psychological study of a sensitive young girl.

ADDITIONAL WORK: Wildwood, 1946.

ABOUT: National Cyclopedia of American Biography (1952).

JOHNSON, OWEN MC MAHON (August 27, 1878-January 27, 1952). For biographical sketch and list of earlier works and references, see TWENTIETH CENTURY AUTHORS, 1942.

* * *

Owen Johnson died at sixty-three, after a long illness, at his home in Vineyard Haven, Mass., where he had lived for the last five years of his life.

His career had been political rather than literary after 1931; he was an unsuccessful candidate for nomination as Democratic Congressman in 1936 and 1938, and actively supported Franklin D. Roosevelt's election campaigns.

Although some of his later novels (notably *The Salamander*) received favorable critical attention, it was for "the Lawrenceville stories" that he was known. The New York *Times* said: "Mr. Johnson's hilarious tales delighted generations of American boys from the class of 1909 onward, but the serious probing of his satire into the social structure of boarding schools and colleges stirred widespread discussion among parents and educators before the first World War."

ADDITIONAL WORK: Prodigious Hickey; a Lawrenceville Story (juvenile) 1946.

ABOUT: Scientific Monthly January 1946; New York Times January 28, 1952.

JOHNSON, PAMELA HANSFORD (May 29, 1912-), English novelist and critic writes: "I was born in London, south

Elliott Erwitt

of the Thames, and educated at the Clapham County Secondary School. I began writing at an extremely early age and published miscellaneous verse at the age of fourteen or so, and onwards. At eighteen I went to work for four years at the London office of the Central Hanover Bank and Trust Company. At twenty-two I had completed my first novel, *This Bed Thy Centre*, and decided to make literature a career. This first novel was published in America in 1935. Since then I have written fourteen novels, the best known of which are *An Avenue of Stone, The Trojan Brothers, The Philistines*, and *Catherine Carter*. I have written a critical study of Thomas Wolfe, published in the U.S.A. under the title *Hungry Gulliver*, a British Council essay on Ivy Compton-Bur-

nett, and have done feature programmes and talks for the Third Programme on Marcel Proust, on whom I am planning a long critical work.

"I have been a book critic since 1936, working mostly for *John O'London's Weekly*, the *Daily Telegraph* and the *Sunday Chronicle*. I am a frequent broadcaster on various programmes connected with literature —this year [1952] on the Sunday 'Critics.'

"My grandfather was Charles E. Howson, for twenty-five years treasurer to Sir Henry Irving, and both my mother and my aunt appeared in Irving's productions. (My aunt went with him on his second American tour.) I grew up so much in the atmosphere of theatrical reminiscence and handled so many souvenirs of the Lyceum of Irving's day that I finally decided, in *Catherine Carter*, to try to recreate some of that past for myself.

"I was married first in 1936 to Gordon Stewart, by whom I have a son and a daughter. In 1950 I married the English novelist C. P. Snow; our son was born in 1952. After a lifetime in London I have now gone to live in the country, in the small town of Clare, in the county of Suffolk."

* * *

Miss Johnson writes that "*The Philistines*, which I think may be my best novel, is not yet available in the U.S.A." She has also written a play, *Corinth House*, which was produced at the New Lindsey Theatre Club in 1948, broadcast in 1949 and 1950, and televised in 1950. *An Impossible Marriage* (1955) was described by John Nerber in the New York *Times Book Review* as "a finely drawn story, sensitive to the imperceptible nuances which, step by step, mark the growing failure of two individuals who, in striving for completion, become only more apart and separate."

PRINCIPAL WORKS: This Bed Thy Centre, 1935; World's End, 1937; Too Dear for My Possessing, 1940; Winter Quarters, 1943; The Trojan Brothers, 1944; An Avenue of Stone, 1947; Thomas Wolfe: A Critical Study, 1947 (in U.S.: Hungry Gulliver); A Summer to Decide, 1948; The Philistines, 1949; Ivy Compton-Burnett, 1951; Catherine Carter, 1952; Corinth House (play) 1954; An Impossible Marriage, 1955.

ABOUT: Current Biography 1948.

JOHNSON, ROBERT UNDERWOOD (January 12, 1853-October 14, 1937). For biographical sketch and list of works and references, see TWENTIETH CENTURY AUTHORS, 1942.

* * *

ABOUT: Banta, R. E. Indiana Authors and Their Books.

JOHNSTON, Mrs. ANNIE (FELLOWS)

(May 15, 1863-October 5, 1931). For biographical sketch and list of works and references, see TWENTIETH CENTURY AUTHORS, 1942.

* * *

ABOUT: Banta, R. E. Indiana Authors and Their Books.

JOHNSTON, DENIS (June 18, 1901-),

Irish playwright, was born in Dublin, of Ulster Presbyterian stock; his father, William John Johnston, was an Irish Free State judge. He attended Merchiston School at Edinburgh, Christ's College, Cambridge, where he received the Master of Laws degree in 1923; and came to America as a Pugsley Scholar to study at the Harvard Law School. It was here he first became interested in playwriting, but was refused admittance to George P. Baker's 47 Workshop. A similar refusal met him when he returned to Dublin, wrote a play (1926) and submitted it to the Abbey Theatre (1928). Lady Gregory turned it down with such strenuous objections that he re-named the play *The Old Lady Says 'No.'* However, the Abbey Theatre directors did subsidize the play's first production, by the Dublin Gate Theatre.

This play, characteristic of one side of Johnston's playwriting, was expressionistic, and as he said in an interview, a "symphonic form of dramatic presentation . . . a romantic play with choral interludes." Curtis Canfield described Johnston's methods in an article in the New York *Times* in 1934 and in an anthology of Irish drama, *Plays of Changing Ireland.* "The Old Lady Says 'No,'" writes Canfield, "follows the structional pattern of Strindberg's *A Dream Play* by placing the action within the subconscious mind of the leading character. We look on Dublin life through the refracted vision of a stunned actor, and it is a nightmare. . . . Expressionism is commonly a fusion of music, poetry, dancing, symbols, and subjective action. . . . The action . . . [here] takes place in the few seconds required by the Doctor to fetch a rug for the prostrate Actor."

Johnston (after practicing law in England and Ireland) joined the Dublin Gate Theatre, a small experimental company, as an actor and playwright. He was their director from 1931 to 1936.

His next play, *The Moon in the Yellow River,* displayed another facet of Johnston's playwriting, a more conventional realistic one. It was performed at the Abbey in 1931, and brought to Broadway by the Theatre Guild. "This brilliant piece of Irish satire . . . full of laughter, full of observation, strongly dramatic at one moment and touched with delicate pathos the next," was W. A. Darlington's descriptive note in the London *Daily Telegraph.* After seeing the Theatre Guild production, Richard Lockridge remarked: "It alternates flashes of divination with long, often tedious, passages of economic philosophizing and the whole is punctuated with pistol shots and explosions."

Johnston's most recent plays are: "The Golden Cuckoo" (written in 1938), "The Dreaming Dust" (1939), and "Weep for the Cyclops" (1940). In the winter of 1953 his *Blind Man's Buff* (on which he collaborated with the late Ernst Toller) was produced in London.

For many years he worked with the B.B.C. as program director and in television, and during the war years was a radio war correspondent, the first to broadcast from enemy-held territory—reporting from Yugoslavia. Coming to the United States in 1947, he rewrote plays for "Theatre Guild on the Air" for more than a year and, after six months in Ireland, again came to the United States to teach at Amherst College and at Mount Holyoke. Since 1950 he has been at the latter college, and is director of dramatics.

Elinor Hughes writing in the Boston *Sunday Herald* in 1948 described him as "a tall, lean, good looking man with a shock of iron gray hair, a slight Irish brogue . . . and a decided twinkle in his eye." His first wife was Shelah Kathleen Richards, then a member of the Abbey Players. They were married in 1928 and had two children. His second wife is Betty (Chancellor) Johnston, who was one of the Gate Players. Married in 1945, they have three children, and live in South Hadley, Mass. Johnston's recreation is sailing.

PRINCIPAL WORKS: The Moon in the Yellow River and, The Old Lady Says 'No,' 1932; Storm Song and, A Bride for the Unicorn 1935; Blind Man's Buff (with E. Toller) 1938; The Golden Cuckoo, and Other Plays, 1954.

ABOUT: Canfield, C. Plays of Changing Ireland 1936; Boston Sunday Herald January 25, 1948; Mount Holyoke Alumnae Quarterly May 1951; New York Herald Tribune May 1, 1935; New York Times November 25, 1934; New York World-Telegram May 6, 1935.

JOHNSTON, Sir HARRY HAMILTON
(June 12, 1858-July 31, 1927). For biographical sketch and list of works and references, see TWENTIETH CENTURY AUTHORS, 1942.

JOHNSTON, MARY (November 21, 1870-May 9, 1936). For biographical sketch and list of works and references, see TWENTIETH CENTURY AUTHORS, 1942.

JOHNSTON, MYRTLE (March 7, 1909-). For autobiographical sketch and list of earlier works and references, see TWENTIETH CENTURY AUTHORS, 1942.

* * *

Myrtle Johnston writes from Canford Cliffs, Dorset: "My eyesight is bad and prevented my enlisting in the Auxiliary Territorial Service in 1942. I therefore spent the War years working in a branch of the Home Office which had a responsibility for organizing the civil side of the military preparations for the invasion of Normandy. During this period I deliberately ceased to be a creative writer. My first post-war novel, *A Robin Redbreast in a Cage*, a dramatic inquiry into the nature of guilt and crime, won a recommendation from the British Book Society and was published in 1951 in the United States. I have just finished writing 'Lorelle,' a modern love story with a poetic theme, which I hope soon to publish [1952]."

ADDITIONAL WORK: A Robin Redbreast in a Cage, 1950.

JONAS, CARL (May 22, 1913-), American novelist, writes: "I was born Carl Stebbins Jonas, in Omaha, Nebr., the youngest

Cosmo-Sileo

of three children: brother August F., who is now a surgeon in Erie, Pa., and sister Mary Elizabeth, who is now Mrs. Harold Clifford of Omaha. My father, August Frederick Jonas, was of German extraction. He became professor of surgery at the University of Nebraska Medical School and chief surgeon of the Union Pacific Railroad. My mother was Jesica Stebbins, born in Hastings, Minn., where her father, Columbus Stebbins, was owner, publisher, and editor of the Hastings *Gazette* which I believe is still published as a weekly.

"I was educated in the Omaha public school system for the most part: Henry W. Yates School for the grades, Omaha Central High School for three and a half years of high school. Then I went east to school and attended Phillips Exeter Academy in Exeter, Mass., for one year, and Governor Dummer Academy in South Byfield, Mass., from which I graduated, for another. I attended Williams College in Williamstown, Mass., for four years and graduated in the class of 1936, B.A. and a major in English literature.

"I spent the following year in travel. Spent the summer and fall in Europe traveling mostly by bicycle, the winter and spring in Asia traveling third class mostly, worked my way on ships, and came home again to Omaha after about a year's absence.

"At this time I began trying to write, but not very successfully and quite shyly. I worked as a cub reporter on the Omaha *World Herald*. In 1938 I went to Chicago and became a free lance radio writer. In the spring of '39 I went on to New York still free lancing radio scripts and lived there most of the time until December 1941 when I went home and shortly after New Year's enlisted as an apprentice seaman in the United States Coast Guard. I participated in the initial amphibious landings on Amchitka, Tarawa, Saipan, and Okinawa. I was separated from the service in September 1945 as a second class boatswain's mate. I wrote my first published book while I was still in the Coast Guard, most of the first draft while on board the U.S.S. 'Arthur Middleton' and the final drafts while stationed at the Love Point Light in Chesapeake Bay. This was the fifth novel I had written. Since the war I have been engaged entirely in writing book-length fiction.

"In 1945 I returned to Omaha. I was married in 1946 to Lydia Tukey, also of Omaha. We came to Aspen which has been our home since then."

* * *

After writing two novels which were for the most part mildly praised by the critics and totally ignored by the public, Carl Jonas published *Jefferson Selleck*, which immediately became both a critical and a popular success. A relentlessly detailed portrait of an American businessman, now dying, the novel was advertised as a *Babbitt* of the 1950's. If this is correct, James Hilton observed, comparing Jonas with Sinclair Lewis, the former is "a gentler satirist, no less observant of the middle-western scene, but as eager to admire as to blame. . . ." Howard Mumford Jones found that *Jefferson Selleck* lacked the burlesque of *Babbitt*. "But it is warm, human, enjoyable. Without being profound and without being philosophical, it is a just picture of a characteristic American life."

PRINCIPAL WORKS: Beachhead on the Wind, 1945; Snowslide, 1950; Jefferson Selleck, 1952; Riley McCullough, 1954.

ABOUT: Saturday Review January 26, 1952.

JONES, ELI STANLEY (January 3, 1884-), American clergyman, missionary, and writer on religious subjects, was born in  Clarksville, Md., and educated at the City College of Baltimore and at Asbury College, in Wilmore, Ky. While still in college he decided to go abroad as a missionary, and in 1907 he went to India under the Methodist Mission Board. He was a pastor of an English church in Lucknow while studying the native language. He then became a district missionary, working particularly among the low castes in India. After his return from his first furlough, he began his work among the educated classes of India, a work which he has carried on for thirty-six years. Among his close friends were Dr. Rabindranath Tagore, the Indian Christian poet, and Mahatma Gandhi.

On one of his trips to America, in 1924, Dr. Jones gave addresses which were later published as *The Christ of the Indian Road*. This volume went into about one million copies and was translated into about thirty languages. Of his other books, the one most widely known is *Abundant Living*. This has gone into over seven hundred thousand copies. Hundreds of newspapers in America published this a page a day for a year as a devotional.

Dr. Jones was elected a bishop of the Methodist church in 1928 at Kansas City, Mo., but after twenty-four hours he resigned in order to continue his work as a missionary and evangelist to India. Since the war he has been spending six months in America and six months in the East. Every other year he goes to Japan for three months. He has established a Christian Psychiatric Center at Lucknow. He has an 'ashram,' a place of spiritual retreat, at Sattal in the Himalayas where every year a group from all over India —Indian and foreign—gather to cultivate their spiritual lives. He has transplanted these 'ashrams' to the Western world and now has five in America and one in Canada. As Dr. Jones describes it, in these 'ashrams' the members "try not to find an answer but to be the answer in their corporate living. They try to be the New Order in miniature."

Active in a movement for United Church in America, on the basis of a federal union, Dr. Jones gives a month each year for this crusade.

In India, in 1911, he married Mabel Lossing who was also a missionary. They have one daughter, Eunice, who is married to the Reverend J. K. Mathew, executive secretary of the Methodist Board of Missions.

PRINCIPAL WORKS: The Christ of the Indian Road, 1925; Christ at the Round Table, 1928; The Christ of Every Road, 1930; The Christ on the Mount, 1931; Christ and Human Suffering, 1933; Christ's Alternative to Communism, 1935; Victorious Living, 1936; The Choice Before Us, 1937; Along the Indian Road, 1939; Is the Kingdom of God Realism?, 1940; Abundant Living, 1942; The Christ of the American Road, 1944; The Way, 1946; Mahatma Gandhi: An Interpretation, 1948; The Way to Power and Poise, 1949; How to Be a Transformed Person, 1951; Growing Spiritually, 1953.

ABOUT: Eddy, G. S. Pathfinders of the World Missionary Crusade; Hughley, J. N. Trends in Protestant Social Idealism; Jones, E. S. The Christ of the Indian Road; Kepler, T. S. Journey with the Saints; Current Biography 1940; Time October 20, 1947.

JONES, HOWARD MUMFORD (April 16, 1892-), American educator, poet, and critic, writes: "I was born in Saginaw, Mich., but I grew up in Wisconsin, mainly in La Crosse, where I first began writing the inevitable poetry that marks one's literary adolescence. Some of it got published. Then I went to the University of Wisconsin and after that to the University of Chicago, two facts which cast my lot irrevocably with the academic world. In the academic world I have remained ever since. Probably when I began teaching at Texas in 1916 the gap between the department of English in college or university and the actual living world of letters was greater than it is now; certainly the colleges and universities did not then customarily support poets in residence or give instruction in contemporary literature to the extent that they do today.

"Verse continued in my case, including verse translation, a much neglected and ill-appreciated art in this country. I translated from the German, the Italian, medieval Latin, and some minor tongues. Publications included versions of Heine and of Benelli's *The Love of the Three Kings,* not to speak of two works on the development of lyric poetry in Europe written conjointly with the late Phillip S. Allen of the University of Chicago. I also wrote a number of short stories, one of which, at least, landed in one of those best-short-stories-of-the-year anthologies. It still sometimes appears in collections of weird tales.

"But I suppose my main line of endeavor has been to fulfill, so far as I can, the function of 'man of letters' exemplified by James Russell Lowell and defined by Archibald MacLeish. This means that in addition to specialized contributions to scholarship, principally concerning English literature in the nineteenth century and American literary scholarship over the whole range of our development, I have tried, consciously or not, to present to that smaller segment of the public which really likes serious reading, the results of scholarly investigation and academic discussion, especially of the national letters.

"I have written biography—a life of Tom Moore called *The Harp That Once* is, I think, my favorite book—and I have written books about the relation of American culture to Europe and about various phases of American literature in relation to our national development. The best known of the first type is *America and French Culture,* which received the Jusserand medal, and which has had the curious fate of being customarily cited as *American and French Culture.* Among titles of the second type are *The Theory of American Literature, The Bright Medusa,* and *The Pursuit of Happiness.* I have also done a lot of editorial work of the academic kind, a vast quantity of book reviewing for both general and specialized magazines, and a great deal of lecturing. The problems of higher education and of free speech have concerned me much in these later years, as in *Education and World Tragedy.*

"I have taught at Texas, Montana, North Carolina, and Michigan (among the state universities) and am now at Harvard, where I have been since 1936.

"It seems to me that the development of a prose style which can convey relatively complicated ideas to a general audience without over-simplification and without condescension has been my principal technical aim. It is not easy to do, and I doubt that I have as yet attained it, but as I am inclined to doubt whether the popularizers do very much good, I still struggle towards that distant goal. The popularizers are always trying to make elusive and complex ideas too simple. On the other hand, a great deal of discourse coming out of the colleges and universities and having to do with literary topics seems to me language calculated to conceal thought and even the lack of thought. Somewhere in between these extremes there is room for adult writing on serious questions having to do with the national development and with American culture."

PRINCIPAL WORKS: A Little Book of Local Verse, 1915; Gargoyles (poems) 1918; America and French Culture, 1927; The Romanesque Lyric (with P. S. Allen) 1928; The Life of Moses Coit Tyler, 1933; They Say the Forties—(poems) 1937; The Harp that Once—, 1937; Ideas in America, 1944; Education and World Tragedy, 1946; The Theory of American Literature, 1948; Primer of Intellectual Freedom (ed.) 1949; The Bright Medusa, 1952; The Pursuit of Happiness, 1953.

ABOUT: Christian Science Monitor Magazine April 12, 1947.

JONES, JAMES (November 6, 1921-), American novelist, writes: "I was born at Robinson, Ill., into a family that had lived in that county for several generations, and thus had achieved the social respect and position such families can get only by living in the same place a long time without going broke. My grandfather was a farmer's son from down in the Embarrass (pronounced 'Ambraw') bottoms who could remember sitting on the fence as a boy and chasing bears (I'm sure he said bears) away from the crops. There is still an old family cemetery with big pine trees where the old farm was. Oil was discovered on the farm and my grandfather became a lawyer and moved to town. Eventually, he bought one of the oldest and biggest houses on East Main St. (not quite as good as West Main St.). My father went to Northwestern and became a dentist instead of a lawyer because he wanted to get out of school quicker so he could get married sooner. He would have preferred to be a lawyer. My mother came from Iowa, of an old German family there which had migrated from New York, and was considered a great beauty locally. She would have preferred to remain a great beauty. My parents were, I think, too much in love ever to be happily married, although I did not understand this then. My father took to drink and my mother to religion. This was all right as long as grandfather and the oil money held out. I thus grew up in an atmosphere of hot emotions and boiling recriminations covered with a thin but resilient skin of gentility. I had a brother older and sister younger. They grew up in this same atmosphere, but the brother grew a little of the way up before it started. Then grandfather died and Samuel Insull absconded, less than two months apart and in that order, and the bottom fell out. The big house was lost, the other houses were mortgaged and finally lost; we held onto our house longer but it too was eventually lost. We were forced to move. This was when I was a junior in high school. As a small boy I had accepted our family's social position without ever questioning it or even realizing it was there; I soon learned social prestige, while a very important thing, was still a very ephemeral one, and that, if there is any permanency in this world at all, that is not it. Perhaps this experience gave me a talent for seeing beneath the surface of lives and various social prestiges; certainly it gave me the desire to. When I graduated from high school my father, who had been in the first war and remembered it sentimentally, suggested that I join the Regular Army. Jobs were still hard to get then. I probably could not have held one.

"It seems to me this background, with numerous variations, is a pretty common one with male American writers—both from what I have read of them, and from what I could piece together about them from their work.

"There is no especial reason why I should have become a writer. I did not come of a particularly literary family. I was stationed at Hickam Field in Hawaii when I stumbled upon the works of Thomas Wolfe, and his home life seemed so similar to my own, his feelings about himself so similar to mine about myself, that I realized I had been a writer all my life without knowing it or having written. Once I made up my mind, it seemed inevitable, something that fate had directed ever since my birth. Once I got out of the Army, I started writing and have been writing ever since, urged on by the help and the whip of two very dear friends, Mr. and Mrs. Harry E. Handy of Robinson.

"I write slowly and painfully, inconclusively, going back over it often, never sure what I have written is worth the effort, which is considerable. I am working on another novel. I live in a large house trailer at present and move around over the country, but am building a small home back in Illinois which will have in it, if not all, at least many of my pet

dreams of what to have in a home. But I plan to keep my trailer, too."

* * *

In 1945 the late Maxwell E. Perkins of Scribner's turned down a manuscript from the then unknown James Jones, but, apparently recognizing in him something of the strange and turbulent genius of Thomas Wolfe, he offered an advance on a still unwritten second novel. This grew into the massive and spectacularly successful *From Here to Eternity*, which was an immediate best seller, a Book-of-the-Month Club selection, and won Jones the National Book Award for fiction for 1952. It was sold to Hollywood and made into a motion picture in 1953.

From Here to Eternity is not, strictly speaking, a war novel; it ends with the attack on Pearl Harbor. But it is a story of Army life, a savage and brutal picture of the peacetime Army in Hawaii. The shock-value of the book, its lurid incidents and barracks-room language, contributed of course to its meteoric success. But beyond that, some critics found real and permanent literary value in the book. Few went so far as David Dempsey of the New York *Times* who hailed Jones as "a major new American novelist." Ned Calmer's evaluation of the book, in the *Saturday Review of Literature,* was, however, representative of its critical reception: "For the non-squeamish adult this is the best picture of Army life ever written by an American, a book of beauty and power despite its unevenness, a book full of the promise of great things to come."

PRINCIPAL WORK: From Here to Eternity, 1951.

ABOUT: Life May 7, 1951; New York Herald Tribune Book Review March 4, 1951, October 7, 1951; New York Times Book Review March 25, 1951, May 10, 1953; New Yorker March 17, 1951; Saturday Review of Literature February 24, 1951, February 16, 1952.

JONES, RUFUS MATTHEW (January 25, 1863-June 16, 1948), American Quaker author, was born in the village of China, Maine, the son of Edwin Jones, a pious Quaker farmer, and Mary G. (Hoxie) Jones, the daughter of a Quaker cabinet-maker. "I said 'thee' and 'thy' to everybody and I would fully as soon have used profane words as have said 'you' or 'yours' to any person," Jones once commented. At

Hans Roth

sixteen he was granted a free scholarship in the famous Friends' School in Providence, R.I., now the Moses Brown School. Jones had intended to study law, but as he worked on his thesis for graduation, on mysticism, he knew that "I had here found the field of my life work." In later years he was to write many comprehensive volumes on the subject of mysticism and to demonstrate in what H. H. Brinton calls his greatest contribution to Quaker history, that Quakerism "is not an isolated phenomenon but a movement which took shape and persisted as an integral part of the great current of mystical religion flowing out of a remote past."

In 1885 Jones was graduated from Haverford College. He studied in Paris and Heidelberg, and returned to America to teach at the Friends' School in Providence and later at Haverford, as instructor in philosophy. Remaining at Haverford for more than forty years (1893-1934, emeritus in 1934), Jones made many trips abroad and became "the nearest thing the Friends had to an international spokesman." In 1917 he organized the Friends' Service Committee whose overseas units, under Jones, went into the destroyed areas of northern France and rebuilt villages, later fed German children, put Polish refugees back on their farms and fought the famine in Russia. The work continued after World War I, both abroad and in America. "We do not come to judge or criticize," said Jones, "but to inquire whether there is anything we can do to promote human welfare and to relieve suffering."

He was the author of about fifty books, some describing his boyhood (*Finding the Trail of Life*, 1926; *A Small-Town Boy*, 1941), some a study of mysticism and the history of the Quaker movement. In *The Flowering of Mysticism* Jones wrote of those fourteenth century Christian mystics who came to be known as the Friends of God. "A gracious and scholarly contribution," wrote the *Churchman*; "As a Quaker he appears not only to understand them but to feel at home with them," said *Commonweal*.

Jones received innumerable honors (degrees M.A., D.D., Th.D., LL.D., Litt.D. from many universities), was joint recipient of the Book Award in 1938; and received the Theodore Roosevelt Medal in 1942.

His first wife was Sarah Hawkshurst Coutant, who died leaving him one son; the son died at the age of eleven. In 1902 he married Elizabeth Bartram Cadbury. They had one daughter. In 1948 Rufus M. Jones died, at the age of eighty-five.

PRINCIPAL WORKS: Studies in Mystical Religion, 1909; Spiritual Reformers in the 16th and 17th Centuries, 1914; The World Within, 1918; Later Periods of Quakerism, 1921; Spiritual Energies in Daily Life, 1922; Fundamental Ends of Life, 1924; Finding the Trail of Life, 1926; Trail of Life in College, 1929; Trail of Life in the Middle Years, 1934; Some Problems of Life, 1936; The Flowering of Mysticism, 1939; A Small-Town Boy, 1941.

ABOUT: Fisher, D. F. American Portraits; Haverford College, Rufus M. Jones; Hinshaw, D. Rufus Jones, Master Quaker; Jacob, C. N. Builders of the Quaker Road; Kepler, T. S. Journey with the Saints; Atlantic Monthly June 1947; Current Biography 1941, 1948; Fortune December 1940; New York Herald Tribune March 10, 1940; New York Times June 17, 1948; Newsweek April 28, 1947, March 21, 1951; Reader's Digest April 1940.

JONG. See DE JONG

JORDAN, Mrs. HELEN ROSALINE (ASHTON). See ASHTON, H.

JORDAN, MILDRED (March 18, 1901-), American novelist, writes: "Chicago was my birthplace. I have Swedish ancestry on my mother's  side, and German, on my father's. Perhaps for this reason I have a square jaw, and I've always known where I wanted to go.

"My first novel was begun when I was twelve and bored one day in eighth grade. Page one was peppered with elegant words from Washington Irving's *Sketch Book* which we were studying at the time. When my mother said, 'Mildred, you didn't write that!' I knew I was good, and my future was decided.

"Graduating from the Nicolas Senn High School, I went as a day student to Northwestern University for a year and a half, then on to Wellesley College, from which I got my B.A. in 1922. Before I was married I sold *Volume Library*, a one-volume encyclopedia, from door to door, and taught basketball to a class of Italian boys at Hull House. During these years I wrote many short stories, none of which were published.

"In 1923 I married J. Lee Bausher, a hosiery manufacturer, and we have lived in Reading, Pa., ever since. We have three daughters and a son. My husband and I are both ardent travelers, and as soon as the Statue of Liberty drifts into sight, we're planning our next expedition.

"My one brother is dead. My older sister lives in Chicago, and my father, in his ninetieth year, is living in Florida.

"I have several early novels on an attic shelf. My first published book, *One Red Rose Forever*, saw forty publishers before Alfred A. Knopf accepted it. I'm sure I've set the record for defeat before success. Some people refer to this book as Pennsylvania German because it is a fictional biography of Stiegel, the glass manufacturer. And when *Apple in the Attic* followed (a story of Pennsylvania Dutch farm people), I found myself classified as a Pennsylvania Dutch writer. I was naturally interested in writing about this part of the country which seemed strange to me as a newcomer, but have since turned farther afield; to the French settlement at Asylum, Pa., in *Asylum for the Queen*, and to the Breton peasants in *Miracle in Brittany*. I have written two children's books, but prefer doing adult fiction. Recently, I finished my first play, which was fine discipline. I think better novels would be written if the aspiring novelist would first learn to measure his words in a successful play.

"I've had various hobbies since my marriage. For quite a few years I studied the harp with Edna Phillips, and now and then suffered agonies by playing in public. From childhood on, I've been a sports enthusiast, and in recent years, have become more and more of a tennis addict. Lately I have taken up painting (along with the rest of frustrated America) and some time would like to illustrate a book of my own or do a dust cover.

"I try to be painstaking about my literary work, and would prefer to write one small book that would be a potential classic than produce a dozen best sellers."

PRINCIPAL WORKS: One Red Rose Forever, 1941; Apple in the Attic, 1942; The Shoo-Fly Pie (juvenile) 1944; "I Won't," Said the King (juvenile) 1945; Asylum for the Queen, 1948; Miracle in Brittany, 1950.

ABOUT: Current Biography 1951.

JOSEPHSON, MATTHEW (February 15, 1899-). For biographical sketch and list of earlier works and references, see TWENTIETH CENTURY AUTHORS, 1942.

* * *

Matthew Josephson's recent biographies reflect the two dominant interests of his work —nineteenth century French literature and twentieth century American economics. His studies of Victor Hugo and of Stendhal were highly praised. As in his earlier works on

Zola and Rousseau, Josephson demonstrated in these two literary biographies sound literary judgment, a lucid style, and comprehensive scholarship. André Maurois considered his Hugo study "well informed, well written, well constructed and very fair." His biography of Stendhal was an important factor in the recent American revival of interest in the works of the great French novelist. Josephson's most successful later study in the field of economics was his biography of Sidney Hillman. L. G. Reynolds wrote of the book in the New York *Herald Tribune*: "Not since *The Robber Barons* has Mr. Josephson so effectively focussed the complex political and economic pressures at work over several decades of American history." And Louis Stark, in the New York *Times*, called it "a work which will stand the test of time."

Josephson lives in Sherman, Conn. He was elected to the National Institute of Arts and Letters in 1948.

ADDITIONAL WORKS: Victor Hugo, 1942; Empire of the Air: Juan Trippe and the Struggle for World Airways, 1944; Stendhal: or The Pursuit of Happiness, 1946; (ed. & tr.) Beyle, H. (Stendhal) Memoirs of Egotism, 1949; Sidney Hillman: Statesman of American Labor, 1952.

ABOUT: Saturday Evening Post September 20, 1947.

JOUVENEL. See COLETTE

JOYCE, JAMES (February 2, 1882-January 13, 1941). For biographical sketch and list of works and references, see TWENTIETH CENTURY AUTHORS, 1942.

* * *

ABOUT: Byrne, J. F. The Silent Years; Campbell, J. & Robinson, H. M. A Skeleton Key to Finnegans Wake; Colum, M. G. Life and the Dream; Connolly, C. The Condemned Playground; Edel, L. James Joyce: The Last Journey; Givens, S. (ed.) James Joyce: Two Decades of Criticism; Gogarty, O. Mourning Becomes Mrs. Spendlove, It Isn't This Time of Year at All; Highet, G. The Classical Tradition; Hutchins, P. (ed.) James Joyce's Dublin; Levin, H. *Introduction to* The Portable James Joyce; Tindall, W. Y. James Joyce: His Way of Interpreting the Modern World; Wilson, E. Classics and Commercials.

JUNG, CARL GUSTAV (July 26, 1875-). For biographical sketch and list of earlier works and references, see TWENTIETH CENTURY AUTHORS, 1942.

* * *

Dr. Jung remained in Switzerland during World War II. In 1944 he assumed the chair of medical psychology, especially founded for him, at the University of Basel. A year later he retired to devote full time to his research and writing. One of the fields of his research was alchemy—in which ancient art he found "anticipations of modern psychology." In 1944 his book *Psychology and Alchemy* was published in German. A Jung Institute was founded in Zurich in 1948 to train Jungian analysts and to carry on research in analytical psychology.

Although Jung has written little that is directly concerned with art, his influence in artistic and literary circles is considerable. Many years ago he suggested that the artist, like the neurotic, only more significantly, reproduces the myths which derive from and connect man with the rituals of his primitive past. He described the poet as "the collective *man*, the carrier and former of the unconsciously active soul of mankind." In *The Armed Vision* Stanley Edgar Hyman traces the influence of Jungian psychology on literary criticism, particularly on the work of Maud Bodkin (see sketch above).

Jung and his wife live in a suburban home near Zurich, where he keeps a busy schedule (in 1950 he was reported writing three books simultaneously). There have been heated controversies in the popular and the scholarly journals over Jung's political sympathies during recent years. Hyman quotes numerous passages from Jung's pre-World War II writings which demonstrate pro-Nazi sympathies, but other commentators argue that such charges are unfounded.

ADDITIONAL WORKS IN ENGLISH TRANSLATION: Essays on Contemporary Events, 1947; Essays on a Science of Mythology (with C. Kerenyi) 1949; Psychological Reflections, 1952; Psychology and Alchemy, 1952; Collected Works, 1953.

ABOUT: Glover, E. Freud or Jung; Progoff, I. Jung's Psychology and its Social Meaning; Schaer, H. Religion and the Cure of Souls in Jung's Psychology; Current Biography 1953; Saturday Review of Literature September 6, December 20, 1947, February 21, 1948, July 9, July 16, July 30, September 10, October 15, 1949; Time July 7, 1952.

*JÜNGER, ERNST (March 29, 1895-   ), German novelist and essayist, was born in Heidelberg, son of a chemist and pharmacist of Lower Saxony; his mother came from Franconia. He spent most of his youth in Hanover and the neighboring Steinhuder Meer. In 1913 he ran away from home to join the Foreign Legion in Africa. However, since he was still a minor, his father succeeded, with the help of the Ministry of Foreign Affairs, in having him released, and then promised him participation in a later expedition to the Kilimanjaro in Africa if he would finish school. Before this project materialized,

* yüng'ĕr

World War I broke out. After his emergency graduation, Jünger volunteered and joined the army, to be attached to the Western Front, where he stayed until the end of the war. Fourteen times wounded, the young lieutenant was promoted to leader of a shock troop unit, and was many times decorated for bravery.

The war over, Jünger stayed with the German army, working on a new textbook on military strategy. He quit in 1923 to continue his studies in natural sciences (specializing in insects and cuttlefish) and in philosophy at the Universities of Leipzig and Naples. In 1925 he gave up before graduating and devoted himself to freelance work. He married and moved to Berlin, where together with his brother, Friedrich Georg Jünger, a lyric-writer and critic, he became the center of the gatherings of former army officers heatedly discussing socialism and nationalism. During this period he published a number of articles on political subjects. Towards the end of the Twenties he found himself opposing Hitler who had tried to befriend him. Jünger became friendly with Ernst Nickisch, a National Bolshevik who was one of Hitler's most fervent adversaries. After Hitler's assumption of power in 1933, Jünger left Berlin, refused to join the newly founded Academy of Poets and withdrew entirely from political activities. He changed his residence quite frequently, moved to Goslar, then to Überlingen, to Hanover, Ravensburg, and settled in Wilflingen, a hamlet in the Swabian Jura in 1950. There were also extensive journeys abroad—Italy, Norway, South America, and Africa.

Ernst Jünger has had a stormy career. He has been a controversial figure in German literature since the publication of his first books, shortly after World War I. At that time, when many German intellectuals were drifting toward repudiation of the nationalist-militarist tradition, he wrote as an ardent militarist, enthusiastically describing his military experiences, urging total mobilization and a mystical dedication to war. Although he was not a Nazi and gave no overt support to the establishment of Hitler's National Socialist government, he was, in the words of Louis Clair, "one of the prophets of that nihilism which has contributed not a little to the demoralization and the cynical contempt for values which characterized large parts of the young German generation of pre-Hitler days."

In 1939 Jünger published a novel, *On the Marble Cliffs*, a story of the destruction of a beautiful and peaceful country by barbarian hordes. Why the book was ever published under then-prevailing Nazi censorship, or how Jünger managed to escape imprisonment for it, is a mystery. The only explanation offered is that because the novel is an allegory, "in the grand symbolist manner," the censors apparently missed the point of it. To readers of the novel when it appeared in English translation some ten years later, it was clearly an anti-Nazi work. Nevertheless, Jünger's loyalty to the state was not questioned at the time the book appeared, and he was commissioned a captain in the German army, heading an infantry company in the invasion of France. While in the army Jünger came into active contact with a number of conservative army officers, including General von Stülpnagel, whose bitter disagreements with Hitler culminated in the attempt on the latter's life in July 1944. Jünger was not directly implicated in this *putsch*, but the remarkable pamphlet *Der Friede (The Peace)*, which he had written in 1943 under von Stülpnagel's protection, expressed the sentiments of the rebellion. *Der Friede*, dedicated to the memory of his eighteen-year-old son who was killed in action in Italy was a plea for peace based upon the renunciation of nationalism and the affirmation of the dignity and the responsibility of the individual. Jünger foresaw a federated Europe in which Germany would play an important role (a plan not unlike that of the Western European Union which emerged a decade later)— "Europe unified on the base of Christianity and German predominance, destined to avert Bolshevism."

Jünger's position remains fundamentally ambivalent. He has repudiated his mystical-nihilistic-militaristic German nationalism, but in its place he has offered an equally mystical plea for international peace and understanding, based on the premise that "this war must be won by everybody and should not be lost by anybody." Some commentators hail Jünger's new position as representing "an exemplary 're-education' from paganism to Christian ethics, from German chauvinism to the unity of the West." Others, however, question whether Jünger's emphasis on "fatalism" and the "superhuman" in the conduct of national and international affairs is not an attempt to absolve Germany of its responsibility for National Socialism. His recent work,

the allegorical novel *Heliopolis*, is a more direct and unambiguous expression of his horror of Nazism; but Edouard Roditi writes that it is "unconsciously still permeated with many notions that, though harmless in themselves, can fit dangerously well within the patterns of a totalitarian theology." As a literary stylist—and his recent work illustrates this as powerfully as his earlier writings—Jünger remains a master. His prose has a "spellbinding" quality that, Clara Menck writes, "is not a matter of external form, but part and parcel of his thinking." Victor Lange describes it as "lithe, resolute, unsentimental and radiant."

PRINCIPAL WORKS IN ENGLISH TRANSLATION: Storm of Steel: From the Diary of a German Storm-Troop Officer on the Western Front, 1929; Copse 125: A Chronicle from the French Warfare of 1918, 1930; On the Marble Cliffs, 1948; The Peace, 1948; African Diversions, 1954.

ABOUT: Clair, L. *Introduction to* The Peace; Columbia Dictionary of Modern European Literature; Müller-Schwefe, H. R. Ernst Jünger (in German); Rausch, J. Ernst Jüngers Optik (in German); Stern, J. P. Ernst Jünger; Commonweal March 11, 1949; Deutsche Rundschau May 1950; Menorah Journal July 1943; New Yorker May 21, 1955; Nineteenth Century January 1946; Queen's Quarterly Summer 1947; Review of Politics April 1945, July 1946; South Atlantic Quarterly July 1949, April 1951.

---

*JUSSERAND, JEAN ADRIEN ANTOINE JULES (February 18, 1855-July 18, 1932). For biographical sketch and list of works and references, see TWENTIETH CENTURY AUTHORS, 1942.

* zhüs rän'

KAFKA, FRANZ (July 3, 1883-June 3, 1924). For biographical sketch and list of works and references, see TWENTIETH CENTURY AUTHORS, 1942.

* * *

ADDITIONAL WORKS IN ENGLISH TRANSLATION: The Country Doctor (short stories) 1945; Parables, 1947; Diaries of Franz Kafka (ed. M. Brod) 1948-49; The Penal Colony (short stories) 1948; Letters to Milena (ed. W. Haas) 1953; Dearest Father, 1954.

ABOUT: Columbia Dictionary of Modern European Literature; Eisner, P. Franz Kafka and Prague; Flores, A. (ed.) The Kafka Problem; Goodman, P. Kafka's Prayer; Janouch, G. Conversations with Kafka; Kafka, F. Diaries, Letters to Milena, Dearest Father; Neider, C. The Frozen Sea, Kafka: His Mind and His Art; Tauber, H. Franz Kafka; Warren, A. Rage for Order; Wilson, E. Classics and Commercials; American Scholar Summer 1946; Books Abroad Autumn 1947; Commentary October 1946; Commonweal December 6, 1946; Saturday Review of Literature August 2, 1947; Sewanee Review Spring 1946; Time February 14, 1949.

*KAGAWA, TOYOHIKO (July 10, 1888-).

For biographical sketch and list of earlier works and references, see TWENTIETH CENTURY AUTHORS, 1942.

* * *

In 1945, only a month after Japan's surrender to the Allies, *Time* magazine interviewed Kagawa in Tokyo and reported that "war has not shaken his faith," and that he remained a Christian and a patriotic Japanese. Shabbily dressed, a small man, "with a ready smile, a forthright, friendly personality," Kagawa told reporters that he had been arrested twice by Japanese authorities during the war and was forbidden to preach. He admitted that he had been critical of America in the war years, but pointed out that in the dilemma that faced him as a Japanese, "I had no choice." In 1946 Kagawa was appointed to the Japanese House of Peers. He has continued very active in church work. In 1950 he visited Europe and the United States on a lecture tour.

ADDITIONAL WORKS IN ENGLISH TRANSLATION: (with F. Cole) The Willow and the Bride: Poems and Meditations, 1947; (with others) Songs from the Land of the Dawn, 1949; Meditations, 1950.

ABOUT: Kepler, T. Journey with the Saints; Christian Century March 20, 1946, December 18, 1946, April 2, 1947, August 2, 1950; Commonweal October 5, 1945; Newsweek May 7, 1945, July 24, 1950; Reader's Digest February 1951; Time June 3, 1946, July 24, 1950.

* kä gä'wä

KAHN, ELY JACQUES, Jr. (December 4, 1916-), American journalist and humorist, writes: "I was born and raised in New

York City, where I enjoyed a tranquil, comfortable childhood and where I lived until I got married and began to have children of my own, at which point the city struck me as a ridiculous place for anyone to rear a child in. From sub-kindergarten through senior high school, I attended the Horace Mann School, and drifted on from there to Harvard. I dimly recall some talk on the part of my parents of my becoming a lawyer. As a boy, I had no particular aptitude for writing and no particular interest in it, until I was a junior in high school, when an English teacher who served also as faculty adviser to the student weekly paper stopped me in a corridor one day and suggested that I try out for its staff. The paper was clearly desperate for recruits, since I shortly found myself editor-in-chief. At college, I dabbled fitfully, and without much distinction, in further journalistic enterprises, and I majored in Greek and English literature. Of the two languages, I am at present fluent only in one.

"Toward the end of my senior year in college, under the lash of an instructor in a composition course I had taken because it seemed less taxing than, say, the physical sciences, I did a little writing, and I managed to sell a piece to the *New Yorker*. This was in the spring of 1937. An editor of that magazine wrote me and asked if I would be interested in applying for a full-time job on it. This was obviously a much more agreeable way of getting started in the world than going to law school, so I pursued it. I have been with the *New Yorker* from graduation day on, and after I have written for the magazine for a total of forty-five years, if I last that long, will begin to receive a pension. Since 1937, I have contributed on occasion to quite a few other magazines, but by far the greatest amount of my output has appeared in the *New Yorker*, which suits me fine. For slightly over four years, between 1941 and 1945, I was in the Army, holding various ranks from private through chief warrant officer, and serving in both the Southwest Pacific and Caribbean Theatres. Toward the end of my military career, I met a WAC lieutenant named Virginia Rice, and convinced her and her commanding officer that she ought to become my wife. We have three sons now, the oldest six and the youngest one, and we live at Scarborough, N.Y., in a house that my father, the architect, designed for us two years ago and that we should be owning outright just about the time I start drawing that pension. Since the second World War, I have made two fairly warlike trips abroad as a correspondent for the *New Yorker*—to Germany in 1949, at the time of the Berlin Airlift; and to Korea in 1951."

* * *

E. J. Kahn's first two books were literate and straightforward accounts of his experiences in the Army, full of "wry and self-deprecatory humor." Stanley Edgar Hyman called them "some of the best, most honest and least pretentious war reporting yet published in America." His later writings have often been autobiographical, chronicling small events with what Lisle Bell calls "an irony that is free from venom; a response to life composed of geniality, sharp observation and a sort of deference."

PRINCIPAL WORKS: The Army Life, 1942; G.I. Jungle, 1943; McNair: Educator of an Army, 1945; Fighting Divisions (with M. McLemore) 1945; The Voice, 1947; Who, Me? 1949; The Peculiar War, 1952.

ABOUT: Kahn, E. J. The Army Life, G.I. Jungle; Saturday Review January 12, 1952.

KAISER, GEORG (November 25, 1878-June 1945). For biographical sketch and list of works and references, see TWENTIETH CENTURY AUTHORS, 1942.

* * *

Georg Kaiser died at sixty-six at Ascona, Switzerland, where he had been in voluntary exile since being expelled from the German Academy at the outset of the Nazi regime. His last play contained an indictment of dictatorship.

Kaiser has been called "one of the most significant dramatists of our times." Of his dramatic method, Hugh W. Puckett observed: "Within the atmosphere of expressionism, which is the only environment thinkable for his products, Kaiser evolved a fitting dramatic style of his own which reduces language to a minimum and makes action the real medium for his ideas."

ABOUT: New York Times June 6, 1945; Poet Lore Winter 1946; Theatre Arts April 1942, June 1949.

KALLAS, Mrs. AINO JULIA MARIA (KROHN) (August 2, 1878-). For autobiographical sketch and list of works and references, see TWENTIETH CENTURY AUTHORS, 1942.

* * *

Mme. Kallas lives in Talinn, Estonia. She has published no books in more than twenty years. Her husband, Dr. Oskar Kallas, died in 1946.

KALLEN, HORACE MEYER (August 11, 1882-), American philosopher and educator, was born in Berenstadt, Silesia, Ger-

many, to Jacob David Kallen, a Hebrew scholar and rabbi, and Esther (Glazier) Kallen. The family came to the United States when the boy was five years old. He grew up in Boston, Mass., and attended the Eliot Grammar School and the English High School. He worked his way through Harvard College, graduating *magna cum laude* in 1903.

After graduation he taught English and studied English literature at Princeton University. After two years he returned to Harvard where he concentrated on philosophy and psychology, under William James, George Santayana, Josiah Royce, Hugo Munsterberg and Edwin Holt. He also studied American literature with Barrett Wendell. He spent the academic year 1907-1908 abroad, studying with F. S. C. Schiller in Oxford, and hearing Henri Bergson in Paris. On his return to Harvard, he took his degree of Doctor of Philosophy in philosophy. The title of his dissertation was *Notes on the Nature of Truth.*

From 1908 to 1911 Kallen taught philosophy at Harvard and Radcliffe serving as lecturer and as assistant to James, Santayana and Royce. He also gave courses in logic at Clark University in Worcester, Mass. In 1911 he was called to the University of Wisconsin where he served as instructor in logic and psychology until his resignation in 1918 on an issue of academic freedom. From then until the end of the war he was a member of the Committee on Labor under the chairmanship of Samuel Gompers, and of the Inquiry into Terms of Peace headed by Col. House. He began his service with The New School for Social Research in 1919, with a course on "The International Mind," and has been on the faculty ever since. He is today the only one left of the original staff, which included Charles Beard, Thorstein Veblen, and James Harvey Robinson. When Alvin Johnson set up the school's graduate faculty as a "University in Exile" made up of the foremost social scientists of Germany and other European lands who could be rescued from Nazi persecution, Kallen became the other American member of the faculty, with Johnson an "honorary exile." In 1945 in his turn he was elected dean and re-elected for a second term. Having reached the age of seventy in 1952 he became professor emeritus and was thereupon elected by the trustees of The New School research professor in social philosophy.

Kallen was early attracted to pragmatism and as a philosopher is largely identified with this school whose leaders are William James, John Dewey, and F. C. S. Schiller. He became a younger associate of this group, with special interest in developing a pragmatic philosophy of freedom in relation to religion, to the arts, to education and to culture. William James left his unfinished work *Some Problems in Philosophy* for Kallen to edit. He is also the literary executor of Benjamin Paul Blood. Kallen's faith is organically bound up with his practical experience as a newsboy, a farm laborer, a journalist, an editor, a social worker, lecturer, writer and a teacher. His tasks brought him face to face with problems of political bossism in Boston's Wards 8 and 6, and the connection between such bossism and the public school system. As a youth he met labor problems at first hand in the needle trades as well as on the farm. They made him very sensitive to the relation between labor, leisure and citizenship and the nature of man as a consumer rather than a producer. His residence in one of Boston's social settlements awakened him to the problems of the Americanization of immigrants in terms of group relations, especially the meaning of minority cultures for American life, and led to the philosophy of cultural pluralism with which Horace Kallen is from his earliest writing identified. This philosophy also plays a central role in Dr. Kallen's activities in the American Jewish community and his work in the Zionist movement where he was closely associated with Louis D. Brandeis and Julian W. Mack, in the civil liberties movement and the cooperative movement.

All of Kallen's books are essays in composing the different aspects of his practical experience as well as his professional scholarship into the general outlook of his philosophy of esthetic pragmatism.

Kallen has been active in numerous civic, educational, and cultural activities. In 1950 he was one of the judges of the National Book Award. The New School awarded him the degree of Doctor of Humane Letters, honoris causa, in 1948, and in 1947 on the occasion of his sixty-fifth birthday twenty-four leading scholars presented him with a Festschrift, *Freedom and Experience*. His seventieth was made the occasion of another Festschrift, *Vision and Action*, among the contributors to which were T. S. Eliot, Senator Paul Douglas, Dr. Adelbert Ames Jr., Hu Shih, John Dewey, Benjamin V. Cohen. The American Association for Jewish Education also honored Kallen on his seventieth birthday by presenting him with a Bibliography of his writings (foreword by Milton R. Konvitz) in June 1952. He has been married since 1926 to Rachael Oatman Van Arsdale. They have a son and a daughter. Kallen's recreations are painting surrealist pictures and reading detective stories.

PRINCIPAL WORKS: William James and Henri Bergson, 1914; The Structure of Lasting Peace, 1918; The Book of Job as a Greek Tragedy, 1918; Zionism and World Politics, 1924; Culture and Democracy in the United States, 1924; Education, the Machine, and the Worker, 1925; Why Religion, 1927; Freedom in the Modern World (ed.) 1928; Indecency and the Seven Arts, 1930; College Prolongs Infancy, 1932; Judaism at Bay, 1932; Individualism: An American Way of Life, 1933; A Free Society, 1934; The Decline and Rise of the Consumer, 1936; Art and Freedom, 1942; Americanism and Its Makers, 1945; Ideals and Experience, 1948; The Liberal Spirit, 1948; The Education of Free Men, 1949; Patterns of Progress, 1950; Democracy and True Religion, 1951.

ABOUT: Hook, S. & Konvitz, M. R. (eds.) Freedom and Experience; Ratner, S. (ed.) Vision and Action; Current Biography 1953; Saturday Review of Literature December 17, 1949.

KANE, HARNETT THOMAS (November 8, 1910-), American journalist, novelist, and miscellaneous writer, reports: "I was born in New Orleans, La., and have lived in the South (with time out for travel) and written about it during all of my adult life. Apparently I am one of those people who are doing what they wanted to do all of their lives, and, better than that, enjoying it.  In elementary school I decided to be a writer. In Warren Easton Boys' High School I spent a large part of my time (classtime and later) as an editor of the school paper; as a freshman at Tulane University, New Orleans, I started at once on the college paper, ending as its editor, editor of the school handbook, president of the International Relations Club, member of the school leadership fraternity, Kappa Delta Phi, the journalism fraternities, Sigma Delta Chi, Theta Nu, etc.

"Meanwhile the Sunday editor of the New Orleans *Item* saw one of my stories, and asked me to do regular ones for that local paper. Then the managing editor called me downtown, and offered me a full-time job. My journalism teacher and everybody else advised me *not* to take it; and so I did, and never regretted the decision, though I have still to catch up with my sleep. I worked from 3 P.M. to midnight, got up for an 8 A.M. class and also continued on the school paper. My eyesight probably suffered, but the gray hairs now appearing in my head came much later.

"After getting my bachelor's degree I did a year's graduate work in sociology at Tulane. During this time I covered every assignment on the paper—crime, interviews, labor, finance, welfare, analytical pieces, historical, eventually politics, including Huey Long, with whom I was on good, or cussing, terms. (He tried to get me fired once because I reported that he wore not cotton nightshirts as he told his country followers, but silk pajamas.) On several hours' notice I was assigned to cover the Louisiana political scandals of 1938-40, and fortunately had a ringside seat for a 'great American circus.' Out of this came my first book, *Louisiana Hayride,* which has stayed in print for twelve years to date.

"After the *Hayride* I was urged to give my full time to writing, but remained on the paper for a year or so, then took a leave of absence, and finally resigned. Since then I have done thirteen books, and have two others in preparation. I work regular hours at my office in my home, following Louisiana field-hand hours, from 'kin see to kain't see,' from the time you can see until you can't. The secret of any writing success is, as nearly everybody who writes can agree, the application of the seat of the pants to the seat of the chair. In my writing I have tried to strike a mean between the old moonlight-and-Spanish moss Southern school and the two-headed-baby-in-a-pigsty genre. All of my books to date have been non-fiction or novels based on fact.

"I received two Rosenwald fellowships for research in Southern history, and taught a year at Loyola University of the South, New Orleans, 1943-44. Thus far, anyway, I am unmarried."

PRINCIPAL WORKS: *Non-Fiction*—Louisiana Hayride, 1941; Bayous of Louisiana, 1943; Deep Delta Country, 1944; Plantation Parade, 1945; Natchez on the Mississippi, 1947; Queen New Orleans, 1949; Gentlemen, Swords and Pistols, 1951; Dear Dorothy Dix (biography, with E. B. Arthur) 1952; Spies for the Blue and Gray, 1954. *Fiction*—New Orleans Woman, 1946; Bride of Fortune, 1948; Pathway to the Stars, 1950; The Scandalous Mrs. Blackford (with A. Parry) 1951; The Lady of Arlington, 1953.

ABOUT: Hoehn, M. (ed.) Catholic Authors, II; Current Biography 1947; New York Herald Tribune Book Review December 21, 1947; New York Times Book Review December 4, 1949.

KANG, YOUNGHILL (1903-). For autobiographical sketch and list of earlier works and references, see TWENTIETH CENTURY AUTHORS, 1942.

* * *

Younghill Kang writes from Huntington, N.Y.: "At the time of Pearl Harbor I was taken into the U.S. Army and other government agencies, doing whatever I could for the war effort. And that meant my severance from New York University classes as well as from the curatorial work for the Metropolitan Museum of Art. After V.J. Day I was sent to the Pacific as chief of publica-

tions for the American Military Government, and for a while I was the head of the literature department and a professor at Seoul University, as well as president of Tongyang Waeguko College. I got back to America and my family in 1948. Ever since I have not had any teaching with tenure, although I had been teaching summer sessions at New York University until last year. [Kang has also taught at Long Island University.] Also in 1950 I was called by Yale University to survey the East Asiatic collection in the Sterling Memorial Library and to recommend important books not yet in the library. It has been hard for me to retake my place in American life after World War II, partly because of my restless anxiety about the world situation, particularly the recent Korean events."

Kang is currently at work on a new book, a cultural history of Korea and northeastern Asia. He writes of his native land with sympathy and understanding: "To be a Korean in this world is to be unorthodox. Neither the passionately Russian Koreans nor the passionately American Koreans are very popular in Korea right now. They'd like a Nehru perhaps. They might issue from their shock, terror and hate at some program like that of the quiet Friends. Koreans are a passionate people. Since they are not so much passionate on the surface as underneath, it takes a long time to know them and most Americans have not gotten around to it. This is a very great tragedy, an untold tragedy of horrible ignorance."

Of himself Kang writes: "In this world my distinctively Oriental look has had advantages and disadvantages, more of the latter in America perhaps, more of the former in Asia or even in Europe. In Germany I was more popular than a high-nosed American in the Hitler thirties, because I could be mistaken for a Japanese, the only race descended from the gods outside the Aryans. But in South Korea after V.J. Day, I was always safe from the terrorists and the Japanese-trained Korean police, as others were not, because of my immunity with A.G. cards. On the other hand, all types of Koreans with different political shades would tell me things they felt too ashamed or embarrassed to tell my American colleagues in the same billet. . . . With these advantages I was naturally able to gather a good deal of information on Korea."

ADDITIONAL WORK: (tr.) Maruyama, M. Anatahan, 1954.

ABOUT: United Nations World May 1948.

KANTOR, MACKINLAY (February 4, 1904-). For autobiographical sketch and list of earlier works and references, see TWENTIETH CENTURY AUTHORS, 1942.

* * *

MacKinlay Kantor writes to the editors of this volume: "I got a tremendous kick out of the old sketch which you sent me. The 'good-looking young man with thick blond hair' is now a grandfather, with hair the color of a close-cropped coonskin coat which has been left out in the frost!

"Early in 1943 I was accredited as a war correspondent and went to the European Theatre. After flying for a time with the R.A.F., became attached to the 305th Bomb Group of the U.S. 8th Air Force as a combat correspondent. Flew later with the U.S. 9th Air Force, but returned to finish the war in the E.T.O. with the 8th again.

"Made a somewhat intricate study of both the strategy and tactics of high altitude bombardment, and, at the request of the late General H. H. Arnold, wrote a detailed report on the co-ordination of aerial activities in the European Theatre.

"Following World War II returned to the Air Force at frequent intervals to keep pace with new developments; early in the Korean War I joined the 92nd Bombardment Wing in the Far East and flew many missions there.

"My novel *Glory for Me* was the original story from which was made the motion picture *The Best Years of Our Lives*. During the interim between the two wars I spent a good deal of time in Hollywood as a writer and associate producer. This venture was unsuccessful, and I haven't done any picture work since 1948.

"In 1948 and 1949 I worked with the New York Police Department learning the life and following the routine of a patrolman in the 23d Precinct. [Kantor used these experiences as the background for his novel *Signal Thirty-Two*.]

"I returned to Florida during the winter of 1950-51, and count Sarasota as my permanent home. Late in 1951 the U.S. Air Force called me to active duty as a technical consultant, with the assimilated rank of lieutenant-general. Have worked in this capacity, both in the United States and overseas, periodically ever since.

"My daughter Layne was married to William Shroder of New York in 1949. They are the parents of one child, Michael. My son Thomas is [December 1952] serving in the U.S. Air Force as an aviation cadet in the Observer Program."

ADDITIONAL WORKS: Gentle Annie, 1942; Happy Land, 1943; Author's Choice (short stories) 1944; Glory for Me (novel in verse) 1945; But Look, the Morn (autobiography) 1947; Midnight Lace, 1948; Wicked Water, 1949; The Good Family, 1949; Signal Thirty-Two, 1950; Lee and Grant at Appomattox (juvenile) 1950; Don't Touch Me, 1951; Warwhoop, 1952; Gettysburg (juvenile) 1953; The Daughter of Bugle Ann, 1953; God and My Country, 1954.

ABOUT: Kantor, M. But Look, the Morn; Scholastic November 12, 1945.

KAPEK. See ČAPEK

KAPLAN, HAROLD J. (July 29, 1918-), American novelist, writes: "I spent the first eighteen years of my life in Newark, N.J., in a community largely composed of first and second generation Americans. I was the youngest of a family of seven, including five girls whom I remember most vividly as a closed and mysterious circle. One by one their suitors carried  them off. This sort of thing concerned me much more than the dialectics of foreignness and assimilation, but the fact remains that our parents—my father was a carpenter by trade, and a Social Democrat—were in many ways closer to the politics and the metaphysics of the old world than to the pragmatic construction of the new. I suspect that my friends and I heard a great deal more in our childhood about the catastrophic ideas which had been sweeping Europe than other Americans of our generation have heard during the entire course of their lives.

"Now, of course, we are all in the same boat, a violently rocking one, for our country has entered the main stream of world history. My own small story has some sense, if any, in relation to all that. In 1936 I went out to the University of Illinois, worked as a waiter, salesman, research assistant, between and during school terms—and began, very laboriously, to write. In 1938, lured by a fellowship, I went to the University of Chicago, which was an extremely lively place to be. The educational theories of Mr. Hutchins, the philosophical ideas of Mr. Carnap on one hand and Mr. Maritain on the other, and finally the challenge of campus religious and political groups—all this probably had more effect on my development than my formal studies. The latter I pursued with some diligence up to and including a Phi Beta Kappa key, for I intended to remain at the university as a teacher. But the onset of the war in Europe brought a growing restlessness. I took an M.A. in a great hurry, tried vaguely to join the American Field Service Ambulance Corps and then, after Pearl Harbor, an officer's training school. Declared unfit for these elite outfits, I went east and found a job with the O.W.I., which did not mind my being myopic and, after a few months, sent me to North Africa, along with General Eisenhower and a motley collection of other fellows, civilian and military. At this point, perforce, I began to grow up.

"I had been publishing small things in literary reviews, chiefly in the *Partisan Review.* I had also—at the age of twenty—married Celia Scop. Before I left New York for North Africa, I managed to finish 'The Mohammedans,' which has been much anthologized and translated. But now I stopped writing and plunged into my work at the Psychological Warfare Branch of Allied Force Headquarters, and into the discovery of a world.

"I began writing again several years later in Paris, but I have never been able entirely to abandon the official or public activities which I fell into during the war. I am passionately interested in these activities which all turn, in one way or another, around the spiritual axis of my life, i.e. the dialogue between Europe and America. In my various functions, at UNESCO, at the U.S. Embassy, at the Mutual Security Agency, I have been trying to understand what is transpiring between my country and . . . what? Call it our heritage. I have also been trying to avoid being bureaucratized and dehumanized by organization. And, of course, I've been trying to write.

"To do these things together has been most difficult, at least for me. Even more difficult is to have any way of knowing how one is progressing, if at all. Harper has been kind enough to publish my two novels: *The Plenipotentiaries* in 1949, and *The Spirit and the Bride* in 1951; and both have been republished in England, by Secker & Warburg. Some critics have also been kind, especially in England, but the public has shown no great interest. As for my bureaucratization, I'm afraid that I just barely manage to keep it at bay, and the longer I live in Europe, the more perplexed I am.

"This perplexity, combined with a certain resistance to the moral and political collectivisms of our time, are all that I have for the moment to pass on to my two children—and to my readers, who are only slightly more numerous, alas. But I still manage to hobble about and I hope to have more—more children, more readers and more to pass on—in the years to come."

* * *

H. J. Kaplan's first novel was judged, in the New York *Times*, "a highly accomplished performance . . . a novel of ideas and implications." His earlier writings, the Paris letters in *Partisan Review* and the long story "The Mohammedans," gave evidence of sound technique and craftsmanship. In the two novels he has published to date, Kaplan has shown signs of fulfilling this early promise, although there is still too little of his work available to afford a basis for a thorough critical evaluation.

PRINCIPLE WORKS: The Plenipotentiaries, 1949; The Spirit and the Bride, 1951.

KARIG, WALTER (1898-), American novelist and journalist, was born in a white frame house on Greenwich Street, New York City. His father, an embosser and engraver by trade, soon moved his family to Glen Ridge, N.J., where Walter Karig grew up as a country boy, the oldest of five children. He began to draw pictures at an early age, and after finishing high school,  commuted to the New York School of Fine and Applied Arts. At nineteen he volunteered for military service, but was rejected by all branches of the United States Service because of astigmatism and some deficiency of his teeth. Joining the Foreign Legion at Quebec, he served eighteen months overseas, then joined the Free Polish Army where he became a captain. He returned to America in 1919, and in 1921 found a job with the Newark *Evening News*, where he remained for twenty-one years, from 1934 serving as manager of its Washington bureau. During this period he was writing the Nancy Drew books for girls, the X-Bar-X books for boys, other juveniles, and adult mystery tales—all under various female and male pseudonyms, including "Keats Patrick."

Karig also wrote for magazines and found a lucrative career as a ghost-writer for political figures. In 1935 he took a trip to Europe and the Far East, writing *Asia's Good Neighbor* as a result. When Pearl Harbor was bombed, Karig volunteered for the Navy, but because of his eye trouble was not accepted until six months later. He then began work for the Public Relations Department, and became head of the newly organized Magazine and Book Section. During the war he covered some 15,000 miles of sea duty, mainly to establish air-courier services. After the war he served as Special Chief Deputy of Information in the Navy Department.

In 1945 his novel *Lower than Angels* was published, "a chunk of early twentieth-century Americana." In 1944 *Pearl Harbor to Coral Sea* (Welbourn Kelly, co-author) introduced a series edited by Karig under the comprehensive title, *Battle Report*, about the part played by the United States Navy in World War II, written from official sources. It was necessarily a highly detailed account, but the *New Yorker* called it "perhaps . . . the war book of the year," and *Book Week* said it mixed "chronology, history, humor, pathos, heroism, vision and imagination into a stirring, memorable, inspiring account of a Navy which recoiled from defeat and started on the road back." *Don't Tread on Me* (1954) is a novel about John Paul Jones.

In 1920 Karig married Eleanor Keating Freye, whom he had met as an art student. They live in Virginia, have two daughters, and are both interested in archeology and animals. In 1954 Karig became book editor of the Washington *Post and Times-Herald*. He is described as a "large, muscular man."

PRINCIPAL WORKS: Hungry Crawford, Legionnaire, 1929; Death Is a Tory, 1935; Asia's Good Neighbor, 1937; Lower than Angels, 1945; War in the Atomic Age, 1946; Zotz! 1947; The Fortunate Islands, 1948; Caroline Hicks, 1951; Battle Report (co-author and editor) 6 vols., 1944-1952; Don't Tread on Me, 1954.

ABOUT: Warfel, H. R. American Novelists of Today 1951; New York Herald Tribune Book Review January 8, 1950; Saturday Review of Literature February 16, 1946.

KARLFELDT, ERIK AXEL (July 20, 1864-April 8, 1931). For biographical sketch and list of works and references, see TWENTIETH CENTURY AUTHORS, 1942.

* * *

ABOUT: Columbia Dictionary of Modern European Literature; Uppvall, A. J. *in* Scandinavian Studies Presented to George T. Flom (ed. Larsen, H. & Williams, C. A.).

KATAEV, VALENTIN PETROVICH (1897-). For biographical sketch and list of earlier works and references, see TWENTIETH CENTURY AUTHORS, 1942.

* * *

Valentin Kataev has published several novels in Russian in recent years, but little of his later work has been translated into English. One of his Russian novels (*Za vlast Sovetov*, the title translated as *For the Power of the Soviets*), published in 1949, dealt with the underground wartime activities of the Odessa partisans and is described by Gleb Struve as a well written, exciting story. This novel came under severe criticism, however, by a fellow writer, Mikhail Bubyonnov, for minimizing the role of the Communist Party in the partisan movement and in 1950 it was officially declared a "political blunder" by the Board of the Union of Soviet Writers.

ADDITIONAL WORKS IN ENGLISH TRANSLATION: The Blue Handkerchief (play) 1944; The Wife, 1946; The Magic Flower, 1947.

ABOUT: Columbia Dictionary of Modern European Literature; Guerney, B. G. (ed.) The Portable Russian Reader; Struve, G. Soviet Russian Literature; Scholastic November 6, 1944.

KATZ, H. W. (December 31, 1906-). For biographical sketch and list of works and references, see TWENTIETH CENTURY AUTHORS, 1942.

KAUFMAN, GEORGE SIMON (November 16, 1889-). For biographical sketch and list of earlier works and references, see TWENTIETH CENTURY AUTHORS, 1942.

* * *

A commentator on the history of American drama, E. M. Gagey, suggested in 1947 that a good case might be made for considering George S. Kaufman "our leading playwright." In Kaufman's comedies, he explains, "one can see commercial Broadway at its best." Even the rowdy farces of Kaufman's early days as a playwright, and certainly the more sophisticated later comedies, offer "the American virtues of clear vision, debunking of pretensions, and a sense of humor." From long years in the theatre Kaufman has developed the professional mastery of technique which can give even a minor play the glossy finish of a hit, though three of his later plays—*Bravo* (1948) written with Edna Ferber, *The Small Hours* (1951) and *Fancy Meeting You Again* (1952), both written in collaboration with his second wife, the actress Leueen Mac-Grath (whom he married in 1949)—were failures and closed after very short runs. Nevertheless, even in these plays critics found lively entertainment and satire.

Kaufman's greatest success in recent years was his collaboration with J. P. Marquand on a dramatization of the latter's novel about Boston Back Bay society, *The Late George Apley.* The play opened on Broadway late in 1944 to enthusiastic critical notices, had a long run there and on the road, and was subsequently made into a motion picture. Since 1950 Kaufman has appeared frequently on television panel comedy programs, where his dry wit and sour, slightly pained expression have made him a popular television personality. *The Solid Gold Cadillac,* a comedy of the business world written in collaboration with Howard Teichmann, was an outstanding hit in 1954. It was sold to motion pictures, with Judy Holliday scheduled to play the leading role created by Josephine Hull on Broadway.

ADDITIONAL WORKS: *Dates of Publication*— (with Marquand, J. P.) The Late George Apley, 1946; (with MacGrath, L.) The Small Hours; (with Teichmann, H.) The Solid Gold Cadillac, 1954.

ABOUT: Gagey, E. M. Revolution in American Drama; Morris, L. Postscript to Yesterday; New York Times Magazine September 17, 1944; Saturday Review of Literature June 16, 1945.

KAUFMAN, LENARD (August 20, 1913-), American novelist, writes: "I was born in New York City. The only work I

ever did outside of writing was a job of manual labor which I took on in order to raise money enough to buy a typewriter. That was when I was seventeen.

"My family did not take kindly to my typewriter or my chosen career and I had to steal up to the attic while the rest of the house slept to write my first piece of fiction. Two years later I 'sold' my first short story to a midwest literary magazine for which I received in payment three copies of the magazine. My family didn't find this very encouraging but as far as I was concerned, my literary career had been launched.

"With this achievement behind me I began work on my first novel, *The Lower Part of the Sky,* which was published eight years later. The book took me two years to write

but six years to convince a publisher that it should be published.

"During my unpublished years the typewriter more than paid for itself. It took me through school and the depression years without so much as a blush for commercialism. There was newspaper work, publicity work, radio work. Later, much later, two novels later, it took me even to Hollywood.

"However, both my typewriter and I are happiest here in New York. Unlike most novelists who write best among the soft surroundings of nature, I work best in the busiest and hardest city in the world because I devote myself entirely to my writing and because writing is the loneliest work in the world. Even if you don't know them, it's good to feel there are eight million people outside your door.

"Paradoxically these eight million people have a profound respect for one's privacy which is an aid to the discipline of any writing regimen.

"My own work habits are fairly strict. I write six hours a day, seven days a week, for three weeks. At the end of the third week I stop for three days and drive into the country. I work slowly, averaging about three hundred and fifty words a day. My original draft of a novel—with minor changes—is my final draft. This peculiar method is a result of an average of six months of thinking and planning before a word is put to paper. While I hardly recommend this to other writers it has worked successfully for me in the writing of four novels and a fifth which I am in the process of concluding now."

* * *

Lenard Kaufman has been described as "an alert watcher of the contemporary scene." His forthright, tautly written novels have been shrewd, sometimes deeply moving comments on modern life. His ear, a reviewer remarked in the New York *Times,* "is subtle and true." One of his most admiring critics is Joseph Henry Jackson who has called him "a novelist with a sense of responsibility to himself and to his craft." His style, the *New Yorker* remarked in 1949, "has a nice drive to it, and he knows not only how to pose an interesting moral problem, but how to make a narrative of it."

PRINCIPAL WORKS: The Lower Part of the Sky, 1948; Tender Mercy, 1949; Jubel's Children, 1950; Diminishing Return, 1952.

ABOUT: Warfel, H. R. American Novelists of Today; New York Herald Tribune Book Review November 5, 1950.

KAVAFIS. See CAVAFY, C. P.

KAYE-SMITH, SHEILA (1887-   ). For biographical sketch and list of earlier works and references, see TWENTIETH CENTURY AUTHORS, 1942.

* * *

Sheila Kaye-Smith remained during World War II at her home in Rye, Sussex—an area, she writes, "that has been considered, geographically, the front line" and was subjected to frequent bombing. Partly as a distraction and partly in recognition of grim necessity, she learned to cook during these trying years and developed considerable culinary skill. In *Kitchen Fugue*, an informal cookbook-autobiography ("a ragout of recipes for eating and thinking," as Isabelle Mallet described the book in the New York *Herald Tribune*) she explained her new enthusiasm: "The diversion of the mind into an unfamiliar activity, a secondary yet urgent interest, and the body into a gentle strain, is the best antidote I know to those trials which beset a lonely woman, no longer young, left to deal single-handed with the marvels of science."

In 1943 Sheila Kaye-Smith collaborated with G. B. Stern in the first of their two highly successful Jane Austen studies. These were written as symposia or, more simply, as informal conversations—fresh, spontaneous, witty and perceptive. The London *Times Literary Supplement* described Miss Kaye-Smith's share as "sober, well informed, thoughtful talk." Nowhere, the *Times* continued, are Jane Austen, her life and art, "more firmly placed in their proper historical and social perspective." Miss Kaye-Smith's later novels have demonstrated her substantial if not inspired talents, what Margaret Evans in the New York *Herald Tribune* called "her sound, humane interest in life and her delightfully mature and full-flavored art of recreating it upon the printed page." Her religious writings, Edward Wagenknecht commented in 1952, "are an unfailing source of spiritual strength and insight." Her latest of these, *Quartet in Heaven*, studies of four women who were raised to sainthood in the Catholic Church, was widely praised by non-Catholic as well as by Catholic readers.

Correction: Sheila Kaye-Smith was born in 1887, not 1888 as listed in TWENTIETH CENTURY AUTHORS, 1942.

ADDITIONAL WORKS: *Novels*—Tambourine, Trumpet and Drum, 1943; The Lardners and the Laurelwoods, 1947; The Happy Tree (in England: Treasures of the Snow) 1949; Mrs. Gailey, 1951; The View from the Parsonage, 1954. *Non-Fiction* —(with G. B. Stern) Speaking of Jane Austen (in England: Talking of Jane Austen) 1944; Kit-chen Fugue, 1945; (with G. B. Stern) More About Jane Austen (in England: More Talk of Jane Austen) 1949; Quartet in Heaven, 1952; The Weald of Kent and Sussex, 1953.

ABOUT: Hoehn, M. (ed.) Catholic Authors, I; Kaye-Smith, S. *in* Roming, W. (ed.) The Book of Catholic Authors, Kitchen Fugue.

*KAZANTZAKIS, NIKOS (December 2, 1885-   ), Greek novelist, was born in Crete. He attended the University of Athens, taking a Doctor of Laws degree; in Paris he studied under the philosopher Henri Bergson; and he completed his studies in literature and art during four other years spent in Germany and Italy. He has also lived and traveled in Spain, England, Russia, Egypt, Palestine, China, and Japan. Before the last war, he spent a great deal of his time on the island of Aegina, where he devoted himself to his philosophical and literary work. In 1945 he was for a short time Minister of State in Greece. In 1947-48 he was director of the Bureau of Translation from the Classics of UNESCO.

Of his writing habits he says, "My method of working strangely resembles that of silk worms: I take out of myself the substance of my book. The first version is made with violent rapidity; then begins more slowly the second version; and finally the third one, still more slowly. I usually make three versions." Beginning with a general plan, he changes and reverses material as he writes. He writes with pen and ink and requires "solitude, solitude." He points to Homer, Aeschylus, Bergson, and Nietzsche as those who have influenced him most in his writing. Kazantzakis' works in Greek are numerous and varied—in the fields of philosophy, travel, the drama, and fiction; and he has written a long epic poem on the fortunes of Odysseus which begins where Homer's *Odyssey* ends. This was translated by Kimon Friar for *New Directions*. Some of his writings have appeared not only in Greek, but in English, American, German, and Swedish publications.

It is for his two novels, *Zorba the Greek* (1952) and *The Greek Passion* (1953), that he is best known to the English and American reader. Both books received approval from distinguished critics. Of the first novel the London *Times Literary Supplement*

* kä zän tzä'kĭs

wrote: "Mr. Kazantzakis has breathed into his prose all the warm airs of the Mediterranean, its light, its color, its sadness. But, more surprising, he has created in Zorba one of the great characters of modern fiction. The novel reflects Greek exhilaration at its best. Zorba, pure in feeling, makes havoc of monks, scholarship and the life of withdrawal." *Commonweal* objected: "As in many another philosophical novel, one is convinced that the characters were contrived to illustrate various maxims." But the *Nation* said, "The whole long tale is superbly written . . . and well translated."

The Greek Passion, translated and published a year later, was pronounced a strong novel by most reviewers, but some thought it too "perverse and evil." However, Thomas Mann and Albert Schweitzer approved emphatically. Mann said, "The novel . . . is without a doubt a work of high artistic order, formed by a tender and firm hand, and built up with strong dynamic power. I have particularly admired the poetic tact in phrasing the subtle, yet unmistakable allusions to the Christian Passion story. They give the book its mythical background which is such a vital element in the epic form today." American critics were in general more restrained and uneasy about Kazantzakis' large canvas. Charles J. Rolo said, "For better or worse, *The Greek Passion* has the flavor of a parable enlarged to epic dimensions." But Albert Schweitzer maintained, "Since I was a young boy, no author has made such a deep impression upon me as Nikos Kazantzakis. His work has depth and durable value because he has experienced much and in the human community he has suffered and yielded much."

Kazantzakis loves the sea, music, traveling, and fruit. Gossip and jazz are his two particular dislikes. He has no hobbies. In 1945 he was married to Elèni Samios in Athens; he and his wife live on the French Riviera. Kazantzakis has been several times nominated for the Nobel prize in literature.

PRINCIPAL WORKS IN ENGLISH TRANSLATION: New Directions #13 (1951); Zorba the Greek, 1952; The Greek Passion, 1953.

ABOUT: New Directions #13 (1951); Current Biography July 1955; Time April 20, 1954.

*KAZIN, ALFRED (June 5, 1915-   ), American critic and autobiographer, writes: "I was born in the Brownsville section of Brooklyn, N.Y.—a raw, poor, fascinating immigrant quarter settled largely by Russian and Polish Jews. I spent the first twenty-three years of my life in a world whose poverty and

* kā'zĭn

fierce pieties opened up so many other worlds for me that I am still amazed by my good fortune—and by how long it took me to realize it. My parents were (and still are) working people who encouraged me in every intellectual concern, had me trained in music from the age of seven, kept alive before me the image of the Europe they had left and of the culture to which they aspired.

Arni

From my first conscious moments, I was absorbed in the most intimate problems of the working class, in the fire and color of immigrant life—and perhaps most of all, thanks in part to my parents' quaint, old-fashioned Socialism and to my own traditionalism, in the historic Jewish effort to realize the Kingdom of God in this world. From my father, who had wandered through the West in his early days as an itinerant workman, I absorbed my passionate interest in the American landscape and in every aspect of American history; from my mother, a skilled craftswoman and a person of profound sensibility, I was confirmed in both my natural feeling for art and in my curious tendency to believe that God is not mocked.

"I went to the College of the City of New York during the depression—a crisis which affected my generation in America much more deeply than even the Second War, and in which I learned how alien I felt to the prevailing ethos—whether of middle-class smugness or of Marxist materialism. In my last year at college, I began to do book reviews for magazines and newspapers, and soon after, began to earn my living as a free-lance critic and college teacher. It always astonished me to find myself a professional critic at all; I had little taste for theory, and my own character was not of that judicious and balanced wisdom which normally allows critics to judge writers with perfect correctness. But believing, as I did, that a critic proves himself entirely by the way he writes, and that there is no other way, I studied the critics who were the best writers—from Sainte-Beuve and Matthew Arnold to Edmund Wilson and Van Wyck Brooks—and went on writing in my own fashion. I found that criticism focussed many—if by no means all—of my own urges as a writer: to show literature as a deed in human history, and to find in each writer the uniqueness of the gift, of the essential vision, through which I hoped to penetrate into the mystery and sacredness of the individual soul.

"In 1937, while I was half-heartedly doing a master's essay at Columbia on Gibbon and wondering what would ever become of me, or of the maddening age, I embarked—on the suggestion of Carl Van Doren—on my historical study of modern American literature, *On Native Grounds*. It was characteristic of my slowness in acknowledging my own deepest interests, and of the social pressure of the period in which I wrote, that I did not deal with poetry, but wrote, as I thought of it, a moral history of America from the dark days of the 1880's up to the present. I worked on the book for five absorbed, happy, isolated years—teaching in the evenings at City College and the New School to keep me going, and spending long full days, year after year, in the New York Public Library, the only formal institution of learning in New York where I have ever learned anything. After the book came out, I went through a long, difficult and restless period —I was briefly literary editor of the *New Republic*, a reporter on *Fortune*, taught at Black Mountain College in North Carolina, and finally went to Britain, on a grant from the Rockefeller Foundation, to study the exciting popular education programs in the British army and in the trade union movement. Those were six tremendously exciting months in Britain, at the end of the war, working closely with people whose fierce hunger for knowledge and democratic faithfulness reminded me of the people I had grown up with. After the war, I settled down in Brooklyn Heights again, a neighborhood particularly dear to me because it is so much the center of what New York once was, did an edition of William Blake for the Viking Portable Library, taught summers in the Middle West or in Europe, and finally began a long personal history against the New York background. The first part of this, dealing with childhood, was published in 1951 as *A Walker in the City*."

* * *

Alfred Kazin's *On Native Grounds* was enthusiastically received by most reviewers as a sound, lucid, and discriminating critical survey of American literature. "He is sensitive, sympathetic and informed," Howard Mumford Jones wrote of the author in the *Saturday Review of Literature*. "No one, I think, has been more deft in setting the social

scene for the appearance of literature, in the successive stages of literary development; and no one has more economically marshalled his writers upon that stage." *A Walker in the City*, Kazin's sensitive and evocative reminiscence of his New York childhood—portions of which were first published in *Commentary* and the *New Yorker*—was also highly praised, although some critics objected to its "deficiencies of structure and substance."

PRINCIPAL WORKS: On Native Grounds; An Interpretation of Modern American Prose Literature, 1942; The Viking Portable William Blake (ed.) 1946; F. Scott Fitzgerald: the Man and his Work (ed.) 1951; A Walker in the City, 1951.

ABOUT: Kazin, A. A Walker in the City; New York Herald Tribune Book Review October 7, 1951; Partisan Review March-April 1952; (London) Times Literary Supplement January 8, 1944.

KEABLE, ROBERT (March 6, 1887-December 23, 1927). For biographical sketch and list of works and references, see TWENTIETH CENTURY AUTHORS, 1942.

"KEENE, FARADAY." See JARRETT, C. H.

KEITH, AGNES NEWTON (1901-   ), American memoirist, writes: "I was born in Oak Park, Ill. My father, Joseph Gilbert Newton, a young Englishman, fell in love with my mother, Grace Goodwillie, of Scot and Welsh blood, the first time he saw her. She was leaning over the banister railing to peek at the tall young man in the drawing room below who was talking with  her mother in accents, she thought, from the stage, the only place a broad *a* was tolerated in Chicago. Father could see that Mother's hair was auburn and curly, her features delicately cut and classical, and although her expression at the moment was one of intense curiosity, it changed as he caught her eye to one of slight disdain as better befitted young ladies in 1900. But Father was not to be fooled; he knew at first sight that she was beautiful, kind and good, and throughout forty years of married life he never had reason to change his mind.

"Mother's Scot-Welsh blood combined to make such an ardent American that she refused to marry her British suitor until he became an American citizen. It was election year, the Republicans were in office. Father indicated his intention of voting the Republican ticket if enfranchised, and his citizenship was speedily accomplished in time for a) his marriage, and b) his vote.

"My brother Al was born shortly after, and I less shortly. The first thing we came to understand about our parents was that their devotion to each other was complete, although they were very unlike. The second was that Father was the iron hand and Mother the silk glove, but the hand was frequently led by the glove. Mother never argued; Father was always right, his judgment was sound, his way was best, only she didn't always follow it. And when innocently enough we sometimes arrived at the opposite goal from that indicated by Father, we always understood that Father was still right and the moral victory was his.

"We left Oak Park to go West when I was just old enough to remember the bears in the Lincoln Park Zoo and the great pale mass of scented lilac bushes in our garden. As I look back, it seems to me that we must have traveled to California in a covered wagon, but the record says that we came by train and arrived at Hollywood when it was only a village of sweet smelling citrus groves. Later we moved to Venice, Calif., where I attended high school.

"Perhaps because I became adolescent in the beginning of the divorce age of the U.S.A., the deep affection that my mother and father always showed each other impressed me much more than did their expressions of love for us, their children. It was natural, I felt, for parents to love their children, but in the world in which I was growing up, it was almost unnatural for them to remain in love with each other. The realization of the strength, beauty, and endurance of such a bond between a man and a woman came to me then, and has stayed with me always.

"In 1914 in San Diego I met a boy called Harry Keith who traded postage stamps with my brother. Harry was English and his parents had lived every place, acquiring postage stamps, porcelain, Persian rugs, and cosmopolitan ways at every stop. Harry at the age of fourteen had for us the exotic flavor of the Orient, and the salty tang of many seas. Harry himself only said he wished his people would stop moving about and settle down.

"Harry was quickly established in my heart as secret sorrow when the first World War came, and although he was under age and British he enlisted in the U.S. Navy. At the end of the war he enrolled in forestry school at the University of California in Berkeley, where I was enrolled as a freshman in Letters and Science. Although we fell in and out of love with each other regularly on weekends, we did not at the end of four college years marry and live happily ever after. Instead Harry accepted a forestry post with the government of North Borneo (as a step towards settling down!) while I went to work on a San Francisco newspaper as its lowest paid reporter. After eight months and a substantial raise I had just made up my mind to be the world's finest feature writer when my ambition was dramatically terminated by a madman's murderous blow on my head. This finished my newspaper career and for several years I fought to survive both the physical and mental aftermaths of this accident. In the end I survived, but minus my youthful faith in my own inalienable right to be happy.

"In 1934 Harry wrote to me from Borneo that he was coming through the United States on leave from Borneo. We met again and this time we knew what we wanted. We were married on three days' notice, and I went with him when he returned to Borneo.

"I believe now that it could not have been otherwise, for I cannot conceive of my life without Harry and Asia, to both of whom I became mutually wedded. For me, to die without ever having lived outside the Western Hemisphere would be not to have been born at all. In finding the Orient I found for the first time the Occident, for I learned that neither one alone is a world; only together do the two halves make a whole. Out of my growing wonder and joy in the new dimensions of the world I was discovering came my first book, *Land Below the Wind*.

"In the second World War, Harry and I with our then two-year-old son George were captured by the Japanese and spent four years in Japanese internment camps. From the experiences of those long years, years that were exhausting, self-revealing, disappointing, despairing, but in the end crowned by the single success of survival, came my second book, *Three Came Home*.

"After the war we returned to North Borneo to find our home destroyed, the coastal towns burned, and the entire country depleted. From the events of North Borneo's reconstruction, and from a growing conviction of the mutual dependency of the Orient and the Occident, came a third book, *White Man Returns*.

"In 1951 we said goodbye to North Borneo, and my husband joined the technical aid program of the United Nations (another step towards settling down!), and we are at present living in the Philippine Islands. We have two children, one grown and one growing."

PRINCIPAL WORKS: Land Below the Wind, 1939; Three Came Home, 1947; White Man Returns, 1951.

ABOUT: Keith, A. N. Three Came Home, White Man Returns; Book-of-the-Month Club News April 1947; New York Herald Tribune Book Review October 7, 1951; Publishers' Weekly July 1, 1939; Saturday Review of Literature April 5, 1947; Scholastic March 18, 1940.

KEITH, Sir ARTHUR (February 5, 1866-January 7, 1955), Scottish anthropologist, was born in Old Machar, Aberdeen, Scotland, the son of John Keith and Jessie Macpherson Keith. He was educated at Aberdeen University, at University College, London, and at Leipzig University. Keith was secretary of the Anatomical Society of Great Britain, 1899-1902, and president of the Royal Anthropological Institute, 1912-14. From 1917 to 1923 he was Fullerian Professor of Physiology at the Royal Institution, becoming secretary of the Institution from 1922 to 1926 and treasurer from 1926 to 1929. From 1930 to 1933 he was Rector of Aberdeen University.

Sir Arthur Keith's book *Human Embryology and Morphology,* first published in 1902, has gone into many editions up to the present day. *Essays on Human Evolution* caused the *Saturday Review of Literature* to remark that Keith "is one of the world's great surgical anatomists and physical anthropologists," and in this book "anatomizes the paradox of civilization's antipathy to the fierce forms of war which it has created." "His particular emphasis is that war has been an integral part of the process of human evolution," said the London *Times Literary Supplement;* an "uncomfortable truth," it added. A Darwinian, Sir Arthur once told his students: "Nature keeps her human orchard healthy by pruning. War is her pruning hook."

In 1950 he published his *Autobiography.* It is especially detailed about his first ten years on his father's farm, then tells the story of his struggle to gain an education, his early years as a doctor, his travels in Siam, Palestine, Egypt, and his rise to fame, culminating with his writing of his memoirs on his own farm in his eighties. "It is an intimate record . . . but it is an honest record," wrote the *Spectator.*

Created a knight in 1921, Sir Arthur Keith received many honorary degrees, and was a Fellow of the Royal Society and a Fellow of the Royal College of Surgeons, as well as an M.D. The American anthropologist Earnest A. Hooton, who had studied under Keith some years before at Oxford, wrote of him in 1946: "The name of Sir Arthur Keith deserves to be associated with those of Charles Darwin and Thomas Huxley in the study of the evolution of man."

In 1899 he married Cecilia Gray, who died in 1934. Sir Arthur died at Downe, Kent. At the time of his death, he was master of the Buckston Browne research farm, a surgical experimental station of the Royal College of Surgeons.

PRINCIPAL WORKS: Human Embryology and Morphology, 1902; Ancient Types of Man, 1911; The Human Body, 1912; The Antiquity of Man, 1915; Menders of the Maimed, 1919; The Engines of the Human Body, 1920; The Religion of a Darwinist, 1925; Concerning Man's Origin, 1927; Darwinism and What It Implies, 1928; The Place of Prejudice in Modern Civilization, 1931; Ethnos or the Problem of Race, 1931; New Discoveries Relating to the Antiquity of Man, 1931; The Construction of Man's Family Tree, 1934; Darwinism and Its Critics, 1935; Essays on Human Evolution (in the United States: Evolution and Ethics) 1946; A New Theory of Evolution, 1948; An Autobiography, 1950.

ABOUT: Keith, A. An Autobiography; Illustrated London News April 1, 1950; New York Times January 8, 1955.

KELLAND, CLARENCE BUDINGTON (July 11, 1881-). For biographical sketch and list of earlier works and references, see TWENTIETH CENTURY AUTHORS, 1942.

* * *

At least three generations of American readers have grown up with Clarence Budington Kelland's novels and short stories—some of them humorous and rakish, some of them historical and melodramatic, all of them slight but smooth, surefire entertainment. In 1947 a reviewer in the Chicago *Sun* summed up Kelland's talent as follows: "If you accept his characters (none of whom have any similarity to real persons, living or dead) and his plots (which never even resemble reality), you have to admit that he turns them into a story which hangs together."

Kelland continues active in Republican politics as executive director of the Republican National Committee. His permanent home is in Phoenix, Ariz., but he spends his summers in Port Washington, L.I.

ADDITIONAL WORKS: Sugarfoot, 1942; Archibald the Great, 1943; Heart on Her Sleeve, 1943; Alias Jane Smith, 1945; Land of the Torreones, 1945; Double Treasure, 1946; The Merchant of Valor, 1947; Murder for a Million, 1947; This Is My Son, 1948; Stolen Goods, 1950; The Great Mail Robbery, 1951; No Escape, 1951; The Key Man, 1952; Tombstone, 1952; Dangerous Angel, 1953; Murder Makes an Entrance, 1955.

ABOUT: Van Gelder, R. Writers and Writing; Saturday Evening Post October 14, 1950.

KELLER, ALBERT GALLOWAY
(April 10, 1874-). For biographical sketch and list of earlier works and references, see TWENTIETH CENTURY AUTHORS, 1942.

* * *

Soon after his retirement from Yale, Dr. Keller published a collection of informal personal essays on a variety of subjects, *Net Impressions.* The essays were lively and provocative. A reviewer in the *Christian Century* said of the book: "Keller pulls no punches, likes to take the unpopular side of an argument or to deflate a popular idol, and has a style that sparkles." Since then he has published no new books, but he has contributed articles to a number of periodicals.

ADDITIONAL WORK: Net Impressions, 1942.
ABOUT: Time January 26, 1942.

KELLY, Mrs. ELEANOR (MERCEIN)
(August 30, 1880-). For biographical sketch and list of earlier works and references, see TWENTIETH CENTURY AUTHORS, 1942.

* * *

Eleanor Kelly's latest novels, like her early works, have won her a small but enthusiastic audience. *Richard Walden's Wife,* based slightly perhaps on her own family background, was an historical novel of pioneer days in Wisconsin before and during the Civil War. A colorful, lively narrative, its total effect, in spite of occasional anachronisms, was (in the judgment of the *Christian Science Monitor*) "adventurous and sumptuous." *Proud Castle,* a romantic novel, reminded the New York *Herald Tribune's* reviewer of Mrs. Kelly's Basque stories, because of "the same warmth and zest."

ADDITIONAL WORKS: Richard Walden's Wife, 1950; Proud Castle, 1951.

KELLY, GEORGE EDWARD (1887-).
For biographical sketch and list of earlier works and references, see TWENTIETH CENTURY AUTHORS, 1942.

* * *

More than twenty years ago Joseph Wood Krutch remarked of George Kelly as a playwright that "he commands respect but he cannot quite inspire a genuine enthusiasm." This failing Krutch attributed to "a touch of coldness in his nature, a certain stubborn negativeness in his moral attitude." In the main Krutch's analysis holds true for Kelly's later work as well. He has never written a bad play, but—with the exception of *Craig's Wife*—his plays always just barely miss success. Both *The Deep Mrs. Sykes* (1945) and *The Fatal Weakness* (1946) were considered superior plays by the critics and had reasonably admiring audiences. Both were comedies about middle-aged women who in their egotism had blinded themselves—one into mistakenly suspecting her husband of infidelity, the other into sentimentally and foolishly trusting him. Both, under Kelly's personal supervision, were sleek and smooth productions. *The Fatal Weakness* (which Burns Mantle chose as one of the ten best plays of the season) was especially distinguished by a sparkling performance by Ina Claire in the leading role. Yet neither play was a complete success, in the commercial or the artistic sense. Similarly, Broadway revivals, in 1947, of *Craig's Wife* and, in 1950, of *The Show Off* revealed expert but only mildly entertaining plays.

ADDITIONAL WORKS: *Dates of publication*—The Deep Mrs. Sykes, 1946; The Fatal Weakness, 1947.

ABOUT: Krutch, J. W. *in* Zabel, M. D. (ed.) Literary Opinion in America (1951); Morris, L. R. Postscript to Yesterday; Theatre Arts February 1947.

KELLY, JAMES FITZMAURICE-. See FITZMAURICE-KELLY

KENNEDY, CHARLES RANN (February 14, 1871-February 16, 1950). For biographical sketch and list of earlier works and references, see TWENTIETH CENTURY AUTHORS, 1942.

* * *

Charles Rann Kennedy died of a heart ailment two days after his seventy-ninth birthday, at his home in Los Angeles. He had lived in retirement in California for the last ten years of his life.

The sincerity and lofty purpose behind Kennedy's plays were not realized in their production. Richard Lockridge wrote of a performance of *The Seventh Trumpet,* Kennedy's last play, "Here is earnestness and high intention and a sermon on the side of the angels. And what it comes to on the stage is appalling, incredible emptiness." Perhaps lack of discipline obscured his intention. The *Catholic World* observed: "Feeding his imagination richly on beauty and holiness, Mr. Kennedy curtails no speeches but seems to put down every thought that occurs to him."

ADDITIONAL WORK: Seventh Trumpet (Repertory of plays for a company of three players, no. 7) 1942.

ABOUT: London Times February 18, 1950; New York Times February 17, 1950.

KENNEDY, MARGARET (1896-). For biographical sketch and list of earlier works and references, see TWENTIETH CENTURY AUTHORS, 1942.

* * *

From 1938 to 1950 Margaret Kennedy wrote no work of fiction, a fallow period during which, she says, "I did not want to write fiction . . . and I was not obliged to do so." She comments: "I had twelve years in which to stroll about and look at things, without being obliged to rush off and turn the *chose vue* into the *chose imaginée* in a sort of pressure cooker." Part of this period was World War II, during which Miss Kennedy (Lady Davies) took her three children to the country to live but traveled back and forth herself to London to visit her husband. Their home was destroyed in a bombing attack.

Since 1950 Miss Kennedy has returned to fiction "with great pleasure and zest." She has once again found an eager and enthusiastic audience in both England and America who admire especially the warmth and the quiet, unhurried charm of her novels. Mary Ross observed of her in the New York *Herald Tribune:* "Perhaps because she has written relatively few books, she seems to have had time to savor the persons and circumstances of which she writes, to observe and understand and enjoy small eccentricities, which are not small in their relation to an individual life, to enjoy the contrasts in thought and feeling and action among people whom many would dismiss as merely odd or even ordinary."

Miss Kennedy lives in London. She is described as "rather tall, neither fat nor thin . . . nervous and talkative." Her favorite, among her own books, is her short biography of Jane Austen in the English Novelists Series, because "in it I did exactly what I set out to do." Her writing habits are relatively simple—long periods of thinking, fairly rapid writing ("I probably do a week's thinking to an hour's writing").

ADDITIONAL WORKS: The Feast, 1950; Jane Austen, 1950; Lucy Carmichael, 1951; Troy Chimneys, 1952; Act of God, 1955.

ABOUT: New York Herald Tribune Book Review August 5, 1951, October 12, 1952; New York Times Book Review March 19, 1950.

KENT, LOUISE (ANDREWS) (May 25, 1886-), American novelist and children's writer, reports: "I was born in Brookline, Mass., within five minutes' walk from where I am now sitting, on May 25, 1886. Last year I noticed in the paper that that day was the hottest 25th of May on record, but I have no reason to think that it has ever been considered remarkable in other

Bradford Bachrach

ways. No tablet of bronze is attached to the house, nor do they wreathe the lamp posts with laurel, woodbine, Boston ivy—or even poison ivy—on that auspicious day. This part of Brookline has changed very little since that time: in fact a friend of mine recently suggested that the whole top of this hill should be sliced off—houses, people, clothes, food, furniture—and placed under glass in the Metropolitan Museum. I notice a few differences myself: one of our neighbors had the colonial pillars of her house painted dark green instead of white, thus causing some raising of eyebrows. You may not believe this but I have seen cigarettes smoked by women within 150 yards of my birthplace! TV has raised its tentacles of paper clips over more than one (two is more than one, isn't it?) Victorian mansion. Kitchens that used to be acquainted with beef only in the form of sirloin with Yorkshire pudding, filet mignon with mushrooms, and porterhouse steak, have now found out about hamburg. I have a freezer with some frozen steaks in it myself. You know, the kind with pasteboard between them? You can tell the pasteboard from the steak because it's a different color. Who says we don't have progress in Brookline?

"Some of my ancestors came here on the Mayflower and other uncomfortable vessels, but my father had the excellent judgment to come by the Cunard from England, about 1870.

"I went to school in Brookline and Boston, sometimes in public, sometimes in private schools. I knew how to read and write when I went to school. An attempt was made to teach me arithmetic. After four years I noticed that the teacher, when she did a problem on the blackboard, subtracted from right to left instead of from left to right as I had been doing patiently and with peculiar results. I asked why she did that. Hearty laughter from my fellow mathematicians made this, so far as I remember, my only display of intellectual curiosity. From then on I knew better and was a fine student, always telling the teachers just what they said first. I feel very lucky to have been educated at a time when my thinking was done for me. Children now, I understand, often have to do it for themselves and, as nothing is so tiring as thinking, I am amazed that they seem to have so much energy. Well, youth is a wonderful thing. Too bad grandmothers can't have some of it. . . .

"I seem to have arrived at mentioning being a grandmother rather suddenly. I married in 1912—Ira Rich Kent (1876-1945), editor and publisher. We had three children; all are married and I have seven grandchildren. Since my marriage I have always spent a good deal of time at my husband's old home, Kents' Corner, in Calais, Vt. A good deal of my affection for Vermont is expressed—I hope—in several of my books.

"I am so fortunate as to be still able to enjoy the things I have always liked. People who set their hearts on killing large—or small—animals and climbing difficult mountains ultimately have to settle down by the fireside, which they make, I'm afraid, rather uncomfortable for everyone else. But if your ideal was already the fireside and a good book, you are lucky. I read about a book a day, and as I have a splendid memory—I forget almost as fast as I read—I am frequently able to read *Middlemarch* or *Persuasion* or *The Eustace Diamonds* over again. I still like music, especially symphonic and chamber music, and I think the FM radio is the most civilized feature of our present-day living. I like birds and can still watch them; flowers and can still have the kinds that thrive on neglect; old furniture—I never had anything else; miniature rooms—I can still make them; cooking—I find no difficulty in getting customers to eat it; old china—my houses are practically silted up with it; old friends—and new ones too; new clothes—and old ones of course: after all, I come from Boston.

"I've given up country dances for crewel embroidery and long distance accordion playing for chess. The world is no sufferer from these exchanges, so far as I can tell."

* * *

Most of Mrs. Kent's writings before 1941 were for children. In the adult field, her pleasant and witty novels with their bright New England flavor have won her a large and faithful group of readers. The novels center around "Mrs. Appleyard," a gentle and witty Boston suburbanite matron who shares many characteristics with the author herself. Mrs. Kent is a graduate of Simmons College (B.S. in Librarianship, 1909). One of her earliest writing jobs was as a columnist ("Teresa Tempest") for the Boston *Traveler*. From 1928 to 1931 she wrote for the Boston *Herald*.

PRINCIPAL WORKS: *Juveniles*—Douglas of Porcupine, 1931; Two Children of Tyre, 1932; The Red Rajah, 1933; Jo-Ann Tomboy (with E. P. Butler) 1933; He Went with Marco Polo, 1935; He Went with Vasco da Gama, 1938; In Good Old Colony Times (with E. K. Tarshis) 1941; He Went With Christopher Columbus, 1940; He Went with Magellan, 1943. *Novels*—The Terrace, 1934; Paul Revere Square, 1939; Mrs. Appleyard's Year, 1941; Mrs. Appleyard's Kitchen, 1942; Country Mouse, 1945; With Kitchen Privileges, 1953. *Non-Fiction*—Village Greens of New England, 1948.

ABOUT: Kunitz, S. J. & Haycraft, H. Junior Book of Authors (rev. ed.); Warfel, H. R. American Novelists of Today; Wilson Library Bulletin October 1944.

KENT, ROCKWELL (1882-). For biographical sketch and list of earlier works and references, see TWENTIETH CENTURY AUTHORS, 1942.

* * *

Rockwell Kent's associations with "left-wing" and allegedly pro-Communist political groups have embroiled him in a number of heated controversies. In August 1950, after he had attended peace conferences in Moscow and in other Communist-dominated countries in Europe, the U.S. State Department voided his passport on the grounds that he had "misused" it. Kent protested that he "was only working for peace," and testified later before a congressional committee that he knew "very little about the Communist Party."

In 1953 Kent's name was again in the news when he was called in a Congressional inquiry over books by alleged Communist authors in State Department overseas libraries. Kent refused, under the Fifth Amendment, to state whether or not he was a Communist. At the time of the hearing it was pointed out that a mural by Kent is owned by Congress and hangs in the House

Interstate and Foreign Commerce committee room.

Kent has stated publicly that he does not believe in Russian Communism for America. He defines socialism, in ideals, as simply the Golden Rule and has said: "In both communism and socialism as I have correctly defined them, I believe." Joseph Wood Krutch has suggested as a possible explanation for Kent's political associations that "Mr. Kent believes so strongly in peace, freedom and equality that he is little disposed to criticize or suspect anyone who says tnat he believes in them too."

In 1955 Kent published a long and colorful autobiography, *It's Me O Lord*.

ADDITIONAL WORKS: Rockwell Kent (American Artists Series) 1946; (ed.) World-Famous Paintings, 1947; It's Me O Lord, 1955.

ABOUT: Kent, R. It's Me O Lord; Mahony, B. E. (ed.) Illustrators of Children's Books; Current Biography 1942; Design September-October 1953; New York Times Book Review May 8, 1955; Publishers' Weekly October 7, 1950; Time August 28, 1950, July 13, 1953.

KER, WILLIAM PATON (August 30, 1855-July 17, 1923). For biographical sketch and list of works and references, see TWENTIETH CENTURY AUTHORS, 1942.

* * *

ABOUT: Pafford, J. H. P. W. P. Ker (bibliography).

KERR, SOPHIE (August 23, 1880-). For biographical sketch and list of earlier works and references, see TWENTIETH CENTURY AUTHORS, 1942.

* * *

In numerous novels and magazine stories, Sophie Kerr has continued to display what one reviewer calls "the expert touch in feminine fare." Her work is slight—mainly romances tailored to the patterns of women's magazine fiction. But it contains a perfect combination of the necessary elements—love, suspense, atmosphere, humor; and it has won her a large and devoted audience.

In 1953 Miss Kerr, long an authority on the culinary arts, collaborated on a cookbook, writing about food "with gusto and common sense." She lives in a Manhattan apartment. In 1948 she received an honorary degree from Franklin and Marshall College.

ADDITIONAL WORKS: Jennie Devlin, 1943; Love Story Incidental, 1946; Wife's Eye View, 1947; The Sound of Petticoats, and Other Stories of the Eastern Shore, 1948; As Tall as Pride, 1949; The Man Who Knew the Date, 1951; The Best I Ever Ate (with J. Platt) 1953.

ABOUT: Warfel, H. R. American Novelists of Today.

KERSH, GERALD (1909-), English author and journalist, was born at Teddington-on-Thames, the son of H. L. Kersh and the former Lea Miller.

He was educated at the Regent Street Polytechnic, an extension school, while working at a dozen different kinds of jobs and learning to write. He achieved publication in 1935 with a novel which had to be withdrawn because of several libel suits. In 1940 he joined the Coldstream Guards and was transferred for special war duties in 1942.

He was correspondent for *The People*, a Labour weekly, from 1943, and script writer with the Army Film Unit in 1942. He was with the special Film Division of the Ministry of Information from 1943 to 1944 and was later under contract to M.G.M. as a film writer. He was accredited to the Supreme Headquarters Allied Expeditionary Force in 1944. From 1941 to 1945 he was chief feature writer for *The People* under the pseudonym "Piers England."

He has written more than twenty novels and some hundreds of stories and articles and some poetry, including, "A Soldier—His Prayer." Kersh writes prolifically, and his novels concerned with the underworld or Bohemian life of big cities have been compared with those of Dickens.

Prelude To a Certain Midnight, first published in America, contained characterizations of a group of London Bohemians who are shocked by the brutal murder of an eleven-year old girl. One of their number is guilty but he is never punished.

The New York *Herald Tribune* said: "This novel is wholly successful in its integration of meaning, story and character. The Kersh cosmos and the people who inhabit it carry his insights easily, without forcing. There is a curious relevance even in the mingling of Bohemian and criminal elements, for in Kersh's view both are Nietzschean rebels, obsessed by a wish for freedom and power. The book is unquestionably good reading. In style it is pleasantly informal, as if the author were writing a letter to the reader, and its phrasing is quick and perceptive." The New York *Times* said: "Kersh is not a writer to be recommended to everyone without reservations. If you like him you like him very much, and his nuisance value to those who don't like him is correspondingly great."

In 1943 he married Claire Alyne Pacaud of Quebec, Canada. He lived in the United States from 1950 to 1952, and now makes his home in London. A huge, burly man, Kersh is proud of the fact that one of the ways in which he earned his living, in his pre-literary days, was as a prize fighter. He likes to give away, as souvenirs "for good luck," sixpences or dimes (depending on what country he is in) which he has bent in two with his teeth. He gives as his recreation, "wandering aimlessly around town." This he does, swinging a gnarled walking cane. His walks are punctuated by visits to pubs where he quickly enters into conversation with a widely varied section of the populace, all of whom begin to sound (in his re-telling of the scene) oddly like characters in Kersh novels. He holds an audience enthralled by telling wildly fantastic stories in a roaring deep-bass voice.

PRINCIPAL WORKS: Jews Without Jehovah, 1935; Men Are So Ardent, 1936; Night and The City, 1937; I Got References, 1938; They Die with Their Boots Clean, 1941; The Nine Lives of Bill Nelson, 1941; The Dead Look On, 1942; Brain and Ten Fingers, 1943; Faces in a Dusty Picture, 1943; An Ape, a Dog and a Serpent, 1945; The Weak and the Strong, 1945; Neither Man nor Dog, 1946; Clean Bright and Slightly Oiled, 1946; Sad Road to the Sea, 1947; Prelude To a Certain Midnight, 1947; The Song of the Flea, 1948; Clock Without Hands, 1949; Jack of Swords, 1950; The Thousand Deaths of Mr. Small, 1951; The Brazen Bull, 1952; The Great Wash, 1953; Guttersnipe, 1954.

KESTEN, HERMANN (January 28, 1900-). For autobiographical sketch and list of earlier works and references, see TWENTIETH CENTURY AUTHORS, 1942.

* * *

Hermann Kesten writes: "I reside at New York since May 27, 1940. I am an American citizen. I traveled since 1940 through most of the states of America, Europe outside the Iron Curtain, and in Turkey and Israel. I am a member of the PEN Club of New York, the German Bundesrepublik, the German Academy of Science and Letters in Mainz, and the German Academy of Letters in Darmstadt."

It is as an interpreter of modern Europe and its history that Kesten has best served the American reader in recent years. He has introduced many little-known works of modern European literature in two anthologies. He has published two novels in English about contemporary Germany. One is the symbolic *Twins of Nuremberg*, a story of two sets of real twins whose natures parallel the elements of Good and Evil in Germany between the two world wars. A strange, loosely-organized,

and at times difficult novel, it nevertheless, according to F. T. Marsh, "displays the equipment of a novelist of the first rank." The other, *Happy Man* (with illustrations by George Grosz), is a bitterly ironic story of life in Berlin in the 1920's. Another contemporary novel, *Die Fremden Götter* (Foreign Gods), was published in Holland in 1949 and in Germany in 1950, but is not yet available in English. In his other writings Kesten has turned to the past to illuminate the present—a biographical novel about Queen Isabella of Spain, a biography of Copernicus, and a biography of Casanova.

ADDITIONAL WORKS IN ENGLISH TRANSLATION: The Heart of Europe (ed. with K. Mann) 1943; The Prose Works of Heinrich Heine (ed.) 1943; Copernicus and His World, 1945; The Blue Flower (ed.) 1946; Ferdinand and Isabella: A Novel, 1946; The Twins of Nuremberg, 1946; Happy Man, 1947; Casanova, 1955.

ABOUT: Columbia Dictionary of Modern European Literature.

KESTER, VAUGHAN (September 12, 1869-July 4, 1911). For biographical sketch and list of works and references, see TWENTIETH CENTURY AUTHORS, 1942.

*KEYES, Mrs. FRANCES PARKINSON (WHEELER) (July 21, 1885-). For autobiographical sketch and list of earlier works and references, see TWENTIETH CENTURY AUTHORS, 1942.

* * *

From the young matron who wrote her first novel in moments snatched from household chores, Frances Parkinson Keyes has developed into a professional author whose novels invariably head the best-seller lists and who refers to her writing as "a big business."

In *The Cost of a Best Seller* Mrs. Keyes candidly admits that in spite of the hard work and frustrations it involves, writing is for her the most rewarding of professions, both materially and spiritually. She has an undisputed narrative gift, a wide range of interests and experience to supply colorful detail and background for her novels, and, although often in poor health, unflagging energy and enthusiasm for her work. Virginia Kirkus, in an essay on Mrs. Keyes in the *English Journal*, points out that her work must not be judged in terms of high literary standards which, as a popular novelist, she does not attempt to meet. But by the standards of best-seller fiction, Miss Kirkus writes, "we can be grate-

* Mrs. Keyes writes that her name "should be pronounced like *eyes* with a *k* in front of it, to rhyme with *skies*."

ful that Mrs. Keyes sustains a reasonably high level for the popular novel."

Mrs. Keyes divides her time between New Orleans and her country home in New Hampshire. In New Orleans she lives in historic Beauregard House, doing her writing in converted slave quarters in the rear. She is busy restoring the house, and in 1948 established the Keyes Foundation to carry on restoration work of this nature and also to set up a scholarship fund to aid young authors.

A Roman Catholic convert (she was received into the Church in 1939 at Lisieux, France, where Saint Thérèse had made her First Communion), Mrs. Keyes won the Siena Medal in 1946 as the outstanding Catholic woman of the year; the Diploma of the Amis de Saumur in 1948; the Medal of Honor of the General Council of the Seine in 1950; and the Silver Medal of French Recognition for her aid in the reconstruction of the Benedictine abbey at Lisieux.

ADDITIONAL WORKS: Novels—Crescent Carnival, 1942; Also the Hills, 1943; The River Road, 1945; Came a Cavalier, 1947; Once on Esplanade, 1947; Dinner at Antoine's, 1948; Joy Street, 1950; Steamboat Gothic, 1952; The Royal Box, 1954. Non-Fiction—All This Is Louisiana, 1950; The Cost of a Best Seller, 1950; Thérèse: Saint of a Little Way (rev. ed. of Written in Heaven, 1937) 1950; Bernadette of Lourdes (rev. ed. of The Sublime Shepherdess, 1940) 1953; The Happy Wanderer (verse) 1954.

ABOUT: Hoehn, M. (ed.) Catholic Authors, I; Keyes, F. P. The Cost of a Best Seller; Christian Century December 7, 1949; English Journal June 1951; New York Times Book Review December 10, 1950.

KEYNES, JOHN MAYNARD (June 5, 1883-April 21, 1946). For biographical sketch and list of earlier works and references, see TWENTIETH CENTURY AUTHORS, 1942.

* * *

John Maynard Keynes died of a heart attack at his home in Firle, Sussex, England, at the age of sixty-two.

The economist played a principal role in the re-establishment of peacetime trade and finance following World War II. In July, 1944 he led the British delegation at the conference at Bretton Woods which set up controls for a post-war international monetary authority, and in February 1946 was appointed Governor of the International Monetary Fund and the International Bank for Reconstruction and Development.

Keynes's personality has been described as "radiant, brilliant, effervescent, gay, full of impish jokes." The London *Times* points out that he was "not merely a prodigy of intel-

lect; he had civic virtues—courage, steadfastness and a humane outlook; he had private virtues—he was a good son, a devoted member of his college, a loyal and affectionate friend, and a lavish and unwearying helper of young men of promise."

Although the Keynesian theory of economics gives us, in the words of Lawrence R. Klein, "a set of tools with which to work on the unemployment problem," it does not deal with many other important socio-economic questions. Seymour E. Harris, in whose opinion Keynes' great contribution "was to adapt economics to the changing institutional structure of modern society," observed that he could enlighten men of action by writing with the charm and persuasiveness of (and more brilliance than) Adam Smith, could inspire economists as did the works of Ricardo, and, like Marx, could awaken "an almost religious fervor" for his theories. "In the wide scope of his interests," Harris wrote, "in his eloquence and persuasiveness, in the virtually complete command over economic forums, both of subjects to be discussed and manner of discussing them, in the impression he made upon our quasi-capitalist system, in the influence upon economists and men of action of his day—in these jointly, and probably in each separately, Keynes has not had an equal."

ADDITIONAL WORK: Two Memoirs, 1949.

ABOUT: Cambridge University King's College: John Maynard Keynes: A Memoir; Dillard, D. D. Economics of John Maynard Keynes; Harris, S. E. John Maynard Keynes, (ed.) New Economics: Keynes's Influence on Theory and Public Policy; Harrod, R. F. Life of John Maynard Keynes; Klein, L. R. Keynesian Revolution; Pigou, A. C. John Maynard Keynes, Baron Keynes of Tilton, 1883-1946; Timlin, M. F. Keynesian Economics; Economic Journal March 1947; London Times April 22, 1946; Mind July 1936; New York Times April 22, 1946; Quarterly Journal of Economics November 1951; Social Studies March 1948, November 1948; Time April 29, 1946.

*KEYSERLING, HERMANN ALEXANDER, Graf von (July 20, 1880-April 26, 1946). For autobiographical sketch and list of works and references, see TWENTIETH CENTURY AUTHORS, 1942.

* * *

Count Keyserling died of apoplexy at his home in Innsbruck, in the Austrian Tyrol, at sixty-five. He had been suffering from partial paralysis and from the effects of wartime malnutrition.

Under the Hitler regime, Keyserling's passport was withdrawn, his papers impounded,

* ki'sēr lĭng

and he was forbidden to publish or lecture. Only his world-wide reputation saved him from worse treatment.

"His judgments or generalizations were not often original," noted the London *Times* at the time of his death. "Sometimes they were platitudinous or questionable. He confessed himself an improvisator and boasted of his indifference to facts with disconcerting emphasis. His style, too, was often marred by verbosity and self-importance. Against these faults, however, must be placed a lively intelligence—what a French critic called his *souplesse Slav,* a gift for expressing his intuitive judgments with persuasive ease and conviction, not seldom with real eloquence."

ABOUT: London Times April 29, 1946; New *York Times* April 29, 1946; Publishers' Weekly May 11, 1946; Time May 6, 1946.

KIDD, BENJAMIN (September 9, 1858-October 2, 1916). For biographical sketch and list of works and references, see TWENTIETH CENTURY AUTHORS, 1942.

* * *

ABOUT: Barnes, H. E. (ed.) Introduction to the History of Sociology; Hofstadter, R. I. Social Darwinism in American Thought, 1860-1915.

KILMER, JOYCE (December 6, 1886-July 30, 1918). For biographical sketch and list of works and references, see TWENTIETH CENTURY AUTHORS, 1942.

KING, BASIL (February 26, 1859-June 22, 1928). For biographical sketch and list of works and references, see TWENTIETH CENTURY AUTHORS, 1942.

* * *

ABOUT: Thomas, C. Canadian Novelists, 1920-45.

KINGSLEY, SIDNEY (October 18, 1906-). For biographical sketch and list of earlier works and references, see TWENTIETH CENTURY AUTHORS, 1942.

* * *

A slow, thorough, and deliberate craftsman, Sidney Kingsley has written relatively few plays in recent years, but each play that he has written has been a pronounced artistic and commercial success. In 1943, while he was serving in the U.S. Army, his historical drama *The Patriots* opened in New York. The play was the result of several years of research by Kingsley on the career of Thomas Jefferson and was more than a year in the actual writing. Selecting the critical years

1790 to 1800, Kingsley focussed his drama on the conflict between Jefferson and Alexander Hamilton over the basic philosophy of government in a democracy. It was a slow-moving play. Several critics suggested that it resembled an historical pageant rather than a drama. But, as Stark Young commented: "It is thoughtful, full of warm feeling, and its general content is rich, honest, and noble as regards its application to our day." In May 1943 Kingsley received the New York Drama Critics Circle award for *The Patriots,* with a citation noting its "dignity of material, its thoughtful projection of a great American theme, its vigorous approach to the characters portrayed, and, in spite of certain limitations, its driving final effect on the stage."

Kingsley did not finish another play until 1949. In the interim, he served in the Army and, after his discharge, wrote several motion picture scenarios for M.G.M. In preparation for his next play, *Detective Story,* he spent two years visiting police stations and detective squad rooms in New York. The finished play, which opened in 1949 to critical acclaim (and was later made into a highly successful motion picture), was a gripping portrait of the routine activities of a Manhattan precinct police station, written so realistically and with such fine reportorial detail that John Chapman compared it to a documentary, and *Time* magazine praised the playwright for his "sociologist's researching zeal."

Two years later Kingsley completed what many critics considered his finest recent contribution to the stage—his version of Arthur Koestler's powerful novel on Soviet Communism, *Darkness at Noon.* Kingsley was careful to point out that the play was based on, but not adapted from, Koestler's novel. He took certain liberties with his source, although the essential force of the novel was not diminished in the dramatization. To give the play the necessary dramatic concentration, Kingsley employed a series of flashbacks which traced the history of the protagonist's relations with the Communist Party. He further devised a practical and effective setting, dividing the stage into levels, which permitted many quick changes of scene. For *Darkness at Noon* Kingsley received, for the second time, the New York Drama Critics Circle award. He has also received the Donaldson award for outstanding achievement in the theatre, and the American Academy of Arts and Letters Award of Merit medal for outstanding drama, 1951. In 1954, making a radical change of pace, Kingsley wrote *Lunatics and Lovers,* a broad farce, which was generally well received.

Kingsley and his wife, the actress Madge Evans, live on a fifty-acre farm near Oakland, N.J.

ADDITIONAL WORKS: *Dates of publication—* The Patriots (with M. E. Kingsley) 1942; Detective Story, 1949; Darkness at Noon, 1951.

ABOUT: Chapman, J. (ed.) The Burns Mantle Best Plays of 1948-49; Gagey, E. M. Revolution in the American Drama; Current Biography 1943; Time April 4, 1949.

"KINGSMILL, HUGH." See LUNN, H. K.

KIPLING, RUDYARD (December 30, 1865-January 18, 1936). For biographical sketch and list of works and references, see TWENTIETH CENTURY AUTHORS, 1942.

* * *

ABOUT: Brown, H. Rudyard Kipling; Carpenter, L. R. Rudyard Kipling: A Friendly Profile; Croft-Cooke, R. Rudyard Kipling; Dictionary of National Biography 1931-40; Mott, F. L. Golden Multitudes; Orwell, G. Dickens, Dali, and Others; Christian Science Monitor Magazine November 10, 1945; Saturday Review of Literature January 19, 1946; Time October 25, 1943.

KITTREDGE, GEORGE LYMAN (February 28, 1860-July 23, 1941). For biographical sketch and list of works and references, see TWENTIETH CENTURY AUTHORS, 1942.

* * *

ABOUT: Brown, R. W. Harvard Yard in the Golden Age; National Cyclopedia of American Biography (1948); Thorpe, J. (comp.) Bibliography of the Writings of George Lyman Kittredge.

KLEIN, ABRAHAM MOSES (February 14, 1909-   ), Canadian poet, Joyce scholar, and lawyer, who writes as A. M. Klein, was  born in Montreal, the son of Colmon and Yetta (Morantz) Klein. He graduated from McGill Arts University in 1930; and from the Law School of the University of Montreal in 1933. He was admitted to the Canadian bar that same year as a practicing lawyer.

Garcia Studios

Klein has published four volumes of verse. *Hath Not A Jew*, the first, appeared in 1940 with a foreword by Ludwig Lewisohn. In emphasizing the fact that Klein uses the traditions, history, and folklore of the Jews to give substance and concreteness to his poetic themes, Lewisohn observed, "Klein had the luck . . . to be born into a family and into an environment in which the lore and tradition of our people were things so alive that the quiver of this aliveness . . . has accompanied all his years. . . . He knows the Talmudic sages great and small as he knows the men and women on Saint Lawrence Street in Montreal, and into his English poetic style, even to the wild wit and sparkle of his rhymes, he has transfused their ardors, their dreams, their exquisite goodness, their storming of the very courts of God."

Hath Not a Jew was followed in 1944 by a volume called *Poems*, and by *The Hitleriad*, a satire in verse. The *Saturday Review of Literature*, after remarking that *Poems* "deals with the longest war in history, the war against the Jews," added: "Opening with a book of XXXVI Psalms based on the life of Abraham, and closing with a ballad in quasi-Spenserian stanzas on the pilgrimage of a medieval troubadour in search of the lost Zion, Klein informs the present with the past and the past with the future"; while the London *Times Literary Supplement* (after commenting that the narrative poem at the end showed the influence of Keats) said, "[but elsewhere] his style is simply and often passionately his own."

For his fourth volume, *The Rocking Chair* (1948), Klein was awarded the (Canadian) Governor General's Medal for Poetry.

In 1951 Klein published a novel, *The Second Scroll*, which is the story of a Jewish-Canadian journalist and his efforts to locate a lost relative. One reviewer wrote, "If John Hersey's *The Wall* can be regarded as the outstanding fictional tribute by a non-Jew to the annihilated Jewry of Europe, this apocalyptic volume by A. M. Klein . . . can with greater justification be described as the most profoundly creative summation of the Jewish condition by a Jewish man of letters since the European catastrophe."

Klein's considerable reputation as a Joyce scholar is based on several essays which have appeared in periodicals and which are chapters from a forthcoming work entitled "A Commentary on James Joyce's *Ulysses*." In addition to his work as a Montreal attorney, Klein was, from 1943 to 1946, visiting lecturer in poetry at McGill University. He has traveled through Ireland, France, Italy, Israel, and North Africa. Witty and energetic, Klein has been described as small, rather fat, with a mobile expressive face and a vivacious manner. He and his wife, Bessie Kozlov Klein (whom he married in 1935), have three children, Colman, Sandor, and Sharon.

PRINCIPAL WORKS: *Poetry*—Hath Not a Jew, 1940; The Hitleriad, 1944; Poems, 1944; The Rocking Chair, 1948. *Fiction*—The Second Scroll, 1951.

ABOUT: Régimbal, H. Artistes Israélites au Canada Français.

KLUCKHOHN, CLYDE (January 11, 1905-), American anthropologist, writes:
"I was born in Le Mars, Iowa, then predom-

inantly an English settlement. I would trace my lifelong interest in cultural difference to the fact that I grew up amid the contrast between English and American culture. My father was of German extraction. His grandparents came to the United States in 1848. My mother's people came from English and Scottish forebears who migrated to New England in the early eighteenth century.

"After grade schools in Le Mars I went to Culver Military Academy, graduating in 1921. Since I was only sixteen I took an additional year at the Lawrenceville School in New Jersey. At both schools I was an editor of the school newspapers and literary magazines.

"In the autumn of 1922 I entered Princeton but was forced by illness to leave after a few months. An out-of-door life was recommended for a year or two. My mother had a cousin married to a rancher at Ramah, N.M., and they agreed to receive me. I spent six months there in constant contact with Spanish-Americans and Zuñi and Navaho Indians. This experience—plus the fact that the rancher (Evon Vogt) was a university graduate with a good library and strong intellectual interests—inevitably drew me to anthropology, although it was seven years later before I had any formal instruction in the subject.

"I left the ranch to take a 3,000-mile horseback trip through the Southwest and especially in the Navaho country. In December of 1922 I published my first paper on the Navaho—in *El Palacio*, the journal of the New Mexico State Museum. It isn't a good piece of anthropology nor of writing either, but it was a start. At Christmas time I returned to Le Mars and spent the next nine months in teaching public speaking at the

Le Mars High School and in instructing in swimming at a summer Boy Scout camp. My spare time was devoted to writing a book about my packhorse trip. This was published in 1927.

"The academic years 1924-28 were spent at the University of Wisconsin. My principal literary effort there was as editorial writer for the *Daily Cardinal*. The summers of 1926, 1927, and 1928 were given over to more pack trips in the Southwest with undergraduate friends. These are described in *Beyond the Rainbow*.

"I then went to Oxford as a Rhodes Scholar. For two years I did Latin and Greek (my undergraduate major at Wisconsin was in Greek). But by 1930 I had decided that there wasn't too much left to do in the scholarship of Greek and Latin literature that excited me, and classical archeology struck me as too specialized. For a time I thought of returning to the law which had been my firm choice until I left Princeton. But a few weeks at the Harvard Law School convinced me this was definitely not for me. Finally, therefore, I made the decision for anthropology toward which the accidents of my life and steadily developing interests had steadily been pressing me. So far as I was conscious of my motivations they came down about to these: 'As an anthropologist, I can continue to spend time in my beloved Southwest. I can travel elsewhere and spend a great deal of time out of doors. I can study almost anything about human beings that interests me and consider it as part of my work. I could write about people.'

"For two years I studied anthropology at Vienna, Paris, Oxford, and Madrid. I was also psychoanalyzed in Vienna. In 1932 I was married and became assistant professor of anthropology at the University of New Mexico. I was happy there but had no trade union card (Ph.D.) and so in 1934 came to Harvard. I had every intention of returning to New Mexico, but had a quarrel with the then head of the department of anthropology there and hence accepted an invitation to become an instructor at Harvard. I have been there ever since except for a period of war service in Washington and a post-war period as consultant to General MacArthur's headquarters in Japan. Of course, during summers and sabbaticals there have been field trips to New Mexico and Arizona, travel in Mexico, travel and teaching at the Salzburg Seminar in Europe. I have just returned (October 1952) from four months in Australia, New Zealand, and the Pacific Islands. In Australia I gave the Dyason Lectures for the Australian Institute of International Affairs."

* * *

Clyde Kluckhohn's *Mirror for Man,* a study of what anthropology can do for world peace, received the $10,000 Whittlesey House –*Science Illustrated* award in 1949 as the best book of science for the layman and a book which "contributed most to man's understanding of the world today." Kluckhohn gave one fourth of the prize money to Harvard University to further studies among the Navahos. He had begun work on his book in 1945 on a Guggenheim fellowship. He was married in 1932 to Florence Rockwood, a sociologist, and they have one son.

PRINCIPAL WORKS: To the Foot of the Rainbow, 1927; Beyond the Rainbow, 1933; The Excavation of BC51 (ed. with P. Reiter) 1939; A Bibliography of the Navaho Indians (comp. with K. Spencer) 1940; An Introduction to Navaho Chant Practice (with L. C. Wyman) 1940; Navaho Witchcraft, 1944; The Navaho (with D. Leighton) 1946; Children of the People (with D. Leighton) 1947; Personality in Nature, Society, and Culture (ed. with H. A. Murray) 1948; Mirror for Man, 1949; Navaho Means People (with L. McCombe and E. Z. Vogt) 1951; Culture (with A. L. Kroeber) 1952.

ABOUT: Current Biography 1951; New York Times Book Review March 27, 1949; Newsweek February 14, 1949; Saturday Review of Literature January 29, 1949.

KNIBBS, HARRY (or HENRY) HERBERT (October 24, 1874-May 7, 1945). For autobiographical sketch and list of works and references, see TWENTIETH CENTURY AUTHORS, 1942.

* * *

Harry Herbert Knibbs died at seventy. His stories of Western life were praised for their sense of character and for a dry humor, and were certainly superior to the general run of such stories. Of his poetry, the late William Rose Benét wrote: "Mr. Knibbs writes in an old Western tradition, but he writes flashingly better than most celebrators of the cowboy."

KNIGHT, ERIC (April 10, 1897-January 15, 1943). For biographical sketch and list of works and references, see TWENTIETH CENTURY AUTHORS, 1942.

* * *

Eric Knight was killed during World War II when a transport plane carrying American Army personnel to Africa crashed off the coast of Dutch Guiana. He was forty-five years old.

A major in the Film Unit of the Special Services Division of the United States Army,

Knight wrote the booklet given to American soldiers going to Great Britain. In 1942 he wrote continuity for a film stressing the need for international food planning.

Harrison Smith said of Knight: "The sturdy and homely virtues of England's Yorkshire were bred into his blood and bones, and with them the Yorkshireman's native gift for eloquence and humor. . . . His real genius lay in his love and understanding of men and women." Although his novel *This Above All* was one of the memorable books about the war, Knight wrote to his publisher just before leaving on his last flight, "The big thing is to win this war by killing Germans, not by writing books."

ABOUT: Van Gelder, R. Writers and Writing; New York Times January 22, 1943; Publishers' Weekly September 23, 1944; Saturday Evening Post August 21, 1943; Saturday Review of Literature February 6, 1943; Scholastic September 13, 1943.

KNIGHT, GEORGE WILSON (September 19, 1897-). For biographical sketch and list of earlier works and references, see TWENTIETH CENTURY AUTHORS, 1942.

* * *

G. Wilson Knight returned to England in 1941 as master at the Stowe School in Buckingham. In that same year he produced and acted in his own work, *This Sceptered Isle,* at the Westminster Theatre in London. In 1946 Knight joined the faculty of Leeds University where, until 1951, he produced and acted in a number of classical dramas— *Agamemnon, Athalie, Timon of Athens, King Lear.* He lectured in Jamaica in 1951 for the British Council and the University College of West India, and in the following year he was a visiting lecturer at the University of Cape Town.

Stanley Edgar Hyman calls Knight "one of the most eclectic of modern critics." He has used and acknowledged almost every major contemporary critic. His critical studies, however, are independent and imaginative, and "brilliantly suggestive." In his later work, Hyman finds, he has been so preoccupied with mysticism that he has produced "some of the most fantastic criticism, or rather non-criticism, ever written." In the writings of Shakespeare and Milton, Knight found anticipations of the crises of modern times. Shakespeare in particular he considers the prophetic spokesman for Christian moral leadership in the contemporary world. Knight's thesis, what H. B. Charlton in the *Manchester Guardian* called his "esoteric Christian mysticism," has had little or no influence in present-day literary criticism.

But even where it has been rejected, his observations on individual works have been received with admiration and respect. Eric Bentley has commented that in spite of the obscurity of his system ("nebulous and oracular"), Knight's criticism "is among the best contemporary work in the field."

ADDITIONAL WORKS: Starlit Dome: Studies in the Poetry of Vision, 1941; Chariot of Wrath: The Message of John Milton to Democracy at War, 1942; The Olive and the Sword, 1944; The Dynasty of Stowe, 1945; Hiroshima, 1946; The Crown of Life: Essays in Interpretation of Shakespeare's Final Plays, 1947; Christ and Nietzsche, 1949; Lord Byron: Christian Virtues, 1952; The Mutual Flame, 1955.

ABOUT: Hyman, S. E. The Armed Vision.

KNIGHTS, LIONEL CHARLES (May 15, 1906-   ), English critic, is the son of C. E. Knights and Lois M. Knights. He studied at Cambridge University and began his teaching career in 1933 as a lecturer in English literature at the University of Manchester. He remained at Manchester until 1947 when he became professor of English literature at the University of Sheffield. Knights was a member of the editorial board of *Scrutiny*, a quarterly critical review, until it ceased publication in 1953.

A much-discussed book of Knights' is *Explorations*, published in 1946, comprising essays in criticism mainly on the literature of the seventeenth century. Stanley Edgar Hyman believes that "in it he does invaluable work in insisting on the essentially Gestalt conception of the reader's total complex emotional response as the starting place of criticism rather than any of the traditional critical abstractions like 'character' and 'plot.'" Many critics find Knights' technique excessively analytical, Anthony Powell in the *Spectator* saying of *Explorations*: "An admonition to read the words that Shakespeare wrote, and study them carefully, is no doubt timely; but in attacking one sort of donnishness Mr. Knights sometimes sails dangerously near the shallows of another variety." "It is an excellent thing to have the essays collected in book form," countered Theodore Spencer in the *Saturday Review of Literature*, "for Mr. Knights' criticism has been among the most intelligent written in England during the past fifteen years; his mind is penetrating and original, his style is lucid, and his references illuminating."

In 1936 Knights married Elizabeth M. Barnes; they have a son and daughter and live in Bristol, England.

PRINCIPAL WORKS: Drama and Society in the Age of Jonson, 1937; Explorations, 1946.

ABOUT: Bentley, E. (ed.) The Importance of Scrutiny; Hyman, S. E. The Armed Vision.

*KNITTEL, JOHN (March 24, 1891-   ). For biographical sketch and list of works and references, see TWENTIETH CENTURY AUTHORS, 1942.

* * *

John Knittel lives in Grisons, Switzerland. His novel *Terra Magna* appeared in German in 1948, and the continuing interest in his earlier works is indicated by the number of recent translations into French and Dutch of some of these. None of his later writings has been translated into English.

* nĭt' 'l

KNOX, EDMUND GEORGE VALPY (July 27, 1881-   ). For biographical sketch and list of earlier works and references, see TWENTIETH CENTURY AUTHORS, 1942.

* * *

After nearly thirty years on the staff of the magazine, Edmund Valpy Knox ("Evoe") resigned from *Punch* in 1949. In the years in which he edited it (1932-49), *Punch's* circulation reached an all-time high of 184,000. In 1950 Knox edited an anthology of humorous verse. He lives in London.

ABOUT: Time June 2, 1947.

KNOX, RONALD ARBUTHNOTT (February 17, 1888-   ). For biographical sketch and list of earlier works and references, see TWENTIETH CENTURY AUTHORS, 1942

* * *

Monsignor Knox retired to Lord Acton's estate at Bridgnorth, in Shropshire, in 1939 to prepare his English prose translation of the Vulgate. His version of the New Testament appeared in 1944, of the Old Testament in 1949 and 1950. "I translate it onto a typewriter," he wrote of his work, "trying to forget that anybody has ever translated the Bible into English before. It would give only an ugly, piebald effect if one tried to make a hash of the versions other people have done. My aim is to produce a translation in English (not colloquial but literary English) which is current today, and at the same time to avoid words and turns of phrase which were not equally current in the seventeenth century. The idea is that you want a kind of timeless English." The Knox translation was everywhere praised for its lucidity and readability. The only reservation raised against it concerned its literary quality (in comparison with the Douay and King James versions). Thomas Sugrue wrote: "It does not strike into the heart and set the harps of the mind singing." But, he added, "As a translation . . . into modern English prose it is an excellent work. It reads easily; it clarifies the narrative as it rolls along; its style is smooth and breaks frequently into lyricism; there are phrases here and there of startling grandeur."

During World War II Monsignor Knox headed a committee to provide Catholic books for servicemen. He has continued to preach, lecture, and teach apologetics to numerous student groups—always with marked felicity of style, easy candor, and (as Nash K. Burger remarked) a "pungent blend of humor and learning." In 1950 he was elected a Fellow of the Royal Society of Literature.

ADDITIONAL WORKS: In Soft Garments, 1942; Retreat for Priests, 1946; God and the Atom, 1946; The Mass in Slow Motion, 1948; The Creed in Slow Motion, 1949; Selections from Occasional Sermons (ed. E. Waugh) 1949; Trials of a Translator (in England: On Englishing the Bible) 1949; Enthusiasm, 1950; The Gospel in Slow Motion, 1950; Stimuli, 1951; The Hidden Stream, 1952; A New Testament Commentary, 2 vols., 1953-54; Off the Record, 1954; Retreat for Lay People, 1955. *Vulgate translation*—The New Testament, 1944; The Old Testament, 1949-50.

ABOUT: Current Biography 1950; Hoehn, M. (ed.) Catholic Authors, I; Commonweal December 30, 1949; Newsweek November 15, 1948, May 2, 1949; Saturday Review of Literature February 18, 1950; Time November 27, 1944, September 20, 1948, November 27, 1950, February 11, 1952.

KOBER, ARTHUR (1900-   ). For biographical sketch and list of earlier works and references, see TWENTIETH CENTURY AUTHORS, 1942.

* * *

Arthur Kober was a screen writer in Hollywood from 1941 to 1946. He now lives in New York with his wife and daughter. In 1953 he lectured at the New School for Social Research.

Kober's comedy of summer resort life in the Catskills, *Having Wonderful Time*, was adapted into a musical comedy by Harold Rome and Joshua Logan in 1952 under the title *Wish You Were Here* and had a successful Broadway run. His Bronx heroine Bella was the subject of another book in 1951. For Bella, as Harvey Breit observed, Kober has "a deep paternalistic affection." His readers share this feeling. But Kober's later fictional creation, the kinetic Holly-

wood agent Benny Greenspan, inspires less affection. Although Kober has protested that he likes him, Benny is too deeply and happily enmeshed in the jungle of Hollywood "talent peddling" to win reader sympathy. A large measure of Benny's charm is his talent—like Bella's—for "phrase mangling" and Kober's skill in reproducing it. Kober's stories appear frequently in the *New Yorker*.

ADDITIONAL WORKS: That Man Is Here Again: The Adventures of a Hollywood Agent, 1946; Bella, Bella, Kissed a Fella, 1951.

ABOUT: New York Times Book Review October 28, 1951.

KOCH, VIVIENNE (1914-   ), American critic, writes: "I have always felt autobiography to be a somewhat paradoxical enterprise and have said so in print about the self-revelations of others. This now puts me in the embarrassing position of allowing to myself what I question elsewhere, but I shall try to be military about it. I was born in New York City of a Hun-

Talbot

garian father and mother, who in their backgrounds represented two different European traditions. My mother was a country girl whose father ran a large ranch on the Hungarian *pustas* (plains); my father came of an urban, intellectual family with members dispersed in the various professions. In my childhood, since I was often left in the care of my grandparents, I was bilingual or rather trilingual, for my sister and I had a German nurse. My primary education was in the city public schools where I excelled at verbal arts like dramatics, debating, and writing. I wanted to be an actress and cherished this not altogether ill-founded notion until my sophomore year at college (Washington Square College in New York) when, although I continued to be active in dramatics, the shabby intellectual content of courses in the theatre made me reconsider my choice. From that point on, my major interests both as an undergraduate and subsequently as a graduate student at Columbia University were in literature and philosophy.

"Although university teaching and writing seemed a happy conjunction, the mid-depression years offered scanty opportunity along those lines. My first job, therefore, was in a field for which I had little preparation but, I like to think, some natural aptitude—that of social work. I chose to work in the blighted tenement areas of Harlem where Negroes, newly-arrived Puerto Ricans, and a few remaining Irish-American families tried to meet the desperate challenge of survival. My innocence was a blessing and I sailed blithely into marijuana dens (my first assignment was to 'investigate' one of these), brothels, and dingy hall-bedrooms where single men with extensive jail records sat waiting to establish 'residence' for the relief authorities. In over three years of field work I never had a single unpleasant experience in the crime-ridden streets of Harlem, and I went away with even more affection for the people I had tried to serve than I had come with, but purified of its original sentimentality by a tough and realistic knowledge.

"My first academic job was as an instructor at Mount Holyoke College. I love New England but I found the plethora of women a bit tiresome and spent all my salary weekending in New York. I returned to social work in the capacity of supervisor and trainer of field workers. I left, in a little less than two years, when the inadequacies both of the 'philosophy' of case work (which I had always questioned), and the undemocratic political pressures of my professional setting conflicted too monstrously with my human and intellectual values. I did a brief stint of editorial research and eventually, after a year's holiday as a housewife (the only year of my adult life in which I hadn't a paying 'job'), I began again to teach and write. My critical writing (with the exception of a few schoolgirlish reviews and little mag squibs) really began about 1944 and since then I have devoted as much time to it, away from teaching, as I could. I enjoy teaching and do not, like some writers, think of it as a mere bread-winning chore; but it is honest to add that I resent the drudgery of heavy teaching loads and the relatively low pay with which this challenging profession still rewards its members—ironically enough, with an especial niggardliness at the university level. Among other places, I have taught at Columbia University and the Bread Loaf School of English. I am currently teaching at New York University.

"With the help of various fellowships and awards, I have traveled and studied abroad, mostly in England. I am a declared Anglophile. I recently returned from Europe where I had gone to lecture at the Salzburg Seminar of American Studies in Austria. My students, who were distinguished workers in various literary fields and who represented almost every European country, gave me high hope that the free enquiring spirit of humanism can still be counted on to help save us all from chaos. I want to go back to Europe for a more extended stay as soon as I can.

"My tastes are for exotic food, unaffected people, handsome clothes (when I can afford them), and flowers. I like politics, swimming, dancing, all kinds of jazz and travel. I don't like politicians, contemporary novels (and rarely read them), advertising men (or women), and pretenders to the arts who use the adjective 'creative' in self-description. I admire and seek out vitality, integrity, intensity and a toleration for differences everywhere, in people and in the things they do or make. I have been married and am now divorced."

Principal Works: William Carlos Williams, 1950; W. B. Yeats: The Tragic Phase, 1951.

*KOESTLER, ARTHUR (September 5, 1905-), novelist and journalist, was born in Budapest, Hungary, the son of Henry K. and Adele (Jeiteles) Koestler. His father was a promoter and would-be inventor and Koestler spent his childhood in Hungary, Austria, and Germany. In Vienna he attended the Polytechnic High School and then the University (1922-26). In 1926 he went to Palestine, and after tramping for several months through the Near East, obtained a job as foreign correspondent for the famous Ullstein publications of Germany. After serving as Middle East correspondent (1926-29) and Paris correspondent (1929-30), he was named foreign editor in 1930 of the Berlin newspaper *B. Z. am Mittag* (circ. 190,000). In the summer of 1931 Koestler was the only newsman aboard the Graf Zeppelin on its Arctic expedition.

Erich Hartmann

In December 1931 Koestler joined the Communist Party (from which he parted at the time of the Moscow Trials). In the middle '30's he traveled through Central Asia and spent a year in the U.S.S.R. In 1936, at the time of the Franco revolt, Koestler went to Spain as a correspondent for the London *News Chronicle*. He collected evidence about the extent of German and Italian military aid to the rebels (published in England and France), and managed to get out of insurgent Spain just one hour before a

* kûs′tlĕr

warrant for his arrest was issued (August 1936). Returning to Madrid, he covered the war from Loyalist Spain until, in February 1937, he was captured by the Fascists at the Andalusian front. Condemned to death as a spy, Koestler spent one hundred days in Franco prisons, expecting at any moment to be led out and shot. *Spanish Testament* (1938) is a moving and vivid account of this nightmare. Protests from England held up his execution and in May 1937 he was exchanged for another prisoner and returned to England.

In September 1939, with the outbreak of World War II, Koestler was again on the Continent, this time in France. He was arrested by the French police as a refugee and eventually imprisoned in the notorious detention camp Le Vernet. *Scum of the Earth* (1941) describes the horrible conditions, the difficulties of survival in that camp. Most of us, wrote Koestler, "had been through prisons and concentration camps in Germany, Italy, Eastern Europe, or Spain"; and "a few years ago we were called the martyrs of Fascist barbarism and defenders of liberty. . . . Now we had become the scum of the earth." Koestler was released in January 1940, but it was not until late the next fall that he succeeded, by a circuitous route, in escaping from France to England. In April 1941 he enlisted in the British Army.

Time, reviewing his autobiographical *Arrow in the Blue* (1952), noted: "The importance of Arthur Koestler is the importance of a man caught in the heart of a holocaust who survives to bear witness: K's holocaust was also that of much of European civilization and Koestler has already borne eloquent witness to it in half a dozen political novels."

Darkness at Noon (1941) is Koestler's outstanding work, and it established his reputation as a political novelist. Based on his understanding of the Moscow Trials, the novel dramatizes the tragic plight of Commissar Rubashov, an old Bolshevik, who is arrested by the GPU and persuaded to confess to crimes against the state which he did not commit. Koestler's penetrating depiction of the mentality of the Soviet bureaucracy plus his understanding of and sympathy for the old revolutionary combine, in this book, to create a tragedy which has lost none of its power and meaning for readers today. The novel was a Book-of-the-Month Club selection in America, and ten years later it was produced as a play (adapted from the novel by Sidney Kingsley).

This book was followed by *Arrival and Departure* (1943), a novel dramatizing the political, social, and moral predicament of an ex-Communist in Europe who no longer sees a way to fight for what he believes in; and by *The Yogi and the Commissar* (1945), a book of essays. In commenting on these two books, Philip Rahv characterized Koestler as "the poet and ideologue of the homeless radical." In 1946 *Thieves in the Night* appeared, a book which throws, said the New York *Times,* an "heroic and terrible light on the tragedy of modern Palestine."

In May 1948 Koestler paid his first visit to the United States, lecturing for the International Rescue and Relief Committee. In early June 1948, shortly after the partition of Palestine and in the midst of the fighting between the Jews and the Arabs, Koestler flew to Haifa. *Promise and Fulfillment* (1952) is a report of his experiences there and contains also an account of the Jews in Palestine and their relations to the Arabs and the British between the years 1917 and 1949.

Koestler's latest books have not aroused the same international discussion and interest as did most of his earlier books. *Insight and Outlook* (1949) contains a discussion of the author's theories of art, science and social ethics; *Age of Longing* (1951) is a picture of the Paris international intelligentsia; and *Arrow in the Blue* (1952), which takes the author from his birth to his 27th year, is the first of a promised series of autobiographical volumes. The second, *The Invisible Writing* (1954), carries his story through the seven years of his membership in the Communist Party. Koestler's career, like that of Malraux and Silone, has been two-sided: he has been as much a man of action as he has been a man of letters; but in the last few years his books have not had the same immense topical and timely urgency and appeal.

On his return to this country from Palestine, Koestler lived for a while on an island in the Delaware River, near New Hope, Pa. More recently he has been spending most of his time in England. He has also had a house on the Seine near Fontainebleau, France. Writing for the New York *Herald Tribune* in 1951, Koestler had this to say about Koestler: "Prides himself on being the only writer who twice changed the language in which he writes: from Hungarian to German at the age of seventeen, from German to English at thirty-five. . . . Hobbies: dogs, chess, handyman's jobs, particularly repairing frigidaires and washing-machines. In other words, an ideal husband."

In 1935 Koestler married Dorothy Ascher whom he subsequently divorced. In 1950 he married Mamaine Paget. Friends of his report that he is an expert on fine wines and has a constitutional hatred of policemen. He is a member of the PEN club.

PRINCIPAL WORKS: Spanish Testament, 1938; Gladiators, 1939; Darkness at Noon, 1941; Scum of the Earth, 1941; Arrival and Departure, 1943; The Yogi and the Commissar, 1945; Twilight Bar, 1945; Thieves in the Night, 1946; Insight and Outlook, 1949; The Structure of a Miracle, 1949; Age of Longing, 1951; Promise and Fulfillment, 1952; Arrow in the Blue, 1952; The Invisible Writing, 1954.

ABOUT: Koestler, A. Spanish Testament, Scum of the Earth, Arrow in the Blue, The Invisible Writing; Pritchett, V. S. Books in General; American Mercury October 1952; Commonweal March 9, 1951, June 1, 1951, September 26, 1952; Current Biography 1943; English Journal December 1951; New York Herald Tribune Book Review October 7, 1951; New York Times Book Review April 1, 1951; New Yorker July 26, 1952; Saturday Review September 27, 1952; Time September 22, 1952; 20th Century January 1953; Wilson Library Bulletin November 1942..

*KÖHLER, WOLFGANG (January 21, 1887-), German-American psychologist and author, was born in Reval, Estonia, the son

of Franz Köhler and Minni (Girgensohn) Köhler. He was a student at the *gymnasium* at Wolfenbüttel from 1896 to 1905, and until 1909 attended the Universities of Tübingen, Bonn, and Berlin. While teaching at Frankfurt-am-Main, Germany, he was the director of the anthropoid station at Teneriffe, Canary Islands. His book *The Mentality of Apes,* published in 1925 in English translation, was the outcome of the patient investigations which Köhler and an associate, Kurt Koffka—both exponents of Gestalt psychology—had made at Teneriffe. "Professor Köhler's work will, we think, always be regarded as a classic in its kind and a model for future studies in animal psychology," wrote the (London) *Times Literary Supplement;* and the *New Statesman* added, "This is undoubtedly the most important book on animal psychology which has appeared for many years. It is written by a man who is neither an anthropomorphist nor a mechanist, and yet who com-

* kü'ler

bines the sympathy of the one with the scientific attitude of the other."

As Köhler and others developed the Gestalt theory, their language became more involved and philosophical, and his later books less readable by the general public. The Gestalt psychologists interpreted phenomena as organized wholes rather than as aggregates of distinct parts, and maintained that the whole was greater than the sum of its parts. Begun in Germany, the movement was transferred to the United States in the 1930's. Köhler himself came to America in 1935 and since then has been professor of psychology at Swarthmore College.

In 1938 *The Place of Value in a World of Facts,* a collection of the William James Lectures, given at Harvard in 1934-35, was published. Here he applied his astonishing erudition and vigorous and creative mind to the problems that arise midway between science and philosophy. "The book as a whole is required reading for those intellectually fit to pursue the problems of value in terms of the philosophy of science," declared the *Saturday Review of Literature.*

In 1927 Köhler married Lili Harleman; they have one daughter.

PRINCIPAL WORKS: The Mentality of Apes, 1925; Gestalt Psychology, 1929; The Place of Value in a World of Facts, 1938; Dynamics in Psychology, 1940.

KOHN, HANS (September 15, 1891-), American historian and educator, writes: "I was born in Prague, then a part of the Austrian monarchy and since 1918 the capital of Czechoslovakia. Before this historical change, I had completed my education there, first in an elementary school main-

tained by the Piarist Fathers, then in the classical *gymnasium* in the Old Town of the city, and finally at the German University, the oldest university in Central Europe, where I studied law, political science and philosophy. In the fall of 1914 I was mobilized into an Austrian infantry regiment, underwent a reserve officer's training in Salzburg, and left soon for the Carpathian Mountains to fight the Russians. There I was taken a prisoner of war, and spent thereafter four years and ten months in the Russian empire, first in Turkestan (in famous ancient Samarkand and in the Ferghana province on the Chinese border) and then in Siberia, which I crossed three times from the Urals to the Pacific Ocean. I preserve a happy memory of the fall and winter which I spent, in 1919, in Irkutsk in the cultural division at the headquarters of the Czechoslovak Legion.

"There, witnessing the effects of the war and above all of the revolution, I decided to make the study of history my main field for the future. I regarded the war chiefly as the result of nationalist passions. Thus the subject of nationalism began to fascinate me, and I have remained faithful to it for now over thirty years. Born in the multi-national Hapsburg monarchy, a great laboratory and observation field for national conflicts—in a city which was the vigorous heart of Czech nationalism and which had been for centuries the classical battleground of Germans and Slavs and where all manifestations of life, and all ancient memories made the national struggle ever present, I had already as a student participated in nationalist movements. I was influenced by the neo-romantic nationalism of the German youth of the period, and by the ethical and idealistic trend of Zionism led then by Martin Buber. In Russia I came in contact with Russian civilization and with the nationality problems of that multi-racial empire.

"After my return to Europe in 1920, I first settled in Paris, where I married [Yetty Wohl], moved then to London where we lived for four years, and left in 1925 for Jerusalem and for extended travels in the Near East. In Palestine I joined the small group working for Arab-Jewish understanding, led by Dr. J. L. Magnes. There I studied the national movements of western and southern Asia. I worked for two leading European newspapers, *Frankfurter Zeitung* and *Neue Zürcher Zeitung*, and wrote books. The first book which I published in 1922 is entitled *Nationalismus;* from my interest in Zionist ideology several books derived, especially a lengthy study of Martin Buber; four other books dealt with nationalism in the Middle East and in the Orient.

"In 1931 we decided to leave Palestine, where our son was born. From my studies of history and national character, I chose the United States as our future home, and in the more than twenty years which have since passed, we have always been happy to have become part of the American community. I loved my teaching jobs and my contact with the youth. For fifteen years I taught at Smith College in Northampton, Mass., and I am now teaching at the City College of New York. I was fortunate enough to be invited to teach also at several other American institutions of learning, above all at Harvard, where I taught for two years and for many summers, and where my son graduated. In four books, published between 1937 and 1942, I tried to discuss the implications of the world crisis, an attempt continued in my recent *The Twentieth Century* which presents a synthesis of my views on the conditions of our modern world. But my main concern is the series of books, which, beginning with *The Idea of Nationalism,* tries to analyze this all-pervading force of contemporary history against the background of the intellectual and social development of mankind."

* * *

Hans Kohn has been called "one of the great teachers of our day." In the classroom, on the lecture platform, and in his many books and articles, he has presented trenchant and stimulating analyses of the major political ideas of the day. Crane Brinton, in the New York *Times,* described his political position as follows: "Professor Kohn is fully aware that the twentieth century has not by any means fulfilled the hopes of nineteenth century liberals, but this awareness has not driven him to despair, or to some new creed irreconcilable with the traditions of Western liberalism. He is that rare, and in these days, most useful person, a patient liberal." Kohn's most important works include a number of volumes on nationalism, on which he is probably the greatest living authority, and an impressive history of the political ideas of Western civilization, *The Twentieth Century.*

PRINCIPAL WORKS AVAILABLE IN ENGLISH: A History of Nationalism in the East, 1929; Nationalism and Imperialism in the Hither East, 1932; Nationalism in the Soviet Union, 1933; Orient and Occident, 1934; Western Civilization in the Near East, 1936; Force or Reason, 1937; Revolutions and Dictatorships, 1939; Not by Arms Alone, 1940; World Order in Historical Perspective, 1942; The Idea of Nationalism, a Study in its Origins and Background, 1944; Prophets and Peoples, Studies in Nineteenth Century Nationalism, 1946; The Twentieth Century, a Midway Account of the Western World, 1949; Panslavism, Its History and Ideology, 1953; New German Views on German History, 1953; The Mind of Modern Russia (ed.) 1955.

ABOUT: Annals of the American Academy of Political and Social Science September 1944; Canadian Forum December 1949; Historische Zeitschrift August 1952; Neue Schweizer Rundschau March 1948; Political Science Quarterly June 1931, March 1945; (London) Times Literary Supplement September 26, 1929, October 19, 1946.

KOMROFF, MANUEL (September 7, 1890-). For biographical sketch and list of earlier works and references, see TWENTIETH CENTURY AUTHORS, 1942.

* * *

In recent years Manuel Komroff has written in a variety of forms and on a variety of subjects. His major interests—as reflected in his work—are history (both European and oriental, used as backgrounds for his novels), Christianity (he has published a biography of Christ made up of passages from the four Gospels arranged as a continuous narrative and more recently a highly praised anthology of readings about Christ), and the craft of writing (he has written *How to Write a Novel* and lectured at Columbia University on the technique of the novel). One of the best received of his later books was the auto-biographical reminiscences of his childhood in New York at the turn of the century, *Big City, Little Boy*.

Komroff is a member of many authors' organizations. He was vice president of the Authors' Guild from 1941 to 1943 and from 1937 to 1947 a member of the council of the Authors' League. During World War II he was active in the Overseas Press Club and the War Writers' Board. He was vice-president of PEN from 1945 to 1947 and secretary from 1947 to 1952. In 1947 he represented PEN International Writers at the United Nations. Komroff lives in New York City.

ADDITIONAL WORKS: All in Our Day (short stories) 1942; Don Quixote and Sancho (play) 1942; One Story: The Life of Christ, 1943; Feast of the Jesters, 1947; Echo of Evil, 1948; How to Write a Novel, 1950; Jade Star, 1951; Marco Polo (juvenile) 1952; (ed.) Jesus Through the Centuries, 1953; Big City, Little Boy, 1953; Napoleon, 1954; True Adventures of Spies, 1954.

ABOUT: Komroff, M. Big City, Little Boy.

*KORZYBSKI, ALFRED (July 3, 1879-March 1, 1950), Polish-American writer on semantics, was born in Warsaw, Poland, the  son of Ladislas Hab-dank Korzybski and Countess Helena (Rzewuska) Korzybski, and was educated at the Warsaw Polytechnic Institute. During World War I he served in the Polish Army and was wounded twice. He was also attached to the Intelligence Department of the Russian

Lotte Jacobi

* kôr zĭp′skē

General Staff and was sent to the United States and Canada as an artillery expert. Secretary of the Polish-French Military Commission in the United States, he was a recruiting officer for the Polish-French Army, in the United States and Canada, in 1918. At the League of Nations in 1920 Korzybski served in the Labor Section of the Polish Commission.

His first book, *Manhood of Humanity—the Science and Art of Human Engineering* (1921), sought to show that by mathematical philosophy we can arrive at the true conception of what a human being really is, and that in discovering the nature of man we come to the science and source of ethics. Ordway Tead commented in the *Freeman:* "To engineers it may prove an inspiration and solace; to others it will appear somewhat less novel and less reassuring. But it is a forthright, earnest book by one who has seen a vision and would share it with his fellows." Best-known of Korzybski's works is *Science and Sanity, an Introduction to Non-Aristotelian Systems and General Semantics*, published in 1933. This became the basic text for the Institute of General Semantics, founded in Chicago in 1938 and later moved to Lakeville, Conn., in 1946. In 1948 *Selections from Science and Sanity* was abstracted from the original text for use by teachers and students of semantics. The author had the ability to awaken great enthusiasm in his students and for his ideas, and he had hundreds of followers throughout the world. A pioneer in semantics, he held that too often men get the steps of their thought-speech processes confused, so that they speak before observing and then react to their own remarks as if they were fact itself. As he explained it, general semantics has to do with living, thinking, speaking, and the whole realm of human experience. Life is composed of nonverbal facts, each different from another and each forever changing. He contended that because of Aristotelian thinking habits, which he considered outmoded, men do not properly evaluate the world they talk about and that in consequence, words have lost their accuracy as expressions of ideas, if ever they had such accuracy. His theory was put to practical use in the fields of public, industrial and race relations and wherever misunderstanding among people is due to different values and structures of words. It was employed during World War II in helping psychiatric casualties.

The general reader found it difficult to understand *Science and Sanity*. A reviewer

535

in the New York *Times Book Review* found
Korzybski's discussion of scientific philosophy in its relation to mathematics and higher
physics a bit steep for him, but referred to
"its calculus, its relativity, its biology and
neurology, its anthropology" as "the most
glittering tribute to the intellectual energy
of the 'intelligent layman' ever issued from
a printing press." Even Sidney Hook, the
philosopher, found it difficult reading. He
said in the *Saturday Review of Literature,*
"I believe that Mr. Korzybski's fundamental
position is sound and that his obiter dicta
contain some seminal ideas which undoubtedly will bear the fruit in the minds of others.
But if he had deliberately set about to obscure his primary insight he could not have
proceeded any differently from the way he
has—or succeeded so well."

In 1919 Korzybski married Mira Edgerly,
a portrait painter who survived him upon his
death at Sharon, Conn., at the age of seventy.

PRINCIPAL WORKS: Manhood of Humanity,
1921; Time-Binding, the General Theory (privately
printed) 1926; Science and Sanity, 1933.

ABOUT: American Journal of Psychiatry May
1950; Isis 1950; New York Times March 2, 1950;
New Yorker February 7, 1948; Time February 14,
1949.

*KOSSAK-SZCZUCKA, ZOFIA
(1890-   ), Polish novelist whose books in
English translation are signed Zofia Kossak,

was born in central
Poland, where her
parents owned an es-
tate, and there she
spent her childhood.
She was the daughter
of Thaddeus Kossak
and Anna Kisielnicka
Kossak, who were de-
scended from the old
rural nobility. Her
grandfather, Julius
Kossak, was a well-known painter, and her
two sisters, Maria Pawlikowska and Magdalena Samozwaniec, were writers. Zofia
Kossak was tutored at home, and she says,
"I studied history with zest—literature, the
arts and philosophy helping me in my writing."

During a "little" Russian revolution from
1904 to 1905, her father was arrested. Soon
after the family estate was sold and her family moved to East Poland, then under Russia.
There she lived during World War I, and
there she was married in 1915. She had two
children by this marriage. Her husband died
in 1921.

* kôs'säk shchōōts'kä

536

Miss Kossak began to write at an early
age, and her first book, *The Blaze,* was published in Polish in 1922 and in English in
1927. It was written in the form of a diary,
dealing with life in Poland between 1917
and 1920. In 1922 she went to live in Silesia,
and here she wrote many books still not
translated into English, "The Great and the
Small," "The Battlefield of Liegnitz," "The
Unknown Land," "This Day," and "Golden
Freedom." A book for children, one of several written, has been translated into English
(1929), *Troubles of a Gnome.* Miss Kossak has also written an untranslated religious
book, "God's Fools," and a romantic biography of St. Stanislas Kostka entitled "For
Love."

To gather material for her next novels,
she visited Egypt and Palestine in 1933, and
described her travels in "The Pilgrim Way."
She then wrote and published her trilogy,
Blessed Are the Meek (in English, 1944),
The Leper King (1945), and *Angels in the
Dust* (1947).

In 1939 Poland was occupied by Germany;
Miss Kossak's book "The Unknown Land"
had already been denounced by the Nazis.
She joined the underground Resistance
Movement and wrote for the illegal press.
However, her literary style betrayed her and
she was arrested by the Gestapo and sent
to the Auschwitz concentration camp. After
ten months she was sentenced to death, but
escaped.

Her most recent volume in English translation is *The Covenant* (1951), a novel of the
life of Abraham, the prophet, set against a
detailed picture of life as it was lived in the
Euphrates valley, in the desert and in Egypt
in ancient times. "A sincere, scholarly, and
thought-provoking book," said the New York
Times. "She is a storyteller of uncommon
imagination," wrote the *Saturday Review of
Literature,* "and an indefatigable researcher.
Judging by the translation of her work, she
is no great stylist." Abraham "is a believable
man, a man touched by God," said Thomas
Sugrue in the New York *Herald Tribune
Book Review.*

Miss Kossak now lives in England with
her second husband, Zygmunt Szatkowski,
whom she married in 1924. The *Columbia
Dictionary of Modern European Literature*
says of her, "Kossak is the outstanding
representative of the post-war school of historical fiction in Poland. She was also a leading figure in the Catholic literary renaissance."

PRINCIPAL WORKS IN ENGLISH TRANSLATION: The Blaze, 1927; Troubles of a Gnome, 1929; Blessed Are the Meek, 1944; The Leper King, 1945; Angels in the Dust, 1947; The Meek Shall Inherit (in England: Gift of Nessus) 1948; The Covenant, 1951.

ABOUT: Columbia Dictionary of Modern European Literature; Hoehn, M. (ed.) Catholic Authors, II; Current Biography 1944.

KRAMM, JOSEPH (September 30, 1907-), American playwright, writes: "I was born in Philadelphia, and slightly less than three years later I recited a story called *The Little Gingerbread Man* to an admiring group of relatives and friends. I was told this by my mother; I don't remember the occasion myself. I imagine there was polite applause when I fin-

Peter Perri

ished, and I imagine also that I never quite got over it. I had tasted the blood of theatre.

"At five, I played the father in a playground version of *Hansel and Gretel*. I was a character man from that moment, except for the occasion two years later, when I played Puck in an abbreviated scene from *A Midsummer Night's Dream*.

"My father was a druggist who hated every moment he had to spend in the store. He would read poetry, and write poetry, until someone disturbed his reveries in the laboratory by shouting 'store.' Then he would close his book, or put down his pen, and go forward to sell a two-cent stamp or make a telephone call for someone who didn't know how to use the phone.

"My mother encouraged my interest in theatre. She bought the tickets for the first professional shows I saw. She instilled the feeling I have for music, for the opera—she taught me the poems I recited (many of them written by my father)—she seemed proudest of me when I appeared in high school or college shows. Yet she was shocked when I announced on graduation from the University of Pennsylvania, in June of 1928, that I was going to make the theatre my professional work. She, and my father, too, were positive I was going to be a great lawyer. They never said anything to me about law after I went into the theatre, though I'm sure they felt I had made a terrible mistake. When they died, I was still only a struggling actor after fourteen years in the theatre.

"My first professional acting job was with Mae Desmond's stock company, at the William Penn Theatre in Philadelphia. This was the season of '28-'29. When the company folded after thirteen weeks—and an additional six weeks of abortive effort on a co-operative basis collapsed—I went back to being a newspaper man. I say 'went back' because I had been a newspaper man during my years at the university.

"I joined the Philadelphia *Record* in the spring of '29. In July of that year I took an audition for the apprentice group of Eva Le Gallienne's Civic Repertory Theatre. In August, I was notified I had passed the audition and in September I left the Philadelphia *Record*, and newspaper work, and committed myself to the theatre for life.

"I was lucky enough to stay with Le Gallienne for six years. The experience shaped my understanding of theatre. The work at the Civic, in active repertory, was the kind that actors dream about now, and speak of its realization in terms usually associated with living in some unattainable utopia. Highminded, and low-minded, producers and directors frequently announce plans for repertory, with the same frequency and for the same reasons that a radio or television network will occasionally do what is known as a 'prestige show.' It is one of my ambitions to launch a real repertory company. I'm sure it can be done, and I'm sure it can be commercially successful. And I don't care how many others launch similar projects. I hope they are *all* successful. The more, the better. The theatre could use the stimulation of bee-hive activity.

"Around Christmas time of 1933, in Chicago while on tour with Le Gallienne, I began to write my first play. It was finished in May of '34, placed in a trunk in June, and there it has remained except for occasional periods when I would decide to re-read and revise it. I haven't looked at it now for a number of years.

"When the tour of *L'Aiglon* ended in the spring of '35, I continued to work sporadically as an actor and was fairly lucky. For a while I was on the Federal Theatre Project of the WPA, and this was the closest our country has been to a national theatre. Some wonderful work was accomplished on this project, and millions of Americans saw flesh and blood actors for the first time in their lives.

"From '36 to '43, when I went into the army, I played a number of shows, among them, *Bury the Dead, Golden Boy* (in London); *Liliom* with Ingrid Bergman and Burgess Meredith; Maxwell Anderson's *Journey to Jerusalem*; *Brooklyn, U.S.A.*; and *Uncle Harry*.

"During those years I continued to write. Five more plays, which wound up in the trunk. They will remain there in blessed darkness and serve only to remind me of how difficult it is to write a play.

"When the war broke out I decided to study radio engineering. I preferred the crossed flag insignia of the Signal Corps to the crossed rifles of the Infantry. Radio engineering was as far from any natural aptitude I might possess as an honest crap game on a gambling ship. But I had recited *Boots* as a schoolboy and I wanted no part of 'sloshing up and down again.' It happened, however, that after taking the FCC license exams and becoming a 'first-class radio operator' I got a job as a control room engineer at WNYC. Five months there, and I moved to WNEW. I worked at the station in the daytime, and played in *Uncle Harry* at night.

"Then, the army. I made the Signal Corps, but found myself sloshing up and down again anyhow. I wound up in cryptography, which sounds fascinating and terribly brainy but in which machines did all the brain work and required from me only the use of a typewriter. With a Signal Service Battalion I went to Europe and moved forward with 'Advanced Section, Communications' through France, Belgium, Luxembourg, into Germany, except for a brief period of moving backwards during the 'Bulge.'

"VE Day! The war in Europe was over. For some cryptic reason the cryptographic section of our outfit was needed in the Phillipines, and there we were shipped without a furlough. The atomic bombs, however, had made Japan see the light seventeen days before we reached Manila, and by the time we docked the war was over. In December of '45, I was discharged.

"I had started to write a new play while I was in the army but I didn't finish it until 1947, and by that time the subject matter had become dated. This was the *first* play, the sixth chronologically, to be considered seriously by the powers on Broadway. I had begun to learn my craft as a playwright. 'The Cry of the Watchman' it was called, and it's still a good play, but events in the world have moved so quickly, the subject is no longer valid. Friends have suggested using the characters in another play, but I can't do that. Those people have a life that is right for the circumstances of that play, and it would be impossible for me to transplant them and have them live honestly in other surroundings and with different problems to face.

"In the meanwhile I began a career as a director. I directed summer stock for two seasons at the Sayville Playhouse, on Long Island, in '46 and '47. I started also to teach acting at the Dramatic Workshop of the New School for Social Research, for Erwin Piscator.

"Then came *Hope Is the Thing With Feathers*. This is a beautiful one-act play by Richard Harrity. I directed this play as part of a bill of three one-act plays for ANTA—the American National Theatre and Academy. It was successful. It brought me the first top-flight recognition I had ever received in the theatre. It brought me several other jobs, as well. That was in the spring of '48, and the summer of that year I directed José Ferrer in *Twentieth Century* at Olney, Md., and June Havoc in *Anna Christie* for the Theatre Guild, at Westport, Conn. In the fall I started teaching at the American Theatre Wing.

"The next year, around Christmas time of '49, I began to write *The Shrike*. Eight weeks later it was finished. Twelve weeks after that it was sold. Four times in two years it was optioned and dropped, twice by José Ferrer. Finally, Ferrer bought it for the third time. The contract was signed on a Tuesday afternoon and a week later we were in rehearsal. It was successful in New York with Ferrer, successful on the road with Van Heflin, a failure in London with Sam Wanamaker, and a moderate success in Vienna.

"It won the Pulitzer prize, two Donaldson awards, and the Page One award of the Newspaper Guild of Philadelphia. Another play, 'The Gypsies Wore High Hats,' is ready for production, and a new play is in the works. That's it!"

PRINCIPAL WORK: The Shrike, 1952.

ABOUT: Current Biography 1952; New York Herald Tribune January 13, 1952, May 6, 1952; New York Times February 24, 1952, May 6, 1952; New Yorker February 9, 1952; Saturday Review February 16, 1952.

KRAPP, GEORGE PHILIP (September 1, 1872-April 21, 1934). For biographical sketch and list of works and references, see TWENTIETH CENTURY AUTHORS, 1942.

KRASSNOFF, PETER NIKOLAEVICH (1869-1947). For biographical sketch and list of works and references, see TWENTIETH CENTURY AUTHORS, 1942.

* * *

Peter Krassnoff's death was reported in Valentin Kiparsky's *Norden in den Ryska Skönlitteraturen*, published in Sweden in 1947.

KREBS, RICHARD JULIUS HERMAN. See VALTIN, J.

*KREY, Mrs. LAURA LETTIE (SMITH) (December 18, 1890-). For autobiographical sketch and list of works and references, see TWENTIETH CENTURY AUTHORS, 1942.

* * *

Mrs. Krey writes from Minneapolis, Minn.: "I am seriously engaged and have been, for ten years, on three novels that bear on the period in Virginia (which I regard as one of the most significant in our modern era) from 1765 to 1920. I am also half through a novel on the early mapping by the Spaniards of the Gulf coast in Texas. This work has been prolonged by the obvious necessity for much extensive research in each field and long stay in each area, as well as by various family emergencies." Mrs. Krey has also contributed essays to *The Writer's Handbook* (ed. A.S. Burack, 1942), *Twentieth Century English* (ed. W.S. Knickerbocker, 1946), and the *Southwest Review* (Summer 1951). These, she writes: "contain the best thought of which I am capable on the whole art of fiction, which seems to me a far thing from the usual run of slick novels that are written to be hastily read as escape-pieces or else, perhaps, as mediums for propaganda of one kind or another."

Mrs. Krey points out that her first work did not appear in women's magazines, as TWENTIETH CENTURY AUTHORS, 1942 stated, but in the *American Review* and the *Sewanee Review*, and that *All Tell of Time* was never intended as an "apology for," but as a portrayal of the plantation system as she knew it in Texas.

* krā

*KREYMBORG, ALFRED (December 10, 1883-). For autobiographical sketch and list of earlier works and references, see TWENTIETH CENTURY AUTHORS, 1942.

* * *

Alfred Kreymborg has lectured at many colleges and universities throughout the country. In 1945 he published a collection of his

* "The *eym* in my surname is pronounced *aim*, and the *o* in *borg* is a long vowel."

works from 1912 to 1944, *Selected Poems*. Louis Untermeyer wrote of the collection: "What emanates from these pages and remains after the book is put away is not the poetry itself, not the singing and even searching lines, but the personal warmth, the sensitive and generous spirit of the singer." Other recent publications include a verse allegory, *Man and Shadow*, and the ballad-play *No More War*, which has been translated into several foreign languages including a recent version in Bengali for the international peace festival in Calcutta, India. Kreymborg lives in New York City. He is currently working on a sequel to *Troubadour*, to be called "The New Troubadour: An American Anthology." In 1949 he was elected to membership in the National Institute of Arts and Letters.

ADDITIONAL WORKS: Selected Poems, 1912-1944, 1945; Man and Shadow: An Allegory, 1946; No More War, and Other Poems, 1950.

ABOUT: Poetry July 1945.

KROLL, HARRY HARRISON (February 18, 1888-), American novelist and autobiographer, writes: "I was born in Indiana in 1888. My father was a pathetic scholarly ne'er-do-well who tried farming and failed, and tried day laboring and failed, but kept on because there was nothing else to turn to. My mother was a big strapping dynamic woman with huge vitality, tremendous emotions and scant common sense. We came to Tennessee—my father wanted to find a country where the pigeons would fly into his mouth—when I was six or seven years old. I worked at odd jobs—was a delivery boy, a messenger boy, helped share-crop and clear land; and did not attend school. But I can't remember when I could not read. We drifted down to Alabama when I was eighteen, and about this time, after saw-milling and tramping as a photographer, I quit home and roved about the Gulf coast. I met a school teacher in the pine woods and married her at the age of twenty-three. I went to school a year or so, in a two-teacher backwoods school with sixth grade children, and lived in a tent. I passed the state teachers' examinations of that time and took up rural school teaching.

"It was while I was living in an old log house in the pineywoods that I started writing. I did nine novels and threw them away.

When I was thirty years old, I packed up my wife and one child and went to Nashville to Peabody College and after three years took the bachelor's and four years the master's degrees. Meanwhile I had begun writing juveniles and pulps and supported myself through the last year of college.

"Since then I have taught in Lincoln Memorial University, Cumberland Gap, Tenn., a small Methodist college in Iowa, summer schools at Peabody, and the last eighteen years at the Martin Branch of the University of Tennessee. In all these years I have written many short stories and some twenty novels, some commercial and some artistic, and have published all the way from the pulps to *Atlantic Monthly*."

PRINCIPAL WORKS: Mountainy Singer, 1928; Cabin in the Cotton, 1931; I Was a Sharecropper (autobiography) 1937: Keepers of the House, 1940; The Usurper, 1941; Rider on the Bronze Horse, 1942; Rogues' Company, 1943; Waters Over the Dam, 1944; Fury in the Earth, 1945; Their Ancient Grudge, 1946; Darker Grows the Valley, 1947; Lost Homecoming, 1950; The Long Quest: The Story of John Wesley, 1954.

ABOUT: Kroll, H. H. I Was a Sharecropper; Saturday Review of Literature February 16, 1946; Wilson Library Bulletin January 1945.

KRONENBERGER, LOUIS (December 9, 1904-   ), American critic and novelist, writes: "I was born in Cincinnati, Ohio—the

descendant of German Jews and the child of a 'German' city. Cincinnati, until Prohibition, had a real Germanic stamp to it, of *Turnvereins* and *Bauvereins* and, in almost every suburb, of 'beer gardens' where families went for supper on summer evenings. But my childhood and adolescence were, for all that, pretty standard suburban American. I went to the public schools, I played the usual games (without much skill), collected the usual junk (without much interest), belonged to the usual organizations, the Boy Scouts among them (without much profit). Middle-class life neither enriched nor discommoded me, which isn't to say that it didn't have marked influences on my character. I always read a great deal, though chiefly trash till I got to high school, when I began to read a lot of good poetry and write a lot of bad. I was perhaps sixteen when I started reading all sorts of adult prose —the Russian novelists before most of the English ones, and so on.

"By the time I entered the University of Cincinnati in the fall of 1921, I was committed to becoming a writer, equally from a strong desire to write and from an utter incapacity to do anything else. During my three years at the university I both read and wrote in a degree never equaled since— which is doubtless normal. From the university itself I derived less than I should have: the place was in some ways pretty stodgy, and I belonged to a generation that was all too flip. What came to my ears were the distant murmurs and reverberations of the literary Jazz Age; and what haunted my dreams was a desire to be part of it. What I longed for above all else was New York, and in June 1924 I finally got there. I landed a very minor statistical job on the New York *Times*, and through that the chance to do some very minor pieces for the *Times Book Review*. After a few months I quit the job, as not up my alley, and began to free lance and tutor which, with a little help from home and a measure of bohemianism, kept me going.

"In 1926 I got an editorial job with Boni & Liveright, who—along with Knopf—were for my generation the most glamorous of New York publishers (O'Neill, Anderson, Faulkner, Hemingway, Dreiser were all part, or about to be part, or had just been part, of their list). I stayed there until late 1932, just before the old firm was dissolved: during those years I published a novel (in the form of an imaginary biography) called *The Grand Manner* and wrote a lot of book reviews and some longer critical pieces. After Boni & Liveright collapsed, I became managing editor of a magazine called *Modern Youth*; after *Modern Youth* collapsed, I went to work for Alfred Knopf. Sometime after, I left his staff to join his list—went, in other words, to London to start a book on eighteenth century England which eventually appeared as *Kings and Desperate Men*. In 1936 I went to work for *Fortune*, from which —two years later—I moved to *Time*, where since 1938 I have been drama critic. From 1940 to 1948 I was also drama critic for the newspaper *PM*.

"Since the middle '30's I've written a good deal of literary and theatrical criticism, edited a number of anthologies, written introductions to the work of Johnson, Boswell, Pope, Byron, Defoe, Fielding, Jane Austen, Ben Jonson and others; written another novel, *Grand Right and Left*, and published—from lectures given at Columbia and Brandeis universities—a book on English stage comedy, *The Thread of Laughter*. Winters I live in New York, with my wife [Emmy L. Plaut] and two children, in a small old-fashioned brick house; summers on a Connecticut 'farm' where little is grown but privacy is guaranteed. I've no particular working habits but, like most lazy people, I try to do some work, if only for an hour, every day in the year."

PRINCIPAL WORKS: *Novels*—The Grand Manner, 1929; Grand Right and Left, 1952. *Non-Fiction*—Kings and Desperate Men, 1942; The Thread of Laughter, 1952; Company Manners, 1954; The Republic of Letters, 1955. *Editor*—An Anthology of Light Verse, 1935; An Eighteenth Century Miscellany, 1936; The Reader's Companion, 1945; The Pleasure of Their Company, 1946; The Portable Johnson and Boswell, 1947; George Bernard Shaw: A Critical Survey, 1952; Cavalcade of Comedy, 1954.

ABOUT: Current Biography 1944; Saturday Review May 14, 1955.

KRUIF. See DE KRUIF

KRUTCH, JOSEPH WOOD (November 25, 1893-). For biographical sketch and list of earlier works and references, see TWENTIETH CENTURY AUTHORS, 1942.

* * *

Joseph Wood Krutch became Brander Matthews professor of dramatic literature at Columbia University in 1943. In recent years he has divided his time happily between the New England countryside and the Southwest —a region which he discovered for himself shortly before World War II, fell in love with, and revisited many times. In 1950 he retired from teaching, gave up his post as drama critic of the *Nation* (which he had held since 1924), and moved to Arizona, where he lived for fifteen months for the purpose of staying in a strange place, he writes in *The Desert Year*, "long enough to observe the process by which the strange is transformed into the familiar." In *The Desert Year* Krutch recorded his observations of the desert with all the curiosity and freshness of "his civilized and charming mind" (Paul Horgan in the New York *Times*), and the naturalist Edwin Way Teale called the book "the finest literary work on the natural setting of the Southwest since . . . Mary Austin's *The Land of Little Rain*." His writings on New England—*Twelve Seasons* and *The Best of Two Worlds*—gave similarly joyful testimony to the delights of nature in another region. *The Measure of Man*, a wise and witty discussion of the problems of modern man, won the National Book Award for non-fiction in 1955.

Krutch is recognized as a master of the philosophical or contemplative essay. A sensitive and thoughtful man with an eye for the slightest and humblest detail, he is ideally suited to be a spectator and commentator on nature and man. In this function he writes as a critic (John Mason Brown called him "one of the few genuine critics we have in the big, proud sense of the word"). In *The Measure of Man*, for example, he criticizes contemporary orthodoxies, pointing out that our modern culture has deprived us of the sense of self-responsibility which man must have to make the fateful decisions of our complex age.

ADDITIONAL WORKS: Samuel Johnson, 1944; Henry David Thoreau, 1948; The Twelve Seasons, 1949; (ed.) Great American Nature Writing, 1950; The Desert Year, 1952; The Best of Two Worlds, 1953; Modernism in American Drama, 1953; The Measure of Man, 1954.

ABOUT: Brown, J. M. Still Seeing Things; New York Herald Tribune Book Review October 11, 1953; Saturday Review of Literature May 21, 1949.

KÜLLER. See AMMERS-KÜLLER

KUPRIN, ALEXANDER IVANOVICH (August 1870-October 25, 1938). For biographical sketch and list of works and references, see TWENTIETH CENTURY AUTHORS, 1942.

* * *

ADDITIONAL WORKS IN ENGLISH TRANSLATION: The White Poodle, and The Elephant, 1947.

ABOUT: Columbia Dictionary of Modern European Literature; Guerney, B. G. (ed.) The Portable Russian Reader; Snow, V. Russian Writers.

KYNE, PETER BERNARD (October 12, 1880-). For biographical sketch and list of works and references, see TWENTIETH CENTURY AUTHORS, 1942.

* * *

Peter Kyne has written no novels in recent years, but several of his short stories have appeared in *Collier's* and other popular magazines. In an analysis of his work, published in *PMLA* in 1949, Professor Carl Bode of the University of Maryland shows Kyne's emphasis upon the racial theory in his writings. Only Cappy Ricks, Bode finds, is a "literary creation of any individual importance." His other characters are racial or national stereotypes, based upon the simple theory that (to quote Bode) "what is purebred and Aryan is good; what is hybrid or pigmented is bad."

ABOUT: PMLA March 1949.

*LACRETELLE, JACQUES DE (July 14, 1888-   ). For biographical sketch and list of works and references, see TWENTIETH CENTURY AUTHORS, 1942.

* * *

Jacques de Lacretelle lives in Paris. He is an officer of the Legion of Honor and since 1936 has been a member of the French Academy. His recent works—none of them as yet translated into English—include an account of life in France during the German occupation, *La Longue Nuit* (1945); a novel, *Le Pour et le Contre* (1946); a study of the great French dramatist Racine (1949); and two volumes of travel writings on Greece (1944, 1948).

ABOUT: Dictionnaire Biographique Français Contemporain; Romantic Review April 1950.

* là krĕ tĕl′

"LADY OF QUALITY." See BAGNOLD, E.

LA FARGE, CHRISTOPHER (December 10, 1897-   ). For biographical sketch and list of earlier works and references, see TWENTIETH CENTURY AUTHORS, 1942.

* * *

Christopher La Farge lives on the farm his parents gave him many years ago near Souderstown, R.I. His first wife died in 1945 and in 1946 he married Violet Amory Loomis. They have one son. During World War II La Farge was active in the War Writers' Board and traveled in the Southwest Pacific as a correspondent for *Harper's* magazine.

La Farge is a sensitive and careful craftsman. He writes English, Hamilton Basso observed, "like those cultivated Englishmen who, whatever their other limitations, seem to have an inbred knowledge of how to use words." For a number of years he has been interested in the rarely attempted form of the novel in verse. *Beauty for Ashes*, a love story set in contemporary times in a Rhode Island village, was the third of La Farge's attempts in this genre (earlier ones were *Hoxie Sells His Acres* and *Each to the Other*). His purpose, he explains, is to arrive at a technique "that will make of this a comprehensible form as interesting as the novel in prose and more moving." *Beauty for Ashes* was well received as both a "truly poetic work" and as a compelling and dramatic novel. The integration of verse and novel was complete and, most critics found, satisfying. Richard Sullivan wrote in the

New York *Times*: "One feels that this book is what it is because this is the way it had to be. The particular story, with its particular effects, seems simply to require this particular treatment. . . . Verse does not here stand out as verse: it is merely the means, quite natural and right, of story telling."

ADDITIONAL WORKS: East by Southwest, 1944; Mesa Verde (play in verse) 1945; The Sudden Guest, 1946; All Sorts and Kinds, 1949; Beauty for Ashes, 1953.

ABOUT: Bishop, J. P. Collected Essays; National Cyclopedia of American Biography (1946); New York Herald Tribune Book Review October 11, 1953.

LA FARGE, OLIVER (December 19, 1901-   ). For biographical sketch and list of earlier works and references, see TWENTIETH CENTURY AUTHORS, 1942.

* * *

In 1942 Oliver La Farge joined the U.S. Army Air Transport Command as its chief historical officer. He was discharged from the Army in 1945 with the rank of lieutenant colonel, and in 1949 he published an authoritative and detailed history of the A.T.C., *The Eagle in the Egg*. He also contributed a story of the Arctic rescue of the crew of a Flying Fortress to Bernt Balchen's and Corey Ford's *War Below Zero* (1944). During the war years La Farge put the finishing touches on his autobiography (written several years earlier), *Raw Material*—a book which Maxwell Geismar described as "pleasant, sensitive, sincere . . . a credit to our sheltered classes."

Long a champion of the rights of the American Indians, since 1948 La Farge has been president of the Association on American Indian Affairs (a group he had headed in 1939-42). In 1949 he was named a member of a ten-man advisory committee to the federal government on Indian affairs. Since 1946 La Farge has been a member of the advisory board of the Laboratory of Anthropology at Santa Fe, N.M. His recent writings have centered largely on Indian subjects. His short stories and essays appear frequently in the *New Yorker*, the *Atlantic Monthly*, and other journals. La Farge lives in Santa Fe.

ADDITIONAL WORKS: Raw Material, 1945; Santa Eulalia: The Religion of a Cuchumatán Indian Town, 1947; The Eagle in the Egg, 1949; Cochise of Arizona (juvenile) 1953; The Mother Ditch (juvenile) 1954.

ABOUT: La Farge, O. Raw Material; Current Biography 1953; New York Times Book Review July 24, 1949.

*LAGERKVIST, PÄR FABIAN (May 23, 1891-   ), Swedish novelist, dramatist, and poet, was born in Växjö, a small town in the

Atelje Ugglaaf

southern Swedish district of Småland, the youngest child of Anders Johan Lagerkvist and Johanna (Blad) Lagerkvist, whose ancestors had been farmers. He studied humanistic subjects at the University of Upsala during 1911 and 1912, and made his literary debut in 1912 with some poems in a Socialist paper and his first book, a novella, *Människor* ("People"). Visiting Paris in 1913, he came under the influence of the Fauvist, cubist, and "naïvist" movements in modern painting. This caused him to turn against naturalistic writing, and his poetry and prose of 1914-1916 showed the French influence. With a collection of poems, *Angest* ("Anguish"), Lagerkvist emerged in 1916 as an author of rank, and was the most arresting figure to appear on the Swedish literary scene during World War I.

However, during most of this war, he lived in Denmark, and there he centered his attention on the theatre, writing plays which showed him the disciple of Strindberg, both in technique and theme. In 1919 he was briefly theatre critic for a Stockholm newspaper, but soon devoted himself entirely to his own creative writing. In the '20's he spent a great deal of time in France and Italy. As he thus entered his own thirties, his earlier pessimism began to yield to what someone has called "love, sublimated into a Christian-Platonic mysticism." He continued his poetic works, which became more simple and lyrical, and also wrote prose fiction and philosophical meditations. The autobiographical documents of this period are "Guest of Reality" (1925), and "Life Conquered" (1927).

In the 1930's he became one of the most eloquent and determined critics of totalitarianism, and proposed in place of it a kind of heroic humanitarian idealism. Few of his works have been translated into English, but in 1934 there appeared *The Eternal Smile*, and in 1936 *Guest of Reality* (including *The Eternal Smile* and *The Hangman*). His book *The Dwarf* was published in Swedish in 1944, and in English in 1945. This is an allegorical novel of Renaissance Italy as seen through the eyes of a malevolent court dwarf. English critics compared Lagerkvist's "sav-

* lä'gĕr kvĭst

age insight" to Jonathan Swift's. *Barabbas*, a novel which appeared in English in 1951, was a major literary event. "A remarkable book," commented André Gide, who supplied a letter to the English edition. "Lagerkvist," wrote Charles J. Rolo in the *Atlantic Monthly*, "evokes the early Christian era with a selective realism more telling than any ponderously detailed reconstruction of the past."

Two of Lagerkvist's plays have been included in *Scandinavian Plays of the Twentieth Century*, in the first series (1944)— *The Man Without A Soul*, and in the third series (1951)—*Let Man Live*.

In 1940 he was elected to the Swedish Academy; this group annually awards the Nobel prize for literature. In 1951 the prize was awarded to him. In 1928 he received another important Swedish literary prize; and received an honorary Ph.D. degree in 1941 from the University of Gothenburg.

His first marriage, to Karen Dagmar Johanne Sörensen of Denmark took place in 1918 and was dissolved in 1925. In that year he married Elaine Luella Hallberg, the widow of the noted Swedish painter Gösta Sandels. Shunning publicity, he has lived since 1930 with his family in Lidingö, an island community near Stockholm.

PRINCIPAL WORKS: The Eternal Smile, 1934; Guest of Reality, 1936; The Dwarf, 1945; Barabbas, 1951.

ABOUT: Columbia Dictionary of Modern European Literature; Lagerkvist, P. Guest of Reality; Books Abroad Winter 1952; Catholic World January 1953; Current Biography 1952; English Journal May 1952; New York Times Book Review November 25, 1951; Pacific Spectator Autumn 1952; Saturday Review of Literature December 1, 1951.

*LAGERLÖF, SELMA OTTILIANA LOVISA (November 20, 1858-March 16, 1940). For biographical sketch and list of works and references, see TWENTIETH CENTURY AUTHORS, 1942.

* * *

ABOUT: Allen, W. G. Renaissance in the North; Columbia Dictionary of Modern European Literature; Horn Book March 1949.

* lä'gĕr lŭv

*LAING, ALEXANDER KINNAN (August 7, 1903-   ). For autobiographical sketch and list of earlier works and references, see TWENTIETH CENTURY AUTHORS, 1942.

* * *

Alexander Laing was assistant librarian at Dartmouth College from 1937 to 1950, and

* läng

in 1952 he became educational services adviser to the library. From 1947 to 1952 he was director of the Public Affairs Laboratory of Dartmouth's Great Issues Course. He lives near the college in Hanover, N.H.

Laing's *Clipper Ship Men,* a history of the clipper ship and the men who built her, was highly praised for scholarship and literary style.

ADDITIONAL WORK: Clipper Ship Men, 1944.

*LALOU, RENÉ (September 3, 1889-). For biographical sketch and list of works and references, see TWENTIETH CENTURY AUTHORS, 1942.

* * *

René Lalou lives in Paris. His recent writings—none of them translated into English—include various literary histories (French poetry, the modern French novel, contemporary English literature), a book on the French novelist and essayist Maurice Barrès (1950), and a history of the French theatre since 1900 (1951).

* là lōō′

LA MARE. See DE LA MARE

LAMB, HAROLD (September 1, 1892-). For autobiographical sketch and list of earlier works and references, see TWENTIETH CENTURY AUTHORS, 1942.

* * *

Harold Lamb has spent most of his adult life studying and reconstructing life in Asia in the Middle Ages. He has charted a vast and little-explored field of knowledge and in his many popular books on the age has presented a vivid and richly detailed picture. During World War II, Lamb's special knowledge of Asia and the Near East was of value to the U.S. government. A study he had made on Mongol warfare (with its resemblance to the Nazi method of swift, total war) was required reading in the Army War College. In 1942 he joined the Office of Strategic Services and traveled through the Near and Middle East during the next three years. His interest in Russian history was especially stimulated by his travels, and in 1948 he published two volumes, *The March of Muscovy* and *The City and the Tsar,* which traced the history of Russia from 1400 to the eighteenth century. These proved to be two of the most successful of Lamb's books. Garrett Mattingly wrote in the *Saturday Review of Literature:* "For color and drama and epic movement one can

trust Harold Lamb. He has the storyteller's gift; he knows how to seize the vivid visual detail which calls to the imagination, how to marshal a hurrying crowd of anecdotes . . . how to maintain suspense from one sentence to the next." Lamb was also praised for his scholarship. There have been more academic studies on the subject, P. J. Searles wrote in the New York *Herald Tribune,* "but none which surpass . . . in grasp of trends and clarity in presenting an intricate subject."

Lamb travels extensively in collecting material for his books and always visits the landmarks for his subjects. His permanent home is on the side of a canyon, near Beverly Hills, Calif. He is slim, grey-haired, and "has frequently been mistaken for a British officer."

ADDITIONAL WORKS: Persian Mosaic: An Imaginative Biography of Omar Khayyam, 1943; Alexander of Macedon, 1946; Garden to the Eastward (novel) 1947; The March of Muscovy, 1948; The City and the Tsar, 1948; Suleiman the Magnificent, 1951; Theodora and the Emperor, 1952; Charlemagne, 1954; Genghis Khan and the Mongol Horde, 1954.

ABOUT: Kunitz, S. J. & Haycraft, H. Junior Book of Authors (rev. ed.); New York Times Book Review June 9, 1946; Saturday Review of Literature March 6, 1948, March 17, 1951.

LAMONT, CORLISS (March 28, 1902-). For autobiographical sketch and list of earlier works and references, see TWENTIETH CENTURY AUTHORS, 1942.

* * *

Corliss Lamont lectured in philosophy at the New School for Social Research from 1940 to 1942. In 1943 he taught a course in Soviet Social Institutions at Cornell University. The next year he lectured on the U.S.S.R. in the Social Studies Workshop of the Harvard Graduate School of Education, and from 1946 to 1955 he lectured in philosophy at the School of General Studies of Columbia University. Lamont was chairman of the Congress of American-Soviet Friendship in 1942 and from 1943 to 1946 chairman of the National Council of American-Soviet Friendship. He resigned from the latter chairmanship in June 1946 to devote more time to teaching and writing. In 1952 Lamont was an unsuccessful candidate for United States Senator from New York on the American Labor Party ticket. In October 1954 he was indicted on a charge of contempt of Congress, for refusing to answer questions of a congressional committee headed by Senator Joseph McCarthy.

Peter Viereck has described Lamont as "America's leading intellectual enthusiast for

Communist Russia." Lamont himself describes his position, in the preface to his book *Soviet Civilization*, as an effort "to help stem the tide of misunderstanding between the United States and Soviet Russia and thereby to make some contribution to the enduring peace for which our two peoples and the whole world so yearn."

Lamont calls his philosophical position humanism, which he defines as "a philosophy of joyous service for the greater good of all humanity . . . according to the methods of reason and democracy." This view he has expounded in *Humanism as Philosophy* and in *The Independent Mind*.

Correction: TWENTIETH CENTURY AUTHORS, 1942 stated incorrectly that Lamont has two daughters and two sons. He has three daughters, Margaret Hayes, Florence Parmelee, and Anne Sterling, and one son, Hayes Corliss.

ADDITIONAL WORKS: The Peoples of the Soviet Union, 1946; Humanism as a Philosophy, 1949; The Independent Mind: Essays of a Humanist Philosopher, 1951; Soviet Civilization, 1952.
ABOUT: Lamont, C. The Independent Mind; Commonweal April 11, 1952; Current Biography 1946.

LANCASTER, BRUCE (August 22, 1896-). For biographical sketch and list of earlier works and references, see TWENTIETH CENTURY AUTHORS, 1942.

* * *

Bruce Lancaster is one of the most popular American historical novelists, respected not only for the swiftness and liveliness of his narratives, but also for the soundness and thoroughness of his research. His plots are generally of the cloak-and-dagger tradition; but, P. J. Searle remarked of one of his later novels in the New York *Herald Tribune*, "the novel escapes banality and stands well above the usual run of such tales because of its characterization, atmosphere, and historical fidelity." The comment reflects the critical consensus on Lancaster's work. "Even melodrama," Searles continued, "has a certain dignity when the author is a skilled craftsman."

In 1955 Bruce Lancaster turned his expert hand to a work of straight history with *From Lexington to Liberty*, subtitled The Story of the American Revolution. Lancaster "'writes as an historian," commented John K. Hutchens in the New York *Herald Tribune*, "but with a novelist's eye for character, color, motive . . . details."

ADDITIONAL WORKS: Trumpet to Arms, 1944; The Scarlet Patch, 1947; No Bugles Tonight, 1948; Phantom Fortress, 1950; Venture in the East, 1951; Blind Journey, 1953; From Lexington to Liberty (non-fiction) 1955.
ABOUT: Van Gelder, R. Writers and Writing; Warfel, H. R. American Novelists of Today.

LANCASTER, OSBERT (1908-), English humorist and cartoonist, was born in London, the son of Robert Lancaster and Clare Bracebridge (Manger) Lancaster. His father was killed in World War I, and he was brought up by his mother. He was educated at Charterhouse School and Oxford, where he received an honors degree in English literature. He was

Cecil Beaton

destined for the Bar and indeed sat for several law exams, failing in all of them once and in Roman law twice. Abandoning all thought of the law, he studied at the Slade School of Art, where he acquired a certificate for stage design, a distaste for painting in oils and a wife, Karen, second daughter of Sir Austin Harris, whom he married in 1933. They have one son and one daughter.

For a time he worked on the staff of the *Architectural Review*. His first book, *Progress at Pelvis Bay*, was a collection of satirical drawings done for that paper. John Betjeman said of this book: "My only fear for this wonderful book is that some town councils may get hold of it and take it literally. It is terrible to think that copies of it will be studied in a hundred years' time when the buildings it ridicules have mercifully collapsed." This was followed by a short illustrated history of architecture, *Pillar to Post*, and some years later by a sequel dealing with interior decoration, *Homes, Sweet Homes*.

In 1939 he started to contribute small cartoons to the London *Daily Express*, a daily assignment which, save for two years during the war, he has kept up ever since. A selection of these pocket cartoons is collected in book form every year, and "Osbert Lancaster types," i.e.: guardees, A.T.S. (Women's Auxiliary Forces) brigadieresses, and rotund clubmen became a familiar fixture of British humor.

At the outbreak of World War II, Lancaster went first to the Press Censorship bureau and then to the Foreign Office News Department. In 1944 he was sent to the British Embassy in Athens as First Secretary. *Classical Landscape with Figures* was the result of his deployment to Greece. Val Gielgud, reviewing this book in the New York *Herald Tribune*, called it "probably the most entertaining and the best informed travel book of the last ten years."

On his return to England in 1946, Osbert Lancaster resumed his daily cartoon in the *Express* and joined the editorial board of the *Architectural Review*. In 1948 he recorded for his two children the involuntary exploits of young William Littlehampton, "the reluctant crusader," under the title *The Saracen's Head*, which the *New Yorker* found "an extremely enjoyable kidding of the Middle Ages." In *Drayneflete Revealed* (published in the United States as *There'll Always Be a Drayneflete*), he parodied the history of the "progressive" city of Drayneflete from the Bronze Age to the vision of the New Drayneflete as seen by its enlightened planners. The text and drawings are sprightly and amusing, with an unobtrusive content of shrewd literary and social satire.

All Done from Memory is a tender and nostalgic reminiscence of the author's childhood in England just before World War I. Lancaster's purpose was to erect a small plaque "to a vanished world"—the world of the English upper middle classes. Nevertheless, Osbert Lancaster must have been a sophisticate from the cradle, for his diverting illustrations of the period have the familiar, suave, Lancaster wittiness.

PRINCIPAL WORKS: Progress at Pelvis Bay, 1936; Our Sovereigns, 1936; Pillar to Post, 1938; Homes, Sweet Homes, 1939; Pocket Cartoons, 1940; New Pocket Cartoons, 1941; Classical Landscape with Figures, 1947; The Saracen's Head, 1948; There'll Always Be a Drayneflete (in England: Drayneflete Revealed) 1950; Lady Littlehampton and Friends, 1952; All Done from Memory, 1953.

LANDAU. See ALDANOV

LANDON, MARGARET DOROTHEA (MORTENSON) (September 7, 1903-),
American author, was born in Somers, Wis.,  the daughter of Annenus Duabus Mortenson and Adelle Johanne (Estbourg) Mortenson. She attended high school in Evanston, Ill., and college at Wheaton College, Ill., where she received a B.A. in 1925. For a year she taught school at Bear Lake, Mich. In 1926 she married Kenneth

Perry Landon, a Presbyterian missionary with educational interests. In 1927 the Landons went to Siam—now Thailand—where they remained until 1937. Mrs. Landon was principal of the Trang Girls' School there for five years.

In Siam Margaret Landon heard much of a strong-minded Welsh woman, Anna Leonowen, who became, in the eighteen-sixties, secretary to Siam's King Mongkut and governess to his sixty-odd children. Mrs. Leonowen had tried to introduce into the royal court Western ideals of freedom. Her two books, published in England in 1870 and 1872, were available—though out of print— and Mrs. Landon read them and found them fascinating: *The English Governess at the Siamese Court* and *The Romance of the Harem*. It was on these memoirs that Margaret Landon based her story, *Anna and the King of Siam*, published in 1944, a choice of the Literary Guild, and a best seller. As additional background for the writing, Mrs. Landon had obtained copies of several old letters from Mrs. Leonowen's granddaughter, and in the Library of Congress had discovered King Mongkut's letters, published in Siamese.

Although not fiction, *Anna and the King of Siam*, according to Harry Hansen, reads like a "refreshing historical novel." Sterling North found the book "a 'natural,' drawing upon the richest vein of untapped material discovered in years. The author's prose lacks professional polish, but the facts of Anna Leonowen's life are sufficiently fascinating to camouflage this lack." The book was made into a motion picture and, under the title *The King and I*, was a hit musical-comedy (1951) with music by Richard Rodgers and book and lyrics by Oscar Hammerstein. *Anna and the King* is a version for young people of the original book.

The Landons live in Washington, D.C., and Margaret Landon's only recent book has been *Never Dies the Dream*, a novel which appeared in 1949. "The plot is elusive and relatively unimportant," wrote Virginia Kirkus; "Miss Landon is not inherently a novelist, but she does leave the impress of place and people on her readers." She is five feet seven and one-half inches tall, of average weight, with attractive, regular features, deep-set blue eyes, and light brown hair. She has four children.

PRINCIPAL WORKS: Anna and the King of Siam, 1944; Anna and the King, 1947; Never Dies the Dream, 1949.

ABOUT: Current Biography 1945; New York Herald Tribune June 29, 1944, October 25, 1944; New York World-Telegram June 29, 1944.

LANE, FERDINAND COLE (1885-   ), American geographer and writer on nature, reports: "I was born on a Minnesota wheat

farm, just across the Red River from North Dakota. When my father's various enterprises ended in bankruptcy we drifted to Minneapolis, then to Akron and Canton in Ohio, and on to Lowell, Mass. We came to Truro, on Cape Cod, when I was seven years old, largely because we could live so cheaply there. For six years I attended a district school under the shadow of Hog's Back Church. We then moved to Marion where I graduated from Tabor Academy. The next seven years were spent at Boston University where I earned my living as well as my education by performing a variety of odd jobs. After completing my academic work, I studied for higher degrees and took some courses in the Law School. Meanwhile, I found time to go on a vagabonding cruise to the western Mediterranean, arriving in London with nineteen cents. During my graduate years I was employed, on part time work, by the Massachusetts Commission of Fisheries and Game where I held the position of assistant biologist. My labors involved experiments with shell fish and other branches of oceanography and in writing scientific reports. Weak lungs then sent me to Alberta where I passed six months in a log cabin on the remote frontier.

"Returning to Boston, I secured employment with the *Baseball Magazine* and was soon appointed editor. I held that position for twenty-seven years, located most of the time in New York City. I also did syndicate work and much ghost writing. While I loved the thrill of the game and prized the many interesting characters I was able to meet, sports writing was always a vocation, never an avocation. I also traveled rather extensively, visiting southern Europe, Northern Africa, and the Near East.

"I left New York so that I might give the balance of my life to more congenial tasks. A rambling Cape Cod house, 150 years old, on the shore of Wellfleet Bay was 'home,' although I was absent much of the time. Several winters were spent in Florida and the better part of three years in Georgia. At Piedmont College I started a school of journalism and took over the departments of history and philosophy. I also lectured at several other colleges and many clubs. But I have always found travel the best of all diversions and educations. My roving tours carried me to the Andes and the Inca ruins of Peru. I traveled by auto all over the United States and into Canada and Mexico. Even more instructive was a leisurely eight months cruise around the world in a trading steamer with a Chinese crew. On this voyage of discovery I indulged in two of my hobbies —collecting sea shells and studying Oriental customs and beliefs. Later I spent six months in the British Isles and the various countries of Western Europe. My more recent writings have been largely devoted to some thirty odd articles for encyclopedias and a series of books on global geography. I have been happily married for thirty-eight years and my wife shares my many interests. Although I am losing the argument with Father Time, as the years pass too swiftly, I still find life a continuous adventure, more interesting than any of its accomplishments."

PRINCIPAL WORKS: The Mysterious Sea, 1947; The World's Great Lakes, 1948; The Earth's Grandest Rivers, 1949; The Story of Mountains, 1950; The Story of Trees, 1952; All About the Sea, 1953; All About the Insect World, 1954.

LANE, Mrs. ROSE (WILDER) (December 5, 1887-   ). For biographical sketch and list of earlier works and references, see TWENTIETH CENTURY AUTHORS, 1942.

* * *

Rose Wilder Lane's only recent book is an informal discussion of man's struggle against authority, *Discovery of Freedom*. The critics found it a stimulating but confused and confusing book. Bernard De Voto considered it "certainly on the side of the angels and it is certainly exciting reading, but it calls for a constant exercise of critical and historical control." From 1943 to 1945 Mrs. Lane edited the National Economic Council's *Review of Books*.

ADDITIONAL WORK: Discovery of Freedom, 1943.

LANGDON-DAVIES, JOHN (1897-   ). For biographical sketch and list of earlier works and references, see TWENTIETH CENTURY AUTHORS, 1942.

* * *

John Langdon-Davies was a war correspondent in Spain from 1936 to 1938 and in Finland in 1940. From 1941 to 1944 he was honorary commandant of the South-Eastern Army Fieldcraft School. He was the founder of the Foster-Parents Scheme for

European Children. For many years a science correspondent for daily newspapers, Langdon-Davies has in his latest books written extensively on medical history for the layman. His history of the Westminster Hospital was praised by the London *Times Literary Supplement* as a "well-constructed story." Langdon-Davies was married to his third wife, Patricia Kipping, in 1949. They have one son.

ADDITIONAL WORKS: Home Guard Fieldcraft Manual, 1942; American Close-Up: Portrait of an Ally, 1943; Achievement in the Art of Healing, 1945; Conquer Fear, 1948; Russia Puts the Clock Back, 1949; Westminster Hospital, 1719-1948, 1952; Gatherings from Catalonia, 1953; Seeds of Life, 1955.

LANGER, SUSANNE KATHERINA (KNAUTH) (1895-), American philosopher and esthetician, was born of German  parentage in New York City. Graduating from a French school in Manhattan, she went to Radcliffe where she received her M.A. and a Ph.D. After a brief period of study at the University of Vienna, she returned to Radcliffe and remained there for fifteen years as a tutor in the philosophy department. She was married in 1921 to William Leonard Langer, a professor of history, by whom she had two children. They were divorced.

The great English mathematician and philosopher Alfred North Whitehead, who taught at Harvard for many years, was Mrs. Langer's friend and tutor, leading her into a long and profound study of symbolic logic. In her first published work *The Practice of Philosophy*, she established her position: "The problem of methodology which was (and still is) in academic vogue, and the conflict of 'isms' that seems to be every student's chief inheritance, still predominated over the ideas that were in the making, and which were to reach their real development only through the liberation of mind that comes from training in logic: the growth of abstractive techniques and imagination."

Some of the ideas first stated in this book were developed later in *Philosophy in a New Key,* a provocative study in the symbolism of logic, of language, of myth and art, which found an extraordinarily wide circulation for a book of this nature in a paper-back edition. Reviewing the book in 1942, the late Irwin Edman wrote: "The vista Mrs. Langer opens of an approach to the whole of life through the rationalities of art and music, as well as the explicit logic of words, constitutes a really generative idea. I suspect Mrs. Langer has established a key in terms of which a good deal of philosophy these next years may be composed."

Susanne Langer has taught courses at Wellesley and Smith, and has been a member of the faculty at the University of Delaware and New York University; since 1945, she has taught at Columbia University. Her more recent work, *Feeling and Form: A Theory of Art,* was written on a grant from the Rockefeller Foundation through Columbia. This book, drawing for evidence on the materials of art and the creative processes of artists, carries to mature development the author's thesis that art is a part of the life process—a continuing symbolic transformation of experience, not a poor substitute for action, but a basic human need.

PRINCIPAL WORKS: The Practice of Philosophy, 1930; Introduction to Symbolic Logic, 1937; Philosophy in a New Key, 1942; Feeling and Form: A Theory of Art, 1953.

LANGER, WILLIAM LEONARD (March 16, 1896-), American historian, was born in Boston, Mass., the son of Charles Rudolph Langer and Johanna (Rockenback) Langer. He attended Harvard University, where he took his Ph.D.; and spent one year at the University of Vienna. In 1927 he began to teach at Harvard, and since 1936 has been  Coolidge Professor of History there. However, there have been absences from teaching, as when Langer served during World War II as director of research, Office of the Coordinator of Information, 1941-42, in Washington; and as Chief of the Research and Analysis Branch, Office of Strategic Services, 1942-46. In 1946 he was special assistant to the Secretary of State, for Intelligence; and from 1950 to 1952 assistant director of the Central Intelligence Agency. The Medal for Merit was awarded him in 1946, and the honorary degree of LL.D. given by Harvard University in 1945.

His first publication concerned his service in the 1st Gas Regiment, United States Army, in World War I: written by Sergeant William L. Langer and Private Robert B. MacMullin, it was called *With "E" of the First Gas* (1919). However, as an eminent historian his career begins with *The Franco-Russian Alliance* (1929), which received the respect and approval of critics. Two titles, intended as companion works, *European Alliances and Alignments 1871-1890* and (in two volumes) *The Diplomacy of Imperialism 1890-1902*, followed, establishing him before the public as an unusually gifted diplomatic historian. "No writer has unraveled more brilliantly the peculiar complexities of the period," wrote Frederick L. Schuman of the latter work, "or presented more lucidly the tangled themes of the cacophonous symphony of power, prestige, and profits, of empire, war, and catastrophe." "The reading of so dense a narrative is not easy. Mr. Langer demands active cooperation from his reader," added the *Christian Science Monitor*, while admiring Langer's work tremendously.

Our Vichy Gamble, a history of American relations with France during the years 1940 to 1942, appeared in 1947. Because Langer had been an O.S.S. official, and had had access to secret files of the State Department, the O.S.S. and the Army, it was authorized by the State Department, yet was quite independent in its judgments and evaluations. "It gives a factual account, readable, entertaining, exciting, frequently depressing, of how and why Washington chose and clung obstinately to Pétain, Darlan and the Vichy fascists," commented the *New Republic*.

Most recently Langer has been co-author of two important companion volumes: *The Challenge to Isolation* and *The Undeclared War* (both with S. Everett Gleason). These are the first of several planned volumes on American foreign policy before and during World War II. "It is history for historians," said the New York *Times*. The authors were able to use unpublished letters, diaries, and notes, as well as State Department files.

Susanne (Knauth) Langer, the philosopher, was his first wife. They were married in 1921 and had two children. In 1943 he married Rowena Morse Nelson. The Langers' home is in Cambridge.

PRINCIPAL WORKS: The Franco-Russian Alliance, 1929; European Alliances and Alignments, 1931; The Diplomacy of Imperialism, 1935; Our Vichy Gamble, 1947. *With S. Everett Gleason*: The Challenge of Isolation (1937-1940) 1952; The Undeclared War (1940-1941) 1953.

ABOUT: Time April 14, 1947.

LANGNER, LAWRENCE (May 30, 1890-). For biographical sketch and list of earlier works and references, see TWENTIETH CENTURY AUTHORS, 1942.

* * *

Lawrence Langner served during World War II as secretary to the National Inventors Council, a group which he had organized in 1940 to serve as a clearing house for inventions relating to warfare. His patent attorney practice is a thriving one, and Langner devotes a fair share of his crowded schedule to it. But his major interest, and the work for which the public knows him best, is the Theatre Guild which, in the 1940's, under the co-direction of Langner and Theresa Helburn, was revitalized with some of the most successful productions in its history (notably *Oklahoma!* and *Carousel*, the Rodgers and Hammerstein musicals). Langner was also the guiding spirit behind two other important theatrical ventures—the Westport Country Playhouse in Westport, Conn., a center of professional summer theatre, and the weekly radio (and later television) series "Theatre Guild on the Air." He has also drawn up plans for an American Shakespeare Festival Theatre, to be modeled on the Elizabethan Globe Theatre and conducted along the lines of the festival produced annually at Stratford-on-Avon in England.

Langner and his wife Armina Marshall, who is associate director of the Theatre Guild, live in New York City and have a summer home in Connecticut. In 1951, in summing up at the conclusion of his autobiography, *The Magic Curtain*, Langner wrote: "A self-appraisal of over thirty years' work in the Theatre Guild leaves me with the feeling that there will never be a time when the work is done. Fortunately, though we grow old, the theatre continues to be eternally young. . . . Our generation has worked hard throughout long and busy lives, to influence the American theatre from time to time in the direction of the eternally great in art. To the extent to which we have succeeded, we shall have laid a foundation on which the theatre of the future can build."

ADDITIONAL WORK: The Magic Curtain, 1951.

ABOUT: Langner, L. The Magic Curtain; Current Biography 1944; New York Times Magazine January 12, 1947; New Yorker October 1, 8, 1949; Saturday Evening Post January 6, 1945; Saturday Review of Literature July 22, 1944.

*LARBAUD, VALÉRY (August 29, 1881-). For biographical sketch and list of works and references, see TWENTIETH CENTURY AUTHORS, 1942.

* * *

In 1951, on the occasion of his seventieth birthday, the city of Vichy honored Valéry Larbaud with an exposition of his books and correspondence. The scope of Larbaud's learning and cultural interests is enormous. Although never a popular writer, he has had a marked influence on French literature—primarily through his translations which introduced to France the work of numerous foreign authors. As Frederick Lehner pointed out in *Books Abroad*, Larbaud "overcame French nationalism," that is, he bridged the gap between the nations by his translations and linked one foreign people to another.

It is significant that one of Larbaud's most recent works should have been a study of the "patron" of translators, St. Jerome (*Sous l'Invocation de Saint-Jérome*, 1946). Like most of his other works, this book is veiled intellectual autobiography. In one section he discusses the obligation of the translator to suppress his own individual personality in the interests of producing a translation faithful to both the spirit and the letter of the original. In 1949 Larbaud's correspondence with André Gide was published in France.

ADDITIONAL WORK IN ENGLISH TRANSLATION: Poems of a Multimillionaire, 1955.
ABOUT: Columbia Dictionary of Modern European Literature; Dictionnaire Biographique Français Contemporain; Books Abroad Winter 1952; Revue de Littérature Comparée October 1951.

* lår bō′

LARDNER, RING (March 6, 1885-September 25, 1933). For biographical sketch and list of works and references, see TWENTIETH CENTURY AUTHORS, 1942.

* * *

Of Ring Lardner's four sons, one—John Lardner—is the well-known author, sports columnist, and war correspondent. Two of his sons were killed—James while fighting for the Loyalists in Spain and Dave in a jeep crash while a World War II correspondent in Germany. Ring Lardner, Jr., a successful screen writer, served a one-year prison term in 1950 for refusing to tell a congressional committee whether or not he was a member of the Communist Party.

ABOUT: Mencken, H. L. A Mencken Chrestomathy; Seldes, G. Introduction to The Portable Ring Lardner; Coronet March 1951.

LARKIN, OLIVER WATERMAN (August 17, 1896-), American author and art historian, was born in Medford, Mass., the son of Charles Ernest Larkin and Kate Mary (Waterman) Larkin. Both sides of the family are of New England descent and his father was known as an antique dealer and collector throughout the Merrimack Valley for fifty years. Oliver W.

Larkin grew up in Medford and in Georgetown, Mass., where he graduated from the Perley Free School in 1914. At eighteen he was already interested in painting, drawing, and dramatics. Entering Harvard College he majored in French and Latin, and won several scholarships. In 1918 he received his Bachelor of Arts degree, and was elected to Phi Beta Kappa. During World War I he served as a private in the Medical Corps of the 73rd Infantry Regiment.

Returning to Harvard in 1919, Larkin received in that year his M.A., and two years later became assistant in fine arts, remaining at Harvard for three years in this capacity. When he was twenty-eight years old, in 1924, he began teaching art at Smith College and today heads their art department. The author of numerous articles and book reviews, Larkin set out in 1944 to write his major work, *Art and Life in America*. Starting with a mass of notes, he wrote and rewrote the text at least four times. This survey of American art from its beginnings in the seventeenth century up to 1945 traces the development of painting, sculpture, architecture, and to a lesser extent, the minor arts, as related to the general social and cultural background. A 547-page volume, *Art and Life in America* was published in 1949 and awarded the Pulitzer prize in history (1950) —the first time that a book devoted to the visual arts had won this prize.

Though Oscar Handlin in the *Magazine of Art* protested that Larkin had not accounted for the "melancholy meagerness of our achievement" in the United States, most critics found the book praiseworthy. "By far the finest general history of the visual arts in America that has yet been written," said the San Francisco *Chronicle*, "and one that might very well supersede all other general histories. It does not supersede specialized studies; but should be used as a springboard toward them."

Married in 1925 to Ruth Lily McIntire of Dedham, Mass., Larkin has one son, Peter Sidney, who in 1950 was stage designer and technician for the Wellesley College theatre. Larkin himself directed plays and designed scenery for Lincoln House, a settlement house in Boston, back in 1919, and still maintains this interest, directing for the Northampton Players and making puppets and producing marionette shows. Known as "Pete" to his friends, Larkin has been characterized as "unassuming." He is five feet four inches tall and weighs one hundred and sixty-five pounds; his hair and eyes are brown. Politically he lists himself as "independent."

PRINCIPAL WORK: Art and Life in America, 1949; Samuel F. B. Morse and American Democratic Art, 1954.

ABOUT: Current Biography 1950; New York Herald Tribune May 2, 1950; New York Times May 2, 1950.

LA ROCHE. See DE LA ROCHE

LARSEN, JOHANNES ANKER. See ANKER LARSEN

LA SERNA. See GÓMEZ DE LA SERNA

LASKI, HAROLD JOSEPH (June 30, 1893-March 24, 1950). For biographical sketch and list of earlier works and references, see TWENTIETH CENTURY AUTHORS, 1942.

* * *

Harold Laski died in a London hospital at fifty-six. Three months earlier he had continued to teach at London University's School of Economics while suffering from pneumonia; later, during an influenza attack, the collapse of one lung resulted in death.

In June 1946 he served as chairman of the first annual conference of the British Labour Party held after that party took office. In 1947 he resigned as chairman of the international subcommittee of the party, and two years later resigned from its executive committee.

Laski was called by John Chamberlain "a good journalist, an excellent publicist, an able and amusing speaker and a stimulating teacher of political theory." Edmund Wilson pointed out that he was "not only a well-equipped scholar and an able political thinker but a fighter for unpopular ideals whose career as a whole is an example of singularly disinterested devotion." Of his own political position Laski once wrote: "The devil is not as red as he is painted. His evilminded socialism is nothing more than the logical development of Jeffersonian democracy in the twentieth century."

In 1953 the letters exchanged between Laski and Oliver Wendell Holmes were published in two volumes, edited by Mark De Wolfe Howe. The correspondence proved to be "a fascinating mirror of the men, events and thought-currents of that troubled age between the wars, and of two great minds at work and at play" (W. H. Stringer, in the *Christian Science Monitor*). The letters revealed Laski in all his mercurial brilliance and his intellectual inconsistency and they shed great light on his personality.

ADDITIONAL WORKS: Reflections on the Revolution of Our Time, 1943; Faith, Reason and Civilization, 1944; American Democracy, 1948; Trade Unions in the New Society, 1950; Reflections on the Constitution, 1951; The Holmes-Laski Letters, 1953.

ABOUT: Deane, H. A. The Political Ideas of Harold J. Laski; The Holmes-Laski Letters; Martin, K. Harold Laski; Commonweal April 7, 1950; Journal of Politics February 1948; Life August 19, 1946; London Times March 25, 1950; Nation December 21, 1946, January 4, 1947, April 1, 1950, April 29, 1950; New York Times March 25, 1950; Saturday Evening Post May 18, 1946; Time December 9, 1946, April 3, 1950.

LASKI, MARGHANITA (October 24, 1915-   ), English novelist and critic, writes: "I was born in London at the home of my grandfather, Dr. Moses Gaster, then Chief Rabbi of England. When I was two, my father was invalided out of the army, and we went to live in Manchester where he practiced as a barrister. I went to an excellent school there run by C. P.  Scott of the *Manchester Guardian* and got a very good education. When I was thirteen my father became a King's Counsel, and we moved to London where I went to St. Paul's, a horrible travesty of a boys' Public School; I passed the appropriate exams and got no real education at all. I left at sixteen, spent a year learning to be a dress-designer, decided I wasn't good enough, and managed to get into Somerville College, Oxford, at a day's notice and without any entrance exam —a feat unsurpassed in the annals of the college. I had a wonderful time at Oxford, went to thousands of parties and studied Anglo-Saxon philology. Indeed, I meant to be a philologist, but my tutor said I would be a better journalist, so a journalist I obediently became.

"I met my husband (who is now my publisher) at Oxford, married him in Paris when I was twenty-one, and spent the pre-war years traveling around Europe with him as far and as often as we could afford. During the war I did nursing, ran a dairy farm, worked in Intelligence, and had two children. It was while I was in the hospital after the second was born that I wrote my first novel, *Love on Super-Tax*, which was very successful. I then wrote a second which was published pseudonymously and this was very successful too. Next I did an anthology for children called *The Patchwork Book* which reviewers said will become a classic, and wrote a critical study of the works of Mrs. Ewing, Mrs. Molesworth and Mrs. Hodgson Burnett. *Tory Heaven* (or *Toasted English*) is my third novel, and I have finished two others, a very sad one called *Little Boy Lost*, and *The Village*. Between times I write articles for *Vogue* and such papers. My principal interests are eating, traveling, and wearing nice clothes. I never had any early struggles, my career having always run with what I sometimes feel must be ominous smoothness, and I like my life very much."

* * *

Miss Laski is the niece of the late Harold Laski. Her husband is the English publisher John Howard.

PRINCIPAL WORKS: Love on the Super-Tax, 1944; To Bed with Grand Music, 1946; The Patchwork Book (ed.) 1946; Tory Heaven; or Thunder on the Right (in U.S.: Toasted English) 1948; Little Boy Lost, 1949; Mrs. Ewing, Mrs. Molesworth, and Mrs. Hodgson Burnett, 1950; The Village, 1952; The Victorian Chaise-Longue, 1954.

ABOUT: Current Biography 1951.

LASSWELL, HAROLD DWIGHT

(February 13, 1902-   ), American author, was born in Donnellson, Ill., the son of Rev.

Yale News Bureau

Linden Lasswell, a Presbyterian minister, and Anna (Prather) Lasswell. A scholarship, won in a competitive examination, in history and English, brought Lasswell to the University of Chicago in 1918; he took his Ph.B. degree in 1922, and in 1926 his Ph.D., writing as his dissertation *Propaganda Techniques in the World War* (1927).

He also did graduate work in London, Geneva, Paris, and Berlin.

First teaching at the University of Chicago as a political scientist (1922-1938), he resigned in 1938 to assume a position at the Yale School of Law, where he has remained ever since. A nationally-known authority on the psychology of public opinion, he is one of a small group of scholars prominent in a field other than law who have been appointed to the faculty of the Yale Law School in order to broaden and extend the limits of legal training. He is interested in helping lawyers to "improve the intellectual tools of the decision-making process."

His work is not restricted to academic circles for he has served in various advisory capacities for the Federal Communications Commission, the U.S. State Department, the U.S. Justice Department; and has been director of War Communications Research of the Library of Congress since 1939. In 1946 he was named to a national committee to advise the State Department on international broadcasting.

In his many publications and speeches, Lasswell has warned against the evils of a possible garrison state in this country. At the New York *Herald Tribune* Forum in 1948 he said, "By the energetic application of the principle of civilian supremacy, we can guard against the perils of a garrison-police state and conserve the physical and moral resources of our nation." In a talk in 1950 at Yale he pointed out that the current tendency of governments to curtail the freedom of the press for security reasons, could, when coupled with further restrictions of information, stifle the democratic process.

The most important intellectual influences upon him, Lasswell reports, were the philosophic orientation of Whitehead, the psychoanalytic method introduced by Freud, and the challenging perspectives of Marx. He has written a great number of books—in 1946 alone there were eleven titles which he authored or co-authored.

In 1949 Yale awarded Lasswell an honorary M.A. degree; in the same year he received a joint award for research in journalism from the Sigma Delta Chi professional fraternity.

Lasswell is unmarried. He is six feet tall, weighs 185 pounds, has gray eyes and graying brown hair. He is a member of the Presbyterian Church and belongs to no political party.

PRINCIPAL WORKS: Propaganda Techniques in the World War, 1927; Psychopathology and Politics, 1930; Politics: Who Gets What, When, How, 1936;

Democracy Through Public Opinion, 1941; World Politics Faces Economics, 1945; The Analysis of Political Behavior, 1948; Power and Personality, 1948; National Security and Individual Freedom, 1950.

ABOUT: Current Biography 1947.

LASSWELL, MARY CLYDE (LUB-BOCK) (February 8, 1905-   ), American novelist, was born in Glasgow, Scotland, the

daughter of William Robinson Lubbock and Mary Clyde (Caskey) Lubbock. Her parents were American citizens; her great-grandfather, Colonel Thomas S. Lubbock, was the founder of the original Texas Rangers, and her great grand-uncle Frank R. Lubbock, Civil War governor of Texas. Her early childhood was spent in Brownsville, Tex., a town largely Mexican in population, where she learned to speak Spanish before English. Later she wrote her only serious novel, *Bread for the Living*, about the town: "It wasn't a funny book and so it wasn't liked," she said. Except for this serious novel, her works have been humorous. "I may be a humorous writer, but I feel seriously about my characters," she told Harvey Breit in the New York *Times Book Review*. "What is funny must be, I think, very close to tragedy."

In 1930 she took a B.S. degree from the University of Texas, and taught for a time. In 1942 her big success, *Suds in Your Eye*, was published. It was a gay story—illustrated by George Price—of three elderly ladies living in a Southern California junk yard and making life a thing of joy to all around them with their humor and their cold beer. "Their story is hilariously funny, uproariously beguiling," said the New York *Times*. The book sold 300,000 copies. It was dramatized in 1943 by Jack Kirkland, and while not a success on Broadway, has been netting the authors royalties from amateur productions: $25,000 for one summer.

This book was followed by *High Time* and *Mrs. Rasmussen's Book of One-Arm Cookery*—the latter the result of communications from servicemen and women overseas who wanted the recipes for the dishes Mrs. Lasswell wrote about in her novels.

Tooner Schooner continued the adventures of the original hilarious trio of ladies in *Suds in Your Eye*. The New York *Times*

felt the humor of this book suffered badly "from excesses of vulgarity," but the *Library Journal* remarked, "For sheer fun hard to beat. Recommended."

Mary Lasswell married Clyde Lasswell, U.S.N., in 1938, and now lives in Newport, R.I.

PRINCIPAL WORKS: Suds in Your Eye, 1942; High Time, 1944; Mrs. Rasmussen's Book of One-Arm Cookery, 1946; Bread for the Living, 1948; One on the House, 1949; Wait for the Wagon, 1951; Tooner Schooner, 1953.

ABOUT: Warfel, H. R. American Novelists of Today 1951; New York Times Book Review December 18, 1949; Saturday Review of Literature March 17, 1951.

"LATHAM, O'NEILL." See O'NEILL, R. C.

LATOURETTE, KENNETH SCOTT (August 9, 1884-   ), American religious historian and Sinologist, writes: "I was born in Oregon City, Ore.

My father and mother, Dewitt Clinton and Rhoda Ellen Scott Latourette, were college classmates and both had taught in colleges before their marriage. Their home, therefore, was one of culture, and good books abounded.

Yale News Bureau

Their parents had 'crossed the plains' by covered wagon, so I was of pioneer stock. My father was a lawyer and banker, and until my senior year in college I planned to follow him. The home was also deeply religious, and it was that, together with the literary atmosphere, which most molded me. I was educated in the public schools of my native town, and from there went to what is now Linfield, a college with which the family had close ties. There I took my first degree, a B.S., and in my last year, after much emotional stress, from a sheer sense of duty decided to become a missionary. After a year with my father in business I went to Yale, entering in senior year. There I took a B.A. and, having decided to go into the teaching phase of foreign missions and having been asked to join the staff of Yale in China, then in its infancy, I remained at Yale in the Graduate School, and took an M.A. and a Ph.D. in history, having as much work in Far Eastern and especially Chinese history as was then available.

"After a year (1909-1910) of travel through the colleges and universities of the

United States and Canada for the Student Volunteer Movement for Foreign Missions, I joined (1910) the staff of Yale in China in Changsha, the capital of the mid-China province Hunan, giving much of my time to the study of the language. At the end of the first year I became seriously ill, and after several months of attempts at a cure, I returned (1912) to the United States, hoping to go back to China in a few months. However, recovery proved slow; it was two years before I could do part time work, and eventually my physicians advised against renewed residence in China.

"During the years 1914-16, while completing my convalescence, I had a part time appointment in the history department of the faculty of Reed College in Portland, Ore. For the following five years I taught history in Denison, and, having been ordained to the Baptist ministry, for the last three years of that time I was also chaplain of the university. I then (1921) went to Yale with primary assignment to the Divinity School, with the title of Professor of Missions. In 1927, because of my interest in Far Eastern history, the title was enlarged to Professor of Missions and Oriental History. I have been at Yale ever since. Because of the age limit, I became emeritus in 1953 and am expecting to stay on at Yale, devoting much of my time to research and writing.

"True to my background and interests, my primary writing has been in the history of Christianity, especially the history of missions, and my secondary interest has been in Far Eastern and particularly Chinese history. In these fields I have written over thirty volumes. In addition to my teaching and writing, I have served on many boards, committees, and scholarly societies outside New Haven. Some of these have been for the promotion of Far Eastern studies. More have been connected with the world-wide outreach of the Christian churches, among them the World Student Christian Federation, the Student Volunteer Movement, the International Missionary Council, and the World Council of Churches."

PRINCIPAL WORKS: The History of Early Relations Between the United States and China, 1784-1844, 1917; The Development of China, 1917; The Development of Japan, 1918; A History of Christian Missions in China, 1929; The Chinese, Their History and Culture, 1934; A History of the Expansion of Christianity, 6 vols., 1937-1945; A Short History of the Far East, 1946; A History of Christianity, 1953; Challenge and Conformity, 1955.

ABOUT: Journal of Theological Studies July-October 1946; London Times Literary Supplement August 3, 1946.

LATTIMORE, OWEN (July 29, 1900-   ), American Sinologist, was born in Washington, D.C., but spent his childhood and most of his young manhood in China, where his father, David Lattimore, was in the educational service of the Chinese government. When the boy was twelve years old, he was sent to school in Switzerland, and in 1915 he entered the St. Bees School in Cumberland, England, from which he was graduated four years later.

Lattimore returned to China and in 1920 took a newspaper job in Shanghai. After two years he began work for an export firm, where his interest in China's frontier dependencies, from Manchuria to Tibet and Turkestan, was stimulated. In 1926 Lattimore gave up his job to explore and write about this territory. In the same year he married Eleanor Holgate, author of several books (but not to be confused with Eleanor Frances Lattimore, his sister, who writes children's books), who had also lived and worked in China for a number of years. The couple spent their honeymoon traveling native style—by horseback, camel train, and sled—across the hinterland of Mongolia through Chinese Turkestan. In 1929 Lattimore's travels and researches were financed by a fellowship from the Social Science Research Council. For the three years following he studied in Peiping and traveled in Inner Mongolia, first on a fellowship from the Harvard-Yenching Foundation and later on a Guggenheim fellowship, which was renewed for a second year in 1932. Lattimore continued his studies in China until 1937, when the Japanese occupation made life there too difficult. He returned to the United States with his wife and his son, David, to become director of the Walter Hines Page School of International Relations at Johns Hopkins University.

Lattimore's reputation as an expert on Chinese affairs and his fluency in several oriental languages brought him to the attention of President Roosevelt during World War II, and in 1941 the President recommended him for the post of political adviser to Generalissimo Chiang Kai-shek. Lattimore remained with the Generalissimo for six months. In 1942 he returned to the United States to become a deputy director of the Office of War Information, in charge of

Pacific operations, with headquarters in San Francisco. In 1944 he was back in the East, visiting China and Siberia with Vice-President Henry Wallace's diplomatic party. Early in 1945 he resigned from the O.W.I. to resume his teaching at Johns Hopkins, only to be called back into service, later in that same year, by President Harry Truman to act as special adviser to an economic mission to Japan. Again he returned to his teaching, and again he was recalled, in 1950, this time as chief of a United Nations technical aid exploratory mission to Afghanistan.

Until 1950 Lattimore was little known outside government and academic circles. His books on China had all been highly praised for their scholarship and their sound grasp of Chinese political and economic problems. He contributed articles, in his field of specialization, to newspapers, the *Atlantic Monthly, New Republic, Asia, Virginia Quarterly Review,* and many specialized journals. From 1934 to 1941 he was editor of *Pacific Affairs,* published by the Institute of Pacific Relations. In all these connections he was a quiet, unassuming man, described by interviewers as "tactful and self-effacing," in every respect the typical academic figure. Then suddenly in 1950 Lattimore was catapulted into the sensational publicity of a congressional investigation. Senator Joseph McCarthy accused him of being the "top Russian espionage agent in the United States" (he later modified the charge to "one of the top espionage agents"). Lattimore found himself in the midst of a violent political controversy. He described his experiences in his book *Ordeal By Slander.* Charges against him were investigated and then dismissed by the Tydings Committee, but a short time later the controversy was refueled with charges by Louis Budenz, an ex-Communist, who testified that Lattimore was or had been a Communist, working under Communist discipline. In 1951 the Senate Internal Security Committee reopened the case as part of a general inquiry into the Institute of Pacific Relations. A year later a Washington grand jury indicted Lattimore on seven counts of perjury, arising out of his testimony. In 1954 and in 1955 a federal court dismissed two of the charges on the grounds of vagueness. On June 28, 1955 the Justice Department dropped all charges against him.

PRINCIPAL WORKS: The Desert Road to Turkestan, 1929; High Tartary, 1930; Manchuria, Cradle of Conflict, 1932; The Mongols of Manchuria, 1934; Inner Asian Frontiers of China, 1940; Mongol Journeys, 1941; America and Asia, 1943; Solution in Asia, 1945; China, A Short History (with E. Lattimore) 1947; Situation in Asia, 1949; The Pivot of Asia, 1950; Ordeal by Slander, 1950.

ABOUT: Boas, G. & Wheeler, H. (eds.) Lattimore the Scholar; Flynn, J. T. The Lattimore Story; Lattimore, O. Ordeal by Slander; Current Biography 1945; Nation February 7, 1953; New York Times Book Review August 13, 1950; Saturday Review of Literature April 19, 1949.

LATTIMORE, RICHMOND ALEXANDER (May 6, 1906-). American classical scholar, translator, and lyric poet, writes:

"I was born in Paotingfu, China, where my father was teaching in a government university. With the exception of a family trip to Europe in 1913, I spent the first fourteen years of my life in China. I neither saw the inside of a school nor learned profoundly about China or the Chinese; but my parents, especially my father, gave us children a thorough grounding in literature and languages, which for me included Greek and Latin. In 1920 my mother took me and my three sisters to settle in Berkeley, Calif. There, two years later, I graduated from high school with an undistinguished record. Meanwhile, my father accepted a position at Dartmouth, and the summer of 1922 found all of my family, with the exception of my brother Owen, settled in Hanover.

"I entered Dartmouth with almost no ambition except the desire to be a good athlete; but I almost automatically majored in Greek and Latin, and began to write poems, critical essays, stories, and one long-since-incinerated novel. I emerged from college wanting to be a writer rather than a scholar; I have spent the rest of my life since then learning that the two can be the same, and trying to make good what I learned. The decisive step was taken in 1926, when I accepted an academic position instead of free lancing, unskilled labor, or going to sea. I was at Illinois two years as instructor and graduate student, at Wabash for one. While there I applied independently for a Rhodes Scholarship and got it. After the Oxford (Christ Church) years came one of unemployment, spent in research for my thesis; then Illinois again, and a Ph.D.; a year at the American Academy in Rome; and finally a position in Greek at Bryn Mawr, where (with three years out for the Naval Reserve) I have been ever since. I married Alice Bockstahler in 1935, and we have two sons, Steven and Alexander.

"My first year of graduate work with Oldfather and Perry showed the essential nonsense, for me, of planning to teach for bread-and-butter and write for a career. No teaching without scholarship; no scholarship without real scholarship. The years at Illinois and Oxford were spent in learning and re-learning fundamentals. These years also showed me that I had not the talent, nor actually the will, to write novels, short stories, or dramas. But the process of studying and interpreting texts, with its impasses and its constant surprise in solution, is strangely the same for me as the process of writing lyric poetry. So I went on writing learned articles and reviews, and poems too, and I always shall. For a while the poems were bookish, made of stuff skimmed from the surfaces of Greek literature, Anglo-Saxon and Old Norse heroics, and every kind of philosophy. I changed my whole style in 1933, and changed because I had to, but what precipitated the change was Dick Eberhart's caustic criticism of a long and conspicuously unsuccessful metaphysical poem on which I had spent years. He told me to be concrete; since then, I have been more concrete than Dick ever was or will be.

"Not that I could be called a successful original poet. My creations are thinly sprayed through the pages of an awfully select group of periodicals. I suppose I am principally a translator now. I began translating seriously in my thirties, with Pindar. My purpose from now on is to keep my activities, pedagogic, domestic, athletic, and in the first and second degree creative, all in some kind of practical harmony. Work now in progress: study of Herodotus and history; translating and editing the Greek tragedies (with David Grene); more lyrics."

PRINCIPAL WORKS: Themes in Greek and Latin Epitaphs, 1942. *Translations*—Some Odes of Pindar, 1942; The Odes of Pindar, 1947; The Iliad of Homer, 1951; The Oresteia of Aeschylus, 1953.

ABOUT: Accent Spring 1943; Hudson Review Autumn 1952; Kenyon Review Autumn 1952; Poetry September 1947.

*LATZKO, ADOLPH ANDREAS (September 1, 1876-   ). For biographical sketch and list of works and references, see TWENTIETH CENTURY AUTHORS, 1942.

* * *

On last reports (1948), Andreas Latzko was living in Salzburg. No information is available on his recent writings.

* läts'kō

*LAURENTS, ARTHUR (July 14, 1918-   ), American playwright, writes: "My own biographical interest is not dates, names, places so much as emotions, ideas, interests: how they were formed, why they were changed, where they are going. However, the matter of a biographical dictionary tends more to a sort of careeristic laundry list. Hence— mine:

"I was born on Bastille Day, 1918, in Brooklyn. My father was a lawyer, my mother had been a school teacher and by the time I was four, I had a very pretty sister. We were middle middle-class, the differentiating factor being the humor and intelligence of both parents.

"At eleven or twelve, I wrote my first short story, completely in dialogue: apparently I always wanted to be a playwright. I later studied playwriting at Cornell University where I learned one generalization—the way to learn to write is to write—and one specific: never begin a play with the telephone ringing—why, I don't know.

"After college, I sold linen in a department store and was fired for sleeping behind the counter. I took an evening course in radio writing at New York University and wrote an original half-hour play *(Now Playing Tomorrow)* which was immediately bought by the Columbia Workshop (they paid me the amount of my tuition: $30). I wrote and sold one or two more radio scripts, and then a night club act. The latter was one of those hopefully bright, satirical abbreviated revues which young people were doing at the time. To get paid, I had to appear in the act, thereby killing for all time any desire I had to perform. The act had a brief success but self-consciousness forced me to quit. Another radio script paid my way to California where I stayed for six months (in radio) until I was drafted.

"For over four years I had a varied army career, ranging from truckdriver to, finally, propagandist. There was a range to that, too. I wrote scripts for the C.B.S. program *The Man Behind the Gun*, a recruiting 'Communorama' for Western Electric war workers, training films and army radio programs: a show a week for half a year of *Army Service Forces Present*, and for over a year for *Assignment Home*. It is an enormous strain

* "Name is pronounced with stress on first syllable."

to write what amounts to a new one-act play every week for almost two years, particularly when you are both trying to say something and to write well. But it is also wonderful training and discipline. During the last few months of that period, I also wrote *Home of the Brave* (I now wonder when) which was not actually produced until I was out of the army.

"After that, another play, *Heartsong,* which died out of town after overly-extended death rattles. Debt sent me back to Hollywood where I did the screenplay for *Rope,* worked on *The Snake Pit,* collaborated on the film version of *Anna Lucasta,* and was partially responsible for a fiasco entitled *Caught.* Another play, *The Bird Cage,* followed without too much success; then a trip to Europe which resulted in *The Time of the Cuckoo* [as motion picture, *Summertime*].

"I think the theatre is finally shaking off the Ibsen influence, leaning more toward Chekhov and heading straighter toward what must be its next phase of development: technically freer, more inwardly emotional and less outwardly naturalistic. At present, I am working on a new play and hope, someday, to write one I really like and see it produced as I really want."

PRINCIPAL WORKS: Home of the Brave, 1946; The Bird Cage, 1950; The Time of the Cuckoo, 1953.

ABOUT: Saturday Review October 18, 1952.

*LAVER, JAMES (March 14, 1899-). For autobiographical sketch and list of earlier works and references, see TWENTIETH CENTURY AUTHORS, 1942.

* * *

James Laver writes from London: "The war brought to me, as to so many, a break in life. The [Victoria and Albert] Museum was closed and after a year in H.M. Treasury, I started on a campaign of public speaking on behalf of the National Savings Movement. Made 750 speeches in coal mines, factories, market places, etc., all over England. When peace came I returned to my duties at the Victoria and Albert Museum, of which I am now the Senior Keeper.

"Rather to my regret my writing has been more and more turned in the direction of expertise; I have produced a number of books on the history and philosophy of dress, and many people seem, unfortunately, to think of it as my sole interest. In September 1952, I presided over the First International Congress for Costume and the Arts at

* lā'ver

Venice. Other interests, however, appear in my book on Nostradamus, in *Drama, Its Costume and Decor,* and in various monographs on English country houses. I have done a great deal of lecturing and broadcasting, including television. I have not published any more novels, plays or poems. Perhaps when I retire from my official duties in six years' time I shall be able to get back to more leisurely and imaginative work."

ADDITIONAL WORKS: The Ladies of Hampton Court, 1942; Fashions and Fashion Plates, 1943; 19th Century French Posters (ed.) 1944; Letter to a Girl on the Future of Clothes, 1946; Nineteenth Century Costume, 1947; Hatchards of Piccadilly, 1947; Isabella's Triumph (ed.) 1947; Eating Out, 1947; Homage to Venus (ed.) 1948; British Military Uniforms, 1948; Paintings by Michael Ayrton, 1948; Style in Costume, 1949; The Shape of Things: Dress, 1950; Titian, 1950; Setting Children Free, 1950; Early Tudor Costume, 1951; Children's Fashions in the 19th Century, 1951; Drama: Its Costume and Decor, 1951; The Fertile Image, 1951; Holkham Hall, 1951; Seventeenth and Eighteenth Century Costume, 1951; The Pleasures of Life: Clothes, 1952; Mellerstain, 1952; First Decadent: The Strange Life of J. K. Huysmans, 1954.

LAVERTY, MAURA (KELLY) (May 15, 1907-), Irish novelist, was born in Rathangan, County Kildare, Ireland, the daughter of Michael  Kelly and Mary Ann (Treacy) Kelly. Part of her girlhood was spent on her grandmother's farm, the "Derrymore House" described in her novels. Later she was sent to the Brigidine Convent in Tullow, County Carlow, to study to be a teacher. Soon after leaving the school in 1925, she went to Spain as a governess in a wealthy family in Madrid. Having little liking for such occupation, she relinquished it to serve as a secretary to the Princess Bibesco. Later she became a foreign correspondent in the Banco Calamarte, and then had a job on a Madrid daily, *El Debate.* Returning to Ireland in 1928, she wrote articles and poems, became editor of a woman's magazine, and then a broadcaster for the Irish Broadcasting Company. In 1928 she married James Laverty, a journalist.

Her first book owes its existence to the memories evoked by the author's perusal of an Irish cookbook. As Mrs. Laverty scanned the recipes, she recalled the delectable dishes prepared in her grandmother's kitchen, "and inevitably . . . memories of the people associated with these things." The resulting

Never No More, an autobiographical novel dealing with life in a village in County Kildare as it revolved around "Gran," is filled with a "rich sense of life, enough humor to salt a dozen books, skill with incident, and understanding." The New York *Times* considered it "a book written as only one of Irish blood could write it; breathing a civilization that has never succumbed to industrial strain or to over-exigencies of modernity."

Her second novel, *Touched by the Thorn,* though banned by the Irish censors, received the Irish Women Writers' award in the year of its publication. The *Manchester Guardian* called it an "absorbing and charmingly written narrative of the Irish countryside," while the *New Yorker* said of it, "Not an important book, but nevertheless a tender human one with lovely Irish dialect singing through it." In her third novel, *No More than Human,* Mrs. Laverty drew on her experiences in Spain. The book contains the character of Delia Scully, whose earlier life is related in *Never No More.* Her fourth volume was a children's book, *Gold of Glanaree,* and her fifth a novel, *Liffey Lane.* Many reviewers found the latter sentimental, or "the Irish equivalent of a 'soap opera,'" but they praised its sense of reality, understanding, and warmth: "a born story teller," said the *Saturday Review of Literature,* and the *New Yorker* praised "her appealing use of the lovely Irish speech." In the San Francisco *Chronicle,* Edith James wrote: "Miss Laverty knows the mind and heart of a child and makes a thing of beauty out of a sordid Dublin slum background."

The Lavertys live in Dublin with their two daughters. Mrs. Laverty, described in 1947 as of medium height, brown-haired and gray-eyed, lists her interests as fishing and "trying out new recipes."

PRINCIPAL WORKS: Never No More, 1942; Touched by the Thorn (in England: Alone We Embark) 1943; No More than Human, 1944; Gold of Glanaree (in England: Cottage in the Bog) 1945; Kind Cooking (a cookbook) 1945; Liffey Lane (in England: Lift up Your Gates) 1947; Green Orchard, 1949.

ABOUT: Hoehn, M. (ed.) Catholic Authors, I; Laverty, M. Never No More, No More than Human; Current Biography 1947.

LAVIN, MARY (June 11, 1912-), American-Irish novelist and short story writer, was born in East Walpole, Mass., the only child of Thomas and Nora (Mahon) Lavin. Though born in the United States, she has spent most of her life in Ireland, going there on a visit at the age of ten. When she was fourteen, her father was put in charge

of Bective House, an estate in County Meath. She attended the Bird School in East Walpole, studied at the Loreto Convent, Stephens Green, Dublin, and received her M.A. degree in 1937 from the National University of Ireland, where she was awarded first-class honors for her thesis on Jane Austen. Miss Lavin began a study of Virginia Woolf, intending to  continue for a Ph.D. This project was interrupted by a visit to the United States for four months, and on her return to Ireland in 1938 she wrote a short story, "Miss Holland," which was published by Seumas O'Sullivan, poet-editor of the *Dublin Magazine.* Lord Dunsany read it, invited her to send other stories to him and volunteered to write a preface for a collection of them. This collection became *Tales from Bective Bridge* (1942) and received the James Tait Black Memorial Prize in England. The book consisted of ten short stories about Ireland and Ireland's people, with an enthusiastic preface by Lord Dunsany. Many comparisons were made to Katherine Mansfield and Kay Boyle by reviewers. "Mary Lavin is a born short story writer," said the *Saturday Review of Literature;* "there are excellent and impressive pieces."

Mary Lavin's novel *The House in Clewe Street,* a study of three generations of a middle-class Irish family, was published in 1945 after serialization in the *Atlantic Monthly* under the title of "Gabriel Galloway." "There are no clichés either of phrasing or of feeling here. Laughter is behind these lines always," said *Book Week,* "sometimes elaborately elephantine, sometimes as delicate as the tread of a small animal that you have scarcely noticed until it has passed you by. . . . [A] fine novel." The New York *Times* commented, "Because Miss Lavin's characters and art lack tragic proportions the conclusion of her novel is thin and strained. But the weakness of the ending is remarkable chiefly because of the vigor of the first two-thirds of the story." Other short story collections have followed, and a novel, *Mary O'Grady* (1950). Dunsany has written of Miss Lavin's work: "To me she seems reminiscent of the Russians more than any other school of writers, and, with the exception of the gigantic Tolstoy, her searching insight into the human heart and vivid appreciation of the beauty of the fields are worthy in my opinion to be mentioned beside their work."

Miss Lavin says her only occupation besides writing is "housekeeping and minding my children." Her husband, William Walsh, is a Dublin lawyer and they have three daughters. They bought a farm in County Meath and live at Bective House. She is a member of the Irish Academy of Letters.

PRINCIPAL WORKS: Tales from Bective Bridge, 1942; The Long Ago, and Other Stories, 1944; The House in Clewe Street, 1945; The Becker Wives, and Other Stories, 1946; At Sallygap, and Other Stories, 1947; Mary O'Grady, 1950; A Single Lady, and Other Stories, 1951.

ABOUT: Hoehn, M. (ed.) Catholic Authors, I; Wilson Library Bulletin November 1945.

LAVRIN, JANKO (February 10, 1887-), British critic and biographer, writes: "The principal fact about my life is that most of

my work has been done in two countries which have nothing to do with the country of my birth. One was Russia before 1917, and the other England from 1917 onwards. I was born in the Slovene region of former Austria (Julian Alps), now a part of Yugoslavia. My elementary and secondary education took place in Austria. After matriculating, I went to visit friends in Russia. I decided to continue my studies there, but also spent some time at the University of Oslo, paying frequent visits to Helsinki. In this way I was able to get an idea of life, not only in Russia, but also in Scandinavia. In 1913 I made an extensive journey through the whole of Europe and returned to Petersburg immediately after the Balkan war. In those days I wrote critical essays and articles mainly in Russian and Slovene.

"When the first World War broke out I was invited to join the staff of the biggest Russian newspaper and was sent as a war correspondent to the Serbian front. In Serbia I had some very interesting experiences and came near to losing my life in the retreat with the Serbian army (through Albania down to Greece) in the early winter of 1915. My experiences appeared in book form in Russian at the end of 1916 while I was recuperating in Salonica. In Corfu I continued my work as war correspondent until the autumn of 1917. In the early autumn of that year I was on my way back to St. Petersburg when the Bolshevist revolution broke

out. When I reached London, the situation was so confused that I decided to wait for a while in England. Finally, for various reasons, I remained in London. Here I got into touch with the *New Age* under R. A. Orage and joined the staff. I wrote for it a number of articles and essays, mostly on literary topics.

"In the autumn of 1918 I became university lecturer at Nottingham. It was there that I developed my literary activities, one of my aims being to combine literary criticism with a psychological and philosophical approach. My early books were on Dostoevsky, Tolstoy, Nietzsche, Ibsen, and other writers. Most of those books were later republished in an enlarged form. I also contributed articles to various periodicals, both English and American. Having been made professor of Russian at Nottingham University, I enlarged the Russian section into the Slavonic department. In 1928 I married the artist Nora Fry, and we have two sons, John and David. My wife and I have made a number of extensive journeys, especially in the Balkans. In 1937 I became a naturalised British subject. My literary activities became intensified during the second World War when I was on the staff of the European service of the B.B.C. as broadcaster and superviser of languages. After the war I resumed my literary and other connections with my native Slovenia. It was since 1942 that some of my books have appeared in America, from whence I have received further commissions upon which I am now engaged. In the autumn of 1952 I retired from academic work, and my present status is that of emeritus professor of Nottingham University."

PRINCIPAL WORKS: Studies in European Literature, 1930; Aspects of Modernism, 1936; An Introduction to the Russian Novel, 1942; Dostoevsky, 1943; Tolstoy, 1944; Pushkin and Russian Literature 1947; From Pushkin to Mayakovsky, 1948; Nietzsche, 1948; Ibsen, 1950; Gogol, 1952; Goncharov, 1954.

"LAWLESS, ANTHONY." See MACDONALD, P.

LAWRENCE, DAVID HERBERT (September 11, 1885-March 2, 1930). For biographical sketch and list of works and references, see TWENTIETH CENTURY AUTHORS, 1942.

* * *

ADDITIONAL WORKS: The First Lady Chatterley, 1944; Letters to Bertrand Russell (ed. H. Moore) 1948; Prelude: His First and Previously Unrecorded Work, 1949; The Later D. H. Lawrence (ed. W. Y. Tindall) 1951; Sex, Literature and Censorship (essays) 1954.

ABOUT: Aldington, R. D. H. Lawrence: Portrait of a Genius But . . . ; Bynner, W. Journey with Genius, 1951; Fay, E. Lorenzo in Search of the Sun; Hoffman, F. J. & Moore, H. (eds.) The Achievement of D. H. Lawrence; Jarrett-Kerr, W. R. D. H. Lawrence and Human Existence; Kenmare, D. Firebird: A Study of D. H. Lawrence; Moore, H. T. The Life and Works of D. H. Lawrence, The Intelligent Heart: The Story of D. H. Lawrence; Rowse, A. L. The English Past; Trilling, D. *Introduction to* The Portable D. H. Lawrence; West, A. D. H. Lawrence; Woolf, V. The Moment, and Other Essays.

LAWRENCE, HILDA, American author, was born in Baltimore, Md., the daughter of John and Martha Bevan (Strayer) Kron-miller. She attended Baltimore schools and a finishing school—a "very conservative day school for girls" —in Rochester, N.Y. After graduation she took a job at Johns Hopkins reading to a professor whose eyesight was failing, then went on to New York City where she settled for twenty years, handling the clippings for the Macmillan Company. There followed work at *Publishers' Weekly.* In 1924 she married Reginald Lawrence, a playwright; they were divorced.

About this time she became interested in radio and wrote some dramatic sketches for Jane Cowl, eventually supplying scripts for Rudy Vallee's show and other variety programs. Because she enjoyed detective stories herself, she was drawn to write one. Her first book, *Blood upon the Snow*, was accepted twenty-four hours after she submitted it to an agent in New York; the critics were enthusiastic. "Here's horror and mystery served up in writing, rich and smooth as pre-war cream," wrote Meyer Berger in the New York *Times*. "Miss Lawrence creates a horror atmosphere with good skill, the hard way, with a light touch that leaves no brush marks. A few snowflakes, the mere suggestion of sinister sounds, the barest hint of screaming silence, and the reader's hackles come away from his collar."

Her second book, *A Time to Die*, was called by the *New Yorker* "an excellent job, well written, and with very fine small-town atmosphere." Some of the critics were less friendly toward *Duet of Death*, a volume offering two novels in one cover. "Slick-magazine stuff," protested the *New Yorker*, but the New York *Times* found them

"Grade-A shockers. They inspire hair-raising fear in a genteel, immensely effective way."

Hilda Lawrence's novels have been translated into French, Czech, Swedish, Danish and Norwegian. She has drawn upon a fund of stories and anecdotes told her by her father and other relatives years ago, and harmless incidents from her family's daily life have often been developed into murders and melodramatic situations. One of the things she has tried to achieve is a "homey" quality, something "that will be understood by every woman over sixty who belongs to a lending library." Dorothy Sayers is her favorite mystery writer. Blonde, blue-eyed, she has been described as a fragile, pretty woman, who looks incapable of imagining the sustained violence she is able to think up. She writes in longhand and revises on the typewriter.

PRINCIPAL WORKS: Blood upon the Snow, 1944; A Time to Die, 1945; The Pavilion, 1946; Death of a Doll, 1947; Duet of Death (Composition for Four Hands, and The House) 1949.

ABOUT: Current Biography 1947; Saturday Review of Literature February 17, 1945.

LAWRENCE, JOSEPHINE (1897?-). For biographical sketch and list of earlier works and references, see TWENTIETH CENTURY AUTHORS, 1942.

* * *

Josephine Lawrence is still only a part-time novelist. The other part of her time is devoted to newspaper work in Newark, N.J. In 1946 she began a weekly book column for the Newark *Sunday News*. Since 1940 she has been married to Artur Platz. In the more than two decades in which she has been writing novels, Miss Lawrence has followed a strict but simple pattern. Her characters and their problems are simple, matter-of-fact, everyday ones. Kelsey Guilfoil in an article on her in the *English Journal*, calls her "the chronicler of the commonplace, the recorder of the ordinary, and the mirror of the common people." Her admirers point out, however, that her work rings true. It lacks profundity and artistic style, but it sometimes reaches to the heart of the human situation. Guilfoil writes: "Few novelists have ranged so far in showing us that the masses of humanity are endowed with an immense courage and that, though the weakling may snivel or retreat into insanity or suicide, heroism of a quiet and unspectacular nature is the norm of human existence."

ADDITIONAL WORKS: There Is Today, 1942; Tower of Steel, 1943; Let Us Consider One Another, 1945; Double Wedding Ring, 1946; The

Pleasant Morning Light, 1948; My Heart Shall Not Fear, 1949; The Way Things Are, 1950; The Picture Window, 1951; Song in the Night, 1952; The Web of Time, 1953; The Gates of Living, 1955.

ABOUT: Warfel, H. R. American Novelists of Today; English Journal September 1949; Newsweek September 4, 1950.

LAWRENCE, THOMAS EDWARD (August 16, 1888-May 19, 1935). For biographical sketch and list of works and references, see TWENTIETH CENTURY AUTHORS, 1942.

* * *

ADDITIONAL WORK: The Home Letters of T. E. Lawrence and His Brothers, 1954; The Mint, 1955.

ABOUT: Aldington, R. Lawrence of Arabia; Dictionary of National Biography 1931-1940; Garnett, D. Preface to The Essential T. E. Lawrence; Kiernan, R. H. Lawrence of Arabia; Lawrence, T. E. The Home Letters; Robinson, E. Lawrence the Rebel; Smith, C. S. Golden Reign: Story of My Friendship with Lawrence; Mercure de France May 1949; Time December 10, 1951; Virginia Quarterly Review October 1945.

LAWSON, JOHN HOWARD (September 25, 1895-). For autobiographical sketch and list of earlier works and references, see TWENTIETH CENTURY AUTHORS, 1942.

* * *

John Howard Lawson writes from San Fernando, Calif.: "From 1942 to 1947, I was engaged in motion picture work. The films which I wrote during this period were *Action in the North Atlantic, Sahara, Counterattack,* and *Smashup*. In 1947, my motion picture career—at least as far as the Hollywood industry is concerned—was rudely interrupted by the much-publicized attack which was made on me and other film writers, actors and directors by the House Committee on Un-American Activities. The Committee forced me to devote a great deal of time to legal and political controversy. But the issues involved in the case intensified my interest in our country's culture and traditions and inspired greater literary effort. I completed an analysis of the history and technique of filmwriting in 1949; it was published as an additional part of my book on playwriting, which was reissued as *The Theory and Technique of Playwriting and Screenwriting*. The first volume of my work on the cultural history of the United States appeared in 1950, entitled *The Hidden Heritage*. I have just completed another book on

films which is about to be published under the title *Film in the Battle of Ideas*. A new play is also near completion."

* * *

In April 1948 Lawson was found guilty of contempt of Congress for refusing to say, before the House Un-American Activities Committee, whether or not he was a Communist. After a two-year legal battle, he began a one-year prison sentence in June 1950.

ADDITIONAL WORKS: The Theory and Technique of Playwriting and Screenwriting (rev. ed.) 1949; The Hidden Heritage, 1950.

ABOUT: New York Times June 10, 1950; Time April 26, 1948.

*LAXNESS, HALLDÓR KILJAN (April 23, 1902-), Icelandic novelist and essayist, was born in Reykjavík, Iceland. Christened Halldór Gudjónsson, he later took his writing name, LAXNESS, from the name of his father's inland valley farm where he spent the years of his boyhood. He was educated at the Icelandic Latin School and for a single winter season attended the *gymnasium* in Reykjavík where he made friends

with a number of promising young writers. His first story, "Child of Nature," was published in 1919 when he was seventeen years old.

Traveling through Scandinavia, he wrote short stories for a Copenhagen newspaper, went on to Germany, Austria, France, and in 1923 lived for more than a year in a monastery in the Duchy of Luxembourg, where he was converted to Catholicism and wrote his novel, *At the Holy Mountain*. This intense interest in religion took him next to London where he studied under the Jesuits, then to Lourdes and Rome; he produced several books rooted in a Catholic theme before he arrived at a state of philosophical disillusionment over what he called "the incompatibility of the fundamental principles of Christianity and those of human life." His first major novel, *The Weaver of Cashmere*, written in Taormina, Sicily, in 1925, expressed this violent shift in his point of view. Published in 1927 and strongly autobiographical in tone, it touched off a controversy which has been compared to the furor which greeted Sinclair Lewis' *Elmer Gantry* in this country.

* läks'něs

After a few years of wandering through the countryside of his own Iceland, he journeyed to America in 1929, living in Canada, San Francisco and Hollywood, where he became a good friend of Upton Sinclair. An article commemorating Sinclair's fiftieth birthday, written for the Icelandic press, in addition to several articles socialist in tone which criticized American culture, led to a demand for his deportation; however, he returned to Iceland before any action was taken. In 1930 he married and settled down in Reykjavík, where he has lived ever since except for brief intervals on the Crimean Riviera (living on royalties from his sales in the Soviet Union), in Republican Spain and in Nazi Germany.

In 1931 and 1932 Laxness published his two-part novel, *O Pure Vine* and *Bird of the Shore*, turning now to his native land for subject matter. Translated into several languages including English, as *Salka Valka*, this book brought him unqualified recognition. The Icelandic government, which grants annual stipends to established writers, awarded Laxness such a grant.

With the publication of *Independent People* in 1934, he reached full stature as the foremost novelist of his country, although here too he continued to be a storm center, criticized by the conservative press, praised by the Left. In this country, *Independent People* was enthusiastically received as a Book-of-the-Month Club choice in 1946. An epic novel of peasant life in Iceland, it was described in the *Saturday Review of Literature* as "a hard but truly great novel, which goes far to explain an entire nation."

Laxness has sometimes been called a Communist. Although politically active in his own country both as a commentator and an organizer, he speaks of himself as a "leftist socialist—not a Communist." In 1953 he was awarded the Stalin prize for literature. The following year, according to the Stockholm press, he was with Ernest Hemingway a candidate for the Nobel prize, which in the final decision went to the American novelist.

Author of six novels and a number of important essays, Halldór Laxness is both satirist and prophet, critic and poet, for his own people. Although he deals often in naturalistic materials, he is never a strict realist. His work is conceived in essentially symbolic terms and written in the great epic tradition.

PRINCIPAL WORKS IN ENGLISH TRANSLATION: Salka Valka, 1936; Independent People, 1946.

ABOUT: Book-of-the-Month Club News August 1946; Books Abroad Summer 1954; Current Biography 1946.

LEA, FANNY HEASLIP (October 30, 1884-January 13, 1955). For biographical sketch and list of earlier works and references, see TWENTIETH CENTURY AUTHORS, 1942.

* * *

Fanny Heaslip Lea died at her home in New York City at the age of seventy. Her stories and poems appeared from time to time in the *Woman's Home Companion, Good Housekeeping*, and other popular magazines. Her last novels, like her earlier works, were slight, frothy romances catering to the tastes of the reader who wants escape and relaxation.

ADDITIONAL WORKS: Sailor's Star, 1944; The Devil Within, 1948; Verses for Lovers, 1955.

*LEA, TOM (July 11, 1907-   ), American novelist and artist, writes: "I was born in El Paso, Tex., where my father was an attorney and mayor of El Paso during the border troubles of the Mexican Revolution. I was educated in the El Paso public schools, and most of my boyhood summers were spent on ranches in Lincoln and Grant Counties of New Mexico, and Culberson County, Tex. After graduating from El Paso High School in May 1924, I went to the Art Institute of Chicago and studied there for two years. My maestro there was John Norton; after leaving the Institute, I worked as an apprentice in Norton's mural studio, did some mural commissions of my own, and worked as a commercial artist in Chicago until 1933. During that time I made a trip to Italy and spent a few months in Tuscany and Umbria studying the works of the pre-Renaissance frescoists. From 1933 to 1936 I lived on a hill about eleven miles from Santa Fe, N.M., painting, working part time at the Laboratory of Anthropology. In 1936 I returned to my home town, El Paso, where I still live.

McElroy

"In the period from 1936 until World War II, I painted a number of murals, a few easel pictures, and did a good deal of illustrating both in books and in magazines. Some of my murals can be seen in the Post Office Department Building, Washington, D.C.; Federal Court House, El Paso; State of Texas Building, Dallas; Branigan Memorial

* "Pronounced as in *sea, tea, pea.*"

Library, Las Cruces, N.M.; Post Offices at Seymour, Tex., Odessa, Tex., Pleasant Hill, Mo.

"I did book illustrations for such volumes as J. Frank Dobie's *Apache Gold and Yaqui Silver* and *The Longhorns* and for a number of items from the private press of the typographer Carl Hertzog. I illustrated stories in magazines like *The Saturday Evening Post.* In 1941 I was the first war artist to go overseas for *Life* magazine, and I was aboard a destroyer in the North Atlantic patrol off Labrador the day of Pearl Harbor. I worked as a war artist and correspondent for *Life* during the entire course of the war, serving on assignments in the North Atlantic, South Pacific, North African, European, Middle East, and China-Burma-India theatres of operations. I traveled more than 100,000 miles outside the U.S., and at the invasion of Peleliu Island hit the bloody beach with the first assault waves of the 1st Marine Division.

"Up to the age of forty I was a painter and aside from caption material accompanying my paintings in *Life,* and a few pieces privately printed by Carl Hertzog, I had never written anything. But I had always wanted to try my hand at it. After the war, traveling in Mexico, I put away my sketch book, got a scratch pad, and started on a book. The result was *The Brave Bulls* published in April 1949. From January 1950 to February 1952 I worked on a novel about the Texas-Mexico border around El Paso in the 1880's which was published under the title *The Wonderful Country.* That's my published work, to date. I've never done any magazine stories with the exception of a couple in the *Southwest Review* and the *Atlantic Monthly.* I usually make drawings to go with my text. At present I am working on a long book of non-fiction, the history of the King Ranch in south Texas. It will also have some drawings. I live in a house on the slope of the mountain overlooking El Paso and the Rio Grande valley with Mexico on the other side. My studio is built in my backyard. I am married and my son Jim is too."

* * *

A latecomer to literature, Tom Lea has had both critical and popular acclaim. His *The Brave Bulls* holds its place beside Hemingway's *Death in the Afternoon* for its vivid picture of bull fighting in Mexico.

PRINCIPAL WORKS: The Brave Bulls, 1949; The Wonderful Country, 1952.

ABOUT: Saturday Review of Literature April 23, 1949, February 11, 1950, November 15, 1952; Time October 16, 1950.

LEACOCK, STEPHEN BUTLER (December 30, 1869-March 28, 1944). For autobiographical sketch and list of earlier works and references, see TWENTIETH CENTURY AUTHORS, 1942.

* * *

Stephen Leacock died in the General Hospital at Toronto, Canada, following a throat operation. He was seventy-four. The first four chapters of an autobiography on which he was working at the time of his death were published posthumously.

A. P. Herbert called Leacock "the greatest humorist of the age." Of his dual career as humorist and economist the London *Times* said: "To Leacock it was given to have always a cap and gown in his cupboard as well as a cap and bells. He frequently contrived to wear both costumes at once, with original and striking effect."

ADDITIONAL WORKS: Canada: the Foundations of Its Future, 1941; Montreal: Seaport and City, 1942; Happy Stories Just to Laugh At, 1943; How to Write, 1943; Last Leaves (essays) 1945; While There is Time: The Case Against Social Catastrophe, 1945; Leacock Roundabout, 1946; The Boy I Left Behind Me, 1946.

ABOUT: Leacock, S. B. The Boy I Left Behind Me; Phelps, A. L. Canadian Writers; Catholic World June 1944; London Times March 30, 1944; New York Times March 29, 1944; Queen's Quarterly Summer 1946; Time April 10, 1944.

LEAF, MUNRO ("John Calvert") (December 4, 1905-). For autobiographical sketch and list of earlier works and references, see TWENTIETH CENTURY AUTHORS, 1942.

* * *

Munro Leaf writes from Old Greenwich, Conn.: "Enlisted in Army April 1942 as lieutenant and left in January 1946 as major, having served in U.S. and European Theatre.

"While in Army (not in line of duty) wrote a very unorthodox and funny but effective field manual on malaria called *This Is Ann* (short for anopheles mosquito). This was used by Army, Navy, Merchant Marine, and Australians.

"Aside from children's books have done some writing of pamphlets in support of Marshall Plan and Committee on the Present Danger. Other 'adult' performance—collaboration with Dr. William C. Menninger on *You and Psychiatry.* Children's books *Let's Do Better* and *Fair Play* widely translated for use in Point Four Program by State Department.

"Thoroughly enjoy writing and being my own boss."

ADDITIONAL WORKS: Health Can Be Fun, 1943; Gordon the Goat, 1944; 3 and 30 Watchbirds, 1944; Let's Do Better, 1945; How to Behave and Why, 1946; Gwendolyn the Goose (by "John Calvert") 1946; Sam and the Superdroop, 1948; Boo, Who Used to Be Scared of the Dark, 1948; You and Psychiatry (with W. C. Menninger) 1948; Arithmetic Can Be Fun, 1949; History Can Be Fun, 1950; Geography Can Be Fun, 1951; Reading Can Be Fun, 1953.

ABOUT: Kunitz, S. J. & Haycraft, H. Junior Book of Authors (rev. ed.); New York Herald Tribune Book Review November 13, 1949.

LEAF, WALTER (November 28, 1852-March 8, 1927). For biographical sketch and list of works and references, see TWENTIETH CENTURY AUTHORS, 1942.

LEAVIS, FRANK RAYMOND (July 14, 1895-), English critic and teacher (who publishes as F. R. Leavis), was born in England in 1895. He began his formal education at the Perse School, and completed it at Emmanuel College, Cambridge, where, as a scholar, he took both the Historical and English Tripos, and received his Ph.D. In 1932 he founded the literary review *Scrutiny*, which he edited until it ceased publication in 1953. Since 1936, he has been a Fellow of Downing College, Cambridge, and University Lecturer in English.

Leavis combines close textual criticism with predominantly moral, or social-moral, principles of evaluation. His analyses and judgments of English poetry are for the most part contained in two books, *New Bearings in English Poetry*—which concentrates on the work of T. S. Eliot, Pound, and Hopkins—and *Revaluation: Tradition and Development in English Poetry*. In the introduction to the latter, Leavis writes that both books were conceived and planned at the same time, for, he says, "An account of the present of poetry, to be worth anything, must be from a clearly realized point of view, and such a point of view, if it is critically responsible, must have been determined and defined as much in relation to the past as to the present." The earlier book the *Saturday Review of Literature* called "a book without fear, the best book of sheer criticism of verse . . . since the lifetime of Coleridge"; and in the *Spectator*, Richard Church said that Leavis was "passionately sincere in his devotion to the cause of keeping literature abreast of the metamorphoses of life."

The Great Tradition: George Eliot, James and Conrad contains Leavis' views on the novel. He includes Jane Austen at one end of the tradition, with D. H. Lawrence at the other. A novel, for Leavis, must justify itself as art "in the realized concreteness that speaks for itself and *enacts* its moral significance." Conrad, he says, "is a greater novelist than Flaubert because of the greater range and depth of his interest in humanity and the greater intensity of his moral preoccupation." He is certain that "Dickens was a great genius and is permanently among the classics . . . but the genius was that of a great entertainer, and he had for the most part no profounder responsibility as a creative artist than this description suggests."

As an educator, Leavis says that the study of English literature can and should be a central discipline for university students. In 1943 he published *Education and the University* (which also includes his early essay, "Mass Civilization and Minority Culture"). Eric Bentley, who has edited a collection of *Scrutiny* articles and reviews, summarizes Dr. Leavis' thesis in these terms: "Learning to read well would be a discipline, a discipline of what Gourmont . . . called the sensibility, that is, a discipline of the intellect and feeling taken—as they must be taken, in the arts —together."

In reviewing *The Great Tradition* for the *New Yorker*, Lionel Trilling said, "Mr. Leavis's moral feeling . . . is everywhere to be found as a shaping and strengthening element in his criticism. . . . We have the energy of his protestantism, which has made him so notable and stormy a figure in English letters —a man of disciples and enemies, the teacher who has made the relatively new and obscure Downing College a dissident center of English studies at Cambridge. . . ; the educational reformer who has made a frontal attack on the academic methods of literary instruction; the editor who, in his quarterly review, *Scrutiny*, has fostered a critical movement of considerable power at the same time that he himself has developed into one of the most formidable of modern critics."

In 1929 Leavis married Queenie Dorothy Roth (also a critic of note). The Leavises live at Cambridge, with their two sons and one daughter.

PRINCIPAL WORKS: Mass Civilization and Minority Culture, 1930; D. H. Lawrence, 1930; New Bearings in English Poetry, 1932; For Continuity, 1933; Culture and Environment (with D. Thompson) 1933; Revaluation: Tradition and Development in English Poetry, 1936; Education and the University, 1943; The Great Tradition: George Eliot, James and Conrad, 1948; The Common Pursuit, 1952. *Editor*— Towards Standards of Criticism, 1933; Determinations, 1934; Mill on Bentham and Coleridge, 1950.

ABOUT: Bentley, E. *Introduction to* The Importance of Scrutiny; Hyman, S. E. The Armed Vision; New Yorker September 24, 1949; Virginia Quarterly Review July 1948

LEBLANC, MAURICE (1864-November 6, 1941). For biographical sketch and list of works and references, see TWENTIETH CENTURY AUTHORS, 1942.

*LE CORBUSIER (or, JEANNERET-GRIS, CHARLES-EDOUARD) (October 6, 1887-), Swiss architect, artist, and  author, was born in La Chaux-de-Fonds, in the French-speaking part of Switzerland, the son of Georges-Édouard Jeanneret, a watchmaker, and Marie-Charlotte Amélie Perret. To learn his father's trade, he studied at a school of arts and crafts at La Chaux-de-Fonds between 1900 and 1904. At the age of eighteen he supervised a group of fifteen students entrusted with building a house for their professor; Le Corbusier has claimed it had the first corner windows used on the Continent. He then traveled in Italy studying early medieval art and in 1908 entered the studio of Joseph Hoffman in Vienna, but did not like the Viennese Secession style and departed for Paris. There Auguste Perret, a pioneer in ferroconcrete construction, accepted him as an apprentice. Two years later he went to Berlin to study industrial art, and to Asia Minor, Greece, and Rome, on a tour financed by the school at La Chaux-de-Fonds. On his return to Switzerland in 1911, Le Corbusier constructed a house for his father. After three years as an interior designer in Switzerland, Le Corbusier went to Paris and, being unable to find work as an architect, became a factory manager. In 1916 he designed another house in his home town which became famous for its fluid, open use of space and plan. During World War I he studied civic planning; and after the war (1919) helped found the review *L'Esprit Nouveau*, which continued publication until 1925.

In 1921 Le Corbusier became a full-time architect, due to the failure of the factory in which he was employed. At the same time he adopted his maternal grandfather's name, Le Corbusier, as his architectural pseudonym, reserving the name Jeanneret for his paintings. He formed a partnership with his cousin, Pierre Jeanneret, and within the next few years they built many houses. Some of Le Corbusier's famous designs are those for the

* lĕ kôr bü zyā'

Palace of the League of Nations (1927), for Moscow buildings (1928-31), and for the City of Refuge for the Salvation Army in Paris (1930-31). Both the French and Russians criticized his "profligate" use of glass, till it was proved he was right about its practicality. Housing 1600 people, the Le Corbusier housing project in Marseilles was named by him the "Radiant City." The apartments are neat, and only one room in each has windows. A leading opponent, once a Le Corbusier enthusiast, said the government could have built two comfortable houses with windows on all sides and the privacy of one's own separate house, for the cost of every apartment in the "radiant city." "I like the Marseillais," answered Le Corbusier. "They yell a lot. . . . Why do you want sunshine in the bathroom when you are in it only in the morning and at night. It will be the coolest building in Marseilles." The architect, said Joseph A. Barry in the New York *Times,* "works out his architectural conception of the good life from his Paris atelier in a former Jesuit convent . . . , in a cell with no windows." An American who had lived in one of the architect's private homes in 1923 recently described its designer as "a functionalist who seems to function differently from the rest of us."

His architectural theories were published in *Toward a New Architecture* (1923; in English, 1927). A house, he said, should be "a machine to live in." He is an exponent of efficient urbanized existence lived in vertical skyscrapers constructed on geometric rather than organic principles—a purely intellectual concept which is modified by his insistence on "sun, space, and silence." He was consultant on projects for housing in Algiers, Antwerp, Barcelona, and Stockholm. He worked in South America also, where several republics retained him to plan their cities. In 1935 he visited the United States and deplored the absence of landscaped parks around the skyscrapers. Since 1950 Le Corbusier has spent much time in India, where he designed an entire city—Chandigarh, the capital of the East Punjab, a state newly formed by the partition of India in 1947.

Le Corbusier has a high forehead, writes the *New Yorker,* "an egg-shaped head, and he likes dark suits and blue shirts. When he reads, writes, paints, or works on architectural plans, he wears heavy-framed spectacles that make him look like an owl." He divides his day into three parts, the morning for painting, the afternoon for architecture, and the evening for writing. He has had more than ten books published. In 1930 he married Yvonne Jeanne Victorine Gallis, and now lives in Paris. The lack of understanding shown his work by French municipal authorities for several years caused him to refuse a proffered ribbon of a chevalier of the Legion of Honor, but he is now an officer of the Legion of Honor. In 1945 the French Ministry of Reconstruction appointed him technical consultant to the supreme council of city planning, and he planned the rebuilding of various areas. He has received many honors including an honorary doctor's degree from the University of Zurich.

PRINCIPAL WORKS IN ENGLISH TRANSLATION: Toward a New Architecture, 1927; The City of Tomorrow and Its Planning, 1929; Aircraft, 1935; Le Corbusier et Pierre Jeanneret 1910-1929, 1937; Concerning Town Planning, 1947; UN Headquarters, 1947; When the Cathedrals Were White, 1947; Home of Man (co-author) 1948; New World of Space, 1948; Four Routes, 1948; Le Corbusier, Architect, Painter, Writer, 1948; The Marseilles Block, 1953; Oeuvre Complète 1946-52 (text in English, French, German) 1953.

ABOUT: Bardi, P. M. Critical Review of Le Corbusier; Le Corbusier, Le Corbusier, Architect, Painter, Writer; Architectural Review January 1947; Current Biography 1947; New York Times June 4, 1950; New Yorker April 26, May 3, 1947, April 30, 1955; Nineteenth Century March 7, 1948; Royal Architectural Institute of Canada Journal May 1953; Royal Institute of British Architects Journal February 1953, April 1953; School Arts January 1946.

LEDWIDGE, FRANCIS (June 19, 1891-July 31, 1917). For biographical sketch and list of works and references, see TWENTIETH CENTURY AUTHORS, 1942.

* * *

ABOUT: Fortnightly December 1945.

LEE, MANFRED. See QUEEN, E.

LEE, Sir SIDNEY (December 5, 1859-March 3, 1926). For biographical sketch and list of works and references, see TWENTIETH CENTURY AUTHORS, 1942.

"LEE, VERNON." See PAGET, V.

LEECH, MARGARET (November 7, 1893-), American author, was born in Newburgh, N.Y., the daughter of William Kernochan Leech and Rebecca (Taggart) Leech. After graduating from Vassar in 1915, she took a job with Condé Nast, "writing trouble-shooter letters to *Vogue* subscribers whose copies had not arrived." During World War I she worked for a number of fund-raising organizations, including Anne

Morgan's American Committee for Devastated France, and eventually joined its staff and went abroad. While in Europe she wrote articles for American newspapers and magazines.

Returning to the United States in the early Twenties, Miss Leech wrote two novels, *The Back of the Book* and *Tin Wedding*. In 1927 she collaborated with Heywood Broun on a biography of *Anthony Comstock, Roundsman of the Lord,* which became the first choice of the Literary Guild. Each author signed the chapters separately. *The Feathered Nest,* a novel, presented a further aspect of American family life. "Psychologically the book is sound. As fiction, however, the theme cannot be anything but unpleasant," wrote the *New Republic.* The theme concerned a rich, idle mother who was determined to keep her hold upon her sons at any cost.

After writing a play with Beatrice Kaufman, *Divided by Three,* produced in the fall of 1934, Miss Leech began working on the book that brought her most critical acclaim: *Reveille in Washington 1860-1865.* Using the New York Public Library, and to a lesser extent the Library of Congress and other Washington libraries, the author alternated periods of research with periods of writing, studied photographs, and read hundreds of old newspapers, memoirs, letters, and government reports. After more than five years of arduous labor, *Reveille in Washington* appeared in 1941, a picture of life in the city of Washington during the Civil War years—the people, the places, and the events. The whole panorama of Washington society and military organization is sketched on a broad and detailed canvas. Clifton Fadiman declared that the work placed Miss Leech "at once among the eminent historians of America," though the *Yale Review* felt the book was not documented properly for an historical work. However, most critics found it "lively and picturesque," with a "brilliance in scene, and universality in insight." A best seller, it was chosen for the Book-of-the-Month in September 1941, and received the Pulitzer prize of 1942 for the most outstanding work in the field of historical writing.

In 1928 Miss Leech married Ralph Pulitzer, son of the founder of the Pulitzer prizes; her husband died in 1939. They had one daughter. Robert van Gelder has described

Margaret Leech as "a tall, attractive woman, very pleasant in talk." She now lives in New York City.

PRINCIPAL WORKS: The Back of the Book, 1924; Tin Wedding, 1926; Anthony Comstock, Roundsman of the Lord (with Heywood Broun) 1927; The Feathered Nest, 1928; Reveille in Washington, 1941.

ABOUT: Van Gelder, R. Writers and Writing; Harper's March 1942; New York Post September 5, 1941; New York Times May 5, 1942; New York Times Book Review September 14, 1941; Saturday Review of Literature August 30, 1941, May 9, 1942; Wilson Library Bulletin October 1941.

LE GALLIENNE, RICHARD (January 20, 1866-September 15, 1947). For biographical sketch and list of works and references, see TWENTIETH CENTURY AUTHORS, 1942.

* * *

Richard Le Gallienne died in his sleep, at eighty-one, in his villa at Mentone in the south of France. Living in Paris at the time of the German occupation, he fled to southern France, and little was heard of him until, in 1945, word was received that he and his wife were safe and well at Monte Carlo.

The London Times has noted that he "had an authentic talent, and much of his verse was graceful, shapely, and keenly felt, yet he was capable, on occasion, of departures from good taste and infelicity of expression." The Times adds that he was "an accomplished and versatile critic and essayist, yet on the whole his prose was the prose of a decadent period, and over-florid. Yet when all this is said, Le Gallienne will be long remembered for his melodious versification, his very considerable imaginative penetration, and his knowledge of what was good in letters."

ABOUT: London Times September 16, 1947; New York Times September 16, 1947; Time September 22, 1947.

*LÉGER, ALEXIS ST. LÉGER ("St.-J. Perse") (May 31, 1887-). For biographical sketch and list of earlier works and references, see TWENTIETH CENTURY AUTHORS, 1942.

* * *

The first poem written by Léger in America, Exil, appeared in Poetry in 1942. It was his first published work since Anabase in 1924. All of his unpublished writings in the years 1924 to 1942 were stolen and destroyed by the Nazis during their occupation of Paris. Since 1940 Léger has lived in Washington, D.C. where he came, at Archi-

* lă zhä′

bald MacLeish's invitation, to work at the Library of Congress. He remains in Washington as a private citizen. (Ralph Thompson wrote in the New York Times Book Review that he is "almost certainly the most admired French poet-in-residence since the days of Ambassador Paul Claudel.") His French citizenship was revoked during the Pétain regime, but in 1945, with the re-establishment of the French government, his rights and privileges were restored.

In 1944 the French text and the English translation of his Eloges were published in the United States, and five years later his Exil (text and translation) appeared in the Bollingen Series, followed by Vents (Winds) in the same series in 1953. A new long poem, Amers, was published in the Nouvelle Revue Française in 1954. Living as an alien in a foreign land, Léger has nevertheless found his place in America. He is still highly honored in his native land, but he has actually bridged the gap between his land and other lands, his language and other languages. He writes in French. He has said: "Even if I were not an essentially French animal, of essentially French clay (and my last breath, like the first, will be chemically French), the French language would still be my only imaginable home." The voice of his poetry, as Katherine Garrison Chapin observed in the Sewanee Review, is French and can be fully appreciated "only by ears attuned to French." But, she continues, "its breadth and power extend beyond the frontiers of language. It is outside of time and space, having neither region nor era." His influence spreads far beyond national boundaries. In 1950 an issue of the French quarterly Les Cahiers de la Pléiade was dedicated to him, and it contained articles of tribute by poets and critics of many nationalities— French, English, Spanish, German, Italian, Swiss. Among the contributing authors were André Gide, Paul Claudel, T. S. Eliot, Stephen Spender, Archibald MacLeish, and Allen Tate.

In Léger the man, as in his poetry, Allen Tate, who first met him in 1943, found "a self-mastery which directs, controls, and illuminates." Writing of Vents, Tate said that it would take its place "as a landmark in modern poetry in any language." He continued: "The beautiful symmetry of the form, the precision of image, and the presence of a cold and passionate intelligence, combine in a quality of insight which is not of the provincial rationalism of our time. It reaffirms the greater tradition of the tragic consciousness."

ADDITIONAL WORKS IN ENGLISH TRANSLATION: Eloges, 1944; Exile, 1949; Winds, 1953.

ABOUT: Cahiers de la Pléiade Autumn 1950; Columbia Dictionary of Modern European Literature; Dictionnaire Biographique Français Contemporain; MacLeish, A. and others in Léger, A. Exile; Nation May 13, 1944; New Republic September 4, 1944; New York Times Book Review July 17, 1949; Poetry September 1949, January 1950, October 1951; Saturday Review of Literature July 16, 1949; Sewanee Review April 1945, January 1952; Time September 6, 1943.

*LEGOUIS, ÉMILE HYACINTHE (October 31, 1861-October 16, 1937). For biographical sketch and list of works and references, see TWENTIETH CENTURY AUTHORS, 1942.

* lē gwē′

LEHMANN, JOHN (June 2, 1907-). For autobiographical sketch and list of earlier works and references, see TWENTIETH CENTURY AUTHORS, 1942.

* * *

John Lehmann writes from London: "In 1946 John Lehmann left the Hogarth Press and founded the publishing firm of John Lehmann Limited, with his sister Rosamond Lehmann as co-director. *Penguin New Writing*, the paper-back successor to the original *New Writing*, after phenomenal wartime sales, ceased publication in 1950. Mr. Lehmann started in 1952 a literary radio-magazine on the B.B.C. Third Programme, called 'New Soundings,' the first of its kind. He is a member of the poetry panel of the British Arts Council, of the publications panel of the British Council, and a Fellow of the Royal Society of Literature."

John Lehmann's various editions of selections from *New Writing* have introduced readers to some of the best of contemporary writing. *New Writing*, as the late Demetrios Capetanakis pointed out, never cultivated the eccentric, the "novelty for novelty's sake" element in the arts. Of its contributors Capetanakis wrote: "Writing was a most serious matter to them. The 'new' they asked from literature was not novelty, but a healthier, more human world."

Early in 1953, owing to difference of opinion over future policy, Lehmann left the publishing firm of John Lehmann Limited. He had been unsuccessful in an effort to buy out the printers who owned the controlling interest in the firm. In 1954 he began publishing a new literary monthly, *The London Magazine*. Sections from his autobiography have appeared in *New World Writing*.

ADDITIONAL WORKS: Forty Poems, 1942; The Sphere of Glass, 1944; Shelley in Italy (ed.) 1947; Poems from New Writing (ed.) 1946; French Stories from New Writing (ed.) 1947; The Age of the Dragon, 1951; English Stories from New Writing (ed.) 1951; The Open Night, 1952; Edith Sitwell, 1952; Pleasures of New Writing (ed.) 1952.

ABOUT: Capetanakis, D. Shores of Darkness; New World Writing, No. 5 (1954), No. 7 (1955); Publishers' Weekly January 17, 1953.

LEHMANN, ROSAMOND (1903-). For biographical sketch and list of earlier works and references, see TWENTIETH CENTURY AUTHORS, 1942.

* * *

Rosamond Lehmann has fulfilled the promise she showed so markedly at twenty-four with her first novel, *Dusty Answer*. Her talent is a quiet but substantial one. With *The Ballad and the Source* in 1944, a finely-wrought story of a dominant old lady as seen through the eyes of an adolescent girl, she wrote what Richard Watts in the *New Republic* hailed as "a beautiful, impressive and strangely moving romantic novel by one of the most important writing talents of our time." Other critics qualified their endorsement of the novel by pointing out that it was a tour de force, lacking in "moral passion" (Diana Trilling's phrase), marred by what the London *Times Literary Supplement* called "artificial imaginative texture." But they were agreed that it was a novel of real distinction. There was similar agreement on her later books, the short stories collected in *The Gipsy's Baby* and the novel *The Echoing Grove*. Miss Lehmann herself is perhaps the fairest critic of her own work. In an interview in 1953 she described her writing method as a "half-trance," in which she covers page after page. She is, she says, "a kind of preserving jar in which float fragments of people and landscapes, snatches of sound [but] there is not one of these fragile shapes and serial sounds but bears within it the explosive seed of life."

ADDITIONAL WORKS: The Ballad and the Source, 1944; The Gipsy's Baby, and Other Stories, 1946; The Echoing Grove, 1953.

ABOUT: Bowen, E. Collected Impressions; New York Herald Tribune Book Review June 14, 1953.

LEHMANN, RUDOLPH CHAMBERS (January 3, 1856-January 22, 1929). For biographical sketch and list of works and references, see TWENTIETH CENTURY AUTHORS, 1942.

LEIGHTON, CLARE VERONICA HOPE (1900-). For biographical references, see TWENTIETH CENTURY sketch and list of earlier works and AUTHORS, 1942.

* * *

Clare Leighton has lived in the United States since 1939. In 1950 she was elected to membership in the National Institute of Arts and Letters. Her home is in Woodbury, Conn. Much of her recent writing and illustrating has been concerned with the American scene. Her book on the American South, *Southern Harvest*, revealed not only the literary and pictorial artist but, as Katherine Woods pointed out in the New York *Times*, "an artist in awareness," sensitive to "the common quality of man's earth-sustained living." Her "chalk and prose poem" to rural America in *Give Us This Day* was an equally felicitous tribute to her adopted country. "It is impelled," wrote George R. Stewart, "by an intense sincerity and a profound and all-embracing love of humanity, of the beasts of the field, and even of the field itself." In quite another vein, Miss Leighton has written a candid portrait of her mother, writer of thrillers for the London *Daily Mail*, and the lively Edwardian age in which she lived—*Tempestuous Petticoat*.

ADDITIONAL WORKS: Southern Harvest, 1942; Give Us This Day, 1943; Tempestuous Petticoat: Story of an Invincible Edwardian, 1947; Where Land Meets Sea, 1954.

ABOUT: American Artist February 1955; Christian Science Monitor Magazine October 21, 1950.

*LEMAÎTRE, JULES (August 27, 1853-August 5, 1914). For biographical sketch and list of works and references, see TWENTIETH CENTURY AUTHORS, 1942.

* * *

ABOUT: Columbia Dictionary of Modern European Literature.

* lĕ mâ'tr'

*LEMARCHAND, JACQUES (1908-), French novelist, was born in Bordeaux. After studying in the religious schools of that city, he spent some time in Morocco in the uniform of the Zouaves. Returning to his native city Lemarchand tried his hand successively at medicine, law, and letters, but found no real satisfaction in any of these. Restless, he went to Paris, where he tried different professions—teaching, writing fiction, tutoring—to support himself. He was in the army from 1939 to 1940. Demobilized in 1940, he remained idle until 1944 when he

* lĕ màr shän'

became drama critic for the paper *Combat*. He has continued to write drama criticism and he is now affiliated with the publishing house of Editions Gallimard for which he does editorial work.

Lemarchand began his professional writing career in 1935 with a novel, *R.N. 234*, and he published another novel, *Conte de Noël*, in 1938. It is his post-war work, however, the novels *Parenthèse* and *Geneviève*, which have won him a following not only in France but in England and the United States as well. Lemarchand does not seek a popular audience. His work is arch, brittle, sophisticated. *Parenthèse*, or *Parenthesis*, the story of a young man's visit to the provincial town where he had grown up, was a brief, seemingly casual novel, told in spare, economical detail. One reviewer felt that it could not properly be called a novel, but rather "a clever exercise M. Lemarchand has done to show how supple his fingers are." The novel was something of a "comedy of manners," and while it had much of the sparkle of that form, it also reflected some of the harsh, cold cynicism and mockery of it too. Thus Charles Poore, in the New York *Times*, found it marred by "unfortunate preciosity, born of pushing his cleverness too far."

Similarly, his novel *Geneviève* was found too precisely analytical to be really effective. This story of a romantic triangle, wrote the London *Times Literary Supplement*, "is done with nice intelligence but is too slight of substance to leave any very satisfying impression."

PRINCIPAL WORKS IN ENGLISH TRANSLATION: Genevieve, 1947; Parenthesis, 1947.

*LENGYEL, EMIL (April 26, 1895-). For autobiographical sketch and list of earlier works and references, see TWENTIETH CENTURY AUTHORS, 1942.

* * *

Emil Lengyel writes: "During the war I lectured in United States army camps as a civilian lecturer. When American forces entered Berlin in 1945 they found a list of some three thousand persons whom the Nazis were to take into custody after the invasion of England. The list was headed by Winston Churchill, and one of the few non-Britishers

* lĕn'gyĕl

on the list was I, who evidently had incurred the Nazis' wrath by my biography of Hitler.

"After the war I spent several summers in the Middle East, writing feature stories for the Toronto *Star Weekly*. I rose through the ranks at the School of Education, New York University, promoted assistant professor, then associate professor, and finally professor of education. I also offered courses at the New School for Social Research, while lecturing all over the country."

Lengyel's long and detailed history of Siberia, published in 1943, was considered a valuable contribution to our knowledge of the region. It was translated into half a dozen foreign languages. He prepared a high school textbook, *America's Role in World Affairs*, for Harper's American Way Series, and a study of the contributions Hungarians have made to American life, *Americans from Hungary*, for Lippincott's Nations of America Series. Lengyel has written short volumes on Eastern Europe and Israel for the Foreign Policy Association's Headline Books. His latest work is a full length study of the Middle East, *World Without End*.

ADDITIONAL WORKS: Siberia, 1943; America's Role in World Affairs, 1946; Americans from Hungary, 1948; Eastern Europe Today, 1949; Israel: Problems of Nation Building, 1951; World Without End, 1953.

ABOUT: Current Biography 1942.

*LENORMAND, HENRI-RENÉ (May 3, 1882-February 17, 1951). For biographical sketch and list of earlier works and references, see TWENTIETH CENTURY AUTHORS, 1942.

* * *

Henri-René Lenormand died at his home in Paris at the age of sixty-eight.

Prolific as a playwright, and author of stories and poems, Lenormand's first novel appeared just before his death. Published in the United States under the title *Renée*, it was well received by the critics. Lenormand "ranks high among the dramatists of psychological refinement," according to the London *Times*. Ben Ray Redmond said: "He knew how to create characters, how to build scenes, how to sustain interest and communicate excitement. He was a master of dialogue. He had the gift of brilliant brevity."

ADDITIONAL WORKS IN ENGLISH TRANSLATION: Renée, 1951; Rising, 1952.

ABOUT: France Illustration March 3, 1951; London Times February 19, 1951; New York Times February 17, 1951.

* lê nôr män'

LEONARD, WILLIAM ELLERY (January 25, 1876-May 2, 1944). For biographical sketch and list of earlier works and references, see TWENTIETH CENTURY AUTHORS, 1942.

* * *

William Ellery Leonard died of a heart attack, at sixty-eight, at his home in Madison, Wis. A year after his death a new volume of his poems was published—*Man Against Time, An Heroic Dream*, having for its theme the love of an aging husband for a younger wife.

His last published poem was, as were many of his creative works, autobiographical; Ruth Lechlitner found it "interesting not for its form but for its genuine emotion frankly and revealingly expressed." William Rose Benét wrote of Leonard: "Obviously the man was a scholar; but he was above all one of the most outspoken and moving poets of our time; hater of all forms of injustice and human tyranny . . . a modern poet with a social conscience as burning as that of Shelley. He wrote fearless and beautiful poetry. That should be said of him; and all the trumpery sensationalism should be swept away. He was a champion of mankind."

ADDITIONAL WORK: Man Against Time, An Heroic Dream (poem) 1945.

ABOUT: Gregory, H. & Zaturenska, M. History of American Poetry; National Cyclopedia of American Biography (1947); New York Times May 3, 1944; Poetry February 1946; Saturday Review of Literature May 13, July 8, 1944.

*LEONOV, LEONID MAKSIMOVICH (June 1, 1899-). For autobiographical sketch and list of earlier works and references, see TWENTIETH CENTURY AUTHORS, 1942.

* * *

Leonid Leonov is one of the most highly honored of Soviet writers. A member of the Praesidium of the Union of Soviet Writers, he has twice received the Stalin prize for literature. Outside the Soviet Union, his work is also known and admired—though nothing by him has appeared in English translation since soon after the end of World War II. A loyal Communist who cleaves to the party line, he nevertheless avoids the writing of mere propaganda. Edmund Wilson said of him in 1944: "Leonov has a novelist's interest in the crude mixed materials of life and a literary sophistication very rare in Soviet fiction." In his best work Leonov portrays the underdogs of life, the "humiliated and injured," with insight and

* lyĭ ô'nôf

compassion. "This compassionate note . . . allies Leonov with Dostoevsky," Gleb Struve writes, "and makes him fit in well with the main tradition of Russian literature." Samuel H. Cross points out, however, in the *Columbia Dictionary of Modern European Literature*, that where Dostoevsky's basic philosophy was one of "salvation through suffering," Leonov "pursues a more materialistic and infallible solution." Leonov lives in Moscow.

ADDITIONAL WORKS IN ENGLISH TRANSLATION: (with A. Korneichuk & K. Simonov) Four Soviet War Plays, 1944; The Road to the Ocean, 1944; Chariot of Wrath, 1946; The Badgers, 1947.

ABOUT: Columbia Dictionary of Modern European Literature; Hackett, F. On Judging Books; Struve, G. Soviet Russian Literature 1917-1950; Wilson, E. Classics and Commercials; Atlantic Monthly March & May 1947.

LERNER, MAX (December 20, 1902-   ). For autobiographical sketch and list of earlier works and references, see TWENTIETH CENTURY AUTHORS, 1942.

* * *

Max Lerner writes from New York City: "In the decade 1942-52 I continued my work in both journalism and academic life. I left Williams College in 1943 and worked for six years as editorial writer for the now defunct newspaper *PM* and later the equally defunct New York *Daily Star*, on which I wrote a column. Since 1949 I have been writing a four-a-week for the New York *Post*. Two volumes containing selected columns have appeared—*Public Journal* (1945) and *Actions and Passions* (1949). In addition, I have taught a course regularly at the New School for Social Research since 1944. And I am at present professor of American Civilization at Brandeis University, Waltham, Mass. My recent books in the academic field are *The Mind and Faith of Justice Holmes*, and *The Portable Veblen*; also editions of Machiavelli's *Prince* and *Discourses* and Aristotle's *Politics*, and Adam Smith's *Wealth of Nations* in the Modern Library. I am at present completing a rather ambitious and comprehensive analysis of contemporary civilization to be called 'America as a Civilization.' I am an enrolled member of the Democratic Party and have voted Democratic at each presidential election since 1928. But my basic interests are not with political organization but with ideas."

ADDITIONAL WORKS: Public Journal, 1945; Aristotle's Politics (ed.) 1943; The Mind and Faith of Justice Holmes (ed.) 1943; The Portable Veblen (ed.) 1948; Actions and Passions: Notes on the Multiple Revolution of Our Times, 1949.

ABOUT: Current Biography 1942; New Republic April 16, 1945.

*LEROUX, GASTON (1868-April 16, 1927). For biographical sketch and list of works and references, see TWENTIETH CENTURY AUTHORS, 1942.

* lĕ rōō'

LESLIE, Mrs. DORIS (OPPENHEIM). For autobiographical sketch and list of earlier works and references, see TWENTIETH CENTURY AUTHORS, 1942.

* * *

Doris Leslie's most successful recent work has been in the field of fictional biography. She has done books on Chopin (*Polonaise*), Lady Arabella Stuart (*A Wreath for Arabella*), Abigail Hill (*That Enchantress*), and George IV as Prince Regent (*The Great Corinthian*). "Light weight" biography, to use the London *Times Literary Supplement*'s phrase, these books make no pretense at being serious social history, but they have been highly praised for their lively and vivid portraits of the times and characters with which they deal. In *The Great Corinthian*, said the *Atlantic Monthly*'s reviewer, she "painted a vastly animated canvas of the period," writing "popular biography of the highest order. It is first-rate historical writing and choice entertainment, a stylish work whose scholarship is invested with color and movement and wit."

During World War II Doris Leslie was an air raid warden. She lists her recreations as chess and the rearing and exhibiting of prize bulldogs. In 1951 her husband, Dr. Walter Fergusson Hannay, was knighted.

ADDITIONAL WORKS: Polonaise, 1943; Folly's End, 1944; The Peverills, 1946; A Wreath for Arabella, 1948; That Enchantress, 1950; The Great Corinthian, 1952; A Toast to Lady Mary, 1954.

"LESLIE, HENRIETTA." See SCHÜTZE, G. H. R.

LESLIE, Sir SHANE (September 29, 1885-   ). For autobiographical sketch and list of earlier works and references, see TWENTIETH CENTURY AUTHORS, 1942.

* * *

Sir (John Randolph) Shane Leslie succeeded his father to the baronetcy in 1944. He lives at Castle Leslie in Glaslouch, Ireland, where he writes and pursues his favorite interests of archeology and forestry.

ADDITIONAL WORKS: The Irish Question for English Readers, 1946; Salutation to Five, 1951; Cardinal Gasquet, A Memoir, 1953; Lord Mulroy's Ghost: A Play for an Irish National Theatre, 1954.

ABOUT: Hoehn, M. (ed.) Catholic Authors, I.

LEVERSON, ADA (1865-1936), English

LEVERSON, ADA (1865-1936), English novelist, belonged to London's world of wealth and fashion, and was the friend of artists and writers, from Oscar Wilde to Osbert Sitwell. Her six novels, published between 1907 and 1916, belong to the Edwardian era; all six of them have been reissued in recent years (1950-51). "As a conversationalist Ada Leverson must have been enchanting," said John Mason Brown, reviewing the reissue of *The Limit* in the *Saturday Review of Literature*. "Her novel is a joy." She "whips the gossamer froth of her material into well turned bons mots, delightful barbs, and titillating feminine anguishes all in a perfection of good taste," wrote the Springfield *Republican* of this book.

The author married early, becoming Mrs. Ernest Leverson. Her only son died when he was a small boy. A daughter, Violet, is married to Guy Wyndham and lives in London. Two sisters of hers were Mrs. Sydney Schiff, whose husband wrote novels under the name Stephen Hudson, and Mrs. Vincent Seligman. The Schiffs were intimate friends of Marcel Proust, many of whose most interesting letters were addressed to them. Puccini wrote hundreds of letters to Mrs. Seligman which were recently published.

Osbert Sitwell has written a long reminiscence of Ada Leverson, a chapter in his *Noble Essences*. She had first met Wilde, she told Sitwell, "through an anonymous parody she had written of *Dorian Gray*. This skit had attracted his attention, and had amused him. He had written to the author, who had suggested a meeting, and when this took place Wilde had been amazed to find it was a woman who entered the room. Before long, she had become one of his intimate circle; he often dined with her and her husband at their house." She was of the few of Wilde's friends who stood by him through his trials, during his imprisonment, and after his release. At a time when she was contributing sketches and parodies to *Punch*, *The Yellow Book*, and other journals, he said, "You have all the equipment of a writer, my dear Sphinx, except pen, ink, and paper." Her first novel, *The Twelfth Hour*, was published years after his death. Wilde had once described her as "the wittiest woman in the world."

In her later years she spent much time abroad, particularly in Italy where she passed the winters in company with the Sitwells. In Osbert Sitwell's memoir of this time, he writes—she was then in her fifties—"She had grown distressingly deaf. . . . She usually wore now in the daytime a flowing black cloak, and a black hat with a rather wide brim, shading well her eyes which were blue and often suffused with smiles. Though the lines of her face were serious, her general and natural expression was a smile, not caused by any wish to mock, but by some absurdity she had detected in the world at large. . . . She was both self-possessed and timid. . . . Her conversation was artificial, in several senses elusive, chaotic and often captivatingly absurd. . . . One of the traits she showed, and which no doubt she retained from more lively days, was a certain impatience or arrogance. . . . She spent a large part of her time in reading—especially in the morning; mostly she read Flaubert and his contemporaries, and Proust, and many other French writers."

After returning to London from Florence, she was struck down by illness in the hotel in which she was staying. She died at seventy-one.

PRINCIPAL WORKS: The Twelfth Hour, 1907; Love's Shadow, 1908; The Limit, 1911; Tenterhooks, 1912; Bird of Paradise, 1914; Love at Second Sight, 1916.

ABOUT: Boulestin, M. Myself, My Two Countries; Pearson, H. Oscar Wilde; Sitwell, O. Noble Essences; Newsweek August 27, 1951; Saturday Review of Literature September 1, 1951; Time August 27, 1951.

*LEVI, CARLO (November 29, 1902-)

*LEVI, CARLO (November 29, 1902-), Italian novelist, political journalist, and painter, was born in the north Italian city of Turin. His father, Ercole Levi, was a merchant and amateur painter; his mother, Annetta Treves Levi, was the sister of a Socialist Party leader who opposed Mussolini.

At twenty Carlo Levi was already a serious, energetic, and versatile young man: a medical student at the University of Turin, he was also a painter, a contributor to a political review founded and edited by his close friend Piero Gobetti (who was later killed by the Fascists), and a member of the anti-Fascist underground. Although

* lä′vē

he received his M.D. in 1924 and then worked for a while as a medical research assistant at the University of Turin, he soon, in his own words, "abandoned the practice of medicine in order to devote himself to painting."

Levi was called up for a year's military service in 1925; by 1928 he was in Paris; and between 1929 and 1933, his paintings were successfully exhibited in a series of one-man shows held in Turin, Milan, Rome, Genoa, London, and Paris. As a painter, although his earliest canvases were neo-classic, he soon became a post-impressionist; his paintings are colorful landscapes and still-lifes.

In Paris Levi helped found the secret, anti-Fascist, Italian Action Party, and was a co-founder and director of the underground publication *Giustizia e Libertà* (Justice and Liberty). In 1933, after his return to Italy, he was arrested for anti-Fascist activity and rearrested in 1934, but both times he was released after a few months for lack of evidence. In 1935, however, he was again arrested—this time charged with opposition to Mussolini's projected invasion of Ethiopia—imprisoned in the Regina Coeli prison in Rome, and sentenced in August 1933 to a three-year term of exile in the isolated malaria-infested village of Gagliano in southern Italy.

Levi's famous book, *Christ Stopped at Eboli*, a book which he did not write until nine years later, is the story of his year of exile in the remote and primitive village of Gagliano. The title, wrote Levi in his introduction, came from the peasants who told him: "We're not Christians—Christ stopped short of here, at Eboli." The book was a best-seller both in America and in Italy, where it was first published in 1945 and where it won two prizes, one of which was the first Arianna Mondadori del Corriere Lombardo prize. In reviewing it, the American Catholic magazine *Commonweal* observed: "Carlo Levi loved these men and women and it is possible in reading his extraordinary and eloquent account to forget the dismal horror of their lives." So many of the half-starved peasants were dying of malaria that Levi began to practice medicine in Gagliano, and though he was officially ordered to stop, he nevertheless continued in secret. He served only one year of his three-year term of exile, for in the summer of 1936, after the fall of the Ethiopian capital of Addis Ababa, Mussolini proclaimed a general amnesty for political prisoners.

When World War II began in 1939, Levi was in France working on an essay which was later included as a chapter in *Paura della Libertà* (1946)—American title, *Of Fear and Freedom*. After the capture of Paris, he fled to Cannes; and shortly after Italy entered the war in 1941, he returned secretly to his native land; he was jailed for two months in Florence and then disappeared into the underground where he became a leader of the resistance movement in the province of Tuscany. Between December 1943 and July 1944 he wrote *Christ Stopped at Eboli.* In 1944 he undertook the editorship of the daily *Nazione del Popolo*, which was published in Florence as an organ of the National Liberation Committee. When hostilities ceased, he went to Rome as chief editor (1945-46) of *Italia Libera*, the Action Party daily paper.

Levi has published three books, of which *Christ Stopped at Eboli* has been by far the most popular. The *New Yorker*, reviewing *Of Fear and Freedom*, said: "Although it is divided into orderly chapters, headed 'Sacrifice,' 'Slavery,' 'Blood,' and so on, it is really a sustained metaphysical prose poem, sharply didactic and humming with thoughts, conceits, and twists in logic." *L'Orologia*, or *The Watch*, is set in Rome in the confused days immediately following the liberation. Although American reviewers found parts of this book remarkably vivid and enlightening —especially the street scenes—most of them agreed that it was somewhat diffuse in its panoramic scope, and not too clear in its evaluation of the Italian political scene.

In the spring of 1947, when *Christ Stopped at Eboli* was published in America, Levi traveled here for two and a half months under the sponsorship of the American Society for Cultural Relations with Italy, and while he was here an exhibit of his paintings was held at the Wildenstein Galleries in New York City.

Currently, Levi writes and draws regularly for many Italian newspapers and periodicals (*L'Italia Libera, L'Italia Socialista*, etc.). He lives in Rome where, in his own words, he has a studio on the top floor of a "magnificent old seventeenth century palace" from which he can see the whole city. He keeps a cat, a turtle, and a ping-pong table; and there is an owl, "Graziadio," which he has painted so often that it has almost become his signature. He has been called witty, jolly, and gallant; and he was described in the New York *Post* as "a stocky man of medium height with wild brown hair, civilized vital blue eyes and a quiet manner of expression."

PRINCIPAL WORKS IN ENGLISH TRANSLATION: Christ Stopped at Eboli, 1947; Of Fear and Freedom, 1950; The Watch, 1951.

About: Current Biography 1952; New Statesman and Nation May 8, 1948; New York Herald Tribune Book Review October 7, 1951; New York Post June 19, 1947; Saturday Review of Literature June 30, 1951.

*LEVIN, HARRY** (July 18, 1912-), American scholar and critic, writes: "Thus far I have been more of a reader than a writer,  a perennial student who continues his studies by calling himself a teacher. I am not ungrateful for the mild destiny that has allowed me to live by reading books, talking and occasionally writing about them. I can only trust that relative detachment from the painful distractions of our time finds some justification in long-range perspective.

"The circumstances of my birth and boyhood in Minneapolis, Minn., were comfortable and fairly typical. Since the age of sixteen, when I entered college, my life has been associated in one way or another with Harvard University. I studied under Kittredge, Lowes, and especially Babbitt; I had courses with Whitehead and, later, the inestimable privilege of his friendship; and when T. S. Eliot returned to his alma mater, he added personal kindness to the intellectual stimulus that his writings had already given my generation. After graduating in 1933, my *wanderjahr* was a first-hand introduction not only to Europe, which I had glimpsed before, but to the twentieth century, from which my bookishness had pretty well sheltered me. Since then my focal points have been the connection between literature and society and the continuity between past and present.

"My academic career has consisted of opportunities and responsibilities which have come so close to each other, it luckily seems, that I have had no occasion for ambitions or disgruntlements. As an early member of Harvard's Society of Fellows, I was allowed to do everything except take the doctorate; and as a would-be humanist, I was especially challenged by my scientific colleagues to demonstrate the method involved in my subject. In my teaching of English I started from Shakespeare and Elizabethan drama, to which I return as often as I can. But I am conscious of progressively moving toward the modern period, the novel, and France— where, for the present year [1952-53] I am visiting professor at the Sorbonne.

* lĕ vĭn'

"Perhaps because my father was born in Germany and brought to this country as a child, perhaps because my wife was born in Russia and emigrated from the other direction, Europe has always loomed large upon my horizon, and literary study has meant comparative literature. The authors whom I have tried most to follow are those who have done the most to develop the ranges and artistic techniques at their command—notably James Joyce, who prompted my little book about him by writing a friendly note to my publisher after I had been rash enough to review *Finnegans Wake*. My ultimate hope is for a kind of criticism which, while analyzing the formal and esthetic qualities of a work of art, will fit them into the cultural and social pattern to which it belongs."

Principal Works: The Broken Column: A Study in Romantic Hellenism, 1931; Ben Jonson: Selected Works (ed.), 1938; James Joyce: A Critical Introduction, 1941; Perspectives of Criticism (ed.), 1950; The Overreacher: A Study of Christopher Marlowe, 1952.

LEVIN, MEYER (October 8, 1905-). For autobiographical sketch and list of earlier works and references, see Twentieth Century Authors, 1942.

* * *

Meyer Levin writes: "To bring my biography up to date, I finally did get a job in Hollywood, one of those seven-year contracts at Columbia, but it came just before Pearl Harbor, and I couldn't see myself sitting in Hollywood during the war, so I quit at the first six-month option time and went to Washington. I was a writer-producer-director for O.W.I. films for about a year and a half, all the time trying to get abroad. Finally I quit the film section and entered the Psychological Warfare Division, was sent to London, and assigned to write about films for the captive populations of Europe. Later I became a front line reporter for P.W. and later I quit the unit to become a war correspondent for the Overseas News Agency, with the principal assignment of discovering the fate of the Jews of Europe. I brought out the first survivor lists from Buchenwald and other concentration camps. Shortly after the war I went to Palestine to cover the terrorist troubles and also to write and film the first full-scale Palestine feature, *My Father's House*. I produced it with Herbert Kline and also wrote it as a novel. A picture-book of the same story was called *If I Forget Thee*.

"Immediately upon completion of *My Father's House* I left for Europe and spent a year filming the underground exodus to Israel, from Warsaw to Haifa. This was something of an adventure, including several arrests, and stealing our negative out of Prague after the Communist coup. Also stealing some of it from the British when they arrested us aboard an illegal ship. However, the entire body of material was saved for history.

"In 1951 I produced a play of mine, *The Good Old Days*, in an American summer theatre venture in Paris. Since then I have been living in New York. I was divorced from Mabel Schamp Foy in 1944; I married Tereska Szwarc, daughter of a Paris sculptor, in 1948. Besides my first son, Jonathan, we have Tereska's daughter by her first marriage, Dominique, and our son, Gabriel."

ADDITIONAL WORKS: My Father's House, 1947; If I Forget Thee, 1947; In Search, 1950.

ABOUT: Levin, M. In Search.

LEVY, HYMAN (March 7, 1889-). For biographical sketch and list of earlier works and references, see TWENTIETH CENTURY AUTHORS, 1942.

* * *

Hyman Levy was made head of the department of mathematics and mechanics at the Imperial College of Science and Technology in London in 1946. From that year until 1952 he was also dean of the Royal College of Science. He writes mainly on mathematical and aeronautical subjects and contributes articles on science and scientific philosophy to a number of journals.

ADDITIONAL WORKS: Elementary Mathematics, 1942; Social Thinking, 1945; (with E. E. Preidel) Elementary Statistics, 1945; (with E. A. Baggott) Numerical Solutions of Differential Equations, 1950.

LEWIS, ALUN (July 1, 1915-March 1944), Welsh poet and short story writer, taught as a young man in a Welsh secondary

John Petts

school, and when World War II came, joined the British Army. In 1941 he was still stationed in England, but in 1942 was sent to India as a lieutenant. "Thinking back on my own writing," wrote Lewis in a letter published after his death, "it all seemed to mature of a sudden between the winter of 1939 and the following autumn." War and love, he said, were the crucial influences. He and his wife, Gweno Lewis, had been married before he left for India.

In 1942 two books were published, *Raiders' Dawn, and Other Poems* and *The Last Inspection*, a book of short stories. Both received favorable reviews. The *Spectator* wrote, "Of the younger poets Alun Lewis is outstanding. His poems are for the most part simple personal statements . . . not remarkable for great power or imagination, but they are often moving in their direction and sincerity, and the verse has a delightful musical, singing quality." Of the stories, the *Weekly Book Review* said, "To his book of short stories . . . he brings the poetic perception and language inherited from his native heath and the sympathetic observation of a man interested in the nuances of human relationships under war conditions."

A second collection of poems, *Ha! Ha! Among the Trumpets*, was published posthumously in 1945. As Robert Graves tells it in his introduction to the volume, Lewis sent him a manuscript of poems and asked him to read it "and decide for him how much should be included and whether any re-writing was needed. In doubtful cases his wife Gweno was to have the casting vote." Graves replied with suggestions, and Lewis wrote him just before he left for Burma, saying he had sent the finished manuscript to his publisher and thanking Graves for his ideas. "It's substantially as you advised," said Lewis, "but I've added some new poems also." In the same letter he referred to his service in the Far East: "Meanwhile I learn to fire a revolver with either hand and try to suppress the natural apprehension of the flesh at a thing so long delayed and postponed and promised and threatened." He spoke of the title of his new book: "I've taken a sardonic title for the poems from Job 39, *Ha! Ha! Among the Trumpets*." On its publication the *New Yorker* commented that the poems "project background and emotion with a rough vigor and a tragic tone, proving that Lewis was already in full command of his powers at the age of twenty-eight." He was killed in Arakan, Lower Burma, in March 1944.

In the Green Tree (1949) includes a selection of the letters, mostly from India, written to his family and six uncollected short stories. The stories show a remarkable achievement, while the letters serve as an interesting commentary on his life and work during this period. In one of the diaries returned with his effects, he writes: "I have kept abreast of the tide, I the inveterate writer, abreast of my other self, the busybody, in the long letters home and in the poems. The letters are *journaux intimes* coloured more than is legitimate with the warmth of the ego when it is speaking to one who, it knows, receives its words with love, and its values then are intenser than the tame proportioned values of the public figure. The poems are even more biased and bigoted. The poet in one sees only a little of it all. Sees what I do not see in daily ways, what I do not talk about when I discuss the future, what I exclude from my hopes for a better world." These letters explore the scenes and the moods from which Lewis' Indian prose and verse emerged.

PRINCIPAL WORKS: The Last Inspection, 1942; Raiders' Dawn, 1942; Ha! Ha! Among the Trumpets, 1945; In the Green Tree, 1949.

ABOUT: Graves, R. Introduction to Ha! Ha! Among the Trumpets; Rowse, A. L. The English Past, Preface to In the Green Tree.

LEWIS, CLIVE STAPLES ("Clive Hamilton") (November 29, 1898-), English novelist and essayist, was born in Belfast, Ireland, the son of  A. J. Lewis, a solicitor of that city, and Flora Augusta (Hamilton) Lewis. His mother died when he was a child. Following a year at Malvern College, he was privately educated by W. T. Kirkpatrick, the former Headmaster of Lurgan College. In 1918 he became a scholar at University College, Oxford. During the first World War he served as a second lieutenant in the Somerset Light Infantry, and was wounded in the back—"oddly enough by an English shell," as he says. In 1924 he became a lecturer at University College, and a year later fellow and tutor of Magdalen College, Oxford, where he now lectures on English literature.

Under the pseudonym of Clive Hamilton, Lewis published his first book, Dymer, in 1926, reissued in 1950. Dymer is a long narrative poem in rime royal, which shows Lewis' early gift of satire and his idealism. In 1933 appeared The Pilgrim's Regress, an allegorical apology for Christianity, reason, and romanticism. The Allegory of Love attracted considerable critical and scholarly attention, and won the Hawthornden prize. Its theme is "the slow evolution of the passion of romantic love, and the slow evolution of the literary expression of that passion through the Middle Ages." Most reviewers found the book "learned, witty, and sensible." Out of the Silent Planet, a tale of life on the planet Mars, was described by Time as "sub-Wellsian fantasy, tinted with irony and as pitted with morality as Pilgrim's Progress." Others have called it "a story of strange fascination." It involves the kidnapping of a Cambridge philologist by two scientists, a Fascist-minded physicist and a gold-hunting materialist, who take him in a space ship to another planet. When the inhabitants of that planet finally order the two evil scientists to depart, the philologist decides to return to Earth with them, in order to help counteract the evil intentions of men like them, and to convert humans "from the conception of Space to the conception of Heaven." The Problem of Pain, which followed in 1940, was a straight exposition of the Christian position toward suffering. Here Lewis insists that the universe may not be evil because the Ruler of it believes in discipline.

In 1942 Lewis won wide acclaim with the publication of The Screwtape Letters. An elderly Devil named Screwtape writes a series of letters to his ambitious young nephew, Wormwood, on the best way of winning to eternal perdition the soul of a certain "patient" living in the world today. Wormwood, helped along by war conditions, is inclined to go all out for "spectacular wickedness." But his wiser uncle keeps reminding him that the safest road to hell is "the gradual one": the real thing that matters is "the extent to which you separate the man from the Enemy (God)." Unfortunately for Wormwood, his victim escapes him when "snatched into salvation by a bomb" during an air raid on London. The Manchester Guardian wrote: "In a book of any length satire easily topples over into farce and any levity in the treatment of such a subject would be fatal. Mr. Lewis never fails. The book is sparkling yet truly reverent, in fact a perfect joy, and should become a classic." According to C. E. M. Joad, "Mr. Lewis possesses the rare gift of being able to make righteousness readable."

In 1943 Christian Behavior and Perelandra, the latter a parable set on the planet Venus, were published. Beyond Personality was a series of B.B.C. broadcasts on Christian theology. That Hideous Strength and The Great Divorce were further fantasies. In Miracles he discusses historical evidence, and decides that the question whether miracles occur can never be answered by experience. To him Christianity is the story of a great miracle, and he himself believes in them. "Probably none of his books so clearly reveals his own religious outlook," writes one reviewer.

"I gave up Christianity at about fourteen," says Lewis. "Came back to it when getting on for thirty. Not an emotional conversion: almost purely philosophical. I didn't *want* to. I'm not in the least the religious type. I want to be let alone, to feel I'm my own master; but since the facts seemed to be just the opposite I had to give in."

Lewis is unmarried and is described as a shy, sensitively poetic, scholarly man. He likes "sitting up till the small hours in someone's college rooms talking nonsense, poetry, theology, metaphysics over beer, tea, and pipes." In recent years he has written a number of children's books.

PRINCIPAL WORKS: The Pilgrim's Regress, 1933; The Allegory of Love, 1936; Out of the Silent Planet, 1938; Rehabilitations, 1939; The Personal Heresy (with E. M. W. Tillyard) 1939; The Problem of Pain, 1940; The Screwtape Letters, 1942; A Preface to Paradise Lost, 1942; Broadcast Talks (reprinted as The Case for Christianity) 1942; Perelandra, 1943; Christian Behavior, 1943; Abolition of Man, 1943; Beyond Personality, 1944; That Hideous Strength, 1945; The Great Divorce, 1945; Miracles, 1947; Weight of Glory (in England: Transposition) 1949; English Literature in the Sixteenth Century, 1954. *Children's Books*—The Lion, the Witch and the Wardrobe, 1950; Prince Caspian, 1951; The Voyage of the Dawn Treaders, 1952; The Silver Chair, 1953. *As "Clive Hamilton"* —Dymer, 1926.

ABOUT: Walsh, C. C. S. Lewis; Catholic World July 1948; Christian Century December 25, 1946; Current Biography 1944; Time September 8, 1947.

LEWIS, DAY. See DAY LEWIS

LEWIS, DOMINIC BEVAN WYNDHAM (1894-). For biographical sketch and list of earlier works and references, see TWENTIETH CENTURY AUTHORS, 1942.

* * *

D. B. Wyndham Lewis has for a number of years been writing the humor column for the London *News Chronicle* under the name "Timothy Shy." A sparkling and impudent satirist, he has been described by another London newspaper, the *Observer,* as "one of those gay dogs who most enjoy barking at the hand that feeds them." James E. Tobin, in an article in *Catholic World,* called him "the master of satiric delight," and said that he writes in the tradition of the great Catholic satirists — Chesterton, Belloc, Baring, and Monsignor Ronald Knox.

Like so many writers of humor, Lewis has a serious side to his writing career. He is a careful and conscientious historical biographer. In 1944 he published his colorful and scholarly biography of Ronsard, on which he had worked for nine years. With this volume, Katherine Brégy wrote in *Commonweal,* "the mantle of Hilaire Belloc . . . seems to have fallen on his shoulders." This was followed by an affectionate biography of James Boswell, which the *New Yorker* called "a brilliant portrait of a man and his era," and a collection of polished and urbane character sketches in *Four Favourites.*

During World War II Lewis was a member of the Home Guard in London where his city residence was bombed. He has a country home in Somerset.

ADDITIONAL WORKS: Ronsard, 1944; The Hooded Hawk: or The Case of Mr. Boswell, 1946 (reprinted in 1952 as James Boswell); Four Favourites, 1948; The Soul of Marshal Gilles de Raiz, 1952. *As "Timothy Shy"*—(with R. Searle) The Terror of St. Trinian's, 1952.

ABOUT: Hoehn, M. (ed.) Catholic Authors, I; Catholic World January 1945; Time April 24, 1944.

LEWIS, Mrs. ETHELREDA (189?-August 1, 1946). For biographical sketch and list of works and references, see TWENTIETH CENTURY AUTHORS, 1942.

* * *

Ethelreda Lewis died at her home in Port Alfred, Cape Province, South Africa. She left one son and one daughter.

Although nearly one hundred biographical projects were proposed to her following the phenomenal success of the *Trader Horn* books, that success was never repeated. J. P. L. Snyman has spoken of the "lyrical beauty of the prose, delicacy of feeling and appreciation of nature" in Mrs. Lewis' novels, adding: "Although her books do not give the impression of deliberate purpose, Ethelreda Lewis studies the disturbing influence which the impact of civilization exerts on certain types of people."

ABOUT: Snyman, J. P. L. The South African Novel in English; London Times August 2, 1946; New York Times August 2, 1946.

LEWIS, JANET (August 17, 1899-), American poet, novelist, and short story writer, reports: "I was born in Chicago at the turn of the century and spent my first twenty years there or in Oak Park. I attended the Oak Park High School, like Mr. Ernest Hemingway. It was a good school. I acquired an A.A. at Lewis Institute and a Ph.B. at the University of Chicago and then went to France for slightly over half a year, where for a time I worked as a clerk in the Passport Bureau of the American Consulate in Paris. I worked also for a few months as

proofreader for the *Redbook* magazine in Chicago, taught at Lewis Institute for one quarter. From 1923 until 1927 I spent most of my time in Santa Fe, N.M., where I married Yvor Winters. We came to California in the fall of 1927, where my husband has been associated with Stanford ever since, first as a graduate student and now as professor of English. We have two children, a girl and a boy. The household also includes at the moment five Airedales and three cats. My husband has some standing as a breeder of Airedales; two of the dogs are AKC champions. In 1950 I visited Paris again, for the first time in thirty years, on a Guggenheim fellowship for creative writing.

"My father was Dr. Edwin Herbert Lewis, a teacher of English, a novelist, a poet, and a very learned man. What I owe him is incalculable and I cannot begin to express it here, but I can note that I received my basic education in English prose from him, and also the entire background and chief inspiration for *The Invasion* which, I hasten to add, is not a novel but a narrative of events concerning the Johnstone family of St. Mary's. The year I was born my father built a cabin on an island in the St. Mary's River, at a spot called Sailor's Encampment, roughly midway between Mackinac and Sault Ste. Marie. Except for three summers spent at the seashore in Rhode Island, our family went to Encampment every year for the long holidays. The descendants of the Johnstone family then living at Encampment were dear and esteemed friends of my family through all my childhood.

"At the University of Chicago I belonged to the Poetry Club sponsored chiefly, I believe, by Robert Morss Lovett. Elizabeth Madox Roberts was also a member at that time, together with Glenway Wescott, Maurice Lesemann, Pearl Andelson, Edward Sherry, John Toigo, Kathleen Foster, and others, whose friendship became important to me; through this group, some time later, I met Yvor Winters. Miss Harriet Monroe, Mrs. William Vaughn Moody, Mrs. Edith Foster Flint, and other writers and patrons of the arts were very kind to this group.

"I have lived a life rather lacking in 'events,' but with a rich, and, in the main, a very happy background. This sort of life does not provide a very interesting brief biography. The interest is chiefly in the background, which can't be treated briefly and still be interesting.

"*The Wife of Martin Guerre* and *The Trial of Sören Qvist* are based on old and very famous cases of circumstantial evidence.

I am at present working on another case of circumstantial evidence, less famous, and far less amply documented. It was to look into the background of this third case that I visited Paris in 1950. I have given up guessing how long it will be before this last book is finished."

PRINCIPAL WORKS: The Invasion, 1932; The Wife of Martin Guerre, 1941; Against a Darkening Sky, 1943; Good-Bye, Son, and Other Stories, 1946; The Trial of Sören Qvist, 1947. *Poetry*—The Wheel in Midsummer, 1927; The Earth-Bound, 1946.

ABOUT: Warfel, H. R. American Novelists of Today; Poetry January 1947.

LEWIS, SINCLAIR (February 7, 1885- January 10, 1951). For biographical sketch and list of earlier works and references, see TWENTIETH CENTURY AUTHORS, 1942.

* * *

Sinclair Lewis died in Rome a month before his sixty-sixth birthday. The immediate cause of death was paralysis of the heart, the culmination of a long series of heart and lung ailments.

Most of his later years were spent in Europe, except for a visit to the United States in 1949. As Mark Schorer has said: "Driven all his life, all over the world, from house to house, by his unmanageable restlessness, he was, perhaps, never at home, only always wishing to be." He finished writing his last novel, *World So Wide,* in Florence in March 1950, and set out on what was to have been a long trip throughout Europe. After three months of travel, illness forced him to settle in Rome, where he worked intensively on poems until his death. Lewis' close friend Harrison Smith has described him as "a brilliant and dynamic man, deeply concerned with social problems, generous, restless, often unhappy," whose most obvious trait was a morbid fear of loneliness.

Maxwell Geismar has called Lewis' novels "a remarkable diary of the middle class mind in America." When his great talents for story telling and for mimicry were fired with the passionate sincerity of a crusader, the result was the novels of the Twenties, which were, as Perry Miller has noted, "in the guise of ferocious attacks upon America, celebrations of it." Vincent Sheean has called him "violently American"; Lewis wrote of the expatriate hero of his last novel: "he knew then that he was unalterably an American; he knew what a special and mystical experience it is, for the American never really emigrates but only travels; perhaps travels for two or three generations but at the end is still marked with the giant image of Tecumseh."

ADDITIONAL WORKS: Gideon Planish, 1943; Cass Timberlane, 1945; Kingsblood Royal, 1947; The God-Seeker, 1949; World So Wide, 1951; From Main Street to Stockholm: Letters of Sinclair Lewis 1919-1930 (ed. H. Smith) 1952.

ABOUT: Gray, J. On Second Thought; Lewis, S. From Main Street to Stockholm; Morris, L. R. Postscript to Yesterday; Schorer, M. Two Houses, Two Ways, in New World Writing 4; Van Gelder, R. Writers and Writing; American Scholar Spring 1954; Atlantic Monthly February 1946, April 1951, June 1951; Christian Century January 24, 1951; College English November 1951; Commonweal June 6, 1947, April 6, 1951, April 20, 1951; Hobbies April 1951; Life January 22, 1951; Nation February 24, 1951; New Republic April 2, 1951; Newsweek May 26, 1947; New York Herald Tribune Book Review September 2, 1951; February 10, 1952; New York Times February 5, 1950, January 11, 1951, February 10, 1952, June 15, 1952, October 28, 1954; New Yorker September 22, 1951; Publishers' Weekly December 20, 1947, January 26, 1952; Saturday Evening Post March 31, 1951; Saturday Review of Literature May 24, 1947, June 6, 1947, January 27, 1951, March 3, 1951; Time January 22, 1951; The Writer June 1951.

LEWIS, WYNDHAM (1886-). For biographical sketch and list of earlier works and references, see TWENTIETH CENTURY AUTHORS, 1942.

* * *

In 1940 Wyndham Lewis came to America. He spent the next eight years traveling in Canada and in the United States and was for a time adviser to the Library of Congress. He returned to England in 1948. Just at about this time a revival of interest in Lewis' work, both his painting and his writing, began. *Time* magazine accounts for this revival, in part at least, by the fact that "Britons have become more used to Lewis' honest vehemence, more conscious of the truths wrapped up in it." He lives in England now. Since 1949 he has been gradually losing his sight. He faces the prospect of blindness with courage and humor and says of his fate as a painter: "I have often thought that it would solve a great many problems if English painters were born blind."

As a writer Lewis continues to be outspoken, needling, at times exasperating, but unfailingly stimulating. He scorns the large popular audience and writes independently. In his autobiographical *Rude Assignment,* an eccentric, informal book which rambles loosely but brilliantly from one subject to another, he says proudly, "I am what is described as a highbrow." Three of his works of fiction have had recent American publication—his novel *The Revenge for Love* (pub-

lished originally in England in 1937), a collection of satirical stories on life in England under the Labour government, *Rotting Hill,* and the powerful novel of an English professor living in Canada, *Self-Condemned.*

ADDITIONAL WORKS: Anglosaxony, 1943; America and Cosmic Man, 1948; Rude Assignment: A Narrative of My Career Up-to-Date, 1950; Rotting Hill, 1951; Self-Condemned, 1954.

ABOUT: Kenner, H. Wyndham Lewis; Lewis, W. Rude Assignment; Newton, E. In My View; New Statesman and Nation May 7, 1949; New Yorker June 4, 1955; Time April 14, 1952.

LEWISOHN, LUDWIG (May 30, 1882-). For biographical sketch and list of earlier works and references, see TWENTIETH CENTURY AUTHORS, 1942.

* * *

An ardent Zionist, Ludwig Lewisohn was editor of the *New Palestine* from 1943 to 1948. He has taught English at Brandeis University in Waltham, Mass., since the University opened in 1948. In 1955 he was named librarian at Brandeis. Lewisohn has published two novels and several works of non-fiction in recent years. His novels have had poor reviews, but his essays—on Jewish affairs and on poetry—have been praised. He is strongly opinionated and outspoken. Joshua Kunitz wrote in the New York *Herald Tribune:* "Mr. Lewisohn seems to have a narcissistic fondness for the gadfly method, and gadflies are not noted for their moderation." As George F. Whicher pointed out, however (in writing of Lewisohn's *The Magic Word*): "No one can read these studies without being stimulated by the genuine respect for human and humane values that inspires whatever Mr. Lewisohn writes, even when it seems most wrongheaded."

ADDITIONAL WORKS: Breathe Upon These (novel) 1944; Anniversary (novel) 1948; (ed. & tr.) Goethe: The Story of a Man, 1949; The American Jew: Character and Destiny, 1950; The Magic Word: Studies in the Nature of Poetry, 1950; In a Summer Season (novel) 1955.

ABOUT: Hoffman, F. J. Freudianism and the Literary Mind; Kazin, A. On Native Grounds.

*LEY, WILLY, (October 2, 1906-), American scientist and writer on science, writes: "I was born in Berlin, Germany, in 1906. The date was the 2nd of October and my family at a somewhat later date, never failed to point out that this was also the birthday of Field Marshal von Hindenburg. That it also happens to be the birthday of Marshal Foch of France and of Mahatma Gandhi of India was something

* 1ā

they either did not know or were reluctant to mention. My mother was a native Berliner too, but my father came from Königsberg in

Olga Ley

East Prussia to which he returned after the First World War which he spent in a P.O.W. camp on the Isle of Man. It so happened that my parents were in London when that war broke out. I was in Berlin all the time, living with relatives and attending in proper and prescribed order four years of municipal grade school before being entered on the rolls of an advanced school, also in Berlin.

"A possible future biographer will have a hard time finding family background for either the scientific or the literary side of my inclinations and activities. My mother's family consisted largely of employees (called 'officials' in Germany) of the German Evangelical (Lutheran) Church, with a number of unimportant craftsmen such as cabinet makers thrown in. My father was a business man (wine merchant), his father a blacksmith and the nearest approach to artistic occupation in the whole family was one of my father's brothers who was an assistant band leader in the German army.

"My scientific activities began with playing hookey from Sunday School; it so happened that the Museum of Natural History was not quite a block from the church I was supposed to attend. Like every future author or scientist I ever heard of, I was an omnivorous reader, first in German only and then, as schooling progressed, in Latin, French, and English too. At about the age of ten I got a bad mark in school because we had been asked to write a composition dealing with our future professions and the reasons for the choice. Instead of writing about something 'secure' and 'approved,' say, postal inspector or doctor, I stated that I wanted to be an explorer. My first interests were astronomy, zoology and, a little distance behind, botany. This was superseded by paleozoology and paleobotany; the past periods of earth's geological history fascinated me no end, and still do. By the time I was ready to graduate from high school I was sure that I would become a geologist and I planned my studies accordingly. Since my father had meanwhile returned from the Isle of Man, I went to Königsberg to study, being, of course, preoccupied with the local phenomenon: amber.

Those years found expression at a fairly recent date in the first two chapters of my book *Dragons in Amber.*

"Regular study was handicapped by the inflation and such incidents as the failure of my father's business (indirectly due to the inflation), but the biggest and, as it turned out, most permanent interruption was the appearance of a scientific book which prophesied the possibility of space travel. I saw it in 1925 (it had originally been published in 1923) and in 1927 I was among the founders of the German 'Society for Space Travel.' In 1929 I became vice-president of that society and co-editor of its monthly journal. In 1934 the society dissolved somewhat stormily under the Hitler regime and half a year later I left for the United States. Some five years after my arrival I met a slight and pretty girl by the name of Olga who combined quadri-lingual literacy with a ballet career and also with scientific interests and art ability. She became Mrs. Ley very quickly and has helped me no end ever since, not only as a companion but actively with library research and by illustrating some of my books and articles. I am a citizen of the United States since 1944 and also the father of two daughters, named Sandra and Xenia.

"I suppose that I should add a few words about my present ambitions, both scientific and literary. The scientific side is easy to tell: I want to contribute to the future conquest of space and would like to be held responsible to some extent for the coming age of space travel. The literary side is best explained by stating my firm belief that no scientific fact or theme is too difficult to be explained to the intelligent outsider. If somebody says that this or that cannot be explained to the layman I understand this to mean that this person either does not have enough factual knowledge or else insufficient skill as an interpreter; often both. In all my books, whether on extinct or living animals, or on rockets and space travel, I have always acted on the belief that my readers will be interested if the story is well told. But I also believe that, in order to tell a story well, you have to tell the *full* story, including sideissues and ramifications.

"As for future projects: two more books in the field of natural history are outlined by now. And then, if I find the time, I'll finish up research begun twenty years ago for a comprehensive (and not too popular) 'History of the Rocket Principle.'"

* * *

Willy Ley's first book was a small paperbacked volume titled *Die Fahrt ins Weltall*

(Trip into Space), 1926, an early exposition of space travel theory. He wrote several other books in German—among them a biography of the Swiss natural historian Conrad Gesner von Zürich (published in 1929). He also contributed to and edited a symposium on space travel called *Die Möglichkeit der Weltraumfahrt (The Possibility of Space Travel)*, 1928. Ley's first American book, the product of thirteen years of research, was *The Lungfish and the Unicorn*, an encyclopedic collection of animal myths and the scientific facts on which, he feels, many of these myths are based. Since 1947 Ley has been consultant to the office of technical services of the United States Department of Commerce, and from 1944 to 1948 he was a research engineer for the Washington Institute of Technology at College Park, Md. He has contributed many articles to popular and scientific journals and lectures widely, to both professional and lay audiences.

PRINCIPAL WORKS IN ENGLISH: The Lungfish and the Unicorn, 1941; Days of Creation, 1941; Bombs and Bombing, 1941; Shells and Shooting, 1942; Rockets, 1944; Rockets and Space Travel (rev. ed. of Rockets) 1947; The Lungfish, the Dodo, and the Unicorn (rev. ed. of Lungfish and Unicorn) 1948; Conquest of Space, 1949; Dragons in Amber, 1951; Rockets, Missiles, and Space Travel (rev. ed. of Rockets and Space Travel) 1951; Lands Beyond (with L. S. DeCamp) 1952; Mystery of Other Worlds Revealed (with others) 1953; Engineers' Dreams, 1954.

ABOUT: Current Biography 1953; New Outlook October 1934; New York Times Book Review July 22, 1951.

LIDDELL, HART, BASIL HENRY
(October 31, 1895-). For biographical sketch and list of earlier works and references, see TWENTIETH CENTURY AUTHORS, 1942.

* * *

Captain Liddell Hart's stimulating and informative writings on military history and strategy were of special interest to readers during and after World War II. In 1945 he interviewed the German generals detained in England after the war, and several years later he published the results of this study in *The German Generals Talk*, which Hanson Baldwin praised as "a study of great importance and interest, indispensable to anyone who wants to know what really went on during World War II." His most widely read and discussed book in recent years was *The Defence of the West*, a survey of the West's chances of survival in the event of a war with Russia. A provocative work written for a general audience rather than for military specialists, the book was praised as a vigorous and sobering presentation of the facts. Major George Fielding Eliot called it a book "well worth the attention of every American citizen—indeed, of every citizen of the free world."

Captain Liddell Hart married Kathleen Sullivan Nelson in 1942. It was his second marriage. He lives in Buckinghamshire and lists as his recreations "discussion, table tennis, chess, the history of fashion and habit."

ADDITIONAL WORKS: This Expanding War, 1942; Thoughts on War, 1944; What Don't We Learn from History? 1944; Revolution in Warfare, 1947; The German Generals Talk (in England: The Other Side of the Hill) 1948; The Defence of the West, 1950; (ed.) Rommel, E. The Rommel Papers, 1950; (ed.) Wheeler, W. Letters, 1952; Strategy: The Indirect Approach, 1954.

ABOUT: Saturday Review August 28, 1954.

LIDIN, VLADIMIR (1894-). For biographical sketch and list of works and references, see TWENTIETH CENTURY AUTHORS, 1942.

* * *

Vladimir Lidin was a war correspondent from 1941 to 1944 on various sectors of the Russo-German front and wrote numerous war stories. He lives in Moscow and is a member of the Union of Soviet Writers. None of his later work has appeared in English translation.

ABOUT: Columbia Dictionary of Modern European Literature; Struve, G. Soviet Russian Literature 1917-1950.

LIEBLING, ABBOTT JOSEPH (October 18, 1904-), American journalist, who signs his work A. J. Liebling, was born in New York City, the son of Joseph Liebling, a prosperous New York furrier, and Anna (Slone) Liebling. He attended Dartmouth College and Columbia Graduate School of Journalism, graduating in 1925. He worked eight months for the

Ray Platnik

New York *Times* and was fired, then for about four years for the Providence (R.I.) *Journal* and *Evening Bulletin*. Since 1935 he has been on the staff of the *New Yorker*, and from 1939 to 1944 was its correspondent in France, England, and North Africa. He had spent a year, earlier, at the Sorbonne, and has been a Francophile as long as he can remember.

The first of his books, *Back Where I Came From,* is a sketch of New York City. "In his way," wrote a reviewer, "a humorous, skeptical, warm-hearted way—Mr. Liebling is something of a kindly Zola, wandering through the many, many levels of New York life and setting down his notes . . . as a seasoned, sensible friend. His humor is sharp, but it grows out of understanding and kindliness toward all sorts and conditions of human beings. . . ." A more recent volume, a pen-portrait of Chicago, originally published as a *New Yorker* "profile," stirred controversy, though most reviewers agreed it made good reading. Liebling describes "the vast anonymous pulp of the city, plopped down by the lakeside like a piece of water-logged fruit. Chicago after nightfall is a small city of the rich who have not yet migrated, visitors, and hoodlums, surrounded by a large expanse of juxtaposed dimnesses." A former Chicagoan, M. L. Rosenthal, writing in the *New Republic,* said, "This is surface journalism which can be most effective when it highlights a revolting situation vividly and wittily, and can be appallingly obtuse when it touches unfamiliar territory. Mr. Liebling writes well, in the *New Yorker's* well-known neutrally satiric vein."

Liebling's *Honest Rainmaker* is a study of Colonel John R. Stingo, a somewhat fabulous, though real, figure of the contemporary sporting world.

Liebling is distinguished not only for his books but for his occasional profiles, book reviews, and sharp analyses of "the wayward press" in the *New Yorker.* His first marriage was to Ann Beatrice McGinn in 1934. They were divorced in 1949, and in that year he married Lucille Hille Spectorsky. They live in New York City. He is described, by *Editor and Publisher,* as "a paunchy, padded, amiable man . . . a voracious reader, and eater."

PRINCIPAL WORKS: Back Where I Came From, 1938; The Telephone Booth Indian, 1942; The Road Back to Paris, 1944; The Wayward Pressman, 1947; Chicago: The Second City, 1952; Mink and Red Herring, 1949; The Honest Rainmaker, 1953.

ABOUT: Editor and Publisher August 14, 1948; New York Times Book Review June 22, 1952; Time November 10, 1947.

LIEPMANN, HEINZ (1905-). For autobiographical sketch and list of earlier works and references, see TWENTIETH CENTURY AUTHORS, 1942.

* * *

Heinz Liepmann (or Liepman, as styled by his most recent American publisher) remained in New York until 1948 when he returned to Germany. He is now married and living in Hamburg. He has published one novel since the war, *Case History,* the story of a dope addict and the efforts of a psychiatrist to cure him. Dr. Liepmann has also written several magazine articles in recent years. One of these, published in the *Menorah Journal* in 1947, is a grim and tragic report on the plight of the surviving Jews who remained in Germany during and after the war.

ADDITIONAL WORK: Case History, 1950.

LIN, YU-T'ANG (1895-). For autobiographical sketch and list of earlier works and references, see TWENTIETH CENTURY AUTHORS, 1942.

* * *

Lin Yu-t'ang took an active part in the United Nations' educational and cultural organization UNESCO, of which he headed the arts and letters division in Paris in 1948. After less than a year in the post, however, he resigned. ("It was an organization," he said, "where seven hundred people wrote each other letters and read them and got paid for it, and I had to get out or lose my mind.") He remained in France until 1952, living most of the time in Cannes, "where the leisurely pace of a French Riviera town just suited me." Early in 1954 he was appointed chancellor of the new Chinese University in Singapore. On that occasion the New York *Times* commented in an editorial: "We shall be sorry to lose from the American scene a witty and wise writer, speaker and philosopher. He has, happily, been with us so long that we count him almost as one of our very own." In April 1955 Lin Yu-t'ang and his staff whom he had personally selected left the new university before it had opened its doors, as the result of a disagreement with the trustees on policy. A lump settlement of $100,000 was accepted by the departing group, most of whom, including Dr. Lin, planned to return to the United States.

ADDITIONAL WORKS: Between Tears and Laughter, 1943; Vigil of a Nation, 1945; Gay Genius: Life and Times of Su Tungpo, 1947; Chinatown Family, 1948; On the Wisdom of America, 1950; Miss Tu, 1950; (tr.) The Widow, The Nun, and The Courtesan: Three Novelettes from the Chinese, 1951; Famous Chinese Short Stories Retold, 1952; The Vermillion Gate (novel) 1953; Looking Beyond, 1955.

ABOUT: Lewis, J. Other Men's Minds; American Mercury August 1950; College English January 1947; New York Herald Tribune Book Review October 11, 1953; New York Times January 24, 1954; New York Times Book Review August 22, 1954; New Yorker February 3, 1945.

LINCOLN, JOSEPH CROSBY (February 13, 1870-March 10, 1944). For biographical sketch and list of earlier works and references, see TWENTIETH CENTURY AUTHORS, 1942.

* * *

Joseph C. Lincoln died at seventy-four of a heart ailment. Death came at his home in Winter Park, Fla. Although in his last years he lived chiefly in Florida and at Villanova, Pa., he never relinquished the home at Cape Cod, scene of his forty books.

Consistently popular with a large audience during his long career, Lincoln combined competent workmanship with salty characters and readable stories. The *Saturday Review of Literature* once noted: "The story is well put together. The joiner work hardly shows. It doesn't really matter that the intellectual content could be reduced to a platitude, or that the moral involved is somewhat shopworn. Mr. Lincoln never leads his reader to expect too much—and he never disappoints him."

ADDITIONAL WORK: The Bradshaws of Harniss, 1943.

ABOUT: McCue, J. W. Joe Lincoln of Cape Cod; Orcutt, W. D. From My Library Walls; New York Times March 11, 1944; Publishers' Weekly March 18, 1944; Saturday Review of Literature March 18, 1944; Scholastic May 1, 1944.

LINCOLN, VICTORIA ENDICOTT (October 23, 1904-   ), American novelist and short story writer, reports: "I was born in Fall River, Mass., a mill town built upon a hill overlooking Narragansett Bay. My family were manufacturers of textile machinery and had been over several generations. I was educated in the public schools there, and at Radcliffe. Upon graduating, in 1926, I married a Harvard classmate, Isaac Watkins. We were separated in 1932 and divorced in the following year. In 1934 I married Victor Lowe, then a graduate student in the field of philosophy which he now teaches at the Johns Hopkins University. I have one child by the first marriage, two by the second, and one grandchild. While I have done a fair amount of traveling, the better part of my life has been lived on the East coast and in the Middle West of the United States.

Blackstone

"From the time I could first hold a pencil and print words, I have taken it for granted that it was my business in life to be a writer. As a poet I have had an appreciative audience of one, namely Victoria Lincoln. As a novelist and short-story writer I have communicated with a considerably wider field."

* * *

February Hill, Victoria Lincoln's best-known novel, enjoyed considerable popularity as a novel and later as a play and motion picture, *The Primrose Path.* It was a pleasant, unconventional book — a strange but wholly entertaining mixture of tough-minded realism and lighthearted humor—which Lewis Gannett compared, within one sentence of his review, to *The Postman Always Rings Twice, Mrs. Wiggs of the Cabbage Patch,* and *Tobacco Road!* Since *February Hill,* whatever there was of the Cain-Caldwell element in her writing has disappeared, and in its place there is engaging freshness, disarming humor, and sensitive observation—especially of children and young people.

PRINCIPAL WORKS: February Hill, 1934; Grandmother and the Comet, 1944; The Wind at My Back, 1946; Celia Amberley, 1949; Out from Eden, 1951; The Wild Honey, 1953.

ABOUT: Warfel, H. R. American Novelists of Today; Good Housekeeping October 1947; New York Herald Tribune Book Review October 7, 1951; New York Times Book Review December 2, 1951, May 10, 1953; Wilson Library Bulletin March 1945.

LINDBERGH, Mrs. ANNE SPENCER (MORROW) (1906-   ). For biographical sketch and list of earlier works and references, see TWENTIETH CENTURY AUTHORS, 1942.

* * *

Anne Morrow Lindbergh contributes poems occasionally to the *Atlantic Monthly* and other periodicals. Her recent books are the novelette *The Steep Ascent,* the story of an air journey made by an American woman and her British aviator husband, and an intensely personal and introspective study of the problems of woman, *Gift from the Sea.* The novelette was praised for its delicacy, sensitivity, and poetic feeling. It was more than an exciting adventure story, Beatrice Sherman wrote in the New York *Times.* "Its charm and grace are rooted in the fabric of the author's mind and in the fruit of her philosophy." *Gift from the Sea,* Elizabeth Gray Vining observed in the New York *Times,* was "the work of a sensitive, tensile, original mind [which] probes delicately into questions of balance and relationship in the world today."

Charles A. Lindbergh's autobiography, *The Spirit of St. Louis,* won the Pulitzer prize for biography in 1954. The Lindberghs live in Darien, Conn.

ADDITIONAL WORK: The Steep Ascent, 1944; Gift from the Sea, 1955.

ABOUT: Adams, J. Heroines of the Sky.

LINDSAY, HOWARD (March 29, 1889-), American playwright, writes: "I was born in Waterford, N.Y. When I was  three, my family moved to Atlantic City, N.J., where my mother's brother published a newspaper. A teacher of elocution who advertised in my uncle's paper failed to pay her bill. I was sent to work it out. This condition continued for about four years and I have always believed it was these early experiences as an elocutionist that made me determined to become an actor.

"When I was twelve we moved again, to Dorchester, Mass. There I was graduated from the Edward Everett Grammar School in 1903 and the Boston Latin School in 1907. Following this I spent a year at Harvard—and I use the word *spent* advisedly. After a six months course at the American Academy of Dramatic Arts, New York City, I joined a touring company of *Polly of the Circus.* I toured with this company for three years.

"An unsuccessful dip into the silent pictures in California was followed by some difficult months of occasional work in vaudeville, burlesque, repertoire and the lecture platform. Then I caught on in a subordinate role with the eminent star of that period, Margaret Anglin. I was with her company for five years as stage manager, actor, and eventually stage director. It was the kind of education not available to the stage aspirant of today.

"World War I took me to France. I rose rapidly to the rank of corporal. During the next ten years after leaving the army I was concerned chiefly with the staging of plays. I should perhaps mention *Dulcy* and *To the Ladies,* the first two plays written by the team of George S. Kaufman and Marc Connelly; *The Poor Nut,* one of the early plays of J. C. Nugent and his brilliant son, Elliott Nugent. Also plays by Owen Davis, Booth Tarkington and many others.

"A somewhat secondary ambition of mine was to be a writer. As soon as I went into the theatre, naturally I started to write plays. I did this with considerable persistence, although with very little encouragement. Finally I caught on to what kind of lines were most easily spoken by actors and to what kind of scenes affected an audience. Early in the '20's I had some success with the writing and the 'doctoring' of vaudeville acts. I met a young man similarly engaged, Bertrand Robinson, and we decided to collaborate on a full-length play. We wrote three, all of which were produced: *Tommy* in 1927; *Your Uncle Dudley* in 1929; and *Oh Promise Me* in 1930.

"Came the talkies and I joined the 'gold rush' to the picture studios of California. It was my good fortune to fail in my first attempt to write for the movies. I returned to New York and the staging and writing of plays. In 1934 I had the great good fortune to start a collaboration with Russel Crouse which has lasted until this day."

* * *

The most successful result of the Lindsay-Crouse collaboration was *Life With Father,* their dramatization of Clarence Day's sketches, which ran five seasons in New York. Lindsay himself played Father and co-starred with him as Mother was his wife, Dorothy Stickney. In 1946 the Lindsay-Crouse political comedy *State of the Union* was awarded the Pulitzer prize for drama.

PRINCIPAL WORKS: *(Date of production)*—She Loves Me Not, 1933; A Slight Case of Murder (with D. Runyon) 1935. *With R. Crouse*—Anything Goes, 1934; Red Hot and Blue, 1936; Hooray for What, 1937; Life With Father, 1939; Arsenic and Old Lace, 1940; Strip for Action, 1942; State of the Union, 1945; Life With Mother, 1948; Call Me Madam, 1950; Remains to Be Seen, 1951; The Prescott Proposals, 1953.

ABOUT: Barnett, L. K. Writing on Life; Cosmopolitan October 1948; Current Biography 1942; Esquire July 1949; New York Times Magazine January 13, 1946; Saturday Evening Post May 27, 1944; Theatre Arts February 1944; Time November 26, 1945.

LINDSAY, JACK (1900-). For autobiographical sketch and list of earlier works and references, see TWENTIETH CENTURY AUTHORS, 1942.

* * *

Jack Lindsay writes from Halstead, Essex: "I was called up in 1941 and served in the British Army 1941-45. The first two years I was a signalman in the Signal Corps; then passing through London on leave I was told by a friend that the War Office wanted a scriptwriter for the new army theatre being formed by A.B.C.A. I rang up the producer MacOwan, then a captain in charge of the project, saw him, and to my surprise was transferred to the job. So from 1943 to 1945 I was in the War Office—the only private in it! As for reasons of establishment I was officially an 'actor' in the group, though in fact doing a major's job. As a result I had a room all of my own while colonels were huddled together, and brigadiers treated me with great respect. (I don't suppose this is of world-shattering import, but amusing to recall.)

"In the War Office I thus learned a lot about drama-techniques, especially of the experimental kind we used. I have used this since in film-scripts, especially for documentary films, and for a full-length documentary play on mining staged at the Scala Theatre in 1946—as well as for radio scripts.

"Since the war I have written some historical novels, of which *Fires in Smithfield* was the most successful, and am now turning to the contemporary scene with an effort to apply the method of the historical novel as worked out by me—i.e. attempting to define the basic structure of a given social scene and the typical figures of that scene without schematisation. At the same time I have been carrying on my work in the field of pure scholarship, mainly concerned with the period of breakdown and transformation of classical culture. I have published *Song of a Falling World*, which deals with the Latin poets of the years 350-650 A.D., and *Byzantium into Europe*, a lengthy examination of Byzantine history with particular reference to cultural developments. I have attempted to show that up to the eleventh to twelfth centuries the key to European developments must be sought in Byzantium, where the essential transformations of the Graeco-Roman world into the medieval world go on.

"I now live in this charming village [Halstead] with its twelfth century keep and church, in an old farmhouse, where I seem at last to have solved the problem of where to keep my large number of books."

ADDITIONAL WORKS: *Novels*—We Shall Return, 1943; Beyond Terror, 1943; The Barriers Are Down, 1945; Hullo Stranger! 1945; A Time to Live, 1946; Fires in Smithfield, 1949; The Passionate Pastoral, 1951; Betrayed Spring, 1953; The Rising Tide, 1953. *Poems*—Into Action, 1942; Second Front, 1944; The Clue of Darkness, 1949; Three Letters, 1950. *Miscellaneous*—Complete Poems of Catullus (tr.) 1948; Song of a Falling World, 1949; Marxism and Contemporary Science, 1949; Charles Dickens, 1950; A World Ahead, 1950; Byzantium into Europe, 1952; Civil War in England, 1954.

LINDSAY, NORMAN (February 23, 1879-). For biographical sketch and list of earlier works and references, see TWENTIETH CENTURY AUTHORS, 1942.

* * *

The senior member of the writing Lindsay family has continued to produce his slight, humorous, and frothy novels, short stories, and essays, when he is not busy painting or drawing political cartoons. He lives in New South Wales.

ADDITIONAL WORKS: The Cousin from Fiji, 1946; Halfway to Anyway, 1947; Dust or Polish, 1950.

ABOUT: Roderick, C. A. Twenty Australian Novelists.

LINDSAY, THOMAS MARTIN (October 18, 1843-December 6, 1914). For biographical sketch and list of works and references, see TWENTIETH CENTURY AUTHORS, 1942.

LINDSAY, *VACHEL (November 10, 1879-December 5, 1931). For biographical sketch and list of works and references, see TWENTIETH CENTURY AUTHORS, 1942.

* * *

ABOUT: Gregory, H. & Zaturenska, M. History of American Poetry, 1900-1940; Harris, M. City of Discontent; Mims, E. Christ of the Poets; American Literature January 1948; Pacific Spectator Summer 1949; Quarterly Journal of Speech April 1947; Saturday Review of Literature October 20, 1945; Scholastic February 25, 1946; Yale Review Summer 1943.

* vă'chĕl

LINKLATER, ERIC (1899-). For biographical sketch and list of earlier works and references, see TWENTIETH CENTURY AUTHORS, 1942.

* * *

Some hint of the extraordinary energy of Eric Linklater is given in the first chapter of his autobiographical *A Year of Space*. In the winter of 1950-51, he writes, he was working on a novel *(Laxdale Hall)* "that had previously defeated my endeavour to give it the shape I wanted," and a translation of Jean Anouilh's *La Répétition*. Of the latter—and Linklater knew no French—he says: "I undertook the translation . . . because, at first sight, it seemed beyond my strength, and I thought it ridiculous that it should be; and after wearisome days with grammar-book and a large dictionary I found some keys to a forgotten syntax, I caught the tail of an idiom as it vanished like a

585

lizard into the crevice of a wall and worked with increasing pleasure."

Having finished these jobs, Linklater went to Sweden for a holiday and there he received a request from the British government to go to Korea to write a history of the campaign. Linklater's experience during World War II with the public relations division of the War Office had well prepared him for the job. He subsequently toured other parts of Asia and Australia and reported on these experiences in *A Year of Space*.

Linklater's nimble, astringent wit has won him a large audience in the United States as well as in Britain. Whether he writes fantasy (some of his works, *A Spell for Old Bones* for example, might be called adult fairy tales; others are written especially for children), satirical novels of contemporary society (like *Laxdale Hall*), or suspense thrillers (like *Mr. Byculla* which has, as James Hilton wrote, "a morbid theme bittersweetened with wit"), he is "good company." Robert L. Duffus remarked of him in the New York *Times*: "He is civilized . . . he makes one think without causing pain—and what writer could do more than that?"

Linklater and his wife live in Nigg, not far from Aberdeen, Scotland, in a splendid old house, larger than he needs. "I bought a big house," he said, "because I couldn't afford a little one." He has subsequently discovered, as he confesses in *A Year of Space*, that the repairs and management of the house are very demanding jobs. From 1945 to 1948 Linklater was rector of Aberdeen University. In the spring of 1954 he received the Order of the British Empire from Queen Elizabeth II.

ADDITIONAL WORKS: The Raft, and Socrates Asks Why: Two Conversations, 1942; The Great Ship, and Rabelais Replies: Two Conversations, 1944; Crisis in Heaven (play) 1944; The Wind on the Moon (juvenile) 1944; Private Angelo, 1946; The Art of Adventure, 1947; Sealskin Trousers, and Other Stories, 1947; The Pirates in the Deep Green Sea (juvenile) 1949; A Spell for Old Bones, 1950; Two Comedies: Love in Albania; and To Meet the MacGregors, 1950; Mr. Byculla, 1950; Laxdale Hall, 1951; A Year of Space, 1953; The House of Gair, 1954; The Sultan and the Lady, 1954.

ABOUT: Linklater, E. A Year of Space.

LINTON, RALPH (February 27, 1893-December 24, 1953), American anthropologist, died at sixty of a heart ailment, in New Haven, Conn. Several months before his death he wrote to the editors of this volume: "I was born and reared as a Quaker and did my undergraduate work at Swarthmore College. In the summer of my junior year I made my first archeological field trip. Dur-

ing the next few years I alternated between academic work and archeological expeditions to Guatemala and the Southwest with time out for the first World War in which I served in the 42nd (Rainbow) Division.

White Studio

"In 1920 I went to the Marquesas Islands for two years. This marked a turning point in my interests. I discovered that the study of living societies was much more interesting than archeology and that it was easy to live on close and friendly terms with people of different culture. In 1922 I took a post with what was then the Field Museum of Natural History in Chicago and in 1925 went to Madagascar as their one-man Captain Marshall Field Madagascar Expedition. In this year I also received my scientific union card in the form of a Ph.D. from Harvard. The next two and a half years were spent in Madagascar and East Africa. I traveled several thousand miles on safari and described my experiences in a series of articles which were published in the *Atlantic Monthly*.

"In 1928 I joined the faculty of the University of Wisconsin where I prepared what I still regard as my *magnum opus, The Study of Man*, a book which was a considerable departure from the anthropological writings of the period. In 1934 I married a Madison girl, Adelin Sumner Briggs. In 1937 I joined the faculty of Columbia University. Here I became interested in the study of personality and culture. Dr. Abram Kardiner and I carried on joint seminars on the subject for some years and I collaborated with him on two books, *The Individual and His Society* and *Psychological Frontiers of Society*. I found my own conclusions increasingly divergent from his and finally embodied these in *The Cultural Background of Personality*.

"Incidental activities during this period included serving as editor of the American Anthropologist and the Viking Fund Publications in Anthropology, and the writing of numerous scientific articles.

"In 1946 I accepted an appointment as Sterling Professor of Anthropology at Yale. Since that time my wife and I have collaborated in a number of small popular books.

"In spite of numerous books and articles I have never considered myself an author in the ordinary meaning of the term. My real interests have been scientific rather than literary.

"Fortunately, as an ethnologist I have always been able to combine business with pleasure and have found my greatest satisfaction in friendships with men of many different races and cultures. I consider as my greatest accomplishments that I am an adopted member of the Comanche tribe, was accepted as a master carver by the Marquesan natives and executed commissions for them in their own art, am a member of the Native Church of North America (Peyote) according to the Quapaw rite, became a properly accredited *ombiasy nkazo* (medicine man) in Madagascar, and was even invited to join the Rotary Club of a middle western city."

PRINCIPAL WORKS: The Material Culture of the Marquesas Islands, 1923; Ethnology of Polynesia and Micronesia, 1926; The Tanala, A Hill Tribe of Madagascar, 1933; The Study of Man: An Introduction, 1936; The Individual and His Society (with A. Kardiner) 1939; Acculturation in Seven American Indian Tribes (ed.) 1940; The Cultural Background of Personality, 1945; The Science of Man in the World Crisis (ed.) 1945; Psychological Frontiers of Society (with A. Kardiner) 1945; Arts of the South Seas (with P. Wingert and R. D'Harnoncourt) 1946; Man's Way from Cave to Skyscraper (with A. Linton) 1947; Most of the World (ed.) 1949; We Gather Together: the Story of Thanksgiving (with A. Linton) 1949; Halloween (with A. Linton) 1950; The Lore of Birthdays (with A. Linton) 1951; The Tree of Culture, 1955.

ABOUT: New York Times December 25, 1953.

LIPPMANN, WALTER (September 23, 1889-). For biographical sketch and list of earlier works and references, see TWENTIETH CENTURY AUTHORS, 1942.

* * *

Walter Lippmann has been the subject of a scholarly book-length study by David E. Weingast and of a three-part profile in the *Saturday Review* by John Mason Brown. He has been analyzed and re-analyzed as the "dean" of American political journalists. The readers of his syndicated column take him seriously, as he in turn takes his job seriously. "He does not write unless he knows what he is writing," the late Harold Ickes said of him. Perhaps his major distinction as a political journalist in an age of bitter political controversy is that he is as widely respected by those who differ with his views as by those who agree with them. Lippmann has sharp critics, however, who have pointed with special eagerness to his many political inconsistencies and shifts in judgment. But to all these objections Harold Ickes answered: "He may even have the appearance

at times of being inconsistent. Who has not, who has gone through life with an open mind, constantly seeking for that which is true and good and never hesitating to accept what appears to be the better, through fear of being jeered at for seeming inconsistencies?" And Weingast pointed out that Lippmann is to be read with skepticism, "with the feeling that his views are the serious reflections of a highly literate, well-informed mind, but also with the feeling that he has been wrong before and will very likely err again." Nevertheless, Weingast concludes his estimate, "Walter Lippmann has dignified his calling by the tirelessness of his labors, by the high literary quality of his writing, and the industry with which he has pursued facts. He has come close to being the scholar in journalism."

United States Foreign Policy: Shield of the Republic was a critical study of American foreign policy over the first forty years of the twentieth century. Some reviewers objected that this brief, precise and lucid little book oversimplified the complex issues of foreign policy. In spite of this failing, which he complained of, Carl Becker found it "a most trenchant and illuminating analysis of 'the order of power' in the world today, of the position of the United States in that order, and of a proper foreign policy in the circumstances." Of another major work, *Essays in the Public Philosophy*, a critical examination of democracy, Erwin D. Canham observed: "One can give only a poor concept of the power and challenge of the book—of its magnificently lucid appeal for a return to the spiritually scientific principles of government and society which animated the men who organized the American Republic and put its faith and its rights into words."

John Mason Brown described Lippmann in 1954 as "a lean, dark-haired, fastidiously dressed man of sixty-four who takes scrupulous care of himself, appears ten years younger than he is, and lives and works in a charming Georgetown house which is as beautifully ordered as his daily routine." That routine provides for a phenomenal amount of work done at a serene and dignified pace—newspaper reading, writing the column, handling a voluminous correspondence, research, working on a new book, reading, hobbies (currently carpentry), and a busy Washington social life.

ADDITIONAL WORKS: United States Foreign Policy: Shield of the Republic, 1943; United States War Aims, 1944; The Cold War: A Study in United States Foreign Policy, 1947; Isolation and Alliances: An American Speaks to the British, 1952; Essays in the Public Philosophy, 1955.

ABOUT: Weingast, D. E. Walter Lippmann; American Mercury March and May 1945; Antioch Review September 1951; New Statesman and Nation February 23, 1946; Publishers' Weekly July 24-31, 1943; Saturday Review April 24, May 1, May 8, 1954.

"LLEWELLYN, RICHARD." See LLEWELLYN LLOYD, R. D. V.

LLEWELLYN LLOYD, RICHARD DAVID VIVIAN ("Richard Llewellyn") (1907?-   ). For biographical sketch and list of earlier works and references, see TWENTIETH CENTURY AUTHORS, 1942.

* * *

Richard Llewellyn has written only three novels since 1939. Of these the most successful, next to *How Green Was My Valley,* was *None But the Lonely Heart* (also made into a motion picture), which Llewellyn completed while in the Army (lieutenant, then captain in the Welsh guards) in World War II. Two weeks after he finished the book, Llewellyn's company was sent to North Africa. *None But the Lonely Heart* was set not in Wales but in the London slums and is a realistic and sympathetic story of a young cockney boy who becomes a petty criminal. Reviewers were divided in their opinions on the novel. Some hailed it for "its variety, originality, and earthy and lyrical richness." Rose Feld, in the New York *Times,* called it "a masterpiece of characterization . . . as richly and robustly peopled as Dickens or Hugo in their portrayals of the submerged." Others, however, objected that it was sentimental and monotonous. Diana Trilling reported in the *Nation* that she had found it a disappointing book—"full of genuine pathos and technical virtuosity but at the same time forced in its sentiment and over-elaborate in its writing."

Llewellyn's later novels—*A Few Flowers for Shiner,* which humorously recounts the adventures of a cockney soldier with the British 8th Army in Italy; and *A Flame for Doubting Thomas,* the story of an American university professor who gets involved in managing an amusement pier—were not well received. "It's a long way from the green valley of Llewellyn's childhood to honky-tonk land, and much of his talent seems to have been mislaid en route," the *Library Journal* observed.

Llewellyn was described by Harvey Breit in 1950 as "a wiry fellow, hard as a nut, tough as a tack, with a jaunty attitude and a snappy speech, a bit mettlesome for most company, and an anger that rises fast, though it is more witty than bitter." At that time Llewellyn had just returned from an extensive lecture tour of the United States. He likes to travel, visited South Africa in 1952, spent considerable time in Argentina (where he went in 1949 to trace descendants of Welsh colonists who had settled in Patagonia in the eighteenth century) and is almost constantly on the move.

ADDITIONAL WORKS: None But the Lonely Heart, 1943; A Few Flowers for Shiner, 1950; A Flame for Doubting Thomas, 1953; The Witch of Merthyn, 1955.

ABOUT: New York Herald Tribune Book Review February 19, 1950; New York Times Book Review April 9, 1950; Time October 4, 1943.

LLOYD, RICHARD LLEWELLYN. See LLEWELLYN LLOYD, R. D. V.

LOAN. See VAN LOAN

LOCKE, ALAIN LE ROY (September 13, 1886-June 9, 1954). For autobiographical sketch and list of works and references, see TWENTIETH CENTURY AUTHORS, 1942.

* * *

Alain Locke died in New York City at sixty-seven after an illness of six weeks. His death occurred just a year after his retirement from Howard University where he had taught for over forty years. He had published no books in recent years but had contributed articles to *Phylon* and other journals.

ABOUT: Current Biography 1944; New York Times June 10, 1954; Time June 29, 1953.

LOCKE, WILLIAM JOHN (March 20, 1863-May 15, 1930). For biographical sketch and list of works and references, see TWENTIETH CENTURY AUTHORS, 1942.

LOCKHART, Sir ROBERT HAMILTON BRUCE (September 2, 1886-   ). For biographical sketch and list of earlier works and references, see TWENTIETH CENTURY AUTHORS, 1942.

* * *

Robert Bruce Lockhart was knighted in 1943. During World War II he served with the political intelligence department of the Foreign Office from 1939 to 1940. From 1940 to 1941 he was British representative to the provisional Czechoslovak government in London. And from 1941 to 1945 he was deputy under-secretary of state in the Foreign Office and director-general of the political warfare branch. He married Frances Mary Beck in 1949.

Lockhart travels widely and has reported on his recent travels in *My Europe.* C. L. Sulzberger wrote in his review of this book in the New York *Times*: "Cultivated, inquisitive, open-minded and fond of travel, [the author] made the most of the very remarkable opportunities presented to him for an interesting life and his own aptitude for reminiscence and observation." Another of his more successful books, in the United States as well as in Britain, was his poignant tribute to the memory of the Czech leader Jan Masaryk. He has also written an entertaining and informative history of Scotch whiskey.

ADDITIONAL WORKS: Comes the Reckoning, 1947; My Rod, My Comfort, 1949; The Marines Were There, 1950; Jan Masaryk: A Personal Memoir, 1951; Scotch, the Whiskey of Scotland in Fact and Story, 1951; My Europe, 1952.

LOCKRIDGE, Mrs. FRANCES LOUISE (DAVIS). See LOCKRIDGE, RICHARD

LOCKRIDGE, RICHARD (September 25, 1898-). For biographical sketch and list of earlier works and references, see TWENTIETH CENTURY AUTHORS, 1942.

* * *

The writing Lockridges are as busy and successful a pair of collaborators as any in the field. Their murder mysteries, in all editions, have sold well over a million copies. The perennially energetic and agreeable Norths continue to flourish (on radio and television, as well as in books). In addition, beginning with *Think of Death* in 1947, the Lockridges have proved that they can write successful mystery stories without the Norths. They have created a new fictional detective hero, Captain Heimrich, who, in spite of certain mannerisms and fidgets to which some critics objected, has emerged, Anthony Boucher writes, as "a believable character of major stature; a patient and shrewd detective, an understanding human being, and even, surprisingly, a serious social thinker."

The Lockridges have occasionally worked independently of each other. Frances Lockridge, an active member of the child placing and adoption committee of the New York State Charities Aid Association, wrote (with Sophie Theis) an informative book on adoption. Richard Lockridge collaborated with George H. Estabrooks, a psychologist, on an exciting spy story about the Nazis in the United States in 1942, *Death in the Mind.*

He also performed solo, in the psychological suspense novel *A Matter of Taste.* Judged by reviews and volume of sales, however, the Lockridges are happiest in their collaborations. In recent years these have included, in addition to their mystery stories, several lovingly written and informative books on cats (some of these written for children), sprinkled with anecdotes based on their own collection of Siamese cats. The cats—and the Lockridges—live in Lewisboro, near Ridgefield, Conn.

PRINCIPAL WORKS: *By Richard Lockridge*—Death in the Mind (with G. H. Estabrooks) 1945; A Matter of Taste, 1949. *By Frances Lockridge*—Adopting a Child (with S. Theis) 1947. *By Richard & Frances Lockridge*—Hanged for a Sheep, 1942; Death Takes a Bow, 1943; Killing the Goose, 1944; Payoff for the Banker, 1945; Murder Within Murder, 1946; Death of a Tall Man, 1946; Untidy Murder, 1947; Think of Death, 1947; Murder Is Served, 1948; I Want to Go Home, 1948; The Dishonest Murderer, 1949; Spring Your Web, Lady! 1949; Cats and People, 1950; Murder in a Hurry, 1950; Foggy, Foggy Death, 1950; Murder Comes First, 1951; A Client Is Canceled, 1951; The Proud Cat, 1951; Dead as a Dinosaur, 1952; Death by Association, 1952; Death Has a Small Voice, 1953; Stand Up and Die, 1953; Curtain for a Jester, 1953; The Lucky Cat, 1953; The Nameless Cat, 1954; A Key to Death, 1954; Burnt Offering, 1955.

ABOUT: Publishers' Weekly August 12, 1950.

LOCKRIDGE, ROSS FRANKLIN, Jr. (April 25, 1914-March 6, 1948), American novelist, was born in Bloomington, Ind., to

Ross Franklin and Elsie Lillian (Shockley) Lockridge. Both his parents were native Hoosiers, graduates of Indiana University, and members of Phi Beta Kappa. His father—author of two books on regional history, *A. Lincoln* (1930) and *Old Fauntleroy Home* (1939)—was a speech teacher and later became head of the department of public speaking at Indiana University. Young Ross was raised in various Indiana towns. When he was ten, the family moved back to Bloomington where he attended high school and began writing verse for the school literary magazine. His proficiency in shorthand and typing in high school made him Indiana's state champion, and his skills proved a real aid years later in the extensive research which he was obliged to do for his novel *Raintree County.*

In 1931 Lockridge entered Indiana University, where he majored in English. In his junior year he went abroad to study in Paris, financed in part by a scholarship from the Institute of International Education. He took his B.A. in 1935 with "high distinction" and in the following year began teaching English at the university and simultaneously working on his Master's degree. This he received in 1939. He remained at Indiana another year on a scholarship for advanced study, and in 1940 received a fellowship to study at Harvard.

By this time Lockridge was married (to Vernice Baker, in 1937) and the father of a two-year-old son. He moved his family to a three-room apartment in the Back Bay section of Boston and began to write a long epic poem. The rejection of this poem by publishers prompted him to make a major decision about his career. He resolved to turn his efforts toward writing more salable material, and in 1941 began work on an historical novel which became *Raintree County*. To support himself and his family he took a teaching job at Simmons College in Boston. During the next seven years, Lockridge worked on the book. Three more children were born to the Lockridges and they all lived in the three-room apartment together with the steadily-growing pile of manuscript pages. In the last stages of work on the book, for over a year and a half, Mrs. Lockridge typed the revised drafts. In April 1946 the novel was submitted to a publisher. Several months later it was accepted for publication, but still another year was spent in editing the manuscript. Six months before its official publication it won the highly lucrative Metro-Goldwyn-Mayer semi-annual novel award. At last, in January 1948, *Raintree County* was published. It became a Book-of-the-Month Club choice, an immediate best seller, and skyrocketed the young author to sudden and sensational success.

Raintree County is set in the community of Waycross, Raintree County, Ind., and takes place in a single day, July 4, 1892. Out of the events of this day, in a series of flashbacks, Lockridge constructed in rich detail the lives, public and private, of a group of citizens of the town. A lusty, full-blooded novel (criticized by clergymen, in particular, for its frankness of language), its 1,066 pages were so crowded with incident and detail that one critic referred to it as Lockridge's "encyclopedia Americana," in which the author "has bludgeoned and blasted the reader with everything that happened to his Raintree inhabitants and to the nation for fifty-three years." Condensation and selectivity, the critics suggested, would have im-

proved the book, but essentially—as many of them pointed out—they might have deprived it of its great appeal, its vitality and robustness. Howard Mumford Jones remarked, in the *Saturday Review of Literature*, "It is . . . repetitious, overly 'organized,' reminiscent of a variety of predecessors, 'literary' in the wrong sense, and too dependent upon source material. But the breath of life sweeps through its voluminous pages; and it may be that *Raintree County* marks at last the end of a long slump in American fiction."

Lockridge did not long enjoy the wealth and fame which the novel brought him. He moved his family back to Bloomington, where he built a new house. Meanwhile, the strain of many years of work on the book began to show. An intense man, burning with what a friend described as "a boyish eagerness that never relaxes," he suffered a nervous breakdown. In March of 1948, only two months after his book was published, and only a few weeks before his thirty-fourth birthday, he committed suicide.

PRINCIPAL WORK: Raintree County, 1948.

ABOUT: Book-of-the-Month Club News December 1947; Current Biography 1948; New York Times March 8, 1948; Saturday Review of Literature June 12, 1948, February 12, 1949; Time January 2, 1948.

LODGE, Sir OLIVER JOSEPH (June 12, 1851-August 22, 1940). For biographical sketch and list of works and references, see TWENTIETH CENTURY AUTHORS, 1942.

* * *

ABOUT: Dictionary of National Biography 1931-40; Low, A. M. They Made Your World.

LOFTING, HUGH (January 14, 1886-September 26, 1947). For autobiographical sketch and list of earlier works and references, see TWENTIETH CENTURY AUTHORS, 1942.

* * *

Hugh Lofting died at his home in Santa Monica, Calif., at sixty-one. Just before his death he completed a final Dr. Dolittle story for his young son Christopher Clement.

Hugh Walpole once called the Dr. Dolittle books "a work of genius—the first real children's classic since Alice." Helen Dean Fish, who felt that the Doctor was "a character so deeply realized that the vein of imagination never wore thin," quoted Lofting's belief that nothing must be allowed to interfere with the entertaining quality of a story. Of his success in fulfilling this intention the London *Times* said: "Imagination, fantasy and humour combined in his work to produce children's stories which became really popular with the audience for which they were intended."

Corrections: Lofting's first wife, Flora Small, died in 1927, not 1917, as given in TWENTIETH CENTURY AUTHORS, 1942. He married Katherine Harrower in 1928 and she died in the same year. In 1935 he married Josephine Fricker, by whom he had the son Christopher Clement, mentioned above.

ADDITIONAL WORKS: Victory for the Slain, 1942; Dr. Dolittle and the Secret Lake, 1948; Dr. Dolittle and the Green Canary, 1950.

ABOUT: Kunitz, S. J. & Haycraft, H. (eds.) The Junior Book of Authors (rev. ed.); Mahony, B. E. & others (comps.) Illustrators of Children's Books; Horn Book September 1948; London Times September 30, 1947, November 23, 1951 (Children's Book Supplement); New York Times September 28, 1947; Saturday Review of Literature January 10, 1948.

LOFTS, NORAH (August 27, 1904-   ). For autobiographical sketch and list of earlier works and references, see TWENTIETH CENTURY AUTHORS, 1942.

* * *

Norah Lofts writes from Bury St. Edmunds, England: "I'm afraid I haven't much to add to the biography; in 1942 I had a son. [Mrs. Lofts then lists her publications since 1942—see below.] At least I have been busy! And if there is a slight disproportion between production of family and trade, I hasten to add that the boy seems to flourish."

Mrs. Lofts has become a specialist in the historical romance, but unlike many of her contemporaries in that field, she is more concerned with the psychology of her characters than with their swashbuckling adventures. The results sometimes strike her readers as contrived and superficial, but never as dull. Kate O'Brien once commented on ". . . the unaffected ease of her writing . . . and her general talent for good, natural narrative," and Beatrice Sherman in the New York *Times* said, "Norah Lofts has the almost uncanny gift of writing about olden times as if she had lived in them."

Most of Mrs. Lofts' novels are set in the early nineteenth century, an era which she recreates with careful and vivid detail. She has been equally successful, however, with the background of the Middle Ages in *The Luteplayer*, the story of Richard the Lionhearted and his minstrel Blondel, and with Biblical times in *Women of the Old Testament*, a series of "psychological portraits," and *Esther*, the story of the great Hebrew queen. *Bless This House*, a chronicle of an English house and family over more than three centuries, was a Literary Guild Selection in April 1954. "An extraordinarily engrossing book," Sara Henderson Hay wrote of it in the *Saturday Review*, "carefully and ingeniously plotted and beautifully written. Norah Lofts is a born storyteller." Another reviewer commented that the author "writes with grace and beauty and a dramatist's sense of the pattern of her tale."

Following the death of her first husband, Geoffrey Lofts, Mrs. Lofts married Dr. Robert Jorisch in 1949. She and her husband made their first visit to America in 1954.

ADDITIONAL WORKS: The Brittle Glass, 1942; Michael and All Angels, 1943; Jassy, 1944; The Golden Fleece, 1944; To See a Fine Lady, 1945; Silver Nutmeg, 1947; A Calf for Venus, 1949; Women of the Old Testament, 1949; Esther, 1950; The Luteplayer, 1951; Bless This House, 1954.

LOHRKE, EUGENE WILLIAM (April 8, 1897-May 17, 1953). For autobiographical sketch and list of works and references, see TWENTIETH CENTURY AUTHORS, 1942.

* * *

Eugene Lohrke died in Westerly, R.I., after a long illness. He was fifty-six. Several months before his death he wrote to the editors of this volume: "My present residence is in Mystic, Conn. I held a commission as major in the war and served overseas in England and North Africa. I was retired from active service in 1945, and then served in the English Department of Upsala College, East Orange, N.J., and for two years as a script writer for the Voice of America. My literary activities since the war have been decidedly feeble, but I expect to resume writing shortly."

ABOUT: New York Times May 18, 1953.

LOMAX, ALAN (January 31, 1915-   ), American folklorist, interrupted his studies at the University of Texas in 1933 to go on his first trip with his father, **JOHN AVERY LOMAX** (September 23, 1867-January 26, 1948), to record folk songs from the people who actually sang them. With a tent, and in an old car, they headed for the Brazos bottoms and the prison camps. The resulting songs were deposited in the newly constituted Archive of American

Folk Song in the Library of Congress, and John A. Lomax was made its first curator. In the years from 1933 to 1935, father and son prepared and published their first collaborations, *American Ballads and Folk Songs* (1934) and *Negro Folk Songs as Sung by Lead Belly, king of the twelve-string guitar players of the world, long-time convict in the penitentiaries of Texas and Louisiana* (1936).

The elder Lomax was born in Goodman, Miss., the son of James Avery Lomax and Susan (Cooper) Lomax. When his family moved to the Texas frontier, they went by horse and ox wagon, and Lomax could hear the cowboys, along the old trail, singing to quiet their cattle at night. Later, when he entered the University of Texas, he took with him a trunkful of songs and ballads; but he found his English professor considered them worthless examples of the crudity of America, and he was told to study the English ballads instead. It was in New England that his American ballads first met with great enthusiasm. When Lomax went to Harvard to get his M.A. (1907), he showed them to Barrett Wendell and George Lyman Kittredge, who arranged for Lomax to receive a Sheldon traveling fellowship. This enabled him to spend three years collecting cowboy songs, ballads, Negro songs, and spirituals. His first publication was *Cowboy Songs and Other Frontier Ballads*, 1910, which contained the first printing of such popular songs as *Get Along, Little Dogie*. This was followed by *Book of Texas* (with H. Y. Benedict) in 1916, and *Songs of the Cattle Trail and Cow Camp* in 1919. Except for these, and his 1947 autobiography, *Adventures of a Ballad Hunter*, John A. Lomax's books found a co-editor and co-compiler in his son, Alan. At the age of eighty John A. Lomax died in Greenville, Miss. He was survived by his second wife, Ruby Terrill Lomax, whom he had married in 1934.

Alan Lomax was born in Austin, Tex. His mother was Bess Baumann (Brown) Lomax; he was one of four children. An excellent student, he was graduated *summa cum laude* from the University of Texas in 1936, and pursued graduate studies at Harvard and Columbia University. Between 1933 and 1942, he collected folk music, with the aid of recording machines, throughout the United States, as well as in Haiti and the Bahamas. He has lectured, written and pro-

duced folk music documentaries for C.B.S. and B.B.C., made extensive recordings in England, Scotland, and Ireland, and edited record albums. In 1937 he married Elizabeth Harold; they have one daughter and live in New York City. From 1937 to 1942 he was assistant in charge of the Archive of American Folk Music. With his father he co-edited several collections, including revised editions of his father's earliest works.

Six feet tall, with dark brown eyes and a wide forehead, Alan Lomax was described as "deep chested and thick set" by Harvey Breit in an interview in 1950 at the time *Mister Jelly Roll*, "the fortunes of Jelly Roll Morton, New Orleans Creole and inventor of jazz," was published. Lomax told Breit that he was working on a book to be called, "From a Great Dark River." "The main people in it are a washwoman, a preacher, a convict and a race record artist." He uses a recording machine instead of a notebook, and—asked if he did much editing—replied: "A lot. It's mostly piecing together, not losing the stream." In the projected book, "The convict tells his tale with the passion of a Dostoevsky. It's thorny prose, very thorny, but it has lots of levels. I believe it will help to transform writing, which has reached a kind of dead end."

PRINCIPAL WORKS: By *John A. Lomax*: Cowboy Songs, 1910; Book of Texas (with H. Y. Benedict) 1916; Songs of the Cattle Trail and Cow Camp, 1919; Adventures of a Ballad Hunter, 1947. By *Alan Lomax*: Fourteen Traditional Songs from Texas (with R. T. Lomax) 1942; Mister Jelly Roll, 1950. By *John and Alan Lomax*: American Ballads and Folk Songs, 1934; Negro Folk Songs, 1936; Our Singing Country, 1941; 111 Best American Ballads: Folk Song U.S.A., 1948.

ABOUT: *John A. Lomax*: Etude March 1948; Journal of American Folklore July 1948; New York Times January 27, 1948; Saturday Review of Literature September 22, 1945. *Alan Lomax*: American Library Association Bulletin September 1, 1940; Christian Science Monitor Magazine March 8, 1941; Current Biography 1941; Etude April 1940; New York Times Book Review July 23, 1950; Southwest Review Winter 1934, January 1938; Time November 26, 1945.

LONDON, JACK (January 12, 1876-November 22, 1916). For biographical sketch and list of works and references, see TWENTIETH CENTURY AUTHORS, 1942.

* * *

ABOUT: Foner, P. S. (ed.) Jack London, American Rebel; Garst, D. S. Jack London, Magnet for Adventure; Morris, L. R. Postscript to Yesterday; Mott, F. L. Golden Multitudes; Whipple, T. K. Study Out the Land; Hobbies February 1946; New Yorker February 26, 1944; Newsweek December 15, 1947.

LONG, GABRIELLE MARGARET VERE (CAMPBELL) (October 29, 1886-December 23, 1952). For biographical sketch and list of earlier works and references, see TWENTIETH CENTURY AUTHORS, 1942.

* * *

Mrs. Gabrielle Margaret Long died in London at sixty-six.

The extent of her published work will probably never be known exactly, since she wrote under six or possibly ten pseudonyms, but something over 150 books are credited to her. She once said that the adoption of a new pen name aided her in assuming a new personality when writing in a different vein.

Her most celebrated authorship, that of the historical novels based usually on actual criminal cases, which she wrote under the name of "Joseph Shearing," was a closely guarded secret until 1942. Although there has been sharp divergence of opinion about the "Shearing" works (E. L. Woodward referred to "an irritating style, a poor choice of words, and the use of cheap effects," while Phil Stong, among others, called their author, in 1941, "the best serious writer of high romance now publishing"), their admirers have been ardent. As Will Cuppy put it, "The novels and characters known as the work of Joseph Shearing have for some years been the shouting point of a rabid cult including the cash customers and critics and running the gamut from able-bodied mystery reviewers to such persons as Rebecca West and William Roughead."

An American admirer who met Mrs. Long in London in 1950 described her as "reserved but charming, ageless."

ADDITIONAL WORKS: *As "Joseph Shearing"*— Lucile Clery: A Woman of Intrigue (in England: Forget Me Not) 1932; Moss Rose, 1934; Spider in the Cup (in England: Album Leaf) 1934; Angel of the Assassination, 1935; Golden Violet: Story of a Lady Novelist, 1936; Lady and the Arsenic, 1937; Orange Blossoms (short stories) 1938; Blanche Fury: or, Fury's Ape, 1939; Aunt Beardie, 1940; Crime of Laura Sarelle, 1941; Spectral Bride (in England: The Fetch) 1942; Airing In a Closed Carriage, 1943; Abode of Love, 1945; So Evil My Love (in England: For Her to See) 1947; Mignonette, 1948; Within the Bubble, 1950; To Bed at Noon, 1951. *As "Marjorie Bowen"*— Church and Social Progress: An Exposition of Rationalism and Reaction, 1945; The Bishop of Hell, and Other Stories, 1949; Life of John Knox, 1949. *As "George Preedy"*—Courtly Charlatan: The Enigmatic Comte de St. Germain, 1942; Lady in a Veil, 1943; Fourth Chamber, 1944; Nightcap and Plume, 1945; No Way Home, 1948; Sacked City, 1949.

ABOUT: New York Times December 27, 1952; Saturday Review of Literature October 31, 1942, July 10, 1948; Wilson Bulletin November 1942.

LONG, HANIEL (March 9, 1888-). For autobiographical sketch and list of earlier works and references, see TWENTIETH CENTURY AUTHORS, 1942.

* * *

In 1929 Haniel Long moved to Santa Fe, N.M., where he still lives. His *Interlinear to Cabeza de Vaca's Relation of His Journey from Florida to the Pacific*, originally published in 1936, was re-issued in 1944 under the title *The Power Within Us*, published in England under the same title, and in Germany titled *Die Kraft In Uns*, in 1950. A collection of his poems, *The Grist Mill*, was described by John T. Frederick as having "such integration of form and substance as makes for lasting satisfaction." Long has also published a deeply personal and sensitive interpretation of the writings of St. Augustine. He contributed a chapter on Santa Fe to *Rocky Mountain Cities* (ed. R. B. West, 1949). An edition of Long's *Pensées (Gedanken)* was recently published in Germany.

ADDITIONAL WORKS: Grist Mill (poems) 1945; Letter to Saint Augustine, 1950.

ABOUT: Commonweal February 12, 1943; Saturday Review of Literature March 16, 1946.

*LONGSTREET, STEPHEN ("Thomas Burton," "Paul Haggard," "David Ormsbee," pseuds.) (April 18, 1907-), American

novelist, scenarist, playwright, and miscellaneous writer, writes: "I was born Henry Stephen Weiner Longstreet in New York City. As a writer I shortened my name, but this has caused some confusion and I am often wrongly listed as  Weiner or Wiener. At the age of two weeks I was moved to New Brunswick, N.J., where my father tried farming, real estate, running stores and shops, with not too much success. I grew up in New Brunswick and have used it as a background for many of my novels.

* "The matter of the proper use of my name is amusing, causing most library heads to list my books under a name I never used. The fault among others is H. W. Wilson's, I hear, who at one time decided I was Philip Wiener. I have no idea where this information came from. It was picked up by the Library of Congress and even by *Time* in one of its reviews, and while I at first tried to correct this, it was much too big a job. A stupid mistake can never be corrected, it appears, and I now take pleasure in confusing people who try to find my books on library shelves. Fifty per cent of them will find me listed under L, the other half under WI. My name is still Henry Stephen Weiner Longstreet, and on books, Stephen Longstreet, as being shorter and looking much better in print, besides saving ink and paper."

My Broadway play *High Button Shoes* is the story of myself and my family in New Brunswick in the year 1913.

"I hung around Rutgers and then Harvard for a while and then went to study art at the New School of Fine and Applied Art (Parsons) where I graduated in 1929 after a three years' course. My education had been wide but without much purpose and I have only gone deeply into things that interest me. In Europe I studied painting in Paris, London, and Rome, and came back to America in the big depression a modern artist when the country was going for the out-house-Americana of Benton, Wood and Curry and their school. Being too modern to sell, I turned magazine artist and cartoonist for the *New Yorker*, *Life* (the comic magazine), *College Humor*, *Saturday Evening Post*, *Collier's*, and many others.

"In 1933 I married Ethel Joan Godoff, well known concert piano player. In 1937 I began to rewrite the stage play *The Front Page* as a radio version, and for ten years I wrote for John Barrymore and many others for radio. Also in 1937, under the pen name of 'Paul Haggard,' I began to write detective novels. For several years I wrote these, then became bored and gave up writing who-dun-its and can no longer even read them. In 1940 I wrote my first serious novel; it was a best seller called *Decade*, and its success turned me into devoting a great deal of my time to serious writing.

"In 1941 I went to Hollywood to do a screen version of my novel *The Gay Sisters*. I stayed on in California and now live in Beverly Hills with my wife and two children, Joan and Harry Stephen. I have written the following motion pictures in whole or part: *The Gay Sisters, The Jolson Story, Stallion Road, Uncle Harry, Silver River, Greatest Show on Earth, Duel in the Sun, Houdini, Stars and Stripes Forever*.

"In 1942 I was an editor on *Time* magazine and also served as motion picture critic for the *Saturday Review of Literature*. In 1948 I got the *Billboard* Award for *High Button Shoes* as the best play of the year. That year too I got the *Photoplay* Gold Medal Gallup Poll Award for *The Jolson Story*, as the most popular motion picture of the year. I am literary critic on the Los Angeles *Daily News* and teach a course called 'Advanced Writing' at the Los Angeles City College.

"For the last ten years I have been working on a large book on the history of art, 'The Picture Makers.' I have never given up painting and am the founder, with three other painters, of a new school of American painting called 'The Functionists West.' Our motto is, 'The function of the painter is to paint.' He has been doing almost everything else these days. The first big Functionists show was held at the Los Angeles Art Association, and shows are planned in Washington and New York [1953].

"As a writer it is interesting to note that 'pocket books' have sold millions of copies of my books, in some cases changing the titles of the books. *Sound of an American* became *Two Beds for Roxane*. I think the novel as we know it is on its way out, to be replaced by a paperbacked cheap book which will sell in the hundreds of thousands. Books cost too much money and too much of the cost is in paper and board. My writing habits are simple. I write every day, have about four books in work at all times, take a long time to think out my material and rewrite it about four times. I am a storyteller and like people and feel the novel must remain a storyteller. My favorite review is from *Time*: 'Stephen Longstreet is the most readable of American writers. . . .'

"My first short stories were printed in *Esquire* magazine, and have been reprinted in collections for years. 'No Peace With the Sea,' a long short story, is still rolling along. It has just been picked again for Charles Grayson's new collection, *The Fourth Round*. I also wrote short stories for *Cosmopolitan* and others, but gave it up when I found the American magazine market that paid a living wage was only interested in formula and watered-down material. However, I have been writing for *Gourmet* magazine for about ten years, doing an average of about eight short stories a year for them. I enjoy the hard work of writing, but the curse of the business is lecturing. Every writer must get out at least twelve times a year and talk some place, to clubs, readers, or colleges, and that is not very rewarding; the author doesn't appear very normal at such times and often feels like a rare animal behind bars being shown off."

PRINCIPAL WORKS: *Novels*—Decade, 1940; The Golden Touch, 1941; The Gay Sisters, 1942; The Land I Live, 1943; Stallion Road, 1945; Three Days, 1947; The Crystal Girl, 1948; The Pedlocks, 1951; The Beach House, 1952; The Lion at Morning, 1954. *Non-Fiction*—The Last Man Around the World, 1941; The Last Man Comes Home, 1942; Nine Lives With Grandfather, 1944; Free World Theatre: Nineteen New Radio Plays (ed. with A. Oboler) 1944; The Sisters Liked Them Handsome (dramatized as High Button Shoes) 1946; A Hundred Years on Wheels, 1952; The World Revisited, 1953. *As "Thomas Burton"*—And So Dedicated, 1940; Bloodbird, 1941; The Great Grab, 1941. *As "Paul Haggard"*—Crime on the Cuff

1936; Dead Is the Doornail, 1938; Death Talks Shop, 1938; Death Walks on Cat Feet, 1938; Poison from a Wealthy Widow, 1938. *As "David Ormsbee"* —Sound of an American, 1942; Chico Goes to the Wars, 1943.

ABOUT: Wilson Library Bulletin 1944.

LONSDALE, FREDERICK (February 5, 1881-April 4, 1954). For biographical sketch and list of earlier works and references, see TWENTIETH CENTURY AUTHORS, 1942.

* * *

Frederick Lonsdale died in London at seventy-three.

He continued almost to the end of his life to write what Brooks Atkinson once called "highly varnished comedy about upper class sin." Lonsdale himself defined comedy as "tragedy averted." "Every play I have done," he said, "was conceived and thought out as tragedy and written as comedy."

The playwright has been characterized by Walter Kerr as "a man of polished flippantry, witty about trifles and iconoclastic about everything else."

ABOUT: Nathan, G. J. Theatre Book 1950-51; Christian Science Monitor March 18, 1950; Commonweal November 4, 1950; New York Times April 6, 1954; New Yorker October 23, 1943, November 4, 1950; Theatre Arts December 1943, November 1946, January 1951; Time November 6, 1950.

LOON. See VAN LOON

LOOS, ANITA (April 26, 1893-). For biographical sketch and list of earlier works and references, see TWENTIETH CENTURY AUTHORS, 1942.

* * *

An interviewer in 1951 described Anita Loos as having "a timeless look." The mere mention of her name, the sight of her small, lively face framed in bangs and a short black bob, conjure up the past—the roaring Twenties, the John Held cartoon, the flapper, and the racoon coat. But Miss Loos has endured with little sign of wear long past the Twenties and in the 1950's found herself enjoying a hearty success, with two plays running on Broadway, several motion pictures in production, and a novel on the presses.

Miss Loos' return to the East and the Broadway theatre was marked in 1946 with a production of her comedy *Happy Birthday*. She wrote the play especially for her friend the actress Helen Hayes, who had confessed to her that, after years of playing Queen Victoria and Harriet Beecher Stowe, she was "fed up with being noble." In

Happy Birthday Miss Loos created the character of a mousy, small-town girl whose inhibitions are suddenly and startlingly released after she takes a few drinks. With Miss Hayes' expert portrayal of the heroine, the play was a complete success and had a long Broadway run. This was merely a preliminary, however, to the rousing success of the musical version of Miss Loos' *Gentlemen Prefer Blondes*, which opened in New York in 1950 and had a long run, a triumphant tour, and was subsequently made into a motion picture. The flapper age had by 1950 taken on something of the quaint charm of an antique shop, but this fact did not dampen but rather seemed to arouse the enthusiasm of the public. In 1951 Miss Loos adapted *Gigi*, Colette's novel, for the stage, and had another hit to her credit.

A Mouse Is Born, Miss Loos' first novel in nearly a quarter of a century, was published in 1951. A satire on life in Hollywood, this novel, like *Gentlemen Prefer Blondes*, is told in the form of letters written by a scatter-brained, semi-literate young Hollywood starlet. Miss Loos' long residence in Hollywood gave her the material for an amusing and authoritative picture of life there, but reviewers agreed that *A Mouse Is Born* lacked the "staying power" of the earlier *Gentlemen*.

Miss Loos lives most of the year in a New York apartment. Her husband, John Emerson, an invalid for many years, lives in California. She follows a busy and unusual schedule—rising to begin work around 4 A.M. and retiring soon after dinner-time.

ADDITIONAL WORKS: *Plays*—Happy Birthday, 1947; Gigi (dramatized from novel by Colette) 1952. *Novel*—A Mouse Is Born, 1951.

ABOUT: New York Herald Tribune Book Review May 6, 1951; New York Times Book Review May 6, 1951; New Yorker December 28, 1946; Theatre Arts November 1950; Time August 26, 1946.

LORCA. See GARCÍA LORCA

LOTHAR, ERNST (October 25, 1890-), German-American novelist, was born in Brunn, Moravia, the son of Dr. Joseph L. Mueller, a lawyer, and Johanna (Wohlmuth) Mueller. The boy was sent to Vienna to be educated. While a student he received the second prize in a short story contest conducted by the Vienna *Neue Freie Presse*. In 1910 he began to write poems and novels, publishing his first book at the age of twenty. His father wanted him to have a career as a jurist, and after taking a Ph.D. and LL.D. at the University of Vienna, he

became a public prosecutor in the Austrian Ministry of Justice, and later a councilor for the Ministry of Education.

However, Lothar continued his writing and in 1918 won first prize in a contest for the best war novel with "The War Lord" (1918). Four years later Lothar gave up the law to devote himself entirely to writing, and was drama critic and columnist for the *Neue Freie Presse*, which had given him his first encouragement in fiction writing. Between 1922 and 1932 he produced seventeen books: novels, essays, and poems. His interest in the theatre increased and he staged and directed classical dramas at the Vienna Burg-Theater. In 1935 he succeeded Max Reinhardt as owner and director of the Theater in der Josefstadt.

Being outspoken in his condemnation of Hitler and National Socialism, Lothar was put on the Gestapo blacklist, and when the *Anschluss* became a reality in 1938, he escaped to Switzerland with a false passport. He went on to Paris, and then brought his wife and daughter to the United States in the spring of 1939.

His novels are of a documentary type, mingling truth and fiction. Lothar is an author who believes that "every true novel transmits and is the history of its time." When he came to the United States he already had a public here, for three of his books had been published in translation in the 1930's: *The Clairvoyant, Little Friend,* and *The Loom of Justice.* His novel of 1941, *A Woman Is Witness,* was selected by the Book League. This story is cast in diary form, a woman's diary said by the publishers to be authentic. "When you put down the book you are surprised that people speak English around you, that faces are calmly bent over their meals and voices have an even, unexcited pitch," wrote one reviewer. "The story is pathetically real," commented the *New Yorker,* finding it under- rather than over-written.

Lothar lectured on the drama for one summer at Bard College, N.Y., and then became professor of the history of the drama at Colorado College and staged plays for the Drama Club there. In the evenings he worked on *Beneath Another Sun* which was a Literary Guild selection in 1943. "Despite the stereotyped nature of the main char-

acters," said the *Saturday Review of Literature,* "the story is vividly told and packed with action. An abundance of minute detail manages fairly well to balance the fantastic and melodramatic elements of the yarn." Between 1946 and 1948 Lothar lived in Europe as United States Theatre and Music Officer for Austria. There he completed his novel *Return to Vienna,* which was praised in part and in part called melodramatic. "There's a lot of grim, exact detail about life in Austria," wrote the *New Yorker,* "but Mr. Lothar becomes somewhat overtheatrical about his hero's problem of whether to be loyal to that land or to America."

In 1933 Ernst Lothar married Adrienne Gessner, the actress. His two daughters by a previous marriage are deceased. The author is of medium height and weight, with black eyes and hair, and has been a great traveler in Europe and also in the United States. As favorite books he names the Bible and the works of Goethe and Emerson. In 1944 he became a United States citizen.

PRINCIPAL WORKS IN ENGLISH TRANSLATION: The Clairvoyant, 1931; Little Friend, 1933; The Loom of Justice (in England: The Mills of God) 1935; A Woman Is Witness: a Paris Diary, 1941; Beneath Another Sun, 1943; The Angel with the Trumpet, 1944; The Door Opens, 1945; The Prisoner, 1945; Return to Vienna, 1949.

ABOUT: Warfel, H. R. American Novelists of Today; Current Biography 1947.

"LOTI, PIERRE" (pen-name of Julien Viaud) (January 14, 1850-June 10, 1923). For biographical sketch and list of works and references, see TWENTIETH CENTURY AUTHORS, 1942.

* * *

ABOUT: Columbia Dictionary of Modern European Literature; Mauriac, F. Men I Hold Great; Saurat, D. Modern French Literature; France Illustration February 19, 1949, January 21, 1950.

*LOUŸS, PIERRE (December 10, 1870-June 4, 1925). For biographical sketch and list of works and references, see TWENTIETH CENTURY AUTHORS, 1942.

* * *

ABOUT: Columbia Dictionary of Modern European Literature; Nineteenth Century April 1950.
* lwē

LOVECRAFT, HOWARD PHILLIPS (August 20, 1890-March 15, 1937), American fantasist, was born in Providence, R.I., to Winfield Scott and Sarah (Phillips) Lovecraft. August Derleth, his biographer, says that his father died of paresis, after spending his last years in a sanatorium. Lovecraft was raised by his mother who was, Derleth writes, "determined to shelter her son from the rigors and dangers of life." He was a  precocious child—by his own account "very peculiar and sensitive, always preferring the society of grown persons to that of other children. I could not keep away from printed matter. I had learned the alphabet at two, and at four could read with ease. . . ." His main interest during his childhood was in the sciences, and his earliest writings were on scientific subjects. At sixteen he was contributing a monthly article on astronomy to the Providence *Tribune*.

Poor health prevented Lovecraft from attending college. He spent most of his life in Providence where he lived with his mother and aunts. He supported himself very meagerly by ghost writing and working as a revisionist. His first published story, "The Alchemist" (written in 1908), appeared in the *United Amateur* (a publication of the United Amateur Press Association in which Lovecraft took an active interest) in 1916, and from that time forward his work appeared in little magazines like the *Vagrant* and *Home Brew*. Lovecraft was not assured of a regular market for his stories, however, until his story "Dagon" was published in the magazine *Weird Tales* for October 1923. Recognition was still slow in coming, but by the late 1920's his work was being reprinted in anthologies of horror stories, and two of the stories had honorable mention in the O'Brien collections. By far the greatest number of his stories was published in *Weird Tales;* others in *Amazing Stories, Astounding Stories,* and *Tales of Magic and Mystery.* He published only one book in his lifetime, and his reputation remained obscure until the late 1940's when his friend the author August Derleth and others began collecting his works.

Lovecraft was married in 1924 to a writer, Mrs. Sonia Greene, of New York City. He lived with his wife in Brooklyn for a little less than two years and they were divorced in 1929. When he separated from his wife Lovecraft returned to Providence which he left thereafter only to make several short winter trips south. Because he liked to write at night, he would draw the shades and work by electric light even during the day. He lived a solitary life but kept up a voluminous correspondence. Derleth says he was a brilliant letter writer. He was never satisfied with his own writing, feeling that "it was touched with commercialism and fell too far short of what he intended it to be." Always in poor health, he became seriously ill in 1936 and died in 1937 of cancer and Bright's disease.

A shy, withdrawn, imaginative, and physically delicate person, sensitively aware of the fact that he was ugly and socially ill-at-ease, Lovecraft lived in his imagination rather than in reality. His literary masters were, first and foremost, Poe, then Arthur Machen, Algernon Blackwood, M. R. James, Walter de la Mare, Lord Dunsany—all artists in fantasy and the macabre. He was obsessed with the idea of the past and filled with loathing of the present. His special historical passion was the eighteenth century, and he wrote a considerable amount of poetry in imitation of eighteenth century verse.

Lovecraft's stories, as Derleth points out, fall into two classes—tales of fantasy, somewhat along the lines of Lord Dunsany's work; and tales of horror, "of cosmic outsideness, after a pattern which, though a compound of Poe, Machen, [Robert W.] Chambers, and Bierce, manifests the influence of Arthur Machen and Algernon Blackwood, and yet manages to remain individually Lovecraftian to such an extent that it has influenced many another writer in the genre." With the current vogue of science fiction and the wide appeal of stories of "other worlds," some of Lovecraft's work—especially his stories of the Cthulhu Mythos, concerned with "dislocation of time and space"—have taken on new interest. Of these Lovecraft wrote: "All my stories, unconnected as they may be, are based on the fundamental lore or legend that this world was inhabited at one time by another race who, in practising black magic, lost their foothold and were expelled, yet live on outside ever ready to take possession of this earth again." In these stories he developed a complete mythology and geography—a wild, weird, yet curiously impressive flight of the imagination. The Cthulhu Mythos placed Lovecraft securely in the great tradition of American horror writing, along with Poe and Bierce.

A taste for Lovecraft's work is special and definitely an acquired one. He has many enthusiastic admirers. A veritable "Lovecraft cult" has developed in the past decade. Edmund Wilson, however, insists that he "was not a good writer . . . quite second-rate." His greatest weakness as a writer was one which he recognized himself—a tendency toward melodrama. His strength, T. O. Mabbott points out, was his narrative gift. "Lovecraft was an original in the Gothic tradition," Derleth writes. "He was a skilled writer of supernatural fiction, a master of the macabre who had no peer in the America of his time. . . . By his own choice he was in letters, as in his personal existence, an outsider in his time."

PRINCIPAL WORKS: The Shadow Over Innsmouth, 1936; The Notes & Commonplace Book Employed by the Late H. P. Lovecraft, 1938; The Outsider and Others, 1939; Beyond the Wall of Sleep, 1943; The Weird Shadow Over Innsmouth and Other Stories of the Supernatural, 1944; Marginalia, 1944; The Best Supernatural Stories of H. P. Lovecraft, 1945; The Dunwich Horror, 1945; Something About Cats and Other Pieces, 1949; Haunter of the Dark and Other Tales, 1951; The Case of Charles Dexter Ward, 1952.

ABOUT: Derleth, A. H.P.L.: A Memoir; Essays by various hands in Lovecraft, H. P. Best Supernatural Stories, Beyond the Wall of Sleep, Marginalia, Something About Cats; Wilson, E. Classics and Commercials.

LOVEJOY, ARTHUR ONCKEN (October 10, 1873-), American philosopher and author, was born in Berlin, the son of

Johns Hopkins Magazine

Rev. W. W. Lovejoy of Boston and Sara Agnes Oncken of Hamburg, Germany. Lovejoy was educated at the University of California, Harvard University (where he took a master's degree), and the University of Paris. In 1899 he began teaching at Stanford University. Two years later, in 1901, he moved to Washington University in St. Louis, and after a brief stay at the University of Missouri, taught for twenty-eight years at Johns Hopkins. In 1938 he retired as professor of philosophy emeritus. In the course of his career, Lovejoy was also a lecturer at Harvard and the University of London. The Great Chain of Being (1936) is by ·some regarded as his most significant work. Comprising a series of addresses given at Harvard, it deals with the conception of the world as accepted down to the close of the eighteenth century, a conception combining the three principles of plenitude, continuity and gradation—as stemming from Plato, Aristotle, and the Neo-Platonists. William P. Montague, writing an appreciation of Lovejoy in 1948, said: "Lovejoy has sometimes been taken to task for being over-critical and insufficiently constructive in his writings. Regardless of

whatever measure of truth may be contained in this appraisal, one cannot read a book like The Great Chain of Being without being impressed by the depth and extent of his learning, and the originality with which he applied it to the subject in hand."

Essays in the History of Ideas is Lovejoy's most recent publication. As Stanley E. Hyman puts it, the history of ideas is a philosophic field largely invented and preempted by Lovejoy; it is the tracing of the unit ideas of philosophies through intellectual history. This work of scholarship has made a real contribution to literary criticism, and has influenced the critical writings of F. O. Matthiessen and Kenneth Burke, for example. Theodore Spencer, reviewing the Essays, commented on the interest and importance to the literary student of Lovejoy's new insight into our intellectual heritage: "He has made us aware of past schematizations, discriminations and conflicts so that not only are we directly fascinated and illumined by the analytical pictures of the past. . . , we are also indirectly influenced as we reflect on our present situations in the light of the past he has revealed."

Lovejoy has received many honorary degrees, LL.D. and Litt.D. He has been associated as editor with the Journal of the History of Ideas. In 1948 a former student wrote, "Professor Lovejoy . . . has changed little in a quarter-century. Perhaps his Prussian-cut hair and goatee are whiter, though they were iron-gray even in 1923. His speech is as clipped and precise (and frequently as devastating) today as when I first heard him. His eyes are still . . . steel blue." The author lives in Baltimore, and is unmarried.

PRINCIPAL WORKS: The Revolt against Dualism, 1930; Primitivism and Related Ideas in Antiquity (with George Boas) 1935; The Great Chain of Being, 1936; Essays in the History of Ideas, 1948.

ABOUT: Hyman, S. E. The Armed Vision; Journal of the History of Ideas October 1948.

LOVELACE, Mrs. MAUD (HART) and DELOS WHEELER (April 25, 1892- and December 2, 1894-). For autobiographical sketch and list of earlier works and references, see TWENTIETH CENTURY AUTHORS, 1942.

* * *

The Lovelaces write: "In the years since 1942, the Lovelaces have collaborated, still happily, on one more book—a collection of pre-Columbian South American Indian legends called The Golden Wedge.

"Through the 'forties, while assistant city editor of the New York *Sun,* D.W.L. wrote a syndicated column, 'Who's News Today,' and also found time (1944) for a biography of General 'Ike' Eisenhower which was later (1952) revised. When the *Sun* became part of the *World-Telegram and Sun* (1950), D.W.L. became a staff writer on the latter newspaper until he resigned (1952) to give all his time to writing. He is busy on a novel at the Lovelace home (still Garden City, but he and M.H.L. are talking California).

"M.H.L. does not know when she will get at a novel again. Her book for children, mentioned so casually in the autobiographical sketch in TWENTIETH CENTURY AUTHORS, proved to be the first of a highly successful series. Sales will soon reach the 300,000 mark, and letters from readers, six to sixteen, pour into the Lovelace home from every state in the union.

"The Betsy-Tacy stories are based on M.H.L.'s own youth in Mankato, Minn. This pleasant town, called Deep Valley in the books, has become a mecca for eager children. Many, although not all, of the characters in the series are real people and take pleasure in identifying themselves. September 1952, Betsy, Tacy, and Tib had a reunion, the first meeting of the three in thirty-four years.

"The childhood memories which grew into this series were first told to the Lovelace daughter, Merian, as bedtime stories. The latest title, *Betsy and the Great World,* indicates how far the heroine has progressed, and Merian is now a Phi Beta Kappa, *cum laude,* graduate of Smith. She majored in Latin-American affairs, has traveled south of the border, and speaks Spanish like one to the hacienda born. She says it all sprang from the dinner table talk when her parents were working on the above-mentioned *Golden Wedge.*"

ADDITIONAL WORKS: *By Maud Hart Lovelace* —Betsy and Tacy Go Over the Big Hill, 1942; Down-Town, 1943; Heaven to Betsy, 1945; Betsy in Spite of Herself, 1946; Betsy Was a Junior, 1947; Betsy and Joe, 1948; Carney's Houseparty, 1949; Emily of Deep Valley, 1950; The Tune Is in the Tree, 1950; The Trees Kneel at Christmas, 1951; Betsy and the Great World, 1952; Winona's Pony Cart, 1953. *By Delos Wheeler Lovelace*— General 'Ike' Eisenhower, 1944; Journey to Bethlehem, 1953.

ABOUT (Maud Hart Lovelace): Kunitz, S. J. & Haycraft, H. Junior Book of Authors (rev. ed.)

LOVELACE, DELOS WHEELER. See LOVELACE, M. H. & D. W.

LOVETT, ROBERT MORSS (December 25, 1870-   ). For biographical sketch and list of earlier works and references, see TWENTIETH CENTURY AUTHORS, 1942.

* * *

All his long life a "fighting liberal," one who has insisted on putting into practice his ideals about freedom and equality, Robert Morss Lovett has been the center of many stormy controversies. Through all of these he has emerged, in the public consciousness, as that rarest of figures—the independent thinker, well-meaning, sometimes perhaps wrong-headed, but always a man of firmness and integrity. Thus it was, as Milton Mayer wrote in *Harper's,* "more in sorrow than in anger" that in 1943 the United States Congress cut off his salary as governmental secretary of the Virgin Islands. (In 1946 the Supreme Court decided that the earlier action in terminating an executive office by cutting off the salary attached to it was illegal, and that Lovett's claim for wages should be paid.) Lovett's dismissal followed upon a denunciation of him by Representative Martin Dies as "an irresponsible, unrepresentative crackpot radical bureaucrat."

After he left the Virgin Islands, Lovett became professor of English at the University of Puerto Rico, where he remained until 1946. He then returned to the United States and settled in Lake Zurich, Ill., some forty miles from Chicago. Here he lives with his wife. "I am in an elegiac period," he wrote in 1948, "all for the quiet ending."

In the storm and stress of Lovett's political career there is a tendency to overlook that more important phase of his life—the years he spent as a scholar and a teacher. As he writes in his autobiography, *All Our Years:* "The best of my life has been given to education in the broader sense, including work with various organizations to promote peace and social welfare. As I look back I realize that my students have been the chief justification of my existence."

All Our Years is Lovett's only recent book. It was favorably received and praised especially for its humor, candor, and modesty. George Mayberry suggested that it might become "a minor classic," and Francis Hackett said in the New York *Times:* "This is a highly significant book. What Congress calls 'un-American activity' has in this book an exponent as American as Bunker Hill. . . . Yet being in no manner a self-seeker, having no rancor in his nature, his generous and robust career is not only fascinating but arresting at a juncture where a deadlock with communism may mean war."

ADDITIONAL WORK: All Our Years, 1948.

ABOUT: Lovett, R. M. All Our Years; Current Biography 1943; Harper's July 1946; New Republic September 27, 1943, April 24, 1944.

LOWELL, AMY (February 9, 1874-May 12, 1925). For biographical sketch and list of works and references, see TWENTIETH CENTURY AUTHORS, 1942.

* * *

ADDITIONAL WORK: (with F. Ayscough) Correspondence of a Friendship, 1946.

ABOUT: Ayscough, F. & Lowell, A. Correspondence of a Friendship; Brooks, V. W. Chilmark Miscellany; Gregory, H. & Zaturenska, M. History of American Poetry; Rollins, H. E. & Parrish, S. M. Keats and the Bostonians; Arizona Quarterly Summer 1952; Scholastic March 11, 1946.

LOWELL, ROBERT (March 1, 1917-   ), American poet, writes: "I was born in Boston and lived there during my youth, except

Arni

for several periods spent in Washington and Philadelphia where my father was stationed as a naval officer. I attended St. Mark's School and Harvard College for two years. Since my interest was writing poetry, a friend suggested that I go to Kenyon College, in Ohio, to study with John Crowe Ransom. This was a happy decision for me, and I graduated from Kenyon, having majored in classics there. Later I spent some time at Louisiana State University and worked for a short time with a New York publisher. During World War II, I was a conscientious objector and served a jail sentence. My first book of poems was *Land of Unlikeness*. Most of the poems were included in my second volume, *Lord Weary's Castle*, published in 1946. In 1951 I published a third volume of poetry, *The Mills of the Kavanaughs.*

"In 1947-48 I was Consultant in Poetry at the Library of Congress. I have held a Guggenheim fellowship and an Institute of Arts and Letters grant. During these years I have also lectured in poetry and creative writing at the State University of Iowa, the Kenyon School of English and the Salzburg Seminar in American Studies in Austria. Three years ago I went to Europe for the first time, traveled and lived all over the continent, and

made a visit to Turkey and Greece. I returned just recently [1953] for a second term of teaching at Iowa.

"I am married to the writer Elizabeth Hardwick."

* * *

Robert Lowell received the Pulitzer prize for poetry in 1947 for *Lord Weary's Castle*. He is a member of the famous Lowell family —a great-grandnephew of James Russell Lowell and a distant cousin of Amy Lowell. He received a B.A. from Kenyon College in 1940. In the same year he entered the Roman Catholic Church. His first wife was the novelist Jean Stafford.

Allen Tate, in his introduction to Lowell's first volume of poems, wrote: "There is no other poetry today quite like this. . . . Lowell is consciously a Catholic poet. . . . The style is bold and powerful and the symbolic language has the effect of being willed." Randall Jarrell commented, after publication of *Lord Weary's Castle*: "I can think of no one younger than Auden who has written better poetry than Robert Lowell's." Jarrell was particularly impressed with the dramatic qualities of his poetry, its concreteness, the poet's "odd and imaginative Catholicism" ("essentially literary, anthropomorphic, emotional"), and his sense of construction. "Mr. Lowell is a thoroughly professional poet, and the degree of intensity of his poems is equalled by their degree of organization. Inside its elaborate stanzas, the poem is put together like a mosaic: the shifts of movement, the varied pauses, the alternation in the length of sentences, the counterpoint between lines and sentences, are the outer form of a subject matter that has been given a dramatic, dialectical internal organization." One or two of the poems in *Lord Weary's Castle*, Jarrell suggested, "will be read as long as men remember English."

PRINCIPAL WORKS: Land of Unlikeness, 1944; Lord Weary's Castle, 1946; The Mills of the Kavanaughs, 1951.

ABOUT: Current Biography 1947; Life May 19, 1947; Nation January 18, 1947; Poetry January 1953.

LOWENTHAL, MARVIN (October 6, 1890-   ). For autobiographical sketch and list of earlier works and references, see TWENTIETH CENTURY AUTHORS, 1942.

* * *

Marvin Lowenthal lives in Sparkill, N.Y. For the past several years he has been editor of the *American Zionist* monthly. The "recent book" referred to in his sketch in the 1942 volume of TWENTIETH CENTURY AU-

THORS as *New York: The City Washington Knew* was published in 1943 under the title *This Was New York: The Nation's Capital in 1789.*

ADDITIONAL WORK: (with F. K. Monaghan) This Was New York, 1943.

LOWES, JOHN LIVINGSTON (December 20, 1867-August 15, 1945). For biographical sketch and list of works and references, see TWENTIETH CENTURY AUTHORS, 1942.

* * *

John Livingston Lowes died in Boston, Mass., at seventy-seven.

W. A. Neilson has noted Lowes' extraordinary store of knowledge in many fields, his persistent curiosity and his "intellectual passion." *The Road to Xanadu* is, as Neilson has said, "a triumphant justification of the type of scholarship of which he was now the most distinguished and most widely recognized exponent in America." Lowes united, in the words of Babette Deutsch, "the special equipment of the scholar and a style so rich and allusive as to touch with life even the more barren tracts of exposition."

ABOUT: Carnegie Foundation for the Advancement of Teaching. 41st Annual Report, 1946; Speculum July 1946.

*LOWNDES, Mrs. MARIE ADELAIDE (BELLOC) (1868-November 14, 1947). For autobiographical sketch and list of earlier works and references, see TWENTIETH CENTURY AUTHORS, 1942.

* * *

Marie Belloc Lowndes died at the home of her daughter, Countess Iddesleigh, at Eversly Cross, Hampshire, England. She was seventy-nine.

Her series of autobiographical books—*I, Too, Have Lived in Arcadia, Where Love and Friendship Dwelt,* and *Merry Wives of Westminster*—has been called by May Lamberton Becker "one of the greatest memoirs of our time." James Barrie is said to have believed that every novel and short story which Mrs. Lowndes wrote would some day be dramatized. The chief distinction of her work probably lies in her power of characterization. In the words of the London *Times,* "what really interested her as a novelist were the relations of men and women. It could also be truly said that the world was her parish."

ADDITIONAL WORKS: Where Love and Friendship Dwelt, 1943; Merry Wives of Westminster,

* loundz

1946; The Passing World (reminiscences) 1948; She Dwelt With Beauty, 1949.

ABOUT: Lowndes, M. B. Where Love and Friendship Dwelt; Merry Wives of Westminster, The Passing World; Hoehn, M. (ed.) Catholic Authors, I; London Times November 15, 1947; New York Times November 15, 1947.

LOWRY, MALCOLM (July 28, 1909-), English novelist, was born in Merseyside, England, the son of a cotton broker and the grandson of a wind-jamming sea captain. From his tenth to his fourteenth year he was isolated from reading, writing, and playing games by chronic ulceration of the cornea of both eyes. After a successful operation he went to Leys School, Cam-

bridge, where his housemaster was W. H. Balgarnie, the original of James Hilton's Mr. Chips. He took up golf and became a junior champion. Inspired by reading Eugene O'Neill, he left school and worked his way to China on a sailing ship. Returning to England, he became enthusiastic over the work of Conrad Aiken and made a trip to Massachusetts to meet the poet. In 1929 he entered Cambridge University; in 1932 he was graduated. That year the manuscript of his first novel, after being accepted by a London firm, was lost when an editor's suitcase was stolen. No carbon existed but in three months the author rewrote the novel and it was published with the title *Ultramarine.* A small notice appeared in the (London) *Times Literary Supplement,* stating that the book "reads less as a novel than as the first expansion of shorthand notes taken with a view to making a novel out of a new experience." The story, concerning a literate young man aboard a tramp steamer, expressed thoughts which sounded as if "reproduced from a recording machine," said the reviewer. "If the art of writing is imitation the author has mastered it; if reconstruction enters it he has yet some way to go."

Lowry went to France, and then came to the United States. Here he wrote, between visits to Mexico, three novels, one of them *Under the Volcano.* All three were rejected. He began a third version of *Under the Volcano;* meanwhile his house burned down. The manuscript was finally completed on Christmas Eve 1944 in the bar of a pub on Lake Ontario. When it was finished the author began to rebuild his house with his own hands, with the help of his wife. Exhausted from the effort the two went to Mexico for a rest. There the news reached them of the acceptance, in England and America, of the final draft of his novel. *Under the Volcano* was published in 1947.

"The story itself is dolorous and simple; its complexities are in its radiations. It begins in 1939, in November . . . in Mexico. Two melancholy, tired, and sensitive men . . . [talk] of a man whom they have not seen for exactly a year," wrote John Woodburn in the *Saturday Review of Literature,* concluding: "I am of the opinion, carefully considered, that *Under the Volcano* is a work of genius." Mark Schorer in the New York *Herald Tribune Book Review* commented: "Mr. Lowry writes with superb vigor and dash and he creates, through his style no less than through his acute capacity for sensuous observation, a novel of opulent texture and consequently resonant meaning." In 1954 Lowry was at work on a collection of novellas and short stories, to be entitled "Hear Us Oh Lord from Heaven Thy Dwelling Place."

Lowry has shipped to sea many times and might have been found at various periods in his life in China, Russia, the Barbados, Paris, Mexico, and British Columbia. While at Cambridge some of his first work as a writer was published by Edward J. O'Brien in his *Best Short Stories.* He is married to the writer Margerie Bonner. They live in British Columbia.

PRINCIPAL WORKS: Ultramarine, 1933; Under the Volcano, 1947

ABOUT: New World Writing No. 3; Saturday Review of Literature February 22, 1947.

LOWRY, ROBERT JAMES (March 28, 1910-   ), American novelist and short story writer, reports: "My father grew up on a  farm in the West Virginia mountain country and left it at seventeen to get himself a job on the railroad in Cincinnati, Ohio. He still has the job, and he and my mother, one of a German immigrant carpenter's twelve children, still live in the same old house with the same old attic where I started writing, in a kind of savage and desperate and romantic way, when I was nine. Some of the stories were published in the local paper. I went on writing and publishing them from then to now.

"Sameness bored me at ten and I tried filling my life with guinea pigs, chickens, dogs, lizards, turtles, fish, and alligators. It went on boring me at twelve and I went rabbit hunting. I tried going without a coat in midwinter at fourteen, and I tried a crewcut at sixteen. I tried reading Kant and not seeing a soul for days; and I tried playing football and not reading anything for days. Not even Kant.

"I followed an older sister, Ruth, through grade school and through high school. Thanks to Dostoevsky, Swift, Schopenhauer, Sherwood Anderson, Maupassant, Hemingway, Gogol, and Mark Twain, as well as a few puzzled educators and elders, I got an education in spite of my feelings about compulsory schooling and confinement in general. At the University of Cincinnati I organized and edited a literary magazine during my freshman year, and fell in love with a girl who thought taking a look at the world might be a good idea. We made it to Little Rock before her mother caught up with her.

"I went on alone—through the Southwest, finally to New York City. Lived and wrote there for a few months, and almost starved. Then went back to Cincinnati where I bought a printing press, taught myself printing, and started publishing Little Man books—illustrated pamphlets by myself and others that nobody had seen the likes of before.

"Then I got married (at twenty-two, to a social worker six years older); then I got drafted (into World War II). The next three years, three months and three days were spent as an infantryman, a topographic draftsman and an Army newspaper editor in the United States, Africa and Italy. After the war I went to New York, divorced my wife, found publishers for the novel and book of stories I'd begun in the Army, and worked a year as production manager for New Directions and another year as book critic for *Time.* I've remarried, have a boy named David, and since 1945 have lived my life and written my books in New York, Michigan, Italy, and Connecticut. Some of the things I care about are writing, women, prizefights, conversation, children, and moving around. One of the things I know is that you write a book in three big jumps: first you write it to explain it to yourself, then you write it again to explain it to somebody else, then you take out all the explanations and let it stand for what it is."

PRINCIPAL WORKS: Casualty, 1946; Find Me in Fire, 1948; The Big Cage, 1949; The Wolf that Fed Us (short stories) 1949; The Violent Wedding, 1953; Happy New Year, Kamerades! (short stories) 1954.

ABOUT: Aldridge, J. W. After the Lost Generation; Warfel, H. R. American Novelists of Today; American Mercury February 1947; Antioch Review Fall 1949; The New Yorker April 23, 1949; Time October 24, 1949.

LUBBOCK, PERCY (June 4, 1879-   ).
For biographical sketch and list of earlier works and references, see TWENTIETH CENTURY AUTHORS, 1942.

* * *

Percy Lubbock returned to Italy after World War II and lives in Lerici. In 1952 he received the Commander Order of the British Empire. His long-awaited book on Edith Wharton was published in 1947. The book was based largely upon personal recollection and written with a discretion and gentility which made for interesting but not completely informative reading. Edmund Wilson describes it as "a real portrait, carefully composed with every brush-stroke studied." But he objects that "the concrete questions that one would have to have answered in order to understand Edith Wharton's career are mostly ignored or evaded by Mr. Lubbock." John Farrelly remarked in the *New Republic* that Lubbock "writes with an exquisite discretion that matches his fine, courteous style, and the resultant tone is one of awe mixed with a determination not to say any more than he has to."

The recent revival of interest in the works of Henry James and Edith Wharton has created new interest in Lubbock's critical works on these authors. The last half of W. H. Graham's remark in the *National Review* in 1943 that Lubbock "is indeed a word master, but seemingly unappreciated" needs modification, since Lubbock is today recognized as a keen critic of modern fiction and one of the initiators of the current critical study of the novel as a literary and aesthetic form. A new edition of his *The Craft of Fiction* was published in England in 1954.

ADDITIONAL WORK: Portrait of Edith Wharton, 1947.

ABOUT: Wilson, E. Classics and Commercials; National Review August 1943.

LUCAS, EDWARD VERRALL (1868-June 26, 1938). For biographical sketch and list of works and references, see TWENTIETH CENTURY AUTHORS, 1942.

* * *

ABOUT: Dictionary of National Biography 1931-1940.

LUCE, CLARE BOOTHE. See BOOTHE C.

*LUDWIG, EMIL (January 25, 1881-September 17, 1948). For biographical sketch and list of earlier works and references, see TWENTIETH CENTURY AUTHORS, 1942.

* * *

Emil Ludwig died in his sleep, at sixty-seven, at Ascona, Switzerland, where he had maintained a home for many years. He had suffered from a heart ailment for two years. He had been a Swiss citizen since 1932; in his native Germany his books were burned during World War II and he was declared an enemy of the Nazi state.

Ludwig had completed a book of memoirs, and at the time of his death was at work on a biography of Alexander and Karl William von Humboldt, German scientists and world travelers, and had begun research on a life of King David.

Although he also wrote plays, poetry, and novels, it was his biographies which brought him popularity. Mary M. Colum called him "a high-class journalist with a strong scent for the human interest in every man's story." The duality which gave him wide popular appeal but only limited critical acclaim is defined by Leonard Woolf: "His analysis of historical events and of character and motive is nearly always intelligent and often brilliant while he is also painstaking and not afraid of being laborious. . . . Where he attempts a synthetic picture, it tends to be commonplace, obvious, or mechanical. This is partly due to a streak of sentimentality and banality in his whole outlook."

ADDITIONAL WORKS: Stalin, 1942; Beethoven, 1943; How To Treat the Germans, 1943; Torch of Freedom: Twenty Exiles of History (ed. with H. B. Kranz) 1943; Mackenzie King: a Portrait Sketch, 1944; Of Love and Life, 1945; Othello, 1947.

ABOUT: Books Abroad Spring 1949; London Times September 20, 1948; New York Times September 19, 1948.

* lo͞ot'vĭk

LUHAN, Mrs. MABEL (GANSON) DODGE (February 26, 1879-   ). For biographical sketch and list of earlier works and references, see TWENTIETH CENTURY AUTHORS, 1942.

* * *

Mabel Dodge Luhan lives in Taos, N.M. With her husband, Tony, she visited New York in 1945. There, interviewed by the *New Yorker*, she reported that she had recently completed a novel which she called "Let's Get Away Together." This book has not yet been published, but in 1947 Miss Luhan did publish *Taos and Its Artists*, an introduction to forty-nine artists who have lived and worked in Taos, together with reproductions of some of their works.

ADDITIONAL WORK: Taos and Its Artists, 1947.

ABOUT: Stein, G. Selected Writings; New Yorker May 5, 1945; Time May 5, 1947.

LUMPKIN, GRACE. For biographical sketch and list of works and references, see TWENTIETH CENTURY AUTHORS, 1942.

* * *

Grace Lumpkin has published no books in recent years. Her name has come up in recent congressional investigations of left-wing organizations. Miss Lumpkin testified in April 1953 that she had written Communist propaganda under pressure many years earlier, but that she had never joined the Communist Party, and that she broke with Communism in 1941. Whittaker Chambers wrote of her in Witness in 1952: "Grace Lumpkin, now a devout woman whose days are filled with good works, had been a close fellow-traveler who broke from the Communist movement after me." Chambers further says that at the time he was preparing his own dramatic break from the party, Miss Lumpkin, who had for many years been a friend of Mrs. Chambers, lent him all her savings.

ABOUT: Chambers, W. Witness; New York Times April 2, 1953.

LUNN, HUGH KINGSMILL (1889-May 15, 1949). For autobiographical sketch and list of earlier works and references, see TWENTIETH CENTURY AUTHORS, 1942.

* * *

Hugh Kingsmill Lunn died at Brighton, England, at fifty-nine.

An unusual and moving memoir of the writer, whose work was published under the name of Hugh Kingsmill, has been written in the form of letters exchanged by his friends and collaborators, Hesketh Pearson and Malcolm Muggeridge. The London Times, pointing out his prolific production of literary journalism, biography, parodies, and anthologies, declared that "there was not a great deal, perhaps, that was original in his style of biography," but adjudged him "a versatile, energetic and entertaining author and critic."

ADDITIONAL WORKS: The Poisoned Crown; 1944; Talking of Dick Whittington (with H. Pearson) 1947; Progress of a Biographer, 1949.

ABOUT: Pearson, H. & Muggeridge, M. About Kingsmill; London Times May 17, 1949; New York Times May 17, 1949.

LUSTGARTEN, EDGAR MARCUS (May 3, 1907-), English novelist and criminologist, writes: "Born in Manchester, England, I was an only child. My father was a successful lawyer and no one doubted that I, too, was destined for the law. My propensity for scribbling stories, which manifested itself at an indecently early age, was regarded as a sign of lively imagination but no more.

Douglas Glass

"I went to the Manchester Grammar School and to Oxford, where I became president of the Union (proving that I possessed at least one asset to lawyers, a fluent tongue). Within a few weeks of leaving the University, I was called to the Bar, and resettled myself in Manchester where I began to practice.

"Work came in gratifyingly, and by the time of my marriage (1932) I was a busy advocate. At the same time I continued to scribble, for no very obvious financial reason, but from some sort of inner compulsion. Lacking the time to attempt any large-scale literary work, I wrote for the radio—short plays, features, song-lyrics—under a nom de plume. But I had no conscious notion of exchanging my established role of lawyer for an uncertain role as writer. The war, however, completely changed my life. I gave up legal practice (fully intending to return to it in peace-time), moved from Manchester to London, and for more than five years, as a member of the B.B.C.'s wartime staff, I was engaged in various forms of counter-propaganda.

"As the war drew near its close and the pressure of B.B.C. work relaxed a little, I began to occupy my spare time with the writing of a novel. As it progressed, the thought gradually took shape in my mind—if this book succeeds, I'll take the risk; I'll abandon my comfortable position in the law and try to create a fresh career as author.

"That first novel was A Case to Answer, (U.S. title: One More Unfortunate). It achieved a success I had not dared to hope for, and ever since I have been a professional writer and journalist, tending to specialise in stories of crime, both real and fictional, but not detective stories. At the present moment, I am engaged on a biography of the famous English advocate, Sir Patrick Hastings [1952].

"I have no fixed methods of work, though I try to keep regular hours. In fact, though,

I often find myself writing at the most unexpected times and in the least convenient places—in pubs, in taxis, even while walking in the street.

"I write slowly and rather painfully; a fair output is seven hundred words a day. But as I am psychologically inhibited from starting any sentence until I am satisfied with the sentence that precedes it, there is never much rewriting or revision. When the last line is penned, the book is really done."

PRINCIPAL WORKS: Novels—A Case to Answer (in U.S. One More Unfortunate) 1947; Blondie Iscariot, 1948; Game for Three Losers, 1952. Fact-crime—Verdict in Dispute, 1949; Defenders' Triumph, 1951; The Woman in the Case, 1955.

LYND, Mrs. HELEN (MERRELL). See LYND, R. S.

LYND, ROBERT (April 20, 1879-October 6, 1949). For biographical sketch and list of earlier works and references, see TWENTIETH CENTURY AUTHORS, 1942.

* * *

Robert Lynd died at his home in London at seventy. Three years before his death he was awarded an honorary degree of Doctor of Literature from Queen's University at Belfast.

The essayist has been described by his friend, the late Desmond MacCarthy, as "a good man—sensible, laughter-loving, humble, kind." His wide range of interests was noted by Richard Church, who called Lynd "a liberal humanist . . . set firmly, and on principle, in the centre of his own tolerance." An imaginative quality in his newspaper work lifted it above the level of "the hand-to-mouth work of journalism," in the words of J. B. Priestley, who characterized him as "one of the best miscellaneous prose writers of our generation, an essayist of rare charm, an acute, witty, yet tolerant critic."

ADDITIONAL WORKS: Both Sides of the Road, 1943; Things One Hears, 1945; Essays on Life and Literature, 1951; Books and Writers, 1952.

ABOUT: Church, R. British Authors (1948); New Statesman and Nation October 15, 1949; New York Times October 7, 1949.

LYND, ROBERT STAUGHTON (September 26, 1892-). For biographical sketch and list of works and references, see TWENTIETH CENTURY AUTHORS, 1942.

* * *

Robert Lynd has been professor of sociology in the graduate school of Columbia University since 1931. He has published no books in recent years, but contributes articles to various social science journals. Mrs. Lynd also publishes articles in the journals. They live in New York City.

LYONS, EUGENE (July 1, 1898-). For biographical sketch and list of earlier works and references, see TWENTIETH CENTURY AUTHORS, 1942.

* * *

Eugene Lyons edited the American Mercury from 1939 until June 1944 when he became editor of a new pocket-sized magazine, Pageant. In 1945 he became a roving editor of the Reader's Digest, a post he retained until 1952. During all of this period he has contributed articles more or less regularly to the American Mercury.

Lyons has gone the complete cycle from Communist-sympathizer to anti-Communist. He is now, as he has been for many years, a bitter and uncompromising foe of Communism. Hans Kohn, discussing Lyons' Our Secret Allies (in which he argues that the best hope for overthrowing the Communist government is to encourage the Russian people to revolt against it) points out that although Lyons writes with authority and knowledge on his subject, his conclusions are weak. "He demands from us the same all-out commitment practiced by the Communists and forgets that such an all-out, either-or attitude is incompatible with the character of the West." Lyons' political stand in general might be described as ultra-conservative. In 1948 he wrote a biography of ex-President Herbert Hoover which, though praised for its marshaling of the facts in Hoover's life, was generally challenged for its uncritical and hero-worshipping attitude toward him. Bert Andrews complained in the Saturday Review of Literature that Lyons "pours it on too thick," and Time remarked that in spite of his rather desperate efforts to make Hoover appear warm and human, "he remains an unbending, inaccessible man." Lyons lives in New York City.

ADDITIONAL WORKS: Our Unknown Ex-President: A Portrait of Herbert Hoover, 1948; Our Secret Allies, 1953.

ABOUT: Current Biography 1944; Newsweek June 2, 1947; Reader's Digest October 1948.

LYTTON STRACHEY. See STRACHEY

"MAARTENS, MAARTEN." See SCHWARTZ, J. M.

*MAASS, EDGAR (1896-), historical novelist, grew up in Hamburg, Germany, where his father had wandered from Holland

to start a business importing Para rubber from South America. At seventeen years of age he joined the army and fought in France for four years, being wounded twice. After the war he studied chemistry and medicine as a disciple of Hans Fischer, Nobel prize winner for 1930. He was much interested in the history of art, mostly through the influence of Oswald Spengler, who had been his mathematics teacher. The period of the rise of consideration for human rights in Europe has been Maass' interest since youth. After his university years in Germany he spent several years in Spain and France studying the rise of seventeenth century humanitarian movements in these countries.

Maass received a doctorate in chemical engineering from the University of Munich in 1923, and thereafter held several positions in industrial chemical factories. Coming to the United States in 1926 to install machinery for a rubber concern, he liked the country so much that he decided to remain. He became an American citizen in 1933.

Maass's first book was *Don Pedro and the Devil*, a novel of chivalry declining. Some critics felt that the scene, sixteenth century Spain, was more effective than the characterization, but the book was generally praised. "Perhaps the highest quality is the sense it conveys of the past," said the *Atlantic Monthly*. "What is really worth your attention," said Clifton Fadiman in the *New Yorker*, "is the boldly colored world in which Pedro makes his nerveless and forgettable gestures."

There has followed a succession of popular historical novels, particularly *Imperial Venus*, a study of Napoleon's favorite sister, and *World and Paradise*, a romance of the Thirty Years' War. A reviewer in the Chicago *Sunday Tribune* described the story of *Lady at Bay* as "an absorbing one of amorousness that never entirely offends good taste, and that holds attention through the element of suspense, skillfully maintained to the end."

After working as chief chemist for a prominent chemical company many years, Dr. Maass retired in 1945 to devote all his time to writing. He lives in New Jersey with his wife and one son.

* màs

PRINCIPAL WORKS: Don Pedro and the Devil, 1942; The Dream of Philip II, 1944; Imperial Venus, 1946; The Queen's Physician (in England: Garnet Cross) 1948; World and Paradise, 1950; Lady at Bay, 1953.

MABBOTT, THOMAS OLLIVE (July 6, 1898-). For autobiographical sketch and list of earlier works and references, see TWENTIETH CENTURY AUTHORS, 1942.

* * *

Thomas O. Mabbott writes: "I became full professor of English at Hunter College in 1946, and was editor-in-chief of the *Numismatic Review*, New York, during 1943-48. In 1951 I brought out a selection of Edgar Allan Poe's works as a small textbook. Maybe I should add to my sketch that I am still collecting notes for my edition of Poe's works. I have a new hobby in the study of linguistic theory; now that I don't have to pass courses in philology, I enjoy them."

ADDITIONAL WORKS: (ed.) Poe, E. A. Selected Poetry and Prose (ed., Modern Library College Editions) 1951.

MABEE, CARLETON. See MABEE, F. C.

MABEE, FRED CARLETON (1914-), American biographer, who writes under the name Carleton Mabee, was born in the French Concession at Shanghai, China. His father was born Canadian, and his parents became naturalized Americans. "On demand, however," he writes, "I can report myself an American of pre-Revolutionary vintage. The first of my family on the continent was the French Huguenot, Gaspard Mabille, of old Dutch New York. Of his descendants who have made a noise on this continent the two noisiest have been writers: Hamilton Wright Mabie, once an editor of *Outlook*, and Janet Mabie, magazine story writer."

He was educated in China and America, graduated from Bates College, and took a doctor's degree at Columbia University. In the course of his career Mabee has been a truck-driver, information agent for a travel bureau, and teacher. His first book, *The American Leonardo*, a life of Samuel F. B. Morse, won the Pulitzer award for biography in 1944. "Few persons have left as much material for the biographer as has Morse,"

said Mabee. "I have followed him into New Hampshire, looking in attics and antique shops for portraits that he painted on wood at fifteen dollars. I have followed him too into the homes of the Charleston waterfront and found some of the portraits that have justified art critics calling Morse the Stuart of his generation. Morse and his family were articulate as well as dexterous. His father was the 'father of American geography'; his brothers were newspaper editors; he himself wrote some thirty books and pamphlets; and the whole family saved its letters. When acclaim for his telegraph catapulted Morse into fame, he was alternately hailed and excoriated in the press across the nation, complicating the task of the biographer. Members of his family, owners of his paintings all over the country, art dealers and galleries, libraries and museums have generously supplied the rich details that make possible a candid, human study."

The American Leonardo, published in 1943, found general approval, though the *New Republic* complained that the title was "pretentious"—"for despite a busy, crowded life, Morse is a rather unimpressive figure." Waldemar Kaempffert in the New York *Times* commended this "scholarly biography in which a distinguished artist and inventor is socially related to his time." Kaempffert said that Mabee showed Morse not as the "perfect hero" which one biographer, Samuel I. Prime, presented, or the "grasping monopolist" that Horace Greeley accused him of being, or the "snob and charlatan that his defeated rivals in telegraphy pictured. . . . It is a very human Morse that emerges from Mr. Mabee's pages."

PRINCIPAL WORK: The American Leonardo, 1943.

ABOUT: Saturday Review of Literature May 6, 1944.

MABIE, HAMILTON WRIGHT (December 13, 1845-December 31, 1916). For biographical sketch and list of works and references, see TWENTIETH CENTURY AUTHORS, 1942.

* * *

ABOUT: Van Dyke, H. *in* American Academy of Arts and Letters Commemorative Tributes, 1905-1941.

MACAULAY, ROSE. For biographical sketch and list of earlier works and references, see TWENTIETH CENTURY AUTUORS, 1942.

* * *

In 1951 Rose Macaulay received an honorary Doctor of Letters degree from Cambridge University. She lives in London, but spends as much time as possible in travel—Portugal, Spain, Southern France, and Italy—in the Mediterranean reigon which she loves so deeply. Most of her recent writings have been travel books in which she has attempted to evoke the spirit of the Mediterranean past. In the opening pages of *The Fabled Shore* she writes: "All the way down this stupendous coast I trod on the heels of Greek mariners, merchants, and colonists, as of trafficking Phoenicians, conquering Carthaginians, dominating ubiquitous Romans, destroying Goths, magnificent Moors, feudal counts, princes and abbots. History in Spain lies like a palimpsest, layer upon layer, on the cities, on the shores, on the old quays of little ports."

The first novel by Miss Macaulay to appear in ten years was *The World My Wilderness*, which the London *Times Literary Supplement* found the most moving book she had ever written. It revived the theme she had introduced nearly a quarter of a century before in *Crewe Train*—the barbarian (in this case a young girl who has been raised in France during the war) at odds with civilized society. Less humorous than her earlier books but equally deft and engaging, *The World My Wilderness*, Virgilia Peterson noted, was "written with poignancy, with memorable descriptions, with a lovely cadence of language and with warmth of heart."

ADDITIONAL WORKS: They Went to Portugal, 1946; The Fabled Shore, 1950; The World My Wilderness (novel) 1950; The Pleasure of Ruins, 1952.

ABOUT: Frierson, W. C. The English Novel in Transition.

MAC CARTHY, Sir DESMOND (1878-June 8, 1952). For biographical sketch and list of earlier works and references, see TWENTIETH CENTURY AUTHORS, 1942.

* * *

Desmond MacCarthy died at Cambridge, two days after the university had conferred on him an honorary degree of Doctor of Letters. He had been knighted in 1951. A conversational wit with a "genius for friendship," MacCarthy was described as "wise, just, deep, generous, acute and fearless" by Cyril Connolly, who added, "As a man, he was as ideal a companion as the breed produced." Under his pseudonym of "Affable Hawk" the critic brought to his work high seriousness, a remarkably wide range of reading, sensitive judgment, interest in new writing, and a great respect for high literary standards. W. T. Scott has observed that "one feels a great deal of wit and wisdom in the man: a man not gifted to write in new ways but able to pursue the genteel tradition of criticism with freshness."

ADDITIONAL WORKS: Romains, J. Death of a Nobody (trans. with S. Waterlow) 1944; Shaw, 1951; Shaw's Plays in Review, 1951; Memories 1953; Portraits, 1954; Humanities, 1954; Theatre, 1955.

ABOUT: Cecil, D. *Preface to* MacCarthy's Humanities; MacCarthy, D. Memories; London Times June 9, 1952; New York Times June 9, 1952; Saturday Review August 1, 1953.

MC CARTHY, JUSTIN HUNTLY (1860-March 21, 1936). For biographical sketch and list of works and references, see TWENTIETH CENTURY AUTHORS, 1942.

MC CARTHY, MARY (1912-   ), American novelist and short story writer, reports: "My life-history is printed on a rather polychrome background:

Kevin McCarthy

my mother's father, a Western lawyer of New England ancestry, my mother's mother, a lively Jewish beauty from San Francisco, where her parents were forty-niners; my father's parents, second or third generation Irish farm-settlers who got rich in grain elevators in Minnesota. I was born in 1912 in Seattle, to Therese Preston and Roy Winfield McCarthy, who met at a coastal resort in a summer vacation of the Univeristy of Washington, where my mother was an undergraduate and my father was in the law school. Both my parents were handsome, winning and romantic; their marriage was opposed by both families, partly for religious reasons, and partly because my father was an invalid, with an invalid's febrile vitality. He had a bad heart, and it was prophesied, from the first, that he would die young and leave his wife with a pack of children. He evaded this prophesy, in the flu of 1918, by taking my young mother with him when he died and leaving the question of the four children to be dealt with by his relations. We, my three younger brothers and I, spent five years together in Minneapolis, in the custody of a severe great-aunt and her sadistic husband. Two blocks away, my McCarthy grandparents, dwelling in sumptuous middle-class style, instilled in us the contrast between wealth and penury by occasional treats and vacations; it was thought beneficial that we should know we were orphans and fitted for a different destiny than our well-tended cousins. Today, some of my relations allege my literary successes and my brother Kevin's career as an actor as proof that the harsh formula followed in our upbringing produced results; nevertheless, I cannot feel grateful. Nor do I believe that artistic talent flowers necessarily from a wounding of the stem on which it grows, as in some gardening-operation where a plant is slashed to make it branch.

"At any rate, when I was eleven, I was rescued from the Minneapolis home by my mother's father, Harold Preston, a distinguished Seattle lawyer, former State Senator and local Bar Association president, framer of the first Workmen's Compensation Act to be passed in the United States, an act which served as a model for later legislation. A conception of probity and public service was implanted in me by him, together with a certain legalistic temper. To these endowments were added a passion for outlay and a dislike of injustice: my Minneapolis heritage. My vehement, flamboyant nature occasioned my grandfather much worry, self-control and tight-lipped caution being almost a religion with him, as with many Yankees. He was not, however, thrifty, and I owe to his large-handedness and to an inheritance, later, from my other grandfather a very good education, at Forest Ridge Convent in Seattle, at Annie Wright Seminary in Tacoma, and finally at Vassar College. During the course of these first years spent with him and my grandmother in Seattle, I lost my religious faith, very easily, and began to read a great deal—the old sets in my grandfather's library, Dickens, Frank Stockton, Sienkiewicz, Bret Harte, Tolstoy, Bulwer-Lytton, along with the latest volumes from the circulating library: Ben Hecht, Carl Van Vechten, Mencken, Cabell, Aldous Huxley.

"In boarding-school, this reading was widened to include much poetry. The discovery of Latin and, in college, of the Elizabethans provided two of those shocks of self-recognition that make us, in adolescence, elect what we are or shall be. Latin came to me very fluently, probably because of my Catholic training, but I felt as if I had known it in another incarnation. Hence writing with a Latinate turn, compressed, analytic, and yet having a certain extravagance or oratorical flourish sounded in my ears like a natural, spoken language. This did not apply to the neo-classic authors, Milton or Pope, or, for that matter, to Horace, who always affected me as a sort of one-man classic revival in his own day—what one might call an export author. I graduated from Vassar in 1933, full of Juvenal, Martial, Catullus, Shakespeare, Nashe and Greene, and began to write book reviews for the *Nation* and the *New Republic*. This became an initiation into the radical movement, specifically, the anti-Communist splinter groups. I became an editor and theatre critic of *Partisan Review* and was myself a great partisan of Trotsky, who possessed those intellectual traits of wit, lucidity and indignation which I regarded, and still regard, as a touchstone. I did not, however, join the Trotskyist sect, but lived a bourgeois life, writing articles, stories and finally novels, and having one son, Reuel Wilson, born in 1938. When I was divorced from Edmund Wilson, I taught for a short time at Bard College and at Sarah Lawrence. This awakened me, slowly, to the fact that cleverness is not a substitute for knowledge—a discovery which belatedly, sometimes happily, sometimes uncomfortably, is altering the course of my life. I was married to Bowden Broadwater in 1946; we live in the country, close to a very good library, and read with a certain gluttony which now and then overreaches itself."

* * *

Mary McCarthy has won a reputation for hard-biting satire. Her novels have generally been praised for their vigorous lampooning of contemporary American intellectualism, for their lucid style, and their "acute wit and the malice to propel it." Like much fine satire, her work—particularly *The Oasis*, the story of an attempt to establish a utopian community, and *The Groves of Academe*, a novel about the clash between an idealistic, "liberal" college president and an unscrupulous professor—is "relentlessly unpleasant." The microscopic lens and the scalpel would appear to be an indispensable part of her professional equipment. Robert Halsband (in *Saturday Review of Literature*) wrote of her collection *Cast a Cold Eye*: "Her brief incisive pieces are etched with corrosive acid, it is true; but they still have a savage honesty, a bristling sensibility, and at bottom a pitiless humanity." Her "satiric manner," Alice Morris observed in the New York *Times*, "is based on a stunning, narrowly aimed accuracy rather than an exaggeration."

PRINCIPAL WORKS: The Company She Keeps, 1942; The Oasis, 1949; Cast a Cold Eye, 1950; The Groves of Academe, 1952.

ABOUT: New Republic March 31, 1952; New Yorker December 4, 1948, December 15, 1951; Publishers' Weekly May 16, 1942; Reporter December 22, 1953, January 5, 1954; Wilson Library Bulletin May 1955.

MC CORMICK, Mrs. ANNE (O'HARE) (1882?-May 29, 1954). For biographical sketch and list of works and references, see TWENTIETH CENTURY AUTHORS, 1942.

* * *

Anne McCormick died in Doctors' Hospital in New York City at seventy-two.

Described as "the shyest of celebrities" and a "soft-spoken, grandmotherly" woman who liked to minimize the dramatic, Mrs. McCormick was awarded the Laetare Medal of Notre Dame University and the Siena Medal of Theta Phi Alpha in 1944, the International Altrusa Distinguished Service Award in 1945, the Chi Omega National Achievement Award in 1946, the Theodore Roosevelt Distinguished Service Medal in 1950, and the William the Silent Award for Journalism in 1952. From 1946 to 1948 she was a delegate to the United Nations Educational, Scientific and Cultural Organization.

The New York *Times* has said that its distinguished reporter's "keen analysis and interpretation were crisp and markedly free of fuzziness and guess work. . . . She brought light without heat to her readers out of increasingly complex material and international politics."

ABOUT: Hoehn, M. (ed.) Catholic Authors, I; Sapieha, V. Eminent Women; Catholic World May 1944, July 1947; New York Times May 30, 1954; Newsweek March 20, 1950; Saturday Review June 19, 1954; Time August 28, 1944, March 22, 1948, January 10, 1949.

MC CRAE, JOHN (November 30, 1872-January 28, 1918). For biographical sketch and list of works and references, see TWENTIETH CENTURY AUTHORS, 1942.

MC CRONE, GUY (1898-), Scottish novelist, writes: "I was born in Birkenhead, England, in 1898, of Scottish parents. A temporary job had taken my father there, and the household went with him. But I spent my early childhood running in the woods and farmlands of central Ayrshire. I describe this pleasant countryside in my books. It is the Burns country. Our nearest village was Mauchline, where Robert Burns first took up house with his wife, Jean Armour. The poet's haunts are well known

to me, and his Ayrshire Scots is very familiar in my ears.

"I have no illustrious ancestors. But one of my family interests me. He was my grandfather's cousin, a certain John Macrone (writing the name thus) who went to London, established himself at 3, St. James Square, became a publisher, encouraged the young Charles Dickens to collect his first newspaper pen sketches, and published them under the Macrone imprint as *Sketches by Boz*.

"I went to school in Glasgow, passing the entrance examination for Cambridge, England, in the middle of World War I. But being ineligible for the army, I went to scrub floors and sell cigarettes in soldiers' Y.M.C.A. in Normandy and Paris. When the war was ended, I duly went up to the university, where I took a degree in economics as it was intended I should be a business man.

"I began writing after I married in 1931. I had the good fortune to have the script of my first novel read by Michael Sadleir, himself a distinguished biographer, novelist and publisher. He invited me to London, then tore my work to pieces, neither showing mercy nor predicting a future for it. It was a shattering experience; but I pulled myself together, came home to Glasgow, rewrote my book and sent it back to him. He replied almost at once that he congratulated me on being able to take instruction, that he was pleased with what I had done and would like to publish. It was on Sadleir's suggestion that I wrote a trilogy, *Red Plush*, which was chosen as Book-of-the-Month in New York for December 1947.

"People have asked me why I continue to write almost exclusively about my own kind of people, my own city of Glasgow and the countryside in which I was reared. Here is my reason. I had not gone far with the study of the novel before I saw that a novelist, especially if he has a recording talent and not a talent for fantasy, writes best about the place that has been his home; that is, the home of his childhood and adolescence. I found endless examples of this among other writers. I believe in travel and wide horizons, of course. But in the end these mostly serve only to put the novelist's home background into the right proportion for him. And it is there, I firmly believe, that his creative talent can be used with the greatest force."

PRINCIPAL WORKS: The Striped Umbrella, 1937; Duet for Two Merklands, 1939; Red Plush (in England: Wax Fruit: a trilogy—Antimacassar City, The Philistines, The Puritans) 1947; Aunt Bel, 1949; The Hayburn Family, 1952.

ABOUT: Saturday Review of Literature November 22, 1947.

MC CULLERS, Mrs. CARSON (SMITH) (February 19, 1917-). For autobiographical sketch and list of earlier works and references, see TWENTIETH CENTURY AUTHORS, 1942.

* * *

Carson McCullers is widely recognized as one of the most distinguished of younger American writers. She is not a prolific writer, nor does she show any great breadth or variety in her choice of subjects. But within the small, lonely, lost world which she has created in her fiction, she moves with sure and steady artistry. Probably her most remarkable achievement to date is *The Member of the Wedding*, which she wrote originally as a novel and later dramatized into one of the most successful plays of the 1950 theatrical season. (Still later, in 1952, it was made into a motion picture.) *The Member of the Wedding* succeeds in that most difficult of tasks—the portraying of the agonizing period of adolescence (in this case a summer in the life of a twelve-year-old motherless girl)—with sympathy, tenderness, insight, and—perhaps most important—a sense of the ineffable sadness of growing up. Critics have spoken of the "odd, dreamlike character of her work," of "its nightmarish intensity" and its extreme, almost morbid, sensibility. Back of these qualities of mood and atmosphere is a sound literary talent. Dayton Kohler cites the following as "qualities which distinguish the born writer" in Mrs. McCullers' work: "the ability to recreate with fidelity and rich complexity a world of sense impressions, an intimation of the mystery surrounding our circle of awareness, and a technique giving form and meaning to the raw lump of experience."

Mrs. McCullers herself dramatized *The Member of the Wedding* and managed to retain, and even amplify, in the dramatic framework the pathos and charm of the book. (No small measure of credit for the success of the play was due to the cast—Julie Harris as Frankie, the tormented adolescent, Ethel Waters as Berenice, the understanding Negro servant, and Brandon de Wilde as the lonely child visitor, John Henry). It was an unusual play, following none of the regular patterns of commercial theatre. As Mrs. McCullers explained it: *"The Member of the Wedding* is unconventional because it is not a *literal* kind of play. It is an *inward* play and the conflicts are inward conflicts. The antagonist is not personified, but is a human condition of life; the sense of moral isolation." Nevertheless it proved to be a commercial success, had a long Broadway run, and received both the Donaldson Award and the New York Drama Critics Prize.

In 1951 Mrs. McCullers published an omnibus volume which included her three novels, her short stories, and the novelette from which the volume took its title, *The Ballad of the Sad Café*. She is a fellow of the American Academy of Arts and Sciences and has twice received Guggenheim awards. Her husband, J. Reeves McCullers, died in 1953.

ADDITIONAL WORKS: The Member of the Wedding (novel) 1946, (play) 1951; The Ballad of the Sad Café, 1951.

ABOUT: English Journal October 1951; New York Herald Tribune Book Review June 17, 1951; Theatre Arts April 1950.

MC CUTCHEON, GEORGE BARR
(July 26, 1866-October 23, 1928). For biographical sketch and list of works and references, see TWENTIETH CENTURY AUTHORS, 1942.

* * *

ABOUT: Banta, R. E. Indiana Authors and Their Books.

"MC DIARMID, HUGH." See GRIEVE, C. M.

MAC DONAGH, THOMAS (1878-May 3, 1916). For biographical sketch and list of works and references, see TWENTIETH CENTURY AUTHORS, 1942.

MAC DONALD, BETTY (BARD) HESKETT (March 26, 1908-), American memoirist and humorist, was born Anne Elizabeth Campbell Bard in Boulder, Colo., the daughter of Darsie Campbell Bard and Elsie Tholimar (Sanderson) Bard. Her father's work as a mining engineer took the family to some of the more rugged mining towns of North America—in Mexico, Idaho, and Montana. When the author was nine the family went to Seattle, Wash., and in this city she lived until shortly after her marriage. She was given instruction in singing, ballet, piano, French, dramatics, bodybuilding exercises, cooking, shooting—and roof-painting. Her formal education was received at the Roosevelt High School in Seattle, and then at the University of Washington where she planned to major in art. But at the age of seventeen she fell in love

with "tall, very handsome" Robert Eugene Heskett, and the next year, 1927, they were married. After a time in Seattle where Heskett was an insurance salesman, they bought a forty-acre ranch for four hundred and fifty dollars and tried to raise chickens— a saga told in detail in *The Egg and I*. A few years later, in 1931, Betty MacDonald was separated from her husband, and they were later divorced. They had two daughters.

She now turned to a business career, beginning as a secretary. Not long afterward, she became the only woman labor adjuster in the National Recovery Administration, and two and one-half years later began work for the procurement division of the United States Treasury Department. Having contracted tuberculosis (the subject later of *The Plague and I*), she was forced to spend the months between September 1938 and June 1939 in Firland Sanatorium; but in October 1939 she returned to the business world as supervisor of publicity for the National Youth Administration, a position she held till 1942.

In 1942 she married a Scotsman, Donald Chauncey MacDonald, returned to being a housewife, and began to write. *The Egg and I*, reminiscences of the chicken ranch in the Olympic mountains, was first published in serial form in the *Atlantic Monthly*, and in 1945 in book form. Ten days after the book was reviewed the publisher prepared for five printings totaling sixty-one thousand copies; soon after, the number of copies passed the million mark. "Her story is extremely funny," said the *New York Herald Tribune*, "and the picture she paints in crisp and good humor of loneliness, endless work and the overrated rigors of the simple life, is appealing." "The book crackles with the innocent deviltry of acorns hitting the roof-tops," wrote Grace Frank in the *Saturday Review of Literature*.

In *Anybody Can Do Anything* Mrs. MacDonald describes her experiences and those of her sister (the writer Mary Bard), job-hunting and job-losing during the years of the depression. *Onions in the Stew* tells of her life on an island in Puget Sound, to which she and her family moved during the war when housing was scarce. She has written several humorous children's books, and boasts four grandchildren who enjoy them. At present she and her husband live in Carmel Valley, Calif. She has auburn hair and green eyes, and is five feet seven inches tall.

PRINCIPAL WORKS: The Egg and I, 1945; Mrs. Piggle-Wiggle, 1947; The Plague and I, 1948; Mrs. Piggle-Wiggle's Magic, 1949; Anybody Can

Do Anything, 1950; Nancy and Plum, 1952; Onions in the Stew, 1955.

ABOUT: Current Biography 1946; Life March 18, 1946; New York Herald Tribune Book Review October 8, 1950; New York Times Book Review December 5, 1948; Publishers' Weekly March 17, 1951; Saturday Evening Post June 17, 1950; Saturday Review May 14, 1955.

MAC DONALD, PHILIP (189?-   ). For biographical sketch and list of earlier works and references, see TWENTIETH CENTURY AUTHORS, 1942.

* * *

Philip MacDonald has lived in the United States since 1931, working most of his time as a scenarist in the Hollywood studios. He is married and lives in Beverly Hills, in a house accessible only by hillside cable car, his publishers report. He has written few books in recent years, but his reputation as a detective story writer is still secure. Reviewing his *Something to Hide* in 1952, Anthony Boucher wrote: "MacDonald is at once a craftsman of writing, whose prose, characterization and evocation of mood (comic or terrible) might be envied by the most serious literary practitioner, and a craftsman of plot technique, whose construction and misdirection should delight (and startle) Carr or Christie."

ADDITIONAL WORKS: The Dark Wheel (with A. B. Correll) 1948; Something to Hide (short stories) 1952; Guest in the House, 1955.

MACDONELL, ARCHIBALD GORDON (November 3, 1895-January 16, 1941). For biographical sketch and list of works and references, see TWENTIETH CENTURY AUTHORS, 1942.

* * *

ADDITIONAL WORK: The Fur Coat (play) 1943.

MC FALL, Mrs. FRANCES ELIZABETH. See GRAND, S.

MACFALL, HALDANE (July 24, 1860-July 25, 1928). For biographical sketch and list of works and references, see TWENTIETH CENTURY AUTHORS, 1942.

MC FEE, WILLIAM (June 15, 1881-   ). For autobiographical sketch and list of earlier works and references, see TWENTIETH CENTURY AUTHORS, 1942.

* * *

In 1946 William McFee published his reminiscences of life aboard tramp steamers more than thirty years before, under the title *In the First Watch*. "A rewarding book," Jennings Rice wrote of it, "deliberately unromantic in tone but filled with mellow wisdom and an honest nostalgia for days that are no more." McFee retired Chief Engineer Spenlove from the English merchant marine, but did not abandon him as a literary subject. He appears again, living quietly but not uneventfully in his English countryside home, in the novel *Family Trouble*. McFee himself lives in Roxbury, Conn.

ADDITIONAL WORKS: Ship to Shore, 1944; World's Great Tales of the Sea (ed.) 1944; In the First Watch (autobiography) 1946; Family Trouble, 1949; The Law of the Sea (non-fiction) 1950; The Adopted, 1952.

ABOUT: McFee, W. In the First Watch; Warfel, H. R. American Novelists of Today.

MC GINLEY, PHYLLIS (March 21, 1905-   ), American poet and author of children's books, was born in Ontario, Ore., the daughter of Daniel McGinley and Julia (Kiesel) McGinley; the family moved to Colorado and Utah when the author was very young. At one time Phyllis McGinley and her brother were the only pupils at a rural Colorado school. She was educated at  the Sacred Heart Academy, Ogden, Utah, and attended the Universities of Utah and California. After teaching for one year in Utah, Miss McGinley went east to New York, on the strength of having sold several poems and having written an operetta for children. She held an assortment of odd jobs in New York, ranging from writing copy for an advertising agency and teaching school in New Rochelle to writing on the staff of *Town and Country*.

"I'd always written verse," she says, "since at the age of six I went introspective and turned out this little stunner:

Sometimes in the evening
    When the sky is red and pink
I love to lie in a hammock
    And think and think and think.

Which must be the beginning of my life-long preference for composing my stuff in a horizontal position."

Her first book was a volume of poems, *On the Contrary*. While they fell into the category of "light verse," said the New York *Times*, "she has instinctively grasped the fact that light verse, so called, must also suggest that modicum of truth which saves the poem from mere buffoonery." Several other collections of poems followed.

"A warm heart, an observant eye, a witty style and an open mind constitute excellent equipment for a poet," notes the New York *Times;* and *Time* remarks that her work "in praise of normal things . . . is disarmingly pleasant." Much of her verse appears first in the *New Yorker.*

In 1944 Miss McGinley made her debut as a children's writer with *The Horse Who Lived Upstairs.* Many others followed, including her alphabet-in-rhyme *All Around the Town* and *Make-Believe Twins,* informal verses arranged typographically as prose.

Of herself she has said: "My eccentricities are few—putting sugar in my soup is the only one I can think of at the moment—and I'm what is known in the trade as a 'good, reliable worker.' That is, I always make a deadline. I am not very prolific and labor painstakingly over every piece I do." In 1937 she married Charles Hayden and they live in Larchmont, N.Y., with their two daughters. In 1948 she wrote lyrics for a revue called *Small Wonder,* and she wrote the film narration for *The Emperor's Nightingale,* a movie of 1951. In 1955 she was elected to the National Academy of Arts and Letters.

PRINCIPAL WORKS: On the Contrary, 1934; One More Manhattan, 1937; A Pocketful of Wry, 1940; Husbands Are Difficult, 1941; The Horse Who Lived Upstairs, 1944; The Plain Princess, 1945; Stones from a Glass House, 1946; All Around the Town 1948; The Most Wonderful Doll in the World, 1950; Blunderbus, 1951; The Horse Who Had His Picture in the Paper, 1951; A Short Walk from the Station, 1951; The Make-Believe Twins, 1953; The Love Letters of Phyllis McGinley, 1954.

ABOUT: Kunitz, S. J. & Haycraft, H. Junior Book of Authors; Current Biography 1941; New York Herald Tribune Book Review December 16, 1951, October 24, 1954; New York Times Book Review December 9, 1951; Saturday Review September 18, 1954; Scholastic September 29, 1947.

MAC GRATH, HAROLD (September 4, 1871-October 30, 1932). For biographical sketch and list of works and references, see TWENTIETH CENTURY AUTHORS, 1942.

*MACHEN, ARTHUR (March 3, 1863-December 15, 1947). For biographical sketch and list of earlier works and references, see TWENTIETH CENTURY AUTHORS, 1942.

* * *

Arthur Machen died in a nursing home at Beaconsfield, England, at eighty-four.

* măk'ĕn

Living quietly in the country for the last fourteen yars of his life, Machen had done no creative writing for many years. In 1943 a committee which included Bernard Shaw, Max Beerbohm, and T. S. Eliot was formed to help ease his straitened circumstances.

Far Off Things and *Things Near and Far* have been called by J. M. Cohen "one of the best pieces of autobiographical writing of the century." Philip Van Doren Stern pointed out that a taste for Machen's elaborate and polished style, subtle thinking, and rich imagery must be acquired. His art, said Stern, "is firmly based on the belief that the mystical interpretation of life is the only one worth holding. Machen is the artist of wonder, the seeker for something beyond life and outside of time, the late-born disciple of early Christianity who sees the physical world as the outer covering of a glowing inner core that may someday be revealed."

ADDITIONAL WORKS: Handy Dickens: Selections from the Works of Charles Dickens (ed.) 1941.

ABOUT: Gekle, W. F. Arthur Machen, Weaver of Fantasy; Atlantic Monthly May 1947; London Times December 16, 1947; New York Times December 16, 1947; Saturday Review of Literature March 20, 1943; Spectator July 20, 1951.

MC HUGH, VINCENT (December 23, 1904-). For autobiographical sketch and list of earlier works and references, see TWENTIETH CENTURY AUTHORS, 1942.

* * *

Vincent McHugh writes: "I worked for the *New Yorker,* writing non-fiction shorts and an occasional lead book review, until the summer of 1943. I continued to teach the Technique of the Novel and other courses in the Division of General Education at New York University until the end of 1943. During some of this period, from late 1942 until August 1943, when it was dissolved by congressional action, I worked as a writer-director for the Office of War Information, Bureau of Domestic Motion Pictures, writing the narration and in some cases directing such pictures as *Mission Accomplished, Day of Battle, 4F, Soldier from the Tropics,* and *Caribbean Patrol.* I also did odd jobs—some of them very odd indeed—for the Writers' War Board.

"In the summer of 1943 my novel *I Am Thinking of My Darling* was published. The book was leased to RKO Pictures, and in the spring of 1944 I went to Hollywood as a contract writer for Paramount Pictures, where I did additional dialogue for the

Mitchell Leisen production, *Practically Yours,* and the treatments for several originals never produced. I found Hollywood an inoffensive but more or less typical one-industry town. My option was renewed, but since I had been thoughtful enough to provide myself with an escape clause I did escape at the end of the minimum ten weeks. In Washington I got an assignment to the central Pacific as a special merchant marine correspondent, at a salary of one cent a month plus found from the port of departure and war-area bonus. I signed on the SS Grange Victory as deck musician (a fictitious rating in wartime) and sailed from Hueneme to Pearl Harbor, the Marshalls, and Guam, returning to San Francisco on November 4, 1944. There, and after August 1945 in New York, Halesite, and Huntington Bay Hills, I worked on a novel, *The Victory,* which required approximately a million words in sea-diary notes and outlines, research, and actual writing. Meantime I had brought out a book of poems, *The Blue Hen's Chickens,* which was almost immediately impounded by the New York Society for the Suppression of Vice. The Appellate Division in New York City refused to return an indictment.

"In 1945 I was divorced, and married Adeliza Sorenson of St. George, Utah. During the first six months of 1948 I worked as a research assistant to Dean Paul A. McGhee at the Division of General Education at New York University. In July of that year I moved to Albuquerque, N.M., and during that summer lectured at Claremont College and taught at the Writers' Conference at Boulder. In December 1948 I moved to Denver and taught writing and other courses at the Community Institute (later College) of the University of Denver. At intervals between 1948 and 1952 I taught (again) at the Writers' Conference in the Rocky Mountains, at the University of Kansas City, the University of Missouri, and the University of New Hampshire. In 1950 my *Primer of the Novel* was published. During this period I also contributed many sea stories and novelettes to *Argosy Magazine.* In December 1952 I moved to San Francisco."

* * *

McHugh's novel *The Victory* was praised for its sound, restrained writing. The *Saturday Review of Literature* called it "a remarkable and laborious job," and the *Atlantic Monthly* found that it had "the pace and texture of life."

ADDITIONAL WORKS: I Am Thinking of My Darling, 1943; The Blue Hen's Chickens (poems) 1947; The Victory, 1947; Primer of the Novel, 1950.

ABOUT: Publishers' Weekly October 25, 1947.

MC ILWAIN, CHARLES HOWARD (March 15, 1871-). For biographical sketch and list of earlier works and references, see TWENTIETH CENTURY AUTHORS, 1942.

* * *

In 1944 Charles Howard McIlwain was George Eastman Visiting Professor at Oxford University. He retired from Harvard in 1946, but has continued active in scholarship. In the academic year 1948-49 he lectured at Princeton. He is an honorary fellow of Balliol College, Oxford, trustee emeritus of Princeton University, and a member of numerous scholarly societies. He has honorary degrees from Harvard, the College of Wooster, Chicago, Rutgers, Princeton, Oxford, and Colgate. He lives in Auburndale, Mass.

ADDITIONAL WORK: (with R. Pound and others) Federalism as a Democratic Process, 1942.

MAC INNES, HELEN (October 7, 1907-), Scottish-American novelist, writes: "I was born in Glasgow, Scotland, the only daughter of Donald and Jess McInnes. When I was about five we went to live in the residential town of Helensburgh where there were good schools, an accent on open-air life, and an abundance of scenery. The town lies at the entrance to the Gare-

Dorothy Wilding

loch on the broad estuary of the Clyde; behind the town are the hills and moors leading to Loch Lomond, and to the west lie the mountains and lochs of the Western Highlands. It was an ideal setting for young children— we grew up with a quick eye for wild flowers (there were prizes at school for the best collections), for paths through the woods that then edged the town, for trees that were an achievement to climb, for trails that would take us safely through heather and bog. To balance this physical freedom, our manners were strictly disciplined at home, our minds were severely educated in the old Scots tradition (give a child as much work as possible— it can learn more than you think), and our Sundays were completely Presbyterian. I attended the Hermitage School, co-educational, which had a reputation for thorough teaching and hard learning. By the time I entered Glasgow University, I had had six years of Latin and French as well as three years of German; English included the reading of Chaucer, Maths meant analytical geometry and trigonometry, History had included European and Ancient Roman, Geography was world-wide; and I had had six years of Science and of Art. I played the piano and was on the school hockey team. It was all a very strange mixture indeed. I had passed the entrance examinations to Glasgow University at the age of sixteen, but I postponed going there for one year and attended the Girls' High School in Glasgow during that waiting period.

"Our family came back to live in Glasgow when I began classes at the university. In my first week as a freshman, I met Gilbert Highet, who was then a sophomore. Seven years later, after he had completed his degrees at Glasgow and then at Oxford, we were married. But meanwhile, I took an M.A. degree concentrating on French and German, with English and Moral Philosophy and Geology on the side. I played in the university tennis team, took part in the annual college show, and worked part-time in my final year as a cataloguer in the university library on a collection of early-printed books which needed some knowledge of Latin, French, and German. In the next few years I worked in the university library, and then with the Education Authority of Dumbartonshire where my job was to choose the books that were sent out to the libraries in that county—both in rural and industrial areas, and then at University College in London where I took a postgraduate course in librarianship. I played on the University College tennis team, read an enormous quantity of contemporary books, and went to concerts.

"In 1932, in the middle of the depression, Gilbert Highet and I were married on the strength of his first job, a fellowship at St. John's College in Oxford. In 1933, our son Keith was born. When he was old enough to let us travel in the long summer vacations, we began translating books from German to pay for these travels. They were a mixture of the usual museums and churches, combined with climbs through the Tyrol and the Dolomites. We traveled in France, Belgium, Bavaria, Austria, northern Italy, Spain, and Majorca. I was still reading and discussing books, but as yet had made no attempt to write one. My leisure in Oxford was taken up by acting with various college societies, including the Experimental Theatre and the Dramatic Society, in plays by Cocteau, Pirandello, Shaw, and Shakespeare.

"In 1937, my husband was invited for a year to Columbia University in New York. After some months, he was offered a permanent appointment there as Professor of Latin and Greek, and we decided to accept it. In 1938, we left Oxford and removed our entire possessions across the Atlantic to settle happily in New York. Late in 1939, I started my first serious attempt at novel-writing, although my self-confidence wasn't yet strong enough to let anyone (except my husband, of course) know that I was writing. To this day, I still don't like to talk about what I am writing, and even my husband has only the vaguest idea of my story until he reads the manuscript.

"After the war and my husband's demobilization from the British Army, we felt we were then free to take out our First Papers. We became American citizens in 1951. My husband is now [1953] Anthon Professor of Latin at Columbia, and book-critic for *Harper's* magazine. We live in New York City, and our son is now at Harvard. We still have our enthusiasm for music—we play two pianos. And we still like to travel. In recent years, we have visited many parts of the United States, from Vermont to New Orleans, from Virginia to California, from Montana to New Mexico. We know some of the Middle West, Colorado, Wyoming (where we lived on a ranch for three months), and much of New England. We have visited Yosemite, Yellowstone, Glacier National Park, and the Indian Ceremonial Dances at Gallup. We enjoy holidays that are complete contrasts to our city life, and the higher the mountains, the better."

PRINCIPAL WORKS: Above Suspicion, 1941; Assignment in Brittany, 1942; While Still We Live, 1944; Horizon, 1945; Friends and Lovers, 1947; Rest and Be Thankful, 1949; Neither Five Nor Three, 1951; I and My True Love, 1953; Pray for a Brave Heart, 1955.

ABOUT: Van Gelder, R. Writers and Writing; New York Times Book Review April 8, 1951; Wilson Library Bulletin September 1942.

MAC INTYRE, CARLYLE FERREN

(July 16, 1890-). For autobiographical sketch and list of earlier works and references, see TWENTIETH CENTURY AUTHORS, 1942.

* * *

C. F. MacIntyre writes from Chapalita, Jalisco, Mexico: "During World War II I was an engineer in the shipyards where I once canceled a contract, saving the government 12,000 bucks—and was severely reprimanded for losing my employer his 10 per cent cost plus. I spent 1948-50 in Europe, working on translations of material for forthcoming books: Tristan Corbière, Mallarmé, more Rilke, and *Faust* II. 1951-1952 have been spent in Mexico while I have prepared a book on the Mexican abbess, Sor Juana Inés de la Cruz.

"I like the bullfights, the guitars, tequila, and the señoritas. I am making a big collection of Mexican toys—they·shame your plastic dime-store stuff. I've got part of an old chateau in the Jura and expect to get back there on the next move. I have had ten other cars, neither rattly nor old, since the one mentioned in the earlier sketch."

ADDITIONAL WORKS: *Translations*—Baudelaire, C. One Hundred Poems from' Les Fleurs du Mal, 1947; Rilke, R. M. Life of the Virgin Mary, 1947; Verlaine, P. Selected Poems, 1948; Corbière, T. Selections from Les Amours Jaunes, 1953.

MC INTYRE, JOHN THOMAS (November 26, 1871-May 21, 1951). For biographical sketch and list of earlier works and references, see TWENTIETH CENTURY AUTHORS, 1942.

* * *

John Thomas McIntyre died at seventy-nine, at the Presbyterian Hospital in Philadelphia, after an illness of several months.

Although critics deplored the unremitting harshness of most of his naturalistic novels and stories, N. L. Rothman praised his "proven talent for swift delineation and for the setting down of bald, true talk," and R. B. Macdougall found that he wrote "with such a discriminating economy that the result is power, no matter what the mood or material."

ADDITIONAL WORK: Young Patriots at Lexington, 1949.

ABOUT: New York Times May 22, 1951.

MC INTYRE, OSCAR ODD (February 18, 1884-February 13, 1938). For biographical sketch and list of works and references, see TWENTIETH CENTURY AUTHORS, 1942.

MAC IVER, ROBERT MORRISON (April 17, 1882-   ), Scottish-American sociologist, writes: "I was born in Stornoway in the outer Hebrides off the west coast of Scotland and went directly from the local school to the University of Edinburgh, which was a new idea at that time. After graduating from there with first class honors in classics I went on a scholarship to Oriel College, Oxford, taking first class honors in both first and second parts of the major

Manny Warman

examination in a program that contained classical literature, philosophy, ancient history, a little political science, etc. From there I went as lecturer in political science to the University of Aberdeen and succeeded in persuading the authorities to give me at the same time a lectureship in sociology—the first and the last lectureship in sociology that, so far as I know, has ever been held at the university, though I have not kept in touch with recent changes there. However, during that period I found my work very much cramped by the professor of moral philosophy, a situation which you can only understand if you know that at the time in the Scottish universities all lectureships were under the aegis of one of the seven old established chairs, or professorships, in the faculty of arts and my lectureship was within the field of the professor in question. He was a strong Hegelian in philosophy and I wrote some articles very critical of Hegelianism. To extricate myself from this situation I accepted a position to which I was invited at the University of Toronto as professor of political science, and since political science in that university was given a very inclusive meaning, I did all I could to develop the sociological side of things, especially when in after years I became chairman of the department of political science.

"However, the conditions there did not permit any large development of sociological studies and I went from there to a professorship in sociology at Barnard College. That was in 1927, at a time when the department of sociology at the university was in a somewhat powerless condition. Consequently, the following year I was invited to become chairman of the department of sociology at Columbia and we went through a rather long period of reorganization there. That however is another story.

"Ever since my coming to Columbia I have been actually engaged in two departments because from the beginning I gave the courses in political theory in the department of public law and government. I have always held the belief that the department frontiers should not be taken seriously and that particularly in the social sciences these may become often artificial barriers to the development of major subjects that refuse to be confined within departmental walls. During the past two years' retirement from the department of sociology I remained as a special lecturer in the department of public law and government. I have also in recent years conducted a series of investigations, including a study of the work and relationships of Jewish agencies operating in the field of community relations and a study that is now occupying me concerned with the problems of academic freedom in the United States."

* * *

R. M. MacIver is widely regarded as one of the outstanding contemporary American sociologists and political philosophers. His writing has been called "forceful, concrete, and sensible." Of his *Democracy and the Economic Challenge,* five lectures delivered at the University of Michigan in 1950, James P. Warburg remarked: "This reviewer cannot remember ever having seen so much wisdom and understanding of the present-day world compressed into so small a space."

PRINCIPAL WORKS: Community, 1917; Labor in the Changing World, 1919; Elements of Social Science, 1921; The Modern State, 1926; Society, 1931; Leviathan and the People, 1939; Social Causation, 1942; Towards an Abiding Peace, 1943; The Web of Government, 1946; The More Perfect Union, 1948; The Ramparts We Guard, 1950; Democracy and the Economic Challenge, 1952.

ABOUT: Berger, M. & others (eds.) Freedom and Control in Modern Society; Ginsberg, M. Recent Tendencies in Sociology; Saturday Review of Literature February 1, 1947.

MACKAIL, DENIS (June 3, 1892-). For biographical sketch and list of earlier works and references, see TWENTIETH CENTURY AUTHORS, 1942.

* * *

Denis Mackail's light-hearted novels and essays have won him a large following in England, but his work is little read in the United States. A London *Times Literary Supplement* review of one of his novels, *Upside-Down, or Love Among the Ruins,* well describes all his writing: "Mr. Mackail ambles along in his own inimitable fashion, touching in with a few deft strokes a character here, a situation there. . . . It is all quite excellent entertainment."

His humor is hearty, facetious, inclined to overstatement at times. His autobiography, *Where Am I? or, A Stranger Here Myself,* is a lively, informal, and quite rambling book which reveals far more about the personality of the author than about the biographical details of his life. Mackail lives in the Chelsea section of London. His wife, Diana Granet,
· died in 1949.

ADDITIONAL WORKS: Life with Topsy, 1942; Upside-Down; or, Love Among the Ruins, 1943; Ho! or, How It All Strikes Me, 1944; Tales for a Godchild, 1944; Huddleston House, 1945; We're

Here, 1947; Our Hero, 1948; Where Am I? or, A Stranger Here Myself, 1948; By Auction, 1949; Her Ladyship, 1949; It Makes the World Go Round; or, Saint Valentine's Day, 1950.

ABOUT: Mackail, D. Where Am I? or, A Stranger Here Myself.

MACKAIL, JOHN WILLIAM (August, 1859-December 13, 1945). For biographical sketch and list of earlier works and references, see TWENTIETH CENTURY AUTHORS, 1942.

* * *

John William Mackail died at his home in London at eighty-six.

His *Life of William Morris* has been called one of the best of English biographies. In his distinguished classical studies he had, in the words of the London *Times,* "at once the wide range and the unity of grasp which characterized the best Victorian scholars." Although he was noted chiefly for his fine scholarship and his active championship of classical education, "what filled his mind and what he strove to convey to others," according to Cyril Bailey, "was the true love of poetry, which he sometimes felt was being lost in the mass of academic analysis."

ADDITIONAL WORKS: Nichols, B. Poems (ed.) 1943.

ABOUT: Bailey, C. John William Mackail, O. M.; London Times December 14, 1945.

MC KAY, CLAUDE (September 15, 1890-May 22, 1948). For biographical sketch and list of earlier works and references, see TWENTIETH CENTURY AUTHORS, 1942.

* * *

Claude McKay died in Chicago hospital at fifty-seven; he had been ill for several years.

A few years before his death he repudiated his earlier left-wing connections. In 1942 he joined the Catholic Church, and for the last five years of his life he lived in Chicago doing research for the National Catholic Youth Organization. His last book of poems was published in 1942.

Max Eastman called McKay "the first great lyric genius his race produced." Horace Gregory and Marya Zaturenska wrote, "McKay's talents, even in their earliest expression, were overripe, and his facility in writing verse probably exhausted his resources before he could find a mature and memorable expression of them. McKay's lyrical gifts were genuine, and were perhaps of a higher quality than he realized."

Correction: a footnote in the third printing of TWENTIETH CENTURY AUTHORS, 1942

(1950) incorrectly gave the year of McKay's death as 1949.

ADDITIONAL WORK: Selected Poems, 1953.

ABOUT: Barton, R. C. Witnesses for Freedom; Drier, H. American Literature by Negro Authors; Eastman, M. *in* Collected Poems of Claude McKay; Gloster, H. M. Negro Voices in American Fiction; Gregory, H. & Zaturenska, M. History of American Poetry; Hoehn, M. (ed.) Catholic Authors, I; New York Times May 24, 1948; Opportunity Magazine Fall 1948; The Progressive February 1953.

*MAC KAYE, PERCY (March 16, 1875-). For autobiographical sketch and list of earlier works and references, see TWENTIETH CENTURY AUTHORS, 1942.

* * *

On his seventieth birthday, in 1945, Percy MacKaye was honored by a national testimonial from the National Arts Club. Three years later he won the $5,000 fellowship award of the Academy of American Poets for "his creative contributions over half a century, in association with his wife and fellow-poet, Marion Morse MacKaye." In 1949 MacKaye's masterwork, the tetralogy *The Mystery of Hamlet, King of Denmark —or What We Will*, was produced at the Pasadena Playhouse in California, a production he describes as "the largest continuous four-fold production of a single dramatic work in the history of the theatre since the ancient Greek productions at Athens." While completing this work, after the death of his wife, he lived alone in a country cottage in Massachusetts.

The tetralogy consists of four verse plays covering the action leading up to the beginning of Shakespeare's tragedy. They deal with the early years of the marriage between King Hamlet and Gertrude, the jealousy of Claudius and his love for Gertrude, the childhood of Prince Hamlet, the murder of the king, and the naming of Claudius as his successor. The protagonist is King Hamlet, and Yorick is brought back to life to play the court fool. MacKaye has explained that the theme of his drama is "the interplay of love and revenge, and what man wills as it affects his destiny." It was his purpose in the plays, he continues, "to attempt a dramatic elucidation not only of Shakespeare's tragedy, but of tragic eras, past and present, as seen by an American poet of the theatre today."

MacKaye lives in New York City. He is currently editing the journal of Marion Morse MacKaye.

* mă kī′

ADDITIONAL WORKS: What Is She? 1942; I Met God Walking Leisurely, 1943; The Mystery of Hamlet, King of Denmark—Or What We Will (The Ghost of Elsinore, A Fool in Eden Garden, Odin Against Christus, The Serpent in the Orchard) 1950; Discoveries and Inventions, 1950; Poog's Pasture: The Mythology of a Child, 1951; Poog and the Caboose Man, 1952.

ABOUT: Publishers' Weekly December 25, 1948; Survey April 1949; Theatre Arts July 1949, July 1950.

MC KENNA, STEPHEN (February 27, 1888-). For biographical sketch and list of earlier works and references, see TWENTIETH CENTURY AUTHORS, 1942.

* * *

Stephen McKenna served with the Ministry of Economic Warfare from 1939 to 1940. He continues to be little known as a novelist and writes for a small but enthusiastic audience. He lives in Lincoln's Inn when in London and has a country home at Waltham-St. Lawrence in Berkshire. His favorite recreation is walking.

ADDITIONAL WORKS: Mean, Sensual Man, 1943; Reginald McKenna: A Memoir, 1948; Not Necessarily for Publication, 1949; Pearl Wedding, 1951; Life's Eventime, 1954.

MC KENNEY, RUTH (November 18, 1911-). For autobiographical sketch and list of earlier works and references, see TWENTIETH CENTURY AUTHORS, 1942.

* * *

Ruth McKenney and her husband, Richard Bransten, spent the war years in Washington, D.C. where their daughter, Eileen, was born. (They also have two sons—one by Bransten's first marriage, and the other the son of her sister Eileen and her husband, novelist Nathanael West, both killed in an auto accident.) In 1944 the Branstens went to Hollywood to write motion picture stories. After a year they decided that although they could make a small fortune writing for the screen, they hated Hollywood, and they packed up and returned to the East, settling in Westport, Conn. In 1947 they went abroad and settled in Brussels. The delights and difficulties of their emigration were described by her in a series of articles for *Holiday* magazine. These were collected and published as a book, *Far, Far from Home*. The family later moved to London; in 1950 they returned briefly to New York before settling in France.

My Sister Eileen remains Miss McKenney's most enduring work. In 1953, after going through the evolution from book to Broadway play to motion picture, it was made into a musical comedy and enjoyed another long Broadway run as *Wonderful Town.* When writing about herself and her family—as she has done in recent years in *The Loud Red Patrick, Love Story,* and *Far, Far from Home*—Ruth McKenney has had almost universal critical acclaim for honesty, humor, and warmth. The critics were far less friendly to her long, serious novel *Jake Home,* a study of a labor leader. Probably the most succinct review is by the author herself. In her autobiographical *Love Story* she writes: *"Jake Home* comes under the live-and-learn department in my checkered career. Parts of it are not too bad, here and there, but the general effect is pious." *Love Story,* Miss McKenney's account of her marriage and her life since that time, was a lively, at times humorous, at times sentimental, book. In it she describes her growing disillusion with left-wing activities. Harry Sylvester, in the New York *Times,* described the book as the story "of the transition of a militant left-winger into a petty bourgeois."

ADDITIONAL WORKS: Jake Home, 1943; The Loud Red Patrick, 1947; Love Story, 1950; Here's England (with R. Bransten) 1950; All About Eileen, 1952; Far, Far from Home, 1954.

ABOUT: Current Biography 1942; McKenney, R. Love Story, Far, Far from Home.

MACKENZIE, Sir COMPTON (January 17, 1883-). For autobiographical sketch and list of earlier works and references, see TWENTIETH CENTURY AUTHORS, 1942.

* * *

Sir Compton Mackenzie write from Wantage, Berkshire: "In 1946 I was invited by the Indian Government to write the history of the part played by the Indian Army in the Second World War. From 1946-48 I visited every battlefield in the Western Desert, Italy, Burma, Assam, Malaya, Hong Kong, Syria, and Eritrea, besides traveling all over India. I drove all the way from Brahmaputra to Singapore, a journey which is not likely to be repeated for many years. Since I returned from the East I have done a great deal of broadcasting, besides playing a part in the film based on my book *Whisky Galore* (*Tight Little Island* in America). In June 1952 I was knighted by Queen Elizabeth II, and it is worth recording that I hold the commission of her great-great-grandmother, Queen Victoria, as a second-lieutenant."

Corrections: Sir Compton writes, "My original name was and remains Edward Montague Compton Mackenzie. I also object to the statement that *The Windsor Tapestry* was attacked for its attitude towards the reigning family. One or two Grub Street hacks may have thought they were currying favour by saying this, but I cannot believe that I should have received the accolade of knighthood from Her present Majesty if I had criticized the reigning family."

His date of birth is 1883, not 1882.

ADDITIONAL WORKS: *Fiction*—Monarch of the Glen, 1941; Keep the Home Guard Turning, 1943; North Wind of Love (in U.S.: Again to the North) 1945; Whisky Galore (in U.S.: Tight Little Island) 1947; Hunting the Fairies, 1949; The Rival Monster, 1952. *Non-Fiction*—Mr. Roosevelt, 1943; Wind of Freedom, 1943; Dr. Beneš, 1946; Eastern Epic, I, 1951; I Took a Journey, 1951; The House of Coalport, 1951; The Savoy of London, 1954.

ABOUT: Church, R. British Authors (1948); Hoehn, M. (ed.) Catholic Authors, I; Mackenzie, C. *in* The Saturday Book, 1950; Commonweal May 2, 1952; The Spectator September 14, 1951.

*MC KEON, RICHARD PETER (April 26, 1900-), American educator and author, was born in Union Hill, N.J., the son of

Kay Carrington

Peter Thomas McKeon and Mathilda (Hirschfield) McKeon. He studied at Columbia University, taking a B.A. in 1920 and an M.A. eight months later. His master's thesis was a study of Tolstoy, Croce, and Santayana. After three years of study in Paris (1922-25), he received two degrees, Diplome d'Etudes Supérieures from the University of Paris and Diplome d'Elève Titulàire from the Ecole des Hautes Etudes. From 1925 to 1929 he was an instructor in philosophy at Columbia, and in 1928 took his Ph.D. there. His doctor's thesis was a study of Spinoza. After being an assistant professor at Columbia from 1929 to 1935, McKeon went to the University of Chicago where he was dean of the Division of the Humanities from 1935 to 1947. Since then he has been Distinguished Service Professor of Philosophy and Greek at that institution. Member of the U.S. Delegation to the General Conference of UNESCO, McKeon went to Paris in 1946, to Mexico City in 1947, and to Beirut, Lebanon, in 1948, to attend meetings of the organization.

His first book was *The Philosophy of Spinoza: the Unity of His Thought.* "Not the least of Mr. McKeon's contributions is the clarity and comprehensiveness with which he surveys the historical sources of a philosophy, for all its complexities so clear and self-con-

* mà kē'ŏn

tained that one forgets it has sources at all," wrote Irwin Edman in the New York *Herald Tribune Book Review*. "There is a sober directness about the style that puts the book in the realm of literature as well as scholarship." The *Nation* objected that the book was over-scholarly, but Lionel Trilling, in the New York *Evening Post*, commended McKeon's "admirable grave prose." *Freedom and History* appeared in 1952, subtitled "The Semantics of Philosophical Controversies and Ideological Conflicts," a book studying the meanings which important words carry over from the systems of philosophers into ordinary speech. "This is semantics at its best and philosophical analysis at its best," said J. A. Mourant.

"We face a *philosophic* problem," wrote McKeon in 1953, "of formulating the organization and interrelations of our knowledge and our values, the interplay of our ideas and our ideals, the influence of our new sciences in providing means for the solution of old problems and in laying the beginnings of new problems, and the distortions and misapplications of what is called scientific method and of what is claimed as democratic practice. That philosophic problem is inseparable from the *educational* problems of equipping men with abilities and insights to face the new problems of our times and to use the instrumentalities with wisdom and freedom."

McKeon received an honorary degree, Litt.D., from the Jewish Theological Seminary of America in 1942, and Doctor *honoris causa* from the University of Aix, Marseilles, in 1951. In 1930 he married Clarice Muriel Thirer; they have two sons and a daughter and live in Chicago.

PRINCIPAL WORKS: The Philosophy of Spinoza, 1928; (ed. & tr.) Selections from Medieval Philosophy, 1929-30; (ed.) The Basic Works of Aristotle, 1941; Freedom and History, 1952; Thought, Action, and Passion, 1954.

ABOUT: Finkelstein, L. (ed.) Thirteen Americans.

MACKINTOSH, ELIZABETH ("Gordon Daviot," "Josephine Tey") (1897-February 13, 1952), Scottish novelist and playwright, was the daughter of Colin Mackintosh and Josephine (Horne) Mackintosh. She used the two pen names Gordon Daviot and Josephine Tey during her writing career. "I was born and educated in Inverness, Scotland," she wrote, "where I attended the Royal Academy. Destined for a university, I stuck my toes in and refused to continue what I had been doing for the previous twelve years. I balked, too, at art —my talent is on the shady side of mediocre

—and settled for a course in physical culture and have never regretted it. I trained at the Anstey Physical Training College in Birmingham for three years and have earned my living all over England as a physical training instructor." However, she did eventually give up teaching to keep house for her father near Loch Ness and pursue her writing.

Angus McBean

Her first book was *The Man in the Queue,* published in 1929 under the pseudonym Gordon Daviot. It was the first in which the portrait of Inspector Grant, familiar now from the "Tey" novels, was drawn. The first presentation of "Josephine Tey" came in 1936 with *A Shilling for Candles;* whereupon the pen name was abandoned until 1947 when she published another mystery novel, *Miss Pym Disposes.* From 1929 to 1946, Miss Mackintosh was chiefly busy with plays, in which she was extremely successful. *Richard of Bordeaux* (published 1933), a play in two acts, was a smash hit with John Gielgud in the lead, and ran for over a year. "Mr. Daviot [*sic*]," said the *Saturday Review of Literature* in reviewing the play, "has succeeded in avoiding the stencils used by most English historical dramatists. Instead of aping Shakespeare or Shaw, or the routine pageant-master episodes of Drinkwater, he has written a straightforward and intensely alive drama in prose that is colloquial without being slangy." Several novels and a biography *Claverhouse* also appeared under the Daviot signature.

When she returned to the mystery story, Miss Mackintosh "began to use as an alias the name of my Suffolk great-great-grandmother, Josephine Tey." "I am persuaded," writes James Sandoe, "that, although not of equal merit or skill among themselves, they [the Tey books] all share as a company this warm persuasiveness that gives them so affectionate a place in memory and that they comprise a solid place in the history of the detective story because they are as congenial as a witty friend and a hearth fire on a snowy day." At the time of Miss Mackintosh's death, he again spoke of the "special quality of warmth" that made Josephine Tey's novels so unusual and so memorable.

Of *The Daughter of Time* Anthony Boucher said in the New York *Times,* "No superlatives are adequate; simply mark this down as one of the best, not of the year, but of all time." Of *Miss Pym Disposes* the *Saturday Review of Literature* remarked, "Very English, very feminine, elegantly written, leisurely, amusing, penetrating, and adequately suspenseful—with thumping terminal ending. Good." Inspector Grant's last case will be found in *The Singing Sands*, published posthumously in 1952. "The manuscript was found among her effects, apparently only just completed," writes her publisher.

Elizabeth Mackintosh died in London at the age of fifty-five.

PRINCIPAL WORKS: *As "Gordon Daviot"*— Man in the Queue, 1929; Kif, 1929; Expensive Halo, 1931; Richard of Bordeaux, 1933; The Laughing Woman, 1934; Queen of Scots, 1934; Claverhouse, 1937; The Stars Bow Down, 1939; Leith Sands, and other short plays, 1946; The Privateer, 1952; Plays by Gordon Daviot, 3 vols., 1953. *As "Josephine Tey"*—A Shilling for Candles, 1936; Miss Pym Disposes, 1947; The Franchise Affair, 1949; Brat Farrar, 1949; To Love and Be Wise, 1950; The Daughter of Time, 1951; The Singing Sands, 1952.

ABOUT: New York Herald Tribune Book Review March 9, 1952; New York Times February 14, 1952; Newsweek September 7, 1953; Unicorn Mystery Book Club News v. 2, no. 10, 1950.

MC LAUGHLIN, ANDREW CUNNINGHAM (February 14, 1861-September 24, 1947). For autobiographical sketch and list of works see TWENTIETH CENTURY AUTHORS, 1942.

* * *

Andrew Cunningham McLaughlin died of pneumonia at eighty-six at his home in Chicago.

A tribute in the *American Historical Review* said: "Always more interested in ideas and institutions than in men and events, he was at his best when tracing, from seventeenth century England through the colonial period and into the stream of our national life and thought, the evolution of concepts, practices, and governmental forms basic to American constitutionalism."

ABOUT: National Cyclopedia of American Biography (1950); American Historical Review January 1948; New York Times September 25, 1947.

MC LAVERTY, MICHAEL (1907-), Irish novelist, was born in County Monaghan, but spent most of his life in Belfast. He was educated at St. Malachy's College and later at Queen's University, both in Belfast. Having taken a master of science degree in mathematics and experimental physics in 1933, he adopted teaching as a

profession and in his spare time began to write short stories. His first story was published that same year. Several of his short stories have appeared in anthologies, both in England and America, and he is today considered one of the foremost novelists in Ireland.

Charles H. Halliday

Part of his boyhood was spent on Rathlin Island, off the coast of County Antrim; and out of the lives of the people of that island and of Belfast, he has created his work. The first novel, *Call My Brother Back*, contrasts the lyrical life of Rathlin with that of the anti-Catholic, anti-Nationalist life prevailing in Belfast. "This is a distinguished book," wrote the *Christian Science Monitor*. "The prose is luminous, astringent, free of rhythmic mannerisms." *Commonweal*, while praising his other work as a short story writer, thought he was going to be one of those doomed to "meet defeat in the novel." Most reviews, however, were favorable.

The idea for his second novel, *Lost Fields*, which he considers his best work, was derived from an essay written in the Belfast school where he taught: a boy wrote a short description of his grandmother, who had come to the city to live with her poor relations and longed for her old life in the country. Of this book Edwin Muir wrote, "It is hard to describe the charm and beauty of this story which deals with people twisted into the shapes of poverty. . . . Mr. McLaverty is a born artist." *In This Thy Day* and *The Three Brothers* were both chosen by the Catholic Literary Foundation for distribution to its members. Of the last, John Woodburn said in the *Saturday Review of Literature*, "This honest, unspectacular little novel, if it does not necessarily stir the blood, commands respect and steadily enlists the sympathies. Mr. McLaverty writes always well and at times beautifully." The scene of *Truth in the Night* is an island off the coast of Ireland and the story concerns a young widow. "Quietly powerful, vivid, masterfully indirect work," said *Commonweal*; "a beautiful illumination of life," said the New York *Times*.

McLaverty has also published two volumes of short stories, *White Mare* and *The Game Cock*. He lives in Belfast.

PRINCIPAL WORKS: Call My Brother Back, 1939; Lost Fields, 1941; White Mare, 1943; In This Thy Day, 1945; The Game Cock, 1947; The Three Brothers, 1948; Truth in the Night, 1951; School for Hope, 1954.

ABOUT: Hoehn, M. (ed.) Catholic Authors, I.

MACLEAN, CATHERINE MACDONALD,

British biographer and novelist, is the daughter of a schoolmaster, Kenneth

Alexander Maclean. She was educated at Muir-of-Ord and Dingwall Academy, at Edinburgh University under George Saintsbury, at Cherwell Hall, Oxford, and at University College, London. From 1917 to 1937 she lectured at Edinburgh University, then at Bristol University, and for six years at the University of Wales; but in 1938 she gave up lecturing for writing. Her essays have appeared widely in various periodicals in England. *Alexander Scott, Montgomerie, and Drummond of Hawthornden as Lyric Poets* was her first book. It was awarded the Lord Rector's Prize. *Dorothy and William Wordsworth* and *Dorothy Wordsworth, the Early Years* followed. There was moderate approval among critics of her first Wordsworth biography, but greater enthusiasm for the second, which Herbert Gorman in the New York *Times* described as "a full-bodied, meticulously documented and graciously written narrative of a life whose importance was implicit in its interior gestures. This is the hardest type of biography to write, for it calls for a high sensitivity on the part of the biographer. Miss Maclean, however, vindicates herself as a biographer and her right to her subject by the careful and yet sensitively intuitive manner in which she has handled her book." In 1943 Miss Maclean published *Born Under Saturn*, a biography of William Hazlitt; she shows him as a small boy emigrating to America with his sturdy nonconformist father in 1783 at the age of five; tells of the life there and the Hazlitt family's return to England a few years later; carries him through his schooling in a nonconformist college; follows his struggles in London and Paris to become a painter; and traces his own emergence as one of the champions of liberty in his day.

Miss Maclean has written three books of stories of Scottish refugee children during World War II: *Seven for Cordelia, The Tharrus Three*, and *Farewell to Tharrus*,

H. N. van Wadenoyen

published between 1941 and 1944. "These sketches, of children evacuated from the slums of Edinburgh and Glasgow to a farm in the Highlands, have moved me by the humor and vigor and honesty with which they are written," said Rachel Field. "These are not sentimentalized pen-and-ink children . . . but highly individualized young people, tough of hide and tongue, yet refreshingly sound of heart and spirit. . . . A book as sturdy and fresh and unpretentious as a sprig of heather."

Most recently, Miss Maclean has published a selection of Hazlitt's essays, *Hazlitt Painted by Himself*, with an introduction by herself. She has been given the degree of D.Litt. and is a Fellow of the Royal Society of Literature. Her recreations are walking and gardening. She lives in Surrey, England.

PRINCIPAL WORKS: Alexander Scott, Montgomerie, and Drummond of Hawthornden as Lyric Poets, 1915; Dorothy and William Wordsworth, 1927; Dorothy Wordsworth, the Early Years, 1932; Seven for Cordelia, 1941; Born Under Saturn, 1943; The Tharrus Three (*in England*: Three for Cordelia) 1943; Farewell to Tharrus, 1944; (ed.) Hazlitt Painted by Himself, 1948.

MACLEISH, ARCHIBALD (May 7, 1892-). For biographical sketch and list of earlier works and references, see TWENTIETH CENTURY AUTHORS, 1942.

* * *

Few poets have so fully and so sensitively reflected the widesweeping social and intellectual currents of the modern age as has Archibald MacLeish. An expatriate in the Twenties, a political liberal "rediscovering" America in the Thirties, a government official in the Forties, and a college professor in the Fifties, MacLeish is a kind of mirror of his times. He has tried, as Kimon Friar observed, "in an age that foredooms such an attempt to almost certain failure, to unite the inner and the outer man, the poet and the man of action." For his effort—and for his readiness to accept his share and more of the buffets and brickbats inevitable in twentieth century political life—he has won the sympathy and admiration of a large public. His reward has been literary honors of the highest rank—the Pulitzer prize (which he received for a second time in 1953), the Bollingen prize, and the National Book Award. But these, it should be emphasized, were for his poetry; and it is for this, rather than for his stormy political career, that MacLeish will be remembered. He is primarily a poet, Friar says, "a man of passion and compassion, a craftsman of integrity." It is true, James P. Southworth writes of him, that "his most insistent subject is political, but he is not political in the party sense of the word, but in its larger connotation of the problem of man's relation to society."

MacLeish held high political office during the administration of President Franklin D. Roosevelt. He was the target of much criticism from newspapers and congressmen for his liberal political views and for his intellectualism (at one congressional investigation an irate senator demanded that he "explain" some of his poetry). Actually, as many observers have pointed out, much of this criticism though directed at MacLeish was actually aimed at President Roosevelt and the New Deal. He was Librarian of Congress from 1939 to 1944. In addition, he organized and for a year (1941-42) directed the war-time Office of Facts and Figures. For another year (1942-43) he was assistant director of the Office of War Information. From 1944 to 1945 MacLeish was assistant Secretary of State. When World War II ended, he became active in the organization of UNESCO and served as chairman of the American delegation to the first general conference of UNESCO in Paris in 1946. In 1949 MacLeish was invited to Harvard to become Boylston professor of rhetoric and oratory, one of the oldest and most highly honored professorships offered by an American university. He teaches a course in expository writing, one in poetry, and another in creative writing.

Although MacLeish finds teaching hard work, he delights in the long summers and leaves of absence which it gives him for writing. Of special interest to him currently is writing for the stage, television, and radio. He has already written a number of highly successful verse plays for radio. ("The radio is perhaps the best medium for the verse play," he comments, "for it requires the ear alone.") In 1952 MacLeish's *Collected Poems 1917-1952* was published. In the long-range, backward view, his work emerged as sound and impressive. Richard Eberhart, in the New York *Times*, called the volume "a major achievement in American letters. . . . There is something basically lithe, wiry, direct and clear-seeing about his talent." I. L. Salomon wrote in the *Saturday Review*: "The masculinity of his lines, the magnificent rhythms of his blank verse, his *terza rima* adaptations, his technical accomplishment in many verse forms, and his perfection in the use of the simplest iambics are paradigms of excellence." And Kimon Friar observed in his review of the book for the *New Republic* that in lyric poems—the

elegy, love poems, poems on man's relation to the mysteriousness of the universe—"he has given us undoubted masterpieces." It was for this volume that MacLeish received his second Pulitzer prize, the Bollingen prize and the National Book award—all honoring the book as the best volume of poetry published in 1952.

ADDITIONAL WORKS: A Time to Act: Selected Addresses, 1943; American Story: Ten Broadcasts, 1944; Act Five, and Other Poems, 1948; Poetry and Opinion: The Pisan Cantos of Ezra Pound, 1950; Freedom Is the Right to Choose: An Inquiry into the Battle for the American Future, 1951; Collected Poems 1917-1952, 1952; This Music Crept by Me upon the Waters (verse play) 1953; Songs for Eve, 1954.

ABOUT: Southworth, J. G. Some Modern American Poets; Waggoner, H. H. The Heel of Elohim; New Republic December 15, 1952; New York Times Book Review December 7, 1952; Poetry March 1945; Saturday Review of Literature December 23, 1944; Time December 25, 1944.

MAC LENNAN, HUGH (March 20, 1907-   ), Canadian novelist, writes: "Though I was born in Cape Breton and grew up in Halifax, I seldom thought of myself as a Canadian until I went to Oxford where I was constantly confused with American Rhodes scholars by the British who thought we all talked alike. In my own mind I am primarily a Nova Scotian, a fact

Nakash, Montreal

which other Canadians find amusing and other Nova Scotians take for granted. I note this habit of mind only because it probably explains more about me as a writer than any long set of facts I could list, for Nova Scotians have always maintained a point of view like island people, sensible of being akin to all parts of the world that are touched by blue seas. They are far less concerned with being politically and geographically part of a continent-wide country to which they are tied by a mere isthmus less than fifteen miles wide.

"I was twenty-one when I first left Halifax. I had just won a Rhodes scholarship to represent Canada-at-large after graduating from Dalhousie University with honors. My three succeeding years at Oriel College, Oxford were the happiest of my life. During the long vacations I crisscrossed Europe either by motorbike, by third-class carriage or (across Greece) on foot. I learned German at Freiburg and in Italy spent most of my time at Lerici on the Gulf of Spezia. And finally I returned to Halifax in 1932 to the full impact of the depression.

"Princeton offered me a graduate fellowship, so I chose the cloisters in lieu of hunting a job in the wider world, and in 1935 I received a Ph.D. During those three years I also wrote two novels, both based upon a youth's-eye view of the state of the world and both laid in European countries. Fortunately neither was published, though the second was accepted by two different publishers, each of whom folded mysteriously—but not before I had been persuaded to rewrite the whole story three times. We learned the meaning of humility in those days and it did us no harm. I also learned how to write, and eventually what to write about, and I am still learning. So much for the depression.

"Today I am trying to teach university upperclassmen something about style in prose writing, from Bacon to Hemingway, from Donne to Rebecca West. These youngsters were all born during the years I spent at Princeton, and I find it a continuing challenge to try to bridge the gap between their attitude toward the world and the point of view of those of us who came to maturity during the Thirties. They expect the quick, easy success, and many of them get it. Certainly their dispositions are better than ours as a result.

"In the autumn of 1935 I accepted the only job I could get in Canada, teaching Latin at a boys' school in Montreal. In 1936 I married Dorothy Duncan, a graduate of Northwestern University, and we have lived in Montreal ever since. Being married to an American has many advantages for a Canadian; it is always a stimulation and sometimes a goad. It was my wife who first made me realize that there was no known contemporary fiction being written in Canada, and what I must do about it. As a result *Barometer Rising*, a novel of Halifax at the time of the great explosion of 1917, was published in New York in 1941.

"Two years later I was offered a Guggenheim fellowship to complete my second novel, a story based upon the relationship of the two peoples who make up the Province of Quebec, and in 1945 I was able to give up teaching boys who had no wish to learn Latin, to devote all my time to lecturing and writing. I have been awarded at different times three Governor-General's prizes, a counterpart of the Pulitzer prizes except that no money changes hands. In 1951 I was offered an associate professorship in the English department of McGill University on a part-time basis, and while I undertook the work somewhat reluctantly because of its demands on my time, I have carried on with it enthusiastically.

"During 1952—these are things which it seems one must mention—I was honored by the University of Western Ontario with the presentation of a D.Litt. and by the Province of Quebec with what used to be known as the Prix David, first prize for all works published in the English language by a resident of Quebec during the past five years."

PRINCIPAL WORKS: Barometer Rising, 1941; Two Solitudes, 1945; The Precipice, 1948; Cross-Country (essays) 1949; Each Man's Son, 1951.

ABOUT: Thomas, C. Canadian Novelists, 1920-1945; Phelps, A. L. Canadian Writers; Book-of-the-Month Club News February 1945; Canadian Book-of-the-Month Club News December 1944; Current Biography 1946; Publishers' Weekly November 10, 1941; Vogue May 15, 1951.

MAC MANUS, SEUMAS (1869-). For autobiographical sketch and list of earlier works and references, see TWENTIETH CENTURY AUTHORS, 1942.

* * *

Seumas MacManus now lives in the United States most of the time, although he also maintains a home in Donegal. He has been visiting lecturer at many American colleges and universities. His later collections of Irish folklore have been warmly received. James Kelly writes (in the New York *Times*) that MacManus' work will be the favorite always of "the young in heart who have longed for a return to the imagery and make-believe of a good story in the hands of a craftsman who knows how to set a mood before he begins."

ADDITIONAL WORK: Heavy Hangs the Golden Grain, 1950; The Bold Heroes of Hungry Hill, 1951.

ABOUT: Hoehn, M. (ed.) Catholic Authors, I; New York Herald Tribune Book Review October 7, 1951; Saturday Review of Literature December 27, 1947.

*MAC NEICE, LOUIS (September 12, 1907-). For autobiographical sketch and list of earlier works and references, see TWENTIETH CENTURY AUTHORS, 1942.

* * *

Louis MacNeice writes from London: "1941—joined the staff of the B.B.C. as script-writer and producer and have remained in this position till now, except for an eighteen-month secondment 1950-51 to the British Council as Director of the British

* măk nēs'

Institute in Athens. Based in London during World War II. Since then have made quite a few visits abroad—to France, Norway, Italy, and India."

One of the group of brilliant young "poets of social protest" in the 1930's, Louis Mac-Neice has, in later and more conservative years, continued to write a poetry distinguished for its variety and—in spite of lapses which have been variously described as "exasperating jargon," "little more than shrewd comments on life strung together in rhyme," and "incredible buffoonery"—its sparkling wit. Politics, a London *Times Literary Supplement* reviewer pointed out, has vanished from his work—"What appears to have taken its place is a development, not of politics, but of the moral outlook which in earlier days found a release in political solutions." In this later verse the *Times* finds a new dimension—a poetry "richer in variety and internal associations, mature in its detachment and arrangement of material and purer in its form." Significantly, the most highly praised of MacNeice's later poems (in *Ten Burnt Offerings*) are those of classical and Biblical reference, where the severity of style and concentration of feeling produce at times work of "great elegance and considerable power," Dudley Fitts observed in the New York *Times*. A reviewer in the *Nation* wrote: "Those who answer to the poem as a self-entering, self-generating, self-sealing form as organically alive as music may well find this the most exciting book of the year or of the decade."

In 1951 MacNeice published his translation of Goethe's *Faust*. Prepared originally for radio broadcasting, MacNeice's version is an abridgment of the poem to about two-thirds its original length. To prepare the translation, MacNeice—who admitted to "having next to no German"—had the help of a German scholar. The results were in the main successful—"an accurate and animated version," the *Times Literary Supplement* called it, particularly effective in its rendering of the colloquial, doggerel verse of parts of Goethe's original. In 1954 MacNeice was at work on a long contemporary poem in several cantos.

ADDITIONAL WORKS: Springboard: Poems 1941-1944, 1944; Christopher Columbus: A Radio Play, 1944; The Dark Tower, and Other Radio Scripts, 1946; Holes in the Sky: Poems 1944-1947, 1948; Collected Poems, 1949; Goethe's Faust, Parts I and II (trans. & abridged) 1951; Ten Burnt Offerings, 1952; The Penny that Rolled Away (juvenile) 1954.

ABOUT: Nation October 13, 1945; Poetry January 1944, June 1944, August 1949, May 1954; (London) Times Literary Supplement August 8, 1952; Saturday Review of Literature January 29, 1949.

MC NEILE, HERMAN CYRIL ("Sapper") (1888-August 14, 1937). For biographical sketch and list of works and references, see TWENTIETH CENTURY AUTHORS, 1942.

* * *

ABOUT: Dictionary of National Biography 1931-1940.

*MAC ORLAN, PIERRE (originally Pierre MacOrlan Dumarchais or Dumarchey) (February 28, 1882-). For autobiographical sketch and list of works and references, see TWENTIETH CENTURY AUTHORS, 1942.

* * *

Pierre MacOrlan, who has been called the precursor of modern French romanticism, was elected to the Académie Goncourt on January 30, 1950. He lives quietly in the country at St. Cyr-sur-Marin, but comes to Paris for meetings of the Academy. In recent years he has written several novels, none of them translated into English. In 1946 his collected poems were published in two volumes.

ABOUT: Columbia Dictionary of Modern European Literature; Dictionnaire Biographique Français Contemporain; France-Asie March 1952; France Illustration February 11 & 18, 1950.

* måk ôr län'

MC WILLIAMS, CAREY (December 13, 1905-), American journalist, writes: "I was born on a cattle ranch near Steamboat Springs, Colo. My father, Jerry McWilliams, was a pioneer cattleman, having come to northwestern Colorado from Missouri not too long after the town of Steamboat Springs was established, which was around 1876. My mother, born in Iowa, had moved to Kansas  and then to Denver with her family and had come to northwestern Colorado as a school teacher. For some years my father represented the thirteenth senatorial district in the Colorado State Senate.

"As a boy, I spent the summers on the ranch and winters in Steamboat Springs or in Denver where I attended the Wolfe Hall Preparatory School. I graduated, however, from the Steamboat High School, and enrolled as a freshman at the University of Denver. After my father's death, I moved to Los Angeles with my mother and my brother, Casley McWilliams. The year, as I recall, was 1922. In Los Angeles I attended the University of Southern California, graduating from the law school in 1927. Until 1938 I was engaged in the practice of the law. During these years I had occasion to become interested in a number of social problems—notably the problems of racial and other minority groups and of migratory workers. In 1938 Governor Culbert L. Olson appointed me chief of the Division of Immigration and Housing, an agency of the state government that was directly concerned with migratory farm labor camps. At the time of this appointment I gave up the general practice of the law.

"I joined the staff of the *Nation* as a contributing editor in January 1945, and since April 1951 have served in the New York office—first as associate editor and more recently as editorial director. While a student at the University of Southern California I served on the campus daily and edited *The Wooden Horse*, the college literary magazine.

"By and large the magazine articles and books that I have written deal with social problems in which I first became interested after I had begun to practice law. However, I have long been interested in California and the West and have written a number of books and magazine articles on themes related to this interest.

"In politics, I consider myself an independent liberal although I have always been a member of the Democratic Party and have served in the administration of a Democratic governor of California."

* * *

Carey McWilliams' *Factories in the Field*, a thoroughly documented study of migratory workers in California, was published only a few months after the appearance of John Steinbeck's novel on the same subject, *The Grapes of Wrath*, and helped to focus the attention of the American public on the plight of these people. *Ill Fares the Land* extended his study of migrant workers to all parts of America and was a powerful exposition of their economic problems. In these and later books McWilliams has studied various minority groups in American society. He writes with passionate indignation of the persecution of racial and social minority groups—Negroes, Mexicans, Chinese and Japanese, Indians, Puerto Ricans. His books have been praised for their courage and honesty, and he is considered a good reporter, with an eye for relevant facts and details.

PRINCIPAL WORKS: Ambrose Bierce: A Biography, 1929; Louis Adamic and Shadow America, 1935; Factories in the Field, 1939; Ill Fares the Land, 1942; Brothers Under the Skin, 1943; Prejudice, 1944; Southern California Country, 1946; A Mask for Privilege: Anti-Semitism in America, 1948; North from Mexico: The Spanish-Speaking People of the United States, 1949; California: The Great Exception, 1949; Witch Hunt: The Revival of Heresy, 1950.

ABOUT: Current Biography 1943; Newsweek October 16, 1944; Time May 24, 1943.

MACY, JOHN ALBERT (April 10, 1877-August 26, 1932). For biographical sketch and list of works and references, see TWENTIETH CENTURY AUTHORS, 1942.

*MADARIAGA, SALVADOR DE (July 23, 1886-). For biographical sketch and list of earlier works and references, see TWENTIETH CENTURY AUTHORS, 1942.

* * *

During World War II Madariaga broadcast weekly to Spanish America over the B.B.C. He also made frequent broadcasts in English and twice a month in Spanish for the Spanish Service of the Radiodiffusion Française. When the war ended, Madariaga served in numerous international organizations of a non-official character. He was especially active in UNESCO until, he writes, "I resigned owing to the admission of Franco Spain." He lives in England.

Madariaga's writings, whether on literary or political subjects, have never failed to stimulate heated controversy. One of his more recent—his biography of Bolívar (completing his New World trilogy, *Columbus* and *Hernán Cortéz*) proved to be a "literary bombshell that caused Spain and Latin America to go to war again, with plenty of ink spilled on both sides" (Marcelle Michelin in *Books Abroad*). Madariaga did his copious research for the book in Venezuela, Bolívar's birthplace and the center of the struggle for South American independence. He was fully aware of the reverence in which Bolívar is held in Latin America. In his book, however, he portrayed him with a "lethal psychiatric scalpel," as "nothing but a vulgar imitator of Napoleon with dreams of reigning over a South American empire." His method, like Lytton Strachey's in his portraits of the Victorians, resulted in stimulating and entertaining reading, but many critics complained that it was not "objective biography." The Latin American reaction was one of shock

* mä thä ryä'gä

and outrage. Argentina's Ministry of Education banned the book and its Bolívar Society condemned the author as an "historical fifth columnist." In North America and in England, however, *Bolívar* met a friendlier reception. Claude G. Bowers wrote in his review of the book in the New York *Times*: "*Bolívar* is a brilliant achievement, charming in style, penetrating in its interpretations of men and motives. Though the myths are destroyed, the real man emerges still, one of the most dramatic and fascinating figures of the history of the Western Hemisphere."

ADDITIONAL WORKS: Heart of Jade (novel) 1944; Victor, Beware, 1946; The Rise of the Spanish American Empire, 1947; The Fall of the Spanish American Empire, 1947; On Hamlet, 1948; Bolívar, 1952; Portrait of Europe, 1952.

ABOUT: Books Abroad Autumn 1953; Columbia Dictionary of Modern European Literature; New York Herald Tribune Book Review October 12, 1952.

MADELEVA, Sister MARY. See WOLFF, M. E.

MADGE, CHARLES (October 10, 1912-), English poet and sociologist, writes:
"I was born in South Africa where my father  was one of Milner's young men in the period of reconstruction following the Boer War. My father was killed in the First World War and I was brought up in England where I won a scholarship to Winchester College and later to Magdalene College, Cambridge, where I was a pupil of I. A. Richards. I owe much to him and his work in reconciling the outlook of the poet and the scientist. Later, T. S. Eliot helped me to publish my poems and to get my first job as a newspaper reporter on the London *Daily Mirror*. I left this job to start the quasi-sociological organization known as Mass-Observation and was joint author, with Tom Harrisson, of a number of books which resulted from this work. When World War II started, I left Mass-Observation and with the encouragement of the late Lord Keynes directed a survey of wartime saving and spending among wage-earners in a number of industrial cities.

"At the end of the war I joined the publishing firm of Pilot Press and edited the *Target for Tomorrow* series of volumes on post-war reconstruction. In 1947 I was appointed social development officer at Stevenage, one of the New Towns which are intended to decentralize population and industry from London, my task being to act as a sociologist-executive on an equal footing with the other chief officers of the Development Corporation. There were frustrating delays in the building of the town and in 1950 I was appointed to the new chair of social science at Birmingham University.

"Meantime I have continued to write poetry and have a third volume now in preparation. My first wife was the poetess Kathleen Raine. My present wife has published four novels under the name of Elizabeth Lake."

PRINCIPAL WORKS: *Ed. with T. Harrisson*—Mass-Observation, 1937; First Year's Work, 1938, Britain by Mass-Observation, 1939, War Begins at Home, 1940; The War-Time Pattern of Saving and Spending, 1943; Industry After the War, 1943; Pilot Guide to the General Election, 1945. *Poetry*—The Disappearing Castle, 1937; The Father Found, 1941.

ABOUT: Nature July 15, 1950.

MAETERLINCK, MAURICE, Comte (August 29, 1862-May 6, 1949). For biographical sketch and list of earlier works and references, see TWENTIETH CENTURY AUTHORS, 1942.

* * *

Maurice Maeterlinck died of a heart attack at eighty-six. Death came at his villa, the Château d'Orlamonde, on the French Riviera, where he had lived since returning to France from a seven-year stay in the United States.

Arriving in this country a penniless war refugee in 1940, the author found here a declining market for his works. At his leave-taking in 1947 he sued his publishers, Dodd, Mead & Company, for $250,000 for having made "no reasonable effort to sell and market the books" and for having allowed "unauthorized abridgments." The suit was withdrawn the following year. At the time of his death he was at work on an autobiography to be entitled "Blue Bubbles."

The varied and redoubtable problems which attracted Maeterlinck have been noted by Constant Burniaux—"moral and social, psychological and metaphysical: instinct, death and immortality, the littleness and solitude of man in the universe; space, time, God." His studies in these fields represent "poetic exploration" rather than a well-coordinated and original philosophic system, as pointed out by S. A. Rhodes, who adds: "In his symbolist theatre, however, he was the creator of a spiritual and idealistic art, a drama of the soul, which has had universal appeal and influence."

This considerable influence, in the words of the London *Times*, "has been felt not so much in the schools as in the hearts of people responsive to his suggestion of the inward peace and dignity to be wrested from life in a mechanistic age."

ADDITIONAL WORK IN ENGLISH TRANSLATION: The Great Beyond, 1947.

ABOUT: Mahony, P. Magic of Maeterlinck; Muldoon, S. J. Psychic Experiences of Famous People; Nizer, L. Between You and Me; Books Abroad Autumn 1949; France Illustration May 21, 1949; London Times May 7, 1949; Mercure de France June 1949; New Statesman and Nation May 14, 1949; New York Times May 7, 1949; Publishers' Weekly August 23, 1947, April 10, 1948; Time May 16, 1949.

MAILER, NORMAN (January 31, 1923-), American novelist, writes: "I was born in Long Branch, N.J., and lived

Robert Frank

there until the age of four at which time my parents moved to Brooklyn, N.Y. If there is a particular place I think of as home, it is probably New York City, and most specifically, Brooklyn. I went to public school there, graduated from Boys High School in 1939, and entered Harvard the same year with the idea in mind of becoming an aeronautical engineer. Somewhere in the course of my freshman year I became interested in writing, and in the following twelve months I must have written twenty or twenty-five short stories, climaxed for me by winning *Story* magazine's college contest for 1941 by a story titled "The Greatest Thing in the World." I have often thought that the peculiar juxtaposition of a Brooklyn culture and a Harvard culture have had the most external importance I could name in making me wish to write. I graduated from school in 1943, my idea of being an engineer forgotten, and during an inexplicable delay of eight months while I waited to go into the army, I wrote a novel about a mental hospital, called, as I remember, "A Transit to Narcissus." It was a romantic, morbid, twisted, and heavily tortured work which went possibly to twenty publishers before I realized that it was not going to be published. I mention it in this small detail because I suspect that if it had not been for the experience of the army (that invaluable experience for the writer of a situation which he cannot quit when he so chooses), I should have continued to write

books in very much that style. For those readers who may have been somewhat confused by the great difference in my two published novels, *The Naked and the Dead* and *Barbary Shore*, it may help to explain that I have long suffered from an inability to combine the best of two quite separate attitudes about the writing of novels: briefly, the romantic and the realist.

"To continue with my biography, I was married to Beatrice Silverman of Chelsea, Mass., in March 1944 shortly before entering the army, and we were divorced in 1951. My ex-wife and myself have a daughter named Susan, born in Los Angeles in August 1949. I was in the army for a little over two years, and being an indifferent soldier, I succeeded in getting myself shunted through a range of army jobs, which included a Field Artillery surveyor, a clerk, a rifleman, and finally a cook. I was overseas for some eighteen months in Leyte, Luzon, and Japan, and was discharged in May 1946 with the paramount obsession of writing a novel about the war. *The Naked and the Dead* is the result, and the book was written and rewritten in fifteen months at a rate of speed which seems rather fantastic to me now. After it was completed I spent a year in France trying to start another book, and was to spend still another year in traveling—Vermont, Los Angeles, New York—before I could begin real work upon it. The second novel, *Barbary Shore*, had the doubtful distinction of receiving possibly the worst reviews of any serious novel in recent years. It was the product of intense political preoccupation and a voyage in political affairs which began with the Progressive Party and has ended in the *cul-de-sac* (at least so far as action is concerned) of being an anti-Stalinist Marxist who feels that war is probably inevitable, and that both the Soviet Union and the United States are driven to war as an answer to problems which may be solved in no other way.

"I suppose that the virtue I should like most to achieve as a writer is to be genuinely disturbing, and by this I mean no easy reliance upon material which is shocking or brutal in itself, but rather effects which come from being truly radical, from going to the root of whatever is written about, so that life—which I believe is always disturbing if it is indeed seen—may serve as the gadfly to complacency, institution, and the dead weight of public taste. It is, I believe, the highest function a writer may serve, to see life (no matter by what means or form or experiment) as others do not see it, or only partially see it, and therefore open for the reader that literary experience which comes uniquely from the novel—the sense of having one's experience enlarged, one's perceptions deepened, and one's illusions about oneself rendered even more untenable. For me, this is the highest function of art, precisely that it is disturbing, that it does not let man rest, and therefore forces him so far as art may force anything to enlarge the horizons of his life. It is my hope that the body of the work I have done and intend to do will fulfill that purpose in its own small way."

* * *

The Naked and the Dead was one of the most impressive novels that emerged from World War II. Maxwell Geismar, writing in the *Saturday Review of Literature*, hailed it as "a substantial work," and its author as "a new novelist of consequence." An "encyclopedic" record of men in battle, it presented a vivid and harrowing picture of modern war. John W. Aldridge wrote of it: "On page after page and in episode after episode, it is Mailer's magnificent reportorial sense, his gift for evoking the tactile sense of a scene, that sustains the book and that will keep it alive at least as long as the events it describes live in the memory."

PRINCIPAL WORKS: The Naked and the Dead, 1948; Barbary Shore, 1951.

ABOUT: Aldridge, J. W. After the Lost Generation; Current Biography 1948; New York Times Book Review August 15, 1948, June 3, 1951; New Yorker October 23, 1948; Saturday Review of Literature May 8, 1948, February 12, 1949.

*MAIS, STUART PETRE BRODIE (July 4, 1885-). For biographical sketch and list of earlier works and references, see TWENTIETH CENTURY AUTHORS, 1942.

* * *

S. P. B. Mais, as a glance at his bibliography will indicate, is one of the busiest and most productive of contemporary English authors. Most of his writings have been travel books. These, in the opinion of the critics, are solidly researched, informative, and entertaining. When not traveling in England or abroad in search of material, Mais lives in Oxford.

ADDITIONAL WORKS: The Home Counties, 1943; The Book of Food, 1944; Youth After the War, 1944; The English Scene Today, 1948; I Return to Scotland, 1948; I Return to Switzerland, 1948; I Return to Ireland, 1948; The Best in their Kind, 1949; I Return to Wales, 1949; Little England Beyond Wales, 1949; Who Dies? 1949; The Riviera, 1950; I Loved You Once, 1950; Come Love,

Come Death, 1951; Arden and Avon, 1951; Madeira Holiday, 1951; Britannia, 1651-1951, 1951; Norwegian Odyssey, 1951; The Story of Oxford, 1951; We Wander in the West, 1951; Winter Sports Holiday, 1951; Buffets and Rewards (autobiography) 1952; Austrian Holiday, 1952; The Channel Islands, 1953; The Happiest Days of My Life, 1953; The Isle of Man, 1954; (with G. Mais) Italian Holiday, 1954.

ABOUT: Mais, S. P. B. Buffets and Rewards.

MAJOR, CHARLES (July 25, 1856-February 13, 1913). For biographical sketch and list of works and references, see TWENTIETH CENTURY AUTHORS, 1942.

*MALAPARTE, CURZIO (1898-), Italian author and journalist, was born at Prato, a small town near Florence. His mother was Italian, his father was German, and his real name was Kurt Suckert. He had little formal education. At sixteen he enlisted in the Garibaldian League, and he fought on the French front before Italy entered World War I (May 23, 1915); he then volunteered for the Italian army, fighting with the Alpine Troops until he was wounded at Bligny in 1918.

When the Italian Fascist Party was founded in 1919, Malaparte was one of its earliest members; after the march on Rome in October 1922, and Mussolini's accession to power, Malaparte's career progressed rapidly. He published a collection of Fascist poetry, stood in well with the Duce, and finally became the editor of Turin's influential newspaper, *La Stampa.*

In 1931 he got into trouble with some important Fascists—Malaparte later claimed the trouble was ideological, but others have said it was personal. In a letter to the New York *Times Book Review* in 1952 Malaparte said that he had been arrested by the Fascists and, after eight months in jail in Rome, was sentenced to five years on the island concentration camp of Lipari. He was freed in 1938 and two years later sent as a correspondent with the German army in Russia. Malaparte claimed that he was in frequent conflict with the Fascists and the Nazis and many times jailed by them. "My position is strongly against any form of totalitarianism," he wrote.

* māz

* mä lä pär′tĕ

Malaparte, the author of two volumes of poetry, two plays, and a score of books, is best known for *Kaputt* and *The Skin*, both of which were published after the end of World War II. During the war Malaparte, with the rank of captain, was a special correspondent for the Milan paper *Corrière della Sera,* and *Kaputt* is an autobiographical account of some of the more horrible and grotesque of his war experiences. In the introduction, he presents a short history of his work on the book: he began it in the summer of 1941 in the village of Pestshanka in the Ukraine; resumed work on it in Poland and while on the Smolensk front in January and February 1942; and finished it, except for the last chapter, during the two years he spent in Finland. He was in Finland in 1943 when he heard the news of Mussolini's fall; he at once flew back to Italy with the manuscript, where he was arrested, released on the intervention of friends, and went to Capri, "where I awaited the arrival of the Allies and where in September 1943, I finished the last chapter of *Kaputt.*"

When the Allies arrived, Malaparte did liaison work with the Italian liberation forces; he was arrested by the British but released when a British newsman vouched for him; and at the end of the war, he toured Germany on a special mission for the Allied Psychological Warfare Branch.

Robert Pick, in reviewing *Kaputt* for the *Saturday Review of Literature,* said, "I suppose the thing to do is to read it as fiction based on facts. You may also call it a fantasy about factual themes. But whatever you call it you won't escape the strange, grisly beauty of these stories"; and *Time* said, "Whatever their worth as history, these tenuously connected yarns have the quality of horrible legends recited against the feverish background of Europe's moral decay."

Despite the opposition of many anti-Fascists of long-standing, *Kaputt,* translated into ten languages, was a sensational best seller on the Continent. Malaparte followed it up with another and equally successful book, again in the form of autobiographical memoirs: *The Skin* covers the period 1943-45 and takes its author and a group of U.S. officers on what *Time* called "a macabre tour of the gutters of war-time Naples."

Malaparte has a taste for the paradoxical and the bizarre, the shocking and the gruesome anecdote. Long well-known in certain cosmopolitan circles as a raconteur, since the war he has gained a popular audience, but more in Europe than in America. His sales have brought him fortune as well as fame and he lives luxuriously in a villa on the island of Capri.

PRINCIPAL WORKS IN ENGLISH TRANSLATION: Coup d'Etat, The Technique of Revolution, 1932; Kaputt, 1946; The Skin, 1952.

ABOUT: Malaparte, C. Kaputt, The Skin; New York Times Book Review November 11, 1952; Saturday Review of Literature November 16, 1946, November 22, 1952; Time November 11, 1946, October 13, 1952.

*MALAQUAIS, JEAN PAUL (April 11, 1908-   ), French novelist, writes: "It is quite possible that I shall write my next book, or a play, or whatever it may be, directly in English, My first verses were in Polish, and so was my first, unpublished novel, but all my published work up to now I have written in French. I was the son of a college professor in the city of Warsaw, where I was born. My early youth is overshadowed by the image of my father lost in a book. When we went for a walk, my brother and I thought we were with father, but father was with his books. At the family table he wedged a book against a pile of books while eating his meal. In the afternoon, when he took his nap on the couch, he'd cover his face with a book. He was an extremely shy man, and if ever he indulged in any controversies at all it must have been with the ideas of his authors. His reserve was such that I don't remember him ever paying a compliment to his wife and two sons. I was about eighteen when I left home, and were I to put on paper the sum of our conversations during all those years I would be at a loss to fill in five double-spaced pages. I am quite positive that he never read fiction or poetry, and even when I became a writer he didn't show the slightest interest in my work. However, when we met some ten years after I left home, he was keenly probing my general ideas, though somewhat from an abstract point of view, as if I were after all another of his books. He was then a mild-mannered, middle-aged gentleman, whose broad culture made me feel like a little boy.

"Mother was altogether of a different type. She was sentimental, spontaneous, idealistic, always ready to meet people, to chatter for the sake of chattering, forever in love with a blade of grass, or the moon, or the stars—of which she knew all the exciting names. She wept reading Dostoevsky, laughed through

* mà là kā′

her tears reading Cervantes. Sometimes she would pick up one of father's books, but try as hard as she may she could make nothing of it: there were no real people in Kant, nobody suffered in a page of Descartes, not a soul was merry or sad in a volume of formal logic. It must have pained her, this incapacity of hers to grasp the meaning of her husband's world. It was, in a way, as if he were leading a secret life of his own, from which she was barred. Never were two beings more opposed temperamentally and intellectually, and both have left me with their particular imprint.

"Up to the time I was drafted into the French Army, in 1939, the longest I used to remain in one single place was a few weeks. I ran wild with curiosity about the world. There were not enough skies and faces and scents to satisfy my lust for life. New experiences grew old before I could exhaust them, and I was always on the move to catch up with myself. Wherever I went, all over Europe, in Asia, in Africa, I would dream of crossing into new lands, meanwhile working at odd jobs to keep body and soul. I was in turn farm and factory hand, miner, clerk, sailor, circus performer, accountant, assistant movie director, script writer, dish-washer, mechanic, carpenter, electrician, semi-professional chess-player, longshoreman. . . . Yet, somehow, I managed to keep up with my studies. Like my father, I was an unsatiated reader: there was always a book bulging in my pockets. André Gide had my first short story published in a literary magazine, and I was on a hospital bed in Paris when the galleys of my first novel were delivered to me. In December 1939, while in the army, I was the recipient of one of the foremost French literary awards, the Prix Théophraste Renaudot. In 1941 I was awarded the Prix de la Guilde du Livre, Lausanne, Switzerland.

"In June 1940 I was taken prisoner by the Germans and eventually escaped. In the fall of 1942 I managed to leave France, went through Spain, boarded ship in Cadiz, landed in Venezuela. In March 1943 I came to Mexico, and on the Fourth of July 1946 I came to the United States on an immigration visa. It was my second trip to this country. That same year I got a grant from the National Institute of Arts and Letters. In 1947 I went to France, traveled in Belgium, Holland, Switzerland, Germany, and in 1948 I was back in the States, teaching at New York University and the New School for Social Research and lecturing occasionally in other colleges and universities. In 1949 I held a Guggenheim fellowship while I was working on a book. My books, essays, short stories, poems, were translated and published in the United States, England, Hungary, Mexico, Brazil, Argentina, and in many international magazines. On the 15th of December 1952 I became an American citizen."

PRINCIPAL WORKS IN ENGLISH TRANSLATION: Men from Java (in U.S.: Men from Nowhere) 1941; War Diary, 1944; World Without Visa, 1948; The Joker, 1954.

ABOUT: Columbia Dictionary of Modern European Literature; Malaquais, J. War Diary; New Yorker January 29, 1944; Saturday Review of Literature February 5, 1944; Time May 24, 1948.

"MALET, LUCAS." See HARRISON, M. ST. L. K.

*****MALINOWSKI, BRONISLAW** (April 7, 1884-May 16, 1942). For biographical sketch and list of earlier works and references, see TWENTIETH CENTURY AUTHORS, 1942.

* * *

ADDITIONAL WORKS: Freedom and Civilization, 1944; Scientific Theory of Culture, and Other Essays, 1944; Magic, Science and Religion, and Other Essays, 1948.

ABOUT: Gluckman, M. Analysis of the Sociological Theories of Bronislaw Malinowski; Redfield, R. in Malinowski, B. Magic, Science and Religion; American Anthropology July 1943; Journal of American Folklore July 1943.

* mä lē nôf'skē

MALONE, DUMAS (January 10, 1892-), American historical biographer, was born in Coldwater, Miss., the son of John W. Malone and Lillian (Kemp) Malone. Though he grew up in Mississippi, he has since lived in New England, Virginia, Washington, and New York; and found a wide and intimate knowledge of the "Jefferson country" through his travels and research both here and in France.

Blackstone

Educated at Emory University (B.A.) and Yale (M.A. and Ph.D.), he taught at Yale and the University of Virginia, was for seven years director of the Harvard University Press, and is now professor of history at Columbia University.

Malone's *Jefferson and His Time,* of which two volumes have already been published, stemmed out of his years at Virginia, where he first became interested in Jefferson, the "Father of the University." When completed, the four-volume work will be the first full-length portrait of Thomas Jefferson and his era since Henry Randall's massive "Life," published before the Civil War. In *Jefferson the Virginian*, Malone recreated the first forty-one years of Jefferson's life, taking him to his departure for France in 1784. In *Jefferson and the Rights of Man*, he told the story of the eventful middle years in the life of Jefferson — his ministry to France, his service as Secretary of State in President Washington's first cabinet, and the beginnings of his long struggle with the Federalists. "There is no pedantry or obscure involvement in petty detail," was the comment of the *American Historical Review* on Volume I. "The work represents American historical scholarship at its very best." The late Harold Laski observed that "if the next three volumes are of the same quality, we shall have, at last, a biography . . . that is worthy of its exciting subject."

The appearance of Volume II brought similar approval: "On the whole, this second volume exceeds the favorable impression made by the first. . . . The first working days of the new republic are treated in illuminating detail," wrote Arthur Schlesinger, Jr., in the New York *Times Book Review*.

Malone is known also for his outstanding work as editor-in-chief of the *Dictionary of American Biography*, volumes VII to XX. All his writing has been historical and biographical. In 1925 Malone married Elisabeth Gifford. They have three children and live in New York City.

PRINCIPAL WORKS: The Public Life of Thomas Cooper, 1926; Saints in Action, 1939; Edwin A. Alderman, 1940; Jefferson and His Time: Jefferson the Virginian, 1948, Jefferson and the Rights of Man, 1951.

ABOUT: Saturday Review of Literature April 10, 1948.

*MALRAUX, ANDRÉ (November 3, 1901-). For biographical sketch and list of earlier works and references, see TWENTIETH CENTURY AUTHORS, 1942.

* * *

André Malraux enlisted in the French tank corps as a private at the outbreak of World War II. He was captured by the Germans, escaped, and became a leader of the guerillas in the French Resistance. He was wounded while fighting in Normandy, recovered, and was decorated with the British Distinguished Service Order. In 1945 he joined the staff of General de Gaulle as Minister of Information. In the turbulent political arena of post-war France he has continued loyal to de Gaulle, serving as his leading propagandist. His activities have involved him in bitter political struggles—the shutters on his study windows are scarred with bullets fired by a would-be assassin in 1947. Theodore H. White has described his great power as a political speaker: "Whoever has seen Malraux on a platform, his hands suddenly transformed into claws that tear at the air as his voice winds up with a fantastic, hypnotic eloquence to sweep an audience of thousands into a frenzy, knows that in naming this man as director of his national propaganda General de Gaulle has chosen the most effective rabble-rouser in France."

There is another Malraux who looms more impressively in modern intellectual life—Malraux the philosopher of art. In 1949-50 his great work, on which he spent more than fifteen years, *Le Psychologie de l'Art*, was published in three volumes. A revised, single-volume edition appeared in Paris in 1951 as *Les Voix de Silence*; and in 1953 Stuart Gilbert's English translation, *The Voices of Silence*, was published in the United States. Within a year of its publication, the French edition sold more than any other book ever published on the plastic arts in France. The five-hundred carefully chosen and skillfully reproduced illustrations to Malraux's text, plus the enormous breadth and depth of his knowledge of his field, made it one of the most valuable books written in recent years on art esthetics. "What survives for us in the great arts of the past," Malraux writes, "is the indefeasible inner voice of civilizations that have passed away." Essentially, as Irwin Edman pointed out in his review in the New York *Herald Tribune*, the book is "a philosophy of civilizations as they express themselves and constantly remake themselves in created forms. . . . It is an extraordinary celebration of the patrimony of the art of the past." Malraux's art history, Francis Henry Taylor of the Metropolitan Museum of Art warns, is "pure Apocrypha," but Taylor, nevertheless considers the book "one of the most stimulating, penetrating and sensitive inquiries that has ever been written."

Malraux visited the United States for the first time in a number of years in 1954, to attend the International Congress on Art History and Museology, sponsored by the Metropolitan Museum of Art. At that time Lewis Nichols interviewed him for the New York *Times* and described him as "a thinnish, slightly built man in his early fifties, with dark hair, pushed back, and a cigarette which

* mål rō'

droops from his mouth in repose but is used manually for emphasis while making a point." Malraux lives in a Paris suburb with his third wife, Marie-Madeleine Malraux, widow of his half-brother Roland Malraux. They were married in 1948. His second wife, the writer Josette Clotis, whom he married early in the war, was killed in a railway accident in 1945. They had two sons. His health shattered by years of intense activity and by his war injuries, Malraux nevertheless continues to work at fever-pitch. Genêt (Janet Flanner), who wrote a two-part profile on him for the *New Yorker* in 1954, says of him: "In France, Malraux is one of the flashing company of great modern literary adventurers who made tours of personal destiny, were deliberate participants in nations' crises, and wrote parts of their own legends."

Correction: Malraux was born in 1901, not 1895, as given in TWENTIETH CENTURY AUTHORS, 1942.

ADDITIONAL WORKS IN ENGLISH TRANSLATION: (with J. Burnham) The Case for de Gaulle: A Dialogue, 1948; The Psychology of Art (three volumes) 1949; The Voices of Silence, 1953.

ABOUT: Columbia Dictionary of Modern European Literature; Dictionnaire Biographique Français Contemporain; Frohock, W. André Malraux and the Tragic Imagination; Rahv, P. Image and Idea; Canadian Forum June 1948; Commonweal May 4, 1951; Life June 7, 1948; New York Times Magazine February 15, 1953; New Yorker November 6, 13, 1954; Time June 16, 1947.

MALTZ, ALBERT (October 28, 1908-). For autobiographical sketch and list of earlier works and references, see TWENTIETH CENTURY AUTHORS, 1942.

* * *

Albert Maltz wrote a number of successful screenplays, produced from 1942 to 1948—*This Gun for Hire, Destination Tokyo, Pride of the Marines, The House I Live In* (a short film on racial relations, for which he received an Academy Award), and *The Naked City*. He was president of the Western Regional Council of the Authors League of America from 1947 to 1948. In 1950 he received the award of the Commonwealth Club of California for literature and, in 1952, the Normandy Pen Award in the short story. A second child was born to Maltz and his wife in 1942.

In 1947 Maltz, along with nine other prominent Hollywood writers, was indicted for contempt of Congress for refusing to tell the House Un-American Activities Committeè whether or not he was a Communist. He served a prison term from June 28, 1950, to April 3, 1951.

ADDITIONAL WORKS: *Novels*—The Cross and the Arrow, 1944; The Journey of Simon McKeever, 1949. *Essays*—The Citizen Writer, 1950.

ABOUT: Warfel, H. R. American Novelists of Today; New Republic April 29, 1946, May 13, 1946.

MANFRED, FREDERICK FEIKEMA ("Feike Feikema") (January 6, 1912-), American novelist, writes: "Frederick Feikema Manfred was born on a farm southwest of Rock Rapids, Iowa, just a few miles from the Minnesota and the South Dakota borders. (This country has since been named Siouxland by him.) His six-foot-four father, Feike Feikes Feikema VI,

Marilyn Bruette

once a Siouxland farmer but now living in Artesia, Calif., is of West Frisian descent, Franeker, The Netherlands. His six-foot mother, Aeltsje (Alice) von Engen, is of East Frisian and Saxon ancestry. Her people originally came from Emelkamp in Northwest Germany though they emigrated to U.S.A. from The Netherlands. FFM has five brothers, Edward John, Floyd, John Garrett, Abben Clarence, Henry Herman, all over six-foot-three. (Edward is still on a farm in Siouxland, Floyd is an accountant with a Minneapolis firm, John is a skilled mechanic and owns and runs a filling station near Los Angeles, Abben is a skilled mechanic also near Los Angeles, and Henry is in law in Minneapolis.) FFM has no sisters. He is the oldest of the brothers, the tallest (six-foot-nine), and the heaviest (250). At the age of twelve he graduated from a parochial (Calvinistic) school (Doon Christian School, Doon, Iowa). At sixteen he graduated from a parochial (Calvinistic) high school (Hull Academy, Hull, Iowa). During his high school days he often stayed home months at a time to help his father on the farm, and after graduation from high school worked full time on the farm for two years. His mother Alice died in 1929. At eighteen he left the farm country for the first time and went to college at Calvin College, Grand Rapids, Mich. He graduated with a Bachelor of Arts degree and a teacher's life certificate in 1934. He worked a good share of his way through school, played basketball, was a member of various literary, philosophy, and dramatic clubs, was an avid reader, wrote poetry, helped edit the college magazine, *The Chimes*.

"From '34 to '37 he hitchhiked over the country, from the Atlantic to the Pacific, from New York City to Los Angeles, stopping off now and then to take on all sorts of jobs to pay his way: factory hand, filling station attendant, weekly newspaper editor, salesman, bus boy, hired hand, professional basketball player, driver, carpenter, painter, harvest hand. During those three years he continued his hungry reading in economics, political science, psychology, science, and literature in such libraries as he found on the way; also wrote poetry and prose sketches whenever he had a moment to himself. In May of 1937 he finally landed a steady job as a reporter on the old Minneapolis *Journal*. At about the same time he began to write novels in his spare time. He was fired in January 1939, possibly because of his union activity (he helped organize the American Newspaper Guild), possibly because of his politics (in his spare time he worked for the re-election of Elmer Benson as Farmer-Labor governor of Minnesota), more possibly because he was an indifferent reporter (sometimes getting too interested in a story, sometimes not getting interested enough). He next tried social service work (under Harold E. Stassen the newly elected Republican governor who defeated Benson), then public opinion survey work—all the while still writing in his spare time. At last, in April of 1940, due to malnutrition, overwork, heartache, he broke down with tuberculosis. He took the cure at Glen Lake Sanatorium, Oak Terrace, Minn., and threw off the infection in a relatively short while, at one time gaining 104 pounds, 175 to 279, in four months. Of sanatorium life, FFM has written: It saved me as an organism and helped make me a writer. It taught me how to live both as a natural animal and as musing human being. It drilled into me an early-to-rise, catnap-at-noon, early-to-bed kind of health discipline. It also gave me two 'free' years to think about where I had been, where I was, and where I might go. It gave me a chance to take a deep breath and a good look around before plunging forward into the battle again.

"He left the sanatorium in March 1942. In July of '42 he joined the editorial staff of *Modern Medicine*, Minneapolis. On October 31, 1942, Halloween, he married Maryanna Shorba, a graduate in journalism from the University of Minnesota at Minneapolis. He left his job at *Modern Medicine* in January of '43 when he found too great a conflict between medical writing and creative writing. He felt that if he was to develop his own particular style as an American of Old Frisic-Anglo-Saxon descent, if he was to write his individual kind of prose, Manfredean (Man'fre-de'an) prose, he had to avoid Latinate vocabulary. He next helped Hubert H. Humphrey run for mayor. (Humphrey later became the Democratic U. S. Senator from Minnesota.) In June of '43 FFM quit all work and decided it was now or never as a writer. He was given a University of Minnesota Writing Fellowship in 1944; a renewal in 1945. His first work, a novel, *The Golden Bowl*, which he wrote seven times, each time from scratch, was published in September of 1944 in St. Paul, Minn. This work won for him a $1,000 grant-in-aid from the American Academy of Arts and Letters. His second work, *Boy Almighty*, was published in November of 1945. His third work, a novel, *This Is the Year*, which many consider one of the finest novels ever written by an American, was published in March 1947. His fourth work, a novel, *The Chokecherry Tree*, was published in April of 1948. His fifth work, a trilogy, *World's Wanderer*, was completed in the fall of 1950. FFM was awarded a writing fellowship from the Field Foundation, Inc., through the University of Minnesota Graduate School in 1948-49, still another fellowship from the Andreas Foundation in 1949-50. As part of the 1849-1949 Minnesota Territorial Centennial celebration he was honored, along with the writers Sinclair Lewis and Robert Penn Warren, as one of the state of Minnesota's 100 Living Great. He held the position of writer-in-residence at Macalester College in St. Paul from the fall of 1949 to the spring of 1952, where he conducted a seminar in fiction writing. FFM lives in the country southwest of Minneapolis on a ten-acre place he has named Long Look. His home and his study are both high on a bluff and he can look many miles down the Minnesota River Valley toward Siouxland. He has two daughters, Freya and Marya. He cultivates a garden, an orchard, and a vineyard on his farm; occasionally pastures part of the land to grassers. His hobbies are reading, small bull sessions, playing the piano, painting, baseball, walking (sauntering) alone, driving alone. While he likes traveling in the plains, he especially likes driving through mountainous country, 'where Old Man Reality really shows his hand.' "

* * *

From 1944 to 1951 Manfred wrote under the pen name of Feike Feikema. In the latter year he published a long statement explaining his reasons for his change to Frederick Manfred. Mainly this was in order to anglicize the name. Also, he explained: "The Anglo-American tongue persistently and invariably pronounced *Feike* as either *Fyk-ee* or *Feek-ee* when it was *Fy-kah*, and pronounced *Feikema* as either *Fy-keem-ah* or *Fee-keem-ah* when it was *Fy-kah-ma*, whereas it pronounced the syllables of *Frederick* and *Manfred* with ease."

Manfred's first novels were largely autobiographical, distinguished for a style which one reviewer described as "a mixture of crudest realism and sensitive poetry." His later works, drawing heavily upon the same Siouxland background, were relatively more objective, although the giant farm boy hero of the trilogy *World's Wanderer* certainly mirrors the author himself. The rich detail of Manfred's language and the overwhelming and undisciplined flow of his narrative inevitably suggested comparison with Thomas Wolfe. Like Wolfe's work, his suffers from lack of selectivity, much of it being, as Granville Hicks pointed out, "a literal reproduction of Mr. Feikema's experiences." But also, like Wolfe's, it has a vigor and vitality which can sometimes dazzle the reader. "The commonplace and the melodramatic, the banal and the would-be poetic, lie side by side," Hicks wrote of his novel *The Giant*. "The trouble is that Mr. Feikema has been unable to communicate his passion and seriousness, principally because he cannot command the necessary resources of style."

PRINCIPAL WORKS: The Golden Bowl, 1944; Boy Almighty, 1945; This Is the Year, 1947; The Chokecherry Tree, 1948; World's Wanderer, a Trilogy: The Primitive, 1949; The Brother, 1950; The Giant, 1951; Lord Grizzly, 1954.

ABOUT: Current Biography 1950; Minnesota Quarterly Fall 1949; Publishers' Weekly May 3, 1952.

MANIFOLD, JOHN (1915-), Australian poet and musicologist, writes: "The Australian Manifolds are from the English branch of the family;  presumably there is some connection with the Irish Manifolds—who also have Australian descendents—but it is too far back to be traceable. My great-grandfather transferred his entire family from Cheshire to 'New South Wales' early in the last century, being among the very first white settlers in what is now the state of Victoria. The family has stuck close to pastoral farming in the same district ever

since; farmers and soldiers, all of them. I have a strong suspicion that the wrong John Manifold is writing this. It is my father who is the author of those remarkable pamphlets on soil-chemistry, not I.

"I was born in 1915, raised in the 'third homestead,' went to Geelong Grammar School and later on a scholarship to Cambridge. It was the headmaster, J. R. Darling, who first awoke my interest in modern literature. At almost the same moment I discovered music for myself—without disrespect to those who had been trying to make me like music ever since I was seven or so! I wrote verses and played the trombone, sitting in the school orchestra beside my brothers who played the trumpet and the tenor horn.

"French and German have long been 'almost native' languages with me. I took my degree in languages at Cambridge, and spent vacations on the Continent. It was the alarming spread of Fascism in Europe that completed my conversion from an ill-informed nationalism, and led me eventually to join the Communist Party in 1937.

"I was working in Germany when war broke out in 1939. I made my way back to England under rather uncomfortable conditions. In 1940 I married Katharine Hopwood, my fellow-student of languages at Cambridge, and was almost immediately called-up into the infantry. In December 1940, owing to the heavy losses in officers at Dunkirk, I was commissioned into the Intelligence Corps. Served on home defence, in Africa, with the Second Army in Holland and Germany. One wound, no decorations.

"My first pamphlet of verses in 1941 did very little towards making me a reputation; but my contributions to Keidrych Rhys' anthology *Poems from the Forces* caught the eye of the American critic Oscar Williams, to whose generous endeavours I owe the publication by John Day in America and by Dennis Dobson in London of my *Selected Verse*. I am extremely happy that my verses have brought me into contact with several very fine musicians—Alan Bush, Daniel Gregory Mason, Alexander Jemnitz, Sandor Veress, Doreen Jacobs, Robert Gill and Aubrey Bowman among them. I felt even more honoured when the eminent German man of letters Wilhelm Lehmann, found some of my sonnets worth translating: isolated poems of mine have also been done into French and into Polish. My friend Major Nicholas Tkatchuk of the Red Army undertook to get a Russian translation made, but the Russians had more urgent things to do at the time.

"Most of my published work since the war has been on musical research; principally on the history of musical instruments. Some of my conclusions appear in "Music in the English Theatre 1561 to 1711" [as yet unpublished]. Other papers and articles have been contributed to *Music & Letters, Keynote, the Canon,* and the *Australian Musical Times.* I have also made editions of some English and French instrumental music of the sixteenth and seventeenth centuries.

"At present I am collecting and re-printing Australian folktunes, songs and dances; and writing a sort of ballad-opera in collaboration with the dramatist Nancy Macmillan (Mrs. Geoff Wills). Also trying to run an amateur group of chamber-musicians, writing music for them, lecturing on (and singing) Australian folk-music, growing vegetables, speaking at Communist meetings, playing the recorder, guitar, bassoon and didgeridoo, and helping my wife to educate our two aggressively charming and healthy children.

"*Likes*:—classical, pre-classical, and some modern music; the Australian poets of the 1860s to 1890s and some of the moderns; the traditional ballads, Anglo-Scottish, Irish and Australian; modern French and Spanish poetry; good crime novels; wines, particularly claret; cheese, particularly Danish Blue; the Marx Brothers; cats.

"*Dislikes*:—romanticism; dogmatism; 'the American way of life.'"

* * *

The critical reaction to the American publication of Manifold's *Selected Verse* was mixed. Individual poems were singled out for praise, although the work as a whole was judged undistinguished. Louise Bogan commended "his plain dislike of sham and cruelty and his occasional bright song," and George Snell welcomed "a vigorous new talent from Australia, mature and lyrical."

PRINCIPAL WORKS: *Poetry*—Death of Ned Kelly, and Other Ballads, 1941; Trident (with H. Nicholson & D. Martin) 1944; Selected Verse, 1946. *Prose*—The Amorous Flute: An Unprofessional Handbook for Recorder Players, 1948.

MANN, ERIKA (November 9, 1905-). For biographical sketch and list of earlier works and references, see TWENTIETH CENTURY AUTHORS, 1942.

* * *

Erika Mann returned to Europe with her father in 1952 and lives with him near Zurich, Switzerland.

ADDITIONAL WORK IN ENGLISH TRANSLATION: Gang of Ten, 1942.

MANN, HEINRICH (March 27, 1871- March 12, 1950). For autobiographical sketch and list of earlier works and references, see TWENTIETH CENTURY AUTHORS, 1942.

* * *

Heinrich Mann died at seventy-eight, of a heart attack, at Santa Monica, Calif.

His wife had died in 1944. Mann was described by a friend during the last few years of his life as a "lonely, old, aggressively witty" but unembittered gentleman. He was working on an autobiography.

Largely underrated and unappreciated in the United States, Mann's works were reissued and honored in Germany after World War II. Death prevented his projected return to his native land to serve as president of the newly-organized Academy of the Arts in East Berlin. At his grave, tribute was paid by Lion Feuchtwanger: "If nothing remained of Heinrich Mann but his books, they would stand as a monument to his memory far into the remotest future. But more than that remains of him. We have the record and the example of a great life."

Mann, who has been called "a visionary of the reason," was characterized by William K. Pfeiler as "a champion of a new European humanism and a passionate fighter for intellectual and political freedom, the master at times of an original, expressive and cultured style."

ADDITIONAL WORKS IN ENGLISH TRANSLATION: Little Superman (in England: Man of Straw; published as The Patrioteer, 1918) 1944; Small Town Tyrant (previously published as The Blue Angel, 1932) 1944.

ABOUT: Books Abroad Summer 1944, Summer & Autumn 1950; New Republic March 25, 1946, April 24, 1950; New York Times March 13, 1950; Saturday Review of Literature March 16, 1946; South Atlantic Quarterly April 1951.

MANN, KLAUS (November 18, 1906- May 21, 1949). For autobiographical sketch and list of earlier works and references, see TWENTIETH CENTURY AUTHORS, 1942.

* * *

Klaus Mann died of a heart attack, at forty-two, at Cannes, France.

He had become a United States citizen in 1943, and served in the United States Army (December 1942 to October 1945) as a correspondent of *Stars and Stripes.* In New York after the war he founded and edited the literary magazine *Decision.*

Klaus Mann's autobiography records the dramatic change in his life (just before the advent of Hitler) from the role of critic and interpreter to that of a man of action. He demanded "greater political awareness on the part of today's younger writers." His novels, stories, essays, and memoirs reflect, in the words of the London *Times,* "the uneasy mind of those young Germans who, tricked by the false dawn of the years following the 1914-18 war, sought to create a new world, but found that the vision imposed by the earlier generation of great Danish, Austrian, and German writers, on the one hand, and the conflicts and breakdowns in the society of Europe, on the other, were too strong for them to overcome.

ADDITIONAL WORKS IN ENGLISH TRANSLATION: André Gide and the Crisis of Modern Thought, 1943; Heart of Europe (ed. with H. Kesten) 1943; Pathetic Symphony: a Novel About Tchaikovsky, 1948.

ABOUT: Commentary June 1950; Mercure de France November 1949; Nation January 9, 1943; New York Times May 23, 1949.

*MANN, THOMAS (June 6, 1875-). For biographical sketch and list of earlier works and references, see TWENTIETH CENTURY AUTHORS, 1942.

* * *

Thomas Mann moved to southern California in 1941, living in a colony of German exiles which included Bruno Walter, Arnold Schönberg, and Franz Werfel. There, under "the Egyptian sky of California," he completed his Joseph tetralogy with *Joseph the Provider*—"one of the great imaginative efforts of our time," as William Phillips described it in the *Nation.* In contrast to the view he held in his early years that the artist is non-political and should remain aloof from political controversy, Mann has interested himself more and more deeply in political activity. He became a United States citizen in 1944. During the war years he toured the United States lecturing and meeting large groups of people. He made a series of appeals to the German people over the B.B.C., and identified himself willingly and generously with numerous liberal causes. As a result, Mann made bitter enemies. When, in 1949, he returned to Germany to accept a Goethe prize in Frankfurt-am-Main, he also crossed into the Eastern or Soviet zone to accept a second Goethe award in Weimar. For this he was severely criticized. In 1952 Mann left the United States to make his permanent home in Switzerland, near Zurich.

On the occasion of his seventy-fifth birthday, Mann announced that he had no intention of writing an autobiography. "I prefer to transmute my life into my work. It is only

* Died August 12, 1955.

the work which really interests me." He has often been compared with that literary giant of an earlier century, Goethe. Like Goethe, he seeks out and cultivates the grotesque and the obscure—a source of considerable irritation to some of his readers. But also, like Goethe, he rarely fails in what he sets out so ambitiously to do. Drawn irresistibly to the same legendary theme that was Goethe's lifework, he wrote his own version of *Dr. Faustus,* the hero a tormented twentieth century intellectual, the scene modern Germany, doomed to decline and eventual ruin. Mann's enormous erudition, his digressions, his complexity of style and symbols, his fondness for the mystical and the eccentric, all contributed to make *Dr. Faustus* the most difficult of his books and probably the least satisfying of them as a novel. Yet, as Henry Hatfield points out, it cannot be dismissed simply as an ambitious failure. Hatfield suggests that it belongs, "like the second part of Goethe's *Faust,* with vast late works which although only partially successful contain an enormous variety of riches."

In the course of his search through all manner of obscure and recondite sources for material for *Dr. Faustus,* Mann read the old legend of Pope Gregory in the *Gesta Romanorum.* The story, with its themes of incest and redemption, fascinated him. He found it again, retold in Middle High German by Hartmann von Aue, and from this source primarily he developed his witty and audacious *The Holy Sinner.* Stephen Spender called the book "a small masterpiece"; others dismissed it simply as a clever and thoroughly entertaining tour de force. But there was complete agreement that this was a work of real distinction. There was far less unanimity of opinion on Mann's recent novel *The Black Swan,* a short and, for him, relatively simple story of a middle-aged woman's passion for a younger man. Since the aging heroine was German, the young hero American, analogies were inevitably drawn to the modern political scene—the impact of a vigorous America upon a decaying Europe. But— in the judgment of most critics—the symbolism was cloudy, the writing stilted and unnatural, and the subject one which failed to move most readers. Some critics who had long looked for signs of a decline in Mann's talents cited *The Black Swan* as a powerful example. Others, however, judged it merely a slighter work than average for him. No later work can diminish his stature as one of the major writers of this century, along with Joyce, Proust, and Gide. Charles Neider wrote of him: "His craftsmanship, his artistic dedication, the scope of his accomplishment, his creation of characters and 'worlds,' the variety of his achievement, the substance and weight, the 'tone' of his work, are all strongly predisposing factors to this judgment." Mann himself inclines to take a self-deprecating view of the matter. Writing in the New York *Herald Tribune* in 1951 he vigorously denied that there was any trace of "Olympian demeanor" about him or that his writing was elevated, prophetic, or ponderous. "My endeavor is to make the heavy light; my ideal is clarity. . . . I feel myself to be primarily a humorist."

Of himself personally Mann wrote: "I live a retired life. Except when I travel, I see few people. I am concerned solely about the tasks that accrue to me, one from the other. I give no thought to the public and to success; and when success comes, it is a coincidence, like a bolt from the blue—or rather: I myself am completely taken aback; for I have never yet sent forth a book without being convinced that it was unreadable."

As Mann approached his 80th birthday (June 1955), all Germany paid him honor. He spoke in both East and West Germany; his native city, Lübeck, granted him honorary citizenship. In excellent health, he planned to start work on the second part of his latest novel, *The Confessions of Felix Krull, Confidence Man*.

ADDITIONAL WORKS IN ENGLISH TRANSLATION: Selected Essays, 1941; Order of the Day: Political Essays and Speeches, 1942; Listen, Germany! 1943; Moses (novelette) *in* The Ten Commandments, ed. A. L. Robinson, 1943 (reprinted as Tables of the Law, 1945); Joseph the Provider, 1944; Essays of Three Decades, 1947; Doctor Faustus, 1948; The Holy Sinner, 1951; The Black Swan, 1954.

ABOUT: Brennan, J. G. Thomas Mann's World; Columbia Dictionary of Modern European Literature; Connolly, C. The Condemned Playground; Hatfield, H. Thomas Mann; Letters, F. J. H. Introduction to Thomas Mann; Neider, C. (ed.) The Stature of Thomas Mann; Atlantic Monthly January 1953; Current Biography 1942; Harper's October 1950; National Cyclopedia of American Biography (1946); New York Herald Tribune Book Review October 7, 1951; New York Times Book Review May 29, 1949, June 11, 1950, June 5, 1955; Saturday Review of Literature June 14, 1947, October 30, 1948, June 3, 1950: Sewanee Review Summer 1946; South Atlantic Quarterly January 1946.

MANNHEIM, KARL (March 27, 1893-January 9, 1947), German sociologist, was born in Budapest, the son of Gustav Mannheim and Rosa Eylenburg. He studied philosophy, languages and social sciences in the Universities of Berlin, Freiburg, and Heidelberg; and was appointed to the chair of sociology at the University of Frank-

furt. Because of the political situation in Germany, Mannheim was removed from this position in 1933, and went to Britain to lecture and to write.

From 1933 to 1945 he was lecturer in sociology at the London School of Economics (University of London). At the time of his death in 1947 he was professor of sociology and education at the Institute of Education in London.

Mannheim's approach to sociology, his editor Paul Kecskemeti points out, was dominated by the idea of "structure." "It was the 'structure' of social reality, and the position of individuals and groups within this 'structure,' which determined thinking and action and guided it into intelligible channels." Mannheim believed that contemporary political, social, and economic forces were leading civilization into dangerous courses, but that these dangers could be averted and controlled by the adoption of the principle of social planning (though he warned against the dangers of 'over-planning'—bureaucracy and the suppression of individual liberties).

Of his translated work *Ideology and Utopia,* the *Economist* wrote, "Professor Mannheim's challenging analysis, first written seven years ago in German, is here presented to English readers with an excellent introductory chapter on the approach to the problem: the sociology of human thought." *Man and Society in an Age of Reconstruction* appeared in 1940. "Nowhere else can one find such a complete, up-to-date and well-reasoned analysis of the inevitability of planning, good and bad, and of its techniques," wrote Julian Huxley; and T. S. Eliot added in the *Spectator*: "This is, in fact, a book which everyone seriously interested in the future of our society ought to read; and being the work of a mind not only powerful and learned, but intelligent and widely cultivated, and possessed of urbanity and wisdom, it is profitable reading quite independently of our prejudices either for or against the science of which the author is an exponent."

In 1943 Mannheim published what became one of the most widely discussed of recent contributions to sociological literature, *Diagnosis of Our Time, Wartime Essays of a Sociologist*. Somewhat critical, C. E. M. Joad wrote of this volume, "When you have swallowed the pomposities and stripped away the platitudes, you come upon an underlying sanity which rises on occasion to the height of wisdom and which enables you to understand the massive scale of Dr. Mannheim's reputation."

From his personal acquaintance with Mannheim, John Middleton Murry has said that while one felt Mannheim to be a heroic figure, at the same time "one felt that he was profoundly tired, his heart as it were soaked through with the weariness of bitter disappointment; yet he was indefatigable, determined to spend himself to the uttermost, in his mission of spreading awareness of the human predicament."

Illness prevented Mannheim from accepting the chairmanship of the European section of the United Nations Educational, Scientific and Cultural Organization, for which he had been designated. He died in London at the age of fifty-three. His wife, whom he married in 1921, was Dr. Julia Lang.

PRINCIPAL WORKS IN ENGLISH TRANSLATION: Rational and Irrational Elements in Contemporary Society, 1934; Ideology and Utopia, 1936; Man and Society in an Age of Reconstruction, 1940; Diagnosis of Our Time, 1943; Freedom, Power and Democratic Planning (with others) 1950; Essays on the Sociology of Knowledge (ed. P. Kecskemeti) 1952; Essays on Sociology and Social Psychology (ed. P. Kecskemeti) 1953.

ABOUT: Murry, J. M. Katherine Mansfield and Other Literary Portraits; American Journal of Sociology May 1947; American Sociological Review June 1947; Discovery February 1947; International Bureau of Education Bulletin 21, 1947; Nature February 22, 1947; New York Times January 10, 1947; Social Research September 1947.

MANNIN, ETHEL EDITH (October 11, 1900-), English novelist and essayist.

NOTE: This biography, at the request of the writer, supersedes the sketch which appeared in TWENTIETH CENTURY AUTHORS, 1942.

Miss Mannin writes: "Born London, eldest daughter of Robert Mannin and Edith Gray. Educated state school; left at fourteen with a scholarship for a course of commercial training; at fifteen was stenographer to leading advertising agency, Charles F. Higham, Ltd. At seventeen was co-editor, with Mr. (later Sir) Charles Higham, of the old theatrical and sporting paper the *Pelican*. Published first novel, *Martha*, 1922; came to the fore with third novel, *Sounding Brass*, a satire on the advertising world, in 1924. *Confessions and Impressions* published 1929, and the sequel to it, *Privileged Spectator*, in 1938. In 1952 is the author of thirty novels, five volumes short stories (the latest, *The Wild Swans*, being modern versions of ancient Irish legends), nine volumes of travel and

memoirs (the latest being *Moroccan Mosaic,* and best known, *South to Samarkand,* the story of a forbidden journey to Russian Turkestan), two volumes of child education, and four volumes of politics and ethics. The travel books include a book on present-day India and Pakistan, under the title *Jungle Journey.* The latest addition to the memoirs, by the end of 1952, is a monograph on the late Robert Mannin, under the title *This Was a Man.* The best-known of the novels is the 'Catholic' novel with the Augustinian title, *Late Have I Loved Thee,* which has had a success in America and in England, and has been translated into French, German, Italian, Dutch; but the author wishes to emphasize that she is not a Catholic, not likely to become one, being a Rationalist. The latest novel published in America was *At Sundown the Tiger,* which has an Indian background. The author discounts as immature all novels published before *Linda Shawn.*

"The author married J. A. Porteous, by whom she has a daughter, in 1919; in 1938 she married the author Reginald Reynolds. In the Thirties she was for some years a member of the Independent Labour Party, but after the Spanish Civil War, in which she worked with Emma Goldman and the Spanish and London anarchists organizing meetings in London, she adopted the pacifist-anarchist position which she still firmly maintains and is not now a member of any party or organization. Her novel *Red Rose* is based on the life of Emma Goldman.

"Hobbies: gardening, walking, entertaining friends. Lives nine miles out of London, and also has a cottage in the far West of Ireland, the country of her ancestors on her father's side."

PRINCIPAL WORKS: *Fiction*—Martha, 1922; Hunger of the Sea, 1924; Sounding Brass, 1925; Pilgrims, 1927; Green Willow, 1928; Crescendo, 1929; Children of the Earth, 1930; Ragged Banners, 1931; Green Figs (short stories) 1931; Linda Shawn, 1932; Venetian Blinds, 1933; Dryad (short stories) 1933; Men Are Unwise, 1934; The Falconer's Voice (short stories) 1935; Cactus, 1935; The Pure Flame, 1935; Women Also Dream, 1937; Rose and Sylvie, 1938; Darkness My Bride, 1938; Julie, 1940; Rolling in the Dew, 1940; Red Rose, 1941; The Blossoming Bough, 1942; Captain Moonlight, 1942; No More Mimosa (short stories) 1943; Proud Heaven, 1944; Lucifer and the Child, 1945; Dark Forest, 1946; Late Have I Loved Thee, 1948; Every Man a Stranger, 1949; Bavarian Story, 1950; At Sundown the Tiger, 1951; The Wild Swans, and Other Tales Based on the Ancient Irish, 1952; The Fields at Evening, 1952; Lover Under Another Name, 1954. *Non-Fiction*—Confessions and Impressions (autobiography) 1929; Commonsense and the Child, 1931; All Experience, 1932; Forever Wandering, 1935; South to Samarkand, 1936; Women and the Revolution, 1938; Commonsense and the Adolescent,

1938; Privileged Spectator (autobiography) 1939; Christianity—or Chaos? 1940; Commonsense and Morality, 1942; Bread and Roses: An Utopian Survey and Blue Print, 1944; Comrade, O Comrade, 1947; Connemara Journal, 1948; German Journey, 1948; Jungle Journey, 1950; This Was a Man, 1952; Moroccan Mosaic, 1953; Two Studies in Integrity, 1954.

ABOUT: Mannin, E. Confessions and Impressions, Privileged Spectator, Connemara Journal, This Was A Man; Bookman August 1926.

MANNING, ADELAIDE. See "COLES, M."

MANNING, FREDERIC (1887-February 22, 1935). For biographical sketch and list of works and references, see TWENTIETH CENTURY AUTHORS, 1942.

* * *

ABOUT: Dictionary of Australian Biography.

MANSFIELD, KATHERINE (October 14, 1888-January 9, 1923). For biographical sketch and list of works and references, see TWENTIETH CENTURY AUTHORS, 1942.

* * *

ADDITIONAL WORK: Letters to John Middleton Murry, 1913-1922 (first complete edition) 1951.

ABOUT: Alpers, A. Katherine Mansfield; Berkman, S. L. Katherine Mansfield; Cather, W. On Writing; Clarke, I. C. Katherine Mansfield; Eustace, C. J. An Infinity of Questions; Friis, A. Katherine Mansfield; Lawlor, J. A. Mansfieldiana (bibliography); Lawlor, P. A. Mystery of Maata; Mansfield, K. Letters to John Middleton Murry; Murry, J. M. Katherine Mansfield, and Other Literary Portraits; Fortnightly April 1948; New Republic January 7, 1952; New Statesman and Nation February 2, 1946; Saturday Review of Literature March 19, 1951; Southwest Review Summer 1953.

MANTLE, BURNS (December 23, 1873-February 9, 1948). For biographical sketch and list of earlier works and references, see TWENTIETH CENTURY AUTHORS, 1942.

* * *

Burns Mantle died at his home in Forest Hills, N.Y., at seventy-four. The cause of death was cancer of the stomach; he had been ill for two months.

Retiring as drama critic of the New York *News* in 1943, Mantle had continued to contribute occasional columns as "critic emeritus," and to edit the annual compilation of *Best Plays* which Joseph Wood Krutch called the "labor of love for which he will be remembered as long as the history of the American theatre remains interesting." He

was the first critic admitted to membership in the Players Club. Regarding himself as a reporter rather than a critic, Mantle combined, said Eugene Burr, "an acute and perceptive mind and a feeling for the theatre, an understanding of its problems, a love for its workers, a gentleness of attitude that at the same time refused to tolerate the cheap, the shoddy or the inept."

ADDITIONAL WORKS: *Editor*—Best Plays (annual vols. through 1947); Best Plays of 1899-1909, and The Year Book of the Drama (with G. P. Sherwood) 1944.

ABOUT: Current Biography 1944; New York Times February 10, 1948; Newsweek August 23, 1943.

MARCELIN, PIERRE. See THOBY-MARCELIN, P.

"MARCH, WILLIAM." See CAMPBELL, W. E. M.

MARE. See DE LA MARE

*MARITAIN, JACQUES (November 18, 1882-   ). For biographical sketch and list of earlier works and references, see TWENTIETH CENTURY AUTHORS, 1942.

* * *

During World War II Jacques Maritain and his wife Raïssa lived in New York City, where he taught at Columbia University, and then in Princeton, N.J., where he taught at the university. He also traveled frequently to Toronto to lecture at the Pontifical Institute of Medieval Studies. In 1945 General de Gaulle, then head of the provisional government of liberated France, offered him the post of French ambassador to the Vatican. After some hesitancy, Maritain accepted the appointment. "It seems to me," he commented just before his departure for Rome, "that I shall have there in the shadow of the Chair of Peter some opportunity to pursue, in thought as in action, the philosophical study of those problems and relationships between the spiritual and the temporal which has been my task for many long years." Maritain spent the next three years in Rome. In 1948 he returned to Princeton where he remained until his retirement, as professor emeritus, in 1953.

Charles Fecher described Maritain in 1952 as slightly stooped, somewhat heavier than in earlier years, with thick white hair and a deep and powerful voice. One of the most highly honored and respected of contempo-

* mà rē tăn'

rary religious philosophers, he is neither solemn nor austere. He is known for his humor, his lightness and informality, a serenity which, Fecher writes, "only long years of intense intellectual preoccupation could have effected." A stimulating teacher and lecturer and a gifted stylist in his writing, Maritain has today almost as many admirers outside the Catholic faith as within it. The Protestant theologian Reinhold Niebuhr speaks of his charm and grace as a person. "There is a quality of character in Maritain one would define as 'saintly' if that word had not such various connotations." As a philosopher Jacques Maritain has exercised an important influence in American thought. It is largely through his efforts—and those of his fellow countryman Etienne Gilson—that there has been a rebirth of interest in the philosophy of Saint Thomas Aquinas, in scholasticism, and in philosophical realism. Maritain has been one of the strongest influences in the current revival of religious thought in American intellectual circles. His appeal has spread even beyond the Catholic Church because, as George Barker suggests, he speaks in "the secular voice." C. J. Eustace writes: "Maritain maintains that philosophy is not removed from the common life of man. The most profound philosophical questions are those which the common sense of mankind asks for an answer. The answers that Maritain proposes appeal to so many people because they open up the heart of experience, struggling toward a truth not of logic alone, but of life."

Maritain's recent writings have reflected the clarity and profundity which mark all his work. Of his *Creative Intuition in Art and Poetry* a reviewer remarked: "The range of its poetic knowledge is as impressive as the brilliance of its metaphysical flights."

ADDITIONAL WORKS IN ENGLISH TRANSLATION: Saint Thomas and the Problem of Evil, 1942; Art and Poetry, 1943; Education at the Crossroads, 1943; Twilight of Civilization, 1943; Christianity and Democracy, 1944; The Dream of Descartes and Other Essays, 1945; Formal Logic, 1946; The Person and the Common Good, 1947; (with J. Cocteau) Art and Faith: Letters, 1948; Existence and the Existent, 1948; Man and the State, 1949; The Philosophy of Nature, 1951; The Range of Reason, 1952; Creative Intuition in Art and Poetry, 1953; Approaches to God, 1954.

ABOUT: Fecher, C. A. The Philosophy of Jacques Maritain; Hoehn, M. (ed.) Catholic Authors, I; Maritain, J. Art and Faith; Maritain, R. We Have Been Friends Together, Adventures in Grace; Morgan, C. Liberties of the Mind; Columbia Dictionary of Modern European Literature; Catholic World February, March 1946; Commonweal February 9, 1945, June 11, 1954; Current Biography 1942; Personalist October 1948; Thomist 1943; Time May 31, 1948.

MARKHAM, EDWIN (April 23, 1852-March 7, 1940). For autobiographical sketch and list of works and references, see TWENTIETH CENTURY AUTHORS, 1942.

* * *

ABOUT: American Academy of Arts and Letters, Commemorative Tributes, 1905-1941; Library Journal June 15, 1942; Pacific Historical Review September 1944.

MARKS, JEANNETTE AUGUSTUS (August 16, 1875-). For autobiographical sketch and list of works and references, see TWENTIETH CENTURY AUTHORS, 1942.

* * *

Jeannette Marks has continued active in little-theatre work and in numerous social and literary societies. From 1942 to 1947 she was chairman of the New York State branch of the National Woman's Party. She lives in Westport, on Lake Champlain, N.Y.

MARKS, PERCY (September 9, 1891-). For biographical sketch and list of earlier works and references, see TWENTIETH CENTURY AUTHORS, 1942.

* * *

Percy Marks writes for the so-called "popular" market—slick fiction of no intrinsic literary value, but smoothly plotted and lightly constructed. The critics dismiss his work as slight, but he has an enthusiastic reading public. He lives in Hamden, Conn.

ADDITIONAL WORKS: Knave of Diamonds, 1943; Shade of Sycamore, 1944; Blair Merriman, 1949.

*MARQUAND, JOHN PHILLIPS (November 10, 1893-). For biographical sketch and list of earlier works and references, see TWENTIETH CENTURY AUTHORS, 1942.

* * *

J. P. Marquand, his wife, and their three children live in Cambridge, Mass. In recent years he has also lived in New York City, in Greenwich, Conn., in the old Marquand place at Kent's Island just outside Newburyport, and on Treasure Island, a three and one-half mile island in the Bahamas. As a writer Marquand has had something of the Midas touch. *Life* magazine called him "the most successful novelist in the United States" —a phrase which suggests not only the financial rewards but the praise and admiration

* mär kwŏnd'

he has had from book reviewers and the reading public. His later novels have without exception been long-term best sellers; several of them have been made into motion pictures—two of them, *The Late George Apley* (dramatized by Marquand and George S. Kaufman) and *Point of No Return* (dramatized by Paul Osborn), have been among the most sparkling Broadway successes of recent years.

Philip Hamburger, in his profile of Marquand (told in the manner of a Marquand novel), has his reporter-interviewer reflect: "Marquand could write. He could write like a breeze." He writes rapidly and easily (some thirty novels and serials by 1952 and innumerable articles and short stories), and he can be read rapidly and easily, so easily indeed that there is always a danger of dismissing Marquand as merely a writer of "slicks." Actually, as Granville Hicks pointed out in a study of Marquand in *Harper's*, beneath the smooth, bright surface of his fiction, there is a rich vein of social irony and a sound basis in modern sociology. (Hicks cites Marquand's indebtedness to W. Lloyd Warner's extensive sociological studies of Newburyport.) With the Pulitzer prize-winning *Late George Apley*, he pinpointed the small, snob-bound world of Boston society. In later books Marquand has continued to focus on the relatively homogeneous New England society, but he has begun to move beyond the rigid social stratifications and to explore the overlapping of class lines, the shuttlings back-and-forth, that characterize modern society. Probably his most interesting recent novel, *Point of No Return*, is a shrewd and skillful dissection of the social structure of the "lower upper class," struggling for a firm foothold on a higher rung of the social ladder. The scene of *Point of No Return* is New York and the fashionable suburbs, but in a series of flashbacks the hero, a young bank executive, goes back to his New England hometown, obviously Newburyport, which Marquand draws with an understanding and reality that surpass the charts and statistics of the sociologists' studies. "He is a social novelist of great talent," writes Hicks, "and neither his slick past nor his successful present should blind us to that fact. It is true that he keeps close to the surface. . . . On the surface, however, he has a mastery that is not to be underestimated."

Marquand's son by an earlier marriage published a novel, *The Second Happiest Day*, in 1953 under the name John Phillips.

ADDITIONAL WORKS: So Little Time, 1943; Repent in Haste, 1945; B.F.'s Daughter (in England: Polly Fulton) 1946; (with G. S. Kaufman) The Late George Apley (play) 1946; Point of No Return, 1949; Melville Goodwin, U.S.A., 1951; Thirty Years (collected fiction and non-fiction) 1954; Sincerely, Willis Wayde, 1955.

ABOUT: Hamburger, P. J. P. Marquand, Esq.; Van Gelder, R. Writers and Writing; Current Biography 1942; Harper's April 1950; Life November 8, 1948; New York Herald Tribune Book Review April 19, 1953; New York Times Book Review April 24, 1949, February 27, 1955; Saturday Review January 26, 1952; Time March 7, 1949.

MARQUIS, DON (July 29, 1878-December 30, 1937). For biographical sketch and list of works and references, see TWENTIETH CENTURY AUTHORS, 1942.

* * *

archy and mehitabel, a short jazz opera by George Kleinsinger based on Don Marquis' sketches, was produced in New York late in 1954 and later recorded with considerable success.

ABOUT: Middleton, G. These Things Are Mine; Morley, C. Introduction to The Best of Don Marquis (1946); American Mercury March 1947; Atlantic Monthly November 1946; Harper's March 1950.

MARRIOTT, CHARLES (1869-). For biographical sketch and list of earlier works and references, see TWENTIETH CENTURY AUTHORS, 1942.

* * *

Charles Marriott retired as art critic of the London *Times* in 1940. He broadcasts occasionally for the B.B.C. His only recent writing is a pamphlet on British handicrafts, written for the British Council. Marriott's second wife died in 1949. He lives in a London suburb.

ADDITIONAL WORK: British Handicrafts, 1943.

MARSH, NGAIO (April 23, 1899-). For autobiographical sketch and list of earlier works and references, see TWENTIETH CENTURY AUTHORS, 1942.

* * *

Ngaio Marsh received the Order of the British Empire in 1948. During the war years she joined the Red Cross Transport Unit in New Zealand and became head section leader. She has been producer since 1944 of the D. D. O'Connor Theatre Management, is active in repertory theatre work, and, in 1948, was honorary lecturer in drama at Canterbury University College. Miss Marsh lives in Christchurch, New Zealand.

Her highly literate "whodunits" continue to win praise, not only as examples of neatly plotted detection, but as novels in their own right. "The important things about Miss Marsh," L. A. G. Strong wrote in the *Spectator*, "are that she writes extremely well, and that her characters are not types subservient to a plot, but real people." She has been especially praised for the authenticity of the settings of her books—whether these settings be New Zealand (where her pictures of Maori life are noteworthy), London high society, or the theatre and backstage life which she knows so well.

ADDITIONAL WORKS: Colour Scheme, 1943; Died in the Wool, 1945; Final Curtain, 1947; A Wreath for Rivera (in England: Swing, Brother, Swing) 1949; Night at the Vulcan (in England: Opening Night) 1951; Spinsters in Jeopardy, 1953; Scales of Justice, 1955.

ABOUT: Saturday Evening Post March 8, 1947.

MARSHALL, ARCHIBALD (September 6, 1866-September 29, 1934). For biographical sketch and list of works and references, see TWENTIETH CENTURY AUTHORS, 1942.

MARSHALL, BRUCE (June 24, 1899-). For biographical sketch and list of earlier works and references, see TWENTIETH CENTURY AUTHORS, 1942.

* * *

Although Bruce Marshall's earlier *Father Malachy's Miracle* had been a very successful book, it was not—by his own admission—"until I was again serving in the second World War that I became financially successful as a novelist." On the outbreak of war, Marshall returned to England from Paris, where he had lived and practiced accountancy for a number of years. (He had married Mary Pearson Clark, a Scot, in Paris in 1928; they have one daughter.) Marshall joined the British Army, was assigned to the Royal Army Pay Corps, and by the time the war ended he was lieutenant-colonel in the Displaced Persons Division of the British Element of the Allied Commission for Austria. Out of this latter experience, incidentally, Marshall drew material for *The Red Danube (Vespers in Vienna)*, which was a Book-of-the-Month Club selection in America and was filmed by M.G.M. Probably his most successful recent novel was *The World, the Flesh and Father Smith*, also a Book-of-the-Month selection, a warmly humorous novel of clerical life in Scotland which some reviewers found even better than *Father*

Malachy's Miracle. On the basis of this novel and some of his other recent works, Christopher Morley paid him this tribute: "Bruce Marshall is full of mockery; he succumbs sometimes to merely carnal or spiritual comedy, but he is never morbid or mean. He is one of my favorite lay priests because he relishes the farce and terror of man." Marshall lives with his wife and their six cats in the south of France.

ADDITIONAL WORKS: Yellow Tapers for Paris, 1943; All Glorious Within (in U.S.: The World, the Flesh, and Father Smith) 1944; George Brown's Schooldays, 1946; The Red Danube (in U.S.: Vespers in Vienna) 1947; To Every Man a Penny, 1949; The White Rabbit, 1952; The Fair Bride, 1953; Only Fade Away, 1954.

ABOUT: Hoehn, M. (ed.) Catholic Authors, I; New York Herald Tribune Book Review October 11, 1953; New York Times Book Review January 18, 1948.

MARSHALL, EDISON (August 28, 1894-), American novelist, writes: "My father, George Edward Marshall, of Illinois frontier stock, studied law, taught school, and came to publish a daily paper in Rensselaer, Ind. He married Lille Blood Bartoo, out of New England; I was born in Rensselaer and lived there until I was thirteen, when my father, fifty-seven, re-

Vernon Gould

tired, sold his newspaper, and became a fruit-grower in beautiful Rogue River Valley in Oregon. But frost, hail, wind, blight, San José scale, codling moth (all terms of horror to me to this day) and the tantrums of the market brought the sheriff on to our front porch. He did not actually get inside, but the cold wind of poverty rattled the windows and gave us the scare of our lives. I resolved that whatever I did in life, first and foremost it must make us a bountiful living.

"At seventeen I was convinced I could write. Trying it a little in my first year in college, I sold a story to *Argosy*. In 1916, age twenty-one, I undertook it as a career. I could not fool around; I had to prove it in one year or try something else. That year I sold a story to the *Saturday Evening Post*, three to the *American*, and several to the pulps.

"Uncle Sam supported me in 1918 without the slightest useful return and even created me a shavetail. Heaving a happy sigh, I got back to the typewriter early in 1919. That year I wrote 'The Elephant Remembers,' which may be the most widely-read story in English written in this century (it was in *Literature and Life* and other school-text books by the score, so that uncounted millions of students could not get out of reading it) and 'The Heart of Little Shikara,' which won the O. Henry Memorial Prize in 1921.

"Obsessed by the outdoors to a degree of passion that would floor Freud, I began to write short stories, novelettes, and novels with wilderness settings. What I think happened was, I did not know enough about civilized settings to employ them well—I was still an unbelievable rustic, in spite of marrying a civilized girl, Agnes Flythe, of Augusta, Ga.—and I made myself go mad over the wild so I could be a successful author. Big-game hunting did give me terrific thrills. I followed it for seventeen years, to Africa, French Indo-China, Alaska, Burma, India. I became, oddly enough, an expert tiger-hunter. Through some romance, I hunted them on foot.

"In these years I graduated from the pulp magazines to the so-called slicks. Dozens of serials, all laid in Alaska or the Far East, appeared in *American, Good Housekeeping, Cosmopolitan*, etc.; and then, to my great delight, I found time to write short stories of deeper themes. In 1937, both the wolf and the sheriff were definitely barred from our door. I was no longer quite such a country-jake. That same year, a magazine editor I liked to write for, W. F. Bigelow, retired. So I renounced the magazine serial with its stock characters, editorial direction, and crippling technique, and resolved to spend the rest of my writing years at writing novels.

"The first was *Benjamin Blake*, Literary Guild for 1941, which made a dashing movie, *Son of Fury*. The next was *Great Smith*, a biographical novel of Captain John Smith, and perhaps my most considerable work. These and later novels were laid in far countries and dealt mainly with adventure. The least successful was the one laid nearest home —no farther than the Carolina low-country.

"I scoured deeper with my last two books, *The Viking*, whose hero was the folk-hero, Ogier the Dane, and *Caravan to Xanadu*, a big book-club winner. Living in Augusta, Ga., not only out of the world but out of my times, avoiding New York, Hollywood, and all contacts and pressures that could breach my dreams (a social delinquent if one ever was), reading poetry and biography but no novels but my own, fishing or shooting three days a week with a soft-voiced, dark-skinned attendant-companion, I hope to write vigorously for two more decades. If so, I will have made something like a record—more than fifty years of good living from my pen alone, and a long lifetime spent at absolutely no other (except a year's soldiering) gainful occupation."

PRINCIPAL WORKS: The Heart of Little Shikara, and Other Stories, 1922; Benjamin Blake, 1941; Great Smith, 1943; The Upstart, 1945; Shikar and Safari: Reminiscences of Jungle Hunting, 1947; Yankee Pasha, 1947; Castle in the Swamp, 1948; Gypsy Sixpence, 1949; Infinite Woman, 1950; Love Stories of India, 1950; The Viking, 1951; Bengal Tiger, 1952; Caravan to Xanadu, 1953; American Captain, 1954.

ABOUT: Marshall, E. Shikar and Safari; National Cyclopedia of American Biography (1952); Warfel, H. R. American Novelists of Today.

MARSHALL, LENORE (GUINZBURG) (September 7, 1897-), American poet and novelist, writes: "On my father's side of the family were several generations of liberal journalists and other professional people, on my mother's a streak of art took various shapes; behind me lies a background that has given a sense of kinship to the past and my childhood  took for granted books, music, pictures. I was born in a brownstone house in New York City, daughter of Henry A., and Leonie (Kleinert) Guinzburg. The strongest influence of my youth was a fine painter aunt, Herminie Kleinert, who awoke my imagination by her own perception of beauty, and indeed although she is dead, her integrity, courage, devotion, her response to form and color in nature, to sensitivity and honor in human beings are still the same living lights that I cherish. Rearing as an early milestone is, aged three, the summer sight of an apple tree hung with gay green balls and of making an instant poem about it; at eight I filled a notebook with verses and illustrations and decided to become a writer. Evidently there were no doubts or difficulties *then!*

"Schooling in New York; received an A.B. from Barnard College where I wrote the graduation poem, was literary editor, etc. Fresh out of college came marriage to James Marshall, soon there were babies, Ellen and Jonathan. Domesticity absorbed me; book reviews here and there were a compromise into which was bottled the wish to write my own books; with delay an unhappy literary inferiority complex set in. In order to overcome this when the children were launched in school I took a job in a publishing house, trying to build a backward bridge to my lost world of artistic direction. I was a reader, then editor; the high point of those years came in picking up, among the hundreds of nondescript manuscripts, one entitled 'The Sound and the Fury' by an obscure man named William Faulkner and feeling after the first pages as though penetrated by a physical force of words, and I rushed in greatest excitement to the head of the firm announcing that I had discovered a work of genius. When the firm dissolved, an interlude followed as poetry editor of a magazine; a few of my poems had meanwhile been written and were appearing; at last I got down to what I had always longed to do and my first novel was soon accepted.

"But writing never comes easily to me; it is a tense necessity, blessed when it turns out, hellish otherwise. A conflict continues between two consciences, two loves, the human deep attachments with their consequent involvements to a group of people including grandchildren now and to external causes, and toward the stream of work which has its own isolated single inner existence. There is, however, no conflict between writing poetry and fiction, although prose, it seems to me, can be forever revised and improved whereas a poem, the most satisfying of expressions, ought to be altogether right and when it is not right is altogether wrong. The theme of my novels and of the new one on which I am working and of any, I suppose, that I will ever do is the secret drama of the forward moving soul seeking its own truth, struggling to fulfill its own goal, learning to come to terms with its passion, its dream, to meet its destiny by burning to its brightest core what it wills to survive of itself, to climb through shadows and rocks to its own air, to reach, perhaps—and if so everything is worth while—its vista of light. My poems are varied in subject dealing with love, nature, grief, war, metaphysical concepts.

"I am interested in people and ideas. I am an inveterate notetaker; jot in notebooks and scraps of paper observations that are raw material from which I draw. I am neat and organized and find this a drawback to a strong flow of productivity, but I cannot help it. Favorite reading to which I return constantly: Tolstoy, Proust, Henry James, Dostoevsky, E. M. Forster, poetry from Shakespeare and Blake to the moderns.

"Since youth I have been a pacifist in the sense of a belief that war never accomplishes its stated nobler ends but leaves more problems than it solves; have worked for peace and for minority rights and am politically a so-called 'Liberal.' I joined the Quakers, in whose attitudes toward living I find a spiritual meaning and purpose and faith where I feel at home. My time is divided between New York, which I hate and fear, and a farm in New Hope, Pa.; although division is disrupting and I cart manuscripts and broken sentences back and forth I choose the city because my family reside there, the country because I can dig in my garden, walk through woodland and fields, and receive an eternal refreshment and delight."

PRINCIPAL WORKS: Only the Fear, 1935; Hall of Mirrors, 1937; No Boundary (poems) 1943.

ABOUT: Book-of-the-Month Club News July 1935.

MARSHALL, ROSAMOND VAN DER ZEE (October 17, 1900-), American novelist, was born in New York City to Charles

and Florence (Hudson) Botsford, both writers. She attended schools in the United States until the age of twelve, when she was taken to Europe and was entered in the Lycée des Jeunes Filles in Dijon, France. Private tutors continued her English-language education at home. She attended high school in Vienna and matriculated in the University of Munich, where she studied languages, history, philology and literature. During her student years she became interested in mountaineering and holds an unbroken record for women of twenty-two new routes with amateur guides in the Swiss, French, and Italian Alps. She also climbed in the Polish Tatra. In Italy she married an artist and lived in Rome for several years. After a divorce, she married Albert Earl Marshall of New York City. She has one daughter.

She began to "write," she says, at the age of three when her first poem appeared in the New York *World*. Stories, playlets, poems were followed by her first historical novel in a setting of the French Revolution, written at the age of fourteen. She later wrote many popular novels in French that were published in Belgium, under a nom de plume. Her first published novel in the English language, *None But the Brave* (1942), for young people, won her the New York *Herald Tribune*

Spring Book Award. It is the story of the Netherlands' revolt against the tyranny of Spain in the sixteenth century.

Miss Marshall divides her time between Southern California and her Vancouver Island farm, where she raises French miniature silver poodles and enjoys the sport of salmon fishing. A hard worker, she rises early, writes for four or five hours conscientiously and then devotes the rest of the day to her friends and her hobbies.

Rosamond Marshall's fame as a writer for young people has been quite overshadowed by the phenomenal success of her historical romances for adults. The first of these, *Kitty* (made into a motion picture), set the pattern for a continuing series of lively, lusty novels, robust picaresque entertainment, which have had sales (in paper-back reprints) ranging from a million and a half to three million.

PRINCIPAL WORKS: Kitty, 1943; Duchess Hotspur, 1946; Celeste, 1949; Laird's Choice, 1951; Jane Hadden, 1952; Bond of the Flesh, 1952; The General's Wench, 1953; The Loving Meddler, 1954; The Dollmaster, 1954; Rogue Cavalier, 1955. *Juveniles*—None But the Brave, 1942; The Treasure of Shafto, 1946.

ABOUT: Current Biography 1942; New York Herald Tribune Book Review May 10, 1942; Publishers' Weekly May 9, 1942.

"MARTENS, PAUL." See SOUTH-WOLD, S.

"MARTIN, ABE." See HUBBARD, F. Mc K.

MARTIN, EDWARD SANDFORD (January 2, 1856-June 13, 1939). For biographical sketch and list of works and references, see TWENTIETH CENTURY AUTHORS, 1942.

MARTIN, EVERETT DEAN (July 5, 1880-May 10, 1941). For biographical sketch and list of works and references, see TWENTIETH CENTURY AUTHORS, 1942.

* * *

Everett Dean Martin died at his home in Claremont, Calif., at sixty as the result of a heart attack. He had been on the staff of Claremont College as professor of social philosophy.

Evans Clark, noting the brilliance of style, easy rhythm, and provocative freshness of Martin's writing, called him one of the most gifted popular writers in the non-fiction field. He has the faculty of distilling the dry detail of the laboratory and the technical report into a refreshing and stimulating draft for the mind of the average man." His *Meaning of a Liberal Education* was characterized by F. P. Keppil as "by all odds the most important contribution to the understanding of adult education which has thus far been made in the United States."

ABOUT: New York Times May 11, 13, 1941.

MARTIN, Mrs. HELEN (REIMEN-SNYDER) (October 18, 1868-June 29, 1939). For biographical sketch and list of works and references, see TWENTIETH CENTURY AUTHORS, 1942.

MARTIN, VIOLET FLORENCE ("Martin Ross") (June 11, 1865-December 21, 1915). For biographical sketch and list of works and references, see TWENTIETH CENTURY AUTHORS, 1942.

* * *

ABOUT: Bushnell, G. H. From Papyrus to Print; Higginson, A. H. British and American Sporting Authors; Pritchett, V. S. The Living Novel; Commonweal October 3, 1947.

*MARTIN DU GARD, ROGER (1881-). For biographical sketch and list of earlier works and references, see TWENTIETH CENTURY AUTHORS, 1942.

* * *

During World War II, Roger Martin du Gard lived quietly in unoccupied France, "maintaining a dignified silence in face of the 'New Order,'" Howard Rice wrote. He lives now in Paris and has a country home in Normandy. His novel *Jean Barois*, published in France in 1913, made its first appearance in an English translation (by Stuart Gilbert) in 1949. A rich and mature study of a free thinker who finally returns to the church, *Jean Barois* was as timely in 1949 as it had been in 1913. Albert Guérard commented in his review of the book: "Rogert Martin du Gard thinks, and compels us to think. He does not offer a ready-made solution; he is neither an iconoclast nor an apologist. Truth is complex and finely shaded. The way out of the maze cannot be imposed; it must be sought within." *The Postman*, a translation of an early novel, is a somber study of village life.

Martin du Gard's most important recent work is his brief but very revealing memoir of the late André Gide. Of all the many personal recollections of Gide which have appeared, Justin O'Brien remarked, "none

* màr tăn dü gàr'

depicts the man and his spirit more faithfully than these too few pages of Martin du Gard."

ADDITIONAL WORKS IN ENGLISH TRANSLATION: Jean Barois, 1949; Recollections of André Gide, 1953; The Postman, 1955.

ABOUT: Columbia Dictionary of Modern European Literature; Dictionnaire Biographique Français Contemporain; New York Times Book Review April 24, 1949; Time May 9, 1949.

*MARTÍNEZ RUIZ, JOSÉ ("Azorín") (June 8, 1873-). For biographical sketch and list of works and references, see TWENTIETH CENTURY AUTHORS, 1942.

* * *

Universally recognized as "one of the great literary figures of twentieth century Spain," Azorín lives with his wife in an apartment in Madrid, within easy walking distance of the Museum of the Prado, which he often visits, and the Park of the Retiro. He follows a strict schedule, rising and writing in the long quiet hours of the early morning, walking and reading in the afternoon, and retiring soon after eight at night. Marguerite C. Rand, who visited him in 1952, reported in *Books Abroad* that he was "very alert, interested in the modern world and in current literature." He was fascinated by moving pictures (which he regards as a new art form), by painting (El Greco, Rubens, Rembrandt, Cézanne), and by contemporary French writers—especially the late André Gide.

Azorín has been highly honored in his native land. In 1947-48 the first eight volumes of his *Obras Completas* (complete works) were published in Spain. Also in 1947 the city of Madrid held a public meeting in his honor and the book dealers of the city held a ten-day exposition of his works. Of Azorín's achievement Marguerite C. Rand wrote: "Azorín's work is a vast panorama of the Spanish world, of her literature, art, landscapes, people, a work truly Spanish but also universal in the beauty of its artistry and in its spiritual overtones."

ABOUT: Granell, M. Estética de Azorín; Krause, A. Azorín, the Little Philosopher; Books Abroad Spring 1953.

* mär tē′näth rōō ēth′ (ä thō rēn′)

*MARTÍNEZ SIERRA, GREGORIO (May 6, 1881-October 1, 1947). For biographical sketch and list of earlier works and references, see TWENTIETH CENTURY AUTHORS, 1942.

* * *

* mär tē′näth syĕr′rä

Gregorio Martínez Sierra died in Madrid at sixty-six of an intestinal tumor. He had returned to Spain a month before his death, after several years of voluntary exile in Buenos Aires.

The London *Times* has noted that his countrymen found in his plays, which were the best-known portion of his prodigious literary output, some "spiritual affinity" with Cervantes, notably in his "serene treatment of fools." In the plays, which ranged from farce to carefully wrought character studies, the *Times* found that "the old virtues seemed new and wise because of the shrewd sense, the fresh apprehension, the loving laughter with which he saw them."

ABOUT: Columbia Dictionary of Modern European Literature; London Times October 3, 1947; New York Times October 2, 1947; Theatre Arts June 1944.

*MARTÍNEZ ZUVIRÍA, GUSTAVO ADOLFO ("Hugo Wast") (1883-). For autobiographical sketch and list of works and references, see TWENTIETH CENTURY AUTHORS, 1942.

* * *

Martínez Zuviría lives in Argentina. He is married and has twelve children. Since 1931 he has been director of the National Library of Buenos Aires. In 1941 he was appointed "Federal Interventor" of the Argentinian province of Catamarca, serving during a period of government crisis until the officials of the province could be duly elected. In 1943 he became Minister of Justice and Public Instruction and initiated new legislation, re-introducing the teaching of religion in the public schools (the teaching of religion had been banned in 1884).

As "Hugo Wast," he has written some twenty-five novels and a number of nonfiction works on Catholicism. His novels—swift-moving and colorful—have been translated into many languages and are frequently used, in their original Spanish, as textbooks in American colleges.

ABOUT: Hoehn, M. (ed.) Catholic Authors, I.

* mär tē′näs sōō vē rē′ä

MARVIN, FRANCIS SYDNEY (August 6, 1863-November 14, 1943). For autobiographical sketch and list of works and references, see TWENTIETH CENTURY AUTHORS, 1942.

* * *

Francis Sydney Marvin died at eighty.

Dominated by the idea of the unity of Western civilization, Marvin wrote to emphasize that thesis. The London *Times* has noted that he was "deeply learned in political history and in the records of science and philosophy, and his gift of synthesis enabled him to plan a short book in which every sentence was weighty with knowledge and relevance."

ABOUT: Isis 1945; John Rylands Library Bulletin March 1944; London Times November 17, 1943.

MARY MADELEVA, Sister. See WOLFF, M. E.

MASEFIELD, JOHN (June 1, 1878-). For biographical sketch and list of earlier works and references, see TWENTIETH CENTURY AUTHORS, 1942.

* * *

Looking back across some sixty years of a distinguished literary career, John Masefield wrote in his autobiographical *So Long to Learn*: "Now that I am coming to an end, I wish to try to set down what matters have been helpful to me in the work of my choice that has filled my days. That work has been the finding, framing and telling of stories, in verse and prose, according to the tale and the power within me. I have done, and have enjoyed, much other work of different kinds, yet always with the love (and the hope) of story-telling deep within me, as the work beyond all other work, to which my nature called."

Thus modestly, with characteristic good humor and serenity, Masefield summed up his career. In spite of illness in recent years he has continued active in writing verse, plays, and autobiography. As Poet Laureate of England, he has produced the occasional poetry required of him, but his most memorable work remains the sparkling and spontaneous poems and stories he writes about the rugged but essentially simple and lyrical life of the sea and the farm country he knew as a boy. Hugh I'Anson Fausset wrote of his poem *Wonderings* in 1943: "His words are not great poetry, but they are vigorous and from the heart."

Masefield lives at Burcote Brook, near Abingdon. In 1947 the novel *Passion Left Behind*, by his son Lewis Masefield (killed in action in 1942) was published with a preface by Masefield.

ADDITIONAL WORKS: *Poetry*—Generation Risen, 1942; Land Workers, 1943; Wonderings, 1943; On the Hill, 1949; (ed.) My Favourite English Poems, 1950; Poems: Complete Edition, 1953. *Plays*—The Play of Saint George, 1948. *Essays and Miscellaneous*—New Chum, 1944; A Macbeth Production,

1946; Thanks Before Going: Notes on Some of the Original Poems of Dante Gabriel Rossetti, 1946; Badon Parchments, 1947; A Book of Prose Selections, 1950; So Long to Learn, 1952.

ABOUT: Bishop, J. P. Collected Essays; Masefield, J. New Chum, So Long to Learn; Mim, E. Christ of the Poets; Spark, M. John Masefield; Christian Science Monitor Magazine November 2, 1946, December 23, 1950; New York Times Magazine October 24, 1948; Saturday Review of Literature May 20, 1950, July 22, 1950; Time February 27, 1950.

MASON, ALFRED EDWARD WOODLEY (1865-November 22, 1948). For biographical sketch and list of earlier works and references, see TWENTIETH CENTURY AUTHORS, 1942.

* * *

A. E. W. Mason died at his home in London at eighty-three, after a year's illness. Both his physical and his creative energy were prodigious; in his late seventies he was still an ardent climber and yachtsman, and the books of his later years were greeted with critical acclaim. At the time of his death he was working on a historical memoir of Admiral Blake, Commonwealth soldier and sailor.

The London *Times* has pointed out that not only was Mason one of the most successful popular writers of his period, but he was also "a writer of admirable quality, a craftsman of superlative skill, economy and finish." He was "a first class story-teller," wrote Kate O'Brien, and "a literary writer who remained true to the graceful, careful style which he made his own."

ADDITIONAL WORKS: Musk and Amber, 1942; The House in Lordship Lane (mystery) 1946.

ABOUT: London Times November 23, 1948; New York Times November 23, 1948.

MASON, VAN WYCK (November 11, 1897-). For autobiographical sketch and list of earlier works and references, see TWENTIETH CENTURY AUTHORS, 1942.

* * *

Van Wyck Mason served from 1943 to 1945 in Europe with Supreme Headquarters Allied Expeditionary Force and in 1945 became a colonel. He received many honors for his war service, including the Croix de Guerre and the Legion of Honor. During the war, under the name "Frank W. Mason," he wrote several lively wartime adventure stories for young readers. When the war ended he returned to his home in Riderwood, Md., from which he travels six days a week to his Baltimore office. Here, following a strict, business-hours schedule, he writes or does research for his books. Mason alternates between historical novels (he is especially interested in naval history) and murder mysteries (centered around his hero-detective Colonel North). He has been phenomenally successful. In his whole writing career, John K. Hutchins reports in the New York *Herald Tribune*, he has sold everything he has written, with the exception of two short stories. Reviewers describe his work as slick, smooth, and professional. His plots may be tailored to formula, his characters uncomplicated, but his research is extensive and the finished product is almost invariably lively and enjoyable reading.

ADDITIONAL WORKS: Rivers of Glory, 1942; (ed.) The Fighting American (stories) 1943; Saigon Singer, 1946; Eagle in the Sky, 1948; Cutlass Empire, 1949; Dardanelles Derelict, 1949; Valley Forge: 24 December 1777, 1950; Proud New Flags, 1951; Himalayan Assignment, 1952; The Golden Admiral, 1953; The Winter at Valley Forge (juvenile) 1953; Blue Hurricane, 1954; Two Tickets for Tangier, 1955. *As "Ward Weaver"*—End of the Track, 1943. *As "Frank W. Mason"*—Q-Boat, 1943; Pilots, Man Your Planes! 1944; Flight into Danger, 1946.

ABOUT: Lewis, J. Other Men's Minds; Van Gelder, R. Writers and Writing; New York Herald Tribune Book Review May 27, 1951; New York Times Book Review February 15, 1948.

MASON, WALT (May 4, 1862-June 22, 1939). For biographical sketch and list of works and references, see TWENTIETH CENTURY AUTHORS, 1942.

MASPERO, Sir GASTON CAMILLE CHARLES (June 23, 1846-June 30, 1916). For biographical sketch and list of works and references, see TWENTIETH CENTURY AUTHORS, 1942.

* * *

ABOUT: Journal of Egyptian Archaeology December 1947.

MASSINGHAM, HAROLD JOHN (March 25, 1888-August 22, 1952). For autobiographical sketch and list of earlier works and references, see TWENTIETH CENTURY AUTHORS, 1942.

* * *

Harold John Massingham died at his home in Buckinghamshire, England, at sixty-four.

He had published about fifty books, plays and pamphlets. A "passionate advocate" of the spiritual value of living close to nature, the life he lived was, said the London *Times*, "consciously a background for the finely wrought literature he poured forth in abundance." An article in the *Times Literary Supplement*, written just before his death,

voiced the opinion that Massingham, who had been for many years "a voice crying—albeit in beautiful prose and well-balanced language —in a wilderness," might now, by virtue of England's recent tendency to return to small-scale farming, find himself "translated from the character of a reactionary dreamer lamenting over an idealized rural past . . . into that of a prophetic revolutionary."

ADDITIONAL WORKS: Field Fellowship, 1942; Remembrance (autobiography) 1942; Men of Earth, 1943; Tree of Life, 1943; This Plot of Earth, 1944; Natural Order (ed.) 1945; Wisdom of the Fields, 1945; Where Man Belongs, 1946; Small Farmer (ed.) 1947; The Englishman's Year, 1948; Curious Traveller, 1950; Faith of a Fieldsman, 1951.

ABOUT: Massingham, H. J. Remembrance, The Englishman's Year; London Times August 25, 1952; London Times Literary Supplement August 29, 1952; New York Times August 24, 1952; Time October 3, 1949.

MASTERS, EDGAR LEE (August 23, 1868-March 5, 1950). For biographical sketch and list of earlier works and references, see TWENTIETH CENTURY AUTHORS, 1942.

* * *

Edgar Lee Masters died in a convalescent home in Philadelphia at eighty-one. He and his wife had lived in virtual seclusion for many years in New York's Hotel Chelsea. In 1944 he was taken to Bellevue Hospital suffering from pneumonia and malnutrition; the Authors' League came to his financial assistance, and in 1946 the Academy of American Poets awarded him a $5,000 fellowship.

The poet was described in his later years by Cyril Clemens: "His fluffy hair, his gold-rimmed-spectacled eyes, his ruddy cheeks and his frank mid-Western manner, reminded one of a typical mid-Western farmer." There were dissimilar sides to his personality, corresponding to dissimilar aspects of his work; editorially, the *Saturday Review of Literature* observed that "he was a cynic whose temper was easily aroused, occasionally long-winded and dull—his mind, to quote William Rose Benét, was informed and independent, and his speculations on life and philosophy were original." Of his volumes of poetry following *Spoon River Anthology*, Louis Untermeyer pointed out that they were "queerly assembled mixtures of good, bad and derivative verse," and his novels "in their mixture of sharp concept and dull writing, were as uneven as his verse." Untermeyer added that "in spite of his repetition and rhetoric, Masters' work is a continual if irritable quest for some key to the mystery of truth and the mastery of life."

His fame will certainly rest on *Spoon River Anthology*, a milestone in American literature, in which, as Horace Gregory and Marya Zaturenska have observed, "it was as though thousands of restless, defeated, anonymous souls had suddenly found their voices."

ADDITIONAL WORKS: Illinois Poems, 1941; Along the Illinois (poems) 1942.

ABOUT: Gregory, H. & Zaturenska, M. History of American Poetry; National Cyclopedia of American Biography (1951); Van Gelder, R. Writers and Writing; Hobbies August 1950; New York Times August 17, 1949; Newsweek April 22, 1946; Saturday Review of Literature March 25, 1950.

MASTERS, JOHN (1914-), English novelist, was born in Calcutta, India, the son of a captain in the 16th Rajputs, was edu-

George Cserna

cated in England (boarding school, Wellington, and Sandhurst, the British West Point) from 1919 to 1934, then returned to India to serve his apprenticeship with a British regiment. A year later he was accepted into the 4th Gurkha Regiment of the Indian Army; between periods of routine training and study, he saw action on the Razmak Frontier from 1936 to 1938, in Baluchistan in 1939, and in the Middle East in 1941. He left his division in 1942 for more training at the Staff College. As a Brigade Major with General Wingate's Chindits, and later Chief of Staff to the 19th Indian Division, he was in action in Burma in 1944-45; his division captured Mandalay and Maymo, and Masters received the D.S.O., O.B.E., and a mention in dispatches. After the war he was assigned to teach mountain and jungle warfare at the British Staff College in England.

The Indian Emancipation took place in 1947. Under the terms of the new constitution, there was no longer a place for Masters in the Indian Army, so with his wife and children he came to the United States, which he had visited on a long furlough in 1938. He now lives in New York City, and is a naturalized American citizen.

The fifth generation of his family to serve Their Britannic Majesties in India, Masters grew up amid the echoes of the world which Kipling immortalized. He has sought, in his

novels, to recount in a series of adventure stories the history of the British in India. Following the fortunes of one family, the Savages, through the entire period gives a continuity, in his historical tales, to some aspects of Anglo-British relations from 1600 to 1947. Thus far Masters has dealt with the Indian Mutiny of 1857 (*Nightrunners of Bengal*), the years of the murderous Thugs (*The Deceivers*), the tense situation with Russia in the 1880's (*The Lotus and the Wind*), the period just before the Indian Emancipation in 1947 (*Bhowani Junction*), and seventeenth century India and Tibet (*Coromandel!*). The series, according to Masters' plan, will contain thirty-odd novels.

Lewis Gannett, reviewing *Bhowani Junction* in the New York *Herald Tribune*, finds "something of Kipling's story-telling passion, of Kipling's sensuous awareness of the sounds and smells and colors of India, and also of Kipling's belief in the white man's burden," in Masters' work; but thinks Kipling might be considered more modern, and less race-conscious, in his outlook on India than Masters. *Bhowani Junction*, writes Gannett, is 'an action-packed yarn of mutiny and murder, Communist trickery and old-school-tie gallantry in 1946, when the British were about to leave India. . . . Despite its brilliant flashes of color and its touches of condescending sympathy, [it] seems oddly out of date in A.D. 1954." *Coromandel!* was described by the New York *Times* as "wildly implausible" escape-fiction.

Although conceding that his work is wholly fiction, John Masters has said, "I hope [it] is also a work of history, because I have tried to give the 'feel' of the times and a sense of historical perspective."

PRINCIPAL WORKS: Nightrunners of Bengal, 1951; The Deceivers, 1952; The Lotus and the Wind, 1953; Bhowani Junction, 1954; Coromandel! 1955.

ABOUT: New York Herald Tribune March 26, 1954; New York Times Book Review March 28, 1954.

MATHER, FRANK JEWETT (July 6, 1868-November 11, 1953). For biographical sketch and list of works and references, see TWENTIETH CENTURY AUTHORS, 1942.

* * *

Frank Jewett Mather died in Princeton, N.J., after a short illness, at eighty-five. He had retired as director of the Princeton University Museum of Historic Art in 1946.

The art scholar has been characterized as "a wise and humane spirit, and a versatile one," by S. Lane Faison, Jr., who adds that

Mather's general histories of painting have been "read more widely than any other books on painting by an American scholar."

ABOUT: Art Digest December 15, 1953; New York Times November 12, 1953; Princeton University Museum of Historic Art Record Fall 1946.

MATSON, NORMAN HÄGHEJM
(1893-   ). For biographical sketch and list of works and references, see TWENTIETH CENTURY AUTHORS, 1942.

* * *

Norman Matson has published no books in recent years, but his short stories appear from time to time in the *Atlantic*, the *Saturday Evening Post, Good Housekeeping*, and other magazines.

MATTHIESSEN, FRANCIS OTTO
(February 19, 1902-April 1, 1950). For autobiographical sketch and list of earlier works and references, see TWENTIETH CENTURY AUTHORS, 1942.

* * *

F. O. Matthiessen committed suicide in Boston at forty-eight. A note left at his death declared that "as a Christian and a socialist believing in international peace, I find myself terribly oppressed by the present tensions." He was on leave from his teaching duties at Harvard, and had just completed a critical biography of Theodore Dreiser.

Commenting on Matthiessen's appearance before a Massachusetts legislative committee investigating "un-Americanism," the *Christian Science Monitor* observed that "he belongs to a tradition of stubborn independence and resolute catholicity of thought which is nothing if not American."

Perhaps his greatest value as a critic, biographer and teacher lay in what Bernard Bowron called his "commitment to scholarship as a special and indispensable kind of social action." His writing has been praised for its sharp, clear expression, its penetration to the essence of its subject, but above all for its skill in establishing the relationship of literature to society. George Mayberry has said: "Although his devotion to art was austere, beneath his work was the organic principle from Coleridge and Emerson: 'He brought the whole soul of man into activity.'"

A novel by May Sarton, *Faithful Are the Wounds* (1955), is apparently based on the tragic conflicts and death of Matthiessen.

ADDITIONAL WORKS: Henry James: The Major Phase, 1944; Melville, H. Selected Poems (ed.) 1944; James, H. American Novels and Stories (ed.) 1947; James H. Notebooks (ed. with K. Mur-

dock) 1947; The James Family, 1947; From The Heart of Europe, 1948; Oxford Book of American Verse (ed.) 1950; Theodore Dreiser (American Men of Letters series) 1951; The Responsibilities of the Critic (essays) 1952.

ABOUT: Huberman, L & Sweezy, P. M. (eds.) F. O. Matthiessen; Catholic World September 1950; Christian Science Monitor December 9, 1950; New Republic April 24, 1950, June 19, 1950, October 27, 1952; New Statesman and Nation April 29, 1950; New York Times April 2, 1950; Time April 10, 1950.

MAUDE, AYLMER (March 28, 1858-
August 25, 1938). For biographical sketch and list of works and references, see TWENTIETH CENTURY AUTHORS, 1942.

* * *

ABOUT: Dictionary of National Biography 1931-1940.

*MAUGHAM, ROBERT CECIL RO-
MER (May 17, 1916-   ), English journalist and novelist, who signs his works Robin Maugham, is the nephew of Somerset Maugham and the son of Viscount Maugham. He was educated at Eton and Trinity Hall, Cambridge, where he read English literature and law. He studied for the bar and is a barrister of Lincoln's

Fayer

Inn. In August 1939 he joined up as a trooper in the Inns of Court Regiment. Commissioned in the County of London Yeomanry in the spring of 1940, he fought in the Western Desert campaign with the Eighth Army, and was mentioned in dispatches. Wounded in June 1942 and down-graded medically, he joined the Middle East Intelligence Centre and worked throughout the Middle East until invalided out of the Army with the honorary rank of captain in 1944 and a fifty per cent disability pension.

Meanwhile, during almost a year spent in the hospital with a head injury, he wrote his first book, *Come to Dust*. "I know of no other book which gives the outsider so vivid and particularised a sense of this form of fighting," said Graham Greene. The book sold out immediately, and since the state of his health made it impossible for Maugham to practice law, he decided to become a writer. During the years 1946-50 he traveled extensively in the Middle East to gain material

* môm

651

for his travel books. He has also lectured to the Royal Institute of International Affairs, to the Royal Empire Society, and to Ashridge College, on Middle Eastern affairs. After a journey in the desert of Transjordan with General Glubb, Commander-in-Chief of the Transjordan Armies, Maugham wrote *Nomad*.

His next novel, *The Servant*, came out in 1948 and was called by the New York *Times*, "a masterpiece of writing, a minor work of art." *North African Notebook* and *Line on Ginger* followed. The latter was made into a movie (*The Intruder*), Maugham helping on the movie script. The story is that of James Merton's search for a former war comrade, Ginger. In his quest he meets other members of his tank unit, all greatly changed in the post-war years. James Stern wrote in the New York *Times*, "As readable and exciting as any thriller, *Line on Ginger* suffers nevertheless from one of its author's principal virtues: speed. There are gaps in this whirlwind, often slick, narrative which make the reader wish to raise questions." "Plotting is the thing Mr. Maugham does best," said the *Saturday Review of Literature*, but felt "Mr. Maugham has no intention of ever getting mixed up personally or emotionally with the people he writes about."

One of his plays, *The Rising Heifer*, has been performed at Margo Jones' theatre in Dallas. In 1953 Maugham was in England working on a film script of three of his short stories.

PRINCIPAL WORKS: Come to Dust, 1945; Nomad, 1947; Approach to Palestine, 1947; The Servant, 1948; North African Notebook, 1948; Line on Ginger, 1949; Journey to Siwa, 1950; The Rough and the Smooth, 1951; Behind the Mirror, 1955.

*MAUGHAM, WILLIAM SOMERSET

(January 25, 1874-). For biographical sketch and list of earlier works and references, see TWENTIETH CENTURY AUTHORS, 1942.

* * *

In 1949, in the preface to his *A Writer's Notebook*, W. S. Maugham wrote: "Now I am an old man, I can be no one's rival, for I have retired from the hurly-burly and ensconced myself not uncomfortably on the shelf. Any ambition I may have had has long since been satisfied. . . . I have done what I wanted to do and now silence becomes me. I am told that in these days you are quickly forgotten if you do not by some new work keep your name before the public, and I

* môm

have little doubt that it is true. Well, I am prepared for that. When my obituary notice appears at last in the *Times*, and they say: 'What, I thought he died years ago,' my ghost will gently chuckle."

No prophecy could have been further from the truth than Maugham's. Five years later, on his eightieth birthday, he was—if such a thing is possible—even better known, certainly more widely known, than he had been in 1949. A slightly younger contemporary of his, Frank Swinnerton, wrote in 1954: "Mr. Maugham is passing into old age amid the cheers of youth and the happy envy of his contemporaries. Since his mind is full of irony I am sure that his pleasure in apotheosis is much sweetened by amusement." In June of that year, Queen Elizabeth II named him a Companion of Honour. Six months earlier he had celebrated his eightieth birthday in London, mellow, but hard at work on a volume of essays and busy with plans for the future. His permanent home is on the French Riviera, at Cap Ferrat, to which he returned at the end of World War II. He lives in France because his health (he was seriously ill in 1951) demands a relatively mild climate. Whenever possible he travels. He has made frequent visits to the United States, where he lived for a considerable time during World War II. On a visit here in 1946 he presented the Library of Congress with the manuscript of *Of Human Bondage*. In 1952 he visited Athens and Istanbul and in 1954 he was in London, looking forward to trips to Spain and Italy.

Maugham announced some time ago that he had written his last play, his last novel, his last short story. In recent years he has devoted himself primarily to the writing of critical essays. The subjects of these have reflected his enduring interests—painting and literature—and a wide variety of his miscellaneous interests. The reader of the essays is captivated not by their profundity but by their charm and urbanity. As Nicholas Joost pointed out in *Commonweal*: "The tone throughout is that of gentle, ever so slightly sardonic litotes, lightened occasionally by a ripple of cool amusement, a warm glint of recollected affection." His literary tastes are eminently conservative, respectable, and impeccable. He has written prefaces for his own selection of the ten great novels of the world (*War and Peace, The Brothers Karamazov, Père Goriot, Madame Bovary, The Red and the Black, David Copperfield, Wuthering Heights, Pride and Prejudice, Tom Jones, Moby Dick*), and of these prefaces John W. Aldridge remarked: "He views the novels he has selected with the practised eye of the professional writer and the keen sense of appreciating the best in them of the professional reader."

Of Maugham's later novels, only one had anything like the popular success of his earlier works. This was *The Razor's Edge*, a character study of a young American whose search for meaning in life takes him ultimately to India and a saintly Indian mystic. The book was more admired for its atmosphere and its minor characters (especially the sharply drawn American expatriate uncle of the hero) than for its plot and major characters. It was a success nevertheless, as Joseph Warren Beach pointed out, largely thanks to "Maugham's usual deftness and ingenuity of manipulation," and after a long career as a best-seller, it was made into a motion picture. *Then and Now*, an historical novel with Niccolò Machiavelli its hero, and *Catalina*, also historical and dealing with the miraculous cure of a crippled Spanish girl, were both disappointments.

The richest source of Maugham's recent popularity has only indirectly been his writing. Rather it has come through the adaptation of his plays and short stories for radio, television, and motion pictures. The most famous such adaptation is the hardy perennial *Rain*, which only as recently as 1953 was again made into a motion picture. In 1948 four of his short stories were filmed and shown in a single feature, *Quartet*. So successful was this venture that two more such films—*Trio* and *Encore*—were made. Meanwhile, some of his short stories were adapted for television in a weekly series in 1950 and proved ideally suited for the new medium. Maugham himself made his movie debut in *Quartet*, speaking a prologue and a commentary between the stories. On his visit to the United States in 1950 he made a number of short films to introduce his television series. Maugham has thus become a public figure, known far beyond literary circles. The motion picture screen has captured his appearance and his personality impressively—elegant, urbane, the voice slightly hesitant, the face a bland, wrinkled mask—and also the spirit of his stories—brilliant, witty, ironic, and, beneath their sleek and glittering exterior (and this *Quartet* captured particularly well), the rugged, brutal honesty of his work and its restrained but unmistakable compassion.

ADDITIONAL WORKS: *Fiction*—The Hour Before the Dawn, 1942; The Razor's Edge, 1944; Then and Now, 1946; Creatures of Circumstance (short stories) 1947; Catalina: A Romance, 1948. *Essays*—Great Novelists and Their Novels, 1948;

A Writer's Notebook, 1949; The Vagrant Mood, 1952; The Art of Fiction: An Introduction to Ten Novels and Their Authors, 1955.

ABOUT: Connolly, C. The Condemned Playground; Maugham, W. S. A Writer's Notebook, The Vagrant Mood; Van Gelder, R. Writers and Writing; Wescott, G. *Introduction to* The Maugham Reader; American Mercury January 1950; College English December 1946; Commonweal July 7, 1944, September 16, 1949, December 3, 1954; Contemporary Review February 1950; Fortnightly November 1950; Harper's October 1947; Life November 20, 1950; New York Times Book Review January 16, 1949; New York Times Magazine January 23, 1949, January 24, 1954; New Yorker December 30, 1944, January 6, 1945, August 27, 1949, October 29, 1949, October 28, 1950; Saturday Review January 23, 1954; Theatre Arts February 1945.

MAULDIN, WILLIAM HENRY (October 29, 1921-), American cartoonist and author who signs his work as Bill Mauldin, was born on a farm in Mountain Park, N.M., the son of Sidney Albert Mauldin and Edith Katrina (Bemis) Mauldin. His father had been badly gassed in World War I and afterwards "found the going tough." As a boy Bill Mauldin had rickets

and thus was forced to spend most of his sickly, lonesome childhood in bed, looking out of the window and watching the other children at play. He drew countless pictures of himself riding ponies in cowboy chaps and ten-gallon hats, or shoveling coal into a locomotive firebox. When he was graduated from grammar school as valedictorian of his class, however, he finally received the horse for which he had longed. He never finished high school.

In 1938 the parents of the "scrawny, cocky" seventeen-year-old artist were divorced, and he and his brother went to Phoenix, Ariz. There Bill joined the R.O.T.C. and was made a corporal. In high school he had sold his first drawing to the La Luz Pottery Company in New Mexico. When he sold his next drawing, he invested the five dollars in a correspondence course in cartooning, but did not receive a diploma. Determined to be a professional cartoonist, Mauldin borrowed three hundred dollars from his maternal grandmother and entered the Chicago Academy of Fine Arts, working his way by painting signs and illustrating menus. Back in Phoenix, he began to send out "gag" sketches to national magazines, but they all came back. In 1940 he briefly found a job with a local political cartoonist, drawing "smear posters" for twenty-five dollars each. Then he enlisted in the Arizona National Guard at a time when volunteers did not have to pass a physical examination. Five days later the Arizona Guard was federalized, and Mauldin who "couldn't have passed the first doctor," found himself in the Army—he was eighteen. At this time he began doing the training cartoons which appeared in the *News* of the 45th Division before it went overseas. Later these cartoons were printed by the Oklahoma University Press in a volume called *News of the 45th*, edited by Don Robinson, with "art by Bill Mauldin." A second book of his cartoons was published in Italy, *Mud, Mules and Mountains* (about 1944), and sold 300,000 copies to the Fifth Army in Italy. *Sicily Sketchbook* was printed in a shop in Palermo, and *This Damn Tree Leaks* (1945) also in Italy.

After Mauldin became a sergeant, the editors of *Stars and Stripes* arranged to have him transferred to their staff. At Salerno he was wounded and awarded the Purple Heart. During that hard winter of 1943-44, he traveled between the two bitterest fronts of the Italian campaign, Cassino and Anzio. At one time on the verge of military arrest (for his cartoons), Mauldin was championed by General Mark W. Clark. Later General George S. Patton declared the cartoons injurious to morale and threatened to ban *Stars and Stripes* from his area unless Mauldin made his men less grimy; General Eisenhower (who liked the cartoons) and Patton and Mauldin even met to discuss the problem.

Up Front, a Mauldin book with 30,000 words of text, was published in 1945, and chosen by the Book-of-the-Month Club. Mauldin was awarded the Pulitzer prize in May 1945 for a cartoon in his *Up Front with Bill Mauldin* series, captioned "Fresh, spirited American troops, flushed with victory"—a drawing of bedraggled American soldiers in pouring rain. The *New Republic* said, "Mauldin . . . writes almost exactly as he draws . . . half brat and half sage . . . he has put together the one indispensable book that any one man has so far published about Americans in action in this war." The sole dissenter, the *Nation*, denounced the book as "a sort of comic strip dedicated to the proposition that war is funny"; but the general opinion was one expressed by William Rose Benét in the *Saturday Review of Literature*, that Mauldin's words "show him as uncompromising a truth-teller with the typewriter

654

as with the pencil. His text has the same biting humor that has gone into his drawings of weary, unshaven, sardonic dogfaces."

Mauldin acted in two films, *Teresa* and *The Red Badge of Courage*. He became national commander of the American Veterans Committee in 1953. "The thing that appeals to me about A.V.C.," he told the *New Yorker*, "is that it's a veterans' organization opposed to veterans' organizations. It has the motto, 'Citizens first, veterans second.' " In the same interview the *New Yorker* described him as "amazingly youthful, with crew-cut hair . . . , and ears that jut out."

In 1942 he was married to Norma Jean Humphries; they had two sons and were divorced in 1946. He and his second wife, Natalie Sarah Evans, whom he married in 1947, live in Rockland County, N.Y., and have three sons. "My house has an unattached stone garage building I have converted to a working room. There I spend a large part of my time drifting aimlessly between a drawing board and a typewriter."

PRINCIPAL WORKS: Star Spangled Banter, 1944; Up Front, 1945; Back Home, 1947; A Sort of a Saga, 1949; Bill Mauldin's Army, 1951; Bill Mauldin in Korea, 1952.

ABOUT: Drewry, J. E. More Post Biographies; Parks, G. Camera Portraits; Infantry Journal June 1946; New York Herald Tribune Book Review October 7, 1951; New Yorker December 26, 1953; Time July 7, 1947.

*MAURIAC, FRANÇOIS (October 11, 1885-   ). For biographical sketch and list of earlier works and references, see TWENTIETH CENTURY AUTHORS, 1942.

* * *

With the death of André Gide in 1951, François Mauriac stepped easily and securely into the position of the greatest living French novelist. In 1952 he received (as Gide had only five years earlier) the ultimate literary honor—the Nobel prize in literature. No two literary figures would appear on the surface more unlike than Mauriac—the austere, rigidly self-disciplined, orthodox and devout Catholic—and Gide—the free-thinking flouter of conventional morality. Yet no two literary figures in modern France share so completely a single obsessive concern with man's moral being. "They appear as one," Wallace Fowlie writes, "in their awareness of man's deepest problems." The world of their novels—in spite of the vast differences in their points of view—is essentially the same: it is the battlefield on which man fights his eternal struggle between good and evil.

* mô ryàk'

Mauriac's dedication to this solemn theme has, until recent years, reduced the size of his audience and involved him in frequent controversy. "The faith, the sensual imagination, and the psychology of sin have existed side by side in his works," an editorial in *Commonweal* observed in 1952. "As a result some of the pious have been scandalized, a few of the sophisticated have been amused, and others, notably Mauriac himself, have been troubled." He writes almost compulsively—his ambition being, he says, "to write one book, just one, that would absolve me from writing any others. I have never begun a novel without hoping that it would be that one." He is intimately bound up with his work and long ago became aware "that nothing pertaining to my time would find its way into my work unless I had first encountered it in myself." Hence, he says, "many critics see in me a poet who expressed himself by means of the novel." It is as a novelist then, rather than as a poet, that Mauriac is known today. Although he himself prefers his poetry above all his other work, he admits that "it was fiction, and not poetry, which released in me that irrepressible confidence, that cry of the inspired man which he is powerless to contain." Out of that passionate inspiration he has created what *Commonweal* calls "a 'Christian literature' in the only sense in which it can ever exist—a literature which treats of man as he indeed is, fallen, but which does not stop at the fact of the fall, but sees beyond it to its infinite immensity and the possibility for its infinite redemption."

During the German occupation of France, Mauriac identified himself courageously with the Resistance. He wrote a *Cahier Noir* for the clandestinely published *Editions de Minuit*. He contributed to *Les Lettres Françaises* and wrote and signed his name to many anti-German articles. After the war he emerged as a powerful literary and political influence, writing for *Figaro, Figaro Littéraire,* and *La Table Ronde.* Where he had been earlier little read in England and America, he now became a figure of considerable importance, and new editions and translations of his works and numerous critical articles on him appeared.

Mauriac lives in Paris but spends considerable time at his wife's country home in Vémars, an old village only twenty miles from Paris. Nona Balakian, who visited him there in 1951, described him as "a vigorous man, despite his failing voice (the result of an operation) and a slight, not unbecoming stoop." To another interviewer in 1952 he appeared "slim, active and possessed of a fighting spirit."

ADDITIONAL WORKS IN ENGLISH TRANSLATION: *Fiction*—The Unknown Sea, 1948; The Desert of Love, and The Enemy, 1949; That Which Was Lost, and The Dark Angels, 1951; The Weakling, and The Enemy, 1952; The Loved and the Unloved, 1952; The Frontenac Mystery, 1952; The Mask of Innocence, 1953; Flesh and Blood, 1955. *Non-Fiction*—The Eucharist, 1944; Saint Margaret of Cortona, 1948; Proust's Way, 1950; Men I Hold Great, 1951; Letters on Art and Literature, 1953.

ABOUT: Columbia Dictionary of Modern European Literature; Dictionnaire Biographique Français Contemporain; Fowlie, W. Clowns and Angels; Garaudy, R. Literature of the Graveyard; Greene, G. The Lost Childhood; Hoehn, M. (ed.) Catholic Authors, I; Jarrett-Kerr, M. Francois Mauriac; Liebling, A. J. The Republic of Silence; Mauriac, F. Letters on Art and Literature; Pell, E. E. François Mauriac in Search of the Infinite; Commonweal July 27, 1951, November 21, 1952, May 15, 1953, July 16, 23, 1954; New York Times Book Review September 23, 1951, November 30, 1952; Sewanee Review July 1948.

MAURIER. See DU MAURIER

*MAUROIS, ANDRÉ (1885-). For autobiographical sketch and list of earlier works and references, see TWENTIETH CENTURY AUTHORS, 1942.

* * *

André Maurois was a captain in the French Army, attached to British General Headquarters, in 1939-40. After the fall of France, he and his wife came to the United States. They lived in New York City and in Kansas City, where Maurois taught at the University of Kansas City, and his stay in this country is described in two autobiographical volumes, *I Remember, I Remember* and *From My Journal.* In 1943 Maurois went to North Africa as a volunteer with the Allied forces. He returned to France in the summer of 1946 and settled at his home in Paris. Here he follows a close schedule of writing in the morning and research in the afternoon: "As I live just opposite the Bois de Boulogne, I take a long walk every day. I never write after dinner; I go to the theatre or to the movies. But my favorite form of relaxation is a pleasant dinner with a few friends . . . and good table talk." During his stay in the United States, Maurois wrote several books on American history (some of them for younger readers). In the main reviewers found these readable, "pleasantly styled," sympathetic, but neither profound nor—for American readers at least—particularly illuminating. In the field of literary biography— where he had won much of his earlier fame

* mô rwà′

—Maurois has produced some highly praised works in recent years. His study of Marcel Proust was called by Joseph Wood Krutch "the best single volume on the subject," and Henri Peyre deemed it "comprehensive, impartial, well informed." His scholarly and thoroughly absorbing study of George Sand, *Lélia*, was judged by many critics the finest biography he has ever written. "In reading *Lélia*," Laurent LeSage wrote in the *Saturday Review*, "I felt that Maurois had indeed called back the spirit of this great French woman of letters to relive her wonderful tempestuous life—although by literary skill rather than occult power, for André Maurois has over many years made of biography a virtual communion with the departed great."

Maurois has always been interested in a wide variety of activities besides his own literary work. In the United States he lectured, traveled, attended all kinds of meetings—political and social—all of these activities carried on with enthusiasm and lively curiosity. Back in France he followed the same course—lecturing, taking part in the meetings of the French Academy, and even (in 1950) devising and writing a radio program for French audiences on the subject of marriage. Called "The Marriage Professor," it was based on the idea of the professional marriage counselor—an idea to which Maurois was introduced during his tour of American universities.

ADDITIONAL WORKS IN ENGLISH TRANSLATION: Frédéric Chopin, 1942; I Remember, I Remember, 1942; The Miracle of America, 1944; The Seven Faces of Love, 1944; Woman without Love (novel) 1945; Franklin, the Life of an Optimist, 1945; Washington, the Life of a Patriot, 1946; From My Journal (in England: My American Journal) 1948; A History of France, 1949; Proust: Portrait of a Genius (in England: Quest for Proust) 1950; The Return of Dr. O'Grady, 1951; Lélia, the Life of George Sand, 1953; Cecil Rhodes, 1953; Alexandre Dumas, 1955.

ABOUT: Columbia Dictionary of Modern European Literature; Dictionnaire Biographique Français Contemporain; Fremantle, A. Introduction to The Maurois Reader (1949); Maurois, A. I Remember, I Remember, From My Journal; New York Herald Tribune Book Review May 7, 1950, October 11, 1953; Newsweek April 10, 1950.

MAWSON, CHRISTOPHER OR-LANDO SYLVESTER (1870-November 4, 1938). For biographical sketch and list of works and references, see TWENTIETH CENTURY AUTHORS, 1942.

MAXTONE GRAHAM, Mrs. JOYCE (ANSTRUTHER). See STRUTHER, J.

MAXWELL, WILLIAM (August 16, 1908-), American novelist, was born in Lincoln, Ill., the son of William Keepers Maxwell and Eva (Blinn) Maxwell, of old American stock long settled in New England, Virginia, and Kentucky. William Maxwell, the author, grew up with his two brothers in a large pleasant house with a sheltering yard and very tall trees. Their

mother died when he was ten. When he was fourteen, the family moved to Chicago, and he finished high school there. Several summer vacations were spent on a farm near Portage, Wis., at which Zona Gale and her friends were frequent guests. "I am only beginning," he writes, "to understand how much, in the way of literary taste and craftsmanship, I received from her." In 1930 he was graduated from the University of Illinois, and won a scholarship offered by the Harvard Club of Chicago. After a year at Cambridge, Mass., he returned to the University of Illinois where for the next two years he taught freshman composition, tutored an entire fraternity house, and browsed around in medieval French and English literature. In 1933 he gave up teaching in order to write novels, and wandered from a beautiful old farm in Wisconsin to the Railroad Men's Y.M.C.A. in New York; to the West Indies; to the MacDowell Colony at Peterborough, N.H.; to Urbana, Ill.; and back to the Wisconsin farm. For ten years he was an editor of the *New Yorker*.

His first book, *Bright Center of Heaven*, appeared in 1934, and was praised by Zona Gale, Christopher Morley, Mary Colum, and Robert Hillyer. "Written with richness as well as clarity," said the critic in the New York *Herald Tribune*. "Behind the accomplishment of this novel there is sensitiveness and artistry of considerable stature." Maxwell's next novel, *They Came Like Swallows* was a Book-of-the-Month Club choice and received the Friends of American Writers award. The *New Statesman and Nation* called it "a sensitive, wistful reminiscence of family life, very intimate and pathetic, with some acute observation which, between one dab of the handkerchief and the next, is actually very delightful." Fanny Butcher said in the Chicago *Tribune*, "The children are as real as any in literature."

Maxwell's third novel, *The Folded Leaf*, was a study of the friendship of two boys,

Lymie, the studious type, and Spud, the extrovert. The story begins in high school, affording a record of middlewestern life in the '20's, and takes the boys on to college. Maxwell avoids sentimentality on the dangerous subject of adolescence. His deeply-felt understanding and sympathy were praised by the critics. "This drama of the immature, with no background more glamorous than middle-class apartments and student fraternity houses," wrote Edmund Wilson, "is both more moving and more absorbing than any of the romantic melodramas which have been stimulated by the war."

In 1946 a fantasy for children, *The Heavenly Tenants*, was found less satisfying by reviewers, but his 1948 novel, *Time Will Darken It*, brought praise. The *Saturday Review of Literature* said he has "a strong flair for poetic imagery, for a well-turned, thoughtful phrase." With this novel, Brendan Gill suggested, Maxwell entered his major phase as a novelist.

In 1945 Maxwell married Emily Gilman Noyes, and they live in Yorktown Heights, N.Y. He is brown-eyed, brown-haired, and of medium height; he describes himself as home-loving, enjoying gardening and swimming. Among his favorite authors are Virginia Woolf, E. M. Forster, and T. S. Eliot.

PRINCIPAL WORKS: Bright Center of Heaven, 1934; They Came Like Swallows, 1937; The Folded Leaf, 1945; The Heavenly Tenants, 1946; Time Will Darken It, 1948.

ABOUT: Warfel, H. R. American Novelists of Today; Current Biography 1949.

MAXWELL, WILLIAM BABINGTON

(1866-August 4, 1938). For biographical sketch and list of works and references, see, TWENTIETH CENTURY AUTHORS, 1942.

MAYNARD, THEODORE

(November 3, 1890-   ), Anglo-American poet, biographer, historian, and critic, writes: "I was

born of English missionary parents in Southern India, where I spent the first ten years of my life, enjoying the inestimable privilege of getting virtually no schooling before going to England for my education. As I had been brought up in an intensely religious atmosphere, I was led to study for a while (in the United States) for the Con-

gregationalist ministry. Returning to England (as a hand on a cattle boat) with the intention of studying for the Unitarian ministry, I 'supplied' occasionally as a preacher in Unitarian churches before my reading led me, in 1913, into the Catholic Church—and, indeed, into the Dominican novitiate, where I spent seven months.

"Partly drawn out by World War I, my eyesight only permitted service in the Ministry of Munitions. By this time I had begun to write for various weekly reviews, principally for the *New Witness* under Cecil and G. K. Chesterton; when my first book of poems appeared in 1915 the elder Chesterton wrote an introduction for it, in which G. K. labelled me 'a poet of colour' and found in me a mixture of whimsicality, pugnacity and (of all things in the world!) asceticism. In 1918 I married Sara Casey, whose brother a few years ago was appointed editor of the London *Times*, and who was herself the author of a novel, several books for children, and a play produced at the Abbey Theatre. In 1920 I came to the United States on a lecture tour, and, on the strength of the literary work I had done, which by then included three volumes of verse, a collection of essays, a book on modern poetry and a very bad novel, I was given a professorship in a California college, and for the next sixteen years taught, my principal later positions being at Fordham and Georgetown. Meanwhile, as I had obtained no degrees, I rectified the matter (while teaching, lecturing far and wide, and publishing a steady stream of poems, magazine articles, and books of various types), going on until I had obtained my Ph.D. at the Catholic University of America. After explaining in Mencken's *Mercury* why I had not become an American, I changed my mind and was naturalized.

"When my wife died, in 1945, I was myself only given a year to live, but I falsified the doctor's predicitons, wrote a couple of books in a sanatorium by dictating them into an ediphone, and then married again, this time Kathleen Sheehan, a former student of mine. As my seven children had grown up, my wife and I built a small house on Manhasset Bay at Port Washington, N.Y., where, though I am obliged to lead the quiet life of a semi-invalid, I nevertheless continue to write."

* * *

Among Maynard's thirty-odd books, probably the most important are *De Soto and the Conquistadores*; *The World I Saw*, described by Father Herbert Walker as "the most complete autobiography of a conversion since the *Apologia* of Newman"; *The Story of Amer-*

ican Catholicism, which Maynard rates as his greatest achievement; and *The Reed and the Rock,* which several critics consider his best book. Maynard became vice-president of the Catholic Poetry Society of America at the time of its founding, more than twenty years ago; since 1948 he has been president of the organization.

PRINCIPAL WORKS: *Poetry*—Laughs and Whiffs of Song, 1915; Drums of Defeat, 1917; Exile, and Other Poems, 1928; Man and Beast, 1936; Not Even Death, 1941; Collected Poems, 1946; Last Garland, 1949. *Prose*—Carven from the Laurel Tree, 1919; The Divine Adventure (novel) 1921; De Soto and the Conquistadores, 1930; Preface to Poetry, 1933; The Odyssey of Francis Xavier, 1936; The World I Saw (autobiography) 1938; Apostle of Charity: Life of St. Vincent de Paul, 1939; Queen Elizabeth, 1940; The Story of American Catholicism, 1941; The Reed and the Rock: Portrait of Simon Bruté, 1942; Orestes Brownson: Yankee Radical, Catholic, 1943; Pillars of the Church, 1945; Too Small a World: Life of Francesca Cabrini, 1945; Mystic in Italy: Life of St. Philip Neri, 1946; The Humanist as Hero: Life of Sir Thomas More, 1947; The Fire Was Lighted: Life of Rose Hawthorne Lathrop, 1948; Richest of the Poor: Life of St. Francis of Assisi, 1948; Henry the Eighth, 1949; The Crown and the Cross: Thomas Cromwell, 1950; Through My Gift: Life of Frances Schervier, 1951; Saints for Our Time, 1952; The Catholic Way, 1952; The Better Part: Life of Teresa Demjanovich, 1952; The Catholic Church and the American Idea, 1953; The Long Road of Father Serra, 1954; St. Benedict and His Monks, 1954; Bloody Mary, 1955.

ABOUT: Hoehn, M. (ed.) Catholic Authors, I; Maynard, T. The World I Saw; Noyes, A. *Introduction to* Collected Poems of Theodore Maynard.

MAYNE, ETHEL COLBURN (187?-April 30, 1941). For biographical sketch and list of works and references, see TWENTIETH CENTURY AUTHORS, 1942.

MAYO, KATHERINE (1868-October 9, 1940). For biographical sketch and list of works and references, see TWENTIETH CENTURY AUTHORS, 1942.

MEAD, MARGARET (December 16, 1901-   ). For biographical sketch and list of earlier works and references, see TWENTIETH CENTURY AUTHORS, 1942.

* * *

During World War II Margaret Mead wrote pamphlets for the Office of War Information and served (1942-45) as executive secretary of the committee on food habits, the National Research Council. She was a visiting lecturer at Teachers College, Columbia University (1947-51), and has served as consultant on mental health, as a member of

the committee on research of the mental health division of the National Advisory Mental Health Council of the United States Public Health Service. She is a member of numerous scholarly associations, including the American Anthropological Society, the New York Academy of Science, and the American Academy of Arts and Sciences. Since 1942 she has been associate curator of the American Museum of Natural History.

Of her recent books, probably the best known is *Male and Female,* a study of sex differences and similarities based in part on her observations of the natives of seven Pacific islands. Readers trained in anthropology objected that the book contained too many broad generalizations and, as David Riesman put it, "a too-great receptivity to concepts from the whole panorama of the human sciences." But the majority of reviewers and readers found it a brilliant if turbulent book. As Bernard Mishkin suggested in the New York *Times:* "It may be that the author's views ought not to be judged scientifically but should be taken for what they are—brilliant insights, momentary illuminations of what may lie behind a culture."

Dr. Mead lives in New York City but spends much of her time in travel—on field trips and lecture tours. In 1953 she led another expedition to New Guinea.

ADDITIONAL WORKS: And Keep Your Powder Dry: An Anthropologist Looks at America, 1942; (with G. Bateson) The Balinese Character: A Photographic Analysis, 1942; Male and Female, 1949; Mountain Arapesh, 1938-49; Soviet Attitudes toward Authority, 1951; Growth and Culture, 1951; (ed. with N. Calas) Primitive Heritage, 1953.

ABOUT: Sapieha, V. Eminent Women: Yost, E. American Women of Science; Current Biography 1951; New York Times Book Review October 30, 1949; Saturday Review of Literature October 15, 1949.

MEERSCH. See VAN DER MEERSCH

*MEIER-GRAEFE, JULIUS (June 10, 1867-July 1935). For biographical sketch and list of works and references, see TWENTIETH CENTURY AUTHORS, 1942.

* mī'er gräf

MENCKEN, HENRY LOUIS (September 12, 1880-   ). For autobiographical sketch and list of earlier works and references, see TWENTIETH CENTURY AUTHORS, 1942.

* * *

In January 1941 H. L. Mencken gave up his regular column in the Baltimore *Sun* and a few years later he told Roger Butterfield, who was interviewing him for *Life* magazine, "I stopped writing about so-called public questions." He devoted himself then to completing the last installment of his autobiography, *Heathen Days*, and to work on the supplements to *The American Language*. But though Mencken gave up writing his astringent comments on the world in general, he did not hesitate to pronounce them on occasion. In 1946, after a period of bemused silence during World War II, he spoke out oracularly: "People are in a state of imbecility. The country is a wreck. Don't ask me for the remedy. It's always been my function to name the disease."

There was a marked revival of interest in Mencken and his work after the war. A new generation, too young to remember the "Mercurial Mencken" of the Twenties, was now introduced to the "Monumental Mencken" of the Forties (the epithets are Jacques Barzun's). He made a series of recordings for the Library of Congress, wrote sketches for the *New Yorker*, was the subject of a *Life* profile, and of two full-length biographies. His Supplement I to *The American Language* was described by Richard Watts as "a wonderful combination of scholarship, festivity, social history, Tory crotchets, political and literary feuding, industry, genuine love of country, unashamed bias, humor, commentary on the world, compendium of American manners, and anthology of Mencken prejudices." Three years later when Supplement II appeared, Allen Walker Read called it "one of the lasting monuments of American scholarship," and the late Robert J. Menner wrote: "He has been the great educator of the American people in the significance of their own language." In 1949 *A Mencken Chrestomathy* was published. This volume contained Mencken's selection of his out-of-print writings, going back to his *Smart Set* days, and some notes that had never before been published.

Mencken suffered a cerebral thrombosis late in 1948. He has never fully recovered from this illness and lives now as an invalid at his home in Baltimore.

ADDITIONAL WORKS: Heathen Days, 1943; The American Language: Supplement I, 1945; Christmas Story, 1946; The American Language: Supplement II, 1948; A Mencken Chrestomathy, 1949.

ABOUT: Brooks, V. W. The Confident Years; Farrell, J. T. *in* New World Writing #6 (1954); Kemler, E. The Irreverent Mr. Mencken; Manchester, W. R. Disturber of the Peace; Morris, L. R. Postscript to Yesterday; West, H. F. Mind on the Wing; Atlantic Monthly January 1946; Catholic World September 1946; Life August 5, 1946; New Republic July 3, 1950; New York Herald Tribune Book Review July 3, 1949; New York Times January 11, 1954; New Yorker July 9, 1949, January 20, 1951; Saturday Review of Literature April 3, 1948, August 6, 1949; Time July 11, 1949, January 8, 1951.

MENEN, AUBREY (1912-), English novelist and essayist, was born in London. His father is an Indian domiciled in England since 1908, and his mother is Irish. He was educated at University College, London, where he was discovered as a writer by the late H. G. Wells who, reading a portion of a dramatization by Menen of his *Shape of Things to Come*, gave Menen  permission to dramatize the whole work. This led to his becoming dramatic critic of the *Bookman* and director of the (London) Experimental Theatre, where he wrote and produced several plays.

In 1939 he went to India on a visit to the Nawab of Bhopal, the ruler of a leading Indian State. This visit was interrupted by the outbreak of war, and Aubrey Menen took over the organization of war publicity through the radio. Writing and broadcasting in English, he became the leading radio personality in India. His programs, in spite of the political opposition of nationalist parties to anything supporting the war, had the largest following in Indian radio history. At the end of the war he was sent at his own request on a special mission to a remote jungle tract in western India as an officer of the political department to the government of India. He returned to England in 1946, but was recalled to India to organize the production of documentary and educational films under the auspices of the J. Walter Thompson Company, of which he was an executive.

Since 1947 he has devoted all his time to writing. His first novel, *The Prevalence of Witches*, was an instant success. The scene is in a remote part of India, called Limbo, where civilization has hardly penetrated. A Limbodian chieftain is accused of murder under the British Civil law, although according to his own law the deed was no crime. Three educated Englishmen, an American missionary and a questionable Swami attempt to see justice done. The *New Yorker* said of this book: "The author is of mixed Irish and East Indian ancestry, which may explain the unusual quality of his genius, at once impudent, ironic and profound. In any event,

Mr. Menen has given us a novel of remarkable wit and originality and full of philosophical implication, which are all but concealed beneath his farcically contrived situation and his prodigality of epigram." The *New Republic* said that it offers "some of the most adroit and exhilarating, not to say adrenaline, satirical writing since Shaw."

His second novel, *The Stumbling Stone,* was described by one reviewer as "a sardonic, witty and provocative picture of professional do-gooders confronted by a really saintly man." A slighter effort than *The Prevalence of Witches,* it was nevertheless expert light satire.

In *The Backward Bride; A Sicilian Scherzo,* Menen turned to another country he knows well, Italy, where he now makes his home (in Amalfi). The novel presents a young Sicilian bride and her intellectual bridegroom on their honeymoon in London and Paris and their return to Italy. Along the way, the author pokes fun at various modern theories from existentialism to psychoanalysis. *The Duke of Gallodoro* describes an Italian author who settles in the village of Gallodoro and helps a violent little waif, Peppin, to prove himself the bastard son of the Duke. In *Dead Man in the Silver Market,* thirteen autobiographical sketches, Menen discusses a subject he is peculiarly well qualified to tackle—the psychopathology of nationalism. His mother was incorrigibly Irish, his father a member of one of the most racially arrogant and exclusive castes in India, and Menen's own Public School education in England instructed him in social snobbery. With sophistication he shows how absurd each of these cherished nationalisms appears in the light of the others. "This is perhaps the wittiest and funniest essay in autobiography and philosophy that has been published in our era," wrote the *Christian Science Monitor.* "How does he do it?"

In 1955 Menen published his modern retelling of the ancient Hindu classic *The Ramayana.* Keeping in mind that the author of the original work was "not a philosopher but . . . a skeptical realist," Menen retold the story with sparkling wit and sardonic humor. "It exerts the appeal of common sense," Gouverneur Paulding wrote of his version; another reviewer described it as "a delightful cross between *Candide* and *The Decameron.*"

PRINCIPAL WORKS: The Prevalence of Witches, 1948; The Stumbling Stone, 1949; The Backward Bride, 1950; The Duke of Gallodoro, 1952; Dead Man in the Silver Market, 1953; The Ramayana Retold 1954.

ABOUT: Menen, A. Dead Man in the Silver Market.

MENNINGER, KARL AUGUSTUS

(July 22, 1893-   ). For autobiographical sketch and list of earlier works and references, see TWENTIETH CENTURY AUTHORS, 1942.

* * *

In 1941 the various activities of the Menninger Clinic were consolidated and expanded with the establishment of The Menninger Foundation, a non-profit organization for training, research, and public education in psychiatry and psychology. Since 1946 Dr. Karl Menninger has been director of the Department of Education and Dean of the Institute of Psychological Medicine of the Foundation. He has held many other educational and professional posts in recent years —including executive offices in the American Psychiatric and the American Psychoanalytic Associations, the National Committee for Mental Hygiene, the National Mental Health Foundation, and the United States Public Health Service. He teaches in both the graduate and medical schools of the University of Kansas and at Washburn Municipal University in Topeka. From 1945 to 1948 he was manager of the Winter Veterans Administration Hospital, also in Topeka, one of the outstanding psychiatric training centers in the United States, where he is now senior consultant in psychiatry.

The work of the Menninger Foundation has been widely publicized. *Newsweek* reports that "in three decades, the term 'the Menningers' has grown to mean the world's best-known psychiatric center." Some measure of this growing popular interest in the Foundation's work has been due to Dr. Karl Menninger's writing. In the preface to *Love Against Hate,* where his announced purpose is to set forth "simply and specifically the basic conflict of human life and of our civilization," he says frankly that his book is aimed at any intelligent reader, professional or non-professional, even at the risk of having the work dismissed as "mere popular science." More recently he contributed to the perennial psychiatry "versus" religion controversy. Writing in the Chicago Theological Seminary *Register* in 1951, Dr. Menninger explained that he saw no irreconcilable conflict between the two. Describing himself as "a life-long Presbyterian," he cited parallel practices in religion and psychiatry.

Dr. Menninger has one child by his second marriage—a daughter, Rosemary, born in 1947.

ADDITIONAL WORKS: Love Against Hate (with J. L. Menninger) 1942; Guide to Psychiatric Books (with G. Devereux) 1950.

ABOUT: National Cyclopedia of American Biography (1946); Current Biography 1948; Newsweek April 17, 1950; Saturday Evening Post November 15, 1947; Survey Graphic September 1947; Time April 16, 1951.

MERCER, CECIL WILLIAM ("Dornford Yates") (August 7, 1885-). For biographical sketch and list of earlier works and references, see TWENTIETH CENTURY AUTHORS, 1942.

* * *

Cecil Mercer was recommissioned in the British Army in 1942 and served from 1942 to 1943 with the East Africa Command. In 1944, with the rank of major, he joined the Southern Rhodesian military forces. After the war he settled in Umtali, Southern Rhodesia.

As "Dornford Yates," Mercer continues to spin his lively adventure yarns—the preposterousness of which, Milton Crane observed, is redeemed "by the verve and excitement by which the puppets are manipulated."

ADDITIONAL WORKS: Period Stuff, 1942; An Eye for a Tooth, 1943; The House that Berry Built, 1945; The Berry Scene, 1947; Red in the Morning (in U.S.: Were Death Denied) 1947; Cost Price (in U.S.: The Laughing Bacchante) 1949; Lower than Vermin, 1950; As Berry and I Were Saying, 1952.

ABOUT: Usborne, R. Clubland Heroes.

*MEREZHKOVSKY, DMITRY SERGEYEVICH (August 2, 1865-December 10, 1941). For biographical sketch and list of works and references, see TWENTIETH CENTURY AUTHORS, 1942.

* * *

ABOUT: Columbia Dictionary of Modern European Literature; Snow, V. Russian Writers; Yarmolinsky, A. (ed.) A Treasury of Russian Verse.

* měr ěsh kôf'skĭ

MERRIAM, CHARLES EDWARD (November 15, 1874-January 8, 1953), American political scientist, was born in Hopkinton, Iowa, where the Merriams lived just across from the Lenox College campus. He has written in an autobiographical essay: "Assume Margaret Campbell Kirkwood, a school teacher fresh from Scotland. Assume the Yankee, Charles E. Merriam, Sr., from Massachusetts—Corporal Merriam, postmaster . . . merchant . . . banker . . . Presbyterian elder Merriam"—his parents. In 1895 Merriam took his B.A. degree at the State University of Iowa, after study-

ing economics and politics there; he studied at Columbia and earned his M.A. in 1897 and his Ph.D. in 1900, also studying at the Universities of Berlin and Paris. His thesis, published in 1900, was the *History of the Theory of Sovereignty since Rousseau.* Beginning to teach in the department of political science at the University of Chicago in 1900, Merriam remained there, becoming a full professor in 1911 and the chairman of the department in 1923.

In 1905 he decided to enter the Chicago political arena. Among many other duties, he served as secretary of the harbor commission, investigated Chicago's revenues for the City Club, was an alderman and investigated municipal finances, exposing large-scale graft within the city government. An advocate of the direct primary as well as other reforms, the professor was persuaded to become a candidate for mayor in 1911, won the Republican nomination but lost the election by a narrow margin. What he learned as a "participant-observer" in the city's struggles is told in *Chicago: A More Intimate View of Urban Politics.*

He was on numerous academic committees, and launched studies into such significant aspects of his field as non-voting, propaganda, leadership, and political psychology. In 1935 he was concerned with the development of administrative standards and practices through the agencies of responsible officials organized for that purpose, as in the Public Administration Clearing House in Chicago.

Between 1919 and 1932 Merriam made many visits to European cities, particularly seeking answers to questions involving the development of citizenship, for he had been commissioned to organize and edit a series of studies on this subject. These were published in 1931 under the title *The Making of Citizens: A Comparative Study of Methods of Civic Training.* In 1932, in the midst of brewing political tumult in Berlin, Merriam wrote *Political Power: Its Composition and Incidence.* Later, in *The Role of Politics in Social Change,* he "undertook to shear through the struggle between individualism and collectivism by attacking the doctrine of economic fatalism upon which both of them rested." Again, in *Prologue to Politics,* he emphasized the importance of man's reason and will as opposed to pessimism and violence in working toward the ideal state. In his later works Merriam continued to examine both the practical and the ideal aspects of democratic government. *Systematic Politics*, his last book, was described by a reviewer as "a *Summa* of one of America's most prominent political scientists."

For ten years Merriam served on the planning boards established during the Roosevelt Administration, including the National Resources Planning Board, which was often sharply attacked and finally dissolved in 1943. Merriam felt, nevertheless, that long-range national planning was making progress in this country.

After his retirement from the University of Chicago in 1940, until his death in 1953, Merriam continued to write books. From 1944 to 1947 he was a member of the University's Commission on Freedom of the Press. He received many honorary degrees, and in recognition of his services as commissioner from America on Public Information in Italy in 1918, he was made by the Italian Government a commander of its Order of the Crown (1921).

In 1901 he married Elizabeth Hilda Doyle; they had four children, the youngest of whom, Robert E. Merriam, is now active in Chicago political life and was defeated as Republican candidate for mayor of the city in 1955.

PRINCIPAL WORKS: History of the Theory of Sovereignty Since Rousseau, 1900; History of American Political Theories, 1903; Primary Elections, 1908; American Political Ideas 1865-1917, 1920; American Party System, 1922; New Aspects of Politics, 1925; Four American Party Leaders, 1926; Chicago, 1929; The Making of Citizens, 1931; Written Constitution and the Unwritten Attitude, 1931; Political Power, 1934; Civic Education in the United States, 1934; The Role of Politics in Social Change, 1936; New Democracy and the New Despotism, 1939; Prologue to Politics, 1939; What Is Democracy? 1941; On the Agenda of Democracy, 1941; Public and Private Government, 1944; Systematic Politics, 1945.

ABOUT: White, L.D. The Future of Government in the United States (essays in his honor) 1942; American Historical Review April 1953; American Political Science Review June 1953; Current Biography 1947, 1953; National Municipal Review February 1953; New York Times August 29, 1943, January 9, 1953; School and Society January 17, 1953.

MERRICK, LEONARD (1864-August 7, 1939). For biographical sketch and list of works and references, see TWEN-TIETH CENTURY AUTHORS, 1942.

* * *

ADDITIONAL WORK: The Leonard Merrick Omnibus (ed. Leslie Merrick) 1950.

MERRILL, STUART FITZRAN-DOLPH (August 1, 1863-December 1, 1915). For biographical sketch and list of works and references, see TWEN-TIETH CENTURY AUTHORS, 1942.

* * *

ABOUT: Columbia Dictionary of Modern European Literature.

MERTON, THOMAS (FATHER M. LOUIS) (1915-), American poet and religious writer, was born in Southern France. His father, a landscape painter, was English and his mother an American Quaker. He grew up in France, England, and the United States and studied at Cambridge and at Columbia University (B.A. 1939, M.A. 1939). For one semester he taught English at Columbia in the Extension Division and wrote book reviews for the New York *Times* and *Herald Tribune*. Concerned over the social and economic injustices of modern life, he joined a young Communist group. Later he worked at a Catholic settlement house in Harlem. In 1938 he joined the Roman Catholic Church. His first book of poems, *Thirty Poems*, was written in "the first flush of his conversion" and won favorable comment. Of his second volume of verse, *Figs for an Apocalypse*, the *Yale Review* remarked that "Merton has become more doctrinal, more the Catholic poet in this book, but his verse is as powerful as ever." Reviewers found the poems in *Tears of the Blind Lions* somewhat labored and obscure but even so, as R. G. Davis observed, they showed "tremendous vigor and great pictorial beauty."

In 1941 Merton entered the Trappist monastery of Gethsemani in Kentucky. He later became ordained a priest, and is known in the order as Father M. Louis. The profound spiritual experiences which impelled the twenty-six year old poet to enter the severe discipline of the Trappist monastery, after having led a full and worldly life, are related in his autobiography, *The Seven Storey Mountain*. This book was published in 1941 and immediately became a best seller. The New York *Herald Tribune* said, "The fervor of his progress to the Trappist monastery at Gethsemani is deeply moving. It is a difficult matter to write about, but I think there will be many who, however alien the experience may remain to them personally, will put the narrative down with wonder and respect." The *New Yorker* remarked that, 'Although non-religious readers are apt to find Merton's youthful helling around and subsequent remorse something less than the stuff of a major battle between the forces of good and evil, and to be disconcerted by a sense of a direct and personal relationship with God, St. Joseph and the Virgin Mary, much of the book is eloquent and all of it is high spirited and undisputatious . . . rare qualities in the literature of converts."

His next book, *The Waters of Siloe*, describes life within the monastery. It is a lucid though somewhat discursive account of the history of the Cistercian order, with special emphasis on the foundations in the United States and a description of the founding of the Order during the twelfth century. Some of the most brilliant and fascinating passages in the book deal with the men, saintly and less saintly, brilliant and dun-colored, who molded the Cistercian spirit and sustained it.

Seeds of Contemplation is a book of meditation, of which the *Journal of Religion* said; "It is as if a breath of air from the country blew in your face, bringing the accompaniment of singing birds and running streams." The *New Republic* found that "Merton's moral values, religious attitude and complete absence of scientific outlook place him with the mystics of the past. In spirit this book is in line with the *Cautelas* and the *Avisos* of St. John of the Cross, the *Meditations* of Guido the Carthusian and similar books of contemplation. What keeps him from wishing to be compared with the authors of these classic mystical works is his genuine humility."

Merton's recent book *The Sign of Jonas*, based upon his journal, is a continuation of his autobiography. Father Louis tells of receiving a wire from his publisher on the acceptance of the *Seven Storey Mountain* and of his astonishment and mixed emotions at its record-breaking history in the following years. The book gives an extraordinary glimpse into six years of a way of life that has seldom been seen from the inside, into the daily round and contemplations of a monk who is a gifted writer.

The Very Reverend Dom Aelred Graham, also a Benedictine monk, has described Thomas Merton as "a modern man in reverse." He writes: "Merton can speak effectively to his contemporaries because he is one of them. Despite his enthusiasm for what he conceives apostolic Christianity to have been and the glories of the Middle Ages, he is no medievalist in love with the past. He is a modern man—" But he is also, as Dom Aelred points out, a mystic, withdrawn into an intensely spiritual and personal world. "His theology is a projection into his writing of a personal experience."

PRINCIPAL WORKS: *Poems*—Thirty Poems, 1944; Figures for an Apocalypse, 1947; Tears of the Blind Lions, 1949. *Prose*—The Seven Storey Mountain, 1948; The Waters of Siloe, 1949; Seeds of Contemplation, 1949; What Are These Wounds? 1950; The Sign of Jonas, 1952; The Last of the Fathers: Saint Bernard of Clairvaux, 1954; No Man Is an Island, 1955.

ABOUT: Merton, T. The Seven Storey Mountain, Seeds of Contemplation, The Sign of Jonas; Atlantic Monthly January 1953; Catholic World February 1948; Commonweal May 13, 1955; Life May 23, 1949; Newsweek September 19, 1949.

MERWIN, SAMUEL (October 6, 1874-October 17, 1936). For biographical sketch and list of works and references, see TWENTIETH CENTURY AUTHORS, 1942.

MERZ, CHARLES (February 23, 1893-). For autobiographical sketch and list of works and references, see TWENTIETH CENTURY AUTHORS, 1942.

* * *

Since 1938 Charles Merz has been an editor of the New York *Times*. He is a trustee of the Russell Sage Foundation and the Guggenheim Foundation. He lives on Gracie Square, in New York City.

ABOUT: Current Biography 1954.

METCALFE, JOHN (1891-). For autobiographical sketch and list of earlier works and references, see TWENTIETH CENTURY AUTHORS, 1942.

* * *

John Metcalfe writes from London: "Was demobilized from the R.A.F. in 1946. Novel entitled *All Friends Are Strangers* published in England in 1948. Of this Frank Swinnerton writes: 'A fascinating novel, rich in humor, powerful realism, human oddity, and sheer original genius. It will enchant all who can appreciate its grim pleasantries.' I have a further novel well on the way, also another volume of short stories."

Correction: John Metcalfe and Evelyn Scott were married in 1930, not 1928.

ADDITIONAL WORK: All Friends Are Strangers, 1948.

MEW, CHARLOTTE (November 15, 1870-March 24, 1928). For biographical sketch and list of works and references, see TWENTIETH CENTURY AUTHORS, 1942.

* * *

ADDITIONAL WORK: Collected Poems of Charlotte Mew, 1954.

ABOUT: Munro, A. *Preface to* Collected Poems of Charlotte Mew; Swinnerton, F. *The Georgian Literary Scene, 1910-1935*; Nineteenth Century July, 1948.

MEYNELL, Mrs. ALICE CHRISTIANA (THOMPSON) (August 17, 1847-November 27, 1922). For biographical sketch and list of works and references, see TWENTIETH CENTURY AUTHORS, 1942.

* * *

ABOUT: Connolly, T. L. (ed.) Alice Meynell Centenary Tribune, 1847-1947; Meynell, Sir F. *Introduction to* Essays of Alice Meynell (centenary ed., 1947); National Book League, Alice Meynell, 1847-1922; Sackville-West, V. *Introduction to* Prose and Poetry of Alice Meynell (centenary ed., 1947); America October 18, 1947; Catholic World November 1947.

MEYNELL, VIOLA (1886-). For biographical sketch and list of earlier works and references, see TWENTIETH CENTURY AUTHORS, 1942.

* * *

Viola Meynell lives in Pulborough, Sussex, where her husband, John W. Dallyn, has farmed for many years. She has remained very active in literary circles in London and has done considerable creative writing as well as collecting and editing the papers and memoirs of her literary family. In 1952 she published a memoir on the famous friendship between her father and the gifted poet Francis Thompson—a volume which reviewers praised as a valuable reconstruction of the life and personality of Thompson—"the one true way of dealing with Francis Thompson outside his poetry" (London *Times Literary Supplement*).

ADDITIONAL WORKS: (ed.) Letters of Sir James M. Barrie, 1942; First Love, and Other Stories, 1947; Ophelia, 1951; Francis Thompson and Wilfred Meynell, 1952.

ABOUT: Hoehn, M. (ed.) Catholic Authors, I.

*MICHAÉLIS, KARIN (March 20, 1872-January 11, 1950). For biographical sketch and list of earlier works and references, see TWENTIETH CENTURY AUTHORS, 1942.

* * *

Karin Michaelis died, at seventy-seven, at her home in Copenhagen. She had returned to her native country at the end of World War II, having spent the war years in the United States in active support of the Free Danish movement. In 1946 she was made an honorary citizen of the island of Thuroe, her birthplace, where in pre-war years she had established a community for refugees from Nazi Germany. The fortune she had made from her books was spent helping others, and in her last years she waged a struggle with poverty.

Ernestine Evans called her "a force to reckon with, as artist and as journalist." J. Claudi, who considers her the greatest Danish woman author, speaks of her "unusual gift for creating woman characters," and adds, "Her imagination is sparkling, and her very style and choice of words have a feminine quality."

ADDITIONAL WORK: Little Troll (autobiography, with L. Sorsby) 1946.

ABOUT: Claudi, J. Contemporary Danish Authors; Michaelis, K. Little Troll; New York Times January 12, 1950.

*MICHAUX, HENRI (May 24, 1899-), Belgian poet and painter, was born in Namur, Belgium, of middle-class parents: his father was a lawyer, his religion was Roman Catholic. But only the beginning of Michaux's life was so unexceptional. Very little is known of his childhood or of his education. He attended a Jesuit school. There were hints of ill health and he was sent

Gisèle Freund

into the country to grow stronger. His own account of this in the autobiographical fragment "Portrait of A" is bizarre: "But the doctors, by setting at him furiously with the fixed idea they have about the necessity of eating and of natural needs, having sent him far away into the strange mob of rascally, smelly peasants, succeeded in conquering him a little. . . . Perfection gone, nutrition came, nutrition and comprehension came. At the age of seven he learned the alphabet and ate."

Such a child had to become the unpredictable young man. Having read and studied constantly for years, especially in mystical literature, at twenty he revolted against his introspective life and went to sea on a collier. The hard months as a sailor on this voyage around North and South America did not mitigate the urge for travel that marks the rest of his life and his writings as well. In the Twenties Michaux traveled as a passenger to South America where he wrote *Ecuador*. A later trip to the Far East produced the better known and wholly individualistic travel book *A Barbarian in Asia.* In recent years he has traveled in Egypt and in Ireland.

The characteristic move of the artist—to Paris from wherever else—followed the first voyage. Henceforward Michaux chose to be French by adoption. In Paris he soon established sympathetic connection with both the arts he was to practice through the poetry of Lautréamont in particular, according to Richard Ellmann, Michaux's translator, and through the art of Paul Klee, Masson and Max Ernst. He slowly and unobtrusively became a member of the literary aristocracy of the city. Between 1937 and 1939 he edited the mystical review *Hermès.* He was in Brazil for a few months after World War II broke out, but he returned to Paris in 1940 and spent the war there and in the south of France. In 1943 he married Marie Louise Ferdière, who died in an accident in 1948. Michaux's *Nous Deux Encore* (1948) is devoted to this most important and tragic relationship. He continues to live in Paris now. His paintings—gouaches and water colors—are regularly exhibited; his poetry, especially since the war, has an international audience; he is one of the favorite poets of the young in France now, though painting has become his chief interest. His life retains a deliberate aloofness.

This sense of distance is carried over into Michaux's poetry and paintings. The poet is usually above the scene; the dramatic characters and even the countrysides are distant from those of the ordinary world. But this strangeness is alleviated by a sense of both compassion and humor in the poet. It is translated too by a persistent concreteness and simplicity of expression; these qualities overshadow the deliberate formlessness of the "prose poem." Ellmann points out that two major themes are nothingness and the millenium—both unreachable and almost unimaginable. Yet these themes are embodied in comic characters like Plume; in tangible, if grotesque, beasts; in the physical, if nightmarish, activity of contests, quarrels and voyages. The real world slips out of grasp, but in the fantastic world which replaces it, impulses are still, and often ridiculously, human; objects like berets and melons are quite recognizable.

Michaux's view of life is original but comparable to that of the surrealists and to that of Kafka. André Gide states that in his poetry Michaux "abandons his whole being to the impulse in a way that recalls Nietzsche's saying: 'In our dreams only are we completely sincere.' ... He excels in making us feel intuitively both the strangeness of natural things and the naturalness of strange things." By this reversal of the expected, Michaux achieves, like Kafka, a re-examination of all customs, standards and emotions which he sees as the monsters created by man to destroy himself.

PRINCIPAL WORKS IN ENGLISH TRANSLATION: A Barbarian in Asia, 1949; Selected Writings (L'Espace du Dedans) 1951.

ABOUT: Bertele, R. Henri Michaux; Ellmann, R. *Introduction to* Michaux's Selected Writings; Gide, A. Découvrans Henri Michaux; Poetry January 1953.

MICHENER, JAMES ALBERT (February 3, 1907-), American novelist, and journalist, writes: "I was brought up in Bucks County, Pa., the poor man's Connecticut. My distinguished neighbors— Pearl Buck, S. J. Perelman, Oscar Hammerstein, Moss Hart, Budd Schulberg, and George S. Kaufman— all are johnny-come-latelys to this part of the world and are known by us natives as foreigners.

Blackstone

"A list of the jobs I held as a young man sounds like a travesty of a political biography of a man running for the presidency, but unique were the time I spent in a traveling show as leading man opposite Drew Pearson's sister and the time I spent in a poor house.

"Athletic prowess, which I now refer to as legendary but which was rather mediocre, gained for me a scholarship to Swarthmore, from which I was suspended numerous times, from which I graduated *summa cum laude,* and from which I got one thing which made the major difference in my life: a traveling fellowship permitting me to study in Europe. In all, I attended nine universities in America and Europe and became both an academic bum and a confirmed traveler.

"My intellectual life has been a long vacillation between English literature and the social sciences. Had I applied myself to either, I might have become an educated man, but I could never decide between abstract thought and practical social applications. Nor can I yet. At age twenty-eight I abruptly ceased being an English teacher and started from scratch to become a historian, serving three years later as visiting professor of history at Harvard's School of Education. As a writer I have persisted in my uncertainty, alternating between novels which could charitably be considered literature and world reporting which by another stretch of objective standards might be called history.

"This vacillation explains why I envy so many living writers. As a lover of good novels, I envy those masters of the pen who write better than I; and as a trained social scientist I envy those real scholars who know the facts about those subjects upon which I write and upon which I am often so inadequately informed.

"My only talent would seem to be a literary scientific sense of what my world is all about. In 1940 I lectured that we would be at war in the Pacific shortly. In 1945 I wrote that Asia must become our major problem and that we would probably be at war with China one day. And in 1950 I pointed out that all the turmoil in Asia would shortly be repeated in Africa. My wrong guesses, which would fill the remainder of this volume, I have conveniently forgot.

"The facts of my life reproduce my vacillation: English teacher (1929-36); history teacher (1937-41); a kind of literary editor at the Macmillan Company (1941-1949); naval historian in the South Pacific (1944-46). My war record was quite undistinguished and all I accomplished could have been done much better by a capable girl secretary, except for one week in Tahiti.

"I have been extraordinarily lucky in my life. I held scholarships almost without interruption from age seventeen and all my adult travel has been paid for by someone else. I have also been unusually fortunate in my writing and in my friendships with gifted people.

"My interest in Asia and the Pacific dates far back into my childhood, but I must admit that of the earth's countries the only two on which I might be considered a minor expert are Scotland and Mexico, about which I have never written. I have had the good fortune to visit most of the islands in the Pacific south of the equator and to have traveled widely in Asia.

"I think of myself primarily as a novelist and consider my forays into non-fiction as preparation and research for fiction; but whenever I have been writing fiction too long I experience an insatiable longing to be writing something which may explain Asia and the Pacific to my fellow Americans.

"I have only one bit of advice to beginning writers: be sure your novel is read by Rodgers and Hammerstein."

* * *

Michener's *Tales of the South Pacific* was awarded the Pulitzer prize for fiction in 1948.

In 1949 it came to Broadway as *South Pacific*, with music and lyrics by Richard Rodgers and Oscar Hammerstein 2d and with Mary Martin and Ezio Pinza in the starring roles—one of the most successful threatical ventures of recent years. His novels *Return to Paradise, The Bridges at Toko-ri*, and *Sayonara* were great popular favorites. The first two were made into motion pictures. In 1954 he published a collection of exquisite Japanese color prints, under the title *The Floating World;* to these he added a lively and informative history of the art of Japanese prints.

PRINCIPAL WORKS: Tales of the South Pacific, 1947; The Fires of Spring, 1949; Return to Paradise, 1951; The Voice of Asia, 1951; The Bridges at Toko-ri, 1953; Sayonara, 1954; The Floating World, 1954.

ABOUT: College English (also English Journal) October 1952; Current Biography 1948; New York Herald Tribune Book Review May 20, 1951, October 7, 1951; New York Times Book Review May 16, 1948, May 22, 1949, July 12, 1953.

MIDDLETON, GEORGE (October 27, 1880-). For biographical sketch and list of earlier works and references, see TWENTIETH CENTURY AUTHORS, 1942.

* * *

In 1947 George Middleton published his autobiography, *These Things Are Mine*. A crowded, somewhat digressive but thoroughly informative book, it was well received. John K. Hutchens wrote in the New York *Times*: "His approach and style [are of the theatre], frequently extravagant and exclamatory, in the manner of a performer addressing an audience. Which, as a matter of fact, is exactly what Mr. Middleton is doing, with warmth and skill and as much candor as one has a right reasonably to expect."

Since 1942 Middleton has been a copyright and trade expert with the Office of Alien Property of the United States Department of Justice. He lives in New York City.

ADDITIONAL WORK: These Things Are Mine, 1947.

ABOUT: Middleton, G. These Things Are Mine.

MIDDLETON, RICHARD BARHAM (October 28, 1882-December 1, 1911). For biographical sketch and list of works and references, see TWENTIETH CENTURY AUTHORS, 1942.

MILES, JOSEPHINE (June 1911-), American poet and scholar writes: "My parents grew up in Chicago; my mother was of a German professional family which came to

America in mid-nineteenth century, my father of an English business family which came in the mid-seventeenth. They came to California first for my father's insurance business when I was a year old, and again when I was five because of my severe arthritis. The deserts and beaches of Southern California were as much home to us as the city. My brothers and I went to school

Estelle Keech

at Latona Avenue Grammar and Los Angeles High School, and then they to Stanford and I to the new University of California at Los Angeles. I wrote first for the *St. Nicholas* League, then for high school clubs and annuals, then for college literary magazines.

"In 1933 the growing interest in the philosophy of language, in the work of Jespersen, Sapir, Richards, Barfield, and Empson, seemed so important to me that I began graduate study in the department of English in the University of California at Berkeley, where I received a Ph.D. in 1938 and am now a professor. My studies have all been concerned with language, and include *The Vocabulary of Poetry* and *The Continuity of Poetic Language,* as well as essays in various quarterlies and collections.

"The teaching of writing and research is in itself so absorbing a job that there is only a little time left for the seacoast and the country, and San Francisco, and even for other work. In 1948 I helped edit an anthology, *Criticism, the Foundations of Modern Literary Judgment;* and with Barnhart and Hungerland and other faculty-graduates of the University of California am now editing a quarterly of research and comment called *Idea and Experiment.*

"Since the publishing of *Trial Balances* by Ann Winslow in 1935 [an anthology in which Miss Miles' poems were first published] I have had three volumes of poems published, the most recent being *Local Measures,* 1946, as well as poems in *Poetry, Kenyon Review, Sewanee Review, Nation, Furioso,* and a number of collections. And I have worked with the aid of Shelley Award, Phelan, A.A.U.W. and Guggenheim fellowships, not to mention the friends and family who have aided me in countless other ways. My present concern is world literature, the terms of reason and value in the languages of the world."

* * *

Josephine Miles' poetry reflects something of the discipline and the keen, analytic approach to language which mark her scholarship. Dudley Fitts writes: "Her way with words is brilliant; the control or rhythm, the arrangement of rime and assonance, the answering of stanza to stanza—everything is elaborately and even intensely worked out." But Fitts finds in her verse an extraordinary and perhaps excessive "preoccupation with technic." Similarly, the *New Yorker* objects that in her later poetry she has "become more interested in language than in the reality it describes."

Miss Miles' studies in poetic language—in which she analyzes and compares the poetic vocabularies of different periods in literary history—have forcefully demonstrated her hypothesis that "every poem is bound to its time and yet shares the major vocabulary of all English poetry." Of her *Continuity of Poetic Language,* Vivienne Koch wrote: "In terms of scope, weight, information, and knowledgeability [it] . . . is likely to become a landmark in modern criticism."

PRINCIPAL WORKS: *Poetry*—Lines at Intersections, 1939; Poems on Several Occasions, 1941; Local Measures, 1946. *Prose*—The Vocabulary of Poetry, 1946; Criticism, the Foundations of Modern Literary Judgment (ed. with others) 1948; The Continuity of Poetic Language; Studies in English Poetry from the 1540's to the 1940's, 1951.

ABOUT: Poetry February 1940, March 1952; Time October 9, 1939.

*MILLAR, GEORGE REID (September 19, 1910-   ), Scottish memoirist and novelist, writes: "I was born in a turreted stone country house to the north of Glasgow, and my earliest recollections are of my father leaving home to fight as a cavalry officer, and of our family excursions as camp followers into an England that seemed luscious, sunbathed, and virile. My father had

John Vickers

a hard war in Flanders, and did not long survive it; long enough, though, to teach us four children to look at pictures, buildings, horses, and the shelves of libraries. My mother sent me to one of the more expensive Scottish boarding schools. It was a good school. I was unhappy there; but the times between terms, always in Ayrshire or in the Highlands, running wild, were wonderful.

* mĭl lär'

"At Cambridge, reading architecture, I took a good 'first' my first year, a middling 'second' my second, and scraped a 'third' my third. I was a turbulent undergraduate who did a lot of work on the river, rowing, and a lot of climbing in and out of college after closing hours. Then I worked in a London architect's office, but the hours at a desk, the chattiness of my fellow-draughtsmen, stifled me. So I began to write, for newspapers, because I seemed unequipped to do anything else. At one period I ran away from journalism, and went as a deck hand on a freighter out of Glasgow to the Pacific coast, and also worked on a salvage ship.

"I left the sea because I wanted to fight in the Spanish Civil War, but I happened to get married, and had to earn a living, so became a reporter again, first on the *Daily Telegraph* in Fleet Street, then for Lord Beaverbrook's lively *Daily Express*. I was in the Paris office of the *Express* when the Second World War broke, and I was very glad to become a soldier.

"In 1941, then a junior officer in a crack regiment of motorised infantry, I was captured by Rommel's wonderful Afrika Korps in the Libyan Desert, and handed over to the Italians. I can say honestly that I enjoyed my twenty months of incarceration in Italy, perhaps the loveliest country on earth; and it was there, when so many around me were repressed and miserable, that I found I could live for writing, if not by it.

"In 1942, after several attempts and adventures, I escaped from prison, and after crossing Germany, France, and Spain, I got home in time to be trained as a saboteur, and was parachuted near Besançon, in France, before D-Day. My unusual war experiences gave material for my first two books, which wrote themselves, and enabled me to leave newspapers and work on my own.

"Each of my books I regard with the strongest distaste and aversion—once it is written. But I hope to do better, to improve indeed by working and living hard. I get my personal adventures now on horseback and in small boats, and with the latter I have seen much of Europe since the war. The difficulties of Europe make me aggressively European, and I have been Francophile since I first knew France at the age of eighteen. Literary circles do not interest me, and I have no wish to model myself on any living writer, for I am more interested in the sixteenth, eighteenth, and nineteenth centuries than in this one. My two favourite writers are the Englishman Gibbon, and the American Prescott."

PRINCIPAL WORKS: Waiting in the Night (in England: Maquis) 1945; Horned Pigeon, 1946; My Past Was an Evil River (novel) 1946; Isabel and the Sea, 1948; Through the Unicorn Gates, 1950; A White Boat from England, 1951; Siesta, 1953; A Crossbowman's Story, 1955.

ABOUT: Millar, G. R. Horned Pigeon, Isabel and the Sea; Current Biography 1949; Time January 14, 1946.

MILLAY, EDNA ST. VINCENT (February 22, 1892-October 19, 1950). For biographical sketch and list of earlier works and references, see TWENTIETH CENTURY AUTHORS, 1942.

* * *

Edna St. Vincent Millay was found dead in the isolated house near Austerlitz, N.Y., where she had lived alone since the death of her husband a year earlier. Her death, which came at fifty-eight, was the result of a heart attack.

The poet, who was called by John Ciardi "the creator of her own legend," has been described by Dorothy Thompson as "a whimsical genius, sometimes as petulant and imperious as the child Cleopatra whom Caeser first met in Egypt; sometimes a witch, with a trace of the sinister; stormy, turbulent and as unreckonable as the sea—her native element; sometimes a lost and tragic soul." Mary M. Colum speaks of "her warmth of heart, her generosity, her compassion for the beaten, the downtrodden."

Horace Gregory and Marya Zaturenska believe that Miss Millay's great success was based on her "creation of a literary personality" whose poetry seemed, more often than not, "a literary exercise in the release of feminine emotion," and predict that "it will probably introduce other generations of girls and young women to the phenomena of an adolescent self-discovery in terms of poetry." If the intensity of the poems of romantic and rebellious youth of the Twenties declined in her graver concern with "the bewildered and self-torturing human spirit" in the Thirties and the more socially conscious work of the Forties, it may be partly because, as Ciardi has said, "having outgrown her youth, Edna Millay had outgrown the one subject she could make exciting," partly because of her "hampering and sometimes destructive role of unofficial feminine laureate," in the words of Louise Bogan. Robert Hillyer has declared that *Mine the Harvest*, a collection of new poems published after the author's death, is her finest book and "strongest claim to immortality"—but this was not the general view.

At her best, Miss Millay expressed a "passion for identification with all of life which few poets in her generation have possessed; she has made ecstasy articulate and almost tangible," wrote Louis Untermeyer. The publication, four years after her death, of *Mine the Harvest*, poems she had written between 1939 and 1950, offered a new opportunity for re-evaluation of her work. In these last poems reviewers found "flashes of power," though, as John Ciardi remarked: "The talent, nevertheless, remains self-dramatizing." Robert Hillyer observed of the book: "The clear sayings, the sure and unpretentious metrical technique, the singing lines bring the poet back from death in the full stature of her genius."

ADDITIONAL WORKS: Murder of Lidice, 1942; Collected Lyrics, 1943; Letters (ed. by A. R. Mac-Dougall) 1952; Mine the Harvest, 1954.

ABOUT: Gregory, H. & Zaturenska, M. History of American Poetry; Sheean, V. Indigo Bunting; Wilson, E. The Shores of Light; Ladies' Home Journal January 1951; Life October 30, 1950; Nation December 30, 1950, April 19, 1952; New Republic March 12, 1951, April 23, 1951; New York Times October 20, 1950; Newsweek October 22, 1951; Saturday Evening Post November 25, 1950; Saturday Review of Literature November 11, December 2, December 9, December 16, 1950, February 17, 1951; Theatre Arts December 1942.

MILLER, Mrs. ALICE (DUER) (1874-August 22, 1942). For biographical sketch and list of works and references, see TWENTIETH CENTURY AUTHORS, 1942.

* * *

ADDITIONAL WORKS: Cinderella, 1943; Hit and Run, 1943; Selected Poems, 1949.

ABOUT: Miller, H. W. All Our Lives; Hackett, F. On Judging Books; Commonweal July 27, 1945; Current Biography 1941; Publishers' Weekly September 16, 1944; Saturday Review of Literature July 21, 1945.

MILLER, ARTHUR (October 17, 1915-), American playwright and novelist, writes: "I was born in the Harlem section of Manhattan.

My father was a well-to-do manufacturer with little education, my mother the daughter of a manufacturer. He was brought to this country as a small boy from a small town in Austria. She was born here. I attended the same public school in Harlem from which she had graduated, and had many of the same teachers.

"Until the age of seventeen I can safely say that I never read a book weightier than

Tom Swift, and *Rover Boys,* and only verged on literature with some of Dickens. I was more interested in football, hockey, and just plain fooling around. I was a poor student, and failed many subjects—algebra three times. When my name became known through my writing, my high-school teachers leafed through the records, found my name, sure enough, but none of them even vaguely recalled me. I passed through the public school system unscathed.

"The first writing I remember doing was a description of a fountain pen. I simply desired to write and that happened to be the one object to fasten my thoughts to. A book that changed my life was *The Brothers Karamazov* which I picked up, I don't know how or why, and all at once believed I was born to be a writer. This was after I had graduated from high school, and was working in a warehouse on Tenth Avenue in Manhattan. On the subway to and from work I began reading, and concurrently saving my money to go to school, for our family fortunes had gone with the boom.

"I entered the University of Michigan partly by virtue of my writing, for the school had turned me down on the basis of my weird scholastic record. After several very emotional letters, however, they gave me a try. I entered under the disguise of a journalism student, for I dared not speak of writing aloud. For one thing I couldn't even spell yet and I knew I was perfectly innocent of any academic knowledge, although I did know a good deal about automobiles, ice skating, and what it was to work for a living.

"I wrote my first play in the ten days of spring vacation. I had seen but one play in my life and had read the tragedies of Shakespeare. The play won several prizes and made me confident I could go ahead from there. It left me with the belief that the ability to write plays is born into one, and that it is a kind of sport of the mind, as though one had to be knocked on the head in a certain way before one could practice the craft. I certainly have never met anyone who learned playwriting. However, at Michigan I studied under Professor Kenneth T. Rowe who was a great help in an emotional way, giving confidence to face a profession so notorious for its failures. I wrote two plays a year at school, won several money prizes, returned to New York, wrote more plays, did radio stuff for a living, got my first production and a flop, wrote a novel, *Focus,* and wrote *All My Sons, Death of a Salesman, The Crucible,* half a dozen short stories, and between each the beginnings of other plays which I can't even remember anymore.

"I have had various trials and adventures, got married to Mary Slattery and have Robert, five, and Jane, eight, a house in Brooklyn and a place in the country. I have traveled whenever possible, to Europe mostly, but my subject is here and my heart as well.

"I care about all my plays, but the only story I like is 'Monte Saint Angelo,' published in *Harper's* and *Prize Short Stories of 1951*. My aim is what it has been from the beginning—to bring to the stage the thickness, awareness, and complexity of the novel."

* * *

Arthur Miller's *Death of a Salesman* received the Pulitzer prize for drama in 1949. This moving and powerful study of the salesman Willy Loman, a small man swallowed up in a world of sham and hollow values, caught the imagination of the American theatre public as few serious contemporary American dramas have done. In several respects, John Gassner wrote, "it represents a culmination of American playwrights' efforts to create a significant American drama. The play carries forward the struggle to create a realistically critical expression of American life, to present the common man as the center of dramatic interest, to find more expressive dramatic forms than the realistic technique permits, and to develop a poetic drama rooted in American speech and manners."

In *The Crucible* Miller turned to the American past, to the dark days of the witchcraft trials in Salem in 1692, to explore the question of liberty of conscience. Although the critics found this a forceful play, written with intense personal conviction, they were generally agreed that it was inferior to *Death of a Salesman*. Nevertheless, as John Mason Brown pointed out: "If *The Crucible* lacks the depth and fire of these earlier and better plays by Mr. Miller, it can claim one indisputable virtue. It is about something that matters. . . . It has its jabbing lines and forceful single scenes written with the vigor one associates with Mr. Miller."

PRINCIPAL WORKS: Situation Normal, 1944; Focus (novel) 1945. *Plays (dates of publication)*—All My Sons, 1947; Death of a Salesman, 1949; Henrik Ibsen's An Enemy of the People: An Adaptation, 1951; The Crucible, 1953.

ABOUT: Atkinson, B. Broadway Scrapbook; Brown, J. M. Still Seeing Things; Gassner, J. Treasury of the Theatre; Nathan, G. J. Theatre Book of the Year, 1948-49; Current Biography 1947; Saturday Evening Post July 16, 1949; Saturday Review January 31, 1953; Theatre Arts June 1947; Time February 21, 1949.

MILLER, CAROLINE (August 26, 1903-). For biographical sketch and list of earlier works and references, see TWENTIETH CENTURY AUTHORS, 1942.

* * *

Caroline Miller is married to Clyde H. Ray, Jr., and lives in Waynesville, N.C. Her only novel in recent years is *Lebanon,* a story of a young Georgia girl in the early nineteenth century. Generally the critics agreed that the book sustained the promise of her prize-winning *Lamb in His Bosom,* but that the later novel was somewhat more strained and less spontaneous. Sara Henderson Hay wrote in the *Saturday Review of Literature* that Lebanon, the heroine of the book, is more like a character in a folk tale than a flesh-and-blood woman. "Perhaps this is what Mrs. Miller wished to do, but there is a quality of unreality about this book, not entirely due to the fact that it deals with a period which has faded into the realm of romance. It is because, I think, Mrs. Miller has been more concerned with the style of her writing than with the characters she was writing about."

ADDITIONAL WORK: Lebanon, 1944.

ABOUT: Warfel, H. R. American Novelists of Today.

MILLER, HENRY (December 26, 1891-). For autobiographical sketch and list of earlier works and references, see TWENTIETH CENTURY AUTHORS, 1942.

* * *

Henry Miller toured the United States in 1940, recording his impressions in *The Air-Conditioned Nightmare.* He settled in Beverly Glen, Calif., in 1942, dividing his time between his writing and his painting in water colors, but living in such poverty that he published an appeal—for old clothes and water color materials—in the *New Republic.* A short time later a friend offered him a cabin in the mountain country of Big Sur, near Carmel, Calif., and here Miller moved in 1944. Big Sur has since become the scene of a new literary and artistic colony, of which Miller is the nucleus. Also in 1944 he married Martha Lepska. They have two children —a daughter, Valentin, and a son, Tony.

Since his return to the United States Miller has won wider recognition than he has ever had before. More of his books have had American publication, and there is a growing interest in and respect for his outspoken observations on contemporary life and literature. In *The Books in My Life,* the first volume in a projected series on his intellectual life-history, Miller listed the books that have influenced him most. The astonishing variety of his choices (ranging from Rider Haggard's *She* and *Peck's Bad Boy* to the works of Dostoevsky, from Marie Corelli to Henry Adams) reflects something of the variety of the man himself.

In 1948 Edwin Corle wrote: "There is no refuting the fact that with James Joyce and D. H. Lawrence off the stage, Henry Miller assumes the mantle of the most controversial writer of our times." This is probably the only non-controversial statement that can be made about Miller who, by virtue of his exuberance, his iconoclasm, his "bohemian desperado" (Philip Rahv's phrase), inspires in most of his readers either a passionate admiration or an acute antipathy. In 1940, with a new World War beginning and the sickness of totalitarianism spreading over Europe, the late George Orwell found Miller's "Whitmanesque" enthusiasm, his hearty acceptance of the universe, "out of date." He wrote: "Miller is simply a hard-boiled person talking about life, an ordinary American businessman with intellectual courage and a gift for words." But nine years later Lawrence Durrell, writing in *Horizon,* reached a very different conclusion about Miller: "There is much that is below his highest standard, to be sure, much that is careless, ill-judged, rash, splenetic, shapeless, overstated. . . . These defects are the peculiar defects of his particular type of genius. But they should not blind us to his positive qualities. Judged by his best work he is already among the great contemporary writers."

ADDITIONAL WORKS: Max and the White Phagocytes, 1938; Sunday After the War, 1944; The Air-Conditioned Nightmare (2 vols.: vol.II Remember to Remember) 1945-47; The Smile at the Foot of the Ladder, 1948; The Books in My Life, 1952.

ABOUT: Corle, E. *in* Miller, H. The Smile at the Foot of the Ladder; Fraenkel, M. The Genesis of Tropic of Cancer; Miller, H. Sunday After the War, Of-By-and-About Henry Miller, The Books in My Life; Moore, N. Henry Miller; Orwell, G. Such, Such Were the Joys; Porter, B. The Happy Rock, Henry Miller: A Chronology and Bibliography; Rahv, P. Image and Idea; West, H. Mind on the Wing; Commonweal December 12, 1947; Horizon July 1945; New Republic December 4, 1944; Time December 24, 1945.

MILLER, MARY BRITTON ("Isabel Bolton") (August 1883-   ), American novelist, writes: "My father was Charles P. Miller, a New York lawyer of distinction. My mother was Grace Rumrill of Springfield, Mass. I was born the youngest of five children at New London, Conn., in the summer of 1883, only five minutes, so legend goes, after my sister. This participa-

tion in identical twinship is the most valuable experience of my life. It is the source of whatever insight into human nature or response to the beauties and mysteries of the natural world I may possess. To live accompanied by another creature whose image resembled one's own precisely and whose response to everything experienced appeared to be simultaneous and identical made the

Leja Gorska

years of my childhood curiously intense and important. Both of my parents died of pneumonia and within an hour of each other in the fourth year of my life. The five children went then to live in Springfield in the home of our grandmother who died shortly after our arrival. We remained in her home under the guidance and guardianship of our uncle and aunt, Mr. and Mrs. James Rumrill. The house was ample and the surrounding grounds, elm trees, grape arbors and orchards were, to put it mildly, delightful. We spent a large part of our summers with our uncle and aunt at their country place outside of New London, Conn., and here again the beauties of nature—ocean, sky, and meadows, contributed most richly to the memories of childhood.

"In my fourteenth year my twin sister was drowned. After this there seems to be a kind of blotting out of life—everything became dim, unreal, artificial. I went to boarding school in Cambridge, Mass., where I seem to have learned practically nothing at all. My formal education is as flimsy as cambric. I hated to study and was treated with sufficient indulgence to make this unnecessary. I acquired, and without guidance, a passionate love for literature, especially for poetry. I soaked it all up in a self-indulgent and undisciplined manner. This private and passionate perusal of good books, however, constitutes the brawn and sinew of my educational experience. Upon leaving boarding school life was desultory, a few years in New York followed by a few years in Springfield and later considerable travel in Europe. Three years in Italy were of profound importance. I grew to appreciate Italian art and literature and above all I loved the intense physical beauty of the Italian landscape. In 1911 New York became my permanent home. I lived awhile at the Greenwich House settlement where I was a volunteer worker. After that I did off and on a good deal of voluntary social work. I had apartments here and there but mostly in Greenwich Village.

"In 1928 Macmillan published my first book of verse, *Songs of Infancy,* under my own name, Mary Britton Miller. After this I continued to write and occasionally publish slender volumes of poems, *Menagerie, Without Sanctuary, Intrepid Bird.* In 1930 I started to write my first novel, *In the Days of Thy Youth.* It was published by Scribner's in 1943. The spring of the same year Scribner's published my long poem *The Crucifixion.* Finding it impossible to continue with my novel which I had intended to turn into an autobiographical trilogy, I abandoned the project and made up my mind to try a book as different as possible from the first and completely divorced from the facts of my own life. When this was finished I decided, as I had completely changed my manner of writing, to endow myself with a new name as well as a new style. When Scribner's published *Do I Wake or Sleep* I assumed the nom de plume of Isabel Bolton. Since this I have published under that name *The Christmas Tree* and *Many Mansions.* I hope that life will give the lady an opportunity to write a few more novels, as she has not yet nearly written herself out."

* * *

The "discovery" of the novelist Isabel Bolton was largely Edmund Wilson's. In a *New Yorker* review of *Do I Wake or Sleep* he called special attention to the book and gave it high praise. "Miss Bolton has learned from Henry James, and from the school of Henry James, the device of the sensitive observer who stands at the center of the action and through the filter of whose consciousness alone the happenings of the story reach us. . . . But in general the style of *Do I Wake or Sleep* seems to have been influenced most by the poetic impressionism of Virginia Woolf. . . . The story has life and moves." Her later novels have revealed the same elegance and precision of style and (though some reviewers have found her emotional range limited) a "deep sensitivity of perception and obvious sincerity." Her prose, Charles J. Rolo wrote, "is precise and packed with feeling, marvelously evocative, faultlessly accented in its elaborate rhythms."

PRINCIPAL WORKS: Songs of Infancy and Other Poems, 1928; Menagerie, 1928; Without Sanctuary, 1932; Intrepid Bird, 1934; In the Days of Thy Youth, 1943; The Crucifixion, 1944; Do I Wake or Sleep, 1946; The Christmas Tree, 1949; Many Mansions, 1952.

ABOUT: New York Herald Tribune Book Review March 27, 1949.

MILLER, MAX (February 9, 1901-). For autobiographical sketch and list of earlier works and references, see TWENTIETH CENTURY AUTHORS, 1942.

* * *

Max Miller writes from La Jolla, Calif.: "I was in the Navy in the Second World War (three and a half years) until the end. I was in the Pacific and wrote *Daybreak for Our Carrier* (our only islands out there at the time—our carriers). Then I was ordered clear across the world again for the Normandy and Southern France invasions, which I recorded in *The Far Shore.* Then back to the Pacific for the clean-up which is recorded in *It's Tomorrow Out Here.*

"Naturally, after having been in two wars by this time, and not being a professional warrior, these things do predominate in my mind. I wrote some civilian books after the war ended. Then when the Korean smash occurred I was called back in again with my former rank of lieutenant commander, and was in Korea within a week from the time the summons came. I wrote about the Navy in Korea in a book, *I'm Sure We've Met Before.* In the meantime (and now a Commander) I have been in the Mediterranean with the Sixth Fleet and wrote *Always the Mediterranean,* then back to the Pacific where I seem to be going all the time, to Southeast Asia. I am recording that now, as I always think that whatever isn't recorded for the public hasn't happened."

ADDITIONAL WORKS: The Land Where Time Stands Still, 1943; Daybreak for Our Carrier, 1944; The Far Shore, 1945; It's Tomorrow Out Here, 1945; The Lull, 1946; The Town With the Funny Name, 1948; No Matter What Happens, 1949; I'm Sure We've Met Before, 1951; The Cruise of the Cow, 1951; Always the Mediterranean, 1952.

ABOUT: Miller, M. No Matter What Happens; Newsweek April 3, 1950.

MILLER, PERRY GILBERT EDDY (February 25, 1905-), American literary critic, scholar, and educator, was born in Chicago, the son of Eben Perry Sturgis and Gertrude (Eddy) Miller. He was educated at the University of Chicago, from which he received a Ph.B. in 1928, and a Ph.D. in 1931. Since then, except for three years in the U.S. Army (1942-45), he has taught at Harvard College where he was first appointed as an instructor in 1931, as an

Harvard Crimson

associate professor in 1939, and as a full professor of American literature in 1946.

Perry Miller has been a pioneer in recording and interpreting early New England literature and theology. By his work, both as an author and as an editor, he has restored for the contemporary reader an important part of the American heritage. With a scholar's persistent and exhaustive concentration on source books and diaries, and with a thinker's imaginative understanding, Perry Miller, in a series of books, has succeeded in dispelling many of the prejudices held by contemporary readers about seventeenth century New England. He has shown that the conventional, narrow, one-sided notion of the Puritan and Puritanism as being mainly a matter of blue-laws and grim moral earnestness is contrary to the historical reality; and he has made the dramatic ideological conflicts of the Founding Fathers and their immediate descendants accessible and meaningful to a twentieth century audience.

His most widely read and best-known works are the two volumes, *The New England Mind, From Colony to Province* (published in 1939 and reprinted in 1953), and *The New England Mind, the Seventeenth Century.* The *Saturday Review of Literature* said of volume one: "Mr. Miller has written a fascinating and indispensable book for all Americans who are interested in the genealogy of their own ideas"; and Reinhold Niebuhr, reviewing volume two for the *New Republic,* observed: "Miller is a meticulous scholar, who has mastered the documents of the age. . . . But he is no pedant, which is to say that he superimposes upon the science of history the imagination of the artist."

By judicious editing of the original texts, and by his own skillful commentary, Miller has called up many famous figures—in anthologies such as *The Puritans* and *The Transcendentalists;* in the two books dealing with Jonathan Edwards (1948 and 1949), the first of which was part of his doctoral thesis; in *Roger Williams,* which was published in the Makers of the American Tradition series. The New York *Herald Tribune,* reviewing *Roger Williams,* remarked: "Perry Miller, alone of American scholars of today, can reclothe the dry bones of New England theology with flesh, and make the issues of those days seem vital."

As a teacher, Perry Miller has been able to communicate heartily and infectiously his own enthusiasm. He has been influential in showing that an understanding of New England's culture is necessary to all students of American literature; and he has been among the foremost teachers and scholars who have labored during the past two generations to make American literature an independent field and not merely a colonial branch of English literature.

Perry Miller and his wife, the former Elizabeth Williams whom he married on September 12, 1930, have spent the better part of a quarter of a century at Harvard. His political tenets are those of a liberal democrat. Believing that American intervention was necessary in World War II, when it came, he was eager to serve in the armed forces. He was in the army from 1942 to 1945, first as a captain, then as a major attached to the O.S.S. in London. Several years later he returned abroad, and spent thirteen months as a visiting lecturer in Continental universities. He has been described as a tall, attractive man with a square broad face; and as a man with an informal, out-going, hearty personality. He is also known as a baseball fan, a persistent rooter for the Boston Red Sox.

During 1953-54 Professor Miller was at the Institute for Advanced Study, Princeton, N.J. He is a member of the Massachusetts Historical Society, the Colonial Society of Massachusetts, the American Antiquarian Society, and the Modern Language Association.

PRINCIPAL WORKS: Orthodoxy in Massachusetts, 1933; The Puritans (with T. H. Johnson) 1938; The New England Mind from Colony to Province, 1939; (ed.) Edwards, J. Images or Shadows of Divine Things, 1948; Jonathan Edwards, 1949; The Transcendentalists, 1950; Roger Williams, 1953; The New England Mind, the Seventeenth Century, 1954.

MILLER, RENÉ FÜLÖP. See FÜLÖP-MILLER

MILLIN, Mrs. SARAH GERTRUDE (LIEBSON) (1889-). For autobiographical sketch and list of earlier works and references, see TWENTIETH CENTURY AUTHORS, 1942.

* * *

Mrs. Millin's husband died in 1952. She lives in Johannesburg, and remains probably the most vigorous and successful interpreter of the history and customs of South Africa currently writing. American audiences know her best for her recent historical novels, *King of the Bastards* and *The Burning Man.* Her style, as Robert Lowry pointed out in the New York *Times,* is "lush at times, but more often her phrasing is frugal and her viewpoint is distant." James Hilton found "a sombre nobility" in *The Burning Man* and "a clear, clenched prose, with never a word wasted." In 1951 Mrs. Millin published a new version of her history of South Africa, first published in 1926 as *The South Africans.* It proved a timely and compelling book—"and one of great beauty," the *New Yorker* added. It was generally recognized as a definitive study of the people and politics of South Africa.

ADDITIONAL WORKS: World Blackout, 1944; The Reeling Earth, 1945; Pit of the Abyss, 1946; Sound of the Trumpet, 1947; Fire Out of Heaven, 1947; Sound of the Trumpet, 1947; Seven Thunders, 1948; King of the Bastards, 1949; The People of South Africa, 1951; The Burning Man, 1952.

ABOUT: Snyman, J. P. L. The South African Novel in English.

MILLIS, WALTER (March 16, 1899-   ).

For biographical sketch and list of earlier works and references, see TWENTIETH CENTURY AUTHORS, 1942.

* * *

Since 1924 Walter Millis has been on the staff of the New York *Herald Tribune.* He lives in New York City with his second wife, Eugenia Benbow Sheppard, whom he married in 1954. In addition to his newspaper assignments, Millis contributes articles to various magazines and in recent years has published several highly praised books of political analysis. *The Last Phase,* a brief and objective report on the defeat of Nazi Germany, was written originally for the Office of War Information, to be distributed in conquered Germany. His account of the background of the Pearl Harbor attack, *This Is Pearl!* was praised by the *New Yorker* as "an admirably straightforward and concise review of Japanese-American relations, with a minimum of editorializing." In 1951 Millis published his edition of the diaries of the late Secretary of Defense James Forrestal. Because of the secret and confidential nature of much of the material, dealing as it did with United States defense and wartime policies, Millis was obliged to take considerable editorial liberties with it—omitting, selecting, and condensing. Although some reviewers of the book regretted that such liberties had to be taken, most agreed that the results were nevertheless rewarding and informative. H. B. Hinton said (in the *Saturday Review of Literature*) of Millis' work: "By consulting other records, by reading other memoirs, and by thorough research into the public problems of the period, he has been able to supply interpolatory text to piece the fragments into a highly readable whole."

ADDITIONAL WORKS: The Last Phase: The Allied Victory in Western Europe, 1946; This Is Pearl! The United States and Japan 1941, 1947; (ed.) Forrestal, J. Diaries, 1951.

MILLS, CHARLES WRIGHT (August 28, 1916-   ), American sociologist, writes: "As a writer, I have always tried, although in different ways, to do just one thing: to define and dramatize the essential characteristics of our time. Whether I have written of labor leaders or farmers, of business executives or Puerto Rican migrants, of office workers, housewives or workingmen  —I have tried to see them as actors in the drama of 20th Century USA. I have often failed in this, and no doubt will again, but that is what I am trying to do.

"Intellectually, I have passed through two rather distinct biographical phases: first, social philosophy and a rather full absorption in the classics of the social studies; second, an intensive period, in the middle Forties, of empirical research. At the present time, I am in the process of combining these interests into a workable style of reflection. Although technically trained in 'social science,' I am, in practice, indifferent to the specialized trivialities and pretentious rituals towards which so many in these disciplines now drift.

"Here are my vital statistics: Born in Waco, Texas, of middle-class English and Irish parentage; boyhood in Sherman, Fort Worth, and Dallas. Public schools, with an early interest in architecture. One unhappy year, 1934-5, at Texas A. & M. Then the University of Texas, to receive the B.A. and M.A. degrees in philosophy and sociology in 1939. Charles D. Oldright Fellow in Philosophy, 1937-8; Departmental Fellow in Logic, 1938-9; Phi Beta Kappa. No participation in any of the usual extracurricular college activities. A research fellowship to the University of Wisconsin in 1939; the Ph.D. in the department of sociology and anthropology; a teaching fellowship during 1940-41.

"In 1941, appointed associate professor of sociology at the University of Maryland; in 1945, briefly, special business consultant to the Small War Plants Corporation, traveling and preparing a Senate committee print. In 1945, also, awarded a John Simon Guggenheim Fellowship, and appointed to Columbia. Until 1948, director of the labor research division of the Bureau of Applied Social

Research at Columbia University. Directed studies of personal influence and mass communications in a midwestern city, of Puerto Ricans in New York City, 1947-8, of health needs for the United Automobile Workers, C.I.O., in the spring of 1948. Since then, several private commercial studies of mass communication.

"Apart from writing and teaching, my major activities include farming, photography, and wood-working. With my wife, Ruth Harper, I have rebuilt and expanded an old house, building in a wood-working shop and photographic darkroom, as well as a small barn and detached writing room. Around this rig, which is in Rockland County, forty miles from New York City, we run a six-acre subsistence farm, producing about half our foodstuffs. We hope in a year or so to increase that to eighty per cent."

* * *

C. Wright Mills' best known work is *White Collar*, an analysis of the morals, mores, and manners of the American middle class. It was Mills' intention (and the reviewers of the book agreed that he succeeded in this) "to avoid the thick facts and thin meanings of the usual sociological work, but also the thin facts and thick meanings of the usual 'literary treatment' of social affairs." The result was a challenging and disturbing picture of this large segment of the American public, "the product of solid thinking and good writing," Ben B. Seligman wrote in the *New Republic,* "exhibiting a perception of society that is not often met with in works of this kind."

PRINCIPAL WORKS: From Max Weber: Essays in Sociology (ed. & tr. with H. H. Gerth) 1946; New Men of Power, America's Labor Leaders (with H. Schneider) 1948; Puerto Rican Journey (with C. Senior & R. Goldsen) 1950; White Collar: America's Middle Classes, 1951.

MILLS, ENOS ABIJAH (1870-September 21, 1922). For biographical sketch and list of works and references, see TWENTIETH CENTURY AUTHORS, 1942.

MILN, Mrs. LOUISE (JORDAN) (March 5, 1864-September 22, 1933). For biographical sketch and list of works and references, see TWENTIETH CENTURY AUTHORS, 1942.

MILNE, ALAN ALEXANDER (January 18, 1882-). For biographical sketch and list of earlier works and references, see TWENTIETH CENTURY AUTHORS, 1942.

* * *

From his country home in Sussex, an aging but in no way dispirited A. A. Milne wrote in 1952:

> In a farmhouse old by centuries
> This so happy an adventure is
> Coming (so I must suppose,
> Now I'm 70) to a close.
> Take it all, year in, year out,
> I've enjoyed it, not a doubt.

The phrase "year in, year out" provided the title for his recent collection of personal essays—a characteristic work which, in the words of the *Times Literary Supplement,* "while demonstrating the versatility of its author, confirms his erudition, his wit and his liberalism." Milne remains one of the best loved of contemporary English authors—for his warm and engaging verse, for his "bland and agile" prose, and (although he has written no new ones in recent years) for his literate and thoroughly entertaining plays. But essentially, and perhaps ironically, it is his writing for children for which readers know and love him best.

> When I wrote them, little thinking
> All my years of pen-and-inking
> Would be almost lost among
> Those four trifles for the young.

These have managed to survive the atomic age and the formidable threats of television and comic books. Christopher (Robin) Milne, very much grown up now, was wounded in Italy in World War II, returned to England, and was married in 1948.

ADDITIONAL WORKS: Chloe Marr (novel) 1946; The Birthday Party, and Other Stories, 1948; The Norman Church (poems) 1948; A Table Near the Band (short stories) 1950; Year In, Year Out, 1952.

ABOUT: Kunitz, S. & Haycraft, H. Junior Book of Authors (rev. ed.); Milne, A. A. Year In, Year Out; Swinnerton, F. The Georgian Literary Scene (sixth ed.); Life February 19, 1951; New York Herald Tribune Book Review October 12, 1952; New York Times Magazine July 25, 1943.

*MINNIGERODE, MEADE (June 19, 1887-). For biographical sketch and list of earlier works and references, see TWENTIETH CENTURY AUTHORS, 1942.

* * *

Meade Minnegerode lives in Essex, Conn., where during World War II, he was active in home defense in the Ground Observer Corps. In 1945 he became associated with the R. W. Cramer Company of Centerbrook, Conn. His only recent book is a work on philately.

ADDITIONAL WORK: (with R. Lesgor) Cancellations on French Stamps of the Classic Issues, 1849-1876, 1948.

* mĭn'ĭ gĕ rōd

MIRSKY, DMITRY SVYATOPOLK
(formerly Prince) (1890- ?). For biographical sketch and list of works and references, see TWENTIETH CENTURY AUTHORS, 1942.

* * *

According to Gleb Struve's report, D. S. Mirsky got into trouble with Soviet authorities soon after his return to Russia in 1932. His surprise conversion to Communism a year earlier seemed to many who knew him "a natural result of his love of intellectual mischief and his instinctive nonconformism." After two years in the Soviet Union, during which he was highly honored, a critical article he wrote was attacked "by some orthodox Communist critics." A year later he was arrested "on unspecified charges." He was released after a few months but "removed from Moscow." Struve writes: "The latest ascertainable news about him was that he was editing a local newspaper in some out-of-the-way town in Siberia. In 1936 and 1937 his signature still appeared under some articles in Soviet publications, but apparently they were articles written before his 'mishap.' After that his name was never mentioned, and it is not known whether he is alive or not."

ABOUT: Struve, G. Soviet Russian Literature 1917.-50.

*MISTRAL, GABRIELA (LUCILA GODOY ALCAYAGA) (April 7, 1889-),
Chilean poet and educator, was born in the

small town of Vicuña, daughter of Jerónimo Godoy Villanueva and Petronila Alcayaga. She is of Spanish and Basque descent with "probably more than a touch of Indian." Her father was the village school teacher and *pallador* or minstrel, who composed verses for festivals.

Lucila attended the village high school and at the age of fifteen became a teacher, educating poor children in rural areas. She later went to the Pedagogical College at Santiago and became a secondary school teacher. In 1912 she was appointed inspector and professor of Castilian in the Liceo de Los Andes for six years.

The young teacher won rapid recognition as a poet. In 1907 she had written *La Voz de Elqui*, her first long poem, inspired by a

* mēs träl'

tragic love affair. In 1914 her three *Sonnets of Death* won first prize—a laurel crown and gold medal—awarded by a writers' society in Santiago. She had submitted these poems under the pseudonym "Gabriela Mistral" honoring two poets she deeply admired: the Italian Gabriel d'Annunzio and the Provençal, Frédéric Mistral.

From 1918 to 1922 she was director and professor of Spanish in three schools successively. On the invitation of the Mexican government, she was commissioned by the government of Chile to reorganize the Mexican libraries and rural schools. During this official visit to Mexico she was deeply impressed by the problems of the Indian masses. She dedicated a school named in her honor, delivered lectures and had her children's songs set to music by a famous composer.

Upon her return to Chile, she was named Chile's delegate to the League of Nations' Institute of Intellectual Cooperation. In 1931 she came to the United States as professor of Spanish history and literature at Barnard College. In 1933 she was appointed Chilean consul in Madrid, and later served her country in Lisbon, Genoa, and Naples. In 1947 she became consul at Santa Barbara, Calif.

The poet's first volume was published not in her native Chile, but in New York City. Dr. Federico Onís, professor of Spanish literature at Columbia University chose her book, *Desolación*, to be published by the Spanish Institute in New York. *Ternura* (Tenderness) was published during the poet's sojourn in Spain. This was followed by three more books in 1930, *Preguntas* (Questionings), *Nubes Blancas* (White Clouds) and *La Oración de la Maestra* (The Prayer of the Schoolmistress).

In 1945 she was awarded the Nobel prize for literature. *Time* magazine called her "the lioness of social Stockholm" on this occasion, and described her as a tall, handsome woman, with strong features, short hair, a dark complexion and "a captivating smile." The style of Mistral's poetry is direct and personal, her imagery is rich and earthy and her words simple and vigorous. Her chief literary influences were the Bible, Tagore, the Mexican Amado Nervo, and the Nicaraguan Rubén Darío. She is an ardent Catholic but an "avowed anti-clerical." The critic Findlayson found in her poetry, "a unique delicacy, a gentle resignation, an inclination that is spontaneously ethical." Her best-known poems, universally sung in South America, *Canciones de Cuña* (Lullabies) and *Rondas de Niños* (Children's Songs) reveal her profound love of children. In her work she has glorified the mission of the teacher and expressed "a universal maternal instinct for children, the poor and the unfortunate." She has said of herself, "I am a Christian, a total democrat. I believe that Christianity in its profoundest social sense can free the peoples of the world."

PRINCIPAL PUBLICATIONS IN ENGLISH TRANSLATION: *in* Blackwell, A. S. (ed.) Some Spanish-American Poets, 1938.

ABOUT: Hoehn, M. (ed.) Catholic Authors, I; Peers, E. A. Gabriela Mistral; Commonweal December 5, 1941; Current Biography 1946; Free World February 1943; Living Age November 29, 1924.

MITCHELL, JAMES LESLIE ("Lewis Grassic Gibbon") (February 13, 1901-February 21, 1935). For biographical sketch and list of works and references, see TWENTIETH CENTURY AUTHORS, 1942.

* * *

ABOUT: Baker, D. V. (ed.) Modern British Writing.

MITCHELL, MARGARET (1900-August 16, 1949). For biographical sketch and list of earlier work and references, see TWENTIETH CENTURY AUTHORS, 1942.

* * *

Margaret Mitchell died at Atlanta, Ga., of injuries received when a speeding automobile struck her as she and her husband crossed a street. She was forty-nine years old. Private funeral services were extended by means of loud speakers to hundreds of people in the street mourning Atlanta's "greatest and most beloved citizen."

A few months before her death Miss Mitchell compiled statistics on *Gone With the Wind*: 3,800,000 copies printed in the United States; still selling, thirteen years after publication, at the rate of 50,000 copies a year; banned and burned by the Nazis; about 2,000,000 authorized and an uncounted number of pirated copies printed in twenty-one other countries. The motion picture, several times revived, remains a screen classic.

Although its author once wrote, "I know good work and I know good writing, and I didn't think mine good," it remains true that, as Harrison Smith has said, "for this generation and perhaps another to follow, the first and only work of an unknown woman remains the most popular novel in the world." In the opinion of J. Donald Adams, *Gone With the Wind* differs from most "synthetic concoctions" in historical fiction because "its author, a vibrantly alive human being to begin with— one who lived close to life—wrote from com-pulsion about a story that mattered to her greatly."

ABOUT: Mott, F. L. Golden Multitudes; Collier's October 22, 1949, December 10, 1949; Harper's Magazine February 1949; Hobbies October 1949; Life August 29, 1949; New York Times August 17, 1949, August 28, 1949; Saturday Review of Literature September 16, 1944, September 3, 1949, September 17, 1949; Publishers' Weekly September 16, 1944.

MITCHISON, Mrs. NAOMI MARGARET (HALDANE) (November 1, 1897-). For autobiographical sketch and list of earlier works and references, see TWENTIETH CENTURY AUTHORS, 1942.

* * *

Naomi Mitchison writes from London that her 1942 sketch "dates a lot, especially the photograph! My husband has been a Labour Member of Parliament since 1945, and I got onto the Argyll County Council in the same year. I never became a J.P. as I seem to have intended in the last paragraph. But I am a member of the Highlands and Islands Advisory Panel. I'm also one of the executives of the Authors' World Peace Appeal. I went to Russia again this year [1952]— though no fellow-traveller! Cripps and Lansbury are both dead. Not sure who I would put now. Bevan??"

ADDITIONAL WORKS: The Bull Calves, 1945; Men and Herring (with D. Macintosh) 1949; The Big House, 1950; Lobsters on the Agenda, 1952; Travel Light, 1952; Graeme and the Dragon, 1954; Swan's Road, 1954.

MITFORD, NANCY (November 28, 1904-), English novelist and biographer, writes: "My father was the second son of an English peer; my mother was a beauty. Second sons, in England, are given no money and I was born in a poor London slum. As my father insisted on keeping seven bloodhounds and a pony for me to ride, it was all rather a squash. How-

Dorothy Wilding

ever, during the first war against the Germans my father's eldest brother was killed and my father became Lord Redesdale. After this we lived in a large house in the Cotswolds. I had five sisters and one brother. My father and mother, illiterate themselves, were against education and we girls had none, though we were taught to ride and to speak French. My brother went to Eton.

"There are some brains in my family all the same. We had two clever grandfathers, Lord Redesdale who spoke every European language as well as Chinese and Japanese, and had a great love of art, and Thomas Gibson Bowles, the wildly eccentric Member of Parliament for King's Lynn. Bertrand Russell is a first cousin of my grandmother; my Redesdale grandfather was first cousin of the poet Swinburne.

"I grew up as ignorant as an owl, came out in London and went to a great many balls. Here I met various people who were not ignorant at all—I made friends with a set of people which included Messrs. Henry Green, Evelyn Waugh, John Betjeman, Sir Maurice Bowra and the brilliant Lord Berners (who appeared, at his own request, in *The Pursuit of Love*, as Lord Merlin). Very soon I became an intellectual snob. I tried to educate myself, read enormously and wrote a few indifferent novels. I married a man whose favorite reading is the Greek and Roman classics.

"When the war broke out I became manager of Heywood Hill's bookshop, Mr. Hill himself having been called up. For the first time in my life I worked hard, at regular hours; I cannot say that I liked it but the discipline which was imposed made it possible for me to write much better books. *The Pursuit of Love* which I wrote in 1945 was immediately a best seller. I left the bookshop and came to live in Paris where I have settled permanently and where I am continuing my education."

* * *

Miss Mitford has been married since 1933 to the Hon. Peter Rodd. She came to the attention of American readers with the publication of her *Pursuit of Love*, and since then her novels ("comedies of manners," as they have been described) have delighted American as well as British readers. The charm of her work, the London *Times Literary Supplement* writes, is "her own talent for personal and social mockery. Within the narrow and comfortable limits of the world she describes . . . her wit and her gift for detecting the absurdities of character have had full scope." Her satire, Phyllis McGinley pointed out, has elegance and malice—"It is all quite funny and rather frightening."

In 1953 Miss Mitford's adaptation of André Roussin's comedy *The Little Hut* was a hit of the London theatrical season. An American production of the play, however, ran only briefly.

PRINCIPAL WORKS: Highland Fling, 1931; Christmas Pudding, 1932; Wigs on the Green, 1935; Pigeon Pie, 1940; The Pursuit of Love, 1945; Love in a Cold Climate, 1949; The Blessing, 1951; Madame de Pompadour, 1954. *Translations*— La Fayette, M. The Princess of Cleves, 1950; Roussin, A. The Little Hut.

ABOUT: Beaton, C. & Tynan, K. Persona Grata; Book-of-the-Month Club News October 1951; New York Times Book Review July 10, 1949; The Observer May 11, 1952.

*MIZENER, ARTHUR MOORE (September 3, 1907-   ), American biographer and critic, writes: "I was born and brought up in the middle-sized city of Erie, Pa., and so spent my young manhood in a social environment which represented with great charm and some completeness the characteristic life of the American '20's. We went to country-club dances Saturday

Fran Hall

nights to scorn the elderly locker-room Babbitts and to live in a labyrinth of romantic intrigue and prohibition illegality which it astonishes and embarrasses me to remember but which was certainly immensely exciting at the time. The fine grasp of the quality of that life in the writers of the '20's is, I think, what first drew me to them.

"In 1922 I went away to school, to The Hill, where I got the beginnings of an education for which I remain very grateful. From there, in 1926, I went to Princeton and, thanks to the friendship of a very great teacher, Willard Thorp, discovered the life of literature. I still remember saying to my mother, when I was a sophomore, 'My God, they pay people for reading books and talking about them!' Despite my profession's habitual complaints about being underpaid I still retain some of that astonishment (why don't we have to pay them to listen?). After graduation I went to Harvard for graduate work, the Harvard of Kittredge and Lowes and a visiting professor named I. A. Richards. Richards is the other great teacher I have known; he shook us all up most wonderfully. Classes at Harvard ran around fifty students so I went back to Princeton after I got my M.A. to complete my graduate work. In 1934 I began teaching at Yale, from which I was fired in 1940 (not moral turpitude, as that verb may suggest; just 'not good enough'). I then taught for five years at Wells College, from which I moved to the chairmanship of

* mĭ´znĕr

the English Department at Carleton College in 1945 and from there came to Cornell in 1951 as a professor of English. Rosemary Paris and I were married in 1936; we have one child, a daughter.

"I began writing as what I suppose would now be called a 'New Critic' with articles in the old *Southern Review*, the *Sewanee* and the *Partisan*. It didn't do me any good: 'Do you,' said an elderly Yale professor, more hurt than angry, 'think that a scholar, who is committed to the ideal of objectivity, ought to write for something called *The Partisan Review*?' I owe a good deal to two great editors of reviews, Allen Tate and John Ransom; they showed me what criticism ought to be and everything I write is another unsuccessful attempt to realize that ideal.

"About 1946 my wife, who was tired of having to listen to me talk about Scott Fitzgerald, suggested to Houghton Mifflin that I write a life of Fitzgerald for them. I spent a good part of the next five years doing so, with a good deal of moral support from Budd Schulberg who, I discovered, was working on *The Disenchanted* just across the river from Princeton, in Bucks County. The best future I can imagine for myself is one which contains just enough time free from teaching to allow me to do more work as marvelously exciting as was that work on Fitzgerald."

PRINCIPAL WORKS: The Far Side of Paradise, A Biography of Scott Fitzgerald, 1951.

ABOUT: New York Herald Tribune Book Review January 28, 1951, October 7, 1951; New York Times Book Review January 28, 1951; Saturday Review of Literature January 27, 1951.

MOLLOY, ROBERT (January 9, 1906-), American novelist, writes: "I was lucky, from the novelist's standpoint, in spending my boyhood in a highly individual city, which, as readers of several of my books may know, was Charleston, S.C., where the Atlantic Ocean divides to form the Ashley and Cooper Rivers (or vice versa). After we moved North, though, in the second year of World War I, about all we did was laugh at the unprogressiveness of the old city and the peculiarities of numerous inhabitants. I never dreamed of writing about them.

Larry Colwell

"Long before we migrated, however, I had made attempts at fiction. The first was written on adding machine tape. It was modeled on that sterling boy's author, Horatio Alger, Jr. I began a *de luxe* copy of the first chapter —all these youthful novels end, with few exceptions, with the first chapter—in white ink on the last page of the family photograph album. It begins, 'Jim Brown was a bad boy' and, as mechanical difficulties put an end to the second edition right there, that's all I can quote. But it shows that I had the makings of a moralist.

"In New York I decided to study music seriously. I had already made a start in Philadelphia. That didn't work out too well, but musical interests really made a reader out of me. After graduation from high school I indulged a taste for languages, too, in my spare time, and then at the suggestion of one of my former teachers I tried 'literature.' I wrote two novels. Both were unpublished, but the second encouraged me to look for work at a publisher's from which it had been returned with a pleasant letter of rejection. I got some reading of manuscripts on the strength of my knowledge of European languages and a translation or two. That was in the early part of the depression. Book reviewing followed, then work on the *Columbia Encyclopedia*, and then I was on the staff of the New York *Sun*, finally becoming its literary editor.

"A few years before this I had, after a long layoff, returned to writing fiction. A couple of short stories in manuscript led to the suggestion of a novel about my home city and I wrote one which, with a few changes, became *Pride's Way*. The Literary Guild selected it and I left newspaper work.

"Since then I've been a free lance with the usual ups and downs. I have written and published five books, two of them novels about Charleston, one a nonfiction book about the city, and two novels with settings in New York. A fifth novel, now [1953] being redrafted, is also about Charleston.

"I've written short stories, humorous and serious, for the big circulation magazines and have briefly taught writing. My novels suffer, with certain readers, from my determination not to be one of those solemn asses to whom memorials are erected. Nevertheless, there is an underlying seriousness about my fiction, and in the novels I have not compromised, consciously at least, for the sake of popularity. The most serious, though lightened by what I hope is humor, was the least successful. I have not yet been 'criticized.' Reviewers have delighted me and maddened me, and I have a few real fans who are a salve to my ego. The *American Yearbook* called *Pride's Way* a minor masterpiece and

I was pleased with that. I think of myself as a novelist of the rather absurd frustrations of life. I don't expect to run out of material."

PRINCIPAL WORKS: *Novels*—Pride's Way, 1945; Uneasy Spring, 1946; The Best of Intentions, 1949; Pound Foolish, 1950; A Multitude of Sins, 1953. *Non-Fiction*—(tr.) Gallegos, R. Doña Bárbara, 1931; Charleston: A Gracious Heritage, 1947.

ABOUT: Current Biography 1948; New York Sun May 15, 1945; Saturday Review of Literature February 16, 1946.

MOLNAR, FERENC (January 12, 1878-April 1, 1952). For biographical sketch and list of works and references, see TWENTIETH CENTURY AUTHORS, 1942.

* * *

Ferenc Molnar died at Mt. Sinai Hospital in New York City, after a long illness, at seventy-four.

For the twelve years before his death his long, narrow room at New York's Plaza Hotel was the headquarters for a select group of Hungarian and international literati, and the "zestful, white-haired gentleman" was well known in the neighboring restaurants (he disliked to go far afield) as a prodigious conversationalist and wit.

Characterizing Molnar's work as polished, dexterous, and frivolous, Joseph Remenyi believes that his best-known play, *Liliom*, discloses "secrets of Molnar's talent which he neglected or could not recapture in most of his other plays." As a whole, his plays never rose to the level of "supreme literary art" in spite of "skilled technique, their ingeniousness, and in some instances their brilliancy."

S. N. Behrman wrote: "Molnar's theme is himself and he has taken his society right along with him over the footlights and confided to it expansively in stage whispers." His later plays, though not matching his earlier ones, had worldly charm. They revealed, with some pathos, his attachment "to a world where nothing is quite so important as knowing what brand of champagne to order."

ADDITIONAL WORKS: Delicate Story: a Comedy (English text by Gilbert Miller) 1941; Blue-Eyed Lady, 1942; Captain of St. Margaret's (in England: Captain Magnificent) 1945; Farewell My Heart, 1945; Companion in Exile: Notes for an Autobiography, 1950; Stories For Two, 1950; Romantic Comedies: Eight Plays, 1952.

ABOUT: Middleton, G. These Things Are Mine; Molnar, F. Companion in Exile; American Mercury April 1945; London Times April 3, 1952; New York Times April 2, 1952; New Yorker May 25, June 1, June 8, 1946; Publications of the Modern Language Association December 1946; Saturday Evening Post October 16, 1948.

MONCRIEFF. See SCOTT-MON-CRIEFF

MONKHOUSE, ALLAN NOBLE (May 7, 1858-January 10, 1936). For biographical sketch and list of works and references, see TWENTIETH CENTURY AUTHORS, 1942.

MONRO, HAROLD EDWARD (March 14, 1879-March 16, 1932). For biographical sketch and list of works and references, see TWENTIETH CENTURY AUTHORS, 1942.

* * *

ADDITIONAL WORK: The Silent Pool, and Other Poems (ed. A. K. Monro) 1942.

ABOUT: Dictionary of National Biography 1931-40; Poetry September 1942.

MONROE, HARRIET (1860-September 26, 1936). For biographical sketch and list of works and references, see TWENTIETH CENTURY AUTHORS, 1942.

* * *

ABOUT: Colum, M. M. Life and the Dream; Gregory, H. & Zaturenska, M. History of American Poetry, 1900-1940.

*MONSARRAT, NICHOLAS (March 22, 1910-   ), English novelist, was born in Liverpool, England, the son of Dr. Keith Waldegrave Monsarrat, a distinguished surgeon, and Marguerite (Turney) Monsarrat. He grew up in Liverpool, was sent to Winchester and then to Trinity College, Cambridge, where he took his honors law degree in 1931. Two years in a Nottingham solicitor's office convinced him that the law was not what he wanted for his life's work. With his typewriter and a half-finished novel he went to London to begin the career of a freelance writer. His first three books, *Think of Tomorrow*, *At First Sight*, and *The Whipping Boy*, had a moderate success. A play, *The Visitors*, was produced with Greer Garson as leading lady.

His introduction to American readers came with the publication of an American edition of his fourth novel, *This Is the Schoolroom*, detailing the experiences of an able young Englishman during four impressionable years. Monsarrat served in the navy during World War II, and attained the rank of lieutenant commander, commanding three escort vessels,

* mŏn'sär rät

a corvette and two frigates. Out of this experience he wrote four books of non-fiction including *H. M. Corvette*, of which the *New Republic* said, "The experience of patrolling, convoying merchantmen, and chasing subs has been related many times during the war, but never with the excellence of *H. M. Corvette*."

Leave Cancelled was a short novel detailing the twenty-four-hour honeymoon of a British officer and his young bride. Its frankness provoked violent reactions of both praise and censure. Jennings Rice in the New York *Herald Tribune* found it "utterly frank without sordidness, bitter-sweet without self-pity, tender without sentimentality," but Hamilton Basso said in the *New Yorker,* "Needn't take up too much of our time. . . . I felt damned embarrassed and I got no enjoyment out of listening in."

The Cruel Sea, published in 1951, achieved great popularity, most reviewers praising Monsarrat's depiction of "the intolerable, exhausting ferocity of the great North Atlantic storms or the equally intolerable menace of a calm and beautiful night with a U-boat wolf pack on the flank," but the author's understanding of the human heart seemed to some less profound than his knowledge of the sea. *The Cruel Sea* was made into a successful motion picture in 1953.

The Story of Esther Costello centers on an Irish girl, stricken blind, deaf, and dumb in an accident, who is taken up by an American woman, as benefactress, exploited and then murdered. The *Library Journal* wrote, "It will be a shocking story to many who have faith in all charitable organizations but it is one that needs telling." The *New Statesman and Nation* condemned it as "a pointless and ugly piece of work . . . dingy sensationalism," but *Time* found it "a skillfully written attack."

From 1946 to 1953 Monsarrat was director of the United Kingdom Information Office in Johannesburg, South Africa, and now holds a similar position in Ottawa, Canada. He has traveled widely in most European countries, Africa, and North America. His wife, formerly Miss Philippa Crosby of Johannesburg, has had a distinguished career in journalism. They have one son and live in Ottawa. In 1951 Monsarrat received the Heinemann Foundation Prize for Literature and was elected a Fellow of the Royal Society of Literature.

PRINCIPAL WORKS: Think of Tomorrow, 1934; At First Sight, 1935; The Whipping Boy, 1937; This Is the Schoolroom, 1940; H. M. Corvette, 1942; East Coast Corvette, 1943; Corvette Command, 1944; Leave Cancelled, 1945; H. M. Frigate, 1946; Depends What You Mean by Love, 1947; My Brother Denys, 1948; The Cruel Sea, 1951; The Story of Esther Costello, 1953.

ABOUT: Current Biography 1950; New York Herald Tribune Book Review August 26, October 7, 1951; New York Times Book Review August 19, 1951.

MONTAGU, ASHLEY (June 28, 1905-), Anglo-American anthropologist, writes: "I was born in London, England. At fifteen I won a first prize in a literary competition;  this consisted of one book, which I selected: William McDougall's *Introduction to Social Psychology.* That book did not determine my interest in human nature, but it powerfully reenforced it. At the University of London, I prepared myself by getting a good grounding in the biological sciences, and I think I was the first student ever to study physical anthropology in the University. At the same time I studied psychology, cultural anthropology, and sociology. What a galaxy of stars my teachers were! Elliot Smith, Woollard, and Arthur Keith in anatomy, Starling in physiology, Spearman and Flugel in psychology, Perry, Seligman, Westermarck, and Malinowski in cultural anthropology, and Ginsberg in sociology. In 1927 I came to the United States in order to study palaeontology with W. K. Gregory at Columbia and the American Museum of Natural History. Aften ten months in New York I decided that America was the place where the work I wished to do could best be done. I spent a delightful year in Florence, Italy, waiting for my visa as a permanent resident of the United States, and returned to New York in August 1930. In 1931 I became assistant professor of anatomy at New York University and also anthropologist to the Division of Child Research. I taught Child Growth and Development at the New School for Social Research in 1931, and ever since have been conducting researches into the way man got to be the way he is now, in all his wonderful variety.

"In September 1931 I married Marjorie Helen Peakes, of Weston, Mass. We have three children, Audrey, Barbara, and Geoffrey. In 1934-37 I studied cultural anthropology with Franz Boas and Ruth Benedict at Columbia and was awarded a Ph.D. in that subject in the latter year. In 1938 I became associate professor of anatomy at Hahnemann Medical College and Hospital in

681

Philadelphia, and moved from there to become chairman and professor of anthropology at Rutgers University in 1949. I became an American citizen in 1940. Politically I would describe myself as an independent liberal.

"Not long ago someone asked one of my friends what my specialty was. The reply was: 'I should say that Ashley Montagu's specialty is versatility.' I do seem to be interested in an awfully large number of things. I'm afraid I have that kind of mind, but fundamentally my principal interest is human beings. This interest has involved me in such diverse, yet unified, activities as being a member of international committees on the standardization of anthropometric techniques; digging for fossil man in Kent; the study of fossil man; the study of the unborn human foetus; the re-examination of the concept of race; and what has, perhaps, given me the greatest pleasure, helping to draft the UNESCO Statement on Race in 1949-50."

* * *

Ashley Montagu's sound and lucid writings on race, human intelligence, and a variety of subjects concerning man and his place in the world, are respected by scholars and laymen alike. Probably his most popular book is *The Natural Superiority of Women*, designed, he writes, "to bring the sexes closer together, not to set them apart by placing one above the other."

PRINCIPAL WORKS: Coming into Being among the Australian Aborigines, 1937; How to Find Happiness and Keep It, 1942; Man's Most Dangerous Myth: the Fallacy of Race, 1942; Introduction to Physical Anthropology, 1945; Adolescent Sterility, 1946; Edward Tyson, M.D., F.R.S. (1650-1708), and the Rise of Human and Comparative Anatomy in England, 1943; On Being Human, 1950; Statement on Race, 1951; On Being Intelligent, 1951; Darwin, Competition, and Cooperation, 1952; The Natural Superiority of Women, 1953; The Meaning of Love (ed.) 1953; Immortality, 1955; The Direction of Human Development, 1955.

ABOUT: Book Find News 112-113; New York Herald Tribune Book Review April 26, 1953; Time April 21, 1941.

MONTAGUE, CHARLES EDWARD

(January 1, 1867-May 28, 1928). For biographical sketch and list of works and references, see TWENTIETH CENTURY AUTHORS, 1942.

MONTGOMERY, LUCY MAUDE (November 30, 1874-April 24, 1942). For autobiographical sketch and list of works and references, see TWENTIETH CENTURY AUTHORS, 1942.

*MONTHERLANT, HENRY DE, Comte

1893-). For autobiographical sketch and list of earlier works and references see TWENTIETH CENTURY AUTHORS, 1942.

* * *

Henry de Montherlant was a war correspondent in the first year of World War II, with a French infantry regiment, and was slightly wounded. When the Germans were victorious, he went to the south of France. In 1941 he published a book of essays (*Le Solstice de Juin*, not translated into English) at first banned by the Germans but later authorized by them. For a time during the occupation he apparently turned against his own people and made his peace with the enemy. According to the *Columbia Dictionary of Modern European Literature* he was "the one prominent French author who during the tragic occupation of his country in the Second World War welcomed and adulated the enemy *pour le plaisir de trahir*, to use his own words—for the sheer pleasure of betraying." But in 1944 he was in trouble with the Germans and his apartment was searched by the Gestapo. During most of the war, from 1942 to 1945, he worked with the Swiss Red Cross for French war victims. In 1942 his play *La Reine Morte* (translated as *Queen After Death or How to Kill Women*) was produced at the Comédie Française. His *Maître de Santiago* was produced in Paris in 1947 and *Demain Il Fera Jour* (*Tomorrow the Dawn*) in 1949. These plays, along with two others, were published in America in 1951.

It is not surprising that anyone of so perverse and cynical a nature as Montherlant should have shocked and offended large numbers of readers. His hedonism, his pride, his anti-feminism, his preoccupation with death, his scorn for conventional social values —all of these qualities have made him enemies. And yet Montherlant remains one of the most highly regarded of contemporary French writers. Haakon Chevalier writes in the *Columbia Dictionary*: "Admirably disciplined, with a rare aesthetic integrity, he is a master of character delineation and possesses psychological insight, trenchant wit, and a grasp of the subtlety and complexity of contemporary social relationships." And Henri Peyre commented: "Montherlant is a well nigh infallible writer of French prose. . . . He seeks greatness, proclaims it without fear of ridicule; and he forces one to confess that he reaches it." The seeming perverseness and inconsistency of his work

* môn těr län'

may, as Jonathan Griffin points out, be the result of "a sincerity more searching than that of most ordinary people and wholly worthy of an artist."

ADDITIONAL WORK IN ENGLISH TRANSLATION: The Master of Santiago and Four Other Plays, 1951.

ABOUT: Beauvoir, S. de, The Second Sex; Bowen, E. Collected Impressions; Columbia Dictionary of Modern European Literature; Dictionnaire Biographique Français Contemporain; Griffin, J. *Preface to* Montherlant's The Master of Santiago.

MONYPENNY, WILLIAM FLAVELLE (August 7, 1866-November 23, 1912). For biographical sketch and list of works and references, see TWENTIETH CENTURY AUTHORS, 1942.

MOODY, WILLIAM VAUGHN (July 8, 1869-October 17, 1910). For biographical sketch and list of works and references, see TWENTIETH CENTURY AUTHORS, 1942.

* * *

ABOUT: Gregory, H. & Zaturenska, M. History of American Poetry, 1900-1940; Veeder, G. N. Concerning William Vaughn Moody (privately printed, 1941); Witham, W. T. Panorama of American Literature; American Literature May 1951.

MOORE, FRANK FRANKFORT (May 15, 1855-May 11, 1931). For biographical sketch and list of works and references, see TWENTIETH CENTURY AUTHORS, 1942.

MOORE, GEORGE (February 24, 1852-January 20, 1933). For biographical sketch and list of works and references, see TWENTIETH CENTURY AUTHORS, 1942.

* * *

ABOUT: Bowen, E. Collected Impressions; Clark, B. H. Intimate Portraits; Dictionary of National Biography 1931-40; Gaunt, W. The Aesthetic Adventure; Gregory, H. The Shield of Achilles; McCullough, B. W. Representative English Novelists; Woolf, V. Death of the Moth; Atlantic Monthly December 1950; Modern Language Notes April 1947; Nineteenth Century Fiction March & June 1954.

MOORE, GEORGE EDWARD (November 4, 1873-), English philosopher, writes: "I was born at Upper Norwood, which is a southern suburb of London. My father was Daniel Moore, M.D., but he had quite ceased to practice as a doctor by about the

time when I was born. My mother's maiden name was Henrietta Sturge; she was a member of the well-known Quaker family of the Sturges, and was a niece of its best known member, Joseph Sturge. I had two elder sisters and two elder brothers, and two younger sisters and one younger brother. My eldest brother, Thomas Sturge Moore, became well known both as a poet and for his wood-cuts; and my second brother, D. H. Moore, was elected in 1894 to a Fellowship at Trinity College, Cambridge, for Physics. I attended Dulwich College as a day-boy for ten years and two terms, starting in January 1882, as soon as I was eight years old; and during my last two years there I was Captain of the School. In December 1891 I was elected to a Major Scholarship for Classics at Trinity College, Cambridge; and I started residence there in the following October. In June 1894 I got a First in Part I of the Classical Tripos; and in the following January won the Craven University Scholarship, which is for Classics. In June 1896 I got a First Class, with distinction, in Part II of the Moral Sciences Tripos. My teachers in philosophy had been Henry Sidgwick, James Ward, G. F. Stout, and McTaggart.

"In 1898 I won a fellowship at Trinity by a philosophical dissertation. This elapsed in 1904, and I then lived first for three and a half years in Edinburgh, and then for another three and a half at Richmond, Surrey, working at philosophy. In 1911 I was appointed to a lectureship in Moral Science at Cambridge and continued to hold it till in 1925 I was elected to one of the two Cambridge professorships of philosophy, and thereupon was elected again to a fellowship at Trinity. In 1916 I married Dorothy Ely; and we have two sons, Nicholas and Timothy, of whom the former is a poet and the latter a composer. My wife's father, G. H. Ely, was one of the two men, who, under the pseudonym, very well known at one time to English boys, of 'Herbert Strang,' collaborated in producing a long series of adventure stories for boys.

"In 1920 I was chosen to edit, from the beginning of 1921, the philosophical quarterly *Mind*, and I continued to edit it till the end of 1947, when, owing to the fact that my health had become uncertain, I thought it wisest to resign. In 1939, having reached the age of sixty-five, I was compelled by the university statutes to retire from my professorship; and in the ensuing Michaelmas term, I delivered, by invitation, a series of eight lectures at Oxford—one every week. In 1940 I was invited to come for one semester, as visiting professor, to Smith College, Mass., U.S.A.; when there, I was invited to come for the next semester to Princeton; the second semester in 1941 I spent at Mills College, Oakland, Calif., until the middle of December; in the two semesters of 1942 I was at Columbia University, New York; then for one semester in 1943 at Swarthmore, Pa.; and finally till May, 1944, for two more semesters at Columbia University. I returned to my home at Cambridge in May, 1944, and in June, 1951, King George VI conferred on me the Order of Merit."

* * *

The actual output of Professor Moore's lifetime of dedication to philosophical study numbers only some four volumes. But the scope and depth of his work and his influence have been enormous, and he is widely recognized and honored as "one of the most eminent philosophers and mathematicians of our time." His most important work, the *Principia Ethica*, published in 1903, has influenced several generations of students and philosophers and was compared, by the late Lord Keynes, with the dialogues of Plato. He wrote of Moore's chapter on "The Ideal" —"I know of no equal to it in literature since Plato. And it is better than Plato because it is quite free from *fancy*. It conveys the beauty of the literalness of Moore's mind, the pure and passionate intensity of his vision, *un*fanciful and *un*dressed up." A writer in the London *Times Literary Supplement* suggested in 1953 that it was with Socrates, rather than with Plato, that Moore should be compared, for like Socrates he raises those simple but devastatingly rational questions which go to the very root of the thinking of his contemporaries: "And even in their characters Socrates and Moore resemble each other, not least in that simplicity which seems so childlike and then suddenly anything but childlike. To conservatism and respectability all thought has always been dangerous, but of all dangers the greatest has always come from those very rare people who have applied a childlike simplicity and divine common sense to religion, philosophy, ethics, and politics."

PRINCIPAL WORKS: Principia Ethica, 1903; Ethics, 1912; Philosophical Studies, 1922; Autobiography and "Reply to My Critics" *in* The Philosophy of G. E. Moore (ed. P. Schilpp) 1942; Some Main Problems of Philosophy, 1953.

ABOUT: Harrod, R. F. The Life of John Maynard Keynes; Keynes, J. M. Two Memoirs; Schilpp, P. (ed.) The Philosophy of G. E. Moore; The Listener August 27, 1953; (London) Times Literary Supplement August 28, 1953.

MOORE, MARIANNE CRAIG (November 15, 1887-). For autobiographical sketch and list of earlier works and references, see TWENTIETH CENTURY AUTHORS, 1942.

* * *

Marianne Moore sends the following corrections to her 1942 sketch. She taught commercial subjects—stenography, typing, bookkeeping, commercial English, commercial law, etc.—at the Carlisle Indian School, not just stenography alone. Her first volume, *Poems* (1921), was published by Bryher (Winifred Ellerman, then Mrs. Robert McAlmon) and H. D., not by Robert McAlmon. There is no *h* in "Schofield"; Scofield Thayer is the name. And, Miss Moore writes, "My hair is not 'auburn' now." She suggests "grey" or "silver mink."

In the past decade Marianne Moore's work has received many honors: in 1944 the Contemporary Poetry's Patrons' Prize and the Harriet Monroe Poetry Award, presented by the University of Chicago; in 1945 a Guggenheim fellowship in creative writing; in 1946 a joint grant of $1,000 from the American Academy of Arts and Letters and the National Institute of Arts and Letters; in 1947 she was elected to the National Institute of Arts and Letters; in 1951, for her *Collected Poems*, she was awarded the Bollingen prize in poetry; in 1952 the National Book Award and the Pulitzer prize for poetry; and in 1953 the Gold Medal for Poetry of the National Institute of Arts and Letters.

Critical comment on Miss Moore's poetry has been almost uniformly favorable. She is a "poet's poet," a craftsman of marvelously polished technique. But more than that, as Randall Jarrell has pointed out, "There is so much of a life concentrated into, objectified on, these hard, tender, serious pages, there is such wit and truth and moral imagination inhabiting this small space, that we are surprised at possibility, and marvel all over again at the conditions of human making and being. What Miss Moore's best poetry does, I can say best in her words: it 'comes into and steadies the soul'; so that the reader feels himself 'a life prisoner, but reconciled.' "

Miss Moore, the author of several sensitive and perceptive critical essays herself, has made her own critical comment on her work. Speaking before the National Book Association, in January 1952, she said: "To be trusted is an ennobling experience; and poetry is a peerless proficiency of the imagination. I prize it, but am myself an observer; I can see no reason for calling my work poetry except that there is no other category in which to put it." In poetry, she continued, "understatement is emphasis. In poetry metaphor substitutes compactness for confusion and says the fish moves 'on winglike foot.' It also says—and for 'it' I had better say Confucius—'If there be a knife of resentment in the heart, the mind will not attain precision.' That is to say, poetry watches life with affection."

ADDITIONAL WORKS: Nevertheless, 1944; Collected Poems, 1951; The Fables of La Fontaine, 1954; Predilections (essays) 1955.

ABOUT: Frankenberg, L. Pleasure Dome; Gregory, H. & Zaturenska, M. History of American Poetry, 1900-1940; Current Biography 1952; New Republic April 7, 1952; New York Herald Tribune Book Review October 7, 1951; New York Times January 12, 1952; New York Times Book Review May 16, 1954; New Yorker November 11, 1944; Partisan Review November-December 1952; Saturday Review February 2, 1952; Time December 10, 1951.

MOORE, MERRILL (September 11, 1903-), American poet and psychiatrist, was born at Columbia, Tenn. His father was

John Trotwood Moore, novelist, historian, poet, and state librarian for Tennessee; his mother was Mary Brown Daniel Moore, who succeeded her husband in the same position after he died in 1929. Merrill Moore attended public schools and prepared for college at Montgomery Bell Academy in Nashville. He graduated from Vanderbilt University in Nashville, B.A. in 1924 and M.D. in 1928. From the latter year until 1935 he served at the Boston City Hospital and the Massachusetts General Hospital. He began his psychoanalytic training with Dr. William Herman in 1931, continued it with Dr. Hanns Sachs from 1934 to 1938. He has taught neurology, neuropathology and psychiatry, and since 1950 he has been clinical associate in psychiatry at the Harvard Medical School.

Fabian Bachrach

Dr. Moore set up private practice in Boston in 1935. During World War II he was a major in the U.S. Army and served in New Zealand and in the South Pacific as a psychiatric consultant. In 1946, with the rank of lieutenant-colonel, he was sent to China on an army mission. At the end of the year he received his discharge, but he remained in the organized reserve with the rank of colonel. Returning to civilian life, Dr. Moore resumed his practice in Boston. He is married to Ann Leslie Nichol of Nashville, Tenn., and they have four children. His hobbies are iris-growing, shell-collecting, photography, swimming, and the study of languages. His published medical articles run to more than 150 titles, dealing with various aspects of neurology and psychiatry, particularly the treatment of alcoholism.

Like a fellow poet, Dr. William Carlos Williams, Moore divides his time between a medical practice and the writing of poetry. Verse has been his avocation for many years, starting back in his college days when he was a member of the "Fugitive Group" which published a poetry magazine, The Fugitive, in Nashville. He describes his writing, in proper psychiatric terms, as a "compulsive addiction" to the sonnet form and says that writing sonnets is his own "occupational therapy." His daily average is from two to five sonnets. He believes that the sonnet form has long been the victim of "a paralyzing Petrarch-Shakespeare fixation." His own sonnets he calls "illegitimate" and they follow a 4-5-5 or 2-2-4-4-2 pattern of his own devising. "My sonnet," he explains, "has an Italian father and an English mother, and it is a hybrid." In his home in Squantum, Mass., Dr. Moore has a "Sonnetorium," where he keeps the more than 100,000 sonnets he has written and "treated." As William Carlos Williams describes his work: "He has broken through the blinding, stupid formality of the thing and gone after the core of it; not of the sonnet, which is nothing, but of the sonnet *form*, which is the gist of the whole matter."

Other critics have described Moore's work as "informal" and "conversational." The *Saturday Review of Literature* wrote of him: "Dr. Moore, unlike poets who attempt to edit and excise their own daily production, offers us everything and bids the reader select for himself. And there is some rich poetry embedded in these diagnostic statements."

PRINCIPAL WORKS: The Noise that Time Makes, 1929; Six Sides to a Man, 1935; Poems from The Fugitive, 1936; Sonnets from The Fugitive, 1937; Sonnets from New Directions, 1938; Ego, 1938; M: One Thousand Autobiographical

Sonnets, 1938; Some Poems for New Zealand (pub. in Wellington, N.Z.) 1944; Clinical Sonnets, 1949; Illegitimate Sonnets, 1950; Case Record from a Sonnetorium, 1951; More Clinical Sonnets, 1952; Verse Diary of a Psychiatrist, 1954; The Dance of Death, 1955.

ABOUT: Wells, H. W. The American Way of Poetry; New York Times Book Review January 23, 1949, July 15, 1951, December 16, 1951; Poetry October 1935, June 1939, April 1952.

MOORE, OLIVE. For autobiographical sketch and list of works and references, see TWENTIETH CENTURY AUTHORS, 1942.

MOORE, THOMAS STURGE (March 4, 1870-July 18, 1944). For biographical sketch and list of works and references, see TWENTIETH CENTURY AUTHORS, 1942.

* * *

T. Sturge Moore died, at seventy-four, in a nursing home in Windsor, England.

His work was never as widely popular as its admirers believed it deserved to be, perhaps, suggested Lascelles Abercrombie, because of "his peculiar intellectual individuality and his occasional obscurities," but his influence was great on many poets of a younger generation. John Masefield called him "a poet and artist of rare gifts, a critic of delicate discrimination, a scholar of art and a man of loyal and devoted friendship."

His poetry has been characterized as "idiosyncratic, sometimes pleasingly so," by William Rose Benét, while a reviewer writing in the New Statesman and Nation declared that "no poet certainly who has accepted the traditional world of classic myth, in which English imagination has found itself, has vivified so familiarly the older mind of paganism."

ADDITIONAL WORK: W. B. Yeats & T. Sturge Moore: Their Correspondence, 1901-1937 (ed. U. Bridge) 1953.

ABOUT: Gwynn, F. L. Sturge Moore and the Life of Art; Yeats, W. B. & T. Sturge Moore: Their Correspondence; Asiatic Review July 1947; London Times July 20, 1944; New York Times July 21, 1944.

MOOREHEAD, ALAN (July 22, 1910-), Australian journalist and travel writer, reports: "I was born in Melbourne, Australia, the second son of a journalist [Richard Moorehead], and after an education at school and university in Australia I left for Europe at the age of twenty-five. I have been traveling ever since. During the last World War I was attached to the British

and American armies as a war correspondent in the East and in Europe. Since then I have been writing books and occasional magazine articles. Once for a short time I took a job with the British Ministry of Defence in London. I have a wife and three children and latterly we have been living partly in London and partly in Italy. Most of my books are either biographies or accounts of my own travels and experiences; but I dislike writing very much and do as little as I can."

* * *

Alan Moorehead's first book was a report based on his coverage for the London Daily Express of the British campaigns in Africa and the Middle East in World War II, Mediterranean Front. In the following year he published two more volumes continuing this account and ultimately he combined the three in African Trilogy. The series was regarded by many reviewers as one of the finest jobs of military reporting of the war. V. S. Pritchett wrote of Moorehead: "Not only has he a fine control of language, a constant curiosity that keeps him ferreting out the campaign every minute of his time and a stimulating judgment, but he has a balanced sense of perspective. He knows how to relate small incidents to the whole."

Since the end of the war Moorehead has divided his time between travel writing and straight reporting of the kind that distinguished The Traitors, a study of three members of the atomic spy ring. His lucid and deft travel sketches appear frequently in the New Yorker and are written in what Serge Hughes describes in Commonweal as "a smooth polished pattern [in which] a situation is elongated into a narrative, the narrative broken by what appears to be almost gossipy rambling, and both narrative and asides are gradually and neatly intertwined."

Moorehead took his B.A. at Melbourne University. From 1930-35 he was on the staff of the Melbourne Herald. He then became foreign correspondent for the London Daily Express in Spain, France, Italy, and the Balkans. In 1939 he married Lucy Milner. They have two sons and a daughter.

PRINCIPAL WORKS: Mediterranean Front, 1942; A Year of Battle (in U.S.: Don't Blame the Generals) 1943; The End in Africa, 1943; Eclipse,

1945; Montgomery: A Biography, 1946; Rage of the Vulture (novel) 1948; Villa Diana, 1951; The Traitors, 1952; Rum Jungle, 1954; A Summer Night (novel) 1955.

*MORAND, PAUL (March 13, 1888-   ). For biographical sketch and list of works and references, see TWENTIETH CENTURY AUTHORS, 1942.

* * *

Paul Morand was in England at the time of the outbreak of World War II as head of the French Mission on Economic Warfare. He was French Minister Plenipotentiary in London in 1940; in 1943 he represented France as Minister in Bucharest and in 1944 he was French Ambassador at Berne. His recent writings—none of them translated into English—include studies of Proust and of Giraudoux, works on political affairs, and his own journal of his memoirs as an ambassador. He lives in Paris and has homes in Vevey, Switzerland, and in Morocco.

ABOUT: Columbia Dictionary of Modern European Literature.

* mô rän'

*"MORAVIA, ALBERTO" (pseudonym of Alberto Pincherle) (November 28, 1907-   ), Italian novelist, was born in Rome.

He had little formal education beyond grammar school. At sixteen he fell ill with tuberculosis and spent two years in a sanitorium where he learned English and French and started to write. A large part of his first novel, *Gli Indifferenti,* was written in bed. The book was published in 1929, when the author was twenty-two. It brought him immediate fame. Influenced by French realism, as well as by such modern Italian writers as Pirandello, Tozzi, and Svevo, the book manifested the grim, hopeless realism which appears to be a fundamental outlook of Moravia. Its first English translation, in 1932, called *The Indifferent Ones,* was, in Moravia's words, "so badly translated that no one paid any attention to it." A new and better translation appeared in 1953 as *The Time of Indifference.* "It is a very exciting, complex book," reported the *New Yorker.* "Moravia . . . drains its possibilities, dramatic and moral, to the lees," Frances Keene wrote

* mō rä'vē ä

in the New York *Times.* "His ear for dialogue, for the rhythm of seemingly pointless banter, gives us the very edge of each one's weaknesses. There are no false passages even in the monologues of this book, which tears open today, as it did more than twenty years ago, the fourth wall of many a sterile ménage."

An established and successful writer in his twenties, Moravia traveled extensively and lived abroad in Paris, London, Mexico, New York, Peking, and Athens. His permanent home remained Italy, although he was from time to time in difficulty with Fascist authorities. His novel *La Mascherata* (later translated as *The Fancy Dress Party*), completed in 1940, was a spirited satire on an easily identifiable Fascist dictator. The manuscript was submitted, as required by law, to the Fascist Ministry of Popular Culture where ultimately it was read by Mussolini. To Moravia's considerable surprise, Mussolini ordered the book published. A month later, however, it was withdrawn. Moravia spent the early years of the war living on Capri. When the Germans occupied Italy in 1943, he went into hiding in the mountains for nine months until the Allies arrived. He now lives in Rome, with his wife, novelist Elsa Morante, whom he married in 1941.

In post-war Italy, Moravia's grim and compelling fiction assumed a new and even greater importance. He first achieved popularity in America with a not entirely characteristic work, *Woman of Rome,* the story of a prostitute, which was admired chiefly because it managed to avoid the obvious pitfalls of a work of that nature, sensationalism and sentimentalism. With more recent novels he has come to be regarded as one of the foremost of contemporary European novelists. With *Conjugal Love,* a sharply observed study of a marriage, Charles Rolo wrote in the *Atlantic,* Moravia achieves "something of the sex-consciousness of D. H. Lawrence, minus Lawrence's sex-mysticism. Moravia's powerful sensuality is altogether spontaneous and forthright, free of any taint of staginess; and his shrewd insight into the psychology of sex never sounds like clinical analysis." *A Ghost at Noon,* another study of married love, showed Moravia "at the peak of his power, still young in years and well rooted in experience," Paolo Milano said in the New York *Times.*

Moravia's great popularity both in Italy and abroad suggests, as Thomas G. Bergin writes, "that he has more than regional significance and belongs by right of achievement to that rather select group of writers who have something to say that other men, regardless of national barriers, want to hear."

Moravia writes every day between nine and noon. He works spontaneously: "When I sit at my table to write, I never know what it's going to be till I'm under way. I trust in inspiration, which sometimes comes and sometimes doesn't. But I don't sit back waiting for it. I work *every* day." He spends his afternoons and evenings reading, walking, visiting with friends, or attending the theatre. He is interested in writing for the stage and has dramatized his own *Time of Indifference* and *The Fancy Dress Party*. He has also done some writing for motion pictures. In 1952 Moravia was elected an officer of the French Legion of Honor.

In April 1955 Moravia visited the United States as a guest of the State Department. To Lewis Nichols of the New York *Times Book Review* he suggested another Steinbeck: "There is the same matter-of-fact, down-to-earth manner, the quizzical approach to the patter of slogans, the view that life is pretty good and should be lived." Moravia reported that he had just completed a play about Beatrice Cenci's patricide trial in 1599 and was projecting a new novel on "the memories of a procurer."

PRINCIPAL WORKS IN ENGLISH TRANSLATION: The Indifferent Ones, 1932 (The Time of Indifference, 1953); Wheel of Fortune, 1937; The Fancy Dress Party, 1947; Woman of Rome, 1949; Two Adolescents (in England: Agostino) 1950; The Conformist, 1951; Conjugal Love, 1951; Bitter Honeymoon, and Other Stories, 1954; A Ghost at Noon, 1955.

ABOUT: Columbia Dictionary of Modern European Literature; Atlantic Monthly February 1955; Books Abroad Autumn 1950; New York Herald Tribune Book Review October 7, 1951; New York Times Book Review August 3, 1950, April 17, 1955; New Yorker May 7, 1955; Paris Review Summer 1954; Virginia Quarterly Review Spring 1953.

MORDAUNT, Mrs. EVELYN MAY (CLOWES) ("Elinor Mordaunt," "A. Riposte") (1877?-June 25, 1942). For autobiographical sketch and list of earlier works and references, see TWENTIETH CENTURY AUTHORS, 1942.

* * *

Evelyn Mordaunt died at Oxford, England. Her birthdate is uncertain; she was probably between sixty-five and seventy years old at her death.

The London *Times* has noted that her caustic pen and eloquent tongue were at the service of those she thought deserving, and attributes the success of her writing to "the intense and vital interest she took in life."

Percival Serle has said that her novels were "competent and interesting. Possibly her best work was put into her short stories, often showing a grim sense of tragedy and humor."

ADDITIONAL WORKS: Blitz Kids, 1941; Here Too Is Valour, 1941; To Sea! To Sea!, 1943.
ABOUT: London Times June 27, 1942.

MORE, PAUL ELMER (December 12, 1864-March 9, 1937). For biographical sketch and list of works and references, see TWENTIETH CENTURY AUTHORS, 1942.

* * *

ABOUT: Thorp, W. (ed.) Lives of Eighteen from Princeton; Wilson, E. The Triple Thinkers; Young, M. O. Paul Elmer More: A Bibliography.

"MORESBY, LOUIS." See BECK, L. M. A.

MORGAN, CHARLES (January 22, 1894-). For biographical sketch and list of earlier works and references, see TWENTIETH CENTURY AUTHORS, 1942.

* * *

Charles Morgan served with the British Admiralty in World War II with intervals in France and the United States. He was W. P. Ker lecturer at the University of Glasgow in 1945 and Zaharoff lecturer at Oxford University in 1948. In 1953 he was elected president of the International PEN, succeeding the late Benedetto Croce. Morgan lives in London.

Morgan ceased to be drama critic for the London *Times* in 1939, but in subsequent years he has been contributing a series of critical essays to the *Times Literary Supplement* under the pseudonym of "Menander." These were collected in *Reflections in a Mirror*. Although they were written during the grim days of World War II, the essays were calm, mellow, and pleasantly meditative. The late Donald Stauffer wrote of the book: "It reflects the sweetness, the tolerance, the freedom, the tentative judgments, the consciousness of large and spiritual issues that have made the great democracies . . . enduring." Several years later Morgan published another collection of essays, *Liberties of the Mind*, which reflected far less intellectual tranquillity and a deep anxiety about the imminent danger, in the present age, of the loss of freedom of the mind and moral choice.

Morgan's later novels have been well received. Their style is measured, "elegant and chaste," as one critic described it, and they are generally works of high professional competence. One of these, *The River Line,* was dramatized and produced at the Edinburgh Festival in 1952. His play *The Burning Glass,* dealing with the moral dilemma confronting a scientist whose discoveries might be used to destroy civilization, was a London success in 1953 but ran only briefly in New York.

ADDITIONAL WORKS: *Novels*—The Judge's Story, 1947; The River Line, 1949; Breeze of Morning, 1951. *Essays and Miscellaneous*—The House of Macmillan (1843-1943) 1943; Reflections in a Mirror, 1944, Second Series 1946; Liberties of the Mind, 1951; The Burning Glass (play) 1954.

ABOUT: Van Gelder, R. Writers and Writing; Commonweal July 13, 1945; Hibbert Journal October 1949.

MORGAN, WILLIAM FREND DE. See DE MORGAN

MORGENTHAU, HANS JOACHIM
(February 17, 1904-   ), German-American political scientist, was born in Coburg, Germany, the son of Lud-

wig Morgenthau and Frieda (Bachmann) Morgenthau. After attending the University of Berlin, he received degrees *summa cum laude* from the University of Munich (1927) and the University of Frankfort (1929). In 1932 he did graduate work at the Graduate Institute for International Studies at Geneva. Morgenthau was admitted to the bar in 1927, and practiced law from 1927 to 1930. Varied occupations followed: he became an assistant to the law faculty at the University of Frankfort (1931), the acting president of the Labor Law Court, Frankfort (1931-33), instructor in political science at the University of Geneva (1932-35), professor of international law at the Institute for International and Economic Studies, and lecturer for the Union of Spanish Societies for International Studies in Madrid, Spain (1935-36). Coming to the United States in 1937, he was an instructor in government at Brooklyn College between 1937 and 1939, and an assistant professor of law, history, and political science at the University of Kansas City from 1939 to 1943. He was admitted to the Missouri bar. Since 1943 he has taught at the University of Chicago in the political science department, a full professor since 1949.

Morgenthau's first work appeared in Germany in 1929, when he was twenty-five years old, a study of "The International Jurisdiction, Its Nature and Its Limits." Many books on law and political science have since been published; those in English are listed below. Some books were written with other scholars, —*Twentieth Century Political Thought* and *The H-Bomb.* Of his *In Defense of the National Interest,* a critical examination of American foreign policy, the New York *Times* said, "Hans J. Morgenthau, professor of political science at the University of Chicago, is an American scholar and citizen whom Hitler's tyranny drove to the United States in 1937. . . . His book is a swiftly written, eleventh-hour plea to his countrymen to throw off the four intellectual errors of post-war diplomacy—Wilsonian Utopianism, Dumbartian Legalism, Trumanian Sentimentalism, and Neo-Isolationism. He urges us to analyze the national interest unemotionally in terms of power and its use."

Aside from teaching at the University of Chicago and being visiting professor at other universities, Morgenthau lectured at the Air War College and the Army War College from 1950 to 1952; he was a consultant to the Department of State in 1949 and 1951. Since 1950 he has been director of the Center for the Study of American Foreign Policy.

In 1935 he married Irma Thormann. They have two children and live in Chicago. In 1943 Morgenthau became an American citizen.

PRINCIPAL WORKS: Scientific Man vs. Power Politics, 1946; Politics among Nations: the Struggle for Power and Peace, 1948; In Defense of the National Interest (in England: American Foreign Policy) 1951; (ed.) Germany and the Future of Europe, 1951.

MORISON, SAMUEL ELIOT (July 9, 1887-   ), American historian, writes: "I was born in the home of my Eliot grandparents, 44 Brimmer Street, Boston, where, marvelous to relate, my wife and I are now living. My mother, Emily M. Morison, was the only surviving child of Samuel Eliot, historian and educator, and his wife Emily Marshall, née Otis; my father, John

U.S. Navy Photo

H. Morison, Harvard 1878, was a younger son of Nathaniel H. Morison, scion of a Peterborough, N.H., family who moved to

Baltimore in mid-century and became the first provost of the Peabody Institute.

"Reared in an atmosphere where scholarship, religion and social graces were happily blended, I proceeded by the normal routes of a classical day school and a church boarding school (St. Paul's) to Harvard, where a galaxy of distinguished professors such as Channing, Hart, Haskins and Merriman awakened my latent taste for history. After graduating *cum laude* in 1908 I was given a year's study in Paris by my parents; then returned to the Harvard Graduate School and took my Ph.D. in 1913. The dissertation was published as *The Life and Letters of Harrison Gray Otis*.

"From 1914, when I had a temporary position at the University of California, I have been teaching American history steadily; mostly at Harvard, but also at Oxford, as first incumbent of the new Chair of American History, 1922-25.

"My constant aim has been to write history and historical biography in a manner that would be both authentic and interesting. This is explained in a pamphlet, 'History as a Literary Art,' which is republished in *By Land and By Sea*, a book of my collected essays. Francis Parkman has been my model. I have always endeavored to *live* and *feel* the history that I write. For example, take my three most successful books: *The Maritime History of Massachusetts* was a product both of research and of my hobby of sailing along the New England Coast. In preparation for *Admiral of the Ocean Sea, a Life of Christopher Columbus*, I made voyages to the West Indies and across the Atlantic in sailing vessels, checking Columbus's routes, methods and landfalls. And for *The History of U.S. Naval Operations in World War II* (nine volumes published 1947-54 and five to come), I obtained a commission in the United States Navy, took part in many operations (six combat stars, Legion of Merit with combat clasp), and learned at first hand how the navy fights.

"I have written but one textbook, *The Oxford History of the United States*, which, in partnership with Henry Steele Commager, has been enlarged into *The Growth of the American Republic*, of which the latest edition is 1950. Apart from the maritime, my chief historical interests have been the history of early New England and of the classical culture transplanted by the Puritans.

"The usual prizes given to historians (Pulitzer, Bancroft, Loubat, Jusserand) have been won; the usual memberships in historical and other learned societies conferred; as well as honorary degrees from Harvard,

Yale, Columbia, Trinity, Amherst, Williams, Union and Oxford. I joined the Democratic Party when first voting in 1912, and left it forty years later to support General Eisenhower; but have never found time to take part in public affairs.

"My first wife, Elizabeth S. Green of Boston, died in 1945. All our four children are grown up, and three are married. In December 1949 I married Priscilla Barton of Baltimore, nineteen years my junior; since then we have enjoyed traveling together to the Mediterranean and the Far East to visit the scenes of the late war. We sail together in the summer and are hopefully planning to build a summer home in Maine. Thus my life has been renewed and I have enough writing projects on hand to keep me busy for another twenty-five years."

* * *

Samuel Eliot Morison received the 1942 Pulitzer prize in biography for his life of Christopher Columbus, *Admiral of the Ocean Sea*.

PRINCIPAL WORKS: The Life and Letters of Harrison Gray Otis, 1913; The Maritime History of Massachusetts, 1783-1860, 1921; Oxford History of the United States, 1927 (rev. with H. S. Commager as The Growth of the American Republic, 1930); An Hour of American History, 1929; Builders of the Bay Colony, 1930; Tercentennial History of Harvard College and University: I (Founding of Harvard College) 1935, II (Harvard College in the Seventeenth Century) 1936; Three Centuries of Harvard, 1636-1936, 1936; Puritan Pronaos (lectures) 1936; The Second Voyage of Christopher Columbus, 1939; Portuguese Voyages to America in the Fifteenth Century, 1940; Admiral of the Ocean Sea, 1942; The History of United States Naval Operations in World War II: I (The Battle of the Atlantic) 1947, II (Operations in North African Waters) 1947, III (The Rising Sun in the Pacific) 1948, IV (Coral Sea, Midway, and Submarine Actions) 1949, V (The Struggle for Guadalcanal) 1949, VI (Breaking the Bismarcks Barrier) 1950, VII (Aleutians, Gilberts, and Marshalls) 1951, VIII (New Guinea and the Marianas) 1953, IX (Sicily-Salerno-Anzio) 1954; Ropemakers of Plymouth, 1950; By Land and by Sea (essays) 1953; (ed.) The Parkman Reader, 1955.

ABOUT: American Historical Review January 1951; Atlantic Monthly August 1950; Current Biography 1951; Life March 25, 1940, May 22, 1944; New York Herald Tribune Book Review August 5, 1951, October 11, 1953; New York Times May 4, 1943; New York Times Magazine March 15, 1942; Newsweek November 20, 1950; Time August 28, 1939, March 2, 1942.

MORLEY, CHRISTOPHER DARLINGTON (May 5, 1890-). For autobiographical sketch and list of earlier works and references, see TWENTIETH CENTURY AUTHORS, 1942.

* * *

Christopher Morley's retirement from the staff of the *Saturday Review of Literature* in 1941 was no symbolic gesture of retirement from American letters. On the contrary, Morley has continued his merry and lively career with poetry, novels, essays, some radio work (he participated in the impromptu "Transatlantic Radio Quiz" from 1944 to 1947), travel abroad and judging new books for the Book-of-the-Month Club. Whitney Balliett writes that he regards himself primarily "as a poet who was overpraised in his early career and underpraised in his maturity." It is true that his name is probably less widely known in the 1950's than it was in the 1920's and '30's. But he retains a loyal and devoted following. "He is still spreading his special brand of robust, nineteenth century bookishness," Balliett writes, "and he is still experimenting, both with his style and subject matter." Harry Gilroy wrote (in the New York *Times*) of his collection of essays, *The Ironing Board:* "The man revealed is a delightful, gently mad virtuoso of language, an old Rhodester careening along on an Oxford mixture of Chaucer, Shakespeare and Max Beerbohm, the Augustan age, George Gissing, a dash of French argot and Sherlock Holmes."

Morley lives in Roslyn Heights, N.Y.

ADDITIONAL WORKS: *Novels*—Thoroughfare, 1942; The Man Who Made Friends With Himself, 1949. *Poetry*—The Middle Kingdom, 1944; Spirit Level, 1946; Old Mandarin, 1947; Ballad of New York, New York, 1950; Gentlemen's Relish, 1955. *Essays and Miscellaneous*—(ed.) Bartlett's Familiar Quotations (rev. ed.) 1948; The Ironing Board, 1949.

ABOUT: Van Gelder, R. Writers and Writing; Hobbies August 1949; New York Times Book Review July 31, 1949; Saturday Review December 26, 1953.

MORRIS, LLOYD (September 23, 1893-August 8, 1954). For autobiographical sketch and list of earlier works and references, see TWENTIETH CENTURY AUTHORS, 1942.

* * *

Lloyd Morris died of cancer in New York City at the age of sixty. At the time of his death he was probably better known as a social historian than as a biographer and essayist. With *Postscript to Yesterday,* a study of cultural and social life in the United States from 1896 to 1946, and its sequel, *Not So Long Ago,* which traces the social and cultural effects on American society of the automobile, the movies, and the radio, he made what Gerald W. Johnson called "a distinct contribution to popular understanding of the popular mind." His most successful book of recent years, both in the United States and in England, was a social history of New York City since 1850, *Incredible New York*. He also wrote a social history of aviation and a study of the American theatre.

In his sketch in TWENTIETH CENTURY AUTHORS, 1942, Morris remarked that he had worked in all branches of the literary craft except verse and drama. That omission was partly corrected in 1942 when he collaborated with John Van Druten on the comedy *The Damask Cheek,* produced on Broadway with Flora Robson in the leading role. Morris lived in New York. During the World War II he served in the Office of Censorship, as he had done in World War I. In 1951 he was a member of the fiction jury of the National Book Award committee.

ADDITIONAL WORKS: Threshold in the Sun (autobiography) 1943; The Damask Cheek (with J. Van Druten) 1943; Postscript to Yesterday, 1947; Not So Long Ago, 1949; William James, 1950; Incredible New York, 1951; Ceiling Unlimited: The Story of American Aviation (with K. Smith) 1953; Curtain Time, 1953.

ABOUT: Morris, L. Threshold in the Sun; New York Herald Tribune Book Review November 27, 1949, October 11, 1953; New York Times August 10, 1954.

MORRIS, WRIGHT (1910-), American novelist, writes: "I was born in Central City, Nebr., and the first ten years of my life were  spent in the whistle stops along the Platte Valley to the west. The books I have written, and hope to write, are apt to bear, on close examination, the stamp of an object made on the plains. This circumstance will not explain why I am a writer, but it will help to explain why I write as I do, and throw light on the tension it is the nature of writing to examine and relieve. I am not a regional writer, but the characteristics of this region have conditioned what I see, what I look for, and what I find in the world to write about. So I believe in shearing off. In working and in traveling light. I like a minimum of words arranged for a maximum effect. I can examine this sentiment, this personal bias, but I cannot dispense with it. When I do a thing right, this is how it will be done. As the writer in the South inclines toward the baroque, and strives for the symbolic ornamental cluster, the writer on the plains is powerfully inclined to shear the ornament off. If he does not, it is no longer an ornament.

"Objects, what few there are on the plains, acquire a dense symbolical significance, and certain simple artifacts have a functional and classic purity. The windmill, the single plow, the grain elevator, the receding horizon, are both signs and symbols at the same time. They speak for themselves. They would rather talk than be talked about. The man who loves these things, whether he knows it or not, is a photographer. Such books as *The Inhabitants* and *The Home Place* grew out of the plains just as I did, and they are experimental in the way I am also an experiment.

"I got away from the plains in time to share in the Capone era in Chicago, and empty several wastebaskets on Charles Lindbergh when he came down Clark Street. It may have been Lindbergh that led me to see America first. I saw it, nearly all of it, in a series of madcap odysseys that were perilous, foolish, inspired and strangely fashionable. A lot of madmen were footloose on the open road. One of these jaunts, softened to meet the standards of the armchair fictional traveler, is honestly recorded in *My Uncle Dudley*, my first book. I'm afraid it all seems very long ago. But very fresh, with a morning look that makes it seem even longer, as if all the giants in the earth belonged with the Greeks. Somewhere, *some*where there is a Marmon with a piece of flannel underwear serving as a clutch, and an almost new Hohner harmonica under one of the seats. I was playing *Bye, Bye Blackbird* the morning the rear end dropped out. The corners of my mouth are sore when I think of it.

"On one of these adventures I saw Pomona College, a green oasis in southern California, and in college I discovered that life began in Paris, on the left bank. So I went off to Paris and many other places where life was both beginning and ending, and then, like a good exile, I came home and married the girl. She was Mary Ellen Finfrock, of Cleveland, and she seemed to be favorably impressed with the notion, which I had picked up somewhere, that I was meant to be a writer of books. We settled down to do this in California, where we had gone to school and knew how to live cheaply, but it was nearly seven years before the writer published a book. What was it about? Seeing America first.

"I have been doing that, in one way or another, ever since. On the wall behind my desk is a map of the United States showing the green and fertile east, the brown and arid west, the great mountains and the plains, the rivers and the harbors, the places we have been and the places we haven't, and there are markings on this map indicating those that belong to us. Silver Plume, in Colorado; Wellfleet, on the Cape; a short stretch of rolling plains near Lone Tree, Nebr.; several mesas north of Gallup, several green valleys in Utah, a mountain or two in the Sierras and the Tetons, and a very large half acre of ground, with birds, bees and termites, here in Wayne, Pa. There is also a ranch house and a mortgage on it, both all ours."

* * *

In 1954, with the publication of *The Huge Season*, Wright Morris was hailed as "probably the most original young novelist writing in the United States" (Mark Schorer, in the New York *Times*). A serious and ambitious writer, he has improved steadily from book to book, writing with skill, wit, and maturity. Harvey Curtis Webster (in the *Saturday Review*) called him "an expert photographer as well as an expert craftsman," and Schorer (who is reminded of Sherwood Anderson by Morris' recent work) regards him as "a master of the comic and deeply sensitive to the most inarticulate of American sorrows."

PRINCIPAL WORKS: My Uncle Dudley, 1942; The Inhabitants, 1946; The Man Who Was There, 1948; The Home Place, 1948; The World in the Attic, 1949; Man and Boy, 1950; The Works of Love, 1951; The Deep Sleep, 1953; The Huge Season, 1954.

ABOUT: Warfel, H. R. American Novelists of Today; Life July 26, 1948; New York Herald Tribune Book Review June 3, 1951; New York Times Book Review August 28, 1948, June 10, 1951.

MORRISON, ARTHUR (1863-December 4, 1945). For autobiographical sketch and list of works and references, see TWENTIETH CENTURY AUTHORS, 1942.

* * *

Arthur Morrison died at Chalfont St. Peter in England at the age of eighty-two.

In retrospect, his novels of life in London's slums emerge as minor classics, of far more importance than his detective stories. V. S. Pritchett said of the former: "They are written from the inside and they have extraordinary merit; *The Hole in the Wall* strikes me as being one of the minor masterpieces of the last forty years."

ABOUT: London Times December 5, 1945; New Statesman and Nation January 22, 1944.

MORRISON, THEODORE (1901-), American poet and novelist, writes: "Born in Concord, N.H., in 1901, I pass (cheerfully, on my part) for a New Englander, though my father was born in Ohio and my mother in Philadelphia. I attended public schools in Concord, N.H., and in Brockton and Lynn,

John Brook

Mass., received my A.B. degree from Harvard in 1923, and an honorary Litt.D. from Middlebury College in 1951. I married Kathleen Johnston in Washington, D.C., in 1927, while I was putting in five years of editorial work for the Atlantic Monthly Company, after two years of teaching freshman English at Harvard. We have a daughter, Anne Guthrie, and a son, Robert Henry. In 1930 I came back to Harvard, eventually took over as director of the freshman English course in which I had first taught as an instructor, and am now lecturer on English, meaning that I teach upper class courses in composition. In 1932 I became director of the Middlebury College Writers' Conference at Bread Loaf, Vt. In this country I have managed to see something of the West coast and Florida, and outside it I have spent one summer in Europe and several in Nova Scotia. But most of my life since college has been spent in Cambridge, Mass., and in recent summers in Vermont. I have lived the outwardly quiet life of a teacher and writer, and any fruits of it that may be of any interest are in my books or in students whom I may have been fortunate enough to help or at least not to hinder.

"When I was younger I wrote a modest number of magazine articles and essays; one, 'Dover Beach Revisited,' which originally appeared in *Harper's,* has been frequently reprinted in collections of readings for college freshmen. But for twenty years or more I wrote chiefly verse; I was a poet or nothing, unless a novelist in preparation. At the same time I always loved what Dryden called "the other harmony of prose," and was concerned with prose fiction both in teaching and in thought. I served my apprenticeship to plot and characterization in narrative poems, or as reviewers sometimes called them, novels in verse. When I finally published an honest-to-God novel, *The Stones of the House,* I was fifty and more, a circumstance that did not escape comment, though it did not seem altogether unnatural to me. I expect that from here on in I shall try to become a novelist, not merely the author of the novel. But in a life of infinite leisure or boundless energy, one of the things I should certainly do would

be to go back to the latest of my verse narratives, *The Dream of Alcestis,* and try once more to make of it what I wish I had been able to make it when it appeared, what on some pages I almost think it threatened to become."

PRINCIPAL WORKS: *Poetry*—The Serpent in the Cloud, 1931; Notes of Death and Life, 1935; The Devious Way, 1944; Chaucer (ed. and tr.) 1949; The Dream of Alcestis, 1950. *Novel*—The Stones of the House, 1953.

ABOUT: Library Journal February 15, 1953; New York Herald Tribune Book Review March 1, 1953.

MORROW, Mrs. HONORÉ (MC CUE) WILLSIE (1880-April 12, 1940). For biographical sketch and list of works and references, see TWENTIETH CENTURY AUTHORS, 1942.

MORTON, HENRY CANOVA VOLLAM (1892-). For biographical sketch and list of earlier works and references, see TWENTIETH CENTURY AUTHORS, 1942.

* * *

H. V. Morton resigned as special writer for the *Daily Herald* in 1942. He now devotes full time to travel and to writing his books on travel and religious subjects. Morton was one of the few journalists who accompanied Winston Churchill in 1941 to his historic Atlantic meeting with Franklin D. Roosevelt. His travels have taken him in recent years to South Africa, the Near East, and Spain. Morton's readers, wrote Horace Sutton in the *Saturday Review of Literature,* "will certainly be able painlessly to absorb most of the guide-book details without guide-book tedium." His method, as reviewers have pointed out, is unique. His first-person narrative moves swiftly and easily. He never hurries the reader who accompanies him but also he never bores him with tedious stops. These qualities give his books what Wilmott Ragsdale, in the New York *Times,* called "the illusion of racy narrative."

ADDITIONAL WORKS: Atlantic Meeting, 1943; I Saw Two Englands, 1943; In Search of South Africa, 1948; In Search of London, 1951; In the Steps of Jesus, 1953; A Stranger in Spain, 1955.

MOTLEY, WILLARD (July 14, 1912-), American novelist, was born in Chicago, where he attended grammar and high school, and established something of a reputation as a football player. Half-back was his position, and "The Little Iron Man" his sports-page nickname. That among other things almost took him to college; but, as he phrases it, "my funds and my 135 pounds were not enough." So Motley set out to study the world, not books. "As far as

Lee

writing is concerned I went through several periods starting with trying to write short stories for pulp sports magazines," he said. "I even tried writing 'confessions.' Finally I moved to the slums of Chicago after being bored in the middle-class neighborhood in which I was reared and there discovered myself and the sort of thing I wanted to put on paper."

He has crossed the continent several times by various means—to New York on a bicycle, by jalopy to California where he lived some months on Catalina Island, by riding his thumb and the brake-rods all over the West. He has known the juke joints, the Negro sections, the hobo camps and the flophouses of several dozen states; he even served a jail sentence in Cheyenne, Wyo.—thirty days for vagrancy. Here, there, and everywhere he has worked at whatever job came to hand, being among other things a migratory laborer and ranch hand, short-order cook, dishwasher, salesman of Christmas cards, coal hiker, football coach, baker's helper, waiter, janitor, chauffeur, handy man, window washer, plasterer's helper, stock clerk, order clerk, animal caretaker, laboratory technician, "artist" (painting decorative brandy bottles), photographer, radio script writer, interviewer for the Chicago Housing Authority, and writer for the Office of Civilian Defense.

In 1947 his best-selling first novel, *Knock on Any Door,* was published. Representing some six years of actual writing, rewriting, and revising, the original draft ran to about 500,000 words; and many more than that were written, and excised, in putting together the final version of some 240,000 words. *Knock on Any Door,* not autobiographical, is a realistic story of a Chicago boy whose early tendencies towards decency were slowly beaten down by his contacts with life along Chicago's streets—among the poolrooms and honkytonks. The *New Republic* found it finer than anything by Dreiser—"there is a greater artistry here, more sensitivity to the trials of the human personality and more richness of detail and description. . . . Some may be repelled by the sordid lives it portrays, but none can come away from it without a feeling

of sympathy for the Italian youth turned gangster." An extraordinary and powerful new naturalistic talent herewith makes its debut in American letters," said the New York *Times.* The novel was made into a motion picture.

In 1951 a second novel was published, *We Fished All Night,* a story of three young men in Chicago politics and labor circles before and after the second World War. The New York *Times'* reviewer said, "Willard Motley has a magic with words and, to the extent that words make the result, lays you under a spell. He has an ear for speech, and his dialogue, while often gross, is speech as people speak it."

Willard Motley did not corner all the artistic talent in the family: an older brother, Archibald John Motley, Jr., studied painting in Paris on a 1929 Guggenheim fellowship, returned to have a one-man show in New York, and has attained stature in the art world.

"I like writing late at night," says Motley, "and when the story is coming good generally work from twelve to fourteen hours a day until I hit a cold spot. Then there are several days when I loaf and wait for the story to take hold of me again. I think that I most enjoy sitting in bars, restaurants, etc., watching people, listening in on their conversations and wondering about them, who they are, what their lives are."

PRINCIPAL WORKS: Knock on Any Door, 1947; We Fished All Night, 1951.

ABOUT: Warfel, H. R. American Novelists of Today; New York Herald Tribune Book Review October 7, 1951; New York Times Book Review July 13, 1947; Saturday Review of Literature February 14, 1948.

MOTT, FRANK LUTHER (April 4, 1886-), American social historian, writes: "I was born in a small Quaker community near the town of What Cheer, Iowa. Two years later my father, David C. Mott, bought the *Patriot,* a weekly paper in What Cheer. My first newspaper job was folding papers after school on the *Patriot's* press day. Thereafter I worked

on my father's various newspapers while going to school, learning to set type by hand when I was eleven years old, in the office of the Tipton (Iowa) *Advertiser.*

"Finishing high school at Audubon, Iowa, I attended Simpson College three years and the University of Chicago one year, receiving a bachelor's degree from Chicago in 1907. I went to Chicago to study law; but in going to my law classes I had to pass the open windows of the university press, and the smell of printer's ink on damp sheets made me so homesick for printing offices that I gave up the law for journalism.

"After ten years of active newspaper work in Iowa, I decided to get into educational work. I had the crazy idea that life in a college faculty would afford more time for writing than newspaper work had. I was to learn that when you are afraid to let go of your full-time job, the only way you can write is by sacrificing your leisure. That is not as bad a way of life, however, as it sounds.

"But I got a master's degree at Columbia, and at long last a doctor's, and then headed the English department at Simpson for a couple of years, until I got a bid from the State University of Iowa. I was there twenty years, first in the English department, and then as director of the School of Journalism. I was dean of the University of Missouri's School of Journalism nine years, becoming emeritus in 1951. I was in France and Japan during parts of 1945-47 on War Department missions.

"Began writing short stories about the time I left active newspapering, but my output in this kind is pretty lean. My best known stories were 'The Man With the Good Face,' published in the *Midland,* O'Brien, and many anthologies, and 'The Phantom Flivver,' a *Saturday Evening Post* story. I was associated with John T. Frederick in editing and publishing the *Midland,* 1925-31.

"About 1925 the fascination which magazines had always held for me since childhood days when free copies of the best of them came to the printing office and piled up in my room at home, resulted in a project for a comprehensive history of American periodicals. Three fat volumes of that work are now on the shelves, a fourth is in the works, and two more are projected. A Pulitzer prize for American history, given to the second and third volumes, was encouraging. I took time out to do a history of the American newspaper, and then, to round out my own study of popular literature, I did a history of best sellers in America called *Golden Multitudes.*

"I like digging in libraries, digging in the garden, painting in oils, reciting verse, observing the tremendous energy of my grandchildren."

PRINCIPAL WORKS: Rewards of Reading, 1926; History of American Magazines, 1930; American Journalism: A History of Newspapers in the United States, 1690-1940, 1941; Golden Multitudes, 1947; The News in America, 1952.

ABOUT: Current Biography 1941; Editor and Publisher March 17, 1951; Publishers' Weekly May 6, 1939; Saturday Review of Literature May 6, 1939.

MOTTRAM, RALPH HALE (October 30, 1883-). For autobiographical sketch and list of earlier works and references, see TWENTIETH CENTURY AUTHORS, 1942.

* * *

R. H. Mottram concluded his sketch in the 1942 volume with the statement that he was prepared to back his convictions "as a reserve officer if necessary." Ten years later he writes from Norwich, England: "Since those words were written it has been necessary. I served in the Home Guard until general release and watched my sons take an active part in the R.A.F. and Royal Navy. We still feel the use of force is futile, but that to stand aside and watch what we should have had to watch was worse than futile. Now I am fit only for Civil Defence but have undertaken that."

ADDITIONAL WORKS: *Fiction*—The Corbells at War, 1943; Visit of the Princess, 1946; The Gentleman of Leisure, 1948; Come to the Bower, 1949; One Hundred and Twenty-Eight Witnesses, 1951; The Part That Is Missing, 1952; Over the Wall, 1955. *Miscellaneous*—Buxton, the Liberator (biography) 1946; Through Five Generations: History of the Butterley Company (with C. Coote) 1950; The Broads (topography) 1952; Window Seat, or Life Observed, 1954.

ABOUT: Mottram, R. H. Window Seat, or Life Observed.

MOWRER, EDGAR ANSEL (March 8, 1892-). For biographical sketch and list of earlier works and references, see TWENTIETH CENTURY AUTHORS, 1942.

* * *

Edgar Ansel Mowrer was deputy director of the Office of Facts and Figures, later the Office of War Information, from 1941 to 1943, and traveled widely in Europe and Asia during World War II. His political analyses, which appear in his books and in magazine articles, are highly regarded as shrewd, sound, and stimulating. He strikes sparks, as one reviewer pointed out, and challenges the reader to think. In his *Nightmare of American Foreign Policy* he criticized the international policies of the United States from 1918 to 1948 in what Charles Rolo, in the *Atlantic,* described as "a biting and admirably succinct study of the mistakes made between wars." In *Challenge and Decision* he urged that the United States take the lead in forming a Peace Coalition and an ultimate federation of non-Communist countries.

Mowrer lives in Washington, D.C.

ADDITIONAL WORKS: The Nightmare of American Foreign Policy, 1948; Challenge and Decision, 1950.

ABOUT: Saturday Review of Literature November 6, 1948; Time January 22, 1945.

MUIR, EDWIN (May 15, 1887-   ). For autobiographical sketch and list of earlier works and references, see TWENTIETH CENTURY AUTHORS, 1942.

* * *

To American readers who knew Edwin Muir best for his translations (with his wife Willa Muir) of the novels and stories of Franz Kafka, the publication of his *Collected Poems* in 1953 came as something of a revelation. In these poems—"unspectacular in outward show," Horace Gregory called them —Muir demonstrated a directness and meditative power so profound and moving that Gregory said of him, "Since the death of W. B. Yeats, no mature poet of Celtic origins has made so impressive a contribution to modern literature." Richard Eberhart points out that Muir is "a philosophical poet. He serves the art not as an innovator . . . but as a wise man speaking plain English, preserving a simple diction. . . ."

Muir lives in Dalkeith, Scotland, where since 1950 he has been Warden of Newbattle Abbey College.

ADDITIONAL WORKS: The Narrow Place (poems) 1943; Poles in Uniform, 1943; The Voyage, and Other Poems, 1946; Essays on Literature and Society, 1949; The Labyrinth, 1949; Collected Poems, 1953; Autobiography, 1954.

ABOUT: Muir, E. Autobiography; New York Times Book Review April 5, 1953; Poetry January 1950.

MUIR, JOHN (April 21, 1838-December 24, 1914). For biographical sketch and list of works and references, see TWENTIETH CENTURY AUTHORS, 1942.

* * *

ADDITIONAL WORK: The Wilderness World of John Muir (ed. E. W. Teale) 1954.

ABOUT: Brooks, V. W. A Chilmark Miscellany; Colby, W. E. *Introduction to* Muir's Studies in the Sierra (1950); Hunt, R. D. California's Stately Hall of Fame; Wolfe, L. M. Son of the Wilderness; Audubon Magazine May 1945; Hobbies August 1951; Natural History February 1946; Reader's Digest September 1949; Scientific Monthly February 1946; Time July 30, 1945.

*MUKERJI, DHAN GHOPAL (July 6, 1890-July 14, 1936). For biographical sketch and list of works and references, see TWENTIETH CENTURY AUTHORS, 1942.

* mŏŏ′kĕr jē

MULFORD, CLARENCE EDWARD (February 3, 1883-   ). For autobiographical sketch and list of works and references, see TWENTIETH CENTURY AUTHORS, 1942.

* * *

Hopalong Cassidy, the stalwart western hero created by Clarence Mulford back in 1907, seventeen years before the author had even taken a trip West, has by now become a national hero, thanks to motion pictures and television. Hopalong was "reborn" in 1934, when Paramount Pictures cast a former silent picture star, Bill Boyd, in the title role and filmed a series of Hopalong pictures, all following a strict formula of hard-riding action and high-minded heroic behavior on the hero's part. As of 1949 sixty-six Hopalong pictures had been made, although Mulford had written only twenty-eight Hopalong books. A new impetus was given the Hopalong craze with television, which brought the Hopalong films into millions of American homes.

Hopalong's creator, whose name is probably not known to more than a handful of his fans, lives quietly in Fryeberg, Me., with his fine collection of Western Americana and of ship and stage coach models.

ABOUT: Life September 12, 1949.

MULLER, HERBERT JOSEPH (July 7, 1905-   ), American critic and scholar, writes: "My chief stock in trade as a teacher and a writer has been a catholicity of interest, unhampered — or undirected—by any felt need of finality, ultimate certainty, the absolute. I am pleased to label it liberalism but cannot represent it as a hard-won wisdom. With me it is a matter of simple temperament; so I assume it was formed in my simple, unexciting, abnormally normal youth.

"I was born of middle-class parents in the middle-class suburb of Mamaroneck, N.Y. When my memories begin we were living in the Bronx, where I grew up happily and heedlessly. Because of my father's poor health we moved to the country every few years, to farm for a year; in the country an innocent boy from the Bronx learned the facts of life but still suffered no growing pains to speak of. At length I entered Cornell University, with the familiar vague dream of becoming a writer and almost as vague an ambition to be a high school teacher of Spanish. Not until my graduation in 1925 did I discover that what I really wanted to do was teach English in college. I thereupon managed to return to Cornell for an A.M., and in 1926 became an instructor in English there. Meanwhile the death of my father had obliged me to work on the side. I continued to spend my summers working in New York, since I contributed to the support of my family and instructors' salaries were especially low at that time. I enjoyed my various jobs— in factories, banks, railroads, brokerage houses, and large corporations—if only because they gave me the comforting knowledge that my enthusiasm for the academic life was a genuine preference, not a mere incapacity for 'practical' affairs.

"In 1932 I acquired the necessary Ph.D. Two years later I married Janet Bailey, a former student who had always smiled at the right moments in my class, and the next year moved to Purdue University, with which I have been connected ever since. In 1939 a Guggenheim fellowship finally enabled me to travel—my chief pleasure apart from writing. When the outbreak of the war forced us to leave France we went to Mexico, which remains one of my favorite summering places. After Pearl Harbor I spent two years in Washington, one as an administrative officer in the State Department, another on the editorial staff of a confidential weekly magazine issued by the War Production Board. (It now appears that I was one of the few people in Washington who never met either Alger Hiss or Whittaker Chambers.) In 1946-47 I served as visiting lecturer in American literature at the University of Istanbul, and in 1951-52 returned for a similar engagement, under a Fulbright grant.

"As a writer, my course has also been unplanned, and might be called either spontaneous or haphazard. The interest in the novel and in principles of literary criticism that produced my first book, *Modern Fiction,* led me naturally into the backgrounds of modern literature, to such subjects as semantics, the relations of science and literature, and the philosophy of modern science; the gradual outcome was *Science and Criticism.* My short book on Thomas Wolfe was written under

contract but grew out of an earlier chapter, as well as a memorable few days I spent with Wolfe. My latest work, *The Uses of the Past,* resulted from my experience in Istanbul. I became fascinated by Byzantine history, for its own sake (it is a hard subject to work into an ordinary conversation); my effort to make sense of this strange history led me back into the Greco-Roman world, to other societies, and ultimately to the philosophy of history.

"Since I remain a professor of English, I am a little embarrassed to find that I have unwittingly become a kind of miniature H. G. Wells. I hope to become a simple literary critic again. At the moment, however, I am absorbed in the extraordinarily rich, diverse history of Asia Minor, the great bridge and battleground between East and West."

PRINCIPAL WORKS: Modern Fiction, 1937; Science and Criticism, 1943; Thomas Wolfe, 1947; The Uses of the Past, 1952.

MUMFORD, LEWIS (October 19, 1895-). For autobiographical sketch and list of earlier works and references, see TWENTIETH CENTURY AUTHORS, 1942.

* * *

Lewis Mumford writes from Amenia, N.Y.: "From 1935 onward I worked steadily at the Renewal of Life Series, whose four volumes were not completed till the publication of *The Conduct of Life* in 1951. During this period I became increasingly preoccupied with the rising menace of fascism and departed from the usual neutralism and pacifism of the Thirties by publicly urging, as early as 1935, that the United States declare its intention of fighting on the side of the democracies, in case of attack by any of the totalitarian powers. This attitude crystallized in an article, 'Call to Arms,' which came out in the *New Republic* in May 1938, four months before Munich; and it was further developed in a series of articles, pamphlets, and books, notably *Men Must Act* (1939) and *Faith for Living* (1940). In the latter year I was a member of the City of Man group, formed by G. A. Borgese, and helped write its original manifesto.

"After the war I was concerned to create an understanding of the moral problems and military embarrassments resulting from our wartime decision to adopt the fascist method of extermination bombing, a decision made even more fatal by the later invention of the atom bomb; and since 1945 I have published a series of articles on this subject, mainly in *Air Affairs.* During this period I took an increasingly active part in education, first as a member of the Board of Higher Education in New York, 1935-1937; then as member of the Commission on Teacher Education of the American Council on Education, 1938-1944; as professor of humanities at Stanford University, 1942-1944; as visiting professor in architecture, North Carolina State College, 1948-1952; and visiting professor of land and city planning, University of Pennsylvania, 1951-. Though my 'Skyline' in the *New Yorker* has stereotyped me, for many people, as an architectural critic, my main work during the past fifteen years has been within the fields of education, politics, religion and philosophy. In 1947 I gave the Earl Lectures at the Pacific Institute of Religion, and in 1951 the Bampton Lectures at Columbia University."

* * *

Estimates of Louis Mumford's work range widely from James T. Farrell's judgment that it is characterized by "fuzziness, obscurantism, mixture of the grandiose and the trivial," to Van Wyck Brooks' view that "he carries on, like no one else living in America today, the tradition of Emerson, Whitman, and William James." Mumford's major achievement up to this time has been his work in the philosophy of civilization, the four volumes of the Renewal of Life Series *(Technics and Civilization, The Culture of Cities, The Condition of Man,* and *The Conduct of Life).* Here he makes his urgent plea for the "transformation of the self and of all organizations," for the "moral renewal" which can save the world from calamity.

In a very different vein from Mumford's philosophical writings is his *Green Memories,* an "affectionate and restrained" biography of his son Geddes, who was killed in action, at nineteen, in World War II.

ADDITIONAL WORKS: The Condition of Man, 1944; City Development, 1945; Values for Survival, 1946; Green Memories, 1947; The Conduct of Life, 1951; Art and Technics, 1952; In the Name of Sanity, 1954.

ABOUT: Farrell, J. T. League of Frightened Philistines; Commonweal October 30, 1942; Current Biography 1940; Fortnightly December 1946; Harper's June 1952; New Republic April 22, 1945; Newsweek May 22, 1944; Saturday Review of Literature September 22, 1951; Time June 8, 1942, December 13, 1948.

MUNDY, TALBOT (April 23, 1879-August 5, 1940). For autobiographical sketch and list of works and references, see TWENTIETH CENTURY AUTHORS, 1942.

* * *

ADDITIONAL WORK: I Say Sunrise, 1947.

MUNRO, HECTOR HUGH ("Saki") (December 18, 1870-November 13, 1916). For biographical sketch and list of works and references, see TWENTIETH CENTURY AUTHORS, 1942.

* * *

ABOUT: Gregory, I. Lady Gregory's Journals, 1916-1930.

MUNRO, NEIL (June 3, 1864-December 22, 1930). For biographical sketch and list of works and references, see TWENTIETH CENTURY AUTHORS, 1942.

MUNROE, KIRK (September 15, 1850-June 16, 1930). For biographical sketch and list of works and references, see TWENTIETH CENTURY AUTHORS, 1942.

MUNSON, GORHAM BERT (May 26, 1896-). For autobiographical sketch and list of earlier works and references, see TWENTIETH CENTURY AUTHORS, 1942.

* * *

Gorham Munson continues to combine the activities of author, editor, and teacher. He is vice-president and editor of the publishing firm of Hermitage House, in New York. He conducts courses in professional writing at the New School for Social Research and teaches summers at various writers' conferences. Most of his own published work in recent years has been on the subject of writing. His *The Written Word*, subtitled "How to Write Readable Prose," was praised as a practical and valuable guide for the beginning writer, Joseph Henry Jackson finding it "the best book yet written for the individual who wants to write . . . for publication and who is willing to work hard."

ADDITIONAL WORKS: Aladdin's Lamp: The Wealth of the American People, 1945; The Written Word, 1949; The Writer's Workshop Companion, 1951; Best Advice on How to Write (ed.) 1952.

*MUNTHE, AXEL MARTIN FREDRIK (1857-February 11, 1949). For biographical sketch and list of works and references, see TWENTIETH CENTURY AUTHORS, 1942.

* * *

Axel Munthe died at ninety-one, in the Royal Palace at Stockholm, where for ten years he had been the house guest of King Gustav V. San Michele, his home in Capri which gave its title to his best known book, was converted into a museum, with proceeds going to charity.

* mŭn'tĕ

Munthe's many-sided character has been described in *Nation and Athenaeum* as being that of a "realist and mystic, scientist and poet, caustic philosopher and kindly essayist. Above all he is the apostle of pity."

ABOUT: Munthe, G. & Uezkull, G. The Story of Axel Munthe; France Illustration February 26, 1949; London Times February 12, 1949; New York Times February 12, 1949.

MURPHY, GARDNER, (July 8, 1895-   ), American psychologist, was born in Chillicothe, Ohio, the son of Edgar Gardner and Maud (King) Murphy. He was educated at the Hotchkiss School in Connecticut, at Yale (B.A. 1916), at Harvard (M.A. 1917), and at Columbia (Ph.D. 1923). In 1917 he interrupted his graduate studies in psychology to serve in France for two years with the A.E.F. Murphy began his teaching career while a graduate student at Columbia in 1921, with the rank of lecturer. In 1925 he became an instructor, in 1929 an assistant professor. In 1940 he left Columbia to become professor of psychology at City College in New York. Murphy is now director of research for the Menninger Foundation in Topeka, Kans. He has been married since 1926 to the former Lois Barclay, who frequently collaborates with him on his books. They have two children.

In 1932 Murphy received the Butler Medal from Columbia University for his studies in experimental social psychology. He is a member of many scholarly societies and in 1943-44 served as president of the American Psychological Association. Murphy has not sought to become a popularizer of psychology. The largest body of his writing is serious scholarship, and it is as a specialist in personality study that he has won his reputation. In recent years, he has become increasingly interested in social psychology. Typical of his recent work is *Human Nature and Enduring Peace,* a symposium which he edited for the Society for the Psychological Study of Social Issues. In this book Murphy and a group of fellow psychologists attempted to apply their specialized knowledge to politics and public affairs. Ordway Tead described the work, in *Survey Graphic,* as "psychological insight of a high order brought to play upon the most urgent problems at home and abroad, with the proffer of specific suggestions of great utility in political, international, educational, and related fields." More recently Murphy and his wife visited India on a UNESCO mission to study social tensions. He reported the results of their trip in *In the Minds of Men,* a thoughtful and thought-provoking book

which Louis Fischer praised as "a uniquely absorbing volume that delves deeply and profitably into the lives of 360 million Indians."

Murphy's studies in human psychology, particularly in personality, have been widely praised for their sound and substantial scholarship and for the lucid and readable style in which they are written. He has summed up his work in this field as follows: "To write about personality in such a way as to help in clarifying the little that we know and to show its possible relations to the vast and confused domain that we do not yet understand—this is my aim." In the judgment of his students and his fellow psychologists, he has fully realized that aim.

PRINCIPAL WORKS: Historical Introduction to Modern Psychology, 1929; (with L. B. Murphy) Experimental Social Psychology, 1931; (with F. Jensen) Approaches to Personality, 1932; General Psychology, 1933; (with R. Likert) Public Opinion and the Individual, 1938; Human Nature and Enduring Peace (ed.) 1945; Personality: A Biosocial Approach to Origins and Structure, 1947; Introduction to Psychology, 1951; In the Minds of Men, 1953.

ABOUT: Hackett, F. On Judging Books; National Cyclopedia of American Biography (1952).

MURRAY, GILBERT (January 2, 1866-   ). For biographical sketch and list of earlier works and references, see TWENTIETH CENTURY AUTHORS, 1942.

* * *

In retirement at his home on Boar's Hill, near Oxford, Gilbert Murray continues active, reading, writing, translating, and annotating. In 1950 he completed his translation of Aristophanes' comedy *The Birds.* From time to time he returns to Oxford to lecture on classical subjects or on that other favorite interest of his, the need for an international organization to promote world peace. In 1941, when he received the Order of Merit, the London *Times* commented that he "might equally have earned it by his success in transmitting the light of Hellas to a generation that is forgetting the Greek tongue—or by the noble failure of his long works for peace." The photographer Alfred Eisenstaedt who photographed him for *Life* magazine in 1952 described him as "a man with a great feeling for other people—a very great man and very humble."

ADDITIONAL WORKS: Greek Studies, 1946; From the League to the UN, 1948; Stoic, Christian and Humanist, 1950.

ABOUT: Life January 14, 1952; Time March 13, 1950.

MURRAY, THOMAS C. (1873-), Irish playwright, who prefers to be known as T. C. Murray, writes: "In January, 1873 I first

Lafayette, Dublin

saw the light. I was the seventh of a family of which four others were destined to follow. The place was the small town of Macroom, Co. Cork. There I had my early schooling. In '91 I went to St. Patrick's College, Dublin, to study for a career of teaching. After two years in St. Patrick's I was sent adrift a fully fledged schoolmaster. I taught in Cork City and in several rural schools. During these years I wrote continuously for professional journals and reviews on various aspects of education in Ireland. My interest in drama was first awakened during my college course through a study of Racine's *Athalie,* one of the prescribed French texts in the curriculum. To this day I find myself on entering any great cathedral recalling its majestic opening line—*Into this gracious temple thus I come,/Prostrate, adoring.*

"I followed with intense interest the Irish literary movement which led to the foundation of the National Theatre. In 1910 I wrote *Birthright* for the Abbey Theatre. Its instant success both in Dublin and in London astonished me. On the first American tour of the Abbey company which began in Boston, it formed with short plays by Synge and Lady Gregory the opening bill. Professor Weygandt in his book, *Irish Plays and Playwrights,* wrote—'Many who saw *Birthright* in America were moved by it more than by any other play in the repertoire of the company, and I have heard more than one whose supreme interest is the theatre say that it was the best play new to America presented there during the winter of 1911-12.'

"*Maurice Harte,* which had its first production at the Royal Court Theatre, London, in 1912, prompted W. B. Yeats to say— 'If Mr. Murray gives us more plays equal in intensity to *Maurice Harte,* then we shall deserve, perhaps, as much attention from history as any contemporary theatre.'

"In 1915 I was appointed headmaster of the Model Schools, Inchicore. There followed a succession of plays, *Spring, Aftermath, The Pipe in the Fields, Autumn Fire, The Blind Wolf, A Flutter of Wings, Michaelmas Eve, Illumination,* and a novel *Spring Horizon.*

"In response to an invitation from Yeats and A.E. (George Russell), I became one of the Foundation members of the Irish Academy of Letters of which George Bernard Shaw was president, and for many years I was a member of the Film Censorship Appeal Board. At fifty-nine, after seventeen years as Headmaster of the Model Schools, I retired. Two years ago [1950] the National University conferred on me an honour of which I was painfully aware I was undeserving, the Doctorate of Letters. Should the Author of Life extend my lease a little longer I shall in mid-January '53 have reached the eightieth milestone on my pilgrimage.

"An unadventurous career, but with the ever pressing cares of school, and of a family of five, a life which has had its measure of mortal joys and sorrows."

PRINCIPAL WORKS: *Plays*—The Wheel of Fortune, 1909; Birthright, 1910; Maurice Harte, 1912; Sovereign Love, 1917; The Briery Gap, 1917; Spring, 1918; Aftermath, 1922; Autumn Fire, 1923; The Pipe in the Fields, 1927; The Blind Wolf, 1928; A Flutter of Wings, 1929; Michaelmas Eve, 1932; A Stag at Bay, 1934; A Spot in the Sun, 1938; Illumination, 1939. *Novel*—Spring Horizon, 1937.

ABOUT: Hoehn, M. (ed.) Catholic Authors, I; Morgan, A. E. Tendencies of Modern English Drama; Robinson, L. The Irish Theatre; Weygandt, C. Irish Plays and Playwrights.

"MURRAY HILL." See HOLLIDAY, R. C.

MURRY, JOHN MIDDLETON (August 6, 1889-). For autobiographical sketch and list of earlier works and references, see TWENTIETH CENTURY AUTHORS, 1942.

* * *

John Middleton Murry writes from Diss, England: "In December 1952 a postscript is required. I became a pacifist—I now believe I was mistaken—during the Second World War, and edited the pacifist journal *Peace News* from 1940 to 1946. I am ashamed to say I had no conception of the horrors of Nazism. Belsen opened my eyes: and I saw that pacifism, however sincere, is merely playing into the hands of Fascist or Communist totalitarianism. However, I was more fortunate than most pacifists in that my main effort during the war was to found an agricultural community. This, after many vicissitudes, survives and flourishes."

In 1951 Middleton Murry published a new edition of Katherine Mansfield's letters. This volume includes a number of personal and intimate letters which had not been included in the extensive collection published in 1929.

ADDITIONAL WORKS: Christocracy, 1942; Adam and Eve, 1944; The Free Society, 1948; The Challenge of Schweitzer, 1948; Looking Before and After, 1948; The Mystery of Keats, 1949; Katherine Mansfield and Other Literary Portraits, 1949; John Clare, and Other Studies 1950; The Conquest of Death, 1951; Katherine Mansfield's Letters to John Middleton Murry (ed.) 1951; Community Farm, 1952; Jonathan Swift: A Critical Biography, 1954.

*MUSIL, ROBERT (1880-1942), Austrian novelist, was born in Klagenfurt, Carinthia, Austria, and educated at a cadet school. At  the age of twenty-six he published his first novel, in German, which dealt with the inner and the outward conflicts of adolescence. It was warmly received, and having already given up a lectureship in civil engineering, Musil similarly abandoned an academic career in philosophy to devote himself to writing. He had had a variety of educations—military, engineering, philosophy —and also a variety of jobs—editor, civil servant, drama critic. "But even a part-time job as librarian in Vienna proved to be so damaging to his writing that it had to be given up," recalls his stepdaughter, Mrs. Anne Rosenthal of Philadelphia. What resulted was the support of Musil and his work by contributions from numbers of people in a systematic way; he accepted this as necessary for the artist.

Musil published two collections of short stories in German, in 1911 and 1923, an expressionistic drama in 1921, and a comedy in 1923. His most serious work, however, was The Man without Qualities, which appeared in German in 1930 (Vol. I), 1933 (Vol. II), and 1942 (Vol. III). After the Anschluss he went voluntarily into exile and his books were banned in Germany. In Switzerland he continued to work on The Man without Qualities, until his death in 1942 in Geneva. On this book he spent twenty years. It is of enormous length: 365 pages were brought out in English translation in 1953, and were said to be only one-half of the first volume and about one-fifth of the total. In a future definitive edition, twenty unrevised chapters will be included.

The author was called by the London Times Literary Supplement, "the most im-

* moo'sil

portant novelist writing in German in this half-century" and "one of the least known writers of the age." Musil himself had not the slightest doubt about his own talent and felt that recognition of his books might have to wait one hundred years. Of the English publication of The Man without Qualities, the first of four projected volumes, V. S. Pritchell commented in the New Statesman and Nation. "It is a wonderful and prolonged firework display, a well-peopled comedy of ideas, on the one hand; on the other, an infiltration into the base areas of what we call 'the contemporary predicament.'" Musil's style is "closely argued," as Commonweal put it, adding, "Yet he is consistently penetrating, observant, and witty, and he is often refreshingly epigrammatic." "He is digressive and even prolix," wrote the New York Herald Tribune Book Review. "He often seems to be emptying his mind (or notebook) of all the essays he ever intended to write instead of busying himself with his novel, but he usually has something to say that sounds fresh and provocative." His work is often compared, in range and intelligence, with Proust and Joyce. "Readers expect one to tell them of life itself, not of life as it is reflected inside the heads of literature and of men," wrote Musil in a notebook of 1932. "But that is justifiable only in so far as that reflection is merely a faint transfer, a worn convention. I am trying to give them the original."

PRINCIPAL WORK: The Man without Qualities, I, 1953, II, 1954; Young Törless, 1955.

ABOUT: Columbia Dictionary of Modern European Literature; Newsweek June 8, 1953; Saturday Review of Literature June 6, 1953.

MUZZEY, DAVID SAVILLE (October 9, 1870-). For biographical sketch and list of earlier works and references, see TWENTIETH CENTURY AUTHORS, 1942.

* * *

David S. Muzzey has been emeritus professor of history at Columbia University since 1940. He lives in Yonkers, N.Y. In recent years he has written textbooks and articles on history and ethics (he is leader emeritus of the Ethical Culture Society). In 1951, in Ethics as a Religion, he wrote what one reviewer called "the best and most lucid statement of humanistic idealism as a substitute for supernaturalistic theology to appear in recent times."

ADDITIONAL WORKS: (with Krout, J. A.) America, A World Power, 1898-1944, 1944; A History of Our Country, 1945; Ethics as a Religion, 1951.

MUZZY, BERTHA. See BOWER, B. M.

MYERS, GUSTAVUS (March 20, 1872-December 7, 1942). For autobiographical sketch and list of works and references, see TWENTIETH CENTURY AUTHORS, 1942.

* * *

Gustavus Myers died at his home in New York City, after a long illness, at seventy. He never recovered from a collapse suffered upon the completion, four months before his death, of the *History of Bigotry in the United States*, on which he had worked for seventeen years. He had been obliged to divide his time between the painstaking research on which he built his books and the journalistic writing from which he made a living.

The New York *Times* observed that his work "was wholly without the flame and the thunder that make of the literature of exposure a popular success. His own method was one of exhaustive and patient research summed up in straightforward narrative which let the facts speak for themselves."

Correction: In the third printing of TWENTIETH CENTURY AUTHORS, 1942, Myers' death date was incorrectly given as December 7, 1943.

ABOUT: New York Times December 9, 1942; Saturday Review of Literature July 31, 1943.

MYERS, JOHN MYERS (January 11, 1906-), American novelist and regionalist, writes: "I was born in Northport, Long Island, the off-shoot of Southern parents and of Irish ancestry. In subsequent years, given to some moving around on the parental part, I got my early education from the family library and running loose in the woods. Later I had to do with several colleges, traveled about both in this country and abroad, and found a number of ways of making an indifferent living. These eventually included newspaper work, farming, advertising, soldiering, editing, college teaching and publishing. Somewhere in the course of those pursuits I married Charlotte Shanahan of Louisville, and I have two youngsters as lagniappe for that good fortune.

"I had early determined to write, and worked at it, but it took quite a few years for my capacities to come within spitting distance of my ambition. Meanwhile I had branched out from the general study of literature into sundry particular fields. Several of these have directly influenced all my work.

"Interest in the classics and Celtic folklore pushed me from two directions into a bout with medieval literature, of which *The Harp and the Blade* was the chief result. Enthusiasm for Elizabethan rogue and pamphlet literature in general turned into *Out on Any Limb*. A liking for the literature of the old Southern frontier was translated as *The Wild Yazoo*.

"Although these have been referred to as historical novels by most reviewers, nothing was further from the intent, or, I believe, the fact. No historical characters or events played a part in any of them, and in each case the effort made was to reproduce the literary spirit of the period rather than to create costume pageantry of the more usual sort.

"This general aim was carried to its logical conclusion in *Silverlock*, in which literary criticism, dealing with a score of literatures and thirty centuries, was the driving force of an adventure story. The form chosen for this romance, and for two, in particular, of the novels, was vernacular narrative, illuminated at intervals with verse.

"For my most recent enthusiasm, the written history and lore of the West, I have so far not too much to show, though I have contributed a couple of factual chronicles to this body of writing: *The Alamo* and *The Last Chance: Tombstone's Early Years*. It is my feeling that the makings of a great cyclic literature lie virtually undisturbed here; the stuff is so rich in the potentialities of its matter, while the achieved fulfillment, my own work by no means excepted, has been deadly pedestrian. However, I believe I have discovered a way to wake the fire in one corner of this great wood, and am now engaged in giving it a try in a work tentatively called 'Tales of Rough Country'."

PRINCIPAL WORKS: The Harp and the Blade, 1941; Out on Any Limb, 1942; The Wild Yazoo, 1947; The Alamo, 1948; Silverlock, 1949; The Last Chance: Tombstone's Early Years, 1950; Doc Holliday, 1955.

ABOUT: Warfel, H. R. American Novelists of Today.

MYERS, LEOPOLD HAMILTON (September 6, 1881-April 8, 1944). For autobiographical sketch and list of works and references, see TWENTIETH CENTURY AUTHORS, 1942.

* * *

Leopold Myers died at his home at Marlow, Buckinghamshire, England, at sixty-two.

It has been said that the publication of Lady Murasaki's *Tale of the Genji* in English "released" Myers' best work by providing him with the setting of the Mogul Empire in which his last four books were laid. The author's "liberalism of thought, ardor for justice, and sympathy in contact" have been praised by T. W. Earp. He was handsome, elegant, and a delightful conversationalist.

Two of the last series of books, *Strange Glory* and *Pool of Vishnu*, have been called modern fiction on its highest level, and, in the opinion of R. E. Roberts, Myers' "grasp of modern problems, personal and political, his insight into character, his delicate sense of the values of life, his tolerant justice . . . are, I think, so remarkable that he can be named with the greatest of those who have chosen to express their ideas in fiction."

ABOUT: Commonweal October 19, 1945; London Times April 10, 1944; New Statesman and Nation April 29, 1944; New York Times April 11, 1944.

*NABOKOV, VLADIMIR VLADIMIROVICH (1899-   ), Russian-born novelist, poet, and memoirist, was born in St.

Clayton Smith

Petersburg, into a family of old Russian nobility. His paternal grandfather had been state minister of justice under two czars; his maternal great-grandfather a president of the Academy of Medicine; and his father a famous liberal statesman, one of the leaders and founders of the Constitutional-Democratic (Liberal) Party and a member of the First Duma. Young Vladimir was educated at the Prince Tenishev Gymnasium in St. Petersburg and at Trinity College, Cambridge University. He graduated from Cambridge in 1922, having specialized in Romance and Slavic languages. Between 1922 and 1940 Nabokov lived in Germany and in France. His main activity during this period was writing poetry and prose. His first novels were published in Russian and in German and later works were translated into French, Swedish, Italian, Czech, Spanish and English. All Nabokov's earlier works were written in Russian, and he gradually emerged

* nä′bô kôf

as a major émigré Russian writer (his books were banned in the Soviet Union). In 1940 he came to the United States and in 1945 he became an American citizen. Since coming to America, Nabokov has switched from the Russian language to English and all the books that he has published since his arrival in this country have been written in English. His style is rich and lucid. George Snell wrote that his memoir, *Conclusive Evidence,* "is one of the most accomplished stylistic achievements of any émigré writer; in fact it would be difficult to think of two or three writers to whom English is native who could match it in any degree." More than one reviewer has compared him to Joseph Conrad, as a foreign-born writer who was able to master and write in English. Nabokov himself dislikes the comparison. "I am not at all displeased in a literary way," he comments: "That isn't what I mean. The point is Conrad had never been a Polish writer, he started right in as an English writer. I had had a number of books in Russian before I wrote in English."

Nabokov combines his literary career with college teaching. In the summer of 1941 he taught Russian literature and a course in creative writing at Stanford University. From 1941 to 1948 he taught at Wellesley College. In the latter year he accepted an associate professorship in Russian literature at Cornell University, on the faculty of which he has remained ever since. Of the three courses he teaches, two are given in English and one of these is devoted to the European novel. During the spring semester of 1952 he was a visiting lecturer at Harvard, where he taught Humanities 2 ("The Novel") and Russian literature. In 1943 and again in 1952 he was awarded a Guggenheim fellowship for creative writing. In 1951 he received an award from the American Academy and National Institute of Arts and Letters. He is married and has one son.

Nabokov's greatest interest, next to literature, is entomology. He is a recognized authority on certain groups of diurnal lepidoptera and has claimed the discovery of several new species of butterfly since he has come to the United States. In 1948 he was research fellow in entomology at Harvard's Museum of Comparative Zoology, and in 1949 he published a study with the formidable title *Neartic Members of the Genus Lycaeides Hubner.* His less scientific but, for the general public, infinitely more charming and readable essays and short stories appear frequently in the *New Yorker, Partisan Review,* the *Atlantic Monthly,* and *Harper's.* He also translates from the Russian and has published translations of the poetry of Pushkin and Lermontov.

PRINCIPAL WORKS: Camera Obscura (in U.S. Laughter in the Dark) 1936; Despair, 1937; The Real Life of Sebastian Knight, 1941; Nikolai Gogol, 1944; Bend Sinister, 1947; Nine Stories, 1947; Conclusive Evidence: A Memoir, 1951.

ABOUT: Columbia Dictionary of Modern European Literature; Nabokov, V. Conclusive Evidence; Books Abroad Autumn 1954; New York Times Book Review July 1, 1951; Time June 16, 1947.

NAMIER, Sir LEWIS BERNSTEIN (June 1888-), British historian, was born in Russia. He attended school in England, including Balliol College, Oxford, where Arnold J. Toynbee was also studying at the time. The year 1913 found Namier engaged in business in the United States, but when World War I broke out, he joined the British Twentieth Royal Fusiliers as a private. In 1915 he moved on to war jobs in the British propaganda and information offices, and between 1918 and 1920 served in the political intelligence department of the Foreign Office. Except for another two-year period in business, he then pursued historical research, writing and teaching, lecturing at Oxford (1920-21) and at Manchester University (1931-53). Between 1929 and 1931 he was Political Secretary of the Jewish Agency for Palestine.

Much of Namier's fame comes from his pioneer studies of the political history of eighteenth century England, but he has also produced several books more recently on contemporary subjects. "The breadth and diversity of his writings reflect in part the experience of a life which has combined scholarly pursuits with an interest in public affairs," writes Catherine Strateman Sims in *Some Modern Historians of Britain*. Namier himself relates in the preface to *The Structure of Politics at the Accession of George III* that his initial researches into the eighteenth century dealt principally with the history of the United States colonies in those days; but an American scholar induced him, instead, to study the history of England at that period. While concentrating on the House of Commons in this early book, the author's frame of reference is always the moral, ethical, and political conceptions of the eighteenth century. Namier possesses in a high degree, writes the *Political Science Quarterly*, the indispensable characteristic of a good historian, "a never-lapsing consciousness of the unlikeness between past and present."

The question of political parties is discussed in more detail in Namier's 1930 volume, *England in the Age of the American Revolution*, in which he asserts that while there was a Whig and a Tory "mentality," organized parties in the modern sense did not exist in 1760. "There is a touch of something unique in Mr. Namier, a new method of tasting the intellectual pleasures of history," wrote G. M. Trevelyan of this book. "The worst of it is that, like life itself, it is involved and long-drawn-out, and I doubt if it will keep every reader's full attention through the whole volume, though it will excite him over the early chapters." "His style," said the New York *Times*, "is marked by lucidity and the poise of the historian who is more interested in the truth than in shadowy rationalizing."

A more recent work, *Avenues of History*, is a collection of Namier's essays, and an admirable introduction to his more serious volumes. "They are what an introduction should be—polite, not too solemn, charming, yet exact," said Gerald W. Johnson in the *New Republic*. Namier married Iulia de Beausobre in 1947. He is a naturalized British subject, and was knighted in 1952.

PRINCIPAL WORKS: Germany and Eastern Europe, 1915; The Structure of Politics at the Accession of George III (2 vols.) 1929; England in the Age of the American Revolution, 1930; Skyscrapers, and Other Essays, 1931; Additions and Corrections to Sir John Fortescue's Edition of the Correspondence of King George the Third, 1937; In the Margin of History, 1939; Conflicts: Studies in Contemporary History, 1942; 1848: the Revolution of the Intellectuals, 1946; Facing East, 1947; Diplomatic Prelude 1938-1939, 1948; Europe in Decay: a Study in Disintegration 1936-1940, 1950; In the Nazi Era, 1952; Avenues of History, 1952.

ABOUT: Ausubel, H. (ed.) Some Modern Historians of Britain; Universal Jewish Encyclopedia.

*NARAYAN, R. K. (October 10, 1906-), Indian novelist, writes: "I was born in Madras and my earlier years of education were completed there, later studied in a high school in Mysore in which my father was a headmaster. I had my college education in Maharaja's College, Mysore, and graduated from it in 1930. I married in 1934, lost my wife in 1939, and  spent a greater part of my following years in bringing up my daughter, Hema, who is now seventeen. I now live in Mysore with my mother and brothers. My first book *Swami*

* nä rä′yån

and *Friends* was published in 1935. Besides my books I have several hundred short stories and sketches which are still to be published in volume form and which have been appearing in the Sunday issue of the *Hindu* of Madras for which I write regularly. I have been writing for this paper since the beginning of my career. My recreations are music and long walks.

"I owe my literary career to Graham Greene's interest in my work. He has encouraged and backed me up for nearly twenty years now, although so far we have never met! But it seems to make no difference. I consider Graham not only the finest writer but the finest and most perfect friend a man can have in this world."

* * *

R. K. Narayan's works were introduced in the United States in 1952 with the publication by an American university press of his humorous and ironic novel *The Financial Expert*. This novel was hailed by the critics, but almost completely ignored by the public. In introducing a second novel by him, the poignant and at least partly autobiographical *The English Teacher*, his American publishers candidly admitted that they were changing the title to *Grateful to Life and Death* in an effort to catch the public eye. The simple story of an Indian teacher of English literature, of his lovely wife who dies tragically, and of their daughter, was widely praised. Anne Fremantle wrote in *Commonweal* that it was a brilliant tour de force, "as perfect as it is pure," a vivid and detailed picture of life in modern India and a touching story with universal appeal. Graham Greene, who introduced Narayan's work to British readers some years ago, has commented on the vitality of his portraits of Indian life: "Whom next shall I meet in Malgudi [the scene of several of his novels]? This is the thought that comes to me when I close a novel of Mr. Narayan's. I don't wait for another novel. I wait to go out of my door into those loved and shabby streets and see with excitement and a certainty of pleasure a stranger approaching, past the bank, the cinema, the haircutting saloon, a stranger who will greet me I know with some unexpected and revealing phrase that will open a door on to yet another human existence."

PRINCIPAL WORKS: Swami and Friends, 1935; Bachelor of Arts, 1937; The Dark Room, 1938; The English Teacher, 1945 (pub. in U.S. as Grateful to Life and Death, 1953); The Astrologer's Day, and Other Stories, 1947; Mr. Sampath, 1949; The Financial Expert, 1952.

ABOUT: Greene, G. *Introduction to* The Bachelor of Arts, The Financial Expert; Life and Letters December 1948.

NASH, OGDEN (August 19, 1902-). For biographical sketch and list of earlier works and references, see TWENTIETH CENTURY AUTHORS, 1942.

* * *

In 1953 a new collection of Ogden Nash's verse, *The Private Dining Room*, was published, and this proved the occasion for some extensive critical reappraisal of his work. Nash is unchallenged in his role of leading American writer of humorous verse. He is probably the most quoted of contemporary American poets, with a larger and more appreciative audience than any other poet. Over the quarter century during which he has chronicled his adventures with the trivia and the non-trivia of daily existence, he has inevitably mellowed. He is a grandfather; the marriage of his elder daughter in 1951 was covered by *Life* which printed on opposite pages the poem he had written to her when she was one and the poem he had written as "the father of a bride, aged nineteen." In *The Private Dining Room*, Ben Ray Redman observed in the *Saturday Review*, Nash "begins to refer to himself as a dear old gentleman; he is baffled by the younger generation." But, Redman concludes happily, "these are pleasures in which he does not indulge to excess. There is still a sharp sting in the tail of the smiling scorpion. May it never grow less."

In 1943 Nash collaborated with S. J. Perelman on the book of the highly successful musical *One Touch of Venus*. He has, in recent years, toured the United States extensively, lecturing and giving readings, and he has recorded many of his poems. His home is in Baltimore, Md.

ADDITIONAL WORKS: Good Intentions, 1942; (with S. J. Perelman) One Touch of Venus (play) 1944; Many Long Years Ago, 1945; Musical Zoo, 1947; Versus, 1949; Parents Keep Out, 1951; The Private Dining Room, 1953.

ABOUT: Blair, W. Horse Sense in American Humor; Frankenberg, L. Pleasure Dome; Holiday December 1952; Life October 29, 1951; New York Herald Tribune Book Review December 24, 1950; Saturday Review April 11, 1953.

NASON, LEONARD HASTINGS (September 28, 1895-). For biographical sketch and list of earlier works and references, see TWENTIETH CENTURY AUTHORS, 1942.

* * *

Leonard Nason saw active duty in the United States Army during World War II with the rank of lieutenant-colonel. He was with the armed forces on the initial landings in North Africa, served as military governor of the Rabat District in 1942, and participated in the Allied invasion of the continent of Europe. He holds honorary decorations from the Moroccan government and a Purple Heart and Silver Star. Since the end of the war he has returned to his writing career, contributing verse to the Chicago *Tribune* under the pseudonym "Steamer," and short stories to *Adventure*, the *Saturday Evening Post*, and other magazines. His adventure novel *Contact Mercury* was praised by the *Saturday Review of Literature* as "top grade spy stuff."

ADDITIONAL WORKS: Contact Mercury, 1946.

NATHAN, GEORGE JEAN (February 14, 1882-). For autobiographical sketch and list of earlier works and references, see TWENTIETH CENTURY AUTHORS, 1942.

* * *

From 1942 to 1951 George Jean Nathan published annually a series called *The Theatre Book of the Year*, each volume containing his impressions (his reviews of the year, revised and enlarged) of the theatrical season, with vital statistics on the production, the cast, the run of each play. But *The Theatre Book* is more than a collection of drama reviews. The *New Yorker's* drama critic, Wolcott Gibbs, found the series "the most engaging body of light critical writing available in this country now." Another fellow drama critic, John Mason Brown, wrote in his review of one of the volumes: "I doubt if in the whole history of the stage any of its more distinguished critical servitors have written about it for so many years with such sustained high spirit and intelligence as Mr. Nathan has done."

Now past seventy, Nathan reviews plays for King Features National Syndicate of Newspapers and for the magazine *Theatre Arts*. He lives, as he has for more than forty-five years, in a cluttered hotel apartment in the heart of New York's theatre district. He is called "the dean" of American drama critics, but nothing of the austerity of that title is reflected in his witty, impudent, highly prejudiced and always lively style, nor in what Charles Angoff calls "the magnificent irrepressibility" of his spirit. In a characteristic passage from the foreword to *The Theatre Book, 1949-1950*, Nathan wrote: "I am not so chipper as I once was, for all some seeming external evidence to the contrary. I work as hard as ever I did, or at least I think I do, but I sometimes say to myself that, since I have already done what I con-

sider to be my share, I am foolish to do so and not take life a little easier. But I don't listen to myself and grunt and groan and plod on nevertheless."

In June 1955 Nathan was married at sea to the actress Julie Haydon.

ADDITIONAL WORKS: Encyclopedia of the Theatre, 1940; Theatre Book of the Year, 1942-1951; Beware of Parents: A Bachelor's Book for Children, 1943; The World of George Jean Nathan (ed. C. Angoff) 1952; The Theatre in the Fifties, 1953.

ABOUT: Angoff, C. *in* The World of George Jean Nathan; Brown, J. M. Seeing Things; Frick, C. The Dramatic Criticism of George Jean Nathan; O'Casey, S. Rose and Crown, The Flying Wasp; Van Gelder, R. Writers and Writing; Current Biography 1945; New York Herald Tribune Book Review May 18, 1952; New York Times Book Review May 11, 1952; New Yorker October 22, 1949; Time May 12, 1952.

NATHAN, ROBERT (January 2, 1894-). For biographical sketch and list of earlier works and references, see TWENTIETH CENTURY AUTHORS, 1942.

* * *

"People think me wishy-washy, a gentle and sentimental writer, and use the word *whimsical* on me. I'm about as whimsical as a scorpion." Thus an exasperated but good-humored Robert Nathan expressed himself to an interviewer in 1950. He has written more than twenty-five novels, nearly all of them great popular successes. Under the light-hearted fantasy of his stories, there lurks from time to time a sharp edge of satiric wit and, as Evelyn Eaton described one of his books, he tosses his assorted characters "on his poet's two-pronged fork of pitying wit." He candidly admits his dislike of "highbrow" art and "intellectual" writing, and makes no pretense of being anything but what he is—a skillful craftsman. His predilection for whimsey and fantasy has been at once his greatest gift and his greatest handicap. At best his pleasant fables are gentle and heart-warming. At less than best they are cloying, sentimental, and artificial. Charles Lee wrote of *The Train in the Meadow*: "The whole effect is that of a story that has been machined out of plastics instead of poetry; it whirrs but it wants wings." His poetry has been described as "adroit." It is bold and direct, "seldom great poetry," Virginia Kirkus remarked, "but it does not pretend to be." One of his most popular poems is the wartime ballad "Dunkirk," which like Edna Millay's "The Murder of Lidice" was an unusually effective propaganda piece.

Nathan was married to Clara May Burns in 1951. This was his fifth marriage (his fourth wife was Janet MacMillen Bingham).

He spent seven years in Hollywood writing for the films and lives in Los Angeles, spending his summers on Cape Cod, at Truro.

ADDITIONAL WORKS: But Gently Day, 1943; Journal for Josephine, 1943; Morning in Iowa (poem) 1944; Darkening Meadows (poems) 1945; Mr. Whittle and the Morning Star, 1947; Long After Summer, 1948; The River Journey, 1949; The Green Leaf: Collected Poems, 1950; The Married Look (in England: His Wife's Young Face) 1950; Innocent Eve, 1951; Jezebel's Husband and Sleeping Beauty: Two Plays, 1953; The Train in the Meadow, 1953; Sir Henry, 1955.

ABOUT: Van Gelder, R. Writers and Writing; Warfel, H. R. American Novelists of Today; New York Times Book Review May 7, 1950.

"NAYLOR, ELIOT." See FRANKAU, P.

NAZHIVIN, IVAN FEDOROVICH
(1874-1940). For biographical sketch and list of works and references, see TWENTIETH CENTURY AUTHORS, 1942.

NEALE, JOHN ERNEST (December 7, 1890-), English biographer and historian, was born in Liverpool, England, and was ed-

ucated at Liverpool University and University College, London. He became Astor Professor of English History at the University of London, succeeding A. F. Pollard, the great Tudor historian, in 1927; Neale came from the chair of modern history at Manchester, where he had succeeded another distinguished historian, H. W. C. Davis. His first book was *Queen Elizabeth*, published in 1934; it was chosen by the Book Society as the book-of-the-month, became a best-seller, and was awarded the James Tait Black Memorial Prize as the best biography of the year. "Professor Neale has written not a psychological study of Elizabeth," commented the *New Statesman and Nation*, "nor an interpretation of the sixteenth century, but a first-rate literary biography. His book will help to revivify interest in a great epoch." The New York *Times* found the book "entirely delightful, witty and gallant in defense, and nothing better has been said on the side of Elizabeth, on this side idolatry." In addition to separate publication in America, the book has been translated into eight foreign languages.

In 1943 Neale published a short study of *The Age of Catherine de Medici*. This was followed by *The Elizabethan Political Scene, The Elizabethan House of Commons,* and *Elizabeth I and Her Parliaments, 1559-1581.* Renowned in historical circles for his researches in Elizabethan parliamentary history, Professor Neale was a member of the Treasury Committee appointed by Baldwin's government in 1929, under Colonel Wedgwood's chairmanship, to report on the personnel and politics of the House of Commons between 1264 and 1832. He is a trustee of the London Museum, a fellow of the British Academy, and holds the honorary degree of Doctor of Letters from the University of Wales. Among other distinctions he has delivered the Ford Lectures at the University of Oxford, and the Raleigh Lecture at the British Academy.

In 1932 he married Elfreda Skelton. They have one daughter, and live in London.

PRINCIPAL WORKS: Queen Elizabeth, 1934; The Age of Catherine de Medici, 1943; The Elizabethan Political Scene, 1948; The Elizabethan House of Commons, 1949; Elizabeth I and Her Parliaments 1559-1581, 1953.

NEIHARDT, JOHN GNEISENAU (January 8, 1881-). For autobiographical sketch and list of earlier works and references, see TWENTIETH CENTURY AUTHORS, 1942.

* * *

John G. Neihardt collected the five epic songs he had worked on since 1912, on the opening of the Missouri territory, in *Cycle of the West,* a volume that struck some of its readers in 1949 as strangely "old-fashioned," but nevertheless "authentic and genuine." Harvey Breit wrote of him: "He is an unfinished and unpolished writer and, worst of all, falls into dreadful archaisms. But he is a writer of immense vitality, who, at the same time, has a quite precise feeling about the frontier and the frontiersmen he considers and records." From 1944 to 1948 Neihardt served in the Office of Indian Affairs, and in 1951 he published a sympathetic study of Indian life in his novel *When the Tree Flowered.*

Neihardt lives at Skyrim Farm, near Columbia, Mo. Since 1948 he has been poet in residence and lecturer in English at the University of Missouri, from which he received an honorary Litt.D. in 1946. He has been vice president for the Middle West of the Poetry Society of America, and Chancellor of the Academy of American Poets. In 1943 he was elected to the National Institute of Arts and Letters.

ADDITIONAL WORKS: Poetry—Cycle of the West, 1949. Fiction—When the Tree Flowered, 1951.

NEILSON, WILLIAM ALLAN (March 28, 1869-February 13, 1946). For biographical sketch and list of works and references, see TWENTIETH CENTURY AUTHORS, 1942.

* * *

William Allan Neilson died at seventy-six of coronary thrombosis. Death came on the campus of Smith College, to which the former president had returned two months earlier to write a history of the college. The work was finished the day before his final illness.

Advocate of progressive educational theories, active in support of civil liberties, as witty as he was scholarly, Neilson has been described by Marjorie Hope Nicolson, his co-worker for many years, as "a belated Elizabethan . . . in his immense zest for life, his gusto, his vitality, his exuberant personality. He seemed to me the last of those Renaissance men who knew everything."

The annual report of the Carnegie Foundation for the Advancement of Teaching speaks of his "enlivening penetration in the classroom, the breadth and depth of his learning, and his kindliness to all with whom he came in contact," and declares that his "scholarship was thorough, never pedestrian, always brilliantly stimulating."

ADDITIONAL WORKS: (ed.) We Escaped: Twelve Personal Narratives of Flight to America, 1941.

ABOUT: American Scholar Autumn 1946; Atlantic Monthly November 1946; Carnegie Foundation for Advancement of Teaching 41st Annual Report 1945-46; London Times February 15, 1946; National Cyclopedia of American Biography (1947); New York Times February 14, 1946; Time February 25, 1946.

*NEMEROV, HOWARD (1920-), American poet and novelist, writes: "I was born in New York City, and lived there until 1937

when, on graduation from the Fieldston School, I went to Harvard, graduating (1941) in nice time for a summer vacation before entering the war. From 1941-1945 I was employed by the R.C.A.F. and the U.S.A.A.F., and after training in Canada and England did a tour of operations as pilot of Beaufighter aircraft with the 236th Squadron, Coastal Command. R.A.F., based in Lincolnshire and assigned to attack enemy shipping.

* něm'ĕr ŏff

During this time I married Margaret Russell, of Croydon, and we have one child, David (1950). After the war we lived in New York City for a year, during which time I completed my first book of verse, which came out in 1947, and composed a novel, which did not come out at all. Just as a want of money became noticeable I was offered an instructorship at Hamilton College, which I held for two years, going in 1948 to the faculty of Bennington College in Vermont, where I am still.

"The above somewhat bald chronology convicts me, if we may count the armed forces as a school, of having been at school almost steadily from the age of five; a career which I have heard held to be the worst possible one for a person pretending to imaginative writing. Whether it is so in fact I cannot of course say; I have seen dangers in the academic life, but so are there dangers everywhere; and I think to have seen one advantage, that teaching absorbs a good deal of one's bent for explaining things—a doubtless praiseworthy trait which, however, in my opinion, ought to be allowed the least possible play in writing fictions whether in verse or in prose."

* * *

Howard Nemerov is a frequent contributor of short stories, poems, and essays to the *New Yorker, Atlantic, Hudson Review, Kenyon Review, Partisan Review,* and *Poetry.* His two novels have been pungent satires. Diana Trilling called *The Melodramatists* "a considerable first novel—literate and entertaining, with a nice satiric barb." *Federigo, or The Power of Love* was another sharply-etched portrayal of "the Hamlets who write advertising copy, of the women whose modern handbook is Freud on the one hand and *Vogue* on the other," as H. F. West wrote in the New York *Times.*

Nemerov's verse has been described, by Milton Crane in the New York *Times,* as "the work of an original and sensitive mind, alive to the thousand anxieties and agonies of our age." Although the critics have found some of his poems marred by "an intrusive verbal cleverness," his work is generally considered vigorous and original. In 1955 Nemerov received the *Kenyon Review* Fellowship in Fiction. Under the fellowship he planned to work on a new novel and short stories.

PRINCIPAL WORKS: *Poetry*—The Image and the Law, 1947; Guide to the Ruins, 1950; The Salt Garden, 1955. *Novels*—The Melodramatists, 1949; Federigo, or The Power of Love, 1954.

ABOUT: New Leader August 6, 1949; Sewanee Review Winter 1952.

*"NERUDA, PABLO" (pseudonym of Ricardo Eliezer Neftalí Reyes Basoalto) (July 12, 1904-   ), Chilean poet, was born in Parral, Chile, son of José del Carmen Reyes, a rugged, ill-tempered railroad worker, and Rosa de Basoalto, who died of consumption when the boy was three years old. He attended the local schools and the *liceo* of nearby Temuco without distinguishing himself in any subject, but showing a marked inclination for poetry writing. This he had to conceal at all costs as his relatives, rough country folk, had no use for poets. When at the age of fifteen he sent his first batch of poems to the magazine *Selva Austral,* he signed "Pablo Neruda," not knowing that there was already a famous Neruda—the Czech short story writer Jan Neruda.

Because of his lack of interest in agricultural work or manual labor, the delicate youngster was sent to Chile's most famous teachers' college, the Instituto Pedagógico in Santiago. Here, however, he evinced no interest in his studies, preferring to spend his time in the cafés talking literature. In 1921 he entered the poetical jousts celebrated annually at Santiago at the coming of spring, and won first prize with his "La canción de la fiesta." The award opened to Neruda Santiago's numerous circles of vanguard poets. He was then seventeen and soft-singing, and the raucous "ultraism" was the rage. He observed, he learned, he streamlined his form. However, no "new" elements are discernible in his next work, *Crepusculario,* which, though published in 1923, belongs to his provincial days; he considers it "naïve and devoid of all literary merit," contrary to current opinion which has accepted it as a Chilean classic. The change in his style and mood seems the more radical with the appearance, the following year, of *Veinte Poemas de Amor y una Canción Desesperada.* A fresh original approach to the old theme of love, this volume represents to many the beginnings of "Nerudism," i.e. a characteristic Neruda now freed from the honeyed melody of Rubén Darío. It remains to this day one of the finest books of verse in the Spanish language. Several difficult experimental works followed the *Veinte Poemas:* the hermetic *Tentativa del Hombre Infinito* (1925) and a collection of prose poems, *Anillos* (1926)

* nā rōō'dà

in collaboration with Tomás Lago, director of the Museum of Popular Arts; *El Habitante y su Esperanza* (1926), which despite the publishers' optimistic label, "A Novel," is but a series of disjointed prose sketches; and, finally, the verbal storm of *El Hondero Entusiasta* (1933), evincing the influence of Uruguay's mystic poet Carlos Sabat Ercasty.

By 1925 Neruda had adumbrated his most original vein in the poems "Galope muerto" and "Serenata": "These poems pointed out to me the kingdom of my personality. With great serenity I discovered that I had succeeded in possessing a territory indisputably mine." This is the trend he followed for the next few years, years of great spiritual concentration spent in foreign countries. For in 1927 Neruda went to Rangoon (Burma) as consul, a position he occupied thereafter in Colombo (Ceylon) 1929, Batavia (Java) 1930, with visits to Indo-China, China and Japan. On a return trip in an old freighter lasting seventy-five days via Cape of Good Hope and the Straits of Magellan, he wrote many extraordinary poems: "Monzón de mayo," "El fantasma del buque de carga," "Tango de viudo." These and many other poems written in the course of years in his totally new technique and with the aroma of exotic climes constituted the first volume of *Residencia en la Tierra* (translated into English as *Residence on Earth*), published in 1933 by the Editorial Ercilla (Santiago de Chile), a milestone in the history of Spanish poetry. Neruda was then consul in Buenos Aires and soon he left for Madrid, also as consul, and there he went on preparing Volume II of *Residencia,* enjoying now the admiration of a brilliant group of Spanish poets, including Alberti, García Lorca, Altolaguirre, Aleixandre, etc., with whom he edited "El Caballo Verde," a stimulating poetry journal which stopped suddenly with its sixth issue when the Civil War broke out in July 1936.

The Spanish Civil War shook the poet deeply and changed him from an esoteric poet to a political poet. While traveling back to Chile, Neruda wrote *España en el Corazón* (Spain in the Heart), "a hymn to the glories of the people at war," which was set in type and printed by the Spanish Republican soldiers on the battlefront. A de luxe edition appeared in Madrid on November 7, 1938, the second anniversary of the defense of Madrid.

In 1939 Neruda was active in Paris helping the Spanish refugees, finally chartering a boat and bringing it filled with refugees to Chile. In that year the Chilean government appointed him secretary to the Chilean Em-

709

bassy in Mexico City, and later consul, 1941-1944. During this time Neruda had been gestating a long, ambitious poem which was to be called "Canto General de Chile" (an excerpt of which appeared in 1943), but as time passed the idea broadened to include the whole of America.

After his return to Chile, he was elected to the Senate as a Communist. Late in 1947 letters by Neruda appeared in newspapers in Venezuela and in Mexico charging that the Chilean President González Videla had "sold out" Chile to the United States for financial aid and had started a reign of terror against the Chilean Communist Party. President Videla immediately began action to strip Neruda of his senatorial immunity and to impeach him. A violent political controversy arose over the issue. The New York *Times,* January 25, 1948, observed: "The Communist problem in Chile and in a sense throughout South America, is currently best symbolized by the case of the Communist Senator Pablo Neruda, which has become something of a *cause célèbre* up and down the West Coast." Neruda carried his case to the Chilean Supreme Court, but the Court upheld President Videla. After several unsuccessful attempts to flee the country, Neruda escaped to Mexico.

From February 1948 to January 1949 Neruda worked intensively on his *Canto General* which, according to many critics, is his masterpiece. It was made public on April 3, 1950, in the home of the architect Carlos Obregon Santacilia in Mexico City, where he and his two illustrators, Diego Rivera and David Alfaro Siqueiros, signed the copies. The huge volume, which abounds in brilliant poems, is a thoroughly political book tracing the history of man's exploitation from the most remote ages to the present. One of its most eloquent moments, "Alturas de Macchu-Picchu" (Summits of Macchu-Picchu) is available in English translation.

With the victory in 1953 of the anti-González Videla forces, Neruda returned to his native country. In contrast to the young poet, who was thin, almost emaciated, and dressed in black, the present Neruda, just past his fiftieth year, looks like a prosperous traveling salesman: fat and friendly, a connoisseur of good wines and delicate food. He recites in a heavy monotone, quite impressive in the enumerative passages. He has made several phonograph records of his recitals. His home is always open to his friends and in it can be seen one of the world's finest collections of seashells. His admirers know that a gift of seashells is most dearly appreciated by the poet. Amongst the poets in his library, his love and admiration go to Blake (whom he once translated into Spanish), Whitman, Alberti, and Mayakovsky. In December 1953 he was named one of the winners of the Stalin Peace Prize.

WORKS AVAILABLE IN ENGLISH: Poems *in* New Directions Yearbook (ed. J. Laughlin) 1941; Selected Poems (privately printed, Washington, D.C.) 1941; Poems *in* Anthology of Contemporary Latin American Poetry (ed. D. Fitts) 1942; Residence on Earth, 1946.

ABOUT: Alonso, A. Poesía y estilo de Pablo Neruda; Books Abroad April 1941; Bulletin of Bibliography January 1950; Inter-American May 1943; Poetry May 1943, January 1945, June 1947, May 1952; Revista Iberoamericana February 1944.

NESBIT, EDITH ("E. Nesbit") (August 15, 1858-April 22, 1924). For biographical sketch and list of works and references, see TWENTIETH CENTURY AUTHORS, 1942.

* * *

ABOUT: Horn Book November 1948; Saturday Review of Literature November 14, 1942.

NEUMANN, ALFRED (October 15, 1895-October 3, 1952). For autobiographical sketch and list of earlier works and references, see TWENTIETH CENTURY AUTHORS, 1942.

* * *

Alfred Neumann died in Lugano, Switzerland, while on a lecture tour, a few days before his fifty-seventh birthday. He had lived in the United States for three years before his death and had become an American citizen.

His most successful work was in the field of the historical novel in which, however, as Frank Spiecker has noted, he used the past "to symbolize present political situations and human problems." He was equally successful, however, in a contemporary setting in his novel *Six of Them,* a study of life in Nazi Germany. "As a novel it has many defects," the *Manchester Guardian* observed, "but as a piece of earnest and exceedingly well-informed writing it holds the attention throughout by its comprehension and delineation of the human beings involved." Kenneth Fearing, writing in the New York *Times,* found the book "topheavy with moral ultimates," but nevertheless "filled with a fresh clairvoyance of real people facing seemingly endless terror."

ADDITIONAL WORKS IN ENGLISH TRANSLATION: Six of Them, 1945; Look Upon This Man, 1950.

ABOUT: Columbia Dictionary of Modern European Literature; Current History August 1942; New York Times October 4, 1952.

NEUMANN, ROBERT (May 22, 1897-). For autobiographical sketch and list of earlier works and references, see TWENTIETH CENTURY AUTHORS, 1942.

* * *

With *Mr. Tibbs Passes Through* (1943) Robert Neumann began writing in English in a style described variously as "tortured" and "cracking under a cartload of adjectives," and as having "an individuality that gives his prose an added sharpness." Neumann himself writes that he had become alarmed at his virtuoso fluency in German, and to correct this he created an idiom which "also expresses German rhythm, German construction, and yet should and could be translated into German—however, not by myself."

His recent novels have all dealt starkly and strikingly with problems of wartime and post-war Europe. Kate O'Brien described his *Children of Vienna* as "a terrible report in which factual truth takes on the universal truth of parable." Because Neumann is an ironist, his work is sometimes misunderstood and misinterpreted. A comprehensive article on him in the German magazine *Der Spiegel* stated, for example, that his hostility toward Communism was colder and more detached than Arthur Koestler's. The reason for this, Neumann explains in a letter from London, is that "I never was a Communist and never cooperated with them. I am a middle-of-the-road Socialist of, say, the Attlee variety, and my 'anti-Americanism' alleged by *Der Spiegel* is a pure invention and has never gone beyond such criticism among friends as might come from Attlee himself. The allegedly 'most anti-American' *Children of Vienna* was published by Dutton's (staunch Republicans, I think); the film rights were sold to a Hollywood company, and your Office of War Information asked me for authorization to distribute the book in the American zones of Germany and Austria and in South Korea."

Neumann has recently become active in the motion picture business, having acquired an interest in a film company, Film Group, Inc., for which he has written scenarios. He plans to produce screen adaptations of several of his novels.

ADDITIONAL WORKS: The Scene Is Passing (in U.S.: Mr. Tibbs Passes Through) 1942; Inquest, 1945; Children of Vienna, 1946; Blind Man's Buff, 1949; Insurrection in Poshansk, 1952; Shooting Star (pub. 1932 as On the Make), and Circe's Island: Two Short Novels, 1954.

ABOUT: Neumann, R. Mit Fremden Federn (Munich, 1949); Der Spiegel August 1952; Les Temps Modernes January 1950.

NEVINS, ALLAN (May 20, 1890-). For biographical sketch and list of earlier works and references, see TWENTIETH CENTURY AUTHORS, 1942.

* * *

Allan Nevins was a special representative of the Office of War Information in Australia and New Zealand during World War II. From 1945 to 1946 he was chief public affairs officer at the American Embassy in London. He returned to the United States and to his teaching duties at Columbia University, with his permanent home in Bronxville, N.Y., and a summer home in Windham, Vt. Nevins has continued to travel and to lecture widely both in the United States and abroad. In 1952 he was visiting professor at Hebrew University in Jerusalem. Of his work he said in 1950 that he preferred writing history to writing biography because the former "seems to me more complex, important, difficult, and therefore more interesting." His recent historical studies have centered on the American Civil War. His two-volume *Ordeal of the Union* won both the Scribner Centenary Prize and the Bancroft Prize. He has continued this study with a work on Lincoln and plans to continue it up through 1877. Nevins has also taken the lead in a number of editorial projects in American history (among them the Chronicles of America series, published by Yale University) and in establishing an "Oral History" project which has recorded the voices of prominent contemporary figures. More recently he completed a comprehensive and heavily documented study of Henry Ford.

ADDITIONAL WORKS: America in World Affairs, 1941; (with L. M. Hacker) The United States and its Place in World Affairs, 1918-1943, 1943; (with F. Weitenkampf) A Century of Political Cartoons, 1944; (with H. S. Commager) A Short History of the United States, 1945; Ordeal of the Union, 1947; (with J. A. Krout) Greater City: New York, 1898-1945, 1948; The Emergence of Lincoln, 1950; The New Deal and World Affairs, 1950; The United States in a Chaotic World, 1950; Ford: the Times, the Man, the Company, 1954.

ABOUT: New York Herald Tribune Book Review October 8, 1950; Saturday Review of Literature October 18, 1947.

NEVINSON, HENRY WOODD (1856- November 9, 1941). For biographical sketch and list of works and references, see TWENTIETH CENTURY AUTHORS, 1942.

* * *

ADDITIONAL WORKS: Thomas Hardy, 1941; Visions and Memories (ed. E. Sharp) 1944; Essays, Poems and Tales (ed. H. N. Brailsford) 1948.

ABOUT: Murray, G. Introduction to Visions and Memories.

NEWBOLT, Sir HENRY JOHN (June 6, 1862-April 19, 1938). For biographical sketch and list of works and references, see TWENTIETH CENTURY AUTHORS, 1942.

* * *

ADDITIONAL WORKS: Life and Letters (ed. M. Newbolt) 1942.

ABOUT: Dictionary of National Biography 1931-40; Newbolt, H. J. Life and Letters (ed M. Newbolt).

NEWBY, PERCY HOWARD (June 25, 1918-), English novelist, who signs his work P. H. Newby, writes: "I was born at Crowborough, Sussex, England. Raised in the Midlands and South Wales my earliest memories are of the mining valleys. But Worcestershire, more particularly the part of the county lying between the Malvern Hills and Bredon, is the place to which I owe allegiance. Here I attended Hanley Castle Grammar School and, a little out of the area I have defined, St. Paul's College at Cheltenham.

Robin Adler

"In July 1939 I was called up for militia training and went to France with the British Expeditionary Force in the October of that year. My unit was among the last to be evacuated from France; we sailed out of St. Nazaire on June 16, 1940. In January 1941, we went to Egypt. After service, mainly in the delta and Canal Zone, I was seconded to the Fouad I University in Cairo as lecturer in English literature. This took place in December 1942, and I held this post until leaving Egypt in June 1946. Living in Egypt, outside Europe and the Christian tradition, was probably the best thing that could have happened to me as a writer.

"My first novel, *A Journey to the Interior*, was published on December 3, 1945 (in England) and a number of others followed at intervals of twelve months. In 1946 I was given one of the Rockefeller Foundation Atlantic Awards; in 1948 I was given the Somerset Maugham Prize. Since 1949 I have been a member of the British Broadcasting Corporation's Talks Department. In 1945 I married Joan Thompson and we have a daughter, Sarah Jane, born in 1947."

* * *

P. H. Newby is regarded as one of the most promising of the younger English novelists. Anthony West of the *New Yorker* calls him "the only English writer with anything approaching genius to be produced by his generation so far." His writings have been compared to those of Virginia Woolf (for craftsmanship) and, for general competence and readability, to Evelyn Waugh and Graham Greene. There is actually a closer resemblance to the work of E. M. Forster in Newby's novels—in the element of mystery (not in the detective story sense), the sudden and seemingly irrational outbursts of violence, the use of understatement and restraint. As an artist, however, Newby attempts to keep himself independent and free of "commitments." He told an interviewer in 1953: "I'm a liberal in my thinking, in the sense that E. M. Forster is, and I dislike absolute beliefs, dogma, the kind of thing Koestler calls 'the tyranny of the absolute.' As a Christian, I believe that man is a supernatural being, but that's as far as I'll go."

Newby and his family live in Buckinghamshire. On his visit to America in 1953 he was described as "wearing correct tweeds and a detached, abstracted manner," and looking "more like a classics instructor in a boys' school . . . than the much-traveled cosmopolitan he is."

PRINCIPAL WORKS: A Journey to the Interior, 1945; Agents and Witnesses, 1947; Mariner Dances, 1948; Maria Edgeworth (English Novelists Series) 1950; The Young May Moon, 1950; A Season in England, 1951; A Step to Silence, 1952; The Retreat, 1953. *Juveniles*—The Spirit of Jem, 1947; The Loot Runners, 1949.

ABOUT: Current Biography 1953; New York Times Book Review April 19, 1953.

NEWHOUSE, EDWARD (November 10, 1911-), American novelist and short story writer, reports: "I was born in a suburb of Budapest, Hungary. My father was an inspector of detectives in that city but, having held the job through one political regime too many, he lost it shortly after the first World War. My family came to the United States when I was twelve. I attended Public School 30 in New York and Townsend Harris Hall Prep, acquiring some command of the English language on East 84th Street and in the Yorkville Branch of the Public Library. In school, my interests were primarily athletic.

"Until the age of eighteen, I don't believe I crossed the city limits of New York for more than a few hours at a time. My concepts of life and civilization in the rest of the United States derived mostly from the works of Upton Sinclair and the pages of the *New Masses.* My associations were with young people in the orbit of the Communist Party. Though temperamentally disinclined to join organizations, I thought of myself as a Communist and of formal education as a bourgeois conspiracy to blunt my revolutionary purpose. At seventeen, I turned down the offer of a four-year athletic scholarship to college, and began to contribute high-octane fiction to the *New Masses.* At eighteen, I left New York and spent some nine months in hopping on and off freight trains through the United States and Mexico; in retracing my path, I find I covered almost 20,000 miles.

"Back in New York, I published two childish novels of the genre known, for some reason, as proletarian. They were exceedingly well received by all sorts of people who might have known better.

"Unequipped to handle any skilled job, even if one had been available during the Depression, and seeing myself described by Lincoln Steffens, in a magazine, as 'the first authentic and eloquent literary voice of America's next generation,' I naturally continued to take advantage of the fact that there were no municipal ordinances against impersonating a writer.

"I ran true to form. The Moscow Trials left me without any political moulds to pour into, and I had to set about learning to write of things as they appeared to my own untrained eyes. At the age of twenty-four, I contributed my first story to the *New Yorker.* Since then, almost all my short fiction has appeared there. Like many other writers, I owe a lot to that magazine's managing editor, G. S. Lobrano, and to the late Harold Ross.

"During World War II, I spent three and a half years in the Army Air Forces, serving, in the grades from private through major, as drill and gunnery instructor, flight control and intelligence officer, and on General H. H. Arnold's staff. The Air Corps was very good to me though I didn't always know it at the time, and very good for me, too. I hold a commission in the U.S.A.F. Reserve.

"Since the war, I have lived in Nanuet, Rockland County, N.Y., with my wife, my son and my daughter. We live here mostly because there is a fine school in the village.

I read, for pleasure, four or five hours a day. I spend much more time with my children, now ten and six, than any other father I've ever known. I don't get nearly enough writing done. I don't attend movies or plays or listen to the radio or view television or dine out much or play cards. When pressed, I am capable of producing a sound game of badminton."

* * *

Edward Newhouse "stands high in the ranks of contemporary short-story writers," Granville Hicks wrote in 1951. His work shows mastery of the form, and what Richard Harrity has described as "an accurate ear, an infallibility of character and a discerning eye for telling incident."

PRINCIPAL WORKS: *Novels*—You Can't Sleep Here, 1934; This Is Your Day, 1937; The Hollow of the Wave, 1949; The Temptation of Roger Heriott, 1954. *Short Stories*—Anything Can Happen, 1941; The Iron Chain, 1946; Many Are Called, 1951.

ABOUT: Book-of-the-Month Club News February 1949; Wilson Library Bulletin May 1937.

NEWMAN, ERNEST (November 30, 1868-) For biographical sketch and list of earlier works and references, see TWENTIETH CENTURY AUTHORS, 1942.

* * *

Ernest Newman has contributed music criticism to the London *Sunday Times* since 1920. It would be impossible to estimate the number of readers in America and in England who owe their introduction to opera to Newman's comprehensive studies. Music critics have objected to Newman's "ostentatiousness and pompousness" as a writer and have disagreed sharply with him on points of interpretation, but, as B. H. Haggin pointed out in his review of *More Stories of Famous Operas* in 1943, "even with faults and deficiencies that limit its usefulness, it is probably the best of its kind." Haggin considers Newman a "critic with powers of insight and intellect that one is bound to respect and admire."

Newman completed his monumental four-volume study of Richard Wagner in 1946. Like the preceding volumes, Hans Kohn commented in the New York *Times*, the final volume "is based on painstaking scholarship, written with an easy grace and a sense of humor, and animated with a deep though not uncritical love of its hero." In 1949 he published a detailed study of Wagner's operas—their scores, the sources of the libretti, and Wagner's method of composition.

ADDITIONAL WORKS: More Stories of Famous Operas, 1943; Opera Nights, 1943; The Life of Richard Wagner, vol. IV, 1946; Wagner Operas (in England: Wagner Nights) 1949; Seventeen Famous Operas, 1955.

ABOUT: Haggin, B. H. Music in The Nation; Newsweek May 27, 1946.

NEWMAN, FRANCES (September 13, 1888-October 22, 1928). For biographical sketch and list of works and references, see TWENTIETH CENTURY AUTHORS, 1942.

NEWTON, ALFRED EDWARD (1863-September 29, 1940). For biographical sketch and list of works and references, see TWENTIETH CENTURY AUTHORS, 1942.

* * *

ABOUT: Atlantic Monthly December 1943.

*NEXØ, MARTIN ANDERSEN (June 26, 1869-June 1954). For biographical sketch and list of works and references, see TWENTIETH CENTURY AUTHORS, 1942.

* * *

Martin Andersen Nexø died in Dresden at eighty-five. He had been living in East Germany since 1951. In 1949 (when he was living in Holte in Denmark) his eightieth birthday was celebrated at a national festival in Copenhagen.

"The first and the greatest of Danish proletarian writers," as Jorgen Claudi has called him, he introduced the working class into his country's literature "with such warmth as to break all doctrinaire bonds." He was not a self-conscious stylist, Edwin Björkman said, but developed his style "out of the colloquial language of the streets and the slums."

Frankly propaganda for his Communist ideas, Nexø's most effective contributions to the cause he served were, J. B. C. Watkins has pointed out, "at the same time his finest artistic achievements"—his novels of *Pelle* and *Ditte*. Joseph Wood Krutch called these "magnificently real and balanced because he has succeeded in picturing human depravity without relenting and human goodness without sentimentality." At his best, Lawrence S. Thompson wrote, Nexø "has portrayed the social processes he knew so intimately with an inspiration and a genius that have found no home in the totalitarian states produced by these changes."

ABOUT: Claudi, J. Contemporary Danish Authors; Heepe, E. & Heltberg, N. (eds.) Modern Danish Authors; Books Abroad Autumn 1954.

* nĭk'sû

714

NICHOLS, BEVERLEY (September 9, 1899-). For biographical sketch and list of earlier works and references, see TWENTIETH CENTURY AUTHORS, 1942.

* * *

During World War II Beverley Nichols spent a year in India as a correspondent of the British syndicate of the Allied newspapers. He reported on his experiences there in a controversial and provocative book, *Verdict on India*. On his return to England, he bought an old house in the suburbs of London, where he settled down to devote himself to his two major interests—gardening and writing. Nichols has chronicled his experiences with his house and garden in *Merry Hall* and in *Laughter on the Stairs*—both of these full of the irrepressible humor that characterized his earlier writings. He resumed his autobiography, begun in 1926 with *Twenty-Five*, with a sequel, *All I Could Never Be*, a chatty account of the years up to the outbreak of World War II. The book had "style and tartness" and "a certain wayward charm," James Hilton commented. "It is the answer both of and to the bright young man who thirty years ago knew just what he wanted to be—and in large measure succeeded."

ADDITIONAL WORKS: Verdict on India, 1944; The Tree that Sat Down, 1945; The Stream that Stood Still, 1948; All I Could Never Be, 1949; Mountain of Magic: A Romance for Children, 1950; Merry Hall, 1951; Laughter on the Stairs, 1954; No Man's Street, 1954.

ABOUT: Nichols, B. Verdict on India, All I Could Never Be, Merry Hall, Laughter on the Stairs; Time March 17, 1952.

NICHOLS, ROBERT MALISE BOWYER (September 16, 1893-December 14, 1944). For autobiographical sketch and list of earlier works and references, see TWENTIETH CENTURY AUTHORS, 1942.

* * *

Robert Nichols died at Cambridge at fifty-one.

His friend Charles Morgan has said that he was "the most comprehensible because the most natural of seers. This was what he meant when he spoke of himself as a romantic realist." The critical disfavor which was largely his lot is attributed by the London *Times* to two factors; his refusal to make "concessions to fashions," and the fact that "the originality of his mind poured itself out in drama, satire and song with an erraticism that submitted to no categories." The *Times* adds that "there was in his wildness an ardour that Byron would have honored and Shelley loved."

ADDITIONAL WORKS: Such Was My Singing (Poems 1915-1940) 1942; (ed.) Anthology of War Poetry; 1914-1918, 1942.

ABOUT: Morgan, C. Reflections in a Mirror, Second Series; London Times December 18, 1944; New York Times December 19, 1944.

NICHOLS, ROY FRANKLIN (March 3, 1896-   ), American historian, writes: "I was born in Newark, N.J., son of Franklin Co-

riell and Anna Cairns Nichols. I did my undergraduate work at Rutgers and took my Ph.D. at Columbia University. In the course of this latter activity I married a fellow student, Jeannette Paddock. At Columbia, my mentor was the late Professor William A. Dunning, who directed my interest in political history into the realm of the activities of the Democratic Party on the eve of the Civil War. My doctoral dissertation was an intensive examination of the behavior of that party, which became a book entitled *The Democratic Machine, 1850-54.* As I was finishing this, there was a great vogue of biographical interest which was sweeping the country in the 1920's, and I wrote a biography of Franklin Pierce. By the time I had finished this I had become deeply interested not only in political history, but in the problem of historical causation. I was concerned primarily with the contribution which political activists had made to the temporary breakdown of our democratic procedures. The result was a book, *The Disruption of American Democracy,* which made an intensive examination of the simultaneous dissolution of the Democratic Party and the Union, 1856-1861. This book was awarded the Pulitzer prize in history in 1949. In collaboration with Dr. J. P. Nichols, I have written *The Growth of American Democracy, The Republic of the United States,* and *A Short History of American Democracy.*

"I served as instructor at Columbia University from 1921 to 1925. In the latter year I came to the University of Pennsylvania, where I have been assistant professor, 1925-1930, professor, 1930- , and, since 1952, dean of the Graduate School of Arts and Sciences. I was visiting professor at Columbia University, 1944-1945, and visiting professor of American History and Institutions at Cambridge University, England, 1948-1949. I was one of the founders of the Pennsylvania Historical Association and served as its president. I likewise have held the presidencies of the Pennsylvania Federation of Historical Societies and the Middle States Council for the Social Studies, and am president of the Genealogical Society of Pennsylvania. I was elected to the Council of the American Historical Association 1943-1947 and to its Executive Committee. The American Historical Association has continued me as one of the historians on the Social Science Research Council for some nineteen years, and I am at present Chairman of its Board. I was appointed by Governor James as a member of the Pennsylvania Historical Commission, 1941-1944. I am a member of the American Philosophical Society, one of the Council of the Historical Society of Pennsylvania, and a trustee of Rutgers University."

PRINCIPAL WORKS: The Democratic Machine, 1850-1854, 1923; Franklin Pierce, 1931; The Disruption of American Democracy, 1948; Historical Study of Anglo-American Democracy, 1949. *With J. P. Nichols*—The Growth of American Democracy, 1939; The Republic of the United States, 1942; A Short History of American Democracy.

ABOUT: Current Biography 1949.

NICHOLSON, KENYON (May 21, 1894-   ). For biographical sketch and list of earlier works and references, see TWENTIETH CENTURY AUTHORS, 1942.

* * *

Kenyon Nicholson lives in Raven Rock, N.J. In recent years two of his plays have had Broadway productions. One of these, *Apple of His Eye* (written with Charles Robinson), ran for more than three months in 1946. The story of a simple farmer who is a widower and embarks on a new romance, it was considered a slight but entertaining play and was successful primarily for a brilliant performance by the late Walter Huston in the leading role. In 1951 Nicholson's *Out West of Eighth* ran for a fleeting four performances. John Chapman commented in his review of the season: "Mr. Nicholson saw great possibilities for fun in a play about rodeo cowboys quartered in a hotel near Madison Square Garden, but he was unable to get these possibilities out into the open on a stage."

ADDITIONAL WORK: (with C. Robinson) Apple of His Eye: A Comedy, 1946.

715

NICHOLSON, MEREDITH (December 9, 1866-December 21, 1947). For biographical sketch and list of works and references, see TWENTIETH CENTURY AUTHORS, 1942.

* * *

Meredith Nicholson died in a diabetic coma, at eighty-one, at Indianapolis. He had retired from his diplomatic career in 1941. His second marriage was dissolved by divorce in 1943.

The best of Nicholson's picaresque novels are now, according to Earl Walbridge, "as fresh, charming, and inventive in quality as the day they were published."

ABOUT: New York Times December 22, 1947; Saturday Review of Literature February 7, 1948.

NICHOLSON, NORMAN (1914-), English poet and playwright, writes: "I was born at Millom, a small mining town on the

coast of Cumberland, backed on the east by some of the barest and loneliest fells of the English Lake District, where most of the farmers and quarrymen are descended from the Viking settlers who came from Ireland and Iceland in the ninth and tenth centuries. Millom, though its foundations go back to the Middle Ages, is a nineteenth-century town, springing like a tree from the large deposits of iron ore in the local rock. It is a curiously isolated spot, blocked off from the rest of England on three sides by the sea and on the fourth by the mountains. Because of this it has developed a strange, independent, ingrown vitality which gives its people a sense of belonging both to a community and to a place.

"I give this description of my home because it seems to me more important towards the understanding of my work than any mere biographical details, since it is this sense of community, of an organic relationship between man and his environment, which is my main theme. I attended local schools until I was sixteen, when after a breakdown in health, I spent two years in the New Forest, since which my life has been comparatively quiet and retired. Round about the age of twenty-three, I became reconverted to Christianity, and it was in the excitement of this that I first began to write verse, drawing my imagery sometimes from the Bible but more often from the physical world about me, whether as seen in a rare flower or a back street.

"I consider myself primarily a poet, though I have written a good deal both of literary criticism and of topography. In 1945 I was asked to write a play for Martin Browne's famous series of 'Plays by Poets' at the Mercury Theatre, London, since when I have been specially interested in the return of poetry to the theatre, aiming my plays, however, not at the sophisticated public of the West End, but at small, thoughtful audiences in the provinces. My first play, *The Old Man of the Mountains*, a transcription of the story of Elijah into a setting in modern Cumberland, has been produced many times in the North of England and has been translated into Welsh by the Arch-Druid. A new play, *A Match for the Devil*, about Hosea, the prophet who married a harlot, was sent on tour (1953) by the Religious Drama Society of Great Britain."

* * *

As a lifetime resident of Cumberland and the English Lake District, Nicholson writes in the historical shadow of William Wordsworth, to whom, Amos Wilder has said, he can pay homage, though he writes "in a strange, modern style," with a turn "towards the surrealistic treatment of nature." His symbolism is heavily Biblical and, Nicholson himself explains in *Man and Literature*, "in its emphasis on the value of imaginative experience it is a reaction against scientific materialism." In his verse drama, Raymond Williams suggests, Nicholson is indebted primarily to the plays of T. S. Eliot—both for the philosophy of Christian orthodoxy which permeates them and for a verse which attempts to combine the natural rhythms of speech with the poetic rhythm of dramatic verse. His novel *The Fire of the Lord*, a somber picture of life in a Cumberland village, was found to be of considerable promise, though overwritten. The *Saturday Review of Literature* observed: "In the dignity of its conception, however, it belongs with books of quality and accomplishment."

PRINCIPAL WORKS: *Poetry*—Five Rivers, 1944; The Old Man of the Mountains (verse play) 1946; Rock Face, 1948; Prophesy to the Wind (verse play) 1950; Pot Geranium, 1954. *Prose*—Man and Literature, 1943; The Fire of the Lord (novel) 1944; The Green Shore (novel) 1947; H. G. Wells, 1950; Cumberland and Westmoreland, 1950; William Cowper, 1951; The Lakers, 1955.

ABOUT: Ross, A. Poetry 1945-1950; Stanford, D. The Freedom of Poetry; Wilder, A. Modern Poetry and the Christian Tradition; Williams, R. Drama from Ibsen to Eliot.

NICOLL, ALLARDYCE (June 28, 1894-   ). For biographical sketch and list of earlier works and references, see TWENTIETH CENTURY AUTHORS, 1942.

* * *

Allardyce Nicoll served with the British Embassy in Washington during World War II. In 1945 he returned to England and became professor of English at Birmingham University. Since 1951 he has been director of the Shakespeare Institute at Stratford-upon-Avon. He is also a trustee of the Shakespeare Birthplace Trust at Stratford and is editor of the *Shakespeare Survey,* an annual survey of Shakespeare scholarship which has been published since 1948. Nicoll's work on the history of the English drama remains among the soundest and most comprehensive in the field. In 1946 he brought that history up to 1900 in a two-volume study of late nineteenth century drama—described by George Freedley in the New York *Times* as "a fine if not exciting work which brings the result of enormous research, of careful scholarly thought, of genuine devotion to an ideal, to the student, the historian and the writer." He has also published an ambitious one-volume history of world drama from ancient times down to the contemporary period (John Gassner called it "the most thorough work of its kind in the English language") and a brief popular introduction to Shakespearean drama.

Nicoll is married to Josephine Calina, author of *Scenes of Russian Life, Shakespeare in Poland,* and other books.

ADDITIONAL WORKS: A History of Late Nineteenth Century Drama, 1850-1900, 1946; World Drama, from Aeschylus to Anouilh, 1949; Shakespeare: An Introduction, 1953.

NICOLL, Sir WILLIAM ROBERTSON (October 10, 1851-May 4, 1923). For biographical sketch and list of works and references, see TWENTIETH CENTURY AUTHORS, 1942.

NICOLSON, Mrs. ADELA FLORENCE (CORY). See HOPE, L.

NICOLSON, Sir HAROLD GEORGE (1886-   ). For biographical sketch and list of earlier works and references, see TWENTIETH CENTURY AUTHORS, 1942.

* * *

Sir Harold Nicolson represented West Leicester in the House of Commons from 1935 to 1945. He joined the Labour Party in 1947. During World War II he was parlia-

mentary secretary to the Ministry of Information from 1940 to 1941 and from 1941 to 1946 a governor of the B.B.C. Since 1952 he has been chairman of the committee of the London Library. He is a Fellow of the Royal Society of Literature and in 1953 was created Knight Commander of the Victorian Order by Queen Elizabeth II.

In addition to his many social and political activities, Sir Harold has in recent years written a number of highly praised biographies, histories and miscellaneous works. Outstanding among these are his study of the Congress of Vienna, in which he reduces the complex political maneuverings of the Napoleonic era to a narrative that one reviewer described as "remarkable for its clarity, its sense of historical proportion, its illuminating character sketches and the ease with which it flows"; his biography of Benjamin Constant; and his biography of King George V of England, an official biography which nevertheless avoided (as Crane Brinton pointed out in the New York *Herald Tribune*) "the dullness, undue reverence and unnecessary reticence so often associated with such biographies."

ADDITIONAL WORKS: The Desire to Please: Hamilton Rowan and the United Irishman (vol. 2 of In Search of the Past) 1943; Friday Mornings, 1941-44, 1944; The Congress of Vienna, 1946; The English Sense of Humour: An Essay, 1946; Comments, 1944-48; Benjamin Constant, 1949; King George V, 1953; The Evolution of Diplomatic Method, 1954.

ABOUT: Wilson, E. Classics and Commercials; Commonweal December 10, 1943; New York Herald Tribune Book Review October 9, 1949.

*NIEBUHR, REINHOLD (June 21, 1892-   ). For autobiographical sketch and list of earlier works and references, see TWENTIETH CENTURY AUTHORS, 1942.

* * *

Reinhold Niebuhr has been called by *Time* magazine "the number one theologian of United States Protestantism." One of the most articulate and effective of present-day theologians, Niebuhr is the spokesman in America of Protestant orthodoxy ("neo-orthodoxy," as some have called it, although Niebuhr himself objects to the term), emphasizing in his writings, his lectures, and his sermons the importance of the Christian dogma of original sin, the recognition of the essentially sinful and tragic nature of man. Niebuhr sees modern man as a complex creature, living "in the paradox of his freedom and his finiteness." Because he believes that man's spiritual dilemma is intimately

* ne͞ʹbŏŏr

717

bound up with his problems as a member of modern society, Niebuhr has explored in his recent writings the whole field of human history and social change. W. E. Garrison wrote, in the *Christian Century,* that his *Irony of American History* was "filled with penetrating analyses of many aspects of modern civilization and its present tensions," and Peter Viereck described the book as "a brilliant philosophical synthesis of his social conscience with his other-worldly conscience."

Niebuhr has been active in a variety of social and political organizations. A former pacifist, he associated himself with many anti-Nazi groups during World War II. In 1944 he became vice-chairman of the Liberal Party of New York. He has urged the church to take a strong stand in the fight for social justice and is generally identified with the liberal, anti-Communist movement in the United States. He is a stimulating teacher and lecturer, with a rapid delivery that reflects his quickness and energy of mind. *Time* describes him as "hawk-nosed and saturnine . . . a cheerful and gracious (though conversationally explosive) man." He lives with his family in New York, where he has taught at Union Theological Seminary since 1930. His wife lectures on religion at neighboring Barnard College. In 1953 he was elected to the National Institute of Arts and Letters.

ADDITIONAL WORKS: The Children of Light and the Children of Darkness, 1944; Discerning the Signs of the Times, 1946; Faith and History, 1949; The Irony of American History, 1952; Christian Realism and Political Problems, 1953; The Self and the Drama of History, 1955.

ABOUT: Carnell, E. J. The Theology of Reinhold Niebuhr; Davies, D. R. Reinhold Niebuhr, Prophet from America; Fisher, D. C. American Portraits; Current Biography 1951; National Cyclopedia of American Biography (1946); Christian Century March 26, 1953; Nation April 20, 1946; New York Herald Tribune Book Review October 11, 1953; New York Times Book Review May 8, 1949; Reporter January 13, 1955; Saturday Review April 5, 1952; Time March 8, 1948, February 19, 1951.

NILES, Mrs. BLAIR (RICE) (188?-).
For biographical sketch and list of earlier works and references, see TWENTIETH CENTURY AUTHORS, 1942.

* * *

Blair Niles' intimate knowledge of Latin America was put to good service in her anthology *Journeys in Time.* A collection of writings by travelers in Latin America from the days of the Conquistadors until 1942, with commentaries and biographical profiles by Mrs. Niles, it was praised by Mason Wade in *Commonweal* as "the most absorbing and revealing single volume on the intangibles of

Latin America which has come this reviewer's way." And H. R. Hayes wrote of the book in the New York *Times:* "She has skillfully arranged her text to capture that aspect of Latin America which most appeals to the love of adventure in all of us, the haunting sense that the southern continent is somehow the last citadel of the unknown."

In other recent writings Mrs. Niles has divided her attention about equally between Latin American and North American history. *Passengers to Mexico* was a "biographical history," told as a swift-moving narrative, of the tragic reign of Maximilian and Carlotta in Mexico. On the North American scene she has published a revised and enlarged edition of her book on the James River (originally published in 1939) and an informal biography of George Washington, entitled *Martha's Husband.* Mrs. Niles lives in New York City. She received the Gold Medal of the Society of Woman Geographers in 1944 and was a member of the international jury in the Latin American prize novel contests of 1941 and 1943.

ADDITIONAL WORKS: Passengers to Mexico, 1943; The James: from Iron Gate to the Sea, 1945; Journeys in Time, 1946; Martha's Husband: An Informal Portrait of George Washington, 1951.

ABOUT: Warfel, H. R. American Novelists of Today.

NIMS, JOHN FREDERICK (1913-), American poet, writes: "I was born in Muskegon, Mich. My father, Frank McReynolds Nims, was of New England stock for the most part English, though the name itself was brought to America by a French Huguenot émigré, Godfrey Nims (or probably Nîmes) who settled in Deerfield, Mass., in the seventeenth century, where one can still see the house he built soon after the terrible Indian massacre that wiped out most of his family. The parents of my mother, Anne McDonald, were born in Ireland; they had come to America to settle in Wisconsin.

James Harjie Connelly

"My own childhood was spent in Muskegon, a quite ordinary childhood without unusual griefs or exultations: in the summer there were picnics on the brilliant shores of Lake Michigan or dusty baseball games in the ball park across the street from us; in the winter there was skating on the ponds or a ragged kind of skiing in the dunes, or there was the exciting gloom of the public library, where I found Howard Pyle's *King Arthur* stories, a series about boyish adventures at Shiloh and Antietam, and chronicles of Boy Scouts at Crater Lake or Dismal Swamp. Nothing precocious in my reading, unless it was the fact that even as a child I read poetry for pleasure. One of my earliest memories is of my father's lugubrious rendering of *Break, Break, Break*.

"When I was about twelve we moved to Chicago, where I finished grammar school not far from the district James T. Farrell has described, though if Studs Lonigan's world was around me, I was largely unaware of it. In those years I wrote verses (one to congratulate Lindbergh on conquering the Atlantic) and thought of being an architect or an artist. For four years I went to Leo High School, also on the South Side of Chicago. Most of the students and all of the teachers were Irish; some of the latter were very fine indeed, perhaps especially a Latin teacher (also the basketball coach) who read Virgil to us with contagious enthusiasm. In high school I continued to write some verses, but my real love during these years was tennis: no July afternoon was too sultry for hours on the court, hardly a December day too cold, if the snow could be cleared from the asphalt with broom or shovel.

"After high school I was given a scholarship to De Paul University, which I attended for two years as a pre-law student. I continued to do some writing, particularly under a very gifted freshman teacher, but my chief scholastic interests were the Greek and Latin classes. The next two or three years were clouded by vague illness that kept me off the tennis courts but gave me more time for reading and writing. Twice I was out of school for a semester (I was now at Notre Dame); I spent the enforced leisure reading Keats, Spenser, and the Greek poets, writing juvenile sonnets that seemed to me quite wonderful, and walking for long afternoons among the Michigan orchards and cornfields.

"After a year of teaching English and Latin at a preparatory school in Portland, Ore., I returned to Notre Dame for my A.B. degree, with a thesis on Horace (1937) and my M.A. degree, with a thesis on Milton's prose (1939). In that year I became an instructor in English there and began further graduate work at the University of Chicago in comparative literature: the history and theory of tragedy in Greek, Latin, French, and English. My major field was Elizabethan and Jacobean drama; I was given my Ph.D. degree in 1945. Except for one year of teaching at the University of Toronto (St. Michael's College) I have been a member of the faculty of the University of Notre Dame since 1939.

"During college and since college I had been writing poetry, which about 1940 began to appear in *Poetry* (Chicago) and in such other 'little' magazines as *Accent* and *Western Review*. For a few years, beginning about 1945, I was one of the editors of *Poetry* and wrote most of the critical supplements that were designed as classroom material. In 1951 I began to write some short stories, chiefly during a summer spent at Yaddo (Saratoga Springs, N.Y.). In the winter of 1952 I began a translation of the poetry of St. John of the Cross, who seems to me, quite apart from his greatness as a mystic, one of the most dazzling of poets.

"In 1947 I married Bonnie Larkin; we have three small sons. At present (1953) we are living in St. Margherita Ligure on the Italian Riviera; I am giving lectures in Milan on contemporary American poetry."

* * *

On the publication of the first volume of John Frederick Nims' poems, the late William Rose Benét wrote that his work "seems to me to rank high among modern verse." The flaws in his early work, as Dudley Fitts pointed out, "are those of much young poetry . . . epigrammatic insistence . . . an overvivacity of diction, as though the poet were in constant dread of being detected in a commonplace." Louise Bogan commented: "Sharp-sighted and keen-witted though he is, Nims does not release us, as he should into the world of the imagination." His second volume, *A Fountain in Kentucky*, was very favorably received, and at least one of the poems, "The Masque of Blackness," was, in Richard Wilbur's judgment, an achievement in its own right and "evidence that its author is making a transition toward a richer poetic method." I. L. Salomon said of him in the *Saturday Review of Literature:* "A Catholic poet, he is not pietistic; a student of the classics, he is not a prissy stuffed-shirt. No subject is too mean for him to transmute into poetry. In his esthetic the poem is the becoming, the substance of his material determining its organic form."

PRINCIPAL WORKS: *in* Five Young American Poets: Third Series, 1944; The Iron Pastoral, 1947; A Fountain in Kentucky, and Other Poems, 1950.

ABOUT: Hoehn, M. (ed.) Catholic Authors, II; Poetry November 1950; Saturday Review of Literature March 22, 1947, March 11, 1950; University of Kansas City Review Winter 1947.

Soichi Sunami

*NIN, ANAÏS, American novelist, writes: "Born in Paris. Father Spanish pianist composer Joaquin Nin. Mother, Rosa Culmell, French-Danish singer and society woman. Brought up in atmosphere of travel, musical life. At age of nine, due to separation of parents, brought to the United States and sent to public school. Rebelled against standardization and decided to be self taught after grammar school. Owes education to public libraries. At twenty married American banker and artist Hugh Guiler, who later became well-known engraver and film maker as Ian Hugo. Lived in Europe after marriage until outbreak of war in 1940, returned to the United States. In France wrote her first three books: a study of D. H. Lawrence, *The House of Incest, Winter of Artifice*. In America no publisher interested in her. Bought her own press and published her own books for four years: *Under a Glass Bell, Winter of Artifice, This Hunger,* and reprint of *House of Incest*. Attracted attention of Edmund Wilson in *New Yorker*. Then *Ladders to Fire* and *Children of the Albatross* were published by commercial publishers, recently *The Four-Chambered Heart* and *A Spy in the House of Love*. She considers herself an international writer, but she is an American citizen and is often included in anthologies of American writers. She has no permanent residence and travels constantly."

* * *

Anaïs Nin's strange chronicles of the subconscious, written in an esoteric and imaginative prose, have brought her the attention of a small but highly literate public. At the outset, as she explains in her sketch above, she was obliged to publish her books herself, on a secondhand foot-power press, illustrated with her husband's engravings. In recent years, however, her work has been published by commercial presses. Her writings defy easy classification and have been called "autobiographical fantasy" and "literary surrealism." Edmund Wilson describes her novels as "half short stories, half dreams, and they mix a sometimes exquisite poetry with a homely realistic observation. They take place in a special world, a world of feminine perception and fancy." Miss Nin herself says: "I am in the difficult position of pre-

* nēn

senting stories which are dreams and of having to say: But now, although I give you these, I am awake!" Her published novels have all been part of one long "spiritual biography" or diary, evolving around the character of a young dancer named Djuna who acts as a kind of "sensitive register" to the whole flow of human experience about her. The effect achieved is not unlike that of the dance, evoking "the grace-in-motion and the elegant patterns, the emotional directness and the dreamlike aura, of a classical ballet." Robert Gorham Davis wrote of her work: "What Miss Nin records are subjective states, configurations of character, the fields of electric tension, movement and resistance in human relationships. She defines these with elegance and insight."

Miss Nin is pale and slender, with brown-red hair and green eyes. When not traveling, she lives in Greenwich Village, New York City. Her favorite recreations are music and dancing.

PRINCIPAL WORKS: Winter of Artifice, 1939; Under a Glass Bell, 1944; Ladders to Fire (Pt. I, This Hunger, 1945) 1946; Children of the Albatross, 1947; The House of Incest, 1949; The Four-Chambered Heart, 1950; A Spy in the House of Love, 1954.

ABOUT: Laughlin, J. (ed.) New Directions 1942; Nin, A. On Writing *and* Burford, W. The Art of Anais Nin, *in* Outcast Chapbooks, no. 11 (1947); Current Biography 1944.

NIVEN, FREDERICK JOHN (March 31, 1878-January 30, 1944). For autobiographical sketch and list of earlier works and references, see TWENTIETH CENTURY AUTHORS, 1942.

* * *

Frederick John Niven died in a Vancouver hospital at sixty-five. His last work was a trilogy of novels presenting a fictional history of the Canadian West; the third volume was unfinished at the time of his death.

Desmond Pacey, while feeling that Niven's novels tend to be "overweighted with theme and history," praised his ability to describe scenery in prose that is "clean, sparse and yet vivid." The comparative liveliness of the characters of his early Scottish novels as against those of his later novels of Canada has been noted by Edward A. McCourt, who adds that "in spite of his comparative failures he is much the most competent historical novelist to write of the Canadian West."

ADDITIONAL WORKS: Under Which King? 1943; The Transplanted, 1944.

ABOUT: Pacey, D. Creative Writing in Canada; McCourt, E. A. The Canadian West in Fiction; London Times February 1, 1944; New York Times February 16, 1944.

NOCK, ALBERT JAY (1873?-August 19, 1945). For biographical sketch and list of earlier works and references, see TWENTIETH CENTURY AUTHORS, 1942.

* * *

Albert Jay Nock died while on a visit to Wakefield, R.I., at seventy-two. His home was in New Canaan, Conn. Before his death, Nock, who had scrupulously kept most details of his personal life secret, destroyed all his notes and papers except a few letters and an autobiographical manuscript later published as *Journal of Forgotten Days*.

A previous autobiography, *Memoirs of a Superfluous Man*, was a "discursive, cantankerous, and wholly delightful book." Clifton Fadiman, in reviewing it, wrote: "Mr. Nock is a highly civilized man who does not like our civilization and will have no part of it. I have not since the days of the early Mencken read a more eloquently written blast against democracy or enjoyed more fully a display of crusted prejudices." As he grew older, he spoke "with increasing stridency." His detestation of "the state, bureaucracy, and Franklin D. Roosevelt," the *New Yorker* observed, robs his later writings "of the urbanity he praised so highly." Although Nock once said that he never aspired to write "any but plain, idiomatic English," his style was, in the words of Frank W. Garrison, "distinguished, humorous and incisive."

ADDITIONAL WORKS: Memoirs of a Superfluous Man, 1943; Journal of Forgotten Days, 1948; Letters (1934-1945) 1949.

ABOUT: Nock, A. J. Journal of Forgotten Days, Letters; Current Biography 1944; Newsweek October 4, 1943; New York Times August 20, 1945; Time January 31, 1949.

NORDAU, MAX SIMON (1849-1923), Austrian litterateur, philosopher, and Zionist, was born in Budapest, the son of Rabbi Gabriel Südfeld and Rosalie Sara Nelkin Südfeld. He studied medicine, but had early shown a literary bent. At sixteen he contributed regularly to a newspaper, and for six years acted as editor of the "Pester Lloyd" newspaper.

In 1873 he received his M.D. degree and went to Vienna to discharge his conscription duties as military surgeon. He later spent about six years traveling throughout Europe, as correspondent for several newspapers, and wrote two travel books on social conditions he had observed. In 1878 he returned to Budapest where he practiced medicine. In 1880 he settled permanently as a physician in Paris. In collaboration with Ferdinand Gross he wrote his first drama *Die Journalisten* (*The Journalists*) and in 1882 his medical degree was confirmed by the University of Paris.

In 1883 appeared the first of his controversial studies of the mental and moral pathology of modern civilization, which were to make him famous: *Conventionelle Lügen der Kulturmenschheit*, which was translated as *Conventional Lies of Our Civilization* in London in 1895. This book was banned in Russia and Austria because of Nordau's attacks on the royal families and social systems of those countries. The next two books were *Paradoxes* and *The Ailment of Our Century*.

Nordau's two-volume book *Entartung* (*Degeneration*) provoked a European storm of literary controversy. In this book Nordau strove to demonstrate that many authors and artists manifest the same mental characteristics as the criminal and the insane. This book was answered in England by G. B. Shaw who in *Sanity of Art* (1908) angrily described Nordau as "one of those remarkable cosmopolitan Jews who go forth against modern civilization as David went against the Philistines or Charles Martel against the Saracens, smite it hip and thigh without any sense of common humanity with it," and charged that Nordau had "trumped up an indictment of its men of genius as depraved lunatics."

Nordau's four-act social drama *Das Recht zu Lieben* (*The Right to Love*) was produced in Berlin, Russia, and Italy. In 1900 he wrote a tragedy, *Dr. Kohn*, dealing with the problem of intermarriage.

Living in France, Nordau was deeply disturbed by the Dreyfus case and the problem of anti-Semitism. When Theodore Herzl founded the political Zionist movement as a solution to the Jewish problem, Max Nordau became one of his first and most ardent supporters. At the First Zionist Congress in Basel in 1897, Herzl was elected president of the movement and Nordau vice-president. After this he devoted all of his lecturing and journalistic ability to helping the oppressed Jews in Eastern Europe, and working towards the political establishment of an autonomous Jewish state in Palestine. 'The Zionist movement was not invented by us," he wrote. "It originated among the Jews of the backward countries. Our brethren there suffer and cry out for help. We hasten to their side. Their masses are unorganized; we seek to remedy that. They stammer their complaints in an obscure tongue. We lend them the world's languages." In this mission, Nordau's non-Jewish wife was his chief source of inspiration and encouragement. His two daughters, Anna and Maxa (a painter), later wrote their father's biography which is a record of the beginning of the Zionist movement.

In 1923, just as he was making plans to visit the new Jewish Palestine which he had helped bring into existence, Nordau died in Paris. His ashes were buried in Tel Aviv.

WORKS IN ENGLISH TRANSLATION: Degeneration, 1893; The Right to Love, 1894; A Comedy of Sentiment, 1895; Conventional Lies of Our Civilization, 1895; Paradoxes, 1895; The Ailment of the Century, 1895; The Shackles of Fate, 1902; Zionism and Anti-Semitism, 1905; Zionism, Its History and Its Aims, 1905; Max Nordau to His People, a Summons and a Challenge, 1941.

ABOUT: Jewish Encyclopedia; Nordau, A. & M. Max Nordau, a Biography; Shaw, G. B. Sanity of Art.

"NORDEN, CHARLES." See DURRELL, L.

NORDHOFF, CHARLES BERNARD

(February 1, 1887-April 11, 1947). For autobiographical sketch and list of earlier works and references, see TWENTIETH CENTURY AUTHORS, 1942.

*   *   *

Charles Nordhoff died of a heart attack at his home in Santa Barbara, Calif., at sixty.

His best work is so inextricably linked to that of his collaborator, James Norman Hall, that it is impossible to speak of its quality except in the plural. As *Time* magazine has said, "Nordhoff and Hall are highly skilled, careful, straightforward literary artisans. Their main purpose is to tell a good story excitingly."

ADDITIONAL WORKS: *With James Norman Hall* —Botany Bay, 1941; High Barbaree, 1945.

ABOUT: New York Times April 12, 1947; Time· January 19, 1942.

NORMAN, CHARLES (May 9, 1904-),

American poet, painter and biographer, writes: "I was born in Russia, the youngest of six sons. My earliest poems were about the sea, possibly because of the unforgotten voyage I had made from Europe to America at the age of five. How fortunate for me to have been no older when my mother set out for the New World, where my father awaited

us; for I was thrust into a Manhattan school almost at once. I grew up in New York City, where I attended New York University; years later, I taught a course in Shakespeare there.

"At eighteen I made another voyage, this time as an ordinary seaman on a freighter bound for South America. Masefield was my passion then, but Masefield was soon to give way to Marlowe. I left the United States twice more—for a sojourn of approximately two years in Paris when I was twenty-one; and as an infantry officer in World War II.

M. Morehouse

"It was while I was in London, on my way to Paris, that a chance purchase in a book store gave direction to my life. The book was Leslie Hotson's *The Death of Christopher Marlowe.* For twelve years, during which most of my time was at the disposal of others—The North American Newspaper Alliance, The Associated Press, Time, Inc., the newspaper *PM*—I worked on a life of Marlowe, laying it aside only during my Army service. When it was accepted for publication, and another contract was offered me for a life of Shakespeare, I left *PM* resolved never to hold down another job. This was in 1946, and I have abided by my decision, with its occasional inconveniences. I have also written a teen-age version of my life of Shakespeare entitled *The Playmaker* of *Avon*, and several children's books.

"As for my painting, which sporadically engrosses all my time, I had a one-man show at the Julien Levy Gallery on 57th Street, New York City, in January 1940, and a second exhibition, November-December, 1953, at the RoKo Gallery in Greenwich Village. I have managed, nevertheless, to retain something of an amateur's view, for I still dislike to part with my pictures. My palette is limited to four or five colors, with white and yellow predominating. I have striven for form without abstraction, believing that in a time of disorder the artist is the guardian of form."

PRINCIPAL WORKS: *Poetry*—Poems, 1929; The Bright World, 1930; The Savage Century, 1942; A Soldier's Diary, 1944. *Biography*—The Muses' Darling: The Life of Christopher Marlowe, 1946; So Worthy a Friend: William Shakespeare, 1947; Mr. Oddity: Samuel Johnson, LL.D., 1951; The Pundit and the Player: Dr. Johnson and Mr. Garrick, 1951; Shepherd of the Ocean: Sir Walter Raleigh, 1952; Rake Rochester, 1954; To a Different Drum (Thoreau) 1954. *Miscellaneous*—The Case of Ezra Pound, 1948; The Well of the Past (novel) 1949; Dominick Dragon (novel) 1951.

NORRIS, CHARLES GILMAN (April 23, 1881-July 25, 1945). For biographical sketch and list of earlier works and references, see TWENTIETH CENTURY AUTHORS, 1942.

* * *

Charles Norris died in the Palo Alto, Calif., hospital at sixty-four. He suffered from a heart ailment for a year, and had been critically ill for four months.

R. A. Cordell noted Norris' competent workmanship, accurately drawn backgrounds and undeniable power, but added that his books "always have a certain naïveté which gives a romantic cast to these earnest studies of our time meant, one is sure, to be wholly realistic." However, as Sterling North pointed out, Norris did dare to tackle major social themes, so that "if he has fallen somewhat short of complete success, his failure is of greater importance than many a lightly won victory."

ADDITIONAL WORKS: Flint, 1944.

ABOUT: New York Times July 26, 1945; Publishers' Weekly August 11, 1945; Time August 6, 1945.

NORRIS, FRANK (March 5, 1870-October 25, 1902). For biographical sketch and list of works and references, see TWENTIETH CENTURY AUTHORS, 1942.

* * *

ABOUT: Ahnebrink, L. The Influence of Emile Zola on Frank Norris, The Beginnings of Naturalism in American Fiction; Geismar, M. Rebels and Ancestors; Kazin, A. On Native Grounds; Marchand, E. L. Frank Norris; Snell, G. D. Shapers of American Fiction; American Literature March 1953; New Republic May 5, 1947.

NORRIS, Mrs. KATHLEEN (THOMPSON) (July 16, 1880-). For biographical sketch and list of earlier works and references, see TWENTIETH CENTURY AUTHORS, 1942.

* * *

Although Kathleen Norris' fiction is slight, conventional, and sentimental, reviewers have found in her later work the same qualities of honesty, directness and simplicity which they admired in her earlier writing. She has sought and has found a ready and eager audience. In 1945 she wrote a radio "soap opera" series, *Bright Horizon*, and of her radio scripts she commented characteristically, "I feel they are reaching the very heart of American women . . . and that's where I want to be." Several years later she told an interviewer: "I write what I would like to read—what I think other women would like

to read. . . . I have no knowledge of those dark forces which fascinate modern writers. I write for people with simple needs and motives because I am like that myself."

Mrs. Norris lives in Palo Alto, Calif. Her husband, Charles Norris, died in 1945.

ADDITIONAL WORKS: An Apple for Eve, 1942; One Nation Indivisible (poem) 1942; Corner of Heaven, 1943; Burned Fingers, 1945; Mink Coat, 1946; Over at the Crowleys', 1946; The Secrets of Hillyard House, 1947; High Holiday, 1949; Morning Light, 1950; Shadow Marriage, 1952; Miss Harriet Townshend, 1955.

ABOUT: Hoehn, M. (ed.) Catholic Authors, I; Taves, I. Successful Women; Collier's November 20, 1948; New York Times Book Review February 6, 1955; Time April 9, 1945.

NORTH, JESSICA NELSON (1894-). For autobiographical sketch and list of earlier works and references, see TWENTIETH CENTURY AUTHORS, 1942.

* * *

Jessica Nelson North writes from Downers Grove, Ill.: "Since 1942 I have published one volume of poetry, *Dinner Party*. I am at present conducting poetry seminars for the adult education branch of the University of Chicago. Magazine publication since 1942 includes the *Atlantic Monthly, Story, Saturday Evening Post*, and *Poetry*. I am no longer on the staff of *Poetry* but continue my interest as a guarantor."

ADDITIONAL WORK: Dinner Party (poems) 1942.

NORTH, STERLING (November 4, 1906-). For autobiographical sketch and list of earlier works and references, see TWENTIETH CENTURY AUTHORS, 1942.

* * *

Sterling North writes: "I am currently the literary editor of the New York *World Telegram and Sun* with a syndicated book review column appearing in twelve major newspapers. My two most successful books to date are *So Dear to My Heart*, which Disney made into a full-length technicolor movie and which has sold in all editions and translations more than one million copies, and the more recent *The Birthday of Little Jesus* which sold 1,000 copies a day the first season and was reprinted in eighty important newspapers during the Christmas season of that year, often in full color.

"My wife and I and our two children, David and Arielle, live in a house we designed ourselves beside our own little lake and waterfall near Morristown, N.J. We have deer, foxes, raccoons and all sorts of birds on the property, but some murderer shot the only bear."

ADDITIONAL WORKS: Midnight and Jeremiah (juvenile) 1943; Speak of the Devil (ed. with C. Boutell) 1945; So Dear to My Heart (novel) 1947; Reunion on the Wabash (novel) 1952; The Birthday of Little Jesus (juvenile) 1952.

ABOUT: Current Biography 1943; Editor and Publisher September 24, 1949; Time February 25, 1946.

NORTHROP, FILMER STUART CUCKOW (November 27, 1893-), American scholar and philosopher, writes:

Yale News Bureau

"The younger son of Marshall Ellsworth Northrop and Ruth Cuckow Northrop, I was born in Janesville, Wis., where I spent my early life. In 1915, after majoring in history, I was graduated from Beloit College and moved to New York to do social work. I stayed in New York until I entered the graduate school of Yale University in 1916. Having finished the requirements for an M.A. in philosophy, I enlisted in the Army in 1918 as a private and received my discharge as a second lieutenant in 1919. The year 1919 was also the date of my marriage to Miss Christine Johnston, the daughter of Mr. and Mrs. John Walton Johnston of Manchester, N.H. Shortly after our marriage we left for Hong Kong, China, where I was education secretary of the international committee of the YMCA.

"Due to an academic turn of mind I left China to study at Harvard for a Ph.D. in philosophy. I took my M.A. in 1922. Awarded a Harvard traveling fellowship for 1922-1923, I took my family to Europe where, during the summer of 1922, I studied at the University of Freiburg, Germany, and worked with Husserl. In the fall we went to Cambridge where I attended Trinity College as a research student under McTaggart. I also worked with James Ward, W. E. Johnson and G. E. Moore at Cambridge and studied under Alfred North Whitehead at the Imperial College of Science and Technology in London.

"Returning to the United States we moved to New Haven where I began my teaching in 1923 as an instructor in the department of philosophy of Yale University. The following June I was awarded a Ph.D. by Har-

vard for my dissertation, 'The Problem of Organization in Biology.' In 1932 I received a Guggenheim fellowship which I used for two-thirds of the academic year at Trinity College, Cambridge, and for the other third at the University of Göttingen. At Cambridge I attended the lectures of Hardy and Littlewood on number theory and the theory of functions and of Wittgenstein on philosophical analysis. At Göttingen I read in the library of the Mathematical Institute on the historical and logical foundations of modern mathematics. Also in 1932 I was appointed professor of philosophy at Yale, the position I held until 1947 when I received my present appointment as Sterling professor of philosophy and law in the department of philosophy and the Yale Law School.

"In 1940 Silliman College, the last of the ten residential colleges at Yale to be completed, was opened and I was appointed as master. In 1947, wanting more time for research work, I retired from my mastership and since then have received from the Viking Fund, now the Wenner-Gren Foundation for Anthropological Research, grants which released me from part of the normal teaching load for research and graduate teaching in the philosophy of culture and world law. Thanks to such grants a field trip was made to South Asia in 1950 and 1951. The editing of Ideological Differences and World Order and the writing of The Taming of the Nations were the results of such grants. Another grant made possible a similar research trip to continental Europe and Turkey in 1952 and to South America in early 1953.

"While continuing my earlier teaching at Yale, visiting professorships were also held at the Universities of Iowa, Michigan, Hawaii, Virginia and the National University of Mexico. In 1949 the Order of the Aztec Eagle was awarded me by the Mexican Government for the portrayal of Mexico in The Meeting of East and West. A Mexican publisher also brought out a Spanish edition of this work. Japanese and German translations have also been published.

"In the early summers of 1939 and 1949 I was a member of the East-West Philosophy Conference at Honolulu. In August 1949 I inaugurated, under the auspices of the Australian Institute of International Affairs and the University of Melbourne, the series of ten annual lectureships by different Europeans or Americans under the Dyason Trust.

"Two technical books, Science and First Principles and The Logic of the Sciences and the Humanities preceded The Taming of *the Nations.* Technical articles in natural and social science, the philosophy of science and the philosophy of culture and of law appeared in diverse popular and technical journals.

"I enjoy traveling, the sports of any people and especially baseball in the case of the United States. In the summer in New Hampshire I enjoy landscape, a doubles in tennis and leisurely swimming when the pressure of reading, writing or proofreading does not otherwise occupy my time. I also like people, except before breakfast or when they insist upon talking nothing but shop in vacation time."

* * *

F. S. C. Northrop's monumental *Meeting of East and West* was an analysis of the philosophical, political, economic and religious ideologies of the Western world and of Asia in an effort to arrive at a synthesis of values common to both worlds. Ordway Tead, reviewing it for the *Saturday Review of Literature,* praised the book as "a rich mine of ideas . . . intellectual statesmanship of a high order of incisiveness." *The Taming of the Nations,* subtitled "A Study of the Cultural Bases of International Policy," was an examination of the philosophical foundations of modern civilization in the search for the principles of a basic foreign policy by which the nations of the world could live, and it concludes with Northrop's proposals for a positive foreign policy for defending the free world through the United Nations.

PRINCIPAL WORKS: Science and First Principles, 1931; The Meeting of East and West, 1946; The Logic of the Sciences and the Humanities, 1947; (ed.) Ideological Differences and World Order, 1949; The Taming of the Nations, 1952; European Union and United States Foreign Policy, 1954.

ABOUT: Murphy, A. E. *in* Essays in Political Theory Presented to George H. Sabine (ed. M. R. Konvitz & A. E. Murphy); Sorokin, P. A. Social Philosophies of an Age of Crisis; Tute, Sir R. C. After Materialism—What?; Journal of the History of Ideas April 1948.

NORWAY, NEVIL SHUTE (January 17, 1899-). For biographical sketch and list of earlier works and references, see TWENTIETH CENTURY AUTHORS, 1942.

* * *

Nevil Shute Norway had little time to enjoy his retirement (in 1938) from the managership of his airplane construction company. When World War II broke out he was commissioned in the Royal Naval Volunteer Reserve becoming lieutenant commander in 1941. He did war work for the British Admiralty until 1945. After the war

he moved to Australia where he lives at Langwarrin, Victoria. He has been married since 1931 to Frances Mary Heaton and they have two daughters.

The two sides of his personality—Nevil Shute Norway, business executive and aeronautical engineer, and Nevil Shute, popular novelist—are caught in his autobiography *Slide Rule,* which Roger Pippett described in the New York *Times* as "the fascinatingly factual record not so much of a writer's apprenticeship as of a' man who has always liked to do two jobs at the same time." As a novelist Shute enjoys a high degree of popularity in England and America. He has been called "a master of the easy, insidious style which practically reads itself." He is a writer, as the London *Times Literary Supplement* points out, of "high moral purpose and happy ending," and his method is "that of a highly skilled entertainer." His most recent novels have been set in Australia, which he depicts in vivid and loving detail.

ADDITIONAL WORKS: Pastoral, 1944; Most Secret, 1945; Vinland the Good, 1946; Chequer Board, 1947; No Highway, 1948; The Legacy (in England: A Town like Alice) 1950; Round the Bend, 1951; The Far Country, 1952; In the Wet, 1953; Slide Rule, 1954; The Breaking Wave, 1955.

ABOUT: Shute, N. Slide Rule; Current Biography 1942; New York Times Book Review May 30, 1954.

NOVELLO, IVOR (January 15, 1893-March 6, 1951), British actor, dramatist and composer, was born in Cardiff, Wales, the son

of David Davies, an accountant, and Clara Novello Davies, a singing teacher. He was educated at Magdalen College School, Oxford, and between 1905 and 1911 was a chorister of Magdalen College. Having studied composition under a private tutor, he published his first song when he was fifteen, and at twenty-one wrote "Keep the Home Fires Burning," which made him both rich and famous. Overnight he became a national idol. *Time* has said, "He was not only Britain's Ziegfeld but also Britain's Valentino, and for a while her Jack Barrymore too; added to which he was one of the most successful song writers of his day, and a maker of light comedies second only to Noel Coward." Among his songs are "Dreamboat," "We'll Gather Lilacs," and about sixty others.

"His songs were among Britain's most popular," wrote the New York *Times*.

At the age of twenty-eight he made his first appearance on the stage. He began his work as actor-manager in 1924 with the production of *The Rat*, written by himself in collaboration with Constance Collier. Author of innumerable plays, he took a leading role in many of them, including *Party, Fresh Fields, Proscenium, Flies in the Sun, Sunshine Sisters*. In 1926 he played the title role in Molnar's *Liliom* in England. In 1930 he appeared at the Shubert Theatre in New York in *Symphony in Two Flats*, his own play. The year 1931 he spent in Hollywood, writing and acting. He then resumed his stage career in London, appearing in some twenty plays, many of them his own composition. Of his work during the '30's, the British theatre critic W. A. Darlington has said, "We in London have learned to know Novello as a very considerable man in the theatre who has proved himself capable of writing a series of large-scale romantic melodramas which kept the Drury Lane open at the time when no other writer could produce even one really successful piece there. Without Mr. Novello, Drury Lane is a white elephant; with him it is a gold mine. He writes plays, composes music and acts the principal male parts. Anybody who can do this successfully is a craftsman of the highest order." In 1944 Novello visited the English forces in Normandy with a play, and in 1947 he took a play to South Africa. In World War I he had served in the Royal Naval Air Service (1914-18).

Novello made his home in London. He died at fifty-eight, following a thrombosis.

PRINCIPAL WORKS: The Rat, 1927; The Truth Game, 1929; Proscenium, 1934; Fresh Fields, 1934; Full House, 1936; Comedienne, 1938; Glamorous Night, 1939; We Proudly Present, 1947.

ABOUT: Macqueen-Pope, W. J. Ivor, the Story of an Achievement; Noble, P. Ivor Novello, Man of the Theatre; Illustrated London News March 10, 1951; Life March 26, 1951; London Sunday Times March 11, 1951; London Times March 7, 1951; Musical America March 1951; New York Times March 6, 1951; Scotsman March 7, 1951; Time October 6, 1947, September 10, 1951.

NOYES, ALFRED (September 16, 1880-).

* * *

The first two printings of TWENTIETH CENTURY AUTHORS (1942 and 1944) incorrectly reported that Alfred Noyes' *Voltaire* (1936) had been condemned and then ordered revised by the Catholic Church. This error was corrected in the third printing of TWEN-TIETH CENTURY AUTHORS in 1950. As Noyes himself relates the facts in his autobiography, *Two Worlds for Memory* (1953): an anonymous letter denouncing the book provoked the misunderstanding and "the temporary suspension of the book" by the Supreme Congregation of the Holy See. The matter was investigated by Cardinal Hinsley who, in April 1939, issued a letter "stating that the competent authorities desired no deletions whatever in the text of the book." Noyes adds that he was later told that Cardinal Pacelli, who became Pope Pius XII, "had declared the charges against the book to be nonsensical."

In 1940 Alfred Noyes visited Canada on a coast-to-coast lecture tour. In 1941 he came with his family to the United States, where he lectured at universities all over the country. He received honorary degrees from Syracuse University in 1942 and from the University of California at Berkeley in 1944. Noyes lived in California for several years. He gave a course of thirty lectures at Berkeley and moved on from there to another branch of the University of California, at Santa Barbara. Meanwhile his eyesight, which had troubled him for many years, began to fail, and in spite of a series of operations, he now has only partial vision. He returned to England in 1949 and lives at Lisle Combe on the Isle of Wight, "where I know every part of the ground, every slope and every tree."

ADDITIONAL WORKS: The Edge of the Abyss (lectures) 1942; Poems of the New World, 1942; The Secret of Pooduck Island (juvenile) 1943; Collected Poems, 1947; Horace: A Portrait, 1947; Daddy Fell into the Pond, and Other Poems for Children, 1953; Two Worlds for Memory, 1953.

ABOUT: Noyes, A. Two Worlds for Memory; Hoehn, M. (ed.) Catholic Authors, I; Catholic World September 1951; Contemporary Review April 1951; Publishers' Weekly July 8, 1944; Time September 5, 1938; Universe (London) March 31, 1939.

NYE, RUSSEL BLAINE (February 17, 1913-), American biographer and historian, writes: "I was born in Viola, Wis., the younger son of Charles H. and Zelma Nye. My father's family were State of Maine men who came West in the Forties, my mother's German immigrants who arrived in Wisconsin in the Eighties. After my mother's death in 1915 I lived chiefly with my paternal grandparents, and after my father's death in 1922 with my aunt in Viroqua, Wis., where I completed high school. Viroqua is the center of heavily-populated

Norwegian territory, sharply divided during my youth by followers of LaFollette the elder and of stalwart Republicanism; I there-fore grew up with a working knowledge of Norse and a decided partisanship for progressive politics. Constant contact with my grandparents, who were loaded with tales of Lincoln, Grant, Bryan and other major figures, gave me, I think, an early strong awareness of history.

"I attended Oberlin College, majoring in English literature simply because I liked it, and received the B.A. in 1934. I returned to Wisconsin for an M.A. in English at the University in 1935, spending the next year teaching at a small college in upper Michigan. In 1936 I received a teaching assistantship in English at Wisconsin and worked on a Ph.D. degree until 1939, when I left to take an instructorship in English at Adelphi College on Long Island. In 1938 I married Kathryn Chaney, a graduate student in French; we have a son, Peter William. During my graduate work I came under the influence of Harry Hayden Clark and William B. Hesseltine, whose courses in American literature and history convinced me that this was my permanent field of interest. Since my grandfather lived by three books—Webster's *Unabridged*, the Bible, and George Bancroft's *History of the United States*—I chose Bancroft as the subject of my doctoral dissertation, which was completed and the degree awarded in 1940.

"After arriving at Michigan State College as an English instructor in 1940, I received a fellowship in biography from Alfred A. Knopf, who encouraged me to recast my dissertation into a full-dress study, which won a Pulitzer prize in 1945. A Rockefeller grant enabled me to spend a year free from teaching for work on the relationship between civil liberties and the abolitionist controversy in the three decades preceding the Civil War. Similarly, a grant from the Newberry Library gave me time to write a study of Midwestern progressive politics, a subject that has fascinated me since boyhood. At present I am working on an American history for British readers. [Nye is now head of the English department at Michigan State College in East Lansing.]

"I find writing very hard work, and usually revise and rework materials five to seven times, hoping to develop the accurate and readable style I consider essential to historical writing. I don't think the historian of ideas can or should strive to be completely neutral. There is, I believe, right and wrong in the past, and I think that the writer must make moral choices in his judgment of man and movements. The sweep of history, the wave of events, is the thing the writer must catch, nor should he miss the larger pattern of the past in the welter of detail."

PRINCIPAL WORKS: George Bancroft: Brahmin Rebel, 1944; Fettered Freedom: Civil Liberties and the Slavery Controversy, 1949; Midwestern Progressive Politics, 1951; (ed.) The Modern Essay, 1952; William Lloyd Garrison and the Humanitarian Reformers, 1955.

ABOUT: Current Biography 1945; New York Herald Tribune May 8, 1945; Publishers' Weekly May 23, 1942.

OBOLER, ARCH (December 6, 1907-), American radio writer and playwright, was born in Chicago, Ill., the son of Leo Oboler and Clara (Obeler) Oboler. His boyhood ambition was to be a naturalist, and his bedroom became a zoo of turtles, frogs, and the like. At the age of ten he wrote and sold a story suggested by this menagerie. In high school in Chicago he continued to  be interested in the world of science, and went on to the University of Chicago, enrolling in a course in electrical engineering. While still a student he wrote a fantasy called "Futuristic"; the National Broadcasting Company bought it and used it in 1934 as a salute program in ceremonies opening Radio City in New York. In 1935 Oboler wrote radio plays for various screen stars, and from 1936 to 1938 contributed to *Lights Out*, an after-midnight horror series. In the spring of 1938 he came from N.B.C.'s Chicago studio to New York with the recorded script of his play *The Ugliest Man in the World*. N.B.C. was so impressed that they launched the series *Arch Oboler's Plays*, dramas of realism, fantasy, comedy, satire, and tragedy. Oboler is said to have been the first to develop the monologue and stream-of-consciousness method for radio use.

His *Fourteen Radio Plays*, published in 1940, included an essay by Oboler on "The Art of Radio Writing." "The very first premise," he wrote, "for good radio writing should be actually having something to say that hasn't been said before quite in the manner in which you say it." Ruth Lechlitner in *Books* complained that Oboler's fourteen plays did not fulfill this premise, but A. N. Williams in the *Saturday Review of Literature* wrote: "Radio has come of age. . . . This first volume of radio plays is tangible proof of this adulthood, and that the acceptance of it has begun." While Oboler has always had his strong advocates among the public and in the radio profession, when the *Oboler Omnibus* appeared in 1945 the literary critics were unconvinced. "On the air there is no denying the impact of his passionate seriousness, enhanced as it is by his skill as a director," said James Fuller in the New York *Times*; "But with the cooling-off process between performance and publication, the clichés emerge, as from a campaign speech revisited." Oboler's radio technique is that of a good storyteller, employing a clearly defined situation, recognizable human speech, clear-cut characters, and suspense and climax. His plays "move invariably toward a resounding final cliché," Richard Match observed in the New York *Herald Tribune*, but he "remains a hard-biting radio writer."

Besides writing and directing movies for M.G.M., such as *Escape*, *Bewitched*, and *The Arnelo Affair*, he wrote, directed and produced the first feature three-dimensional movie, *Bwana Devil* in 1952, a tale of railroad building in Africa. Bosley Crowther, reviewing it in the New York *Times*, found the story hackneyed, and downright old-fashioned. "To be sure, *Bwana Devil* is a first try, done at comparatively small expense and probably never presumed by Mr. Oboler to excite the public interest that it has. One should therefore not judge it too harshly nor be too disappointed by the fact that it turns out to be almost as footless and tame as its two weary lions."

Dark-haired, energetic, and small in stature, Oboler likes to wear old clothes. He says he has dreamed some of his plays, and that he gets inspiration for others by listening to the music of great composers. In 1945 he won the Peabody Award for radio drama. He married Eleanor Helfand, has four sons, Guy, David, Steven, and Peter, and lives in Malibu, Calif.

PRINCIPAL WORKS: Everything Happened to Him; the Story of Tex Rickard (with M. E. Rickard) 1936; Fourteen Radio Plays, 1940; Ivory Tower, and Other Radio Plays, 1940; Plays for Americans, 1942; This Freedom, 1942; (ed., with S. Longstreet) Free World Theatre, 1944; Oboler Omnibus, 1945.

ABOUT: Current Biography 1940; Variety Radio Directory.

O'BRIEN, EDWARD JOSEPH HARRINGTON (December 10, 1890-February 25, 1941). For biographical sketch and list of works and references, see TWENTIETH CENTURY AUTHORS, 1942.

* * *

ADDITIONAL WORKS: *Edited*—Best British Short Stories, 1938-40; Best Short Stories, 1938-41.

ABOUT: Hoehn, M. (ed.) Catholic Authors, I.

O'BRIEN, FREDERICK (1869-January 9, 1932). For biographical sketch and list of works and references, see TWENTIETH CENTURY AUTHORS, 1942.

O'BRIEN KATE (December 3, 1897-). For biographical sketch and list of earlier works and references, see TWENTIETH CENTURY AUTHORS, 1942.

* * *

Kate O'Brien's great interest in Spanish history and Spanish culture was nowhere better reflected than in her novel based on the political and romantic intrigue in the court of Philip II of Spain, *That Lady* (published in America as *For One Sweet Grape*). In her heroine, the proud and lovely Castilian princess Ana de Mendoza, she created a memorable dramatic figure, and the work as a whole was described in the *Spectator* as "a novel of much beauty and fascination, at once subtle and satisfying." Two of *That Lady's* most enthusiastic readers were the actress Katherine Cornell and her husband, the producer Guthrie McClintic, who asked Miss O'Brien to dramatize the book for them. (She had previously dramatized two of her novels—*The Anteroom* and *The Last of Summer*.) After three years of hard work, Miss O'Brien completed the dramatization, which was produced in New York in December 1949 with Miss Cornell in the leading role. The play, however, did not enjoy anything like the novel's success. Although the critics admired Miss Cornell's interpretation of the role, they found the play heavy and ornate. John Chapman described it as "a rather dull and tearful fragment of history." In 1955 it was made into a motion picture starring Olivia De Havilland.

Miss O'Brien herself told an interviewer in 1949 that she preferred writing novels—in which medium the writer has more freedom and flexibility—to writing plays. Her next novel, *The Flower of May*, once again demonstrated how expert she is in the form. The story of a young Irish convent-bred girl in early twentieth century Europe, it was a delicate and sensitive portrait, "a novel of fine sensibility and splendid, persuasive power," Riley Hughes wrote. In this book, *Commonweal* observed, the author "realizes with new ease that maturity of craftsmanship which readers of her work have come to expect from one of Ireland's most distinguished novelists."

In 1949 Miss O'Brien visited New York. She makes her home in Ireland and, on the 1949 visit, announced to an interviewer, with "only the subtlest trace of an Irish brogue," that "I am going to spend my old age in peace in County Galway."

Correction: Miss O'Brien was born in 1897, not 1898, as given in TWENTIETH CENTURY AUTHORS, 1942.

ADDITIONAL WORKS: The Last of Summer, 1943; For One Sweet Grape (in England: That Lady) 1946; That Lady (play) 1949; Teresa of Avila, 1951; The Flower of May, 1953.

ABOUT: Hoehn, M. (ed.) Catholic Authors, I; New York Times Book Review December 4, 1949.

O'CASEY, SEAN (1880-). For autobiographical sketch and list of earlier works and references, see TWENTIETH CENTURY AUTHORS, 1942.

* * *

With *Sunset and Evening Star* Sean O'Casey published the sixth and presumably final volume of his autobiography, a colorful and turbulent story that well reflects the personality of the man himself. In an earlier volume, *Inishfallen, Fare Thee Well*, describing his break with Ireland and the Abbey Theatre, he had written: "It was time for Sean to go. He had had enough of it. He would be no more of an exile in another land than he was in his own. He was a voluntary and settled exile from every creed, from every party, and from every literary clique." In a sense, O'Casey has remained an exile, living in England (in Totnes, Devon, until 1954 when he moved to St. Marychurch, near Torquay, on the Devon coast) and writing his plays which, though they have many devoted admirers, have not in recent years had any considerable popular success.

"It has been O'Casey's fate," John Gassner writes, "to be always pushing his skiff of talent against the current." Partly at least, this is due to the marked shift from the powerful "living texture" of the earlier plays like *Juno and the Paycock* and *The Plough and the Stars* to an increasing reliance on symbolism and fantasy in the later plays like *Red Roses for •Me* and *Cockadoodle Dandy*. Partly, according to Gassner, it is due to changing and narrowing tastes in the the-

atre: "Our spiritually diminished theatre in a spiritually diminished world cannot quite assimilate his particular genius . . . his wild humor of words and farcical action, his vast anger, and his vast love."

O'Casey calls himself a Communist, but he makes it clear that this is a personal rather than a political philosophy with him. Of the Communists he has said: "They drive me mad. They know nothing but what they read in their little pamphlets." Four of his autobiographical volumes are banned in Ireland. In March 1955, however, his new play, *The Bishop's Bonfires*, was produced in Dublin. O'Casey himself described it as "a play about the ferocious chastity of the Irish, a lament for the condition of Ireland, which is an apathetic country now. . . ." Anticipating a repetition of the famous riot at the première of *The Plough and the Stars* in 1926, city officials stationed police around the theatre for this opening. There was a flurry of shouts, boos, and hisses, but no actual violence. The play itself was considered brilliant in spots, but not so "inflammable" as *The Plough and the Stars.* W. A. Darlington reported to the New York *Times* that the characters of the comedy "have much the flavor, though something less than the abounding life, of the great O'Casey characters of the early plays and bear the authentic O'Casey seal."

Corrections: O'Casey's date of birth is 1880, not 1884. He has a young daughter, Shivaun, as well as the two sons mentioned in the 1942 sketch.

ADDITIONAL WORKS: *Plays*—Red Roses for Me, 1942; Oak Leaves and Lavender, 1946; Cockadoodle Dandy, 1949; Collected Plays, 1949-1951, 1951; Selected Plays (introd. by John Gassner) 1954. *Autobiography*—Drums Under the Windows, 1945; Inishfallen, Fare Thee Well, 1949; Rose and Crown, 1952; Sunset and Evening Star, 1954. *Essays*—The Flying Wasp, 1937.

ABOUT: Gregory I. Lady Gregory's Journals; Kavanagh, P. The Story of the Abbey Theatre; Koslow, J. The Green and the Red; O'Casey, S. Drums Under the Windows, Inishfallen, Fare Thee Well, Rose and Crown, Sunset and Evening Star; America June 11, 1949; New Republic March 20, 1944; New York Times March 6, 1955; New York Times Book Review December 26, 1948; Nineteenth Century and After April 1946; Theatre Arts January 1950, June, July, August 1951, December 1952, September 1953; Time March 14, 1955; (London) Times Literary Supplement September 21, 1951.

O'CONNOR, FRANK (pseudonym of Michael O'Donovan) (1903-), Irish man of letters and the author of many witty and moving volumes of short stories, was born in Cork, the son of Michael and Mary O'Donovan. He attended the Christian Brothers school in Cork, but his family was

poor and unable to give him a university education. That did not discourage the young writer, however, who already at twelve had

put together a "collected edition" of his work, consisting of poems, biographies, and essays on Irish history.

His early work, states O'Connor, was written in Gaelic, a language which he knew at first only by ear from the lips of

Louis Faurer

his grandmother before studying it systematically. He worked as a librarian, first in County Cork and then in Dublin, a profession which allowed him the time and energy to educate himself and to develop as a writer. "Æ" (George Russell) accepted many of O'Connor's early stories for publication in the *Irish Statesman*, and in 1931, he called the young author the most important "find" among Irish writers since James Stephens. In 1931 O'Connor's first volume, *Guests of the Nation*, was published; and the title story was reprinted in the *Atlantic Monthly*, the first of the many O'Connor stories which have since appeared in American magazines (currently in the *New Yorker*).

In Dublin, O'Connor was for a time one of the directors of the famous Abbey Theatre, an experience which gave him, he has said, "a lasting passion for techniques." But although he collaborated on a number of plays, his particular art was then and has remained the short story. Yeats once said that O'Connor was "doing for Ireland what Chekhov did for Russia," a grand enough compliment to please any writer but especially O'Connor, who has said that Chekhov had what he himself strove for: "the completely organic form." "Story telling," wrote O'Connor, "is the nearest thing one can get to the quality of a pure lyric poem. It doesn't deal with problems; it doesn't have any solutions to offer; it just states the human condition."

American critics and readers have been delighted, amused, and surprised by O'Connor's statement of the human condition. They have found his sense of humor equalled only by his sense of reality and the warmth and richness of his character delineation. H. C. Webster's comments on *The Stories of Frank O'Connor* are typical: "Long or short, every tale in this book," he writes, "is a treasure, a joy in its subject, in its characters, in their colorful language, and in the manner in which, without a seeming mite of effort, the author holds your most attentive interest."

Besides his many volumes of short stories, O'Connor has published several books of verse, a critical study of Turgenev—"one of my early great loves, and he will be one of my last great loves"—and a study of Michael Collins and the Irish Revolution.

Mr. O'Connor is a handsome man with the charming accent, the contagious sparkle and the wit of the true Irishman. He prefers to write in the mornings, sometimes in the evenings, but to leave the afternoons free to cycle or walk about, looking in bookshops, talking to the people he meets. He is interested in architecture and has cycled through most of Ireland, and large parts of England and France; and his one complaint about America is that it doesn't have cycling tracks. He is also something of a student of eighteenth century music. Mr. O'Connor has two sons and a daughter by a first marriage to Evelyn Bowen. In 1953 he married Harriet Rich, an American girl from Annapolis, Md.

PRINCIPAL WORKS: Guests of the Nation, 1931; The Saint and Mary Kate, 1932; The Wild Bird's Nest, 1932; Bones of Contention, 1936; The Big Fellow, 1937; Three Old Brothers, 1937; Lords and Commons, 1938; Fountain of Magic, 1939; Dutch Interior, 1940; Three Tales, 1942; A Picturebook, 1942; Crab Apple Jelly, 1944; The Midnight Court, 1945; Towards an Appreciation of Literature, 1945; Selected Stories, 1946; Irish Miles, 1947; Art of the Theatre, 1947; The Common Chord, 1947; Southern Ireland, 1950; Traveler's Samples, 1950; More Stories, 1954. *Plays*—In the Train, 1937; The Invincibles, 1937; Moses' Rock, 1938; Time's Rocket, 1939; The Statue's Daughter, 1940.

ABOUT: Bruce, H. A. *in* In Our Heritage; New York Herald Tribune Book Review August 24, 1952, October 12, 1952; New York Times Book Review August 24, 1952.

O'CONNOR, WILLIAM VAN (1915-   ), American critic, writes: "I was born in Syracuse, N.Y., the second of four children. My father's family were residents of New York but my mother's people were Canadian, of Scotch-Irish stock. I took my B.A. (1936) and M.A. (1937) from Syracuse University, then went with my elder brother, Donald, to Columbia to do fur-

ther graduate work, he in economics, I in English. Both of us taught in the New York area while taking courses at Columbia. The orthodox graduate school approach to literature, despite the presence of some good teachers, troubled me no little, but I didn't know how to formulate my dissatisfaction beyond observing that it seemed strange to find such a decided animus between scholars on the one hand and poets, novelists and critics on the other. While teaching at Ohio State in 1940-41 I came upon the critical writing which was later to be called 'new criticism.' This seemed to promise a union of literary and scholarly interests. The next year I was fortunate enough to get an instructorship at Louisiana State, while Cleanth Brooks, Robert Penn Warren and Robert Heilman were still teaching there and the *Southern Review* was putting up a struggle for its last few months of existence.

"At L.S.U. I met and married Mary Allen, a South Carolinian, who was also teaching in the English department. That winter and spring, with army induction awaiting me, we collaborated on *Climates of Tragedy*, published by the L.S.U. Press. In the Army I was stationed at a number of bases in the United States, finally shipping to New Guinea, where I spent a year, and to the Philippines, where I spent a second year. In New Guinea I learned that time can look like milk glass and came to feel that Conrad's view of the natural world was the most reasonable one.

"At Milne Bay and Hollandia I became friends with Karl Shapiro, whose poetry I had read and felt to be peculiarly the voice of my generation. Being able to talk and correspond with him helped me maintain and develop my interest in modern poetry and criticism.

"Back in the U. S. I rejoined my wife who was teaching at the University of Missouri, and became acquainted with our daughter, Willa Van, whom I had seen on brief occasions as a baby. On a postwar Rockefeller Fellowship I wrote *Sense and Sensibility in Modern Poetry*, using it as a dissertation at Columbia, with Professors Lionel Trilling, Marjorie Nicolson and William York Tindall serving as my advisors. While doing this book I became a member of the staff in English at the University of Minnesota, when Joseph Warren Beach was still chairman and Robert Penn Warren was directing the program in writing. At present I am associate professor and director of graduate studies in English. In Minneapolis our second child, Ellen Lee, was born.

"During its first year of existence I was executive editor of *American Quarterly*. Besides writing *The Shaping Spirit* and contributing to a number of literary journals I have edited *Forms of Modern Fiction: Essays Collected in Honor of Joseph Warren Beach*; collaborated with Leonard Unger on a college textbook for the study of poetry; and co-edited with Frederick Hoffman the six-volume survey *Twentieth Century Literature in America*, contributing *An Age of Criticism, 1900-1950* to the latter series. Like all writers of critical volumes I am privately committed to the notion that I can write fiction and poetry—but thus far there is nothing that could be offered to a jury as evidence."

PRINCIPAL WORKS: Sense and Sensibility in Modern Poetry, 1948; The Shaping Spirit: A Study of Wallace Stevens, 1950; An Age of Criticism, 1900-1950, 1952.

ABOUT: A Southern Vanguard 1947; New Mexico Quarterly Spring 1951.

ODETS, CLIFFORD (July 18, 1906-). For biographical sketch and list of earlier works and references, see TWENTIETH CENTURY AUTHORS, 1942.

* * *

John Mason Brown pointed out in 1950: "Mr. Odets' career can be said to have got off to a poor start if for no other reason than that it started off too well. It did not work up to a climax; it began with one." Again and again, from *Golden Boy* in 1937 to *The Big Knife* in 1949, Odets tried to recapture the spirit that had given his early plays their brilliant distinction (what John Gassner called their "vibrant intimacy and authentic theatrical ring"). Invariably the reviewers and audiences alike were dissatisfied. Meanwhile Odets had moved to California, where he wrote scenarios and directed motion pictures. The most frequently offered explanation for his slackening in powers was that Hollywood—with its easy rewards and cheap commercialism—had corrupted him. Interestingly enough, Odets offered this same theory to explain the defections of the hero of his play *The Big Knife*, a Broadway actor who becomes a movie star. John Gassner said that in this play Odets "deliberately chose Hollywood as a symbol for everything deteriorative and unscrupulous in our society; he returned to the *Golden Boy* theme of how a materialistic, success-worshipping world corrupts the soul. He overlooked the weak character of his hero in his zeal to transfer the guilt to society; he made equations without considering whether the terms were right."

Even Odets' sharpest critics, however, were quick to point out that whatever the weaknesses of his later plays, they never failed to stimulate interest and theatrical excitement. In this respect they were agreed that his talent was intact. They were also agreed that essentially Odets was suffering "from the defects of his merits, that his great passion has led to straining, his moral earnestness to rhetoric, his originality to defections from good sense." When these merits could be sufficiently disciplined, they argued, he would again write good plays.

That prediction seemed to gain a measure of verification in 1950 when his *The Country Girl* (which he also directed) was produced on Broadway to generally enthusiastic critical notices. A play about backstage life, the story of an actor with a weakness for liquor who makes a "comeback" thanks to the help of his wife, it was Odets' most successful play in more than a decade and gave evidence of a newly awakened and reinvigorated talent. John Chapman wrote: "This play shows a new depth in the author's work, for he has approached his three principal characters from within themselves; the externals of society—in this case, the society of the theatrical world, which Odets knows intimately—have little to do with the events of the play." The play had a long run on Broadway, toured successfully, and was sold to motion pictures. In 1955 his *The Flowering Peach*, a re-telling of the legend of Noah in terms of Jewish family life, was produced on Broadway and received mixed reviews.

Odets married the actress Bette Grayson in 1943. She died in 1954. They had two children. In 1952 Odets testified before a House Un-American Activities Committee hearing that he had been a member of the Communist Party for eight months in 1934 and quit the party because it tried to force him to write according to a 'party-line' pattern.

ADDITIONAL WORKS: The Big Knife, 1949; The Country Girl, 1951.

ABOUT: Mersand, J. American Drama since 1930; Morris, L. R. Postscript to Yesterday; Saturday Review of Literature December 9, 1950; Theatre Arts July 1949, December 1950; Time February 10, 1947.

O'DONNELL, PEADAR (February 22, 1893-), Irish novelist.

This biography supersedes the one which appeared in TWEN-TIETH CENTURY AUTHORS, 1942.

Peadar O'Donnell, born in County Donegal, Ireland, was one of a peasant family of eleven children. He was educated at the local National School, becoming a monitor (student-teacher) at fourteen or fifteen, and received his teacher training at St. Patrick's College, Drumcondra, Dublin, 1911-13. He returned to County Donegal as a National Teacher. In his second job he obtained a

new school building by surreptitiously knocking down the old one. In 1916 he became principal of the school on the island of Arranmore, Donegal. A strike among potato-harvesters in Scotland resulted in his being asked to go there and report back to the migratory workers of Arranmore, who did not wish to become scabs. After looking at conditions in Scotland, he gave up teaching to become an organizer for the Irish Transport and General Workers' Union. Speaking against conscription in 1918 brought him into conflict with the British authorities; he joined the Irish Republican Army and became the commanding officer of the Donegal Brigade in March of 1921. He sided with the anti-Treaty forces in the Civil War of 1922, was captured at the taking of the Four Courts, Dublin, spent some time under sentence of death as a hostage for the good behavior of his native county, took part in a forty-one-day hunger strike, and finally escaped from Harepark Camp, County Kildare, in 1924.

O'Donnell began to write in jail, and his first novel, *Storm*, a story of the Anglo-Irish War, appeared in 1925. In 1927 he was in jail again for agrarian agitation. When he got out, he went with his wife Lil—whom he had married soon after his 1924 escape—to the South of France, where he wrote *The Way It Was with Them*. He also became involved with European agrarian movements and presided over the European Peasant Congress in Berlin in 1930. He supported De Valera in the 1932 election, but soon after turned against him. In 1934 he quit the I.R.A. because of its Fascist tendencies and founded the Irish Republican Congress with George Gilmore. He vigorously opposed General O'Duffy's Blueshirt movement, was in Spain when the Spanish War broke out, and returned to Ireland to combat pro-Franco propaganda with first-hand information. He refused to take sides in World War II, condemning both German Fascism and British imperialism. In 1942 he was appointed Adviser on Migratory Labour to the Irish Department of Industry and Commerce, visiting Britain frequently to observe conditions among Irish workers there. Business manager of *The Bell* magazine from its foundation in 1940, he became editor in 1946, discontinued publication in 1948, and revived it in 1950. His only play, *Wrack*, was first performed at the Abbey Theatre in 1932. He lives in Dublin.

PRINCIPAL WORKS: Storm, 1925; Islanders (in U.S.: The Way It Was with Them) 1927; Adrigoole, 1928; There Will Be Fighting (in U.S.: The Knife) 1930; The Gates Flew Open (autobiography) 1932; Wrack (play) 1933; On the Edge of the Stream, 1934; Salud: An Irishman in Spain (non-fiction) 1937.

ABOUT: O'Donnell, P. The Gates Flew Open; Nineteenth Century December 1936; Time June 14, 1948.

ODUM, HOWARD WASHINGTON

(May 24, 1884-November 8, 1954), American sociologist, was born in Bethlehem, Walton County, Ga., the son of William Pleasants Odum and Mary Ann (Thomas) Odum. He received his B.A. from Emory College (Ga.) in 1904 and his M.A. from the University of Mississippi in 1906. Two Ph.D.s were acquired: one from Clark University in 1909 and one from Columbia University in 1910. During Odum's long career of teaching, he was co-principal of Toccopola (Miss.) School (1904-05), instructor at the University of Mississippi (1905-08), fellow at Clark University (1908-09), research expert with the Philadelphia Bureau of Municipal Research (1910-12), a professor of educational sociology at the University of Georgia (1912-19) and superintendent of its Summer School for Teachers (1916-19), director of the bureau of home service camps and camp cities, Southern Division of American Red Cross (1918), dean of the School of Liberal Arts at Emory University (1919-20), and Kenan Professor of sociology at the University of North Carolina since 1920. He remained at the latter institution for over thirty years, taking time out to be visiting professor at the University of Washington (1942) and Silliman Fellow at Yale (1946-47).

In presenting Odum with the Oliver Max Gardner Award in 1953, the University of North Carolina said: "Dr. Odum has always placed emphasis upon opportunities rather than problems, upon 'the South at its best,' as he is wont to say. He was one of the early students of the place of the Negro in the life of the South and the place of the South in the life of the Negro." For his adopted state of North Carolina, Odum served as president of the Conference for Social Service, chairman of the Commission on Interracial Cooperation, chairman of the Emergency Relief Administration, chairman of the Civil Works Administration, chairman of a crime commission, consultant to the State Board of Public Welfare, secretary of the State Planning Board, and a member of the Prison Advisory Board. He was also president of the Southern Regional Council from 1944 to 1946. His contribution in these fields, and chiefly in that of race relations, was recognized by the award of the Catholic Conference of the South in 1943, and by the Bernays Award in 1945. Among his honorary degrees was an LL.D. from Harvard, given in 1939.

Odum's printed works included some fifty-five books and monographs and more than one hundred and sixty articles. In 1947 was published *The Way of the South*, subtitled "Toward the Regional Balance of America." The *Nation* reviewed this volume negatively, saying in part: "It mixes history and sociology, rhapsody and catalogue, impressionism and scholarly abstraction, in a totally unreadable pastiche." But the *Yale Review* felt it was an excellent book for the general reader, presenting as it did "the range and richness of Professor Odum's thought." His definitive work, *American Sociology*, the story of sociology in the United States, came out in 1951, a book over five hundred pages in length. "A mature, vastly informative, and pre-eminently generous book," was the opinion of H. E. Barnes in the *American Sociological Review*. "Odum has lived through most of the period he describes and probably has known personally or by correspondence almost all the men with whom he deals," said *Social Forces*. "Perhaps this is what makes the material come alive."

In 1910 Odum married Anna Louise Kranz of Hendersonville, Tenn.; they had three children. He was described as modest and humane, with an incalculable optimism in the face of any difficulty. As a serious avocation, Odum worked for some thirty years in developing a special strain of Jersey cattle for which he received, in 1948, the Master Breeders Award from the American Jersey Cattle Club. He died in Raleigh, N.C., at the age of seventy.

PRINCIPAL WORKS: Social and Mental Traits of the Negro, 1910; Sociology and Social Problems, 1925; The Negro and His Songs (with G. B. Johnson) 1925; Approach to Public Welfare and Social Work (textbook) 1926; Negro Workaday Songs (with G. B. Johnson) 1926; Man's Quest for Social Guidance, 1927; Rainbow Round My Shoulder, 1928; Wings on My Feet, 1929; An American Epoch, 1930; Cold Blue Moon, 1931; Southern Regions of the United States, 1936; American Social Problems, 1939; Race and Rumors of Race, 1943; The Way of the South, 1947; American Sociology, 1951.

ABOUT: New York Times November 10, 1954.

OEMLER, Mrs. MARIE (CONWAY)
(May 29, 1879-June 6, 1932). For biographical sketch and list of works and references, see TWENTIETH CENTURY AUTHORS, 1942.

*O'FAOLÁIN, SÉAN (February 22, 1900-). For biographical sketch and list of earlier works and references, see TWENTIETH CENTURY AUTHORS, 1942.

* * *

In recent years Séan O'Faoláin has turned away from the writing of novels (though he has continued to write short stories) and has devoted himself largely to essays, biography, and travelogues. He has become one of the best known interpreters of modern Irish life, and his writings on Ireland and its people, while anything but flattering and rosy-tinted, are widely praised outside Ireland as realistic and sympathetic interpretations. Within Ireland O'Faoláin invariably stirs up tempests when he writes. Nevertheless he is respected for his candor and his courage. Walter O'Hearn said of him in *Commonweal* (October 28, 1949): "When Mr. O'Faoláin sets about the myths with which Irishmen warm their hearts at patriotic gatherings, he reminds you a little of a strong-armed boy at a county fair, throwing balls at the target and hitting the crockery too." The main targets of O'Faoláin's criticism of his country are the "clergy-inspired" censorship (especially the puritanical extremes involved in the banning of such Catholic authors as Graham Greene and Evelyn Waugh) and the insularity and provinciality of the country. He advised young Irishmen (*Commonweal* July 10, 1953) to "follow my own practice, to get out of Ireland as often as possible in order to keep their sense of perspective; and, contrary to my own foolish practice, to avoid controversy." In an even more blunt and widely publicized article in *Life* (March 16, 1953) called "Love Among the Irish" (which appears also in a volume of essays edited by J. A. O'Brien, *The Vanishing Irish*, 1953), he deplored the atmosphere of "celibacy and censorship" in Ireland which, he feared, produces "racial decay" and is sapping the nation of its vitality.

O'Faoláin lives in Killiney, in County Dublin. He is married and has a son and a daughter. For all his criticism of Ireland, he finds that his roots there are deep and permanent. In 1952 he wrote: "It is a gregarious place but not too distracting; and it has one great virtue—it drives one howling

* ō f(w)ä´lŏn

with boredom out of it from time to time; and it lures one back, gently, insistently, until it drives one mad again—and so *da capo*." Since the end of World War II he has traveled extensively in Europe (particularly in Italy) and in the United States. He gave a series of lectures on contemporary literature at the Graduate School of Princeton University in 1954, and it was on this visit that an interviewer described him as "a medium-height man of fifty-four, silver-rim glasses, soft, Irish voice, who looks like the school teacher he once was in County Wicklow."

Irish Sagas and Folk-Tales, by the author's wife, Eileen O'Faoláin, a retelling of old heroic legends and chimney-corner tales, appeared in 1954.

Corrections: O'Faoláin is a member of the Irish Academy of Letters, not the Irish Royal Academy, as given in TWENTIETH CENTURY AUTHORS, 1942. In the list of his Principal Works, *The Great O'Neill* (1942) appears under fiction. It is a biography of Hugh O'Neill, second Earl of Tyrone.

ADDITIONAL WORKS: Teresa, and Other Stories, 1947; The Man Who Invented Sin, and Other Stories, 1948; The Short Story, 1948; The Irish: A Character Study, 1949; A Summer in Italy, 1950; Newman's Way, 1952; An Autumn in Italy, 1953.

ABOUT: Hoehn, M. (ed.) Catholic Authors, I; Commonweal October 28, 1949, July 10, 1953; New York Herald Tribune Book Review October 12, 1952, April 4, 1954; New York Times Book Review June 13, 1954; Time August 8, 1949.

O'FLAHERTY, LIAM (1897-), Irish novelist.

This biography supersedes the one which appeared in TWENTIETH CENTURY AUTHORS, 1942.

Liam O'Flaherty was born in the Aran Islands, a year before Synge's first visit there. He was educated free by the Holy Ghost Fathers from the time he was thirteen, as a postulant for the priesthood. He studied at Rockwell College, County Tipperary, at Blackrock College, County Dublin, and at the Dublin diocesan seminary (Holy Cross College, Clonliffe), where he finally gave up the idea of taking Orders. He entered University College, Dublin, but left after a short time to join the Irish Guards. He was six months in France in World War I and was shell-shocked at Langemarck in September 1917. His injuries kept him in the hospital for many months and he was discharged with a disability pension.

After a period of convalescence at home, O'Flaherty began to travel. His journey took him most of the way round the world. He was a stoker and deckhand, a beachcomber, hobo and lumberjack. He visited his brother in Boston and held various jobs in New York. After two or three years of wandering he returned to Ireland, rested and recuperated once more on Aran. In 1922 at the head of a group of unemployed workers, he seized a public building in Dublin and hoisted the red flag. As a result he was driven out of Ireland by the government and he fled to England. There his first novel *Thy Neighbour's Wife* was written and accepted for publication by Edward Garnett, D. H. Lawrence's editor. *The Black Soul*, and *Spring Sowing* (short stories) followed. In Dublin that year he met Margaret Barrington, and they were married in 1926. His novel *The Informer* took the world by storm in 1925. Ten years later in a movie version it was equally successful. No work of his has since equaled it in popularity, but *Skerrett* and *Famine* are considered finer novels. Of the latter William Plomer wrote: "It is a magnificent assertion of sympathy with the perpetual struggle of the mass of humanity for bread, freedom, and civilisation." Some of O'Flaherty's best work is contained in his short stories.

O'Flaherty went to Hollywood to help John Ford make the motion picture version of *The Informer*. Since then he has written little by comparison with his earlier prodigious output. He has lived mainly in the United States. In 1938 he visited France for the making of a French film from his novel *The Puritan*, and he returns to Aran periodically, report Mercier and Greene in their anthology of Irish prose, for "fresh contact with his first and best subject-matter, the fauna—human and otherwise—of his native place." He completed *Insurrection*, his fourteenth novel, there.

PRINCIPAL WORKS: Thy Neighbour's Wife, 1924; The Black Soul, 1925; Spring Sowing (short stories) 1926; The Informer, 1926; The Tent and Other Stories, 1926; The Martyr, 1927; Life of Tim Healy (biography) 1927; The Assassin, 1928; Tourist's Guide to Ireland, 1929; The Fairy Goose and Other Stories, 1929; The House of Gold, 1929; Two Years (autobiography) 1930; I Went to Russia (non-fiction) 1931; The Puritan, 1932; Skerrett, 1932; The Wild Swan and Other Stories, 1932; Shame the Devil, 1934; Hollywood Cemetery, 1935; The Short Stories of Liam O'Flaherty, 1937; Famine, 1937; Land, 1946; Two Lovely Beasts, and Other Stories, 1948; Insurrection, 1950.

ABOUT: O'Flaherty, L. Two Years; Mercier, V. & Greene, D. 1000 Years of Irish Prose: Bookman (London) January 1930; London Mercury December 1937; Nuova Antologia September 16, 1934; Revue des Deux Mondes June 15, 1934; Saturday Review of Literature May 25, 1946.

OGBURN, WILLIAM FIELDING (June 29, 1886-   ), American sociologist, writes: "The atmosphere of my childhood in Georgia, like that of my forefathers in Virgina, instilled in me an appreciation of manners, character, family status, the deprecation of money as such, and the obligation to fight for honor. Women were angels, and chivalry was admired as much as boasting was  condemned. My father, planter and merchant, died in 1890 when I was four. Then began my long struggle to resist a dear mother's beautiful but excessive love. To the successful outcome, I attribute my strong devotion to objective reality, my antipathy to the distorting influence of emotion, my appreciation of the normal, and a liking for extroverts.

"I got along fast in schools to end as a graduate student in Columbia University in my early twenties. There I married a girl with whom I went horseback riding in the Southern moonlight, who bore us two sons. In this strange world of big Northern cities I saw that standards crumbled and virtues were forgotten in the bitter competition for success, the bitch goddess, as Henry Adams called it.

"There continued my efforts to adjust. I had previously rejected the escape of the artist, and I never felt the call of religion. My protest took the course of radicalism, though for that I was not maladjusted enough, or too cautious. Curiously I found comfort in anthropology, where reading about the variety of customs of primitive peoples showed me that the social order need not be a tyranny over our biological nature.

"I gave up social action after six years of it while teaching on the Pacific coast. I saw I could not do well both in promoting social movements and in teaching. Instead I turned to science. Perhaps the scientific method applied to society could do as much for our social environment as it had done to the material world. Various later activities outside universities, such as directing the study of social trends under President Hoover, were advisory and compatible with social science.

"Not being very ambitious, I spent much time wandering, in the realm of ideas. I taught anthropology, economics, history, political science, social psychology, statistics on international relations at Princeton University, the University of Chicago, and Oxford University. Adventure in ideas was more attractive than in action. It was the pursuit of ideas that took me on various travels in Europe and in the Far East.

"The search for adjustment, the devotion to science, the advocacy of the new and better, all channeled into the study of social change. That great men were found to be the media rather than the prime movers of change has not left me frustrated. For I have found a measure of personal adjustment through work, sports, aesthetic interests, friends, family life, travel and hobbies. Such achievements have been facilitated by good health, freedom from poverty, the reliance upon thinking to keep me out of undue difficulties, and luck."

* * *

W. F. Ogburn retired from the University of Chicago in 1951, after more than twenty years of teaching there. From 1933 to his retirement, he was Sewell L. Avery Distinguished Service Professor of Sociology. Ogburn is regarded as the "top social statistician in the United States." He was a consultant to the federal government in the administrations of Presidents Hoover and Franklin Roosevelt. On his retirement he was quoted in *Time* as saying: "I want to spend three months seeing every athletic event in Chicago, then I want to go to all the movies, then I would like to spend several years traveling. . . . Then I want to write." Since then he has served as lecturer at the University of Calcutta, in 1952, and in 1952-53 as visiting professor at Nuffield College, Oxford.

PRINCIPAL WORKS: Progress and Uniformity in Child Labor Legislation, 1912; Minimum Wage and Cost of Living, 1918; (ed.) Social Change, 1927-1934; (ed. with A. A. Goldenweiser) Social Sciences and Their Interrelations, 1927; The Economic Development of Post-War France (with W. Jaffe) 1929; You and Machines, 1935; Sociology (with M. F. Nimkoff) 1940; (ed.) American Society in Wartime, 1943; The Social Effects of Aviation, 1946.

ABOUT: Current Biography February 1955; Time June 25, 1951.

OGILVIE, ELISABETH (May 20, 1917-   ), American novelist, writes: "I was born to American parents of Scottish stock, and spent a very pleasant little-girlhood in Dorchester, Mass., doing what most little girls of my background were doing; my days were taken up with school, dancing lessons, Sunday school, roller-skating on those lovely wide old-fashioned sidewalks, making Valentines, hanging Maybaskets, and playing dolls. I don't believe anybody expected me to be a writer, though I read a good deal and very

easily from the age of five. A family of extroverts in many ways, we were also a reading family. They might have expected me to be a dancer.  The yearly recitals were the high point of my existence; I was merely bored by the dull routine of lessons, but blossomed ecstatically under the glow of footlights. It wasn't until I started to learn to be a writer that I realized the uses of drudgery.

"My first thoughts of writing came when I was in high school. By that time we had moved to Quincy, Mass., and I was going to North Quincy High School, whose English department was of a very high caliber. There was a great emphasis on writing in all the grades from the seventh to the twelfth, and most of the teachers were eager to encourage any signs of talent. In the senior grades, when we were urged to think seriously about our careers, this encouragement took a positive form. Our grammatical training was very stiff; we had also to do much précis-writing, and, besides the bi-weekly themes that were required all through high school, we had to write fairly adult analyses of the books we read, taking apart their structure and their methods of characterization. I believe my first lessons in technique for writing novels were learned in those days. I began writing for the school magazine, which came out often, so I learned young about writing to a deadline. And as editor in charge of stories and poems from the junior school, I had to learn how to be critical. The standards were extremely high, and the teachers in charge wouldn't let us drag our toes, so to speak. I didn't go to college, but I feel that I received a solid foundation for my craft in high school, and some useful habits of study.

"After high school, backed by my mother, I was able to take a university extension course, 'Writing for Publication,' taught by Donald MacCampbell, a young man just starting out as a literary agent. We formed an association which has lasted ever since. He helped me to develop an objective attitude toward my own work and to stop feeling that to cut out one sentence was to lop off one of my fingers. This is the most difficult lesson for a writer, for the nature of the critter is to be sensitive.

"The writing of my first novel, *High Tide at Noon*, was a stormy period, but the reviews were worth all the strife. That was in 1944. Because of that book, I was able to join with some congenial friends in buying part of an island off the Maine coast, and have lived and worked there ever since. *High Tide* was followed by *Storm Tide* and then by *The Ebbing Tide*, the three forming a trilogy of the Bennett family. They have been published in England and Denmark. My next book, *My World Is an Island* (non-fiction) described our discovery of this island and our misadventures in settling, and *Rowan Head* was a novel with a mainland background. Both these books have been published in England, and *Rowan Head* will be published in France.

"I have done a few short stories for *Woman's Day* magazine, but don't sell short stories as often as I'd like to. The successful ones have come to me by inspiration and must be done all at once, like a good water color. But in writing a novel, I like a rough, flexible outline so that I can be sure of what is to be accomplished in the course of the book.

"The island where I live, Gay's Island, in the mouth of the St. George River, is almost my chief interest outside of my work, for there is always some new spot to be discovered on it, or something new to be done to the garden or the house. I say 'almost' because I am a Foster Parent to a twelve-year-old Italian boy, and that is engrossing and satisfying.

"Though I have a yearning to see other countries, particularly England and Scotland, I love Maine and can find endless material everywhere I turn."

PRINCIPAL WORKS: High Tide at Noon, 1944; Storm Tide, 1945; The Ebbing Tide, 1947; Rowan Head, 1949; My World Is an Island, 1950; The Dawning of the Day, 1953; Whistle for a Wind, 1954.

ABOUT: Ogilvie, E. My World Is an Island; Current Biography 1951.

O'GRADY, STANDISH (JAMES) (September 18, 1846-May 18, 1928), Irish author, was born in Castletown Berehaven, County Cork, Ireland, the son of a Church of Ireland clergyman. He attended Tipperary Grammar School, and in 1864 entered Trinity College in Dublin. After a distinguished undergraduate career, during which he excelled in oratory, essay-writing, and almost every game and sport then popular, winning a scholarship in classics, O'Grady graduated B.A. in 1868. He then studied law and was called to the Irish Bar in 1872,

but practiced for only a short time.

His later work as an author was first suggested to him in 1869, when he spent a day in the library of a country house and discovered the first Irish history he had ever read — O'Halloran's. There followed years of enthusiastic reading in Irish history and legend, especially the latter. Meanwhile he turned from law to critical writing, and

J. B. Yeats

from that to an attempt to recreate ancient Irish literature in a readable form. O'Grady's *History of Ireland* appeared in two volumes (1878, 1880), one dealing with Ireland's heroic period and the other with Cuchulain and his contemporaries; these books became the foundation stones of the literary revival. In 1881 he published *History of Ireland: Critical and Philosophical*, the first volume of a work left unfinished. It has been remarked by some critics that the earlier *History* should be considered an epic rather than history.

O'Grady next wrote many novels and tales, based primarily on Irish history of the Elizabethan period; two of these are *The Bog of Stars* and *The Flight of the Eagle*. His career is full of ironies, for while he brought Old Irish literature to life for the modern reader, he himself hardly knew the language at all. When the Irish Literary Theatre sought to dramatize the legends he had helped to popularize, he objected to the dramatizations as "degrading Irish ideals."

Among other things, O'Grady was a working journalist and an ardent student of politics. He began as a Tory, urging that the landlords take the lead once again in Irish affairs (see his *Toryism and the Tory Democracy*), but ended as an advocate of Guild Socialism in A. R. Orage's magazine *The New Age*. As owner and editor of the *Kilkenny Moderator*, a small-town newspaper, he printed and published his own and others' books, and from 1900 to 1906 published the *All Ireland Review*, a literary weekly. Many years before his death he left Ireland permanently; he died at Shanklin, Isle of Wight, when eighty-one years old.

PRINCIPAL WORKS: History of Ireland, vols. 1 & 2, 1878-1880; Early Bardic Literature of Ireland, 1879; History of Ireland: Critical and Philosophical, 1881; Crisis in Ireland, 1882; Toryism and the Tory Democracy, 1886; Red Hugh's Captivity: Ireland in the Reign of Elizabeth, 1889; Finn and His Companions, 1892; Story of Ireland, 1893; Bog of Stars, 1893; The Coming of

Cuchulain, 1894; The Chain of Gold, 1895; In the Wake of King James, 1896; Lost on Du Corrig, 1896; Ulrick the Ready, 1896; The Flight of the Eagle, 1897; All Ireland, 1898; In the Gates of the North, 1908; The Departure of Dermot, 1917; Selected Essays and Passages, 1918; The Triumph and Passing of Cuchulain, 1919.

ABOUT: Boyd, E. A. *Introduction to* Standish O'Grady: Selected Essays and Passages, Irish Renaissance, Appreciations and Depreciations; Mercier, V. & Greene, D. H. 1000 Years of Irish Prose; O'Grady, H. A. Standish James O'Grady: The Man and the Writer.

O'HARA, JOHN (January 31, 1905-   ). For biographical sketch and list of earlier works and references, see TWENTIETH CENTURY AUTHORS, 1942.

* * *

In 1949 John O'Hara published his first novel in eleven years. During that interim he had written a number of short stories which once again demonstrated his talents as a "social commentator," his faculty (as H. M. Robinson pointed out) "for catching the shape, tempo, and color of American words as they leave the speaker's mouth," and producing in his work "a teeming index of American manners, events, and characters." The new novel, *A Rage to Live*, was an immediate best-seller; by the official publication date more than 75,000 copies had been sold. A tumultuous and sprawling story, a portrait of a small Pennsylvania town and of the amorous adventures of one of its upper-class matrons, *A Rage to Live* was O'Hara's most ambitious work. "The earlier books were special books about specialized people," O'Hara told an interviewer, "but this is the big one, the over-all one." Most reviewers agreed that the book was vigorous and exciting, especially in its portrait of the town. But few of them found any real literary significance in it. A. C. Spectorsky described it in the New York *Times* as "a portrait with no apparent purpose, no special depth, and no discoverable literary or artistic function." *Time*'s reviewer objected to its "lack of final meaning, of implicit comment on human experience by which the reader subconsciously finds the true measure of all fiction." The critical reaction to O'Hara's next novel, *The Farmers Hotel*, was even more divided. This was a brief, crisply written story of a group of people who are marooned by a snowstorm. The *New Yorker* found it "alive and talking . . . short, assured, and contrary . . . all wonderful, except for the odd, violent ending." But Charles J. Rolo in the *Atlantic* judged it a "studiously pointless piece of fiction, which betrays the belief that a novelist's function is to emulate a camera wired

for sound," and James Kelly, in the *Saturday Review of Literature*, found it "empty of real personality and warmth." *Sweet and Sour* is a collection of articles on books and people reprinted from the author's column in the Sunday edition of the Trenton (N.J.) *Times-Advertiser*.

O'Hara's later work has probably added little to his stature as a writer, but his earlier writings have shown unusual powers of endurance. *Appointment in Samarra* was recently reprinted in a Modern Library edition, and the musical comedy based on his *Pal Joey* stories was revived in 1952 with great success. O'Hara lives in Princeton, N.J. He said of himself in 1951: "I seem to have settled down a bit, but that is not to say that I do not have an occasional outburst. I am married and have a six-year-old daughter with the mellifluous name, Wylie O'Hara." In 1955, after the death of his second wife, Belle Wylie, he married Katharine Barnes Bryan.

ADDITIONAL WORKS: Pipe Night (short stories) 1945; Here's O'Hara, 1946; Hellbox (short stories) 1947; A Rage to Live, 1949; The Farmers Hotel, 1951; Sweet and Sour (non-fiction) 1954.

ABOUT: Bishop, J. P. Collected Essays; Van Gelder, R. Writers and Writing; Wilson, E. Classics and Commercials; Collier's February 5, 1954; New York Herald Tribune Book Review August 29, 1949, October 7, 1951; New York Times Book Review August 21, 1949, September 4, 1949; Saturday Review of Literature May 18, 1946.

O'HARA, MARY (pseudonym of Mary O'Hara Alsop Sture-Vasa) (July 19, 1885-), American novelist, spent the first summer of her life at a New Jersey summer resort, her childhood in Brooklyn Heights, N.Y., her young married life in Los Angeles, Calif., ten middle years on a Wyoming ranch, four years in Santa Barbara, Calif., and in 1948 returned to the East, purchased a property in Monroe, Conn., and made that her home.

Marion Stevenson

She writes: "For generations back, apparently, our family—Alsops, Springs (Gardiner Spring of the Brick Church, New York), Dennys (Father Denny, Jesuit priest), Edwards (Jonathan and Timothy), Penns (William) and Fells—have been adventurers of the spirit, always searching their souls, never hesitating to declare the truth as they see it, even at the cost of becoming wanderers and exiles. My father, Reese Fell Alsop, the young son of a Philadelphia Quaker family, was attending Haverford College when he received an inner 'call' that caused him to abandon his church and the legal career he was planning and enter the Episcopalian ministry.

"My earliest recollections are of the big house in Brooklyn Heights and my father's church, St. Ann's. We were a family of several generations, for my mother died when I was six and my grandmother, Mrs. James Walton Spring (Mary O'Hara Denny) and some aunts came to live with us. I was one of four children. My soul searchings began in childhood. I was taught religion at Sunday school, in church, at prayer meetings, at chapel (in school), and at daily morning prayers in our own home. So much piety, it seemed to me, was bound to take most of the fun out of life. Besides, looking around, I felt I did not really believe the articles of the Creed, and at fourteen I made a declaration to this effect at morning prayers.

"At nineteen, I became engaged to a third cousin, Kent Kane Parrot, who was also an agnostic. We were married, went to Los Angeles to live, and had two children. The failure of this marriage and the ensuing loneliness and unhappiness made me believe that there were no human solutions to human problems. I had chosen and taken my own way and failed, and this failure seemed to me one that embraced all possibilities. I sank into despair. But the soul searching continued ever more deeply.

"There around me in California current thought was bubbling with ideas derived from India and Tibet, brought to this country by the missionary efforts of Hindu Swamis and Yogis. That modern psychological thought has to a considerable extent followed yoga philosophy is now well known, but it was new to me then. And if this was religion, it was a most interesting kind. I loved the physical exercises designed to perfect balance, strengthen the body and prolong youth. On the wide California beaches, sunburned American boys and girls practiced the deep breathing, the strange postures. I loved the mental exercises to achieve control of the mind, for, obviously, right thinking comes before right doing; and right feeling before thinking; and willing before feeling. Heretofore religion had told me what to do even against my will. Now I had to see what I must think—feel—will. And learn and practice new techniques which would enable me to do it.

"So I was introduced to the *interior* life, and gradually, through years of study and reading, beginning with the *Upanishads* and ending with the Early Christian Fathers, I

came to understand that it was the foundation of all true religion of whatever church or denomination. Meanwhile I had found work of a congenial kind as a writer in a moving picture studio. (Musical composition and writing had been my two gifts since earliest childhood.) I had a successful Hollywood career, which was terminated when my second husband, Helge Sture-Vasa, took me to a Wyoming ranch. Here I wrote the three books about the wild horse on the plains of the American 'West,' *My Friend Flicka, Thunderhead, Green Grass of Wyoming,* which opened the door for the spate of horse books which has poured out upon the public ever since. Those books sold millions of copies, were translated into all modern languages, and read all over the world.

"As my children grew up, I saw that my abandonment of any form of external religion was robbing them of something they would need as they went through life, something I needed too; for in Wyoming there were no 'Lectures on Hindu Mysticism' such as I had attended in California; no 'Guru' to advise me. I saw that a universal church was a necessity. Since my study of the Early Christian Fathers, I had held the opinion that the Roman Catholic Church had preserved more of the doctrines of antiquity than the Protestant. I applied to the Ecclesiastical Court for an annulment of my first marriage. When this was granted, I entered the Church. Shortly after, I obtained a decree of divorce from my second husband.

"After returning to the East in 1948 I wrote *The Son of Adam Wyngate,* a book which dealt with the trials of the spirit, and combined the religious philosophies of the East and the West, as I had come to do in my own life."

PRINCIPAL WORKS: My Friend Flicka, 1941; Thunderhead, 1943; The Green Grass of Wyoming, 1946; The Son of Adam Wyngate, 1952; Novel in the Making (non-fiction) 1954.

ABOUT: Current Biography 1944; Hoehn, M. (ed.) Catholic Authors, II; O'Hara, M. Novel in the Making; New York Herald Tribune Book Review April 6, 1952; Newsweek March 31, 1952.

"O. HENRY." See HENRY, O.

O'HIGGINS, HARVEY JERROLD (November 14, 1876-February 28, 1929). For biographical sketch and list of works and references, see TWENTIETH CENTURY AUTHORS, 1942.

O'KELLY, SEUMAS (1881-1918), Irish author, was born in Loughrea, County Galway, Ireland. His father was a grain-buyer and carrier. After finishing his education at the local Catholic secondary school, St. Brendan's College, O'Kelly began to write for a country newspaper; in 1903 he became editor of the *Southern Star*, published in Skibbereen, County Cork. Presently he moved nearer Dublin and became editor of the *Leinster Leader*, Naas, County Kildare. A member of the Gaelic League, he at this time met Arthur Griffith and other prominent Dublin authors and journalists; he joined Sinn Fein when it was founded.

O'Kelly's first book, *By the Stream of Killmeen*, was published in 1906. A collection of short stories and sketches, it was generally undistinguished, but a few years later he contributed some admirable short stories to the *Irish Weekly Independent*. At the same time he was writing plays, which were at first ignored by the Abbey Theatre. Finally, in 1910, he won their approval with his third play, *The Shuiler's Child*. Other Abbey plays by O'Kelly are *The Bribe*, which was published in 1914, *The Parnellite* of 1917, and *Meadowsweet* of 1919.

Around 1911 he had a severe attack of rheumatic fever, from which his heart was permanently weakened. He resigned from the *Leinster Leader* in 1912 to become editor of the *Dublin Saturday Post*, but his poor health forced him to give up this position. In 1915 he retired to Naas with an older sister and a young nephew and devoted himself to free-lance writing. His novel *The Lady of Deerpark*, and a collection of short stories, *Waysiders*, both appeared in 1917. Of the latter the *Athenaeum* wrote, "He brings home to the reader, with poignant force, the tragedies of the humble in those desolate wilds, even the tragedies of dumb beasts suffering from the callousness and heedlessness of man. Simple as they are, the tales have unquestionable power."

In 1918 Arthur Griffith was imprisoned, and O'Kelly went to Dublin, thus risking his health, to edit the Sinn Fein paper *Nationality*. In November of that year some British soldiers, celebrating the Armistice, broke into the *Nationality* office and began committing acts of vandalism. O'Kelly's efforts to resist them were too much for his overstrained heart; he died at his desk a few hours later. After his death three collections of early short stories were published, as well as an unfinished and unrevised novel, *Wet Clay* (1922). O'Kelly's last completed work, the long short story, *The Weaver's Grave*, is by some accounted his masterpiece.

PRINCIPAL WORKS: By the Stream of Killmeen, 1906; The Shuiler's Child, 1910; Three Plays: The Home Coming; The Stranger; The Matchmakers, 1912; The Bribe, 1913; Waysiders, 1917; The Lady of Deerpark, 1917; The Golden Barque and, The Weaver's Grave, 1919; The Leprechaun of Killmeen, 1919; Hillsiders, 1921; Wet Clay, 1922.

ABOUT: Crone, J. Concise Dictionary of Irish Biography; Mercier, V. & Greene, D. H. 1000 Years of Irish Prose; O'Kelly, M. Memoir *prefixed to* "The Parnellite," *in* The Leinster Leader, 1919.

OLDFIELD, CLAUDE HOUGHTON

("Claude Houghton") (1889-). For autobiographical sketch and list of earlier works and references, see TWENTIETH CENTURY AUTHORS, 1942.

* * *

"Claude Houghton" writes from London that his novels have been translated into many languages—Czech, Dutch, Danish, Swedish, Spanish, German, Rumanian, etc. Among admirers of his work he lists the late Jan Masaryk, Dean Inge, P. G. Wodehouse, J. B. Priestley, Frank Swinnerton, and Henry Miller. His novel *I Am Jonathan Scrivener*, originally published in 1934, was televised in the United States on "Studio One" in December 1952. "My ambition," Houghton writes to the editors of this volume, "is to succeed with my best work."

ADDITIONAL WORKS: Six Lives and a Box, 1943; Passport to Paradise, 1944; Transformation Scene, 1946; The Quarrel, 1948; The Birthmark, 1950; The Enigma of Conrad Stone, 1952; At the End of the Road, 1953; The Clock Ticks, 1954.

OLIVER, GEORGE. See ONIONS, O.

OLIVER, JOHN RATHBONE (January 4, 1872-January 21, 1943). For biographical sketch and list of works and references, see TWENTIETH CENTURY AUTHORS, 1942.

* * *

John Rathbone Oliver died at seventy-one, after a three-years' illness, at the McLean Hospital in Waverly, Mass.

The most winning characteristic of his published works, whose royalties went to educate men for the ministry and for medicine, was the reflection in them of the personality of the author. J. H. Holmes has called him "one of the remarkable figures of our time. His nature is rich, his life abundant, his sympathies wide and full, his love of men and human things a native grace of his pure spirit."

Oliver used the pseudonym "John Roland" for some of his early published work.

ABOUT: New York Times January 22, 1943; Time February 1, 1943.

*OLIVIER, EDITH (1879?-May 10, 1948). For biographical sketch and list of earlier works and references, see TWENTIETH CENTURY AUTHORS, 1942.

* * *

Edith Olivier died at her home at Wilton in Wiltshire, England. She spent most of her life in Wilton, of which she was mayor for several terms, and drew most of her literary material from her native county.

Her writing seems, according to the London *Times*, "somewhat reminiscent of a remote fashion" (Cyril Connolly found a resemblance to Jane Austen), but she wrote "with humour and spirit." Characteristics of her work noted by *New Statesman and Nation* are "a persuasive certainty, a consummate sense of circumstance and an unerring feeling for temperament."

ADDITIONAL WORKS: Night Thoughts of a Country Landlady, 1943; Four Victorian Ladies of Wiltshire, 1945; Wiltshire (County Books Series) 1951.

ABOUT: London Times May 12, 1948.

* ō lĭv'ĭ ēr

OLLIVANT, ALFRED (1874-January 19, 1927). For biographical sketch and list of works and references, see TWENTIETH CENTURY AUTHORS, 1942.

OLSON, CHARLES (December 27, 1910-), American poet and critic, writes: "My shift is that I take it the present is  prologue, not the past. The instant, therefore, Is its own interpretation, as a dream is, and any action—a poem, for example. Down with causation (except, see below). And yrself: you, as the only reader and mover of the instant. You, the cause. No drag allowed, on either. Get on with it.

"In the work and dogmas are: (1) How, by form, to get the content instant; (2) what any of us are by the work on ourself, how make ourself fit instruments for use (how we augment the given—what used to be called the fate); (3) that there is no such thing as duality either of the body and the soul or of the world and I, that the fact in the human universe is the discharge of the many (the multiple) by the one (yrself done right, whatever you are, in whatever job, is the thing—all hierarchies, like dualities, are dead ducks).

"I am still, at 40, hugely engaged with my parents, in fact more engaged with them now than with that I spent so much time on in my 20's and 30's: society, and other persons (why I was in education, government and politics so long). So, first, I tell you their names and places, to indicate how I am of the heterogeneous present and not of the old homogeneity of the Founders, and the West.

"My father was born Karl Joseph Olson, in Sweden, and his name probably reflects a story in the family that they were Hungarians on my grandmother's side. He was carried to the States at five months.

"My mother was Mary Hines, and Yeats told me (on the grounds of my grandfather, who was the immigrant, 'born in Cork and brought up in Galway') that my mother's aunt must have been his 'Mary Hines,' the beloved of the blind poet Raftery and 'the most beautiful woman in all Western Ireland.' It was rough on my mother when I found this out at 18—my father and I never let her forget the fall from grace, that she was only the most beautiful woman in South Worcester, Mass.

"But what strikes me (and I now suspect has much more governed the nature of my seven years of writing than I knew) is, the depth to which the parents who live in us (they are not the same) are our definers. And that the work of each of us is to find out the true lineaments of ourselves by facing up to the primal features of these founders who lie buried in us—that this is us, the Double-Backed Beast. (Didn't Hesiod call his genealogy of the gods and men 'the work of the days,' that next oldest poem of the old culture to Homer's two?)

"There are only two live pasts—your own (and that hugely includes your parents), and one other which we don't yet have the vocabulary for, because the West has stayed so ignorant and the East has lived off the old fat too long. I can invoke it by saying, the mythological, but it's too soft. What I mean is that foundling which lies as surely in the phenomenological 'raging apart' as these queer parents rage in us.

"I have spent most of my life seeking out and putting down the 'Laws' of these two pasts, to the degree that I am permitted to see them (instead of the boring historical and evolutionary one which the West has been so busy about since Thucydides) simply because I have found them in the present, my own and yours, and believe that they are the sign of a delightful new civilization of man ahead.

"Now, I spend most of my time studying the Sumerians and Mayans, transposing the poems and inscriptions they left. The will to cohere in both these people is what I see in us, in now. I do not mean collectivism, though I am not at all so uncomfortable in the face of it, and of quantity, as those of my contemporaries seem to be who are stuck with the old soul, and quality, and who back up, for sanctions, to those walls which have been a comfort for man in the East and the West since 1500 B.C. (The American Indian lies outside that comfortable box just as much, I'd argue, as the Americans now do, despite Western appearance. I meant it, in *Ishmael*, that we are the last first people.)

"Therefore I find it awkward to call myself a poet or a writer. If there are no walls there are no names. This is the morning, after the dispersion, and the work of the morning is methodology: how to use oneself, and on what. That is my profession. I am an archeologist of morning. And the writing and acts which I find bear on the present job are (I) from Homer back, not forward; and (II) from Melville on, particularly himself, Dostoevsky, Rimbaud, and Lawrence. These were the modern men who projected what we are and what we are in, who broke the spell. They put men forward into the postmodern, the post-humanist, the post-historic, the going live present, the 'Beautiful Thing.'"

* * *

The more routine and conventional details on Charles Olson are as follows: he was born in Worcester, Mass., "uneducated" (he writes) at Wesleyan, Yale, and Harvard (B.A. 1932, M.A. 1933). He has taught at Clark University and (1936-1939) at Harvard. The chief intellectual disciplinarians for him in those years were Frederick Merk and Edward Dahlberg. Olson's first publication was an essay, "Lear and Moby Dick," which appeared in *Twice-A-Year* in 1938. The essay established his bases, as it were, in Melville and Shakespeare, and was the germ of his book *Call Me Ishmael*, a study of the literary influences upon Melville during the writing of *Moby Dick*. Olson has been the recipient of two Guggenheim fellowships. In 1952 he received a grant from the Wenner-Gren Foundation to study Mayan hieroglyphic writing in Yucatan. In recent years he has taught at Black Mountain College in North Carolina.

PRINCIPAL WORKS: Call Me Ishmael, 1947; Apollonius of Tyana (dance-play) 1951; Mayan Letters (ed. R. Creeley) 1953. *Poetry*—Letter for Melville, 1951; In Cold Hell and Thicket, 1953; The Maximus Poems, 1-10, 1953.

O'MALLEY, Lady MARY. See BRIDGE, A.

O'NEILL, EUGENE GLADSTONE (October 16, 1888-November 27, 1953). For biographical sketch and list of earlier works and references, see TWENTIETH CENTURY AUTHORS, 1942.

* * *

Eugene O'Neill died in his Boston apartment, of bronchial pneumonia, at sixty-five. The playwright had suffered for several years from Parkinson's disease, a form of palsy which prevented him from writing. His son by his first marriage, Eugene O'Neill, Jr., who had become a noted Greek scholar, teacher, and writer in his own right, committed suicide in 1950. The elder O'Neill's will specifically cut off the children of his second marriage, his son Shane and his daughter Oona, now Mrs. Charles Chaplin.

As Edith J. R. Isaacs has described the playwright: "With his close friends and his co-workers he was simple, lovable, openhearted. But he was shy, high-strung, nervous, thoughtful, eternally perplexed, hardworking and distinctly over-productive."

Several of his later plays remain unproduced, including those of a cycle dealing with the rise and fall of an American family, "A Tale of Possessors Dispossessed," written during a twelve-year period spent on the west coast (1934-1946). Some of these he is said to have destroyed, convinced that their dramaturgy was faulty. An autobiographical play, "Long Day's Journey into Night," is not to be produced until twenty-five years after the author's death.

O'Neill's place and value in the history of the theatre are still to be determined, but his serious purpose, his high standards, his rebellion against theatrical conventions will assure him of a position of importance. George Jean Nathan, O'Neill's staunchest critical supporter, said in 1946 that he was the "foremost dramatist in the American theatre" because of "his ability to delve into and appraise character, his depth of knowledge of his fellow man, his sweep and pulse and high resolve, his command of a theatre stage and all its manifold workings, and his mastery of the intricacies of dramaturgy." Acknowledging his preeminence, Harold Clurman ascribed it to his having written "consistently as an artist," and added the qualification that "O'Neill is not a great *writer*; he is a *playwright* of a very high order." Any final evaluation of his work will probably weigh the quality of his writing against his exalted purpose. Although his "fierce willingness to grapple with the imponderables" has been evident in his poorest as well as his best plays, as John Mason Brown has pointed out, "O'Neill's own tragedy, and ours, has been that though he possesses the tragic vision he cannot claim the tragic tongue."

ADDITIONAL WORKS: The Iceman Cometh, 1946; Lost Plays, 1950; A Moon for the Misbegotten, 1952.

ABOUT: Engel, E. A. The Haunted Heroes of Eugene O'Neill; Gray, J. On Second Thought; Morris, L. E. Postscript to Yesterday; Zabel, M. D. Literary Opinion in America; America December 14, 1946; American Mercury October 1946, December 1946; American Scholar Summer 1947; Collier's October 26, 1946; Life October 14, 1946; New Republic February 4, 1952; New York Times September 12, 1946, October 6, 1946, November 28, 1953; New Yorker February 28, March 6, March 13, 1948; Poet Lore Summer 1946; Saturday Review of Literature October 19, 1946, August 6, 1949, June 17, 1950, September 9, 1950; Theatre Arts October 1946, July 1950, February 1951; Time October 21, 1946.

O'NEILL, ROSE CECIL (1874-April 1944). For biographical sketch and list of works and references, see TWENTIETH CENTURY AUTHORS, 1942.

* * *

Rose O'Neill died at sixty-nine. She had returned in 1937 to her farm home in the Ozark Mountains, near Springfield, Mo., where she died. Her estate of over $1,000,000 was witness to the popularity of her creation of the Kewpie doll.

Of the writing which she took seriously, that of her novels, the Boston *Transcript* said, "Rose O'Neill's words prove as malleable as the clay that is also her interpretive medium. One may or may not be charmed by the characterization, but one cannot fail to be enthralled by the sheer beauty of the expression."

ABOUT: Horine, M. M. Memories of Rose O'Neill; Hobbies June 1946; New York Times April 7, 1944; Saturday Review of Literature June 3, 1944; Time April 17, 1944.

ONIONS, OLIVER (1873-). For biographical sketch and list of earlier works and references, see TWENTIETH CENTURY AUTHORS, 1942.

* * *

In 1945, in a review of Oliver Onions' *Story of Ragged Robyn*, the *Times Literary Supplement* pointed out that Onions' work has been much neglected in England (and certainly in America). Partly, the review suggested, this was his fault: "He has dab-

bled a little too obstinately, almost too calculatingly, perhaps, in the bizarre." But, it continued, even his less successful work reflects "something of the firm poetic insight and essentially tragic vision he has made his own."

In all his recent novels Onions has written of "a vanished way of life," seeking out the darker corners of the English past—the later Middle Ages, the wild, lonely Welsh March, the marshlands and the moors. *The Story of Ragged Robyn*, a curious adventure in seventeenth century England, was praised by the *Times* as "a beautiful piece of fiction, rare in quality and charged with a force of poetic suggestion resolved from the uncomprehending terrors of the mind to which it is difficult to give a name." *Poor Man's Tapestry*, which won the James Tait Black Memorial Prize, had the Wars of the Roses for its background and recreated in faithful and beautiful detail the husbandry, the crafts, and the monastic custom of fifteenth century England.

ADDITIONAL WORKS: The Story of Ragged Robyn, 1945; Poor Man's Tapestry, 1946; Arras of Youth, 1949; A Penny for the Harp, 1951; Bells Rung Backwards, 1953.

ABOUT: Swinnerton, F. The Georgian Literary Scene 1910-1935.

OPPENHEIM, EDWARD PHILLIPS (1866-February 3, 1946). For biographical sketch and list of earlier works and references, see TWENTIETH CENTURY AUTHORS, 1942.

* * *

E. Phillips Oppenheim died at seventy-nine at his home on the Channel island of Guernsey, to which he had returned after World War II.

Undisputed holder of the title of most popular and most prolific writer of thrillers, Oppenheim produced an average of more than three novels a year for over fifty years, in addition to innumerable short stories. William Dana Orcutt has called him "a natural story teller, gifted with unusual power of observation and fired with imagination."

ADDITIONAL WORK: Mr. Mirakel, 1943.

ABOUT: Orcutt, W. D. From My Library Walls; London Times February 4, 1946; New York Times February 4, 1946, February 24, 1946; Time February 23, 1942.

OPPENHEIM, JAMES (May 24, 1882-August 4, 1932). For biographical sketch and list of works and references, see TWENTIETH CENTURY AUTHORS, 1942.

ORAGE, ALFRED RICHARD (January 22, 1873-November 5, 1934). For biographical sketch and list of works and references, see TWENTIETH CENTURY AUTHORS, 1942.

* * *

ABOUT: Dictionary of National Biography 1931-1940.

*ORCZY, EMMUSKA, Baroness (1865-November 12, 1947). For biographical sketch and list of earlier works and references, see TWENTIETH CENTURY AUTHORS, 1942.

* * *

Baroness Orczy died in London at eighty-two.

The writer, whose full name was Emma Magdalena Rosalia Maria Josefa Barbara Orczy Barstow, spent five years of World War II living next door to the Nazi Gestapo headquarters in Monte Carlo. Her husband died there in 1943. Her villa was bombed by the R.A.F. just before the town was liberated. She returned to England and spent her last years in a secluded country home at Henley-on-Thames.

She had, as the New York *Herald Tribune* has pointed out, "a natural gift for swift narration, a vivid imagination and an appropriately flamboyant style." Although her "Scarlet Pimpernel" was not a profound creation, and Baroness Orczy "could hardly be classed as a serious student of history or a writer of outstanding originality," in the words of the London *Times,* "nevertheless both became household names for a grateful multitude." The "Scarlet Pimpernel" has reappeared over the years in motion picture versions and, for a time, in a radio series based upon new adventures of her hero.

ADDITIONAL WORKS: Pride of Race, 1942; Links in the Chain of Life (autobiography) 1947; Will o' The Wisp, 1947.

ABOUT: Orczy, E. Links in the Chain of Life; London Times November 13, 1947; Saturday Review of Literature January 26, 1946.

* ôr'tsĭ

ORENBURGSKY, SERGEY GUSEV (1867-). For biographical sketch and list of works and references, see TWENTIETH CENTURY AUTHORS, 1942.

* * *

At last reports Orenburgsky was living in New York City. He has published no books in recent years.

ABOUT: Snow, V. Russian Writers: A Bio-Bibliographical Dictionary.

O'RIORDAN, CONAL O'CONNELL (April 29, 1874-June 18, 1948). For biographical sketch and list of works and references, see TWENTIETH CENTURY AUTHORS, 1942.

* * *

Conal O'Connell O'Riordan died at his home in Ealing, England, at seventy-four.

The novelist and playwright has been described as very small, frail-looking and crippled, and as a witty, wise and exceptionally well informed conversationalist. His last years were spent in seclusion. The London *Times* says he wrote with a "sense of ironic tragedy which in his best work underlies and counterbalances the dazzling comedy."

ABOUT: London Times June 21, 1948; New York Times June 19, 1948.

"ORMSBEE, DAVID." See LONG-STREET, S.

*ORTEGA Y GASSET, JOSÉ (May 9, 1883-). For biographical sketch and list of earlier works and references, see TWENTIETH CENTURY AUTHORS, 1942.

* * *

Ortega y Gasset remained in voluntary exile from Spain for some twelve years, living during that time in France, South America, and Portugal. In 1949 he returned to Madrid to found a free institute of philosophy and cultural science. At his first lecture he was greeted with wild enthusiasm. He had apparently made his peace with the Franco government. Little changed in appearance, "still the erect and fastidious intellectual," he said of himself: "If there is something that characterizes my life, it is that I have had to struggle with the world's dramatic future—the future always tending to shake the ground of the present on which I had my feet." He still struggles, he says, with a "passion which is the most vivid I find in my heart. I would call it intellectual love."

Ortega's researches in recent years have concentrated heavily upon the philosophy of history. History is for Ortega the basic reality, Ernst Curtius writes in *Partisan Review.* "Stars, plants, and animals have nature. Man, instead of nature, has history. Hence it is the task of thought to raise history to a system." Ortega himself has not attempted to devise this system. Instead he has been content to point out and to analyze those trends in human history which are relevant to his thesis. His *Concord and Liberty* is a collection of four essays on this general

* ôr tä'gä ē gä sĕt'

theme. William Barrett wrote of it: "Ortega remains above all a passionate and unreconstructed aristocrat. The intellectual tradition to which he remains faithful is the high Brahmanism of German academic thought, with all its great merits and its shortcomings."

Ortega y Gasset is recognized as the finest prose stylist writing in Spanish today. "His sentences shoot out like arrows and strike square in the center of the target," Curtius writes. "We have the feeling that we are seeing things for the first time, and simultaneously the feeling that we are seeing them in their true image."

ADDITIONAL WORKS IN ENGLISH TRANSLATION: The Mission of the University, 1944; Concord and Liberty, 1946; The Dehumanization of Art; and, Notes on the Novel, 1948.

ABOUT: Sanchez Villaseñor, J. Ortega y Gasset, Existentialist, 1949; Columbia Dictionary of Modern European Literature; Partisan Review March 1950; Romanic Review December 1949; Time June 10, 1946, January 17, 1949.

ORTON, WILLIAM AYLOTT (February 9, 1889-August 13, 1952), Anglo-American economist and educator, was born in

Bromley, Kent, England, the son of William Amor Orton and Emma (Aylott) Orton. He was educated at Cambridge University, graduating with a B.A. in 1919 and an M.A. in 1922; and at the London School of Economics, graduating with an M.Sc. in 1921 and a D.Sc. in 1946. From Boston College he received an LL.D. in 1948. Orton was a staff officer with the industrial relations department of the British Ministry of Labour from 1919 to 1922. In the latter year he came to the United States as professor of economics at Smith College, a post he held until his death. During World War I, as a lieutenant in the British Army, he served in Egypt and France (1914-17) and, after being wounded in action, he worked in the War Office, London (1917-19).

He wrote many books on economics and social conditions, and in 1945 published The Liberal Tradition, a study of the social and spiritual conditions of freedom. "A professor's book," reported the Library Journal, "with many quotes and some personal opinions reported as God's truth. Timely as to theme and references, opposed to excess nationalism." "This is a serious book," said Book Week, "in spite of the constant play of wit—sometimes quiet, sometimes fiery—which enlivens all its pages." Orton "gives the impression of opposition to rule by the masses and lack of faith in their ability to govern," was Current History's objection. "The book is more likely to promote intolerance between races and religions and sects, than to further the cause of liberalism." But Pitirim A. Sorokin found it "a truly thoughtful, stimulating, and careful analysis of the liberal tradition." Reinhold Niebuhr admitted to "a tremendous initial enthusiasm which was gradually dissipated as concluding chapters failed to maintain the profundity of insight promised in the earlier chapters. . . . One feels that he is not completely committed to the liberal tradition and that he is prepared to show that American liberalism might well borrow some of the virtues of true conservatism," which Niebuhr describes (in Orton's view) as "reverence for the past, appreciation of organic forms, communal unity, and constitutional continuity."

In a later book, The Economic Role of the State, Orton's aim is a "recurrence to fundamental principles." George Soule in the New York Times found him "unnecessarily antagonistic to the application of science to human problems"; but the American Economic Review while "highly skeptical of some of Professor Orton's practical conclusions," called the book "wise and witty" and said "old-fashioned liberals will read this slim volume with pleasure."

In 1917 Orton married Olmen Marlais Moment of London, and they had two children, twins. In 1946 he became a Roman Catholic. Orton took leaves of absence from Smith College from time to time, to serve as visiting professor at the University of California, Amherst, Williams, and other colleges. He died while vacationing at Damariscotta, Maine.

PRINCIPAL WORKS: Prelude to Economics, 1932; America in Search of Culture, 1933; Last Romantic (autobiographical novel) 1937; Twenty Years' Armistice 1918-1938, 1938; The Liberal Tradition, 1945; Challenge of Christian Liberalism, 1946; The Economic Role of the State, 1950.

ABOUT: Hoehn, M. (ed.) Catholic Authors, II; New York Times August 16, 1952.

"ORWELL, GEORGE" (pseudonym of Eric Blair) (1903-January 21, 1950). For autobiographical sketch and list of earlier works and references, see TWENTIETH CENTURY AUTHORS, 1942.

* * *

George Orwell, who had suffered from tuberculosis for three years, died at forty-six in a London nursing home. His first wife had died in 1945; eight months before his death he married Sonia Brownell. The last few years of his life were spent in a quiet rural atmosphere in Hertfordshire, where he wrote critical articles for the London *Observer* and the London *Times*. His "satirical fable" *Animal Farm* was made into a cartoon motion picture in 1954, and a British television production in the same year of his novel *Nineteen Eighty-Four*, a sensational projection of a possible future totalitarian state, resulted in a furor of public reaction.

V. S. Pritchett, who has called Orwell "the conscience of his generation" and speaks of his "fast, clear, grey, bitter prose with its arguing ring and satirical asides," feels that "his limitation was that he was not so much a novelist as a writer of vivid, arguing monologues." Orwell himself said that he had been forced by the age in which he lived into becoming "a sort of pamphleteer," and declared, three years before his death, "what I have most wanted to do throughout the past ten years is to make political writing into an art." He has been characterized as a radical in politics but a conservative in feeling, who, in the words of Geoffrey Ashe, "sought for the roots of the dying decencies."

The first annual award by *Partisan Review*, given for a distinguished body of work, went to Orwell in 1949 with the notation that his writing "has been marked by a singular directness and honesty, a scrupulous fidelity to his experience that has placed him in that very valuable class of the writer who is a witness to his time."

ADDITIONAL WORKS: Animal Farm: A Fairy Story, 1945; Dickens, Dali and Others, 1946; Nineteen Eighty-Four (novel) 1949; Shooting an Elephant (essays) 1950; Such, Such Were the Joys (essays) 1953.

ABOUT: Orwell, G. Such, Such Were the Joys; Trilling, L. The Opposing Self; Antioch Review March 1947; Commentary March 1952; Commonweal June 1, 1951, January 28, 1955; Fortnightly June 1951; New Republic February 20, 1950; New Statesman and Nation January 28, 1950; New York Herald Tribune June 12, 1949; New York Times June 12, 1949, January 22, 1950, February 5, 1950; New Yorker January 13, 1951; Nineteenth Century March·1950; Partisan Review October 1949, May 1950; Poetry November 1949; Saturday Review of Literature June 11, 1949, February 4, 1950; Spectator August 29, 1947.

OSTENSO, MARTHA (September 17, 1900-   ). For autobiographical sketch and list of works and references, see TWENTIETH CENTURY AUTHORS, 1942.

* * *

Martha Ostenso lives near Brainerd, Minn. She is married to Douglas Durkin. In evaluating her recent work, reviewers are agreed

that she is at her best "when she writes about the land and those who really love it," as she did in *O River, Remember,* an historical novel about two pioneer families, which Sterling North considered "the best novel [she] has written since *Wild Geese.*" Her more recent books have been judged as slighter efforts, but she is always spoken of as a competent writer who has a real skill in portraying the details of simple rural life.

ADDITIONAL WORKS: (with E. Kenny) And They Shall Walk (biography of Sister Kenny) 1943; O River, Remember, 1943; Milk Route, 1948; The Sunset Tree, 1949.

ABOUT: Thomas, C. Canadian Novelists, 1920-45; Warfel, H. R. American Novelists of Today.

"O'SULLIVAN, SEUMAS." See STARKEY, J.

O'SULLIVAN, VINCENT (November 27, 1872-   ). For biographical sketch and list of works and references, see TWENTIETH CENTURY AUTHORS, 1942.

*OURSLER, FULTON (January 22, 1893-May 24, 1952), American journalist, novelist, mystery writer, and playwright, was born in Baltimore, the son of William C. Oursler, a line superintendent for the United Railways and Electric Company of Baltimore, and Lillian Phillips (Sappington) Oursler, both of whose families were among the earliest settlers in Maryland. Fulton Oursler left public school without finishing the eighth grade. He worked as a water-boy for a construction gang, assisted on a butter and egg route, and was a packer in a department store. For two years he was a clerk in a Baltimore law office at a salary of three dollars a week. He supplemented this income by giving sleight-of-hand performances at club and lodge entertainments. With the law firm, Oursler was supposed to "read law" with the idea of becoming an attorney. Instead, with the help of the president of Baltimore City College, he read good literature, getting also the rudiments of French and German, and many other studies. The reading of great books made him decide to become a writer, and he obtained a job as a cub reporter on the Baltimore *American*.

Oggiano

* ourz′lĕr

When he left for New York in 1918, it was to join the staff of the New York *Music Trades* as news editor. He began the work on a Monday morning, and on Wednesday afternoon he was appointed managing editor. During the next four years, Oursler was also writing short stories and articles for a variety of magazines, mostly the pulps. In 1920, after selling many stories to Macfadden publications, he was invited to join the staff; two weeks later he was in complete editorial charge, and for the next twenty years remained supervising editor of all the Macfadden magazines, including *Metropolitan, Physical Culture, True Story,* and *True Detective.* He took an important interest in detection of criminals, and on three occasions made the graduating address before the National Police Academy of the F.B.I. From 1931 to 1942, Oursler was editor-in-chief of *Liberty;* and in 1944 he became a senior editor of the *Reader's Digest.*

He also was a frequent speaker on the radio, during the war speaking nightly as "The People's Reporter," answering questions from listeners concerning current news; and was a vacation replacement for Walter Winchell, Lowell Thomas, and Bishop Fulton Sheen.

Oursler wrote some thirty volumes, plus several in collaboration with other authors. As "Anthony Abbot" he wrote eight mystery stories, between 1930 and 1948; he wrote a number of plays and a number of novels. He is today best known for his retelling of the New Testament in *The Greatest Story Ever Told.* This was begun in 1935, after Oursler's first visit to Palestine. In 1934 he wrote *A Skeptic in the Holy Land,* the least successful of his books. This failure he attributed to the fact that his mind was undergoing a change while he was writing, and in the final chapter he was much less a skeptic than in the first. He had come to the conclusion that democracy was possible only to men worthy of its great responsibilities—men of character; and he believed that Jesus had taught the highest concepts of human character. Because much of the growing generation had not read the Bible, he decided to write a life of Christ in popular modern style. The task took eleven years. As he read the works of the Early Fathers, Oursler began the trail that led him eventually to adopt the Roman Catholic faith. His retelling of the Bible stories, however, are acclaimed by Protestant ministers and by rabbis as well as by Catholic leaders. His *A Child's Life of Jesus* and *The Greatest Story Ever Told* are available in both Protestant and Catholic editions. Of the last-named book the New York *Times* said, "The stories are simply written and can be read as entertainment, as introduction to the gospel story or as commentary. The important thing is that they present in modern form an account of those dramatic, long-past, seemingly obscure events that have somehow changed the world." The book has sold over 2,175,000 copies, including the pocket-sized edition. It was syndicated in more than one hundred and fifty newspapers, and has been translated into many languages.

Oursler traveled and lectured in all of the forty-eight states, and in other countries. He received many honors and degrees, including the annual award of Catholic Institute of the Press, 1951, a Freedom Award for a *Reader's Digest* article, 1951, and a Cardinal Gibbons medal of the Catholic University of America Alumni, 1951. He was a member of many clubs, and a trustee of the Carnegie Fund for Needy Authors.

His first marriage was to Rose Keller Karger in 1911; they had two children. His second wife was Grace Perkins, the writer, whom he married in 1925, and two children were born of this marriage. A novel by his son Will Oursler, *New York, N.Y.,* was published in 1954.

Oursler died in New York City of a heart attack. At the time of his death he was working on *The Greatest Faith Ever Known,* published posthumously.

PRINCIPAL WORKS: Behold This Dreamer, 1924; Sandalwood, 1925; Stepchild of the Moon, 1926; Poor Little Fool, 1928; The True Story of Bernarr Macfadden, 1929; The World's Delight, 1929; The Great Jasper, 1930; Joshua Todd, 1935; A Skeptic in the Holy Land, 1936; Three Things We Can Believe In, 1942; The Precious Secret, 1947; The Greatest Story Ever Told, 1949; Why I Know There Is a God, 1950; Modern Parables, 1950; A Child's Life of Jesus, 1951; The Greatest Book Ever Written, 1951; The Greatest Faith Ever Known, 1953; Lights Along the Shore, 1954.

ABOUT: Hoehn, M. Catholic Authors, I; O'Brien, J. A. Road to Damascus; Current Biography 1942, 1952; New York Times May 25, 1952.

OUSPENSKY, P. D. See USPENSKII, P. D.

OVERSTREET, HARRY ALLEN (October 25, 1875-). For biographical sketch and list of earlier works and references, see TWENTIETH CENTURY AUTHORS, 1942.

* * *

Probably the most popular of "popularizers" of contemporary psychology and sociology, Harry A. Overstreet has devoted the years since his retirement from college teaching to promoting adult education. He has done this by sponsoring and affiliating with such organizations as The Town Hall of New York City and the American Association for Adult Education, by extensive lecturing, and by the writing of books and magazine articles which present the problems of modern social thought in simple, direct, and eminently readable terms. The most successful of his recent books is *The Mature Mind,* a Book-of-the-Month Club selection and a best seller for more than a year after its publication. By 1952 close to half a million copies had been sold. Some critics have complained that Overstreet's work "oversimplifies" the complex nature of his material. *Time* magazine objected to its "psychological nostrums and all-too-truisms" which give readers "the heady sensation of doing mental push-ups by the dozen." But as Morris L. Ernst describes his work (in a review of *The Great Enterprise* in the *Saturday Review*): "He has garnered and presents in simple language some of the advances and new techniques developed in the fields of psychology and psychiatry for dealing with the interrelationship of individuals. . . . He fills in the interstices with wise, temperate, and calm observations. . . . He gives evidence of his talent for treating complicated material with pleasant observations."

Overstreet and his wife Bonaro, who in addition to her own teaching and writing collaborates with him on many of his books and frequently shares the lecture platform with him, winter at Mill Valley, Calif., and spend their summers in Bennington, Vt.

ADDITIONAL WORKS: The Mature Mind, 1949; Where Children Come First: A Study of the P.T.A. Idea (with B. Overstreet) 1949; The Great Enterprise, 1952; The Mind Alive (with B. Overstreet) 1954.

ABOUT: Book-of-the-Month Club News Summer 1949; Current Biography 1950; New York Herald Tribune Book Review October 12, 1952; Saturday Review August 9, 1952.

OVERTON, GRANT MARTIN (September 19, 1887-July 4, 1930). For biographical sketch and list of works and references, see TWENTIETH CENTURY AUTHORS, 1942.

OWEN, WILFRED (March 18, 1893-November 4, 1918). For biographical sketch and list of works and references, see TWENTIETH CENTURY AUTHORS, 1942.

* * *

ABOUT: Sitwell, O. Noble Essences; Swinnerton, F. The Georgian Literary Scene, 1910-1935; Fortnightly November 1944.

OXENHAM, JOHN (1852-January 24, 1941). For autobiographical sketch and list of works and references, see TWENTIETH CENTURY AUTHORS, 1942.

* * *

ADDITIONAL WORK: Selected Poems (ed. C. L. Wallis) 1948.

ABOUT: Oxenham, E. I. John Oxenham, Scrapbook of John Oxenham; Parr, O. K. My Chief Knight: John Oxenham.

PAASSEN. See VAN PAASSEN

*PACH, WALTER (July 11, 1883-). For autobiographical sketch and list of earlier works and references, see TWENTIETH CENTURY AUTHORS, 1942.

* * *

Walter Pach lives in Washington Square, New York City. His first wife, Magdalene Frohberg Pach died, and in 1951, in Athens, Greece, he married Nikifora Loutsis. In 1948 Pach published *The Art Museum in America,* a history and study of art museums in relation to American art and society. The volume, called by Huntington Cairns "the best rationale of the American museum, and indeed of museums generally, that has yet been put forward," also contained valuable lists of collections of the most important museums in the United States. Pach's work, Cairns writes, "has an informal richness which can come only from years of first-hand study."

ADDITIONAL WORK: The Art Museum in America, 1948.

* "My family retains the original German or Dutch pronunciation of the *ch* at the end of our name; it does not exist in English, but is the same as that of the great composer Bach."

PACKARD, FRANK LUCIUS (February 2, 1877-February 17, 1942). For biographical sketch and list of works and references, see TWENTIETH CENTURY AUTHORS, 1942.

* * *

ABOUT: Thomas, C. Canadian Novelists, 1920-1945.

PAGE, ELIZABETH (August 27, 1889-). For autobiographical sketch and list of earlier works and references, see TWENTIETH CENTURY AUTHORS, 1942.

* * *

Elizabeth Page writes from Manchester, Vt.: "In 1943, on my mother's death, I returned to our family home in Vermont where I still live. From December 1945 until January of 1948 I worked with the American Friends Service Committee, having a position in the Philadelphia headquarters which gave me the privilege of visiting the International Friends Centers in eleven countries of Europe in 1946."

Also in 1946 Elizabeth Page published another historical novel, *Wilderness Adventure*, a story of frontier life and adventure in early colonial America.

ADDITIONAL WORK: Wilderness Adventure, 1946.

PAGET, VIOLET ("Vernon Lee") (October 1856-February 13, 1935). For biographical sketch and list of works and references, see TWENTIETH CENTURY AUTHORS, 1942.

* * *

ADDITIONAL WORK: The Snake Lady, and Other Stories, 1954.

ABOUT: Gregory, H. *Introduction to* The Snake Lady, and Other Stories; Commonweal June 25, 1954; Cornhill November 1944; Dictionary of National Biography 1931-1940; Publications of the Modern Language Association September 1953.

PAIN, BARRY ERIC ODELL (September 28, 1864-May 5, 1928). For biographical sketch and list of works and references, see TWENTIETH CENTURY AUTHORS, 1942.

PAINE, ALBERT BIGELOW (July 10, 1861-April 9, 1937). For autobiographical sketch and list of works and references, see TWENTIETH CENTURY AUTHORS, 1942.

PAINE, RALPH DELAHAYE (August 28, 1871-April 29, 1925). For biographical sketch and list of works and references, see TWENTIETH CENTURY AUTHORS, 1942.

PAKINGTON, HUMPHREY (September 8, 1888-). For biographical sketch and list of earlier works and references, see TWENTIETH CENTURY AUTHORS, 1942.

* * *

Humphrey Pakington lives in the small town of Holt, near Worcester. He has continued active in the London architectural firm of Pakington and Enthoven. At the beginning of World War II, he re-enlisted in the Navy and served until the end of the war on the staff of the commander-in-chief of the Western Approaches. In 1942 he was awarded the Order of the British Empire.

Pakington's placid, leisurely-paced, and deftly-written novels have won him an admiring audience in the United States as well as in Great Britain. His scene is usually England of the 1890's and the turn of the century, his characters the solid country gentry. Amy Loveman, writing of *Aston Kings*, found "delightful wit" in it, and described the book as "civilized writing about civilized people presented through the imagination of an author who is sophisticated without being 'smart' and who obviously finds delight in observing his fellows." Pakington's most popular books in recent years are his novels (sometimes described as "social comedies") *The Washbournes of Otterley* and its sequels, *Young William Washbourne* and *Farewell to Otterley*, a chronicle of the lives of several generations of an English country family, from 1845 to modern times.

ADDITIONAL WORKS: Aston Kings, 1946; The Washbournes of Otterley, 1948; Young William Washbourne, 1949; Farewell to Otterley, 1951; The Brothers Bellamy, 1953; Willoughby Carter, 1953.

PALMER, FREDERICK (January 29, 1873-). For autobiographical sketch and list of earlier works and references, see TWENTIETH CENTURY AUTHORS, 1942.

* * *

Frederick Palmer has concentrated on military subjects in his later writings. *It Can Be Done This Time* was a plea for the establishment of universal peace through the cooperation of the major powers. His authoritative and informative biography of General Pershing, on whose staff he had served in World War I, was highly praised. Donald Armstrong, in *Saturday Review of Literature*, called it "a labor of love" which "achieves a high degree of objectivity."

During World War II Palmer was an observer with the British Army in France in 1940 and with American forces in Germany and the Pacific in 1945. He lives in Charlottesville, Va.

ADDITIONAL WORKS: It Can Be Done This Time, 1944; John J. Pershing, General of the Armies, 1948.

PALMER, GEORGE HERBERT (March 19, 1842-May 7, 1933). For biographical sketch and list of works and references, see TWENTIETH CENTURY AUTHORS, 1942.

* * *

ADDITIONAL WORK: Academic Courtship: Letters of Alice Freeman and George Herbert Palmer, 1886-87, 1940.

PALMER, JOHN LESLIE. See "BEED-ING, F."

PANTER-DOWNES, MOLLIE (August 25, 1906-   ). For biographical sketch and list of earlier works and references, see TWENTIETH CENTURY AUTHORS, 1942.

* * *

Mollie Panter-Downes continues as London correspondent for the *New Yorker*, a post she has held since 1939, writing her "quietly perceptive" reports on life in England. Occasionally she contributes a short story to the *New Yorker*. Some of her most distinguished writing was done during the World War II bombings, when she went up to London from her fifteenth-century country home in Surrey, toured the city, visited everything from the House of Commons, the theatres, and the concert halls, to the bombed-out slums, and reported all this to her American readers with sensitivity and restraint.

Miss Panter-Downes is better known as a literary figure in the United States than in her own country where, *Time* magazine points out, she is "almost a literary unknown." Her recent books have tended to bridge the gap between British and American readers. *Watling Green*, a children's book, was written in the form of a letter from an English girl to an American girl, describing pre-war and wartime life in a small English town. *One Fine Day* was a simple and gently muted story of a day in the life of an English woman. Rosemary Benét said of it in *Saturday Review of Literature*: "This is an English view . . . but it is a moving picture and the nostalgia for other more peaceful days translates itself into our own idiom and our own experience."

In 1947 Miss Panter-Downes and her husband, Clare Robinson (then an official in the German control office in London), visited the United States. She was described as "a slender, friendly woman . . . who seemed as unaffected as her correspondence."

ADDITIONAL WORKS: Watling Green (juvenile) 1943; One Fine Day, 1947.

ABOUT: Time March 3, 1947.

*PANZINI, ALFREDO (December 31, 1863-April 10, 1939). For biographical sketch and list of works and references, see TWENTIETH CENTURY AUTHORS, 1942.

* * *

ABOUT: Columbia Dictionary of Modern European Literature.

* pän tsě′nē

*PAPASHVILY, GEORGE and HELEN, American humorists and essayists, collaborators on the best-selling *Anything Can Happen*, sent in separate sketches for this volume. **GEORGE PAPASHVILY** (August 23, 1898-   ), writes: "I was born in Kobiankari, Georgia, in the Caucasus. No schools, or at least no free schools, existed there during my childhood so my father  paid a prince a bag of grain to teach me the letters of the alphabet and how to write my name. At the age of eight I was apprenticed to a leather worker to learn braiding and ornamenting of crops. Later I added another trade, sword making, to my first one. At sixteen, following the outbreak of World War I, I joined the Russian Army and served in Persia, Armenia, and Turkey with the newly organized and very rudimentary air corps.

"After the war I wanted more technical training in aviation, so I left Georgia and came to New York. Without the language or any formal education it was difficult to find the kind of job and training I wanted. I worked at many things—odd jobs in New York, in the automobile factories in Detroit, in a steel mill in Pittsburgh, as a movie extra in Hollywood, selling box lunches in San Francisco. Like many immigrants I had planned to stay in the United States only long enough to learn the new skills and save some money and then go home, but after I had been here a short time and especially after I met an American girl, Helen Waite, whom I later married, I decided to make the U.S. my permanent home and became a naturalized citizen. My wife, Helen Waite Papashvily, and I have collaborated on four books: *Anything Can Happen, Yes and No Stories, Thanks to Noah,* and *Dogs and People.*

"In 1943 I began to do sculpture, first in wood and later in stone, and since 1946 I have devoted all my time to this work and have exhibited in group shows at the National Academy in New York City, the National College of Fine Arts in Washington, D.C., the Boston Museum of Fine Arts, the Pennsylvania Academy of Fine Arts and in two one-man shows, Allentown (Pa.) Museum of Art, 1951, and the Philadelphia Art Alliance, 1953."

* på påsh vē′lē

HELEN (WAITE) PAPASHVILY

(December 19, 1906-   ), writes: "My maternal grandparents, Scotch Irish immigrants, and my father's family, Vermonters, were all lured west in the early days of the gold rush. I was born in Stockton, in the San Joaquin Valley of California, the youngest child of Herbert Waite and Isabella Findlay Lochhead Waite. I graduated from the local grammar and high school and in 1927, while still attending college at the University of California at Berkeley, I began working in a campus book store. In 1929, I opened a shop of my own.

"After marriage to George Papashvily, we lived in New York where I did bibliographical research, collected books for two private libraries, and began to write, though not very often to sell, short stories, juveniles, and nonfiction articles. In 1935 we bought a farm near Quakertown, Pa., where we still live. From 1939 to 1950 I owned and managed the Moby Dick Bookshop, Allentown, Pa.

"It had often seemed to me that some of my husband's experiences as an immigrant would make good stories, and I tried to set them down just as he told them. We sent one of these sketches to *Common Ground,* a magazine published by the Common Council for American Unity, and the editor, M. Margaret Anderson, accepted it and urged us to write others. At the suggestion of Elizabeth F. Lawrence, an editor of Harper and Brothers, this material was developed into a book, *Anything Can Happen,* published in 1945 and a selection of the Book-of-the-Month Club for January of that year.

"Our second book, *Yes and No Stories,* was a collection of Georgian folk tales as remembered by my husband and set down by me. Our third book, *Thanks to Noah,* was the story of the animals in our life, the bear and the dogs my husband grew up with in the Caucasus and the dogs that have shared our life on our farm."

* * *

Anything Can Happen was described by the *Saturday Review of Literature* as "an interesting psychological case-study in the adjustment of the alien, . . . written with the rich enjoyment and humor that the author felt." It was made into a motion picture, with José Ferrer playing George Papashvily.

PRINCIPAL WORKS: Anything Can Happen, 1945; Yes and No Stories, 1946; Thanks to Noah, 1951; Dogs and People, 1954.

ABOUT: Papashvily, G. & H. Anything Can Happen; Current Biography 1945; Book-of-the-Month Club News November, December 1944; New York Times Book Review December 31, 1944; Publishers' Weekly January 27, 1945.

*PAPINI, GIOVANNI (January 9, 1881-   ). For biographical sketch and list of earlier works and references, see TWENTIETH CENTURY AUTHORS, 1942.

* * *

Giovanni Papini lives in Florence. In spite of failing eyesight, he has continued to write busily and with the same stormy, restless brilliance which characterized his earlier work. A practicing Catholic, he has nevertheless provoked criticism from Catholic sources for "exaggerations, inaccuracies and theological shortcomings." His recent book *The Devil* provoked heated controversy. His *Letters of Pope Celestine VI to All Mankind*—purporting to be written by a non-existent pope about the state of the world—were found, by Anne Fremantle in *Commonweal,* to contain "a disagreeable amount of personal advertising." But, Miss Fremantle continued, the letters "contain some lovely laments for the living, written in moving and lyrical prose. . . . They are empty of bitterness, intensely charitable, and generally wise." His biography of Michelangelo offended some critics by its length, its pretentiousness, and a style which Charles J. Rolo described in the *Atlantic* as "inflated, cliché-ridden, and bespattered with silly statements presented as portentous thoughts." But still others admired the vigor and imagination reflected in the work. Thomas Craven wrote in the New York *Herald Tribune:* "Unfearful of the magnitude of the subject and undeterred by the imposing accumulations of authoritarian lore and esthetic explication, he proceeds with trenchant conviction and sustaining spiritual insight to build up one of the most plausibly conceived and rigorously fortified studies of the great Florentine thus far to appear—and by all odds the most engaging."

It will be some time before the bitter controversies over Papini's works and his equally brilliant but erratic personality die down enough to permit a thorough evaluation. Meanwhile, Marie Buffa's comment on him (in the *Columbia Dictionary of Modern European Literature*) is one of the fairest estimates: "Papini with his vast ambitions and hasty renunciations remains a typical representative of a period disturbed by great events. His works voice the moods of a whole generation of Italians, a generation that

* på pē′nē

fed too eagerly on abstractions, that hated its masters too cordially, that often sought the short cut to success and the achievement of sound culture, a generation which, nevertheless, struck not a few chords of spiritual revival that echoed through the world."

ADDITIONAL WORKS IN ENGLISH TRANSLATION: Letters of Pope Celestine VI to All Mankind, 1948; (with others) Florence, Flower of the World, 1951; Michelangelo: His Life and His Era, 1952; The Devil, 1954.

ABOUT: Columbia Dictionary of Modern European Literature; Hoehn, M. (ed.) Catholic Authors, I; Livingston, A. Essays on Modern Italian Literature; Books Abroad Spring 1948; Catholic World June 1951.

*PARES, Sir BERNARD (March 1, 1867-April 17, 1949), English writer and authority on Russia, was born in Surrey, the son of

a country squire who was an ardent follower of the liberal Prime Minister Gladstone. Sir Bernard was educated at Harrow and at Trinity College, Cambridge. Between 1904 and 1914 when World War I began, he visited Russia annually and continued his studies of Slavonic languages.

As foreign correspondent for British newspapers he attended sessions of the Duma (Russian Parliament) and established himself as a shrewd observer of the many changes that were brewing beneath the surface of Europe's last great feudal state. He witnessed many of the principal events of the first Russian revolution, 1904-1907, and in collaboration with Professor Samuel N. Harper of Chicago University, interviewed practically all those who had taken part in Russian politics of the time. In 1907 he was one of several persons who organized the School of Russian Studies at the University of Liverpool. During World War I he was an expert on Russian affairs with the British War Office and was attached to the Third Army of Russia until the Czarist regime collapsed in 1917. Attached to the Russian Red Cross, he won the Medal and Soldier's Cross of St. George.

When the Bolsheviks moved toward power, Sir Bernard took the stand taken by his country and its allies in favoring the conservative Kerensky party, feeling certain that the Bolsheviks planned to take Russia out of

* pârz

the war. Before the final resistance to the Bolsheviks collapsed, Sir Bernard was with Admiral Kolchak in Siberia. When he returned to England in 1919 he was knighted for his services to Russia.

Although Sir Bernard did not visit Russia again for seventeen years, he kept in close touch with developments there. From 1918 he was director of the School for Slavonic and East European Studies at the University of London. When the Soviet Union again opened its doors to him in 1936, he found Russia to be a "country ruled by Communists who have ceased to practice Communism." In books, magazine and newspaper articles, he strove to interpret the Soviet Union to the English-speaking world, but in so doing he gained the ill will of the Soviet authorities because he said several times that he believed that Communism would not endure in Russia in its present form.

For many years Sir Bernard believed that Russia and the nations of the West could be brought together by mutual understanding. In his last years he was compelled to modify this view. The Literary Gazette, an official Soviet publication, described him in 1948 as "an eighty-year-old man enraged to the extreme, to the state of marasmus (progressive emaciation)" and asserted that he was not, as he claimed to be, a "friend" of the Soviet Union, but a "White Guard counter-revolutionary and spy—the same as he was thirty years ago."

Sir Bernard lived in the United States from 1942 until his death. He lectured at the New School For Social Research and at Sarah Lawrence College and was a radio commentator. In 1948 his autobiography, The Wandering Student, was published and was well received. He had written nearly a dozen detailed studies of Russian affairs and in 1923 had edited the letters of the Czar and the Czarina. He died in New York in 1949.

Sir Bernard married Margaret Dixon in 1901 and they had five children, the first letters of whose names spell his last name: Peter, Andrew, Richard, Elizabeth, and Susan. Peter Pares is in the Foreign Office in London, Major Andrew Pares is in the British Army. Professor Richard Pares of the department of history, Edinburgh University, contributed an introduction to the definitive edition of his father's famous and classic book, A History of Russia, revised and reset after Sir Bernard's death.

PRINCIPAL WORKS: Russia and Reform, 1907; Day by Day with the Russian Army, 1916; The Letters of the Czar and Czarina, 1923; A History of Russia, 1926; My Russian Memoirs, 1931; Moscow

Admits a Critic, 1936; The Fall of the Russian Monarchy, 1939; Russia and the Peace, 1944; The Wandering Student, 1948.

ABOUT: Pares, B. The Wandering Student; New York Times April 18, April 25, May 4, 1949.

*PARETO, VILFREDO (August 15, 1848-August 19, 1923). For biographical sketch and list of works and references, see TWENTIETH CENTURY AUTHORS, 1942.

* * *

ADDITIONAL WORK IN ENGLISH TRANSLATION: The Ruling Class in Italy Before 1900, 1950.

ABOUT: Columbia Dictionary of Modern European Literature; Ginsberg, M. Reason and Unreason in Society; Schumpeter, J. A. Ten Great Economists from Marx to Keynes.

* pä rá′tō

PARKER, Mrs. DOROTHY (ROTHS-CHILD) (August 22, 1893-). For biographical sketch and list of earlier works and references, see TWENTIETH CENTURY AUTHORS, 1942.

* * *

After a number of years of screenplay writing in Hollywood, Dorothy Parker has recently made two new attempts at writing for the theatre. (An early effort was her collaboration with Elmer Rice in 1924 on an unsuccessful play, Close Harmony). With Ross Evans in 1949 she wrote The Coast of Illyria, a play based on the life of the English essayist Charles Lamb. It was produced by Margo Jones in Dallas, Texas, and was well received, but never reached Broadway. In 1953 her play Ladies of the Corridor (written with Arnaud d'Usseau) had a moderately successful Broadway run. The story of a group of aged and aging women who live in a residential hotel in New York, it was a gloomy but vivid picture of aimless and empty lives. Wolcott Gibbs, reviewing the play for the New Yorker, suggested that Mrs. Parker, "who is in the habit these days of irritably deprecating her reputation as a wit, is responsible not only for the precise and deadly wit that frequently punctuates the script but also for the acute understanding of human loneliness, cruelty, stupidity, and occasional glowing, unpredictable fortitude that gives the characters their intermittent flashes of absolute fidelity to life."

It is certainly true that Dorothy Parker has made no effort to keep alive her reputation as a wit—the sparkling, sophisticated personality that Alexander Woollcott once described as "so odd a blend of Little Nell and Lady Macbeth." The fact remains that it is for her brittle and ironic humor that she is best remembered and most admired. The publication of an anthology of her writings in 1944 caused several reviewers to remark on its evocation of the spirit of the 1920's. But, Edward Weeks observed in the Atlantic, "As we see the work in toto, with its laughter, its wit, its silly sophistication, and its heartburn, we realize that there are limitations, the chief of them being a lack of depth and a lack of cordiality." Edmund Wilson saw more permanent value in her work: "She is not Emily Brontë or Jane Austen, but she has been at some pains to write well, and she has put into what she has written a voice, a state of mind, an era, a few moments of human experience that nobody else has conveyed."

In 1951 Dorothy Parker was cited, along with more than 300 other writers, professors, actors, and artists, by the House Un-American Activities Committee for her affiliation with what the committee designated as left-wing and "Communist-front" organizations. She and her husband, Alan Campbell, were divorced in 1947 and remarried in 1950.

ADDITIONAL WORKS: (ed.) The Portable F. Scott Fitzgerald, 1945; (with A. d'Usseau) Ladies of the Corridor (play) 1954.

ABOUT: Adams, F. P. Foreword to Collected Stories of Dorothy Parker (1942); Gray, J. On Second Thought; Maugham, W. S. Introduction to The Portable Dorothy Parker (1944); Wilson, E. Classics and Commercials; Woollcott, A. in The Portable Woollcott; Scholastic May 7, 1945.

PARKER, Sir GILBERT, Bart. (November 23, 1862-September 6, 1932). For biographical sketch and list of works and references, see TWENTIETH CENTURY AUTHORS, 1942.

* * *

ABOUT: Dictionary of National Biography 1931-1940; Friden, G. The Canadian Novels of Sir Gilbert Parker.

PARKER, LOUIS NAPOLEON (October 21, 1852-September 21, 1944). For biographical sketch and list of works and references, see TWENTIETH CENTURY AUTHORS, 1942.

* * *

Louis Napoleon Parker died in Devonshire, England, at ninety-one.

The playwright has been characterized as a "shrewd and indefatigable craftsman" by the New York Herald Tribune, which added that his works were "theatrically sound, though his plots were old-fashioned and his history at times freely handled."

ABOUT: New York Herald Tribune September 22, 1944; New York Times September 22, 1944.

PARRINGTON, VERNON LOUIS (August 3, 1871-June 17, 1929). For biographical sketch and list of works and references, see TWENTIETH CENTURY AUTHORS, 1942.

* * *

ABOUT: Hyman, S. E. The Armed Vision; Trilling, L. The Liberal Imagination.

PARRISH, ANNE (November 12, 1888-). For autobiographical sketch and list of earlier works and references, see TWENTIETH CENTURY AUTHORS, 1942.

* * *

Anne Parrish still lives in Peaceable Street, Georgetown, Conn., in her home "Quantness" (not "Quaintness" as incorrectly given in TWENTIETH CENTURY AUTHORS, 1942.) Her husband, the author Joseph Titzell, died in 1943. Miss Parrish has since published three books for adult readers, the novels *Poor Child* and *And Have Not Love,* and the story of the Negro slave leader Harriet Tubman, *A Clouded Star.* She has also written and illustrated a juvenile, *The Story of Appleby Capple,* of which Louise Seaman Bechtel has said: "It is the distillation of a most charming mind, amusing itself with weaving together its over-acute observations of much of the world's loveliness into a witty dream-search with a beautiful, happy ending." The idea for the book grew out of a letter game she and her brother, Dillwyn Parrish, had played as children.

ADDITIONAL WORKS: Poor Child, 1945; A Clouded Star, 1948; The Story of Appleby Capple (juvenile) 1950; And Have Not Love, 1954.

ABOUT: Mahoney, B. E. Illustrators of Children's Books; Warfel, H. R. American Novelists of Today; Horn Book January-February 1951; Saturday Review of Literature November 11, 1950.

PARRY, Sir CHARLES HUBERT HASTINGS, Bart. (February 27, 1848-October 7, 1918). For biographical sketch and list of works and references, see TWENTIETH CENTURY AUTHORS, 1942.

PARSHLEY, HOWARD MADISON (August 7, 1884-May 19, 1953). For autobiographical sketch and list of earlier works and references, see TWENTIETH CENTURY AUTHORS, 1942.

* * *

H. M. Parshley died of a heart attack in Northampton, Mass., at sixty-eight. Several months before his death he wrote to the editors of this volume: "Since 1942 I have continued as professor of zoology at Smith College, retiring at the end of the academic year 1951-52 but pursuing my various interests as before. Three years ago I entered a new field, for me, undertaking to translate and edit a great work on woman and her situation in the world, *The Second Sex,* by the French writer Simone de Beauvoir, published early in 1953. I have also translated a more definitely zoological work, *The Life and Habits of Wild Mammals,* by F. Bourlière, professor in the University of Paris.

"As for the double bass, I have been playing professionally for some years in the Springfield Symphony Orchestra and also in various amateur orchestras in this region. I may add for the record that I have published four articles in the *Ford Times* and have written a chapter on 'Research in Sex Behavior' for *Sex in Our Culture,* edited by Dr. A. Stone and Gladys Groves."

ADDITIONAL WORKS: Translations—Beauvoir, S. de, The Second Sex, 1953; Bourlière, F. The Life and Habits of Wild Mammals, 1954.

ABOUT: New York Times May 20, 1953.

PARSONS, GEOFFREY (September 5, 1879-). For biographical sketch and list of earlier works and references, see TWENTIETH CENTURY AUTHORS, 1942.

* * *

Geoffrey Parsons retired as chief editorial writer of the New York *Herald Tribune* in 1952 and in the same year became that newspaper's chief editorial adviser. In recent years he has received honorary degrees from Franklin and Marshall College and from Louisville University. Parsons lives in New York City.

Geoffrey Parsons, Jr., was a war correspondent and later European correspondent for the New York *Herald Tribune* until 1950 when he became chief of press and public relations for NATO in Paris. He contributes articles to the *New Yorker, Saturday Evening Post,* and other magazines.

ADDITIONAL WORK: Black Chattels: The Story of the Australian Aborigines, 1946.

PARSONS, WILFRID (March 17, 1887-). For biographical sketch and list of earlier works and references, see TWENTIETH CENTURY AUTHORS, 1942.

* * *

In 1940 Father Parsons became professor of political science at the Catholic University of America. In 1948 he published *First Freedom,* in which he considered the subject of church and state in the United States and suggested the substitution of the terms "distinction and co-operation" for "separation and unity." *Catholic World* praised the book as "well documented and clearly written." Father Parsons lives in Washington, D.C.

ADDITIONAL WORK: First Freedom: Considerations on Church and State in the United States, 1948.

ABOUT: Hoehn, M. (ed.) Catholic Authors, I; Parsons, W. *in* The Book of Catholic Authors (ed. W. Romig).

PARTRIDGE, BELLAMY (1878-). For biographical sketch and list of earlier works and references, see TWENTIETH CENTURY AUTHORS, 1942.

* * *

Bellamy Partridge has followed his memorable *Country Lawyer* with a number of warmly nostalgic books recalling the peaceful and abundant (though not quite idyllic) days of the early twentieth century. "It's the seemingly inconsequential that creates a feeling for the times," he told an interviewer. He records the small details, but the ones which best suggest the distinct flavor of a period. Stanley Walker said of him: "He has the small town man's restraint, the tolerance of the intelligent countryman, together with a sly humor and an eye for all sorts of trivial but revealing little things. He brings back a transition period with complete faithfulness."

The most successful of Partridge's later books have been memoirs and works of reminiscence and social history. His novel *January Thaw*, which describes the misadventures of a New York couple who buy a country house in Connecticut, was a rambling farce, "bathed in light and humor," N. L. Rothman wrote in *Saturday Review of Literature*. The book was dramatized by W. E. Roos and had a brief run as a play in New York in 1946. *Big Freeze*, a more serious historical novel, was praised for its rich period detail. Partridge's history of the automobile in American life, *Fill 'Er Up!*, won commendation as a rare combination of entertainment and social history.

Partridge lives with his wife and their two children in Connecticut, close enough to New York for frequent visits. He writes mornings, and spends his summer afternoons gardening and the winter ones shoveling snow or cutting firewood. "It's a good life," he says, "for the industrious and ambitious."

ADDITIONAL WORKS: Excuse My Dust, 1943; January Thaw, 1945; (with O. Bettmann) As We Were: Family Life in America, 1850-1900, 1946; Big Freeze, 1948; The Old Oaken Bucket, 1949; Salad Days, 1951; Fill 'Er Up: The History of Automobiles, 1952; The Ainsley Case, 1955.

ABOUT: Partridge, B. Salad Days; Warfel, H. R. American Novelists of Today; New York Herald Tribune Book Review October 7, 1951; New York Times Book Review May 6, 1951.

PARTRIDGE, ERIC (HONEYWOOD)
(February 6, 1894-), British man of letters and lexicographer, writes: "I was the first white child born in Waimata Valley, Poverty Bay, New Zealand, where I remained until late in 1907. The family then moved to the Darling Downs, Queensland, Australia. At the age of sixteen I began to earn my living as a schoolteacher. In March 1914 I went to the University of Queensland, but after one year I enlisted as an infantryman in the Australian Forces and served both in Gallipoli and on the Western Front: all very educational. In 1919-early 1921 I continued my university course and then did postgraduate work at Oxford. (Degrees: B.A., 1st Class Honours, and by thesis, M.A., University of Queensland; B.Litt., University of Oxford; but almost never use them, the University of Life having been so very much more important.)

"After two years of lecturing at the Universities of Manchester and London in English literature, I founded in 1927 a small publishing firm, which I directed until December 1931. Finally I did what I should have done long before: became a professional writer, mostly on the subject of English—usage, composition, grammar; slang and cant; clichés, jargon, punctuation, etc; and since mid-1947, especially etymology. Indeed, I am writing—not compiling—'An Etymological Dictionary of Modern English,' along entirely new lines; but unless I obtain some financial assistance I'll probably never finish it: original work in etymology attracts no sympathy from those foundations which think that sociology and science are the only things that matter.

"In 1940 I enlisted in the British Army; was invalided out in January 1942. After ten tedious months as a civilian, I re-enlisted, but in the Royal Air Force, where I laboured mightily with the pen. I found World War II no less instructive than World War I: both were invaluable in aiding me to acquire a thoroughly practical knowledge both of spoken English and of how language really does work—not how so many pundits say it works.

"Perhaps I should add that in 1925 I married Dora Vye-Parminter; we have a daughter, born in 1933. We live in London. And finally, I'm not ashamed to say I 'love' my work in language and enjoy writing on language."

* * *

Eric Partridge's work, the *Spectator* remarked in 1949, "always combines true scholarship with a pungent originality, and his books have the double merit of being not only valuable to the student but also prodigiously entertaining to the common reader." To the formidable science of philology he brings enthusiasm, imagination, and a sense of humor. Of his most important work, *A Dictionary of Slang and Unconventional English from the Fifteenth Century to the Present Day*, Edmund Wilson wrote: "Not only is the Partridge dictionary a comprehensive work of reference, in which all the information is presented crisply and clearly, but it also makes interesting reading as a picture of English society that brings out strikingly the class stratifications." Similarly, his *Dictionary of the Underworld* and his collection of the slang of the British armed forces in World War II are solid contributions to the study of society and the social trends and upheavals which language reflects.

PRINCIPAL WORKS: *Essays*—Literary Sessions, 1932; Journey to the Edge of Morning, 1946; Words at War, Words at Peace, 1948; Here, There and Everywhere, 1950; From Sanskrit to Brazil, 1952. *Dictionaries and Linguistic Studies*—Songs and Slang of the British Soldier (with J. Brophy) 1930; Slang Today and Yesterday, 1933; Words, Words, Words, 1933; Name This Child, 1936; A Covey of Partridge, 1937; Dictionary of Slang and Unconventional English, 1937; A World of Words, 1939; Dictionary of Clichés, 1940; Slang, 1940; Usage and Abusage: A Guide to Good English, 1942; Dictionary of Abbreviations, 1943; Dictionary of R.A.F. Slang, 1945; Shakespeare's Bawdy, 1947; English: A Course for Human Beings, 1949; Name Into Word, 1949; Dictionary of the Underworld, British and American, 1950; British and American English Since 1900 (with J. W. Clark) 1951; The Shaggy Dog Story, 1953; You Have a Point There: A Guide to Punctuation, 1953; The Concise Usage and Abusage, 1954.

ABOUT: New Yorker August 4, 1951; Time January 30, 1950.

PASSOS. See DOS PASSOS

PASTERNAK, BORIS LEONIDO-VITCH (1890-), sometimes called "Russia's greatest living poet," was born in Mos-

cow, the son of Leonid and Rosa (Kaufman) Pasternak. His family was a cultivated one: his father was a well-known painter, and his mother was a musician. One of his childhood idols was Scriabin, the famous composer, who was a family friend. Music, he says, was his first love, and he thought for a long time that he might become a composer; but, as he describes it in his short autobiography *Safe Conduct:* "Music, with which I

was still only postponing a parting, was already becoming interwoven with literature."

Pasternak attended a Moscow *gymnasium*, and then entered Moscow University to study law. He became so interested in ideas, however, that he finally broke off his studies of both music and law and went to Germany to pursue his study of philosophy under Hermann Cohen at Marburg. He returned to Russia and his "beloved Moscow" in the winter of 1912-13, after a summer trip to Italy; and his first book of poems, *Twin in the Clouds*, appeared in 1914.

When World War I broke out, Pasternak was caught up in the literary fervor of the groups of young Futurist and Symbolist poets in Moscow. "The sun beat sweetly on the pavement," he writes, "twisted like fine mauve sweet peas. It was May 1914. Historic changes were so near! But who thought of them?" The second year of the war, Pasternak, who had broken his leg as a boy and could not serve in the army, left for the Urals where he worked in a factory. He finished his second volume of poems, *Over the Barriers*, in 1916; and in 1917, he wrote most of the poems for *My Sister, Life*, perhaps his most important volume, which was first published in 1922. He returned to Moscow soon after the February revolution; and was later employed in the library of the Commissariat for Education.

"There is hardly a critic," writes A. Kaun in *Soviet Poets and Poetry,* "who questions the superb quality of Pasternak's art, his originality, the striking freshness of his imagery and similes, the simplicity and, at the same time, subtlety of his words—ordinary conversational speech which acquires under his pen unexpected meaning and precision of shades." Between 1922 and 1932, Pasternak published a number of volumes of poetry, as well as two of prose—*Aerial Ways*, a collection of four short stories, three of which were written during the war; and *Safe Conduct*, his short autobiography which ends with the suicide of his friend, Mayakovsky, the Futurist poet and a national figure in the early years of the revolution. The first collected edition of Pasternak's work was published in Russia in 1933, and was reprinted in 1936.

For the past twenty years, Pasternak has published little original work: *In Early Trains*, a small volume of poems, appeared in 1942; and in 1954, a second volume (which has not yet been translated or commented upon abroad). But he has published a number of exceptionally fine translations into Russian of the works of foreign poets, as well as of poets writing in one of the other hundred-odd tongues included in the Soviet Union. He has translated works of Goethe, Kleist, Hervegh and the German expressionists, Verlaine, Ben Jonson, Swinburne, Shelley, and others. His translations of Georgian lyricists, writes Kaun, "have aroused public endorsement and emulation"; and his translations of Shakespeare, which include *Hamlet, Othello, Antony and Cleopatra,* and *Romeo and Juliet,* have been especially popular with his Russian readers.

Few details about Pasternak's personal life have been published abroad. He married as a young man and his wife's first name was Zhenia; and it is clear from the early autobiography that they had at least one son.

PRINCIPAL WORKS IN ENGLISH TRANSLATION: Childhood, 1941; Collected Prose Works, 1945; Selected Poems, 1946; Selected Writings, 1949.

ABOUT: Kaun, A. Soviet Poets and Poetry; Slonim, M. Modern Russian Literature; Yarmolinsky, A. (ed.) Treasury of Russian Verse; Poetry July 1950.

PATCHEN, KENNETH (December 3, 1911-). For autobiographical sketch and list of earlier works and references, see TWENTIETH CENTURY AUTHORS, 1942.

* * *

Kenneth Patchen writes from San Francisco: "Major operation on spine in 1951 after many years' incapacitating illness: necessary money raised through a fund committee-ed by T. S. Eliot, W. H. Auden, Archibald MacLeish, and Thornton Wilder; among those who took part in poetry readings for the fund were E. E. Cummings, Marianne Moore, William Carlos Williams, Edith Sitwell. At moment living in California, after long residence in New York and Connecticut."

In spite of illness and financial reverses, Kenneth Patchen has managed to publish poetry and prose at the rate of better than one volume a year. The quality of his work is, however, uneven: critics frequently finding his books full of brilliant flashes of talent, but curiously disappointing as a whole. Of his satiric novel *Memoirs of a Shy Pornographer,* for example, Diana Trilling wrote that it "never does fulfill the promise of its opening." Similarly, Delmore Schwartz wrote of Patchen's *Selected Poems* in 1947: "Patchen has a real poetic talent. It comes to nothing because he has no respect for poetic form, no concern about the meaning of words, and no way of judging the value of his emotions."

Two years later, with the publication of Patchen's *Red Wine and Yellow Hair,* Dudley Fitts observed "a faint but distinct recrudescence of the artistic drive and intelligence that characterized his first book." Ruth Lechlitner commented on these poems that Patchen had turned from his "surrealist experimentation" of recent volumes to a greater care for the form and integration of a poem. The result, she wrote, is "a volume of emotional honesty and mature significance of intent too rarely found in the poetry of our time."

ADDITIONAL WORKS: The Teeth of the Lion, 1942; Cloth of the Tempest, 1943; Memoirs of a Shy Pornographer (novel) 1945; An Astonished Eye Looks Out of the Air, 1946; Sleepers Awake (prose) 1946; Pictures of Life and Death, 1946; They Keep Riding Down All the Time (prose) 1946; Selected Poems, 1946; Panels for the Walls of Heaven (prose-poems) 1947; See You in the Morning (novel) 1948; Red Wine and Yellow Hair, 1949; To Say if You Love Someone, 1950; Orchards, Thrones, and Caravans, 1952; Fables and Other Little Tales, 1954; The Famous Boating Party, and Other Poems in Prose, 1954.

ABOUT: Miller, H. Patchen, Man of Anger and Light; Arizona Quarterly Autumn 1951; New Mexico Quarterly Summer 1951; New Republic December 3, 1945; Poetry February 1944, August 1947, November 1949; Saturday Review of Literature April 12, 1947, March 22, 1949.

PATERSON, Mrs. ISABEL M. (BOWLER). For autobiographical sketch and list of earlier works and references, see TWENTIETH CENTURY AUTHORS, 1942.

* * *

Early in 1949 Isabel Paterson retired from the staff of the New York *Herald Tribune Weekly Book Review* and gave up her column, "Turns With a Bookworm." She lives now in Princeton, N.J. In 1943 Mrs. Paterson published *The God of the Machine* which, she writes, is "a book on political economy as engineering."

ADDITIONAL WORK: The God of the Machine, 1943.

ABOUT: Thomas, C. Canadian Novelists, 1920-1945; Publishers' Weekly March 12, 1949.

"PATIENT OBSERVER, THE." See STRUNSKY, S.

*PATON, ALAN (STEWART) (January 11, 1903-), South African novelist, was born in Pietermaritzburg in the province of Natal, South Africa. He went to school at the Pietermaritzburg College, and having done well in mathematics and English decided to graduate in the former. Afterwards he took a second degree in education, and embarked on a career as a schoolmaster. As a young man he taught in the country village of Ixopo, and there he married Doris, daughter of G. E. Francis; they

* pā'tŭn

have two sons, David and Jonathan, born in 1930 and 1936 respectively. He was an enthusiastic school teacher and thought it one of the best jobs in the world. His love of literature persisted, and he wrote at least two novels which he later consigned to the wastepaper basket.

Blackstone

In 1935 he started on a new chapter when he was appointed principal of the Diepkloof Reformatory, near Johannesburg, which with other reformatories had just been transferred to the National Education Authority. This grim and severe institution he converted into a modern training school, poorly equipped perhaps, when compared with similar places in the world, but using physical freedom as its prime reward and reformatory instrument, and using the removal of freedom as its prime corrective. Diepkloof Reformatory cared for from six to seven hundred African boys, and was the biggest institution of its kind in the whole continent. He proved to his satisfaction that the amount of corporal punishment used in such an institution bore no relation whatever to the number of offenses, and secondly that the amount of absconding at such an institution bore, or appeared to bear, an inverse relation to the amount of freedom.

Towards the end of the war of 1939-1945, having been refused permission to leave his post, he decided to visit the prisons and reformatories of countries like Sweden, England, the United States of America and Canada. To make this possible he sold his old insurance policies and bought new ones. It was on this journey while in Trondheim, Norway, that he began to write his *Cry, the Beloved Country*. He finished it in San Francisco some three months later. Some chance-met friends, the Aubrey Burnses of California, read his story and found him a publisher before he left for South Africa. His novel was published in 1948 and was well reviewed. Maxwell Anderson translated it into the opera *Lost in the Stars*, with music by Kurt Weill, and London Films made a picture with the same name as the book.

Paton retired from Diepkloof Reformatory and went to live on the south coast of Natal, where he wrote many articles about South African affairs. In 1951, while he was in England in connection with the London Films picture, he started a second novel, *Too Late the Phalarope*. This was a Book-of-the-Month choice in the United States.

In 1953 he and his wife went to work at the Toc H T.B. Settlement, at Botha's Hill, Natal. There he is responsible for the gardening and for providing occupation for these African patients who are near to the time when they must return to some kind of normal life.

Paton was one of a number of people who formed the Liberal Association of South Africa, which recently emerged as a political party. It challenges the racial theories of white supremacy and offers to extend the rights and responsibilities of the South African society to all civilized men. He is also president of the Transvaal association of Non-European Boys' Clubs, in whose work he took a very active part during his principalship of Diepkloof Reformatory, and the honorary commissioner of Toc H, Southern Africa, an association which renders service of all kinds to all sections of the South African community.

Paton writes: "It is my conscience that urges me to take some part in public life, whereas my inclinations urge me to write, not articles but stories. When I tell interviewers about this they write of the grim inner conflict which is going on inside me. In actual fact it is not a conflict at all, but I must add it is an unmitigated nuisance to try and meet the ever-opposing demands of two parts of myself, neither of which I would disown. Maybe I shall not do too badly after all if I insist on going off by myself when I want to produce another story. Many interviewers find me very grim; this is largely because I find interviewing a very grim business."

* * *

The foregoing sketch was sent to the editors of this volume by Alan Paton from the T.B. Settlement in Natal where he and his wife continue to serve the sick and oppressed colored peoples of South Africa. Probably the greatest service he has done for these people was the writing of *Cry, the Beloved Country*, one of the few novels which have come out of South Africa to stir the emotions of readers all over the world. The story of a Zulu minister from Ixopo who comes to Johannesburg to find his sick sister and discovers that she has become a prostitute and his own son has become a murderer, it was written with simple dignity and eloquence, and with restraint and compassion. James Stern, in the *New Republic*, hailed it as "one of the best novels of our time" and Orville Prescott, in the *Yale Review*, called it "the finest I have ever read about the tragic plight of black-skinned people in a white man's world." Paton's second novel, *Too Late the Phalarope*, was a study of the stern social morality of the Afrikanders and of the tragedy which falls upon a white man's family when he has an affair with a native girl. Reviewers found it too a deeply moving and compassionate novel, but some objected to its Biblical style as becoming at times stilted and monotonous. Alfred Kazin wrote in the New York *Times*: "With his delicacy, knowledge, and tact he can bring out the human values inherent in a social situation, and thus force the subject on our attention. What he cannot do is to perplex and awaken us to more than is immediately given by the situation itself. The humanity of his work and the limitations of his fiction are clearly marked in *Too Late the Phalarope*."

PRINCIPAL WORKS: Cry, The Beloved Country, 1948; Too Late the Phalarope, 1953; The Land and People of South Africa, 1955.

ABOUT: Snyman, P. The South African Novel in English; College English April 1953; Current Biography 1952; Hibbert Journal April 1952; Life November 14, 1949; New York Herald Tribune Book Review November 6, 1949, October 11, 1953; New York Times Book Review November 20, 1949.

PATRICK, JOHN (May 17, 1906?-), American playwright, was born John Patrick Goggan in Louisville, Ky. His grandfather, an Irish immigrant named O'Goggan, sold pianos to the cattle barons of the South and West. Patrick dropped the Goggan name and adopted his present one legally years ago. Tragically separated from his parents when a child, he was cared for by aunts and sent to one Southern boarding school after another; in most of them he remembers being cruelly beaten in the name of education. After attending Holy Cross College in New Orleans, and Harvard and Columbia, he began writing in earnest. He initiated his literary career as a script writer for the National Broadcasting Company, and in the Thirties spent some time in Hollywood. Patrick has written a dozen or more films, including *The President's Lady* and *Three Coins in the Fountain*.

The playwright's first production on Broadway was *Hell Freezes Over* in 1935. It was a drama about an airship forced down in polar regions, and gave Joshua Logan his first job of directing. This play failed commercially, as did the second, *The Willow and I*, in 1942. In March 1942 Patrick joined the American Field Service as an ambulance driver, and was assigned to the British Army, first with Montgomery's 8th Army in North Africa, then in Syria and finally in India and Burma. He found, he said, that "wherever you go, the army of occupation there tends to resent the people of the country they're in. It's discouraging but it's true. I'm guilty of it too." Patrick's first successful play, *The Hasty Heart*, was produced in 1944 and published in 1945. He thought about the play for two years and finally found a chance to write it when he got aboard a transport in the Pacific to come home on furlough. Written in longhand in just twelve days, it was sent to Howard Lindsay and Russel Crouse on a Friday and accepted on Monday. They produced it for a run of 204 performances. In *The Hasty Heart* Patrick wanted to show "the importance of man's acknowledgment of his interdependency. We must see this or the shrewd and ruthless will get us involved in more wars." The plot emanated from his experiences as an ambulance driver in wartime. Reviewing the published volume, John Mason Brown wrote in the *Saturday Review of Literature*, "In spite of its shortcomings as literature, *The Hasty Heart* does what it sets out to do behind the footlights. It is more than sentimental. However it overstates them, its basic concern is those emotions which, especially among men in wartime, resist statement. This is the source of its truth no less than of its effectiveness."

Patrick's next three plays, all produced and all published, did not succeed; but *The Teahouse of the August Moon*, a dramatization of Vern Sneider's novel, which came to Broadway in 1953, was a great triumph. A month after its opening it was bringing Patrick $2,100 a week, and would continue to do so as long as it ran at capacity. Touring companies and foreign productions have made it one of the most successful plays of the modern theatre. The plot tells of the attempts of the American occupation forces in Okinawa to inculcate the ideals of democracy in an Oriental village. The delight of the play, wrote Brooks Atkinson, "goes beyond its pleasantly ironic story. As a piece of theatre writing it is extraordinarily fresh. In the theory of art, form and content are identical, i.e., the content provides the form. But the marriage of form and content is seldom as happy as it is in the case of this comedy."

Patrick is unmarried. He avoids cocktail parties and formal gatherings of any nature and lives on sixty-five acres of woodlands and field in Rockland County, N.Y., a farm called "Hasty Hill." He finds farm life healthy in more ways than the physical. "When I get up in the morning I make some notes," he told Harry Gilroy. "If things go well I go to work at the typewriter. If not I get out the tractor and yank out some more trees around the plowed field. I make notes while I do that and pretty soon I go back to the typewriter. But I never work more than two hours at a stretch."

PRINCIPAL WORKS: The Willow and I, 1943; The Hasty Heart, 1945; The Story of Mary Surratt, 1947; The Curious Savage, 1951; Lo and Behold! 1952; The Teahouse of the August Moon, 1954.

ABOUT: Look June 29, 1954; New York Herald Tribune May 4, 1954; New York Times December 31, 1944; May 5, 1954; New York Times Magazine November 15, 1953; PM January 3, 1945.

PATTEE, FRED LEWIS (March 22, 1863-May 6, 1950). For biographical sketch and list of works and references, see TWENTIETH CENTURY AUTHORS, 1942.

* * *

Fred Lewis Pattee died at eighty-seven, after two years of illness, at his home in Winter Park, Fla. His wife had died in 1943.

Pattee's autobiography, published four years after his death, emphasized his successful struggle for the academic recognition of American literature as distinct from English literature. Richard Eberhart characterized the autobiography as "a stolid, rather humorless" work with "sprightly moments," valuable as a picture of the period of the author's early life.

W. L. Werner and Arlin Turner have spoken of Pattee's "happy facility in presenting the details of research in a popular style and the sincere American spirit which illuminated his defense of our literature and his histories of it."

ADDITIONAL WORK: Penn State Yankee (autobiography) 1954.

ABOUT: Pattee, F. L. Penn State Yankee; American Literature January 1951; New York Times May 7, 1950.

PATTEN, GILBERT ("Burt L. Standish") (October 25, 1866-January 16, 1945). For biographical sketch and list of works and references, see TWENTIETH CENTURY AUTHORS, 1942.

* * *

Gilbert Patten died in his sleep, at seventy-eight, at the home of his son in Vista, Calif.

Although none of his later attempts to revive interest in his dime-novel characters succeeded, the fact remains that for the first twenty years of his career Patten was one of the most widely read writers in the world. Stewart H. Holbrook has said of Patten's best known creation, "Frank Merriwell," "I can think of no other fictional characters so real to my generation as those who peopled the Merriwell saga."

ABOUT: Holbrook, S. H. Little Annie Oakley and Other Rugged People; Hobbies September 1942; National Cyclopedia of American Biography (1948); New York Times January 17, 1945; Newsweek January 29, 1945; Reader's Digest January 1953; Saturday Review of Literature December 22, 1945; Scholastic March 25, 1946.

PAUL, ELLIOT HAROLD (February 11, 1891-). For biographical sketch and list of earlier works and references, see TWENTIETH CENTURY AUTHORS, 1942.

* * *

Joseph Henry Jackson once described Elliot Paul's own special style of reporting as "a matter of basic fact strained through a highly imaginative mind, colored by the author's highly developed sense of anecdote, and shaped by his personal sensitivity to people and places." Nowhere has this talent been better demonstrated than in the series of autobiographical books that Paul is writing, part of a whole work to be called "Items on the Grand Account." So far Paul's rambling memoirs (which reminded one reviewer of Laurence Sterne's technique in *Tristram Shandy*) have covered six volumes (including two earlier books—*The Life and Death of a Spanish Town*, 1937, and *The Last Time I Saw Paris*, 1942) and have brought him up only through his young manhood. Actually, however, they have been focused less on Paul than on the host of oddly assorted people he remembers and recreates in these volumes. A New York *Times* reviewer commented that this large cast of characters, with their rowdy, ribald adventures, confront the reader "with the question of where autobiography ends and fiction begins." The question really matters little, the reviewer continued, because "Paul is a vivid and sensitive recorder of nature, a warmhearted viewer of human frailties, and a superb story-teller."

ADDITIONAL WORKS: I'll Hate Myself in the Morning; and, Summer in December, 1945; Paris, 1947; Springtime in Paris, 1950; Murder on the Left Bank, 1951; The Black Gardenia, 1952; Waylaid in Boston, 1953; Understanding the French, 1955. "Items on the Grand Account"—Linden on the Saugus Branch, 1947; Ghost Town on the Yellowstone, 1948; My Old Kentucky Home, 1949; Desperate Scenery, 1954.

ABOUT: Paul, E. Linden on the Saugus Branch, Ghost Town on the Yellowstone, My Old Kentucky Home, Desperate Scenery; New York Times Book Review September 11, 1949; Saturday Review of Literature July 24, 1948.

PAUL, LOUIS (December 4, 1901-).

For autobiographical sketch and list of earlier works and references, see TWENTIETH CENTURY AUTHORS, 1942.

* * *

In 1948 Louis Paul's dramatization of his novel *Breakdown*, a study of a young woman who becomes an alcoholic, was produced on Broadway as *The Cup of Trembling*, with Elisabeth Bergner in the leading role. Paul has also written plays for television. Although he has written a number of serious novels, he is probably better known today for his light novels, *A Husband for Mama* and *A Father in the Family*, both humorous and pleasantly sentimental family stories. He lives in Huntington, Long Island.

ADDITIONAL WORKS: This Is My Brother, 1943; The Ordeal of Sergeant Smoot, 1943; Breakdown, 1946; Summer Storm, 1949: A Husband for Mama, 1950; A Father in the Family, 1951; The Man Who Came Home, 1953.

ABOUT: Warfel, H. R. American Novelists of Today.

*PAVESE, CESARE (1908-1950), Italian

novelist, poet, critic, and translator, was born in San Stefano Belbo, a small town in Pied

mont in north Italy. As a young man he moved to the city of Turin. Only fourteen when Mussolini seized power, Pavese's early career was stifled and blocked by Fascism. Unable to express his own attitudes and point-of-view directly, he devoted himself to scholarship and study, publishing for the most part translations and critical essays.

The young Pavese was especially excited and moved by the democratic vistas of American literature. "At that point, American culture became something very serious and precious to us," he said later. And he was able, under the guise of literary criticism, to attack the Fascist outlook and way of life. Between 1930 and 1940, Pavese translated many American authors including Melville,

* pä vě′sě

Sherwood Anderson, Gertrude Stein, Hemingway, Dos Passos, and Faulkner. Melville's classic, *Moby Dick*—Pavese's translation appeared in 1931—was one of his favorite books, the subject of several of his essays, and a novel which influenced him profoundly as an author. Pavese's critical judgments and interpretations of American authors have been a dominant influence in establishing the frame of reference and the way in which American literature has influenced and does influence contemporary Italian literature. Paolo Milano, commenting on Pavese's achievements, has written: "Both as translator and as essayist, Cesare Pavese probably did more than any single man to make American literature known, loved, and imitated in Italy."

Although Pavese was always watched with suspicion by the Fascist authorities, he was not actually arrested until 1935 when Mussolini was tightening up his political dictatorship for his campaigns in Abyssinia. Jailed for a short time, he was then confined for some months on an island off Naples. Released, he returned to Turin. In 1936 his first book of poems appeared entitled *Lavorare Stanca* (To Work Is Tiring); and in 1941, his first short novel, *Paesi Tuoi* (On Native Ground).

In 1943 Pavese fled to the hills of his native Piedmont and lived for two years among the Partisans in that Nazi-occupied territory. His experiences then brought him into the ranks of the Communists. And he has tried in his work to harmonize what Milano calls his "lyrical and elegiac temperament" with the political commitments which he felt were necessary.

Pavese emerged in postwar Italy as a major literary figure. Between 1946 and his tragic suicide in the fall of 1950, the bulk of his work was published; and he was a winner of the coveted literary award, the Premio Strega. Of seven short novels written during those years, *Il Compagno* (The Comrade, 1947), *Tra Donne Sole* (Among Women Alone, 1948), and *La Luna e i Falò* (*The Moon and the Bonfires*, 1950) are reputed to be the best. Pavese's favorite of his own books was *Dialoghi con Leucò* (Dialogues with Leuko, 1949), a series of poetic meditations on classical myths which Leslie Fiedler in an article on Pavese in the *Kenyon Review* called, "surely his most beautiful, his most achieved effort." His diaries, 1935-1950, entitled *Il Mestiere di Vivere* (The Art of Living) were published posthumously as was also a late book of love lyrics, *Verrà la*

Morte e Avrà i Tuoi Occhi (Death Will Stare at Me out of Your Eyes).

The only one of Pavese's works which, to date, has been translated and published in America is *The Moon and the Bonfires*. Pavese himself has said that the theme of all his books is "the rhythm of what happens." The New York *Times* after characterizing the theme of this novel as the familiar one of the "native's return," said that Pavese "who spiritually 'came home' from his imaginary journey to an America which here symbolizes the bleakness and dissociation of modern life, sees it as a human rather than a social tragedy and portrays it with an economy of words and in a vein of compassion which make him that rare true writer who can convey to us a place and its people with intensely deep feelings."

Pavese committed suicide at the age of forty-two; and there were immediate charges and counter-charges that his death was or was not the result of political disillusionment or of personal instability and an unhappy love for the American actress C., to whom his last novel was dedicated. Leslie Fiedler, commenting on his death, says that ". . . for the Italians, his death has come to have a weight like that of Hart Crane for us, ? meaning that penetrates back into his own work and functions as a symbol in the literature of an age."

PRINCIPAL WORK IN TRANSLATION: The Moon and the Bonfires, 1953.

ABOUT: Milano, P. *Introduction to* The Moon and the Bonfires; Kenyon Review Autumn 1954; New Republic May 4, 1953.

PAXSON, FREDERICK LOGAN (February 23, 1877-October 24, 1948). For biographical sketch and list of earlier works and references, see TWENTIETH CENTURY AUTHORS, 1942.

* * *

Frederick Logan Paxson died in a Berkeley, Calif., hospital following an operation, at seventy-one. He had been appointed professor emeritus of history at the Universtiy of California after his retirement from active teaching in 1947.

The third volume of Professor Paxson's most widely known work, *American Democracy and the World War*, was published in the year of his death. H. S. Commager, commenting on the earlier volumes, did not find the work unusually brilliant or profound, but did find it remarkable "for the moderation of its judgment, the balance and proportion of its treatment, the shrewdness and

thoughtfulness of its interpretation, the clarity of its style."

ADDITIONAL WORKS: The Great Demobilization, and Other Essays, 1941; American Democracy and the World War (vol. 3) 1948.

ABOUT: New York Times October 25, 1948.

PAYNE, PIERRE STEPHEN ROBERT (December 4, 1911-), English poet, novelist, and journalist, who signs his work "Robert Payne," writes:

"My mother comes from Provence and my father from a family of shipwrights in Portsmouth, England. There seems to have been some Irish blood on the English side, and there is a legend of descent from Tom Paine. I have never been able to discover whether it is true. On the French side there is a legend that the family is descended from the Princes of Polignac, but all that we know for certain is that we come from the village of Polignac near Le Puy, where for generations the family consisted of small inn-keepers and lace-makers. Some time ago I was delighted to discover that it was a Prince of Polignac who ordered the arrest of Tom Paine in Paris, and I like to think that the account is now settled.

"My earliest memories are of the south of France and of ships, and in a very real sense those are the memories which have continued into my writing. From France I learned to love the sunlight, castles, vineyards, peasants; from England came the overwhelming passion for ships. So my youth was a struggle between the two, and I think that in later years those differences which I discovered between France and England were somehow equated to the differences I found between Asia and the West. For me Asia was always as feminine as France, and somehow lit with the light of the Provençal sun.

"Half my childhood was spent in visits to France. For the rest there was a succession of schools. We were not rich, and so I ran away with scholarships and became a monstrously proficient scholar in Latin and Greek, and something of a mathematician—the mathematics went with the ships, and the ancient languages with France. There was a wonderful bust of Plato above my locker at St. Paul's School, and I think this decided the issue. Though I have still a very great fondness for mathematics and hope some day to write a definitive life of Evariste Galois, I decided after taking the entrance examination at Greenwich on naval architecture that I should devote myself to writing, and so it has been, though there have been vicissitudes on the journey.

"I spent three years in South Africa, lapping up the sunlight, studying the classics at the Diocesan College in Rondebosch and then swinging over to mathematics and pure science at Capetown University. Afterwards there followed a brief eighteen-month sojourn in a shipyard at the height of the depression, and that cured me, I think, of any lingering desire to continue to build ships. So I went to Liverpool University and studied modern European languages, learning Danish, German, Italian and Russian reasonably well, but I was stumped by Polish and very nearly broke my head over it. Afterwards I became an income-tax inspector for another year and a half—a period I prefer to forget. Then I wandered over Europe, studying briefly at the Sorbonne and at Munich University, got caught up in an attempt to assassinate Hitler and visited the Spanish battlefronts for an English newspaper. Spain was wonderfully exciting, but when the Republicans retreated over the border, I was exhausted and ill, and when my father, who had become the civilian head of the naval base, invited me to Singapore I went there. I had seen Vienna fall, and watched the crumbling of the Spanish Republic. There seemed more hope in the East. I traveled through Java, wandered through Bali, and at the outbreak of the war became a shipwright once more at the naval base. Later I was an armament officer, and placed in charge of camouflage. I think I could have camouflaged the naval base reasonably well, but the war came before we had even begun to put our plans into operation. I saw the 'Prince of Wales' and 'Repulse' go out to sea, and I was on the docks when the survivors returned.

"By this time I knew a little Chinese. A week after the Pacific War broke out, the British Ministry of Information decided to send me to China. It was the time when Clerke-Kerr was the British ambassador, and I was appointed by him cultural liaison officer—an appointment which did not please the ambassador's successor, with the result that I escaped from the embassy into the Chinese universities, and stayed with them until August 1946. An account of those years is given in *Forever China* and *China Awake*. I wrote and edited an enormous number of books during this period. It was a time of immense intellectual striving, and of this time I like to remember most the great scholar Wen Yi-tuo, who was killed by the Kuomintang government a few days before I left China forever. Afterwards I traveled through India, and since then, except for short visits to England, France and Persia, I have lived in the United States, first in the San Fernando Valley and then at Montevalle, Ala., where I am author-in-residence at a woman's college. Recently I have been making documentary films."

* * *

Robert Payne began writing at the age of seven, with a story called "The True Adventures of Princess Sylvia," and has been writing ever since. Several of his novels were published in England under pseudonyms. His diary of three years of life in China, *Forever China*, brought him instant acclaim in America, as did his novel on life in modern China, *Torrents of Spring*, of which John Cournos wrote: "China lives in Payne's pages as it does in few books."

PRINCIPAL WORKS: Singapore River, 1940; David and Anna, 1941; Forever China (in England: Chungking Diary) 1945; The Torrents of Spring, 1947; (ed.) The White Pony: An Anthology of Chinese Poetry, 1947; The Revolt of Asia, 1947; The Yellow Robe, 1947; China Awake, 1947; The Rose Tree (poems) 1948; The Blue Nigger, 1948; Sun Yat-Sen, 1946; The Bear Coughs at the North Pole, 1947; Zero, the Story of Terrorism, 1950; Mao Tse-tung, Ruler of Red China, 1950; The Wanton Nymph, 1951; Red Lion Inn, 1951; The Young Emperor, 1951; The Fathers of the Western Church, 1951; General Marshall, 1951; Red Storm over Asia, 1951; Journey to Persia, 1952; The Great God Pan: A Biography of the Tramp Played by Charles Chaplin, 1952; Blood Royal, 1952; The Chieftain, 1953; Alexander the God, 1954. *As "Valentin Tikhonov"*—The Mountains and the Stars, 1937. *As "Robert Young"*—The War in the Marshes, 1937; A Young Man Looks at Europe, 1939. *As "Richard Cargoe"*—The Tormentors, 1950; Maharajah, 1951.

ABOUT: Payne, R. Forever China, China Awake; Current Biography 1947.

PEABODY, JOSEPHINE PRESTON (May 30, 1874-December 4, 1922). For biographical sketch and list of works and references, see TWENTIETH CENTURY AUTHORS, 1942.

PEARSE, PADRAIC HENRY (November 10, 1879-May 3, 1916). For biographical sketch and list of works and references, see TWENTIETH CENTURY AUTHORS, 1942.

* * *

Correction: Pearse's bi-lingual preparatory school Sgoil Eanna or St. Enda's was incorrectly given as St. Edna's in the sketch and list of principal works in TWENTIETH CENTURY AUTHORS, 1942.

ABOUT: Colum, M. Life and the Dream; Catholic World October 1945.

PEARSON, DREW (December 13, 1896-), American journalist and political commentator, was born in Evanston, Ill. His

Hessler

father was Paul Martin Pearson, a Quaker professor who became governor of the Virgin Islands and was later unseated after a Senate investigation. Young Pearson graduated from Swarthmore in 1919 and went abroad as a director of postwar relief in the Balkans, where a town was renamed Pearsonavatz in his honor.

Coming back to the United States in 1921, he taught industrial geography for a year at the University of Pennsylvania before he started traveling again. He spent time in Japan, China, and the Philippines as a seaman, and later lecture-toured through Australia and New Zealand. Here, unexpectedly enough, he began his career as a newspaper columnist with a contract from a syndicate for papers in Australia, India, and South Africa. For the next six years he managed to juggle at least three separate careers: teaching again briefly, this time at Columbia; traveling through Japan and China to Tibet; interviewing the leading political figures of Europe and writing for American newspapers and magazines. As foreign editor of the *United States Daily* he covered the Geneva Naval Conference, and in 1928 accompanied Secretary of State Kellogg to Paris and President Coolidge to Havana.

The phase of his career by which he is best known began in 1929 when he was attached to the Washington Bureau of the Baltimore *Sun*. In 1931 he collaborated with Colonel Robert S. Allen, then on the *Christian Science Monitor*, to write a book called *Washington Merry-Go-Round*. First published anonymously and full of the political gossip "which the Capital loves to whisper but hates to see in print," the book stirred up a lively scandal, got its two authors fired from their jobs, and established them as successful political commentators. Again collaborating with Allen, Pearson inaugurated a candid, "inside-view" newspaper column, *Washington Merry-Go-Round*, which in the ten years from 1932 to

1942 became one of the most widely-read columns in the country. When Allen was recalled to active military service in 1942, Pearson continued as sole author of the column.

Pearson and Allen's first best seller was followed by a sequel and several other books trimmed to the same journalistic pattern. Describing himself anonymously in the first *Merry-Go-Round*, Pearson wrote: "Drew Pearson, the *Sun's* expert on foreign affairs, has the reputation of knowing more about the State Department than most people who run it, and to a considerable extent this is true." This quote is a fair sample of his style, which has been praised as sharp and criticized as shoddy, and an indication of his method. He has continued to give the political news from the boys-in-the-backroom. There has scarcely been a period in recent years in which he has not been involved in heated and sometimes violent controversy. In 1950 he was involved in a brief scuffle with Senator Joseph McCarthy, and two weeks later he was beaten up by a Washington lawyer whom he had frequently criticized in his column. Though staunchly liberal, he has from time to time antagonized some of the great liberal leaders. Both Franklin Roosevelt and Harry Truman, though generally friendly to him, called him a liar. His career as a crusading journalist and commentator flourished, however, in the glow of all this publicity, until 1952 when his radio sponsors began dropping away. At last, in 1953, he lost his regular network show, but he has continued to reach a wide audience by selling his programs, recorded on tape, to many individual stations.

Pearson has been described as tall, mild-mannered, "with thinning, light brown hair, a sparse mustache and earnest mien," but as *Time* magazine pointed out in a profile on him in 1948, "the mild manner camouflages a tough, diamond-hard core." He lives in Georgetown and has a farm in Maryland. His first marriage took place in 1925 to Countess Felicia Gizycka, daughter of the late Eleanor ("Cissy") Patterson, owner of the newspaper chain which included the Washington *Times-Herald* where Pearson's column appeared. They had one daughter and the marriage ended in a friendly divorce. Pearson and Mrs. Patterson, his former mother-in-law, continued on good terms until they split over politics during the New Deal days—Pearson being pro-New Deal and Mrs. Patterson violently opposed to it. Pearson's column was dropped from the *Times-Herald*.

In 1936 he married Luvie Moore, formerly a movie reviewer for that paper.

PRINCIPAL WORKS: *With R. S. Allen*—Washington Merry-Go-Round, 1931; More Merry-Go-Round, 1932; Nine Old Men, 1936; Nine Old Men at the Crossroads, 1937. *With C. Brown*—The American Diplomatic Game, 1935.

ABOUT: Drewry, J. E. (ed.) More *Post* Biographies; Collier's July 30, 1949; Current Biography 1941; Time December 13, 1948.

PEARSON, EDMUND LESTER (February 11, 1880-August 7, 1937). For biographical sketch and list of works and references, see TWENTIETH CENTURY AUTHORS, 1942.

PEARSON, HESKETH (1887-   ), English biographer, writes: "I was a biographer at the age of fourteen, but did not know it till  I was forty. As a boy I wrote a magazine for home consumption, and most of the contents were described as 'Summarys *(sic)* of Famous Men's Lives.' At school I was a complete failure at everything I did not wish to learn, and as I wished to learn very little I left with about as much knowledge as I had picked up for pleasure, and one scholastic achievement to my credit: I scored *nought* in an algebra exam, probably a record at Bedford School. My form-master was staggered, but I took it in my stride.

Robin Adler

"My parents wanted me to go into the Church, my family tree being a sort of ecclesiastical rabbit warren, but I showed no aptitude for anything and was shoved into a city shipping office, where I was quite useless and utterly bored by bills of lading, share certificates, and all the other things I was supposed to understand but which were totally meaningless to me. Two years of this were two years too many for my employers as well as myself, and inheriting some money at the age of twenty-one I went forth to see the world, starting with Mexico, as I wished to be reminded of nothing that in the least resembled the City of London.

"Having roamed Mexico, the United States and Canada, I returned to England minus my inheritance and spent a couple of very enjoyable years at Brighton mismanaging my brother's motor business so effectually that it was soon in liquidation. After that I went on the stage, not only because I had become mad on Shakespeare but because it was the easiest and pleasantest way of earning a living.

"Then came the war of 1914-18. I joined up in the ranks, and after three years of unpleasantness in Mesopotamia and Persia closed my military career as a captain.

"Returning to the stage after the war, I began to write books, my first appearing in 1921. Soon I got tired of being cast for parts in modern plays, when all I wanted to do was to play Shakespeare's villains; and in 1931 I left the stage in order to devote myself to the writing of biographies, which I then realised was my true vocation. I managed to keep my family by writing a certain amount of journalism and working for a firm of advertising consultants. My first biography was of Erasmus Darwin, one of my ancestors, but it did not sell well. My second, of Sydney Smith, was a moderate success and put me, as it were, on the biographical map, though many publishers had shied at it because I was in full reaction against the Strachey school which was then extremely popular in England and the United States. My first success came with my 'Life of Bernard Shaw,' and since then my biographies of Oscar Wilde, Dickens and Disraeli have been 'sellers.'

"By disposition I am lazy, and nothing but an inexhaustible interest in extraordinary characters could have overcome my natural indolence and resulted in fourteen full-length biographies."

* * *

Hesketh Pearson has been called "a light-handed biographer who conceals careful scholarship behind a delightfully readable style." His biographies are not definitive works, but they reveal their subjects as human and engaging personalities.

PRINCIPAL WORKS: Ventilations: Biographical Asides, 1930; Doctor Darwin, 1930; The Smith of Smiths, 1934; The Fool of Love: William Hazlitt, 1934; Gilbert and Sullivan, 1935; Labby: Henry Labouchere, 1937; Tom Paine, 1937; Thinking It Over, 1938; The Hero of Delhi: John Nicholson, 1939; G.B.S.: A Full-Length Portrait, 1942; Conan Doyle, 1943; Oscar Wilde, 1946; The Last Actor-Managers, 1950; Dickens: His Character, Comedy, and Career, 1949; Dizzy: The Life and Personality of Benjamin Disraeli, 1951; The Man Whistler, 1952; Sir Walter Scott, 1955.

ABOUT: New York Herald Tribune Book Review May 15, 1949; New York Times Book Review May 15, 1949; Saturday Review March 21, 1953.

PEARSON, KARL (1857-April 27, 1936). For biographical sketch and list of works and references, see TWENTIETH CENTURY AUTHORS, 1942.

* * *

ABOUT: Dictionary of National Biography 1931-1940.

PEATTIE, DONALD CULROSS (June 21, 1898-).

For autobiographical sketch and list of earlier works and references, see TWENTIETH CENTURY AUTHORS, 1942.

* * *

Donald Culross Peattie writes: "In the period since your last record of me, the chief event in my professional life has been my association with the *Reader's Digest* as a 'Roving Editor.' As a result, the range both of my work and of my personal living has been greatly broadened. My contributions to the magazine have been largely in the fields of nature, history, and biography, and research in these subjects has carried me, with my wife as co-worker, back and forth across the country and into many of its most colorful corners, as well as to many lands in Europe. When we are at home, it is in Santa Barbara, Calif."

The Peatties are a writing family (see Louise Redfield Peattie and Roderick Peattie below). With his son Noel, then aged seventeen, Donald Culross Peattie wrote *A Cup of Sky*, essays on natural history.

ADDITIONAL WORKS: Journey into America, 1943; Immortal Village, 1945; American Heartwood, 1949; A Cup of Sky (with N. Peattie) 1950; A Natural History of Trees of Eastern and Central North America, 1950; Sportsman's Country, 1952; A Natural History of Western Trees, 1953; Lives of Destiny, 1954.

ABOUT: Christian Science Monitor Magazine September 23, 1950; Current Biography 1940.

PEATTIE, Mrs. LOUISE (REDFIELD) (June 14, 1900-).

For autobiographical sketch and list of earlier works and references, see TWENTIETH CENTURY AUTHORS, 1942.

* * *

Louise Peattie writes: "The only volume I have published since your last report is *Ring Finger* [a novel]. However, I continue to contribute to periodicals, and above all to work closely with my husband, so that much of my professional life is anonymous but no less rewarding."

ADDITIONAL WORK: Ring Finger, 1943.
ABOUT: Good Housekeeping October 1950.

PEATTIE, RODERICK (August 1, 1891-),

American geographer and essayist, writes: "I was born in Omaha, Neb., on a very hot night in August, 1891. [He is the older brother of Donald Culross Peattie, the naturalist.] My parents were Robert Burns Peattie and Elia W. Peattie, who were both editors of the Omaha *World Herald* and my

mother was very active in creating women's clubs throughout the new west. At the age of five, I chose to live in Chicago where my parents in the end became editors of the Chicago *Tribune,* that being before the days of Colonel McCormick. They became very definitely associated with the literary, artistic, and dramatic life of that city, and my mother guided the reading public of Chicago in those days through her literary editorship. In 1910, I attended the University of Chicago and later got my Doctor of Philosophy degree from Harvard University. I began with the study of geology under some distinguished masters but switched to geography in the end.

"In my undergraduate days, I began writing and had articles accepted by the literary magazine of which I was editor-in-chief. After a splurge of my articles, the magazine failed. In my freshman year, I fell in love with Margaret Rhodes and that story is best told in *The Incurable Romantic.* This is my autobiography and in most books of that sort the authors state that in 1722 they were married to Amelia Seymore or somebody and then do not mention her again. *The Incurable Romantic* is mainly a book telling the influence of Margaret on my life, for I married her in 1917. In World War I, I became a master engineer of the first Flash Ranging Section in France, one who is on the staff of the colonel but we had no colonel. I fought an easy war and received a citation from General Pershing. I suppose for being on time to mess call.

"In 1919, I was teaching at Williams College as an associate professor. I was then called to Ohio State University where I have been ever since, a thorn in the side of this conservative community. My wife decided that I should do a major post-doctoral research and I chose the geography of mountains as my subject. I had been to Europe, once as a vagabond and once as a soldier; now I went on a trip of eighteen months and later returned for nine months. During that time, I did field work in mountains and read in the important university libraries. Then after ten years at work here I produced *Mountain Geography.*

"My teaching has developed a slant, as in my writing, toward the popularizing of geography. For this reason, I was asked to teach in the summer time at Clark, Northwestern,

Wisconsin, and California. In popularizing my subject, I have written some fifty articles and a dozen books. They have been translated into foreign languages, Braille, and one on records in the Library of Congress. I have been the editor of the American Mountain Series.

"In World War II, after service in this country, I went to South Africa as head of the O.W.I. and as a special envoy to that land. I then was called home because of the illness of my wife. She died in 1946. I married, a year later, Ruth Cavett.

"My three children were born of Margaret: Roderick Elia was born while I was at the front in World War I and is married to Lisa Redfield; Anne is married to John Wood; and Michael Ransome has returned from Korea wearing an Air Medal. I have a mountain home in Vermont which I love very dearly and I am jealous of activities which prevent me from going there."

PRINCIPAL WORKS: New College Geography, 1932; Rambles in Europe, 1934; Geography in Human Destiny, 1940; The Incurable Romantic, 1941; Look to the Frontiers, 1944; Struggle on the Veld, 1947.

ABOUT: Peattie, R. The Incurable Romantic.

PEEL, DORIS NANNETTE (February 27, 1909-). For biographical sketch and list of earlier works and references, see TWENTIETH CENTURY AUTHORS, 1942.

* * *

Doris Peel worked in New York with the British Information Services during World War II. She joined the staff of the *Christian Science Monitor* as special correspondent at the United Nations Conference at San Francisco and subsequently became book editor of the *Monitor*. In 1949 she was sent on a special assignment to Germany, to report on the attitudes and outlook of the young people there. She returned to Germany in 1951, exploring not only the Western side of the Iron Curtain but also Soviet-controlled East Germany. Miss Peel's book on these experiences was *The Inward Journey*, a personal and deeply felt portrait of the minds and emotions of young Germans. Erwin Canham of the *Christian Science Monitor* called the book "an extraordinarily vivid poet's picture," and reviewers generally agreed that it was a sensitive study, more impressionistic perhaps than politically illuminating, but nevertheless penetrating and informative.

ADDITIONAL WORK: The Inward Journey, 1953.
ABOUT: Newsweek October 12, 1953.

PEFFER, NATHANIEL (June 30, 1890-). For biographical sketch and list of earlier works and references, see TWENTIETH CENTURY AUTHORS, 1942.

* * *

Nathaniel Peffer is professor of international relations at Columbia University. In 1952 he went to Australia for a year as visiting professor at the University of Queensland. His *America's Place in the World*, a reasoned and scholarly analysis of American policy, urged American participation in a world community of nations. Articles by Peffer appear frequently in the New York *Times Magazine*, *Harper's*, the *New Republic*, the *Foreign Policy Bulletin*, and other periodicals. He lives in Essex, Conn.

ADDITIONAL WORKS: A Basis for Peace in the Far East, 1942; America's Place in the World, 1945.

*PÉGUY, CHARLES-PIERRE (January 7, 1873-September 5, 1914), French poet and essayist, was born at Orléans. He was ten months old when his father died, and he was brought up by his mother and grandmother, who earned a meager living by mending rush chairs. From his childhood, Péguy was immersed in the legend of Joan of Arc, who had rallied the French  forces at Orléans four centuries earlier. He grew up on the outskirts of the city, among the peasants of the district; thus his celebration of French peasantry as representative of the best in France was based on intimate acquaintance with their way of life. His education was exceptional for a child of his origins: he was recognized as a promising student and was awarded a scholarship to the Lycée d'Orléans; from there he went to Paris to prepare for entrance to the Ecole Normale Supérieure. After a year of study, he enlisted for military service, at the completion of which he returned to Paris, with a scholarship to the Lycée Louis-le-Grand and a grant for residence at the Collège de Sainte-Barbe, where he made life-long friendships.

In 1894 he entered the Ecole Normale Supérieure, where, according to a fellow student, "he was the one subject of all conversation" because of his passionate convictions and his air of authority. He was later to describe himself at this period as "that ardent,

* pã gē′

gloomy, stupid young man." Among the lecturers were Henri Bergson, in philosophy, and Romain Rolland, in the history of art; the librarian Lucien Herr spoke to Péguy of Socialism, and particularly of the Socialist Party; Jean Jaurès, an alumnus of the school, often dropped in to talk with the students. At this time Péguy considered himself an atheist and a revolutionary Socialist, although he never really allied himself with the Socialist Party. He took a leave of absence from school in 1895, and spent the year at his mother's house in Orléans. He resumed his studies in 1896, but a few months before the examinations he announced his intention of marrying. In October 1897 he married Charlotte Baudouin, the sister of his dear friend Marcel Baudouin.

In December 1897 he published *Jeanne d'Arc*, a dramatic poem on which he had been working secretly. He enlisted the financial support of his fellow students for this project. Eight hundred copies were printed, but only one was sold. It was an extraordinary work, handsomely printed, but very disconcerting in that the text was broken by blank spaces, sometimes for entire pages. It was, in many circles, an object of ridicule.

With his wife's dowry and ardent support, Péguy opened a Socialist bookstore and publishing concern in the heart of the Paris Latin Quarter. Inaugurated, significantly, on May 1, 1898, it was a center of activity, particularly of supporters of Dreyfus. From the financial point of view, the venture was a failure, and Péguy let it go out of his hands.

The year 1900 marked an important event: the founding of the *Cahiers de la Quinzaine* (Fortnightly Notebooks), edited and published by Péguy. He was the author of many of the *Cahiers* and wrote prefaces to the works of other writers. Romain Rolland, Anatole France, and Jean Jaurès were among the contributors. Most of the subscribers paid little attention to Péguy's writings, which they tolerated between volumes of Rolland's *Jean-Christophe*.

"A brave man," said Péguy, "for the sake of the truth breaks with his friends and his interests," and Péguy felt himself forced to break with many of his friends, especially with those active in the Socialist Party. The atheism of his school-days was abandoned, too, and in 1908 he announced to a friend that his faith was restored, that he was a Catholic. Péguy's Catholicism, like so many aspects of his personality, was paradoxical: he could not be received into the Church since his marriage was sanctioned only by civil authority, and Madame Péguy, of a family of free-thinkers, refused baptism for herself and their children. Though he could not attend Mass, he continued to pray. After his death, his family, of their own free will, asked for baptism.

Péguy said that he "could go on writing of Joan of Arc for twenty years," and, in fact, he did so for sixteen years. In 1910 appeared *Le Mystère de la Charité de Jeanne d'Arc*, published as a *Cahier*; he had filled in the blanks of his earlier work, which has sometimes been called the Socialist *Jeanne d'Arc*. This was followed in October 1911 by *Le Porche du Mystère de la Deuxième Vertu* and in March 1912 by *Le Mystère des Saints Innocents*.

In his last years, he devoted more time to his poetry and less to pamphlet-writing. *La Tapisserie de Sainte-Geneviève et de Jeanne d'Arc* and *La Tapisserie de Notre-Dame* appeared in 1912. *Ève*, his last long poem, was unfavorably received because of its difficulty, but the concluding stanzas of the final section, *Morts Parallèles de Sainte-Geneviève et de Jeanne d'Arc*, are now among the best-know work of Péguy.

Péguy was killed in action at Villeroy, on the first day of the Battle of the Marne.

His poetry celebrates the glory and greatness of France; patriotism and faith go hand in hand, and it is always the sentiment and its heroic expression that mattered most to him. Despite his involvement in the events of his day, Péguy thought of himself as belonging to an older period. He decried the modern spirit, politics, and money values, and deplored the absence of the old-fashioned virtues.

"Péguy's style," wrote André Gide, "is like that of very ancient litanies. It is like Arab chants, like the monotonous chants of heath and moor; it is comparable to the desert; . . . Péguy's style is like the pebbles of the desert which follow and resemble each other so closely, one so much like the other, but yet a tiny bit different; and with a difference which corrects itself, recovers possession of itself, repeats itself, seems to repeat itself, stresses itself, and always more clearly; and one goes ahead. What do I need with more variety!"

Critical attention and acclaim came only after Péguy's death. His early *Jeanne d'Arc*, considered unreadable, was staged by the Comédie Française in 1924. *Ève*, adapted for rendition by two speakers, was presented at the Théâtre Français.

PRINCIPAL WORKS IN ENGLISH TRANSLATION: Basic Verities, 1943; God Speaks, 1945; Men and Saints. 1947.

ABOUT: Green, J. *Introduction to* Péguy's *Basic Verities*; Halévy, D. Péguy and the Cahiers de la Quinzaine; Mabille de Poncheville, A. Vie de Péguy; Maritain, R. Les Grandes Amitiés; Rolland, R. Péguy; Rousseaux, A. Le Prophète Péguy; Roussel, J. Mesure de Péguy; Tharaud, J. & J. Notre Cher Péguy; Servais, Y. Charles Péguy; Commonweal November 10, 1950.

*PEI, MARIO (1901-), American linguist, writes: "I was born in Rome, Italy. When I was seven, my parents decided to

come to America, and my education, barely begun in one language, was continued in another. This was the real foundation of my multilingual background—mental comparisons between my native and my adopted tongue. My elementary training at the parochial school of St. John Evangelist in Manhattan wound up with the winning of the Mooney Medal for English composition and of a scholarship to Xavier High School. Here, for four years, my education continued, with Latin, Greek and French aplenty. During my summer vacations I worked—one summer in a law office, another in a bank, a third in a Fifth Avenue jewelry shop.

"On graduating, at seventeen, I was offered a sixth-grade class to teach in Xavier Grammar School. This was the beginning of a teaching career that has never been interrupted since. For seven years I taught by day and studied at night in the evening session of City College, from which I received an A.B. degree in 1925, with a *magna cum laude* and a Phi Beta Kappa key. But since 1923 I had been teaching Romance languages in the day session of the college. This went on, while I acquired a Ph.D. at Columbia in Romance philology and comparative linguistics, which came in 1932. The number of languages, living, dead and half-alive, that came within my purview at this period probably comes close to the 2796 said to be in spoken use today. In 1937 Columbia University called me to teach Romance linguistics, to which was later added the course in the World's Chief Languages in which students are trained to recognize and have some acquaintance with thirty or forty of the globe's leading tongues.

"My travels include nearly a year spent in Havana, in 1920-21, as the private tutor of the nephews of Cuba's President Menocal,

and four European summers, when I revisited my native land and made the acquaintance of France, Switzerland, Germany, Spain, Portugal, Austria, Yugoslavia, Hungary and Greece.

"I am active in professional language-teaching circles, and have held office in the American Association of Teachers of French, American Association of Teachers of Italian, and American Federation of Modern Language Teachers' Associations. I am associate editor of *Romanic Review* and *Symposium,* and a prolific writer of articles and book reviews for both professional and popular journals. During and after the war, I did writing and broadcasting in half a dozen languages for the O.W.I., O.S.S., Voice of America and Radio Free Europe, ultimately getting tangled with the Russians, who devoted a five-column article in *Literaturnaya Gazeta* to my (to them) nefarious activities.

"My interests are predominantly linguistic, but with a literary angle. The medieval literatures, particularly the Old French *chansons de geste,* have always fascinated me, and in my first historical novel, *Swords of Anjou,* the themes of those legendary epics are interwoven in a fashion that I hope will be acceptable to the modern reading public."

PRINCIPAL WORKS: The Language of the Eighth-Century Texts in Northern France, 1932; The Italian Language, 1941; Languages for War and Peace, 1943; The American Road to Peace, 1945; French Precursors of the Chanson de Roland, 1948; The World's Chief Languages, 1948; The Story of Language, 1949; The Story of English, 1952; Swords of Anjou (novel) 1953; All About Language, 1954; (with F. Gaynor) Dictionary of Linguistics, 1954.

ABOUT: American Magazine March 1943; Catholic Digest June 1946; Collier's October 13, 1951; Columbia Alumni News November 1950; Life January 9, 1950; New York Herald Tribune Book Review December 21, 1952.

*PENNELL, JOSEPH STANLEY (July 4, 1908-), American novelist, writes: "I was born in Junction City, Kans., when it was

still a 'tough' town. For the place is three miles from Fort Riley; and all famous cavalry regiments— including the Seventh —knew 'Junktown' well. The 'Wild West,' however, had gone. By the time I began to notice things most of the towns-

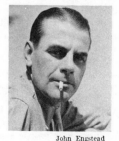

John Engstead

people had forgotten James Butler Hickok.

* pā

* "My name is pronounced to rhyme with *kennel.*"

And I do not remember the saloons and bawdy houses of my native town. Nevertheless, when I left the town in 1947 there were still respectable women of earlier generations who would not walk down the 'saloon side' of Washington Street.

"My Grandfather Pennell served with the North Carolina troops in the War-Between-the-States; and my Grandfather Stanley fought in the Ninety-Fifth Pennsylvania Volunteers (Goslin's Zouaves) in the Civil War. My great-grandfather on my mother's side, a major in the Fifteenth Iowa Volunteer Infantry, went through the battle of Shiloh and the Atlanta campaign. I am both a Rebel and a Damyankee.

"I was educated in St. Francis Xavier's School, the Junction City High School, Kansas University and Pembroke College, Oxford University. I chose Pembroke College because it was known (and still is) as one of the most 'literary' of English speaking colleges.

"As a newspaper reporter, I 'broke in' on the Denver Post, worked for the St. Louis Post-Dispatch, the Kansas City Star, the Los Angeles Examiner and the Los Angeles Post-Record. I was, for a couple of years, managing editor of the Huntington Park Signal (California). During hard times, I worked for the radio station KMOX of St. Louis (as everything from end man in the minstrel show to continuity writer and announcer for the Farm Hour), taught in the John Burroughs School and acted in a St. Louis stock company. (Even now I occasionally see a former fellow player on a movie screen.) After I had finished The History of Rome Hanks, I joined the army and served for two years as a private and subsequently a second lieutenant of anti-aircraft artillery. Rome was published while I was still in uniform.

"As far back as I can remember I have always wanted to be a maker of things. I think it was at Kansas University that I began to think of myself as a writer, a maker of books. It was, however, much later, in time and burned manuscripts, when I began to write Rome Hanks. That book took more than five years of my time. I read scores of other books, looked at many others and searched long in divers obscure corners of obscurity. For my grandfathers had told me little of their part in the Civil War: my Grandfather Stanley had recollected a thing or two—but he always exploded into a rage of fine cuss words when he began to tell of how the Rebels let maggots get into his wound when he was a prisoner on Bell Isle. And Grandfather Stanley and Grandfather Pennell called each other 'Mr. Stanley' and 'Mr. Pennell' whenever they met.

"Aside from the newspaper stories I wrote, I published an article on Americans at Oxford in the North American Review and some verse in Miss Harriet Monroe's Poetry: A Magazine of Verse. These, I believe, were my start. I now live, with my wife, Virginia Horton Pennell, on Tillamook Head, a promontory overlooking the Pacific Ocean."

* * *

Joseph Stanley Pennell wrote his first novel, The History of Rome Hanks and Kindred Matters, at Junction City, Kans., and finished it just before his induction into the army. The book caused an immediate stir. Reviewers were sharply divided in their opinions of it, but there were enough who praised it so highly that it became a best seller overnight. Sales were further stimulated when it was banned in Boston for "vulgarity." A sprawling novel which shifts back and forth in time from the contemporary scene to the Civil War, Rome Hanks was the story of a young man who searches back into the past to learn the histories of his great-grandfather and his grandfather. The book had many faults, Hamilton Basso pointed out in the New Yorker—"chaotic, undisciplined, and formless, it is extravagant and sentimental, its prose is so emotionally overcharged that it often sputters all over the place." Despite these faults, Basso continued, it struck him "as being a work of unusual talent, and . . . the best novel about the Civil War I have read, with the natural exception of The Red Badge of Courage." Pennell's second novel, The History of Nora Beckham, continued the story of Rome Hanks, but was a far quieter novel, faithfully detailing life in a small town in Kansas at the turn of the century.

PRINCIPAL WORKS: The History of Rome Hanks, 1944; The History of Nora Beckham, 1948.

ABOUT: Burlingame, R. Of Making Many Books; Perkins, M. Editor to Author: Letters (ed. J. H. Wheelock); Current Biography 1944.

PERCY, WILLIAM ALEXANDER (May 14, 1885-January 21, 1942), American poet and memoirist, was born in Greenville, Miss., the son of the late United States Senator LeRoy Percy and Camille (Bourges) Percy. He was graduated from the University of the South (Sewanee) in 1904, and from the Harvard Law School in 1908. Thereafter he joined his father in legal practice, and played some part in various subsequent political campaigns—particularly his father's campaign for election to the Senate in 1912. He was also one of the leaders in

Wynn Richards

the successful fight against the Ku Klux Klan when the hooded organization tried to win political power in Greenville in 1922. When the Mississippi flood of 1927 swept down over the state, covering an area as large as Rhode Island to a depth of ten feet, Percy, as chairman of the local Red Cross unit, had the summer-long task of feeding and caring for the 120,000 people, many of them Negro field-hands, who were left homeless by the catastrophe. He was known as an "unreconstructed Southerner" who sharecropped his 3,343 acres and maintained that sharecropping, properly administered, was a good system.

Percy traveled extensively in England, France, Greece, Japan and Samoa. In World War I he was a member of Herbert Hoover's Belgian Relief Commission, and was decorated for his services by King Albert. Later he obtained a commission in the United States Army—he was a small, slightly-built man, and had to go on a diet for a month to build up his weight to the required minimum—and ended his services as a captain. He was awarded the Croix de Guerre with gold star.

A collection of poems, *Sappho in Levkas,* was his first book. It was followed by three other books of verse, *In April Once, Enzio's Kingdom,* and *Selected Poems.* After his death in 1942, the *Collected Poems* was published, composed of all previous books: "No poem has been omitted or revised." Of this collection, *Book Week* found the poetry "literary and derivative in the least desirable sense of that double-edged word. . . . At times Percy overcame his self-conscious writing, and when he did some simple charming lyrics resulted." "Percy considered himself a poet," commented Willard Thorp in the New York *Times;* "what he wrote in verse seemed to him more essentially himself than anything he said or did. Yet he deliberately stood aside from the poetic movements of his time."

In 1941 his autobiography, *Lanterns on the Levee,* recollections of a planter's son, appeared, and the reviews were decidedly favorable. The *New Republic* commented: "You may not agree with all Mr. Percy says, but you have rarely heard his side stated with so

much wisdom, gentleness and wit. . . . Set this down as a very creditable swan song"; but Carl Sandburg and Roark Bradford spoke with stronger approval, the latter asserting, "Will is one of those rare geniuses who are at once honest, informed and articulate. His impressions of his own life in America's most complex social and economic locality are sane, cruel, disillusioning and beautiful."

Percy died of a hemorrhage at his home in Greenville. A life-long bachelor, his immediate survivors were three orphaned cousins to whom he had acted as foster-father.

PRINCIPAL WORKS: Sappho in Levkas, and Other Poems, 1915; In April Once, 1920; Enzio's Kingdom, 1924; Selected Poems, 1930; Lanterns on the Levee, 1941; Collected Poems, 1943.

ABOUT: Percy, W. A. Lanterns on the Levee; Current Biography 1942; New York Times January 22, 1942.

PERELMAN, SIDNEY JOSEPH
(1904-). For biographical sketch and list of earlier works and references, see TWENTIETH CENTURY AUTHORS, 1942.

* * *

S. J. Perelman has written with success for the motion pictures and for the stage (with Ogden Nash he wrote the book for the musical comedy *One Touch of Venus*), but his most devoted audience is composed of the readers of the *New Yorker* and *Holiday* magazine, where his sketches usually appear first, before they are published in book form. Perelman roams widely and wildly in his search for material. He parodies anything from advertising, movies, and current drama, to himself as the world-weary traveler. and *bon vivant.* One of his most admired recent series was "Cloudland Revisited," an account of his reactions on re-reading and re-viewing some of the more lurid best sellers and motion pictures of his youth—*The Sheik, Three Weeks, Replenishing Jessica,* etc.

In an interview in 1953 Perelman said that the writers who influenced him most were Ring Lardner, Robert Benchley, Stephen Leacock, George Ade, and James Joyce (whom he considers "*the* great comic writer of our time"). Perelman's admiration for Joyce is especially interesting in view of his own brilliant command of language, his use of a prodigious and recondite vocabulary which—for many readers—is the chief fascination of his work and the crowning glory of his humor. As his *alter ego,* who signed himself "Sidney Namlerep," said in his introduction to the Modern Library edition of his work: "In his pages proliferate all the weird grammatical flora tabulated by H. W. Fowler in his *Modern English Usage*—the Elegant Variation, the Facetious Zeugma, the Cast-Iron Idiom, the Battered Ornament, the Bower's-Bird Phrase, the Sturdy Indefensible, the Side-Slip, and the Unequal Yoke-fellow."

As many reviewers of his work have pointed out, Perelman cannot be "devoured in one gulp," and a reading straight through of one of his collections leaves an impression of mere virtuosity, strained and forced. But taken singly, his sketches remain some of the best comic writing being done in America today. "The sheer cubic volume of his vocabulary," Lee Rogow wrote in the *Saturday Review of Literature* in 1950, "his stock of pungent slang, his feeling for literary parody, his choice of the least probable word, all make his style . . . tantalizing and attractive." All of Perelman's recent books have been illustrated with wild but distinctly appropriate caricatures by Al Hirschfeld.

Since the end of World War II, Perelman has made two round-the-world trips, reported in *Westward Ha!* and *The Swiss Family Perelman*. In between trips, his home is in Bucks County, Pa.

ADDITIONAL WORKS: The Dream Department, 1943; Crazy Like a Fox, 1944; (with O. Nash) One Touch of Venus (play) 1944; Keep It Crisp, 1946; Acres and Pains, 1947; Westward Ha! or, Around the World in Eighty Clichés, 1948; Listen to the Mocking Bird, 1949; The Swiss Family Perelman, 1950; The Ill-Tempered Clavichord, 1952.

ABOUT: New York Herald Tribune Book Review January 11, 1953; Saturday Review of Literature July 8, 1944.

*PÉREZ DE AYALA, RAMÓN (August 9, 1880-   ). For biographical sketch and list of works and references, see TWENTIETH CENTURY AUTHORS, 1942.

* * *

Pérez de Ayala lives in Buenos Aires. He has written little in recent years, but new editions and collections of his work appear frequently in Spain, where he is a member of the Royal Spanish Academy. In *Who's Who* he lists his recreations as "duty and life in itself."

Correction: The birthdate of Pérez de Ayala is 1880; not 1881, as given in TWENTIETH CENTURY AUTHORS, 1942.

ADDITIONAL WORK IN ENGLISH TRANSLATION: Selections from Peréz de Ayala (comp. & ed. N. B. Adams & S. A. Stoudemire) 1945.

ABOUT: Columbia Dictionary of Modern European Literature.

* pā'rāth thā ä yä'lä

*PÉREZ GALDÓS, BENITO (May 10, 1843-January 4, 1920). For biographical sketch and list of works and references, see TWENTIETH CENTURY AUTHORS,

* * *

Recent publication of English translations of some of Pérez Galdós' novels has stimulated new interest in the work of this important Spanish author. In a review of *The Spendthrifts* in *New Statesman and Nation*, V. S. Pritchett suggested that he was the only nineteenth century Spanish novelist "who escapes to some extent from Spanish provincialism and can be compared with European figures [Pritchett suggests Balzac and Dickens]. He has a large range of scene and character; he has been beyond the Pyrenees; he is a social moralist." He was not so much interested in portraying strong individual characters as in drawing a class or a group. Gerald Brenan writes: "He is a social historian who aimed at giving the pattern of a society and, what is more, of a society which he regarded as corrupt and frivolous."

ADDITIONAL WORKS IN ENGLISH TRANSLATION: The Spendthrifts, 1951; Torment, 1952.

ABOUT: Berkowitz, H. C. Pérez Galdós, Spanish Liberal Crusader; Brenan, G. Literature of the Spanish People, *Introduction to* Galdós' The Spendthrifts; Columbia Dictionary of Modern European Literature; Hispanic Review October 1946; New Statesman and Nation December 15, 1951; Romanic Review February 1950.

* pä'räth gäl dōs'

PERRY, BLISS (November 25, 1860-February 13, 1954). For biographical sketch and list of works and references, see TWENTIETH CENTURY AUTHORS, 1942.

* * *

Bliss Perry died at a hospital in Exeter, N.H., after a brief illness, at ninety-three.

Of his three-fold contribution to American literature appreciation—as critic, editor and as teacher—it is the third role for which he will probably be best remembered. His critical writing, notably his early appreciation of Walt Whitman and his studies of Emerson (of whom, it has been said, he "knew as much as any living scholar"), was "of the kind to contribute to good teaching," in the words of Rollo Walter Brown. Brown has described Perry's teaching at Harvard: "His own aliveness had an extraordinary contagion. It was in his earnestness, as if the literature he discussed were a matter of life and death—as he knew it was."

ABOUT: Stone, I. & Kennedy, R. (eds.) We Speak For Ourselves; Atlantic Monthly June 1954; New York Times February 15, 1954.

PERRY, GEORGE SESSIONS (May 5, 1910-), American novelist and regionalist, writes: "I was born at the corner of Green and Davilla Streets, Rockdale, Milam County, Texas, where I still live except in the summers, which my wife, Claire Hodges Perry, and I usually spend in Guilford, Conn. After graduating from Rockdale High School I attended three institutions of higher learning: Southwestern University at Georgetown, Texas; Purdue; and Houston University, Houston, Texas. In none did I ever graduate from the freshman class. Between attending Purdue and Houston University, I made one trip to Europe as a deck boy on a freighter and another as a passenger on a liner. On the latter trip I remained in North Africa for six months, just pleasantly passing the time.

"Once my college career had ground to a halt, I began writing and wrote a half dozen unpublishable novels. I then turned to the short story and soon began to sell them to the *Saturday Evening Post*, as well as to other magazines, but primarily to the *Post*. During the war I turned to non-fiction. As a war correspondent I represented the *New Yorker* in North Africa, the *Saturday Evening Post*, as a Navy correspondent, in the invasion of Sicily and southern France.

"I was co-script writer of one movie for Paramount: *Arkansas Traveler*, starring Bob Burns. I was co-author of a play titled *My Granny Van*, produced by Miss Margo Jones in her Dallas theatre-in-the-round. I would guess I have written considerably over a hundred magazine stories in all, counting fiction and non-fiction as well. Portions of this work have been reprinted in a dozen or so anthologies, but are only recently beginning to be transposed into television shows.

"If I have an avocation, it is growing Hereford cattle, which for the past five years I have been doing on a modest scale in Milam County, Texas. I am also fond of raising bird dogs, hunting upland game and fishing."

* * *

Along with J. Frank Dobie, George Sessions Perry is the best known of contemporary Texas writers. Resembling the Texan of the legend, Perry is "a big fellow, jolly, good-humored," with a hearty sense of humor. His first published stories were full of lively rural atmosphere, and it was this spirit of jaunty, robust humor and courage which distinguished his novel *Hold Autumn in Your Hand*, a story of a year in the life of a poor Texas farmer. This novel won the National Book Award of 1941. It was described by Clifton Fadiman as "a miniature *Grapes of Wrath* seen through optimistic glasses," and Beatrice Sherman wrote in the New York *Times* that it was "a fine book—a wholesome and heart-warming combination of ventures and problems on the land, with a racy mixture of earthy humor." It was made into a motion picture under the title *The Southerner*.

PRINCIPAL WORKS: The Walls Rise Up, 1939; Hold Autumn in Your Hand, 1941; Texas, A World in Itself, 1942; (with D. C. Disney) Thirty Days Hath September, 1942; (with I. Leighton) Where Away: A Modern Odyssey, 1944; Hackberry Cavalier, 1944; Cities of America, 1947; Families of America, 1949; My Granny Van, 1949; The Story of Texas A. and M., 1951; Tale of a Foolish Farmer, 1951.

ABOUT: Perry, G. S. Tale of a Foolish Farmer; Saturday Evening Post April 3, 1954, May 15, 1954; Texas Parade October 1952.

PERRY, RALPH BARTON (July 3, 1876-). For biographical sketch and list of earlier works and references, see TWENTIETH CENTURY AUTHORS, 1942.

* * *

In 1953 Ralph Barton Perry published *Realms of Value: A Critique of Human Civilization*, a comprehensive study which he considers his "major effort." This work began in 1926 with his *General Theory of Value*, at the time a pioneer study in a field which has since become a central one in philosophical study. Professor Perry is one of the most highly honored of American philosopher-scholars. He retired from Harvard's department of philosophy in 1946, becoming professor emeritus. In 1945 he gave the Lowell lectures in Boston (published as *One World in the Making*), and in 1946-48 he was Gifford lecturer at the University of Glasgow. In recent years he has received honorary degrees from Colby College, the University of Pennsylvania, and Harvard. His home is in Cambridge, Mass.

Perry described himself in 1951 as an incorrigible "do-gooder." "I do not, of course mean that I do good, but that I am obliged, for peace of mind, to imagine that I am trying to do good. . . . My world has to be the sort of world in which despite the reality of evil there is always a chance for good. . . . I dislike cynicism, despair and arrogance, and the great personal influences of my life have come from such men as my father in early years, and Charles W. Eliot,

William James and other colleagues and friends in my later life, all of whom were moralists at heart if not by profession."

ADDITIONAL WORKS: Our Side Is Right, 1942; Puritanism and Democracy, 1944; Hope for Immortality, 1945; One World in the Making, 1945; Characteristically American, 1949; The Citizen Decides: A Guide to Responsible Thinking in Time of Crisis, 1951; Realms of Value, 1953.

ABOUT: New York Herald Tribune Book Review October 7, 1951.

"PERSE, ST.-J." See LÉGER, A.

PERTWEE, ROLAND (1885-). For autobiographical sketch and list of earlier works and references, see TWENTIETH CENTURY AUTHORS, 1942.

* * *

Roland Pertwee has written several novels and plays in recent years, but American readers know his work best in his scripts for such popular British motion pictures as *Madonna of the Seven Moons* and *They Were Sisters.* He lives in Kent.

ADDITIONAL WORKS: Pink String and Sealing Wax (play) 1945; The Paragon (play) 1949; The Islanders, 1950; Rough Water, 1951; Young Harry Tremaine, 1952.

PETERKIN, Mrs. JULIA (MOOD) (October 31, 1880-). For biographical sketch and list of works and references, see TWENTIETH CENTURY AUTHORS, 1942.

* * *

Julia Peterkin lives in Fort Motte, S.C., at her plantation home, Lang Syne. She has published nothing in recent years.

ABOUT: Southern Folklore Quarterly June 1946.

PETERSON, HOUSTON (December 11, 1897-). For autobiographical sketch and list of earlier works and references, see TWENTIETH CENTURY AUTHORS, 1942.

* * *

Houston Peterson writes: "During the war I spoke to numerous service groups, organized the Commencement Day committee of the Victory Book Campaign, and for no bellicose reason at all, nearly died of pneumonia and jaundice. In June 1946 I resigned from the Cooper Union after arranging and chairing more than five hundred meetings during eight years, but I have continued to teach philosophy at Rutgers University.

"*Poet to Poet: A Treasury of Golden Criticism,* which I edited with William S.

Lynch, did not prove as charming for many others as it did for us. But my *Great Teachers: Portrayed by Those Who Studied Under Them* has brought me invitations to speak before thousands of teachers, and has appeared in a Japanese translation and in a talking version for the blind.

"Since my former communication my tennis has declined deplorably, but I have taken up bowling with warmth and some success. My wife and I continue to live in Greenwich Village, but instead of two Cairn terriers and a small monkey, we now boast a noble cat and two miniature schnauzers."

Houston Peterson is pictured as a teacher in *The Ivy Years,* by Earl S. Miers, Jr., and as a forum leader in *Fine Tooth Comb,* by "Paul" (P. M. Hollister).

ADDITIONAL WORKS: *As Editor*—Poet to Poet (with W. S. Lynch) 1945; Great Teachers, 1946; A Treasury of the World's Great Speeches, 1954.

PETERSON, ROGER TORY (August 28, 1908-), American nature writer, was born in Jamestown, N.Y., the son of Charles Gustav Peterson and Henrietta (Bader) Peterson. He attended the public schools, and when his seventh-grade science teacher organized a Junior Audubon Club, the whole future of his life was determined. From the age of eleven, the outdoor world formed the hub about which his life revolved. His drawing ability became apparent, and his art career began by attendance at classes of the Art Students' League in New York (1927-28) and the National Academy of Design (1929-31). Weekends he roamed the fields and woods with an energetic group of young ornithologists.

As an instructor in science and art at Rivers School, Brookline, Mass., from 1931 to 1934, he began his first *Field Guide to the Birds.* In praising it, John Kieran in the New York *Times* said, "It is distinctly for amateurs, beginning or advanced. . . . It is, in fact, a fine compendium of 'field marks' and the 'field mark' is as helpful to the wandering bird student as the highway signs are to a motoring tourist." From 1934 on he was engaged in bird painting and the illustration of bird books. He has illustrated several books written by other authors, among them *Arizona and Its Bird Life*; and has contributed to books such as *The Audubon*

Guide to Attracting Birds (1941) and *A Field Guide to the Birds of Britain and Europe* (1954).

Roger Tory Peterson is on the administrative staff of the National Audubon Society in charge of educational activities, and the editor of the Houghton Mifflin Field Guide Series. He has received the Brewster Memorial Medal from the American Ornithologists Union (1944) and the John Burroughs Medal (1950). He received an honorary D.Sc. from Franklin and Marshall College in 1952. During World War II (1943-45) he served in the United States Engineer Corps.

His marriage in 1936 to Mildred Warner Washington ended in divorce. In 1942 he married Barbara Coulter. They live in Glen Echo, Md., and have two sons. His hobbies are photography and travel. In the writing of his *Field Guide to Western Birds* he traveled 20,000 miles.

PRINCIPAL WORKS: A Field Guide to the Birds, 1934; Junior Book of Birds, 1939; A Field Guide to Western Birds, 1941; Birds over America, 1948; How to Know the Birds, 1949; Wildlife in Color, 1951.

PETRIE, Sir CHARLES ALEXANDER, 3d Bart.

(September 28, 1895-   ), English historian, was the son of the first Baronet of Carrowcarden and Hannah (Hamilton) Petrie. First educated privately, Petrie went on to Corpus Christi College, Oxford, where he took a master's degree. He was foreign editor of the *English Review* from 1931 to 1937, associate editor of the *Empire Review* in 1940-41, and editor of the latter from 1941 to 1943. In 1945 he became managing editor of the *New English Review,* remaining in this post until 1950. During World War I he served with the Royal Garrison Artillery, being attached to the War Cabinet Office in 1918-19.

Petrie said that *The Stuart Pretenders,* which appeared in the United States in 1933, was "an attempt to tell the story of Jacobitism, not as a romance, but as a definite political movement." "Petrie's approach," wrote the *American Historical Review,* "is in harmony with the growing current tendency to reappraise conservative forces and characters so unsympathetically treated by Whigs of the last century. But at times he is swayed by his reactionary zeal toward

very dubious results." While agreeing that Petrie writes wholly from the point of view of a Royalist, if not of a legitimist, the London *Times Literary Supplement* said, "but what is told is told well, by a practised hand and with the enthusiasm of a critical devotee —a good combination." The *Annals of the American Academy of Political and Social Science* noted of *Monarchy in the Twentieth Century*: "Sir Charles Petrie has produced here an important piece of historical writing. He is a master in his field."

Created baronet in 1918, Petrie is also Knight of Order of Civil Merit (Spain), and has received the Commendatore Order of Crown of Italy, and Commander Order of George I (Greece). His first marriage was to Ursula Gabrielle Dowdall in 1920. They had one son, and were divorced in 1926. His second marriage was in 1926 to Jessie Cecilia Mason. They have one son. Petrie lives in London, and since 1945 has been editor of the *Household Brigade Magazine.*

PRINCIPAL WORKS: The Story of Government (in England: History of Government) 1929; George Canning, 1930; Mussolini, 1931; The Stuart Pretenders; a History of the Jacobite Movement 1688-1807 (in England: The Jacobite Movement) 1932; Monarchy, 1933; William Pitt, 1933; The British Problem, 1934; Spain, 1934; The Four Georges: A Revaluation of the Period from 1714-1830, 1935; Walter Long and His Times, 1936; Bolingbroke, 1937; Lords of the Inland Sea, 1937; The Stuarts, 1937; The Chamberlain Tradition, 1938; Louis XIV, 1938; Life and Letters of the Right Hon. Sir Austen Chamberlain, 2 vols., 1939-40; Joseph Chamberlain, 1940; Twenty Years' Armistice—and After, 1940; When Britain Saved Europe, 1941; Diplomatic History, 1713-1933, 1946; Earlier Diplomatic History, 1492-1713, 1949; Chapters of Life, 1950; Monarchy in the Twentieth Century, 1952; The Marshal Duke of Berwick, 1953.

ABOUT: Petrie, C. A. Chapters of Life.

PETRIE, Sir WILLIAM MATTHEW FLINDERS

(June 3, 1853-July 28, 1942). For biographical sketch and list of works and references, see TWENTIETH CENTURY AUTHORS, 1942.

* * *

ABOUT: Sorokin, P. A. Social Philosophies of an Age of Crisis; Smith, S. Sir Flinders Petrie; Quarterly Review October 1945.

PETROV, EUGENE

(November 30, 1903- July 2, 1942). For biographical sketch and list of works and references, see TWENTIETH CENTURY AUTHORS, 1942.

* * *

ABOUT: Columbia Dictionary of Modern European Literature; Gurney, B. G. (ed.) Portable Russian Reader; Struve, G. Soviet Russian Literature, 1917-1950.

*PETRY, ANN (October 12, 1911-), American novelist, writes: "I was born in Old Saybrook, Conn., the youngest of two  children of Peter C. and Bertha J. Lane. I grew up in Old Saybrook, one of the loveliest villages in New England. It is situated at the mouth of the Connecticut River, at the point where the river empties into Long Island Sound, so that the town is almost an island, bordered as it is by the river, the Sound, and filled with small coves and inlets. My mother was a chiropodist, my father was a druggist. After I graduated from high school (in Old Saybrook) I attended the College of Pharmacy of the University of Connecticut, graduated, passed the State Board, and then worked in drug stores in Lyme and Old Saybrook.

"After this rather brief career in pharmacy, I married and went to New York, lived in Harlem for ten years, worked on two Harlem newspapers, and continued to write short stories and collect rejection slips. During this long apprenticeship, I read autobiographies of writers, studied history, sociology, psychology, (self-imposed courses of study, in which I was my own instructor). Finally enrolled in Professor Mabel L. Robinson's deservedly famous course in the short story at Columbia University, I worked on an experiment in education being conducted in one of the elementary schools in New York, shortly afterwards sold my first short story to the *Crisis*.

"After the publication of this story, I began work on my first novel—only because I received a letter from Houghton Mifflin asking if I were working on a novel, and, if I were, if I would be interested in entering it in their Fellowship Award Contest. Two years later, I submitted *The Street* to Houghton Mifflin. The book was awarded the 1945 Houghton Mifflin Fellowship Award for fiction.

"I have one child, a daughter, Elisabeth Ann. Thought I knew a lot about children until I had one of my own, and, of course, I made the usual discovery, that I knew nothing at all about them. It is quite easy to be objective about other people's children—it is almost impossible to be objective about one's own.

* pē′tri

776

"Slowly, over the years, I have become convinced (and here I admit to bias) that the most dramatic material available to a writer in this country is that which deals with the Negro, and his history in the United States. This material is rich, varied, and comparatively untouched, reaching back as it does to the seventeenth century freedman or runaway slave or plantation hand, early ancestor of the mid-twentieth century doctor or lawyer or school teacher.

"I have no literary gods—as such. I find that I reread Dickens, Balzac, Faulkner, Proust—though I doubt that I can offer an explanation as to why I reread them. I like the ordinary garden variety of cat, old-fashioned flowers, old houses, modern painting."

* * *

Mrs. Petry has said that in her novels she has tried to show Negroes as human beings rather than as "types" who fit into special categories in a "problem novel." Her first novel, *The Street*, reflected her intention to show the inhabitants of Harlem "as people with the same capacity for love and hate, for tears and laughter, and the same instincts for survival possessed by all men." In subsequent novels she has continued to emphasize the dramatic and emotional problems of her characters over the problems of race conflict, with the result, Arna Bontemps wrote of *The Narrows* in 1953, that her work "resists classification as a 'Negro novel'" and can be judged upon its own artistic merits.

PRINCIPAL WORKS: The Street, 1946; Country Place, 1947; The Drugstore Cat, 1950; The Narrows, 1953.

ABOUT: Current Biography 1946; PM March 3, 1946; The Writer July 1948; Opportunity Spring 1946.

PHELPS, WILLIAM LYON (January 2, 1865-August 21, 1943). For biographical sketch, and list of works and references, see TWENTIETH CENTURY AUTHORS, 1942.

* * *

William Lyon Phelps died at his home in New Haven, Conn., at seventy-eight, following a cerebral hemorrhage. He had maintained a strenuous schedule of public appearance until shortly before his death. A William Lyon Phelps Memorial in the form of annual accessions of new books to be added to the personal library which he left to Yale was announced in December, 1943.

Phelps has been described as "a generous and ardent spirit, full of charm and rich in kindliness and wisdom," by Joseph J. Reilly.

Although he was the author of more than twenty-five books and innumerable miscellaneous writings, he has been called "the most unbookish of men." Henry Seidel Canby said that "Billy Phelps was not a scholar in the strict sense, though he was widely read; he was too good-natured to be a critic of the first water. But he was a great, I think a very great, teacher."

Corrections: The following corrections should be noted in the William Lyon Phelps sketch in TWENTIETH CENTURY AUTHORS, 1942. In the list of his principal works, *Human Nature in the Bible,* 1925, should read *Human Nature and the Gospel.* In the list of works about him, the reference to *Saturday Review of Literature* August 28, 1933 should be dropped.

ABOUT: Barber, F. H. Fellow of Infinite Jest; Reilly, J. J. Of Books and Men; Stone, I. & Kennedy, R. (eds.) We Speak For Ourselves; Christian Century September 1, 1943; Library Journal March 1, 1944; New York Times August 22, 1943; Publishers' Weekly December 25, 1943; Saturday Review of Literature September 4, 1943; Scientific Monthly December 1943; Time August 30, 1943.

PHILLIPS, DAVID GRAHAM (October 31, 1867-January 24, 1911). For biographical sketch and list of works and references, see TWENTIETH CENTURY AUTHORS, 1942.

* * *

ABOUT: Banta, R. Indiana Authors and Their Books, 1816-1916; Morris, L. R. Postscript to Yesterday; Thorp, W. (ed.) Lives of Eighteen from Princeton; Bulletin of Bibliography May-September 1948.

PHILLIPS, HENRY WALLACE (January 11, 1869-May 23, 1930). For biographical sketch and list of works and references, see TWENTIETH CENTURY AUTHORS, 1942.

PHILLIPS, STEPHEN (July 28, 1868-December 9, 1915). For biographical sketch and list of works and references, see TWENTIETH CENTURY AUTHORS, 1942.

PHILLPOTTS, EDEN (November 4, 1862-   ). For biographical sketch and list of earlier works and references, see TWENTIETH CENTURY AUTHORS, 1942.

* * *

Eden Phillpotts has had what is probably one of the longest and most productive careers in the history of English literature. He has been called "the dean of Britain's living novelists." In the half century and more since he has been writing, he has published over 250 books, working in a variety of forms —poetry, plays, mysteries, regional novels— and producing on an average of two books a year. American readers are still largely unfamiliar with Phillpotts' writings. In 1953, however, the University of California at Los Angeles acquired a collection of some two hundred of his books. These were mainly his Dartmoor novels, set in the region which he knows and loves and has recorded faithfully for many years. He is at his best, the London *Times Literary Supplement* observed, when he writes of Dartmoor—"and he writes with great feeling, for to those dark and lonely uplands of Devon he has always remained faithful."

In 1951 Phillpotts wrote a book of personal reminiscences, not an autobiography but a collection of random recollections of the personalities and events of his long lifetime, *From the Angle of 88.* His home is in Exeter.

ADDITIONAL WORKS: Flower of the Gods, 1942; Miniatures (poems) 1942; Museum Piece, 1943; The Changeling, 1944; They Were Seven, 1945; Drums of Domball, 1945; Quartet, 1946; There Was an Old Woman, 1947; Widecombe Fair, 1947; The Enchanted Wood (poem) 1948; The Fall of the House of Heron, 1948; Address Unknown, 1949; Dilemma, 1949; The Waters of Walla, 1950; Through a Glass Darkly, 1951; From the Angle of 88 (memoirs) 1951; The Secret Woman, 1952; George and Georgina, 1952; The Hidden Hand, 1952; His Brother's Keeper, 1953; One Thing and Another, 1954.

ABOUT: Girvan, W. (ed.) Eden Phillpotts: An Assessment and a Tribute; Phillpotts, E. From the Angle of 88.

PICKTHALL, MARJORIE LOWRY CHRISTIE (September 14, 1883-April 19, 1922). For biographical sketch and list of works and references, see TWENTIETH CENTURY AUTHORS, 1942.

* * *

ABOUT: Percival, W. P. (ed.) Leading Canadian Poets; Thomas, C. Canadian Novelists, 1920-1945.

PICKTHALL, MARMADUKE (April 7, 1875-May 19, 1936). For biographical sketch and list of works and references, see TWENTIETH CENTURY AUTHORS, 1942.

* * *

Marmaduke Pickthall's "explanatory translation" of the Koran remains the only English translation approved by conservative Muslims. An inexpensive paper-bound edition of the work was published by the New American Library in 1953.

ABOUT: New York Times Book Review October 4, 1953.

PIDGIN, CHARLES FELTON (November 11, 1844-June 3, 1923). For biographical sketch and list of works and references, see TWENTIETH CENTURY AUTHORS, 1942.

*PILNYAK, BORIS (October 14, 1894-   ). For biographical sketch and list of works and references, see TWENTIETH CENTURY AUTHORS, 1942.

* * *

Little has been heard of Boris Pilnyak in recent years. Gleb Struve reports a rumor that he got into difficulties with the Russian government and was arrested and shot in 1937; but this has never been confirmed. According to recent issues of the *International Who's Who* he is still alive and lives in Moscow. There is no record of his having published any writings since the late 1930's.

ABOUT: Columbia Dictionary of Modern European Literature; Struve, G. Soviet Russian Literature, 1917-1950.

* pyĭl y' nyàk'

PINCHERLE, ALBERTO. See "MORAVIA, A."

PINCKNEY, JOSEPHINE (January 25, 1895-   ), American novelist, was born in Charleston, S.C., the daughter of Thomas Pinckney and Camilla (Scott) Pinckney. She attended Ashley Hall in Charleston, and studied English at Charleston College, Columbia University, and Radcliffe College. Her literary career began with the writing of poetry, and her first book was *Sea-Drinking Cities*, a volume of poems. She has been steeped in the peculiar and mysteriously haunting beauty of the Low Country of South Carolina, but her approach is not a sentimental one. She has been interested, in Charleston, in the contrast between the survivors of the southern aristocracy and the new, vigorous generation engaged in trade and manufacturing. In addition to her writing, she has found time to help found the Society for the Preservation of Spirituals and the Poetry Society of South Carolina, and is a trustee of the Charleston Museum.

Arni

Miss Pinckney's first novel, *Hilton Head*, appeared in 1941, an historical novel about a young surgeon in Charleston. *Three O'Clock Dinner*, also portraying Charleston, was a Literary Guild Selection. *"Three O'Clock Dinner* is a delight," Bucklin Moon said in *Book Week*. "It is charming, witty and written with a sensitivity that is only on occasion pretentious. If it is brittle, it is at the same time brilliant. But above all it is readable, in a way that all too few novels are readable." "A thoroughly satisfying novel," wrote William Du Bois in the New York *Times*; "Miss Pinckney's success with an old formula shows us how good old formulas can be when they are processed by a knowing hand. . . . All in all, it is a complete tour of Charleston, and a beautifully planned tour de force as well."

Great Mischief was a Book-of-the-Month choice. In *My Son and Foe*, the *Times* (London) *Literary Supplement* thought, as did some other critics, that her characters were "too tenuous," but others found "a high degree of competence" (Chicago Sunday *Tribune*) and "unassuming artistry" (New York *Herald Tribune Book Review*). Dorothy Canfield Fisher has called Miss Pinckney "one of our most gifted American authors."

She received the honorary degree of Doctor of Letters from the College of Charleston, and resides in that city.

PRINCIPAL WORKS: Sea-Drinking Cities, 1927; Hilton Head, 1941; Three O'Clock Dinner, 1945; Great Mischief, 1948; My Son and Foe, 1952.

ABOUT: Warfel, H. R. American Novelists of Today; Antiques May 1946; New York Herald Tribune Book Review January 20, 1952.

PINSKI, DAVID (April 5, 1872-   ). For biographical sketch and list of works and references, see TWENTIETH CENTURY AUTHORS, 1942.

* * *

David Pinski moved to Israel in 1950. He is a member of the editorial staff of *Davar* in Tel Aviv. His home is in Haifa.

* * *

ABOUT: Who's Who in World Jewry (1955).

*PIRANDELLO, LUIGI (June 28, 1867-December 10, 1936). For biographical sketch and list of works and references, see TWENTIETH CENTURY AUTHORS, 1942.

* * *

ABOUT: Bentley, E. In Search of Theatre; Columbia Dictionary of Modern European Literature; Fergusson, F. The Idea of a Theatre; Krutch, J. W. 'Modernism' in Modern Drama; Lamm, M. Modern Drama; Nicoll, A. World Drama; Theatre Arts May 1952.

* pē rän dĕl'lō

PITKIN, WALTER BOUGHTON (February 6, 1878-January 25, 1953). For biographical sketch and list of earlier works and references, see TWENTIETH CENTURY AUTHORS, 1942.

* * *

Walter Pitkin died at seventy-four, after a brief illness, in Palo Alto, Calif., where he had lived since his retirement from the faculty of the Columbia University Graduate School of Journalism in 1943. His first wife died in that year; several years later he married Katharine B. Johnson, who had been his secretary since 1925.

Of Pitkin's autobiography, published in 1944, R. L. Duffus observed that it was infused with "a sardonic humor, operated by a keen mind. . . . There are flashes of light in his pages. But no sweetness." The New York *Times* characterized him as "a crusading, opinionated, provocative and iconoclastic person."

ADDITIONAL WORKS: Escape from Fear, 1940; On My Own (autobiography) 1944; Best Years; How To Enjoy Retirement, 1946; The Road to a Richer Life, 1949.

ABOUT: Pitkin, W. B. On My Own; Current Biography 1941; New York Times January 26, 1953.

PITTER, RUTH (November 7, 1897-). For autobiographical sketch and list of earlier works and references, see TWENTIETH CENTURY AUTHORS, 1942.

* * *

Ruth Pitter writes from London that she and her partner, Kathleen M. O'Hara, gave up their arts and crafts business when World War II began and took war jobs: "They were office jobs, but I took on an evening shift once a week in a machine shop as well, just to help, at a shilling an hour. I learned a lot in that shop. I shed bitter tears there, but it was nothing to miss. It was a very dirty factory indeed, but I added rheumatism and dermatitis to my experiences. 'Lousy dump, but lovely people,' was the general verdict, which I endorse. My partner got sick and had to leave, but I stuck it till September 1945.

"We couldn't start the business again, for there were no adequate supplies, and our skilled people were scattered to the winds. So we let the workshop and do what we can in our own rooms. My plan now is to leave London as soon as possible, and to make a home in the country with Kathleen O'Hara near Oxford, where the climate is milder and where one will be in touch with friends in the University. K. O'Hara has retired from trade and has been painting pictures with considerable success. I have been carrying on with the commercial painting by myself since January 1949, making a passable living by British standards, but not adding to my capital at all, owing to heavy taxation. I work very long hours, as one must do to sell handwork at commercial prices, and what with that and my share of the chores, I haven't had time for anything else since the war. Using our living-room as a workshop, I am not alone enough to compose much, and —let's be honest—I am feeling that recession of the lyrical impulse so common in middle-aged poets. So a few poems, articles, and lectures represent my output for the last seven years. I have a very small book of new poems (*The Ermine*) in the press now, and last year I published a collection of serious poems from *A Trophy of Arms, The Spirit Watches,* and *The Bridge,* under the title *Urania,* with a title page by Joan Hassall. I hope also to publish in the coming year a new edition of *A Mad Lady's Garland,* with illustrations also by Joan Hassall, but this will depend a good deal on her commitments.

"At present I should describe myself as rather over medium height, fattish but athletic, with rather mousy shortish wavy hair worn parted at the side, and very dark blue-grey eyes."

In 1954 Ruth Pitter received a Heinemann Foundation award for her book *The Ermine*.

ADDITIONAL WORKS: Rude Potato, 1941; The Bridge: Poems 1939-1944, 1945; On Cats, 1947; Urania, 1951; The Ermine: Poems 1942-1952, 1953.

ABOUT: Gilbert, R. Four Living Poets; Watkin, E. I. Poets and Mystics.

*PLIEVIER, THEODOR (February 17, 1892-March 12, 1955), German novelist (whose last name is sometimes spelled Plivier), was born in Berlin, the son of a poor file-cutter. From the age of twelve young Plievier earned his own way in life. He went to sea, and during World War I served in the German navy on patrol boats, mine-sweepers, and the privateer "Woolf."

Photo Maywald

His first book to be published in English, *The Kaiser's Coolies,* is an autobiographical narrative of those years and paints a grim pic-

* plē vēr'

ture of the conditions which led to the general mutiny of 1918 in which Plievier took an active part. Eugene Lohrke wrote of the book in the *Nation*: "Lacking in all ordinary richness of style, Plievier's crude, flimsy prose takes strength from the lean force of his own conviction, and his battle of Jutland . . . is assuredly one of the remarkable prose epics that the Great War has produced."

In the years between the two World Wars, Plievier won considerable reputation in Germany for his books, most of them based on his own experiences as a seaman sailing all over the world. The only sample of these in English is his *World's Last Corner,* which combines material from two of his novels on the adventures of a German sailor in a South American port. Described as an "idealist" who was "devoted to the concept of the dignity of the human being and the blessing of unfettered freedom," he was active in the Berlin League of Proletarian Revolutionary Writers and outspoken in his opposition to Nazism. In 1933 he left Germany. A year later his German citizenship was revoked by the Nazis, in the same order that also stripped Albert Einstein of his citizenship. Hoping to find fulfillment of his political ideals in Communism, Plievier settled in Russia, but soon become dissatisfied with that government. The New York *Times* reported in his obituary that he wanted to leave Moscow as early as 1936 but had no opportunity until World War II ended. Then he returned to Germany, first to the Soviet Zone until 1947 when he took refuge in United States-occupied Bavaria. He spent his last years in Baden, near the Swiss border, and died at sixty-three of a heart attack.

Plievier is known best to English and American readers for his stirring and powerful novels on the Russian-German fighting during World War II—*Stalingrad* and *Moscow.* His sympathies were of course with the Russian armies, but as a German he felt a deep personal involvement in the terrible fighting. "It is my own people, and as one of them I saw the battlefields myself, in my own hands I held those wretched records taken from dead bodies—the letters and diaries—and I spoke with the prisoners of war and undertook to describe what happened on the Volga as a turning point not only in our military, but also in our moral history." Robert Gorham Davis in the New York *Times* hailed *Stalingrad* as " the most impressive novel of the second World War yet to appear in Europe." In its clinical realism, its stark picture

of the chaos and moral disintegration caused by war, the book reminded more than one reviewer of the classic of World War I, Remarque's *All Quiet on the Western Front. Moscow,* though it did not in the critical consensus measure up to the standards of *Stalingrad,* was nevertheless a powerful book. R. D. Charques described it in the *Spectator* as "an unrhetorical book, firmly disciplined in narrative power, but shattering in its illustration of the error and irresponsibility which go with the strategic and tactical direction of battle."

Opposed to war and to tyranny in any form and exiled from his native land for many years, Plievier nevertheless remained faithful to his German origin. In 1948 he was quoted as saying of the political situation in Germany: "We are standing at the crossroads—not only we but the other nations too, and yet we Germans more than the others. . . . The tyranny born of our own soil, of our own work, and of our own impotence has left us poor and disgraced after its ignominious collapse. . . . But for us to sign ourselves away to East or West would be total self-destruction. Awareness, a real national feeling, and love of this country of our forefathers should keep us from a death from which there would be no resurrection."

PRINCIPAL WORKS IN ENGLISH TRANSLATION: The Kaiser's Coolies, 1931; The Kaiser Goes, the Generals Remain, 1933; Revolt on the Pampas, 1937; Stalingrad, 1948; The World's Last Corner, 1951; Moscow, 1953.

ABOUT: Contemporary Review October 1953; New York Times March 14, 1955.

*PLOMER, WILLIAM CHARLES FRANKLYN (December 10, 1903-).

For autobiographical sketch and list of earlier works and references, see TWENTIETH CENTURY AUTHORS, 1942.

* * *

William Plomer served during the war years, 1940-45, with the British Admiralty. He was commissioned to write the libretto for Benjamin Britten's opera *Gloriana,* performed during the coronation celebration for Queen Elizabeth II in 1953.

A reviewer for the *Times Literary Supplement,* discussing a new edition of Plomer's *Sado,* compared him to E. M. Forster. Like Forster, his reputation "rests upon a body of work done in comparative youth." And like Forster's *Passage to India,* two of his novels, *Turbott Wolfe* and *Sado,* explore the conflict of different cultures and the obstacles to sym-

* *"Plomer* is pronounced to rhyme with *rumour,* not with *Homer."*

pathetic understanding between them. Finally, Plomer, like Forster, "has seldom if ever engaged to write out of the necessity of keeping the pot boiling or his name before the public." His only novel of recent years, *Museum Pieces,* is an ingratiating satire on British society, which reveals him, H. F. West wrote in the New York *Times,* as "a remarkably able novelist—intelligent, witty, with a true sense of style, and possessing in real measure Meredith's comic spirit."

Correction: the volume *Visiting the Caves,* 1936, in the list of William Plomer's principal works is a collection of verse, not short stories.

ADDITIONAL WORKS: Double Lives (autobiography) 1943; Four Countries (stories) 1949; Museum Pieces (novel) 1952; A Shot in the Park (poems) 1955.

ABOUT: Plomer, W. Double Lives; (London) Times Literary Supplement October 5, 1951.

PLUNKETT, EDWARD JOHN MORTON DRAX. See DUNSANY

PLUNKETT, JOSEPH MARY (November 1887-May 3, 1916). For biographical sketch and list of works and references, see TWENTIETH CENTURY AUTHORS, 1942.

PODMORE, FRANK (February 5, 1855-August 14, 1910). For biographical sketch and list of works and references, see TWENTIETH CENTURY AUTHORS, 1942.

POIRIER, LOUIS. See "GRACQ, J."

POLLARD, ALBERT FREDERICK (December 16, 1869-August 3, 1948). For biographical sketch and list of works and references, see TWENTIETH CENTURY AUTHORS, 1942.

* * *

Albert Frederick Pollard died at his home at Milford-on-Sea, Hampshire, England, at seventy-eight. Before his death he had amassed extensive material on which he planned to base a history of the Reformation Parliament.

One of Pollard's great contributions was as "a teacher, and as an inspirer and organizer of learning in others." The *American Historical Review* has said of his achievement in founding the Institute of Historical Studies in London: "No single thing has done more to give history its proper place."

Both as writer and teacher he worked to establish a healthy balance between high standards of scholarship and high standards of reporting the results of scholarly research. As the London *Times* put it, "Pollard both taught and proved that history should be readable."

ABOUT: American Historical Review January 1949; English Historical Review April 1949; London Times August 5, 6, 13, 25, 1948; New York Times August 5, 1948.

POLLOCK, CHANNING (March 4, 1880-August 17, 1946). For autobiographical sketch and list of earlier works and references, see TWENTIETH CENTURY AUTHORS, 1942.

* * *

Channing Pollock died at his summer home at Shoreham, Long Island, N.Y., at sixty-six, of cerebral thrombosis. His wife had died five months earlier. Until shortly before his death he continued his very active life, traveling, lecturing and contributing articles to Hearst and other publications. In 1945 a revised edition of his autobiography was published containing four new chapters.

Campaigning against the tawdry and salacious in literature, against racial and religious intolerance and the abridgment of individual liberties, Pollock "worked ceaselessly through most of his mature life," as the New York *Times* has indicated, "to make his opinion known and to accomplish something by the weight of that opinion."

ADDITIONAL WORK: Harvest of My Years (autobiography) 1943.

ABOUT: Pollock, C. Harvest of My Years; National Cyclopedia of American Biography (1948); New York Times August 18, 1946.

POLLOCK, Sir FREDERICK, 3rd Bart. (December 10, 1845-January 18, 1937). For biographical sketch and list of works and references, see TWENTIETH CENTURY AUTHORS, 1942.

* * *

ABOUT: Brogan, D. W. American Themes; Dictionary of National Biography 1931-1940; Shientag, B. L. Moulders of Legal Thought.

POLLOCK, WALTER HERRIES (February 21, 1850-February 21, 1926). For biographical sketch and list of works and references, see TWENTIETH CENTURY AUTHORS, 1942.

POLNAY, PETER DE. See DE POLNAY, P.

*PONTOPPIDAN, HENRIK (July 24, 1857-August 21, 1943). For biographical sketch and list of works and references, see TWENTIETH CENTURY AUTHORS, 1942.

* * *

Henrik Pontoppidan died at his home in Charlottenlund, Denmark, at eighty-six.

In his fight for educational progress, freedom from hypocrisy and the triumph of scientific materialism, Pontopiddan excoriated his fellow Danes, in much of his writing, for complacency and tolerance of abuses; however, his volume of memoirs, published late in his life, was "mellow and kindly in tone." Alfred Werner called him "Denmark's greatest representative of naturalism and realism."

His wide knowledge of many parts of his native country and of various classes and groups of her people was reflected faithfully in his work. Hanna Astrup Larsen observed that "the future historian will be able to reconstruct Denmark for the last three-quarters of a century from the novels of Henrik Pontoppidan."

ABOUT: American Scandinavian Review September 1943; Columbia Dictionary of Modern European Literature; London Times August 24, 1943; New York Times August 22, 1943; Saturday Review of Literature September 4, 1943.

* pŏn tŏp'ē dän

POOLE, ERNEST (January 23, 1880-January 10, 1950). For biographical sketch and list of earlier works and references, see TWENTIETH CENTURY AUTHORS, 1942.

* * *

Ernest Poole died of pneumonia, at sixty-nine, at his home in New York City.

Although Poole lived what M. R. Werner has called "a full and useful life of romantic groping," and continued writing until shortly before his death, his best work remains his first novel, *The Harbour*. Harry R. Warfel praised its "journalistic crispness and sense of urgent speed," and John Chamberlain called it the outstanding American proletarian novel. His later works, both in fiction and non-fiction, were praised by the reviewers for their "simple, ingratiating charm."

ADDITIONAL WORKS: Giants Gone; Men Who Made Chicago, 1943; Great White Hills of New Hampshire, 1946; Nancy Flyer: A Stagecoach Epic, 1949.

ABOUT: Warfel, H. R. American Novelists of Today; New York Times January 11, 1950.

POORTEN. See SCHWARTZ

POPE-HENNESSEY, Dame UNA (BIRCH) (1876-August 16, 1949), English biographer, was the oldest daughter of Sir Arthur Birch, K.C.M.G. (Knight Commander of St. Michael and St. George). She married Maj.-Gen. Ladislaus H. R. Pope-Hennessey in 1910. Her first biographical work was an essay, *Mary Stuart,* followed by numerous other studies. On the appearance of her biography of Edgar Allan Poe in 1934 some of the critics applauded her characteristic detachment from her subject and others lamented it. "Mrs. Pope-Hennessey is competent and she has gone to the best authorities. She has not intruded unduly in arguing her conception of Poe's character," commented Herbert Gorman in the New York *Times.* "Her primary value is her foreign birth and outlook which make it possible for her to view Poe's career and mind in a detached manner." But Sean O'Faoláin, in the *Spectator,* was disturbed at times by the highly judicial style: "In such a biographer," he added, "a somewhat over-warm admiration for Poe's work is a welcome offset to the strange calm with which she describes what to others must seem the details of a terrible and harrowing life."

One of her best known works was *Charles Dickens,* an exhaustive and controversial volume that appeared in 1945; in America it was chosen as the April 1946 selection of the Catholic Book Club. Providing an extensive study of Dickens, the work showed him against his contemporary background, including his experiences with his writing, his rise from obscurity to international fame, and his relations with his family, friends, and others. *The Christian Science Monitor* called it "an admirable book, clear, comprehensive, readable, impressing one as sound and unbiased in its judgments—although, for the most part, Dame Una Pope-Hennessey is content to let the reader form his own opinions from the facts."

The author was created D.B.E., Dame Commander Order of the British Empire, in 1920 in recognition of her volunteer work in London during World War I. She had two sons, John and James, who survived her, both of whom are writers. Her husband, a military man, published articles and books on military matters, and died in 1942 at the age of sixty-seven. Until her death at the age of seventy-three Dame Una Pope-Hennessey had lived in London, but she had traveled much abroad, accompanying her husband on his military assignments to Ireland, Berlin, Leningrad and Washington D.C. She was a convert to the Catholic faith.

PRINCIPAL WORKS: Mary Stuart, 1911; Early Chinese Jades, 1923; Three English Women in America, 1929; The Laird of Abbotsford: An Informal Presentation of Sir Walter Scott, 1932; Edgar Allan Poe, 1809-1849, 1934; Closed City, 1938; Agnes Strickland, 1940; Durham Company, 1941; Charles Dickens, 1945; Jade Miscellany, 1946; Canon Charles Kingsley, 1948; Sir Walter Scott, 1948.

ABOUT: Hoehn, M. (ed.) Catholic Authors, II; New York Times August 18, 1949.

POPPER, KARL RAIMUND (July 28, 1902-), Austrian philosopher and social scientist, writes: "I was born in Vienna on  the anniversary of the death of the composer I love best. My father was a barrister: he had taken over the practice from his friend and partner, the last liberal burgomeister of Vienna. He was a poet, an excellent classical scholar, and a historian, particularly interested in the Hellenistic period to which a considerable part of his library of over ten thousand books was devoted. My mother was very musical. She had heard Brahms, Liszt, and Bülow, and she played Mozart and Beethoven very simply and beautifully. She told me that even as a child I reacted against Wagner's music. The background of my childhood was our home in the heart of Vienna, so close to St. Stephan's Cathedral that, when its main door was open, we could see from our windows far into the church.

"The breakdown of the Austrian Empire which followed the First World War, the famine, the hunger riots in Vienna, and the inflation, have often been described. They destroyed the world in which I had grown up. I was sixteen when the war ended, and hopeful and eager for a better world. I had always disliked the so-called *gymnasium* (the secondary school which led to a matriculation examination for which one could not sit before the age of eighteen), and I decided to leave it, late in 1918, and to study on my own. I enrolled at the University of Vienna, first as a non-matriculated student.

"It was a time of upheaval. Few of us seriously thought of a career—there was none. We studied for the sake of studying. I was particularly interested in mathematics and physics: it was the time when Einstein's theory of gravitation had its first great success.

"At about that time, late in 1919, I formulated for myself the problem (and a solution of it) which I still believe is both the most practical and the deepest problem in the philosophy of science—that of distinguishing between a science, such as astronomy, and a pseudo-science, such as astrology. (I have called this the 'problem of demarcation'; it should not be confused with the positivists' attempts to distinguish between meaningful and meaningless propositions.) I have described how I was attracted to this problem in a lecture 'Philosophy of Science—A Personal Report,' to be published in a forthcoming book of essays.

"I was, however, not entirely one-sided in my interests. I felt that I ought to be able to work with my hands. I became a cabinet-maker's apprentice, and I still possess an elaborately ornamented certificate stating that I have successfully served my apprenticeship. I cannot say that I was happy as a cabinet-maker. I found it extremely difficult to concentrate on the work I was doing. My mind turned to other problems, especially to problems of the theory and philosophy of music. It was during that time, while working at the cabinet-maker's bench, that I conceived some of the more important ideas of my philosophy of science; they were, largely, influenced by my philosophical speculations about the development of European music. I became a member of the Schönberg Circle, in order to become acquainted with modern music; but the final result was only an increased dislike of it, and a greater appreciation of the old masters up to Schubert.

"In 1923 I sat for my teacher's certificate, and I got a temporary job as a social worker, looking after wayward youngsters. (I had been interested in this work since I was seventeen, when I met Alfred Adler and worked for a time in one of his advisory clinics for difficult children.) It was a hopeless task under the conditions then prevailing, and I stuck to it only for about a year. At about this time I published my first paper, in the field of the philosophy of education. In 1925 I became for the first time a full-time student at the University of Vienna and at the Institute of Education of the City of Vienna. Scholarships were unknown then, but I could earn something by coaching for university examinations. During my whole university career, I attended few courses, and profited from even fewer; nevertheless, I learned a great deal from some of my teachers, and was very much influenced by them, especially by Schlick, Bühler, and Gomperz, but nearly exclusively by their books rather than by any lectures. Personal contacts between professors and students were rare.

"At this time I began to work on the problem of dogmatic and critical ways of thinking, and its connection with the problem of induction; I wrote a thesis about it (for the certificate of the Institute of Education), another for my Ph.D. (which I took in 1928), and a third on the axiomatic method of geometry for my secondary school teacher's certificate. No doubt, I sat for too many examinations. But by that time I wanted to become a teacher, and examinations might count when jobs became available again.

"In 1930 I got a job as a secondary school teacher. In the same year I married a colleague [Josefine Anna Henninger]. I continued with my philosophical studies, and I began to prepare for publication some of the results of the work I had been doing since 1919. This activity was partly stimulated by hearing, first through Professor Gomperz, and then through their publications, of the work of the Viennese Circle of Philosophers which had become a more or less recognized body by 1929. From the beginning I was attracted by their interest in the philosophy of science, but I disagreed with their positivistic tendencies. What divided me most strongly (it still does) from my positivistic friends was that I believed that there are genuine problems to be solved, and secrets to be discovered, while they believed that everything is on the surface—that there is no depth. Moreover I felt that I had arrived, from a very different angle, at the solution of some of the problems whose existence they were denying. This made me decide to publish my ideas. I wrote two books, of which the first is still unpublished, while the second (*Logik der Forschung*, i.e. The Logic of Discovery) was published in 1934 (with the imprint of 1935), after a very brief outline of it had been published in 1933.

"Before writing my first book, I never dreamt of an academic career, only of a career as a school teacher. But even my first unpublished book had considerable influence in academic circles, and some of its results were referred to at length in *Erkenntnis*, the journal of the Viennese Circle. In 1934, I was invited to attend an international philosophical conference in Prague, and after the publication of my book, *Logik der Forschung*, I was invited, in 1935-36, to give lectures in Paris, London, Cambridge, and Copenhagen; I also received an invitation to lecture in several Polish universities, and one to go for a year as a guest lecturer to Cambridge. But before I could do this, I received, on Christmas Eve 1936, a letter informing me of my appointment to a University lectureship in Christchurch, New Zealand. It was there that I heard, in March 1938, the news of Hitler's occupation of Austria; this made me decide to write what became *The Open Society and Its Enemies*, which may be roughly described as a critical survey of the problems of political philosophy. (Its original title was 'False Prophets—Plato, Hegel, Marx,' but this was judged too narrow.) Material for this book had been accumulating ever since 1919.

"In May 1945, while still in New Zealand, I was appointed to a readership in logic and scientific method in the University of London (tenable at the London School of Economics). Although looking forward to London, I was sorry to leave some very good friends behind in New Zealand. I was made a professor of logic and scientific method in the University of London in January 1949, and in 1950 I spent three very happy months in the United States, where I delivered the William James Lectures at Harvard. I also gave lectures in the University of Chicago, Yale, Columbia, and Princeton.

"The problems which have interested me most of the time were problems of the philosophy of science. Apart from the problems of induction (which I believe I solved in the Twenties) I am still interested in the old great problems of philosophy which, I hold, can be reformulated in new ways—the status of physical theories, the problems of probability, the body-mind problem, the problem of individuality, and the problem of freedom."

PRINCIPAL WORK IN ENGLISH TRANSLATION: The Open Society and Its Enemies, 2 vols., 1945.

ABOUT: Wild, J. D. (ed.) The Return to Reason; Hibbert Journal July 1949; Philosophical Review October 1951.

"PORLOCK, MARTIN." See MACDONALD, P.

PORTER, Mrs. ELEANOR (HODGMAN) ("Eleanor Stewart") (1868-May 23, 1920). For biographical sketch and list of works and references, see TWENTIETH CENTURY AUTHORS, 1942.

* * *

ABOUT: Good Housekeeping July 1947.

PORTER, Mrs. GENE (STRATTON) (August 17, 1868-Dcember 6, 1924). For biographical sketch and list of works and references, see TWENTIETH CENTURY AUTHORS, 1942.

* * *

ABOUT: Banta, R. Indiana Authors and Their Books; Harper's October 1947.

PORTER, HAROLD EVERETT ("Holworthy Hall") (September 19, 1887-June 20, 1936). For biographical sketch and list of works and references, see TWENTIETH CENTURY AUTHORS, 1942.

PORTER, JEANNETTE STRATTON. See PORTER, G. S.

PORTER, KATHERINE ANNE (May 15, 1894-). For autobiographical sketch and list of earlier works and references, see TWENTIETH CENTURY AUTHORS, 1942.

* * *

Katherine Anne Porter's first full-length novel, "No Safe Harbor," and her study of Cotton Mather, both announced in her 1942 sketch, are still unfinished. But in the years since then she has published a collection of short stories, *The Leaning Tower,* and a collection of her critical writings, *The Days Before.* These two volumes, and the continued and increasing interest in her short stories—especially *Pale Horse, Pale Rider* and *Flowering Judas*—have established Miss Porter securely in the first rank of contemporary American writers of fiction. It is not only in the technical mastery of her medium—the precision, the subtlety, the poetic sensibility of her prose—that she rises above so many of her contemporaries. She has, in addition, what Glenway Wescott called "a kind of style of the mind, rather than the voice or the eye, never perceptibly a manner." Her stories, Edmund Wilson says, "show us human relations in their constantly shifting phases and in the moments of which their existence is made."

In 1943 Miss Porter was elected a member of the National Institute of Arts and Letters, and in the following year she was named Fellow in Regional American Literature of the Library of Congress. She has an honorary Litt. D. from the Woman's College of the University of North Carolina, was guest lecturer in literature at Stanford University in 1949, and was one of six delegates representing American literature at the International Festival of Twentieth Century Arts in Paris in 1952.

Miss Porter was divorced from Albert Russell Erskine, Jr., in 1942. She lives in New York City. From time to time she has gone to Hollywood to write motion picture scenarios, the latest of which is a screen treatment of Margaret Irwin's *Young Bess.* Of her work in progress she writes to the editors of this volume: "Several things; but no more promises, no more announcements of publication. When things get finished, I shall publish, as usual."

ADDITIONAL WORKS: The Leaning Tower, and Other Stories, 1944; The Days Before (essays) 1952.

ABOUT: Wilson, E. Classics and Commercials; Young, V. A. *in* American Thought 1947; College English April 1953; New York Herald Tribune Book Review October 12, 1952; Publishers' Weekly November 22, 1952.

PORTER, WILLIAM SYDNEY. See HENRY, O.

POST, MELVILLE DAVISSON (April 19, 1871-June 23, 1930). For biographical sketch and list of works and references, see TWENTIETH CENTURY AUTHORS, 1942.

POSTGATE, RAYMOND WILLIAM (November 6, 1896-). For autobiographical sketch and list of earlier works and references, see TWENTIETH CENTURY AUTHORS, 1942.

* * *

Raymond Postgate writes from London: "Took over editing *Tribune* in 1940, to save it from Communists who had captured it and were using it to denounce Finnish imperialist war on Soviet Russia. Left in 1942 to become government servant in Board of Trade and Ministry of Supply; became controller of business machines. Left government service 1948; left Knopf's 1949.

"Since then has become an authority on gastronomy and founded and run the 'Good Food Club,' an organisation of some 20,000 British gourmets who report upon the cuisine, wines, and service in British hotels and restaurants. He has published annually since 1951 the *Good Food Guide,* which contains accounts of the establishments that members have approved, amounting in 1952 to rather over 700. He is president of the club, as well as editor of the *Guide,* and is a peer of the 12th-century Jurade of St. Emilia, and has broadcast from Bordeaux (and of course from London) frequently. He was also selected to revise and bring up to date H. G. Wells' *Outline of History.* He has no connection now with the *New Republic.*"

ADDITIONAL WORKS: Somebody at the Door (novel) 1943; (ed.) Boswell, J. Conversations of Dr. Johnson, 1949; (ed.) Morrison, H. S. Peaceful Revolution, 1949; (ed. and rev.) Wells, H. G. Outline of History, 1949; Plain Man's Guide to Wine, 1951; Good Food Guide, 1951—; Life of George Lansbury, 1951; The Ledger Is Kept (novel) 1953.

POTTER, STEPHEN (February 1, 1900-), English humorist, is the son of Frank Collard and Elizabeth (Reynolds) Pot-

Baron

ter. "I was at Westminster School and Merton College, Oxford, both noted for vast and almost incalculable age (of foundation)," writes Potter. "My early career is somewhat nil, as I did not start really working until I was about thirty-five, but I was a part-time lecturer in Literature at various universities and the only word I invented before Gamesmanship was quite a valuable one, I think, namely 'Eng. Lit.' which means the racket, the flummery, the techniques and the gambits of English Literature teaching, which I describe in *The Muse in Chains*. My first novel, *The Young Man*, had no plot, no characters, and no action (all this seemed O.K. in 1928)." Elsewhere Potter has said this novel had "no anything, you know, just observations: a man put on his mackintosh and then took it off." But to return to his autobiographical sketch: "I wrote the first book on D. H. Lawrence—rather a distinction—edited the *Nonesuch Coleridge,* and then wrote a book on Coleridge. I think this book *(Coleridge and S.T.C.)* is my best work. From 1935 to 1945 I churned out an enormous number of programmes for the B.B.C., to my great personal pleasure and interest. Nobody took much notice of these programmes till I started working with my old friend Joyce Grenfell [the actress] on a series called 'How'—'How to Woo,' 'How to Go to the Theatre,' 'How to Blow Your Own Trumpet,' etc. These programmes were successful and continued off and on for about ten years.

"I have written no poetry and no anthologies, and one play which got as far as a read-through by a Sunday Society and is perhaps the only play which has died on the first rehearsal. I write walking up and down (is that possible?). The writer who I think has influenced me most in my satirical series is Herbert Farjeon, brilliant writer of revues, old friend, now dead. I believe his work is little known in the States in spite of his U.S. ancestry.

"My favorite recreation is playing golf at a medium handicap, and I can prove that it is better to be medium standard than high or low. As to military or naval service, I held a commission in the Special Reserve of the Coldstream Guards for a brief period in that not very dangerous year, 1919.

"I am inclined to family pride as my wife, Mary Potter, is reasonably said to be one of the four or five best women artists in the country. My first son has just got through Oxford more smoothly than I ever did, and my second son served in Korea (he volunteered)."

* * *

Potter's satirical books, *Theory and Practice of Gamesmanship, or the Art of Winning Games without Actually Cheating, Some Notes on Lifemanship, One-upmanship,* being some account of the activities and teaching of the Lifemanship correspondence college of one-upness and gameslifemastery, have enjoyed a great popularity. Of the last-named, the *Spectator* wrote, "A man less witty than Mr. Potter might have worked his devices to death; it is far otherwise with the Master of Station Road, Yeovil. On he goes, continually scintillating, and rarely probing into his victim without a preliminary anaesthetic of good-humour."

In 1951 Potter toured the United States, visiting most of the large cities from New York to California. His home is in Aldeburgh, Suffolk.

PRINCIPAL WORKS: The Young Man (novel) 1929; D. H. Lawrence, a First Study, 1930; Coleridge and S.T.C., 1935; The Muse in Chains, a Study in Education, 1937; Theory and Practice of Gamesmanship, 1947; Some Notes on Lifemanship, 1950; One-upmanship, 1952; Sense of Humour, 1955.

ABOUT: New York Times Book Review May 20, 1951.

*POTTLE, FREDERICK ALBERT (August 3, 1897-), American scholar and critic, writes: "I was born in Lovell, Maine, the second of six children, my father being a farmer. When I was two years old my father bought a farm in Otisfield, Maine, some twenty-five miles away, and in Otisfield I grew up. I was never a really expert farmer or woodsman, but I did for years all

Yale News Bureau

the tasks expected of a Maine farm boy: for example, I learned to drive oxen, which must be a rare accomplishment among present-day professors at Yale. I obtained my early education in an ungraded, one-room public school

* "My name is pronounced just as it is spelled. It is a French name, and in France is spelled Potel, but it has now been Anglicized a long time. (My ancestor Christopher Pottle arrived in Massachusetts in 1674.)"

in Otisfield, and when I was a little past twelve entered the public high school in the neighbouring town of Oxford. The principal was a graduate of Colby College, and steered into Colby most of the boys and girls who went on beyond high school. I entered Colby when I was sixteen and graduated when I was a couple of months short of twenty. Most of the men at Colby had to help support themselves. I worked for three years as janitor in a women's dormitory, and in my senior year was a very inefficient assistant in the department of physics. My undergraduate major was in chemistry, and I had intended to do graduate work in that subject, but in the second half of my senior year I came by accident on the poems of Shelley, suffered a violent conversion, and decided instead to devote my life to literature. On graduation in June 1917 I took a job teaching English and history at Hebron Academy, Hebron, Maine, but in December of that year enlisted in the Medical Corps of the U.S. Army. I was assigned to Evacuation Hospital No. 8, which trained at Fort Oglethorpe, Ga., and went to France in the spring of 1918. We were established at Juilly near Meaux during Belleau Woods and the summer offensives of 1918, and then moved to Petit Maujouy, near Verdun, for the St. Mihiel and Meuse-Argonne fighting. I held a rating as surgical assistant, and worked in the operating room. After the armistice we went into Germany and did post-hospital work for American troops in Mayen, near Coblenz. In the spring of 1919 I left my outfit and went to the A.E.F. University at Beaune, where I taught chemistry. I came home as a casual, and was discharged at Camp Devens in July 1919.

"During 1919-20 I taught history and economics (later chemistry) and coached debating in the Deering High School, Portland, Maine. In the autumn of 1920 I married Marion Isabel Starbird, of Oxford, Maine, whom I had known in high school and college, and entered the Yale Graduate School. My wife, who had taken a course in library science after graduating from Colby, had already been in New Haven a year as cataloguer in the library of the Law School.

"My plan in entering Yale was to fit myself to be a poet or novelist, but I fell in love with learning and consented to dwindle into a scholar. I took my M.A. in June 1921, and for the next two years taught debating and public speaking at the University of New Hampshire. My daughter Annette was born in July 1921 and died the next year. I returned to Yale in the autumn of 1923, received my Ph.D. in June 1925, and have been teaching at Yale ever since. I was promoted to full professor in 1930, and have been Sterling Professor since 1944.

"My first book (a very bad one) was my M.A. essay *Shelley and Browning,* published in 1923, fortunately in a very small edition. In 1929 I published at the Yale Press a history of Evacuation Hospital No. 8 entitled *Stretchers: the History of a Hospital on the Western Front,* and at the Oxford Press a revision of my Ph.D. dissertation entitled *The Literary Career of James Boswell.* My choice of a subject was largely accidental: I wanted to work under Professor Chauncey B. Tinker, and he happened to mention one day that the bibliography of Boswell needed investigation. The appearance of my book in the spring of 1929 determined my later career. Lt.-Col. Ralph H. Isham had purchased the first installment of the Boswell papers from Lord Talbot de Malahide in 1926 and 1927, and had launched an expensive limited edition under the editorship of the English essayist Geoffrey Scott. Mr. Scott died suddenly of pneumonia in the summer of 1929, and Colonel Isham asked me to complete the project. I have been working with Boswell ever since, and have brought out more volumes by or about the biographer of Johnson than I like to contemplate.

"My son Christopher was born in 1932, my son Samuel in 1934. In 1941 I gave the Messenger lectures at Cornell, publishing them the same year with the title *The Idiom of Poetry* (revised and enlarged edition 1946). When Yale acquired the Boswell papers in 1949, I was made chairman of the editorial committee, and have since that time brought out from the papers three volumes of wide circulation.

"I ordinarily teach a full schedule at Yale: one undergraduate and two graduate courses. Though I am known outside Yale principally as an eighteenth-century scholar, I do more teaching at Yale in the Romantic period. I was Public Orator of Yale in 1942 and 1945. I hold honorary degrees from the University of Glasgow (LL.D., 1936), from Colby College (Litt.D., 1941), and from Rutgers University (Litt.D., 1950), and have twice been a Guggenheim Fellow (1945-1946, 1952-1953). I am an Episcopalian, a member of Alpha Tau Omega and Phi Beta Kappa; of the Elizabethan Club (New Haven), the Grolier Club, and Ends of the Earth (New York); the Johnson Club, and the Johnson Club of London. I am a Trustee of Colby College and the General Theological Seminary, and a Chancellor of the Academy of American Poets.

"My wife (who holds an M.A. in English from Yale) has worked at various times with me in the Boswell project, and since the autumn of 1949 has been working full-time cataloguing the manuscripts."

PRINCIPAL WORKS: The Literary Career of James Boswell, 1929; Stretchers, the Story of a Hospital on the Western Front, 1929; The Idiom of Poetry, 1941. Editor—The Private Papers of James Boswell, vols. 7-18, 1930-34; (with C. H. Bennett) Boswell's Journal of a Tour to the Hebrides, 1936; Boswell's London Journal, 1762-1763, 1950; Boswell in Holland, 1763-1764, 1952; Boswell on the Grand Tour: Germany and Switzerland, 1764, 1953; Boswell on the Grand Tour: Italy, Corsica and France, 1765-66, 1955.

POUND, EZRA LOOMIS (October 30, 1885-   ). For autobiographical sketch and list of earlier works and references, see TWENTIETH CENTURY AUTHORS, 1942.

* * *

Ezra Pound returned to the United States in 1945 after nearly forty years as a voluntary exile in Europe. He returned as a prisoner of the United States government, arrested on the charge of treason. The bases for the charge were the radio broadcasts he had made from Italy in strong support of Fascism and Nazism and in condemnation of the war efforts of the United States and its allies. When Italy fell to advancing American armies, Pound was arrested and imprisoned in a camp near Pisa, where he wrote the poems which were to comprise the later controversial Pisan Cantos. He was flown to Washington to stand trial for treason, but before the trial got under way he was examined by four alienists. In the judgment of these examiners: "He is abnormally grandiose, is expansive and exuberant in manner, exhibiting pressure of speech, discursiveness and distractibility. . . . He is, in other words, insane." On the basis of this report he was declared "of unsound mind" in 1946 and committed to St. Elizabeth's Hospital, on the outskirts of Washington. The treason charges still stand, and if Pound is ever released from the hospital, he must face trial on them.

At the hospital Pound "works constantly, reads interminably," and sees many visitors. He moves, one visitor reported in 1954, "with the athletic vigor of a young man in excellent condition." According to his old friend the poet William Carlos Williams, in 1950, Pound has never budged from his basic position on money control (see TWENTIETH CENTURY AUTHORS, 1942). As Williams describes him: "The man is sixty-five

now and has grown heavier during the past year. His reddish hair, beard and moustaches have been permitted to grow wildly at random—the long hairs framing his unchanged features half-ludicrously, half-frighteningly, to resemble the face of the beast in Cocteau's well-known film."

The case of Ezra Pound was not closed with his commitment to a hospital for the mentally ill. If anything, he has become a more controversial figure since then. The controversy has flared up twice in recent years with heated and bitter debate. In 1946 Bennett Cerf, head of the publishing firm of Random House, announced that he had asked Conrad Aiken to omit Pound's poems from a Modern Library edition of famous English and American poetry which he was editing. Aiken agreed to this only on condition that a statement be included in the book that this omission reflected the wishes of the publisher and not of the editor. Cerf was sharply criticized for taking this stand and printed many letters which he had received on the subject in his column in the Saturday Review of Literature. Upon reconsideration, he reversed himself, and in the Saturday Review of Literature, March 16, 1946, he announced that although he was in no way altering his dislike and disapproval of Pound, his decision "was an error in judgment." The main reason for his change of attitude, he said, was his fear of setting a precedent, that this kind of action might lead "straight to the sort of censorship and assumption of the right to tell others what they should and should not read."

In 1948 Pound's Pisan Cantos, part of the monumental epic poem on which he had been working for more than two decades, was published. In February 1949, Pound was named winner of the newly-established Bollingen-Library of Congress Award of $1,000 for the best poetry by an American citizen published during 1948. Among the judges (all Fellows in American Letters of the Library of Congress) were T. S. Eliot, W. H. Auden, Allen Tate, Robert Penn Warren, and Katherine Anne Porter. Recognizing that their choice was likely to arouse opposition, the judges made a statement which read in part: "To permit other considerations than that of poetic achievement to sway the decision would destroy the significance of the award and would in principle deny the validity of that objective perception of value on which any civilized society must rest."

The first and loudest challenge to the award was raised by Robert Hillyer in an article in the Saturday Review of Literature,

June 11, 1949, who protested that Pound's poems "are the vehicle of contempt for America, Fascism, anti-Semitism, and, in the prize-winning *Pisan Cantos* themselves, ruthless mockery of our Christian war dead." Hillyer further suggested that the "expatriate" T. S. Eliot, for many years Pound's friend and associate, wielded too much influence on the Bollingen committee and should be forced to resign. The judges issued a statement denying Hillyer's charges, and the dispute continued—not only in literary and in academic circles, but in the newspapers, popular magazines and in Congress. Ultimately, as a result of the dispute, the Library of Congress discontinued its practice of judging of Bollingen prizes, and this function was transferred to Yale University.

One result of the Bollingen controversy was that it brought Pound wider publicity than he had ever had before, and it stimulated a revived interest in his work. From the many critical re-appraisals of recent years he has emerged as a major figure in twentieth century literature and one of the most influential poets of the age. He will never be widely read, nor—beyond a group of loyal friends—is it likely that he will ever be personally admired. But his life has been dedicated to literature and to the promotion of the best in literature. T. S. Eliot wrote in 1946: "Pound did not create the poets: but he created a situation in which, for the first time, there was a 'modern movement in poetry' in which English and American poets collaborated, knew each other's works, and influenced each other."

ADDITIONAL WORKS: The Pisan Cantos, 1948; Selected Poems, 1949; Patria Mia, 1950; Letters, 1907-1941, 1950; (ed. & trans.) The Great Digest, and The Unwobbling Point, by Confucius, 1951; The Translations of Ezra Pound, 1953; The Spirit of Romance (essays) 1953; Literary Essays, 1954; The Classic Anthology Defined, by Confucius, 1954.

ABOUT: Bishop, J. P. Collected Essays; Espey, J. J. Ezra Pound's Mauberley; Frankenberg, L. Pleasure Dome; Highet, G. The Classical Tradition; Kenner, H. The Poetry of Ezra Pound; Leary, L. (ed.) Motive and Method in the Cantos of Ezra Pound; MacLeish, A. Poetry and Opinion; Norman, C. The Case of Ezra Pound; Pound, E. Letters; Russell, P. (ed.) An Examination of Ezra Pound; Watts, H. H. Ezra Pound and the Cantos; Wertham, F. The Road to Rapallo; Weyl, N. Treason; Williams, W. C. Autobiography; Commentary April, July 1951; Current Biography 1942; New Republic October 3, October 17, 1949; Partisan Review April, May 1949; Poetry September 1946, January 1949; The Reporter February 2, 1954; Saturday Review of Literature February 9, March 16, 1946, September 4, October 2, 1948, June 11, 1949.

POWELL, ANTHONY (DYMOKE) (December 21, 1905-   ), English novelist, writes: "I was born in London, only child of Lieutenant-Colonel P. L. W. Powell, C.B.E., D.S.O., a regular officer in the Welch Regiment, whose family came from the Welsh Border, though the branch to which we belong has not lived in that part of the country for a century and a  half. My mother, Maud Mary, daughter of E. L. Wells-Dymoke, comes of a Lincolnshire family. As my father was a serving soldier, my childhood was spent in the various places where he was stationed, which later included Finland when he was sent on a military mission there in 1924. After a day school in London and a boarding school in Kent, I went to Eton in the summer of 1919. Some account of my time there is given in *The Old School,* a symposium edited by Graham Greene in 1934. I left Eton in 1923, and went up to Balliol College, Oxford, reading history and coming down with a B.A. degree in 1926. On leaving Oxford I entered the London publishing house of Duckworth, who published my first novel, *Afternoon Men,* in 1931, which was followed by *Venusberg, From a View to a Death,* and *Agents and Patients.* In December 1934 I married Lady Violet Georgiana Pakenham, daughter of the 5th Earl of Longford. I left publishing in 1936 and for a time wrote a signed review column for the London *Daily Telegraph* (a job to which I have returned on several subsequent occasions), together with other journalism. After a period on the scenario side of Warner Brothers' company in Great Britain, I traveled to Hollywood via Panama and tried, though unsuccessfully, to find employment in the film business. In 1939 my novel *What's Become of Waring?* appeared and I began to make some notes on a biography I was contemplating of John Aubrey, the seventeenth century writer and antiquary. When war broke out in 1939, as a member of the Officers' Emergency Reserve, I was commissioned in December in a territorial battalion of the Welch Regiment, and served as an infantry second lieutenant for eighteen months. In August 1941 I was transferred to the Intelligence Corps, and served as liaison officer at the War office with the Polish, Belgian, Czechoslovak, Luxembourg, and finally

French forces, having been promoted major in 1943. After being demobilized in September 1945, I set to work on my life of John Aubrey, which appeared in 1948 with the title of *John Aubrey and His Friends.* In the following year I published a selection from Aubrey's works. Since then I have been at work on a series of linked novels to be called 'The Music of Time.' There are to be at least six of these volumes of which the first is *A Question of Upbringing* and the second *A Buyer's Market.* I have two sons, born in 1940 and 1942 respectively, and have recently moved from London, where I spent all my adult life, to a Regency house called 'The Chantry' near Frome in Somerset on the Wiltshire border. I have traveled fairly extensively in Europe, including Russia."

* * *

Since 1951, the year of publication of his *A Question of Upbringing,* Anthony Powell has enjoyed great popularity in both Britain and the United States as a master ironist, quite capable of holding his own with Evelyn Waugh and Henry Green in the writing of social comedy. The London *Times Literary Supplement* says of him: "Mr. Powell is, mercifully, a writer without a 'message,' either philosophical, religious, or political; he is content to examine without comment, and to illustrate through character in action, the changes in human nature brought about by the changing face of the social order in which we live: in other words, he is attempting to fulfill the novelist's only true function." Yet he is not merely a comic writer. Underlying his wildly improbable plots, Charles J. Rolo points out in the *Atlantic,* "there is a serious scrutiny of human weakness—a scrutiny which is trenchant but humane."

PRINCIPAL WORKS: Afternoon Men, 1931; Venusberg, 1932; Mr. Zouch: Superman: From a View to a Death, 1933; Agents and Patients, 1936; What's Become of Waring? 1939; John Aubrey and His Friends, 1948; A Question of Upbringing, 1951; A Buyer's Market, 1952; The Acceptance World, 1955.

ABOUT: New Statesman and Nation June 28, 1952; Newsweek December 8, 1952, March 9, 1953; (London) Times Literary Supplement February 16, 1951.

POWELL, DAWN (November 28, 1897-). For autobiographical sketch and list of earlier works and references, see TWENTIETH CENTURY AUTHORS, 1942.

* * *

Dawn Powell writes from New York City: "I have spent—(*misspent* is the word)— much time in the last ten years working with producers on musical comedies and plays. I have traveled in Haiti, spent a winter in Paris, another in Key West. My articles and book criticisms have appeared in the *Nation, Harper's Bazaar,* New York *Evening Post,* and other periodicals. Short stories from the *New Yorker, Story, Mademoiselle, Cosmopolitan, Collier's* and *Today's Woman* were collected in *Sunday, Monday and Always,* published here and in England. I have worked on television scripts for the Columbia Broadcasting System's 'Studio One.'

"My husband and I live in a large, dark duplex apartment near Washington Square, but I have a sunny work-room on the roof from where I can watch the riveters and wreckers at present tearing down the whole block. Although it seems that my beloved city is being pulled down around my ears, our own life seems singularly untouched by progress. I have never had an automobile, mixmaster, Bendix, television set, or pressure cooker, and have the same two maids we had twenty-five years ago, the same ignorance of mechanics and games, even many of the same friends. However, I like progressive jazz, modern music, radio crime programs, night disk jockeys, and the United Nations Building."

* * *

Of Dawn Powell's novel *The Wicked Pavilion,* C. J. Rolo wrote in the *Atlantic Monthly:* "The loves, quarrels, dishonorable schemes, and misadventures of Miss Powell's people form a narrative in which the going is always lively and unpredictable—a bittersweet commentary on a raffish section of Manhattan life."

ADDITIONAL WORKS: My Home Is Far Away, 1944; The Locusts Have No King, 1948; Sunday, Monday and Always (short stories) 1952; The Wicked Pavilion, 1954.

ABOUT: Van Gelder, R. Writers and Writing; Warfel, H. R. American Novelists of Today.

POWERS, JAMES FARL (July 8, 1917-), American short story writer, writes: "I was born in Jacksonville, Ill., and spent my youth in that state, in Rockford, Quincy, and Chicago. For a time I was employed in bookstores in Chicago, and published my first stories at that time (1943) in *Accent,* a literary quarterly. I dedicated my book, *Prince of Darkness, and Other Stories* to the editors of that magazine, in grateful acknowledgment of their patience

Carl Fritz

with me. I have since received help of the same sort (which I, more than most writers, seem to need and benefit from) from one of the editors of the *New Yorker,* where my latest stories have appeared. In recent years, I have lived in Minnesota (St. Paul and St. Cloud), in Wisconsin (Milwaukee, where I taught writing courses at Marquette University), and in Ireland (Co. Wicklow, where I worked on a novel). In 1946, I married Betty Wahl, a writer whose work appears in the *New Yorker.* We have two children, Katherine and Mary. I have been a Guggenheim Fellow (1948) and in the same year received a grant from the National Institute-American Academy of Arts and Letters."

* * *

J. F. Powers' short story "Lions, Harts, Leaping Does" first appeared in *Accent* magazine and was then selected for the *O. Henry Prize Stories of 1944.* With this single story Powers won recognition as a young writer of extraordinary skill and promise. In his most successful stories he has drawn heavily upon his Catholic background, and his portraits of the life of the Catholic clergy are outstanding for their wry humor and their brilliant perceptions—"interesting not only for their acuteness," Henry Rago wrote in *Commonweal,* "but for the mass of dense particulars which they penetrate." V. S. Pritchett tersely summed up his estimate as follows: "Mr. Powers is above all an intelligent writer, with a gift for recording natural speech: he is poetic without being poeticising, and he has a notably wide range of characters and a fine sensibility to atmosphere. . . . He has, as a general rule, the indispensable gift of being unexpected in every line without straining for literary effects."

PRINCIPAL WORK: Prince of Darkness, and Other Stories, 1947.

ABOUT: Hoehn, M. (ed.) Catholic Authors, II.

POWYS, JOHN COWPER (October 8, 1872-   ). For biographical sketch and list of earlier works and references, see TWENTIETH CENTURY AUTHORS, 1942.

* * *

John Cowper Powys lives in Dorset, England. He is the last surviving of the three writing brothers of the distinguished Powys family. His wife died in 1947.

Powys continues to write with vigor, humor, and imagination. In his eightieth year he produced two novels which were widely admired in Great Britain and in the United States. One of these, *Porius,* was a murky romance of North Wales in the fifth century and involved much recondite detail on Arthurian legend and druidical rites—all of which, the *Times Literary Supplement* suggested, "will induce in the reader a pleasant sensation of controlled nightmare." The other novel, *The Inmates,* was a love story involving two inmates of an insane asylum. Harrison Smith, in the *Saturday Review,* called it "an astonishing and fascinating novel," and John Nerber, in the New York *Times,* wrote of it: "There is a kind of warmth and understanding here, a Gothic irony, and beyond this, a comic and inverted point of view, which makes the book not only palatable but a delightful Sunday excursion in the monkey-gardens at Bedlam." Powys has also published in recent years a spirited study of François Rabelais and several volumes of essays, many of these concerned with his personal philosophy of life.

ADDITIONAL WORKS: The Art of Growing Old, 1944; Dostoievsky, 1947; The Obstinate Cymric: Essays 1935-47, 1947; Rabelais, His Life, 1948; Porius: A Romance of the Dark Ages, 1951; The Inmates, 1952; In Spite Of: A Philosophy for Everyman, 1953.

ABOUT: Wilkinson, L. U. The Brothers Powys (pamphlet).

POWYS, LLEWELYN (August 13, 1884-December 2, 1939). For biographical sketch and list of works and references, see TWENTIETH CENTURY AUTHORS, 1942.

* * *

ADDITIONAL WORKS: Letters (ed. L. U. Wilkinson) 1943; Swiss Essays, 1947; Advice to a Young Poet, 1949.

ABOUT: Brooks, V. W. A Chilmark Miscellany; Elwin, M. Life of Llewelyn Powys; Martin, E. W. The New Spirit; Powys, L. Letters, Advice to a Young Poet; Wilkinson, L. U. The Brothers Powys (pamphlet).

POWYS, THEODORE FRANCIS (1875-November 27, 1953). For biographical sketch and list of earlier works and references, see TWENTIETH CENTURY AUTHORS, 1942.

* * *

T. F. Powys died at his home at Sturminster, England, at seventy-seven. He had been a semi-invalid for several years.

The London *Times* has called him "a writer who achieved a completely characteristic expression of a profoundly individual response to life." His work is possibly the most original of that of the three celebrated Powys brothers. "A maker of myths," as Charles Prentice characterized him, his stories treat of "the general and the unalterable, with subtlety of thought and feeling, and with simplicity of presentation. Wisdom and humor are embedded in them. They are delicate, wiry and human."

Perhaps the best description of his method is in his own pregnant sentence, quoted by L. U. Wilkinson: "I like best a story about ordinary people, and then, for something odd to come in."

ADDITIONAL WORKS: Bottle's Path, and Other Stories, 1946; God's Eyes A-Twinkle (short stories) 1947.

ABOUT: Powys, T. F. God's Eyes A-Twinkle (preface by C. Prentice); Wilkinson, L. U. The Brothers Powys (pamphlet); London Times November 28, 1953; New York Times November 28, 1953.

*PRAED, Mrs. ROSA CAROLINE (MURRAY-PRIOR) (March 27, 1851-April 13, 1935). For biographical sketch and list of works and references, see TWENTIETH CENTURY AUTHORS, 1942.

* * *

ABOUT: Dictionary of Australian Biography; Roderick, C. A. In Mortal Bondage.

* präd

*PRATOLINI, VASCO (October 19, 1913-), Italian novelist, writes: "I was born in Florence, on the second floor of  a house with high windows which looked out on the Via de Magazzini (Street of the Merchants) at the corner of the Piazza della Signoria (Florence City Hall), which sufficed nevertheless to keep me from seeing a fifth of the street. On the other side of the wall opposite was the Bargello and, at the foot of my street, the Tower of the Priors and the presumed house of Dante —a spot which tourists know well, and which permitted me to call myself a 'Florentine of the first circle.' But soon, as a matter of fact from the age of ten, I sank to living in the houses and in the streets of the 'little people,' my contemporaries. The Pratolini family, unable to keep the walls of our house about them when it was put up for sale, were driven out by the new owner. From then on I grew up steeped in the life of Sanfrediano and Santa Croce, of Canto alla Briga and

* prä tō lē'nē

792

Canto ai Quattro Leoni (Corner of the Four Lions): more and more I identified myself with the people of these quarters whose self-appointed chronicler I would one day become. Suffice it to say that as the son of working people, I did not have and did not look for schooling. When I was eight I sold caramels in the public theatres of Florence, the 'National,' the 'Alfieri,' and the 'Summer Follies,' where my father was a waiter and served the people in the stands and the actors in their dressing-rooms. At twelve I became apprenticed at a printer's; at twenty, my somewhat uncertain health led me to forsake the typesetter's bench for that of a vendor of iced drinks in the Piazza Madonna degli Aldobrandini. In front of my stand I had for a view the Medici Chapel, so even this place was ideal for opening the eyes to art and the romance of history.

"Two years in a sanatorium from 1935 to 1937, from which I emerged completely restored in health, gave me the opportunity to ask myself how much truth and how much wishful thinking there was in my already strong desire to attempt literature. In the sanatorium I wrote my first short story entitled 'A Memorable Day,' which formed the most important part of the little book of essays and stories, my first, which was published in 1941. From that time on I have had a book published practically every year with the exception of the period from 1943 to 1945 when the vicissitudes of my country caused me to become a minor and obscure combatant on the periphery. I had already gone to Rome at the end of 1940 and during the German occupation of Italy's capital I directed the Resistance in the capacity of sector head of the Flaminian Quarter and Ponte Milvio under the battle-name of 'Rodolfo Casati.' "

* * *

Vasco Pratolini is one of a number of young Italian authors who have served as a kind of sensitive register to the turmoils and upheavals of contemporary Italian life. He records the degrading and demoralizing effects of poverty, war and Fascism upon a people he knows and loves. The results are often shocking and brutal but, Hamilton Basso said of his work, it "is not the same old kettle of naturalistic fish. It has a quiet, gentle, completely unsentimental compassion that lifts it high above the rather dehumanized plane that realistic and naturalistic writing in this country so often rests on." Probably the most deeply felt and personal of his novels is The Naked Streets, set in the Florence slums of the 1930's in which Pratolini himself grew up. Frederic Morton said of it in the New York *Herald Tribune*: "Mr. Pratolini's forte is not the projection of single personalities. . . . What he does achieve, with an almost blunt simplicity, is . . . the evocation of the togetherness shared by all the folk in Santa Croce as they support one another against the burden of their days."

PRINCIPAL WORKS IN ENGLISH TRANSLATION: A Tale of Poor Lovers, 1949; A Hero of Our Time (in England: A Hero of Today) 1951; The Naked Streets (in England: A Tale of Santa Croce) 1952.

ABOUT: New York Times Book Review June 19, 1949.

PRATT, EDWIN JOHN (February 4, 1883-), Canadian poet, writes: "Born in Western Bay, Newfoundland, son of John

Ralph MacDonald: Eaton's

and Fanny (Knight) Pratt; received high school education at St. John's, Nfld.; taught school in a remote northern settlement of the Island; entered Victoria College in the University of Toronto, Canada; after graduation joined the staff of

philosophy and psychology, pursuing postgraduate studies at the same time ending with a Ph.D., 1916. To supplement a small stipend, a few summers were spent in Western Canada, farming, running a local mail, and selling books on commission. Married Viola Whitney, 1919: has one daughter, Mildred Claire. The following year, appointed to the staff of English in Victoria College: still there.

"Elected Fellow of the Royal Society of Canada, 1930; editor of the *Canadian Poetry Magazine* (1936-1943); awarded the Lorne Pierce Gold Medal of the Royal Society of Canada (1941) and the University of Alberta Medal (1952). Honorary degrees: D.Litt. (Manitoba and McGill Universities— 1945 and 1949); LL.D. (Queen's University, 1948); D.C.L. (Bishop's University, 1949). Awarded C.M.G. in the King's Birthday Honor List (1946)."

* * *

E. J. Pratt, Canada's most famous contemporary poet, is the son of a Methodist minister and himself an ordained clergyman. His earliest verse was Wordsworthian, full of the haunting echoes of the rugged Newfound-

land fishing village where he grew up, and—to quote him—"full of theories and reflections of theories about life . . . bald, very bald generalizations—practically the whole cargo of the department of philosophy as it existed twenty years ago in the University of Toronto." Reflecting, perhaps, his shift from the philosophy department to the department of English literature, his verse became increasingly vivid and concrete. It was not until he was past forty, however, that Pratt found the forms and the idiom for which he was best suited. With the collection *Titans*, and the short epic poem about a whale, "The Cachalot," which begins the volume, Pratt was clearly marked as a poet of the first rank. Since then his poetry, most of it narrative, has been praised for its robust humor, originality, and vitality. Pratt has said of his work: "Poetry ought to be, at least in part, the expression of a grand binge, making for healthy physiological releases where the world for a time is seen backside-up, and the poet becomes gloriously emancipated from the thralldoms of day-by-day routine."

The late E. K. Brown described Pratt as a convivial man, "never so much himself as when he sits at the head of his table with half a dozen men around him, a great fowl before him, and vigorous, easy conversation in the air." His place in contemporary Canadian letters is unique, and he serves as a bridge between the elder and younger poets, between tradition and experiment, between creative writers and scholar-teachers in the universities. "The essence of his genius," Brown wrote, "is a deeply original thing. . . . It is perhaps too easy for those who talk with Pratt to forget that this man of unconsidered speech and homespun exuberant manner is a distinguished poet: to the unreflecting he may too often seem just one of the boys; but the reflecting know that only the outer rings of the man are penetrable, and that at the core is a secret life, the life of one who is not lonely only because he is self-sufficient."

PRINCIPAL WORKS: Newfoundland Verse, 1923; The Witches' Brew, 1926; Titans, 1926; The Iron Door, 1927; The Roosevelt and the Antinoe, 1930; Verses of the Sea, 1930; Many Moods, 1933; The Loss of the Titanic, 1935; The Fable of the Goats, 1937; Brebeuf and His Brethren, 1939; Dunkirk, 1940; Still Life, 1943; Collected Poems, 1944; They Are Returning, 1945; Behind the Log, 1947; Towards the Last Spike, 1952.

ABOUT: Brown, E. K. On Canadian Poetry; Percival, W. P. (ed.) Leading Canadian Poets; Phelps, A. L. Canadian Writers; Wells, H. W. & Klinck, C. F. Edwin J. Pratt, the Man and His Poetry; College English May 1946; Current Biography 1946; Northern Review (Canada) February-March, April-May 1952.

PRATT, FLETCHER (1897-   ), American journalist, science fiction writer, and specialist on military and naval affairs, writes:

"Fletcher Pratt was born in Buffalo. After a wholly undistinguished period of schooling which extended through one year of college, went to work for a public library. First writing was as a result of this, when he became librarian for the Curtiss Airplane Company, and in connection with this, edited their house organ.

Erich Hartmann

"In 1919 this brought him to New York, and he worked for various trade journals until 1923, when he began to free-lance, principally for trade journals, but also for naval and military publications. Wrote no fiction until 1927, when the appearance of the first of the science fiction magazines, *Amazing Stories*, started him on that line. In 1931, the apartment where he and his wife [Inga Stephens] lived in New York burned out; they used the insurance money for a two-year stay in Paris, where she studied painting and he studied languages and cryptography. He wrote some articles for magazines and did a good deal of translating during this period.

"After his return to America, his first published book came out in 1934, a history of the Madison administration and the War of 1812. In the meanwhile, he continued to do a good deal of work for military and naval publications and for true crime magazines. Various other books followed the first at the rate of about one a year, a rate speeded up in the late 1930's, when he again began to write science fiction and fantasy.

"The accident of being a writer on military topics made him a war correspondent during World War II, and in this capacity he was in the North Atlantic, Caribbean, South Atlantic and Pacific with the Navy. Has been on the staff of the Bread Loaf Writers' Conference since 1938."

* * *

Fletcher Pratt is best known as a writer on military affairs, but he has, as an interviewer in the New York *Herald Tribune* put it, written books "on almost everything you can think of from the Napoleonic wars to Japanese card games." He is a pioneer in the field of science fiction writing and in recent years has turned to the juvenile field, with books on history for teen-age readers. Pratt

calls himself "a literary mechanic," works a five-day-week, keeping strict business hours, and comments on his career: "As I grow older, I have developed an invincible repugnance to not writing for money." In spite of the machine-like regularity with which he turns out his books, Pratt manages to write in a fresh and vigorous style and, D. M. Potter wrote in the *Saturday Review*, his work reflects "a keen sense of wartime atmosphere and a gift for vivid portrayal and trenchant statement."

PRINCIPAL WORKS: *History and Strategy*—The Heroic Years: Fourteen Years of the Republic, 1934; Ordeal by Fire: An Informal History of the Civil War, 1935; Hail Caesar! 1936; The Navy, a History, 1938; The Road to Empire, 1939; Sea Power and Today's War, 1939; Secret and Urgent: The Story of Codes and Ciphers, 1939; Fighting Ships of the U.S. Navy, 1941; America and Total War, 1941; What the Citizen Should Know About Modern War, 1942; The Navy Has Wings, 1944; Night Work: Story of Task Force 39, 1946; The Empire and the Sea, 1946; The Fleet Against Japan, 1946; (with R. Bailey) Man and His Meals, 1947; The Marines' War, 1948; The Empire and the Glory: Napoleon Bonaparte, 1949; Eleven Generals, 1949; Preble's Boys, 1950; The Third King, 1950; War for the World, 1950; The Monitor and the Merrimac, 1951; Stanton, Lincoln's Secretary of War, 1953. *Novels and Science Fiction*—The Cunning Mulatto, and Other Cases of Ellis Parker, 1935; (with L. S. De Camp) The Land of Unreason, 1942; The Well of the Unicorn, 1948; Double in Space: Two Novels, 1951; Double Jeopardy, 1952; Undying Fire, 1953; (with L. S. De Camp) Tales from Gavagan's Bar, 1953.

ABOUT: New York Herald Tribune Book Review November 11, 1951; Saturday Review of Literature January 15, 1949.

PRATT, THEODORE ("Timothy Brace," pseud.) (1901-   ), American novelist, writes: "I was born in Minneapolis Minn., from where my family moved when I was fourteen to New Rochelle, N.Y. There, summers during high school, I worked as a reporter on a local daily newspaper, getting to fires on my bicycle soon after the engines arrived. That fixed me, for, also

with being editor of the school paper, I have never since wanted to be anything except a writer.

"This held good through two years at Colgate and two at Columbia, during which I contributed to college publications and second-rate magazines. Being fearfully bored by mathematics and Latin, I refused to take them and instead became a special student, not interested in a degree. I took only courses that attracted me and thus obtained something of an education for my particular purpose. During a year after college I held three jobs at once, as a playreader, staff reader for a movie company, and newspaper columnist. I saved enough money to spend a year in Europe, mostly in Paris.

"Returning to the United States I married and in 1929 went back to Europe to live in various countries with my bride. For four years we lived there very comfortably on the proceeds from an average monthly article for the *New Yorker*, a happy time. In 1933, after I wrote an article for Henry Mencken's *American Mercury* about conditions in the Spanish tourist resort of Majorca, our house was attacked by a mob and the government requested my absence from Spain.

"Back home I began to write novels, going to Florida to settle, where I now live at Boca Raton. I soon found the background of the state fascinated me. I have visited virtually every inch of it, have been lost in what is now the Everglades National Park, nearly killed in a hurricane, and once was threatened with lynching by some tough Glades characters after I did a piece for *The Saturday Evening Post* about juke joints in their section. I have accumulated close to a million words of notes about the state during the process of writing nine of my twenty-two books about Florida. Adding to this a play, *Big Blow*, I dramatized from one of the Florida books, which ran for six months on Broadway, and innumerable articles and stories in forty-odd magazines, including 'The Owl That Kept Winking' in *The Best Short Stories of 1945*, I claim to have written more about Florida than any other author, past, present and possibly future. It is a source of great gratification to me that my Florida trilogy, *The Barefoot Mailman*, *The Flame Tree*, and *The Big Bubble*, is now required reading in a number of Florida universities. I am at present writing my tenth novel about the state and also writing an outdoor drama about its history."

* * *

Theodore Pratt is a smallish man, almost a bantam-weight. He is known for successfully publicizing his Florida books in his adopted state by having his Florida trilogy listed on a sign placed in the front license plate space of his car. As early as 1950 he began to publish his books almost exclusively as original 25c and 35c paperbacks. In this form his works now often sell a million copies apiece. Four of his novels have been made into movies, each keeping the author's original title.

PRINCIPAL WORKS: Spring from Downward, 1933; Not Without the Wedding, 1934; Big Blow, 1936; Mercy Island, 1941; Mr. Limpet, 1941; Mr. Winkle Goes to War, 1943; The Barefoot Mailman, 1943; Thunder Mountain, 1944; Perils in Provence (short stories) 1944; Miss Dilly Says No, 1945; Valley Boy, 1946; Mr. Thurtle's Trolley, 1947; The Flame Tree, 1950; The Tormented, 1950; Cocotte, 1951; The Big Bubble, 1951; Handsome, 1951; The Golden Sorrow, 1952; Seminole: A Drama of the Florida Indian, 1953; Smash-Up, 1954. *As "Timothy Brace"*—Murder Goes Fishing, 1936; Murder Goes in a Trailer, 1937; Murder Goes to the Dogs, 1938; Murder Goes to the World's Fair, 1939.

ABOUT: Warfel, H. R. American Novelists of Today.

PRAZ, MARIO (September 6, 1896-   ), Italian scholar and critic, writes: "My name, pronounced in Italy with a final hard *z*, sounds odd for an Italian writer; it is a Franco-Provençal name, common enough in the Aosta valley, the word meaning nothing more formidable than 'field'; for people accustomed to consider Italian as a harmonious language, flowing with liquid  vowels, it is certainly a harsh name. My father's family originated from Zermatt (Valais, Switzerland), crossed the Alps about 1535 and settled in the village bearing their name near Nus, in the St. Barthélemy district. Had custom decided that one should be called after one's mother's name, I could have sported a very harmonious Di Marsciano, a name as high-sounding and noble as the family to which it belongs, which can be traced back to a Farolfo who lived in the eighth century. For centuries the counts Di Marsciano owned lands round Orvieto; their two palaces in Orvieto belong nowadays one to the state, the other to the clergy, and the splendor of the family is very much a thing of the past. A cross between Piedmont and Central Italy, I was born in Rome, passed the first four years of my life in Switzerland, lost my father when I was four, and was educated in Florence, where my mother's family lived after my grandfather's retirement from the army. As I lived in Florence during the formative years, until 1923, no wonder I consider myself a Tuscan by election, and Tuscan is the accent of my speech.

"Like many young Italians, when my vocation was still unsettled, I studied law; and the study of a subject I did not like helped me to find my true interests which were all literary and artistic; at first I thought I would become a Greek scholar, but fortunately I quarreled with my professor, a leading authority in the field of classical studies, of whom later I became a friend, Giorgio Pasquali. I say fortunately because, having turned to English studies, I was able three years after taking my Ph.D. in 1923, to obtain a scholarship for England; for one year I worked in the British Museum preparing my volume on the metaphysical poets, then I was appointed to the chair of Italian (a senior lectureship) in Liverpool where I spent most of the following eight years. I say 'most,' but my English colleagues did not think it was enough, because I had the habit of fleeing the place (can anyone blame me?) at every holiday to travel abroad. Thus I came to know all Western Europe, and in 1928 published a book on Spain which interested Knopf; however, my *Unromantic Spain*, offering a far from orthodox view of Spanish picturesqueness, was not a success, and was soon remaindered. In those two first books, the one on Donne and Crashaw, and the other on the legend of Spain, lies the originary nucleus of my subsequent production, because while the metaphysicals led me to the study of emblems, Barrès' slogan about Spain, *du sang, de la volupté, de la mort*, made me interested in decadent literature and its roots. This subject proved very congenial —a psychoanalyst would tell you why—and the result was the best-known of my books, whose Italian title (*La Carne, la Morte e il Diavolo nella Letteratura Romantica*), better than the English (*The Romantic Agony*), reveals its origin.

"As a professor of Italian in England (after Liverpool, I was professor of Italian Studies in Manchester, 1932-34) and of English in Italy (in Rome from 1934 on), I have written on a quantity of subjects of comparative literature; my family life also, as long as I had a wife by my side, from 1934 to 1945, was astride two countries, because my ex-wife is English and my daughter ought to speak both languages (in fact, being educated in England, she has forgotten her Italian, and she never stays long enough with me in Italy to pick it up again). One of the reasons of disagreement with my wife was my passion for Empire furniture. This mania dates back from the time when, as a young man, I received a fatal present in the form of an Empire bed: I liked it so much (it must have stirred some hidden chord in me), that I decided to accompany it with cupboard, writing desk, etc, in the same style, with the result that now I am supposed to have the best collection of Empire furniture in Italy (which is not really so important as it sounds). I embodied my passion for Empire in book form, but since the book, *Neoclassical Taste*, appeared during the war and was soon out of print, very few people know it abroad. From about that period dates my career as an essayist, though my earliest work, a translation of the *Essays* of Charles Lamb (1924) is ultimately responsible for this later development. The *Essays of Elia* were a seed that took nearly fifteen years to blossom; but now, with my several volumes of essays (*Fiori Freschi, Motivi e Figure, La Casa della Fama, Lettrice Notturna*), I am best known in Italy as an essayist. That does not mean that I have abandoned my professorial interests; *La Crisi dell'Eroe nel Romanzo Vittoriano*, published in 1952, is a less spectacular, but no less learned production than *The Romantic Agony*. I am internationally minded and fortunately I was prevented from taking part in any fight by a limp, which, with a few other minor characteristics, I have in common with a much greater man than me, Byron. I certainly must have degenerated from my mother's family, because they were most of them soldiers. In 1952 I visited the United States for the first time; I have written on my American tour a number of essays which will be eventually collected together with other travel impressions."

PRINCIPAL WORKS IN ENGLISH TRANSLATION: Macchiavelli and the Elizabethans, 1928; Unromantic Spain, 1930; The Romantic Agony, 1933; Studies in Seventeenth Century Imagery, 1939; (ed.) An English Miscellany, 1950.

ABOUT: New York Times Book Review July 15, 1951; New Yorker October 11, 1952; (London) Times Literary Supplement February 19, 1931, August 31, 1951; September 5, 1952.

"PREEDY, GEORGE." See LONG, G. M. V. C.

PRESCOTT, HILDA FRANCES MARGARET (February 22, 1896-), British historian and novelist, was born in Latchford, Cheshire, the daughter of a Church of England clergyman, the Rev. James Mulleneux Prescott, and his wife Margaret. After attending the Wallasey High School in Cheshire, she went to Lady Margaret Hall, Oxford, on a Jephson scholarship and took her B.A. there. She then did research in medieval history at Manchester University under the late Professor T. F. Tout and received M.A. degrees from both Manchester and Oxford. For a few years after her graduation from Oxford, Miss Prescott taught at Manchester and Pendleton High Schools and at Wallasey High School. In 1923 she gave up teaching to devote herself to writing. Since that time she has done occasional coaching and lecturing at Lady Margaret Hall, St. Hugh's College, and King's College, Newcastle-on-Tyne.

Ramsey & Muspratt

H. F. M. Prescott's first books were historical romances set in the Middle Ages. She has also tried her hand, with some success, at a detective novel, *Dead and Not Buried*. Her main interest remained history, however, especially the turbulent period of the later Middle Ages and the early days of the Reformation. In 1940 her first major historical work, a biography of Mary Tudor, was published in England under the title *Spanish Tudor*. It was awarded the James Tait Black prize in 1941 and was widely acclaimed for its scholarship, its fairness, and its fluent and dramatic presentation. Of the revised and expanded second edition, published as *Mary Tudor*, Helen C. White remarked in *Commonweal*: "If this . . . is a sobering book to read, it is also a fascinating one, thanks to the author's power of invoking the look and feel of a vanished moment, and of summing up a very complicated matter in a pithy sentence or two."

In 1940 Miss Prescott began work on *The Man on a Donkey*. The book was conceived rather simply as the story of an ignorant servant girl who has a vision of Christ as a man riding on a donkey. A year later Miss Prescott moved to the north of England to join her brother. Here in Yorkshire she found the scene for her historical panorama—the nunnery of Marrick which had managed to survive the destruction of monasteries and convents ordered by Henry VIII—and the birthplace of the Pilgrimage of Grace and its courageous leader Robert Aske. Combining these and many other lines of narrative, she completed, after seven years of work, a massive and compelling book which was hailed as the finest historical novel of many years, "the almost perfect historical novel," as one reviewer called it. The *New Statesman and Nation* hailed the book as a unique achievement: "It blends fine scholarship with great literary imagination and it has a sweep and a breadth that one had forgotten could belong to the historical novel." In the United States

The Man on the Donkey received a Christopher Award in 1953.

During the time that she was writing the novel, Miss Prescott served as county organizer of the Red Cross Hospital Libraries in Northumberland. From 1943 to 1948 she was vice principal of St. Mary's College in the University of Durham. She is unmarried and lives alone with a fox terrier in an eighteenth century cottage in Charlbury, a short distance from Oxford. An interviewer described her in 1953 as "one of those ageless looking women. She has short brown hair and a face as narrow as those seen in medieval stained-glass windows, with a high-arched nose and fine brown-green eyes."

PRINCIPAL WORKS: The Unhurrying Chase, 1925; The Lost Fight, 1928; Bernardet the Troubadour's Flamenca: A Translation from the French Provençal, 1930; Son of Dust, 1932; Dead and Not Buried, 1938; Spanish Tudor, 1940 (2d ed., Mary Tudor, 1953); Friar Felix at Large: A Fifteenth Century Pilgrimage to the Holy Land, 1950; The Man on a Donkey, 1952.

ABOUT: Time September 22, 1952; Washington (D.C.) Sunday Star October 4, 1953.

*PRÉVOST, MARCEL (May 1, 1862-April 8, 1941). For biographical sketch and list of works and references, see TWENTIETH CENTURY AUTHORS, 1942.

* * *

ABOUT: Columbia Dictionary of Modern European Literature.

* prā võ′

PRICHARD, HESKETH VERNON HESKETH (November 17, 1876-June 14, 1922). For biographical sketch and list of works and references, see TWENTIETH CENTURY AUTHORS, 1942.

PRIESTLEY, JOHN BOYNTON (1894-), English novelist, essayist, and dramatist.

NOTE: This biography, at the request of the writer, supersedes the sketch which appeared in TWENTIETH CENTURY AUTHORS, 1942.

J. B. Priestley was born in Bradford, Yorkshire, the son of a schoolmaster. Throughout the First World War, from 1914 to 1919, he served in the infantry, starting in the ranks and becoming commissioned later, and was three times wounded. After the war he went to Trinity Hall, Cambridge, where he took honors in English literature, modern history, and political science. He had been writing steadily and contributing articles, etc., to London and provincial papers ever since he was sixteen, and indeed helped to keep himself at Cambridge by his writing. In 1922 he came to London and quickly established himself as a reviewer, critic, and essayist, doing a great deal of periodical work and publishing two or three books a year as well. These included two volumes in the "English Men of Letters" series, a short history of the English novel, *The English Comic Characters,* and several books of essays.

Priestley still returns occasionally to the essay form by which he first established himself, as in his recent and very successful collection, *Delight.* As a novelist his first great success was *The Good Companions,* by which he helped to popularize the long novel and which is still one of the best selling novels of this century. It was followed by the almost equally successful *Angel Pavement,* and among other novels which he has published since then are *Faraway, Wonder Hero, Daylight on Saturday* and, most recently, *Bright Day* and *Festival.* Notable too among Priestley's works are those which combine personal history with social criticism such as *English Journey, Midnight on the Desert* and its sequel, *Rain Upon Godshill.* All have been translated into many different languages and published in all manner of editions: their total sales run into millions.

In 1932 Priestley began a new career as a dramatist with *Dangerous Corner,* which has since been played all over the world. Unlike his novels, which are traditional in manner, his plays are often experimental in form. He has run his own producing company and directed two London theatres and has produced nearly thirty plays, of which the most important are *Eden End, Time and the Conways, I Have Been Here Before, Music at Night, Johnson Over Jordan, An Inspector Calls,* and *Dragon's Mouth,* a dramatic quartet which he wrote in collaboration with Jacquetta Hawkes; although it is the comedies like *Laburnum Grove* and *When We Are Married* which have had the longest runs. Priestley has been called a master of dramatic construction, but his plays have stimulated much controversy and criticism along with the praise.

Priestley is one of the few English writers who are equally good as broadcasters, and his Sunday night radio talks were immensely popular, as were his wartime commentaries to a vast number of listeners all over the world. He has occasionally written and appeared in special radio feature programs, and has also written plays for television, but he has not had the time to experiment in these mediums as much as he would like to do.

Since the war, Priestley has given much time to public affairs. He was a United Kingdom delegate to two UNESCO conferences, chairman of the British Theatre Conference, and was chairman of the council on the London Philharmonic Orchestra and a director of the *New Statesman and Nation.* Politically, although at times in former years he has strongly supported the Left, his sympathies have lately moderated and swung back toward the Center. At heart—as a newspaper profile of him recently pointed out—he is really an old-fashioned English radical.

Priestley has traveled extensively in Europe and the East and especially in the United States, where he loves above all Arizona and the Southwest. Some Americans suppose him to dislike their country, chiefly because he freely criticizes it—as indeed he does everything else—but actually, he maintains, he has a great affection for the United States and knows a great deal about its life, history, and literature.

In July 1953 he was married to the author Jacquetta Hawkes. From two earlier marriages he has five daughters, four of whom are married (one to the Dutch author Jan de Hartog), and a son. He has a flat in the Albany, Piccadilly, in the heart of London, but spends much time in his country house on top of a hill in the Isle of Wight where he has a magnificent view of the sea and the cliffs, and where he includes farming among his other activities. Although Priestley calls himself a lazy man, few would agree with him, for in addition to much writing in so many different forms, dealing with a large correspondence, seeing people, reading widely, playing or listening to music, he still likes a vigorous game of lawn tennis and finds time for a wide variety of other interests, including his favorite hobby of photography.

PRINCIPAL WORKS: *Novels*—Adam in Moonshine, 1927; The Old Dark House (in England: Benighted) 1927; The Good Companions, 1929; Angel Pavement, 1930; The Town Major of Mirancourt, 1930; Faraway, 1932; Wonder Hero, 1933; They Walk in the City, 1936; The Doomsday Men, 1938; Let the People Sing, 1940; Blackout in Gretley, 1942; Daylight on Saturday, 1943; Three Men in New Suits, 1945; Bright Day, 1946; Jenny Villiers, 1947; Festival at Farbridge (in U.S.: Festival) 1951; The Magicians, 1954; The Other Place (stories) 1955; Low Notes on a High Level, 1955. *Plays*—Laburnum Grove, 1933; The Roundabout, 1933; Three Plays and a Preface (Dangerous Corner, Eden End, Cornelius) 1935; Duet in Floodlight, 1935; Bees in the Boat Deck, 1936; Spring Tide (with George Billam) 1936; Mystery at Greenfingers, 1937; People at Sea, 1937; Time and the Conways, 1937; I Have Been Here Before, 1938; When We Are Married, 1938;

Johnson Over Jordan, 1939; They Came to a City, 1944; Desert Highway, 1944; How Are They at Home? 1945; An Inspector Calls, 1945; Music at Night, 1947; The Long Mirror, 1947; The Golden Fleece, 1948; The Linden Tree, 1948; Ever Since Paradise, 1949; Home Is Tomorrow, 1949; Bright Shadow, 1950; Dragon's Mouth (with J. Hawkes) 1952. *Essays and Miscellaneous Prose* —Brief Diversions, 1922; Papers from Lilliput, 1922; I For One, 1923; Figures in Modern Literature, 1924; The English Comic Characters, 1925; Essayists Past and Present, 1925; Fools and Philosophers, 1925; George Meredith, 1926; Talking, 1926; Open House, 1927; Thomas Love Peacock, 1927; Too Many People, 1928; Apes and Angels, 1928; The English Novel, 1928; English Humor, 1928; The Balconinny and Other Essays, 1929; Self-Selected Essays, 1932; Four-in-Hand (essays and fiction) 1934; English Journey, 1934; The Beauty of Britain, 1935; Midnight on the Desert, 1937; Rain Upon Godshill, 1939; Britain Speaks, 1940; Postscripts, 1940; Out of the People, 1941; Theatre Outlook, 1947; Delight, 1949; Low Notes on a High Level: A Frolic, 1954.

ABOUT: Church, R. British Authors (1948); Clarke, D. W. Modern English Writers; Pogson, R. J. P. Priestley and the Theatre; Bookman May 1931; Bookman (London) September 1930; Forum May 1940; Hibbert Journal January 1939; London Mercury July 1932; New York Times Book Review April 22, 1951, May 30, 1954; New York Times Magazine January 4, 1948; Queen's Quarterly February 1941; Saturday Review of Literature March 7, 1931.

PRINGLE, HENRY FOWLES (August 23, 1897-). For biographical sketch and list of earlier works and references, see TWENTIETH CENTURY AUTHORS, 1942.

* * *

Henry Pringle taught journalism at Columbia University from 1932 to 1943. During World War II he held various editorial posts with the Office of War Information, the air force, and the office of the Secretary of War. In 1944-45 he was a Guggenheim fellow. In recent years Pringle has written articles for the *Saturday Evening Post* and other magazines. With his second wife, Katherine Douglas Pringle (whom he married in 1944 after a divorce from his first wife), he is writing a dual biography of Theodore Roosevelt and Woodrow Wilson. The Pringles live in Washington, D.C.

PRIOR, JAMES (1851-?). For biographical sketch and list of works and references, see TWENTIETH CENTURY AUTHORS, 1942.

PRITCHETT, VICTOR SAWDON (December 19, 1900-), English novelist and literary critic who writes as V. S. Pritchett, was born in Ipswich, to Sawdon Pritchett and Beatrice (Martin) Pritchett. After at-

tending a number of schools, including Alleyn's School in London, he went to work, first in the leather trade and then as a commercial traveler and shop-assistant. In France in the 1920's he got a job as a newspaper correspondent, moving on to Spain and Morocco. Commissioned to do several pieces on Spain, a country which, he said later, "always has had a very

Elliott Erwitt

powerful effect on me," he stayed on there for a couple of years, and in 1929 with the publication of *Claire Drummer* and *Marching Spain*, his career as an author began.

Interviewed by the New York *Times* when he was in America in 1954, V. S. Pritchett said he had written "six or seven novels," four collections of short stories, two books on Spain, and three volumes of criticism. His early novels, though they made his reputation in England, were not equally successful here, where his reputation has remained primarily that of a critic.

As a fiction writer, Pritchett, a great admirer of Dickens, has had a style and point-of-view that have been consistently even, unpretentious, and lightly satirical, although the subject matter and décors of his novels have ranged widely. For example, *Elopement Into Exile*, one of his earliest, is the romantic drama of a young and beautiful English girl who elopes to Spain with an Anglo-Spaniard; *Dead Man Leading* is the adventure story of a young man searching for his father who was lost years before in a jungle in South America; while *Nothing Like Leather* is about a businessman and is set in the grayness of industrial England; and his recent novel *Mr. Beluncle* is a suburban satire which the New York *Times* called "high comedy," adding that "most of the characters are absurd or dreadful or both, but they fascinate us because they do not let us escape without admitting how much we have in common with them."

As a critic, Pritchett uses one of the traditional modes of English criticism, that of the familiar essay, a method which goes back to writers like William Hazlitt and Charles Lamb, and which approaches literature from the point-of-view of a man of belles-lettres, rather than from the more specialized point-of-view of a scholar or of a formal analyst of literary structure and techniques. Shortly after World War II, V. S.

Pritchett was for two years the literary editor of the *New Statesman and Nation*, and he has continued to write a weekly column for the journal entitled *"Books In General."* In recent years, he has also been a frequent contributor to American periodicals and especially to the New York *Times Book Review Section.*

Three collections of his critical essays have been published: *In My Good Books, The Living Novel*, and *Books in General.* Readers and reviewers, both English and American, have been delighted with the variety of his interests and insights. The London *Times Literary Supplement*, reviewing *The Living Novel*, called V. S. Pritchett "that rare being, the man of balanced sensibility with a mind particularly open to the unexpected echo which good books of the past strike off our own time"; while Willard Thorp, reviewing *Books in General* for the *New Republic*, said that Pritchett is "one of the best critics writing in English. . . . [His] pages are full of delightful surprises—of insight, judgment, and real wisdom."

Pritchett has traveled a great deal. "I was mad on walking when I was young," he said, when he was interviewed by the New York *Times* on his last visit to America. "That's a peculiar custom of the English. I came over here once and walked from Johnson City, Tenn. to Asheville, N.C., a hundred miles of rugged mountain hiking. I was young and wanted to see the world." On his last visit over here in the fall and early winter of 1953-54, he lectured on the comic element in the English novel for the Christian Gauss Seminars in Literary Criticism at Princeton University in New Jersey; but he also found time to visit the mid-West where he took an hour's icy tramp with the defeated Democratic presidential candidate, Adlai Stevenson. Princetonians say that no one can read Dickens as wonderfully as Pritchett can; and that his energy, wit, and good humor are inexhaustible. The New York *Times*, in describing him, said: "He is composed primarily of smile, pipe, wispy hair and glasses, and he has the laugh of a man who will seek out a good joke."

V. S. Pritchett married Dorothy Roberts of Welshpool, Montgomeryshire. He has two children, and resides permanently at Andover, in Hampshire. His club is the Savile.

PRINCIPAL WORKS: *Fiction*—Claire Drummer, 1929; Elopement Into Exile, 1932; The Spanish Virgin (short stories) 1932; Dead Man Leading, 1932; Nothing Like Leather, 1935; You Make Your Own Life (short stories) 1938; It May Never Happen (short stories) 1947; Mr. Beluncle, 1951.

Non-Fiction—Marching Spain, 1933; In My Good Books, 1942; The Living Novel, 1947; Books in General, 1953; The Spanish Temper, 1954.

ABOUT: London Times Literary Supplement October 19, 1951; New York Times Book Review April 25, 1954.

PROKOSCH, FREDERIC (May 17, 1908-). For autobiographical sketch and list of earlier works and references, see TWENTIETH CENTURY AUTHORS, 1942.

* * *

Frederic Prokosch worked with the Office of War Information from 1942 to 1945, spending two years of that period in Stockholm. From 1947 until early 1953 he lived in Rome and held a Fulbright fellowship at the University of Rome in 1951-1952. From Rome he wrote to the editors of this volume: "In general I find my statements in your 1942 edition still hold good."

After a long absence Prokosch returned to the United States early in 1953. To a New York *Times* interviewer he reported some of his impressions: on the favorable side, "the sense of things changing, of potentiality of possibilities"; on the less favorable, the young writers who "want the rewards without the trials and the struggle." When reminded that he wrote his own first novel, *The Asiatics*, at twenty-three, Prokosch replied, "Ah, yes, but that was a time when to be young and successful wasn't so chic."

The characteristic note of Prokosch's work was summed up by Virginia Kirkus in a review of his *Chosen Poems*: "a lyric beauty, a sense of tragedy, a fluid emotion, and above all a sense of things happening in a dream." In both his poetry and in his novels there is this same poetic and dreamlike quality. At times, however, as Babette Deutsch writes of his poems and other critics have noted in his novels, his work "suffers from a tendency to become verbose, literary, soft and damp."

ADDITIONAL WORKS: The Conspirators, 1943; The Age of Thunder, 1945; The Idols of the Cave, 1946; Chosen Poems, 1947; Storm and Echo, 1948; Nine Days to Mukalla, 1953.

ABOUT: Bishop, J. P. Collected Essays; Warfel, H. R. American Novelists of Today; New York Times Book Review March 29, 1953.

PROTHERO, Sir GEORGE WALTER (October 14, 1848-July 10, 1922). For biographical sketch and list of works and references, see TWENTIETH CENTURY AUTHORS, 1942.

PROTHERO, ROWLAND EDMUND.
See ERNLE

*PROUST, MARCEL (July 10, 1871-November 18, 1922). For biographical sketch and list of works and references, see TWENTIETH CENTURY AUTHORS, 1942.

* * *

ADDITIONAL WORKS IN ENGLISH TRANSLATION: Maxims, 1948; Letters (ed. M. Curtiss) 1949; Letters to a Friend (ed. A. & E. Henderson) 1949.

ABOUT: Bibesco, M. L. Veiled Wanderer: Marcel Proust; Brogan, D. W. French Personalities and Problems; Capetanakis, D. The Shores of Darkness; Chernowitz, M. E. Proust and Painting; Coleman, E. The Golden Angel; Columbia Dictionary of Modern European Literature; Fardwell, F. V. Landscape in the Works of Marcel Proust; Green, F. C. The Mind of Marcel Proust; Haldane, C. Marcel Proust; Hindus, M. The Proustian Vision; Lindner, G. D. (comp.) Marcel Proust; March, H. The Two Worlds of Marcel Proust; Mauriac, F. Proust's Way; Maurois, A. Proust: Portrait of a Genius; Proust, M. Letters, Letters to a Friend; Turnell, M. The Novel in France; Atlantic Monthly October 1948; Contemporary Review June 1950; New Yorker December 8, 1951; Nineteenth Century January 1950; Time February 21, 1949; Twentieth Century January 1951.

* prōost

*PROUTY, Mrs. OLIVE (HIGGINS) (1882-   ). For biographical sketch and list of earlier works and references, see TWENTIETH CENTURY AUTHORS, 1942.

* * *

Olive Higgins Prouty lives in Brookline, Mass. Her husband died in 1951. Her latest novels have concerned one well-to-do family, the Vales of Boston, and their emotional and psychological problems. Critics agree that although Mrs. Prouty occasionally wrenches the long arm of coincidence, she nevertheless writes honest and readable novels. Her most famous work remains *Stella Dallas*. In soap-opera form, with added episodes, of course, Stella has flourished for some two decades on the radio.

ADDITIONAL WORKS: Home Port, 1947; Fabia, 1951.

ABOUT: Warfel, H. R. American Novelists of Today.

* prou'ti

PRYCE, RICHARD (1864-May 30, 1942). For biographical sketch and list of works and references, see TWENTIETH CENTURY AUTHORS, 1942.

"PRYDE, ANTHONY" (pseudonym of Agnes Russell Weeks) (1880-   ). For biographical sketch and list of earlier works and references, see TWENTIETH CENTURY AUTHORS, 1942.

* * *

ADDITIONAL WORKS: (with R. K. Weekes) Alda Abducted, 1942.

*PUSEY, MERLO JOHN (February 3, 1902-   ), American journalist and biographer, writes: "The desire to write took possession of me in youth as soon as I discovered the joys of reading Dickens, Mark Twain, and Shakespeare. But the possibility of writing for publication seemed as remote as Mars. Born in a little 'Mormon' ranching community (Woodruff, Rich

Harris & Ewing

County, Utah), second among the eight sons of J. Sidney and Nellie (Quibell) Pusey, I grew up in an environment in which books were scarce, most of the families were poor, and the climate was severe. My earliest jobs were herding and milking cows, clerking in my father's country store, driving the derrick team in the hayfields, and later driving a mowing machine and a 'bullrake.' Probably the most exciting moments of my life came in the runaways I experienced on the seat of a potentially murderous mowing machine at the age of fifteen.

"In 1918 I broke away from this rural background for two years of schooling at the Latter-Day Saints University in Salt Lake City, paying my way out of earnings from ranch jobs in the summer months and by borrowing. In the second year I was chosen editor of the school's biweekly newspaper, and this led, after my graduation, to a proofreading job with the *Deseret News* in Salt Lake City. Within a few months I was advanced to the status of a cub reporter, and in 1926 became assistant city editor.

"About a year after getting my foot in the door of journalism, I resumed my schooling with afternoon and evening classes at the University of Utah, working almost a full day as a reporter to pay my way. I received an A.B. degree in 1928 and was elected to Phi Kappa Phi, honorary scholarship fraternity. In September of the same year I married Dorothy Richards of Salt Lake, and we

* pū'zĭ

set forth on an adventurous honeymoon that ended four weeks later in Washington, D.C. For a brief period I worked as a copyreader on the Washington *Daily News* and then went to the Washington *Post* as an editorial writer, a new experience.

"A few years later I began to write occasionally for the national magazines. From 1931 to 1933 I worked part time for the Senate Finance Committee as expert for the majority while continuing my newspaper work, and from 1939 to 1942 I taught a night class in journalism at the George Washington University. My first experience in the book field came in 1937 when I turned out, in twenty-two nights of toil, a 105-page volume on President Roosevelt's attempt to pack the Supreme Court. My next effort, an exposé of the United States' voteless stepchild, the District of Columbia, was not published. During the Second World War my survey of the overextended Federal Government was published under the title *Big Government: Can We Control It?*

"Shortly after this volume appeared in 1945 I induced the retired Chief Justice of the United States, Charles Evans Hughes, to give me access to his papers and a long series of interviews with the object of writing his biography. This proved to be a most fascinating experience. Over a period of two and a half years I visited Mr. Hughes regularly and had an opportunity to review with him in detail every major event in his career. Six years of research and writing went into this book. Published in 1951, it won the Pulitzer prize and the Tamiment Institute award for biography and one of the two Bancroft awards in history. It also won for me an honorary degree (Doctor of Letters) at the Brigham Young University at Provo, Utah.

"Throughout these extra-curricular ventures I have continued to write editorials for the *Washington Post.* I was made associate editor in 1945, and have been acting editor through most of the last year. In June, 1952, I suffered painful burns when a quart of powder I was attempting to dispose of burst into flames with me on the leeward side; but my burns have healed and the itch to write is still in my fingers."

PRINCIPAL WORKS: The Supreme Court Crisis, 1937; Big Government: Can We Control It? 1945; Charles Evens Hughes, 2 vols., 1951.

ABOUT: Current Biography 1952; New York Herald Tribune May 6, 1952; New York Times May 6, 1952; Washington (D.C.) Post May 6, 1952.

PUTNAM, HOWARD PHELPS (July 9, 1894-1948). For biographical sketch and list of works and references, see TWENTIETH CENTURY AUTHORS, 1942.

* * *

Phelps Putnam died at fifty-four from a stroke. He had suffered from asthma for several years before his death.

The late Stephen Vincent Benét noted the poet's significant progression from an early rich lyricism "to a complex symbolism that attempts to organize, in terms of vision, some of the leading philosophical ideas of the age." It is possible that the vastness and complexity of his conception prevented completion of *The Earthly Comedy,* on which Putnam worked for years.

The poet's scholar-friend F. O. Matthiessen wrote that "his best passages, both those of lyric delicacy and those of realistic acidness, still look as good as they did twenty years ago. . . But Putnam's eloquence was that of the rhapsode, so cloudily full that it inescapably deliquesced after lines whose magnificence defied the lightning."

ABOUT: Kenyon Review Winter 1949.

PUTNAM, Mrs. NINA (WILCOX) (November 28, 1888-   ). For biographical sketch and list of earlier works and references, see TWENTIETH CENTURY AUTHORS, 1942.

* * *

Mrs. Putnam contributes articles to a number of popular magazines—*Collier's, American Mercury, Reader's Digest,* etc. Her only book-length work in recent years is a romance written for teen-age girls.

ADDITIONAL WORK: Lynn, Cover Girl, 1950.
ABOUT: Collier's April 20, 1946.

PUTNAM, PHELPS. See PUTNAM, H. P.

PUTNAM, SAMUEL (1892-January 17, 1950), American biographer, translator, and critic, was born in Rossville, Ill. His addiction to exotic tongues dates back to age nine, when an old German shoemaker in the central Illinois village where he was born taught him a few Bavarian words. At twelve he was studying Latin and Greek, and in a hayloft shortly after, he peeked into Rabelais—the reason some years later for his sojourn in France among the "lost generation." His translation of the works of Rabelais came out in 1929, and utilized colloquial speech instead of academic vocabulary.

Putnam's translation of Latin in high school classroom won for him a scholarship to the University of Illinois, but frail health prevented him from obtaining a degree. He left the university to join the staff of the Chicago *Evening Post* where from 1920 to 1926 he served as literary and art critic. Immersed in the "Chicago Renaissance" of the Twenties, he was founder and editor of *Youth,* which started the "young magazine" craze. In another little magazine, *This Quarter,* he introduced James Farrell's work.

Joseph Stella

From 1927 to 1934 Putnam lived in Paris, studying at the Sorbonne. During this period he wrote several books, besides doing translations. He contributed art criticism to newspapers, and an Italian letter to the *Saturday Review of Literature.* In 1928 was published *François Rabelais, Man of the Renaissance,* a spiritual biography, and in 1935 *Marguerite of Navarre* appeared, which won critical praise. *Paris Was Our Mistress* was subtitled Memoirs of a Lost and Found Generation. "Mr. Putnam," wrote the New York *Times,* "is not satisfied with merely setting down the facts of the pilgrimage to Montparnasse. His glimpses into the lives of the exiled greats and near-greats are interesting enough, and rewarding. The real value of this book lies in his attempts to search for the causes, both immediate and primary, of expatriation."

After Putnam returned to America in 1933, he devoted most of his literary efforts to South American works. His translation of two Brazilian classics, *Rebellion in the Backlands* and *The Masters and the Slaves,* won him honorary membership in the Brazilian Academy of Letters. In 1947 he was awarded the Pandia Calogueras award of one thousand dollars by Brazil. From 1935 until his death Putnam was editor of the Brazilian literature section of the *Handbook of Latin American Studies,* published by the Library of Congress. In 1946 he lectured at the University of Brazil on comparative literature.

Putnam died at his home in Lambertville, N.J.; he had been in bad health for years, and dangerously ill several times, but his zestful publications had continued. He was said to be the most talented American translator of his generation, and his work as critic and historian was distinguished. Publication of his translation of *Don Quixote* in 1949 climaxed more than fifteen years of work, and he was translating the novellas of Cervantes at the time of his death.

Putnam had founded and edited the *New Review,* a periodical, and had written literary columns for the *Daily Worker* and the *New Masses,* but had broken with the Communist Party in 1944. His wife, Riva Sampson Putnam, and a son, Hilary, survived him.

PRINCIPAL WORKS: François Rabelais, Man of the Renaissance, 1928; Glistening Bridge: Leopold Survage and the Spatial Problem in Painting, 1929; World of Jean de Bosschère, 1932; Marguerite of Navarre, 1935; Paris Was Our Mistress, 1947; Marvelous Journey, 1948. *Principal Translations*—Rabelais, F. Extant Works, 1929; Mauriac, F. The Desert of Love, 1929; Cocteau, J. Enfants Terribles, 1930; Pirandello, A. As You Desire Me, 1931, Horse in the Moon, 1932, Tonight We Improvise, 1932; Aretino, P. Works; Duhamel, G. Fortunes of the Pasquiers, 1935; Cervantes, M. de, The Ingenious Gentleman, Don Quixote de La Mancha, 1949.

ABOUT: Putnam, S. Paris Was Our Mistress; Américas March 1950; Books Abroad Summer 1950; New York Herald Tribune January 18, 1950; New York Herald Tribune Book Review October 2, 1949; New York Times January 18, 1950; Saturday Review of Literature September 24, 1949; Time October 3, 1949.

PYLE, ERNEST TAYLOR (ERNIE)

(August 3, 1900-April 18, 1945), American journalist, was born on a farm near Dana, Ind., the son of William C. and Maria Pyle. Although — or perhaps because—his father made him help out with the farm chores at a very early age, Pyle never had a taste for farming. He was a good student, and after three months' duty in the

Navy just before the Armistice, he entered Indiana University. There he was an editor on the student daily. His real understanding of newspaper work came, he said, from his work on that daily in 1921. Kirke Sampson's great report on the burial of the Unknown Soldier, which won Sampson the Pulitzer prize, moved Ernie to tears. It gave him a goal to work toward. It was while he was at the university that Japan's Waseda University invited a baseball team from an American college, and Pyle shipped along as a bellhop. After college (he neglected to graduate though he always meant to go back and finish the few necessary credits), Pyle went to work for the La Porte (Indiana) *Herald.* That apprenticeship was followed by a job on the Washington (D.C.) *Daily News.*

In the summer of 1926 he married Geraldine Siebolds, a Minnesota girl who was a clerk in the Civil Service Commission in Washington. She became "that girl who rides beside me," famous to his readers. They quit their jobs in 1926 and toured the country in a Ford roadster, finishing up in New York, where Pyle worked briefly for the *Evening World* and the *Evening Post*. He soon returned to Washington and his old paper, the *News*, and from 1928 to 1932 he wrote a column of aviation news. He knew all the great fliers of that period, and he developed at this time his skill in presenting the personal, human side of events. In 1932, he became managing editor of the *News*; but at the end of three years he persuaded the paper to let him write a column as a wandering correspondent. The column began on August 10, 1935 and was published in all Scripps-Howard papers.

Ernie Pyle and his wife Jerry crossed the country thirty-five times. They saw each state in the Union at least three times, traveling by plane, horseback, mule back, boat, truck and train. His search for material took him to Canada, Hawaii, Alaska and through the South American countries. He wrote of the leper colony at Molokai and of Devil's Island in French Guiana. He rode a freight truck day and night from Denver to Los Angeles and a bus from San Francisco to New York. In 1941 he was in London, and his account of the London air bombardment of January 1st excited so much attention that readers and critics believed it the "best column of the year." A few months later his book *Ernie Pyle in England* was published. It is in this year—1941—that he was described as "an inconspicuous little man with thinning hair and a shy, pixy face."

He joined the combined American-British expedition in North Africa, lived with the soldiers, sharing their rations and their hardships in camp and on the march. More than any other American war correspondent he became the sympathetic spokesman for the common soldier and he was beloved by all. He was called "Ernie" by privates and generals alike. Congress passed the "Ernie Pyle" bill raising the base pay of combat soldiers ten dollars a month. In 1943 his African dispatches were reprinted in a book, *Here Is Your War*, which immediately became a best seller. "This is not a book of memories, revived and polished on a sunny terrace in Connecticut. It was written behind rocks scarred by snipers' bullets, in pup tents, foxholes and dugouts," wrote the New York *Times*. "It concerns only what came within the range of Pyle's vision." Edward Weeks said in the *Atlantic Monthly*: "It took weeks of reading his daily dispatches to realize that he was assembling a magnificent mosaic right before our eyes."

After several months with the 5th American army in Italy, Pyle returned to England in early 1944 to await the invasion of France. Going into Normandy on D-Day plus one, he remained with the American forces until after the liberation of Paris and then returned to America for a rest in Albuquerque, N.M., which had been his home for several years. During this period his third book, *Brave Men*, was published. Early in 1945 Pyle joined the campaign in the Pacific with the U.S. Navy and Marine Corps. He was ashore in the Ryukyus Islands—on Ie-jima —not far from Japan, with the 77th infantry division when he met his death by Japanese machine-gun fire. He was buried on the island.

He was awarded posthumously the U.S. Medal for Merit, and his name was given to a Liberty ship, a B-29 Superfortress and a large theatre in Tokyo. An honorary M.A. degree offered him by Harvard University was never conferred, as death intervened. In 1944 he had been awarded a Pulitzer prize for distinguished correspondence.

His Pacific dispatches were published in book form, posthumously, in 1946 as *Last Chapter*. And another collection, this time of his pre-war writings, was also published posthumously, *Home Country*.

He and his wife were divorced in 1942, but were remarried by proxy while Pyle was in North Africa.

PRINCIPAL WORKS: Ernie Pyle in England, 1941; Here Is Your War, 1943; Brave Men, 1944; Last Chapter, 1946; Home Country, 1947.

ABOUT: Barnett, L. K. Writing on Life; Brown, J. M. Seeing Things; Miller, L. G. Ernie Pyle Album, Story of Ernie Pyle; Pyle, E. T. Last Chapter; Coronet April 1950; Current Biography 1941; National Cyclopedia of American Biography (1947).

"QUEEN, ELLERY" (pseudonym of Frederic Dannay, October 20, 1905- and Manfred B. Lee, January 11, 1905-). For biographical sketch and list of earlier works and references, see TWENTIETH CENTURY AUTHORS, 1942.

* * *

Ellery Queen celebrated his silver anniversary in 1954 with the publication of *The Glass Village*, a mystery novel in which, incidentally, Queen himself (for the first time) does not appear. On this occasion, collaborators Dannay and Lee summed up their accomplishments as eighty books, of which twenty-eight were novels and the others collections of stories, anthologies, juveniles, and editorial projects. This count does not include their operation of *Ellery Queen's Mystery Magazine,* founded in 1941, one of their most successful ventures (in it they have published seven Nobel and seventeen Pulitzer prize winners in works of detection, crime and mystery). Their method of work is a simple and efficient one. They told an interviewer in 1954: "One of us does the plotting, the other does the writing. It doesn't make any difference which. . . . We kind of try to top each other. It's a collaboration, but also a competition."

Manfred B. Lee, "heavy-set and jovial," lives in Connecticut. He married Kaye Brinker in 1942 and has seven children. Frederic Dannay, "slight and quiet," lives with his family in Westchester.

ADDITIONAL WORKS: *As "Ellery Queen"*—(ed.) The Detective Short Story: A Bibliography, 1942; (ed.) Sporting Blood: Great Sports Detective Stories, 1942; There Was an Old Woman, 1943; (ed.) The Misadventures of Sherlock Holmes, 1944; (ed.) 101 Years' Entertainment: Great Detective Stories, 1841-1941, 1945; The Murderer is a Fox, 1945; (ed.) Rogues' Gallery: Great Criminals of Modern Fiction, 1945; (ed.) Great Women Detectives and Criminals, 1946; (ed.) Queen's Awards, 1946—; (ed.) To the Queen's Taste, 1946; (ed.) Murder by Experts, 1947; (ed.) Twentieth Century Detective Stories, 1948; Ten Days' Wonder, 1948; Cat of Many Tails, 1949; Double, Double, 1950; The White Elephant Mystery, 1950; (ed.) The Literature of Crime, 1950; Calendar of Crime (short stories) 1952; The King Is Dead, 1952; The Scarlet Letters, 1953; The Glass Village, 1954; Queen's Bureau of Investigation, 1954. *By Frederic Dannay, as "Daniel Nathan"*—Golden Summer, 1953.

ABOUT: Boucher, A. Ellery Queen: A Double Profile (pamphlet); Life November 22, 1943; New York Times Book Review August 15, 1954; Publishers' Weekly November 20, 1943.

*QUENEAU, RAYMOND (February 21, 1903-   ), French poet and novelist, was born in Le Havre. He was educated at the *lycée* in Le Havre and went on to Paris for his university studies, taking his degree in philosophy. Queneau worked for a time in a bank, but he was soon drawn into a literary career in Paris. He joined the publishing firm of Editions Gallimard—with which he is still associated—as a reader. Meanwhile he had become interested in the then flourishing surrealist movement, contributing to the journal *La Révolution Surréaliste,* and surrealism left a strong imprint upon all his later work.

* kě nŏ'

Queneau's first book appeared in 1933, but it was not until the publication of his autobiographical verse-narrative *Chêne et Chien* (Oak and Dog) in 1937 that he made his mark as a writer of real distinction and originality. He is most admired as a wit—bold, impudent, and brilliant. What strikes his readers is his seemingly limitless invention and his inexhaustible erudition. He is a scientist and a mathematician as well as a poet. In his *Petite Cosmogonie Portative* (A Little Portable Cosmogony) he attempted to survey in verse the development of life, from the first atom through the coming of man and the machine, using the epic form and the neo-classical alexandrine line. It was an audacious undertaking, but one which he managed to carry through with extraordinary agility. However serious his subject matter, he retains a lightness of touch in his verse as though (as Maurice Saillet pointed out in *Mercure de France*) he were writing first to amuse himself and only second for an audience. His *Exercices de Style,* a retelling in some ninety different rhetorical styles of a single simple incident, for example, was described in the London *Times Literary Supplement* as a work of "pure wit." For some readers, the reviewer continued, such things "leave an after-taste of sophistication which irritates the palate. But the book as a whole is both original and funny." Most of Queneau's verse is bantering, burlesque, even grotesque. Some of it has been put to music. But like many a wit and satirist, he has at times startled his readers with lovely and simple lyrics written primarily for children.

The same audacity and ingenuity that distinguishes Queneau's verse has also shaped his fiction. He is at one and the same time a light and a serious novelist. His novels have been found deficient in form, abstract rather than dramatic, mocking and ironic. But they have also been praised for their vitality, their precision, their "mastery of understatement." The first of his novels to be published in English was *A Hard Winter,* the story of a love affair between a French army officer and an English girl during World War I. The *Times Literary Supplement* found that in spite of a poor translation, "an effect of considerable artistry is none the less conveyed to the reader." The only one of his works published in the United

States to date is *Skin of Dreams* (in an excellent translation by H. J. Kaplan), which the New York *Times* described as "a mixture of fairy tale and off-color story."

Queneau, a stocky, dark-haired man, is married and lives in Paris. In addition to his creative writing, he has edited a number of works of philosophy and has written on art criticism and many other subjects for *La Nouvelle Revue Française, Les Temps Modernes,* and other journals. His own literary preferences give some inkling of his unpredictable and stimulating personality: "My favorite poets are Rutebeuf, Villon, Boileau, Chénier, Péguy. I have imitated them with all my heart (also several others) and I hope that this is apparent in these poems, where it is a question of a little of all, it doesn't matter what, of death, for instance."

PRINCIPAL WORKS IN ENGLISH TRANSLATION: A Hard Winter, 1948; Skin of Dreams, 1948; Pierrot, 1950; *Introduction to* Miró *in* Masterpieces of French Painting Series, 1952.

ABOUT: Dictionnaire Biographique Français Contemporain; France Illustration March 24, 1951; Mercure de France February 1951.

QUENNELL, CHARLES HENRY BOURNE. See QUENNELL, M. C.

QUENNELL, Mrs. MARJORIE (COURTNEY) (1884-). For biographical sketch and list of works and references, see TWENTIETH CENTURY AUTHORS, 1942.

* * *

Mrs. Quennell was curator of the Geffrye Museum in London until 1941. Since then she has done some work as an illustrator and continues to paint for recreation. She was in the United States in 1950, living in Melrose, Mass. At present her home is in Lewes, Sussex. TWENTIETH CENTURY AUTHORS, 1942 incorrectly stated that she had only one son, the writer Peter Quennell, and a daughter. Another son was killed in World War II.

QUENNELL, PETER COURTNEY (March 9, 1905-). For biographical sketch and list of earlier works and references, see TWENTIETH CENTURY AUTHORS, 1942.

* * *

Peter Quennell edited the *Cornhill Magazine* from 1944 to 1951. He also edits *History Today* and contributes reviews to the "Books in General" column of the *New Statesman and Nation.* Quennell's literary-

biographical essays have won him high praise among both English and American readers. Charles J. Rolo describes him in the *Atlantic* as "a man of taste, intelligence, and wit, who wears his learning urbanely and writes with fluency and grace." V. S. Pritchett wrote of his *The Profane Virtues,* studies of four great eighteenth century figures (Boswell, Gibbon, Sterne, Wilkes): "Mr. Quennell stands at a measured distance from his models at just the right point between formality and intimacy. His grasp of character is complete, his response to life immediate, his judgment is sane, without being phlegmatic." Quennell lives in London.

ADDITIONAL WORKS: Time Exposure (with C. Beaton) 1941; Profane Virtues: Four Studies of the Eighteenth Century (in England: Four Portraits) 1945; John Ruskin: Portrait of a Prophet, 1949; The Singular Preference, 1953.

QUICK, HERBERT (October 23, 1861-May 10, 1925). For biographical sketch and list of works and references, see TWENTIETH CENTURY AUTHORS, 1942.

*QUILLER-COUCH, Sir ARTHUR THOMAS ("Q") (November 21, 1863-May 12, 1944). For biographical sketch and list of earlier works and references, see TWENTIETH CENTURY AUTHORS, 1942.

* * *

Sir Arthur Thomas Quiller-Couch died at his home in Fowey, Cornwall, at eighty, two months after he had been injured by a jeep while walking near his home.

Versatile and prolific, he published more than twenty novels, twelve volumes of short stories, twelve volumes of literary studies, six books for children and two volumes of verse, in addition to the several anthologies he edited and a quantity of miscellaneous journalistic prose.

Criticized by some as a "mere sentimental popularizer of literature," "Q" was praised by the London *Times* for having, in his teaching, "opened many closed doors, and freed literature, as an educational subject, from pedantic philology."

His biographer and editor, F. Brittain, speaks of the high standards he maintained in his own writing, and adds, "His chief contribution to English letters was his style, in which there lives again the chivalrous, hospitable 'Q' who loved bright colors, dressed with great care, was accurate but not pedantic, and refused ever to be hurried."

* kwil′ẽr kōōch′

ADDITIONAL WORKS: Cambridge Lectures (Everyman's Library) 1943; Memories and Opinions (unfinished autobiography) 1944; Shorter Stories, 1944; Q Anthology, 1949.

ABOUT: "Q": Memories and Opinions; Brittain, F. Arthur Quiller-Couch; Willey, B. Q Tradition; London Times May 13, 1944; New York Times May 13, 1944; Spectator May 19, 1944; Time December 6, 1948.

QUINN, ARTHUR HOBSON (February 9, 1875-). For autobiographical sketch and list of earlier works and references, see TWENTIETH CENTURY AUTHORS, 1942.

* * *

Arthur Hobson Quinn retired as John Welsh Centennial Professor at the University of Pennsylvania in 1945, but has remained on the faculty as emeritus professor and special lecturer. He was joint editor with Edward O'Neill of a two-volume collection of the works of Edgar Allan Poe, and, with K. B. Murdock, Clarence Gohdes, and George F. Whicher, wrote and edited *The Literature of the American People,* which received a medal for the best book of 1951 from the Athenaeum Club of Philadelphia. Professor Quinn lives in Bala-Cynwyd, Pa.

ADDITIONAL WORKS: Poe, E. A. Complete Poems and Stories (ed. with E. O'Neill) 1946; A Treasury of Edith Wharton (ed.) 1950; The Literature of the American People, 1951.

ABOUT: Hoehn, M. (ed.) Catholic Authors, I.

QUINTERO. See ALVÁREZ QUINTERO

RABINDRANATH TAGORE. See TAGORE

RABINOWITZ, SOLOMON J. ("Shalom Aleichem"*) (February 18, 1859-May 13, 1916). For biographical sketch and list of works and references, see TWENTIETH CENTURY AUTHORS, 1942.

* * *

The continued and ever-increasing popularity of the writings of Sholom Aleichem is testified to by the number of English translations and studies of his works that have appeared in recent years. In 1943 Maurice Samuel published *The World of Sholom Aleichem,* a picture of Jewish life in Russia in the late nineteenth century, based on Aleichem's writing, which introduced the author to a large non-Jewish public. Subsequently, translations of some of his short stories and novels again demonstrated his warm humor

* shälōm' (or shŏ'lĕm') älä'kĕm

and his rich but never self-pitying sympathy. Through his work, Marvin Lowenthal wrote in a review of his *The Old Country,* "we can understand why his own people by the millions have laughed and cried and sworn by his name." In 1953 a group of actors offered a small off-Broadway production called *The World of Sholom Aleichem* which consisted of three short plays about Jewish life. Only one of these was by Aleichem, but the title and the spirit of the whole production were a tribute to him. This modest theatrical undertaking proved to be one of the greatest successes of the season and played in New York and in Chicago for many months, and later in London.

ADDITIONAL WORKS IN ENGLISH TRANSLATION: The Old Country, 1946; Inside Kasrilevke, 1948; Tevye's Daughters, 1949; A Sholom Aleichem Panorama (ed. M. Graftstein) 1949; Wandering Star, 1952; The Adventures of Mottel, the Cantor's Son, 1953; The Great Fair, 1955.

ABOUT: Columbia Dictionary of Modern European Literature; Samuel, M. The World of Sholom Aleichem; Commentary August, September 1946, December 1949, October 1950, September, December 1953; New Republic April 6, 1953.

*RADIGUET, RAYMOND (June 18, 1903-December 12, 1923). For biographical sketch and list of works and references, see TWENTIETH CENTURY AUTHORS, 1942.

* * *

Raymond Radiguet's sensitive novel of a love affair between an adolescent school boy and a young married woman, *Devil in the Flesh,* was made into a distinguished motion picture in France in 1948, with Gerard Philippe and Micheline Presle in the leading roles. The film was very successful in America, and its release stimulated new interest in the writings of this remarkable boy, of whom François Mauriac wrote: "Such as it is, his work is enough for us, his elders; the cause is clear, that child was a master."

ADDITIONAL WORKS IN ENGLISH TRANSLATION: Count d'Orgel (trans. as The Count's Ball, 1929) 1953.

ABOUT: Cocteau, J. *Preface to* Count d'Orgel; Columbia Dictionary of Modern European Literature; Huxley, A. *Preface to* Devil in the Flesh (1949); Mauriac, F. Men I Hold Great; Cornhill Spring 1947; France Illustration January 10, 1953; Time March 30, 1953.

* rà dē gĕ'

RAGLAN, FITZ ROY RICHARD SOMERSET, 4th Baron (June 10, 1885-), English folklorist and anthropologist, better known as Lord Ragland, was born in London, the eldest son of the third Baron Rag-

lan and Lady Ethel Jemina Ponsonby. His education and early career cut close to the pattern of his family tradition and his class

—Eton and Sandhurst, the Grenadier Guards, service in Hong Kong, 1912 and 1913, in the Sudan, 1913 to 1918, and in Transjordan, 1918 to 1921—but his later interests and his writings are most certainly his own; original, controversial and, for a member of the British aristocracy, mildy eccentric.

When he was in the Sudan, Lord Raglan became interested in cultural anthropology, writing a number of articles on the Lotuko tribe. On his return to England in 1921 after the death of his father, he retired from active service and divided his time between the duties of the baronetcy and his increasingly profound interest in anthropology. This was an interest sharply critical in edge, more apt perhaps in cutting to pieces some of the whole-cloth assumptions of earlier scholars than in fitting together new evidence. He did, however, in his most important work, *The Hero,* amass a vast amount of valuable material to support his bold thesis that the figures and events of myth have no basis in history, but are rather the actor and the acts in a universal dramatic ritual.

Since 1926 Lord Raglan has been living at Cefntilla Court, some 1100 acres presented by public subscription as a memorial to the first Lord Raglan, a hero of the Crimean war. Here he writes on anthropological and political subjects, takes part in county affairs, and from time to time journeys the 150 miles to London for debates in the House of Lords. He is married to the Hon. Julia Hamilton and has two sons and two daughters.

As a member of the Royal Anthropological Institute, Lord Raglan is a frequent contributor to its monthly journal, *Man.* He has published half a dozen books, two of which, *The Hero* and *Jocasta's Crime,* a study of incest, have had considerable attention in this country, less from anthropologist than from critics and poets interested in the relations between myth, ritual and basic patterns of human thinking. Stanley Edgar Hyman considers his *The Hero,* a study of traditional heroes in various cultures, "one of the most important and little-appreciated books of our time."

Raglan's writings are not only learned, but extraordinarily witty, and can be read for their intellectual entertainment value as well as for their contributions to folklore. He is, as the *London Times* has called him, a kind of "Till Eulenspiegel, deftly at work among the doctors."

PRINCIPAL WORKS: Jocasta's Crime, An Anthropological Study, 1933; The Science of Peace, 1933; If I were Dictator, 1934; The Hero: A Study in Tradition, Myth and Drama, 1936; How Came Civilization?, 1939; Death and Rebirth, 1945; The Origins of Religion, 1949; Monmouthshire Houses (with Sir Cyril Fox) Vol. I, 1951; Vol. II, 1953.

ABOUT: Hyman, S. E. The Armed Vision.

RAHV, PHILIP (March 10, 1908-), American critic and editor, was born at Kupin in the Ukraine. His family emigrated to America while he was still a boy in his teens (1922), settling in Providence, R.I., where he went to high school. Always fascinated by books and ideas, he was an early rebel against his provincial background, and emerged in the Thirties as a left-wing theorist and polemicist.

Sylvia Salmi

Rahv began his career in New York City during the depression, supporting himself with various odd jobs including a brief fling as a car salesman, and a span on the W.P.A. writers' project. During this period he contributed articles and reviews to magazines like the *Nation, New Republic, New Masses, New Leader,* and the *Southern Review.* In 1933, as a member of the John Reed Club, he was one of the original founders of the magazine *Partisan Review,* which was called by T. S. Eliot, a decade later, "America's leading literary magazine."

The first issue of *Partisan Review* appeared in February 1934: in it the editors dedicated themselves to revolutionary aesthetics, Marxist thinking, and good will toward the Soviet Union. The Communist Party, although it did not finance the magazine (officially it was a John Reed Club publication), dominated the editorial board. In the months following, however, the editorial battles were increasingly fierce between those who could and those who could not accept the "cultural party line." In this battle, Rahv and his friend and co-editor William Phillips were allies, and as they not only did most of the actual work of getting out the magazine, but also organized the lectures and parties which raised funds to finance it, in the end they gained control. When in 1936 radical movements all over the world were shocked by the tragic spectacle of the first Moscow Trials, *Partisan Review* suspended publication; and when it reappeared in late 1937, it was with a "completely renovated editorial staff and policy." "Our own politics at the time," write Rahv and Phillips in a statement in *The Partisan Reader* (1946), "might be summed up as a kind of independent and critical Marxism: independent of all party organizations and programs, and critical insofar as we were inclined to re-examine the entire course of socialism in order to understand its present plight. It goes without saying that we were intransigently anti-Stalinist."

For twenty years *Partisan Review* has been an important forum for American intellectuals. In its pages have appeared such symposia as *The New Failure of Nerve* (1943), *The Future of Socialism* (1947), *The State of American Writing* (1948), *Religion and the Intellectuals* (1950). And it has brought many young writers to the attention of publishers, readers, and critics—poets such as Elizabeth Bishop, Delmore Schwartz, Randall Jarrell, Karl Shapiro, and Robert Lowell; novelists such as Eleanor Clark, Mary McCarthy, Isaac Rosenfeld, Jean Stafford, and Saul Bellow.

In 1949 Rahv published *Image and Idea*, a collection of his critical essays about writers—James, Hawthorne, Tolstoy, Kafka, Dostoevsky, and others. As an historical critic of literature (primarily fiction), Rahv emphasizes the social, cultural, and intellectual milieu which influences art and is in turn influenced by it. This is an active, living relationship, he has said, and too many critics tend to consider poems, stories, and novels as the dead works of dead men.

About *Image and Idea*, Richard Chase wrote in the *Nation*, "what one admires about Rahv's critical method is his abundant ability to use such techniques as Marxism, Freudian psychology, anthropology, and existentialism toward his critical ends without shackling himself to any of them"; and R. G. Davis in the New York *Times* said, "The way in which he has tried to comprehend his own very representative political and ethical evolution through a reassessment of American and European writers has made *Image and Idea* one of the most clarifying of recent books of criticism."

Rahv has been employed as a literary consultant by several publishing firms, and as editor of *The Great Short Novels of Henry James* and *The Bostonians* was one of the persons responsible for the James revival. He has taught in the Adult Extension division of New York University, and is one of the senior fellows of the School of Letters of Indiana University. In 1950 he was awarded a Guggenheim fellowship in criticism.

Heavy-set, with a powerful personality, Rahv is a good lecturer, a cogent and forceful arguer. In 1941 he married Nathalie Swan, an architect, and they live in New York City.

PRINCIPAL WORKS: *Criticism*—Image and Idea: Fourteen Essays on Literary Themes, 1949; *Editor* —The Great Short Novels of Henry James, 1944; The Bostonians by Henry James, 1945; The Short Novels of Tolstoy, 1946; The Partisan Reader: Ten Years of Partisan Review: 1934-1944 (co-editor W. Phillips) 1946; Discovery of Europe: The Story of American Experience in the Old World, 1947; Great Russian Short Novels, 1951; The New Partisan Reader, 1953 (co-editor W. Phillips); Stories in the Modern Manner, 1954 (co-editor W. Phillips).

RAINE, KATHLEEN (June 14, 1908-), English poet, writes: "I was born in one of the ugliest of the London suburbs. My father was then the English master at a new secondary school, newly come from Durham University, where he had won for himself an education, by means of scholarships, which his father, a coal miner, could not have given him. My mother's family was Scots, and much of my childhood, including most of the First World War, was spent with my maternal grandparents and with an aunt who was, like my mother and most of her sisters, village schoolmistress in a remote hamlet in Northumberland, north of Hadrian's Wall. (I myself was intended for the same profession.) The noble country and dignified way of life among the still feudal community of farmers and shepherds of Northumberland was then, and has since remained for me, the epitome of all that I have ever loved. Since the age of ten, when I finally returned to the suburb, I have lived in exile.

"My father devoted his leisure to preaching and lecturing in the non-conformist churches of the district; but to me the suburb was nothing more than an image of life at its vulgar worst, to set beside my memories of the Scottish border-country that I loved. I had only one thought—to escape; and since I could not return to the past, I proceeded, on scholarships, to Girton College, Cambridge, where I read natural sciences, specializing in botany and zoology. There my first poems were published in the undergraduate magazine *Experiment,* edited (amongst others, since distinguished) by William Empson, J. Bronowski, and Humphrey Jennings. These, and others then and now my friends, were pupils of Professor I. A. Richards, then at the height of his fame. There was no sharp distinction at that time in Cambridge between scientists and students of the humanities, and I believe that even the least of us (amongst whom I number myself) preserved to this day a certain dispassionate clarity of thought, or, at all events, a respect for such thought.

"After Cambridge I married Charles Madge (poet and now professor of sociology) but left him soon after, retiring, with my son and daughter at the beginning of the Second World War, to the Border country, where my neighbors were Michael Roberts and his wife, Janet Adam-Smith, to whom I owe much. Here I wrote the poems published in *Stone and Flower.* Financial necessity drove me back to London, but I have written almost no poems there, seizing, however, every opportunity of returning to Cumberland, Northumberland, and Scotland, where alone I am able to feel myself anything other than an exile or a caged wild creature. My mind, such as it is, and the friendships of the mind, belong to Cambridge; but my imagination loves nothing and no one outside that wild and remote country to which I hope someday to be allowed to return, when all my debts to life elsewhere have been paid.

"My debt to the suburbs I try to repay by lecturing to evening class students at Morley College during most winters. The years since Cambridge have been a dream of unreality and suffering, for the most part self-caused. But that suffering, together with the beauty of the world I knew as a child, and to which I have since several times been permitted to return has alone made me a poet, if poet I may be called. I am at present working on the symbolic thought of William Blake. If I live to be old, I would wish to study Vedantic and Buddhist metaphysics, but that may never be."

* * *

In 1943 Kathleen Raine wrote in an essay: "Facts we know enough. We must understand rather states of mind." As a scientist as well as a poet, she knows the divisive and destructive consequences of present-day knowledge—"Knowledge dissolves contours," she wrote, "but only faith creates them." Her verse, as Evan Owen points out in *Poetry* magazine, "is a revelation of the poet's search for the faith and the love that will integrate; that will weld all the broken particles of modern life into the perfection of a rose, a tree." Her technique and craftsmanship have been highly praised, but it is mainly for the mystical and visionary qualities of her poetry, its pure immediacy, what Kimon Friar described as "a crystalline fire which recalls some of the early poems of William Blake," that she is regarded as one of the most distinguished of contemporary English poets. Dudley Fitts wrote of her volume *The Pythoness*: "She is a craftsman of a very high order; and if she were no more than this, she would still be a refreshing phenomenon in an age of slick, mechanical technique. She is her own Pythoness: a seer."

PRINCIPAL WORKS: Stone and Flower, 1943; Living in Time, 1946; The Pythoness, and Other Poems, 1949; The Year One, 1951.

ABOUT: Rexroth, K. (ed.) The New British Poets; Poetry April 1952.

RAINE, WILLIAM MAC LEOD (June 22, 1871-July 25, 1954). For biographical sketch and list of earlier works and references, see TWENTIETH CENTURY AUTHORS, 1942.

* * *

William MacLeod Raine died of a heart attack in a Denver hospital. He was eighty-three.

Until shortly before his death he continued writing his extremely popular Westerns, "packed with fast action, suspense and excitement and surpassingly well written," in the words of G. W. Harris, who placed him "in the very front rank of writers of Western fiction."

ADDITIONAL WORKS: Damyank, 1942; Hell and High Water, 1943; Courage Stout, 1944; Who Wants to Live Forever, 1945; Clattering Hoofs, 1946; Cry Murder, 1947; This Nettle Danger (in England: Top Rider) 1947; Bandit Trail (in England: Outlaw Trail, 1948) 1949; He Threw a Long Shadow, 1949; Ranger's Luck, 1950; Saddletramp, 1950; Jingling Spurs (in England: His Spurs A-Jingling) 1951; Saddlebum, 1951; Challenge to Danger, 1952; Justice Comes to Tomahawk, 1952; Dry Bones in the Valley, 1953.

ABOUT: New York Times July 26, 1954.

RALEIGH, Sir WALTER ALEX-ANDER (September 5, 1861-May 13, 1922). For biographical sketch and list of works and references, see TWENTIETH CENTURY AUTHORS, 1942.

* * *

ABOUT: Gordon, G. S. Lives of Authors.

"RAMÓN." See GÓMEZ DE LA SERNA, R.

*RAMUZ, CHARLES FERDINAND (1878-May 23, 1947), French-Swiss novelist, was born in Cully, Switzerland, a small town on Lake Geneva in the canton of Vaud. He studied at the University of Lausanne, in 1902 moving to Paris where he lived in obscurity for twelve years. During this time he wrote four volumes of poetry, eight novels and two collections of short stories, but these did not attract attention beyond a small circle of his friends and admirers. As he explained in *Raison d'Être*, published in 1914, he made the momentous decision to return to Cully. and it was there that he began his long and successful career as a writer.

After 1914 he wrote over twenty volumes of fiction, stories of the peasants, winegrowers, small craftsmen, fishermen, and others of his own canton. Ramuz readily admitted the presence in his novels of regional peculiarities of language, and conceded that the word order is often logical rather than grammatical. His first book to appear in English translation, *The Reign of the Evil One*, was compared to Synge's *The Playboy of the Western World*. The New York *Times* remarked on the author's "talent as a narrator" and his "sympathetic understanding of both the inner and the outer existence of that Swiss peasantry which is so little known to the majority of American readers." The New York *Herald Tribune* objected that after the first chapters "Ramuz, the metaphysician and mystic, banishes Ramuz the novelist. From what promised to be a novel evolves chaotic morality."

In *The End of All Men*, published in English in 1944 with an introduction by Denis de Rougemont, several reviewers found

* rà müz′

only "a series of disconnected scenes played by unrelated characters," but A. H. Fuller in the Springfield *Republican* said: "Reflection on the book will bring conviction of its imaginativeness, inventiveness and power." B. R. Redman in the *Weekly Book Review* described the "famous Ramuz style . . . with its syntactical eccentricities, its provincialism, archaisms, neologism, ellipses, missing verb and Biblical echoes," and congratulated the translator, Allan Ross Macdougall, for rendering into English the style of a man "who would write like a painter."

In 1947, at the age of sixty-nine, Ramuz died in Switzerland following an operation. He had been considered for the Nobel prize in 1945.

PRINCIPAL WORKS IN ENGLISH TRANSLATION: The Reign of the Evil One, 1922; Beauty on Earth, 1929; The End of All Men (in England: Triumph of Death) 1944; When the Mountain Fell, 1947; What Is Man (sel. from three of the author's works) 1948; Life of Samuel Belet, 1951.

ABOUT: Columbia Dictionary of Modern European Literature; Emporium July 1947; French Review March 1948; Modern Language Review October 1947; New York Times May 25, 1947; Nineteenth Century and After September 1947.

RAND, AYN, American novelist, was born in Petrograd, Russia. "When she first arrived in America," wrote *House and Garden*, "Russian-born Ayn Rand stood spellbound before Manhattan's steel-sprung skyscrapers. Later in California, she chose to live and write in an all-steel house, elemental in form, dynamic in color. Surrounded by flowering shrubs and exotic trees, the house inside is peacock blue." Miss Rand's most famous work, *The Fountainhead*, a novel published in 1943, had as its hero an architect and iconoclast.

"When I am questioned about myself," she wrote in a Letter to the Readers of *The Fountainhead*, "I am tempted to say, paraphrasing Roark: 'Don't ask me about my family, my childhood, my friends or my feelings. Ask me about the things I think.' It is the content of a person's brain, not the accidental details of his life, that determines his character. My own character is in the pages of *The Fountainhead*....

"I decided to be a writer at the age of nine—it was a specific conscious decision—I remember the day and the hour. I did not start by trying to describe the folks next door—but by inventing people who did things the folks next door would never do. . . . I left home when I was quite young and have been on my own ever since. My life has been 'single-tracked,' or anything anyone wishes to call a life consciously devoted to a conscious purpose. I have no hobbies. I have few friends. I do not like to 'go out.' I am unbearable—to myself and others—when I stay too long away from my work. Nothing else has ever mattered to me too much. The only exception to that last line is my husband, Frank O'Connor. *The Fountainhead* is dedicated to him. He is my best proof that people such as I write about can and do exist in real life.

"I have never studied writing nor taken any formal course in literature. I did have a college education, but whatever I learned I had to learn by myself and in my own way. I did not attempt to write professionally until I knew what I was doing and felt that I was ready. I sold the first screen story, the first stage play and the first novel I ever wrote. The screen story was called *Red Pawn* and was bought by Universal Pictures. The play was *The Night of January 16th*, which ran on Broadway in the season 1935-36. The novel was *We, the Living*, published in 1936.

"Yes, I've had a hard struggle before, between and after these jobs. I had to earn my own living before I could start writing. After I started, I had to earn my living whenever the money I made by writing was exhausted. I did all sorts of odd jobs: I have been a waitress, an office clerk, a reader for film companies. I could not concentrate on a business career, but had to take such jobs as could be held temporarily and would leave me free to write in my spare time."

We, the Living described three young people of independent spirit in Soviet Russia who are destroyed by the totalitarian dictatorship. Of *The Fountainhead* she said: "It was rejected by twelve publishers who declared that it had no commercial possibilities, it would not sell, it was 'too intellectual,' it was 'too unconventional,' it went against every alleged popular trend." Its popularity came from "single individual readers who discovered it of their own choice, who read it on their own initiative and recommended it on their own judgment." The book aroused much controversy both on an intellectual and on an artistic level. "Its background seems authentic enough," wrote August Derleth, "and Miss Rand pursues her thesis without devia-

tion and with good characterization and enough action to satisfy even the most exacting. . . . [Yet] Miss Rand's writing manner . . . is offensively pedestrian, pockmarked with short, clipped staccato sentences." Lorine Pruette in the New York *Times* took quite a different view: "Ayn Rand is a writer of great power. She has a subtle and ingenious mind and the capacity of writing brilliantly, beautifully, bitterly. . . . It is a long but absorbing story."

PRINCIPAL WORKS: The Night of January 16th; a comedy-drama in three acts, 1936; We, the Living, 1936; Anthem, 1938; The Fountainhead, 1943.

ABOUT: Warfel, H. R. American Novelists of Today; House and Garden August 1949; Saturday Review of Literature February 22, 1947.

RANDALL, JAMES GARFIELD (June 24, 1881-February 20, 1953), American historian, died of leukemia, at seventy-one, in Champaign, Ill. Several months before his death, he wrote to the editors of this volume: "I was born in Indianapolis, was graduated from Butler College, and studied at the University of Chicago for the doctor's degree in history, which was granted in 1911. Among those I well remember at the University of Chicago were William Rainey Harper and, with much affection, William E. Dodd. Since 1920 I have been on the faculty of the University of Illinois, having served prior to that as teacher at Illinois College, University of Michigan, Syracuse University, Butler College, Roanoke College (Salem, Va.), and Richmond College (Richmond, Va.). To this may be added summer teaching appointments at Chicago, Duke, Pennsylvania, Columbia, Harvard, and the University of California at Los Angeles.

"This sounds like an academic record, but I do not attach to myself any such term as 'professional historian.' One does not speak of a professional physicist. It is sufficient to say physicist or geologist, and so through the various branches of learning. Though not assuming that it is deserved, I will be content with the word 'historian' without any qualifying adjective. Not all of my work has been limited to the campus. In 1918-19 I worked on the staff of the United States Shipping Board and I have served as president of the Mississippi Valley Historical Association

(1939-40), the Illinois State Historical Society (1945-46), and the American Historical Association (1951-52).

"My writing has been chiefly concerned with Lincoln and the Civil War. Elaborate masses of manuscript and published material have been sifted, after which the effort has been to put the result in presentable form. So voluminous has been the material that, in order to spare the reader, a great deal has been left in the inkpot. In interpreting Lincoln there has been no mere repetition of familiar patterns. In cases where a careful study of the evidence plainly requires it, the treatment in my books has run counter to established popular notions. Lincoln has not been pictured as a provocative war maker in 1861; Britain has not been represented as 'siding with the Confederacy'; and the Herndon version of the Ann Rutledge tale has been subjected to critical historical analysis. Emphasis has been placed upon Lincoln's liberal views, akin to those of Jefferson. My wife, Ruth Painter Randall, a Virginian, has prepared a life of Mrs. Lincoln under the title *Mary Lincoln: Biography of a Marriage* (1953). I have contributed articles to a number of magazines, including the *American Historical Review*, the New York *Times Magazine*, and the *North American Review*.

"I live in a small five-room apartment in Urbana, Ill., in an old part of town near the University campus. Since the apartment is too small for books, it holds only those that remain after much shifting. A study room in the University Library holds other books and files. By the use of photostats and microfilms the resources of widely scattered collections over the country, in which I have done research, are made available in Urbana."

* * *

J. G. Randall retired in 1949, after thirty-two years of teaching at the University of Illinois. He was regarded as one of the nation's foremost authorities on the life of Abraham Lincoln. At the time of his death he was at work on the fourth and final volume of his monumental *Lincoln the President*, of which Jay Monaghan wrote in the New York *Times*: "It is a profound study to be read with pleasure and referred to later for unimpeachable facts. Here is the last word on Lincoln's life and problems during his most crucial year." In December 1951 Randall was elected president of the American Historical Association.

PRINCIPAL WORKS: Confiscation of Property During the Civil War, 1913; Constitutional Problems Under Lincoln, 1926; The Civil War and Re-construction, 1937; Lincoln the President: Springfield to Gettysburg (2 vols.) 1945; Midstream (vol. III) 1952; Lincoln the Liberal Statesman, 1947.

ABOUT: Thomas, B. T. Portrait for Posterity: Lincoln and His Biographers; American Historical Review July 1953; New York Herald Tribune Book Review October 12, 1952; New York Times February 22, 1953; Time July 4, 1949.

RANDOLPH, VANCE (February 23, 1892-), American folklorist, writes: "I was born in Kansas, educated in Massachusetts, spent most of my adult life in the Ozark Mountains of Missouri and Arkansas. Carl Sandburg and Margaret Larkin turned my attention to folksongs in the 1920's, and I have been collecting songs and tales and superstitions and wisecracks ever since. I am a Democrat, an Episcopalian, a widower, an Elk, a member of the American Legion. I was once president of the Arkansas Folklore Society. I have written several books and papers about Ozark folklore."

Randolph's birthplace was Pittsburgh, Kan., and he was the son of John Randolph and Theresa (Gould) Randolph. Attending the Kansas State Teachers College, he received a B.A. in 1914, then went on to Clark University (Mass.), where he took an M.A. in 1915. From 1922 to 1924 he pursued graduate studies at the University of Kansas, teaching psychology part of the time. His first book was *The Ozarks*, published in 1931. "Mr. Randolph gives a vivid and veracious account of the customs, industries, manner of life, sports, speech and songs of the Ozark hillman," wrote the *Christian Century*. A more recent volume, *We Always Lie to Strangers*, was called a priceless collection of tall tales. "For thirty years," said the Chicago *Sunday Tribune*, "he has hunted, eaten, fished, loafed and drunk moonshine with the hill people, scribbling bits of their conversation, folklore and superstitions on scraps of paper which he slyly tucked into his pockets as he smoked and listened. This latest book, *We Always Lie to Strangers*, is by far the neatest and best organized of the lot." Carl Carmer has said Randolph is clearly not only a master-teller but a master-listener as well, or he could not have gathered his material so well as he has.

The author has been a scenario writer for Metro-Goldwyn-Mayer (1933-34), an assistant state supervisor of the Federal Writers

Project (1936-37), and a field worker for the Archive of American Folksong, Library of Congress (1941-43). In World War I he was a private in the infantry, and is a member of the Disabled American Veterans as well as of the American Legion. His wife, Marie Wardlaw Wilbur Randolph, whom he married in 1930, is deceased. He lives in Eureka Springs, Ark.

PRINCIPAL WORKS: The Ozarks, 1931; Ozark Mountain Folks, 1932; From an Ozark Holler, 1933; Ozark Outdoors (with G. W. Von Schriltz) 1934; Camp on Wildcat Creek, 1934; Hedwig (novel) 1935; Camp-Meeting Murders (with N. Clemens) 1936; (ed.) An Ozark Anthology, 1940; Ozark Folksongs (4 vols.) 1946-50; Ozark Superstitions, 1947; We Always Lie to Strangers, 1951; (comp.) Who Blowed Up the Church House? 1952; Down in the Holler: A Gallery of Ozark Speech (with G. P. Wilson) 1953; The Devil's Pretty Daughter, and Other Ozark Folk Tales, 1955.

RANSOM, JOHN CROWE (April 30, 1888-). For biographical sketch and list of earlier works and references, see TWENTIETH CENTURY AUTHORS, 1942.

* * *

John Crowe Ransom has been Carnegie professor of poetry at Kenyon College since 1937. He has taught summers at the Kenyon School of English and at the School of Letters of Indiana University, and he has lectured at many American colleges and universities. His major contribution to American criticism has been made through the *Kenyon Review*, which he has edited since 1939. In 1951 he received the Bollingen prize in poetry and the Russell Loines award in literature from the American Institute of Arts and Letters.

Ransom has published only a few new poems in recent years, but they have been sufficient to confirm the critical estimate that he is one of the most accomplished poets of modern times. The late Theodore Spencer wrote of his *Selected Poems* in 1945: "The best poems in this volume remind us again that he occupies an enviable and special place, a permanent place, in contemporary American poetry." And Randall Jarrell observed: "In Ransom's best poems every part is subordinated to the whole, and the whole is realized with astonishing exactness and thoroughness. Their economy, precision, and restraint give the poems, sometimes, an individual but impersonal perfection; and Ransom's feel for the exact convention of a particular poem, the exact demands of a particular situation, has resulted in poems different from each other and everything else, as unified, individualized, and unchangeable as nursery rhymes." It is as a critic, however,

that Ransom is best known and most influential. He is the founder and leader of the Kenyon School—literally a school where the most distinguished critics have come to teach and lecture, and, less literally, that phase of contemporary criticism, usually designated as the "New Criticism," which seeks to study poetry in terms of its structure (the logic of the poem) and its texture (the detail of the poem), quite apart from its historical and social contexts.

On the occasion of Ransom's sixtieth birthday, Allen Tate and Robert Penn Warren collected a series of papers by various critics (many of them his former students) on his achievement, and these were published in an issue of the *Sewanee Review* (Summer 1948). Here Tate wrote: "He has kept before us the example of a classically educated intelligence; he has been unremitting in the zeal and integrity with which he has explored possibilities of an Aristotelian criticism of the poetic disorder of our age."

ADDITIONAL WORKS: A College Primer of Writing, 1943; Selected Poems, 1945; (ed.) The Kenyon Critics: Studies in Modern Literature, 1951.

ABOUT: Hyman, S. E. The Armed Vision; Jarrell, R. Poetry and the Age; Winters, Y. The Anatomy of Nonsense; New Republic August 13, 1945; Poetry January 1946; Sewanee Review Summer 1948, Spring 1950.

RANSOME, ARTHUR (January 18, 1884-). For autobiographical sketch and list of earlier works and references, see TWENTIETH CENTURY AUTHORS, 1942.

* * *

Arthur Ransome has continued the adventures of the children of the Swallows and Amazons series in two more volumes, *The Picts and the Martyrs* and *Great Northern?* Of these lively stories of sailing, adventure, and nature lore, May Lamberton Becker wrote: "Few authors have the satisfaction of knowing that their next book will be a classic, but the saga of Swallows and Amazons is so firmly established in children's literature that a new volume takes at once its place in the canon." The London *Times Literary Supplement* summarizes his work as "firm, intelligent, in tune with twentieth-century mentality and well written."

Ransome has an honorary Litt.D. from the University of Leeds, conferred in 1952. In 1953 he received the C.B.E. (Commander of the Order of the British Empire).

Corrections: TWENTIETH CENTURY AUTHORS, 1942, incorrectly stated that Ransome was unmarried. He was married in 1909 to

Ivy Constance Walker. This marriage was dissolved, and in 1924 he married Eugenia Shelepin. In the list of his principal works, read *Portraits and Speculations* for *Ports and Speculations,* 1913.

ADDITIONAL WORKS: The Picts and the Martyrs, 1943; Great Northern? 1947; (ed.) Slocum, J. Sailing Alone Around the World *and* Voyages of the Liberdade, 1948; (ed.) McMullen, R. T. Down Channel, 1931, 1949; Knight, E. F. The Falcon on the Baltic, 1951; (ed.) Knight, E. F. The Cruise of the Alerte, 1952.

ABOUT: Kunitz, S. J. & Haycraft, H. Junior Book of Authors (rev. ed.); Publishers' Weekly October 27, 1945, December 1, 1945.

*RAPHAELSON, SAMSON (March 30, 1896-   ), American playwright, reports: "I was born in New York City. I lived with my

grandparents in clean and well-fed poverty until I was eleven, when I joined my parents in Chicago. High school in Chicago. Then two years of miscellaneous jobs, including journalism on City News Service. Then four years at the University of Illinois, where it was not difficult to earn one's way. By that time I had written and sold some short stories. I also was quite active in journalism on the Illinois campus.

"After college, I worked with some advertising agencies in Chicago, wrote short stories, taught a semester at my alma mater. Then I went to New York and worked on the *Times* as reporter for almost a year. I left the *Times* to become vice-president of a small advertising agency, where I stayed from 1922 to 1925. In 1925 I wrote *The Jazz Singer.* It was produced with George Jessel in the starring role and ran three years. In 1927 I married Dorothy Wegman. We have a son, Joel, born in 1928, and a daughter, Naomi, born in 1930.

"My savings were wiped out in 1930, and I went to Hollywood, where I wrote many pictures with Ernst Lubitsch and one picture, *Suspicion,* with Alfred Hitchcock. In the meantime, I was writing plays: *Young Love,* produced in 1928 starring Dorothy Gish, *The Magnificent Heel,* produced (briefly) in 1929 by Horace Liveright. In 1939, after having written and lived through the productions of *The Wooden Slipper, Accent on Youth* and *White Man,* I undertook the direction of my play *Skylark,* which starred Gertrude Law-

* rä′fĕl sŭn

rence. After that I directed all my plays, including *Jason* and *The Perfect Marriage.* My last play, *Hilda Crane,* a tragedy, starring Jessica Tandy, produced in 1950, is an exception; it was directed by Hume Cronyn.

"I have written some thirty or forty short stories for magazines like *Good Housekeeping* and the *Saturday Evening Post.* One of these, originally published in *Good Housekeeping,* was included in Martha Foley's *Best American Short Stories, 1947.* In 1948 I spent a semester as visiting professor at the University of Illinois, teaching a special course in playwriting. A stenographer kept a record of the conversation between the students and me. This record, enormously revised and edited, I made into a book, *The Human Nature of Playwriting.*

"In recent years I have begun a serious study of photography, am spending a good deal of my time in the making of black-and-white photographs ('still,' not movie) and plan to work professionally in the field of photography."

PRINCIPAL WORKS: *Plays (dates of publication)*—The Jazz Singer, 1925; Young Love, 1928; The Wooden Slipper, 1933; Accent on Youth (published with White Man) 1935; Skylark, 1939; Jason, 1942; The Perfect Marriage, 1945; Hilda Crane, 1951; The Human Nature of Playwriting, 1949.

ABOUT: Brown, J. M. Broadway in Review; Theatre Annual 1943.

RASCOE, BURTON (October 22, 1892-   ). For biographical sketch and list of earlier works and references, see TWENTIETH CENTURY AUTHORS, 1942.

* * *

Burton Rascoe left the staff of the *American Mercury* in 1941 and from 1942 to 1946 wrote drama criticism and editorials for the New York *World-Telegram.* His only recent book is a continuation of his autobiography, *We Were Interrupted,* which carries his life story up through the 1920's. The *New Yorker* described the book as "an anecdotal social history of an era to which distance is lending an increasing enchantment, abounding in names of the famous and marked by Mr. Rascoe's customary enthusiasm, mordant humor, and airy disregard for accuracy."

Rascoe lives in New York City. In 1941 he was enrolled in the Oklahoma Hall of Fame.

ADDITIONAL WORK: We Were Interrupted, 1947.

ABOUT: Rascoe, B. We Were Interrupted; Newsweek May 27, 1947; Saturday Review of Literature October 18, 1947, February 28, 1948.

*RAUSCHNING, HERMANN (1887-).

For biographical sketch and list of earlier works and references, see TWENTIETH CENTURY AUTHORS, 1942.

* * *

Hermann Rauschning became an American citizen in 1948. In recent years he has lived in Gaston, Ore., farming and raising cattle. His first postwar book, *Time of Delirium*, analyzed some of the dangers of the world scene in 1946—especially the problems facing Germany. In general American reviewers found his book timely but in places obscure and confused. "Many of his insights show a genuine profundity," Henry Bamford Parkes observed, but he found points of contradiction in Rauschning's argument. E. W. Fox wrote of it in the New York *Times*: "Oracular in tone, with a tendency toward metaphysical phraseology, its most striking characteristic is the frankness, almost brashness, with which its author draws conclusions from his rich store of prejudice and opinion. Without the slightest inhibition, for example, he equates democracy and economic privilege or defends Italian Fascism as essentially democratic in inspiration." Another book by Rauschning, *Deutschland zwischen West und Ost* (*Germany Between East and West*) was published in Germany in 1950.

ADDITIONAL WORK IN ENGLISH TRANSLATION: Time of Delirium, 1946.

ABOUT: Catholic World March 1947.

* roush'ning

RAWLINGS, Mrs. MARJORIE (KINNAN) (August 8, 1896-December 14, 1953). For biographical sketch and list of earlier works and references, see TWENTIETH CENTURY AUTHORS, 1942.

* * *

Marjorie Kinnan Rawlings died at fifty-seven, in St. Augustine, Fla., of a cerebral hemorrhage.

At the time of her death she was working on a biography of Ellen Glasgow; Mrs. Rawlings' last novel, *The Sojourner*, suggested by memories of her grandfather, was called "a good novel—a solid novel," with moments of inspired writing, by Louis Bromfield, who agreed with most critics that it did not have "the fire and the feeling" of her greatest success, *The Yearling*.

She has been called "the adopted sister of regionalism" by James Gray, who pointed out that although the Florida backwoods which formed the setting of most of her work was not her native heritage, she possessed that "gracious and receptive sympathy which discovers in a primitive and apparently uncomplicated way of life its own subtleties, its own delicate distinctions in the field of morality, its own complexities of impulse."

ADDITIONAL WORKS: Cross Creek Cookery, 1942; Jacob's Ladder, 1950; The Sojourner, 1953.

ABOUT: Gray, J. On Second Thought; Current Biography 1942; New York Times December 16, 1953; Publishers' Weekly November 18, 1944, June 29, 1946, October 2, 1948, April 1, 1950.

RAYNOLDS, ROBERT (April 29, 1902-). For autobiographical sketch and list of earlier works and references, see TWENTIETH CENTURY AUTHORS, 1942.

* * *

Robert Raynolds writes from Newton, Conn.: "During the recent war I worked as a machinist in two Connecticut factories. During 1949, 1950 and 1951 I taught courses in the novel and the short story at Columbia University."

In 1952 Raynolds wrote "A Novelist's Code" for the New York Herald Tribune *Book Review*, part of which reads: "I have three desires when I begin to write a novel: to tell a good story, to affirm that life is good, and to find and say in the course of the work more of the truth about our human mind and heart and soul than I knew when I began it."

Since 1944 Raynolds has published five novels. Of these, *The Sinner of Saint Ambrose* has been by far the most successful since his first novel, *Brothers in the West*. A long historical novel based on the struggles between the early Christian Church and the late Roman Empire, the *Sinner of Saint Ambrose* received generally enthusiastic reviews and was a Book-of-the-Month Club choice. F. H. Bullock found the novel "a spacious fictional version of the *Decline and Fall*," lively, eminently readable, and full of "brilliant detail," and Edmund Fuller, of the *Saturday Review*, called it "a distinguished and important book." An earlier novel, *Paquita*, set in nineteenth century Mexico, was described as "a lurid romance," with all the clichés of that form. Nevertheless, the *Library Journal* praised it for "vivid descriptions, exciting narrative, . . . excellent portrayal of tumultuous Mexico."

ADDITIONAL WORKS: May Bretton, 1944; The Obscure Enemy, 1945; Paquita, 1947; The Sinner of Saint Ambrose, 1952; The Quality of Quiros, 1955.

ABOUT: Warfel, H. R. American Novelists of Today; Book-of-the-Month Club News Midsummer 1952; New York Herald Tribune Book Review August 17, 1952, October 12, 1952.

REA, LORNA (SMITH), Lady (June 12, 1897-   ). For biographical sketch and list of works and references, see TWENTIETH CENTURY AUTHORS, 1942.

* * *

Lady Rea lives in London, with a country home in Eskdale, Cumberland. During World War II she served with the Women's Voluntary Services. Her husband, Philip Russell Rea, became Baron of Eskdale in 1937 and received the Order of the British Empire in 1946. He is an active member of the Liberal Party.

READ, Sir HERBERT EDWARD (December 4, 1893-   ). For autobiographical sketch and list of earlier works and references, see TWENTIETH CENTURY AUTHORS, 1942.

* * *

Sir Herbert Read writes that he has returned to his native Yorkshire, but is still involved in literary and artistic activities in London. The scope of these activities is so wide that, Richard McLaughlin commented, some of his admirers hail him as "one of the most notably persuasive influences upon his age," "a genius too fertile to be constrained within the categories of one art." On the other hand, he is little known outside England and even there, McLaughlin writes, "it is only in recent years that Read has been read by any but an intellectual politico-literary group."

In his preface to a new edition of *The Innocent Eye* in 1947, Sir Herbert wrote, "I have come to believe that the highest manifestation of the immanent will of the universe is the work of art." A few years later, introducing his collection of essays entitled *The Philosophy of Modern Art,* he said: "I believe that among the agents or instruments of human evolution, art is supremely important. I believe that the aesthetic faculty has been the means of man first acquiring, and then refining, consciousness." Primarily, and in spite of the variety of fields in which Sir Herbert has worked, he remains an aesthetician. From 1940 to 1942, when on appointment to the University of London as a Leon Fellow, he developed his theory of education, urging that the creative arts receive the major emphasis in democratic education. Some time later he criticized UNESCO for assuming that culture is merely "concrete material" that can be "bartered like butter or steel."

As a critic, Sir Herbert Read is generally regarded as sound and stimulating. Stanley Edgar Hyman cites his "sympathetic attention to every new current of thought and every youthful artist." As a poet, his work has what Rolfe Humphries calls "a quiet excellence." R. P. Blackmur finds that his verse "belongs more to the history of sensibility between the two wars than it does to the history of poetry." Similarly, Conrad Aiken comments that his poetry "reflects the mind of an intelligent and sincere liberal, but sometimes one feels that it is the work of one who is a poet by determination rather than instinct."

In 1953 he was knighted by Queen Elizabeth on her New Year's Honors List.

Correction: Sir Herbert Read has five children, a son by his first marriage, and three sons and a daughter by the second.

ADDITIONAL WORKS: Education for Art, 1943; The Politics of the Unpolitical, 1943; A Coat of Many Colours (essays) 1945; World Within a War (poems) 1945; The Grass Roots of Art, 1946; Collected Poems, 1947; Coleridge as Critic, 1949; The London Book of English Verse (ed. with B. Dobrée) 1949; Education for Peace, 1949; The Philosophy of Modern Art, 1952; The True Voice of Feeling (essays) 1953; Anarchy and Order, 1954.

ABOUT: Treece, H. (ed.) Herbert Read; Harper's June 1947; Poetry July 1945, November 1945, February 1948; Saturday Review of Literature June 28, 1947, December 11, 1948; Time June 23, 1947, May 3, 1948.

READ, OPIE PERCIVAL (December 22, 1852-November 2, 1939). For biographical sketch and list of works and references, see TWENTIETH CENTURY AUTHORS, 1942.

REDDING, JAY SAUNDERS (October 13, 1906-   ), American novelist and educator, writes: "I was born, the third of what was to be a family of seven children, in Wilmington, Del. My parents, Lewis Alfred and Mary Ann (Holmes) Redding, were far from being either rich or poor. Both were religious, of profound Christian faith, but 'faith without works' is no good. So they  worked—my mother at home, my father at many things, but principally at his job in the postal service which was the steady source of our income. My parents taught their children to work too. I remember the first three of us in the evening after dinner washing and drying the dishes while our mother sat on the step that led down from the dining room and read aloud to us. She loved to read and we loved to listen to Hans Christian Andersen, Paul Dunbar, Longfellow, Shakespeare, 'The Tragic Story of the Titanic' and selections from the *World's Famous Orations,* including Greek and Roman orations. We were taught the declining art of elocution. My brother, a lawyer, still does a lot of speaking, but it's a different art now.

"College education was preordained. My parents had attended Howard University, and my sisters went there. My brother and I went to Brown in Providence. It was at college that I began to give serious attention to writing, not as a career but because I liked it; though only heaven knows why, since even then the effort used to tear me apart. But I wrote reams and reams, and got taken on the *Brown Literary Quarterly,* and worshipped Sid (S. J.) Perelman, who was on the *Brown Jug,* and read everything, and finally, in my senior year, got a letter from H. L. Mencken telling me to try again, and another letter from Eugene Jolas, way over in Paris, telling me that *transition* was going to publish my story, 'Delaware Coon.'

"That was in 1928. Though I wrote a novel and a great deal in notebooks, I did not try for publication again until the late '30's. Things were pretty exciting, for meantime I got married and then almost immediately I got fired from a very pretentious and conservative institution for being 'radical.' So for three years my wife and scholarships supported my graduate studies at Brown and Columbia. In 1938 I went back into the literary market, got things published here and there and worked on my first book nights—every night after I'd read my freshmen's themes. That book was published in 1939. Four others (five counting one I co-edited last year) have followed, but all but one were written between four and eleven A.M., before my classes began.

"As a writer I feel that my first obligation is to truth. Since life is tragically short, there is only so much truth that one can experience and know about in the wholly personal and intimate way that is necessary to the writer. Thus my subject-matter is restricted. But I understand that even the little truth that one can know is generally unpleasant, and in so far as I have told the truth in them my books have not been pleasant. I myself do not go along with the popular judgment on truth. Certainly truth is the only real thing we have to live by. I call myself a realist. I never take intention for performance. I am not tolerant: I don't believe in tolerance. Some of my critics say that I'm an idealist.

"I'm a double-two writer. Using a pencil, I write what I think I want to say, slow sentence by slow sentence, on a white pad. When a paragraph seems right, still using pencil, I transfer it to a legal-size yellow pad. Changes are always made in this transfer. When the whole work is done in this manner I swing around to the typewriter, and the transfer from pencil to pica brings changes. The final transcript represents a fourth effort. I've never cost my publishers a penny in proof changes.

"I am still married and have two sons, one of whom is a freshman at Brown. The other is eight years old. I've been on the faculty of Hampton Institute for ten years, with one year off on a Guggenheim fellowship, with half a year off as visiting professor at Brown, and [in November 1952] am just back after several months off working for the Department of State on an assignment in India. With the usual painful slowness, I am now working on two books, one a novel and the other on my India experiences."

* * *

In 1942 J. Saunders Redding's *No Day of Triumph,* a report of his observations of Negro life in the South, was hailed by Wallace Stegner as "perhaps the sanest and most eloquent study of the Negro American that has appeared." Since then he has written sympathetically but also objectively of the problems of the Negro in America. His novel *A Stranger and Alone,* the story of a half-Negro, half-white boy who betrays his Negro friends, was written with great passion and conviction. Coleman Rosenberger said of it in the New York *Herald Tribune:* "It is an angry book, but one in which the anger is controlled and made purposeful. It is written with both insight and skill." His moving and deeply personal *On Being Negro in America* was described by R. W. Logan in the *Nation* as "one of the most effective statements in recent literature of the constant conflict experienced by the Negro between his reactions as a normal human being and those which life in America requires of him."

PRINCIPAL WORKS: To Make a Poet Black, 1939; No Day of Triumph, 1942; They Came in Chains, 1950; A Stranger and Alone (novel) 1950; On Being Negro in America, 1951; An American in India, 1954.

ABOUT: Barton, R. C. Witnesses for Freedom; Redding, J. S. No Day of Triumph, On Being Negro in America; New York Herald Tribune Book Review July 16, 1950; New York Times Book Review March 5, 1950; Saturday Review of Literature February 17, 1951.

REED, DOUGLAS (1895-). For biographical sketch and list of earlier works and references, see TWENTIETH CENTURY AUTHORS, 1942.

* * *

Douglas Reed has traveled extensively as a free-lance correspondent in recent years. In 1944 he was in Normandy covering the Allied landings. He traveled in Africa in 1947-48 and spent considerable time in South Africa. In 1949 and again in 1951-52 he toured the United States and Canada. Reed's later books have been written in the same controversial and disturbing spirit as his earlier works. He has lashed out against what he considers to be the great "menaces" to Christian society—Communism and political Zionism. The "grand design of the twentieth century," as he sees and describes it in *Somewhere South of Suez*, is the destruction of Christianity and the enslavement of the white races. In the United States he found ominous symptoms of the same conspiracy and he detailed these in his book on America, *Far and Wide*. Of this volume the London *Times Literary Supplement* observed: "His perfervid zeal on behalf of, and faith in, Anglo-Saxondom mars what, with economy of words and a wider judgment, might have been a notable book."

ADDITIONAL WORKS: All Our Tomorrows, 1942; Downfall (play) 1942; Lest We Regret, 1943; From Smoke to Smother, 1948; Rule of Three, 1950; Somewhere South of Suez, 1950; Far and Wide, 1951; The Prisoner of Ottawa: Otto Strasser, 1953. *Novels*—Next Horizon, 1945; Galanty Show, 1947; Reasons of Health, 1949.

ABOUT: Reed, D. From Smoke to Smother.

REED, JOHN (October 22, 1887-October 19, 1920). For biographical sketch and list of works and references, see TWENTIETH CENTURY AUTHORS, 1942.

* * *

ABOUT: Madison, C. A. Critics and Crusaders: A Century of American Protest.

REEDY, WILLIAM MARION (December 11, 1862-July 28, 1920). For biographical sketch and list of works and references, see TWENTIETH CENTURY AUTHORS, 1942.

REESE, LIZETTE WOODWORTH (Janaury 9, 1856-December 17, 1935). For biographical sketch and list of works and references, see TWENTIETH CENTURY AUTHORS, 1942.

* * *

ABOUT: Gregory, H. & Zaturenska, M. History of American Poetry, 1900-1940

REEVE, ARTHUR BENJAMIN (October 15, 1880-August 9, 1936). For biographical sketch and list of works and references, see TWENTIETH CENTURY AUTHORS, 1942.

* * *

ABOUT: Hoehn, M. (ed.) Catholic Authors, I.

REGLER, GUSTAV (May 25, 1898-). For autobiographical sketch and list of earlier works and references, see TWENTIETH CENTURY AUTHORS, 1942.

* * *

Gustav Regler lived in Mexico until the end of World War II, when he returned to his parental home in Germany. There he published a novel in 1947 and a book on Mexico (these have not appeared in English translation), and is working on new novels.

ADDITIONAL WORKS IN ENGLISH TRANSLATION: The Bottomless Pit (poems in English and German) 1943; Wolfgang Paalen, 1946.

*REICH, WILHELM (March 24, 1897-), the father of "Orgonomy . . . the science of cosmic Orgone Energy," for years a storm center in the combined fields of psychotherapy and biophysics, was born in Austria, the son of a well-to-do farmer. A childhood spent on his father's farm, close to the natural rhythms of plant and animal breeding, reinforced his later, adult insist-  ence upon the unitary nature of all being and of the strictly biological and sexual bases of man's emotional life.

After obtaining his M.D. from the University of Vienna in 1922, Dr. Reich undertook postgraduate work in neuropsychiatry. Vienna was in the early 1920's experiencing the tumultuous birth pangs of the new science of psychoanalysis. Dr. Reich early identified himself with this movement; in 1920 he attained membership in the Vienna Psychoanalytic Society, under Sigmund Freud. He was Freud's first clinical assistant at the Psychoanalytic Polyclinic from its foundation in 1922 until 1928; and was subsequently closely identified with other psychoanalytic centers. From 1927 through 1930, Wilhelm Reich wrote and lectured extensively on the social origin of the neuroses at mental hygiene centers in Vienna, and con-

* rīĸ

tinued this work in Berlin until the rise of Hitler forced him to flee Germany in 1933. One product of his early thinking along the lines of sex reform was his book *The Sexual Revolution* (English edition). In 1946 the first English translation of his *Mass Psychology of Fascism* (1933) appeared.

After 1934 it was apparent that Reich was no longer moving with the mainstream of psychoanalysis; and he was excluded from the International Psychoanalytic Association. He was later invited by the Norwegian association to re-enter, but refused to do so. However, much of his early work has by now been at least partly absorbed, like the ideas developed in his book *Character Analysis,* in which the rigidity and blockings of the neurotic character were shown to be reflected in the body in various types of spasms and muscular armoring.

In Denmark, where he first settled in his flight from Germany, and later in Norway, Dr. Reich lectured on the need for greater sexual freedom and continued his experimental work on the bio-electrical nature of sexual impulses; and he has elaborated and extended the scope of these studies since coming to the United States in 1939. For the first two years after arriving in this country he lectured at the New School and established an Orgone Energy Laboratory at Forest Hills, N.Y. This laboratory now has a permanent home in "Orgonon," in the Rangeley Lakes district of Maine.

The Function of the Orgasm contains the heart of Dr. Reich's theories of "orgastic potency." In this book, he pursues the idea that the ability to experience a complete sexual orgasm, and the resulting release from nervous tension, is always lacking in neurotic individuals (i.e., nearly everybody brought up in contemporary "repressive" cultures). The healing of neurotics is to be accomplished by substituting for the "character armoring" that constricts them an un-neurotic set of traits known as the "genital character." The necessity of not repressing childhood sexuality is stressed as a means of preventing neuroses in future generations.

The Cancer Biopathy (1948) carries on the experimental work on "orgone energy," the basic form of "primordial cosmic energy," which permeates the universe and governs all living matter. Re-charged in the individual at the moment of orgasm, the stasis of orgone energy results in a host of diseases which afflict modern man, including, notably, cancer. On the social level, the failure to achieve the genital character results in "emotional plague," a wide range of destructive tendencies culminating in totalitarianism and nuclear warfare (cf. his *Listen, Little Man!,* 1948).

Any further attempts to present the impact of Dr. Reich's writings must refer to the special, highly private vocabulary he has evolved with his "new science of Orgonomy." Whether, as adverse critics have maintained, this consists in an attempt to pour old wine into new scientific test-tubes, or whether a fresh modulation of contemporary vocabulary is really necessary in order for new scientific concepts to assert themselves (as the word "libido," "id," "repression," accompanied Freud's explorations into man's nature) is only one example of the type of problems that Dr. Reich's controversial work awakens.

Dr. Reich is powerful-looking with a thatch of white hair and the massive shoulders of a man who has done physical labor in his youth.

PRINCIPAL WORKS IN ENGLISH TRANSLATION: The Sexual Revolution, 1945; The Function of the Orgasm (revised ed.) 1948; The Cancer Biopathy, 1948; Listen, Little Man! 1948; Character Analysis (revised ed.) 1949; Ether, God and Devil, 1951; The Oranur Experiment, 1951; Cosmic Superimposition, 1951.

ABOUT: Fenichel, O. The Psychoanalytic Theory of Neurosis; Fliess, R. The Psychoanalytic Reader, 1948; Bibliography on Orgonomy 1920-52 (Orgone Institute Press) 1953; New Republic May 26, 1947; New York Post Magazine September 5, 1954.

Note: For comprehensive information, the reader is referred to the Orgone Institute Press, Rangeley, Me., publishing house of the Wilhelm Reich Foundation, which is preparing extensive biographical material on Wilhelm Reich's life and work.

REID, FORREST (June 24, 1876-January 4, 1947). For biographical sketch and list of earlier works and references, see TWENTIETH CENTURY AUTHORS, 1942.

* * *

Forrest Reid died at Warrenpoint, in Northern Ireland, at seventy.

His nearly twenty novels were distinguished by "his fine psychological insight, the wide range of his sympathy, and his excellent style," commented the London *Times,* which adds that "the effect of his fantasy resembled the soaring ribs and arches of late Gothic architecture whose delicacy was obvious but whose strength was no less clear."

ADDITIONAL WORKS: Retrospective Adventures, 1941; Young Tom: or, Very Mixed Company, 1944; Milk of Paradise: Some Thoughts on Poetry, 1946.

ABOUT: London Times January 7, 1947; New York Times January 6, 1947.

*REIK, THEODOR (1880-), Viennese-born psychoanalyst and author, became a pupil of Sigmund Freud in 1910. He com-

pleted his first doctor's dissertation on psychoanalysis in 1911 and took his medical degree from the University of Vienna in 1912. In 1914 he won first prize for the best paper on applied psychoanalysis, which was awarded by Freud. For many years he was lecturer at the Vienna Psychoanalytic Institute, and he also lectured in Berlin and at The Hague, Holland. He came to the United States in 1938 and is now an American citizen.

A favorite pupil of Freud, Reik in his book *Listening with the Third Ear* discusses the causes which drove Freud towards his discovery of psychoanalysis. He conducts this rather on the same lines as Freud's examination of Leonardo da Vinci. Then he makes an excursion into self-analysis. The main body of the book is devoted to a detailed description of a number of cases which he treated during thirty-seven years of active practice. He stresses the importance of the creative intuition of the psychoanalyst, the "third ear" with which he senses the unspoken and unconscious thoughts of the patient.

Although he has remained a devoted disciple of Freud, Reik differs with some of the ideas of orthodox Freudianism. "The psychoanalytical mirror shows human nature as grotesquely sexual," he writes critically in his book *The Psychology of Sex Relations.* He denies that all neuroses have a sexual origin and states categorically that there is no such thing as sublimation of the sexual urge. According to Reik's "neo-psychoanalysis," all neurosis is caused by a weakness in the ego. "A neurosis is an emotional disturbance caused by a shake-up of the self-trust and self-confidence of a person." He does not believe love to be an offshoot of the sex-drive, but rather "a rival of it, fighting it and finally uniting with it."

In his autobiography, *Fragment of a Great Confession,* Reik recounts how, at the age of eighteen, following the death of his father, he developed a compulsion to read every word ever written by the poet Goethe. He discusses the psychoanalytic reasons for this

* rīk

compulsion and then discusses the psychoanalytic problems of literature and of writers. In *The Secret Self: Psychoanalytic Experience in Life and Literature* he continues his reminiscences and divulges still more about his own personality, problems, inner experiences, unconscious emotions and methods. He selects mundane cases from his files which link his insights obtained in analytic practice to others from the literature of Shakespeare, Goethe, Heine, Schiller, and Anatole France.

In *The Haunting Melody; Psychoanalytic Experiences of Life and Music* he turns to music, another deep interest of his. He describes autobiographically his associations with the opening chorale from the last movement of Gustav Mahler's 2d Symphony, and the search for the hidden meaning of the Mahler theme to him. "In giving us the history of this piece of detective work," said the New York *Herald Tribune's* reviewer, "Reik has many true and original things to say about life, love, death and the confusing creature, man."

Dr. Reik is married to Marija Cubelic and lives in New York City. He has three children.

PRINCIPAL WORKS IN ENGLISH TRANSLATION: Ritual: Psycho-Analytic Studies, 1931; Unknown Murderer, 1936; Surprise and the Psychoanalyst, 1937; From Thirty Years with Freud, 1940; Masochism in Modern Man, 1941; A Psychologist Looks at Love, 1944; Psychology of Sex Relations, 1945; Listening with the Third Ear, 1948; Fragment of a Great Confession, 1949; Dogma and Compulsion, 1951; The Secret Self: Psychoanalytic Experiences in Life and Literature, 1952; Haunting Melody: Psychoanalytic Experiences in Life and Music, 1953.

ABOUT: Reik, T. Fragment of a Great Confession.

*REMARQUE, ERICH MARIA (1897-). For biographical sketch and list of earlier works and references, see TWENTIETH CENTURY AUTHORS, 1942.

* * *

Erich Remarque became a United States citizen in 1947. He divides his time now between his home on Lake Maggiore in Switzerland and his permanent home in New York City. Remarque has lived in the United States since 1939. During much of that time he traveled around the country, always moving with him his splendid art collections of nineteenth century French painting, antique Persian rugs, and Chinese figurines. He is a quiet, soft-spoken men who does not seek publicity but who has nevertheless managed

* rĕ märk'

to capture and retain the curiosity and interest of a large public. The three novels that he has published in recent years have had greater popular than critical success. *Arch of Triumph,* the story of a love affair between a German refugee doctor and an actress, set in the tense and tragic days of Paris just before the outbreak of World War II, had a tremendous sale and was made into a motion picture. The critics agreed generally that it was serious and absorbing book, but many were revolted by its brutality and sensationalism. "Powerful writing and many fine touches of characterization are clotted for want of selection," Edward Weeks observed of it in the *Atlantic.* In *Spark of Life* Remarque presented a grim and terrible picture of a German concentration camp—a "fictional documentary," as one reviewer described it, less flamboyant than *Arch of Triumph* but, some readers found, more moving. With *A Time to Love and a Time to Die* he told a quieter story, though his setting was still World War II, that of a young German soldier and his sweetheart and their effort to forget the war during his three-week furlough. A restrained and unpretentious treatment of a simple theme, the novel was at its best in its picture of life in a war-devastated city. But, Robert Gorham Davis pointed out in the New York *Times:* "The inner realities do not measure up to the outer ones. Instead of being made more intense and complex by the violences which surround it, the love affair takes on some of the unreality of the ruined city itself, seen at night with only the moon to light it."

ADDITIONAL WORKS IN ENGLISH TRANSLATION: Arch of Triumph, 1946; Spark of Life, 1952; A Time to Love and a Time to Die, 1954.

ABOUT: Columbia Dictionary of Modern European Literature; Gray, J. On Second Thought; Van Gelder, R. Writers and Writing; New Yorker November 6, 1943; May 12, 1945; Saturday Review May 22, 1954; Time November 8, 1943.

*REMIZOV, ALEXEY MIKHAILO-VICH (1877-). For biographical sketch and list of earlier works and references, see TWENTIETH CENTURY AUTHORS, 1942.

* * *

Remizov was last reported living in Paris. Only one of his books has appeared in English in recent years, but he has continued to publish books in Russian, and the number of French translations of his works suggests that there is considerable interest in his work in France.

* ryä′myĭ zôf

ADDITIONAL WORK IN ENGLISH TRANSLATION: On a Field Azure, 1947.

ABOUT: Columbia Dictionary of Modern European Literature; Struve, G. Soviet Russian Literature 1917-1950; Books Abroad Autumn 1954.

"RENN, LUDWIG." See VIETH VON GOLSSENAU

*REPPLIER, AGNES (April 1, 1858-December 15, 1950). For biographical sketch and list of works and references, see TWENTIETH CENTURY AUTHORS, 1942.

* * *

Agnes Repplier died of a heart ailment, at her apartment in Philadelphia, at ninety-two. She had been in ill health for several years.

Her rank in the dwindling company of pure essayists has been adjudged by Charles A. Brady to be below that of the "great British masters of her chosen genre" but "high among the American essayists"; he calls her style "the delicate quintessence of sound sense and sounder sensibility."

Sainte-Beuve's tribute to Mme. de Sévigné has been quoted in Miss Repplier's regard: "She had a knowledge of the world and of men, a lively and acute appreciation both of the becoming and the absurd." Joseph J. Reilly adds that she "championed those ideals of thought and conduct by which the dignity and grace of life are maintained and its inalienable values reaffirmed."

ABOUT: Hoehn, M. (ed.) Catholic Authors, I; Reilly, J. J. Of Books and Men; Stokes, G. S. Agnes Repplier, Lady of Letters; America February 3, 1951; Catholic World July 1951; Commonweal December 10, 1948; New York Times December 16, 1950; Saturday Review of Literature April 30, 1949; Southern Atlantic Quarterly April 1945.

* rĕp′lēr

REXROTH, KENNETH (December 22, 1905-), American poet, writes: "I was born in South Bend, Ind. Father, Charles Marion Rexroth, the son of a plumber, George Rexroth, and a schoolteacher, Mary Moore. Mother, Delia Reed, daughter of Charles Reed, a horse-trader, and Mary Newman, a foster child and servant. All these grandparents were of very old American stock, predominantly Pennsylvania Dutch in origin. Remote ancestors were Men-

nonites, Brethren, Schwenckfelders. Many were active in early abolitionist, suffrage, and socialist movements in America. My great grandparents were all pioneers on the advancing edges of the old Northwest.

"My early childhood was spent in Elkhart, Ind.; Battlecreek, Mich.; Toledo, Ohio; Chicago, Ill., and on various farms in the Midwest. My mother died when I was ten, my father took to drink, lost his job in a Chicago wholesale drug house, and became a factory hand in Toledo. When I was thirteen, he too died. I lived with relatives for three years, mostly my mother's sister and mother in Chicago—Fifty-fifth and the El, the locale of Studs Lonigan. From thirteen on, I had to support myself. I managed a couple of years of high school, but left in a row over military training. At fifteen or sixteen I moved to the Bohemian district of Chicago, the Near North Side, and joined the I.W.W. For the next five years I hoboed around the country, soap-boxing for the I.W.W., working at every imaginable sort of job, mucker, harvest hand, forest patrolman, packer, factory hand, fruit picker, insane asylum attendant. Winters I spent in Chicago or New York. I knew most of the people in the arts and the radical movement, the Chicago underworld, the 'New Negro,' the founders of Jazz, etc., etc.,—the world of the Twenties which so excites this generation in retrospect. Meanwhile, I took various courses at the New School, the Art Students League, and the Chicago Art Institute. None of them, except the Art Institute, which I had attended since childhood, ever taught me anything. I am self-educated.

"In 1927 I married 'Andrée Dutcher' (Myrtle Schaefer) a young abstract artist. That summer we came to San Francisco, and I have lived there ever since. For the next several years I was active in the John Reed Club, trade union, and unemployment movements all supposedly under the 'leadership' of the Communist Party, but in those days, in the Far West, actually dependent on the collaboration of ex-I.W.W.'s. At Hitler's seizure of power I quit this collaboration, except for some activity in the trade unions at the time of the San Francisco general strike. Since then I have been consistently anti-political—an anarchist and war resister. During World War II, I was a conscientious objector, and though just too old for the draft, worked as an attendant in the San Francisco psychopathic hospital. In 1940, Andrée Rexroth died and I married Marie Kass, a nurse. In 1948 we separated. In 1949 I married Martha Larsen, a student. We have one child, Mary, born in 1950.

"I was one of the first abstract painters in America, and have had one-man shows in Los Angeles, Santa Monica, New York, and San Francisco. Since I have lived in the West much of my time has been spent in the High Sierras. I am a skier and climber. My creative writing is done in the mountains, too."

* * *

In 1945 Vivienne Koch remarked of Kenneth Rexroth's The Phoenix and the Tortoise: "Quietly, but with a solid sense of direction that is rare, Kenneth Rexroth, once active in the Objectivist movement, has arrived at a poetic maturity that is marked at once by passion and by control." His early poems, as his collection The Art of Worldly Wisdom strikingly illustrated, were eccentric, heavily influenced by surrealism and the experimental forms so popular in the 1920's. In recent years, however, as Dudley Fitts wrote in 1949, "the reader will find adumbrated the firm control, the brilliant wit, the quick ear, and the deep humanistic passion that characterize Mr. Rexroth's mature work. He is often difficult, at times perversely so; but he is always the convinced, absorbed artist."

Rexroth's The Dragon and the Unicorn is a free-ranging journal in verse of a year of travel in Europe, described by Richard Eberhart in the New York Times as "a grand tour of the whole sensibility of the author . . . a fabulous voyage."

PRINCIPAL WORKS: In What Hour, 1940; The Phoenix and the Tortoise, 1944; The Art of Worldly Wisdom, 1949; The Signature of All Things, 1949; (ed.) New British Poets: an Anthology, 1949; Beyond the Mountains (verse plays) 1951; The Dragon and the Unicorn, 1952.

ABOUT: New York Times Book Review February 15, 1953; Poetry February 1945, June 1950, September 1951.

REYMONT, WLADYSLAW STANISLAW (May 6, 1868-December 5, 1925). For biographical sketch and list of works and references, see TWENTIETH CENTURY AUTHORS, 1942.

* * *

ABOUT: Columbia Dictionary of Modern European Literature.

REYNOLDS, QUENTIN JAMES (April 11, 1902-), American journalist, was born in New York City, the son of James J. Reynolds, principal of a public school in Brooklyn, and Katherine (Mahoney) Reynolds.

When Quentin was three years old, the family moved to Brooklyn. There he attended public schools, then Manual Training High School, and Brown University at Providence, R.I. He played football, became heavyweight boxing champion of the college, and was a crack member of the swimming team. During his summer vacations Reynolds worked on newspapers, until graduation in 1924. After attending Brooklyn Law School, he soon returned to newspaper work, writing for the Brooklyn *Times,* later for the New York *Evening World,* during the day and studying law at night. After receiving the law degree he became reporter, rewrite man and sportswriter for the *Evening World* until the newspaper died; he then joined the staff of the *World-Telegram* and from there went to the International News Service. After an assignment in Germany in 1933, he joined the *Collier's* staff, writing articles and short stories. During World War II he spent some time in France and in London, doing the commentary on two films, *London Can Take It* and *Christmas under Fire.*

R. D. Englund

In 1941 he published a book about wartime England which became a best seller—*The Wounded Don't Cry.* "It is a journalist's book from start to finish," said the New York *Times,* "a book of flashes, sharp, racy, significant: one of the very good books of its kind." "The author is a master of vivid description without the use of many adjectives or high-sounding phrases," added the Springfield *Republican.* "Short sentences, simple words, and the author's emotion and the reader's aroused imagination complete the story." It was at this time that Reynolds accompanied W. Averell Harriman to Moscow as press officer; he remained six months, leaving in protest against the Soviet censorship. When Reynolds got back to the United States he learned he had been awarded a prize by the Communist *New Masses,* and finding that Fitzpatrick, the cartoonist, and other non-Communists had likewise been honored, he attended the award dinner. Asked to speak, he launched into a tirade against Soviet censorship, his address being received in stony silence. Over ten years later, in 1954, Reynolds was awarded what some believe to be the largest libel award ever made, $175,001, in his suit against Westbrook Pegler and two Hearst corporations. It stemmed from a column Pegler wrote in 1949 charging Reynolds with being pro-Communist, "yellow," and an "absentee war correspondent during World War II."

Reynolds covered war fronts in North Africa, Sicily, Salerno, Teheran, Palestine, as well as in the Southwest Pacific area. In 1948 he spent several months in Europe and the Middle East, gathering material for articles. He has been vitally interested in Palestine and then Israel, in 1950 raising some thirty million dollars, making forty-five speeches and twenty radio appeals. A strong supporter of Franklin D. Roosevelt, Reynolds —though born a Brooklyn Democrat—became an Eisenhower follower and wrote a personal story about him for *Life.* Although he had received many requests from magazines for an intimate authorized story, Eisenhower would not cooperate unless Reynolds was the writer. When the story was finished and Eisenhower was asked to check it, he refused, saying that during the war years he had never found it necessary to check any story by Reynolds and would not do so now.

In 1953 Reynolds was briefly involved in a literary hoax, for which, however, he was not blamed. He went to Canada to interview and write the story of one George DuPre, who claimed to have been a secret service agent in World War II. The book was published as *The Man Who Wouldn't Talk,* and shortly after its publication it was revealed that DuPre's adventures had been sheer fabrication—a revelation which astonished Reynolds apparently quite as much as it did the reading public. The book was nevertheless a success as fiction if not as fact.

Reynolds holds honorary degrees from the University of Western Ontario, Brown University, and the Brooklyn Law School. He is six feet one inch tall, convivial, and a hearty eater. In 1942 he married Virginia Peine, an actress. Reynolds lives in Bedford Village, N.Y.

PRINCIPAL WORKS: (With S. J. Perelman) Parlor, Bedlam and Bath, 1930; The Wounded Don't Cry, 1941; London Diary, 1941; Don't Think It Hasn't Been Fun (in U.S.: Convoy) 1941; Only the Stars Are Neutral, 1942; Dress Rehearsal, 1943; The Curtain Rises, 1944; Officially Dead, 1945; 70,000 to One, 1946; Leave It to the People, 1949; Courtroom, 1950; The Wright Brothers (juvenile) 1950; Custer's Last Stand (juvenile) 1951; The Battle of Britain (in England: R.A.F. and the Blitz of London; juvenile) 1953; I, Willie Sutton (as told to Reynolds) 1953; The Amazing Mr. Doolittle, 1953; The Man Who Wouldn't Talk, 1953; The F.B.I. (juvenile) 1954; Headquarters, 1955.

ABOUT: Murrow, E. R. This I Believe; Rechnitzer, F. E. War Correspondent; Current Biography 1941; Esquire June 1941; New York Herald Tribune Book Review June 18, 1950; United Nations World April 1951.

REYNOLDS, REGINALD (1905-), British man of letters, says of himself: "There are two of me. No. 1. was born at

Glastonbury (Somerset) of a Quaker family, went to the Friends School, Saffron Walden (England) and Woodbrooke College, Birmingham. After an inglorious interlude in the family business No. 1. went to India in 1929 and worked with Gandhi. Subsequent activities included Secretaryship of the No More War Movement (1932-37) and one year as Field Secretary, Friends Peace Committee (1951-52). No. 2. evolved about 1943—a satirist and student of historical by-ways. Both are still living and married to Ethel Mannin.

"Works by No. 1.: *White Sahibs in India, The Wisdom of John Woolman, A Quest for Gandhi*, and innumerable articles.

"Works by No. 2.: *Cleanliness and Godliness, Og and Other Ogres, Beards, Beds.*

"I have edited other volumes which do not appear to come under either category and are unimportant, anyway. No. 1. has traveled again to India (1949-50) and other places, is active and very conscientious. No. 2. is to be found at the British Museum, in bed, or drinking coffee in some part of Chelsea. No. 1. is a public speaker on serious subjects, such as religion and politics. No. 2. talks a great deal, though seldom in public, which is fortunate, but he sometimes breaks loose on the radio."

* * *

Reynolds' *White Sahibs in India*, a history of the English occupation of India, raised a storm of protest on its publication in 1937. It contained a foreword by Nehru. The London *Times Literary Supplement* wrote that "Mr. Reynolds has largely destroyed his own case by overstating it." The *New Statesman and Nation* was similarly negative in its opinion of what it called "the most unqualified indictment of the British system since the days of H. M. Hyndman."

To the other phase of Reynolds' writing, as exemplified by *Beards, Their Social Standing, Religious Involvements, Decorative Possibilities and Value in Offence and Defence*

Through the Ages, the critics have been favorable in their comments. "Some time back," wrote the New York *Herald Tribune's* reviewer "Mr. Reynolds added to the salty learning and gayety of life by his study of *Cleanliness and Godliness.* He's done it again in *Beards,* and the masculine population, bearded and clean-shaven, solemn owls and merry wits, will lap it up." "For those who find amusement in this kind of thing—and I must say I'm one of them," J. H. Jackson said in the San Francisco *Chronicle*, "*Beards* will be first-rate entertainment."

In *Cairo to Cape Town*, subtitled "a pilgrimage in search of hope," Reynolds returned to what he calls his No. 1 literary personality. "Many travelers have crossed Africa by foot, car, boat, oxwagon and airplane," commented John Barkham in the New York *Times*, "but few have told of it with so trenchant a tongue. In the current battle of books on Africa this one stands out for the refreshing iconoclasm of its author and the toe-stubbing forthrightness of its viewpoint."

PRINCIPAL WORKS: White Sahibs in India, 1937; Why India? 1942; Cleanliness and Godliness, 1943; Og and Other Ogres (verse) 1946; The Wisdom of John Woolman, 1949; Beards, 1949; To Live in Mankind: A Quest for Gandhi (in U.S.: A Quest for Gandhi) 1951; Beds, 1951; Cairo to Cape Town, 1955.

"RHODE, JOHN." See STREET, C. J. C.

RHODES, EUGENE MANLOVE (January 19, 1869-June 27, 1934). For biographical sketch and list of works and references, see TWENTIETH CENTURY AUTHORS, 1942.

* * *

ABOUT: Atlantic Monthly June 1949; Newsweek November 7, 1949.

RHODES, JAMES FORD (May 11, 1848-January 22, 1927). For biographical sketch and list of works and references, see TWENTIETH CENTURY AUTHORS, 1942.

* * *

ABOUT: Saveth, E. N. American Historians and European Immigrants; New England Quarterly September, December 1948; Saturday Review of Literature April 3, 1948.

*RHYS, ERNEST (July 17, 1859-May 25, 1946). For autobiographical sketch and list of works and references, see TWENTIETH CENTURY AUTHORS, 1942.

* * *

Ernest Rhys died in a London nursing home at eighty-six.

* rēs

His own writing career was overshadowed by his editorial work. He was "a distinguished poet," in the words of Wilfred Gibson, "who devoted most of his life to so noble an enterprise as the production of the incalculably valuable Everyman's Library."

His two autobiographical books showed him to be, as H. W. Boynton called him, "a friendly and ardent soul—a true cherisher and nourisher of the fine art of living."

ABOUT: London Times May 27, 1946; New York Times May 26, 1946; Saturday Review of Literature June 22, 1946.

RICE, Mrs. ALICE CALDWELL (HE-GAN) (January 11, 1870-February 10, 1942). For biographical sketch and list of works and references, see TWENTI-ETH CENTURY AUTHORS, 1942.

* * *

ADDITIONAL WORK: Happiness Road, 1942.
ABOUT: Wilson Library Bulletin April 1942.

RICE, CALE YOUNG (December 7, 1872-January 24, 1943). For autobiographical sketch and list of earlier works and references, see TWENTIETH CENTURY AUTHORS, 1942.

* * *

Cale Young Rice committed suicide at his home in Louisville, Ky. He was seventy years old.

Of his autobiography, which described "an almost idyllic bookish life," the London *Times Literary Supplement* observed that it lacked "that poetic perception of the infinite" and could not escape a charge of "some triviality, or at any rate disproportion." A review of Rice's *Stygian Freight* in the *Literary Supplement* characterized his poetry as failing "to the extent that he shirks the problem of translating real life into terms of the imagination and so of poetry. . . . His realism in certain poems has undeniably a stark power, and in some of his shorter lyrics he criticizes life with some poetic insight."

ADDITIONAL WORKS: Best Poetic Work (ed. L. L. Rice) 1943; New Approach to Philosophy, 1943.
ABOUT: National Cyclopedia of American Biography (1948); New York Herald Tribune January 25, 1943; Publishers' Weekly February 20, 1943.

RICE, ELMER L. (September 28, 1892-). For biographical sketch and list of earlier works and references, see TWEN-TIETH CENTURY AUTHORS, 1942.

* * *

Although in recent years Elmer Rice has written no play which measures up to the artistic success of *The Adding Machine*, or—with the exception of *Dream Girl*—the popular success of *Street Scene* and *Counsellor-at-Law*, he has managed to maintain his reputation as one of the most serious and important of contemporary American playwrights. This has been the result, in part at least, of his work with the Playwrights' Company, which he helped to found in 1938, the Dramatists' Guild, and other groups which reflect his view that the theatre is not merely a place of "escapist" entertainment, but a forum "for discussion in emotional and dramatic terms of problems that affect the lives and happiness of millions."

Rice's great earnestness—his eagerness to plunge into any cause in which he feels deep ethical and moral issues are involved—has perhaps cost him some easy popularity, but he shows little sign of compromising. In 1951, for example, he came to the defense of actors whose allegedly left-wing associations were now causing them to lose their jobs in radio and in television. He resigned, with a loud cry of protest, from the Playwrights' TV Theatre, a group of dramatists (including Robert Sherwood, Maxwell Anderson, Eugene O'Neill) whose works were performed on a television program the sponsor of which, Rice charged, barred actors because of their political beliefs. He wrote in an open letter: "I have repeatedly denounced the men who sit in the Kremlin for judging artists by political standards. I do not intend to acquiesce when the same procedure is followed by political commissars who sit in the offices of advertising agencies or business corporations."

Of Rice's recent legitimate plays, only one, *Dream Girl*, 1945, had an extended run. A "fantastic comedy," based on the dream life of a lively but average girl, the play was praised as a vehicle for the splendid acting of Betty Field (Mrs. Rice in private life) in a leading role which kept her on stage for all but two minutes of the action. Miss Field has also acted in several other plays by Rice. In 1943 she starred in his *A New Life,* a serious and moderately successful drama (the climax of which was a scene in the delivery room of a maternity hospital) about a conflict between a young wife and her husband's "capitalistically conscious" family. Other recent plays by Rice have had only brief Broadway runs and have followed fairly conventional patterns (although *Not for Children,* a comedy, involved the relatively little-used idea of a play about the making of a play). In 1947 the late Kurt Weill wrote the music and Langston Hughes the lyrics for a very effective opera based upon *Street Scene.*

Rice and Betty Field were married in 1942 after his divorce from his first wife. They have two sons and a daughter and live on a farm in Connecticut.

ADDITIONAL WORKS: *Plays (dates of publication)*—A New Life, 1944; Dream Girl, 1946; The Grand Tour, 1952; The Winner, 1954. *Novel*—The Show Must Go On, 1949.

ABOUT: Current Biography 1943; Mersand, J. American Drama Since 1930; Collier's August 31, 1946; New York Times Magazine September 12, 1943, January 12, 1947, February 2, 1947; Theatre Annual 1948-49; Theatre Arts May 1949; Time November 26, 1951.

RICH, LOUISE DICKINSON (June 14, 1903-   ), American memoirist, writes: "I was born in Huntington, Mass., and have

Eric Schaal

lived all my life, with the exception of two years of exile that I spent teaching in New Jersey, in one or another of the four northern New England states. I was educated by the Massachusetts public school system, starting in kindergarten and ending—as far as formal education goes—by being graduated from the Massachusetts State Teachers' College, at Bridgewater. My father was editor of the local weekly paper, so my only sister and I felt that we belonged to the literary tradition, an attitude fostered by our family connection with the poetess, Emily Dickinson. I intended, therefore, to become an author when I got around to it. However, as soon as I embarked upon the teaching for which I had been prepared, I discovered that the correcting of sophomore themes and the daily expounding of the virtues of a comma preceding a non-restrictive clause do not put one into the frame of mind conducive to creative writing. My career, so-called, was postponed to some future and unspecified date, and I spent the interim reading practically anything I could lay hands on; and to this day I believe that the best preparation for the writer is enthusiastic living plus omnivorous reading.

"In 1934 I met and married Ralph Eugene Rich, a Bostonian who had retired to Forest Lodge, at Middle Dam, in the center of the Rangeley Lake region in northwest Maine. Since I couldn't prevail upon him to live any-

where else, I perforce made that my home, too, and I have lived there ever since. My two children were born there, and, eleven years after we were married, my husband died there. I am bound to the place by ties no power on earth can sever. It was there that I began to write. Since the nearest neighbor is two miles away, and there is no road connecting our lake-bound home with what we call the Outside, I had and have plenty of uninterrupted time to devote to the typewriter.

"Working on the principle that to write at all convincingly, you must restrict yourself to that material about which you know something, I wrote about our life in this remote and uncivilized and beautiful corner of the country. My first book, *We Took to the Woods,* was well enough received—it was a Books-of-the-Month Club selection—so that I continued the chronicle of the Rich tribe in three others:—*Happy the Land, My Neck of the Woods,* and *Only Parent.* I have also written two books of fiction for teenagers, *Start of the Trail* (a *Herald Tribune* Award winner), and *Trail to the North.* These deal in a thinly disguised manner with the country and the people that I know and love, as do also most of the short stories and articles of mine which have appeared from time to time in magazines.

"When census takers ask me what my occupation is, I am somewhat at a loss. I tell them that I am a widow, a mother, a father-substitute, and a writer. They usually just put down *housewife;* and all things considered, that's about as nearly accurate as possible."

PRINCIPAL WORKS: We Took to the Woods, 1942; Happy the Land, 1946; Start of the Trail, 1949; My Neck of the Woods, 1950; Trail to the North, 1952; Only Parent, 1953; Innocence Under the Elms, 1955.

ABOUT: Rich, L. D. We Took to the Woods, Happy the Land, My Neck of the Woods, Only Parent, Innocence Under the Elms; Current Biography 1943; New York Herald Tribune Book Review October 8, 1950.

RICHARDS, IVOR ARMSTRONG (February 26, 1893-   ). For biographical sketch and list of earlier works and references, see TWENTIETH CENTURY AUTHORS, 1942.

* * *

I. A. Richards was director of the Harvard Commission on English Language Studies from 1939 to 1944. In the latter year he became professor of English at Harvard. His permanent home is at Magdalene College,

Cambridge, but for the past decade and more he has lived in Cambridge, Mass.

Richards is credited, "in the most literal sense," with having founded modern literary criticism, with the publication in 1924 of his *Principles of Literary Criticism.* More than two decades later, Stanley Edgar Hyman wrote that it is still "an important and continually influential text." A pioneer work in the study of literature as experience, the book was an attempt "to develop criticism as an 'applied science,' with the dual function of analyzing both the interpretive and the evaluative experiences." Richard's influence on other literary critics—most particularly on William Empson and Kenneth Burke—has been enormous. In England (and to a large degree in America), Hyman remarks, "almost no contemporary critic has written without being touched by Richards at some point."

Since the mid-1930's, however, Basic English has absorbed most of Richards' interest, to the exclusion of literary criticism. In 1942 he published an abridged edition of Plato's *The Republic* in Basic, and this volume received much attention. A year later his *Basic English and Its Uses* urged the adoption of the system, not only internationally as an aid to better understanding among nations, but also as a useful tool in the understanding of our own literature. He enlarged upon his thesis in *Nations and Peace,* stating the case for world government in a Basic vocabulary of less than 400 words. Commentators on Richards' work in Basic are generally agreed on the usefulness of the method in teaching the English language to foreigners. But they are sceptical of its value or its feasibility as an international or supra-national language. James Burnham remarked in the New York *Times* in 1947: "Mr. Richards is not free of the common fallacy of semanticists: the belief that confusions of language are the cause of our troubles, and that linguistic clarity will therefore save us. The truth is closer to the reverse. It is we who confuse our language. It is too easy to make words our scapegoat."

ADDITIONAL WORKS: Basic English and Its Uses, 1943; Learning Basic English (with C. Gibson) 1945; Nations and Peace, 1947.

ABOUT: Harding, D. W. *in* The Importance of *Scrutiny* (ed. E. Bentley); Hyman, S. E. The Armed Vision; James, D. G. *in* Critiques and Essays in Criticism (ed. R. W. Stallman); Tate, A. On the Limits of Poetry; Ethics January 1949; Partisan Review February 1950; Time December 31, 1945.

RICHARDS, Mrs. LAURA ELIZABETH (HOWE) (February 27, 1850-January 14, 1943). For autobiographical sketch and list of works and references, see TWENTIETH CENTURY AUTHORS, 1942.

* * *

Laura Elizabeth Richards died at her home in Gardner, Me., at ninety-two.

Until a few months before her death she continued to write verse; it was her nonsense verses for children which prompted Louis Untermeyer to declare that "one of her hands turns a moonstruck hurdygurdy; the other fingers the pipes of Peter Pan."

Reviewing her life, Arthur Colton has said: "The culture which came to Mrs. Richards by inheritance, the insatiable love of books, the tradition of service, the standards of thought and conduct which belong and give grace to the best of New England, she has maintained and passed on."

ABOUT: Horn Book July 1941, March 1943; New York Times January 15, 1943.

RICHARDSON, DOROTHY M. (1882-). For autobiographical sketch and list of works and references, see TWENTIETH CENTURY AUTHORS, 1942.

* * *

Dorothy Richardson lives very quietly in England and has published nothing in recent years. Her work is little read today, although its extraordinary significance in the development of the modern English novel is widely acknowledged. Her technique—the free flowing of experience in an attempt to record the entire contents of a human mind—is her own invention. W. Y. Tindall writes: "Thoughts, feeling, images from the senses, and the endless, inexplicable irrelevancies that constitute waking life and complicate it by pursuing several simultaneous courses—in short, the rich confusion described by Bergson and William James as our immediate reality—became her material, and fidelity to this rich confusion provided her technique." This lack of disciplined selection and structure has had results at times "monotonous and aesthetically unsatisfying," but no reader concerned with the development of modern fiction can afford to overlook Miss Richardson's work.

ABOUT: Tindall, W. Y. Forces in Modern British Literature; Life and Letters April, May, November 1946; Pacific Spectator Winter 1954.

RICHARDSON, HENRY HANDEL
(1880?-March 20, 1946). For autobiographical sketch and list of earlier works and references, see TWENTIETH CENTURY AUTHORS, 1942.

* * *

Henry Handel Richardson died at her home in Hastings, Sussex, England. She had been in ill health during most of her adult life. Her first name has been incorrectly given as "Henrietta"; the full name was Mrs. Ethel Florence (Lindesay Richardson) Robertson.

Until shortly before her death she was engaged in writing an autobiographical memoir (she completed it to 1895, the year of her marriage), which C. Hartley Grattan called "a fascinating and invaluable book for those who regard Henry Handel Richardson's novels as among the greatest in English of her time."

Reticent as she was about personal publicity, many facets of Mrs. Robertson's personality and philosophy are relatively unknown to her reading audience, as Bruce Sutherland has pointed out; he mentions specifically her "courage, realism, style, vulgarity, intellectuality." Her "steadiness of vision and sobriety of judgment allied to very exceptional imaginative power" have been noted by Frank Swinnerton, who added that "the method is so quiet that its merits and in fact the essential imaginativeness of the work, may be missed by those eager for display; a little formal as to style, it has not the pace and brilliance of the best very modern exhibitions of life. But the touch is unerring."

ADDITIONAL WORK: Myself When Young, 1948.
ABOUT: Palmer, N. Henry Handel Richardson; Richardson, H. H. Myself When Young; Swinnerton, F. The Georgian Literary Scene; New York Herald Tribune Book Review July 21, 1946; New York Times March 21, 1946; South Atlantic Quarterly January 1950.

RICHMOND, Mrs. GRACE LOUISE
(SMITH) (1866-). For biographical sketch and list of works and references, see TWENTIETH CENTURY AUTHORS, 1942.

*RICHTER, CONRAD (October 13, 1890-). For autobiographical sketch and list of earlier works and references, see TWENTIETH CENTURY AUTHORS, 1942.

* * *

* rĭk′tēr

In the decade 1940-1950 Conrad Richter published his trilogy of American pioneer life in the novels The Trees, The Fields, and The Town. For the latter he received the Pulitzer prize in 1951. Of these three novels, The Trees, Richter feels, is the one that is most alive. He still receives letters from readers all over the world who are reading it for the first time. Each of the novels stands on its own as an independent work, but read in a series they reveal a unity of design. "Together," Dayton Kohler writes, "they probably give us our truest picture of the everyday realities of frontier life."

More than a simple realist, however, Richter probes deeply into the myth and the mind of the pioneer. As Frederic I. Carpenter points out, "His pioneers live not only as actual adventurers but also as explorers of the primeval past and the racial unconscious." His recent novel The Light in the Forest, for example, is told from the point of view of a fifteen-year-old white boy who, for eleven years of life, has been a captive of an Indian tribe. Now rescued and restored to his family, the boy rebels against this civilization and tries to return to his Indian captors, only to discover in the end that there is an eternal and irreconcilable conflict between the two worlds. Richter says that one of the purposes of the novel is "to point out that in the pride of our American liberties we're apt to forget that already we've lost a good many to civilization. . . . Perhaps if we understood how those First Americans [the Indians] felt toward us even then and toward our white way of life, we might better understand the adverse, if perverted, view of us by some African, European, and Asian peoples today."

In addition to the Pulitzer prize, other recent honors awarded Richter are a gold medal for literary achievement from the Society for the Libraries of New York University (1942), an honorary Litt.D. from Susquehanna University (1944), and the Ohioana Library Medal (1947). He lives part of the year in Pine Grove, Pa., and part in the West.

ADDITIONAL WORKS: The Free Man, 1943; The Fields, 1946; Always Young and Fair, 1947; The Town, 1950; The Light in the Forest, 1953; The Mountain on the Desert: A Philosophical Journey, 1955.
ABOUT: College English February 1947, November 1950; Commonwealth Magazine May 1947; Current Biography 1951; New Mexico Quarterly Winter 1945; New York Herald Tribune Book Review April 30, 1950; Saturday Review May 16, 1953; Wilson Library Bulletin December 1942.

RIDGE, LOLA (1883-May 1941). For biographical sketch and list of works and references, see TWENTIETH CENTURY AUTHORS, 1942.

* * *

ABOUT: Gregory, H. & Zaturenska, M. History of American Poetry, 1900-1940.

RIDING, LAURA. See JACKSON, L. R.

RIESENBERG, FELIX (April 9, 1879-November 19, 1939). For biographical sketch and list of works and references, see TWENTIETH CENTURY AUTHORS, 1942.

RIESMAN, DAVID (September 22, 1909-), American social scientist, writes: "I was born on Spruce Street, the doctors'  street in Philadelphia as it then was, the eldest of three children of Dr. David Riesman, practicing internist and professor of clinical medicine at the University of Pennsylvania. My father prided himself on his versatility, my mother, Eleanor (Fleisher) Riesman, a Bryn Mawr graduate, on her intellectuality. I attended Penn Charter, a Quaker preparatory school in downtown Philadelphia, where the arts were neglected, the classics emphasized. Considered too young when I graduated to go to Harvard College, I spent a year at the Evans School in Tucson, Ariz., where I did a lot of camping and wrote rather sardonic pieces for the humor magazine. My father wanted me to be a doctor and I concentrated in bio-chemical sciences as a Harvard undergraduate. I found more stimulation in history and literature courses and in my work as one of the editors of the Harvard *Crimson*.

"Graduating in 1931, I went on to Harvard Law School more out of aimlessness than out of any passion for the law. During my law school years I became acquainted with Professor Carl J. Friedrich of the Harvard government department. Together we bought and started to run a dairy farm near Brattleboro, Vt. Friedrich introduced me to political and social science, and encouraged in me (as did some of my law school teachers, notably Felix Frankfurter and James A. McLaughlin) the thought, previously alien, that I might be suited to teaching and intellectual life. I became an editor of the *Harvard Law Review* and, in time free from law school duties, studied government, economics, and American history. Graduating in 1934, I went back for a fellowship post-graduate year to continue these latter pursuits. During my last law school year and also in this graduate year I had a little opportunity to do some teaching, filling in for professors who had gone to work for the New Deal in Washington.

"There is no need here to go into all the details of my legal career: I practiced law in Boston and taught law at the University of Buffalo and spent a year in the New York County District Attorney's office. I was moderately good at these things—and moderately unhappy, unhappy because I found myself increasingly attracted to the "newer" social sciences and to the breeds of men and women who were working in them. In my spare time I took courses at the Washington School of Psychiatry (in New York), worked with Erich Fromm for a number of years, and read widely in psychoanalytic and sociological materials. And as I studied and began to write in these fields, I found sympathetic colleagues mainly outside the law. Perhaps the same spirit of adventure which had led me as a student to spend a summer with the Grenfell Mission in Labrador, or to visit the Soviet Union, or to take a camping trip without guides in the Canadian bush north of Timagami—where we got lost and found again by search-planes—led me quite out of the law and into my present position as professor of the social sciences at the University of Chicago.

"The shift, however, was made easier by virtue of the accident that I spent the years from 1943 to early 1946 as an official of Sperry Gyroscope Company, where I had the chance to get out of my system the kind of executive energies many lawyers have: I was reassured of my desire to return to academic work by my taste of success as a businessman and consequently I have not been tempted by opportunities to take other administrative jobs. And the shift was eased financially for my family of four children (I had married Evelyn Hastings Thompson, of Brookline, Mass., in 1936) by an inheritance from my mother, who died in 1945; I could accept the smaller salary and lower rank that entry into a new field occasioned. My ambition was no less than to become an all-around social scientist, familiar with sociological and psychological materials as well as with economic and political and historical ones. I could not have done better than to land as I did in the College at the University of Chicago, among a group of enterprising colleagues who sought a similar scope and were engaged in building it into a teaching program in general education.

"However, until I had actually directed a research project of my own, and designed interviews and done them, and had seen what was involved in coding and interpreting interview material, I did not even begin to feel at home under my new designation of social scientist—and indeed I go on learning under the inspiring guidance of my colleagues. The Committee on National Policy, an interdepartmental group at Yale, gave me the chance to do research on American character and communication in 1948 and 1949, out of which grew *The Lonely Crowd* and *Faces in the Crowd;* this time it was the Yale group who were venturesome, for I was still untried. Now it is the Committee on Human Development at the University of Chicago, which has brought me in to help direct a study of urban life, with emphasis on aging. For that committee and for another interdepartmental group, the Committee on Communication, I have given seminars on Leisure in America and on Popular Culture in collaboration with my colleague Reuel Denney, longtime friend, tennis companion, and fellow student of the various 'brow' levels of American culture.

"In the summers I relax from the very demanding nature of teaching and academia generally, to play with my two boys and two girls, who now range in age from nine to fourteen, and to do the kind of reading and reflecting which busy winters prevent; I refuse to budge from the Vermont dairy farm which, with mechanization and competent help, runs with few of the crises which used to plague us."

* * *

Within a few years of its publication, *The Lonely Crowd*, a lengthy, detailed, scholarly study of "social-character formation" of the middle-class urban American, had become a best seller in a paper-bound edition, a popular book and a modern classic—all this in spite of the fact that some critics had objected to its "overabundance of jargon and unnecessarily obscure terminology." The reason for its phenomenal success, Jacques Barzun suggested, was that "Mr. Riesman not only describes but also explains. He never forgets that he lives among those he has studied and that before reducing them to types he has felt their feelings and understood their thoughts." Riesman's method is that of the historian and

the sociologist combined. "His command of the literature relevant to his varied topics is encyclopedic, and his imagination is like Zeus' thunderbolts, far-darting," Barzun wrote.

PRINCIPAL WORKS: Civil Liberties in a Period of Transition, 1942; Democracy and Defamation, 1942; (with others) The Lonely Crowd: A Study of the Changing American Character, 1950; (with N. Glazer) Faces in the Crowd: Individual Studies in Character and Politics, 1952; Thorstein Veblen: A Critical Interpretation, 1953; Individualism Reconsidered and Other Essays, 1954.

ABOUT: Cahiers Internationaux de Sociologie, XII (1952); Current Biography January 1955; The Griffin, I (1952); New York Times Book Review June 13, 1954; Time September 27, 1954.

RIGGS, LYNN (1899-June 30, 1954). For biographical sketch and list of earlier works and references, see TWENTIETH CENTURY AUTHORS, 1942.

* * *

Lynn Riggs died at Memorial Hospital in New York City, after a brief illness, at fifty-four. He had been working on a first novel which was unfinished at the time of his death.

In 1936 Richard Watts, Jr. called Riggs "one of the most provocative talents in the current American theatre," and declared that there was invariably in his work "the hint of a rich and lyric folk quality, of a true feeling for atmosphere and period, and of an original and sensitive mind." In spite of this promise the playwright never achieved a major success in the theatre except through *Oklahoma!*, which was based on his play *Green Grow the Lilacs*. Robert Littell had described the earlier play as "full of rich, free humor, salty poetry, and . . . reckless tenderness."

Collaborating for the first time, at the suggestion of the Theatre Guild, which had produced *Green Grow the Lilacs,* Richard Rodgers and Oscar Hammerstein (Riggs was not involved in the adaptation) created in *Oklahoma!* "virtually a new art, writing of real people, with book, ballets and songs growing out of the reality of the people," in the words of the New York *Times.* The musical made theatre history, running for 2,202 performances in its original Broadway run, netting a profit of $5,000,000 in its first ten years, and setting new standards in the musical theatre.

ADDITIONAL WORKS: Four Plays, 1947; Hang On to Love, 1948; Toward the Western Sky, 1951.

ABOUT: New York Times July 1, 1954; Time July 12, 1954; Variety July 7, 1954.

*RILKE, RAINER MARIA (December 4, 1875-December 29, 1926). For biographical sketch and list of works and references, see TWENTIETH CENTURY AUTHORS, 1942.

* * *

ADDITIONAL WORKS IN ENGLISH TRANSLATION: Letters, 2 vols., 1945-48; Five Prose Pieces, 1947; The Lay of Love and Death of Cornet Christopher Rilke, 1949; Letters to Benvenuta, 1951; Letters to Merline, 1951; The Life of the Virgin Mary (new trans. by S. Spender) 1952; His Last Friendship: Letters, 1952; From the Remains of Count C. W. (poems) 1952.

ABOUT: Bowra, C. M. The Heritage of Symbolism; Columbia Dictionary of Modern European Literature; Fausset, H. I. Poets and Pundits; Graedner-Hattingberg, M. Rilke and Benvenuta; Heerikhuizen, F. W. Rainer Maria Rilke: His Life and Work; Holthusen, H. E. Rilke: A Study of His Later Poetry, 1952; Kenmare, D. *in* Modern British Writing (ed. D. V. Baker); Mises, R. & others, Rilke in English: A Tentative Bibliography (1947); Purtscher, N. Rilke: Man and Poet; Rilke, R. M. Letters, Letters to Benvenuta, Letters to Merline, His Last Friendship; Contemporary Review December 1945; Dublin Review July 1946; Partisan Review January 1949.

* ríl'kĕ

RINEHART, Mrs. MARY (ROBERTS) (1876-). For biographical sketch and list of earlier works and references, see TWENTIETH CENTURY AUTHORS, 1942.

* * *

Mary Roberts Rinehart published her sixty-first book, *The Swimming Pool*, in 1952. This novel, like her most famous early ones, was a mystery romance. But Mrs. Rinehart insists that she has never written a detective story. "I'm not primarily interested in clues. I'm primarily interested in people and their motivations." Her advanced age and poor health (she has had several heart attacks) have necessarily curtailed her activities in recent years, but she reads avidly and writes methodically. "Writing is the hardest work in the world. When I'm working, I lead a very disciplined life." She lives in New York, in a large apartment overlooking Central Park. Her summer home in Bar Harbor, Maine, was destroyed in the fire that swept the island in 1947. In that same year Mrs. Rinehart figured prominently in a private drama as exciting as any she had described in her novels. Her cook, a man who had been in her service for twenty-five years, suddenly went berserk and attempted to murder her. She was rescued by other servants in the house, and the cook later committed suicide.

ADDITIONAL WORKS: Alibi for Isabel, and Other Stories, 1944; The Yellow Room, 1945; The Light in the Window, 1948; My Story (new and enlarged ed.) 1948; Episode of the Wandering Knife, 1950; The Swimming Pool, 1952.

ABOUT: Rinehart, M. R. My Story (1948); Life February 25, 1946; New York Herald Tribune Book Review February 3, 1952; New York Times Book Review February 3, 1952.

RITTENHOUSE, JESSIE BELLE (1869-September 28, 1948). For biographical sketch and list of works and references, see TWENTIETH CENTURY AUTHORS, 1942.

* * *

Jessie Belle Rittenhouse died at seventy-eight. She left her library and a large collection of letters from writers to Rollins College, where she had lectured for several years.

G. M. Whicher has pointed out that in her autobiography, as in her lectures, one found the "same clear and animated expression, the same earnestness and candor of spirit, and, above all, the same glowing enthusiasm for the cause of poetry, and living poetry at that."

ABOUT: New York Times September 30, 1948; Saturday Review of Literature October 30, 1948.

RIVES, AMÉLIE. See TROUBETZKOY, A. R.

ROBERTS, CECIL ("Russell Beresford") (1892-). For biographical sketch and list of earlier works and references, see TWENTIETH CENTURY AUTHORS, 1942.

* * *

Cecil Roberts was described by Roger Pippett (in the New York *Times*) in 1953 as "a survival from the eighteenth century . . . an interesting amalgam of the snob and the man of feeling." He is a writer of considerable grace and charm. His prose—whether in his travel books or in his novels—is "relaxed and relaxing." As a novelist probably his greatest fault is that, as Isabelle Mallet observed, he "is too gentlemanly an observer to inquire about the secret motives of his protagonists." As a travel writer he is sometimes superficial but unfailingly sensitive and stimulating. "Every journey was rich and rewarding and the horizon ever receding," he has said of his own experiences, and the statement well reflects his freshness and enthusiasm.

Roberts spent six years lecturing in the United States with a British mission during and just after World War II. His impressions of this country are recorded in *And So to America*. When not traveling, he makes his home in Alassio, Italy.

ADDITIONAL WORKS: The Labyrinth, 1944; So Immortal a Flower, 1944; And So to America, 1947; Eight for Eternity, 1948; And So to Rome, 1950; A Terrace in the Sun, 1951; One Year of Life, 1952; The Remarkable Young Man, 1954.

ABOUT: Roberts, C. One Year of Life.

ROBERTS, Sir CHARLES GEORGE DOUGLAS (January 10, 1860-November 26, 1943). For biographical sketch and list of earlier works and references, see TWENTIETH CENTURY AUTHORS, 1942.

* * *

Charles G. D. Roberts died in a Toronto hospital, at eighty-three, as the result of a cardiac condition. He was married to Joan Montgomery a month before his death.

As the London *Times* has pointed out, "While much of his work was merely popular, the best of it will not be soon forgotten." His primary distinction was as the "father of Canadian literature," exemplified in his own poetry dealing with the pastoral Canadian scene, and in his influence on the emergence of a national literature in the early days of the Dominion. Lorne Pierce has called him the first Canadian writer "to make a definite, conscious and sustained break with the past, as well as a conscious, deliberate and sustained dedication to the future of his country."

ADDITIONAL WORKS: Canada Speaks of Britain (poems) 1941; (ed.) Flying Colours (patriotic verse) 1942.

ABOUT: Brown, E. K. On Canadian Poetry; Percival, W. P. (ed.) Leading Canadian Poets; Pomeroy, E. M. Sir Charles G. D. Roberts; Thomas, C. Canadian Novelists; London Times November 29, 1943; New York Times November 27, 1943; Saturday Review of Literature March 4, 1944.

ROBERTS, ELIZABETH MADOX (1886-March 13, 1941). For biographical sketch and list of works and references, see TWENTIETH CENTURY AUTHORS, 1942.

* * *

ABOUT: Van Doren, M. The Private Reader; Southwest Review Autumn 1954.

ROBERTS, KENNETH LEWIS (December 8, 1885-). For biographical sketch and list of earlier works and references, see TWENTIETH CENTURY AUTHORS, 1942.

* * *

Kenneth Roberts has written only one historical novel in recent years, *Lydia Bailey*, an action-packed story set against a background of the native uprisings in Haiti under Toussaint L'Ouverture. For the most part he has devoted himself to his own rather special, sometimes seemingly eccentric, interests. According to his friend, the late Ben Ames Williams, these include—besides American history and all things relating to the state of Maine—raising ducks, reclaiming sour land, power lawn mowers, dogs, painting with oils or water colors, and divining rods. The latter interest has been the subject of two of Roberts' later books—*Henry Gross and His Dowsing Rod* and *The Seventh Sense*. He believes firmly in the power of the dowsing rod to locate underground springs, and in these books, Robert P. Tristram Coffin pointed out, he "advances the cause of folklore as the basis of the science of living."

In 1949 Roberts published his literary autobiography, *I Wanted to Write*. His life, as portrayed in this book, vividly demonstrates his thesis that "no one can become a writer of any standing unless he learns to drive himself incessantly and ruthlessly." The book was loosely organized, rambling and in some places even repetitious, but, as W. K. Rugg pointed out in the *Christian Science Monitor:* "The book would not be Kenneth Roberts' if it were not vigorous, downright, full of enthusiasms and antipathies, and sharply amusing." Roberts lives in Kennebunkport, Maine.

ADDITIONAL WORKS: Lydia Bailey, 1947; I Wanted to Write, 1949; Henry Gross and His Dowsing Rod, 1951; The Seventh Sense, 1953.

ABOUT: Lewis, J. Other Men's Minds; Roberts, K. I Wanted to Write; Williams, B. A. *Introduction to* The Kenneth Roberts Reader (1945); Life October 4, 1948.

ROBERTSON, ARNOT. See ROBERTSON, E. A.

ROBERTSON, EILEEN ARBUTHNOT (1903-). For autobiographical sketch and list of earlier works and references, see TWENTIETH CENTURY AUTHORS, 1942.

* * *

E. Arnot Robertson's wartime novel, *The Signpost*, was a sensitive story of a wounded English aviator and a French refugee girl who spent an idyllic week in a village in Ireland. The novelist Kate O'Brien found that the Irish setting of the book "has the effect of toning down Miss Robertson's customary assurance of judgment to a new speculativeness; it neutralises the well-known acidity and induces a warm, odd generosity." When the war ended, she took a job lecturing to British forces in Central Europe and North Africa. She was in Greece for much of the Greek Civil War and drew upon her experiences there in her recent, highly praised novel about a group of refugees, *Devices and Desires.*

In 1947 E. Arnot Robertson became involved in a legal battle with the American motion picture company of Metro-Goldwyn-Mayer. As film critic for the British Broadcasting Company, she had broadcast a series of sharp-tongued reviews of their pictures which prompted the company to bar her from their previews and to ask the B.B.C. "to silence a voice that was completely out of touch . . . unnecessarily harmful to the film industry." Miss Robertson filed a libel and slander suit against M.G.M. and was awarded £1,500 damages by the court. The film company appealed the decision; the appeal was upheld; and in 1950 Miss Robertson took the case to the House of Lords which decided in favor of the decision of the Court of Appeals. Although she had lost her case, she had a sound moral triumph. More than £7,000 was reportedly collected from newspapers and private donors to finance her legal fight, and the *New Statesman and Nation* commented upon the outcome of the case: "Miss Robertson was right to fight the case because of the immense importance of checking, at its very inception, any threat to the critic's freedom."

Miss Robertson is the wife of Sir Henry Turner, General Secretary of the Commonwealth Press Union. She lives in London.

ADDITIONAL WORKS: The Signpost, 1943; Devices and Desires, 1954.

ABOUT: New York Herald Tribune Book Review October 24, 1954; Newsweek July 28, 1947; Publishers' Weekly March 25, 1950; Time July 28, 1947.

ROBERTSON, MORGAN (September 30, 1861-March 24, 1915). For biographical sketch and list of works and references, see TWENTIETH CENTURY AUTHORS, 1942.

ROBINS, ELIZABETH (1862-May 8, 1952). For biographical sketch and list of works and references, see TWENTIETH CENTURY AUTHORS, 1942.

* * *

Elizabeth Robins died at Brighton, England, at an advanced age. She had come to the United States in 1940, during World War II, but returned to her home at Backset Town in Sussex in 1945.

She possessed, in the words of the London *Times,* "beauty and social charm that drew to her orbit many friends famous in their day and since." Some of these friendships are recorded in her lively autobiography and in her exchange of letters with Henry James.

Her novels were written with "a style that is simple and direct, often illuminated with a pleasant sense of comedy," according to the Boston *Transcript.* Isabel Paterson observed that she could not produce a book "devoid of distinction and the saving grace of readability."

ABOUT: London Times May 9, 1952; New York Times May 9, 1952; Pacific Spectator vol. 3, No. 1 (1949).

ROBINSON, EDWIN ARLINGTON (December 22, 1869-April 6, 1935). For biographical sketch and list of works and references, see TWENTIETH CENTURY AUTHORS, 1942.

* * *

ADDITIONAL WORKS: Letters to Howard George Schmitt (ed. C. J. Weber) 1943; Untriangulated Stars: Letters to Harry de Forest Smith (ed. D. Sutcliffe) 1947.

ABOUT: Barnard, E. Edwin Arlington Robinson, A Critical Study; Bates, E. W. Edwin Arlington Robinson and His Manuscripts; Bishop, J. P. Collected Essays; Brooks, V. W. A Chilmark Miscellany; Fussell, E. S. Edwin Arlington Robinson; National Cyclopedia of American Biography (1947); Neff, E. E. Edwin Arlington Robinson; Robinson, E. A. Letters to Howard George Schmitt, Untriangulated Stars; Southworth, J. G. Some Modern American Poets; Waggoner, H. H. The Heel of Elohim; Winters, Y. Edwin Arlington Robinson; Modern Language Notes January 1946; New Republic December 6, 1948; Publishers' Weekly November 22, 1947; South Atlantic Quarterly October 1944, January 1946; Time March 8, 1948, February 11, 1952.

ROBINSON, HENRY MORTON (September 7, 1898-   ), American novelist and poet, writes: "I was born on Beacon Hill, Boston, a few hundred yards from the State House, and attended public schools in the nearby suburb of Malden until the outbreak of World War I. In April 1917, I volunteered in the U.S. Naval Reserve and served twenty-two months on destroyers and Navy rifle-ranges. After the war I entered Columbia, received degrees of A.B.

Halsman

('23), M.A. ('24), and for three years thereafter was instructor in English in Columbia College. It was my good fortune to be first a student and later a colleague of John Erskine during those exciting years when he was launching his Great Books program.

"I enjoyed teaching but could not disown the deeper wish to be a full-time writer. I took a small house in Woodstock, N.Y., and for the next ten years barely supported myself and growing family by writing short stories and articles, as well as two volumes of poetry and three books of non-fiction. In 1937 I joined the staff of the *Reader's Digest* as associate editor, later becoming senior editor. During these editorial years (1937-45) I wrote two books: *Fantastic Interim,* and (in collaboration with Joseph Campbell) *A Skeleton Key to Finnegans Wake,* a full-length commentary on James Joyce's last and most difficult work.

"In 1945 I decided to devote the rest of my life to creative writing. Of the novels written during this period, *The Cardinal* is perhaps the best known; it has been translated into fifteen modern languages including the Japanese. My most recent publication was a fourth volume of verse: *The Enchanted Grindstone,* 1952. I am now working on a long novel entitled 'Water of Life' which traces the fortune of an American whiskey-making dynasty between 1885 and the present.

"After writing daily for thirty years one might reasonably expect that the task would become easier. For me it grows more difficult. Increasing skill and profounder experience seem unable to close the widening gap between creative vision and actual performance. Occasionally, after rewriting a page, a chapter, or an entire book, ten or even twenty times, sheer desperation obliges me to let it go, still imperfect, to the printer. I believe that my books will always be written the hard way. A study of the lives of other writers that I admire (Joyce, Conrad, Wolfe) leads me to suspect that my professional difficulties are neither unique nor hopeless."

* * *

Robinson's best selling *The Cardinal,* a story of the career of a Roman Catholic priest, was praised as a novel of "remarkable virtuosity," in which, as one reviewer pointed out, "the ecclesiastical robes of its principal characters are never used to obscure their individual, human qualities and relationships."

Robinson has been married to Gertrude Ludwig since 1926, and they have three children.

PRINCIPAL WORKS: *Poetry*—Children of Morningside (novel in verse) 1924; Buck Fever, 1929; Second Wisdom, 1936; The Enchanted Grindstone, 1952. *Novels*—The Perfect Round, 1945; The Great Snow, 1947; The Cardinal, 1950. *Miscellaneous*—Stout Cortez, 1931; Science vs. Crime, 1935; Public Virtue, Private Good, 1937; (with J. Campbell) A Skeleton Key to Finnegans Wake, 1939; Fantastic Interim, 1943.

ABOUT: Hoehn, M. (ed.) Catholic Authors, II; Current Biography 1950; New York Herald Tribune Book Review April 16, 1950; Saturday Review of Literature April 12, 1947.

ROBINSON, JAMES HARVEY (June 29, 1863-February 16, 1936). For biographical sketch and list of works and references, see TWENTIETH CENTURY AUTHORS, 1942.

* * *

ABOUT: Hendricks, L. V. James Harvey Robinson: Teacher of History; Journal of Higher Education January 1949; Journal of the History of Ideas April 1947; Saturday Review of Literature June 7, July 26, 1947.

ROBINSON, LENNOX (October 4, 1886-). For biographical sketch and list of earlier works and references, see TWENTIETH CENTURY AUTHORS, 1942.

* * *

Lennox Robinson has written several comedies in recent years, but probably his most important work is his study of the Abbey Theatre, its history, and its place in Irish life. In this connection he has edited the journals of Lady Gregory and compiled an "official" history of the Abbey, assembling all production details, casts, and other factual data. The latter book disappointed some reviewers who found it a "colorless . . . patchwork of personal reminiscences, of quotations from old records and newspaper clippings." But, as the *Times Literary Supplement* pointed out, this was a commissioned history, not an elaborate critical estimate of the Abbey's achievement. Most reviewers agreed with the *Spectator's* judgment that the book was "an admirable piece of historical writing within the limits Lennox Robinson proposed to himself, and it must remain a standard reference work of the Abbey's first fifty years during its second fifty." Robinson lives in Monkstown, Co. Dublin.

ADDITIONAL WORKS: Towards an Appreciation of the Theatre, 1945; (ed.) Lady Gregory's Journals, 1916-1930, 1947; Palette and Plough, 1948; Ireland's Abbey Theatre, 1899-1950, 1951. *Plays*—Pictures in a Theatre, 1947; The Lucky Finger, 1949; Speed the Plough, 1952.

ROCHE, ARTHUR SOMERS (April 27, 1883-February 17, 1935). For biographical sketch and list of works and references, see TWENTIETH CENTURY AUTHORS, 1942.

ROCHE. See DE LA ROCHE

RODGERS, WILLIAM ROBERT (1909-), Irish poet, was born in Belfast, Ireland. After taking his degree at Queens

Nigel Henderson

University, Belfast, he studied for the ministry of Loughgall Presbyterian Church, County Armagh. Rodgers is said to have not written a poem until he was twenty-nine years old. His first book, *Awake! and Other Poems*, appeared in England in 1941 creating the kind of stir that greets a new poet. Rodgers' extreme use of alliteration was early criticized, and while his poetry was thought to have a winning energy and vitality, his taste was frequently questioned. "With more economy," wrote Stephen Spender, "he would be a wholly delightful, if somewhat spasmodic poet. With more thought the development of his poems would be strong and sweeping. As it is, his lines tend to arrest the attention, and then fail to develop beyond what is vivid and striking. Sometimes the ends of poems seem arbitrary and prosaic." Since 1946 Rodgers has been a scriptwriter and producer for the B.B.C., his verse programs having included "Easter in Europe" and "Europe in Festival." In 1947 he published *Ulstermen and Their Country*, a prose work; and in 1952 *Europa and the Bull, and Other Poems*. In the latter, Kathleen Raine found his style "greatly influenced by Hopkins and Dylan Thomas and it is never dull, never flat—except when he has something to say of a philosophic nature, when he drops into bathos—but this seldom happens." Stephen Spender followed up his earlier estimate with this statement about *Europa and the Bull*: "Mr. Rodgers is an uneven poet, sometimes vivid and visual, sometimes vulgar. Everyone though should read him, because he is a poetic phenomenon." In spite of disagreement of opinion, there is always an enthusiastic audience for Rodgers' books of verse.

In 1951 he was elected to the Irish Academy of Letters to fill the vacancy caused by the death of Bernard Shaw.

PRINCIPAL WORKS: Awake! and Other Poems, 1941; Ulstermen and Their Country (prose) 1947; Europa and the Bull, and Other Poems, 1952.

ABOUT: Rexroth, K. (ed.) The New British Poets.

RODMAN, SELDEN (February 19, 1909-), American poet, editor, and art critic, writes: "Selden Rodman was born in New York City.

Maja Wojciechowska

While at Yale he helped found and edit (with William Harlan Hale) the magazine *The Harkness Hoot*. After graduation in 1931 and a year in Europe he and Alfred M. Bingham started the monthly political magazine *Common Sense*, which they edited together until their induction into the army in 1943. During the war Rodman served in an automatic weapons battalion and as a master sergeant in the foreign nationalities section of the Office of Strategic Services. After the war he returned to Haiti—his play *The Revolutionists* had been produced in Port-au-Prince by the Haitian government, on which occasion the order of Commander in the Haitian Legion of Honor had been conferred upon him—to become co-director of the Centre d'Art. In 1949-51 he initiated the mural painting movement in Haiti and directed the decoration of the Episcopal Cathedral of St.-Trinité in Port-au-Prince by nine primitive artists. As president of the Haitian Art Center of New York he organized exhibitions of the work of the Haitian artists throughout the United States and Europe. He is married to Maja Wojciechowska, daughter of the wartime chief of staff of the Polish Air Force and herself an author (*'Ti André Goes to Market*). They live with their daughter, Oriana (born 1951), in Oakland, N.J., where Rodman is presently doing editorial work for *New World Writing* and *Perspectives USA* and working on a book about religious art to be entitled 'The Eye of God.'"

* * *

Selden Rodman's work has been singularly varied and independent of conventional literary styles and influences. He has gone his own way, Peter Viereck remarks. "Belonging to no clique, he has never had a claque. The books he himself has written are little known, in contrast with the books he has edited." His verse ranges from a long dramatic-narrative poem on the life of T. E. Lawrence and the narrative *The Airmen,* through the verse drama of *The Revolutionists* (which Jeremy Ingalls called "a permanent contribution to the small library of notable American drama") to a poetic diary, *The Amazing Year, May 1, 1945-April 30, 1946.* His writings on art have been praised as sound, scholarly, and sensitively written. Probably his most successful book in this field is his biography of the artist Ben Shahn, based on long talks between the author and his subject reported "with almost Boswellian fidelity." J. T. Flexner wrote of the book in the New York *Times:* "Like some of the best American artistic biographies of the past, Rodman's biography of Shahn is in itself a work of art."

PRINCIPAL WORKS: *Poetry*—Mortal Triumph, 1932; Lawrence: The Last Crusade, 1937; The Airmen, 1939; The Revolutionists, 1942; The Amazing Year, 1947. *Prose*—Horace Pippin: A Negro Painter in America, 1947; Renaissance in Haiti, 1948; Portrait of the Artist as an American: Ben Shahn, 1951; Haiti: The Black Republic, 1954. *Anthologies*—A New Anthology of Modern Poetry, 1938, 1946; The Poetry of Flight, 1941; (with R. Eberhart) War and the Poet, 1946; 100 American Poems, 1948; 100 Modern Poems, 1949.

RODÓ, JOSÉ ENRIQUE (July 15, 1871-May 1, 1917). For biographical sketch and list of works and references, see TWENTIETH CENTURY AUTHORS, 1942.

* * *

ABOUT: Davis, H. E. Latin American Leaders; Henríquez-Ureña, P. Literary Currents in Hispanic America.

*ROETHKE, THEODORE (1908-), American poet, writes: "I might manage to write an anecdotal and perhaps even semi-engaging and mildly witty account of my life; but of what importance is it that I grew up in and around a beautiful green-house owned by my father and uncle; that I hated high school and Michigan and Harvard (in spite of fine teachers like Strauss, Campbell, Rice, I. A. Richards and others); that I have taught in various colleges and coached tennis; worked in a pickle factory for several seasons; have lived, alter-

* rĕt′kĕ

nately, very quietly and then foolishly and violently; that I have been called 'as good a steak cook as Brancusi' by William Carlos Williams; and that the kids at Bennington in a burst of misdirected generosity called me 'the best teacher we ever had'; that my books have been treated with astonishing generosity by good critics and poets and the young; that the English seem to like me even better; and that I mean almost nothing (except for a handful of personal friends) to the people of my own state, to the man in the street—and desire that regard most passionately; that I am much interested in oral presentation.

"All such details, and others like them, seem particularly trivial and vulgar in my case because I have tried to put them down in poems, as barely and honestly as possible, symbolically, what few nuggets of observation and, let us hope, spiritual wisdom I have managed to seize upon in the course of a conventional albeit sometimes disordered existence. I have tried to transmute and purify my 'life,' the sense of being defiled by it, in both small and formal and somewhat blunt short poems, and, latterly, in longer poems which try in their rhythms to catch the very movement of the mind itself, to trace the spiritual history of a protagonist (not 'I,' personally), of all haunted and harried men; to make in this series (now probably finished) a true and not arbitrary order which will permit many ranges of feeling, inc'.ading humor.

"I began, like the child, with small things. I had had no interest in verse after an intense period of pleasure in nursery rhymes in English and German and songs my mother and my nurse sang me. I really wanted, at fifteen and sixteen, to write a beautiful, a 'chiseled' prose as it was called in those days. There were books at home and I went to the local libraries (and very good ones they were for such a smallish town); read Stevenson, Pater, Newman, Tomlinson, and those maundering English charm boys known as familiar esssayists. I bought, on my own, editions of Emerson, Thoreau, and, as God's my witness, subscribed to the *Dial* when I was in the seventh grade. I was strong for anthologies of great thoughts, including Elbert Hubbard; and had such deep interest in the short story that I started buying the O'Brien anthologies in 1920 when I was twelve. (You could make money in the short story!)

"My first verses, and dreadful they were, I sold for $1. About a year later when I was moping through the Harvard Yard one night,

I saw a man I thought might be Robert Hillyer. I said boldly, 'Pardon me, Sir, I think I have some poems you might like.' A look of pain came over his face. 'Come to my office at eleven,' he said. I did, complete with fur coat and a fancy suit (those Harvards weren't going to have it over me!). Ushered in by his secretary, he took the verse, started reading. Suddenly he wheeled in his chair. 'Any editor who wouldn't buy these is a fool!' he said. I was overwhelmed (though I had thought so too!). There were only three poems, but Ridgely Torrence of the *New Republic* and George Shuster, then of *Commonweal*, did buy two of them.

"I felt I had come to the end (really the beginning) of a trail. I had learned how to get high grades, but that seemed meaningless. Now I didn't have to go into advertising (I had written at eighteen copy which had been used in national campaigns), or the law. I wasn't just a spoiled sad snob. I could write and people I respected printed the stuff.

"It took me ten years to complete one little book, and now some of the things in it seem to creak. Still, I like about ten pieces in it. Writers were extraordinarily generous to me in a very personal way in this long incubation, particularly in what *not* to do. Let me name some: W. H. Auden, Louise Bogan, Malcolm Cowley, Babette Deutsch, Rolfe Humphries, John Holmes, Stanley Kunitz, Douglas Moore, A. J. M. Smith, William Carlos Williams, and latterly, Kenneth Burke, Edith Sitwell, and many students. These people, maybe without realizing it, spoke with absolute candor and often with great insight; they often kept me from going down blind alleys or wasting what time I had for writing better.

"I write this down because it is a matter rarely mentioned. I owe much less, I believe, to the *work* of contemporaries than to their qualities as men and women. And that debt is immense."

* * *

Theodore Roethke is professor of English at the University of Washington. Previously he taught at Lafayette, Pennsylvania State, and Bennington. In 1945 he was awarded a Guggenheim fellowship. *Poetry* has honored him twice, with the Eunice Tietjens prize (1947) and the Levinson award (1951). In 1952 he was granted a fellowship by the Fund for the Advancement of Education and an award by the American Academy of Arts and Letters. In 1954 he

received the Pulitzer prize for poetry with his volume *The Waking*. He is a member of Phi Beta Kappa. A sojourn in Italy followed his marriage in January 1953 to Beatrice O'Connell of Winchester, Va.

In appearance Roethke is big (six feet three), ruddy blonde, lumbering, but his bulk and gait are deceptive, for despite his two hundred pounds-plus he is remarkably agile and quick-reflexed, as anybody who has ever opposed him on a tennis court will testify. "A dancing bear" is his image-identification. At both Lafayette and Pennsylvania State colleges he served as varsity tennis coach.

"Mr. Roethke is instantly recognizable as a good poet," wrote W. H. Auden. "Many people have the experience of feeling physically soiled and humiliated by life; some quickly put it out of their mind, others gloat narcissistically on its unimportant details; but both to remember and to transform the humiliations into something beautiful, as Mr. Roethke does, is rare." According to Stanley Kunitz, "The ferocity of Roethke's imagination makes most contemporary poetry seem pale and tepid in contrast. Even his wit is murderous.... What Roethke brings us is news of the root, of the minimal, of the primordial. The sub-human is given tongue; and the tongue proclaims the agony of coming alive, the painful miracle of growth."

PRINCIPAL WORKS: Open House, 1941; The Lost Son and Other Poems, 1948; Praise to the End! 1951; The Waking, 1953.

ABOUT: Roethke, T. *in* Mid-Century American Poets, ed. by John Ciardi; New York Times May 5, 1954; Poetry July 1941, January 1949; Sewanee Review January 1950.

ROGERS, SAMUEL (September 5, 1894-). For autobiographical sketch and list of earlier works and references, see TWENTIETH CENTURY AUTHORS, 1942.

* * *

Samuel Rogers writes from Madison, Wis.: "During World War II, I represented the American Field Service in Wisconsin. As a relaxation, unable to concentrate on 'serious' literature, I wrote three mystery stories. In 1950 I represented the United States, as a guest of the French government, at the centenary of the death of Balzac in Paris. That same year I was appointed a Chevalier in the order of the French Legion of Honor (La Légion d'Honneur)."

ADDITIONAL WORKS: Don't Look Behind You, 1944; You'll Be Sorry, 1945; You Leave Me Cold, 1946; Balzac and the Novel, 1953.

ROGERS, WILL (November 4, 1879-August 15, 1935). For biographical sketch and list of works and references, see TWENTIETH CENTURY AUTHORS, 1942.

* * *

In 1949 Donald Day published a selection from Will Rogers' writings as the humorist's *Autobiography*. The book was highly praised as a faithful portrait of Rogers and a real "manual of American humor."

A motion picture, *The Story of Will Rogers*, was made in 1951 with Will Rogers, Jr. (a former Democratic congressman from California) portraying his father.

ADDITIONAL WORKS: Autobiography (ed. D. Day) 1949; How We Elect Our Presidents (ed. D. Day) 1952.

ABOUT: Garst, D. S. Will Rogers: Immortal Cowboy; Hagedorn, H. Americans: A Book of Lives; National Cyclopedia of American Biography (1947); Rogers, B. B. Will Rogers; Rogers, W. Autobiography; Coronet January 1950; Good Housekeeping November 1947; Holiday April 1951; Life May 27, 1946, July 18, 1949, January 23, 1950; Saturday Review of Literature October 15, 1949; Scholastic October 27, 1948; South Atlantic Quarterly July 1951.

"ROHMER, SAX" (pseudonym of Arthur Sarsfield Wade) (1883-). For autobiographical sketch and list of earlier works and references, see TWENTIETH CENTURY AUTHORS, 1942.

* * *

Sax Rohmer and his wife, a former British actress, are living in White Plains, N.Y. He plans to spend the rest of his life in the United States.

A *New Yorker* correspondent reported that his health "continues excellent in the face of persistent rumors that he's been dead for years," and described him as "small, gray, nervous, affable, and shy about revealing his age." The immortal Dr. Fu Manchu has undergone considerable transformation in the post-World War II era. "He's still villainous and unscrupulous," Rohmer said, "but he's flat out against the Communists and trying to help democracy. In the old days, you know, he was all for personal power." Rohmer has written a play—so far unproduced—based on Fu Manchu's adventures. Several of his later novels have been serialized in *Collier's*.

Early in 1955 it was reported that Rohmer had sold to Republic Pictures the TV, radio, and film rights to Dr. Fu Manchu for $4,000,000. "Jolly good thing for me right now," he was quoted as saying, "because I've been most improvident all my life. I've never been secure, even though I've made a million or two out of Fu Manchu. . . . Editions have gone on for twenty-one years and they're still coming out, published everywhere, in every language, but I couldn't keep track of the money. I just gave up and spent it."

ADDITIONAL WORKS: Seven Sins, 1943; Bimbashi Baruk of Egypt (in England: Egyptian Nights) 1944; The Shadow of Fu Manchu, 1948; Hangover House, 1949; The Sins of Sumuru, 1951; The Slaves of Sumuru, 1952; Virgin in Flames, 1953; The Moon Is Red, 1954.

ABOUT: Collier's May 15, 1948; New York World-Telegram January 21, 1955; New Yorker November 29, 1947.

"ROLAND, J." See OLIVER, J. R.

ROLFE, FREDERICK WILLIAM SERAFINO AUSTIN LEWIS MARY ("Baron Corvo"), (July 22, 1860-October 26, 1913). For biographical sketch and list of works and references, see TWENTIETH CENTURY AUTHORS, 1942.

* * *

The first American edition of Baron Corvo's *The Desire and Pursuit of the Whole* appeared in 1953 and stimulated new interest in the perverse and fascinating figure of Frederick Rolfe. The book, like the personality of the author, was at once intriguing and repulsive. Its literary merits were challenged by some of the critics, but the style was generally praised as distinctive for "verbal exuberance, exotic learning, and richness of abuse and invective." Anthony West wrote in the *New Yorker*: "It is one of the most mean-spirited books ever written, but the fascinations of its flawless nastiness from the psychological point of view are a very inadequate compensation for its almost complete lack of literary merit." A. J. A. Symons, on the other hand, found considerable literary merit in this book. *"The Desire and Pursuit* is an incongruous compound of an exquisite, romantic dream-tale with undramatic and sordid details from Rolfe's life." When all the adverse criticism has been weighed, Symons continued, "it remains an admirable and astonishing book, a characteristic product of its author's genius, full of his unflagging zest for life and phrases, with hundreds of memorable and beautiful passages and sentences."

ABOUT: Auden, W. H. & Symons, A. J. A. Foreword and Introduction to The Desire and Pursuit of the Whole (1953); Life and Letters February 1947.

*ROLLAND, ROMAIN (January 29, 1866-December 30, 1944). For autobiographical sketch and list of earlier works and references, see TWENTIETH CENTURY AUTHORS, 1942.

* * *

Romain Rolland died at seventy-eight at his home in the French village of Vézelay.

Because of his anti-Nazi activities the Vichy government imposed house arrest on him during the occupation of France, but he was able to continue working throughout the war years. The fruit of these final years was a book based on the life of Charles Péguy, with whom he had been closely associated; the result Denis Saurat called "his true masterpiece."

Although in his championship of the oppressed he wrote "with burning sincerity and a brilliant pen," Harrison Smith has noted that "his novels and his volumes on art and music will outlive his reputation as a political actionist," with *Jean-Christophe* remaining his most significant work. His credo has been summarized by W. Hunter Beckwith as centering on the principle "that all art manifestations should convey moral truth, which for him seems to be faith in humanity, a pantheistic religion, and continued insistence on the virtues of great artists."

ADDITIONAL WORKS IN ENGLISH TRANSLATION: The Journey Within, 1947; Essays on Music, 1948.

ABOUT: Aronson, A. Romain Rolland; Columbia Dictionary of Modern European Literature; Rolland, R. The Journey Within; Saurat, D. Modern French Literature; Christian Century January 17, 1945; London Quarterly Review January 4, 1946; Mercure de France March 1951, December 1952; New York Times January 2, 1945; Saturday Review of Literature January 6, 1945, January 13, 1945.

* rô län′

*RØLVAAG, OLE EDVART (April 22, 1876-November 5, 1931). For biographical sketch and list of works and references, see TWENTIETH CENTURY AUTHORS, 1942.

* * *

ABOUT: Scholastic February 28, 1951.

* rôl′väg

*ROMAINS, JULES (August 26, 1885-). For autobiographical sketch and list of earlier works and references, see TWENTIETH CENTURY AUTHORS, 1942.

* * *

* "The *J* in Jules must be pronounced as in the French word *jour; ules* as in *bulle;* and *mains* in Romains as in *main* or *demain.*" zhül rô mäN′

Jules Romains writes from Paris: "The outbreak of war in September 1939 was a mortal blow to the ideal for which I had not ceased to struggle since my youth. Up to the last moment I tried desperately to believe that a new war was avoidable, persuaded as I was (and still am) that if men work together to prevent a catastrophe, the causes of which lie in humanity itself, they have a good chance of succeeding. But since this war had come, and since I knew that we were on the right side, it was necessary to win it. That is why I undertook various missions for the French government, which I described later (in the United States) in my series of articles entitled 'Seven Mysteries of Europe.' Alas, I saw quickly that France, poorly prepared and still more poorly supported by her friends and allies, could not long resist Nazi Germany. When the collapse came, I thought that if I wanted to work constructively, by my own means which are the pen and the word, for the victory of free peoples, I could do so only in a country which was free itself. Taking my young wife with me, but leaving behind everything that we possessed, I fled to seek the hospitality of the United States.

"I want to say here how grateful I am for the welcome that I received in the United States. It is a country that I had admired very much before, but, in spite of the sad circumstances, I was happy to have had the occasion to live there for a length of time, no longer as a traveler but as a resident. I had many friends there; I added to the number. And, while living in New York, I made an effort to know regions of the country that I had not known before. I think I can say without bragging that I now know more parts of the United States than most Americans know.

"As soon as I arrived in New York, in July 1940, I got in touch with the local representative of the Free French with whom I did not cease working until the liberation of France. That did not prevent me from continuing my personal work. At the request of the *Saturday Evening Post,* I wrote, on my experiences of the last few years, the series of articles mentioned above, and which appeared later in book form under the title *Seven Mysteries of Europe.* A little later I published a book on the United States, *Salsette Discovers America.* And I continued to work on *Men of Good Will.*

"As the guest of several universities, I enlarged my knowledge of the very congenial university centers. Also during this period

I went for the first time to Canada and to Cuba. Invited early in 1942 by the University of Mexico City to give a course, I went with my wife to Mexico where we stayed until the end of the war, not without long and frequent visits to the United States. In Mexico City, in October 1944, I finished the twenty-seventh (thirtieth in the American edition) and last volume of *Men of Good Will*, which was for me, if I may say so, an important date, because I had often asked myself, in the course of those terrible years, if I would have the strength and courage to finish this long work. I also wrote, during this period, several works—two plays, two long short stories (*Nomentanus le Réfugié* and *Bertrand de Ganges*), etc.

"I returned to France for the first time at the beginning of 1945. In spite of the joy of finding myself again in my country and of seeing Paris intact, I had the sadness of learning that my apartment was occupied by other people (and to find an apartment in Paris since the war is a more than difficult problem) and that the Gestapo had laid violent hands on everything I possessed: furniture, paintings, objects of art, books, papers, etc. Nothing was left but our house in Touraine. I returned to America to settle various affairs, as much in Mexico as in the United States; then I was rather seriously ill for a long time, and it was not until the beginning of the summer of 1946 that my wife and I were able to return to settle permanently in France. Meanwhile I had been elected a member of the French Academy.

"At first we had to live in a hotel; then finally we settled in the apartment in which we are still living today, and which we furnished as quickly as possible. My life has gradually taken on again the rhythm it had before the war, divided between Paris, Touraine, and travel in France and abroad. I have renewed contact with those countries of Europe which are on this side of the Iron Curtain (including Berlin); I returned to North Africa and Egypt, and I am preparing to go for the first time to the Far East. Unfortunately I have been able to return to the United States only once during this period (in the autumn of 1950).

"Since my return to France I have published a volume of poems, *Pierres Levées;* some short stories, the most important of which, published in volumes, are: *Le Moulin et l'Hospice, Violation de Frontières, Démêlés avec la Mort et le Temps;* two volumes of essays, one on politics, *Le Problème N° 1,* the other literary, *Saints de Notre Calendrier.* Many of my works have been revived by the Paris stage and played in Europe."

* * *

With *The Seventh of October,* Jules Romains completed his monumental *Men of Good Will* series. The twenty-seven volumes cover a twenty-five-year period from 1908 to 1933, with a multitude of characters and a scene that ranges widely over European history, from the pre-World War I era to the rise of Nazism and Fascism. The critical summing-up of this ambitious project was in general an expression of disappointment that the later volumes had not fulfilled the promise of the earlier ones. The critic Wallace Fowlie feels that their genre is properly lyricism rather than the novel: "The poet of *La Vie Unanime* has recapitulated his first themes, but the action into which he has forced them is so diffuse that the force and unifying focus which action in a novel should have are subordinated to effects of lyric quality."

ADDITIONAL WORKS IN ENGLISH TRANSLATION: "Men of Good Will" Series—Work and Play (Mountain Days, Work and Play) 1944; The Wind Is Rising (Gathering of the Gangs, Offered in Evidence) 1945; Escape in Passion (Magic Carpet, Françoise) 1946; The Seventh of October, 1946.

ABOUT: Fowlie, W. Clowns and Angels; Gray, J. On Second Thought; Saurat, D. Modern French Literature; American Scholar Spring 1948; France Illustration July 15, 1950; Newsweek November 25, 1946; Saturday Review of Literature December 7, 1946; Time January 24, 1944.

ROMANOV, PANTELEIMON SERGE-YEVICH (1884-April 30, 1938). For biographical sketch and list of works and references, see TWENTIETH CENTURY AUTHORS, 1942.

* * *

ABOUT: Columbia Dictionary of Modern European Literature; Struve, G. Soviet Russian Literature, 1917-1950.

ROSENBERG, ISAAC (November 25, 1890-April 19, 1918). For biographical sketch and list of works and references, see TWENTIETH CENTURY AUTHORS, 1942.

* * *

ADDITIONAL WORK: Collected Poems (ed. G. Bottomley & D. Harding) 1949.

ABOUT: Sassoon, S. *Foreword to* Collected Poems; Commentary January 1949; Poetry April 1946.

ROSENFELD, MORRIS (December 28, 1862-June 21, 1923). For biographical sketch and list of works and references, see TWENTIETH CENTURY AUTHORS, 1942.

ROSENFELD, PAUL (May 4, 1890-July 21, 1946). For autobiographical sketch and list of earlier works and references, see TWENTIETH CENTURY AUTHORS, 1942.

* * *

Paul Rosenfeld died at St. Vincent's Hospital in New York City following a heart attack. He was fifty-six. During the later years of his life he had been a frequent contributor to *Kenyon Review, Commonweal, Tomorrow,* and other periodicals.

Among many friends attesting to his extraordinary generosity and loyalty, Marianne Moore has called him "a figure best praised by his own myriad chivalries, drudgeries and masteries . . . a son of consolation, a son of imagination, the man of deeds."

He made a lasting contribution to our literature of musical criticism, in the opinion of Alfred Frankenstein, as "a galvanizer of musical enthusiasm" and "a seeker and affirmer of the creative spirit." Literary pretensions were subordinated in his work to critical verities; William Carlos Williams said that he "sacrificed his style for the truth of his observations and his career for those loyalties, personal and impersonal, for which he will be remembered and honored."

ADDITIONAL WORK: *Editor*—Sherwood Anderson Reader, 1947.

ABOUT: Mellquist, J. & Wiese, L. (eds.) Paul Rosenfeld: Voyager in the Arts; Commentary February 1948; Commonweal August 15, 1947; Modern Music Summer 1946; Nation August 17, 1946; New York Times July 22, 1946.

ROSMAN, ALICE GRANT. For biographical sketch and list of works and references, see TWENTIETH CENTURY AUTHORS, 1942.

* * *

Alice Grant Rosman has published no books in recent years. A confirmed Londoner, she lists her recreations as "motoring, traveling, and returning to London, especially the last."

ROSS, ALAN (May 6, 1922-), English poet, critic, and travel writer, reports: "I was born in Calcutta, where my father was leader of the European Party in the Bengal Legislative Assembly. On my father's side I am of pure Scottish descent, while my mother, the daughter of a colonel in the Indian Army, comes from a Franco-Irish family whose home was near Dijon. I spent my childhood moving between India, France, Italy and England. I went to schools in Cornwall and Sussex, then to Haileybury and St. John's College, Oxford. At Oxford I played cricket and squash rackets for the university and when there was time, read Modern Languages. After eighteen months, however, I joined the Royal Navy. The next five years were spent mostly at sea. I was for various periods based in Iceland and Russia, doing convoy work in a destroyer, and later on, as a staff officer attached to a destroyer flotilla, took part in the attacks on Europe. After the end of the war I was in Germany for a year on the staff of the British Naval Commander-in-Chief.

Thea Umlauff

"In 1947 I was granted an Atlantic Award for Literature by the Rockefeller Foundation, and the same year published my first book of poems, *The Derelict Day.* Many of these had appeared in literary reviews during the war, in John Lehmann's *New Writing,* the *New Statesman and Nation,* the *Listener,* etc. In 1948 I published *Time Was Away,* a travel book about Corsica, illustrated by the painter John Minton.

"In 1949 I married. I was working for the British Council, but left it in 1950 for full-time writing. I reviewed fairly regularly, for the *New Statesman,* the *Times Literary Supplement,* and *Tribune,* and also did a number of broadcasts. I managed also to travel a good deal. I went to Bagdad as personal assistant to Sir Charles Darwin and Dr. A. E. Morgan, when they went there on a government mission in 1949. I spent some months in Spain, Elba, and the Gulf of Naples, writing a book of prose and verse about the latter under the title of *The Gulf of Pleasure.* In 1950 I published *The Forties,* an illustrated book about the war decade, and in the same year *Poetry 1945-50,* a critical essay on contemporary English verse. The longer criticism I was writing justly reflects my literary interests. Two essays were published in *Horizon* on Scott Fitzgerald and Nathanael West, articles in the *Times Literary Supplement* on St. Exupéry, W. H. Auden and Ernst Jünger.

"I had always been interested in sport, and cricket and soccer have given me as much pleasure as anything in my life. In 1950 I began to write regularly on these two games for the *Observer*.

"My recent work has included a translation of Philipe Diolé's *L'Aventure Sous-Marine*, and an introduction to Charles-Louis Philippe's *Bubu of Montparnasse*. I am now [December 1952] writing a travel book about a journey through Sardinia, to be called 'The Bandit on the Billiard Table,' and hope soon to publish a new volume of poetry."

PRINCIPAL WORKS: The Derelict Day, 1947; Time Was Away, 1948; The Forties, 1950; The Gulf of Pleasure, 1951; Poetry 1945-50, 1951; The Bandit on the Billiard Table, 1954.

"ROSS, BARNABY." See "QUEEN, E."

"ROSS, J. H." See LAWRENCE, T. E.

"ROSS, LEONARD Q." See ROSTEN, L. C.

"ROSS, MARTIN." See MARTIN, V. F.

ROSS, NANCY (WILSON) (November 22, 1907), American novelist, writes: "I am descended from Norman-English, Irish and Scotch ancestry and I was born and grew up in the Pacific Northwest. I consider this happenstance of my early geography to be of considerable importance in my personal history. To live near the rhythms of tide-water, and always within sight of snow-capped peaks is bound to have an effect on any imaginative child. Also my early environment created in me an enduring interest in Nature, Indians, and Orientals, and my writings frequently reflect these influences. Both of my parents were bookworms and I have read constantly and avidly all my life. To my father I owe the will to pursue the idea for the idea's sake. To him I also owe an ever-growing interest in the study of comparative religion.

Marcus Blechman

"I have done two non-fiction studies of the part of America where I was born: *Farthest Reach: The Story of Oregon and Washington* and *Westward the Women*, an unsentimental study of women pioneers. (This latter has led to the accusation that I am a feminist, which is perhaps the truth, though I tend to agree with the estimate of American women as, in general, 'our greatest unused national resource.')

"In the novel *I, My Ancestor*, I also made direct use of Far Western landscape and Indian myths as a part of the book's thematic material. Yet I do not consider myself in any sense a regional writer—nor do I want to be considered one, for I dislike 'religion of place' and hope always to extend any regional material beyond the bounds of the purely local. Actually as much of my life has been lived away from the Pacific Northwest as in it, and I know the woods of the Adirondacks and the deserts of Arizona almost as well as Puget Sound beaches and forests.

"I attended the University of Oregon and later the *Bauhaus* in Germany. The latter was an advanced school of contemporary art and architecture which Hitler closed as 'dangerous.' My experiences during the 1930's while living through the rapid Nazi destruction of the 'New Germany' made a profound effect on me. An article I wrote while a student, 'A German Main Street,' appeared in the *Saturday Evening Post*. This article, which turned out to be prophetic, created a great deal of heated controversy at the time, though in retrospect it seems mild indeed.

"It appears to be a part of my individual fate pattern to see countries just before, or during, drastic changes. Thus—after Germany—in 1939, I visited Japan, Korea and Peking, and saw ways of life which have since disappeared. During World War II I flew, as a special writer assigned to the Air Corps, over all of the European and North African theatres of war. Now, as I write this piece, in May 1953, I have just returned from a trip around the world, during which I visited Pakistan, India, Ceylon, Thailand, Burma, French Indo-China, Hong-Kong and Japan.

"My most successful novel from the point of view of sales and wide distribution was *The Left Hand Is the Dreamer*. This novel was bought for publication in fourteen countries. It dealt with the theme of the penalty of prolonged immaturity on the part of an American woman. My latest novel, *Time's Corner*, is a fictional study of types of modern 'escape.' In it I used the extreme example of drug addiction as a way of 'exploding the frame' of the theme of attempted withdrawal from the problems of daily life. The setting of this novel was laid in an Anglican House of Retreat.

"I am at present working on a 'Primer on Buddhism for the Western World.' My recent trip to the Far East was taken in pursuit of the material for this book. I wished particularly to see, at first hand, some of the great relics of Buddhist art and architecture in the Orient.

"Next to writing, my chief interest has always been in art. I have made a modest collection of modern paintings and sculpture, and Far Eastern art objects. I have also lectured and written in the field of art criticism. I am married to Stanley Young, the publisher and playwright. I have three stepchildren. We live in Old Westbury, Long Island."

* * *

Nancy Wilson Ross was born in Olympia, Wash., the daughter of Robert James and Lydia May (Giles) Wilson. She was educated in the West and took her B.A. from the University of Oregon. Her first marriage, to Charles Walton Ross, Jr., ended in divorce, but she retained the name for her professional signature. Her recent novels have been singled out for praise for their seriousness and sensitivity. Critics have found them literate and intelligent works which sometimes miss "complete success by being overambitious" (James Stern in the New York *Times*) but never fail to make stimulating reading.

PRINCIPAL WORKS: *Novels*—Friday to Monday, 1932; Take the Lightning, 1940; The Left Hand Is the Dreamer, 1947; I, My Ancestor, 1950; Time's Corner, 1952. *Non-Fiction*—Farthest Reach: Oregon and Washington, 1941; Westward the Women, 1944; The WAVES: The Story of the Girls in Blue, 1945; Joan of Arc (juvenile) 1953.

ABOUT: Current Biography 1952; New York Herald Tribune Book Review February 26, 1950, October 12, 1952; New York Times Book Review February 23, 1947, January 29, 1950; Saturday Review of Literature February 8, 1947.

*ROSTAND, EDMOND (April 1, 1868-December 2, 1918). For biographical sketch and list of works and references, see TWENTIETH CENTURY AUTHORS, 1942.

* * *

ABOUT: Columbia Dictionary of Modern European Literature; Contemporary Review July 1948.

* rôs tän´

ROSTEN, LEO CALVIN ("Leonard Q. Ross") (April 11, 1908-). For autobiographical sketch and list of earlier works and references, see TWENTIETH CENTURY AUTHORS, 1942:

* * *

Leo Rosten writes from New York that his book on the movies, *Hollywood: The Movie Colony, The Movie Makers,* received excellent reviews which "got lead space in the Sunday book sections—but the Sunday was December 7, 1941. The next day I was called to Washington. At one time or another I served on (or as) the research staff, the President's Committee on Administrative Management; chief, Motion Picture Division, National Defense Advisory Commission; assistant to Lowell Mellett, administrative assistant to President Roosevelt; chief, Motion Picture Division, Office of Facts and Figures; deputy director, Office of War Information; special consultant to the Secretary of War's office.

"In the fall of 1945 the War Department sent me to Europe on a special mission involving the morale of American troops in France and Germany. I returned to America to become a consultant to the Rand Corporation, a research project of the Air Forces. In 1949 I moved to Springdale, Conn., and became special editorial adviser to Gardner Cowles, editor and publisher of *Look* and *Quick.*

"For ten years I have written one melodrama a year. For these coffer-liners I use the pseudonym Leonard Ross, without the Q. Many of these exercises in technique became movies; many were published in magazines as serials. They include: *The Dark Corner, Sleep, My Love, Miss Wheelwright Discovers America, All Through the Night, The Washington Angle (They Got Me Covered), Double Dynamite, Dateline: Europe, The Velvet Touch, The Conspirators,* and *Cory.* I wrote the original story and screen play for *Walk East on Beacon.*

"I am a faculty associate at Columbia University and have lectured at Stanford, New York, Yale, UCLA, the New School for Social Research. I am currently engaged in research on communications and symbolism.

"The first reporter who interviewed me was a bright young lady who was 6'1" tall. She reported to *Time* magazine: He is short, dark, serious-looking, with black eyes under heavy lids. I happen to be 5'8" high, my eyes are brown, and I have never had any difficulty in raising my lids.

"I am a member of Phi Beta Kappa, the American Political Science Association, the Academy of Political and Social Science, the American Association for the Advancement of Science, the American Sociological Society. I have traveled extensively on the continent of Europe. My books have been published in England and in French, Spanish, Swedish, and Czech translations.

"I have three children—a son and two daughters. My other hobby is photography."

ADDITIONAL WORK: (ed.) A Guide to the Religions of America, 1955.

ROSTEN, NORMAN (January 1, 1914-), American poet and playwright, reports: "My parents were immigrants—a marvelously  madcap mother and an intensively introspective father, which may have had something to with my becoming a writer. Though it could as well have been the depression of the Thirties, when I sat in a room for month after month and began to write out of idleness and desperation.

"My first ten years were spent on a farm in upstate New York. I attended a little red schoolhouse and fell in love with a girl named Marie. That is all I remember of my childhood.

"The farm burned down, the family moved to New York City and finally migrated southward through Brooklyn to Coney Island. I shall never know why, but it was undoubtedly my mother's attraction to the Byzantine. There, realism and romanticism were curiously one, and to this day, to my despair, I find myself unable to clearly separate them.

"Friends are always surprised to discover that I have actually lived in Coney Island, as though the place were unreal. It is, but people have lived there since the early 1600's.

"My early influences were a winter seascape and the throbbing summer carnival. With the works of Chekhov, Sandburg, and MacLeish thrown in.

"Out of school without much visible future (Brooklyn College '35, with New York University for an M.A.), I decided to teach English, but failed to pass a grammar exam. Bored and brooding, I wrote an imitation Chekhov play about some Brooklyn peasants, won a year's playwriting scholarship at the University of Michigan, and began writing plays and poetry with some seriousness. At Michigan, I had a verse drama successfully produced and, upon leaving (1938), I won the Avery Hopwood award in both poetry and drama. I don't recall exactly, but I believe I lived at least two years on that $1500.

I was lucky with awards. I worked next for the New York Federal Theatre (W.P.A.), a great institution of the Thirties which gave a writer $22 a week and some dignity, and was ultimately destroyed by an idiot Congress. I turned to radio and wrote some of the pioneer verse plays to be produced in this medium. My first Broadway play had opened and almost immediately closed. My first book of poems was issued in the Yale Series of Younger Poets (1940). A Guggenheim fellowship encouraged me on a second book. I wrote, for some time during the Forties, rather extensively for radio. With the war, I contributed much special material for the U.S.O., Council for Democracy, Writers War Board, O.W.I., Armed Forces Radio, etc. In 1945 I received an award from the American Academy of Arts and Letters for my 'exploration of the Radio as a new medium for poetry.'

"My most ambitious work, a book-length narrative poem dealing with the Alcan Highway and the drama of roadmaking, was published in 1946. I kept at my plays, meanwhile; the options were many but productions few.

"I've lived in Brooklyn most of my life. In 1940 I married Hedda Rowinski, a Connecticut émigré, and we have a daughter entitled Patricia.

"After five volumes of poetry and some ten plays (three produced), I think, at forty, I can agree with my fellow poet Louis MacNeice:

Do I prefer to forget it? This middle stretch
Of life is bad for poets; a sombre view
Where neither works nor days look innocent
And both seem now too many, now too few."

* * *

Some years ago Norman Rosten said of his work: "What I am concerned with most in my poetry is the external world and its action, for the beliefs and heroisms of that world are, finally, the sources of poetry. I do not belong to that school which holds to the curious belief that poetry is written for poets and should be as difficult and obscure as possible. Poetry . . . should neither exhaust nor confuse, but invigorate and clarify." His poetry is vigorous and dramatic. Harry Roskolenko wrote in *Poetry* in 1953 that he "plays his socially attuned harp with varied technical skill, for he has the true lyric touch when he doesn't pluck a lot of outdated dialectical discords." John Ciardi observed that Rosten's "talent in language is simplicity, directness and a colloquial ear.

There are few gems of diction to be culled from his writing; the line, rather, moves stagewise—spoken and out."

PRINCIPAL WORKS: *Poetry*—Return Again Traveler, 1940; The Fourth Decade, 1943; The Big Road, 1946; Songs for Patricia, 1951; The Plane and the Shadow, 1953.

ABOUT: Current Biography 1944.

*   *   *

ROTH, CECIL (March 5, 1899-   ), British historian, writes: "I was born in London in 1899, the youngest son of a scholarly merchant, Joseph Roth,  and his wife, Etty Jacobs, and educated at the City of London school. In the summer of 1917 I was called up for military service, and was sent to France in the following year. In January 1919 I went up to Oxford as an Exhibitioner at Merton College, and remained on and off, somewhat drably, for five years, reading history, and obtaining a first class in the final examination. Meanwhile I had come to be interested in the Italian Renaissance and chose the last Florentine Republic of 1527-30 as the subject for my doctorate thesis. This was published in 1925 and though it sold unexcitingly, had some moral success, being translated into Italian and adding a new term to Florentine historiography. But, in the profession of history, the Italian Renaissance is no longer the scholastic asset that it was in the last century, and I failed to obtain my appointment.

"While working in Italy, however, I had happened to acquire a mass of original documents illustrating ghetto life, and I employed some of my leisure in straightening these out and writing a few articles based on them. Thus I entered into the field of Jewish history, which in due course absorbed me. When the post of Reader in Jewish Studies was established in Oxford in 1939, I thus became its first incumbent. Meanwhile, I had trotted about the world: lecturing in America, collecting manuscripts and objects of art in the Latin countries, obtaining some first-hand knowledge of Palestine and the Arab lands. In 1945, I went to Italy to lecture to the British (and U.S.) troops, and to my horror found myself pitchforked into lecturing also in ̄Hebrew and Italian: I gave in fact the first public lecture by an outsider after the war in the historic University of Bologna, on Anglo-Florentine relations in the

Middle Ages. A memorable lecture-tour to the forces in Egypt and Greece, and for educational purposes in South Africa, followed in the next year. In the course of my half-dozen American trips, I have lectured I think in nearly every state. But my main occupation has been writing. Apart from my journalistic work between 1924 and 1939, I have published, I am afraid, hundreds of 'learned' articles in various scholarly periodicals and something like thirty separate books, several of which have been translated into foreign languages (including French, Spanish, Hebrew, Italian, Serb-Croat). They deal with various aspects of Italian and Jewish history, especially in England and the Latin countries. I have also tried my hand at a novel, which fortunately did not receive much notice."

PRINCIPAL WORKS: The Last Florentine Republic, 1925; A History of the Jews in Venice, 1930; Donato Giannotti: Lettere a Piero Vettori (with R. Ridolfi) 1932; History of the Marranos, 1932; The Life of Menasseh Ben Israel, 1934; A Short History of the Jewish People (in U.S.: A Bird's Eye View of Jewish History) 1935; The Jewish Contribution to Civilization, 1938; A History of the Jews in England, 1941; The Jews of Medieval Oxford, 1951; The Life of Disraeli, 1952; Personalities and Events in Jewish History, 1954.

ROTH, JOSEPH (September 2, 1894-May 1939). For biographical sketch and list of works and references, see TWENTIETH CENTURY AUTHORS, 1942.

*   *   *

Ward Powell, of the University of Colorado, who is working on a study of Joseph Roth, points out that there is some question over whether Roth committed suicide. Powell writes: "True, he had several times contemplated it, but he declared that his religious beliefs always held him back. In the accounts of his death which I have been able to find— as in Hermann Linden, *Joseph Roth: Leben und Werk, Ein Gedächtnisbuch* (1949), or the tribute in the Paris periodical *Das Neue Tage-Buch* at the time of his death—there is no suggestion of suicide. Roth was an alcoholic, and I think it can be assumed that he slowly drank himself to death."

ABOUT: Columbia Dictionary of Modern European Literature; Books Abroad January, October 1944.

ROTHENSTEIN, Sir WILLIAM (January 29, 1872-February 14, 1945). For biographical sketch and list of earlier works and references, see TWENTIETH CENTURY AUTHORS, 1942.

*   *   *

Sir William Rothenstein died at his home in Stroud, Gloucestershire, England at seventy-three. His health had been seriously affected by the strain of extensive flying during World War II when, as unofficial artist attached to the Royal Air Force, he made about two hundred service portraits and drawings.

In both the later painting and the autobiography, Basil Taylor has noted Rothenstein's "failure to catch fire, to re-create his obviously powerful and sympathetic response to people in terms of line or words." He played an important role in the English art world, and Peter Munro Jack called him "an indefatigable one-man committee of the fine arts in England."

ABOUT: London Times February 15, 1945; New Statesman and Nation May 20, 1950; New York Times February 15, 1945.

*ROUGEMONT, DENIS DE (September 8, 1906-   ), Swiss man of letters, was born in Neuchâtel, son of Georges and Alice (Bovet) de Rougemont. He took his degree in literature, after studying at the Universities of Neuchâtel, Vienna, and Geneva, and began his teaching career as a lecturer at the University of Frankfurt-am-Main in 1935. In 1936 he went to Paris as editor of *Nouveaux Cahiers* and remained there until the outbreak of World War II. Rougemont had contributed articles on culture, literature, and social history to a number of scholarly journals in Europe and in North and South America and had won an international reputation even before 1940. In 1941 he came to America and taught at the Ecole Libre des Hautes Etudes in New York for a year. In 1942-43 he was a script writer for the Office of War Information. He spent some time late in 1945 at Princeton University. When the war ended, he returned to France. He lives at Ferney, in Ain, near the Swiss border, where Voltaire once made his home. In 1950 he became director of the Centre Européen de la Culture. He has received many honors and prizes, among them the Gottfried Keller prize, the Prix Rambert, and the prize of the Schiller Foundation.

Rougemont has been characterized as "an international mind." His thought is broad and dynamic; he sees the deeper, philosophical implications of modern life. He writes of the atomic bomb, for example (in *The Last Trump*): "The Bomb is not dangerous at all. It is only a Thing. What is horribly dangerous is man. It is he who made the

* rōōzh moN'

Bomb and is getting ready to use it. The control of the Bomb is an absurdity. Committees are formed to restrain it! It is as if suddenly people threw themselves on a chair to prevent it from rising to smash the china. If they leave the Bomb alone, it is clear it won't do anything, it will remain quiet in its box. Tell them to stop talking nonsense. What is needed is *a control of man*."

The best known of his works are the essay *Penser avec les Mains* (Think with the Hands), on the crisis of modern culture and its political repercussions; *Journal d'un Intellectuel en Chomage* (Journal of an Unemployed Intellectual), a study of France between the two wars; *The Heart of Europe*, a book on Switzerland; and *Love in the Western World*, a study of the theory and practice of love in Western European literature from the Tristan legend down to modern times. George N. Shuster described this last book in *Commonweal* as "a worthy essay in fundamental Christian moral apologetic" and called the author "an extraordinarily able writer. His pages have spice as well as meat." The London *Times Literary Supplement* observed: "This is a brilliant book with unusual qualities of penetrative vision and a lively style. . . . A great deal of what Mr. de Rougemont says is fair statement in the light of scholarship, and fair comment in the light of psychology."

One of the most stimulating of his books is *The Devil's Share*, a study of the diabolic element in modern society. It may be true, as the *New Yorker* pointed out that "his lesson is, in substance, simply the old Christian lesson that good and evil are opposing forces in the heart of every man and woman." But, Anne Fremantle wrote in *Commonweal*: "This book is a little masterpiece of witty restatements of many truths that we have neglected and forgotten to our peril. It is all the better for saying nothing new, for there is nothing new to say on the subject of sin."

PRINCIPAL WORKS IN ENGLISH TRANSLATION: Love in the Western World 1940; The Heart of Europe (with C. T. Muret) 1941; The Devil's Share, 1945; The Last Trump, 1947.

ROUGHEAD, WILLIAM (February 1870-May 11, 1952). For biographical sketch and list of earlier works and references, see TWENTIETH CENTURY AUTHORS, 1942.

* * *

William Roughead died at eighty-two in Edinburgh, Scotland.

His accounts of true crimes, which combined, as William Lyon Phelps once pointed out, "the accuracy of court records with the art of the creative novelist," were the result of eloquence, scholarship, enthusiasm and "a mildly pawky humor." Deploring the "popular approach" in crime writing, Peter Hunt has said that Roughead "never once debased the currency, and for that reason, more than any other, he will survive time and the salvage drive." His last book, *Classic Crimes,* has been called "the cornerstone of any library of crime."

ADDITIONAL WORKS: Art of Murder, 1943; Nothing But Murder, 1946; Classic Crimes (selection from earlier works) 1952.

ABOUT: Bridie, J. *Preface to* Roughead, W. Classic Crimes; Russell, L. Saturday Book (1951); New York Herald Tribune May 11, 1952.

ROURKE, CONSTANCE MAYFIELD
(November 14, 1885-March 23, 1941). For autobiographical sketch and list of works and references, see TWENTIETH CENTURY AUTHORS, 1942.

* * *

ABOUT: Hyman, S. E. The Armed Vision.

*ROUSSET, DAVID (January 18, 1912-), French journalist, was born in Roanne (Loire). After completing his education

(*licencié es lettres* in philosophy), he traveled through all of Europe and North Africa, and spent some time working for the Loyalist government in Spain during the Spanish Civil War. On returning to France, he became political and economic correspondent for the American publications *Time* and *Fortune.* When World War II broke out, he was exempted from military service and continued his career as a journalist, but after France fell to the German invaders, he became active in the French Resistance.

As he reports in a letter to the editors of this volume: "David Rousset was known as an anti-Fascist before the war. During the occupation of France he took part in two Resistance networks: that of Velet-Thermopyles (Fighting French Forces) and the 'Vengeance' movement. He helped to organize at Brest secret groups of anti-Hitler German soldiers. For this activity he was arrested in Paris by the Gestapo on October 16, 1943.

* rōō sä'

Thirty German soldiers were shot in this affair, and David Rousset was deported with four other French comrades. First incarcerated at Fresnes, he was sent to the camp at Compiègnes, then to Buchenwald, in 1944. He left Buchenwald to help form the base of a new camp at Porta Westphalica. Then toward the middle of March 1944, he was sent to the camp of Neuengamme, near Hamburg, and from there in the first days of April to Elmstedt, where he worked in the salt mines for a year. In April 1945 the Elmstedt camp was evacuated before the advance of Allied troops to Wöbbelin, near Ludwigslust. He returned to Paris in May 1945 suffering from typhus.

"In 1946 he published his first book, *L'Univers Concentrationnaire* (which won the Théophraste Renaudet prize for that year). In 1947 he published *Les Jours de Notre Mort.* In 1948 he published a little work entitled *Le Pitre Ne Rit Pas* (The Clown Does Not Laugh), which is a selection of official Nazi texts demonstrating how the totalitarians behaved in daily life. In 1949, collaborating with Jean-Paul Sartre and Gérard Rosenthal, he published a work entitled *Entretiens sur la Politique,* concerning French political problems. In 1951, with Rosenthal and Theo Bernard, he did *Pour la Vérité sur les Camps Concentrationnaires,* which is an account of the suit he filed against *Lettres Françaises* in 1950. In two months, in the French press alone, 3,000 articles were published on this suit. Arthur Koestler, in his preface to *Conspiracy of Silence* by Alexander Weissberg, describes the case as follows: 'In 1950 a political trial was held in France which became a European sensation and ended in a decisive defeat for the Communists. Technically, the trial was a libel suit brought by the writer David Rousset against the Communist weekly *Les Lettres Françaises* which had accused Rousset of falsifying a text from the Soviet penal code. The real purpose of the trial was to expose the facts about the Russian terror regimes, its prisons and forced labour camps.'

"On November 12, 1949, Rousset published in *Figaro Littéraire* an open letter under the title: 'An Appeal from David Rousset to Former Deportees of the Nazi Camps.' The letter immediately had repercussions: violent controversies broke out among the Resistance groups and those of the deportees, as well as in the international press. For several months the French, Belgian, and Swiss press devoted a considerable number of articles to this affair. The

Communist deportees having refused to accept the proposal of an international commission of inquiry on the existence of concentration camps in the world, divisions took place in France and in Germany which isolated the Communists in Resistance circles and deportee groups, groups which in effect they had considered their monopoly.

"The first result was the creation of the French commission of inquiry. The commission of Spanish Republicans who lived in Nazi camps formed almost immediately, then the Belgian commission, the Dutch, and finally the German. Germany, Belgium, Republican Spain, Holland, Norway, the Saar, and Denmark have replied to Rousset's appeal. Thus was constituted the Commission Internationale contre le Régime Concentrationnaire, whose headquarters are in Brussels, representing 100,000 former deportees in Nazis camps, organized in their national federations. Under Rousset's inspiration this commission effected in 1951 in Brussels a public inquiry into the Soviet concentration camps.

"In May 1952 the International Commission sent to Spain a delegation of inquiry which visited twenty-five prisons or internment camps. At the same time another delegation of the Commission was sent to Greece where they were able to visit all the internment camps in existence.

"Finally, at the demand of the Chinese Syndicate, in December 1952 the International Commission decided to interest itself actively in labor camps in China."

* * *

Rousset's *L'Univers Concentrationnaire* has been translated into English, Italian, and Dutch. A personal record of his sixteen months in German concentration camps, it is a calmly reasoned, analytical report of the psychology of Nazism in which such camps flourished. Irving Howe wrote of the book: "It is the most terrifying of all the reports on the concentration camps, even though it recounts the fewest atrocities; and . . . it is written by a man of fine feeling and genuine talent who has the capacity to shape his emotion and increase its power by restraint." Donald Davidson called it "an amazingly honest, penetrating and skillfully written book . . . an indispensable source book for those who would understand our times and degredations."

PRINCIPAL WORK IN ENGLISH TRANSLATION: The Other Kingdom (in England: A World Apart) 1947.

ABOUT: Dictionnaire Biographique Français Contemporain, II; Time July 8, 1946.

ROWSE, ALFRED LESLIE (December 4, 1903-), English historian, was born at St. Austell, Cornwall, and attended elementary and county schools there. He grew up in Cornwall and "spent the next part of my life discovering England and the English—they have a very different life from mine. People overseas may not know how important these differences are." Rowse  attended Christ Church, Oxford, and is now a Fellow of All Souls College at Oxford. This is the best possible environment for writing large books, he finds. "I go to earth, bury myself, shut myself up for two or three years. . . . These rooms of mine in the quiet of an Oxford quadrangle—gardens all round and within sight of the Bodleian Library—are admirable for that purpose. In all the distraction of the modern world one can only get big books written by an intense concentration."

His first book was *On History,* published in 1927. His wish has always been to avoid the "cold-mutton" aspect of so many history books, defining history as "life looked back over in the perpective of time." Of *The English Spirit: Essays in History and Literature,* the New York *Times* wrote: "Apparently slight sketches, but sketches conveying a tremendous amount of reference and suggestive detail." *Time* commented: "Professor Rowse's ardent patriotism is never offensive —partly because of his style, which is finished and yet with a deliberately rough texture, like good tweed, and partly becaue of his humor."

A popular and successful book was *The England of Elizabeth.* While the *Spectator* thought it "churlish and foolish to dwell on what may appear to be defects and forget the undoubted merits of this striking contribution to literature," H. R. Trevor-Roper wrote in the *New Statesman and Nation:* "Certainly Mr. Rowse will not please everyone. His style is highly personal, sacrificing the older virtues of firmness and clarity to a vivid, intemperate, sometimes irritating impressionism. It is sometimes arch, sometimes angular, sometimes shrill." Despite what the reviewer terms Rowse's "intellectual arrogance . . . his worship of Philistine high spirits, his romantic admiration of the English, the successful, the upper classes," he evaluates the book as "the best and most scholarly account of Elizabethan society." Rowse believes in going to see the places one writes about, living in the homes the people one writes about lived in, handling the objects they loved, looking at their portraits, their tombs, hearing their music. Today, he believes, is America's "Elizabethan Age."

His degrees include an M.A. and a D.Litt.; he is a Fellow of the Royal Society of Literature.

PRINCIPAL WORKS: On History, 1927; Science and History: A New View of History, 1928; Politics and the Younger Generation, 1931; Question of the House of Lords (pamphlet) 1934; Queen Elizabeth and Her Subjects (with G. B. Harrison) 1935; Mr. Keynes and the Labour Movement, 1936; Sir Richard Grenville of the Revenge, 1937; Poems of a Decade 1931-1941, 1941; Tudor Cornwall, 1941; A Cornish Childhood (autobiography) 1942; The Spirit of English History, 1943; Poems Chiefly Cornish, 1944; The English Spirit, Essays in History and Literature, 1944; West-Country Stories, 1945; Poems of Deliverance, 1946; The Use of History, 1946; The End of an Epoch, Reflections on Contemporary History, 1947; The England of Elizabeth, 1950; The English Past, Evocations of Persons and Places, 1951; An Elizabethan Garland, 1953; (translation and completion) History of France by Lucian Romier, 1953.

ABOUT: Rowse, A. L. Confessions, in Saturday Book (ed. Leonard Russell, 9th annual issue, 1949), A Cornish Childhood; Saturday Review of Literature July 28, 1951.

ROY, GABRIELLE (1909-), French-Canadian novelist, was born in St. Boniface, Manitoba, the youngest of eight children in

a French-Canadian family of pioneer stock. She attended the convent, St. Joseph Academy, at St. Boniface, and then went on to Teachers Training School at Winnipeg, Manitoba. Teaching school, she saved her money to go to London to study for

Annette & Basil Zarov

the stage, and at the same time became a member of the Cercle Molière which won the French Trophy in Ottawa at dramatic festivals on two occasions. In 1937 she sailed for Europe to study drama, staying in Paris, London, and in a region of Provence. She had, however, been writing since she was twelve years old and when some of her short stories were published with success, she decided to revert to her earlier ambition to become an author. On returning to Canada in 1939, she settled in Montreal, and made her living writing stories and feature articles for the Canadian papers and magazines. She

wrote a series of studies of Canadian life for *Le Bulletin des Agriculteurs;* but each year managed to take two or three months to work on her novel, *The Tin Flute* (original French title, *Bonheur d'Occasion*). A Literary Guild selection in 1947, *The Tin Flute* was the story of a large Canadian-French family, living in the poverty-stricken Saint-Henri quarter of Montreal: "a story unsalted by tears or laughter, a story without blitheness," said the San Francisco *Chronicle,* "yet you will be glad you read it. Miss Roy offers no solution to the problems she sets forth. She is no reformer. She is an artist with a point of view." "Except that it has a tougher fibre and an almost complete lack of humor, the book may remind you of *A Tree Grows in Brooklyn* as it tells its story of an affectionate, not at all grim, family's life in a Montreal slum," wrote the reviewer in the *New Yorker.*

Her next book, *Where Nests the Water Hen,* also translated from the French, included two stories about simple people living far from civilization in Manitoba. "Miss Roy's earlier story of the Montreal slums," said the *Canadian Forum,* "was not nearly so charming—but it was a far more penetrating study of human motives and emotions." Other reviewers mentioned the book's lacking somewhat the substance or depth of the first, but—perhaps characteristically—were more lyric in their praise of the new: "warm, human, endearing, and fundamental" (*Commonweal*), "warmth and sincerity and charm" (New York *Herald Tribune Book Review*), "a rare book that will lift the heart with its innocent gaiety and warm the mind with its wisdom" (Chicago *Sunday Tribune*).

Miss Roy was awarded the Medal of the French Academy, and a prize by the French-Canadian Academy, as well as the Prix Femina (France, 1947). She lives in Montreal and has been married since 1947 to Marcel Carbotte.

PRINCIPAL WORKS IN ENGLISH TRANSLATION: The Tin Flute, 1947; Where Nests the Water Hen, 1951.

ABOUT: Books Abroad Summer 1948; Newsweek April 21, 1947; Royal Society of Canada, Proceedings and Transactions 1948; Saturday Review of Literature February 14, 1948; Time March 17, 1947.

ROYCE, JOSIAH (November 20, 1855-September 14, 1916). For biographical sketch and list of works and references, see TWENTIETH CENTURY AUTHORS, 1942.

* * *

ADDITIONAL WORK: Logical Essays (ed. D. S. Robinson) 1951.

ABOUT: Brown, R. W. Harvard Yard in the Golden Age; Brown, S. G. (ed.) The Social Philosophy of Josiah Royce; Cohen, M. R. Studies in Philosophy and Science; Cotton, J. H. Royce on the Human Self; Kraushaar, O. F. *in* Classic American Philosophers (ed. Fisch, M. H. & others); McElroy, H. C. Modern Philosophers; Smith, J. E. Royce's Social Infinite; Werkmeister, W. H. History of Philosophical Ideas in America.

ROYDE-SMITH, NAOMI GWLADYS.

For biographical sketch and list of earlier works and references, see TWENTIETH CENTURY AUTHORS, 1942.

* * *

Naomi Royde-Smith's novels are little read in the United States, but in England she is one of the more popular of the so-called "women's" novelists. Her work is generally slight, smoothly plotted, full of detail. In the judgment of the London *Times Literary Supplement,* she "writes gracefully and with telling ease." She duplicated something of the success of her early biography of Julie Lespinasse (*The Double Heart,* 1931) with another biography of a French figure, this time the nineteenth century poet Maurice de Guérin, which she published as *The Idol and the Shrine* in 1949.

ADDITIONAL WORKS: Mildensee, 1943; Fire-Weed, 1944; The State of Mind of Mr. Sherwood, 1946; Love in Mildensee, 1948; The Iniquity of Us All, 1949; The Idol and the Shrine, 1949; Rosy Trodd, 1950; The New Rich, 1951; She Always Caught the Post, 1953; All Night Sitting (play) 1954; Melilot, 1955.

RUCK, BERTA (1878-).

For autobiographical sketch and list of earlier works and references, see TWENTIETH CENTURY AUTHORS, 1942.

* * *

Berta Ruck lives in North Wales. In recent years—in addition to writing her pleasant, frothy romances—she has lectured to the British armed forces in the adult education program and to women's institutes. To the list of her recreations of country walks and swimming (she writes in 1954 that she "still takes a daily dip in the sea throughout the winter), she now adds "travel by air whenever possible."

ADDITIONAL WORKS: Bread and Grease Paint, 1943; Intruder Marriage, 1944; She Danced in the Ballet, 1948; Gentle Tyrant (in England: Love and Apron Strings) 1949; Joyful Journey, 1950; Hopeful Journey, 1950; The Rising of the Lark (in England: Song of the Lark) 1951; Love at a Festival, 1951; Blind Date (in England: Marriage Is a Blind Date) 1953; Fantastic Holiday, 1953; The Men in Her Life, 1954; We All Have Our Secrets, 1955.

RUGG, HAROLD ORDWAY (January 17, 1886-   ), American educator, was born in Fitchburg, Mass., the son of Edward Francis Rugg and Merion Abbie (Davidson) Rugg. He attended the Fitchburg high school, leaving it in 1902 to work as a weaver in a textile mill. He managed to get to Dartmouth and there took his B.S. in 1908 and a degree from the Thayer  School of Civil Engineering (Dartmouth) in 1909. Beginning as a teacher of civil engineering, Rugg was an assistant at Dartmouth in 1908, and taught thereafter at James Millikin University and the University of Illinois. Having taken his Ph.D. in education and sociology at the latter institution, he went on to the University of Chicago in 1915 as an instructor in education. In 1920 he became a professor of education at Teachers College, Columbia, where he has remained, since 1951 as emeritus professor. Teacher, lecturer, editor, and author of numerous books, Rugg also found time to serve on numerous commissions and survey committees.

It was around 1920 that he acquired the idea that American life could be presented to pupils in an integrated way rather than by the study of isolated fragments of history, economics, and geography. The social science textbooks that resulted have sold millions of copies and have been used in thousands of schools, chiefly in small towns. A book written for an adult audience, *The Great Technology,* reflected his engineering interests as well as his concern with education, and made him a subject for controversy. "The author presents his ideas with commendable orderliness, clarity and unperturbed logic fixed upon a single goal," wrote the New York *Times;* but by 1934 Rugg had the unhappy experience of finding himself listed in Elizabeth Dilling's *Red Network.* To charges of Communism he has stated that he is not and never has been either a Communist or a Socialist. Yet a year or two later Rugg was branded "pro-Soviet" on the floor of Congress, and in 1939 the campaign against him, and his influence on the young, began in earnest. By 1941 his books had been banned in several American communities. Their public burning had been proposed in one or two places, and in the town of Bardner, Ohio, a few were shoved into the furnace after a school meeting. However, many eminent people rose to his defense, and his publishers announced that sales of his books had actually increaed.

That Men May Understand is Rugg's autobiography, the story of his "twenty-two-year battle to bring into the schools a full account of American life—its deficiencies and problems as well as its magnificent achievements." In 1952 *The Teacher of Teachers* appeared. Here, wrote *Booklist*, "an important controversialist in education urges the younger teachers of education to follow what he terms the creative path of the Great Tradition . . . based on new theories of society, human behavior, and esthetics."

An enthusiastic and cherubic-looking man, Rugg lives in Woodstock, N.Y., with his third wife, the former Elizabeth May Howe Page, whom he married in 1947. His earlier marriages were to Bertha Miller in 1912 and to Louise Krueger in 1930. He has a son by his second marriage and two adopted children by his first.

In 1952-53 Rugg was a Fulbright lecturer in Egypt; he served as visiting professor at the University of Puerto Rico in 1953-54.

PRINCIPAL WORKS: Experimental Determination of Mental Discipline in School Studies, 1916; Statistical Methods Applied to Education, 1917; Primer of Graphics and Statistics for Teachers, 1925; Syllabus of the Course in the Psychology of the Elementary School Subjects, 1926; Introduction to American Civilization (rev. ed. called Our Country and Our People, 1938) 1929; History of American Civilization, Economic and Social, 1930; Changing Civilizations in the Modern World (rev. ed. called Changing Countries and Changing Peoples, 1938) 1930; Culture and Education in America, 1931; History of American Government and Culture, 1931; Introduction to Problems of American Culture (rev. ed. called Community and National Life, 1940) 1931; Changing Governments and Changing Cultures, 1932; The Great Technology, 1933; American Life and the School Curriculum, 1936; America's March toward Democracy, 1937; Conquest of America, 1937; That Men May Understand, 1941; Now Is the Moment, 1943; Foundations for American Education, 1947; The Teacher in School and Society (with B. M. Brooks) 1950; The Teacher of Teachers, 1952.

ABOUT: McKinnon, H. R. Changing Our Children: Harold Rugg's Crusade to Remodel America; Rugg, H. That Men May Understand; Current Biography 1941; National Cyclopedia of American Biography (1946); PM September 22, 1940; Publishers' Weekly September 28, 1940; Time September 28, 1940; Time September 9, 1940, June 25, 1951.

RUGGLES, ELEANOR (June 24, 1916-), American biographer, writes: "I was born in Boston, Mass., though the 'proper Bostonians' wouldn't admit me as one of them since my mother came from Cincinnati, Ohio, and my father from Hanover, N.H. From my mother's side the blood of the Scotch dominies boils in my veins. My great-grandfather and great-grand-uncle wrote a series of schoolbooks, the 'McGuffey Readers,' that taught the alphabet along with moral maxims to generations of Middle Westerners.

"I went to Vassar College where I took dramatics courses with Hallie Flanagan and John Houseman, and English composition with the late Alan Porter. Mr. Porter introduced me to the poetry of Gerard Manley Hopkins and my work on Hopkins led me on to write about John Henry Newman. The life of Edwin Booth attracted me because I've always loved the theatre. I studied acting in London with the great lady of dramatic teachers, Elsie Fogerty, and was one of the directors of the Duchess County Players, a summer theater in Poughkeepsie, N.Y. All three of my heroes—Hopkins, Newman, and Booth—not only had genius but were affirmative-minded and courageous men, who won out in their struggles with exacting lives and passionate, difficult temperaments. Because of this (here my Scotch blood speaks) I find them more interesting to write about than the fascinating decadents.

"I was married in 1941 to Robert Semmes O'Leary, an editor of the *New England Journal of Medicine*, and now lead the life of a college-town housewife—combining housework with going to concerts and reading omnivorously (I also like television)—in a typical college-town, elephant-gray frame house in Cambridge, Mass."

* * *

Whether she writes of the intense religious struggles of Hopkins and Newman or of the turbulent life and career of the great actor Edwin Booth, Eleanor Ruggles has the rare gift of combining authentic scholarly research with a graceful narrative skill. Her book on Booth is regarded as the definitive critical biography, and it sold well in the popular field. In 1955 it was made into a motion picture. Less well-known but even more highly praised are her lucid and learned studies of the Anglican converts to Catholicism, Hopkins and Newman. These are not "definitive" works, but, as the late Theodore Spencer remarked of her work on Hopkins, the author presents her facts in a straightforward and economical way, she is both sensitive and impartial, and . . . has written as good a book as we are likely to have."

PRINCIPAL WORKS: Gerard Manley Hopkins: A Life, 1944; Journey into Faith: The Anglican Life of John Henry Newman, 1948; Prince of Players: Edwin Booth, 1953.

ABOUT: Book-of-the-Month Club News February 1953; New York Herald Tribune Book Review March 29, 1953; New York Times Book Review March 8, 1953; Saturday Review February 28, 1953.

RUIZ. See MARTÍNEZ RUIZ

*RUKEYSER, MURIEL (December 1913-). For autobiographical sketch and list of earlier works and references, see TWENTIETH CENTURY AUTHORS, 1942.

* * *

Muriel Rukeyser published her first work in prose, a biography of the American physicist Willard Gibbs, in 1942. Her book was hailed as one of the finest biographies of the year. The *New Yorker* wrote: "Her emphasis is on the contours of his mind, the qualities which make him 'the type and emblem of the imagination in America.' Her fine book interprets Gibbs as an example of the profoundly American search for unity."

Her later poetry has shown uneven but positive development in the direction of "rhetorical intensity" and in "the purely musical aspects of her writing," M. L. Rosenthal has observed. According to Richard Eberhart, her *Selected Poems* of 1951 demonstrated her "grasp of the essential, her practice of positive speech." These poems certainly reflect the richness and variety of experience on which she constantly draws. Her emotional response to these experiences, she writes in her prose work *Life in Poetry*, is one "which accepts a world of process, a dynamic universe of time and growth relations." The faults of her work, Rosenthal points out, are those of romantic overstatement: "the unearned triumphant conclusion, the occasional muddy emotionalism that can blur the phrasing almost to a blot." But it is in this same tradition of lyric romanticism, Rosenthal finds, that she has done her best work. "Shelley's 'Ode to the West Wind,' Whitman's 'Out of the Cradle Endlessly Rocking,' Lawrence's 'New Heaven and Earth' are of this order of romantic rhetoric—universal, prophetic, organic. Such works are Muriel Rukeyser's best tradition and point to her finest possibility."

* rōō′ki sĕr

In 1942 Miss Rukeyser received a $1000 award from the American Academy of Arts and Letters and the National Institute of Arts and Letters. In 1943 she won a Guggenheim fellowship. She lives in New York City.

ADDITIONAL WORKS: Beast in View, 1944; The Green Wave, 1948; Elegies, 1949; Life of Poetry, 1949; Orpheus, 1949; Selected Poems, 1951.

ABOUT: Ciardi, J. (ed.) Mid-Century American Poets; Current Biography 1943; Gregory, H. & Zaturenska, M. A History of American Poetry, 1900-1940; Rosenthal, M. L. *in* New Directions 14; Poetry January 1943, December 1948.

RUNYON, DAMON (October 4, 1880-December 10, 1946). For biographical sketch and list of earlier works and references, see TWENTIETH CENTURY AUTHORS, 1942.

* * *

Damon Runyon died at Memorial Hospital in New York City at sixty-two. Cancer of the throat had necessitated removal of his larynx a year earlier; thereafter communication with his many friends during their nightly gatherings at Lindy's restaurant had been by means of written notes. At his request, Runyon's body was cremated and his ashes were dropped from a plane over Manhattan. He had been divorced from his second wife in 1946.

Shortly after his death, at the instigation of his friend Walter Winchell, the Damon Runyon Memorial Fund for Cancer Research was established.

Damon Runyon, Jr., published a "sad, odd, revelatory" book about his father in 1954, in which he wrote: "My father's whole approach to life, including family, was the same as his fictional counterpart in his short stories, the anonymous narrator 'I,' who attempted to remain the detached observer of the passing crowd." Runyon's style, so individual that "Runyonese" and "Runyonesque" have entered the vocabulary, and his choice of subjects have been taken seriously enough to be considered examples of "literary regionalism" by Svend Riemer: "Damon Runyon has achieved the crystallization of attitudes which we are accustomed to associate with urbanism." John Lardner has pointed out that "as he went along, he learned to exchange straight writing for oblique writing, ideas for pictures of ideas, and heard speech for manufactured speech."

It was Runyon himself who furnished us with one of the clearest insights into his work in a review of his own *Short Takes*, in which he said: "As a study in the art of carrying water on both shoulders, of sophistry, of writing with tongue-in-cheek, and of intellectual dishonesty, I think it has no superior since the beginning of time. . . . He has one not easily acquired trick which is conveying a thought by indirection. He makes it appear that he is not personally responsible for the thought, but there it is. . . . I tell you Runyon has subtlety but it is the considered opinion of this reviewer that it is a great pity the guy did not remain a rebel out-and-out, even at the cost of a good position at the feed trough."

The extraordinarily successful musical comedy *Guys and Dolls,* first produced in 1950, was based largely on the short story "The Idyll of Miss Sarah Brown" in *Runyon à la Carte.* Written by Jo Swerling and Abe Burrows, with music and lyrics by Frank Loesser, it had long runs in both New York and London and was sold to Samuel Goldwyn for a motion picture for a reported down payment of $1,000,000 plus 10% of its gross earnings over $10,000,000. John Chapman described it as "cynical, with Runyon's cool amusement at a weird and fanciful assortment of seamy characters; yet it is not tough and is notably free from dirt."

ADDITIONAL WORKS: Runyon à la Carte, 1944; Short Takes, 1946; Poems for Men, 1947; Trials and Other Tribulations, 1948; Runyon First and Last (selected stories) 1949.

ABOUT: Runyon, D. Runyon First and Last (*Foreword by* C. Kinnaird); Runyon, D. Jr. Father's Footsteps; Weiner, E. H. The Damon Runyon Story; Collier's March 11, April 22, 1950; Current Biography 1942; Editor and Publisher February 18, 1950; Newsweek May 20, 1946, December 23, 1946, September 20, 1948; New York Times December 11, 1946, December 22, 1946; New Yorker August 27, 1949; Time June 24, December 23, 1946, February 23, 1948, August 1, 1949.

RUSSELL, BERTRAND ARTHUR WILLIAM, 3rd Earl Russell, Viscount Amberley (May 18, 1872-). For biographical sketch and list of earlier works and references, see TWENTIETH CENTURY AUTHORS, 1942.

* * *

In 1950 Bertrand Russell received the Nobel prize for literature, "in recognition of his many-sided and significant authorship, in which he has constantly figured as a defender of humanity and freedom of thought." No contemporary philosopher has captured the interest and the admiration of so wide an audience, in the English-reading world, as Russell has. His greatest and probably most enduring work (on which he collaborated with the late Alfred North Whitehead) is the least-read of all his writings, the *Principia Mathematica.* But it is not for his work as a theoretical mathematician that he is so famous and so widely honored. Rather, it is for his unswerving faith in humanity and in the power of human reason. Humanism as a religion, Russell wrote in 1943, does not satisfy his emotions. "And yet I am unable to believe that, in the world as known, there is anything that I can value outside human beings, and, to a much lesser extent, animals. Not the starry heavens, but their effects on human percipients, have excellence; to admire the universe for its size is slavish and absurd; impersonal non-human truth appears to be a delusion. And so my intellect goes with the humanists, though my emotions violently rebel."

Russell wrote in 1951 that he was "enjoying a serene old age." Serenity, however, has not been the keynote of his life, and there has rarely been any extended period in which he has not been involved in one turbulent controversy or another. In 1940, living in the United States at the time, he signed a five-year contract to lecture at the Barnes Foundation in Merion, Pa. Upon his dismissal from the lectureship in 1942 he sued for breach of contract and was awarded $20,000 in damages. (These lectures, incidentally, were the basis for his witty and challenging *History of Western Philosophy.*) In 1944 Russell returned to England with a fellowship at Trinity College, Cambridge. Here he completed the book which has been described as his "philosophical testament," *Human Knowledge: Its Scope and Its Limits.* In this book Russell approached as closely as he has ever done a systematic philosophy. The scope of the book, Sidney Hook observed in his review, was enormous. "All the central issues in contemporary philosophy, from the theory of meaning to the nature of space-time are discussed with . . . characteristic incisiveness, technical skill and imagination." Since the publication of *Human Knowledge,* Russell has written little "pure" philosophy and has concentrated on political writing and fiction. He remarked, more whimsically perhaps than accurately, in 1951: "My intelligence, such as it is, has been steadily decaying since the age of twenty. When I was young I liked mathematics. When this became too difficult for me I took to philosophy, and when philosophy became too difficult I took to politics. Since then I have concentrated on detective stories."

His recent essays are marked by the same qualities that distinguished his earlier work— a witty, lucid, and urbane style, a vigorous intellect, and an erudition that can be simultaneously graceful and leviathan. At eighty-one he made his debut as a writer of fiction, with five mannered but pleasantly diabolical stories of the supernatural, *Satan in the Suburbs*. In person as well as in intellect he remains vigorous and energetic. On the occasion of his becoming an octogenarian he wrote: "I am convinced that survival is easier for those who can enjoy life, and that a man who has sufficient vitality to reach old age cannot be happy unless he is active."

On this same occasion Russell gave a radio and television interview for British and American audiences. Trim and erect, "with a fine head of white hair and a face that is at once sharply Voltairean and gently humane" (as Maurice Cranston described him in the *Spectator*), he spoke simply and candidly about himself and the world around him. He offered no sibylline prophecies, only the balanced and rational outlook of a man who has spent his life in the search for truth: "I think one of the troubles of the world has been the habit of dogmatically believing something or other, and I think all these matters are full of doubt and the rational man will not be too sure that he is right. I think that we ought always to entertain our opinions with some measure of doubt."

In 1952 Russell was divorced by his third wife, the former Patricia Spence (by whom he had had one son). Later that same year he married Edith Finch of New York. His home is in Richmond, Surrey.

ADDITIONAL WORKS: History of Western Philosophy, 1945; Human Knowledge: Its Scope and Limitations, 1948; Authority and the Individual, 1949; Unpopular Essays, 1950; The Impact of Science on Society, 1951; New Hopes for a Changing World, 1951; Satan in the Suburbs (short stories) 1953; Human Society in Ethics and Politics, 1955.

ABOUT: Lawrence, D. H. Letters to Bertrand Russell; Leggett, H. W. Bertrand Russell; McElroy, H. Modern Philosophers; Schilpp, P. A. (ed.) The Philosophy of Bertrand Russell; Atlantic Monthly August 1952; Canadian Forum December 1948; Current Biography 1951; Life May 26, 1952; New York Herald Tribune Book Review October 7, 1951; New York Times November 11, 1950; New York Times Magazine July 8, 1951, May 18, 1952; Saturday Review of Literature November 25, 1950; Spectator May 16, 1952; Time November 20, 1950.

RUSSELL, CHARLES EDWARD (September 25, 1860-April 23, 1941). For biographical sketch and list of works and references, see TWENTIETH CENTURY AUTHORS, 1942.

* * *

ADDITIONAL WORK: Pioneer Life in Early Iowa: A Sketch of the Life of Edward Russell by His Son, 1941.

ABOUT: Morris, L. R. Postscript to Yesterday.

RUSSELL, GEORGE WILLIAM ("AE") (April 10, 1867-July 17, 1935). For biographical sketch and list of works and references, see TWENTIETH CENTURY AUTHORS, 1942.

* * *

ABOUT: Bose, A. C. Three Mystic Poets; Colum, M. Life and the Dream; Dictionary of National Biography 1931-40; Asiatic Review April 1948; Atlantic February 1943; Fortnightly January 1949.

RUSSELL, JOHN (April 22, 1885-). For biographical sketch and list of works and references, see TWENTIETH CENTURY AUTHORS, 1942.

RUSSELL, MARY ANNETTE (BEAUCHAMP) RUSSELL, Countess ("Elizabeth") (1866-February 9, 1941). For biographical sketch and list of works and references, see TWENTIETH CENTURY AUTHORS, 1942.

* * *

ABOUT: Saturday Review of Literature February 10, 1945.

RYALL, WILLIAM BOLITHO. See BOLITHO, W.

*SABATINI, RAFAEL (1875-February 13, 1950). For biographical sketch and list of earlier works and references, see TWENTIETH CENTURY AUTHORS, 1942.

* * *

Rafael Sabatini died at seventy-five in Adelboden, Switzerland, where he was spending the winter. He had lived for the last ten years in Herefordshire, England. He was survived by his widow; his son Rafael was killed in a motor accident in 1927.

The wide popularity of his swashbuckling historical novels could be attributed to his talent for constructing "a compact and exciting plot" and "the playing of a lively imagination upon facts gathered in the course of many hours of research," in the opinion of the London *Times*. Beyond these factors, he brought "a confident, dramatic sweep and an unfailing boldness of romantic colour to every setting or period which he attempted";

* sä bä tē′nē

the *Times* adds that "if the result was not history, it was first-class storytelling."

ADDITIONAL WORKS: King in Prussia, 1944; Birth of Mischief, 1945; Turbulent Tales (short stories) 1946; The Gamester, 1949.

ABOUT: London Times February 14, 1950; New York Times February 14, 1950; Scholastic February 22, 1950.

*SACHS, CURT (June 29, 1881-), German-born musicologist, writes: "Curt Sachs, music historian, author, and educator, was

born in Berlin, Germany. He took his bachelor's degree in 1900 and his Ph.D., in art history, archeology, music history, and philosophy, from Berlin University early in 1904. After fifteen years of scholarly activity, he was appointed in 1919 professor of music history, at the National Academy of Church and School Music, as well as curator of the Museum of Musical Instruments. Besides, he was a board member of the National Museums and of the National Radio. These activities were interrupted only for lecture tours in Germany and abroad, for the installation of music exhibitions here and there, and in 1930, for serving the Cairo government in the restoration of Arabo-Egyptian music. Three years later, the Hitler regime dismissed him from all his positions. He accepted a gracious invitation by the French government (backed by the Rockefeller Foundation and spent four years at the anthropological museum, which since has changed its old name Trocadéro into Musée de l'Homme. In 1937, New York University appointed him visiting professor in its Graduate School of Arts and Sciences, and he emigrated with his family to the United States. Sachs is still connected with N.Y.U. and, as a lecturer, with Queens College. A position as a consultant to the New York Public Library was ended in 1952. After the war, he also taught summer classes at Harvard, Ann Arbor, Columbia, Berkeley, and Los Angeles. For two years, he was the national president of the American Musicological Society and is now a member of its executive board.

"His printed work consists essentially of twenty-eight books and about 180 papers. He started from the musical history of his home-

* säks

856

town, but turned soon to the history of musical instruments, which he freed from merely technical interests and transformed into a branch of culture history. From the instruments, he found the way to primitive, oriental, and ancient music and achieved a fusion of music with anthropology and archeology. The close relationship of music with motion led him to writing *A World History of the Dance* (which has been published in German, English, French, and Spanish) and, as his latest book, to a history of rhythm and tempo. Alongside with these interests, he was fascinated by the ideal of a unified history of all the arts, in which each one has played a well determined role of its own within a lawful whole. The attempts at such unification resulted ultimately in his book *The Commonwealth of Art.*

"Besides books and papers, Sachs created the audible material for the teaching and learning of music history. In 1930, he published a smaller collection of phonographic recordings under the title of *2000 Years of Music* (recently re-published on long-playing records); and in 1934, he started, as the musical and musicological director, the voluminous 'Anthologie Sonore,' which is still being continued in Paris."

PRINCIPAL WORKS: World History of the Dance, 1937; The History of Musical Instruments, 1940; The Rise of Music in the Ancient World, East and West, 1943; The Commonwealth of Art, 1946; Our Musical Heritage (in England: A Short History of World Music) 1948; Rhythm and Tempo, a Study in Music History, 1953.

ABOUT: Current Biography 1944; Musical Quarterly July 1941.

SACKVILLE-WEST, EDWARD (November 13, 1901-). For autobiographical sketch and list of earlier works and references, see TWENTIETH CENTURY AUTHORS, 1942.

* * *

Edward Sackville-West lives in Wimborne, Dorset. He was associated with the Features and Drama section of the B.B.C. during the World War II, working mainly on poetry broadcasts. His own poetic drama *The Rescue* was written especially for radio and was broadcast in 1943 with a musical score by Benjamin Britten. For many years Sackville-West reviewed records regularly for the *New Statesman* and for the *Gramophone,* and he is co-author of two books on record collecting. He is currently a director of the Royal Opera House, Covent Garden.

A recent collection of Sackville-West's critical essays, *Inclinations,* was described by Leonard Bacon as "a pleasant book by a pleasant man, who writes with ease and authority and certainly not as the scribes. . . . He obviously is passionately devoted to literature, as he is to music and painting."

Correction: Edward Sackville West is a first cousin, not a nephew, of the writer V. Sackville-West.

ADDITIONAL WORKS: The Rescue, 1945; Inclinations, 1949; The Record Guide (with D. Shawe-Taylor) 1951; The Record Year (with D. Shawe-Taylor) 1952.

ABOUT: Hoehn, M. (ed.) Catholic Authors, II.

SACKVILLE-WEST, VICTORIA MARY (March 1892-). For biographical sketch and list of earlier works and references, see TWENTIETH CENTURY AUTHORS, 1942.

* * *

V. Sackville-West continues to be acknowledged one of the most interesting and adroit of contemporary British women authors. In 1947 her long poem *The Garden* received the Heinemann prize. In 1953 her novel *The Easter Party,* though it was not received with general enthusiasm, proved to be a stimulating and provocative book. A study of a group of people visiting for the weekend at a beautiful English country house, it was told with such restraint and detachment that some readers found its characters cold and lifeless. Nevertheless, as the London *Times Literary Supplement* pointed out: "If she has not fulfilled in *The Easter Party* all that she there seems to propose, the fact of seeming to propose so much is an earnest of her range of thought." She has tried her hand at the detective story with *The Devil at Westease*—a novel in which, the critics agreed, the author's fine style far excelled the original but somewhat improbable plot—and has written a history of nursery rhymes. Probably her most successful book of recent years was her biographical study of two Carmelite saints, St. Teresa of Avila and St Thérèse of Lisieux, *The Eagle and the Dove.* An Anglican herself, she won praise from both Catholics and non-Catholics for her lucid and sympathetic treatment of her subjects.

Miss Sackville-West was named Companion of Honour in 1948. She lives with her husband, the author Sir Harold Nicolson, at Sissinghurst Castle in Kent. Both their sons have taken up careers in publishing: Lionel Benedict Nicolson being editor of the *Burlington Magazine* and author of several books on painting, and Nigel Nicolson a director of the publishing house of

Weidenfeld and Nicolson and author of a history of the Grenadier Guards.

ADDITIONAL WORKS: The Eagle and the Dove, 1943; The Women's Land Army, 1944; (comp. with H. Nicolson) Another World Than This, 1945; The Garden (poems) 1946; The Devil at Westease, 1947; Nursery Rhymes, 1947; In Your Garden, 1951; The Easter Party, 1953; In Your Garden Again, 1953.

ABOUT: Mercure de France March 1949.

*SADLEIR, MICHAEL (December 25, 1888-). For autobiographical sketch and list of earlier works and references, see TWENTIETH CENTURY AUTHORS, 1942.

* * *

Michael Sadleir writes: "I live near Windsor in a small eighteenth century house, with a dairy farm of 150 acres managed by my wife. In 1951 my nineteenth-century novel collection was purchased *en bloc* by the University of California [in Los Angeles] and was catalogued and described by me in a two-volume bibliography. I am an ex-president of the Bibliographical Society, and a member of the Roxburghe and Grolier Clubs. My elder son was killed in active service at sea in 1940; his brother and sister are both married, with children."

ADDITIONAL WORKS: Things Past, 1944; Forlorn Sunset (novel) 1947; Michael Ernest Sadler: a Memoir by His Son, 1949; Nineteenth Century Fiction: a Bibliographical Record, 1951.

ABOUT: College and Research Libraries April 1952; The Library December 1944.

* săd'lĕr

*ST. EXUPÉRY, ANTOINE DE (June 29, 1900-July 1944). For biographical sketch and list of earlier works and references, see TWENTIETH CENTURY AUTHORS, 1942.

* * *

Antoine Marie Reger de St. Exupéry was reported "missing in action" on July 21, 1944. He was forty-four. His American publishers had brought him to the United States after the fall of France, but he felt impelled to rejoin his old flying squadron in North Africa in April 1943. Grounded because of his age, he participated as an instructor until the summer of 1944, when he was assigned to make lone reconnaissance flights from Italy over southern France. He did not return from the sixteenth mission.

He has been called (by James Gray) "perhaps the most consistent and most vigorous of all the poet-philosophers who undertook to be the preservers of the European con-

* săN-tāz zü pā rē′

science." His philosophy has been summarized by his biographers Richard Rumbold and Lady Margaret Stewart as that of a humanist: "He believed—unfashionable as it sounds today—in the self-sufficiency of human virtue, recognized the possibilities open to man as a spiritual and creative being, and extolled the values of friendship, love, responsibility, compassion and beauty." These ideas are the subject of *Letter to a Hostage,* expressed in "an evocation of moods and feelings." *The Little Prince* (written, as was *Letter to a Hostage,* while he was in America), a fantasy about the visit of a Prince from Asteroid B-612 to the earth, has been interpreted both as a poetic allegory for adults and as a fairy story for children. *Wisdom of the Sands* (published in France as *Citadelle* in 1948) is a collection of notebooks, hypothetically the voice of the monarch of a desert empire, written by the author over many years. "St. Exupéry's mystique has here turned political," commented the late Irwin Edman. "What in the vocabulary of politics would sound like the grimmest authoritarianism, presented in the diction of God, Love and the Infinite seems to suggest the deliverance of a religious prophet, a dedicated mystic."

Summing up St. Exupéry's career, Edman wrote: "It is difficult to think of another writer who so artfully—and ardently—united the Homeric simplicity of action recounted in quickening images with the meditations of a mind all steady lucid flame. It is as if by some alchemy of spirit a poet, a philosopher and an expert aviator were fused into one person."

St. Exupery's widow, Consuelo de St.-Exupéry, published an autobiographical work, *Kingdom of the Rocks,* in 1946.

In 1954 the Bibliothèque Nationale in Paris held a memorial exhibition of St. Exupéry's manuscripts and mementoes.

ADDITIONAL WORKS: Airman's Odyssey (Wind, Sand and Stars; Night Flight; Flight to Arras) 1943; The Little Prince, 1943; Letter to a Hostage, 1943; Wisdom of the Sands (published in France as Citadelle) 1950.

ABOUT: Chevrier, P. Antoine de Saint-Exupéry; Gray, J. On Second Thought; Rumbold, R. & Stewart, M. The Winged Life—A Portrait of Antoine de Saint-Exupéry, Poet and Airman; Columbia Dictionary of Modern European Literature; Commonweal October 19, 1945; France Illustration August 6, 1949; French Review March 1946, December 1950; New York Times January 19, 1941, August 10, 1944; Publishers' Weekly December 23, 1944, April 13, 1946; Time August 14, 1944, October 16, 1950.

"ST.-J. PERSE." See LÉGER, A.

ST. JOHN ERVINE. See ERVINE

ST. JOHN GOGARTY. See GOGARTY

"ST. LÉGER-LÉGER." See LÉGER. A.

SAINTSBURY, GEORGE EDWARD BATEMAN (October 23, 1845-January 28, 1933). For biographical sketch and list of works and references, see TWENTIETH CENTURY AUTHORS, 1942.

* * *

ADDITIONAL WORKS: George Saintsbury: The Memorial Volume, A Saintsbury Miscellany (ed. Oliver, J. W. & Muir, A.) 1945; Last Vintage: Essays and Papers (ed. Oliver, J. W. & others) 1950.

ABOUT: Dictionary of National Biography 1931-40; Oliver, J. W. (ed.) George Saintsbury: The Memorial Volume, Last Vintage; Wilson, E. Classics and Commercials; New Statesman and Nation September 14, 1946; Nineteenth Century November 1945; Saturday Review of Literature February 23, 1946; Spectator July 21, 1950.

"SAKI." See MUNRO, H. H.

*SALINAS, PEDRO (November 27, 1892-December 4, 1951), Spanish poet and critic, was born in Madrid, Spain, the son of Pedro and Soledad Salinas, and was educated at the Instituto de San Isidro, Madrid (B.A.) and at the University of Madrid (Ph.D. 1918). Lecturer in Spanish at the Sorbonne from 1914 to 1917, in 1918 he became a professor at the University of Seville. Between 1933 and 1936 he was executive secretary of the Universidad Internacional de Santander. Salinas left Spain at the outbreak of Civil War in 1936, and in that same year established residence in the United States. He taught at Wellesley College in Massachusetts, lectured at many colleges and universities in the United States, and taught in Mexico, Puerto Rico, and various South American cities. From 1947 until his death he was Professor of Spanish Literature at Johns Hopkins University.

His first book was *Presagios,* poems, published in 1923, but not translated into English. Salinas believed that the external world is for the poet a sort of formless life, and the poet's task, his joy, consists in giving it

* sä lē'näs

order and sense. Salinas' own poetry is made up of psychological subtleties, his images built upon concepts or ideas rather than sensations. "The poet places himself before reality . . . in order to create something else," he wrote in *Reality and the Poet in Spanish Poetry,* a prose critical work.

Several of his works of poetry have been translated by Eleanor L. Trumbull, published with Spanish and English on opposite pages. These are *Lost Angel, and Other Poems, Truth of Two, and Other Poems, Zero,* and *Sea of San Juan.* Of the latter José Garcia Villa wrote in the New York *Times*: "In this reviewer's opinion, Salinas' work excels the better known Federico García Lorca's in many ways. . . . Salinas' poems are rich, complex and full of reverberations —a finer, more cultivated instrument." "One of the most powerful and original poets of our day," Robert P. Tristram Coffin said of him. Angel del Río wrote (in the *Columbia Dictionary of Modern European Literature*) in summary of Salinas' achievement: "A typical representative of the many-sided contemporary spirit, he is both international and very Spanish in character and taste; a man awakened to the realities of his time and an artist of subtle intellectual—almost abstract— inspiration."

Salinas was given an honorary Litt.D. degree by Middlebury (Vt.) College, and was created Knight, Legion of Honor, France, in 1933. He married Margarita Bonmati in 1915, and they had two children. He died in Boston after a two-months' illness, and his body was flown to Puerto Rico for a state funeral at San Juan at the request of Governor Luis Muñoz Marín.

"There was nothing about his personal appearance that would lead one to believe he was a Spaniard," wrote Lowell Dunham in a reminiscence in *Books Abroad.* "He was a rather heavy-set man, with shoulders that were beginning to stoop; he had more of the coloring and appearance of a good, comfort-loving Austrian burgher than of a hard-bitten son of Castile. . . . Don Pedro was a lover of good wine, good food, good living, and good conversation. Stimulated by them he blossomed forth with all the play of a brilliant and scintillating mind that was always in evidence, creative, energetic, and original."

PRINCIPAL WORKS IN ENGLISH TRANSLATION: Lost Angel, and Other Poems, 1938; Reality and the Poet in Spanish Poetry, 1940; Truth of Two, and Other Poems, 1940; Zero, 1947; Sea of San Juan, 1950.

ABOUT: Columbia Dictionary of Modern European Literature; Books Abroad September 1952.

*

SALINGER, JEROME DAVID (1919-), American novelist and short story writer, writes: "Born in New York City. Have lived in and around New York most of my life. Educated in Manhattan public schools, a military academy in Pennsylvania, three colleges (no degrees). A happy tourist's year in Europe when I was eighteen and nineteen. In the Army from '42

Lotte Jacobi

to '46, two and a half years overseas (in Europe). I was with the Fourth Infantry Division, as a staff sergeant, through five campaigns, from D-Day to the end of the war. I'm now living in Westport, Conn.

"I've been writing since I was fifteen or so. Published my first story in 1940, when I was twenty-one, in *Story.* At the time, it seemed like a late start. My short stories have appeared in a number of magazines over the last ten years (*Harper's, Saturday Evening Post, Collier's, Esquire, Cosmopolitan, Story, Good Housekeeping, Mademoiselle*), mostly—and most happily—in the *New Yorker.*

"I'd like to say who my favorite fiction writers are, but I don't see how I can do it without saying why they are. So I won't.

"I'm aware that a number of my friends will be saddened, or shocked, or shocked-saddened, over some of the chapters of *The Catcher in the Rye.* Some of my best friends are children. In fact, all of my best friends are children. It's almost unbearable to me to realize that my book will be kept on a shelf out of their reach."

* * *

J. D. Salinger's first book, *The Catcher in the Rye,* was a best-seller, a Book-of-the-Month Club choice, and one of the most highly praised novels of recent years. For Salinger, a modest and conscientious young man who shuns publicity, the success of the book was almost as embarrassing as it was gratifying. *The Catcher in the Rye*—a sensitive study of an adolescent boy adrift in New York—combined humor and pathos. It is told in the first person by the semi-sophisticated and startlingly articulate young hero.

The novelist William Maxwell reports that Salinger works "with infinite labor, infinite patience, and infinite thought for the technical aspects of what he is writing." Salinger himself admits that he finds writing "a hard life." But, he adds, "it's brought me enough happiness that I don't think I'd ever deliberately dissuade anybody (if he had talent) from taking it up. The compensations are few, but when they come, if they come, they're very beautiful."

Reviewing his collection of short stories, Eudora Welty wrote in the New York Times: "J. D. Salinger's writing is original, first rate, serious and beautiful. . . . From the outside [his stories] are often very funny; inside, they are about heartbreak, and convey it; they can do this because they are pure." William Peden observed in the *Saturday Review*: "Salinger is an extreme individualist with a pleasing disregard for conventional narrative form and style. He possesses a saving grace of humor which makes even his somber stories very pleasant reading."

PRINCIPAL WORKS: The Catcher in the Rye, 1951; Nine Stories (in England: For Esmé—with Love and Squalor, and Other Stories) 1953.

ABOUT: New York Herald Tribune Book Review August 19, 1951; Saturday Review of Literature July 14, 1951, February 16, 1952.

*SALMINEN, SALLY (April 25, 1906-   ). For autobiographical sketch and list of works and references, see TWENTIETH CENTURY AUTHORS, 1942.

* * *

Sally Salminen writes from her home in Denmark: "There is hardly anything to add [to the 1942 sketch], as no other books have been translated into English. Perhaps it would be of interest to mention that after the war, from 1946 until 1951, S. S. has, at short intervals, mostly lived in France. A novel, which is going to have the title 'Prins Efflam' and is laid in a fishing village in Brittany, is at this time (January 1953) under preparation and will during this year appear in four of the Scandanavian languages."

Miss Salminen adds that the story, reported in the 1942 sketch, that her former employers in the United States invited her to be their guest before she returned to Europe is "a very sentimental and romantic but altogether false tale." Furthermore, she comments, if she ever said that writing poetry was "a kind of sickness that one gets over," this was not her "unchangeable opinion." She adds, "I am now happily engaged in poetry. For evidence, I can mention that I recently (November 1952) had an essay on poetry in *Berlingske Aftenavis* (a Copenhagen evening paper)."

* sàl'mĭ nĕn

SALTEN, FELIX (September 6, 1869-October 8, 1945). For autobiographical sketch and list of earlier works and references, see TWENTIETH CENTURY AUTHORS, 1942.

* * *

Felix Salten died at seventy-five, after a long illness, in Zurich, Switzerland, in exile from his native Austria.

His undoubted talent was occasionally subject to his "journalistic flair for word making," in the opinion of Alfred Werner, who adds: "Nevertheless, if we separate the yellow mica from the genuine gold, there is enough left of the latter to secure for Salten a lasting monument in the field of Austrian literature." John Chamberlain said of him: "he has the gift of a tender, lucid style. His observation is next door to marvelous, and he invests the fruits of this observation with pure poetry."

ADDITIONAL WORKS: Forest World, 1942; (ed.) Fairy Tales From Near and Far, 1945; (comp.) Favorite Animal Stories, 1948; Jibby the Cat, 1948; Little World Apart, 1948.

ABOUT: Columbia Dictionary of Modern European Literature; New York Times October 9, 1945; Saturday Review of Literature November 3, 1945.

SALTER, JAMES ARTHUR, 1st Baron of Kidlington (March 15, 1881-   ). For biographical sketch and list of earlier works and references, see TWENTIETH CENTURY AUTHORS, 1942.

* * *

Arthur Salter, now Lord Kidlington, has held so many official positions in the British government that he has been called the "civil servant par excellence." In World War II he headed the British Shipping Mission to the United States and was a member of the British Supply Council in North America. When the United States entered the war he represented Great Britain on the Anglo-American Combined Shipping Adjustment Board. In 1944 he became senior director deputy general of UNRRA. He returned to London in 1944 and in 1945 became chancellor of the Duchy of Lancaster. From 1947 to 1948 he served as chairman of the advisory council of the International Bank. After the Conservative government returned to power, he was Minister of State for Economic Affairs from 1951 to 1952 and from 1952 to 1953 he was Minister of Materials. During that same period he represented the Ormskirk Division of Lancashire in the House of Commons.

His only recent book, *Personality in Politics*, was a collection of portraits of distinguished British and American political leaders whom he had known personally in his long and active career. The *Manchester Guardian* described it as an "animated book," written by "a man of independent and penetrating mind with a terse and vivid style." For many years known as "one of the world's great bachelors," he married Mrs. Arthur Bullard in Washington, D.C., in 1940. In 1944 he was named Knight Grand Cross of the Order of the British Empire. In 1953 he was created 1st Baron of Kidlington.

ADDITIONAL WORK: Personality in Politics: Studies of Contemporary Statesmen, 1947.

ABOUT: Current Biography 1944; Time April 14, 1941.

SALTUS, EDGAR EVERTSON (October 8, 1855-July 31, 1921). For biographical sketch and list of works and references, see TWENTIETH CENTURY AUTHORS, 1942.

SAMPSON, GEORGE (April 6, 1873-February 1, 1950), English editor and essayist, was born in London. "You must picture me," he wrote in "A Boy and His Books" in *Seven Essays*, "as the youngest of a small middle-class family, having neither poverty nor riches." His older sister taught him to read, for although he was free to come and go as he pleased, he was forbidden to go to school. "The doctor forbade this emphatically: 'He is much too delicate; his brain is too active already.' How often did I hear these words repeated to visitors, who never failed to comment on my delicate appearance and pale face." When he was eleven years old, he attended Southwark P.T. School and then Winchester Training College. A great reader even as a child, Sampson became a distinguished man of letters and a high authority on the teaching of English. A point stressed in all his educational writings and all his books is that literature is a thing to be enjoyed, that great poetry or prose has to be loved first and studied afterwards. He was actively interested in many educational groups, was a member of the Cambridge Advisory Committee on Religious Instruction, of the Departmental Committee on the Teaching of English in England, and honorary general secretary of the English Association. For many years he was an inspector of schools for the London County Council. He received an honorary M.A. degree from St. John's College, Cambridge.

Sampson's rewriting and digest of fifteen volumes of the Cambridge history, *The Concise Cambridge History of English Literature* was enthusiastically received by many critics. "Mr. Sampson's book is a masterpiece. It has knowledge, it has wit, it has shape and order, it has irony," wrote Harold Hobson in the *Christian Science Monitor*. "It is, moreover, exceedingly modest." When *Seven Essays* appeared, Wilson Follett commented in the New York *Times*: "This essayist is no mere thick-and-thin lover of the past; but he does have the sense of history, which is the sense of balance. Neither is he ever merely contentious, though he does not hesitate to diagram his aversions by way of the indirect approach to his deeper affections."

For recreation Sampson enjoyed music, travel, and reading. He lived in Sussex, until his death in February 1950.

PRINCIPAL WORKS: A Day with Felix Mendelssohn-Bartholdy, 1910; Cambridge Readings in Literature (ed.) 1918; English for the English 1921; The Cambridge Book of Prose and Verse (ed.) 1924; Cambridge Lessons in English, 1926; The Concise Cambridge History of English Literature, 1941; The Century of Divine Songs, 1943; Seven Essays, 1947.

ABOUT: Sampson, G. Seven Essays; London Times Educational Supplement March 10, 1950.

SAMPSON, RICHARD HENRY ("Richard Hull") (September 6, 1896-). For autobiographical sketch and list of earlier works and references, see TWENTIETH CENTURY AUTHORS, 1942.

* * *

"Richard Hull" writes from London that he served from September 1939 to July 1940 with the Territorial Battalion (mentioned in the 1942 sketch), "when it was decided that his age made him unsuitable for service overseas. He was released from the Army and employed by the Admiralty as a chartered accountant to investigate the cost of government contracts. He is still so employed."

Correction: Richard Henry Sampson was born September 6, not 16, 1896.

ADDITIONAL WORKS: And Death Came Too, 1942; Left-Handed Death, 1946; Last First, 1947; Until She Was Dead, 1949; A Matter of Nerves, 1950; Invitation to an Inquest, 1950; The Martineau Murderers, 1953.

SAMUEL, MAURICE (February 8, 1895-), American journalist, novelist, man of letters, writes: "The place of my birth is Macin, a townlet in Rumania, opposite Braila on the Danube; the city of my boyhood and youth is Manchester, in England; and I have lived my adult life with New York as a base, Palestine (now Israel) as its opposite, and a lot of countries and cities popping in and out of my life. One

would think that with all the traveling I have done—fifty to seventy-five thousand miles in a normal year—I must have a wanderer's blood in me. But except for the exhaustion it sometimes brings, I could swear that it is the world which passes in panorama before me, while I observe and note and write. The fact is that I *do* write almost anywhere: on trains, planes, and ships, in hotels, rondavels and motels. I have a portable typewriter and earplugs. The act of traveling I practically ignore; and when I'm in the new place I adjust myself to listen, and then to write. That is, when I am not lecturing.

"The dominating interest of my life has been the riddle of the Jewish episode—some three or four thousand years old now—in the history of the planet. Most of my books have been devoted to one facet or another of this riddle. I have written about Jews lightly, seriously, grimly, satirically, passionately, lovingly—but always in the form of essays. In these essays I pose the question of the meaning of the Jew, his place in the ethical evolution of society, his self-fulfillment in his communities and in his reconstructed homeland, and the continuation of his trajectory into the future.

"When I break away from this dominating interest, I usually write novels; and afterwards I discover that the theme had had something to do with a moral problem which occupied me in one of my Jewish essays. Thus critics of my novel *Beyond Woman* observed that the non-Jewish characters were Jewish. And in the Italian Renaissance novel *Web of Lucifer* I was actually concerned with the birth of modern Fascism—the matrix of anti-Semitism—as exemplified in Macchiavelli and Cesare Borgia. My most recent novel, *The Devil That Failed,* is a parable of the man trapped in a totalitarian state and unable to establish his identity; but it might also be the parable of the Jew trapped by history and struggling to find out what and who he is.

"In addition to the portentous foregoing works I have some lighter literary essays, like *The World of Sholom Aleichem* and *Prince of the Ghetto,* in which I try to reconstruct the vanished Yiddish-speaking civilization of Europe from the works of its leading writers. In these, as in my other books, my preoccupation is with the meaning behind realities, the spirit which speaks through the acts and characters of men and women.

"I don't anticipate any change in my habits and interests, except as I am overtaken by senility. I am full of ideas for new books, but they will deal with the old themes, which I find inexhaustible."

* * *

Maurice Samuel lived for ten years (1929-1939) in Palestine, and has revisited Israel frequently since then. He knew the late Chaim Weizmann well and in the course of his career has been in contact with "practically every Jewish community between Jordan and the Golden Gate, between Manchester and Cape Town." In 1944 the *Saturday Review of Literature* awarded him a prize for his book *The World of Sholom Aleichem,* which was considered the best contribution of the year toward improving intergroup relations. In addition to his own writing, he has made numerous translations from the Yiddish, including books by Sholem Asch and I. J. Singer. Samuel married Gertrude Kahn in 1921. They have one daughter, now married.

PRINCIPAL WORKS: The Outsider, 1921; Whatever Gods, 1922, You Gentiles, 1924; What Happened in Palestine, 1929; On the Rim of the Wilderness, 1931; Jews on Approval, 1932; Beyond Woman, 1934; The Great Hatred, 1940; The World of Sholom Aleichem, 1943; Harvest in the Desert, 1944; Web of Lucifer, 1947; Prince of the Ghetto, 1948; The Gentleman and the Jew, 1950; The Devil That Failed, 1952; Level Sunlight, 1953.

ABOUT: Samuel, M. The Gentleman and the Jew.

SANBORN, PITTS (1878-March 7, 1941). For biographical sketch and list of works and references, see TWENTIETH CENTURY AUTHORS, 1942.

SANDBURG, CARL (January 6, 1878-   ). For biographical sketch and list of earlier works and references, see TWENTIETH CENTURY AUTHORS, 1942.

* * *

On January 6, 1953, Carl Sandburg's seventy-fifth birthday, he was honored at a dinner in Chicago attended by more than five hundred people. The day was proclaimed "Carl Sandburg Day" in Illinois by Governor Adlai Stevenson. There were press conferences, autographing sessions, cocktail parties, and radio appearances for the poet. A representative of King Gustav VI of Sweden decorated him with the Commander Order of the Northern Star. Three days later Sandburg returned to Galesburg, Ill., where he read poems and sang ballads before a large audience of enthusiastic admirers in the Congregational Church. Honored as one of the greatest of living American poets and probably the only American "national" poet, Sandburg moved through these ceremonies with dignity and simplicity. The best tribute to his achievement is his writing itself. His work reflects his personality with rare accuracy—unaffected, direct, rugged, full of common sense and warm humor. "He celebrates what is best in us, and recalls us to our heritage and our humanity," Henry Steele Commager wrote of him in 1950. "A poet," Sandburg writes, "explains for us what for him is poetry by what he presents to us in his poems. . . . There is no escape. There stands the work of the man, the woman, who wrought it. We go to it, read it, look at it, perhaps go back to it many a time, and it is for each of us what we make of it."

In recent years Sandburg has written more prose than poetry. His first novel, *Remembrance Rock*, was not successful. Over a thousand pages long, it was an attempt to tell the story of America from Pilgrim days through the Civil War—"a measured epic of the quest for individual freedom and self-realization," one reviewer described it. Its weakness lay perhaps in the loftiness of the theme and its essentially non-dramatic nature. Perry Miller wrote in the New York *Times*: "The effect is to show, unmistakably, some of the things a Bard falls short of—when he tries to construct a novel out of no more intelligible or dramatic a comprehension of the past than his blind assurance that 'Life goes on.'" His first attempt at autobiography, however, was widely admired. This was *Always the Young Strangers* and covered the period of his childhood to young manhood in Galesburg—a warm, rambling, and honest account, "authentic Americana, as faithful a picture of a small town in the Middle West sixty years ago as a Currier & Ives lithograph, a chapter in the history of this country," wrote Earnest Elmo Calkins in the *Saturday Review*. Sandburg has also continued his Lincoln scholarship. One of the most painstaking of his tasks in this field was the cutting down of his six-volume biography into a single volume of 762 pages, published in 1954. "His portrait of Abraham Lincoln," Robert E. Sherwood remarked, "whether in one volume or six, is a monument that will stand forever—a monument to subject and author alike."

During World War II Sandburg wrote a series of newspaper columns and did radio broadcasts for the Office of War Information. He makes many public appearances reciting his own poems and singing folk ballads, and since the advent of television he has reached an even wider audience in televised interviews. His home is in Flat Rock, N.C.

ADDITIONAL WORKS: Storm Over the Land: A Profile of the Civil War Based on Lincoln: The War Years, 1942; Home Front Memo, 1943; Remembrance Rock (novel) 1948; Lincoln Collector: The Story of Oliver R. Barrett's Great Private Collection, 1949; Complete Poems, 1950; (ed.) The New American Songbag, 1950; Always the Young Strangers (autobiography) 1952; Abraham Lincoln: The Prairie Years and The War Years, 1954; Prairie-Town Boy (taken from Always the Young Strangers) 1955.

ABOUT: Gregory, H. & Zaturenska, M. History of American Poetry, 1900-1940; Lewis, L. It Takes All Kinds; Lorimer, S. The Will to Succeed; Sandburg, C. Always the Young Strangers; Thomas, B. P. Portrait for Posterity; Lincoln and His Biographers; Christian Science Monitor Magazine July 19, 1947, September 2, 1950; English Journal April 1950; New York Herald Tribune Book Review October 8, 1950; New York Times Book Review January 4, 1953; Publishers' Weekly January 17, 1953; Saturday Review January 17, 1953.

SANDERSON, IVAN TERRANCE (January 1911-   ). For autobiographical sketch and list of earlier works and references, see TWENTIETH CENTURY AUTHORS, 1942.

* * *

Ivan T. Sanderson has become a United States citizen. Writing with a deep personal love of nature and a keen sense of the drama of natural history, Sanderson has been able to convey to his readers "his own feeling for the beauty and wonder of life in the wild" (Elizabeth Hodges, in the New York *Times*). Sanderson does most of the illustrations for his books. He has been described as "a tireless Nature-promoter." He travels extensively on expeditions to collect specimens for zoos and museums, lectures, gives radio talks, and in recent years has become a well-known television personality.

ADDITIONAL WORKS: (ed.) Animal Tales, 1946; How to Know the American Mammals, 1951; The Silver Mink, 1952.

ABOUT: Mahoney, B. E. (comp.) Illustrators of Children's Books; Von Hagen, V. W. Green World of the Naturalists.

*SANDOZ, MARI (1901-   ). For autobiographical sketch and list of earlier works and references, see TWENTIETH CENTURY AUTHORS, 1942.

* * *

Mari Sandoz writes from New York City: "Since 1942 I have published several books and added to my shorter publications, which

* săn dŏz' mä'rī

863

had varied from *North American Review* to *Ladies' Home Journal.*

"Since my college days I have worked with students of writing courses, later on the staff of writers' conferences, and, from 1947 on, I have conducted the advanced short story and novel writing courses in the eight-weeks' Writers' Institute at the University of Wisconsin in their summer sessions. In 1950 the University of Nebraska gave me an honorary Doctor of Literature. I am a member of the Authors Guild of the Authors League of America; the Association on American Indian Affairs, and on the board of associate editors of their *The American Indian*; the New York Posse of The Westerners, etc."

Miss Sandoz' biography of the Oglala Sioux chieftain, Crazy Horse, and her earlier book, *Old Jules*, were hailed by Wallace Stegner as "two of the great stories of the West . . . written in the spirit of the sagas, with a scrupulous regard to truth and history." In *Cheyenne Autumn* she tells the poignant saga of a band of Indians who set out in 1878 from Indian Territory, where they had been sent by the American army, to return to their native haunts in the Yellowstone. "Actually," wrote August Derleth in the Chicago *Sunday Tribune,* "Mari Sandoz does more than just tell the story. With her customary skill, she manages to recreate a man, a scene, an event, a page from history, so that through her prose this great struggle of a small band of homesick, mistreated, half starved Indians against the military might of a major nation takes on the stature of an American epic."

The governor of Nebraska proclaimed August 23, 1954, "Mari Sandoz Day" in honor of the publication of her book *The Buffalo Hunters,* the story of the slaughter of the American buffalo and the social impact of this upon the West.

ADDITIONAL WORKS: Crazy Horse, 1942; The Tom-Walker (fiction) 1947; Cheyenne Autumn, 1953; The Buffalo Hunters, 1954; Winter Thunder (fiction) 1954.

ABOUT: Publishers' Weekly August 7, 1954; Saturday Review August 21, 1954.

SANSOM, WILLIAM (January 18, 1912-   ), British novelist and short story writer, reports: "I was born, and soon began writing. The pattern is all too familiar. The worried baby, the shy child, schooldays spent avoiding the ball, the first rungs of the commercial ladder—indeed, in a bank—and then the revolt that ended not in a garret but an advertising agency. The skeleton of fact supporting this well-worn tissue

stands as follows: Birth in 1912, an English public school, a commercial bank in the City of London. There were intermissions abroad —a time spent studying German at Bonn, travels in Spain and Hungary and other European countries.

"The war extracted me from advertising, I served as a London fireman, and the Blitz taught me to write seriously. Hitherto I had dabbled with 'formula' magazine stories and so forth, always bearing an audience in mind, without success. The suddenly more serious texture of life, and the foreshortened expectation of it, impelled me to write down what I really thought rather than what I imagined people wanted. Thus, with no thought of publication I was immediately published. And then went on writing regularly for English literary periodicals—*Horizon, New Writing,* the *Cornhill,* etc.

"On demobilisation I secured a good position in a film company, writing scripts. It was comfortable—but had it all that much point? —I was thirty years old and it seemed a case of 'now or never.' I left the job and risked the purely literary life, drawing in all horns and accepting the garret.

"In 1946 and again in 1947 I was awarded literary prizes by the Society of Authors. In 1951 was elected a Fellow of the Royal Society of Literature."

* * *

Although he has not as yet written any single novel which the critics have considered a major work, William Sansom is generally recognized as one of the most able and interesting of the younger British novelists and short story writers. Harvey Breit said of him in the *Atlantic:* "His language is quietly distinctive, effortless, and exact. He sees with an unrestrained and a fresh eye. He has superb control of his material and he doesn't try what he can't do." Sansom is unmarried. A quiet, reflective man, he lives alone in London, has a garden which he cheerfully neglects, and in *Who's Who* lists his favorite recreation as "watching." He gets his ideas for his writing mainly from self-searching: "I ask myself, what do I really know about? What type of person do I really know? To be truthful, it starts a little before that, with a place or a thing.

I wanted to write about the district here where I had lived ten years. I wrote about it in *The Body.*" Sansom has a photographic eye for detail, "a telling selectivity and a vivid imagination which invests landscape or the machine with emotional life and with symbolic suggestiveness," Charles J. Rolo wrote in the New York *Times.* Eudora Welty has said of him: "He makes you see, hear, taste, touch and smell to his order. . . . Mr. Sansom's descriptive power is a steady fireworks."

PRINCIPAL WORKS: *Novels*—The Body, 1949; The Face of Innocence, 1951; A Bed of Roses, 1954. *Short Stories*—Fireman Flower, 1944; Three, 1946; Something Terrible, Something Lovely, 1948; The Passionate North, 1950; A Touch of the Sun, 1952; Pleasures Strange and Simple, 1953. *Miscellaneous*—South: Aspects and Images from Corsica, Italy and Southern France, 1948.

ABOUT: London Times Literary Supplement August 29, 1952; New York Times Book Review August 7, 1949, August 12, 1951; Saturday Review of Literature February 11, 1950.

---

*SANTAYANA, GEORGE (December 16, 1863-September 26, 1952). For autobiographical sketch and list of earlier works and references, see TWENTIETH CENTURY AUTHORS, 1942.

* * *

George Santayana (Jorge Augustín Nicolás de Santayana) died in his sleep of cancer of the stomach at eighty-eight. Living in Rome at the outbreak of World War II, he applied for asylum at the Convent of Santo Stefano Rotondo on the Celian Hill, where the Blue Sisters of the Little Company of Mary, a British order, allowed him to live during the war years. He remained there for the rest of his life, living almost monastically, reading, writing, receiving occasional visitors, seldom leaving his small room. During the last year of his life his sight and hearing failed. He was buried, at his request, in unconsecrated ground in the Verano Catholic Cemetery. There were no religious rites at the funeral; Daniel Cory, his close friend and literary executor, read Santayana's own brief *Epitaph.*

Dominations and Powers, the fruit of many years of meditation and writing, was published a year before his death. Subtitled "Reflections on Liberty, Society and Government," it deals rather with "metapolitics" than with specific conditions in the nations of the world. The late Irwin Edman said that there was "no book on political philosophy remotely like this in its lordly and patrician detach-

* sän tä yä′nä

ment, in its setting of politics in the grand context of matter and spirit, in its relating of government to the great forces in nature and to the delicate intimacies of spirit."

The third volume of Santayana's memoirs was published, at his direction, only after his death. The autobiographical volumes reveal much of the man who combined what Edmund Wilson called "one of the highest examples of flexible international intelligence" and, in the words of Joseph Wood Krutch, "an arrogant assumption that he is above and beyond the hopes and fears as well as the obligations of other men."

Santayana once described himself as a "recalcitrant materialist." It has been said that he belonged less to the tradition of technical philosophy than to that of "general humane insight," and the core of his philosophy lay in his belief "that everything is material in its basis and ideal in its possible career." Much of the persuasiveness of his work can be attributed to the brilliance of his style. Edman said that his prose had "a marble precision and a dreamy suggestiveness." His prose and his poetry share, as Horace Gregory points out, "an absence of concrete imagery, a pure, limpid diction, great intellectual charm, graceful cadences and the implied desire to contemplate man and his destinies wisely—but at a distance."

Found among his papers when they were released by the Spanish Embassy at Rome a year after his death was a remarkably objective self-appraisal, "The Idler and His Works," written between 1942 and 1944, in which he says: "In spite of being so much in sympathy with the sages, I am well aware of not having been one of them. As a person I was too self-indulgent and not heroic enough: as a writer I was too miscellaneous; as a thinker I was born at the wrong time and bred in the wrong way . . . yet for my own happiness I was philosophical enough. In a commonplace psyche I kept alive a spark of pure spirit which cast an impartial light, as far as it could reach, over the *universitas rerum.*"

ADDITIONAL WORKS: Realms of Being (one vol.) 1942; The Idea of Christ in the Gospels, or, God in Man, 1946; Dialogues in Limbo; with Three New Dialogues, 1948 (first listed 1925); Dominations and Powers: Reflections on Liberty, Society and Government, 1951; The Poet's Testament (poems and plays) 1953. *Autobiography*—Persons and Places, 1944; The Middle Span, 1945; My Host the World, 1953.

ABOUT: Brown, R. W. Harvard Yard in the Golden Age; Fausset, H. I. Poets and Pundits; Fisch, M. H. & others (eds.) Classic American Philosophers; Gregory, H. & Zaturenska, M. A History of American Poetry; Lamont, C. The Independent Mind; McElroy, H. C. Modern Philosophers; Santayana, G. Persons and Places, The Middle Span, My Host the World; Slochower, H. No Voice Is Wholly Lost; American Mercury July 1945, November 1951, March 1953; Atlantic Monthly April 1953; Commonweal October 24, 1952, October 31, 1952; Educational Record October 1949; Life August 7, 1944, October 6, October 13, 1952; New Republic April 20, 1945; New York Times May 9, 1948, August 14, 1949, September 28, October 1, 1952; New Yorker May 5, 1945, April 6, 1946, August 25, 1951; Newsweek May 7, 1951; Publishers' Weekly April 28, 1945; The Reporter April 28, 1953; Saturday Review of Literature April 21, 1945, May 12, 1951, May 15, 1954; Time April 23, 1945, March 25, 1946, September 27, 1948, May 7, 1951; Virginia Quarterly Review, 21, No. 3, 1945; Wilson Library Bulletin September 1950.

SANTEE, ROSS (1888-   ), American regionalist and novelist, writes: "Born in Iowa, Thornburg—five miles north of What Cheer

and twenty miles east of Oskaloosa; family Quakers on both sides. My father died when I was a baby. Mother and two older sisters made up the family, it was an integrated group. Father's people had gone to Iowa in a covered wagon. There were several long tables of the Santee clan at the Old Settlers' picnics at Coal Creek. Mother was a Penrose from Ohio. Mother had gone out to Iowa to visit a sister, that was where she met my Dad. Father's people laughed a lot, but on Mother's side they were the stiffnecked variety.

"Raised the usual juvenile disturbances as a boy; interested in any kind of athletics, but I think hunting and trapping were the real love as a boy. Always liked to draw, but about the only pictures I saw were McCutcheon's cartoons in the old Chicago *Record*.

"Moved to Moline, Ill., when I was sixteen; spent the last two years of high school there. Athletics and learning to shoot a good game of pool were my main interests, although the library in Moline was a joy since it was the first one I'd ever been in.

"The river, of course, meant Huck Finn, Tom Sawyer. It was there I first read everything Mark Twain had written. The river itself was something in those days; the log rafts were still coming down and I came to know many of the old men who spent their lives on the river. Among other things I flunked in high school was drawing. I had no interest in drawing flowers and still life

setups when I could see the old river rolling from the classroom.

"I spent four years at the Chicago Art Institute, went there with the idea of becoming a cartoonist; worked backstage in most every theatre in the Loop; slung hash in as many places; worked a broom at the Institute for my tuition. New York was the next move.

"Frank Casey, art editor of *Collier's*, bought the first drawing I sold in New York. I sold a few to *Judge*, peddled some to the newspapers. That first year was tough. I interviewed more office boys than I did editors. Worse yet, I'd lost interest in doing cartoons.

"At night I'd prowl the streets of New York, then try to put down what I'd remembered with a brush. One morning Tom Benton saw a lot of these sketches on the floor. He didn't like the cartoons I was doing any more than I did, but these sketches interested him since they were simple, forthright statements. He sent me down to the public library to look up Daumier. That changed everything. When I walked back up to the old Lincoln Square Arcade that night I knew I was through making any drawings except what I wanted to do.

"For several years Mother had been living with a married sister in Globe, Ariz.; they'd been wanting me to come. I had no idea of ever going to work for a cow outfit, but I had to have a job.

"I wrangled horses mostly, and the doggone country had got hold of me. I wasn't exactly strange to cowboys, either. As a small boy in Iowa, one of our nearest neighbors owned a big stock farm; they brought in the Longhorns from Montana, sometimes by the trainload; sometimes half a dozen cowpunchers wintered there, mostly Texans via Montana, I heard all the old songs, and I can still remember the scrape of the fiddle when they sang, 'Natchez Under the Hill.'

"Things rocked along for several years—with a year out, killing mosquitoes at Camp Bowie, Texas, in the first unpleasantness, where I got eight dollars and ten cents a month and never made Pfc. But along with my weakness for pool I had a liking for poker, both stud and draw. So I got out of the army with six hundred dollars. I worked through the fall roundup; went up to Chicago 'to winter,' as the cowboys say, and O'Donnell, editor of a little magazine, *Cartoons*, bought most everything submitted.

"The late George Bellows was teaching at the Art Institute that winter so I went to one of his night classes. He liked the drawings I was making and talked me into trying New York again. So I went back to Arizona, worked through the spring and fall roundups; bought a cap, a pair of flat-heeled shoes, tightened my belt and headed for New York.

"Frank Casey was now editor of *Life*; Charles Dana Gibson had just bought the magazine. Frank was one of the few art editors I'd remembered who left a good taste in my mouth, so I went up to see him. Frank bought some drawings and, besides, he talked me into going down to see Crump, who was editor of *Boys' Life* at that time. Mr. Crump wanted me to do some stories. At first I said No; Tom Craven was a friend of mine and Tom had written ten years and made just twenty dollars. I said it was bad enough to be a lousy artist without taking on more misery. But Crump was insistent; so I wrote a little incident that had happened at the ranch and made a couple of drawings for it—that was what he wanted, something to tie the drawings down. He gave me twenty-five dollars for the piece.

"About that time I went into the old *Leslie's* to try to peddle some drawings. William Morris Houghten, who was editor, liked the drawings and asked if I'd ever written anything. I laughed, told him I'd just sold two lousy stories to a boys' magazine. He said, 'Bring in one of those "lousy" stories and let me see it.'

"Then *Century* bought six or seven pages of drawings without any text. And about that time 'Spike' Hunt came back from Europe. Spike has older-brothered me ever since we met in Chicago in 1908. I talked Spike into going back to Arizona with me and doing a story about a real cow outfit, and the Rodeo at Payson where they built the corral at the head of the street an' turned the calves right down the street; they rode the broncs there, too, and had the horse races down the main street. Spike was high on the idea, and he was coming home with me. Then he was sent to Haiti and the whole thing blew up.

"When I went over to *Century* to pick up some drawings they asked what I was going to do when I went home. I said, 'First thing is the Rodeo at Payson, then I'm going back to the ranch to work.' When I told them a little about the Payson Rodeo they asked me not only to make the pictures but write the piece. Well, this is the way it all started.

"Until I was married, in 1926, I split the time between the ranch in Arizona and New York. I never worked for any outfits except the Bar F Bar and the Cross S. Most of their range was on the San Carlos Apache Reservation. In the early '20's both outfits went broke—with the drouth and the drop in prices. Then the range was turned back to the Apaches, and the white outfits all moved off.

"Now I hope this covers what you want. I don't know whether it's pertinent or not, but that's the way it was. Right now as we're putting this down, I can see the old trail from Globe that went to the Bar F Bar. All the old-timers are gone; some of the kids I worked with are old men with white hair. Globe, itself, has changed, there're no horses at the rack now.

"This Arizona country, Globe and Gila County, has been the setting for most everything I've ever written—most of the short stories, 'Men and Horses,' 'Cowboy,' 'Apache Land,' and 'The Bubbling Spring'; the setting of 'Hardrock and Silver Sage.' Only the hills haven't changed. It's almost forty years since I rode up the old trail that evening to the Bar F Bar—and, after all, forty years is a long time."

PRINCIPAL WORKS: Men and Horses, 1926; Cowboy, 1928; Pooch, 1931 (published in 1934 as Spike: The Story of a Cowpuncher's Dog); Sleepy Black: Story of a Horse, 1933; The Bar X Golf Course, 1933; Apache Land, 1947; The Bubbling Spring, 1949; Rusty: A Cowboy of the Old West, 1950; Hardrock and Silver Sage, 1951; Lost Pony Tracks, 1953.

ABOUT: Santee, R. Lost Pony Tracks; Saturday Review of Literature November 11, 1950.

"SAPPER." See MC NEILLE, H. C.

*SARETT, LEW R. (May 16, 1888-August 17, 1954). For autobiographical sketch and list of earlier works and references, see TWENTIETH CENTURY AUTHORS, 1942.

* * *

Lew Sarett died in Gainesville, Fla., at sixty-six. Several months before his death he wrote to the editors of this volume: "In 1953 I became professor emeritus at Northwestern University and established my home in Gainesville, Fla. I am now serving as visiting professor of speech at the University of Florida. My first wife, Margaret Husted, died February 27, 1941. On April 19, 1946, I married my present wife, Alma Johnson." Of his two children by his first marriage, Sarett wrote that his son, Dr. Lewis H. Sarett of Princeton, N.J., is famous for his

* sä rĕt'

synthesis of the miracle drug cortisone; his daughter is now Mrs. John M. Stockdale, of Estherville, Iowa.

In 1950 Lew Sarett became regional vice-president of the Poetry Society of America, to represent the South.

Correction: In the list of works about Lew Sarett the reference to the *American Magazine* should read February and March 1926, not 1936.

ADDITIONAL WORK: Speech: A High School Course (with W. T. Foster & J. H. McBurney) 1943.

ABOUT: New York Times August 18, 1954.

SAROYAN, WILLIAM (August 31, 1908-). For biographical sketch and list of earlier works and references, see TWENTIETH CENTURY AUTHORS, 1942.

* * *

William Saroyan served in the U.S. Army in World War II. He drew heavily upon the experience in his satiric novel *The Adventures of Wesley Jackson*, a book which was described as "the first anti-war novel of World War II." For most readers, however, it was simply another eccentric, warm-hearted Saroyanesque fantasy. Thomas Sugrue remarked of it: "The war was too big a piece of viciousness for him to leaven. The evil behind it was too raw and strong. Mr. Saroyan needs a smaller and less complicated environment and a problem which will submit more easily to love and friendship and the soft, sweet tears of Wesley Jackson on a young summer night."

In none of his later writings has Saroyan captured the hearts and imagination of the public as he had done in *The Daring Young Man on the Flying Trapeze* or *The Time of Your Life*. Reviewers have complained that "Saroyan pathos is close to bathos." At their most sharply critical, however, they have conceded that he can on occasion rise to great heights. One of the most representative critical evaluations of him was made by Kelsey Guilfoil in the Chicago *Tribune* in 1950: "It has been my belief for a long time that William Saroyan is a man who doesn't know how to write and doesn't know what to write, but who, by a virtue of a great and compassionate feeling for the frailties of human aspirations, combined with a somewhat artless skill in the weaving of words, manages now and then to produce a masterpiece." To strike a balance, there remains Saroyan's own critical estimate: "I am so innately great that by comparison others who believe they are great or act as if they believe they are great

seem to me to be only pathetic, although occasionally charming."

In 1943 Saroyan married Carol Marcus. They had two children, Aram and Lucy, and were divorced in 1949. Saroyan continues to live in California and has an office in Beverly Hills where, he announced in 1951, "my intention is to earn a great deal of money." That intention was fulfilled, in part at least, the same year, when Saroyan turned song writer and—in collaboration with his cousin, Ross Bagdasarian—wrote a song which became an overnight sensation on juke boxes and on the radio—"Come On-a My House."

Saroyan's most popular play, *The Time of Your Life*, was revived at New York's City Center for a limited engagement early in 1955.

ADDITIONAL WORKS: Dear Baby (short stories) 1944; The Adventures of Wesley Jackson, 1946; The Assyrian, and Other Stories, 1950; Twin Adventures: The Adventures of William Saroyan, a Diary [and] The Adventures of Wesley Jackson, 1950; Rock Wagram, 1951; Tracy's Tiger, 1951; The Bicycle Rider in Beverly Hills (autobiography) 1952; The Laughing Matter, 1953. *Plays*—Get Away Old Man, 1944; A Decent Birth, A Happy Funeral, 1949; Don't Go Away Mad, 1949; Hello Out There, 1949; Sam Ego's House, 1949.

ABOUT: Feibleman, J. K. Aesthetics; Gray, J. On Second Thought; Saroyan, W. Twin Adventures, The Bicycle Rider in Beverly Hills; Wilson, E. Classics and Commercials; Van Gelder, R. Writers and Writing; American Mercury September 1943; Commonweal April 28, 1950; New York Herald Tribune Book Review October 1, 1951.

SARTON, GEORGE ALFRED LÉON (August 31, 1884-), Belgian-American historian and philosopher of science, writes:

"George Sarton was born in Ghent (Belgium). Educated at the Athenaeum and University of Ghent. After obtaining his doctorate in mathematics in 1911, he dedicated his life to the study of the history and philosophy of science. In 1915,  he came to the United States; in 1918, he was appointed an associate of the Carnegie Institution of Washington and could devote all his time to his chosen work. From 1916 on, he did some teaching in Harvard University, but it was the Carnegie Institution which made the accomplishment of his task possible. He is now professor emeritus of the History of Science in Harvard University.

"He founded *Isis*, an international quarterly concerning his studies, in 1912, and was

Fabian Bachrach

its editor until 1952; in 1936, he founded *Osiris* to accommodate longer memoirs on the subject."

* * *

George Sarton has been described as "the most eloquent and convincing prophet of the value of the history of science as a discipline, and the man best qualified on the history itself." His monumental *Introduction to the History of Science*, the first volume of which appeared in 1927, is the definitive work in the field, covering the subject from ancient times through the Renaissance. Sarton has devoted his life to bridging the gap between science and the humanities. "No such division existed in the time of Plato and Aristotle and during the Renaissance," he explained in an interview in the *New Yorker* in 1952, "but today scientists and humanists are like cats and dogs. It's partly because science has made such strides. Well, it was a crazy thing to do—I could have made a good living as a professor of mathematics and I had an income of only five thousand francs a year—but I did it."

Sarton was married in 1911 to Eleanor Mabel Elwes of London, who died in 1950. Their daughter (Eleanor) May Sarton, the novelist and poet, has recently written a series of essays on her childhood for the *New Yorker*. Out of these pleasant and sensitive memoirs, her father emerges as a man of charm, vast erudition, and total dedication to his life's work. Sarton is a member of numerous scholarly societies, holds honorary degrees from many American and European universities, has twice received the Prix Binoux from the Académie des Sciences of Paris, and was decorated Knight of the Order of Leopold, Belgium, in 1940.

PRINCIPAL WORKS: Introduction to the History of Science (3 vols. in 5) 1927-1948; The History of Science and the New Humanism, 1931; The Study of the History of Science, 1936; The Study of the History of Mathematics, 1936; The Life of Science, 1948; Horus, Guide to the History of Science, 1952; History of Science: Ancient Science through the Golden Age of Greece, 1952; Galen of Pergamon, 1954; Ancient Science and Modern Civilization, 1954.

ABOUT: Montagu, M. F. Ashley (ed.) Studies and Essays in the History of Science and Learning Offered in Homage of George Sarton; Current Biography 1942; Isis, vol. 44 (1953); New Yorker November 28, 1952, January 9, February 6, April 3, 1954.

SARTON, MAY (May 3, 1912-), American poet and novelist, writes: "I was born in Wondelgem, Belgium, but I do not remember anything about Belgium then as we were driven out as refugees from the German invasion in 1914. My father, Belgian by birth, is the historian of science, George Sarton. My mother was English. We became naturalized Americans in 1924. It is strange to me to think that I would be a writer in French, if it had not been for World War I. As it was I soon forgot my French, as we spoke English at home for my father's sake, and I had to learn French later like

Peter Rossiter

any other American child. Belgian writers are divided into those 'of the Flemish tongue' and those of 'the French tongue.' George Sarton and I seem to be Belgian writers 'of the English tongue.' I believe this was all lucky as I'm convinced that English is the best language for poetry in the world.

"My chief education was at the Shady Hill School in Cambridge, at that time an open-air school. Writing in mittens perhaps explains the illegibility of my hand. But I had the great good fortune there as a small child to be taught poetry by a genius, Agnes Hocking. Poetry became my passion then and has never ceased to be so. From Shady Hill School I went on to high school at the Cambridge High and Latin. My graduation in 1929 was the end of any formal education, because for the next eight years I thought that theatre was to be my life. I entered Eva Le Gallienne's Civic Repertory Theatre as an apprentice when I was seventeen, worked there in small parts and finally became a member of the company and director of the Apprentice Group. When the Civic Repertory closed, I tried to keep together a group of the students and we rehearsed and played together as The Associated Actors Theatre for the next three years. All this was a kind of education, different perhaps from college, but I believe now immensely valuable to me as a writer, and I do not regret it.

"The year my little company disbanded my first book of poems came out, and from that time on I have been wholly concerned with writing. I have had all kinds of jobs, from film script writing at the Office of War Information to extensive lecturing on poetry in colleges all over the country, and more recently have been for three years Briggs-Copeland Instructor in Composition at Harvard University. But these jobs were only for the purpose of buying time for my own writing.

"I believe that poetry and novels are a good combination. Poetry comes in spurts whereas after the initial imaginative creation, a novel can and perhaps must be written day after day on a very regular schedule. The novels, so far, have been all laid in Europe where I have gone back many times to find those old roots. But I believe passionately in America and, as time goes on, hope perhaps to build a bridge the other way, and to be one of those writers who contribute to the understanding of the United States in Europe."

* * *

May Sarton has shown rare skill and sensitivity as both poet and novelist. Her poems are mainly lyrics, written with what Wallace Fowlie calls "admirable simplicity." In her *Land of Silence,* Fowlie comments, "she demonstrates a great range of feeling and subject, an unusual strength in describing what comes before her eyes and touches her heart." In some of her later work critics have objected to a thinness of emotional content, a certain facility and a tendency toward the "conventionally literary." But even while raising these objections, Louise Bogan, for one, finds that some of these poems "exhibit her mature power of recognizing the heart of the matter and of expressing it in memorable terms."

Her novels have been highly praised for "an incisive intelligence that never fails to see complexity and never gives in to sentimentality" (so J. H. Raleigh wrote in the *New Republic*). John Nerber, reviewing *A Shower of Summer Days* for the New York *Times,* writes that she "ranks with the very best of our distinguished novelists." Her first novel with an American background, *Faithful Are the Wounds,* was concerned with the suicide of a Harvard professor of English literature, an idealist and political radical whose life and death were strikingly paralleled in real life by the life and death of F. O. Matthiessen, Harvard professor and critic.

In 1952 Miss Sarton received the Reynolds Lyric Award of the Poetry Society of America, and in 1953 she was honored by Bryn Mawr College with the Lucy Martin Donnelly Fellowship of $3,000.

PRINCIPAL WORKS: *Poetry*—Encounter in April, 1937; Inner Landscape, 1939; The Lion and the Rose, 1948; The Land of Silence, 1953. *Novels*—The Single Hound, 1938; The Bridge of Years, 1946; Shadow of a Man, 1950; A Shower of Summer Days, 1952; Faithful Are the Wounds, 1955.

ABOUT: New Yorker January 9, February 6, April 3, 1954.

***SARTRE, JEAN-PAUL** (June 21, 1905-), French philosopher, playwright, and novelist, was born and raised in Paris. He was educated at the Lycée de la Rochelle and the Lycée Louis-le-Grand and entered the Ecole Normale Supérieure in 1925 where he majored in philosophy. In 1929 he completed his studies, with high academic honors, and began his career as a

teacher in the secondary schools. He taught at Havre, Laon, and Neuilly. Also during this period, 1929-34, he traveled and studied abroad—in Egypt, Greece, Italy, and Germany. In Germany in 1933 and 1934 he studied under two of the most influential of contemporary German philosophers, Edmund Husserl and Martin Heidegger. He had also by this time begun his studies of the great nineteenth century Danish philosopher Soren Kirkegaard, who is regarded as the founder of the modern existentialist movement.

In 1935 Sartre returned to Paris and took a teaching post at the Lycée Condorcet. He lived in a small hotel on the Left Bank and began frequenting the cafés of the neighborhood, where he soon attracted around him a circle of young intellectuals. His writings at this time were deeply original psychological studies of the imagination and human emotions. They were brilliant in promise, but they won him no particular recognition. He did, however, reach a larger audience with a series of critical essays on contemporary literature in *La Nouvelle Revue Française.* In these he called attention to (and did much to popularize in France) the writings of a number of American novelists—Faulkner, Caldwell, Hemingway, Dos Passos, and Steinbeck. In 1938 Sartre published his first novel, *La Nausée (Nausea)*, and a year later a collection of short stories, *Le Mur (The Wall)*, both reflecting the bitter pessimism and despair of man who finds himself in a universe where "nothing, absolutely nothing, justifies his existence."

In September 1939 Sartre entered the French army as a private. In June 1940, with the collapse of France, he was taken prisoner by the Germans on the Maginot line. After nine months of imprisonment, during which he wrote and directed plays for his fellow prisoners in the camp, he was released. He returned to Paris and joined

* sär'tr'

the Resistance movement, writing for such underground publications as *Les Lettres Françaises* and *Combat*. His first play, *Les Mouches* (*The Flies*), was produced in Paris in 1943. A re-telling of the classical Orestes legend of a man who takes upon himself the responsibility of avenging his father's death, the play's powerful message of freedom and resistance to tyranny somehow eluded the Nazi censors. A year later came the production of his play *Huis Clos* (*No Exit*), which pictured Hell as a cheap and dingy hotel room where three people (two women and a man) "are forever condemned to each other's presence." At about the same time Sartre published his 700-page philosophical treatise *L'Etre et le Néant* (Being and Non-Being) and the pamphlet *L'Existentialisme Est un Humanisme* (Existentialism Is Humanism), giving the now vastly enlarged circle of his disciples a concrete philosophical text for the existentialist movement.

When World War II ended and France was liberated, Sartre immediately won international reputation as the leading intellectual of post-war France, and existentialism became the most publicized and fashionable philosophy of the age. Sartre and his associates, best known of whom is Simone de Beauvoir, had their headquarters at the Café de Flore, which soon became a center of tourist attention. The movement attracted many young disciples and, particularly in the period 1944-50, had an enormous influence upon writers and artists.

Existentialism has been defined as "the philosophy which declares as its first principle that existence is prior to essence." As opposed to the idea that there is purpose, plan, and meaning in human existence, existentialism—as Sartre expounds it—argues that man "is alone, abandoned on earth in the midst of his infinite responsibilities, without help, with no other aim than the one he sets himself, with no other destiny than the one he forges for himself on this earth." Human existence is thus a void, a total frustration. Man exists, but for this there is no more reason than for his non-existing. This existence is in itself freedom, but (to quote Margaret Walker in the *Yale Review*, Winter 1953) "not freedom conceived as a gift, condition, or property so much as a task, a responsibility devolving upon the individual himself." Thus arises the famous existentialist phrase that man is "condemned to be free." He seeks to escape the responsibilities implicit in this freedom—"to deny," Miss Walker writes, "the implacable necessi-

ties implicit in being a quite unjustifiable creature in a groundless universe." He plunges himself into all kinds of futile activities simply to keep busy, to keep him from coming to this realization of his "alone-ness" in the universe. Only—and here Sartre retrieves himself from the position of total pessimism—by recognizing these facts does man purge himself from the self-deception under which he has been laboring. If he can face the terrible knowledge of his total responsibility and isolation, he may, like the hero of Sartre's novel *Nausea*, "climb out of the abyss of despairing awareness to achieve some form of self-affirmation."

Sartre's fame in America derives largely from the productions of his plays *The Flies, No Exit, Red Gloves,* and *The Respectful Prostitute,* all of them stark and compelling dramas, though generally considered too grim and ambiguous for widespread popularity. He visited the United States in 1945 and in 1946 and lectured at several American universities. In recent years, however, his apparent sympathy for Communism and his overt anti-Americanism have dampened enthusiasm for his work in this country.

In 1946 Sartre founded the review *Les Temps Modernes,* which he has edited ever since. He lives in Paris and is unmarried. Slight in build and balding, he wears thick horn-rimmed glasses. Behind the thick lenses, however, John L. Brown writes in the New York *Times Magazine,* "his glance is sharp, analytical, and responsive." He is said to be a brilliant conversationalist, speaking rapidly and fluently with much gesturing with his ever-present pipe.

PRINCIPAL WORKS IN ENGLISH TRANSLATION: No Exit, and The Flies, 1946; The Reprieve, 1947; Existentialism (in England: Existentialism and Humanism) 1947; The Age of Reason, 1947; Anti-Semite and Jew, 1948; The Chips Are Down, 1948; The Wall (stories) 1948; Emotions, Outline of a Theory, 1948; The Psychology of Imagination, 1948; Nausea (in England: The Diary of Antoine Roquentin) 1949; What Is Literature? 1949; Intimacy (stories) 1949; Three Plays (Dirty Hands, The Respectful Prostitute, The Victors) 1949; Baudelaire, 1950; Troubled Sleep (in England: Iron in the Soul) 1950; Lucifer and the Lord (play) 1953; Existential Psychoanalysis, 1953.

ABOUT: Bentley, E. R. The Playwright as Thinker; Dempsey, P. The Psychology of Sartre; Desan, W. D. Tragic Finale; Garaudy, R. Literature of the Graveyard; Grene, M. Dreadful Freedom; Murdoch, I. Sartre, Romantic Rationalist; Natanson, M. A Critique of Jean-Paul Sartre's Ontology; Columbia Dictionary of Modern European Literature; Current Biography 1947; Dictionnaire Biographique Français Contemporain; Life June 17, 1946; New York Times Magazine February 2, 1947, January 30, 1949; New Yorker

March 16, 1946, August 2, 1947; Partisan Review November 1952; Saturday Review of Literature July 9, 1949, January 20, 1951; Time January 28, 1946; Virginia Quarterly Review Spring 1947; Yale Review Winter 1953.

SASSOON, SIEGFRIED LORRAINE
(September 8, 1886-). For biographical sketch and list of earlier works and references, see TWENTIETH CENTURY AUTHORS, 1942.

* * *

Applying to his own works what Frank Swinnerton describes as the "Malthusian doctrine," Siegfried Sasoon has published only a small amount of poetry in his lifetime. His poems are reflective lyrics, intense and frequently dramatic. A collected volume appeared in 1947.

Sasoon has continued his memoirs (*The Old Century and Seven More Years* and *The Weald of Youth*) with *Siegfried's Journey*, a volume covering the years 1916 to 1920. Written in an unobtrusive but polished and evocative prose, the book, Irwin Edman commented, "is a unique record of a personality whom only England could have in one person: a foxhunting man, a soldier, and a meditative and humorous poet all in one." Sassoon has also written a widely-admired critical biography of George Meredith. He lives in Wiltshire. In 1951 he received the Commander Order of the British Empire.

ADDITIONAL WORKS: Siegfried's Journey, 1945; Collected Poems, 1947; Meredith, 1948.

ABOUT: Sassoon, S. Siegfried's Journey; Swinnerton, F. The Georgian Literary Scene; New Statesman and Nation January 19, 1946.

SAUNDERS, HILARY AIDAN ST. GEORGE. See "BEEDING, F."

SAUNDERS, MARSHALL (April 13, 1861-February 15, 1947). For autobiographical sketch and list of works and references, see TWENTIETH CENTURY AUTHORS, 1942.

* * *

Margaret Marshall Saunders died at Toronto at eighty-five.

Internationally she was known principally because of the wide currency of her book about a dog, *Beautiful Joe*. In her native Canada she was considered one of that country's foremost literary personalities and a popular lecturer on humanitarian and literary topics. Dorothy Howard, speaking of her wit, humor and charm on the lecture platform, has said: "Few women in North America have won so endeared a place in the hearts of countless millions of people." Of her last novel, *Esther de Warren*, the Boston *Transcript* observed that it was written with "too subtle and too charming a humor for the age that adores its smart sayings."

ABOUT: Thomas, C. Canadian Novelists; London Times February 18, 1947; New York Times February 17, 1947; School April 1947; Saturday Night (Toronto) March 1, 1947.

*SAURAT, DENIS (1890-). For biographical sketch and list of earlier works and references, see TWENTIETH CENTURY AUTHORS, 1942.

* * *

In 1950, after nearly a quarter of a century of teaching at King's College of the University of London, Denis Saurat retired and is now emeritus professor. He returned to France and makes his home in Nice.

Professor Saurat's major work of recent years was his exhaustive study of *Modern French Literature, 1870-1940*. It was a controversial book, reflecting the author's rather intense personal feelings (his dislike of André Gide, for example). The London *Times Literary Supplement* said of it: "He assumes in his readers a certain familiarity with his subject, yet there is little to reward the informed for this breathless scamper across one of the most fertile regions of modern literature; as for those seeking guidance, they are likely to be bewildered by too many arresting and disconnected generalizations, which leave them very much where they started, having run very hard indeed." Professor Saurat is active in scholarship in his retirement. In 1954 he published a book in French on William Blake.

ADDITIONAL WORKS IN ENGLISH: Death and the Dreamer, 1946; Modern French Literature, 1870-1940, 1946; Gods of the People, 1947; (ed.) Angels and Beasts: New Short Stories from France, 1947.

* sô rä'

"SAUSER, FREDERIC." See CENDRARS, B.

SAVAGE, DEREK STANLEY (March 6, 1917-), British poet and critic, who signs his works D. S. Savage, writes: "My parents were of the artisan class; but my father became a small business man, and prospered. I was born at Harlow, in Essex, my father then serving in the Army Transport Corps. We moved to Cheshunt, in Hertfordshire, where my father owned two shops, so I had a semi-rural upbringing, and have never loved cities. There was no love or knowledge of

art in our family. We children were brought up to 'know the value of money' and to appreciate something called 'security.' My temperament is funda-

mentally rebellious and freedom-loving, and as a consequence I have always lived in poverty, and have a certain contempt for security. An injury, with complications, at thirteen interrupted my schooling (but I learned nothing at school) and prevented my becoming a merchant sailor as I desired. I went to a commercial college, and was an office-clerk for a time. I worked in a bottle factory, a copper refinery, a bookshop. I became a 'red' and a pacifist and spoke vehemently at street-corners. My poems began to be published from my sixteenth year.

"I formally accepted the Christian faith, after a phase of militant atheism, in 1937, and was confirmed in St. Paul's Cathedral. I married the same year—we have five children. When war came I refused military service as a conscientious objector. I wrote my first book of criticism, *The Personal Principle*, in a condemned cottage, without sanitation or water-supply; when the nearby pumps froze we scraped snow from the ground. Unemployed, lived on the dole for a time, until I obtained work in a hospital. Persecuted by neighbours, payment for the book enabled us to move to Herefordshire, where I worked on the land and wrote the greater part of *The Withered Branch*. In 1947 I was given a two-hundred pound Atlantic Award (Rockefeller Foundation). The house we rented being sold over our heads, we were ejected by the new owners, and came to Cornwall, where we have lived ever since.

"My spiritual bent may be indicated by a life-long preference over the other books in the Bible for the Apocalypse: also Ecclesiastes. A memorable early experience was a reading of *The Pilgrim's Progress* immediately following the painful extraction of several teeth: a sort of initiation. Russian writers have influenced me profoundly. When, at twenty, I first read Berdyaev's *Freedom and the Spirit*, I knew that my own obscure intuitions were for the first time being developed and expressed for me.

"I have not made literature my career, for I have no career. However, my life and writing are in intimate relation. I write slowly, because I do not care to write like a journalist or a teacher, from my being, but like a poet or seer, from my becoming: in my writing, I am in advance of myself, therefore. I've been working for several years on a very exhaustive study of *Hamlet*, entitled 'The Underground Man': and I am just preparing for publication a study of the writer and politics, 'Caesar's Laurel Crown.'

PRINCIPAL WORKS: A Time to Mourn (poems) 1943; The Personal Principle, 1944; The Withered Branch, 1950; Hamlet and the Pirate, 1950.

SAWYER, RUTH (August 5, 1880-). For biographical sketch and list of earlier works and references, see TWENTIETH CENTURY AUTHORS, 1942.

* * *

Ruth Sawyer and her family now live in "Gull Rock," in Hancock, Me. She has continued to draw upon her wide knowledge of the folklore and customs of faraway places, for her tender and charming children's stories—Mexico, Serbia, and Ireland are the scenes of some of her more recent books. One of her books, *The Long Christmas*, appeared in a Dutch translation in 1950; another, *The Least One*, a story of a little Mexican boy, was published in German in 1952 for distribution by the U.S. Army.

ADDITIONAL WORKS: The Least One, 1941; The Long Christmas, 1941; Christmas Anna Angel, 1944; This Is Christmas, 1945; Old Con and Patrick, 1946; The Little Red Horse, 1950; Maggie Rose, 1953.

ABOUT: Kunitz, S. J. & Haycraft, H. (eds.) Junior Book of Authors (rev. ed.).

SAXON, LYLE (September 4, 1891-April 9, 1946). For biographical sketch and list of earlier works and references, see TWENTIETH CENTURY AUTHORS, 1942.

* * *

Lyle Saxon died in New Orleans at fifty-four. He had been ill for several years, and dictated his last book during his illness. A collection of books, pictures and manuscripts from his estate was given to the library of Tulane University as the nucleus of a Lyle Saxon Memorial Collection.

Saxon has been called, by C. J. Finger, "an energetic collector of information who is able to make a faithful narrative exciting." He wrote with "a seemingly effortless spontaneity and finish that is the hallmark of literary craftsmanship," in the words of Edward Larocque Tinker.

Perhaps Saxon's quality is best conveyed in an epitaph placed in the New Orleans newspapers by his friend George Sessions

Perry: "Since it is an old New Orleans custom to print one's feelings in religious matters, and since Lyle Saxon so deeply favored each of these old customs, I'd like to burn this one small candle of congratulations to God Almighty, who now has the rich, the easy, yet exquisite pleasure of the company of this lonely, generous man."

ADDITIONAL WORK: Friends of Joe Gilmore (and Some Friends of Lyle Saxon, by E. Dreyer) 1948.

ABOUT: Saxon, L. Friends of Joe Gilmore; New York Times April 10, 1946; Publishers' Weekly July 6, 1946.

SAYERS, DOROTHY LEIGH (1893-).

For biographical sketch and list of earlier works and references, see TWENTIETH CENTURY AUTHORS, 1942.

* * *

Dorothy Sayers has published no detective novels since the outbreak of World War II. She has concentrated in recent years upon the writings of religious dramas and essays in popular theology. In addition, she has begun work on an English translation of Dante's *Divine Comedy*—the *Inferno* was completed and published in a Penguin edition in 1949 and the *Purgatorio* in 1955. Her purpose, in the translation and in her essays on Dante, has been to bring the poet closer to the common reader. Her translation has been described as a readable, "middle" Dante in English verse.

Of her religious dramas the best known is the series of twelve radio plays on the life of Christ, *The Man Born to Be King*. This cycle was described as "deeply moving and monumental in scope" and formidable in scholarship. Her theological essays are full of wit and style. Like her fellow Anglican C. S. Lewis, she writes of orthodox theology in brisk and vigorous terms, popularizing but never vulgarizing her subject. "The Christian faith," she has said, "is the most exciting drama that ever staggered the imagination of man—and the dogma *is* the drama."

Miss Sayers has residences in London and in Essex. Her husband, Captain Atherton Fleming, died in 1950.

ADDITIONAL WORKS: The Man Born to Be King: Play Cycle on the Life of Christ, 1941; Even the Parrot: Exemplary Conversations of Enlightened Children, 1944; The Just Vengeance (play) 1946; Unpopular Opinions (essays) 1947; Creed or Chaos? (essays) 1947; Four Sacred Plays, 1948; The Emperor Constantine: A Chronicle (play) 1951; Introductory Papers on Dante, 1954. *Dante Translations*—Inferno, 1949; Purgatorio, 1955.

SCARBOROUGH, DOROTHY (1877-November 7, 1935).

For biographical sketch and list of works and references, see TWENTIETH CENTURY AUTHORS, 1942.

SCARFE, FRANCIS (September 18, 1911-),

British poet, critic, and novelist, writes: "I was born at South Shields, in Durham, England. Descended from sea-faring stock I felt myself to be destined for the sea, but perhaps the fact that I could not walk properly for some years owing to rickets gave me an angle on life which turned me into a writer. My father was lost at sea in 1916, and in 1921 or '22 I was sent to the Royal Merchant Seamen's Orphanage in Berkshire, where I spent four years. Those years are described fictionally in my first novel, *Promises*—a book I should like to rewrite closer to fact, which in this case was more interesting than fiction.

"I received my university education at Durham, Cambridge and Paris, and subsequently became senior lecturer in French in Glasgow University, where I now am. My first prose book *Auden and After,* was written in a hurry and had the success that often comes to one's least careful work. I had published a year earlier my first poems, *Inscapes,* and in 1942 *Poems and Ballads.* Being a late developer, and delayed by war service (lieutenant-colonel in the Army Educational Corps), it was not until 1949 that I found myself able to express anything properly in prose. I refer to my novels *Promises* and *Single Blessedness,* which were for me only exercises written with a view to learning techniques. I have since written two other novels, 'Man's Desiring' and 'Violet-Anne,' the first of which I do not intend to publish, the second to appear I hope soon. My life is a constant struggle to keep a balance between my job and my writing. To consolidate the first I've recently written a long book on Paul Valéry, whom I met and admired in 1936; but on the whole I regret having to do anything which prevents me from writing my own stuff. I regard those who have no responsibilities, and who can give themselves entirely to writing, as very fortunate.

"My view of the novel is that one's job is not to turn fact into fiction, but to turn fiction into fact. By this I mean I regard the novelist's task as imaginative; the realistic novel is washed-up; political novels are only journalism; the time has arrived now for what I would call the *poetic novel*.

"I still write poems sometimes (see *Underworlds*), but they tend to be personal. I revolt against the 'impersonal' theories of Eliot and others but haven't space to say why. But I think there will always be some readers who will realise that the thought and feeling of one man affect all men.

"I have blue eyes and wavy lips, if that interests anybody, also short ears and thick hair and a voice on the whole quiet."

* * *

Francis Scarfe married Margarete M. Geisler in 1938, and they have one son. His permanent home is in Oxford.

PRINCIPAL WORKS: *Poetry*—Inscapes, 1940; Poems and Ballads, 1942; Underworlds, 1950. *Novels*—Promises, 1950; Single Blessedness, 1951; The Unfinished Woman, 1954. *Criticism*—Auden and After, 1942; W. H. Auden: A Study, 1949; The Art of Paul Valéry, 1954.

SCHACHNER, NATHAN (January 16-1895-), American biographer, historian, and novelist, writes: "I was born in New York City and attended its public and high  schools. I suppose I was somewhat precocious as a child, since by the age of thirteen I had read with avidity if not complete understanding such works as the *Divine Comedy, Faust, Paradise Lost,* Shakespeare complete, the Greek dramatists, Shelley, Keats and Byron. In spite of these literary passions and the editorship of high school and college magazines, my first turn was toward the sciences. I majored in chemistry, graduating from City College of New York as a Bachelor of Science.

"After several years as chemist with the New York Board of Health and private concerns I shifted to law and, in spite of the interruption of my legal studies by an interval of army life during World War I, received the degree of Juris Doctor from New York University. Thereafter I spent sixteen years as a busy and fairly successful lawyer; but continued to read more in literature and history than in reported cases.

"About 1930, on a dare, I dashed off a story for a science fiction magazine and lo, it was accepted with a request for more. I

was fairly launched on a pulp writing career, snatching moments from my law practice to write hundreds of science, detective, mystery, western and adventure stories. Meanwhile my reading concentrated more and more on history, particularly the medieval scene and early America. The former flowered in a history of the *Mediaeval Universities* which, published simultaneously in England and the United States, achieved a *succès d'estime* if not undue financial rewards.

"My appetite thus whetted, I dropped law and devoted full time to writing. With the single exception of a novelized life of Dante in *The Wanderer,* I have consistently engaged in an examination of American life: including full length biographies of Aaron Burr, Alexander Hamilton and Thomas Jefferson, and a series of historical novels, numerous articles for the general magazines (paid for), learned articles for the learned quarterlies (unpaid for) and assorted book reviews.

"During World War II, I joined the staff of the American Jewish Committee as magazine liaison and editorial consultant in a campaign to promote better group relations in this country and headed an editorial board of prominent writers which offered prizes for the magazine stories best directed toward that end.

"My major avocations besides armchair reading and research have been the development of jet propulsion, travel and photography. I was a founder and charter member of the American Rocket Society, as well as its president. It is an ironic thought that our first experiments in jet fuels and propulsion in 1931 were greeted with brightly satiric editorials in the press and a cold shoulder from government authorities. (Item: the German, Russian and Japanese governments showed deep interest and even offered to become members of the Society.)

"My greatest delight is to pack my car and wander for months—I have explored every nook and cranny of this country, Canada, and Mexico, and have shipped my car to do the same in Europe. There, in out of the way places, the 'big American car' (a Ford) made a sensation.

"My picture collection, black and white and color, is supposed to be quite good. I cannot pass a mountain without attempting to climb it; but in late years my wife has strictly prohibited this form of sport with suitable remarks on my age and general debility. My wife was the former Helen Lichtenstein of New York. We have one daughter, now engaged in market research with the New York *News*. By the time this appears, she will be Mrs. Ludwig Brunner of Miami, Fla."

PRINCIPAL WORKS: Aaron Burr: A Biography, 1937; The Mediaeval Universities, 1938; By the Dim Lamps, 1941; The King's Passenger, 1942; The Sun Shines West, 1943; The Wanderer, 1944; Alexander Hamilton, 1946; Thomas Jefferson, 1951; Space Lawyer, 1953; The Founding Fathers, 1954.

ABOUT: American Historical Review July 1938; New York Herald Tribune May 24, 1942; New York Times November 19, 1951; Saturday Review of Literature June 15, 1946.

SCHAUFFLER, ROBERT HAVEN
April 8, 1879-). For biographical sketch and list of earlier works and references, see TWENTIETH CENTURY AUTHORS, 1942.

* * *

Robert Haven Schauffler's major works of recent years have been biographies of Schumann and Schubert. His study of Robert Schumann, *Florestan,* was divided into two parts: part one being a brisk and colloquial biography, part two a critical discussion of the composer's works. Clearly intended for a popular audience rather than for experts, *Florestan* was an entertaining and informative book and has enjoyed considerable popularity. Schauffler used the same method in his biography of Franz Schubert and again, while not perhaps producing the authoritative and definitive work on the subject, he did offer "the essence of the man and the essence of the musician," as one reviewer put it. And the *Saturday Review of Literature* commented: "It is in fact a charming book, full of delightful minutiae and great good sense."

ADDITIONAL WORKS: Fiddler's Folly and Encores, 1942; Florestan: The Life of Robert Schumann, 1945; Franz Schubert: The Ariel of Music, 1947.

ABOUT: Schauffler, R. H. Fiddler's Folly and Encores.

SCHELLING, FELIX EMANUEL (September 3, 1858-December 15, 1945). For biographical sketch and list of works and references, see TWENTIETH CENTURY AUTHORS, 1942.

* * *

Felix E. Schelling died at his home in Mt. Vernon, N.Y., at eighty-seven. He was survived by his second wife, the former Gertrude Bueb; his first wife died in 1935. He had served as curator of the Horace Howard Furness Memorial Library of Shakespeariana at Mt. Vernon since his retirement from the faculty of the University of Pennsylvania.

A quality of "benign serenity" about his work has been noted by the New York *Herald Tribune Book Review*, which added, "but beneath the smooth surface of his essays there is the firm substratum of scholarship; and if he speaks softly he speaks none the less with authority."

ABOUT: Banta, R. Indiana Authors; Carnegie Foundation for the Advancement of Teaching, 41st Annual Report (1945-46); New York Times December 16, 1945.

SCHEVILL, FERDINAND (November 12, 1868-December 10, 1954), American historian, was born in Cincinnati, Ohio, the son of Ferdinand Schevill and Johanna (Hartmann) Schevill. In 1889 he took his B.A. at Yale, and in 1892 his Ph.D. at the University of Freiburg, Germany. Returning to the United States he began his career of teaching at the University of Chicago

(1892), from which he retired as professor emeritus in 1937. A very popular teacher, Schevill wrote a number of books, one of the best known being *A History of Europe from the Reformation to the Present Day,* first printed in 1925 and since revised and reissued. Although primarily a student of modern history, he also wrote a *History of Florence,* from the founding of the city through the Renaissance. While he kept the political history of the city in the foreground, Schevill did not neglect its literary and artistic contributions. The Boston *Transcript* praised his "insight into tangled situations, his analysis of complex motives, his appraisal of personalities and his ordering of events and movements." The *Christian Century* said, "Professor Schevill's ripe and comprehensive scholarship comes to its finest fruitage in this magnificent work." The book is illustrated with Alinari prints.

In a review of *The Great Elector,* a biographical study of Frederick William of Brandenburg, published in 1947, the New York *Herald Tribune Book Review* pointed to "the masterful analyses, the persuasive style." The New York *Times,* writing of *The Medici,* said: "Not only great skill but wide knowledge was necessary. . . . The pattern emerges not only to tell the story of the past, but to astonish us suddenly with parallels, never obviously drawn, but often obliquely suggested, of what our own times have accomplished, or failed to accomplish, in packed parliaments, bribed committees, broken agreements and vengeful acts."

Schevill's wife was Clara E. Meier, whom he married in 1913. He lived in the Dunes, just outside Chicago, in Michigan City, Ind., until his death at the age of eighty-six.

PRINCIPAL WORKS: Political History of Modern Europe from the Reformation to the Present Day, 1907; Siena, the Story of a Mediaeval Commune, 1909; The Making of Modern Germany, 1916; Karl Bitter, a Biography, 1917; History of the Balkan Peninsula, 1922; A History of Europe from the Reformation to the Present Day, 1925; First Century of Italian Humanism, 1928; History of Florence, 1936; The Great Elector, 1947; The Medici, 1949.

ABOUT: New York Times December 11, 1954.

*SCHICKELE, RENÉ (August 4, 1883-January 31, 1940). For biographical sketch and list of works and references, see TWENTIETH CENTURY AUTHORS, 1942.

* * *

ABOUT: Columbia Dictionary of Modern European Literature.

* shĭk'ĕlĕ

SCHIFF, SYDNEY. See HUDSON, S.

*SCHLESINGER, ARTHUR MEIER (February 27, 1888-). For autobiographical sketch and list of earlier works and references, see TWENTIETH CENTURY AUTHORS, 1942.

* * *

Since 1939 Arthur Meier Schlesinger has been Francis Lee Higginson professor of history at Harvard. He was president of the American Historical Association in 1942, a member of the United States Government's Committee on Records of the War Administration from 1942 to 1946, and a member of the Committee on the Freedom of the Press from 1943 to 1946. In the academic year 1948 to 1949 he was guest professor at the University of Leyden.

Professor Schlesinger has been called "the leading interpreter of America's past." His writings have the quality, rare among historical studies, of "combining sound scholarship and popular appeal." His short history of American etiquette books was said to contain more information on American social history than volumes several times its size. Allan Nevins' comments on a collection of Schlesinger's essays, Paths to the Present, apply well to his work as a whole: "[Schlesinger] does not attempt the elevated flights

* shlä'zĭngĕr

of a Froude or Morley, winging his way nearer the ground. Yet he is always entertaining and instructive . . . and he throws out some general ideas of far-reaching significance."

ADDITIONAL WORKS: Learning How to Behave, 1946; Paths to the Present, 1949; The American as Reformer, 1950; The Rise of Modern America (new edition of Political and Social Growth of the United States) 1951.

SCHLESINGER, ARTHUR MEIER (October 15, 1917-), American historian and biographer, writes: "I was born in Columbus, Ohio. My father [Arthur Meier Schlesinger, see sketch above] was professor of American history successively at Ohio State, Iowa and Harvard; and I grew up in an academic environment, living from 1924 on in Cambridge, Mass. I went to the  Cambridge public schools, then to Phillips Exeter Academy and Harvard, graduating summa cum laude in 1938. I spent the next year—the year between Munich and the war —as a Henry Fellow at Cambridge University; then, for three years, I was a member of the Society of Fellows at Harvard University. In the summer of 1942 I went to Washington to work, first for the Office of War Information and then for the Office of Strategic Services. I went overseas for O.S.S. in the spring of 1944, remaining in Europe for a year and a half and serving in London, Paris and Germany. I was deputy chief of the O.S.S. Reports Board in Paris, and, in the meantime, attained the high rank of corporal in the United States Army.

"My senior honors essay at Harvard provided the basis for my first book, Orestes A. Brownson: a Pilgrim's Progress, a selection of the Catholic Book Club in 1939. As a member of the Society of Fellows, I completed a first draft of a book on Andrew Jackson and his times; this was accepted for publication shortly before I left for Europe in 1944 and was finally published as The Age of Jackson in 1945. It won the Pulitzer prize for history.

"After the war, I spent some time in Washington as a free-lance writer, contributing to such magazines as Life, Fortune, Saturday Evening Post and Collier's. In the fall of 1947 I returned to Cambridge as associate professor of history at Harvard. In the meantime, I had come to feel the urgent necessity for the development of an organization of American liberals which would recognize the true nature of the Communist threat at home and abroad and would at the same time continue the fight for freedom and social progress. In 1946 I wrote a full-length exposure and indictment of the American Communist Party for *Life* magazine. I participated in the founding convention of Americans for Democratic Action in 1947 and have served since as a national vice-chairman. In an effort to explain the importance of an anti-Communist liberal position, I wrote *The Vital Center* in 1949.

"Since returning to Cambridge, I have been primarily occupied in research for a projected work on 'The Age of Roosevelt.' I have also served as a consultant for the Economic Cooperation Adminstration and the Mutual Security Adminstration; and in the 1952 presidential campaign I was a member of Governor Adlai Stevenson's staff. My wife, Marian Cannon, is the author and illustrator of a number of children's books. We have four children, ranging from four to ten years of age [1952]."

PRINCIPAL WORKS: Orestes A. Brownson: A Pilgrim's Progress, 1939; The Age of Jackson, 1945; The Vital Center: the Politics of Freedom, 1949; (with R. Rovere) The General and the President, 1951; (ed. with Q. Howe) A Guide to Politics, 1954.

ABOUT: Current Biography 1946; New York Herald Tribune Book Review September 25, 1949; New York Times Book Review March 10, 1946, September 18, 1949; Saturday Review of Literature September 10, 1949; Time April 29, 1946.

SCHLOSS, ARTHUR DAVID. See WALEY, A.

SCHMITT, BERNADOTTE EVERLY
(May 19, 1886-). For biographical sketch and list of earlier works and references, see TWENTIETH CENTURY AUTHORS, 1942.

* * *

Bernadotte Schmitt writes from Alexandria, Va.: "In 1943 Schmitt joined the U.S. government for war service, first as special consultant to the Secretary of War, then as a member of the Office of Strategic Services, and next as a special adviser in the division of Historical Policy Research of the Department of State. In 1949 he was appointed United States editor-in-chief of *Documents on German Foreign Policy*, 1918-1945, a tripartite enterprise of the British, French, and United States governments for publish-

ing the captured archives of the German Foreign Office, and served until his retirement in July 1952.

"In 1946 he became professor emeritus of the University of Chicago and resigned as editor of the *Journal of Modern History*.

"In 1945 he edited *Poland* in the United Nations Series, contributing one chapter. He also contributed one chapter to *Yugoslavia* in the same series (1949). While serving as historical adviser in the Department of State, he edited two volumes of official documents, one relating to the Treaty of Versailles, the other to the United Nations Conference in San Francisco.

"In his retirement he is writing a volume on the war of 1914-1919 for the series 'Rise of Modern Europe' and plans to write a revision of his book *The Coming of the War: 1914.*

"In 1942 Schmitt was elected a member of the American Philosophical Society, the oldest learned body in the United States (1748)."

ADDITIONAL WORK: Poland (ed.) 1945.
ABOUT: Current Biography 1942.

SCHMITT, GLADYS (May 31, 1909-), American novelist, was born in Pittsburgh, Pa., the first of three children of Henry H. and Leonore (Link) Schmitt. Of her early years she writes: "I took my intellectual nourishment, and perhaps the foreshadowings of my style, from Lutheran doctrine, Lutheran hymns, the Bible, and such glimpses of literature as one gets in the  readers of a public grade school and from kind teachers who are amazed to find in a somewhat colorless pupil a natural concern about grammar." She began writing verse (some of it prize-winning) in grammar school and started her first novel at fifteen. At the University of Pittsburgh, she majored in English and continued to write, now concentrating primarily on fiction. She received her B.A., *magna cum laude*, in 1932 and proceeded to graduate work in English. Meanwhile she had a story accepted by Whit Burnett of *Story* magazine ("House Divided," later developed into the novel *The Gates of Aulis*); a second story was bought by the *Atlantic Monthly*.

In 1933 Miss Schmitt left college, in the middle of the depression, to take a job as typist in the Pittsburgh offices of *Scholastic* magazine. In her spare time she worked away at her short stories and at novels. When *Scholastic* moved its editorial offices to New York in 1939, she went along, by now associate editor of the magazine. Dividing her time between her editorial duties and her writing—and she is a meticulous writer, given to slow and careful revision and polishing—she nevertheless managed to complete her first novel, *The Gates of Aulis*. She submitted the manuscript to the Dial Press, which was offering a $1,000 prize for a novel "of high literary quality that concerns itself realistically with the problems of adjustment which face the young men and women of America today." *The Gates of Aulis* was the unanimous choice of the judges, and it was published in 1942 with considerable critical fanfare. The story of an American family in Pittsburgh, and of their deep personal devotion to each other (the title refers to the sacrifice of Iphigenia—the "complete gift" of oneself—in classical legend), the novel was an immediate success. Its style was poetic and overwrought (Orville Prescott described it as "supercharged" and Lionel Trilling called it "impossibly wordy"), but it was sufficiently serious and intense to convince nearly all the reviewers that this was an important first novel. "Miss Schmitt's writing is astonishingly good," Stanley Edgar Hyman commented in the *New Republic*, "a tactile and heightened prose that is rare enough in modern writing and unbelievable in a first novel." "Her talent," Clifton Fadiman said in the *New Yorker*, "is too much for her theme, whose dimensions are less grandiose than she supposes."

Soon after her first novel was published, Miss Schmitt returned to Pittsburgh to take a teaching post in the English department of the Carnegie Institute of Technology. She has remained there, teaching two sections of a humanities-English course five days a week, reading themes, and counseling the would-be writers among the students. By following a rigid schedule, she has managed to combine teaching with her ambitious writing plans. In 1945 her *David the King*, a massive and learned re-telling of the Biblical story, proved to be both a popular and a critical success. It was selected by the Literary Guild, sold some 900,000 copies, and was translated into Danish, Italian, French, Czech, Portuguese, and Hebrew. Among historical novels it was rated highly. If not on the level of Thomas

Mann or Lion Feuchtwanger (in his Biblical novels), nevertheless, as the *New Yorker* commented, "compared to current historical novelists, she stands among the giants." Louis Untermeyer wrote in the *Saturday Review of Literature*: "Nothing is trivial or facile in these pages; the reconstruction becomes an act of continual creation, fresh and extraordinarily moving."

Gladys Schmitt's labored but sensitive and poetic prose has proved generally more successful in the historical novel than in a contemporary setting. *Alexandra*, the story of an American actress, was disappointing both in its critical reception and in its sales. Her historical novel of early Christianity in Rome, *Confessors of the Name*, was better received. The book was described as "a large, crowded and colorful panorama of the far past," sound and thorough in its research, and serious and conscientious in its recreation of the past. W. T. Scott wrote in the New York *Herald Tribune*: "She has recreated fierce and unrestrained passions by the score and, being a novelist of most serious intention, has quite rightly placed her well-balanced conjectures in the rank of facts."

Miss Schmitt married Simon Goldfield, a musician, in 1937. Her husband reads her manuscripts as she writes and "freely gives too much of his time and energy to discussion of my literary plans and minute criticism of everything I write." They live in Pittsburgh and lead an active social life—"I like music, history, and good talk," she says. But, she adds, "The center of my life is writing."

PRINCIPAL WORKS: The Gates of Aulis, 1942; David the King, 1946; Alexandra, 1947; Confessors of the Name, 1952; The Persistent Image, 1955.

ABOUT: Current Biography 1943; New York Herald Tribune Book Review October 12, November 23, 1952; New York Times Book Review March 17, 1946.

SCHMITZ, ETTORE. See SVEVO, I.

SCHNEIDER, ISIDOR (August 25, 1896-). For autobiographical sketch and list of earlier works and references, see TWENTIETH CENTURY AUTHORS, 1942.

* * *

Isidor Schneider writes from New York City: "Since the listing in the 1942 TWENTIETH CENTURY AUTHORS, I have published one novel and a translation of Maxim Gorky's three autobiographical volumes, *My Childhood, In the World* and *My Universities*, and poems, articles and reviews in various periodicals.

"Direct experience with socially conscious writing as writer, critic and editor has altered my former thinking about it. I have observed that conscious application of one's writing to social ends results in stiff, self-conscious, and more often than not, feeble work. While long-range advancement is served, in various ways, by good writing of every sort, immediate social objectives can be served by a writer only at risk of restricting and ephemeralising his work. I now feel that a writer can discharge his social responsibility, like other men of whatever profession, best as a citizen."

ADDITIONAL WORKS: The Judas Time (novel) 1947; Gorki, M. Autobiography (tr.) 1949.

SCHNITZLER, ARTHUR (May 15, 1862-October 21, 1931). For biographical sketch and list of works and references, see TWENTIETH CENTURY AUTHORS, 1942.

* * *

ABOUT: Clark, B. H. & Freedley, V. History of Modern Drama; Columbia Dictionary of Modern European Literature; Liptzin, S. Germany's Stepchildren; Middleton, G. These Things Are Mine; Nicoll, A. World Drama; Slochower, H. No Voice Is Wholly Lost; Modern Language Review October 1945.

*SCHOLES, PERCY ALFRED (1877-). English musicologist, was born in Leeds, England, the son of Thomas Scholes. He re-

ceived the degrees of M.A. and D.Litt. from Oxford; and later received various honors and degrees: D.Mus. (Oxon.), Litt.D. (Leeds), Dr. ès Lettres (Lausanne), Officer of the Star of Rumania (1930), and others. Scholes was music critic to *The Observer* from 1920 to 1925, and to the B.B.C. from 1923 to 1928. He has been an extension lecturer for the Universities of Oxford, Cambridge, London, and Manchester, and was Frick Lecturer at Pittsburgh in 1928, 1930, 1932. A former music editor for *Radio Times*, he was inspector of music in schools to London University and also inspected for the Board of Education. He was founder and general secretary of the Anglo-American Conference on Musical Education at Lausanne in 1929 and 1931.

Author of innumerable guides and reference books concerning music, he published *The Listener's History of Music* in several volumes, from 1923 to 1929, the first volume "To Beethoven," the second, "The Romantic and Nationalist Schools of the Nineteenth Century," and the third, "To the Composers of Today." *The Great Dr. Burney*, which received the James Tait Black Memorial Prize in 1948, was praised by the *Saturday Review of Literature* as "a work of genial wit, manifold interest, and wide cultural ken." Dr. Scholes' volumes, said the *Manchester Guardian* on this occasion, "are an encyclopedia of music, musicians, and musical opinion in Europe in the eighteenth century clustered around the personal, domestic, and social history of Charles Burney in his encounters with the world and its wife." "Dr. Scholes has [modeled] his work on the leisurely, semi-picaresque eighteenth century novel. . . . In place of the moralizing discursiveness of the novelist, however, Dr. Scholes supplies the meticulous detective work of the scholar. It is a rich cast of characters that passes before us," commented the *Music Library Association Notes*. Of his *The Mirror of Music*, a study of a century of British musical life (1844-1944) as reflected in the issues of the *Musical Times*, the New York *Herald Tribune Book Review* wrote, "Every conceivable aspect of music in the high romantic and modern periods is touched upon and enlivened with lore and accurate data."

Scholes married Dora Wingate; they live at Oxford. His recreations are music, reading and travel, and he is vice-president of the Vegetarian Society, and patron of the League for the Prohibition of Cruel Sports.

PRINCIPAL WORKS: The Listener's Guide to Music, with a Concert-Goer's Glossary, 1919; The Listener's History of Music, 1923-29; A Miniature History of Music for the General Reader and the Student, 1928; The Columbia History of Music Through Ear and Eye, 1930-38; A Miniature History of Opera, 1931; The Puritans and Music: in England and New England, 1934; The Oxford Companion to Music, 1938; The Mirror of Music: 1844-1944, 1947; The Great Dr. Burney, 1948; The Life and Activities of Sir John Hawkins, 1953; God Save the Queen: The History and Romance of the World's First National Anthem, 1954.

*SCHOPFER, JEAN ("Claude Anet") (May 28, 1868-January 9, 1931). For biographical sketch and list of works and references, see TWENTIETH CENTURY AUTHORS, 1942.

* skōlz

* shôp fär' (à në')

SCHORER, MARK (May 17, 1908-), American novelist, critic, and biographer, writes: "I was born in Sauk City, Wis., the

Philip Fein

second of four children of Anna and William Schorer, and educated in the local public schools, the University of Wisconsin (1925-29), and Wisconsin again (1931-36). Three degrees and too many important years. I began writing short stories for publication in 1933 (*Scribner's, Harper's, Story,* etc.) and published a novel, *A House Too Old,* in the year before I took my Ph.D. This novel, like the early stories, used Sauk City as background, but since 1936, I have seldom drawn on that material.

"From the beginning, people have been eager to help me to write. As an undergraduate, I held one of the Zona Gale Fellowships that Miss Gale for a certain period of her life personally administered in the interest of young writers at the university. In my last year as a graduate student, I held the Mary L. Adams Fellowship, which made possible the first sketch of a book I later published on William Blake. Teachers were helpful, too, in their confidence, notably Helen C. White and Clinch Calkins at Wisconsin, and later, at Harvard, Robert Hillyer, who did me the greatest service a teacher of writing can do: he begged me not to go on with a novel that was clearly headed for catastrophe. I didn't.

"In the summer of 1936, I was married to Ruth Page of Madison, Wis., and we have two children, Page and Suzanne. The first was born while I was an instructor in Dartmouth College (1936-37), the second, in my second year as an instructor in Harvard College, where I taught until 1945 as one of the Briggs-Copeland instructors—writers who also wanted to teach; or vice versa. At Harvard, I wrote a novel called *The Hermit Place.* That year I was awarded the Guggenheim fellowship for the Blake book, which was started in Laguna Beach, Calif., continued on a sheep ranch outside Roswell, N.M., on a renewal of my Guggenheim, completed in Cambridge, and published in 1946. In the meantime, I had been publishing stories in many magazines, but chiefly the *New Yorker,* and literary articles in the quarterlies, and book reviews in the newspapers.

Thirty-two of these stories were published in book form under the title *The State of Mind* in 1947.

"By that time I was a professor of English in the University of California, Berkeley, chiefly teaching contemporary literature, critical theory, and story writing. In 1948 I had another Guggenheim renewal to work on a novel in progress and to begin a book on the theory of the novel. I began to be interested in the question of what a novel is as a Fellow of the Kenyon School of English at Kenyon College (now the School of Letters at Bloomington, Ind.), and my work then took the form of a series of lectures delivered before the Princeton Seminar in Literary Criticism in the spring of 1950. The work progresses, but to find out what a novel is, you have to read a great many novels.

"At present [1952] I am enjoying a Fulbright Award in Italy, and my wife and younger child and I will spend the winter here. Just this week, in the dim light of a Florentine *pensione,* I finished the novel mentioned above, on which I have worked for too many summers. Tentative title: 'States of Love and War' [published in 1953 as *The Wars of Love*].

"I am here mainly to complete a critical study of D. H. Lawrence for New Directions ('Makers of Modern Literature' series) and to begin some preliminary work on a life of Sinclair Lewis, the executors of whose estate have restricted all the papers left at the time of his death to my use for this book. Occasionally I will lecture on the novel in Italian universities, and hope to push that book on a little further toward its end. My essays on fiction writers, which in one form or another will be part of this book, have appeared chiefly in the quarterlies, *Kenyon Review, Hudson Review, Sewanee Review,* and in introductions to novels by Defoe, Emily Brontë, D. H. Lawrence, Ford Madox Ford. I have an idea for a novel that may hatch as spring approaches and the evenings grow longer.

"I write criticism rapidly, fiction very slowly, yet I can obviously not afford to put any faith in the old notion that the two do not get along amiably together, or even in the witty remark about 'Those who can,' etc."

PRINCIPAL WORKS: A House Too Old (novel) 1935; The Hermit Place (novel) 1941; William Blake: the Politics of Vision, 1946; The State of Mind: Thirty-Two Stories, 1947; (ed. with others) Criticism: the Foundations of Literary Judgment, 1948; (ed.) The Story: A Critical Anthology; The Wars of Love (novel) 1953.

ABOUT: Vogue August 1947.

SCHREINER, OLIVE EMILIE ALBERTINA (March 24, 1855-December 12, 1920). For biographical sketch and list of works and references, see TWENTIETH CENTURY AUTHORS, 1942.

* * *

ABOUT: Buchanan-Gould, V. Not Without Honour; Snyman, J. P. L. The South African Novel in English; Contemporary Review April 1947.

SCHRIFTGIESSER, KARL (November 12, 1903-), American historian, writes:

Cosmo Sileo

"Karl Schriftgiesser was born in Boston, Mass. His grandfather published a daily and weekly German language newspaper and his father, who died when he was five, was a reporter on Boston newspapers. His mother was of Yankee and Russian ancestry and one of the early kindergarten teachers in that city. Brought up by his Yankee grandmother on the Maine coast and in old Boston, and educated at the famous Roxbury Latin School and for three years in a 'seminary' in Barre, Vt., his New England background outweighed his European antecedents and led him to his interests in American history and politics about which he has written extensively.

"At seventeen he quit school to become a copy boy on the Boston *Post.* In 1924 he became a feature writer for the magazine section of the famous old Boston *Evening Transcript.* For the next ten years he wrote feature articles on every conceivable subject, covered many of the big news events in New England of the 1920's, and contributed articles to such magazines as the *American Mercury,* the *New Yorker,* and the *New Republic.* Through most of this period he assisted the late Edwin Francis Edgett in editing the *Transcript's* book section, interviewing scores of writers for its columns, and writing many critical articles on contemporary literature.

"Shortly after the inauguration of Franklin D. Roosevelt as President he went to Washington to write editorials and a signed column for the Washington *Post.* There he continued his writing about books, but began concentrating more on the contemporary political scene. A difference of political opinion with the publisher led to his resignation, and after a summer spent proving he had no talents as a novelist he joined the reportorial staff of the New York *Times.*

"Assigned to the writing of advance obituaries he wrote hundreds of biographical sketches of leading world citizens, a job of research and writing which led naturally to the writing of his first two books. *Families* was a study of ten outstanding American families, from the Adams family to the Roosevelts. This was followed by *The Amazing Roosevelt Family,* the first over-all history of the famous family which produced two Presidents. His main interests, however, were in the political history of the nation and, in 1944, he wrote a highly critical biography, *The Gentleman from Massachusetts,* of the late Senator Henry Cabot Lodge of Massachusetts, the man most responsible for the defeat of the League of Nations by the U.S. Senate.

"This led to a fuller study of the twelve years of Republican rule in Washington, *This Was Normalcy,* in which Schriftgiesser evaluated the administrations of Harding, Coolidge, and Hoover. In the meantime he had become the book critic for *Newsweek,* a post he held for six years. His research on the politics of the 1920's led him to undertake a study of the pressure groups which influence legislation and the results were published, in 1951, in *The Lobbyists.* During this period and since he wrote extensively, for the New York *Times Book Review,* and elsewhere, on the New Deal and Franklin D. Roosevelt. His liberalism was not acceptable to the postwar management of *Newsweek* and he resigned, in 1950, to devote his time to historical research and writing (mainly on a projected history of the New Deal), and to magazine articles for the *Atlantic Monthly, Collier's,* and the New York *Times Magazine.*

"He is married to the former Ruth Mansfield of Boston, has one daughter, and lives on an old farm near Londonderry, Vt."

PRINCIPAL WORKS: Families, 1940; The Amazing Roosevelt Family, 1613-1942, 1942; Oscar of the Waldorf, 1943; The Gentleman from Massachusetts: Henry Cabot Lodge, 1944; This Was Normalcy, 1948; The Lobbyists, 1951.

ABOUT: New York Herald Tribune Book Review September 16, 1951.

SCHULBERG, BUDD WILSON (March 27, 1914-), American novelist and short story writer, reports: "I was born in New York City, but I never think of New York as my source. While I now live less than

two hours' drive from the city, near New Hope, Pa., I always visit New York as an enthusiastic tourist. My home town, and,

for better or worse, the spring that feeds most of my work, is Hollywood, Calif. My father, B.P. Schulberg, was one of the motion picture pioneers, one of the very first screen writers, associated with the first American director, Porter, as well as with Zukor and Lasky in 1912. Before I was ready for the first grade we were living in Hollywood, where B.P. had gone to take charge of Paramount Studios. From that time, about 1920, until I was ready to come East to prep school and college, some seventeen years later, Hollywood was the only world I knew. The studio backlot was my playground and hundreds of nights I went off to sleep with the drone of interminable story conferences as my lullaby music.

"As a child I suffered from a rather severe speech impediment, and perhaps it was for this reason that I began writing poems and stories at an early age. Somewhere in my files I still have a short story written when I was eleven. My mother had founded the first progressive school in Hollywood and was strong for self-expression; she encouraged me. My father, despite his preoccupation with movie-making, had been a newspaperman and still boasted of the short-story prize he had won in a city-wide contest while he was at City College in New York. In other words, he had never lost his interest in the printed word, and I can remember his reading aloud (that lost entertainment!) the works of Melville, Conrad, Dickens and Stevenson.

"At Los Angeles High School I was better at editing the daily paper and at writing little stories than I was at running the half mile, a feat to which I gave considerable time and effort. In 1932 I came east to Deerfield Academy, by way of preparing for Dartmouth College. It was a significant move for me. I looked around in some wonderment at this green world of the Connecticut Valley. Until that time I must have believed that Western Civilization had its center at the corners of Vine Street and Hollywood Boulevard.

"At Deerfield and at Dartmouth I continued to edit the newspapers and to write.

In my senior year at Dartmouth I won a prize in an inter-collegiate short-story contest. I published a few short stories in little magazines, including a novel in *Story* titled 'Passport To Nowhere.' From this time on, although there were to be a number of Hollywood detours, I considered myself primarily a writer of fiction.

"From 1937 to 1939 I served a term as a sort of apprentice screen writer for movie producers David O. Selznick and Walter Wanger. But during this same period I was writing a series of Hollywood short stories which were published in *Liberty, Collier's* and the *Saturday Evening Post.* One of the first of these was a story called 'What Makes Sammy Run?' In 1939 I left Hollywood, returned to the now familiar Connecticut River, and at Norwich, Vt., just across from Dartmouth College, I completed my first novel, using the title of the short story mentioned above. Much to my surprise, and to that of my publisher, it proved both a critical and a commercial success and has recently been added to the Modern Library.

"After the publication of this novel I spent a half-vacation, half-work year in Mexico writing screenplays, followed by three years in the Navy, working for the Office of Strategic Services in Washington, and in Europe. I was in charge of gathering photographic evidence for the Nuremberg Trials, and was returned to the inactive reserve in 1946.

"From that time until the present, seven years later, I have lived with my wife Victoria and our three children in one of those old stone houses that have endured in Bucks County, Pa. I have written two more novels, one against a background of the prize-fight business, which has always interested me, *The Harder They Fall,* and more recently, *The Disenchanted,* which was drawn from my experience as a 'junior writer' assigned to collaborate with a number of older and well-established novelists and playwrights. Although the protagonist of *The Disenchanted* was generally identified as F. Scott Fitzgerald, and although I had worked with Mr. Fitzgerald and regarded his work with enthusiasm, I actually had made a list of fifteen established American writers whom I had known in Hollywood and whose trials as film writers contributed to my study of a famous American author offering up pieces of himself for money. The theme of success has always fascinated me; each of my novels has been concerned with it; I believe Hollywood is rather an ideal microcosm in which to study it; and for this reason I hope to write more novels about the dream factories and their heterogeneous personnel.

"My hobbies, in no particular order, are fishing, tennis, reading, drinking with friends, jazz, prizefights, racing pigeons, family vacations to the Caribbean. I like all forms of writing, from articles to motion pictures, but of them all I prefer the novel. In a day of increasing taboos, I think it may represent the final redoubt of a truly free enterprise. I like the feeling that it is up to me, that make or break, it is all mine."

* * *

Writing in a vigorous and hard-hitting prose, with a sharp eye for detail and a sharp ear for authentic dialogue, Budd Schulberg became famous as a chronicler of the bright hard world of Hollywood with his memorable and best-selling portrait of an office boy's rise to the position of a motion picture mogul, *What Makes Sammy Run?* He used the same scene for his best-selling novel of a decade later, *The Disenchanted*, the story of the rapid physical and spiritual disintegration of a famous novelist of the 1920's, now reduced to providing a scenario for a Hollywood musical comedy. The resemblance of Schulberg's hero to the late F. Scott Fitzgerald was unmistakable—and Schulberg had worked with Fitzgerald briefly in Hollywood on a scenario for just such a motion picture and with him attended the Dartmouth Winter Carnival where the climax of the book takes place. In between his two novels of motion picture life, Schulberg wrote a novel (and a number of articles and short stories) on prize fighting—where again he knew his background thoroughly and projected it in vivid detail. In 1953 he spent considerable time studying at first-hand conditions among the dock workers around the Port of New York, gathering material for a motion picture scenario. The picture, released in 1954 under the title *On the Waterfront*, proved to be one of the most successful motion pictures of recent years, and Schulberg was highly praised for his sympathetic yet brutally realistic treatment of the story. He received awards from the Academy of Motion Picture Arts and Sciences and from the Writers Guild for his work on the film. In 1951 Schulberg voluntarily testified before a congressional Un-American Activities Committee investigation that he had been a Communist briefly during the 1930's but broke with the party "when Communists sought to dictate how he should write *What Makes Sammy Run?*"

PRINCIPAL WORKS: What Makes Sammy Run? 1941; The Harder They Fall, 1947; The Disenchanted, 1950; Some Faces in the Crowd (short stories) 1953.

ABOUT: Van Gelder, R. Writers and Writing; Current Biography 1951; New York Herald Tribune Book Review October 8, 1950; New York Times March 6, 1955; New York Times Book Review November 5, 1950, May 24, 1953; Saturday Review of Literature October 14, 1950; Time November 13, 1950.

SCHUMAN, FREDERICK LEWIS
(February 22, 1904-). For biographical sketch and list of earlier works and references, see TWENTIETH CENTURY AUTHORS, 1942.

* * *

In recent years Frederick Schuman has been visiting professor at Cornell and at Columbia universities. He lives in Williamstown, Mass., where he is professor of political science at Williams College. In World War II he served as a political analyst for the foreign broadcast intelligence service of the Federal Communications Commission. In 1950-51 he was a Fellow of the Foundation for World Government.

Schuman was one of a number of distinguished American authors and scholars who became involved in the heated controversy over the Cultural and Scientific Conference for World Peace, sponsored by the National Council of the Arts, Sciences, and Professions, held at the Waldorf-Astoria Hotel in New York in April 1949. The conference was labeled by the U.S. State Department as a "Communist sounding board" and was severely criticized by the American press. Schuman, speaking at the final session, was booed by the audience when he suggested that there existed dangers to world peace in both the United States and the Soviet Union: "Most Americans who are convinced disciples of democracy now believe, in all sincerity, and with some reason, that their cherished way of life is threatened primarily by the Soviet Union." After a reply from the Russian author Alexander Fadeyev, Schuman modified his statement and was quoted as saying. "No one in the U.S.S.R. wants war with the U.S." In the following year Senator Joseph McCarthy named him, along with a number of other teachers and scholars, before a Senate Foreign Relations subcommittee for affiliation with alleged left-wing organizations. The committee later issued a report clearing the persons charged.

Schuman's book *Soviet Politics at Home and Abroad* was generally praised for its comprehensive survey of Russian political history, and—the New York *Times* remarked —"like the previous writing of the author [it] is notable for the breadth of its perspective, the vigor of its style and the abundance of its factual contents." Merle Fainsod, writing in the *American Political Science Review,* however, found weaknesses in Schuman's analysis which, he suggested, was vitiated by a curious dichotomy: "Essentially Schuman cannot make up his mind whether the Soviet policy is a dictatorship or whether it embodies a new and higher form of democratic leadership. Writing from the vantage point of a professed adherence to Western liberal values, Schuman seeks at one and the same time to differentiate the U.S.S.R. from the West and to equate its values and objectives with the loftiest aspirations of Western liberalism." Schuman's more recent *The Commonwealth of Man,* a study of the outlook for world government, was generally praised. Albert Guérard found the book "rich and vital. To excess: . . . I cannot believe it was necessary to give us . . . compendious treatises on anthropology and psychoanalysis." Stringfellow Barr called the author "one of the foremost reporter-scholars of our time," peculiarly fitted "for inventory by an extraordinary eye for the relevant, whether in a scholarly treatise or a newspaper."

ADDITIONAL WORKS: Soviet Politics at Home and Abroad, 1946; The Commonwealth of Man, 1952.

ABOUT: Time April 4, 1949.

SCHÜTZE, GLADYS HENRIETTA (RAPHAEL) ("Henrietta Leslie") (1881-July 19, 1946). For autobiographical sketch and list of works and references, see TWENTIETH CENTURY AUTHORS, 1942.

SCHWARTZ, DELMORE (December 8, 1913-). For biographical sketch and list of earlier works and references, see TWENTIETH CENTURY AUTHORS, 1942.

* * *

Delmore Schwartz has made major strides in recent years as poet, short story writer, and critic. In 1943 he published his most ambitious poetic work, *Genesis, Book I,* a long introspective poem—its central figure a sensitive young American of Russian-Jewish extraction growing up in New York City. "Despite occasional garrulous aridity," Frank Jones wrote in the *Nation,* "it suggests as a whole a genuinely tragic view of life." Schwartz's more recent verse appeared, along with some prose pieces, in *Vaudeville for a Princess.* The critics found this later poetry substantial, though not inspired. "There is little of fury or rage, much of philosophic understanding, and a hard-worked control over what is being said," Richard Eberhart observed in the New York *Times.* Something of this same quiet but impressive skill was reflected in the collection of Schwartz's short stories, mainly about middle class Jewish family life, *The World Is a Wedding.* His prose, John Farrelly pointed out in the *New Republic,* seems at first deficient in color and imagery and even monotonous. "But one soon notices in the explicit themes, in the abstract language, in the political references and in the tone of polite discussion, a deliberate direction halfway between traditional fiction and the philosophical dialogue. In a number of instances Schwartz brings it off beautifully." Although Schwartz has not as yet published a full volume of literary criticism, his critical essays frequently appear in *Kenyon Review, Partisan Review,* and other journals, and several of them have been published in recent critical anthologies. His work as a critic is widely respected for its originality and independence and for its general soundness.

Schwartz taught at Harvard from 1940 to 1947. Since then he has lectured at New York University, the Kenyon School of English, the Indiana School of Letters, Princeton, and the University of Chicago. Schwartz has had a distinguished editorial career. He was editor of *Partisan Review* 1943-46 and associate editor 1947-55. In 1952-53 he was associated with *Perspectives,* published by the Ford Foundation, and he serves as literary consultant for New Directions, the publishing firm. In recent years he has received awards from *Poetry* magazine (1950) and the National Academy of Arts and Letters (1953). In 1955 he became poetry editor of the *New Republic,* for which he also writes on motion pictures. In 1949 Schwartz married the writer Elizabeth Pollet. They live, with their two cats, in a white frame farmhouse in the country near Pittstown, N.J.

Corrections: TWENTIETH CENTURY AUTHORS, 1942, incorrectly listed "The Imitation of Life and Other Problems of Literary Criticism" among Schwartz's published works. Also, the year of his birth was incorrectly given as 1914.

ADDITIONAL WORKS: Genesis, Book I, 1943; The World Is a Wedding (short stories) 1948; Vaudeville for a Princess, and Other Poems, 1950.

ABOUT: Commentary December 1950; Harvard Advocate December 1948.

SCHWARTZ, JOZUA MARIUS WILLEM VAN DER POORTEN ("Maarten Maartens") (August 15, 1858-August 3, 1915). For biographical sketch and list of works and references, see TWENTIETH CENTURY AUTHORS, 1942.

*SCHWEITZER, ALBERT (January 14, 1875-   ), surgeon, theologian, musicologist, missionary, philosopher, was born in Kaysers-

berg, Alsace, the son of Louis Schweitzer, a Lutheran minister, and Adele (Schillinger) Schweitzer. He was educated at the University of Strasbourg, at the Sorbonne at Paris, and at the University of Berlin, receiving a Ph.D. in 1899 and an M.D. in 1913, not to mention innumerable honorary degrees in later life. In 1899 he was curate of St. Nicolaus at Strasbourg. Schweitzer was *Privatdozent* at the University of Strasbourg (1902-03); director of seminary, St. Thomas, Strasbourg (1903-06); organist for the J. S. Bach Society of Paris (1903-11); organist, Orfeo Catala, Barcelona; and missionary, surgeon and founder of the hospital at Lambaréné, Gabon, French Equatorial Africa (1913-17, 1924-27, 1929-32, 1933-35, and 1937 to the present). His two addresses are Lambaréné, and Günsbach, near Colmar, Haute-Alsace (France).

As *Time* has described him: "He is a musicologist whose edition of Bach's organ works is a standard text; his biography of Bach has never been surpassed. He is a doctor of medicine whose thirty-six years of selfless pioneering as a missionary to the natives of French Equatorial Africa are a bright highlight in the relations between the white race and the black. He is a philosopher who, like Spengler and Toynbee, has thought deeply about the crisis of Western culture. He is a Protestant minister and Biblical scholar whose historical criticism of the New Testament, early in this century, turned out to be a theological blockbuster. Above all, he is a man who decided to turn his back on the dazzling rewards the world wanted to give him in order to serve his fellow men."

At the age of twenty-one Schweitzer came to this decision: "I would consider myself justified in living until I was thirty for science and art, in order to devote myself from that time forward to the direct service of human-

* shvī'tsĕr

ity. Many a time already had I tried to settle what meaning lay hidden for me in the saying of Jesus: 'Whosoever would save his life shall lose it, and whosoever shall lose his life for My sake and the Gospels shall save it.' Now the answer was found. In addition to the outward, I had now inward happiness." In 1899 when he was twenty-four, his first book, on the religious philosophy of Kant, was published. The book that made his reputation international was *The Quest of the Historical Jesus,* published in English in 1910. He showed Jesus as a man of His own time, thinking and acting within the framework of contemporary Jewish belief.

When in 1905 Schweitzer announced to his parents and a few friends that he was going to take up the study of medicine and spend the rest of his life as a doctor in Equatorial Africa, they protested, saying among other things that he could do much more for the Africans by raising money for them through concerts and lectures. As Schweitzer has told it: "It moved me strangely to see [my friends] so far from perceiving that the effort to serve the love preached by Jesus may sweep a man into a new course of life, although they read in the New Testament that it can do so and found it there quite in order." While he studied for his M.D. at Strasbourg University, he continued to preach, to play the organ, and to write books, one of which was *Paul and His Interpreters* (published in English in 1912). In 1913 he and his wife set out for Africa, a story told in such books as *On the Edge of the Primeval Forest* and *From My African Notebook.* "This is a little book," said the *Saturday Review of Literature* of the latter, "but it is filled with the great kindliness of a missionary who sees Africans as human beings and not merely Christian mortar." In spite of the physical and mental labor as a doctor in this area (some 2,000 cases during his first nine months there), Schweitzer continued to work at his writing. During a long period of internment, as an enemy alien, in French camps from 1914 to 1918, Schweitzer resumed his studies of Pauline theology, published some years later in *The Mysticism of Paul the Apostle.* When World War I ended, he spent several years traveling and giving lectures and organ recitals all over Europe. In 1923, while in Europe for advanced medical studies, he published the first two volumes of his work on the philosophy of civilization, *The Decay and Restoration of Civilization* and *Civilization and Ethics.*

In 1912 he had married Helène Marianne Bresslau, the daughter of a well-known

Strasbourg historian; she planned for their life in Africa by becoming a trained nurse. The Schweitzers have one daughter, Rhena, born in 1919 on Schweitzer's birthday. His humility, forbearance, and friendliness are always noted by interviewers. As to religion, he subscribes to no creed and has no patience with theological distinctions. His religious thinking defies any precise labeling. In 1949 on the occasion of the Goethe bicentennial celebration here (and because funds were promised the Lambaréné hospital), Schweitzer made his first visit to the United States, where he was pleased to find that "people here are almost as disorganized and leisurely as they are in Europe."

The Nobel Peace Prize was awarded to Dr. Schweitzer in 1952.

PRINCIPAL WORKS IN ENGLISH TRANSLATION: The Quest of the Historical Jesus, 1910; J. S. Bach, 1911; Paul and His Interpreters, 1912; The Mystery of the Kingdom of God, 1914; On the Edge of the Primeval Forest, 1922; Christianity and the Religions of the World, 1923; The Decay and the Restoration of Civilization, 1923; Civilization and Ethics, 1923; Memoirs of Childhood and Youth, 1925; The Mysticism of Paul the Apostle, 1931; The Forest Hospital at Lambaréné (in England: More from the Primeval Forest) 1931; Out of My Life and Thought, An Autobiography, 1933; Indian Thought and Its Development, 1936; From My African Notebook (in America: African Notebook) 1938; Goethe, 1948; A Psychiatric Study of Jesus, 1948.

ABOUT: Exman, E. & Anderson, E. The World of Albert Schweitzer; Feschotte, J. Albert Schweitzer: An Introduction; Gollomb, J. Albert Schweitzer, Genius in the Jungle; Hagedorn, H. Prophet in the Wilderness; Joy, C. R. and Arnold, M. Africa of Albert Schweitzer; Kepler, T. S. Journey with the Saints; Kraus, O. Albert Schweitzer, His Work and His Philosophy; Murry, J. M. Challenge of Schweitzer; Northcott, C. Venturers of Faith; Oursler, F. Why I Know There Is a God; Oxnam, G. B. Personalities in Social Reform; Ratter, M. C. Albert Schweitzer, Life and Message; Roback, A. A. Albert Schweitzer Jubilee Book; Rosen, G. and Caspari-Rosen, B. 400 Years of a Doctor's Life; Salmon, D. Jungle Doctor; Schweitzer, A. Memoirs of Childhood and Youth, Out of My Life and Thought; Seaver, G. Albert Schweitzer, a Vindication; Current Biography 1948; Ecumenical Review Winter 1950; Etude December 1950; Life October 6, 1947, July 25, 1949; New York Times Book Review July 17, 1949; New York Times Magazine January 13, 1952; New Yorker November 20, 1954; Rotarian March 1952; Saturday Review of Literature June 17, 1950, May 2, 1953; Spectator February 18, 1949, November 6, 1953; Time July 11, 1949.

SCOLLARD, CLINTON (September 18, 1860-November 19, 1932). For biographical sketch and list of works and references, see TWENTIETH CENTURY AUTHORS, 1942.

SCOTT, DUNCAN CAMPBELL (August 2, 1862-December 19, 1947). For autobiographical sketch and list of earlier works and references, see TWENTIETH CENTURY AUTHORS, 1942.

* * *

Duncan Campbell Scott died at his home in Ottawa, Canada, at eighty-five.

As with many Dominion poets, Scott's subjects were generally the conflicts between man and nature, in which "the dominant mood is heroic endurance," in the words of Desmond Pacey, who asks: "Is it too much to suggest that in these quietly powerful poems, seldom brilliant but always competent in style and solid in substance, we catch an authentic glimpse of the Canadian spirit at its finest?"

The late E. K. Brown called Scott "one of the chief masters of Canadian literature." He was at his best in writing of the Indians to whom he devoted most of his professional life in the Canadian Civil Service. "Of all Canadian poets," Brown wrote, "indeed of all Canadian imaginative writers, he has best succeeded in making great literature out of such distinctively Canadian material."

ADDITIONAL WORKS: In the Village of Viger, 1945; Circle of Affection, 1947; Walter J. Phillips (Canadian Art series) 1947; Selected Poems (ed. by E. K. Brown) 1951.

ABOUT: Brown, E. K. On Canadian Poetry; Percival, W. P. Leading Canadian Poets; Thomas, C. Canadian Novelists, 1920-1945; Canadian Forum August 1948; New York Times December 20, 1947; Royal Society of Canada Transactions (1948).

SCOTT, EVELYN (January 17, 1893-   ). For autobiographical sketch and list of earlier works and references, see TWENTIETH CENTURY AUTHORS, 1942.

* * *

Evelyn Scott wrote from London in 1952 that she "has been unable to publish anything for ten years beyond three or four poems and precisely three criticisms. In 1937 she signed with Charles Scribner's a contract for a novel on the French Revolution; but Scribner's has relinquished the contract as obsolete and useless, so long has been the passage of time since this novel—still uncompleted—was begun; and so difficult has been the struggle for mere survival made by Evelyn Scott and her present and second husband, John Metcalfe, during their financial stranding in Britain; which began when he was demobilized from R.A.F. service."

The manuscript of the novel on the French Revolution, to which Miss Scott refers above, disappeared, "with every indication of theft," she notes, while she was living in Canada where her husband was serving with the R.A.F. Work on this volume and on another novel was interrupted by wartime and family difficulties. She and her husband returned to London during the blitz. Here she completed the first version of a novel, "Escape Into Living," and a volume of poems. Miss Scott comments that the paper shortage of the post-war years and the increased publishing costs dimmed the prospects of publishing these books. She rewrote the novel, deleting many pages, "an aesthetically destructive gesture, made against creative conscience and injurious in effect." In 1951 she again rewrote the book and restored many of the cuts in a new version, as yet unpublished.

Miss Scott sends the following additional data: she was born Elsie Dunn, in Clarksville, Tenn. She dropped the name Elsie and substituted Evelyn before her majority, when it became her legal Christian name. Her first husband, Cyril Kay Scott (Frederick Wellman) is the well-known painter (whose autobiography, *Life Is Too Short* was published in 1943), and their son, Creighton Scott is also a painter and writer. In 1954 Miss Scott returned to the United States.

SCOTT, WINFIELD TOWNLEY (April 30, 1910-), American poet, writes: "The question, though irrelevant, is so frequent

that perhaps I should begin by answering it: No, I am not related to the famous U. S. general whose name I bear. Some of my American ancestry dates from 1620, but for the most part it is Scots-English—farmers and millworkers who settled in New England in, I think, the 1840's. Nobody even remotely literary or even 'artistic,' barring Job Townsend and John Goddard, cabinet-makers now revered by antiquarians. One of my grandfathers was a good shoe manufacturer, the other a good hardware storekeeper, and my father at various times in his life was employed by both.

"Like Mark Twain, I was born under Halley's Comet (a few days after he also died under it). That was in Haverhill, Mass., but I lived my first ten years in Newport, R. I. Then back to Haverhill. I attended public schools in both cities. I believe I was a very quiet little boy for there were always old ladies who told me stories: I must have sat a great deal. I became a very bookish little boy

and soon—I don't know how soon, but before I was ten—I began scribbling stories and had only the one ambition, to 'be an author.' In Haverhill High School the ambition became specific when we were assigned *The Rime of the Ancient Mariner:* I was dazzled as by sudden revelation. Then and there I thought poetry the most wonderful thing in the world, and I still think so. My own first poems (*not* among the most wonderful, however I may have then felt about them) were printed in the high school paper and, presently, in *Scholastic* magazine.

"My year of graduation from Brown University, 1931, was a year of frightening economic depression, but I had the great luck of a part-time job assisting the literary editor of the Providence *Journal*, for which, as an undergraduate, I had been writing book reviews; and though now and then I had other part-time work—such as ghost-writing speeches and a brief spell of teaching at Brown—I continued on the *Journal* in its book and movie and radio departments for twenty years, the last ten as its literary editor. In 1951 I resigned to have my writing time to myself. I still do a few book reviews for various publications and now and then a literary essay, but my principal concern continues to be poetry.

"I have had—and I think this is generally true in the field—neither extremes of fortune: some difficulties of publication, but so far temporary ones; some awards and honors. I take it as axiomatic that the attempt to create poetry, as a career, never receives indubitable proof of success; never, certainly, in one's lifetime.

"I have always lived in New England and, except for a summer in the British Isles and the Netherlands, have traveled very little. Since 1951 I have lived year-round in a seventeenth century house, to which we have added a big-windowed mid-twentieth century wing, in the little Connecticut town of Hampton. I have been twice married: in 1933 to Savila B. Harvey and, after a divorce in 1946, to Eleanor Metcalf. I have three children. Non-athletic, I like to walk: New York streets, country roads and woods, and the floor. It is still a pleasant necessity to sit a great deal."

* * *

Winfield Townley Scott has kept close to home in his choice of poetic material—drawing mainly upon the New England scene, its history and traditions. The results have been a quiet but sharply realized poetry—"always interesting," Marshall Schacht wrote in *Poetry* in 1942, "because the writer is always intelligent, aware and unpretentious—not swayed by last year's social consciousness, or this year's attitudes toward this and that." More recently Selden Rodman wrote of him in the New York *Times:* "It is encouraging to find a real craftsman working in the mainstream of American poetry—and working it steadily toward mature accomplishment."

PRINCIPAL WORKS: Elegy for Robinson, 1936; Biography for Traman, 1937; Wind the Clock, 1941; The Sword on the Table, 1942; To Marry Strangers, 1945; Mr. Whittier, and Other Poems, 1948.

ABOUT: Providence Journal May 6, 1951.

SCOTT-MONCRIEFF, CHARLES KENNETH (September 25, 1889-February 28, 1930). For biographical sketch and list of works and references, see TWENTIETH CENTURY AUTHORS, 1942.

SEABROOK, WILLIAM BUEHLER (February 22, 1886-September 20, 1945). For biographical sketch and list of earlier works and references, see TWENTIETH CENTURY AUTHORS, 1942.

* * *

William Seabrook took his own life with an overdose of sleeping pills at his farm in Rhinebeck, N. Y. He was fifty-nine. He was survived by his third wife, the former Constance Kuhn; his second marriage ended in divorce in 1941.

He has been characterized by Clifton Fadiman as "a man who has spent his life doing the unconventional and writing about it. He has sometimes written pretty well, sometimes not so well. If he were a first-rate literary artist, he could make his oddities and defiances add up to something. As it is, his disregard for convention, instead of interesting us by its amorality, too often amuses us by its absurdity." He has earned "his own place among contemporary travellers," in the words of Paul Allen, by his "verve and his paradox," and by his ability as an accomplished raconteur.

ADDITIONAL WORK: No Hiding Place: An Autobiography, 1942.

ABOUT: Seabrook, W. B. No Hiding Place; New York Times September 21, 1945; New Yorker October 31, 1942; Newsweek November 2, 1942.

SEAGER, ALLAN (February 5, 1906-), American novelist and short story writer, reports: "I was born in Adrian, Mich., a small town. Both my grandfathers had settled in the region after the Civil War. Beauman Seager, a Vermonter and a cousin of President Benjamin Harrison, had taken up bounty land. John Allan, an English orphan boy educated at the Blue Coat School had come to this country as a bricklayer in time to be a soldier. My father was a traveling salesman who knew the whole Mississippi Valley. Sherwood Anderson said he was one of the best story-tellers he ever heard and "if you have any talent, it comes from him." It was my mother, however, who read to me young and gave me an interest in books. None of my kinfolk was literary in any sense.

"When I was about ten, we moved to Memphis, Tenn. Hating the place as a Yankee, solemnly reading a hundred pages a day aside from my school work, composing a few worthless, unshowable poems, I wanted to write but I thought there was a special way to do it that someone could show me. No one did (no one ever does) either there or at the University of Michigan where it is not study or classrooms I remember, rather a frieze of pretty girls and long aimless journeys in cars at night. I did, however, make Phi Bete and a Rhodes Scholarship in my senior year.

"From my English grandfather I had expected a journey to England to be, in a sense, a return. I was mistaken. It was a foreign country more so than the France, Spain, Germany, and Switzerland I visited in the holidays. It was at an English pub, however, that I began to write, The Crown, East Hanney, Berks. I was stuck there the summer because I had no money and I spent it on a story Sir John Squire bought for the *London Mercury.* I felt then I had a start.

"Returning to New York in the midst of the depression I was fortunate to be hired as an assistant to Frank Crowninshield on *Vanity Fair.* The magazine was dying but I published several stories in it and I learned enough about New York from Crownie's assignments to know that it was not my city. I came to teach part-time at the University of Michigan and except for one year at Bennington College and a year in Hollywood I have been there ever since. Meeting students, young, hopeful, uncorrupt, is a continuing refreshing experience from which I have learned any amount.

"Once I would have hesitated to say that the novel is the conscience of the middle class but when I remember my own, *Equinox, The Inheritance,* and *Amos Berry,* I discover that I believe it. A pleasure of middle-age is the acceptance of one's own origins, whatever one has pretended, however ambivalent the bonds. If I can say anything about the sources of my own work, I believe they lie in the tensions of that ambivalence.

"I live in a village full of maple trees, Tecumseh, Mich., and I drive the twenty-six miles to Ann Arbor three times a week. My wife, whom I married in 1939, is a beautiful, patient woman, the mother of two beautiful little girls from whom I am learning everything I know all over again."

PRINCIPAL WORKS: Equinox, 1943; The Inheritance, 1948; The Old Man of the Mountain (short stories) 1950; Amos Berry, 1953.

ABOUT: Warfel, H. R. American Novelists of Today.

SEAMAN, SIR OWEN (September 18, 1861-February 2, 1936). For biographical sketch and list of works and references, see TWENTIETH CENTURY AUTHORS, 1942.

* * *

ABOUT: Dictionary of National Biography 1931-1940.

SEAVER, EDWIN (January 18, 1900-). For autobiographical sketch and list of earlier works and references, see TWENTIETH CENTURY AUTHORS, 1942

* * *

In 1944 Edwin Seaver published the first of a series of collections of new, heretofore unpublished writings by Americans, *Cross Section.* Seaver, as editor, had to choose from thousands of manuscripts submitted for each volume. Among the better-known writers who contributed were Langston Hughes, William March, Shirley Jackson, and Jessamyn West. Avoiding the esoteric tendencies of some of the "little" magazines and the conventional slickness of the "popular" magazines, *Cross Section* was praised for the freshness and vigor of its contents. Some critics objected, however, that Seaver's choices ran too much to stories of violence, brutality, and futility. The last volume of *Cross Section* appeared in 1948 and contained, among other selections, a chapter from Norman Mailer's novel *The Naked and the Dead*, which became a bestseller when published complete later that year.

ADDITIONAL WORKS: *Editor*—Cross Section: A Collection of New American Writing, 1944, 1945, 1947, 1948; The World's Great Love Novels, 1944; Pageant of American Humor, 1948.

SEAWELL, MOLLY ELLIOT (October 23, 1860-November 15, 1916). For biographical sketch and list of works and references, see TWENTIETH CENTURY AUTHORS, 1942.

SEDGWICK, ANNE DOUGLAS (March 28, 1873-July 19, 1935). For biographical sketch and list of works and references, see TWENTIETH CENTURY AUTHORS, 1942.

* * *

ABOUT: Bowen, E. Collected Impressions; Sedgwick, E. (comp) Atlantic Harvest.

SEEGER, ALAN (June 22, 1888-July 4, 1916). For biographical sketch and list of works and references, see TWENTIETH CENTURY AUTHORS, 1942.

SEELEY, MABEL (HODNEFIELD) (March 25, 1903-), American detective story writer, reports: "No one ever mistakes me for anything but what I am, a Middle Westerner. The first six years of my life were spent in Minnesota— I was born there, at Herman—the next five in Illinois, the next five in Iowa, the next three in Wisconsin. In 1921, as a high school senior, I was  back in Minnesota, happy to be there. Except for a few years in Chicago, between 1926 and 1929, I stayed in Minnesota until 1949.

"In my family I early discovered the uses of story telling; as the eldest of six children it was soon my job to ride herd. My father is a librarian with a scholarly love for books and language, my mother a member of a clan whose delight is to gather in swarms for family meals and family yarning-sessions. No other stories in the world, for me, have the flavor of those told by the descendants of Norwegian pioneers. What I learned at the family knee was that the most absorbing, the most amazing, the most amusing of all organisms are *people,* and experience hasn't changed this attitude.

"An early taste of being read came at Ellsworth, Wis., where I wrote 'High School News and Notes' for the Ellsworth *Record.* In St. Paul I met one of the big pieces of luck in my life; Mary Copley was one of my English teachers. She not only chuckled appreciatively—what note is more musical?—

over my writing efforts, but got me a St. Paul College Club Scholarship, which took me to the University of Minnesota in 1922. There luck burst over me a second time: Mary Ellen Chase was then on the Minnesota English staff. Callow I may have been, but not so much so I didn't turn up in each course taught by Miss Chase; to this day she has a splendor in my mind that no one else touches. Also at Minnesota I was on the board of the *Minnesota Quarterly,* and in 1926, on graduating, was married to a fellow editor, Kenneth Seeley.

"The two of us set sail for Chicago, he to do graduate work at the University of Chicago, I to take a copy job in advertising. Millions of words later, in 1936, I retired from a profession paced too fast for me, determined never to put pencil to yellow paper again. A year later I was at work on *The Listening House.*

"Why did I choose mysteries for a major interest? Perhaps because I'd found them such a useful anodyne, perhaps because I have a natural relish for horror. If I had a premise, it was that terror would be more terrible, horror more horrible, when visited on people the reader would feel were real, in places he would recognize as real. This hasn't changed, either.

"Mysteries exist only within very rigid limitations; sometimes I find these confining. Twice so far I've tried out the wider spaces of the straight novel; I've enjoyed the freedom. But I've never been able to say 'no more of the other.' In this year of 1953 I'm living at Burbank, Calif., with son Gregory who now is ten. Working. On a mystery."

PRINCIPAL WORKS: The Listening House, 1938; The Crying Sisters, 1939; The Whispering Cup, 1940; The Chuckling Fingers, 1941; Eleven Came Back, 1943; Woman of Property, 1947, The Beckoning Door, 1949; Stranger Beside Me, 1951; The Whistling Shadow, 1954.

ABOUT: Warfel, H. R. American Novelists of Today.

*SEGHERS, ANNA (1900-). For biographical sketch and list of earlier works and references, see TWENTIETH CENTURY AUTHORS, 1942.

* * *

Anna Seghers' *The Seventh Cross* was one of the most successful of all anti-Nazi novels. In the United States it was a best seller, a Book-of-the-Month Club choice, and was made into a motion picture. Two more of her novels have appeared in English translation, but these have not enjoyed the popularity

of *The Seventh Cross.* After the war, Anna Seghers returned to Germany. She lives in East Berlin. In recent years she has identified herself more and more with left-wing political thought, and in 1951 she received the Stalin Peace Prize.

ADDITIONAL WORKS IN ENGLISH TRANSLATION: Transit (in England: Transit Visa) 1944; The Dead Stay Young, 1950.

ABOUT: Columbia Dictionary of Modern European Literature; Slochower, H. No Voice Is Wholly Lost; Current Biography 1942.

SEID, RUTH. See "SINCLAIR, J."

SEITZ, DON CARLOS (October 24, 1862- December 4, 1935). For biographical list of works and references, see TWENTIETH CENTURY AUTHORS, 1942.

*SELDES, GEORGE (November 16, 1890-). For autobiographical sketch and list of earlier works and references, see TWENTIETH CENTURY AUTHORS, 1942.

* * *

George Seldes writes from Norwalk, Conn.: "I learned, to my astonishment [from the 1942 sketch], that I was listed as a sociologist (as well as a journalist). Don't know a thing about sociology. I was for ten years an editor and publisher, an employer, I met a payroll, and I was perhaps even a capitalist; but sociologist, never!

"The p.s. says I was 'reared' in Vineland, N.J. I went to high school there; it is the nearest town to our farm in Alliance, N.J.— a utopian colony founded by my father. (It has ceased to exist, thanks to rural free delivery.) As to my (also Gilbert's) parents: my father's father came from Odessa, in the Ukraine; my mother's parents came from Strasbourg, France, shortly after the Franco-Prussian War. My father was a Freethinker, and we were brought up in that 'faith.'

"My newsletter *In Fact* reached a high of 176,000. In 1948 I visited Western and Iron Curtain countries and wrote a series of articles for it. Up to that year I had been redbaited generally; but owing to my interview with Tito, and reports favorable to Yugoslavia and anti-Cominform and anti-Moscow, my newsletter was bitterly attacked by the Reds. Between these two attacks my circulation fell to 55,000 and I quit then because we were losing $500 a week. I refused gifts, subsidies, the idea of 'associates' or group or party sponsorship. When I quit

* zā′gărs

* sĕl′dĕs

I still had about the total circulation of the two leading liberal publications in America: the *Nation* and the *New Republic.*

"I have just completed a book published as *Tell the Truth and Run,* a personal history of forty years of American journalism. Not an autobiography, but a record of adventures and meanings."

ADDITIONAL WORKS: Facts and Fascism, 1943; One Thousand Americans 1947; The People Don't Know, 1949; Tell the Truth and Run, 1953.

ABOUT: Seldes, G. Tell the Truth and Run; Current Biography 1941.

SELDES, GILBERT VIVIAN (January 3, 1893-). For biographical sketch and list of earlier works and references, see TWENTIETH CENTURY AUTHORS, 1942.

* * *

Gilbert Seldes has been called "the most articulate and thoughtful commentator on American entertainment arts." In 1950, more than a quarter of a century after the publication of his *The Seven Lively Arts,* Seldes published a shrewd analysis of the three mass arts of the contemporary scene—movies, radio, and television—in *The Great Audience.* Here Seldes recanted his earlier theory that the audience is always right and presented a critique that is, as Jack Gould of the New York *Times* described it, "timely, constructive and controversial."

Seldes has become an expert on television drama. In the pioneer days of the medium, from 1937 to 1945, he directed television programs for the Columbia Broadcasting System, and he has written many television scripts and a textbook on writing for television. He reviews television and radio shows for the *Saturday Review* and has his own radio program of critical comment on plays, movies, radio, and television.

Correction: Seldes' marriage to Alice Wadhams Hall took place in 1924 not 1934, as reported in TWENTIETH CENTURY AUTHORS, 1942.

ADDITIONAL WORKS: The Great Audience, 1950; Writing for Television, 1952.

SÉLINCOURT. See DE SÉLINCOURT

"SELKIRK, JANE." See CHAPMAN, M.

SELTZER, CHARLES ALDEN (August 15, 1875-February 9, 1942). For biographical sketch and list of works and references, see TWENTIETH CENTURY AUTHORS, 1942.

*SENDER, RAMÓN J. (February 3 1902-). For autobiographical sketch and list of earlier works and references, see TWENTIETH CENTURY AUTHORS, 1942.

* * *

Florence Hall Sender (Mrs. Ramón Sender) writes from Albuquerque, N.M.: "Ramón Sender came to the United States on a Guggenheim fellowship in 1942. He married Florence Hall in 1943. He became an American citizen in 1946. He has lectured at Amherst College, Harvard University, Denver University and Ohio State University, and has contributed to *Kenyon Review, Partisan Review, View, Harper's, Books Abroad, New Leader,* New York *Times Book Review, New Mexico Quarterly,* etc. Since 1947 he has been professor of Spanish literature at the University of New Mexico. Following publication of *The King and the Queen* in May 1948, the Associated Press named him Author of the Week. A new novel, *El Verdugo Afable,* has recently been published in Santiago, Chile, as well as a series of critical articles on Valle-Inclán in *Cuadernos Americanos* (Mexico). Just now [December 1952] he is finishing the second volume of his autobiography, "El Taller del Lego," sequel to *Chronicle of Dawn.*"

Mrs. Sender sends the following corrections to the 1942 sketch: "His only imprisonment took place during the Primo de Rivera dictatorship, when he was held without trial and released after intervention by the Press Association of Madrid. He was never arrested in Huesca, or exiled from there, nor was he ever the leader of any revolutionary movement, though he was implicated in that movement. He did not leave Spain in 1937 except briefly to establish his children in France. In the spring of 1938 he visited this country as an official lecturer for the Spanish Republic, returning to the front. He left Spain for the last time late in 1938. And, *Time* magazine to the contrary, there is nothing in either his background or career to make anyone familiar with him mistake him for Malraux' Manuel."

* * *

The noted Spanish critic Arturo Barea considers Sender "the only important novelist of the young pre-Civil War generation." In his recent novels, as well as in his earlier work, as William L. Fichter points out, "his art draws its strength from a deep consciousness of social wrongs and from sympathies with man's long, painful, upward struggle." At the same time, however, Sender does not write

* sän dĕr'

"social" novels, in the popularly understood sense of the term. His later works are essentially symbolic and metaphysical. Alfred Kazin, reviewing Sender's *Dark Wedding,* writes: "He is like the Surrealists, and shares their aridity to this extent: what he gives us is more the idea of the fantasy than its concreteness." Sender's artistic development in the past decade has been well summarized by Barea—"Ramón Sender's work in exile began with novels of nostalgic self-discovery; the mystical element that had always been there under a cover of realistic symbols has grown strong, and his last novels are expositions of ideas in a style which oscillates between the poetic and the didactic."

ADDITIONAL WORKS IN ENGLISH TRANSLATION: Dark Wedding, 1943; Chronicle of Dawn, 1944; The King and the Queen, 1948; The Sphere, 1949.

ABOUT: Columbia Dictionary of Modern European Literature; Books Abroad Autumn 1940, Spring 1953; Bulletin of Bibliography September 1950-January 1951; Hispania February 1951.

SERGE, VICTOR (1890-November 18, 1947), Russian author, was born Victor Lvovich Kibalchick in Brussels; his parents

were revolutionary exiles. Serge's childhood was spent in Belgium and England, and as a young man he worked as a photographer and draftsman as well as journalist and translator. In 1913 he made a defense of anarchist principles which, in connection with an assassination case directed against a number of anarchists at the time, served to put Serge in the penitentiary for several years. In 1917 he joined the revolutionary attempt of the Catalonians in Spain, having gone to that country to work with the syndicalists and anarchists there. Arrested by the Clemenceau government while on a trip through France to Russia, Serge was exchanged in 1919 for a French officer who had been arrested in Russia. In Petrograd he soon joined the Communist Party and was sent by it on dangerous undercover missions abroad. For many years he also held the post of managing editor of the official world publication *Communist International.* Later becoming an active spokesman for the Trotskyist opposition, he was expelled from the Communist Party in 1928 and exiled to Siberia. His punishment led many world literary figures, including André Gide, to protest vigorously to the Soviet government. After eight years Serge

was permitted to leave Russia. He went to France, and on the fall of France went to Mexico, the only country to offer him a haven. Until his death he hoped in vain for a United States visa.

Serge's principal works on the Soviet Union are *From Lenin to Stalin* and *Russia Twenty Years After.* As a highly-placed and important member of the Communist International, he was well equipped to write on Soviet history and politics. The author of several novels in French and English, he wrote *The Long Dusk,* published just before his death. In 1950 appeared the posthumous work *The Case of Comrade Tulayev,* a novel said by the *Christian Science Monitor* to be "in the great tradition of the European novel. It is the Human Comedy of a police state. . . ." Thought by some critics to be wordy, it was nevertheless called a stark, terrible picture of modern Russia. "Gide has described the sense of failure which surrounded Serge, his nervousness, his purely Russian morbidity and delicacy," wrote Robert Payne in the New York *Times,* "but in the novel there are no traces of what he called 'Serge's instinctive sense of failure.' In the novel Serge found himself. Here at last, writing when he was very ill, he showed his power."

At fifty-seven, in his home in Mexico City, Serge died of a heart attack. At this time he was a democratic socialist, opposed to totalitarianism of every variety.

PRINCIPAL WORKS: From Lenin to Stalin, 1937; Russia Twenty Years After (in England: Destiny of a Revolution) 1937; The Long Dusk, 1946; The Case of Comrade Tulayev, 1950.

ABOUT: Steinberg, J. (ed.) Verdict of Three Decades; New York Times November 20, 1947.

SERNA, ESPINA DE. See ESPINA

SERNA, GÓMEZ DE LA. See GOMEZ

SERVICE, ROBERT WILLIAM (January 16, 1876?-). For autobiographical sketch and list of earlier works and references, see TWENTIETH CENTURY AUTHORS, 1942.

* * *

In 1950 Robert W. Service announced from his home on the Riviera, "My hobby is longevity." As Geoffrey T. Hellman pointed out in a *New Yorker* profile on him in 1946, the fact that he is alive "has been a source of pleasurable astonishment to a growing number of people on this continent during the past few years." Although Service has continued to publish his poems, he is so exclusively identified with one poem, "The Shooting of

893

Dan McGrew," which in turn is so exclusively identified with the bygone era of Alaskan gold-rush days, that many readers find it hard to believe that he is still alive and active.

Service has lived in France for more than forty years. In June 1940 he and his French wife (Germaine Bourgoin) and their daughter Iris left their home in Brittany only a few hours ahead of the advancing German armies. He came to Canada and then to the United States, settling in Hollywood where he wrote his autobiography, *Ploughman of the Moon*. The book, which brings the account up to World War I, revealed "an astonishing life," crowded with adventure. But Service made no attempt to put the record straight on particular details. There is not a single date given, not even his birth date, which has been variously recorded as 1874, 1876, and 1877.

When World War II ended, Service returned to France. He retains his British citizenship. In his home on the Riviera he completed a second volume of autobiography and continues to write poetry. Hellman describes him as "a clean-shaven, short, handsome, ruddy-faced man with bushy gray hair and a slight Scotch burr. He is polite, modest, gentle in manner, and rather formal in conversation. He is proud of his youthful appearance, and this, as well as his tendency toward vagueness, often makes him misstate his age."

ADDITIONAL WORKS: Ploughman of the Moon, 1945; Harper of Heaven, 1948; Songs of a Sun-Lover, 1949; Rhymes of a Roughneck, 1950; Lyrics of a Low Brow, 1951; Rhymes of a Rebel, 1952.

ABOUT: Hellman, G. T. How to Disappear for an Hour (also in New Yorker March 30, April 6, 1946); Percival, W. P. (ed.) Leading Canadian Poets; Phelps, A. L. Canadian Writers; Service, R. W. Ploughman of the Moon, Harper of Heaven; Thomas, C. Leading Canadian Novelists; Reader's Digest October 1951; Time May 6, 1946, October 2, 1950.

SETON, ANYA (1916?-), American novelist, writes: "I was born in New York City in the old Beaux Arts Studio Apartments behind the Public Library, which may explain my early and growing passion for libraries and research! I think that every idea, productive one, that I've ever had, has come to me while standing bemused in the stacks of some library, and to the patience and efficiency of librarians I am extremely grateful.

"I was born into a writing family. My father, Ernest Thompson Seton, wrote (and illustrated) some forty books. My mother, Grace Gallatin Seton, has written a dozen.

So the career had no glamor for me whatsoever, and I determined to be a physician instead. This ambition died early, for I married at eighteen and at once produced two babies, but all my life I have had a lively interest in medicine and worked in hospitals and clinics particularly mental hygiene clinics, social service—and I was a nurse's aide for some years during and after the war.

"I was an only child and had a rather unorthodox upbringing. It included life (with Indians and Boy Scouts and Woodcraft) on my father's large estate in Cos Cob, Conn., five extended trips to Europe, and three to the Far West. I learned French before I did English, was taught by governesses, travel, and a really formidable amount of reading, until I finally reached a private school and graduated from it. College plans were also erased by the early marriage, but I then lived two years at Oxford with my husband and took courses there.

"During my twenties I experimented rather drearily with short stories and verse, but it was not until 1937 that I suddenly determined to write and sell. It took nineteen months of effort and disappointment until I sold my first short story, and then a few more. But short stories are not natural media for me and it wasn't until I conceived the idea of *My Theodosia*, a biographical novel about the daughter of Aaron Burr, that I found what I wanted to do.

"Research is a joy to me, and the interpretation of actual characters in the light of actual events: the authentic, and I hope vivid, reconstruction of certain phases of the past. So far, my five novels have all dealt with Americana, the one I am now [1952] working on is English, fourteenth century England and about real people. This one has taken three years of research and two trips to England, and is a long long pull, but it is of great interest to me as a subject [published in 1954 as *Katherine*, this was the story of Katherine Swynford, Chaucer's sister-in-law, and the wife of John of Gaunt].

"Willa Cather's work has probably influenced me more than any other writer, yet there is Katherine Mansfield, and Dickens, and the inimitable Jane. My life is predominantly domestic. I married (Hamilton M. Chase) a second time, and we have a daughter, and except for necessary travel in search of material, I live in a little house on the Sound in the same Connecticut town where I lived as a child."

PRINCIPAL WORKS: My Theodosia, 1941; Dragonwyck, 1944; The Turquoise, 1946; The Hearth and the Eagle, 1948; Foxfire, 1951; Katherine, 1954; The Mistletoe and Sword, 1955.

ABOUT: Current Biography 1953; Warfel, H. R. American Novelists of Today; New York Herald Tribune Book Review October 24, 1954.

SETON, ERNEST THOMPSON (August 14, 1860-October 23, 1946). For biographical sketch and list of earlier works and references, see TWENTIETH CENTURY AUTHORS, 1942.

* * *

Ernest Thompson Seton died at eighty-six at his home in Seton Village, Santa Fe, N.M. His physical and intellectual powers were remarkable for his age; shortly before his death he completed his forty-second book and was planning a 10,000-mile lecture tour. He was survived by his second wife, the collaborator of his later years, the former Julia (Moss) Buttree, and their adopted daughter Beulah. His daughter by his first marriage, Anya Seton (see sketch above), continues her successful career as a novelist. Seton Village, with its magnificent 2500-acre tract of land, its adobe "castle" and fine library, remains as a memorial to Seton, who was generally known as "The Chief" to a host of friends and admirers.

Seton has been characterized by *Time* magazine as "a man who, in an age of sweeping mechanization, had loved the natural earth, its seasons and its creatures, with rare intensity and an unusual power to communicate his vision to others."

ADDITIONAL WORKS: Arctic Prairies, 1943; Santana, The Hero Dog of France, 1945; Ernest Thompson Seton's America (ed. by F. A. Wiley) 1954.

ABOUT: Mahoney, B. E. Illustrators of Children's Books; Current Biography 1943; National Cyclopedia of American Biography (1950); New York Times October 24, 1946; Reader's Digest September 1946; Time November 4, 1946.

"SEUSS, DR." See GEISEL, T. S.

SEYMOUR, Mrs. BEATRICE KEAN (STAPLETON). For biographical sketch and list of earlier works and references, see TWENTIETH CENTURY AUTHORS, 1942.

* * *

Beatrice Kean Seymour's favorite subject recently appears to be the upper middle-class family saga. Her novels are sound and perceptive. She identifies herself closely with her themes—too closely, the London *Times Literary Supplement* felt of *Family Group,* a novel about a war-tired family in 1945. This book, the reviewer wrote, "falls short of animation and substitutes a too trivial verisimilitude for a larger truth." In most of her novels, however, the *Times* observed, "sympathetic insight gives her people a warmth of actuality which makes the reader genuinely curious to know what actually happens to them; and what does happen has the ring of truth."

ADDITIONAL WORKS: Return Journey, 1942; Bride of May, 1943; Joy as It Flies, 1944; The Tumbled House, 1946; Family Group, 1947; Children Grow Up, 1949; The Second Mrs. Conford, 1951; The Wine Is Poured, 1953.

"SHALOM ALEICHEM." See RABINOWITZ, S. J.

SHANNON, FRED ALBERT (February 12, 1893-   ). For autobiographical sketch and list of earlier works and references, see TWENTIETH CENTURY AUTHORS, 1942.

* * *

Fred A. Shannon writes from Urbana, Ill.: "In 1941 I became a full professor of history at the University of Illinois, and I have remained at that rank since that date. In 1945 my volume in the Rinehart series on economic history of the United States appeared, its title being *The Farmer's Last Frontier.* Two years later I published *The Civil War Letters of Sergeant Onley Andrus.* Since then, aside from working on a volume for Harper's 'Rise of the American Nation,' as yet unfinished, I have been just doing the usual professorial duty of publishing occasional articles in the reviews. In 1952 I was made vice-president of the Mississippi Valley Historical Association."

ADDITIONAL WORKS: The Farmer's Last Frontier, 1945; Civil War Letters of Sergeant Onley Andrus (ed.) 1947.

SHAPIRO, KARL JAY (November 10, 1913-   ), American poet, critic and editor, writes: "I was born in Baltimore, Md. Baltimore was the birthplace of my parents and of my brother and sister. Our grandparents emigrated from East Europe in the 1880's.

"I attended public schools in Baltimore, Virginia, and Chicago, and these places have remained home to me off and on during my life. I entered high school in Norfolk, Va., and graduated from one in Baltimore. I matriculated at the University of Virginia in 1932 but continued, several years later, at Johns Hopkins in Baltimore. My army train-ing took place in Virginia in a section of the state which I had been familiar with since childhood. Part of my early schooling took place in Chicago; in later years I returned there to teach in Chicago universities and to edit *Poetry, a Magazine of Verse.*

"My interest in poetry dates back to my high school years. We possessed a large undiversified library in our home, and it was a natural occupation for us to read and try to write. My brother, who was a year older than I, had won several literary prizes for essays, fiction and poetry while in high school and at college. I emulated him. The first poem of any seriousness which I can remember writing was a sonnet in praise of Gandhi. Later, at the University of Virginia, I did poorly in my studies because of my greater interest in writing verses. On leaving the university, which I did against the protests of my family, I devoted myself to this pursuit. I was permitted to study alone for several years, and it was during this unusual period of freedom that I began to develop my work in my own way.

"During this time of self-study I wrote many long poems and plays in verse, nearly all of which I later destroyed. In 1935 I collected a few of my shorter poems and had them published at the Waverly Press in Baltimore. The volume bore the title *Poems* and it was not reviewed or noticed by writers.

"From 1935 to 1937 I worked at various jobs in Baltimore and in 1936 traveled for a short period to Tahiti. The following year, through the assistance of Dr. Hazelton Spencer at Johns Hopkins, I received a scholarship to continue my studies at that university. After two years, however, I found it necessary to raise money to continue, and I enrolled as a salaried library student at the Pratt Library in Baltimore. Toward the end of my first year at the Library I was drafted (March, 1941) into the Army, no deferment being permitted at that time.

"During my first year in the Army I completed a series of poems which I had begun in 1938; these I now began to publish in literary magazines. New Directions offered to publish this group of poems in an anthol-ogy for young poets, and I consented. My war service took me overseas in 1942 and I served three years abroad in Australia, New Guinea and the surrounding islands."

"During my overseas life, my fiancée, Evalyn Katz, moved to New York in order to find a publisher for my work. At this venture she was extraordinarily successful. In 1942 she edited *Person, Place and Thing* for Reynal and Hitchcock. In 1944 she edited a new collection to be called *V-Letter*, a book which won the Pulitzer prize the following year. A third volume, *Essay on Rime*, was printed in 1945. Meanwhile, I had published a limited edition of a small collection of my own in Sydney; it was called *The Place of Love*. This book contained a number of poems which appeared in my American books and more which I felt were not worth reprinting. In addition to supervising the publication of my books, Evalyn Katz acted as my literary agent in sending poems to magazines, appearing at literary functions in my behalf, and generally furthering my literary career. On my return to America in 1945 we were married in Baltimore.

"The book called *Essay on Rime* perhaps merits a note. It is a critique of modern poetry, written in blank verse. It was written in New Guinea and in the Dutch East Indies. Part of the pleasure of writing the essay lay in recollecting notes which I had gathered before the war and trying to piece them together into a coherent whole. Certain errors of fact in the poem can be laid to this manner of composition also. By and large, the essay is a comment on the pretentiousness of modern poetry vis-à-vis its myth-making, its self-consciousness about culture and history, and its techniques of symbolism and metaphysics. The book was widely acclaimed on the whole, but it aroused the enmity of the literary avant-garde—as, in fact, it was calculated to do.

"In 1947, after living a year in Connecticut, I was appointed to the Library of Congress as Consultant in Poetry. This was an annual appointment, and the following year I was invited to join the faculty of the Johns Hopkins University as lecturer. *Trial of a Poet* was published in 1947 and contained a masque about the plight of the poet who comes into conflict with society.

"In 1950 I was invited to edit *Poetry, a Magazine of Verse,* and I resigned my post as associate professor in writing at Hopkins and moved to Chicago. In that city I also taught writing classes at Loyola University and later at the University of Iowa. In 1952 I lectured in Austria at the Salzburg Seminar in American Studies. In 1953 I delivered a series of lectures at the University of Nebraska which were published as a book under the title of *Beyond Criticism*. These lectures elaborate the thesis of *Essay on Rime* and fix as the two chief schools of modernism which seem to me deleterious: Mythic and Historic Poets, the one using poetry as a substitute religion and the other as social propaganda. In opposition to these I posit 'human' poetry, or poetry which is the fullest expression of personality. In 1953 I received a Guggenheim Fellowship and lived in Rome with my family for several months. A volume *Poems 1940-53* was published at that time.

"There are three children in my family: Katharine, born in New York in 1946, John Jacob, born in Baltimore in 1948, and Elizabeth, born in Chicago in 1950."

* * *

In 1941 when a group of Karl Shapiro's poems appeared in New Directions' *Five Young American Poets,* he was hailed as one of the most interesting of the younger American poets. Louise Bogan predicted at that time that "his work will become a sort of touchstone for his generation." During the war years his poetry ripened and matured to the point where, Conrad Aiken wrote of *V-Letter,* "Shapiro thinks with his feelings, thinks with his imagination, and the result is a curious and delightful poetic analysis or criticism of the given theme." Stephen Spender, while detecting in his verse "elements of crudeness and insensitivity which make him vulnerable to the purist approach," nevertheless concluded that "he is a poet of rare intellectual strength, he has an exceptional power of being able to think of a poem as a single idea." More recently, in reviewing his *Poems, 1940-1953,* Babette Deutsch observed: "His interest in his immediate surroundings, together with his verbal facility, set him apart from those of his fellows who stand in the street damning a disjointed world, and apart, too, from those spinning word-webs in an ivory corner of a prefabricated tower. Yet he is acutely conscious of the predicament of the poet in our time, and has written about it repeatedly." Early in 1955 Shapiro went to the University of California at Berkeley on a teaching assignment, still retaining his title as editor of *Poetry.*

PRINCIPAL WORKS: Poems, 1935; *in* Five Young American Poets, 1941; Person, Place and Thing, 1942; V-Letter, 1944; Essay on Rime, 1945; Trial of a Poet, 1947; Beyond Criticism (lectures) 1953; Poems, 1940-1953, 1953.

ABOUT: College English February 1946; Current Biography 1944; Publishers' Weekly March 23, 1946; Western Review Spring 1954.

SHAPLEY, HARLOW (November 2. 1885-). For biographical sketch and list of earlier works and references, see TWENTIETH CENTURY AUTHORS, 1942.

* * *

Harlow Shapley was director of the Harvard Observatory from 1921 to 1952, when he became Paine Professor of Astronomy at Harvard. In 1947 he became president of the American Association for the Advancement of Science. He has received many honorary degrees in recent years—from New York University, the Universities of Copenhagen, Delhi, Hawaii, and Mexico; holds membership in numerous scholarly and professional organizations; and has received, among many other medals and awards, the Pope Pius IX prize, the Calcutta Science Society medal, the gold medal of the Indian Association for the Cultivation of Science, and the Mexican Order of the Aztec Eagle.

As a result of his membership in several organizations of allegedly "left-wing" political nature, Dr. Shapley's name has been frequently mentioned in congressional investigations of subversive activity in recent years. He was chairman of the National Council of the Arts, Sciences, and Professions, which, in April 1949, sponsored the Cultural and Scientific Conference for World Peace.

ADDITIONAL WORKS: Galaxies, 1943. *Editor (with others)*: Treasury of Science, 1943; Readings in the Physical Sciences, 1948.

ABOUT: Fisher, D. C. American Portraits; Science February 14, 1947; Newsweek January 20, 1947; Science Illustrated January 1949; Scientific Monthly March 1947.

SHARP, DALLAS LORE (December 13, 1870-November 29, 1929). For biographical sketch and list of works and references, see TWENTIETH CENTURY AUTHORS, 1942.

SHARP, MARGERY (1905-). For biographical sketch and list of earlier works and references, see TWENTIETH CENTURY AUTHORS, 1942.

* * *

Margery Sharp worked for the Armed Forces' Education Program during World War II, while her husband, Major G. L. Castle, served in the British Army. They now live in London, just off Piccadilly, "only occasionally casting an eye toward the country."

Miss Sharp's bright, frequently zany, but always entertaining brand of fiction has won her large and enthusiastic audiences in both England and the United States. Her most all-around successful novel of recent years was *Cluny Brown,* the story of a parlormaid whose avocation was plumbing and whose unconventional but charming behavior won her a distinguished Polish author for a husband. The book was a best seller and was made into a motion picture. Her more ambitious novel of social life in England from the last days of the Victorian age to modern times, *Britannia Mews,* was also made into a motion picture. Every one of her recent novels has had good reviews and good sales. The secret of her success may well be, as the London *Times Literary Supplement* pointed out in 1953, that her writing "shows no trace of her own labour, so that she seems to find no difficulty in putting into words precisely what she wishes to say. What she has to tell is nothing very profound: it is simply a first-rate narrative. For hers is the most fundamental of the literary arts, the art of the confident and experienced story-teller; and her self-confidence is catching."

ADDITIONAL WORKS: Cluny Brown, 1944; Britannia Mews, 1946; The Foolish Gentlewoman, 1948; Lise Lillywhite, 1951; The Gipsy in the Parlour, 1954.

ABOUT: New York Herald Tribune Book Review October 7, 1951; New York Times Book Review October 13, 1946.

SHAW, GEORGE BERNARD (July 26, 1856-November 2, 1950). For biographical sketch and list of earlier works and references, see TWENTIETH CENTURY AUTHORS, 1942.

* * *

George Bernard Shaw died at his home at Ayot St. Lawrence at ninety-four. Seven weeks earlier he had broken his thigh in a fall, while cutting the limb off a tree; the shock activated a latent kidney-bladder infection, and it was from the effects of this that he died. Following the death of his wife in 1943 there had been little change in his life; he seldom left Ayot St. Lawrence, but continued to write and carry on his normal activities.

His ninetieth birthday occasioned international celebration. A dinner in New York City assembled many notable figures and launched the publication of *G.B.S. 90,* a collection of tributes and studies of various aspects of this many-faceted man. *Buoyant Billions,* his last full-length play, was produced in Zurich in 1948 "before a respectful if uncomprehending audience." In 1949 he published *Sixteen Self-Sketches,* which Hesketh Pearson believes to be "the only example in history of a readable book by a nonagenarian." He began a new play just before his

ninety-second birthday, and was said to be working on a "light comedy" up to the time of the accident which resulted in his death.

Shaw's interest was always primarily in what Maurice Colbourne has called his "hobbies"—his economic and political theories, creative evolution, spelling reforms, vegetarianism, etc.—rather than in the plays through which he sought to give these ideas to a wide public. His pose of the arrogant, self-advertising clown, distressing to many friends and target for enemies, may well have been, as Eric Bentley believes, "a deliberate strategy in an utterly altruistic struggle" to better the world by gaining audience for his ideas. And if as he grew older he assumed the stature of an institution, it was not, William Irvine has pointed out, because Shaw grew more worldly but "because the world has become more Shavian."

The transition from the "well-made" Victorian play to the theatre of ideas was aided at the turn of the century by Shaw's critical attacks on fashionable drama and his championship of Ibsen in England, as well as by his own plays, which startled early audiences by applying classical techniques to modern subjects. Pearson has said: "He gave back mind to the drama, awakened the social conscience of his age, made entertainment serve the cause of religion, proved that historical figures are as human and interesting as our own contemporaries, and recreated in the theatre what had long been absent from it: an atmosphere of intelligent gaiety and good-fellowship."

Few public figures have been the subject of as much criticism, analysis, explanation, speculation, description as Bernard Shaw. As John Mason Brown has said, "This astonishing Mr. Shaw has been greater than anything even he has written." But the playwright himself wrote: "I have had no heroic adventures. Things have not happened to me: on the contrary it is I who have happened to them; and all my happenings have taken the form of books and plays. Read them, or spectate them; and you have my whole story."

After Shaw's death an effort to raise funds for the conversion of his home to a public memorial failed to win popular support, and the property at Ayot St. Lawrence eventually passed into private hands.

ADDITIONAL WORKS: Everybody's Political What's What? 1944; Selected Novels, 1946; The Crime of Imprisonment, 1946; Ellen Terry and Bernard Shaw: A Correspondence (ed. C. St. John) 1949; Shaw on Vivisection (ed. G. H. Bowker) 1949; Sixteen Self-Sketches, 1949; Buoyant Billions: A Comedy of No Manners in Prose, 1950;

London Music in 1888-89, 1951; Bernard Shaw and Mrs. Patrick Campbell: Their Correspondence (ed. A. Dent) 1952.

ABOUT: Bentley, E. R. Bernard Shaw; Brown, J. M. Seeing Things; Clarke, W. George Bernard Shaw: An Appreciation and Interpretation; Fuller, E. George Bernard Shaw; Gregory, Isabella, Lady Gregory's Journals, 1916-1930; Irvine, W. The Universe of G. B. S.; Joad, C. E. M. Shaw; Kronenberger, L. (ed.) George Bernard Shaw: A Critical Survey; Laing, A. M. (ed.) In Praise of Bernard Shaw; MacCarthy, D. Shaw; MacCarthy, D. Shaw's Plays in Review; Patch, B. E. Thirty Years with George Bernard Shaw; Pearson, H. G. B. S.: A Postscript; Shaw, G. B. Sixteen Self-Sketches; Ward, A. C. Bernard Shaw; Wilson, E. The Triple Thinkers; Winsten, S. Days With Bernard Shaw; Winsten, S. (ed.) G. B. S. 90: Aspects of Bernard Shaw's Life and Work; Winsten, S. Shaw's Corner; American Mercury January 1946; The Christian Science Monitor October 8, 1949; Current Biography 1944; Fortnightly February 1953; London Times November 3, 1950; Nation July 27, 1946; New Statesman and Nation November 18, 1950; New York Times February 16, 1947, August 29, 1948, November 2, 1950; New Yorker July 31, 1948, April 14, 1951; Nineteenth Century August 1946; Saturday Review of Literature November 18, 1950; Spectator November 10, 1950; Theatre Arts April 1948, January 1953; Time November 13, 1950; Publishers' Weekly June 15, 1946, August 3, 1946. Bibliography—Ward, A. C. Bernard Shaw (Bibliographical Series of Supplements to British Book News).

SHAW, IRWIN (1913-). For autobiographical sketch and list of earlier works and references, see TWENTIETH CENTURY AUTHORS, 1942.

* * *

Irwin Shaw writes from Paris: "During the war I served in Africa, England, France, and Germany. After the war, produced two plays, *The Assassins* and, with Peter Viertel, *The Survivors*. Both failed. In the field of the novel I've published *The Young Lions* and *The Troubled Air*. In addition I've published four books of short stories. A short story of mine 'Walking Wounded' won the O. Henry Memorial Prize in 1944.

"I'm married, have one son, now [December 1952] aged nearly three, and am at present living in Europe."

Irwin Shaw's long-awaited first novel, *The Young Lions*, was one of the most important American novels to come out of World War II. It was widely read and widely criticized —largely, perhaps, because so much had been expected from Shaw on the promise of his short stories and plays. Few readers questioned the impressiveness, the compassion, and the eloquence of the novel. What was found faulty, however, was its loose structure, the abstract and (to some readers) contrived symbolism of the three leading char-

acters—the New York intellectual-liberal, the American Jew, and the Nazi soldier—and the essentially shallow and oversimplified presentation of profound social and moral ideas. "Mr. Shaw," Edward Weeks wrote of the book in the *Atlantic*, "portrays his characters from the outside, and his brush, though lively enough, paints in bold outline and often in conventional colors." The most severe indictment of *The Young Lions* is John Aldridge's: "Everything about the book has an air of prefabrication and contrivance. . . . The result is not a novel in the true sense but a piece of propaganda designed to give us not a man but a social problem."

Less sprawling in its structure and scope than *The Young Lions*, though equally important in its theme, was *The Troubled Air*, which considers the dilemma of a well-meaning American liberal faced, on the one hand, with the threat to civil liberties of witch-hunting investigations and, on the other hand, with an equally sinister threat from the Communists themselves. Lionel Trilling found that however admirable the political motives behind it, *The Troubled Air* "gives little pleasure as a work of fiction." Still, Trilling feels, it is an interesting book, as all of Shaw's work has been interesting, because "he always *does* observe and always *does* feel, and even when he is facile in observation and sentiment he is not insincere. And . . . he has established himself in a position which guarantees at least the historical or sociological or cultural interest of whatever he writes."

ADDITIONAL WORKS: Sons and Soldiers (play) 1944; The Assassin (play) 1946; Act of Faith, and Other Stories, 1946; The Young Lions, 1948; Mixed Company (short stories) 1950; Report on Israel, 1950; The Troubled Air, 1951.

ABOUT: Aldridge, J. After the Lost Generation; Commentary December 1948; Current Biography 1942; New York Herald Tribune Book Review October 7, 1951; Saturday Review of Literature February 12, 1949, June 9, 1951.

SHAW, THOMAS EDWARD. See LAWRENCE, T. E.

SHEARING, JOSEPH. See LONG, G. M. V. C.

SHEDD, MARGARET COCHRAN (1900-), American novelist and short story writer, writes: "Born in Urumia, Persia, where my parents, and my grandparents before that, were Presbyterian missionaries. My childhood was more than usually happy because it was free, and so it remains in my memory set there far away and lovely in the dark frame of the violence which came immediately after I was sent away to United States for school—the First World War  which, for that part of the world, meant massacre by the Kurds and Turks, death of my parents, and extermination of the native people that I had grown up with and loved, and destruction of the place which had been our family home. I believe this search for another home has motivated much of my writing. Living in Persia also gave me the respect for bi-linguality, and, retroactively, some understanding of its effect on a writer and on writing. This probably motivates the work I am presently doing in Mexico.

"I was educated in the United States, went to Stanford University. In 1931 I began to write. At that time we (my husband, Oliver Michael Kisich, one child, and I) lived in the deep bush in British Honduras. There was nothing at all for me to do. Writing seemed a better alternative. The first piece I wrote was for *Theatre Arts* magazine, and it was accepted; and so, with this little encouragement, the thing began which has been happening to me for twenty-two years now—the certainty that life without writing doesn't amount to much and that conversely, the life of a writer is the happiest there is. I wrote a first book, about British Honduras and its lonely, terrible and beautiful jungles, under contract to a publishing house which went broke before the book was published. I then wrote my first novel, *Hurricane Caye,* without contract and in great discouragement, and it was published in 1941. Meantime we had been living in Central America and the West Indies as much as we had in the United States. Bringing up children (three total) in primitive places does not leave much time for writing. I had got into short stories, which in many ways are the medium I love most of all.

"The Latin countries became a substitute for the childhood home I lost, perhaps because the people are very lovable, maybe because of the multitude of dogs barking at night or because roofs are flat and usable, both in Persia and in these countries. Anyway in 1950 I got interested in working with Mexican and American writers in a bi-lingual writing enterprise. I am presently Director of Centro Mexicano de Escritores, which is largely sponsored by the Rockefeller Foundation. This takes about half the year. We have both creative writers, including some of the best in Mexico, and research fellows. The Centro is presently expanding into some experiment in the theatre and into bi-lingual publishing.

"However, the main thing for me remains my own writing. I am presently [1953] engaged in short stories, with a novel projected for next year. I might add to the above that precisely because I had lived so much outside the United States, I used my last novel, *Return to the Beach,* to explore what may be called, in cliché, the American heritage. Living half time out of the United States gives me an especial appreciation of my own country, maybe; anyway I wanted very much to understand what it is we believe in as Americans. My own ancestors were involved in every war and every westward push America has had. I wanted to know what they and I believed and believe in."

PRINCIPAL WORKS: Hurricane Caye, 1942; Inherit the Earth, 1945; Return to the Beach, 1950.

ABOUT: Warfel, H. R. American Novelists of Today.

SHEEAN, VINCENT (December 5, 1899-   ). For biographical sketch and list of earlier works and references, see TWENTIETH CENTURY AUTHORS, 1942.

* * *

Vincent Sheean was an intelligence officer in the United States Air Corps during World War II. He served with Allied forces in the North African and Italian landings and was then sent on to the Far East to report on B-29 operations. On this mission he visited India for the first time and was so deeply moved by the country and its people that he made it the scene and the subject of some of his later books. Upon his return from the East, Sheean was released from the service and began an assignment as war correspondent for *Red Book* magazine. In this capacity he covered the last phase of the war. When the war ended, Sheean returned to the United States and covered the organizing of the United Nations at the San Francisco conference in June 1945. His wartime experiences are reported in *This House Against This House.*

Since then Sheean has written a variety of books—novels, memoirs, and biography. An earnest and serious writer, he has not matched the success of his earlier and memorable *Personal History* and *Not Peace But a Sword.* His later books have been criticized for loquaciousness and sometimes pretentiousness.

Walter Millis' comment upon *This House Against This House* was characteristic of much critical writing on him: "The reporting is superb. The philosophy, on the other hand, seems disjointed and sometimes a little tedious, showing a tendency to mistake a rich prose style, a wealth of allusion and a good deal of at least dubious history for essential content. A little too much of that, and one begins to run into the law of diminishing returns."

Sheean is as his best as a reporter—sensitive, subjective yet sufficiently objective to give a vivid and generally accurate account. His biography of Gandhi, for example, was as deeply revealing of Sheean's own progress to faith as it was of the spiritual life of the Indian leader. Many reviewers commented upon Sheean's remarkable insights into Hinduism and the sympathy of his approach to his subject. In his novels, however, these same qualities present difficulties, slowing down the action with "philosophical excursions." *Rage of Soul*, which deals with the impact of Indian mysticism upon a sophisticated American couple, was described by F. H. Bullock in the New York *Herald Tribune* as an "effort to present esoteric ideas in an attractive fashion with not altogether successful results."

ADDITIONAL WORKS: Between the Thunder and the Sun, 1943; This House Against This House, 1946; A Certain Rich Man (novel) 1947; Lead, Kindly Light, 1949; Indigo Bunting: A Memoir of Edna St. Vincent Millay, 1951; Rage of Soul (novel) 1952; Thomas Jefferson (juvenile) 1953; Lilly (novel) 1954; Mahatma Gandhi, 1955.

ABOUT: Sheean, V. Between the Thunder and the Sun, This House Against This House; New York Herald Tribune Book Review July 31, 1949; Saturday Review of Literature July 16, 1949.

SHEEN, FULTON JOHN, Bishop (May 8, 1895-), American Catholic cleric and apologist, was born in El Paso, Tex., the son  of Newton Morris Sheen and Delia (Fulton) Sheen. His name was Peter at baptism, but he took the name of John at the time of confirmation and then, later on, adopted his mother's maiden name as his first name. When he was still a small child, the family moved to Peoria, Ill., where Sheen attended St. Mary's School and Spalding Institute. In 1917 he took a B.A. at St. Viator College in Kankakee, Ill., an M.A. there in 1919, and went on to St. Paul (Minn.) Seminary. In 1919 he was ordained a priest for the Diocese of Peoria. At the Catholic University of America he received two theological degrees, S.T.B. and J.C.B., and took his Ph.D. at Louvain University, Belgium, in 1923. In 1934 he was appointed Papal Chamberlain with the title of Very Reverend Monsignor, being raised to the title of Right Reverend Monsignor the following year, and becoming a Bishop in 1951 (Titular Bishop of Caesariana and Auxiliary to the Archbishop of New York).

A teacher at the Catholic University of America in Washington, D.C., from 1926 to 1950, the winner of many medals and prizes, the recipient of honorary degrees, Sheen preached from 1930 to 1945 on the Catholic Hour each Sunday over N.B.C., and from 1931 to 1945 also preached at St. Patrick's Cathedral, New York City. He now conducts a popular radio and television program called "Life Is Worth Living." He is a contributor to *Commonweal, America,* and *New Scholasticism,* and the author of more than one book each year since 1925. Sheen has been responsible for the conversion of many prominent people, among them Heywood Broun, Clare Boothe Luce, Grace Moore, Fritz Kreisler. He has been called "the most persuasive speaker for Roman Catholicism in America today." In 1950 he became national director of the Society for the Propagation of the Faith, an international organization which allocates funds to Catholic missionaries.

One of Sheen's chief concerns is the subject of Communism, which he considers the primary enemy of religion and of mankind. During the Spanish Civil War he supported Franco, and before World War II denounced any alliance with Soviet Russia, opposing aid to that country during the war. One of his books dealing with this subject appeared in 1948, *Communism and the Conscience of the West.* The *Canadian Forum* found its picture of liberalism a "caricature" and wondered "whether the author's real enemy is not this liberalism rather than the Communism which forms part of the title of the book"; but the New York *Times* reported it "an exceedingly careful and accurate analysis."

Of *Peace of Soul* the Chicago *Sun* said, "The writing is clear and forceful, the logic frequently brilliant, but the intellectual workout brooks no distractions. This is a rewarding experience for any reader." One of Sheen's many collections of broadcast sermons, *Life Is Worth Living* (1953), is "lightened by wonderful humor and a touch of beauty," according to the Chicago *Sunday*

Tribune. "Complex ideas are reduced to living room conversation, so that any thoughtful member of the family may understand them."

A remarkably handsome man, with a compelling voice and searching gray eyes, Sheen is a popular speaker as well as writer.

PRINCIPAL WORKS: God and Intelligence in Modern Philosophy, 1925; Religion without God, 1928; The Life of All Living, 1929; The Divine Romance (rev. ed.) 1930; Old Errors and New Labels, 1931; Moods and Truths, 1932; Way of the Cross, 1933; Seven Last Words, 1933; Hymn of the Conquered, 1933; The Eternal Galilean, 1934; Philosophy of Science, 1934; The Mystical Body of Christ, 1935; Calvary and the Mass, 1936; The Moral Universe, 1936; The Cross and the Beatitudes, 1937; Communism, Opium of the People, 1937; The Cross and the Crisis, 1938; Liberty, Equality and Fraternity, 1938; Rainbow of Sorrow, 1938; Victory over Vice, 1939; Freedom under God, 1940; Whence Come Wars, 1940; Seven Virtues, 1940; War and Guilt, 1941; Declaration of Independence, 1941; For God and Country, 1941; God and War, 1942; Peace, 1942; Armor of God, 1943; Crisis in Christendom, 1943; Divine Verdict, 1943; Philosophies at War, 1943; Seven Pillars of Peace, 1944; Love One Another, 1944; Seven Words to the Cross, 1944; You, 1945; Seven Words of Jesus and Mary, 1945; Preface to Religion, 1946; Characters of the Passion, 1946; Jesus, Son of Mary, 1947; Light Your Lamps, 1947; Communism and the Conscience of the West, 1948; Philosophy of Religion, 1948; The Modern Soul in Search of God, 1948; The Love that Waits for You, 1949; Peace of Soul, 1949; Lift Up Your Heart, 1950; Three to Get Married, 1951; The World's First Love, 1952; The Seven Last Words, 1952; Life Is Worth Living, 1953, second series, 1954; The Way to Happiness, 1954; The Way to Inner Peace, 1955.

ABOUT: Adams, J. C. More Than Money; Baker, G. I Had to Know; Hoehn, M. A. (ed.) Catholic Authors, I; Nizer, L. Between You and Me; Catholic Library World April 1941; Catholic World September 1938; Collier's January 24, 1953; Current Biography 1951; Life April 6, 1953; New Republic February 1, 1939; New York Herald Tribune September 14, 1950, November 22, 1950; New York Times September 13, 1950, September 14, 1950; Reader's Digest June 1947; Scribner's Magazine May 1941; Theatre Arts December 1952; Time March 11, 1940, April 18, 1949, April 14, 1952.

SHELDON, CHARLES MONROE (February 26, 1857-February 24, 1946). For biographical sketch and list of works and references, see TWENTIETH CENTURY AUTHORS, 1942.

* * *

Charles M. Sheldon died at a hospital in Topeka, Kans., as the result of a cerebral hemorrhage, two days before his eighty-ninth birthday.

The world sale of his tract-novel *In His Steps*, generally estimated as upwards of 30,000,000, probably did not exceed 6,000,000 according to Frank Luther Mott, authority

on "best-sellers." Mott has said of the book that "as literature it is nothing less than amateurish; as a social document, it has first-rate importance." The *Christian Century* called Sheldon "one of the most effective Christian publicists this country has ever known."

ABOUT: Henrichs, H. F. (ed.) In His Steps Today by C. M. Sheldon (memorial ed.) 1948; Mott, F. L. Golden Multitudes; Christian Century March 13, 1946; National Cyclopedia of American Biography (1948); New York Times February 25, March 10, 1946; Publishers' Weekly March 2, 1946.

SHELDON, EDWARD BREWSTER (February 4, 1886-April 1, 1946). For biographical sketch and list of works and references, see TWENTIETH CENTURY AUTHORS, 1942.

* * *

Edward Sheldon died of coronary thrombosis, at his home in New York City, at sixty. His mother, who died in 1949, bequeathed $100,000 for the establishment of a Sheldon Memorial theatre collection at the Harvard University library.

The playwright who, in his youth, was "a man of exceptional talent, of brilliant mentality, of striking personality (in the words of Dorothy Black Hamill), was eventually rendered blind and almost completely paralyzed by the arthritis which struck him in his early thirties. Yet from his bed in his penthouse apartment in New York he wielded an exceptionally powerful influence through his advice and collaboration with his many friends in the literary and theatre world.

"All who knew him," Anne Morrow Lindbergh has said, "were fired by his sustained gallantry, were quickened by the unquenchable flame of his spirit, were overcome by his princely prodigality of heart. And you had only to walk into his room to be won by his chivalrous courtesy."

ABOUT: Clark, B. H. Intimate Portraits; Lotz, P. H. (ed.) Unused Alibis; National Cyclopedia of American Biography (1948); London Times April 13, 1946; New York Times April 2, 1946; Reader's Digest January 1947.

SHELLABARGER, SAMUEL (May 18, 1888-March 21, 1954), American biographer and novelist, died at his home in Princeton, N.J., of a heart attack. Several months before his death, he wrote to the editors of this volume: "I was born in Washington, D.C., and, since my parents died during my infancy, was brought up there in the house of my paternal grandfather, the Hon. Samuel Shellabarger, a member of Congress during the Civil War, for a time Minister to

Portugal, and a well-known lawyer. My grandfather was born in 1817 and my grandmother in 1828, so that, during my boyhood, I was especially under the influence of that generation with its traditional standards and with its memories which extended to the early days of the Republic. I consider this influence paramount in my life.

"Two events of my youth are perhaps worth recording because they helped to determine my later interests. As a boy of twelve, I attended a performance of Sardou's *Dante,* with Sir Henry Irving in the title role. For some reason or other, I decided then, if possible, to become a writer; and, unlike most boyish enthusiasms, this remained constant throughout the years. Afterwards, in 1903, I first toured Europe; and the impressions of London, Paris, and Rome at the turn of the century became indelible in my mind and have left a nostalgia for the past which has colored my historical writing.

"Educated at private schools, I graduated from Princeton in 1909, and, having chosen the academic profession, set out for Germany in order to study for a doctor's degree. A couple of years later, however, it seemed more expedient to obtain this degree in America, and I entered the graduate school at Harvard in 1911.

"From 1914 until 1917, I was an instructor in English at Princeton. During the First World War, I served in the Ordnance and Military Intelligence and spent a year at the end of the war as assistant military attaché to our legation in Stockholm. Upon returning to Princeton, I spent the next four years as assistant professor in English. In 1922, I resigned from the university and moved with my family to Lausanne, Switzerland, where I remained for the ensuing five years, occupied with writing and travel. Two additional years were spent in France and England. During this period, I wrote a biography, *The Chevalier Bayard,* and a couple of novels.

"Upon returning to America in 1931, we resided for a while in Washington, then settled in Princeton, where I continued for the next seven years to write biography and fiction: the life of Lord Chesterfield, a number of mystery stories and romances. In 1938, I was appointed headmaster of the Columbus School for Girls in Columbus, Ohio. I have always been interested in education and I

consider the eight years I spent there as among the most creative and valuable of my life. My duties, however, did not prevent continued writing. It was during this period that I wrote *Captain from Castile.* I returned to Princeton in 1946. Since then I have written two novels: *Prince of Foxes* and *The King's Cavalier.* I am now engaged on another historical novel laid in the eighteenth century.

"In 1915, I married Vivan G. L. Borg, a native of Sweden. We have had two sons and two daughters. My first son, Robert, died in infancy. My second son, John Eric, was killed in World War II. My eldest daughter, Ingrid Rivera, married William H. Rea of Pittsburgh; and her sister, Marianne Jenner, married John Jeppson of Worcester, Mass. I have now five grandchildren. I am an Episcopalian and a Republican. During the 1952 campaign, I was chairman of Princeton Citizens for Eisenhower-Nixon."

* * *

Samuel Shellabarger, whom the New York *Times* called "one of the most popular historical novelists of modern times," earned more than $1,500,000 from the four historical novels he wrote in the nine years before his death. Motion pictures were made of two of these books—*Captain from Castile* and *Prince of Foxes.* Long before he turned to writing popular fiction, Shellabarger had won critical acclaim for his scholarly biographies of Lord Chesterfield and the Chevalier Bayard. He carried over to his novels some of the habits of meticulous research which he had acquired in his academic work, and the swashbuckling, glamorous, and romantic stories had the respect of historians and, for all readers, as Lillian De La Torre wrote, afforded "a rich and reliable measure of the pleasure proper to the historical novel, the pleasure of living vicariously in a past time." His gifts, Harrison Smith remarked in the *Saturday Review,* "are commensurate with the task he sets for himself. His narrative style is lively and simple; his characters, although they are necessarily stereotyped, are not period costumes with sawdust inside, but something resembling flesh and blood."

PRINCIPAL WORKS: *Biography*—The Chevalier Bayard, 1928; Lord Chesterfield, 1935. *Novels*—Captain from Castile, 1945; Prince of Foxes, 1947; The King's Cavalier, 1950; Lord Vanity, 1953.

ABOUT: Current Biography 1945; New York Herald Tribune Book Review December 9, 1951, October 11, 1953; New York Times March 22, 1954; New York Times Book Review July 27, 1947.

SHEPARD, BENJAMIN HENRY JESSE FRANCIS. See GRIERSON, F.

SHEPARD, ODELL (July 22, 1884-   ).
For biographical sketch and list of earlier
works and references, see TWENTIETH
CENTURY AUTHORS, 1942.

* * *

Odell Shepard was elected Lieutenant Governor of Connecticut in 1940, but was defeated for re-election in 1942. In 1946, after
twenty-five years of teaching there, he resigned from Trinity College, charging that
the new president of the college had refused
to grant him a leave of absence. Since then
Shepard, in collaboration with his son Willard
O. Shepard, has written two highly praised
historical novels. The first of these, *Holdfast
Gaines,* covered the period of the American
Revolution to the early 1800's, its hero being
a young Indian. Reviewers found the book
"an unusually ambitious and unhackneyed
novel, combining conscientious research with
"a feeling for the poetic turbulence" of the
period (Herbert Lyons, in the New York
Times). The Shepards' second collaboration
was an account of the War of Jenkins' Ear,
told from the point of view of the eighteenth
century English gentleman-of-letters Horace
Walpole—an elaborate and fanciful framework for a richly detailed historical narrative.
Shepard lives in Waterford, Conn.

ADDITIONAL WORKS: *With W. O. Shepard—*
Holdfast Gaines, 1949; Jenkins' Ear: A Narrative
Attributed to Horace Walpole, 1951.
ABOUT: Time May 13, 1946.

**SHERIDAN, Mrs. CLARE CONSUELO
(FREWEN)** (1885-   ). For biographical sketch and list of earlier works and
references, see TWENTIETH CENTURY
AUTHORS, 1942.

* * *

Clare Sheridan lived in Galway, Eire, for
several years after World War II. In 1954
she was living in Algeria. She also maintains a home in London. She has published
little in recent years. In 1943 *My Crowded
Sanctuary,* an informal collection of memoirs
and personal reflections, revealed what the
London *Times Literary Supplement* described
as the "wayward and vivid expression of an
engaging personality." The book reflected
Mrs. Sheridan's many lively interests, from
gardening to spiritualism. The *Times* wrote:
"Events, spiritual adventures, descriptions,
meditations, recollections follow one another
pell-mell in these pages, but always with
instinctive artistry." Mrs. Sheridan's son
Richard died shortly before the outbreak of
World War II. She has a daughter.

ADDITIONAL WORKS: The Mask, 1942; My
Crowded Sanctuary, 1945.
ABOUT: Sheridan, C. My Crowded Sanctuary.

SHERMAN, STUART PRATT (October
1, 1881-August 21, 1926). For biographical sketch and list of works and
references, see TWENTIETH CENTURY
AUTHORS, 1942.

SHERRIFF, ROBERT CEDRIC (June 6,
1896-   ). For biographical sketch and
list of earlier works and references, see
TWENTIETH CENTURY AUTHORS, 1942.

* * *

In recent years R. C. Sherriff has written
a number of motion picture scenarios—including the screen adaptations of F. L.
Green's powerful novel *Odd Man Out* and
of W. S. Maugham's short stories in *Quartet.*
He has also written several novels and stage
plays. Of his recent plays, *Home at Seven*
was the most successful and had a long run
in London.

In 1950 Sherriff announced that he was
refusing an offer of $10,000 to write a script
for Hollywood because British income taxes
would absorb all but a fraction of the sum:
"It didn't seem worth while putting in four
or five months of very hard work for a sum
I could make as a jobbing gardener—or collecting refuse in cans, for that matter." He
said that he would continue to write for only
four months of the year and would farm for
the rest of the year. Sherriff has a home in
Surrey and a farm in Devon.

ADDITIONAL WORKS: *Novels*—Chedworth, 1944;
Another Year, 1948; King John's Treasure, 1954.
Plays—Miss Mabel, 1949; Quartet (screen-play)
1949; Home at Seven, 1950; The White Carnation,
1953.
ABOUT: Christian Science Monitor Magazine
July 29, 1950; Time March 27, 1950.

SHERWOOD, ROBERT EMMET (April
4, 1896-   ). For biographical sketch and
list of earlier works and references, see
TWENTIETH CENTURY AUTHORS, 1942.

* * *

A three-time winner of the Pulitzer prize
for drama, Robert E. Sherwood received his
fourth Pulitzer prize, this time in history, in
1949 for his masterful study *Roosevelt and
Hopkins: An Intimate History.* This work
developed out of a long and brilliant association between Sherwood and President Franklin D. Roosevelt, which began in 1940 when
Sherwood campaigned for him. In the war
years which followed, Sherwood was an unofficial member of the White House staff.
He headed the overseas branch of the Office
of War Information and served for a time
as special assistant to the Secretary of War
and the Secretary of the Navy. He is credited

with writing many of Roosevelt's finest speeches (along with Roosevelt himself and Judge Samuel Rosenman). After the end of the war and the deaths of Roosevelt and Harry Hopkins, Sherwood began work on the forty filing cases of papers left by the latter. "I had to present as accurately as possible the extraordinary drama of those lives and of that tremendous period," he said. He spent some thirty months of steady, full-time work on the book and published it as a long (nearly 1,000 pages) and serious work, with no eye to the popular market. To his surprise, it became a best-seller, proving to be not only the most intimate and illuminating study of the late President and his administration yet published, but also an engrossing and dramatic human portrait. John Mason Brown called it "his finest drama and the most titanic in scale he has so far written." Its richness, Henry Steele Commager wrote in the New York *Times*, "will be the delight of the journalist and the arsenal of the historian." In addition to the Pulitzer prize, the book received the Bancroft prize for distinguished writing in American history, was named Book of the Year by the *Saturday Review of Literature*, and received the Gutenberg award of the Book Manufacturers' Institute.

To relax after the strenuous work involved in *Roosevelt and Hopkins*, Sherwood collaborated with Irving Berlin and Moss Hart in writing the musical comedy *Miss Liberty*. He also completed and prepared for Broadway production the last play by Philip Barry (who died in 1949), *Second Threshold*. His scenario for the motion picture *The Best Years of Our Lives* won an Academy award. Recently Sherwood has been writing for television.

ADDITIONAL WORKS: Roosevelt and Hopkins: An Intimate History, 1948; (ed.) Barry, P. Second Threshold, 1951.

ABOUT: Brown, J. M. Still Seeing Things; Fisher, D. C. American Portraits; Nizer, L. Between You and Me; Collier's April 30, 1949; New York Times Book Review February 13, 1949; Saturday Review of Literature October 23, 1948.

*SHIEL, MATTHEW PHIPPS (July 21, 1865-February 17, 1947). For autobiographical sketch and list of earlier works and references, see TWENTIETH CENTURY AUTHORS, 1942.

* * *

M. P. Shiel died at a hospital at Chichester, England, at eighty-one. He had lived at Horsham, Sussex, for several years.

The New Testament study *Jesus*, of which he wrote in TWENTIETH CENTURY AUTHORS,

* shēl

1942, was finished in Sepember 1946; between that time and his death six months later half the manuscript was "mysteriously mislaid," according to his biographer, A. Reynolds Morse. An error in the earlier TWENTIETH CENTURY AUTHORS sketch is pointed out by Morse: Shiel's first wife was Carolina Garcia Gomez, who died about five years after their marriage; about fifteen years later he married Mrs. Lydia (Fawley) Jewson, from whom he separated in 1929.

There are admirers of his work who consider Shiel "one of the greatest writers ever to use the English language." Certainly his work deserves to be more widely known than it is. E. M. Benson called his novels "a glorious excursion into the incredible," and a Boston *Transcript* reviewer observed, "Here is the sheer abandon of an imagination that is hypnotic, that sweeps the reader along on a winging brilliancy of phrasing that is as irresistible as magic."

The London *Times* has said that "he tossed the world about in his dreams, not with a juggler's detachment, but with a sense now bitter, now exultant, of the tragedy and splendour that enwrap the *mysterium tremendum* of existence. At his slacker moments a 'shocker,' perhaps, at his tenser, poet, seer, and 'flaming genius,' as the late Sir Hugh Walpole once said of him."

ADDITIONAL WORKS: Above All Else, 1943; Best Short Stories (ed. J. Gawsworth) 1948; Science, Life and Literature, 1950.

ABOUT: Morse, A. R. Works of M. P. Shiel; Shiel, M. P. Science, Life, and Literature (foreword by J. Gawsworth); London Times February 20, 1947; New York Times February 18, 1947; Time June 30, 1947.

SHIELS, GEORGE (1886-September 19, 1949), Irish playwright, only once saw a performance of one of his plays. It was from an invalid chair in the wing of the Belfast Opera House that he saw *Professor Tim* acted. But he frequently listened to broadcasts of his works. One of the most prolific dramatists writing for the Abbey Theatre, Shiels had his first effort, a  one-act comedy, *Bedmates,* accepted by the Irish group in 1921. Then came a succession of plays that were immediate and great successes. The audience came to his bright and simple comedies, as well as to the more serious work of his last period, in greater numbers than even to O'Casey's early masterpieces on

Dublin slum life. Though perhaps the only man who wrote plays especially for the Abbey Theatre and its company, Shiels never visited either the Abbey or Dublin.

In Canada in 1913 he received an injury in a Canadian railway accident that crippled him for life; yet his cheerful attitude did not change. Returning from Canada, he wrote short stories based on his experiences there. When the stories succeeded, he decided to become a playwright.

Popular with comedies, Shiels turned to serious topics in his last phase as a dramatist; seriousness is reflected in *The Rugged Path* and *The Summit*, the fifteenth and sixteenth plays which he wrote for the Abbey Theatre. Produced in 1940, *The Rugged Path*, which deals with peasant conflict and murder, ran eight weeks at the Abbey despite the theatre's policy at the time of weekly or fortnightly runs. A year later the author wrote a sequel in *The Summit*, which was slightly less successful. Both plays have been frequently revived. Published together in 1942, these two plays, "so far as an alien can judge," wrote *Books*, "are almost painfully truthful, and also rich in character types. But they are more restricted in appeal than the plays which started the Abbey on its career, and they are far less infused with poetry or imagination."

After a long illness Shiels died in Ballymoney, Northern Ireland, at the age of sixty-three.

PRINCIPAL WORKS: Bedmates, 1922; Professor Tim, and Paul Twyning, 1927; Two Irish Plays: Mountain Dew, and Cartney and Kevney, 1930; New Gossoon, 1936; Passing Day, and The Jailbird, 1937; The Rugged Path, and The Summit, 1942; Fort Field, 1947; Grogan and the Ferret, 1947.

ABOUT: New York Times September 21, 1949.

SHIRER, WILLIAM LAWRENCE

(February 23, 1904-   ), American journalist and novelist, was born in Chicago, the son of Seward Smith Shirer and Bessie Josephine (Tanner) Shirer. His father was a lawyer and at one time an assistant U.S. district attorney. Shirer attended Coe College in Cedar Rapids, Iowa, and in 1925 received his degree. Determining upon graduation to spend some time in Europe, he borrowed funds and sailed from Montreal on a cattle-boat. The same year he obtained a job writing

* shīr′ĕr

906

copy for the Paris edition of the Chicago *Tribune*, and the next year became foreign correspondent for that paper, covering various European capitals (1926-33). While in Paris he took courses at the Collège de France in European history.

A skiing accident in the Alps in 1932 cost Shirer the loss of sight in one eye and he temporarily left the newspaper work to spend the year 1933 in free-lance writing, while living on the Catalan coast of Spain. During this period he wrote his autobiography, which he destroyed, and a novel on the Indian civil disobedience movement—he had met Gandhi in India. This novel has not been published. He returned to Paris in 1934 to work on the New York *Herald*, and then went to Berlin as correspondent for the Universal News Service (1935-37). Up to 1937 he had been stationed in Paris, London, Berlin, Vienna, Geneva, Rome, the Balkans, the Near East and India. During that period he was a newspaper correspondent and later, as a foreign radio correspondent (from 1937 until the end of World War II), he was stationed in Vienna, Geneva, Berlin, London, Paris, Rome, etc. Part of the time between 1941 and 1948, Shirer was a radio commentator in the United States as well as abroad.

His first and most popular book was published in 1941, *Berlin Diary*, the journal of a foreign correspondent between 1934 and 1941. The first entry in the book is January 11, 1934, when the author was vacationing in Spain; the last is December 13, 1940, written on board the ship which was bringing him back to America. "He is a man of letters," said Edward Weeks in the *Atlantic Monthly*: "He writes with the power and beauty, with the anger and pity, that comes straight from the incandescent movements he lived through. . . . He lets the evidence speak, and his stark quotation of the German headlines is one of his most skillful strokes." Max Fischer in *Commonweal* wrote: "I myself lived in Germany till the fall of 1935. . . . Reading *Berlin Diary 1934-1941*, I am of course eager to learn how the Berlin atmosphere has changed since the days of my farewell," but he found Shirer's interest in "headlines" a reflection of his being "just the typical newspaperman, whose interests are restricted to his profession. I admit he is an excellent reporter, but his book seems to me rather sterile."

Shirer's novel *Stranger Come Home* is a story about one Raymond Whitehead, a foreign correspondent who comes home to America after World War II to broadcast news analyses for the Federal Broadcasting Company. His former boss in Europe has become a vice-president of the network. The foreign correspondent gets involved in a controversy with an anti-Communist Senator named O'Brien, heading a much-publicized committee, and he is fired by "F.B.C." Shirer insisted that his characters were imaginary; but, as *Commonweal* pointed out, William L. Shirer, Columbia Broadcasting System foreign correspondent, came home to America at the close of the war to broadcast news analyses, found his former boss in Europe, Edward R. Murrow, had become vice-president in charge of news and public affairs for the network, and a controversy developed over the amount of personal opinion to be included in his broadcasts; this controversy led to Shirer's resignation. "If a reader does not live in a political vacuum," adds *Commonweal*, "he will read this book as a passionately-written, sincere polemical work."

Shirer is a member of the editorial board of *United Nations World* and a member of the French Legion of Honor. Coe College awarded him an honorary degree, LL.D., in 1941; the George Foster Peabody Award was presented to him in 1946 for his excellence in interpreting the news. Shirer married a Viennese, Theresa Stiberitz, in 1931; they have two daughters. His hobbies are puttering around his farm in Connecticut and listening to Beethoven, Mozart, and chamber music. He also likes football, the sea, mountains, Rembrandt, El Greco, and Van Gogh.

PRINCIPAL WORKS: Berlin Diary, 1941; End of a Berlin Diary, 1947; Midcentury Journey, 1952; The Challenge of Scandinavia, 1955. *Novels*—The Traitor, 1950; Stranger Come Home, 1954.

ABOUT: Murrow, E. R. This I Believe; Shirer, W. L. End of a Berlin Diary; Commonweal June 18, 1954; Current Biography 1941; National Cyclopedia of American Biography (1952); New York Herald Tribune Book Review October 8, 1950; Saturday Review of Literature September 27, 1947, May 29, 1954.

---

*SHOLOKHOV, MIKHAIL ALEKS-ANDROVICH (May 24, 1905-). For biographical sketch and list of earlier works and references, see TWENTIETH CENTURY AUTHORS, 1942.

* * *

Mikhail Sholokhov's major work, completed in 1941, *The Silent Don*, remains probably the most popular single work in Soviet literature. Sholokhov himself has received many honors, including the Stalin prize and the Order of Lenin. During World War II he wrote some war stories and sketches, but his war novel, on which he was reported work-

* shô′lŭ kôf

ing, has appeared only in fragments, and none of it has been translated into English.

On his fiftieth birthday in May 1955 Sholokov was honored by an official state celebration in Moscow. Russian newspapers and magazines printed articles about him, and an entire issue of *Literaturnaya Gazeta* was devoted to his life and work.

ADDITIONAL WORK IN ENGLISH TRANSLATION: Soviet War Stories, 1944.

ABOUT: Buck, P. N. Directions in Contemporary Literature; Spector, I. The Golden Age of Russian Literature; Struve, G. Soviet Russian Literature 1917-1950; Current Biography 1942; New York Times May 24, 1955; Time February 9, 1948.

SHORTER, CLEMENT KING (July 19, 1857-November 19, 1926). For biographical sketch and list of works and references, see TWENTIETH CENTURY AUTHORS, 1942.

SHOTWELL, JAMES THOMSON (August 6, 1874-). For biographical sketch and list of works and references, see TWENTIETH CENTURY AUTHORS, 1942.

* * *

In 1943 James T. Shotwell became chairman of the board of directors of the newly established United Nations Association, which was campaigning for the entry of the United States into a permanent world organization for collective security. He served as consultant to the U.S. Department of State in planning the various post-war meetings which led to the Dumbarton Oaks and the San Francisco conferences. His book *The Great Decision* was a lucid and judicious study of the causes of war and the plans for an international organization to prevent war. Long associated with the Carnegie Endowment for International Peace, he became its president in 1949 and its president emeritus in 1950. After more than forty years of teaching at Columbia University, he retired in 1942 as Bryce professor of international relations. He lives in New York City.

In 1954 Professor Shotwell published a volume of his collected poems, many of them expressing his strong conviction that world peace can be attained. Reviewers found the poems graceful and "written with authority." J. S. Bixler said of the volume in the *Saturday Review*, "It offers an eloquent statement of triumphant belief."

ADDITIONAL WORKS: The Great Decision, 1944; (with M. M. Laserson) Poland and Russia, 1919-1945, 1945; Balkan Mission, 1949; (with M. Salvin) Lessons on Security and Disarmament from the History of the League of Nations, 1949; Poems, 1954.

ABOUT: Current Biography 1944.

*SHRIDHARANI, KRISHNALAL JE-
THALAL** (September 16, 1911-), Indian man of letters, writes: "The only unusual thing about my
career is that through
literary pursuits I
have become a man of
two worlds; it is the
fate of high caste
Hindus to become
'twice born,' but my
rebirth has been un-
conventional. I ac-
quired some recogni-
tion as a Gujarati
(one of the major Aryan languages of India)
poet and playwright at the age of twenty
when my *The Banyan Tree* (*Vadalo*, written
in jail) came out, but by the time I was
twenty-five and in America, English, which
was my second language from kindergarten,
had become my medium of expression. Even
today, six years after the native's return,
I continue to write in English and only
occasionally in Gujarati, which gives me a
much wider reading public not only in the
English-speaking world but also in India;
even Gujaratis read English. And although
most of my books in English have been of
the non-fiction variety, the two novels I have
recently completed are in English, and I feel
as much at home in English as in my mother-
tongue while writing fiction. It is a different
story with poetry; I continue to write poems
in Gujarati and stories in English. This dual
literary nationality often makes me fall between two stools, but often enough it brings
to my English writings the flavour of the
East, and to my Gujarati writings the cerebra-
tions of the West.

"It was at the height of the Gandhian Age
in Gujarati literature and when I was eleven
that my first poem was accepted by a literary
magazine. The fact needs underscoring because my writings both in Gujarati and in
English up to 1947, the year India became
independent, echo the throbs of the new movement led by Gandhi to revive ancient springs
of emotion and to equate our heritage with
those of the proudest peoples in the West.
Not that what I wrote was propaganda and
not art. But even art became suspect in the
eye of the ruling race and the press that
printed and published my play, *A Flicker of
the Flame* (*Zabakjyot*), had to pay a heavy
security for better behaviour in future. My
novel, *I Shall Kill the Human in You* (*Insan
Mita Dunga*, a story of jail life) was pro-
scribed.

* shrid'hä rä nē   krish'nä läl

"I had the satisfaction of partly illustrating
my first published book, a poetic play; my
earlier ambition was to be a painter. At poet
Rabindranath Tagore's Santiniketan (abode
of peace) I wrote *The Suttee* (*Padmini*), a
play based on a fable from our Rajput history which dramatizes the conflict of ethical
values and arrives at a conclusion diametrical-
ly opposite to the one reached by Maurice
Maeterlinck in *Monna Vanna*. The poems
written during this period show Tagore's influence in their musical cadence if not in their
imageries.

"Thousands of miles away from Tagore's
abode of peace where gazelles moved as
freely as pupils, I had the greatest fun writing
My India, My America amidst the sky-scrap-
ing canyons which squeeze the New York
sky into narrow ribbons. Three years of
notes required two additional years of writing
down comparisons and contrasts between the
East and West in the intimate terms of my
experience. It was a deeply disturbing experience also, as the balance is slow in coming.
But the balance happily is slowly coming not
only within me but to our age whose main
problem is not dictatorship and the like but
the impact of one culture on another."

* * *

Readers of *My India, My America* will
remember that Dr. Shridharani is five feet,
five inches tall, light complexioned, has big
dark eyes, and for daily exercise practices
Shirsasan, or standing on his head for three
minutes. He is a popular lecturer in America.
In 1950, he married Sundari (Bhavnani), a
famous classical dancer of India, who runs
an art academy in New Delhi. He first came
to the United States in 1934. He toured the
country in a jallopy, and studied here at New
York University (M.A. 1935) and at Columbia University (M.S. 1936, Ph.D. 1940).

G. L. Mehta, Indian Ambassador in Washington and a writer in Gujarati, wrote of
Dr. Shridharani's first published play, *The
Banyan Tree*: "You are likely to be regarded
as a Philistine if you go to Gujarat without
reading *Vadalo*." Rear-Admiral H. E. Yar-
nell remarked of *My India, My America*: "I
have always admired two great writers for
their ability to write better in an alien language—Joseph Conrad and Lin Yutang.
Shridharani is the third on my list."

PRINCIPAL WORKS IN ENGLISH: War Without
Violence, 1939; My India, My America, 1941;
Warning to the West, 1942; The Mahatma and
the World, 1946; The Big Four of India, 1951;
(with others) The General Knowledge Encyclopedia, 1953.

ABOUT: Shridharani, K. My India, My America; Asia October 1941; Current Biography 1942.

SHUSTER, GEORGE NAUMAN (August 27, 1894-   ). For biographical sketch and list of earlier works and references, see TWENTIETH CENTURY AUTHORS, 1942.

* * *

President of Hunter College, New York, since 1939, George N. Shuster has in recent years won national and international recognition not only for his work in American higher education, but for the active part which he has taken in international education. During World War II he was an adviser to the U. S. Department of State on cultural relations, and when hostilities ended in 1945, he headed an historical commission to Germany. Also in 1945 he was an adviser to the American delegation to the London Conference on International Education, and in 1946 he was a delegate to the UNESCO conference in Paris. Since 1948 he has been chairman of the board of trustees of the Institute of International Education. Shuster is probably best known today for his part in the re-education of postwar Germany. Since 1945 he has been sent to that country on many government assignments. In 1950-51 he was Land Commissioner for Bavaria.

Shuster contributes articles to *Commonweal* and other magazines. Much of his recent writing has been concerned with the problems of freedom of thought and religion in Communist-dominated countries.

ADDITIONAL WORKS: (ed.) The World's Great Catholic Literature, 1942; (with A. Bergstrasser) Germany: A Short History, 1944; Religion Behind the Iron Curtain, 1954.

ABOUT: Finkelstein, L. (ed.) American Spiritual Autobiographies; Hoehn, M. (ed.) Catholic Authors, I; Roming, W. (ed.) A Book of Catholic Authors; Business Week April 29, 1950; Time February 28, 1944.

"SHUTE, NEVIL." See NORWAY, N. S.

SIDGWICK, ETHEL (December 20, 1877-   ). For biographical sketch and list of works and references, see TWENTIETH CENTURY AUTHORS, 1942.

* * *

Ethel Sidgwick has published no books in recent years. She lives in Oxford, England.

SIEGFRIED, ANDRÉ (April 21, 1875-   ). For biographical sketch and list of earlier works and references, see TWENTIETH CENTURY AUTHORS, 1942.

* * *

André Siegfried remained in Paris through World War II. In reply to reports of anti-American statements, he has written the editors of this volume: "I have always been a friend of the United States and have never hesitated to say so, even during the Nazi occupation." In 1944 Siegfried was elected to the French Academy. He is now honorary professor at the Collège de France. Siegfried lives in Paris and in addition to his many books, writes articles for *Figaro, Revue des Deux Mondes,* and other journals.

Siegfried's recent works include geographies and travel books, a biography of his father, and essays on contemporary life. In 1955, a full generation after his *America Comes of Age* (1927), he published a new study of American society, *America at Mid-Century.* Sharply critical of some aspects of that society, the book provoked lively discussion in the American press. Reviewers found it inaccurate in some details and "erratic in coverage." Nevertheless, they agreed that it was a valuable reflection of contemporary European attitudes toward America—"a bit too muted and wistful to be fully effective," Arthur Schlesinger Jr. wrote in the New York *Times,* "but still deeply revealing of mounting European apprehensions about the direction in which American life is moving." "His curiosity and verve have never flagged," Allen Nevins wrote of Siegfried in the *Saturday Review:* "With a first-hand knowledge of America going back nearly sixty years . . . he has imbibed the true spirit of American life and ways."

ADDITIONAL WORKS IN ENGLISH TRANSLATION: The Mediterranean, 1948; Switzerland: A Democratic Way of Life, 1950; African Journey, 1950; Nations Have Souls, 1952; The Character of Peoples, 1952; America at Mid-Century, 1955.

ABOUT: Dictionnaire Biographique Français Contemporain; Saturday Review June 11, 1955.

SIERRA. See MARTINEZ SIERRA

SIGERSON, DORA (August 16, 1866-January 16, 1918). For biographical sketch and list of works and references, see TWENTIETH CENTURY AUTHORS, 1942.

*SILLANPÄÄ, FRANS EEMIL (September 16, 1888-   ). For biographical sketch and list of works and references, see TWENTIETH CENTURY AUTHORS, 1942.

* * *

Sillanpää has written several books in Finnish in recent years, but none of these has appeared in English translation. His address is given as Helsinki.

* sĭl'län pǎ

909

*SILONE, IGNAZIO (May 1, 1900-).
For autobiographical sketch and list of earlier works and references, see TWEN-TIETH CENTURY AUTHORS, 1942.

* * *

Ignazio Silone writes from Rome: "After the liberation, Silone took an active part in Italian political life, as manager of the journal *Avanti!*, as member of the Constituent Assembly, as leader of the left wing of Italian Democratic Socialism. In 1950 he retired from political life and took up his literary activities. He is president of the Italian PEN Club, vice-president of the International PEN, member of the executive body of the International Congress for Freedom of Culture, correspondent for the American Academy of Arts and Sciences."

Silone sends the following corrections and additions to his 1942 sketch: His name was originally Secondo Tranquilli. He adopted his pseudonym to spare members of his family from Fascist persecution. After the liberation Silone took his pseudonym for his legal name. In 1944 he married the Irish writer Darina Laracy, who translated into English his novel *A Handful of Blackberries*. He speaks French, Spanish, and German.

In an autobiographical essay which he contributed to Richard Crossman's *The God That Failed*, Silone described the subtle but powerful influences that drew him into the Communist Party (he calls his joining "a conversion, a complete dedication"), and his growing disillusionment with the party and final break from it. At the conclusion of the essay, Silone reaffirms his faith in Socialism which, he writes, "has remained more alive than ever in me. In its essence, it has gone back to what it was when I first revolted against the old social order; a refusal to admit the existence of destiny, an extension of the ethical impulse from the restricted individual and family sphere to the whole domain of human activity, a need for effective brotherhood, an affirmation of the superiority of the human person over all the economic and social mechanisms which oppress him."

ADDITIONAL WORKS: And He Hid Himself (play) 1945; A Handful of Blackberries, 1953.

ABOUT: Columbia Dictionary of Modern European Literature; Crossman, R. (ed.) The God That Failed; Scott, N. A. Rehearsals of Discomposure; Slochower, H. No Voice Is Wholly Lost; Harper's November 1949; Nation August 26, 1944; New Republic August 24, 1942; New York Times Book Review December 6, 1953; New Yorker September 8, 1945; Saturday Review October 24, 1953; Wilson Library Bulletin October 1942.

* sē lō′nā

*SIMENON, GEORGES (February 13, 1903-), Franco-Belgian novelist.

NOTE: This biography, at the request of the writer, supersedes the sketch which appeared in TWENTIETH CENTURY AUTHORS, 1942.

Mrs. Georges Simenon sends the following biography of her husband: "Born in Liège, Belgium, on Friday, February 13, of a middle-class family. His mother, who was superstitious, had his birth registered as of the twelfth. His father was an insurance salesman. To round out the family income, his mother took in lodgers, mostly foreign students of the University.

"College education. Had to leave college abruptly, in his last year, upon father's death. He was sixteen years old. His mother, who dreamed of keeping shop for him, tried to make a baker of him and started him as an apprentice. He soon rebelled and clerked for a while in a book store. An avid reader, he made the mistake of correcting his boss on a point of literary history in front of a client, and was promptly fired.

"So, in his first pair of long pants, bought for the occasion, he hied himself to the publisher of the biggest local newspaper, who, amused, hired him on trial and assigned him to the police court beat. One month later, young Simenon was starting a column in the paper, which he kept up for the next three years, along with police reports, lectures, civic ceremonies which he variously covered, as is the custom in provincial territory. Went through military training in the cavalry.

"At twenty, left for Paris. After buying all the current pulp magazines and novels, started to write stories of all kinds for the most varied reading public. Wrote some three hundred, under seventeen pen-names. Soon discovered that, at the rate of eighty pages a day, he was earning enough money to buy a car, hire a chauffeur, own a yacht, and so forth. But, in his mind, this was only a means of meeting all kinds of people and of traveling extensively. Because he thought that he could not start to write serious works before knowing the world at large, he decided that he might achieve this goal around the age of forty.

"At twenty-seven, in 1930, he started to write what he called semi-literary novels, the Maigret series. By the end of the first year, they were translated in eighteen languages. But, after the twentieth story, he decided that he was due to try his hand at more serious works and to enter the literary field proper.

* sēm nôn′

"From then on he wrote some 150 novels, which he calls 'plain novels,' i.e., without the prop of police detection. He also wrote a play, which he adapted from one of his recent books, *The Snow Was Black.* Thirty-nine of his novels were made into movies, in France and/or England and America.

"He is still writing some five or six novels a year, one or two being detective stories which he continues to write not only as a relaxation and a kind of limbering exercise, but through a sort of loyalty to Maigret himself. After all, Maigret was very kind to him, not only in the book market, but on every major radio and television network of the United States and Europe (France, England, Belgium, Luxembourg, Italy, Switzerland, Algeria, Morocco, Norway, etc.) Not one day goes by without broadcasts of his works.

"Came to America in 1945 and lived at various times in New York, Florida, Arizona, California, and is now settled in Lakeville, Conn., where he lives in an old restored farmhouse with his wife, two sons, and a daughter.

"Of Dutch and Breton blood, still a Belgian citizen but American permanent resident, he and his family plan to live on in America, but with frequent sojourns in Europe."

* * *

The judgment of André Gide some years ago that Simenon was "perhaps the greatest and most truly 'novelistic' novelist in French literature today" was not much altered as late as January 13, 1948, when Gide wrote of Simenon in his *Journal*: "He writes for the 'vast public' to be sure, but delicate and refined readers find something for them too as soon as they deign to take him seriously. He makes one reflect; and this is close to being the height of art."

Simenon's literary development has been little short of spectacular. He has moved with ease and extraordinary success from pulp fiction to urbane detective stories (his detective-hero Maigret is as famous in France and Belgium as Sherlock Holmes is in England and America) to psychological novels which reveal him, Otis E. Fellows writes in the *Saturday Review*, "as a writer with a keen insight into human motivation, a masterful talent for depicting atmosphere and oddities of personality, and a faculty for telling stories that grip the attention."

Simenon writes in French and turns out novels more rapidly than his publisher can print them. Currently his novels appear two to a volume. The bulk of his work has not yet been translated in the United States. Brendan Gill estimates that of the 155 novels Simenon has published under his own name, about 110 are still unavailable in English. These numbers do not include the volumes published under pseudonyms—"Georges Sim" and others—a total which *Time* judges roughly to be about 350. Simenon's present writing schedule calls for a minimum of six novels a year—two of these Maigrets, two "half-hard novels," and two "hard" ones.

PRINCIPAL WORKS IN ENGLISH TRANSLATION: The Crime of Inspector Maigret, 1932; The Death of M. Gallet, 1932; The Strange Case of Peter the Lett, 1933; Introducing Inspector Maigret, 1933; The Crossroad Murders, 1933; Inspector Maigret Investigates, 1933; The Triumph of Inspector Maigret, 1934; The Patience of Maigret, 1940; Maigret Travels South, 1940; Maigret to the Rescue, 1941; Maigret Keeps a Rendezvous, 1941; Maigret Sits It Out, 1941; Maigret and M. Labbé, 1941; In Two Latitudes, 1942; Affairs of Destiny, 1942; The Man Who Watched the Trains Go By, 1942; Tropic Moon, 1943; Havoc by Accident, 1943; Escape in Vain, 1944; The Shadow Falls, 1945; Blind Alley, 1946; First Born, 1947; Black Rain, 1947; Chit of a Girl, 1949; Wife at Sea, 1949; Poisoned Relations, 1950; The Snow Was Black, 1950; Strange Inheritance, 1950; Maigret on Holiday, 1950; Strangers in the House, 1950; Heart of a Man, 1951; Window Over the Way, 1951; Girl in His Past, 1952; House by the Canal, 1952; Act of Passion, 1952; Burgomaster of Furnes, 1952; Satan's Children, 1953; No Vacation for Maigret, 1953; Inspector Maigret and the Strangled Stripper, 1954; Inspector Maigret and the Killers, 1954; Strangers in the House, 1954; The Magician, and the Widow, 1955; Maigret in New York's Underworld, 1955.

ABOUT: Bishop, J. P. Collected Essays; Haycraft, H. Murder for Pleasure: The Life and Times of the Detective Story; Narcejac, T. Le Cas Simenon; Annales Politiques et Littéraires September 1, 1933; Cahiers du Nord Nos. 2, 3, 1939; New Republic March 10, 1941; New York Herald Tribune Book Review August 6, 1950, October 7, 1951; New York Times Book Review May 28, 1950; New Yorker January 24, 1953; Publishers' Weekly December 2, 1939; Saturday Review February 21, 1953; Time July 2, 1951.

*SIMMEL, GEORG (March 1, 1858-September 26, 1918), German sociologist, was born in Berlin, the youngest of seven children. His father, who was a partner in a well-known chocolate factory, died when Simmel was a boy. A guardian was appointed, a friend of the family who was the founder of an international music publishing house. This man left Simmel a considerable fortune which permitted him to lead the life of a scholar. As to Simmel's mother, she is reported to have been temperamental and domineering.

When he graduated from the *gymnasium*, he went on to the University of Berlin to

* zĭm′ĕl

911

study history. Here he changed to philosophy as his major, and for his second "minor" in his doctoral examination he chose medieval Italian and made a special study of Petrarch. In 1881 Simmel received his doctor's degree with a dissertation on "The Nature of Matter according to Kant's Physical Monadology," and from 1885 to 1900 was a *Privatdozent*—which is a lecturer unpaid except for student fees—in philosophy at the University of Berlin. From 1900 to 1914 he continued there as a professor—"professor extraordinary," an honorary but unremunerative title. Then, at the age of fifty-six, in 1914, he was called to Strasbourg as a full professor. Four years later he died.

Simmel's reputation as a speaker and thinker was great, but some critics thought his spirit negative. On one occasion, in 1908, when Max Weber had not succeeded in obtaining a professorship at Heidelberg for Simmel, Simmel remarked in a letter: "What you write has not surprised me. . . . In certain circles the idea exists that I am an exclusively critical, even a destructive spirit, and that my lectures lead one only to negation. . . . My lectures, as, for many years, all my work, tend exclusively toward the positive, toward the demonstration of a deeper insight into world and spirit, with complete renunciation of polemics and criticism in regard to divergent conditions and theories." Simmel lectured and wrote on a wide range of subjects, primarily sociology, philosophy of history, ethics, general philosophy, philosophy of art, philosophy of contemporary civilization, and metaphysics.

In his early *Die Probleme der Geschichtsphilosophie*, published first in 1892, Simmel took the position that such general concepts as progress, general welfare, freedom and society, which were being used by philosophers of the period, were inadequate. For him neither society nor group is imbued with genuine unity; the individual alone is real. One critic, A. Vierkandt, has said that often in Simmel's sociological writings he merely piles up examples, drawn from the most varied periods and cultures, without really digesting them, and that therefore they may seem amateurish in character.

The largest body of translated work is *The Sociology of Georg Simmel*, which appeared

in 1950. "Simmel's influence in sociology," wrote Meno Lovenstein in the *American Economic Review*, "has been quite large and there is a rather extensive literature on him. Still, until the appearance of Professor Wolff's translation, only a small and scattered part of his writing was available in English. His major works in philosophy and ethics—and a great one in economics—have yet to be translated. We should be particularly grateful for Professor Wolff's smooth and scholarly rendition of two of Simmel's major sociological treatises." "This volume of Simmel," added the *American Sociological Review*, "is or should be indispensable for any sociologist, social psychologist, political scientist."

In 1918, knowing that he was fatally stricken with cancer of the liver, Simmel went to the Black Forest to finish his last work, a book on his metaphysics of life, *Lebensanchauung*.

PRINCIPAL WORKS IN ENGLISH TRANSLATION: The Sociology of Georg Simmel, 1950; Conflict, and The Web of Group Affiliations, 1955.

ABOUT: Abel, T. F. Systematic Sociology in Germany; Spykman, N. J. Social Theory of Georg Simmel; Vierkandt, A. Encyclopedia of the Social Sciences; Wolff, K. H. *Introduction to* The Sociology of Georg Simmel.

SIMMONS, ERNEST JOSEPH (December 8, 1903-), American biographer and specialist in Russian literature, writes: "It

is sometimes true that academicians are often frustrated writers, and it occasionally happens that writers are frustrated academicians — Gogol had ambitions to be a famous professor of history, but he failed and became a great writer instead. Whatever the degree of frustration involved on both scores, I have managed to write a sizable number of books while at the same time leading a very active life as a professor of Russian literature at a large university. Of course, the two are not incompatible, and for some, writing had better remain an avocation in a world where its devotees may face the risk of penury as the price of commercial failure.

"The desire for security, no doubt, played an unconscious part in the selection of a profession with a salary, for a very insecure childhood in a large poverty-stricken family left its scars and its fears. It is more than a twice-told tale of American life. One of five children of emigrant English and Scotch parents, I was born in Lawrence, Mass., a mill town of mixed population and unstable economy. The death of my father, when I was five, threw the whole burden of the support of the family on my mother, an heroic Scotch woman, who never flinched in her duty to her children. Perhaps as an escape from dull, impoverished surroundings, I sought refuge in the luxury of omnivorous, undisciplined reading. A new world opened up. I began to scribble poetry and short stories, getting them published in the high school paper. I became a fiery defender of the downtrodden, the condemned, the atheist. At fifteen I wrote a small book, with the pretentious title—'Three Great Iconoclasts: Spinoza, Paine, and Ingersoll.' Fortunately, no publisher found it irresistible, though apparently a theological student at Harvard did years later, for he purloined the manuscript.

"The glittering grail of a college education obsessed me. Getting through high school had meant odd jobs late afternoons and evenings; surviving through seven years of Harvard from the A.B. to the Ph.D was a feat of financial legerdemain, made possible only by part-time work, scholarships, and hard physical labor during the summers. Then came teaching in English and Russian literature at Harvard, Cornell, and finally at Columbia, where I am head of the department of Slavic languages and professor of Russian literature at the Russian Institute.

"The writing itch does not always survive such competition, but I was determined. Research trips to Russia during its more interesting early phases of revolutionary development (1928, 1932, 1935, 1937) provided me with rich experiences, and close study of the great Russian classics gave me plenty of inspiration. I continued to turn out arty but unsalable short stories and then a long novel, based on my experiences in Russia, which had in it perhaps more of Dostoevsky than the stuff of contemporary life. My literary agent liked it, the publishers didn't and ordered revisions; in the end no one was satisfied.

"After publishing a purely scholarly book, I turned to biographical writing which had always fascinated me. In those days the Strachey school of biography had reached the point of the widely popularized studies of Maurois, such as his *Ariel*, the biography of Shelley. Fact was often sacrificed to subjective impressionism and the reality of life to sheer sensationalism. It seemed to me that a biography did not have to be dull simply because it was factual and the product of exhaustive research. All the art of the novelist could be employed but in such a way as never to falsify the objective facts of life in constructing a narrative pattern that would be at once absorbing without being unfaithful to the subject.

"In this spirit I wrote my biography of the great poet Pushkin, after three years of research, part of it conducted in Russia. Months of effort by my agent resulted in numerous rejections which might be summed up in the language of one of them: 'A most readable book, but who the hell is Pushkin?' In despair I took a copy of the manuscript to a university press. The day before it was accepted by them I received a telephone call from my agent that the Literary Guild had taken the book! A long moral struggle ensued. The publisher connected with the Guild tried to force the issue by agreeing to take my novel as well, although they clearly did not think much of it. The university publisher won out. They published the book in a handsome edition and I lost a lot of money.

"I next turned to literary criticism in an extensive study of the notebooks of Dostoevsky in an effort to describe in much detail the creative art of a great writer. This book was an exciting task, for I learned a great deal about the art of writing in moving around so intimately in the creative laboratory of a genius such as Dostoevsky. Meanwhile I had embarked on what was to be a major effort—to put my biographical theories to the test in writing a definitive life of Leo Tolstoy. Seven years of exacting research and endless writing and polishing went into this behemoth, and the result was a book of some eight hundred pages, just about half of what I originally wrote. And this had further to be boiled down to about half again for its serialization in the *Atlantic Monthly*. But it was all worth it, for apart from the material rewards, I obtained much spiritual and intellectual satisfaction in portraying faithfully and objectively, in all its magnificent proportions and accomplishments, the life of one of the greatest men in modern times.

"At present, ever-increasing administrative and academic work seriously interferes with my writing. I spend much of my time in nursing along the manuscripts of my students, and my own literary efforts are reduced to reviews, magazine articles, editing, and writing introductions to the books of others. However, at least two long-delayed books are slowly gestating, but these may remain trade secrets for the present."

913

PRINCIPAL WORKS: English Literature and Culture in Russia, 1934; Pushkin, 1937; Dostoevsky: The Making of a Novelist, 1940; Tolstoy, a Biography, 1946; (ed.) The USSR: A Concise Handbook, 1947; (ed.) Through the Glass of Soviet Literature, 1953.

ABOUT: Publications of the Modern Language Association (PMLA) June 1954.

SIMONDS, FRANK HERBERT (April 5, 1878-January 23, 1936). For biographical sketch and list of works and references, see TWENTIETH CENTURY AUTHORS, 1942.

*SIMONOV, KONSTANTIN MIK-HAILOVICH (1915-), Soviet author and journalist, was born in Leningrad

Sovfoto

in 1915, in the middle of World War I during which his father was lost (presumed killed). After some elementary schooling at Saratov on the Volga, the fifteen-year-old Konstantin went to work to support his mother and himself. From 1930 to 1935, he worked in a factory as a turner's mechanic; but he was already interested in a literary career, and some of the poems he wrote then were posted on the walls of his factory. In 1934 he entered the Literary Institute of the Writer's Union; two years later he became a professional writer; and in 1937 he was graduated from the Institute. In 1939 Simonov was sent to the Far East to cover the battle of Khalkhin Gol in Outer Mongolia.

In June 1941 Simonov was sent to the front as an army correspondent; and in the course of World War II, he reported from almost all of the Russian battle-fronts, and became one of the most famous of war correspondents. His accounts of battles, of the courage and heroism of the civilian population, of the life of the soldiers at the front, were printed in both Red Star, the Russian army newspaper, and in Pravda. Simonov was awarded the Order of the Red Banner, as well as medals for Khalkhin Gol, Stalingrad, Odessa, and Moscow.

From the Black Sea to the Sea of Barents (translated and published in England with the title No Quarter) contains stories of the war; and Stalingrad Fights On is a collection of his front-page despatches.

* sĕ'mŭn ôf

Several of Simonov's plays were produced in Moscow during the war. His first pre-war play, A Story About One Love (about an Arctic explorer), had been a failure (1940); but his second, A Fellow From Our Town (1942), which dealt with the transformation of an unimportant man into a daring tank driver, was a spectacular success, and was awarded the Stalin prize of 100,000 rubles. About The Russian People, another play continuing the lives of some of the main characters in A Fellow From Our Town, Nemirovich-Danchenko, then director of the Moscow Art Theatre, said: "In these stern days of war, it is difficult to over-rate the significance of The Russian People as art. . . . Art must teach the people to hate the dark and terrible forces of Fascism which threaten humanity and its culture." This play, as adapted by Clifford Odets, was produced by the Theatre Guild in New York during the winter of 1942-43. (Another Simonov play, The Whole World Over, a post-war comedy about the housing shortage, was produced in New York in 1946-47 (adapted by Thelma Schnee).

Days and Nights, a novel about the heroic and desperate defense of Stalingrad, was published in America in 1945. The book begins as its hero, Captain Saburov, enters Stalingrad, where the Germans have already succeeded in capturing large parts of the city, and ends, seventy days and nights later, as Captain Saburov hears the rumbling of the Russian cannon to the North which heralded the beginning of the great Russian winter offensive, the pincer movement which eventually cut off and destroyed so many of Hitler's troops.

Harrison Smith, reviewing the novel for the Saturday Review of Literature, wrote: "Simonov has accomplished two remarkable feats in his novel. . . . First, that a war novel of such stature should have appeared so soon after hostilities ceased . . . . [second] that a modern Russian novel should speak the universal human language of suffering and heroism without a single trace of the usual Soviet propaganda. It is no wonder that Days and Nights has swept over Russia and is regarded there as the best novel of the war."

Simonov has also published a book of poems, With Her and Without Her, most of which are lyrics written to his wife during the war. In 1946 he was elected a Deputy to the Supreme Soviet.

PRINCIPAL WORKS IN ENGLISH TRANSLATION: No Quarter, 1943; The Russian People (play) 1944; Four Soviet War Plays (with others) 1944; Days and Nights, 1945; The Whole World Over (play) 1947.

ABOUT: Struve, G. Soviet Russian Literature 1917-50; Yarmolinsky, A. Y. (ed.) A Treasury of Russian Verse; New York Times Book Review May 19, 1946; Saturday Evening Post June 28, 1947, January 6, 1951.

SIMPSON, GEORGE GAYLORD (June 16, 1902-   ), American writer on science, reports: "I was born in Chicago, youngest of

three children and only son of Joseph A. and Helen (Kinney) Simpson, but we soon moved to Wyoming and then to Colorado. My earliest memories are of Denver, where most of my formative years were spent. My father was engaged principally in land de-

Fabian Bachrach

velopment, irrigation, and mining in Utah and Colorado. Trips with him and summers spent in the mountains gave me wide knowledge and enduring love of the Rocky Mountain region, which I still consider my real home. Except for one year in Piedmont, Calif., I attended the Denver public schools, and I entered the University of Colorado in 1918. Family reverses caused me to leave the university in 1919 and to spend a year working in Chicago and then bumming my way from one job to another in the South and West. In 1920 I was able to return to the University of Colorado, and in 1922 I transferred to Yale University, where I was graduated in 1923.

"Doting elders thought I had a talent for writing and especially for versifying. I accepted their judgment and entered college with the naïve notion of learning to be a poet. I soon found that for me, at least, knowledge is more important than self-expression and that substance in writing is more important than manner. The learning of new truths is far more satisfying than the restating of old ones, and I was increasingly drawn to scientific research as a career. As an undergraduate I determined to study the history of life and the principles of its evolution, the subjects to which I have ever since devoted myself with no regrets. This aim motivated transfer to Yale, where I continued in the graduate school and was given a Ph.D. in 1926. After a year of post-doctorate research abroad, mostly in the British Museum, I joined the staff of the American Museum of Natural History, New York, where I still am.

"At the museum I busied myself especially with basic paleontological research, collecting, identifying, and describing fossils, mostly fossil mammals. This work involved numerous expeditions throughout the United States and in South America. Most interesting, perhaps, were two long journeys through the heart of Patagonia (1930-31, 1933-34) and another to the then virtually unknown and still wild and beautiful forests and peaks of Venezuelan Guiana (1938-39). Research produced a great deal of scientific rather than literary writing, the number of my technical articles now being well over three hundred.

"As the years have passed, my interests have not changed in focus but have broadened in scope. I have not lost sight of basic technical research, but I have tended more and more to seek a synthesis of knowledge of life and its history and to try to present such knowledge to a wider audience than that of my specialized colleagues. If the label 'author' fits me at all, it is for several books written from this point of view. My career, such as it is, has been scientific rather than literary and has been symbolized by the usual tokens of reasonably successful research: honorary degrees (Yale, Princeton, Glasgow, Durham, Oxford), medals (from the National Academy of Sciences, Geological Societies of America and of France, and others), and fellowships or honorary memberships (National Academy of Sciences, American Philosophical Society, American Academy of Arts and Sciences, Academy of Sciences of Venezuela, Zoological Society of London, and others). I have lectured widely in the United States and also in Argentina, Venezuela, Australia, Egypt, England, and France.

"Aside from more than twenty-five years on the staff of the American Museum, I have taught as a part-time professor at Columbia University since 1945. I also spent two unpleasant years as an intelligence officer (captain and major) in combat zones in the Mediterranean.

"I have been married twice, secondly and permanently to Dr. Anne Roe, a research psychologist. Thanks to four daughters, our stock of grandchildren is rapidly increasing. We have built a home in the mountains of New Mexico, where we spend as much time as my duties permit."

PRINCIPAL WORKS: Attending Marvels, a Patagonian Journal, 1933; (with A. Roe) Quantitative Zoology, 1939; Los Indios Kamarakotos (Tribu Caribe de la Guayana Venezolana) 1940; Tempo and Mode in Evolution, 1944; The Meaning of Evolution, 1949; Horses, 1951; The Life of the Past, 1953; The Major Features of Evolution, 1953.

ABOUT: Saturday Review April 18, 1953; Scientific Monthly June 1947.

SIMPSON, HELEN DE GUERRY (1897-October 1940). For biographical sketch and list of works and references, see TWENTIETH CENTURY AUTHORS, 1942.

* * *

ABOUT: Dictionary of Australian Biography; Roderick, C. A. Twenty Australian Novelists.

SINCLAIR, Mrs. BERTHA (MUZZY). See BOWER, B. M.

SINCLAIR, HAROLD (May 8, 1907-). For autobiographical sketch and list of earlier works and references, see TWENTIETH CENTURY AUTHORS, 1942.

* * *

Harold Sinclair's only novel of recent years is *Music Out of Dixie*, a book which closely reflects his interest in and appreciation of jazz. It is, moreover, a sound and moving portrayal of New Orleans around the time of World War I and of a lonely young Negro boy growing up in Storyville. Harnett T. Kane said of it: "For the first time, a strong and honest novel has been derived from the rich materials of New Orleans jazz."

ADDITIONAL WORK: Music Out of Dixie, 1952.

"SINCLAIR, JO" (pseudonym of Ruth Seid) (July 1, 1913-), American novelist and playwright, writes:  "I was born in Brooklyn, N.Y. My parents were still scuffling for a living in the 'Promised Land,' a struggle which had begun for them in Russia the day they were born. Poverty, persecution, hope; these must have been the whips that changed their lives.

"Emigration was a frightened but insistent dream to Jews in those days. My father, a carpenter, and my mother, a seamstress, went with a large group from their village to the Argentine, in South America, to work land belonging to a wealthy baron who paid all expenses and promised a living. Their first child was born there, and the living stayed harsh. They went back to Russia. There another child was born, and there, somehow, the dream was replenished. Persecution, poverty, hope; the old words were still there, made a louder and louder sound until the next step was taken. The carpenter and his family came to the United States, to a big

city this time. Three more children were born, and the living stayed harsh.

"When I was three, the carpenter took his last step of wandering. We landed in Cleveland, Ohio, and stayed. The rest is uneventful: a family becomes part of a community. We went to school, we graduated and went to work the following day; no money or energy enough for college. Some of us married; maybe the carpenter's grandchildren will go to college.

"I was the youngest child. I grew up in the melting-pot neighborhoods of a large industrial city, played and went to school with other second-generation kids. Our parents had come from Russia, Italy, Hungary—and from Atlanta, Ga. We were white and colored, and whereas the dreams were shouted in the dirty stone streets in many languages and slurred dialects, and we kids knew all of them, our own dreams were told in our own language—English, Midwest near-slums variety.

"What makes a person want to write? The old wandering in the bloodstream? The dreams or the pushing around which began long, long ago, and continued in another land, were repeated in any neighboring house? I started writing in high school, and I've been trying ever since.

"For a living, I typed and filed, I made boxes in a knitting mill and read proof for telephone directories, edited a trade magazine, worked on W.P.A. editing and writing projects, was secretary to a calendar-and-novelty boss, wrote publicity for the American Red Cross during a war. Evenings and weekends, I wrote short stories, finally began the first fumbling novel, sold that first story, went on writing. The carpenter was amazed, incredulous, full of a kind of jeering laughter. A writer? The carpenter's wife shrugged: who ever heard of such a thing?

"One day the first novel was published. It had won a literary contest, it had made quite a bit of money. The carpenter and his wife, much older and very tired with all the struggling and scuffling, held the book in their hands. They looked at the money. Then they said, with a kind of dazed happiness: 'In America, anything can happen.'

"Maybe the old dream had run its gamut, finally. Such dreams can move worlds, they say."

* * *

In 1946 Jo Sinclair's first novel, *Wasteland*, won the $10,000 Harper prize contest for the novel which offered the best study of some aspect of American life. *Wasteland*, the story of a second-generation American who tries to conceal his Russo-Jewish heritage, was, according to the late Thomas Sugrue, "the story of a predominantly Anglo-Saxon culture and the differences it presents to people reared in the peasant societies of Slavic and Latin countries. . . . It is a powerful, solemn story as Miss Sinclair tells it, gently and with understanding." The framework of the novel is a series of visits by the protagonist to a psychiatrist, and while the form seemed to some reviewers essentially a tour de force, and at times more a case history than a novel, they were agreed that "the book has an honesty and a sincerity of purpose which lifts it above the general run of novels." In her second novel, *Sing at My Wake*, Miss Sinclair showed herself again a compelling story teller, although the book did not have the popular success of *Wasteland*. Long interested in the theatre, she wrote a play, *The Long Moment*, in 1950.

PRINCIPAL WORKS: Wasteland, 1946; Sing at My Wake, 1951.

ABOUT: Current Biography 1946; New York Times Book Review January 6, 1946; Publishers' Weekly January 5, 1946.

SINCLAIR, MAY (1865?-November 14, 1946). For biographical sketch and list of works and references, see TWENTIETH CENTURY AUTHORS, 1942.

* * *

May Sinclair died at her home near Aylesbury, Buckinghamshire, England.

Before her final illness she was deeply interested in many progressive causes, in the methods of the writing craft, and in philosophical idealism, in addition to her interest in spiritualism. The London *Times* described her prose as "evocative, well-wrought, and distinguished," and called her "a novelist of keenly analytical intellect, a careful and finished stylist, and the possessor of a comprehensive imaginative grasp of character."

ABOUT: Frierson, W. C. The English Novel in Transition; Swinnerton, F. The Georgian Literary Scene; London Times November 15, 1946; New York Times November 15, 1946.

SINCLAIR, UPTON BEALL (September 20, 1878-   ). For biographical sketch and list of earlier works and references, see TWENTIETH CENTURY AUTHORS, 1942.

* * *

No matter how many books Upton Sinclair publishes, Alfred Kazin remarked in *On Native Grounds* in 1942, "he will remain a touching and curious symbol of a certain old-fashioned idealism and quaint personal romanticism that have vanished from American writing forever." The vigorous muckraking which characterized Sinclair's early books has given way, in recent years, to a kind of modern-day myth-making; his indestructible hero Lanny Budd moves through the panorama of contemporary history with the timeliness of a daily newspaper headline and the verisimilitude of a newsreel. Lanny Budd is both historian and history-maker, an associate of Franklin D. Roosevelt and every great historical figure of the 1930's and '40's. There may be readers of the future, George Bernard Shaw suggested, who will seek to understand the twentieth century not by reading the newspaper files but by reading the Lanny Budd, or, as Sinclair prefers to call them, the "World's End" series. On the question of the literary merit of these novels there has been some controversy. The early volumes in the series were vigorous and passionately sincere records of the major political events of our time. *Dragon's Teeth*, the third volume and the first to treat of Nazism, won the 1942 Pulitzer prize for fiction. Their weaknesses are essentially those inherent in the polemical novel—naïveté, "non-dimensional" characterizations, a tendency to editorialize and to oversimplify. "The machinery creaks," R. L. Duffus wrote in a review of *Wide Is the Gate*. "But one tends to forget the machinery and the inventions for the simple reason that Mr. Sinclair is a story-teller, and that he tells his story, as he sees it, for the good of humanity. This last attribute doesn't make a novelist, but it does turn a good plotsmith into a writer one dare not ignore."

In 1949 Sinclair announced, with the publication of *O Shepherd, Speak!* that this, the tenth volume, would conclude the series. He had spent ten years of "incessant labor" on "World's End"—"There were few times when the work was out of my mind for a single day." But in 1953 Sinclair resurrected Lanny Budd and sent him to Washington, Hollywood, and the capitals of Europe for further adventures, including kidnapping by the Russians; and there are no signs that Lanny is contemplating retirement from the international scene.

Relaxing between volumes of "World's End," Sinclair has written a novel, a play, and a book of personal philosophy. The novel, *Another Pamela*, was a twentieth-century re-telling of Richardson's eighteenth-century epistolary novel. The play, *The Enemy Had It Too*, was a science-fiction

917

type of fantasy, dealing with visiting Martians and the almost decimated human race. The book of philosophy (for which he had great difficulty in finding a publisher), *A Personal Jesus,* was an imaginative re-interpretation of the life of Christ; "a personal testimony of a free-thinking idealist," A. P. Davies wrote of it in the New York *Times,* "with a colorful imagination and a warm love of the true and the good."

Sinclair lives in Buckeye, Ariz.

ADDITIONAL WORKS: *"World's End" Series*—Wide Is the Gate, 1943; Presidential Agent, 1944; Dragon Harvest, 1945; A World to Win, 1946; Presidential Mission, 1947; One Clear Call, 1948; O Shepherd, Speak! 1949; The Return of Lanny Budd, 1953. Giant's Strength (play) 1947; Another Pamela; or, Virtue Still Rewarded, 1950; The Enemy Had It Too (play) 1950; A Personal Jesus, 1952.

ABOUT: Kazin, A. On Native Grounds; McWilliams, C. Southern California Country; Parrington, V. L. American Dreams; New York Herald Tribune Book Review August 7, 1949; New York Times Book Review September 8, 1946, February 9, 1947; Saturday Review of Literature May 17, 1947, August 13, 1949.

SINCLAIR-COWAN, Mrs. BERTHA (MUZZY). See BOWER, B. M.

SINGER, ISRAEL JOSHUA (November 30, 1893-February 10, 1944). For autobiographical sketch and list of works and references, see TWENTIETH CENTURY AUTHORS, 1942.

* * *

I. J. Singer died at his home in New York City, following a heart attack, at fifty.

The Brothers Ashkenazi, his most notable work, was called (by Philip Rahv) "the most important novel of Jewish life so far published in English." The strength of Singer's work lay, as Milton Rugoff has observed, in his "extraordinary knowledge of varieties of human beings, and that ability to seize upon the significant traits in character and to present them with a minimum of strokes and a maximum of power."

I. J. Singer's younger brother, Isaac Bashevis Singer, born in Radzymin, Poland, in 1904, is also a writer of distinction. After a traditional Jewish education, he attended a rabbinical seminary in Warsaw, and then began to write fiction in Hebrew, later turning to Yiddish. He published short stories and book reviews in *Die Literarische Bletter, Die Yiddische Welt, Globus,* and other magazines. Since coming to the United States in 1935, he has been on the staff of the *Jewish Daily Forward.* His short stories have appeared in translation in *Partisan Review, A Treasury of Yiddish Stories,* and *More Stories in the Modern Manner.* His first novel, *Satan in Goray,* originally published in Yiddish in 1935, is scheduled for publication in English in 1955. A translation in 1950 of his second novel, *The Family Moskat* (1945), was a selection of the Book Find Club and was awarded the Louis Lamed Prize. Both of Isaac Bashevis Singer's novels have been translated into Hebrew.

ABOUT I. J. Singer: Current Biography 1944; New York Times February 11, 1944.

SINGMASTER, ELSIE (August 29, 1879-). For autobiographical sketch and list of earlier works and references, see TWENTIETH CENTURY AUTHORS, 1942.

* * *

Elsie Singmaster lives in Gettysburg, Pa., and continues to write with sensitive affection about the region in which she has spent so much of her life. Her only departure from this subject matter was a fictionized biography of Thaddeus Stevens, who—as it happened—also lived in Pennsylvania, though he was not a native of the state. The book was praised as a "completely adult biography," distinguished for its sympathetic and forthright presentation of a complex political personality.

ADDITIONAL WORKS: I Speak for Thaddeus Stevens, 1947; The Isle of Que, 1948; I Hear of a River: The Story of the Germans in Pennsylvania, 1948; Pennsylvania's Susquehanna, 1950.

ABOUT: Warfel, H. R. American Novelists of Today.

SITWELL, Dame EDITH (1887-). For biographical sketch and list of earlier works and references, see TWENTIETH CENTURY AUTHORS, 1942.

* * *

The striking personality of Edith Sitwell has sometimes in recent years overshadowed the sound and serious accomplishment of her work as a poet. In America particularly she is probably better known for her extraordinary dress and appearance—which an interviewer described in 1948 as "characterized by a marble complexion, lively, squinty eyes, a Plantagenet nose, a red velvet turban, and considerable stature—five feet eleven"—than for her writing, although she has an admiring and strongly articulate audience on both sides of the Atlantic.

The American première of *Façade,* her "entertainment" in verse and music (by William Walton), took place in 1949 at the Museum of Modern Art in New York City.

She read her verse from the fourth floor of the museum into a microphone which carried her voice down to the basement auditorium. When the performance was over, she came down, in white satin, a brocaded cape, and turban, to accept the enthusiastic applause—quite a different reception from the one the work originally had in London twenty-five years earlier, when the audience laughed at it and the critics ridiculed it. Since then Dr. Sitwell (as she is now called) has visited the United States frequently and given many readings, including one of *Macbeth*, in which she was Lady Macbeth to Glenway Wescott's Macbeth. In 1954 she went to Hollywood to write a motion picture scenario.

Recognized as one of the most eminent English women poets of her time, Edith Sitwell writes what Horace Gregory has called "poetry in the great tradition." In her work, Katherine Anne Porter observes, there is "the true flowering branch sprung fresh from the old, unkillable roots of English poetry; with the range, variety, depth, fearlessness, the passion and elegance of great art." Her poems are more effective read aloud than silently—especially as read by Dr. Sitwell herself. In print they appear sometimes overly oracular; and the sibylline quality which has become characteristic of her manner produces "symbolism in capital letters . . . an overdressed monotony and a certain hollowness" (L. F. Duchene in the *Manchester Guardian*). Louise Bogan wrote: "Miss Sitwell is so skillful and so dazzling that she almost persuades us that spiritual intensity follows upon verbal intensity, which may or may not be true."

In recent years Dr. Sitwell has received many honors—including three doctorates (Leeds 1948, Durham 1948, Oxford 1951) and election to the American Institute of Arts and Letters. In June 1954 she was named Dame Grand Cross of the Order of the British Empire by Queen Elizabeth II. Like her brothers, she makes no effort to conceal her delight in the widespread celebrity of the Sitwells after many years of neglect and adverse criticism. She favors a strictly sedentary existence: "I detest walking more than anything in the world. I read the whole time when I am not working at poetry." One of her favorite recreations, according to *Who's Who*, is "silence."

ADDITIONAL WORKS: *Poetry*—Green Song, and Other Poems, 1944; Shadow of Cain, 1947; Song of the Cold, 1948; Canticle of the Rose: Poems 1917-1949, 1949; Façade, and Other Poems, 1920-1935, 1950; Gardeners and Astronomers: New Poems, 1953; Collected Poems, 1954. *Prose*—A Poet's Notebook, 1943; Fanfare for Elizabeth, 1946;

A Notebook on William Shakespeare, 1948. *Miscellaneous*—(comp.) Book of the Winter (poems and prose) 1950; (ed.) American Genius (anthology of prose and poetry) 1951.

ABOUT: Sitwell, O. Left Hand, Right Hand, The Scarlet Tree, Great Morning, Laughter in the Next Room, Noble Essences; Swinnerton, F. The Georgian Literary Scene (1910-35); Villa, J. G. (ed.) A Celebration for Edith Sitwell; Wykes-Joyce, M. Triad of Genius; Harper's March 1949; Life December 6, 1948; New Yorker November 6, 1948, January 29, 1949, November 18, 1950; Saturday Review of Literature January 14, 1950, December 19, 1953.

SITWELL, Sir OSBERT (December 6, 1892-). For biographical sketch and list of earlier works and references, see TWENTIETH CENTURY AUTHORS, 1942.

* * *

On one of his recent visits to the United States, of which he has made several accompanied by his sister Edith, Sir Osbert Sitwell was described as "a tall, ruddy, friendly, informal man." He is the official chronicler of his distinguished and extraordinary family. The five volumes he has written covering that history have been both critical successes and best sellers. He is as well known in the United States as he is in England, and his lectures and recorded readings are in great demand.

Sir Osbert's entry in recent editions of *Who's Who* is in itself a small literary gem. Here he writes: "For the past thirty years has conducted, in conjunction with his brother and sister, a series of skirmishes and hand-to-hand battles against the Philistine. Though outnumbered, has occasionally succeeded in denting the line, though not without damage to himself. Advocates compulsory Freedom everywhere, the suppression of Public Opinion in the interest of Free Speech, and the rationing of brains without which innovation there can be no true democracy." And he adds: "Has lectured extensively in public and private." His recreations are "thinking for himself, speaking for others, not receiving letters and not answering them."

The above well illustrates the iconoclastic spirit which made the Sitwells such colorful figures in the Twenties. But their continued and increased popularity in recent years indicates the presence of more than mere daring and surface brilliance. Osbert Sitwell is recognized today as a prose writer of unusual grace and richness and as a sharp critic of society. He is, as Jocelyn Brooke pointed out in the *New Statesman and Nation,* "that rare bird, a writer whose whole output seems the product of literary maturity." Evelyn Waugh

919

has measured him as follows: "The interest of Sir Osbert's fame is that it rests on a lifetime of uninterrupted development and enrichment. His natural growth has continued into late middle age so that his latest book has always been his best. He acquired his reputation first, then seriously settled down to earn it."

Sir Osbert's family memoirs began with *Left Hand, Right Hand* in 1944 and continued through *Noble Essences* in 1950. Neither the author nor his readers would attempt to deny the literary and aristocratic "snob" appeal of these books. They are, as Cecil Roberts observed of the first volume in the series, "compact of charm, culture and urbanity . . . a vivid tapestry of the English scene, as fascinating in its embroidery, its minor panels of heraldry, as in its main theme." Sir Osbert's achievement in reconstructing the leisurely and luxurious world of the late-Victorian and Edwardian era is no small one. He brings that period to life, Donald Stauffer wrote, "with a completeness that the average biographer, not being also an imaginative artist, does not even dream can exist."

ADDITIONAL WORKS: *Memoirs*—Left Hand, Right Hand, 1944; The Scarlet Tree, 1946; Great Morning, 1947; Laughter in the Next Room, 1948; Noble Essences, 1950. *Essays and Short Stories*—Letter to My Son, 1944; Sing High, Sing Low: Essays, 1944; The True Story of Dick Whittington: A Christmas Story for Cat Lovers, 1946; Death of a God, and Other Stories, 1949; Wrack at Tidesend (stories) 1953; Collected Stories, 1953; The Four Continents, 1954. *Poetry*—Four Songs of the Italian Earth, 1948; Demos the Emperor: A Secular Oratorio, 1949; England Reclaimed: A Book of Balearics, 1949.

ABOUT: Sitwell, O. See *Memoirs* above; Swinnerton, F. The Georgian Literary Scene (1910-35); Wykes-Joyce, M. Triad of Genius; Atlantic Monthly April 1951; Life December 6, 1948; New York Herald Tribune Book Review October 8, 1950; New York Times Magazine November 30, 1952; New Yorker November 6, 1948; Saturday Review of Literature January 1950, December 19, 1953.

SITWELL, SACHEVERELL (1897-).
For biographical sketch and list of earlier works and references, see TWENTIETH CENTURY AUTHORS, 1942.

* * *

Sacheverell Sitwell visited the United States for the first time on a lecture tour in 1952. Like his brother Osbert and his sister Edith, he has scorned easy popularity and has cultivated what his sister once called, in describing the family, "the remote air of a legend." Like his brother and sister, ironically, he has won more fame for this apparent in-

difference to conventional success than for the actual content of his work.

A writer of versatility and urbanity, of vast erudition and the most eclectic tastes, Sacheverell Sitwell is better known for his prose—especially his art criticism—than for his poetry. Most critics have found his verse beautiful but structurally weak, giving "the feeling of a brilliant improvisation rather than of a sharply conceived whole," Richard Ellmann remarked of his *Selected Poems* in *Poetry* magazine. The London *Times Literary Supplement,* however, considers him "a poet of major significance"—"his work contains mysterious atmospheres, subtle feeling, the ever-changing lights and temperatures of the surrounding airs." His art criticism has been described as "a marvel of sustained imaginative, pictorial, and interpretive writing" (Eric Forbes-Boyd, in the *Christian Science Monitor*). Probably the most interesting and representative of his books in this field is *The Hunters and the Hunted,* in which Sitwell roams freely from fact to fantasy, from Picasso to Mozart, with incidental notes on hunting and birds of paradise. It is a book strongly marked by dilettantism, J. W. Rogers observed in the *Saturday Review of Literature*—"well-nigh incomprehensible to anyone who is not capable of esthetic feeling and a culture broad enough to ferret out at least a portion of the all-too-passing obscure allusions. . . . But it reflects an eager mind of high quality."

ADDITIONAL WORKS: The Homing of the Winds, and Other Passages in Prose, 1942; Splendours and Miseries, 1943; The Hunters and the Hunted, 1948; The Netherlands, 1948; Morning, Noon and Night in London, 1948; Selected Poems, 1948; Theatrical Figures in Porcelain, 1949; Spain, 1950; Selected Works, 1953; Portugal and Madeira, 1954.

ABOUT: Sitwell, O. Left Hand, Right Hand, The Scarlet Tree, Great Morning, Laughter in the Next Room, Noble Essences; Swinnerton, F. The Georgian Literary Scene (1910-35); New Yorker November 8, 1952; Poetry July 1949; Saturday Review of Literature March 19, 1949, December 19, 1953.

SIWERTZ, SIGFRID (January 24, 1882-).
For autobiographical sketch and list of works and references, see TWENTIETH CENTURY AUTHORS, 1942.

* * *

Sigfrid Siwertz is one of the most honored and admired of contemporary Swedish writers. He is a member of the Swedish Academy and serves on the Nobel committee. An accomplished stylist, he has been specially praised for his "plastic and colorful prose."

Siwertz has published about fifty books—only two of which are available in English translation. His recent writings include novels, essays, and memoirs. He lives in Stockholm.

ABOUT: Columbia Dictionary of Modern European Literature.

SKINNER, CONSTANCE LINDSAY
(1882-March 27, 1939). For biographical sketch and list of works and references, see TWENTIETH CENTURY AUTHORS, 1942.

* * *

Since 1940 the Women's National Book Association has annually presented a Constance Lindsay Skinner Award to a woman for "outstanding contribution to the world of books."

ABOUT: Thomas, C. Canadian Novelists, 1920-1945.

SKINNER, CORNELIA OTIS (May 30, 1901-), American humorist and actress, was born in Chicago, the daughter of the  actor-manager Otis Skinner and Maud (Durbin) Skinner, an actress until her marriage. She attended the Baldwin School in Bryn Mawr, Pa., where her mother at one point volunteered to coach the Baldwin girls in a Shakespearean production. "Cornelia's Lady Macbeth had made her a leader in the club," her father wrote in an article in the New York *Herald Tribune.* "Once started, the spark of her ambition burned steadily. From her preparatory school she departed with high honors and entered Bryn Mawr.... She immediately found herself in the midst of the dramatic activities of the college. She shared in the writings of the class plays and burlesques.

"In the summer before her sophomore year George Tyler organized a company for a short season in Washington. I suggested that he make a place for my daughter in its ranks and give her a first taste of the real theatre.... The experiment was interesting and she made a professional debut. The call of the stage grew more insistent after two years at Bryn Mawr. I was convinced that if she was really going to act, a continuance of her studies would be useless. So Cornelia and her mother sailed for a year's residence in Paris. Instruction in acting, daily exercises in diction

and vocal training, a course of lectures in French literature at the Sorbonne, attendance at the classic and modern plays, attainment of fluency in French conversation—these constituted the routine of her Paris days." Cornelia Otis Skinner herself adds to her father's account, "I took private lessons from Dehelly, a *sociétaire* of the Comédie Française [and] rebelled at the heavy dose of classicism and the stylized method of performing that had not changed since the time of Molière." But when she wrote to her father, he replied, "Don't make fun of it. It's a grand old school to learn—*and then forget!*" To acquire some grounding in more modern methods she enrolled in a dramatic school run by Jacques Copea, of the Théâtre du Vieux Colombier.

"I was to produce Blasco Ibáñez' *Blood and Sand* at the Empire Theatre in New York," said her father. "In the part of a languid Spanish aristocrat in that play my daughter made her real entrance on the stage [1921]. She realized the part.... At its conclusion I said to her '... from now on you must work out your own destiny.'" Miss Skinner appeared in a number of plays, but longed for something more. "In her college days," wrote her father, "she had written monologues on intimate subjects and impersonated them to the delight of teachers and fellow students. Three years in the theatre had given her its technique and taught her the power of projecting. She could people her stage with her own creations and be a whole company in herself. Not until much later did the idea develop of recording the impressions of contemporary life which she discovered. The result was a series of sketches, humorous, pathetic, tender and satirical, which her photographic eye had caught. She had found her medium, she was her own dramatist and impersonator."

Later she pioneered in offering an historical costume drama with only one actress performing it, *The Wives of Henry VIII,* followed by *The Empress Eugénie* and *The Loves of Charles II;* in *Mansion on the Hudson* and *Edna His Wife* she again acted alone. In *Candida* she appeared for the first time as a star with full company; the next plays were *Theatre, The Searching Wind,* and *Lady Windermere's Fan.* After these her major theatrical activity became the preparation of *Paris '90,* produced in 1952, a full-length solo drama about various women—mostly entertainers—as portrayed in the posters and canvases of Toulouse-Lautrec. Miss Skinner has also appeared on the screen, radio, and television.

Meanwhile Cornelia Otis Skinner was writing books. Her first, *Tiny Garments,* was published in 1932. "Nothing is dearer to a woman," said the author, "than a nice long obstetrical chat." This humorous volume was followed by *Excuse It, Please!, Dithers and Jitters,* and *Soap Behind the Ears.* All four books have more recently been collected into an omnibus called *That's Me All Over.*

The first book to achieve wide fame was *Our Hearts Were Young and Gay,* written in collaboration with Emily Kimbrough. The book sold over one million copies. There followed *Family Circle,* which Edward Weeks of the *Atlantic Monthly* described as "affectionate, uncritical, the chronicle of a talented, uneccentric trio." *Nuts in May,* a collection of articles, all but one of which had appeared in the *New Yorker,* came out in 1950. "Delightful and vigorous," wrote Richard Blakesley in the Chicago *Sunday Tribune.* "In it the reader shares Miss Skinner's giddy joy of living. It is a picture of a woman who apparently never has an idle moment."

She was awarded an honorary Doctor of Letters from the University of Pennsylvania in 1938, and another honorary degree from New York University in 1942. The author has been described as a tall, almost stately woman, with black hair and humorously cynical eyes. She married Alden S. Blodget in 1928, and they have one son, Otis Skinner Blodget, better known as "Dick" to her readers. She lives in New York City.

PRINCIPAL WORKS: Tiny Garments, 1932; Excuse It, Please! 1936; Dithers and Jitters, 1938; Soap Behind the Ears, 1941; Our Hearts Were Young and Gay (with E. Kimbrough) 1942; Popcorn, 1943; Family Circle (in England: Happy Family) 1948; Nuts in May, 1950; Bottoms Up, 1955.

ABOUT: Collier's March 3, 1934; Current Biography 1942; New York Herald Tribune Book Review September 24, 1950, October 8, 1950; New York Times May 11, June 8, October 26, 1941; Newsweek September 6, 1948; Time December 20, 1937.

SKLAR, GEORGE (1908-), American novelist and playwright, reports: "I was born in Meriden, Conn., within sound of a munitions plant, where my father worked as a gun assembler. Now, some forty years and three thousand miles removed, that sound, increasingly ominous, is still with me—although I have never given up the hope that man will some day learn to do without his arsenals.

"At Meriden High School, after I had won an essay contest on the subject of the Child Labor Amendment, I added writing to the imposing list of careers which were the shifting subjects of my Algeresque fantasies. I also fancied myself as a budding young

movie critic, and the publication of some half dozen letters—very technical disquisitions on the then silent art—in Richard Watts' movie column in the New York *Herald Tribune* seemed to confirm a definite leaning toward writing.

"Even at that optimistic age, I was aware that it wasn't a very practical way of earning a living. Being very realistic, I decided I'd teach—of all things, Latin—and devote spare time and summers to writing. So I majored in the classics at Yale and wrote one-act plays on the side. One of them, an expressionistic piece called *Pity* was produced by the Yale Dramat and received with such enthusiastic applause by a very undiscriminating Derby Day audience that I was then and there lost to the teaching profession. That, plus the fact that I graduated with the Class of '29 into a depression economy which would have none of teachers, nor, it seemed, anything else.

"So, having tried the practical and found it to be highly impractical, I switched horses. I enrolled in Professor George Pierce Baker's famous 47 Workshop in playwriting at the Yale department of drama. While there, in collaboration with Albert Maltz, I wrote a play called *Merry Go Round.* It was produced simultaneously at the University Theatre and on Broadway. Five other plays followed, all produced between the years 1932-1939. I then signed a writing contract with Columbia Pictures and sweated out a four-year stretch, which, aside from salary, I regretted.

"In 1945, I turned to the writing of novels, a medium which I increasingly prefer. *The Two Worlds of Johnny Truro* appeared in 1947; *The Promising Young Men* in 1951; and *The Housewarming* in 1953. I am now at work on my fourth.

"My work would probably be described as of the realistic school. I believe that a writer should reflect the times and society in which he lives and, more importantly, the aspirations of the human heart. I live in Los Angeles with my wife and three children; work six days a week, on a regular schedule, slowly and painfully."

* * *

George Sklar's plays, written in collaboration with Albert Maltz and Paul Peters and produced during the 1930's by the non-profit group Theatre Union, were forceful "proletarian" dramas. Probably the most effective of these was *Stevedore,* a melodramatic but genuinely moving protest against racial discrimination and a plea for closer cooperation between black and white workers. His novels, on the other hand, are polished, sophisticated character studies, set against a background of Hollywood or Eastern society. But they show a distinct influence of his earlier career, with their easy, natural dialogue, and the same "hard-driving pace" that marked the plays.

PRINCIPAL WORKS: *Plays (dates of production)*—Merry Go Round (with A. Maltz) 1933; Stevedore (with P. Peters) 1934; Parade (with P. Peters) 1935; The Life and Death of an American, 1939; Laura (with V. Caspary) 1946. *Novels* —The Two Worlds of Johnny Truro, 1947; The Promising Young Men, 1951; The Housewarming, 1953.

SLADE, CAROLINE (BEACH) (October 7, 1886-), American novelist, was born in Minneapolis, Minn.

Gustave Lorey

At·the age of seven she moved with her family to Saratoga Springs, N.Y., where she has lived ever since. For many years Mrs. Slade was a county social worker, and the subject of her books is the plight of those who must live under public welfare of one kind or another. During her work with the County Board of Child Welfare and the Children's Court, she trained and supervised many students from Skidmore College in their field work. She is the wife of John A. Slade, lawyer and a former lecturer on legal subjects at Skidmore, now a trustee of the college and president of the Corporation of Yaddo in Saratoga Springs.

Mrs. Slade is now retired from social work. She lives a quiet and secluded life with her husband on the old Slade farm, near Saratoga Springs. Here she has written articles and short stories for a number of popular magazines and her popular "social-work novels." These have been translated into several foreign languages and have sold well in England and in Europe, as well as in the United States. Mrs. Slade's first novel, *Sterile Sun,* was described as "the bitter fruit" of her long experience as a social worker. The story of four girls who are driven by social and economic circumstances into prostitution, it was praised by James T. Farrell as "an important social document and a moving piece of writing." In later novels she considered the problems of the unem-ployed, the families on relief, wayward girls, and many other victims of the vast and often cold and cruel social structure of modern life. Her stories are sometimes brutal and shocking, but they are written with such warmth and compassion and with so much obvious understanding of the social problems involved, that they emerge as works of genuine literary distinction. Diana Trilling wrote of her novel *Lilly Crackell:* "I have no particular fondness for fiction as reform, and there were even moments when I found *Lilly Crackell* tedious. But in the current flood of propaganda novels compounded of Hollywood-*Life* sentimentalized generalities, a book like Mrs. Slade's shines out for its old-fashioned zeal for decency." Mrs. Slade has said of her own work that in spite of ill health, she is always "ready to do battle with welfare set-ups, organizations and workers for the right of individuals to maintain a good way of life, even while on relief."

PRINCIPAL WORKS: Sterile Sun, 1936; The Triumph of Willie Pond, 1940; Job's House, 1941; Lilly Crackell, 1943; Margaret, 1946; Mrs. Party's House, 1948.

ABOUT: Warfel, H. R. American Novelists of Today.

SLATER, HUMPHREY (1906-), English novelist, was educated at Sedbergh and Tonbridge Schools, and then studied painting at the Slade

School of Art, London, where he was awarded scholarships and prizes. In 1930 he spent some months in the U.S.S.R. and in 1932 in Germany was involved in anti-Nazi politics and Berlin street battles. Later he traveled in France and Spain as a political journalist. He fought on the Republican side in Spain (1936-38), and was appointed Chief of Operations, International Brigade.

In 1940 he initiated, with Tom Wintringham, the training of the Home Guard at Osterley, England. He also served as an anti-aircraft gunner, went through an infantry O.C.T.U., was promoted to captain, and was then appointed instructor in tactics with the rank of major. Slater wrote two books on military strategy and tactics. In 1944 he was invalided out of the service.

In addition to essays in philosophy and the arts, Slater has written several novels, the first of which was *The Heretics,* the parallel stories of three children involved in the Children's Crusade of the twelfth century and three twentieth century English students in the Spanish Civil War. Here, said the *Christian Century*, the author "has achieved a style remarkable for its compactness and cool detachment, and has virtually created a new form of fiction." *"The Heretics* is a book which can be quickly read, but which remains in the mind, making its point, fastening its implications, impressing its inescapable truth, long after it is put aside," wrote Thomas Sugrue in the New York *Herald Tribune Book Review.* "All who are heretics will want to read it and teach it and preach it; all who are not heretics will want to burn it. As Mr. Slater so expertly demonstrates, the situation remains the same."

Slater's second novel was *Conspirator.* The weaknesses of this novel were felt to be certain implausibilities of characterization, which were, however, well concealed by a brilliantly melodramatic manipulation of plot. The New York *Times* wrote, "Mr. Slater is gifted with dramatic insight, acute observation and a sure-footed literary style—economical, graceful, tinged with satire, and suggestive of a gentler, more political Evelyn Waugh. But as a novel, *Conspirator* splits down the middle. . . . The warm human interest of personal relations vanishes; instead we have a dissection of ideology." Latest of Slater's novels is *Calypso,* published in 1953. "Though he does not fully succeed . . . ," wrote the (London) *Times Literary Supplement,* "his novel is delightful to read, successful in the portrait of Calypso herself and in what is far more difficult—the sketch of a young poet in whose genius the reader can believe."

PRINCIPAL WORKS: The Heretics, 1946; Conspirator, 1948; Calypso, 1953.

SLAUGHTER, FRANK GILL (February 25, 1908-), American novelist, writes: "I was born in Washington, D.C., but when I

was about five years old, my family moved to the old home on a farm about twelve miles north of Oxford, N. C., in the Piedmont section, where we raised tobacco and corn. My father was a rural mail carrier, operating several farms, a sawmill, and

Underwood & Underwood

some other enterprises. Since I was rather small to walk three miles each way to a country school, my mother taught me until I was ready for the sixth grade, which I entered at the age of nine. I was always studious and an omnivorous reader, traits which have stood me in very good stead as a writer of historical novels, where much research is necessary. Even today, I find that I enjoy the research for my novels more than any other part of my work.

"At fourteen I graduated as valedictorian from the Oxford High School and at eighteen *magna cum laude* from Duke University, being a member of Phi Beta Kappa at seventeen. At twenty-two, I received my M.D. from Johns Hopkins Medical School and spent four years in surgical training at the Jefferson Hospital, Roanoke, Va. There I met Jane Mundy. We were married in June 1933 and have two sons, Frank, Jr., and Randolph Mundy. In 1934 I came to Florida to practice surgery and was associated with a group clinic until I entered the army as major M.C. in July 1942. Promoted to lt. col. in March 1944, I served at Camp Kilmer, N.J. and on a hospital ship out of Los Angeles. In 1938 I became a Fellow of the American College of Surgeons and in 1940 was certified as a Specialist in Surgery by the American Board of Surgery.

"I began writing as a hobby in 1935 and wrote 250,000 words a year for five years, earning $12, roughly five cents a week. My first novel, *That None Should Die,* was published in 1941 and has been translated into ten foreign languages, as have most of my other books. *Spencer Brade, M.D.* followed, then *Air Surgeon, Battle Surgeon* and *A Touch of Glory,* written while in military service. While studying surgery of the Civil War, I became interested in that period and wrote *In a Dark Garden,* a world best seller, now in its second million. At this time I gave up medical practice to write and lecture. There followed: *The Golden Isle, Sangaree, Divine Mistress, The Stubborn Heart,* and *Fort Everglades;* I then turned my attention to the Biblical period with a novel about St. Luke titled *The Road to Bithynia; East Side General,* a modern day novel of a New York Hospital; *The Galileans,* a novel of Mary Magdalene; and *Storm Haven,* another Civil War novel laid in Florida. In the non-fiction field I have published *The New Science of Surgery, Medicine for Moderns,* and *Immortal Magyar,* a biography of Semmelweis, conqueror of childbed fever.

"I live in Jacksonville, Fla., and work at my home in one of its suburbs near the St. Johns River. I am an elder in the Riverside Presbyterian Church. Summers I live on Lake Geneva in Keystone Heights, Fla. In addition to publishing a novel a year, I write articles, do radio broadcasting, serve on various boards, and do some magazine fiction. My two Biblical novels are part of a long-range series that will number four or more. I also write a weekly historical article for *Florida Suntime* and experiment with plays, none of which have been produced, plus boating, camping and water skiing.

"Writing, I think, is one of the most satisfying occupations one could have. Through it I reach millions of people, since many of my books have a larger sale in foreign countries than they do in America. I now have ten foreign publishers in addition to my American publishers."

PRINCIPAL WORKS: That None Should Die, 1941; Spencer Brade, M.D., 1942; Air Surgeon, 1943; Battle Surgeon, 1944; A Touch of Glory, 1945; In a Dark Garden, 1946; The Golden Isle, 1947; Sangaree, 1948; Divine Mistress, 1949; The Stubborn Heart, 1950; Fort Everglades, 1951; The Road to Bithynia, 1951; East Side General, 1952; The Galileans, 1953; Storm Haven, 1953; The Song of Ruth, 1954; The Healer, 1955; Apalache Gold, 1955. *Non-Fiction*—The New Science of Surgery, 1946; Medicine for Moderns, 1947; Immortal Magyar, 1950.

ABOUT: Current Biography 1942; New York Times Book Review September 29, 1946.

SLESINGER, TESS (July 16, 1905-February 21, 1945). For biographical sketch and list of works and references, see TWENTIETH CENTURY AUTHORS, 1942.

* * *

Tess Slesinger died at the Cedars of Lebanon Hospital in Los Angeles, after an illness of six months, at thirty-nine.

The reviews which greeted Miss Slesinger's *The Unpossessed* spoke generally of the "extraordinary promise" of this first novel by a young writer. Robert Cantwell called it "one of the very best of recent American novels." Herschel Brickell said it "has faults, and obvious ones, but it also manifests a very real and brilliant talent." During her ten years in Hollywood she appears to have written little except motion picture scripts. She and her husband Frank Davis completed the screen treatment for Betty Smith's *A Tree Grows in Brooklyn* shortly before her death.

ABOUT: New York Times February 22, 1945; Publishers' Weekly March 10, 1945.

*SLICHTER, SUMNER HUBER (January 8, 1892-), American economist, was born in Madison, Wis., the son of Charles Sumner Slichter and Mary Louise (Byrne) Slichter. His father was a professor of mathematics in the University of Wisconsin

* slĭk'tēr

Graduate School, and later he became dean. Slichter attended high school in Madison, graduating in 1909, and then went to the University of Munich for one year. Returning to the United States, he studied at the University of Wisconsin as an economics major, in 1913 taking a bachelor's degree and a year later a master's. From the University of Chicago in 1918 he received his Ph.D. Enlisting in the U.S. Army the same year, he soon became a lieutenant.

Michael L. Meier

After the war Slichter began teaching at Princeton (1919-20), then at Cornell (1920-30), and finally at Harvard (1930-). Since 1940 he has been Lamont University Professor there. *Fortune* has called Slichter "the public's economist, labor's economist and the businessman's economist." The author of numerous popular and scientific articles, he invented the phrase "laboristic economy" to describe American capitalism. The emphasis in his economic writings is on problems of labor-management relationships. In 1919 he urged management to adopt a policy of understanding toward labor and of employing a well-trained labor administrator who would be invested with authority. In the early 1930's Slichter called for the establishment of a federal labor board. In the 1940's he suggested the regulation of both unions and management, and made specific suggestions in this regard. He testified in 1947 before the House Labor Committee in favor of legislation establishing compulsory arbitration. From 1935 to 1938 he was a member of the Social Science Research Council, and from 1942 to 1951 chairman of the research advisory board of the Committee for Economic Development. Since 1946 he has been economic advisor to Incorporated Investors. In 1947-48 he was chairman of the advisory council on Social Security of the United States Senate.

The Turnover of Factory Labor, his first book, appeared in 1919, and he has written many volumes since. His *Union Policies and Industrial Management* is considered "one of the leading books on collective bargaining." Of his *What's Ahead for American Business* the *Christian Science Monitor* said: "The lay person doesn't need a course in economics to find this book rewarding." "From beginning to end," wrote Ray Hickok in the *Saturday Review of Literature*, "the book moves rapidly and freshly. That constitutes its chief charm and will, we hope, provide this particular professor with a sizable audience. His teaching is easy to take and is decidedly needed among our economic illiterates."

Slichter has brown eyes and white hair, is five feet ten and a half inches tall. *Time* once quoted him as considering himself politically "a Wisconsin liberal—a conservative liberal that does not go off half-cocked." He married Ada Pence in 1918, and they have two sons; they live in Cambridge, Mass. Slichter's brother, Louis Byrne Slichter, is a well-known geophysicist.

PRINCIPAL WORKS: The Turnover of Factory Labor, 1919; Modern Economic Society, 1931; Towards Stability, 1934; Union Policies and Industrial Management, 1941; Economic Factors Affecting Industrial Relations Policy in National Defense, 1941; Social Security after the War, 1943; Present Savings and Postwar Markets, 1943; Trade Unions in a Free Society, 1947; The Challenge of Industrial Relations, 1947; The American Economy: Its Problems and Prospects, 1948; What's Ahead for American Business, 1951.

ABOUT: Current Biography 1947.

SMART, CHARLES ALLEN (November 30, 1904-). For autobiographical sketch and list of earlier works and references, see TWENTIETH CENTURY AUTHORS, 1942.

* * *

Charles Allen Smart writes from Chillicothe, Ohio: "Just before the war, with rising prices, I increased my farming operations largely and actually made money. In May 1942 I enlisted as an apprentice seaman, USNR, and became a signalman, then quartermaster. serving entirely in the LST's, including the New Guinea, Normandy, and Okinawa can.paigns. I was commissioned a lt. (jg) and then made lt., being released as such in September 1945. During the war I had to sell our larger farm and all our livestock. When I returned, prices were very high for going back into farming, more machinery was necessary, and I was a bit tired. In February 1946 I became writer-in-residence at Ohio University, Athens, Ohio, sixty miles east of my home, and held this position until February 1953. In 1947 Random House published my novel *Sassafras Hill*, which was also published in Sydney, Australia, and in digest, and in Swedish, in Stockholm. Since then, I have been floundering a bit in my writing. As a part of the celebration of its Sesquicentennial in 1954, Ohio University will produce (and publish) an historical play by me called 'The Green Adventure.'

"To go back to your sketch: I never was very tall or fair. My height is 5' 8½" and I am now grizzled. The Chillicothe Little Theatre folded up just before the war, and the historical play already mentioned is my only present connection with the theatre. In 1949 my wife and I had six months in Mexico, where I studied painting, my hobby ever since."

ADDITIONAL WORK: Sassafras Hill, 1947; The Green Adventure (play) 1954.

SMEDLEY, AGNES (1894-May 6, 1950). For biographical sketch and list of earlier works and references, see TWENTIETH CENTURY AUTHORS, 1942.

* * *

Agnes Smedley died in a nursing home in Oxford, England. She had been engaged in writing a book about General Chu Teh, Commander-in-Chief of the Chinese Communist Army.

In 1949 General Douglas MacArthur's headquarters in Tokyo issued charges that Miss Smedley was "a spy and agent of the Soviet government." She denied the charges and asked for a chance to answer them in court. Shortly afterward United States Army headquarters in Washington said there was "no proof" of the charges and that their issuance had been a *"faux pas."* At the time of her death, however, the House Committee on Un-American Activities had reopened the case and had suggested her return from England for questioning.

Of Miss Smedley's personality, Hilda Selwyn-Clarke has said: "She had so much wit, so much gaiety, such generosity in her friendships." Her books were written "with a disdain for the outward flourishes of literary ornament," in the words of T. A. Bisson, but he added that her work "constitutes one of those inimitable pages of life experience which lays bare the reality of contemporary historical developments." Her last book, *Battle Hymn of China,* was called (by Mark Gayne) "an earthy, honest, powerful book by a good woman. . . . Miss Smedley may be intemperate and intolerant, but she is honest, and this honesty underscores every line."

Correction: Miss Smedley was born in 1894, not 1890, as given in TWENTIETH CENTURY AUTHORS, 1942.

ADDITIONAL WORK: Battle Hymn of China, 1943.

ABOUT: Venkatachalom, G. Profiles; Christian Century March 2, 1949; Current Biography 1944; Nation February 19, 1949; New Republic May 29, 1950; New Statesman and Nation May 20, 1950; New York Times May 9, 1950; Newsweek May 28, 1951; Publishers' Weekly March 5, 1949.

SMITH, ALFRED ALOYSIUS. See HORN. A. A.

SMITH, ARTHUR COSSLETT (January 19, 1852-May 22, 1926). For biographical sketch and list of works and references, see TWENTIETH CENTURY AUTHORS, 1942.

* * *

ABOUT: Saturday Review of Literature May 18, 1946.

SMITH, ARTHUR JAMES MARSHALL (1902-   ), Canadian poet, critic, and editor, writes: "I was born in Montreal and edu-

cated at McGill University and at Edinburgh University, where I worked under Sir Herbert Grierson, receiving a Ph.D. degree for a thesis on the metaphysical poets of the Anglican church in the seventeenth century. As an undergraduate at McGill I was one of the founders and editors of the *McGill Fortnightly Review* (1926-27), which introduced the new poets of the 'Montreal School' who were instrumental in bringing modern cosmopolitan poetry into Canada, and I contributed verse and criticism to the *Canadian Forum*, the *Nation*, and the *Dial*. Since 1929 I have been a college teacher of English and after various brief excursions into Indiana, Nebraska, and South Dakota, I became a member of the English department at Michigan State College, where I am now a professor. I continued to contribute verse to such magazines as *Hound and Horn*, the *Adelphi*, *New Verse*, *Twentieth Century Verse*, and *Poetry*, receiving *Poetry's* Harriet Monroe Memorial Prize in 1941. A volume of poems, *News of the Phoenix*, was published in 1943 and was awarded the Governor General's Medal for the best Canadian book of verse of the year. I traveled across Canada in 1941 and '42 on a Guggenheim fellowship and prepared a critical and historical anthology of Canadian poetry, *The Book of Canadian Poetry*, which was published in 1943. A new and enlarged edition was brought out in 1948. At the present time I am preparing a larger collection of Canadian prose literature, much of the initial work having been made possible by grants from the Rockefeller Foundation. I spend some part of each year in Canada. In 1946

I delivered the Founders' Day Address at the University of New Brunswick and since then have taught in the summer schools at the University of Toronto and Queens University, Kingston. I have also taught in the summer at the University of Washington. I have published two anthologies of poetry outside the Canadian field: *Seven Centuries of Verse,* a collection of poems for college students, which surprised me by selling nearly fifteen thousand copies, and *The Worldly Muse,* an anthology of 'serious light verse' compiled for fun, which, though the *Nation* called it 'an altogether delightful anthology,' is not nearly so well known as I could wish."

* * *

The late E. K. Brown considered A. J. M. Smith a central figure among contemporary Canadian poets. His verse, Brown pointed out, is severe, almost austere (he described his *News of the Phoenix* as "a proud, hard, noble and intense book")—but not without sharp, satiric humor. Smith himself urges his fellow poets to set the highest standards for themselves, to read widely and intensively, and to remember "that poetry does not permit the rejection of every aspect of the personality except intuition and sensibility. It must be written by the whole man. It is an intelligent activity, and it ought to compel the respect of the generality of intelligent men. If it is a good, it is a good in itself."

PRINCIPAL WORKS: News of the Phoenix, 1943; Exploring Poetry (with M. L. Rosenthal) 1955. *Editor*—The Book of Canadian Poetry, 1943; Seven Centuries of Verse, 1944; The Worldly Muse, 1951.

ABOUT: Brown, E. K. On Canadian Poetry; Collin, W. E. The White Savannahs; Percival, W. P. (ed.) Leading Canadian Poets; Canadian Forum February 1944.

SMITH, BETTY (WEHNER) (December 15, 1904-   ), American novelist and playwright, was born in the Williamsburg section of Brooklyn, N.Y.,

the daughter of John C. Wehner—son of Irish immigrants—and Catherine (Hummel) Wehner—daughter of German immigrants. She attended P.S. 23 in Greenpoint, and read nearly all the books in the little public library on Leonard Street. She learned to cook, sew, and to dance at the Jackson Street Settlement, acted in several amateur plays at the

Williamsburg Y.M.C.A., but her formal education ended with graduation from the eighth grade. At the age of fourteen she started to work, finding jobs in various factories, offices and stores in New York and Brooklyn.

At an early age she married a Brooklyn boy, a law student at the University of Michigan. Two daughters were born a year apart, Nancy and Mary Smith. When the children were old enough to attend kindergarten, she received permission to audit several English courses at the university, eventually being admitted as a special student. Because she had not graduated from high school, or attended high school at all, she could not take the regular undergraduate courses, but was permitted five hours' work per week. And although not a candidate for a degree, she competed for the Avery Hopwood Award and won it in drama. It was during this period at the university (1927-30) that she began to have her one-act plays published, and became a feature writer on a Detroit paper. From 1930 to 1934 she attended Yale Drama School, taking a course under George P. Baker. On leaving Yale, she became a member of the Federal Theatre, and met playwright Paul Green who suggested she come to Chapel Hill, N.C., and write. She was given a Rockefeller fellowship in playwriting by the University of North Carolina, and a year later a Rockefeller Dramatists Guild fellowship. During this time she wrote and published seventy-five one-act plays and five full-length ones, some of them in collaboration. She won many awards and some of her one-act plays are used as class texts.

In her spare time Betty Smith was writing a novel. A page a day, it took her three years to write. This was *A Tree Grows in Brooklyn,* published in 1943, which became an immediate best seller and a book club selection. It has been translated into sixteen languages, and sales have reached nearly three million copies: one of the ten best sellers of all time. It was made into a motion picture and a Broadway musical comedy.

"A remarkably good first novel," wrote the *New Yorker.* "The author sees the misery, squalor, and cruelty of slum life but sees them with understanding, pity, and sometimes with hilarious humor." Five years later, her second novel, *Tomorrow Will Be Better,* was published. It too had a Brooklyn locale, but lacked the poignancy and the warm humor of the earlier book. It nevertheless rang with conviction and authenticity and was generally well received.

Betty Smith was at one time on the faculty of the University of North Carolina, and is still a consultant to graduate students in the department of drama. During the summers she makes guest appearances in Paul Green's *The Lost Colony;* she has been an actress in stock and summer companies. A few days before the publication of *A Tree Grows in Brooklyn,* she married Joseph Piper Jones, an assistant editor of the Chapel Hill *Weekly,* but then a private in the army. They were divorced in 1951.

PRINCIPAL WORKS: A Tree Grows in Brooklyn, 1943; The Boy Abe (one-act play) 1944; Tomorrow Will Be Better (in England: Streets of Little Promise) 1948; A Tree Grows in Brooklyn (a musical play; with George Abbott) 1951.

ABOUT: Warfel, H. R. American Novelists of Today; Current Biography 1943; Life June 6, 1949; New York Times Book Review August 22, 1948; Saturday Review of Literature August 21, 1948.

SMITH, CHARD POWERS (November 1, 1894-). For autobiographical sketch and list of earlier works and references, see TWENTIETH CENTURY AUTHORS, 1942.

* * *

Chard Powers Smith writes from Cornwall, Conn.: "My *Ladies Day,* like *Artillery of Time* (1939), had a fine press, but, unlike *Artillery of Time,* it was not a bestseller. In 1943 I published two small war novels, one of merely current interest, and the other, *Turn of the Dial,* a valuable book for the long run but a failure in immediate sales. It may have been too strong medicine, for it showed with some precision how Hitler's methods were learned from American advertising. In 1946 I moved out of fictionized history a little closer to real history with *The Housatonic* in the Rivers of America series, again a critical success and again a bestseller. It did me the great service of introducing me to the history of New England, especially to the Puritans who have been so absurdly villified by debunking historians, especially Charles Beard and James Truslow Adams.

"Since 1946, I have had two aims, which I retain. One is to finish the three-generation trilogy which *Artillery of Time* introduced (Civil War generation), *Ladies Day* continued (the '80's and '90's) and which needs finishing with the story of my—the 'Lost' —generation. I have made two starts at this novel, and each has been unsatisfactory, perhaps through the conscious proximity of my other aim. This is to write a real history of New England culture, from the Atlantic to the Pacific, and from 1620 to date. It has never been done, and it is the story of the stronger of the only two true cultures this country has produced, the other being that of the Old South. In pursuance of this aim, I took an M.A. at Columbia and have been doing some teaching. [The book was *Yankees and God*, published in 1954.]

"Meanwhile I have become a professing Christian, combining two approaches that are not as incompatible as is sometimes supposed. Emotionally and ecclesiastically, I have become a Quaker. [Smith is a trustee of the Friends Seminary and the Brooklyn Friends School, both in New York.] But intellectually, I am a Calvinist. I am of those who believe that America's only hope is in a great Christian awakening, not only emotionally but intellectually as well."

* * *

Yankees and God, a long but lively history of the New England cultural pattern, was acclaimed for both its scholarship and its style. The *Christian Science Monitor* wrote: "This is a rambunctious, opinionated, idiosyncratic, difficult, and delightful book. Mr. Smith is a passionate Puritan rising to the defense of a stout-hearted Puritan culture. . . ."

ADDITIONAL WORKS: He's in the Artillery Now, 1943; Turn of the Dial, 1943; The Housatonic, Puritan River, 1946; Yankees and God, 1954.

ABOUT: Warfel, H. R. American Novelists of Today.

SMITH, Lady ELEANOR FURNEAUX

(1902-October 20, 1945). For autobiographical sketch and list of earlier works and references, see TWENTIETH CENTURY AUTHORS, 1942.

* * *

Lady Eleanor Smith died in London, after a long illness, at forty-two. She had never married. In 1931 she and her sister were converted to Catholicism.

Her friend Cecil Beaton has paid tribute to her "dynamic enthusiasm and sparkling passions," adding: "In the company of someone with so unbiased an eye and so original a mind as hers one was always stimulated to discover further interests and unexpected joys in everyday existence." In her novels of circus and gypsy life she exhibited what Charles Marriott called "a special and apparently constitutional turn for the flamboyant in type and character." With a lively imagination and great story-telling skill she could, Isabelle Mallet says, continue to produce "vivid entertainment out of the familiar but unfaded material."

ADDITIONAL WORKS: Caravan, 1943; Magic Lantern, 1945; British Circus Life, 1948.

ABOUT: Hoehn, M. (ed.) Catholic Authors, I; London Times October 22, 1945, October 24, 1945; New York Times October 21, 1945.

SMITH, ERNEST BRAMAH ("Ernest Bramah") (1869?-June 27, 1942). For biographical sketch and list of works and references, see TWENTIETH CENTURY AUTHORS, 1942.

SMITH, HARRY ALLEN (December 19, 1907-   ), American humorist, who publishes under the name H. Allen Smith, writes: "I am an Egyptian in the sense that I was born in that part of Illinois known as 'Egypt.' I have expended a good many units of energy explaining to people that the H. stands for Harry. One of nine children, I grew up in Illinois, Ohio, and Indiana. On finishing

Editta Sherman

the eighth grade I went to work as a chicken picker in a poultry house (hens, 2½ cents, roosters, 3 cents) then became a shoeshine boy and sweeper-up of used hair in a barber shop. At this period of my life I despised Horatio Alger, Jr.

"From the barber shop I moved to my first newspaper job as proofreader. Soon I became a reporter and later an itinerant newspaperman in Indiana, Kentucky, Florida, Oklahoma, Colorado, and, in 1929, New York. I worked five years for the United Press and five years for the *World-Telegram*. In 1939 I wrote a book and in 1940 I wrote another. Their publication led me to seek employment as a crossing guard for a railroad. Before I could make such a connection, a man asked me to put together some flippant newspaper reminiscences and these were published under the title *Low Man on a Totem Pole*. People lost their heads. They bought it. I quit newspapering and wrote another one, *Life in a Putty Knife Factory*. Madness seized the populace. They bought it.

"Up to the beginning of the Eisenhower Era, I produced fifteen books. Three of these were novels, including *Rhubarb* which was made into a motion picture. One was an anthology of humorous stories and essays, *Desert Island Decameron*.

"I am generally referred to as a humorist although a good many people think of me as a suppuration, or worse. There appears to be nothing I can do about this latter crowd. I don't believe, if it came right down to it, that I would push them off cliffs. Yet I feel that they are entitled to the sleep that is eternal, starting right away.

"Since 1945 I have lived in Westchester County, forty miles from Manhattan. I have been married to the same party since 1927 and have a grown son who is a chemical engineer and a daughter who is married. I have two major hobbies: my grandson, born in 1952, and playing low-brow, i.e., popular, music on the Hammond organ. I am a baseball fan, a Mark Twain fan, a James Thurber fan, a Mencken fan and a Bertrand Russell fan. I believe that the human race will shortly blow itself up and I am already at work weaving the handbasket which shall serve as my transportation into the after-world."

* * *

Bergen Evans, in an essay on H. Allen Smith introducing an anthology of his writings, *The World, the Flesh, and H. Allen Smith* (1954), places his subject squarely in the long tradition of Midwest American humorists, from Davy Crockett through Mark Twain, Finley Peter Dunne, George Ade, Kin Hubbard, etc. Smith's specialty—one which developed quite naturally from his career as a newspaper feature writer—is the collecting of odd, "wacky" characters. Fred Allen has called him "the screwballs' Boswell" and the "biographer to the dispensable man." Although he sometimes tries to conceal it, he sympathizes with the frustrated, the defeated, and the hopeless. Evans writes: "Nobility and absurdity are often intertwined and the pathetic and the ludicrous are frequently inseparable." His humor is hearty, boisterous and ribald. "There are no clichés in his writing and no acceptance of the reports or opinions of others where he can see and judge for himself. He doesn't tell lies, not even noble lies. He keeps his humor pure, in a way that some of his critics cannot even comprehend, by being honest."

PRINCIPAL WORKS: Robert Gair, 1939; Mr. Klein's Kampf, 1940; Low Man on a Totem Pole, 1941; Life in a Putty Knife Factory, 1943; Lost in the Horse Latitudes, 1944; (ed.) The Desert Island Decameron, 1945; Rhubarb, 1946; Lo, the Former Egyptian, 1947; Larks in the Popcorn, 1948; We Went Thataway, 1949; People Named Smith, 1950; Mister Zip, 1952; Smith's London Journal, 1952; The Compleat Practical Joker, 1953; The Rebel Yell, 1954.

ABOUT: Evans, B. Introduction to The World, the Flesh, and H. Allen Smith; Smith, H. A. Low Man on a Totem Pole; Van Gelder, R. Writers and Writing; Collier's August 10, 1946; Current Biography 1942; New York Times Book Review June 12, 1949; Saturday Review June 26, 1954.

SMITH, JUSTIN HARVEY (January 13, 1857-March 21, 1930). For biographical sketch and list of works and references, see TWENTIETH CENTURY AUTHORS, 1942.

SMITH, LILLIAN EUGENIA (December 12, 1897-   ), American novelist and student of race relations, writes: "I was born in Jasper, Fla. There were nine of us who grew up in a big old rambling house set under great oaks heavy with Spanish moss, in a small Florida town just across the Georgia line. My mother's people were rice planters near St. Mary's; my father's  family were pioneer folk who settled southwest Georgia and helped drive the Seminoles into Florida. Both families had had slaves; both thought slavery wrong.

"I began writing 'books' about the time I learned to read them. Making up a life different from my own which I did not quite accept. Asking questions which no one would answer, perhaps because they could not. 'Where did I come from? . . . where was I going? . . . what is eternity?' I must have been a nuisance of large dimensions for I remember my Sunday School teacher firmly laying down the law that never must I ask about eternity again in Sunday School. So I tried to find my answers in our library. I read Shakespeare one day, *Elsie Dinsmore* the next, *Pilgrim's Progress* the next. I had read all of Shakespeare's plays by the time I was ten or eleven years old. And though I had not found the answers to my questions I had found something very wonderful that made me know the magic of words and poetry at an age when it almost got into my bloodstream.

"And then one day I discovered music. Every one in my family played or sang. I was used to music; but one day, it became something for me. And though I continued my love for books, music was my ardent passion for the next twelve years. I was dedicated in that awful way in which a passionate child can give herself. I practiced hours each day. Bach, Beethoven, Chopin, and trivial composers too held me in a kind of thralldom. It was a beautiful flight. Then suddenly, I was once more absorbed in words, writing, books.

"In between times, I went to college, to Peabody Conservatory in Baltimore; I taught music for three years in Huchow, China; I came home and was secretary to a city manager of a south Florida city and played the organ in a church. Then I took over my father's summer camp for girls which happened to be the first private camp to open in

Georgia. It was in the mountains close to North Carolina, and I still live on top of the mountain at the old camp site. I directed it for twenty-four summers. It became a camp known for its creative activities: music, sculpture, the children's theatre; and for the success it often had in dealing with the emotional problems of its children.

"While I had this camp, I also edited and published a magazine (for ten years) called *South Today*. This psychically rewarding and financially impoverishing venture began with twelve pages and twenty-five subscribers and ended as a hundred-page magazine with 10,-000 subscribers. But I abandoned the project in 1946 in order to give all of my time to writing.

"My first two novels were never published. One was about missionaries in China; the other was a family chronicle. My third novel was *Strange Fruit*, published in 1944. It was turned down by seven publishers all of whom said it was interesting but not 'salable.' The eighth publisher accepted it immediately. *Strange Fruit* sold around three million copies in this country without benefit of book clubs. It has been translated into fifteen languages. Has received the Constance Lindsay Skinner Award, the Page One Award, was listed fourth 'best novel of the decade' and sixteenth 'best book of the decade' in The H. W. Wilson Company's *The Best Books of the Decade 1936-45*.

"In 1949, *Killers of the Dream* was published. This book was an experiment in the joint autobiography of a person and her region: a searching out of the creative and destructive forces at work in a culture and in the lives of the children who grow up in it. It received the Southern Authors' Award for 1950 and was cited by American Library Association as one of the 'Fifty Best Books of the Year' in their annual list.

"I am now completing for fall (1953) publication a non-fiction book called 'I Went on a Journey' [published as *The Journey*]. A personal book, drawing heavily on my own experiences as I search for an image of the human being that I can believe in. I have worked for seven years on my novel tentatively called 'Julia.' Still unfinished.

"In 1950, I received the honorary degree of Doctor of Letters from Oberlin College and that of Doctor of Humane Letters from Howard University. I have taught at the Writers' Conference at the University of Indiana and at the University of Colorado."

* * *

The tragedy of racial segregation in the South has rarely been treated more graphically and dramatically than it was by Lillian Smith in *Strange Fruit*. This novel about the love of a Negro girl and a white man was one of the most controversial books of recent years. Banned in Boston and in most of Massachusetts, it became the subject of a test case when the author Bernard De Voto arranged with a Cambridge bookseller to purchase the book openly. The case against De Voto was dismissed, but the bookseller was fined $200. The attendant publicity—and further attempts to ban the book in Detroit and in New York City—did nothing to harm the sale of the book and probably contributed to its great success. A work of passionate conviction and sincerity, *Strange Fruit* did not show extraordinary literary brilliance. Malcolm Cowley wrote of it: "Miss Smith seems to lack the specifically literary gifts of William Faulkner, . . . or Carson McCullers; and it is possible that her talents will lead her eventually into some other field than the novel. But she has done something in this book that nobody did before her; she has shown that a lynching was intimately connected with the life of a whole community; that it explains and condemns a whole social order."

Cowley's guess that Miss Smith's talents might lead her into other fields than the novel proved to be a good one. In the books which have followed *Strange Fruit*, she has addressed the reader directly and presented the racial problem without dressing it in story form. *Killers of the Dream*, an attempt to probe the psychological bases of prejudice, and *The Journey*, a spiritual autobiography, were both praised for their compassion and conviction. Of the latter A. Powell Davies wrote in the New York *Times*: "Here is a book that lives and breathes, a fearless encounter with reality, a mind-stretching experience."

Miss Smith is unmarried. She lives on Old Screamer Mountain, on the site of the camp she ran for many years, near the little town of Clayton, Ga. A slight and soft-spoken woman with grey hair and "rich blue eyes," she has in her face, Dorothy Dunbar Bromley once wrote, "the tranquility of spirit which comes from listening to the pines on the mountain top."

PRINCIPAL WORKS: Strange Fruit, 1944; Killers of the Dream, 1949; The Journey, 1954; Now Is the Time, 1955.

ABOUT: Smith, L. The Journey; Current Biography 1944; Common Ground Autumn 1943; Collier's January 28, 1950; New York Herald Tribune Book Review October 30, 1949; New York Times Book Review December 12, 1954.

SMITH, LOGAN PEARSALL (October 18, 1865-March 2, 1946). For biographical sketch and list of earlier works and references, see TWENTIETH CENTURY AUTHORS, 1942.

* * *

Logan Pearsall Smith died at his home in the Chelsea section of London at eighty. The controversial *Recollections of Logan Pearsall Smith* by Robert Gathorne-Hardy has set forth the record of a sixteen-year relationship between Smith and his "perpetual apprentice" which emphasized Smith's deterioration into a manic-depressive state in his later years. Ernestine Evans characterized the book as "moving, frightening, a precise account of a mental disease, set down with both objective and subjective detail."

Smith has been described by Paul Dinkins as "the exclusively literary man" who was "in constant mental flight from the real facts and issues of experience," but his friend Cyril Connolly has attributed to him "a perpetual warm, ironical appreciation of life heightened by a never-failing passion for the best in literature and the human heart."

His *Trivia* revealed, "with cool self-mockery," Edmund Wilson said, "his old-fogyism, his timidity, his snobbery, his envy, his respect for money, his capacity for being a bore, as well as the touching aspiration, the Quakerish sobriety and purity, of his worship of literature." George Santayana called the same work "delightfully vivid and humorous" and "a document of importance." Smith's ultimate attitude may best be expressed in his own phrase, used late in his life: "To set a chime of words ringing in the thoughts of a few fastidious people is the only thing worth living for."

ADDITIONAL WORK: All Trivia: Trivia, More Trivia, Afterthoughts, Last Words (new edition) 1945.

ABOUT: Gathorne-Hardy, R. Recollections of Logan Pearsall Smith; Russell, J. (ed.) Portraits of Logan Pearsall Smith Drawn from His Letters and Diaries; Atlantic Monthly June 1946; Catholic World November 1950; London Times March 4, 1946; New York Times March 3, 1946; New Yorker May 27, 1950; Spectator January 26, 1951; Time December 10, 1945, April 24, 1950.

SMITH, Mrs. MARY PRUDENCE (WELLS) (July 23, 1840-December 17, 1930). For biographical sketch and list of works and references, see TWENTIETH CENTURY AUTHORS, 1942.

SMITH, NAOMI. See ROYDE-SMITH

"SMITH, S. S." See WILLIAMSON, T. R.

SMITH, SHEILA. See KAYE-SMITH

SMITH, THORNE (1893-June 21, 1934). For biographical sketch and list of works and references, see TWENTIETH CENTURY AUTHORS, 1942.

SMITH, WALLACE (1888-January 31, 1937). For biographical sketch and list of works and references, see TWENTIETH CENTURY AUTHORS, 1942.

SMITTER, WESSEL (1894-November 7, 1951). For biographical sketch and list of works and references, see TWENTIETH CENTURY AUTHORS, 1942.

* * *

Wessel Smitter died in Eureka, Calif., as the result of a heart attack he suffered while he was chopping redwoods. He was fifty-seven. Smitter was on a visit from his home in southern California to the northern part of the state to gather material for a novel. He left his widow, Mrs. Faith Smitter, and three children.

His literary reputation must rest on his two published novels. Louis Paul said of the first, *F.O.B. Detroit*, "It is strong stuff and full of profound sympathy, and constitutes a social document." The second, *Another Morning*, was called "a fine and moving story" by Ruth Gruber, while Wallace Stegner pointed out that "this novel is important because it transplants the typical frontier virtues from a dead past to a living present and future."

ABOUT: New York Times November 9, 1951; Wilson Library Bulletin January 1952.

SNAITH, JOHN COLLIS (1876-December 8, 1936). For biographical sketch and list of works and references, see TWENTIETH CENTURY AUTHORS, 1942.

SNOW, CHARLES PERCY (October 15, 1905-), English novelist and scientist who signs his work C. P. Snow, was born in Leicester. The childhood of Lewis Eliot in his novel *Time of Hope* is in part autobiographical. His father was William Edward Snow, an unsuccessful businessman, and his mother, Ada Sophia (Robinson) Snow. He has three brothers. Since his family was poor, Snow has said: "I first

made my way in the most practicable career open to me, as a professional scientist. Getting through the university (University College, Leicester) on  scholarships, I did research in physics at Cambridge (Ph.D. 1930), became a Fellow of Corpus Christi College (Cambridge) and continued in scientific work and college administration through the Thirties. At this time I had

Lotte Jacobi

published my first works." Snow tutored at Corpus Christi from 1935 to 1940 and from 1938 to 1940 was editor of *Discovery*. He was also editor of the Cambridge Library of Modern Science.

During World War II, Snow was the chief of scientific personnel for the Ministry of Labour and was rewarded with the C.B.E. (Commander of the British Empire) in 1943. Immediately after the war, in 1945, he was appointed civil service commissioner, a post he still holds. He has also been physicist-director of the English Electric Company.

Snow's first book was a humorous detective story, *Death Under Sail*, in 1932. In 1935 *The Search* appeared. The *New Statesman and Nation* described it as "the story of a scientist, a well-known crystallographer, of his rise from indigence to eminence and of his decline from scientific eminence to hard-won matrimonial felicity." The novel was generally well received with special praise for its characterization of the scientific world but with some criticism of the weakness of its characters. Beatrice Sherman wrote, in the *New York Times*, that it was "a meaty, stimulating novel which deserves and demands a careful reading," and the late William Rose Benét found it "superior to the average modern novel in that it deals more with the intellectual and less with the purely emotional and physical."

In 1935 Snow first conceived the ambitious idea for a ten-novel series attempting to picture English life over a long period of modern life. He did not actually begin this project until after World War II; by 1955 he had completed four separate but interrelated novels as part of a series to be called "The New Men." The first to be published, *The Light and the Dark,* is a character study of a young Cambridge don who attempts to curb his dark moods by promiscuity, alcohol, concentration on his studies, and religion. He joins the Royal Air Force at the

outbreak of the war and is killed in action. The New York *Times* expressed the general opinion of the critics: "Several of the minor characters come alive; some of the incidents, such as the forming of academic cliques within the college, are vivid. But the dominant characters are essentially sterile. They move like puppets, with the handler behind the platform exhorting us to consider the unique qualities and problems of his actors." The *Spectator* characterized the novel as "the work of a civilized, sensitive author who writes for readers like himself."

In the second novel in the series, *Time of Hope*, the narrator of *The Light and the Dark*, Lewis Eliot, relates the story of his own childhood and youth, his training in law, and his unhappy marriage. Harrison Smith in the *Saturday Review of Literature* wrote that "the pages illuminating Eliot's inner nature . . . can stand with the finest examples of the novelist's or the biographer's art; one unconsciously thinks of Rousseau and Emma Bovary."

The Masters is also narrated by Eliot, and this time he describes the conflicting forces aroused in the faculty over the election of a new master in one of the Cambridge colleges. The *New Yorker* declared: "Mr. Snow's writing is slow, sure and shrewd, and powerful enough to draw the reader entirely into his closed, almost airtight world of scholars and their families." The London *Times Literary Supplement* concluded its review thus: "There can be no doubt that *The Masters* gives an excellent account of at least one side of university life, upon which Mr. Snow is to be warmly congratulated." *The Masters* was chosen as the English Book Society Fiction Choice for July 1951.

In these novels—and in the most recent of them, *The New Men*—Snow has shown a keen awareness of the moral dilemmas of the scientists in the atomic age. He is also as keenly aware of the dilemmas faced by the novelist in a science-dominated age. In an article in the New York *Times Book Review,* January 30, 1955, he points out that science has had a devitalizing effect upon all contemporary arts—"not because it is evil or inhuman, but simply because it has been so overwhelmingly successful." With the discovery of the atom bomb, however, Snow finds a growing pessimism and a new humility among the scientists—a spirit in which scientists and novelists can learn from each other—"and the novel can take on a new authority and a new lease on life." In the future, he suggests, novels will be more closely related to man and his environment.

"For the novel only breathes freely when it has its roots in society."

Blue-eyed, fair-haired C. P. Snow is six feet tall and weighs 175 pounds. On July 14, 1950 he married the well known English novelist and critic Pamela Hansford Johnson. They have one son, Philip Charles Hansford Snow. They live in Clare, Suffolk, in eastern England. Snow has neither political nor church affiliations. He is a fiction reviewer for the London *Sunday Times*.

PRINCIPAL WORKS: Death Under Sail, 1932; New Lives for Old, 1933; The Search, 1935; Strangers and Brothers, 1940; The Light and the Dark, 1948; The Time of Hope, 1949; The Masters, 1951; The New Men, 1954.

ABOUT: Current Biography 1954.

SNOW, EDGAR PARKS (July 19, 1905-). For autobiographical sketch and list of earlier works and references, see TWENTIETH CENTURY AUTHORS, 1942.

* * *

Edgar Snow worked for the *Saturday Evening Post* as its first correspondent assigned to cover the U.S. Army in 1941. In 1942 he joined the staff of that journal, and from 1943 to 1952 was an associate editor. After Pearl Harbor, Snow became the *Post's* first "world correspondent" and went overseas, accredited to the U.S. Army, first to India and China, then to the Soviet Union, Iran, North Africa and Britain. He was in the Soviet Union most of 1944. In the last year of the war Snow was a correspondent in Britain, France, Germany, and Austria. With Jack Bell (then of the Chicago *Daily News*) he was the first American correspondent to enter liberated Vienna.

As post-war correspondent for the *Post* Snow covered events in Britain, France, Switzerland, the Soviet Union, Arabia, India, Burma, Thailand, Indo-China, China, Japan, the Philippines, Korea (1945-49). In 1950 he went to Mexico on an assignment for the *Post*. In addition to his writings for the *Post*, Snow has contributed articles to other journals, among them the *Nation* and the *Reporter*. His report on the Soviet Union, China, and India in the early years of the war, *People on Our Side*, was a Book-of-the-Month Club selection in 1944. His two books on the Soviet Union were well received. Of *Stalin Must Have Peace*, H. E. Salisbury wrote in the New York *Times* in 1949: "His study is the most penetrating analysis of the Soviet which has yet appeared in the American press."

Snow writes that his own views on domestic and foreign policy were close to those of the late Franklin D. Roosevelt who, he feels, was the greatest man he has ever met. (Among other famous men, Snow has interviewed Winston Churchill, Harry Truman, Dwight Eisenhower, Ibn Saud, Chiang Kaishek, Mao Tse-tung, Gandhi, and Nehru). He points out further that as early as 1937 he had depicted the Chinese Communists as revolutionaries, aiming to establish a proletarian dictatorship.

In 1949 Snow was divorced from Helen Foster ("Nym Wales") and married to Lois Ann Wheeler. They have two children.

ADDITIONAL WORKS: People on Our Side, 1944; Pattern of Soviet Power, 1945; Stalin Must Have Peace, 1947.

ABOUT: Deadline Delayed (Overseas Press Club of America); Current Biography 1941; New Republic March 3, 1947; Time December 17, 1945.

SOBY, JAMES THRALL (December 14, 1906-), American art critic, writes: "I was born and grew up in Hartford, Conn. Attended Williams College, where I became interested in illustrated books, particularly those done by the leading Parisian artists — Picasso, Matisse, Bonnard, Rouault, etc. After two years I decided to leave college for Paris  and there, in the late 1920's, began to collect contemporary paintings. Returned to Hartford and became a partner in the bookshop of Edwin Valentine Mitchell and took part in various staff capacities in the activities of Hartford's remarkable art museum, the Wadsworth Atheneum. I continued to collect modern paintings and sculptures, both European and American, and began to write articles about living artists and, presently, some books about the latter. Gravitated more and more toward New York City. Was on the staff of the Museum of Modern Art for several years, beginning in 1942, and have since continued to serve on various of the museum's committees. Since 1946 have been art critic for the *Saturday Review of Literature* and have continued to write articles and books on art, past and present; at present am chairman of the editorial board of the *Magazine of Art*. I live in New York City, which seems to me an extraordinarily vital art center.

"I am more and more convinced what we all think of as 'modern' art is of vast and enduring importance, though only in its fine examples, since no work of art is automatically valid because of the era to which it belongs. Also, I've always believed that an understanding of contemporary art must be accompanied by devotion to the art of the past. Hence I've tried to spend as much time on art-historical research as on the modern field. My one serious complaint about the state of the arts in America is that too many professional critics, myself included, tend to become over-involved in executive art tasks of one kind and another, thus not allowing themselves enough time for the tiring but I think inescapable chore of trying to write about painting, sculpture and the graphic arts."

* * *

James Thrall Soby married Melissa Wadley in 1952. They have one son. Soby has been described as "one of the most discerning writers on modern art." His art appraisals, the *New Yorker* writes, "are unfailingly wise and enlightening, and he has exceptional ability at describing the evocative effect of an artist's work."

PRINCIPAL WORKS: After Picasso, 1935; The Early Chirico, 1941; Salvador Dali, 1941; Tchelitchew, 1942; Romantic Painting in America (with D. C. Miller) 1943; Georges Rouault, 1945; Ben Shahn, 1947; Contemporary Painters, 1948; Twentieth Century Italian Art (with A. H. Barr) 1949.

ABOUT: Carnegie Magazine September 1952.

*SOLOGUB, FEDOR (1863-December 5, 1927). For biographical sketch and list of works and references, see TWENTIETH CENTURY AUTHORS, 1942.

* * *

ABOUT: Columbia Dictionary of Modern European Literature; Lavrin, J. Introduction to the Russian Novel; Struve, G. Soviet Russian Literature 1917-1950; Yarmolinsky, A. (ed.) A Treasury of Russian Verse.

* sŭ lŭ gōōp'

SOMERVILLE, EDITH ANNA OE-NONE (1861-October. 9, 1949). For biographical sketch and list of earlier works and references, see TWENTIETH CENTURY AUTHORS, 1942.

* * *

Edith Oenone Somerville died at her home at Castletownshend in County Cork, Ireland. Some obituaries reported her age as ninety-one, others eighty-eight.

Her writing career, as well as her other many interests, continued to the end of her life; the manuscript of her last work reached her publisher shortly before her death. The London *Times* has called her "a woman of strikingly individual character and wit."

An early novel of the many written in collaboration with her cousin "Martin Ross" (Violet Martin), *The Real Charlotte*, is generally conceded to be their best. Lord David Cecil called it "a masterpiece, a classic: one of the very few novels of the first rank that has appeared in England during this century." But the series of humorous books which began with *Some Experiences of an Irish R. M.* are the most widely popular of their books throughout Great Britain. The London *Times* places them "on a plane of comedy not attained by any Irish writer before or since. Even in their most boisterous moments these stories hold an essence which flows deeper than the laughter."

ADDITIONAL WORKS: (with "Martin Ross") Happy Days! 1946; Maria, and Some Other Dogs, 1949.

ABOUT: Cummins, G. Dr. E. OE. Somerville, a Biography; Higginson, A. H. British and American Sporting Authors; Commonweal October 3, 1947; London Times October 10, 1949; New Statesman and Nation December 2, 1944; New York Times October 10, 1949. *Bibliography*—Hudson, E. Bibliography of the First Editions of the Works of E. OE. Somerville and Martin Ross.

"SOMERVILLE & ROSS." See SOMERVILLE, E. A. O. and MARTIN, V. F.

SORENSEN, VIRGINIA (EGGERT-SEN (February 17, 1812-), American novelist, writes: "My great-grandparents all came West with the Mormon pioneers, the Danish half of them directly from conversion in Denmark. I was born in Provo, Utah, to Helen (Blackett) and Claude E. Eggertsen. Provo is dominated by two great things — the memory of Brigham  Young, after whom the Mormon University there is named, and by Mount Timpanogas, one of the highest peaks of the Wasatch Range of the Rocky Mountains. Both of these have been of increasing importance in my life and my writings, although during the last twenty years I have lived in California, Colorado, Indiana, Michigan, Alabama, and Pennsylvania. About history I have a curious feeling of presentness, perhaps because in Utah 'long ago' is no more than yesterday. In my childhood I actually heard stories of the long trek and of the settlement of our town from people who had experienced it all.

"I was educated in public schools in Utah and graduated from Brigham Young University. By then I had spent one year away from the mountains, studying writing at the University of Missouri. Returning to Brigham Young to graduate was the first of many returns, and I do not speak of journeys away and back again, but of constant returns in my stories. Whether in Utah or not, I find myself at my desk constantly living in her climate and with her history and her people. The chief meaning of my other homes, I believe, has been complementary—they serve for comparison, to complete with what I believe to be the virtue of objectivity my particular view of the people to whom I belong.

"While still an undergraduate I was married in the Salt Lake Temple to Frederick Sorensen of Mendon, Utah. I received my diploma and my baby daughter Elizabeth during the same week in June, 1934. For the next five years my husband taught and studied at Stanford University, in Palo Alto, Calif., and our son, Frederick Walter, was born there in 1936. Taking care of the two babies and a typical graduate-student apartment took up my days, but I wrote a good deal at night and managed to audit one evening course in poetry writing from Yvor Winters. My chief output was a three-act verse-play about an old legend of Timpanogas. During those years I also completed a first novel which is still happily in manuscript. It was a sort of exposé of the difficulties encountered by my own 'depression generation' and I still keep it around as a particularly private piece of Americana which serves to keep alive the 'good anger' of idealistic student days.

"Before we left Stanford, properly PhDeified (as my husband puts it), we had decided to live in as many places as possible. This ambition was more than continental to begin with, but aside from short sojourns in Mexico whenever we could afford it, we have so far lived only in the United States. Our first two stops were both in the Midwest, close to the beginnings of Mormonism. Visiting the early homes of our wandering grandfathers in Illinois and Missouri and Ohio, we found of special fascination the old city of Nauvoo, Ill., on the Mississippi, and I soon was at work on a novel about a lady who lived and died there as the city itself lived and died. It was published under the title of *A Little Lower than the Angels*.

"My next three novels were about Mormons in the West and all traced the relationships of men and environment, of generation and generation. The problems of rootlessness entered somehow into every story. In 1946 I had my first real years of freedom for study and writing, receiving a Guggenheim fellowship. Intending to complete a study of a Mormon apostate who had cut an important figure in the Gold Rush and had lived for many years in Sonora, Mexico, I went to Guaymas and to the Yaqui Indian villages beyond. There I found my hero much belittled by the wonderful people he had tried to exploit. At first only curious, I was presently fascinated by the Yaquis, and wrote their story into a novel called *The Proper Gods*. This novel, like all the others, was concerned with roots and rebellion, with age and youth, for I had begun to see these as the universal themes they are.

"In my work-in-progress I have returned once more to Utah, though at present writing in Pennsylvania. My setting is once more a mythical place I have made out of the three Utah valleys I love most—Utah, Sanpete, and Cache."

* * *

Virginia Sorensen has written extensively and with great knowledge and understanding of the Mormon communities of the past and the present. Her style is simple, direct, and uncluttered, and she has been especially praised by reviewers for her gift "for exactly the right phrase, her superb awareness, and her discriminating intelligence."

PRINCIPAL WORKS: A Little Lower than the Angels, 1942; On This Star, 1946; The Neighbors, 1947; The Evening and the Morning, 1949; The Proper Gods, 1951; Curious Missie (juvenile) 1953; Many Heavens, 1954; The House Next Door, 1954.

ABOUT: Current Biography 1950.

SORLEY, CHARLES HAMILTON (May 19, 1895-October 13, 1915). For biographical sketch and list of works and references, see TWENTIETH CENTURY AUTHORS, 1942.

*SOROKIN, PITIRIM ALEXANDRO-VICH (January 21, 1889-   ), Russian-born sociologist, writes: "Eventfulness has possibly been the most significant feature of my life-adventure. In a span of sixty-three years I have passed through several cultural atmospheres: pastoral-hunter's culture of the Komi, agricultural and then urban culture of Russia and Europe, and finally, the me-

* sŏ'rŭ kyĭn

galopolitan technological culture of the United States. Starting my life as a son of a poor itinerant artisan and peasant mother, subsequently I have been a farmhand, itinerant artisan, factory worker, clerk, teacher, conductor of a choir, revolutionary, political prisoner, journalist, student, editor of a metropolitan paper, member of Kerensky's cabinet, an exile, professor at Russian, Czech, and American universities, and a scholar of an international reputation. No less eventful has been the range of my life-experience: joy and sorrows, successes and failures of normal human life, I fully tasted six imprisonments—three under the Czarist and three under the Communist regimes; the unforgettable experience of a man condemned to death and daily during six weeks, expecting his execution by the Communist firing squad. I know what it means to be damned and praised, to be banished or to lose one's brothers and friends in a political struggle, and, in a modest degree, I have experienced also the blissful grace of a creative work.

"These life-experiences have taught me more than innumerable books I have read and lectures I listened to.

"Born and reared among the Komi, Ugro-Finnish people on the North of Russia, up to the eleventh year of my life, I did not see even a small town. Incidentally I learned to read and write, incidentally became a pupil of a 'normal school,' and at age of ten, father and mother dead, I became 'independent,' penniless, but free to chart my life-course. Earning my living, subsequently I was a student of a teachers' college, arrested and imprisoned four months before graduation for my political activities in 1906. Then a starving and hunted revolutionary, student of a night school, of the Psycho-Neurological Institute, and of the University of St. Petersburg. Two more imprisonments gave me a first-hand experience in criminology and penology—the field of my graduate study and then of my first professorship. Besides several papers, in my junior year I published my first volume: *Crime and Punishment, Service and Reward* (1913). In 1916 I received magister's degree in criminal law; in 1922, the degree of Doctor of Sociology from the University of St. Petersburg. With the explosion of the Russian Revolution I became one of the founders of the Russian Peasant Soviet (dispersed by the Communists), editor of a metropolitan paper, the *Will of the People,* member of the Council of the Russian Republic, a secretary to Prime Minister Kerensky, and a leading member of the Russian Constituent Assembly (dispersed by Communist government). From the beginning of the revolution I vigorously fought Lenin, Trotsky, Kamenev and other Communist leaders. For this reason I was arrested January 3, 1918, and imprisoned for four months in the Russian 'bastille,' fortress of Peter and Paul. Released, I resumed my struggle with the Communists and was one of the group which engineered the overthrow of the Communist government in Archangel in 1918. In October 1918, I was again arrested and condemned to death by the Communist government of Vologda province. After six weeks of waiting to be shot, by Lenin's order I was freed and returned to my academic activity at the University of St. Petersburg. There I became the founder, first professor, and chairman of the department of sociology. During the years 1920-22 I published five volumes in law and sociology. In 1922 I was again arrested and, finally, banished by the Soviet government. A few days after my arrival in Berlin, my good friend President Masaryk invited me to be a guest of Czechoslovakia. I stayed there for some nine months. Having received an invitation from the Universities of Illinois and Wisconsin to lecture there on the Russian Revolution, in November 1923 I came to the United States, and in 1924 was offered professorship by the University of Minnesota. After six years of a happy work there, I was invited to be the first professor and chairman of sociology department at Harvard. Since 1930 I have been living and working in this great university.

"In 1948 Mr. Eli Lilly and the Lilly Endowment by their own initiative kindly offered $120,000 for my studies of how to make human beings less selfish and more creative. This generous offer led to the establishment of Harvard Research Center in Creative Altruism in 1949, which I am directing now. In 1930 I became a naturalized American citizen.

"During the years of my being in America, honorary memberships in several academies of science and arts, presidency of the International Institute of Sociology, honorary doctorates and similar distinctions have been granted to me. During the same years I have published, besides many scientific papers, some twenty-one substantial volumes. Most of these volumes have been translated into many languages: my *Contemporary Sociological Theories* into eleven main languages of mankind, *Crisis of Our Age* into eight, other volumes into lesser number of languages. All in all, so far, I have twenty-nine translations of my published volumes. With an elapse of time the translations go on *crescendo*. Rapidly grows also the already considerable literature about my theories. In recent years books began to be published and Ph.D. theses written about my books.

"In 1917 I was happily married and have two sons—graduate and undergraduate students at Harvard. My main recreations are now: my professional creative work, enjoyment of great music, my azalea-rhods-lilac-rose garden, grown by my and my family's labor, and each spring enjoyed by several thousands of visitors, and various forms of outdoor recreation: camping, mountain-climbing, fishing, etc.

"I have also been lucky in having a warm friendship with many a simple and eminent person. If I have had many a sorry and trying experience, I have also had a full measure of the purest and meaningful happiness. Both have made my life worth living."

* * *

In March 1955 it was announced that Dr. Sorokin would retire from teaching at Harvard University on August 31. He planned, however, to continue as director of the university's center for research in creative altruism.

PRINCIPAL WORKS IN ENGLISH: Leaves from a Russian Diary, 1924 (enlarged ed., 1950); The Sociology of Revolution, 1925; Social Mobility, 1927; Contemporary Sociological Theories, 1928; (with C. Zimmerman) Principles of Rural-Urban Sociology, 1929; (ed.) A Source Book in Rural Sociology, 3 vols., 1930-31; Time-Budgets of Human Behavior, 1939; Social and Cultural Dynamics, 4 vols, 1937-41; The Crisis of Our Age, 1941; Man and Society in Calamity, 1942; Sociocultural Causality, Space, Time, 1943; Russia and the United States, 1944; Society, Culture and Personality, 1947; Reconstruction of Humanity, 1948; Altruistic Love: A Study of American Good Neighbors and Christian Saints, 1950; Social Philosophies of an Age of Crisis, 1950; (ed.) Explorations in Altruistic Love and Behavior, 1950; S.O.S.: The Meaning of Our Crisis, 1951; (ed.) Forms and Techniques of Altruistic and Spiritual Growth, 1954; The Ways and Power of Love, 1954.

ABOUT: Bartlett, R. M. They Work for Tomorrow; Cowell, F. R. History, Civilization and Culture; Sorokin, P. Leaves from a Russian Diary; Current Biography 1942; New York Times March 24, 1955.

*SOULE, GEORGE HENRY (June 11, 1887-). For autobiographical sketch and list of earlier works and references, see TWENTIETH CENTURY AUTHORS, 1942.

* * *

George Soule left the *New Republic* in 1936 and has since devoted his time to writing and teaching. He was visiting professor of economics at Rutgers University, 1948-49, professor of economics, during summer sessions, at Columbia University, 1948-52, and since 1949 has been teaching economics at Bennington College.

In 1952 Soule published his economic history of the United States, entitled *Economic Forces in American History*. Several reviewers found the earlier sections less valuable than the chapters on twentieth century economics. Here, Louis M. Hacker wrote, the book "constitutes the best analysis we have of the contemporary American economic scene." Soule has also written economic studies of Latin America and Great Britain. He is a Fellow of the American Association for the Advancement of Science and a member of the American Economic Association. He is married to Dr. Flanders Dunbar, and they have one daughter, Marcia Winslow Dunbar-Soule, born in 1941.

ADDITIONAL WORKS: America's Stake in Britain's Future, 1945; Prosperity Decade, 1947; Introduction to Economic Science, 1948; Economic Forces in American History, 1952; Ideas of the Great Economists, 1952; Economics for Living, 1954.

ABOUT: Current Biography 1945.

* sōl

SOUTHWOLD, STEPHEN ("Neil Bell") (1887-). For biographical sketch and list of earlier works and references, see TWENTIETH CENTURY AUTHORS, 1942.

* * *

In 1950 the London *Times Literary Supplement* estimated that "Neil Bell" had written thirty-five novels in the past twenty years. "As a writer, Mr. Neil Bell can scarcely be accused of a lack of vitality or inventiveness; his output is likewise tremendous . . . but these are qualities which, unless curbed by the most rigorous self-discipline, lead to over-abundance of subject matter and a consequent diffusion of interest on the part of the reader." His novels are invariably competent and frequently ingenious. They have had considerable popularity in Britain.

ADDITIONAL WORKS: As "Neil Bell"—Peek's Progress, 1942; Cover His Face: A Novel of the

Life and Times of Thomas Chatterton, 1943; Child of My Sorrow, 1944; The Handsome Langleys, 1945; Alpha and Omega (short stories) 1946; Romance in Lavender, 1946; Forgive Us Our Trespasses, 1947; The Governess at Ashburton Hall, 1948; Immortal Dyer, 1948; Scallywag, 1949; Who Was James Carey? 1949; I Am Legion, 1950; The Inconstant Wife, 1950; Dark Page, 1951; Three Pairs of Heels: A Novella and Twenty-Four Short Stories, 1951; Flowers of the Forest, 1952; One of the Best, 1952; The Secret Life of Miss Lottinger: A Novella and Twenty Short Stories, 1953; Custody of the Child, 1953; Who Walk in Fear, 1953; Many Waters, 1954.

"SOUZA, ERNEST." See SCOTT, E.

*SPAETH, SIGMUND (April 10, 1885-   ). For autobiographical sketch and list of earlier works and references, see TWENTIETH CENTURY AUTHORS, 1942.

* * *

Sigmund Spaeth writes from New York City: "I have never used the middle name of Gottfried since I was fifteen years old. (It was forced upon me in the publication of my doctoral thesis, and the New York Public Library insisted on keeping it on index cards, but it is not my name.) I don't know where the story started that I was ever a 'ditch digger.' Nor have I ever been an army captain, although I was in YMCA uniform in the First World War and did a lot of entertaining and song-leading in the Second, besides editing *A Guide for Army Song Leaders*. Obviously I no longer play baseball (or even tennis), but I swim from the beach in front of my cottage in Westport (on Long Island Sound)."

Since 1948 Sigmund Spaeth has been national chairman of radio, television, and motion pictures for the National Federation of Music Clubs. Spaeth has turned his hobby of music into a full-time career. As a popularizer of classical music, he has reached the public through almost every means of communication—books, newspapers (he writes a syndicated column, "Music for Everybody"), magazines (currently he reviews records for *Theatre Arts* magazine), records, radio, and television. He is the senior member of the "Metropolitan Opera Quiz," on the air since 1940, and has had his own "Tune Detective" radio program.

ADDITIONAL WORKS: Fun With Music, 1941; A Guide to Great Orchestral Music, 1943; At Home with Music, 1945; A History of Popular Music in America, 1948; Dedication: The Love Story of Clara and Robert Schumann, 1950; Opportunities in Music, 1950.

ABOUT: Current Biography 1942.

* späth

SPEARMAN, FRANK HAMILTON (September 6, 1859-December 29, 1937). For biographical sketch and list of works and references, see TWENTIETH CENTURY AUTHORS, 1942.

SPENCE, LEWIS (November 25, 1874-March 3, 1955), Scottish folklorist and poet, died in Edinburgh at eighty. Some months before his death he wrote to the editors of this volume: "I was born at Broughty Ferry, near Dundee, Scotland, and was educated at the Collegiate School there. My relatives were surgeons, editors, and shipbuilders. My paternal grandfather,  James Spence, was professor of surgery at Edinburgh University and surgeon to Queen Victoria in Scotland. I made a resolution to become a writer at an early age, but my parents were unfriendly to the design, so I took a course in dentistry. After a few years of dental study I abandoned it and commenced to write, chiefly poetry and articles on folklore. My prentice efforts met with a poor reception and I turned to journalism, and joined the staff of the *Scotsman*, Edinburgh, in 1899, as a sub-editor. In that year I married Helen Bruce, and have four children, two of whom are successful journalists. In 1906 I was appointed news editor of the *British Weekly*, London, and remained there for four years.

"Leaving London in 1909, I returned to Edinburgh to take up the career of a free lance and soon established a firm footing, contributing articles to many newspapers and journals of importance. Apart from journalistic work, my efforts have been directed into two distinct channels: the writing of verse, both in English and Scots, and research into the mythology and antiquities of ancient Central America. As regards the first, I resolved so long ago as 1910, to try to 'rescue' the Scottish tongue from the sadly degenerate condition into which it has fallen. This I sought to achieve by composing verses in its dialect strengthened and embellished by the addition of words and phrases taken from the old Court Scots which was in general use until the period of the union of the crowns of England and Scotland in 1603. The endeavour attracted considerable attention, chiefly from the circumstance that it synchronized with my political campaign to secure parliamentary self-government for Scotland (1920-31)˙ which culminated in the establishment of the National Party of Scotland in 1929. Since that time a new school of poetry has arisen in Scotland, with the membership of which I am not in communion and with whose efforts I find myself in little sympathy because of what I conceive to be its infringements of the linguistic properties.

"So far as my Americanist studies are concerned, these have naturally been carried on under difficulties well-nigh insuperable. Residing in Scotland thousands of miles distant from those countries in which the remains of the civilizations in which I was interested are to be found (Mexico and Central America) and unable because of indifferent health to visit them, I resolved to confine myself to research into their traditional and mythological aspects alone. For five-and-twenty years I worked ceaselessly at the compilation of my major work, *The Gods of Mexico*, which was published in 1923 and is now recognized as a standard book of reference on the subject. I have also produced several other publications dealing with Mexican and Mayan antiquities, the titles of which I append below.

"My more general works on the mythologies of other races, Egyptian, Babylonian and more especially the Celtic, have enjoyed a world-wide circulation, as have those in which I have dealt with the origins of magic and occult belief.

"At present, because of advanced age and failing health I am compelled to live in a manner more or less retired, although my literary output has been in no wise restricted by such conditions."

PRINCIPAL WORKS: *Poetry*—Le Roi d'Ys, 1910; Songs Satanic and Celestial, 1913; The Plumes of Time, 1926; Collected Poems, 1953. *Americanist Studies*—The Civilization of Ancient Mexico, 1911; Myths of Mexico and Peru, 1913; The Gods of Mexico, 1923; The Magic and Mysteries of Mexico, 1930. *Mythology*—Introduction to Mythology, 1918; The Myths of Ancient Egypt, 1913; The Problem of Atlantis, 1924; The Fairy Tradition in Britain, 1948; The History and Origins of Druidism, 1950. *Magic and the Occult*—An Encyclopedia of Occultism, 1920; The Magic Arts in Celtic Britain, 1945; Second Sight: Its History and Origins, 1951.

ABOUT: New York Times March 4, 1955.

SPENCER, CLAIRE (April 20, 1899-).

For biographical sketch and list of works and references, see TWENTIETH CENTURY AUTHORS, 1942.

SPENCER, ELIZABETH (July 19, 1921-), American novelist, writes: "The events of my life are completely unremarkable. It seems to me there must be somebody exactly like me living in every small Mississippi town, perhaps in every Southern town. However: I was born in Carrollton, Miss., a town of 500 people, but with, I believe, more than normal share of

history and legend, or perhaps more than the usual number of old people around to remember it. As a young child, I was sick a good deal and was read to. Later I disliked everything but Edgar Rice Burroughs and never read with much pleasure until I finished college. But I cannot remember a time when I did not make up stories and from the time I was nine I was writing them down with intense pleasure. This impulse was not suggested to me by my family, though they always praised and encouraged me. Both my parents came of farming families who had lived in Carroll County, Miss., since the early 1830's. My father's family has, in later generations, combined business with farming; my mother's family, the McCains, have tended to select military careers. I have one brother, a doctor now serving with the Navy.

"I was sent to a small denominational school, Belhaven College, in Jackson, Miss., and upon graduation there was awarded a scholarship to Vanderbilt University in Nashville, Tenn. Here it was my good fortune to study with Donald Davidson, a great teacher, whose encouragement and help have meant more to me and to others of his students than any of us are qualified to say.

"My study at Vanderbilt (1942-43) was followed by some lean years. I had got my B.A. degree in English and my M.A. degree in English: there was nothing to do but teach. I taught one year at a junior college in Senatobia, Miss.; another at Ward-Belmont School in Nashville. Then, dissatisfied, I resigned to work as a newspaper reporter on the Nashville *Tennessean*. This kind of writing was still not what I wanted. I had earlier, during my senior year in college, started a novel, never titled, never finished, and mercifully never published. Poor and inept as it was, certain characters from it did not forsake me. I at last shut my eyes and jumped: resigned from the paper, cleaned my portable, and bought a ream of paper. I had been sending out short stories which met with complimentary notes but no takers. I was determined to try another novel. The old characters, and some new ones, took their places in a new plan. A year later, at Donald Davidson's suggestion, an editor from Dodd, Mead, David M. Clay, asked to look at my work in progress. What little I could show him received favorable attention; he asked that more be sent when it was ready. I sent a second section in due time and received a contract in return. This novel, *Fire in the Morning*, was published in 1948 and was accorded wide praise—perhaps too much, a mixed blessing.

"In 1948 I joined the faculty of the University of Mississippi where I am still employed in half-time teaching—one class in creative writing. In 1952 my second novel, *This Crooked Way*, was published. In the interim I have written a few short stories, one published in the *Virginia Quarterly Review* in Summer 1950, titled 'Pilgrimage.' It was listed by Matha Foley as one of the year's best. Last spring (1952) I was awarded $1000 by the National Institute of Arts and Letters.

"At present I am engaged in writing another novel. I do not feel that my work to this date has anything tremendous to offer. Older writers whom I admire have generously accorded me such encouragement, especially Eudora Welty and Robert Penn Warren. It is always the next thing I am writing that I hope will be the fine one."

PRINCIPAL WORKS: Fire in the Morning, 1948; This Crooked Way, 1952.

ABOUT: Warfel, H. R. American Novelists of Today.

SPENCER, THEODORE (July 4, 1902-January 18, 1949), American poet, critic, and teacher, was born at Villanova, Pa. He was

Fabian Bachrach

named after his father, the vice-president and general manager of the Bell Telephone Company in Philadelphia. His father died in 1905 and Theodore and his sister grew up with their mother, Helena Carroll Frazier, in Haverford where he attended Haverford Academy. He entered Princeton (class of '23) where he was a member of the dramatic club, and an editor of the undergraduate magazine. After graduation, he continued his studies at Cambridge, England (B.A., 1925), and then at Harvard (Ph.D.,

1928). In England, he acted in some of the Marlowe Society productions of Elizabethan plays; and his doctoral thesis, written under Professor Kittredge, was on Elizabethan tragedy.

In 1927 Spencer became a tutor at Harvard, and in 1929 he gave his first course. In 1939 when his appointment as an assistant professor ended, Spencer was the first American ever elected to the post of permanent lecturer in English literature at Cambridge, England. But the war prevented his departure, and in 1940 he became an associate professor at Harvard, and in 1946 Boyleston Professor of Rhetoric and Oratory (a famous chair first held by John Quincy Adams in 1806).

Spencer wrote poems all his adult life, and when he died in 1949, he had just finished correcting the proofs of *An Acre in the Seed*, a slim volume of sestets. His poetry was lyrical and metaphysical, following the models provided by W. B. Yeats and T. S. Eliot. *Poems: 1940-1947* included much of the work published in two earlier volumes, *The Paradox in the Circle* and *An Act of Life*. The latter volume included three long philosophical poems which Spencer read when he was Phi Beta Kappa poet—in 1942 at the College of William and Mary, and in 1943 at Tufts and at Harvard.

As a critic, Spencer was most concerned with the philosophical implications of literature, although he was also a brilliant exponent of the dramatic technique of Shakespeare, and of the dramatic situation implicit in most of the great lyric poems of English literature. He published two books of criticism, *Death and Elizabethan Tragedy* and *Shakespeare and the Nature of Man*. The second, wrote F. O. Matthiessen, "grew naturally from his big undergraduate course on Shakespeare, as well as from a series of Lowell lectures. In his earlier book he had been occupied with the conflicting attitudes towards life from which Elizabethan tragedy had sprung. Now he broadened his survey to outline the Renaissance world-view, and to describe the tension which is resolved in Shakespeare's tragedies, the tension between the forces of order and the forces making for chaos."

Spencer combined the role of a man of letters with an academic career in a way which showed the two occupations were naturally congenial. A scholar in Elizabethan literature, he was also an authority on the contemporary novel, the contemporary theatre, and modern poetry. He had one son, John, by a first marriage to Anna Murray; in 1948, he married Eloise Bergland Worcester. He was a member—at one time, the president—of the College English Association, a Fellow in American Letters at the Library of Congress, a trustee of the Boston Athenaeum, of the New England Conservatory of Music, and of Wellesley College.

"His stylish clothes and bright bow ties, the lifelong fondness for playing the piano as a delight to himself and his friends, the eager knowledge of birds which can be seen also in his poems, the verve with which he read Shakespeare aloud, the capacity for throwing himself into each new enthusiasm—all these things had seemed to keep him younger than middle age," wrote F. O. Matthiessen shortly after the death of his friend and colleague.

Spencer died of a heart attack at forty-six. T. S. Eliot, a personal friend, paid tribute to him when he gave the first Theodore Spencer Memorial Lecture at Harvard.

PRINCIPAL WORKS: *Prose*—Death and Elizabethan Tragedy, 1946; Shakespeare and the Nature of Man, 1942. *Poetry*—The Paradox in the Circle, 1941; An Act of Life, 1944; Poems: 1940-1947, 1948; An Acre in the Seed, 1949.

ABOUT: Matthiessen, F. O. Theodore Spencer, 1902-1949, *in* Responsibilities of the Critic; Atlantic Monthly November 1948; Saturday Review of Literature August 5, 1944, March 20, 1948.

SPENDER, STEPHEN (February 28, 1909-). For biographical sketch and list of earlier works and references, see TWENTIETH CENTURY AUTHORS, 1942.

* * *

Probably the two most interesting developments in Stephen Spender's career in recent years are his final and complete rupture with the Communist Party and the increasing importance of his prose writing. He has been called "as truly representative of his generation as it is possible to be," and the course of his evolution from brilliant young radical poet to sober, mature man-of-letters is peculiarly characteristic of the era 1930-1950. At eighteen, he writes in *World Within World*, "I could not reconcile my ideals either with myself or with the world. I was tormented by the feeling that nothing was as it should be, single and clear and pure." By becoming a Communist, he believed, "I could become another kind of social projection. I would be 'on the side of history' and not 'rejected' by it." In time, however, he came to understand the importance of the individual—"Within even a good social cause, there is a duty to fight for the pre-eminence of individual conscience . . . and the individual must not be swallowed up by the concept of

social man." In 1951 he writes that he has at last learned "both to accept myself and to aim beyond myself."

Spender records his total disillusionment with Communism in *The God that Failed*. In his autobiography he sums it up as follows: "When I considered the existing injustices and the future destruction which were involved in the system in which I lived, I longed to be on the side of the accusers, the setters-up of world socialism. But at this stage, having shifted the center of the struggle within myself from the bourgeois camp to the Communist one, I failed to find myself convinced by Communism. Even when I had accepted in my own mind the possibility of having to sacrifice everything I gained by living in a bourgeois society, I still could not abandon my liberal concepts of freedom and truth."

Spender remained associated with the magazine *Horizon*, of which he had been a founder, until 1941. Although he respected and admired *Horizon*'s editor, Cyril Connolly, he did not agree with him on policy: "I, who started out with concern for planning post-war Britain, defending democracy, encouraging young writers, and so forth, was disconcerted to find myself with an editor who showed little sense of responsibility about these things." When the war ended, he began to travel extensively and spent considerable time in the United States, lecturing and visiting colleges and universities all over the country. Some of his most interesting writings have been his reports on his post-war travels. In *European Witness* he described his visit to the British zone of Germany in 1945. It was not his intention to offer a shrewd political analysis of the troubled European scene. Rather, he wrote an impressionistic, candid, and sensitive report. "He has a genuine and sincere liberal optimism that will not allow him to think so badly of human nature," the *Spectator* observed. "Everything he writes," Edmund Wilson said in the *New Yorker*, "has the charm of a natural appetite for the highest art and a natural sympathy with human beings." In 1952 he visited Israel and wrote a discerning account of his tour in *Learning Laughter*. But probably his most interesting and effective prose writing of recent years is his autobiography, *World Within World*, a painfully honest memoir which the late Irwin Edman described as "the almost novelistic reconstruction of a personality and . . . a lyric meditation."

Spender's later poetry has been received with respect but with little enthusiasm. "Mr.

Spender may be in a minor phase," Frank Jones wrote in *Poetry* in 1949, "but it is that of a major poet." What has been lost, some critics argue, is his impressive lyric style, its moving simplicity and its actuality. "His tendency toward the large subject, the magniloquent line, and the baroque point of view," said the *New Yorker*, "often throws his music as well as his thought out of gear." What remains, however, is his passionate sincerity. Babette Deutsch described him in 1947 as "a man who is working, not too successfully, but sensitively and responsibly, toward an undertanding of his and our difficult world."

Spender was a fireman during World War II with the National Fire Service. In 1941 he married the pianist Natasha Litvin; they have a son and a daughter and live in London. In 1953 he became co-editor, with Irving Kristol, of *Encounter*, an international monthly magazine sponsored by the Congress for Cultural Freedom.

ADDITIONAL WORKS: *Poetry*—Poems of Dedication, 1946; Returning to Vienna, 1947; Edge of Being, 1949; Collected Poems, 1928-1953, 1955. *Prose*—European Witness, 1946; World Within World, 1951; (ed.) Europe in Photographs, 1951; Learning Laughter, 1952; The Creative Element, 1954.

ABOUT: Capetanakis, D. Shores of Darkness; Crossman, R. H. (ed.) The God that Failed; Spender, S. World Within World; Commonweal May 11, 1951; New York Herald Tribune Book Review October 11, 1953; New York Times Book Review September 14, 1947, March 13, 1955.

*SPENGLER, OSWALD (May 29, 1880- May 8, 1936). For biographical sketch and list of works and references, see TWENTIETH CENTURY AUTHORS, 1942.

* * *

ABOUT: Bentley, E. R. A Century of Hero-Worship; Hughes, H. S. Oswald Spengler: A Critical Estimate; Muir, E. Essays on Literature and Society; Sorokin, P. A. Social Philosophies in an Age of Crisis; Slochower, H. No Voice Is Wholly Lost; Steiner, R. Oswald Spengler, Prophet of World Chaos; Atlantic Monthly April 1948; Dublin Review July 1944; Foreign Affairs October 1942.

* shpĕng'lĕr

*SPEWACK, Mrs. BELLA (COHEN) (March 25, 1899-) and **SAMUEL** (September 16, 1899-). For autobiographical sketch and list of earlier works and references, see TWENTIETH CENTURY AUTHORS, 1942

* * *

The most successful recent collaboration ·of the Spewacks was the sparkling musical

* spē'wăk

play *Kiss Me, Kate,* for which Cole Porter wrote the music. *Kiss Me, Kate* had a long run on Broadway in 1949-1950, toured the United States, and was produced in London, with Samuel Spewack as director, in 1951. In 1953 it was made into a motion picture. The Spewacks also worked together on the screenplay *Weekend at the Waldorf* (1945) and the play *Woman Bites Dog* (1946), and their adaptation of Albert Husson's *La Cuisine des Anges,* which they called *My Three Angels,* was one of the comedy hits of the 1953 season. In 1955 their comedy *Festival* had a short run on Broadway.

Samuel Spewack's first solo venture as a playwright since his marriage was a farce-comedy, *Two Blind Mice,* spoofing the intricacies of Washington bureaucracy. Produced in New York in 1949, it had mixed reviews but a long run. In the following year another comedy of his, *Golden State,* produced by Bella Spewack, had uniformly unfavorable reviews. Far more successful, however, was his whimsical comedy *Under the Sycamore Tree,* which was produced in London in 1952 starring Alec Guinness.

During World War II Spewack directed the domestic film unit of the Office of War Information in 1942 and was press attaché in 1943 to the United States Embassy in Moscow for the Moscow Conference. After the conference, he headed the Russian Division for the overseas office of the O.W.I. More recently he prepared a feature-length documentary film, *This Is Russia,* for the United States Army Air Force. Spewack's experiences in the Soviet Union provided the material for his satiric novel about wartime life in Moscow, *The Busy, Busy People.*

Bella Spewack did a broadcast series for the American Broadcasting Company on the work of UNRRA and reported on conditions abroad from London, Paris, Berlin, Prague and Geneva.

Corrections: The Spewacks were married in Brooklyn in 1922, not in Berlin as previously stated. "I am sure I do not know," writes Samuel Spewack, "where you gathered the information that we 'both held radical economic views in youth and both have now abandoned them.' Since we did not hold radical economic views in youth, we have never abandoned them."

ADDITIONAL WORKS: *By Bella and Samuel Spewack*—Woman Bites Dog, 1947; My Three Angels, 1953. *By Samuel Spewack*—The Busy, Busy People (novel) 1948; Two Blind Mice, 1949; Golden State, 1951; Under the Sycamore Tree (*in* Plays of the Year, ed. J. C. Trewin) 1953.

ABOUT: Theatre Arts December 1949.

*SPEYER, Mrs. LEONORA (VON STOSCH) (November 7, 1872-). For autobiographical sketch and list of earlier works and references, see TWENTIETH CENTURY AUTHORS, 1942.

* * *

Leonora Speyer has published one volume of verse in recent years and she continues active in the work of the Poetry Society of America. In 1955 the Society awarded her its Gold Medal for Distinguished Achievement. Of her latest poems, which are simple and melodic lyrics, W. B. C. Watkins wrote in the New York *Times*: "This is the kind of poetry which is for the most part taught in schools, and there is nothing here which anyone should fail to understand. This does not mean that Mrs. Speyer writes down to her public. She writes, with the genuine skill of long practice in traditional idiom, exactly what she wants to write and what many will want to hear."

ADDITIONAL WORK: The Slow Wall: Poems, together with Nor Without Music, 1946.

* spī'er

SPINGARN, JOEL ELIAS (May 17, 1875- July 26, 1939). For biographical sketch and list of works and references, see TWENTIETH CENTURY AUTHORS, 1942.

*SPITTELER, CARL (April 24, 1845- December 28, 1924). For biographical sketch and list of works and references, see TWENTIETH CENTURY AUTHORS, 1942.

* * *

ABOUT: Columbia Dictionary of Modern European Literature; Lange, V. Modern German Literature, 1870-1940; Deutsche Rundschau January 1951.

* shpĭt'ĕ lĕr

SPRIGG, CHRISTOPHER ST. JOHN ("Christopher Caudwell") (1907-March 5, 1937). For biographical sketch and list of works and references, see TWENTIETH CENTURY AUTHORS, 1942.

* * *

ADDITIONAL WORKS: The Crisis in Physics, 1939; Further Studies in a Dying Culture, 1949. ABOUT: Hyman, S. E. The Armed Vision.

SPRIGGE, ELIZABETH (1900-). For autobiographical sketch and list of earlier works and references, see TWENTIETH CENTURY AUTHORS, 1942.

* * *

Elizabeth Sprigge writes from London: "In 1942, because of my knowledge of Swedish, I was called to the Ministry of Information, London, as Swedish specialist, where I remained until nearly the end of the war. In 1948 I went to Sweden to collect material for my biography *The Strange Life of August Strindberg,* which was published for his centenary in 1949. This book led to my lecturing widely on Strindberg and making new translations of his plays for the B.B.C. and for theatres and publishers. I also began lecturing and giving readings of Gertrude Stein, for whose work I have a great admiration and consider it should be better known over here. The 48 Theatre Group, of which I was a director, produced her *Yes Is for a Very Young Man,* and through this I came to know Alice B. Toklas in Paris.

"In the winter of 1949 I became a director of London's newest experimental Theatre Club, the Watergate, and worked there until 1951. I am now living in a little old house in London and writing, translating, and reading Scandinavian books for publishers. I have six grandchildren, three boys and three girls."

ADDITIONAL WORK: The Strange Life of August Strindberg, 1949.

SPRING, HOWARD (February 10, 1889-). For autobiographical sketch and list of earlier works and references, see TWENTIETH CENTURY AUTHORS, 1942.

* * *

Howard Spring sends the following additions and corrections to his 1942 sketch: "Cornwall is the background of much of Mr. Spring's recent writing. He has lived in that county, in the port of Falmouth, since leaving London. During the troubles which broke out after the 1914 war, he was a special correspondent of *Manchester Guardian* in Ireland, and what he saw there was effectively used in *My Son, My Son!* which, like his later novel *Fame Is the Spur,* was made into a motion picture. His English, he says, he owes largely to Cobbett's *Grammar.* In his teens he attended night classes with a view to matriculation at London University, but he never sat the examination. The deepest literary influence upon his work would appear to be that of Dickens, his favorite novelist since childhood. His recently published novel *The Houses in Between* (1951), was a choice of the Book-of-the-Month Club in America. In 1941 when Mr. Winston Churchill crossed the Atlantic to meet President Roosevelt off the Newfoundland coast, Spring was one of the two English writers chosen to accompany him."

* * *

The influence of Dickens to which Howard Spring refers above has been noted by many of his readers. Sometimes the results have not been completely happy. Of *The Houses in Between,* a panoramic novel of English life from the reign of Queen Victoria up to 1948, the novelist James Hilton wrote: "Almost everything happens to somebody some time or another, and though this may be statistically defensible in a whole century's annals of a large family, it does not prevent a modern reader's feeling that the story is in some places too plotful and melodramatic." On the other hand, Spring's colorful, leisurely-paced, thickly-peopled and -plotted novels have enormous popular appeal and the quality Hilton called "dogged readability."

Spring has written a volume which supplements his two earlier autobiographical works —*And Another Thing,* an account of his own religious experiences.

ADITIONAL WORKS: *Novels*—Hard Facts, 1944; Dunkerleys, 1946; There Is No Armour, 1948; The Houses in Between, 1951; A Sunset Touch, 1953. *Non-Fiction*—And Another Thing, 1946.

ABOUT: Church, R. British Authors (1948); Spring, H. And Another Thing; Current Biography 1941; Saturday Review of Literature April 13, 1946.

SQUIRE, Sir JOHN COLLINGS (April 2, 1884-). For biographical sketch and list of earlier works and references, see TWENTIETH CENTURY AUTHORS, 1942.

* * *

Sir John Collings Squire, one of the most powerful of the London critics and for many years book reviewer in chief of the *Observer,* now contributes reviews regularly to the *Illustrated London News.* As a critic he is fair and generally moderate in tone. Frank Swinnerton says that he is "in literature a conservative with a strong bias in favour of novelty." His own writings belong to an earlier period—World War I and just after. At that time he was an influential poet, the center of a group sometimes called the "Squirearchy," who wrote in the tradition of Keats, Tennyson, and Bridges. His parodies brought him popularity, but it is his serious poetry on which his permanent reputation will rest. Of this work Swinnerton observed: "It is eloquent and vigorous, but not especially unfamiliar in sentiment and diction. . . . He is boldly sincere (and lacking in finesse) in both writing and speaking." The London *Times Literary Supplement* observed in 1948 that his poetry may be dated—"But it will also be perceived that it lies in the main river

of the English poetic tradition as canalized by the Romantics of the last century."

ADDITIONAL WORK: Selected Poems, 1948.

ABOUT: Swinnerton, F. The Georgian Literary Scene (1910-35).

STAFFORD, JEAN (July 1, 1915-), American novelist, was born at Covina, Calif., and spent her childhood both there

Erich Hartmann

and in Colorado where her family later moved. Her father, John Richard Stafford, was at one time a reporter and also the author of a number of Western stories. In Colorado, Jean Stafford attended the State Preparatory School at Boulder; and in 1936 she graduated M.A. from the University of Colorado. The next year she spent abroad, studying in Heidelberg, Germany.

On her return, she taught for a year at Stephens College, Columbia, Mo., and later spent a year in Tennessee where she worked for the *Southern Review.* These were years of apprenticeship for Miss Stafford, who was a severe critic of her own work; she wrote and discarded several novels before she began *Boston Adventure,* which she worked on for four years.

A popular and critical success, *Boston Adventure* is the story of Sonia Marburg, daughter of a chambermaid who works in a summer hotel for the rich, and of her patroness, the Bostonian Miss Pride, who employs Sonia and takes her into Boston society. In the *Saturday Review of Literature,* one critic remarked, "Miss Stafford is a commanding talent, who writes in the great tradition of the English novel"; other reviewers commented on the richness and smoothness of her style, and on the haunting power of her observations and perceptions. For this book, Miss Stafford was given *Mademoiselle's* Merit Award for outstanding achievement in 1944. In 1945 she won a Guggenheim fellowship, and also a thousand-dollar award from the American Academy and National Institute of Arts and Letters.

Since then Miss Stafford has published two more novels, *The Mountain Lion* and *The Catherine Wheel.* The *New Yorker* called *The Mountain Lion* "a second novel that is hard to match these days for subtlety and understanding. . . . A sharply focussed study rather than a broad exploration of adolescence, written wittily, lucidly, and with great respect for the language." And of *The Catherine Wheel, Commonweal* said, "Miss Stafford has written a novel to compel the imagination and nurture the mind. She has also written one in which pity and terror combine to reach us in the secret, irrational places of the heart."

Besides her novels, Miss Stafford has written numerous short stories appearing in the *New Yorker, Harper's Magazine, Atlantic Monthly, Kenyon Review, Harper's Bazaar, Sewanee Review, Partisan Review,* and *Mademoiselle.* Ten of these (six reprinted from the *New Yorker*) were collected in the volume, *Children Are Bored on Sunday.* One reviewer said her stories had "implacable finality"; and *Time* called them "ten small monuments to minor tragedy." They miss complete success, however. Paul Pickerel wrote in the *Yale Review*: "The pieces are overwrought both in an emotional sense and in the sense that they are decked out in too much verbal embroidery."

Miss Stafford has been married twice. Her first husband was Robert Lowell, well-known poet, and a great-grandson of James Russell Lowell; her second, Oliver Ormerod Jensen, who was at one time a staff photographer for *Life* and the editor of several picture-books.

Since her college days, Miss Stafford has lived in Massachusetts, Missouri, Louisiana, Tennessee, Maine, Connecticut, and New York City. She once listed her favorite authors as Henry James, Jane Austen, Flaubert, and Dostoevsky. Even on short acquaintance, her vivid face and vivacious conversation are unforgettable.

PRINCIPAL WORKS: Boston Adventure, 1944; The Mountain Lion, 1947; The Catherine Wheel, 1952; Children Are Bored on Sunday, 1953.

ABOUT: Hackett, F. On Judging Books; Current Biography 1951.

STALLINGS, LAURENCE (November 25, 1894-). For biographical sketch and list of earlier works and references, see TWENTIETH CENTURY AUTHORS, 1942.

* * *

Laurence Stallings' only play of recent years is *The Streets Are Guarded,* which ran for twenty-four performances in New York in 1944. A war play, this time set in the Pacific in World War II, it contained here and there the vigor and rowdy humor of his memorable *What Price Glory?* but it was weakened, the critics agreed, by a heavy-handed mysticism and seriousness which, George Jean Nathan wrote, "crept into his writing like a dank mist and has cast a pallor over most of it."

"STANDISH, BURT L." See PATTEN, G.

"STANTON, SCHUYLER." See BAUM, L. F.

STAPLEDON, WILLIAM OLAF (May 10, 1886-September 6, 1950). For autobiographical sketch and list of earlier works and references, see TWENTIETH CENTURY AUTHORS, 1942.

* * *

Olaf Stapledon died at his home in Cheshire, England, of coronary occlusion, at sixty-four.

In 1949 he was the only delegate from Great Britain given a visa by the United States Embassy to attend a Conference for World Peace held in New York by the National Council of the Arts, Sciences and Professions. The conference had been labeled a "Communist sounding board" by the U.S. State Department.

His last work, *The Opening of the Eyes,* completed and edited by his wife from notes, is a rather mystical statement of the conclusion of his life-long search for a philosophical truth. It is not quite accurate to describe his novels as "science fiction"; E. V. Rieu has called them cosmic "histories of the future." As one of the few really creative intelligences working in his medium, he has been "an inspiration to good writers and a veritable quarry to hacks," in the words of Basil Davenport, who added: "William Olaf Stapledon was not a great poet, nor even in some conventional respects a very good novelist; but he was a mythmaker, and as such he was unique. In his chosen field, his books stand absolutely unequaled in their combination of intellectual brilliance, imaginative sweep, and tragic dignity."

ADDITIONAL WORKS: Beyond the 'Isms, 1942; Darkness and the Light, 1942; Sirius; a Fantasy of Love and Discord, 1944; Death into Life, 1946; Youth and Tomorrow, 1946; Flames, a Fantasy, 1947; Worlds of Wonder (including Flames, Death into Life, Old Man in a New World) 1949; Man Divided, 1950; The Opening of the Eyes, 1951; To the End of Time: The Best of Olaf Stapledon, 1953.

ABOUT: Stapledon, O. The Opening of the Eyes (preface by E. V. Rieu); To the End of Time (preface by B. Davenport); London Times September 8, 1950; New York Times September 8, 1950.

STARK, FREYA MADELINE (1893-).

For biographical sketch and list of earlier works and references, see TWENTIETH CENTURY AUTHORS, 1942.

* * *

Freya Stark's years of first-hand knowledge of the Middle East were put to the service of the British government during World War II. Her assignment was to help hold the Arab world to the Allied cause. To do this she conceived the idea of the Brotherhood of Freedom, an organization to educate and prepare the Arabs for their coming freedom. Since the Nazis were also engaging in widespread propaganda to woo the Arabs to their side, Miss Stark and her organization had a hard fight on their hands. She traveled through almost all of the Arab world, frequently in convoys under fire from Nazi planes. Her plan won many members, including some 35,000 in Egypt alone.

Miss Stark makes her permanent home in Asolo, Italy. Since the end of the war, she has written extensively on Arab problems and on her own experiences in the Near East. Her sympathy for the region and the people, her knowledge and understanding, and her sensitive prose style allow her to stand along with Charles M. Doughty and T. E. Lawrence as one of the great Western authorities on the subject. Probably her most interesting writings are her volumes of autobiography, carrying her story up to the time of World War II. In 1947 Miss Stark married Stewart Henry Perowne, long active in the British Foreign Service and also an expert on Middle and Near-East affairs.

ADDITIONAL WORKS: Letters from Syria, 1942; Arab Island, the Middle East, 1939-1943 (in England: East Is West) 1945; Perseus in the Wind, 1948; Traveller's Prelude, 1950; Beyond Euphrates, 1951; The Freya Stark Story (condensation of three vols. of autobiography) 1953; Ionia: A Quest, 1955.

ABOUT: Stark, F. Perseus in the Wind, Traveller's Prelude, Beyond Euphrates, The Freya Stark Story; Collier's April 8, 1944; Newsweek January 17, 1944.

STARKEY, JAMES SULLIVAN ("Seumas O'Sullivan") (1879-). For autobiographical sketch and list of earlier works and references, see TWENTIETH CENTURY AUTHORS, 1942.

* * *

"Seumas-O'Sullivan" continues to edit the *Dublin Magazine,* which he founded. He lives in Dublin and is vice president of the Irish Academy of Letters. His recent works include poetry and essays. In America he is best know for his poetry—minor verse, "in the true, uninvidious sense of the word," Horace Reynolds described it. "It is the verse of a man who deals with the retired corners and the edges of life, not with the clashes on the high road." He is steeped in the Celtic spirit, the tradition of Yeats and "AE". In his best work, F. J. Hynes pointed out in the *Saturday Review of Literature,* "the pure music of his language is enchanting and his mystical understanding of the secret life of the poplars, hazel bushes, sedges, and meadows is eerie."

ADDITIONAL WORKS: Essays and Recollections, 1944; Dublin Poems, 1946; Rose and Bottle, and Other Essays, 1946; Translations and Transcriptions (verse) 1950.

ABOUT: Saturday Review of Literature November 30, 1946.

STARKIE, ENID, English biographer and literary critic, is the daughter of the Rt. Hon. W. J. M. Starkie, Litt.D., who was Resident Commissioner of National Education for Ireland. Miss Starkie attended the Alexandra School and Alexandra College, Dublin, the Royal Irish Academy of Music, as a pupil of Michele Esposito, and went on to Somerville College, Oxford, and the Sorbonne. For two years she was a lecturer at University College, Exeter, was appointed to a lectureship in French literature at Somerville College, and later to a University lectureship in French literature at Oxford. Since 1934 she has been a Fellow of Somerville College.

Of her *Baudelaire,* published in 1933, Peter Quennell wrote, "Her standpoint is scholarly, but brisk and maternal—so much so, that a hint of patronage is apt to intrude." Most reviewers found the book overlong, and verging on the academic in style, but as the *Spectator* said, "Its full and objective presentation of the sources, its clear arrangement, and the fascination of the subject combine to make it thoroughly readable." "This is the most complete and best informed life of Rimbaud that I have read," said Cyril Connolly of Miss Starkie's *Arthur Rimbaud.* "Miss Starkie has had access to new material and brought a critical sense unhampered by preconceived ideas to the understanding of it."

The author knew Gide personally, and her short study of him, *André Gide,* was published in 1954. "These sixty close-packed pages add up to a striking account of Gide's complex and wayward personality; Dr. Starkie's personality is discreetly and continuously present," commented the *Times* (London) *Literary Supplement.*

Enid Starkie's degrees and honors include an M.A., a D.Litt.Oxon., Chevalier de la Légion d'Honneur, Docteur de l'Université de Paris, and Lauréate de l'Académie Française. She is a Fellow of the Royal Society of Literature. Her home is in Oxford; her recreation music.

PRINCIPAL WORKS: Baudelaire, 1933; Arthur Rimbaud in Abyssinia, 1937; Arthur Rimbaud, 1938; A Lady's Child, 1941; André Gide, 1954; Petrus Borel, the Lycanthrope, 1954.

STARKIE, WALTER FITZWILLIAM
(August 9, 1894-). For autobiographical sketch and list of earlier works and references, see TWENTIETH CENTURY AUTHORS, 1942.

* * *

Walter Starkie writes from Madrid: "I am corresponding member of the Royal Spanish Academy of History, also special lecturer in the University of Madrid. In 1948 I made a lecture tour in Austria and Italy; in 1950, a lecture tour in Central and South America, with lectures at the following universities: Mexico, Colombia, Lima, Santiago, Buenos Aires, Montevideo, etc." Mr. Starkie is the representative in Spain of the British Council.

ADDITIONAL WORKS: Menéndez Pidal, R. The Spaniards in Their History (tr.) 1950; In Sara's Tent's, 1954.
ABOUT: Hoehn, M. Catholic Authors, I.

STARRETT, VINCENT (October 26, 1886-). For biographical sketch and list of earlier works and references, see TWENTIETH CENTURY AUTHORS, 1942.

* * *

Vincent Starrett writes from Chicago: "Late in 1942 I became book columnist of the Chicago *Tribune,* a position I still hold. I am at present [December 1952] writing my autobiography."

John T. Winterich describes the items of Starrett's column as "salty, urbane, informative, shrewd, pungent, witty, thoroughly readable paragraphs." In his poetry, as the late William Rose Benét pointed out, Starrett is a humorist rather than a wit. "In contrast to the popular light verse of today," Elizabeth Drew writes, "which depends for its effect on the attitude of pure irony, and the use of unexpected vocabulary, Mr. Starrett

expresses richer and mellower attitudes and a personality more in the round."

ADDITIONAL WORKS: *Poems*—Autolycus in Limbo, 1943; Sonnets, and Other Verse (Brillig) 1949. *Essays*—Books and Bipeds, 1947. *Miscellaneous*—Case Book of Jimmie Lavender (short stories) 1944; World's Great Spy Stories (ed.) 1944; Murder in Peking, 1946.

STAUFFER, DONALD ALFRED (July 4, 1902-August 8, 1952), American critic and educator, was born in Denver, Colo., the son of Alfred Vincent and Carrie Ella (Macdonald) Stauffer. He attended Princeton University where he was the valedictorian of the Class of '23, and where he obtained his master's degree in 1924. As a Rhodes scholar, he then continued his studies at Oxford University, England, also winning a Guggenheim fellowship before he had completed the work for his Ph.D., which he received in 1928.

Orren Jack Turner

In the English department at Princeton, Stauffer was first appointed to an instructorship in 1927; to an assistant professorship in 1931; and to a full professorship in 1945. At the time of his death in 1952, he had been for some years chairman of Princeton's department of English, and the previous April he had received the appointment to the Woodrow Wilson Professorship of Literature, a chair which had been vacant since the death of Princeton's Dean Robert K. Root in 1946.

Stauffer was a remarkably able and versatile man, and it has been said that he liked to think of himself as a Renaissance man. Certainly he devoted himself as few modern men can to being not only a teacher, but also a novelist, a poet, and a critic; during the war he was an officer in the U.S. Marines; and afterwards he proved himself to be an excellent administrator. He sometimes startled undergraduates by announcing: "The purpose of the English department is to help you in the business of living." He was an inspiring lecturer, and he knew how to awaken the interests and stimulate the abilities of his students. He also had much to do with widening the curriculum of English studies at Princeton, making room for criticism as well as scholarship, and for courses in the present of literature to balance the scholar's concern with the past of literature. An apt instance was his enthusiastic sponsorship of the "Creative Art" program enabling Princeton students to study as apprentice-writers under modern critics such as R. P. Blackmur.

The range and variety of Stauffer's interests is exhibited also in his critical work. He had an early interest in biography, and his first published work, in 1930, was the monumental two-volume study, *English Biography Before 1700*; it was followed in 1941 by *The Art of Biography in Eighteenth Century England*. He edited the anthology *The Intent of the Critic*, which included essays by Edmund Wilson and others. In 1946, he published *The Nature of Poetry*, "a critical examination of the structure, texture, and meaning of English poetry, with examples running from Spenser to Yeats"; in 1949 *The Golden Nightingale*, five essays about the poetry of W. B. Yeats, a book which Robert Hillyer, writing in the New York *Times*, called "a model of criticism, clear, compressed and enthusiastic"; and in 1952 *Shakespeare's World of Images*, a subject which Professor Stauffer treated not only as a poet but also as a moralist and as a humanist.

During World War II, Stauffer volunteered for the Marines, serving three years, from 1942 to 1945. His wartime record included some fifteen months in the South and Southwest Pacific as a captain and major in air combat intelligence. Among his poems is a volume entitled *Brother, This Is War*.

In 1946, the year after his return to civilian life, Stauffer wrote, in twenty-seven days, a novel he had been thinking about for ten years, *The Saint and the Hunchback*. This is a delightfully comic medieval fantasy about two seventh century monks, Odo and Aelfric, who set out for Europe in a miraculously floating stone coffin to convert the heathen barbarians to Christianity. Reviewers called it "a diverting tale," "mellow and mature prose," "a rare combination of philosophical and theological thought."

Professor Stauffer has been described as a man of medium height with a round face and a game leg; as very amusing and witty; as a man both genial and stubborn; and in his youth, a great mountain climber. He was informal and friendly. His death, when he was only fifty, came as a great shock to his many friends. He died of a heart attack at Oxford, England where he had been, during the academic year 1951-52, the Eastman Professor from the United States to Oxford University. Stauffer had lectured at a great many colleges and universities other than Princeton; he had also taught summer sessions at the University of Colorado and at Bread Loaf. He was a member of the editorial board of the *American Scholar;* a member and former president of the Princeton Chapter of Phi Beta Kappa; an active member of the Modern Language Association; and a member of the Nassau Club, Princeton, N.J.

PRINCIPAL WORKS: English Biography Before 1700, 1930; The Art of Biography in Eighteenth Century England, 1941; (ed.) Wilson, E. & others, The Intent of the Critic, 1941; The Nature of Poetry, 1946; The Saint and the Hunchback, 1946; Poetry and the Easy Life, 1948; The Golden Nightingale, 1949; Shakespeare's World of Images, 1952.

ABOUT: Publications of the Modern Language Association February 1952.

STEAD, CHRISTINA ELLEN (July 17, 1902-). For autobiographical sketch and list of earlier works and references, see TWENTIETH CENTURY AUTHORS, 1942.

* * *

Christina Stead went to Hollywood in 1943 to write scripts for M.G.M. She has also taught a workshop course in the novel at New York University. In recent years she has lived in England. The distinguishing marks of her talent were listed by one reviewer as "her sure knowledge of financial intrigue, her talent for making distasteful characters come distastefully alive, and her needling, admirably unsentimental prose." Her recent novels, especially *A Little Tea, A Little Chat* and *The People with the Dogs*, have been praised for these qualities, but have seemed less substantial than her early work.

ADDITIONAL WORKS: For Love Alone, 1944; (ed. with W. Blake) Modern Women in Love, 1945; Letty Fox, Her Luck, 1946; A Little Tea, A Little Chat, 1948; The People with the Dogs, 1952.

ABOUT: Roderick, C. A. Twenty Australian Novelists.

STEARNS, HAROLD EDMUND (May 7, 1891-August 13, 1943). For biographical sketch and list of earlier works and references, see TWENTIETH CENTURY AUTHORS, 1942.

* * *

Harold Stearns died in a hospital in Hempstead, Long Island, after an illness of several months, at fifty-two.

Neither the literary quality nor the material in his early "repudiation" and later "rediscovery" of America impressed the critics. As Carl Van Doren said, "He needed thirteen years and a long exile to become aware of the obvious America." But his autobiography was called "another *New Grub Street,* good enough to rank with Gissing's," by E. S. Bates. *Time* pointed out that "the pattern of denial and reaffirmation that he wove into his life—the rejection of American values and then a sober reexamination of them—was part of the social pattern of his time."

ABOUT: New York Times August 14, 1943; Publishers' Weekly August 28, 1943; Time August 23, 1943.

STEED, HENRY WICKHAM (October 10, 1871-). For biographical sketch and list of earlier works and references, see TWENTIETH CENTURY AUTHORS, 1942.

* * *

Wickham Steed took an active part in the wartime work of the British Broadcasting Company. His broadcasts on world affairs were heard over the B.B.C. until 1947 and have been published in book form. Steed lives in Oxford.

ADDITIONAL WORKS: That Bad Man: A Tale of the Young of All Ages, 1942; Words on the Air, 1938-1945, 1947.

STEEGMULLER, FRANCIS ("Byron Steel," "David Keith") (July 3, 1906-), American biographer and translator, writes:  "I was born in New Haven of Connecticut parents and attended the public schools of Greenwich. My first two books were written while I was a student at Columbia College, and soon thereafter I began to contribute to the *New Yorker.* Some of my stories still appear in that magazine, and for a time I was a member of its staff, writing 'Talk of the Town.'

"Two of my principle interests are the psychology of the creative process, and the art and nature of painting. The first is evidenced in my books on Flaubert and Maupassant, the second in my biography of James Jackson Jarves, a fascinating, little-known nineteenth century American art critic and collector whose collection of Italian primitives hangs in the Yale University art gallery.

"After trying my hand at various kinds of novels, including a series of mysteries, I finally wrote *States of Grace.* It discusses, rather lightly, uncharitable behavior in supposedly

religious circles, and it achieved the distinction of receiving two reviews in the same issue of a Roman Catholic newspaper—one for and one against.

"In 1935 I married the painter Beatrice Stein. We live in an apartment in New York but spend part of our time in France."

* * *

As a writer Francis Steegmuller manifests not simply a split personality, but three distinct personalities—the author of light, humorous sketches which appear frequently in the *New Yorker,* the scholar-biographer-editor specializing in nineteenth-century French literature, and as "David Keith" the author of a number of fast-paced and diverting murder mysteries (he won the Red Badge Mystery prize in 1940). It is as the biographer of Flaubert and Maupassant that Steegmuller is best known. He writes of French literature, V. S. Pritchett has commented, "with sympathy and acuteness, though sometimes in indifferent prose." Of his edition and translation of Flaubert's letters, the late Irwin Edman wrote: "There emerges cleanly the portrait of a great literary artist."

PRINCIPAL WORKS: O Rare Ben Jonson, 1928; Java-Java, 1928; Sir Francis Bacon, 1930; The Musicale, 1930; America on Relief (with M. D. Lane) 1938; Flaubert and Madame Bovary, 1939; A Matter of Iodine, 1940; A Matter of Accent, 1943; States of Grace, 1946; French Follies and Other Follies, 1946; The Blue Harpsichord, 1949; Maupassant, A Lion in the Path, 1949; (tr.) Venturi, L. Impressionists and Symbolists, 1950; The Two Lives of James Jackson Jarves, 1951; (ed. & tr.) The Selected Letters of Gustave Flaubert, 1953.

ABOUT: New York Times Book Review October 2, 1949.

STEEL, Mrs. FLORA ANNIE (WEBSTER) (April 2, 1847-April 12, 1929). For biographical sketch and list of works and references, see TWENTIETH CENTURY AUTHORS, 1942.

STEELE, WILBUR DANIEL (March 17, 1886-). For biographical sketch and list of earlier works and references, see TWENTIETH CENTURY AUTHORS, 1942.

* * *

With his recent writings Wilbur Daniel Steele has all the more firmly established his position in the first rank of contemporary American storytellers. His work is sound and solid. It may lack the flashes of brilliance and wit that mark some of the more "modern" short stories, but it reflects sober craftsmanship and serious purpose. He has been praised for his novels on the West.

G. W. Allen, in the New York *Times*, called *That Girl From Memphis* "a contribution toward our understanding of American folk-lore, mores and social history," and other reviewers have pointed out that he writes of the West with directness and laconic humor. He remains, however, more successful in the short story than in the longer narrative, in which, the *Saturday Review* remarks, "he tends to sprawl, and the narrative force with which he builds individual scenes is vitiated by his failure to supply inevitable connections between the various scenes." His short stories are carefully planned, each designed to be, he says, "a condensation of life."

Steele was described in 1950 as "medium tall, bony and slight, and profoundly shy." He lives in Lyme, Conn., only rarely visiting nearby New York City. He writes slowly and methodically: "Words for me are very difficult. They're always fighting me. . . . I'm in a pure funk the whole time I'm writing."

ADDITIONAL WORKS: That Girl from Memphis, 1945; Best Stories, 1946; Diamond Wedding, 1950; Their Town, 1952.

ABOUT: National Cyclopedia of American Biography (1946); New York Herald Tribune Book Review July 23, 1950; New York Times Book Review August 6, 1950.

STEEN, MARGUERITE. For autobiographical sketch and list of earlier works and references, see TWENTIETH CENTURY AUTHORS, 1942.

* * *

Marguerite Steen writes: "The war destroyed her London home and after five wandering years (principal sport, bomb-dodging), she bought the eighteenth century cottage in Berkshire—from which nothing would induce her to return to London. Her recreations are traveling—so far as a British travel allowance permits—the collection of all-white china and porcelain, Negro literature, and making a new home. Elected a Fellow of the Royal Society of Literature, 1951."

Marguerite Steen's trilogy about the Flood family, which began with her best-selling *The Sun Is My Undoing* (1941), was completed in *Twilight on the Floods* and *Jehovah Blues*. Neither of these later novels, carrying the history of the great shipping family of the Floods down to modern times, enjoyed the popular success of the first volume. Most of the reviewers found them too rich and lurid. "It is a brilliant accomplishment," Harrison Smith wrote of *Twilight on the Floods*, "but the reader is finally surfeited and stunned as if he had been gorged with an enormous dinner." That Miss Steen's technique with the historical novel was still sure and masterly, however, was demonstrated in *The Swan*, a relatively restrained story of provincial life in England in the early nineteenth century. Here her impressive research and her ability to bring the past to vivid life produced what James MacBride, writing in the New York *Times*, considered "historical novel-writing as it is almost never practiced today, real to the last lace transparency, the last all-male oath."

Correction: Omitted from the list of Miss Steen's works in the 1942 edition was *Stallion*, 1931.

ADDITIONAL WORKS: William Nicholson (biography) 1943; Bell Timson (in England: Rose Timson) 1946; Twilight on the Floods, 1949; Granada Window, 1949; The Swan, 1951; Jehovah Blues, 1952; Anna Fitzalan, 1953; The Bulls of Parral, 1954.

ABOUT: Report to Writers May 1953.

STEFÁNSSON, VILHJÁLMUR (November 3, 1879-). For biographical sketch and list of earlier works and references, see TWENTIETH CENTURY AUTHORS, 1942.

* * *

After more than half a century of study and exploration of the Arctic, Vilhjalmur Stefánsson is probably the greatest living authority on that region. His vast library of some 34,000 or more items was acquired by Dartmouth College in 1953. From 1932 to 1945 Stefánsson was an adviser on northern operations to Pan-American Airways. His studies proved to be of value to the United States government during World War II when his *Arctic Manual*, originally prepared for the Air Force in 1935, was reprinted for general circulation. In 1947 he became editor of the "Encyclopedia Arctica" project sponsored by the Office of Naval Research, and in the same year he became Arctic consultant to Dartmouth College. In addition to his books on all matters relating to the polar regions, he writes extensively on diet, continuing to proclaim the virtues of an all-meat diet. Perhaps the best evidence in support of his thesis is his own alert and vigorous personality. Now in his middle seventies, he continues his work with undiminished energy and enthusiasm.

ADDITIONAL WORKS: Arctic Manual, 1944; The Arctic in Fact and Fable, 1945; Not by Bread Alone, 1946; (ed.) Great Adventures and Explorations, 1947.

ABOUT: Hanson, E. P. Stefánsson, Prophet of the North; Canadian Forum January 1943; Current Biography 1942; New Yorker February 12, February 26, 1949.

STEFFENS, LINCOLN (April 6, 1866-August 9, 1936). For biographical sketch and list of works and references, see TWENTIETH CENTURY AUTHORS, 1942.

* * *

ABOUT: Feibleman, J. K. Aesthetics; Madison, C. A. Critics and Crusaders: A Century of American Protest; Morris, L. R. Postscript to Yesterday; Commentary February 1952; South Atlantic Quarterly January 1949.

STEGNER, WALLACE EARLE (February 18, 1909-). For autobiographical sketch and list of earlier works and references, see TWENTIETH CENTURY AUTHORS, 1942.

* * *

Wallace Stegner writes: "I left Harvard in 1945 to become professor of English and director of the Creative Writing Center at Stanford University. My present home is Los Altos, Calif., in the hills behind Stanford.

"*One Nation* [a collection of pictures and text prepared with the editors of *Look* magazine] won the Houghton Mifflin Life-in-America award and shared the *Saturday Review*'s Anisfield-Wolfe award in 1945. Three of my short stories have won O. Henry prizes, the latest one being 'The Blue Winged Teal,' which won first prize in 1950. In 1950 and again in 1952 I have held Guggenheim fellowships, and in 1950-51 my wife and I were sent around the world on a literary reconnaissance of Asia by the Rockefeller Foundation and Stanford University. At present [December 1952] I am completing a biography of Major John Wesley Powell, the explorer of the Colorado River and the founder of many of Washington's government bureaus [published in 1954 as *Beyond the Hundredth Meridian*]. Since 1945 I have been West Coast editor for Houghton Mifflin Company, in addition to my teaching at Stanford."

Wallace Stegner regularly edits collections of the distinguished short stories produced in his advanced creative writing courses at Stanford. His own fiction is quiet, restrained, craftsmanlike, and powerful. Probably his most successful novel is *The Big Rock Candy Mountain*, a study of a family's struggles in the West during the first half of the twentieth century. Orville Prescott wrote: "This is a sound, solid, intelligent, interesting novel, a good story and an excellent interpretation of an important phase of American life."

ADDITIONAL WORKS: The Big Rock Candy Mountain, 1943; One Nation (with the editors of *Look*) 1945; Second Growth, 1947; The Women

on the Wall (short stories) 1950; The Preacher and the Slave, 1950; Beyond the Hundredth Meridian, 1954.

ABOUT: New York Herald Tribune Book Review October 8, 1950; Publishers' Weekly March 21, 1945; Saturday Review of Literature August 17, 1946.

STEIN, GERTRUDE (February 3, 1874-July 27, 1946). For biographical sketch and list of earlier works and references, see TWENTIETH CENTURY AUTHORS, 1942.

* * *

Gertrude Stein died at the American Hospital in Neuilly, France, at seventy-two. The immediate cause of death was cancer. Her long illness had been aggravated by the hardships of the war years in occupied France.

Miss Stein and Alice B. Toklas lived throughout the German occupation in the village of Culoz. When the American Seventh Army entered Culoz in August 1944, and again three months later when she returned to her Paris apartment, Miss Stein found herself surrounded by American soldiers to whom she was both a legend and a friend from home. *Brewsie and Willie*, published a week before her death, records "the legend of the G.I. as it was being lived and created" in post-war Europe. In *Wars I Have Seen* she wrote her account of life in occupied territory in World War II, and in *Paris France* she celebrated the end of the war with a portrait of her adopted country. She had planned to return to the United States in the fall of 1946.

The many questions about her own work are not yet answered; of her influence on the work of others there is no question. Leo Lerman has said: "Everyone who writes must be more explicit because of her writing both intelligibly and unintelligibly"; he adds that "she made many mad and many thought her ridiculous and a phony but she made everyone with any sense think."

A negative reaction has been expressed by Katherine Anne Porter, who says: "Her judgments were neither moral nor intellectual, and least of all aesthetic; indeed, they were not even judgments, but simply her description from observation of acts, words, appearances giving her view; limited, personal in the extreme, prejudicial without qualification, based on assumptions founded in the void of pure unreason." On the other hand, as John L. Brown has observed, "Her tastes and intuitions have been triumphantly confirmed by the years: the obscure painters she once collected now dominate French art, and the young American writers who were first known in Paris through her efforts have determined the directions of contemporary French prose."

One of the best descriptions of her purpose and method was furnished by the author herself (speaking in the third person): "Gertrude Stein in her work has always been possessed by the intellectual passion for exactitude in the description of inner and outer reality. She had produced a simplification by this concentration, and as a result the destruction of associational emotion in poetry and prose."

ADDITIONAL WORKS: Wars I Have Seen, 1945; Brewsie and Willie, 1946; Selected Writings (ed. C. Van Vechten) 1946; Four in America, 1947; In Savoy: or, Yes Is for a Very Young Man (play), 1947; Mother of Us All: an Opera, 1947; Blood on the Dining Room Floor, 1948; First Reader, and Three Plays, 1948; Last Operas and Plays (ed. C. Van Vechten) 1949; Things as They Are (novel) 1950; Two: Gertrude Stein and Her Brother (Yale Edition of the unpublished writings of Gertrude Stein, vol. 1) 1951; Mrs. Reynolds; and Five Earlier Novelettes (Yale Edition) 1952; Bee Time Vine (Yale Edition) 1953.

ABOUT: Miller, R. S. Gertrude Stein: Form and Intelligibility; Rogers, W. G. When This You See, Remember Me; Stein, G. Selected Writings (Introduction by C. Van Vechten), Wars I Have Seen; Sutherland, D. Gertrude Stein: A Biography of Her Work; Commonweal October 25, 1946; Harper's December 1947; Hobbies October 1947; Life October 2, 1944, August 18, 1947; New York Times July 28, 1946, September 15, 1946, August 6, 1950; New Yorker August 10, 1946, May 31, 1947; Poetry November 1946; Reporter October 13, 1953; Saturday Review of Literature August 10, November 2, 1946, May 27, 1950; Time August 26, 1946, August 16, 1948.

STEIN, LEO (May 11, 1872-July 29, 1947), American critic, brother of Gertrude Stein, was born in Pittsburgh, Pa. His family was both wealthy and cultivated and as a child he

traveled in most of the countries of western Europe. He attended Harvard University where he studied with Charles Eliot Norton and with William James; and in 1897 he went to Johns Hopkins to study biology.

In the early 1900's he settled in Paris, where his sister joined him in 1904; and Leo was, to quote the New Yorker, "one of the earliest buyers of the Ecole de Paris, in the days when the names of Cézanne, Picasso, and Matisse were merely cues for laughter." The Stein salon was a literary and artistic center, and many of its frequenters have since become famous. An account of those Paris days is given by Gertrude in her Autobiography of Alice B. Toklas, and a quite different version by Leo in his papers and journals published posthumously.

The ABC of Aesthetics, Leo's first book, was not very successful. In America the reviewers found it much too personal, flighty, and dense, although the Theatre Arts Monthly said, "He analyzes emotion and feeling, and discusses distortion, composition and pictorial seeing in a way that illuminates the approach of a modern painter to his art."

Appreciation: Painting, Poetry and Prose, his second book, published only a few weeks before he died, was quite generally praised. Lloyd Morris wrote in the New York Herald Tribune that "his pages are studded with trenchant analyses, urbane wit, and vivid anecdotal reminiscence, and these make his book one of the most exciting of recent commentaries on the art of our times"; the Nation called it a "charming, informative, and human book"; and the Chicago Daily News commented that he "puts his points before one with the orderliness of a mature intellect that has become impatient of any ritualistic stunt of language."

In 1913 Leo Stein, having quarreled with his sister Gertrude, moved to Florence where he lived near his friend Bernard Berenson; although he returned to the United States during World War I, he did not remain here; in 1920 he married Nina Auzias, and shortly afterwards settled at Settignano in Italy, which was his home until his death.

Van Wyck Brooks, writing of Leo Stein in The Confident Years, observed that he was a voracious reader, "a critic born, or, as one should say, a philosopher who thought about pictures almost too much to paint them, whose impressions, whether of art or nature, or the poetry he discussed so well, were instantly transmuted in his mind into ideas and reflections," and, "a twentieth-century Amiel who found himself late in life, when he wrote with serenity, lucidity, distinction and grace." Of his lighter side, Brooks says, "He liked to test new methods of cooking and dancing, inventing fresh combinations of rhythms, pies that had never been heard of and novel and unique variations of the flapjack and the pancake."

Leo Stein died in 1947 at the age of seventy-five. In 1950 Journey into the Self, a selection from his letters, papers, and journals edited by Edmund Fuller with an introduction by Van Wyck Brooks, was published. J. W. Krutch stated in the Nation that the book "adds significantly to the documents concerning a much-studied group of between-wars intellectuals"; and in the New York *Times* J. J. Sweeney wrote: "Thanks to Stein's own frankness and the sensibility of the editing, we see the gradual working out of . . . [his] critical approach. . . . We witness his lifelong struggle with deep-seated neuroses, which were only conquered in his last years. . . . The result is a volume that sums up an unusual individual, his contribution and his tragedy."

PRINCIPAL WORKS: The ABC of Aesthetics, 1927; Appreciation: Painting, Poetry and Prose, 1947; Journey Into the Self, 1950 (ed. E. Fuller).

ABOUT: Stein, L. Journey into the Self; Brooks, V. W. *in* The Confident Years: 1885-1915; Frank, D. D. The American Jungle; New York Times July 2, 1950.

STEINBECK, JOHN (February 27, 1902-   ). For biographical sketch and list of earlier works and references, see TWENTIETH CENTURY AUTHORS, 1942.

* * *

It is a frequently made critical observation that there are two John Steinbecks. Carlos Baker has suggested that some day there may be a critical study called "The Two Masks of John Steinbeck," referring to the comic and the tragic masks which he has worn alternately in his writing career. In his novels W. H. Frohock finds "a maximum of two emotional attitudes, one compounded of some delight and much compassion toward the people he writes about, the other of compassion and wrath." His greatest novel, *The Grapes of Wrath*, reflects the latter. Nothing that he has written since then has matched it in power and beauty, although his retelling of an old Mexican folktale in *The Pearl* had something of its dignity and noble simplicity. Only once in recent years has Steinbeck attempted a really ambitious novel. This was *East of Eden*, a long, realistically detailed saga of a California family. The book was a best seller and was made into a motion picture, but its reception from the critics was curiously mixed, ranging from Mark Schorer's pronouncement that it was the best of Steinbeck's novels and a "strange and original work of art" to Charles Rolo's judgment that, although it began promisingly, the novel degenerated rapidly. "The improbabilities grow more flagrant, the sentimentality thicker, the intellectual naïveté more exasperating."

At the opposite pole from the extreme of passionate intensity that was *East of Eden*, Steinbeck has written in recent years several warm, earthy, and humorous novels in the tradition of his earlier *Tortilla Flat*. These include *Cannery Row* and its sequel, *Sweet Thursday*, with their miscellaneous but vivid assortment of benign outcasts—bums, prostitutes, thieves, drunkards—mixed together in what Carlos Baker described as "Steinbeck's confectional blend of satire and sentiment, of cracker-barrel philosophizing and the comic mystique." Also in this category was his much debated novel *The Wayward Bus*, a *Grand Hotel* type of novel in which a group of bus passengers, stranded overnight in a roadside gas station, are studied. Steinbeck's modern-day pilgrimage, presented in the frankest language of literary naturalism, was interpreted by some readers as allegory. These readers, Norman Cousins wrote in an editorial in the *Saturday Review of Literature*, found it "an artful and commanding attempt to point to the greatest tyranny of all—the self-torture of self-inflicted restraints, the surface adherence to artificial values of morality." Others, however, received it simply as "an amusing, absorbing, superficial novel" (as Bernard De Voto described it). Still others thought it dreary and prurient—"a sermonizing book," said J. M. Lalley in the *New Yorker*, "which those who are not of Mr. Steinbeck's priapic persuasion may find fairly tedious."

Over the years several of Steinbeck's novels have been dramatized very successfully for stage and motion pictures. In 1950 he made an attempt to write directly for the stage in a play-novelette, *Burning Bright*. A "morality play," with four characters who are "legendary arch-types of folklore" rather than men and women, it was generally dismissed by the critics as mystical, vague, and dull. The play was, however, distinguished for its imaginativeness, and it has been revived from time to time by non-professional groups.

Steinbeck is not a regional writer, but he is associated primarily with California in his work, and he writes of that state with the mixture of love, poetry, cynicism, and outright bitterness which a man can have only for his native region. Nevertheless by adoption Steinbeck is a New Yorker. He has lived in many places, California, Mexico, Europe, but it is in New York City only, he says, where he finds both the privacy and the friendliness that he seeks in a home place. In 1953 he wrote: "The only explanation I can think of to describe my feeling about the city is that if you have lived in New York no place else is good enough. New York is the world with every vice and blemish and beauty and there's privacy thrown in. What more could you ask?"

During World War II, Steinbeck did special writing assignments for the U.S. Army Air Forces. In 1943 he went to Europe as a correspondent for the New York *Herald Tribune*. Since the war ended he has traveled extensively and reported on his travels for several magazines and newspapers. In 1948 his visit to Russia with the photographer Robert Capa was described in a straightforford and unpretentious book, *Russian Journal*. In 1943, after a divorce from his first wife, Steinbeck married Gwyn Conger, by whom he had two sons. His third marriage was to Elaine Scott in 1950.

ADDITIONAL WORKS: Cannery Row, 1945; The Pearl, 1947; The Wayward Bus, 1947; Russian Journal, 1948; Burning Bright: A Play in Story Form, 1950; East of Eden, 1952; Sweet Thursday, 1954.

ABOUT: Frohock, W. H. The Novel of Violence in America; Gannett, L. *Introduction to* The Portable Steinbeck; Gray, J. On Second Thought; Morris, L. R. Postscript to Yesterday; American Mercury May 1947; Antioch Review September 1947; Atlantic December 1945; New York Times Magazine (supplement) February 1, 1953; Saturday Review of Literature February 15, March 8, 1947, October 28, 1950.

---

*STEKEL, WILHELM (1888-June 25, 1942) Austrian pioneer psychoanalyst, was born in Bukovina, then Rumania. In his

autobiography he describes his father as an orthodox Jew who later became a freethinker, of a benevolent and easy-going nature, and his mother as a bookish woman who "instinctively recognized what I learned after many years of psychoanalytical experience—the value of training by love."

Stekel was a slow schoolboy, living in a world of daydreams. At fourteen, however, his intellectual strength asserted itself. He shot up to the top of his class and started to write poetry and music. He later studied medicine at the University of Vienna, underwent military service at Czernowitz, and started working in the Krafft-Ebing Clinic.

In order to afford to marry his fiancée, Malvina, after a six years' engagement, Stekel gave up his research work at the clinic and went into private practice as a physician in Vienna. He had two children, a son who became a well-known composer-

* shtā′kĕl

conductor, and a daughter who became a painter. His marriage, however, was unhappy and ended in divorce.

While a private practitioner in Vienna, Stekel called on Freud, whose theories interested him. Freud suggested that he himself analyze Stekel. "My treatment lasted not more than eight sessions. I told Freud my life history and he expressed his surprise about the fact that I had so few repressions." Stekel became a qualified psychoanalyst and Freud started sending him patients. He became an intimate member of the first circle of psychoanalysts who met at Freud's house and founded the Psychoanalytical Society. His autobiography sheds light on the personalities of these men and reveals their bitter feuds.

Stekel quarreled with Freud when Freud proposed Jung as a life-long president of the Psychoanalytical Society. "Dear Master," wrote Stekel, "I am afraid that in a short time you will see you have sacrificed your most faithful collaborator for an ungrateful one. Jung will not remain a Freudian for long."

Stekel seceded from the Society and, with Adler, founded an independent psychoanalytical magazine, *Die Psychoanalysische Zentralblatt,* in which to publish their researches. Freud founded *Imago* magazine. Stekel asserts that he first told Freud of the concept of the "death instinct" and that "Freud later adopted some of my discoveries without mentioning my name." Stekel disapproved of long psychoanalytical treatments, claiming to cure most of his patients in six months. "Freud expects from the patient most of his enlightenment. Stekel attempts to obtain his enlightenment through independent exploration of the material, through intuitive grasp of the patient's character." He called his technique "Active Analytic Therapy."

During World War I, Stekel worked as neurologist-psychiatrist in a large war hospital in Vienna. He married his second wife, Hilda, whom he trained to be an analyst. She carried on his work after his death. During the 1920's he came to the United States and lectured before the Neurological Society of Chicago. He returned to Europe and for sixteen years was director of medicine at the University of Vienna. When Hitler invaded Austria, Stekel came to England as a refugee. At the outbreak of World War II he had an unhappy time as an "enemy alien." At the same time, his health began to fail. As a physician he watched the progress of his disease and in 1942, when he judged he was about to become helpless, alone in a London hotel, he took his life.

PRINCIPAL WORKS IN ENGLISH TRANSLATION: Sex and Dreams, 1922; Beloved Ego, 1922; Disguises of Love, 1922; Depths of the Soul, 1923; Peculiarities of Behavior, 1924; Frigidity in Women, 1925; Impotence in the Male, 1927; Sadism and Masochism, 1929; Sexual Aberrations, 1930; Marriage at the Crossroads, 1931; Primer for Mothers, 1931; Bi-Sexual Love, 1933; Homosexual Neurosis, 1933; Technique of Analytical Psychotherapy, 1939; Interpretation of Dreams, 1943; Compulsion and Doubt, 1949; Autobiography, 1950; Auto-Eroticism, 1950; Conditions of Nervous Anxiety and Their Treatment, 1950; Patterns of Psychosexual Infantilism, 1952.

ABOUT: Stekel, W. Autobiography; Look May 7, 1940.

STEPHENS, JAMES (February 2, 1882-December 26, 1950). For biographical sketch and list of earlier works and references, see TWENTIETH CENTURY AUTHORS, 1942.

* * *

James Stephens died at his London home at sixty-eight. He had suffered from gastric ulcers for years, but his death was unexpected. During World War II he dissociated himself from Ireland's neutrality, writing to the London *Times* to declare himself an Irishman who wished "to elect himself an Englishman for the duration." The British government granted him a civil pension in 1942.

Stephens has been described by Frank Swinnerton as having "an old face—a droll face," across which constantly stole "a little dry, quiet, melancholy smile," and a mind which was "quick, rich, unhesitating." His friend James Joyce (the two writers were born in the same hour) once said that if he died before *Finnegans Wake* was finished, the only man capable of finishing it was Stephens.

A revised collection of Stephens' poems published in 1954 prompted Randall Jarrell to say that "Stephens is such a human and appealing poet that one rather winks at his faults." Gerald Bullett speaks of the poetry's "luminous and limpid clarity of diction, its satisfying rhythms, and its delicate flavor of irony." His prose has been called "nut-flavored, sinewy-supple, antic, high-colored," by Charles A. Brady. Certainly his work was unclassifiable and unique; it gave delight to many readers. Swinnerton has said: "First it is a tale, and then it is philosophy, and then it is nonsense; but all these qualities are so merged and, for the reader, confounded, that the effect is one of profound laughter."

Correction: Stephens was married, contrary to the statement in TWENTIETH CENTURY AUTHORS, 1942; he had two children.

The award given him for his *Deirdre* was the Tailteann Gold Medal, incorrectly reported in the 1942 edition as the Tallman Medal.

ABOUT: Swinnerton, F. The Georgian Literary Scene, 1910-1935; America January 20, 1951; Arizona Quarterly Summer 1953; London Times December 27, 1950; New York Herald Tribune Book Review August 10, 1947; New York Times December 27, 1950; Saturday Review of Literature March 22, 1947; Time January 8, 1951.

STEPHENS, ROBERT NEILSON (July 22, 1867-1906). For biographical sketch and list of works and references, see TWENTIETH CENTURY AUTHORS, 1942.

* * *

ABOUT: Saturday Review of Literature January 31, 1948.

STERLING, GEORGE (December 1, 1869-November 17, 1926). For biographical sketch and list of works and references, see TWENTIETH CENTURY AUTHORS, 1942.

* * *

ABOUT: Dickson, S. San Francisco Is Your Home; Gregory, H. & Zaturenska, M. History of American Poetry, 1900-1940.

STERN, GLADYS BRONWYN (June 17, 1890-). For biographical sketch and list of earlier works and references, see TWENTIETH CENTURY AUTHORS, 1942.

* * *

After the destruction of her London flat by an incendiary bomb in 1940, with the loss of all her possessions including about 2,000 books, G. B. Stern moved to the country and resolved that "I would live bare and travel light." Like all resolutions, this one was soon broken, and, complete with collections of all sorts, Miss Stern returned to London where she now lives for at least half of each year, in rooms at the Albany, just a few yards from Piccadilly Circus. She also owns a country house with a garden, of which she is "fatally fond."

It has been suggested that G. B. Stern as a personality is likely to survive G. B. Stern the novelist. In her informal and engaging volumes of memoirs, reminiscence, random and frequently idle chatter, she reasserts, as Richard Altick pointed out in the New York *Times*, "the importance and the dignity of the individual whim." She is observant but not analytical. F. H. Bullock wrote in the New York *Herald Tribune*: "She understands human nature as a novelist should, and she presents it . . . with more overt intentness on the how of its behavior than the why. But underneath the bright chatter runs the richly colored, sure thread of her knowledge." Her recent novels, like her more personal writings, have been slight in structure and theme, nowhere so ambitious as her earlier *Matriarch* series, but full of warmth and spirit. She admits now that she was "never very keen on *The Matriarch* books." —perhaps because they were too close to actual fact. Her own favorite among her works is her book on Robert Louis Stevenson, *No Son of Mine* (a confirmed "rereader," she is regarded as an authority on Jane Austen and on Stevenson). Next to that she lists her novels *The Rueful Mating* and *Ten Days of Christmas* and her series of memoirs. In 1947 Miss Stern became a Catholic, and she describes her conversion in *All in Good Time.*

ADDITIONAL WORKS: Dogs in an Omnibus, 1942; Trumpet Voluntary, 1944; (with S. Kaye-Smith) Speaking of Jane Austen, 1944; Reasonable Shores, 1946; No Son of Mine, 1948; Benefits Forgot, 1949; A Duck to Water, 1949; (with S. Kaye-Smith) More About Jane Austen, 1949; Ten Days of Christmas, 1950; The Donkey Shoe, 1952; A Name to Conjure With, 1953; Johnny Forsaken, 1953; All In Good Time, 1954; Robert Louis Stevenson, 1954.

ABOUT: Stern, G. B. Benefits Forgot, A Name to Conjure With, All in Good Time; New York Herald Tribune Book Review October 12, 1952.

STERN, PHILIP VAN DOREN (September 19, 1900-), American novelist, historian, and anthologist, writes: "I was born

in Wyalusing, Pa., a little village on the Susquehanna River, but grew up in New Jersey, where I was graduated from Rutgers in 1924. (In 1940 the university gave me an honorary doctorate for my work on Lincoln.) I had been interested in science, particularly chemistry, during my pre-college days, but a summer in a chemical laboratory cured me of that. I turned to the liberal arts and at graduation was offered an instructorship in English. I refused it and went into advertising during the pioneer days of radio. I made a lot of money, but chucked the job in 1926 and went to Europe. During my advertising work I had become increasingly interested in printing and wrote a book on typography. On the strength of it, I got a job as designer for Alfred A. Knopf and then with Simon and Schuster. Once in the publishing business, where I had always wanted to be, I began to write.

"I edited the papers of Thomas De Quincey, did a mystery under the name 'Peter Storme,' and then wrote my first historical work, *The Man Who Killed Lincoln,* which was taken by the Literary Guild. I thought I could earn a living from writing, so I resigned from Simon and Schuster and edited *The Life and Writings of Abraham Lincoln.* Then I began work on a long historical novel of the Abolition period, *The Drums of Morning.* I ran out of money before I finished it and returned to publishing on a part-time basis with Pocket Books, Inc. I edited half a dozen anthologies for them, one of which sold more than a million copies. When the war came, I left there to join the Office of War Information, where I was editor and then on the planning board. In 1943 I became general manager for Editions for the Armed Services, a non-profit organization that issued 122,000,000 paper-bound books for the troops overseas.

"In 1944 a short story I had written as a Christmas booklet for distribution to my friends, under the title 'The Greatest Gift,' was bought by the movies and made into Frank Capra's first post-war picture, *It's a Wonderful Life.* After the war, I returned to Pocket Books, where I became vice-president in charge of editorial work and printing production. In 1946, I again had a chance to try to earn a living from writing when a motion picture company offered me a fabulous option for a novel about Lola Montez. I left Pocket Books and began work, but by the time the book was finished, the bottom had dropped out of Hollywood, so I returned to publishing, this time in the printing end, where I have been ever since. Recently I have become fascinated by boats and boating, as a result of which I invented a new almanac."

* * *

Philip Van Doren Stern's interests are many and varied—Lincoln and the Civil War era, typography, photography, automobiles, mystery stories, and almost anything directly or indirectly related to the literary scene.

PRINCIPAL WORKS: An Introduction to Typography, 1932; The Man Who Killed Lincoln, 1939; The Drums of Morning, 1942; The Greatest Gift, 1944; Lola, 1949; Love Is the One with Wings, 1952; A Pictorial History of the Automobile, 1903-1953, 1953. Edited—The Selected Writings of Abraham Lincoln, 1940; The Midnight Reader, 1942; The Moonlight Traveler, 1943; The Portable Poe, 1945; Travelers in Time, 1947.

ABOUT: Warfel, H. R. American Novelists of Today; Wilson Library Bulletin May 1943.

STERNE, Mrs. EMMA (GELDERS)
May 13, 1894-). For biographical sketch and list of earlier works and references, see TWENTIETH CENTURY AUTHORS, 1942.

* * *

Emma Gelders Sterne writes: "The war years were spent in Cambridge, Mass. Writing pamphlets for the Office of War Information and later for the United Nations left little time for creative work. But I did manage to do two more books, *We Live to Be Free,* a study of the rise of democratic thought, and *Incident in Yorkville,* a wartime novel for teenagers, before the stress of those eventful years engulfed my writing entirely.

"My husband and I returned for a brief span to our country home in Connecticut, and for five years I taught at the Thomas School in Rowayton, Conn. My path back to writing lay through textbook editing. For the first group of the American Heritage Series, published by Aladdin Books, I wrote *Printer's Devil.* I am now editing the American Heritage Series and have had the pleasure of guiding through the press my story of the Amistad captives, *The Long Black Schooner,* finished after ten years of interruption! I am now living and working in New York City. Grandchildren—five of them—fill hours and thoughts that gardens once held in a busy life."

ADDITIONAL WORKS: We Live to Be Free, 1942; Incident in Yorkville, 1943; Printer's Devil, 1952; The Long Black Schooner, 1953.

STEVENS, JAMES FLOYD (November 25, 1892-). For biographical sketch and list of earlier works and references, see TWENTIETH CENTURY AUTHORS, 1942.

* * *

James Floyd Stevens writes from Seattle, Wash.: "Now I am an associate member of the Society of American Foresters and an honorary life member of the College of Forestry, University of Washington, Alumni Association. Other honorary life memberships are in the Friends of the Seattle Public Library and the Concatenated Order of Hoo-Hoo—a lumbering fraternity. And now I am a member of Plymouth Congregational Church, Seattle, of Seattle Post No. 1 of the American Legion, and of the public relations committee of the Seattle Chamber of Commerce. A trustee of the Washington State Forestry Conference and of the Keep Washington Green Association, Inc., I still wear the Democratic Party label, but I have

become the most Republican-voting Democrat extant."

Stevens' memorable *Paul Bunyan* was published in an Armed Services edition during World War II, and total sales were estimated at 200,000 in 1948. In recent years he has published one adult novel, *Big Jim Turner,* set in the West in the early 1900's, and two juveniles.

ADDITIONAL WORKS: Paul Bunyan's Bears, 1947; Big Jim Turner, 1948; Tree Treasure, 1950.

*STEVENS, WALLACE (October 2, 1879-). For biographical sketch and list of earlier works and references, see TWENTIETH CENTURY AUTHORS, 1942.

* * *

Wallace Stevens continues to list his profession in *Who's Who in America* as "insurance," and he has since 1916 spent every workday at his desk in the imposing offices of the Hartford Accident and Indemnity Company where he is a vice-president. The same entry in *Who's Who in America,* however, states that he won the Bollingen prize for poetry in 1950, was elected to the National Academy of Arts and Letters in 1946, and it lists the volumes which have made him one of the most distinguished of contemporary American poets—"America's chief conjuror," Marianne Moore has called him, "as bold a virtuoso and one with as cunning a rhetoric as we have produced." In 1950 and again in 1955 he won the National Book award for poetry. In 1955 he won the Pulitzer prize for poetry for his *Collected Poems.*

Stevens himself rejects the Jekyll-Hyde, work-by-day and poetry-by-night split which his career suggests. "I prefer to think I'm just a man, not a poet part time, business man the rest." On his seventy-fifth birthday, when his *Collected Poems* was published, he was described as "tall, heavy without being ponderous," with "a close-cropped gray crewcut"—openly defying, both in spirit and in appearance, the stereotypes of poet and businessman. He writes his poems on slips of paper, often on walks from his house to the office, has his secretary type them, and then puts them aside for later revision. Although a keen and sensitive critic of poetry, he has no solemn poetic credo, regards himself as "just a run of the mine person," and says simply: "The only value to yourself in respect to any poem is that it shall be true. To me, poetry is a very important sanction to life—life from which traditional sanctions are disappearing."

Stevens has been called a "poet's poet." He has never sought a popular audience and,

* Died August 2, 1955.

with the exception of a few widely anthologized poems, he has been little read except by connoisseurs. "In his poetry," William Van O'Connor writes, "the careful craftsmanship of the symbolists . . . finds its best American experession." His work reflects a deliberate estheticism. O'Connor writes: "Stevens in his own way and for his own purposes and subject learned how to employ the language of ambiguity, the modulated tones of stressed and unstressed sounds, evocative rhythms, the shifts of light and shadow, the interaction of theme and symbol, and the mysterious luminousness of metaphor newly caught. Controlling the elegance of his lines are a rich sensibility and a wonderfully quick intelligence." He is an intellectual poet—subtle, witty, paradoxical. His poems sometimes challenge and defy literal exegesis. They are, as Samuel French Morse pointed out, "a triumph of the imagination." For him, O'Connor says, "the imagination is the agency that creates values." In an age which decries imagination and is dominated by 'reality' and 'rationality' Stevens seeks to create "a truth that cannot be arrived at by the reason alone, a truth that the poet recognizes by sensation."

ADDITIONAL WORKS: Notes Toward a Supreme Fiction, 1942; Three Academic Pieces, 1947; Transport to Summer, 1949; Primitive Like an Orb, 1948; Auroras of Autumn, 1950; The Necessary Angel (essays) 1951; Collected Poems, 1954.

ABOUT: Gregory, H. & Zaturenska, M. A History of American Poetry, 1900-1940; Moore, M. in Zabel, M. D. (ed.) Literary Opinion in America (1951); O'Connor, W. V. The Shaping Spirit; Rajan, B. (ed.) Modern American Poetry: Focus Five; Winters, Y. The Anatomy of Nonsense; College English April 1955; English Literary History December 1949; Modern Philology May 1946; New York Herald Tribune Book Review October 24, 1954; New York Times Book Review October 3, 1954; Partisan Review September 1949; PMLA September 1951; Poetry December 1949; Saturday Review December 4, 1954; Yale Review March 1955.

STEVENSON, BURTON EGBERT (November 9, 1872-). For autobiographical sketch and list of earlier works and references, see TWENTIETH CENTURY AUTHORS, 1942.

* * *

Burton E. Stevenson writes: "Returned from a long vacation at Monte Carlo in late August 1939 and settled down to a compilation which he determined should be as scholarly, accurate and comprehensive as he could make it, The Home Book of Proverbs, Maxims and Familiar Phrases. He spent nearly ten years at this task, checking every quotation with the original, using in every case

the original language as well as the English translation (except of course such languages as Chinese and Arabic), and carefully dating every quotation in order that the development of the proverb in question, from its first vague form to its final finished one, could be clearly seen. This book, a tome of over 2800 double-column pages, was published in 1948.

"To round out the series, Mr. Stevenson then turned to the Bible, and in 1949 published The Home Book of Bible Quotations, a hefty double-columned volume of 650 pages. There seemed to be no more worlds to conquer, but he finally decided to do his Shakespeare over again from the beginning. He had never been satisfied with the original book, into which he had crammed so much extraneous detail that its chief appeal was to Shakespeare students and reference libraries, rather than to the general public.

"So he went to work again, reading Shakespeare very carefully from the first page to the last, and managed to put together a book equally comprehensive but in more compact form, which could also be printed in less expensive textbook form for school use. As soon as it is finished, he plans to go to Monte Carlo again for a long stay, and perhaps write a book about the Littoral with special reference to his experiences in the Casino over the past thirty years, or perhaps another mystery story, of which several of his older ones were laid in this locale. Or perhaps he will call it a day and lay aside his pen for good. He was eighty years old last November [1952], and the idea has occurred to him occasionally that it is about time to quit.

"Mr. Stevenson is still librarian of the Chillicothe Public Library, having completed his fifty-third year in that position last September, which is perhaps a record. It is worth remarking that the library, which was established in 1848, has had only three librarians, all of them men (another record?). He is a member of the National Institute of Arts and Letters and of the Century Club in New York. He has lived for more than fifty years in a rambling old house on a hill overlooking Chillicothe and the Scioto valley. From spring to fall he spends a part of his days, like Candide, cultivating his garden and looking after his vines and hundred fruit trees growing on the three acres surrounding his home. He is fond of mystery stories, reads one almost every night, and thinks on the whole that the English writers in this genre are better and more literate than their American confreres. He works only a few hours a day, but remarks, 'It is astonishing how much one can get done in fifty years, working only an hour or two a day.' His forty novels, mystery stories, children's stories and what not, added to the 15,000 pages or so of his compilations seem to prove that this is true."

ADDITIONAL WORKS: Home Book of Proverbs, Maxims, and Familiar Phrases (ed.) 1948; Home Book of Bible Quotations (ed.) 1949.

STEVENSON, DOROTHY EMILY (D. E. Stevenson) (1892-). For autobiographical sketch and list of earlier works and references, see TWENTIETH CENTURY AUTHORS, 1942.

* * *

D. E. Stevenson lives at Moffat, in Dumfriesshire, Scotland. Her sprightly heroine "Mrs. Tim" flourishes, and her adventures have been the subject of two recent novels. "Miss Buncle" is now "Mrs. Abbott." The second and third volumes of Miss Stevenson's trilogy on life in the Scotch border country—*Vittoria Cottage, Music in the Hills,* and *Shoulder the Sky*—were selections of the People's Book Club in the United States. She has written that "the first aim of a storyteller must be to entertain his audience." Her novels achieve this aim—warm, happy, and pleasantly sentimental, "ideal summer and escape reading," in Virginia Kirkus' judgment.

ADDITIONAL WORKS: Crooked Adam, 1942; The Two Mrs. Abbotts, 1943; Celia's House, 1943; It's Nice to Be Me (poems) 1943; Listening Valley, 1944; The Four Graces, 1946; Mrs. Tim Gets a Job, 1947; Kate Hardy, 1947; Young Mrs. Savage, 1948; Vittoria Cottage, 1949; Music in the Hills, 1950; Shoulder the Sky (in England: Winter and Rough Weather) 1951; Mrs. Tim Flies Home, 1952; Five Windows, 1953; Blow the Wind Southerly, 1954; Charlotte Fairlie, 1954.

STEWART, ALFRED WALTER (1880-July 1, 1947). For biographical sketch and list of earlier works and references, see TWENTIETH CENTURY AUTHORS, 1942.

* * *

Alfred Walter Stewart died at his home in Belfast, Ireland, at sixty-six. He had for several years borne an extremely painful heart affliction with notable stoicism. He left his wife and one daughter.

In 1944 he retired from the chairmanship of the department of chemistry of Queen's University at Belfast (he was appointed professor emeritus) and devoted himself entirely to writing.

For manny years the composition of the "J. J. Connington" mystery books, begun almost as a hobby, had been carried on late at night after a full day of teaching. The mysteries depend, as E. R. Punshen has said, "upon the ingenuity of their plots and the logical development of their theme rather than upon any subtlety of characterization, brilliance of style, or novelty of background." As a teacher, Stewart "endowed his students with something of his own critical powers and independent thought," in the words of S. Smiles, while as a scholar and scientist his "wide culture enabled him to view science against the larger background of human endeavour."

ADDITIONAL WORKS: Alias J. J. Connington (autobiographical) 1947. As "J. J. Connington"— Jack-in-the-Box, 1944; The Dangerfield Talisman, 1945; Commonsense Is All You Need, 1947.

ABOUT: Stewart, A. W. Alias J. J. Connington; Chemical Society Journal March 1948; London Times July 3, July 4, 1947; Nature July 26, 1947.

STEWART, DONALD OGDEN (November 30, 1894-). For biographical sketch and list of works and references, see TWENTIETH CENTURY AUTHORS, 1942.

* * *

In recent years Donald Ogden Stewart has written a number of screen plays, including *Life With Father, Cass Timberlane,* and *Edward, My Son.* His only recently-produced stage play was a comedy, *How I Wonder,* which had a brief Broadway run in 1947, starring Raymond Massey. Stewart lives in California.

ABOUT: Current Biography 1941.

STEWART, GEORGE RIPPEY (May 31, 1895-), American novelist and miscellaneous writer, reports: "My family goes back chiefly to Scotch-Irish origins, though with strong English and some French and Dutch strains. I was born in Sewickley, Pa. My boyhood was spent in the small town of Indiana, Pa. My family moved to California in 1908. I graduated from Pasadena High School in 1913, and in the same year entered Princeton, the traditional college of my mother's family. I graduated in 1917, with a major in English, fairly near the head of the class scholastically but not otherwise distinguished.

"In May 1917, I enlisted in the U.S. Army Ambulance Service. I never got overseas, but the Army taught me a lot.

"In March 1919, I was discharged from the Army, and that fall I began graduate work in the English department at the University of California. For the next fifteen years I was definitely academic. I took an M.A. (California, 1920), and a Ph.D. (Columbia, 1922). I was an instructor at the University of Michigan (1922-23), and then went to the English department at Berkeley as an instructor.

"During the next decade and more I lived a pleasantly academic life. I was married (Theodosia Burton, in 1924), and the father of two children (Jill, 1925, and John Harris, 1928). I published a book, *The Technique of English Verse*, and many scholarly articles, such as 'The Meaning of *Bacheler* in Middle English.'

"My first book on a 'general' list was my life of Bret Harte. In the next few years the universities were caught in the depression, and advancement was slow and the situation discouraging. Partly for these reasons I turned to non-academic writing with *Ordeal by Hunger*, a thoroughly historical, non-fictional book, but meant for the general reader. Its good reception encouraged me to take the next step and write a historical novel —*East of the Giants*.

"From that time on, I have lived a rather complicated life, being all at once a professor, a novelist, and a writer of non-fiction. As might be expected from my background, however, my novels have had a strongly authentic basis, and *Storm* and *Fire* have been used as reading in university courses on meteorology and forestry. On the other hand, *Man* was a selection of the Non-Fiction Book Club, even though it makes use of many fictional devices. I consider *Names on the Land* my most important contribution to scholarship, and it is, I think, my own favorite among my books. *Storm* and *Fire*, however, remain the most popular, and have been widely translated.

"I like to experiment, and various attempts (not always very successful with the public) are *Doctor's Oral*, *Earth Abides* (much more successful abroad than here), and *Sheep Rock*, the most unusual of all, with a devoted but small group of admirers. I am also experimenting with plays, and in *U.S. 40* have made a trial at relating photography with writing.

"I worked for a while on a Navy project in World War II. Four of my books appeared in Armed Services editions.

"In 1950, collaborating with a group of my colleagues, I published *The Year of the Oath* in connection with the oath-controversy at the University of California.

"From October 1952 to January 1953 I was Fulbright Professor of American Literature and Civilization at the University of Athens.

"I plan to continue writing both fiction and non-fiction, and to remain as professor of English at the University of California, teaching one term a year."

PRINCIPAL WORKS: The Technique of English Verse, 1930; Bret Harte, 1931; Ordeal by Hunger, 1936; John Phoenix, 1937; East of the Giants, 1938; Doctor's Oral, 1939; Storm, 1941; Names on the Land, 1945; Man, An Autobiography, 1946; Fire, 1948; Earth Abides, 1949; (with others) The Year of the Oath, 1950; Sheep Rock, 1951; U.S. 40, 1953; American Ways of Life, 1954; To California by Covered Wagon (juvenile) 1954.

ABOUT: Van Gelder, R. Writers and Writing; Current Biography 1942; New York Times Book Review October 23, 1949.

STEWART, JOHN INNES MACKINTOSH ("Michael Innes") (September 30, 1906-). For autobiographical sketch and list of earlier works and references, see TWENTIETH CENTURY AUTHORS, 1942.

* * *

John I. M. Stewart taught at Adelaide University in Australia until 1945. From 1946 to 1948 he was lecturer in Queen's University, Belfast. He now lives in Oxford, where he has been a student of Christ Church College since 1949. The Stewarts have three sons and two daughters.

As "Michael Innes," Stewart continues to turn out his literate and urbane novels of suspense and detection. Something of the liveliness of his fiction carries over into his scholarship, and his *Character and Motive in Shakespeare*, in which he sharply attacks some contemporary Shakespeare criticism, was praised by G. W. Stonier of the *New Statesman and Nation* as "a first-rate piece of criticism."

ADDITIONAL WORKS: *As John I. M. Stewart*— Character and Motive in Shakespeare, 1949. *As "Michael Innes"*—The Daffodil Affair, 1942; Unsuspected Chasm, 1943; Appleby's End, 1945; From London Far, 1946; What Happened at Hazelwood? 1946; Night of Errors, 1947; The Case of the Journeying Boy, 1949; Hawk and the Handsaw, and Mysterious Affair at Elsinore (*in* Three Tales of Hamlet, ed. with R. Heppenstall) 1950; Paper Thunderbolt (in England: Operation Pax) 1951; One Man Show (in England: Private View) 1952; Appleby Talking, 1954; Dead Man's Shoes, 1954; Mark Lambert's Supper, 1954; The Man from the Sea, 1955.

STICKNEY, TRUMBULL (June 20, 1874-October 11, 1904). For biographical sketch and list of works and references, see TWENTIETH CENTURY AUTHORS, 1942.

* * *

ABOUT: Commonweal August 16, 1946.

STILL, JAMES (July 16, 1906-   ). For autobiographical sketch and list of works and references, see TWENTIETH CENTURY AUTHORS, 1942.

* * *

James Still lives in Wolfpen Creek, Bath, Ky. He served in Africa and the Middle East with the U.S. Army Air Force from 1942 to 1945. Still received a Guggenheim fellowship in 1946 and in the following year an award from the Academy of Arts and Letters and the National Institute of Arts and Letters with the citation: "For his gift of style and mastery of character and scene." He contributes verse and fiction to the *Atlantic Monthly, Yale Review, Virginia Quarterly Review*, and other journals, and his short stories have appeared in *The Best American Short Stories* of 1946, 1950, and 1952.

ABOUT: The English Journal March 1942; Virginia Quarterly Review October 1946.

STOKER, BRAM (1847-April 20, 1912). For biographical sketch and list of works and references, see TWENTIETH CENTURY AUTHORS, 1942.

* * *

ABOUT: Irving, L. Henry Irving.

STONE, Mrs. GRACE ZARING ("Ethel Vance") (January 9, 1896-   ). For autobiographical sketch and list of earlier works and references, see TWENTIETH CENTURY AUTHORS, 1942.

* * *

Captain Ellis S. Stone, Grace Zaring Stone's husband, writes from Taormina, Sicily: "Since my retirement from the Navy for physical disability in 1945 we have maintained a flat in New York, with long summers in a charming colonial place we have owned for many years in Stonington, Conn. After thirty-six years of marriage, during which she followed me in the travels incident to a naval career, we now do a great deal of wandering about the world for pure pleasure. We are presently [December 1952] abroad, planning to return to Stonington next summer after a year and a half in Europe. For the past few years Mrs. Stone has been a

member of the Council of the Authors League, is treasurer of the Committee for Cultural Freedom, and is a Fellow of the Royal Society of Literature (Great Britain)." Captain Stone sends the following corrections to the description of his wife: "She is of medium height rather than tall, her hair is chestnut rather than 'dark curly' and her eyes are blue as the skies rather than 'hazel.'"

Both *Escape* and Mrs. Stone's later novel *Winter Meeting* were made into motion pictures. Two of her recent books, *Winter Meeting* and *The Grotto*, were serious psychological novels, written with sensitivity and restraint. *The Secret Thread*, less favorably received by the reviewers, was, according to the London *Times Literary Supplement*, "a competent but unexciting thriller."

ADDITIONAL WORKS: Winter Meeting, 1946; The Secret Thread, 1948; The Grotto, 1951.

ABOUT: Time November 16, 1942.

STONE, IRVING (July 14, 1903-   ). For autobiographical sketch and list of earlier works and references, see TWENTIETH CENTURY AUTHORS, 1942.

* * *

Irving Stone writes: "In 1945 I sold my ranch in Encino on a hilltop because I now had two children—my son Kenneth was born in April 1942—and since we were alone on the hilltop and the children had no playmates, we moved into Beverly Hills where they could find their friends out on the street. We bought a very old, black Spanish castle and converted it into a steel and glass modern to house our very interesting collection of modern paintings and sculpture.

"In 1943 I published *They Also Ran*, which was the story of all the men who were defeated for the presidency, starting with Henry Clay and coming down through the chapter on Thomas E. Dewey. During the second half of the writing of the book, which took me a full two years, I made myself literally ill with apprehension that the theme was in much too minor a key to attract serious attention. I was therefore delighted when upon publication I received the best press I had had since *Lust for Life* and found that the book was taking a permanent place for itself not only on the shelves of university libraries but on city editor desks as well, and was being used as almost an object lesson in practicing political circles.

"In 1944 I published *Immortal Wife*, a biographical novel about Jessie Benton Fremont with whom I had fallen in love in 1924 while a student at the University of California. I had read about her over a period of twenty years and had always hoped someone would write a novel about her. Howver, when I saw that no one else would, and finally managed to convince myself that I could write a book about a woman, I undertook the task myself. *Immortal Wife* proved to be my most successful book, remaining in the top five on the best-seller lists for some fifteen months and earning me a much wider public among American readers than I had ever enjoyed before.

"In 1947 *Adversary in the House,* a biographical novel about Eugene V. Debs, was published. In 1949 I published *Passionate Journey,* a biographical novel about John Noble, an American painter, unknown, who lived one of the most interesting lives of any of our contemporary artists. In 1950 I published *We Speak for Ourselves, a Self-Portrait of America,* including excerpts from outstanding autobiographies of over sixty Americans, representing every time, class, and professional level in our history.

"At the present time [December 1952] I am in the middle of a biographical novel about Mary Todd Lincoln and Abraham Lincoln [published in 1954 as *Love Is Eternal*]. This book, along with *The President's Lady* [a novel about Rachel and Andrew Jackson, made into a motion picture in 1953] and *Immortal Wife,* concludes a trilogy of great American women I've had in mind and in work for the past ten years."

ADDITIONAL WORKS: They Also Ran, 1943; Immortal Wife, 1944; Adversary in the House, 1947; Earl Warren, 1948; Passionate Journey, 1949; We Speak for Ourselves: A Self-Portrait of America (ed. with R. Kennedy) 1950; The President's Lady, 1951; Love Is Eternal, 1954.

ABOUT: Warfel, H. R. American Novelists of Today.

STONG, PHILIP DUFFIELD (January 27, 1899-). For biographical sketch and list of earlier works and references, see TWENTIETH CENTURY AUTHORS, 1942.

* * *

Phil Stong's address is still the East—Washington, Conn.—but the subject matter of his books is still primarily the Middle West. When he strays away from it—as he did for example in *Marta of Muscovy,* a fictionized biography of Catherine the Great—the results are entertaining but not thoroughly successful. "There are times," the *New Yorker* wrote of this book, "when his prose has a slightly amazed look, as if he were watching the ascent of his heroine through the eyes of one of the rustics in *State Fair.*" Probably his most popular books of recent

years are the series of stories he has done in collaboration with the illustrator Kurt Wiese —*Censored, the Goat, Positive Pete, Hirum, the Hillbilly.* These have been aptly described as "family books": intended mainly for children, they actually appeal to the whole family. *State Fair* remains his most memorable book. It has twice been made into a motion picture, the later version a musical comedy. In 1953 Stong published a sequel to the novel. This was *Return in August* and took up the romance between the farm girl and the newspaper man twenty years later.

ADDITIONAL WORKS: One Destiny, 1942; Missouri Canary, 1943; Censored, the Goat, 1945; Marta of Muscovy, 1945; Jessamy John, 1947; Positive Pete, 1947; The Prince and the Porker, 1950; Forty Pounds of Gold, 1951; Hirum, the Hillbilly, 1951; Return in August, 1953; Mississippi Pilot: With Mark Twain on the Great River, 1954; Blizzard, 1955.

STORM, HANS OTTO (July 29, 1895-December 11, 1941). For autobiographical sketch and list of works and references, see TWENTIETH CENTURY AUTHORS, 1942.

* * *

ADDITIONAL WORKS: Three Days Reckoning, 1941; Of Good Family, 1948.

ABOUT: Storm, H. O. Of Good Family.

STOUT, REX (December 1, 1886-). For autobiographical sketch and list of earlier works and references, see TWENTIETH CENTURY AUTHORS, 1942.

* * *

During World War II Rex Stout emerged as one of the most active and successful "mobilizers of public opinion" in American life. With characteristic zeal, he threw himself into the work of numerous committees for the democratic cause. He distinguished himself particularly as a platform orator and radio debater, broadcasting for the Council for Democracy, Freedom House, and on the Columbia Broadcasting System's "Our Secret Weapon" series. He was chairman of the Writers War Board, 1941-1946. When the war ended, Stout turned with equal enthusiasm to debates on postwar policy toward Germany, atomic warfare, and, his special interest, world federation. Since 1941 Stout has been chairman of the Writers Board for World Government. He was president of the Authors Guild from 1944 to 1946, and since 1951 he has been president of the Authors League of America.

Nero Wolfe still flourishes with undimmed luster, his exploits being recorded currently in about two volumes a year. There is little physical resemblance between the author and his hero, but, as the late Alva Johnston demonstrated in a *New Yorker* profile, there is a striking identification of the spirit between them. Johnston wrote: "Nero is a unique personality because Stout is. Nero is odd and a trifle grotesque because he has all the foibles and peculiarities of the man inside of him. . . . The fat detective can't help being a knowing and versatile operator, since he gets his stuff from the variegated experiences of the author."

ADDITIONAL WORKS: Not Quite Dead Enough, 1944; The Silent Speaker, 1946; Too Many Women 1947; And Be a Villain, 1948; Trouble in Triplicate, 1949; The Second Confession, 1949; Three Doors to Death, 1950; In the Best Families, 1950; Curtains for Three, 1951; Murder by the Book, 1951; Triple Jeopardy, 1952; Prisoner's Base, 1952; The Golden Spiders, 1953; Three Men Out, 1954; The Black Mountain, 1954.

ABOUT: Van Gelder, R. Writers and Writing; Current Biography 1946; New York Times Book Review November 15, 1953; New Yorker July 16, July 23, August 20, 1949; Newsweek October 30, 1944.

STOWE, LELAND (November 10, 1899-) American journalist, was born in Southbury, Conn., the son of Frank Philip

Stephen Fay

Stowe and Eva Sarah (Noe) Stowe. He was graduated from Wesleyan University in 1921 with a B.A. degree, and started his newspaper career with the Worcester (Mass.) *Telegram*. The following year, 1922, he joined the staff of the New York *Herald*. From 1924 to 1926 he was news editor of Pathé News. Stowe has spent two-thirds of the past twenty-four years as a foreign correspondent, in peace and war, on five continents. His reputation as an authority on international affairs developed during his years of experience as a foreign correspondent between the two world wars. From 1926 to 1935 he covered numerous League of Nations sessions, the World Disarmament and Economics conferences and events from Britain to Rumania while serving as Paris correspondent on the New York *Herald Tribune*. In 1936 he accompanied President Roosevelt to the Pan-American conference in Buenos Aires. He later reported the 1938 Pan-American conference in Lima and then investigated Nazi spy activities in Lima, Bolivia, and Panama. During World War II he served with the armies of seven different nations and colonies, was overseas three and one-half years. In 1940 his world scoops on the German occupation of Oslo and the British defeat in Norway won international attention. He was a featured war correspondent of the Chicago *Daily News* from 1939 to 1943; of the A.B.C. Network and the New York *Post* Syndicate from 1944 to 1945. Since the war Leland Stowe has been a commentator on the A.B.C. and M.B.S. networks, and has reported from Europe for American magazines. His feature articles now appear in *This Week* magazine, the Toronto *Star Weekly*, and leading American newspapers.

Nazi Means War was Leland Stowe's first book, published in 1933, which the *Economist* called "an impartial and convincing account of the militarization of Nazi Germany." Frederick L. Schuman in the *New Republic* also cited it as "an excellent account of Nazi militarism by a careful and reflective journalist." "Mr. Stowe has produced a thought-provoking little book," wrote the *Spectator*, "particularly for those who look at the militant tone given to all German official education and propaganda, and are disinclined to discount it all by the observations about sorely-needed discipline and physical training." Numerous timely books followed; and in 1952 *Conquest by Terror*, the story of satellite Europe, countries behind the Iron Curtain. "Mr. Stowe has written a book to alarm the West," said the New York *Herald Tribune Book Review*.

In 1930 Stowe won the Pulitzer prize for the exceptional accuracy of his reports on the four-months' Young Reparations Conference in Paris. He has also been awarded the medal of the University of Missouri School of Journalism and the medal of Sigma Delta Chi, honorary journalistic fraternity — both in 1941. Only one other journalist has ever won all three of these American awards for foreign correspondence.

At college Stowe earned his letter as a cross-country runner. Years later he hiked ten miles through mud and snow over a mountain range near Trondheim, Norway, to reach the Swedish border and file his exclusive story of the Nazi invasion

In 1924 he married Dr. Ruth F. Bernot, like himself a New Englander. They have two sons, both born in Paris while Stowe was Paris correspondent (1926-35).

PRINCIPAL WORKS: Nazi Means War, 1933; No Other Road to Freedom, 1941; They Shall Not Sleep, 1944; While Time Remains, 1946; Target: You, 1949; Conquest by Terror, 1952.

ABOUT: Murrow, E. R. This I Believe; Current Biography 1940; National Cyclopedia of American Biography (1952); Newsweek May 5, 1947.

STRACHEY, EVELYN JOHN ST. LOE
(October 21, 1901-). For biographical sketch and list of earlier works and references, see TWENTIETH CENTURY AUTHORS, 1942.

* * *

When World War II broke out, John Strachey broke with the Communist Party and took an active part in his country's war effort. After two years as an air raid warden in London, he joined the Royal Air Force as a public relations officer in 1941 and later as a radio commentator over the B.B.C. When the war ended, Strachey rose rapidly in political office as a member of the new Labour government. In the general elections of 1945 he was elected to the House of Commons to represent Dundee and was appointed Under-Secretary for Air. In 1946 he was appointed Minister of Food, a post which he held for the next four years during a period of critical food shortage in Britain. It was not an office which would bring great popularity with it. Strachey was obliged to extend strict rationing during the post-war period in the face of a popular demand for relaxation of restrictions.

Strachey's problems were complicated by his long-standing sympathy for left-wing and Communist causes. In 1950, when Prime Minister Clement Atlee promoted him to Secretary of State for War, one British newspaper attacked him as "an avowed Communist." This was strongly denied by Strachey and many others, but the suspicion remained and seriously complicated his work. When the Labour government was voted out in 1951, Strachey remained in Commons as a member for West Dundee. He lives in Abridge, Essex.

In 1952 Strachey published a novel, *The Frontiers,* which had been written in 1942 but was refused at that time by the war censors who thought the book so realistic that it might endanger the lives of pilots shot down behind enemy lines. When it appeared a decade later, the book proved to be a loosely organized but sensitive story of a British pilot shot down over occupied France. Herbert Mitgang summed up critical opinion when he wrote in the New York *Times:* "The result is a novel that at times talks itself into fictional hot water, that says some philosophical things well, but that is often dragged down by the weight of its own erudition."

ADDITIONAL WORKS: Socialism Looks Forward, 1954; The Frontiers (novel) 1952.

ABOUT: Current Biography 1946; New Yorker March 15, 1947; Time June 10, 1946, March 13, April 17, 1950.

STRACHEY, GILES LYTTON (March 1, 1880-January 21, 1932). For biographical sketch and list of works and references, see TWENTIETH CENTURY AUTHORS, 1942.

* * *

ADDITIONAL WORKS: Collected Works, 6 vols., 1948; Literary Essays, 1949; Biographical Essays, 1949.

ABOUT: Beerbohm, M. Lytton Strachey; Carver, G. Alms for Oblivion; Clemens, C. Lytton Strachey; Dictionary of National Biography 1931-1940; Johnstone, J. K. The Bloomsbury Group; Srinivasa Iyengar, K. K. Lytton Strachey; Swinnerton, F. The Georgian Literary Scene (1910-35); Nation August 5, 1944.

STRACHEY, JOHN. See STRACHEY, E. J. St. L.

STRACHEY, LYTTON. See STRACHEY, G. L.

STREET, CECIL JOHN CHARLES
("John Rhode") (1884-). For biographical sketch and list of earlier works and references, see TWENTIETH CENTURY AUTHORS, 1942.

* * *

"John Rhode" continues to write prolifically, but details of his life remain obscure. His detective novels and his expert sleuths, Dr. Priestley and Superintendent Waghorn, have a devoted following in the United States as well as in England.

"I find Rhode readable enough even at his dullest," Anthony Boucher remarked. The detective work is sound and the plotting neat. He proceeds in workmanlike fashion. James Sandoe wrote: "It is a mode nostalgic, mildly soporific . . . but comfortingly free of distressed damsels or of sub-literate hardboiled eggs."

ADDITIONAL WORKS: Dead of the Night (in England: Night Exercise) 1942; Dead on the Track, 1943; Death Invades the Meeting, 1944; Men Die at Cyprus Lodge, 1944; Too Many Suspects (in England: Vegetable Duck) 1944; Secret of the Lake House (in England: Lake House) 1946; Shadow of a Crime (in England: Bricklayer's Arms) 1946; Death in Harley Street, 1946, Experiment in Crime (in England: Nothing But the Truth) 1947; Death of an Author, 1948; Shadow of an Alibi (in England: Telephone Call) 1948; Links in the Chain, 1948; Blackthorn House, 1949; The Fatal Garden (in England: Up the Garden Path) 1949; Double Identities (in England: Two Graphs) 1950; Affair of the Substitute Doctor (in England: Dr. Goodwood's Locum) 1951; The Last Suspect, 1951; Secret Meeting, 1951; Death in Wellington Road, 1952; Death at the Dance, 1952; The Mysterious Suspect, 1953; The Case of the Forty Thieves, 1953; The Dovebury Murders, 1954; Death on the Lawn, 1955; Grave Matters, 1955.

STREET, JAMES (October 15, 1903-September 28, 1954), American novelist, collapsed and died of a heart attack, just after

Editta Sherman

addressing a meeting of the North Carolina Associated Press Broadcasters in Chapel Hill. Street was fifty. Several months before his death, he sent the following sketch to the editors of this volume: "My full name is James Howell Street and I was born in the sawmill village of Lumberton, Miss., the second son of John Camillus Street and William Thompson Street, and my mother's name, unusual or not, is correct. My father was a lawyer, a liberal Roman Catholic in an ultra-Protestant environment.

"I was reared at Laurel, Miss., and at fourteen, was a part-time reporter on the Laurel *Daily Leader*. At eighteen and after an eleventh grade education, I was on my own as a reporter for the Hattiesburg, Miss., *American*.

"There I married Lucy Nash O'Briant and in 1923 became a Baptist minister and for no explanation that I can offer. I was pastor of churches in St. Charles, Mo., Lucedale, Miss., and Boyles, Ala. I was unfitted, emotionally and religiously, for the Baptist ministry and gave it up in 1925 and became news editor of the Pensacola, Fla., *Journal*.

"Then to the *Arkansas Gazette* in Little Rock, Ark., and then to the Associated Press. As correspondent and feature writer for the Associated Press I worked in all the Southern states and, in 1933, I went to New York for that organization and soon as a feature writer. On this job, I wrote my first book, *Look Away*, and that's what the public did and rightly so.

"I began writing short stories while working as a reporter for the New York *World-Telegram* and the first of these, *Nothing Sacred*, was made into a movie in 1938 and, in 1953, was basis for the musical comedy *Hazel Flagg*.

"I became a free-lance writer in 1938, moved to Old Lyme, Conn., and wrote articles and short stories, including *The Biscuit Eater* which also was a movie and later a book. My first novel was *Oh, Promised Land*. It was written in 1940, and I've been at my trade ever since.

"I am a professional writer of short stories, articles and novels and my work is far more popular with the public than with serious

critics, the only exceptions being *The Biscuit Eater* and *In My Father's House*.

"We have three children and three grandchildren and live in Chapel Hill, N.C. I am a little man with white hair and had rather talk than write, and do it much better. I stammer when I get intense. I enjoy good comrades, good tobacco and good stories. I collect books, walking sticks, pipes and am an electric train enthusiast, a green-thumb flower grower and a front porch farmer. My ambition is to write a *good* book and my only serious regret is that I did not go to school more.

"I am an Episcopalian, although the public seems to think I am a Baptist because I have written about that community. Politically, I am independent liberal, everlastingly espousing lost causes and following hopeless ones. My friends say I am pugnacious and aggressive, but they seem not to mind."

* * *

A reviewer once described James Street's work as "of little literary significance but of immense popular appeal." He was most successful in his writings on Southern life (particularly those dealing with children or drawing upon his own experiences as a Baptist minister); but in every field he wrote with a sure professional touch.

PRINCIPAL WORKS: Look Away, 1936; Oh, Promised Land, 1940; In My Father's House, 1941; The Biscuit Eater, 1941; Tap Roots, 1942; By Valour and Arms, 1944; Short Stories, 1945; The Gauntlet, 1945; Tomorrow We Reap, 1949; Mingo Dabney, 1950; The High Calling, 1951; The Velvet Doublet, 1953; The Civil War (non-fiction) 1953; The Revolutionary War (non-fiction) 1954; Good-bye, My Lady, 1954; James Street's South (ed. J. Street, Jr.) 1955.

ABOUT: Van Gelder, R. Writers and Writing; Current Biography 1946; New York Times September 29, 1954.

STREET, JULIAN LEONARD (April 18, 1879-February 19, 1947). For biographical sketch and list of earlier works and references, see TWENTIETH CENTURY AUTHORS, 1942.

* * *

Julian Street died at his home in Lakeville, Conn., at sixty-seven. He was writing a motion picture script at the time of his death. The *Saturday Review of Literature* observed that "his is a cultivated style and an urbane acquaintance with the lesser ironies of life, and he knows how to handle the material he chooses."

ADDITIONAL WORK: Men, Machines and Morals, 1942.

ABOUT: National Cyclopedia of American Biography (1948); New York Times February 20, 1947.

*STREIT, CLARENCE KIRSHMAN
(January 21, 1896-). For autobiographical sketch and list of earlier works and references, see TWENTIETH CENTURY AUTHORS, 1942.

* * *

A new edition of *Union Now* was published in 1949 with an introduction by Senator Estes Kefauver. In the light of the then current discussions of the North Atlantic Treaty, the question of the veto power in the United Nations Security Council, and the conflict between the Western democracies and the Communist-dominated Eastern powers, the book had special timeliness. Streit testified before hearings of a subcommittee of the Senate Foreign Relations Committee in 1950 on the North Atlantic Treaty.

L. A. Mander wrote of *Union Now* in the *American Political Science Review* in 1949: "Streit's contribution, whatever its limitations, has been one of great importance, and much in his work remains extremely challenging." August Heckscher called it "a book with a life of its own, one of the very few in any generation that rise above the influences which gave them birth to shape and to direct the future." Since 1946 Streit has been editor of the magazine *Freedom & Union.* He lives in Washington, D.C.

ADDITIONAL WORKS: Union Now with Britain, 1941; Hafiz in Quatrains (rev. ed. of Tongue of the Hidden, 1928) 1946; Union Now (rev. and enlarged) 1949; The New Federalist (ed. with others) 1950; Freedom Against Itself, 1954.

ABOUT: Current Biography 1950; Time March 27, 1950.

* strīt

STRIBLING, THOMAS SIGISMUND
(March 4, 1881-). For biographical sketch and list of works and references, see TWENTIETH CENTURY AUTHORS, 1942.

STRINDBERG, AUGUST (January 22, 1849-May 14, 1912). For biographical sketch and list of works and references, see TWENTIETH CENTURY AUTHORS, 1942.

* * *

ADDITIONAL WORK IN ENGLISH TRANSLATION: Queen Christina, Charles XII, Gustav III, 1955.

ABOUT: Bentley, E. R. The Playwright as Thinker; Columbia Dictionary of Modern European Literature; Martin, E. W. L. (ed.) The New Spirit; Mortensen, B. M. E. & Downs, B. W. Strindberg; Nicoll, A. World Drama; Sprigge, E. The Strange Life of August Strindberg; Books Abroad Autumn, Winter 1940; Theatre Arts May 1949, February 1950; Yale Review September 1949.

STRINGER, ARTHUR JOHN ARBUTHNOTT (February 26, 1874-September 14, 1950). For biographical sketch and list of earlier works and references, see TWENTIETH CENTURY AUTHORS, 1942.

* * *

Arthur Stringer died at his home in Mountain Lakes, N.J., at seventy-six, after a long illness.

His last work was a biography of Rupert Brooke, based in part on material which had been gathered by the late Richard Halliburton. Although he wrote motion picture scripts, poetry, plays and Shakespearean criticism (an early study of *King Lear* is used as a standard reference), it is for his more than fifty novels and his more than one hundred magazine serials and short stories, most of them based on adventures in the Canadian wilds, that he is known. As a New York *Times* reviewer put it, "Arthur Stringer has staked out a fictional domain of his own in the Canadian Northwest, which he knows intimately, and he writes of it convincingly and entertainingly."

ADDITIONAL WORKS: Shadowed Victory (poem) 1943; Star in a Mist, 1943; The Devastator, 1944; New York Nocturnes (poems) 1948; Red Wine of Youth: a Life of Rupert Brooke, 1948.

ABOUT: Percival, W. P. (ed.) Leading Canadian Poets; Thomas, C. Canadian Novelists; New York Times September 15, 1950.

STRODE, HUDSON (October 31, 1893-). For autobiographical sketch and list of earlier works and references, see TWENTIETH CENTURY AUTHORS, 1942.

* * *

Hudson Strode writes: "At the University of Alabama Hudson Strode lectures on Shakespeare and gives a nationally famous course in advanced fiction writing. In the past twelve years students from his class have published more than twenty-five novels and also numerous short stories, mostly in quality magazines, several of them being national prize-winners.

"Strode lectures extensively and gives dramatic readings of Shakespeare's tragedies. He has lectured from Amherst to San Antonio and from Richmond to San Francisco, and in Sweden, Italy, and Brazil. In the spring of 1941 he bought twenty acres of woodland five miles from Tuscaloosa and built a Swedish modern house with a separate studio. He and his wife are devoted gardeners and interested in metaphysics. The Strodes have never owned a radio, and they are still driving their first car, a 1941 Olds-hydramatic.

"At present Strode is at work on a biography of Jefferson Davis, president of the Confederacy. At Commencement in 1952 the University of Alabama conferred upon Strode an honorary degree of Doctor of Letters."

ADDITIONAL WORKS: Timeless Mexico, 1944; Now in Mexico, 1947; Sweden: Model for a World, 1949; Denmark Is a Lovely Land, 1951.

ABOUT: Alabama Librarian January 1952; Pathfinder April 1950; Newsweek March 20, 1950; Time July 30, 1945.

STRONG, ANNA LOUISE (November 14, 1885-). For biographical sketch and list of earlier works and references, see TWENTIETH CENTURY AUTHORS, 1942.

* * *

Anna Louise Strong spent 1944-45 in Russia and Poland, entering the latter country with the Soviet armies. In 1946-47 she traveled through Communist China and Manchuria, reporting on her observations there in syndicated newspaper columns and in two books. These were uniformly sympathetic to the Communist governments, but—as many reviewers pointed out—in spite of their unmistakable political bias, interesting, informative, and challenging reading. In 1949, while she was in Moscow seeking to enter China again, she was arrested and charged with espionage—much to her own amazement and that of the rest of the world who knew her long-time sympathies with Communism. Deported by the Russians, she returned to the United States in March 1949 and was summoned to testify before a U.S. Grand Jury investigating espionage. At that time she publicly denied that she was a member of the Communist Party. In 1955 the Russian government announced that it was withdrawing all charges against Miss Strong and that she would be allowed to re-enter the country if she wished.

In recent years Miss Strong has lived in California. For a while she published a mimeographed paper called *Today* in which she commented on news events with no apparent change in her political views.

ADDITIONAL WORKS: The Russians Are People, 1943; Wild River (novel) 1944; The Peoples of the U.S.S.R., 1944; I Saw the New Poland, 1946; Tomorrow's China, 1948; The Chinese Conquer China, 1949.

ABOUT: Current Biography, 1949; Nation April 9, 1949; New York Herald Tribune February 20, 1949; New York Times March 5, 1955; Reporter April 7, 1955; Time February 28, March 7, April 4, 1949.

STRONG, LEONARD ALFRED GEORGE (March 8, 1896-). For autobiographical sketch and list of earlier works and references, see TWENTIETH CENTURY AUTHORS, 1942.

* * *

L. A. G. Strong's activities include, besides the writing of numerous books (novels, verse, essays and drama), broadcasting, preparing radio and television scripts, acting for the B.B.C., teaching "verse-speaking" at one of the principal drama schools in London, lecturing, and serving as a director for the London publishing firm of Methuen, Ltd. His recent published works reflect this variety of interests, ranging from literary criticism to crime stories. In this latter field, which Strong entered only in 1942, he has had particular success, winning praise for his humor, admirable plotting, and adroit characterization. In 1944, in *All Fall Down*, Strong introduced to detective story fans the composer-sleuth Inspector Ellis McKay—"of all the inspectors of fiction's Scotland Yard the man I would most enjoy meeting," wrote Anthony Boucher. Of his sympathetic and enlightening book on James Joyce, *The Sacred River*, James Stern wrote, "there has been no study more informative, more lucid and more intelligent." Strong received the James Tait Black Memorial Prize for his collection of short stories *Travellers*. He lives in Frensham, Surrey.

Correction: Strong's mother's maiden name was Marion Jane Mongan, not Mangan.

ADDITIONAL WORKS: *Fiction*—The Bay, 1942; The Director, 1944; Travellers, 1945; Trevannion, 1948; Darling Tom, 1952; The Hill of Howth, 1953. *Crime Stories*—Slocombe Dies, 1942; All Fall Down, 1944; Murder Plays an Ugly Scene (in England: Othello's Occupation) 1945; Which I Never, 1950. *Miscellaneous*—An Anthology of Modern Verse (ed. with C. D. Lewis) 1941; A Tongue in Your Head, 1945; The Sacred River, 1949; The Writer's Trade, 1953; The Story of Sugar, 1954; Personal Remarks, 1954.

STRUNSKY, SIMEON (July 23, 1879-February 5, 1948). For biographical sketch and list of earlier works and references, see TWENTIETH CENTURY AUTHORS, 1942.

* * *

Simeon Strunsky died, at sixty-eight, at the Princeton, N.J., Hospital. He had been ill for several months. His wife died in 1945.

His later books carried on Strunsky's quiet love affair with New York City and with America. H. M. Jones called him "that rarity, a normal observer of American things." In *Two Came to Town*, published a year before his death, he speculated on the results of a visit of Hamilton and Jefferson to New York City during a session of the United Nations General Assembly.

An "earnest Socialist" at seventeen, Strunsky called himself a "Tory" in later years, clinging to "an old-fashioned belief that America is a pretty good country for its plain people." Amy Loveman has characterized him as "a happy union of wisdom and nobility," engaged in "a constant and searching effort to arrive at truth."

The New York *Times*, for which he wrote "Topics of the Times" for fifteen years, observed editorially: "His style, like his personality (and indeed it was his personality), was a perfected instrument, but it was also the whole man—honest, sincere and benevolent."

ADDITIONAL WORKS: No Mean City, 1944; Two Came to Town, 1947.

ABOUT: New York Times February 6, 1948; Saturday Review of Literature October 21, 1944, February 21, 1948; Time September 18, 1944, February 16, 1948.

STRUTHER, JAN (June 6, 1901-July 20, 1953). For biographical sketch and list of earlier works and references, see TWENTIETH CENTURY AUTHORS, 1942, under **Maxtone Graham, Mrs. Joyce (Anstruther).**

* * *

Jan Struther died in the Presbyterian Hospital in New York, after a brief illness, at fifty-two.

She spent the World War II years in the United States, lecturing extensively for the benefit of British War Relief, and remained in this country; in 1948 she married Adolf Kurt Placzek, a member of the library staff at Columbia University (her marriage to Anthony Maxtone Graham having ended in divorce). She had been working on a semi-autobiographical book before her death.

Miss Struther is said to have taken a detached view of her widely-known creation, "Mrs. Miniver," and to have declared that she was "not a proper writer." The London *Times* agrees that "the felicity and assurance of her craftsmanship was not matched by a strong creative urge," but adds that "whatever she wrote, whether poetry or prose, had a trim excellence, an agreeable flavor, and a point. . . . Miss Struther had, in addition to felicity of style, considerable perception and an urbane sense of comedy."

ADDITIONAL WORK: Pocketful of Pebbles, 1946.

ABOUT: Van Gelder, R. Writers and Writing; London Times July 21, 1953; New York Times July 21, 1953.

STUART, FRANCIS (April 29, 1902-   ). For autobiographical sketch and list of earlier works and references, see TWENTIETH CENTURY AUTHORS, 1942.

* * *

TWENTIETH CENTURY AUTHORS, 1942 incorrectly stated that Francis Stuart fled to Germany in 1940. According to his entry in *Who's Who 1950*, he lectured on English and Irish literature at the University of Berlin from 1939 to 1944. After the war he was "mistakenly imprisoned" in the French zone of Austria. He is at present living in France. The best known of his recent works is the novel *Redemption*, its hero an Irishman living in Berlin during the bombings of World War II. The book has been described as "a study of the sexual and spiritual urges which Stuart sees as the motivating forces of human conduct" and the reviewers generally found it an overwrought but fascinating work.

ADDITIONAL WORKS: The Pillar of Cloud, 1948; Redemption, 1949; The Flowering Cross, 1950; The Wild Wings, 1951; Good Friday's Daughter, 1952; The Chariot, 1953; Pilgrimage, 1955.

STUART, HENRY LONGAN (1875-August 26, 1928). For biographical sketch and list of works and references, see TWENTIETH CENTURY AUTHORS, 1942.

STUART, JESSE (August 8, 1907-   ). For autobiographical sketch and list of earlier works and references, see TWENTIETH CENTURY AUTHORS, 1942.

* * *

Jessie Stuart writes from Riverton, Ky.: "In World War II, I was in the Navy. I did boot-training at Great Lakes Naval Training Station where I was made seaman 2d class. Later I was commissioned lt. j.g., and served during the war in the United States Naval Reserve. I have traveled over the United States and have lectured at colleges, university and teacher groups—Harvard, Columbia, Vanderbilt, Peabody College for Teachers, the universities of Illinois, Kentucky, West Virginia, Florida, etc. I have been given three honorary degrees, Doctor of Literature, University of Kentucky, 1944; Doctor of Humanities, Lincoln Memorial University, 1950; Doctor of Literature, Marietta College, 1952.

"In addition to my books I have had many short stories, poems, and articles published. Halsey P. Taylor, graduate student at the University of Southern California, did his thesis on my short stories. He listed 190 stories from 1934 to 1951. One of my collections, *Men of the Mountains,* won the Academy of Arts and Sciences Award of $500. Then I have had numerous articles published and many, many poems. Also, I have the most triple-starred stories in the late Edward J. O'Brien's collections of the *Best Short Stories.* One year, 1939 I believe it was, I had eighteen triple-starred stories. At present I have twenty-three short stories in secondary and college English textbooks, which is almost a record for an American author, living or dead.

"We live here, my wife Naomi, our daughter Jane, on the land where I was born in W-Hollow. We live in the house where I lived as a child when my parents rented this farm. Lived here when I was nine and left when I was twelve. Later I bought this place and we used the house for housing cattle, corn and hay, for barnroom was scarce at that time with 500 sheep, 60 head of cattle, and 3 mule teams. But in the meantime I got married and my wife loved the old house, so we put the cattle out and went to work. It is our home today. We have 723 acres of land here now, most of it is in timber. We farm, raise corn, hay, and tobacco, but we no longer have sheep, and we don't have as many cattle as we once had here. We also have two dogs, Birchfield, a cocker, and Fleetwind, a young foxhound."

* * *

Jesse Stuart's novel *Taps for Private Tussie* sold over a million copies, was a Book-of-the-Month Club selection, was published in eight foreign countries, and won the Thomas Jefferson Southern Award of $2500. MGM bought the motion picture rights. His autobiographical *The Thread That Runs So True,* an account of his experiences as a teacher in Kentucky and Ohio, was selected as the best book of 1949 by the National Education Association and is widely used in schools of education all over the country. Stuart writes that "it has brought me more mail than my other thirteen books combined."

ADDITIONAL WORKS: Taps for Private Tussie (in England: He'll Be Coming Down the Mountain) 1943; Mongrel Mettle, 1944; Album of Destiny (poems) 1944; Foretaste of Glory, 1946; Tales from the Plum Grove Hills, 1946; The Thread That Runs So True (autobiography) 1949; Hie to the Hunters, 1950; Clearing in the Sky, 1950; Kentucky Is My Land (poems) 1952; The Beatinest Boy, 1953; The Good Spirit of Laurel Ridge, 1953; A Penny's Worth of Character, 1954.

ABOUT: Stuart, J. The Thread That Runs So True; American Magazine May 1951; Christian Science Monitor Magazine December 30, 1950; Life December 6, 1943; New York Herald Tribune Book Review October 8, 1950; New York Times Book Review July 16, 1950; Poetry June 1945; Saturday Review of Literature February 16, 1946; Time September 26, 1949.

STURE-VASA, MARY ALSOP. See O'HARA, M.

SUCKOW, RUTH (August 6, 1892-). For autobiographical sketch and list of works and references, see TWENTIETH CENTURY AUTHORS, 1942.

* * *

Ruth Suckow's only recent book is *Some Others and Myself,* seven sketches about Iowan characters, of whom she has in the past written so successfully, with a memoir of her own father, a Congregationalist minister.

The stories, Anzia Yezierska wrote in the New York *Times,* "have the quiet realism that distinguishes all Ruth Suckow's work. As always she is more interested in capturing the essence of character than in plotting a story." There is no noticeable shift in tone when she turns from her fictional characters to writing about her own parents, for whether she deals with fact or fiction, she writes with dignity and simplicity.

ADDITIONAL WORK: Some Others and Myself, 1952.

ABOUT: Suckow, R. Some Others and Myself.

*SUDERMANN, HERMANN (September 30, 1857-November 22, 1928). For biographical sketch and list of works and references, see TWENTIETH CENTURY AUTHORS, 1942.

* * *

ABOUT: Columbia Dictionary of Modern European Literature; Nicoll, A. World Drama.

* zōō′dĕr män

*SUGIMOTO, Mme. ETSU (INAGAKI) (1874-June 20, 1950). For autobiographical sketch and list of works and references, see TWENTIETH CENTURY AUTHORS, 1942.

* * *

Etsu Sugimoto died at her home in Tokyo at seventy-six.

Her books, which were "tender, charming and graceful" in their style, gave many readers in this country their first insight into life in Japan. As E. H. Walton said of her last novel, written in 1940, "Very delicately, very tactfully, Mrs. Sugimoto supplements the headlines." Several years after publication of her *Daughter of the Samurai,* its publisher noted that it was "the most continuously successful book of non-fiction on the Doubleday-Doran list."

ABOUT: New York Times June 22, 1950.

* soō gē mō′tō

*SUGRUE, THOMAS (May 7, 1907-January 6, 1953), American journalist, author, critic, was born "an Irish Catholic in a family  of political Democrats in a Connecticut community which was Yankee, Protestant, and Republican." The community was Naugatuck, where he went to school and worked for two years in a bank before he left New England to attend Washington and Lee University. With an M.A. in English literature, he began his journalistic career in 1930 as a reporter first on the Naugatuck paper, and then on the New York *Herald Tribune*. Four years later he joined the *American Magazine*, traveling for two years in foreign countries as a roving reporter, before he returned to New York to join the permanent staff of the magazine.

Sugrue was thirty years old when he was stricken with seriously disabling arthritis. He went to Clearwater, Fla., in the fall of 1938 and, in spite of great physical handicaps, wrote his first novel, *Such Is the Kingdom*, a story of life in a Connecticut factory town seen through the eyes of a boy in an Irish Catholic family. The book was well received, several critics comparing the author's work with that of James Farrell. During this period he also became a close friend of Edgar Cayce, the Kentucky mystic and healer, whose life story he told as a ghost-writer in *There Is a River*, a Literary Guild selection in 1943.

During the war years Sugrue worked with Colonel Edmund W. Starling on *Starling of the White House*, published in 1946. A year later he found himself well enough to resume an active life and returned again to New York where he lectured, did book reviews, conducted a radio program, and worked for Marshall Field on a stillborn publishing venture. He also collaborated with Eddie Condon on a book about jazz, *We Called It Music*.

In the fall of 1948 Sugrue went to Israel to find material for a book, *Watch for the Morning*, published two years later. A final book, *A Catholic Speaks His Mind*, was completed shortly before the author's death from a complication of his old ailment. His illness was diagnosed as an unusual form of paralysis at the New York Hospital for Joint Diseases where he died following an operation. He left a widow, Mary Margaret

* shŭ grōō′

(Ganey) Sugrue, and a daughter, Patricia Ann. Writing of his varied and always lively career, the *Saturday Review* called him "one of the ablest reporters of our time."

Sugrue's most interesting book remains his autobiography, *Stranger in the Earth*, published in 1948, which chronicles the author's quest for insight and integrity, and does much to illuminate a complicated personality in the light of his many interests.

PRINCIPAL WORKS: The Crowning of Technocracy (with John Lardner) 1933; Such Is The Kingdom, 1940; There Is a River, 1943; Starling of the White House (with E. W. Starling) 1946; We Called It Music, 1947; Stranger in the Earth, 1948; Watch For the Morning, 1950; A Catholic Speaks His Mind, 1952.

ABOUT: Current Biography 1948; Sugrue, T. Stranger In The Earth (autobiography); New York Herald Tribune Book Review October 15, 1950; New York Times January 7, 1953.

SULLIVAN, FRANK (September 22, 1892-). For biographical sketch and list of earlier works and references, see TWENTIETH CENTURY AUTHORS, 1942.

* * *

Frank Sullivan's quiet but wildly humorous essays appear frequently in the *New Yorker* and other magazines. His subject matter is human society in general, and he satirizes, lampoons, and otherwise holds the mirror up to humanity. The late Irwin Edman pointed out that humorous essays like Sullivan's "have far more serious commentaries to make on contemporary life and morals than many of our most pontifical moral analyses."

Sullivan lives on "the ancestral half-acre" in Saratoga Springs, N.Y. "When Saratoga gets too quiet," he comments, "I go to New York and when New York gets too noisy I come back to Saratoga. In this state of contented oscillation I hope to end my days." In 1953 he reviewed his life as follows: "Since I reached voting age I have survived three wars (two hot, one cold, none ended) and one depression (hot) and am still here, on guard with my little wooden sword against whatever lies around the corner."

ADDITIONAL WORKS: A Rock in Every Snowball, 1946; The Night the Old Nostalgia Burned Down, 1953.

ABOUT: Edman, I. Under Whatever Sky; New York Herald Tribune Book Review October 11, 1953.

SULLIVAN, JOHN WILLIAM NAVIN (January 22, 1886-August 11, 1937). For biographical sketch and list of works and references, see TWENTIETH CENTURY AUTHORS, 1942.

SULLIVAN, MARK (September 10, 1874-August 13, 1952).

SULLIVAN, MARK (September 10, 1874-August 13, 1952). For biographical sketch and list of works and references, see TWENTIETH CENTURY AUTHORS, 1942.

* * *

Mark Sullivan suffered a heart attack on his farm at Avondale, Pa., and died in the Chester County (Pa.) Hospital. He was seventy-seven. From 1945 he lived at Avondale, where he continued writing his daily syndicated column until the day of his death.

The six volumes of *Our Times* will remain an invaluable first-hand record for future historians, although Sullivan himself was, as Charles Seymour noted, "probably too good a journalist to be a good historian."

His day-to-day political reporting and counseling undoubtedly helped "mould a measure of the political thinking of his time," and gave him, in Charles Fisher's words, the status of "prophet, analyst, philosopher and Grand Old Man of conservative journalism."

ABOUT: Fisher, C. Columnists; New York Herald Tribune August 15, 1952; New York Times August 15, 1952.

SULLIVAN, RICHARD (November 29, 1908-)

SULLIVAN, RICHARD (November 29, 1908-), American novelist and short story writer, reports: "I was born in Kenosha, Wis.  My parents—Thomas A. Sullivan and Rose A. Pitts — were both born in Kenosha County, as were three of my grandparents. My Irish and German descent, half and half, is common in the American Middlewest in this century, though not before. My father was a retail merchant—dry goods—in Kenosha. I went to St. James grammar school and to Kenosha High School. At various periods I intended to become a professional baseball player, an inventor, a major general, a magician, and a holder of assorted other high places. I did not intend to become a writer. By the time I was through high school I had settled emphatically for art, which I then conceived as solely concerned with the painting of pictures. I took a couple of classes at the Art Institute of Chicago for a summer; and then started off as a freshman at the University of Notre Dame. By a mistake I was put into a Liberal Arts program rather than the Fine Arts for which I had signed up. Mistakes can be providential, when one looks back on them. At the time they merely kept one going to the Art Institute during the summers. At Notre Dame two very memorable yet entirely different teachers separately and successively got me interested in another kind of art, verbal rather than pigmentary. I tried seriously to write something real and good. But I still wanted to paint. After I graduated from Notre Dame in 1930 I went back to the Art Institute's autonomous adjunct, the Goodman School of Drama, to try to combine, in the theatre, a pair of now rather urgent intentions.

"This is difficult, this tracing out in brevity of a single little line amidst all the complicated tangle of the past. There was a depression. There were a lot of things which need now to be remembered and rendered in words. There are many lines which should be traced.

"In 1932 I married Mabel Constance Priddis, born in Kenosha; we went to Europe for a few months; our elder daughter Jill was born in Kenosha; I worked there in my father's store, and free lanced radio plays and wrote Wild West and G-man thrillers for kids; also, I published a few serious and decent stories. In 1936 I came to Notre Dame to teach in the department of English. I've been here ever since. Our younger daughter, Molly, was born in South Bend. My first novel was published in 1942. In the ten years since then there have been three other novels, a collection of short stories, and a book about the University of which I am a member. I am at the moment [November 1952] in the final stages of work on a new novel. There are some more stories, long ones and short ones, in the making.

"For what it's worth, I must mention that I have personally experienced no conflict between writing and teaching.

"I suppose that all I've written has risen out of the fact of my curiously having been alive in a given region during the first half of a given century. I mean that it seems to me I'm tied down—without objection—to place and time; and I feel that to my place and time, and to the human beings of this time and place, this region and its people, I owe as a writer simple fidelity. I would like to render, in fiction, these people in this time and region with precision and justice and a rightful measure of affection."

PRINCIPAL WORKS: Summer After Summer, 1942; The Dark Continent, 1943; The World of Idella May, 1946; First Citizen, 1948; The Fresh and Open Sky (short stories) 1950; Notre Dame (non-fiction) 1951; 311 Congress Court, 1953.

ABOUT: Hoehn, M. (ed.) Catholic Authors, I; Warfel, H. R. American Novelists of Today.

"SULLIVAN, SEUMAS O'." See STARKEY, J.

SUMMERS, MONTAGUE (April 10, 1880-August 8, 1948). For autobiographical sketch and list of earlier works and references, see TWENTIETH CENTURY AUTHORS, 1942.

* * *

Rev. Montague Summers died suddenly at Richmond in Surrey, England, at sixty-eight.

However one may look askance at his firm belief in the existence of witchcraft and his preoccupation with the supernatural, this was only one side of his nature. His critical and editorial work formed a "distinguished contribution to scholarship," as the London *Times* has pointed out. The late Richard Le Gallienne once declared of Summers' authority in the Restoration drama that he had achieved "so lonely an eminence in his own field that he alone is qualified to be his own final critic."

He was, in the words of the London *Times*, "in every way a 'character,' and in some sort a throwback to the Middle Ages."

ADDITIONAL WORKS: Witchcraft and Black Magic, 1946; Physical Phenomena of Mysticism, 1950.

ABOUT: Strachey, G. L. Literary Essays; London Times August 11, 1948; New York Times August 11, 1948.

SUTRO, ALFRED (August 7, 1863-September 11, 1933). For biographical sketch and list of works and references, see TWENTIETH CENTURY AUTHORS, 1942.

* * *

ABOUT: Dictionary of National Biography 1931-1940.

*"SVEVO, ITALO" (pseudonym of Ettore Schmitz) (December 19, 1861-September 13, 1928). For biographical sketch and list of works and references, see TWENTIETH CENTURY AUTHORS, 1942.

* * *

ABOUT: Columbia Dictionary of Modern European Literature; Pritchett, V. S. Books in General; Roditi, E. *Preface to* Svevo's As a Man Grows Older (2nd ed., 1949.)

* svà'vō

SWANSON, NEIL HARMON (June, 30, 1896-). For autobiographical sketch and list of earlier works and references, see TWENTIETH CENTURY AUTHORS, 1942.

* * *

Neil Harmon Swanson has been executive editor of the Baltimore *Sun, Evening Sun,* and *Sunday Sun* since 1941. In 1946 he directed and edited the news enterprise which brought the *Sun* the Pulitzer prize. He was in charge of the establishment of the *Sun's* television station, WMAR-TV. He is also vice-president of the A. S. Abell Company, publishers.

Swanson has continued work on his ambitious project of books covering the settlement of the eastern half of the United States. *The Perilous Fight,* dealing mainly with the fighting in Maryland in the War of 1812, was a fresh and lively retelling of history, based closely on contemporary sources. *The Unconquered* dealt with the Pontiac Indian uprising. Richard Match, in the New York *Times,* describes it as "a good old-fashioned settlers-versus-redskins, man-the-stockades-lads frontier melodrama." It was made into a motion picture by Cecil B. DeMille.

ADDITIONAL WORKS: The Perilous Fight, 1945; The Unconquered, 1948.

ABOUT: Warfel, H. R. American Novelists of Today.

SWEENEY, JAMES JOHNSON (May 30, 1900-), American art critic and museum director, was born in Brooklyn, N.Y., the son of Patrick M. and Mary (Johnson) Sweeney. He received his B.A. degree from Georgetown University in Washington, D.C., in 1922 and spent the following years studying abroad: at Jesus College, Cambridge, from 1922 to 1924, the Sorbonne in  1925, and the University of Siena in 1926. During these years he contributed verse and art criticism to the *Irish Statesman,* the New York *Times,* and *Cahiers d'Art,* and he was art correspondent for the Chicago *Evening Post* and *Art World.* In 1927 he married Laura Harden. They have five children—Ann, Sean, Siadhal, Tadhg, Ciannait.

In 1933-34 Sweeney was director of an exhibition of twentieth century painting and sculpture at the University of Chicago. In 1935, after spending some months in Europe collecting materials, he directed an exhibit of African Negro art for the Museum of Modern Art. He has also directed exhibitions of the works of Miró, Calder, Mondrian, and Stieglitz for the museum, and in 1945-46 he was director of its department of painting and sculpture. Since then he has directed exhibits in Virginia (for the Biennial Exhibition), Toronto (a Picasso show), Paris (twentieth century masterpieces, at the Musée d'Art Moderne), and London (at the Tate Gallery). He also selected the exhibition of Alexander Calder's sculpture and installed the American Pavilion at the Biennial Exposition in Venice. Since 1948 he has been vice president of the International Art Critics Association. He has lectured on American art at Salzburg and in the season 1950-51 he gave a fortnightly radio broadcast on art, literature, and the theatre over Radio Eireann, Dublin. Deeply interested in contemporary literature, Sweeney was associate editor of *transition* from 1935 to 1938. Since 1948 he has been an advisory editor of *Partisan Review.* In 1952 he was reported to be working on a study of T. S. Eliot's poetry.

In 1952 Sweeney was appointed director of the Solomon R. Guggenheim Museum (formerly the Museum of Non-Objective Art) in New York City. Under his leadership the Museum has expanded its collection and put on a number of successful exhibitions.

PRINCIPAL WORKS: Plastic Redirections in Twentieth Century Painting, 1934; (ed.) African Negro Art, 1935; Joan Miró, 1941; Alexander Calder, 1943; (ed.) Three Young Rats, and Other Rhymes, 1944; Stuart Davis, 1945; Marc Chagall, 1946; Henry Moore, 1947; African Folk Tales and Sculpture (with P. Radin) 1952; Antoni Gaudi (with J. L. Sert) 1953.

ABOUT: Hoehn, M. (ed.) Catholic Authors, II; Art Digest November 1, 1952· Current Biography March 1955.

"SWIFT, ANTHONY." See FARJEON, J. J.

SWING, RAYMOND (March 25, 1887-   ), American news commentator and author, was born in Cortland, N.Y., the son of Albert Temple Swing and Alice Edwards (Mead) Swing. He was educated at Oberlin—both at the College and at the Conservatory of Music (non-graduate)—and in 1906 began newspaper work in Cleveland. From there he went to Orville, Ohio, and then joined, successively, several midwestern papers. In 1913 he was sent to Berlin as correspondent for the Chicago *Daily News*; one of his scoops there was a story of the mysterious large-bore gun that was shelling Liège. He left this job and returned to the United States in 1917, and in 1918 became an examiner with the War Labor Board. After serving as Berlin correspondent, this

time for the New York *Herald,* from 1919 to 1922, Swing then became director of foreign service for the *Wall Street Journal* for two years. For ten years (1924-34) he was in the London bureau of the Philadelphia *Public Ledger* and the New York *Evening Post,* and from 1934 to 1936 on the editorial board of the *Nation.* A news commentator on American affairs for the B.B.C. from 1935 to 1945, he was also a commentator on the Mutual Broadcasting System from 1936 to 1945, and for the American Broadcasting Company from 1942 to 1948. During this period he was one of the best known American radio commentators. In 1945 he received the Peabody Award for his radio work. Between 1948 and 1950 he turned to lecturing, but in 1950 he reported over WOR as commentator, and over the Liberty network in 1950-51. More recently he has been an overseas reporter for the Columbia Broadcasting System.

As an author he started out—in his twenties—writing sonnets for *Outlook* and the *Literary Digest.* His first book was published in 1935, *Forerunners of American Fascism,* portraits of five American leaders who have been defined as demagogues. George E. Sokolsky said Swing "spoils his book by distortion," but Lewis Gannett in the New York *Herald Tribune* found "Mr. Swing's book full of fresh and realistic perspectives. . . . He has good eyes." In 1946 *In the Name of Sanity* appeared. George Soule found this discussion of the political aspects of the atomic bomb "vivid, logical, forceful."

In 1912 Swing married Suzanne Morin of Paris; they had a son and a daughter; and were divorced. His second marriage, in 1920, was to Betty Gram of Portland, Ore., whom he met in Berlin where she was studying voice. "Gram" which Swing used as a middle name for many years, is thus the maiden name of his second wife, who feministically refused to abandon it; he now calls himself Raymond Swing. By this marriage there were three children, two boys and a girl. His third marriage took place in 1945 to Mary S. Hartshorne.

Swing has received several honorary degrees, including an honorary M.A. from Harvard in 1942. In 1946 he was the chairman of the board of directors of Americans United for World Government. As a radio commentator and lecturer, Swing speaks in a friendly, quiet, painstaking manner, somewhat pedagogical in tone. His relaxations are ping pong, bridge, piano playing, listening to concerts and playing poker. He has written several classical compositions for the piano but is very modest about them and never intends to have them published.

PRINCIPAL WORKS: Forerunners of American Fascism, 1935; How War Came, 1939; Preview of History, 1943; In the Name of Sanity, 1946; (ed.) This I Believe, 1954.

ABOUT: Fisher, D. F. American Portraits; Atlantic Monthly July 1945; Current Biography 1940; Nation January 24, 1948.

SWINNERTON, FRANK ARTHUR
(August 12, 1884-). For autobiographical sketch and list of earlier works and references, see TWENTIETH CENTURY AUTHORS, 1942.

* * *

Frank Swinnerton writes from Old Tokefield in Surrey: "From 1937 to 1942 (inclusive) I was chief novel reviewer to the London Observer; and from October 1949 I have written the weekly article signed 'John O'London' in John O'London's Weekly. I do not edit the paper. My predecessors in this work were Wilfred Whitten and Robert Lynd."

In the introduction to a new edition of Tokefield Papers, published in 1949, Frank Swinnerton wrote: "I have lived, not inertly, through sixty-five years of strange and terrible events, without losing zest for life, but gaining what seems to me to be worth having, a sense of proportion, or what (respecting myself) has been variously called sense, tolerance, and sagacity." These qualities of sense, tolerance, and sagacity characterize Swinnerton's work. He points out with good humor that critics sometimes damn his novels with the term 'competence,' but it is essentially the solid competence of his craft that distinguishes his fiction. Charles Lee has called him "one of England's most dependable story tellers."

Swinnerton's essays are rambling and chatty, packed with odds and ends of information and reminiscences of the literary London of H. G. Wells and Arnold Bennett. They are written to the liking (as the Manchester Guardian put it) "of those who value tolerance, humour, and a subtle and discerning insight into human nature."

ADDITIONAL WORKS: A Woman in Sunshine, 1944; Faithful Company, 1948; The Cats and Rosemary (juvenile) 1948; The Doctor's Wife Comes to Stay, 1949; A Flower for Catherine, 1951; The Bookman's London (essays) 1952; An Affair of Love (in England: Master Jim Probity) 1953; A Month in Gordon Square (novel) 1953.

ABOUT: Church, R. British Authors (1948); Swinnerton, F. Tokefield Papers (1949); Newsweek March 6, 1950.

SYKES, CHRISTOPHER (November 17, 1907-), English writer of fiction and essays, was born in Yorkshire, the second son of the late Sir Mark Sykes. He was educated at Downside, Christ Church, Oxford, and the Sorbonne. After serving as a junior officer at the British Embassy in Teheran, he studied at the School of Oriental Studies and returned to Persia and  Afghanistan in 1933 to study the campaigns of the 1914-18 war in the interior of Persia and Central Asia. He was a correspondent for the London Times in Teheran in 1934. From 1936 to 1939 he wrote for the Spectator and the Observer. During World War II, he served in General Headquarters, Middle East, in Cairo, Persia and Palestine, and lastly in the Special Air Service. He won the Croix de Guerre and was mentioned in dispatches. After the war he worked for the B.B.C. and from 1949 to 1952 he was literary editor of the English Review.

Sykes' novel Answer to Question 33 is set in England and the Middle East and the subject is loyalty, which he was later to treat at greater length in essays. The hero, Kirkby, is called by a friend to a session in the House of Commons concerning an Italian woman, Donna Isabella, who was broadcasting anti-British propaganda from Moscow. Isabella was a once ardent admirer of all things British, whose love had turned to bitterness. L. A. G. Strong, reviewing this book in the Spectator, wrote: "The writing is intelligent and humane, the characters are well observed and, what is rarer, understood, and the whole story gives that feeling of inevitability which means that the writer's imagination has been deeply stirred and has made sense of its disturbance."

Four Studies in Loyalty, published in the same year, consists of four essays, picturing different types of loyalty. The first sketch depicts the author's great-uncle and namesake, Christopher Sykes, who was an intimate friend of Edward VII, and whose loyalty to his king survived countless jokes played on him, and the loss of his fortune (spent in entertaining the king). The second sketch is of a Persian, whose adoration of England, and especially of Oxford, which he fancied he had attended, dominated his life. The third sketch presents the author's friend, the English writer, Robert Byron. The fourth sketch pictures the members of the French Resistance movement living in a small town near the place where the author himself landed by parachute during the war. The book was very well received.

In 1950 a book of short stories appeared, *Character and Situation*. Evelyn Waugh wrote in his introduction: "The stories presented here are typical of his talents. All have a foreign setting; all have great variety. If I had to name the particular qualities of his work, I should put this, Variety, first. There are many writers who confine themselves to one narrow milieu and fret away book after book with its problems. Not so Mr. Sykes. Secondly, I should put Independence. He is obviously not writing for a particular market.... Thirdly, I should put something which is not easy to define in a single word. It is almost the gift of seeing events *'sub specie aeternitatis.'*"

This book was followed in 1953 with *Two Studies in Virtue*. The first of these essays, "A Study of the Religious Movements of the Nineteenth Century" is based on the story of Richard Sibthorp, an English clergyman who passed back and forth from Anglicanism to Roman Catholicism several times. The second essay, "The Prosperity of His Servant" is a study of the origins of the Balfour Declaration in 1917, and deals, among other Zionists, with the author's father, Sir Mark Sykes. The *Spectator* commented: "The author, the talented son of a brilliant and distinguished Roman Catholic Zionist, handles both impacts with sympathetic objectivity, couched in the urbane tradition, but not in imitation of, Lytton Strachey and Harold Nicolson."

Christopher Sykes is married to the daughter of Sir Thomas Russell Pasha, and has one son. He lives in Dorset.

PRINCIPAL WORKS: Wassmuss, The German Lawrence, 1936; Innocence and Design (with R. Byron) 1936; Stranger Wonders, 1937; High-Minded Murder, 1944; Answer to Question 33, 1948; Four Studies in Loyalty, 1948; Character and Situation, Six Short Stories, 1950; Two Studies in Virtue, 1953.

ABOUT: Hoehn, M. (ed.) Catholic Authors, II.

SYKES, GERALD (1903-), American novelist, was born in Ontario, Canada, attended Culver Military Academy and then went on to the University of Cincinnati. During World War II, Sykes served with the Office of War Information and the State Department, having formerly been a newspaperman for the Kentucky *Post*. Sykes is

that fortunate novelist whose second novel received far more praise than his first. Harvey Breit, on the occasion of the republication of *The Center of the Stage* in a twenty-five-cent edition (1954), spoke of Sykes as a writer who becomes more expert and strong as he goes along, and who stands for the lucid and rational against the abdominal school that abounds. "Novelist Sykes," wrote *Time* of the same book, "has an enviable gift for writing cultivated dialogue and intelligent reflection; his book, even in its limp spots, reveals the controlling presence of a grown-up mind."

Buffie Johnson

The author of articles in the *New Republic, Partisan Review, Hound and Horn,* the *Nation, United Nations World,* and other periodicals, Sykes published his first novel, *The Nice American,* in 1951. With rare general consent, the critics felt the novel held praiseworthy ideas which were not very well expressed, and that interest lay in the ideas rather than in plot and characters. The London *Times Literary Supplement* remarked that it was accustomed to slick American novels in which plot and dialogue flow easily but where ideas are trite or nonexistent. "Mr. Gerald Sykes reverses this process," it said; although "some of its obvious imperfections should not blind readers to the importance of its theme." "In fictional terms," noted *Commonweal*, "it has little more emotional impact than the North Atlantic treaty."

Sykes' second novel, *The Center of the Stage,* a study of the marriage of an actress, was highly praised. "One of the most exciting novels I have read in a long time," said George Freedley in the *Library Journal.* And Chad Walsh wrote in the New York *Times*: "Of the novelists now coming to the fore, Gerald Sykes is one of the most promising and exciting. He is that rare being, a thoroughly civilized writer, devoid at the same time of preciousness and affectation."

The Children of Light was a timely picture of the dilemmas of an intellectual trying to participate in present-day political life. Granville Hicks commented: "He examines the conditions of contemporary life with bold realism, and, instead of complaining, he seeks for strategies by which the intellectual can maintain his freedom and integrity." The novel was weakened by ambiguities and inconsistencies, Hicks found, but it remained more vital than many faultless novels. "Mr. Sykes writes of the world we live in—and writes of it with remarkable poise and understanding."

Gerald Sykes is married to the former Buffie Johnson. They have a daughter and live in East Hampton, N.Y.

PRINCIPAL WORKS: The Nice American, 1951; The Center of the Stage, 1952; The Children of Light, 1955.

SYLVESTER, HARRY (January 19, 1908-), American novelist and short story writer, reports: "The real landmarks in any-

Stephen Baldanza

one's life lie within. A man's birthplace and travels are meaningful only in that they may have helped shape and mark him. That I was born in Brooklyn, worked for newspapers and traveled and lived in many parts of the hemisphere seem less to me than that I was raised as a Roman Catholic.

"To begin an autobiographical note with a reference to religion may seem gauche but since the Catholic Church has been the central theme of almost all of my serious writing, I cannot write of myself as a writer without making clear my relation to that Church, past and present. I wrote three serious novels about the Church in the United States because I was emotionally and intellectually committed to it and felt it to be the highest and best authenticated 'Way.' A concern with a society operating within the framework of the Catholic Church and deeply affected by its precepts is not one common to writers in the United States. It is a concern common to French writers and as much as I consciously patterned myself on anyone in the early days, I did so on Georges Bernanos.

"My first and third novels have been called anti-clerical, which should have surprised no one, as they were intended to be anti-clerical. The second novel is more affirmative and represents a final venture into writing of religious mysticism. For years I considered myself to be a Catholic troubled by the corruption within the Church although not by its central ideas.

"In 1947 I was asked to deliver a lecture at a school in Chicago on 'Problems of the Catholic Writer.' I agreed to try to do so and in writing my lecture began a process that brought into consciousness doubts more serious than those engendered merely by an occasional androgynous cardinal. The lecture was well-received at this school sponsored by a liberal bishop. Only a few local protests were heard until some weeks later the lecture was published in the Atlantic Monthly. The many letters, the numerous angry, astonished and occasionally vicious replies in the Catholic press to what I had thought of only as a somewhat weary statement of problems with which I had lived and under whose pressures done my writing for fifteen years, forced me to consider the possibility that between myself and my variously excited critics, one of us was not a Catholic and that it might be me. Other letters, including some of the friendly ones, suggested that I was already out of the Church or on the way out.

"I discovered this to be true. Not everyone, like Paul, has the moment of his conversion or disconversion marked for him. I do not know exactly when I left the Catholic Church although I know that I am out of it permanently and irrevocably. For those interested in such details, I last 'attended the Sacraments' in a church whose name I have forgotten in a suburb of Lima, Peru. The month was March, 1949, the disconversion intellectual. I cannot accept the Church's teaching on such basic matters as transubstantiation, the assumption of the Virgin, or the infallibility of the Pope. I do believe that great aboriginal truths lie at the roots of Christianity but that in its formative decades some dreadful error involving misinterpretation or expediency, like a mistake made early in a long algebraic equation, conditioned and invalidated all that followed. There is no other explanation for a church finding its way from the Sermon on the Mount to the four hundred thousand dead of the Inquisition.

"There might have been more books, better written, if there had not been an almost constant financial pressure requiring me to sell over the years about 150 short stories, most of which I would rather not have written, in order to raise my children and find occasional free months in which to accomplish the novels. Recently, I have returned to journalism as a more honorable and less debilitating way of supporting them.

"The sense of freedom and release which has steadily grown since leaving the Church is worth whatever I may have paid for it. I do not know the course of books I have yet to write for they will flow from different wells than those already written."

* * *

Harry Sylvester, son of Harry Aaron and Margaret (Curtin) Sylvester, was born in Brooklyn, N.Y., and educated at Notre Dame (B.A. 1930). He wrote for the New York *Herald Tribune*, the New York *Post*, and the Brooklyn *Daily Eagle* until 1933, when he gave up newspaper work to free lance. In the years which followed, his work appeared in *Commonweal, Collier's, Cosmopolitan, Esquire, Story*, and many other magazines. Several of his short stories appeared in the O. Henry and O'Brien collections. His most successful novel has been *Moon Gaffney*, a story of a young liberal Catholic whose political activities bring him into conflict with a political machine and with his Church. Francis Downing in *Commonweal* found the novel "beautifully and wonderfully done. His, now, is a sure and great talent." Brendan Gill, in the New York *Times*, was less enthusiastic about its literary merits, but he was impressed with its ringing sincerity and conviction. "Reading it, one knows and is grateful for the fact that it wasn't written in order to win a $300,000 movie prize contest, but to say something. It does say something." Sylvester married Rita Ryall Davis in 1936. They have four children.

PRINCIPAL WORKS: Big Football Man, 1933; Dearly Beloved, 1942; Dayspring, 1945; Moon Gaffney, 1947; All Your Idols (short stories) 1948; The Golden Girl, 1950.

ABOUT: Hoehn, M. (ed.) Catholic Authors, I; Warfel, H. R. American Novelists of Today; New York Herald Tribune Book Review July 6, 1947.

*SYMONS, ALPHONSE JAMES ALBERT** (1900-August 26, 1941), English man of letters who signs his work A. J. A. Symons, grew up in a suburb of London. After a prosperous period, his family had financial reverses, and Symons was obliged to work as an apprentice to a firm of fur dealers for three years. This impressed him with a sense of humiliation far beyond anything his family realized. Julian Symons, in his biography of his brother, has published a letter written to

* sǐm'ǔnz

the girl whom A. J. A. Symons later married. "At an incredibly early age (fourteen)," the letter reads in part, "I left school and left home, and a drudgery by no means as extreme as that Dickens endured, but still dreadful to memory, began. (It meant labor from 8 to 8). All I will say of it is that it lasted three years, during which time I went home only for weekends, that I learned a great deal, that I was utterly lonely. All that I know, I taught myself. At school, such as it was, I certainly surprised my masters, and those three years of apprenticeship were for me years of solitary study among people who, though they had started level with me, could not take from me the consciousness of attainments and abilities infinitely superior. (During this space I gained my knowledge of furs. This is the only hint I will give you.) About that time, I first became imbued with the idea that I could write, and that I could build and shape my life as an architect plans a house, selecting and rejecting the material to hand." At the time he wrote this letter he was twenty-one.

Symons worked as secretary and director of the First Edition Club of London, and was described as a lean young man, talking in a rich, deep voice, with brown eyes flashing brightly behind thick horn-rimmed spectacles. He became a bibliographer, and this sobered his youthful romanticism (writes his brother) and "put him out of sympathy with the best art and writing of his time, so that he could draw no sustenance from them." A believer in dandyism, Symons left unfinished a biography on Oscar Wilde. He found it difficult to write, and studied psychoanalysis to find an explanation and cure.

When his biography of the African explorer, *H. M. Stanley*, appeared in 1933, the London *Times* found the book sane, accurate and readable rather than lively or vivid, but the Springfield *Republican* said, "This book is well-written despite its brevity and makes excellent reading for those interested in exploration and in extraordinary personalities." Symons' best-known work, *The Quest for Corvo*, "An Experiment in Biography," is a study of the eccentric-writer Frederick Rolfe, who called himself the Baron Corvo. "Fascinating the book is," wrote R. P. Blackmur in the *New Republic*, "not because its subject is presented as a whole with a character to explain its fate, but because the fragments of personality and incident, vivid in themselves and pressing upon the reader, remain partly undisclosed and have often no satisfying context whatever. There are hints, notes, tokens and signs, and there are gaps, some of them indicated as sufficiently horrible, which the reader cannot help putting dramatically together." *The Quest for Corvo* is generally regarded as one of the most brilliant of modern biographies.

Symons married Gladys Weeks in 1924; they were divorced in 1936. He died in 1941 after an illness, beginning in 1939, which was marked by partial paralysis. Baffling to physicians, the cause was discovered after his death to be a haemangioma of the brain stem, a lesion of a blood vessel which is not necessarily dangerous, unless it occurs—as did his—in the nervous system.

PRINCIPAL WORKS: Bibliography of the First Editions of Books by William Butler Yeats (comp.) 1924; Frederick Baron Corvo (privately printed) 1927; Anthology of 'Nineties Verse (comp. & ed.) 1928; Emin, Governor of Equatoria, 1928; H. M. Stanley, 1933; The Quest for Corvo, 1934.

ABOUT: Symons, J. A. J. A. Symons: His Life and Speculations.

*SYMONS, ARTHUR (February 28, 1865-January 22, 1945). For biographical sketch and list of works and references, see TWENTIETH CENTURY AUTHORS, 1942.

* * *

Arthur Symons died at his home in Wittersham, England, at seventy-nine.

It is probable, as Arnold B. Sklare has said, that if Symons' mental breakdown in 1908 had not left "a mind which had never wholly healed," his critical development would have been great. His early exposition of the theory of symbolism in art, his introduction of foreign authors to English readers, and his ability "to express 'the unique reality of the object' while making new beauty of the writer's own intuitions" (in the words of the London *Times*), were greater contributions than his own poetry or criticism.

Richard Jennings has said: "I think that all the later part of his work should be forgotten. But it should not be forgotten that he was a 'period' poet by no means negligible, a poet praised by his admired master Walter Pater for his 'fine qualities of style, his fine scholarship, his dramatic hold on life'; a sensitive critic or rather *describer* of books, places, pictures, music and action. What he lacked was that part of genius we call originality."

ABOUT: Journal of Aesthetics June 1951; London Times January 25, 1945; New York Times January 26, 1945; Nineteenth Century March 1945; Saturday Review of Literature April 7, 1945; Time February 5, 1945.

* si'mŭnz

*SYMONS, JULIAN (1912-), British poet, biographer, and critic, writes: "Born in London, and has lived in England since then. Followed a variety of commercial occupations, including secretary to an engineering company, advertising copywriter and executive. For the last five years has lived dangerously as a free-lance writer and book reviewer. From 1946 contributor of  regular weekly column, 'Life, People—and Books' to the Manchester *Evening News*, evening paper of the *Manchester Guardian*. Regular contributor also to left-wing weekly *Tribune*, for a short time literary editor of that paper, and closely associated with most of its political views. Has a wife, two children, a house with sunroof overlooking a village green in Kent.

"Before the war, founded and edited *Twentieth Century Verse* (January 1937 to September 1939), a 'little' magazine which introduced some of the younger English poets, and showed an interest—at that time unfashionable in England—in American poetry. In 1945 dug out of a dusty drawer a near-comic detective story called *The Immaterial Murder Case,* posted it to a publisher, and took the first step on a literary treadmill. Has thus two separate literary reputations, highbrow and commercial; the first buttressed by various critical articles in magazines and by biographies of brother A. J. A. Symons (author of *The Quest for Corvo,* bibliographer, gastronome and dandy) and Thomas Carlyle; the second by a number of stories which attempt, no doubt vainly, to blend the values of a serious novel with the excitement of a thriller."

* * *

Julian Symons writes a brisk, straightforward, and constantly interesting prose, whether his subject be a formidable literary figure like Thomas Carlyle or Charles Dickens, or a cloak-and-dagger type of mystery melodrama. His "serious" works of biography, while of no great depth, serve as excellent introductions. Gordon N. Ray wrote of his book on Carlyle: "For the most part Mr. Symons makes his way through the jungle of nineteenth-century social history with ease and adroitness." And the *New Statesman and Nation* considered his study

* sĭm'ŭnz

of Dickens "the best short introduction to the greatest of English novelists that exists." His "thriller" novels are full of spirited action. Anthony Boucher said of *The Broken Penny* that the author "lets himself go on a full-scale Ambler-Hitchcock thriller and, without the least sacrifice of brilliance in prose and insight, shows a superb command of every trick in the repertory of the spy melodrama."

PRINCIPAL WORKS: *Poetry*—Confusions About X, 1939; The Second Man, 1944. *Biography and Criticism*—A. J. A. Symons, His Life and Speculations, 1950; Charles Dickens, 1951; Thomas Carlyle, 1952. *Detective Stories*—The Immaterial Murder Case, 1945; A Man Called Jones, 1947; Bland Beginning, 1949; The 31st of February, 1950; The Broken Penny, 1953; The Narrowing Circle, 1954.

ABOUT: Scarfe, F. Auden and After.

SYNGE, JOHN MILLINGTON (April 16, 1871-March 24, 1909). For biographical sketch and list of works and references, see TWENTIETH CENTURY AUTHORS, 1942.

*TABORI, GEORGE (1914-), Hungarian-British novelist, was born in Hungary, the son of Cornelius Tabori, "king of Hungarian reporters."

When he was eighteen, his family, trying to protect him from the writing profession, persuaded him to leave Budapest and go into the hotel business. In 1932, while Hitler was making his first speeches, Tabori worked in Berlin's fashionable Hotel Adlon, as kitchen cleaner, assistant cook, and waiter. He then became bartender, waiter, and captain at a little hotel and café on the Kurfuerstendam, until February 1933, when the Storm Troopers broke up this meeting place of intellectuals and liberals. At this point he returned to Budapest and the Hotel Ritz as desk clerk. Later he became a travel manager for a London travel agency and conducted de luxe tours of the Continent. In 1935, however, determining to be a writer, he announced this unwelcome news to his family, and his father found him a job on a Hungarian magazine.

In 1937 Tabori repaired to England where, like Conrad and Koestler, he adopted the new language for his writing. He finds it an advantage. "You don't write in clichés, be-

* tǎ bô rē'

cause you don't know them." When the war came he worked as a correspondent for a Hungarian newspaper, for the United Press, and then became wartime B.B.C. broadcaster from Israel and Egypt. While he was there he married, in 1942, a psychiatric social worker, also an exile, who had been sent from Germany as an orphan to a children's village in Israel.

Tabori worked on his first novel, *Beneath the Stone*, during the war, and it was published in 1945. This book, and his two following novels, were best sellers in post-war London and a moderate success in America. His fourth novel, *The Caravan Passes*, was praised as a rich and violent book, of trenchant ideas, stormy action, and urgently human beings. "Tabori writes provocatively," said Vance Bourjaily in the *Saturday Review of Literature*, "writes strong narrative, and has the indispensable gift which makes a novelist good: everyone on whom his writing touches, be it only for a paragraph, comes to life." His English style is greatly admired; he has been said to write with the unlabored eloquence and reckless accuracy of a poet.

In 1949 Tabori came to America and found Hollywood a disillusioning experience, though America seems to him "a magnificent laboratory for an artist. The conflicts and tensions are sharper and richer than in any of the countries I have so far visited." He thinks Hungary "the loneliest country in Europe," and America also characteristically a country of lonely people. Tabori's play, *Flight into Egypt*, produced on Broadway in 1952, dealt with a refugee family en route to America who decide finally to go back and help rebuild their native country, rather than take flight to a new country. In 1953 his play *The Emperor's Clothes*, a study of the conflicts faced by an intellectual in a totalitarian state, had a brief Broadway run. Tabori also collaborated on the script of *The Young Lovers*, an English motion picture released in 1954.

He has been described as a gentle, easy person with a sly smile and a sardonic humor, who "looks like a caricature of himself since all his features—the attenuated neck, the narrow face, the straight sandy hair worn long and sandy mustache worn short (both in correct R.A.F. style), the beak nose, large ears and small chin, the close-togetherness of the gray eyes—are strongly exaggerated." Tabori says: "I have gone through two world wars, three revolutions, and a number of minor upheavals. Sixty per cent of my family were killed by the Nazis." His father was one of fifty leading journalists whom the

Nazis caught in their first dragnet, and one of those finally killed at Auschwitz. In 1954 Tabori married the actress Viveca Lindfors.

PRINCIPAL WORKS: Beneath the Stone (in England: Beneath the Stone the Scorpion) 1945; Companions of the Left Hand, 1946; Original Sin, 1947; The Caravan Passes, 1951.

ABOUT: New York Times Magazine March 9, 1952.

TAGGARD, GENEVIEVE (November 28, 1894-November 8, 1948). For autobiographical sketch and list of earlier works and references, see TWENTIETH CENTURY AUTHORS, 1942.

* * *

Genevieve Taggard died in a New York hospital just before her fifty-fourth birthday.

She had retired from teaching to continue writing at her home in Jamaica, Vt. In May 1948 she received an award from the American Academy of Arts and Letters "in recognition of creative work" but was too ill to attend the presentation ceremony. A record of poetry reading by Miss Taggard was issued in 1953 by The River Press in East Jamaica, Vt. The Dartmouth College Library has an extensive collection of printed works in all forms, including juvenilia, also much material about the writer and some manuscripts. The Genevieve Taggard Papers in the New York Public Library include correspondence and manuscripts. Additional manuscripts are in the Lockwood Memorial Library, Buffalo, N.Y.

The late William Rose Benét spoke of "the shy irony, the genuine mirth, the 'scorn of scorn'" in her work, and of the poet herself he said: "I think of Genevieve Taggard as a free spirit. She was beautiful. She was feminine. . . . She reminded me of the spirit of a stream, changeable (though not in the deep things), impetuous, impatient, and meditating and lonely."

The quality of her poetry has been called "brilliant, various and warm" by J. R. Caldwell. "I know of no poet to whom the lyric gift appears more native. Her words are lithe, eager, and beforehand. They move to suit her purposes with a suppleness that seems, in these bleak and muscular days, almost illicit." There is strong evidence in her work of her sensitivity to social injustice. She said, "I have refused to write out of a decorative impulse. . . . I hope I have written poetry that relates to general experience and the realities of our time." Near the end of her life she wrote: "In the little church my parents attended in Honolulu I was impressed with the text, 'I am come that ye might have

life and have it more abundantly. When we sat listening I had only to move my eyes from the minister to see outside the flowering vines and colored trees of abundance. . . . I have never ceased to think that the text, taken literally, should be the aim of all governments. I am not interested in anything else and, come to think of it, neither are you, dear reader. . . . I am still forced to write. No matter how happy or fortunate our personal lives, the great cause still remains—it is 'the misery of the world that will not let us rest.'"

ADDITIONAL WORKS: Monologue for Mothers, 1929; Falcon, 1942; A Part of Vermont, 1945; Slow Music, 1946; Origin: Hawaii, 1947.

ABOUT: Stauffer, D. A. Poets at Work; Taggard, G. Origin: Hawaii; Wilson, E. The Shores of Light; Bennington College Alumnae Quarterly Spring 1949; Nation December 11, 1948; New York Herald Tribune November 9, 1948; New York Times November 9, 1948; Sarah Lawrence Alumnae Magazine Fall 1948; Saturday Review of Literature December 14, 1946, November 20, 1948.

*TAGORE, Sir RABINDRANATH (May 6, 1861-August 7, 1941). For biographical sketch and list of works and references, see TWENTIETH CENTURY AUTHORS, 1942.

* * *

ADDITIONAL WORKS IN ENGLISH TRANSLATION: Two Sisters, 1944; Three Plays: Mukta-dhara, Natir Puja, Chandalika, 1951; A Tagore Testament, 1955.

ABOUT: Anand, M. R. in The New Spirit (ed. E. W. L. Martin); Aronson, A. Rabindranath Through Western Eyes; Bose, A. C. Three Mystic Poets; Estborn, G. The Religion of Tagore in the Light of the Gospel; Fausset, H. I. Poets and Pundits; Ghose, D. N. Rabindranath Tagore; Narasimhan, R. (ed.) Gurudev Tagore; Paul, R. I. Tagore and His Life Campaign; Ray, B. G. The Philosophy of Rabindranath Tagore; Sen Gupta, S. C. Great Sentinel: A Study of Rabindranath Tagore; Sykes, M. Rabindranath Tagore; New Era July 1949.

* tä'gōr, rà bēn'drà nät

"TAINE, JOHN." See BELL, E. T.

TALLANT, ROBERT (April 20, 1909-   ), American novelist and regionalist, writes: "I was born in New Orleans, the son of James Robb Tallant and Lucy Texada (Magruder) Tallant. My father died when I was sixteen. After high school I went to work in a bank as a 'runner,' from which position it was assumed by my relatives I would rise rapidly to vice-president. Although I did not like bank work much, I did have some fun, for I used to play hookey between runs and go to movies, so that I probably made the slowest runs of any bank runner then extant. However, for

some reason, I was soon promoted and became a teller—it may have been only that they thought it best to put me in a cage—where

Philip Stiegman

I remained for some years, during which time the only fun I had was when I was once held up by bank robbers. I got out of the cage and out of work when the banks crashed. After that I was a young man caught by the Great Depression, with no profession and no training that could be useful in making a living during times so difficult. I once estimated that I had nineteen jobs in five years during this period, none of which I could tolerate.

"Yet I didn't decide to become a writer until 1937, when I was already twenty-eight, an advanced age at which some writers are today publishing their memoirs and making farewell appearances. Until now I don't know the reason for my decision to be an author, except that I had always been highly imaginative, was an avid reader, and had always thought a man who had a book published was superior to all other human beings. Anyway, I bought a writer's magazine, discovered that manuscripts should be submitted typed on one side of the page only, doublespaced, and then I went out and bought a secondhand typewriter for five dollars, which was truly possible in those days. Since my mother was born on a plantation, and there were a lot of family stories, I started writing a novel about a southern plantation. It seemed to end in a few chapters, so I threw it away, and I've never written about a southern plantation since. Then I began writing short stories, and after selling the first one I wrote (for six dollars) I was definitely encouraged. During the next five years I wrote around five hundred, of which I sold, or gave away to 'little' magazines and university quarterlies, about sixty.

"In 1940, needing a job, for the stories were not earning me a real living, I managed to attach myself to the Louisiana Writers' Project as an editor. The late Lyle Saxon, then the dean of Louisiana writers, was its state director, and I had met him casually a few times before he became my boss. In fact he was the first book writer I ever met, and at that first meeting I trembled visibly with sheer awe. Later, after we became close friends, he told me that he had been under the impression that I was ill.

"During the months I spent on the project I did the final writing of *Gumbo Ya-Ya, A Collection of Louisiana Folk Tales*, from data that had been collected by scores of project research workers. This was edited by Saxon and Edward Dreyer for publication, but was not published until 1945 because of the coming of World War II.

"When the war came I went to work in the New Orleans Office of Censorship. Rejected by the draft, I remained there until late in 1945, when wartime censorship ended, and by which time I was a department head. During this period I wrote *Voodoo in New Orleans*, working at night and on Sundays, and began my first novel, *Mrs. Candy and Saturday Night*. In October 1945 I was transferred by the government from the closing censorship office to the Social Security Office. In November, on a Sunday, Lyle Saxon telephoned me and suggested we go to New York that night. We went, and when I returned I resigned from the Social Security Office. Since then I have devoted all my time to writing books.

"I have now written fourteen books, and these in seven or eight years. I write fast when I work, and never do a complete second draft although I sometimes re-do pages. Somehow I also manage to loaf a good deal, but always am afflicted with an acute sense of guilt when I do, which at times can be almost painful physically. All my books have been about life in the South, and almost all 'have in some way concerned New Orleans. I have published four non-fiction books, five novels, and two juveniles. I have two novels and another juvenile completed and accepted for publication yet to appear. At present [June 1953] I am at work on a new novel, a third about Mrs. Candy of my first novel.

"I am unmarried. Politically I am a liberal Democrat. I was reared a Methodist, but am not now a church member. I do not care much about traveling, but like to stay here in New Orleans, although I realize it would be better for me to get around more. I hate sports and games, including parlor games. I like parties, and eating and drinking. I don't like historical novels much, but prefer modern ones, usually those of a humorous and/or satirical sort. For sheer escape and wonderment I dote on science fiction, but I've never attempted to write it. I will not do any public speaking, and radio and television appearances terrify me when I am coerced into making them. If my writing has been influenced by anyone it is probably by such diverse authors as Norman Douglas, Evelyn Waugh, Somerset

Maugham, William March, and by the conversation of Lyle Saxon."

PRINCIPAL WORKS: *Novels*—Mrs. Candy and Saturday Night, 1947; Angel in the Wardrobe, 1948; Mr. Preen's Salon, 1949; A State in Mimosa, 1950; Southern Territory, 1951; Love and Mrs. Candy, 1953; Mrs. Candy Strikes It Rich, 1954. *Non-Fiction*—Voodoo in New Orleans, 1946; Mardi Gras, 1948; The Romantic New Orleanians, 1950; The Pirate Lafitte and the Battle of New Orleans, 1951; Ready to Hang, 1952; The Louisiana Purchase, 1952.

ABOUT: Current Biography 1953; New York Times Book Review December 10, 1950.

TAPPAN, EVA MARCH (December 26, 1854-January 30, 1930). For biographical sketch and list of works and references, see TWENTIETH CENTURY AUTHORS, 1942.

TARBELL, IDA MINERVA (November 5, 1857-January 6, 1944). For biographical sketch and list of works and references, see TWENTIETH CENTURY AUTHORS, 1942.

* * *

Ida Tarbell died of pneumonia, at the Bridgeport (Conn.) Hospital, at eighty-six.

In 1943 she went to Tucson, Ariz., where she served as consulting editor to an Arizona literary magazine *Letters*, and lectured at the University of Arizona. She was living with her sister at Easton, Conn., at the time of her death.

Miss Tarbell was, as Lloyd R. Morris has said, "a scholar by temperament and a research historian by training." Although some of her work has been outmoded, she was a pioneer in impartial, objective and exhaustive investigation. R. L. Duffus has said that the words in which she can be described are old-fashioned ones: "intelligence, simplicity, unselfishness, utter lack of vanity, energy, conscientiousness, kindness, imagination. . . . Together they add up to a truly American species of genius."

ABOUT: Morris, L. R. Postscript to Yesterday; Thomas, B. P. Portrait for Posterity; New York Times January 7, 1944; Time January 17, 1944.

TARDINEAU, RENÉ MARIE AUGUSTE. See BOYLESVE, R.

TARKINGTON, BOOTH (July 29, 1869-May 19, 1946). For autobiographical sketch and list of earlier works and references, see TWENTIETH CENTURY AUTHORS, 1942.

* * *

Booth Tarkington died at his home in Indianapolis at seventy-six. He had been ill for two months.

In 1942 the Roosevelt Memorial Association gave the Roosevelt Distinguished Service Medal to Tarkington for his "service to American literature in depicting the life of the Middle West." The Howells Medal of the American Academy of Arts and Letters was awarded to him in 1945. He left an unfinished novel which was published posthumously with a foreword by his wife, Susannah Tarkington, in which she stated the serious core of his philosophy as a writer: "The truth and mystery of human nature have been his chief concern." In 1943 the Pasadena Community Playhouse presented a "Tarkington cycle" consisting of six of his more than twenty plays.

Noting that he was "incurably sentimental," *Time* has paid tribute to his "pleased ear for U. S. speech; an effortless way of evoking familiar things" and his ability to spin out a plot "at his sardonic leisure." A *New Yorker* writer called him "an extraordinarily observant novelist" who "often wrote with a happy grace that has no precise counterpart in American letters." Although his biographer, James Woodress, believes that Tarkington was a far greater writer than is generally recognized, Orville Prescott notes in the New York *Times* that "Tarkington was too amiable, too humorous, too gentle in his satire, and he wrote far too many mediocre books to please modern critical tastes."

ADDITIONAL WORKS: Kate Fennigate, 1943; The Image of Josephine, 1945; Show Piece, 1947; Three Selected Short Novels (Walterson; Uncertain Molly Collicut; Rennie Peddigoe) 1947; Your Amiable Uncle; Letters to His Nephews, 1949.

ABOUT: Woodress, J. Booth Tarkington; New York Times May 20, 1946, April 22, 1955; New Yorker June 1, 1946; Publishers' Weekly August 8, 1942; Time January 27, 1947.

TATE, ALLEN (November 19, 1899-). For autobiographical sketch and list of earlier works and references, see TWENTIETH CENTURY AUTHORS, 1942.

* * *

Allen Tate edited the *Sewanee Review* from 1944 to 1947. During this same period and until 1950 he was Fellow in American Letters of the Library of Congress, having earlier (1943-44) had the Chair of Poetry there. He lectured at New York University from 1947 to 1951, but spent the academic year 1949 in Chicago as visiting professor of humanities at the University of Chicago. Since 1951 he has been professor of English at the University of Minnesota and Senior Fellow of the Indiana School of Letters.

Tate received a $1,000 award for service to American letters from the National Institute of Arts and Letters in 1948 and a year later was elected a member of that group. In 1952 he became senator-at-large for Phi Beta Kappa. He was one of seven American representatives at the International Exposition of the Arts (Congress for Cultural Freedom) in Paris in 1952 and in the same year was a member of the American delegation to the UNESCO Conference on the Arts in Venice. In 1954 he lectured on modern poetry in Rome.

Since the publication of *Reason in Madness* in 1941, Tate has been recognized as one of the most important of contemporary American critics. His name has been variously associated with the literary movement of "Southern Agrarianism," some years ago, and, more recently, with the "New Criticism." He has worked closely with such fellow poet-critics as John Crowe Ransom, Robert Penn Warren, and Cleanth Brooks, like them approaching the literary text with careful concentration and producing precise and illuminating interpretations. But Tate has always maintained a degree of independence from "schools" of criticism. His recent collection of critical essays, *The Forlorn Demon*, written after his conversion to Roman Catholicism in 1950, reflects new influences. Delmore Schwartz writes: "Almost throughout the book Mr. Tate has drawn upon Catholic and Thomist doctrine to organize his impressions and deepen his perceptions in a new way—a way which makes possible a great range of sympathy, a mature lucidity, and a prose style which is various and powerful."

A similar growth and development has been observed in Tate's recent poetry. Vivienne Koch suggests that in his latest poems he is making a complete break from the Southern school, from traditionalism and classicism, and in his new independence producing "the most enduring, vital, and original poetry . . . [he] is capable of writing." Especially significant, she finds, is his poem "Seasons of the Soul" (published in *Poems, 1922-1947*) with its "religio-ethical purpose" —"tragic, sensuous, lyrical, and deeply compassionate." Of Tate's latest collection of verse Frederick Morgan wrote in the *Hudson Review*: "Mr. Tate has done more than add a few very good poems to the language . . . .; this poetry has attained the stature at which it must inevitably be assessed in its totality, at which even the less successful poems take on importance for the understanding of the whole."

ADDITIONAL WORKS: *Poetry*—The Vigil of Venus (trans. of Pervigilium Veneris) 1943; The

Winter Sea, 1945; Poems, 1922-1947, 1948. *Essays* —On the Limits of Poetry, 1948; The Hovering Fly, 1949; The Forlorn Demon, 1952. *Miscellaneous* —The House of Fiction (ed. with C. Gordon).

ABOUT: Hoehn, M. (ed.) Catholic Authors, II; Hyman, S. E. The Armed Vision; Koch, V. *in* Modern American Poetry (ed. B. Rajan); Atlantic Monthly November 1948; Hudson Review Summer 1948; Nation April 21, 1945; Poetry September 1945; Sewanee Review Autumn 1948; South Atlantic Quarterly April 1948.

TAWNEY, RICHARD HENRY (1880-). For biographical sketch and list of earlier works and references, see TWENTIETH CENTURY AUTHORS, 1942.

* * *

R. H. Tawney is now retired, with the rank of emeritus professor, from the University of London, where he taught economic history from 1931 to 1949. He lives in Gloucestershire. One of the most distinguished and influential of contemporary historians, Tawney's reputation rests solidly upon his two major works, *The Acquisitive Society* and *Religion and the Rise of Capitalism*. In recent years he has written mainly essays and articles for periodicals. As a Fabian Socialist, he has been a moderating but a firm influence. While urging the socialization of the economic system, he also emphasizes the need for guarding the political and civil liberties of the individual: "The serious danger is . . . not that democracy may be sacrificed to the reckless pursuit of economic fredom," he said in 1944. "It is that the establishment of the conditions of such freedom may be too long delayed, and that the failure to achieve it may discredit democracy." In reading Tawney's essays, Noel Annan remarked in the *Manchester Guardian*, "one becomes imperceptibly aware that his gentle reflections evoke a vision of society which is neither utopian nor doctrinaire and is more durable than those of other more voluble writers because it is founded on common sense and knowledge of how human beings can reasonably be expected to behave."

ADDITIONAL WORKS: The Attack (essays) 1953.

ABOUT: Ausubel, H. & others (eds.) Some Modern Historians of Britain; Tawney, R. H. The Attack.

TAYLOR, BERT LESTON ("B.L.T.") (November 13, 1866-March 19, 1921). For biographical sketch and list of works and references, see TWENTIETH CENTURY AUTHORS, 1942.

TAYLOR, DEEMS (December 22, 1885-   ). For biographical sketch and list of earlier works and references, see TWENTIETH CENTURY AUTHORS, 1942.

* * *

Deems Taylor's pleasant, informed and eminently sensible comments on serious music have had the widest possible circulation. From 1936 to 1943 he was the intermission speaker on the Sunday afternoon broadcasts of the New York Philharmonic Symphony. He has also appeared, with witty and urbane musical observations, on the Metropolitan Opera broadcasts, *Information Please!*, and many other programs. From 1942 to 1948 he was president of the American Society of Authors, Composers and Publishers (ASCAP), of which he is now a member of the board of directors. He has composed several orchestral works in recent years, including *Marco Takes a Walk, Elegy for Orchestra*, and the *Restoration Suite*.

Taylor's writings, like his radio comments, are light in substance, intended for a wide popular audience rather than for specialists. One of his recent books was a "non-musical" pictorial history of the movies. Another was *Some Enchanted Evenings*, a cheerful study (which Taylor called a "story," not a "biography") of Richard Rodgers and Oscar Hammerstein II, the extraordinarily successful musical comedy composers. Taylor was married in 1945 to Lucille Watson Little.

ADDITIONAL WORKS: Ramuntcho: Lyric Drama in Three Acts, 1941; (with others) A Pictorial History of the Movies, 1943; Moments Musical, 1949; Music to My Ears, 1949; Some Enchanted Evenings, 1953.

ABOUT: Ewen, D. American Composers Today; Reis, C. Composers in America; Étude April 1949.

TAYLOR, ELIZABETH (COLES) (July 3, 1912-   ), English novelist, writes: "Born in Reading, Berkshire, England. Educated at

the Abbey School, Reading—a school which carries on the name of an eighteenth-century school, run by French refugees, at which Mrs. Sherwood, Miss Mitford, and Jane Austen were pupils.

"As a young child I began to write stories and always wanted to be a novelist; but I earned nothing from writing until after I was thirty. When I left school, worked as a governess and, later, in a library—and continued to write in my spare time. I learnt so much from these jobs and have never regretted the time I spent at them.

"I married when I was twenty-four, John William Kendal Taylor; and we have a son, Renny, and a daughter, Joanna. Living, during the war, a lonely life in the country, while my husband was in the Royal Air Force, I wrote the first of my published novels—*At Mrs. Lippincote's*. My short stories have been printed, for the most part in the *New Yorker*; but also in *Harper's Bazaar* and *Harper's* magazine. A study of the novels of I. Compton-Burnett appeared in the English *Vogue*.

"I live in the country, in the village of Penn, Buckinghamshire. I dislike traveling, I love London; but not to live in. Village-life, with its wider differences—in every social sense—seems a better background for a woman novelist, and certainly more congenial to me. In towns, one tends to select one's friends. In the country, they are chosen for one—and if they rarely have the same interests as oneself, so much the better; so much the richer.

"I suppose that I have no hobbies, although I am interested in painting. I like to have a house full of children to cook for; and as many cats sitting in front of the fire as possible. I love England and it would be painful to me to consider living in any other place. I find so beautiful, harmonious and evocative, its landscape, style, tradition, even its climate. I should like to feel that the people in my books are essentially English and set down against a truly English background."

* * *

Elizabeth Taylor's work belongs to that fine English tradition of "novels of sensibility." If she reminds readers of Elizabeth Bowen, Virginia Woolf, and even of Jane Austen, the resemblance is one of spirit, rather than any kind of conscious imitation on Mrs. Taylor's part. Her prose, the American novelist Elizabeth Janeway has commented, "is one of the most beautiful and exact instruments of precision in use today." She writes with meticulous care and craftsmanship. "Sometimes," she says, "a sentence in its evolution takes a whole page of scratching out." The result is precise and delicate, but—some reviewers find—too quiet and unemphatic to hold the reader's attention completely. R. D. Charques, of *the Spectator*, considers it "style without a great deal of substance," lacking the sheer compelling force of storytelling. Mrs. Taylor's own preference in reading is for "books in which practically nothing ever happens," and some of her critics find this taste too well reflected in her writing. But the basic validity of her work has not been challenged. Gerald Sykes wrote in the New York *Times* in 1954: "At all times Mrs. Taylor conveys a profoundly healthy tenderness with a consummate economy of style. She has a woman's unfooled realism and sympathy, and uses them to give quiet enjoyment to all who believe, despite our estranging new conveniences, that man is still the best show of all."

PRINCIPAL WORKS: At Mrs. Lippincote's, 1946; Palladian, 1947; A View of the Harbour, 1947; A Wreath of Roses, 1949; A Game of Hide-and-Seek, 1951; The Sleeping Beauty, 1953; Hester Lilly, and Twelve Short Stories, 1954.

ABOUT: Current Biography 1948; New York Herald Tribune Book Review October 11, 1953.

TAYLOR, PETER HILLSMAN (1917-),

American novelist and short story writer, was born in Tennessee, and attended schools

in Nashville, St. Louis, and Memphis. In 1940 he graduated from Kenyon College, and his first published work was a poem printed in the *Kenyon Review* that spring. This was followed the next year by three stories in the *Southern Review*. After serving in World War II, Taylor taught for several years at the Woman's College of the University of North Carolina, at Greensboro. He now teaches at Kenyon College.

His stories have appeared in the *New Yorker*, the *Sewanee Review*, and the *Kenyon Review*. In 1948 his first book, *A Long Fourth, and Other Stories*, appeared, consisting of seven stories about urban, middle-class life in the upper South of today. It was called by the *New Yorker* "an excellent collection, particularly notable for a vein of unobtrusive humor and for a complete lack of the regional chauvinism that Southern authors so frequently exhibit when writing about their own." Hubert Creekmore in the New York *Times* added, "At thirty he has produced a book at once entertaining, perceptive, and well written."

Taylor's first novel, *A Woman of Means*, was published in 1950. "It is a short novel," noted Robert Penn Warren, "but there is such a vividness of characterization and such a sense of the depth and complication of event that the effect is one of a full-bodied narrative." *The Widows of Thornton*, published

four years later, was a collection of nine stories and received wide approval from critics. Taylor's comedy is quiet, his drama subtle and generally muted. Passion, violence and the more extreme aberrations are absent from his fiction. Except in a one-act play which is part of this book, and in a few of the briefer stories, his narrative method consists more of summary, of distilled reminiscence, than of dialogue and action. Dan Wickenden in the New York *Herald Tribune Book Review* referred to Taylor as "possibly the most interesting and accomplished new writer to have come out of the South in the last ten years."

In 1950 Taylor was awarded a Guggenheim fellowship.

PRINCIPAL WORKS: A Long Fourth, and Other Stories, 1948; A Woman of Means, 1950; The Widows of Thornton, 1954.

ABOUT: North Carolina Authors.

TAYLOR, PHOEBE ATWOOD ("Alice

Tilton") (May 18, 1909-). For biographical sketch and list of earlier works and references, see TWENTIETH CENTURY AUTHORS, 1942.

* * *

Phoebe Atwood Taylor's recent detective stories, like her earlier ones, are distinguished for ingenuity and humor. Her rustic Cape Cod detective Asey Mayo flourishes, and, as "Alice Tilton," she continues to chronicle the adventures of Leonidas Witherall. The ingredients of Miss Taylor's success were listed by the late Will Cuppy as "high excitement, top-drawer detectivism and enough honest-to-goodness fun to take the kinks out of your system for quite some time."

ADDITIONAL WORKS: Three Plots for Asey Mayo, 1942; Going, Going, Gone, 1943; The Proof of the Pudding, 1946; Punch With Care, 1946; Asey Mayo Trio, 1946; The Diplomatic Corpse, 1951. As "Alice Tilton"—File for Record, 1943; Dead Leonidas, 1944; The Iron Clew (in England: The Iron Hand) 1947.

TAYLOR, Mrs. RACHEL (ANNAND)

1876-). For biographical sketch and list of earlier works and references, see TWENTIETH CENTURY AUTHORS, 1942.

* * *

Rachel Taylor's only published work of recent years is *Renaissance France*. She lives in London, and lists her recreations as novel reading and conversation. In 1943 she received an LL.D degree from Aberdeen University.

ADDITIONAL WORKS: Renaissance France, 1949.

TEALE, EDWIN WAY (June 2, 1899-   ), American naturalist writes: "The two most important dates in my writing life are June 2, 1899 and October 15, 1941. On the first, I was born in Joliet, Ill. On the second, I finally was able to begin doing what I had wanted to do from boyhood, be a free-lance author of nature books. Between those two dates, I graduated from Earlham College, B.A. 1922, and Columbia University, M.A. 1927; acted as editorial assistant to Dr. Frank Crane and worked for thirteen years as staff feature writer for *Popular Science Monthly*.

Bachrach

"As a small boy, the Old Testament character I envied most was Noah—all those animals and only one human being! Wild things, even down to the smallest insect, have fascinated me as long as I can remember. When I earned my first box camera by picking 20,000 strawberries on my grandfather's farm, Lone Oak, in the Indiana dune country, the first thing I snapped was the picture of a baby cottontail rabbit. I early began filling little notebooks with 'nature observations' and the year I was nine I completed a whole unpublished book of twenty-four chapters called 'Tales of Lone Oak.' I spelled it Tails.

"To the image of the baby rabbit, I have since added—with more expensive cameras—25,000 nature negatives. Most of my books have been illustrated with my own photographs. For fifteen years, as an aid to studying and photographing small subjects, I maintained an insect garden in an old orchard on a Long Island hillside, planting things that would attract insects to the spot. The story of this garden is recorded in *Near Horizons*. In gathering the material for other books, I have spent a night during bird migration at the top of the Empire State Building, have lived in a trapper's cabin in the Maine woods and have followed the spring north, keeping pace with its advance from Florida to Canada. To get material for the book on which I am now [March 1953] working, my wife and I traveled 28,000 miles through thirty-nine states.

"Like most authors I know, I love research. It puts off the actual writing. For me, writing never gets any easier. I put in long days when working on a book, beginning frequently at 5 and sometimes at 4:30 A.M. I write slowly, rewrite much, do a great deal of checking for accuracy. Most of my work is done at a twenty-five-year-old flat-topped desk that was made for me in a carpenter shop in Chesterton, Ind., with a fourteen-year-old tabby cat, Silver, curled up under the lamp beside me. This desk and this cat have been companions of mine during the writing of ten books.

"The year after I graduated from Earlham, I married Nellie Donovan, of Indianapolis, Ind. Our only son, David, was killed on the Moselle River, in Germany, in March 1945, while on a reconnaisance patrol ahead of the Third Army.

"As for myself, I am six feet tall, have the kind of a memory that never forgets a face and never remembers a name, get along fairly well with the human race and believe that such simple foods as oatmeal and dates, whole kernel hominy and pumpkin pie are the highest achievements of culinary art. The authors I reread most often are Henry Thoreau, W. H. Hudson, Thomas Hardy and Joseph Conrad. For me, the greatest 225 words in literature are the first seven verses of the twelfth chapter of Ecclesiastes."

* * *

Edwin Way Teale's writings, illustrated with his own photographs, reflect a happy blend of the scientist's zeal for exact detail with the poet's enthusiasm for natural beauty. His style is candid and simple. What makes his books outstanding among the works of contemporary naturalists is their sense of positive delight in and sympathetic understanding of everything he sees in nature. R. C. Murphy says of him: "He enjoys his own outdoor experiences with irrepressible gusto; and happily his written record sounds as though it had been set down for his own delectation."

Teale is a large, hearty man with "a rollicking sense of humor." John Kieran, a fellow naturalist, writes that his outstanding qualities are "physical energy, intellectual integrity and a never-failing enthusiasm in the pursuit and enjoyment of knowledge of nature."

PRINCIPAL WORKS: Grassroot Jungles, 1937; The Golden Throng, 1940; Byways to Adventure, 1942; Near Horizons, 1942; Dune Boy, 1943; The Lost Woods, 1945; Days Without Time, 1948; North With the Spring, 1951; The Circle of the Seasons, 1953; (ed.) The Wilderness World of John Muir, 1954.

ABOUT: Teale, E. W. Dune Boy; Audubon Magazine May-June 1952; Collier's February 26, 1949; New York Herald Tribune Book Review October 7, December 2, 1951; Wilson Library Bulletin December 1943.

TEASDALE, SARA (August 8, 1884-January 29, 1933). For biographical sketch and list of works and references, see TWENTIETH CENTURY AUTHORS, 1942.

* * *

ABOUT: Gregory, H. & Zaturenska, M. History of American Poetry, 1900-1940; Library Journal February 15, 1942.

TERHUNE, ALBERT PAYSON (December 21, 1872-February 18, 1942). For autobiographical sketch and list of works and references, see TWENTIETH CENTURY AUTHORS, 1942.

* * *

ABOUT: Terhune, A. M. S. The Bert Terhune I Knew; National Cyclopedia of America Biography (1948).

TETERNIKOV, FEODOR KUZMICH. See SOLOGUB, F.

"TEY, JOSEPHINE." See MACKINTOSH, E.

*THARAUD, JÉRÔME (May 18, 1874-January 28, 1953) and **THARAUD, JEAN** (May 9, 1877-April 9, 1952). For biographical sketches and list of works and references, see TWENTIETH CENTURY AUTHORS, 1942.

* * *

Jean Tharaud died in a Paris hospital, of a heart ailment, at seventy-four. His brother Jérôme died eleven months later, at his country home at Varengeville-sur-Mer, on the Normandy coast, at seventy-eight.

The younger brother had followed the elder into membership in the French Academy in 1946. On the occasion of Jérôme's admission in 1940, he was welcomed as "a reporter of great merit" by Georges Duhamel, who added: "Thanks to men of your stamp, reporting has taken its place as a type of literature, and, I may add, literature of a most vivid and effective kind." The tribute may be taken as applying to both members of this inseparable partnership whose work, in the view of the London *Times,* made a "rich and distinctive contribution to French literature."

ABOUT: Columbia Dictionary of Modern European Literature; London Times April 10, 1952, January 30, 1953; New York Herald Tribune April 10, 1952, January 29, 1953; New York Times April 10, 1952, January 29, 1953.

* tà rō'

THAYER, TIFFANY ELLSWORTH (March 1, 1902-   ). For autobiographical sketch and list of earlier works and references, see TWENTIETH CENTURY AUTHORS, 1942.

* * *

Tiffany Thayer edits the magazine *Doubt,* published by the Fortean Society, which he founded nearly a quarter of a century ago. He is active in publishing and advertising, having worked as a radio writer with the J. Walter Thompson Agency from 1938 to 1948, and, since then, as an associate of Sullivan, Stauffer, Colwell, and Bayles.

ADDITIONAL WORKS: *Editor*—33 Sardonics I Can't Forget, 1946; Adults' Companion, 1948.

THAYER, WILLIAM ROSCOE (January 16, 1859-September 7, 1923). For biographical sketch and list of works and references, see TWENTIETH CENTURY AUTHORS, 1942.

*THIESS, FRANK (1890-   ). For biographical sketch and list of earlier works and references, see TWENTIETH CENTURY AUTHORS, 1942.

* * *

Frank Thiess remained in Germany throughout World War II, but there is no evidence that he was a Nazi before or during that period. The *New Statesman and Nation* described him in 1946 as "a liberal novelist with one or two brave books (as well as some compromises) to his credit." In 1946 Thiess became involved in a controversy with Thomas Mann over the question of the war guilt of the German people. Mann had refused an invitation to return to Germany and had stated that he could not trust writers who had voluntarily remained in Germany during the Nazi regime. Thiess answered in behalf of the German anti-Nazis who had remained in their native land, reporting that these people "have found in themselves a spiritual resistance . . . out of which a new Germany must arise."

Only one of Thiess' recent books, a novel, *Neapolitan Legend,* has appeared in English translation since the end of the war. He has published many books on many subjects in Germany, however — novels, literary and music criticism, books on the theatre, on German politics and history. He lives in Darmstadt and also has a residence in Bad Ausee, Austria.

ADDITIONAL WORK IN ENGLISH TRANSLATION: Neapolitan Legend, 1949.

ABOUT: New Statesman and Nation March 16, 1946.

* tēs

THIRKELL, Mrs. ANGELA (MAC-KAIL) (January 30, 1890-). For biographical sketch and list of earlier works and references, see TWENTIETH CENTURY AUTHORS, 1942.

* * *

Angela Thirkell visited the United States in 1949 to lecture at Columbia and Yale universities and to visit her eldest son and his family in Canada. She was described on that visit as "tall, slender, with a fine-line, well-bred air . . . [suggesting] Tenniel's Alice, but grown up." Her sparkling and seemingly inexhaustible chronicles of Barsetshire life have won her a devoted following in the United States as well as in Britain. Possibly it is the revival of interest in the novels of Barsetshire's nineteenth century inventor, Anthony Trollope, which has increased interest in her work. (Some Thirkell-devotees would doubtless suggest that it is Thirkell who stimulated interest in Trollope.) In any case, she has carried her genteel, snobbish, and solidly British characters through World War II, post-war readjustments, the Labour government, and the coronation of Queen Elizabeth II with hardly a ripple in the smooth surface of her narrative. She is humorous, gentle, satiric, malicious (Phyllis McGinley speaks of her "charm of malice—the malice of the family group"), and indefatigable. Reviewers frequently observe that her material is thin and her treatment of it superficial. But her admirers continue to find freshness and sparkle in each new book.

ADDITIONAL WORKS: Growing Up, 1943; The Headmistress, 1945; Miss Bunting, 1946; Peace Breaks Out, 1947; Private Enterprise, 1948; Love Among the Ruins, 1948; The Old Bank House, 1949; County Chronicle, 1950; The Duke's Daughter, 1951; Happy Return, 1952; Coronation Summer, 1953; Jutland Cottage, 1953.

ABOUT: New York Herald Tribune Book Review August 14, 1949, October 8, 1950; New York Times Book Review August 21, 1949.

*THOBY-MARCELIN, PHILIPPE (December 11, 1904-), and MARCELIN, PIERRE (August 6, 1908-), Haitian novelists, are brothers. Following Haitian custom, Philippe Thoby-Marcelin has prefixed his mother's maiden name to his own. Both were born in Port-au-Prince. They are members of a family of proud literary tradition in Haiti, and were educated privately in Catholic schools; much of their education came informally in their home in Port-au-Prince, where the distinguished literary and political figures of Haiti often gathered. Their novel Canapé-Vert, written

* tō bē' mär slăn'

in the standard French spoken by educated Haitians rather than in the Creole patois, and translated into English by Edward Larocque Tinker, was the first piece of Haitian fiction ever translated into English and served as a brilliant introduction of Haitian literature to the English-reading world. Edmund Wilson wrote that "it gives us an inside picture of the Negro population of Haiti which, so far as I know, is unique, and which will be of special interest to anyone with an appetite for finding out how other kinds of human beings live." Since 1949 Philippe Thoby-Marcelin has lived in Washington, D.C., where he is a French translator at the Pan-American Union. His younger brother lives in Haiti.

Philippe Thoby-Marcelin writes to the editors of this volume: "Born in Port-au-Prince, the heir to a family political and literary tradition. One of his ancestors, Boisrond-Tonnerre, was the author of the Act of Independence (January 1, 1804) and for this fundamental text, as well as his Memoirs, is considered the 'initiator of Haitian literature.' His maternal grandfather, Armand Thoby (1841-99), besides being an important statesman, attained eminence as a writer. So did Frédéric Marcelin (1848-1917), a cousin on the paternal side and the creator of the Haitian realistic novel. His father too, Emile Marcelin (1874-1936), in addition to having a political career which culminated in the post of Minister of Finance, was a novelist and literary critic.

"Although he hasn't followed his elders in the political field, Philippe Thoby-Marcelin has devoted himself to writing. His first medium was poetry, of which he produced five volumes: Lago-Lago (1924-30), La Négresse Adolescente (1928-31), Le Jour et la Nuit (1932-41) Dialogue avec la Femme Endormie (1940), A Fonds Perdu (1943-48).

"He was also active as a critic and has borne the responsibility for much of Haiti's renaissance in the arts and was a leader in the avant-garde literary movement there. A member of the group which centered around La Revue Indigène, he took a strong stand against the imitation of French writing which had been the custom of most of his forebears. The tenets of this circle were frankly nationalistic and stemmed from the belief that their cultural heritage was the strongest weapon against any deleterious influences from abroad. By writing as Haitians, speaking the languages of their own people and their own times, they strove to encourage a respect for values native to their country.

"It was not until his late thirties that, in collaboration with his brother Pierre, Philippe Thoby-Marcelin started to write a series of three novels which made them known abroad, mainly in the United States, Latin America, Great Britain, France—and the first Haitian novelists to be translated into English and Spanish. Their first novel, *Canapé-Vert*, was awarded the prize in the second Latin-American contest (1943) by John Dos Passos, Ernesto Montenegro, and Blair Niles. In 1951 they were each granted a fellowship by the Guggenheim Foundation."

PRINCIPAL WORKS IN ENGLISH TRANSLATION: Canapé-Vert, 1944; The Beast of the Haitian Hills, 1946; The Pencil of God, 1951.

ABOUT: Wilson, E. *Preface to* The Pencil of God; Saturday Review March 3, 1951.

THOMAS, AUGUSTUS (January 8, 1857-August 12, 1934). For biographical sketch and list of works and references, see TWENTIETH CENTURY AUTHORS, 1942.

THOMAS, *DYLAN (October 27, 1914-November 9, 1953). For biographical sketch and list of earlier works and references, see TWENTIETH CENTURY AUTHORS, 1942.

* * *

Dylan Thomas died in New York City at thirty-nine. In the United States primarily to read his own and other poetry in some forty university towns (he had made similar tours in 1950 and 1952), he intended to work on the libretto of an opera with Stravinsky before returning to Wales. Stricken with a cerebral ailment in his New York hotel room, he died three days later in St. Vincent's Hospital.

He was survived by his wife, Caitlin Macnamara Thomas, his daughter Aeron, and two sons, Llewellyn and Colm. A Dylan Thomas fund was established by British and American friends to assist his family; funds were raised in Wales to return his body to his home village of Laugharne, where he was buried.

In the last few years of his short life, occasional pieces written for the British Broadcasting Company, scripts for documentary films and several short stories account for a

* dï'làn

body of writing which, though considerably less distinguished than his poetry, has been described by his compatriot Gwyn Jones as "matured, abundant, exact, rhythmic and pictorial prose (and *joyful* prose)." His "Welsh-singing" voice provided what amounted to an additional career—reading and speaking over the B.B.C., the American poetry-reading tours, and the making of two long-playing recordings of readings from his own work. *Under Milk Wood,* a dramatized chronicle of life in a Welsh village, has been given reading performances in the United States and over the B.B.C.

To a great degree, Thomas' personality was reflected in his writing. Horace Gregory has remarked that in his poetry, "with a greater consistency than any of his immediate contemporaries, he has held to the impulses and dictates of his wit and his imagination, which are always spirited and unashamedly 'romantic.' " The key to the personality was probably what Richard Eberhart called "innocence after experience," and was described by A. G. Prys-Jones when he said: "Beneath his saloon panache and the brittle half-truths, the extravagant *obiter dicta* which he threw off like brilliant sparks in bar-rooms and lecture-halls, there lay just beneath the surface —the clear still waters of a child-like innocence."

Edith Sitwell described Thomas: "He was not tall, but was extremely broad, and gave an impression of extraordinary strength, sturdiness and superabundant life. (His reddish-amber curls, strong as the curls on the brow of a young bull, his proud, but not despising, bearing, emphasized this.) Mr. Augustus John's portrait of him is beautiful, but gives him a cherubic aspect, which though pleasing, does not convey, to the present writer at least, Dylan's look of archangelic power. In full face he looked much as William Blake must have looked as a young man. He had full eyes—like those of Blake—giving at first the impression of being unseeing, but seeing all, looking over immeasurable distances."

The body of Thomas' poetry is not large; he wrote only six poems in the last six years of his life. But shortly before his death John Davenport said, prophetically, "If he were never to write another line, there is enough here to justify his place in the canon of English poetry." At almost the same time Philip Toynbee called him "the greatest living poet in the English language," and Herbert Read declared his work "the most absolute poetry that has been written in our time." Calling him the most powerful and most sensational of the younger British poets, Louis Untermeyer has said: "In a tragically short life he recorded his 'individual struggle from darkness toward some measure of light' in a language so genuinely impassioned, so buoyantly persuasive that, though intemperate in pitch, it is exuberantly irresistible."

ADDITIONAL WORKS: New Poems, 1943; Deaths and Entrances, 1946; Selected Writings, 1947; Poems, 1950; In Country Sleep, And Other Poems, 1952; Collected Poems, 1953; The Doctor and the Devils (motion picture script) 1953; Quite Early One Morning (prose) 1954; Adventures in the Skin Trade, and Other Stories, 1955.

ABOUT: Frankenberg, L. Pleasure Dome; Grigson, G. Harp of Aeolus; Olson, E. The Poetry of Dylan Thomas; Thomas, D. Quite Early One Morning, Selected Writings (see introduction by J. L. Sweeney); Treece, H. Dylan Thomas; American Scholar October 1948; Atlantic Monthly February 1954; Commonweal March 26, 1954; Life and Letters November 1946; London Times November 28, 1952, November 10, 1953; Mademoiselle February 1954; New Republic April 29, 1946; New Statesman and Nation November 14, 1953; New World Writing Nos. 5, 7; New York Times May 14, 1950, February 17, 1952, November 10, 1953, November 22, 1953; Time April 6, 1953; Twentieth Century February 1953.

THOMAS, EDWARD (March 3, 1878-April 9, 1917). For biographical sketch and list of works and references, see TWENTIETH CENTURY AUTHORS, 1942.

* * *

ADDITIONAL WORK: Prose (ed. R. Gant) 1948.

ABOUT: Thomas, H. Introduction to Thomas' Prose (1948).

THOMAS, LOWELL JACKSON (April 6, 1892-). For biographical sketch and list of earlier works and references, see TWENTIETH CENTURY AUTHORS, 1942.

* * *

Lowell Thomas has broadcast his news commentary for nearly a quarter of a century. His brisk but calm and reassuring voice has become a kind of radio institution. During World War II he traveled around the world, broadcasting from Europe, India, the Philippines, Iwo Jima and China. In 1945 he received the A. I. du Pont award for the best news broadcasting of the year.

In 1949, accompanied by his son, Lowell Thomas, Jr., Thomas made an expedition to Tibet at the invitation of the Dalai Lama. Their trip (described by the younger Thomas in Out of This World) was exciting and informative—and particularly hazardous for the elder Thomas who fell from a horse in the Karo Pass and was saved from falling over a precipice only by the quick action of his son.

Thomas lives on a farm in Pawling, N.Y., from which he makes most of his broadcasts when he is not traveling. In addition to his broadcasting and his writing (mainly magazine articles now), Thomas produced the extremely successful three-dimensional motion picture innovation Cinerama and is chairman of the board of the Cinerama Company.

ADDITIONAL WORKS: These Men Shall Never Die, 1943; (with F. R. Thomas) Pageant of Romance, 1943; Back to Mandalay, 1951.

ABOUT: Thomas, L. J., Jr. Out of This World; Atlantic Monthly July 1945; Coronet June 1949; Current Biography 1952; Newsweek October 13, 1947; Reader's Digest December 1948.

THOMASON, JOHN WILLIAM (February 28, 1893-March 12, 1944). For biographical sketch and list of earlier works and references, see TWENTIETH CENTURY AUTHORS, 1942.

* * *

Col. John William Thomason, Jr. died in the Naval Hospital at San Diego, Calif., at fifty-one. He had been chief of the American Republic section of the Navy Department in Washington, D.C. from 1940 to 1943; at the time of his death he was with the amphibious training command of the Pacific Fleet. He was made a full colonel in 1941.

His last book, —And a Few Marines, has been called "a colorful and entertaining volume of tales" by Maxwell Geismar, who characterized its author as "a sort of unique liaison officer between the Army and the arts and the people in that exchange of notions which make a democracy go." The late William Rose Benét said of Thomason's work: "In pen, pencil or watercolor, the free stroke conveying movement and life, which is the mark of the artist born, was always his. As he drew, so he wrote . . . his stories were intensely alive."

ADDITIONAL WORK: —And a Few Marines, 1943.

ABOUT: National Cyclopedia of American Biography (1947); New York Times March 13, 1944; Saturday Review of Literature March 18, 1944.

THOMPSON, DOROTHY (July 9, 1894-). For biographical sketch and list of earlier works and references, see TWENTIETH CENTURY AUTHORS, 1942.

* * *

Since 1941 Dorothy Thompson's columns have been carried by the Bell Syndicate. She also does a monthly editorial column for the Ladies' Home Journal. She lives in New York City with her third husband, Maxim Kopf, whom she married in 1943.

In recent years Miss Thompson has taken a more mellow view of national and international affairs. In 1945 Dixon Wecter called her a "vigorous and intellectual valkyrie." She is today no less vigorous and intellectual, but the "valkyrie" aspect of her personality has softened and almost disappeared. She is less strenuous and emotional; but she remains a speaker and a writer of great conviction and effectiveness. Dorothy Canfield Fisher has observed that next to Mrs. Franklin D. Roosevelt, she is "the most widely known living American woman." Her only book of recent years is *Listen, Hans,* a discussion of the problems of post-war Germany. Part of the book consisted of radio addresses that had been broadcast on short wave by Miss Thompson to Germany.

ADDITIONAL WORK: Listen, Hans, 1942.

ABOUT: Fisher, D. C. American Portraits; Atlantic Monthly July 1945; Collier's June 23, 1945; Newsweek October 20, 1944, April 21, 1947; Saturday Evening Post April 16, 1949; Saturday Review of Literature June 10, September 2, 1944.

THOMPSON, EDWARD JOHN (1886-April 28, 1946). For biographical sketch and list of earlier works and references, see TWENTIETH CENTURY AUTHORS, 1942.

* * *

Edward John Thompson died at his home in Bedlow, Buckinghamshire, England, at sixty. He had held the post of Spalding Senior Research Fellow of Oriel College, Oxford, since 1936. His elder son, Major W. F. Thompson, was a hero of World War II who was killed while assisting partisans behind the battle lines in Bulgaria.

Thompson has been praised for his statesmanship, his judgment as a critic of contemporary literature, and his mastery of English prose, and described as "a genius, not without a touch of the waywardness of genius." A friend, writing in the London *Times,* called attention to his contribution to India as an "historian who disinterred truth from the perishing archives of India, a novelist who painted the Indian scene in brilliant colors."

A selection of his poems published in 1944 showed, in the words of the London *Times,* "how genuine and deep-seated was his inspiration." John Stigall has said that "the elegance of his style is comparable with his meticulous honesty."

ADDITIONAL WORKS: Essex and Elizabeth, a play, 1943; Making of the Indian Princes, 1943; One Hundred Poems, 1944; Robert Bridges, 1844-1930, 1944.

ABOUT: London Times April 29, 1946, May 4, 1946; New York Times April 29, 1946.

THOMPSON, JAMES MATTHEW (September 27, 1878-), English historian, was born in the Iron Acton Rectory, Gloucestershire, the son of Catharine (Paget) Thompson and the Rev. H. L. Thompson, Rector of Iron Acton at the time, and later Vicar of St. Mary's, Oxford. He was educated at Winchester and at Christ Church, Oxford, becoming a curate at St. Frideswide's, Poplar, in 1903 at the age of twenty-five. From 1904 until 1938 he was a Fellow of Magdalen College, specializing in modern French history. He also served at Oxford as Dean of Divinity, Home Bursar, and Vice-President. From 1945 to 1947 he edited the *Oxford Magazine.*

Thompson's *Robespierre,* published in 1935 in two volumes, is one of his major works. Some reviewers felt dissatisfied with Thompson's analysis of Robespierre's psychology, but the book was hailed by the *Manchester Guardian,* for one, as "the best life of Robespierre in any language," and many other critics praised the patient and exacting scholarship that went into it. Thompson "investigates with scrupulous fidelity even the most unimportant facts; and he never rejects or accepts evidence without giving his reasons," was part of the commendation given by Leonard Woolf in the *New Statesman and Nation.*

Thompson has written several highly praised books on various aspects of the French Revolution. His study of Napoleon was termed "lively and original" by the *Spectator.* He has also published a collection of his poems and a philosophical essay in verse. In 1952 he returned to a favorite subject with his *Robespierre and the French Revolution.* "Mr. Thompson is by far the most learned and most eminent English historian of the French Revolution," said the London *Times Literary Supplement.* "This may not be the last word on Robespierre, and Mr. Thompson would be the first to deny that it can be: but it is a more coherent and penetrating judgment of him than most that have enjoyed common currency."

In 1913 Thompson married Mari Meredyth Jones, daughter of the Vicar of Penmaenmawr; they had one son. He and his wife live in Oxford.

PRINCIPAL WORKS: Through Facts to Faith, 1912; Lectures on Foreign History 1494-1789, 1926; Historical Geography of Europe 800-1789, 1929; Leaders of the French Revolution, 1929; Notes on the French Revolution, 1934; Robespierre, 1935; French Revolution, 1943; Collected Verse, 1939-46, 1947; Spider's Web: a Philosophical Essay in Verse, 1949; Napoleon Bonaparte: His Rise and Fall, 1951; Robespierre and the French Revolution, 1952; Louis Napoleon and the Second Empire, 1954.

THOMPSON, SYLVIA (September 4, 1902-). For biographical sketch and list of earlier works and references, see TWENTIETH CENTURY AUTHORS, 1942.

* * *

Sylvia Thompson lives in London. Her recent novels have been characteristically delicate, even tenuous, in plot, but have been distinguished by what Sara Henderson Hay described, in the *Saturday Review of Literature*, as her "sensitive and perceptive character portrayal and her limpid and beautiful prose style." The most ambitious of these later novels is *The Candle's Glory*, a study of the emotional and spiritual conflicts of a sensitive Catholic woman and her young daughter.

ADDITIONAL WORKS: The People Opposite, 1948; The Candle's Glory, 1953.

THOMSON, EDWARD WILLIAM (February 12, 1849-March 5, 1924). For biographical sketch and list of works and references, see TWENTIETH CENTURY AUTHORS, 1942.

THOMSON, GEORGE DERWENT (August 19, 1903-), English classical scholar, was the son of William Henry Thomson and Minnie Thomson. He

was educated at Dulwich College, London, and King's College, Cambridge, and was a Fellow of King's College from 1927 to 1933 and from 1934 to 1936. Since 1937 he has been professor of Greek at the University of Birmingham. As a classical scholar, translator, and author, Thomson has employed a Marxist viewpoint. In *Aeschylus and Athens, a Study in the Origins of Drama*, Thomson denies "at the outset the possibility of objective truth or historic impartiality," notes the *Classical Review*, and maintains "that the study of Aeschylus ought itself to have a social or political motive." The reviewer felt this dislocated his understanding at many points. *Science and Society* called the same book the most stimulating of recent studies devoted to the poets of Greece. "It is packed with solid achievement," wrote the critic A. D. Winspear. "Its formulations are in many cases brilliantly incisive and illuminating." In a characteristic reply to this review, Thomson protested that the critic "praises my book too highly." Stanley Edgar Hyman points out

that in his critical system Thomson is primarily indebted to the late Christopher Caudwell and his Marxist criticism. Like Caudwell, Thomson sees the origin of poetry in the collective primative rituals of the harvest ("utilizing a combination of Marxism and the Cambridge anthropological approach," Hyman writes). In spite of certain extremes in his position, Hyman finds his work generally "informed, brilliant, and invaluable."

The editor and translator of Aeschylus' *Prometheus Bound* and *Oresteia,* and the translator from the Irish of M. O'Sullivan's *Twenty Years A-Growing*, Thomson has also published a book on Greek lyric metre (in 1929), one on Marxism and poetry (in 1945), and volume 1, *The Prehistoric Aegean* (1949), of "Studies in Ancient Greek Society." Of this volume, the London *Times Literary Supplement* said, "This is an extremely important and serious study. Professor Thomson describes his task as 'to reinterpret the legacy of Greece in the light of Marxism.' In so far as this leads him to bring anthropology and the economic interpretation of history to bear on early Greece it is wholly admirable; but his occasional use of 'bourgeois' as an expletive and his occasional attribution of political motives to earlier scholars will seem to many to be blemishes. They must not be allowed to obscure the true value of his work."

In 1934 Thomson married Katharine Fraser Stewart; they have two daughters and live in Birmingham, England. Since 1947 he has been a member of the executive committee of the Communist Party of Great Britain.

PRINCIPAL WORKS: Greek Lyric Metre, 1929; Aeschylus and Athens, 1941; Marxism and Poetry, 1945; Studies in Ancient Greek Society, vol. 1, The Prehistoric Aegean, 1949.

ABOUT: Hyman, S. E. The Armed Vision.

THOMSON, Sir JOHN ARTHUR (July 8, 1861-February 12, 1933). For biographical sketch and list of works and references, see TWENTIETH CENTURY AUTHORS, 1942.

* * *

ABOUT: Fraser, ... Half-Hours with Great Scientists.

THOMSON, VIRGIL (November 25, 1896-). For biographical sketch and list of earlier works and references, see TWENTIETH CENTURY AUTHORS, 1942.

* * *

One of the most distinguished of contemporary American composers, Virgil Thomson is also an urbane, if sometimes controversial, writer on music. *Time* magazine calls him "America's most readable, and perhaps its best, music critic." He is a real literary craftsman. His columns of criticism for the New York *Herald Tribune* (from which he resigned in 1954) were collected in several volumes, and these reflect, writes Moses Smith in the New York *Times,* an "extraordinarily high level of sheer literary competence, to say nothing of his brilliance, wit, keen judgment, and knowledge of his subject."

Thomson has composed for the opera, the concert hall, and the motion picture. Some of his most effective compositions have been his scores for the documentary films made by Pare Lorentz—*The Plow that Broke the Plains* and *The River*—and for Robert Flaherty's *Louisiana Story.* These are frequently played in concert form. In 1947 his second opera to a text by Gertrude Stein, *The Mother of Us All* (about Susan B. Anthony and the fight for woman suffrage), was produced at Columbia University in New York and was praised by the critics as "adroit, entertaining, and expressive." His earlier *Four Saints in Three Acts* was revived in New York, to considerable critical acclaim, in 1952.

‾ɪONAL Works: The Musical Scene, 1945; ¹⁻ɪng Music, 1948; Music, Right

Composers To-
ᴅᵉis, C.

my parents, both of whom originally came from Maine, overlooked the fact that one of my two older brothers, later a distinguished psychologist, already had the initials, E. L. [His brothers were Edward Lee Thorndike, educator and psychologist, compiler of the Thorndike Century Dictionary, and Ashley Horace Thorndike, literary historian, whose biographical sketch appears in TWENTIETH CENTURY AUTHORS, 1942.] When in 1902 I came as a graduate student in history (Ph.D., 1905) to Columbia University, where E. L. was already a professor, and especially when I became chief clerk under Fred Keppel, then secretary of the University, in 1905-06, this gave rise to endless confusion, so that I dropped my first name and have been simply Lynn Thorndike ever since.

"The itinerant system of the Methodist ministry involved change of residence to Lowell and Roxbury, Mass., Providence, R.I., Lynn again, Springfield, Mass., and Lynn, *noch einmal,* whence I left home for college at Wesleyan in Middletown, Conn. There I was a member of the Phi Nu Theta fraternity, and also achieved Phi Beta Kappa, and an A.B. *magna cum laude.* I had not been outside of New England until, shortly before graduation, I paid a preliminary visit to New York.

"The most dramatic incident of my boyhood occurred when in the seventh grade of grammar school in Springfield. The class, of
· ᵀ was the youngest member, had not
‾ᵃˡˡ. and the principal, Elias
‾‾ⁱˡ War veteran with
·‾n wielded a
: us a scare.
, he stood in
ked anyone in
: would be pro-
ͺ to stand up. I
.rs of the class
in order of their
Two girls and I
ee top seats in the
ᴊell Rogers headed
Ada Rosenberg sat
· behind me. Since
the class were not
no one in that row
ᴃut neither did anyone
.e next.
I thought, 'they always
ɾ-fifths of a class.' And
for some or all of those
ᴀg rows to rise. But even
ᴅ to do so; I was the only
Psychiatrists will tell you

that this made me aloof from, not to say scornful of, my fellowmen. It certainly did not make me popular with my classmates. However, not only at the end of the school year did I receive a double promotion into the ninth grade, skipping the eighth, but so did seven or eight of the modest cowards who had kept their seats.

"Although I played baseball with the other boys in vacant lots, reading and writing were my chief pastimes. At college I failed to make the literary monthly, but Caleb T. Winchester, professor of English literature, heartened me greatly by saying that I had a style of my own, and I took several essay prizes. As a graduate student I earned my way for two years by tutoring and the third year had a fellowship to live on.

"In 1906-07 I taught at the University School, Cleveland, and, after two years at Northwestern University in Evanston, Ill., returned to Cleveland for fifteen years at Western Reserve University. Whenever I felt a little blue, all I needed to put me in the best spirits again was to walk past the grim buildings of the University School and remind myself that I was no longer connected with it. In 1924 I was called to Columbia and gave graduate courses in intellectual history there until I became professor emeritus in 1950.

"At Northwestern I became associated with a faculty group—Locy, Crew, and Libby —interested in the history of science, and also played the card game, 'skat,' with them. At Cleveland I continued to play 'skat,' and, when the American Historical Association met there in 1920, organized the first session devoted to the history of science in this country. Next year the American Association for the Advancement of Science followed suit, and soon afterwards the History of Science Society was founded. I served as its president in 1928-29. I was one of the founding fellows of the Mediaeval Academy of America, and of l'Académie Internationale d'Histoire des Sciences; and am a member of the American Philosophical Society and a corresponding member of l'Académie des Inscriptions et Belles-Lettres, as well as of other learned associations. In 1930 Wesleyan awarded me the honorary degree of Doctor of Humane Letters.

"Upon graduation from college I weighed only 130 pounds. Fifteen or twenty years later, when I could afford to dine at university clubs instead of boarding houses, my weight slowly but steadily increased to a trifle over 200.

"My first trip to Europe was in the summer of 1909, when I landed in Glasgow and made the grand tour through southern Scotland, England, Rouen and Paris, Switzerland, down the Italian peninsula to Naples and back, Germany and Holland. I have been there nineteen times since, sometimes for a half year, and have worked in many libraries and especially with medieval Latin manuscripts, although of late the investigation of magic and experimental science in the sixteenth centuries has called chiefly for reading of printed books. In addition to the following list of books, I have contributed more than two hundred articles and seventy reviews to over sixty periodicals representing varied fields of learning and human interest."

PRINCIPAL WORKS: The History of Medieval Europe, 1917; A History of Magic and Experimental Science, 6 vols., 1923-41; A Short History of Civilization, 1926; Science and Thought in the Fifteenth Century, 1929; A Catalogue of Incipits of Medieval Scientific Writings in Latin, 1937; University Records and Life in the Middle Ages, 1944; (ed.) The Herbal of Rufinus, 1945; (ed. & tr.) The Sphere of Sacrobosco and Its Commentators, 1949; (ed.) Latin Treatises on Comets Between 1238 and 1368 A.D., 1950.

ABOUT: Isis, vol. 33 (1942).

THURBER, JAMES (December 8, 1894-). For biographical sketch and list of earlier works and references, see TWENTIETH CENTURY AUTHORS, 1942.

* * *

In 1949 T. S. Eliot, reviewing James Thurber's work, described it as "a form of humor which is also a way of saying something serious." At the bottom of his humor, Eliot found a serious and profound criticism of life. Most of Thurber's readers may not take so solemn a view of his work, but they would certainly agree with Eliot's pronouncement: "His writings and also his illustrations are capable of surviving the immediate environment and time out of which they spring. To some extent they will be a document of the age they belong to."

In 1951 Thurber celebrated his twenty-fifth year as a contributor to the *New Yorker*. Most of his stories, essays, and cartoons still appear first in that magazine, and in his quiet, modest but completely devastating way, he has identified himself with the *New Yorker* over the years and, along with E. B. White, he has, as *Time* reported, "pretty much set the tone of the magazine." Thurber has no imitators. His humor is unique, but it is also adaptable. It has succeeded on the stage (a revival of *The Male Animal* was a hit of the 1952 season), in the motion pictures (Danny Kaye starred in a film version of *The Secret Life of Walter Mitty* and plans are under way for a full-length motion picture based on his writings and drawings), and even in television (an operatic version of *The Thirteen Clocks* in 1954 was highly praised). In 1955 three of Thurber's stories, adapted for the stage by Paul Ellwood and St. John Terrell, were presented at the Theater de Lys in New York under the title *Three by Thurber.*

Thurber lives in an old house in West Cornwall, Conn. He is now almost blind, having lost all but one-eighth vision from his remaining eye. In 1953 his wife, on whom he depends heavily for assistance, was ironically threatened with blindness herself, but her sight was saved by an operation. His handicap has slowed down Thurber's pace—he is a painstaking reviser and rewriter—but it has not materially affected his output. In the decade 1940-50, for example, he wrote and published more than he had done in any earlier decade. More important, it has not blunted the razor-sharpness of his wit nor dampened the engaging charm and tranquility of his fairy tales. In 1950 he wrote: "My one-eighth vision happily obscures sad and ungainly sights, leaving only the vivid and the radiant, some of whom are my friends and neighbors. My pleasures are clean and simple. I like to sit around at night holding untenable positions against logical and expert assault, playing the match game, listening to ball games on the radio, and romping with my wife and daughter and our female French poodle who is nine but doesn't look a day over five. She thinks she is a human being and not a dog, and no one is allowed to let her look into a mirror."

ADDITIONAL WORKS: Men, Women and Dogs, 1943; Many Moons, 1943; The Great Quillow, 1944; The White Deer, 1945; The Beast in Me and Other Animals, 1948; The Thirteen Clocks, 1950; The Thurber Album, 1952; Thurber Country, 1953.

ABOUT: Beaton, C. & Tynan, K. Persona Grata; Friedrich, O. *in* Discovery #5; Thurber, J. The Thurber Album; Van Gelder, R. Writers and Writing; Commonweal March 9, 1945; Ladies' Home Journal July 1946; Life February 19, 1945; New York Herald Tribune Book Review October 8, 1950; New York Times Book Review June 29, 1952; New York Times Magazine December 4, 1949; Poetry December 1943; Time July 9, 1951.

THURSTON, ERNEST TEMPLE (September 23, 1879-March 19, 1933). For biographical sketch and list of works and references, see TWENTIETH CENTURY AUTHORS, 1942.

* * *

Correction: On page 1405 of TWENTIETH CENTURY AUTHORS, 1942, Katherine Cecil Madden Thurston's name is incorrectly given as Katherine Cecil Alden.

THURSTON, Mrs. KATHERINE CECIL (MADDEN) (April 18, 1875-September 5, 1911). For biographical sketch and list of works and references, see TWENTIETH CENTURY AUTHORS, 1942.

THURSTON, Mrs. TEMPLE. See THURSTON, K. C. M.

THWAITES, REUBEN GOLD (May 15, 1853-October 22, 1913). For biographical sketch and list of works and references, see TWENTIETH CENTURY AUTHORS, 1942.

*TIETJENS, EUNICE STRONG (HAMMOND) (July 29, 1884-September 6, 1944). For autobiographical sketch and list of works and references, see TWENTIETH CENTURY AUTHORS, 1942.

* * *

Eunice Tietjens died in Chicago at sixty.

Her place in the American poetry scene is assured as a "warm personality, remarkable for its range of interests" and her "vigorous and refreshing" attitude toward life, in the words of Philip Horton, rather than for her own work. Of her poetry, *Outlook* noted its "quiet charm," and observed that "while it has no spontaneous lyric impulse the emotion is usually genuine."

ABOUT: New York Times September 7, 1944.

* tē′jĕns

*TILLICH, PAUL JOHANNES (August 20, 1886-   ), German-born theologian, is the son of a Lutheran pastor, Johannes Tillich, and Mathilde (Dürselen) Tillich. He was born in Starzeddel, Kreis Guben, Prussia, and was educated in a *gymnasium* in eastern Brandenburg, where his father became the diocesan superintendent of a group of parishes, and in Berlin. He studied theology at the Universities of Berlin, Tübingen and Halle, and received his Ph.D. from the University of Breslau and the Licentiate in Theology from Halle, with his theses for both degrees on the subject of Schelling's philosophy of religion. In 1912 Tillich was ordained a minister of the Evangelical Lutheran Church. During World War I he was

* til′lĭk

a chaplain with the German forces. He was bitterly opposed to the war itself and when hostilities ended, he took an active part in the establishment of a German republic. Meanwhile he began teaching theology at the University of Berlin, 1919-24, and at the Universities of Marburg, Dresden, Leipzig and finally at Frankfurt-am-Main. His liberal, humanitarian views brought him into sharp conflict with the rising Nazi regime, and in 1933 he lost his professorship at Frankfurt. "I had the great honor and luck," he said, "to be about the first non-Jewish professor dismissed from a German university."

Tillich came to the United States in 1933 and has made his home here ever since. He became a naturalized citizen in 1940. From 1933 to 1954 he was on the faculty of the Union Theological Seminary in New York. During this period he traveled widely, in the United States and abroad, on lecture tours. In 1953 he went to Edinburgh to deliver the Gifford lectures on theology, and in 1948 and again in 1951 he returned to Germany to lecture. Since the end of World War II his teachings have become very popular in Germany and many of his English writings are now being translated and published there. In 1954 he was appointed to the faculty of the Divinity School of Harvard University. Of medium height and build, reserved in manner but warm and friendly, Tillich is married to Hannah Werner. They have a son and a daughter.

One of the greatest of contemporary Protestant theologians, Paul Tillich has sought to clarify the meaning of Christianity in the light of the needs and dilemmas of modern man. In his more than twenty-five books he has studied the relation of religion to politics, art, sociology, philosophy, and psychology. His work, write Charles W. Kegley and Robert W. Bretall, constitutes "a kind of Protestant *Summa* for our time," in that it "most fully gathers up the strands of all that is best in secular thought, and unites them with the truths of God's self-disclosure." His major work, *Systematic Theology*, on which he has worked for three decades, holds as its thesis that Protestant theology can, "without losing its Christian foundations, incorporate strictly scientific methods, a critical philosophy, a realistic understanding of men and society, and powerful ethical principles and motives." He believes that any division between philosophy and theology would be impossible, "for, whatever the relation of God, world, and man may be, it lies in the frame of being; and any interpretation of the meaning and structure of being as being unavoidably such

has consequences for the interpretation of God, man, and the world in their interrelations."

Reviewing his career, in an autobiographical introduction to *The Theology of Paul Tillich*, Tillich considered how his life compared with the world of his predecessors in the last generation. One thing emerged clearly, he writes: "We are not scholars according to the pattern of our teachers at the end of the nineteenth century. We were forced into history in a way which made the analysis of history and of its contents most difficult. Perhaps we have had the advantage of being nearer to reality than they were. Perhaps this is only a rationalization of our shortcomings. However this may be, my work, although humanly speaking not yet finished, has come close to its end."

PRINCIPAL WORKS IN ENGLISH: The Interpretation of History, 1936; (with others) The Christian Answer, 1945; The Protestant Era, 1948; Shaking the Foundations, 1948; Systematic Theology, I, 1950; The Courage to Be, 1952; Love, Power, and Justice, 1954; The New Being, 1955.

ABOUT: Kegley, C. W. & Bretall, R. W. (eds.) The Theology of Paul Tillich; Soper, D. W. Major Voices in American Theology; Tillich, P. The Interpretation of History, The Protestant Era; Current Biography 1954; New York Herald Tribune Book Review March 8, 1953; New York Times June 4, 1950; Newsweek May 17, 1954; Time October 20, 1952.

TILLYARD, EUSTACE MANDEVILLE WETENHALL (1889-), English scholar-critic, writes: "Born Cambridge, grew up with University in background. Attended Perse School and learnt Latin and Greek by Rouse's 'direct method.' Head of school and captain of hockey and cricket. Classical scholar of Jesus College, Cambridge, first classes in  Classical Tripos. B.A. 1911 and studentship to British School of Archaeology, Athens; travel in Greece and Turkey. 1912 got access to Hope Collection of Greek antiques, long closed to students; began cataloguing vases there. College elects me Fellow. 1914 War catches me with catalogue unfinished. Volunteer, serve first with infantry France, surviving nine months trench warfare. Transfer to Salonika Force because of languages, spend rest of war there on Intelligence. Captain, with military O.B.E., Greek Military Cross. Return Cambridge University 1919, transfer from Classics to recently created English

Tripos, then becoming University Lecturer in English. Helped by wife (college girl who drove ambulance in France and Salonika) finish vase catalogue. But real tastes literary. Helped build up English School at Cambridge along with I. A. Richards and others. Began critical writing with anthology of Lamb's criticism. Turned to early love, Milton, and wrote the book on him that gave me standing as scholar-critic. From Milton turned to epic in general on which am still engaged, other business having intervened. Demand from Sorbonne for lecture on Shakespeare diverted me to him; also found Shakespeare's history plays were epic in spirit and had to be dealt with before could write on English epic proper. Three books on Shakespeare and two on English Renaissance. Second World War found me too old for service except in Home Guard and created shortage of college administrators. Became Senior Tutor of Jesus College, Cambridge and in 1945 Master.

"I address most of my books to educated reader not to professional scholar; deplore growing gap between scholar and public.

"I like travel and have been east as far as the river Euphrates and west as far as Vancouver. Gave Alexander Memorial Lectures at Toronto University and Turnbull Memorial Lectures at the Johns Hopkins University. Civil honours include degree of Litt.D. at Cambridge, honorary membership of Modern Language Association of America, and Fellowship of British Academy.

"I like open air and exercise and intend to continue to walk and cycle till stopped by infirmity.

"I vote Liberal when there is a candidate, but my only active intervention in politics has been on behalf of Federal Union and United Europe."

* * *

E. M. W. Tillyard, one of the most eminent of Elizabethan scholars, is admired for the ingenuity and enthusiasm of his scholarship as well as for its depth. Henry W. Wells has said of him: "Few contemporary critics write with as much wisdom and as little pedantry as E. M. W. Tillyard. . . . His breadth is academic in the best sense of the word."

PRINCIPAL WORKS: The Hope Vases, 1923; Milton, 1930; Poetry Direct and Oblique, 1934; Shakespeare's Last Plays, 1938; The Miltonic Setting, 1938; (with C. S. Lewis) The Personal Heresy, 1939; The Elizabethan World Picture, 1943; Shakespeare's History Plays, 1944; Five Poems, 1470-1870, 1948; Shakespeare's Problem Plays, 1950; Studies in Milton, 1951; The English Renaissance, Fact or Fiction, 1952; The English Epic and Its Background, 1954.

"TILTON, ALICE." See TAYLOR, P. A.

TINDALL, WILLIAM YORK (March 7, 1903-), American critic and literary historian, writes: "I was born in Williamstown, Vt. My father, a country doctor, complete with horse and buggy, was a Vermont Democrat; my mother, a former New York City schoolteacher, came from Kutna Hora, in what is now Czechoslovakia. Her desire for New York accounts  for my middle name. I attended the public schools of Montpelier, Vt., until 1918 when, upon the removal of the family to New York City, I entered a high school in Hell's Kitchen. Later, in Columbia College, where the pressures were less intense, I was moved by the lectures of John Erskine to specialize in literature rather than in journalism as I had intended. By the aid of the Proudfit fellowship I added a year of graduate work in English. My teaching career began at Washington Square College in 1926. Tom Wolfe was a colleague there; and Greenwich Village provided an even more liberal education than Hell's Kitchen or Morningside Heights.

"In 1931 I became an instructor in the Graduate School at Columbia, where I have taught ever since. My full professorship came in 1950. In 1932 I went to the British Museum for a year on a Cutting fellowship to study seventeenth-century preachers. My doctoral dissertation on John Bunyan was published in 1934. Since then I have lectured on contemporary English literature, conducted seminars in the field and a discussion group in difficult texts. Since 1940, with the aid of this group, I have explored Finnegans Wake. Besides Joyce my special interests have been D. H. Lawrence and Yeats, on whom I have written a number of articles, prefaces, and books. At present [November 1952] I am preparing a book on symbolism. For a year or so, apparently as a result of virus pneumonia, I was a poet. Eight of my poems appeared in little magazines and two of them made the Accent Anthology, but the infection diminished and I sang no more.

"In 1937 I married Cecilia Kramer of Ohio. We have one daughter, Elizabeth, and she has a cocker spaniel. As for politics: I voted for Coolidge, but since that time I have been a Democrat. For a year I served Tammany

Hall as a county committeeman, but the voters of my district denied me a second term."

* * *

Probably the best known of W. Y. Tindall's works is his *Forces in Modern British Literature,* a survey, with critical evaluations, of contemporary British literature. "The presentation of so much material with zest and clarity and conciseness is an awe-inspiring accomplishment," Robert Hillyer wrote in the New York *Times.* His book on Joyce was highly praised for its fresh and concisely written interpretations, and his study of D. H. Lawrence, with its memorable title *D. H. Lawrence and Susan His Cow,* was a humorous but also an informative exposition of that novelist's intellectual background.

PRINCIPAL WORKS: John Bunyan, Mechanick Preacher, 1934; D. H. Lawrence and Susan His Cow, 1939; Forces in Modern British Literature, 1947; James Joyce: His Way of Interpreting the Modern World, 1950; (ed.) The Later D. H. Lawrence, 1952.

TINKER, CHAUNCEY BREWSTER
(October 22, 1876-). For biographical sketch and list of earlier works and references, see TWENTIETH CENTURY AUTHORS, 1942.

* * *

Chauncey Brewster Tinker retired from the English department of Yale University in 1945 after more than forty years of teaching there. He has remained at the university, however, living at Davenport College, surrounded by his collection of books and Boswelliana, and serving as keeper of rare books at the Sterling Memorial Library. It was in part through his efforts and interest in Dr. Samuel Johnson and his biographer Boswell that Yale acquired the invaluable Boswell papers, discovered after so many years at Malahide Castle in Ireland.

Tinker has two reputations—one as a popular lecturer (Ben Ray Redman described his lectures as "intelligent without profundity, instructive without pedantry . . . uncommon common sense based on learning that is lightly carried"), the other as a serious scholar-teacher. In the latter capacity Tinker trained several generations of Yale students, including many of the university's most distinguished alumni. He was a stern teacher and a strict disciplinarian, but his courses were always crowded, and his students idolized him. In 1949 a group of these students paid him a tribute in a collection of studies made in his honor and appropriately titled *The Age of Johnson.*

ADDITIONAL WORK: Essays in Retrospect, 1948.

ABOUT: Lewis, W. S. *in* The Age of Johnson (ed. F. W. Hilles); Tinker, C. B. Essays in Retrospect; Time March 28, 1949.

TINKER, EDWARD LAROCQUE (September 12, 1881-). For autobiographical sketch and list of earlier works and references, see TWENTIETH CENTURY AUTHORS, 1942.

* * *

Edward Larocque Tinker writes from New York City: "Mr. Tinker is one of the chancellors of the American Antiquarian Society, to which he gave his collection of French Imprints of Louisiana, probably the most complete yet made; and he presented to the Houghton Library of Harvard the letters, manuscripts, and association copies of Lafcadio Hearn upon which he based his biography of that author. His library on the history and Creole dialect of Haiti enabled him to translate *Canapé Vert,* a novel of the peasant life of that country written by Pierre Marcelin and Philippe Thoby-Marcelin.

"In 1943 the Carnegie Endowment for International Peace sent Mr. Tinker to Mexico to give a course on American literature at the National University, which later conferred on him the degree of Professor Extraordinario. Two years later he went to Uruguay and Argentina as exchange lecturer under the auspices of the Department of State. While in South America he made an important collection of books on the gaucho and published a monograph on *The Cult of the Gaucho and the Birth of a Literature,* and followed it with *Los Jinetes de las Américas y la Literatura por Ellos Inspirada* (1951), a comparative study of the gaucho, vaquero, and cowboy, accompanied by a long bibliography, published in Buenos Aires. An English version followed in 1953 under the title *The Horsemen of the Americas and the Literature They Inspired.* In the same year *Creole City* appeared, an informal history of New Orleans and various facets of its life.

"Mr. Tinker is a trustee of the Museum of the City of New York and of the French Institute of New York, a member of the Council on Foreign Relations and of the Society of American Historians, as well as a corresponding member of the Hispanic Society. He has an LL.D. from Middlebury College."

ADDITIONAL WORKS: The Cult of the Gaucho and the Birth of a Literature, 1948; The Pennells (privately printed) 1951; The Horsemen of the Americas and the Literature They Inspired, 1953; Creole City, 1953.

ABOUT: Antiquarian Bookman May 10, 1952.

TODD, MABEL LOOMIS (1858-October 14, 1932). For biographical sketch and list of works and references, see TWENTIETH CENTURY AUTHORS, 1942.

* * *

ADDITIONAL WORK: *Edited, with M. T. Bingham*—Dickinson, E. Bolts of Melody, 1945.

TODD, *RUTHVEN (June 14, 1914-   ), British-born poet, editor, novelist and essayist, writes: "I was born in Edinburgh, Scotland, the eldest of ten children of W. J. W. Todd, A.R.S.A., architect, and Christian (Craik) Todd. My ancestry is mixed, Scottish, English, Irish, Spanish and French. Literary ancestors on my father's side include Sir Walter Scott and Henry

Laura Beaujon

Mackenzie, 'The Man of Feeling,' and on my mother's side the Scottish man of letters, George Lillie Craik, whose son married Dinah Mulock, author of *The Little Lame Prince* and *John Halifax, Gentleman,* and Sir Henry Craik, the educator and politician, who wrote a history of English literature, a life of Jonathan Swift, and other books.

"This literary background had, I fear, little influence on me as a child. I wanted to paint and it was assumed that I would follow my father as an architect. At Fettes College, Edinburgh, I succeeded in winning the school prize for painting, and also contributed verse to the *Fettesian;* during several vacations I worked in my father's office, but found little to attract me in architecture, so, at the age of sixteen, I entered the Edinburgh College of Art, studying painting. I quickly discovered that I had technical facility but no originality and gave up painting to work as a farm-laborer on the Isle of Mull, off the West of Scotland. During the two years I spent there I devoted my spare time, such at is was, to writing poems, and my first poems were published in the *Bookman,* having been sent there by Mr. Geoffrey Grigson, the editor of *New Verse.* I next spent a short time in Edinburgh, as assistant editor of the *Scottish Bookman,* and then went to London. During the Thirties I wrote many poems, publishing them in such papers as *New Verse, Twentieth Century Verse,* the *Listener, Poetry,* etc. As a method of staying alive I did anything that came along, working in art galleries (including the First International Sur-

* "Ruthven *is pronounced* riven—*rhyming with* driven."

realist Exhibition in 1936, and a gallery that specialized in pottery), as a tutor, as John Lehmann's secretary in the Hogarth Press, as a publisher's reader and so on.

"At the outbreak of war I worked for a short time on the embryonic *Horizon,* and then joined the Civil Defense, from which I was ejected as unfit for service in 1942. After that I worked for a while in a bookstore, Zwemmer's, in the Charing Cross Road, and, after a flying-bomb damaged my London flat, retired to live in a farm house in Essex. There I lived by writing extremely poor detective novels, at terrific speed, under the pseudonym of 'R. T. Campbell.' All this time I had been working on William Blake and his paintings, and, with the aid of a Pilgrim Trust grant, I visited the United States in 1947; for a short while I worked, teaching creative writing at Iowa State University, a thing I had no right to do on a visitor's visa, so I left the United States for six weeks, returning as a permanent resident in 1948. In 1952 I married."

* * *

Ruthven Todd has been described by Mark Schorer as "a brilliant poet and a distinguished novelist and . . . a gifted exemplar of the long British tradition of amateur scholarship." A glance at the list of his works will indicate the variety of his interests and the wide range—from poetry to children's books, from scholarly studies to spy thrillers. In 1954 he received a citation from the National Institute of Arts and Letters for his "loving devotion to natural history."

PRINCIPAL WORKS: *Poetry*—Until Now, 1940; The Acreage of the Heart, 1944; The Planet in My Hand, 1947; A Mantelpiece of Shells, 1955. *Novels*—Over the Mountain, 1939; The Lost Traveller, 1942; Loser's Choice, 1953. *Non-Fiction*—The Laughing Mulatto: The Story of Alexandre Dumas, 1940; (ed.) Alexander Gilchrist's Life of William Blake, 1942; Tracks in the Snow, 1946; (ed.) Redgraves' A Century of Painters of the British School, 1947; The Tropical Fish Book, 1953. *Juveniles*—Space Cat, 1952; Trucks, Tractors and Trailers, 1954.

ABOUT: Stanford, D. The Freedom of Poetry.

TOLLER, ERNST (December 1, 1893-May 22, 1939). For biographical sketch and list of works and references, see TWENTIETH CENTURY AUTHORS, 1942.

* * *

ADDITIONAL WORK IN ENGLISH: Commentaries from unpublished papers *in* Saturday Review of Literature May 20, 1944.

ABOUT: Columbia Dictionary of Modern European Literature; Slochower, H. No Voice Is Wholly Lost; Willibrand, W. A. Ernst Toller and His Ideology; Contemporary Jewish Record October 1943; Encounter October 1953.

TOLSTOY, ALEXEY NIKOLAEVICH

(December 29, 1882-February 22, 1945). For biographical sketch and list of earlier works and references, see TWENTIETH CENTURY AUTHORS, 1942.

* * *

Alexey Tolstoy died at sixty-two in Moscow. Penicillin needed for his treatment during his final illness was contributed by a U.S. medical mission in Europe.

Soviet Russia's most honored writer, Tolstoy had received the Order of Lenin and was an Academician, as well as a member of the Supreme Soviet of the U.S.S.R. Samuel H. Cross has cited him as an example of "a gifted middle-class intellectual who worked his way through to a sympathetic understanding of the socialist environment and carved out for himself a dominant position among proletarian writers." Until shortly before his death he was engaged in work on the third part of his biography of Peter the Great.

It was reported in 1944 that next to Lenin and Gorky, Alexey Tolstoy was the most widely read author in Russia. The London *Times* ascribed his popularity to "his fertility as a storyteller and his mastery of a form of prose which was never far in its effects from the spoken language."

ADDITIONAL WORKS IN ENGLISH TRANSLATION: My Country, 1944; Russian Tales for Children, 1944; Nikita's Childhood, 1945; The Making of Russia, 1945; The Road to Calvary, 1945; The Golden Key, 1947; Selected Stories, 1949.

ABOUT: Bunin, I. Memories and Portraits; Columbia Dictionary of Modern European Literature; Guerney, B. G. (ed.) Portable Russian Reader; Snow, V. Russian Writers; American Slavic Review October 1950; London Times February 26, 1945; New York Times February 24, 1945; Time May 27, 1946.

TOMLINSON, HENRY MAJOR

(1873-   ). For biographical sketch and list of earlier works and references, see TWENTIETH CENTURY AUTHORS, 1942.

* * *

In 1953 H. M. Tomlinson celebrated his eightieth birthday with the publication of a slim volume of autobiographical essays, *A Mingled Yarn*. In one of these essays, titled "On Being Out of Date," he explains that he is scarcely aware of old age. "The weight of the years is as light as a packet of minutes," he writes. Tomlinson would be the first to admit that he belongs to the past, with his childhood memories of Carlyle and Stevenson and Queen Victoria, when travel was uncomplicated by passports and visas. "There was nothing but the yarns of messmates, and nothing to be seen but the sky and the ocean,

and at night the shadow of a masthead sweeping to and fro among the stars." Nevertheless, even while Tomlinson grumbles at the devastating inroads of "progress," he writes with what one reviewer described as "a continuing freshness from the essentials of human and natural existence." In Tomlinson's words: "It is exhilarating to be alive and still trying to write English. Besides, one returns to youth with one's grandchildren, to start growing up all over again."

Tomlinson's reputation rests solidly upon his sensitive and evocative travel essays. Although he has written excellent novels, he is essentially a reflective and descriptive writer, and he is at his best in his short and exquisitely written essays. He is essentially a poet, Lloyd Morris pointed out—"a topographer of the spirit, not of the globe." Although he has written much about the sea, he remains a "landsman," one who, Frank Swinnerton writes, "has been to sea a number of itmes, and into the jungle too, taking with him a mildness of manner, a warmly coloured pen, a dry yet fluty Cockney voice, and an eye and sensitiveness rare among professional writers."

ADDITIONAL WORKS: Old Junk, 1945; Turn of the Tide, 1945; Morning Light (novel) 1946; The Face of the Earth, 1950; Malay Waters, 1950; The Haunted Forest, 1951; A Mingled Yarn, 1953.

ABOUT: Swinnerton, F. The Georgian Literary Scene (1910-35); Tomlinson, H. M. A Mingled Yarn; Von Hagen, V. C. Green World of the Naturalists; Atlantic Monthly November 1943; New York Herald Tribune Book Review October 7, 1951.

TORRENCE, FREDERIC RIDGELY

(November 27, 1875-December 25, 1950). For autobiographical sketch and list of earlier works and references, see TWENTIETH CENTURY AUTHORS, 1942.

* * *

Ridgely Torrence died in the Lenox Hill Hospital in New York, at seventy-five, after a three-months' illness. His wife, Olive Howard Dunbar, who was also a writer, died January 6, 1953, at seventy-nine.

Torrence's *Poems*, issued in 1941, was awarded the Shelley Memorial Prize, and the following year he was named poet of the year by the National Poetry Center. In 1947 he received the Fellowship of the Academy of American Poets, an honor which carries with it a grant of $5,000.

Torrence was "a fine poet and a spirit at once perceptive, humane and reconciled," in the words of Rolfe Humphries. John Holmes has said: "A firm, grave strength, and a fully matured certainty, lighted and warmed by both human compassion and spiritual vision, distinguish the poetry of Ridgely Torrence."

ADDITIONAL WORKS: (ed.) Branch, A. H. Last Poems, 1944; The Story of John Hope, 1948.

ABOUT: New York Times December 26, 1950; Publishers' Weekly May 3, 1947; Time September 1, 1952.

*TOVEY, Sir DONALD FRANCIS (July 17, 1875-July 10, 1940), British musicologist, and composer, was born in Eton, the

youngest son of Duncan Crookes Tovey (at that time an assistant master at Eton, later rector of Worplesdon, Surrey) and Mary (Fison) Tovey. Both parents were unmusical but had literary gifts. At eight years of age Donald Tovey is said to have embarked on musical composition, and it was the acuteness of his 'ear' in childhood, and the correlation of pitch heard and pitch sung that attracted the notice of Miss Sophie Weisse (later a headmistress of a girls' school). She alone educated the boy until he was nineteen, and he never went to an ordinary boys' school. During this period he was also sent to Walter Parratt for counterpoint lessons, later to James Higgs, and at thirteen to Charles Hubert Parry, to whom he always referred as 'my master.' In 1894 Tovey went to Balliol College, Oxford, and in that same year appeared at Windsor as pianist with Joseph Joachim, the great violinist. In 1898 he graduated B.A. with classical honors. Launched by Miss Weisse in a series of classical chamber concerts in 1900 in London, Tovey became a pianist in the first rank among players of his day, though he never embarked upon a virtuoso's career. In 1914 he became Reid Professor of Music at Edinburgh University, where he remained until his death in 1940. He was a conductor of the Reid Orchestra.

As a composer he wrote, consciously, in the idiom of the German classics. His opera, *The Bride of Dionysus*, was produced in Edinburgh in 1929, and his compositions have been performed in European and American cities as well as in England. Although known chiefly as a musical historian and commentator, Tovey was also deeply interested in the writing of general prose. He planned books, but never made a whole one himself. He had dreams of a complete

* tō'vĭ

treatise of musical instruction in four volumes, but wrote none of it. He wrote prose to assist the occasion of music, to expound music, or to clarify it, and he was surprised, and not entirely pleased, at his universal acceptance as a writer. His writings are generally classed as "occasional." His *Essays in Musical Analysis* were, for example, written as commentaries for programs and then collected.

Tovey's first marriage was annulled, and in 1925 he married Clara Georgina Wallace, of Edinburgh. There were no children. Tovey was a tall, large man. He was slender and ascetic-looking in youth, but became more robust in appearance as he grew older. In later life he suffered an increasing rheumatic disability of the hands, which crippled him in his last years. He visited the United States in 1924, 1925, 1926, and 1928. Awarded a doctorate of music by decree of convocation at Oxford in 1921, he was elected an honorary fellow of Balliol in 1934, and was knighted in 1935.

PRINCIPAL WORKS: Beethoven's Ninth Symphony in D Minor, 1927; Companion to Beethoven's Pianoforte Sonatas, 1931; A Companion to "The Art of Fugue," 1932; Musical Form and Matter, 1934; Essays in Musical Analysis (6 vols.) 1935-39; Normality and Freedom in Music, 1936; The Main Stream of Music, 1938; A Musician Talks, 1941; Some English Symphonists (a selection from Essays in Musical Analysis) 1941; Walter Parratt (with Geoffrey Parratt) 1941; Essays in Musical Analysis: Chamber Music, 1944; Musical Articles from the Encyclopedia Britannica, 1944; Beethoven, 1944.

ABOUT: Grierson, M. Donald Francis Tovey; Walker, E. *Preface to* Tovey's A Musician Talks; Dictionary of National Biography 1931-1940; Music Review February 1942; Music Teachers National Association Proceedings 1951.

TOWNE, CHARLES HANSON (February 2, 1877-February 28, 1949). For biographical sketch and list of earlier works and references, see TWENTIETH CENTURY AUTHORS, 1942.

* * *

Charles Hanson Towne died at the Flower-Fifth Avenue Hospital in New York City, at seventy-two.

He had what Joseph Auslander called "a positive passion for people as people; a positive genius for people as friends." An autobiography published in 1945 recorded that many of these friends were among America's outstanding literary figures.

ADDITIONAL WORKS: So Far, So Good (autobiography) 1945; Testament of Love: A Sonnet Sequence, 1945.

ABOUT: Towne, C. H. So Far, So Good; New York Times March 1. 1949.

TOYNBEE, ARNOLD JOSEPH (April 14, 1889-). For biographical sketch and list of earlier works and references, see TWENTIETH CENTURY AUTHORS, 1942.

* * *

During World War II, Arnold Toynbee directed foreign research for the Royal Institute of International Affairs, an organ of the British Foreign Office. Since the war ended, he has remained with the institute to edit its political history of the war. He lives in London (with weekends and summers in his country home), spends his mornings writing at home, his afternoons at the Institute. His busy schedule allows him no time for reading except on weekends—"I am always healthily hungry to read, and am never doped by too much of it." He has made several visits to the United States on lecture tours. In 1945 he and his wife, Rosalind Murray, were divorced, and in the following year he married Veronica M. Boulter, his research assistant.

Toynbee completed his ten-volume *A Study of History* in 1954. His work has been called "a major contribution to modern thought," and is generally accorded a place alongside Gibbon's *Decline and Fall of the Roman Empire* and Spengler's *Decline of the West* as one of the really great works of intellectual history. Unlike his predecessors in the field, however, Toynbee has a popular following as well as a scholarly audience. A one-volume abridgment of his work, published in 1946, appeared on the best-seller list; and on his visit to the United States in 1954 Toynbee was interviewed by the press, radio and television and was generally lionized. D. W. Brogan has observed that his ideas are "now in public domain." This is not to suggest that his work has met with universal agreement and endorsement. On the contrary, it has been sharply disputed on individual points and on its overall theses. Toynbee's emphasis upon religion in the course of history (he defines history as "a vision . . . of God revealing Himself in action to souls that are sincerely seeking Him"), his opposition to militarism and nationalism, his hypothesis that there is "form" in society (based on many features that he finds common to all societies)—all these and numerous other points have been challenged by historians as illogical, untrue, or unrealistic. As Richard Chase pointed out, however, in an article in the *American Scholar*: "Great and persuasive theorists—Marx, Freud, Toynbee —do not exert their strongest influence because of the logical tightness of their theories,

but rather because they fill an unconsciously felt vacuum with the force and urgency of their moral passion." The particulars of his arguments prove in the long run to be relatively unimportant. The *Manchester Guardian* commented in 1947: "The high qualities of Mr. Toynbee's great work lie rather in his poetic vision, in his freedom from the trammels of time and space, and in the Olympian sweep of his glance across the centuries."

ADDITIONAL WORKS: A Study of History (abridged in one vol. by D. C. Somervell) 1946; Christianity and Civilization, 1949; Civilization on Trial, 1948; Prospects of Western Civilization, 1949; The World and the West, 1953; A Study of History, vols. 7-10, 1954.

ABOUT: Barnes, H. E. *Introduction to* A History of Sociology; Sorokin, P. Social Philosophies in an Age of Crisis; American Mercury June 1947; American Scholar July 1947; Current Biography 1947; Harper's February 1947; New York Herald Tribune Book Review October 8, 1950; New York Times Book Review July 10, 1949; Saturday Review of Literature May 1, 1948, October 2, 1954; Time March 17, 1947; Virginia Quarterly Review October 1950.

TOYNBEE, PHILIP (June 25, 1916-), English novelist, writes: "I was born at Oxford in the middle of the First World War, son of Professor Arnold Toynbee, the historian, and grandson of Professor Gilbert Murray, translator of Euripides. My earliest, and very vague memory is of Armistice Day, 1918, in London when I walked, or was wheeled, across the  Thames and saw flour-coated millers dancing in a ring to celebrate the war's ending. All my early memories are of London, where we lived, and of Yorkshire where my mother's family owned a large house in which we spent our summer holidays.

"I grew up in an atmosphere of scholarship, and until at least the age of seventeen I revolted against this by doing badly at school and refusing to read anything except the adventure stories. At that age I began to rebel in a different way, by running away from Rugby School and declaring myself a Communist. This led to the threat that I should not go to Oxford unless I won a scholarship there—which was assumed to be impossible. It was this assumption which made me work hard for the first time in my life, and the result of my perverse endeavours was that I won a scholarship to Christ Church College, and entered the university in the summer of

1935. I joined the Communist Party during my first term, and most of my three years at Oxford were spent in political activity of one sort or another. I became, for example, the first, and so far the only, Communist president of the Oxford Union (debating) Society.

"Disillusioned by the Soviet-Nazi pact in 1939, I left the Communist Party and became what I have remained ever since—an anti-Communist supporter of the Labour Party. But politics, of which I had such a thorough dose during my Oxford years, have long ceased to be my primary interest. By the beginning of the war, when it seemed almost too late to do anything about it, I had decided that my real interest was in writing. I had already published a novel while I was at Oxford, but this had simply been *the* novel which everyone is said to have it in him to write. It had been strictly and naïvely autobiographical. I wanted now to *think* about my novels before I wrote them.

"The war interfered at first. I was in the army—for a short and mutually unsatisfactory period in the Brigade of Guards—and little opportunity was given me for writing the thoughtful novels which I'd planned. But by 1941 I had been seconded to a ministry in London, and was living in a pleasant flat with my wife, whom I had married in 1939. This period produced two novels—*School in Private* and *The Barricades*, the second of which was published in the United States. I was also contributing frequent stories and articles to *Horizon*, and had become a novel reviewer on the *New Statesman and Nation*.

"After the war my wife and I went to live on the Isle of Wight, where I wrote *Tea with Mrs. Goodman* (published in America under the title *Prothalamium*). This was an experimental novel, and easily the most important of my publications up to this time.

"In 1950 I joined the staff of *The Observer* and was sent to the Middle East as their correspondent. My first marriage had been dissolved, and I married again in Teheran. On my return I bought a cottage in Suffolk, where I am still living, and I wrote my second experimental novel, *The Garden to the Sea*. I am now [June 1953] at work on a memoir of two friends who were killed in the war [published as *Friends Apart* in 1954]. I am still employed by the *Observer*."

* * *

Philip Toynbee's earliest novels were sharp, ironic, and brittle portraits of modern life. "Mr. Toynbee is an intellectual," V. S. Pritchett wrote of *The Barricades*, "supple-minded, sensitive, witty, brilliant—too brilliant, one might say, for all his characters." With *Prothalamium*, subtitled *A Cycle of the Holy Grail*, he broke away from conventional forms, in a subjective manner reminiscent of some of the early poems of T. S. Eliot and the novels of Virginia Woolf and James Joyce, to tell a story through the consciousness of seven guests at a modern tea party. The reviewers found the results brilliant but bewildering. In the *New Yorker*'s judgment: "The wraithlike tale flowing underneath the contemporary story is suggested with subtlety and considerable delicacy of invention, but for this sort of thing to be really effective the main narrative must be of more expertly fashioned and solid stuff than Mr. Toynbee's fanciful work." His later novel, *The Garden to the Sea*, proved to be an even more baffling excursion into the subjective, but readers who accepted it as a purely experimental work found it stimulating and entertaining. Robert Gorham Davis said of it in the New York *Times*: "Mr. Toynbee writes a carefully studied poetic prose of considerable rhetorical and imagistic intensity. It steadily requires and often rewards close reading."

PRINCIPAL WORKS: The Savage Days, 1937; School in Private, 1941; The Barricades, 1944; Prothalamium (in England: Tea with Mrs. Goodman) 1947; A Garden to the Sea, 1953; Friends Apart: A Memoir of Esmond Romilly and Jasper Ridley in the Thirties, 1954.

TRACY, HENRY CHESTER (August 26, 1876-). For autobiographical sketch and list of works and references, see TWENTIETH CENTURY AUTHORS, 1942.

* * *

Henry C. Tracy writes from Hollywood, Calif.: "In 1942 I was made head of the book department in *Common Ground*, program of the Common Council for American Unity, New York City, concerned with promoting better relations among the many national and racial groups in the United States. I held this position for six years, and at the same time continued my work with the book groups. The excessive reading and reviewing required, and the confinement involved, injured my eyes and health to such an extent that although I resigned the position, I soon after lost my eyesight completely. This might seem to end my career as a writer and critic. However, since recovering a degree of health and some progress in touch typing, I have begun to do some creative writing and am also at work on a series of studies of birds, including a now completed monograph on the 'Great Birds of Asia Minor.'"

TRAIN, ARTHUR CHENEY (September 6, 1875-December 22, 1945). For biographical sketch and list of earlier works and references, see TWENTIETH CENTURY AUTHORS, 1942.

* * *

Arthur Train died at Memorial Hospital in New York City at seventy. He had been ill for a year. A week before his death he was re-elected president of the National Institute of Arts and Letters, an office he had held since 1941.

The degree to which Train was able to approximate the reality of the American scene and character was illustrated when, upon publication in 1943 of the "autobiography" of Ephraim Tutt, lawyer hero of fourteen of Train's books, the author discovered the "seemingly incredible but certainly appalling fact" that multitudes of people refused to be convinced that Mr. Tutt was not a living person. Scores of letters were received by the publishers from "old friends," "distant relatives," would-be clients; *Who's Who* invited him to its pages; an irate reader sued for fraud learning that the book was fiction.

Truly, as the *Saturday Review of Literature* has said, Mr. Tutt was "more real, more typically true to the legal personality than life itself . . . the best known of American lawyers."

ADDITIONAL WORKS: Yankee Lawyer: the Autobiography of Ephraim Tutt, 1943; Mr. Tutt Finds a Way, 1945.
ABOUT: Van Gelder, R. Writers and Writing; New York Times December 23, 1945; Newsweek September 13, 1943; Publishers' Weekly May 27, 1944; Saturday Evening Post April 8, 1944; Saturday Review of Literature January 5, 1946; Time September 20, 1943.

TRAUBEL, HORACE L. (December 19, 1858-September 8, 1919). For biographical sketch and list of works and references, see TWENTIETH CENTURY AUTHORS, 1942.

* * *

ADDITIONAL WORK: With Walt Whitman in Camden, vol. 4, January 21-April 7, 1889 (ed. S. Bradley) 1953.
ABOUT: Commonweal January 7, 1955.

TRAVEN, B. For biographical sketch and list of earlier works and references, see TWENTIETH CENTURY AUTHORS, 1942.

* * *

The closely-guarded secret of B. Traven's identity has been at least partly penetrated. Both *Life* and *Time* magazines have identified him and even published photographs of a man who "may be" the author, but the details of his biography remain shrouded in mystery. This much is generally accepted: that he is American, born in the Middle West of Swedish parents in about 1890, that he had little formal education, went to sea early, and settled in Mexico. His name is believed to be Berick Traven Torsvan. Another theory, though it is not so widely held, was advanced in the *New Republic* in 1947 by Manfred George. George insisted that Traven was German-born and that he writes in German. In pre-Hitler Germany, George says, "Traven was admired not only as a novelist but also as a courageous political writer." His name originally was Marut (an editor years ago mis-read his signature as "Traven"), and he was a revolutionary who escaped from Germany in 1919.

Interest in Traven's identity was stimulated in 1948 with the release of a motion picture version of *The Treasure of the Sierra Madre*. Directed by John Huston and starring Walter Huston and Humphrey Bogart, it was a brilliant study of human greed and one of the finest motion pictures of recent years.

ADDITIONAL WORK IN ENGLISH TRANSLATION: The Rebellion of the Hanged, 1952.
ABOUT: Life March 10, 1947, February 2, 1948; New Republic March 24, 1947; Time August 16, 1948, April 21, 1952.

TRAVERS, PAMELA L. (1906-). For autobiographical sketch and list of earlier works and references, see TWENTIETH CENTURY AUTHORS, 1942.

* * *

P. L. Travers writes from London to the editors of this volume that the statement that the scene of two of her books was the Great Barrier Reef is incorrect and that she has never written about the Reef. She adds: "P. L. Travers dislikes personal publicity and believes that an author should be as anonymous as possible, indeed, that only in this way can an author continue to write books in peace."

Two more Mary Poppins books have appeared in the past decade and these are in the same spirit of happy fantasy and nonsense as the earlier ones. Though written for children, they also have an enthusiastic adult audience. The philosopher Irwin Edman commented on *Mary Poppins in the Park* that it is "at once poetry and fun and wisdom."

ADDITIONAL WORKS: Mary Poppins Opens the Door, 1943; Mary Poppins in the Park, 1952.
ABOUT: Kunitz, S. J. & Haycraft, H. (eds.) Junior Book of Authors (rev. ed.); New York Herald Tribune Book Review October 12, 1952.

TREECE, HENRY (1912-), English
novelist and miscellaneous writer, reports: "I
was born in the West Midlands of England,

of Welsh extraction
originally. I went to
school at Wednesbury
Grammar School in
Staffordshire, where I
won the science prize
for two years in the
senior school. Then
followed a scholarship
to Birmingham Uni-
versity, where I took
a poor degree in 1933,
and where I played hockey for the third
eleven and boxed for the university as a
welterweight. I was captain of university
boxing in 1932. At the same time I acted, in
occasional small and violent parts, with the
university dramatic society; but in the main
was more interested in the unacademic, mundane things—like weight-lifting and playing
the piano in various small dance-bands. We
played anywhere, from country clubs to
Saturday night dives, where gangs of hooli-
gans sometimes began fights in the middle of
the floor.

"At this time my attitude to life was
robust rather than aesthetic, and I spent most
weekends on the River Severn in Shropshire,
with roaming unliterary strong-arm friends,
expending surplus energy brawling and swimming over weirs.

"In 1933 I spent a period in Spain and
there became flamenco-conscious. My musical
taste switched from blues to Scarlatti and de
Falla, and I found as much to admire in a
matador as in a world heavyweight champion.

"Back home I accepted a post as officer
at a Home Office School for delinquents in
Leicestershire, where I learned how to make
adolescents wash but not how to stop them
reading comic papers in church.

"With great relief I then found a post as
English master at Cleobury Mortimer College
in the most beautiful area of Shropshire, a
Tudor school with a love for the old traditions. There, one summer afternoon in 1934,
looking down from Titterstone Clee Hill
across the patchwork fields that lead to Wales,
I first realized that I was perhaps a poet, and
began to write seriously. There too I met
Mary Woodman, whom I married in 1939.

"In 1935 I became English master at Tyne-
mouth School, a public school in Northumberland, at which time I came to know the late
Michael Roberts, a fine poet and critic. Now
my verse began to appear in the little magazines and in 1938 I first became acquainted
with Dylan Thomas, about whom I later pub-

lished a critical estimate, which did neither of
us much good!

"In the same year I met J. F. Hendry, a
Scots philosopher and poet, with whom—and
with the encouragement of Sir Herbert Read
—I helped to found a Romantic literary movement which was known as the 'New Apocalypse' and which attracted many of our poet-
contemporaries. In the three anthologies
which we published (*The New Apocalypse*;
The White Horseman; *The Crown and the
Sickle*) we made a stand against all forms of
totalitarianism—an unusual literary attitude at
that time—asserted man's right to free expression and the artistic need for an organic
mythos to express the age we lived in.

"When the war broke out, Hendry and I
joined the armed forces and this group lost
its coherence. I served with the Royal Air
Force for five years, largely as an intelligence
officer in Bomber Command. Then, in the
early war years, and largely through the
agency of Sir Herbert Read, I met Stefan
Schimanski—then personal secretary to Lord
Wedgewood—and there began a literary
partnership which lasted until Schimanski was
killed in an air-crash in 1950 on his way to a
journalistic assignment on the war-front in
Korea.

"With Schimanski I edited first a magazine,
Kingdom Come, and later a literary bi-yearly,
Transformation, the 'party line' of which was
Personalism (i.e. man's right to attain to and
express the dignity of which God had made
him the custodian). About this time, 1942,
T. S. Eliot began to take an interest in and
to publish my poetry; while the late George
Orwell, who was working with the B.B.C.,
introduced me to broadcasting. I was also
working now at short stories and began to
find them appearing in various publications in
Britain and the U.S.A.

"After my demobilisation in 1946 I turned
more seriously to radio, and when I had
served some apprenticeship at writing talks,
stories and topographical features, wrote
verse-dramas for radio. These allowed me to
express myself more broadly, and to use the
elements of narrative and character which
straight poetry precluded. During these years
I completed the radio trilogy, *The Dark
Island*, *The End of a World* and *The Tragedy
of Tristram*, all based on archetypal Celtic
themes. Recently I moved on to the 'strong'
drama of realism in the radio play, *Maguire*,
which deals with life during a drought on a
remote African farm.

"The inevitable development then followed:
having learned by poetry and the short story
to manipulate words, and by drama to construct forms, I turned to the novel, using the

title of my earlier radio play, *The Dark Island*, for my first novel.

"At the time of writing, I find the novel a most satisfying literary form: it allows the poet to exercise his talent with as much licence as he wishes, and the dramatist to employ as big a cast and as many changes of scene as he needs. It lets the writer create the film he would love to see, but which no director could afford to make. It has this advantage over radio that a book is durable, whereas the word once spoken, however exciting while the vibration lasts, soon passes from the memory. I ask only that my novels should entertain; my evangelical days are now so far away that I would not wish to persuade anyone of anything, except perhaps the multiplicity of man's mind.

"As senior English master at Barton-on-Humber Grammar School, and as the father of a boy and a girl, I am naturally interested in children and have latterly written radio plays and stories for them, usually based on historical themes.

"Since the end of the war my only excursion from the small Lincolnshire market town where I now live has been to the United States, where, in the winter of 1950, I spent five weeks, covering New York theatre for the *Manchester Guardian*, and lecturing at the Poetry Center and at the University of Buffalo.

"Although I am a strong monarchist and an inflexible European, I regard the United States as my second spiritual home. I shall never forget that a press in Illinois published my first book of poems; that a New York publisher first brought out my *Collected Poems* and that another has so enthusiastically received me in my most recent status, as a novelist. I can never forget, or adequately repay, the heart-warming hospitality which I received on my first visit to the United States. Both as writer and as person, these things are of the greatest importance to me."

PRINCIPAL WORKS: *Poetry*—Towards a Personal Armageddon, 1940; Thirty-Eight Poems, 1940; Invitation and Warning, 1942; The Black Seasons, 1945; Collected Poems, 1946; The Haunted Garden, 1947; The Exiles, 1952. *Fiction* —I Cannot Go Hunting Tomorrow (short stories) 1946; The Dark Island, 1952; The Rebels, 1953; Boy of the Belgae, 1953. *Essays*—Herbert Read, 1944; How I See Apocalypse, 1946; Algernon Charles Swinburne, 1948; Dylan Thomas, 1949.

ABOUT: Fraser, G. S. & Melville, R. The White Horseman; Scarfe, F. Auden and After; Spender, S. Poetry Since 1939.

TRENCH, HERBERT (November 26, 1865-June 11, 1923). For biographical sketch and list of works and references, see TWENTIETH CENTURY AUTHORS, 1942.

TRENT, GREGORY. See WILLIAMSON, T. R.

TRENT, WILLIAM PETERFIELD (November 1862-December 7, 1939). For biographical sketch and list of works and references, see TWENTIETH CENTURY AUTHORS, 1942.

* * *

ABOUT: Journal of Southern History May 1949.

TREVELYAN, GEORGE MACAULAY (February 16, 1876-). For biographical sketch and list of earlier works and references, see TWENTIETH CENTURY AUTHORS, 1942.

* * *

One of the fairest summaries, and a very modest one, of G. M. Trevelyan's long and distinguished career is his own, recorded in an autobiographical essay in 1949: "I have not been an original but a traditional kind of historian. The best that can be said of me is that I tried to keep up to date a family tradition as to the relation of history to literature, in a period when the current was running strongly in the other direction towards history exclusively 'scientific,' a period therefore when my old-fashioned ideas and practice have had, perhaps, a certain value as counterpoise." In 1949 Trevelyan wrote that he was "too old to write another serious history book." Since that time, however, he has written a number of learned and charming essays, including the Clark Lectures, published as *The Layman's Love of Letters*. The *New Statesman and Nation* observed of this volume: "Dr. Trevelyan belongs in spirit to that golden generation of critics . . . in whom a keen literary appetite blended with a powerful and detailed knowledge of men and affairs."

Shortly before he reached sixty-five, when his professorship at Cambridge was due to end, Trevelyan was appointed Master of Trinity College, thereby remaining at the university until his retirement in 1951. His home is still in Cambridge, and he is active in university and community affairs. In 1953 he delivered the Clark Lectures at Trinity College. Since 1946 he has been High Steward of the Borough of Cambridge and since 1949 Chancellor of the University of Durham.

ADDITIONAL WORKS: Trinity College: An Historical Sketch, 1943; Autobiography and Other Essays, 1949; Illustrated English Social History, vol. 4: The Nineteenth Century, 1950; A Layman's Love of Letters, 1953.

ABOUT: Trevelyan, G. M. Autobiography and Other Essays; Life January 14, 1952; Time September 19, 1949.

TREVOR-ROPER, HUGH REDWALD

(January 15, 1914-), English historian, was born in Glanton, Northumberland, England,

the elder son of Dr. B. W. E. Trevor-Roper. He received his education at Charterhouse and Christ Church, Oxford. He was a Fellow of Merton College, Oxford, before the war, and in 1945 was appointed a Student of Christ Church, Oxford. Both before and during the war Trevor-Roper traveled fairly widely in western Europe.

His first book was published in 1940, *Archbishop Laud, 1573-1645*. But his fame came with *The Last Days of Hitler*, which appeared when the fate of Hitler was causing interesting speculation throughout the world. The author was a British Intelligence Officer at the time he was sent, under official orders, to collect the material used in this book. The investigation uncovered a great deal of evidence about a dark period of history, and all this was used in *The Last Days of Hitler*, including interviews with those who witnessed the events and hitherto secret documents. "The author has an inquisitive mind and a flair for the well-rounded phrase," wrote the Chicago *Sun Book Week.* "He can marshal the facts as well as any lawyer to prove a point, but he can also sustain interest by skillful writing." The *Manchester Guardian* commented: "It may be a poor compliment to say of an historical work that it is more readable than a novel, but in this case it is true." The book discussed not only the question of Hitler's death, but the plot of July 20, 1944, Hitler's routine, health, and character, his relations with the generals, Goebbels' program of universal destruction, Himmler's fantastic character and maneuvers, Goering's fall, and Bormann's intrigues.

In 1953 Trevor-Roper returned to the field of his special interest, Elizabethan history, with *The Gentry, 1540-1640*. In the same year he contributed an introductory essay on the mind of Adolf Hitler to the publication of Hitler's *Secret Conversations, 1941-44.*

PRINCIPAL WORKS: Archbishop Laud, 1573-1645, 1940; The Last Days of Hitler, 1947; The Gentry, 1540-1640, 1953.

TRILLING, LIONEL (July 4, 1905-),

American critic and scholar, writes: "Lionel Trilling was born in New York City, the son of David W. and Fannie (Cohen) Trilling. He attended the public schools of the

city and in 1925 was graduated from Columbia College. In 1926 he took his Master of Arts degree in English literature at Columbia University and taught for a year at the University of Wisconsin. After returning to New York he taught at Hunter College until his appointment as instructor of English at Columbia in 1932. He took his doctorate at the university in 1938,

Robert Christie

his dissertation being his first published book, *Matthew Arnold.* He passed through the usual academic grades (assistant professor 1939, associate professor 1945) and since 1948 he has been professor of English, giving courses in the literature of England and America in Columbia College and in the Faculty of Philosophy.

"Mr. Trilling's first published work, a short story, appeared in 1925 in The *Menorah Journal*, to which he subsequently contributed other stories as well as essays and reviews. He was one of the group of young writers who reviewed extensively and with terrifying authority for the literary section of the New York *Evening Post* when it was under the generous editorship of Harry Dounce. His later critical writing has appeared in the *Nation*, the *New Republic*, the *Times Book Review*, *Partisan Review* and the *Kenyon Review*. He is a member of the advisory boards of the two latter periodicals. With John Crowe Ransom and F. O. Matthiessen, he was one of the organizers of the Kenyon School of Letters at Kenyon College, and he has continued to serve as one of the Senior Fellows of the School, which has now become the School of Letters—Indiana University.

"In 1943 Mr. Trilling published *E. M. Forster*, a critical study of the Britsh novelist which had its part in making Forster's work known in this country. His novel, *The Middle of the Journey*, appeared in 1947, and a collection of his critical essays, *The Liberal Imagination*, in 1950. He has published a few short stories, of which two, 'Of This Time, of That Place,' and 'The Other Margaret,' have become especially well known and have been frequently reprinted.

"Mr. Trilling is married to Diana Trilling, who is known for her critical writing. They have one son and they live in New York."

* * *

One of the most thoughtful and stimulating of contemporary American scholar-critics.

Lionel Trilling has been highly praised for his lucid, imaginative, and scholarly essays and lectures. Milton Wilson wrote, in *Canadian Forum*, that "he perpetually stimulates the reader to revise and reorganize his own values, he shows us (to use his own terms) the work of art functioning as subject as well as object, with an existence of its own beyond our partial comprehensions." Trilling's only novel, *The Middle of the Journey*, a quietly-told but effective study of the conflicts, in present-day America, faced by liberals and by former Communists, was described as "a novel of ideas." Morton Dauwen Zabel wrote of it in the *Nation*: "A brilliant example of a new mode of fiction, one whose function in the moral dilemmas of our age his acute critical sense has seen, and whose claims on the imaginative resources of his generation the finely controlled, humanly faithful art of this novel demonstrates. It is a book that brings the best critical intelligence now discernible in America into play with an absolutely honest creative talent."

Of Trilling's second collection of critical essays, *The Opposing Self*, Harry Levin said: "Other critics may push esthetic perception or historical scholarship somewhat further, but their writing often seems dry and technical; whereas Mr. Trilling's is increasingly and deservedly popular because he has the courage to be a moralist."

PRINCIPAL WORKS: Matthew Arnold, 1939; E. M. Forster, 1943; The Middle of the Journey (novel) 1947; The Liberal Imagination, 1950; The Opposing Self, 1955.

ABOUT: New York Times Book Review February 13, 1955; Saturday Review of Literature February 14, 1948.

TRIOLET, ELSA. See ARAGON, L.

*TROUBETZKOY, AMÉLIE (RIVES), Princess (August 23, 1863-June 15, 1945). For autobiographical sketch and list of works and references, see TWENTIETH CENTURY AUTHORS, 1942.

* * *

Princess Amélie Troubetzkoy died in Charlottesville, Va., after a long illness, at eighty-one.

The New York *Times* noted: "Few American women writers of her generation achieved such a sensational literary success." She possessed what the Boston *Transcript* has called an "exceptional knowledge of life and a distinctive skill in its presentation."

ABOUT: New York Times June 17, 1945; Publishers' Weekly July 7, 1945.

* tro͞o byĕts koi'

TRUMBO, DALTON (1905-   ). For biographical sketch and list of earlier works and references, see TWENTIETH CENTURY AUTHORS, 1942.

* * *

Dalton Trumbo wrote a number of successful screen plays in Hollywood during the 1940's—among them, *A Guy Named Joe*, *Thirty Seconds Over Tokyo*, and *Our Vines Have Tender Grapes*. In 1949 his play *The Biggest Thief in Town* was produced in New York. In its original form the play, which concerns the unethical practices of an undertaker, had been, as Trumbo pointed out, "two plays in one—a serious piece and a comedy." Out-of-town tryout audiences, he said, "howled at the comedy and displayed such ominous hostility to the serious portions that we cut the latter entirely out." The result, when it came to Broadway, was a broad farce which the critics found clumsy and tasteless. It ran for only thirteen performances.

Trumbo's left-wing activities brought him under the scrutiny of congressional investigating committees and—as he later claimed—resulted in his being blacklisted by motion picture companies. Called before the House Un-American Activities committee in 1948, he refused to state whether or not he was a Communist. As a result, he was charged with contempt of Congress, fined $1,000, and sentenced to one year in prison. After a long legal battle he began serving the sentence in 1950. He entered prison with another author, John Howard Lawson, who was convicted on similar charges.

ADDITIONAL WORKS: A Guy Named Joe (novelization by R. M. White of Trumbo's screen play) 1944; The Biggest Thief in Town, 1949.

ABOUT: New York Times June 10, 1950; Theatre Arts January 1950, July 1950.

TUCKER, BENJAMIN RICKETSON (1854-June 22, 1939). For biographical sketch and list of works and references, see TWENTIETH CENTURY AUTHORS, 1942.

* * *

ABOUT: Madison, C. A. Critics and Crusaders.

TULLY, JIM (June 3, 1888-June 22, 1947). For biographical sketch and list of earlier works and references, see TWENTIETH CENTURY AUTHORS, 1942.

* * *

Jim Tully died in Hollywood at fifty-nine as the result of a heart malady from which he had suffered for two years. He was survived by his third wife, Mrs. Myrtle Tully.

Louis Kronenberger has described Tully's writing at its best as "a succession of direct, hard blows straight from the shoulder. The prose has the defiant blare of trumpets; all of it is speed and force and action. . . . It is not art. But it is the creative and compelling journalism of a creative mind." The author's friend Frank Scully, referring to the dichotomy between the "hard-boiled" novels on which Tully's reputation rests and the motion picture fan magazine articles from which he made an additional fortune, spoke of "the mass of bilge and enduring literature that his pen has turned out impartially and the public has paid for generously."

ADDITIONAL WORK: A Dozen and One, 1943.
ABOUT: Scully, F. Rogues' Galley; Tully, J. A Dozen and One (Introduction by Damon Runyon); New York Times June 23, 1947.

TUNIS, JOHN ROBERTS (December 7, 1889-). For autobiographical sketch and list of earlier works and references, see TWENTIETH CENTURY AUTHORS, 1942.

* * *

Raymond Swing observed, in an article in the *Saturday Review* in 1954, that John R. Tunis has done more than any other American author to promote the cause of sports in a democratic society. "He not only has been one of the most successful sport writers for boys, but the only outstanding writer in the field who can make fair play compete for interest with winning a game." Tunis has written more than twenty-five books and his sales are well over half a million. What delights his readers—and they are mainly young boys—is his knack of creating honest excitement, combined with his expert knowledge of every sport he writes about. What delights Swing, in addition, is his ability to arouse in his readers "a better sense of true sportsmanship and of the elements that make strength of character."

ADDITIONAL WORKS: The Keystone Kids, 1943; Lawn Games, 1943; Yea! Wildcats! 1944; A City for Lincoln, 1945; The Kid Comes Back, 1946; Highpockets, 1948; Son of the Valley, 1949; Young Razzle, 1949; The Other Side of the Fence, 1953; Go, Team, Go, 1954; Buddy and the Old Pro, 1955.
ABOUT: Library Journal December 15, 1943; Saturday Review June 19, 1954.

TURNBULL, Mrs. AGNES (SLIGH) (October 14, 1888-). For autobiographical sketch and list of earlier works and references, see TWENTIETH CENTURY AUTHORS, 1942.

* * *

Agnes Sligh Turnbull's two latest novels, both dealing with the lives of Protestant ministers, have been best sellers. Of the first of these, *The Bishop's Mantle*, E. D. Doyle remarked in the San Francisco *Chronicle*: "This is no nambly-pamby narrative of a sticky-good parson." Instead, as Virginia Kirkus wrote, it is "a book which fulfills the demand for a worthwhile story which is also inspirational." Similarly, *The Gown of Glory*, though more nostalgic and sentimental than its predecessor, was a solid story, told (to quote Charles Lee) "with an old-fashioned richness of episode and emotion." Both novels were bought for motion pictures.

Mrs. Turnbull received a degree of Litt.D. from Westminster College in 1945. Her home is in Maplewood, N.J.

ADDITIONAL WORKS: The Bishop's Mantle, 1947; The Gown of Glory, 1952.
ABOUT: Warfel, H. R. American Novelists of Today; Publishers' Weekly January 5, 1952.

TURNER, FREDERICK JACKSON (November 14, 1861-March 14, 1932). For biographical sketch and list of works and references, see TWENTIETH CENTURY AUTHORS, 1942.

* * *

ABOUT: Commager, H. S. The American Mind; Saveth, E. N. American Historians and European Immigrants; American Scholar October 1949; Mississippi Valley Historical Review December 1943; Wisconsin Magazine of History March 1948.

TURNER, WALTER JAMES (October 13, 1889 or 1890-November 18, 1946). For autobiographical sketch and list of earlier works and references, see TWENTIETH CENTURY AUTHORS, 1942.

* * *

W. J. Turner died in London of a cerebral hemorrhage. He had been literary editor of the *Spectator* since 1942. During the last years of his life he edited a series of volumes giving a panoramic view of British life and culture under the title *Britain in Pictures*.

Jacquetta Hawkes, the writer, a friend of Turner's, observed that his personality ranged from "sometimes excessive violence" to "the most subtle delicacy. . . . There was in his reactions to life nothing in any way automatic or second-hand; he responded completely, simply, directly."

W. B. Yeats once wrote that Turner "thinks that the horror of the world is in its beauty. Beautiful forms deceive us, because if we grasp them, they dissolve into what he calls 'confused sensation'; and destroy us because they drag us under the machinery of nature; if it were possible he would, like a Buddhist, or a connoisseur, kill, or suspend desire. He does not see men and women as the puppets of Eliot's poetry, repeating always the same movements, but as the reflections of a terrible Olympus."

ADDITIONAL WORKS: Fables, Parables and Plots, 1943; The English Ballet, 1945; Fossils of a Future Time? (poems) 1946; Exmoor Village, 1947. *Editor*—Panorama of Rural England (in England: Englishman's Country) 1944; Pictorial Guide to Many Lands (in England: British Commonwealth and Empire) 1944; Romance of English Literature (in England: Impressions of English Literature) 1945; Treasury of English Wildlife (in England: Nature in Britain) 1946; Aspects of British Art, 1947; British Adventure, 1947; British Craftsmanship, 1951.

ABOUT: London Times November 20, 1946; November 23, 1946; Spectator November 22, 1946.

TUVE, ROSEMOND (1903-), American scholar, writes: "I was born in a small South Dakota town between the Big Sioux and the prairies. My father was a mathematician, president of a small Lutheran college (Augustana) then located at Canton, and my mother taught music at the same college. My four grandparents had severally come from Norway as pioneers, escaping from rigors of one sort or another, a too dominating state church or a sea-captain's hard life or too much family, and we children were taught to think that America was synonymous with freedom, and that each man's own mind and spirit was the measure of his excellence. I suppose it was as a corollary to this that we understood that the one thing no sensible man occupied his head with was money, either making or keeping or spending it. Except of course for 'education.' In the small rural college community these astonishing generalizations stood up rather better against the wear of experience than one could expect.

"Since the only kind of books I write, or will write, are those which concern what other men have written, and I would gladly keep myself out of them if I could, the details of my own life have the less relevance. But why people write at all, or keep on once they start, is always a puzzle, and in my case probably the only interesting one. I suppose one persists in writing my kind of books because one becomes curious when very young, and cannot stay away from certain authors and kinds of problems and pleasures. As the third child among four I chiefly did what my three brothers thought was important, such as learning the Morse code to take down their wireless messages, and playing in neighborhood gangs, but I learned without noticing it before I was ten to care about most of the things I have since thought or written about—and no doubt was equally inescapably made ready to miss the rest. My father said long passages of Shakespeare and Tennyson and the New Testament to me while we hoed the peas, or tried in the face of my stubborn docility to make me willing to do my arithmetic the 'prettier' way by algebra instead of following the book, and for years on Sunday afternoons told me a story (indifferently concerned with the fortitude of St. Polycarp martyr or the floods from which my pioneer grandmother rescued my uncles) which I was allowed to rework into a 'composition,' after supper. I was brought up on everyone in the family of six (but especially my mother) reading aloud to all the others who had 'things they had to do,' incessant singing in parts, mostly of Bach chorales and hymns, and vast terrains, summer and winter, of leisure that was completely unscheduled — except for Shakespeare 'on Chatauqua' in July, endless hot afternoons without sight of a person, 'staking the cow' along the road-edges where the grass outlasted the dry Dakota summer, and training her to stay content with one staking per chapter of a book, and in winter except for school or town 'operettas' and a debating team that tried out all the same subjects as the men's Monday night Athenian Society. Barring the old Reo, we had nothing that cost anything, but no one took our time.

"We had less and less money but thought nothing of it; but when I was fifteen, some months after my father died, we hurriedly picked up the household in mid-year and moved to Minneapolis to put safely into the University of Minnesota my next oldest brother, now a physicist with the Carnegie Institution, to prevent him from saving the family fortunes by going on the boards with a Chicago opera company; in another year I went on like my two elder brothers into the university, paying for it mostly by a job in which I put three trees into three holes in a Christmas card of which inexplicable thousands were needed to satisfy the demands of the country. I stopped off after my sophomore year to teach 4th and 5th grades in a tiny prairie town, returned with joy and (having become enamored of medieval literature) gave up the Christmas cards and addressographs to be student assistant to Friedrich Klaeber, who taught me to respect philology, then to Thomas Raysor, who tempered the ideas I had got about Romantic poets from reading Babbitt; I took my B.A. in 1924, and acting on the family principle and with their reckless advice borrowed a thousand dollars to go to Bryn Mawr for graduate work, first as Scholar and then as Fellow. When I was given a Bryn Mawr European fellowship I took out two years to pay my debts, teaching at Goucher and going to Johns Hopkins; then adding an A.A.U.W. fellowship went into residence at Somerville College, Oxford. There I swam among the Bodleian manuscripts—a sort of imrama for anyone working as I was on medieval subjects—and did the B.Litt. courses and viva, but being unable to complete my residence returned to teach three years at Vassar, finish the Bryn Mawr Ph.D., and teach three more summers at the Bryn Mawr School for Women Workers in Industry, an experience which left me forever (I hope) left of center, at least of where this country has taken to placing the center.

"I then returned in 1932, to France to see a book through the press in Paris, and to work and write in Oxford, London and Ireland; after a second year living mostly with friends in a village in Somerset, I came to Connecticut College in 1934. On various leaves I have gone back to England to work or Italy and France to sit and stare, taught refugees in a Quaker seminar at Black Mountain, held a visiting lectureship in Renaissance literature at the University of Minnesota. Three divorces that have become accepted in modern American intellectual life I have been unable to accede to because of the faith of those I lived among when I was young: that between scholarship and criticism, that between research or writing and teaching (these I saw unified too often to believe then inimical), and most important that between science and the humanities. I first read Milton and Eliot through aloud in a laboratory, and the philosophy to which I was introduced in a scientific household filled with the arguing friends of three brothers in mechanical engineering, physics, and chemistry, was not naturalistic positivism. Among dozens of scientific friends I learned to expect one combination (whose recurrence finally led me to relate it to the nature of their discipline): music, humility, and intellectual courage (except, alas, in politics). These are what I pay allegiance to in poetry; what they leave out—the poet's eye for truth in figure— I see as threatened rather by those more potent enemies who despise all four; I only

write so that the poets may be heard better, being more potent than the enemies, if we do not bind them while they sleep. I suppose everyone who does this brings his own cord to it, to be cut by the next."

PRINCIPAL WORKS: Seasons and Months: Studies in a Tradition of Middle English Poetry, 1933; Surveys of Scholarship in the Field of the Renaissance, 1943; Elizabethan and Metaphysical Imagery: Renaissance Poetic and Twentieth Century Critics, 1947; (ed.) Palingenius' Zodiake of Life, 1947; A Reading of George Herbert, 1952.

ABOUT: Accent Autumn 1953.

TWEEDSMUIR. See BUCHAN

TYLER, PARKER (1907-   ), American poet and critic, writes: "As to life, Thomas Z. Tyler and Eva (Parker) Tyler gave it to me. The place was New Orleans. The reason was love. And I can never cease being as grateful for all the particular facts of it as I am critical of all the general. For life imposes on us, with primal desire and its endless satisfactions, the strange and  cleansing negative of criticism. My maternal grandfather was a newspaper editor who achieved public prominence in Louisiana. His spirited daughter, who was to be my mother, married a member of an old South Carolina family with impressive forebears. Our little family (with one other child, Phyllis) soon became nomadic. Urban and suburban America unfolded for our innocence like one of the original prairies or forests here.

"Our fortunes were uneven. Revelation of the daily was certainly novel and often interesting—especially (for me) those dusky theatres where living pictures unrolled on a flat screen. I vacillated between the work of books and the image of the film screen. Extraordinarily self-fixated, I turned on myself a pitiless criticism and imbued myself with a steely ambition to do something with life besides live it. That is, I meant to contribute to the things of the world. My adolescence, in retrospect, seems to have been unusually painful—perhaps because my family was so inward and so complacent in a tight moral sense. I suddenly became an actor in a little-theatre, the Cleveland Playhouse. Before that, I had put certain lyrical daydreams into verse. And I had abandoned, in Chicago, my formal education in the very middle. Only one thing seemed to face me: New York with all its mysteries and glory.

"Today it is merely factual for me to say that I rushed at evérything in New York and therefore had to turn back on many things before I could say' I had profited by experiencing them. My oldest friend, Charles Henri Ford, provided the first little magazine of those that soon represented for me the literary heights. But I had already contributed precocious book reviews to weeklies and even read manuscripts for a publisher. As an advance-guard poet, I took Ezra Pound, William Carlos Williams, E. E. Cummings for my masters, and attained print in *transition.* I was published and encouraged even by the conservative organ, *Poetry,* where now I am one of the active 'old contributors.' With nods from Eliot and Pound, I issued my own anthology of modern verse. If I have a venial sin, it was and is impatience.

"Then came Ford's internationally inflected *View* (1940-47) and I was given *carte blanche* to write almost anything. The dance, painting, literature, the movies, all appeared as grist for aesthetic-philosophic speculation, and I wrote on them all. Out of this came the fruit of my childhood initiation in the movie-house: my first book on the cinema; and also, analogously, my first full-length poem showing the influence of the movies on my imagination. Friends deep and light, dangerous and hale, had come, stayed, gone; returned. Life seemed only practice for expression in my chosen media. Of course, public appreciation had a good deal to do with my main pursuit of film criticism. I was delighted to become, in *Kenyon Review,* an interpreter of film to an elite interested primarily in literature.

"One day, lately, I realized that I have concentrated so much on work, to the slighting of social activity, that I could tell a poet I had lost sight of for years that I am virtually a recluse. Well, not quite. The basic spiritual gesture is what counts; then criticism, with its myriad lights, can only help show the way through the purlieus of the common soul that both engulfs and separates men from each other . . . in life as in books. But love and creation remain the torch-bearers."

* * *

Iris Barry described Parker Tyler's *Hollywood Hallucination* as "the first book in its field to deserve the name of creative criticism." Eric Bentley considers him "one of the most interesting writers on the movies in America today." Bringing to motion pictures his background in modern art and poetry, Tyler writes highly individualistic interpreta-

tions. Some of his readers find his work obscure, dogmatic, and esoteric, but serious students of the motion picture as an art form find him informative and challenging. In 1952 *The Screen,* a play by Tyler described as "a metaphysical comedy," was produced in New York by the Artists' Theatre. Richard Hayes, reviewing it for *Commonweal,* wrote: "Mr. Tyler's mind is elusive, sophisticated and Freudian in orientation. He writes at this point with more feeling for the stage than knowledge of it. . . . [It] nonetheless introduces a stimulating and sophisticated intelligence into our theatre."

PRINCIPAL WORKS: *Poetry*—The Metaphor in the Jungle, 1940; The Granite Butterfly, 1945; Yesterday's Children, 1947. *Prose*—(with C. H. Ford) The Young and Evil, 1933; The Hollywood Hallucination, 1944; Magic and Myth of the Movies, 1947; Chaplin: Last of the Clowns, 1948.

ABOUT: Barry, I. *Preface to* P. Tyler's The Hollywood Hallucination; Hoffman, F. J. (and others) The Little Magazine; Miller, H. Sunday After the War; Accent Spring 1946; Commonweal May 22, 1952; Kenyon Review Winter 1948; Sewanee Review Summer 1947.

TYNAN, KATHARINE (January 23, 1861-April 2, 1931). For biographical sketch and list of works and references, see TWENTIETH CENTURY AUTHORS, 1942.

* * *

ABOUT: Dictionary of National Biography 1931-1940; Hoehn, M. (ed.) Catholic Authors, I; Yeats, W. B. Letters to Katharine Tynan.

TYRRELL, GEORGE (February 6, 1861-July 15, 1909). For biographical sketch and list of works and references, see TWENTIETH CENTURY AUTHORS, 1942.

ULLMAN, JAMES RAMSEY (November 24, 1907-   ), American novelist, writes: "A New Yorker to begin with (and probably to end with), I was born on West 90th Street and such roots as I have are anchored firmly in Central Park. Attended Ethical Culture School, Andover and Princeton, emerging from the last in 1929 with the usual B.A. My senior thesis, *Mad Shelley,* won a  prize and was subsequently published—which encouraged me in my hope for a writing career—and after graduation I took off for Paris, with the twin purposes of getting a job as foreign correspondent and writing the Great American Novel. Neither materialized, however, and I returned to New York, arriving on the day of the 1929 stock market crash.

"After much pavement-pounding I found a reporter's job on the now defunct Brooklyn *Standard Union* and held it for two years. On the side I tried my hand at play-writing. Two of my efforts were tried out in summer theatres, but none (just as well, no doubt) reached Broadway. In the process, however, I made many theatrical contacts, and in 1933, to my considerable surprise, found myself no longer a newspaperman but a producer of plays. During the next few years I had a hand in ten New York productions. One of them, *Men in White*, won the Pulitzer prize for 1934; two, *The Milky Way* and *Blind Alley*, were modest successes; the rest are best forgotten. After demobilizing myself from the commercial theatre I spent two hysterical but fascinating years as an executive of the WPA's Federal Theatre Project. And at last in 1939, I got back to what I had always wanted to do (and should have been doing) : i.e., writing.

"I had already, in off hours, done a travel book, *The Other Side of the Mountain*, based on a trip I had made across the Andes and down the Amazon. Now, as a full-time author, I wrote short stories and articles for the magazines and a history of mountaineering called *High Conquest*. Came 1941, Pearl Harbor—and an interruption. The army wanting no part of me (near-sightedness), I joined the American Field Service as an ambulance driver. Served for eighteen months with the British Eighth Army in Africa—from El Alamein through to Tunisia.

"Returning home, and to writing, I concentrated on the novel and produced, over the next several years, *The White Tower, River of the Sun* and *Windom's Way*, all three of which were lucky enough to be book-club selections.

"Over the years I have managed to escape occasionally from the desk and lead something of a double life as traveler and mountaineer, venturing as far afield as Brazil and Hawaii, Russia and South Africa, the Alps and the Andes. And, inevitably, my love of far and high places has strongly influenced my writing. As far back as I can remember, my fondest dream has been to have a try at Mount Everest; but, at the age of forty-five, I am afraid it will remain just that.

"Now married for the second time. Have two almost grown sons and two smaller stepchildren. Since 1949 headquarters have been in Bermuda, which I find a fine place to (1)

live, (2) write, (3) bring up the younger ones sans TV."

* * *

Although James Ramsay Ullman has written on a variety of subjects and his novels have been set in a variety of locales, he is most widely known as a specialist in mountains and mountain climbing. His best-selling novel *The White Tower*, a tense and dramatic story of the ascent of a mountain in the Alps, was especially praised for its vividly detailed descriptions of climbing. His nonfiction survey of mountain climbing, *High Conquest*, was hailed by Clifton Fadiman in the *New Yorker* as "among the finest popular histories (at least in English) of its subject." Its sequel, *The Age of Mountaineering*, which brings the survey up to date, was described by a fellow mountain climber, Justice William O. Douglas, as "a beautiful narrative of the conquests of mountains that is as exciting as fiction."

PRINCIPAL WORKS: *Fiction*—The White Tower, 1945; River of the Sun, 1950; Windom's Way, 1952; The Island of the Blue Macaws (short stories) 1953; The Sands of Karakorum, 1953; Banner in the Sky, 1954. *Non-Fiction*—The Other Side of the Mountain, 1938; High Conquest, 1941; Kingdom of Adventure: Everest, 1947; The Age of Mountaineering, 1954; (with Tenzing of Everest) Tiger of the Snows, 1955.

ABOUT: Ullman, J. R. The Other Side of the Mountain; Current Biography 1945; New York Herald Tribune Book Review January 21, October 7, 1951; New York Times Book Review January 21, 1951; Saturday Review of Literature February 16, 1946.

*UNAMUNO Y JUGO, MIGUEL DE (September 29, 1864-December 31, 1936). For biographical sketch and list of works and references, see TWENTIETH CENTURY AUTHORS, 1942.

* * *

ABOUT: Balseiro, J. A. Blasco Ibáñez, Unamuno, Valle-Inclán, Baroja: Cuatro Individualistas de España (in Spanish) ; Barea, A. Unamuno; Columbia Dictionary of Modern European Literature; Hispanic Review July 1944, July 1950, October 1951; Nation December 1, 1945; South Atlantic Quarterly July 1950.

* ōō nä mōō'nō ē hōō'gō

UNDERHILL, EVELYN (1875-June 15, 1941). For biographical sketch and list of works and references, see TWENTIETH CENTURY AUTHORS, 1942.

* * *

ADDITIONAL WORKS: Letters (ed. C. Underhill) 1943; Collected Papers (ed. L. Menzies) 1946; Shrines and Cities of France and Italy (ed. L. Menzies) 1949; Of the Love of God (ed. L. Barkway & L. Menzies) 1954.

ABOUT: Kepler, T. S. Journey With the Saints; Underhill, E. Letters, Collected Papers.

*UNDSET, SIGRID (May 20, 1882-June 10, 1949). For autobiographical sketch and list of earlier works and references, see TWENTIETH CENTURY AUTHORS, 1942.

* * *

Sigrid Undset died at her home in Lillehammer, Norway, after suffering a paralytic stroke, at sixty-seven.

She returned from the United States to her liberated homeland in 1945, and lived quietly in her medieval logwood house during the last years of her life. In 1947 King Haakon VII conferred upon her the Grand Cross of St. Olaf; no other woman not of royal blood had ever received this honor. During her stay in America she had received honorary degrees from Rollins College (1942) and Smith College (1943).

Fru Undset's greatest achievements were the epic novels in which she (in the words of Donald Douglas) "bodied forth the medieval world with [the] richness and fulness of indisputable genius." Both in these and in the studies of modern life there is a timelessness, a "sense which seizes on what is peculiar to one period and writes it with what is true of every period," as Louis Kronenberger noted. Charles A. Brady said that she "reconciled in art two clashing planes of human experience: the plane of serene acceptance; the plane of passionate conviction and no less passionate protest."

Although most of her work is available in excellent translations, it is interesting to note the description of her style by Alrik Gustafson, who can speak from knowledge of the original language: "Her style is simply a striking individual illustration of what Newman once happily called 'a flowing out of thought into language'; it is a style determined in every detail by Sigrid Undset's characteristic habits of mind—the sombre massiveness with which her spirit broods over the essentially sad yet not ignoble materials of human experience."

ADDITIONAL WORKS: Sigurd and His Brave Companions: A Tale of Medieval Norway, 1943; (ed.) True and Untrue, and Other Norse Tales, 1945.

ABOUT: Allen, W. G. Renaissance in the North; Columbia Dictionary of Modern European Literature; Hoehn, M. Catholic Authors, I; Van Gelder, R. Writers and Writing; Winsnes, A. H. Sigrid Undset; America July 2, 1949; Books Abroad Winter 1950; Catholic World September 1949, November 1949; London Times June 13, 1949; Mercure de France August 1949; New York Times June 11, 1949; Saturday Review of Literature June 25, 1949.

* ōōn'sĕt

*UNRUH, FRITZ VON (May 10, 1885-   ). For biographical sketch and list of earlier works and references, see TWENTIETH CENTURY AUTHORS, 1942.

* * *

Fritz Von Unruh settled in New York City during World War II and has made his permanent home in that city. When the war ended, he returned to Germany and in 1948, still weak after a serious operation, he addressed a group in Frankfurt on the one hundredth anniversary of the Frankfurt Assembly. His speech was a passionate plea to the German people to recognize and admit their common guilt in Nazism and to resist any further attempts to stifle their freedom. In that same year Unruh received the Goethe prize for his contributions to German literature. Since then he has occasionally broadcast to Germany from the United States over the Voice of America short wave stations.

In New York, with characteristic energy and vitality, Unruh threw himself into new work. He studied English, lectured, took up painting, and wrote his novel *The End Is Not Yet*, an intense and dramatic story of man's struggle for freedom. George N. Shuster called the book "the first convincing evocation of the spirit of Nazism from inside the German culture itself," and Robert Breuer, in *Books Abroad*, commented: "It is the solid and profound record of Unruh's personal experience and culminates in a fearless condemnation of totalitarian ideology in all its forms." His later novel, *The Saint*, was based on the life of Catherine of Siena.

ADDITIONAL WORKS IN ENGLISH TRANSLATION: The End Is Not Yet, 1947; The Saint, 1950.

ABOUT: Kronacher, A. Fritz von Unruh; Columbia Dictionary of Modern European Literature; Books Abroad Summer 1951, Spring 1955; Saturday Review of Literature October 30, 1948; Time May 31, 1948.

* ōōn'rōō

UNTERMEYER, JEAN (STARR) (1886-   ), American poet, writes: "I was born in Zanesville, Ohio, and educated at its public schools and the Putnam Seminary until I was a little over fifteen years old. Then I was sent to Mrs. Alexander Kohut's School on West 58th Street in New York City to prepare for college. While my childhood impressions are the ones that remain most vividly in my mind, I became aware at an early age of the constricting nature of a provincial environment. I longed, with a vast thirst, for the great ocean of life, even though I might be only a little fish, afloat or aswim in those waters. Of course, in my ignorance, it was not in the form of a minnow that I imaginatively saw myself. My first love in the arts was music. I began to study piano  when I was barely six years old. Had I had sufficient talent and time I would have preferred to be a composer above all else.

"As a child I was a voracious and undiscriminating reader, but not particularly of poetry. Yet, what I now feel was my first dedication to poetry came with the writing, at about the age of twelve, of an essay called 'Dreamers and Doers.' It was in prose, but it posed an ethical problem that has never been completely solved.

"My first poems as an adult were written in secret. Undoubtedly, they germinated in the ferment of what we now call the American Renaissance. The most representative poets of that movement were among the closest friends of my husband and myself and were often in our home for readings and discussions. My poems, hidden for more than three years, were accidentally discovered by my husband, Louis Untermeyer, who was enthusiastic about them and it was he who sent them out to magazines. My first publisher, B. W. Huebsch, now senior member of the Viking Press, but then an independent publisher, took several poems away with him, unbeknown to me, and on my birthday sent me a dummy copy of a book with several of my poems printed in it and with a letter which read, in part: 'May I have the honor of publishing your first book of poems? They will add brilliance to my candles' flame.' (His colophon was then the Menorah, or seven-branched candlestick.) This first book was called *Growing Pains*. The second was *Dreams Out of Darkness*, the third, *Steep Ascent*, the fourth *Winged Child*, the fifth *Love and Need*. *Love and Need* was really my Collected Poems in which I had reprinted all I wished to keep of the former four volumes and added twenty new poems.

"Meantime to go back: in 1924, after fifteen years of preparation, I made my debut in Vienna—and later in that year in London —as a *lieder* singer, with gratifying success. Unhappy circumstances after my return to America in 1925, after a two-year sojourn in Europe, made the continuance of my musical career a practical impossibility.

"In 1928 I translated Oscar Bie's *Schubert the Man* from the German. That was the book chosen as the official *life* for the Schubert Centenary. During the summers of 1936-37 I taught at the Writers' Conferences at Olivet College, Olivet, Mich. In the winter of 1940 I was invited to take the chair of creative literature at Olivet College. This lectureship had been founded in the name of Ford Madox Ford and he was the first to honor it. Other writers who served there, besides myself, were Sherwood Anderson and Katherine Anne Porter.

"From 1940 to 1945, the year of its publication, I worked exclusively on the translation of Hermann Broch's *The Death of Virgil* and in 1946 was asked to come to the German Club at Yale University to talk about it. This it gave me great pleasure to do.

"From 1948 through 1951 I taught and lectured at The New School, 66 West 12th Street, New York. From time to time I review books. I am a member of the Authors' League, the Poetry Society of America, and PEN.

"My marriage to Louis Untermeyer was finally and legally dissolved by divorce in 1951. We were married on January 23, 1907. Our only child, Richard Starr Untermeyer, was born in December of that year, and died in 1927, just a month after his nineteenth birthday.

"I forgot to mention above, in speaking of my education, that I did begin special work at Columbia University, but that I found the prospect of marrying Louis Untermeyer more exciting than continuing in college. No doubt that too was an education."

PRINCIPAL WORKS: Growing Pains, 1918; Dreams Out of Darkness, 1921; Steep Ascent, 1927; (tr.) Bie, O. Schubert the Man, 1928; Winged Child, 1936; Love and Need, 1940; (tr.) Broch, H. The Death of Virgil, 1945.

UNTERMEYER, LOUIS (October 1, 1885-). For biographical sketch and list of earlier works and references, see TWENTIETH CENTURY AUTHORS, 1942.

* * *

During World War II, Louis Untermeyer was an editor for the Office of War Information and the Armed Services Editions. His recent writings have been mainly reviews, articles, and prefaces to the many anthologies he edits. Allen Tate considers his famous series of *Modern American Poetry* "the best omnibus anthology of contemporary American poetry," and Horace Gregory and Marya Zaturenska point out that Untermeyer "was the first to recognize the importance of the anthology in voicing a critical survey of his chosen field."

Untermeyer lives in Brooklyn. He married Bryna Ivens, his fourth wife, in 1948. His tangled marital affairs were in the news in 1950 when Esther Antin, his former wife, asked the courts to declare her his legal wife. The courts ruled that his marriage to Jean Starr was still valid, and they were finally divorced in 1951.

ADDITIONAL WORKS: The Wonderful Adventures of Paul Bunyan: Now Retold, 1945; Makers of the Modern World, 1955. *Anthologies*—The Book of Noble Thoughts, 1946; A Treasury of Laughter, 1946; Anthology of the New England Poets, 1948; (with R. E. Shikes) Best Humor Annual 1949-1952; A Book of Living Verse, 1949; The Magic Circle, 1952.

ABOUT: Gregory, H. & Zaturenska, M. A History of American Poetry, 1900-1940; Time June 12, 1950.

UPFIELD, ARTHUR WILLIAM (September 1, 1888-) Australian novelist, writes: "I see myself in a sailor suit, playing

Austin-Murcott

with red-coated soldiers on an immense carpet patterned in light-brown and black. I play quietly because seated before the fire are three dozing Queen Victorias. Each wears a black dress, a white shawl and a white lace bonnet. I am released from the ban of silence when the grandfather clock strikes four and the starched maid brings in the afternoon tea.

"Those three ladies progressively reared me on *Alice in Wonderland, The Sky Pilot, The Pickwick Papers*. The grandmother and her two sisters passed on with the real Victoria, and the next phase in my life began when I returned to the home of my parents who were in business, and who had four other sons. This phase was influenced strongly by Nick Carter, Sexton Blake, Sherlock Holmes, Edward VII, and Uncle William, in that order.

"Uncle William was a retired butcher, of cubic proportions and rich. He was passionately interested in historical sites and relics, and on arrival, would commandeer my services as companion-guide, hire a cab by the day, and begin an Upfield tour at the Blue Post Inn, made eternally famous by *Midshipman Easy*. Between pubs we would visit the home of Charles Dickens, the museum, the bedroom at the George Hotel where Nelson last slept ashore, and the fort outside which the great Buckingham was stabbed. And so on and so forth in that very home of English

history—Portsmouth. Impinged on the background of this phase were the writings of H. G. Wells, William le Quex, and Max Pemberton.

"When I left the small and quite unimportant public school my record was top in history and geography in all tests, and bottom in every other subject. There was never the slightest variation. I hated grammar, and to this day find spelling irksome: i.e. Upfield's sample of *khaki—karkee*. When Lord Northcliffe, on being asked why he never learned shorthand, and replied: 'Why waste my time? I can hire people to write shorthand,' I was given my reply to this spelling racket.

"At the beginning of my indenture to a surveyor and estate agent, I had completed two 100,000-word 'novels.' During the apprenticeship, it was assumed that I would pass three examinations. I failed all three, but did complete a 150,000-word 'novel' detailing the subjugation of the world by the Yellow Peril.

"Thus early it was clear to my father that his money had been wasted and I never would become a surveyor. Dickens, Doyle, Dumas, Pemberton, and Uncle William had combined to produce a character for which there was no place in sedate England, and I was shipped to Australia as being the farthest country but one from England, and which even then had an efficient police force.

"For the next sixteen years my life was influenced by sheep, cattle, riding camels, war, women, gold, opals, delirium tremens, and, fortunately, Mary.

"Mary was a genuine colonial pioneer, the wife of a man who owned 60,000 acres and 10,000 sheep, etc. She drilled it into me that I was going nowhere of importance very fast, that I was industriously building a mountain of regrets, and that my salvation *might* lie in the exercise of the only talent she could observe.

"It was due to Mary that I began writing with ambition to make something of the rest of my life. I sent an article on trapping for fur to the *Wide World* magazine, and received a cheque and a commission to write a series of articles. I wrote a thriller the theme of which was a home for murderers run by a millionaire murderer. This was accepted by Hutchinson & Co., London, and the contract required three optionals. I raced to the great mining town of Broken Hill where I was drunk for a solid month and was rescued by Mary's husband and put to work by Mary on the optionals.

"There came a half-caste horse breaker who had gone to a university from high school, and who, as though inevitably, had been reclaimed by the bush. He liked James Joyce: I liked Edgar Wallace. He loved poetry: I loved brandy. His greatest attribute was patience, never more greatly exercised than with me. He taught me to read the Book of the Bush. He revealed the eternal war within himself, as example for me. He did not know, or did I, the influence he was to exert on my career as a writer.

"Now for twenty-five years I have earned my living solely with the pen. Running books is infinitely better as a gamble than running horses. Writing is easier work than riding a horse all day in the sun, or gouging for opals, and to-day I am what I am through and because of the influence of women on my life. Which is why I have never been able to portray an evil feminine character. At sixty, and with no more than five grey hairs, I look back to those famous authors, the Queen Victorias and Uncle William, my mother and Mary, and of them all the two who influence me most in this present phase of life is Partner Jessica and Detective-Inspector Napoleon Bonaparte."

* * *

Arthur Upfield's writings on Australia range from serious articles on the topography and history of the continent (in 1948 he headed a party of experts who made a 6,000-mile expedition to northern and western Australia for the Australian Geographical Society) to solid, "meaty," expertly-plotted detective stories (his hero is the half-caste Detective-Inspector Bonaparte). Upfield was born in Gosport, England, the eldest of five sons of a draper, James Oliver Upfield and Annie (Barmore) Upfield. In Australia he has had a lively and varied career, which has provided invaluable background for his writings —sheepherder, cowhand, soldier, gold miner, fur trapper. In 1935 he was appointed a Justice of the Peace. He is married, has a son, and lives in Victoria. He describes himself as follows: "Physical Features: Height 5′ 10″. Weight 150. Dark-brown hair. Hazel eyes. Crooked nose. Straight mouth. Quick in speech. *Mental Defects:.* Quick temper. Arrogance. Impatience, excepting with one subject—writing. Improvident."

PRINCIPAL WORKS: The House of Cain, 1929; The Barrkee Mystery, 1929; Beach of Atonement, 1930; Sands of Windee, 1931; A Royal Abduction, 1932; Gripped by Drought, 1932; Wings Above the Diamantina (in U.S.: Wings Above the Claypan) 1936; Winds of Evil, 1937; Mr. Jelly's Business (in U.S.: Murder Down Under) 1937; Mystery of Swordfish Reef, 1939; The Bone Is Pointed, 1938; Bushranger of the Sky (in U.S.: No Footprints in the Bush) 1939; Death of a Swagman, 1945; The Devil's Steps, 1946; An Author Bites the Dust, 1948; The Mountains Have a Secret, 1949; The Widows of Broome, 1950; The Bachelors of Broken Hill, 1951; The New Shoe, 1951; Venom House, 1952; Murder Must Wait, 1953; Death of a Lake, 1954; The Sinister Stones, 1954.

ABOUT: Current Biography 1948.

*USPENSKII, PETR DEMIANOVICH

(1878-1947), Russian author, was born in Moscow. The family's name is sometimes spelled as Ouspensky.  Both his parents were cultured people. His father was in the Survey Service, but his main hobbies were the arts and mathematics, especially the study of the fourth dimension. Uspenskii once said that certain characteristics were determined in him at the age of six through reading two of the classics of Russian literature, Lermontov's *Hero of Our Time* and Turgenev's *A Sportsman's Sketches.* As a boy he had a strong attraction toward poetry and painting, and always considered them the highest forms of art. At twelve he developed an interest in natural sciences, at thirteen an interest in dreams, which led him to a study of psychology. At sixteen he discovered Nietzsche, at eighteen he began to travel and to write, and before he was twenty he began the serious study of science. At this time, he said, he was very anarchistically inclined and made up his mind never to pass any examinations or take a degree.

Traveling to the Near East, he studied occult literature, published several books and lectured. In 1913 he went to Egypt, Ceylon, and India and did not return to Russia until after the beginning of World War I. In Moscow among a small group of people, instructed by a Caucasian Greek named George Ivanovitch Gurdjieff, Uspenskii found that philosophical system for which he had been searching in the occult literature of the East. At the time of the Russian revolution, Uspenskii decided at once to leave Russia. He lived as an exile in Constantinople, and when the war ended went to England. This was in 1921, and there he collected groups of students about him and continued to write.

Tertium Organum, translated from the Russian, was published in England in 1920 and in America in 1922. Called by its author "a key to the enigmas of the world," it ran through many editions. Introducing glimpses of the occult world into our conception of

* ōō spĕn′skĭ

life, it was based on scientific investigation and personal observation. It included such chapters as "Mathematics of the Infinite" and "The Mystery of Time and Space." *A New Model of the Universe* presented a conception of the world in which purely spiritual discoveries were placed side by side with purely materialistic-scientific ones. It dealt with subjects ranging from yoga to Einstein's relativity, with the Gospels, the study of dreams, and a new theory of a six-dimensional universe. *In Search of the Miraculous* was described by Thomas Sugrue as "a fascinating collection of conversations and ideas, with a portrait of Russia in 1917 which surely is unique," while the New York *Times* characterized it as "lengthy, repetitious . . . yet . . . fascinating and provocative." Published only a few weeks after his death, *The Strange Life of Ivan Osokin* showed Uspenskii, known for his works of philosophical speculation, turning to the novel form to expound his doctrine of temporal recurrence. "He believed that everything in life repeats," wrote Stephen Stepanchev in the New York *Herald Tribune Book Review*, "and in order to change the cycle a man must first change himself, a feat of character of which, generally speaking, he is incapable. Ouspensky clothed his determinism in what is essentially a philosophical fable. . . . But the work is not successful as fiction."

In 1923 he was described as "a very solid man of medium height, with closely cropped gray hair," and wearing very strong glasses over which he sometimes peered nearsightedly. During World War II he moved to America, but returned to England after the war ended, a sick man, and died in 1947 at Virginia Water, Surrey, England, at the age of sixty-nine. His wife survived him.

PRINCIPAL WORKS: Tertium Organum, 1920; A New Model of the Universe, 1931; The Strange Life of Ivan Osokin (novel) 1947; In Search of the Miraculous, 1949; The Psychology of Man's Possible Evolution, 1950.

ABOUT: Bragdon, C. Merely Players; Landau, R. God Is My Adventure; Uspenskii, P. In Search of the Miraculous; Walker, K. M. Venture with Ideas; Publishers' Weekly October 25, 1947; Wilson Library Bulletin December 1947.

*

USSHER, ARLAND (September 9, 1899-), Irish philosopher and critic, writes: "I grew up on my grandfather's estate of Cappagh in West Waterford, where—unlike W. B. Yeats' Sligo of half a century earlier —the Gaelic was still a spoken tongue; and the old-style story-teller, with his courtly pre-Christian sagas, could still be met with. I quickly picked up the language, to the un-

comprehending amazement of 'County neighbours'; though it was not, alas, till many years later—and when much had perished beyond recall—that I put together my two volumes of Gaelic colloquialisms. I may thus claim to have been present at the death of an old culture: an experience of some interest today, when we are likely to see the extinction of many another culture

—but, for the same reason, not to be taken too tragically.

"My parents were liberal intellectuals, who always felt themselves, unquestioningly, to be a part of the British ruling class in an enlightened era; so that an act of injustice anywhere in the world—a massacre of Armenians, a pogrom in Russia—affected them with a sense of almost personal responsibility. A cabinet minister should be spoken to about it, a committee formed, and so forth. I have inherited, I believe, their sense of responsibility without their optimism. I have always felt that, simply by being born, one has 'joined the racket' and taken on oneself the burden of the world's guilt. And as I believe neither in Heaven nor in Utopia, I see redemption and finality only in a possible esthetic view of life and history. As a philosopher, I should define the human problem in these terms: to *see* the world in order to stop it, and to stop it by seeing it.

"In my English school at Abbotsholme, Derbyshire, I learnt little; but the headmaster, Cecil Reddie, a student of German metaphysics and also of the mystics, gave a powerful prod to my intelligence. Upon leaving, I was sent to Trinity College, Dublin, and afterwards to St. John's, Cambridge; but about this time a friend happened to lend me an unpublished (now lost) work of D. H. Lawrence, and its impact on me was such as totally to preclude my working for a degree in either university. Since then I have lived on a small income in Waterford and Dublin — with intervals abroad — trying to hammer out a new *esthetic* philosophy, which should carry on the work of our great Irish thinker, George Berkeley.

"I have published (privately) two volumes of philosophical essays, which are little known. My books on more popular topics, on the other hand, have had fair success; but they are not the works which contain my more personal—or if one wish eccentric—speculations.

"Philosophy today, it seems to me, stands where the art of painting did a century ago: it has become an academy-monopoly, and has not as yet got its Impressionist movement—though I see hope in Existentialism. Philosophers (for I scarcely count the Pragmatists as such) have not yet learned that 'the Absolute is dead.' The classical philosophies, it might be suggested, set up a single Absolute Truth like a lamp-stand in a room, and tried to explain all things by its light; for us that lamp-stand is smashed, and we must rediscover the contents of our world gropingly, like a man in a dark house striking one match after another. Thus the short essay and aphorism (like the repeated spurt of a match) seem to me a better method in philosophy than the old-fashioned 'system,' and more appropriate to the 'faceted' modern way of seeing. My hope is for a revival of the essay, which at present suffers under the aspersion of belle-lettrism and literary trifling."

* * *

Arland Ussher, a Protestant Irishman living in Dublin, has written of Catholic Ireland with objectivity and detachment. His *The Face and Mind of Ireland* has been called, by Oliver St. John Gogarty, the "most fair-minded book on Ireland" that he has ever read. His insights into the literature of his countrymen are particularly fresh and profound. Horace Reynolds said of his studies of Shaw, Yeats, and Joyce: "Mr. Ussher writes with learning, wit, clarity and imagination. If at times he is capriciously personal, if occasionally he is seduced into ornament by his virtuosity in analogy, the caprice is often engaging, the ornament exciting and amusing." In addition to his literary criticism, Ussher has done a considerable amount of writing in Gaelic and has translated from the Gaelic the eighteenth-century poem *The Midnight Court*. He lives in Dublin.

PRINCIPAL WORKS: Postscript on Existentialism, and Other Essays, 1946; The Twilight of the Ideas, and Other Essays, 1948; The Face and Mind of Ireland, 1949; The Magic People: An Irishman Appraises the Jews, 1950; Three Great Irishmen: Shaw, Yeats, Joyce, 1952.

VACHELL, HORACE ANNESLEY (October 30, 1861-January 10, 1955). For biographical sketch and list of earlier works and references, see TWENTIETH CENTURY AUTHORS, 1942.

* * *

Horace Vachell died in Bath, England, at ninety-three. During his last years he lived in Dorset with his daughter and his grandchildren. Though well into his nineties, he continued to write with energy and enthusiasm. In 1954 his one-hundredth book was published. "My ninth decade," he observed in *More Notes from Methuselah*, "has been tranquil and happy." His last writings were a series of volumes of memoirs, actually rambling, anecdotal jottings. They revealed a genial, lively old man, full of mellow good humor, though they were of only slight literary significance.

ADDITIONAL WORKS: The Wheel Stood Still, 1943; Hilary Trent, 1944; Averil, 1945; Farewell Yesterday, 1946; Now Came Still Evening On (memoirs) 1946; Eve's Apples, 1947; Rebels, 1947; The Hill, 1947; Quiet Corner, 1948; Children of the Soil, 1948; Twilight Grey, 1948; Golden Slippers, 1949; In Sober Livery (memoirs) 1949; Methuselah's Diary (memoirs) 1950; More from Methuselah (memoirs) 1951; Quests: The Adventures and Misadventures of a Collector, 1954.

ABOUT: Higginson, A. H. British and American Sporting Authors; Vachell, H. Now Came Still Evening On, In Sober Livery, Methuselah's Diary, More from Methuselah; New York Times January 11, 1955.

*VALÉRY, PAUL (October 30, 1871-July 20, 1945). For biographical sketch and list of earlier works and references, see TWENTIETH CENTURY AUTHORS, 1942.

* * *

Paul Valéry died of a heart ailment, at his home in Paris, at seventy-three.

Ironically for one who sought solitude and non-attachment, and who often declared he was not a man of letters, his last twenty-five years were spent as a public figure both in national affairs and as the "official literary figure" of France. Among his activities were participation in the administration of the Mediterranean University Center at Nice, presidency of the League of Nations Committee for Intellectual Cooperation (1936), and a professorship in poetry at the Collège de France (1937-44). Following the liberation of France he presided over the Comité National des Ecrivains, which published the review *Les Lettres Françaises*.

From 1940 to 1944 Valery worked on the first two parts of a projected dramatic trilogy on the Faust theme. He left hundreds of notebooks of unpublished writing, with instructions that they were not to be consulted for fifty years.

Valéry had married Jeanne Gobillard in 1900. His son François has written a perceptive sketch of the poet in which he says, "My father was not a man of letters. . . . He dealt as a man of action with the things of the

* và lã rē'

spirit." André Gide, who remained Valéry's warm friend even though the points of view and the personalities of the two men were as far apart as possible, has told us that "Valéry 'plays' life as you play a game of chess which must be won; and as he writes his poems, placing the needed word exactly where it is needed, in the same way that you advance a pawn." His interest was always in the process rather than in the product. As Elizabeth Sewell has said, "He was always watching himself making poetry, watching his mind thinking and making a form and structure out of its thoughts."

Valéry's poetry is usually called "difficult." C. M. Bowra has noted that "he writes for the few" but that for those who can understand its subtleties his work "is representative of the age in which it was written, scientific and sceptical of transcendental hypotheses but willing to admit that in the varied pattern of life there is much that calls for wonder." Although it is as a "philosophical poet" that he will be known, according to Charles Weir, Jr., "there is no doubt that he is a great poet on any grounds, a master of metrical effects and of language, capable of expressing the most abstract themes with a restrained richness of sensuous imagery almost unrivaled in French poetry."

In the opinion of Jackson Matthews, future times will see "that the figure of Paul Valéry stands for his age, as Voltaire and Hugo stand for theirs. As hero and symbol of the mind he is of their stature."

ADDITIONAL WORKS IN ENGLISH TRANSLATION: Monsieur Teste (first published in 1925) 1947; Degas Dance Drawing, 1948; Reflections on the World Today, 1948; Selected Writings, 1950; Dance and the Soul, 1951.

ABOUT: Bowra, C. M. The Heritage of Symbolism; Columbia Dictionary of Modern European Literature; Highet, G. The Classical Tradition; Sewell, E. Paul Valéry; Suckling, N. Paul Valéry and the Civilized Mind; Valéry, P. Monsieur Teste (see note by J. Matthews); Atlantic Monthly February 1952; Books Abroad Spring 1946; French Review February 1946, January 1947; London Times July 21, 1945; New Statesman and Nation August 11, 1945; New Writing & Daylight 1946; New York Times July 21, 1945; Nineteenth Century September 1945; Poetry October 1945, August 1950; Saturday Review of Literature November 8, 1947; Sewanee Review Spring 1946; Southern Atlantic Quarterly October 1946.

*VALLE-INCLÁN, RAMÓN MARÍA DEL (October 28, 1866-January 5, 1936). For biographical sketch and list of works and references, see TWENTIETH CENTURY AUTHORS, 1942.

* * *

* vä′lyä ēng klän′

ABOUT: Balseiro, J. A. Blasco Ibáñez, Unamuno, Valle-Inclán, Baroja: Cuatro Individualistas de España; Columbia Dictionary of Modern European Literature; Jimenez, J. R. *in* Hispanic American Institute Studies (University of Miami, Fla.), no. 2, 1941.

VALLENTIN, ANTONINA (1893-). For biographical sketch and list of earlier works and references, see TWENTIETH CENTURY AUTHORS, 1942.

* * *

Antonina Vallentin lives in Paris, and from her windows has a view of the rooftops of the city across the Bois de Boulogne. Writing is for her "a habit which has become a tyranny," and she works at it with great intensity. Miss Vallentin's biographies are highly respected. Her recent subjects include the statesman Mirabeau, the painter Goya, the author H.G. Wells, and scientist Albert Einstein. In the preparation of these books she has done painstaking research. Moreover, as Albert Guérard pointed out, she has "the most essential gift of the biographer, sympathy." The most personal of her recent books is *The Drama of Albert Einstein,* for she was for many years a close friend of the Einstein family. The difficult job of presenting Einstein's personality, as well as his achievement, was done, the *New Yorker* remarked, "with dignity and good taste."

ADDITIONAL WORKS IN ENGLISH TRANSLATION: Mirabeau, 1948; This I Saw: The Life and Times of Goya, 1949; H. G. Wells: Prophet of Our Day, 1950; The Drama of Albert Einstein, 1954; El Greco, 1955.

*VALTIN, JAN (December 17, 1905-January 1, 1951), German political writer, was born Richard Julius Herman Krebs. *Out of the Night,* his autobiography, was one of the most highly publicized books of the 1940's and sold over 1,000,000 copies. Published as the anonymous autobiography of a former German secret agent of the Communist International, it was a sensational

Eliason

exposé of his activities as an agent for both the Communists and the Nazis. Many reviewers questioned the complete authenticity of the book. Valtin himself was quoted as saying that he "put into the story some things that happened to other people, not in order to make them appear my life, but as typical

* väl tăN′

of the totalitarian way." Details of Valtin's life have remained obscure. His later books, including two novels, were praised for the grim power and vividness of his style, although none of them matched the popularity of *Out of the Night*.

Physically Valtin was large and rugged-looking. His voice was described as "by turns quiet and stormy," and he was in great demand as a lecturer. He became an American citizen in 1947. At the time of his death, of pneumonia, in 1951 he was living on a farm in Maryland with his third wife and their three children.

The following sketch was written several years earlier: "I was born in the German Rhineland, Since my father was a German sea captain, the family traveled with the skipper to China, Singapore, South Seas, Dutch East Indies. At the outbreak of World War I the family was in Genoa, and when Italy declared war on Germany, we fled across Switzerland into Germany. After a childhood absence of ten years, I entered the 'Fatherland' at the age of eleven.

"I left home at the age of fifteen, immediately after the 'Peace of Versailles,' to go to sea and sailed four years on windjammers and tramp steamers. I returned again to Germany in 1923, when the country was in the throes of a wild and uncontrolled inflation. In 1923, I joined the German Communists and fought on the barricades of the Hamburg insurrection during the autumn of the year. The revolutionists were defeated and I fled the 'Fatherland' for the U.S.

"I served under the American flag in 1924 and 1925 and went to Hawaii and a number of Latin American countries. I returned to Germany, where things had quieted down, and then visited Russia. After the Russian visit I traveled to the Far East as a courier of the Communist International. In Shanghai (1926) I embarked for the United States, as a stowaway, and arrived in San Francisco. Three months later I was in San Quentin Prison, Calif., convicted for assault. This period of life formed the subject matter of my book, *Bend in the River*, published in New York in 1942.

"I was released in 1929 and returned to Germany. There Hitler and his Nazis were struggling bloodily toward power. I joined the most militant and violent anti-Hitler group, the Communist Party of Germany (1930). My travels as a revolutionist took me to France, Belgium, Holland, Russia, England, Scandinavia, and other countries, during 1931 and 1932. I was in Germany when Hitler came to power. When the Reich-stag burned and the German horror began, I went underground. In November 1933 I was arrested by the Gestapo for treason against the Hitler regime. I was sentenced to thirteen years' imprisonment in 1934. After four years spent in various concentration camps, I escaped. My wife, also imprisoned as an anti-Nazi, died. I fled to Copenhagen, where Russian secret service agents insisted that I should work for them. I refused. I had enough of politics; I thought it was time to look for a home. As a result, Nazi police hunted me as a Communist, and Russian police hunted me as a Nazi.

"In March 1938, I came to America again as a sailor aboard a British ship. I jumped ship, ill and penniless, in Norfolk, Va., and made my way to Manhattan. The next two years I worked at manual labor in New York. Again I began to write—a personal account of life under totalitarian rule. In 1940 I moved into a tent, and then into a garage in a New England wood, and there I finished my first book. I called it *Out of the Night*.

"Since 1941 it has sold a million copies in a dozen languages. It was published in Yiddish and it was published in China. It was fought over, acclaimed, attacked, and it was outlawed in Germany, Italy and Russia. Goebbels broadcast against it over Radio Berlin, and Moscow campaigned against it viciously. American Communists launched a campaign to have me deported from the U.S. to Germany and death. I lectured all over the U.S. during 1942, sold war bonds, and volunteered for the Army at the ripe old age of thirty-eight. In November 1942, through a Communist trick, I was arrested and placed on Ellis Island among captured Nazis and Japanese—and it took me six months to bring the matter to the attention of the Attorney General of the U.S., who then ordered my release.

"From 1943 to 1945 I served in the U.S. army. I fought in New Guinea and in the Philippines with the 24th Infantry Division (Leyte, Mindanao, Corregidor, etc.), and graduated from rifleman to combat reporter and several medals, among them the Bronze Star for heroism in action. While overseas, I wrote the book *Children of Yesterday*, a day-by-day account of tropical warfare. In 1946 I wrote my first novel, entitled *Castle in the Sand*.

"Other activities since the war include: winning my U.S. citizenship in 1947 after an incessant nine-year struggle, on the basis of my war record. Conducted a search all over defeated Germany for my lost son (lost in 1937, when I escaped from Germany, at which time Hitler's police seized the child, then four, as a hostage)—and found him, skinny, ragged, but in good spirits; I brought him to the U.S. for a very personal job of 're-education.'"

PRINCIPAL WORKS: Out of the Night, 1941; Bend in the River, and Other Stories, 1942; Children of Yesterday, 1946; Castle in the Sand, 1947; Wintertime, 1950.

ABOUT: Valtin, J. Out of the Night; Van Gelder, R. Writers and Writing; Current Biography 1941; New York Times January 3, 1951; Newsweek January 15, 1951; Saturday Evening Post February 3, 1951.

VAN AMMERS-KÜLLER. See AMMERS-KÜLLER

"VANCE, ETHEL." See STONE, G. Z.

VANCE, LOUIS JOSEPH (September 19, 1879-December 16, 1933). For biographical sketch and list of works and references, see TWENTIETH CENTURY AUTHORS, 1942.

*VAN DER MEERSCH, MAXENCE (1907-January 14, 1951). For biographical sketch and list of earlier works and references, see TWENTIETH CENTURY AUTHORS, 1942.

* * *

Maxence Van Der Meersch died at forty-three, at his home in Le Touquet, on the Normandy coast, where he had lived in retirement with his wife and two children for the last few years of his life.

The novel *Bodies and Souls* was called by Warren Ramsay "one of the most important and least superficially adroit novels to come out of France recently." The complexity of significant detail in his work was often admirable but occasionally overwhelming. Alfred Kazin has praised his humanist viewpoint, and says that "his best effects are gained by his gentle but meticulous descriptions of suffering." Frequent comparison has been made between his work and that of Tolstoy. Kazin points out that Tolstoy "knew that you cannot describe collective destiny without speculating about it clearly and rationally," and that the lack of this element in Van Der Meersch's work "is why his novels do not rise to the level of tragedy."

ADDITIONAL WORKS IN ENGLISH TRANSLATION: Fishers of Men, 1947; Bodies and Souls, 1948; Poor Girl, 1949; The Bellringer's Wife, 1951.

ABOUT: Van Der Meersch, M. Fishers of Men (Introduction by J. Fitzsimons); London Times June 16, 1951; New York Times June 16, 1951.

* vän dĕr märs

VAN DE WATER, FREDERIC FRANKLYN (September 30, 1890-), American novelist and miscellaneous writer, reports:

"An instinct for imitation and a monumental incomprehension of mathematics were the major forces that thrust me into the writing profession. My maternal grandmother, Mary Virginia Terhune, wrote for seventy-odd years under the pen-name of 'Marion Harland.' Her three children: Christine Terhune Herrick, Virginia Terhune Van de Water, and Albert Payson Terhune all were successful authors. Their example must have influenced me. Certainly, I inherited their inability to accomplish anything but the simplest processes of arithmetic.

"I was born in Pompton, N.J., the son of Frederic Franklyn and Virginia (Terhune) Van de Water. Though years of residence in Vermont have not eradicated native belief that my surname is indicative of foreign birth, my earliest Van de Water ancestor came to New Amsterdam almost a century before the first permanent dwelling was raised on Vermont soil.

"Public schools in New Jersey and New York City gave me my preparatory education. In 1912, when, conforming to my Terhune inheritance, I had acquired all the mathematics conditions available at New York University, Columbia providentially established its School of Journalism which required no knowledge of geometry or calculus. I was graduated from the school in 1914, worked briefly thereafter as a reporter on the New York *American* from 1915 to 1922, led a protean existence on the New York *Tribune*, serving at one time or another as reporter, special writer, night city editor, columnist and pinch-hitting now and then as literary or theatrical critic.

"Meanwhile, I had married Eleanor Gay of New York, October 4th, 1916, and our son, also Frederic Franklyn, had been born. Some ambition and more economic pressure impelled me in my spare time to edit a state police magazine and write a book that my psychiatrist-employer signed. In 1921, my own first volume was published: *Grey Riders*, a history of the New York State Police, an organization in which I still hold the rank of honorary-sergeant.

"In 1922, I left full-time employment on the *Tribune* and began a disheveled but generally rewarding career as a free lance, running a book column on the *Tribune* and later on the *Evening Post,* undertaking assignments for a number of magazines and selling to these and others on my own initiative a rather appalling number of serials, short stories, articles and verses. Possibly I am most distinguished in my profession by the fact that though I have written mysteries, novels, histories, biographies and a number of books that can be most accurately listed as essays, I am one working-author who at no time in his creative life ever has even attempted to write a play.

"Since 1934, when we left Manhattan with brief and non-recurrent regret, my wife and I have lived on a Vermont hillside farm that still shows every indication of being our permanent home. Most of my work that has been done here has concerned itself, directly or indirectly, with my adopted state. Though in the eyes of my native neighbors I continue to be 'city folks,' Vermont has been kind to us; its charity being best exemplified by the degree of Doctor of Humane Letters conferred on me by Middlebury College in 1952."

PRINCIPAL WORKS: *Fiction*—Horsemen of the Law, 1926; The Eye of Lucifer, 1927; Elmer 'n' Edwina, 1928; Hurrying Feet, 1928; Still Waters, 1929; Alibi, 1930; Havoc, 1931; Plunder, 1933; Thunder Shield, 1933; Hidden Ways, 1935; Death in the Dark, 1937; Mrs. Applegate's Affair, 1944; Fool's Errand, 1945; The Sooner to Sleep, 1946; Reluctant Rebel, 1948; Catch a Falling Star, 1949. *History*—Gray Riders, 1921; The Social Ladder (with M. Van Rensselaer) 1924; The Reluctant Republic; Vermont, 1724-1791, 1941; Lakes Champlain and George, 1946; The Captain Called It Mutiny, 1954. *Biography*—The Real McCoy, 1931; Glory Hunter: A Life of General Custer,' 1934; Rudyard Kipling's Vermont Feud, 1938. *Essays*—A Home in the Country, 1937; We're Still in the Country, 1938; Fathers Are Funny, 1939; The Circling Year, 1940; Members of the Family, 1942; In Defense of Worms, 1949. *Travel*—The Family Flivvers to Frisco, 1927.

ABOUT: Warfel, H. R. American Novelists of Today; Wilson Library Bulletin September 1945.

"VAN DINE, S. S." See WRIGHT, W.

VAN DOREN, CARL CLINTON (September 10, 1885-July 18, 1950). For biographical sketch and list of earlier works and references, see TWENTIETH CENTURY AUTHORS, 1942.

* * *

Carl Van Doren died, at sixty-four, in a Torrington, Conn., hospital, as the result of a heart attack. His second marriage had ended in divorce in 1945.

In 1948 he published an account of the drafting and ratification of the Federal Constitution (*The Great Rehearsal*) which Stringfellow Barr characterized as "in the great tradition of historical writing." His last original book, *Jane Mecom,* an account of the life of Benjamin Franklin's sister, was called by J. H. Powell "the most extraordinary he ever wrote" in craftsmanship and artistry.

Howard Moss, who called Van Doren "probably America's most popular biographer," has said: "His virtues, honesty, clarity and tolerance are rare. His vices, occasional dullness and a somewhat monotonous rhetoric, are merely, in most places, the reverse coin of his excellence." His value to American letters lay less, as Louis Kronenberger has said, "in anything permanently important he has done" than in his "having shown much good sense, much alert appreciation, much clear thinking; in having played a real part in a movement that roused and educated American readers and raised the standards of American culture."

ADDITIONAL WORKS: Mutiny in January, 1943; Carl Van Doren: Selected by Himself, 1945; American Scriptures (with C. L. Carmer) 1946; The Great Rehearsal, 1948; Jane Mecom, 1950; (ed.) Letters of Ben Franklin and Jane Mecom, 1950.

ABOUT: American Antiquity Society Proceedings October 1950; Nation July 29, 1950; New York Times July 19, 1950; Saturday Review of Literature January 17, 1948, July 29, 1950.

VAN DOREN, MARK (June 13, 1894-). For biographical sketch and list of earlier works and references, see TWENTIETH CENTURY AUTHORS, 1942.

* * *

In recent years Mark Van Doren's published work has strikingly demonstrated his extraordinary versatility. He has written poetry, fiction, criticism, and biography (as well as editing a large number of anthologies) —all of this crowded into a tightly-packed schedule of teaching and lecturing. Since 1942 he has been full professor of English at Columbia University (where he has taught since 1920), and since 1937 he has lectured at St. John's College and taken part in the administration of the college. (His *Liberal Education* was a spirited defense of the "Great Books" curriculum of St. John's.) In addition he has taken part in the activities of authors' associations, radio panels, the American Academy of Arts and Letters, and the National Book and Author War Bond Committee (during World War II). He writes, he says, "by fits and starts"—with long intervals between books; but when he begins to write, he works rapidly. He does most of his writing during summer vacations and sabbaticals on his farm in Connecticut. During the rest of the year he lives in New York City.

Van Doren's poems were described by one reviewer as "the natural and satisfying product of an always questioning, questing, curious and loving intelligence." His maturity, his warm sympathy for man and nature, and his deceptively simple style ("layered in many depths," I. L. Salomon wrote of it, "the artifice hidden, the art revealed") have reminded many of his readers of Robert Frost. His fiction is slight—evocative but lacking in strong narrative interest. His literary criticism is aimed at the general reader, not the scholar and specialist. Essentially it consists of "appreciations," rather than critical analysis. To his best critical essays he brings, Carlos Baker points out, "a warmth of epithet, a crisp precision of definition, and a luminousness of poetic insight."

ADDITIONAL WORKS: *Poetry*—The Seven Sleepers, 1944; The Country Year, 1946; The Careless Clock, 1947; New Poems, 1948; Spring Birth, 1953; Selected Poems, 1954; Mortal Summer, 1954. *Criticism and Biography*—Liberal Education, 1943; The Noble Voice, 1946; Nathaniel Hawthorne, 1949; Introduction to Poetry, 1951. *Fiction*—Tilda (novel) 1943; Short Stories, 1950; Nobody Say a Word, and Other Stories, 1953.

ABOUT: Bishop, J. P. Collected Essays; New York Herald Tribune Book Review March 15, October 11, 1953; Saturday Review of Literature April 30, 1949.

VAN DRUTEN, JOHN WILLIAM (June 1, 1901-   ). For autobiographical sketch and list of earlier works and references, see TWENTIETH CENTURY AUTHORS, 1942.

* * *

In 1953 John van Druten published a candid and "stage-wise" account of his craft in *Playwright at Work*. In the first chapter of the book, he sums up his own record as a playwright as "almost fifty-fifty in its successes and failures." Although a straight statistical list of his works would confirm this statement, the extraordinary popular success of about half these plays—from *Young Woodley* through *The Voice of the Turtle, I Remember Mama, Bell, Book and Candle,* and *I Am a Camera* (winner of the Drama Critics Award of 1952)—far outbalances the debit side of the ledger. Of all these the most successful was *The Voice of the Turtle,* produced in 1943, which George Jean Nathan described as "a comedy that for smoothness, wit, humorous understanding and all-around satisfaction has not been surpassed on the local stage for several seasons." Working with only three characters and a dramatically slight situation involving a soldier on weekend leave and the young actress in whose apartment he spends the weekend, van Druten nevertheless managed to avoid the clichés of the merely "well-made" play, and the result was genuinely sparkling, romantic, and urbane. It had a long run on Broadway starring Margaret Sullavan and Elliott Nugent, a nation-wide tour, and was later made into a motion picture.

Several of van Druten's recent plays have been adaptations of books. Most memorable are *I Remember Mama,* a warmly nostalgic portrait of life in a Norwegian-American family, based on Kathryn Forbes' sketches, *Mama's Bank Account,* and *I Am a Camera,* van Druten's dramatization of Christopher Isherwood's *Berlin Stories.* Both these plays have a definite link with the past and with reality (in both the action is projected through a writer-narrator who recalls some episodes of his past), but van Druten proved himself equally expert with sheer fantasy in *Bell, Book and Candle,* a happy if incongruous blend of modern drawing-room comedy with the theme of witchcraft.

Van Druten has directed the Broadway productions of all his own recent plays, and he directed the famous Rodgers and Hammerstein musical *The King and I.* He has also written a number of motion picture scenarios, including several adaptations of his plays for the screen. In 1944 van Druten became a naturalized American citizen. He lives on a ranch in Thermal, Calif., but regularly spends several months of each year in New York.

ADDITIONAL WORKS: *Plays* (dates of publication)—The Damask Cheek (with L. R. Morris) 1943; The Voice of the Turtle, 1944; I Remember Mama, 1945; The Mermaids Singing, 1946; The Druid Circle, 1948; Make Way for Lucia (based on novels of E. F. Benson) 1949; Bell, Book and Candle, 1951; I Am a Camera, 1952; I've Got Sixpence, 1953. *Miscellaneous*—Playwright at Work, 1953.

ABOUT: Morris, L. R. Postscript to Yesterday; van Druten, J. Playwright at Work; Current Biography 1944; New York Times Book Review January 25, 1953.

VAN DYKE, HENRY (November 10, 1852-April 10, 1933). For biographical sketch and list of works and references, see TWENTIETH CENTURY AUTHORS, 1942.

ABOUT: Jones, E. D. Royalty of the Pulpit.

VANE, SUTTON (1888-   ). For biographical sketch and list of works and references, see TWENTIETH CENTURY AUTHORS, 1942.

VAN LOAN, CHARLES EMMET (June 29, 1876-March 3, 1919). For biographical sketch and list of works and references, see TWENTIETH CENTURY AUTHORS, 1942.

VAN LOON, HENDRIK WILLEM (January 14, 1882-March 10, 1944). For autobiographical sketch and list of earlier works and references, see TWENTIETH CENTURY AUTHORS, 1942.

* * *

Hendrik Willem Van Loon died at his home in Old Greenwich, Conn., at sixty-two. He had been ill with a heart ailment for several months; his life was undoubtedly shortened by his strenuous activities during World War II in behalf of the war effort here and in support of his beleaguered homeland. These consisted of the writing of pamphlets and articles, making speeches, and the establishment of a short-wave radio station from Boston to the Netherlands, over which he broadcast as "Uncle Hank." In 1942 the exiled Queen Wilhelmina conferred on him the Order of the Netherlands Lion.

By a curious circumstance, Van Loon was married four times to three wives. In 1927 his second marriage to Helen Criswell was dissolved by divorce and he married Frances Goodrich, an actress. Within the year he was again divorced and remarried Miss Criswell.

At the time of his death he had ten writing projects in preparation. One was an autobiography, *Report to Saint Peter,* of which the completed fragment pertaining to his boyhood in the Netherlands was published posthumously.

F. Fraser Bond described the writer as a "big, lusty, generous, vital, industrious, Renaissance person." His enormously popular books (it has been estimated that more than 6,000,000 copies of his works had been sold at the time of his death) were characterized by the late William Rose Benét as "a huge enthusiastic flood of history, biography, geography, high fooling, and conversation about the arts."

ADDITIONAL WORKS: Life and Times of Simon Bolivar, 1943; Thomas Jefferson, 1943; Adventures and Escapes of Gustavus Vasa, 1945; The Story of the Bible, 1946; Report to Saint Peter, 1947; Ships and How They Sailed the Seven Seas, 1947.

ABOUT: National Cyclopedia of American Biography (1947); Van Loon, H. W. Report to Saint Peter; New York Times March 12, 1944; Publishers' Weekly December 2, 1950; Reader's Digest September 1952; Saturday Review of Literature March 18, 1944, June 15, 1946; Survey Graphic April 1944.

*VAN PAASSEN, PIERRE (1895-). For biographical sketch and list of earlier works and references, see TWENTIETH CENTURY AUTHORS, 1942.

* * *

Pierre van Paassen returned to the ministry in 1946—not of the Dutch Reformed Church into which he was born, but of the Unitarian Church. In Unitarianism he found the same freedom for which he had fought in Europe. He is not attached to any church, but preaches all over the country. The two causes for which he fights most strongly from the pulpit are still political liberalism and Zionism, believing as he does that "the pursuit of the Kingdom of God, as preached by the prophets of Israel and as exemplified by Jesus, is the road the democracies must follow if they are to survive the challenge of Communism and prove the validity of their philosophy."

ADDITIONAL WORKS: The Forgotten Ally, 1943; Earth Could Be Fair (reminiscences) 1946; The Tower of Terzel (novel) 1948; Why Jesus Died, 1949; Jerusalem Calling! 1950.

ABOUT: Van Paassen, P. Earth Could Be Fair; Time January 21, 1946, March 17, 1947.

* văn pà'sĕn

VAN TYNE, CLAUDE HALSTEAD (October 16, 1869-March 21, 1930). For biographical sketch and list of earlier works and references, see TWENTIETH CENTURY AUTHORS, 1942.

*VAN VECHTEN, CARL (June 17, 1880-). For biographical sketch and list of earlier works and references, see TWENTIETH CENTURY AUTHORS, 1942.

* * *

Carl Van Vechten has kept to his announcement, made some years ago, that he would write no more books, but he has edited two volumes of Gertrude Stein's works, for which he wrote valuable and sympathetic introductions. He now devotes most of his time to photography and to his collections of manuscripts, books, recordings, and photographs. In 1941 he gave his extensive collection of materials by and about Negroes, the James Weldon Johnson Memorial Collection, to Yale University and in the same year he founded the Carl Van Vechten Collection at the New York Public Library. In 1944 he gave a splendid musical library, the George Gershwin Memorial Collection, to Fisk University. In 1949 he made additional gifts of books and music to Fisk. George R. Schuyler wrote in *Phylon* that Van Vechten "has done

* văn vĕk'tĕn

more than any single person in this country to create the atmosphere of acceptance of the Negro."

ADDITIONAL WORKS: *Edited*—Stein, G. Selected Writings, 1946; Stein, G. Last Operas and Plays, 1949.

ABOUT: Gloster, H. M. Negro Voices in American Fiction; Jonas, K. W. Carl Van Vechten, a Bibliography; Lueders, E. Carl Van Vechten and the Twenties; Phylon, vol. 11 (1950); Time March 6, 1944.

VAN VOGT, ALFRED ELTON (April 26, 1912-   ), Canadian-American science fiction writer, reports: "I was born a Canadian.

My origin is Dutch, my great grandfather on my father's side having settled near what is now Portland, Ore., about 1860, although his family moved to the province of Manitoba in Canada. As a child I lived in the prairie province of Saskatchewan, and it was there that I first ran into the very curious assumption that the world around me was full of common people. This was never said in so many words. It was just understood that greatness or extra value as a human being existed only among the dead, or else it was an attribute of someone far away, whom one never met. I grew up feeling the full weight of my insignificance, and slowly, slowly, began to build up my ego. Receiving no help from the environment, I withdrew from it into a world of imagination which was particularly illuminated by science fiction stories which I read in the British *Chum* magazine, and later in *Amazing Stories*, when it was edited by Hugo Gernsback, its founder.

"Looking back, I would not exchange my countryside childhood for a city existence at that time but as I grew older, there was no place in the country to hide. The first feel of the big city streets filled what was then an undefinable need in me, to be swallowed up by bigness. I felt safer in the city, but presently this environment also got too close to me, and again I pulled back out of sight behind a solid phalanx of fiction—not only science fiction. From this comparatively secure environment, I began a creative writing activity based upon a certainty that I was a writer; that no one had ever thought to deny, they not understanding the enormous egotism of it. I didn't understand it either. But I knew I was a writer; other people

simply didn't have enough data to know differently, so it was taken for granted.

"I moved innocently and unhindered along this open channel, and presently at the age of twenty sold the first short story I ever completed, a confession-type story which was purchased by the *True Story* group of magazines. I sold a few more stories of this type, and then wrote some radio plays, and then some love stories, and then became a business paper representative for western Canada, and then in January 1939 grew interested again in science fiction (after an eight-year absence from the field even as a reader). I wrote and sold a science fiction novelette, *Black Destroyer*, the first of a series which a couple of years ago I revised into a novel, *The Voyage of the Space Beagle*.

"A characteristic, much-commented on in many of my stories, has been: a man who does not know who he is goes in search of himself. The question of identity is never more than partially answered. The most interesting example of such a search is *The World of Ā*, where the philosophic-logic system of General Semantics, as developed by Alfred Korzybski, is presented in story form. This book has been my bestseller, it having gone to about fifteen thousand copies to date.

"At one time, my science fiction protagonists were human mutations (outstanding example: *Slan*), but I no longer consider such physical alterations necessary, being convinced that human beings need only be freed from false assumptions in order to achieve the highest goals.

"I have published twelve books (nine novels and three collections), and have been anthologized about thirty times. I have written (in collaboration with Charles Edward Cooke, Los Angeles hypnotherapist) 'Handbook of Hypnosis for Therapy'—not yet published—and I am interested in, and a proponent of, the techniques and theory of L. Ron Hubbard as described in his dianetic books, feeling that they represent the first real breakthrough in this field since Freud.

"In 1939, I married Edna Mayne Hull, also a writer, daughter of the late J. T. Hull, Canadian newspaper editor and a wheat pool executive. Under the name of E. Mayne Hull, she has published a number of science fiction and fantasy short stories and serials, and we share a collection of fantasy stories under the title: *Out of the Unknown*.

"In my writing, I strive for a fine balance between feeling and factualness, idealism, and reality. One of these days, I hope to carry this approach into a novel of present day life.

"A few final details: I was born in Manitoba. My father is an attorney. My wife and I now live in Los Angeles (since 1944), and early in 1952 achieved the greatest prize of the twentieth century: American citizenship."

* * *

The British novelist and critic Angus Wilson considers A. E. Van Vogt perhaps the most promising of all serious science fiction writers—a view shared by many science fiction enthusiasts. Wilson writes: "He seems equally at home with all the richest themes of the genre: the mathematics and physics of space travel, the strange mutations and symbiosis of imagined life in other stellar systems, cybernetics and the robot, and the vast possibilities of extra-sensory perception. To this he adds a subtle political sense with an ardent humanistic ethic." Van Vogt's best-praised novel is *Slan,* a story of the human race's attempt to subdue another race, the "slans." Anthony Boucher called it "an exciting melodrama, a fascinating study in scientific conjecture."

PRINCIPAL WORKS: Slan, 1946; The Book of Ptath, 1947; The Weapon Makers, 1947; The World of Ã, 1948; Out of the Unknown (with E. Mayne Hull) 1948; The Voyage of the Space Beagle, 1950; The House that Stood Still, 1950; Masters of Time, and Changeling, 1950; The Weapon Shops of Isher, 1951; Away and Beyond, 1952; Destination: Universe! 1952; The Mixed Men, 1952.

ABOUT: Warfel, H. R. American Novelists of Today.

VAUGHAN, HILDA (1892-). For biographical sketch and list of earlier works and references, see TWENTIETH CENTURY AUTHORS, 1942.

* * *

Hilda Vaughan and her husband, the author Charles Morgan, spent two years in the United States in the early years of World War II. They returned to England and now make their home in London. Miss Vaughan's recent books have, like all her work, drawn upon her knowledge of and love for Wales and its people. *Pardon and Peace* was a love story distinguished for its vivid and moving portrayal of Welsh country folk. *Iron and Gold,* however, a retelling of an old Welsh legend of a marriage between a mortal and an immortal, was somewhat weakened by an excess of the haunting atmosphere of the region, suffering from what the London *Times Literary Supplement* called "the over-sweetness of the Celtic twilight without its authenticity."

ADDITIONAL WORKS: Pardon and Peace, 1943; Iron and Gold, 1948; The Candle and the Light, 1954.

ABOUT: Adam, G. F. Three Contemporary Anglo-Welsh Novelists.

VEBLEN, THORSTEIN BUNDE (July 30, 1857-August 3, 1929). For biographical sketch and list of works and references, see TWENTIETH CENTURY AUTHORS, 1942.

* * *

ABOUT: Commager, H. S. The American Mind; Daugert, S. M. The Philosophy of Thorstein Veblen; Duffus, R. L. The Innocents at Cedro; Gambo, J. S. Beyond Supply and Demand; Lerner, M. *Introduction to* The Portable Veblen (1948); Madison, C. A. Critics and Crusaders; Mencken, H. L. A Mencken Chrestomathy; Morris, L. R. Postscript to Yesterday; Riesman, D. Thorstein Veblen: A Critical Interpretation; Schneider, L. Freudian Psychology and Veblen's Social Theory. American Scholar October 1946; Antioch Review September 1947; Fortune December 1947.

VECHTEN. See VAN VECHTEN

*VEILLER, BAYARD (January 2, 1869-June 16, 1943). For biographical sketch and list of works and references, see TWENTIETH CENTURY AUTHORS, 1942.

* * *

Bayard Veiller died in Doctors' Hospital in New York City, after an illness of several months, at seventy-four. For several years before his death he had lived on his farm in Darien, Conn. He was married twice; his second wife, Martin Vale, a writer in her own right, collaborated with him on his last play, *Courtesan in Green,* written in 1942.

Burns Mantle called Veiller "one of the picturesque figures of the American theatre" who wrote some "tingling and adroit melodramas." John Mason Brown has said: "He has had fun. . . . His days have been passed fully, with zest, and excitingly. If he does not appear to have stopped often to ask himself just where the procession was going in which he has found himself, he has none the less enjoyed it and contributed to its color."

ABOUT: National Cyclopedia of American Biography (1947); New York Times June 17, 1943.

* vā yā'

*VENTURI, LIONELLO (1885-), Italian art historian and critic, writes: "Born in Modena, studied in Rome and became Ph.D., 1907. Traveled in Europe from Spain to Russia before 1914. Was appointed assistant director and then director of the galleries of Venice, Rome, and Urbino. At the beginning of 1915 he became professor of art history at Turin University. His lecturing there was not regular before 1918 because he participated in the war, was

* vän tŏŏ′rē

permanently wounded and got a silver medal of military merit. From 1918 to 1931 he built up in Turin a successful school of art  historians on the following principles. He realized that the method prevailing in teaching art history was unilateral and faulty. The erudition was very great, the progress in the knowledge of details was amazing, but the interpretation of a work of art as art was lacking everywhere. In art history, history had slowly annihilated art. To modify this condition of things he based his teaching on three principles: 1) art history must be identified with art criticism in order to harmonize the exposition of historical facts with esthetic judgment; 2) the history of ancient art must become a consciousness of actual taste, by judging the works of art of the past through the experience of the art in the making, the contemporary art; 3) the principles of art criticism must be drawn not from the last esthetic theory but from the knowledge of the whole history of esthetics and art criticism.

"While writing books and articles to support these principles, he was required, like all Italian professors, by the government of an oath of faithfulness to Fascism. He refused, was dismissed and left Italy to settle in Paris from 1932 to 1939 and in New York from 1939 to 1945. While in France he dedicated himself to the study of Cézanne and other French painters of the Impressionistic and Symbolistic periods, and generally of the nineteenth century. His attention in the painting of the twentieth century was focused on Rouault and Chagall.

"In America he was visiting professor at the Johns Hopkins University, Baltimore (1940), at the University of California, Berkeley (1941), Mexico University, Mexico City (1942) and Ecole Libre des Hautes Etudes, New School for Social Research, New York (1943-44).

"In 1945 he was recalled by the democratic government of Italy and appointed professor of history of modern art at Rome University."

* * *

Lionello Venturi's art criticism reflects a rich intellectual background and a deep devotion to his subject. The American art critic Clement Greenberg considers him "one of the few serious and informed art critics now alive." Venturi's style is graceful, almost deceptively simple, and his approach to each work of art is fresh and sympathetic. He judges, he says himself, "on a norm which is not fixed once and for all and applied to each work and to every artist, but which is derived from a reconstruction of each artistic personality." In America the best-known of his works is his two-volume history of modern art, *Modern Painters* and *Impressionists and Symbolists*. Of the latter volume Dorothy Adlow wrote in the *Christian Science Monitor*: "He has a fine perception of the temperament, the peculiar intellectual and emotional drives of the artists. He quotes critics; he quotes the artist. He can be intellectually analytical and humbly appreciative."

PRINCIPAL WORKS IN ENGLISH TRANSLATION: A History of Art Criticism, 1936; Botticelli, 1937; Art Criticism Now, 1941; Paul Cézanne's Water Colors, 1943; Marc Chagall, 1945; Painting and Painters, 1946; Modern Painters, 1947; (ed. with S. F. Kimball) Great Paintings in America, 1948; Impressionists and Symbolists, 1950; Italian Painting (with R. Skira-Venturi) 3 vols., 1950-52; Piero della Francesca, 1954.

*VERCEL, ROGER (1894-   ). For biographical sketch and list of earlier works and references, see TWENTIETH CENTURY AUTHORS, 1942.

* * *

The sea, the cold, misty, half-Celtic background of Brittany, and the dark regions of the human heart are the material of Roger Vercel's powerful novels. He writes with rich and sure knowledge of the Breton fishing villages and their strong and stern-minded people. He knows the sea and its ways well; more important, he knows (in Walter Havighurst's phrase) "the deep waters of human emotion." His novels are vigorous, economical, and emotionally restrained, sometimes even taut. They may lack the intellectual depth of the novels of Gide or Mauriac, but, as Richard Plant pointed out in the New York *Times* in 1950, they possess "the robustness and virility found in all good practitioners of French realism."

Vercel still makes his home in the quiet little town of Dinan. He is retired from teaching now and devotes his time to writing.

ADDITIONAL WORKS IN ENGLISH TRANSLATION: Madman's Memory, 1947; Northern Lights, 1948; The Eastern Fleet, 1950; Ride Out the Storm, 1953.

* věr sěl'

"VERCORS." See Bruller.

*VERGA, GIOVANNI (1840-1922), Italian novelist, master of *verismo* (realism), was born in 1840 in the Sicilian city of Catania. His family were established landowners, members of the upper bourgeoisie, and Verga was given a good education with private tutors and classes at a private institute. Besides their residence in Catania, the family had a summer home near the Southern village of Vizzini, and it was there that the Vergas fled to escape the French sacking and looting of Catania in 1848, and the horrors of the cholera plagues of 1854 and 1855.

The young Verga was excited by the patriotic fervor of the times: Italy did not emerge as a modern nation-state until after the unification of 1859-60 (which included Sicily); and Verga's paternal grandfather had been a liberal, a *carbonaro*, and a deputy to the first Sicilian parliament of 1812. This grandfather was the hero of Verga's first work, the four-volume *Carbonari della Montagna*, which endures now only as a curiosity; for at fifteen, Verga was already determined to be a writer, and at twenty, when the time came for him to attend the university and take the customary law degree, he balked and was able to persuade his father to finance, instead of a degree, the publication of this novel.

In 1865 Verga went to Florence, the cultural and, for a brief span, the political capital of Italy; moving later (1870) to Milan. For the better part of fifteen years, he lived in the north, writing fashionable and very popular *romanzi*, tales of sensual passion, of duels and intrigues, of northern gallants and their ravishing ladies, novels of "elegance and adultery," as Verga later called them. These early works (*Eva, Tigre Reale, Eros*, etc.), most of them published between 1870 and 1876, were written, not in Verga's native Sicilian, nor in the more flexible standard Italian of his later work, but in Tuscan, the language of the cultivated Florentines. *Nedda* (1874), a story about a Sicilian peasant girl is the one exception of this period, and though the fashionable critics of the time found it somewhat vulgar, later critics have marked it as the first expression of Verga's real genius.

* vär'gä

It was not until Verga turned back to Sicily and found a new subject matter in the lives of the peasants and fishermen he had known as a youth that he wrote his great works. After 1876, he began to spend more and more of his time in Sicily (though he did not give up his house in Milan until 1880): for four years he published nothing, then in 1880, *Vita dei Campi*, in 1881 his famous novel, *I Malavoglia*, and in 1883, *Novelle Rusticana*. With these books, Verga had become the great realist and the master of an Italian prose which could express the conversational style, the vivid proverbs and metaphors of the Sicilian people. (In the late 1920's, D. H. Lawrence translated *Vita dei Campi — (Cavalleria Rusticana and Other Stories)*, *Novelle Rusticana (Little Novels of Sicily)*, and a later work, *Mastro-don Gesualdo*; and in 1953 a much-needed new translation of *I Malavoglia* was published under the title *The House by the Medlar Tree*.

I Malavoglia was to be the first of a projected series of novels on different social levels, collectively entitled *I Vinti* (The Conquered or Defeated); in *I Malavoglia* the struggle is for survival, on other levels it was to be for wealth, for social position, and finally for political power and dominion; for Verga, the world as we are born into it is the implacable victor, and individuals the inevitable victims. The Malavoglia, a family of Sicilian fishermen, lose first their boat, then their house, and finally their honor. V. S. Pritchett, in an essay on Verga, says of this book: "Though it is generally described as a tragedy, it is rather a pungent, spluttering vivid picture of life."

In 1888, Verga published *Mastro-don Gesualdo*, but after that, except for a few plays based on some of his most famous stories, he wrote almost nothing. He lived in retirement at Catania, and on his eightieth birthday was honored by being made a Senator. When he died in 1922, he was given an official funeral. Although, strictly speaking, Verga is a nineteenth century author, the modernity of his writing and the current interest in his work in English translation seem to justify his inclusion in the present volume.

PRINCIPAL WORKS IN ENGLISH TRANSLATION: The House by the Medlar Tree (tr. W. D. Howells) 1890, (tr. E. Mosbacher) 1953; Cavalleria Rusticana, and Other Tales of Sicilian Peasant Life (tr. A. Streetell) 1893, (tr. D. H. Lawrence) 1928; Under the Shadow of Etna (tr. N. H. Dole) 1896; Mastro-Don Gesualdo (tr. D. H. Lawrence) 1923; Little Novels of Sicily (tr. D. H. Lawrence) 1925.

ABOUT: Bergin, T. G. Giovanni Verga; Pritchett, V. S. Books in General, The Living Novel; New Republic January 11, 1954; Time May 4, 1953.

*VERHAEREN, ÉMILE (May 21, 1855-November 27, 1916). For biographical sketch and list of works and references, see TWENTIETH CENTURY AUTHORS, 1942.

* * *

ABOUT: Columbia Dictionary of Modern European Literature; Modern Language Notes April 1947.

* vĕr hä′rĕn

VERONA, GUIDO DA (1881-1939). For biographical sketch and list of works and references, see TWENTIETH CENTURY AUTHORS, 1942.

"VESTAL, STANLEY." See CAMPBELL, W. C.

*VIDAL, GORE (October 3, 1925-   ), American novelist, writes: "I was born at the United States Military Academy, West  Point, N.Y., where my father was instructor in aeronautics. Shortly after my birth he left the army to pioneer two national airlines and to serve as Roosevelt's Director of Air Commerce. My childhood was spent in Washington, D.C., much of the time in the house of my maternal grandfather, the blind senator, T. P. Gore, a scholarly, witty man who represented Oklahoma from statehood (1907) to 1937. He had a vast library and he was read to constantly by his family and secretaries. I was pressed into service at seven, not only as reader but as guide: I would lead him onto the floor of the Senate, on one occasion barefoot, to the delight of the Capitol guards who were quite informal in the summer days of twenty years ago.

"I graduated from the Phillips Exeter Academy, New Hampshire, in 1943, enlisting that same year in the army where I served without distinction until 1946. A number of obscure convolutions turned me into a warrant officer and, as such, I was first mate aboard an army freight-supply ship in the Aleutians. While making the dreary run from Chernowski Bay to Dutch Harbor week after week, I composed, slowly, in longhand, in a gray ledger marked Accounts, *Williwaw*. I was then nineteen.

* vĕ däl′, gôr

"*Williwaw* was published after my discharge in 1946. It did not receive any dispraise which is of course a spoiling thing for a young man. The next book, rapidly written, was as well received and I found myself hailed as one of the ornaments of a brave new generation. Wisely, I left the country for Guatemala. There, in the ruins of a monastery, I composed my third and fourth books, not leaving Central America until 1947, after a nearly fatal attack of hepatitis.

"The third novel was a wicked popular novel called *The City and the Pillar*. Despite some stunning bad writing, it had a rude power and honesty which has kept it alive for some years now. I was just twenty-one when I finished it and I earnestly believed that truth without artifice would prevail. The publication of this novel fortunately relieved me of the 'spokesman for his generation' label: I could now revel, if I chose, in a wild Byronism for I was everywhere attacked as vicious, decadent, un-American, the author of the worst novel ever written.

"Somewhat bemused, I left the country again, traveling this time to Europe and North Africa. I was gone two years and I was happiest in Italy (the Vidals were a Venetian family who came to the United States in the 1860's). I wrote, read, thought; I met many strangers and some venerable men, among them Santayana and Gide. Gradually, reluctantly, I realized that the manner of my early books was not adequate to support a vision of any but the meaner sort, and I flattered myself that I had something of curious importance to communicate. Until 1948 I wrote in what I call 'the national manner': a flat, precise realism derived from Crane and Hemingway. With *The City and the Pillar* I attempted to do something of my own, and failed. Not until *A Search for the King* and *The Judgment of Paris* was the voice suddenly my own, for better or worse: I was able at last to project with it the themes which most concerned me, those elusive richer variations which cannot, one might say, be whistled.

"I have been called a war writer, a Southern writer, a decadent writer. I am, I suggest, none of these. I have led a bookish life and the influences upon me are more ancient than modern. I am not one of those who see in a recently dead writer, no matter how noble, the proud shape of a final art. I have been a student of Petronius and Apuleius, Peacock and Meredith, as well as of that grand but unpopular line which amuses itself with ideas and wit, with an irreverence for whatever 'truths and verities' are currently regnant. I detest dogma. I believe it possible, mandatory, to function without absolutes: to realize *simultaneously* that though life is human relationships, splendid in human terms, all our games, nonetheless, are essentially irrelevant in the impersonal universe. I suspect it is this double sense which I have tried most to communicate: the 'yes' at the center of the 'no.' In art one orders reality while existing in a universe whose order, if any, is inscrutable. To convey a private small vision of this large paradox is the reason for my writing, for the main work which is just beginning, or so I like to think."

* * *

Gore Vidal, the youngest of a group of novelists who came to prominence after World War II, has—as John W. Aldridge points out in *After the Lost Generation*—"already produced as large and varied a body of work as many of his contemporaries may be expected to produce comfortably in a lifetime." His first novel, *Williwaw*, a tense and controlled story of a group of Army men on a cargo ship in the Aleutian Islands, was successful primarily because, Aldridge suggests, it reflected the talents "of a very young man who has experienced a great deal and had the good sense to write only of what he knows, can clearly see, and unthinkingly understand." His later novels show greater depth and freer experimentation. They range from *The City and the Pillar*, a frank, shocking, but sympathetically handled study of homosexuality, to veiled historical allegory and myth in *A Search for the King* (the search is Blondel's, for King Richard I) and a modern-dress version of *The Judgment of Paris*.

PRINCIPAL WORKS: Williwaw, 1946; In a Yellow Wood, 1947; The City and the Pillar, 1948; The Season of Comfort, 1949; A Search for the King, 1950; Dark Green, Bright Red, 1950; The Judgment of Paris, 1952; Messiah, 1954. *As "Edgar Box"*—Death Before Bedtime, 1952.

ABOUT: Aldridge, J. W. After the Lost Generation; Wagenknecht, E. Cavalcade of the American Novel; Life June 2, 1947; Kenyon Review Autumn 1947; New York Herald Tribune Book Review October 8, 1950; New York Times Book Review January 22, 1950.

*VIÉLÉ, EGBERT LUDOVICUS (May 26, 1863-November 12, 1937). For biographical sketch and list of works and references, see TWENTIETH CENTURY AUTHORS, 1942.

* * *

ABOUT: Columbia Dictionary of Modern European Literature.

* vyā lā'

"VIÉLÉ-GRIFFIN, FRANCIS." See VIÉLÉ, E. L.

*VIERECK, GEORGE SYLVESTER (December 31, 1884-), German-born poet, novelist, and political writer, reports: "I have been called 'the stormy petrel of American literature.' I am. My life has always been stormy. At my birth, in Munich, the shot of a late reveler landed in the bed in which I was born.

"Always ahead of my time, I arrived two months before I was expected. My mother was born in San Francisco. She was my father's first cousin. Her father, Wilhelm Viereck, a contemporary of Carl Schurz, came to the U.S. in 1849, aided by my paternal grandmother, Edwina Viereck, who was said to be the 'most beautiful actress Berlin had seen in one hundred years.' Her bust in the Royal Playhouse was destroyed in World War II by precision bombers.

"I was eleven when my father, also a stormy petrel, decided to emigrate to the U.S. At one time in his career, he was a Socialist member of the German Diet. Incarcerated with Bebel, the chief of the party, for one year, he discovered that he did not believe in 'the dictatorship of the proletariat, and quit. I was astonished to find his picture and the exchange of his letters with Marx in the Marx-Engels Museum in Moscow. Engels, co-author of the *Communist Manifesto*, was a witness at the wedding of my parents in London.

"We are a literary family, breeding books like rabbits. My father, Louis Viereck, was the author of several scholarly volumes. My wife edited several educational books. Genius is hereditary in our family. My son, George Sylvester II, who fell at Anzio in defense of the U.S., published a symposium, *Before America Decides*, at Harvard. My son, Peter Viereck, historian and poet, received the Pulitzer prize for his verse.

"At the age of twelve, I wrote a theosophical essay, based, no doubt, on my reading of esoteric books. At fourteen I dashed off in a school notebook 'Eleanor, the Autobiography of a Degenerate,' in German. The book, dedicated to Emile Zola, and fortunately unpublished, now reposes in the archives of Professor Alfred Kinsey.

* vēr'ĕk

"My first little sheath of verse containing a baker's dozen of German poems, with a preface by Ludwig Lewisohn, created a stir. I was hailed as a 'wonder child.' When the distinguished playwright, Ludwig Fulda, came to U.S., he carried back with him all my German verse and persuaded Goethe's publisher, Cotta, to issue the book. That was in 1906.

"My first book of English verse, out one year later, *Nineveh and Other Poems*, created a furor. I was hailed as America's poet of passion and the liberator of American poetry from the shackles of Puritanism. A conceited brat, I decided to become an American classic. The literary supplement of the New York *Times* devoted two successive front pages to the youthful prodigy (1907). Poe, Whitman, Swinburne, Rossetti, Wilde, Lord Alfred Douglas, Heine and a now almost completely forgotten woman poet, Marie Madeleine, were my poetic progenitors.

"While I was still a college boy, my friend and advisor, James Huneker, secured a publisher for my *Game at Love and Other Plays*. These rather sophisticated dramulets were not intended for the stage. Nevertheless one of them was produced in Japan. The College of the City of New York granted me the indulgences latterly reserved only for athletes. I won my B.A. in 1906, in spite of my lamentable failure in chemistry, physics and mathematics. The president of the college, John H. Finley, procured for me a job on the editorial staff of *Current Literature*. I was associate editor of that magazine for nearly ten years. I also edited a magazine of my own, *The International*, which did spade work in introducing divers daring European authors to the American public. I was literary editor of a German-language magazine *Der Deutsche Vorkaempfer*, published by my father.

"It was always my ambition to be a living link between the country of my birth and the country of my adoption. Like two great men who gave me their confidence and their friendship, Theodore Roosevelt and Emperor Wilhelm II, I held that the future of Western civilization rested upon the cooperation of the three countries to which I owed most, the United States, England and Germany. Two World Wars thwarted my efforts and almost wrecked me.

"One week after the first World War broke out, newsstands blazoned forth my magazine, *The Fatherland*, advocating fair play for the Central Powers. It became a powerful organ of public opinion and within a few months achieved a circulation of 100,000. When the U.S. broke with Germany, it became the *American Monthly*.

"In spite of my staunch support of the American war effort, I was decried as an isolationist and a pro-German. I was boycotted by the war party. Five celebrated authors banded themselves together under the slogan, 'Never Again Viereck.' My verse was dropped from anthologies and my name from *Who's Who in America*. I was expelled from the Poetry Society of America which owed its existence largely to my efforts and from the Authors' League. I was now a poet without a license.

"My English friends, Wells, Zangwill, Chesterton, Douglas, Shaw, Le Gallienne, Frank Harris, and others remained unaffected by war hysteria. I was almost lynched but not jailed in World War I, in spite of rumors to the contrary.

"I remained in the dog house for almost ten years. It was only then that my name was restored to *Who's Who*. Much to my surprise I found myself riding on the crest of the wave. I became an interviewer de luxe for such publications as the *Saturday Evening Post*, the Hearst papers, and *Liberty*. I was advisory editor of *Liberty* for nearly ten years. With Paul Eldridge, I wrote the Wandering Jew series (1928, 1931, 1932) which proved a best seller over many years and is still being republished both in this country and in England. The German edition was burned by the Nazis in their first auto-da-fé.

"I interviewed many of my greatest contemporaries, Foch, Joffre, Hindenburg, Clemenceau, Shaw, Hauptmann, Einstein, Henry Ford, Schnitzler, Freud, Hitler, Mussolini, etc. Wilhelm II, then in exile in Doorn, became my friend. I collaborated with him on many articles published under his name throughout the world. I exploited my World War experiences in a book on propaganda, *Spreading Germs of Hate*. My friendship with Freud bore fruit both in my novels and in *My Flesh and Blood, A Lyric Autobiography with Indiscreet Annotations*. My correspondence with Wilhelm II was acquired by Harvard University. Yale has added to her collection my letters from Colonel House, and microfilms of my letters from the 'Columbus of the Unconscious' are preserved in the Freud Archives in the custody of the Library of Congress.

"World War II brewed more trouble for me. I made every attempt to keep my country, America, out of the war. The atrocity stories that were beginning to seep in, seemed to me mere repetitions of similar tales with which propaganda regaled us in World War I. I had no hesitation to act as library advisor to the German Library of Information. The world has forgotten that a great British statesman, Lloyd George, after a visit to the Fuehrer in 1936, called him 'the German George Washington.' Churchill praised him 'as a bulwark against Bolshevism.' He said in 1938 that he wished England would find a Hitler to lead her back to power if she ever were defeated in war. Is it surprising that I did not evaluate the pathological aspect of Hitler's genius? I first interviewed him in 1923 when he was still comparatively obscure, I wrote 'This man, if he lives, will make history for better or for worse.' He did both. I called him 'the overcompensation of Germany's inferiority complex.'

"Under the influence of war psychosis, I was indicted and eventually sent to prison under an obscure clause of an act of Congress that had to be rewritten after my trial to make it intelligible. After my release, G.B.S. wrote in one of his characteristic notes, 'I say, G.S.V., they have let you out after five years. You seem to have stood it with extraordinary spirit. Most martyrs are duds.' I do not claim to be a martyr. My incarceration has broadened the circle of my experience. I can well say with Terence, 'I am a man; nothing human is alien to me.' My contact with murderers, thugs, thieves, etc. on terms of complete social equality inspired my novel, *All Things Human*, published under the pen name of 'Stuart Benton' in the United States and under my own name in England. *Men Into Beasts*, recently published under my own name, candidly reflects the tensions of prison life. After my conviction I was ousted once more from *Who's Who* and most periodicals remain closed to me. Having been buried before, I calmly await my second resurrection.

"I have been discussed in many books and periodicals too numerous to cite. I figure as Forrest Quadratt in four volumes of Upton Sinclair's 'Lanny Budd' series, and as Strathcona, a decadent poet in Sinclair's *Metropolis*, published a generation ago. In T. Everett Harre's *Behold the Woman*, I am the poet Almachus. Various writers, including John Roy Carlson, author of *Under Cover*, have found me a convenient target. I figure quite innocently in *The Great Beast*, a recent biography of Aleister Crowley, who once edited *The International* for me. Professor Tansill in *Back Door to War* deals with me in a scholarly and impartial manner."

PRINCIPAL WORKS: *Poetry*—Nineveh, and Other Poems, 1907; Songs of Armageddon, 1916; My Flesh and Blood: A Lyric Autobiography with Indiscreet Annotations, 1931. *Plays*—A Game at Love, and Other Plays, 1906. *Fiction*: The House of the Vampire, 1908; All Things Human, 1949; Gloria, 1952; The Nude in the Mirror, 1949; *with P. Eldridge*—My First 2000 Years, 1928, Salome, the Wandering Jewess, 1931, The Invincible Adam, 1932, Prince Pax, 1933. *Non-Fiction*—Confessions of a Barbarian, 1910; The Viereck-Chesterton Debate, 1915; Roosevelt, A Study in Ambivalence, 1919; (as "George F. Corners") Rejuvenation, 1923; An Empress in Exile, 1928; Glimpses of the Great, 1930; Spreading Germs of Hate, 1931; The Strangest Friendship in History: Woodrow Wilson and Col. House, 1932; The Temptation of Jonathan, 1938; Seven Against Man, 1941; Men into Beasts, 1952.

ABOUT: Current Biography 1940.

VIERECK, PETER ROBERT EDWIN
(August 5, 1916-), American poet and political writer, was born in New York City, the son of George Sylvester Viereck and Margaret (Hein) Viereck. He is a fourth-generation American. The elder Viereck attracted notoriety during both World Wars for his pro-German writings, views which his son emphatically did not

Eric Stahlberg

share. After attending public schools in New York City, Peter Viereck went on to the Horace Mann School for Boys, from which he graduated in 1933. In 1937 he graduated *summa cum laude*, with a B.S. degree and a Phi Beta Kappa key, from Harvard, and he won a Henry fellowship for study at Oxford University (1937-38). He returned to Harvard for graduate work in history, receiving an M.A. in 1939 and a Ph.D. in 1942. His first book, *Metapolitics, from the Romantics to Hitler*, was published in 1941 and was hailed by Thomas Mann as a work of "profound historical and psychological insight," and described in the *Saturday Review of Literature*, as "the best account of the intellectual origins of Nazism available to the general reader."

During World War II Viereck served as a sergeant in the African and Italian campaigns. In 1945 he became an instructor in the U.S. Army University at Florence; he married Anya di Markov in Rome; they have two children.

Viereck is widely recognized as one of the leading spokesmen for the "New Conservatism." Defining conservatism as "revolt against revolt," he urges liberals and conservatives alike to combine their "halves of the truth" against the "whole lies of their enemies," Fascism and Communism, and he charges that the twentieth century liberal intellectual movement betrayed itself in failing to fight Stalinism as vigorously as it fought Hitlerism. Viereck's ideas have been described as brilliant, provocative, and paradoxical. His attack on liberal intellectuals is balanced, as even his "liberal" critics point out, by attacks on right-wing demagogues and politicians who use anti-Communism as a weapon to beat down all opposition to their views. Will Herberg, in *Commonweal*, wrote of Viereck's *Shame and Glory of the Intellectuals*: "Mr. Viereck is a poet and critic doubling as historian and social philosopher. He is therefore able to combine a scholarly control of his material and a scrupulous documentation with a really original insight and a gift of fresh, if sometimes forced, expression."

Viereck's Pulitzer prize-winning volume of verse, *Terror and Decorum*, was characterized by Selden Rodman as "so rich in experimental vigor, so full of new poetic attitudes toward civilization and its discontents, so fresh and earthy in its reanimation of the American spirit, that it seems to offer endless possibilities of development." His later poems have been less enthusiastically received. Rodman suggests that he is not a lyric poet and that his great gifts "are in the realm of the didactic, the meditative, and perhaps the pastoral." While recognizing the flashing wit of his verse, M. L. Rosenthal objects to the "endless slogans, the precious credos, the saucy banalities about poetry and this harsh world, etc., etc." Louise Bogan suggests that "much of his originality seems to be stiffening into eccentricity." Anne Fremantle observed of his collection *First Morning*: "Too many of the poems are marred by Dr. Viereck's combined will to preach and to be pert."

Peter Viereck taught at Smith College in 1947-48 and since 1948 has been professor of modern European and Russian history at Mount Holyoke College. He received a Guggenheim fellowship in 1949 and a year earlier won the Eunice Tietjens prize for poetry. In 1955 he occupied the newly-founded Chair in American poetry and civilization at the University of Florence on a Fulbright grant. In 1956 he is scheduled to hold the Elliston Chair in Poetry at the University of Cincinnati.

PRINCIPAL WORKS: *Poetry*—Terror and Decorum, 1948; Strike Through the Mask! 1950; The First Morning, 1952. *Prose*—Metapolitics, 1941; Conservatism Revisited, 1949; Shame and Glory of the Intellectuals, 1953; Dream and Responsibility, 1953.

ABOUT: Current Biography 1943; Poetry May 1954.

* * *

*VIETH VON GOLSSENAU, ARNOLD FRIEDRICH ("Ludwig Renn") (April 22, 1889-   ). For autobiographical sketch and list of earlier works and references, see TWENTIETH CENTURY AUTHORS, 1942.

* * *

"Ludwig Renn" writes from Berlin: "For two years I taught modern European history at the University of Morelia in Mexico. In 1941 I was called to Mexico City as president of the Free German Movement in Mexico. In this position I remained till the end of the Second World War. During this time I studied anthropology and archeology and wrote about my experiences as a young officer in the book *Adel im Untergang* (Aristocracy in Decay).

"In 1947 I returned to Germany and got a professorship in anthropology at the Technical University in Dresden, until I was called in 1951 to the German Academy of Fine Arts in Berlin. This was a period of intensive literary work. In 1950 my book *Morelia* was published, in 1952 *Vom alten und neuen Rumänien* (About Ancient and New Rumania). In preparation are the books 'Casto García Roza, Schicksale eines Spanischen Metallarbeiters' (Adventures of a Spanish Metal Worker); 'Krieg ohne Schlacht' (War Without Battle), a novel about the Second World War; 'Meine Kindheit und Jugend' (My Childhood and Youth), and others."

Correction: The German title of the book *Death without Battle* is *Vor Grossen Wandlungen*.

ABOUT: Columbia Dictionary of Modern European Literature.

* "The pronunciation of my name is difficult only in 'Vieth' which is pronounced like the English word *feet*."

*VILLA, JOSÉ GARCÍA (August 5, 1914-   ), American poet, writes: "Born in Manila, Philippines, of Philippine parentage.

His father was a doctor and was chief of staff for General Aguinaldo in the Philippine revolution against Spain. Villa came to the United States in 1930 and attended the University of New Mexico, from which he graduated. He did post-graduate work at Columbia University. He is now a permanent resident of the United States.

* vĭ'lä

1035

"While an undergraduate at New Mexico he wrote short stories and edited a little magazine *Clay*, which published the early work of Saroyan, Caldwell, William March, David Cornel DeJong, etc. Edward J. O'Brien, the short story critic, was his first literary encourager and reprinted several of his stories in *The Best Short Stories* annuals, dedicating the 1932 volume to Villa. Scribner's later published a collection of these stories.

"Although the short story form was his first literary interest, Villa felt later that it was not his proper métier, as he was not interested in outward events and his tendency was toward more and more concision. He therefore undertook the study of poetry seriously and from 1933 onwards he delved intensively into English and American poetry. He wrote a great deal but did not publish anything until 1942, when his book of poems *Have Come, Am Here* appeared. It received warm recognition and later Villa was awarded a Guggenheim fellowship and the $1,000 poetry award of the American Academy of Arts and Letters.

"Villa has always been interested in technical experiment and in *Have Come, Am Here* he introduced a new rhyming method which he calls 'reversed consonance.' In his next book, *Volume Two*, he introduced the 'comma poems' where the comma is employed as a modulator of line movement. Both experiments are explained in notes to be found in the books.

"Recently someone remarked to Villa that he found Villa's poetry 'abstract,' contrary to the general feeling for detail and particularity that characterizes most contemporary poetry. Villa comments: 'I realize now that this is true; I had not thought of my work in that light before. The reason for it must be that I am not at all interested in description or outward appearance, nor in the contemporary scene, but in *essence*. A single motive underlies all my work and defines my intention as a serious artist: The search for the metaphysical meaning of man's life in the Universe—the finding of man's selfhood and identity in the mystery of Creation. I use the term *metaphysical* to denote the ethic-philosophic force behind all essential living. The development and unification of the human personality I consider the highest achievement a man can do.'"

* * *

José García Villa is generally considered to be the first-ranking poet of Filipino origin writing today. Edith Sitwell has hailed him as "a poet with a great, even an astounding,

and perfectly original gift." His early poems were enthusiastically received by the critics for their freshness and "imaginative singularity." With his second volume of verse, however, and its collection of his "comma poems" and various other "typographical *jeux d'esprit*," as Louise Bogan described them in the *New Yorker*, he met with some scepticism and considerable disapproval of what David Daiches called his "mannerism and self-parody." Nevertheless, Daiches continued, "He retains the poet's eye and the poet's ear, and the best poems in this volume have the sharp colors, the cunning verbal precision, and that almost Blake-like combination of innocence and outrage which his earlier poems showed so markedly."

Villa was married in 1946 to Rosemarie Lamb, and they have two children. In 1953, on a Bollingen fellowship, he began work on "a theory of poetry." He is small, dark, delicate-featured.

PRINCIPAL WORKS: Footnote to Youth (short stories) 1933; Have Come, Am Here, 1942; Volume Two, 1949.

ABOUT: O'Brien, E. J. *Introduction to* Villa's Footnote to Youth; Pacific Spectator Summer 1952; Scholastic February 17, 1947.

VILLARD, OSWALD GARRISON
(March 13, 1872-October 1, 1949). For biographical sketch and list of earlier works and references, see TWENTIETH CENTURY AUTHORS, 1942.

* * *

Oswald Garrison Villard died at his home in New York City, following a stroke, at seventy-seven. He had been in ill health for several years.

His crusading career continued until shortly before his death; his last two works were a study of journalism ("what was once a profession but is now a business"), and a plea for free trade as a key to "a free world." The World War II years were embittered by his uncompromising pacifism; Lewis Gannett has said that Villard "walked through them armed with the consciousness of rectitude."

S. K. Ratcliffe, who called him "extraordinarily resolute, consistent and courageous," pointed out that, "despite the vigor, and rigor, of his opinions, he was a master of the difficult craft of objective reporting."

ADDITIONAL WORKS: The Disappearing Daily: Chapters in American Newspaper Evolution, 1944; (ed.) Villard, H. Early History of Transportation in Oregon, 1944; Free Trade—Free World, 1947.

ABOUT: America October 15, 1949; Journal of Negro History January 1950; Nation October 8, 1949, July 22, 1950, September 16, 1950; New Statesman and Nation October 15, 1949; New York Times October 2, 1949.

*VILLIERS, ALAN JOHN (September 23, 1903-). For autobiographical sketch and list of earlier works and references, see TWENTIETH CENTURY AUTHORS, 1942.

* * *

Alan Villiers writes: "Mr. Villiers was awarded the Portuguese Camões Prize for Literature for 1952 for his book *The Quest of the Schooner Argus*. He is a governor of the *Cutty Sark* Preservation Society, trustee of the National Maritime Museum, chairman of the Records Committee of the Society for Nautical Research and member of the Council. He is a Commander of the Portuguese Order of St. James of the Sword and holds the British Distinguished Service Cross for his work at the Normandy landings. Since the end of the war, he has commanded the sail training-ship Warspite for the Outward Bound Sea School, made a dory-fishing voyage to the Grand Banks and Greenland fishing grounds, sailed the bark Sagres.

"In 1940 he married, secondly, Nancie Wills, of Melbourne, Australia. They have two sons and a daughter and live at Oxford, England."

The voyage to the fishing grounds of Greenland and the Grand Banks referred to above was the subject of Villiers' *Quest of the Schooner Argus* which proved to be a valuable contribution to the history of primitive deep-sea fishing as well as lively reading for the arm-chair adventure enthusiast. Similarly, his *Monsoon Seas*, a "biography" of the Indian Ocean, combined impressive historical detail with a variety of colorful sea stories. Joseph Henry Jackson wrote: "Few could tell it with the vigorous sweep that Villiers gives his narratives, and fewer still have the personal knowledge to give the narrative the depth he does." His autobiography, *The Set of the Sails*, a summing up after more than three decades of sailing, is a tribute to the sea as a way of life—free, unregimented, unmechanized.

Villiers frequently visits the United States on lecture tours which he illustrates with his own color films. He is a lieutenant commander in the Royal Naval Volunteer Reserves.

ADDITIONAL WORKS: The Coral Sea, 1949; The Set of the Sails, 1949; The Quest of the Schooner Argus, 1951; Monsoon Seas, 1952; And Not to Yield, 1953; The Way of a Ship, 1953.

ABOUT: Villiers, A. The Set of the Sails; Newsweek January 10, 1949; New York Herald Tribune Book Review February 6, 1949; Time January 24, 1949.

* "The way I pronounce my name is Vill-yers, with the accent on the first syllable."

*VITTORINI, ELIO (July 23, 1908-), Italian novelist, writes: "I was born at Siracusa, Sicily. My father was a railroad employee, and we used to live most of the time in small railway stations, with grilled windows, surrounded by desert country. In one of these stations I read the very first book that ever made a deep impression on me: *Robinson Crusoe*. I didn't have much  schooling: five years of primary schools, and three years at an accountants' school. At seventeen, however, after several previous attempts, I left school, and, six months afterwards, found myself working on road building. In 1927 I helped build a bridge near Udine.

"I had also started, however, to write some stories. I sent one of these to a small review: they published it. Later, I became a steady contributor to a small Florentine magazine, *Solaria*, which was published by our cooperative financial and literary efforts. There I published almost all the short stories which later on, in 1931, were collected to form my first book, *Piccola Borghesia*.

"I was then living in Florence (since 1930), having left my work with the road company, and correcting, instead, proofs at a Florentine daily, called *La Nazione*. It was then that I got to learn English: an old typographer, who had been abroad, taught me.

"In 1934 an Italian publisher printed, translated by me, a novel by D. H. Lawrence. Soon afterwards, I fell ill, with a severe lead-intoxication, and I was forced to leave my job at the paper. However, I had discovered that I could live by doing translations, and from then on, up to 1941, I made a living by translating: Lawrence, Poe, Faulkner, Defoe, and many stories: Hemingway, Saroyan. These I used to publish in various papers and magazines, with short critical introductions. At that time, I also introduced several English and American poets to Italy: T. S. Eliot, W. H. Auden, Louis MacNeice.

"In 1936 I had started *In Sicily*: it was published, in installments, by a new Florentine magazine, *Letteratura*, which had taken the place of *Solaria*. I finished the book two years later, in the autumn of 1938. A first edition of 300 copies had good critical notices, but caused me no trouble. Then a commer-

* vēt tō rē'nē

cial publisher risked a 5,000 copies' edition: it was sold out in a month: a second one, again of 5,000, went at once: but at this stage the same papers that had praised my book in their review section, started to attack it bitterly in their front page articles. In 1942 I was summoned by cable to the headquarters of the [Fascist] Party in Milan: they threatened to throw me out of the party because I had written the book: when, at last, my turn to speak came up, I pointed out that I couldn't possibly be thrown out, since I wasn't a member of the party. Incredible as it may seem, they apologized, and let me go.

"The book went through six clandestine editions, and was translated into German (in Switzerland) and into French. Finally, in 1943, the party caught up with me, and I was arrested: from the windows of my cell I saw Milan burning after the bombardments. In September 1943 the prison commander set us all free again before the Germans walked in. But our files were not destroyed, and I had to go into hiding. The life we led during the German Occupation would deserve to be told: it had the same importance, for me, as that first reading of *Robinson Crusoe*. However, I came out of the fight for liberty without knowing how to pull a trigger.

"I didn't know when I went underground, and, as time passed, I got more and more ashamed of admitting my ignorance. In July 1945 I published my second novel *Uomini e No*, which I had written during the lulls of the 'Liberation' war. It was translated into French, German, and into other minor languages, but not into English, and not into Russian.

"At the beginning of 1947 my third book came out, *Il Sempione Strizza l'Occhio al Frejus* (*The Twilight of the Elephant*): there are a good many translations of this, too. In 1948 I published an older book, written in 1933-35: *The Red Carnation*, which has been translated into more languages than any other one of my books, except *In Sicily*. In 1949 I published what, so far, is my latest novel *Le Donne di Messina*. I am rewriting this at present [1953], and no foreign translations are therefore available."

* * *

Among the "new" Italian novelists who have come into prominence since the end of World War II, Elio Vittorini offers, in his work, "the most determined effort to estimate the Fascist experience" (Irving Howe in the *New Republic*). His best-known novel in America is *The Red Carnation*, a strangely tender story of an adolescent's love affair in Mussolini's Italy. His young hero is drawn to Fascism. "His experience," Howe writes, "becomes a mirror for the desperate emptiness and braggadocio that lay just beneath the surface of Fascism." Although *The Red Carnation* has had the deepest political interest of Vittorini's works, *In Sicily* has been praised as a more artistic novel. This simple story of a young man's brief visit to his birthplace has been called by Robert Penn Warren "a remarkable, quite beautiful and original little book." One of its most enthusiastic admirers was Ernest Hemingway who wrote a preface to the American edition. Another admirer was Stephen Spender. Many reviewers saw in it the influence of Hemingway and Steinbeck.

Vittorini lives in Milan and supplements his income from his novels by serving as an adviser to several publishing houses. He is an admirer and student of American writing and has been reported at work on a history of American literature.

PRINCIPAL WORKS IN ENGLISH TRANSLATION: In Sicily, 1949; Twilight of the Elephant, 1951; The Red Carnation, 1952.

ABOUT: Hemingway, E. *Preface to* Vittorini's In Sicily; Mercure de France January 1951; New Republic August 4, 1952; Saturday Review of Literature February 11, 1950.

---

*VIZETELLY, FRANK HORACE (April 2, 1864-December 20, 1938). For biographical sketch and list of works and references, see TWENTIETH CENTURY AUTHORS, 1942.

* vĭz ĕ tĕl′ĭ

VOLLMER, LULA (d. May 2, 1955). For autobiographical sketch and list of works and references see TWENTIETH CENTURY AUTHORS, 1942.

* * *

Lula Vollmer died at her home in Macdougal Alley, in New York's Greenwich Village. In recent years she had written short stories, published in the *Saturday Evening Post* and *Collier's*, and radio programs. In 1949 she wrote "The American Story," a radio series, for the National Association of Manufacturers.

Miss Vollmer was born in Keyser, N.C., the daughter of William Sherman and Virginia Vollmer. She was survived by two sisters.

ABOUT: New York Times May 3, 1955.

VON GOLSSENAU. See VIETH VON GOLSSENAU

*VON HAGEN, VICTOR WOLFGANG
(February 29, 1908-   ), American naturalist,
biographer, and explorer, writes: "I was born

Charles Daugherty
in St. Louis, Mo., de-
scendant of noble Ger-
man émigrés who
came to America and
St. Louis in 1844. My
father being a paper-
chemist with a paper-
mill I was brought up
in a paper-world,
which influence was
to provide me with
the stimulus for my
second expedition—a paper search in Mexico
for primitive paper-making and eventually
my most important book (*The Aztec and
Maya Papermakers*, 1943). After an education, mostly in private schools in America
and England, I was immediately torn (and
still am) between literature and science, between the active life of an explorer and the
contemplative life of a writer. I read widely
and voraciously. But my second expedition
—this time to Mexico (1931-33) at the age
of twenty-three—and my research into the
origins and technics of primitive Mexican
paper-making gave me the direction I needed
and henceforth I devoted all my explorations
and all my books and articles to the subject
of the Americas. An expedition to Ecuador
and the Galapagos Islands (1934-36) gave
me the material for my first book. *Off With
Their Heads* (1937) dealt with the head-
hunters; it was supposed to be worldly and
ironic; it apparently was neither for one
critic said of it 'There is no substitute for
good writing.'

"The need for craftsmanship in writing now
assailed me and on my fourth expedition, this
time to capture in Honduras (1937-38) the
legendary Quetzal Bird, I availed myself of
the critics' ban and did a little better on the
new books. But still I was writing panoramic
travel books with an overlay of science. So
it was that my *South America Called Them*
(1945), a biography of four famous natural-
ist-explorers of South America, opened up
the world that I wanted. I had found, at last,
the large canvas that I needed to bridge the
conflict of my own world: literature and science. Through my explorations of the Americas from Mexico to Chile I would cover all
the historical ground of the explorer-natural-
ists and I would recast their own experiences
and discoveries and so do a new history, a
different history of the Americas. This I am
now doing. Of the projected eight volumes,

* fŏn hä'gĕn

three have been published and a fourth, the
life of the American explorer-archeologist
E. G. Squier (with aid of a Guggenheim
grant), is about ready. The other four are
in various stages of completion. But I am
happily thrown off occasionally from this by
such as the intrusion of Manuela Saenz, the
fiery mistress of Simon Bolívar, of whom I
did a biography as *The Four Seasons of
Manuela;* and I am going nicely astray by
translating and editing the memoirs of J. B.
Boussingault, a now little-known but fascinating nineteenth century chemist-explorer
in South America. In the main whoever
sets foot in the Americas and represents the
zeitgeist becomes grist for my literary mill.
In the main I seem to lean toward men of
action rather than men of contemplation and
that is why I have not written the biography
of William Prescott—as I should.

"The adventure of and within the Americas; the impression that this continent left
on the myriad of travelers, explorers, scientists; the books that came out of this and
which shaped our American history (I use
America in its full continental sense), is the
fundamental animating theme of my interests
—my published books and my projected
books. I dare say it will keep me occupied
for a little while. Since I cannot yet be said
to write literature it would be a mis-use of
the term to speak of my 'literary influences';
influences however have been many: irony
from the French, seriousness from the German, stimulation from the Spanish, and as
would be natural, direction from personal
friendships. A long friendship (only through
correspondence) with George Santayana from
1930 until his death led me to a broad reading
in philosophy much helped by his suggestions; a personal friendship with Van Wyck
Brooks—in whose house I briefly lived—
brought about another change of interest and
through his urging the authoring of two books
in which there was much about the North
American scene and which forced me to read
deeply into epochs I knew only dimly.

"I am now (1953-1955) leading an expedition in Peru for the American Geographical Society in an attempt to rediscover the
Inca Highways, and that should keep me out
of publishers' circles long enough not to hear
them say 'You publish too much.' "

* * *

When not on expeditions to study archeo-
logical sites in Central and South America,
Victor Von Hagen lives in Westport, Conn.
On his current expedition studying the Inca
Highway (his reports on this trip appear
from time to time in the New York *Times*

1039

and other newspapers), he is accompanied by his wife, Silvia Hofmann-Edzard, whom he married in 1951. An earlier marriage to Christine Brown ended in divorce. They had one daughter. Carleton Beals considers Von Hagen "our best scholar and best writer in the field he has chosen." His books range from technical scientific studies to lively romantic biography like *The Four Seasons of Manuela*, and—Beals finds—"all are careful, honest books, mostly well-written and interesting. Several are brilliant and delightful."

PRINCIPAL WORKS: Off With Their Heads, 1937; Ecuador the Unknown, 1939; Quetzal Quest, 1939; Treasure of Tortoise Islands, 1940; Jungle in the Clouds, 1940; Aztec and Maya Papermakers, 1943; South America Called Them, 1945; South American Zoo, 1946; Maya Explorer, Life of John Lloyd Stephens, 1947; (ed.) Green World of the Naturalists, 1948; Frederick Catherwood, Archt., A Biography, 1950; The Four Seasons of Manuela (with C. B. Von Hagen) 1952.

ABOUT: Current Biography 1942; New Yorker January 3, 1953.

VON HEIDENSTAM. See HEIDENSTAM

VON HOFMANNSTHAL. See HOFMANNSTHAL

VON HORVATH. See HORVATH

VON KEYSERLING. See KEYSERLING

VORSE, Mrs. MARY MARVIN (HEATON). For autobiographical sketch and list of earlier works and references, see TWENTIETH CENRURY AUTHORS, 1942.

* * *

Mary Heaton Vorse lives in Provincetown where she has made her home for more than forty years. In her book *Time and the Town*, she wrote: "If Provincetown were wiped out —my house and my town gone—I would be as vulnerable as a hermit crab without its shell. Wherever I go I carry Provincetown around with me invisibly."

She has published no full-length books in recent years, but she writes on unions and labor problems for magazines (an article by her on the United Automobile Workers of America appeared in *Harper's*, July 1954); she is on the staff of the Magazine Institute, a correspondence school which teaches writing.

ADDITIONAL WORK: Time and the Town, 1942.
ABOUT: Kempton, M. Part of Our Time; New Republic July 13, 1942.

VOTO. See DE VOTO

WADDELL, HELEN JANE (May 31, 1889-). For biographical sketch and list of earlier works and references, see TWENTIETH CENTURY AUTHORS, 1942.

* * *

Helen Waddell's exquisite translations from the medieval Latin and her books on medieval life have won her an enviable reputation for sound and perceptive scholarship. In 1947 she delivered the W. P. Ker Memorial Lecture at the University of Glasgow, later published as *Poetry and the Dark Ages*. Her *Stories from Holy Writ* is a retelling of Bible stories. These had originally appeared, some thirty years earlier, in a small missionary magazine. The book showed that, in addition to her scholarly talents, Miss Waddell had the rare gift, as C. B. Mortlock pointed out in the *Spectator*, "of communicating her delight in ancient narratives to the minds and hearts of young children."

ADDITIONAL WORKS: Poetry in the Dark Ages, 1948; Stories from Holy Writ, 1949.

WADE, ARTHUR SARSFIELD. See "ROHMER, S."

*****WAGENKNECHT, EDWARD CHARLES** (March 28, 1900-), American critic, biographer, and anthologist, writes:

"I was born in Chicago and grew up on the West Side. I decided to be a writer when I first read *The Wizard of Oz;* I was about six years old at the time. Nobody greatly encouraged this insane idea until I got my fourth grade teacher, Miss Mary  Dwyer, at the Plamondon School. Miss Dwyer made me promise to send her a copy of my first book, a promise which was kept.

"When I was halfway through high school, we moved to Oak Park, where both Oak Park High School and the Oak Park Public Library became important factors in my development. I became locally 'famous' as a public speaker and graduated in 1917 as valedictorian of my class, which was also Ernest Hemingway's class.

"So far as scholarship goes, I consider myself essentially a product of the University of Chicago, in the days when John M. Manly

* wäg'ĕn ĕkt

was head of the department of English. From the University of Chicago I received both the Ph.B. and the M.A. degree. (My Ph.D. I took at the University of Washington, while I was teaching there.) The greatest single influence upon me at Chicago was that of Edith Rickert, the only person I have ever encountered whom I could honestly describe as both a great scholar and a great teacher. Besides the universities already mentioned, I have taught at Illinois Institute of Technology and at Boston University, where I have been professor of English since 1947. In 1932 I married Dorothy Arnold, of Seattle. We have three sons.

"During my high school days I became greatly interested in essays and criticism, and particularly in the work of Agnes Repplier and Samuel McChord Crothers. Dr. Crothers influenced my career when he advised me to try to break in first as a book reviewer. I followed his advice literally and was reviewing for the *Atlantic Monthly* and the *Yale Review* when I was in my early twenties. I have since reviewed for nearly all the important American book-reviewing media. Since 1944 I have been a featured reviewer for the Chicago *Sunday Tribune Magazine of Books*.

"More important than this, however, was my association with Gamaliel Bradford, through whom I acquired a 'method.' I used the Bradford 'psychography' in my books on Dickens, Mark Twain, and Jenny Lind. My preoccupation, in later years, with the history of the novel has taken me away from psychography, but I intend to return to it in a series of books in which I hope to make use of the rich literary deposits in the Boston area, relating to New England writers.

"Because I was distressed by the amount of time it took me to write the history of the English and American novel, I determined to try to keep on the market by editing anthologies. The result was that I produced fourteen of them, the most successful of which was *The Fireside Book of Christmas Stories*. I have enough ideas in mind now to keep me busy until I am a hundred, but I shall probably not be able to carry them all out.

"I have no theories about writing except that I think people should write about what they care for. I compose directly upon the typewriter, and what I can do at all, I can do at any time and under any circumstances. I would much rather write than eat. I believe that waiting upon 'inspiration' is a lazy man's excuse and that 'writers' conferences' are for people who do not want to write but prefer

to talk about writing. All my work has long roots in my own experience: I wrote about Jenny Lind, for example, because she was a family tradition from the time my grandfather heard her sing. I try to steep myself in my material; I take copious notes, but much of what finally reaches the printed page was not in my notes at all. I have never begun a book or an article with a preconceived theory, and I do not consider myself to have much control over the final end product."

PRINCIPAL WORKS: Lillian Gish: An Interpretation, 1927; Values in Literature, 1928; Geraldine Farrar: An Authorized Record of Her Career, 1929; Utopia Americana, 1929; A Guide to Bernard Shaw, 1929; The Man Charles Dickens: A Victorian Portrait, 1929; Jenny Lind, 1931; Mark Twain: The Man and His Work, 1935; Cavalcade of the English Novel, 1943; Cavalcade of the American Novel, 1952; Preface to Literature, 1954. *Editor*—The College Survey of English Literature (with others) 1942; Six Novels of the Supernatural, 1944; The Fireside Book of Christmas Stories, 1945; The Story of Jesus in the World's Literature, 1946; When I Was a Child, 1946; The Fireside Book of Ghost Stories, 1947; Abraham Lincoln: His Life, Work, and Character, 1947; The Fireside Book of Romance, 1948; A Fireside Book of Yuletide Tales, 1948; Joan of Arc: An Anthology of History and Literature, 1948; Murder by Gaslight, 1949; The Collected Tales of Walter de la Mare, 1950; An Introduction to Dickens, 1952.

WAITE, ARTHUR EDWARD (October 2, 1857-May 19, 1942). For autobiographical sketch and list of works and references, see TWENTIETH CENTURY AUTHORS, 1942.

WAKEMAN, FREDERIC (December 26, 1909-   ), American novelist, was born in Scranton, Kan., the son of Don Conklin Wakeman and Myrtle (Evans) Wakeman. His native town was twenty miles south of Topeka and "well within the orbit of the late William Allen White." Frederic Wakeman's father was a newspaperman, who later went into politics and then into government service.  After finishing high school, Frederic Wakeman spent what John Selby called "a *wanderjahr*, in the course of which he trouped with a Santa Fe telegraph gang and worked in a railway mail terminal in Kansas City." He then entered Park College in Parkville, Mo., and emerged in 1933 with a B.A. degree. In 1934 he began as an advertising copywriter, later becoming account executive for an advertising agency. When he was thirty-two years old, in 1942, he enlisted in the Navy and served as lieutenant until his medical discharge in 1943. From this experience he wrote his first novel, *Shore Leave*. Wakeman had always wanted to be a novelist. Before the war he had already begun two books, and put them aside because he could not spark them with the tempo he feels is essential to fiction writing today, if that fiction is to find and hold an audience.

In 1945 he accepted a script-writing job with M.G.M., but for reasons of health went to Cuernavaca, Mexico, taking his family with him, and remaining there until 1946. In two months he wrote *The Hucksters*, an exposé of the advertising business, which became a best-seller. "Quite a book, quite a book!" wrote the New York *Times Book Review*. "The only other novelist who could have done justice to Evan Lewelyn Evans and his soap business is Charles Dickens." Most reviewers praised the satire of the book, and almost unanimously deplored the love story. Both *The Hucksters* and his later novel *The Saxon Charm* were made into motion pictures.

Tall and brown-eyed, Wakeman has been said to have the look, eager and boyish, of a midwestern collegian, from crew cut to flashing smile. He writes rapidly, and tries to keep everything "on a level of action—an illusion like that of the theatre—no introspection, no beautiful periodic sentences." He sees his books as a succession of scenes acted out by people, and not as "messages."

In 1934 he married Margaret Keys, whom he met at college. They have two children.

PRINCIPAL WORKS: Shore Leave, 1944; The Hucksters, 1946; The Saxon Charm, 1947; The Wastrel, 1949; Mandrake Root, 1953.

ABOUT: Warfel, H. R. American Novelists of Today; Current Biography 1946; New York Times Book Review August 4, 1946, September 7, 1947.

WALEY, ARTHUR (1889-   ). For biographical sketch and list of earlier works and references, see TWENTIETH CENTURY AUTHORS, 1942.

* * *

Arthur Waley's studies and translations of Chinese literature have established him as the foremost Sinologist of his time. His work combines a felicitous style with exhaustive scholarship and is widely read in both Britain and the United States. Waley was made a Commander of the Order of the British Empire in 1952. He is a Fellow of the British Academy, an honorary Fellow of King's College, Cambridge, and has an honorary degree

from the University of Aberdeen. He lives in London and lists skiing as his favorite recreation.

ADDITIONAL WORKS: Chinese Poems (translations) 1946; The Life and Times of Po Chu-i, 1950; The Poetry and Career of Li Po, 1950; The Real Tripitaka, 1952.

WALKER, MILDRED (May 2 1905-   ), American novelist, writes: "I was born in a parsonage in Philadelphia. Since I always saw my father sitting at his desk writing his Sunday sermons, I, too, used to sit at a desk and 'write.' I grew up with the feeling that I was well acquainted with Paul and Peter and Luke, not as Biblical figures but as people, and that the Prophets of the  Old Testament were good friends of my father. The cadence and phraseology of the Bible were inextricably mixed with our daily living. We 'laid up treasures in heaven where neither moth nor rust corrupts'; we 'looked to the hills from whence cometh our help.' We 'worked for the night was coming.' There was always a sense of drama in parsonage living and the singing mystery of words.

"Perhaps because ministers' families are only transient tenants of parsonages, I gave my first loyalty to Vermont where my grandparents on both sides had been born, and where we *owned* a small house. There was a barn loft where I wrote and an old trunk, lined with an 1847 newspaper, that I filled and am still filling with unwanted manuscripts.

"After finishing Germantown High School, I graduated from Wells College in Aurora, N.Y., with an English prize that was completely counterbalanced by a law suit for writing about one of the villagers (by name), and with the intoxicating idea of writing novels.

"In 1927, as the wife of a young surgeon (Ferdinand Ripley Schemm) in a lumber town on Lake Superior, I found a new world. Here our first child was born. In the three years there, I wrote verse, short stories and several beginnings of a novel and fed them to an understanding base-burner, called the Duchess. I finally finished a novel, with an autobiographical background, of course, and sent it to ten publishers before retiring it to the trunk.

"For the next three years, while my husband was instructor in the medical school at the University of Michigan, I worked for my master's degree in English. Here our second child was born and I wrote a second novel, this time about life in that Lake Superior mill town, and called it *Fireweed*. It had the luck to win an Avery Hopwood award and find its way to publication. It did more, it gave me hope when I needed it badly.

"We 'came West' in 1933 and have been living since that time in Montana, where my husband is a cardiologist. Our third child was born here, and we have put down our roots.

"My novels have been laid in the parts of the country that I have known, Vermont, the Middle West, and Montana, but my interest has never been in writing a novel about any certain region except as it affects the characters I am writing about. Since I myself have followed the familiar folk pattern of 'going West' I am interested in the effect of that pattern on individuals now that the geographical frontier is gone and the pattern has become a symbol. I still find the idea of writing a novel intoxicating but each one seems harder work; perhaps because literary taste and self-criticism continually run ahead of capacity and realization."

* * *

Mildred Walker and her family live on a ranch a few miles from Great Falls, Mont., where her husband, Ferdinand R. Schemm, is a specialist in internal medicine. Her books have been described as "mature and intelligent." They are simple and unpretentious stories, and she frequently draws upon her own background for authentic detail and flavor. Perhaps the highest praise that has been given her is the following tribute, written by a reviewer of her *The Brewer's Big Horses* in 1940: "Miss Walker must be taken seriously not only as a 'woman novelist' or as a 'regional novelist,' but purely as a novelist." One of her most successful novels was *The Southwest Corner*. A simple story of an old Vermont woman who hires a companion, it was told with restraint but with deep feeling. A dramatization of the book ran briefly in New York in 1955 with Eva Le Gallienne in the leading role and was also performed on television.

PRINCIPAL WORKS: Fireweed, 1934; Light from Arcturus, 1935; Dr. Norton's Wife, 1938; The Brewers' Big Horses, 1940; Unless the Wind Turns, 1941; Winter Wheat, 1944; The Quarry, 1947; Medical Meeting, 1949; The Southwest Corner, 1951; The Curlew's Cry, 1955.

ABOUT: Current Biography 1947; Warfel, H. R. American Novelists of Today.

WALKLEY, ARTHUR BINGHAM (December 17, 1855-October 8, 1926). For biographical sketch and list of works and references, see TWENTIETH CENTURY AUTHORS, 1942.

WALLACE, EDGAR (December 1875-February 10, 1932). For biographical sketch and list of works and references, see TWENTIETH CENTURY AUTHORS, 1942.

* * *

ABOUT: Swinnerton, F. The Georgian Literary Scene (1910-35).

WALLAS, GRAHAM (1858-August 10, 1932). For biographical sketch and list of works and references, see TWENTIETH CENTURY AUTHORS, 1942.

* * *

ABOUT: Barnes, H. E. Introduction to the History of Sociology; Dictionary of National Biography 1931-1940.

WALLER, MARY ELLA (March 1, 1855-June 15, 1938). For biographical sketch and list of works and references, see TWENTIETH CENTURY AUTHORS, 1942.

WALLING, ROBERT ALFRED JOHN (January 11, 1869-September 4, 1949). For autobiographical sketch and list of earlier works and references, see TWENTIETH CENTURY AUTHORS, 1942.

* * *

R. A. J. Walling died, at eighty, at his home in Plymouth, England. His wife had died a year earlier. To the time of his death he continued as managing director of the *Western Independent*, a Sunday newspaper in Plymouth. His last work, published posthumously, was a history of Plymouth which the London *Times Literary Supplement* called "the best of the histories of the town, certainly the most well-written and readable."

The mystery stories by which Walling was chiefly known in this country, centering around the detective named Tolefree, have been praised by Will Cuppy for their "high, wide and handsome deducing, continuous suspense, and a solution that satisfied," as well as for their "comforting English and lifelike characters."

ADDITIONAL WORKS: Corpse by Any Other Name (in England: Doodled Asterisk) 1943; Corpse Without a Clue, 1944; Late Unlamented, 1948; The Corpse With the Missing Watch, 1949; Story of Plymouth, 1950.

ABOUT: London Times September 6, 1949; New York Times September 18, 1949.

WALMSLEY, LEO (1892-). For autobiographical sketch and list of earlier works and references, see TWENTIETH CENTURY AUTHORS, 1942.

* * *

Leo Walmsley writes from Cornwall: "I am at present engaged on a sequel to my autobiographical novel *Love in the Sun,* to be called 'The Golden Waterwheel,' and I am now actually living in the wooden ex-Kaiser's war army hut described in *Love in the Sun,* not more than three miles away from the mansion of Daphne du Maurier's Menabilly, and Daphne and her husband and family are still among our closest friends."

Leo Walmsley's varied interests—marine biology, flying, traveling, movie making—and his warm and friendly personality were well represented in his autobiography, *Turn of the Tide.* In his writings there is always reflected the close and enthusiastic observation of all living things that is so characteristic of the biologist. A reviewer in the London *Times Literary Supplement* describes this quality as "the eye that does not demand magnitude for primary stimulation and is rewarded by the significance underlying everyday happenings and by 'the thrilling sequence of action in small creatures.'"

During the World War II, Walmsley served with the Royal Flying Corps in East Africa. In 1946 he dramatized his novel *Sally Lunn* for production by the Arts Council.

ADDITIONAL WORKS: British Ports and Harbours, 1942; Turn of the Tide (in England: So Many Loves) 1944; Master Mariner, 1948; Invisible Cargo, 1952.

ABOUT: Walmsley, L. Turn of the Tide.

*WALN, NORA (June 4, 1895-). For biographical sketch and list of works and references, see TWENTIETH CENTURY AUTHORS, 1942.

* * *

Nora Waln has published no books in recent years, but she has been busy traveling and writing for the magazines. She has lived, since the end of World War II, in China, Japan, and Europe. In 1945 she became European correspondent for the *Atlantic Monthly* and made extended trips to Austria, Hungary, and Czechoslovakia. In 1946 she returned to the United States for her first extended stay in this country for more than two decades. At this time she published, in the *Atlantic,* a

* wôl

chapter from a book-in-progress on the Quaker Rufus Jones. She was soon traveling again, however. As correspondent for the *Saturday Evening Post,* she was attached to General MacArthur's headquarters in the Far East from 1947 to 1951, spending six months on the Korean battlefields. She is currently a European correspondent for the *Atlantic Monthly.* Her permanent home is in Buckinghamshire, England, and her recreations are cooking, riding, and flying.

ABOUT: Atlantic Monthly June 1947.

WALPOLE, Sir HUGH (1884-June 1, 1941). For biographical sketch and list of works and references, see TWENTIETH CENTURY AUTHORS, 1942.

* * *

Correction: TWENTIETH CENTURY AUTHORS, 1942 incorrectly stated that Walpole was educated at Oxford University. He attended Cambridge.

ADDITIONAL WORKS: Katherine Christian, 1943; Mr. Huffam, and Other Stories, 1948.

ABOUT: Hart-Davis, R. Hugh Walpole; Swinnerton, F. The Georgian Literary Scene (1910-35); Time August 18, 1952; Twentieth Century May 1952.

WALSH, MAURICE (May 2, 1879-). For autobiographical sketch and list of earlier works and references, see TWENTIETH CENTURY AUTHORS, 1942.

* * *

Maurice Walsh writes: "I still live on the foothills of the Dublin Mountains within sight of the sea, and only two bombing planes came over. My red-hared wife died in 1941, God rest her. I now live in a small cottage with a grandson and a housekeeper to look after me. The number of my grandchildren has risen now to a dozen; ten of them live not far away, and pocket money reaches quite an appreciable sum every Saturday."

Orville Prescott has said, "If you never enjoyed Buchan, Stevenson, or Dumas, you probably won't care for Walsh." As Prescott has suggested, it is primarily in the art of the romancer, the spinner of tales, that Walsh excels. Whether he writes a straight detective novel or the charming dialect stories of his native Ireland, his technique is sure and his humor is rich. A reviewer for the New York *Times* wrote in 1951: "It would seem that neither time nor wars nor gloomy forebodings can subdue the romantic spirit of Maurice

Walsh." His short story "The Quiet Man" was made into one of the most successful films of 1952.

ADDITIONAL WORKS: The Spanish Lady, 1943; Nine Strings to Your Bow (in England: The Man in Brown) 1945; Damsel Debonaire (in England: Castle Gillian) 1948; Trouble in the Glen, 1950; Son of a Tinker (short stories) 1952; Take Your Choice (short stories) 1954.

ABOUT: Hoehn, M. (ed.) Catholic Authors, I.

*WALTARI, MIKA TOIMI (September 19, 1908-   ), Finnish novelist, writes: "I was born in Helsinki. My father was a clergyman  and idealist: among the offices he held was that of prison chaplain in Helsinki. He died early, when I was five. We were poor at home. My mother brought up and schooled her three sons on her small pay as civil service clerk. The most deeply stamped memories I retain from my childhood are of the first World War, the Finnish civil war of 1918 and the ensuing famine.

"I passed the university matriculation examination in 1926 and first studied theology. However, my literary career had started the same year I entered school and in 1929 I passed the candidate of philosophy (Master of Arts) examination. My first literary efforts were poems and a collection of stories, published when I was seventeen.

"After that I traveled for a while, studied in Paris, worked in a publishing company, translated books, reviewed books, edited an illustrated weekly and even wrote some movie scenarios. All that time I kept publishing one or two books a year, novels, short stories, plays and some poetry. My greatest artistic success before the wars was due to my novel *Vieras mies tuli taloon (A Stranger Came to the Farm)* which won a first prize in a competition in 1937 and afterwards was translated into eleven European languages. In October 1952 it appeared also in the United States. In 1938 I started living entirely by my pen, but during the Finnish Winter War (1939-40) and in the following war of 1941-44 I was doing military service at the governmental information center. After the wars I lived wholly aside from public life and engaged myself in historical research. My principal work so far, *The Egyptian*, was written in 1945 and published in the United States in 1949. It has also been translated

* väl'tä ri

into ten languages (Swedish, Norwegian, Danish, German, French, English, Spanish, Dutch, Japanese, Portuguese, and Italian). In a certain sense I consider this novel as the sum of my literary efforts and experiences. The research work for it took more than ten years.

"I have knocked about in most of the countries of Europe. The cities dearest to me are Helsinki, Paris, and Istanbul. Spiritually I feel a European as much as a Finn. I am happiest when allowed to work in peace. I have separated myself from all social intercourse. In wintertime I live in Helsinki or travel. The summers I spend in the country writing.

"Of my family I may mention that I married at twenty-two, which was the most sensible act of my life. In addition to my wife our family consists of one daughter, who recently passed her matriculation examination and published her first novel *Cafe Mabillon*, and one dachshund. I like small dogs, show people, and the modern art of painting.

"That would be my life in a few words: I am neither a preacher nor a fighter by nature. But if there is any program or tendency to be found between the lines in the books I write nowadays, it is: individual liberty, humaneness, tolerance."

*   *   *

Mika Waltari first became interested in ancient Egypt during the 1930's when he wrote a drama about the Pharaoh Akhnaton which was performed at the National Theatre in Helsinki in 1938. His novel *Sinuhe, Egyptiläinen* was published in Finland in 1945. Four years later an English translation of it was published in the United States as *The Egyptian*. It was an instant success, a best seller, and a Book-of-the-Month Club choice. In 1954 an elaborate Cinemascope film version of it was released. The novel was especially remarkable for its vast historical detail (it was abbreviated by about one-third in its translation). Though much of this detail was lurid and sensational, the book remained (wrote Gladys Schmitt in the New York *Times*) "an earnest attempt to tell an honest story—successful at least in that it brings a dead age to life again."

PRINCIPAL WORKS IN ENGLISH TRANSLATION: The Egyptian, 1949; The Adventurer (in England: Michael the Finn) 1950; The Wanderer, 1951; A Stranger Came to the Farm, 1952; Moonscape (stories) 1954; A Nail Merchant at Nightfall, 1955.

ABOUT: Current Biography 1950; New York Herald Tribune Book Review October 8, 1950; Newsweek September 25, 1950; Saturday Review of Literature August 20, 1949.

WARBURG, JAMES PAUL (August 18, 1896-   ), American publicist, writes: "Although being the seventh generation in a family of bankers and, therefore, predestined to that career, I have wanted to be a writer ever since I can remember.

Raymond K. Martin

"The Warburgs lived in Hamburg, Germany, ever since they moved to that Hanseatic city from the little Westphalian town of Warburg, some time in the sixteenth century. My mother was a native New Yorker and I have always held it against her that she allowed me to be born in Germany before she persuaded my father to move to this country and become an American citizen.

"However, the transatlantic nature of my early childhood had certain advantages, such as growing up multilingually and establishing a feeling of world citizenship at an early age. It also had the disadvantage of going to school here but spending every summer vacation until I was seventeen in Europe. These annual family migrations were due to my father's maintenance of his European business affiliations, especially with the century-old family firm of M. M. Warburg & Co., until 1914, when he was appointed to the first Federal Reserve Board by President Wilson.

"After the war, in which I served as a naval aviator, I entered the banking business and this, again, caused me to make at least one trip a year to Europe, until after my father's death in 1932, I made up my mind to leave the banking profession. The immediate cause of the break was my being drafted by President Roosevelt as one of his financial advisers during the early part of the New Deal. This did not last long, because, while in basic sympathy with the New Deal, I became an outspoken critic of the Roosevelt monetary policies.

"From 1935 to the present—except for service during World War II—I have been a student of international affairs. During World War II, I had charge of American propaganda policy in the European Theatre.

"The first writing venture that I can remember was an essay on Lincoln, written when I was attending grammar school in New York. This effort won some sort of minor prize in a New York *Times* competition. At Middlesex School, in Concord, Mass., I became editor of the *Anvil* and at Harvard I was one of the editors of the *Crimson*. My

one and only scientific piece was published during World War I by the U.S. Navy. This, a dissertation on compass navigation, resulted from my more or less accidentally inventing a new type of compass for use in aircraft.

"During my fifteen years as banker, I wrote a number of books and pamphlets dealing with financial matters and industry. I also wrote verse, some of which was published in magazines and in two slender volumes. Writing poetry has been a lifelong avocation. During the same period I wrote some extremely bad plays, none of which ever saw the light of day, but as a lyric-writer for popular songs I did achieve a modest success. A few of my lyrics still occasionally haunt me on the radio, particularly one very uninspired song, called 'Fine and Dandy.'

"My recent life has been devoted almost entirely to international affairs. I have worked as a free-lance reporter and commentator, with a large part of each year spent in informing myself abroad and writing and lecturing at home. My work has been mostly of a pamphleteering nature, directed toward the development of a more creative American foreign policy.

"Although much more in sympathy with the post-war Democratic administrations than with the Republican opposition, a long series of books and pamphlets, as well as magazine articles, have expressed a growing dissent from a foreign policy which has seemed to me too negatively preoccupied with Russia, too unimaginative and too inflexible. I have been particularly concerned with our policy as to Germany, which has seemed to me a tragic series of blunders.

"Wherever I have expressed criticism, I have tried to present concrete alternatives which seemed to me more likely to lead to enduring peace. I have frequently been called an idealist and accused of making impractical suggestions. This has not troubled me, because I believe that, in the world of today, foreign policy must concern itself with *what should be* as well as with *what is*.

"Almost all of my books have been most generously reviewed here and abroad. Some of them have been translated into foreign languages. A few have achieved the best-seller lists, but only one—in my opinion, the worst book I have written—reached well into six-figure sales.

"I do not feel that my work has had any impact whatever upon American foreign policy, though it may, in a modest way, have prepared the soil of public opinion for a more enlightened and world-minded policy in the future."

* * *

Since the end of World War II, James P. Warburg has traveled extensively in Western Germany, and his writings on the problems of German reconstruction are recognized as authoritative and hard-hitting. Warburg has homes in New York City and in Greenwich, Conn. He has three daughters by his first wife, Katharine Fuller Swift, whom he married in 1918. They were divorced in 1934 and in 1935 he married Phyllis Baldwin Broome. This marriage ended in divorce and in 1948 he married Joan Melber, by whom he has a son and a daughter. Warburg continues active in his many business and financial interests. He is a director of the Bank of The Manhattan Company, the Bydale Company, the Fontenay Corporation, and the Polaroid Corporation. He is also a trustee of the Juilliard School of Music and a director of the New York Philharmonic Society. His recreations are tennis, trout fishing, and painting.

PRINCIPAL WORKS: Acceptance Financing, 1921; Three Textile Raw Materials, 1923; The Money Muddle, 1934; It's Up to Us, 1934; Hell Bent for Election, 1935; Still Hell Bent, 1936; Peace in Our Time? 1939; The Isolationist Illusion, 1940; Our War and Our Peace, 1941; Foreign Policy Begins at Home, 1944; Unwritten Treaty, 1945; Germany —Bridge or Battleground, 1947; Put Yourself in Marshall's Place, 1948; Last Call for Common Sense, 1949; Faith, Purpose, and Power, 1950; Victory without War, 1951; How to Co-Exist without Playing the Kremlin's Game, 1952; Germany: Key to Peace, 1953; The United States in a Changing World, 1954. Poetry—And Then What? 1931; Shoes and Ships and Sealing Wax, 1932; Man's Enemy and Man, 1942.

ABOUT: Current Biography 1948.

WARD, BARBARA (May 23, 1914-), English journalist and writer on international affairs, was born in York, England, the eldest

daughter of Walter Ward and Teresa Mary (Burge) Ward, but was brought up in the seaside town of Felixstowe, near Ipswich, where her father practiced as a solicitor. He is said to have "inclined" toward the Quaker creed; his wife, however, was a

Dorothy Wilding

devout Roman Catholic, and their children were brought up in the mother's faith. Barbara Ward accordingly received her early education at the neighboring Convent of Jesus and Mary, Felixstowe. At the age of fourteen she wrote a two-hundred-thousand-

word novel "about two wonderful countesses of seventeenth century France." ("I have a horrible facility with words," she comments.) At fifteen she was sent to Paris for two years of study at the Lycée Molière and at the Sorbonne, and at seventeen to Germany for a year at a college in Jugenheim. In 1932, when she was eighteen, she entered Somerville College, Oxford, as an exhibitioner, and three years later took a "first" in "Modern Greats," the equivalent of a summa cum laude Bachelor's degree in politics, philosophy, and economics. Gifted with a "pleasant soprano voice," Miss Ward at first looked forward to a musical career, and at Somerville was a member of the operatic society and of a madrigals group, as well as secretary of the dramatic society; she was also considered a good fencer and rider.

When she left Oxford she accepted a postgraduate Vernon Harcourt scholarship enabling her to study abroad for three summers, while giving university extension lectures during the winters to workers' groups. In 1938 her first book appeared, a brief study of the colonial question entitled The International Share-Out. In 1939 she joined the staff of the weekly The Economist, becoming foreign editor in 1940. In this same year Miss Ward became an enthusiastic crusader for the Sword of the Spirit movement initiated by the late Cardinal J. H. Hinsley, the aim of which she has defined as "to remind English Catholics of the fifth precept of Pope Pius' encyclical which inveighed against the division of the world into have and have-not nations."

A governor of B.B.C. from 1946 to 1950, Miss Ward was known to millions for her broadcasts on "Brains Trust," the British counterpart of "Information Please." Both as a speaker, and as the author of numerous articles and books, she is distinguished by the clarity with which she can make complex issues intelligible to the general public. To Americans she is known as a lecturer not only on economic topics but on the role of Catholicism in the modern world.

In 1950 she married Robert G. A. Jackson, an economist, formerly an Assistant Secretary General of the United Nations. After a recent journey to her husband's native Australia, she went with him to the Gold Coast of Africa, where they are now living. Barbara Ward is of medium height, pretty, disarmingly modest in demeanor, and a gay and widely informed conversationalist. She writes fast, drafting articles in pencil, because she cannot type or dictate. She has a host of friends, mostly politicians, diplomats, scientists, and intellectuals.

PRINCIPAL WORKS: The International Share-Out, 1938; (with others) Hitler's Route to Bagdad, 1939; Russian Foreign Policy, 1940; Italian Foreign Policy, 1941; (with others) A Christian Basis for the Post-War World, 1942; Turkey, 1942; The West at Bay, 1948; Policy for the West, 1951; Faith and Freedom, 1954.

ABOUT: Hoehn, M. (ed.) Catholic Authors, I; Current Biography 1950; Newsweek April 7, 1947; Saturday Review November 20, 1954; Time May 19, 1947.

WARD, MARY AUGUSTA (ARNOLD) (Mrs. HUMPHREY WARD) (June 11, 1851-March 24, 1920). For biographical sketch and list of works and references, see TWENTIETH CENTURY AUTHORS, 1942.

* * *

ABOUT: Dictionary of Australian Biography; Mott, F. L. Golden Multitudes; New Statesman and Nation August 23, 1947; Spectator June 8, 1951.

WARD, MARY JANE (August 27, 1905-), American novelist, writes: "I was born in Fairmount, Ind. My parents, Marion Lockridge and Claude Arthur Ward, brought my sister and me to Evanston, Ill., in 1915. After graduating from the Evanston High School, I attended Northwestern University for two years. Then I studied art and worked briefly at a variety of jobs. I took piano lessons for some ten years and although I can't play now as I did in my early teens when I won a year's scholarship at a Chicago conservatory, I find playing the piano a pleasant relaxation.

"In 1928 I married Edward Quayle, a statistician whose avocation is painting. Except for a period of four years divided between New York City and a farm forty miles west of Chicago, our headquarters have been in Evanston.

"I didn't settle down to serious writing until after my marriage. I've had a dozen short stories and articles published, have done book reviews and a little reporting of lectures and musical events, but my chief interest is in the field of the novel.

"*The Snake Pit* was a dual selection of the Book-of-the-Month Club for April 1946, and it has had sixteen foreign translations. The motion picture based on this novel received the Robert Meltzer and the Screen Writers Guild

awards for 1948. In 1949, I received an Achievement Award from the Women's National Press Club, 'for outstanding accomplishment in Mental Health.'

"I am a member of the Unitarian church, the Society of Midland Authors, the National Association for Mental Health and the Illinois Society for Mental Health. Recently I have been doing some speaking for groups especially interested in mental illness problems.

"I keep to a fairly regular writing schedule but whenever there's a chance, we go fishing."

* * *

The Snake Pit was Mary Jane Ward's third published novel (the fourth she had written). Her early career had been a struggle all the way. In 1941 she suffered a nervous breakdown and spent nine months in a mental hospital. It was this experience which provided the background for her extraordinary novel *The Snake Pit*, a poignant, quietly told but deeply revealing picture of life in a mental hospital. Her later novels, though not matching the great popularity of *The Snake Pit*, have been well received by the critics and the public alike; and she has been especially admired for what Pamela Taylor, in the *Saturday Review*, describes as her "sensitive and compassionate insight into feminine psychology." Miss Ward is slender and soft-spoken. She has dark auburn hair and, according to a friend's description, "the quickest, most oddly penetrating, yet friendly brown eyes in the world."

PRINCIPAL WORKS: The Tree Has Roots, 1937; The Wax Apple, 1938; The Snake Pit, 1946; The Professor's Umbrella, 1948; A Little Night Music, 1951; It's Different for a Woman, 1952.

ABOUT: Warfel, H. R. American Novelists of Today; Current Biography 1946; New York Times Book Review April 14, 1946.

WARD, WILFRID PHILIP (January 2, 1856-April 9, 1916). For biographical sketch and list of works and references, see TWENTIETH CENTURY AUTHORS, 1942.

* * *

ABOUT: Neill, T. P. They Lived the Faith.

WARNER, REX (March 9, 1905-). For biographical sketch and list of earlier works and references, see TWENTIETH CENTURY AUTHORS, 1942.

* * *

Many of Rex Warner's recent writings have developed out of his work as an educator. A specialist in classical literature, he has taught in England, in Egypt, and in Greece. From 1945 to 1947 he was director of the

British Institute in Athens. Some of his most valuable works have been translations from Greek literature — Aeschylus' *Prometheus Bound*, Euripides' *Hippolytus* and *Helen*, Xenophon's *Anabasis*, Ovid's *Metamorphoses*. His translations were praised for their vigor and for their sound, but unobtrusive, scholarship. It is for his novels, however—his vivid and intense allegorical studies of modern life—that Warner remains best known. "He is the only outstanding novelist of ideas whom the decade of ideas produced," V. S. Pritchett wrote. "He is the only English novelist to make original and imaginative use of the three-cornered struggle between Fascism, Communism and Democracy." Neither his *Return of the Traveller*, the story of an English soldier killed in World War II and returning to ask "Why was I killed?" nor his *Men of Stones*, the story of life in a political prison ruled by a tyrannical but brilliant madman, has won the critical acclaim that his earlier novels received. They have been found stimulating and imaginative, but also cold ("algebraically stylish" was James Hilton's phrase for *Men of Stones*), lacking in dramatic intensity and coherence.

Warner's first wife was Frances Chamier Grove, whom he married in 1929, and by whom he had two sons and a daughter. His second wife is Barbara, Lady Rothschild. They were married in 1949 and have a daughter. His home is in Oxford.

ADDITIONAL WORKS: Return of the Traveller (in England: Why Was I Killed?) 1944; The English Public Schools, 1945; The Cult of Power (essays) 1946; Men of Stones, 1949; John Milton, 1950; Men and Gods (translations from Ovid's Metamorphoses) 1950; Views of Attica and Its Surroundings, 1950; Greeks and Trojans, 1951; Escapade, 1953; Eternal Greece, 1953; The Vengeance of the Gods, 1954.

ABOUT: Pritchett, V. S. *in* Modern British Writing (ed. D. V. Baker); Saturday Review of Literature January 11, 1947.

WARNER, SYLVIA TOWNSEND (December 1893-). For biographical sketch and list of earlier works and references, see TWENTIETH CENTURY AUTHORS, 1942.

* * *

Sylvia Townsend Warner's subtle and substantial talents as a novelist have won her considerable respect in both England and the United States. She is not a "popular" writer, nor is she, on the other hand, a "coterie" writer, but she holds a position somewhere between the two. Her work is serious, mature, and artistic. It is also witty, its seriousness lightened by shrewd but genuine humor. In *The Flint Anchor*, a chronicle of the lives of a nineteenth century English family dominated by a tyrannical father, she combined (C. J. Rolo wrote in the *Atlantic*) "a solidity and a subtlety of feeling, a fusion of warmth and wit and quietly biting shrewdness, that are reminiscent of the art of Jane Austen." Her earlier *The Corner That Held Them* was a masterly recreation of life in a medieval English convent. Of this novel Robert Gorham Davis wrote in the New York *Times:* "Miss Warner is not exploiting the past for romance or quaintness, to escape something or find something or sell us medievalism, but rather to deepen our sense of the common human lot, its limits and possibilities."

ADDITIONAL WORKS: A Garland of Straw (short stories) 1943; Museum of Cheats (short stories) 1947; The Corner That Held Them, 1948; Somerset, 1949; The Flint Anchor, 1954.

WARREN, AUSTIN (July 4, 1899-   ), American critic and scholar, writes: "I was born in Waltham, Mass., ten miles from Boston, where my city-born father tried variously to earn a living. As I was entering high school, he yielded to his steady desire—about which there was nothing Utopian or doctrinaire: only an instinctive fondness for animals and an archaic versatility—  and moved his family to a country village north of Concord.

"The Stow high school, with a male principal and two women assistants, gave me a sound education in Latin and German. The two centers of my life, however—neither of them shared by my parents—were music and religion. I taught myself to play the piano; then had the instruction of an excellent teacher who paid a weekly visit to Stow. Ecclesiastically the village was divided between the Unitarians and the Evangelicals, to which later I adhered.

"College was—by my grandmother's choice —Wesleyan, in Connecticut. Our admirable German-trained professors had assembled an admirable library. In my years (1916-20), alas, they were all nearing retirement and too old and remote for concern with teaching the few students desirous of education. Partly taught by an older student, I chiefly taught myself by systematically reading through the alcoves of the almost unfrequented library. I remember discovering Emily Dickinson and Jane Austen, Swedenborg, and Albrecht Dürer.

"For the next six years, I alternated teaching and studying—the 'studying' at Harvard and at Princeton. My one great 'official' teacher was Irving Babbitt; but I had, during those years, two unofficial teachers—philosopher-theologians; and then, as always, I learned from all my contemporary friends whatever they lovingly knew: French poetry, for example, from Wallace Fowlie; contemporary American poetry from John Wheelwright and Howard Blake.

"Since taking my doctorate at Princeton in 1926, I have taught in universities, for the last fifteen years chiefly graduate students in age between twenty and thirty; but all through my professional life I have been primarily a teacher—a 'coach' of creative writers and critics rather than of academic scholars.

"It is difficult to earn an honest livelihood as a teacher and still write; but in our competitive world there is, it would seem, no easy and honest way to live while writing. My chief resource is my steady conviction that I can't be an honest teacher without managing time for writing: a New England justification for what I would do anyway had I independent means.

"I have been a copious writer. During my twenties I wrote and published theology. In the next ten years I disciplined myself to scholarly research, on the specious ground that, having proved to scholars that I was a scholar, I would then be at liberty to be a critic. The last ten years have gone to literary criticism and literary theory. I trust to live to publish an autobiography, a novel, a thin book of rich and meticulous poems, and a 'philosophy of religion.' "

* * *

Austin Warren has taught at the University of Kentucky, Boston University, the University of Iowa, and since 1948 at the University of Michigan. In addition he has taught summers at Wisconsin and at New York University, and has been a fellow of the Kenyon School of English and of the School of Letters of Indiana University. In 1950 he held a Guggenheim fellowship. Warren's volume of critical essays *Rage for Order* was highly praised. "These essays," Mark Schorer wrote in the New York *Times*, "are in themselves the product of a coherent and civilized intelligence. . . . They do honor . . . to contemporary criticism, no less than contemporary education, and it is gratifying to observe how intimately these two have come together." With René Wellek, Warren has written one of the most important books of recent years on contemporary literary criticism—*Theory of Literature*, which the late Donald Stauffer described as "the most ordered, ranging and purposeful attempt made in some time toward keeping the study of literature at once intelligent and liberal."

PRINCIPAL WORKS: Alexander Pope as Critic and Humanist, 1929; The Elder Henry James, 1934; (ed.) Hawthorne: Representative Selections, 1934; Richard Crashaw: A Study in Baroque Sensibility, 1939; Rage for Order: Essays in Criticism, 1948; Theory of Literature (with R. Wellek) 1949.

WARREN, CHARLES (March 9, 1868-August 16, 1954). For biographical sketch and list of earlier works and references, see TWENTIETH CENTURY AUTHORS, 1942.

* * *

Charles Warren died at his home in Washington, D.C., at eighty-six.

His last public function was as a member of the President's War Relief Control Board, from 1943 to 1946. In 1942 he published *Odd Byways in American History*. A reviewer said: "It is refreshing to learn that so serious a historian as Charles Warren, when he wishes, can turn aside to pursue an intriguing story down some side-lane of the past for sheer entertainment."

ADDITIONAL WORK: Odd Byways in American History, 1942.

ABOUT: New York Times August 17, 1954.

WARREN, ROBERT PENN (April 24, 1905-). For autobiographical sketch and list of earlier works and references, see TWENTIETH CENTURY AUTHORS, 1942.

* * *

Since 1943 Robert Penn Warren has worked in three distinct fields of literary activity with marked success in all of them—creative writing (both the novel and poetry), literary criticism, and education (as teacher and author-editor, with Cleanth Brooks, of college textbooks in rhetoric and literature). He is best known today as a novelist, author of several of the most powerful and significant American novels of recent years—*At Heaven's Gate*, a novel of the present-day South; the Pulitzer prize-winning *All the King's Men*; and a rich and ambitious (to many critics overly ambitious) historical novel *World Enough and Time*. Outstanding among these is *All the King's Men*, a study of the rise and fall of an American political dictator, the ruthless and dynamic Willie Stark. This novel—swift-moving, violent, and timely (the resemblance of Willie Stark to the late Huey P. Long was much commented upon)—had a wide popular appeal.

But critics have also recognized more enduring values in *All the King's Men*. Warren's works, Eric Bentley says, "have to be taken as serious moral documents"—the constant theme of them, according to Bentley, is "self-knowledge." As Frederick Brantley writes, Warren shares a task with Joyce, Hardy, Faulkner, Melville and Conrad in striving "to illuminate the tragic experience by presenting it imaginatively in the light of the conflict of self, the private struggle in a world of public action to achieve self-definition."

In like manner a sense of moral seriousness and depth informs Warren's poetry and literary criticism. Of the former, Louise Bogan has commented upon "his complex perceptions and the modern poetic style working brilliantly together on subjects which perceptive modern poets keep coming back to: obscure psychological guilt and corruption, sadism, obsession—dissimulated under the fixed pattern of modern life and everyday conformity." His long dramatic poem *Brother to Dragons* is a remarkable achievement, major in scale and theme. Among his most widely read and discussed critical writings are the essay on *The Ancient Mariner* and the essay "Pure and Impure Poetry," first delivered as a lecture at Princeton in 1942.

In addition to the Pulitzer prize for fiction which he received in 1947, Warren was a co-winner of the Shelley Memorial prize for poetry in 1942, winner of the Southern prize in 1947, a Guggenheim fellowship in 1947-1948, and the Meltzer award of the Screen Writers Guild in 1950. The motion picture version of *All the King's Men* was named the best film of 1949 by the Academy of Motion Picture Arts and Sciences.

Warren was professor of English at the University of Minnesota from 1942 to 1950. From 1944 to 1945 he served as poetry consultant of the Library of Congress. In 1950 Warren was visiting professor at Yale University and a year later joined the faculty of the Yale Drama School as professor of playwriting. He was divorced in 1951 and in 1952 married the writer Eleanor Clark. They have one daughter. Warren writes of himself to the editors of this volume: "Still an unreconstructed New Dealer but stop a good way this side of idolatry for FDR. Even so, he was better luck that we had a right to expect."

ADDITIONAL WORKS: *Poetry*—Eleven Poems on Same Theme, 1942; Selected Poems, 1923-1943, 1944; Brother to Dragons, 1953. *Criticism*—Coleridge's Rime of the Ancient Mariner, 1946. *Fiction*—At Heaven's Gate, 1943; All the King's Men, 1946; Blackberry Winter (novelette), 1946; The Circus in the Attic, and Other Stories, 1948; World Enough and Time, 1950. *Textbooks (ed. with C*

Brooks)—Understanding Fiction, 1943; Modern Rhetoric, 1949; Fundamentals of Good Writing, 1950.

ABOUT: Bentley, E. *in* Forms of Modern Fiction (ed. W. V. O'Connor); Brantley, F. *in* Modern American Poetry (ed. B. Rajan); O'Connor, W. V. *in* Southern Vanguard (ed. A. Tate); Accent Spring 1953; Nation November 25, 1944; New York Herald Tribune Book Review July 2, 1950, October 11, 1953; New York Times Book Review July 2, 1950, August 22, 1953; Saturday Review of Literature June 24, 1950; Sewanee Review January 1945; South Atlantic Quarterly October 1948.

WASSERMANN, JAKOB (March 10, 1873-January 1, 1934). For biographical sketch and list of works and references, see TWENTIETH CENTURY AUTHORS, 1942.

* * *

ADDITIONAL WORK IN ENGLISH TRANSLATION: Alexander in Babylon, 1949.

ABOUT: Blankenagel, J. C. The Writings of Jakob Wassermann; Columbia Dictionary of Modern European Literature; Journal of English and Germanic Philology April, July 1951.

"WAST, HUGO." See MARTÍNEZ ZUVIRÍA, G. A.

WATKIN, LAWRENCE EDWARD (December 9, 1901-). For autobiographical sketch and list of works and references, see TWENTIETH CENTURY AUTHORS, 1942.

* * *

Lawrence E. Watkin writes from Burbank, Calif.: "Early in 1942 I joined the naval reserve and as a lieutenant commander headed the naval aviation training manuals unit at Washington. My associates and I devoted ourselves chiefly to 'Sense Manuals,' and probably represented the strangest and most unmilitary group ever gathered together in one room: Roark Bradford (*Green Pastures*), Robert Lewis Taylor (*New Yorker*), W. C. Fields and Churchill biographies), Hannibal Coons ('Dear George' stories), John Faulkner (*Men Working*), Jesse Stuart (*Taps for Private Tussie*). After duty in the Pacific, I left the Navy late in 1945 and came to Hollywood, learning the screen writer's trade in brief assignments at Goldwyn's, Columbia, and Warner Brothers. Since 1947 I have worked for Walt Disney, and, in addition to originals, have sole screen credit on the live-action technicolor productions *Treasure Island*, *Robin Hood*, and *Sword and the Rose*.

"Scouting stories for Disney has taken me into the little-traveled parts of Ireland and Spain, and my family and I know London better than we do Hollywood."

WATKINS, VERNON PHILLIPS (June 27, 1906-), Welsh poet, writes: "I was born at Maesteg, South Wales. From the

Tal Jones

first I was accustomed to hear the Welsh language as my parents, who normally talked English, spoke Welsh whenever it was preferable for me not to understand them. Instead of becoming bilingual, as my parents were, I grew up under the spell of the English poets, who began to influence me when I was six or seven years old. I gradually collected the English poets, and by the time I was twelve I had most of the great poets and read them with undiscriminating enthusiasm.

"After a year at the Swansea Grammar School, I went to a preparatory school in England, then to Repton, and then to Magdalene College, Cambridge. At Repton and Cambridge I studied modern languages. The influence of the English poets had always persisted, but I became interested in all the European poets, and in poets all over the world. I was able to study the ancient Welsh poets with my father's help, and my mother helped me with Welsh as well as German. As a child I had many holidays in France, and my last two years at school and my year at Cambridge were given chiefly to the study of French and German. I had always written poetry, but I now tried to translate poetry from those languages.

"In 1925 I left Cambridge and became a clerk in Lloyds Bank. I wrote a great deal of poetry at this time and in the years following, but it was not until the Thirties that I began to understand the nature of my poetry and to find a style for it. I had written at least a thousand poems when I first met Dylan Thomas in 1935, and he certainly helped me to cut from my own style what belonged to other people's. In our approach to poetry and in our method of composition we were unlike, but in our belief and findings there was great affinity, and we became close friends. In 1939 I met Yeats, whose poetry I admired more than that of any other contemporary.

"Many writers experience a turning-point, after which it is impossible to go back. When I had this experience it left me opposed to the idea of publishing what I wrote. I was persuaded to publish by a friend. My first published poems which I value were printed in the first number of the magazine *Wales* in 1936. After this I contributed poetry frequently to this review as well as to *Life and Letters, Horizon, The Listener, Poetry* (London), and many other reviews in England and America.

"I served in the Air Force during the war, first as a policeman and then on special duties, rising unaccountably to the rank of flight-sergeant. I married in 1944 and have two sons and a daughter."

* * *

Vernon Watkins draws upon Welsh material and legend in his poetry, and he writes with something of the bardic spirit of that tradition. Nevertheless, as some of his reviewers have pointed out, "he is essentially an English poet in the great tradition." The themes of which he writes are relatively few and simple. "The central experience of these poems," the London *Times Literary Supplement* writes of *The Death Bell*, "is a sustained wonder at the glories of the created world, told in twin and merging moods of rhapsodic acceptance and grave meditation." He is at his best, Anthony Hartley observes in the *Spectator*, in his ballads, full of action and solid imagery—"when he allows his meaning to emerge from concrete description without trying to be abstract or to impose symbols from without."

PRINCIPAL WORKS: The Ballad of the Mari Lwyd and Other Poems, 1941; The Lamp and the Veil, 1945; The Lady With the Unicorn, 1948; Selected Poems, 1948; The North Sea (trans. from H. Heine) 1951; The Death Bell, and Other Poems, 1954.

ABOUT: Poetry December 1948.

WATSON, Sir WILLIAM (August 2, 1858-August 13, 1935). For biographical sketch and list of works and references, see TWENTIETH CENTURY AUTHORS, 1942.

* * *

ABOUT: Dictionary of National Biography 1931-1940.

WATTS, Mrs. MARY (STANBERY) (November 4, 1868-). For biographical sketch and list of works and references, see TWENTIETH CENTURY AUTHORS, 1942.

WAUGH, ALEC (July 8, 1898-). For biographical sketch and list of earlier works and references, see TWENTIETH CENTURY AUTHORS, 1942.

* * *

Alec Waugh saw active service in World War II with the British Army. He joined the Dorset Regiment, with which he had served in World War I, in 1939, went to France in 1940, to the Middle East in 1941, and from 1942 to 1945 served with the Persia and Iraq Command. When the war ended, he retired with the rank of major.

Waugh's reputation, in the United States particularly, has been overshadowed by the great success of his brother Evelyn. In his own right, Alec Waugh is an expert, if somewhat conventional, novelist, a facile raconteur, and, in his travel writings and biography, a keen reporter.

ADDITIONAL WORKS: His Second War, 1944; The Sunlit Caribbean (in U.S.: The Sugar Islands) 1948; Unclouded Summer (novel) 1948; (comp.) These Would I Choose, 1949; The Lipton Story, 1950; When the Clock Strikes Twice, 1951; Guy Renton, 1952.

WAUGH, ARTHUR (August 24, 1866- June 26, 1943). For biographical sketch and list of works and references, see TWENTIETH CENTURY AUTHORS, 1942.

* * *

Arthur Waugh died at his London home at seventy-six. He was survived by his wife and two sons, the authors Alec and Evelyn Waugh.

The London *Times* has said of the elder Waugh, who was chairman of the publishing house of Chapman and Hall, Ltd., up to his death: "He had a keen gusto for life and literature, and the literary recollections of his own life are a valuable contribution to the history of the period. In his own person he combined a real feeling for art with an aptitude for business and a shrewd judgment of his colleagues and assistants."

ABOUT: London Times June 28, 1943; New York Times June 28, 1943.

*WAUGH, EVELYN (October 1903-). For biographical sketch and list of earlier works and references, see TWENTIETH CENTURY AUTHORS, 1942.

* * *

In 1944 Edmund Wilson, a critic later none too friendly to him, described Evelyn Waugh as "the only first-rate comic genius that has appeared in England since Bernard Shaw." Waugh first won his fame in Britain and the United States as an audacious satirist whose portraits of the fast-living high society of the 1920's and '30's were hilarious but also stingingly true. (Wilson cited his ability "to combine the outrageous with the plausible without offending our sense of truth.") In

* wó

only one novel, *A Handful of Dust,* was there any hint of Waugh as a serious social critic and even here it was glossed over by the swiftness and the polish of the narrative. In 1945, however, Waugh astonished his readers with *Brideshead Revisited,* a frankly serious novel about the decline of an aristocratic English Catholic family. Many reviewers considered it Waugh's finest book. John K. Hutchens wrote in the New York *Times*: "*Brideshead Revisited* has the depth and weight that are found in a writer working in his prime, in the full powers of an eager, good mind and a skilled hand, retaining the best of what he has already learned. It tells an absorbing story in imaginative terms." Others objected, however, that the book was a Catholic tract. This in itself was no cause for criticism, for in the post-World War II era the success of the work of Graham Greene and François Mauriac was a frank recognition of the validity of the religious, especially the Catholic, theme in the modern novel. But what was resented in Waugh's treatment of the theme was his extreme conservatism (some critics called it "snobbery"). "Its comedy," the London *Times Literary Supplement* observed, "is always engulfed in the last resort in the author's asseveration of Catholic doctrine, in his sentiment of the aristocratic or oligarchic English past, in his feeling for whatever may be thought to be a corrective for the idea of progress."

Brideshead Revisited became a best seller. In the United States, where it was a Book-of-the-Month Club selection, it brought Waugh a large and enthusiastic public. He visited this country on a lecture tour and was widely acclaimed. In the April 8, 1946, issue of *Life* magazine he devoted several pages to answering questions about himself and his work for his admirers. Conservatively dressed, bland and cherubic in appearance, his manner sardonic, he brought to life the spirit of his work. One interviewer described him as looking "a little like a boyish Winston Churchill." On his American visit in 1946 Waugh announced that in his future books he would follow two aims—"a preoccupation with style and the attempt to represent man more fully, which, to me, means only one thing, man in his relation to God."

With only one of his later novels has Waugh shown any substantial evidence of the old hard, satiric brilliance. This was *The Loved One,* a farcical satire set in a de luxe funeral park in Hollywood. Although the humor of *The Loved One* was based on a series of macabre shocks and was itself in the same questionable taste as the mortuary establishment it was satirizing, it was nevertheless, as Orville Prescott described it, "brilliantly amusing satire," and, in Wolcott Gibbs' words, "as rich and subtle and unnerving as anything its author has ever done." *Scott-King's Modern Europe* and "Love Among the Ruins" (a short story first published in America in *Commonweal* and later included in the volume *Tactical Exercise*) were timely and topical satires, but, most critics agreed, they lacked humor and inventiveness. Of the former, a political satire about a mythical but easily identifiable European country, the late George Orwell remarked that "it lacks the touch of affection that political satire ought to have."

Waugh enlisted in the Royal Marines at the outbreak of World War II. He later shifted to the Commandos (with the rank of major), was parachuted into Yugoslavia, and narrowly escaped death in the crash of a transport plane. His war experiences served as the basis for two recent novels—*Men at Arms* and *Officers and Gentlemen,* described as "diabolically bland satire on the infinitely varied manifestations of the martial spirit." He lives in Gloucestershire with his wife and six children, three sons and three daughters. In 1946 he wrote of himself characteristically: "I live in a shabby stone house in the country, where nothing is under a hundred years old except the plumbing and that does not work. I collect old books in an inexpensive, desultory way. I have a fast-emptying cellar of wine and gardens fast reverting to the jungle. I am very contentedly married. I have numerous children whom I see once a day for ten, I hope, awe-inspiring minutes."

ADDITIONAL WORKS: Work Suspended: Two Chapters of an Unfinished Novel, 1942; Brideshead Revisited, 1945; When the Going Was Good (travel sketches) 1947; The Loved One, 1948; Scott-King's Modern Europe, 1949; Helena, 1950; Men at Arms, 1952; The Holy Places (non-fiction) 1953; Tactical Exercise (stories) 1954; Officers and Gentlemen, 1955.

ABOUT: Hoehn, M. (ed.) Catholic Authors, I; Linklater, E. The Art of Adventure; O'Brien, J. A. (ed.) The Road to Damascus; O'Donnell, D. *in* The Kenyon Critics (ed. J. C. Ransom); Wilson, E. Classics and Commercials; Atlantic Monthly October 1954; Commonweal March 3, 1950; Fortnightly March 1952; Life April 8, 1946; New York Times Book Review March 13, 1949, November 19, 1950; Saturday Review of Literature June 26, 1948; South Atlantic Quarterly April 1949.

WAY, ARTHUR SANDERS (February 13, 1847-September 25, 1930). For biographical sketch and list of works and references, see TWENTIETH CENTURY AUTHORS, 1942.

* * *

ABOUT: Dictionary of Australian Biography.

WEAVER, JOHN VAN ALSTYN (July 17, 1893-June 14, 1938). For biographical sketch and list of works and references, see TWENTIETH CENTURY AUTHORS, 1942.

WEBB, Mrs. BEATRICE (POTTER) (January 22, 1858-April 30, 1943) and **WEBB, SIDNEY,** 1st Baron Passfield (July 13, 1859-October 13, 1947). For biographical sketch and list of earlier works and references, see TWENTIETH CENTURY AUTHORS, 1942.

* * *

Beatrice Webb died in her sleep, after an illness of about ten days, at the Webb home at Passfield Corner, Liphook, England. She was eighty-five. Four years later her husband Sidney Webb died, also at Passfield Corner, at eighty-eight. On December 12, 1947, at the suggestion of George Bernard Shaw, their ashes were interred in Westminster Abbey.

Although they lived in retirement during the last few years of their lives, the Webbs continued to exert considerable influence upon younger generations, particularly upon the leaders of the British Socialist movement, of which Sidney Webb has been called "the main architect." Beatrice continued to write, until a few days before her death, the diaries in which she recorded the story of their remarkable intellectual and literary "partnership."

R. H. Tawney called the Webbs "historical figures, and figures whose stature increases as their world recedes," and felt that simplicity and magnanimity were their most striking characteristics. "The combination of worldly wisdom with personal unworldliness, though rare, is not unknown. The Webbs possessed it in more than ordinary measure."

Probably the greatest single concept for which they fought was what Beatrice Webb described as "a legally enforced 'minimum standard of life'"; the establishment of national minimums of income, health, housing, leisure, etc. Lord Beveridge has said that "Britain today would have been very different from what it is if there had been no Sidney and Beatrice Webb. For more than fifty years they were a ferment in society, bringing new ideas to men's minds, bringing new organizations and institutions to birth."

ADDITIONAL WORKS: *By Beatrice Webb*—Our Partnership (ed. by B. Drake & M. I. Cole) 1948; Diaries, 1912-1924 (ed. by M. I. Cole) 1952.

ABOUT: Cole, M. I. Beatrice Webb, Social Services and the Webb Tradition, (ed.) The Webbs and Their Work; Oxnam, G. B. Personalities in Social Reform; Tawney, R. H. Beatrice Webb; Webb, B. Diaries, Our Partnership; Canadian Forum June 1948; Contemporary Review August 1948; Economic Journal September 1948; Labour Monthly November 1947; Life January 12, 1948; London Times May 1, 1943, October 14, 1947; Nation November 8, 1947; New Statesman and Nation October 18, 1947, October 25, 1947; New York Times May 1, 1943, October 14, 1947; Political Quarterly January 1948; Saturday Review of Literature November 1, 1947; Time April 12, 1948; Universities Quarterly February 1950.

WEBB, Mrs. MARY GLADYS (MEREDITH) (March 25, 1881-October 8, 1927). For biographical sketch and list of works and references, see TWENTIETH CENTURY AUTHORS, 1942.

* * *

ADDITIONAL WORKS: Fifty-One Poems Hitherto Unpublished in Book Form, 1946.
ABOUT: Armstrong, M. Introduction to The Essential Mary Webb (1949): Atlantic Harvest (ed. E. Sedgwick); Swinnerton, F. The Georgian Literary Scene (1910-35).

WEBB, SIDNEY. See WEBB, B.

*WEBER, MAX (1864-1920), German sociologist and political economist, came from a highly cultured and prosperous portion of the  German upper middle class. His father was prominent in the politics of the National Liberal Party in the time of Bismarck and was for many years a member of the Reichstag. As a child Max Weber was brought up in Berlin, and as a young man he studied law, receiving an appointment as *Privatdozent* at the University of Berlin. He had first entered upon the study of law under the aegis of the historical school, and his early views were in conscious opposition against the 'formalism' of the neo-Kantian philosophy of law. This in turn led him beyond mere interest in the history of legal institutions as such, and his early studies in this field, principally an essay on the decline of the Roman Empire and an economic history of the ancient world, emphasize the dependence of law on economic and technological background.

Weber became professor of economics at the University of Freiburg, then went on to a chair of economics at Heidelberg. After

only a brief tenure in this position, his health broke down, leading to his resignation from the professorship and a cessation of productive work for almost four years. During the most fruitful years of his life as a writer, he lived as a private scholar in a state of semi-invalidism in Heidelberg. It was not until near the end of World War I that he accepted a temporary appointment at the University of Vienna, and then, in 1919, a regular appointment at Munich. He died suddenly of pneumonia in his second semester at the latter institution, at the height of his intellectual powers.

Weber was always torn between his interest in active politics and his scholarly pursuits. He sat on the committee which submitted the first draft of the Weimar Constitution and is said to have been responsible for the provision for the popular election of the president, although as a youth he had belonged to the Pan-German League and sympathized with its conservative program. Both in his emphasis on economic rather than formal legal factors, and in his concern with the genesis of "capitalism" in the western world, Weber took a course which brought him into close contact with the Marxist position. But this he found uncongenial, being convinced of the important role of "ideas" in the explanation of great historical processes. Insistent on rigorous objectivity in historical research, he could not tolerate the metaphysical "cloudiness" of idealistic philosophers of history. "It may perhaps be said," writes his translator and editor Talcott Parsons, "that it is out of his insight into and conviction of the inadequacy both of German historical economics and jurisprudence and of Marxism to solve the problems he had become interested in that Weber launched on the development of an independent line of broad theoretical analysis in the social field, in particular into the development of a science of 'sociology.'" Weber's *The Theory of Social and Economic Organization* gives his discussion of the fundamental concepts of sociology, of sociological categories of economic action, and of types of authority. When *Methodology of the Social Sciences* appeared in 1949, the *American Journal of Sociology* said, "There has been, up to now, no abler, more penetrating writing on the problem of 'Evaluation' in social science than that of Max Weber." Weber's mind was continually developing throughout his life, and he explicitly repudiated the desire to set up a 'system' of scientific theory and never completed a systematic work. Yet there are important systematic elements in his thought. Many years after his death his work is still current and of considerable influence on contemporary sociologists."

PRINCIPAL WORKS IN ENGLISH TRANSLATION: General Economic History, 1927; Protestant Ethic and the Spirit of Capitalism, 1930; From Max Weber: Essays in Sociology, 1946; Theory of Social and Economic Organization, 1947; Methodology of the Social Sciences, 1949; Hindu Social System, 1950; Religion of China: Confucianism and Taoism, 1951; Ancient Judaism, 1953; On Law in Economy and Society, 1954.

ABOUT: Mayer, J. P. Max Weber and German Politics; Parsons, T. Introduction to Weber's The Theory of Social and Economic Organization; Robertson, H. M. Aspects of the Rise of Economic Individualism; Encyclopedia of the Social Sciences; Church History December 1950; Rural Sociology September 1946; Social Research June 1947.

WEBSTER, ELIZABETH CHARLOTTE (1914?-1946), Scottish novelist,

was ill from childhood with bronchial asthma. In her native Edinburgh her respiratory troubles kept her from school; she once estimated that her total attendance could not have been more than five days. Her sister, close companion, and fellow writer, Mary Morison Webster, has said that the circumstance of illness stimulated Elizabeth C. Webster to read "automatically," and confined her to a bedroom which, "because she was so intuitively wise, became the Mecca for friends and relatives requiring witty conversation or general advice on all matters, particularly those pertaining to affairs of the heart." Both girls were very poor, and apparently because of her delicate health and South Africa's softer climate, Elizabeth C. Webster and her sister went to Johannesburg. Here she completed three novels, the best known being Ceremony of Innocence, a novel of life in a South African Anglican convent and the havoc wrought there by a psychic novice. Published after her death, this book, by some thought "polemical," caused cries of "infidel!" to be raised. The London Times regretted the "bitterness and occasional brutality of the style," while the Saturday Review of Literature said, "A delicious, audacious, truly civilized, and altogether wonderful book . . . only a dull eye will fail to see the deep religiousness, at once militant and humble, which underlies the stinging wit and relentless irony." The book received a prize given by the Afrikaans Press Bureau,

and was reputedly accorded the most enthusiastic press reception of any book ever published in that country up to that time. "If you can imagine," wrote Diana Trilling, "a first-rate novelist of social manners—urbane, witty, a fine stylist, an acutely satiric but sympathetic observer of social behavior—who at the same time is concerned to hypothecate man's ultimate fate, you perhaps have some notion of Miss Webster's unusual gift."

Having spent two years writing Ceremony of Innocence, Elizabeth C. Webster finished it just three days before she was struck down by pneumonia; she died less than a week later at the age of thirty-two.

PRINCIPAL WORKS: Bullion, 1933; Expiring Frog, 1946; Ceremony of Innocence, 1949; High Altitude, a Frolic (with M. M. Webster) 1949.

ABOUT: Saturday Review of Literature February 11, 1950.

WEBSTER, HENRY KITCHELL (September 7, 1875-December 9, 1932). For biographical sketch and list of works and references, see TWENTIETH CENTURY AUTHORS, 1942.

* * *

ABOUT: Newberry Library Bulletin December 1946.

WEBSTER, JEAN (July 24, 1876-June 11, 1916). For biographical sketch and list of works and references, see TWENTIETH CENTURY AUTHORS, 1942.

WECTER, DIXON (January 12, 1906-June 24, 1950), American historian and author, was born in Houston, Tex., the son of

John Joseph Wecter and Eugenia (Dixon) Wecter. His father, an employee of the Southern Pacific Railroad, died when the boy was four, and afterward his mother earned a living for her family by teaching junior high school. Wecter grew up on the

Rio Grande during the era of Pancho Villa, and liked to recall how his window was once shattered by a trooper's bullet. He attended Baylor University, graduating in 1925, and a year later took his M.A. at Yale. In 1928 he went to Oxford as a Rhodes Scholar and there received his B.Litt. In 1936 he took a Ph.D. at Yale, and was later awarded honorary degrees by Rockford College and Baylor University.

He taught at the University of Denver and the University of Colorado, and in 1937 married one of his students, Elizabeth Farrar; they had no children. From 1939 to 1949 he was professor of English at the University of California at Los Angeles. In 1945 he was visiting professor in American history at the University of Sydney and was the first professor to teach that subject in Australia. From 1946 to 1949 he served as chairman of research at the Huntington Library at San Marino, Calif.; in 1949 he moved to the Berkeley campus of the University of California to occupy the Byrne Chair of United States History.

Wecter's first book, *Saga of American Society, a Record of Social Aspiration 1607-1937,* was published in 1937, a serious piece of work, recording skillfully, wittily, and benignly a phase of American civilization. The author had been greatly influenced by the social historian Arthur M. Schlesinger. Many other books followed, the last being *Sam Clemens of Hannibal,* a posthumous publication in 1952. As an associate editor of *The Literary History of the United States,* Wecter had written the chapter on Mark Twain, and this won him the editorship of the Mark Twain Estate, a position he held from 1946 until his death in 1950. Besides editing three books on Twain, including his letters, Wecter had time to complete the first draft of volume one of a projected biography. He died in Sacramento, Calif., very suddenly and unexpectedly of a heart attack, at the age of forty-four. The job of putting the book into shape for publication fell to his wife. On the publication of *Sam Clemens of Hannibal,* Bernard De Voto wrote of the author, "He was the right man for Mark's biography: toughminded but intuitive, a literary scholar who was also a man of letters, a brilliant historian, a first-rate writer, a mind adept at interpreting American experience and sensitive to the subtleties and contradictions of Mark Twain." The book, Edward Weeks wrote in the *Atlantic,* "is a delightful tonic to the American spirit. Its warmth, its honesty, its exuberance are balm to the mind."

PRINCIPAL WORKS: Saga of American Society, 1937; Edmund Burke and His Kinsmen, 1939; The Hero in America, 1941; Our Soldiers Speak, 1775-1918 (with W. Matthews) 1943; When Johnny Comes Marching Home, 1944; The Age of the Great Depression, 1948; Changing Patterns in American Civilization (with others) 1949; Sam Clemens of Hannibal, 1952.

ABOUT: American Antiquarian Society Proceedings October 1950; Current Biography 1944, 1950; New York Times January 4, September 18, 1944, June 26, 1950; Pacific Historical Review August 1950; Saturday Review of Literature July 17, 1948, July 8, 1950, August 30, 1952.

*WEDEKIND, FRANK (July 24, 1864-March 9, 1918). For biographical sketch and list of works and references, see TWENTIETH CENTURY AUTHORS, 1942.

* * *

ABOUT: Columbia Dictionary of Modern European Literature; Lange, V. Modern German Literature.

* vä'dĕ kĭnt

WEEKLEY, ERNEST (1865-May 7, 1954). For autobiographical sketch and list of works and references, see TWENTIETH CENTURY AUTHORS, 1942.

* * *

Ernest Weekley died at eighty-nine. He had spent his last years in Putney, a London suburb. During these years he wrote no new books but published new editions of his popular *Words Ancient and Modern* (1947) and *The English Language* (1953).

ABOUT: London Times May 8, 1954.

WEEKS, EDWARD AUGUSTUS, Jr. (February 19, 1898-   ). For biographical sketch and list of works and references, see TWENTIETH CENTURY AUTHORS, 1942.

* * *

Edward Weeks has edited the *Atlantic Monthly* since 1938. The policy of the magazine in recent years (as *Time* magazine summarized it) has been one of "less literature for literature's sake, more issue-grappling articles." Its circulation has increased until, in 1943, it was larger than that of any other magazine in its class. In 1947 the magazine celebrated its ninetieth anniversary. Although he has written only one book, Weeks is a widely known literary figure—both for his editorship and for the sound and perceptive book reviews which he writes for the *Atlantic.* He was for two years, 1940-41, a radio commentator, and he is a popular lecturer, witty, urbane, and devoted to the cause of literature. Weeks is active in civic and educational work. He is an overseer of Harvard University, a trustee of Wellesley College, and a member of the corporation of Northeastern University. He is a fellow of the American Academy of Arts and Sciences and since 1942 has received honorary degrees from Williams College, Middlebury College, the University of Alabama, Dartmouth, and Bucknell.

ADDITIONAL WORK: (ed.) The Pocket Atlantic, 1946.

ABOUT: New York Public Library Bulletin June 1950; Publishers' Weekly October 15, 1949; Time November 3, 1947.

WEIDMAN, JEROME (August 4, 1913-). For biographical sketch and list of earlier works and references, see TWENTIETH CENTURY AUTHORS, 1942.

* * *

Jerome Weidman worked for the Office of War Information during World War II. Shortly after the war ended, he wrote *Too Early to Tell*, a broad satire of a mythical wartime government agency called the Bureau of Psychological Combat, which drew rather obviously upon his own experiences in the O.W.I. In his later novels Weidman has to some extent modified the hard realistic manner of his early novels; he has also sacrificed some of the shock-value which made those novels popular successes. *The Price Is Right*, the story of an ambitious newspaperman's fight to get ahead in his career, had much of the brash vigor of *I Can Get It for You Wholesale*, but the general effect was not successful. "Weidman is clever about people without being really wise about them," Lee Rogow wrote in the *Saturday Review of Literature*. "The emotional penetration and the understanding of the sources of human ethics are essentially superficial."

Weidman is a hard-working writer, an expert story teller, and a shrewd observer of modern life. The seriousness of his literary ambitions is reflected in a note which he prepared for the New York *Herald Tribune* in 1953: "In almost three decades of intensive reading, much of it devoted to the hope of picking up a few pointers for what Hemingway has called the serious trade of novel writing, only two men have ever taught me anything really helpful. Conrad is one. James Gould Cozzens is the other. To be able to write as well as either of them seems to me to be as much as a man can ask."

In 1942 Weidman married Peggy Wright; they have two sons. Their home is in Westport, Conn., but they travel frequently. In 1953 they were in Europe.

ADDITIONAL WORKS: The Lights Around the Shore, 1943; Too Early to Tell, 1946; The Captain's Tiger (short stories) 1947; The Price Is Right, 1949; The Hand of the Hunter, 1951; The Third Angel, 1953; Your Daughter Iris, 1955.

ABOUT: Warfel, H. R. American Novelists of Today; New York Herald Tribune Book Review October 11, 1953.

WEIGALL, ARTHUR EDWARD PEARSE BROME (November 20, 1880-January 20, 1934). For biographical sketch and list of works and references, see TWENTIETH CENTURY AUTHORS, 1942.

*WEIL, SIMONE (February 3, 1909-August 24, 1943), French mystic and writer, was born in Paris. The daughter of a well-to-do doctor, she early identified herself with the underprivileged part of society. As a little girl during World War I, she refused to eat sugar because the soldiers at the front were deprived of it, or to wear warm socks because the children of  the workers went bare-legged. Extremely precocious in her studies of literature and science, she quoted passages of Racine at six, and obtained her *baccalauréat ès lettres* with distinction at fifteen. She attended the Lycée Victor Duruy and prepared for the Ecole Normale Supérieure at the Lycée Henri IV.

At the Ecole Normale Supérieure she worked under Alain, the well-known philosopher and essayist who recognized in her "a power of thought which was rare." After passing her *agrégation* in philosophy in 1931, she was appointed to the secondary school for girls at Le Puy. Strongly interested in politics at this time, she held liberal, humanitarian views. For a time she had sympathy for communism, but she never joined the Communist Party, and she was critical of Stalinism. In Le Puy she walked in picket lines, contributed to the *Révolution Prolétarienne* review, and refused to eat more than the unemployed workers could buy on relief. When the school board threatened to take away her license for this radical activity, she told them she would consider the revocation of her license "the crown of her career."

This early martyrdom was not granted to her, however. In 1934 she took a year's leave from teaching to work in the Renault automobile factory, in Paris, in order to experience more fully the working people's life. Despite severe and constant migraine headaches, she refused any comfort which would make her lot different from that of the factory girls. Her conclusions about the uprooted life of the workers are contained in her book *Enracinement (The Need for Roots).*

In 1936 she went to Barcelona to share the suffering of the Spanish Republican Army for several weeks on the Catalonian front, experiencing to the very depths of her being the calamity of war. Accidentally burned, she was rescued by her parents who took her to Portugal for convalescence. In a cathedral

* vil

in Portugal, while listening to a Gregorian chant during the worst of agony of a migraine headache, she had her first mystical experience. "In a moment of intense physical suffering when I was forcing myself to feel love, but without desiring to give a name to that love, I felt, without being in any way prepared for it (for I had never read the mystical writers), a presence more personal, more certain, more real than that of a human being, though inaccessible to the senses and the imagination."

After this, she became convinced that social and political action was mere *"ersatz Divinity"* and turned her search in the direction of religion itself. Although her parents were Jewish, Simone Weil had been brought up in a thoroughly secular and non-religious atmosphere. In 1940, when Paris was occupied by the Germans, she went to Marseilles with her parents, and there met the Reverend Father Perrin who was then at the Dominican Convent at Marseilles. She had conversations with Father Perrin who brought her to the very threshold of the Roman Catholic Church, which she never entered. In a beautiful image, she described herself as the bell which tolls to bring others to Church. Her book, *L'Attente de Dieu (Waiting for God)* contains her letters to Father Perrin and her "spiritual autobiography" in which she explains her reasons for refusing baptism at his hands.

In the south of France, Simone Weil engaged in agricultural work, while continuing her studies of Greek and Hindu philosophy and widening her knowledge of Sanskrit. In May 1942 she finally agreed to accompany her parents to America. She soon returned to England where she worked for the Free French and tried desperately to be allowed to be parachuted into France to join the resistance movement. Although weak and sick, she refused to eat any more than the rations allowed her countrymen in occupied territory. On August 24, 1943, she died in Ashford, England. The main cause of her death, medical authorities said, was "voluntary starvation."

The remarkable career of Simone Weil in the twentieth century recalls the lives of some of the saints and mystics of the Middle Ages. E. W. F. Tomlin writes: "If Simone Weil has any claim to sanctity, it lies not in her conversion at a particular time, but in the steady convergence of her whole being upon a point which throughout life she kept clearly in view." Grasping the essential rootlessness of modern man, which has driven him toward idolatry ("State worship in the totalitarian society"), she wrote in *The Need for Roots* what many critics consider to be one of the most brilliant intellectual works of the twentieth century. Physically she was a pathetic figure, thin, pale, indifferent as to clothing, usually wearing an old cloak, a beret, and large horn-rimmed spectacles. Tomlin writes: "In a surviving photograph she bears some resemblance to the inmate of a concentration camp; but on closer inspection, we notice that the features are serene and without blemish, and the mouth, half smiling, almost beautiful." Her influence upon modern thought is considerable and is constantly growing. In a world dominated by the sense "of being poised on the edge of an abyss," Simone Weil has perhaps a greater relevance "than the most subtle of Existentialists."

PRINCIPAL WORKS IN ENGLISH TRANSLATION: Waiting For God, 1951; Gravity and Grace, 1952; The Need for Roots, Prelude to a Declaration of Duties Toward Mankind, 1952.

ABOUT: Davy, M. M. The Mysticism of Simone Weil; Tomlin, E. W. F. Simone Weil; Weil, S. Waiting for God; Catholic World, June 1952; Commentary January 1951; New Republic August 18, 1952; New Yorker May 13, 1950; Nineteenth Century July 1950; Time January 15, October 1, 1951.

WEINSTEIN, NATHAN WALLENSTEIN. See WEST, N.

WEISKOPF, FRANZ (1900-   ), Czechoslovakian novelist, was born in Prague, which was then a provincial capital of the Hapsburg empire. In 1917 he was mobilized for service with a Hungarian regiment of the Imperial and Royal Army. At the end of the war he went back to the *gymnasium* to resume his interrupted studies in history, literature, and philosophy. In 1923 a doctor's degree was conferred upon him by the University of Prague. His initial literary venture was a play, *Foehn*, produced when he was still a student. In 1923 a first book, a volume of poetry, was published, and since that time Weiskopf has written a number of books of verse, short stories, essays and novels, several of which were burned in Hitler's literary bonfires. In 1939 the author came to the United States, living and writing in New York. *Dawn Breaks*, his first novel in English translation, was based on the German invasion of Slovakia and the peasants' sabotage of the attack. Telling his tale

Fred Stein

graphically, Weiskopf was found by the critics to have written well and movingly of the people he knew so intimately.

Children of Their Time continued a series of novels begun with his *Twilight on the Danube,* dealing with an old patrician family of Prague. "*Children of Their Time* has perspective and an authentic bite," wrote Virgilia Peterson in the New York *Herald Tribune Book Review.* "If it lacks design—because its final shape is still to be determined in a later book—its purpose is clear." She compared it with Romains, saying that "while Romains's objectivity might give future historians a more accurate photograph of our times, the righteous indignation of a Weiskopf would give them an insight into our hearts. For Weiskopf believes in humanity and suffers to see it fail."

Weiskopf's books have been translated into many languages. He is the editor of an anthology of Czechoslovakian writings, *Hundred Towers.* By 1949 he had returned to Czechoslovakia where he was named, successively, Ambassador to Sweden; Minister Plenipotentiary, Embassy of Czechoslovakia, Washington, D.C.; and Ambassador to Communist China.

PRINCIPAL WORKS IN ENGLISH TRANSLATION: Land without Unemployment (ed. with E. Glaeser) 1931; Dawn Breaks, 1942; Firing Squad, 1944; Hundred Towers (ed.) 1945; Twilight on the Danube, 1946; Children of Their Time, 1948.

WELLES, SUMNER (October 14, 1892-), American diplomat and author, was born in New York City, the son of Benjamin Welles and Frances (Swan) Welles. "I was born and brought up in the New York City of the mauve decade—a city that no longer exists except in distant memory. After Groton and Harvard I went on a six months' safari in East Africa and then returned to the United States to enter the American Foreign Service," Welles wrote in 1951. "I served three years in Japan when Japan still possessed liberal political and social forces. . . . But at that stage my chief interest had for some time been the improvement of inter-American relations and the development of that Regional Organization of American States that has now come into being."

Karsh, Ottawa

Tokyo was his first diplomatic post, from 1915 to 1917, after which Welles was transferred to Buenos Aires. Here he studied Spanish and became proficient in the language. In 1920 he returned to Washington, becoming chief of the Latin-American Affairs Division. From this period came his first book, *Naboth's Vineyard,* an account of the Dominican Republic between 1844 and 1924. Best known for his later work with Franklin D. Roosevelt, Welles assumed responsibility with this administration first as Ambassador to Cuba, then as Assistant Secretary of State, and finally as Under-Secretary of State. Before France fell, Welles went to Europe on a fact-finding mission and conferred with Hitler, Mussolini, Daladier, and Chamberlain, among others. He conversed with each man in his own language. The following year he accompanied President Roosevelt to his Atlantic Charter meeting and had a part in drawing up that document. Resigning the post in 1943, Welles devoted himself to lecturing and writing, producing the unusually popular book *The Time for Decision* in 1944. England's *New Statesman and Nation* said, "Mr. Sumner Welles . . . has written a book which is not merely a best-seller but by far the most important work on American foreign policy in the last twenty-five years, and by far the most far-sighted plan for the post-war world that has emerged from World War II." "His book would have benefited by editorial pruning," commented the *Saturday Review of Literature,* "and his style of writing—in contrast to his eloquent speeches—retains too many overtones of formal diplomatic statements to be always effective. But his book is crammed with mature and stimulating comment."

In 1951 appeared *Seven Decisions That Shaped History,* a freshly informative account of the war years, with a final chapter summing up United States foreign policy in the years following the war. "The real importance of the book," stated Samuel Grafton, writing in the *New Republic,* "lies in its defense of the man of vision who was the wartime President; in its stiffness and awkwardness, as it comes from the pen of a cool man stirred by proximity to greatness, it carries more force than many a stereotyped tribute from others in the Roosevelt political family."

Welles has been president of Freedom House since 1952, and has served as editor-in-chief of the Foreign Policy Series published by the Harvard University Press. His tastes in reading are chiefly history, biography, and books that deal with the more recent developments in foreign relations. Most of the year he lives in Maryland on the Potomac River not far from Washington, but his writing is done largely during the summer in Maine or during the winter in Florida. Welles is said to be a formal and austere person, possessed of an inflexible will. His figure is tall, correct, disciplined. He is a hard worker. In December 1948 he had a near escape from death when he collapsed, of an apparent heart attack, while on a walk on his country estate. He lay for eight hours in the freezing cold before he was rescued.

Welles' first marriage was to Esther Slater; they had two sons. His second marriage was to Mathilde Townsend who died in 1949. Since 1952 he has been married to Harriette Post.

PRINCIPAL WORKS: Naboth's Vineyard, 1928; United States and the World Crisis, 1941; World of the Four Freedoms, 1943; The Time for Decision, 1944; Intelligent American's Guide to the Peace (ed.) 1945; Where Are We Heading? 1946; Cooperation Between Canada and the United States in the Search for World Peace, 1947; We Need Not Fail, 1948; Seven Decisions That Shaped History 1951.

ABOUT: Karsh, Y. Faces of Destiny; Current Biography 1940; New York Herald Tribune Book Review October 7, 1951; Saturday Review of Literature June 12, 1948; Time January 3, 1946.

WELLMAN, PAUL ISELIN (October 14, 1898-   ), American novelist and historian, writes: "A somewhat unusual childhood left no very great impress on me, unless it had something to do with cultivating my imagination. I was born in Enid, Okla., my parents, Dr. Frederick C. Wellman, and Lydia (Isely) Wellman, having moved to the newly opened Cherokee Strip soon after their marriage. My father, a physician with a brilliant mind, who became noted in both scientific and artistic fields, came from an old American family, the progenitors of which settled in Jamestown from Devonshire England about 1627, moving west through Virginia, Kentucky and Missouri with the frontier. My mother was of Swiss stock, with musical and literary tastes and profound religious convictions. These factors combined to send my parents to Africa when I was less than a year old, my father to become expert in tropical medicine, my mother to do mission work among the Bantu natives of Angola. I spent my first ten years in West Africa, save for brief 'furloughs' in England and once in the United States, and spoke the native tongue, Umbundu, before I spoke English.

"Returning to this country with a younger brother to go to school, I lived three years with an aunt, Miss M. Alice Isely, then a teacher in a non-Mormon school in Utah. It might be supposed that out of the African experiences, which were rich in episode and color, I might have used something in my writings, but save for one brief section in The Iron Mistress nothing of this kind has ever appeared. I sometimes question myself as to why the early part of my life seems to have been lived by someone other than myself. Emotional trouble, growing out of the incompatability of my parents, who were divorced when I was fourteen, may be the explanation. In any case the whole African part of my life, though I have the clearest memories of it, seems almost shut out of my mind as creative source material.

"Not so my life in America, every part of which has contributed to my interests and authorship. With my aunt I lived successively in Salt Lake, Provo, and Vernal, Utah—the latter town just then emerging from the primitive frontier stage. For a year I was in Washington, D.C., where my father was connected with the Smithsonian Institution. After the break-up of our family, I went with my mother, two younger brothers and a sister, to Cimarron, a small hamlet in western Kansas, an area just beginning to turn from the cowboy to the plowman, and worked on farms and cattle ranches. There I knew some of the veterans of the Indian fighting and trail-driving West, who still were living.

"This period was the genesis of my three historical works, Death on the Prairie, Death in the Desert, and The Trampling Herd, and also 'The Spanish Southwest' on which I am now [1952] engaged. Such novels as Jubal Troop, and Broncho Apache also had their beginnings in the interests started in those days.

"I graduated from the University of Wichita in 1918, and went into the army, the First World War being then in progress, serving in 1918 and 1919. After the war I devoted the next twenty-five years of my life to the newspaper field, an ideal career because it is an eventfully episodic one in which to gather a vast fund of experience and material for writing.

"Though I found newspaper work interesting, and did my best to excel in it, I always desired to do more important writing. While holding down full-time jobs as city editor and later editorial writer on various newspapers, including the Kansas City Star, I wrote and published my first seven books. Inevitably this dual career of intensive work on the newspaper by day, followed by equally intensive work on authorship at night, brought about a physical breakdown. The doctors told me I must give up either journalism or authorship. I did not find the choice difficult, and in 1944 resigned from the Kansas City *Star* and went to Los Angeles with my wife —I had married Miss Laura Mae Bruner in 1923—and our son, Paul I. Wellman, Jr., who is now a successful industrial engineer.

"After two years of screenplay writing at Warner Brothers and Metro-Goldwyn-Mayer, I settled down at last to writing of novels and historical works without any other deviating demands on my time and thought. Such books as *The Walls of Jericho, The Chain,* and *The Bowl of Brass* came out of my newspaper experience, and my historical interests resulted in *The Iron Mistress, The Comancheros, Angel with Spurs,* and *Female.*

"For the history and background of this country, its varied peoples, and its uniquely magnificent characteristics I have an almost spiritual reverence, and these are my central interests. Mrs. Wellman is of immense help to me, particularly with suggestions in handling feminine characters in my novels. My viewpoints are liberal and tolerant in most matters. I concede the right to others to have their own opinions, but I also maintain my right to my own. By religion I am an Episcopalian, by politics a Democrat. My recreations are a cattle ranch in Oregon, in which I have a partnership; fishing when I can get to it; and extensive reading.

"I work in the mornings, starting early and writing until after luncheon, seven days a week. My theory is that style should be clear, simple, yet varied enough to be interesting, and I have no sympathy with self-concious ornamentations or obscurities in writing which are sometimes affected, and which only serve to confuse the reader. In every book I seek to add something of interest, perhaps even of value, to my reader's knowledge of his country, his people, and his world."

* * *

Wellman's father writes and paints under the name Cyril Kay Scott. His brother Manley Wade Wellman is an author.

PRINCIPAL WORKS: *Non-Fiction*—Death on the Prairie, 1934; Death in the Desert, 1935; The Trampling Herd, 1939; Glory, God, and Gold, 1954. *Fiction*—Broncho Apache, 1936; Jubal Troop, 1939; Angel With Spurs, 1942; The Bowl of Brass, 1944; The Walls of Jericho, 1947; The Chain, 1949; The Iron Mistress, 1951; The Comancheros, 1952; Female, 1953.

ABOUT: Warfel, H. R. American Novelists of Today; Current Biography 1949; New York Times Book Review February 16, 1947; Saturday Review of Literature March 19, 1949.

WELLS, CAROLYN (187?-March 26, 1942). For biographical sketch and list of works and references, see TWENTIETH CENTURY AUTHORS, 1942.

WELLS, HERBERT GEORGE (September 21, 1866-August 13, 1946). For biographical sketch and list of earlier works and references, see TWENTIETH CENTURY AUTHORS, 1942.

* * *

H. G. Wells died at his London home in Regent's Park at seventy-nine. He had been ill for several months.

The man who at one time was probably the most widely read author in the world continued his ardent crusading to the end of his life. Three years before his death he earned a doctorate in science at the London University by writing a thesis on personality. A year later he published, in limited edition, a "contemporary memoir upon human behavior" ('42 to '44) castigating many public figures. The conservative London *Times* deplored the "rising intolerance" of his old age as "fascinating but horrible." Other critics, like E. L. Woodward, found that "Mr. Wells, angry, not always scientific, and at times a little rattled, is more worth reading than anyone else now writing."

Personally, as in his writing, he was a "difficult" but enormously persuasive man. George Bernard Shaw, whose close friendship with Wells withstood innumerable differences, said, "He was the most completely spoiled child I have ever known . . . yet H. G. had not an enemy on earth. He was so amiable that though he raged against all of us none of us resented it. . . . What a charmer he was!"

H. L. Mencken called his mind "really one of the most extraordinary that England has produced in our time. It moves swiftly and daringly and overlooks little that lies along its path. It has an insatiable acquisitiveness, and a great deal of originality. Day in and day out, it buzzes with ideas, good, bad, and indifferent." Although he himself disclaimed the title of "author" and proclaimed his work "just high-class journalism," some of his novels were certainly the product of a creative artist. The two words most frequently applied to his career are "prolific" (the London *Times* called him "this irrepressible non-stop genius") and "versatile" (Clifton Fadiman spoke of "Wells the world-citizen, Wells the world-planner, Wells the world-encyclopedist" as well as Wells the artist). A third characteristic was the unity underlying this fecund variety of work; unity based on his plea for rational control of the material forces released by modern man, which could lead toward progress and without which he believed mankind faced doom and destruction.

If much of his writing seems "dated" it is because, as Fadiman pointed out, "His aim was to make us aware of our time—its perils and its promises. That accomplished, we were no longer very much aware of Wells himself." Somerset Maugham tells us that in his last years Wells was "a disappointed man" and "had had his day." However, in that day he had achieved what Julian Huxley defined as "nothing less than having done more than any single man in the present century to alter the current of modern thought, and to alter it in a progressive direction."

ADDITIONAL WORKS: Crux Ansata: An Indictment of the Roman Catholic Church, 1944; '42 to '44, 1944; Happy Turning: A Dream of Life (also called Mind at the End of Its Tether) 1945.

ABOUT: Brome, V. H. G. Wells; Church, R. British Authors; Coates, J. B. Leaders of Modern Thought; Gray, J. On Second Thought; Nicholson, N. H. G. Wells; Orwell, G. Dickens, Dali and Others; Salter, Sir J. A. Personality in Politics; Swinnerton, F. The Georgian Literary Scene 1910-1935; Vallentin, A. H. G. Wells: Prophet of Our Day; Van Gelder, R. Writers and Writing; Atlantic Monthly May 1951; Commonweal September 27, 1946; Hibbert Journal July 1948; London Times August 14, 1946; London Times Educational Supplement August 17, 1946; London Quarterly Review January 1947; New Statesman and Nation August 17, 1946; New York Herald Tribune October 20, 1946; New York Times August 14, 1946, August 25, 1946; Saturday Review of Literature August 31, 1946, March 13, 1948, April 11, 1953; Spectator (London) August 16, 1948; Time August 26, 1946, November 6, 1950.

WELTY, EUDORA (April 13, 1909-), American short story writer and novelist, was born in Jackson, Miss., the daughter of Christian Webb Welty and Mary Chestina (Andrews) Welty. Her father was the president of a southern insurance company. Katherine Anne Porter has described Miss Welty's family as "cheerful and thriving. She seems to have got on excellently with both her parents and her two brothers." She attended the Mississippi State College for Women from 1925 to 1927, the University of Wisconsin, where she received her B.A. in 1929, and Columbia University, where she studied advertising in 1930-31. Although Eudora Welty began writing as a

Kay Bell

child, her first ambition was to become a painter. After her schooling and a quick try at advertising ("I quit advertising because it was too much like sticking pins into people to make them buy things that they didn't need or really much want"), she settled in Jackson and began to write. Her first published story was in a "little" magazine, *Manuscript*, in 1936.

With her first book, *A Curtain of Green*, a collection of her stories with an introductory preface by Miss Porter, Miss Welty was acclaimed by the critics. The *New Yorker* wrote: "Miss Welty's short stories are deceptively simple. They are concerned with ordinary people, but what happens to them and the manner of the telling are far from ordinary. Miss Welty builds up to her climax with force and economy, using no unnecessary words and making no false starts. A fine writer and a distinguished book." With the books that followed, Miss Welty continued to garner critical praise. Like her fellow Mississippian and author William Faulkner, she has lived most of her life in the region where she was born and has drawn upon that region for nearly all her work. "She gets her right nourishment from the source natural to her—her experience so far has been quite enough for her and of precisely the right kind," Miss Porter writes.

Eudora Welty did not publish a full-length novel until 1946, *Delta Wedding (The Robber Bridegroom*, a fantasy, was a novella). *Delta Wedding*, a quietly told story of Southern family life, was hailed by Granville Hicks as "a triumph of sensitivity" and "one of the finest novels of recent years . . . because Miss Welty's sensibility is equal to the burden she has imposed upon it."

Some critics have objected to the narrowness of her scene, its almost exclusive concentration upon one small region and its inhabitants. Even Hamilton Basso, who greatly admires her work, has admitted: "I am not sure that anyone not moderately familiar with the South can fully appreciate Miss Welty's accomplishment." Granville Hicks, however, argues that "she proves, as the good regionalists have always proved, that the deeper one goes into the heart of a region, the more one transcends its geographical boundaries." With *The Ponder Heart*, a short novel which first appeared in the *New Yorker* in December 1953, she demonstrated vividly that there are still vast resources to draw from in her southern scene. This boisterous story, told in the first person by a garrulous woman about her soft-hearted and soft-headed uncle, was an immediate success. It is "one of Miss Welty's lighter works," V. S. Pritchett remarked, "but there is not a mistake in it."

In May 1944 she was awarded a $1000 prize by the American Academy of Arts and Letters, and in 1955 the Howells Medal (awarded every five years by the Academy for "the most distinguished work of American fiction"—viz., *The Ponder Heart*—published in that period). She had previously twice won the O. Henry Memorial prize for the short story. Miss Welty is blonde and five feet ten inches tall. She writes easily and naturally and with complete enjoyment. "I certainly never think of who is going to read it. I don't think of myself either—at least, I don't believe I do. I just think of what it is that I'm writing. That's enough to do."

PRINCIPAL WORKS: A Curtain of Green, 1941; The Robber Bridegroom, 1942; The Wide Net, 1943; Delta Wedding, 1946; Music from Spain, 1948; The Golden Apples, 1949; The Ponder Heart, 1954; The Bride of the Innisfallen, 1955.

ABOUT: Porter, K. A. *Preface to* E. Welty's A Curtain of Green; Scherman, D. E. & Redlich, R. Literary America; Van Gelder, R. Writers and Writing; Current Biography 1942; English Journal November 1952; New York Herald Tribune Book Review August 21, 1949; Saturday Review of Literature August 27, 1949.

WENDELL, BARRETT (August 23, 1855-February 8, 1921). For biographical sketch and list of works and references, see TWENTIETH CENTURY AUTHORS, 1942.

WENDT, GERALD (March 3, 1891-   ). For autobiographical sketch and list of earlier works and references, see TWENTIETH CENTURY AUTHORS, 1942.

* * *

Gerald Wendt writes from the UNESCO offices in Paris: "In 1942 I became science editor of Time, Inc., thus counsellor in science for the editors of *Time, Life, Fortune,* and *The March of Time,* but left in 1946 to assist the McGraw-Hill Publishing Company in launching the new monthly *Science Illustrated,* as editorial director. It was the first major American effort to establish a popular magazine of science above the adolescent level and attained a monthly circulation of 650,000 within three years but failed for lack of adequate advertising support. By this time my experience with the media of popular education in science and my devotion to the cause were sufficient to lead me to accept an invitation from the United Nations Educational, Scientific and Cultural Organization in Paris to take charge of the Division of Teaching and Dissemination in the Department of Natural Sciences. This involves the improvement of science instruction in schools and colleges throughout the world, the incorporation of science into elementary and 'fundamental' education, popular education by means of exhibits, films and radio, the organization in many countries of science clubs for youth, the dissemination of science news by the diverse media of mass communication, and the study and wide discussion of the social consequences of science."

* * *

Dr. Wendt was divorced in 1938 and in 1947 married Anne Dolores Powers. He has continued his writing on science (usually unsigned) in the *UNESCO Courier, UNESCO Features, UNESCO World Review,* and *UNESCO Science News,* which are translated into many languages and reprinted throughout the world. He is also editor of UNESCO's quarterly *Impact of Science on Society* and has continued his annual lecture tours of the United States.

ADDITIONAL WORKS: The Atomic Age Opens, 1945; Atomic Energy and the Hydrogen Bomb, 1950.

WENTWORTH, PATRICIA (pseudonym of Mrs. George Oliver Turnbull), British detective story writer, writes: "Patricia Wentworth comes of an old army family. Her father was a distinguished general, and she is married to a soldier. She began her literary career by writing historical novels, with the first of which, a romance of the French Revolution, she won an open  prize for the best first novel. It scored an immediate success, and has been used as a textbook for students. Later she turned to the romantic thriller, her first book in this style, *The Astonishing Adventure of Jane Smith,* being hailed as quite a new departure in detective fiction. Her books are in continuous demand at the libraries and attract a widening public. It is her aim to portray ordinary, convincing human characters in extraordinary circumstances, and in this she has been told that she succeeds. Miss Silver, who knits her way through one mystery after another and flavours detection with moral maxims, is quite unlike any one else in this field and has become a favourite."

* * *

A glance at the list of works below will indicate the astonishing prolificness of Miss Wentworth. "The bountiful Miss Wentworth," James Sandoe wrote in 1954, "supplies a measure full to overflowing, always much the same draught and usually agreeable, teasing, soothing." Her detective-heroine, the genteel Miss Maud Silver, is one of the most popular of all fictional detectives—a paragon of refinement and good sense. Miss Wentworth herself shuns publicity. Born Dora Amy Elles, daughter of Lieutenant-General Sir Edmund Roche Elles, she married Lieutenant-Colonel George Dillon, who died in 1906. In 1920 she married Lieutenant-Colonel George Oliver Turnbull; they have one daughter. Miss Wentworth lives in Surrey. Her recreations are reading, gardening, music and motoring.

PRINCIPAL WORKS: A Little More Than Kin, 1911; The Devil's Wind, 1912; The Fire Within, 1913; Queen Anne Is Dead, 1915; The Astonishing Adventure of Jane Smith, 1923; The Red Laquer Case, 1924; The Annam Jewel, 1925; The Black Cabinet, 1926; The Dower House Mystery, 1926; The Amazing Chance, 1927; Hue and Cry, 1927; Will-o'-the-Wisp, 1928; Anne Belinda, 1928; Fool Errant, 1929; Marriage Under the Terror, 1929; The Grey Mask, 1929; A Kingdom Lost, 1930; Coldstone, 1930; Beggar's Choice, 1931; Danger Calling, 1931; Nothing Venture, 1932; The Red Shadow, 1932; Outrageous Fortune (in England: Seven Green Stones) 1933; Walk With Care, 1933; Fear by Night, 1934; Red Danger, 1934; The Blindfold, 1935; Red Stefan, 1935; Hole and Corner, 1936; Dead or Alive, 1936; The Case Is Closed, 1937; Down Under, 1937; Mr. Zero, 1938; Run! 1938; The Lonesome Road, 1939; The Blind Side, 1939; Rolling Stone, 1940; Account Rendered (in England: Who Pays the Piper?) 1940; In the Balance (in England: Danger Point) 1941; Weekend with Death (in England: Unlawful Occasions) 1941; Pursuit of a Parcel, 1942; The Chinese Shawl, 1943; Miss Silver Deals with Death (in England: Miss Silver Intervenes) 1943; The Clock Strikes Twelve, 1944; The Key, 1944; Silence in Court, 1945; She Came Back (in England: The Traveller Returns) 1945; Beneath the Hunter's Moon (poems) 1945; Pilgrim's Rest, 1946; The Latter End, 1947; The Wicked Uncle (in England: Spotlight) 1947; The Case of William Smith, 1948; Miss Silver Comes to Stay, 1949; The Catharine-Wheel, 1949; The Brading Collection, 1950; Through the Wall, 1950; Anna, Where Are You? 1951; The Ivory Dagger, 1951; Ladies' Bane, 1952; Watersplash, 1952; The Pool of Dreams (poems) 1953; Out of the Past, 1953; The Vanishing Point, 1953; The Silent Pool, 1954; The Benevent Treasure, 1954.

*WERFEL, FRANZ V. (September 10, 1890-August 26, 1945). For biographical sketch and list of earlier works and references, see TWENTIETH CENTURY AUTHORS, 1942.

* * *

* vĕr'fĕl

Franz Werfel died at his home in Hollywood at fifty-four. He was survived by his wife, Anna Mahler Werfel, the widow of the noted composer Gustav Mahler. His death was the result of a third heart attack; the other two had taken place two years earlier, and, according to Gustav O. Arlt, had changed the author's perspective on his last book, Star of the Unborn. Completed a few days before Werfel died, the book is (in Arlt's words), "the uninhibited account of one who has made his final reckoning with the world and who looks back in retrospect on his own life and upon his contemporaries."

In 1944 S. N. Behrman's "American version" of Werfel's play Jacobowsky and the Colonel was produced in New York by the Theatre Guild with Elia Kazan as the director, and was very successful. Later that same year a play by Ladislaus Bus-Fekete and Mary Helen Fay, based on Werfel's novel Embezzled Heaven, starring Ethel Barrymore, was less enthusiastically received. The motion picture made from The Song of Bernadette won five Motion Picture Academy Awards and launched the acting career of Jennifer Jones.

The unevenness in the quality of Werfel's work taken as a whole, which led Commentary to call him "a writer of enormous talent who yet fell continuously into the second-rate," is explained by Heinz Politzer as due to "an exuberant boyishness that surrendered itself wholly to every possible source of inspiration, and to his journalistic dependence on his subject matter." His plays, according to Wolfgang Paulsen, "belong to the best of modern German dramatic literature," and Eric Bentley said of the Poems (published in 1945), "If they are not quite major poetry, they are in their way as good as anything in German poetry since the generation of George and Rilke."

Politzer has commented: "Like Baroque literature, his work made a public affair of faith, of the mystery of life and death, of ecstasy and repentance—did this by the seduction of words, the melody of language, by the modern dexterity with which he reported metaphysical problems and experience." For many of his readers it is as an eloquent idealist that he will be remembered. As Harrison Smith said, "The world has lost in him one of its most inspired, emotional writers, a champion of the dignity of man on earth, and a believer in his place in heaven."

ADDITIONAL WORKS IN ENGLISH TRANSLATION: Between Heaven and Earth, 1944; Jacobowsky and the Colonel: Comedy of a Tragedy, 1944; Poems, 1945; Star of the Unborn, 1946.

ABOUT: Columbia Dictionary of Modern European Literature; Lange, V. Modern German Literature; Liptzin, S. Germany's Stepchildren; Parrington, V. L. American Dreams; Slochower, H. No Voice is Wholly Lost; American Magazine March 1945; Books Abroad October 1945; Christian Century January 10, 1945; Commentary March 1950; Contemporary Jewish Review April 1945; London Times August 28, 1945; Saturday Review of Literature September 8, 1945, March 2, 1946; Theatre Arts July 1944.

WERTHAM, FREDRIC (1895-), German-born psychologist, writes: "Since adolescence I have been a voracious reader and interested in literature. I think it was literature that led me to psychiatry. And psychiatry led me back to literature.

Gordon Parks

"I was born in Germany and educated there and in England. My training in medicine was also partly in Germany, partly in England. My post-graduate studies in neurology and psychiatry were in Munich, Vienna, Paris, and London. In 1921 I came to the United States to work under Professor Adolf Meyer at Johns Hopkins, where I stayed for seven years, teaching and doing research. I was the first American psychiatrist to be awarded a research fellowship by the National Research Council (Washington, D.C.). In 1932 I organized and directed the first psychiatric clinic in a major court where all convicted felons got a psychiatric examination about which a report was made to the judges. Since then my main psychiatric interest has been the practice and organization of psychotherapy in mental hygiene clinics. I have become acquainted with the personal, sexual, social and bureaucratic difficulties of innumerable people. And I plan to write about that some day. My interest in psychoanalysis started through my personal acquaintance with Freud after the First World War; my training in it came from Dr. Horace Westlake Frink, whom Freud regarded as his best American pupil. I have been director of some of the largest clinics in the country, the mental hygiene clinic of Bellevue Hospital and that of the Queens Hospital Center. I also organized two free clinics on my own, the Quaker Emergency Service Readjustment Center, devoted entirely to the psychotherapy of sexual difficulties (most of which were homosexual), and the Lafargue Clinic. I started that in 1946 in the heart of a slum area in Harlem. The Lafargue Clinic fulfilled such a need that from the day it opened we were swamped with patients. However, we have never been able to get any endowment from any individual or any organization and are still dependent upon very small contributions from well-wishers all over the country. None of the staff gets paid. Aside from these clinics, I have been practicing psychiatry and psychoanalysis in New York for some twenty years.

"My first book, The Brain as an Organ, is entirely technical, being a textbook of neuropathology. Dark Legend, which appeared first in 1941, is a factual story in literary form. It deals with a seventeen-year-old boy who committed matricide. I found that no psychiatric nor psychoanalytic study of such a case had been made before and was impressed by the fact that this untutored boy of the slums used expressions paralleling those of Orestes and Hamlet in high tragedy. The British edition had censorship trouble and could not be published for a few years. My next book, The Show of Violence, also is a factual description. In it I present the details of a few of the many murderers I have psychiatrically studied and discuss the whole question of murder and insanity. The main point of that book is that we could prevent violence if we wanted to. My latest book deals with the same subject in another field. It is called Seduction of the Innocent and is the first complete independent study of a type of literature that has become the greatest publishing success in all history, the comic book. A condensation of this book appeared in the Ladies' Home Journal for November 1953.

"I wrote a study of Ezra Pound called The Road to Rapallo. In The World Within, an anthology of short stories with psychiatric subjects edited by Mary Louise Aswell, I wrote an introduction, on 'Psychiatry and Literature,' and an analytic comment on each story. A type of literature—for that is what I think it should be—much neglected at present is the book review. The essay-review is one field where literature and social criticism can help to reestablish the often-broken link between life and literature. I have written book reviews for the New Republic, New York Times Book Review, psychiatric and legal journals, Saturday Review, etc. My essay on Tolstoy has elicited so much comment that it has reinforced my opinion that the prevention of violence is on many people's minds."

* * *

Dr. Wertham is one of the best known of contemporary psychologists. His books are widely read by laymen as well as by experts in the field. In addition, he has been called upon from time to time to testify in sensational murder trials. An authority on crime, especially among young people, Dr. Wertham holds that murder is "an index to the state of the society in which it occurs." The large crime rate in our own society, he believes, reflects a general social callousness toward human dignity and human life; and his powerfully-written books on criminal psychology have been an attempt to educate the public to a better understanding of crime and its prevention. He has long been an active crusader against crime comic books which, he argues, have a pernicious influence upon children and young people. After making a careful study of these comic books and interviewing children who read them, he presented a shocking but thoroughly documented attack on them in *Seduction of the Innocent*. Charles Wright Mills wrote of the book in the New York *Times*: "Dr. Wertham's cases, his careful observations and his sober reflections about the American child in a world of comic violence and unfunny filth testify to a most commendable use of the professional mind in the service of the public."

Dr. Wertham lives in New York City. He is tall, grey-haired, with "deep, intense blue eyes." He is married to Florence Hesketh, a sculptress.

PRINCIPAL WORKS: The Brain as an Organ, 1934; Dark Legend, 1941; The Show of Violence, 1949; The Road to Rapallo, 1949; Seduction of the Innocent, 1954.

ABOUT: Pinner, M. & Miller, B. F. (eds.) When Doctors Are Patients; Current Biography 1949; New Republic June 3, 1946; New York Post November 1, 1946; Newsweek May 9, 1949; Saturday Review of Literature May 7, 1949; Time February 18, 1946, December 1, 1947.

WESCOTT, GLENWAY (April 11, 1901-). For autobiographical sketch and list of earlier works and references, see TWENTIETH CENTURY AUTHORS, 1942.

* * *

Glenway Wescott writes from Hampton, N.J.: "Perhaps I should speak of myself now with a sharper sense of humor, a turn of phrase less melancholy, than in 1942. On the other hand, my prognosis of further production of volumes of fiction is less optimistic or less ambitious. Evidently I felt then that I had mastered the narrative art, so that it would be easy for me to narrate a great deal. Perhaps I should call myself a man of letters rather than a novelist. In the past decade I have produced only one novel, *Apartment in Athens*, a Book-of-the-Month Club selection in the spring of 1945.

"Having been found ineligible for the selective service, I wanted some other part in the tragic necessity of the war. Living in Germany in 1921-22, and traveling there from time to time after that, I had made friends with Germans of all sorts; and it seemed to me that I had an understanding of certain mysteries of the German mentality and Central European history out of which Nazism developed, and that in the form of a novel this might serve a useful national and international purpose. So many Americans were having to fight and to sacrifice in ignorance. I first attempted a tale of the fall of France, but I found that unwritable, perhaps because the French spirit seemed to fluctuate too much, and my imagination likewise; and in what information came to me I could not see the wood for the trees. Then I happened to meet a hero of the Greek underground who was visiting this country on a secret mission, and although I had never been to Greece even as a tourist, I was inspired by his account of the German occupation of Athens to begin all over again, with Greek everyman and everywoman and everychild instead of my familiar, too familiar French.

"Since the war I have published nothing in book form except two fairly important critical studies, introductions to *The Maugham Reader* (1950) and to *Short Novels of Colette* (1951).

"I am now at work on a novel of remembrances of Europe, especially Paris in the twenties, to be entitled 'A Hundred Affections.' I have also undertaken one other ambitious volume, 'The Small World,' an account of my education and foreign travel, famous friends and worldly influences. Two further volumes, non-fiction, I keep still about. I am an incorrigibly copious letter-writer, and doubtless I have wasted time in that way and in more or less parallel ways."

* * *

Apartment in Athens is a story of a middle-class Greek family in whose apartment a Nazi officer is billeted. Through the simple and spare lines of the narrative emerges a powerful study of war and defeat and their effects on the lives of decent and dignified human beings. "I have not read any other book—either of fiction or of direct documentation—," Edmund Wilson wrote, "which has given me the feeling of starving and stifling, of falling back on interior positions, constructing interior defenses, reorganizing and redirecting, behind a mask of submission, the whole structure and aim of one's life, as *Apartment in Athens*." Eudora

Welty called it "a work of art in the true sense." She praised especially its "moderateness, lack of exaggeration, serenity."

Correction: *Fear and Trembling* (1932), listed in TWENTIETH CENTURY AUTHORS, 1942 among Wescott's principal works as a volume of short stories, is a collection of essays.

ADDITIONAL WORK: Apartment in Athens, 1945.

ABOUT: Warfel, H. R. American Novelists of Today; Wilson, E. Classics and Commercials.

WEST, ANTHONY (1914-), English critic and novelist, was born in England, the son of H. G. Wells and Rebecca West.

Madame Yevonde

"At school I was a rather unsuccessful student. . . . I never went to a university and have never acquired any sort of certificate or diploma." Although in about 1932 West himself began a four-years' vagabondage about the world, he decries a bohemian life as injurious to the young writer. "Take your sensitivity and vision through the normal working world," he advises, "and don't begin writing too soon." In 1937 West started to write reviews for Raymond Mortimer, editor of the *New Statesman and Nation*, and when the war broke out he was that journal's regular critic of new fiction. Unable to be in combat service because of a past history of tuberculosis, West was employed during World War II by the British Broadcasting Corporation, and remained at this task until 1946 when he resigned to begin work on a novel. In 1936 he had married; this marriage was later dissolved. There were two children.

His first novel, *On a Dark Night* (in the United States, *The Vintage*), was published in England in 1949. "An earnest book," wrote the *Manchester Guardian*, "full of the bitterness of twentieth-century disillusionment." Although the novel was criticized by some reviewers for the fault of grandiose imagery, it was generally praised for the quality of its writing. In 1950 West came to America, and has since settled in Stonington, Conn., with his second wife, Lily West; he has applied for United States citizenship. His reasons for coming to America are many. "I was a painter to start with, and at seventeen I fell in love with America through the eye for its dynamic landscape, primary colors, clear air—unlike England's, which blur definition." And among the further reasons,

"Under the pressure of economics, England has for a short-term policy forsaken liberalism for statism; I find the narrowing of the intellectual climate involved repulsive. America is still fundamentally liberal, and the spirit is alive." These and many other feelings add up to his change of allegiance to what he calls "my America, my new found land." He believes that the concept of the individual as a fragment of the divine being is a more creative one than that of the individual either as a freebooter or as the component of a state or society.

A book reviewer for *Time* and the *New Yorker*, West has written a guide book, *Gloucestershire*, as well as a book on D. H. Lawrence. His most recent novel was *Another Kind*, which met with critical disfavor, though individual scenes or chapters were praised. The London *Times Literary Supplement* found the minor characters well delineated, and the descriptions of places and scenes excellent.

PRINCIPAL WORKS: Gloucestershire, 1939; On a Dark Night (in the United States: The Vintage) 1949; Another Kind, 1951; D. H. Lawrence, 1951; The Crusades (juvenile) 1955.

ABOUT: Saturday Review of Literature January 14, 1950, February 17, 1951.

WEST, JESSAMYN, American novelist, was born in Indiana, but has lived in California since she was six years old. She at-

Kay Bell

tended a small Quaker college, Whittier College, in southern California and there married a classmate, H. M. McPherson. After graduation she went to England to study, and on her return attended the University of California. Discovering that she had tuberculosis of the lungs, Miss West spent some years in bed, where she began to write in a notebook. She writes reclining, a habit she acquired in the sanatorium and still prefers.

Her first book, *The Friendly Persuasion*, consisted of gently humorous sketches about the life of a family of Quakers living in Indiana about the time of the Civil War. The book had no comprehensive plot, but was praised for its vivid picture of a country household. "None of the characters, not one, is a puppet," wrote the *Weekly Book Review*. "The writing is now like the running of a brook and now like the stillness of a forest pool. Miss West's style is full of surprises, vivid metaphors, odd turns of plot, yet she is never disconcerting, over-ingenious, or repetitive." In 1948 she published an opera script based on an original conception of Raoul Pène DuBois for portraying the life of Audubon in a musical drama; the book was called *Mirror for the Sky*.

Miss West's second novel was *The Witch Diggers*, a rowdy and macabre book which one reviewer defined as "Indiana, 1899, Brueghel." The scene of *The Witch Diggers* is a "poor farm" in southern Indiana. The novel received high praise for its evocation of a mood of horror and violence, for its faithful detailing of the life of the period, for its craftsmanship and its honesty. Eudora Welty wrote of it in the New York *Times*: "This is a good, long, warm, generous, and curious novel. Its detail rounded and rich, an enormous number of vigorous characters abounding, it is a physical panorama concerned morally with man's infatuation with plans and calculations, from the noblest of them to the maddest and most useless and hopeless, and how this infatuation distorts, ruthlessly opposes, and even dooms his powers of love."

In quite another vein was Jessamyn West's series of stories of the adolescence of a charming young girl, *Cress Delahanty*. Cress first appeared in stories in the *New Yorker*. She is a warm-blooded, sensitive and intelligent girl, caught by Miss West in the painful and bewildering moment between childhood and maturity. Reviewing the book in the New York *Herald Tribune*, Dan Wickenden observed: "Miss West possesses a refreshing sanity, an essential earthiness, a robust sense of humor; and because she is a born writer, and a good one, she illuminates even the most commonplace material with her own particular magic."

Miss West was described by David Dempsey in the New York *Times* in 1954 as "a red-haired, copper-complected woman on the youngish side of middle age." She is a Quaker. Because her husband's business requires that he travel, she is often alone—"which she thinks is ideal from the point of view of getting things done but a limitation on the gregarious instincts that may keep a writer from going stale." In an effort, therefore, to get a "sense of community" with other writers, she frequently teaches at summer writing conferences.

PRINCIPAL WORKS: The Friendly Persuasion, 1945; Mirror for the Sky, 1948; The Witch Diggers, 1951; Cress Delahanty, 1953.

ABOUT: New York Herald Tribune Book Review February 18, October 7, 1951; New York Times Book Review January 3, 1954.

WEST, NATHANAEL (1906?-December 21, 1940). For biographical sketch and list of works and references, see TWENTIETH CENTURY AUTHORS, 1942.

* * *

ABOUT: Wilson, E. Classics and Commercials; Atlantic Monthly September 1950; Faulkner Studies Summer 1953; Newsweek September 4, 1950; Theatre Arts August 1951.

WEST, REBECCA (December 25, 1892-). For biographical sketch and list of earlier works and references, see TWENTIETH CENTURY AUTHORS, 1942.

* * *

Rebecca West's distinguished reporting of the post-war treason trials of Lord Haw-Haw and others who collaborated with the enemy during World War II has won her the reputation of the foremost woman journalist of Great Britain and the United States. American readers first read her accounts of the treason trials in the *New Yorker* magazine. These were later collected and published under the title *The Meaning of Treason*, a volume as remarkable for its rich and beautiful style as it was for its brilliant and penetrating analyses of the accused men. She reports "in depth," *Time* magazine observed, "a depth whose winding recesses of character, situation and context she divines by the play of unusually acute instincts and intuitions guided by an eye for significant detail. And she floods the planes of her perception with the generous human warmth of a womanly nature and a culture-crowded brain that gives to the meanest fact a new perspective."

Of *A Train of Powder*, another collection of essays "on the problem of guilt and punishment in our time," William L. Shirer wrote: "She has raised journalism to a high art, breathing into it a depth, a poetry, a subtlety and an understanding and compassion for human beings."

In 1949 Miss West was made a Commander in the Order of the British Empire. She lives with her husband, Henry Maxwell Andrews, on a farm in Buckinghamshire, close enough to London for her to continue to fulfill her journalistic assignments for British and American newspapers. Now in her sixties, she is a handsome woman, with flyaway grey hair and piercing dark eyes that light "a face that is impressive with mature intelligence."

ADDITIONAL WORK: The Meaning of Treason, 1947; A Train of Powder, 1955.

ABOUT: Saturday Review of Literature December 6, 1947; Time December 24, 1945, December 1, December 8, 1947.

WEST, SACKVILLE-. See SACK-
VILLE-WEST

WESTERMARCK, EDVARD ALEX-
ANDER (November 20, 1862-Septem-
ber 3, 1939). For biographical sketch
and list of works and references, see
TWENTIETH CENTURY AUTHORS, 1942.

"WESTMACOTT, MARY." See CHRIS-
TIE, A.

WESTON, CHRISTINE (GOUTIERE)
(August 31, 1904-   ), Anglo-American novelist and short story writer, reports: "I was

born in Unao, in the
United Provinces of
India. There were five
of us—three boys and
two girls. My parents
[Georges and Alicia
(Wintle) Goutiere]
were born in India;
my father's people
were French indigo-
planters, my mother
the daughter of an
English army officer. For many years my
father, who had become a naturalised Englishman, was an officer in the Indian Imperial Police. Later he went to London,
where he retired from the Police and studied
for the bar. He returned to India and practised as a barrister until his death in 1921.
Except for brief visits to England as a child
I lived in India until my marriage in 1923.
The country of one's childhood is always pre-
dominant in one's memory: India is a beautiful, brown, kindly land, and notwithstanding
all the perils of life in the tropics, it is a
fine country for any child to grow up in. I
was fortunate, too, in my parents, whose attitude towards the natives was quite different
from the attitude of most English people.

"The war of 1914 intervened between me
and the customary English education. My
oldest brother was already in school in England: I was destined for a convent in Bruges,
Belgium, my younger brother for Douai College. We were to have sailed from India on
the S.S. Persia, which was sunk by the Germans, I think early in 1915. My parents
sent me to a convent school in the hills. It
was a school run by English, German, and
Irish nuns. My father, whose radical spirit
had long since revolted against official discipline, apparently retained vestiges of his
French Catholic upbringing. He hoped that
his oldest daughter would acquire certain of

the gentle and lady-like arts, amongst which
he classed music and beautiful needle-work.
I acquired neither. In fact I acquired absolutely nothing except the Catholic ritual and
a desperate loathing for my teachers and most
of my classmates. My aversion to convent
life became chronic, and I kept running away
until my parents withdrew me. I had been a
peripatetic boarder for almost four years. I
had learned to read at the age of four and
was writing stories and poems at four and a
half. I marvel, now, at the almost anarchic
freedom of those days. However, when much
later my father discovered my taste for
penny thrillers he offered me the use of his
professional library, which included a whole
series of famous English trials. I think this
was during one of my legal winter holidays
from the convent. I must have been about
twelve. There are two books whose color,
weight, shape and content are forever fixed in
my memory: Plutarch's Lives and The Trial
of Eugene Aram.

"As I grew up I helped my father in his
law work. Our house was always filled with
odds and ends of humanity. One might suppose that in a country so large and a society
so diverse the net impression would be confused and blurred. On the contrary, every
face and every personality emerged vivid in
that strong light. I can still see the long,
shady, pillared verandah outside my father's
study. Rows of jutas (native shoes) left
outside, like boats tied up to a wharf. In
India people remove their shoes, not their
hats, when they enter a house. From inside
the great airy room came the chant of voices
and the click of a typewriter where the
Mohammedan clerk was taking down dispositions.

"In 1923 I married an American [Robert
Weston] and came to the United States. I've
lived in Maine ever since."

* * *

Christine Weston writes of contemporary
India with sure knowledge. E. M. Forster
said in 1950: "Mrs. Weston writes seriously,
carefully, compassionately; she is not interested in the glamorous East or in the boosting
of this or that political creed; she writes for
those who are emotionally involved in the
country and who love it." Probably her best-
known work is Indigo, a novel which has
been compared to Forster's own A Passage
to India for its authenticity and its understanding of the complexity of India's problems. Mrs. Weston was described in 1950 by
Harvey Breit as "a comely woman, in her
middle forties . . . simple, forthright and
gentle, though not sentimental." She received

a Guggenheim fellowship in 1940. Many of her short stories have appeared in the *New Yorker* and other magazines.

PRINCIPAL WORKS: Be Thou the Bride, 1940; The Devil's Foot, 1942; Indigo, 1944; Bhimsa, the Dancing Bear (juvenile) 1945; The Dark Wood, 1946; There and Then (short stories) 1947; The World Is a Bridge, 1950.

ABOUT: New York Times Book Review April 16, 1950; Wilson Library Bulletin December 1943.

WEYER, CONSTANTIN. See CON-STANTIN-WEYER

WEYGANDT, CORNELIUS (December 13, 1871-). For autobiographical sketch and list of earlier works and references, see TWENTIETH CENTURY AUTHORS, 1942.

* * *

Cornelius Weygandt has been emeritus professor of English at the University of Pennsylvania since 1942. He lives in Germantown, Pa. In 1946 he published his autobiography, *On the Edge of Evening*, a warm and rambling volume of reminiscence. At the conclusion of the book he wrote: "I have had enough of many things in life, of the city, of the theatre, of lecturing. I have not had enough of writing, of listening to music, of country contentments. I hope I am privileged to live on the Wissahickon Hills to the end. I could not be happy where there are houses just across the street and lack of elbow room about the house. The little things, as all my life long, are still the most of life to me."

ADDITIONAL WORKS: Heart of New Hampshire, 1944; On the Edge of Evening, 1946.

ABOUT: Weygandt, C. On the Edge of Evening; Saturday Review of Literature August 3, 1946.

* wī′gănt

WEYMAN, STANLEY JOHN (August 7, 1855-April 10, 1928). For biographical sketch and list of works and references, see TWENTIETH CENTURY AUTHORS, 1942.

WHARTON, Mrs. EDITH NEWBOLD (JONES) (January 24, 1862-August 11, 1937). For biographical sketch and list of works and references, see TWENTIETH CENTURY AUTHORS, 1942.

* * *

ABOUT: Gray, J. On Second Thought; Jessup, J. L. Faith of Our Feminists; Lubbock, P. Portrait of Edith Wharton; Morris, L. R. Postscript to Yesterday; Nevius, B. Edith Wharton; Quinn, A. H.

Introduction to The Edith Wharton Treasury (1950); Snell, G. D. Shapers of American Fiction; Wilson, E. Classics and Commercials; New Statesman and Nation January 20, 1945; Partisan Review July 1951.

WHEELER, WILLIAM MORTON (March 19, 1865-April 19, 1937). For biographical sketch and list of works and references, see TWENTIETH CENTURY AUTHORS, 1942.

WHEELOCK, JOHN HALL (September 9, 1886-). For autobiographical sketch and list of earlier works and references, see TWENTIETH CENTURY AUTHORS, 1942.

* * *

John Hall Wheelock succeeded the late Maxwell E. Perkins as a senior editor of Charles Scribner's Sons, and in 1950 he edited and wrote the introduction to an edition of Perkins' letters. Wheelock contributes poetry to the *New Yorker, Virginia Quarterly Review, Harper's Magazine,* and other periodicals. He was married in 1940 to Phyllis de Kay Bury, daughter of the late Charles de Kay, poet and art critic. His home is in New York City.

The statement in Mr. Wheelock's sketch in the 1942 volume that "his recurrent themes are loneliness, lost love, and nostalgia for the past" should be modified, he writes. "I have written poems that would fall in the first two categories—none that I know of that would answer to the third—but they form a very small proportion of my work, which is in the main metaphysical and concerned, to use the words of one critic, with 'the mystery, the beauty, the sadness and the unity of life'— especially the last." The influence on his work of Shelley and Swinburne is marked, Mr. Wheelock agrees (though with Swinburne only in the early books), but "Seeger's work is entirely opposite in method and point of view from mine." He continues: "My first book was published in 1905, some fifty years ago, and it is true that I belong to the generation preceding the one which has since made poetic history. At the time that my first books appeared they were distinctly in the contemporary movement, and certainly the range of my poems, both in subject matter and form, has been far from narrow."

ADDITIONAL WORKS: The Face of a Nation: Poetical Passages from the Writings of Thomas Wolfe (ed.) 1939; Editor to Author: Letters of Maxwell E. Perkins (ed.) 1950.

WHETHAM, W. C. D. See DAMPIER, W. C.

WHIBLEY, CHARLES (December 9, 1859-March 4, 1930). For biographical sketch and list of works and references, see TWENTIETH CENTURY AUTHORS, 1942.

WHITE, EDWARD LUCAS (May 18, 1866-March 30, 1934). For biographical sketch and list of works and references, see TWENTIETH CENTURY. AUTHORS, 1942.

WHITE, ELWYN BROOKS (July 11, 1899-). For biographical sketch and list of earlier works and references, see TWENTIETH CENTURY AUTHORS, 1942.

* * *

The late Irwin Edman, a distinguished essayist in his own right, proclaimed early in 1954, in a review of *The Second Tree from the Corner,* that E. B. White "is the finest essayist in the United States." The statement will probably go unchallenged — unless the challenger be White himself, with his gentle but firm mockery of accolades and superlatives. Edman continued: "He says wise things gracefully; he is the master of an idiom at once exact and suggestive, distinguished yet familiar. His style is crisp and tender, and incomparably his own."

White's long association with the *New Yorker*—and the fact that in his crisp editorials for the "Talk of the Town" he is its veritable spokesman — has identified him in the minds of many readers so closely with the magazine that they may visualize him as the bland and supercilious Eustace Tilley himself, who decorates the cover every spring. Actually he has a sharply defined literary personality quite distinct from the magazine. Through its pages he has indeed become the spokesman of the bemused, worldly yet strangely hopeful and wide-eyed contemporary urban generation. But even there his work bears the mark of his independence and individuality. He is a humorist, but he is also (and sometimes simultaneously) serious. "Humor," he once observed, "plays close to the big, hot fire which is truth and the reader often feels the heat." His brief comments in "Talk of the Town" on world affairs, the need for world government, and on national and local politics are sounder and more lucid than many long and lofty political studies. He thinks, as Edman remarked, "in terms of the wide and simple fact of our common humanity." His books for children, *Stuart Little* and *Charlotte's Web* (which like all the best children's books are read with greater delight by adults than by children) have become modern classics. Of *Charlotte's Web* Eudora Welty wrote: "The book has liveliness and felicity, tenderness and unexpectedness, grace and humor and praise of life, and the good backbone of succinctness that only the most highly imaginative stories seem to grow."

ADDITIONAL WORKS: Stuart Little, 1945; The Wild Flag, 1946; Here Is New York, 1949; Charlotte's Web, 1952; The Second Tree from the Corner, 1954.

ABOUT: Van Gelder, R. Writers and Writing; College English April 1946; New York Times Book Review January 17, 1954; Saturday Review November 15, 1952.

WHITE, HELEN CONSTANCE (November 26, 1896-). For autobiographical sketch and list of earlier works and references, see TWENTIETH CENTURY AUTHORS, 1942.

* * *

Helen C. White has taught English at the University of Wisconsin since 1919. She has also held visiting professorships to Barnard College and to Columbia University. She has been active in the United States Commission for UNESCO, the American Council on Education, and numerous other educational, religious, and social organizations. From 1941 to 1947 she was president of the American Association of University Women. Among the many honors she has received are the Laetare Medal from Notre Dame University in 1942, the Siena Medal in 1944, and the Distinguished Achievement Award of the Radcliffe Alumnae Association, and she has honorary degrees from a number of colleges, including Rockford, Wilson, and Smith.

Both her fiction and her works of scholarship are distinguished for their sound and sympathetic humanism. A handsome woman with a keen sense of humor and an extraordinary capacity for work, she relaxes by reading detective stories.

ADDITIONAL WORKS: Social Criticism in Popular Religious Literature of the Sixteenth Century, 1944; Dust on the King's Highway (novel) 1947; Tudor Books of Private Devotion, 1951; (ed., with others) Seventeenth Century Verse and Prose, I, 1951; The Four Rivers of Paradise (novel) 1955.

ABOUT: Hoehn, M. (ed.) Catholic Authors, I; Warfel, H. R. American Novelists of Today; Current Biography, 1945.

WHITE, NELIA GARDNER (November 1, 1894-), American novelist, writes: "I can think of no better training for the life of a writer than that of living in a Methodist parsonage in the early part of this century. Andrews Settlement, Little Genesee, Ceres, Pulteney, Cameron, Canaseraga, Knoxville—

all were little towns, so small that you could see their pattern clearly, if you would, could know all the people, see their relationship to the whole. Ministers' children are unafraid of change, yet aware of the value of roots. They are used to making homes in all sorts of houses, with other people's furniture. They are not afraid of society because they have always felt secure even inside what would nowadays be called poverty, but which never seemed like poverty then because there was always a margin for books, for friendships, for music and hospitality. No matter how limited the materials with which we worked, we clung to an ideal. This is a security far beyond any offered by money. Nearly all ministers' children I know have rebelled against orthodoxy. This rebellion seems to me normal and good, coupled as it nearly always is with a never-lost idealism. No writer can ever be worth his salt if he is not a questioner, a doubter. This does not mean he can have no standards by which to live, but only that his approach to life must forever be a question. The how and the what and the why of living are his business.

"Out of this background, plus two years at Syracuse University and two more at Emma Willard Kindergarten School, I began to write. First I wrote stories for kindergarten-age children and articles on how to bring up children for a kindergarten journal. Then I knew how very well to bring up children. When I had two of my own I made a few changes in my approach to the matter. But I have been writing ever since, countless short stories and novelettes, books for children, books for adults. I started out in a green, blind way, with no agent, no real knowledge of writing, but my youth had made me ambitious and unafraid and I was pleased but not too surprised when I sold what I wrote. I know now that I was lucky, and that the gift of words that came to me from my father and mother was a greater gift than I realized then. I know, too, that there is no end to learning how to write and that your living is tied inexorably to your writing. I know now how immeasurably richer my life has been because I blindly chose this work. The discipline, the ever-widening interests entailed, the joy of creating characters that seem like flesh and blood people—all these are gifts the business of writing gives the

writer. I have heard a number of writers say they hate writing. I do not hate it; I love it. It is hard work, calls for tremendous concentration, involves endless disappointments, and there is always the knowledge that your vision exceeds your grasp, but these things are part of the challenge, the excitement of writing. I raise my brows in doubt when writers say they hate to write.

"It would be futile to discuss all my books. Some are not worth discussing. *Daughter of Time*, a fictionized biography of Katherine Mansfield, was a labor of love. It involved a long journey to England and the continent for material, made some wonderful friends for me. *No Trumpet Before Him* won the Westminster prize and was perhaps responsible for my receiving the Arents award for literature from Syracuse University. During the last war I was in England with several other writers observing England in wartime, afterwards writing various stories that grew out of this experience. Now, in an old farmhouse on a back road in western Connecticut, we again begin to put down roots. Our son, with the same heritage of questioning and idealism, studies Polynesian culture in Tahiti. Up in the old schoolhouse at the corner our daughter has established a thriving library, for which she begged books, and neighbors built shelves and painted walls. My husband interests himself in civic affairs. It is a long way back to parsonage days but my security comes still from the same things, love of family, books, music, work."

* * *

Nelia Gardner White was born in Andrews Settlement, Pa., one of five children of John Adrian and Anna (Jones) Gardner. Her father was a Methodist minister. She studied at schools in New York and Pennsylvania, attended Syracuse University and the Emma Willard Kindergarten School in Syracuse. In 1917 she married Ralph Leon White, a lawyer. Her most successful book to date is *No Trumpet Before Him*, the story of a young country minister, which won the Westminster Press award in 1947. Her work has been called mature and "well contrived." Jane Voiles writes in the San Francisco Chronicle: "Mrs. White has complete mastery of the formula novel. She holds your interest even though you know, more or less, what is going to happen."

PRINCIPAL WORKS: Jen Culliton, 1927; David Strange, 1928; Tune in the Tree, 1929; Hathaway House, 1931; Mrs. Green's Daughter-in-Law, 1932; This Is My House, 1933; A Family Affair, 1934; The Fields of Gomorrah, 1935; Daughter of Time, 1942; Brook Willow, 1944; No Trumpet Before Him, 1948; The Pink House, 1950; The Woman at the Window, 1951; The Merry Month of May, 1952; The Spare Room, 1954; The Thorn Tree, 1955; *Juveniles*—Mary, 1925; Marge, 1926; And Michael, 1927; Joanna Grey, 1928, Kristin, 1929; Toni of Grand Isle, 1930; Boy of Scott's Corners.

ABOUT: Warfel, H. R. American Novelists of Today; Current Biography 1950.

WHITE, PATRICK (May 28, 1912-   ).
For autobiographical sketch and list of earlier works and references, see TWENTIETH CENTURY AUTHORS, 1942.

* * *

Patrick White writes from New South Wales, Australia: "Since the war my life has been practically uneventful. I returned to Australia, to a small property at Castle Hill, about twenty-five miles from Sydney, where I breed Schnauzers, Saanen goats, cultivate olives and citrus fruit, grow vegetables, and live more or less off my own produce.

"A novel, *The Aunt's Story*, was published in New York and London in 1948. A French translation of *Happy Valley* and an Italian one of *The Aunt's Story* have appeared. French translations of the latter and *The Living and the Dead* are in preparation. Some time after the war a play, *Return to Abyssinia*, was produced in London.

"For the last three years I have been working on a novel and expect I shall take several more years to finish it on account of the great amount of other work that has to be done."

The Aunt's Story, a study of a plain woman "whose instincts are greater than her adaptability to life," was a curious combination of wit and pathos which puzzled and disappointed some reviewers as much as it delighted others. Hamilton Basso called the book a "distinguished success." Diana Trilling, on the other hand, found it dull and unconvincing, although she conceded that it had "some striking visual moments" and a "superb" final scene.

ADDITIONAL WORK: The Aunt's Story, 1948.

WHITE, STEWART EDWARD (March 12, 1873-September 18, 1946). For biographical sketch and list of earlier works and references, see TWENTIETH CENTURY AUTHORS, 1942.

* * *

Stewart Edward White died at the University of California Hospital in San Francisco, following an operation, at seventy-three. The last seven years of his life he spent in retirement at his estate in Burlingame, Calif., largely occupied in writing the books which he declared were "dictated" to him by his wife after her death.

In his novels and travel books, he "carried to millions the thrills of his own adventurous life," in the words of the New York *Times*. "A pioneer by inheritance and instinct, he possessed a brilliant talent for interpreting the spirit of pioneering to newer generations."

ADDITIONAL WORKS: Anchors to Windward, 1943; Speaking for Myself, 1943; Daniel Boone (juvenile) 1946; The Saga of Andy Burnett (includes Long Rifle; Ranchero; Folded Hills; Stampede) 1947; With Folded Wings, 1947; The Job of Living, 1948.

ABOUT: White, S. E. The Job of Living (Introduction by L. F. Kimmel), Speaking for Myself; New York Times September 19, 1946.

WHITE, TERENCE HANBURY (May 29, 1906-   ). For biographical sketch and list of earlier works and references, see TWENTIETH CENTURY AUTHORS, 1942.

* * *

T. H. White writes: "My history as a writer is one of pure good luck, like winning a series of sweepstake tickets. Born in India, of British parents, I was educated at Cheltenham College in England and at Cambridge University, where I took first class honours with distinction in the English tripos. I earned my living as a schoolmaster at Stowe, while trying to establish a literary reputation, with books written in the vacations. At the age of thirty, I realised that if I stayed any longer I should remain a schoolmaster forever, so I resigned from Stowe, on a capital of £100 which I had saved, and went to live in a labourer's cottage in the middle of a wood, at a rental of five shillings a week. My next book, *The Sword in the Stone*, was chosen by the Book-of-the-Month Club. After some years of comparative opulence, I was again reduced to a capital of £100 but this time in a shepherd's cottage on top of a mountain, and at no rental, for it had been lent to me by David Garnett. At that point another of my books, *Mistress Masham's Repose*, was again chosen by the Book-of-the-Month Club. I now live in a small house on an island in the English Channel, and funds are beginning to run low. I have perfect confidence that I shall shortly win the Irish Sweep, or be left a few million dollars by an anonymous benefactor, or be given the Nobel prize for something or other. Success in popular literature is a matter of good luck assisted by bad writing.

"Behind my façade as a wage-earning novelist, there has persisted for as long as I can remember a genuine passion for learning: not only for reading history or translating mediaeval Latin, but for learning to fly aeroplanes or catch salmon or train falcons or plough with horses or fence with foils or paint pictures or for anything else which needs the lovely effort of knowledge."

ADDITIONAL WORKS: Mistress Masham's Repose, 1946; The Elephant and the Kangaroo, 1947; The Age of Scandal: An Excursion through a Minor Period, 1950; The Goshawk, 1952; The Scandalmonger, 1952; (ed. & tr.) The Book of Beasts, 1954.

WHITE, WALTER FRANCIS (July 1, 1893-March 21, 1955). For autobiographical sketch and list of earlier works and references, see TWENTIETH CENTURY AUTHORS, 1942.

* * *

Walter White died in New York City at sixty-one of a heart attack. Secretary of the National Association for the Advancement of Colored People since 1931, he had been one of the most active and effective forces in American life in the cause of equal rights for Negroes. The New York *Times* called him "the nearest approach to a national leader of American Negroes since Booker T. Washington." His efforts to establish job equality for Negroes in World War II led to the establishing, by President Franklin D. Roosevelt, of a Fair Employment Practices Committee. During the war also he traveled to Europe as a correspondent for the New York *Post*. In 1945 he was a consultant to the organizing conference of the United Nations, and in 1948 he went to Paris as a consultant to the United States delegation to the U.N. General Assembly. He was active in many civic and national organizations and also managed to find time for writing. *Rising Wind* was his report on the status of the Negro soldier abroad during World War II. His autobiography, *A Man Called White*, was a stirring review of the Negro's struggle for his rights, as well as a personal history.

White was divorced from his first wife and in 1949 married Poppy Cannon.

ADDITIONAL WORKS: Rising Wind, 1945; A Man Called White, 1948.

ABOUT: Gloster, H. M. Negro Voices in American Fiction; White, W. A Man Called White; New York Times March 22, 1955; New Yorker September 4, 11, 1948.

WHITE, WILLIAM ALLEN (February 10, 1868-January 29, 1944). For autobiographical sketch and list of earlier works and references, see TWENTIETH CENTURY AUTHORS, 1942.

* * *

William Allen White died in Emporia, Kan., just before his seventy-sixth birthday.

He had been ill for more than a year. His son, William Lindsay White (see sketch below), succeeded his father as editor and publisher of the *Emporia Gazette* and completed the autobiography that the elder White left unfinished.

The man who became the symbol of middle-class, Middle Western, small-town America has been described, by Walter Johnson, as "a strange mixture of broad, kindly tolerance and small, narrow provincialism—a composite American." F. W. Pick has said: "White was a good man and a successful man. . . . His zest for life in all its manifestations—gushing yet always charming—found expression in his writings. His style is like the man: expansive, bubbling over, gay and gaudy."

ADDITIONAL WORKS: Autobiography, 1946; Selected Letters, 1899-1943 (ed. by W. Johnson) 1947; Letters of William Allen White and a Young Man (with G. B. Wilson) 1948.

ABOUT: Fisher, D. C. American Portraits; Hinshaw, D. Man from Kansas; Johnson, W. William Allen White's America; Lewis, L. It Takes All Kinds; Morris, L. R. Postscript to Yesterday; Van Gelder, R. Writers and Writing; White, W. A. Autobiography, Selected Letters; Contemporary Review January 1947; Kansas Magazine 1947; New York Times January 30, 1944; Newsweek February 10, 1947.

WHITE, WILLIAM ANTHONY PARKER. See "BOUCHER, A."

WHITE, WILLIAM LINDSAY (June 17, 1900-), American journalist and author, was born in Emporia, Kan., the son of the celebrated journalist, William Allen White, and Sallie (Lindsay) White. He attended Emporia High School, Kansas State University (1918-20), and Harvard University, from which he graduated in 1924. After this he worked on his father's

Arni

newspaper, made two trips to Europe, served one term in the Kansas State Legislature (1931-32), and acted as the Republican county chairman in 1933. His first impression of international affairs was gained at the age of eighteen when he accompanied his father to the Versailles Peace Conference. As a reporter he began on his father's Emporia *Gazette* in 1914. In 1935 he was on the staff of the Washington *Post*, and in 1937 with *Fortune* magazine.

During the winter of 1940-41, White was in England as a correspondent. He went through some of the worst bombings of the war, and that experience and his adoption of a three-year-old English orphan are recounted in *Journey for Margaret*. This book was extremely popular, and was followed by *They Were Expendable*. Telling the story of the part played by a squadron in the Philippine campaign in World War II, it was an unusual literary form, a book-length interview. The *New Yorker* termed it "a short, grim, glorious book"; it enjoyed great popularity.

During the war White also visited Europe, spent a month in Berlin, covered the Finnish War, visited the Scandinavian and Allied sides of the lines and the Balkans, and received the Headliners award for the best radio broadcast of 1939, which was made under fire on Christmas Day from the Mannerheim line.

White has been a prolific writer. Of his *Queens Die Proudly*, an account of the flying fortresses in World War II, Clifton Fadiman commented : "A powerful piece of reporting with the fine, solid ring of truth. The book's accounts of air action are as clean-cut and exciting as any the war has evoked, and while there is plenty of the technical detail that Mr. White handles so skillfully, the figures of the human beings behind the machines are always projected in clear outline." *Land of Milk and Honey* purported to be the story of a young Russian who escapes when the plane returning him to Russia crashes. "That it is a reliable analysis of the mind of the younger generation in Russia is open to doubt," wrote Gerald W. Johnson. "It doesn't account for the durability of Russia." And other critics agreed. "The book is, of course, interesting for its glimpse of life on the other side," said the *New Yorker,* "but one cannot help suspecting that Mr. White has touched it up here and there for the purposes of drama." In 1953 *Back Down the Ridge* appeared. "A short, choppy book," remarked the New York *Times*, "that nevertheless conveys something of the horrors of front-line combat and of the magnificent work of the Army's medical teams."

In 1931 White married Katherine Klinkenberg, former Kansan, of *Time* magazine. He is an associate director of the American Civil Liberties Union, and since 1950 has been a member of the Board of Overseers of Harvard University. He was described some years ago as being tall, round-faced, almost bald, and mild-mannered, with a notable resemblance to his father.

PRINCIPAL WORKS: What People Said, 1938; Journey for Margaret, 1941; They Were Expendable, 1942; Queens Die Proudly, 1943; Report on the Russians, 1945; Report on the Germans, 1947; Lost Boundaries, 1948; Land of Milk and Honey, 1949; Bernard Baruch, Portrait of a Citizen, 1950; Back Down the Ridge, 1953.

ABOUT: Van Gelder, R. Writers and Writing; Current Biography 1943; New York Times Book Review November 1, 1942; Saturday Evening Post October 18, 1941; Time January 31, 1944.

WHITEHEAD, ALFRED NORTH

(February 15, 1861-December 30, 1947). For biographical sketch and list of earlier works and references, see TWENTIETH CENTURY AUTHORS, 1942.

* * *

Alfred North Whitehead died at his Cambridge, Mass., home, following a stroke, at eighty-six. In 1945 he received Britain's Order of Merit, considered the highest honor in the field of learning. Felix Frankfurter described him as having "a benign and beautiful presence, a voice and diction that made music of English speech, humor that lighted up dark places, humility that made the foolish wiser and evoked the wisdom of the taciturn."

His greatest contribution to the history of thought was his "philosophy of organism," which he defined as concerned with "the becoming, the being and the relatedness of actual entities." To express his new and often complex ideas he virtually created a new vocabulary, etymologically sound, but adding to the layman's difficulty in reading his work. The London *Times* observed that "no man ever clothed such profound thoughts in such obscure language." On the other hand, he was a master of vivid aphorism and subtle wit, and, as Justice Frankfurter noted, "No one who is ready to read serious books can fail to find luminous charm in his nontechnical writings."

The New York *Times* characterized him, editorially, as "a distinguished scholar who regarded himself as a Victorian, but who belonged so very much to our time that he could discuss relativity and the quantum theory with the best mathematical physicists and suggest common-sense approaches to cosmology and matter that deserve more attention than they have received."

ADDITIONAL WORKS: Essays in Science and Philosophy, 1947; Wit and Wisdom (quotations— ed. by A. H. Johnson) 1947; Alfred North Whitehead: An Anthology (selected by F. S. C. Northrop and M. Gross) 1953; Dialogues of Alfred North Whitehead, 1954.

ABOUT: Beer, S. H. The City of Reason; Ely, S. L. The Religious Availability of Whitehead's God; Emmet, D. M. Alfred North Whitehead; Foley, L. Critique of the Philosophy of Being of

Alfred North Whitehead in the Light of Thomistic Philosophy; Hammerschmidt, W. W. Whitehead's Philosophy of Time; Johnson, A. H. Whitehead's Theory of Reality; Mack, R. D. Appeal to Immediate Experience; McElroy, H. C. Modern Philosophers; Shahan, E. P. Whitehead's Theory of Experience; Wells, H. K. Process and Unreality; Werkmeister, W. H. History of Philosophical Ideas in America; Whitehead, A. N. Essays in Science and Philosophy, Wit and Wisdom (see introduction by A. H. Johnson); Whittaker, E. T. Alfred North Whitehead; American Scholar Winter 1946; Atlantic Monthly May 1948; London Times December 31, 1947; Mind April 1948; Nation February 14, 1948; New Statesman and Nation January 10, 1948; New York Times December 31, 1947, January 1, 1948, January 8, 1948; Science March 12, 1948; Time May 12, 1947, January 12, 1948.

WHITEING, RICHARD (July 27, 1840-June 29, 1928). For biographical sketch and list of works and references, see TWENTIETH CENTURY AUTHORS, 1942.

WHITLOCK, BRAND (March 4, 1869-May 24, 1934). For biographical sketch and list of works and references, see TWENTIETH CENTURY AUTHORS, 1942.

WICKENDEN, DAN (March 24, 1913-), American novelist, writes: "I'm a first-generation American, born [Leonard Daniel Wickenden] of English parents, in Tyrone, Pa., where my father had a position as chemist with the West Virginia Pulp & Paper Company. Later he became laboratory chief of the New York office, and my earliest memories are mostly of Long Island, at a time when Flushing ran off at the edges into a wonderful country of farms and fields and great tracts of swampy woodland.

"Those early years were sharply divided from all the rest by a voyage to England that followed the end of my elementary schooling. By the time we came home I had turned fourteen, and we moved out to Manhasset, where I started high school. I'd always wanted to write, and had always written; but now I sometimes wrote middles and ends as well as beginnings, and began to bother magazines with manuscripts. This habit became ingrained during four years at Amherst College, where I majored in English, played character parts with the Masquers, and spent a good deal of my spare time roaming about the countryside—I've always liked weathers and landscapes.

"In the fall after graduation in 1935, I sold a one-act play and a short story, in rapid succession, to magazines that have since gone out of existence, and tried to believe that I had become an author. For some eighteen months I was also a commuter and an employee of the Columbia Broadcasting System; but after the acceptance, in 1937, of my second serious attempt at a novel, I began trying to support myself by writing alone.

"For a few years I succeeded, after a fashion, and in the summer of 1940 set out on a 15,000-mile journey through much of the United States and Mexico. This confirmed a passion for scenery on the grand scale and aroused an interest in the Indians of the Americas that has continued ever since. Poverty began to pinch, though, and early in 1942 I went to Michigan and became a reporter for the Grand Rapids *Press*. This job, too, lasted for about eighteen months, and it was a good and stimulating experience; but I wasn't writing any fiction, so toward the end of 1943 I cut loose again and returned to the East and to free lancing.

"A period of prosperity made possible two long sojourns in Guatemala, with which I became infatuated, but where I got no writing done. Since 1945, home base has been Westport, Conn., where there are neither mountains nor Indians, but which has its advantages and isn't completely suburban yet.

"In 1951 I was married to Hermione Hillman of Grand Rapids, and a son named David was born in 1952. Wife and child are far more important than the six published novels behind me, and most of the time I still don't really feel like an author; but I continue to hope that I may someday write a book which will seem good to me even after it is in print."

* * *

It is perhaps the best tribute to Dan Wickenden's success as a novelist that he has proved, Mary McGrory writes in the New York *Times*, "that it is possible to be warmhearted without being mawkish and wholesome without being insipid." His novels have been described as "soft-spoken," suggesting the unpretentious and unobtrusive manner in which Wickenden writes. Generally his subject matter is contemporary American family life, recorded faithfully and understandingly. When he moves to stranger and more exotic scenes (Guatemala, for instance, in *The Dry Season*), his work remains thoughtful and intelligent, although some reviewers find that it loses something of its power and charm. In one of his most recent novels, *The Red Carpet*, a story of a young man who comes to New York from a small town in the Middle West and has his first taste of "bohemian" life, Wickenden showed a gift for hearty humor. F. H. Bullock described the book in the New York *Herald Tribune* as "a bubble of pure delight, blending deliciously all the subtle, wise, literary sophistication of these our times with the innocence of a poem by William Blake."

PRINCIPAL WORKS: The Running of the Deer, 1937; Walk Like a Mortal, 1940; The Wayfarers, 1945; Tobias Brandywine, 1948; The Dry Season, 1950; The Red Carpet, 1952.

ABOUT: Prescott, O. In My Opinion; Warfel, H. R. American Novelists of Today; Current Biography 1951; New York Herald Tribune Book Review October 8, 1950, June 15, 1952.

WICKHAM, ANNA (1884-   ). For biographical sketch and list of works and references, see TWENTIETH CENTURY AUTHORS, 1942.

WIDDEMER, MARGARET. For autobiographical sketch and list of earlier works and references, see TWENTIETH CENTURY AUTHORS, 1942.

* * *

Margaret Widdemer lives in New York City. In addition to her writing, she devotes considerable time to teaching and lecturing on fiction and creative writing in general. She was a member of the Writers' Conference at the University of New Hampshire from 1941 to 1943 and of the Chatauqua Writers' Conference from 1947 to 1949.

Although Miss Widdemer considers poetry the most important part of her work, she is best known today as a writer of light romantic fiction. Several of her recent books have been historical novels. *Red Cloak Flying*, a story of the Jacobite rebellion and the American colonial period of 1745 to 1747, was set in the Adirondack country where Miss Widdemer spends her summers. The characters in the novel, the New York *Herald Tribune* wrote, "incline toward ornate speech and sweepingly romantic gesture, but the author subordinates ornament to emotion. She has created a colorful novel of the period."

ADDITIONAL WORKS: Constancia Herself, 1945; Lani, 1948; Red Cloak Flying, 1950; Lady of the Mohawks, 1951; Prince in Buckskin, 1952; Basic Principles of Fiction Writing, 1953; The Golden Wildcat, 1954.

ABOUT: Warfel, H. R. American Novelists of Today.

*WIECHERT, ERNST EMIL (1887-August 24, 1950), German novelist and poet, was born in a remote part of East Prussia, the son of a forest ranger. When he was eleven years old, he was sent to school in Königsberg, where he continued academic studies and took his degree. Later teaching in secondary schools left him dissatisfied, and influenced by Russian and Scandinavian writers, he wrote his first novel, *Die Flucht* (1916), which terminated in the suicide of the hero. During World War I Wiechert served on the Eastern and then on the Western front, and was wounded in France. The war did not change his views of life, and in his novel *Jedermann* (1931) he gave expression to the experience of endless waiting, the emptiness which scars the soldier's mind. After the war he did not at first go back to teaching, but instead withdrew into the forest of his homeland. Several novels appeared in the Twenties; in them he turned to ideas of redemption through the universal suffering from which love is born.

In 1933 and 1936, by which time Wiechert had become an active supporter of Pastor Niemoeller, he delivered two addresses at the University of Munich. Himmler was said to have been in the audience at the last lecture and to have been responsible for his five months' internment in the concentration camp of Buchenwald in 1938. Although after his release he was forbidden to publish anything and his house was under observation by the Gestapo, Wiechert continued to write. He became best known through his novels, *Die Madg des Jürgen Doscozil* (1932) and one translated into English in 1936 as *The Baroness*. Reviews of the latter show the disparate views taken of Wiechert's work; they are perhaps in part influenced by the relations between England and America and Germany at the time. "The novel, we are told, has been enormously popular in Germany," said the London *Times Literary Supplement* of *The Baroness*. "Its sham poetry and sham mysticism of the soil are less likely to appeal to English readers." "A work of hifalutin pietism, written in a fake biblical-symbolic style, full of a lyrical and disgusting *simplesse*," was the view taken by Lionel Trilling in the *New Republic*. "A reticent and quietly lovely book," wrote E. H. Wal-

* vĕ′kĕrt

ton in the New York *Times.* "Herr Wiechert has an extraordinary capacity for describing wild, dark, windy forests and fruitful fields . . . he gives his characters a half-legendary stature and dignity." In the post-war period, however, English translations of Wiechert's novels met with increasing critical sympathy and admiration. *The Forest of the Dead,* the deeply personal story of a sensitive German's reaction to imprisonment in a concentration camp, made probably the deepest impression of any of his novels. "He has hitherto not been one of Germany's greatest writers," George Shuster wrote in the New York *Herald Tribune,* "though he has been knotty, sincere and complex in the manner of his best countrymen. But this book one does not hesitate to call great." In 1953 *Missa Sine Nomine,* a religious novel, was published. It was begun in the winter of 1949 and completed early in 1950, and among other themes suggests that we accept the inevitable and unknown in the firm belief that good exists, that God wills the right, and man is destined to strive towards that right. In 1947 Wiechert had moved to Switzerland. In the fall of 1949 he made his only visit to the United States as a guest lecturer at Stanford University for one month. An observer described him then, in his sixties, "with his high-domed, softly tinted head with its fringe of long white hair, and with his long Düreresque hands," seeming to personify his own mission as an apostle of peace.

It has been postulated by Alfred Werner in *Commentary* that the Nazis' relative leniency toward Wiechert up to the spring of 1938 is explained by the fact that his novels glorified life in the villages and forests, and that he was born in East Prussia, cradle of Junkerism and nationalism. Actually Wiechert's family was a mixture of German, Slavic, Lithuanian, and French blood. According to Werner, "He suffered social ostracism because, while technically married, he lived in 'sin' with a woman who was estranged from her husband. . . . After the death of his first wife, the poet was able to marry the woman with whom he had been living."

Wiechert died at his home in Staefa on Lake Zurich in his sixty-third year.

PRINCIPAL WORKS IN ENGLISH TRANSLATION: The Baroness, 1936; The Forest of the Dead, 1947; The Girl and the Ferryman, 1947; The Poet and His Time (non-fiction) 1948; Earth Is Our Heritage, 1951; Missa Sine Nomine, 1953.

ABOUT: Books Abroad Summer 1950; Columbia Dictionary of Modern European Literature; Commentary August 1951; Commonweal March 11, 1949; New York Times August 26, 1950.

WIGGIN, Mrs. KATE DOUGLAS (SMITH) (September 28, 1856-August 24, 1923). For biographical sketch and list of works and references, see TWENTIETH CENTURY AUTHORS, 1942.

* * *

ABOUT: Hunt, R. D. California's Stately Hall of Fame; Horn Book November 1950.

WILBUR, RICHARD (March 1, 1921-   ), American poet, writes: "My father, the artist Lawrence Wilbur, came east from Omaha to New York; my mother, Helen Purdy, came north from Baltimore. I spent the first two years of my life, or so I am told, in what was to be the shadow of the George Washington Bridge; then we moved to New Jersey. My parents

Walter R. Fleischer

rented a pre-Revolutionary stone house in North Caldwell, in one corner of the large country estate of a retired English manufacturer, and in this pocket of resistance to suburbia (since infiltrated) my brother Lawrence and I grew up among woods, orchards, corn-fields, horses, hogs, cows and hay-wagons. A friend recently remarked that my poems are unfashionably favorable toward nature, and I must blame this warp on a rural, pleasant and somewhat solitary boyhood.

"I began to write poems very early. Doubtless the fact that my father was an artist encouraged and legitimized this activity, and I suspect that I inherited a facility with words from my mother's family: her father was an editor of the Baltimore *Sun,* and *his* father, an itinerant editor and publisher, had founded some forty Democratic newspapers in his wanderings. My first poem was called 'That's When the Nightingales Wake.' There are, of course, no nightingales in New Jersey, and the poem was a pure verbal and rhythmic exercise, drawing not at all upon my eight years' experience.

"At high school I wrote editorials; at Amherst College I edited the newspaper, and anticipated a career in journalism. The summers were passed in vagrancy; I toured most of the forty-eight states by freight-car. Poetry did not seem a primary occupation, and my poems for the most part continued to be diversions with other people's nightingales. Amherst's excellent instruction in

English literature was more likely to produce, immediately, an awakened critical intelligence than an aroused poetic faculty; and it was not until World War II took me to Cassino, Anzio and the Siegfried Line that I began to versify in earnest. One does not use poetry for its major purposes, as a means of organizing oneself and the world, until one's world somehow gets out of hand. A general cataclysm is not required; the disorder must be personal and may be wholly so, but poetry, to be vital, does seem to need a periodic acquaintance with the threat of Chaos.

"I had married Charlotte Ward in 1942, and after the war we went to Cambridge, where I attended Harvard's graduate school, receiving the M.A. in 1947. During the next three years I was a member of the Society of Fellows of Harvard University, and since 1950 have taught in its department of English, living in nearby Lincoln with my wife and three children (Ellen, Christopher, Nathan). In 1946 a friend sent a packet of my poems to Reynal and Hitchcock, and that venturesome house—very much to my surprise—brought out *The Beautiful Changes* in the following year. My second book, *Ceremony*, like the first a collection of lyrics, was published by Harcourt, Brace in 1950. There is hardly space here in which to characterize my work, little of it as there is; as regards technique, a critic has called me one of the 'New Formalists,' and I will accept the label provided it be understood that to try to revive the force of rhyme and other formal devices, by reconciling them with the experimental gains of the past several decades, is itself sufficiently experimental."

* * *

Richard Wilbur has received both the Harriet Monroe and the Oscar Blumenthal prizes from *Poetry* magazine. In 1952 he went to New Mexico on a Guggenheim fellowship, and in May 1954 he was named winner of the $3,000 Prix de Rome fellowship of the American Academy of Arts and Letters. Randall Jarrell considers Wilbur "a delicate, charming, and skillful poet," limited only by too great a self-imposed restraint ("Mr. Wilbur never goes too far, but he never goes far enough"). Nevertheless, Jarrell believes that he is "the best of the quite young poets writing in this country." David Daiches wrote of him in 1951: "Mr. Wilbur's poetry is sensuous, musical and speculative, a combination of qualities to make him a poet worth reading and watching."

PRINCIPAL WORKS: The Beautiful Changes, 1947; Ceremony, and Other Poems, 1950.

ABOUT: Jarrell, R. Poetry and the Age; Mademoiselle August 1953; New York Times May 7, 1954; Poetry January 1948; April 1953; South Atlantic Quarterly November 1951.

WILDE, PERCIVAL (March 1, 1887-September 19, 1953). For biographical sketch and list of earlier works and references, see TWENTIETH CENTURY AUTHORS, 1942.

* * *

Percival Wilde died at the University Hospital in New York, at sixty-five, after being stricken with a heart attack at the Lambs Club. He had been in ill health for three years.

In the last two decades of his life, Wilde turned from the one-act play to a new field, that of the mystery novel, in which he won high praise. Of *Inquest,* published in 1940, Marian Wiggin said, "[It] is one of the best stories I have ever read. It is not nearly so much a mystery story as it is a study in character conflicts. As such it is superb." *Tinsley's Bones,* two years later, was called "the year's most intelligently hilarious mystery yarn" by *Time.*

As a dramatist, Wilde made the transition from stage to radio and television, and in 1951 a new edition of *The Craftsmanship of the One-Act Play* was issued, revised to include these media. Harold Brighouse said that Wilde's plays "are various, they never forget to be dramatic, and their economy of words is remarkable," and that they indicate "skill in climax, vigor in invention, discipline in words."

ADDITIONAL WORKS: Bridge Blackouts (based on articles by S. T. Bigelow) 1942; Tinsley's Bones, 1942; P. Moran, Operative, 1947.

ABOUT: New York Times September 20, 1953; Saturday Review of Literature March 10, 1951.

WILDER, ROBERT (January 25, 1901-), American novelist, writes: "At the age of twelve or thirteen I won a school prize of a dollar for a short story and this seemed such an easy touch that I decided to make a career of writing. Off and on for some forty years, in various fields, I have pursued this goal and, as Somerset Maugham once confessed, I am frequently astonished by the fact that I am a writer and that it never seems to get any easier; the last book being as hard to write as the first.

"I was born of a Spanish mother and a Scotch father in Richmond, Va., where at the time my father was working at one of his several careers. He was still going to college after I was born and at different times was a

lawyer, a Presbyterian minister, a doctor and, finally, a dentist. Essentially a mechanic at heart he found in dentistry that which appealed to him, returning to his boyhood home, at Daytona Beach, Fla., to open an office and to rear a family. I went through the grade and high schools at Daytona Beach until late in 1917 when, stretching my age a bit, I enlisted in the army for World War I and eventually found myself a member of the S.A.T.C. at Stetson University, in DeLand, Fla. At the conclusion of the war I decided that I was too old to go back to school and went to New York where I found a job behind the soda fountain in a Liggett's drug store. A year of this made the academic field seem more attractive and I enrolled at Columbia University. I sold a short story then to a magazine, *Telling Tales*, for which I was paid $75. That really cinched the literary life.

"Finishing at Columbia I found a job with a theatrical press agent, Dixie Hines. I remained with him for four years, learning the business and finally branching out on my own, handling the publicity for such stars of the day as Irene Bordoni, Helen Menken, Claudette Colbert, Raquel Meller, and such producers as A. H. Woods, Ray Goetz, the Shuberts, Sam Harris, Charles Wagner and others. At this time I married Sarah Adams Peters, daughter of a well-known illustrator. Theatrical publicity is an uneasy living at best and then the National Broadcasting Company offered me a job, directing the publicity of a nationwide tour which A. H. Rothafel (Roxy) and 'his gang' were making. At the conclusion of this I went with radio Station WOR in charge of publicity and remained there for seven years until a change of ownership landed me on the street along with several other executives.

"By then Sally and I had a son, Robert Wallace Wilder, and I took the first job I could find, re-write on the lobster trick of the New York *Sun*. I was graduated from this to a daily column of my own, 'On the Sun Deck,' which I wrote for almost nine years. Newspaper work, I decided, was fun if you could afford it. I couldn't. The alternative was to write myself out of it. I wrote two plays, both produced on Broadway,

Sweet Chariot and *Stardust,* which didn't make much money for anyone concerned. Then I started my first novel, *God Has a Long Face,* which G. P. Putnam's Sons bought on the face of a half-completed manuscript. This was followed by *Out of the Blue,* a reporter's diary, and then I wrote *Flamingo Road,* first as a novel, then as a play for Broadway, produced by Roland Stebbins, and then as a motion picture for Joan Crawford.

"By then I could see daylight and left the *Sun* to work for myself. I went to Hollywood under contract for Metro-Goldwyn, then did a trick of two years for Paramount and later a picture for Warner Brothers. I like pictures and Hollywood but decided that the only way to cope with them was to keep a book ahead. I wrote steadily, publishing nine novels in eleven years.

"Unfortunately, I don't have a backlog of rejected manuscripts which could be reworked and marketed now. I have never written anything which hasn't sold. My writing habits are simple. Once started on a novel I do a thousand words a day; no more and no less. Sometimes they're not always good and I have to re-do them the next day before I start work on the new quota. This, however, works out better for me than saying I'll work so many hours a day. After all, you can sit in front of a typewriter for eight hours and never write a line.

"For the past three years I have made my home in Mexico where, in addition to my other activities, I also serve as correspondent for the Miami *Herald.*"

PRINCIPAL WORKS: God Has a Long Face, 1940; Flamingo Road, 1942; Out of the Blue, 1943; Mr. G. Strings Along, 1944; Written on the Wind, 1946; Bright Feather, 1948; Wait for Tomorrow, 1950; And Ride a Tiger, 1951; Autumn Thunder, 1952; The Wine of Youth, 1955.

ABOUT: Warfel, H. R. American Novelists of Today.

WILDER, THORNTON NIVEN (April 17, 1897-). For biographical sketch and list of earlier works and references, see TWENTIETH CENTURY AUTHORS, 1942.

* * *

Thornton Wilder, as Brooks Atkinson once remarked of him, "takes his own time as a writer." He works hard but publishes little. What he does publish, however, has the distinction of being as sound and as significant as any important literary work done in America today. He won his third Pulitzer prize (his second in drama) in 1943 with his high-spirited allegorical comedy of man's struggle for survival, *The Skin of Our Teeth*. In 1948 his richly imaginative novel on the life of Julius Caesar, *The Ides of March*, was hailed as a work of brilliant craftsmanship, "a short, witty and extremely serious book," the London *Times Literary Supplement* described it. More recently he has translated Jean-Paul Sartre's *The Victors* into English (1949) and revised his earlier play, *The Merchant of Yonkers*, into *The Matchmaker*, produced with considerable success in London and at the Edinburgh Festival of 1954.

Wilder was briefly involved in a literary controversy over charges that *The Skin of Our Teeth* was plagiarized from James Joyce's *Finnegans Wake*. In point of fact, Wilder, a great admirer of Joyce's work, was indebted to the novel in his play, but no issue of plagiarism was involved. The play is wildly eccentric, skipping over some five thousand years of man's history, indifferent to theatrical conventions. Stark Young described it as "a kind of cosmic variety show." But it was also a heartening and frequently brilliant comedy and a memorable event in the contemporary American theatre. In June 1955 *The Skin of Our Teeth* was produced in Paris, starring Helen Hayes and Mary Martin, as a feature of "Salute to France," the cultural exchange program of the American National Theatre and Academy.

Professionally Wilder regards himself as a teacher rather than a writer, and he has indeed devoted more time to teaching than to writing. He is a cultural ambassador for the United States, frequently lecturing and teaching abroad. In 1941 the U.S. State Department sent him to South America on an educational mission. In 1942 he entered the Army Air Corps Intelligence division as a major and saw service in Italy. After the war he resumed teaching. He was Charles Eliot Norton Professor of Poetry at Harvard in 1950-51 and in 1953 he was in Germany, Austria, and Switzerland lecturing on writing. Wilder's home is in a suburb of New Haven. He spends what spare time he has reading in the Yale Library in the many fields of his interests, ranging from Joyce and Kirkegaard to archeological and medical journals.

ADDITIONAL WORKS: The Skin of Our Teeth (play) 1942; The Ides of March (novel) 1948.

ABOUT: Current Biography 1943; New Yorker December 26, 1942; Saturday Review of Literature December 19, 26, 1942, January 2, 9, February 13, 1943, February 21, 1948; Theatre Arts January 1943; Time December 28, 1942, January 12, 1953.

WILENSKI, REGINALD HOWARD

(March 1887-), English artist, art critic, and art historian, writes: "The basis of my work as an art critic is experience in art schools and practice as a professional portrait painter and draughtsman; I have never used art-critical writings by others. The basis of my work as art-historian is personal study in the museums of various countries; I use other people's art-historical writings to find factual data, never to find art-historical theories. My books and other writings, for good or evil, are thus at any rate my own.

"I was born in London. My father, a naturalised British subject, born in Russian-Poland, was a merchant in the City of London. My mother was English. Neither had artistic interests or talents, though visits to the opera, concerts or the theatre were weekly routine on Saturday evenings. I won a scholarship at St. Paul's School and a special drawing prize for a set of life-size charcoal portraits when I was sixteen. I went as a Commoner to Balliol College, Oxford, and worked in London art schools in vacations; then came art schools in Munich and Paris and then my own studio in London. I was never much good as an artist but I was good enough to find out that 'modern' art is much more difficult than sheer representational painting and good enough to get hung in reputable exhibitions in London and Paris and efficient enough to make the wherewithal by portrait painting for a tour round Italy. When the Germans began the 1914 war I closed my studio and went into a government office. Between the wars I worked as an art critic on a number of London papers and for a time I was London correspondent for the Paris *L'Amour de l'Art*. I wrote my first art-critical book, *The Modern Movement in Art* in 1925-1927; and my art-historical books *Dutch Painting* and *French Painting* and *English Painting* between 1928 and 1933; I worked on *Modern French Painters* from 1935 to 1939. All these were published in London and the U.S.A., and revised editions have appeared in recent years. I have also done some art-historical teaching (Bristol University 1929 and 1930, Manchester University 1933-39, 1945, and 1946), and written one biography, *John Ruskin*. In the second German war I was seconded from Manchester University to a government department and later to the foreign service of the British Broadcasting Corporation. Since 1946 I have been preparing a book on Flemish Painting (two volumes, 1000 plates); my publishers expect to lose money on it as they have financed my studies, but they hope as I do that it will bring them credit. In these years also I have been general editor of the series of art monographs with colour plates called *Faber Gallery*.

"I married in 1914 a wise and beautiful girl who has written a good novel called *Table Two* [Marjorie Harland Wilenski] and made money in business and attempted unsuccessfully to breed a champion English bulldog. Our recreation formerly was motoring in France, Italy and Spain. Now it is our garden in Berkshire."

PRINCIPAL WORKS: The Modern Movement in Art, 1927; Introduction to Dutch Art, 1929; (with P. G. Konody) Italian Painting, 1929; A Miniature History of Art, 1930; French Painting, 1931; The Meaning of Modern Sculpture, 1932; Outline of French Painting, 1932; Outline of English Painting, 1933; John Ruskin, 1933; Masters of English Painting, 1934; The Study of Art, 1934; Modern French Painters, 1940; Faber Gallery Series—Manet, 1945; Degas, 1945; Royal Portraits, 1946; Mantegna, 1947; Renoir, 1948; Seurat, 1951; Douanier Rousseau, 1953.

WILKINS, MARY ELEANOR. See FREEMAN, M. E. W.

WILKINS, WILLIAM *VAUGHAN (March 6, 1890-), British novelist, writes: "I was born in London of stock representing

Howard Coster

all the races in the British Isles—English, Scottish, Welsh and Irish. When I started life as a journalist I broke away from a family tradition of taking holy orders in the Church of England, or entering the profession of architecture—my great-grandfather, a Royal Academician, built the National Gallery and University College, London, and a distant forebear, Chrysostom Wilkins, was assistant to Sir Christopher Wren in the building of St. Paul's Cathedral.

"I had astonishingly good luck, for when I was twenty-four years old I was made editor of the London *Daily Call*, creating an age record in Fleet-Street journalism, I believe. Well, I went away to the wars—service in Egypt, Palestine, and France—and when I came back, at the end of 1919, my paper was

* *"Vaughan* is pronounced *vorn."*

defunct, and I had to start all over again. I eventually became the assistant editor of the London *Daily Express*—of which the owner, manager, and editor were Canadians!

"In 1936 I sickened of journalism: I told myself that I would write a book. I did. In a lonely house in the Welsh mountains, in a freighter on the Atlantic, in my uncle's home at Lake Charles, La., at my cousin's ranch in Texas—I have many more relations in America than in England—and in a tall old building in London, overlooking the Thames, with recollections of Samuel Pepys, the diarist, and David Copperfield.

"The book—it was called *And So—Victoria* became a best seller in America and England and on the Continent; was translated into German, Spanish, Italian, Hungarian, Danish, Dutch, Norwegian, and Swedish; and was bought for filming by Metro-Goldwyn-Mayer.

"It was not the first novel that I had written: that was an effort called, 'When and If,' written many years before in my scanty spare time, and so bad that I purpose using the back of the manuscript as scribbling paper. It was not even my first book published: that was a monograph on the eighteenth century industrial revolution in England, published in 1925, which I have vaguely regretted since.

"The outbreak of World War II had a serious effect on my output, and it was five years before my next novel appeared. It is extraordinarily difficult to write books in a house shaken by the crash of falling bombs, and in the intervals of military duty with the Home Guard, and of work as a billeting officer for refugees.

"With one single exception all my novels have been historical, ranging roughly over the hundred years 1737-1837. The amount of research involved is very considerable; for the book which I have just completed, *Fanfare for a Witch*, I have had to read twenty specialized works, apart from those I have consulted for confirmatory detail or as a check. It may be that I am getting lazy, but I *should* like to be allowed to write another modern story."

* * *

Vaughan Wilkins, as he signs his novels, has attained wide popularity in Britain and in the United States. His works are perhaps more accurately designated historical romances than straight historical novels, for they heavily emphasize adventure, swift action, and vivid characterization. An American reviewer once described his technique as follows: "Mr. Wilkins writes briskly and breezily, obviously enjoying the rustling velvets and brocades, the snuff-taking and skull-cracking, the niceties and nastinesses of diplomacy and armour, as thoroughly as he may, with confidence, expect his readers to enjoy him." Wilkins lives in Herefordshire. He married Mary Powell in 1930 and they have two sons.

PRINCIPAL WORKS: And So—Victoria, 1937; (ed.) Endless Prelude, 1937; Seven Tempest, 1942; Being Met Together, 1944; After Bath, 1945; Once Upon a Time, 1949; City of Frozen Fire, 1950; Crown Without Sceptre, 1952; A King Reluctant, 1953; Fanfare for a Witch, 1954.

WILKINSON, Mrs. MARGUERITE OG-DEN (BIGELOW) (November 15, 1883-January 12, 1928). For biographical sketch and list of works and references, see TWENTIETH CENTURY AUTHORS, 1942.

WILLARD, JOSIAH FLYNT (January 23, 1869-January 20, 1907). For biographical sketch and list of works and references, see TWENTIETH CENTURY AUTHORS, 1942.

* * *

ABOUT: Morris, L. R. Postscript to Yesterday.

WILLEY, BASIL (July 25, 1897-), British scholar, writes: "I was born in London, where I lived until I was called up for World

War I. My father was William Herbert Willey, eldest son of a Cornish Wesleyan minister; my mother was Alice Ann Le Gros, a Jersey woman, through whom I am descended from the old Jersey family of de Carteret. It was in honour of a member of this family, Sir George Carteret, a Royalist admiral in the time of our seventeenth century civil wars, that New Jersey received its name. Carteret had defended the Island of Jersey against the Parliamentary forces, and in return for his services he was granted a piece of land between the Hudson and Delaware Rivers, to be held by him of the Crown as 'Lord Proprietor' at a rent of £5 a year.

"When I was demobilized in 1919 I went up to Cambridge (where I had already won a history scholarship), and I have lived and taught there ever since. My first book, *The Seventeenth Century Background*, was published in 1934, and the following year I be-

came a Fellow of Pembroke College. The second, *The Eighteenth Century Background*, appeared in 1940; the third, *Nineteenth Century Studies*, published in 1949, had previously formed the substance of a course of lectures at Columbia University, where I was visiting professor 1948-49.

"In 1946 I had succeeded Sir Arthur Quiller-Couch as King Edward VII Professor of English Literature at Cambridge; in 1947 I was elected Fellow of the British Academy, and in 1948 I received from Manchester University the honorary degree of Litt.D. My most recent publication was *Christianity, Past and Present*, which reproduced a series of lectures delivered for the Cambridge Faculty of Divinity in 1950. In 1953 I was privileged to spend another semester in the United States, this time at Cornell University. While I was there I also lectured at twelve other universities, and afterwards traveled extensively, on holiday, to the Pacific coast and in New England. At other times I have also lectured in France, Ireland, Switzerland and Denmark. Looking back over this outwardly uneventful life, I cannot but think myself singularly fortunate. Happy in my early home, happy again in my marriage [to Zélie Murlis Ricks in 1923], blessed with two sons and two daughters (all of them charming people, and two of them already happily married), and living for the best part of my life in one of the loveliest cities on earth, I have indeed much to be thankful for. And as if this were not enough, I have the entry into two other worlds: music (in which I am instinctively more at home than in my own chosen field of letters), and the English countryside—of which I am a devoted lover and explorer—particularly the Lake District which I visit constantly for the good of both body and soul."

* * *

Basil Willey has won his reputation not only for the soundness of his scholarship, but for the lucidity and urbanity of his literary style. V. S. Pritchett wrote of his *Nineteenth Century Studies*: "Cool, placid, economical, sensitive and self-effacing, he writes with the beguiling simplicity of great learning, keeping his subjects in the foreground, himself almost concealed. His sympathy is continuous; as always in the best criticism, it is a form of curiosity, so that the great pleasure (and value) of his inquiry is that it really does disclose more and more of his subject."

PRINCIPAL WORKS: The Seventeenth Century Background, 1934; The Eighteenth Century Background, 1941; Nineteenth Century Studies, 1949; Christianity, Past and Present, 1952.

WILLIAMS, BEN AMES (March 7, 1889-February 4, 1953). For autobiographical sketch and list of earlier works and references, see TWENTIETH CENTURY AUTHORS, 1942.

* * *

Ben Ames Williams collapsed and died of a heart attack while engaged in a curling contest in Brookline, Mass. He was sixty-three. Just two months before his death he wrote to the editors of this volume in comment on the 1942 sketch: "It is no longer true—if it ever was—that my stories are 'always cheerful.' As for 'pretensions to literature,' literature and pretensions do not go together."

In 1943 Williams told Robert van Gelder that he felt he was "no born writer," but one who succeeded by virtue of sheer energy, persistence, and hard work. He spent some twenty years in the research for, and four and a half years in the writing of, *House Divided*, a long and ambitious historical novel on the Civil War which was on the best seller lists for several months. Also best sellers were his novels *The Strange Woman* and *Leave Her to Heaven*—both made into motion pictures.

ADDITIONAL WORKS: Amateurs at War (ed.) 1943; Leave Her to Heaven, 1944; It's a Free Country, 1945; House Divided, 1947; Fraternity Village, 1949; Owen Glen, 1950; The Unconquered, 1953.

ABOUT: Van Gelder, R. Writers and Writing; Warfel, H. R. American Novelists of Today; Collier's May 28, 1949; Hobbies May 1953; New York Herald Tribune Book Review October 8, 1950, February 22, 1953; New York Times February 5, 1953; New York Times Book Review August 24, 1947.

WILLIAMS, CHARLES (September 20, 1886-May 15, 1945), English man of letters, was born in London, of Welsh ancestry, the

son of R. W. Stansby Williams, a translator and poet. After attending St. Alban's School, Williams studied for two years at the University of London until his money ran out. He took a job with a small publishing house and continued to study evenings at the Workingmen's College. Years later, in spite of a lack of formal academic degrees, he was appointed a lecturer at Oxford University and awarded an honorary M.A. He married Florence Conway in 1917 and they had one son.

Williams spent most of his adult life working as an editor of the Oxford University Press. He also taught and lectured. In addition to all these activities, he published some thirty-eight books—drama, poetry, biography, theology, criticism, fiction—edited anthologies, translated, and wrote numerous prefaces and miscellaneous essays. He was capable of grinding out mere potboilers and of writing inspired and profound treatises. His novels the work for which he is best known today, are exercises in the supernatural, full of daring theological speculation, but they have the plots of thrillers. He was a deeply religious man, an Anglican. He was also deeply interested in witchcraft and in the occult. He might almost be called a mystic except, as T. S. Eliot points out, "If a mystic means a man wholly detached from this world, detached from private affections and public activity, a man wholly dedicated to contemplation, then the term does not fit." Geoffrey Parsons writes of him: "Williams lived and breathed in a world that knew no sharp dividing line between natural events and spiritual events." Eliot said that he was "a man who was always able to live in the material and spiritual world at once, a man to whom the two worlds were equally real because they are one world. So while his novels are constantly flashing with religious insight, his religious books communicate a good deal of the excitement of a sensational novel."

In England Williams became the center of a coterie of distinguished admirers, a group which included T. S. Eliot, W. H. Auden, C. S. Lewis, and Dorothy Sayers. It was his presence, apparently, as well as his writing which inspired such intense admiration. "He lectured eloquently and inspiringly—on literature, on religion. He had a rare talent for communicating his faith, his excitement, to his audience," Parsons writes. Physically he was most unprepossessing. T. S. Eliot describes him as "a plain, spectacled man of rather frail physique, who made no attempt to impress anybody." When he began to speak, however, he was transfigured. Then, C. S. Lewis recalls, "his presence was one of the stateliest I have ever seen. . . . He gave to every circle the whole man; all his attention, knowledge, courtesy, charity, were placed at your disposal." In America Williams was almost completely unknown until the posthumous publication of some of his novels and the tributes of his English admirers won him a small but enthusiastic audience here. His best known novels are *Descent into Hell, War in Heaven,* and *All Hallows' Eve*—all of them moving back and forth with extraordinary ease and rapidity from the natural world to the supernatural. They are imaginative, strikingly original, profoundly Christian. What his work as a whole has to offer, T. S. Eliot writes, "is no mere moral teaching, no mere theory of doctrine. It is a work of imagination, based upon real experience of the supernatural world which is just as natural to the author as our everyday world."

PRINCIPAL WORKS: The Silver Stair (poems) 1912; Poems of Conformity, 1917; Divorce (poems) 1920; Windows of Night (poems) 1924; The Myth of Shakespeare, 1928; Poetry at Present, 1930; Heroes and Kings, 1930; War in Heaven (novel) 1930; Many Dimensions (novel) 1931; Three Plays, 1931; The Place of the Lion (novel) 1932; Greater Trumps (novel) 1932; The English Poetic Mind, 1932; Reason and Beauty in the Poetic Mind, 1933; Shadows of Ecstasy (novel) 1933; Bacon, 1934; James I, 1934; Rochester, 1935; The Rite of the Passion, 1936; Thomas Cranmer of Canterbury (play) 1936; Descent into Hell (novel) 1937; He Came Down from Heaven, 1938; Taliessin Through Logres (poems) 1938; Judgment at Chelmsford (play) 1939; Descent of the Dove, 1939; Religion and Love in Dante, 1941; Witchcraft, 1941; The Forgiveness of Sins, 1942; The Figure of Beatrice, 1943; Region of the Summer Stars (poems) 1944; House of the Octopus (play) 1945; All Hallows' Eve (novel) 1945; Flecker of Dean Close, 1946; Seed of Adam, and Other Plays, 1948; The Arthurian Torso (with C. S. Lewis) 1948.

ABOUT: Sayers, D. & others, Essays Presented to Charles Williams; Eliot, T. S. Preface to Williams' All Hallows' Eve (1948); Atlantic Monthly November 1949; Catholic World October 1950; The Listener December 19, 1946; Time November 8, 1948.

WILLIAMS, EMLYN (November 26, 1905-). For biographical sketch and list of earlier works and references, see TWENTIETH CENTURY AUTHORS, 1942.

* * *

Several plays by Emlyn Williams were produced in London during and after World War II, but none of these matched the success of his earlier The Corn Is Green and Night Must Fall. It is as an actor, a keen and sensitive interpreter of a variety of characters, that Williams is best known today. To a large British and American public he is primarily the re-incarnation of Charles Dickens, whose works he has presented in a series of highly acclaimed dramatic readings. These developed out of his nightly readings to his children from Bleak House. In 1951 he gave his first public Dickens reading in a London theatre, and this proved so successful that he brought his one-man show to America in 1952 where it was also a hit. With a characteristic flair for theatrical effectiveness, Williams duplicated in every possible detail the readings which Dickens himself gave on his popular tours nearly a century ago. In formal Victorian dress suit and frilled shirt, with beard and wavy hair, and a lectern that was a duplicate of the one Dickens had designed for his own readings, Williams read from Our Mutual Friend, Dombey and Son, Pickwick Papers, A Tale of Two Cities, etc. American audiences know him also for his part in Lillian Hellman's Montserrat (in 1949) and for his many motion picture roles —in The Stars Look Down, Major Barbara, Another Man's Poison, and Dolwyn. Recently he has been giving readings from the works of the late Dylan Thomas.

ADDITIONAL WORKS: Plays—Morning Star, 1942; Druid's Rest, 1944; The Wind of Heaven, n.d.; Spring, 1600, 1946; Trespass, 1947; Pepper and Sand, 1948; Accolade, 1951; Readings from Dickens, 1953.

ABOUT: Current Biography 1952; Esquire November 1941; Life March 3, 1952; Theatre Arts January 1948, March 1952.

WILLIAMS, JESSE LYNCH (August 17, 1871-September 14, 1929). For biographical sketch and list of works and references, see TWENTIETH CENTURY AUTHORS, 1942.

* * *

ABOUT: Egbert, D. D. & Lee, D. M. Princeton Portraits.

WILLIAMS, MICHAEL (February 5, 1877-October 12, 1950). For biographical sketch and list of works and references, see TWENTIETH CENTURY AUTHORS, 1942.

* * *

Michael Williams died in Hartford, Conn., at seventy-three.

His own writing was, in the opinion of Murray Godwin, "intelligent, earnest, and tolerant." His most positive contribution to his chosen cause of liberal Catholicism was his editorship of the Commonweal. That publication said of its first editor, "He was in the front rank of those who fought for social justice. He fought with all the charm and exuberance and warm friendliness of his whole personality, but he really fought."

Correction: Williams was born in 1877, not 1878, as given in TWENTIETH CENTURY AUTHORS, 1942.

ABOUT: Hoehn, M. (ed.) Catholic Authors, I; America October 28, 1950; Commonweal October 27, 1950; New York Times October 13, 1950.

WILLIAMS, OSCAR (December 1900-). For autobiographical sketch and list of earlier works and references, see TWENTIETH CENTURY AUTHORS, 1942.

* * *

Oscar Williams writes from New York City: "Your biographical note of 1942 is slightly inaccurate: I am married to Gene Derwood, the painter and poet. Also, my glasses are *not* perched precariously on a long nose! It's 1952, and they haven't fallen off yet!

"I am at present the General Editor of the Little Treasury series being published by Charles Scribner's Sons, and I have lectured at many universities, including Iowa, California, Utah, Missouri, Washington (Seattle), British Columbia, Wayne, etc."

As originator and editor of the Little Treasury series, Oscar Williams was called by the poet Robert Lowell "probably the best anthologist in America." In these collections Williams has brought together a valuable selection of the great poems in the English language from Chaucer down to the present day. Henry Rago has commented on the "atmosphere of ease and enjoyment—almost the presence of a gentle and cheerful host," which is Williams' special editorial contribution to these volumes. In addition, as Archibald MacLeish has pointed out, Williams renders a service to the art of poetry in America by "his generous encouragement of the work of younger and less-known men."

Williams has published two collections of his own verse in the past decade. Primarily a poet of the city, Williams writes with vigor and enthusiasm, displaying (to quote John Malcolm Brinnin) "a wide dexterity in the use of forms and a spectacular imagination." In one volume, *That's All that Matters*, Conrad Aiken found a range from "his very best and most brilliant things" to "a fascinating exhibit of his very worst." But Dylan Thomas, viewing his work as a whole, praised him as "a very real and important American poet. . . . His powerful imagery and unique personal idiom add a permanent page to American poetry."

Gene Derwood died in 1954. A collection of her poems was published in 1955.

ADDITIONAL WORKS: *Poems*—That's All That Matters, 1945; Selected Poems, 1947. *Anthologies* —The War Poets, 1945; The New Poems Series, 1940, 1942, 1943, 1944; A Little Treasury of Modern Poetry, 1946; A Little Treasury of Great Poetry, 1947; A Little Treasury of American Poetry, 1948; A Little Treasury of British Poetry, 1951; Immortal Poems of the English Language, 1952; (ed.) F. T. Palgrave's The Golden Treasury, 1953; The Pocket Book of Modern Verse, 1954.

ABOUT: Atlantic Monthly October 1947; New York Herald Tribune Book Review October 14, 1945; Poetry December 1945.

WILLIAMS, TENNESSEE (March 26, 1914-), American playwright, novelist, and short story writer, reports: "I was born in the Episcopal rectory of Columbus, Miss., an old town on the Tombigbee River which was so dignified and reserved that there was a saying, only slightly exaggerated, that you had to live there a whole year before a neighbor would smile at you on the street. As my grandfather, with whom we lived, was the Episcopal clergyman, we were accepted without probation. My father, a man with the formidable name of Cornelius Coffin Williams, was a man of ancestry  that came on one side, the Williams, from pioneer Tennessee stock and on the other from early settlers of Nantucket Island in New England. My mother was descended from Quakers. Roughly there was a combination of Puritan and Cavalier strains in my blood which may be accountable for the conflicting impulses I often represent in the people I write about.

"I was christened Thomas Lanier Williams. It is a nice enough name, perhaps a little too nice. It sounds like it might belong to the sort of writer who turns out sonnet sequences to Spring. As a matter of fact, my first literary award was twenty-five dollars from a woman's club for doing exactly that, three sonnets dedicated to Spring. I hasten to add that I was still pretty young. Under that name I published a good deal of lyric poetry which was a bad imitation of Edna Millay. When I grew up I realized this poetry wasn't much good and I felt the name had been compromised, so I changed it to Tennessee Williams, the justification being mainly that the Williamses had fought the Indians for Tennessee and I had already discovered that the life of a young writer was going to be something similar to the defense of a stockade against a band of savages.

"When I was about twelve, my father, a traveling salesman, was appointed to an office position in St. Louis and so we left the rectory and moved north. It was a tragic move. Neither my sister nor I could adjust ourselves to life in a midwestern city. The schoolchildren made fun of our Southern speech and manners. I remember gangs of kids following me home yelling 'Sissy!' and home was not a very pleasant refuge. It was a perpetually dim little apartment in a wilderness of identical brick and concrete structures with no grass and no trees nearer than the park. In the South we had never been conscious of the fact that we were economically less fortunate than others. We lived as well as anyone else. But in St. Louis we suddenly discovered there were two kinds of people, the rich and the poor, and that we belonged more to the latter. If we walked far enough west we came into a region of fine residences set in beautiful lawns. But where we lived, to which we must always return, were ugly rows of apartment buildings the color of dried blood and mustard. If I had been born to this situation I might not have resented it deeply. But it was forced upon my consciousness at the most sensitive age of childhood. It produced a shock and a rebellion that has grown into an inherent part of my work. It was the beginning of the social-consciousness which I think has marked most of my writing. I am glad that I received this bitter education for I don't think any writer has much purpose back of him unless he feels bitterly the inequities of the society he lives in. I have no acquaintance with political and social dialectics. If you ask what my politics are, I am a Humanitarian.

"I entered college during the great American depression and after a couple of years I couldn't afford to continue but had to drop out and take a clerical job in the shoe company that employed my father. The two years I spent in that corporation were indescribable torment to me as an individual but of immense value to me as a writer for they gave me first-hand knowledge of what it means to be a small wage-earner in a hopelessly routine job. I had been writing since childhood and I continued writing while I was employed by the shoe company. When I came home from work I would tank up on black coffee so I could remain awake most of the night, writing short stories which I could not sell. Gradually my health broke down. One day coming home from work, I collapsed and was removed to the hospital. The doctor said I couldn't go back to the shoe company. Soon as that was settled I recovered and went back South to live with my grandparents in Memphis where they had moved since my grandfather's retirement from the ministry. Then I began to have a little success with my writing. I became self-sufficient. I put myself through two more years of college and got a B.A. degree at the University of Iowa in 1938. Before then and for a couple of years afterwards I did a good deal of traveling around and I held a great number of part-time jobs of great diversity. It is hard to put the story in correct chronology for the last ten years of my life are a dizzy kaleidoscope. I don't quite believe all that has happened to me, it seems it must have happened to five or ten other people.

"My first real recognition came in 1940 when I received a Rockefeller fellowship and wrote *Battle of Angels,* which was produced by the Theatre Guild at the end of that year with Miriam Hopkins in the leading role. It closed in Boston during the try-out run but I have re-written it a couple of times since then and still have faith in it. My health was so impaired that I landed in 4F after a medical examination of about five minutes' duration. My jobs in this period included running an all-night elevator in a big apartment-hotel, waiting on tables and reciting verse in Greenwich Village, working as a teletype operator for the U.S. Engineers in Jacksonville, Fla., waiter and cashier for a small restaurant in New Orleans, ushering at the Strand Theatre on Broadway. All the while I kept on writing, writing, not with any hope of making a living at it but because I found no other means of expressing things that seemed to demand expression. There was never a moment when I did not find life to be immeasurably exciting to experience and to witness, however difficult it was to sustain.

"From a $17 a week job as a movie usher I was suddenly shipped off to Hollywood where M.G.M. paid me $250 a week. I saved enough money out of my six months there to keep me while I wrote *The Glass Menagerie.* I don't think the story, from that point on, requires any detailed consideration.

"If I can be said to have a home, it is in New Orleans where I've lived off and on since 1938 and which has provided me with more material than any other part of the country. I live near the main street of the Quarter which is named Royal. Down this street, running on the same tracks, are two street-cars, one named 'Desire' and the other named 'Cemetery.' Their indiscourageable progress up and down Royal struck me as having some symbolic bearing of a broad nature on the life in the *Vieux Carré*—and everywhere else for that matter . . . that's how I got the title."

* * *

The title referred to above was, of course, *A Streetcar Named Desire* which, along with his earlier *The Glass Menagerie,* established Tennessee Williams as one of the most distinguished of contemporary American playwrights. Both plays had long and highly successful runs on Broadway, on tour, and in motion picture versions. *The Glass Menagerie,* a compassionate and imaginative drama for which Williams drew heavily upon his early life in St. Louis, won the New York Drama Critics' Circle award in 1945 as the best American play of the season. In 1947 his deeply moving study of the mental and moral disintegration of a Southern belle, *A Streetcar Named Desire*, proved to be one of the really major theatrical successes of recent years. Brooks Atkinson wrote in the New York *Times*: "Out of a few characters he can evoke the sense of life as a wide, endlessly flowing pattern of human needs and aspirations. . . . He is an incomparably beautiful writer," and John Mason Brown hailed it as "an achievement of unusual and exciting distinction." With *Summer and Smoke*, produced in 1948, Williams again wrote a sensitive study of a frustrated young Southern woman, but the play was judged to be more tenuous in theme and execution than the powerful *Streetcar*. In *The Rose Tattoo*, produced in 1951, his heroine, an Italian woman living in a small Louisiana town, was a stronger, more vigorous and earthy personality than Williams had heretofore created, better able to cope with the challenges of her life; but he treated her with the same sympathy and penetrating understanding. In 1953 Williams turned from these studies of feminine psychology to fantasy and allegory with *Camino Real*, a tender but bizarre play whose characters included a dying prize fighter and Lord Byron. The play was not a commercial success, and the critics were sharply divided over it, some acclaiming it the best play he had ever written, others condemning it outright. *Cat on a Hot Tin Roof*, Williams' powerful portrait of a wealthy Southern planter and his family, was a major play of the 1955 theatrical season and won the New York Drama Critics Circle award for that year.

Williams has been described as "small, blue-eyed," with a boyish grin, a gentle voice, and "a certain shy charm." He is unmarried. He takes himself and his work seriously. "Every artist," he has said, "has a basic premise pervading his whole life, and that premise can provide the impulse in everything he creates. For me the dominating premise has been the need for understanding and tenderness and fortitude among individuals trapped by circumstance."

He has twice received the Pulitzer prize for drama—in 1947, for *A Streetcar Named Desire*, and in 1955, for *Cat on a Hot Tin Roof*.

PRINCIPAL WORKS: *Plays (dates of publication)*—Battle of Angels, 1945; The Glass Menagerie, 1945; Twenty-Seven Wagons Full of Cotton, and Other One-Act Plays, 1946; You Touched Me (with D. Windham) 1947; A Streetcar Named Desire, 1947; American Blues: Five Short Plays, 1948; Summer and Smoke, 1948; The Rose Tattoo, 1951; Camino Real, 1953. *Fiction*—One Arm, and Other Stories, 1948; The Roman Spring of Mrs.

Stone, 1950; Hard Candy: A Book of Stories, 1954; One Arm, and Other Stories, 1954.

ABOUT: Barnett, L. B. Writing on Life; College English October 1948; Current Biography 1946; Harper's July 1948; New York Times Magazine December 7, 1947; New Yorker April 14, 1945; Theatre Arts February 1946.

WILLIAMS, VALENTINE (October 20, 1883-November 20, 1946). For autobiographical sketch and list of earlier works and references, see TWENTIETH CENTURY AUTHORS, 1942.

* * *

Valentine Williams died in a New York City hospital at sixty-three. He had come to this country from England a month earlier for medical treatment.

Since 1943 he had divided his time between Hollywood and London as a screenwriter associated with Sir Alexander Korda, and had continued writing and acting for radio in both countries. Eugene Lyons has said that Williams "brought to each of his many vocations and avocations a lusty appetite for life, a keen mind, and a fine appreciation of the nuances of people, places, and events." His mystery and adventure stories exhibit fine craftsmanship and a strong dramatic sense, and are peopled with well-conceived human beings. The London *Times* observed: "Gifted, traveled, and urbane, he had as a writer qualities which raised him well above the normal level of those who supply the market of his choice."

ADDITIONAL WORKS: Courier to Marrakesh, 1945; Skeleton Out of the Cupboard, 1946.

ABOUT: Hoehn, M. (ed.) Catholic Authors, I; London Times November 21, December 3, 1946; New York Times November 21, 1946.

WILLIAMS, WILLIAM CARLOS (September 17, 1883-). For autobiographical sketch and list of earlier works and references, see TWENTIETH CENTURY AUTHORS, 1942.

* * *

In 1946 William Carlos Williams published the first of the four books of his major poetic work *Paterson*. The poem has been called his "personal epic." It has grown out of his very roots—his home, his profession, his country, the image embodying what he calls "the whole knowable world about me." In his autobiography Dr. Williams explains that he selected Paterson, an industrial city on the Passaic River with a rich background of colonial history and a population reflecting the characteristic American racial and cultural mixture, because he wanted to write about what he knew best and most concretely.

"That is the poet's business. Not to talk in vague categories but to write particularly, as a physician works, upon a patient, upon the thing before him, in the particular to discover the universal." Dudley Fitts has called the work "an *Ars Poetica* for contemporary America." Robert Lowell sees it as "Whitman's America, grown pathetic and tragic.... No poet has written of it with such a combination of brilliance, sympathy, and experience, with such alertness and energy."

Dr. Williams' recent prose work includes his autobiography, a collection of short stories, *Make Light of It*, and a novel, *The Build-Up*, final volume of a trilogy with *White Mule* (1937) and *In the Money* (1940). His prose is casual, colloquial, at times slangy and commonplace, but "fullbodied" and warm with compassionate love for humanity. It brims, W. T. Scott wrote, "with the sense of the living day." But it is in his poetry that Dr. Williams has achieved his greatest stature. I. L. Solomon sums up his achievement thus: "The essentiality of Dr. Williams lies in his approach to the poem, his union of idea and form, and his unceremonious insistence that the things seen spring alive imaginatively by the proper distillation of emotion into words." Vivienne Koch finds a continuity in his work, over its span of more than four decades, in the search for the knowledge of self. "It is not extravagant to say that Williams throughout all his difficult and passionate explorations has sought precisely that: to know of his situation what it does to him and with him and thus, in the end, to discover *its* nature, and so, perhaps, his own."

Long known only to a small group of readers, Dr. Williams (though by no means a "popular" poet) has recently received a number of honors in recognition of his work. In 1948 he received the Loines Award of the National Institute of Arts and Letters and in 1950 he was elected a member of that group. Also in 1950 he received the National Book Award for poetry. In 1952 he was appointed Consultant in Poetry to the Library of Congress (though he did not occupy the office owing to an attack on his politics), and in 1953 he and Archibald MacLeish were named double winners of the Bollingen prize in poetry for 1952, awarded by the Yale University Library. Dr. Williams has honorary degrees from the University of Buffalo (1946), Rutgers University (1950), Bard College (1950), and the University of Pennsylvania (1952).

ADDITIONAL WORKS: *Poetry*—The Wedge, 1944; Paterson (Books I-IV) 1946-1951; Clouds,

Aigeltinger, Russia, &c., 1948; Collected Later Poems, 1950; Collected Earlier Poems, 1951; The Desert Music, and Other Poems, 1954. *Play*—A Dream of Love, 1948. *Prose*—Make Light of It (short stories) 1950; Autobiography, 1951; The Build-Up (novel) 1952; Selected Essays, 1954.

ABOUT: Frankenberg, L. Pleasure Dome; Koch, V. William Carlos Williams; Rahv, P. Image and Idea; Williams, W. C. Autobiography; New York Herald Tribune Book Review October 8, December 17, 1950; New York Times Book Review January 15, 1950; Poetry May 1952; Saturday Review March 15, 1952; Yale Review Spring 1952.

WILLIAMS-ELLIS, Mrs. AMABEL (STRACHEY) (1894-   ). For biographical sketch and list of earlier works and references, see TWENTIETH CENTURY AUTHORS, 1942.

* * *

Amabel Williams-Ellis has continued to follow (and sometimes to combine) her three major literary interests—writing for children, writing social history, and writing popularizations of scientific subjects. She is a wellinformed, witty, and invariably stimulating writer. If her work is intellectually rarely above the reading level of the popular magazines, it is nevertheless sound and informative. The *Spectator* observed that "Mrs. Williams-Ellis does not suffer from the highbrow delusion that no work on a social topic can be valuable unless addressed strictly to a Third Programme Audience." She lives, as she has for many years, in Llanfrothen, North Wales. Her son was killed in action in World War II.

ADDITIONAL WORKS: Women in War Factories, 1943; Princesses and Trolls: Twelve Traditional Stories Retold, 1950; The Art of Being a Woman, 1951; (with E. S. Cooper-Willis) Laughing Gas and Safety Lamp, 1951; Headlong Down the Years, 1952.

WILLIAMSON, Mrs. ALICE MURIEL (LIVINGSTON) (1869-September 24, 1933). For biographical sketch and list of works and references, see TWENTIETH CENTURY AUTHORS, 1942.

WILLIAMSON, C. N. See WILLIAMSON, A. M. L.

WILLIAMSON, HENRY (1897-   ). For biographical sketch and list of earlier works and references, see TWENTIETH CENTURY AUTHORS, 1942.

* * *

Henry Williamson, one of the most gifted of contemporary writers on natural history, lives very quietly on a farm in Norfolk, shunning publicity and working away at his sensitive and perceptive books on country and animal life. The most successful of his recent pastoral novels was *The Phasian Bird,* the story of a cock-pheasant growing up on an English farm. Williamson's fidelity of observation was especially remarkable in this book. "Mr. Williamson," T. M. Longstreth wrote in the *Christian Science Monitor,* "watches with such intentness and patience and that sympathetic union with nature which made a Wordsworth but is almost unknown to city man, that his eye notes everything and holds it in his heart."

Other recent books by Williamson include three autobiographical novels — *The Sun in the Sands, Tales of a Devon Village,* and *Life in a Devon Village,* the latter two being largely rewritings of his earlier *The Village Book* and *The Labouring Life,* but affording as Malcolm Elwin points out, "an astonishing study of a literary artist's development through fifteen years of maturing reflection." In 1947 *The Gold Falcon,* originally published anonymously in 1933, was reissued.

ADDITIONAL WORKS: The Sun in the Sands, 1945; Life in a Devon Village, 1945; Tales of a Devon Village, 1945; The Gold Falcon (second ed.) 1947; (ed.) Anthology of Modern Nature Writing, 1948; The Phasian Bird, 1948; The Scribbling Lark, 1949; The Dark Lantern, 1951; Donkey Boy, 1952; Tales of Moorland and Estuary, 1953; Young Phillip Madison, 1953.

ABOUT: Elwin, M. *in* Modern British Writing (ed. D. V. Baker); New York Times Book Review September 19, 1948.

WILLIAMSON, THAMES ROSS (February 7, 1894-). For biographical sketch and list of earlier works and references, see TWENTIETH CENTURY AUTHORS, 1942.

* * *

In recent years T. R. Williamson has made his home in Ashland, Ore. His novels continue to reflect a high degree of professional competence. His *Christine Roux,* a story of a French novice who leaves her convent for the secular world, was praised for its delicacy and warmth of feeling. His non-fiction work on Alaska, *Far North Country,* though criticized by some reviewers for errors of fact, was nevertheless generally received as a lively and sympathetic treatment of the subject.

ADDITIONAL WORKS: Far North Country, 1944; Christine Roux, 1945; The Gladiator, 1948.

ABOUT: Warfel, H. R. American Novelists of Today.

WILLINGHAM, CALDER (1922-), American novelist, was born in Atlanta, Ga., of an old Southern family. He attended Darlington School in Rome, Ga., the famous Southern military academy the Citadel, and the University of Virginia, before coming up to New York City at the age of twenty-one, in 1943. Four years later, with the publication of his first novel, *End as a Man,* he emerged as an *enfant terrible* of modern fiction, arousing heated critical dissent and nearly entangling his publishers in a morals suit. *End as a Man,* a violent and vitriolic study of life in an unnamed military academy in the South, was alternately

Hella Heyman

praised and attacked for its naturalistic rendering of the texture of the cadets' lives and its too-faithful reproduction of their daily speech. "It reads," said one unfavorable critic, "with the imbecile monotony of scrawls on lavatory walls." However, James T. Farrell, the archdeacon of American naturalism, admired the book for its "complete realism." And many readers came to understand that the author was attempting a larger moral interpretation of the scene he had so vividly called to life; a decision concurred in by the court on May 25, 1947, when it dismissed obscenity charges against The Dial Press brought by the New York Society for the Suppression of Vice.

After such notorious beginnings, Willingham's later literary efforts have continued to awaken decided responses, pro and con, in his readers. His output has been high; by the age of thirty-two he had already published five works of fiction and produced one play. In 1950 his second novel, *Geraldine Bradshaw,* appeared. This novel, which had Chicago as its locale, delineated the story of a hotel bellboy's pursuit of a girl elevator operator. This single-minded sex chase is drawn unsparingly; again, Willingham brought his characters, for all their limited interests and motivation, vividly to life. The following year, in 1951, a collection of twenty-five humorous sketches, satires, fables, and realistic narratives was published under the title, *The Gates of Hell.* This collection allowed the writer to demonstrate a wider variety of themes and potentialities than his work had indicated previously.

Reach to the Stars, published in 1952, the story of another bellhop's experiences, this time in a hotel in Hollywood, was considered a brilliant, but "plotless" excursion, consisting of a series of scenes like variations on a single theme. *Natural Child,* a departure in some ways from his other novels, was also published in 1952. This was a study of young persons living on the fringe of pseudo-Bohemian society in New York, working out their lives and loves with reference to metropolitan goals and strivings. It has been considered by some critics the author's most mature achievement to date.

On September 15, 1953, Willingham's dramatization of his first book, *End as a Man*, opened at the Theatre de Lys, an off-Broadway playhouse in New York City. The play scored a hit at once, partly for the way the sadistic cadet, Jocko de Paris, was brilliantly brought to life by the actor Ben Gazzara. The following month the play moved uptown to the Broadway theatre district. On the day the play opened Willingham was married to Jane Bennett of Brooklyn. It was Willingham's second marriage, his previous one having terminated in divorce.

The play version of *End as a Man* was completed in hiding in his brother's fish-packing plant in Maryland. Willingham is not planning to write any longer in New York, he has told reporters. "Success is always dangerous," he announced to William Hawkins of the New York *World-Telegram*; "and early success is deadly. . . . What I went through writing my second book shouldn't happen to a 'dawg.' A prisoner in the electric chair couldn't have had it worse." Willingham is tall, lanky, aggressively red-headed, and speaks in the accents of his native South. He has confessed to his publisher a fondness for New Orleans jazz and Beethoven; a hatred for critics, even admiring ones; and an inability to read any other works except his own. He believes all writers really feel that way. "You can write or read," he says. "I write."

PRINCIPAL WORKS: End as a Man, 1947; Geraldine Bradshaw, 1950; The Gates of Hell, 1951 (short stories); Reach to the Stars, 1952; Natural Child, 1952; To Eat a Peach, 1955.

ABOUT: New York Herald Tribune Book Review February 16, 1947, June 17, 1951; New York Times Book Review May 25, 1947; New York World-Telegram September 14, 1953; Saturday Review of Literature February 16, 1947.

WILLISON, GEORGE FINDLAY (July 24, 1896-), American historian, writes: "Born of Scottish parents in Denver, Colo., I grew up on the outskirts of the city, roaming the neighborhood and the inviting open prairie for miles around even as a small child. City children in those days enjoyed a far-ranging freedom of foot—and with that, a degree of social freedom, and intellectual as well — which the automobile with its whir of death-dealing traffic has destroyed. We did not have to wait for an adult hand to lead us across the street into new adventure.

"Though still desirous of becoming a second Ty Cobb, I did my first serious writing in high school—and never was I more serious. In Latin we were reading Cicero, and I grew so tired of his pomposities, so disgusted with his whining self-righteousness and really dirty digs at Catiline, that I decided to come to the defense with a rousing appeal and silence Cicero forever. It was a long and ambitious work, and not without fruit, leading me to my first acquaintance with the real learning process, seeking sources, weighing evidence, throwing away the second-hand, and with the deep pleasures and high excitements of slowly shaping a creation of one's own. Instead of asking me to read the historic paper to the class, the teacher handed it back a few days later, with scarcely a glance at me as she remarked, 'You seem to have spent a great deal of time on this, which is probably the reason you are not doing so well in what you should be doing.' What I should have been doing, indeed!—which was to toss her to the lions, along with Cicero.

"At the University of Colorado, I 'majored' —as the phrase ran—in Greek, a very rewarding choice. First, for the language and the literature itself, a constant revelation and delight. Second, for the rare spirit that lighted my steps, the late Dr. George Norlin, one of the great Grecians of his day, a humanist in his every fibre.

"As I was usually the only one in the class, we met as we pleased and talked not merely of the text before us, but of everything from Greek games and the cult of Aphrodite to *The Spoon River Anthology* and World War I then raging. A sharp and sensitive critic, a fine writer himself, a wise man of the world, Dr. Norlin was a university in himself, and I know he went to the Elysian Fields to join Aristophanes, Aeschylus, Herodotus, Sappho, and his many old friends there.

"After a stint in the army in 1918, I was named, by good fortune, a Rhodes Scholar and lived abroad for four years—largely in Oxford, London, Paris, and Heidelberg— which opened a new world of both the flesh and the spirit to a still rather naïve youth from the Rockies. Officially, I 'read' history, economics, and political science, but I managed to read as widely in other fields—in English and French literature especially.

"In 1928, after several misguided years in journalism, I went to St. John's College, Annapolis, Md., to teach Greek, Latin (but not Cicero), and related subjects. The next year I joined the staff of the experimental Hessian Hills School at Croton on Hudson, N.Y., remaining there till 1935, when I resigned to get on with my own work. Meantime, I had married Florence Hauser; had a son, Malcolm; and written *Here They Dug the Gold,* a chronicle of gold rush days and early boom towns in Colorado. Just after the book appeared—the Depression had come— the publisher failed, went bankrupt, collapsed, and the book was buried in the debris. Resurrected as a reprint in 1935, it soon went down again in another bankruptcy.

"Removing from Croton to Provincetown, Cape Cod, where living was pleasant and cheap, I completed a study of war as a social and economic institution, which came out in 1936. My luck still held—the publisher collapsed. With all of those who were desperately trying to earn a mere subsistence in the arts and crafts, I welcomed the W.P.A. Federal Arts Program, becoming in 1938 a national editor in the Washington office of the Writers' Project, working chiefly on the American Guide Series, an education in itself. After Pearl Harbor, I transferred to the Civil Aeronautics Administration, as writer-editor, and early in 1944 joined the publicity staff of the Democratic National Committee, remaining there till the summer of 1946.

"In Washington I had continued with my own writing as time from the job allowed. In 1940 appeared *Let's Make a Play* (the publisher didn't collapse) and in 1945, a group biography of the Pilgrims, *Saints and Strangers,* which was well received by the critics and in the bookshops, later chosen as a dividend by the Book-of-the-Month Club. This windfall enabled me to acquire a modest country place in up-state New York, above Albany, where I have since lived and worked —except for 1950, when I was with the United Nations, in Publications, and the first half of 1952, when I was again in Washington, with Senator Estes Kefauver in his campaign for the Democratic presidential nomination.

"In 1946, I revised and added some recently disclosed material to my first book, *Here They Dug the Gold,* which found readers at last, even in Britain, where it became, surprisingly, a book club choice. Since then, I have completed *Behold Virginia: The Fifth Crown,* a critical history of the Old Dominion down to 1776, a Book Find Club selection, and *The Pilgrim Reader.*

"For a new series, Mainstreams in American History, I am at work on a volume dealing with the colonization of our eastern shores down to 1700 or slightly thereafter. When that is completed, I intend a book on the theocrats of the Massachusetts Bay Colony, with whose ideologies and practices I have long been concerned.

"In short, my mature interests are strung on this thread—the American people, where they came from, how they got here, and how they have fared along the way in all respects."

PRINCIPAL WORKS: Here They Dug the Gold, 1931; Why Wars Are Declared, 1935; (ed.) Let's Make a Play, 1940; Saints and Strangers, 1945; Behold Virginia, 1951; (ed.) The Pilgrim Reader, 1953.

ABOUT: Current Biography 1946.

WILSON, ANGUS (August 11, 1913-), British writer of fiction, reports: "My full name is Angus Frank Johnstone-Wilson. I was born at Bexhill, Sussex. My father was William Johnstone-Wilson and my mother formerly Miss Maude Caney. She came from Durban, Natal, South Africa, and when the first World War was ended we visited there and I spent three years of  my childhood there. On our return I went to Westminster School and subsequently to Merton College, Oxford, where I studied medieval history. After two years in which I did numerous jobs such as tutoring, secretarial work, catering and running a restaurant and acting as social organizer, I went to the Department of Printed Books, British Museum. In the 1939 war I was employed at the Foreign Office and since my return to the British Museum I have first worked on replacing as many as possible of the three hundred thousand books destroyed here during the bombing, and subsequently as deputy superintendent of the Reading Room.

"It had always been my intention not to write books. I used to say that too many people wrote and I still do. However, during the 1939 war I suffered a nervous breakdown and on my return to London I felt that I could only find satisfaction in life if I gave myself an additional interest. For this reason I began to write short stories, working only at weekends. These stories, luckily for me, turned out successful and formed the first volume which was published in England in 1949 called *The Wrong Set.* I have continued

Paul Moor

to be a weekend writer only and have subsequently published another volume of short stories, *Such Darling Dodos,* an examination of the novels of Emile Zola, entitled *Emile Zola,* and last my novel, *Hemlock and After.* Next year I will publish a satirical work on the 1920's entitled *For Whom the Cloche Tolls.* I contribute reviews and literary articles to many of the periodicals here including *Horizon, The Observer, New Statesman and Nation, The Listener,* the *Times Literary Supplement* and the *Sunday Times.* I have also broadcast literary talks on the Third Programme and recently, a small imaginary autobiographical play. Although my work has been well received both in England and in the United States, it has been generally criticized for its savage characterization and the unpleasantness of the persons portrayed. In general critics have found it satisfactory to describe the work as satirical. I do not myself feel that this is a satisfactory description except in so far as I like to use irony as my approach. To me the characters do not appear degraded and depraved, but simply realistic accounts of people as they are, and I feel that the general desire that some characters should be faultless is unhealthy and untrue and that to portray characters without saying all that must be said against them is patronage and not praise. I also believe very strongly that if the novel is to recover its strength in the modern world it must, though not returning to the nineteenth century standards, once more acquire that generality which belonged to the great nineteenth century novels and it is for that reason I do not hesitate to mix satire, social realism, farce, melodrama, and tragedy in one work. It has been criticized as an impossible method, but I believe this is only because people are no longer familiar with the wide generalized approach of the last century. Finally I believe that if the novel is to recover from the anemia which has beset it since the 1920's, it must once more cover a wide, social canvas."

* * *

The writer to whom Angus Wilson is most frequently compared by the critics is Evelyn Waugh. Like Waugh, he writes in a crisp prose style, with sure malice and acid-edged contempt for sham and pretension. He is, however, his own master and not an imitator. His two volumes of short stories have won him an enthusiastic reading public in both Britain and the United States, and with his first novel, *Hemlock and After,* he became one of the most promising of the younger, post-World War II generation of British novelists. The London *Times Literary Sup-*

plement described this novel as "an ambitious book, and essentially a moral one, a savage exposure of corruption in a disintegrating society," and L. A. G. Strong, in the *Spectator,* called it "an important novel on a major theme."

PRINCIPAL WORKS: The Wrong Set, and Other Stories, 1949; Such Darling Dodos, and Other Stories, 1950; Hemlock and After, 1952; Emile Zola, 1952; For Whom the Cloche Tolls: A Scrapbook of the Twenties, 1954.

ABOUT: (London) Times Literary Supplement August 29, 1952.

WILSON, CHARLES MORROW (June 16, 1905-), American regionalist, son of Joseph Dickson and Mattie Morrow Wilson, both deceased, was born at Fayetteville, Ark., the youngest of three children. He grew up on a small farm in the Arkansas Ozarks, near the town of Fayetteville, there attended public grade school and high school, and in 1926 was graduated from the Uni-

Affiliated Photo: Conway

versity of Arkansas with the degree of Bachelor of Arts, with literature and philosophy his major studies. During his final three years in college he earned his way as a correspondent for three newspapers, *Arkansas Gazette,* St. Louis *Post-Dispatch* and the *Christian Science Monitor.* After graduation he went immediately into newspaper reporting, serving stints with the St. Louis *Post-Dispatch,* an ambiguous interval with the New York *World,* and almost three years with the New York *Times.* During that period and thereafter, Wilson wrote for a wide variety of magazines and reviews.

His theme has been preponderantly that of rural life and problems in the United States. In 1935, Wilson went to the tropics and thereafter spent principal portions of twelve years in agricultural work and reporting in Central America, South America, the West Indies, and Africa. He returned to home pastures, to a farm in the Arkansas Ozarks, near Fayetteville, in June 1952, and there resides.

Wilson has said of himself: "My relations are a bizarre mixture of lawyers, farmers, and politicians. But personally I never thought seriously of any occupation other than writing. Under duress I have been other things; a highway worker for six months, a junior corporation executive for several years, and throughout most of my youth and about ten years of my adult life a farmer of meager sorts, and for brief intervals a lecturer at colleges and universities, a historian and archeologist solely as hobbies. My ambition is to write good books of Americana. My grandfather, Alfred M. Wilson, a lawyer-politician and a cavalry colonel in the Confederate Army has been my personal beacon and lighthouse. His lifelong ambition was that of rendering good service to American Indians. He got around to realizing this when, at seventy-one, he was made attorney for the Cherokee Commission. At the tender age of eighty-two he took over for the Governor's Commission which finally made the Indian Territory into the State of Oklahoma. At eighty-six my grandfather reported that he was beginning to feel he was getting somewhere. I still have hopes."

PRINCIPAL WORKS: Acres of Sky (novel) 1930; Backwoods America, 1934; Meriwether Lewis of Lewis and Clark, 1934; The Rabble Rouser (novel) 1936; Roots of America: A Travelogue of American Personalities, 1936; Aroostook: Our Last Frontier, 1937; Country Living: Plus and Minus, 1938; Ginger Blue (novel) 1940; Landscape of Rural Poverty: Corn Bread and Creek Water, 1940; Challenge and Opportunity: Central America, 1941; Ambassadors in White: The Story of American Tropical Medicine, 1942; Trees and Test Tubes: The Story of Rubber, 1943; Man's Reach (novel) 1944; Middle America, 1944; (ed.) New Crops for the New World, 1945; Oil Across the World, 1946; Liberia, 1947; Empire in Green and Gold: The Story of the American Banana Trade, 1947; One Half the People: Doctors and the Crisis of World Health, 1949; The Tropics: World of Tomorrow, 1951; Butterscotch and the Happy Barnyard, 1953.

WILSON, EDMUND (May 8, 1895-).

For biographical sketch and list of earlier works and references, see TWENTIETH CENTURY AUTHORS, 1942.

* * *

In 1944 Edmund Wilson succeeded Clifton Fadiman as book reviewer for the *New Yorker*. He held this post for the next four years, and continues to contribute reviews, as well as feature articles, to that magazine. In contrast to Fadiman's urbane, breezy, and genial handling of new books, Wilson tackled his job belligerently, sometimes irritating readers with his iconoclasm (his attack on the detective story, for example, caused a major flurry of excitement) and sometimes mystifying them with his profound erudition. Nevertheless, his reviews were probably the most stimulating and vigorous criticism that has appeared in a popular American periodical in recent years.

Because he has made his living mainly by writing for periodicals, Wilson calls himself a journalist. If that is what he is, Perry Miller commented in the *Nation* in 1951, "then his is journalism in the grand historic manner of Johnson and Sainte-Beuve." Whether or not Wilson's "journalism" is "literary criticism" is a matter of some debate. He is popularly regarded as the outstanding contemporary American critic, and his writings, from *Axel's Castle* down to *The Shores of Light*, are basic texts for any reader in the field of contemporary criticism. However, as Delmore Schwartz has pointed out: "We do not get from his ostensibly critical essays the strict formal analysis, which is one kind of traditional literary criticism; we do not get the reformation, correction, and extension of taste, which is another important kind; nor do we get the propagation of the leading ideas of an age, which is a third kind. . . . If we look for literary judgment in Wilson, we find a singular weakness and lack of critical pioneering."

Perhaps the most accurate description of Wilson's place in criticism is Stanley Edgar Hyman's in *The Armed Vision*. Hyman calls him a "translator" or interpreter, who serves today as the much needed "conduit between the obscure or difficult work and the reader." He suggests that Wilson is a popularizer. It should be added, however, that he is not one who merely reduces or vulgarizes literature to make it attractive to large numbers of people, but one who interprets, explains, analyzes, and draws upon his own impressive background of erudition to illuminate the text at hand.

Wilson's major contribution to American letters has been his criticism rather than his creative writing. He has written little verse in recent years. His plays have been received with respect, though not with enthusiasm. *The Little Blue Light* (which was produced professionally in New York in 1951), a satirical comedy on American society in the future, was praised as an ingenious intellectual exercise, suffering, however, Francis Fergusson remarked, "from the weaknesses of all Wellsian, Shavian or Huxleyan fantasy: the difficulty of competing with the daily newspaper." His collection *Five Plays*, published in 1954, contained only one new play, "Cyprian's Prayer," an allegorical fairy-tale about a sorcerer's apprentice. By far the most publicized of his works was his collection of first-person stories, *Memoirs of Hecate County*, which, a few months after its publication in 1946, was banned by the Court of Special Sessions as obscene. A few reviewers pointed out that the volume contained several fairly distinguished short stories, but the inclusion of one lengthy, highly erotic story brought the book a notoriety which it would otherwise never have had.

After a divorce from novelist Mary McCarthy, Wilson married Elena Thornton in 1946. They have a daughter.

ADDITIONAL WORKS: Notebooks of Night (verse and prose) 1942; (ed.) The Shock of Recognition, 1943; (ed.) Fitzgerald, F. S. The Crack-Up, with Other Uncollected Pieces, 1945; Memoirs of Hecate County, 1946; Europe Without a Baedeker, 1947; Classics and Commercials, 1950; The Little Blue Light (play) 1950; The Shores of Light, 1952; Five Plays, 1954.

ABOUT: Hyman, S. E. The Armed Vision; Schwartz, D. *in* Accent Anthology (ed. K. Quinn & C. Shattuck); Antioch Review December 1946; Current Biography 1945; Nation October 16, 1948, January 27, 1951; New York Times Book Review November 2, 1952; Sewanee Review April 1948.

WILSON, FLORENCE ROMA MUIR.
See WILSON, R.

WILSON, FORREST (January 20, 1883-May 9, 1942), American biographer, was born in Warren, Ohio, the son of James Forrest

Wilson and Harriet Rose (Larned) Wilson. He began his writing career as a newspaper reporter in Cleveland, and from 1910 to 1916 represented the Scripps newspapers in Washington, D.C., as a correspondent. In the latter year he toured South America, and during World War I served as a captain in the chemical warfare division. After the war he worked with the Assistant Secretary of War, Benedict Crowell, in the preparation of historical data on the war; the two co-authored *How America Went to War*, a six-volume opus published in 1921. At this time Wilson wrote under the name of Robert Forrest Wilson.

As European correspondent for *McCall's* magazine from 1923 to 1927, he lived in Paris during that time, and until 1930, contributing articles and short stories to magazines, co-authoring a play, *Blessed Event*, which appeared on Broadway in' the early 1930's, and publishing such books as *Paris on Parade*, a study of the spirit of the French capital. Of this book the Boston *Transcript* said, "Mr. Wilson does more than describe. He does more even than interpret. He makes the very stones of Paris human." *A Rich Brat* was a novel about Paris dressmaking; *How to Wine and Dine in Paris* reprinted some chapters from *Paris on Parade* and

added two new ones. For the novel Wilson had dropped the Robert from his name.

Twelve thousand miles of travel, mainly in the South and Southwest, and several years of research went into the writing of his biography of Harriet Beecher Stowe, *Crusader in Crinoline*. The reviewers approved, and Herbert Gorman noted in the New York *Times*: "The color of the times is excellently communicated with the development of his subject, and in achieving this art of presentation he has surrounded Mrs. Stowe with all the panoply, emotions, and constant stir of the long years through which she lived. She is never in a vacuum, as it were, but always moving, speaking and gesturing through her own times." The Pulitzer prize of 1942 was awarded him for the best American biography; a few days later, at the age of fifty-nine, he died at his home in Westport, Conn.

Wilson married Katherine Deniston Dewey in 1907; they had one daughter, now Mrs. Denny Markas of Hollywood. His second marriage was to Marie Humphreys.

PRINCIPAL WORKS: How America Went to War (with B. Crowell) 1921; Living Pageant of the Nile, 1924; Paris on Parade, 1925; A Rich Brat, 1929; How to Wine and Dine in Paris, 1930; Crusader in Crinoline, 1941.

ABOUT: New York Times May 5, May 11, 1942.

WILSON, HARRY LEON (May 1, 1867-June 29, 1939). For biographical sketch and list of works and references, see TWENTIETH CENTURY AUTHORS, 1942.

WILSON, JOHN DOVER (July 13, 1881-), British Shakespearean scholar, was born in London, son of the scientific artist Edwin Wilson, of Cambridge. He attended Lancing College and entered Cambridge University, Gonville and Caius College, as a history scholar. In 1902 he was Members' prizeman, in 1904 Harness prizeman (the latter for his essay on John Lyly). In 1903 he took his B.A. and second class in the history tripos, and in 1908 he received his M.A. Wilson began his teaching career as assistant master in the Whitgift Grammar School in 1904. For three years, 1906-09, he was in Finland lecturing at the University of Helsingfors. From 1909 to 1912 he taught at Goldsmiths' College, University of London, and from 1912 to 1924 he served as His Majesty's Inspector of adult education. He returned to the University of London, King's College, in the latter year as professor of education. In 1935 he moved to Edinburgh as Regius professor of rhetoric and English literature at the University of Edinburgh, a post he held until 1945. During this period he visited both Oxford and Cambridge on guest lectureships. Wilson married Dorothy Baldwin in 1906. They had two daughters and a son; the latter died in active service in World War II.

J. Dover Wilson's lifetime interest in Shakespeare was kindled in his undergraduate days by Alfred Ainger, who in 1900-01 gave the Clark lectures on Shakespeare at Cambridge (the same series in which Wilson himself gave his Falstaff lectures in 1942-43). "For one tranced listener," he writes in his preface to *The Fortunes of Falstaff*, "that 'merry-cheeked' old man with the silver hair opened a book that has never since been closed." In pursuit of his interest, Wilson has become one of the most distinguished of contemporary Shakespearean scholars. Probably his most important contributions are in the field of textual criticism (he is an editor of the New Cambridge edition of Shakespeare's works), where his intensive study of Elizabethan handwriting has helped him especially in the reconstruction of Shakespeare's text. At times his critical judgments have proved extreme, if not faulty. Oscar James Campbell observed that sometimes "his craving for critical adventure carried him beyond the reach of Shakespeare's text," and W. W. Greg once described his theories as the "careerings of a not too captive balloon in a high wind." His attempt to elucidate some of the mysteries in the plot of *Hamlet* (in *What Happens in Hamlet*) was a daring exercise of imagination as well as scholarship, but as the London *Times Literary Supplement* commented in its review of the book: "Imagination is no bad quality in the interpreter of high tragedy, especially when its eye is so firmly held to the object as in this book." Wilson himself writes of his book (in *The Fortunes of Falstaff*): "An editor of Shakespeare, who tries to do his duty, has . . . not only to explain the text and explain the language of his author, but also to imagine, as vividly as his knowledge and powers allow, every action and situation in the play he is engaged upon, as it would, or might, be represented by an Elizabethan company in an Elizabethan theatre."

Not quite so controversial as Wilson's views on *Hamlet* is his re-interpretation of Falstaff and the "Henry plays" in *The Fortunes of Falstaff*. Here his point of departure is the traditional interpretation of Falstaff and Prince Hal as lovable old rascal and suddenly reformed and self-righteous young prince— the view propounded by the nineteenth century scholar Andrew Bradley. "A new Fal-

staff stands before me," Wilson writes, "as fascinating as Bradley's, certainly quite as human, but different; and beside him stands a still more unexpected Prince Hal." Wilson sees Falstaff drawn as "an impossible companion for a king and governor, however amusing as jester to the heir apparent," a force of evil who is ultimately resisted by the prince. His theory was not received by the critics as the last word on the subject, but it was generally felt that he had cast new and valuable light on these plays.

Wilson was made a Companion of Honour in 1936. He is a Fellow of the British Academy, an honorary Fellow of Gonville and Caius College, and has many honorary degrees. He is a trustee of Shakespeare's birthplace and of the National Library of Scotland. His home is in Midlothian, Scotland.

PRINCIPAL WORKS: John Lyly, 1904; (comp.) Life in Shakespeare's England, 1911; Poetry and the Child, 1916; (with A. W. Pollard & others) Shakespeare's Hand in the Play of Sir Thomas More, 1923; (ed.) The Poetry of the Age of Wordsworth, 1927; (ed.) The Schools of England, 1928; Six Tragedies of Shakespeare, 1929; The Essential Shakespeare, 1932; The Manuscript of Shakespeare's Hamlet and the Problems of its Transmission, 1934; What Happens in Hamlet, 1935; Leslie Stephen and Matthew Arnold as Critics of Wordsworth, 1939; The Fortunes of Falstaff 1943; John Charles Moore Smith: Memoir, 1945; A. W. Pollard: Memoir, 1948; (with T. C. Worsley) Shakespeare's Histories at Stratford, 1951, 1952.

WILSON, MARGARET (January 16, 1882-). For autobiographical sketch and list of works and references, see TWENTIETH CENTURY AUTHORS, 1942.

WILSON, PHILIP WHITWELL 1875-), British journalist, biographer, and novelist, was born in Westmorland, England. His father, I. Whitwell Wilson, was a justice of the peace for Westmorland. His mother, Annie (Bagster) Wilson, was the daughter of Jonathan Bagster, Bible publisher. Young Wilson was educated at Kendal Grammar School and  at Clare College, Cambridge, where he was president of the Cambridge Union Society. He began his career in journalism before the turn of the century as editor of the *Granta* magazine from 1897 to 1899. For the next two years he was editor of the *Railway Herald*. In 1906 he was elected to Parliament as a Liberal, representing South St. Pancras, and he served until 1910. Returning to journalism, he became a member of the press gallery of the House of Commons and covered parliamentary sessions for twelve years.

Most of P. W. Wilson's long career has been devoted to reporting on American life for British readers and to writing and lecturing on British life for American audiences. He was American correspondent for the London *Daily News* for twenty-one years. Since the early 1920's he has lived in the United States and has been on the staff of the New York *Times*. His first wife, whom he married in 1899, was Alice Collins of Rhode Island; she died in 1939. They had three sons and two daughters. In 1944 Wilson married Mary Elizabeth Cross of New Jersey, and she died in 1951. He lives in Riverdale, New York City.

Wilson's first books were religious works —a product of his own deep religious faith supplemented by considerable research and what one reviewer described as "an intelligent imagination." His thesis was a simple one (as stated in *Is Christ Possible?*): "For individuals and nations, is life possible without Christ? Christ is not only possible but inevitable. There is none other who meets the need." He also wrote biographies—the best known being his biography of Evangeline Booth of the Salvation Army which, the New York *Times* observed, "has charm, vitality, sincerity, and its restrained emotion gives now and then a touch of eloquence to its rapidly flowing narrative." The book which perhaps most closely reflects Wilson's personality is *Newtopia*, "an assortment of comments upon every phase of our present troubled world." The book was published soon after the beginning of World War II, but its outlook, though realistic, remained cheerful. "The author has a sense of time, space, and men living that lifts him above the doubts that oppress most of us," Leon Whipple remarked in *Survey Graphic*. The late Simeon Strunsky said of the book : "It is a report on the state of the world grounded in understanding rather than in formula."

In his most recent books Wilson has moved to an entirely new field—mystery story writing—and he has been distinctly successful in it. His stories have been highly praised for their nicely balanced combination of mystery, detection, romance, and humor.

PRINCIPAL WORKS: The Christ We Forget, 1917; The Vision We Forget, 1921; A Layman's Confession of Faith, 1924; Unofficial Statesman: Robert C. Ogden, 1924; Explorer of Changing Horizons: William Edgar Geil, 1927; Simon, the Cross-Bearer, 1929; William Pitt the Younger,

1930; Is Christ Possible? 1932; General Evangeline Booth, 1935; The Romance of the Calendar, 1937; The Meaning of Moody, 1938; Newtopia: The World We Want, 1941; Bride's Castle, 1944; The Black Tarn, 1945; The Old Mill, 1946.

WILSON, ROMER (1891-January 11, 1930). For autobiographical sketch and list of works and references, see TWENTIETH CENTURY AUTHORS, 1942.

"WINCH, JOHN." See LONG, G. M. V. C.

WINSLOW, ANNE GOODWIN, American novelist and short story writer, was born in Memphis, Tenn., the daughter of William W. and Mary Frances (Blythe) Goodwin.  She was brought up in the country and did not attend school, but was educated at home under the supervision of her father, whom she has described as "a scholar in the old-fashioned sense, a lover of classic languages and literature and fond of applying them to the most casual and modern events. His theory was that a child needed only the will to read and the books that were congenial. In this way, I came off with a very unbalanced sort of culture, but the very kind I like to live with—my mind being furnished to suit my taste." She married an Army officer, E. Eveleth Winslow, with whom she traveled widely, both in the United States and abroad. They had two children, Randolph and Mary. Mrs. Winslow lived in Switzerland and in Italy for some time, and it was during her stay abroad that she began writing poetry. Her poems appeared in *Harper's*, the *Century*, *Scribner's*, and the *Atlantic Monthly*. They were collected in a volume in 1925, *The Long Gallery*, which the critics found to be the work of "a graceful but limited talent."

Mrs. Winslow's first published prose work, *The Dwelling Place*, a volume of memoirs, did not appear until 1943. It had been written at her family home in Raleigh, Tenn., in the long years of loneliness after her husband's death in 1928. Her intention in *The Dwelling Place*, Mrs. Winslow wrote, was "to give something of the feeling of the life that has gone on about me in this place . . . to throw a little light on one corner of the American scene." This Mrs. Winslow succeeded in doing, and the book was praised as "delicately humorous and wisely observant." These same qualities of mellowness, humor, and charm have marked her fiction, which began appearing in 1945. Her work is always redolent of the past — quiet, gentle, elusive. The plots are slight, the characters genteel and reserved, the style simple but exquisitely polished. Her work has frequently been compared to that of Henry James, but, as Diana Trilling has suggested, "Mrs. Winslow is less a conscious disciple of the master than a parallel cultural manifestation." In recapturing a past that seems now so remote and tenuous, she nevertheless manages to avoid the quaintness and preciosity of the "period piece." "Her magic has method in it," C. M. Brown observed in the *Saturday Review of Literature.* "Her indirection never misses the mark, and her touch, fragile to a degree, remains unfailing." Her work, wrote Orville Prescott in the *Yale Review,* embodies "three of the finest virtues of fiction . . . distillation, suggestion, and selectivity."

PRINCIPAL WORKS: The Long Gallery (poems) 1925; The Dwelling Place (memoirs) 1943; A Winter in Geneva, and Other Stories, 1945; Cloudy Trophies, 1946; A Quiet Neighborhood, 1947; It Was Like This, 1949; The Springs, 1949.

ABOUT: Warfel, H. R. American Novelists of Today; Current Biography 1948.

WINSLOW, OLA ELIZABETH. For biographical sketch and list of earlier works and references, see TWENTIETH CENTURY AUTHORS, 1942.

* * *

Ola Elizabeth Winslow was a member of the English department of Goucher College from 1914 to 1944. In the latter year she joined the English department at Wellesley College where she remained until her retirement in 1950. Since then she has taken part in seminars at Radcliffe College during the winter months, and spends the rest of the year at her home in Sheepscot, Maine. *Time* magazine described her, in 1950, as "a prodigious and painstaking worker [who] gently persuaded a whole generation of students to take after her." In 1952 she published her sound and scholarly history of the new England meetinghouse, *Meetinghouse Hill, 1630-1783.* A study of New England religious and social life, it was written, the *Yale Review* observed, "with sympathetic understanding, yet realistically and with a deal of quiet humor."

ADDITIONAL WORK: Meetinghouse Hill, 1630-1783, 1952.

ABOUT: Time July 3, 1950.

WINTER, JOHN KEITH (October 22, 1906-). For autobiographical sketch and list of works and references, see TWENTIETH CENTURY AUTHORS, 1952.

* * *

Little has been heard of Keith Winter in recent years. His play *The Rats of Norway,* which had been a success in England, had a brief and quite unsuccessful run in New York in April 1948; the reviewers generally dismissed it as "a turgid affair concerning repressed and misdirected sex impulses in an English school."

WINTERICH, JOHN TRACY (May 25, 1891-). For autobiographical sketch and list of earlier works and references, see TWENTIETH CENTURY AUTHORS, 1942.

* * *

During World War II, John T. Winterich served on active duty (rising in rank from major to colonel) with the Officers' Reserve Corps in Washington, D.C. He was managing editor of the *Saturday Review of Literature* from 1945 to 1946, and since that time has been a contributing editor. Winterich has continued his bibliographical activities as a member of the editorial board of the *New Colophon.* His lectures and his books on bibliographical subjects are lucid and witty and are read and enjoyed by non-specialists as well as by specialists in the field. From time to time Winterich contributes essays to the *New Yorker.* A series of these, reminiscences of his youth in Providence, R.I., were published in book form as *Another Day, Another Dollar.* Winterich lives in Ossining, N.Y.

ADDITIONAL WORKS: Another Day, Another Dollar, 1947; Three Lantern Slides, 1949; The Grolier Club, 1884-1950: An Informal History, 1950.

ABOUT: Winterich, J. T. Another Day, Another Dollar; New York Times Book Review August 31, 1947.

WINTERS, YVOR (October 17, 1900-). For autobiographical sketch and list of earlier works and references, see TWENTIETH CENTURY AUTHORS, 1942.

* * *

Yvor Winters has written little poetry in recent years, and his *Collected Poems* (1952) contains only eleven or twelve pieces of the last ten years. He has come to be recognized, however, as a critic of major importance and influence: this on the basis of four books— *Primitivism and Decadence, Maule's Curse, The Anatomy of Nonsense* (all three collected in 1947 under the title *In Defense of Reason*), and *Edward Arlington Robinson,* a critical study.

Stanley Edgar Hyman has said: "To the extent that the evaluation of works of art has not become an extinct critical function in our time, credit must be largely due to the redoubtable labors of Yvor Winters." That his evaluations are dogmatic and highly controversial (Hyman calls him "our foremost and perhaps sole representative of Johnsonian criticism") in no way minimizes their interest and significance. Randall Jarrell writes that his "clear, independent and serious talent has produced criticism that no cultivated person can afford to leave unread." His studies of Hawthorne, Melville, and Poe, in particular, are widely respected, although his stated preferences for Jones Very over Emerson, Edith Wharton over Henry James, Robert Bridges over T. S. Eliot—to cite a few examples — have caused equally widespread critical dismay and irritation and have involved Winters in some bitter critical polemics. The fairest estimate of his work is probably R. P. Blackmur's: "Mr. Winters' criticism is powerful, informed, consistent, and for the most part just—with only those errors caused by too great a rigidity in the structure of his intellect. . . . Why is it, then, that his criticism is not in general use? . . . The answer lies in the habits of our age. Mr. Winters' criticism is judicial; we have a horror of judgment because we do not know what it might destroy in our potential selves."

Winters became professor of English at Stanford in 1949. He was a Fellow of the Kenyon School of English from 1948 to 1950 and of the School of Letters of Indiana University. He lives in Los Altos, Calif.

ADDITIONAL WORKS: *Poetry*—Giant Weapon, 1943; Collected Poems, 1952. *Criticism*—Anatomy of Nonsense, 1943; Edward Arlington Robinson, 1946; In Defense of Reason, 1947.

ABOUT: Hyman, S. E. The Armed Vision; Kenyon Review Spring 1944; Poetry November 1943, February 1944; Quarterly Review of Literature Spring and Summer 1944, Winter 1945; Rocky Mountain Review Fall 1944.

WINWAR, FRANCES (May 3, 1900-).

For autobiographical sketch and list of earlier works and references, see TWENTIETH CENTURY AUTHORS, 1942.

* * *

Frances Winwar writes from Middletown Springs, Vt.: "I am writing this from a handsome old house built by the family of the inventor of the horsepower harvester, A. W. Gray. I bought it from royalties obtained from *The Life of the Heart,* a biography of George Sand and her times. It sold best of any of my books.

"In 1942 I was visiting professor at the University of Kansas City. I have also lectured at other universities and for women's clubs. But I much prefer to stay at home and write. My latest book is a novel about Napoleon, *The Eagle and the Rock.* I have also entered the juvenile field. Bennett Cerf asked me to write a book for his World Landmark series—*Napoleon and the Battle of Waterloo.* He has commissioned me to write still another volume in the series on an Elizabethan subject. I am working on it now [1953].

"Besides the *Decameron* I have translated a number of libretti: *Simon Boccanegra, Il Signor Bruschino, Don Carlo, Lucia di Lammermoor,* and *La Traviata* for the Metropolitan Opera Association. I review books for the New York *Times Book Review,* for the *Saturday Review,* and other papers. *The English Journal* has published an article of mine on biography, and also a study of S. V. and W. R. Benét. I have written very few short stories. Some of them have appeared in *Tomorrow.*

"Manuscripts of mine are at Rutgers University (the library) and in the library of Brooklyn College. The original manuscript of *The Immortal Lovers* was laid in the cornerstone of the Armstrong-Browning Library at Baylor University, in Waco, Texas. My books have been translated into some ten European languages."

* * *

Frances Winwar's long-lasting success as a writer of "popular" biography may well be explained by W. S. Lynch's comment on her *Life of the Heart:* "Miss Winwar has made her book as easy to read as a detective story and as clear as a Somerset Maugham novel." Whatever the limitations of her scholarship, she nevertheless manages, writes Howard Moss, to reproduce faithfully "the pertinent facts and attitudes of the period." It is difficult, of course, to draw a line between "romantic biography" and the romantic "historical novel." At times, some reviewers have objected, Miss Winwar's biographies read like novels and her novels read like biographies. But her novel *The Eagle and the Rock* seemed to strike a happy balance. The historian Geoffrey Bruun found that though it was listed as a romantic novel, "it reads like a biographical narrative retold with flair and insight." In his judgment, it is "a work of historical fiction of superior quality and compelling interest."

Miss Winwar and Professor Grebanier were divorced. In 1943 she married Richard Wilson Webb. They were divorced, and in 1949 she married F. D. Lazenby.

ADDITIONAL WORKS: *Novels*—The Sentimentalist, 1943; The Eagle and the Rock, 1953; The Last Love of Camille, 1954. *Biography and History*—The Life of the Heart, 1945; The Saint and the Devil: Joan of Arc and Gilles de Rais, 1948; Immortal Lovers: Elizabeth Barrett and Robert Browning, 1950; The Land of the Italian People, 1951. *Juvenile*—Napoleon and the Battle of Waterloo, 1953; Queen Elizabeth and the Spanish Armada, 1954.

ABOUT: Peragallo, O. Italian-American Authors.

WISE, THOMAS JAMES (October 7, 1859-May 13,1937). For biographical sketch and list of works and references, see TWENTIETH CENTURY AUTHORS, 1942.

* * *

ADDITIONAL WORK: Letters of Thomas J. Wise to John Henry Wrenn (ed. F. E. Ratchford) 1944.

ABOUT: Carter, J. & Pollard, G. The Firm of Charles Ottley, Landon and Company: Footnote to an Enquiry; Dictionary of National Biography 1931-1940; Partington, W. G. Thomas J. Wise in the Original Cloth, 1947; Ratchford, F. E. Review of Reviews, Certain Nineteenth Century Forgeries; Raymond, W. O. Infinite Moment; Wise, T. J. Letters of Thomas J. Wise to John Henry Wrenn; Atlantic Monthly February, May 1945; Hobbies August 1951; Modern Language Notes February 1948; New York Times Book Review July 3, 1949; Publishers' Weekly November 17, 1945.

WISTER, OWEN (July 14, 1860-July 21, 1938). For biographical sketch and list of works and references, see TWENTIETH CENTURY AUTHORS, 1942.

* * *

ABOUT: Saturday Review of Literature August 12, 1944.

*WODEHOUSE, PELHAM GRENVILLE (October 15, 1881-). For biographical sketch and list of earlier works and references, see TWENTIETH CENTURY AUTHORS, 1942.

* * *

Now in his middle seventies, P. G. Wodehouse remains the prototype of the irrepressible and ebullient young-man-about-town. His brief flirtation with Nazism brought him severe criticism. As late as 1944 there were demands in Parliament that he be tried for treason and, for a time, many lending libraries withdrew his books from circulation. But by 1945 he was generally forgiven, his broadcasting for the Nazis dismissed as naïve and

* wŏŏd'hous

foolish but not malicious either in intention or in effect. Wodehouse's defense was: "I never was interested in politics. I'm quite unable to work up any belligerent feeling."

Probably his most persuasive defender was the late George Orwell, who found him no more guilty than a whole generation of his fellow men who lived twenty years behind their times and refused to wake up to the dangers of twentieth century political life until war was upon them. Orwell considered his work charming but dated. The mental atmosphere of his books, he wrote, "shows little alteration since 1925." Wodehouse is still a popular favorite, however, and he has managed to sustain his humor through sixty novels (as of 1955), although the formula is close to threadbare from hard use. But at his best, John Lardner wrote in the *New Yorker* in 1948, he "has a comic richness that makes you laugh out loud no matter how often he repeats his plots and characters."

Wodehouse and his wife now live in "a white-shingled, maroon-shuttered" house on Long Island, after long residence in France. He has been described as "a large, broad fellow, with enormous hands and a gentle face."

ADDITIONAL WORKS: Joy in the Morning, 1946; Full Moon, 1947; Spring Fever, 1948; Uncle Dynamite, 1948; The Mating Season, 1949; Nothing Serious, 1950; Old Reliable, 1951; Angel Cake, 1952; Pigs Have Wings, 1952; (with G. Bolton) Bring on the Girls, 1953; Performing Flea: A Self-Portrait in Letters, 1953; The Return of Jeeves, 1954; Bertie Sees It Through, 1955.

ABOUT: Orwell, G. Dickens, Dali and Others; Swinnerton, F. The Georgian Literary Scene (1910-35); Wodehouse, P. G. Performing Flea; Wodehouse, P. G. & Bolton, G. Bring on the Girls; New York Times Book Review May 11, 1947; New Yorker May 22, 1948; Spectator December 22, 1944; Time August 26, 1946, May 5, 1947.

*WOLF, FRIEDRICH (1888-). For biographical sketch and list of works and references, see TWENTIETH CENTURY AUTHORS, 1942.

* * *

After twelve years of exile from his native land, Friedrich Wolf returned to Germany in 1945 and settled there. He lives near Berlin, and has apparently remained in favor with the Communist government of East Germany. From 1949 to 1951 he headed the diplomatic mission of the German Democratic Republic to Warsaw. His recent books—none of them translated into English—include plays (one of them made into a motion picture), novels, and essays. He has also written film scenarios. In 1952 an eight-volume edition of his collected works was published.

* vōlf

WOLFE, HUMBERT (January 5, 1885-January 5, 1940). For autobiographical sketch and list of works and references, see TWENTIETH CENTURY AUTHORS, 1942.

* * *

ABOUT: Dictionary of National Biography 1931-1940; Menorah Journal January 1943; Spectator October 18, 25, 1946.

WOLFE, LINNIE (MARSH) (1881-September 15, 1945), American biographer, was born in Michigan, educated in Idaho and at

Whitman College (Washington) and Radcliffe College. She taught in high schools in Washington and worked as a librarian in California. It was as a librarian in Los Angeles that Mrs. Wolfe first became interested in studying John Muir. Later, after she had gone to live in Contra Costa County, she met Muir's eldest daughter, Mrs. Wanda Muir Hanna, and some of his old friends. Mrs. Wolfe used to organize pilgrimages of school children to Muir's former home; she also gave a number of radio talks about him. In 1937 she was asked by the Muir heirs to prepare for publication some of his unpublished journals and notes, issued the following year as *John of the Mountains*.

At the invitation of Alfred A. Knopf, Mrs. Wolfe then undertook the writing of John Muir's biography. The research for this work took her across the continent, searching, sifting, and evaluating. The resulting volume, *Son of the Wilderness: the Life of John Muir,* was published in 1945. In that year Mrs. Wolfe died in a Berkeley, Calif., nursing home at the age of sixty-four; her death came after a long illness. In 1946 the book received the Pulitzer prize for biography.

Her only original work, this portrait of the Scotch-American naturalist, geologist, inventor, and explorer was based on all available journals and literary remains. Congratulating the author for bringing together the materials she did, the critics were nevertheless restrained in their praise of the literary result. "Very earnest, very well-documented, and considering the material the author had to work with, rather unforgivably dull," said the *New Republic.* The *Scientific Book Club Review* was more enthusiastic. "Here one finds a well-balanced account of John Muir's life," it wrote, "his far-reaching influence

upon the lives of countless persons, his contributions to science, especially in the field of glacial geology, and his leadership in the conservation movement. . . . Mrs. Wolfe is to be congratulated for her work; she has painted a portrait of a genius who 'comes alive' as her words are read." *Book Week,* in extenuation of the book's limitations, mentioned the difficulties, perhaps, of writing a biography "with the subject's daughters looking over one's shoulders."

PRINCIPAL WORKS: John of the Mountains (ed.) 1938; Son of the Wilderness, 1945.

WOLFE, THOMAS (October 3, 1900-September 15, 1938). For biographical sketch and list of works and references, see TWENTIETH CENTURY AUTHORS, 1942.

* * *

ADDITIONAL WORKS: Gentlemen of the Press (play) 1942; Letters to His Mother (ed. J. S. Terry) 1943; A Stone, A Leaf, A Door: Poems (selected & arranged in verse by J. S. Barnes) 1945; Mannerhouse (play) 1948; Western Journal: A Daily Log of the Great Parks Trip, 1951; Correspondence (with H. A. Watt) 1954.

ABOUT: Adams, A. B. Thomas Wolfe: Carolina Student; Bishop, J. P. Collected Essays; Frohock, W. M. The Novel of Violence in America; Geismar, M. Introduction to The Portable Thomas Wolfe (1946), Johnson, P. H. Hungry Gulliver (in England: Thomas Wolfe); Muller, H. J. Thomas Wolfe; Pollock, T. C. & Cargill, O. (eds.) Tom Wolfe at Washington Square; Preston, G. S. Thomas Wolfe (bibliography); Rubin, L. D. Thomas Wolfe, the Weather of His Youth; Walser, R. The Enigma of Thomas Wolfe; Wolfe, T. Letters to His Mother, Correspondence with H. A. Watt; American Mercury November 1946, April 1947; American Scholar Spring 1953; Atlantic Monthly November 1950; Commentary January 1952; New York Times Book Review August 4, 1946; PMLA September 1949; Revue de Littérature Comparée July 1950; Saturday Review of Literature January 5, 1946, February 7, November 27, 1948, August 11, October 6, 1951; South Atlantic Quarterly July 1950; Virginia Quarterly Review Summer 1946; Yale Review Summer 1946.

WOLFERT, IRA (November 1, 1908-), American journalist and novelist, was born in New York City, the son of Moses and Sophie (Seidl) Wolfert, and was educated in the New York public schools. He began his newspaper career as a copy boy in 1923. Three years later he enrolled at Columbia University's School of Journalism, and paid for his college education by working as a streetcar motorman and as a taxi driver. In 1931, with a college degree and a wife (he married Helen Herschdorfer, a poet, in 1928), Wolfert went to Europe. He found a position in Berlin representing the New York *Post,* but remained there only long enough to see "that the rise of Hitler was inevitable," he writes. The Wolferts returned to New York in 1932, and he became a correspondent  for the North American Newspaper Alliance.

In the course of his newspaper career, Wolfert wrote almost every kind of story—sports, drama criticism, interviews, feature articles. In 1942 he was sent to the Pacific to cover the fighting in the Solomons and Guadalcanal. His eyewitness accounts of battle were collected in his first book, *Battle for the Solomons,* which received the Pulitzer prize for reporting in 1943. Wolfert returned to the United States briefly to complete a second book on the war in the Pacific, *Torpedo 8,* and to recover from malaria. While in this country he completed his first novel, *Tucker's People.* He had earlier published several short stories, two of them selected for O'Brien collections. *Tucker's People,* a realistic novel of the "numbers" racket in a New York City slum, was praised as a mature and understanding book, vivid and melodramatic but also, as Newman Levy wrote in the *Saturday Review of Literature,* "a penetrating and sympathetic novel of frustration and insecurity."

Wolfert next went to the European front in 1944, covering the Normandy landings and the push through France and Belgium into Germany. When the war ended, he went to Hollywood to work as a screen writer. His *American Guerrilla in the Philippines,* a true story of an American naval officer who worked behind enemy lines in the Philippines, was made into a motion picture. In Hollywood, Wolfert writes, "I was being paid in a week what it had taken me twenty-three weeks to earn as a newspaperman, and the money was coming in week after week, gorgeous, stupefying, making me feel like a balloon afloat." Nevertheless, he decided to give it up, and for the next three years he lived on his savings and wrote a novel. The novel, *Act of Love,* the story of a Navy flier and the battle he fights within himself to solve his conflicts, was neither a popular nor a critical success. Reviewers found it earnest but turgid, effective in its descriptions of actual battle but otherwise bogged down in "tortured self-analysis." Nevertheless the book survived after many other wartime novels were forgotten. Wolfert himself continued to think about it and work on it, and in 1954 he published a completely rewritten novel under the same title. Norman Cousins devoted an editorial in the *Saturday Review* to the rewritten novel, congratulating both the author and his publisher—the latter for giving Wolfert "the chance to do what almost every serious novelist who ever lived has dreamed of being able to do: to give added growth and dimension to a book apparently beyond reach." In the years between the two versions of *Act of Love,* Wolfert wrote a long novel about big business, *Married Men.* The book was uneven in quality, but, John W. Aldridge wrote in the *Nation,* "even in its failure it testifies in a major way to the high quality of Mr. Wolfert's intent, the continued purity of his aspiration."

Wolfert, his wife, and their two children live in New York City.

PRINCIPAL WORKS: Battle for the Solomons, 1943; Torpedo 8, 1943; Tucker's People, 1943; American Guerilla in the Philippines, 1945; Act of Love, 1948; Married Men, 1953; Act of Love: Retold Version, 1954.

ABOUT: Current Biography 1943; New York Herald Tribune Book Review October 11, 1953; Saturday Review of Literature January 1, 1949, August 14, 1954.

WOLFF, MARITTA MARTIN (December 25, 1918-), American novelist, was born on Christmas Day at her grandparents' farm in Michigan, when her father was still in France with the A.E.F. She writes: "I was a very lonely child and seldom played with other children. I · attended a one-room rural school, after the best American tradition, and began to write as soon

Ghealey

as I grasped the essentials of penmanship—plays, poems, short stories. My greatest interest as far back as I can remember was in people—anything and everything happening to them."

After attending high school in Grass Lake, Mich., Miss Wolff entered the University of Michigan, at Ann Arbor, intending to study journalism. She soon switched her major to English. At the university she received two minor Hopwood awards for some short stories. In her senior year she wrote her first novel, *Whistle Stop,* a realistic and sordid picture of the seamy side of American small-town life. "I simply wrote down all that I picked up here and there about life and people in various small towns in Michigan." The novel won the major Avery Hopwood award in 1940, the year in which Miss Wolff also received her B.A. and a Phi Beta Kappa key, and was published in 1941. It was an extraordinary novel for a twenty-two-year-old college girl. Critics likened her to Farrell, Steinbeck, and Caldwell.

"Her book has a rich, raw vitality, a fundamental grimness," Edith Walton wrote in the New York *Times*. "In its force, in its vividness, in its lack of sentimentality, in its refusal to compromise with the reader's natural squeamishness, *Whistle Stop* is brilliantly different from the average." A year later *Night Shift,* a story of the struggle of a family in a Michigan industrial town, proved to be a solid work. Its limitations were those of *Whistle Stop*—a lack of discipline and form, a tendency toward the stereotyping of characters, a narrowness of vision. "There is no point in quarreling with Miss Wolff's defined world," N. L. Rothman commented in the *Saturday Review of Literature*. "It is certainly not a false picture, any more than it is a complete one." In her later novels Miss Wolff has continued to write with vigor and understanding of the emotional problems of small people living "on the edge of town" and on the edge of society. *Whistle Stop* remains her most successful novel. Both it and *Night Shift* were made into motion pictures.

In 1943 Maritta Wolff married a fellow Hopwood winner at the University of Michigan, Hubert Standish Skidmore. He died in 1946. In 1947 she married Leonard Stegman, and they live in California with their son Hugh in a house facing the ocean at Pacific Palisades. Miss Wolff is a strikingly pretty woman. Her hobby is jazz; she is an authority on all its phases, history, and exponents and has a large and constantly growing record collection.

PRINCIPAL WORKS: Whistle Stop, 1941; Night Shift, 1942; About Lyddy Thomas, 1947; Back of Town, 1952.
ABOUT: Current Biography 1941.

WOLFF, MARY EVALINE (Sister Mary Madeleva) (May 24, 1887-). For autobiographical sketch and list of earlier works and references, see TWENTIETH CENTURY AUTHORS, 1942.

* * *

Sister Mary Madeleva has been president of Saint Mary's College, in Notre Dame, Ind., since 1934. A gifted author and a stimulating teacher, she has received many honors—including, in 1953, an honorary Litt.D. from Notre Dame University. She is a member of the National Conference of Christians and Jews and is active in many Catholic and non-Catholic educational groups. From 1942 to 1947 she was president of the Catholic Poetry Society of America. Her *Collected Poems*, Katherine Brégy wrote in *Catholic World*, "set a new standard for the poetry of our religious men and women." Her recent essays on Chaucer were gracious and learned, "delicate in their penetration," Theodore Maynard commented, "and written in beautiful prose."

ADDITIONAL WORKS: Addressed to Youth, 1944; Collected Poems, 1947; The Lost Language, and Other Essays on Chaucer, 1951.
ABOUT: Hoehn, M. (ed.) Catholic Authors, I; Catholic Library World February 1950; Scholastic January 12, 1948.

WOLFSON, VICTOR (March 8, 1910-), American playwright and novelist, was born on New York's lower East Side to Adolph and Rebecca (Hoch-stein) Wolfson. His father, who was described as "a handsome and eloquent Russian ex-revolutionary," moved his family out of New York City to an upstate farm while Victor was a child. He was educated in New

Halsman

York City, however, at the Ethical Culture School, and helped meet expenses by working backstage at the Neighborhood Playhouse. Determined to make the theatre his career, Wolfson enrolled at the University of Wisconsin to study at its experimental theatre. He received his B.A. in 1931 and in the following year reached Broadway as assistant stage manager in the highly successful production of Elmer Rice's play *Counsellor-at-Law.* He followed this with other writing, directing, and producing jobs. From 1933 to 1936 he was on the executive board of the Theatre Union. He has also been secretary of the Authors League of America, secretary of the Dramatists Guild, and a lecturer in drama at New York University.

Wolfson's first produced play was an adaptation of Dostoevsky's *Crime and Punishment.* His second play and first commercial success was *Bitter Stream,* a dramatization of Silone's novel *Fontamara,* which ran for sixty-one performances on Broadway in 1936. His most successful play, *Excursion,* was produced in 1937. A pleasant fantasy about an old excursion boat whose captain suddenly decides to take her off on a Caribbean cruise, *Excursion* had a generally enthusiastic reception from the critics, and Burns Mantle selected it as one of the ten best plays of the season. None of Wolfson's later plays has equalled the success of *Excursion. Pastoral,* a comedy set in the Catskill country, had only a very brief run in 1939. *The Family,* a dramatization of Nina Fedorova's novel, was performed seven times after its première in 1943. *Pride's Crossing,* a grim drama of a vicious servant who tries to dominate a household, closed after eight performances in 1950. A better reception was accorded *American Gothic,* Wolfson's dramatization of his novel *The Lonely Steeple.* This was produced off-Broadway, at the Circle-in-the-Square Theatre, under the direction of José Quintero in 1953. Two other plays by Wolfson have been produced outside New York: *Love in the City,* in Cleveland in 1947, and *A Murder in the Family,* at the Berkshire Playhouse in 1952.

Wolfson also writes radio and television plays, short stories (in the *New Yorker, Harper's,* and other periodicals), and in 1945 he published his first novel, *The Lonely Steeple,* an intense psychological melodrama set in New England. Lewis Funke in the New York *Times* called it "an unpretentious debut and within its scope a commendable one." Certain theatrical characteristics that Wolfson brought over from his career as a playwright—mounting suspense, a powerful dramatic climax—added to the effectiveness of the book. In general, Grace Frank wrote in the *Saturday Review of Literature,* this first novel revealed Wolfson as "an accomplished and distinguished craftsman in the art of fiction." His second novel, *Eagle on the Plain,* was a change in pace—a "folk story" of a small and poor backwoods community in the Catskills (where Wolfson himself grew up). The only complaint of the critics—who, for the most part, liked the novel—was that it was "too consciously mellow." Diana Trilling described it as "a fable of freedom . . . at once truly touching and uncomfortably inflated." In 1950 Wolfson made a first and not altogether successful try at detective story writing with *Midsummer Madness,* published under the pseudonym "Langdon Dodge."

Wolfson married Alice L. Dodge in 1942. They have three sons and live in New York City. He writes about five hours a day, relaxes by walking and painting "for fun."

PRINCIPAL WORKS: *Plays*—Excursion, 1937; Pastoral, 1940. *Novels*—The Lonely Steeple, 1945; Eagle on the Plain, 1947; Midsummer Madness (by "Langdon Dodge") 1950.

ABOUT: Saturday Review of Literature July 26, 1947.

WOOD, CHARLES ERSKINE SCOTT
(February 20, 1852-January 22, 1944). For autobiographical sketch and list of earlier works and references, see TWENTIETH CENTURY AUTHORS, 1942.

* * *

Charles Erskine Scott Wood died a month before his ninety-second birthday, at his home near Los Gatos, Calif.

The late William Rose Benét called him "a man of the highest idealism . . . [whose] lifetime [was] devoted to courageous battling for the rights of the underprivileged . . . a poet certainly superior in keenness of intellect to Walt Whitman, if not by any means so voluminous in rhetorical output; and a social satirist of the first order." Five years after his death an edition of his *Collected Poems,* prepared by his wife, Sara Bard Field, and Genevieve Taggard, was published. The volume included some of his scattered published verses, and a play and many poems which he had left in manuscript.

ADDITIONAL WORK: Collected Poems, 1949.

ABOUT: National Cyclopedia of American Biography (1950); New York Times January 24, 1944; Saturday Review of Literature January 29, 1944, March 24, 1945.

WOOD, CLEMENT (September 1, 1888-
October 26, 1950). For autobiographical sketch and list of earlier works and references, see TWENTIETH CENTURY AUTHORS, 1942.

* * *

Clement Wood died at sixty-two, following a stroke, in a Schenectady, N.Y., hospital.

Up to his death he continued to publish miscellaneous writings—verse and prose. Versatility was his outstanding characteristic; his work included songs, novels, histories, poetry, children's books, books on games and amusements, biographies, anthologies, mystery stories, popular works on psychology and dreams and other subjects. The New York *Times* observed: "In his poetry and much of his historical writing, Mr. Wood was an exponent of romanticism and a bitter foe of social and racial injustice. His most signal contribution to American letters, in the opinion of many critics, was his lifelong study of the origins and inspirations of American verse, distilled into a number of highly acclaimed works of literary history."

ADDITIONAL WORKS: Death on the Pampas, 1944; Death in Ankara, 1944; The Corpse in the Guest Room, 1945; Double Jeopardy, 1947; The Eagle Returns (poems) 1947; Desire, and Other Stories, 1950; Strange Fires, 1951.

ABOUT: New York Times October 27, 1950.

WOODBERRY, GEORGE EDWARD
(May 2, 1855-January 2, 1930). For
biographical sketch and list of works and
references, see TWENTIETH CENTURY
AUTHORS, 1942.

* * *

ABOUT: Pritchard, J. P. Return to the Fountains; Columbia University: Addresses at the University Convocation in Honor of George Edward
Woodberry, May 12, 1948 (pamphlet); New England Quarterly December 1951; Saturday Review
of Literature October 28, 1944.

WOODHAM - SMITH, CECIL
BLANCHE (FITZGERALD) ("Janet
Gordon") (1896-   ), English historian, was

born in Tenby, Wales,
the daughter of an
army officer, Colonel
James Fitzgerald, and
his wife, Blanche
Elizabeth (Philipps)
Fitzgerald. Her father,
a descendant of the
old Irish family the
FitzGeralds of Lein-
ster, had served with
his regiment for many
years in India. His stories about military
history, campaigns, and Florence Nightingale's great work stirred her interest even in
childhood. It was many years before she
began work on her biography of Miss Nightingale, but in the intervening time she read
nineteenth century history eagerly, collected
books on the period, and Staffordshire portrait figures of many prominent military and
political figures of the nineteenth century,
and—without actually knowing to what purpose she would put her knowledge—prepared
herself as an authority in the field.

After completing her education at St.
Hilda's College, Oxford, where she read
English Literature, Cecil Fitzgerald worked
in an advertising agency until her marriage
to George Ivon Woodham-Smith, a London
solicitor, in 1928. Managing a Regency house
in London and a small country cottage and
raising two children kept her sufficiently occupied, but she also found time to write a
number of articles, short stories and plays.
None of these had any particular success,
but three of her books were published (under
the pseudonym "Janet Gordon"): *April Sky,
Tennis Star*, and *Just Off Bond Street*.

In 1942, with her children old enough for
school, Mrs. Woodham-Smith almost accidentally stumbled on the subject of her first
historical book. In a dinner table conversation with Michael Sadleir, the bibliophile and
publisher, she revealed such special knowledge

of Florence Nightingale that Sadleir suggested that she write a biography of her.
Mrs. Woodham-Smith promptly set about
mastering the formidable collection of materials—letters, documents, state records, family
papers—on Miss Nightingale. Her job was
enormously complicated by the war; papers
were scattered all over England, and transportation and normal channels of information
were blocked. She did most of her research
at the British Museum, sometimes climbing
over bomb debris to get there, and once
perilously close to a flying bomb that landed
only a few yards from the North Library of
the British Museum where she was working.
After more than six years of work, *Florence
Nightingale, 1820-1900*, was published. It
was hailed by the critics as the long-awaited
definitive Nightingale biography and awarded
the James Tait Black Memorial prize. Based
on contemporary records and family papers
never before made public, it was informative,
sympathetic yet scrupulously fair, and gracefully written. Its picture of hospital conditions, both in military and civilian life, in
mid-nineteenth century England, made it, as
Morton Dauwen Zabel pointed out in the
Nation, "a distinguished social document, not
only beautifully readable but a revelation of
much more than its specific subject."

Her research into the Crimean War for the
Nightingale biography led Mrs. Woodham-
Smith to one of the most dismaying but also
intriguing episodes of British military history,
the slaughter of the Light Cavalry Brigade in
the Battle of Balaclava in 1854. *The Reason
Why*, a non-fiction best seller in both England and America, was her examination of the
historical events involved in this egregious
blunder, but it was also, and more importantly, an absorbing study of the two men most
closely involved in the disaster—Lord Lucan,
who ordered the charge, and Lord Cardigan,
who led it—and of the hopelessly corrupt and
decadent military system in which it happened. "The story she relates," Geoffrey
Bruun observed in the New York *Herald
Tribune*, "will take its place as one of the
most electrifying and dramatic exposés ever
written on the history of the Victorian age."
One indication of the extraordinary success
of the book was the fact that shortly after
its publication the television program Author
Meets the Critics was obliged to cancel plans
for a discussion of it when no critic could
be found to take the "anti-" position and
attack the book. "The reason why" for the
success of Mrs. Woodham-Smith's books is
at least partly suggested in an essay she
wrote on the writing of history (New York
Times Book Review, July 1, 1954): "The

historian's task is to make the past live again, to find out the truth and make it real. He does not need the assistance of novelty to attract his readers, he needs historical imagination, the capacity so to live in the past that it becomes as actual as the present."

Mrs. Woodham-Smith lives in London, doing her writing in a workroom, formerly the nursery, crowded with her collections of nineteenth century books and china. Her children are now grown up. Her daughter (now married) has been presented at Court, and her son is in military service.

PRINCIPAL WORKS: Florence Nightingale, 1950; Lonely Crusader: The Life of Florence Nightingale (juvenile) 1951; The Reason Why, 1954. As "Janet Gordon"—April Sky, 1938; Tennis Star, 1940; Just Off Bond Street, 1940.

ABOUT: New York Herald Tribune Book Review May 9, 1954; Wilson Library Bulletin March 1955.

WOODWARD, WILLIAM E. (October 2, 1874-September 27, 1950). For autobiographical sketch and list of earlier works and references, see TWENTIETH CENTURY AUTHORS, 1942.

* * *

William E. Woodward died, a few days before his seventy-sixth birthday, in Augusta, Ga., while on a visit to his brother. He had been ill for two years. In his autobiography, published three years before his death, Woodward had outlined three novels he intended to write.

Occasionally criticized for literary or scholarly lapses, his books nevertheless attained wide popularity. As Harrison Smith pointed out, "He had the qualities that create success and the instinctive flair for saying the right thing at the right time." Leo Huberman observed that his work indicated "keen insight, a pungent style, and refreshing candor. . . . In the technique of writing for the common man Mr. Woodward had few equals."

ADDITIONAL WORKS: The Way Our People Lived, 1944; Tom Paine: America's Godfather, 1945; The Gift of Life (autobiography) 1947; Years of Madness, 1951.

ABOUT: Woodward, W. E. The Gift of Life; New York Times September 30, 1950; Saturday Review of Literature November 22, 1947.

WOOLF, LEONARD SIDNEY (November 25, 1880-). For autobiographical sketch and list of earlier works and references, see TWENTIETH CENTURY AUTHORS, 1942.

* * *

Leonard Woolf writes: "At the end of the war the Hogarth Press became the Hogarth Press Limited, the directors of which are myself and Harold Raymond, Ian Parsons, and Norah Smallwood, who are three directors of Chatto & Windus."

Woolf lives in Lewes, Sussex. His recent writings have all been in the field of international politics and foreign policy. Since the death of his wife, Virginia Woolf, he has edited three volumes of her miscellaneous essays and short stories and extracts from her diary.

ADDITIONAL WORKS: International Post-War Settlement, 1944; Foreign Policy, 1947; Principia Politica, 1953.

WOOLF, Mrs. VIRGINIA (STEPHEN) (1882-March 28, 1941). For biographical sketch and list of works and references, see TWENTIETH CENTURY AUTHORS, 1942.

* * *

ADDITIONAL WORKS: The Haunted House, and Other Short Stories, 1943; The Moment, and Other Essays, 1947; The Captain's Death Bed, and Other Essays, 1950; A Writer's Diary, 1954.

ABOUT: Bennett, J. F. Virginia Woolf: Her Art as a Novelist; Blackstone, B. Virginia Woolf; Bowen, E. Collected Impressions; Chambers, R. L. The Novels of Virginia Woolf; Daiches, D. Virginia Woolf; Johnstone, J. K. The Bloomsbury Group; Newton, D. Virginia Woolf; Swinnerton, F. The Georgian Literary Scene (1910-35); Woolf, V. A Writer's Diary; Commonweal November 2, 1945; Emporium February 1947; New Republic December 3, 1945; Partisan Review February 1949; South Atlantic Quarterly October 1947.

WOOLLCOTT, ALEXANDER (January 19, 1887-January 23, 1943). For biographical sketch and list of earlier works and references, see TWENTIETH CENTURY AUTHORS, 1942.

* * *

Alexander Woollcott died in New York's Roosevelt Hospital, at fifty-six, after suffering a heart attack in the middle of a radio broadcast of a round-table discussion of Hitlerism. He had had several heart attacks during the preceding three years.

In his role as radio's "Town Crier" he had achieved a vast and devoted audience to whom "the first raconteur and gossip of the day" imparted his ardent enthusiasms and his sometimes malicious resentments. Frankly exhibitionist, he even came in time, as the New York Times observed, to boast of his appearance, "of his 'great paunch'—he weighed 230 pounds; his owlish eyes, peering out from behind horn-rimmed frames, and the tiny mustache which clung to his upper lip."

Woollcott made many enemies and many friends. Beneath "the trappings of his deliberate eccentricities" he was a finer man than he sometimes seemed, in the opinion of his biographer Samuel Hopkins Adams. "In the small commerce of existence, Alexander Woollcott could be unconscionably petty, irascible, impatient, offensive, and inconsistent. Important issues . . . he met with balanced temper, a fine conviction, inflexible courage and principle. But this phase of his personality he doggedly guarded from view."

His literary deficiencies (Charles Angoff has called him a journeyman reporter, a mediocre dramatic critic, and as a literary judge "nearly always offensive to men and women of good taste") were due at least in part to his preference for feeling rather than cerebration. John Mason Brown pointed out that "though admirably equipped to think, Woollcott preferred to feel. Ideas did not interest him as much as people. He rejoiced in personalities and let principles alone." And if his feelings were not profound, they were intense and honest. John Chamberlain called him "an invaluable connoisseur of minor key perfection." Primarily he was, as Brown said, "one of the best yarn-spinners of his time. He was a raconteur who could achieve the miracle of seeming to talk in print."

ADDITIONAL WORKS: Long, Long Ago, 1943; Letters (ed. by B. Kaufman & J. Hennessey) 1944; (ed.) As You Were (anthology) 1943; The Portable Woollcott, 1946.

ABOUT: Adams, S. H. Alexander Woollcott, His Life and His World; Brown, J. M. Seeing Things; Lewis, L. It Takes All Kinds; Philistina (pseud.) Alec the Great; Wilson, E. Classics and Commercials; Woollcott, A. The Portable Woollcott (Introduction by J. M. Brown), Letters; American Mercury August 1945; New Republic June 4, 1945; New Yorker January 30, 1943; New York Times January 24, 1943; Saturday Review of Literature January 19, 1946; Theatre Arts January 1951; Time February 1, 1943, June 11, 1945.

WOOLRICH, CORNELL (William Irish," "George Hopley," pseuds.) (December 4, 1906-), American detective story writer, was born in New York City. His childhood, he says, was more eventful than his adult life. It was spent in Mexico during the revolutions of 1910-1920, and his hobby in those days was collecting used rifle cartridge shells which littered the grounds outside his house. "Nearly every second night at dinner," he writes, "the lights would fail, which meant either that Villa had captured the town from Carranza, or Carranza had captured it from Villa. My memory may be faulty, but the turnover was something terrific. From my own personal point of view, the revolution was pure velvet, as every time there was a new 'triumphal entry,' the

schools would close down for a day or two, until the sporadic shooting had quieted down. I wouldn't have cared if the revolution had never ended."

The revolution ended for young Woolrich, however, when he was sent back to New York to complete his education. He enrolled in Columbia University, taking a degree in 1925. In the same year he launched his writing career—somewhat accidentally—while convalescing from an illness. Having read all the books in the house, he started writing one, "on one of those stray impulses." Ultimately the book, Cover Charge, was published. Up to that time Woolrich had been vaguely interested in becoming a "hoofer," but the first check he received for his book convinced him that writing was to be his career.

Since then Woolrich has written on an average of one book a year. In addition he has contributed to a number of magazines—during the 1920's to College Humor, McClure's, Smart Set, and since then mainly to detective story magazines. He is considered one of the ablest craftsmen in the mystery story field. He has written every variety of crime story—from pure detective fiction to psychological horror stories. John Sutherland, writing in the New York Times, summed up critical opinion on Woolrich when he pointed out that he "rigs his plots with a few inconsistencies, but uses them . . . to ricochet suspense to an almost unbearable pitch."

Woolrich writes in longhand, usually in the afternoons and evenings, then revises and transfers the material to typescript. He does not keep a rigid writing schedule, and can work only when a story is clearly set in his mind. Since the stories often come two or three at a time, with long intervals between them, he says, "the rhythm is very irregular." Some years ago he described his work as "a form of subconscious self-expression . . . and as long as it supports me, I don't bother trying to find out what causes it."

PRINCIPAL WORKS: Cover Charge, 1926; Children of the Ritz, 1927; Times Square, 1929; Young Man's Heart, 1930; The Time of Her Life, 1931; Manhattan Love Song, 1932; The Bride Wore Black, 1940; Black Curtain, 1941; Black Alibi, 1942; Black Angel, 1943; The Black Path of Fear, 1944; Rendezvous in Black, 1948. As "William Irish"—Phantom Lady, 1942; I Wouldn't Be in Your Shoes, 1943; After Dinner Story, 1944; Deadline at Dawn, 1944; Dancing Detective, 1946; Waltz into Darkness, 1947; I Married a Dead Man, 1948; Dead Man Blues, 1948; Blue Ribbon, 1949; Somebody on the Phone (in England: The Night I Died) 1950; Strangler's Serenade, 1951; Eyes that Watch You, 1952. As "George Hopley" — The Night Has a Thousand Eyes, 1945; Fright, 1950.

*WOUK, HERMAN (May 27, 1915-), American novelist and playwright, writes: "At thirty-seven I have published three novels and one play. I entered the literary field at thirty. My background was a New York City boyhood, four years at Columbia College, half a dozen years as a radio writer (I wrote mainly for the comedian Fred Allen), and four years as a naval officer of the line in World War II. I briefly served the U.S. government in 1941 as a dollar-a-year man, producing radio broadcasts to sell war bonds. My service in the Navy included three years at sea in the Pacific. The first ship in which I served, the U.S.S. Zane, an old destroyer-minesweeper, received the unit commendation for its service in the Solomons campaign. My last post was second in command (executive officer) of the U.S.S. Southard, a ship of the same type.

Editta Sherman

"*Aurora Dawn*, my first novel, a short satiric extravaganza about big business in New York, was distributed by a popular book club, thereby enabling and encouraging me to continue writing novels. *The City Boy*, a humorous story of boyhood, was made into a movie, and was recently re-issued in an illustrated edition. *The Caine Mutiny*, an account of U.S. Navy life in World War II, was the first of my stories to achieve any general acceptance. It won the Pulitzer prize for fiction, and continues popular in America and abroad. *The Traitor* (1949), a play of atomic spying, drew criticism from some liberals when it first appeared; this was before the convictions of Alger Hiss and Klaus Fuchs, when the idea that Communists are capable of treason was more controversial than it is now. I have also written moving pictures.

"I try for regular work habits, sitting down pen in hand each day to write a few long yellow pages of the story. The first draft, cut down more or less, has been what I have published previously, and I believe this will be true of the next book, which is now (December 1952) partly done. My wife, Betty Sarah, types my manuscripts and is secretary and bookkeeper of the enterprise. I have read to her every word that I have written."

* * *

* wōk

The Caine Mutiny, probably the most successful of recent novels dealing with World War II, reached the top of the best-seller lists about three months after its publication and remained there for an unusually long period. In 1953 it was estimated that, in the various editions, some 1,750,000 copies were in print. In 1954 two dramatic versions of the novel were appearing simultaneously in New York—a powerful stage adaptation (made by Wouk himself) of one part of the book, *The Caine Mutiny Court Martial*, and a motion picture version of the entire novel.

Wouk lives in New York City with his wife, Betty Sarah Brown, whom he married in 1945, and their young son. His favorite recreation is reading. He admits to a special fondness for Anthony Trollope, from whose autobiography he learned valuable lessons in literary craftsmanship, especially rigorous self-discipline. He is also interested in Hebrew studies, is a member of the board of directors of the Orthodox Jewish Council of Congregations, and has taught courses in literature at Yeshiva University in New York.

PRINCIPAL WORKS: Aurora Dawn, 1947; The City Boy, 1948; The Traitor (play) 1949; The Caine Mutiny, 1951; The Caine Mutiny Court-Martial (play) 1954; Marjorie Morningstar, 1955.

ABOUT: Commentary June 1952; Current Biography 1952; New York Times Book Review September 16, 1951; Saturday Review of Literature February 14, 1948; Vogue February 1953.

WREN, PERCIVAL CHRISTOPHER (1885-November 23, 1941). For biographical sketch and list of works and references, see TWENTIETH CENTURY AUTHORS, 1942.

WRIGHT, FRANK LLOYD (June 8, 1869-), American architect and author, was born in Richland Center, Wis., the son of William Russell Cary Wright and Anna Lloyd (Jones) Wright. His father was a musician and preacher from New England, his mother a school teacher. In 1872, when Wright was three, they moved to Massachusetts, but returned to Wisconsin when Wright was eleven. He attended high school in Madison and went on to the University of Wisconsin, enrolling for courses in civil engineering when he was fifteen.

1109

From the beginning Anna Wright wanted her son to become an architect, but at that time the university offered no courses in architecture. At the age of eighteen, in 1887, Wright left college without graduating and went to Chicago in the role of draftsman. There he completed plans for his earliest executed work, a house for his aunts at Spring Green, Wis., built in 1888. In the latter year Wright entered the office of the most progressive architectural firm in the country, Dankmar Adler and Louis Sullivan. Sullivan is the only architect to whom Wright acknowledges a debt. In 1893, when he was twenty-four, the young architect began an independent practice in Chicago. His innovations became marked in the "Prairie houses," emphasizing strong horizontals and a flow of room with room, which he began to construct in 1900.

In 1910 Wright visited Europe for the first time; in that year a large portfolio of his work was published in Berlin and influenced the younger generation of modern architects in Europe. One of Wright's famous undertakings was the Imperial Hotel in Tokyo, constructed between 1915 and 1922. To withstand earthquakes, he allowed a foundation which floated on a cushion of soft mud. This and other unique innovations permitted the hotel to survive an otherwise disastrous earthquake in 1923. Wright developed, in the 1920's, a new method of construction, using precast concrete blocks threaded through with metal reinforcement. In the latter 1920's his fortunes ebbed, and some critics regarded him as finished.

In 1932 the Taliesin fellowships were organized by Wright as a studio-workshop arrangement for apprentices, who would pay to work with him and assist in his commissions. (Currently, one "Taliesin" is at Spring Green, Wis., for use in summer, and a "Taliesin West" is located at Paradise Valley, Phoenix, Ariz., for winter use. The Taliesin Foundation also maintains a center in San Francisco.) It was in this period of the 1930's that his arguments against the so-called "international style" of the European modernists began; he opposed his own "organic architecture" to what he saw as the mechanistic and anti-democratic "negativities" of the European influence. Much of his time in this decade was devoted to writing and lecturing, and to the publication of several of his most important books. Reviewing his 1931 volume, *Modern Architecture*, *Books* said, "Wright speaks chiefly as a preacher and a poet, in turn brutal and tender, violent and urbane, flippant and intensely serious." "One of the most trenchant and most beauti-

ful books of our time," wrote Sheldon Cheney in the *Saturday Review of Literature*. "Artist and layman alike should read it, for entertainment and for stimulus to new faith, and perhaps just a little for punishment." His *Autobiography* was first published in 1932 and revised and expanded in 1943. Of this later version Clifton Fadiman remarked in the *New Yorker*: "It is extraordinary that a man whose work is so harmonious, so just, so measured, so serene, and so deeply original should, when he takes up his pen, be so unrestrained, so lopsided, so sentimental, and so ridden with clichés. Yet somehow not even his most humorless pomposity can quite disguise the central magnificence of his professional thought on the subject he knows best."

Wright's *Future of Architecture,* published in his eighty-fifth year, contains both new material and some of his major writing of the past. It also sums up his views on art, education, and history. "It is full of quirks and prejudices," commented the San Francisco *Chronicle*. "Now and again, too, he grows mystical; there has always been this streak in him. But few can fail to be stimulated by the ideas here presented."

The architect and his third wife, Olga Lazovich (who came originally from Montenegro) live in Taliesin (Wisconsin) and Taliesin West (Arizona), along with some forty of his apprentices. The Wrights have one daughter, born in 1928. In November 1954, after the Wisconsin Supreme Court ruled that his home in that state was not an educational institution but was subject to local taxation, Wright announced that he was moving out of the state; but a testimonial dinner in February 1955 at Madison, where he received a check for $10,000 to help him pay the back taxes on his studio-home, persuaded him to change his mind. Some 400 persons from Wisconsin and fifteen other states were present at the dinner.

Wright's first wife was Catherine Lee Clark Tobin, whom he married in 1890; they had four sons and two daughters. His second wife was Miriam Noel, a sculptor; they were married in 1922 and divorced in 1927. Wright is five feet eight inches tall, and has white hair, light gray eyes, and a mobile countenance. He collects Oriental art, enjoys music, and plays the piano.

PRINCIPAL WORKS: Japanese Prints: An Interpretation, 1912; Modern Architecture, 1931; Two Lectures on Architecture, 1931; Autobiography, 1932; Disappearing City, 1932; Architecture and Modern Life (with Baker Brownell) 1937; Organic Architecture, the Architecture of Democracy, 1939; Frank Lloyd Wright on Architecture; Selected Writings 1894-1940 (edited by F. Gutheim) 1941;

Autobiography (expanded and brought up to date) 1943; When Democracy Builds (expanded edition of Disappearing City) 1945; Genius and the Mobocracy, 1949; Future of Architecture, 1953; The Natural House, 1954.

ABOUT: Gutheim, F. (ed.) Frank Lloyd Wright on Architecture; Hitchcock, H. (ed.) In the Nature of Materials; Hitchcock, H. R. & Johnson, P. Modern Architects; Karsh, Y. Faces of Destiny; Kaufmann, E. Jr. Taliesin Drawings; Lewis, L. It Takes All Kinds; Morris, R. B. (ed.) Encyclopedia of American History; Sargeant, W. Geniuses, Goddesses and People; Stone, I. & Kennedy, R. (eds.) We Speak for Ourselves; Wijdeveld, H. T. (ed.) Life-Work of the American Architect Frank Lloyd Wright; Wright, F. L. Autobiography; Wright, J. My Father Who Is on Earth; Zevi, B. Frank Lloyd Wright, Towards an Organic Architecture; American Artist May 1951; Américas April 1954; Architectural Forum January 1946; Architectural Review January 1947, August 1949, June 1953; Art Quarterly Summer 1953; College Art Journal Autumn 1946; Current Biography 1941, 1952; Fortune August 1946; Harper's December 1953; House and Garden August 1948; House Beautiful December 1946, August 1948; Life August 12, 1946; New York Times Book Review July 24, 1949, November 1, 1953; New York Times Magazine June 5, 1949, December 27, 1953; New Yorker July 12, 1952, September 26, 1953, October 31, 1953; Saturday Review of Literature November 14, 1953; Theatre Arts July 1949; Time April 1, 1946, July 1, 1946, February 9, 1948.

WRIGHT, HAROLD BELL (May 4, 1872-May 24, 1944). For autobiographical sketch and list of earlier works and references, see TWENTIETH CENTURY AUTHORS, 1942.

*　*　*

Harold Bell Wright died in a La Jolla, Calif., hospital, of bronchial pneumonia, at seventy-two. A month before his death he sold his Escondido ranch home and moved to San Diego.

Without literary aptitude or pretensions, Wright wrote nineteen books whose aggregate sale was over ten million copies. The "artificial flavor" of his novels came primarily from his interest in themes rather than in reality—Grant Overton called him, rather than a novelist, "a moralist, a fabulist, a preacher of sermons, a Sayer, and an Utterer."

His enormous success was partly due to powerful advertising campaigns by his publisher, but also to his deep sincerity, the timeliness of his choice of social problems as subjects, and his understanding of his wide middle-class audience. Frank Luther Mott observed: "Probably America is better off for having read a lot of Harold Bell Wright. His stuff is wholesome, occasionally somewhat stimulating in ideas, and very often picturesque; and millions found it entertaining."

ADDITIONAL WORK: The Man Who Went Away, 1942.

ABOUT: Mott, F. L. Golden Multitudes; Harper's October 1947; New York Times May 25, 1944.

WRIGHT, RICHARD (September 4, 1908-　). For biographical sketch and list of earlier works and references, see TWENTIETH CENTURY AUTHORS, 1942.

*　*　*

Richard Wright gave a vivid account of his years in the Communist Party in an essay in The God that Failed. In a letter to his publisher in 1952 he tersely summed up; "In 1944, when Communism in America was at the apogee of its popularity, I felt personally impelled to terminate my Communist membership which I had held for ten active years. Under my own steam, with no warnings from Hollywood or the Un-American Activities Committee, I broke publicly with Communism and have remained politically inactive since."

Wright, his wife, and their young daughter moved to Paris in 1946 and now make their home there. The intellectual dilemmas of the ex-Marxist continued to plague him. He writes: "I found it urgently necessary to search for a new attitude to replace the set of Marxist assumptions which had in the past more or less guided the direction of my writings." A product of this search is his novel The Outsider, "the first literary effort of mine projected out of a heart preoccupied with no ideological burden save that of rendering an account of reality as it strikes my sensibilities and imagination." The Outsider is a violent and intense novel about a Negro who becomes involved with Communism, commits murder, and is in turn murdered by a member of the party. Reviewers found it a troubled book, uneven, melodramatic but powerful. "The book is bad," the Nation pointed out, "but only as a work of genuine talent can be bad, and nevertheless full of interest." Wright himself acknowledged that in The Outsider he was trying to do what he called "that dreadfully unpopular thing: to depict my sense of our contemporary living as I see it and feel it."

In 1953 Wright visited the African Gold Coast for several months. His report on his journey was published in Black Power, a highly emotional and subjective work which emerges, Michael Clark wrote in the New York Times, "more as a tract than as a considered study." It was, nevertheless, as Walter White commented, an "important, informative and infuriating first-hand account," and its thesis—that "the West is being judged by the events that transpire in Africa"—was one worthy of serious attention.

Wright's most popular book of recent years was his autobiographical *Black Boy,* which covered his childhood and young manhood. The book was a frank and moving human record, as well as a valuable piece of social observation. "It comes out of life, it is a part of life, and it lets a light into places that have not seen this kind of light before," Hamilton Basso said of it in the *New Yorker.* In 1951 Wright played the role of Bigger Thomas in a motion picture version of his *Native Son,* made in Argentina.

ADDITIONAL WORKS: Black Boy, 1945; The Outsider, 1953; Black Power, 1954.

ABOUT: Gloster, H. M. Negro Voices in American Fiction; Slochower, H. No Voice Is Wholly Lost; Wright, R. Black Boy, *essay in* The God That Failed (ed. R. Crossman); Antioch Review June 1945; Life June 4, 1945; Phylon, vol. X (1949).

WRIGHT, RICHARDSON LITTLE (June 18, 1886-   ). For biographical sketch and list of earlier works and references, see TWENTIETH CENTURY AUTHORS, 1942.

* * *

Richardson Little Wright was editor of *House and Garden* magazine for forty-six years, until his retirement in 1950. His essays on a variety of domestic matters—cooking, gardening, home decoration—are informative and entertaining. He has also written a group of devotional exercises growing out of his deep religious faith (he is an Episcopalian)—*A Book of Days for Christians.* Wright lives in West Chatham, Mass. In 1941 he married Gertrude Albion MacCormick.

ADDITIONAL WORKS: The Bed Book of Eating and Drinking, 1943; The Gardener's Tribute, 1949; A Book of Days for Christians, 1951.

ABOUT: New York Herald Tribune Book Review December 4, 1949.

WRIGHT, WILLARD HUNTINGTON ("S. S. Van Dine") (1888-April 11, 1939). For biographical sketch and list of works and references, see TWENTIETH CENTURY AUTHORS, 1942.

* * *

ABOUT: Mellquist, J. The Emergence of an American Art.

WURDEMANN, AUDREY (January 1, 1911-   ). For biographical sketch and list of earlier works and references, see TWENTIETH CENTURY AUTHORS, 1942.

* * *

Audrey Wurdemann has published no volumes of verse in recent years, but she has collaborated with her husband, Joseph Auslander, on two heart-warming and nostalgic novels—one on the Americanization of a Czech family in Wisconsin in the 1890's (*My Uncle Jan*) and the other on a Greek family adjusting to life in Florida (*The Islanders*). She also worked with her husband during World War II on a series of poems celebrating the heroism of the "little people" of the occupied countries of Europe, published in 1943 as *The Unconquerables.*

ADDITIONAL WORKS: *With J. Auslander*—My Uncle Jan, 1948; The Islanders, 1951.

ABOUT: Saturday Evening Post September 25, 1943.

WYLIE, Mrs. ELINOR (HOYT) (September 7, 1885-December 16, 1928). For biographical sketch and list of works and references, see TWENTIETH CENTURY AUTHORS, 1942.

* * *

ADDITIONAL WORKS: Last Poems, 1943.

ABOUT: Colum, M. Life and the Dream; Gregory, H. & Zaturenska, M. History of American Poetry, 1900-1940; Olivier, E. *in* Last Poems of Elinor Wylie.

WYLIE, IDA ALEXA ROSS (1885-   ). For autobiographical sketch and list of earlier works and references, see TWENTIETH CENTURY AUTHORS, 1942.

* * *

I. A. R. Wylie lives on a farm in Belle Mead, N.J. She is a regular contributor to the *Saturday Evening Post, Good Housekeeping, Collier's, Ladies' Home Journal,* and other magazines, and has written a film, *Phone Call from a Stranger.* Her novels are generally well received. Always present in her writing, Andrea Parke finds, are "humor and drama, taste and a quiet emotion."

In the summer of 1942 Miss Wylie made a trip to England in wartime which she described vividly and sympathetically in her book *Flight to England.*

ADDITIONAL WORKS: *Fiction*—Ho, the Fair Wind, 1945; Storm in April (short stories) 1946; Where No Birds Sing, 1947; Candles for Therese, 1951. *Non-Fiction*—Flight to England, 1943.

ABOUT: Wylie, I. A. R. Flight to England; American Magazine August 1948.

WYLIE, PHILIP (May 12, 1902-   ). For autobiographical sketch and list of earlier works and references, see TWENTIETH CENTURY AUTHORS, 1942.

* * *

Philip Wylie describes his life and his personality as "stereotypes." He is a successful popular writer, lives comfortably in Florida, golfs, plays bridge, takes part in civic activities, and leads in general "a very American existence." From time to time, however, he churns up this smooth routine. In recent years he has won a reputation for controversial, hard-hitting, "angry" books. A born skeptic and pessimist, he sees himself with a definite mission as a writer: "By showing the gulf between our pretensions and what we really do, and by predicting where our vanities and follies will lead us, I have tried to throw light behind the curtain we Americans draw across our unconscious minds." In 1954 he told an interviewer, "Myself, I'm no Savonarola. I spend most of my life dancing and fishing. But, damn it, once in a while I like to strike a blow for freedom."

Probably the most controversial of Wylie's books was *A Generation of Vipers*, a survey of American habits and beliefs and a grim warning of the need for logical and realistic thinking. Out of this book came a new term —"momism"—which has won Wylie a kind of ironic immortality as a woman hater. "Momism" was Wylie's tag for the sentimentalizing of the idea of "mother" in American society. Actually, Wylie insists, the brief discussion of "momism" in the book was meant as a joke. Readers took it seriously however, and Wylie found himself the center of a storm of protest and controversy. He was even more severely criticized for a bitter attack on organized religion in his *Essay on Morals*. "He indulges in vast generalizations, some of them platitudes, some obscurely profound, some patently false, most of them intellectually irresponsible," Dr. Frederic Wertham said of the book in the *New Republic*. In spite of such harsh criticism, Wylie is admired in many quarters for his vigorous style, reflecting sincere, if sometimes wrong-headed, conviction.

It is quite another Philip Wylie who writes the pleasant and easy-going Crunch and Des stories and essays on fishing, although even here reviewers detect flashes of the Wylie fighting spirit. He is an intense and serious-looking man—though not without a sense of humor. Lewis Nichols described him in 1954 as "a thinnish man with an air of unpressed dapperness, and an accent suggesting Florida superimposed upon eastern Massachusetts. He is serious about his beliefs, not serious about himself."

ADDITIONAL WORKS: A Generation of Vipers, 1942; The Corpses at Indian Stones, 1943; Night unto Night, 1944; Fish and Tin Fish: Crunch and Des Strike Back, 1944; An Essay on Morals, 1947; Crunch and Des: Stories of Florida Fishing, 1948; Opus 21, 1949; The Disappearance 1951; Three to Be Read, 1952; Denizens of the Deep, 1953; Tomorrow, 1953.

ABOUT: Warfel, H. R. American Novelists of Today; New York Herald Tribune Book Review October 7, 1951; New York Times Book Review July 3, 1949; February 21, 1954; Saturday Review of Literature March 8, 1947.

WYNDHAM, GEORGE (August 29, 1863-June 8, 1913). For biographical sketch and list of works and references, see TWENTIETH CENTURY AUTHORS, 1942.

* * *

ABOUT: Biggs-Davison, J. George Wyndham; Gregory, I. Lady Gregory's Journals, 1916-1930.

*YARMOLINSKY, AVRAHM (January 1 [O.S.], 1890-   ). For autobiographical sketch and list of earlier works and references, see TWENTIETH CENTURY AUTHORS, 1942.

* * *

Avrahm Yarmolinsky writes: "In 1940 Avrahm Yarmolinsky became an alumnus member of Phi Beta Kappa. He lives in New York with his wife, his sons pursuing their careers elsewhere."

As translator, editor, and anthologist, Yarmolinsky has brought a vast amount of otherwise little-known Russian literature to the attention of the American reading public. His *Portable Chekhov*, for which he supplied most of the translations, was praised in the *New Yorker* as a "first-rate collection assembled by a distinguished scholar and translator." He recently published a valuable *Treasury of Russian Verse*, pronounced "excellently edited" by Ernest J. Simmons, which contained a number of poems translated into English by his wife, Babette Deutsch.

ADDITIONAL WORKS: As Editor—Russian Americana, 1943; A Treasury of Great Russian Short Stories, 1944; The Portable Chekhov, 1947; The Heritage of European Literature (with E. H. Weatherly and others), 1948-49; A Treasury of Russian Verse, 1949.

* "Accent second *a* in first name and *i* in last name."

"YATES, DORNFORD." See MERCER, C. W.

YATES, ELIZABETH (December 6, 1905-   ), American novelist and writer of children's books, writes: "It was in Buffalo, N.Y., that I was born and there I went to school—the Franklin School from kindergarten through the twelfth grade. The memorable days of my childhood were the long summers spent on my father's farm in the rich rolling country south of Buffalo. Next to the youngest of seven children, there were always playmates for me as

well as horses and dogs; and there were always tasks. The house was filled with books, and being alone or being read to by my mother was part of our life. I used to go off on my horse for a day at a time, rambling through the countryside, a sandwich in my pocket and the knowledge that any stream would give us both drink; I was never lonely, for there was the horse to talk with and in my head I was writing stories. A year at boarding school followed graduation from the Franklin, a summer abroad, and then three years of work in New York City. During those years I had various jobs, gradually arriving at more and more writing. In the summers I taught riding at girls' camps.

"At twenty-three I married William Mc-Greal, an American whose business was in London. Ten years in England followed with frequent travel in the British Isles and on the Continent. In 1939 we returned to the United States to live in Peterborough, N.H. There we found an old farmhouse which adapted itself happily to our needs, and a farm of fields and woodland which we are endeavoring to bring back to usefulness and production. There are mountains near to climb, forest lakes to swim in, and lovely white villages strong with New England tradition. The garden is my joy; the vegetables, especially, which grow in such abundance that there is always plenty to share with friends, and neighbors. I love good talk, I love the wide warm circle of friends which keeps expanding with the years, but I still love to be alone and it is the hours of working in the garden or the woods that help me to think out stories.

"Morning hours of work are relatively uninterrupted; the rest of the day goes in care of home and family and various oddments of activity. Reading is still my job—books about nature, biography, philosophy; while my mentors of earlier days—Traherne and Blake, Hardy, George Eliot and the Bible—still have much to say to me. There are occasional trips to Boston and New York, to the seashore and the high mountains, to Durham every summer to teach at the Writers' Conference of the University of New Hampshire, or to some city or town to give a talk on books or writing; but it is a quiet life we lead and in it there is time to think—time to enjoy the

things that have always meant much: friends, books and the countryside."

* * *

In 1943 and again in 1950 Elizabeth Yates won New York *Herald Tribune* Spring Festival awards for *Patterns on the Wall* and *Amos Fortune: Free Man*. The latter book also received the 1951 Newbery award of the American Library Association as "the most distinguished contribution to American literature for children" of the year. In both her adult and her juvenile writings, Miss Yates has demonstrated what critics describe as "a gentle, serene faith which often transcends literary limitations," and a "deep belief in man's ultimate humanity to man." Her simple, idealistic writings have sometimes been compared with those of the English novelist Elizabeth Goudge.

PRINCIPAL WORKS: *Novels*—Wind of Spring, 1945; Nearby, 1947; Beloved Bondage, 1948; Guardian Heart, 1950; Brave Interval, 1952; Hue and Cry, 1953. *Juveniles*—Under the Little Fir, 1942; Patterns on the Wall, 1943; Mountain Born, 1943; Once in the Year, 1947; Amos Fortune: Free Man, 1950; Children of the Bible, 1950; A Place for Peter, 1952; (comp.) Your Prayers and Mine, 1954; Rainbow Round the World, 1954.

ABOUT: Kunitz, S. J. & Haycraft, H. (eds.) Junior Book of Authors (rev. ed.); Current Biography 1948; Horn Book July 1951; Library Journal April 1, 1951; National Cyclopedia of American Biography (1952); New York Herald Tribune Book Review October 8, 1950; Publishers' Weekly March 10, 1951.

*YBARRA, THOMAS RUSSELL (October 8, 1880-), American journalist and biographer, was born in Boston, Mass. His father was General Alejandro Ybarra of Caracas, Venezuela, several times governor of six of the states comprising the Republic of Venezuela, and Minister of War and Foreign Affairs; his mother was Ellen Taylor Russell, daughter of Judge Thomas Russell of Boston. For several years Ybarra's father was in business in the United States and the boy was sent to grammar schools in Boston and then to Roxbury and Cambridge Latin schools. After three years at Harvard, he graduated in 1905. He also studied in Venezuela and in Europe.

Arni

Joining the staff of the New York *Times* in 1905, he began as a reporter and became Sunday editor. In 1908 he published a book of ballads called *Davy Jones's Yarns and*

* ĭ bär'à

1114

Other Salted Songs. In 1924 Ybarra became a correspondent in Berlin, in London, and then throughout Europe. He later traveled in North Africa, Egypt, Asiatic Turkey, and South America, and was a correspondent for a time for *Collier's.* Between 1929 and 1932 he published three biographies, on Bolívar, Cervantes, and Hindenburg. The log of his trips became the basis for *America Faces South.* In 1941 his autobiography, *Young Man of Caracas,* covering the first twenty years of his life, appeared, with a foreword by Elmer Davis. It received warm praise from reviewers. "Mr. Ybarra's reminiscences have a light charm of their own," wrote Clifton Fadiman in the *New Yorker,* "and offer an amusing picture of a family that practically all the reviewers, including me, are bound to characterize as the Clarence Days of Caracas." It was a Book-of-the-Month Club selection.

Ybarra's biography of Caruso, subtitled "The Man of Naples and the Voice of God," appeared in 1953. "If the public has made a legend out of the tenor, Mr. Ybarra has done his bit to bring back the man in all his ardor and gusto," wrote Howard Taubman in the New York *Times.* A fast-paced, popular biography, *Caruso* showed Ybarra's flair for human color.

Ybarra married Penelope O'Leary of New York in 1930.

PRINCIPAL WORKS: Davy Jones's Yarns and Other Salted Songs, 1908; Bolivar, the Passionate Warrior, 1929; Cervantes, 1931; Hindenburg, the Man with Three Lives, 1932; America Faces South, 1939; Young Man of Caracas, 1941; Young Man of the World, 1942; Lands of the Andes: Peru and Bolivia, 1947; Caruso, 1953; Verdi, 1955.

ABOUT: Hoehn, M. (ed.) Catholic Authors, I; Ybarra, T. R. Young Man of Caracas; Current Biography 1940.

YEATS, WILLIAM BUTLER (June 13, 1865-January 28, 1939). For biographical sketch and list of works and references, see TWENTIETH CENTURY AUTHORS, 1942.

* * *

ADDITIONAL WORKS: Letters (ed. A. Wade) 1955.

ABOUT: Brooks, V. W. A Chilmark Miscellany; Colum, M. Life and the Dream; Dictionary of National Biography 1931-1940; Ellmann, R. Yeats: The Man and the Mask, The Identity of Yeats; Gogarty, O. St. J. Mourning Becomes Mrs. Spendlove; Gregory, I. Lady Gregory's Journals; Hall, J. & Steinmann, M. (eds.) The Permanence of Yeats; Henn, T. R. The Lonely Tower; Jeffares, A. M. W. B. Yeats: Man and Poet; Kavanagh, P. The Story of the Abbey Theatre; Koch, V. Yeats: The Tragic Phase; Menon, V. K. N. The Development of William Butler Yeats; Moore, V. The Unicorn: W. B. Yeats' Search for Reality; Orwell, G. Dickens, Dali, and Others: Parkinson,

T. F. W. B. Yeats: Self-Critic; Ure, P. Towards a Mythology; Wade, A. A Bibliography of the Writings of W. B. Yeats; Warren, A. Rage for Order; Witt, M. *in* English Institute Essays 1946; Yeats, J. B. Letters to his Son, W. B. Yeats, and Others, 1869-1922; Yeats, W. B. Letters; Life October 25, 1948; Sewanee Review October 1949; Spectator September 24, 1948.

*YEATS-BROWN, FRANCIS CHARLES CLAYPON (August 15, 1886-December 19, 1944). For biographical sketch and list of earlier works and references, see TWENTIETH CENTURY AUTHORS, 1942.

* * *

Francis Yeats-Brown died in London at fifty-eight.

He reentered the British Army during World War II, and in 1943-44 toured the India-Burma war front gathering material for a book. He was also working on a biography of Catherine the Great.

The books concerned with his adventures in the East are his most notable works. Of *Lives of a Bengal Lancer,* E. F. Benson noted that the author was "possessed of that extremely rare faculty of being able to decipher himself without self-consciousness. . . . He gives the impression of a very acute observer noting down and describing with great vividness in a style of excellent clarity a quantity of most interesting happenings external to himself, but all the time he is carving with deft and quiet strokes that image of himself which long before the book is done, stands out complete."

ADDITIONAL WORK: Martial India, 1945.

ABOUT: London Times December 20, 1944; New York Times December 21, 1944; Spectator (London) December 22, 1944.

* yāts'-broun'

*YERBY, FRANK GARVIN (September 5, 1916-   ), American novelist, writes: "The biographical facts are as follows: Born in Augusta, Ga., son of Rufus G. Yerby and Wilhelmina Smythe Yerby—two brothers, one sister; education at Haines Institute, Paine College, A.B. 1937 (both Augusta, Ga.), Fisk University, Nashville, Tenn. M.A. 1938, additional postgraduate study, University of Chicago. Married, March 1, 1941 at New Orleans, La., Flora Helen Claire Williams; four children—Jacques Loring,

Sam Langford

* *"Yerby* rhymes with *derby,* pronounced American style."

Nikki Ethlyn, Faune Ellena, and Jan Keith. Taught, Florida Agricultural and Mechanical College, Tallahassee, Fla., 1939-40, Southern University, Baton Rouge, La., 1940-41. Worked for Ford Motor Company, Detroit, then Fairchild Aircraft, Jamaica, Long Island, during entire war.

"Writing—won special O. Henry Award for first published short story, 'Health Card,' in 1944. *Foxes of Harrow* published 1946, has sold to date more than two million copies in English; translations of it and my other novels now number more than twelve languages exclusive of such English editions as Great Britain, New Zealand, Australia."

* * *

The above account was written in France where Yerby is currently living and where he plans to remain while his children are educated in Switzerland. As a Negro, Yerby has sometimes been criticized for devoting his writing talents to the purely escapist popular historical romance instead of treating contemporary social problems. Sometimes overlooked is the fact that Yerby's first published writings were serious and sensitive stories about Negro life in the South. One of these was "Health Card," a tense, objective account of the humiliation of a Negro couple by military police, and similar stories appeared in *Phylon*, *Tomorrow*, and *Common Ground*. His first published novel, *The Foxes of Harrow*, a romantic story of the ante-bellum South, full of violent action and stock characters, was quite frankly written for the popular market. Its success, however, exceeded the author's most optimistic expectations. Within a year of its publication over a million copies had been sold, and Hollywood had purchased the screen rights. Since then Yerby has written steadily for a popular market. The sales records of his books have been impressive. In the United States alone they have sold more than twelve million copies. They have all been book club selections, and three of them have been bought for motion pictures. Yerby is a hard worker: "I frequently write right around the clock. I work as much as eighteen hours a day. Not only that; I rewrite . . . and not only that: I do a lot of research." He feels that the novelist "has a professional obligation to please his reading public" and, in answer to any implied criticism of his work as "escapist," he states: "The novelist hasn't any right to inflict on the public his private ideas on politics, religion or race. If he wants to preach he should go on the pulpit."

PRINCIPAL WORKS: The Foxes of Harrow, 1946; The Vixens, 1947; The Golden Hawk, 1948; Pride's Castle, 1949; Floodtide, 1950; A Woman

Called Fancy, 1951; The Saracen Blade, 1952; Devil's Laughter, 1953; Bride of Liberty, 1954; Benton's Row, 1954.

ABOUT: Current Biography 1946; New York Times Book Review May 13, 1951.

*YEZIERSKA, ANZIA (1885-   ). For biographical sketch and list of earlier works and references, see TWENTIETH CENTURY AUTHORS, 1942.

* * *

Anzia Yezierska lives in New York City and works as a free-lance writer, doing mainly magazine articles and book reviews. Her only recent book, and the first she had published in nearly twenty years, was an autobiography, *Red Ribbon on a White Horse*, in which Miss Yezierska chronicled her rise from poverty on New York's lower East Side to wealth and success in Hollywood, and her subsequent return to poverty after the Depression of the 1930's. In poverty, in a series of small furnished rooms in New York, she has found a spiritual contentment which was lacking in the world of material success. W. H. Auden described her book as "an account of her efforts to discard fantastic desires and find real ones, both material and spiritual." Lyman Bryson wrote of the book in the New York *Times*: "The fierceness of temperament that has made life so hard for her shows in her writings, which is nervous, direct, and passionate. . . . She tells the disturbing truth about her own soul."

ADDITIONAL WORKS: Red Ribbon on a White Horse, 1950.

ABOUT: Yezierska, A. Red Ribbon on a White Horse; The Reporter January 19, 1954; Saturday Review of Literature November 4, 1950.

* yĕ zyĕr′skà

YORKE, HENRY VINCENT. See GREEN, H.

YOUNG, ELLA (December 26, 1867-   ). For autobiographical sketch and list of earlier works and references, see TWENTIETH CENTURY AUTHORS, 1942.

* * *

Ella Young writes from Oceano, Calif.: "I am still living within sound of the sea, among trees that my hands have planted. *Flowering Dusk*, a sort of autobiography, came into being leisurely here. I called it: 'Things Remembered, accurately and inaccurately,' but many distinguished critics, to whom I am grateful, described it in kinder and more flattering terms. William Benét said it was: 'One of the choicest works of literature in our time.'"

The two worlds in which Ella Young has lived—the real Ireland with its struggles for independence and its great literary renaissance, and the "other world" of the spirit, of mystery and enchantment—are both reflected and recorded in *Flowering Dusk*. Her personal triumph, Kathleen Coyle wrote, is that "she succeeds in giving us the essence of a life that has been lived beautifully, even when the world about her seethed with ugliness." Frances Clarke Sayers once described Miss Young as "a woman like no other: a mystic, a scholar, a priestess of the earth, a wit, and a medium through whom those who read her words are filled with longing for loveliness and with a sorrowing pity for all that goes awry through evil."

Corrections: Miss Young was born in 1867, not 1865, as given in TWENTIETH CENTURY AUTHORS, 1942. She lectured at Alexandra College in Dublin, not at Trinity College.

PRINCIPAL WORKS: (revised list): *Poetry*—Poems, 1906; The Rose of Heaven, 1920; The Weird of Fionavar, 1922; To the Little Princess, 1930; Marzilian, 1938; Seed of the Pomegranate, 1949; Smoke Myrrh, 1950. *Prose*—The Coming of Lugh, 1909; Celtic Wonder Tales, 1910; The Wonder-Smith and His Son, 1927; The Tangle-Coated Horse, 1929; The Unicorn with Silver Shoes, 1932; Flowering Dusk, 1945.

ABOUT: Kunitz, S. J. & Haycraft, H. (eds.) The Junior Book of Authors (rev. ed.); Young, E. Flowering Dusk; Arizona Quarterly Spring 1954; Horn Book May-June 1945.

YOUNG, EMILY HILDA (1880-August 8, 1949). For biographical sketch and list of earlier works and references, see TWENTIETH CENTURY AUTHORS, 1942.

* * *

E. H. Young died at her home at Bradford-on-Avon in Wiltshire, England, at sixty-nine.

Norreys Jephson O'Conor has commented on her gift for "conveying the particular flavor of middle class life and . . . the background of the countryside and of a provincial town." Her last book, published two years before her death, was enthusiastically received. The London *Times* observed, "She brought a shining truthfulness to her observation of ordinary, or seemingly ordinary, personal relationships; she had gaiety and a rich fund of subtle and delicately astringent humour; and her work showed fastidious care . . . and was always admirably finished in craftsmanship."

ADDITIONAL WORK: Chatterton Square, 1947.

ABOUT: London Times August 10, 1949; Publishers' Weekly September 17, 1949; Saturday Review of Literature January 28, 1950.

YOUNG, FRANCIS BRETT (1884-March 28, 1954). For biographical sketch and list of earlier works and references, see TWENTIETH CENTURY AUTHORS, 1942.

* * *

Francis Brett Young died in a Capetown, South Africa, nursing home, following a long illness, at seventy.

His last work was a descriptive piece about South Africa. In 1944 he published a long narrative poem recounting England's history in lyric, ballad, elegy, narrative, and dialogue; the London *Times* called it "a storyteller's poem rather than a poet's poem, though poetry was there."

The *Times* has observed that while he achieved "breadth rather than depth" as a novelist, and "attained a level of performance that just fell short of what might have been hoped for from him," he "possessed a fertile gift of narrative, which he employed with increasing skill and assurance." Frank Swinnerton described his work as "unfailingly mellow, graceful, and delicate. If he does not at any time give an air of sharp actuality to the life he describes, that is probably intentional, for strict realism is not his object. His object is rather to present in tranquility, and with beauty . . . a long, leisurely panorama of England."

ADDITIONAL WORKS: The Island (poem) 1944; Portrait of a Village, 1951.

ABOUT: Swinnerton, F. The Georgian Literary Scene (1910-35); London Times March 29, 1954; New York Times March 29, 1954.

YOUNG, STARK (October 11, 1881-   ). For biographical sketch and list of earlier works and references, see TWENTIETH CENTURY AUTHORS, 1942.

* * *

Stark Young resigned from the staff of the *New Republic* in 1947. A year later, with the publication of *Immortal Shadows*, a collection of his critical essays, he announced that this was "the last writing that I shall do on the subject of the theatre." He has kept faithful to this intention, and his penetrating and illuminating criticism has been sorely missed. "It is a great pity," Walter Prichard Eaton wrote in 1948, "that so keen a mind as Mr. Young's, so catholic a taste and so civilized and wide-ranging a background for appreciation, should no longer contribute to the pitifully small body of drama criticism seriously concerned with our current theatre." Eric Bentley described Young as "a critic in the fullest sense—one who *judges* by *standards* that are not imposed from without but prompted and checked by his own first-rate

1117

sensibility." And he regards his reviews written over the years for the *New Republic* as "some of the best theatre criticism ever written in America or anywhere else." In recent years Young has taken up painting and has exhibited his work in the New York galleries. He has also written an autobiographical study —a collection of quietly-told and charming reminiscences about himself and his family— *The Pavilion.* His translation of Chekhov's *Three Sisters* had a successful off-Broadway production in 1955.

ADDITIONAL WORKS: Immortal Shadows, 1949; The Pavilion, 1951.

ABOUT: Young, S. The Pavilion; Kenyon Review Winter 1950; Nineteenth Century November 1949; Theatre Arts November 1947; Time June 14, 1943, December 13, 1948.

YUTANG, LIN. See LIN YU-TANG

ZABEL, MORTON DAUWEN (August 10, 1901-), American critic and scholar, writes: "I was born in southern Minnesota  (Minnesota Lake), my grandparents and their families having come to that part of America in the early and middle decades of the nineteenth century from Europe, some of them by way of New York and the East, some by way of New Orleans and the Mississippi Valley in the early pioneer years of the Middle West. It was there, a short distance south of Minneapolis, that I spent my childhood, had my early schooling, lost my father when I was thirteen, and prepared for college, first with the intention of going to one of the Eastern universities, but after my father's death with the decision to go to schools nearer home. For three years I attended the Miltary College of St. Thomas at St. Paul, Minn., and then went on to the University of Minnesota, where I took the Master of Arts degree in 1922. I first planned to study medicine, and in fact completed the work of the pre-medical course for the medical school at the University of Minnesota; but it soon became apparent that my real interests lay not in science but in literary and humanistic studies, so at Minnesota I changed and took the master's degree in English literature, studying there under such men as Cecil A. Moore, Joseph Warren Beach, Frederick Klaeber, Richard Burton, E. E. Stoll, and other professors of literature who formed the distinguished depart-

ment of English at that time. In 1922 I moved to Chicago, to teach, and to continue doctoral studies at the University of Chicago, where I worked under John Matthews Manly, Robert Morss Lovett, Charles R. Baskervill, Tom Peete Cross, Sir William Craigie, Edith Rickert, James R. Hulbert, and other scholars, specializing in nineteenth century literature, English and European. I also spent periods of research at Harvard and Columbia. I took the Ph.D. degree in 1933, at Chicago, with a dissertation on *The Romantic Idealism of Art in England: 1800-1850.* Meanwhile I taught for a considerable number of years at Loyola University, Chicago, where in 1928 I became chairman of the department of English; but I also filled visiting professorships at the Universities of Chicago, California, and Northwestern, and lectured at a good many other American universities and colleges.

"My first trip to Europe came in 1922, and others followed in 1924, 1928, 1935, and, after the Second World War, in 1951 and 1954. Some of these were long visits, with study and research work in London and Paris, and travels in most of the western and southern Continental countries. My work as a writer began around 1924, and has continued steadily ever since. This work was in poetry and, at one point, in fiction, but chiefly it was in literary and art criticism, and in scholarship. In 1926 I became acquainted with Harriet Monroe, the founder and editor of *Poetry: A Magazine of Verse.* I began contributing verse and criticism to *Poetry,* and in 1928 Miss Monroe asked me to become her associate editor. This was a fruitful and rewarding association; it brought me the acquaintance of many writers; I contributed, for about twelve years, to every issue of the magazine—editorials, reviews, reports on American and European periodicals, as well as verse. When Miss Monroe died in Arequipa, Peru, in September 1926, on her return journey from the PEN Congress at Buenos Aires, I took over the editorship of *Poetry* and carried it through a difficult year of problems and adjustments. Then, because writing and teaching had first claims, I decided to withdraw from the editorship and its inevitable insecurity. I continued writing for the journals to which I had been contributing. I also served as visiting professor at Chicago, at Northwestern, and at the University of California in Berkeley. I published *Literary Opinion in America* and other books in the following years. And in 1943 a new chapter opened.

"The Department of State in Washington had negotiated with the government of Brazil for the installation of a Chair of North

American Literature at the National University of Brazil in Rio de Janeiro. At the instigation of the Rockefeller Foundation, I was chosen for the post. I had never seriously sent my thoughts in the direction of Latin America, but I decided to undertake the venture. Early in 1944, I went by air— four days of flying in those wartime years— to Rio de Janeiro and saw that fabulous city for the first time. My work soon began—the first and still the only official professorship of American literature on that continent. I inaugurated the *cadeira* and began to make the acquaintance of a new world of writers, friends, and scenes. I had gone to Brazil for nine months; I stayed for two years; and besides my work at the university and at the Instituto Brasil-Estados Unidos, I visited and lectured in São Paulo, Belo Horizonte, Ouro Preto, Porto Alegre, Bahia, and other Brazilian cities. When the two memorable Brazilian years and the delightful experience of living in Rio were over, I spent another five months flying to other South American and Central American countries, lecturing in universities and cultural institutes, and making acquaintance with the whole panorama of Latin American life — Uruguay, Argentina, Chile, Peru, Ecuador, Colombia, Venezuela, Panama, Guatemala, and Mexico. I count this as one of the most revealing and impressive experiences of my life. It was renewed in the summer of 1953, when, again on a cultural mission for the State Department, I returned for three months to Brazil (Rio, São Paulo, Bahia, Belo Horizonte, Ouro Preto, Florianapolis, Porto Alegre), as well as to Argentina, Uruguay, and Peru. And in 1954 I was invited by the Brazilian authorities to return to act as United States delegate to the International Congress of Writers in August, held in connection with the Fourth Centenary Exposition of the city of São Paulo. My fellow American delegates were William Faulkner and Robert Frost. This time I flew to Brazil from Europe, where I was spending a year in travel, lecturing, and research, and had three weeks in São Paulo and Rio to renew old friendships, as well as delightful weeks in Portugal and Spain on my return to London. Thus South America, and particularly Brazil, has become a distinct part of my work and experience. I left behind there two books on American literature—*A Literatura dos Estados Unidos,* in Portuguese, published in Rio (1947), and *Historia de la Literatura Norte-Americana,* in Spanish, published in Buenos Aires (1951)—as a record of my work and as books now widely used in the schools and universities of the southern hemisphere; as well as many articles in the literary journals and reviews, and two anthologies of American literature.

"In 1944 I was awarded a Guggenheim fellowship to aid my literary studies, and in 1955 a $1000 Award from the National Institute of Arts and Letters. I have tried in my work as a writer to combine the study of literature with social and historical studies, as well as with a lifelong interest in art and music. My particular literary heroes, in the nineteenth and twentieth centuries at least, have been writers like Coleridge, Dickens, Arnold, Flaubert, Conrad, Yeats, and Henry James; the poets have claimed my attention as much as the critics and novelists. I became professor of English Literature at the University of Chicago on my return from South America in 1946, and teaching will be my profession, writing my avocation and purpose, for the remainder of my life. I see the critical spirit, the enquiring intelligence, as central to all great literature, imaginative or otherwise, and have made it my object to trace its workings among the western literatures in whatever form it manifests itself. I hope in the future to continue traveling and working in Europe and South America, and to use my experience in those continents toward understanding the thought and art of England and America."

PRINCIPAL WORKS: The Romantic Idealism of Art in England, 1933; The Critical and Popular Background of Art in England, 1937; Shakespeare's Imagery: A Criticism, 1936; The Situation in American Criticism, 1939; Two Years of Poetry, 1939. *Editor:* A Book of Poems (with Harriet Monroe) 1932; Literary Opinion in America, 1937 (new ed. 1951); The Portable Joseph Conrad, 1947; The Portable Henry James, 1951; Samuel Butler's The Way of All Flesh, 1950; Joseph Conrad's The Nigger of the 'Narcissus,' 1951; Joseph Conrad's Under Western Eyes, 1951.

*ZAMACOIS, EDUARDO (February 17, 1873-). For biographical sketch and list of works and references, see TWENTIETH CENTURY AUTHORS, 1942.

* * *

Eduardo Zamacois left Spain in the early 1940's and settled in Latin America. On last reports he was living in Cuba. He has published no new books in recent years.

* thä mä kois'

*ZAMAYATIN, EUGENE IVANO-VICH (1884-1937). For biographical sketch and list of works and references, see TWENTIETH CENTURY AUTHORS, 1942.

* * *

Zamayatin died in France, where he had settled after leaving Soviet Russia, in 1937.

* zà myä'tyĭn

Shortly before his death he published (in Russian) the first part of a novel on Attila. According to Gleb Struve, the full Russian text of his controversial novel *We* (a shortened version of which brought him into disfavor with Soviet officials) was scheduled for publication in 1939, but plans for publishing were abandoned when war broke out, and the book has never appeared.

ABOUT: Struve, G. Soviet Russian Literature, 1917-1950.

ZANGWILL, ISRAEL (February 14, 1864-August 1, 1926). For biographical sketch and list of works and references, see TWENTIETH CENTURY AUTHORS, 1942.

*ZARA, LOUIS (August 2, 1910-   ). For autobiographical sketch and list of earlier works and references, see TWENTIETH CENTURY AUTHORS, 1942.

* * *

Louis Zara writes: "Since 1947 I have been associated with the Ziff-Davis Publishing Company, first in Chicago, now in New York City. I started as the executive editor, was promoted to director of the book division, then to a vice-presidency in the firm. I was editor-in-chief of Ziff-Davis' unique experiment in popular art, the publication *Masterpieces: The Home Collection of Great Art,* now suspended. Since the company no longer publishes books, I am now in charge of various new magazine projects.

"For one year, 1946-47, I was a member of the panel of the 'Stump the Authors' show, which I helped to originate for the American Broadcasting Company network. We did it on radio for twenty-six weeks and also for another twenty-six weeks on television. I was the third member of the story-telling panel.

"At present, in addition to my normal duties, I am planning a new novel, have published a number of new short stories, and have just completed two historical plays: 'Cleopatra the Queen' and 'Caesar.'"

* * *

With the exception of one novel, *Ruth Middleton,* the first volume of a projected trilogy on the life of an American girl, Louis Zara's recent books have been historical novels. These are, in Edward Weeks' words, "rousing historical narrative." Some reviewers have found them over-long, stilted and "ceremonious" in style, but there would be

* "I prefer to have my name pronounced *Zah-ra,* but I don't insist."

little disagreement with Weeks' judgment that they make "engaging reading." Zara's novels are popular in Europe. They have been published in England and, in translation, in Argentina, Norway, and the Netherlands.

Zara's recent novel *Blessed Is the Land,* a story of the first Jews who settled in the New World in 1654, was the fruit of long and painstaking research. The reviewers found it informative, convincing, and well-told.

ADDITIONAL WORKS: Against This Rock, 1943; Ruth Middleton, 1946; In the House of the King, 1950; Rebel Run, 1951; Blessed Is the Land, 1954.
ABOUT: Warfel, H. R. American Novelists of Today; Scholastic October 4, 1943.

*ZATURENSKA, MARYA ALEXAN-DROVNA (September 12, 1902-   ). For autobiographical sketch and list of earlier works and references, see TWENTIETH CENTURY AUTHORS, 1942.

* * *

Marya Zaturenska has been described (by Chad Walsh in the New York *Times*) as "a poet who quietly refuses to put herself into one of the convenient pigeonholes." Her special gift, Walsh wrote in 1954, is meditative lyricism: "Deeply responsive to nature, to love, to all the moments and occasions of life, she celebrates them in their own right. She simultaneously celebrates a hovering and ultimate something of which nature and human moments are the visible images. A strong strain of mystical intuition runs through these poems." In addition to her verse, Miss Zaturenska has done two volumes of prose in recent years. With her husband, Horace Gregory, she wrote *A History of American Poetry, 1900-1940.* In 1949 she published a sensitive study of Christina Rossetti and the Pre-Raphaelite circle. The Gregorys live in Rockland County, N.Y.

ADDITIONAL WORKS: The Golden Mirror (poems) 1944; (with H. Gregory) A History of American Poetry, 1900-1940, 1946; Christina Rossetti, 1949; Selected Poems, 1954.

* zä tŏŏr ĕn'skä

*ZEROMSKI, STEFAN (November 14, 1864-November 20, 1925). For biographical sketch and list of works and references, see TWENTIETH CENTURY AUTHORS, 1942.

* * *

ADDITIONAL WORK IN ENGLISH TRANSLATION: Faithful River, 1943.
ABOUT: Columbia Dictionary of Modern European Literature; Slavonic Review March 1943.

* zhĕ rôm'skĕ

*ZILAHY, LAJOS (1891-), Hungarian novelist and man of letters, was the son of a lawyer. His family belonged to that lesser

nobility which traditionally prepared its sons for the legal profession or for a military career. At sixteen, however, Zilahy was already turning toward literature, and at that time his early poems began to appear in the more important Budapest periodicals. He studied law briefly but soon gave it up to write.

During World War I Zilahy was wounded on the Russian front. It was at this time that his first book appeared, a collection of pacifist verses.

Most of his later books and plays are concerned with war, pleading eloquently for world peace and inveighing against militarism. After he recovered from his injury, Zilahy was unwilling to return to the battlefront because he felt that Hungary was waging war in Germany's interest rather than her own. Whereupon he risked a firing squad by deserting the army.

After the armistice, Zilahy adopted writing as a profession and in the following decade his novels, plays, and essays made his name famous throughout Europe. In 1930 he married the daughter of a former mayor of Budapest, and his only son, Mihaly, was born in 1931. In 1932, when the League of Nations invited a representative author from every nation to prepare an article warning the coming generations against the dangers of war, Zilahy sent an ironic letter which read in part: "I am afraid the League of Nations has misaddressed its invitation. The truth is that I am a passionate supporter of war. In fact I love war. I can hardly wait to receive my wound in the belly and to die in the course of the most excruciating agonies." He suggested that the troops which would be sent out to die should first, in a formal ceremony, execute all the statesmen and industrialists who make war. Zilahy supposed that his letter would be relegated to the wastebasket by the pacifist bloc in the League of Nations. Some months later, however, he received a large parcel from Geneva, Switzerland. His letter, together with the articles of other writers, had been translated into English, French, German, and Italian.

* zĭ′lŏ hĭ

Because his "modest proposal" attracted such wide attention, Zilahy was encouraged to write a play, *The Twelfth Hour,* on this theme. Hungarian audiences gave the play a vociferous and enthusiastic reception, but the most influential general in the Hungarian war ministry was displeased by the play and prohibited its performance.

During his writing career, Lajos Zilahy has produced ten novels and nineteen plays along with several volumes of essays and poems. Most of his novels have been translated into every European language and several of his plays have been produced throughout the world. Two of his plays were produced in New York—*Siberia* (1930) and *The Firebird* (1932). Hollywood has made motion pictures of his *The Virtuous Sin* (1937) and *The Firebird* (1933).

In September 1942 Russian bombers shattered Zilahy's villa in Budapest. Zilahy and his family happened to be spending a few days in the country at that time, but some tenants were living there at the time and two children and a governess were killed. After this escape from death, Zilahy and his wife gave their fortune to the state as a grant for the foundation of an educational institute to train men in the service of humanity, of world peace, and of the highest spiritual ideals. Zilahy's ancestors on one side of his family had been impoverished Protestant ministers for three hundred and fifty years. In a pamphlet published at the time of the founding of the Zilahy Institute, Zilahy stated: "Following the example of my forefathers, I seek to preach the Gospel, and it is impossible to preach the Gospel while accumulating wealth in the process." The pamphlet was noted by the press throughout the world. In 1943, a radio station in New York gave an account of the Zilahy Institute and the ideals it embodied. Later the same facts were broadcast in fourteen languages by the United States Office of War Information.

The German and German-controlled Hungarian press attacked the Zilahy Institute with vehemence for the anti-German implications in its underlying principles. In 1944 the Germans who occupied Hungary sought to arrest Zilahy, but he succeeded in evading them. Under an assumed name, hiding in cellars, he survived the battle of Budapest with his wife and child.

In 1947 they came to the United States to live. Although he had not participated in any Hungarian political movement, the Communist government in Hungary pronounced him a traitor to the "People's Democracy" and blacklisted his works. In 1949, Zilahy's son Mihaly, a student at Harvard, was killed in an accident. Zilahy and his wife now reside in New York City and he is planning to become an American citizen.

Zilahy is known to American audiences for several powerful novels on Hungarian political life. Probably his most ambitious novel is *The Dukays*, a chronicle of an aristocratic Hungarian family. American readers sometimes find the political details of his novels obscure, but his books have been praised for their richness of style, their humor, and their erudition. Of his later novel, *The Angry Angel*, which continues the story of the lives of the Dukays, Charles Lee remarked in the New York *Times*: "It is heavy with the weight of 'historic forces,' it heaves with the convulsions of the twentieth century, it suggests the massiveness of the hour. And yet, despite its Tolstoyan gravities, it is hearty with humor and delicate with soul."

PRINCIPAL WORKS IN ENGLISH TRANSLATION: The Deserter, 1932; Two Prisoners, 1933; The Guns Look Back, 1938; The Dukays, 1949; The Angry Angel, 1953.

ABOUT: New York Herald Tribune Book Review January 30, 1949, May 10, 1953; New Yorker May 21, 1949.

*ZILBOORG, GREGORY (December 25, 1890-   ), American psychiatrist, was born in Kiev, Russia, to Moses and Anne (Braun)  Zilboorg. After graduating from the *gymnasium* in Kiev, he attended the Psychoneurological Institute of Petrograd, from which, in 1917, he received his M.D. degree. His studies were interrupted in 1915 and 1916 for service as a physician in the Russian Army. Calling himself an "intellectual revolutionist," he participated in the short-lived Lvov government, after the deposition of the Czar, as Minister of Labor and held this post also during the brief administration of Alexander Kerensky. In 1918 he became a journalist and edited a daily newspaper until he was forced to leave Russia. In 1919 he came to the United States, becoming a citizen in 1925. He married Ray Liebow of New York (they were divorced in 1946) and they had a son and a daughter.

During his first years in America, Zilboorg supported himself as a lecturer and translator (among his translations are Andreyev's *He*

* zil'boŏrg

Who Gets Slapped and Zamayatin's *We*). His major interest, however, remained psychiatry. In 1926 he received his M.D. from Columbia University and joined the staff of the Bloomingdale Hospital. In 1929-30 he went to Berlin as a member of the staff of the Psychoanalytic Institute there. Since 1931 Dr. Zilboorg has maintained a private practice in New York City. He has also given considerable time to teaching and to clinical work. He has taught at the Catholic University of America, the University of California, and at Johns Hopkins. He is currently teaching at the New York State Medical College in New York City. Since 1948 he has also been a consultant in psychotherapy and research at Butler Hospital in Providence, R.I. He belongs to a large number of scholarly and professional associations, and is secretary of the Section on Legal Aspects of Psychiatry of the American Psychiatric Association.

In addition to many scholarly articles and technical studies, Dr. Zilboorg has written several books on psychiatry which have won him a popular audience. These too are serious studies, not mere popularizations, but they are written in a lucid style, in nontechnical language, and have been praised by the critics as both informative and entertaining. With George William Henry he wrote *A History of Medical Psychology* which, the London *Times Literary Supplement* observed, "combines exactitude with a popular approach to the most intricate problems of medical psychology." His *Mind, Medicine, and Man* was described by one reviewer as "an extraordinary, persuasive, and wide-minded exposition of the Freudian contribution through psychoanalysis." The *Christian Century* commented: "Zilboorg writes with vigor and clarity. He draws upon a rich and varied erudition. He swings his cudgels at prejudice and misunderstanding. He expounds the kernel of psychoanalytic doctrine and applies it explicitly to problems of society, law and religion."

Zilboorg was described some years ago as "small, dark, mustached, with thick-lens glasses that lend him a rather enigmatic expression." He is known for his "waspish wit and fluent conversation." His second wife is Margaret Stone. They have two children.

PRINCIPAL WORKS: The Medical Man and the Witch During the Renaissance, 1935; (with G. W. Henry) A History of Medical Psychology, 1941; Mind, Medicine, and Man, 1943; Sigmund Freud: His Exploration of the Mind of Man, 1951; The Psychology of the Criminal Act and Punishment, 1954.

ABOUT: Current Biography 1941; National Cyclopedia of American Biography (1952).

ZINSSER, HANS (November 17, 1878-September 4, 1940). For biographical sketch and list of works and references, see TWENTIETH CENTURY AUTHORS, 1942.

* * *

ABOUT: National Academy of Sciences: Biographical Memoirs, XXIV (1947); National Cyclopedia of American Biography (1950).

*ZUCKMAYER, KARL (or CARL) (December 27, 1896-). For autobiographical sketch and list of works and references, see TWENTIETH CENTURY AUTHORS, 1942.

* * *

Karl Zuckmayer settled in the United States in 1939 and lived in Barnard, Vt., until 1946 when he returned to Germany. He has resumed his leading position in German literature. In 1949 Eric Bentley called him "the most popular German playwright today." His *The Devil's General*, which he had written in Vermont, was a tremendous success in its German production in 1949. It was the story of a German army officer who, by reason of his sympathy for the Jewish people, came into conflict with the Nazis and was finally driven to suicide. Bentley wrote of the play: "In portraying his German general who is also a human being, Zuckmayer tries as well to paint a panoramic picture of life in Nazi circles during the war. Those who should know commend the accuracy with which he was able, three or four thousand miles away, to reconstruct the truth down to every detail of military and bureaucratic lingo."

In 1952 Zuckmayer received the Goethe prize for his collected works.

ABOUT: Columbia Dictionary of Modern European Literature; Scholastic March 22, 1950; Theatre Arts June 1949.

* tsŏŏk mī'ĕr

ZUGSMITH, LEANE (January 1903-). For autobiographical sketch and list of earlier works and references, see TWENTIETH CENTURY AUTHORS, 1942.

* * *

With her husband, Carl Randau, Leane Zugsmith wrote a mystery story, *The Visitor*, in 1944. The book was praised as a suspenseful and expertly written novel. The Randaus were associated with the newspaper *PM* until 1942. Their home is in Madison, Conn.

ADDITIONAL WORK: *With C. Randau*—The Visitor, 1944.

ZUVIRÍA. See MARTÍNEZ ZUVIRÍA

*ZWEIG, ARNOLD (November 10, 1887-). For biographical sketch and list of earlier works and references, see TWENTIETH CENTURY AUTHORS, 1942.

* * *

Arnold Zweig returned to Germany when World War II ended, after a long exile in Israel. He settled in Eastern Germany where he was hailed as the "grand old man" of German Communist literature. His earlier works, which had been banned by the Nazis, were reprinted; he received many honors and "national" prizes and was made president of the East German Academy of Letters. His only book of recent years is a novel, *The Axe of Wandsbek*, a massive and powerful study of life in Nazi Germany in 1937. American reviewers were generally impressed with the novel. Richard Plant, in the New York *Times*, described it as "the work of a mature story-teller and a wise and philosophical heart," and the *New Yorker* called it "a first-rate novel, constructed with uncommon precision." It was made into a motion picture by an East German studio, but the film was banned by the Communist government.

ADDITIONAL WORK IN ENGLISH TRANSLATION: The Axe of Wandsbek, 1947.

ABOUT: Columbia Dictionary of Modern European Literature; Liptzin, S. Germany's Stepchildren; Slochower, H. No Voice Is Wholly Lost; New York Times Book Review December 7, 1952.

* tsvīk

ZWEIG, STEFAN (November 28, 1881-February 23, 1942). For autobiographical sketch and list of works and references, see TWENTIETH CENTURY AUTHORS, 1942.

* * *

ADDITIONAL WORKS IN ENGLISH TRANSLATION: The Royal Game, 1944; Balzac, 1946; Stefan and Frederike Zweig: Their Correspondence, 1912-1942, 1954.

ABOUT: Arens, H. (ed.) Stefan Zweig: A Tribute to His Life and Work; Columbia Dictionary of Modern European Literature; Liptzin, S. Germany's Stepchildren; Mann, K. *in* Treasury of the Free World (ed. B. Raeburn); Slochower, H. No Voice Is Wholly Lost; Zweig, S. Stefan and Frederike Zweig: Their Correspondence; Books Abroad January 1943, Spring 1946, September 1952; German Quarterly May 1952.